The New York Times

GUIDE TO
ESSENTIAL
KNOWLEDGE

A DESK REFERENCE FOR THE **CURIOUS MIND**

REVISED AND EXPANDED THIRD EDITION

ST MARTIN'S PRESS ☙ NEW YORK

ISBN: 978-0-312-64302-7

First published in the United States by St. Martin's Press

Third U.S. Edition: November 2011
Second U.S. Edition: October 2007
First U.S. Edition: October 2004

10 9 8 7 6 5 4 3 2 1

Please send all questions and comments to:
John W. Wright, General Editor
Box 4580
Grand Central Station
New York, NY 10163

For The New York Times:

Administration: Michael Greenspon, General Manager, News Services; Nancy Lee, Vice President and Executive Editor, News Services and Syndicate; Alex Ward, Editorial Director, Book Development; Mitchel Levitas, Executive Associate.

Featured Writers: Natalie Angier, Pam Belluck, Sandra Blakeslee, Graham Bowley, Jane E. Brody, Elisabeth Bumiller, Kenneth Chang, Celia W. Dugger, Justin Gillis, Michiko Kakutani, Michael Kimmelman, Anna Kisselgoff, Gina Kolata, Sonia Kolesnikov-Jessop, Alastair Macauley, Charles McGrath, Anahad O'Connor, Nicolai Ouroussoff, Dennis Overbye, Jon Pareles, Thom Shanker, Will Shortz, Brian Stelter, Anthony Tommasini, Hal Varian, Nicholas Wade, John Noble Wilford.

Contributors:

This book was assembled and edited by the staff of Elizabeth Publishing and by a group of academic and professional writers.

Elizabeth Publishing:

General Editor: John W. Wright
Executive Editors: Matt Fisher, Lisette Cheresson
Designer: Virginia Norey

Senior Writers and Editors:

Herb Addison (Architecture, Business, Economics); Ariana Brookes (Literature, Music, Reference Library); Ellen Chodosh (Medicine, Music, Dance); Philip Francis (Psychology, Biographies, Sports); Terry Golway (History); Colleen Hamilton, Ph.D. (Literature); C. Alan Joyce; Deborah Kaple, Ph.D. (Government); John Major, Ph.D. (Art, Religion, World History, Languages); David Major, Ph.D. (Anthropology, Chemistry, Economics, Environment, Geography, Religion); Michael Miller (Botany, Computers, Music, Zoology); Robert Murphy (Literature, Biographies); Lincoln Paine (Geography, History, Biographies); Lisa Renaud (Literature); Jenny Tesar (Biochemistry, Biology, Medicine, Nutrition).

Principal Contributors:

Christopher Anderson, Ph.D., Indiana University (Radio and Television); Bryan Bunch (Math, Physics); Richard Carlin (Popular Music, Dance); T. Susan Chang (Food); Michael Coffey (Baseball); Susan Doll (Film); Abigail Elbow (Photography); Alice Finer (Mythology, Biographies); Pete Fornatale (Sports); Kurt Hettler (Sports, Wine); Michael Kaufman, Ph.D., San Jose State University (Astronomy); Christine Leahy (Art, Biographies); Edward O'Donnell, Ph.D., Holy Cross College (American History); John Rosenthal (Business, Finance); Robert Sharp (Major Wars); Michael Signer, Ph.D., J.D. (Law); David Sobel (Geology); Murray Sperber, Ph.D., Indiana University (College Sports); Robert L. Spring (Literature); Karen Tolchin, Ph.D., Florida Gulf Coast University (American Literature); Harvey Wiener, Ph.D., formerly of City University of New York and Adelphi University (Writer's Guide); Thomas Willkens (Philosophy).

Contributing Editors: Jeff Deeney, Andrea Galyean, Anna Kelman, Ben Keene, James McCaffery, Fred Riccardi, George L. Seibel IV, Laura Stickney, Randy Te Velde, Joseph Wiener, Saul Wiener.

Senior Copy Editors: Jerold Kappes, Susan Gamer.

The New York Times

Guide to Essential Knowledge

TABLE OF CONTENTS

INTRODUCTION

BY SAM TANENHAUS

"Nothing in education is so astonishing as the amount of ignorance it accumulates in the form of inert facts," Henry Adams remarks in *The Education of Henry Adams*, his classic autobiography, published in 1907, when its author was sixty-nine. "Adams," he goes on, in the self-mocking third-person address he uses throughout, "had looked at most of the accumulations of art in the storehouses called Art Museums; yet he did not know to look at the art-exhibits of 1900. He had studied Karl Marx and his doctrines of history with profound attention, yet he could not apply them at Paris."

This is the admission not of a man who disdains facts, but of one who had placed inordinate faith in them, though facts of a high order. Anyone who has worked his way through a chapter of *Das Kapital* or looked at the paintings in a single gallery of the Louvre instantly realizes he has entered a world in which facts of a particular kind—ice-hard atoms of observed reality—converge into interlocking systems, often governed by a single unifying principle. Adams, as it happened, hoped to achieve something like this himself. His life ambition was to find or invent a universal law that might bind together all the loose contradictory multiplicities he encountered in his relentless pursuit of truth. The search led him to investigate almost the entire range of available knowledge. A partial list of the disciplines he studied includes biology, geology, mathematics, magnetics, foreign languages, medieval architecture, international diplomacy, Washington politics, global finance, the art of the novel.

In this, Adams was following the dictates of his age's intellectuals. What was the goal of reason if not to uncover the underlying meaning of things—of *all* things—and so achieve an exalted state of being? "Knowledge enormous makes a god of me," John Keats had declared in *Hyperion*, an epic poem, meant to rival *Paradise Lost*, which Keats began and abandoned in his early twenties. True knowledge promised emancipation. This was also true for Marx as well as for others whose work Adams mastered: Charles Darwin, Charles Lyell, Thomas Macaulay. We might add later names, too: Durkheim, Einstein, Freud, Joyce, Picasso, Weber. Each was born in the 19th century. Each was a system-builder, a creator of cosmologies. And each, in his way, was a stepchild of the Enlightenment, the era that gave us the first true compendium of knowledge.

The book you're now holding belongs to this tradition and so, quite properly, signals its debt in the following sentences: "In Paris a group of intellectuals led by Voltaire and Denis Diderot produced the first encyclopedia, which they claimed was based on rational and secular values. The *Encylopédie* consisting at first of 28 volumes was published in 1728 and was an immediate success."

The New York Times Guide to Essential Knowledge, now in its third edition, also encompasses much of the world, and in a single very large volume, though the range of facts is wide and, like its French forerunner, is anchored in its specific historical moment. Thus, the entry on books includes not only a concise survey of the "great works of Western Literature" but also a useful discussion of "Popular" genres, including romance fiction, science fiction and fantasy, and police procedurals. And why not, since today an accomplished "literary" writer like the Irish author John Banville, winner of the prestigious Booker Prize, doubles, under the pseudonym Benjamin Black, as the author of crime fiction?

The planet is more concretely knowable than in the days of Voltaire and Diderot. Eighteenth-century cartographers could only dream of a time when every great river could be measured. The editors of this book not only furnish the numbers, they have also ranked all the major rivers by length and so inform us that the Arkansas and Colorado rivers flow for exactly 1,450 miles, nearly as far as the Ganges (1,560 miles) and the Euphrates (1,510).

Any decent American fact-book should have a roster of Hall of Fame baseball players, complete with essential statistics. Once again, the editors of this book have added telling details. Who knew Paul Waner hit 62 doubles in 1932 or that Larry Doby, the American League's first black player (overshadowed all those years and still today by the legend of Jackie Robinson) was a seven-time All Star and twice led his league in homers?

A good encylopedia must be more than a compendium. If it is to be read, it must be *written*. Here is one choice sentence (from the entry on "Beer Styles and Brewing Nations"), on Bavarian brews: "Hefeweizen or Hefeweissbier, has flavors and aromas that are banana-like, clove-like, or even akin to bubble-gum, while the darker Weizenbock or Weissbock tends to have a bready malt flavor and a caramel sweetness. Both are lightly hopped."

It is fair to ask, with Henry Adams, what all these pleasures add up to, if anything at all. The French encyclopedists, again, offered a distinctive vision. As our latter-day editors note of their antecedents, "Many of these *philosophes* were atheists, although not all of them professed their non-belief in public." Today this non-belief seems ablaze with spiritual purpose, set forth in *Encyclopédie's* most celebrated passage, its "preliminary discourse," composed by the mathematician and philosopher Jean Le Rond d'Alembert, who asked, "Are not the ideas of 'all,' of 'part,' of 'larger,' and of 'smaller,' strictly speaking, the same simple and individual idea, since we cannot have the one without all the others presenting themselves at the same time?" And if so, couldn't this same truth be applied across the widest conceivable spectrum, until "the universe, if we may be permitted to say so, would only be one fact and one great truth for whoever knew how to embrace it from a single point of view"? In other words, the encyclopedists were intent not simply on disproving inherited orthodoxies or ancient superstitions, but on replacing them with a newer, truer revelation.

Are the editors of *The New York Times Guide to Essential Knowledge* also saying something like that? Is this book too meant to defy religious teachings or at least espouse a post-religious position? If so, there's no hint of it in the many pages here on the world's religions, with particular emphasis on the three major monotheisms, or in the discussion of the Books of the Bible, Old Testament and New. Some may think the editors' inclusive ecumenicalism muddles the issue. Others may accuse them of wanting their truth both ways—that is, of being craftily political or politically correct. Diderot and d'Alembert, proud in their ultra-rationalism, at least let us know where they stood. Why can't our 21st-century encyclopedists do the same?

Here's one reason. In many areas the old debates have been exhausted. Of course there remain fervent advocates on both sides (and the most engaged combatants, or fundamentalists, will bristle even at the suggestion that there are "two" legitimate sides). But as a general rule the intellectual climate has changed, the monistic ideal has given way to the pluralistic. This isn't surprising or shouldn't be. Most of us, born in the 20th century and adjusting to the 21st, have learned to distrust monism, whether religious or secular, because it inclines toward absolutism. And the absolutist, we have also learned, is not content to accumulate inert facts. Instead he marshals them in a cause, or crusade, with results that are often catastrophic.

But pluralism poses dangers too. The worst is the discrediting of the very idea of authority—authority in the sense of earned respect (as distinct from power, which is ruthlessly imposed). If our moment has its own secular belief, it is the insistent hope that in the digital age, with more facts available than ever before, the highest authority rests in numerical consensus, whether calculated algorithmically via "visits" and "hits" or computed by "likes" and "follow buttons." It is the doctrine of tabulation. Some "900,000 blog posts, 50 million tweets, more than 60 million Facebook status updates, and 210 billion emails are sent off into the electronic either every day," Eli Pariser estimates in *The Filter Bubble: What the Internet is Hiding from You.* He informs us as well that Eric Schmidt, the Google executive, "likes to point out that if you recorded all human communications from the dawn of time to 2003, it'd take up about 5 billion gigabytes of storage space. Now we're creating that much data every two days."

What this doesn't tell us is how much of this data is either useful or true. Data was once a synonym for facts. Today it is absorbed into the category of "information" where it is entangled with its damaged offspring "misinformation" and "disinformation."

Best, in this discussion of fact, to admit an obvious one: If you type any of the entries found in this guide into Google you'll instantly get information—particles of fact that will direct you to other facts and with luck, deliver the answer you had been seeking. But this book makes a bolder promise. Its proffered information will "guide" us toward "knowledge." This last word says much.

Even the casual browser of this book expresses a form of faith in its editors and contributors, faith in the reliability of the many facts they present and also in the interlocking system they have devised. Expect a good deal from it, but not overly much. Henry Adams, who was quite possibly the best informed American of his time, reminds us continually that his prodigious education amounted to no education at all. "Not that his ignorance troubled him! He knew enough to be ignorant. His course led him through oceans of ignorance; he had tumbled from one ocean into another till he had learned to swim."

To swim is to be in constant motion, taking the facts as we meet them, but always testing them against our own experience, until we arrive at something like the truth.

Sam Tanenhaus is the editor of *The New York Times Book Review* and the author of *Whittaker Chambers: A Biography* and *The Death of Conservatism.*

THE FINE ARTS

ARCHITECTURE

A Brief History of Architecture

Noted architectural historian Spiro Kostof stated: "Architecture, in the end, is nothing more, and nothing less than the gift of making places for some human purpose." This almost deceptively simple definition captures the essence of what we call architecture. The definition is broad enough to include the Paleolithic caves inhabited by early humans, the great Gothic cathedrals, and modern Levittowns of hundreds of nearly identical suburban houses.

The characteristics of individual works of architecture reflect this definition and derive from the interplay of three elements that are inseparable from one another: *purpose*, the reason for the building to exist; *design*, the shape that a building takes in response to its perceived purpose; and *structure*, the way the building is put together out of its constituent parts.

Paleolithic Architecture

The earliest known humans who left evidence of their dwelling places were hunters who followed migratory game herds and did not establish permanent living places. They did, however, seek shelter in caves and huts to which they regularly returned. These primitive dwellings were the earliest beginnings of architecture.

Caves Beginning around 40,000 years ago in Europe, the modern humans who displaced the earlier Neanderthals began to create domestic and ceremonial spaces in caves that were often elaborately decorated with wall paintings. A typical example is the cave at Lascaux in southwestern France, which was inhabited between 10,000 and 20,000 years ago. Not only does it contain evidence of daily life, but its walls are painted with pictures of animals and humans of exquisite sensitivity; these paintings are believed to have had religious or magical significance.

Structures The earliest known structures built by humans (*Homo erectus*) are at Terra Amata in southern France, dating to about 380,000 years ago. The site consists of some 20 huts built of branches held in place by large stones arrayed in oval rings. Small groups of people occupied the encampment regularly each late spring, leaving it abandoned until the following spring.

Ice-age huts built of mammoth bones that would have been covered by hides have been found at many sites in eastern Europe, including a famous example at Mezhirich, Ukraine, dating to about 15,000 years ago.

Neolithic Architecture

A warming climate about 10,000–12,000 years ago brought about the end of the last ice age. Improved techniques of managing game herds and harvesting wild plants led to an increase in population, which in turn required more intensive development of food sources. As people began growing crops and domesticating animals they began to form permanent, settled communities.

Dwellings Neolithic people in many parts of the world built small houses of woven tree limbs, pitched roofs, roof beams held up by supporting posts, and walls filled in with mud. In some places the houses were large enough to accommodate numbers of families, and in other places groups of houses were ringed by stones with paths between them defined by rows of stones.

Monuments In parts of western Europe from the Neolithic period through the Bronze Age and into the Iron Age, people built circular or linear arrays of stone (megaliths) of surprising size and complexity. Many of these ceremonial monuments still exist, the most famous of which is Stonehenge, in southwest England. There, from about 2750 to 1500 B.C., successive builders erected enormous stones in circular formations. There are many theories to explain the purpose of Stonehenge. The inner circles open toward a stone over which the sun rises on the summer solstice. The prodigious effort of construction and the elaborate layout of the stones suggest that Stonehenge must have been a ceremonial place central to the builders' culture.

Western Asian Architecture

In the area of the Tigris and Euphrates Rivers in western Asia, Neolithic settlements became larger, wealthier, and socially more complex. With the rise of civilization beginning about 7500 B.C., people gathered together in cities and produced a profusion of impressive architecture.

Western Asian builders invented construction methods that were as important as their architectural forms. An absence of large stones for building, especially for long beams between columns, forced builders to find other ways of covering wide enclosed spaces. These included the round arch built of voussoirs (wedge-shaped stones or bricks) and the dome. In later times arches and domes would become central to some of the greatest works of architecture.

Towns and Cities The earliest surviving evidence of a town is Jericho on the Jordan River, where settlement began around 7500 B.C. Built largely of mud bricks and in successive waves of construction, the settlement already showed traits that would characterize later cities: a population much larger than prehistoric villages, a perimeter wall to defend against enemies, and public buildings set among private dwellings.

Temples and Ziggurats With the growth of cities, organized, state-sponsored religions appeared, and temples became a key element in the urban fabric. Temples evolved from small shrines in prehistoric villages into one of the most striking forms of architecture, the ziggurat. In its classic form, the ziggurat was a stepped pyramid set on a platform with stairs leading to the summit—a place nearest to heaven—where the supreme god was worshipped. The ziggurat of Ur-Nammu in Ur, built around 2000 B.C., is a well-known example.

In the first millennium B.C., temples of the Assyrian Empire (in present-day Iraq) were elaborately decorated with free-standing stone sculptures and narrative sculptural reliefs. One of the finest monuments of late Mesopotamian architecture, the Ishtar Gate of the Babylonian Empire (ca. 575 B.C., now at the Staatliche Museum, Berlin) is made of blue-glazed brick and decorated with reliefs of bulls and other sacred animals.

Palaces As the social order became more complex, the ruler became more dominant and palaces began to overshadow ziggurats. Huge palaces were built by the Assyrian kings. Rock-cut tombs and cities of the eastern Mediterranean, such as the city of Petra (in present-day Jordan) show Greek influence, as do the buildings of the Persian Empire, rivals of the Greeks. The palaces of Persepolis (in what is now west-central Iran) exemplify the sophistication and imagination achieved by the Persian architects. Built by Darius (ca.550–486 B.C.)

and his son Xerxes (519–465 B.C.), the complex includes both Greek-influenced hypostyle (having roofs supported by columns) temples and palaces and Mesopotamian-style narrative sculptural reliefs.

Egyptian Architecture

At the same time that literate city-states were forming in western Asia, people along the Nile River in northern Africa were also developing an advanced civilization. In contrast to western Asia, there was an abundance of sandstone, limestone, and granite with which to build.

Tombs and Pyramids Early Egyptian kings were considered gods, and their tombs reflect the importance of perpetuating their life after death. One of the first architects of record was Imhotep, who designed the pyramid complex at Saqqara in 2680 B.C. as King Zoser's tomb. Equally famous are the three pyramids at Giza, built about 2570–2500 B.C. The largest and oldest of these, the pyramid of Cheops, was originally 482 feet high and 760 feet square, and occupies about 13 acres. The manipulation of the huge stones used to build these structures required both the large-scale mobilization of labor and the invention of ingenious engineering techniques.

Temples Later pharaohs were buried in more modest tombs, furnished with sculptures and painted pictorial reliefs. For example, the tombs of Mentuhotep, about 2050 B.C., and Queen Hatshepsut, about 1500 B.C., at Deir el-Bahri, are considerably smaller than the pyramids at Giza. The temple replaced the tomb as Egypt's dominant architectural work. The temple of Karnak—dedicated to the sun god Amon—was built in stages over a period from about 1525 B.C. to about 1350 B.C.; Karnak's hypostyle hall is one of the great works of ancient architecture.

Greek Architecture

The architectural building types and orders developed in Greece began a long evolution in European, and eventually American, architecture that continued well into the 20th century. Early Greek building was influenced by both the monumental Egyptian buildings and the use of columns to achieve a powerful visual effect. Greek architects brought the hypostyle building to an unprecedented level of beauty and refinement. An abundance of fine-grained native marble provided them with an excellent building material.

Temples   The most important and influential Greek building was the temple. Greeks believed in a pantheon of gods, and temples were dedicated to individual gods. The temple form began evolving in the 11th and 12th centuries B.C., took its characteristic form during the period beginning in 700 B.C., and reached a high point of refinement after 400 B.C.

Temples in their final form were set on a stylobate, a rectangular platform of three steps. A peristyle, a row of columns, was placed at the periphery. The columns supported a horizontal entablature. At the short ends a triangular pediment closed the ends of the pitched roof. Within the peristyle was a cella, or naos, a structure that housed a statue of the dedicated god or goddess and associated treasures.

Architectural Orders   Greek architects also developed architectural orders called Doric, Ionic, and Corinthian. Each is easily distinguished by its fluted columns.

The Doric order was the first developed, and its column has a simple capital between the shaft and the entablature. The proportion of the width to height is less than in later orders; the effect of a Doric temple is of superbly proportioned solidity. The best known Doric temple is the Parthenon on the Acropolis in Athens (447–432 B.C.), dedicated to the goddess Athena and designed by the architects Callicrates and Iktinos.

The Ionic order denotes a style of columns that have a capital with scroll-like volutes that spread the load where the column meets the entablature. The column is more slender than the Doric, giving Ionic temples a graceful appearance. The Erechtheion (421-405 B.C.) on the Acropolis in Athens, is an example that also includes a porch with carayatids, draped female figures, taking the place of columns that support a roof structure.

The Corinthian order, though not often employed by the Greeks, is distinguished by column capitals with acanthus leaves. The columns are tall and graceful like the Ionic and support Doric or Ionic entablatures interchangeably. One of the few examples is the Olympieion in Athens designed by the Greeks but built by the Romans.

Other Building Types   Though the Greek temple became a seminal icon for future architects, the Greeks developed other building types that provided models for Western architecture. The open-air theater, usually carved from a hillside, consisted of an orchestra, stage, and auditorium. The stadion, an athletic arena, was long and narrow, straight at one end and circular at the other, with tiered rows of seats on three sides. Greek democracy was reflected in the agora, an open-air forum where citizens gathered to hear speeches, discuss issues, shop, and socialize. And sometimes adjoining the agora was the stoa, a simple structure, usually long and narrow, with a flat or pitched roof that housed court sessions, shops, banquets, and public gatherings in general.

Roman Architecture

The Romans were great empire builders and equally great architectural builders. As they conquered societies from western Asia to the Atlantic Ocean, they created daring new structures as they shaped their architecture in the service of an imperial society. Roman ideas about architecture are known from the writings of the architect and theorist Marcus Vitruvius Pollio (46–30 B.C.), whose *Ten Books on Architecture* remains one of the most important works ever written on the subject.

Roman architects copied the true arch, using voussior stones, from Etruscan buildings in the north. The arch and its expanded variants were crucial to the prodigious achievements of Roman architects. Extend an arch in a single direction and the result is a barrel vault; a barrel vault intersected by another barrel vault is a groin vault; an arch rotated through 180° becomes a dome. These structural elements are very common in Roman buildings.

The Italian peninsula provided a variety of building materials, including travertine, tufa, peperino, lava, and marble, as well as sand and gravel. The latter were basic to the Roman invention of concrete, which allowed them to create unprecedented new building forms. Sand mixed with lime and water became very hard and, when shaped by wooden forms, liberated Roman architecture from the limitations of post-and-lintel structures.

Forums   The evolution of Roman forums reflects changes in Roman governance. When Rome became a republic in about 500 B.C., nominally governed by elected representatives, Roman architects adapted the Greek agora for their forums. The Roman Forum in the heart of the city of Rome is the most important of its kind, and its ruins today give a sense of its scope.

As the empire grew through conquest and political power passed from the people to the emperor, later forums were constructed more to impress the populace with the majesty of the emperor than as democratic meeting places. Adjacent to the Roman Forum are the more impressive imperial forums of the Emperors Vespian, Augustus, and Trajan.

Temples   Roman temples began by imitating the Greek peristyle, but with columns that engaged the *cella* instead of standing free. Roman architects freely used the Doric, Ionic, and Corinthian orders, even mixing them on the same building. To the three Greek orders, Roman architects added the Tuscan and Composite orders. Tuscan columns had a plain capital similar to Doric, but were not fluted. Composite capitals blended Ionic volutes with Corinthian acanthus leaves.

The Romans were not bound by past examples, however, and created new architectural forms for worship. The Pantheon in Rome is a round structure with a portico and crowned by a magnificent dome that is just over 142 feet across and 142 feet high. The rotunda was constructed in A.D. 120–127 and, though the building has undergone changes over the years, it is in good condition and preserves the impressive feeling of the great space under the dome.

Baths   The Romans were fond of bathing, and public baths were important elements of civic architecture throughout the empire. Some were enormous and architecturally complex. The buildings enclosed three main rooms visited sequentially by the bathers—the warm room (Tepidarium), the hot room (Calidarium), and the cool room (Frigidarium). Wide barrel-vaulted ceilings covered many of the rooms, and beneath the floor were systems of ducts that brought hot air from nearby furnaces to heat the rooms.

Theaters and Amphitheaters   Other places of diversions for citizens of the Roman Empire were theaters and amphitheaters. Roman theaters were similar to Greek theaters except for the decreased size of the orchestra between the auditorium and the stage. Roman builders also built free-standing theaters instead of carving them out of convenient hills, as with the Theater of Marcellus in Rome, built in 23–13 B.C.

The amphitheater, either round or oval, with seating surrounding the arena, was a Roman invention. The Colosseum in Rome, completed in A.D. 80, seated 50,000 spectators and is a structure of great complexity, including stairs and aisles to the seats, and a labyrinthine system of rooms and passages under the arena for animals, workers, and machinery.

Aqueducts and Bridges   Roman engineers understood hydrodynamics and built large arched aqueducts to carry water across rivers and ravines to large cities throughout their empire. The Aqua Claudio aqueduct (A.D. 38–52) serving Rome is a well-preserved example, as are the Pont du Garde (ca. 19 B.C.) in Nimes, France, and the Segovia aqueduct (ca. A.D. 100) in Spain, in use until the late 19th century. Roman bridges were arched structures similar to aqueducts.

Basilicas   Adjacent to most forums were basilicas, which contained law courts and commercial activities. Basilicas were often rectangular, with the length twice as long as the width, and featured a central nave, two or four lower side aisles, and a circular apse at one or both ends with seating and an altar for sacrifices before ceremonies. Two rows of columns supported the nave ceiling in the four-aisle model, two more rows of columns supported the two-aisle ceiling. Often clerestory windows in the nave walls above the aisles admitted light into the interior. The ceilings were either timber trusses or barrel vaults.

Early Christian and Byzantine Architecture

In the centuries following the death of Jesus of Nazareth the fabric of the Roman Empire began to weaken. As the populace began to convert to Christianity, they needed new places of public worship.

Basilican Churches   In contrast to Greek and Roman temples that enclosed statues of the deities while worshipers gathered outside, Christians brought worshipers indoors. For this they developed the rectangular basilican church, a building creatively adapted from the Roman model.

Romans entered basilicas on the long side, but Christians entered their churches through an atrium, an open colonnaded court at the end. Crossing the atrium, worshipers entered the church proper through a narthex vestibule, into a central nave covered by a timber roof where they heard the services. At the far end was a half-domed apse derived from the Roman apse. In front of the apse was an ambo, or pulpit, for Bible reading and services. Early churches were oriented with the apse facing west while the priest faced east toward the congregation. The basilican church became the basis for Christian churches for centuries thereafter.

Byzantine Architecture   In A.D. 330, the Christian emperor Constantine I moved the capital of the empire to

Byzantium (later called Constantinople, now Istanbul), on the Bosporus Strait. Byzantium offered no good building stones, which forced builders to import marble and other fine stones; it also fostered the use of concrete, which made possible bold new interior spaces.

Byzantine architects found a new expression for Christian worship beyond the rectangular early Christian churches. Borrowing the western Asian dome, they created interiors of soaring spaces. They solved the problem of placing a circular dome over a square space by inventing the pendentive, a triangular piece in the corners to provide the transition between the square and the dome. The outward thrust of the dome was transferred to half-domes at the sides, or to buttresses. Inside, the architects enhanced the effect of the space with glittering mosaics. The supreme example of Byzantine ecclesiastical design is Hagia Sophia, the Church of the Holy Wisdom, in Constantinople; it was designed by the architects Anthemios of Tralles and Isidoros of Miletus, and built in 532–537.

Romanesque Architecture

After the fall of Rome in A.D. 476, the early Christian basilican church underwent gradual changes. Eventually this gave rise to a new form, called Romanesque, that spread rapidly beginning in the 11th century. There was no pure form of Romanesque; each country's culture, available building materials, and climate shaped its version of the Romanesque church.

Italy The spatial organization of Italian Romanesque churches is different from early Christian churches, though they continue a basic basilican plan. The atrium is abandoned in favor of a decorative treatment of the western façade leading directly to the narthex. The transept, an intersecting structure at 90° to the axis of the nave, forms a Latin cross with the nave; the chancel is extended beyond the transept, with the apse terminating the central interior space in the east. Rounded arches and wood-trussed ceilings are carried over from early Christian churches, but barrel vaults now frequently replace timber ceilings. Towers are added either attached or separate from the church.

Italian Romanesque churches, with the availability of fine stones such as marble, were often faced in contrasting colorful marbles and had small windows to filter the bright sunlight. A striking example is Pisa Cathedral, built in 1063–1092. The exterior is faced with alternating bands of red and white marble, and the west façade is enlivened with rows of arcades.

France In the south, French Romanesque churches often had only a nave with no aisles, while in the north there were aisles and a nave. Windows were narrow, especially in the sunny south. Saint Sernin in Toulouse, built in 1080–96, is a well-preserved example of southern French Romanesque; the Abbaye-aux-Hommes in Caen, also known as Saint Etienne, built in 1066–77, is a splendid example of northern Romanesque.

Germany German Romanesque churches differ from Italian and French by including more towers, transepts, and apses at both east and west ends. Windows are larger and roofs steeper to shed winter snow. The availability of suitable stone varied with region and resulted in stone construction in some places and brick in others. A fine example of German Romanesque is Worms Cathedral, built in 1110–81.

Gothic Architecture

In the 12th century, political and religious competition played a major role in the development of a new kind of architecture that came to be called Gothic. While Gothic builders produced many important halls and castles, their supreme achievement was in the equipoise of the elements of architecture—purpose, design, and structure—in Gothic cathedrals.

France Gothic architecture began in France. The kings of France sought to consolidate their power over the monasteries that owed their allegiance to the pope, and they wanted an architectural expression different from the Romanesque monasteries. Just north of Paris, Abbé Suger responded by creating the first Gothic choir at Saint-Denis, begun in 1144.

Three structural elements are at the heart of Gothic cathedrals: the pointed arch, the ribbed vault, and the flying buttress. Gothic builders created an entirely new ecclesiastical expression with these structural elements. Walls, freed from having to support heavy vaults, could be much lighter and pierced by large clerestory windows that could rise to the vaults themselves. The ribbed vaulting and flying buttresses allowed the height of the nave to be built higher and higher. The exteriors of Gothic cathedrals were carved in a delicate profusion of statues, windows, and arcades that often combined with towers on the western end to give a sense of verticality to the whole.

The unique power of the Gothic cathedrals, however, was the result both of their structure and of the interior that the structure created. The great height of the naves, with the pointed vaults and clerestory windows, drew the eyes of worshipers upward toward heaven. Multicolored light filtering through the stained glass windows created a feeling of reverence that was enhanced by the biblical scenes in the windows that served to instruct worshipers.

The choir at Saint-Denis was almost immediately emulated as cities in the Île-de-France, the area surrounding Paris, competed to erect higher and more elegant Gothic cathedrals. First was Chartres (1140–1260), followed by Notre Dame in Paris (1163–1235), Rheims (1212–1300), Amiens (1220–1280), and others.

Germany   French Gothic soon spread across Europe, and in Germany this often took the form of the "hall church," in which the aisles were the same height as the nave. The Frauenkirche in Nuremberg (1354–61) is an example, as is Cologne cathedral (1248–1880).

Spain   Spain enthusiastically embraced Gothic architecture. The result was a number of fine cathedrals and churches in major cities, including Toledo (1226–1493), Burgos (1220–1500), and Seville (1401–1520)—the largest medieval cathedral in Europe.

Italy   With a few exceptions, Italy seemed inhibited by its classical heritage and never caught the spirit of French Gothic, beyond employing pointed vaulting and windows. For example, Siena cathedral (1245–1380), with its thick walls without flying buttresses, lacks the Gothic verticality found elsewhere in Europe. Milan cathedral (1385–1485) in the north (closer to the influence of France and Germany) is a notable exception, with its delicate pinnacles, flying buttresses, and high stained glass windows.

England   After the Norman conquest in 1066, England began importing ideas, words, and architecture from France. The first Gothic cathedral was erected at Canterbury (1174–1400), designed initially by William of Sens (d. ca. 1180) from France. Many Gothic cathedrals and churches followed, among which are Salisbury (1220–58), Westminster Abbey in London (1245–1740), and York Minster (1261–1324). With their lower vaults, extended choirs, and square apses, English Gothic cathedrals have their own character in the canon of Gothic architecture.

Renaissance Architecture

In the late Middle Ages, scholars began to rediscover the classical writings of ancient philosophers and scientists, and there was a growing humanistic rejection of the medieval world, including Gothic architecture. Architects, now considered artists rather than simply master builders like their medieval predecessors, became individually identified with their buildings; many drew inspiration from the classical models of Greece and Rome, and included rounded arches in their designs.

Italy   The problem facing Renaissance architects was to adapt classical models to buildings that did not exist in ancient times. A competition held in 1418 to design a dome to complete the cathedral of Florence that had been begun in 1296 during the Gothic era was won by Filippo Brunelleschi (1377–1446). His design is a masterpiece of blending a Renaissance dome with an Italian Gothic cathedral.

In Rome, St. Peter's Church was begun in 1506 by Donato Bramante (1444–1514). After his death, a succession of architects changed the design several times until Michelangelo Buonarroti (1475–1564) was brought in at the age of 72 to redesign the structure, including the dome.

The Renaissance architect with the longest-lasting influence was Andrea Palladio (1508–1580), who worked in Venice and Vicenza. A number of his villas, including the Villa Capra (1560's)—also known as the Rotonda— set the design for centuries of domestic and public architecture. His influence was also spread by his *Four Books on Architecture*, a theoretical work of idealized buildings that ranks among the most important written works about architecture. In it he implicitly rejected the Gothic style while paying tribute to the Romans—who, he said, "in building well, vastly excelled all those who have [lived] since their time."

France   In France Italian Renaissance architecture became the model for a number of châteaux and palaces, including the Palais de Fountainebleau (1528), designed by Gilles Le Breton (1506?–58). But the transition from Gothic was not always smooth; Saint Eustache in Paris (1532–89), begun as a Gothic church, was finished in Renaissance details, including round arches.

Germany Renaissance architecture came slowly to Germany and had a limited impact there. Heidelberg Castle (1513–1612) had many additions over time that reflect different periods of German Renaissance architecture. Political and religious turmoil in Germany inhibited the building of significant new churches during the 16th and 17th centuries, limiting the influence of the Renaissance style.

Spain Spain's wealth and power rose to its zenith during the Renaissance, and its architects had ample opportunities for major works. King Philip II built the imposing palace of San Lorenzo de El Escorial (1559–84) near Madrid, begun by Juan Bautista de Toledo (?–1567) and finished by Juan de Herrera (1530?–97). Granada cathedral (1529), designed by Diego de Siloe (1495?–1563), is a fine example of a Spanish Renaissance church.

England Renaissance architecture came last to England, and was practiced while the Continent was entering the Baroque period. Inigo Jones (1573–1652) studied in Italy, especially Palladio's buildings, and his subsequent work strongly influenced English Renaissance design. Jones's Banqueting House in London (1619–21) is a famous example of his work. The Great London fire of 1666 provided Christopher Wren (1632–1723) the opportunity to design many parish churches of ingeniously differing designs, as well as Saint Paul's Cathedral (1675–1710), with its monumental western façade, splendid dome, and barrel-vaulted interior.

Baroque Architecture

The term *Baroque* (possibly from the Portuguese word *barroco*, an irregularly shaped pearl) was originally used to mean grotesque, excessive, or bizarre. Baroque architecture created palaces and churches characterized by elaborate and often fanciful decorative elements.

Churches The great Baroque Catholic churches were designed and built after the Counter-Reformation. Giovanni Lorenzo Bernini (1598–1680), one of the great Baroque architects, asserted that churches should "reach out to Catholics in order to reaffirm their faith, to heretics to reunite them with the church, and to agnostics to enlighten them with the true faith." Bernini is best known for the magnificent colonnade (1629–62) that forms the piazza in front of the entrance façade of Saint Peter's.

Baroque architects manipulated interior spaces to be more plastic and flowing than ordered Renaissance spaces. Using stucco, an inexpensive and infinitely malleable material, they created free-flowing surfaces and elaborate decorations that would have been too expensive to carve in marble and other fine stonework.

Francesco Boromini (1599–1667) was one of the most daring in manipulating spaces. His church of San Carlo alle Quattro Fontane (1638–41) in Rome, with its oval plan, curvilinear walls, and dome that flows up from the walls, is a superb example of Baroque architecture.

Palaces and Gardens French Baroque architecture was expressed most characteristically in palaces and their associated gardens. Until the late 17th century, the Louvre in Paris was the king's official residence, and successive kings enlarged it, joined it to the Tuileries palace, and extended an elaborately planned garden, designed by André Le Notre (1613–1700), along the banks of the Seine. The buildings themselves were restrained and classic—hardly the Baroque of Italian churches—but their relationship to the extended garden created a new sense of transition between the city and the palace.

When King Louis XIV decided to move his main residence to Versailles in 1677, he greatly enlarged the existing palace into the largest in Europe. He also commissioned Le Notre to lay out the gardens. The palace and gardens, with their enormous scope and subtle symmetry, became the model for palaces throughout Europe, such as the Hermitage and other palaces along the Neva River in Peter the Great's new Russian capital of St. Petersburg.

The Baroque was succeeded by the Rococo style, even more refined and decorative and often incorporating chinoiserie and other exotic elements. A noted example is Frederick the Great's summer palace, Sans-Souci (1745–47), at Potsdam.

18th- and 19th-Century Architecture

The Age of Enlightenment—led by philosophers and scientists who relied on the power of reason to challenge accepted values and beliefs—had a profound and lasting impact on architecture. No longer were architects and their patrons certain about the immutable models of the Greek, Roman, Gothic, or Baroque builders. Architects of the Enlightenment created a welter of movements, revival styles, and schools that vied with one another for supremacy.

One such movement was neoclassicism, which stripped excess ornament from Baroque forms to reveal their basic geometry. A related movement in Great

Britain was the 18th-century Georgian style of domestic architecture, championed by the brothers James Adam (1728–92) and Robert Adam (1730–94); notable examples are the terraced houses at Bath and the New Town district of Edinburgh. The first half of the 19th century also saw a Gothic revival, such as the English Houses of Parliament (1835–70) by Charles Barry (1795–1860) and Augustus Welby Northmore Pugin (1812–52). In Germany the Gothic revival resulted in the scrupulous completion of Cologne cathedral in the 19th century from medieval designs.

Classicism was not dead during this period, but it took new forms. An important impetus to rethinking classicism was the École des Beaux-Arts in Paris, formed after the French revolution in 1789; it taught that classical forms could be adapted to new kinds of buildings, such as bridges and office buildings. Its students, who came from a number of countries, returned home to produce new buildings in the classical manner. Examples are found virtually everywhere in Europe.

Technology   Until the 19th century, most large buildings were constructed of stone, masonry, and wood. The Industrial Revolution yielded two new materials of great importance to architects: inexpensive iron, and glass produced on a large scale. When iron became cheaper than masonry, some 19th-century architects recognized its expressive potential. For example, Pierre-François-Henri Labrouste (1801–75) designed the library of Sainte-Geneviève (1838–50) and the Bibliothèque Nationale (1854–75) in Paris using classical Roman forms, but with iron construction and ample glass fenestration.

Probably the most striking iron and glass building of its time was the Crystal Palace in London, designed by Joseph Paxton (1803–65) for the Great Exhibition of 1851. Assembled entirely of cast iron members, standard sheets of glass, and wooden supports, the transparent building showed the world that new kinds of architectural experiences were possible using industrial technology.

The Skyscraper   As land prices rose steadily in the heart of rapidly growing cities, there was a need to make maximum use of a given lot. The answer was to build vertically, and the industrial age had provided the means: the development of steel as a construction material, and the invention of the elevator.

The type of building that became known as the skyscraper was born in Chicago, where two visionary architects grappled with the aesthetics of tall building design. William Le Baron Jenney (1832–1907) and Louis Henri Sullivan (1856–1924) pushed their buildings up to new heights and clothed them in ways that plainly celebrated their verticality. Sullivan's Wainright Building in St. Louis (1890–91) epitomizes his famous statement that a tall building "must be every inch a proud and soaring thing." The maxim that "form follows function"—that is, the look of a building must be subordinate to its purpose—is also attributed to Sullivan, and was later taken up by 20th-century architects.

Modern Architecture

Architecture at the dawn of the 20th century underwent a seismic change as significant as any in its history. An American architect and a small group of European architects broke free from historical models and created a new architecture called "modern." This new architecture was enabled by a new material, reinforced concrete, that combined the compressive strength of concrete with the tensile strength of steel and could be shaped into structures that were previously impossible.

Frank Lloyd Wright   A seminal modern architect, Frank Lloyd Wright (1867–1959) paradoxically influenced but stood apart from nearly all of his modernist contemporaries. After serving an apprenticeship with Louis Sullivan, Wright opened his own office in 1893 and began designing houses in the Chicago suburbs. By the early 1900's, he had developed his distinctive Prairie houses with their open plans arranged around large central fireplaces, and hovering hipped roofs parallel to the ground. The Robie House (1906–10) in Chicago is a masterpiece of Prairie design. Wright also produced two major large works that had a lasting impact on European architects, Unity Temple (1904) in the suburb of Oak Park, and the Larkin Company Administration Building (1903–06, demolished) in Buffalo.

Some of Wright's greatest works, which were at odds with orthodox modernism, came after he turned 60 years old. In the 1930's he surprised the architectural world with Fallingwater (1936–38), a country residence in western Pennsylvania with cantilevered reinforced concrete terraces built over a stream, as well as the curvilinear brick Johnson Wax Building (1936–37) in Racine, Wisconsin. His Solomon R. Guggenheim Museum (1956–59) in New York City, with its spiral exhibition ramp, is a major work realized in his last years.

But Wright's Usonian houses, designed in the 1930's to be affordable to middle-class owners, were perhaps his most important achievement. The Herbert Jacobs House (1936) in Madison, Wisconsin, was an early example of his method of conserving of space by allowing the living room-dining room-kitchen to flow into one another without walls. Countless tract homes, including the post-World War II Levittowns, later mirrored his conservation of interior space.

Early European Modernists

In 1910–11 the German publisher Wasmuth brought out two illustrated volumes of Wright's work that caught the imagination of his European contemporaries. European architects quickly grasped the spirit of Wright's rejection of historical models, his free flow of interior spaces, and the beauty of the sensitively proportioned plain exterior surfaces.

Five significant European architects developed a functional approach to design, using modern materials primarily in large commercial buildings: Peter Behrens (1868–1940), who designed a notable turbine factory in Berlin (1908–09); Otto Wagner (1841–1918), who designed Vienna's Post Office Savings Bank (1904–06); Adolf Loos (1878–1933), who designed Vienna's starkly geometric Steiner House (1910); Hendrik Petrus Berlage (1856–1934), who designed the Amsterdam Stock Exchange (1898–1903); and Auguste Perret (1874–1954), who designed the church of Notre Dame in Le Raincy (1922–24).

Bauhaus and the International Style

One of Peter Behrens's young assistants, Georg Walter Adolf Gropius (1883–1969), went on to surpass his mentor in his contribution to modern architecture. His major influence began in 1919, when he founded the Bauhaus in Weimar, Germany, a school that combined craftsmanship with design and brought together artisans, painters, sculptors, and architects.

In 1926 Gropius moved the Bauhaus to Dessau, into a radical new building complex he had designed that was laid out on a pinwheel plan and constructed of concrete, steel, and glass. It became an icon of what came to be called the International Style. The interconnecting buildings were designed to foster the interaction of designers and craftspeople to create mass-produced furniture, utilitarian household objects, and low-cost housing. The ideal of inexpensive mass-produced items was never achieved, but some Bauhaus designs, especially furniture, have ironically become widely sold as luxury items.

The last director of the Bauhaus (appointed in 1930) was Ludwig Mies van der Rohe (1886–1969), born Ludwig Mies. Mies's stature does not rest on his association with the Bauhaus, however, but with his many buildings based on an intense study of new building materials, their aesthetic potential, and the plasticity of architectural space. He developed his ideas in a series of houses built over a 10-year period, culminating in the Tugendhat House (1928–1930) in Brno, Czech Republic. The house stands on a sloping site, constructed of concrete and steel, with carefully defined interpenetrating living spaces, and a glass wall facing the view, part of which retracted to open the interior to the air.

In 1938 Mies became director of the architectural department at Illinois Institute of Technology. There he tested his ideas on the simplification of architectural elements that he summed up in his famous phrase, "less is more." The design idiom he developed at IIT and in later buildings, particularly his bronze Seagram Building (1954–58) on Park Avenue in New York City, influenced building design in hundreds of cities in America and Europe.

Le Corbusier

Born Charles-Edouard Jeanneret-Gris, Le Corbusier (1887–1965) traveled widely and met many early modern architects. He sought to reconcile his deeply felt responses to their work with the historical works he studied in his travels, particularly Greek temples.

In the 1920's, Le Corbusier found a vocabulary for domestic architecture that resulted in one of the great works of modern architecture, the Villa Savoye in Poissy, France (1928–30). Standing alone in a field, the pristine white house is supported on pilotis, slender concrete columns that carry the load of the floors and free the interior to be developed into flowing horizontal and vertical spaces. In a seminal book, *Towards a New Architecture* (1923), he delivered his notorious dictum, "The house is a machine for living in," but his houses were elegant, with hints of classicism, and far from machinelike.

The New Modernists

Classicism and historicism slowly lost the struggle with modernism, and the International Style became synonymous with it. After World War II, modern architecture—broadly defined—was the new orthodoxy.

Building on the works of the old masters, a new generation of architects found a wide range of expression within the modern idiom. These architects include Finnish Hugo Alvar Hendrik Aalto (1898–1976), who began in a strict International Style but later softened his work, as demonstrated by the Baker House dormitory (1947–49) at the Massachusetts Institute of Technology; Eero Saarinen (1910–61), who moved creatively between International Style-inspired designs such as the elegant rectilinear General Motors Technical Center (1948–56) in Warren, Michigan, and the sculptural, birdlike concrete TWA Terminal (1956–62) at Kennedy Airport in New York; Philip Cortelyou Johnson (1906–2005), who worked with Mies on the Seagram Building and established his own modernist credentials with the Glass House (1949) in New Canaan, Connecticut; Minoru Yamasaki (1912–86), who is best known for the twin towers of New York's World Trade Center (1966–73, destroyed); and I.M. Pei (b. 1917), born in China, who practiced in America and found new expressive forms in modernism.

Probably the purest of the new modernists is Richard Alan Meier (b. 1934). Early in his career he established a vocabulary of impeccably white buildings, composed mostly of abstract rectilinear forms, like the Smith House (1965) on Long Island, New York. His Getty Center complex (1989–97) in Los Angeles is the latter-day International Style writ large in a major work.

Beyond Modern Architecture

If modernism, and especially the International Style, had become an orthodoxy following World War II, it was never universally accepted. Though widely practiced in commercial and public buildings, modernism had never caught on in domestic building. Only a few, and usually wealthy, clients could both afford and want to live in the iconic concrete, steel, and glass houses epitomized by Le Corbusier's Villa Savoye. Frank Lloyd Wright, alone among the early giants of modern architecture, continued to produce his Usonian houses for less affluent clients.

Postmodernism   By the 1960's the sense that something important in modernism was missing was captured by Robert Venturi (b. 1925) in his highly influential book, *Complexity and Contradiction in Architecture* (1966). His argument is suggested in his criticism of the aesthetic purity of late modernism: "Less is a bore." Lacking, he said, were elements of the ambiguity found in much of historical building, and this lack risked "separating architecture from the experience of life and the needs of society." His book, together with his designs—including his early Guild House

(1960–63) in Philadelphia and the Vanna Venturi House (1963) in Chestnut Hill, Pennsylvania—were a catalyst for the movement that came to be called postmodern.

Postmodernism is characterized by often outsized fragments of historical orders (such as arches, broken pediments, and keystones) and other incongruous elements appearing on otherwise plain buildings, creating the kind of complexity and contradiction Venturi admired. Good examples of Postmodernism include Philip Johnson's AT&T building (1979) in New York City, with its Chippendale top above a traditional skyscraper design, and Michael Graves's (b. 1934) Team Disney Corporate Headquarters (1986) in Burbank, California, with Disney's Seven Dwarfs serving as enormous caryatids on the entrance façade.

Skyscrapers   The skyscraper continued to evolve during the 20th century, mostly in America, but not in the radical new International Style. Many American architects adopted the Art Deco style—an eclectic combination of Egyptian, Aztec, and other exotic elements—to decorate tall buildings. The Chrysler Building (1928–30) by William van Alen (1882–1954) and the Empire State Building (1930–31) by the firm of Shreve, Lamb & Harmon, both in New York, are conspicuous examples. Rockefeller Center (1929–39) in New York is an arrangement of slablike buildings in restrained Art Deco, designed by a group of leading architects and laid out in a superb urban plan.

In the late 20th century, skyscrapers became a form of competition between nations. The race was on to build the tallest building. Since then a succession of countries have announced the construction of new skyscrapers taller than the last announced building. Though these buildings featured designs that distinguished one from another, height was the predominant element, not bold new designs.

At the same time, other clients hired forward-thinking architects to recosider what a tall building might be. The rise of Hong Kong as a world financial and commercial center provided architects wide latitude to experiment. Among the most creative of their buildings is the Hong Kong and Shanghai Bank Headquarters (1986) by the architect Norman Foster. The interior space is free of any supporting structure but wears its supports on the outside like an exoskeleton. Its unobstructed views of the harbor give it the advantage of good *feng shui*, a traditional design system that includes the belief that enterprises with a direct view of water will prosper.

The DZ Bank Headquarters in Frankfurt am Main (1993) by the firm of Kohn Pedersen Fox Associates is an example of a tall building that is distinctive, but also exceptionally sensitive to its surroundings. Set on a main street along which the city planned a grouping of tall buildings intended to suggest the city's prosperity and to attract tourists, the building subtly reflects nearby office towers with its divisions and breaks. A cantilevered crown at the top identifies it at a distance without overshadowing its partners along the street.

A more recent tall building that is distinctive for its design rather than height is the Central Chinese Television Tower (CCTV) in Beijing (a fire in a nearby building delayed construction and its opening date is uncertain) by OMA, the firm founded by Rem Koolhaas and his colleagues in 1975. The architects avoided what they call "the exhausted typology of the skyscraper" in a "hopeless race for the ultimate height and style." Instead, the building is a folded loop of intersecting structures designed to include production, broadcasting, and administration. The spaces flow into each other and are meant to encourage chance encounters among the workers and the resulting collaboration that is vital to a creative medium.

Architects as Stars Throughout most of history, with a few notable exceptions, architects have labored anonymously. It wasn't until the Renaissance that architects were recognized as true artists to be identified with the buildings they designed. But well into the 20th century very few architects or their buildings were known outside of a comparatively small group of connoisseurs, clients, historians, and architects themselves. About mid-20th century that began to change.

For the first time, commercial developers began to construct buildings that were promoted as being designed by "celebrity architects." Living in an apartment tower or condominium designed by a star architect brought a special cachet. An early example is the 860-880 Lake Shore Drive twin-tower apartments in Chicago (1949) designed by Mies van der Rohe in glass and steel that advertised its world-renowned architect. Though financing was difficult at first, these unconventional buildings have become trademarks of Meis's work and were designated a Chicago Landmark in 1996 and placed on the National Register of Historic Places in 1980. A new way of identifying star architects was created in 1979 that helped to spread their fame: The Pritzker Architecture Prize. Awarded annually to a living architect, or architects, the award was established by the Pritzker family of Chicago and was modeled on the Nobel Prizes. The intention was to create a greater public awareness of buildings and to stimulate greater creativity among architects. The prize has become the ultimate accolade an architect can receive. Now developers or builders can chose among a list of laureates and know that they can't go wrong if they choose one from the list. In New York there are now apartment and condominium buildings advertised as being designed by Richard Meier and Frank Gehry, whose names now have commercial value in the real estate market.

Non-Western Architecture

The non-Western world includes a number of architectural traditions that developed largely independently of one another and, until recent times, of European influence. Major religions, particularly Buddhism and Islam, created distinctive architectural styles that transcend national boundaries.

East Asian Architecture

Beginning in the second millennium B.C., China developed a distinctive form of architecture for palaces and other signficant structures. A raised platform was constructed of compacted earth, on which wooden pillars were erected to support a bracket-work roof shingled with tile. The spaces between the pillars were filled in with brick, stucco, or other materials, but the entire load of the building was carried by its pillars. Palaces and temples built in this style were generally laid out on a north-south axis, with doorways facing southward.

The Forbidden City, a palace complex in the center of Beijing, is the best-preserved group of ancient buildings in China. The great beauty of the individual buildings, the relationship of the buildings to one another, the open spaces between them, and the subtle changes in level both outside and inside the buildings, create one of the greatest of all architectural complexes. It was built during the Ming period (1368–1644), although most existing buildings were built or reconstructed early in the Qing period (1644–1911).

Chinese-style pillar-and-bracket architecture reached

Japan in the sixth century, with the spread of Buddhism to Japan via Korea. The world's oldest surviving wooden buildings (seventh century), at the Horyuji near Nara, exemplify this style. The Phoenix Hall of the Fujiwara family mansion at Uji is the world's only surviving example of a palace in Tang Dynasty (618–907) Chinese style.

Architecture in the Chinese style coexisted in Japan with an older native style, in which rectangular buildings, often with thatched roofs, are raised above ground level on stiltlike pillars; this style survives principally in Shinto shrines. The characteristic Japanese wooden house, with straw-mat floors and internal dividing walls of paper, is a late development, dating from the 14th century. The 17th-century Imperial Villa at Katsura, near Kyoto, is regarded as the epitome of Japanese domestic architecture.

Japan's military heritage is expressed in castle architecture. Rising above the modern city of Himeji is the handsome Shirasagijo (Castle of the White Heron), a fortress built, and rebuilt, from 1333 to 1618. Several moats protect the outer perimeter, while narrow and twisting alleys—exposing invaders to fire from above—lead to the heart of the complex. The Daitenshu (Main Tower) has five exterior levels but seven stories in the interior.

South Asian Architecture

South Asian architecture began with the great Indus Valley cities such as Harappa and Mohenjo-Daro (2500–1500 B.C.). The evolution of religious belief and associated cultural expression, from ancient and elite Brahmanism to later and more popular Hinduism, gave rise to numerous local forms of Hindu temples devoted to various gods; these characteristically were built from stone or brick and had a tall tower above the main entrance gate. In many parts of India, temples, complete with pillars supporting interior ceilings, have been hewn from solid stone; well-known examples (seventh century) are at Mahabalipuram, in the southeastern Indian state of Tamil Nadu.

As Hinduism spread to Southeast Asia from India, it led to the creation of many monumental works of architecture, such as the temple at Prambanan (ca. 900), in central Java, Indonesia. The finest architectural expression of Hinduism in Southeast Asia is the Temple of Angkor Wat in what is now Cambodia. Constructed of sandstone by King Suryavarman II from 1113 to 1150, though not completed during his reign, Angkor Wat was dedicated to the Hindu god Vishnu and its central stepped pyramid represented the cosmic mountain Meru. In the 15th century, Angkor fell to invaders and its temples were abandoned.

The coming of Islam to South Asia, and especially the establishment of the Moghul Dynasty in 1526, added an overlay of international Islamic architecture to the older indigenous forms. (See "Islamic Architecture.")

Buddhist Architecture

Buddhist architecture originated in South Asia, but developed largely outside the Indian peninsula. Its basic form is the stupa, originally a domed temple topped by a narrow spire; this underwent many transformations as Buddhism spread throughout central, eastern, and southeastern Asia.

The domed stupa is substantially preserved in Buddhist architecture in Southeast Asia, for example the bell-shaped shrines atop the mandala-mountain of Borobudur (central Java, Indonesia, ca. 800). The most spectacular example is the great bell-shaped dome, covered with tons of gold leaf, of Shwe Dagon Temple, on a hilltop in the city of Yan'gon (formerly Rangoon), capital of Myanmar (formerly Burma).

In Central Asia and East Asia, the dome of the stupa shrank, and the spire became enlarged, producing the characteristic building known as a pagoda. The Chinese city of Xi'an, once the eastern terminus of the Silk Road, is home to the Great Wild Goose Pagoda. Originally constructed during the Tang Dynasty in A.D. 652 as a square, five-storied pagoda, it was later rebuilt to seven stories. It is 240 feet tall, constructed of brick, and was built to house Buddhist *sutras* (scriptures) brought from India by the monk Xuanzang.

Islamic Architecture

The characteristic Islamic building is the mosque, designed to enclose a large space to hold large numbers of people for communal prayers. The usual design, inherited from Byzantine church architecture, is a square building surmounted by a dome. A mihrab (arched niche) indicates the direction of Mecca, toward which worshipers face while praying. Adjacent to the mosque may be a minaret, a tall tower from which the call to prayer is chanted five times daily. Mosques of this basic design (but with local variations of style) followed the spread of Islam across North Africa to Spain, and across Asia to India, China, Indonesia, and beyond.

The first major surviving Islamic building is the Qubbat al-Sakhra (Dome of the Rock) in Jerusalem. It was originally built by the caliph Abd al-Malik in A.D. 692. Octagonal in shape and surmounted by a dome, it is a transitional building between contemporaneous

Byzantine architecture and later pure forms of Islamic architecture, and was partly modeled on the Holy Sepulchre in Jerusalem (328–336) built by Emperor Constantine I.

After the fall of Constantinople to the Ottoman Turks in 1453, many important Islamic buildings were built in what is now Istanbul, including the Süleymaniye Mosque (1550–57). Commissioned by the sultan Süleyman I (ca. 1494–1566), the mosque was designed by the court architect Sinan (1489–1578), and is a part of a complex that included theological colleges, schools, a hospital, an alms-kitchen, a bath, and the tombs of its founder and his wife. It is a masterpiece of design, engineering, and construction, and the account books that have survived make it the best documented of the great Ottoman buildings.

In India, the Jami' Masjid (Friday Mosque) in Old Delhi is the largest of the many mosques that were built by its Mughal emperors after successive Islamic invasions and migrations. The emperor Shah Jahan (1592–1666), who also built the Taj Mahal, supervised the construction from 1650–56 and regularly attended Friday prayers there during his reign. It can accommodate more than 20,000 worshippers for communal prayers. Also in India, at the center of the city of Jaipur, is the City Palace (1727), which combines elements of Mughal and traditional Rajasthan architecture. It is constructed of pink-colored sandstone and matches the rest of the central buildings in this "pink city." Today the Chandra Mahal (Moon Palace) in the City Palace is still the residence of the Maharaja of Jaipur.

African Architecture

The meaning of the word *zimbabwe* has changed over the years, but came to be used to designate the "ruler's court" or "house"; the largest of all was Great Zimbabwe in what is now the country of Zimbabwe. Though settled by A.D. 500, the great stone walls and mud buildings for which the site is best known were built in the 14th and 15th centuries, and had an estimated population of over 10,000. Scholars believe the stone walls were not for defense but were symbols of the ruler's power. Beginning in the 15th century Great Zimbabwe declined and was eventually abandoned.

In Ghana the remaining Ashanti (or Asanti) traditional buildings are the last examples of the once great Ashanti civilization. The Ashanti reached their height in the 18th century and in the 19th century fought the British colonizers in battles that largely destroyed their villages.

Made of earth, wood and straw, the remaining buildings near the city of Kumasi are vulnerable to the elements.

Indigenous American Architecture

At its height in the sixth century A.D., the city of Teotihuacán, near present-day Mexico City, had an estimated population of 200,000 and was the sixth most populous city in the world. It was laid out on a grand scale along the north-south Avenue of the Dead with the Pyramid of the Moon at the north end and the Temple of Quetzalcóatl at the south end. East of the Avenue of the Dead, and just north of the intersection of the East and West Avenues, is the largest structure, the Pyramid of the Sun, which faces west toward the setting sun. The city collapsed in the seventh or eighth century and its population apparently dispersed.

The city of Uxmal in northern Yucatán, Mexico, is considered by many scholars to be the finest work of Mayan architecture. It is in the Puuk region and flourished from about A.D. 800 to 1000. The conquering Spanish gave its buildings names that do not correspond to their use in Mayan times. Notable among these are the Pyramid of the Magician, the Nunnery, and the Governor's Palace. The complex was laid out to emphasize sight lines between the buildings and to align with astronomical phenomena, including the setting sun on the summer solstice. The Mayans abandoned the site following the Spanish conquest in the 16th century.

Set in a spectacular site in the southern mountains of Peru, Machu Picchu was built by the Incas in the 14th and 15th centuries. Scholars differ on the exact purpose of the site, but its size and the sophistication of its construction indicate its importance in Inca civilization. The inhabitants were supported by agriculture on a series of terraces irrigated by an intricate system of channels and canals to direct rainwater to the fields. After the Spanish conquest in the 16th century the city was abandoned, but was rediscovered and excavated in the 20th century.

In southwestern Colorado, most of the cliff dwellings at Mesa Verde were built by the Anasazi ("ancient enemies") culture from A.D. 1230 to 1240, though they had been living in the area for 500 to 1000 years. They built multiroomed living structures in the eroded cliff sides below a mesa and cultivated the land on the mesa. Their cliff dwellings and structures elsewhere on canyon floors are considered the most elaborate and sophisticated Native American architecture. In the late 13th century the Anasazi abandoned the site for reasons that are still not understood.

The Acoma pueblo in northwestern New Mexico is one of the oldest continuously occupied villages in the United States. It sits atop a mesa and is believed to have been inhabited for a thousand years. In 1598 its original buildings were destroyed by Spanish invaders, but were rebuilt in the early 17th century. Today it is inhabited by families who pass the right to live in individual dwellings down through their youngest daughters.

Glossary of Architectural Terms

agora open area for assemblies, meetings, and markets in ancient Greece.

aisle division of the main structure of Roman basilicas and Christian churches into lateral areas adjacent to, and on both sides of, the nave.

acropolis group of main temples on an elevated section, or hill, in ancient Greek cities.

ambo pulpit or stand in Early Christian or Byzantine churches used for readings.

amphitheater outdoor theater, either round or semicircular, with tiered seats for the audience.

apse semicircular, polygonal, or square end of a Roman basilica or Christian church.

aqueduct means of channeling or carrying water; arched Roman aqueducts carried water over rivers and valleys.

arch curved structure that spans an opening and is usually formed by voussoirs; see *corbeled arch*.

arcade series of arches carried on columns; can be attached to a wall or freestanding.

atrium court with open roof; in Roman houses it included a basin to catch rainwater; in Early Christian churches, a forecourt with colonnade leading to the church entrance; in modern times often a glass-covered interior.

auditorium in an amphitheater, the circular or semicircular area of tiered seats for the audience.

barrel vault continuous semicircular ceiling.

basilica Roman meeting hall with high central nave, clerestory windows, apse, and often side aisles, used for law courts, meetings, and other assemblies; adapted in Early Christian churches; see *basilican church*.

basilican church early Christian church based on the basilica with central nave and clerestory windows, two or four side aisles, an apse at one end, and covered with a timber roof; the basilica remained a basic Christian church building type until modern times.

broken pediment pediment that has a gap where the apex would be.

buttress heavy structure against a wall that carries the outward thrust of a vault or dome down to a lower support or the ground.

cantilever beam or other structural member that projects past its support at one end and is free at the other.

caryatid sculpture of a figure, usually a draped female, used in place of a column.

cathedral church where the bishop presides; other churches in the bishop's area of authority are subordinate.

capital highest part of a column where it meets the entablature; design reflects different architectural orders.

cella room in a classical temple that houses the statue of the god of that temple; same as the Greek *naos*.

chancel extension of a Christian church, usually beyond the transept, that includes the choir and apse.

choir area in the chancel, usually immediately beyond the transept, in which the choir is seated; can also mean the entire chancel.

Classical architecture architecture of ancient Greece and Rome; also applied to later buildings based on Greek and Roman forms.

clerestory windows windows in the walls of a nave that rise above the roofs of the side aisles.

cloister covered and often colonnaded structure in monasteries, with open courtyard in the center, that is reserved for monks or nuns.

colonnade row of columns supporting a beam, entablature, or roof structure.

column cylindrical vertical support member; see *post*.

composite order combination of Corinthian and Ionic orders; the capital has acanthus leaves and scroll volutes.

concrete structural material, composed of cement, water, and aggregate, that can be cast in a multitude of shapes; see *reinforced concrete*.

corbeled arch arch constructed of horizontal stone layers in which each layer projects beyond the one below until they meet at the top of the arch.

Corinthian order Greek order with slim fluted columns and capitals decorated with acanthus leaves.

crossing space created in a basilican church where the nave is intersected by the transept.

cupola small dome, sometimes on a top of a larger dome.

dome circular convex structure that covers an interior space; sometimes mounted on a drum; semicircular domes often cover apses and can also act as buttresses.

Doric order Greek order with sturdy fluted columns and plain capitals.

drum circular or polygonal wall that supports a dome.

elevation projection of a building from one side onto a vertical plane showing the arrangement of windows, roof, etc.; see *plan* and *section*.

entablature horizontal structure supported by columns in classical architecture.

entasis slight convex swelling of the sides of classical columns to counteract the optical illusion that a column with straight sides is slightly thinner in the center than at the top and bottom.

fenestration windows.

fluting vertical grooving of columns and pilasters.

flying buttress detached vertical structure adjacent to vaulting that arches over to the main structure at the point of outward thrust from the vault and carries the thrust down to a lower support; a feature of Gothic cathedrals that permits thin walls and large clerestory windows; see *buttress*.

forum open square in ancient Rome used for assemblies, meetings, and business; often surrounded by a colonnade with adjacent basilica and temple.

groin vault ceiling structure that is formed when one barrel vault intersects another.

hall church church in which the side aisles are as high, or nearly as high, as the nave.

hypostyle room with roof supported by rows of columns.

Ionic order Greek order with slim fluted columns and capitals decorated with scrolls, or volutes.

lintel horizontal beam supported by columns, as in post and lintel construction.

mosaic small, usually rectangular pieces of colored glass or stone set into walls by plaster or mortar and arranged in designs or pictures.

mosque Muslim holy building.

narthex anteroom or vestibule spanning the full width of the building at the entrance to an Early Christian church.

nave in Roman basilicas, the central section higher than the side aisles and illuminated by clerestory windows; in Christian churches, the central section from the entrance to the transept that is usually higher than the side aisles and illuminated by clerestory windows.

naos Greek name for the room in a classical temple that houses the statue of the god of that temple and other treasures; same as the *cella*.

Neolithic the "New Stone" Age beginning in about 8000 B.C., when polished stone tools appeared, settled agricultural communities were formed, and animals were domesticated.

orchestra in ancient Greek and Roman theaters the circular or semicircular area in front of the stage; often used for singing and dancing that accompanied performances on the stage.

orders in classical architecture, the design of columns and entablature according to defined models. See *Doric, Ionic, Corinthian, Composite,* and *Tuscan* orders.

Paleolithic the "Old Stone" Age that began when the first crude stone tools appeared about 750,000 years ago.

pediment originally the triangular structure closing the end of a pitched roof of a classical temple; later used to describe any crowning structure over a door or window; see *broken pediment*.

pendentive curved triangular piece in the corners of a square or rectangular space that forms the transition to a circular drum or dome.

peristyle row of columns that surrounds the outside of a structure such as a temple or the inside of a courtyard.

piazza open paved area in a city surrounded by buildings or other structures.

pilaster flat column attached to a wall, usually for decorative purposes.

By the Architects, for the People: A Trend From the Past

By NICOLAI OUROUSSOFF

When the city planning board in Newark, New Jersey voted to approve construction of a four-block-long mixed-use development, the decision was barely noticed outside a small circle of civic boosters. But it was a turning point in the career of the project's architect, Richard Meier.

For decades Mr. Meier, with his trademark dark suits and leonine white hair, has been a fixture on the New York social scene, where he often rubs elbows with his moneyed clients. And his designs, from second homes in the Hamptons to international art museums, have become known for an almost unbearable, and expensive, refinement. He is the Martha Stewart of the Modernists.

But the Newark development, a complex for middle- and lower-income tenants to be known as Teachers Village, takes Mr. Meier, 75, back to his roots, to a time more than 40 years ago when he devoted as much energy to subsidized housing as to beach houses. Despite the project's modest budget of $120 million, its tautly composed and thoughtfully laid out forms reflect the same intelligence and care found in most of Mr. Meier's work.

Teachers Village is not only the most impressive of several new initiatives in Newark, but also the most dramatic example yet of what is shaping up to be a significant and hopeful trend in architecture. After a long period in which America's greatest talents seemed to work almost exclusively at the service of the wealthy, there are signs that their efforts are trickling down to other segments of society.

If things continue this way, it may actually mean a renewal of architecture's onetime commitment to elevating the lives of ordinary people. Such a renewal is not likely to be as ambitious — some would say naïve — in its social aims as President Lyndon B. Johnson's War on Poverty and the Modernist architecture that was dominant at the time. But it could lead to a fresh engagement with some of the challenges those movements took on, an engagement informed by the lessons of their failings.

Mr. Meier's career in particular neatly reflects the historical ups and downs of the past half century. In the late 1960s, he was approached by the newly created Urban Development Corporation of New York State to design a 523-unit project in the Bronx. As an alternative to the conventional tower-in-the-park model, he created three midrise buildings that were lifted up on columns to invite the neighborhood into their central courtyard.

But by then the backlash against large-scale Modernist housing — and the government programs that paid for it — was in full swing, as even progressive projects like Mr. Meier's failed to deliver on their promises. Modernism of every stripe was condemned, sometimes unfairly, for a tabula rasa approach to planning and insensitivity to local contexts.

Mr. Meier has gone to greater lengths than in the past to merge his new design with its context, not just by breaking it down into several buildings, but also by using strategies like a pedestrian passageway cut between two of the charter schools. In an effort to diminish the monumentality of a building that houses two schools, part of it will be clad in white metal panels, part in brick. And the few existing buildings worth preserving will be restored.

The design incorporates some of the sensibilities that can be found in Mr. Meier's higher-end projects. The apartment buildings include small, open courtyards and outdoor terraces, bringing light deep into their interiors. In each building a ground-floor retail level is conceived as a glass band, imbuing the floors above with an air of weightlessness. This effect is reinforced by the irregular pattern of the apartment windows, which gives the facades a cubist feeling.

If the project succeeds in revitalizing Newark's bleak downtown — or even if it simply manages not to be swallowed up by the decay around it — its most important impact may be to help open eyes again to architecture's potential role in addressing complex urban challenges.

Mr. Meier said, "You always hope what you build has arms, that they reach out and affect others. You want to feel you've done something that allows other positive things to happen."

pilotis columns that support the main structure of a building above the ground, with the ground level left open; often used by Le Corbusier.

plan projection of a building or other area onto a horizontal plane showing the arrangement of rooms, walls, doors, etc.

portico covered entrance supported by columns.

post vertical support member like a column; see *post and lintel*.

post and lintel construction system consisting of columns supporting beams.

Pritzker Architecture Prize An annual award given to "honor a living architect whose built work demonstrates a combination of those qualities of talent, vision, and commitment, which has produced consistent and significant contributions to humanity and the built environment through the art of architecture." Established in 1979 by the Pritzker family of Chicago, the award is modeled on the Nobel Prizes.

refectory dining hall in a religious or secular building.

ribbed vault vaulting that is supported by a system of ribs that support the ceiling between the ribs.

reinforced concrete concrete with steel bars cast in the places where external loads force the concrete to be in tension; the bars absorb the tension, which concrete cannot; elsewhere the concrete absorbs the compression resulting from external loads.

section view, or projection, of a building as if it were cut by a plane vertically or horizontally, showing interior spaces and structure.

stage raised structure in a theater behind the orchestra on which the performance takes place.

stoa roofed portico in ancient Greece with columns in the front and a wall at the back.

stucco plaster material that can be molded into a multitude of shapes; important in Baroque and Rococo buildings.

stylobate raised platform, usually the top step, of a temple or other structure on which the columns are placed.

transept structure that crosses the long axis of a church at 90°; on one side of the crossing is the nave and on the other the chancel.

truss rigid structure made of interlocking triangular members used to span open spaces; early trusses were of timber while later trusses were of iron, steel and other metals.

Tuscan order Roman order with slender columns and plain capitals, without fluting.

vault elongated arch that forms a ceiling or roof.

volute scroll-like form used in the Ionic order.

voussoir wedge or triangular shaped stones that form arches or vaults; see *corbeled arch*.

ziggurat stepped pyramid in ancient western Asia set on a platform with stairs leading to the summit where the supreme god was worshipped.

ART

History of Art in the Western Tradition

Prehistoric and Ancient Art

Prehistoric Art Making art has always been an important part of human society, and the process is older, in fact, than writing or agriculture. The drive to represent the world through pictures may be innate, since wherever traces of early human settlements have been found, the sites nearly always contain works of art. In the past century, several sites were discovered in Europe—especially in France and Spain—that show a variety of prehistoric artwork. Of these, the best known are the extraordinary scenes painted around 15,000 B.C. on the walls of a series of caves at Lascaux in southwest France. The caves feature elegant multicolored murals—some over 20 yards long—of stylized but recognizable animal shapes in active poses and complex groupings. Many of the figures are outlined with black charcoal that was probably applied with moss or hair, and they are colored with mineral pigments such as ochre and iron oxide.

The Lascaux caves contain 600 individual animal figures, including horses, bulls, and stags, as well as a single human figure. Many of the Lascaux animals are drawn along the curves of the rock to suggest three dimensions, but the artists also used such sophisticated effects as layering, perspective, and a combination of frontal and profile poses.

Other important collections of prehistoric painting have been found in the Chauvet cave in France, the Altamira cave in Spain, and the Apollo 11 caves in Namibia. Many appear to have sacred or ceremonial significance and may have been drawn by group leaders to increase success on the hunting grounds, or by shamans attempting to access mystical powers.

Egyptian Art Because Egyptian society was highly stratified, it produced a skilled class of artisans who created and passed down an increasingly refined style of artwork that lasted for more than 2,000 years. Artisan painters were rigorously trained to maintain consistent motifs and techniques for particular applications. Some painters worked solely to color sculptures and relief carvings, while others specialized in murals, and manuscript painters created small-scale works on papyrus. These artisans developed and mastered a variety of materials, including distemper paint (a combination of powdered lime and a gluelike binder) and encaustic (tinted wax paint colored with mineral pigments), and created very stylized and highly symbolic imagery that changed little over the years, but still allowed for individual variation.

The paintings of ancient Egypt are rarely exclusively decorative; most surviving Egyptian paintings use very formal compositions to tell narrative stories. They are symmetrical, often framed by ornate borders, and feature strong outlines filled with flat areas of bold color—especially white, black, brown, red, and blue. A distinctive innovation of Egyptian art is the twisted perspective of human figures which places the head in profile, the torso full forward, and the legs in profile with the left foot forward. Additionally, Egyptian artists combined representational imagery with symbolic pictographs known as hieroglyphics that together related complex narratives and eventually became the basis for written language in the Western world.

By the New Kingdom dynasties (mid-second millennium B.C.), Egyptian art both influenced and was influenced by Mesopotamian and Minoan art. Monumental statues of pharaohs and gods were produced in great numbers, tombs were often decorated with elaborate mural paintings showing scenes from daily life and the afterlife, and portrait sculptures, though stylized, were often highly expressive of the appearance and character of their subjects; a painted limestone portrait bust of Queen Nefertiti (ca. 1360 B.C.) is a famous example.

After Alexander the Great invaded Egypt in 331 B.C., much of Egyptian art was overwhelmed by Hellenistic styles, although local features endured. Hundreds of small portrait paintings on wood, created in the ancient Egyptian style, have been found in the tombs of wealthy citizens of Egypt from the third century A.D.

Art of Ancient Mesopotamia   In what is commonly considered the cradle of Western civilization, the land surrounding the Tigris and Euphrates Rivers hosted a succession of ancient civilizations—including the Sumerians, the Akkadians, the Hittites, the Babylonians, the Assyrians, the second Babylonian empire, and the Persian Empire. They shared a generally similar artistic style that showed a strong interest in the relationship between the natural and divine worlds. Distinctive elements include a loose compositional style and increasingly fantastical combinations of animals and humans to create winged bulls, griffins, and magnificently bearded warrior-kings. While the majority of artworks that have survived from these Mesopotamian civilizations are stone relief sculptures from palaces and small carved cylinder seals, some vases and mural fragments show refined painting techniques that emphasize stylized depictions of plants and animals, as well as exaggerated renderings of human musculature and hair. One of the finest works of Mesopotamian art is the Ishtar Gate of the second Babylonian Empire (612–539 B.C.), a work of blue-glazed faience brick and low-relief sculpture now reconstructed in the State Museum, Berlin. The various cultures of Mesopotamia and adjacent regions were absorbed into the Persian Empire (559–331 B.C.) and influenced its art, as seen, for example, in the elaborate relief sculptures of the ceremonial city of Persepolis (ca. 500 B.C.).

Art of Ancient Greece   The art of the ancient Greeks is generally regarded as the foundation of subsequent European art, although Greek art itself was derived from that of the earlier Minoan civilization of Crete, and influenced by nearby Egyptian and Mesopotamian cultures. But by the seventh century B.C., Greek artists working in vase painting, wall painting, and sculpture had developed these influences into a fully Greek style.

Archaic Painting   While artisans had painted simple geometric and symbolic motifs on pottery for thousands of years, by about 700 B.C. Greek painters created a highly workable black glaze that allowed them to decorate vases with detailed narrative scenes. These paintings were rendered as drawings and then filled in with solid color—the earliest examples are painted with the main figures silhouetted in black against the red clay, but later works (ca. 530 B.C.) were painted black with the figures left in the red color of clay. Many of the first Greek vase painters preferred to illustrate battle scenes and mythological characters like Athena, but later artists also painted commemorations of real-life events like athletic competitions and weddings and even bawdy revelries or comic scenes. The paintings feature some stylized conventions to show details such as musculature, fabric folds, and hairstyles, but also demonstrate a more illusionistic approach to composition than was used in Egypt or Mesopotamia. Greek vase painters, most of whom worked in Athens, became well known as individuals, and many different workshop traditions began to emerge, creating the beginning of the idea of the independent artistic style.

By the end of the fifth century B.C., many Greek artists had turned to wall painting with tempera and were executing complex murals, smaller works on wood panels, and even paintings on parchment, all of which allowed for greater variety of expression and a wider palette of colors than did pottery. Painters used human models to help them create more naturalistic scenes and, although none of the ancient murals survive, the names of several artists and their work are known from historical documents. Apelles was renowned for his skill in drawing and for modeling techniques that gave realistic shape to his figures; Parrhasius used spatial perspective to give the illusion of depth, making his figures stand out from their backgrounds; and Zeuxis is credited with developing the shading technique known as *sfumato* (Italian, "shaded"). It was said that he painted such realistic grapes that birds tried to eat them.

As Greek culture moved into the Classical (480–323 B.C.) and then Hellenistic eras (323 B.C.–A.D. 31), paintings became even less formal and more naturalistic, with dynamic poses, action-filled scenes, and more effort to accurately represent the three-dimensional world with special effects, including *chiaroscuro* (Italian, "light-dark")—the use of contrasting light and shadow to create an illusion of depth. In Italy, however, the Etruscans (early eighth century B.C. to 510 B.C.) shunned these innovations and instead adopted the more conservative and static features shown in the Archaic Greek vases they collected. Etruscan artists adapted many of the older Greek stylistic conventions in their own pottery and tomb paintings.

Archaic Sculpture   By 650 B.C., two types of sculpture were being widely produced: the *Kouros*, or standing male youth, and *Kore*, or standing maiden. They are the first known examples of free-standing statues, unattached to an architectural support. The Kouros statues were slim nudes with stylized features and wiglike hair, standing in a tight pose with clenched fists and the left foot forward. Kore were posed and styled similarly, but clothed. Figural sculptures toward the end of the archaic period often featured a placid expression with a closed-mouthed smile, which became known as the "archaic smile."

In the Archaic period the Greeks also developed a characteristic style of stone temple with an entablature (roof structure) supported by stone columns. They customarily decorated such temples with figurative sculpture, filling the space of the triangular pediment, and creating horizontal bands of decoration known as a *frieze*.

Classical Period (480–323 B.C.) During this period (from the great Greek naval victory over the Persians at Salamis to the death of Alexander the Great), sculpture became much more naturalistic and illusionistic, moving away from the rigid stylizations of the Archaic period. While most statues still represented an idealized beauty, they became remarkably lifelike, with anatomically accurate muscles and skeletal structures. Clothed figures wore drapery that mimicked the appearance of real cloth, with creases and folds. Although today the austere purity of white marble is appreciated as one of the beauties of Greek sculpture, in ancient Greece statues were in fact painted in bright colors to imitate naturalistic colors of skin, hair, and clothing.

One of the most important developments in classical scupture was the introduction of the *contrapposto* pose, in which the sculpted figure stands at ease, resting his weight on one leg and giving the body an asymmetrical and relaxed stance. The famous nude *Kritios Boy* (ca. 480 B.C.) is the earliest known sculpture to exhibit this feature. This pose has been copied repeatedly in other sculptural traditions up to the present day, and as far afield as the Buddhist sculpture of Central and East Asia.

Once Greek sculptors had learned to depict the body at rest, they went on to develop techniques for showing it in motion, in the form of charioteers, discus-throwers, and other active figures. To cite a famous example, the ambitiously conceived marble decorations made for the temple of the Parthenon in Athens (448–432 B.C.) depict many deities in a variety of lifelike poses.

Hellenistic Period (323 B.C.–A.D. 31.) Sculptors in this period (from the death of Alexander to the Roman conquest of Alexandria) continued to develop the realism of classical art, engaging their figures in increasingly dramatic and action-filled poses. The most famous work from this time, *Nike of Samothrace* (ca. 200–190 B.C.) is a victory monument showing a winged goddess descending on the prow of a ship, with a strong headwind pushing her clothing against her body in sensuous and energetic folds. Another significant piece from this period is the *Laocoön Group* (second century B.C. to first century A.D.), which shows the mythical Laocoön and his two sons being attacked by sea serpents.

Etruscan Art The Etruscan city-states dominated northern and central Italy politically and culturally from the early eighth century B.C. to 510 B.C., when the last Etruscan king of Rome was overthrown. The Etruscans spoke a non-Indo-European language, known from numerous tomb inscriptions but not yet deciphered despite many attempts. Their art was strongly influenced by Greek art of the Archaic period, which the Etruscans knew from the Greek colonies that had been established in southern Italy and Sicily beginning around 750 B.C. Etruscan art was profoundly conservative, characterized by marble and bronze sculptures and painted tomb murals that retained the static poses and archaic smiles of Archaic art long after the Greeks themselves had embarked on classical refinements. Akin to Greek art and antecedent to Roman art, the art of the Etruscans remains, like the people who made it, imperfectly understood.

Art of Ancient Rome The Roman republic was founded ca. 509 B.C., after the overthrow of the Etruscan Tarquinian dynasty; two centuries later, Rome controlled the entire Italian peninsula and had begun its expansion into other lands. The Romans were great builders, and in the ensuing centuries they built cities, complete with temples, palaces, baths, arenas, theaters, and civil engineering works such as aqueducts and roads, from Spain to the Near East, and from North Africa to Britain. Roman art, strongly influenced by Etruscan, classical Greek, and Hellenistic art, was closely allied to architecture. Roman leaders supported an array of civic construction projects and saw the value of including great artworks in these new buildings to promote the values and official gods of the republic.

They commissioned Greek and native artists to decorate vast numbers of public buildings and private homes with sculptures, mosaic floors, and colorful murals that covered walls, ceilings, or even whole rooms. Murals were executed using both the secco ("dry") method of painting with watercolors on dry plaster, and the more challenging and durable fresco ("wet") method of applying pigment directly to wet plaster before it dries. Many fine examples of these murals remain—including some preserved in the ashes of Pompeii and Herculaneum after Mt. Vesuvius erupted in A.D. 79. They show four distinct styles of Roman wall painting. In the first, artists applied simple "faux" finishes to create flat blocks of color or to imitate the look of wood or stone; in the second, artists wrapped large murals around entire rooms and tried to extend the visual space beyond the limits of the walls with techniques that nearly achieved true linear perspective; in the third, this illusion of space was traded for flatter images confined to smaller areas and bounded by painted borders; in the fourth, these smaller images were grouped like individual paintings on a wall and executed with illusionistic painting techniques, including false frames.

Following the preferences of their Hellenistic teachers, Roman artists strove toward technical mastery in their desire to create highly naturalistic works. Even small paintings and portraits—usually made on wood using tempera and *encaustic* (wax paint)—show a nuanced approach to portraying figures in a lifelike and realistic manner. The subject matter of these paintings ranged from scenes honoring the civic gods to expansive landscapes, and from architectural scenes to elaborate interiors and still-life paintings. While some critics maintain that the Roman artists were mere imitators of the Greeks—and they did, indeed, copy many Greek works and use them as study aids—Roman painters also made several innovations, such as the development of the landscape as a painting genre and the promotion of *trompe l'oeil* (French, "fool the eye") paintings, which render ordinary objects as accurately as possible in order to create an illusion of three dimensions for the viewer. Unlike the celebrated Greek artists, however, most Roman painters were viewed simply as near-anonymous craftsmen for hire.

Celtic Art   The Celtic peoples occupied much of central and western Europe in the early first millennium B.C., with populations extending through Central Asia as far as what is now western China. Early Celtic art, for example of the Hallstatt and La Tène Cultures (eighth–fifth centuries B.C.), has much in common with the art of the Germanic peoples of northern Europe and the Scythians of the steppe lands of Asia; it is characterized by fantastic, intertwining animal and plant designs on bronze, iron, or gold weapons, jewelry, and various utilitarian and decorative objects. In later La Tène art, Greek influence is both pervasive and totally assimilated to the Celtic "animal style."

The Celtic peoples were absorbed or displaced by the expansion of the Roman Empire and the northern Germanic tribes, surviving as intact cultures only in isolated areas of eastern Europe, Anatolia, Iberia, and westernmost Europe including Britain and Ireland. Celtic art re-emerged with the Christian conversion of Britain and Ireland in the fifth century A.D. Metalwork, enamel painting, and manuscript illumination all employed characteristic Celtic intertwining patterns of knotwork, animals, or stylized plants; a particular innovation of Celtic manuscript art was the elaboration of initial capital letters into fantastic compositions of entwined lines. Few of these illustrated manuscripts have survived. The most highly regarded is the *Book of Kells*, created on the Scottish island of Iona and preserved in Ireland after the Viking destruction of Iona in 807. Later illustrated books, including the "books of hours" popular throughout Europe from the 13th through 16th centuries, preserved many features of the Celtic manuscripts, such as decorated page borders, embellished capital letters, bold outlines, primary colors, and detailed botanical flourishes.

Byzantine Art   The Roman Empire was already in decline when it became a Christian empire under Constantine (ca. 274–337), who founded his capital, Constantinople, on the remnants of the ancient city of Byzantium. The geographic shift of the capital from Rome to Constantinople, as well as the religious shift from paganism to Christianity, provoked a massive cultural change as Christians were freed from the brutal suppression that had inhibited the early church. Constantine and his wealthy followers funded church building and missionary work throughout the region that, in turn, demanded a new style of art. The earliest Christian paintings, such as the murals in fourth- and fifth-century churches, have mostly been lost, but surviving fragments, sculptures, and mosaics from the same era suggest that they generally followed classical Hellenistic and Roman visual conventions and simply substituted New Testament subject matter. However, this was not entirely satisfactory to church leaders, and artists struggled to develop an appropriately reverent style of ecclesiastical imagery that would both honor their faith and instruct new converts.

By the early fifth century, the bishop of Rome was recognized as the primate of the church, but the repeated sackings of Rome by successive waves of barbarians left

Constantinople as the political, economic and, in many ways, spiritual capital of the empire. Freed from Roman influence, the flourishing Byzantine artists were left alone to resolve the dilemmas about how to depict Christ and the saints. These artists rejected naturalism in favor of a more lavish and allegorical approach to painting, which used stylized images with frontal poses, elongated bodies, symbolic hand gestures, large eyes, and round glowing halos. Artists intentionally made their paintings look flat and two-dimensional to remind the viewer that the image was not a representation of an earthly experience but an entry into the spiritual dimension. They generally favored simple palettes of vivid colors, often on a gold background and with specific meaning attached to each color. Most works show a formal composition with an emphasis on symmetry and with figures sized hierarchically, in order of importance. Some small *encaustic* (wax paint) paintings as well as mosaics at St. Vitale in Ravenna (completed 547) and Hagia Sophia in Constantinople (completed 537), give clear evidence of this new style. After the final collapse of the Western Roman Empire in 476, Byzantine art reigned supreme in most of the Christian world, just as Eastern Orthodoxy gained primacy in Christian belief and practice.

Byzantine painters decorated churches, illustrated manuscripts, and created paintings for individual believers, but the most characteristic product of Byzantine and later Orthodox art is the icon—a small, portable image of Christ, the Virgin and Child, or one or more saints. Icons, whether painted on folding wooden panels or combined into large altar screens, were produced in increasing quantities for churches and private chapels beginning in the seventh century and often became objects of devotion in themselves. Icons preserved the distinctively lavish features of larger Byzantine paintings and were often further gilded, heavily framed, and even encrusted with jewels. The small scale of the works encouraged artists to imbue every detail with careful symbolism, lending a rich, dense feeling to even the simplest icon. While icon painting was essentially conservative in style, this slowly changed over the centuries, and later examples show the influence of Italian Renaissance ideas of modeling and perspective.

Islamic Art   Islam, which dates its founding to A.D. 622 (Year 1 of the Muslim calendar), was quickly spread by conquering Arab armies throughout the Middle East and North Africa. A distinctive Islamic style of architecture and art quickly developed to serve the needs of the faithful. Most important was the mosque, designed to hold large numbers of people for communal worship; the usual form was a square or rectangular building with a dome supported by interior columns or pillars. Mosques were built not only in North Africa, the Middle East, and Central Asia, but also in parts of Europe—most notably in Sicily and in parts of Spain (Cordoba, Seville, Granada), as well as, much later, in the Balkans. Because Islam prohibits the depiction of living creatures, its decorative style of architecture relied on foliate, geometric, or calligraphic designs in stone, stucco, brick, or tile; similar ornamentation was used for ceramic and metalwork objects. Chief among the arts of Islam was calligraphy and the decoration of books; finely embellished copies of the *Koran* influenced the Christian art of illuminated sacred books. Through trade, warfare, and conquest, Islamic art influenced both Byzantine art and the revived arts of western Europe in the Middle Ages.

Gothic Art

The crowning of Charlemagne as the Holy Roman Emperor in 800 renewed the vigor of the Roman Catholic Church and eventually that of Western Christian art. Even as the Roman Church broke from the dogma and practice of the Orthodox Church, the desire to spread the Gospel to an illiterate population led Western painters away from the formal and heavily symbolic Byzantine style. Both the art and theology of western Christianity began to emphasize the suffering, Crucifixion, and resurrection of Christ through more narrative artworks. By the 10th century, newly stable feudal monarchies in northern and western Europe were wealthy enough to begin building churches and large cathedrals in what became the Romanesque style, which offered vast wall space and curving vaulted ceilings for murals. Most of these works have been lost, but many of them included scenes from the Old and New Testaments placed on opposite walls, along with a painting of Christ as the focal point of the apse. Stylistically, these murals were similar to the illuminated manuscripts of the era, and there was little attempt at creating perspective. Rather, figures and objects were sized hierarchically and simply layered to suggest their relative distance from the viewer.

As the more intellectual Gothic era emerged in the mid-12th century, a newly rich bourgeoisie joined the nobility and the church as patrons of the arts, commissioning small artworks for their own homes and private chapels. Increased literacy expanded the demand for illustrated books, and the growth of scientific and secular literature encouraged the development of secular themes in art. Even religious works were more open in style and subject matter, with looser compositions and more animated poses. Many cities formed trade guilds for painters, preserving the identity of artists more reliably than ever before, and some artists began signing their works.

The Gothic Style in Italy

In Italy, Duccio di Buoninsegna (ca.1255–ca.1318) used pigment and egg tempera to create richly gilded religious paintings and altarpieces in the tradition of Byzantine icons, but he gave his figures recognizably human gestures and expressions. His pupil Simone Martini influenced many later painters with a soft, expressive style that traded the vivid Byzantine colors and static arrangements for muted tones, dynamically posed figures, and elegant compositions. Giotto di Bodone, a native of Florence, broke further from Byzantine tradition with his masterly church frescoes that placed naturalistically conceived New Testament figures in architectural or landscape settings. Regarded as the first artist in the Gothic tradition to depict nature in a convincingly realistic manner, Giotto's art represents a crucial turning point in the progression of Western art toward the illusionism of the Renaissance. He developed an algebraic method of calculating the appropriate relative sizes of objects in his paintings and also revived the tradition of drawing figures from life. He is best known for his frescoes in the Arena Chapel in Padua, which include *The Lamentation* (1305–06), as well as small panel paintings such as *Madonna* (ca.1310).

The Sienese painter Ambrogio Lorenzetti went further still in breaking conventions and set biblical narrative scenes in realistic Tuscan landscapes. He is best known, however, for his secular fresco cycle *Allegory and Effects of Good and Bad Government* (ca. 1338–1340). While frescoes remained an important form of painting, wooden panel paintings were developed in Italy in the 13th century, and became the dominant form throughout Europe by the 15th century.

Late Gothic Painting in France and the Netherlands

The early 15th century in the Netherlands marks the transition from the last phase of Gothic painting to the first phase of Early Renaissance art. The epitome of the late Gothic style is the *Trés Riches Heures*, an illustrated devotional book created ca. 1413–16 for the Duc de Berry by the Limbourg brothers, Flemish artists working in Burgundy. Their gemlike miniature paintings give an idealized but wholly convincing image of Burgundian life in the High Middle Ages. Another important artist of this transitional period is known as the Master of Flémalle (he may have been Robert Campin, ca.1378–1444), whose paintings imitated reality with revolutionary precision. His *Merode Altarpiece* (ca. 1425–30) was the first known artwork to place the Annunciation scene in a contemporary domestic interior. While Gothic artists had mixed realistic details with fantastical or celestial settings that often did not convey an accurate sense of three-dimensional space, the Master of Flémalle made his figures appear to exist in the same world as the viewer with unprecedented realism. The Master of Flémalle was the first artist to promote oil painting instead of tempera (pigments in an organic emulsion, such as egg yolk), allowing him to use brilliant colors and re-create the nuanced effects of light, which would have been impossible with the less versatile tempera.

The other great Flemish master of the time, Jan van Eyck (1395–1441), used oils to such great effect that he is often regarded as the "Father of Oil Painting." Van Eyck brought exacting attention to human figures and fabrics, which he rendered with rich shading, deep colors, and carefully observed details. He exploited such recent inventions as the glass mirror to help him paint realistic self-portraits and to refine his perspective. Van Eyck painted religious as well as secular works, and he is credited with developing the technique of atmospheric perspective—a gradual changing of tone used to represent objects farther away in the picture space.

Renaissance Art (1400–1600)

The Early Renaissance in Italy

The late Gothic shift toward a more realistic style of painting continued in the Renaissance, which focused more on the immediate and tangible human experience than on an idealized afterlife. The intellectual culture of the Renaissance (literally "rebirth") looked back past the Christian era to classical Greek ideals in literature, philosophy, science, and art—after hundreds of years of iconographic art, naturalism and realism were again en vogue.

The trend toward realism was facilitated when the Italian architect Filippo Brunelleschi developed the mathematical method of linear perspective in about 1415. This approach, which introduced the optical trick of parallel lines receding to a vanishing point, allowed artists and architects to faithfully represent the three-dimensional world, and Brunelleschi's method was quickly taken up by other painters. Combining Brunelleschi's linear perspective with painting techniques such as modeling, the Tuscan painter Masaccio (Tommaso Di Giovanni Di Simone Guidi, 1401–28), produced solid-looking figures that seemed to exist in real spaces. Masaccio's use of tempera meant that his color lacked the virtuosity of van Eyck and the Master of Flémalle, but several Venetian artists, led by Giovanni Bellini, soon adopted the oil paints and rich colors favored by the northern painters.

Technical advances merged with spiritual reverence in the work of Fra Angelico, a Dominican monk whose religious frescoes and panel paintings combine a serenity of mood with precisely modeled figures and clearly defined background elements. Fra Angelico was one of Florence's most sought-after artists of the early Renaissance. He is admired for strong three-dimensional spatial compositions and is best known for fresco cycles at the Vatican and St. Peter's Basilica in Rome, as well as his fresco of *The Annunciation* (1440–50) at the monastery of San Marco in Florence. The Tuscan painter Piero della Francesca published three treatises on mathematics and geometry, and his artwork demonstrates his exacting attention to composition and perspective. Piero's masterwork, *The History of the True Cross* (ca. 1447–1460), also includes the first nocturnal scene in Western art.

Domenico Ghirlandaio placed historical and New Testament characters in settings that combine classical architecture with contemporary domestic detail, and his exquisitely delineated outlines and masterly use of perspective recall, and often surpass, Roman trompe l'oeil paintings, which first attempted to fool the eye with crafty renderings of real-world objects. Secular subjects and portraits became increasingly popular in the late 15th century. The revived interest in both classical realism and pre-Christian mythology inspired Sandro Botticelli to risk the ire of the Catholic Church and paint such pagan-influenced works as *The Birth of Venus* (ca. 1480), now one of the most famous artworks in the world, which depicts a nude Venus rising from the water on a seashell.

As wealth in Europe increased and artists rediscovered Roman innovations, the stage was set for the dramatic leaps forward in the arts and humanities that would be called the High Renaissance.

The High Renaissance   During the period between 1495 and 1520, a rapid progression of artistic accomplishments occurred in Italy. While religious themes were still important, harmonious forms, unified composition and skillful execution—including smooth, nearly invisible brushstrokes—became more important than thematic or moral content. Painters aspired to be faithful to nature through careful observation and life-studies, and a more tolerant attitude from religious leaders allowed a revival of the nude figure.

Leonardo da Vinci, the first great master of the High Renaissance, exemplified the "Renaissance man" interested in everything from mathematics to botany to music. His gesture studies along with his extensive study of human bodies gave his figures great liveliness, and his knowledge of mathematics allowed him to develop a convincing atmospheric perspective exemplified by his *Last Supper* (1492/4–98). He developed new techniques, including a method of shaping figures by imitating the effects of light and shadow rather than with outlines. He also perfected *sfumato*, in which tiny dots in delicately varied shades create a hazy, indistinct atmosphere. These techniques created the poetic qualities of Leonardo's most famous work, the thoughtful *Mona Lisa* (1503–05), whose enigmatic smile is softened by the shadows around her eyes and mouth.

Michelangelo Buonarotti, as diversely talented as Leonardo, was an engineer, poet, architect, and artist, while primarily a sculptor. His *Pietà* (1499) and *David* (1501–04) are considered among the finest sculptures of all time. Michelangelo apprenticed with Ghirlandaio and used his knowledge of anatomy to create a muscular and awe-inspiring painting style. His frescoes for the Sistine Chapel in Rome (1508–12) cover the ceiling with monumental figures in such dramatic Old Testament scenes as "The Creation," in which a gray-bearded God reaches out his finger to impart the spark of life to Adam.

Raphael completed the trinity of High Renaissance masters. Unsurpassed in his technical perfection and in the visual harmony of his works, Raphael's frescoes, especially for the Stanza della Segnatura in the Vatican Palace in Rome (1509–11), are more serene and delicate than those of Michelangelo, seamlessly blending classical composition with devoutly Christian themes. Although Leonardo and Michelangelo were admired for their originality, Raphael's formal symmetry and graceful, expressive figures—as in his *Sistine Madonna* (1512–1514), with its pair of winged cherubs at the bottom—epitomize Renaissance style.

While southern Italian painters focused on composition and form, Venetian artists experimented with the sensuous colors and new effects made possible by oil paints. Giorgione (ca. 1477–1510) employed sfumato to create moody, poetic paintings with glowing light and realistic landscape backgrounds. Titian (ca. 1490–1570) mastered tonal color and developed a rich approach that made him the most famous Venetian painter of the Renaissance. For decades, Titian operated a large studio where assistants would fill in the less important parts of his paintings and was an exceptionally versatile and prolific artist. Over his long career, Titian painted altarpieces—including the bold and dynamic *Assumption of the Virgin* (1516–18)—as well as portraits, religious subjects, and classical scenes such as the *Bacchanal* (ca. 1518). The luminous colors, controlled lighting, and subtle brushwork of Titian's paintings influenced generations of Western painters.

The Northern Renaissance

The Northern Renaissance was a product of intellectual and artistic influences from the Italian Renaissance, strongly modified by the work of northern intellectuals such as the humanist Desiderius Erasmus (1466–1536) and religious reformers, including Martin Luther (1483–1546) and John Calvin (1509–64). After the turn of the 16th century Italian painting began to influence northern Europe. The German artist Matthais Gothardt Neithardt (often known as Grünewald, ca. 1480–1528) was among the first to combine the bold use of color and sharp attention to detail, championed by earlier Flemish masters, with Italian methods like linear perspective. Albrecht Dürer (1471–1528), the foremost northern artist of his time, traveled to Venice and brought both Italian techniques and a Renaissance sensibility to his art.

Albrecht Dürer, the foremost northern artist of his time, traveled to Venice to learn Italian techniques and brought elegance and careful observation to his many religious paintings and self-portraits. Dürer's detailed woodcut prints, such as *St. Jerome in His Study* (1514), were much admired in Italy, and his watercolor paintings were probably the first landscape studies in Western art. Further from Renaissance delicacy, the eccentric Dutch painter Hieronymus Bosch promoted Christian morality with grotesque imagery, disturbing perspectives, and apocalyptic violence. Bosch's complicated religious triptychs, including *The Garden of Earthly Delights* (ca. 1503–04), presented dark allegories about human folly that would later inspire 20th-century Surrealists.

The Northern Renaissance was a product of intellectual and artistic influences from the Italian Renaissance, strongly modified by the work of northern intellectuals such as the humanist Desiderius Erasmus and religious reformers, including Martin Luther and John Calvin. After 1517, the Protestant Reformation curtailed the German tradition of religious paintings, although it still flourished in southern Europe and the Catholic realms of Germany. Luther was indifferent to religious art, but Calvin was actively hostile toward it, so in the Calvinist Netherlands portraiture and secular scenes flourished instead. Hans Holbein the Younger (1497–1543), a German artist working in Switzerland and England, became famous for his monumental, intensely detailed portraits of King Henry VIII and Erasmus. Lucas Cranach painted several portraits of Erasmus, as well as pagan-themed works.

Other northern artists turned toward secular subject matter. Pieter Bruegel the Elder (1525/30–69) painted scenes of peasant life that document the daily life of the time but also suggest allegory. His *Hunters in the Snow* (1565), for example, shows empty-handed men and their dogs returning to a wintry town; the painting's mood invites the viewer to consider symbolic meaning. Albrecht Altdorfer (ca. 1480–1538) also painted landscapes that seem to invite allegorical interpretation. These secular works pointed the way for the development of the landscape and genre painting characteristic of northern art of the next century.

Mannerism

After 1520, as artists strove for increasingly virtuosic effects, a new style emerged in Rome and Florence. Reacting against the idealized naturalism of the High Renaissance, several artists began to intentionally distort the perspectives, figures, colors, and objects in their paintings. The term "Mannerism" was initially used to criticize such works as being artificially "mannered" after certain aspects of Raphael and Michelangelo; however, recently some art historians have considered some of Michelangelo's later work to be of the Mannerist style.

One of the earliest Mannerist paintings, Rosso Fiorentino's (1494–1540) *Descent from the Cross* (1521), abandoned Renaissance balance and harmony for a dizzying composition of discordant colors and sharp angles.

Parmigianino (1503–40) presented otherworldly figures with elongated bodies, improbably smooth skin, and contrived poses in paintings such as *Madonna with the Long Neck* (ca. 1535). Agnolo Bronzino (1503–72) became famous for rigidly elegant portraits with precisely rendered clothing. Tintoretto (1518–94) emulated Titian's color and light but traded naturalism for dynamic and emotional compositions such as his *Last Supper* (ca. 1594), going to great lengths to give the event an everyday setting to contrast with the supernatural aspects of Christ and the angels.

Domenicos Theotocopolous (known as El Greco, 1541–1614) was a controversial artist who worked in both Venice and Spain. His paintings—which include perceptive portraits, turbulent landscapes, and eccentrically iconographic religious scenes—feature elongated figures, vivid and sometimes grotesque colors, and jumbled compositions. However, El Greco's human figures—especially in devotional paintings such as *The Adoration of the Shepherds* (1612–14) and *The Burial of the Count Orgaz* (1586)—seem to glow from an inner light, and his interweaving of form and space greatly influenced Paul Cézanne and Pablo Picasso three centuries later.

Baroque Art (1600–1750)

Known as the "century of genius" for such scientific giants as Galileo, Descartes, and Newton, the 17th century gave rise to a number of movements in the visual arts that had in common an interest in ornament and the play of light. Some, but not all, of these movements are contained within the boundaries of the Baroque movement.

The term *baroque* (possibly from the Portuguese *barroco*, an irregularly shaped pearl) was originally used to mean grotesque, excessive, and bizarre. The Baroque style was characterized by an interest in movement and the dramatic; Baroque artists explored the drama of psychology and emotion, created dramatic decorative flourishes, and made full use of light (contrasted with dark) as a theatrical device.

Italy and the Baroque

In Italy Michelangelo Merisi da Caravaggio (1571–1610) developed a new type of realism known as *naturalism*. He insisted upon using common people as models and placing them in ordinary contemporary settings. He is credited with developing the technique of lighting known as *tenebrism*, produced by a single source of light coming into the picture at a sharp angle, used to enhance dramatic gestures and highlight the most important features of the scene; other parts of the picture were thrown into deep, rich shadows. Especially when applied to biblical scenes, Caravaggio's naturalist techniques were considered shocking and unseemly by many of his contemporaries. One of Caravaggio's best-known followers was Artemesia Gentileschi (1593–1652/3), whose bold use of chiaroscuro and tenebristic lighting lent powerful emotional impact to her paintings.

Other Roman artists developed the style of idealism, derived from the harmonious, idealized aesthetic of Renaissance artists like Raphael. One of the most important advocates of this style, Annibale Carracci (1560–1609), is best known for his ceiling paintings in the Palazzo Farnese, Rome, inspired by Michelangelo's Sistine Chapel frescos. Carracci in turn influenced later generations of artists, notably Giambattista Tiepolo (1696–1770), whose work is a celebration of classically inspired pageantry.

The decorative impulses of Baroque art are found with particular force in Italian sculpture and architecture. Figures are often shown during climactic moments of action, and seem to be fully engaged in the space around them. The work of the ornamentalist Gianlorenzo Bernini (1598–1680) typifies the excesses of Baroque sculpture. Bernini's most famous piece, The *Ecstasy of St. Theresa* (1645–52), shows the saint, whose heart is about to be pierced by an angel's arrow, rising heavenward on wavelike clouds while golden shafts of light come down from above.

The Baroque in Flanders and Holland

Peter Paul Rubens (1577–1640) studied in Italy and brought Baroque painting to northern Europe, reuniting northern and southern styles, much as Dürer had during the Renaissance. Rubens painted grand historical and religious scenes that combined Italian qualities, like warm Venetian color, a sensuous, painterly flourish, and active, almost tumbling compositions, with a typically Flemish attention to realistic detail. In a highly successful career, Rubens was not only a painter but also a scholar, a diplomat, and (like Titian) the proprietor of a vast studio staffed by many assistants.

Dutch artists developed a Baroque style through contact with Rubens and Caravaggio. In middle-class Protestant Holland, the biggest art consumers were prosperous citizens rather than church institutions, and artists sold their work in a market system. Artists created still lifes and landscapes of familiar contemporary objects and places, as well as genre scenes of everyday life—a type of image that soon became popular all over Europe.

Dutch painters found that naturalism in the style of Caravaggio fit in well with the secular northern tradition, and they tended to paint with less of the rosy flourish that characterizes Rubens. Some of the most important Dutch artists of the time include Frans Hals (1581/5–1666), who produced genre scenes, and Rembrandt van Rijn (1606–69), often considered the period's greatest master, who was fascinated with Old Testament scenes and the effects of light, producing dramas of unsurpassed emotional and psychological subtlety. Jan Vermeer (1632–75) was a unique genre painter who painted quiet, contemplative images of everyday domesticity that often feature exquisite renderings of daylight.

The Baroque in Spain Like the Dutch, Spanish artists were influenced by Caravaggio and by the Flemish, developing a tenebristic, realistic style. In devoutly Catholic Spain, religious painting retained its popularity well after it had waned in much of Europe. Francisco de Zurbarán, one of the foremost painters of the Spanish Baroque, is known for his quiet, intense devotional images. The most famous Spanish artist of the time was Diego Velázquez (1599–1660), and his masterpiece, *Las Meninas* (1656), has become one of the best-known works in Western art. A large group portrait centered on Spain's young princess, the painting exhibits a typically Baroque fascination with countless variations in the qualities of light.

The Baroque in France and England A Carracci-inspired classicism came to dominate French Baroque painting, mainly because of the influence of painters Nicolas Poussin (1594–1665) and Claude Lorrain (1604/5–1682). Poussin's classical landscapes and scenes from ancient literature are rendered with restraint, austerity, and a seriousness meant to appeal to the mind instead of the senses, while Lorrain became known for idyllic classical landscapes in which the elements of nature are arranged to produce an ideal beauty. Poussin's followers, known as the Poussinistes, emulated his emphasis on design over color, and they were soon opposed by artists known as Rubénistes, who favored the sensuous, rosy qualities typical of Rubens.

Rococo Toward the end of the Baroque period, the Rubénistes became more popular. Three painters in this style, Jean-Antoine Watteau (1684–1721), François Boucher (1703–70) and Jean-Honoré Fragonard (1732–1806), who painted scenes of merrymaking in lush landscapes, typify the Rococo movement, which mainly affected architecture and the decorative arts in southern Germany, Austria, and Central Europe. The aesthetic favored ornate and playful decorative motifs, often based on themes of water, shells, and other organic sources.

A prominent theme in Rococo art was *chinoiserie*, a decorative style based on Chinese art (particularly painted porcelain) but modified to satisfy a European taste for picturesque exotica. Throughout the 18th century, wealthy patrons indulged their fancies for chinoiserie gardens, pavilions, and pagodas, filled with real or faux Chinese porcelain and lacquerware; the movement stimulated the production of European porcelain and other decorative arts.

The 18th century saw the first internationally important group of English painters since the Middle Ages, all of whom were influenced by the polished hues and idealized detail of the Rococo. They included William Hogarth (1697–1764), famous for painting scenes of biting social commentary, such as *The Rake's Progress*; the portraitist Thomas Gainsborough (1727–88); and the classicist Sir Joshua Reynolds (1723–92).

Early American Painting

The early colonial period in America was not especially friendly to the fine arts: colonists were concerned primarily with survival, and the Puritans rejected even religious art. As a result, many of the first American painters copied 17th-century European conventions; however, as colonists sought to commemorate their new surroundings, realistic portraiture and documentary scenes became popular. Distinctively American art forms emerged by the mid-18th century.

Benjamin West (1738–1820) was the first native-born American to study art in Europe, where he became a leading history painter. West introduced historical accuracy to neoclassical composition with works such as *The Death of General Wolfe* (1770). While painting in England, West founded the Royal Academy of Arts in 1768, where many Americans came to study. John Singleton Copley, like West, exhibited in England. Unlike West, Copley preferred to spend his days in Boston. His painstaking technique and true-to-life details in paintings such as *Watson and the Shark* (1778) made him one of the most influential painters in colonial America. Gilbert Stuart studied with West but returned to the United States, where his naturalistic approach reinvigorated the "Grand Manner" of full-length portraiture. Stuart's unfinished portrait of George Washington (1796) was engraved on the dollar bill. Another of West's pupils, John Trumbull (1756–1843), memorialized the Revolution and inspired generations of history painters with dramatic works such as *The Battle of Bunker Hill* (1786).

Charles Willson Peale (1741–1827) not only painted portraits of American leaders, but was also a curator and scientist. Peale opened a museum exhibiting artwork alongside natural history specimens, and used science as a subject in works such as *Exhuming the First American Mastodon* (1808). His style of scientific naturalism, which combined neoclassical composition with precise observation, became a model for many subsequent artists.

As photographers took over the portraiture trade, American painters followed trappers and surveyors into the wilderness of the 1803 Louisiana Purchase. John James Audubon (1785–1851) used his understanding of biology and botany to make vivid studies of birds, plants, and animals. George Catlin (1796–1872) painted anthropological portraits and hunting scenes of Native Americans, portraying them as noble but endangered peoples. Both Catlin and Audubon published their paintings in books, which gave them widespread appeal.

Neoclassicism and Romanticism (1750–1850)

Neoclassicism   The Neoclassical movement was a revival of the popular Renaissance style based on Classical Greek and Roman art. Neoclassicism was linked with the principles of the Enlightenment, which championed reason as the noblest human attribute; the ideal beauty created by classical artists was thought to exemplify natural law and the principles of reason.

Many artists since the Renaissance had embraced classical values, but the Neoclassical movement differed from previous revivals. It was prompted in part by a series of archaeological discoveries that made much more ancient art accessible to contemporary artists. In addition, the American Revolution of 1776 and French Revolution of 1789 questioned established authority in fundamental ways. The Rococo style of the mid-18th century was seen by intellectuals of the revolutionary era as frivolous and aristocratic. Many artists looked instead to the serious historical and mythological paintings of the Baroque classicist painter Poussin for guidance on how

the classical style could be adopted to modern times.

Neoclassical sculptors, such as Jean Antoine Houdon (1741–1828) and Antonio Canova (1757–1822), created portraits of important contemporary figures such as Napoleon and the Enlightenment thinker Voltaire. They gave their figures a sense of historical importance by portraying them in the costumes typical of classical gods and rulers.

Neoclassical painters also sometimes used this device, recording scenes from recent history with an emphasis on line and structural composition and with figures that reveal an ideal yet austere beauty. The French painter Jacques Louis David (1748–1825) became famous for his portrait of the freshly murdered revolutionary leader Georges Danton, as well as Benjamin West, who staked a claim for the neoclassical heritage of the United States.

Later in the period, the French painter Jean-Auguste-Dominique Ingres (1780–1867) built on David's style, though his images, which have an obsessive neoclassical attention to detail, are often romantic in subject. His portraits of young women, as well as his many paintings of orientalist themes such as the *Odalisque* (1819), celebrate a romanticized ideal of plump, opulent womanhood.

Romanticism   The Romantic movement did not necessarily favor a specific aesthetic; rather, Romanticism is characterized by an approach to art in which emotion is more important than reason. While Neoclassicism and Romanticism seem to follow opposing trends, some scholar argue that Neoclassicism is a romantic revival of the past, and thus simply one phase of Romanticism.

Romanticism began as a trend in literature and was a movement in which the written and visual arts were closely linked, one often serving as inspiration for the other. Romantic artists were attracted to subjects that were thrilling, awe-inspiring, grotesque, and often fanciful. Because Romantic artists believed in the expression of the subjective experiences of the individual, the movement supported any number of styles, including a revival of several older styles. The self-taught English painter William Blake (1757–1827) was strongly influenced by Michelangelo and Dürer; Blake's art reflects a rejection of the Enlightenment ideal of reason in favor of a deeply held mystical vision of God's role in the universe.

Other Romantic artists looked back to the Baroque era for inspiration. Francisco Goya (1746–1828), for example, based his aesthetic on the dramatic lighting and dark palette of Baroque artists Rembrandt and Velázquez. Goya painted gruesome scenes documenting contemporary battles as well as violently thrilling nightmare images. Other important neo-Baroque painters were the French artists Jean-Antoine Gros (1771–1835), Eugène Delacroix (1798–1863), and Théodore Géricault (1791–1834), whose painting *The Raft of the Medusa* depicted shipwrecked sailors in a manner that combined Classical composition with Romantic intensity of emotion.

Romantic Landscape Painting   Romantic artists admired nature for its wild, untamed qualities, believing that people connected with the natural world on an emotional, rather than a cerebral, level. While Neoclassical landscape painters had painted idealized visions of nature, Romantic painters, believing in the importance of sincerity, wanted to capture nature as it was, without altering its most essential qualities.

The French painter Camille Corot (1796–1875) was known for executing entire paintings outdoors, unlike the Neoclassicists, who painted outdoors only to make studies. Corot was highly influential to the Barbizon school of painters, who worked on often loosely painted landscapes and country scenes in and near the village of Barbizon, not far from Paris; the school focused on Théodore Rousseau (1812–67) and is also associated with the realist François Millet (1814–75).

In England, John Constable (1776–1837) and J.M.W. Turner (1775–1851) painted landscapes that focused on fleeting qualities of light and atmosphere, evoking the sublime power of nature. Turner, in particular, emphasized the importance of color over line, in a reversal of the Neoclassical preference, and recalled the sensuous hues of Rubens.

Orientalism   During the early 19th century, European trade and political involvement in the Middle East, North Africa, India, and other parts of what was vaguely known as "the Orient" led to a fascination with artistic portrayals of those lands. Many of the Romantics pursued Oriental themes. Orientalist art combined careful depiction of exotic objects (buildings, costumes, objects of daily use) with wholly imaginary scenes of life in "Eastern" harems and palaces. The Orient was romanticized as colorful, exotic, erotic, and feminine, a place where female nudity could safely be exposed to the evaluating European gaze. The odalisques and harem scenes of Jean Auguste Ingres (1780–1867) contributed to the popularity of the Orientalist genre; other promi-nent Orientalists were Eugène Delacroix (1798–1863) and J. L. Gérôme (1824–1904).

The Hudson River School   The Hudson River School was the most important art movement in 19th-century America. The founders of the movement, Thomas Cole (1801–48) and Asher Durand (1796–1886) painted many of their works in the Hudson River Valley and nearby regions (the Catskill and Adirondack Mountains, Lake George); prior to the opening of the West, this was the most dramatic scenery to be found in the early United States. Other artists associated with the movement, such as the prolific John Frederick Kensett (1816–72), ranged widely among the rivers and mountains of New England and the Middle Atlantic states, and among the rocks and salt marshes of the seacoast from Maine to Long Island. The characteristic features of Hudson River School paintings include an interplay of sky and water, dramatic lighting, picturesque rocks and trees, and a sense of awe created through a comparison of the grandeur of nature with people and buildings depicted as small and insubstantial.

The Hudson River School painters were among the first professionally trained artists in America (except for a few earlier portraitists, notably Gilbert Stuart), and their paintings, many of which were publicly exhibited, would have been the first professional works of art seen by many Americans. Concentrating on landscape painting and the effects of light, the Hudson River School painters were influenced by European landscape painting of the 17th century and also by contemporary European Romantic landscape artists (Constable, Turner, Friedrich). The Americans generally rejected the concept of Romanticism, believing that they were letting the power of nature and the spiritual qualities of the untamed American wilderness speak for themselves, but in retrospect it is clear that they were idealizing a landscape that was already being transformed by agriculture, industry, and a growing network of canals and railroads.

After the Civil War the movement lost some of its coherence, and a number of artists associated with the Hudson River School went on to address other subjects. As early as the 1830's Thomas Cole himself had painted huge allegorical works, notably the five-canvas *The Course of Empire*. Frederic Edwin Church was one of several second-generation Hudson River painters whose fascination with glowing atmospheric light led to a movement called Luminism. Like later Impressionism, Luminism focuses on the effects of light on a subject, generally a landscape; however, Luminism is also characterized by attention to detail and concealed brushstrokes. Church traveled widely and produced such varied scenes as *The Icebergs* (1861) and *The Heart of the Andes* (1859). The expansionist ideas of Manifest Destiny were visible in the Luminist works of German-born Albert Bierstadt, who joined several westward expeditions and returned with awe-inspiring images such as *The Rocky Mountains, Lander's Peak* (1863) and *Sierra Nevada Morning* (ca. 1890). The marine painter Fitz Henry Lane applied the warm pervasive light of Luminism to quiet, mournful seascapes.

Academic Painting

During the 17th and 18th centuries, academies of painting had been established under royal patronage in all of the major capitals of Europe, including Paris, London, Berlin, and Rome. The academies functioned as a kind of artistic civil service, producing paintings to decorate royal palaces and public buildings and to commemorate important national events. The academies also functioned as schools, training painters, sculptors, and other artists in the demanding techniques required to produce large, polished works of art that combined highly realistic details with heroic grandeur of conception. The academies also functioned to grant a sort of official seal of approval on the work of favored artists, who were invited to submit works to annual exhibitions (such as the Salons of Paris and the Burlington House exhibitions of the Royal Academy in London). During the 19th century the academies became bastions of conservative styles such as Historicism and Orientalism. Academic painters such as the French Paul Delaroche (1797–1856) and the English Lord Frederick Leighton (1830–96) were hugely admired in their own time but regarded as hopelessly old-fashioned by later generations. The experiments of Impressionists, Pointillists, Symbolists, and other avant-garde artists of the later 19th century were undertaken in conscious opposition to academic art.

Realism, Impressionism, and Post-Impressionism (1850–1900)

Realism   In the mid-19th century, a group of French painters led by Gustave Courbet (1819–77), reacting against academic tradition, made it their aim to produce objective, unidealized images. Painters such as François Millet (1814–75) and Honoré Daumier (1808–79), chose as their subjects peasants and moments of everyday life pre-

viously considered unworthy of the high art tradition.

American Realism   As national optimism faded in the wake of the Civil War, Winslow Homer (1836–1910) and Thomas Eakins (1844–1916) developed soberly realistic styles that combined documentary objectivity with unsentimental compassion. Homer began his career producing illustrations for *Harper's Weekly*, but unlike most of the other illustrators, Homer depicted everyday camp life rather than battle scenes. Homer's development as an artist was slow but constant: over time his oil paintings became larger, his figures more solitary, and his ability to portray naturalistic detail greater. He produced scores of seascapes exploring the relationship between man and nature, like *Breezing Up* (1876), and *Lost on the Grand Banks* (1885). Known for bold, fluid brushwork and strong compositions, Homer worked extensively in watercolor and helped to popularize the medium with paintings such as *Adirondack Guide* (1894).

Thomas Eakins studied in France but derided the French Academy aesthetic as "affectation" and proclaimed truth as his highest artistic goal. Rejecting formal portraits, Eakins painted his subjects at work, as in *The Gross Clinic* (1875), which shows Dr. Samuel Gross presiding over a surgery. He also startled critics with his vigorous scenes of Philadelphia life, including wrestlers, nude male swimmers and rowers, as in *Max Schmitt in a Single Scull* (1871). In addition to painting, Eakins taught at the Pennsylvania Academy. Eakins stressed anatomy and drawing from live, nude models rather than the traditional methods of using plaster casts of antique sculptures.

Americans Abroad   Although art schools were established in Philadelphia and New York by the mid-19th century, newly affordable travel encouraged many American painters to study or work abroad among the old European masterworks. After studying painting in France, James McNeill Whistler (1834–1903) settled in England, where he had his first success when *Symphony in White No. 1: The White Girl* (1862) was shown at the original Salon des Refuses in 1863. While Whistler's most famous painting might be *Arrangement in Grey and Black: Portrait of the Author's Mother* (1871), it was another painting that caught the attention of the public in the 1870s. In 1877, the British art critic John Ruskin attacked Whistler's painting, *Nocturne in Black and Gold: The Falling Rocket* (1874) in a scathing newspaper review. Whistler responded to this critique by suing Ruskin. While Whistler technically "won" the trial, he was awarded only a farthing and was forced to split the court costs. These costs, along with the money invested in his home, brought Whistler to bankruptcy in 1879.

John Singer Sargent (1856–1925) studied painting in Florence and Paris. His early work shows an interest in landscapes, but as his style and technique matured he moved toward portraiture, as in his highly controversial *Portrait of Madame X* (1884), which boldly captured its subject's haughty sexuality. His mastery of lighting is also evident in works such as *Carnation Lily, Lily Rose* (1886), which shows two young girls hanging lanterns in a garden at dusk. After 1910, Sargent gave up portraiture and devoted the rest of his life to painting murals and landscapes in watercolor, painting more than 2,000 by the end of his career.

The Pre-Raphaelites   In 1848 eight English artists formed the Pre-Raphaelite Brotherhood, a society dedicated to reviving what they considered to be the sincerity and naturalism of the early Renaissance masters, especially those of northern Europe. In eschewing artistic frivolity and adopting a position of moral consciousness in art, they hoped to help reform the ills of modern civilization, and they depicted historical and literary subjects in clear, detailed images that often involved visual symbolism. Members of the original group, including Dante Gabriel Rossetti (1828–82), William Holman Hunt (1827–1910) and John Everett Millais (1829–96) were later joined by other like-minded artists such as William Morris (1834–96) and Edward Burne-Jones (1833–98).

Impressionism   In 1863 a group of innovative French artists, inspired by the Realists and frustrated by the conservative standards of the annual Paris Salon, decided to show their work at the *Salon des Refusés*—an exhibition of artworks that had been turned down for exhibition by the official Salon. The "Refusés" included Édouard Manet (1832–1883), Claude Monet (1840–1926), Edgar Degas (1834–1917), Camille Pissarro (1830–1903), and Paul Cézanne (1839–1906), among many others. They were the key proponents of the radically new style of painting called Impressionism. The artists had been working since the 1860's toward an aesthetic that could capture the essential qualities of an image, such as the shifting effects of light and atmosphere. The term Impressionism itself, coined by a critic, was first used derisively after the artists' group exhibition (1874), referring to Monet's painting,

Impression, Sunrise (1873).

The guiding motive for the Impressionists was to reinvent painting appropriate for the "modern age." Following the Realist lead, Impressionists painted landscapes, scenes of leisure, and urban street scenes, always featuring contemporary settings rather than historical narratives, and painting scenes from direct observation, often *en plein air* (outdoors) rather than in a studio setting.

As the movement developed, distinctive approaches to both color and composition emerged. Traditional painting had long emphasized techniques such as *sfumato* or *chiaroscuro* to create the illusion of depth in a painting using strong, dark, or grayish shadows, but Impressionists attempted to rewrite the rules for color based on scientific study of the qualities of natural light on a subject. The practice of painting *en plein air* resulted in both the increasing tendency to flatten pictorial space and use complementary hues for shadows, both phenomena that appear to the eye under bright sunlight. In addition, many Impressionists interpreted the light and movement of subjects in loose, abbreviated strokes, a drastic change from the classical style of studio painting, which had long prized subtle brushwork. Impressionists also drew heavily from Asian color palettes and compositions, mimicking the elongated pictorial formats, asymmetrical compositions, and aerial perspective found in Japanese printmaking.

Édouard Manet   Manet's reputation as founder of the Impressionists was established by two paintings that were as groundbreaking for their controversial subject matter as for their visual feel. The prevailing bohemian attitude in Paris encouraged Manet and other artists to develop themes, techniques, and subject matter the Academie had long prohibited: the underclass, sex, drugs, unbalanced composition, flattened space, experiments with color and tone, and daring personal style. *Le Déjeuner sur l'Herbe* (1863) depicts a picnic attended by two men in modern attire and a naked woman who is staring confidently at the viewer. This odd, scandalous scene fit nowhere in the traditional subject matter for paintings, which had for nearly a century been concerned with allegorical or mythological themes. Furthermore, Manet had flattened the colors and visual space of the painting; this combination of subtle color palette and confrontational subject matter refuted both the idealized style and traditional content of academic painting. Patrons and critics at the original Salon des Refusés were disgusted, but the

Déjeuner was an immediate sensation among artists. At the next Salon de Paris, Manet exhibited *Olympia* (1864), which depicts a naked prostitute lying on a bed while looking at the viewer, again outraging critics but energizing the Parisian cadre of experimental artists.

Camille Pissarro Impressionist paintings were mostly rejected from official exhibitions such as the Salon de Paris and were roundly criticized for looking unfinished or sloppy. Among Impressionists, Camille Pissarro was key in organizing the group to exhibit on its own, and in 1874 the Impressionist circle held the first show in which five of Pissarro's works were featured (one of which was *The Old Road to Ennery*, 1872) alongside works by Monet, Renoir, Degas, and Berthe Morisot. The show was a critical failure and in the succeeding years several of the original collective dropped out, yet Pissarro remained steadfast. By 1880, he was focusing primarily on figure studies rather than landscapes (*Young Peasant Woman Drinking Her Café au Lait*, 1881). Toward the end of his career, Pissarro experimented with Pointillism but then turned back to series paintings featuring Paris, often working on multiple canvases at the same time.

Claude Monet For many, Monet's paintings typify the visual style of Impressionism. Made *en plein air*, his paintings are composed with unblended colors and short, thick brushstrokes meant to capture specific, fleeting qualities of light. This is easily recognized in Monet's multiple series of paintings, each of which depicts the same subject in several paintings made quickly at various times of day, including those of Rouen Cathedral (1892–94), haystacks (1890–91), and water lilies (painted over 30 years beginning in 1899).

Edgar Degas In the early 1870s, Degas began to develop simplified compositions, partly under the influence of Japanese prints. Unlike his contemporaries, who were experimenting with painting outdoors, Degas continued to work in the studio. Between 1870 and 1873, Degas first began working on studies of ballet rehearsals and performances, including *Dance Class* (1871). In the years to follow, dancers and other performers would become one of Degas most frequently painted subjects, as in *Singer with a Glove* (1878).

Pierre-Auguste Renoir Established as a painter of bourgeois leisure, such as in *Dancing at Le Moulin de la Gallette* (1876), many of Renoir's (1841–1919) paintings are portraits, mostly of well-to-do women and girls, whom he painted with a characteristically cheerful palette and generally flattering compositions, as in *Two Sisters (On the Terrace)* (1881).

Mary Cassatt The American Mary Cassatt (1844–1926) was one of few women to be invited to exhibit with the Impressionists, first in 1879, and again in 1880, 1881, and 1886. Almost all of Cassatt's paintings feature women and children as subjects, rendered in warm colors and soft strokes. She was influential in the development of pastels as a medium, and she was known in Parisian art circles for her drawing talent and her command of asymmetrical composition. After an exhibition of Japanese artists such as Utamaro and Toyokuni in Paris, Cassatt began to shift her emphasis from form to pattern, as seen in works such as *Woman Bathing* (1890).

Post-Impressionism Younger contemporaries took advantage of the new artistic freedoms provided by the original Impressionist rebellion, and in 1884 organized the Société des Artistes Indépendants (Society of Independent Artists), which showed works by more than 400 artists at its first exhibition. In some cases, these new groups and styles were an extension of Impressionist ideas, but in others, they veered off in novel directions. The key movements of this period—Post-Impressionism, Primitivism, Fauvism, Pointillism, Art Nouveau—set the stage for the dramatic evolution that would occur in the arts in the 20th century.

Post-Impressionism generally refers to new styles that arose after the mid-1880s. Where the Impressionists had been a more or less cohesive group related by specific ideas, Post-Impressionism is better thought of as a convenient name, rather than a strict school of thought. Many Post-Impressionists pursued personal stylistic expression, rather than a common methodology or outlook.

Vincent van Gogh (1853–90) By far, the most well known Post-Impressionist artist is the Dutch painter Vincent van Gogh, whose short 10-year career has nonetheless resulted in perhaps the most famous body of work of any painter of the last several hundred years. Almost completely unknown in his lifetime, van Gogh seldom exhibited and sold only a single painting. Although he used some Impressionist techniques, such as short brushstrokes and bright colors, van Gogh's paintings are considered Post-Impressionist because they portray ecstatic highs and lows, unlike most Impressionist works that sought an objective rendering of a scene. Often, van Gogh distorted space, color, and texture in his work, incorporating highly rhythmic, swirling surface patterns in his paintings, as in the famous *Starry Night* (1889), which was painted a year before his suicide.

Paul Gauguin (1848–1903) Often described somewhat misleadingly as a Post-Impressionist, Gauguin was a member of several movements over a short period of time, including Cloissonnism, Synthetism, and Primitivism, all of which favored bright colors, simplified shapes, and compositions that reflected an artist's emotions or opinions. Gauguin was a key proponent of Primitivism, which rejected many aspects of the Western artistic tradition and chose to emulate native styles and subjects from various developing nations. His best-known paintings were created after he abandoned his life and family in Europe and moved to Tahiti, where he used tropical palettes to depict Tahitian women, as in *Tahitian Women on the Beach* (1891) and *Motherhood* (1899).

Georges Seurat (1859–91) Though inspired by the broken brushstrokes and patterned use of color popularized by the Impressionists, Seurat sought to develop a style that was more rational and scientific. Seurat studied optics and color theory, developing a method of painting in small dots of unmixed color placed close to one another, which he called Divisionism (more often referred to as Pointillism). In Pointillist paintings, colors appear to blend together as the viewer steps back from the painting. Seurat's best-known work, *A Sunday Afternoon on the Island of La Grande Jatte* (1884–85), was a triumphant vindication of his theories.

Henri Toulouse-Lautrec (1864–1901) In 1892, three years after completion of the Eiffel Tower crowned Paris's status as the City of Lights, the Moulin Rouge club opened its doors, setting the stage for Henri Toulouse-Lautrec's glamorously lurid, off-rhythm depictions of cancan nightlife, as in his 1892 painting *Au Moulin Rouge*. Toulouse-Lautrec is known for his paintings and posters of dancers, madames, and carousers from Parisian cabarets, and in his work, color, space, and pattern became highly distorted.

Paul Cezanne (1839–1906) While Cezanne used many Impressionist techniques and exhibited with them in 1874, his work focused more on the underlying structures of the objects he painted than on light qualities or observation, and he is often considered a transitional figure in the history of Western painting. By the mid-1890s, Cezanne's paintings had already exhausted Impressionism and Post-Impressionism and were exhibiting something new, a tense frisson of flattened color and space that anticipated the Cubism eventually developed by Pablo Picasso and Georges Braque. This new style, which would greatly influence later abstractionist painters, can be clearly seen in his famous depictions of Montagne Sainte-Victoire from 1898–1900.

Henri Rousseau (1844–1910) Although he never left France nor saw a jungle, Henri Rousseau's paintings mostly depict jungle scenes and are characterized by extremely stylized shapes and Primitivist style. Self-taught and late to painting (he began painting seriously at age 40), Rousseau was often ridiculed during his lifetime, but his works, including *The Repast of the Lion* (1907), are widely popular today.

Art Nouveau The libertine excesses of Parisian nightlife combined with traditional Czech printing style inspired the designer Alphonse Mucha's organic, eroticized illustrations and helped define a new style of decoration coined Art Nouveau. At once lively, stylish, and erotically charged, Art Nouveau washed over Europe under a variety of names and affected several disciplines: in France and England it was shown in the works of the designers Alphonse Mucha and William Morris and illustrator Aubrey Beardsley; in Germany, it was called Jugendstil and was evident in paintings by Egon Schiele and Hermann Obrist; in Spain, it was the funky, organic Modernisme of the architect Antoni Gaudi; in Austria it was the Viennese Secession, a group that included the painter Gustav Klimt and architects Otto Wagner and Joseph Maria Olbrich, whose Secession Hall in Vienna is an early landmark of modern architecture. Art Nouveau would captivate Europe and remain popular for roughly 15 years between 1895 and about 1910.

Symbolism Paul Gauguin's late work made him a leading figure in the Symbolist movement, which involved both literature and art in the late 19th century. The Symbolists, who included the "naïve" painter Henri Rousseau (1844–1910) and Odilon Redon (1840–1916), whose work often featured fantastic imaginary creatures, opposed rationality and materialism and embraced emotion and spirituality. They were followed by a group that called themselves the Nabis, which is the Hebrew word for prophet; their work stressed outline and the bold, simplified use of color. Leading members of the group included Edouard Vuillard (1868–1940), Pierre Bonnard (1867–1947), and the sculptor Aristide Maillol (1861–1944). Amedeo Modigliani (1884–1920), though of a later generation, shared much of their sensibility.

Symbolism was extremely influential to the emotionally charged Expressionist artists at the turn of the last century, including Edvard Munch (1863–1944), whose now-iconic image *The Scream* (1893) depicts a nightmarish vision of a solitary, cartoonlike figure standing under a feverish sky.

Nineteenth-Century Sculpture

The painter Edgar Degas created a scandal when he exhibited his unidealized statue of the *Little Dancer, Aged Fourteen* (1878–81), which included real hair and a ribbon and was considered both ugly and technically bizarre. It nevertheless was a landmark in liberating sculpture from academic formalism. The most influential sculptor of the late 19th century was probably Auguste Rodin (1840–1917). His figures, in unconventional poses and with exaggerated shapes, struck some critics as looking unfinished; this has led some art historians to compare him with the Impressionists, though he was more strongly influenced by the Realists. Rodin's assistant and mistress, Camille Claudel (1864–1943), was also successful at a similarly expressive style.

Modernism

Increasingly pursuing their own creative ideas, artists in the late 19th century began a time of broad experimentation, beginning what is now called the Modernist period, roughly a hundred years from the mid-1860's through the mid-1960's. Beginning with the Impressionists' initial rejection of established academic rules, European modernists supplanted the old definition of art with the new, avant-garde belief that an artist should act as a visionary and forge new cultural trends. As growing numbers of artists began to work outside the confining tastes of the *Academie*, they banded together into groups with shared aims, even while developing individual artistic voices. To the extent that so many artists chose to work within these groups, Modernism is unique among art periods for its profusion of manifestos and movements. Many of these movements were short-lived, but have provided lasting influence on the direction of the arts to the present day.

The movements and styles of the Modernist era can be characterized by several general trends. Many artists moved toward abstraction, gradually abandoning representational images in favor of pure line, color, and form. Artists also took a self-conscious interest in the process of artmaking, emphasizing qualities like brushstrokes and chisel marks that call attention to the actions of the artist. Others introduced new and unconventional materials to their art. Alongside abstraction, several strains of realism

continued to flourish, particularly in the United States.

Two highly important artists of the Modernist era, Pablo Picasso (1881–1973) and Henri Matisse (1869–1954), were to some extent identified with particular schools or trends in painting, but they also defined or anticipated a broad range of new possibilities in art.

Picasso was born in Spain but lived his entire adult life in France. A prodigiously gifted painter, he was able to work in a multitude of styles. His "Blue Period" paintings (1903–06) are tinged with a sad and poetic beauty, emotional tones that he overthrew completely and deliberately with his masterpiece *Les Demoiselles d'Avignon* (1907), which was in effect a modernist manifesto. Influenced by African sculpture, Picasso devoted much of his artistic career to exploring the ways in which solid shapes could be broken down visually into sets of planes; one result was the Cubist movement (see below).

Expressionism

European artists at the turn of the century continued to develop the trends set in motion by the Impressionists and Post-Impressionists, many of which were inspired by the aesthetics of African, Oceanic, and pre-Columbian art. Painters were attracted to the simplified shapes and flat patches of color used by artists like Gauguin, believing that a departure from illusionistic accuracy allowed more room for imaginative and emotional expression. Artists working with these concepts developed a number of styles that can be called Expressionist.

The first, and very short-lived, Expressionist movement became known as the *Fauves*, or wild beasts, because their heavy outlining, loud color schemes, and seemingly clumsy shapes gave viewers the impression that the artists were untrained or primitive. Matisse was the movement's leading participant. Matisse was a mature painter by the beginning of the 20th century, but he helped to forge the modernist sensibility through his vivid sense of color, his skewed use of perspective, and his bold approach to design. Many of Matisse's best-known paintings explore the play of light in settings in southern France and northern Africa. Georges Rouault (1871–1958), later known for his religious paintings, was another.

Another Expressionist movement, the Vienna Secession, was influenced by the Art Nouveau trend in the decorative arts, which favored organic, asymmetrical linear patterns. The leader of the Vienna Secession, Gustav Klimt (1862–1918), mixed abstract geometric decorative motifs with illusionistic objects and figures in his often erotic images.

The lushness of Klimt's paintings contrasts with the austere and pessimistic canvases of the German Expressionists Emile Nolde (1867–1956) and Ernst Ludwig Kirchner (1880–1938). Allied with a group known as Die Brücke (the Bridge), they stressed the ideal of painting as an expression of inner conviction. The same spirit animates the often anguished work of the Austrian Egon Schiele (1890–1918), who died in the great influenza epidemic of 1918.

Cubism The invention of Cubism by Picasso and Georges Braque (1882–1963) was one of the most important developments in early 20th century art. It is a style of painting in which a picture, usually based on a representational image, is depicted in fragmented planes, rendering it highly abstract. An image of a face, for example, might be shown as four different trapezoidal shapes, each trapezoid acting as a frame through which we see parts of the face from different angles. The shifting perspective is said to represent different moments in time.

The visual and theoretical complexity of Cubism was so unprecedented that at first it met with perplexed reactions, even from avant-garde artists. But it quickly became influential to a number of later movements, including Futurism, in which dynamic fragmented images feature subjects of industrialization, speed, and technology. One of its leading practitioners was the Italian painter and sculptor Umberto Boccioni (1882-1916).

Cubism was closely linked with the genre of collage, a work of art in two dimensions, with scraps of paper, cloth and other materials pasted together in a composition. While forms of collage had been in use for some time, Picasso first introduced it as a high-art technique.

Dada and Surrealism For many artists, World War I was the final indictment of bourgeois European culture. In protest to the supposed rationality of modern culture, a group of Zurich artists started the Dada movement, which prized absurdity, nonconformity, and intuition. Dada was avowedly anti-art, which it felt had been complicit in the buildup to the war. Dada art included spontaneous performances, automatic drawing and writing, collage and cut-ups, elements of chance, presentation of manufactured or found objects as art (called "readymades"), and other procedures aimed at outraging or confounding the art establishment. One such technique was called *automatism*, in which artists tried to let their unconscious take control of their actions, hoping to produce artwork free of inhibition. Hans (Jean) Arp (1887–1966), for example, created collages by dropping square pieces of paper onto a single sheet of paper, and glued them in the chance arrangements in which they landed. Other Dadaists made collages piecing together photos cut from newspapers and magazines, inventing the technique of photomontage.

Notable Dadists included Tristan Tzara (1896–1963), Raoul Hausmann (1886–1971), Man Ray (1890–1976), and Francis Picabia (1879–1953), but the most enduring figure has been Marcel Duchamp (1887–1968). Duchamp originally composed paintings in the Cubist style (his 1912 *Nude Descending a Staircase No. 2* is a seminal Cubist painting), but quickly evolved through several artistic ideas. He exhibited the first readymade sculptures (his 1917 *Fountain*, considered one of the pivotal artworks of the 20th century, was a factory-made urinal), developed chance art, conceptual art, installation art, and kinetic art—all trends explored by postmodernist artists in the latter half of the century.

Evolving from Dada, the circle led by the magnetic André Breton (1896–1966) combined *fin-de-siecle* Symbolism with Sigmund Freud's groundbreaking work in psychoanalysis to develop Surrealism, the artistic exploration of repressed desires and the unconscious. The German painter and former Dadaist Max Ernst (1891–1976) produced works such as *The Elephant Celebes* (1921), which features a mechanical elephant and a headless mannequin. Other surrealist artists included René Magritte (1898–1967), Joan Miró (1893–1983), Yves Tanguy (1900–55), and surrealist pop icon Salvador Dali (1904–89).

The New Objectivity As a reaction to the rise of Expressionism, a new German movement called The New Objectivity prized instead distance, form, simplicity and matter-of-factness. Several adherents would establish the most important Modernist laboratory in Europe, the Weimar-era Bauhaus school (1919–33) led by Walter Gropius (1883–1969). The Bauhaus valued the marriage of form and function, practicality, and mass production. The simplified shapes and clean lines of Bauhaus designs have become iconic modernist forms, and are still widely influential today. Bauhaus instructors included well-known painters Paul Klee

(1879–1940), Wassily Kandinsky (1866–1944), László Moholy-Nagy (1895–1946) and Josef Albers (1888–1976), as well as the architect Ludwig Mies van der Rohe (1886–1969). The Bauhaus disbanded with the rise of Nazism in Germany 1933, but Bauhaus-style workshops such as the Wiener Werkstätte in Vienna and De Stijl in the Netherlands carried on the idea.

Realism in the United States   European Modernism did not immediately affect most artists in the United States until the famous Armory Show of 1913 shocked New York audiences with various Post-Impressionist and Modernist styles. American artists at the beginning of the 20th century developed several realist styles, some of which were independent of modernist influence, some of which reacted against modernism, and some of which were influenced by it.

A group of artists known as The Eight or the Ashcan School developed around the artist Robert Henri (1865–1929), painting unglamorous and unadorned scenes of everyday urban life in a loose, painterly fashion that was considered anti-academic. One of Henri's later students, Edward Hopper (1882–1967), disavowed the loose Ashcan style, but adopted the dark undercurrents of the movement in spare, carefully composed paintings of isolated figures in commonplace settings, such as *Night Shadows* (1924), *Early Sunday* (1930), *Gas* (1940) and his most famous work, *Nighthawks* (1942), which depicts four figures inside a New York diner on an otherwise deserted nighttime street.

American Scene Painting   Reacting to an increasingly industrialized culture, some American painters developed a nationalistic and romanticized documentary style after World War I. Expanding the social realism of the Ashcan School, American Scene Painters created representational—if stylized—works featuring easily understandable images of rural and urban life, often inspired by social or political goals.

Influenced by the Mexican muralist Diego Rivera (1886–1957), many of these artists painted public murals during the Great Depression, when their images of stoic farmers and factory workers offered emotional support to the nation. Grant Wood, Thomas Hart Benton, and John Steuart Curry led a Midwestern contingent known as Regionalism, which celebrated the steadfast virtues of small towns. This sensibility is exemplified in Wood's painting *American Gothic* (1930), as well as Benton's mural series *America Today* (1930) and his murals illustrating folk songs such as *The Ballad of the Jealous Lover of Lone Green Valley* (1934).

Working outside the main trends of American art, Georgia O'Keeffe (1887–1986) became widely recognized for her semi-abstracted style and sensual flowing color in paintings of the New Mexico landscape, such as *Cow's Skull with Calico Roses* (1931) and close-up images of flowers including *Abstraction White Rose* (1927) and *Black Iris* (1926).

Art and Politics   In Russia, the 1917 Bolshevik Revolution led to a short-lived explosion of artistic experimentation. In the early days of the Soviet Union, the artists Alexander Rodchenko (1891–1956), El Lissitzky (1890–1941), Vladimir Mayakovsky (1893–1930), and Vladimir Tatlin (1885–1953) helped popularize a movement called Constructivism, which used psychologically charged abstraction to promote pro-revolutionary ideals. The early film pioneer Sergei Eisenstein (1898–1948) utilized the Constructivist vocabulary in pro-revolutionary works such as *Strike* (1925) and *Battleship Potemkin* (1925), which have established a lasting standard for directorial excellence. In the 1930's Soviet Union, Joseph Stalin effected the total takeover of artistic style by the Communist Party. All art was now ordered to exuberantly support the aims of the Bolshevik revolution and the Soviet state, and artists not adhering to the new Socialist Realism style (a mishmash of heroic Realism, Expressionism, and Constructivism) were branded as conspirators. Under Stalin, the legacy of early, experimental post-revolutionary Modernism was suppressed or hidden deep underground.

In 1930's Germany, the Nazi regime expunged Modernist "degenerate art" from the cultural record of the Third Reich. Joseph Goebbels, Hitler's minister of propaganda, saw the psychologically persuasive power of Soviet-style Constructivism, however, and began using it to promote the Reich's interests. Among influential Nazi-era artists were cinematographer and director Leni Riefenstahl (1902–2003), whose *Triumph of the Will* (1934) and *Olympia* (1938) are still hailed as stylistic (if not moralistic) watersheds, and designer Hans Schweitzer (1901-1980), whose propaganda posters crystallized Nazi agitprop style.

Abstract Expressionism: The New York School

World War II left the European artistic scene in a dismal state. Many artists had fled or been killed, or were now living under repressive regimes. Paris, which had been the artistic nexus of the West for over a century, would never regain its former status and relatively few artists returned there after the war. Many of the leaders of prewar avant-garde movements had immigrated to New York City. Furthermore, the catastrophe of war threw the main assumptions of traditional European-style Modernism into a tailspin.

The United States emerged from World War II a financial, military, and cultural power. Many artists who had been associated with the Depression era Works Progress Administration's Federal Art Project (1935–43)—including Jackson Pollock (1912–1956), Lee Krasner (1908–1984), William Baziotes (1912–1963), Willem de Kooning (1904–97), Arshile Gorky (1904–48), Philip Guston (1913–80), and Marsden Hartley (1877–1943)—were part of a growing group of painters living in New York City in the 1930's who took inspiration from jazz and Surrealist improvisation, and began to experiment with abstract painting.

By the early 1940's, Pollock was drawing on the muralist tradition of his teacher, the Regionalist Thomas Hart Benton, and the Mexican painter Diego Rivera to compose physical, abstract paintings on a large scale that seemed to both reflect the European history of Expressionist painting while encapsulating a new, distinctly American point of view. In Pollock's images from the 1940's, figural representation from Jungian psychotherapy gradually vanished into a chaotic haze of dripped and poured paint until, by the time of masterworks such as *Full Fathom Five* (1947), there was only a raw field of movement and action.

The style would come to be called Action Painting or more commonly Abstract Expressionism. Many Abstract Expressionists worked entirely intuitively, painting and repainting over the same composition until it "felt right," and deliberately leaving traces of earlier drafts in the final work. This technique is evident in key works by Dutch-born Willem de Kooning, who painted loosely representational images with impulsive-looking brushstrokes that suggested a frenzy of creation and re-creation, and also in the black-and-white paintings of Franz Kline, which went through a slow evolution to find a precise balance and rhythm.

Also among the Abstract Expressionist group were painters who tended to compose images by positioning areas of color against each other. These so-called Color Field artists included the Latvian émigré Mark Rothko (1903–70), who focused on the effects of large, concentrated fields of color and subtle modulations in hue; Barnett Newman (1905–70), whose paintings usually were composed of one or two vertical stripes on a contrasting background; Robert Motherwell (1915–91), whose generally black-and-white paintings included stacked, totemic shapes, and Clyfford Still (1904–80), whose jagged interlocking areas of color seemed to represent natural forms. These various strains of abstraction became known as the New York School.

Also active at the time was Larry Rivers (1923–2002) who began his career as a jazz saxophonist before becoming a painter; closely associated with de Kooning, he maintained a more representational style than many of the New York Abstract Expressionists, and would remain a prominent painter long into late-century.

Meanwhile, an important Southern outpost of the New York School would revive a Bauhaus-style workshop of ideas. From 1933 to 1956, North Carolina's Black Mountain College hosted some of the brightest postwar luminaries and fomented several new trends. Led by the Bauhaus alumnus Josef Albers, Black Mountain College hosted as instructors visionary Buckminster Fuller (1895–1983), dancer Merce Cunningham (1919–2009), artist/musician John Cage (1912–92), poet Robert Creeley (1926–2005), photographer Aaron Siskind (1903–91), and painters Willem de Kooning, Franz Kline (1910–62), Jacob Lawrence (1917–2000), and Robert Motherwell, along with Bauhaus alumnus architect Ludwig Mies van der Rohe. Black Mountain College saw John Cage's first "happenings," (impromptu performances) and his development of chance music, both presaged by Marcel Duchamp's work of the 1920s. Students of the college included many of the next generation's most famous artists, including painters Robert Rauschenberg (1925–2008), Kenneth Noland (1924–2010), and Cy Twombly (1928–2011), and sculptor John Chamberlain (b.1927).

While some abstract painters, such as Joan Mitchell (1926–92), continued to work with the gesturely, messy brushwork developed by de Kooning, others developed a style that the critic Clement Greenberg called "post-painterly"—a cleaner, simpler, hard-edged approach.

Ellsworth Kelly (b. 1923), for example, painted large, flat geometric shapes, with sober, even lines. A group of painters working in similar modes, but who produced much busier geometric patterns, became part of the Op Art movement, so called because their work was intended to appeal to the optical senses.

Modern Sculpture   Modern sculpture followed many of the same patterns as painting, with artists pursuing abstracted forms. Constantin Brancusi (1876–1957), for example, is famous for his sculptures of simplified bird shapes, while Henry Moore (1898–1986) worked on abstracted human figures, often using large empty spaces or holes within the figure. Other sculptors also explored this use of negative space. Defining empty space with the contours of the sculpture ironically created a sense of shape and volume. This effect mirrored what was happening in painting; in moving toward abstraction, painters had blurred the distinction between foreground and background.

After the development of Cubism, many sculptors applied the principles of Cubist painting to three dimensions, creating figures and objects that seem to be pieced together in such a way that their planes and contours are jagged or broken. Picasso invented a genre of sculpture called *assemblage*, in which existing objects are pieced together. Marcel Duchamp's readymades, which were industrially-created objects displayed as artworks, took this genre one step further.

Other important trends in sculpture included the introduction of welded metal as a sculptural medium. Alexander Calder (1898–1976) invented the mobile, or kinetic sculpture, a hanging metal work with components made of simple abstracted shapes that move in response to air currents.

Postmodernism (1960–)

The stylistic pluralism that characterized the art of the early 20th century continued to broaden after World War II, as the art world increasingly prized experimentation, originality, and self-awareness. By the 1970's many artists and critics claimed that this pluralism was a product of Postmodernism, a movement that, they argued, had superseded the era of Modernism. Postmodernists were skeptical of the purity, optimism, and confidence that defined many Modernist movements, and instead embraced complexity and duplicity in artworks that

nonetheless attempt to be bold and direct. This seeming paradox is at the core of Postmodernist artwork, and it often leaves viewers puzzled rather than engaged.

For the confused, two generalizations are helpful in trying to understand Postmodernist art. First, the most important aspect of a Postmodernist artwork is the concept driving it, not its physical qualities. This came about as a rejection of *formalism*, the belief that the meaning of an artwork is wholly communicated by its composition and materials. For Postmodernist artists, a work of art is always only partially complete; the context, environment and situation of a work of art is what completes it. Second, personal experience, insight, and meaning are more valid than grand collective identities or ideologies. To many post-war artists, the collective horrors of World War II, the rise of mass-media culture, and the splintering of capitalist society had completely invalidated traditional ways of approaching and understanding the world. The way forward was to explore personally idiosyncratic ideas, regardless of their attachment to larger theories.

Postmodernism includes a broad rage of artistic directions and continues to grow, as artists continuously splinter and recombine existing traditions with new ideas. While there are still some schools and formal movements within Postmodernism, a common trait among many Postmodern artists tends to be wariness regarding group manifestoes, and instead a preference for personal theories.

Below are descriptions of some of the most well-known trends. Many of the artists mentioned here have created works that could be described by more than one of the headings listed, as Postmodernism is characterized by an increasing number of hybrids, e.g. "Pop Minimalism" and "Postconceptual Abstraction."

Conceptual art   Beginning in the mid-1950's, artists sought to radically change the way people thought of the categories "painting" and "sculpture" by pushing boundaries to extremes. Many of these artists created highly ephemeral, nontraditional, or intentionally provocative works that were eventually grouped together under the name Conceptual Art. To many artists, it was no longer necessary to think of drawing or painting, for example, as being restrained by a frame, or even by two dimensions.

Furthermore, a prominent view of conceptual art is that the artist need not create the artwork at all. Sol LeWitt (1928–2007), for example, created wall drawings that are represented simply by a written set of instructions—anyone, in theory, can execute them. In a similar vein, Lawrence Weiner's (b. 1942) works usually consist of a simple set of statements printed in large block letters, such as THE JOINING OF FRANCE GERMANY AND SWITZERLAND BY ROPE (1969).

In 1977, sculptor Walter De Maria (b. 1935) buried a vertical, mile-long brass rod in the earth, exposing only a few centimeters at the top to create the work *The Vertical Earth Kilometer*, demonstrating the idea that the greater part of any work of art exists only in the mind of the beholder. He is best known for *The Lightning Field* (1977), which is constructed out of 400 steel rods arranged outdoors in a grid in rural New Mexico.

Even for artists working in more traditional ways, conceptual art offered new possibilities and freedoms. In that sense, all recent artwork that takes advantage of these innovations can be said to be at least somewhat conceptualist, and the tradition of conceptual art can be seen throughout most kinds of Postmodernist artwork.

Performance art   A type of conceptual art called *performance art* had its roots in Surrealism and Dada, and became popular after mid-century. By staging interactive events, artists created work that could not be bought, sold, or owned. Allan Kaprow (1927–2006) put on live multimedia events known as *happenings*—productions involving actors and props engaged in a sequence of not-necessarily narrative events—in the 1950's. Another performance artist, Joseph Beuys (1921–1986), produced "actions" based on his own personal mythology. Increasingly, performance art came to include many kinds of live events, political actions, video art, and participatory sculpture, and is usually documented by photographs, video recordings, or written statements.

Because of its loose, interactive format and connections to dance, theater, and mass media, performance art quickly became the choice medium for politically-oriented artists. In Europe, performance artists drew from the legacy of Situationist International, a political group active in France from 1957–1972 that used direct mobilized actions to disrupt normal daily routines and participated in the general strike that hobbled the country in 1958.

Postmodernist feminist artists have often made pieces that call attention to the lack of recognition traditionally given to female artists, as well as other gender-related issues. For example, Eleanor Antin's (b. 1935) performance artwork *Representational Painting* (1971) records her slowly and deliberately applying makeup, and was intended to call attention to the ways women must conform to expectations of beauty and identity. The collective group Guerrilla Girls used performance art to point out the continuing struggle of women to gain recognition in cultural circles. Wearing gorilla masks to obscure their identities, they became famous for printing propaganda-style posters such as 1989's "Do Women have to be naked to get into the Met Museum?" which features an Ingres nude from the painting *Odalisque*, wearing a gorilla mask. The poster was shown as an ad on the sides of NYC buses. Photographer and filmmaker Cindy Sherman (b. 1954) straddles the line between performance art and other disciplines in work that depicts her sliding between identities as she doffs costumes to recreate scenes from film, as in her series of 69 photographs that make up *Untitled Film Stills, 1977–1980*.

Other performance artists used danger and risk to make their work impactful. West coast performance artist Chris Burden (b. 1946) took the medium to extremes, having himself shot (*Shoot*, 1971) and crucified on the hood of a Volkswagen beetle (*Trans-Fixed*, 1974). Paul McCarthy (b. 1945) famously conducted performances that exhausted his viewers, who watched as he threw himself around a room smeared with ketchup in *Class Fool* (1976) and other performance works.

Minimalism   The tendency toward simple, pure, or geometric forms has been a constant undercurrent in art's history, and whenever it surfaces as a movement it often draws on a mix of influences. Beginning in the 1960's artists expanded this trend with new vigor, taking inspiration from a wide range of sources—among them Bauhaus, Zen Buddhism, Constructivism, folk art styles, automotive design, typography, and architecture.

Under various labels (often devised by critics) such as ABC Art, Literalism, and the Light & Space movement, artists stripped down objects and pictures to bare essentials; the work usually consisted of simplified images or forms that created an impersonal yet grand effect. Minimalist painters used limited palettes, and tended to use simple shapes and direct compositions. For example, Ellsworth Kelly (b. 1923) created large, simplified, brightly colored and shaped paintings such as *Red, Yellow, Blue II* (1965), which is made up of three large panels of color. Isamu Noguchi (1904–88), a Japanese-American sculptor and landscape architect, infused his works with traditional Japanese minimal aesthetic. Primarily focused on drawn grids, Agnes Martin (1912–2004) shared with musical minimalists a concentration on repetition and symmetry in her works, such as *Friendship* (1963), a hand-drawn rectangular grid on gold leaf.

Likewise, sculptors often presented elemental forms to create viewing experiences that resisted easy explanation. A famous Donald Judd (1928–94) sculpture, *Untitled* (1965), for example, consists of a series of identical boxes made of galvanized iron, attached to a wall in a straight line. Robert Irwin (b. 1928) originally began as a painter, and gradually came to use large areas of colored light as his primary medium. Fred Sandback (1943–2003) often used colored yarn to demarcate almost visible, yet empty forms inside a space or room. John McCracken (1934–2011) utilized starkly minimal, but highly polished planks of enameled wood, often leaning against a wall. Richard Serra (b. 1939) became widely famous for enormous, leaning or twisting sculptures made out of imposing sheets of weathering steel such as 1981's *Tilted Arc*, a leaning, 120-foot wall of 12-foot-high steel installed at Federal Plaza in New York City (it was removed in 1989 to much controversy).

Pop

Beginning in the late 1950's artists, examining contemporary popular culture, mimicked the production methods and aesthetics popularized by advertising, sign painting, comic books, and Hollywood. This trend continues unabated in contemporary art, with current artists drawing additionally from the Internet, graffiti, popular film, and computer games.

Andy Warhol (1928–87) used the commercial process of silkscreening to mass-produce images of Campbell's soup cans and celebrities such as Marilyn Monroe. Jasper Johns (b. 1930) painted images of targets and the American flag, while Claes Oldenburg (b. 1929) made large sewn and stuffed sculptures of cake slices and household appliances. Roy Lichtenstein (1923–97) enlarged and reproduced comic book pages, as in *Drowning Girl* (1963).

Described as both a pop and conceptual artist, printmaker, photographer, and painter, Ed Ruscha (b. 1937) first became famous for his ironic, deadpan painting *LA County Museum of Art on Fire*. The work of Jeff Koons (b. 1955) and other later conceptual artists is also sometimes called Pop. Koons conceives of works that are fabricated according to his specifications, but never built by the artist

himself. His piece *Rabbit* (1986) looks like a cheap plastic blow-up toy, but is rendered in elegant and costly stainless steel. British artist Damien Hirst (b. 1965) uses images of pharmceuticals and often includes preserved animals, as in his sculpture *The Physical Impossibility of Death in the Mind of Someone Living* (1991), which includes an embalmed tiger shark in a large vitrine.

Installation and site-specific sculpture

In the 1960's and 70's, sculpture designed to alter the space itself became known by the term *installation*. Such pieces can include objects, sound, performance, and any other element, and they can be temporary or permanent. The artist Nam June Paik (1932–2006), for example, created videos that are displayed on custom-built monitors, arranged in sculptural ensembles suited to specific places. Paik's work can also be described as video art, a genre that became popular as video equipment grew inexpensive and readily accessible. Paik's well-known video piece *Global Groove* (1973) incorporates Korean drummers, Japanese Pepsi commercials, tap dancers, and Allen Ginsberg reading his poetry. Judy Chicago's (b. 1939) installation *The Dinner Party* (1979) features long tables arranged in a triangular shape, with place-settings marked for famous women throughout history.

Site-specific installations in natural outdoor settings, which often make use of natural materials, are known as "earthworks." Robert Smithson (1938–73) is famous for his earthwork *Spiral Jetty* (1969–70), a large stone and earth construction that winds in a spiral shape into Utah's Great Salt Lake. Christo (b. Christo Javacheff, 1935), born in Bulgaria and trained in Paris, is best known for a fabric-based public art in which buildings, bridges, and other large structures are temporarily wrapped in cloth, or temporary linear sculptures of cloth and other materials are created to form part of a landscape; the ephemeral works are extensively documented in drawings and photographs. Two of his best-known works are *Running Fence* (California, 1976), and *The Gates* (Central Park, New York City, 2005). James Turrell (b. 1943)—best known for his highly crafted installations which create planes of colored light that seem to float in space—has been constructing since 1979 one of the largest and most famous earthworks. His *Roden Crater*, near Flagstaff, Arizona, is a 3-mile-wide meteor crater that is being reshaped into a mammoth celestial observatory and sculpture and is scheduled to be completed in 2011.

Caravaggio: An Italian Antihero's Time to Shine

By MICHAEL KIMMELMAN

By at least one amusing new metric, Michelangelo's unofficial 500-year run at the top of the Italian art charts has ended. Caravaggio, who somehow found time to paint when he wasn't brawling, scandalizing pooh-bahs, chasing women (and men), murdering a tennis opponent with a dagger to the groin, fleeing police assassins or getting his face mutilated by one of his many enemies, has bumped him from his perch. That's according to an art historian at the University of Toronto, Philip Sohm, who has studied the number of writings (books, catalogs and scholarly papers) on both of them during the last 50 years. Mr. Sohm has found that Caravaggio has gradually, if unevenly, overtaken Michelangelo.

He has charts to prove it.

The change, most obvious since the mid-1980s, doesn't exactly mean Michelangelo has dropped down the memory hole. To judge from the throngs still jamming the Sistine Chapel and lining up outside the Accademia in Florence to check out "David," his popularity hasn't dwindled much.

But, charts or no charts, Mr. Sohm has touched on something. Caravaggiomania, as he calls it, implies not just that art history doctoral students may finally be struggling to think up anything fresh to say about Michelangelo. It suggests that the whole classical tradition in which Michelangelo was steeped is becoming ever more foreign and therefore seemingly less germane, even to many educated people. His otherworldly muscle men, casting the damned into hell or straining to emerge from thick blocks of veined marble, aspired to an abstract and bygone ideal of the sublime, grounded in Renaissance rhetoric, which, for postwar generations, now belongs with the poetry of Alexander Pope or plays by Corneille as admirable but culturally remote splendors.

Caravaggio, on the other hand, exemplifies the modern antihero, a hyperrealist whose art is instantly accessible. His doe-eyed, tousle-haired boys with puffy lips and bubble buttocks look as if they've just tumbled out of bed, not descended from heaven. Coarse not godly, locked into dark, ambiguous spaces by a strict geometry then picked out of deep shadow by an oracular light, his models come straight off the street. Cupid is clearly a hired urchin on whom Caravaggio strapped a pair of fake wings. The angel in his *Annunciation* dangles like Chaplin's tramp on the high wire in *The Circus*, from what must have been a rope contraption Caravaggio devised.

Rome's art establishment at the turn of the 17th century, immersed in the mandarin froufrou of Late Mannerism, despised Caravaggio for the filthy, barefoot pilgrims he painted at Mary's doorstep. Out to "destroy painting," as Nicolas Poussin, the most high-minded of all French artists, saw it, Caravaggio connected with ordinary people, the ones who themselves arrived barefoot and filthy as pilgrims in Rome. And fortunately for Caravaggio, he also appealed to a string of rich and powerful patrons.

But almost immediately after he died from a fever at 38, in 1610, on the beach at Porto Ercole, north of Rome, his art was written off by critics as a passing fad and neglected for hundreds of years, setting the stage for his modern resurrection. Connoisseurs like Bernard Berenson were still dismissing his work a century ago when Lionello Venturi, Roger Fry and Roberto Longhi, among others, finally revived his reputation as a protomodernist.

"The only way to understand old art is to make it participate in our own artistic life" is how Venturi phrased it in 1925. That Caravaggio left behind no drawings, no letters, no will or estate record, only police and court records, makes him a perfect Rorschach for our obsessions. He was outed in the 1970's by gender studies scholars, notwithstanding the absence of documents to indicate he was gay. Pop novelists and moviemakers have naturally had a field day with his life. Exhibition organizers cook up any excuse ("Caravaggio-Bacon," "Caravaggio-Rembrandt") to capitalize on his bankability. Newly discovered "Caravaggios" test the market every year.

Gifts for a beautiful young Roman nobleman, Tommaso de' Cavalieri, on whom Michelangelo had developed a crush, the drawings were ostensibly supposed to help Cavalieri learn to draw. Imagine Roger Federer handing you a DVD of himself at Wimbledon, saying "Just do this." These are drawings of the most arcane refinement, unearthly beautiful.

Caravaggio, wrestling art back to the ground, distilled scenes into a theatrical instant at which time seems suddenly stopped. That's why his pictures can bring to mind movie stills. The art historian Michael Fried, who has just written a book about Caravaggio, notes the quality of the figures' absorption. Life-size images, they share our space and we theirs, face to face, as another art historian, Catherine Puglisi, has pointed out (something that doesn't happen with Michelangelo's enormous sculptures or his frescoed ceiling that we only see from far away). The immediacy somehow dovetails with the tabloid tawdriness of his biography, with the whole modern celebrity drama.

Figurative and Abstract Painting   Under various names—including Lyrical Abstraction, Post-painterly abstraction, Neo-expressionism, Neo-Geo, and others—post-war and late-20th century abstract painting sought to transcend what painters saw as the limits of *formalism*, the notion highly prevalent during mid-century that a painting's composition was the most important part of its meaning. Increasingly they grappled with the question of how and why, in a contemporary setting, a painter could make pictures that aren't "merely" beautiful or well-designed.

The interdisciplinary foment of Black Mountain College from earlier in the century produced a generation of abstract painters who blurred boundaries between painting and other disciplines, including Robert Rauschenberg (1925–2008), whose "Combine" paintings from the 1950's incorporated newspaper clippings, objects, clothing and photographs affixed to the surface of the painting. Another Black Mountain alumnus, Cy Twombly, used drawing and script in his very large paintings, which often resembled blackboards.

Likewise, later 20th-century representational painting saw many trends. The French painter Jean Dubuffet (1901–85), for example, was inspired by the idiosyncratic aesthetic he found in the art of children and the mentally unstable, and coined the term Art Brut, which sought to promote the artistic styles of untrained or "outsider" artists. In some ways, this trend recalled earlier fascinations of European Primitivists. English painter Francis Bacon (1909–92) painted nightmarish biomorphic forms that jarringly combined realism and abstraction to depict moments of fear and violence.

In another trend in figurative art, Photorealism, artists produced highly illusionistic objects. The paintings of Richard Estes (b. 1932) and Chuck Close (b. 1940) look as detailed and realistic as photographs, and the sculptures of Duane Hanson (1925–96), fiberglass casts made from human models, are at first glance hard to distinguish from real people. Now aided by digital photography and computers, contemporary photorealist painters and sculptors are able to produce uncanny representations of real life objects and scenes.

PHOTOGRAPHY

A Technical History of Photography

The word "photography," from the Greek for "light" and "to draw," was first used by Sir John F.W. Herschel in 1839, a year that also marks the formal beginning of photography as we know it. But the origins of the medium date back long before the word itself was ever used.

First Visions

In the fifth century B.C. in China, the philosopher Mo Ti (ca. 470 B.C.–391 B.C.) made the first recorded observation that light passing through a small hole into a dark chamber created an inverted but exact image of the scene outside the chamber. In the 10th century, an Arabian scholar, Abu 'Ali al-Hasan ibn Al-Haytham (Alhazen) (965–1040), discovered that the image thus seen was made clearer with a smaller hole or aperture. Roger Bacon (ca. 1214–92) in the 13th century and Reinerius Gemma-Frisius (1508–55) in the 16th century made similar observations. The phenomenon these men observed was the basis for the *camera obscura*, formally developed during the Renaissance.

Camera Obscura Initially, a camera obscura (literally "dark room") was an actual room with a tiny opening in one wall that permitted an image of the outside to be projected on the opposite wall. It could then be drawn or traced by the artist standing in the room. A number of 16th-century scholars, including Leonardo da Vinci (1452–1519), Girolamo Cardano (1501–76), Erasmus Reinhold (1511–53) and Gemma-Frisius, all recorded descriptions of camera obscurae; no one knows who first invented the device. By the mid-1550's it was widely familiar to scientists, artists, and magicians; by the 17th century it was a common tool for artists and draftsmen.

Capturing the Image In 1727 Johann Heinrich Schulze (1687–1744) discovered the light-sensitivity of silver salts (especially halides) while experimenting with the production of phosphorous, and called his chalk-silver nitric acid mixture scotophorous ("bringer of darkness"). In the mid-1700's Giacomo Battista Beccaria (1716–81) and Carl Wilhelm Scheele (1742–86) independently discovered the light-sensitivity of silver chloride.

Among the first to use silver salts as an emulsion on an object were Dr. William Lewis and Joseph Priestley (1733–1804), who painted silver nitrate onto bone and recorded the light that hit it. Their work was followed by Josiah Wedgwood (1730–95), the famous British potter, and his son Thomas (1771–1805). Thomas created "sun prints" by putting objects or painted transparencies directly on sensitized paper or leather and exposing them to daylight until the exposed areas darkened. However he had no way to make the images permanent; any further exposure turned the rest of the paper dark.

Niépce and Daguerre Joseph Nicéphore Niépce (1765–1833)—considered one of the two "fathers of photography"—took the next step in recording light. Working with his brother Claude (1763–1828), he used paper sensitized with silver chloride to capture the camera's images. He succeeded in making negative paper images but had no way to make positive prints from them. Soon he discovered a new light-sensitive substance that he called bitumen of Judea (used as a ground when etching copper plates with acid). The bitumen hardened when exposed to light, and Niépce used it to create accurate reproductions of engravings and drawings. The principle Niépce had discovered—differential hardening of a substance on exposure to light—was fundamental to future developments in visual media. Niépce used the process to make positive images from a camera; some consider these heliographs to be the first photographs ever made, but that credit is usually given to Daguerre.

Louis Jacques Mandé Daguerre (1787–1851), a scenic artist, was also working on a way to record the images of a camera obscura, in order to create large and realistic stage sets. Niépce and Daguerre were put in contact by Charles Chevalier (1804–59), Daguerre's lens maker, and between Daguerre's camera design and Niépce's success with light-sensitive chemicals, the two had a productive partnership until Niépce's death.

Daguerre continued working, and by 1837 had made a successful still-life photograph using his new method. He called the finished product a daguerreotype. Daguerreotypes are made beginning with a highly polished silver-plated sheet of copper. The plate is sensitized with iodine to create silver iodide, which is reduced to silver as it is exposed to light. The image is made visible by placing the plate face-down over a box of heated mercury, which combines with the reduced silver to form an image in white mercury tones. The remaining silver iodide is desensitized in a strong solution of sodium chloride (table salt). The finished plates, delicate to the touch, were kept in glass-fronted cases to protect the surface from scratches or smudges.

Talbot

In the 1830's an Englishman by the name of William Henry Fox Talbot (1800–77) was simultaneously arriving at his own way of recording a camera's image, but using paper instead of metal plates. He bathed a sheet of paper first in a weak solution of sodium chloride, and then (when dry) in strong silver nitrate, which reacted to form silver chloride. He made negative contact prints of objects such as leaves and lace. Where the sun hit the paper it turned dark; where it was shadowed by the object it remained light. Talbot (imperfectly) preserved the images by washing the prints in strong sodium chloride or potassium iodide.

He then began using a box camera (nicknamed a "mousetrap" by his wife) with various lenses to create negative pictures, the most famous being of a lattice window in Lacock Abbey (August 1835). He presented his "photogenic drawings" to the Royal Society of London early in 1839, and went on to make even more important contributions to the field of photography (see "Calotype").

Fixing the Image

Sir John F. W. Herschel (1792–1871), knowing of the work of both Daguerre and Talbot, researched ways to preserve photographic images from further light action. In 1819 he had discovered that hyposulfite of soda (now called sodium thiosulfate, but still referred to by photographers as "hypo") dissolved silver salts. In 1839 he applied his discovery to photographic images, using the substance to wash away the unexposed silver salts. He soon gave his process to both Daguerre and Talbot, who could finally make permanent prints.

Improvements

Three major improvements in 1840 made daguerreotype portraiture both practical and economically feasible. Peter Friedrich Voigtländer (1812–78) began marketing a vastly improved lens designed by Josef Max Petzval (1807–91). The new "German lens" let in 20 times more light than the Chevalier lenses that Daguerre had used. Second, daguerreotype plates were made far more light-sensitive by recoating the iodized plates with additional halogens, such as bromine and/or chlorine. John Frederick Goddard (1795–1866) was the first to publish this process, calling the material an "accelerator" or "quickstuff." Finally, gold chloride was used as a toner to darken and stabilize the daguerreotype image, a process invented by Hippolyte Fizeau (1819–96). Together these three improvements brought exposure time down from several minutes to as little as five seconds—little enough time for a person to hold still.

Calotype

Calotypes (from the Greek for "beautiful picture," and sometimes called Talbotypes) were patented by Talbot in 1841, and were based on the fundamental principle of development of a latent image—possibly Talbot's most important contribution to photography. Initially, paper negatives had to be exposed until the image was actually visible. But Talbot discovered that if he bathed his already sensitized (but not yet exposed) paper in "gallo-nitrate of silver" (a mixture of gallic acid and silver nitrate), the paper became far more light-sensitive. He could then expose the paper briefly and bring out the unseen image using a second bath in the same solution. The process finally made paper negatives a feasible option.

Gustave Le Gray (1820–82) improved the calotype in 1851 by waxing the negative paper before sensitizing it. This made it possible to adjust the developing time to correct exposure problems.

Glass Plates

Glass had been suggested as a base for emulsions since 1839, but it wasn't until 1847 that a workable system was devised by Claude Félix Abel Niépce de Saint-Victor (1805–70), a relative of Joseph Nicéphore Niépce. He mixed egg white (albumen) with potassium iodide and sodium chloride, coated a glass plate with this mixture and then immersed the plate in silver nitrate to sensitize it. The plates were developed using gallic and pyrogallic acid.

Collodion

The use of glass plates succeeded with the development of the collodion or "wet-plate" process, invented in 1850 by Frederick Scott Archer (1813–57). Glass plates were coated with a mixture of collodion and potassium iodide, then bathed in silver nitrate to form silver iodide. However, the plates had to be exposed and

Back to the Kodak Moment When Light Was Captured

By MICHAEL KIMMELMAN

Among the earliest photographs William Henry Fox Talbot made was a picture of lace. Talbot placed the lace on a piece of paper he had sensitized with silver salts, then put them both in the sun. After a few minutes he removed the lace. The paper, reacting to the sunlight, retained the impression of the fabric as a silhouette.

Amazing. The image today looks mysterious: a fine, flat, abstract shape, irregular and ghostly. It takes a moment to recognize it. Before that, we assume the intent is art, accustomed as we are to seeing abstract images in museums that way, which was certainly not how Talbot thought about the photograph.

We can only imagine the original magic of it. Vision became a physical object fixed on paper; three dimensions became two not through the intermediary of somebody wrestling with a pencil or brush but directly through nature, and in more detail than anybody, or almost anybody, could match by hand. The famous story is that Talbot, frustrated at his own infelicitous attempts to sketch landscapes while at Lake Como in Italy in 1833, determined to find another way "to cause these natural images to imprint themselves durably."

So photography was born partly as a kind of convenience, a labor-saving alternative to drawing, but also an impersonal machine, dispassionate, unlike the human hand, except that it soon became obvious to Talbot and every other thinking person that photography was still a tool of human manipulation and individual taste.

Nothing can return us to the state of innocence before photography was invented—invented twice, by Talbot and by Louis Jacques Mandé Daguerre, separately, using different techniques. But Talbot's early work can remind us how utterly the world was changed by their invention. Talbot reshaped how people saw their surroundings: photography became, as a visual tool, the threshold between the past and modernity.

Talbot photographed Byronic landscapes and also pensive men sitting in plush armchairs gazing dreamily into the ether. He contrived stagy scenes of laborers, who posed holding saws and hammers or stood beside ladders. Shadowy streets and university buildings, empty (because the photographs required long exposures and so couldn't capture people moving), look ghostly like ruins.

Talbot brought about a world now largely imagined through images people see through a viewfinder, accumulate, hold in their hands. Photographs define the rituals of our lives; they make everyone a potential artist and document reality, while also altering it, because photographs have their own particular truth and integrity. Photographs fragment and dislocate the world, and reduce everything to the same scale.

They also concentrate attention on what the eye might not normally bother to notice, which, when set apart on a sheet of paper, becomes strange, new and beautiful. Talbot made a beautiful photograph of books on shelves, perhaps imitating a still life, perhaps suggesting photography's potential as evidence, legal or otherwise, perhaps implying a self-portrait. Those are Talbot's books, about subjects he studied, and include volumes with articles he wrote in them. We're meant to read the titles on the spines. Do they add up to a diary of a life? The meaning is up to you. Talbot's genius was to raise the different possibilities.

He identified from the start, with what now seems astonishing speed and clarity, photography's implications, which he laid out in *The Pencil of Nature*, the first book illustrated with photographs. This proved a different point: not just that art can be photographed and the photographs dispersed, but that lighting alters the appearance of whatever is in a photograph, as every Hollywood star knows.

Talbot saw the future, in which photography would become an industry. His panorama of the Reading Establishment shows the world's first commercial photographic company to produce prints from calotype paper negatives. He and his associates pose to illustrate photography's potential: a man sits for his portrait; a Velázquez engraving and a maquette of Canova's *Three Graces* await photographers; technicians monitor prints for *The Pencil of Nature*. This is a picture of photographers photographing themselves while preparing the first book of photographs about photography.

Inventions age and are supplanted. Art is constant. Talbot's technique is being replaced by digital technology, but his pictures remain vivid and alluring. The art of his photographs is clearly in the enduring freshness of their wonderment.

developed (in ferrous sulphite) while the collodion was still wet. This meant photographers had to bring a full traveling darkroom or "dark-tent" wherever they went in order to sensitize and process the plates.

Ambrotypes   The collodion process was also used to make direct positives, called Ambrotypes, named in 1854 by Marcus Aurelius Root (1808–88), and patented in the same year by Joseph Ambrose Cutting (1814–67). The process worked on the principle that when camphor and potassium bromide were added to the collodion and a weak negative was made, the exposed areas appeared light in tone; unexposed (and thus empty) areas were dark when the glass plate was held against a black background.

Tintypes   Another popular adaptation of the wet-plate process was the tintype (also called melainotype and ferrotype). The process was invented by Hamilton L. Smith (1818–1903), who assigned the patent in 1856 to his student Peter Neff (1827–1903); manufacture began the same year under the Neffs and Victor M. Griswold (1819–72). Tintypes were made using thin sheets of black-enameled iron instead of glass; the plates were easy to make and not nearly so fragile as daguerreotypes or ambrotypes.

Cartes-de-Visite   A third use of the collodion process was known as the carte-de-visite, and was patented by André Adolphe-Eugène Disdéri (1819–89) in 1854. He used a special camera with a movable plate and four lenses. This allowed four exposures on each half of the plate, for a total of eight poses. The negative was contact printed onto a single paper, which was then cut into the separate images, each of which was mounted onto a 4-by-2-inch mount—the same size as visiting cards, hence the name. These prints were easily produced using unskilled labor, and greatly increased studio productivity.

Early Printing

Daguerreotypes and other metal plate processes produced positive prints on the plates themselves. Glass plate and paper negatives, however, needed to be printed onto paper to achieve the final photograph. The next improvement needed in photography was a feasible and efficient way to make these prints—not only for creating individual photographs, but also for reproducing multiple (and even mass) quantities of a given image, such as for newspapers.

Albumen Paper   Albumen paper, which became the most common printing medium for collodion negatives, was invented in 1850 by Blanquart-Evrard. He mixed potassium bromide and acetic acid with egg white and coated paper with the mixture, then sensitized it in a silver nitrate solution. The paper was exposed to sunlight under a negative, sometimes for several hours, until the image appeared. The prints were then toned and burnished for deeper hues and a glossy surface. Photographers could buy paper with the albumen coating already on it, ready to sensitize, thus contributing to large-scale printing, and massive egg use (more than 60,000 a day in one company alone).

Carbon Printing   Both albumen paper and Talbot's salted paper prints were somewhat unstable and prone to fading. In response in 1856 Adolphe Louis Poitevin (1819–82) devised a non-silver carbon process, based on earlier research by Mungo Ponton (1802–80). Particles of carbon were added to a mixture of gelatin and light-sensitive potassium bichromate. The combined substance hardened differentially on exposure to light beneath a negative, and the unexposed emulsion washed out, leaving a stable carbon-pigmented gelatin image.

The carbon process was greatly improved by Sir Joseph Wilson Swan (1828–1914), with his 1864 carbon transfer process. He coated a sheet of tissue paper with the carbon gelatin, sensitizing and exposing it in the same way as Poitevin. Then using a series of water baths and squeegeeing, Swan transferred the carbon image on the tissue to a blank sheet of paper. Soon the tissues were made with a wide variety of pigments, for prints in over 50 different colors.

Photomechanical Reproduction   In 1852 photogravure was developed, based on work by Talbot. It worked by etching steel plates using gauze or crosshatched glass to break up continuous tone spaces. In 1855 Poitevin perfected photolithography, which relied on the properties of bichromated colloids on stone and their repulsion (after exposure to light) to greasy ink. Collotypes or albertypes were a similar variation, perfected in 1868 by Josef Albert (1825–86). And woodburytypes, invented in 1866 by Walter Bentley Woodbury (1834–85), used bichromated gelatin (like that in carbon prints) as a relief image to create a lead mold, which could then be inked and printed onto paper.

Each of these printing methods was moderately successful; but the real goal was printing images alongside text for newspapers, for example, and so far no technique could reproduce an image using a text-style printing press. Half-tone printing provided the solution. Talbot's mesh idea was used again, in a complex process involving double exposure, bichromated gelatin and etching of metal plates. The result was a plate with clusters of raised dots that together represented the dark tones of the image, and the whole plate could be mounted alongside typeface and printed on a standard press.

Advances in Equipment

Cameras   Sliding box cameras like those used by Daguerre and Talbot were replaced with the first bellows cameras in 1851 by the firm of W. and W.H. Lewis. Their "Lewis Folding Camera" had a sliding rectangular camera box, with an access door, and was connected by a bellows to a fixed front piece fitted with a lens. By the 1860's, cameras were made with rising fronts and swing fronts and backs, allowing adjustments in focus, angle, and perspective.

In 1844 Fredrich von Martens (1809–75) designed the first arc-pivoted camera, which could make panoramics on curved daguerreotype plates. Photographers also used curved glass plates with the collodion process for the same purpose. The "Pantascope camera" was patented in 1862; it rotated the entire camera on a circular base while a collodion plate was pulled past an exposing slot using a system of string and pulleys.

Early Enlargers   Throughout the 1800's, most negatives were contact printed—that is, with the negative directly in contact with the printing paper, creating a print the same size as the negative. However enlargements were occasionally made with the use of " solar cameras," or daylight enlargers. The devices were generally large, often rooftop constructions that allowed sunlight in one end, through a glass or paper negative and a set of lenses, and onto a sheet of albumen paper at the back. The enlargers could be turned and angled to follow the sun during the long exposures needed.

Shutters and Multiple Exposures   In 1834 William Horner created a zoetrope—a strip of sequential pictures viewed through slits in a cylindrical drum to give the illusion of motion (a precursor to modern motion pictures). Eadweard Muybridge (1830–1904) invented one of the first camera shutters in 1869, which he perfected for the use of stop-action photography in 1877. His silhouetted images of horses mid-stride were the first views of their true gait, and defied all previous conceptions—a striking example of photography's ability to show us what

we cannot see. In 1880 he used a similar technique to project pictures onto a screen with a device he called a zoogyroscope or zoopraxiscope.

Celluloid and Film   In 1888 the Eastman Company (later Eastman Kodak) began to produce the first roll film, as opposed to single plates. Long enough for 100 exposures, the film's gelatin emulsion initially had to be transferred from its paper backing to glass before processing. However a year later, the company began to use a new backing substance: celluloid. Developed in the 1860's by John Wesley Hyatt (1837–1920), it was a much more flexible backing that could be manufactured to a .01-inch thickness. Celluloid and roll film became mainstays of photography and made possible the development of motion picture photography.

New Printing Papers   At the same time that gelatin dry plates came into use, new printing papers, manufactured ready for commercial use, were marketed in two major types. "Printing-out papers" required no chemical developing: the image appeared upon exposure. These used a gelatin-silver-chloride emulsion, and in the United States were sold beginning in 1890 as Aristotype and Solio papers. The other type was called "developing-out paper," and needed chemicals to bring the image to view. This silver-bromide emulsion paper was first introduced in 1873, but was not widely used until the 1880's. Along with the improved printing papers came rapid and vast automation of printing by commercial studios.

Evolving Equipment

Along with the wider range of negative materials of the late 1800's came a new series of evolutions in photography equipment. Cameras became more sophisticated, in their design and in individual components like shutters and lenses. And for the first time, indoor photography became possible with the advent of the flash.

View Cameras   In 1895 Frederick H. Sanderson designed a more precise view camera that allowed vertical, horizontal, and swing movement of the front panel. This allowed the photographer to adjust not only focusing distance, but also the angle of the plane of focus, as well as angles of perspective. These design elements continue to be the standard for professional view-cameras today.

Single Lens Reflex and Specialty Cameras   In contrast to these large, somewhat cumbersome cameras, smaller reflex cameras were also manufactured, making possible fast exposure, focusing control, and a large image size. First they were built as twin-lens reflex cameras that used two identical lenses: one exposed the plate; the other, directly above, with an angled mirror that bounced the image up to a horizontal ground glass for framing and focusing.

The introduction in 1902 of single-lens reflex cameras, like the well-known Graflex, allowed photographers to see the exact image they were taking through the lens itself; the mirror swung out of the way during exposure. SLR cameras, as they are now known, became widely used and valuable for a variety of photographic situations. They were light and easy to carry in one's hand or on a tripod, and could be used in the natural field, for news and street photography, and for portraiture.

There were also a variety of so-called "detective" cameras marketed in the 1880's. Fairly inconspicuous to operate, they included novelty versions in the forms of walking sticks, revolvers, books, and binoculars. The most popular was the Kodak, invented and manufactured beginning in 1888 by George Eastman (1854–1932) of the Eastman Company of Rochester.

Shutters Shutters initially took the form of string— or pneumatically-controlled flaps, drops, or sliding plates. Focal-plane shutters, situated between the lens and the plate, followed the window-shade form first designed by Muybridge, and even at this point could make very short exposures. Alternately, between-the-lens diaphragm shutters—a set of metal blades that simulate the iris of an eye—were sometimes attached inside the lens barrel itself. Then in 1904 the Zeiss Company manufactured a compound shutter designed by Friedrich Deckel (1871–1948). This blade shutter worked like a diaphragm shutter, but controlled both the length of exposure and the size of the aperture; it became standard equipment on many hand cameras.

Lenses Progress in lens design came in 1866 with the rapid rectilinear lens, designed independently but simultaneously by Hugo Adolph Steinheil (1832–93) and John Henry Dallmeyer (1830–83) to correct both spherical aberration and some astigmatism. The development in 1886 of barium crown glass by the Schott Glass Works in Germany made possible the first true anastigmat lenses: those that correct distortion both vertically and horizontally. Two of the most popular were the Double Anastigmat or Dagor lens (1893), and Zeiss's

Tessar lens (1902). Dallmeyer also patented the first telephoto lens in 1860.

Lighting and Flashes The first experiments into artificial lighting used electric batteries, which often required exposures of up to 18 minutes; these were replaced beginning in 1864 by magnesium wire and then powder. Blitzlichtpulver, or "flashlight powder," as the most common form was called, created harsh light and clouds of smoke, but remained the primary type of artificial light until after the First World War. In 1925 Dr. Paul Vierkötter encased the magnesium inside a glass bulb, which eliminated the acrid smoke and high contrast. Four years later flash bulbs were made to hold aluminum foil; these popular bulbs were soon synchronized to camera shutters.

Electric flash systems, the precursor of today's electronic flashes, were known as early as the 1852 to be capable of extremely short flashes. In 1938 Harold Edgerton (1903–90) invented a xenon-filled tube for use in his groundbreaking stroboscopic work. Multiple strobe (flash) units that could be placed around a room, independently controlled, and synchronized together, were manufactured for studio photography in the 1940's.

Color

From the early days of photography, prints were sometimes hand tinted or toned to achieve color. But there remained no way to photographically record natural colors. After numerous attempts, success finally came out of scientific research into human vision: the discovery that all color comes from combinations of red, green, and blue light, which can either be added together or subtracted (using filters) to create a full range of colors.

First Color Photographs James Clerk Maxwell (1831–79) made one of the first color photographs in 1861. He photographed a piece of tartan three times, each time through a different filter (a glass filled with either red, green, or blue liquid), and then projected the three images onto a screen through the same filters. The three pictures overlapped and formed a full-color image, in a technique that uses the additive properties of light. Frederic E. Ives (1856–1937) in 1892 invented a more convenient and portable device called a Kromskop, which united the three images without the use of lanterns and liquid filters.

Film and Printing in the 20th Century

Since the First World War, black and white films have become remarkably faster (perhaps as much as 24 million times faster than the daguerreotypes of 1839), and are now available in ratings from ASA 65 to 3200 or more. (ASA is an international film speed rating system based on work by Kodak in the 1940's.) The larger silver halide crystals of faster films work in low-light situations, but produce grainier negatives and prints. Specialty infrared and color-process black and white films are also currently marketed.

Subtractive Color   Until 1925 most color images were produced using the additive theory of color. As early as 1869, a subtractive process was suggested, in separate but simultaneous announcements by Louis Ducos du Hauron (1837–1920), and Charles Cros (1842–88). As in Maxwell's process, three separate photos (called color separation negatives) were taken through red, green and blue filters. This time a black and white transparency was made from each negative, then each slide was dyed or tinted in the complementary color of the filter (cyan, magenta, and yellow). When these three slides were held together, an accurate color image was seen.

Kodachrome   These methods eventually developed into more sophisticated color transparency films, the foremost of which was Kodachrome, invented by Leopold Godowsky (1900–83) and Leopold Mannes (1899–1964). It was the first "tripak" film, which meant the film had three layers of emulsion, each with a primary color filter layer (called a " dye-coupler") that would block out the complementary color. The effect was the same as taking separate photos and reassembling them. But Kodak's new film, released first for movies (1935) then in sheet (1938) and roll film (1942), made unique color positive images from a single instantaneous exposure.

Color Prints   Kodak and another firm, Ansco, both released tripak films that the photographer could process in the darkroom (instead of sending to the company for processing): Ansco-Color film in 1942 and Ektachrome shortly thereafter. In response to the need for true color-negative film—for making multiple prints instead of a single unique positive—Kodak released Kodacolor film in 1941, and then in 1947 released Ektacolor film which the photographer could process by hand.

Modern Cameras

Professional cameras improved and expanded dramatically during the 20th century. Large-format view cameras continued to follow much the same form, but hand-held cameras underwent significant changes. In 1949 the Zeiss-Ikon company introduced the popular Contax-S single-lens reflex camera, the first to use a pentaprism mirror system that allowed eye-level viewing. In 1913 35mm cameras were first designed as a way to use leftover motion picture film. Beginning with the Leica, introduced in 1925, 35mm cameras became the standard of SLR photography. Newer cameras have been further improved by adding features such as: motor drives that advance film and reset the shutter; autofocus lenses; multiple exposure meter settings; auto-bracketing; and a host of electronic features.

The Eastman Brownie camera, introduced in 1900, was a turning point in amateur photography, bringing snapshot photography to the public at large. It evolved by 1963 into the Kodak Instamatic, and in 1973 was adapted as the pocket Instamatic for 16mm film. So-called point-and-shoot 35mm cameras followed, experiencing mass public acceptance and becoming standard items in most American homes.

Instant Photography   The Polaroid Land Camera, invented by Edwin H. Land (1909–91) and introduced in 1948, was groundbreaking: it processed the film inside the camera itself. The camera used special film containing a pod with processing chemicals, which after exposure was squeezed through rollers along with the negative and paper, generating a final print in less than a minute. At first these were black-and-white prints, but in 1962 Polaroid Polacolor film was introduced. A variety of Polaroid cameras and film systems are now used for amateur snapshots, by professionals to test lighting and exposures setups, as well as in some art photography. As innovative as Polaroid was, the company declared bankruptcy in 2002, due in part, many suggest, to the revolution of digital photography.

Digital Photography

In 1969 a new type of semiconductor, called a charge coupled device, or CCD, was developed by George Smith and Willard Boyle of Bell Labs. Roughly a year later, Bell Labs created a solid-state video camera that used this new chip as an image sensor. The original intent was to develop a small, low-powered camera that could be used in a videophone device; by 1975 they were able to demonstrate a CCD camera with image quality sharp enough for broadcast television.

Building on the development of the CCD, in 1972, Texas Instruments patented a film-less electronic camera. The first commercial electronic camera was Sony's Mavica, released in 1981. The Mavica saved images onto a recordable mini disc; the mini disc was then inserted into a video reader that was connected to a television monitor or color printer. Over the next decade Eastman Kodak led the way in developing professional-level cameras, but it took the computer companies to bring them to the consumer.

Consumer-Level Digital Cameras   The first digital camera for the consumer market was introduced in 1994 by Apple. The Apple QuickTake 100 camera connected to any Apple personal computer by means of a serial cable.

Other early consumer digital cameras were the Kodak DC40 and Casio QV-11 (both released in 1995), and the Sony Cyber-Shot Digital Still Camera (1996). Kodak was particularly aggressive in promoting digital photography to a mass market, partnering with Microsoft and Kinko's to place digital image-editing workstations and kiosks in all Kinko's locations. These workstations enabled consumers to edit and print digital photographs, as well as create Photo CD discs. Simultaneously, Kodak partnered with IBM to create an Internet-based image exchange, and Hewlett-Packard marketed the first color inkjet printers designed especially for the printing of digital photographs.

Professional-Level Digital Cameras   In contrast to the typical point-and-shoot consumer-level digital camera, several manufacturers now offer digital single lens reflex (SLR) cameras, similar to SLR film cameras. The professional-level cameras offer a through-the-lens viewfinder, manual adjustment of aperture and lens speed, enhanced depth of field, and faster shutter response. In addition, digital SLRs let photographers use interchangeable lenses; point-and-shoot cameras offer only a single fixed lens. At prices starting under $1,000, digital SLRs are the cameras of choice for professional photographers and advanced hobbyists.

An Art History of Photography

Photography initially came about as a means to make drawing, especially portraits, easier. It was a quicker way of accurately recording a scene and ideally would require no artistic skill. Over time, however, the unique advantages of the medium brought it respect and significance for its own sake.

Daguerreotypes   When the secret of Daguerreotypes was released in 1839, what the French dubbed "daguérrotypomanie" spread like wildfire throughout Europe, England, and the United States. At first, due to the length of exposure time required, most pictures taken were of landscapes, architecture, and especially foreign places. Publisher N. M. P. Lerebours (1807–73) put out a series called *Excursions daguerriennes* between 1840 and 1844; a collection of daguerreotypes taken in locations from the Middle East to North Africa to Niagara Falls. This work, along with that of other traveling daguerreotypists, brought to the west views of a world most had little idea of.

Portraiture   When improvements in the daguerreotype process made portraits feasible, commercial studios opened up in major cities everywhere. Because of the relatively cheap price, almost anyone could have his or her portrait taken. For example, in Massachusetts in one year, 403,626 daguerreotypes were taken. A studio in New York reported taking up to 1,000 portraits a day.

Generally these portraits were simple, posed, and straightforward. However, a few studio photographers added a creative touch, notably Albert Sands Southworth (1811–94) and Josiah Johnson Hawes (1808–1901). Their well-known portrait of the chief justice of the Massachusetts Supreme Court in 1851 used bright overhead lighting—emphasizing his wild hair and the contours of his weathered face.

Calotypes   With the advent of paper calotype negatives came expansion in the uses of photography. David Octavius Hill (1802–70) and Robert Adamson (1821–48) took more than 1,500 photographs of common people across Scotland, including a well-known set of informal portraits of one fishing community. Mostly, however, calotypes continued to be used for landscape and architectural photography.

Folk Portraiture   Wet-plate collodion technology brought photography further into the hands of everyday individuals in the 1800's. Tintypes—easy to make and far less fragile than daguerreotypes—were used, for instance, during the Civil War in America, for soldiers to send home pictures of themselves to their families. Cartes-de-visite swept the Western world with "cardomania." Many people had portraits taken of themselves, and for the first time mass-produced prints of famous people and places were sold widely—for example, 70,000 of the Prince Consort in England in the week after his death.

Early Artistry   It was not all folk art, however. Many Young Romantics in Paris's Latin Quarter were using collodion plates to work artistically. Perhaps the most famous was Nadar, born Gaspard Félix Tournachon (1820–1910), who created artistic and caricature portraits of well-known Parisians for his Panthéon-Nadar (released beginning in 1854). His studio itself became a sort of salon for liberal thinkers in the city, and Nadar went on to explore both air travel and electric lighting for photography.

Other photographers working at the same time included Étienne Carjat (1828–1906), and Antony Samuel Adam-Salomon (1811–81), whose use of high side light on his sitters is to this day known as "Rembrandt lighting," following the painter's style. Napoleon Sarony (1821–96), working in the 1860's, specialized in theatrical photographs, in which he experimented with elaborate props and backdrops, and especially with the attitude of the sitter—exploring the playful and dramatic side of his actor subjects. Julia Margaret Cameron (1815–79) made headshots of her famous friends in which she attempted to show the spirit and "truth" of the people she photographed.

War   Photography's strength of veracity found an outlet in the documentation of war. Roger Fenton (1819–69) in London was one of the first war photographers, working in Crimea. Matthew Brady (1823–96) contributed unique and renowned coverage of the Civil War in America. His photographs provided the public with some of the first views of the destructive and gruesome nature of warfare.

Exploration   In the mid-1800's collodion photography was used throughout North America as part of the United States Geological Survey's exploratory expeditions, including Powell's travels along the Colorado River. William Henry Jackson (1843–1942) took photographs of Yellowstone that were instrumental in getting the area designated as the first National Park in 1872; without his images no one believed the area's shooting geysers, steaming sulfur pools and otherworldly landscape truly existed.

Early Social Documentation   Jacob A. Riis (1849–1914), a police reporter in New York City, was one of the earliest to use his camera as a documentary tool, which he employed to illustrate the misery of immigrant slum life in New York in a way that his writing never could. However, due to the poor photomechanical techniques available at the time (ca. 1890), his photographic work was not recognized until 1947.

Adam Clark Vroman (1856–1916) and Edward S. Curtis (1868–1952) each took their cameras to Native American reservations, making photographic studies of American Indians. Their work served both as sympathetic portraits (Vroman) and as a substantial record of what was by then a dying culture (Curtis).

Pictorial Photography   Starting in 1886 Peter Henry Emerson (1856–1936) led a revolt toward what he called "Naturalistic" or "Pictorial Photography," which paradoxically saw the reproduction of nature as the primary aesthetic goal of photography. He suggested pictures be taken slightly out of focus to mimic the human eye's inability to hold all of a scene in focus at once; critics called these images "fuzzygraphs." In 1891 Emerson reversed his opinions completely, and decided that photography was not in fact art. In an odd twist, he continued to make photographs and publish a photography textbook.

Galleries and Groups   At the end of the 19th century, the fight between photography and art was heating up across Europe. Galleries and groups were beginning to hold controversial juried photography exhibitions, with painters and sculptors as the judges. Before this, photographs had generally been assessed for their technical achievements, not their artistic merits.

A London-based group called the Linked Ring formed in 1892 as an art-focused breakaway from the London Photographic society. The group wanted to free photography from the bondage of science and technology. One member, Alfred Stieglitz (1864–1946), spent his remarkable career working to improve and evolve American photography. As part of this effort, Stieglitz established the Camera Club of New York (1896), and its influential publication *Camera Notes*. The Club held exhibitions featuring work by important new photographers such as Gertrude Käsebier (1852–1934) and Edward Steichen (1879–1973).

In 1902 Stieglitz founded a new group, Photo-Secession, following the German and American avant-garde's mission to separate itself from the academic establishment. The Little Galleries of the Photo-Secession at 291 Fifth Avenue (commonly called "291"), along with the group's publication, *Camera Work*, showcased work by leading photographers, as well as avant-garde artists, including Matisse, Picasso, and O'Keeffe.

Straight Photography   A new style of "straight photography"—photographs that did not try to emulate paintings—began to flourish at this time, with Stieglitz among its advocates. His portraits were considered remarkable for portraying depth of soul and character with perfect technique, but with no pretense or artificiality. Paul Strand (1890–1976) and Edward Weston (1886–1958) furthered the trend, emphasizing form and design and the beauty of everyday objects.

A new group formed in 1934 following in the straight photography tradition. They called themselves group "f/64" in reference to the narrow aperture that produces the greatest depth of field and focal sharpness. The founding members included some of the biggest names in photography: Ansel Adams (1902–84), Imogen Cunningham (1883–1976), John Paul Edwards (1883–1958), Sonya Noskowiak (1905–75), Henry Swift (1891–1960), Willard Van Dyke (1906–86), and Edward Weston. The group's code was strict realism, and soon the designation f/64 came to refer to anyone practicing this style of photography.

Ansel Adams is very famous because of the extraordinarily beautiful photographs he took of the American West. But he is worth noting for several other reasons, including technical innovations and for making photography into an art form accessible to the public. In addition, his "zone system" of exposure and processing was one of the most important developments in photography in the 20th century. By breaking down the tones of a scene into values on a scale from zero to IX and exposing and processing his film based on those values, Adams was able to produce prints with the rich tonal range that has made his images renowned, especially those of Yosemite National Park.

Alternative Views   In the same postwar years, some photographers experimented instead with alternative perspective and abstraction. Alvin Langdon Coburn (1882–1966) and Alexander Rodchenko (1891–1956) created memorable works using novel angles of view, mirrored camera attachments (Coburn) and multiple exposures (Rodchenko). Even further from straight photography's realism were László Moholy-Nagy (1895–1946) and Man Ray (1890–1976). They made true camera-less abstractions called photograms and rayograms, respectively, by placing objects onto light-sensitive paper and exposing to create shadows and shapes. Others found influence in science and motion studies, while followers of the Dada modern painting group and the Bauhaus movement began to create photomontages and photocollages—new work that relied on juxtaposition and contrast to create meaning and messages that were often political or social in nature.

Documentary Photography   Early in the 1900's Lewis W. Hine (1874–1940) made what he called "photo-interpretations" or "human documents." These included series on immigrant workers in New York and Red Cross workers in Europe. Hine intended his work to spread knowledge and improve the human condition. Along with Riis's similar photographic style, Hine's photography ushered in the documentary photography movement that was especially strong during the Great Depression. The Farm Security Administration, created as part of Roosevelt's efforts to assist those devastated by the drought, undertook the documentation of the government's aid efforts and life in rural America in general. The two best-known F.S.A. photographers were Walker Evans (1903–75) and Dorothea Lange (1895–1965), whose stark but sympathetic portraits of farmworkers continue to influence aspiring photographers.

Photojournalism   The release of fast hand-held cameras permitted the first indoor available-light photography, which meant events and meetings could be covered without the intrusive light and smoke of flash powder. This led to a new trend: documentation of the political and social events that shaped history. The camera's ability to capture decisive moments like the Hindenburg disaster (1937) further pushed the use of photography as a news medium. Photography's place in newspapers and journalism was clinched by the invention of the half-tone printing process, which made it possible to print both text and images using the same press. This new form of photography, photojournalism, was pioneered especially by German photographers like Erich Salomon (1886-1944), Felix H. Man (1893-1985), André Kertész (1894-1985), and Alfred Eisenstaedt (1898-1995).

Magazines also played an important role in the development of photojournalism. The founder of *Time* and *Fortune*, Henry Luce (1898–1967), started *Life* magazine in 1936 with the specific intention of incorporating photography into the stories. With the help of staff photographers like Margaret Bourke-White (1904–71), *Life* initiated a new kind of magazine and a new kind of photography, driven by the "mind-guided camera." Instead of capturing a news event that happened to occur, the photographer had a preset assignment; her job was to take all the photographs needed in order to capture the few images that would best tell the story. During World War II, Bourke-White became one the first woman war correspondent and her photos of the war are considered as among the very best of the genre.

Modern Realism   Starting in the 1960's, a branch of art photographers began to focus on what was called the "social landscape." Walker Evans and Harry Callahan (1912–99), working in the 1940's, first established this style, characterized by the straightforward depiction of daily life. Robert Frank (b. 1924) and Diane Arbus (1923–71) were exemplary photographers in this vein—Frank with his extensive documentation of America, and Arbus sympathetically portraying outcast groups. And

Thomas Struth (b. 1954) bridged the gap between art and viewer with his nearly life-size photographs of ordinary people inside museums, churches, and other public places, often observing other photographs, paintings, and sculptures.

Conceptualism   At the same time there emerged a new sense of postmodernism: the idea that the camera could not be an objective or factual viewer. Photographers taking this attitude often used series or juxtapositions of the same object from multiple angles or viewpoints. They also engaged in deliberate manipulations of images, or carried theatrical staging to its limits, to create unreal, bizarre, or simply questioning images. Cindy Sherman (b. 1954), with her disguised self-portraits and mannequin images, is a prime example of a photographer this genre.

With the rise of color and chemical photographic techniques, expressive possibilities expanded even further. The abstract avant-garde styles of the Bauhaus followers grew and flourished in the 1960's and 70's, with techniques whose names hint at their variety: photogenics, crystallography, lightgraphics, luminograms, chemigrams. Together, photographers have drawn on an expanding panoply of methods, all in name of meaningful and conceptual imagemaking.

Glossary of Photographic Terms

additive color the principle that any color can be produced by starting with black (absence of color) and adding proportions of red, green, and blue (RGB) light.

aperture the opening in a camera or camera lens that allows light through, or the size of that opening.

APS (Advanced Photo System) recent type of consumer film, camera, and processing technology that uses drop-in film loading, user-picked picture format, and alternative processing that provides thumbnails, print-format choice, and stores the pictures in the film canister.

autofocus (or AF) a lens designed to set its focus automatically on an object in its view, using sensors. Or a camera equipped to work with AF lenses.

backlight lighting on a subject that comes from behind the subject, often used to create a halo (where the edges of a person's hair are lit) or silhouette effect.

bounce the use of a reflector or reflective surface (such as

a ceiling or wall) to bounce an indirect light source onto a subject, resulting in softer, more diffuse lighting.

bracketing the technique of taking a series of pictures of the same image, with a range of exposures around the 'proper' exposure. Used in situations where there is doubt as to the best exposure, or the image has a wider range of light/dark tones than the film can record.

calotype from Greek "beautiful picture," a print type invented by William Henry Fox Talbot, it uses silver nitrate, gallic acid, and acetic acid to sensitize a paper before exposure, and to develop the picture after exposure. Innovative because it used a latent image—the image could not be seen until development, whereas previous techniques all relied on exposing the paper for long periods until the image was visible.

camera obscura a precursor to modern photographic cameras. Initially a dark room with a hole in one wall, causing an image of the outside to be projected (upside-down and reversed) on the opposite wall. Later designed as boxes with a lens, aperture, and access door.

CCD ("Charge Coupled Device") a wafer-thin piece of hardware covered with tens of thousands of capacitors (or diodes or conductors), used in digital photography to capture an image. Exposure to light builds a charge on each receptor cell, converting the light into an electrical signal, which is then transferred to an amplifier and detector.

CMOS ("Complementary Metal Oxide Semiconductor") an alternate form of digital image capture that works essentially the same as a CCD, used in some brands of digital cameras.

color depth (bit depth) refers to the number of bits (a single on-off choice) used to represent a color in a digital image. 8-bit color (or 1 byte) represents 256 colors (2^8 possible combinations); 24-bit gives approximately 16 million values or colors. Usually refers to a digital image, but also used to show a monitor's capabilities.

contact print a photographic print made by putting a negative in direct contact with light-sensitive material, resulting in a print the exact size of the negative.

Daguerreotype considered the "first" photographs, based on a process devised by Louis Jacques Mandé Daguerre, that used silver-plated copper, iodine, and mercury to form a unique image after exposure to light in a camera.

depth of field the 'depth' or extent of the focal plane of an image—the range of what is in focus. It is determined by the type and focal length of lens used, and the aperture.

emulsion a light-sensitive chemical substance applied to film, paper, plate, or other backing, that receives light and is processed to produce a negative or positive image.

exposure the act of allowing light to reach light-sensitive material, or the amount of light that reaches that material, as modified by shutter speed and aperture size.

f/number also called f-stop, the size of the aperture opening, expressed as a numerical designation, e.g. f/2, f/2.8, etc.

fill the use of light, from a flash or other source, to balance or fill in direct ambient light sources, in order to reduce the contrast between brightly lit and shadowed areas.

filter transparent attachment for camera or enlarger lens used to alter the color, range, or other characteristic of light entering the lens. Examples include (red and yellow) B&W contrast filters, polarizing filters, and special effects filters.

fish eye super wide angle lenses, with nearly infinite depth-of-field, whose angle of view can approach 180 degrees. Views through these lenses results in extreme distortion, like that of a door peep-hole.

focal length the distance between the lens and the focal plane, or sharp object in an image. Combined with the film format, it determines the lens angle of view. With 35mm film, lenses with focal length around 50mm are "normal" (they approximate the view without any lens); less than 35mm are wide angle; and greater than 70 are called telephoto lenses.

halftone process used to print continuous tone photographic images by representing tones as a series of black dots (or CMYK dots for color images); the density of the dots, when viewed from a distance, recreates the scale of grey tones in the image. Devised for reproducing photographs on newspaper printing presses.

large format photography using film in single sheets larger ranging in size from 4 x 5 inches up to 20 x 24 inches. Large format cameras generally have bellows and component to allow swing and pitch adjustments and viewing on a ground glass plate.

lens simple lenses consist of a glass or plastic element that is curved on one or both sides. Most photographic lenses are compound, using between three and 20 elements in order to correct aberrations, allow a sharp focus across the entire picture, and aid in focusing and (in zoom lenses) changing focal length.

luminance the brightness of a surface or image, determined by how much light it emits or reflects. In digital photography, it is a value given to each pixel.

macrophotography also called "close up photography," any photography with magnification of the subject greater than 1:1.

megapixel 1 million pixels. Used as a rating for digital cameras' capture and resolution capabilities.

multiple exposure exposing a single frame of film many times, to show motion or for special effects.

negative a print or piece of film whose tonalities are reversed from the natural scene. Light projected through a negative onto light-sensitive material produces a positive image when that material is processed.

optical zoom the use of multiple lens elements in differential motion to enable a lens to move smoothly between different focal lengths.

overexpose too much light when exposing film; results in a washed out or overly light print.

photogravure from French for "photo engraving," a method of etching copper plates by placing photosensitive material on the plate that hardens differently when exposed to light, then washing away the unhardened material after exposure through a negative, and using acid to etch the exposed copper. The plate is then used to print multiple copies of the photograph, with finer quality than halftone printing. Photogravure was regularly used by Alfred Stieglitz and his followers.

point and shoot hand-held, usually consumer-level cameras with automatic exposure and focusing, and a separate viewfinder.

positive a print or piece of film whose tonalities match that of the natural scene; produced either directly from the camera (as with positive transparencies or slides) or by printing from a negative.

red eye the effect resulting from light from a flash striking the back of a person's retina and reflecting straight back into the camera, causing the irises to look red. This occurs predominantly in low light situations—where pupils are dilated—when the flash is close to the camera.

resolution the sharpness of an image, based on the number and density of pixels; more pixels result in better detail and a higher resolution. Often expressed in dpi or dots per inch.

shutter the mechanical device between a lens and film in a camera that opens to allow light in for a set amount of time. Focal plane shutters are part of the camera body and mimic window shades. Between-the-lens shutters use metal blades and work like the iris/pupil of an eye and adjust not only for time but for the size of the opening.

shutter speed the amount of time a camera shutter stays open to let light onto the film. Expressed in fractions of a second, it ranges in most cameras between 1 (or more) seconds down to 2000 (1/2000th of a second).

SLR (single lens reflex) hand-held cameras in which the viewfinder (what the photographer looks through) shows the actual image through the lens, using a series of mirrors that lift out of the way when the shutter is released. These are the standard cameras for most serious amateur or professional photographers.

speed a rating of the light-sensitivity of film, commonly expressed in ASA ratings.

stereoscope a device used to merge (in viewing) two images of the same scene, taken at slightly different angles, by having each eye view one image, so that together the effect is a three-dimensional view.

stroboscope a special flash unit that fires multiple flashes in rapid succession, used with a moving subject and a long camera exposure, in order to break the motion down into discreet units that are all (usually) recorded on a sngle frame.

subtractive color the principle that any color can be produced by starting with a white light (all colors present), and using cyan, yellow, and magenta (CMY) filters to remove complementary colors. It is the basis for most modern color photography.

telephoto a lens with a focal length generally greater than 70mm (or longer than the diagonal of the film format). The effect is enlargement of the image and a decreased depth of field.

tintype also called melainotype and ferrotype and popular especially during the Civil War, these direct positives were made by coating black-enameled iron sheets with light-sensitive material. Processing stripped away unexposed areas, and the black backing made the image appear positive. Tintypes are fast and easy to make, and so were extremely popular with the public at large.

transparency processed direct positive film. In 35mm format, this is called "slide" film.

TWAIN a data source manager that operates between a driver and a device; the interface standard for scanners, which come with TWAIN drivers to make them compatible with TWAIN-supporting software.

twin lens reflex a camera with two identical lenses, one to expose the film, and the other above it to focus the camera. The distance between the two lenses makes framing of very close subjects more difficult because of parallax error.

underexpose an image that was exposed with too little light. The result is a dark image.

wide angle lenses with a short focal length, generally smaller than the diagonal of the film format. The result is an increased angle of view (the number of degrees from perpendicular to the film that are included in the image), and increased depth of field. The shorter the focal length, the more distorted the image becomes to accommodate the wide angle.

zoetrope a drum-like device with slits in the sides, used to view a strip of images in quick succession so that the subject appears to move.

LITERATURE

World Literature

Literature of the Ancient Western World

Western literature begins with the Babylonian poem *Gilgamesh*, composed probably ca. 2000 B.C. but known most completely from Akkadian-language clay tablets in the library of King Assurbanipal at Nineveh (r. 668–626 B.C.). It presents a mythical account of the exploits of an ancient king of southern Mesopotamia; some of its episodes parallel other accounts in ancient Middle Eastern literature such as the biblical narrative of Noah and the Flood. *Gilgamesh* tells of a king who, through the actions of the gods and his friendship with the "wild man" Enkidu, learns to forsake the tyranny with which he had ruled his subjects. Contemporary with the Gilgamesh epic is a cycle of hymns to the Sumerian goddess Inanna (2000 B.C.), known to the Babylonians as Ishtar and a precursor of the Greek goddess Aphrodite.

The most important work of early Egyptian literature is the *Book of Going Forth by Day* (earliest portions ca. 2300–2100 B.C.; also known as the "Egyptian Book of the Dead"), a collection of incantations and spells (in many different versions) placed in tombs as guides for the dead in their journey to the afterlife. Ancient Egyptian literature is also rich in poetry, including love poems, hymns to the gods, and evocations of daily life, written over a period of many centuries from the late third millennium to the early first millennium B.C. The story of "The Sailor and the Wonder Island," from the Middle Kingdom (2022–1850 B.C.) has some parallels with the later Greek myth of Atlantis. (For the Hebrew Bible, a work of great literary as well as religious and historical importance, see "The Bible.")

Greek literature begins with Homer (ca. 800 B.C.), by tradition a blind poet who composed and sang the two great epic poems, *The Iliad* and *The Odyssey*, that are considered the cornerstones of western literature. The background of both is the Trojan War, believed to have been fought around 1100 B.C. and, according to Homer, caused by the abduction of Helen, wife of the Greek king Menelaus, by Paris, a Trojan prince. *The Iliad* tells the story of the 10-year siege of Troy by the Greeks with all of the action centered on the final year, and the fierce warrior and demigod Achilles as the central character. *The Odyssey* relates the story of Odysseus, a wily Greek leader who after the success of his scheme to penetrate the walls of Troy with a wooden horse, is forced by the god Poseidon to wander for 10 years before he can return home to Ithaca, his beloved wife, Penelope, and his faithful son, Telemachus. Both epics are filled with gripping scenes of war, love, loyalty, and betrayal—all the elements we have come to associate with brilliant stories that help to illuminate the human experience. Although Homer is always credited as the author, some scholars believe they are the work of more than one person.

Another important poet of this period was Hesiod (ca. 700 B.C.), whose poem *Theogony* is a leading source of information about the deities of ancient Greek religion, and whose *Works and Days* celebrates the pleasures of agrarian and pastoral life. Other important early Greek poets were Archilocus (ca. 650 B.C.); Alacaeus (ca. 620–580 B.C.); Sappho (fl. ca. 612 B.C.), the first woman poet known by name; and Anacreon (sixth century B.C.).

Greek literary work of the high classical period was dominated by writing for the theater: the tragedies of Aeschylus, Sophocles, and Euripides, and the comedies of Aristophanes and Menander (see *Drama*). Their contemporary Pindar (518–446 B.C.) was considered the greatest poet of his age, famed for celebratory choral verse (lyric odes), while Demosthenes (384–322 B.C.) was regarded as the greatest orator. Expository prose writing also flourished in classical Greece, reaching hitherto unknown levels of logical and rhetorical power in the histories of Herodotus (ca. 484–425 B.C.) and Thucydides (ca. 470–425 B.C.) and in the philosophical and scientific works of Plato, Aristotle, and Euclid, among many others.

Poetry blossomed in the Hellenic Period that followed the end of the Classical Greek era (conventionally dated to the death of Aristotle). Theocritus (fl. 270 B.C.) was the inventor of the pastoral ode, while Appollonius Rhodius (fl. third century B.C.) wrote epic poetry in Homeric style, including the *Argonautica*. Hundreds of Hellenic poems are preserved in the Greek *Anthology*, which has as its core the first-century B.C. collection *The Garland* edited by the poet Meleager (ca. 140–70 B.C.), and was augmented by a series of editors over the next millennium. Among the many poets represented in the earlier (and generally finer) layers of the anthology, particularly with short, epigrammatic verses, are Callimachus (ca. 300–240 B.C.), Antipater of Sidon (ca. 130 B.C.), Philodemus (110–40 B.C.), and Lucilius (99–55 B.C.).

Latin writing prior to the first century was largely derivative of, or reactive against, Greek literature, and did not cohere into a Latin literature as such. The situation changed drastically in the last century of the Roman Republic, with the lyric love poetry of Catullus (84–54 B.C.) contrasting with the *De Rerum Natura* ("The Nature of Things") and other long expository poems by Lucretius (95–54 B.C.). Latin prose came of age in the works of Cicero (106–43 B.C.) and Julius Caesar (ca. 100–44 B.C.). Virgil (70–19 B.C.), the greatest of the Latin epic poets, is known for his long pastoral poems, the *Eclogues* and the *Georgics*, but especially for his epic masterpiece, the *Aeneid*, which tells the story of the founding of Rome by Aeneas, a prince of Troy driven away by the Greek conquest in the Trojan War.

Horace (65–8 B.C.) was the greatest master of Latin lyric poetry; his *Odes and Epistles* take brilliant advantage of the grammatical complexities and expressive possibilities of Latin. The republican era of Latin literature effectively came to an end with Ovid (43 B.C.–A.D. 19), who forsook an official career for his poetry, and spent the last decade of his life in exile on the Black Sea. His amatory and erotic verse, *Amores* ("The Loves") and *Ars Amatoria* ("The Art of Love"), won him fame and notoriety; his *Metamorphoses* ("Transformations") are meditations on the ceaseless changes that affect gods, humans, and the natural world.

Medieval Europe

The earliest medieval European literature was written in Latin, and, whether prose, poetry, or drama, predominantly expressed Christian themes. Vernacular literature first appeared ca. 800 with the now fragmentary epic in High German, the *Lay of Hildebrand*. Much of Europe's literature before the 12th century, including epics and ballads, was communicated orally, and Old Norse (Norwegian) oral poetry migrated to Iceland, where heroic narratives called "eddas" were written down from ca. 1100 to ca. 1350. France's national epic, the *Chanson de Roland*, appeared ca.

1100, followed during the ensuing century by Spain's *Cantar del Mio Cid* and at the turn of the 13th century by Germany's *Nibelungenlied*.

The Christian romance form, based largely on British-Celtic Arthurian legend, also appeared in 12th-century France, where its leading practitioner was Chrétien de Troyes. In Germany, Wolfram von Eschenbach composed his long great romance *Parzival* about 1220. During this same period lyric poetry was developed by the troubadours in southern France and spread to northern France and to Germany, where its exponents were known as "minnesingers." In the 13th century, allegorical fable and romance arose in France, best represented by the long symbolic poem of courtly love, *Roman de la Rose*.

The French lyric tradition was also picked up in Sicily, where the first sonnets are believed to have been composed in the 13th century, leading to the northward spread of a "sweet new style" and the birth of a great Italian vernacular (Tuscan) literature. Its supreme poetic voice was the Florentine politician Dante Alighieri (1265–1321), creator, in the early 14th century, of one of the transcendent works of world literature, *The Divine Comedy*, an allegorical tour of heaven, hell, and purgatory that embodies all medieval Christianity within the limits of the poet's own time and country.

Dante entitled his poem of three books, 100 cantos, and more than 14,000 intricately rhymed lines simply *La Commedia*, indicating that it was a positive or happy pilgrimage by the poet (representing Dante himself) from darkness, or ignorance, to a glimpse of the ultimate light and truth emanating from the heavenly God. He is guided by the Roman poet Virgil through the nine circles of hell and seven stages of purgatory, all astonishingly imagined and vividly populated by historical persons and the poet's own acquaintances. And when the pagan Virgil can take him no farther, Beatrice, Dante's ideal human, now become celestial, leads him triumphantly, though less dramatically, through the radiant spheres of Paradise.

Later in that century, another Tuscan, Petrarch, wrote a series of sonnets that became for centuries the foundation for that international verse form. His contemporary, Giovanni Boccaccio, produced the volume of tales, *The Decameron*, that is the foundation for all prose storytelling.

After the troubadours, lyric poetry became a profession, consummately practiced in 15th-century France by Francois Villon. In 1499 the first European novel, *La Celestina*, probably by Fernando de Rojas, appeared in Spain.

Renaissance Europe

Literature in the Tuscan dialect flourished during the reign of Lorenzo de'Medici, prince of Florence in the late 15th century; in the 16th century two of the greatest humanistic works appeared: Ludovico Ariosto's epic *Orlando Furioso* (1516), and Baldassare Castiglione's *The Courtier* (1528), a series of dialogues on courtly requirements and behavior. Niccolò Machiavelli's *The Prince* (1513), expressing a ruthlessly pragmatic view of statecraft and centralized power, is one of history's most enduring political treatises. Among the best Italian lyric poets of the 16th century were Torquato Tasso, who also wrote an epic of the First Crusade; and Michelangelo Buonarotti (the great painter and sculptor).

The Italian Renaissance moved to France, where it so influenced lyric poetry that a group of poets known as the Pléiade, led by Pierre de Ronsard (1524–85), reacted by dedicating themselves to writing verse that was more distinctly French. Other important 16th-century French literary figures wrote prose. François Rabelais (1490–1553) composed four extended comic, socially incisive tales about the father-and-son giants Gargantua and Pantagruel between 1532 and 1552. Michel de Montaigne (1533–92) was the first great modern essayist, who commented, from a classical, humanist, skeptical perspective, on a great range of subjects.

In Spain the late 16th century and the 17th century are known as a Golden Age of literature, and its poets, including Garcilaso de la Vega (1503?–36), were also inspired by the Italian tradition. A new genre, the chivalric novel, had arisen early in the 16th century, and led to the great masterpiece of all Spanish literature, Miguel de Cervantes's (1547–1616) *Don Quixote de la Mancha* (1605–15), a mock-chivalric, all-encompassing novel of an idealistic but all-too-flawed "knight's" adventures.

The hero of the novel (in two books—Parts I and II, published a decade apart), is an old gentleman who has been so addled by his reading of romances that he fancies himself a knight and undertakes, in the company of his peasant "squire," Sancho Panza, a mission to spread his noble influence across Spain—a panorama richly and hilariously imagined. This allows the narrator to observe all Spanish society, and ultimately, all humanity, under the dual lenses of illusion and reality, in a work identified as the first modern novel by many and as the greatest novel by some.

Before the Protestant Reformation in the 16th century, Catholic humanist writing, embracing a modern, skeptical view of church organization and materialism, took hold in northern Europe, including Martin Luther's Germany. The greatest humanists were Thomas More in England and, in Holland, Desiderius Erasmus (1466?–1536), who promoted church reform and further challenged the institution in his satirical book *The Praise of Folly* (1509).

17th-Century Europe

In France the 17th century was a period of growing political and cultural influence during which, under rigid state control, literary language and sensibility were refined and confined to an almost doctrinal Classicism. The greatest Classical writers were playwrights of the middle and late century: the tragedians Pierre Corneille and Jean Racine and the comedian Molière (see *Drama*). The leading non-dramatic poets were the satirist (and critic) Nicolas Boileau-Despreaux (1636–1711) and the great fable-writer Jean de La Fontaine (1621–95). Distinguished prose was exhibited in the *Maximes* of François, duc de La Rochefoucauld (1613–80), and the *Pensées* of Blaise Pascal (1623–62). In 1678 Madame de La Fayette (1634–92) produced the first significant French novel, *La Princesse de Clèves*. Nine years earlier, *Simplicissimus*, considered the first German novel, had been published by Hans Jakob von Grimmelshausen (1625–76).

18th-Century Europe

In early 18th-century Germany, French-influenced Classicism brought linguistic and stylistic restrictions such as had been introduced in France. Throughout Europe this would be the Age of the Enlightenment, a time of secular, rationalist vision, when science and humankind were being emphasized more than religion and God.

The Enlightenment was most fully realized in France, where Voltaire (1694–1778) was its dominant voice; his most famous literary work is the satirical tale *Candide* (1759). Another essential figure in this movement was Denis Diderot (1713–84), essayist on the arts and science, novelist, and editor of the 28-volume *Encyclopédie*, the very emblem of the age.

A contemporary writer whose original views departed from those of the Enlightenment was Jean-Jacques Rousseau (1712–78), who exhorted humanity to renounce society and rediscover its natural goodness and equality. His *Social Contract* (1762) incorporates these ideas into a political treatise. In addition, he was the author of an important and influential novel, *La Nouvelle Héloïse* (1761).

The Enlightenment influenced German rationalist and classicist literature, but more important in the country's literary history is the *Sturm und Drang* ("storm and stress") movement that followed as a reaction. Influenced by Rousseau, *Sturm und Drang* emphasized emotion over reason and self-expression over social norms, and it celebrated nature. Its greatest exponent—one of the great figures in all literature—was Johann Wolfgang von Goethe (1749–1832), whose early play, *Götz von Berlichingen* (1773), and novel, *The Sorrows of Young Werther* (1774), were central to the movement. Its other major voice was Friedrich von Schiller (1759–1805), first heard in the 1781 drama *Die Räuber*. Goethe and Schiller both represented a new and more genuine period of German Classicism. Schiller's most famous work is the play *Wilhelm Tell*; Goethe's is the great dramatic investigation of God and man, *Faust* (1808, 1832), a long poem presented in two parts and in a remarkable variety of styles and poetic meters. Goethe's broad and deep sensibility embraced science, music, philosophy, politics, and theology. He changed the Faust legend from that of a man who loses his soul after bargaining with the devil to grow in power and knowledge, to that of one who defeats Satan's claim on him when he reaches beyond wordliness to divine redemption. Goethe's Faust, then, is more than a Romantic rebel; he is a type of the European, or Western, man, whose mind and soul are caught between the self, the created world, and its Creator.

19th-Century Europe

Although the French Revolution of 1789 is the great political event at the source of European Romanticism, the movement in fact arrived sooner in Germany than in France. Early German Romantics were the lyric poet and novelist Novalis, (1772–1801), and Heinrich von Kleist (1777–1811), a poetic dramatist and the most accomplished author of a newly popular form, the novella (*The Marquise of O and Other Stories*, 1810–11). E.T.A. Hoffmann (1776–1822) applied grotesque and supernatural subject matter to this form.

In Germany the philosopher Friedrich von Schlegel (1772–1829) and in France the novelist and literary hostess Madame Germaine de Stahl (1766–1817) advocated a new, and international, literature of feeling. Their wish was fulfilled in France by the poetry of Alphonse de Lamartine (1790–1869) and consummately by the writing of Victor Hugo (1802–85), who gained fame as a poet, a dramatist, and especially a novelist (*Notre Dame de Paris* (1832), *Les Misérables* (1862). Hugo's contribution to a distinguished period of French drama was accompanied by the achieve-

ments of Alfred de Vigny and Alfred de Musset. As a popular historical novelist he was rivaled by Alexandre Dumas *père* (1802–70) who wrote *The Three Musketeers* (1844) and *The Count of Monte Cristo* (1845).

From Britain to Russia, the novel came of age in the 1800's. While George Sand (Amandine Dupin, 1804–76) steadily produced romantic works, French fiction was dominated by a series of extraordinary realistic novelists. The earliest of these, Stendhal (1785–1842), author of *The Red and the Black* (1831), was both romantic and realist, for he wrote vividly but unflinchingly about passion and society. French society, in all its colors and textures, was the special study of Honoré de Balzac (1799–1850), whose prolific output of novels and stories is known as *La Comédie Humaine*. He was followed by the quintessential French realist, Gustave Flaubert (1821–80), whose *Madame Bovary* (1857) depicts a heroine whose illusory romanticism is doomed in a dull provincial world.

French poetry, too, departed from strictly Romantic pathos as the mid-century approached. Perhaps the most original French poetic voice of the century was that of Charles Baudelaire (1821–67), who was also an aesthete, a Symbolist, and in some degree a romantic in his sensitivity to emotional pain and the corruption that infected beauty. His *Fleurs du Mal* (1857) is a landmark of European poetry.

The "Young Germany" movement was an organized reaction against Romantic poetry, and its most significant figure was Heinrich Heine (1797–1856). Although political in outlook—immersed in the French Revolution and critical of German nationalism—he was a splendid love poet and the finest German lyric poet of the century. In France the second half of the century was the period of Symbolist and Decadent poetry, both influenced by Baudelaire. Paul Verlaine (1844–96) belonged to the first movement in his early career and the second in later life. His protégé as a Symbolist (and also his lover) was Arthur Rimbaud (1854–91). The latter's dreamlike verse differed from the elliptically phrased, pessimistic symbolism of his contemporary Stephan Mallarmé (1842–98).

In fiction, the literary movement that succeeded realism was naturalism, which depicted humanity, often in disturbing detail, as determined by nature and environment. Its well-known practitioners were Émile Zola (1840–92) and Guy de Maupassant (1850–93). Zola's Rougon-Macquart sequence of novels, including *Nana* (1880), examined the life of the lower classes. De Maupassant's masterly, brief, often bitter short stories have always been widely read. An important later naturalist was the German playwright, novelist, and poet Gerhart Hauptmann (1862–1946).

Late-19th and 20th-Century Europe

In southern Europe the careers of two major writers straddled the border of the 20th century. Italy's Gabriele D'Annunzio (1863–1938) first made his mark as a sensuous poet in the 1880's, and soon turned to writing novels, then plays. A nationalist and World War I airforce hero. D'Annunzio's reputation is besmirched by his embrace of fascism. A contemporary literary star in Spain was Miguel de Unamuno (1864–1936), a philosopher turned novelist and poet who searched for political and religious certainty.

The leading French poets of the early 20th century were Paul Claudel (1868–1955), a mystical Catholic who was also a major playwright; Paul Valéry (1871–1945), who picked up the Symbolist tradition; and Guillaume Appollinaire (1880–1918), a modernist influenced by Cubist painting. The great novelists were Marcel Proust (1871–1922), whose seven-novel sequence, *Remembrance of Things Past*, published from 1913 until after his death, is one of the greatest achievements in psychological literature; and André Gide (1869–1951), a writer who examined individual freedom (*The Immoralist*, 1902) and increasingly explored technical innovation.

The men widely regarded as Germany's greatest 20th-century poet and novelist, Rainer Maria Rilke and Thomas Mann, were both born in 1875. Like Appollinaire, Rilke (d. 1926) was inspired by modern art and was a strongly visual poet who explored both spirituality and erotic love. Mann (d. 1955), who moved to America during the Nazi regime, was a profound, wide-ranging writer who explored eroticism and the meaning of art in novels such as *The Magic Mountain* (1924).

Mann's contemporary, Hermann Hesse (1875–1962), was a psychological, symbolic novelist whose spiritual interest was directed to the East (*Siddhartha*, 1922). One of the most distinct voices in 20th-century fiction is that of a Czech Jew who wrote in German, Franz Kafka (1883–1924). The nightmarish anxiety that entraps his characters in works such as *The Metamorphosis* (1917) seemed to represent the political and psychological conditions of the age.

In the years before the 1930's civil war, poetry flourished in Spain, including that of two Andalusian poets, Juan Ramon Jiménez (1881–1958; 1956 Nobel Prize), and Federico García Lorca (1898–1936), a compassionate and popular surrealist poet and dramatist who was killed by Revolutionary forces.

The French novel continued to develop in many directions. In the 1920's and 30's two profound Catholic writers, François Mauriac (1885–1970) and Georges Bernanos (1888–1948), emerged, followed by the politically tumultuous works of André Malraux (1901–76), best known for *La Condition Humaine* (1933); and the innovative, sometimes obscene and bigoted, novels of Céline (1894–1961). Soon there appeared the great French existentialist philosopher novelists, for whom modern life was godless and without intrinsic meaning: Jean-Paul Sartre (1905–80), whose first, and most famous, novel was *Nausea* (1938); and Albert Camus (1913–60), whose first, and most famous, novel was *The Stranger* (1942). In 1937 another major writer grouped with the existentialists, the Irishman Samuel Beckett (1906–89), moved to Paris and soon began writing novels and plays in French.

Italy, too, produced important novelists toward the mid-century, including Alberto Moravia (1907–90), a close observer of uprooted modern humanity; and Italo Calvino (1923–85), who wrote in both realistic and fantastic modes. The Spanish novelist Camilo José Cela (b. 1916) won a Nobel Prize in 1989, as did the Italian poet Eugenio Montale (1896–1981) in 1975.

After the Second World War a main current in French fiction was experimental, often depriving the reader of familiar patterns of time, plot, even character—the *nouveau roman*, represented by authors such as Romain Gary (1914–80), Marguerite Duras (1914–96), and Alain Robbe-Grillet (b. 1922). Understandably, German writers examined a society devastated by the experience of Nazism and war. Heinrich Böll (1917–85) and Günter Grass (b. 1927) were internationally popular novelists in the late 20th century. Grass's novel *The Tin Drum* (1961) helped to earn him the Nobel Prize.

Russian Literature

Except for some oral secular poems, the earliest Russian literature, after the introduction of Christianity in 988, was almost entirely religious, until the nation's first great work, the heroic *Song of Igor's Campaign*, was completed in 1187. The first significant work with a known author was a late 14th-century epic imitative of the Igor tale, *Beyond the River Don*, by Sophonia of Ryazin, which celebrated a victory over the Tatars. The following centuries produced some interesting travel writing, more dogmatic religious writing and some political polemics, but Russian literature did not begin to hit stride until Czar Peter the Great welcomed Westernization in the second half of the 17th century. The first theater opened in 1662, and a new poetic style and prose fiction were introduced.

In the 18th century, a specific Russian literary language was developed, codified by Mikhail Lomonosov (1711–65), who was distinguished amid a thriving crop of poets. The first native dramatist was Aleksandr Sumarokov (1718–77). Empress Catherine the Great, whose reign began in 1762, felt the breath of the European Enlightenment and herself wrote plays, though she also punished writers who displeased her.

Romantic poetry was introduced to Russia through the translations and original poems of Vasily Zhukovsky (1783–1852), clearing a path for Russia's greatest poet, Aleksandr Pushkin (1799–1837), who was a superb lyric and narrative poet and a complexly ironic composer of parodies. His most famous works are the great verse-novel *Eugene Onegin*, (1823–31), a tragic tale of love and egotism; and the historical drama *Boris Godunov* (1831).

The first important 19th-century Russian fiction writer, Nikolai Gogol (1809–52), known for his stories and the novel *Dead Souls* (1842), has been hailed as both the first Russian realist and as a comic fantasist. A parade of great prose artists followed. A chief "Westernizer" was Ivan Turgenev (1818–83), a controversial critic of Russian society, best known for *Fathers and Sons* (1862). His contemporary was the brilliant novelist Fyodor Dostoyevsky (1821–81), author of *Crime and Punishment* (1866) and *The Brothers Karamazov* (1880). A more realistic, yet no less profound and emotionally vivid writer was Leo Tolstoy, (1828–1910), whose historical *War and Peace* (1865–69) and passionate *Anna Karenina* (1874–77) are among the world's greatest novels. And the compassionate, moral tales of Anton Chekhov are among the world's best short stories, while his sad, realistic, internationally produced plays are the finest written by any Russian.

Writers such as the novelist and poet Andrei Bely (1880–1934) formed a significant Symbolist movement around the turn of the 20th century. A reactive movement, that of the "acmeists," emphasized precision in poetry. Its principal voice was Osip Mandelstam (1892–1938). He and Maxim Gorky (1868–1936) were the last important writers to express themselves before the Communist revolution of 1917—although Gorky's "social realism" (as revealed in the play *The Lower Depths*, 1902) was in fact a forerunner of Soviet literature.

Bolshevism stifled artistic expression, yet some writing of distinction was produced in the following decades, including the epic novels of Mikhail Sholokhov (1905–84), the stories of Isaac Babel (1894–1940), and the satirical works of Mikhail Bulgakov (1891–1940) and Aleksey Tolstoy (1883–1945). After the death of Josef Stalin a more tolerant period of expression was marked by the 1954 publication of Ilya Ehrenburg's (1891–1967) novel *The Thaw*. Boris Pasternak's (1890–1960) famous *Dr. Zhivago* followed in 1957. And the poems of Yevgeny Yevtushenko (b. 1933) became well known outside his homeland. The powerfully anti-Soviet work of Aleksandr Solzhenitsyn (b. 1918), however, beginning with the novel *A Day in the Life of Ivan Denisovich* (1962), led to his exile in 1974. He later returned to a Russia in which he was free to express his religious beliefs, along with another member of the Tolstoy family, Tatyana Tolstaya (b. 1951), whose spiritually informed short stories continued to move that distinguished Russian form forward.

Latin-American Literature

The effective beginning of literature in Latin America is the appearance in Chile in 1569 of the epic poem *La Araucana* by a native Spaniard, Alonso de Ercilla y Zúñiga (1533–94); it is a tribute to the Indian tribe with whom the Spanish had warred. This pattern was reversed in the 17th century, when a Mexican-born poet, Juan Ruiz de Alarcón (1581?–1639), moved to Spain and became one of that country's greatest dramatists. A much later Mexican, writing near the end of colonial times, José Joaquín Fernández de Lizardi (1776–1827), published the first Latin-American novel, *The Itching Parrot*, in 1816–30.

In the first half of the 19th century the Ecuadorian José Joaquin Olmedo (1780–1847) celebrated the continent's independence movement and its great hero in the poem *La Victoria Junín: Canto a Bolívar* (1825). The Venezuelan-born Andres Bello (1781–1865) wrote poetry about agrarian life. The next generation of poets were primarily Romantics, who expressed the ideal of freedom in an age of political independence. Chief among them were the Argentinians Esetban Echevarría (1805–51) and Domingo Faustino Sarmiento (1811–88), both of whom protested against a tyrannical ruler. And out of their romantic enthusiasm for their land emerged the South American tradition of gaucho (or cowboy) literature, in particular *Martin Fierro* (1872), Argentina's national epic, by José Hernández (1834–86). Meanwhile, in Peru, Ricardo Palma (1833–1919) introduced another traditional Latin-American genre, the historical anecdote.

The novel flourished in the latter part of the century, the most popular being the tragic *Maria* (1867) by Colombia's

Jorge Isaacs (1837–95). Brazil produced several important novelists, including the realists Aluisio Azevedo (1857–1913) and Joaquim Maria Machado de Assis (1839–1908).

As the century drew to a close, writers embraced an experimental style known as *modernismo*. The Mexican poet and story-writer Manuel Guittierez Najera (1859–95) and the Cuban poet (and, in spite of the movement's contrary trend, revolutionary warrior) José Martí (1853–95) were principal initiators. The most important *modernista* was Nicaragua's Rubén Darío (1867–1916), a poet whose influence was felt strongly even in Spain.

Modernismo influenced a group of women lyrical poets in the early decades of the 20th century, including Chile's Gabriela Mistral (1889–1957), who in 1945 became the first Latin American to win the Nobel Prize in Literature. Another Chilean poet, Pablo Neruda (1904–73), would receive that honor in 1971.

Both nonfiction and fiction prose writers in the 20th century were affected by the Mexican Revolution of 1910 and inclined to address economic and social conditions. The outstanding novel of that uprising was Matriana Azuela's (1873–1952) *The Underdogs* (1915). A less prominent uprising was depicted by the Brazilian novelist Euclides da Cunha (1866–1909) in *Rebellion in the Backlands* (1902), which also described the harsh penurious living conditions of provincial people. Such problems were also addressed in a series of "Indian" novels, including *Birds Without a Nest* (1889) by Clorinda Matto de Turner (1852–1909) and *Peru and The Indian* (1935) by Gregorio Lopez de Fuentes (1897–1966) in Mexico.

Many novelists in the first half of the century wrote about the challenges of life in specific environments. Among them, Ricardo Guiraldes (1886–1927) wrote about the gauchos of the Argentine pampas, Jóse Eustasio Rivera (1889–1928) about the Colombian jungle, Manuel Gálvez (1882–1962) about urban social problems in Argentina, and Jorge Amado (b. 1912) about the hardships of cacao-harvesting in Brazil.

Since the 1960's Latin-American literature—fiction, especially—has burst forth with such creativity that the period has been called "El Boom." One of century's greatest Spanish-American writers, Argentina's Jorge Luis Borges (1899–1986), wrote only short tales, poems, and essays. His tales, though—fantastic, symbolic, elusive, and allusive—are something like a new literary form.

The new direction in Latin-American literature can be seen in the surrealism of Guatemalan novelist Miguel Ángel Asturias (1899–1974), a 1967 Nobel laureate. He is linked with the great trend of the time, "Magical Realism," a term introduced by Cuban novelist Alfonso Carpentier (1904–80) and signifying a blend of fantasy and reality. The most thoroughgoing, most widely-read magical realist is Gabriel García Márquez (b. 1928), Colombian author of *One Hundred Years of Solitude* (1967) and a 1982 Nobel winner. Other exponents are the Mexican Carlos Fuentes (b. 1928) and the Chilean Isabel Allende (b. 1942). The most admired Brazilian novel of the last half century is *The Devil to Pay in the Backlands* (1956) by João Guimarães Rosa (1908–67). Peru's leading contemporary novelist is Mario Vargas Llosa (b. 1936) After Neruda, Latin America's premier poet has been Mexico's Octavio Paz (1914–98), who became his country's first Nobel laureate in 1990.

Chinese Literature

The earliest surviving Chinese writings, dating from the 13th century B.C., are divination records inscribed on animal bones and turtle shells ("oracle bones"); despite their considerable historical value, they do not amount to literature in the usual sense of the term. Literary values can be seen in some inscriptions on bronze ritual vessels dating to the Western Zhou period (ca. 1046–771 B.C.), commemorating feasts, wars, royal gifts to aristocrats, and similar events.

Three books represent the foundation of the Chinese literary tradition. The *Shujing* ("Book of Documents"), a collection of historical accounts, contains some material that may date to the early Western Zhou period as well as later materials. The *Chunqiu* ("Chronicle of Springs and Autumns") is a chronicle of the aristocratic state of Lu for the years 722–481 B.C. The *Shijing* ("Book of Poetry") preserves over 300 poems from the Zhou period, comprising liturgical hymns, folk songs, elite poetry, and other types.

These three works were regarded as classics of great literary and moral value by Confucius (Kongzi, 551–479 B.C.), whose own teachings were recorded in the *Lunyü* ("Analects of Confucius") by his followers over a long period of time, ca. 450–250 B.C. The period after about 400 B.C. saw a dramatic increase in the production and circulation of written documents of all kinds, and marks the first great age of Chinese philosophical literature. Important philosophical works include eponymous books by the Confucian followers Mengzi ("Mencius," ca. 387–303 B.C.) and Xunzi (ca. 307–235 B.C.); the *Mozi*, ascribed to a rival of Confucius and compiled in stages ca. 400–200 B.C.; the Daoist classics *Laozi* or *Daodejing* ("The Way and Its Power"), ascribed to the legendary "Lao Dan," sixth century B.C., but actually dating from ca. 320–220 B.C.; and *Zhuangzi*, third century

B.C.; and the works of "Legalist" thinkers Shang Yang ("Lord Shang"), fourth century B.C., and Han Feizi (d. 233 B.C.). Narrative nonfiction and protofiction flourished in such collections as the *Guoyü* ("Narratives of the States"), *Zhanguoce* ("Intrigues of the Warring States"), and the *Guanzi* ("Book of Master Guan"). A southern tradition of poetry is preserved in the *Chuci* ("Elegies of Chu"), the earliest portions of which are ascribed to the statesman-poet Qu Yuan (fourth century B.C.).

In the Han Dynasty (206 B.C.–A.D. 220), most of the works mentioned above were edited into the form in which they are presently known. A tradition of historical writing was established by Sima Qian (ca. 145–90 B.C.) in the *Shiji* ("Records of the Historian") and Ban Biao (A.D. 3–54) and his son Ban Gu (32–92) in the *Han shu* ("History of the [Former] Han Dynasty"); their works served as the model for subsequent official dynastic histories compiled throughout the imperial era. Poetry flourished as folk lyrics were collected and edited by the official Music Bureau, and named poets worked in several genres, including the characteristically *Han fu* ("rhapsody") style of long, rococo narrative verse.

The great age of Chinese poetry was the Tang Dynasty (618–907), during which the principal genre was highly formal *shi* ("regulated verse"). In a time of poetic genius, the greatest figures included Wang Wei (699–761), Li Bo (or Li Bai, 701–762), Du Fu (712-770), the courtesan-poet Xue Tao (768–831), and Bo Juyi (or Bai Juyi, 772–846). The poet and essayist Han Yü (768–824) led a movement in favor of classical simplicity in prose writing. The art of Chinese fiction advanced in the Tang, with the rise of short stories, often ghost stories or "tales of the strange" with Buddhist or Daoist themes.

Poets of the Song Dynasty (960–1279) favored the *ce* ("song lyric") form; the greatest master of the age was Su Shi (or Su Dongpo, 1036–1101). Classical poetry continued to be written into the 20th century, but with few exceptions it failed to match the brilliance of Tang and Song verse. Under the Mongol Yuan Dynasty (1270–1368) writers turned their attention to the theater, and *qu* ("Chinese opera") scripts became a major genre of literary creation.

Fiction, though despised as "vulgar" by the elite, flourished under the Ming (1368–1644) and Qing (1644–1911) dynasties, when China's major novels were written: *Sanguozhi yanyi* ("Romance of the Three Kingdoms") by Luo Guanzhong (ca. 1330–1400); *Shuihu zhuan* ("Water Margin," also called "Outlaws of the Marsh") by Luo Guanzhong and Shi Nai'an (ca. 1296–1370); *Xiyouji* ("Journey to the West")

by Wu Cheng'en (1500–1582), incorporating earlier narratives; the anonymous satirical and erotic classic *Jinpingmei* ("Plum Blossoms in a Golden Vase"), ca. 1618; and the greatest of all, *Hong lou meng* ("Dream of the Red Chamber") by Cao Xueqin (1715–1763).

Following the Republican revolution of 1911, a vernacular literature movement led by Chen Duxiu, Hu Shi, and others led to an outpouring of essays, criticism, translations, and fiction in the new style. The leading master of the new prose was Lu Xun (pen name of Zhou Shuren, 1881–1936), whose short stories helped define an age. Prominent novelists including Ba Jin (pen name of Li Feigan, b. 1904), Guo Moruo (1892–1978), Mao Dun (pen name of Shen Yanbing, 1896–1981), Lao She (pen name of Shu Shuyu, 1899–1966), and Ding Ling (pen name of Jiang Bingzhi, 1904–86) combined social consciousness with a tendency toward romanticism derived from 19th-century Western fiction. The best-known works of these writers include Ba Jin's *Jia* ("Family," 1931) and Lao She's *Luotuo xiangzi* ("Rickshaw," 1936).

Mao Zedong's "Yan'an Talks on Art and Literature" (1943) served notice to artists and writers that their work was expected to serve the interests of the Communist Party; the result was a decades-long literary drought. After Mao's death in 1976, older writers such as Liu Binyan (b. 1925) and Wang Meng (b. 1934) began to write more freely, joined by younger writers such as the novelist Mo Yan (b. 1956; *Red Sorghum* and other novels) and the "misty" poets including Bei Dao (b. 1949) and Mang Ke (b. 1950). A Chinese diaspora literature also began to flourish in the last decades of the 20th century; leading figures include Gao Xingjian (b. 1940, resident of France), author of *Soul Mountain* and other novels; Jung Chang (b. 1952, resident of England), author of *Wild Swans*; Anchee Min (b. 1957, resident of the U.S.), author of *Red Azalea*, and Ha Jin (b. 1956, resident of U.S.), who won the National Book Award for *Waiting* (1999).

Japanese Literature

The foundational works of Japanese literature date from the eighth century A.D. Two works of history, the *Kojiki* ("Record of Ancient Matters," 712, written in Classical Chinese) and the *Nihon shoki* or *Nihongi* ("Chronicle of Japan," 720, written in Japanese) recount the history of Japan from its mythical beginnings and underpin the imperial clan's claim to rule. The *Man'yōshuō* ("Book of Ten Thousand Leaves," ca. 759) is Japan's first anthology of poetry. Its more than 4,500 poems include works in both "long poem" (*chōka*) and "short poem" (*tanka*) form, on a wide range of subjects including bereavement, erotic longing, and other emotion-laden themes.

By the early 10th century, with the publication of the anthology *Kokinshō* ("Ancient and Modern Writings," edited by Ki no Turayuki (ca.868–945) and others, the world of Japanese poetry was and would remain dominated by the *tanka*, verse of 31 syllables arranged in five lines of 5, 7, 5, 7, and 7 syllables. The development of a syllabic script (*kana*) for writing Japanese opened the literary world to women writers (men were expected to write prose in formal Classical Chinese, whereas women could write informally in Japanese). The most celebrated writers of the Heian Period (794–1185) were women, including Murasaki Shikibu (ca. 973–?), author of the *Tale of Genji*; and Sei Shōnagon (ca. 966–?), whose *Pillow Book* gives us an intimate picture of Heian court society. The poetic travel diary (e.g., Ki no Turayuki's *Tosa Nikki*) was a favorite genre of Heian authors.

The establishment of samurai military rule in 1185 led to the popularity of novels with military themes, most famously the *Tale of Heike* (anon., ca. 1240). Zen Buddhism influenced many literary works of the Kamakura Period (1185–1333), including belles-lettres essays by Kamo Chōmei (1155–1216, *Hojoki*, "The Ten-Foot-Square Hut") and Yoshida Kenkō (1283–1352, *Tsurezuregusa*, "Essays in Idleness"). The slow, formal, Zen-influenced musical drama known as *Nō* flourished in the ensuing Muromachi Period (1336–1573), with scripts by Zeami (1363–1443) and Sōami (d. 1545). The popularity of *renga* linked-verse (Sogi, 1422–1502, was its greatest practitioner) led to the development of *haiku*, a 17–syllable, 3–line form (5–7–5, essentially the first three lines of a *tanka*). The *haiku* form developed further during the Tokugawa Period (1601–1868); its finest practitioner was Matsuo Bashō (1644–1694), whose poetic travel diary *Oku no hosomichi* ("Narrow Road to the Interior") is one of the great masterpieces of Japanese literature.

Urban culture flourished during the Tokugawa Period, leading to new markets for popular literature and theater. Ihara Saikaku (1642–1693) was known for "Life of an Amorous Woman" and other racy, satirical stories; Chikamatsu Monzaemon (1653–1725), Japan's greatest playwright, wrote scripts used in both *bunraku* puppet theater and *kabuki* live drama.

With the Meiji Restoration (1868) and the creation of modern Japan, literature changed markedly. Western literary forms influenced the essayist Fukuzawa Yōkichi

(1835–1901), the novelist and critic Mori Ōgai (1862–1922), and others. Yosano Akiko (1878–1942) brought a modernist sensibility to *tanka* poetry in *Midaregami* ("Tangled Hair") and other collections. Other important 20th-century poets include Takamura Kotarō (1883–1956), Nishiwaki Junzaburō (1894–1982), and Ibaragi Noriko (b. 1926).

Twentieth-century Japan also produced many important novelists and short-story writers, including Natsume Sōseki (1867–1916; *Botchan*); Akutagawa Ryōnosuke (1892–1927), whose short story "Rashōmon" was the basis for Kurosawa Akira's famous film; Tanizaki Junichirō (1886–1965; *The Makioka Sisters*); Dazai Osamu (pen name of Tsushima Shuji, 1909–48), who wrote *Ningen Shikkaku* ("Disqualified as a Human"); Kawabata Yasunari (1899–1972, *Snow Country*; *House of the Sleeping Beauties*), who won the 1968 Nobel Prize in Literature; and Mishima Yukio (1925–1970, *Temple of the Golden Pavilion*), who combined literary genius with theatrical right-wing politics.

The postwar generation of Japanese writers includes Abe Kobo (1924–1993, *Woman in the Dunes*); Oe Kenzaburo (b. 1935, *The Silent Cry*), who won the 1994 Nobel Prize in Literature; Murakami Haruki (b. 1949, *A Wild Sheep Chase*); and Banana Yoshimoto (b. 1964, *Kitchen*). Japan today is home to a very diverse and vibrant literary scene.

Indian Literature

The earliest surviving works of literature from the Indian subcontinent are the Vedas. These were written in Sanskrit, and are dated from 1500 to 1200 B.C. Written in verse, the Vedas contain the essential beliefs and laws of Hinduism. The Upanishads, composed between the eighth and sixth centuries B.C. were written as commentaries on the Vedas.

Two epics, the *Ramayana* and the *Mahabharata*, both written in Sanskrit, are the foundations of Indian mythology. The *Ramayana* (Romance of Rama), made up of seven books and probably written around 300 B.C. by Valmiki, tells the story of the life of Rama, from his birth, to his marriage to Sita, through his quest to rescue Sita from captivity by the demon Ravana, and to their reunion. The *Ramayana* is the source of much Indian literature and dance.

The *Mahabharata* (Great Epic of the Bharata Dynasty), composed between 300 B.C. and A.D. 300 and consisting of close to 100,000 verses, tells the story of the great war between the Pandavas and the Kauravas. The *Bhagavadgita*, contained within the *Mahabharata* and probably one of the later additions to the text (thought to have been written in the first or second century A.D.), is written as a dialogue between Prince Arjuna, one of the Pandavas, and Krishna, who acts as his charioteer in battle.

Bankim Chandra Chatterjee (1838–94) is credited with having first introduced European models of narrative structure to Indian literature. Chatterjee's novels, the most memorable of which are written in Bengali, include *Durgesnandini* and *Rajsimha* (1881). The first Indian writer of modern times to achieve international recognition was Rabindranath Tagore (1861–1941). Born in Calcutta, Tagore, who wrote in Bengali, achieved success first as a poet and later as a novelist and painter. His collection *Gitanjali* was published in English translation in 1910. Tagore won the Nobel Prize in 1913.

R.K. Narayan (1906–2001) was one of the first major Indian literary figures to write in English. Much of his work takes place in Malgudi, a fictitious town in South India. Among his novels are *Swami and Friends* (1935), *The English Teacher* (1945), and *A Tiger for Malgudi* (1983).

Salman Rushdie, born in Bombay in 1947, first rose to international prominence with the publication of his second novel, *Midnight's Children* (1981), which uses magical realism to chronicle the history of India after the end of British rule. Rushdie's other works include *The Satanic Verses* (1988), *The Moor's Last Sigh* (1995), and *The Ground Beneath Her Feet* (1999).

The literature of the Indian subcontinent appears today in many languages, including Bengali, Hindi, Tamil, and others. It is, however, those writing in English, many of whom live abroad, who have achieved the greatest international acclaim. Among this group are Amitav Ghosh, born in Calcutta in 1956, whose book *Shadowlines* chronicles the effects of partition; and Arundhati Roy (b. 1961), whose first novel, *The God of Small Things* (1998), won the Booker Prize.

African Literature

A rich and diverse oral literary tradition in Africa extends from the distant past to the present time. Marked by wordplay and musical accompaniment, this tradition comprised myths, folktales, dramas, poems, songs, parables, riddles, and other forms. Since ancient African languages were exclusively oral, written literature on the continent did not begin until Arab conquests in North Africa brought Arabic language and culture to the continent. A poet of African birth, Antar, wrote in Arabic in the sixth and seventh centuries.

The first evidence of indigenous written African literature is in the East African Swahili language in the mid-17th century, and from 1728 there is a manuscript of a Swahili epic, *Ubendi wa Tambuka*. This work, as well as 19th-century poems in the Hausa language of Nigeria, was set down in Arabic script. After the arrival of Europeans, the Latin alphabet was used, and many Africans, including several writers who escaped slavery, wrote in European languages. The most important and thorough early account of the life of a freed slave was published in 1789 by a Nigerian who had been shackled and sent to the American South, and later lived free in England: *The Interesting Narrative of the Life and Adventures of Olaudah Equiano or Gustavus Vassa, the African*. In the late 19th century, the Angolan poet Caetano da Costa Alegre of São Tomé became the first African to write literature in Portuguese.

In the 20th century African writing blossomed in both native and colonial tongues, in fiction, poetry, and drama. The first African writer to be read internationally was Thomas Mofolo of Lesotho (South Africa), who wrote novels in the Sotho language, including *Chaka* (1925), about a Zulu warrior. In 1934 James Mbotela published the first Swahili work of fiction; and beginning in 1939, Olorunfemi Fagunwa of Nigeria wrote a series of groundbreaking novels in Yoruba. Among native-language poets, Tanzania's Shaaban Robert Swahili and South Africa's S. E. K Mqhayi in Xhosa stand out. Perhaps the finest African poet of the first half century was Jean-Joseph Rabéarivelo of Madagascar, who wrote dreamy, imagistic poems in French.

Ironically, the French language gave a voice to a group of writers who expressed alienation from their African roots. These were the poets of the *négritude* movement, which arose in the 1930's, and whose most famous exponent was Léopold Senghor, who would become the first president of Senegal.

A boom in African writing coincided with the independence movement after World War II, and much of the literature is charged with reaction against colonial influence. The principal novelists have written in French and English. In the 1950's, two Cameroonians, Ferdinand Oyono (*Houseboy*, 1956) and Mongo Beti (*The Poor Christ of Bomba*, 1956), wrote novels critical of French cultural impositions; and two Nigerians published important books of fiction in English: Amos Tutuola's folklore-rooted tales have been popular well beyond Africa, and Chinua Achebe's *Things Fall Apart* (1958) became a famous novel about the clash of European and native sensibilities. Among novels in English, the Mau Mau rebellion in Kenya is the background for *Weep Not Child* (1964), by Ngugi Wa Thiong'o; and exile is a theme of South African Es'kia Mphahlele's *The Wanderers* (1971). More recently, the

Nigerian Ben Okri has applied the magic-realism motif in his novels, including *The Famished Road* (1991).

The *négritude* movement in poetry endured into the 1950's and 1960's in the writings of Tchicaya U Tam'si of the Congo and David Diop of Senegal. Agostinho Neto, the first Angolan president, was a leading Portuguese-language poet. Significant English-language poets since the 1960's have included Christopher Okigbo of Nigeria, Okot p'Bitek of Uganda, Kofi Awoonor of Ghana, and Dennis Brutus of South Africa.

Another important Nigerian poet is Wole Soyinka, better known as a playwright and the first African to win a Nobel Prize in Literature (1986). His works, ranging from the comic (*The Lion and the Jewel*, 1963) to the intellectually complex (*Death and the King's Horsemen*, 1975), are inflected by Yoruba culture yet satirically focused on contemporary politics.

Two separate traditions of African writing are the Afrikaans and English literature produced by white South Africans. In the 20th century, Afrikaans literature was distinguished by a strong poetic tradition, particularly the "Poets of the 30's." Another group, the "writers of the 60's," included poets and novelists such as André P. Brink. Better known in the West are the English-language novelists Alan Paton (*Cry, the Beloved Country*, 1948) and two Nobel laureates, Nadine Gordimer (1991) and J. M. Coetzee (2003).

English Poetry

Old English Poetry (ca. 428–1100)

The earliest English, or Anglo-Saxon, poetry celebrated the heroic deeds, physical accomplishments, courage, and success in battle of kings and warriors in the period between the arrival of the Angles and Saxons in the fifth century and their conversion to Christianity in the seventh century. But this poetry does not survive in its original form. The earliest recorded poems, written, like all Old English poetry, in alliterative verse-form, in which sounds at the beginnings of words are repeated in each line, are from the second half of the seventh century: the secular paean to kings, "Widstith"; and the nine-line "Caedmon's Hymn," the first in a centuries-long tradition of English Christian devotional poems. Caedmon, a Northumbrian monk, is the first known English poet. "The Dream of the Rood," in which the rood, or Christ's cross, describes its experience to the dreamer, was written in the early eighth century, and is considered the best example of the Anglo-Saxon devotional poem. While it is often ascribed to the second known English poet, Cynewulf, there is doubt as to whether he is actually its author.

The Heroic Epic The finest example of the Old English heroic epic, a narrative verse form depicting the deeds of a valorous hero, and the longest existing poem of its day, is *Beowulf*, written in the eighth century. *Beowulf* records an older pagan tale of slaying a monster. Set in Scandinavia, it is overlaid with Christian elements, including a judging God and a biblical lineage for the monster Grendel, but remains a celebration of courage and honor, the virtues of a harsh, pre-Christian heroic age. Later examples of heroic poems include the *Battle of Maldon* (undated) and the *Battle of Brunanburgh* (undated).

Middle English Poetry (1100–1500)

Middle English poetry first flourished in the 14th century, although some short lyrical poems, poems of an emotionally expressive nature, appeared as early as the 12th and 13th centuries; and long verse romances, narratives about kings and knights and sexual love, were also written in the 13th century. The elegy and the allegory were also popular during this period.

The Middle English Lyric Examples of anonymous lyrics abound into the 15th century. Among these lyrics, which have themes of nature (especially of springtime), love, and Christian piety, are "The Cuckoo Song" and "Westron Wind." Numerous short ballads, narrative verse meant to be sung or spoken aloud, such as "Barbara Allen," "Lord Randall," and "Sir Patrick Spens," appear from about 1200 to 1700.

Romance, Elegy, and Allegory These three forms rose to prominence in the Middle English period. The romance, a narrative in which knights and other characters of chivalry are the main actors, is exemplified by *Sir Gawain and the Green Knight* (ca. 1380–1400), the story of a brave knight who must defend the honor of King Arthur and his court after its invasion by the mysterious Green Knight. Sir Gawain's testing reveals the limitation of manly virtue and leads him to a religious epiphany. The elegy, a poem of mourning written to commemorate the death of a person and often used as a meditation on death or life, is exemplified by *The Pearl* (ca. 1360), believed to have been occasioned by the death of the poet's daughter. *Sir Gawain* and *The Pearl* are believed to have been written by the same person, but, as is the case with so many works of this period, their author remains anonymous. The allegory, in which virtues or states of being are represented as persons or other objective forms, is exemplified by *Piers Plowman* (ca. 1362), which may have been written, or partly written, by William Langland, of whom little is known. The poem is an account of the Plowman's dream vision of the history of Christianity and its current, somewhat corrupted, state.

Geoffrey Chaucer Considered the first great English poet, Geoffrey Chaucer (ca. 1343–1400) was a Londoner who wrote in a Middle English dialect. His *Canterbury Tales*, a narrative cycle told by 22 richly varied travelers brought together on a religious pilgrimage, is one of the greatest works of English literature—ribaldly comic in parts, yet profound and vivid in its portrayal of medieval life and character. Although Chaucer never completed this work, which he began in 1386, it develops unity and artistic resonance from the interplay, even quarreling, between the characters, and through their tendency to respond to the stories of others in their own stories. Chaucer's other poems include the love story *Troilus and Criseide* (ca. 1385), and *The Parliament of Fowls*.

The Tudor Period (1485–1603)

The era of Tudor England, which began in 1485 with the accession of King Henry VII and lasted through the death of Elizabeth I in 1603, saw a modernizing of the English language, allowing it to reflect the humanist ideas and images of the European Renaissance. Fittingly, the sonnet, the 14-line form first developed in Italy, began to carve its deep impression into English poetry in the 16th century.

The English Sonnet and Blank Verse During the Tudor period, nearly all sonnets were love poems, often expressing disappointment or despair. The earliest English practitioners were Thomas Wyatt (1503–42), a distinguished lyric poet, and Henry Howard, Earl of Surrey (1517–47), who wrote the first sonnets with an "English" rhyme-scheme, which arranged the poem in three four-line sections and one two-line section rather than the Italian pattern of eight and six lines. Howard also composed the first English *blank verse*, unrhymed 10–syllable lines with a regular meter, usually iambic pentameter (a set of an unstressed syllable followed by a stressed syllable, repeated five times). Philip Sidney (1554–86) fol-

lowed Howard with a similarly patterned sequence of love sonnets, *Astrophel and Stella*.

Elizabethan Poetry The greatest nondramatic Elizabethan poet was Edmund Spenser (1552–99), whose romantic and allegorical *The Faerie Queene* (1590–96) is one of the great English epics and stands apart from all other 16th-century narrative poetry. Its six books are each dedicated to a courtly virtue, and its strong ecclesiastical views mark it as the first masterly English Protestant poem. Among Spenser's innovations was the nine-line stanza that is named for him. He, too, wrote a sonnet sequence, *Amoretti*.

The leading Elizabethan dramatists, Christopher Marlowe (1564–93) and, greatest of all English writers, William Shakespeare (1564–1616), were also significant lyric and narrative poets. Marlowe's *Hero and Leander* retold a classical Greek love story. Shakespeare used the Roman poet Ovid as the source of two narrative poems of his early career, the mythological *Venus and Adonis* (1593) and *The Rape of Lucrece* (1594). His 154-sonnet sequence, written in the 1590's and addressed to both a young man and a woman, is the pinnacle of that Elizabethan tradition.

The 17th Century

The turn of the 17th century brought with it the reign of James I (1603–25) and introduced two new traditions in English poetry that would endure until the century's end: the Metaphysical style originated by John Donne and the Cavalier style embraced by the followers of Ben Jonson.

Donne and the Metaphysical Poets John Donne (1572–1631) created a poetry of intellectual and spiritual reaching, which in a later period was labeled "metaphysical." Donne's poetry was witty, and sometimes abrupt in manner, allowing content to take precedence over form. Within his poetry he made unusual imagistic and intellectual connections. Donne, a clergyman, wrote beautiful religious poetry, including the *Holy Sonnets*. But his equally trenchant poems of physical love would inspire others who wrote in this tradition.

Other poets of the Metaphysical school included George Herbert (1593–1633), who approached God with more certainty than Donne, but with similar leaps of imagery. In poems such as "Easter Wings" and "The Altar," he used lines shaped to depict his subject. Richard Crashaw (1613–49), a convert to Catholicism, was influenced by Italian poetry and wrote idiosyncratic, baroque, passionately devotional verse that incorporated notably Italian Catholic flesh-and-blood images. Other members of the Metaphysical school were Henry Vaughan (1621–95), Thomas Traherne (ca. 1636–74), and Abraham Cowley (1618–67).

Jonson and the Cavalier Poets

Ben Jonson (1572–1637), born the same year as Donne, wrote spare, smooth lines modeled on classical poetry that were in striking contrast to those of the Metaphysical poets. Jonson's poems included satires, a celebrated tribute to a great house ("To Penshurst"), and a powerful memorial to Shakespeare. But it was his lyrics addressed to women ("To Celia") that influenced the casual yet polished style of the Cavalier poets. In addition to being a poet, Jonson was also a leading Jacobean playwright.

Jonson was not himself a Cavalier poet in the sense in which Donne was a Metaphysical poet. The term *Cavalier* refers to supporters of Charles I, the king beheaded in 1649 during Oliver Cromwell's Puritan Revolution, eight years after Jonson's death. But the Cavalier poets modeled their work on the classical beauty of Jonson's verse. The first and finest of the Cavalier poets, Robert Herrick (1591–1673), was one of a group of Jonson's companions and admirers who called themselves "Sons of Ben." He and the later Cavaliers were informed by the ideal of courtly love and by upper-class sophistication. Their mostly lyrical poems were witty, and well-crafted. Herrick's lyrics, mainly short and sometimes epigrammatic, were often concerned with the natural things and the females that delighted him. These two subjects were often addressed in the same poem: "To the Virgins, to Make Much of Time" ("Gather ye rosebuds while ye may"); or "Corinna's Going-A-Maying." These direct addresses to women and urges to "seize the day" ("*carpe diem*") were repeated by later Cavalier poets such as Edmund Waller (1606–87; "Go, lovely rose"), John Suckling (1609–42; "Why so pale and wan, fond lover?"), and Richard Lovelace (1618–57; "To Althea, from Prison"). The greatest *carpe diem* poem, "To His Coy Mistress," was composed by Andrew Marvell (1621–78), who wrote in both the Cavalier and Metaphysical traditions. A creator of lyrics, odes, and dialogues that married playful wit with deep significance, he has been called England's most important minor poet.

The Restoration and 18th Century

With the restoration of the monarchy in the person of Charles II in 1660, freedom of expression, in such forms as satire and staged drama, was again possible. The later decades of the 17th century introduced an age of mordant satire and wit that endured into the second half of the 18th century, in which poetry focused on human behavior and political developments. Although the poets of these times were generally unrestrained in their personal attacks, their style was moderated, simplified, and cool, reflecting the peaceful era that followed the heat and turbulence of civil war. Because this period was compared to the post-civil war reign of Augustus Caesar, and because its poetic style was in good part derived from the great Roman poets of that time, it is known as the neoclassical or Augustan period of English poetry. This movement, in the age of rationalism, emphasized order and restraint in imagination, along with an emphasis on human society more than communion with the divine, a belief, in Alexander Pope's words, that "the proper study of mankind is man."

John Milton and the Neoclassical Period

John Milton (1608–74) is considered the most important poet of the neoclassical period. Milton restored a rich and resonant style to English poetry, and, as is true of Spenser in the previous century, his epic poetry sets him apart from the traditions of his time. He produced *Paradise Lost*, considered the greatest English epic, in 1667. In soaring blank verse, *Paradise Lost* presents the fall of Satan and of Adam and Eve, and thus the origin of evil. Although a theological argument with the pronounced intention to "justify the ways of God to men," *Paradise Lost* is a powerfully dramatic and descriptive poem, especially vivid in its portrayal of Satan. A second epic, *Paradise Regained* (1671), describes the redemptive triumph of Christ. In addition to these long poems and the poetic drama *Samson Agonistes* (1671), Milton wrote some of the best English sonnets.

Satire in the Neoclassical Period

Satire rose in full force when Samuel Butler (1612–80) published Part I of *Hudibras*, his three-part ridicule of religious and political nonconformists (i.e., Cromwell and the Puritans) two years after the monarchy returned. This scalding poem is also a burlesque of the romantic idealism expressed in such poems as Spenser's *Faerie Queene*.

The original neoclassicist and finest satiric poet of the period, as well as a leading dramatist, was John Dryden (1631–1700). In earlier decades an "occasional" poet, a celebrator of public events, his career as a satirist began with a mock-heroic poem, "Mac Flecknoe," which lampooned a rival playwright, and continued with his masterpiece,

Absalom and Achitophel (1681), an account of the "popish plot" against King Charles II. Dryden's stylish wit and his mastery of the heroic couplet—pairs of rhymed, 10-syllable lines—greatly influenced later poets. He was also an influential and masterly composer of odes, such as "To Mrs. Anne Killegrew" and "Alexander's Feast."

Best known as a prose satirist, Jonathan Swift (1667–1745), author of the timeless *Gulliver's Travels*, was also a distinguished poet, whether he was mocking his fellow humans or praising his beloved "Stella." However, the title of greatest English satirical poet belongs to Swift's friend Alexander Pope (1688–1744). A neoclassicist and literary descendant of Dryden, whose heroic couplets he picked up and mastered, Pope updated the satirical and didactic forms and styles of the Roman poet Horace. He ridiculed the upper class in the mock-epic *The Rape of the Lock* (1712–14) and contemporary poets in *The Dunciad* (1728); defined the literary principles of the age in *An Essay on Criticism*; and argued for classical order in all things in *An Essay on Man* (1733).

The Late 18th Century and Nature Poetry

Samuel Johnson (1709–84), who, like Swift, is known primarily for his prose (and for his conversation), also made his mark as a poet, particularly with *The Vanity of Human Wishes* (1749). Oliver Goldsmith's *The Deserted Village* (1770), was a reaction against the destruction of small farms and village life as a result of the Enclosure Acts. Its rural theme is indicative of a tendency for poets in the mid and late 18th century to express feelings, often melancholy, about nature or in natural settings. Thomas Gray's "Elegy Written in a Country Churchyard" (1751), a meditation on the anonymity of the rural dead, is a famous example of this trend, and the poem is considered a harbinger of the Romantic movement. William Collins's "Ode to Evening" (1746) is another example of this trend toward nature as a subject. This wave of nature poetry, in fact, began earlier in the century with James Thomson's *The Seasons* (1726–27), and was picked up toward the century's end by William Cowper, particularly in his long poem about country life, *The Task* (1785), and by George Crabbe, whose realistic depiction of poverty and inhumanity in the countryside in *The Village* (1783) is a stark alternative to Goldsmith's idealized view.

The Romantic Period

In the Romantic period, the focus of poetry moved even further away from society, toward nature and the individ-ual expressing inner feelings. Arising in the wake of the French Revolution, Romanticism tilted to the political left, embraced nationalistic yearnings, and expressed rebellious impulses. Its poets reached beyond 18th-century restraints to commune with realities and absolute principles, such as love, beauty, and truth, that existed outside the boundaries of everyday life.

Although the Romantic period in English poetry is traditionally assigned a starting date, 1798, when William Wordsworth and Samuel Taylor Coleridge published *Lyrical Ballads*, groundbreaking Romantic poems had already been written by then by William Blake in England and Robert Burns in Scotland.

The "Pre-Romantics"   William Blake (1757–1827), whose first poems were published in 1783, was a visionary poet-artist who, both in lyrics (*Songs of Innocence*, 1789; and *Songs of Experience*, 1794) and in long prophetic and narrative poems, was characteristically Romantic in his deep concern for economic oppression, his simple diction, and his use of symbolism. Robert Burns, who died in 1796, took plainness of language even further than Blake by producing in Scots dialect the lyrics, especially love poems, for which he is well known.

The First Generation of Romantic Poets   These predecessors notwithstanding, the year 1798 remains a boundary line for the Romantic movement. In a manifesto-like preface to the second edition (1800) of *Lyrical Ballads*, William Wordsworth (1770–1850) explicitly separated poetry's future from its neoclassical past, prescribing that poems should deal with "common life" in "language really used by men," and pronouncing poetry to be "the spontaneous overflow of powerful feelings." These remained qualities of the English Romantic poetry that thrived for the next three decades and lingered until Wordsworth's death.

Wordsworth's output comprised short lyric poems, meditative odes, such as "Tintern Abbey" and "Intimations of Immortality," and long poems, including the masterly, autobiographical *The Prelude*, completed in 1805 but published posthumously. Samuel Taylor Coleridge (1772–1834) also wrote meditative verse but is best known for narrative poems tinged by supernatural effects, particularly "The Rime of the Ancient Mariner," which was published in *Lyrical Ballads*.

The Second Generation of Romantic Poets   The relative brevity of the Romantic era was caused in part by the early deaths of three of its greatest poets of the second generation, Lord Byron, Percy Bysshe Shelley, and John Keats. The eldest of these, Byron (George Gordon, 1788–1824), was a notorious lover and enormously popular writer in his own time, regarded best for his long narrative and satirical poems (*Childe Harold's Pilgrimage*, 1812–18; *Don Juan*, 1819–24) and known for his creation of the rebellious, immoral "Byronic hero." Shelley (1792–1822) was a more philosophical poet who believed in the transforming power of love. He was a composer of lyrics and politically inflected poems such as "Ode to the West Wind," and his advocacy of the romantic impulse to overcome human limitations is well expressed in the title of his great verse-drama *Prometheus Unbound* (1820), which offers the possibility of humanity's moral triumph over evil.

Keats (1795–1821) was a poet of sensuous and emotional experience to whom life was "a vale of soul-making." He pronounced, in "Ode on a Grecian Urn," the quintessentially Romantic sentence: "Beauty is truth, truth beauty." Yet his beautiful works also expressed the sadness that accompanies human yearning.

Sir Walter Scott (1771–1832), a Scotsman who achieved distinction as a novelist and as a narrative lyric poet, is also considered a Romantic poet. Like other Romantics, including Keats, Scott sometimes reached into the medieval past for themes. Other notable lyric poets of the period were Robert Southey (1774–1843), Walter Savage Landor (1775–1864), Leigh Hunt (1784–1859), and the Irishman Thomas Moore (1779–1852).

The Victorian Age (1837–1901)

During the long reign of Queen Victoria, from 1837 to 1901, England was transformed into the most vigorous industrial, capitalist society ever known, and its empire gained its farthest reach. It was an age in which the population shifted from the land to the cities and the advance of science encroached on the ground of religious certainty. These matters roiled the poetic imagination and diversified poetic points of view.

Faith and Doubt in Victorian Poetry   During the Victorian age, religion was subject to experimentation, renunciation, and doubt. The dominant, longest-lived poet of the period, Alfred, Lord Tennyson (1809–92), absorbed, early in his career, the age's uncertainty about material and scientific progress. Tennyson, racked by the death of his best friend, expressed his melancholy and longing for faith in his first successful volume of poems; then, in an extended elegy for that friend, *In Memoriam A. H. H.* (1850), Tennyson embraced faith. Tennyson found further assurance in his country's distant past, most thoroughly explored in his epic *Idylls of the King* (1859–62).

Faith and doubt were also pervasive issues for the other great Victorian poets, Robert Browning (1812–89) and Matthew Arnold (1822–88). As a young man, Browning made the transition from atheism to belief, and he has often been misconstrued as having harbored a Pollyannaish certainty that, as he once wrote, "God's in his heaven— / All's right with the world." In fact, he was a writer of psychological depth, keenly aware of human corruption and fully conscious of the implications of Darwin's science, whose belief in a transcendent God was buffeted from many sides. Arnold is considered the emblematic Victorian poet of doubt and alienation, particularly for his most famous poem, "Dover Beach," in which he spoke hauntingly of an "eternal note of sadness."

Pre-Raphaelites and Others   Between Tennyson and Browning, particularly, there is an obvious dissociation of poetic style. While Tennyson wrote within the great tradition of fluid and sonorous English verse, Browning's diction was more colloquial, his rhythms less regular, and his poetic modes more experimental, all of these traits apparent in his brilliant dramatic monologues, such as "My Last Duchess." Both styles had followers. Dante Gabriel Rossetti (1828–82), for example, leader of the "Pre-Raphaelite" artistic-poetic movement (which advocated an earlier, simpler style of painting than was prevalent at the time) was a poet of rich color and smooth meter. His sister, Christina Rossetti (1830–94), was a lyrical poet of strong religious sensibility. Browning's wife, Elizabeth Barrett Browning (1806–61), was best known for an extended series of love sonnets, as was the later Victorian George Meredith (1828–1909). Edward FitzGerald (1809–83) translated and revised the 12th-century *Rubaiyat of Omar Khayam* (1857–59); his version, recognized for its polished beauty, quickly gained great popularity. Algernon Charles Swinburne (1837–1909), a Pre-Raphaelite in his early career, later became entranced by the sound of words and metrical experiment. Like his contemporary and friend, Matthew Arnold, Arthur Hugh Clough (1819–61), experienced his own bouts of religious skepticism, which he addressed, somewhat ironically, in his verse.

Late Victorian and Early 20th-Century Poetry

In late Victorian times a number of strains ran independently through English poetry. In the 1890's, one of the great novelists of the second half of the 19th century, Thomas Hardy (1840–1928), brought his dark but compassionate vision to the writing of lyric poetry, and over the next 30 years developed into a major poet. In the same decade, A. E. Housman (1859–1936) published a wistful and classically spare volume of lyrics, *A Shropshire Lad* (1896); and the end-of-the-century "decadents," chief among them Oscar Wilde (1854–1900) and Ernest Dowson (1867–1900), rose to prominence. Meanwhile, a poet of an altogether different sensibility and style, Rudyard Kipling (1865–1936), writing rhythmically about the imperial British soldier, emerged and began to win great popularity.

Oscar Wilde, Ernest Dowson, and the Decadents

The term *decadent* refers to a school of writing, most popular in France but present in England as well, in which art took precedence over nature. The Decadents produced poems that rejected Victorian convention and reflected the somewhat antisocial ideal of "art for art's sake." The two most important poets of the British Decadent movement were Oscar Wilde and Ernest Dowson. Dowson, the iconic English Decadent, was a sonorous, incantatory poet who characteristically expressed the loss of love, youth, and beauty, and a weariness with life that may have contributed to his dissipation and early death. Oscar Wilde, whose novel *The Picture of Dorian Gray* exemplifies the Decadent school's preoccupation with art and decay, looked back to the work of Pre-Raphaelites as a model for his verse.

Gerard Manley Hopkins and Sprung Rhythm

The most influential poet of the Victorian age, the Jesuit priest Gerard Manley Hopkins (1844–99), is often not considered a Victorian at all. Because of his extraordinary break with the poetic traditions of his era, and because he was not published until 1918, long after his death, he is instead often grouped among poets of the 20th century. His originality included the development of an irregular "sprung" meter in which poetic feet of varying syllables are used in an attempt to mirror the rhythms of prose, that changed poetic rhythm; a precise diction that was partly invented; and the extensive, forceful use of alliteration. Hopkins's verse is at times bright and at times somber. He is considered one of the language's most powerful religious poets. Like many of his predecessors, he was a great composer of sonnets.

World War I and the End of the Victorian Age

World War I had a profound impact on the direction of English poetry. Kipling's patriotic poems, featuring stoically virtuous troops in India and other far-flung places, yield in modern memory to the palpable expressions of combat experience by England's World War I poets. One of these, Rupert Brooke (1887–1915), still sang patriotically, "there's a corner in of some foreign field / That is forever England"; but others, Wilfred Owen (1893–1918; "Anthem for Doomed Youth"), Siegfried Sassoon (1886–1967), and Isaac Rosenberg (1890–1918), wrote with darker realism and increasing bitterness. Their vivid lines, like the Great War itself, delivered a decisive finish to Victorian times.

The 20th Century after World War I

British poetry after the First World War has been more diverse in style and intention than that of any previous century. The Modernist movement arrived in the 1910's and 1920's. With it came the use of new, irregular meters and forms and an unprecedented range of diction and subjects. These were used to effectively mirror the breaking with the past, the concern with alienation and a fractured world, and the breaking down of England's imperial power that rose after World War I.

Neither of the two most influential figures of "English" poetry in the 20th century were English. William Butler Yeats (1865–1939), an Irishman, is often considered the century's greatest English-language poet (see "Irish Literature"). However it was the work of the American-born and -educated T.S. Eliot (1888–1965), who settled in England in his 20's, that most profoundly shaped the poetry of the English Modernist movement. His technique presented a clear break with the poetic past. Eliot's breakthrough has long been identified with two early poems, "The Love Song of J. Alfred Prufrock" (1915) and *The Waste Land* (1922). In these, Eliot presented fresh, sometimes jarring, images, diverse literary allusions, snatches of conversation, and a variety of scenes in disconnected and ironic juxtaposition. In Eliot's poetry, the spiritual and emotional dislocation of the modern world was represented in form as well as content.

Although Eliot exerted a profound influence on poets of the following generations, not all important 20th-century

British poetry was affected by Eliot's revolutionary innovations. His contemporaries Edwin Muir (1887– 1959), Robert Graves (1895–1985), and D. H. Lawrence (1885–1930) all found ways to address the changing world without using Eliot as their model. Muir, a Scotsman, and Graves each wrote traditional lines with traditional diction but a distinctive voice, and each sought to understand the present in relation to the classical past. Graves, especially, was influenced by Thomas Hardy. Primarily a novelist, Lawrence also produced several books of increasingly significant poetry, expressing the same intimacy with the force and beauty of nature that is reflected in his poetic prose. For a model he looked well past Eliot to the free verse of an earlier, American modernism.

It was the next generation of Modernist poets, those born in the first decade of the 20th century, that owed so much to Eliot. Coming of age in the 1930's, these poets saw a different kind of wasteland from that which Eliot had written of—economic depression—and wrote poetry that leaned sharply to the political left. The finest of these was W. H. Auden (1907–73), who moved to New York early in his life and grew to be a poet with a wide range of concerns who combined technical dexterity with straightforward but eloquent diction. His contemporaries included Stephen Spender (1909–95), who later wrote of his disillusion with communism; and two Irish natives educated in England: C. Day Lewis (1904–72), who would one day be poet laureate, and Louis MacNeice (1907–63), a poet known for his sad and sometimes ironic depictions of modern life.

Dylan Thomas (1914–53), born in Wales, is often included in discussions of the Modernist period. His language was not colloquial or restrained, but energetic, resonant, sensuous, and full of life. In his use of alliteration and original phrasing, Thomas looked back to Hopkins; and in his fashion, Thomas, too, celebrated nature with religious fervor. To Thomas, who incorporated Freudian thought into his poetry, all nature, all sexuality, and all love are linked to death.

New Apocalypse Poetry and "The Movement"

By the mid to late 20th century, British poetry had begun to coalesce into a series of movements. The exuberance and surrealism of Thomas, George Barker (1913–91), and others were placed under the heading of "New Apocalypse" poetry, which was followed in the 1950's by a reaction labeled simply "The Movement" and included Philip Larkin (1922–85), Donald Davie (b. 1922), and Thom Gunn (b. 1929). Their poems were subdued, ironic and "antiromantic." Larkin, like Robert Graves before him, was much influenced by Thomas Hardy, and is regarded as the chief successor to Hardy in the expression of a pessimistic sensibility. Some of Larkin's concerns were shared by John Betjeman (1906–84), poet laureate from 1972 to 1984; and the distinctly "English," nonmodernist tradition that they wrote in has been impressively taken up by the working-class poet Tony Harrison (b. 1937).

Hughes and MacDiarmid   Ted Hughes (1930–98), whose work does not fall neatly into any one school, was Betjeman's successor as poet laureate. Hughes was perhaps the most distinguished English poetic voice of the second half of the 20th century. Greatly influenced by Lawrence, Hughes was a poet of nature, but the nature he wrote of was an often ferocious one, a nature that reveals a deep and troubling undercurrent beneath all creation, including humanity. The chief Scottish poet after Muir was Hugh MacDiarmid (1892–1978), a nationalist, communist, and leader of the "Scottish Renaissance."

Contemporary Irish Poets   In recent times, extraordinary contributions to poetry in English have come from Ireland, particularly Northern Ireland, which has produced Seamus Heaney (b. 1939), winner of the 1995 Nobel Prize and widely considered the finest living English-language poet, and his onetime pupil, Paul Muldoon (b. 1951), who settled in America and received a 2003 Pulitzer Prize.

The English Novel

The English novel emerged in the 18th century. Its forerunners included long prose stories dating back to Roman times and such later classics as Cervantes's *Don Quixote* and Swift's *Gulliver's Travels*. The term *novel*, implying the newness of the form, is derived from the Italian *novella*, which identified realistic medieval prose tales such as those contained in Boccaccio's *Decameron*.

At its most basic level, the novel is defined as an extended prose narrative. Elements of the novel include characterization, plot, and theme. *Characterization* involves the creation and depiction of lifelike characters to act within the narrative. *Plot* involves a series of causally linked events, usually broken into the three-part structure of beginning, middle, and end. *Theme* is the unifying idea behind the novel. Early on, realism was an essential ingredient of the novel, as was the depiction of interior consciousness. In languages other than English, the novel is most often called a *roman*, implying a link to the romances of the Medieval period (see "English Poetry"). Historically, *romans* looked back to a romanticized or magical past for their subjects, whereas novels looked to the realistic present, though these distinctions faded as the forms progressed.

The 18th-Century English Novel

The French novel appeared earlier than the English novel. Madame de La Fayette's *La Princesse de Clèves* (1678), a psychologically detailed love story, is generally thought to have been the first novel in France, and writers in England were able to draw on it as a model for the new form. *Moll Flanders* (1722) by Daniel Defoe (1660–1731), the story of a thieving prostitute, is sometimes considered the first English novel; because *Moll Flanders* lacks a depiction of interior consciousness, the claim belongs more accurately to *Pamela* (1740) by Samuel Richardson (1689–1761), an epistolary novel, or novel written in the form of letters. With the publication of Richardson's highly regarded *Clarissa Harlowe* (1747–48), also an epistolary novel, the English novel had become firmly established as a literary form. Among the innovations that Richardson introduced were a focus on character and moral choice.

Even as Richardson established moral choice as one of the criteria for the novel, his contemporary, Henry Fielding (1707–54), recognizing the form's power for innovation, used it to satirize Richardson's work. Fielding's novel *Shamela* (1741) is a send-up of *Pamela*. Fielding, who is considered the first great English novelist, continued to develop the form throughout his career with picaresque novels—novels that depict the adventures of a rascal through a series of loosely connected episodes—such as *Joseph Andrews* (1742) and *Tom Jones* (1749), both of which depict ordinary English life, and both of which were conceived as "comic epics in prose."

The tradition of great comic fiction established by Fielding was picked up by the Irish-born Laurence Sterne (1713–68), whose *Tristram Shandy*, published between 1760 and 1767, is perversely whimsical in its variety of styles, moods, and devices, and marks the first instance in which development of character and exploration of the inner self take primacy over plot. The Scottish-born Tobias Smollett (1721–71) returned to the episodic tradition in his novels of international land-and-sea escapades and his mature *Humphrey Clinker* (1771), a realistic adventure story set in England and Scotland.

The 19th-Century English Novel

In the 19th century, the novel flourished in Britain, as well as in France, Russia, and the United States. The first important British novelists of the century, the Scotsman Walter Scott (1771–1832) and the Englishwoman Jane Austen (1775–1817), were close contemporaries but radically different in style. Scott was a lyric and narrative poet whose transition to novel writing produced well-plotted romances of Scottish life, as well as introduced the historical novel in Britain. Scott's works include his "Waverley novels" (among them *Rob Roy* and *The Heart of Midlothian*, both 1818; and *Ivanhoe*, 1820, which takes place during the Crusades), the first and most famous of his historical novels. Scott's work was aligned with the Romantic movement then thriving in English poetry. Austen, whose first novel, *Sense and Sensibility*, was published in 1811, wrote completely outside the Romantic movement, producing novels of manners that were largely concerned with the social customs and conventions of provincial society. These stories, which include *Pride and Prejudice* (1813), *Mansfield Park* (1814), *Emma* (1816), and the posthumous, *Northanger Abbey* and *Persuasion* (1817), are masterly in form, witty, satirical, and sharply observant of character and manners.

The Romantic Novel   The Romantic novel reached its pinnacle at the beginning of the Victorian age when, in 1847, the Brontë sisters each published one of the most enduringly popular novels in English literature: Charlotte Brontë's (1816–55) *Jane Eyre* and Emily Brontë's (1818–48) *Wuthering Heights*. Both novels were tales of passionate love. *Wuthering Heights*, Emily Brontë's only novel, is an intense and eerie account of the relationship between a gentlewoman and a Gypsy foundling. It is considered to be one of England's finest examples of the novel for its clarity of structure and streamlined plot.

The Satirical Novel   The satirical novel *Vanity Fair* by William Makepiece Thackeray (1811–61) was published in 1848. Although Thackeray called *Vanity Fair* "a novel without a hero," it has a heroine, of sorts, in Becky Sharp, a winning, though not admirable, character who serves as a vehicle for lampooning the English upper class. Because of its concern with the interior life of its characters, *Vanity Fair* is considered an early forerunner of the psychological novel, a form that would grow in popularity as the 19th century progressed.

Charles Dickens (1812–70), perhaps the most widely read English novelist of all time, had an unmatched genius for creating richly mannered and comic characters, most of whom populate his vividly portrayed, socially diverse London. Raising his voice against poverty and industrial depersonalization, Dickens was, like Thackeray, a great satirist. He was also a brilliant master of plot, though many of his books, written hurriedly in magazine installments, are overly sentimental and structurally flawed. His best-known novel is *David Copperfield* (1850), but his most critically acclaimed works are *Bleak House* (1853), *Hard Times* (1854), and *Great Expectations* (1861).

The Psychological Novel   George Eliot (1819–80), the pen name of Mary Ann Evans, set her novels in small towns far from Dickens's London. Her psychologically probing novels reflect the Victorian uncertainty about religious faith. In them, she presented highly intelligent, fully realized characters with the moral challenge to live meaningful lives. Her novel *Middlemarch* (1872) is sometimes called the greatest English novel because of its scope, its richly drawn characters, and its psychological insight. Other works include *Silas Marner* (1861) and *The Mill on the Floss* (1860). Eliot's work represents the full flowering of the psychological novel.

The Late Victorian Novel   The Victorian age brought with it the expansion of the British Empire, the Industrial Revolution, and breakthroughs in science that created a new understanding of the world. Many novels of this period reflect a loss of certainty and religious consolation and influence. The work of two novelists of the late Victorian age, Thomas Hardy and Henry James, reflect the questions of this changing era.

Thomas Hardy (1840–1928) began his career as a novelist and later turned to poetry. Hardy's novels, which include *The Return of the Native* (1878), *Tess of the D'Urbervilles* (1891), and *Jude the Obscure* (1896), are set in "Wessex," his name for Dorsetshire. In Hardy's worldview, nature is beautiful but harsh, and cosmic fate mocks human aspiration.

Henry James (1843–1916) was born and educated in America but resettled in England at the age of 33. He was fascinated with the schism between the old, genteel, sophisticated world of Europe and the relative innocence of America. In early novels such as *The Portrait of a Lady* (1881) and later ones such as *The Ambassadors* (1903) and *The Golden Bowl* (1904), he explored the psychological complexity of characters on the boundary between the old and new worlds. In his "middle period" he focused on political themes in books such as *The Bostonians* (1886), then wrote a series of short "dramatic" novels such as *What Maisie Knew* (1897), and *The Turn of the Screw* (1898). Among James's innovations was the technique of writing from a character's point of view. He was the originator of the technique of "stream of consciousness" which would so profoundly affect the novel in the 20th century.

The Novel in the 20th Century

The historical events of the 20th century brought with them enormous changes to the development of the novel. The Victorian issues of imperialism, a new social order engendered by the Industrial Revolution, and loss of religious consolation continued to return as literary themes. World War I brought with it a fractured worldview. Experiments in form and subject matter reflected this changing world.

Novels of the Edwardian Age (1901–1914)   During the period between the death of Queen Victoria and the advent of World War I—in England, the Edwardian age—two novelists made concerns about Victorian imperialism the subject matter of their most famous novels. Despite the fact that English was his third language, Joseph Conrad (1857–1924), a Pole, is considered the first great 20th-century English novelist and a masterly prose stylist. His earliest important novels, *The Nigger of the Narcissus* (1897) and *Lord Jim* (1900), and several brilliant novellas, including *Youth* (1902), *Heart of Darkness* (1902), *Typhoon* (1903), and *The Secret Sharer* (1909), are set on the sea. *Heart of Darkness*, his most important work, is especially concerned with the fruits of imperialism. Some of Conrad's finest works, such as *Nostromo* (1904), *The Secret Agent* (1907), and *Under Western Eyes* (1911), are overtly political novels. A master of narrative technique, using, for example, multiple points of view, and of keen psychological insight, Conrad examined the isolation and moral conduct of men confronting the human condition.

E. M. Forster (1879–1970) made his mark between the turn of the century and the end of World War I. Indeed, Forster, who died at 91 in 1970, published fiction only between 1905 and 1924, when his last and best novel, *A Passage to India*, which examines the British Raj, appeared. In this and other social novels, including *A Room with a View* (1908) and *Howards End* (1910), he exposes the barren emotional life of the English middle class and explores the difficulties of personal relationships. Forster was one of several experimental writers and artists collectively known as the Bloomsbury Group, the most famous of whom was Virginia Woolf.

The Early Modern Novel   While many novelists rose to prominence during and just after World War I, two, D. H. Lawrence (1885–1930) and Virginia Woolf (1882–1941), exemplify the novel's shifting subject matter and form.

Lawrence's first major novel was the autobiographical *Sons and Lovers* (1913), followed by *The Rainbow* (1915) and *Women in Love* (1921), and *Lady Chatterly's Lover* (1928). He was a groundbreaker (and enormously controversial) in his celebration of sensuality. Lawrence was an original, impassioned stylist, and a latter-day romantic who scorned social convention and reacted against industrialism and intellectualism that divorced humanity from nature.

Virginia Woolf, E. M. Forster's close associate in the Bloomsbury Group, departed from Forster's traditional storytelling techniques and developed stream-of-consciousness narrative well beyond the innovations of Henry James. Stream of consciousness, in which the reader has access to all aspects of a character's mental processes, allows the reader to experience a character with enormous immediacy and closeness. In the novels *Mrs. Dalloway* (1925), *To the Lighthouse* (1927), and *The Waves* (1931), this style became increasingly poetic and free-ranging, and was a perfect vehicle with which Woolf could examine time,

change, and the interior lives of characters seeking both to know themselves and to form valuable relationships with others. Stream of consciousness was also used by James Joyce (1882–1941) in his masterpiece *Ulysses* (1922).

The Recent English Novel   No writer or group of writers has claimed a preeminent place in English fiction in the period since the 1930's, a time during which novelists writing in English have approached the complex and bewildering modern world from varied political, religious, and geographical directions.

An indication of this variety might begin with two prominent novelists born in the first decade of the 20th century, Evelyn Waugh (1903–66) and Graham Greene (1904–91), both of them Catholic in faith and theme but with altogether disparate political views and literary styles. For Waugh, the leading satirist of his time and a thoroughgoing conservative, the church represented a depth of values rooted in the distant past. After directing his devastating wit at British society in books like *Vile Bodies* (1930) and the British military in *Put Out More Flags* (1942), Waugh wrote his most famous novel, *Brideshead Revisited* (1945), about an aristocratic Catholic family, and a highly regarded trilogy of World War II entitled *Sword of Honour* (1952–61). Greene's road to Catholicism emerged out of the leftist atmosphere of the 1930's. He was a master composer of thrillers and spy stories that he labeled "entertainments," and his more important works are soul-searching novels such as *The Power and the Glory* (1940) and *The Heart of the Matter* (1948).

The century's first years also produced two persistent chroniclers of English society as it changed during their lives: C. P. Snow (1905–80), who between 1940 and 1970 produced a sequence of 11 novels, *Strangers and Brothers*; and Anthony Powell (1905–2000), who from 1951 to 1975 published 12 under the collective title *A Dance to the Music of Time*. Again, these men observed very different worlds. Snow wrote of one man rising from the lower class to political power. Powell, with homage to Marcel Proust, chronicled, with depth and humor, the shifting realities of upper-class life.

George Orwell (1903–50), who eloquently represented the left wing, is more highly regarded as an essayist than as a novelist, but in 1949, the year before his death, he completed the most widely read English novel of the century's second half, *Nineteen Eighty-Four*, his chilling warning against totalitarianism. Five years later, William Golding (1911–93) produced another much-read novel, as chilling in its way—*Lord of the Flies*, a symbolic tale of accumulating cruelty and barbarism among boys stranded on a Pacific island. It was Golding's first novel and is by far his most famous, although he published many more significant novels and won the Nobel Prize in 1983.

During the 1950's, a highly talented, diverse, and bountiful crop of new English novelists appeared. Among them were Muriel Spark (b. 1918–2006), Iris Murdoch (1919–99) and Doris Lessing (b. 1919), none of whom were born in England. The Scottish Spark, like Greene a Catholic convert, shares with him a keen awareness of evil, and focuses on fallen humanity's disturbing misbehavior. Her best-known novel, replicated on stage and in film, is the brief *The Prime of Miss Jean Brodie* (1961). Murdoch, a philosopher turned fiction writer, also examined evil but, much influenced by Plato, might be called a novelist of "the good," a principle that she keeps permanently in view even while depicting the limitations of human nature. Murdoch wove entertaining plots as webs in which characters struggle with the duality of spiritual and sexual yearning. She won early acclaim for *The Bell* (1958) and *A Severed Head* (1961) and wrote novels prolifically thereafter, including *Henry and Cato* (1976) and *The Sea, The Sea* (1978). Lessing came to London from Rhodesia in 1949 and soon wrote the first of five novels in the *Children of Violence* sequence (1952–69), an extended, autobiographically based psychological and social portrait of the character Martha Quest. These and other novels, particularly *The Golden Notebook* (1962) established her as a major feminist writer, as well as a chronicler of the changing sensibilities of her time. She later shifted modes from realism to fantasy in *A Briefing for a Descent into Hell* (1971) and *The Memoirs of a Survivor* (1974) and to science fiction in a series of five novels under the general title *Canopus in Argos* (1979–83).

A group of male novelists who began publishing in the 1950's became known, along with certain playwrights and poets, as the "angry young men," for their protest against the meanness of postwar society and against the old order clinging to its authority. These included Alan Sillitoe (b. 1928), John Wain (1925–94), John Braine (1922–87), and Kingsley Amis (1922–95), who is best known for his sharply amusing first novel, *Lucky Jim* (1954).

In the second half of the 20th century, numerous British novelists arrived in England from points all around the imperial compass. Among them, from Dominica in the Caribbean came Jean Rhys (1890–1979), author of *Wide Sargasso Sea* (1966); from South Africa came Angus Wilson (1913–91), author of *No Laughing Matter* (1967); from Ireland, William Trevor (b. 1928), an accomplished short story writer; from Trinidad, the ethnic Indian V. S. Naipaul (b. 1932), author of *A Bend in the River* (1979); and from India, Salman Rushdie (b. 1947) author of *Satanic Verses* (1988). Notable English novelists currently writing include Margaret Drabble (b. 1939), A.S. Byatt (b. 1936), Ian McEwan (b. 1948), John Banville (b. 1945), and Martin Amis (b. 1949), son of Kingsley.

American Literature

Colonial Period through the 18th Century

Origins   Locating a starting point for the diverse collection of genres and voices known as American literature has provoked lively debate for centuries. The Viking Leif Ericson's voyage to Newfoundland in 1001 became fodder for two Norse fables that might be considered the first texts of North American origin. But many critics now mark America's literary origins with the performance of oral literature by Native Americans such as the Zuni and Navajo, both tribes of the southwest United States. European exploration narratives by such figures as Christopher Columbus (1451–1506) and Alvar Núñez Cabeza de Vaca (1490–1556) gave Europeans a first glimpse of indigenous cultures, but the 18 million indigenous peoples speaking roughly 200 distinct languages in North America at the time had been sharing stories perhaps for millennia.

Not transcribed until the 19th century, these included creation myths and trickster tales (the latter most notably featuring the figure of the coyote), and were woven with natural imagery. The Zuni "Talk Concerning the First Beginning" speaks of a mammalian birth of the world through a "fourth womb," for example.

Literature in the Colonies

Mainstream American literature dates from the early 17th century with the arrival of European settlers in North America, beginning with the small, precariously situated colonial presence in Jamestown, Virginia, founded in 1607. In 1619 passengers on the *Mayflower* arrived in Plymouth, Massachusetts. Like those in Jamestown, these settlers learned survival and agricultural tactics from Native Americans. Diarists recorded the hardships they suffered as well as their encounters with indigenous tribes. Mary White Rowlandson (1637–1711) wrote a captivity narrative about her three-month detention with Native Americans during King Philip's War (1675–78), which became one of the first best sellers from the New World and helped prepare the soil that would later give life to the genre of the western.

The Pilgrims in Plymouth were motivated to leave England in part for Separatist religious causes. As a result, much of the early literature to emerge from the colonies was religious in tone and content. One of the most influential early American men of letters was William Bradford (1590–1657), who served as governor of the Plymouth Colony for a total of 33 years and bestowed upon the settlers the name "Pilgrims." His *Of Plymouth Plantation* reads more like a theological treatise on Christianity than the history it purports to be. The Pilgrims were soon followed by the Puritans, who attempted to create a religious utopia in the Massachusetts Bay Colony. As John Winthrop (1588–1649), the colony's governor for a dozen years, put it (in a nod to the New Testament), they strove to craft "a city upon a hill." Anne Bradstreet (1612–72), who came to the colonies with Winthrop, earned the distinction of being the first colonial subject, male or female, to publish a book of poetry. Indeed, she was one of the first women writing in English to achieve success in the literary market, and her critical reception has endured. Her poetry eschews religious zealotry in favor of a more nuanced treatment of her own spirituality and also treats themes of family life.

John Cotton (1585–1652) established the justification for the Puritan way of life by publishing an influential sermon and contributing a preface to the *Bay Psalm Book* of 1640. Cotton gained recognition for pursuing the case of heresy against Anne Hutchinson (1591–1643) for her doctrinal differences with him and other leaders. Later in the century, a prolific clergyman and poet named Edward Taylor (1642–1729) crafted such works as "The Psalm Paraphrases" and "God's Determinations." In the same era, Cotton Mather (1663–1728) fulfilled his destiny as the grandson of two Puritan leaders and the son of Increase Mather (1639–1723), pastor of the Old North Church and president of Harvard, by writing many influential documents, including a definitive ecclesiastical history of New England, *Magnalia Christi Americana* (1702). Less admirable but equally momentous was his approval of the Salem witch trials in 1692. The sermon form that gained popularity in New England traces its roots to

Cicero's oratory and shares much with other performance arts. Jonathan Edwards (1703–58) stepped forward as the last great religious orator of colonial New England. His "Sinners in the Hands of an Angry God" caused many of those who heard it to swoon with fear, and marked the last time that religious writing would constitute the center of American literature.

18th-Century Enlightenment and Revolution

The most distinctive and enduring voice in colonial America belonged to Benjamin Franklin (1706–90), who subscribed to the Enlightenment faith in the rational, scientific mind. He set in motion the restless American narrative of upward mobility with his autobiography. J. Hector St. John de Crèvecoeur (1735–1813) fueled this narrative by attempting to describe the American character for Europeans in his *Letters from an American Farmer* (1782). Franklin and Crèvecoeur helped colonial Americans articulate a coherent national identity full of patriotism.

The Revolution inspired the political writings of the editor and writer Thomas Paine (1735–1826), who became a leading voice in the revolutionary movement with his pamphlet "Common Sense," published in 1776. In the same year, Thomas Jefferson (1743–1826), who would become the third president of the new United States and was the leading writer of the Revolution, wrote the first draft of the Declaration of Independence, outlining a rational, legal argument for a break with the English throne. It is widely held to be the most vital document of American political letters. Next most important is *The Federalist* (1787–88) of Alexander Hamilton, James Madison, and John Jay, a series of essays urging adoption of the Constitution.

In this climate of revolutionary freedom, Olaudah Equiano (1745–97), who had served masters in America, the West Indies, and England, published the first American slave narrative. The title, *The Interesting Narrative of the Life of Olaudah Equiano, or Gustavus Vassa the African, Written by Himself* (1789), displays pride in the remarkable achievement of reading and writing, which were outlawed for slaves. Equally powerful was the work of another former slave, the poet Phillis Wheatley (1753–84), who earned the distinction of becoming the first published black American.

Early American Novels The most democratic of genres, the novel, flourished on American soil, rapidly catching on with the masses. To their dismay, the elite could not wield control over its widely and quickly disseminated messages. The three most popular novelists of the 18th century were Hannah Webster Foster (1758–1840), Susanna Haswell Rowson (1762–1824), and Charles Brockden Brown (1771–1810), all of whom specialized in the seduction narrative, a particularly troubling form for the arbiters of culture and morals. Many such volumes claimed that the moral contained within their pages would outweigh the perils of the subject matter for their young readers.

The 19th Century

American literature exploded onto the world stage from the turn of the 19th century through the Civil War, as American writers rushed to distinguish themselves from their European forebears and define a distinct American character for themselves. By 1800 Americans found the country charming and baffling by turns. The resulting prose, poetry, and essays expose a complex ambivalence about the same contradictions that Charles Dickens, the Frenchman Alexis de Tocqueville, and other distinguished visitors witnessed, along with a profound thirst for a coherent national identity.

The Role of the Frontier   Frontier mythology emerged to fill what seemed a worrisome void to the country's first citizens—the lack of an artistic and historical identity like the identities cultivated in Europe over millennia. Frontier fiction drew upon forms and characters from travel narratives and captivity diaries, wherein the land and its indigenous occupants could be portrayed as alternately magnificent and brutal and the American could declare his independence over and over again, reinventing himself and his context. The land supported the lofty democratic ideals of a population that soared from 5.3 million in 1800 to 31.4 million ca. 1860.

In the first three decades of the 19th century, novelists such as Washington Irving (1783–1859) and James Fenimore Cooper (1789–1851) furnished portraits of American lands and struggles. Both were masters of the picaresque, a form known for panoramic landscapes, characters from the lower rungs of society, and freedom from convention. *Rip Van Winkle* (1819), Irving's most famous contribution to the American literary canon, is a shrewd metaphor for life in America in the early years following the American Revolution: if a citizen slept too long, he would run the risk of waking to an unrecognizable country.

Cooper's *Leatherstocking Tales*, a series of novels featuring the hero Natty Bumppo (called Hawkeye), were very popular adventure stories about the epic hazards and glories of westward expansion. The sentimental and nostalgic images of the frontier in such novels as *The Last of the Mohicans* (1826) would ignite a collective vision of the contours of a wild and self-reliant American spirit. America gained recognition as a literary entity in its own right when it inspired Noah Webster (1758–1843) to compile the new *American Dictionary of the English Language* (1828), but critics abroad scoffed.

Transcendentalism, Romanticism, and the American Renaissance

Romanticism originated in Germany as a late 18th-century reaction against the cold, clinical mind-set of Enlightenment reason. In the world constructed by the American Romantic writer, the individual reigns supreme, but not at the expense of civility—a departure from European Romantics such as Byron. The Americans imagined a community in which individuality leads to unity, not chaos. The Romantic literary movement in America was informed by Transcendentalism, which blossomed in New England as a reform movement in Unitarianism under the prominent abolitionist minister William Ellery Channing (1780–1842). He argued for the presence of the divine within each human being, who must be trained to listen to intuitive thoughts. The Transcendentalists believed in the unity of God and a divine presence in the world linking nature and people. This marked a departure from New England Calvinism, which cast sin as the defining characteristic of humanity, and from 18th-century Enlightenment rationalism, which renounced spirituality. Transcendentalism built upon the emerging ideals of optimism, opportunity, and self-reliance in the American democracy at a time when the United States was deeply divided on the morality of its laws, particularly those concerning slavery. Romanticism and Transcendentalism characterized an intense flowering of all the literary arts that has inspired critics to refer to the period from about 1830 to 1865 as an "American Renaissance."

The Essay   Transcendentalism found its most direct expression in the essays and other nonfiction works of thinkers and artists centered in Concord, Mass. Ralph Waldo Emerson (1803–82) began his writing career in good-natured defiance of old traditions. In a talk that would ultimately appear in print as "The Divinity School Address" (1838), Emerson declared a break from Harvard's traditional theologians, and he would find himself effectively prevented from sharing his controversial views at the university until after the Civil War. His Transcendental view proposed that God was dead in church but very much alive in nature and the individual.

Emerson's most famous works include *Nature*, published in 1836; and "Self-Reliance," in 1841. As part of the Transcendental Club, he cofounded a periodical called *The Dial*, published from 1840 to 1844, with the free-thinking author of *Women in the Nineteenth Century (1845)*, Margaret Fuller, as a vehicle for the expression of Transcendentalist views.

No single writer better evokes the sights and sounds of Concord, or better uses the natural landscape to promote his philosophy, than Henry David Thoreau (1817–62), Emerson's close friend. Thoreau began his two-year experiment in living at Walden Pond in 1845; writing about it in *Walden* (1854), he advocates a spiritually exuberant but materially spartan life. In 1849 he delineated the platform for peaceful resistance that would inspire future generations, in an essay later titled "Civil Disobedience."

Poetry　The early 19th century saw meaningful innovation in poetry, as well as an exploration and celebration of democratic ideals. The poet William Cullen Bryant (1794–1878), a prominent leader of Unitarianism, is best known for "Thanatopsis," which praised divine nature and inspired Emerson and Thoreau, although he is more often classified with the Knickerbocker School of New York writers than with Transcendentalism's Concord cabal. Bryant helped fashion a distinctly American voice in literature, as did Henry Wadsworth Longfellow (1807–82), who was best known for *Evangeline* (1847), *Hiawatha*, (1855), and "Paul Revere's Ride" (1861).

Walt Whitman (1819–92) offers a poetic voice that may be said to encapsulate and call into being the American character more effectively than that of any other poets of the century, or perhaps of any century. His *vers libre* or "free verse" poems broke away from conventional meters and rhyme. Whitman got his start in journalism with the *Brooklyn Daily Eagle* in 1841, and his poems share with works of journalism a gift for keen observation. In 1855 he first published his magnum opus, *Leaves of Grass*, which he would add to and revise for decades. In this equal-opportunity collection, a prostitute occupies the same poetic space as the president of the United States.

Emily Dickinson (1830–86) seldom left her home in Amherst, Massachusetts, after age 30, but her spiritual searching and devoted observation of nature made her poems very much of their time and place. Her witty, epigrammatic style is also reminiscent of the 17th-century English Metaphysical poets, whom Dickinson admired. At the same time her unlikely images that multiply meanings in tightly worked lyrics anticipate 20th-century poetic trends. With very few exceptions, Dickinson's 1,000-plus extant poems, many written in a burst of creativity around 1860, were not published until after her death, close to the turn of the century.

Edgar Allan Poe (1809–49) left his mark on both poetry and the short story. His was the world of the Romantic individual locked in personal consciousness. In one of the most famous American poems, "The Raven" (1845), Poe's narrator construes the bird's parroted responses as a message of doom, suggesting that humans require no outside source of fear—they most often frighten themselves.

Poe's fascination with the supernatural, alternative realities, and the power of the human mind to perceive and deceive makes his tales early examples of the modern-day horror, science fiction, and detective-story genres. A number of his most famous stories, including "The Fall of the House of Usher," appeared in *Burton's Gentleman's Magazine* while he was its coeditor from 1839 to 1840.

Fiction　The novelist and short-story writer Nathaniel Hawthorne (1803–82) commanded the world's respect for the subtlety of his often melancholic, anxiety-riddled narratives. Hawthorne imagined the recent past of his Puritan and colonial forebears and gave voice to the dark underside of life in the new republic, which was often fraught with alienation and despair. In 1850 he published *The Scarlet Letter*, which, like much of his work, employs rich symbolism and allegory to highlight the profound moral dilemma of evil and guilt: the scarlet *A* for adultery metamorphoses as sympathies shift. The Romantic fiction writers offered nuanced character studies, moving well beyond setting and plot to psychological interiority.

Louisa May Alcott (1832–88) grew up in a world steeped in Transcendentalism. Her father, Bronson Alcott (1799–1888), was a school reformer in Concord and elsewhere and a frequent contributor to *The Dial*. His daughter shared his passion for philosophy and education. She was memorialized as "the children's friend" at her funeral, primarily for *Little Women* (1868), one of the most popular works of children's literature ever published. She has never fallen into obscurity, unlike many other 19th-century women who wrote about the domestic sphere.

The fiction of Herman Melville (1819–91) combines the adventure of the frontier narrative with the symbolism and psychological interiority of Hawthorne's character studies. In Melville's novels—such as *Typee* (1846) and *Moby-Dick; or, the Whale* (1851), and short stories and novellas, such as *Billy Budd, Sailor*, which drew on his own maritime adventures—authority is no guarantee of morality. Both Hawthorne and Melville struggled to make a financial success of writing. At the time of Melville's death in 1891, he had a stronger following in England than in his own country, but since the early 20th century scholars have considered his contribution to American letters virtually unparalleled.

Women's Domestic Fiction

Hawthorne railed against what he called "those damned scribbling women," who wrote domestic or sentimental fiction. While *The Scarlet Letter* was a best seller in 1850, it sold only a few thousand copies; that same year the novelist Susan Warner (1819–85) published *The Wide, Wide World*, whose 14 editions in two years exceeded any previous book's sales in the United States, and became an exceptional publishing sensation in England as well. Domestic or sentimental fiction enjoyed its greatest popularity in America from 1820 through 1870, beginning with Catharine Sedgwick's *New-England Tale* (1822). Stemming from the 18th-century novel of sensibility, the genre promoted reliance on the goodness of human nature and the power of feelings as a guide to proper behavior. It took its place alongside conduct manuals for young girls and women. The stories generally focused on the plight of a heroine in an economically precarious situation whose redemption often comes with self-mastery. In sentimental fiction, sacrifice through marriage, family, and service to God takes precedence over personal happiness, or stands as the fastest route to that happiness.

The novelist Harriet Beecher Stowe (1811–96) resists classification in this genre because her themes transcend the hearth, although her work would be readily accessible to a reading public hungry for sentimental fiction. The sentimental aspects of her writing helped her advocate for causes, primarily for the abolition of slavery. In 1851 *Uncle Tom's Cabin* sold 1 million copies within the year, another unprecedented literary success in the United States.

The Slave Narrative

One slave who found freedom and wrote about his experiences was Frederick Douglass (1818–95), who published *Narrative of the Life of Frederick Douglass, an American Slave: Written by Himself* in 1845. Reading and writing proved the former slave's salvation: Douglass was forced to learn in secrecy and by his wits. He eloquently depicts the dehumanizing effects of bondage, writing what is often considered one of the finest examples of the slave narrative genre. In describing the efforts of an overseer to break his spirit, Douglass turns the tables to show that it was the slaveholders, not the slaves, who were the brutes to be feared. Douglass toured much of the United States and Europe speaking about his experiences and working for the emancipation of slaves.

Another slave who wrote a powerful account of the hazards of life for a black person in antebellum America was Harriet Ann Jacobs (1813–97), also known as Linda Brent, the author of *Incidents in the Life of a Slave Girl* (1861). Jacobs survived her enslavement by hiding in the crawl-space of an attic on her owner's property for several years. She used sentimental conventions to describe the plight of a black woman intent on keeping her virtue in an immensely cruel and dehumanizing system. A spin-off of the slave narrative is the narrative from a "free" black woman. Harriet Wilson (1827–63) published *Our Nig: Or, Sketches from the Life of a Free Black, in a Two-Story White House, North, Showing that Slavery's Shadows Fall Even There*, the first novel by an African-American woman, in 1859. It features the horrible mistreatment of a slave/servant in the North and appealed to the humane sensibilities of white northern women.

Late 19th- through Early 20th-Century Literature

In 1867 the cattle route known as the Chisholm Trail would fuel the genre of the western; and the completion of the Union Pacific–Central Pacific Railroad in 1869 and the Klondike Gold Rush of 1896 would expand the frontiers of America's literary imagination. Alexander Graham Bell's invention of the telephone in 1876 would propel Americans into the future; the advent of motion pictures at the turn of the 20th century would forever alter the production of art and literature both at home and abroad. With a "Rough Rider" for a president in Theodore Roosevelt, who ascended to power in 1901; the advent of Orville Wright's flying machine in 1903; Henry Ford's Model T in 1908; Albert Einstein's theory of relativity in 1905, and a world war lurking on the horizon, the country and the world were hurtling into a new era at the turn of the 20th century—a time of excitement and anticipation as well as conflict, secularism, industrialization, and alienation.

Naturalism   Naturalism depicted the chaos of modern human life with rational, scientific objectivity in an exploration of Darwinian theories of biological and environmental determinism. Like Romanticism, the movement began in Europe and focused on the disadvantaged in society, as in Émile Zola's 1885 novel about French mine workers, *Germinal*. As America became more mechanized, the social radicalism of the trend flourished. Many of its practitioners came of age in the heyday of muckraking journalism, which exposed the horrors of working life at the time. Upton Sinclair (1878–1968) honed his skills in this training ground, telling about factory atrocities of the meatpacking industry in *The Jungle* (1906). Stephen Crane, native of New Jersey, changed the genre of war writing with *The Red Badge of Courage* (1895). His *Maggie: A Girl of the Streets* (1893) depicted the immigrant experience.

The masters of naturalism include Frank Norris (1870–1902), who was born in Chicago but spent most of his life in San Francisco. Theodore Dreiser (1871–1945), a protégé of Norris, was born in Indiana, the ninth child of German immigrants. His concern with the plight of the working class led him to spend most of his life as a socialist; shortly before he died, he joined the American Communist Party. Dreiser's *Sister Carrie* (1900) and *An American Tragedy* (1925) reveal the profound dissatisfactions of the materialist life in an America with a torn social fabric utterly beyond individual control.

The Californian novelist Jack London (1876–1916) explored the potential for adaptation to one's environment in such novels as *The Call of the Wild* (1903) and *White Fang* (1906). He gained equal fame for his real-life adventures and for his literary achievements, becoming the most commercially successful writer of the period.

Realism   The line separating naturalism and realism often seems blurred, but they have quite distinct aims. Realism attempts to capture reality as faithfully as possible, almost photographically. Instead of focusing on the dark and seemingly inevitable chaos in the offing, the real-

ist project concerns itself with the immediate present, the verifiable fact, and the search for truth. With roots in journalism and a lifelong series of editorial positions at literary magazines, Ohio-born William Dean Howells (1837–1920) was best known for *The Rise of Silas Lapham* (1885). Henry James (1843–1916), the scion of an old and powerful New York family, refined psychological interiority into high art, particularly in such works as *The Portrait of a Lady* (1881). His characters occupied high social strata, yet they could cut absurd (though ethically superior) figures next to their European counterparts, especially in *The American* (1877). James reigned over a set of American writers, philosophers, architects, artists, and philanthropists known as the "cosmopolitans," training his eye on the bustling transatlantic traffic of the day. He examined the American character laid bare before the scrutiny and ridicule of ancestral Europe, routinely lampooning its democratic cousin abroad. James's protégée, the Pulitzer Prize-winning novelist Edith Wharton (1862–1937), examined American personalities, mores, and ethics, sharing his fascination with the social elite. She crafted chilling and illuminating portraits of the social order in the United States, most notably in *The Age of Innocence* (1919), *Ethan Frome* (1911), and *The House of Mirth* (1905).

Regionalism   The use of vernacular and dialect aids realist characterization, which trumped plot in the regionalist movement and figured in regional or local-color fiction. The master of vernacular was Missouri-born Mark Twain (Samuel Clemens, 1835–1910), who served as a Confederate soldier. His humor, which he used to depict life on the Mississippi River, demonstrates realism's distinction from the dour naturalist model. His unflinching honesty debunked outmoded ways of thinking about the country. Twain was a great and influential innovator with his frequent use of authentic vernacular language. His work also exemplified popular frontier humor, and *Adventures of Huckleberry Finn* (1884) is often considered to be the best novel produced by an American.

A literary renaissance centered in Chicago flourished at the end of the 19th and start of the 20th century and also challenged the East's literary monopoly. Hamlin Garland (1860–1940) documented the unromanticized truth of pioneer subsistence. Sherwood Anderson (1876–1941) spun character studies set in the quiet desolation of small-town midwestern American life, most famously in *Winesburg, Ohio* (1919). Carl Sandburg (1878–1967), whose *Chicago Poems* emerged in print in 1916, won two Pulitzers.

Vachel Lindsay (1879–1931), of Springfield, Illinois, traveled the country on foot performing his poetry for the masses. *Spoon River Anthology* (1915) by Edgar Lee Masters (1869–1950), conjures up voices of tiny Spoon River in dramatic monologues. The Chicago poets used experimental techniques to animate overlooked members of society.

Late 19th- and early 20th-century regional voices often belonged to women. Willa Cather's *O, Pioneers!* (1913), *My Antonia* (1918), and *Death Comes for the Archbishop* (1927) made high art out of life on the prairie and in the American Southwest. Like Wharton, Cather gave texture and nuance to the life experienced by women as the nation struggled with women's suffrage. In the same vein, Kate Chopin (1851–1904) and Charlotte Perkins Gilman (1860–1935) wrote narratives that illuminated the great dissatisfaction that even affluent women could feel with their lives—dissatisfaction that could lead to mental illness and suicide. Both Chopin's *The Awakening* and Gilman's *The Yellow Wallpaper* appeared in 1899.

In the heyday of regionalism, a group in Nashville, Tennessee, taking its name from a Vanderbilt University literary magazine, *The Fugitive*, launched a challenge to northern values of urban industrial life and cast off the charges of southern racism and provincialism. The "Fugitives" were led by the poet and critic John Crowe Ransom (1888–1974), the poet Allen Tate (1899–1979), and novelist Robert Penn Warren (1905– 89). They were affiliated with New Criticism and attentive to formal patterns.

The South also blossomed with tart, insightful, humorous, and haunting fiction by Katherine Anne Porter (1890–1980), Eudora Welty (1909–2001), and Flannery O'Connor (1925–64). More recently, Wallace Stegner (1909–93) has crafted several brilliant and effective character studies set in the West in *Angle of Repose* (1971) and *Crossing to Safety* (1987).

Modernism and Its Discontents

Modernism reached its height in the 1920's, though it began before World War I and dominated the arts at least through the 1940's. Along with scientists such as Werner Heisenberg and philosophers such as Edmund Husserl, modernists believed that what we call objective reality is shaped by perception. The new human sciences of psychology, anthropology, and linguistics exposed the mental and social dimensions of reality. Artists tried to capture the ways in which dreams, culture, and language color perception. Cubism in painting, with its rejection of three-dimension-al perspective; and jazz in music, with its improvisation and syncopation, began to dismantle familiar structures of visual and aural experience. Modernist writers brought analogous stylistic innovations to the page.

The era's epistemological uncertainty, along with the upheavals of war and technological change, bred anxious despair about the disintegration of Western civilization as well as breathless expectation of a radically different future. Influenced by the technological enthusiasm of the Italian Futurists, Ezra Pound (1885–1972) enjoined aspiring poets to "make it new." Pound presided over the Imagist movement of the 1910's, which ushered in a spare poetic style that broke with traditional prosody and discursive rhetoric. Like the "objective correlative" described by T. S. Eliot (1888–1965), the Imagist poem elicits a reader's emotions through associations in the material world. In addition to writing his own extensive opus, most notably the unfinished long poem of 30 years' labor, *The Cantos,* Pound mentored many important Modernist poets, including Eliot, whose poem *The Waste Land* (1922) famously captures the tenor of Modernism. It is a collage of fragments—myths, legends, symbols, overheard voices—from many different cultures, some in other languages, that its neurotic speaker "shores up against the ruins" of modern urban life.

Many American intellectuals, including Pound and Eliot, sought refuge in Europe from what they saw as the culturally impoverished, socially repressive United States. Gertrude Stein (1874–1946) hosted a number of them, bringing together the artists in her life as much as in her work. An avant-garde poet, fiction writer, and dramatist herself, Stein was also a discerning, forward-looking collector of paintings by the likes of Pablo Picasso and Henri Matisse, and her adopted home in Paris served as a salon for these and other artists, including expatriate Americans such as Ernest Hemingway (1899–1961) and F. Scott Fitzgerald (1896–1940). Stein's phrase for the decimated youth of World War I, the "lost generation," would eventually be applied to such American exiles, whose European adventures are fictionalized in Hemingway's *The Sun Also Rises* (1926) and Fitzgerald's *Tender Is the Night* (1934). Hemingway's journalistic style of direct statement and concrete detail might be compared to Imagist poetry. Writing in a more conventional style, Fitzgerald chronicled the libertine lifestyle of the "roaring" 1920's, with its speakeasies and flappers, in *The Great Gatsby* (1925) and other works.

A Relentless Updike
Mapped America's Mysteries

By MICHIKO KAKUTANI

Endowed with an art student's pictorial imagination, a journalist's sociological eye and a poet's gift for metaphor, John Updike was arguably this country's one true all-around man of letters. He moved fluently from fiction to criticism, from light verse to short stories to the long-distance form of the novel: a literary decathlete in our age of electronic distraction and willful specialization, Victorian in his industriousness and almost blogger-like in his determination to turn every scrap of knowledge and experience into words.

It is as a novelist who opened a big picture window on the American middle class in the second half of the 20th century, however, that he will be best remembered. In his most resonant work, Mr. Updike gave "the mundane its beautiful due," as he once put it, memorializing the everyday mysteries of love and faith and domesticity with extraordinary nuance and precision. In Kodachrome-sharp snapshots, he gave us the 50's and early 60's of suburban adultery, big cars and wide lawns, radios and hi-fi sets, and he charted the changing landscape of the 70's and 80's, as malls and subdivisions swallowed up small towns and sexual and social mores underwent a bewildering metamorphosis.

Mr. Updike's four keenly observed Rabbit novels (*Rabbit, Run*, 1960; *Rabbit Redux*, 1971; *Rabbit Is Rich*, 1981; and *Rabbit at Rest*, 1990) chronicled the adventures of one Harry Rabbit Angstrom—high school basketball star turned car salesman, householder and errant husband—and his efforts to cope with the seismic public changes (from feminism to the counterculture to antiwar protests) that rattled his cozy nest. Harry, who self-importantly compared his own fall from grace to this country's waning power, his business woes to the national deficit, was both a representative American of his generation and a kind of scientific specimen — an index to the human species and its propensity for doubt and narcissism and self immolation.

In fulfilling Stendhal's classic definition of a novel as "a mirror that strolls along a highway," reflecting both the "blue of the skies" and "the mud puddles underfoot," the Rabbit novels captured four decades of middle-class American life. Mr. Updike's stunning and much underestimated 1996 epic, *In the Beauty of the Lilies*, tackled an even wider swath of history. In charting the fortunes of an American family through some 80 years, the author showed how dreams, habits and predilections are handed down generation to generation, parent to child, even as he created a kaleidoscopic portrait of this country from its nervous entry into the 20th century to its stumbling approach to the millennium.

Producing roughly a book or so a year, Mr. Updike tried throughout his career to stretch his imagination. To the novels starring Rabbit—perhaps the self Mr. Updike might have been had he not become a writer—he added a series of books about Bech, another alter ego described as a "recherché but amiable" Jewish novelist afflicted with acute writer's block. While Bech boasted a modest oeuvre of seven books and remained a second-string cult author, his creator was blessed, as he once wrote of Nabokov, with an "ebullient creativity," and his work, too, gave the happy impression of "a continuous task carried forward variously, of a solid personality, of a plentitude of gifts explored, knowingly."

In other novels, Mr. Updike ventured even farther afield. *The Centaur* (1963) infused Joycean myth into its tender portrait of a well-meaning schoolteacher. *The Coup* (1978) conjured up an imaginary African kingdom called Kush and its imperial leader Colonel Ellelloû. And *The Witches of Eastwick* (1984) and its sequel, *The Widows of Eastwick* (2008), depicted heroines who were supernatural sorceresses with the power to conjure and maim. These experiments did not always work. Indeed Mr. Updike's strongest work remained tethered to the small town and suburban worlds he knew firsthand, just as many of his heroes shared the same sort of existential fears the author acknowledged he had suffered as a young man: Henry Bech's concern that he was "a fleck of dust condemned to know it is a fleck of dust," or Colonel Ellelloû's lament that "we will be forgotten, all of us forgotten." Their fear of death threatens to make everything they do feel meaningless, and it also sends them running after God—looking for some reassurance that there is something beyond the familiar, everyday world with "its signals and buildings and cars and bricks."

But if their yearnings after salvation pulled them in one direction, Mr. Updike's heroes also found themselves tempted by sex and romantic misalliances in the here and now. Caught on the margins of a changing morality, unable to forget the old pieties and taboos and yet unable to resist the 60's promise of sex without consequences, these men vacillate between duty and self-fulfillment, a craving for roots and a hungering after freedom. As the author himself once put it, his heroes "oscillate in their moods between an enjoyment of the comforts of domesticity and the familial life, and a sense that their essential identity is a solitary one—to be found in flight and loneliness and even adversity. This seems to be my feeling of what being a male human being involves."

Although Mr. Updike's earliest stories could sound self consciously writerly and derivative—at their worst, O'Hara without the bite, Cheever without the magic—he soon found his own inimitable voice with *Pigeon Feathers* and *Rabbit, Run*. Over the years, the stories and novels tended to track Mr. Updike's own life: couples wooed and wed and went their separate ways, and the hormonal urges of youth slowly became the quiescence of middle age.

In a series of overlapping stories about Joan and Richard Maple (collected in *Too Far to Go*), Mr. Updike created an indelible two-decade-long portrait of a marriage, chronicling how one couple created and then dismantled a life together, while tracing the imprint that time and age left on their relationship. Many of his later stories and novels seemed preoccupied with mortality and the ravages of time, featuring characters grappling with the looming prospect of their own demise with a mixture of anger, grace and resignation and looking back upon their youth in an often cloudy rear view mirror.

Mr. Updike summed up his love of his vocation: "From earliest childhood I was charmed by the materials of my craft, by pencils and paper and, later, by the typewriter and the entire apparatus of printing. To condense from one's memories and fantasies and small discoveries dark marks on paper which become handsomely reproducible many times over still seems to me, after nearly 30 years concerned with the making of books, a magical act, and a delightful technical process. To distribute oneself thus, as a kind of confetti shower falling upon the heads and shoulders of mankind out of bookstores and the pages of magazines is surely a great privilege and a defiance of the usual earthbound laws whereby human beings make themselves known to one another."

In fiction and drama, William Faulkner (1897–1962) and Eugene O'Neill (1888–1953) (see "Drama") may be considered America's modernist masters. Faulkner's *The Sound and the Fury* (1929) exhibits two key innovations of the period: stream-of-consciousness narration and multiple points of view. Depicting the same circumstances from four points of view, the text reads as if it were the transcription of characters' interior monologues, including apparently random thoughts usually omitted from rational discourse. Other renowned works by Faulkner include *Light in August* (1932) and *Absalom, Absalom!* (1936).

The Great Depression of the 1930's made the "high" Modernism of the previous decade seem especially removed from the real hardships of everyday life. Pound's fascist sympathies and anti-Semitism, especially in the years leading up to World War II, confirmed suspicions of modernists' conservative politics at a time when many artists were leaning left. William Carlos Williams (1883–1963), once published as an Imagist poet, began to object to his colleagues' elitism. Instead of the models many in the "lost generation" adopted abroad, he sought a uniquely American voice in his poetry and largely stuck to native shores. Even as he documented the humble and home-grown, however, Williams let the unadorned image speak, in true Modernist style. John Dos Passos (1896–1970) also put Modernist technique in the service of progressive politics. His *U.S.A.* trilogy, which explored the degradations of the economic and social divide under capitalism in the United States between 1900 and 1930, juxtaposed newspaper headlines and popular songs with the stories of his fictional characters in a manner reminiscent of Cubists' collages and the montage style of film, a modern form by definition. Experiences as a manual laborer enabled John Steinbeck (1902–68) to write proletarian novels from the heart. Especially moving and enduring is *The Grapes of Wrath* (1939), the story of a dispossessed farm family fleeing the Dust Bowl for California.

The Beats of the 1950's rejected the establishment in all its guises, including the Modernist literature that had gone mainstream by that time. Although Beat literature employed open forms akin to the Modernists' free verse, the Beats prized uncensored, spontaneous self-expression whereas the Modernists favored an impersonal, crafted lyricism. *Howl* (1956) by Allen Ginsberg (1926–97), for example, seemingly blurts out all aspects of the author's private life—sexual encounters, drug experiments, episodes of mental illness—in incantatory Whitman-esque catalogs. Jack Kerouac (1922–69) so urgently wanted to capture raw moments of inspiration that he typed on continuous rolls of paper parts of *On the Road* (1957), a *roman à clef* depicting the cross-country joyrides of Beats such as Kerouac, Ginsberg, and the novelist William S. Burroughs (1914–97). Kerouac defined this distinctly American group of artists as "beaten" down by the conformist postwar suburban lifestyle and capable of a certain "beatitude" through altered states induced by drugs, sex, music, and Eastern mysticism.

The Harlem Renaissance   African-American writers left the constraints of the slave narrative as they migrated from the rural South searching for opportunity in the cities of the North. In 1892 Frances Harper's sentimental novel *Iola Leroy* was the best-selling of all African-American women's writings of the 19th century. In 1899 Charles Chesnutt (1858–1932) published *The Conjure Woman* and *The Wife of His Youth and Other Stories of the Color Line*, which neatly bridged antebellum and postbellum American life. In 1903 W. E. B. DuBois (1868–1963) contributed a controversial, landmark book called *The Souls of Black Folk* about life and opportunity for African Americans in the United States. By the 1920's, a community in northern New York City known as Harlem had become a mecca for men and women of color, including musicians and artists, spawning what became known as the Harlem Renaissance of culture and artistic expression.

In the vitality of this environment, a number of talented writers flourished, including Langston Hughes (1902–67), the brave poet of such works as *The Weary Blues* (1926); Nella Larsen (1891–1964), best known for her sobering account of the perils of assimilation in America in the 1929 novel *Passing*, and Zora Neale Hurston (1891–1960). Hurston was raised in all-black Eatonville, Florida, to which she returned to do research, having studied with the anthropologist Franz Boaz, and became a folklorist and novelist. She is best known for *Their Eyes Were Watching God* (1937). Additional stars of the Harlem Renaissance include Claude McKay (1889–1948), the poet Countee Cullen (1903–46), and Jean Toomer (1894–1967).

They all paved the way for such masterly novelists and essayists as Richard Wright (1908–60) and James Baldwin (1924–87), who depicted racial struggles throughout the civil rights era. Like many modern writers, James Baldwin spent time in self-imposed exile, particularly in Paris, and his experiences abroad translated into remarkable perspective in his writings. *The Fire Next Time* (1963) takes stock of American race relations on the 100th anniversary of the Emancipation Proclamation. The collection of essays contains a jeremiad to a nation that might self-destruct if it cannot heal its own racial wounds. Martin Luther King Jr., Malcolm X, Maya Angelou (b. 1928), Alice Walker (b. 1944), and Toni Morrison (b. 1931) flesh out Baldwin's portrait of a nation still very much in need of change.

Mid- to Late-20th Century and Beyond

The responsibilities of technology and the challenges of modernity in a diverse democracy have provided most of the fodder for the postmodern American novel. The coming-of-age narrative or bildungsroman began in Germany but caught fire in the United States, perhaps because the nation had come of age rather violently and quickly in the late 19th and 20th centuries. *The Catcher in the Rye* (1951) by J. D. (Jerome David) Salinger (1919–2010) stands as the quintessential 20th-century American bildungs-roman; but Philip Roth (b. 1933), John Winslow Irving (b. 1942), Bernard Malamud (1914–86), Jamaica Kincaid (b. 1949), Amy Tan (b. 1952), Maxine Hong Kingston (b. 1940), and many others have added to the canon. For scope, range, and sheer talent, it is hard to surpass Nobel Prizewinner Saul Bellow (1915–2005) or Vladimir Nabokov (1899–1977), who was foreign-born but captured America's love affair with youth, Hollywood, sex, and materialism in the scandalous

Lolita (1955). Kurt Vonnegut (b. 1922–2007), Norman Mailer (b. 1923–2007), John Updike (b. 1932–2009), John Cheever (1912–82), Raymond Carver (1938–88), Joyce Carol Oates (b. 1938), Tim O'Brien (b. 1946), T. C. Boyle (b. 1948), Barbara Kingsolver (b. 1955), and Don DeLillo (b. 1936) have all shown tremendous talent and courage describing war, prejudice, gender relations, and other topics of great importance in a wild and varied nation.

Postmodernism   A common characteristic of postmodern fiction and poetry is an awareness of the unreliability of representation. Gone is the realist faith in the capacity of writing to capture external reality, but gone too are the Modernists' earnest efforts to document perception. Though postmodern authors may write in a realist mode or use modernist techniques, they often do so self-consciously. This self-consciousness produces a pastiche of styles; a mixing of genres and registers, including allusions to mass culture; adaptations of earlier modes, as in magic realism's interpolation of fantasy interludes amid everyday life; a fascination with chance and randomness; and self-reflexivity, or art about art, called metafiction in the novel. An example of self-reflexivity in poetry is *Self-Portrait in a Convex Mirror* (1975) by John Ashbery (b. 1927), with its central image of a painter painting a distorted reflection of himself while the poet comments on the composition of the poem. The incommensurability of words with what they represent in a poststructuralist universe evinces world-weary resignation, ironic detachment or even giddiness in postmodern literature. Still, the critique of power structures that followed from poststructuralism has helped open the postmodern canon to women and multiethnic authors.

Multimedia approaches and the continued challenges of war and technology, as well as unprecedented and expanding access to art and literary production with the Internet and online publishing, should ensure that the literary landscape will continue to shift radically in the 21st century.

Popular Literature

Popular literature is simply writing read by a wide audience. More pejoratively, literary critics have sometimes used *popular* to distinguish supposedly formulaic and disposable writing from unique and valuable art. Always appealing to readers and lucrative for the publishing industry, popular literature now commands academic regard among scholars of cultural studies.

The history of popular literature is the story of how large numbers of readers have obtained and consumed texts. Books remained largely out of the reach of most people's skills and means until the 18th century, when in England small paper-covered "chapbooks" usually containing 24 pages of oral-tradition folklore were sold by itinerant peddlers called "chapmen." Also called "penny histories," these little books offered much cheaper diversions than the hardback, multivolume, professionally written novels enjoyed by the middle and upper classes at the time. In the 19th century charity schools and compulsory public education created a mass readership in Europe and the United States. This reading public began to look beyond the family Bible for entertainment, and the market responded with gripping tales produced inexpensively for the cash-strapped lower classes. From around 1830 in the United States, family-friendly "story papers" such as *Tip Top Weekly* and the *Fireside Companion* provided romances for women, adventure tales for men, and stories for children, primarily boys, in an affordable newspaper format enabled by the new steam-powered rotary press.

The dime novel of the late 19th century and the pulp magazine of the early 20th combined the hallmarks of popular literature—expendability, irresistibility, and affordability. Dime novels were billed as "Books for the millions!" by their original publisher, Beadle and Adams, and were imitated by many other publishing houses such as the long-lived Street and Smith. Priced between five and 25 cents, these small, approximately 100-page, paper-covered volumes appeared at regular intervals in numbered sequence. This presentation qualified them for periodical-rate postage, which, together with the new transcontinental railway, kept national distribution costs down and the ever-expanding readership among the poor affordably supplied. Publishers also economized by employing a stable of unrecognized, meagerly compensated authors writing anonymously under house pseudonyms. The American frontier was a favorite setting, and recurring heroes such as Deadwood Dick won readers' loyalty. Around the turn of the 20th century, European publishers jumped on the American dime-novel bandwagon, but the parade slowed during World War I and halted entirely by 1933. While the Great Depression contributed to the dime novel's demise, competition from the new mass media of film and radio played a part, too. Readers of little means turned to pulp magazines, which offered more and bigger pages covered with glossy color illustrations at the same price as dime novels. Subsidized by many advertisers and printed on cheap untrimmed wood-pulp paper, the "pulps" saw their heyday in the 1920's and 30's following publisher Frank A. Munsey's early success with the fiction magazine *Argosy* in the 1890's.

Since 1950 or so, popular literature has often been equated with the common paperback genres of western, horror, romance, mystery, fantasy, and science fiction. This division of the field solidified in the days of pulp magazines, when publishers marketed separate periodicals under clearly defined niche titles such as *Western Story*, *Love Story*, *Detective Story*, and *Astounding Science Fiction*. Paperbacks as we know them today first appeared in the 1930's from Penguin Books in England and Pocket Books in the United States. In the tradition of popular literature, these books were designed for low price rather than long life. Portability also made them popular with soldiers in World War II. Reprints of major works by recognized authors appeared in paperback after more expensive hardback editions; however, the often anonymous writers of so-called paperback originals wrote to order for a familiar hero or series. To draw a mass audience, these strictly softcover novels had dramatic cover illustrations and were sold at drugstores and newsstands rather than in bookstores. Mystery, romance, and science fiction remain most steeped in these traditional practices of popular literature. Sometimes dismissed as formula fiction, novels in these genres indeed tend to follow well-established conventions. Fans and scholars alike find varied and complicated functions beneath this apparent simplicity, however. Some note that the very predictability of these books can offer a reassuring anchor amid personal turmoil or cultural upheaval. Such novels can even help to make social change more acceptable—for example, by adapting familiar plots and settings to new roles for women and ethnic minorities. For readers well versed in a favorite genre, aesthetic pleasure lies in observing writers' innovation within conventional constraints.

Mystery Fiction

Urbanization began in Europe and North America about the same time that a mass readership for popular literature emerged. City living kindled the interest of 18th- and 19th-century readers in the new urban crime-fighting organizations. These included the Bow Street Runners in London, the Sûreté Nationale in Paris, and the Pinkerton private investigation agency, which orginated in Chicago. Bookworms seeking a thrill eagerly consumed police accounts such as *Richmond: Or, Scenes in the Life of a Bow Street Runner* (1827); the *Mémoires* (1828–29) of François Eugène Vidocq (1775–1857), first chief of the Sûreté; and the monthly *Police Gazette* of Allan Pinkerton (1819–94). Early mysteries often drew upon characters and cases from real-life police work. English novelist Wilkie Collins (1824–89) modeled Sergeant Cuff in *The Moonstone* (1868) after Scotland Yard detective Jonathan Whicher, who had solved a similar case. Old Sleuth, hero of a fiction series starting in 1872 in the *Fireside Companion* and continuing in the dime novel *Old Sleuth Weekly*, which lasted until 1918, is thought to have been based on Allan Pinkerton.

The greater anonymity afforded by urban life meant that bringing a criminal to justice sometimes necessitated feats of detection that could make for a good story. More than a strong arm, mental muscle began to characterize the quintessential crime fighter. The famous tales of ratiocination featuring C. Auguste Dupin—a dectective created by Edgar Allan Poe (1809–49)—surpasses that of real police officers like Vidocq, whose inferior powers Dupin belittles in "Murders in the Rue Morgue" (1841). In this story, along with two others featuring Dupin, Poe inaugurated a common pattern in mystery fiction: a slower-witted sidekick narrates for mystified readers how a cerebral amateur detective solves an apparently impossible crime mishandled by the police.

Sherlock Holmes The well-known stories of the eccentric savant Sherlock Holmes and the simpler everyman Dr. Watson, written by Sir Arthur Conan Doyle (1859–1930), certainly fit this pattern. A physician himself, Conan Doyle represented crime detection as a diagnostic science, modeling Holmes after one of his own medical school teachers, Dr. Joseph Bell. The first Holmes story, *A Study in Scarlet*, appeared serially in 1887, and Conan Doyle continued to recount the great detective's cases primarily in magazines. Having written these stories out of financial need, the author grew weary of his creations long before the public's appetite for Holmes and Watson was satisfied. "The Final Problem" (1893) attempted to dispense with Holmes, but he soon came back by popular demand for an eventual total of 60 narratives by Conan Doyle himself, not to mention many by imitators and parodists. Conan Doyle's first short-story collection, *The Adventures of*

Sherlock Holmes, appeared in 1892; his most acclaimed Holmes novel is *The Hound of the Baskervilles* (1902). Other novels featuring Holmes include *The Sign of Four* (1892) and *The Valley of Fear* (1915). To this day, Sherlock Holmes and Dr. Watson live on in the imagination of fans who write letters addressed to the fictional detective's address, 221B Baker Street.

Nick Carter One of America's earliest and most enduring detectives, Nick Carter was a figure of great learning and brilliance—like Sherlock Holmes—as well as a man of action, adventure, and strength in the tradition of popular narrative. He debuted in 1886 in story papers, appeared from 1889 to 1915 in his own dime-novel series, *Nick Carter Detective*, which totaled 800 issues, and survived in pulp magazines, paperback originals, radio shows, and movies as late as the 1970's.

Classic Detective Fiction The classic "whodunit" flowered in the 1920's and 30's—sometimes called the "Golden Age" of mystery novels. In the tradition of Poe and Conan Doyle, Golden Age mysteries narrate the intellectual exercise of determining who committed an improbable murder. During the social and economic upheaval of the decades between the wars, the solution of such puzzles offered rationality and order in fiction. Readers also took comfort in the Golden Age's typically upper-class settings, vicariously partaking of financial ease and social privilege. Clichés like "the butler did it in the library" date from this period, when murder infiltrated the English manor house. The era's fictional sleuths operated as leisured amateurs or even hailed from the aristocracy themselves. The grande dame of classic detective fiction, Agatha Christie (1890–1976), introduced the retired inspector Hercule Poirot in *The Mysterious Affair at Styles* (1920). Another writer in Christie's cohort, Dorothy L. Sayers (1893–1957), brought forth a titled detective, Lord Peter Wimsey, in *Whose Body?* (1923). One legacy of the period is today's "cozy" mystery. Often set in a reassuringly predictable English village, a "cozy" treats murder as an unpleasant aberration that an affable amateur can explain. Christie's sleuth Miss Jane Marple, an elderly spinster-knitter of St. Mary Meade, anticipated this trend. The present-day American anglophile Martha Grimes, who titles her stories after English country pubs, preserves the "cozy" conventions most faithfully.

Some of Christie's and Sayers's contemporaries across the Atlantic cultivated Golden Age sensibilities as well.

Writing as a team under the pen name Ellery Queen, the cousins Frederic Dannay (1905–82) and Manfred B. Lee (1905–71) created a literary empire with their codetectives Ellery Queen and his father, Richard Queen. The erudite Ellery is a writer by trade but spends his time helping Richard, a New York City police inspector, solve crimes. The two men lead a refined home life on Manhattan's upper East Side. Beginning with *The Roman Hat Mystery* (1929), Ellery Queen solved crimes in 40 novels and short-story collections, 10 films, a weekly radio show of nine years' duration, and television series and specials. Dannay also lent the famous name to his influential *Ellery Queen's Mystery Magazine*, which fostered the careers of many now legendary mystery writers during his 40-year editorship. Another American author, Rex Stout (1886–1975), found great success with the reclusive genius Nero Wolfe, whose taste for rare orchids and gourmet food places him in the tradition of great Golden Age detectives with their upper-crust trappings.

Hard-Boiled Detective Fiction America's indigenous mystery genre is "hard-boiled" detective fiction. The adjective *hard-boiled* described World War I drill sergeants before being applied to the similarly tough, unsentimental but righteous postwar detectives (or "dicks") of stateside popular literature. Whereas Golden Age novels offered a fantasy of wealth and charm, hard-boiled fiction painted a picture of gritty mean streets, with a lone-wolf private investigator in the environment of organized crime and police corruption during Prohibition. Cynical about the law, such crime fighters operated by their own codes of honor. Like latter-day knights-errant, they enshrined the little guy against fallible institutions and the Depression-era establishment that kept many people down while insulating those at the top from hardship. The hard-boiled style began in the pulp magazine *Black Mask* with the macho man of action Race Williams, created by Carroll John Daly (1885–1958). Originally publishing adventure stories of all kinds, *Black Mask* eventually specialized in detective fiction and became nearly synonymous with the hard-boiled school, especially under editor Joseph T. "Cap" Shaw (1874–1952) from 1926 to 1936. The fast-paced, violent tales of hard-boiled suspense, as opposed to the genteel, intellectual narratives of Golden-Age puzzle solving, arose from America's pulp-magazine roots. *Black Mask* also published stories by Dashiell Hammett (1894–1961) and Raymond Chandler (1888–1959). Along with

Hammett's Sam Spade and Continental Op, Chandler's Philip Marlowe epitomized the hard-boiled hero's tough softness. "Down these mean streets," Chandler's credo went, "a man must go who is not himself mean, who is neither tarnished nor afraid." Perry Mason, the famous lawyer invented by Erle Stanley Gardner (1889–1970), another *Black Mask* regular, plays by his own rules and defends against injustice like any hard-boiled detective. All three writers set many of their cases in the rough-and-tumble world of Los Angeles and San Francisco.

Variations on the hard-boiled style continued during and after World War II. Mike Hammer, the dectective created by Mickey Spillane (b. 1918–2006) is most directly descended from Daly's Race Williams. Hammer's disdain for women harks back to Williams's machismo, and, as his name would suggest, Hammer retaliates against crime with sometimes extreme violence, eschewing the moral high ground of Chandler's hard-boiled ideal. Often called "noir" fiction, many detective stories of the 1940's and 1950's adopted a darker outlook. The protagonists no longer uphold justice and order but find themselves subject to the crime and chaos that surround them. The present-day writer James Ellroy (b. 1948) keeps the noir mood alive by setting novels of cruelty and corruption in Los Angeles during the 1950's.

Police Procedurals and Crime Novels

There are two mystery subgenres that do not focus on a great detective, action hero, or spy. "Police procedurals" document a whole squad's daily grind in solving a case. The 87th Precinct in Ed McBain's procedurals, for example, has five detectives, plus a lieutenant, desk sergeant, and clerk. Writing under the pen name McBain, the New Yorker Evan Hunter (Salvatore A. Lombino, b. 1926–2005) conducted his research in squad cars and crime labs in order to portray police work as realistically as possible. Another subgenre, the crime novel or "whydunit," explores the psychology of a criminal rather than the solution of a crime. Whereas the detective in a whodunit champions justice in a world of distinct right and wrong, the killer in a whydunit may lead an apparently innocuous life in a murkier world of moral ambiguity. Prominent practitioners of the crime novel include expatriate American Mary Patricia Plangman (1921–95), writing as Patricia Highsmith, and the Belgian-born Georges Simenon (1903–89). One of the most prolific and best-selling novelists of all time, Simenon also wrote classic detective fiction about Inspector Jules Maigret of the Paris Sûreté.

Other examples of mystery fiction put a twist on the classic form by varying the age, gender, race, ethnicity, sexual orientation, occupation, or historical context of the crime solver. The adventures of the famous juvenile detectives Frank and Joe Hardy (the Hardy Boys) and Nancy Drew started in 1927 and 1930 under the pen names Franklin W. Dixon and Carolyn Keene, respectively. The Americans Edward L. Stratemeyer (1862–1930) and his daughter Harriet Stratemeyer Adams (1892–1982), as well as many ghost writers employed by the Stratemeyer Literary Syndicate, composed volumes in these ongoing, perennially popular series. The women's movement of the 1970's opened the door for widely known female sleuths of American authors: Sue Grafton (b. 1940) created Kinsey Millhone; Sara Paretsky (b. 1947) created V[ictoria] I[phigenia] Warshawski; and Patricia Cornwell (b. 1956) created Kay Scarpetta. Even before Conan Doyle created Sherlock Holmes, the American Anna Katherine Green (1846–1935), famous for *The Leavenworth Case* (1878) and other Ebenezer Gryce mysteries, brought us two women crime solvers, Amelia Butterworth (Gryce's assistant) and Violet Strange. The African-American author Chester Himes (1909–84) began writing about two black detectives, "Coffin" Ed Johnson and "Grave Digger" Jones, in the language of his adopted country, France, in 1957. These two Harlem crime fighters appeared in seven additional novels in English. Walter Mosley (b. 1952) found considerable success in the 1990's with his series about an African-American investigator, Ezekiel "Easy" Rawlins set in Mosley's hometown, Los Angeles. The Native American Tony Hillerman (b. 1925–2008) conveys Navajo culture through mysteries involving a tribal police captain, Joe Leaphorn; and his sergeant, Jim Chee. The openly gay Dave Brandstetter, an insurance investigator, is the creation of American Joseph Hansen (b. 1923–2004). A boom in mysteries solved by sleuths with alternative sexualities—such as lesbians Cassandra Reilly and Pam Nielsen, created by American Barbara Wilson (b. 1950)—has followed Hansen's early success. British author Edith Mary Pargeter (1913–95), writing as Ellis Peters, set the sleuthing holy man, Brother Cadfael, in the medieval period. Peters's monastic crime solver follows the venerable British tradition of G.K. (Gilbert Keith) Chesterton (1874–1936), who created Father Brown.

Annual awards honoring achievement in all varieties of mystery fiction began in the 1950's. The Mystery Writers of America appoints a committee of its members to choose the year's best novel, which wins an Edgar Allan Poe

("Edgar") award. The Crime Writers' Association of Great Britain has a panel of external critics determine the winner of its yearly Gold Dagger award. Mystery Writers of America has also recognized lifetime accomplishment in mystery writing by Agatha Christie, Rex Stout, Ellery Queen, Erle Stanley Gardner, Georges Simenon, John le Carré, Ed McBain, Tony Hillerman, and Mickey Spillane with its Grand Master award. The Crime Writers' Association bestows a similar honor, the Diamond Dagger.

Romance Novels

Romance once referred to all genres of popular literature in Europe. In medieval times tales intended for a wide audience were called romances because they were written not in Latin, the lingua franca of the elite, but in regional tongues of the common folk such as French, Spanish, and Italian— the romance languages derived from the Roman tongue. Recounting a knight's feats of valor and devotion to his lady, these stories combined action, adventure, and love. Modern romance novels focus more exclusively on a love relationship and often have a female protagonist. This trend evolved during the 17th and 18th centuries as women readers became more common and women writers more popular. Early chroniclers of love such as the Frenchwoman Madeleine de Scudéry (1607–1701) and the English-woman Aphra Behn (1640–89), who fictionalized the sex scandals of their rich and famous contemporaries, were among the first female professional writers. England's Mary de la Rivière Manley (1663–1724) and Eliza Haywood (1693–1756) wrote cautionary tales for the feminine reading public about virgins seduced and abandoned by wealthy and powerful men. Susanna Rowson Haswell (1762–1824) wrote *Charlotte Temple* (1791), a sentimental tale of seduction and betrayal that was an early publishing sensation. It saw nearly 200 editions in America after the author emigrated from England.

Narratives of the 19th and 20th centuries, written by or for women, elaborated on the romantic theme and female focus. A typical plot emerged when the Englishman Samuel Richardson (1689–1761) wrote *Pamela: Or, Virtue Rewarded* (1740), in which a vulnerable but spunky heroine reforms a worldly man and they marry. Set in the authors' native England, these novels also provide templates for the gothic and regency settings of today's historical romance fiction. Eleanor Hibbert (1906–93), writing as Victoria Holt, summoned up the gothic's eerie castles and supernatural events from *Jane Eyre* and its popular precursor *The Mysteries of Udolpho* (1794), written by another Englishwoman, Ann Radcliffe (1764–1823). The novels of the British writer Georgette Heyer (1902–74) recall Austen's genteel English countryside in the 1810's, during the regency of the Prince of Wales, later George IV.

A heroine's romantic adventures ending in marriage became the stock-in-trade for much popular literature of the 19th and 20th centuries. Some of this literature was devoted exclusively to affairs of the heart, such as the longest-running Bertha Clay Library and New Bertha M. Clay Library (1900–32), whose titles refer to a pen name under which different authors wrote. Pulp magazine romances began with Street and Smith's *Love Story* in 1921. Harlequin Enterprises, a Toronto-based publishing company, became synonymous with the mass market romance paperback sold in groceries and drugstores. This publishing house specialized exclusively in romance titles starting in 1964. With the purchase of Simon & Schuster's romance line, Silhouette, in 1985, Harlequin became the only major publisher of traditional series romances. Other numbered series, such as Bantam's "Loveswept" line, market the works of individual authors.

Though the basic formula remains the same, the romance genre has diversified with changing times. The American Kathleen Woodiwiss's *Flame and the Flower* (1972) introduced explicit sex between the virginal heroine and the older love interest. The force of sexual encounters in "bodice-rippers" attracted criticism for normalizing violence against women and implying that women find rape arousing. By the 1980's, cover art reflected the industry's response. Bare-chested muscle-bound men replaced fainting heroines' ripped bodices, and sex scenes became somewhat more consensual. The age gap between partners also closed. Contemporary romances such as those by the American author Nora Roberts, who has placed 69 titles on the *New York Times* best-seller list, often feature older, sexually experienced career women.

Romance fiction dominates popular literature in English today. Defining its genre as novels with a central love story and an emotionally satisfying, optimistic ending, Romance Writers of America (R.W.A.) counts more than 50 million regular readers in North America alone. In 2009, according to the R.W.A., romance fiction sales hit $1.36 billion, and in 2010 romance fiction was ranked number two in overall e-book sales.

Science Fiction and Fantasy

Fantasy became a distinct genre in the 18th century. Rather than depicting people and events as they appear, fantasy invents enchanted locales inhabited by witches, wizards, ghosts, werewolves, vampires, and demons. It includes everything from the work of J. R. R. Tolkien (1892–1973), who created a mythology for his ancestral England, to the horrifying or "dark" fantasy of the American Stephen King (b. 1947).

Science fiction emerged after the scientific revolution. It leads into possible futures or along alternate time streams and features spaceships, ray guns, teleportation, robots, androids, cyborgs, and aliens. Though science fiction's wonders generally do not exist, its writers extrapolate empirical understandings of the physical, biological, or social environment. For example, many scholars credit the Englishwoman Mary Shelley (1797–1851) with writing the first science fiction novel in 1818, when she told the story of Dr. Victor Frankenstein's creation of a monster in a laboratory. Victor's experiments extend 18th-century theories of electricity as the life force, so reanimating a corpse through "galvanism" would have seemed plausible to Shelley's readers. The inventions of fantasy, by contrast, are logically impossible.

As the Industrial Revolution brought technology into the daily lives of millions, science fiction came to dominate speculative literature. Steam-powered factories and railroads transformed the agrarian societies of Europe and the United States so quickly that the present seemed strange and the future likely to become more so. As novelists tried to imagine what lay ahead, some believed technology would be a positive force while others had doubts. France's Jules Verne (1828–1905) started by equipping benign heroes with exciting futuristic machines, beginning with *Five Weeks in a Balloon* (1863), the first of what he called his "scientific-didactic" novels. The misanthropic Captain Nemo in *Twenty Thousand Leagues under the Sea* (1870), however, qualifies Verne's earlier vision of benevolent science. By contrast, his optimistic countryman Edward Bellamy (1850–98) imagined a utopia free from class privilege or sexism in his best seller of 1888, *Looking Backward, 2000–1887*. Bellamy anticipated telephones, television, automobiles, and automated industry transforming society for the better. England's H. G. Wells (1866–1946) responded to him with characteristic gloom in *When the Sleeper Wakes* (1899). Wells projected a future of ever more destructive weapons, a theme also evident in *War of the Worlds* (1898), *The War in the Air* (1908),

and most horrifyingly in *The World Set Free* (1914), which envisions the weaponization of nuclear energy. Even the first of Wells's "scientific romances," as he called them, *The Time Machine* (1895), warned of our planet's ultimate demise.

Both science fiction and fantasy blossomed into popular genres through magazines. In his periodical *Science and Invention*, Hugo Gernsback (1884–1967) included stories involving made-up inventions that he called "scientifiction." Gernsback went on to publish a pulp magazine, *Amazing Stories*, devoted entirely to "science fiction." Gernsback's foundational role is recognized each year with the Hugo Award for best science fiction, still the most prestigious prize, along with the Nebula award, given by the Science Fiction and Fantasy Writers of America. Even before Gernsback's *Amazing Stories* began in 1926, the American author Edgar Rice Burroughs (1875–1950) had been writing about life on Mars, on Venus, and at the center of the Earth for *All-Story, Argosy*, and other general-interest pulps.

"Space opera," a successful formula, pitted good against evil in epic struggles on intergalactic frontiers of human expansion. The American E. E. "Doc" Smith (1890–1965) cultivated a devoted readership for these thrilling action adventures. One of Smith's fans, American John W. Campbell Jr. (1910–71), went on to foster "golden age" of science fiction through *Astounding Stories*, which came under his editorship in 1938. The American authors Robert Heinlein (1907–88); Theodore Sturgeon (1918– 85); Isaac Asimov (1920–93), who was born in Russia; A. E. van Vogt (1912–2000), who migrated from Canada; and many others rallied to Campbell's editorial vision. Campbell's "hard" approach to science fiction insisted on scientific plausibility, and he encouraged philosophical speculation about the human interface with technology. Destined for fame as the author of *2001: A Space Odyssey* (1968), the English-born Arthur C. Clarke (b. 1917–2008) got his start in *Astouding Stories* under Campbell as well. Campbell also raised the profile of fantasy through another pulp, *Unknown*. Only *Weird Tales*, the primary outlet for the legendary fantasist H. P. Lovecraft (1890–1937), exceeds *Unknown* in significance. A number of fantasy writers elaborated on Lovecraft's Cthulhu mythos, a system of gods and demons based in his native New England.

The mushroom clouds that ended World War II fundamentally changed science fiction and fantasy. Writers began to look to the technological future more soberly, and readers wanted to escape into fantastic alternative worlds. Splitting the atom for a superweapon had been a common fictional topic until life and art converged with horrifying results in Hiroshima and Nagasaki. Naive faith in technological progress, or in humankind for that matter, no longer seemed tenable. Pessimism peaked in the 1960's in the British science fiction magazine *New Worlds* under the editorship of Michael Moorcock (b. 1939). His New Wave science fiction abandoned the traditional adventure format to experiment with literary style. Instead of sending a hero into outer space to fight evil and expand civilization, New Wave stories explore the inner space of individuals caught in oppressive societies. Two important New Wave authors are the Englishmen Brian Aldiss (b. 1926) and J. G. Ballard (b. 1930–2009).

The postwar period brought other reactions against the pulp fiction typified by *Amazing* and *Astounding* magazines, the latter of which became *Analog* in 1960. *Galaxy* rose to prominence in the 1950's with a "soft," often satiric turn away from the pulps' swashbuckling technophilia. *The Magazine of Fantasy and Science Fiction* emphasized literary quality, and Isaac Asimov's *Science Fiction Magazine* prized innovation. By appearing in the new digest format and including both science fiction and fantasy, these two publications survived the capture of the popular literature market by paperbacks, which brought the two genres to a new generation. The paperback juggernaut also kept up-and-coming authors such as the Californian Philip K. Dick (1928–82) writing furiously. Often set in a dystopian future California, Dick's novels inspired the "cyberpunk" writers of the 1980's, who combined computers, information theory, and biotechnology with a countercultural edge. The American William Gibson (b. 1948) has provided the prime example with his first novel of cyberspace, *Neuromancer* (1984).

After the age of space exploration and the Internet, science fiction is crossing over into the mainstream and converging with fantasy. Today's realism can look a lot like yesterday's science fiction, and hard scientific speculation no longer defines the genre as it blurs into fantasy. The American Ray Bradbury (b. 1920) has ceased to be regarded as a niche author, for example, even though his most famous novel, *Fahrenheit 451* (1953), first appeared in the science fiction magazine *Galaxy* and he wrote extensively for the fantasy pulp *Weird Tales*. The American Ursula K. LeGuin (b. 1929) has a similar reputation as a literary artist who happens to write science fiction and fantasy. The third in her young-adult *Earthsea* trilogy even won the National Book Award. Crossing over into the mainstream is a sign of the increasing respectability and widening appeal of these two popular genres.

Glossary of Literary Terms

Note: *When discussions of poetic meter arise, universal symbols are used: "–" for a stressed syllable, "◡" for an unstressed syllable.*

acrostic poem in which the initial letters of each line form a word when read downward. When composed in prose, the first letters of each paragraph spell a word.

> *Shining down on our faces*
> *Under the bright blue sky we sit*
> *Nightfall ends its warm embrace*

allegory story in which persons or places represent abstract, often moral, concepts. John Bunyan's *The Pilgrim's Progress*, in which Christian, on his journey to the Celestial City, must pass through such locations as the Slough of Despond and meet such characters as the Giant Despair, is a famous English Christian allegory. One may enjoy an allegorical work of verse or prose for its literal story or for the lesson it implies.

alliteration repetition of one consonant sound at the beginning of words or of stressed syllables.

> *Sally sells seashells at the seashore.*

allusion appeal to the knowledge shared by the author and reader, usually an implicit reference to a preexisting work of literature or, a art, a person, or a historical event.

anamnesis "recalling to mind" (Greek); in a work of literature, a look back to events or people from a previous existence. See also *flashback*.

anapest in poetry, a metrical foot consisting of two unstressed syllables followed by one stressed syllable, giving a sense of galloping or steady motion.

> ◡ ◡ – ◡ ◡ – ◡ ◡ – ◡ ◡ –
>
> *With a leap and a bound the swift Anapests throng.*
> —Samuel Taylor Coleridge, "Metrical Feet"

antagonist in drama or fiction, the character who opposes the main character (protagonist).

antihero character who does not possess the typical traits of a literary hero. An antihero tends to be stupid, clumsy, or unlucky—one for whom heroic deeds seem impossible.

apostrophe technique in which a speaker addresses a

dead, absent, or inanimate subject as if it were present or able to understand.

> *Death, be not proud, though some have call'd thee*
> *Mighty and dreadful, for thou art not so...*
> —John Donne

assonance repetition of the same or similar vowel sounds.

> *She eats each peach with speed.*

bildungsroman "formation novel" (German); a novel that chronicles the development of a hero or heroine from youth to maturity.

blank verse poetic form consisting of unrhymed iambic pentameter lines.

bowdlerize to delete words or passages of a work considered obscene, improper, or unfit for children; named for Thomas Bowdler, who performed this operation on an 1818 edition of Shakespeare.

burlesque most general term for a literary work that uses comic imitation to ridicule persons or events or another literary work. A burlesque of a literary work can be a parody, which applies a serious literary style to a trivial subject; or a travesty, which treats a serious subject in low terms. A burlesque of a person can be a caricature or, if extended, a lampoon.

caesura pause or break within a line of poetry indicated by either punctuation or a natural pause in the syntax. In an analysis of poetic lines, it is indicated by two slashes (//).

> *Of foot and heart, // and did invite*
> *Me to its game.// 'Its seemed to bless*
> *Itself in me;*
> —Marvell, "The Nymph Complaining
> for the Death of her Fawn"

catharsis according to Aristotle in his *Poetics*, the effect that a Greek tragedy has on its audience of purging or relieving the emotions of fear and pity that the play arouses. The term has also been applied to the experience of the tragic hero. At the end of Sophocles's *Oedipus Rex*, for example, Oedipus gouges out his own eyes to purge himself of his sins.

comedy primarily associated with drama, this form originated in Greek antiquity as a means of celebrating fertility and the god Dionysus. Aristotle wrote in his *Poetics* that comedy was the opposite of tragedy in that it deals with everyday life in a humorous way. Frequently comedies start with misfortune and end with pleasure, whereas classical tragedies open with kings or heroes living in a lofty state and end with their misfortune. Forms of comedy include comedy of errors, comedy of manners, romantic comedy, and black comedy.

connotation implied or suggested meaning of a word as opposed to its literal meaning (denotation).

consonance close repetition of consonant sounds.

> *Deep with the first dead lies London's daughter*
> —Dylan Thomas

couplet in poetry, two successive rhyming lines.

> *But if thou live rememb'red not to be,*
> *Die single, and thine image dies with thee.*
> —Shakespeare, sonnet no. 3

dactyl in poetry, a metrical foot consisting of one stressed syllable followed by two unstressed syllables.

$$\_\ \smile\ \smile\ \_\ \smile\ \smile\ \_\ \smile\ \smile\ \_\ \smile\ \smile$$

> *Ever to come up with Dactyl's trisyllable.*
> —Samuel Taylor Coleridge, "Metrical Feet"

denotation most literal meaning of a word.

dénouement unraveling of a plot's complications after the climax of a story.

deus ex machina "god out of a machine" (Latin); originally, the resolution of a plot in Greek tragedy by the intervention a god lowered to the stage on a machine; by extension, the resolution of a conflict or difficult situation, in literature or elsewhere, by any unexpected or contrived device or event (for example, a violent storm). The term is often used pejoratively.

dramatic irony theatrical technique whereby the audience knows something that one or more characters in a play are unaware of, causing anticipation for the moment of revelation. For example, in Shakespeare's comedy *Twelfth Night*, Olivia, a rich countess, falls in love with Cesario, who is actually a woman named Viola disguised as a man.

dramatic unities in classical theory, the requirements for a properly constructed play, particularly a tragedy. Aristotle, in the *Poetics*, insisted upon "unity of action": a plot that is well-ordered, excludes extraneous events, and is focused on the protagonist. Seventeenth-century French neoclassicists, feeling that a play should not strain the limitations of the stage, added that it should possess unity of place (unfolding in one location) and unity of time (taking place within one day).

elegy poem that laments the death of an individual or other sad event.

enjambment one line of poetry running into another, unseparated by end punctuation.

> *Let my left remember, and your right close*
> *And your mouth open near the gate.*
> —Amichai, "If I Forget Thee, Jerusalem"

epic long narrative poem telling the story of heroic characters and often representing critical events in the history of a race or nation. Homer's *Iliad* and *Odyssey* and John Milton's *Paradise Lost* are among the greatest epics.

epigram any terse statement or, in poetry, a brief, usually rhymed, often two-lined, witty observation.

> *Know then thyself, presume not God to scan;*
> *The proper study of mankind is Man.*
> —Pope, *An Essay on Man*

epigraph quotation preceding a literary work or part of a work, indicating a theme for what is to follow and sometimes providing a title.

epiphany term, notably applied in literature to the stories in James Joyce's *Dubliners*, that indicates a sudden realization or revelation taking place in a character, usually at a story's end.

fable story, often satirical or pointed toward a moral, in which animals have human characteristics. Examples are tales by Aesop and La Fontaine and George Orwell's *Animal Farm*.

farce comic drama that relies heavily on "low" comedy. A farce can contain slapstick (physical) comedy, buffoonery, absurd events and situations, and exaggerated characters and personalities. Whereas a classic comedy aims toward a happy ending, a farce primarily seeks to make its audience laugh.

figurative language nonliteral language, also called "figures of speech," used to express meaning or insight. In figurative language, something or someone is often presented as or compared to something that in literal terms is quite different. For specific kinds of figures of speech, see *metaphor, metonymy, simile,* and *synechdoche.*

figure of speech See *figurative language.*

flashback literary device common in modern fiction and drama that uses events from an earlier time to provide additional information about current characters or events.

foot in poetry, a group of syllables forming a metrical unit. Poems traditionally have been written in lines with a spe-cific number of feet in a specific meter. Thus a poem written in iambic pentameter would consist of lines of five feet in iambic meter, that is, five feet containing two syllables, the first stressed and the second unstressed. A four-foot line would be tetrameter; a six-foot line would be hexameter, and so on. When illustrated for the reader, metrical feet are divided by a slash (/).

foreshadowing presentation of clues in a narrative to indicate later events.

free verse in poetry, a form with no regular line length or meter, intended to imitate the rhythms of natural speech.

hamartia ancient Greek term for the tragic flaw in the protagonist of a tragedy, as described by Aristotle. Hamartia is the cause of the hero's downfall. In Greek tragedy, this flaw was often hubris, or pride that leads a character to disregard the superiority or moral authority of a god or gods.

hubris in Greek tragedy, the characteristic of the hero which causes him to ignore warnings by the gods or oppose their commands.

hyperbole extreme exaggeration for rhetorical effect.

> *I told you a million times that I would not be*
> *home on Saturday.*

iamb in poetry, a metrical foot containing an unstressed syllable followed by a stressed syllable. One of the most commonly used metrical patterns, iambs most closely imitate the normal speech pattern of English.

> ˘ _ ˘ _ ˘ _ ˘ _
> *Iambics march from short to long.*
> —Coleridge, "Metrical Feet"

imagery appeal to any of the five senses to create a mental impression for the reader.

irony literary mode, tone, or attitude of which there are many variations, but which fundamentally involves parallel or opposite ways of seeing or knowing that in some way oppose each other. Irony may involve events of which the result is the opposite of what is anticipated, a character's saying one thing but meaning another, or a character's unawareness of a certain situation or fact critical to his or her well-being. Irony may be comic or cosmic, as when the gods control events with intentions that are contrary to those of hopelessly striving characters.

melodrama play in which absolutely good and evil characters are opposed, and in which the evil characters usually threaten the well-being of the good, but, in the end, good survives or triumphs and evil is defeated or punished.

metaphor comparison of two unlike objects or ideas in which the writer states that one is the other.

> *My eyes are flowers for your tomb*
> —Thomas Merton

meter in poetry, the pattern of unstressed and stressed syllables. See *iamb*, *trochee*, *dactyl*, *anapest*, and *spondee*. Lines in a given poem often have a regular number of metrical units, or feet. See *foot*.

metonymy figure of speech in which something represents an entity or person with which it is typically associated.

> *The White House says it will not tolerate such behavior.*

monologue single person speaking alone, especially on stage or in a poem. In a dramatic monologue, such as one written by the Victorian poet Robert Browning, an implied listener is present but silent. See also *soliloquy*.

novel extended (generally, more than 100 pages) work of prose fiction, usually, in distinction from the older romance form, realistic in setting. A novel may have one or more plots, may narrate current or historical events, and almost always contains dialogue between characters. Cervantes's *Don Quixote*, published in early 17th-century Spain, is often considered the first novel. In English, the earliest novels were written in the 18th century.

novella work of prose fiction, longer than a short story but shorter than a novel, and thus often between 50 and 100 pages long. Examples are several works by Joseph Conrad, including *The Heart of Darkness* and *The Secret Sharer*. These are also called short novels or novelettes.

ode long lyric poem, grand in tone and typically marking a ceremonious occasion.

onomatopoeia word used to represent a sound.

> *boom; buzz; plop; woof*

oxymoron combination, for effect, of two inherently contradictory words.

> *Darkness visible*
> —Milton, *Paradise Lost*
> *It was the best of times, it was the worst of times.*
> —Dickens, *A Tale of Two Cities*

parody imitation of a specific work, style, or idea, in which certain characteristics are exaggerated to call attention to the ridiculous nature of what is imitated. See *burlesque*.

pastoral poem literally about shepherds or, more generally, about rural life. It may be lyrical, elegiac, narrative, satir-ical, or dramatic. Spenser's *Shepherd's Calendar* and Milton's *Lycidas* are examples.

pentameter line of poetry containing five metrical units, or feet. See *foot* and *meter*.

personification literary device in which human qualities are attributed to an inanimate object.

> *In the faint moonlight, the grass is singing*
> —Eliot, *The Waste Land*

picaresque term describing a usually satirical story or novel focusing on a rogue (*picaro*) who may serve many masters and often experiences many adventures.

plot sequence of events in a work of fiction, a drama, or a narrative poem.

prose written or spoken language with no restrictions imposed (as in poetry) by rhyme, meter, or length and structure of lines.

roman à clef "key novel" (French), a novel in which the characters portray real people. In some cases, a key to the characters has been published with the book to provide the reader with the true identities of the characters.

romance literary form containing characters who seem removed from the real world by fantasy or improbability. The romance was originally a medieval European literary form narrating, in verse or prose, the adventures of knights and kings, often involving a religious quest and including a love theme. The term is also applied to historical novels such as those of Walter Scott or other unrealistic novels of adventure or love.

saga heroic prose or verse narrative, originally appearing in Norse and Icelandic medieval literature, telling of historical or legendary events, the reigns of kings, or the life of a family.

satire work of literature that pokes fun at an institution or idea. A satire is intended to be critical and humorous, and may also seek to reform what it attacks by forcing those associated with it to see its ridiculous qualities. For example, Horace Miner's satirical article "Body Ritual among the Nacirema" illustrates how the "Nacirema" ("American" spelled backward) pay particular attention to how they look and insist upon ridiculous rituals to make their bodies look better.

setting where and when a story takes place.

simile figure of speech comparing two unlike objects or ideas, generally employing the words *like* or *as*.

> *Helen, thy beauty is to me*

> *Like those Nicae barks of yore*
> —Edgar Allan Poe, "To Helen"

soliloquy in theater, a speech delivered by a character, alone on stage, often expressing his or her deepest thoughts and feelings. The most famous soliloquy is Hamlet's "To be or not to be . . ."— a speech in which he reveals his internal struggle as he contemplates suicide.

sonnet 14-line lyric, rhymed poem, usually in iambic pentameter. The form originated in 13th-century Sicily and was made famous and internationally influential by the Tuscan Petrarch in the 14th century. Although sonnets continue to be written in various rhyme schemes, these poems have traditionally had rhyme patterns called Petrarchan or Italian (divided into an octave rhymed *abbaabba* and a sestet rhymed *cdecde*) and Shakespearean or English (comprising three quatrains and a couplet: *abab cdcd efef gg*). The English sonnet was actually introduced in the 16th century by Henry Howard, earl of Surrey, who, like Petrarch in Italy and several other 16th-century English poets—Wyatt, Sidney, Spenser, and Shakespeare—wrote a sequence of love sonnets.

spondee in poetry, a metrical foot consisting of two consecutive stressed syllables.

> *From long to long in solemn sort*
> *Slow Spondee stalks, strong foot!*
> —Coleridge, "Metrical Feet"

Spondaic feet are used less frequently than the others in poetry and, when used, bring a certain emphasis. These two lines from Coleridge's poem are written in iambs until the last metrical foot.

symbolism literary technique in which an object is used to represent one or more ideas or concepts.

synecdoche representation of the whole of an object using only a part of the object.

> *All hands on deck!*

Here the hands, being the most important parts of bodies being summoned to labor, represent the men.

tone the attitude—comic, somber, ironic—that an author or character expresses.

tragedy first defined by Aristotle in his *Poetics* as a drama that imitates serious and great events, in which a tragic flaw (hamartia) leads to a hero's downfall, and in which the events arouse fear and pity in the audience, followed by a purgation (catharsis) of these emotions. These characteristics remained applicable, but only partly so, as tragedy developed in later cultures, such as Elizabethan and Jacobean England—the time of Shakespeare. The tragedies of that period might include comic elements, and in them the causes of catastrophe are not as sharply defined. Still later, in the 19th century, tragedies would focus on middle-class rather than aristocratic characters, and would not necessarily end with the death of a hero. Tragedy can now be defined as a drama that starts with fortune and happiness and ends with misfortune and displeasure.

tragic flaw See *hamartia*.

tragicomedy play in which gravely serious and lighter elements or scenes are combined, particularly one in which, as in Shakespeare's *Merchant of Venice*, the plot poses danger to the main character but turns toward a happy ending.

trochee (pronounced tro-kee) in poetry, a metrical foot consisting of a stressed syllable followed by an unstressed syllable.

> _ ˘ _ ˘ _ ˘ _
> *Trochee trips from long to short*
> —Coleridge, "Metrical Feet"

vernacular native language. In literature, vernacular refers to works, particularly in medieval times, that were written in the local language or dialect rather than in Greek or Latin.

verse term used to describe the forms and patterns of poetic language, involving any number of specifications of meter, rhyme, and length, and arrangement of lines.

zeugma "yoking" (Greek); literary device in which one word (such as an adjective or a verb) is applied grammatically to two others (such as two nouns).

> *Dost sometimes counsel take—and sometimes tea.*
> —Pope, *The Rape of the Lock*

Zeugma tends to show comic or ironic variation. In the example above, the character is equally businesslike when he takes counsel and relaxed when he takes tea.

Literary Criticism

The Classical Tradition in Literary Criticism and Theory

The Greek philosophers Plato (c. 427–347 B.C.) and Aristotle (384–322 B.C.) framed debates over the nature of language and the uses of literature that dominated literary theory for over two thousand years and that still preoccupy many commentators today. Plato believed that changeable material things imitate unchanging ideal models of these things, which he called "Ideas" or "Forms." Words, fleetingly spoken or written, belong to the material world, and, because they represent other material things, Plato concluded that language is twice removed from the true nature of existence and literary art can thereby deceive its audience. In Plato's utopian society, the Republic, philosophers who seek to understand the Ideas beyond veils of language and material existence would reign, while poets would be banished or drastically demoted from their cultural prominence at the time. Aristotle rated literature more highly. He countered that because a tragedy, for example, strips away the incidentals of an event to make its story timeless, literary art brings its audience closer to universal truths than do the everyday things that words copy.

Both philosophers were influenced by rhetoric, the study of audience that largely comprised literary learning in classical times and later. The Latin poet Horace (65–8 B.C.), for example, coined the watchword of writers through the European Renaissance, namely, that literature should both "teach and delight" its readers. Centuries later, the classical tradition continued in England with Sir Philip Sidney's (1554–86) defense of poetry against Puritan objections to make-believe. Drawing on both Aristotle and Horace, Sidney argued that poetry delights its readers while also teaching principles of right action. Englishman Matthew Arnold (1822–88) similarly pleaded for the salutary power of great literature, measured against what he called "touchstones" such as Dante and Shakespeare, in a rudderless modern age. Following Arnold and his predecessors back to Aristotle, conservative cultural warriors place their faith in the Western canon to teach universal truths and standards that they fear will be lost to student-readers of multicultural, gender-equitable, and popular-culture curricula.

Structuralism

Structuralism transformed not only literary study but also many other fields, including history, anthropology, political science, and psychology. Scholars now often assume that we relate to the world through language and other symbolic systems that operate as languages do. Increasingly interdisciplinary, students of the new human sciences analyze how human beings "construct" their world out of words and images. The resulting structures have become a common object of study.

The structuralist revolution began with the Swiss linguist Ferdinand de Saussure (1857–1913). Earlier linguists had studied how single elements in different languages evolve diachronically, or through time, from a hypothetical common origin. This approach accorded with the assumption, over two thousand years old, that words derive their meaning from a pre-existing ideal or divine order. Saussure believed instead that each language creates its own order and we understand what words mean only as a result of their relationships with other elements in a certain language system. Thus, he emphasized how any language conveys meanings synchronically or within a single period of time. The whole system, or *langue*, became his focus rather than any particular utterance, or *parole*. Saussure's description of the sign broke with the past most radically. Spoken or written words, or signifiers, plus what they mean, their signifieds, are one kind of sign. Signifier and signified, Saussure believed, have only a conventional and arbitrary connection, so, for example, English speakers connect the signifier cat to its signified—the four-legged creature—more because they are in the habit of doing so than because this word has roots in any original language. Binary opposition, the contrast between two linguistic elements, is the fundamental relationship that produces meaning.

Subsequent thinkers used Saussurean linguistics as a model for understanding all the ways in which human activity conveys meanings. Following Belgian-born Claude Lévi-Strauss (1908–2009), structural anthropologists see cultures as systems of signs by which their members communicate such information as political authority, sexual availability, or spiritual attainment. These scholars decode meanings expressed in signs such as dress, ritual, or myth by identifying key binary oppositions. Lévi-Strauss also sought to understand the master code on which all cultures are modelled. The famous phrase titling one of his books, *The Raw and the Cooked*

(1964, tr. 1969), denotes a binary opposition he saw underpinning the myths of many cultures. Like Lévi-Strauss, structuralist literary critics had grand aims of breaking master codes such as the structure of narrative itself. First and most famously, the Frenchman Roland Barthes (1915–80) applied structuralism to the novel in *S/Z* (1970, tr. 1974), whose title refers to a phonetic binary opposition. Barthes also turned structuralist analysis onto elements of his own culture beyond the realm of literature such as wrestling matches and advertisements. Because structuralists see all human activity as systems of signs that operate like languages, nonlinguistic phenomena constitute "texts" whose cultural meanings are available for decoding. Like Barthes, who later became involved in poststructuralism, literary critics today rarely identify themselves as structuralists. Nevertheless, structuralism's lines of influence are still directly evident in folklore, narrative theory, stylistics (the linguistic study of literary effects), and semiotics. A comprehensive term for the study of signs first popularized by the philosopher Charles Sanders Peirce (1839-1914), an American contemporary of Saussure, semiotics now includes the structuralist study of symbolic systems.

Formalism

"Formalist" describes any kind of literary criticism that focuses on the instrinsic features of a poem, play, or novel such as prosody, plot, image patterns, and word choice. Formalist criticism eschews extrinsic matters such as an author's biography, the work's sociohistorical context, or an individual reader's reaction. The dominant critical movements of the first half of the 20th century were formalist, and the most broadly influential of these was called New Criticism. An Anglo-American group of writers and scholars acquired this name when the Southerner John Crowe Ransom (1888–1974) titled his 1941 study of the critical writings of modernist poet T.S. Eliot (1888–1965) and others *The New Criticism*. Ransom's "new" critics were reacting against the "old" critics of the nineteenth century who read works of literature as expressions of authors' unique emotions, imagination, and life events. Adherents to the New Critical school insisted instead on the autonomy of literary works. Seeking a quasi-scientific objectivity for the interpretation of literature, New Critics believed that the words of a poem, for example, and their arrangement, alone, conveyed its meaning.

Deconstruction

Deconstruction has entered the vocabularies of most academic fields, as well as art, media, and design. In practice, deconstructive critics attend to multiple meanings and paradoxes in written texts and other cultural products, often to dissect their value systems. Deconstruction got its name in the 1960s when Algerian-born Jacques Derrida (1930–2004) first read philosophy as if, like literature, it were subject to various interpretations. Derrida challenged three elements of structuralism's then-current theory of how we make meaning. First, contrary to Ferdinand de Saussure's signifiers, which come firmly attached to signifieds, a signifier according to Derrida moves freely, never conveying exactly the same idea in different circumstances. Second, the binary oppositions structuring sign systems tend to assume hierarchized values. For example, we often comprehend what is human by opposing the term to animal. In so doing, we make humans primary and universal and animals secondary, marginal forms of animate being. Third, the hierarchical distinctions in binary oppositions tend to contradict themselves. Contrary to our example, we also consider animals enough like us that we test them in order to understand ourselves. On some level, paradoxically, we think of animals as primary and universal, while humans are secondary, a particular type of animal. Deconstruction does not aim to reverse binary oppositions nor make them more consistent. Rather, reading for multiple meanings and paradoxes sensitizes us to the necessary fluidity of meaning and value.

Structuralists' failure to recognize deconstruction's "freeplay" of signifiers followed from Western culture's understanding of language, which Derrida called logocentrism. For over two thousand years, sages had assumed that meaning derives from an ideal or divine order and therefore that words have inherent meanings. Even Saussure described language as a system apart from particular utterances. Derrida, however, insisted that there is no language apart from what we actually say or write, so there is not even an ideal linguistic order guaranteeing the meanings behind our words. Saussure had become locked in a binary opposition that Derrida found among many thinkers. They all believed that speech represents the primary, universal state of language while writing is secondary and marginal. This perception allowed them to assume correspondences between words and meanings that accord with an ideal order. Spoken words and concepts seem to combine effortlessly for speakers and listeners alike; written words, by contrast, are separated in space and time from the hand and mind that wrote them, sometimes rendering even the writer unable to discern later what was meant. A reader, too, must self-consciously piece together a meaning without those often subconscious contextual cues that seem to make the meanings of spoken words self-evident. By attributing such gaps and uncertainties to writing, and making it subordinate to speech, Western philosophers have ignored the similarities between writing and speech. Signs in both modes depend on many variables in order to make sense. This similarity deconstructs the binary opposition between speech and writing. Putting writing on top, for the moment, as a way to understand how language works, Derrida perceived meanings as changeable and hierarchies unstable among signs of any form.

Deconstructive criticism caught fire in the 1970's and smolders still in much contemporary interpretive work. Because Derrida's theories involved tropes, deconstruction appealed to students of literature. Deconstructive critics tend to do with literary texts what Derrida did with other philosophers' writings. They read closely to discover textual impasses, called *aporia*, where multiple meanings and paradoxes destabilize binary oppositions. Eventually, practitioners tired of confirming Derrida's point that language is slippery. The hotbed of deconstructionist criticism, Yale University's English and comparative literature departments, lost credibility in 1987 when evidence surfaced that former professor Paul de Man (1919–1983) was a Nazi sympathizer in wartime Belgium. This moral scandal fueled charges that deconstruction's indeterminacy of meaning can unhinge language and the world it constructs from enduring values. Nevertheless, deconstructive theory opened the way for most contemporary critical trends.

Poststructuralism

The response to structuralism that began with deconstruction in the 1960's led to a new critical orientation called poststructuralism. Like their theoretical forebears, poststructuralists assume that human languages and cultures construct people's worlds. Believing that the conditions of our lives are not naturally occurring or divinely ordained, poststructuralists study cultural products of all kinds to see what assumptions these texts carry and what

psychic and social ends they may serve. Poststructuralism partakes of structuralism's theoretical innovations but challenges the detached, objective pose of its practitioners.

Ever wary, after deconstruction, that signifiers' meanings change, poststructuralists specify their own context, eschewing definitive interpretations. Because criticism itself contributes to the signifying structures that shape people's lives, poststructuralists also consider the ethics of what they choose to study and how they choose to write about it. Poststructuralist modes within contemporary criticism focus on the reader, the psychology of author and reader, texts' sociohistorical contexts, and the dynamics of class, race, gender, and sexuality.

Feminist Criticism, Gender Studies, and Queer Theory

Feminist critics analyze the ways in which literature and literary institutions reinforce patriarchy, the system that grants men control in public and private affairs. Feminist critics aim to undermine male dominance by recognizing women authors and female ways of writing and reading. This critical orientation coincides with the postwar resurgence of the women's movement, which, after winning the vote, had lain relatively dormant under the pressures of depression and war. The 1949 book *The Second Sex* (trans. 1953), by French philosopher and writer Simone de Beauvoir, traced the history of women's inferior role and explored how male novelists cast men as central characters and women in secondary positions. As the women's movement gained prominence during the 1970's, feminist criticism in the United States and Britain expanded beyond the analysis of misogynist images to include the recovery of a women's literary tradition.

Other critics, especially in France, posited a uniquely feminine language and way of writing. Still others objected to the essentialism of this approach. Under the influence of structuralism and poststructuralism, they believed that the characteristics commonly associated with men and women do not arise from the sex organs—the supposed essence of being male or female. Rather, they found the categories "male" and "female" to be cultural constructions, the products of language and other sign systems, and began to question this binary opposition. Many feminist scholars then shifted their focus from biological sex as a determiner of behavior to gender, an effect of language and culture. Like its cousin cultural studies, gender studies examines texts of all kinds on the assumption that all human activities convey messages. Similarly, Queer Theory scholars consider in a variety of texts how Western culture constructs a distinction between heterosexuality and homosexuality and question this binary opposition.

Marxist Literary Criticism

Karl Marx himself contemplated the role of literature in his socioeconomic theory. Institutions that he called the superstructure of a society, including the arts, religion, and law, reflect the means of production upon which that society depends. For example, the Hungarian Communist Georg Lukács (1885–1971) interpreted Western modernist novels as representing characters' alienation from the products of their labor under capitalism. He believed that such novels reconcile their readers to this state of mind, thus perpetuating an exploitive economic system.

Marxist theorists have long debated the degree to which literature simply reflects and reinforces a society's economic base and the degree to which it can resist the status quo and promote revolution. Some believe that while the upper classes traditionally control the literary marketplace in order to ideologically prop up their privileged social position, in the hands of the lower classes, who would benefit from socioeconomic change, creative works can expose oppression and present alternatives. Knocked from its pedestal, the institution of art itself, some go on to claim, would lose its capacity to dominate a society's thinking. Others believe that resistance lies in literary criticism itself. The critic can analyze how a piece of literature reflects and reinforces the socioeconomic system that produced it. With understanding comes the potential to escape a work's coercive tendencies. After the Cold War ended, Westerners became increasingly comfortable with using Marxism to explore how literature functions within its socioeconomic context.

Cultural Studies, New Historicism, and Postcolonial Studies

Cultural Studies is the apotheosis of the interdisciplinary examination of culture that began with structuralism. For a growing number of scholars, any human activity articulates a culture's values, conflicts, anxieties, and power relationships in conversations known as discourses. Such phenomena as fashion, cuisine, legal systems, architecture, medical procedures, games, ceremonies, public spectacles, and countless others both incidental and monumental are "texts" made up of signs that can be

"read." In this poststructuralist age, cultural studies also takes account of how signifiers shift and multiply meanings. Practitioners of cultural studies acknowledge that different contexts shape different inter- pretations and that their writings participate in their own culture's discourses. Borrowing as much from Marxism as from structuralism and poststructuralism, cultural studies scholars often steer the conversation about cultural phenomena toward a discussion of wealth and power. Cultural studies of contemporary Western culture, such as college classes about Madonna, get publicity in the popular media, but there are allied movements investigating past cultures and non-Western cultures as well.

New Historicism got its name in 1982 when the American scholar of Renaissance literature Stephen Greenblatt (b. 1943) applied this phrase to a collection of pathbreaking essays. He introduced a new approach to the relationship between history and literature. Formerly, a literary scholar might use history to fix the date of a poem's composition or to clarify a novelist's allusions to nonfictional people or events. A historian might use literature as a source alongside other written documents such as speeches, tracts, and newspaper articles. Cultural studies, however, blur these disciplinary boundaries by casting all human artifacts as texts within discourses. A New Historicist in an English department or a cultural historian in a history department might study 18th-century European plays, etiquette manuals, and high-heeled court shoe styles, interpreting all three as expressions of anxiety about class mobility.

Students of the past influenced by cultural studies often look to Michel Foucault (1926–84). This French poststructuralist philosopher of history and social historian emphasized how people of the past experienced the world as it was shaped by human language and symbols. His own studies of insane asylums, prisons, and sexual mores showed how these institutions functioned in past societies' discourses about power.

Scholarship focused on cultural aspects of American and European colonialism became known as postcolonial studies in the 1980's. This varied field includes cultural-studies style inquiry into texts of all kinds. Poems, plays, and novels, no less than colonial laws, travelogues, monuments, museums, and schoolbooks participate in discourses justifying domination. Edward Said, born in Jerusalem in 1935, initiated the study of such discourses. His 1978 book *Orientalism* shows that 19th-century

European writers on the Middle East and Asia, such as linguists, historians, and art connoisseurs, depicted the "Orient" as a zone of irrationality, depravity, and immaturity requiring subjection to Western rationality, virtue, and maturity.

Some studies of postcolonialism focus on cultural texts produced by colonized peoples at home and abroad such as Native Americans and African-Americans. Students of African-American literature inherit a long critical history of its own and hotly debate the appropriateness of contemporary theory deriving from poststructuralism, structuralism, and ultimately Euro- pean philosophy for understanding the African-American experience. Nevertheless, like cultural studies, African-American studies deals with written texts and other cultural products that enable or resist the assertion of power and the unequal distribution of wealth and privilege.

Psychoanalytic Criticism

Psychoanalysis and literary criticism are natural bedfellows. The great psychoanalytic theorists of the twentieth century, Austrian Sigmund Freud (1856–1939), Swiss Carl Jung (1875–1961), and French Jacques Lacan (1901–81), all used literature to illustrate their ideas, beginning with Freud's famous application of the Oedipus myth from ancient Greek tragedy. The later two thinkers built on Freud's basic idea that language, whether it be a slip of the tongue or a folktale, unintentionally expresses the unconscious. In clinic or library both psychoanalysts and literary critics interpret verbal texts to discover hidden meanings.

For the psychoanalytically inclined literary critic of the 1920's and '30's, under the influence of Freud, a literary work was like the author's dreams, which the critic could interpret the latent content of the author's developmental trauma. Psychological complexes also provided handy templates for formal character analysis. In the 1950's Canadian Northrop Frye (1912–91) led a critical movement derived from Jung, who described a collective unconscious expressed in the recurring patterns and images of myth and literature. We process common human experiences, Jung believed, through universal symbols or archetypes such as seasonal death and rebirth. Frye and the archetypal or "myth" critics understood works of literature as expressions of the collective unconscious.

In the 1960's Lacan shook the psychoanalytic world by bringing structuralism to his study of the human psyche.

The structuralist idea that the world as we know it is constructed of sign systems that function like languages led Lacan to posit that the "unconscious is structured like a language." Its contents gain significance through a system of distinctions or binary oppositions, the most important of which is the difference between the conscious self or "subject" and "the Other," meaning other people as well as one's own unconscious. Whereas biological and sexual events mark Freudian developmental stages, recognition of signs and language acquisition are defining moments in Lacanian development.

Lacan's use of linguistic theory also accorded with poststructuralism, which subscribes to deconstruction's view of signifiers as being unstable and having multiple meanings. We are constantly reconstructing ourselves with every utterance so that identity becomes indeterminate, ever-changing, and fragmented. Cherished notions such as individualism and self-determination collapse under Lacan's theories. If we construct ourselves out of sign systems that everyone uses, the building blocks of identity are a shared medium over which we have little personal control.

Early psychoanalytic critics influenced by Lacan tended to read literature as a way to exemplify his psychological concepts. For example, a critic may observe how signs or clues unconsciously left by the murderer in a murder mystery construct an identity, at first indeterminate and fragmentary, against that person's will. Lacan's structuralist approach to the psyche, like structuralism itself, has spread into every field that seeks to understand human interaction. American Fredric Jameson (b. 1934), for example, combines Lacanian psychoanalysis and marxist criticism to understand political, social, and economic relationships propounded by fiction as well as other cultural texts such as architecture. Both Freudian and Lacanian psychoanalysis have fueled feminist criticism and gender studies in their investigations of identity founded on gender and sexuality.

Reader-Response Criticism

The label reader-response groups together many different interpretive practices oriented, like the classical study of rhetoric, toward the reader. Traditional rhetoricians, however, assumed that a text predetermines reader reactions, and so studied texts as a means to sharpen compositional skills. Modern reader-response critics study readers' interpretations as an end in itself. The way in which these critics define readers and the degree to which they attribute meaning to the reader distinguish different approaches. Semioticians, contemporary inheritors of the structuralist science of signs, tend to posit a broad public whose understandings are controlled by a culture's various codes. Some feminist critics, defining textual roles by gender, observe, for example, how male writers impose a masculinist worldview on female readers. Hans Robert Jauss (1921–97) of the German school of reception theory defines readers historically. Texts evolve over time, he believes, as readers' interpretations change. For psychoanalytic reader-response criticism, individual readers recompose texts to satisfy their particular desires, fears, and defenses. American Stanley Fish (b. 1938) stakes the most extreme position. For him, reading is a performance that actualizes otherwise inert marks on a page. Readers, whom Fish defines by their membership in a given community, such as a classroom, negotiate among themselves what counts as a "correct" interpretation. In the second half of the 20th century, poststructuralism created an environment friendly toward variable meanings of texts for different readers; reader-response critics do not all subscribe to poststructuralist theory, however.

Great Works of Western Literature

The following is a selective list of the great works of Western literature. It is by no means a complete representation, but the works we have selected are universally considered to be of the highest quality, and they are among the most widely read. Note that the dates provided are publication dates or first manuscript appearances except for the earliest works from Greece.

(For summaries of 12 of the most popular Shakespeare plays, see "Elizabethan and Jacobean Drama.")

Iliad (ca. 800 B.C.) by Homer

This epic poem is about the 10-year war between the ancient Greeks and the Trojans, supposedly waged around 1100–1000 B.C. This war was prompted by the abduction of Helen, the wife of the Greek king Menelaus, by the Trojan hero Paris. The poem focuses on the wrath of the young Greek warrior Achilles. It was most likely composed around the eighth century B.C. by a man we know today as Homer. Together with its companion, *The Odyssey*, the poems were meant to be sung and were not written down for several hundred years. They are composed in dactylic hexameter (six metric feet per line and two to three syllables per foot); a modern comparison would be *Stars and Stripes Forever*.

Book 1 After nine years of attempting to siege the walled city of Troy (also known as Ilium), frustration, disease, and short tempers rage among the Greek warriors. The Greek leader, Agamemnon, angers Achilles, who then withdraws himself and his followers from the battle and threatens to return to their homeland in Greece.

Book 2 As a ploy to minimize the importance of Achilles in battle, Agamemnon stirs the Greek troops and generals to fierce debate over the pros and cons of continuing the siege or returning to Greece. The conclusion is to continue. A lengthy catalogue of the many ships, their leaders, and their specific points of origin then follows.

Book 3 As the armies prepare for the battle, a decision is made to have Agamemnon's brother and co-leader, Menelaus, engage the Trojan hero Paris in one-on-one combat to determine the war's outcome. Menelaus wins, but the goddess Aphrodite saves Paris, and the war's status appears in doubt.

Book 4 The Greeks consider themselves the victors, but the gods on Mount Olympus, who play an important role in the *Iliad*, debate among themselves and conclude that the war must continue. The war does go on with many anticipated losses of warriors on both sides.

Book 5 The battle proceeds with many Greek and Trojan heroes engaged in mortal combat. Aeneas, a Trojan prince, is introduced by name along with many other warriors and generals. Many Greek gods join in the action, helping both the Trojans and Greeks, but sometimes simply battling among themselves.

Book 6 The gods abandon the battle, leaving the action in the hands of the mortals, and the Greeks begin to dominate the Trojans. Hector, a Trojan prince, prepares himself for battle in full regalia and shares a tender farewell with his wife, Andromache, and their frightened son, Astyanax, virtually knowing he will not return.

Book 7 Hector advances to the battle site and, at the behest of the gods, challenges the Greeks to a one-on-one combat with their warrior of choice. Ajax is chosen by lot.

Their combat lasts through the day and ends with no winner by nightfall. The two show respect for each other and return to their camps. Feasting at both camps prevails through the night.

Book 8 The gods reassemble, and Zeus warns them not to interfere with the warring mortals. The battle resurges on a grand scale with even wise old Nestor attempting to confront the Trojans. The Greeks triumph early but are soon driven back. Night passes with both sides on watchful alert. The gods continue to argue the merits and faults of each side.

Book 9 After the previous day's defeat, some Greek generals again consider abandoning the siege, but Nestor implores them to continue and to appeal to Achilles to rejoin the campaign. Odysseus and Ajax, accompanied by Achilles's old tutor, Phoenix, beg Achilles to return. He rejects them and their offerings of gifts, expressing his hatred for Agamemnon and claims he would not rejoin the fight unless Hector and the Trojans were at the beaches, about to burn the Greek ships.

Book 10 Agamemnon and Menelaus, frustrated over the recent course of the battle, rouse the Greek generals during the night to find someone to infiltrate the Trojan camp. Diomedes and Odysseus are chosen as scouts to determine the Trojan plans. They encounter Dolon, sent by Hector on a similar mission for the Trojans, and discover strategic information on Trojan plans and then kill him, steal several prize Trojan horses, and return to camp.

Book 11 Agamemnon leads the Greek troops in a fierce morning battle. The Trojans are driven back, and Agamemnon slays all he encounters until he himself is wounded and returns to camp. Hector now joins the battle and leads the Trojans to halt the Greeks' progress. Odysseus is wounded in this attack but is saved from death by Menelaus and Ajax. Suddenly, Achilles takes an interest in the battlefield events.

Book 12 With Hector in the lead, the Trojans fight back against the weakened Greeks. They reach a moat and a wall that the Greeks have built to protect the beached ships. A portent—an eagle flying with a snake in his talons—causes hesitation until Hector dismisses its importance. They advance to the seemingly impenetrable wall, and Sarpedon eventually breaches it, allowing the Trojans to rout the Greeks back to the ships.

Book 13 The Greek god Poseidon intervenes on behalf of the Greeks to encourage them to enliven themselves after the defeat and re-engage the battle. This is accomplished, and Hector and his troops are halted. The Greek Idomeneus is stirred to exceptional valor and slays many Trojan warriors, while many other Greeks and Trojans kill and are killed.

Book 14 While Poseidon encourages the Greeks in battle, Zeus favors the Trojans. Hera plans to seduce her husband and uses all her charms, and some borrowed, to soothe Zeus into a deep sleep so Poseidon's help could have more force. The deceit is successful, and the Greeks push the Trojans back, wounding Hector in the process, causing him to withdraw.

Book 15 Zeus awakens and is enraged at what has happened. He berates Hera and has her send the goddess Iris to Poseidon to have him abandon the effort; he also has her send Apollo to Hector to rejuvenate him and send him back to battle. The Trojans take control and drive the Greeks to retreat to the ships, which they heroically defend, although they realize the tide of battle has again changed.

Book 16 With Achilles's blessing, his companion, Patroclus, dons Achilles's armor and leads Achilles's men to drive the Trojans away from the ships and back to the field of battle. Patroclus slays the Trojan hero Sarpedon, thereby enraging Hector, who leads a charge against the Greeks and kills Patroclus in revenge.

Book 17 Patroclus's dead body becomes the focal point of the battle. Menelaus defends the body until Hector advances, whereupon Ajax joins Menelaus to drive Hector back. The struggle goes back and forth, and the horses of Achilles are seen crying over Patroclus's death. His body is returned to the ships, and a messenger is sent to inform Achilles of his friend's death.

Book 18 Achilles is overwhelmed with grief. He is comforted by his mother, the goddess Thetis, and resolves that he will return to the battle to avenge Patroclus. Thetis appeals to the god Hephaestus to forge a new set of armor, which Achilles can don and go back to battle the Trojans. This is done, and Thetis returns to Achilles with the armor.

Book 19 Achilles is delighted. At an assembly of the army, Achilles and Agamemnon reconcile their differences and Achilles is offered many gifts as well as Briseis, the maiden whose theft by Agamemnon caused the rift. The Greek army, with Achilles in front, takes to the battlefield.

Book 20 With Achilles back in the battle, Zeus assembles the gods and permits them to side with their favorite mortals. Achilles and Aeneas face off, but Poseidon saves Aeneas. Achilles then encounters Hector, and each is saved in turn by Athena and Apollo. Achilles then goes on a bloody rampage through the ranks of the Trojans, slaughtering many of the warriors.

Book 21 Achilles slaughters Trojans at the river Xanthus (also known as Scamander), kills many and takes 12 captives in revenge for Patroclus's death. The gods fight among one another, and Achilles continues to fight as the Trojans retreat to the city.

Book 22 With the Trojan warriors within the walls of the city, Hector alone remains outside to battle Achilles. His father, Priam, begs him to reconsider, but Hector remains. Achilles approaches, and fearing for his life, Hector runs around Troy's walls three times as Achilles chases him. They finally confront each other, and Hector is killed. Achilles ties his feet to a chariot and drags Hector toward the Greek ships as Hector's wife, Andromache, and his parents look on in grief.

Book 23 With elaborate ritual, Patroclus's body is cremated in a huge funeral pyre. Many sacrifices are added, including animals, the 12 Trojan captives taken earlier, and locks of Achilles' own hair. The funeral games—a chariot race, a boxing match, a wrestling match, a foot race, one-on-one combat, and a spear-throwing contest—commence.

Book 24 Achilles and Priam remain disconsolate, and the gods offer a solution. Thetis tells Achilles to accept a ransom for the return of Hector's body, and Iris convinces Priam to approach Achilles with valuable gifts. They hold a mutually reverent meeting, and Achilles grants a 12-day truce for the Trojans to prepare a solemn funeral for Hector.

Odyssey (ca. 800 B.C.) by Homer

Homer's epic tale covers the period following the Trojan War and recounts the travels of the Greek warrior Odysseus in the 10 years he takes to return to his homeland, Ithaca. The other surviving Greek warriors are already home, but the god Poseidon has put Odysseus in

several adventurous situations, including a seven-year stay with the goddess-queen Calypso on her island of Ogygia. Through the intervention of the gods, he returns to Ithaca to find his home overrun with suitors of his wife, Penelope, all of whom assume he is dead. Their brashness invokes Odysseus's revenge, resulting in his confrontation with them, allowing him to rejoin Penelope, his household, and his kingdom.

Book 1 Odysseus remains on the island with Calypso, while Athena persuades Zeus to allow him to leave and continue his homeward trek to Ithaca. His son, Telemachus, is visited by the disguised Athena and is advised to dismiss the suitors and seek the whereabouts of his father and to facilitate his return.

Book 2 Telemachus calls for an assembly of the princes of Ithaca as well as the boisterous suitors and warns the suitors to abandon their quest of Penelope since Odysseus will return and punish them all. The suitors dismiss his words and return to Odysseus's palace. Telemachus prepares a ship and crew to search for information about his father.

Book 3 Accompanied by the disguised Athena, Telemachus sails to Pylos, the home of wise old Nestor, who had survived the 10-year siege of Troy. Nestor welcomes them and tells tales of the war itself as well as his knowledge of the fate of many other warriors. He knows nothing of Odysseus and tells Telemachus to question Menelaus at Sparta.

Book 4 Telemachus visits Menelaus and Helen, who tell several tales of the war, including Odysseus's ploy of the wooden horse in which the Greeks entered and besieged the city. He tells of meeting the god Proteus, who related the fate of several returning Greeks, including Agamemnon's fatal homecoming and the imprisonment of Odysseus by Calypso on Ogygia.

Book 5 Odysseus is still on Calypso's island, longing to return home. At Athena's request the gods have agreed that Odysseus may sail to Ithaca and Calypso is persuaded. With her help, he builds a raft and begins the voyage, but Poseidon continues his wrath and Odysseus is storm-driven into the sea. He washes up on the island of the Phaeacians with the help of the goddess Ino.

Book 6 The island is ruled by the peaceful King Alcinous. His daughter, Nausicaa, and her handmaidens go to the shore to wash garments and play ball. Nausicaa chases a missed ball and encounters Odysseus, who pleads with her not to be frightened and begs that she take him to meet her king. She is in awe of him and does as he asks.

Book 7 Odysseus enters the town and is led by a disguised Athena to the palace of King Alcinous and his queen, Arete. As is the custom, he is received as an honored guest. He relates his encounters with Calypso as well as his voyage to their island and the generous aid provided by Nausicaa. They promise him immediate help in returning to his homeland.

Book 8 The following day, Alcinous's men prepare a ship and crew for Odysseus's return, and a great feast is held in the palace. This is followed by sporting events at which Odysseus is invited to participate and does so with amazing success. He is further feted by the lords and their bard, Demodocus, and is given gifts and asked to reveal his identity, and recount his origins, and adventures.

Book 9 Odysseus identifies himself and begins his tale. He had been driven by the wind to the island of the Lotus-eaters, who lived in a perpetual dreamland. He next encountered the giant one-eyed Cyclops, who devoured several of his men before Odysseus, feigning friendship, lulled him to sleep with wine. He and his men then gouged out his eye and retreated to their ship.

Book 10 Odysseus continues his tale, telling how he approached Ithaca but was blown back by the winds and landed on the isle of the Laestrygonians, cannibals who killed most of his men. They then landed on Aeaea, the home of the goddess Circe, who turned many of his men into swine and convinced Odysseus to stay with her in luxury together with his, again human, crew. He leaves with instructions from her to visit Hades and consult the seer Teiresias about his future.

Book 11 Odysseus obeys and confronts Teiresias, who predicts he will encounter more hardships on his journey home but will live long and die in comfort in his homeland. In Hades Odysseus meets his mother, who died while he was at war, as well as many of his comrades-in-arms, and Agamemnon, who tells him of his tragic death on returning to his home and his unfaithful wife, Clytemnestra.

Book 12 Odysseus returns to Circe's island and then sails by the spell-inducing Sirens and the rocks and whirlpool of Scylla and Charybdis, losing six of his men. He lands on the island of the sun god Hyperion, where his men disobediently devour the god's sacred cows, resulting in their death in a storm and leaving Odysseus alone to float to shore on Calypso's island.

Book 13 Alcinous and his court are amazed at Odysseus's tale and present him with gifts before taking him to Ithaca where he is put to sleep. Athena appears to inform him of his location and the state of Penelope and Telemachus. She changes his appearance into that of an old beggar man and sends him to his former swineherd, Eumaeus, while she proceeds to Sparta to send Telemachus home.

Book 14 Odysseus proceeds to Eumaeus's hut, where he is graciously greeted as a stranger. They talk of former times, and the disguised Odysseus relates tales of fictitious adventures; in one he says he encountered Odysseus, who will return to Ithaca. Eumaeus doubts the prediction of the disguised Odysseus and accepts a challenge to reward the old man if Odysseus does indeed return.

Book 15 Athena appears to Telemachus in Menelaus's home and tells him to return to Ithaca and go to Eumaeus's hut. Menelaus and Helen give him gifts, and he sets sail. Meanwhile, Odysseus hears from Eumaeus that his mother is dead and that his father lives on in sorrow. Telemachus lands at Ithaca and proceeds to Eumaeus's hut.

Book 16 Telemachus goes to Eumaeus's hut and sends him to tell Penelope of his return. Athena returns Odysseus to his natural form, and he identifies himself to his son. They conceive plans for Odysseus's return to the palace and for the disposition of the suitors. Eumaeus returns to his hut, and Odysseus is once again transformed into an aged beggar man, so that Telemachus alone knows his true identity.

Book 17 Telemachus returns to town and tells Penelope what he has heard from Nestor and Menelaus as well as prophesies that Odysseus will soon return home. On his way to town, Odysseus sees his old hound, Argus, who recognizes him and joyfully dies. The disguised Odysseus begs among the suitors and is insulted and threatened.

Book 18 Odysseus encounters the beggar Irus, who entices him to hand-battle. Odysseus beats him handily and drives him out of the palace. Penelope appears before the suitors, repeats her mourning for Odysseus and chides them for their use of her household and their failure to provide customary gifts. Odysseus proceeds to further madden the suitors, and Telemachus dismisses them for the night to their own homes.

Book 19 Odysseus instructs Telemachus to remove all weapons from the palace. Penelope sits with the disguised Odysseus, and he assures her that her husband will return shortly. In disbelief she tells him of her plan to have an archery contest among the suitors, the winner to be awarded her hand. Her aged maid, Eurycleia, who nursed Odysseus, bathes his feet, notices a familiar scar, and recognizes him but is forced to secrecy.

Book 20 Odysseus is quietly enraged as he observes the household with servants admonishing him and the suitors continuing to waste his resources while they discuss the murder of Telemachus. He is again insulted at dinner, and another guest warns the suitors that Odysseus is about to appear and reclaim his wife and palace.

Book 21 Penelope confronts the suitors and announces that whoever can string the great bow of Odysseus and shoot an arrow through the openings of 12 ax handles will have her hand in marriage. They each try, but none can even string the bow. Odysseus, still a disguised beggar, asks to try his hand and successfully strings the bow and shoots the arrow through the ax handles to the amazement of all.

Book 22 Shedding his beggarly disguise, Odysseus confronts the suitors, and along with Telemachus kills them one by one. Several beg for mercy, but all, except the bard Pherius, are killed by arrow or spear. Twelve of the household women who slept with the suitors are hanged for their unfaithfulness.

Book 23 Eurycleia, the maid, wakes Penelope to tell her that the aged beggar is Odysseus and that he has shed his disguise and killed the suitors. Penelope has doubts and meets with Odysseus, who proves himself by describing their marital bed, built from an olive tree, a feat unknown to others. He recounts the tales of his return, and they spend the evening in marital bliss.

Book 24 The god Hermes escorts the souls of the dead suitors to Hades with several exchanging words with Agamemnon, Achilles, Patroclus, and Ajax. Odysseus vis-

its his father, Laertes, on his farm; after some disbelief he is elated to see his son again. Relatives and friends of the suitors arm themselves to do battle with Odysseus, who slays 12 of them before calling a truce.

The Theban Plays: *Oedipus the King, Oedipus at Colonus, Antigone* (fifth century B.C.) by Sophocles

The Theban plays constitute three of the seven surviving plays by Sophocles (he is believed to have written 123). Aristotle considered *Oedipus the King* the ultimate example of tragedy, and Sigmund Freud famously drew his theory of the "Oedipal Complex" from its classic plot.

Oedipus the King (Oedipus Rex) The ancient Greek city of Thebes has been hit by a terrible plague. The Theban citizens appeal to King Oedipus, who says that he has sent his brother-in-law Creon to consult the Oracle at Delphi for advice. Creon returns and tells Oedipus the Oracle said that the plague will be lifted when the man who murdered Laius, the former king of Thebes, is expelled from the city. Creon explains that Laius was killed by robbers while traveling to Delphi, and Oedipus curses the murderer and vows to find him.

Oedipus sends for the blind prophet Teiresias, but he refuses to speak about Laius's death. Furious, Oedipus accuses him of being the murderer and of being a false prophet. Oedipus had become king after solving the Sphinx's riddle and thereby ending the city's plague, and he questions Teiresias's inability to solve the riddle himself. Teiresias responds by accusing Oedipus of the murder and also of incest. Teiresias continues, saying that the murderer is an immigrant to Thebes who is actually a native, and that he is both brother and father to his children and the murderer of his own father.

Oedipus accuses Creon of conspiring with the prophet, which he denies. Queen Jocasta, Oedipus's wife and Creon's sister, arrives, and Oedipus tells her of the prophet's words. Jocasta proclaims that all prophecies are false, and as proof she tells him that an oracle had told Laius that he would be murdered by his own son, and that Laius had reacted by sending his three-day-old son to die on a mountainside. But, as Jocasta explains, according to the slave who years later returned with the report of Laius's murder, Laius was murdered not by his son but by robbers at the intersection of three roads. At these words, Oedipus becomes suspicious and asks for more details, and Jocasta says that the murder occurred just before Oedipus came to

Thebes and describes Laius's physical appearance, which resembled Oedipus's.

Now terrified, Oedipus tells Jocasta that his father is King Polybus of Corinth, but that one day an oracle came to Corinth and told him that he was not his father's true son. In response, Oedipus traveled to the Oracle at Delphi, who prophesied that he would sleep with his mother and kill his father. While traveling, Oedipus came to the intersection of three roads, where a coach full of men threatened to drive him off the road. A fight ensued, and Oedipus killed the men. Oedipus explains to Jocasta that he may have killed Laius, and that he wants to ask the slave whether Laius was killed by a band of robbers or by one man.

A Corinthian messenger arrives at the palace and tells Oedipus that his father, King Polybus, has died of old age and that the Corinthians want Oedipus to rule. Oedipus is relieved, since this means he will not kill his father, but he refuses to return to Corinth, because he still fears the part of the prophecy relating to his mother. The messenger, a shepherd, tells him that Polybus was not his real father, explaining that he himself brought baby Oedipus—who had been given to him by one of Laius's herdsman—to the king. Oedipus sends for the herdsman and forces him to reveal that Oedipus was Laius's son, and that he had been ordered by Jocasta to leave Oedipus to die, but had given him to the Corinthian shepherd out of pity for the baby.

Oedipus screams and leaves the stage. A messenger describes what has happened offstage. Inside the palace walls Oedipus has discovered that Jocasta has hanged herself, and he has blinded himself with the pins from her robe. Oedipus now reappears, bleeding. He begs Creon to send him away from Thebes and asks him to look after his daughters, Antigone and Ismene.

Oedipus at Colonus

Wandering Oedipus and his daughter Antigone arrive at Colonus, just outside of Athens. A stranger tells them that they are resting on a sacred grove, and orders them to move. Oedipus refuses and requests the presence of King Theseus of Athens. Oedipus tells Antigone that an oracle told him that this would be his final resting place and that the land and its inhabitants would therefore be blessed. The Elders of Colonus arrive and force Oedipus to reveal his identity. They insist that he leave, but he appeals to Athens's legendary hospitality and is told that Theseus will decide upon his arrival.

Oedipus's daughter Ismene arrives and informs her father that her two brothers are fighting for his throne, and that the younger brother has banished the elder. She says the oracle predicted that the kingdom depends on Oedipus, and that Creon wants him to be buried just outside of Thebes. Theseus arrives and grants Oedipus permission to be buried in the sacred grove. Creon arrives next and tries to convince Oedipus to be buried outside of Thebes. When Oedipus refuses, Creon's guards (who had just kidnapped Ismene) abduct Antigone. Theseus threatens Creon until he releases the women, who are reunited with their father. Oedipus is then visited by his hypocritical elder son, Polyneices, who asks for Oedipus's forgiveness because an oracle said that it would ensure his victory. Oedipus refuses and curses his sons.

Sudden claps of thunder convince Oedipus that his time has come, and he sends his daughters away. A messenger reports that he has died, and Antigone and Ismene decide to return to Thebes.

Antigone

Having returned to Thebes, Antigone decides to disobey King Creon's edict by burying the corpse of her brother Polyneices, who was killed by his younger brother during an attack on Thebes. Despite the penalty of death, Antigone buries her brother and is caught in the act by Creon's guards. Creon sentences her to death, even though she is engaged to his son Haemon, and orders that she be buried alive in a desert cave. The prophet Teiresias warns Creon that this action will result in large-scale mourning and suffering, and Creon's counselors convince him to free Antigone.

Creon arrives at the cave and discovers that Antigone has hanged herself, and that Haemon is lying beside her. Upon seeing his father, Haemon stabs himself and dies. When Creon returns to his palace he discovers that his wife, Eurydice, distraught over the death of her son, has killed herself, cursing Creon with her last breath.

The Oresteia (458 B.C.) by Aeschylus

These three plays by the Greek tragedian Aeschylus were written and performed in the fifth century B.C. and can be thought of as a three-act play with each act (or play) tied to the other by circumstances and flow of plot. The trilogy tells the story of a specific saga centered on the House of Atreus in Argos following the end of the Trojan War.

Agamemnon   After the fall of Troy, the Greek warriors and their leaders return to their homes. Agamemnon, a son of Atreus and brother of Menelaus, returns to his wife, Clytemnestra, and to his kingdom in Argos (Mycenae) as a hero of the war. In vengeance for his sacrificing their daughter Iphigenia to the gods, he is murdered by his wife and her lover, Aegisthus. Clytemnestra and Aegisthus do verbal battle with several older citizens (the chorus), who predict her son, Orestes, will return and avenge his father's death by murdering her.

The Libation Bearers   Several years after the *Agamemnon* ends, Orestes returns, determined to avenge his father's death. He encounters his sister Electra, and a group of slave women (the chorus), who are paying homage to Agamemnon by preparing to pour wine over his grave. Orestes reveals himself to Electra, and it is agreed that Clytemnestra and Aegisthus must be murdered as the killers of their father. Orestes accomplishes the deed and is immediately besieged by guilt and the Furies (the Eumenides), who drive him to near madness for his action.

The Furies   At Delphi Apollo gives refuge to Orestes, promising not to rashly give him up to the Furies (the chorus), who vow never to let him free since he murdered his mother, Clytemnestra. The goddess Athena arranges a trial whereby 12 Athenian men will vote under oath as to Orestes's guilt. The trial proceeds and the final vote ends in a tie, whereupon Athena herself casts a deciding ballot to allow Orestes to go free. Following a heated discussion, Athena promises the Furies they will be kindlier people and live forever in an underground land, overseeing and protecting the land of the Greeks.

Aeneid (30 B.C.) by Virgil

Virgil's epic poem tells the story of the Trojan prince Aeneas and his escape from Troy as the Greeks overtook it. Modeled somewhat after Homer's *Iliad* and *Odyssey* in structure and story line, Aeneas wanders for years on his journey to Italy to found the city of Rome. It is believed that the poem was meant to glorify the emperor Augustus and was written in his time. Like Homer's tales, it is written in dactyllic hexameter and imitates much of Homer's style and phraseology.

Book 1   The author invokes the Muse to tell why the goddess Juno is angry at Aeneas and his men, all Trojan War survivors, and causes them undue hardships on their escape from Troy as they sail to Italy to found the city of Rome. After several years of wandering, Aeneas's ships encounter a tempest and are shipwrecked in Carthage in northern Africa. They are presented to the queen, Dido, and as she was instructed by the gods, they are feasted and offered many gifts. Dido asks that Aeneas tell the tale of the fall of Troy and his subsequent adventures.

Book 2   Aeneas recounts the tale of the fall of Troy; how the Greeks devised the apparent gift of a wooden horse filled with warriors and thereby entered the city. The Trojan Laocoon warned his people not to accept the gift but was ignored and was subsequently attacked and devoured by serpents. At night, after the Trojans had celebrated the victory, the Greeks emerged from the structured horse and besieged and burned the town. Aeneas escaped the burning city with his father, Anchises, and his son.

Book 3   Aeneas goes on to tell how they sailed to Thrace and then to Crete, where they considered settling but were told by Apollo in a dream not to do so and to continue on to Italy. They traveled around Greece and proceeded toward Italy, stopping at several islands for rest and nourishment. They met Andromache, wife of Hector, the great Trojan warrior; she had been taken as a slave from Troy. They then heard a prophecy of their subsequent adventures en route. They reached the shores of Italy, landed on the isle of the Cyclops, and escaped with a Greek shipmate of Ulysses after being threatened by the Cyclops. Aeneas's father, Anchises, died on the journey.

Book 4   Dido falls in love with Aeneas and prepares for marriage. Her suitor, King Iarbas, is displeased and appeals to Jupiter, who sends Mercury to remind Aeneas of his fate: the founding of Rome. Aeneas prepares the fleet to set sail while Dido pleads with him to stay. But Aeneas refuses and Dido decides to take her own life and does so as she sees the ships sailing off.

Book 5   A storm drives Aeneas's ships to the coast of Sicily, where Acestes, a former Trojan, welcomes them with a feast and games in honor of Anchises. These include a boat race, a foot race, a boxing match, an archery contest, and equestrian contests. Many of those in Aeneas's band want to stay in Sicily, and they attempt to burn the ships to do so. The fires are contained, and Aeneas founds a city in Sicily for many of the women, the elderly, and others wishing to remain. He then sets sail for the mainland with the rest of his crew.

Book 6   They reach the coast of Italy, and Aeneas pays tribute to Apollo, asking for a reprieve from their wanderings. A prophetess, the Sybyl of Cumae, alerts Aeneas that in the founding of Rome more trials are yet to come. Aeneas is accompanied by the Sybyl to the underworld to address his father. He encounters many of the Trojan heroes as well as Dido and meets his father in the land of the good, Elysium. Anchises foretells the history of Rome and its eventual greatness through Caesar and Augustus and others.

Book 7   Aeneas and his men arrive in Latium on the banks of the Tiber River and are welcomed by King Latinus, who proposes that Aeneas marry his daughter, Lavinia, to unite the Trojans and the Latins (Italians) and thereby fulfill an omen that predicted she would marry a foreigner. Latinus's wife, Amata, is enraged because she wants her daughter to wed the Italian warrior Turnus. At this time Aeneas's son, Ascanius, kills a favored deer. The Latins are furious and prepare for war with the Trojans.

Book 8   Worried that Turnus has many more men than he, Aeneas, alerted by the god Tiber, goes to Pallanteum, the future site of Rome, and finds allies under King Evander, an old friend of Anchises. At the request of Juno, the god Vulcan forges weapons for Aeneas, whom King Evander provides 400 warriors as well as his own son, Pallas, who is to learn warfare from Aeneas. The shield forged by Vulcan for Aeneas portrays many great moments in the future history of Rome, down to the battle of Actium in Virgil's own time.

Book 9   The Trojans build a wall around their camp to make it more of a fortress. Turnus and his men surround it and become frustrated at not being able to attack the Trojans. Two of Aeneas's warriors, Nisus and Euryalus, leave the camp, sneak through the enemy lines, and kill many of the Latins as they sleep. Turnus's men eventually capture them, kill them, and plant their heads on stakes outside the Trojan walls. Turnus infiltrates the fort and kills many of the Trojans before he is stopped and escapes over the walls.

Book 10   At a council of the gods to learn why the Trojans and Latins are battling, Jupiter tells the feuding gods not to intervene any further. Aeneas and his warriors confront Turnus and his troops; Pallas, King Evander's son, is slain by Turnus, who gloats over the boy's death. In a rage, Aeneas wounds the tyrant Mesentius, and, after

warning his son Lausus to retreat, Aeneas kills him when he refuses and gives the body to the Latins for burial.

Book 11   There is deep mourning for the dead warriors on both sides, and both factions realize the need for a truce. Turnus is the major Latin dissident. Latinus calls a council of leading citizens to discuss peace. They are close to a decision when the news arrives that the Trojans are approaching the city. Many panic, but Turnus arms himself and charges off. Camilla, a warrior maiden, tries to help Turnus in battle but is slain while gloating over the death of several Trojans. Turnus retreats to the city to find help.

Book 12   A truce is arranged, but Aeneas and Turnus agree to a one-on-one battle. Aeneas is wounded by an irate Latin, and Turnus reacts by spearing many Trojans and desecrating their corpses. Venus disobeys Jupiter and heals Aeneas's wound. Aeneas rearms and eventually wounds Turnus, and when he sees that Turnus is wearing a belt stolen from Pallas's body, he kills him. The Trojans and Latins unite to stay in Italy and forswear the Trojan identity.

Beowulf (ca. 1000 A.D.)

This is the first great English poem, the first English epic, and the most important work of literature written in the Anglo-Saxon language. More than 3,000 lines long, the manuscript of the poem is from the late 10th century, but it is believed to have been written in the first half of the eighth century by an anonymous poet who used older poetic sources. Moreover, the action of the poem takes place two centuries earlier, in Scandinavian areas from where some of England's ancestors may have migrated.

Beowulf is a Geat warrior-prince from southern Sweden who arrives surprisingly in Denmark at the mead hall of King Hrothgar to offer his services in conquering the monster Grendel, who has relentlessly been devouring Hrothgar's men. Beowulf succeeds, but Grendel's vengeful mother makes a new deadly attack. Beowulf then hunts her down in her underwater cave, slays her, and decapitates Grendel. Beowulf is richly rewarded and returns to the court of King Hygelac of the Geats, who is a historical figure. He soon succeeds Hygelac as king and rules for 50 years.

In Beowulf's old age, a dragon, angered by the theft of a goblet from its hoard, breathes fire on the Geats, and the hero, with great difficulty, deserted by all but one warrior, kills it, but is killed himself. Beowulf's funeral pyre, accompanied by a prophecy of more suffering for the Geats, ends the poem.

A remarkable characteristic of *Beowulf* is its combination of pre-Christian, heroic sensibility, celebrating honor and courage, depicting a rigid code of vengeance, and invoking an awareness of conquering doom, with a Christian understanding of God and Satan, heaven and hell. To some readers the latter elements seem arbitrarily attached. To others, however—notably Seamus Heaney, a recent translator of *Beowulf*—the two worldviews are accommodated by the poet in a way that deepens the poem's cultural significance and meaning.

The Divine Comedy (1310–14) by Dante Alighieri

This medieval poetic masterpiece was composed in the Florentine dialect in distinct terza rima (triple rhyme) near the end of the poet's life. Precisely and symbolically structured in three "canticas"—*Inferno, Purgatorio,* and *Paradiso,* containing a total of 100 cantos—it is a vividly descriptive, dramatic, allegorical account of the poet's journey through the Christian afterworld, inhabited by identifiable historical and contemporary figures.

It begins with the poet lost in a "dark wood," symbolic of sin, where he is rescued by the Latin poet Virgil, who guides him through the only route of deliverance, the nine circles of hell, which descend to the center of the earth.

Inferno, with its exquisitely imagined tortures, is the most widely read and discussed section of the poem. As the poets proceed, they are blocked by a leopard, a wolf, and a lion, the first of several fierce creatures they will encounter, and must take another path into hell's anteroom, where "the neutrals," who in life took no stand for good or evil, are attacked by wasps. Across the River Acheron, in the First Circle, or limbo, are the virtuous unbaptized, including ancient poets. Circles Two through Five are populated by those guilty of sins of incontinence—the lustful, including legendary lovers such as Paolo and Francesca; the gluttons, watched by Cerberus and wading in mud; the misers and spendthrifts, presided over by Plutus, the babbling god of wealth; and, in the swampy River Styx, the grimy souls who suffer for sins of anger. Three Furies carrying the head of Medusa guard the Sixth Circle, and they must be admitted by an angel to its City of Dis, occupied by heretics. Beyond, in Circle Seven, is the Plain of Fire, where the violent are tortured by fire

and boiling blood. In the 10 "pouches" of the Eighth Circle are found the various fraudulent transgressors, among them thieves and schismatics. Precipitously below the other circles is the Ninth, the Pit of Hell, where the most abject sinners, the traitors, are punished. There, trapped in ice, the giant Lucifer clenches Brutus, Cassius, and Judas Iscariot in his teeth.

Purgatorio depicts the travelers' ascent up a mountain, the ledges of which are occupied by those guilty of one of the seven great sins, who are purified by punishment and gradually proceed toward heaven. Atop Purgatory lies the Garden of Eden, where Virgil yields his function to the blessed Beatrice, who in life had been the object of Dante's transforming love. Their course through the nine spheres of *Paradiso,* bathed in celestial harmony and radiance, involves encounters with angels, saints, and holy warriors and culminates in the poet's ecstatic experience of the Divine.

Canterbury Tales (1387–1400) by Geoffrey Chaucer

The conceit that frames the 22 tales in this poem, composed mainly in rhymed Middle English couplets, is a proposal that each of 30 Christian pilgrims relate two stories each on both the way to and from Canterbury. Despite being far from complete, it provides the most vivid and insightful view ever recorded of English life in the Middle Ages.

A "Prologue" describes the pilgrims, their various occupations and frailties; their stories that follow range from heroic to devout to hilariously ribald. The first, "The Knight's Tale," is a chivalric romance set in ancient Greece. The second is "The Miller's Tale," a comic masterpiece in which a foolish carpenter is cuckolded by a student. This draws an offended response from the Reeve, who has once been a carpenter and proceeds to tell of a thieving miller and his a family. "The Man of Law's Tale" describes the adventures of a noblewoman who is twice banished to sea by two vicious mothers-in-law. The five-times-married Wife of Bath is granted both a prologue, a paean to lust and marriage, and a tale in which a knight must accurately answer "What does a woman love most?" In one of several dramatic linking sections of the poem, the Friar and a Summoner begin to quarrel, and then deliver tales insulting to each other, one of a cheating summoner who is escorted by the devil into hell, the other of a friar who falsely promises prayers for money and receives a humiliating comeuppance. "The Clerk's Tale," reflecting the theme of marriage introduced by the Miller and Wife of Bath, is an account of a humble woman who is mistreated by her noble husband, and it is followed by the Merchant's story of a young woman who is brazenly unfaithful to her blind old husband. Extending this thread, the Franklin tells of a married woman who assigns her lover an impossible labor so that she can be rid of him.

"The Second Nun's Tale" is a pious story about the miracles and martyrdom of St. Cecilia, and is followed by "The Canon Yeoman's Tale," a satirical attack on alchemists. In "The Doctor's Tale," a father kills his daughter, Virginia, at her bidding, so that she can escape the evil judge who pursues her. Tinged with allegory, "The Pardoner's Tale" describes three greedy sinners who set out to slay Death to gain gold, but are murdered by one another. Another husband and wife at odds appear in "The Shipman's Tale," in which a woman borrows money for clothing from a priest, who in turn has borrowed it from her stingy husband. The devotional, albeit anti-Semitic, strain is picked up by the Prioress, who tells of a boy who continues to sing a hymn after he is murdered by Jews.

Chaucer then presents his own stories, the fragmentary "Tale of Sir Thopas," a satire on contemporary romances, and "The Tale of Melibee," somewhat puzzling in purpose, a prose translation of a French story about the propriety of vengeance. The pilgrims return with "The Monk's Tale," actually several stories about the downfalls of mighty or famous men. The next two tales are fables: "The Nun Priest's Tale," about cocky Chauntecleer who is caught by but outfoxes a fox, and "The Manciple's Tale," which ends with a white crow's having his feathers plucked, thus explaining why crows are black. The poem's final "tale," offered by the Parson, is in fact a long sermon on the seven deadly sins and penance.

These self-revealing characters are observed with sympathy and without judgment. A human panoply displayed in a religious context, they demonstrate that spiritual aspiration is never far from fleshly joy and folly.

Don Quixote (Pt. I, 1605; Pt. II, 1615) by Miguel de Cervantes

In this two-part Spanish novel, set in 17th-century Spain, Don Quixote, an aging gentleman overly influenced by chivalric tales, sets out with his servant, Sancho Panza, on a quest for honor and adventure. Told through an ironic narrative voice that purports to recount the adventures of a real man, the novel follows Don Quixote through episode after episode in which he grows more and more befuddled, misunderstanding situations and picking fights all for the sake of defending the honor of the fair Dulcinea.

In Part I, Don Quixote, obsessed with knightly romances, has himself knighted by an innkeeper and convinces Sancho Panza to join him by promising him the governorship of an island. Quixote sets out on his old horse, Rocinante, with Sancho riding on a donkey by his side, to win glory and honor. He hopes to win the love of a peasant girl, upon whom he confers the name Dulcinea del Toboso. Quixote and Sancho have many adventures, including battling with windmills mistaken for giants, dueling with friars, and getting beaten by the servant of a lady.

Part II continues Don Quixote's adventures, but with a different tone. In Part II, Quixote discovers that his own adventures have been written about, but incorrectly, and that tales of his deeds precede him wherever he goes. His desire to prove himself leads him on a further quest. But now Quixote's befuddlement leads to more serious problems both for himself and for other people. Sancho convinces Quixote that Dulcinea has been put under a spell that has turned her into a peasant. A duke and duchess conspire to confuse Quixote further, cruelly setting up trials for him and Sancho that put them both in danger. Eventually, Quixote is vanquished by the Knight of the White Moon, an old friend in disguise trying to end Quixote's journeys, and he ultimately dies of a fever. The narrator tells us that after Quixote's death, chivalry died as well, and that his death marks the end of the era of knights.

Widely considered the first novel, *Don Quixote* demonstrates innovations in narrative style and structural form that are still fresh today.

Paradise Lost (First Edition 1667; Second Edition 1674) by John Milton

This monumental poem is entirely in blank verse, all of it dictated by Milton, a blind poet of extraordinary power. It begins with an invocation to a muse—a nod to classical Greek and Latin epics. Grappling with themes of predestination versus free will, Milton retells the story of mankind's original sin, embellishing heavily on the book of Genesis and creating a richly detailed story involving Satan's own estrangement from Heaven. Milton's complex and compelling portrayal of Satan is considered one of the first literary portrayals of an antihero.

The narrative begins in Hell, where Satan, once a glorious member of God's coterie, and his followers have been banished after rebelling against God. They plot revenge with a scheme to sabotage God's beloved new creations: Earth and humankind. Satan travels to Earth, meeting his offspring, Sin and Death, on the journey. God sees Satan's approach and predicts that humankind will fall from grace. God's Son offers himself as a sacrifice in their place.

Satan deceives the archangel Uriel into ushering him into Paradise, where Adam and Eve share an idyllic existence. Satan overhears Adam reiterating to Eve that God has forbidden them to eat fruit from the Tree of Knowledge. Uriel realizes his error and warns the other archangels of the impostor. Satan is discovered and evicted from Eden.

God sends the archangel Raphael to caution Adam and Eve, reminding them that their own free will determines their destiny. Raphael warns them about Satan's determination to have them disobey God's order. Satan slips back into Paradise, disguised as a serpent. Finding Eve alone, he convinces her to partake from the Tree of Knowledge. Adam is horrified, but decides to join her in mutual doom. Lust is the first manifestation of their fall from God's favor.

God's Son comes to Earth and tells Adam and Eve that the consequences of their disobedience will be a life of pain, toil, and eventual death. Satan returns to Hell, expecting to celebrate, but he and his followers are turned into serpents. Adam and Eve bicker, but resolve to survive by loving each other and serving God.

God sends the archangel Michael to cast Adam and Eve out of Paradise. Michael shows Adam a vision of humankind's future, which will be plagued with sin and grief. But Adam also sees that God's Son will someday provide redemption. Hand in hand, Adam and Eve sadly leave Paradise to begin an uncertain future.

Paradise Lost is considered the definitive epic poem of the English language. A follower of Oliver Cromwell, Milton was persecuted after the Stuart restoration in 1660.

Paradise Regained (1671)

Paradise Regained (1671) The counterpart to *Paradise Lost*, this brief epic poem dramatizes Jesus as the epitome of Christian heroism—the Job-like ability to constantly reaffirm faith in God and resist temptation while enduring increasingly difficult trials. The poem is structured as a series of arguments in which Satan unsuccessfully tries to tempt Jesus. Milton drew inspiration for the poem from the *Book of Job*, and from the accounts of Jesus' temptations in the wilderness in the gospels of Matthew and Luke.

Robinson Crusoe (1719) by Daniel Defoe

Disregarding his father's advice to build a secure, middle-class life in England, Robinson Crusoe runs off to seek his fortune at sea. On his second journey, he is seized by Moorish pirates and enslaved in Africa. He escapes, and a kindly Portuguese ship's captain takes him to Brazil, where he establishes a successful plantation. Crusoe joins a slave-trading expedition, but he is shipwrecked and all of his companions perish.

Marooned alone on a tropical island, Crusoe salvages weapons, tools, and supplies from the ruined ship. Falling ill, he experiences a vision that God has delivered him. After recovering, Crusoe surveys the island and finds a lush valley, where he sets up a home, complete with goat and pet parrot. He fills his days by tending crops and acquiring useful skills. Crusoe builds a boat and attempts to sail away, but nearly perishes. Returning to shore, he is grateful to God for sparing him once again.

After several uneventful years, Crusoe spots a band of cannibals with captives. One of their prisoners breaks away, and Crusoe kills his pursuer. The grateful man vows loyalty to Crusoe, who names his new servant Friday.

Crusoe teaches Friday to speak English and introduces him to Christianity. Friday informs Crusoe that the cannibals saved other survivors from a shipwreck, and they are nearby. Crusoe and Friday build a boat and set off to investigate. They battle with a band of cannibals, and rescue Friday's father and a Spaniard from captivity.

One day an English ship approaches, and its mutinous crew drags the captain ashore. Crusoe and Friday overpower the men and rescue the captain. Crusoe is stunned to realize that a seaworthy ship is at his disposal.

Returning to Europe, Crusoe learns that his Brazilian plantation has made him wealthy. After a perilous overland journey, he returns to England, where most of his family has died. He marries, has children, and is widowed. Eventually he undertakes one last journey to revisit his island, which is now a well-governed Spanish colony.

One of the earliest novels, *Robinson Crusoe* is structured as the fictional "autobiography" of its title character. This classic adventure yarn (likely inspired by the true story of a

Scottish sailor who survived for years on a deserted island) is also a morality tale about humankind's ability to master their surroundings through diligence and Christian faith.

Gulliver's Travels (1726) by Jonathan Swift

When British surgeon Lemuel Gulliver's medical business begins to fail, he takes a job as a ship's doctor and departs for the South Sea. When his ship capsizes, he swims to shore and falls asleep. He awakens to find himself bound by countless tiny threads and surrounded by tiny humans. He learns that he is in the kingdom of Lilliput, a country of tiny and fiercely nationalistic humans. The Lilliputians revere him and eventually use him as a physical defense against nearby Blefuscu, another nation of tiny humans with whom the Lilliputians have a longstanding nonsensical feud. The Lilliputian king eventually convicts Gulliver of treason for extinguishing a palace fire with a stream of his urine, but he is pardoned, and he travels to Blefuscu, where he repairs an old boat and sets sail for England. Soon after returning home to his family, Gulliver sets sail again, and soon finds himself in Brobdingnag, a land of giants. A farmer adopts Gulliver as a pet, then sells him to the queen. Gulliver becomes a favorite of the royal court, but he is continually disgusted by his magnified view of their physical bodies and he is shocked by their ignorance of the outside world. His sojourn ends when an eagle plucks his cage from the ground and drops him into the ocean. He is rescued by sailors and returns to England, only to set sail again. This time his ship is attacked by pirates, and he is set adrift in a canoe, which takes him to the island of Laputa, a floating island that hovers over a land called Balnibarbi. The people of Laputa are scholars and royals who are obsessed with impractical research, and the daily lives of the people of Balnibarbi have been destroyed by these ridiculous pursuits. From there Gulliver travels to a few more foreign lands before eventually returning to England.

On his fourth and final journey, Gulliver sails as the captain of his own ship, but his crew turns on him and he arrives at another foreign country, this one inhabited by Houyhnhnms, rational horses who rule the country but lack any sense of individualism, and Yahoos, animal-like humans who serve the horses. Gulliver is intrigued by the Houyhnhnms and their culture, but he is forced to leave because of his resemblance to the Yahoos. Gulliver finally returns to his native England, where he finds himself repulsed by what he perceives as Yahoo-like tendencies in his wife and children. A broken man, his only comfort is speaking to his horses for several hours each day.

Presented to the reader as the written account of one Englishman's 16-year journey abroad, *Gulliver's Travels* is a satire of British and European culture, politics, colonialism, and of human nature itself. Swift's novel was considered highly controversial when it was published in 1726, in part because of the passages describing bodily functions, and the text was not published in its entirety until 1735.

Pride and Prejudice (1813) by Jane Austen

This novel of manners follows the misadventures and misunderstandings of Elizabeth Bennet and her four sisters as they search for love and marriage in early 19th-century England. Elizabeth, the spirited and intelligent second-oldest Bennet sister, is thrilled when her gentle, shy older sister, Jane, falls in love with Bingley, the new tenant of a nearby estate. Later, Elizabeth takes great offense when she hears Bingley's best friend, the handsome, arrogant Mr. Darcy, criticizing her at a ball.

The Bennet sisters are in the unfortunate position of being unable to inherit their father's estate, which can be passed only to a male heir. The heir to the estate, Mr. Collins, an insufferable bore, comes to visit, and announces that he has decided to marry one of the Bennet sisters. When he settles on Elizabeth, she refuses his proposal, and he marries her good friend Charlotte Lucas.

Elizabeth befriends George Wickham, a member of a militia based in nearby Meryton, and through him hears how he has been mistreated by Darcy. When Bingley unexpectedly leaves for London and all contact with Jane is cut off, Elizabeth blames Darcy. Elizabeth visits Charlotte at her new home on the estate of Lady Catherine de Bourgh, Darcy's aunt. While Elizabeth is there, Darcy comes for a prolonged visit. She is shocked and furious when he makes a profession of his love for her. She refuses him, and he leaves, giving her a letter before he goes. The letter makes clear that he separated Bingley from Jane only because he did not think Jane loved Bingley, and that he and his sister were wronged by Wickham rather than vice versa. Elizabeth begins to rethink her feelings for him.

Elizabeth, on vacation with her aunt and uncle, visits Pemberley, Darcy's estate. She runs into him unexpectedly and finds him greatly changed. She receives word from her family that her youngest sister, Lydia, has run away with

Wickham. Wickham agrees to marry Lydia, but, Elizabeth discovers, only after Darcy intervened, promising Wickham money in exchange for agreeing to marry her. Bingley returns to his country estate. He and Jane become engaged. Darcy visits his friend, and he and Elizabeth finally both admit that they love each other.

An ironic, comic study of the manners and morals of society, this novel praises the virtues of common sense and level-headedness over the prevailing notions of the romantic movement.

Frankenstein (1818) by Mary Shelley

This gothic tale begins with a series of letters from Robert Walton, the captain of a ship headed to the North Pole (presumably during the early 1800's, when the novel was written), to his sister in England. Walton tells his sister that his mission was interrupted by impenetrable ice, and while trapped he spotted a man with a dogsled. The man, Victor Frankenstein, was very weak and Walton took him aboard. In his last letter, Walton tells his sister that Victor has agreed to share his story, and Victor's tale begins.

Victor spends his youth in Geneva in the company of his cousin Elizabeth Lavenza and his friend Henry Clerval. At the University of Ingolstadt, he becomes obsessed with finding the secret of life. After several years, he believes he has the answer, and spends months creating a creature from spare body parts. One night he brings the creature to life, but, horrified by what he has done, he runs out into the streets. He finds Henry and brings him back to his apartment, but the monster has disappeared.

Victor is preparing to return to Geneva when he receives a letter informing him that his brother William was strangled. On his way home, he spots his monster and immediately believes he is the murderer. At home, Victor finds that his adopted sister has been accused. She is executed, and Victor, overwhelmed with guilt, goes to the mountains for solace. One day his monster appears and reveals that he murdered William out of his resentment toward Victor. Sad and lonely, he begs Victor to create a mate for him. Victor agrees and retreats to a desolate island to create the second monster. One night he spots his monster staring through the window, and horrified by his actions, he destroys his new creation. The monster swears revenge and says he will be with Victor on his wedding night.

Victor dumps the remains of his creation in the lake, but wind prevents him from returning to the island, and

he lands ashore at an unknown town. He is arrested for murder, and when he denies the charges he is shown Henry's strangled body. The mark of the monster's fingers is on Henry's neck, and Victor falls ill and is imprisoned. After he is acquitted, he returns to Geneva and marries Elizabeth. On their wedding night, the monster murders Elizabeth. Victor returns home, and his father dies of heartache. Victor vows revenge. He chases the monster northward and narrowly misses catching him. It is then that Victor is discovered by Walton, who concludes the story in letters to his sister. Soon after coming aboard, Victor dies, and a few days later Walton finds the monster weeping over Victor's body. The monster tells Walton of his solitary suffering and, freed by his creator's death, he heads north to die.

Supposedly the result of a ghost-story competition between Shelley, her then-husband, Percy Shelley, and Lord Byron, *Frankenstein* was an immediate best seller and has been adapted for film several times.

The Hunchback of Notre Dame (1831) by Victor Hugo

In 15th-century Paris, Quasimodo, the hunchbacked bell ringer of the cathedral of Notre Dame, has gone deaf because of his job ringing the bells. He was raised at the cathedral by the archdeacon, Claude Frollo, after being abandoned as an infant. Because of his deformities, Quasimodo has been mistreated throughout his life by everyone but Frollo. When Frollo, who is obsessed with the gypsy girl, Esmeralda, asks him to help kidnap her, Quasimodo does so, and when he is arrested for the act, he does not betray his protector. He is publicly humiliated for the kidnapping, and only Esmeralda treats him with kindness. Esmeralda, enchantingly beautiful, is a singer and dancer. She, too, is an orphan, and has spent her life trying to discover who her mother was. She was rescued from the kidnapping attempt by a handsome young officer, Pheobus. She falls in love with him, but is unable to see that he is a dishonorable man. Meeting Phoebus one night, she is horrified to see Frollo jump out of the shadows and stab him. Frollo disappears, leaving Pheobus gravely wounded. When Esmeralda is arrested for Phoebus's attempted murder and for witchcraft, he does not come forward to clear her name. Just before Esmeralda is to be hanged, she is rescued by Quasimodo, who hides Esmeralda inside Notre Dame. When Frollo discovers where she is, he attacks her. She discovers that

Frollo has been obsessed with her for some time. When the army storms Notre Dame to remove and hang Esmeralda, Frollo sneaks her out of the cathedral, but when she refuses to return his love, he turns her over to the army. Esmeralda is hanged. Quasimodo realizes that Frollo is responsible for her death, and he pushes him off the tower of the cathedral. Quasimodo then disappears. The story ends years later, with Esmeralda's skeleton being uncovered in a crypt, and Quasimodo's skeleton clinging to her bones.

Jane Eyre (1847) by Charlotte Brontë

Jane Eyre is a 19th-century British orphan who leaves her old life behind to become a governess in the home of the mysterious and handsome Mr. Rochester. Jane, parentless and penniless, is raised until the age of 10 in the home of her aunt, where she is abused by her older cousins. When she rebels, she is locked in the room in which her uncle died. Terrified and alone, Jane articulates an essential strangeness in herself which keeps her at a distance from other people.

After a physical collapse brought on by her terror, Jane is sent to Lowood Orphan Asylum. Under the supervision of the kind and gentle Miss Temple, Lowood is bearable, despite the cruelty of its director, Reverend Brocklehurst. Jane makes a close friend in Helen Burns, who dies of typhoid fever. Jane remains at Lowood until the age of 18, when she finds a post as governess to Adele, the ward of the wealthy and eccentric Edward Rochester.

Jane quickly warms to her new life at Thornfield, Rochester's home. Rochester is not in residence, and it is three months before he returns. When he does return, Jane quickly falls in love with him. Strange things begin to happen. Rochester's bed curtains catch fire one night. Jane is urged to keep her bedroom door bolted while she sleeps. The mysterious and unfriendly Grace Poole, who lives at Thornfield, seems more and more sinister. Mr. Rochester and Jane become engaged, but on their wedding day it is disclosed that Rochester has another wife, Bertha, who is insane and violent, and he keeps her locked in Thornfield's attic under Grace's care.

Jane leaves Rochester and is eventually taken in by the charitable Rivers siblings, St. John, Mary, and Diana. Eventually St. John asks Jane to marry him and accompany him on his mission to India, but just as she is finally convinced to become engaged, she imagines she hears Rochester's voice calling her. She realizes that she still loves him, and travels to Thornfield, only to discover that Bertha burned Thornfield and Rochester was blinded trying, unsuccessfully, to save her. Rochester and Jane marry.

Jane Eyre brings together elements of the gothic novel—foreshadowing, sense of unknown terror, the supernatural—and the romantic novel, while also providing a detailed portrait of a complex and highly moral woman.

Wuthering Heights (1847) by Emily Brontë

This is the story of the passionate and tumultuous relationship between Catherine Earnshaw, a wealthy and rebellious woman, and Heathcliff, her father's ward, and of the destruction their love brings to two families. When the narrator, Lockwood, moves to Thrushcross Grange, he becomes fascinated with his landlord, the mysterious and misanthropic Heathcliff, resident of Wuthering Heights. Paying a visit to Wuthering Heights, he finds Heathcliff out, and the other residents of Wuthering Heights, Hareton Earnshaw, Catherine Heathcliff, and the servant Joseph, extremely unfriendly. Lockwood, unable to return home because of snow, spends the night. Before falling asleep, he reads the journals of a young girl named Catherine Earnshaw. That night he dreams of a ghostly girl reaching through the window. In his horror, Lockwood screams, waking Heathcliff. Heathcliff cries for Catherine to come back. In the morning, Lockwood returns to Thrushcross Grange, becoming ill on the walk. During his recovery, Lockwood learns the story of Heathcliff from his servant, Ellen.

Catherine and her brother, Hindley Earnshaw, lived at Wuthering Heights. Their father returned one day with a gypsy boy, Heathcliff. Mistreated by Hindley, Heathcliff quickly replaced him in his father's affections. When Mr. Earnshaw died, Hindley, newly married, took over the estate. Catherine and Heathcliff, inseparable, spent their days wandering on the moor. However, Catherine eventually became close to Edgar Linton of nearby Thrushcross Grange. Heathcliff, in love with Catherine and profoundly hurt by her seeming disapproval of him, vanished. Catherine married Edgar. When Heathcliff returned, he married Edgar's sister, Isabella. Meanwhile, Hindley, whose wife died while giving birth to a son, Hareton, became an alcholic. Heathcliff, having moved back into Wuthering Heights, vowed to raise Hareton to be uncultured and uneducated.

Isabella immediately realized that it was a mistake to marry Heathcliff. Eventually she escaped to London and gave birth to a son, Linton. Catherine died giving birth to a daughter, Cathy. When Hindley died, Wuthering Heights passed to Heathcliff. After Isabella's death 13 years later, Heathcliff demanded that Linton be brought to Wuthering Heights. Three years later, with Edgar deathly ill, Linton tricked Cathy into entering Wuthering Heights, and Heathcliff locked her in, refusing to let her leave until she married Linton. Desperate to see her father before he died, Cathy agreed. Edgar died, leaving Thrushcross Grange vacant for a tenant, bringing the story to the present.

Lockwood leaves Thrushcross Grange soon after. On his return a year later, he finds that Linton and Heathcliff eventually died, but not before Heathcliff had a revelation about all the harm he had done. Cathy and Hareton are in love and engaged. There are rumors that Heathcliff and Catherine can be seen wandering the moor together at night.

Wuthering Heights is distinguished by its tight plotting, its emphasis on the supernatural, and in the character of the Byronic hero Heathcliff.

David Copperfield (1849–50) by Charles Dickens

Set in early 19th-century England, and told in the first person, this novel is the story of a boy who tries to maintain his belief in humanity through the hardships and loneliness of an orphan's life and into adult maturity.

David Copperfield's father dies before his birth, and his mother later marries the cruel Mr. Murdstone. As a young boy, David is taken by his beloved servant, Peggotty, to her brother, Daniel's, house, where he meets Ham and Little Em'ly. David is later sent to boarding school where he is befriended by James Steerforth. He returns home on holiday to discover that his mother has had a baby. He next returns after his mother and baby brother have died.

Sent to work in London by his stepfather, David boards with the constantly debt-ridden Mr. Micawber and his family. When the Micawbers leave London, David decides to find his wealthy aunt, Betsey Trotwood. She agrees to oversee his education, and he is sent to school in Canterbury, where he boards with Mr. Wickfield and his daughter, Agnes, and where he becomes acquainted with Wickfield's clerk, the evil Uriah Heep. David comes to abhor Uriah, to respect Agnes greatly, and to worry about Wickfield's drinking. When he leaves their home after finishing school in order to take a trip to visit Peggotty and her family, he runs into Steerforth, who accompanies David on his trip. At Daniel Peggotty's, they discover that Little Em'ly, now the radiantly beautiful Emily, has just become engaged to Ham.

David returns to London and enters an apprenticeship with a proctor, Mr. Spenlow. He becomes reacquainted with Mr. Micawber. David falls in love with Spenlow's daughter, Dora. Hearing that Uriah Heep has insinuated himself still further into Wickfield's business, he learns that Uriah's ultimate goal is to ruin Wickfield and marry Agnes.

Steerforth runs away with Emily, later deserting her, unmarried. Betsey Trotwood loses her fortune and comes to depend upon David. David and Dora marry, but she proves to be a childlike and incompetent homemaker. Emily is saved from a house of prostitution, and Daniel Peggotty makes plans to immigrate to Australia with her.

Through the help of Mr. Micawber, Uriah Heep's criminal actions are exposed. Betsey Trotwood's estate is recovered. The Micawbers also decide to immigrate to Australia, and leave with Emily and Daniel Peggoty. Ham dies while rescuing Steerforth from a shipwreck. Dora dies. David realizes that he loves Agnes, and is finally married to her.

Considered an important contribution to the creation of the bildungsroman, which traces a character from youth to maturity, *David Copperfield* is replete with rich characters and keen sociological observations.

The Scarlet Letter (1850) by Nathaniel Hawthorne

This story within a story takes place in a Puritan settlement in Boston in the late 17th century. It begins with a narrator relating his discovery of a strange manuscript in a Massachusetts customhouse in the mid-19th century. Wrapped in a scarlet, gold-embroidered cloth shaped like the letter "A," the manuscript reveals the story of Hester Prynne, a woman who had lived in the Puritan settlement. After losing his job at the customhouse, the narrator decides to write a novel based on the manuscript.

Hester's tale begins the day she and her infant daughter, Pearl, are led from the town prison to the scaffold, where she is sharply criticized by the town elders. Hester had been sent to Boston by her elderly husband, who stayed behind in Europe to settle his affairs, but inexplicably never arrived. While waiting for him, Hester gave birth to a daughter, proving herself an adulteress. She is made to wear a scarlet "A" on her chest, which, as one man in the watching crowd tells an unfamiliar elderly observer, symbolizes her status.

The elderly observer is Hester's long-lost husband, who had been captured by Native Americans while on his way to Boston, and had just arrived. Vengeful toward Hester and her secret lover, he settles there, takes the name of Roger Chillingworth, and begins to practice medicine. He reveals his true identity to no one, save Hester herself. The years pass, and while living in a cottage on the edge of town, Hester works as a seamstress as Pearl grows up into a stubborn and unusually perceptive child. Arthur Dimmesdale, a kind young minister, helps Hester retain custody of Pearl. Suffering from heart disease, he grows increasingly ill, and Chillingworth, who suspects a psychological connection between the illness and Hester, moves in to care for him. His suspicions are confirmed by a mark on Dimmesdale's chest.

One night Hester and Pearl find Dimmesdale on the scaffold, punishing himself for his sins. Pearl, guessing his true identity, asks him to tell the town that he is her father, but he refuses, and a meteor draws an "A" in the sky. Hester asks Chillingworth to leave Dimmesdale alone, but is unsuccessful. Hester meets Dimmesdale in the forest, and the pair decide to sail to Europe with Pearl in four days. The day before they are to leave, Dimmesdale ascends the scaffold with Hester and Pearl and reveals his true identity—and the scarlet "A" emblazoned on his chest—to the townspeople, then dies suddenly. Chillingworth dies the next year, and Hester and Pearl leave Boston. Years later, following Pearl's marriage, Hester returns. When she dies, she is buried next to Dimmesdale. The two share a headstone engraved with a scarlet "A."

An exploration of sin, hypocrisy, religion, individualism, and America's Puritan roots, *The Scarlet Letter* helped solidify Hawthorne's reputation as an American writer on universal human issues. The novel has been adapted to film several times, and is standard reading in high school classrooms.

Moby Dick (1851) by Herman Melville

The novel's famous opening words, "Call me Ishmael," introduce the narrator of this epic novel about whaling and obsession. In his hope to find a job on a whaling ship,

Ishmael sets out for New Bedford, Massachusetts, and meets Queequeg, a strange tattooed harpooner from the South Pacific. They decide to seek work together and head to Nantucket, then the center of America's whaling industry. There they sign on with the crew of the *Pequod*. The ship's captain, Ahab, is strangely absent; he is recovering from the loss of his leg after surviving a violent attack by a sperm whale.

The *Pequod* sets off with a large and diverse crew. Captain Ahab finally makes an appearance on deck, balancing on a false leg made from a sperm whale's jaw. He declares his intention to hunt down and destroy Moby Dick, the fearsome white whale that took his leg. He nails a gold doubloon to the mast, offering it as a reward to the first man who spots the whale. Most of the crew heartily endorse the mission, though the first mate, Starbuck, expresses misgivings.

As the *Pequod* sails toward Africa, a mysterious group of men emerges from the hold; they are Ahab's private harpoon crew, led by Fedallah. The *Pequod* encounters other ships, whose men share ominous tales of Moby Dick's extraordinary powers and their fatal encounters with him. The *Pequod* successfully hunts other whales, and Ishmael explains the nature of whaling in great detail.

Ahab's relentless obsession deepens. Descending into madness, he casts the whale as the living embodiment of evil, which he presumes to destroy on his own. He forges a harpoon out of steel for the express purpose of killing Moby Dick.

The great white whale is finally spotted, and after an intensive three-day hunt the *Pequod* finds him. The violent encounter is a disaster as Ahab is yanked into the depths by his own harpoon, Moby Dick rams the ship, and the *Pequod* sinks, drowning the entire crew. Ishmael survives, floating on an empty coffin, until another ship rescues him.

Melville's novel is widely regarded as a masterpiece of American literature. Combining elements of several genres, including tragedy and detailed documentary, the novel is ultimately an allegory of man's struggle to dominate nature and confront evil.

Leaves of Grass (1855–92) by Walt Whitman

First published in 1855 and revised and expanded over the next 37 years, this work comprises almost all of the poet's published verse. Whitman wanted to document life in the

United States of America in a new, homegrown style. *Leaves of Grass* went through six revised and expanded editions and eventually consisted of 383 poems divided into 14 sections.

The first edition began with more than 1,000 lines that would subsequently be titled "Song of Myself." This poem expounds Whitman's ideal of democracy based on a profound interconnectedness. It introduces the speaker of *Leaves of Grass* as "no stander above men and women or apart from them" who believes that "[w]hoever degrades another degrades me." Whitman celebrates the physical body and the material world. In poems such as "I Sing the Body Electric," he inventories the corporeal realm and its potential for reproduction, beauty, and pleasure in incantatory lists known as "catalogs." "Children of Adam" and "Calamus" are the most overtly sexual sections. At the center of *Leaves of Grass*, "Drum-Taps" records the poet's Civil War years spent caring for the sick and injured in military hospitals, followed by "Memories of President Lincoln," which features "When Lilacs Last in the Dooryard Bloomed," a famous elegy for the assassinated leader. Having suffered two strokes and become homebound, Whitman acknowledges diminished physical powers but expresses satisfaction with his poetic accomplishment in the closing sections of his masterwork.

Whitman became famous not only as the "good gray poet" but also as a controversial public figure. Under charges of obscenity, he was fired from a government position and his publisher rejected later editions of *Leaves of Grass*. Whitman himself disclaimed homosexual interpretations of his poetry, but this aspect of his life and work is commonly accepted today.

The poetic form of Whitman's exceptionally long lines depends on repeated words and sentence structures rather than rhyme or fixed meter. This innovation opened the door to perhaps the most characteristic feature of 20th-century poetry: free verse. Modernist poets such as Ezra Pound, T. S. Eliot, William Carlos Williams, and Hart Crane inherited Whitman's drive to write new epics defining their time and place. *Leaves of Grass* is widely recognized as the most comprehensive single expression of America's democratic ideals, diverse population, and varied landscape.

Madame Bovary (1857) by Gustave Flaubert

Shy and awkward as a boy, Charles Bovary grows up to be a dull young man. He barely manages to establish himself as a country doctor in a provincial French town. His mother arranges his marriage to an unpleasant widow, who dies and leaves Charles much less money than expected.

Charles then pursues the beautiful Emma Roualt, who has spent years devouring popular novels that leave her yearning for romance. Charles and Emma are married in an elaborate wedding, but Emma quickly finds herself disillusioned and bored to the point of illness. When she becomes pregnant, Charles decides to move in hopes of curing Emma's malaise.

In their new town, Emma meets Leon, who shares her love for romantic novels. Emma gives birth to Charles's daughter, Berthe, but finds motherhood disappointing. She resists Leon and guiltily throws herself into her family duties. Leon gives up and moves to Paris, leaving Emma despondent.

A wealthy neighbor named Rodolphe seduces Emma. Their passionate affair has the town buzzing with gossip, though Charles remains oblivious. After Charles harms a patient through incompetence, Emma becomes even more fixated on Rodolphe. The worldly Rodolphe tires of her and shatters her romantic fantasies. Emma falls deathly ill.

Charles finds himself in serious financial straits by the time Emma recovers. Nevertheless, he takes her to the opera in nearby Rouen, where she encounters Leon. This time Emma throws herself into an affair. She begins borrowing from a moneylender named Lheureux to finance her excursions to Rouen.

Eventually the affair sours under the weight of Emma's emotional excesses. When her debts mount, Lheureux moves to seize her property. Horrified at the prospect of being found out, she begs Leon for help and attempts to sell herself to Rodolphe. Finding no solution, Emma eats arsenic and dies an agonizing death. Charles cherishes her memory for a time, but is crushed to discover letters from her lovers. He dies alone, and Emma's daughter is left an orphan.

Madame Bovary was a pioneering work, both in its stylistic innovations and its realism. Flaubert's rejection of middle-class morality and his frank accounts of extramarital sex provoked a storm of outrage. He and the book's publisher were brought up on charges of violating public morals—and after their acquittal, *Madame Bovary* became a best seller.

Great Expectations (1860–61) by Charles Dickens

This novel combines intrigue, personal growth, and issues of social class as it follows the life of an orphan, Pip, who narrates his story from boyhood to adulthood in 19th-century England. Pip lives with his sister and brother-in-law, Joe, a blacksmith. One afternoon, while visiting his parents' grave, he encounters an escaped criminal. Terrified, Pip agrees to help him by bringing him food and a file. When the man is caught, Pip worries that his help will be discovered, but he is never found out.

Pip is brought to the home of a wealthy and eccentric recluse, Miss Havisham, to read to her. Pip falls in love with Miss Havisham's ward, the beautiful and cold-hearted Estella. Miss Havisham, having been left at the altar as a young woman, has allowed nothing in her house to be changed since that day. She still wears her wedding dress, and the table is still covered with food from her wedding feast. She is consumed with the idea of taking vengeance on men.

Shortly thereafter Pip mysteriously comes into a fortune. He assumes that the fortune is from Miss Havisham, in order to make it possible for him to marry Estella. Mr. Jaggers, Miss Havisham's lawyer, is in charge of Pip's money, and arranges for Pip's education in London.

While in London, Pip becomes friends with Herbert Pocket. Pip spends his money recklessly. He befriends Wemmick, who works with Jaggers. Pip continues to love Estella, and is heartbroken when she marries Bentley Drummle, a man of low character and dim intelligence.

One night Pip returns to his apartment and finds the convict he helped when he was a boy. The convict, Magwitch, has been supplying his fortune, not Miss Havisham. Devastated that he is indebted to a convict, Pip agrees to help Magwitch get out of England, and with the help of Wemmick and Herbert, develops a plan for the escape. Pip discovers that Estella is Magwitch's daughter and that her mother is Jaggers's housekeeper, who was once one of his criminal clients. Pip pays one last visit to Miss Havisham before she dies.

Magwitch is caught during the escape and dies in prison just after Pip tells him that he has a daughter. Pip reunites with Joe. He joins Herbert's firm and prospers abroad. The story ends when, years later, he reunites with Estella, whose husband has died.

Great Expectations is considered one of Dickens's mostly masterfully constructed novels—making up for what it lacks in breadth with a compact narrative, a finely wrought and subtle portrait of its narrator, and with its examination of class issues.

War and Peace (1865–69) by Leo Tolstoy

This sweeping novel covers the lives of several families both in times of peace and in times of war. Combining passionate romance, a historical account of the Napoleonic Wars, and philosophical essays, the story is enormous both in length and scope. It famously opens with a party in which many of the principal characters are introduced, and then focuses primarily on the lives of three people, Prince Andrei Bolkonsky, Pierre Bezhukov, and Natasha Rustov.

Prince Andrei is an arrogant and high-minded member of St. Petersburg's aristocracy, but he perceives the aristocratic world as lacking truth or meaning. He believes that he will find a sense of purpose by joining the military. He leaves his family at their country estate to become an aide-de-camp in the approaching war. While at war, he comes to believe that battle is not a place of glory, but rather a place as empty as the society he has left behind.

Natasha is the beautiful, spirited young daughter of a count who has lost much of his wealth. When she meets Andrei, shortly before he reenters the war, they quickly fall in love. However, before they are married, she is seduced by another man and, in her shame, ends her engagement. Andrei leaves for war, and Natasha is left alone. Andrei is gravely wounded in battle. He and Natasha are united briefly before he dies.

Andrei's friend Pierre, the moral center of the book, is the clumsy, ungainly, illegitimate son of an extraordinarily wealthy man. When his father dies, Pierre inherits his fortune and suddenly becomes a sought-after bachelor. In his innocence, he marries the scheming Elena, who is interested only in his money. Her brother, Anatoly, seduces Natasha. Pierre meets Natasha during the incident and falls in love with her, but does not believe there is any hope of ever having a life with her. Unhappy in his marriage and in search a sense of purpose, Pierre reaches for one philosophical system after another. Retiring to his country estate, he attempts to free his serfs and find a new way to manage his land, but his social experiments lead to disappointment. He separates from Elena, who eventually dies. He joins the army, witnesses the horrors of war firsthand, and experiences a conversion of sorts. He is eventually taken prisoner of war and is forced to participate in the disastrous French retreat from Moscow. He is ultimately freed by the Russians.

Eventually, Natasha comes to love the steadfast Pierre, who has long loved her, and the two marry. In the novel's first epilogue, Natasha's youthful brilliance fades to the drabness of an older married woman, and Pierre has found happiness in domestic life.

In addition to following the three main characters, long sections of the novel are devoted to peripheral or symbolic characters. Among them is Napoleon, who attempts to manage every aspect of battle, and who eventually flees from the disaster his own army faces. Napoleon is contrasted with the Russian general, Kutuzov, who understands that he cannot control the chaos resulting from each small decision made on the battlefield.

War and Peace demonstrates Tolstoy's view that history is shaped not by the decisions of great men but rather by the cascading randomness of small decisions. Like *Anna Karenina*, it shows that a moral and fulfilling life is created through everyday choices and not through grand passions.

Crime and Punishment (1866)
by Fyodor Dostoyevsky

In this novel, set in 19th-century Russia, Raskolnikov, a young intellectual, ponders killing Aliyona Ivanovna, a pawnbroker, not for money, although he is deeply in debt, but for philosophical reasons. He reasons that if he kills her, he will be helping all those that owe her money; he refutes the idea that morality even exists, and thus that the idea of crime exists; and he believes that there are great men who are exempt from the standard rules of moral conduct.

Raskolnikov meets a clerk, Marmeladov, who tells him of his daughter, Sonia, a virtuous girl who has become a prostitute in order to help her family. Raskolnikov receives a letter from his mother telling him that his sister, Dounia, fired after refusing an affair with her employer, Svidrigailov, has become engaged to a wealthy businessman, and that the mother and daughter will soon be coming to St. Petersburg. All around him, Raskolnikov sees people whose lives are filled with suffering. He follows through with the murder, killing Aliyona Ivanovna with an axe, and, when seen at the crime scene by her sister, Lizaveta, kills her as well.

Raskolnikov falls ill, and is cared for by two friends. He is plagued with unease about the murders. He worries about being caught, and about the reasoning behind the crime. He becomes paranoid, convinced that everyone he encounters is conspiring to make him confess. He no longer trusts in the reasoning that led him to kill Aliyona Ivanovna, and cannot decide on the one real reason as to why he committed the crime. A police detective, Porfiry Petrovich, becomes convinced of his guilt, but is unable to prove it.

Marmeladov dies, and Raskolnikov helps his family. He meets Sonia, and is deeply moved by the choices she has made to help her family. Although another man confesses to the murders, Raskolnikov tells Sonia that it was he who killed the women. At Sonia's urging, Raskolnikov turns himself in, and is sentenced to hard labor in Siberia. Sonia accompanies him, and Raskolnikov, at first unrepentant, becomes influenced by Sonia's selflessness and generosity, as well as by a revelatory dream, and eventually comes to truly repent for his crime.

Crime and Punishment exemplifies Dostoyevsky's preoccupation with extreme psychological states of mind, and with philosophical searching and emotional suffering leading to religious redemption.

Anna Karenina (1878)
by Leo Tolstoy

A vibrant woman, Anna Karenina, a member of St. Petersburg's upper class, is married to the emotionally withdrawn Alexei Karenin. During a trip to Moscow, which she takes in order to help convince her sister-in-law, Dolly, to forgive her husband, Stepan Oblonsky, for an affair, Anna meets Count Vronsky, a handsome young cavalry officer. She falls in love with him, and so must choose between a life with Vronsky, in which she would be forced to leave behind her young son, Sergei, and a life in which she would continue to live within a loveless marriage. She chooses Vronsky. The two eventually have a daughter together. When Anna's husband refuses a divorce, the lovers go into exile.

At the same time that Anna's story unfolds, the stories of the Oblonskys and of Konstantin Levin unfold as well. Dolly Oblonsky, married to Anna's irresponsible brother, Stepan, attempts to hold her family together while Stepan recklessly squanders the family's money. Levin, a close family friend, asks Kitty, Dolly's sister, to marry him. When Kitty initially refuses, Levin, heartbroken, devotes himself to the management of his country estate. He becomes more and more attached to the land, finding peace in the rhythms of country life. Eventually, Kitty realizes that she loves Levin. After the two marry, she lives on his country estate with him.

As the years pass, Anna becomes consumed with jealousy, certain that Vronsky no longer loves her. She is unable to love her daughter with the same devotion she feels for the son she abandoned. Vronsky, his career ruined by the love affair and now faced with Anna's increasing paranoia, withdraws from her emotionally and physically, retreating to his mother's home. When he does not respond to a letter that Anna sends him, she kills herself, throwing herself in front of a train. Only when she is lying on the track does she realize that her choices in life were choices that caused her to abandon what would have been true happiness—the steadiness of family life.

Anna Karenina demonstrates Tolstoy's belief in the weight of everyday choices over grand intellectual ideas as holding responsibility for the outcome of a life. It also demonstrates his philosophical rejection of romantic love for the deeper love of family and of land.

Adventures of Huckleberry Finn (1884)
by Mark Twain

This is the story of Huck Finn, an adventurous and free-spirited preteen from Missouri who rafts down the Mississippi River with Jim, a runaway slave desperate to go to the North. To escape his abusive alchoholic father and the kind, but overbearing, townsfolk who wish to civilize him, Huck fakes his own death and runs away to camp out on a nearby island. There he discovers Jim, who has run away after overhearing his mistress's plans to sell him to a slave trader. They are hiding on the island when the river rises, and a house with a dead man inside floats by. Jim discovers that the man is Huck's father, but decides not to tell Huck. Huck, disguised as a girl, goes to town and learns that Jim is a suspect in Huck's "murder," and that the townspeople think Jim is hiding on the island.

To escape discovery, the pair decide to float down the Mississippi River in a raft, hoping to reach Cairo, where they can board a steamship that will take them north to the free states. Their plans are snagged when a dense fog causes them to accidentally pass Cairo in the night, and their problems are compounded when their raft is destroyed. Forced ashore, Jim hides in a swamp while Huck is taken in by a "civilized" family, but the family's longstanding feud with another family results in the slaughter of the men of both families, and Huck and Jim return to the river. Soon after, the pair make the mistake of

rescuing two con artists, who force them to take part in scheming against the inhabitants of the towns they pass. Eventually, Huck and Jim escape their clutches and return to the raft, but the con artists catch up with them and sell Jim into slavery. Huck sets out to free him and discovers that Jim has been sold to Huck's friend Tom Sawyer's Aunt Sally. Huck pretends to be Tom, and when the real Tom arrives he pretends to be his younger brother, Sid. They contrive an elaborate plan to rescue Jim, but are chased and injured by local farmers when they attempt their getaway. In the midst of the chaos, Tom's Aunt Polly arrives at her sister's house and informs the group that Jim's mistress has died and has freed Jim in her will. Jim tells Huck that the dead man in the house was his father, and Aunt Sally offers to adopt and civilize Huck. Fed up with "civilized" life, Huck turns down her offer and decides to set out on his own.

Frequently banned in schools and libraries since the year of its publication, this great American novel is both an adventure story and a scathing satire of antebellum southern society.

Tess of the d'Urbervilles (1891)
by Thomas Hardy

The Durbeyfields are an uneducated peasant family in rural England. When the local parson remarks that their name is derived from "d'Urberville," an ancient noble family, John Durbeyfield decides to cash in. He sends Tess, his beautiful daughter, to make her claim with the local d'Urbervilles (actually a nouveau-riche family that has modified the name to appear aristocratic).

Tess accepts a job on the d'Urberville estate and is soon fending off advances from Alec, the family's playboy son. One night Alec finds her alone in the woods and takes advantage of her. After ending their brief relationship, Tess returns home pregnant. Her sickly child, Sorrow, soon dies.

Hoping for a fresh start, Tess leaves home and becomes a milkmaid. She meets and falls in love with Angel Clare, a minister's son. Tess is tormented by her disgrace, but finally agrees to marry him. On their wedding night, Angel confesses a sexual indiscretion. Assuming that their sins are identical, Tess tells Angel about her past. Disgusted that Tess does not measure up to his standards of purity, Angel leaves for Brazil.

After a brief and miserable return to her family, Tess again searches for work. Alec d'Urberville returns, insisting that he has changed, but Tess rejects him. She throws herself into back-breaking field work, praying that Angel will someday accept her past. When John Durbeyfield dies, Tess's family is left homeless. In desperation, she gives in and becomes Alec's mistress to support her family.

After traveling to Brazil and barely surviving a bout of illness, Angel realizes that he has been unfair. He returns to England, but finds Tess living with Alec. Brokenhearted, Tess is forced to send Angel away. When Alec sneers at her plight, Tess stabs him and runs to Angel, hoping that the murder will somehow redeem her. The couple goes into hiding, then flees to Stonehenge. Just before she is captured by the police, Tess asks Angel to care for her younger sister, Liza-Lu. Angel and Liza-Lu watch outside the prison walls as a black flag signals Tess's execution.

An early modernist writer, Thomas Hardy shocked Victorian audiences by exploring the sexual double standards that victimize women. The novel was originally published in serial form by the *Graphic Illustrated Weekly*, a newspaper that censored the sexual content; a British bishop later burned the book.

The Importance of Being Earnest (1895) by Oscar Wilde

Set in London and the English countryside during the late 19th century, this comedy of errors explores what Wilde perceived as the shallow and hypocritical world of Victorian society. A take on the Victorian melodrama, the play opened at the height of Wilde's success. Just two weeks later, he was publicly accused of homosexuality, which led to his incarceration and eventual death.

Act I   Wealthy young Algernon Moncrieff is at home in his London flat when his friend from the country, Ernest Worthing, drops by. Algernon is expecting his aunt, Lady Bracknell, and his cousin Gwendolen for tea, and Ernest confesses that he has come to town to propose to Gwendolen. Algernon demands that he explain the inscription in his cigarette case, which is addressed to "Uncle Jack" from "little Cecily." Ernest admits that his real name is Jack and that Ernest is the alias he uses to escape the responsibilities of his country estate, which include his ward, Cecily, the grandaughter of the man who adopted Jack when he was a baby. Algernon confesses that he too has an alias, his invalid "friend" Bunbury, whom he uses to escape his city life, and Jack tells him that he is going to "kill" Ernest because Cecily has become too curious. Gwendolen and Lady Bracknell arrive, Jack proposes,

and Gwendolen accepts, saying that she could not marry a man who was not named Ernest as the name "inspires absolute confidence." However, when Jack tells Lady Bracknell that the man who adopted him as a baby found him in a handbag at the train station, Lady Bracknell forbids the engagement.

Act II   Eager to meet Cecily, Algernon travels to Jack's estate, pretending to be Jack's brother, Ernest. Jack arrives home and, because of his own lies, is forced to go along with Algernon. Algernon proposes to Cecily, who accepts because she has always been fascinated by Ernest, in part because of his name. Algernon leaves to ask the rector to change his name. Gwendolen arrives at the estate and is surprised to learn that Ernest has a ward. Cecily explains that Jack Worthing is her guardian and Ernest Worthing is her fiancé. Gwendolen responds that Ernest is her fiancé. Jack and Algernon arrive and are forced to confess.

Act III   Gwendolen and Cecily confront Jack and Algernon, who explain the reasons for their lies, and the women are appeased when the men announce their plans to be christened Ernest. Lady Bracknell arrives, having followed Gwendolen, and again refuses to allow a marriage between Gwendolen and Jack. Algernon tells his aunt that he is engaged to Cecily, and Lady Bracknell refuses this engagement as well, until she learns that Cecily is a woman of means. Jack explains that he will agree to that marriage only if he can marry Gwendolen, at which point the rector arrives. When he mentions Cecily's governess, Miss Prism, Lady Bracknell immediately requests her presence.

Miss Prism, it is revealed, had left Lady Bracknell's sister's house with a baby 28 years prior, and had never returned. Miss Prism admits that she had lost the baby, having accidentally put him in a handbag, which she left at the train station. Jack shows her the handbag in which he was found, and she confirms that it is hers. Jack learns that he was christened Ernest John and that he is Algernon's older brother, thereby discovering that he had been unknowingly telling the truth the entire time. Happily, all embrace as Jack announces that he now understands "the vital importance of Being Earnest."

Heart of Darkness (1902) by Joseph Conrad

Sitting aboard a boat moored on the Thames, Charlie Marlow begins to recount the tale of his harrowing journey through Africa. As a young man craving adventure,

Marlow secured a position as captain of a riverboat steamer plying the Congo; his employer is identified only as "the Company," a Belgian trading concern. On his arrival, Marlow is struck by the brutal treatment meted out by the Company's agents to the local workers.

Marlow is sent to a Company station run by a shifty general manager. Stuck there while his boat undergoes repairs, he hears talk of Kurtz, a wildly successful trader based upriver. Kurtz is said to be idealistic and polished, but dark rumors swirl around his activities.

Marlow sets out to find Kurtz. As his boat plies deeper into the jungle, the crew comes under attack from a band of natives. When they reach Kurtz's outpost, Marlow encounters a wild-eyed Russian, who explains that Kurtz now rules over the natives as a godlike figure, controlling the local ivory supply through bloody raids. Severed heads impaled on fence posts attest to depravity, but the Russian insists that the usual moral judgments do not apply here. Gravely ill, Kurtz is brought out on a stretcher and carried onto the steamship. The Russian reveals that Kurtz ordered the attack on Marlow's boat, hoping to be left to his own devices in the jungle.

Kurtz attempts to escape, but Marlow finds him crawling on his hands and knees back to the native camp. With his mysterious passenger once again secured on board, Marlow turns back toward civilization, but Kurtz is fading. With his last breath, Kurtz whispers "The horror! The horror!"

Marlow returns to Europe and seeks out Kurtz's fiancée. Still in mourning for a man she regarded as virtuous, she begs to know Kurtz's last words. Unwilling to crush her idealism, Marlow lies, telling the fiancée that Kurtz died while calling her name.

This spare novella, an early modernist masterwork, explores the corrupting effects of colonialism on the occupiers themselves. While breaking with Victorian literary traditions, Conrad simultaneously shattered Victorian myths that imperialism was simply a benevolent means for spreading Western civilization. Decades after its publication, *Heart of Darkness* inspired Francis Ford Coppola's 1979 film, *Apocalypse Now*, which used the Vietnam War as its backdrop.

The Metamorphosis (1916) by Franz Kafka

Gregor Samsa is a young traveling salesman who wakes up one morning and discovers that he has transformed into a giant cockroach. His parents and younger sister knock on his door, concerned that he has overslept and is late for work, and when he tries to respond, he realizes that his voice sounds different. Soon his manager arrives, and Gregor, with great difficulty, opens his bedroom door. The manager and family are horrified and lock him in his room, and Gregor grows increasingly depressed. Once the breadwinner for his family, he is now treated with disgust. His parents neglect him, but his sister brings him food and cleans his room.

Gregor's parents and sister are forced to find jobs. His sister begins to neglect him, and his father's temper grows worse. When Gregor attempts to leave his room, his father violently forces him back, and on one occasion he throws a torrent of apples at Gregor, embedding an apple in his back and leaving him badly wounded. Gregor's family takes in lodgers and turns his room into a storage area, and because of his intense sadness he eats less and less and grows weak. One night the lodgers hear Gregor's sister playing her violin, and they ask her to play for them in the parlor. Her music is so beautiful that Gregor cannot help himself from crawling to her. The lodgers see him and, disgusted, announce that they are leaving. Gregor's sister tells her parents that they must accept that Gregor is gone and decide how to get rid of the cockroach. Gregor crawls back into his room and dies later that night. The next morning, the housekeeper informs the family of his death. Gregor's family decides to take a rare day-trip to the countryside, and while riding on the electric tram they suddenly realize that their prospects are far from bleak. The story ends as the parents notice their daughter's physical beauty and then decide it is time to find her a husband.

Although *The Metamorphosis* found only a small audience upon publication, the novella helped to establish Kafka as the voice of 20th-century alienation and existential despair.

The Age of Innocence (1920) by Edith Wharton

This tale of duty versus happiness takes place in late 19th- and early 20th-century New York City. The story opens during an opera, at which flirtatious Newland Archer, a respected and fashionable lawyer, makes eyes at May Welland, who accepts his marriage proposal later that night. Joining May in her box is her cousin, the exotic Countess Ellen Olenska, who was recently estranged from her Polish husband, and who has just returned to New York. Her family decides to give the countess a debutante ball to quell rumors about her fidelity, though Ellen finds their efforts provincial after her time abroad. Since avoiding family scandal is a high priority in their society, Newland is asked to counsel the countess against divorce, but during their increasingly friendly meetings he develops romantic feelings for her, which she reciprocates. He can speak with her candidly, without the propriety that strains his relationship with May. Though she is aware of the growing tension, May does not question her fiancé. Frightened by his feelings for Ellen and terrified of abandoning his social duty, Newland asks May, who is in Florida with her family, if they can be married sooner than planned, but May demurs. Back in New York, just after sharing an intense kiss with Ellen, Newland receives a telegram from May agreeing to marry him as soon as possible, and he finds that he lacks the courage to follow through with his deception.

After a year of marriage, Newland is still infatuated with the countess, and proposes they have an affair. Although it never happens, the family is suspicious and provides the countess with the financial means to return to Europe without returning to her husband. On the night of Ellen's farewell dinner, May tells Newland she confirmed that morning that she was pregnant, and casually, though meaningfully reveals that she informed Ellen of her pregnancy a fortnight earlier. Time passes, and after May's death, Newland travels to Paris with his grown son, Dallas. Dallas tells his father of his mother's deathbed confession that Newland gave up his happiness for their family, and Newland is both shocked and comforted by his wife's insight. Dallas sets up a meeting with the countess, though Newland realizes he has missed the "flower of life," and decides to sit outside her building while his son visits. He watches a butler draw the evening blinds in the countess's room, and returns to his hotel alone.

The novel's ironic title refers to the assumed innocence in an era better characterized by clandestine manipulation and repressed impulses. However, the book was initially not widely understood as criticism. Set in a world of strictly coded social behavior, this novel explores the tensions between the old rich and the nouveau-riche, and satirizes their understanding of sacrifice, obligation, and satisfaction.

Women in Love (1920) by D. H. Lawrence

Set primarily in a small coal-mining town in the English Midlands during World War I, this novel follows the Brangwen sisters, Ursula and Gudren, as they search for love. Ursula and Gudren, both present in Lawrence's earlier novel *The Rainbow*, are independent-minded, artistic, and intellectual free-thinkers. They both teach at the local grammar school. Gudren, an artist, has recently returned from London.

The novel opens with a marriage, to which the groom arrives late. Rupert Birkin, a school inspector, and Gerald Crich, the bride's brother and son of the owner of the coal mine, are both present at the wedding, as is Hermione Roddice. Hermione is obsessively in love with Birkin. Gudren is immediately attracted to Gerald, both because of his good looks and because of his cruel demeanor.

Birkin comes to inspect Ursula's classroom, but their encounter is interrupted by Hermione. She invites Ursula and Gudren to visit her family's estate. During the visit to Hermione's estate, Birkin, strongly attracted to Ursula, ends his romantic relationship with Hermione. Although Ursula and Birkin fall in love with each other, they constantly clash in their ideas about love and independence. Eventually they marry, planning to leave their jobs to live abroad.

Gerald and Birkin become close friends, with a strong homoerotic undercurrent present in their relationship. Gerald and Gudren admit their mutual attraction at a party at the Crich estate, but the evening is marred by the drowning death of Gerald's sister, Diana. Gudren is asked to teach art to his youngest sister, Winifred. When Gerald's long-ill father dies, she and Gerald enter into a relationship. Their relationship is stormy, with Gerald dominating Gudren sexually and emotionally.

Ursula, Birkin, Gudren, and Gerald travel together to the Alps. There Gudren and Gerald's relationship changes. Gudren becomes fascinated with a small, feeble artist, Loerke, and Gerald becomes obsessed with Gudren. Eventually Gerald brutally attacks Gudren and Loerke, and then walks off into the mountains to his death. Gudren stays on the Continent. Ursula and Birkin decide to leave for the warmer climate of Italy and eventually return to England.

Women in Love, whose publication was long delayed because of its frank descriptions of sexuality and its homoerotic themes, examines how the alienation of those living in the modern world interferes with love.

The Waste Land (1922) by T. S. Eliot

A poem of 434 lines in five sections, this touchstone of modernism depicts social, personal, and cultural breakdown in the West after World War I. The waste land's typical inhabitants go about mundane jobs in a featureless urban environment barely interacting with one another. In private life, such alienation results in sexual failure or violence. Nature itself is stricken with drought, and many of the poem's phrases are quotations—literal fragments of a culture in ruins. *The Waste Land* asks, Is there hope for the modern world?

The poem begins "April is the cruellest month"—spring raises the possibility, but not the fulfillment, of nature's rebirth. In the first section, quoting from *Ecclesiastes*, Dante's *Inferno*, and Charles Baudelaire's *Flowers of Evil*, among other sources, Eliot conjures a spiritually vacant, hellish latter-day metropolis. He reminds readers of various disastrous romances from the Western canon—Tristan and Isolde, Antony and Cleopatra, Aeneas and Dido, Adam and Eve—before concluding the second section with an allusion to Ovid's account of the rape of Philomel and a present-day discussion of marital boredom, infidelity, and abortion overheard in a London pub. In the third section, readers encounter Tiresias, the old, blind hermaphrodite and prophet of Greek myth, whom Eliot considered the most important figure in the poem. A gender expert who is reproductively nonfunctional due to age and physiology, Tiresias, physically unable to see, presents his vision of a deadly modern existence. The title of the fifth section, "What the Thunder Said," promises an answer, in metaphorical terms, to the question *The Waste Land* poses. This resolution turns out to be ambiguous at best: thunder is hopeful, but the land remains arid.

Among 434 footnotes, Eliot directs readers to Jessie L. Weston's *From Ritual to Romance*. Weston had traced the medieval Grail legend, one of Eliot's major sources, to a basic fertility myth shared by many cultures. A common original narrative such as this could stitch the modern fabric together, but the poet's use of footnotes emphasizes the inadequacy of any single reader's cultural foundation.

Ulysses (1922) by James Joyce

This long novel, the most prominent landmark in modernist literature, is a 20th-century re-imagining of Homer's *Odyssey*, containing 18 "chapters" that correlate to the episodes in the classical poem. The events, both actual and psychological—in the conscious and unconscious minds of the characters, described in "stream-of-consciousness" style—take place in Dublin between 8 A.M. on June 16, 1904, and 2 A.M. the next day. At the beginning, Stephen Dedalus (representing Odysseus's son, Telemachus), a young writer and self-absorbed aesthete, is living with companions in a seaside tower, having returned to Ireland from the Continent to visit his dying mother. His father is a feckless drunk, and in the day and night that follow, Stephen's actions and thoughts unfold in relation to those of his symbolic father, the "wandering" Jew, Leopold Bloom (Odysseus or Ulysses), a newspaper-ad salesman who has lost a son, and with whose path Stephen will unknowingly intersect during the day. Bloom, the natural man leading a normal life, is first seen at home, where he reads the morning paper while visiting the privy. He attends a funeral, goes to work, and lunches in a pub. Later, he will stroll to a strand where a young woman's tempting incites him to masturbate, an episode based on "Nausicaa" in the *Odyssey*.

Bloom is married to the sensuous and unfaithful Molly, his Penelope, whose trysts with Blazes Boylan sting his thoughts. Yet a visit to a post office reveals an amorous correspondence of his own. Stephen meanwhile teaches a class of inattentive schoolboys and is sent by the headmaster on an errand to a newspaper office, one of several plot elements linking him and Bloom, who meets Stephen's father at the funeral and dines with Stephen's uncle. In the afternoon, Bloom stops in the National Library, where Stephen is discoursing on Shakespeare. But they do not meet until well into the evening. Stephen has been out with friends and is quite drunk; Bloom responds to him with paternal concern and follows him through the now darkened city. They go to a brothel, and their long day climaxes in the extended, hallucinatory, dramatically structured "Nighttown" section, in which their unconscious minds deliver deep truths about their lives and natures. Bloom then brings Stephen home, feeds him, and offers him a bed; but his guest refuses. Bloom retires beside Molly, to whom is given the book's final words, a majestic monologue recounting her life and loves, including her courtship with her husband.

The novel ends with Molly's words, "yes I said yes I will Yes," reinforcing the affirmation of the closest human relations amid life's endless complexity and bottomless depth, despite human weakness and cruelty, and in the face of death, all depicted with unprecedented, and unequalled, linguistic and stylistic virtuosity.

The Great Gatsby (1925)
by F. Scott Fitzgerald

Nick Carraway tells his story. He is a young Yale graduate from a prominent midwestern family who moves to New York in the early 1920's to learn the bond business. After settling in the nouveau riche neighborhood of West Egg, Long Island, Nick visits his cousin Daisy Buchanan and her husband, Tom, who live in the old-money neighborhood of East Egg. While there, he meets Daisy's friend Jordan Baker, a cynical and beautiful professional golfer, who tells him that Tom is having an affair with Myrtle Wilson, whose blue-collar husband owns a garage on the road to Manhattan. Soon after, Nick attends a lavish party at the mansion next door to his house, which is owned by a stylish and popular millionaire named Jay Gatsby. Gatsby and Nick soon become friendly, and Nick becomes intrigued by the young millionaire who has notorious criminals for friends, and whose history and present business dealings are steeped in mystery.

Jordan tells Nick that Gatsby and Daisy had a love affair when they met before World War I. Gatsby asks Nick to help him see Daisy; the love affair is reignited, and Nick soon finds himself entangled in the love affairs of Gatsby, Daisy, Tom, and Myrtle. When Tom learns of Gatsby and Daisy's affair, he forces the entire group to take a trip into New York City, where he confronts Gatsby in a hotel suite. Gatsby begs Daisy to renounce Tom, but she refuses. Daisy and Gatsby drive back to Long Island, with Daisy at the wheel of Gatsby's car, and while driving past Wilson's garage, she accidentally runs over Myrtle Wilson, killing her. Nick urges Gatsby to leave town for his own safety, but Gatsby's love and fear for Daisy keep him from protecting himself. Tom tells Myrtle's husband, George, that Gatsby was the driver who killed Myrtle, and the tormented George shoots and kills Gatsby before killing himself.

The Buchanans conveniently leave town, and disheartened Nick is left to plan Gatsby's funeral, which few attend. Gatsby's father comes to the funeral, and Nick learns the true story of Gatsby's rags to riches rise to wealth and power. Traumatized and now cynical, Nick decides to leave New York, and he ends his "memoir" by reflecting on humankind's inability to escape the past.

With its image of a green light symbolizing frustrated progress and longing, this tale of the Jazz Age is a reflection on the American Dream, the loss of innocence, and the meaning of "greatness."

The Sun Also Rises (1926)
by Ernest Hemingway

Set in Europe between the World Wars, this fictionalized autobiography is one of Hemingway's most admired novels. Jake Barnes is the narrator-protagonist; a self-assured, well-intentioned drifter who, it is implied, was rendered impotent by a war injury. He's desperately in love with Lady Brett Ashley, a beautiful woman and his former nurse, who is engaged to the heavy-drinking American, Mike Campbell.

The story opens in Paris as Jake runs into Brett at a bar. Jake has been spending time with Robert Cohn, a bumbling Jewish writer who also falls in love with Brett, and she and Cohn take off for San Sebastian, Spain. Another war veteran Bill Gorton meets Jake in Paris, and they make plans to take a fishing trip en route to the Running of the Bulls fiesta in Pamplona. Jake meets Brett and Campbell on a train, and tells them they're welcome in Pamplona. Jake and Bill meet Cohn in the south of France, leave him behind to pine for Brett while they fish, and the whole group meets again for the fiesta.

Tensions are high in Pamplona. Mike has learned of Brett's rendezvous in San Sebastian with Cohn, and he sharply mocks Cohn for his undesired advances toward her. At the first event of the festival, 19-year-old Pedro Romero emerges as a bullfighting virtuoso, and a few days later the group runs into him at a restaurant. Brett declares she's fallen in love with Romero, and asks her old buddy Jake to help her snag him.

One night during the festival Cohn drunkenly loses his temper, and in separate incidents gets into fistfights with Jake, Mike, and Romero. Romero refuses to accept his apology. The next day Romero gives Brett the severed ear of the prized bull he kills, and she leaves for Madrid with her new love. Cohn leaves in a state of embarrassment, and everyone else parts ways. Planning to spend a few quiet days in San Sebastian, Jake changes his plans when he receives a telegram from Brett, asking him to join her in Madrid. She is alone, and the book closes with the two of them in a taxi, musing on what "a damned good time" they could have had together. Jake responds that it is "pretty to think so."

The Sun Also Rises exemplifies both Hemingway's unique unadorned style of writing, as well as his ability to create exceptional characters that deftly reveal the major themes of his novels through their actions. Hemingway published the novel under its current title but when a

British publisher bought the rights to issue it in the U.K. they changed the title to *Fiesta*.

To the Lighthouse (1927) by Virginia Woolf

The Ramsays are an upper-class couple vacationing with their eight children and various family friends at their summer home in Scotland, just prior to the start of World War I. Staying with the Ramsays is Lily Briscoe, a 20-something artist whom Mrs. Ramsay hopes to marry off. The first section of the novella, "The Window," breaks down the events of one day, during which Lily begins a portrait of Mrs. Ramsay, and the youngest Ramsay child, James, begs his inattentive philosopher father to take him on a day-trip to the lighthouse across the bay.

The second section, "Time Passes," is a short summary of the next decade of the family's life. One of the Ramsay boys dies in the war, Mrs. Ramsay and one of the daughters die, and the summer home falls into disrepair. Now 10 years since the day recounted in "The Window," Lily Briscoe and some of the Ramsays decide to return, and the housekeepers attempt to return the house to its former glory. In "The Lighthouse," the final section, Mr. Ramsay, his daughter Cam, and his youngest son, James, finally make the trip to the lighthouse. Lily Briscoe watches from the garden, where she adds the last touches to the painting she began 10 years earlier.

Light on plot and heavy on symbolism, *To the Lighthouse* is a modernist text both stylistically and thematically, and most of the action takes place in the minds of the characters. Told through stream-of-consciousness narration, importance is placed less on the events, and more on the meaning behind them—and the meaning of life itself.

The Sound and the Fury (1929) by William Faulkner

Once a proud Mississippi family, the Compsons have seen their wealth and status erode. The Compson brothers (Quentin, Jason, and the severely retarded Benjy) are all obsessed with their headstrong sister, Caddy. Their father is a well-meaning but detached alcoholic, and their mother is a narcissistic hypochondriac. The household is held together by Dilsey, the family's loyal cook.

Caddy grows to be a promiscuous young woman. Benjy has fits of crying when she is out, and Quentin develops a neurotic obsession with his sister's sexuality. Mr. Compson sells off much of the family's property to send Quentin to Harvard, hoping that a prestigious

degree will restore the Compsons' fading name. Caddy becomes pregnant and refuses to identify the father. Quentin, profoundly disturbed by the news, lies to his father that he has committed incest with Caddy, but Mr. Compson dismisses the story.

Caddy marries a banker, who promises the street-smart Jason a job. However, her husband files for divorce and shatters Jason's career prospects when he realizes that she is carrying another man's baby. Meanwhile, Quentin sinks into depression and commits suicide in Cambridge.

Mr. Compson dies shortly thereafter. The Compsons shun Caddy, but agree to raise her daughter, also named Quentin. Jason becomes poisoned with bitterness when he must take a menial job to support the household. To exact petty revenge, he confiscates the money sent by Caddy for her daughter. As Quentin grows up, she develops her mother's rebellious and promiscuous streak. Jason grows increasingly vicious as he attempts to rein her in. She finds the cache of stolen money and runs away, leaving Dilsey to care for Benjy.

Faulkner's dense and challenging masterpiece is split into four chapters, each with a distinct voice. The first three sections unfold in stream-of-consciousness style, with disjointed thoughts and frequent jumps in chronology. The title is taken from a soliloquy spoken by Macbeth in Shakespeare's play of that name: "/tis a tale told by an idiot/full of sound and fury/signifying nothing." This "tale told by an idiot" chronicles a southern family's disintegration into chaos.

The Grapes of Wrath (1939) by John Steinbeck

Set in Oklahoma during the Dust Bowl years of the Great Depression, this classic American novel tells the story of the Joad family, poor farming people forced to seek a new life in the West. Just released from prison, Tom Joad has returned to his family farm when he meets Jim Casy, a preacher who left the ministry to pursue his calling among the people. The Joads' home is deserted; a neighbor reveals that most local families have lost their farms. Tom and Jim find the family at an uncle's house, packing up their meager possessions. The clan sets out in a rickety old truck, joining a mass exodus toward the promised land of California.

The journey is arduous, and Grandpa Joad, bitter over losing his land, dies on the road. Tom's brother-in-law abandons the family, leaving Tom's pregnant sister, Rose of

Sharon. Grandma Joad passes away shortly after arriving in California. Ma Joad fights to keep the family together as they move from one squalid camp to the next, hungry and desperate for work. During a stay in one migrant camp, Tom and his companions scuffle with a local sheriff, and Casy is arrested.

The Joads move to a government camp, where they are well treated. After learning that the police plan to stage a riot as a pretext for clearing out the migrants, Tom averts the danger. When work peters out, the Joads move on. They land fruit-picking jobs, only to learn that they have been hired as scabs to break a strike. Tom again encounters Jim Casy, who is now actively organizing workers. When the police track down and kill Casy, Tom retaliates by killing a police officer.

While Tom goes into hiding, the family takes shelter in a boxcar. The youngest sister, Ruthie, inadvertently reveals that Tom is nearby and wanted by the law. Ma Joad panics and sends Tom away; he bids her farewell, vowing to continue Casy's quest for social justice. Heavy rains set in just as Rose of Sharon gives birth to a stillborn child. Ma Joad leads the family into a dry barn, where they find a man on the brink of starvation. Rose of Sharon offers the dying man the sustenance of her breast milk.

The Grapes of Wrath reveals the hollowness of the American dream for the poor and the dispossessed. Director John Ford created a highly acclaimed film version of Steinbeck's Pulitzer Prize-winning novel in 1940.

1984 (1949) by George Orwell

Set in the then-future, this popular novel tells the story of Winston Smith, a minor bureaucrat who chafes under the rigid control of the Party, the political entity that controls the nation of Oceania. Cameras constantly monitor him, even in his own squalid home. The image of the Party's leader is plastered everywhere, with ominous reminders that "Big Brother is watching you." The Party sets out to implement a language called Newspeak, eliminating all words related to dissent. Sex, individuality, and even subversive thoughts are outlawed.

Despite the risks, Winston records his illicit thoughts in a diary. He becomes convinced that a powerful Party boss named O'Brien is actually a secret member of the Brotherhood, a shadowy opposition group.

In his job at the Ministry of Truth, Winston spends his days doctoring historical records to support the Party's constantly shifting needs. By night, he prowls the bleak neighborhoods where the "proles" live relatively free of surveillance. One day Julia, a beautiful coworker, passes him a love note. They begin a secret affair, renting a room in the prole district. As their relationship progresses, Winston's loathing of the Party deepens.

Winston is summoned by O'Brien, who confirms his membership in the Brotherhood. Enlisting his help in undermining the Party, he gives Winston a copy of the Brotherhood's manifesto. As Winston reads the forbidden book to Julia in their hideaway, soldiers seize the couple, having been tipped off by their landlord, a member of the Thought Police.

Dragged away from Julia, Winston is brought to the Ministry of Love, where O'Brien reveals that he lied to trap Winston. O'Brien subjects Winston to months of brutal torture, finally threatening to unleash a cage of rats onto his face. Confronted with his deepest fear, Winston breaks down completely, begging O'Brien to inflict the horror on Julia instead.

Having utterly degraded Winston and destroyed the couple's illicit relationship, O'Brien releases his prisoner. Winston sees Julia again, but cannot muster any feelings for her. Reprogrammed and broken in spirit, he pledges loyalty to Big Brother.

Orwell paints a dark picture of totalitarianism, showing how governments can employ technology, manipulation, and a state of permanent warfare to control the masses. Several terms from this prescient novel, such as Big Brother, have entered the language as shorthand for state invasions of privacy. The word *Orwellian* itself is used to describe intrusive government actions or deceptive propaganda.

Waiting for Godot (1953) by Samuel Beckett

This two-act play begins as friends Vladimir and Estragon meet by a bare tree. Estragon fusses with his boots while Vladimir examines his hat, and they discuss the Gospel story of the two thieves crucified beside Jesus. Estragon says that he wants to leave, but Vladimir reminds him that they cannot, because they are waiting for someone named Godot. The men wonder if they have the right day and the right place, then discuss splitting up, but decide against it. They consider hanging themselves from the tree, but ultimately decide to wait to hear what Godot has to say.

A man named Pozzo arrives with his slave, Lucky, who is harnessed by a rope around his neck. Pozzo is on his way to the market to sell Lucky, but he stops to talk to Vladimir and Estragon, and Lucky entertains the men by dancing and thinking. After Pozzo and Lucky leave, a boy arrives with a message from Godot. He explains that Godot will not come tonight, but will definitely come tomorrow. After the boy leaves, the men again question whether they should part, but decide to stay together.

The second act takes place the following evening. Vladimir and Estragon again meet by the tree, which now has a few leaves. Estragon cannot remember the previous day, so Vladimir reminds him of the events, and the two talk and take turns donning each others' hats. Pozzo and Lucky enter, but Pozzo is now blind and does not remember meeting Vladimir and Estragon. They ask Pozzo if Lucky will sing for them, but Pozzo says that Lucky is dumb. Pozzo and Lucky leave, and Godot's young messenger arrives. He does not remember meeting the men the previous day, and, as Vladimir predicts, again says that Godot will not be coming that night, but will certainly come the next day.

As the sun sets, Estragon tells Vladimir that he wants to leave. Vladimir reminds him that they have to come back the next day to wait for Godot. They again consider hanging themselves, but do not have any rope. They decide that they will hang themselves the next day if Godot does not arrive, and decide to leave, but instead remain onstage as the curtain closes.

Beckett dubbed his masterpiece a "tragicomedy." Perhaps the most famous example of the "Theatre of the Absurd," and a play in which little happens and little changes, it is at once a vaudeville comedy as well as a serious commentary on the repetitive nature and futility of modern life.

Lolita (1955) by Vladimir Nabokov

Lolita is the jailhouse confession of Humbert Humbert, a darkly handsome European writer tormented by his infatuation with "nymphets." After a failed marriage and several mental breakdowns, Humbert moves to America.

In New England, Humbert rents a room from the widow Charlotte Haze and falls in love with her twelve-year-old daughter Dolores, nicknamed Lo. In order to pursue "my Lolita," Humbert marries Charlotte, who discovers his secret by reading his diary, but is hit by a car before she can leave him.

Humbert takes Lolita on a road trip. He attempts to drug her, but Lolita, already sexually experienced, seduces him instead. They travel the country for a year, during which Lolita becomes increasingly resentful. Humbert enrolls her at a private school, but after a few months she demands they return to the road. Humbert soon realizes that a man is following them. Lolita becomes ill, then leaves the hospital with the mystery man. Humbert retraces their route, but finds only cryptic taunts that the man has written in motel registers.

After another breakdown, Humbert takes up with Rita, a kind but dimwitted woman. Two years later, he receives a letter from "Dolly Schiller" saying that she is married and pregnant and needs money. He visits Lolita and her husband in a dingy shack. She reveals that her clandestine lover was the playwright Clare Quilty, who later kicked her out when she refused his sexual perversions. Humbert knows that he has destroyed Lolita's life, but he still loves her. He gives her $4,000 even though she refuses to come back to him.

Humbert finds Quilty and, in a bumbling confrontation, shoots him several times. Feeling unencumbered by laws, he then drives into oncoming traffic and is arrested. He ends his confession by stipulating that it not be published while Lolita is alive. However, in the preface, a psychiatrist discloses that Humbert died of a heart attack shortly before his trial date, and that Mrs. Schiller died in childbirth a month later.

Although many readers have been scandalized by the taboo subject matter, there are no actual descriptions of sex in Lolita, and the ironic tone and exuberant wordplay are clearly satirical. However, five American publishers rejected the book. After *Lolita*'s publication in Paris, critics argued over whether it was one of the best books of the year, or "sheer unrestrained pornography." Britain and France banned it as obscene, and U.S. Customs held up two shipments. But the first American edition sold 100,000 copies in three weeks and stayed on the *Times* bestseller list for a full year. Nabokov cited it as his favorite work, although he also insisted that "*Lolita* has no moral in tow."

THE PERFORMING ARTS

MUSIC

History of Western Classical Music

The history of Western music is the history of both standardization and increasing sophistication. Over the centuries, composers have learned to combine the 12 pitches of the Western tonal system in increasingly complex ways. Where music from earlier eras was limited to the naturally occurring (*diatonic*) notes of the major or minor scales, modern music is free to incorporate notes and harmonies from outside the natural scale. This approach, known as *chromaticism*, has extended the boundaries of traditional Western tonality—and resulted in new musical forms that challenge musicians and listeners alike.

Early Music (4000 B.C.–A.D. 400)

Archeological findings of ancient instruments demonstrate that humans have made music from the earliest times. While we don't know how this early music sounded, it's clear that Western music, as we know it, evolved from ancient Near Eastern culture.

Ancient Egyptian society regarded music as a gift from the gods. The appearance and the sound of early musical instruments had symbolic significance in Egyptian culture, where music played an important role in religious practice.

Some of the earliest-known instruments were stringed harps and lutes, known to be played in Egypt as early as 4000 B.C.; lyres and double clarinets were played as early as 3500 B.C. and percussion instruments were added to Egyptian orchestral music ca. 2000 B.C., while the tambourine was known to be used by the Hittites ca. 1500 B.C., along with the guitar, lyre, and trumpet.

All ancient Mesopotamian societies—including the kingdoms of Akkadia, Assyria, Babylonia, Chaldea, and Sumeria—made music central to their religious rites and festivals. Starting around 1800 B.C., Babylonian liturgical services were known to include a variety of psalms and hymns. The musical style was *antiphonal*, with two different voices alternating in chant. Instruments of the time included harps, flutes, drums, and lyres.

The earliest-known written music dates to Sumeria, ca. 800 B.C., in the form of a hymn written in cuneiform on a stone tablet. The first-known musical scales, incorporating five and seven tones per octave, began to appear in Babylonian music during the same period.

The central role of music in Hebrew society is documented in the pages of the Bible. Music was known to be a part of both secular and nonsecular Jewish life; the Old Testament tells of trumpet signals in war, of victories celebrated with women's choirs, and of music played in religious festivals. During this period, the Levites were appointed to perform both instrumental and vocal music in the church—using stringed instruments, harps, and cymbals, according to the First Book of Chronicles. Music of this era was primarily *monophonic*, meaning that it contained a single melody line with no harmonic accompaniment.

Greece and Rome   The first European music is that of the ancient Greeks and Romans, dating from roughly 500 B.C. to A.D. 300. Fewer than a dozen examples of Greek music from this period, written in an alphabetical notation, survive. Ancient Greek philosophers believed that music originated from the god Apollo, as well as from the mythological musician Orpheus and other divinities. They also believed that music reflected in microcosm the laws of harmony that rule the universe, and that music influenced human thought and actions.

The Greek philosopher Pythagoras (ca. 580 B.C.–ca. 500 B.C.) discovered the mathematical relationships between specific frequencies and *musical intervals*, using a single-string instrument (called a monochord) to produce the various intervals. For example, two notes whose frequencies form a ratio of 2:1 sound one *octave* apart; a ratio of 3:2 forms an interval of a *fifth*, and a ratio of 4:3 forms a *fourth*. These basic intervals combine to create the modes and scales on which all Western melodies and harmony are based.

Aristotle (384 B.C.–322 B.C.), in his treatise *The Politics*, noted that different musical melodies, modes, and rhythms have different effects on the listener. He argued that since music has the power of forming character, it should be an important part of the education of the young. His student, Aristoxenus of Tarentum (364 B.C.–304 B.C.), in his

Elements of Harmony, formalized the Greek scheme of *modes*, which utilize a limited series of pitches defined by set intervals. These modes predated the modern major and minor scales that came to prominence in the 16th and 17th centuries.

Greek music was primarily *monophonic*, meaning that there was a single melodic line without any harmony or accompaniment. In song, the music duplicated the rhythms of the text; in instrumental pieces, the melody followed the rhythmic patterns of the various poetic feet. The internal structure of Greek music was based on a system of modes, similar to that used in Arab and Indian music today.

The musical principles and ideas developed by the Greeks were preserved by the Romans throughout their history. Roman music was also influenced by the music of the many kingdoms conquered by the Roman Empire. From 27 B.C. to A.D. 192, slave musicians and dancers were recruited throughout the Empire, musical theater flourished, and both Greek and Roman musicians had their own professional organizations.

The Middle Ages (ca. 500–1400)

In the period following the fall of the Roman Empire in 476, the newly emerged Christian Church came to dominate European societies and culture by providing stabilizing institutions and charitable services to the populace. By A.D. 800 the church wielded political as well as spiritual power and as the era's most important institution eventually dictated the destiny of art, literature, and music.

Since the Christian Church exerted such control over all artistic fields, most professional musicians were employed by the church, and most medieval music was created in monasteries. The church was opposed to the paganism associated with ancient Greece and Rome, which led to the decline of Greek and Roman music and the rise of new sacred musical forms, based on the so-called church modes. Both sacred and secular music of the period incorporated both voices and a wide variety of instruments, including the lyre, medieval fiddle (viele), organ, small drums, and bells.

Early Medieval Music and Gregorian Chant   In the early medieval period music was almost exclusively monophonic. The unaccompanied chant called *plainsong* or *plainchant* was performed by ancient monks in the services of the early Christian Church. This chant consisted of Latin words derived from the Roman Catholic mass, set to a simple unharmonized melody using eight tones with set intervals between them. This sequence of notes—called modes—eventually evolved into today's modern scales (do, re, mi, fa, sol, la, ti, do). This style of medieval music was known as *ars nova*. Plainsong eventually evolved into *Gregorian chant*, after Pope Gregory I (b. Italy, ca. 540; d. 604), who encouraged a ritualized use of music by the church. Gregory first ordered the organization and compilation of church chants, titled "antiphonar."

Troubadours and Other Secular Music   By the turn of the second millennium, sacred musical forms were supplemented by a developing folk music tradition. This music typically took the form of poetry set to music, performed on simple string instruments.

Sometime prior to the 11th century, a form of secular music sprang forth in southern France. This music was played and sung by roving poet-minstrels, called *troubadours*, who went from castle to castle, singing songs, telling stories, and otherwise entertaining the lords and ladies of the upper class.

These troubadours introduced the idea of *fin' amours* ("pure love") into Western culture. Their music was simpler in design than that produced in the church of the time. The secular songs of the troubadours were often faster than sacred songs, used the common language of the people (instead of Latin), and were accompanied by string and percussion instruments such as the lyre, fiddle, and drums.

The influence of the troubadours spread northward throughout the Middle Ages, giving rise to their successors, the *trouvères* of France and the *minnesingers* of Germany.

By the dawn of the 14th century a greater range of song forms began to emerge. Many of these forms, such as the *rondeau* and *virelai*, were based on peasant dances. Perhaps the most prolific songwriter of the late Middle Ages was Guillaume de Machaut (ca. 1300–77). Machaut not only composed some 100 songs, he also wrote several masses and *motets* (a sacred vocal form for two to four voices) and was one of the first known composers to explore polyphonic forms.

The Rise of Polyphony   Western music remained monophonic through approximately A.D. 900. At that time many musicians felt the need for music more elaborate than an unadorned melody. The later Middle Ages gave rise to *polyphony*, in which multiple melodic lines are sung simultaneously.

The first polyphonic musical form was known as *organum*, which added an extra voice part sung in tandem with sections of the basic Gregorian chant. In early organum the voice part was sung a fourth or a fifth above (and parallel to) the chant melody. Later variations featured the second voice singing an independent counter-melody; by the early 12th century, organum incorporated three and four separate voices.

Ars Nova Style During the 14th century a major stylistic change occurred. Dubbed *Ars Nova* (Latin for "new art"), this was a more sophisticated music, incorporating a new rhythmic complexity. Composers of Ars Nova created *isorhythm*, patterns of a dozen or more notes, repeated over and over in multiple voices. By layering other melodies over these *isorhythmic* voice parts, composers created intricate polyphonic designs. In these pieces the foundation voice (known as the *cantus firmus*) was typically borrowed from Gregorian chant.

The concepts of Ars Nova and isorhythm led to the development of the *motet*, originally for two voices, in which the ornate upper voice (called the *tenor*) is given a different text from the chant melody. In this respect a motet is like a song accompanied by a tenor. Motets of the medieval period were typically based on sacred texts. The form was expanded late in the 13th century, when three- and four-voice motets were introduced.

The Roman Catholic Mass Polyphony also found its way into the Roman Catholic mass, which had incorporated music—in the form of plainchant—since at least the fourth century. The first known mass cycle was Machaut's *Messe de Nostre Dame*, written in the early 1360's, which set all movements of the mass in four-part scoring.

During the late 14th century composers began to create mass settings in which the movements were musically related to one another. In England, Lionel Power (d. 1445) and John Dunstable (ca. 1390–1453) unified the mass by basing all the movements on the same plainchant *cantus firmus*. By the end of the medieval period these English masses became available in northern Italy; their impact helped to launch the fully unified mass cycle that reigned through the end of the 17th century, and to establish the polyphonic mass as the most serious of musical forms of that period.

Music Notation The rise of polyphony in the late Middle Ages contributed to the development of the modern system of music notation; musicians had to be able to read and perform several different parts simultaneously, hence the need for a precise system of pitch and rhythmic notation. The 11th-century Benedictine monk Guido d'Arezzo (995–ca. 1033) thus conceived of a five-line staff, with each line and space representing a specific pitch; individual notes were represented as square symbols called *neumes*. A system of rhythmic notation was similarly introduced in the late 13th century by German theorist Franco of Cologne (ca. 1240–ca. 1280).

The Renaissance (1420–1600)

Music, like all the arts, flourished during the Renaissance. With the rise of the middle class, more people moved to cities and spent their leisure time attending plays, concerts, and other entertainment. Music became part of the common education, and—thanks to the invention of the printing press (ca. 1450)—sheet music and method books (for lute, recorder, and guitar) were made available to the populace.

The music of the Renaissance, while building on the polyphonic developments of the late Middle Ages, also reflected a reaction against the complexities of Ars Nova. This took the form of simpler, smoother-flowing melodies and harmonies, with less emphasis on highly structured counterpoint. In addition, many new instruments were developed during the Renaissance. These included the viol (predecessor to the modern violin), guitar, harp, recorder, sackbut (predecessor to the trombone), harpsichord, and clavichord.

Renaissance Polyphony Polyphony in the Renaissance period evolved from the independent counterpoint of the early 1400's into a more harmonious form of melody and accompaniment. Renaissance polyphony is characterized by the equal participation of voices in an exchange of motifs and phrases. The contrapuntal music of the Renaissance evolved to rely heavily on a style called "statement and imitation," where the additional voices successfully restate parts of the original melodic idea. When one part imitates another consistently for a relatively long time span, the two voices form what is called a *canon*. One of the foremost proponents of polyphonic music was Josquin Després (1440–1521), who was one of the first to use repetition or imitation of melodies within a composition. He distinguished himself by writing 18 masses, nearly 100 motets, and more than 70 chansons and other secular works.

Church Music Church music in the Renaissance reflected the growing influence of secular music—despite the attempts of Catholic authorities in Italy and Spain to curb what they viewed as the seductive and profane excesses of music. Also key was the impact of the Reformation, and Martin Luther's desire to break with tradition and use songs that could be sung by the whole congregation, not just the choir.

The Latin Mass Perhaps the most important musical form of the Renaissance was the Latin mass, typically composed of five related passages.

The Renaissance-era mass became more elaborate as composers used more voices and instruments, and added more and more ornamentation to the music. Thus the mass became a work of epic proportions, comparable in scope to the symphonies of the 19th century. The master of the Renaissance-era mass was Giovanni Pierluigi da Palestrina (1525–94), whose 104 masses are considered the epitome of the Renaissance mass style. Other notable composers of the period include Guillaume Du Fay (1397–1474) and Tomás Luis de Victoria (1548–1611).

Motet At the beginning of the Renaissance, the motet was a relatively small-scale sacred form, as defined during the late Middle Ages. But as the mass form developed in the 15th and 16th centuries, composers turned to the motet as a vehicle of experimentation. These later motets were full of contrasts, with passages for all voices paired with passages for just two or three voices, or sections in *duple* time (two beats per measure) followed by sections in triple time (three beats per measure). This more sophisticated motet form is best represented by the works of Orlande de Lassus (1532–94), who also emphasized the depiction of individual words in the text, incorporating techniques developed earlier in the madrigal form.

Renaissance Secular Music Secular music in the Renaissance took the form of various types of song. Early song forms were monophonic; later they incorporated various degrees of polyphony and counterpoint, with two or more lines played in contrast to each other.

Chanson The Ars Nova movement of the late Middle Ages, while initially embraced by sacred composers, was also incorporated into the secular music of the early Renaissance period. In particular, the unharmonized melodies sung by 13th-century troubadours evolved during the early 14th century into two- and three-voice pieces called *chansons* (French for "songs"). The type of line repetition used determined the overall form of the music; the most commonly used schemes were the rondeau, the virelai, the ballade, the caccia, and the ballata.

Notable early chanson composers included Du Fay and Gilles de Bins dit Binchois (ca. 1400–60). By the 16th century, the chanson evolved from its simple beginnings to include elaborate contrapuntal melodies and musical allusions to birdcalls, the cries of street vendors, and so forth. Masters of this later form of chanson included Claude de Sermisy (1490–1562) and Clément Janequin (1485–1558).

Madrigal A further song form inspired by the *ars nova* movement was the *madrigal*, which set secular poetic text in arrangements for four to six voices. The first madrigals were sung in Italy at the end of the 13th century; by the 16th century, the form had become more complex, and had spread across Europe to England. Key madrigal composers include Palestrina, Lassus, and, in England, Thomas Morley (1557–1602).

The Baroque Period (1600–1750)

The Baroque period was all about drama and ornamentation, and the music of the Baroque echoed the dramatic styles of the period's fashions and architecture. Simple melodies evolved into flamboyant airs, full of trills and turns and other ornamentation. Elaborate melodies were layered on top of one another, and the concept of chordal accompaniment—with three or more notes played simultaneously under the melody—gained favor. New musical forms came into prominence, incorporating more and different combinations of instruments—and, in the case of opera, encouraging the interplay of voices and instruments.

With the rise of these new genres, the basic concepts of musical structure were transformed. Instead of writing pieces in which all the voices participated equally in the musical activity, Baroque composers often concentrated on the soprano and bass parts, filling in the middle part of the musical space with chords. To many composers the exact spacing of the chords was unimportant, and keyboard players were often allowed to create their own parts—marking the first instances of musical improvisation.

The early Baroque period saw a clear break with the music of the Renaissance. Harmony and counterpoint, in which two or more simultaneous musical lines are played together, replaced simple polyphony, and rich orchestral sound was heard for the first time. Composers also explored new compositional techniques such as dissonance (the jarring quality of two close pitches played simultaneously) and chromaticism, which utilizes all 12 tones within a musical scale, rather than the limited eight tones found in sacred chants.

By the mid-1600's these new resources had become fully integrated into the musical firmament, and in the late Baroque period composers took firm control over the complex forces of tonality by establishing a single emotional quality (called an *affect*) through the course of a piece. During this period the dominant musical forms reached an almost excessive degree of elaborateness, and musical expression became formalized, if not somewhat mechanical in its construction.

Composers   While Palestrina and Claudio Monteverdi (1567–1643) bridged the Renaissance and Baroque eras, the most influential Baroque composers were those of the later period—notably Antonio Vivaldi (1678–1741), Johann Sebastian Bach (1685–1750) and George Frideric Handel (1685–1759), who created music that was virtuosic in its mastery of harmony and tonality.

Antonio Vivaldi was born in Venice, and although he was ordained as a priest, he was employed for most of his working life at the Ospedale della Pietá, an orphanage for girls that developed a highly regarded conservatory of music. Vivaldi wrote 46 operas, most of which are lost, but he is remembered in the annals of music for bringing the concerto to its mature state. A violin virtuoso himself, he wrote close to 500 concertos, intended for use by his students. These were inventive and musically challenging, and allowed students to fully display their talents. The best known of his concertos is *The Four Seasons* (1723).

George Frideric Handel, though German by birth, spent most of his career in England. An accomplished organist and violinist, Handel performed on concert stages in Italy and London. He composed in all genres, writing chamber music and orchestral works such as *Water Music* and *Music for the Royal Fireworks* (commissioned by King George I), he was primarily a vocal composer, writing 40 operas and 20 oratorios. The "Hallelujah Chorus" of his masterwork, *Messiah*, is one of the most recognizable pieces of music in the Western world.

Johann Sebastian Bach, foremost among the Baroque composers, was a true musical genius and the most important member of a large musical family, which included 20 children, most notably Carl Philipp Emanuel (C.P.E.) and Johann Christian, influential composers in their own right. J.S. Bach produced an astounding variety of chamber and orchestral works, including the *Brandenburg Concertos*, as well as a large number of organ and keyboard works. His *Well-Tempered Clavier*, a collection of solo keyboard works is regarded as one of the most important compositions in Western music. Bach wrote most of his great church music when he was Kantor of St. Thomas's Church in Leipzig. These include sacred and secular cantatas, motets, and other large choral pieces, including *St. Matthew Passion*, written for Good Friday vespers services at the church.

Composers of the Baroque era were often employed by the wealthy ruling class as part of what was called the patronage system. As such, the patron paid the composer for each work, and usually decided what kind of piece the composer should write. Even the major composers partook of this patronage; Bach spent several years as Kapellmeister (music director) to Prince Leopold of Anhalt-Cöthen; Handel wrote various works for the duke of Chandos; and Domenico Scarlatti was in the employ of Princess Maria Barbara of Portugal (later queen of Spain) for most of his career.

Musical forms favored by patrons—in essence, the popular music of this era—included dances, preludes, and suites. While writing within these genres could be creatively limiting, the best of the Baroque composers were able to thoroughly explore, and in some cases expand, these and other Baroque-era forms.

Vocal Works   Several genres of vocal music developed during the Baroque era, most of which were sacred in nature. The most significant were the *oratorio* and the *cantata* (see also Musical Forms).

Oratorio   The oratorio form flourished throughout 17th-century Italy, then spread throughout the rest of Europe. Essentially an unstaged opera with sacred text, in oratorio vocal soloists are accompanied by orchestra or instrumental ensemble; singing can be in either recitative or aria style. The first known oratorio, Cavalieri's *Rappresentatione di Anima et di Corpo*, debuted in 1600 in Rome. Notable oratorios were composed by Heinrich Schütz, Bach, Georg Philipp Telemann (1681–1767), Giacomo Carissimi (1605–74), and Handel.

Cantata   Derived from the Italian word *cantare*, "to sing," the cantata emerged in Italy early in the Baroque era, having evolved from the madrigal. Originally a short work for one or two voices and continuo, it evolved into a more substantial series of recitatives and arias with orchestral accompaniment—in essence, a small, unstaged, secular opera.

A chief proponent of the form was Alessandro Scarlatti, who wrote 600 or so cantatas, primarily for solo voice.

Scarlatti bridged recitatives and arias with passages sung midway between the two styles, called *arioso*. Also notable are the cantatas of Handel and Bach; while he was *Kantor* in Leipzig, Bach provided a new cantata every Sunday, close to 300 in all.

Instrumental Works   During the late Baroque period, orchestral music gained popular status in the public concerts that proliferated in many European cities. During this era many of the "modern" orchestral instruments still in use today were first developed. Wind instruments that came to prominence during the Baroque period included the flute, clarinet, oboe, bassoon, trumpet, and French horn. In addition, the entire string family that we know today was developed during the Baroque period—including the violin, viola, cello, and double bass.

The rise of instrumental music served to diminish the importance of sacred musical forms. Before 1600 the church had been the center of musical development, with vocal music dominating. After 1600 the influence of church music began to wane; secular forms such as the *sonata* and the *concerto* gained prominence. Composers began to write music for a specific instrument, such as the violin, rather than music that could be sung or played by any combination of voices or instruments, as had been the case in previous eras.

Sonata   The type of instrumental piece known as the sonata, was one of the most notable developments of the Baroque period. Composed of contrasting sections, the early sonata took the form of a piece for two melody instruments and continuo—typically two violins with cello or harpsichord—called the *trio sonata*. By the late Baroque, this had evolved into the *solo sonata*, for solo instrument and continuo. The Baroque-era sonata was typically in four movements (slow-fast-slow-fast), with the third and fourth movements based on popular dances, such as the *sarabande* and *gigue*.

During the Baroque period the violin was the most popular sonata instrument, although sonatas were written for all variety of instruments, including the oboe, flute, and cello—as well as for solo keyboard. Domenico Scarlatti, for example, wrote more than 500 sonatas for harpsichord, all in single-movement form.

Concerto   The early 18th century saw the rise of the *concerto* form, with its emphasis on solo virtuosity. As developed by Vivaldi, Bach, and their counterparts, the concerto focused on one or more solo instruments supported by the larger orchestra. An earlier influence was

Tomaso Albinoni (1671–1751), who was the first composer to write concertos in three movements.

The *concerto grosso* became popular during the late Baroque era. This form alternated sections for orchestra with sections for a small ensemble within the larger orchestra, called the *concertino*. This form reached maturity in the works of Bach and Vivaldi, most notably those in Vivaldi's first published collection of concertos, titled *L'estro armonico*. Also notable were the works of Handel, especially his 12 *Concerti Grossi* op. 6, for strings and optional woodwinds.

The Classical Period (1750–1820)

Each new period in Western music is marked by a revolt against the conventions of the previous period. This was especially true for the Classical period, in which younger musicians rebelled against the heavy ornamentation and perceived restrictions of Baroque-era counterpoint, as well as the emotionally constraining constructions of Bach and Handel. The musical revolution of the Classical period mirrored the cultural and political revolutions taking place in the last half of the 18th century. This period was host to the American Revolution, the French Revolution, and the Napoleonic Wars; writers such as Voltaire, Rousseau, and Paine challenged conventional political thought, while the Enlightenment helped to diminish the dominance of church on Western society.

Equally significant was the musical revolution of the Classical period. The patronage system of the Baroque era died out and was replaced by public concerts and a newfound freedom of choice in terms of compositional inspiration and form. Polyphony gave way to harmony, counterpoint gave way to melody, and ornamentation gave way to simplicity—and emotional detachment gave way to a more spontaneous and emotional musical expression.

The Classical Style   In the early Classical period, this expression took different forms in different countries. In France the new style was called *rococo* or *gallant* ("courtly"), and bridged the Baroque and the Classical eras by blending a gracefully ornamented melody with chordal accompaniment. In Germany the new style was known as *empfindsamer Stil* ("sensitive style"), and resulted in longer compositions and the development of large orchestral forms, such as the concerto, sonata, and symphony. Italians did not have a name for their new style, although they were also important contributors to the development of the symphony and other new genres.

The music of the Classical era is lighter, clearer, and less complicated, and the melodies themselves are more graceful and lyrical.

The Viennese School The Classical period is widely recognized as an exceptional period in terms of musical achievement. The climax of the era's musical development came at the end of the 18th century, with a group of musicians known collectively as the Viennese classical school.

By the mid-1700's, the city of Vienna had become a magnet to musicians from all of Europe, thanks in part to an abundance of wealthy patrons. This confluence of talent resulted in convergence of musical styles and a melting pot of ideas, out of which emerged the Classical style.

This new style was primarily forged by the three greatest composers living in Vienna at the time: Franz Joseph Haydn (1732–1809), Wolfgang Amadeus Mozart (1756–91), and Ludwig van Beethoven (1770–1827), who bridged the Classical and Romantic periods. These three musical geniuses created a body of work—consisting of majestic sonatas, string quartets, symphonies, and operas—that has for generations defined the term *classical music*.

Franz Joseph Haydn was the most celebrated composer of the early Classical period. Often referred to as "Papa Haydn," he was a key figure in the development of the string quartet, which became the most popular form of chamber music, with its versatile grouping of two violins, viola, and cello, and his Sonata in C Minor no. 36, is rightly said to mark the introduction of the Viennese Classical style. But he is best known as the "father of the symphony," composing an astonishing 104 symphonic works. Haydn spent the early years of his musical career in Vienna, as Kapellmeister for the wealthy House of Esterházy, a noble Hungarian family. His most famous works, however, were written during his two long visits to London. The 12 "London symphonies" (Nos. 93–104) were grander than anything he'd composed in Vienna. The second of these, No. 94 in G—nicknamed "Surprise" because of a sudden loud chord appearing after the tranquil beginning of the second movement—is among the most popular symphonies of the Classical period.

Wolfgang Amadeus Mozart made his own impressive contributions to the symphonic tradition, but was greatly influenced by Haydn's works. Mozart was a master in every form in which he chose to work. He produced at least 626 nearly flawless works including 41 symphonies, 27 string quartets, five violin concertos, and 27 piano concertos. Most of the piano concertos were composed for occasions when Mozart himself was the featured artist, and he introduced the *cadenza*, a virtuoso solo passage designed to display the technical skills of the soloist. Of these, perhaps the most recognized is *Piano Concerto No. 21* (1785), anachronistically known as "Elvira Madigan" following its use in the soundtrack of the 1967 Swedish film of the same name. Among his other familiar and beloved orchestral works are *Serenade No. 13 in G for Strings* (*Eine Kleine Nachtmusik*, 1787), and *Symphony No. 41 in C* ("Jupiter," 1788).

Ludwig van Beethoven was a musical giant whose work was uniquely innovative and influential. His musical output was smaller than that of Haydn and Mozart, but he had considerable freedom as to what and how he composed. In Beethoven's hands, several musical genres—most notably the symphony—reached new heights, featuring longer and more ambitious movements within each piece. He raised the stature of the piano sonata, writing 32 such pieces, most famously No. 14 ("Moonlight") and No. 13 ("Pathetique"). Beginning with his third symphony, the Eroica (1804), Beethoven bridged the cultural divide separating the 18th and 19th centuries. It is double the length of any Mozart symphony and the composer's expressions of idealism, agony and triumph are immediately evident. Beethoven's Ninth Symphony, twice the length of his earlier symphonic works, adds a large choir to the orchestra, and features an elaborate choral setting of Schiller's "Ode to Joy," an optimistic hymn championing the brotherhood of humanity.

The Piano and the Classical Orchestra During the Classical period, instrumental music finally became more important than vocal music. This was due in part to the improved technical quality of instruments that was achieved during this period, as well as to the development of several new and more expressive instruments.

Chief among these new instruments was the *pianoforte* (Italian for "soft-loud"), known simply as the piano. While the first piano was created ca. 1700, it was during the late 1700's that the instrument developed into the form we know today. The piano supplanted previous keyboard instruments such as the harpsichord and clavichord, and was capable of a wider range of dynamics than those earlier instruments could reproduce.

The Classical period also saw the development of the modern orchestra. During the Baroque period the orchestra was dominated by the string section, with wind instruments used only for doubling, reinforcing, and filling in harmonies. By the late 18th century, however, wind instruments were being used for more important and more independent material. The wind instruments were now regarded as equal to the strings in terms of playing the melody, as well as supplying harmony.

Haydn and Mozart helped to standardize the instrumental makeup of the orchestra—pairs of flutes, oboes, clarinets, bassoons, horns, and trumpet, along with the standard first and second violins, violas, cellos, double basses, and timpani. In the Classical orchestra, strings and winds were self-contained, melodically and harmonically independent of each other.

Vocal Works   Even though the emphasis of the Classical period was on new, longer instrumental works, the great composers continued to create both secular and sacred vocal works—in particular, masses and oratorios.

Mass   The mass, as a musical style, continued to flourish in the Classical period, even as it took on more modern stylings. The Viennese composers introduced a more integrated structure to the mass, often merging the *Gloria* and *Credo* into a single section. Haydn employed symphonic techniques alongside more traditional practices, as did Mozart; Mozart's Coronation Mass contains many symphonic devices, as well as an almost-operatic intensity in the solo voices.

Oratorio and Cantata   Sacred and secular cantatas declined in importance during the Classical period. The oratorio, however, increased in popularity. In Italy the most popular type of oratorio was the *oratorio volgare*, a two-part form with Italian (rather than Latin) lyrics. There were two primary types of oratorio in Germany: a dramatic form with biblical themes, and a contemplative form that emphasized sentimental expression. The most notable oratorios of the late Classical period were composed by Haydn. His oratorios—in particular, *Die Schöpfung* ("The Creation") and *Die Jahreszeiten* ("The Seasons")—are poetic celebrations of faith and nature, in a mature symphonic style.

The Romantic Period (1820–1900)

Beginning in the early 19th century, composers began to extend the Classical style in new and unique ways. Instead of adhering to the formal guidelines set forth in the Classical period, Romantic composers followed the inspiration of literary, historical, pictorial, and other nonmusical sources. The emphasis, then, was on the personal expression of emotion and the freedom of form; there were no restrictions on the length of a piece, the number of movements, or the types of instruments or voices used.

This new movement resulted not in revolution, but in evolution—in both the expansion of established musical forms and the creation of new and related forms, such as the *symphonic poem* and German art song (*lieder*). The expansion of expression was seen in the use of unusual chord progressions, sophisticated harmonies and chromaticism, and unexpected modulations. While Romantic music was more complex than anything that came before—and ultimately brought about a disintegration of tonality—it was also infused by grand, sweeping, truly romantic melodies.

Instrumental Works   The Romantic period saw the final evolution of most of the musical instruments used in symphonic orchestras today. Many of these developments—the use of valves on brass instruments, new key systems on woodwinds, and so on—made the instruments much easier to play, which encouraged their greater use in Romantic-era compositions.

Programme Music and the Symphonic Poem   The late Romantic period saw the development of *programme music*—an instrumental work that is associated with an extramusical image or narrative text. Programme music doesn't attempt a literal musical interpretation of the chosen text, but rather provides an impression that the listener can use as a starting point to grasp the poetic idea of the subject. The best-known type of programme music is the *symphonic poem*, an extended orchestral piece in a single movement. Franz Liszt (1811–86) was the most prolific proponent of this new genre, composing 13 symphonic poems that dealt with subjects taken from classical mythology, Romantic literature, and imaginative fantasy. Among these are *Les Préludes* (1848) the *Dante Symphony* (1857), based on the *Divine Comedy*, and the *Faust Symphony* (1857), based on Goëthe's masterwork. Richard Strauss's (1864–1949) *Don Juan* is another notable symphonic poem from this period.

Symphony   While symphonic music of the Romantic era remained faithful to the concept of the Classical symphony, it also responded to the grandeur suggested in Beethoven's later works. Romantic-era symphonies tend to use larger orchestras than in the Classical period, and often incorporate more than four movements. Johannes Brahms (1833–1897) is one master of this new breed of symphony and is considered the true successor to Beethoven, writing sweeping, lush scores with strong personal aspects to them. His four symphonies and his majestic *Violin Concerto* are emblematic of the work of the Romantic period.

Other key symphonic composers of the Romantic period included Felix Mendelssohn (1809–47), Robert Schumann (1810–56), Anton Bruckner (1824–96), and Antonín Dvořák (1841–1904). Bruckner was especially influential; his nine symphonies were on a monumental scale comparable to those of Beethoven, complete with soaring melodies and rich chromatic harmony. Hector Berlioz broke new ground with his *Symphonie Fantastique*, inspired not only by Gothic fiction and Shakespearean drama, but by a Shakespearean actress, Harriet Smithson, for whom he had an uncontrollable passion. The *Symphonie* was the first to use a melodic motif, an *idée fixe* (fixed idea) that recurs in each movement, connecting a large and varied piece into a unified whole.

Vocal Works   Vocal music in the Romantic period explored the same boundaries as the instrumental music of the period—with both shorter, more intimate works and longer, more epic works joining the repertory.

Lieder Music based on poetry was the basis for another new Romantic musical form, the German art song, otherwise known as *lieder* (plural of *lied*, or "song"). In these art songs, composers attempted to portray with music the imagery and moods of the texts—typically 18th- and 19th-century poems. Franz Schubert, a Viennese-born composer, established the lieder as a new art form. In his short life, he wrote more than 600 songs inspired by the lyric poetry written in the late 18th century by Goëthe, Heine, Schiller, and others. His two song cycles are miniature music dramas. *Die Schöne Mullerin* (*The Fair Maid of the Mill*, 1823) is a narrative cycle representing the courtship of a miller's daughter. *Winterreise* (*Winter's Journey*, 1827), is a more contemplative piece that portrays in music nearly every conceivable emotional state.

Sacred Music By the start of the 19th century, new masses were being written largely to celebrate state occasions. These new works—such as Berlioz' *Grande messe des morts*—were typically conceived on a large scale, complete with orchestra and brass bands. In addition, the oratorio gained new prominence, along with similarly epic form, as typified by Mendelssohn's *Elijah* and Berlioz's *L'enfance du Christ*.

Nationalism in Music   The period following the Napoleonic wars gave rise to nationalism, as ethnic groups in many countries struggled for self-determination. Likewise in music, composers in eastern Europe, Russia, and Scandinavia broke away from French and German influences and began to draw on local folk songs, national epics, and peasant dances for their inspiration. The Czech composer Antonín Dvořák wove folk songs and rhythms into symphonic works such as Slavonic Rhapsodies and Slavonic Dances, and incorporated African-American folk music and Native American rhythms into his *Symphony No. 9* (*From the New World*, 1893). Frédéric Chopin, who composed more than 200 technically demanding, het highly lyrical piano works, contributed to the nationalist movement with his polonaises and mazurkas.

Russian composers also sought to establish a uniquely nationalist style. Their contributions include Modeste Mussorgsky's tone poem *Night on Bald Mountain*, and Nikolai Rimsky-Korsakov's *Scheherazade*. Pyotr Tchaikovsky continued to follow the musical traditions of the Continental countries, but incorporated folk material into his work when it fit his larger designs.

The 20th Century

If the Romantic period represented an evolution from the Classical period, the 20th century witnessed a full-fledged musical revolution. The high value placed on individuality and personal expression in the late 1800's grew even more pronounced in the 1900's, with the very fabric of tonality being ripped apart in the search for new and unique musical forms. The defining feature of 20th-century music, then, is the lack of any central defining feature. Although twentieth-century composers continued to work in the mature musical forms of the Romantic period, they represent an enormous range of tastes, skills, and styles; what the general public continues to call "classical music" has splintered into a virtual plethora of competing styles and genres.

Most major composers of the 20th century used and expanded upon the symphonic form, but the modern symphony, however, was likely to incorporate extreme dissonances and jagged rhythms; many composers abandoned traditional tonality to embrace the various experimental styles typical of other 20th-century music.

Gustav Mahler (1860–1911), the Czech-born Austrian composer, was the transitional artist between the Romantic and Modernist periods. Although he drew on the fundamentals of the Romantic period, his work is often considered part of the expressionist movement, in which composers sought to depict extreme states of mind, creating music that could be alternately harsh, violent, dissonant, or passionate. Mahler's symphonies were enormous, both in length—often running more than 90 minutes—and in the size of the orchestra. His *Symphony No. 8* ("Symphony of a Thousand", 1906), calls for a gigantic orchestra, five vocal soloists, a boy's choir, and an adult choir.

Representative of the modern symphonic form are the symphonies of Jean Sibelius (1865–1957). Sibelius's compositions were shorter works for more traditional orchestras; he viewed the form as an abstract drama with a tight internal logic.

Other important symphonic composers of the 20th century include Sergey Rachmaninov (1873–1953), Sergey Prokofiev (1891–1953), and Dmitry Shostakovich (1906–75).

Musical Styles

Composers in the 20th century experimented with all manner of musical styles, expanding on the sophisticated harmonies of the late Romantic period with increasingly radical explorations of chromaticism and non-traditional tonalities.

Claude Debussy and Impressionism Early in the 20th century, Claude Debussy (1862–1918) became fascinated by Eastern music and the whole-tone scale. He helped create a style in which solo and orchestral music is created from subtle blends of sound, similar to the blends of color in the paintings of Monet, Renoir, and other artists within the Impressionist movement. Debussy sought to express in music the impressions created by natural scenes, in works such as *La Mer* (*The Sea*, 1905), *Prélude à l'après-midi d'un faune* (*Prelude to the Afternoon of a Faun*, 1894), and "Clair de Lune" ("Moonlight," from *Suite Bergamesque*, 1905). Although Debussy resisted the idea of a "school" of Impressionism, his influence can be seen in the works of Maurice Ravel (*Bolero*, 1928, *La Valse*, 1920), Manuel de Falla (*Nights in the Gardens of Spain*, 1915), and Ottorino Respighi (*The Fountains of Rome*, 1916).

Chromaticism and the Twelve-Tone Method The gentle sounds of Impressionism contrasted strongly with those of chromaticism. A chromatic note is any note not contained within the primary major or minor scale of a composition and sounds conspicuously out of key when used against a mostly tonal backdrop. In the modern era chromaticism was seen as a giant, innovative leap in music, with adherents including Arnold Schoenberg (1874–1951), Alban Berg (1885–1935), and Anton Webern (1883–1945).

Once any and all notes became fair territory for musical writing, Arnold Schoenberg imposed order from atonal chaos by creating *twelve-tone* music. Twelve-tone music introduces each of the 12 tones of the Western chromatic scale in a predetermined order called a "tone row," which serves as the melodic line. Pioneering works using this method are Schoenberg's *Pierrot Lunaire* (1912), Alban Berg's *Violin Concerto* (1935), and opera *Wozzeck* (1922), and Anton Webern's *Das Augenlicht* (*The Light of the Eye*, 1935).

Microtonality and Polytonality Twelve-tone music led to the development of several similar musical styles, including *microtonality* and *polytonality*. Microtonal music uses the same serial approach as 12-tone, but divides the octave into more and smaller harmonic intervals; polytonality uses more than one tonality simultaneously.

Neo-Classicism In a world of increasingly experimental and eclectic compositions, the style known as *Neo-Classicism* offered a welcome respite from oppressively progressive musical approaches. The neoclassical style marked a return to the classic concept that all elements of a composition should contribute to the overall structure of the piece; it blended formal schemes from the Baroque and Classical eras with a modified sense of tonality that embraced chromaticism and other elements of the Romantic and modern eras.

The foremost proponent of the Neo-Classical style was Igor Stravinsky. Retreating from the experimentation of his earlier works, Stravinsky began, in the early 1920's, to embrace the musical forms and instrumentation of earlier periods. He abandoned the dense chords and shifting meters characteristic of *The Rite of Spring* and other controversial works, substituting a more traditional tonality—although still filtered through modern harmonic sensibilities. His two important works from this period are *Symphony in C* (1940) and *Symphony in Three Movements* (1945) which represent the summation of his neoclassical principles.

Other composers who worked in this style were the Russian composer Sergei Prokofiev (*Symphony No. 1, Classical Symphony*, 1917), the British composer Ralph Vaughan Williams (*Fantasia on a Theme by Thomas Tallis*, 1910, revised 1913, 1919), and the German composer Paul Hindemith (*Sonata for Viola d'Amore and Piano*, 1922).

Serialism *Serialism* is another style that evolved from the 12-tone method emerging in the late 1940's and early 1950's. In this method, pitches, rhythms, and dynamics are presented in a pre-determined fashion.

Olivier Messiaen (1908–1992) pioneered the method of *total serialism*, which applied twelve-tone rules to duration and volume as well, employing it in his *Scale of Durations and Dynamics* (1949). Pierre Boulez (b. 1925) took this form even further, dictating that no pitch, volume, attack, or duration could repeat until the other 11 pitches, volumes, durations, and attacks had occurred. This was music at an extreme limit of rigor and structure and is exemplified by his *Le marteau sans maître* (*The Hammer Without a Master*, 1955). Other influential serial composers include Karlheinz Stockhausen (*Kreuzspiel*, 1951), and the American composer, Milton Babbitt (*Three Compositions for Piano*, 1947).

Interdeterminancy While serialism is highly programmed, later composers believed that some aspects of their music should be left to chance—letting the performer choose which notes to play, or basing some sound choices on the outcome of a random event, such as the rolling of dice. In some cases, proponents of *indeterminancy* use colors and symbols in place of traditional music notation. Two important examples of this method are Earle Brown's *Twenty-Five Pages* (1953), which features a 25-page score which can be played in any sequence by 1–25 pianists, and John Cage's *4'33"* (1952), in which no sound is played at all by the musician. The piece requires the audience to listen to the ambient sounds of the auditorium—the idea being that any collection of sounds, if given focus and attention, has many of the qualities of music.

Minimalism The style known as *minimalism* arose in response to the increasing complexity of both "classical" and popular music forms, including the highly sophisticated type of jazz known as bebop. Minimalism is hypnotic in its repetition, characterized by relatively simple melodies and rhythms employed with diatonic harmony and long pedal points. Chief among the minimalists of the late 20th century are Philip Glass (b. 1937) and Steve Reich (b. 1936), who have both had success with traditional and popular applications of this style, best exemplified by Glass's *Violin Concerto No. 1* (1987), and his operas *Einstein on the Beach* (1975) and *Satyagraha* (1980), and Reich's *Piano Phase* and *Violin Phase* (both 1967).

Musique Concrète In 1948 the engineer and composer Pierre Schaeffer (1910–95) began to use the newly developed magnetic tape recorder to record various everyday sounds, and then combine those sounds in various ways. The result was dubbed *musique concrète* (French,

"concrete music"), as it consisted of "real-world" sounds, rather than the "artificial" sounds of musical instruments.

Electronic Music *Musique concrète* marked the beginning of what we now call electronic music. In this new and developing genre, electronic equipment—including but not limited to computers and synthesizers—is used to generate, modify, and combine all manner of sounds. Early composers of electronic music included Cage, Stockhausen, and Herbert Eimert (1897–1972); this style became more prevalent (and integrated into other musical forms) as newer types of electronic instruments were developed in the later years of the 20th century.

Nationalism and Folk Music *Nationalism* describes serious musical forms that embrace elements of *folk music* native to specific countries. Its greatest 20th-century proponents were the Hungarian composer Béa Bartók and Charles Ives of the United States, both of whom made unusually creative use of national idioms. Bartók drew on the folk music of Central Europe for his inspiration, and the melodies of Hungarian folk tunes and asymmetrical dance rhythms became a hallmark of his work. His six string quartets, written between 1908 and 1939, are considered the summation of his compositional style.

Charles Ives drew his inspiration from his native New England, blending unconventional rhythms and harsh dissonance with familiar hymns and popular tunes. His work was only appreciated later in his life. After he won a Pulitzer Prize in 1947 for his *Third Symphony*, his earlier works, such as *The Unanswered Question* (1908) received more notice.

Other representative works in this style are Vaughan Williams's *A London Symphony* (1913), Leo Janácek's opera *Jenufa* (1904) and Aaron Copland's *Hoe Down* (1942) and *Appalachian Spring* (1944).

American Music and Third Stream While Copland helped to define American "classical" music in the 20th century, other composers further wedded native musical forms (such as blues and jazz) to create an even more complete American musical language. Chief among these architects were George Gershwin (1898–1937) and Gunther Schuller (b. 1925), who coined the term *third stream* for the new musical styles that combined jazz and concert works.

Classical Music in the New Millennium

Although they make use of many techniques from the previous century, composers of classical music today are incorporating elements of all styles of music in their

The 10 Greatest Composers

By ANTHONY TOMMASINI

Here goes. This article completes my project to select the top 10 classical music composers in history, not including those still with us. The argument, laid out in a series of articles, online videos and blog posts, was enlivened by the more than 1,500 informed, challenging, passionate and inspiring comments from readers of *The New York Times*.

To step back for a moment, I began this project with bravado, partly as an intellectual game but also as a real attempt to clarify—for myself, as much as for anyone else—what exactly about the master composers makes them so astonishing. However preposterous the exercise may seem, when I found myself debating whether to push Brahms or Haydn off the list to make a place for Bartok or Monteverdi, it made me think hard about their achievements and greatness.

Ah, greatness. The title essay in Alex Ross's new collection, *Listen to This*, argues that the very term "classical music" makes this vibrant art form seem dead. Indeed, as he writes, "greatness" and "seriousness" are not classical music's defining characteristics; it can also "be stupid, vulgar and insane."

All true. Yet what came through in the comments from readers and, I hope, my articles and videos is that for most of us these composers are not monumental idols but living, compelling presences. Just as we organize our lives by keeping those we love in a network of support, we do something similar with the composers we rely on.

One. My top spot goes to Johann Sebastian Bach, for his matchless combination of masterly musical engineering (as one reader put it) and profound expressivity. I have been thinking more about the perception that he was considered old-fashioned in his day. Haydn was 18 when Bach died, in 1750, and Classicism was stirring. Bach was surely aware of the new trends. Yet he reacted by digging deeper into his way of doing things. In his austerely beautiful *Art of Fugue*, left incomplete at his death, Bach reduced complex counterpoint to its bare essentials, not even indicating the instrument (or instruments) for which these works were composed.

On his own terms he could be plenty modern.

Though Bach never wrote an opera, he demonstrated visceral flair for drama in his sacred choral works, as in the crowd scenes in the Passions where people cry out with chilling vehemence for Jesus to be crucified. In keyboard works like the *Chromatic Fantasy and Fugue*, Bach anticipated the rhapsodic Romantic fervor of Liszt, even Rachmaninoff, and through his chorales alone Bach explored the far reaches of tonal harmony.

Two. The obvious candidates for the second and third slots are Wolfgang Amadeus Mozart and Ludwig von Beethoven. If you were to compare just Mozart's orchestral and instrumental music to Beethoven's, that would be a pretty even match. But Mozart had a whole second career as a path-breaking opera composer. Such incredible range should give him the edge.

Still, I'm going with Beethoven for the second slot. Beethoven's technique was not as facile as Mozart's. He struggled to compose, and you can sometimes hear that struggle in the music. But however hard wrought, Beethoven's works are so audacious and indestructible that they survive even poor performances.

Four? Franz Schubert. You have to love the guy, who died at 31, ill, impoverished and neglected except by a circle of friends who were in awe of his genius. For his hundreds of songs alone — including the haunting cycle "Winterreise," which will never release its tenacious hold on singers and audiences — Schubert is central to our concert life. The baritone Sanford Sylvan once told me that hearing the superb pianist Stephen Drury give searching accounts of the three late Schubert sonatas on a single program was one of the most transcendent musical experiences of his life. Schubert's first few symphonies may be works in progress. But the "Unfinished" and especially the *Ninth Symphony* are astonishing. The Ninth paves the way for Bruckner and prefigures Mahler.

Claude Debussy, who after hundreds of years of pulsating Germanic music proved that there could be tension in timelessness, is my No. 5. With his pioneering harmonic language, the sensual beauty of his sound and his uncanny, Freudian instincts for tapping the unconscious, Debussy was the bridge over which music passed into the tumultuous 20th century.

One who later walked that bridge was Igor

Stravinsky, my No. 6. During the years when *The Firebird* and *The Rite of Spring* were shaking up Paris, Stravinsky was swapping ideas with his friend Debussy, who was 20 years older. Yet Stravinsky was still around in the 1960s, writing serial works that set the field of contemporary music abuzz. One morning in 1971 I arrived at the door of the music building at Yale, on which someone had posted an index card with this simple news: "Igor Stravinsky died today." It felt as if the floor had dropped out from under the musical world I inhabited. Stravinsky had been like a Beethoven among us.

I'm running out of slots. In some ways, as I wrote to one reader, either a list of 5 or a list of 20 would have been much easier. By keeping it to 10, you are forced to look for reasons to push out, say, Handel or Shostakovich to make a place for someone else.

Some musicians I respect have no trouble finding shortcomings in the music of Johannes Brahms. He did sometimes become entangled in an attempt to extend the Classical heritage while simultaneously taking progressive strides into new territory. But at his best (the symphonies, the piano concertos, the violin concerto, the chamber works with piano, the solo piano pieces, especially the late intermezzos and capriccios that point the way to Schoenberg) Brahms has the thrilling grandeur and strangeness of Beethoven. Brahms is my No. 7.

In an earlier installment of this series I tried to weasel out of picking Romantic composers other than Brahms by arguing that the era fostered originality and personal expression above all. To a genius like Frederic Chopin, having a distinctive voice and giving vent to his inspirations were more important than achieving some level of quantifiable greatness.

But the dynamic duo of 19th-century opera, Giuseppe Verdi and Richard Wagner, aimed high. That a new production of a Verdi opera, like Willy Decker's spare, boldly reimagined staging of *La Traviata* at the Metropolitan Opera, can provoke such heated passions among audiences is testimony to the enduring richness of Verdi's works. A production of Wagner's "Ring" cycle has become the entry card for any opera company that wants to be considered big time. The last 20 minutes of *Die Walküre* may be the most sadly beautiful music ever written.

But who ranks higher? They may be tied as com-posers but not as people. Though Verdi had an ornery side, he was a decent man, an Italian patriot and the founder of a retirement home for musicians still in operation in Milan. Wagner was an anti-Semitic, ego-maniacal jerk who transcended himself in his art. So Verdi is No. 8 and Wagner No. 9.

One slot left. May Haydn forgive me, but one of the Vienna Four just had to go, and Haydn's great legacy was carried out by his friend Mozart, his student Beethoven and the entire Classical movement. My apologies to Mahler devotees, so impressively com-mitted to this visionary composer. Would that I could include my beloved Puccini.

I was heartened by the hundreds of readers who championed 20th-century composers like Ligeti, Messiaen, Shostakovich, Ives, Schoenberg, Prokofiev and Copland, all of whom are central to my musical life. Then there is Berg, who wrote arguably the two greatest operas of the 20th century. His Violin Concerto, as I explained in my first video, would make my list of top 10 pieces. I was disappointed that an insignificant number of readers made a case for Britten. I have some advocacy work to do.

I received the most forceful challenges from read-ers who thought that pre-Bach composers simply had to be included, especially Monteverdi. Though Monteverdi did not invent opera, he took one look at what was going in Florence around 1600 and figured out how this opera thing should really be done. In 1607 he wrote "Orfeo," the first great opera. His books of madrigals brought the art of combining words and music to new heights. The Monteverdi contingent is probably right.

But forced to pick only one more composer, I'm going with Bela Bartok, whose work has empowered generations of subsequent composers to incorporate folk music and classical traditions from whatever cul-ture into their works, and as a formidable modernist who in the face of Schoenberg's breathtaking formula-tions showed another way, forging a language that was an amalgam of tonality, unorthodox scales and atonal wanderings.

So that's my list. And now, in an act of contrition, I am beginning a personal project to listen nonstop to recordings of Britten, Haydn, Chopin, Monteverdi, Ligeti and those composers whom I could not squeeze in but whose music carries me through my days.

work, breaking down the boundaries between musical genres and blurring the distinction between popular and serious music.

Twenty-first century music is characterized by its diversity, and the influence of new technology. Polystylism (or musical eclecticism) is a growing trend, in which a composer's body of work as a whole will encompass many different styles.

John Zorn (b. 1953), for example, is an American avant-garde composer who draws from many genres—jazz, punk, klezmer, classical—often incorporating them within a single composition. Among his major concert works are *Songs from the Hermetic Theatre* (2001), featuring four experimental compositions, and *Madness, Love and Mysticism* (2001), his first piece of electronic music.

Julian Anderson (b. 1967), a British composer, incorporates house and club music into his work, alongside elements of Indian and Eastern European folk music. His large-scale *Book of Hours* (2005), written for an ensemble of 20 players, also features live and pre-recorded electronics.

Thomas Adès (b. 1971), is both a contemporary composer and a renowned performer and interpreter of classical works by Schubert, Grieg, Stravinsky and others. One of the trademarks of his own compositions is his innovative use of percussion, incorporating silverware, empty cans, and pots and pans into the ensemble. Among his major orchestral works are *Asyla* (1997), which incorporates house music into one of its movements, and *In Seven Days* (2008), a piano concerto featuring hi-tech imagery on six video screens along with the score.

Magnus Lindberg (b. 1958) is a Finnish composer whose early works show the influence of serialism, and the compositions of Stockhausen and Milton Babbit, but he later began to incorporate the syncopated styles of progressive rock and ethnic music into his compositions. His breakthrough work, *Kraft* (1983–85) uses traditional instrumentation as well as percussion on scrap

metal, and was heavily influenced by punk rock music. His *Clarinet Concerto* (2002) is one of his most popular scores, and in 2009, as composer-in-residence at the New York Philharmonic, he premiered *EXPO*, a large-scale orchestral work.

Women have composed music throughout history, although their contributions have often gone unrecognized. In recent years however, several women have captured the attention of the classical music world, receiving important commissions, prizes, and critical acclaim.

Sofia Gubaidulina (b. 1931) was born in the Tatar Republic of the Soviet Union, and is considered one of the three most important Soviet composers of the post-Shostakovich period, alongside Edison Denisov and Alfred Schnittke. Her compositions show a deep-rooted belief in the mystical properties of music, and is informed by the sounds of rare Asian, Russian and Caucasian folk instruments. Among her major commissions are *Two Paths* ("A Dedication to Mary and Martha", 1999), commissioned by the New York Philharmonic for two solo violas and orchestra and *Light of the End* (2003), commissioned by the Boston Symphony Orchestra. Her most recent work is *In Tempus Praesens* ("In the Present Time, 2007), a violin concerto premiered by Anne-Sophie Mutter.

Jennifer Higdon (b. 1962) is an American composer who won the 2010 Pulitzer Prize for Music for her *Violin Concerto*. Her work ranges across genres from orchestral pieces to chamber music and vocal works. Her composition, *blue cathedral*, is one of the most performed contemporary orchestral works, having been performed by more than 250 orchestras since its premiere in 2000. Although her compositions have moments of dissonance, her audience-pleasing style is fundamental tonal, and shows the influence of 20th century composers such as Aaron Copland, Samuel Barber, Igor Stravinsky and Maurice Ravel.

Opera

Europe in the 17th century was host to a great rise in dramatic theater. In England this revival was led by the works of William Shakespeare and Christopher Marlowe; in France, by Pierre Corneille and Jean Racine. In Italy, however, this movement emerged in a new form that combined drama with music—opera. In practice, opera consists of vocals, using text from a *libretto* (literally, "little book"), with instrumental accompaniment, with the singers typically in costume in an elaborate theatrical production. Most opera lovers would agree that beautiful singing by highly trained artists, accompanied by the musical creations of the greatest composers, produces a theatrical experience unmatched in its emotional intensity by any other art form.

Baroque Origins   The operatic form originated in Florence, Italy, during the Baroque era (1600–1750). It grew out of attempts to recreate the effect of Ancient Greek and Roman dramas in a more modern context. Early operas were referred to as *drama per musica* ("drama through music"), and their plots were typically based on myth, much like their inspiration, the classic dramas of ancient Greece and Rome. The first opera is generally considered to be *Daphne*, composed in 1597 by Jacopo Peri (1561–1633), based on the tale of the god Apollo and his courtship of a nymph named Daphne. Peri's contemporaries in early opera included *Giulio Caccini* (ca. 1545–1618) and *Emilio del Cavalieri* (ca. 1550–1602).

Early operas did not yet fully integrate music and drama. Half-sung passages, called *recitatives*, alternated with orchestral interludes and choruses that commented on the dramatic events. In this style, the music was subservient to the words. By the 1620s a different type of vocal style, known as *aria*, gained prominence. In contrast to the recitative, this style was more expressive and melodious, with the music taking precedence over the words. Over time, the aria became a showcase for virtuoso singing, and it eventually became a self-contained piece for solo voice with orchestral accompaniment.

Claudio Monteverdi (1567–1643) contributed more to the development of the opera form in the 17th century than anyone else. The aria style was used prominently in his later operas, especially *Il ritorno d'Ulisse in patria* (The Return of Ulysses, 1640) and *L'incoronazione de Poppea* (The Coronation of Poppaea, 1642) and he was known for using multiple musical forms in his operas. *Orfeo* (Orpheus, 1607), for example, was one of the first works to combine choruses, dances, madrigals, and duets. In addition to developing the aria, he also introduced a larger and richer-sounding orchestra. His work became a model for the operatic composers who followed and helped to bring opera to the masses, first in Venice and then throughout Europe. By 1700, Vienna, Paris, Hamburg, and London were all centers of operatic activity.

In London, **George Frideric Handel** (1685–1759) composed a series of 42 powerful operas, including *Ariodante, Alcina, Guilio Cesare*, and *Orlando*. He was the first composer to write an Italian opera for the London stage, and in 1719 Handel joined with a group of English nobles to found the Royal Academy of Music, a company dedicated to the production of Italian operas. Handel's operas, like his other compositions, were praised for their high quality of orchestral and vocal writing.

The later Baroque period saw the creation of several different operatic styles, including *opera seria* ("serious opera"), *opera buffa* ("comic opera"), and the French *opèra-ballet*, which merged opera with narrative dance. Jean-Baptiste Lully (1632–87) developed the *tragèdie lyrique* style, emphasizing recitative, and prominent roles for choir, orchestra, and often, dancers.

Classical Opera   Opera underwent many important changes in the Classical era (1750–1820). Italian opera had become a series of overly wrought arias designed to display the talents of the public's favorite singers. As a reaction against this perceived vocal excess, Classical composers cut back on the ornamentation, reintroduced instrumental interludes and accompaniments between arias, and made greater use of choral singing, combining them into unified scenes. The Classical period also saw the decline of serious Italian opera and the rise of lighter forms, such as *opera buffa* and *opéra comique*, forms which used more realistic spoken dialogue interspersed with songs.

Christoph Willibald von Gluck (1714–87) was the most important reformer during the Classical era. In his works, the musical drama was more important than the singers who performed it, and he did away with unnecessary orchestral passages and florid singing. Gluck blended the traditions of Italian and French opera, writing eight operas for the Paris stage, the most important of which were *Orfeo ed Eurodice* and *Iphigénie en Tauride*, which remain in the repertory today.

The reformation movement climaxed in the stage works of **Wolfgang Amadeus Mozart** (1756–91), in which every aspect of the vocal and instrumental portions contributed to the overall plot development and characterization. In Mozart's operas, such as *Le Nozze di Figaro* (*The Marriage of Figaro*, 1786), the music for each character is distinct in tone and style from the other characters, and the action is reflected in the structure of the work. Many of Mozart's operas are known for their hilarious comic aspects, with twisting, farcical plots set to witty music that brought clever characters to life. His mature compositions are distinguished by their melodic beauty, formal elegance, and richness of harmony and texture. He brought the orchestra to the forefront of the opera, incorporating sophisticated orchestral techniques perfected in his other instrumental works. Mozart was a prolific composer, writing 20 operas before his premature death at age 35. His other notable works include *Così fan tutte* (1790), *Idomeneo* (1781), *Don Giovanni* (1787), and his final work, *Die Zauberflöte* (*The Magic Flute*, 1791).

Opera in the Romantic Period

Even with the introduction of new instrumental forms, opera remained the most popular music of the 19th century. During the Romantic period (1820–1900), the art of opera reached its greatest heights, producing grand spectacles with numerous showcases for spectacular singing. In every way, Romantic operas were longer, bigger, and more majestic than their Classical-era counterparts. Characteristic of the new Romantic opera was the French grand opera, typified by Hector Berlioz's epic *Les Troyens* (*The Trojans*, ca. 1856), a five-act opera based on Virgil's *Aeneid*.

In Italy, **Gioachino Antonio Rossini** (1792–1868) introduced a new style known as bel canto (literally, "beautiful singing") which featured complex and ornate melodic lines (which vocalists could ornament at will), simple harmonic structure, and musical numbers that combined to make composite scenes. In the history of opera, Rossini is a transitional figure. His early operas are more Classical in nature, while his later ones are definitively Romantic. His most famous work, *Il Barbiere di Siviglia* (*The Barber of Seville*) was written during a single two-week period in 1816. His other famous opera is *Guillaume Tell* (*William Tell*, 1829), with its memorable overture, the finale of which was popularized as the theme music for the Lone Ranger.

Later in the 19th century, **Giuseppe Verdi** (1813–1901) introduced a new realism and intensity of expression to the form. His operas combined rhythmic vitality with superbly crafted melodies. Verdi eschewed the symphonic leanings of other Romantic-era composers, and exhibited a technical mastery of traditional operatic form. The characters in his 28 operas are as complex as the characters in Shakespeare and other traditional theater. His most popular operas include *Macbeth*, *Rigoletto*, *Il trovatore* (*The Troubador*), *La traviata*, *Aida*, *Don Carlo*, *Otello*, and *Falstaff*.

In Germany, **Richard Wagner** advanced the majestic music drama, which combined elements from Greek tragedy and the symphonies of Beethoven into a dramatic whole that was referred to as *Gesamtkunstwerk* ("Complete Artwork"). His groundbreaking work changed the nature of opera and *Tristan und Isolde* (1859), and the 4-part, 16-hour *Der Ring des Nibelungen* (1869–74)—pushed the boundaries of traditional tonality and propelled the art form to a larger scale. One can easily recognize Wagner's music for its power and size, requiring a huge orchestra and powerful voices that can soar over the orchestra. Wagner's music is harmonically challenging, and his use of extreme chromaticism and shifting tonal centers led directly to the atonal music of the 20th century. Of particular note is Wagner's "Tristan Chord," the first chord used in *Tristan und Isolde*, which was emblematic of Wagner's developing harmonic sense and foreshadowed further harmonic evolution after the turn of the century.

Operetta In stark contrast to Wagner's imposing dramatic operas was the debut of a new, less ponderous musical form called *operetta*. Rooted in the song and dance music of the late 19th century, the operetta was a form of light entertainment that, as practiced by Jacques Offenbach (1819–80) and Johann Strauss (1825–99) was a definite contrast to the often self-consciously "heavy" music of the times. Although Offenbach's best-known work, *Les contes d'Hoffman* (*Tales of Hoffman*, 1881), is a fully operatic work, his *La belle Hélène* (1864) and *Orpheus in the Underworld* (1858), combined political and cultural satire and were hugely popular in France and in the English-speaking world. Strauss's most popular work, *Die Fledermaus* (*The Bat*, 1874) is still regularly performed both in German and in English. While this form was often dismissed as inconsequential and predictable, it proved phenomenally popular among audiences of the time.

The 20th Century   Richard Strauss (1864–1949) bridged the Romantic and modern eras, composing intense works that reflected the tremendous influence of Wagner. His early operas, such as *Salome* (1905) and *Elektra* (1909), were highly dissonant works that built on Wagner's chromatic harmonies. Strauss moderated this harmonic experimentation in his later works, however. The beautifully romantic *Der Rosenkavalier* (1911) embraced a fading romanticism that starkly contrasted to the more atonal musical environment of the early 20th century.

The romantic operas of **Giacomo Puccini** (1858–1924) continued the Italian grand opera tradition of Verdi and Rossini and were marvels of characterization, sentiment, and craftsmanship. The plots of most of his operas feature a tragic female lead—the "Puccini heroine"—who usually dies at the end, thus lending a particularly romantic slant to his works. Puccini's music, while seemingly simple, is actually quite complex. His mastery of melody and genius for orchestration makes his works—including *La Bohème* (1896), *Tosca* (1900), *Madama Butterfly* (1904), and *Turandot* (1926)—among the most popular and beloved in the repertoire.

At the time Puccini's works were dominating the repertory, the influences of the atonal movement were being felt in the opera world as well. Alban Berg's *Wozzeck* (1921), still the most performed work in this style, tells the grim story of a working-class love affair gone bad, ending in the woman's murder by her lover and his suicide. The music is unmelodic but startling and moving nonetheless.

World War II proved to be a turning point for 20th century opera, with postwar composers seeking to revitalize the form that had apparently come to a conclusion with the outbreak of hostilities in Europe. These newer composers, led by **Benjamin Britten** (1913–76), breathed new life into opera by judiciously integrating other 20th-century musical forms into the established opera form. The protagonist in a Britten opera is typically a misfit or outsider pitted against the crowd, and Britten's music reflects this 20thcentury alienation in its unusual and often stark instrumentation. His most famous operas include *Peter Grimes* (1945), *Billy Budd* (1951), and *Death in Venice* (1973).

Contemporary Opera   At the dawn of the new millennium, composers such as **Philip Glass** (b. 1937) and **John Adams** (b. 1947) continued to change the face of opera, introducing multimedia elements, political commentary, and rock music into their work. Both composers employ minimalist techniques, such as constantly repeating musical patterns. Glass's operas include *Einstein on the Beach* (1976) and *Satyagraha* (1980), based on the life of Mohandas Gandhi, and sung in Sanskrit. Adam's most famous operas are *Nixon in China* (1987) and *Doctor Atomic* (2005), which chronicles the building of the atomic bomb. **Thomas Adès** (b. 1971) is considered the most accomplished British musician since Benjamin Britten. *Powder Her Face*, a 1995 chamber opera, gained notoriety for its musical depiction of the sexual acts of Margaret Campbell, Duchess of Argyll, whose escapades scandalized Britain in the 1960s. His first full-scale opera, *The Tempest*, adapted from Shakespeare's play, premiered in 2004.

The Human Voice

The voice is the most versatile and expressive of all musical instruments, employed by composers since the earliest times. Vocal ranges—the span between the highest and lowest notes a singer can produce—have been standardized into four principal groups: from highest to lowest, soprano, alto, tenor, and bass. In opera and some vocal ensembles, the classifications are expanded to include the mezzo-soprano (between the soprano and alto) and baritone (between the tenor and bass).

Within each range, singers are further categorized depending on the texture, power, and flexibility of their voice. The "Fach system," developed in Germany, is often used by opera houses and voice teachers to categorize singers by voice type, or "facher." It is somewhat subjective, and many roles can be sung by more than one "fach."

Soprano   The soprano is the highest female voice. The typical soprano range starts at middle C and goes up two octaves, to the first C above the treble clef staff. The Fach system defines the following types of soprano voices:

Coloratura range: Middle C to the F two octaves above middle C. The highest, lightest and perhaps most "agile" female voice. Comfortable in the highest register and able to perform rapid dazzling passages. Example: Queen of the Night in Mozart's *The Magic Flute*.

Soubrette range: Middle C to the C two octaves above middle C. This is a light, pretty voice often found in younger sopranos. Example: Susanna in Mozart's *The Marriage of Figaro*.

Lyric range: Middle C to the C two octaves above middle C. The "standard" soprano voice. Capable of sustained, melodic singing. Example: Mimi in Puccini's *La Bohème*.

Dramatic range: Middle C to the C two octaves above middle C. Light dramatic sopranos can push their lyric voices to be heard through the orchestra and can take on roles at the high and low end of their range. Example: Butterfly in Puccini's *Madama Butterfly*. Full dramatic sopranos, or Wagnerian sopranos have powerful voices that work well at the lower registers. Examples: Elsa in Wagner's *Lohengrin*; Leonore in Beethoven's *Fidelio*.

Mezzo-Soprano Common in opera but less so in other musical styles, the mezzo-soprano has a similar overall range and quality as a lyric soprano, but with slightly more power in the lower range. The Fach system defines two primary types of mezzo-sopranos:

Lyric/Coloratura range: C below middle C to the B two octaves above middle C. Often cast in "trouser roles" in which women play the parts of young men. Example: Cherubino in Mozart's *The Marriage of Figaro*; Rosina in Rossini's *The Barber of Seville*.

Dramatic range: C below middle C to the B two octaves above middle C. The counterparts to dramatic sopranos, with powerful voices that carry over dense orchestration. Example: Amneris in Verdi's *Aida*.

Alto The alto (short for contralto) is the lower female voice, with a deep and resonant tone. The range of a typical alto starts on the G below middle C, and goes up two octaves, which results in substantial overlap with both the male tenor and the female soprano voices. In classical music, the alto voice can be quite heavy and dark, while in popular music (especially in jazz) this type of voice sounds warm and rich in its depth of tone.

While the Fach system does not define alto voices separately, two voices within the mezzo-soprano range function as alto voices in most vocal forms:

Dramatic contralto range: G below middle C to the B above middle C. This is the traditional alto voice. Example: Erda in Wagner's *Der Ring des Nibelungen*.

Deep contralto range: F below middle C to the A above middle C. A deep and penetrating female voice, with a a darker and richer vocal tone than the typical alto.

Example Ulrica in Verdi's *Un ballo en maschera*.

Tenor The tenor is the highest and probably most popular of the male voices—especially in popular music. The tenor range overlaps significantly with the range of the female alto, and with the male bass. The Fach system defines to primary types of tenor voices:

Lyric/Light Dramatic range: Low C to the C an octave above middle C. Possesses a dramatic upper range that rings out above orchestration. Example: Rodolfo in Puccini's *La Bohème*.

Dramatic/Heldentenor range: B below low C to the C above middle C. Combines the brightness of a lyric tenor with strength in the baritone range; more resonant than a lyric tenor. Examples: Siegfried in Wagner's *Der Ring des Nibelungen*; Otello in Verdi's *Otello*.

Baritone The baritone voice bridges the gap between the tenor and the bass. Although rarely broken out separately in choral music, it is a very "listenable" voice, being rather lyric in quality. It lends itself well to much of the popular repertoire. The Fach system defines two primary types of baritones:

Lyric/Kavalier range: B below low C to the G above middle C. Singers in this category may have a sweet, higher baritone or a powerful, somewhat harsher tone. Examples: Count Almaviva in Mozart's *The Marriage of Figaro*; Don Giovanni in Mozart's *Don Giovanni*.

Bass-Baritone range: From E a half octave below low C to the F or F# above middle C. The range for this voice varies widely according to the role. Examples: Wotan in Wagner's *Der Ring des Nibelungen*; Figaro in Mozart's *The Marriage of Figaro*.

Bass The bass is the lowest and heaviest of the male voices. The bass voice can be very powerful, capable of overwhelming many lighter voices. The Fach system defines two primary bass voices:

Comic Bass range: E a half octave below low C to F above middle C. A lyrical voice used in comedic roles. Examples: Leporello in Mozart's *Don Giovanni*; Don Pasquale in Donizetti's *Don Pasquale*.

Dramatic Bass/Basso Profundo range: From C one octave below low C to F above middle C. This is the lowest of all voices. Examples: Sarastro in Mozart's *The Magic Flute*; King Mark in Wagner's *Tristan und Isolde*.

Musical Forms

Church Music

From the earliest times, music has been associated with religious worship. Many vocal forms have their roots in the music of the Catholic and Protestant Churches.

Anthem The *anthem* is the Protestant Church's version of the Latin motet. In most instances the choir is accompanied by organ; many anthems include passages for vocal soloists, either individually or in combination. Major composers of this form include Henry Purcell and John Blow (1649–1708).

Chorale The *chorale* (in German, *choral*) is a type of unison hymn characteristic of the German Reformed Church. This sacred form resulted from Martin Luther's desire to restore the congregation's role in church services. Most chorales feature simple devotional words set to familiar tunes—either folk songs or the traditional ecclesiastical melodies known as plainsong—intended for singing by the congregation. (This is in contrast to the more formal Catholic mass, which is sung by a separate choir.)

Early Lutheran chorales had much of the free rhythm of plainsong, often mixing duple and triple time. Later chorales employed a more rigid metric scheme. The melody of early chorales was often placed in the tenor voice. During the 17th century the melody moved to the treble voice, and four-part chorales became popular during the 17th and 18th centuries.

One of the most prolific composers for the chorale was J. S. Bach, during the Baroque era. Bach composed some 30 chorales, and reharmonized 400 others. He also used several chorale melodies in his *St. John Passion* and *St. Matthew Passion*.

Conductus A *conductus* is a metrical Latin song, either sacred or secular, for two or three voices. The conductus originated in France during the 12th century, and was superseded by the motet.

Lauda The *lauda* is a religious song not based on liturgical texts, typically performed in either Italian or Latin. This form was popular during the 13th, 15th, and 16th centuries.

Mass The Roman Catholic *Mass* has inspired many great vocal works. The five passages of the Mass that are frequently set for choir or for choir and vocal soloists include the *Kyrie* ("Lord have mercy"), *Gloria in excelsis Deo* ("Glory be to God on high"), *Credo* ("I believe"), *Sanctus* ("Holy, holy"), and *Agnus Dei* ("O Lamb of God"). In some later Masses these five sections are subdivided even further; for example, J. S. Bach divided the *Kyrie* into three parts: *Kyrie eleison* ("Lord have mercy"), *Christe eleison* ("Christ, have mercy"), and a second *Kyrie eleison*.

The earliest polyphonic masses were set in the 14th century, by Machaut. In the 15th century secular tunes were introduced to the Mass as a *cantus firmus*, courtesy of Du Fay and his 15th-century contemporaries. By the end of the 16th century the Mass had evolved into an unaccompanied contrapuntal style, as practiced by Palestrina, Victoria, and William Byrd (1542–1623).

In the 17th and 18th centuries the mass welcomed an increase in solo singing and then, moving into the 19th century, evolved into more of an oratorio style. Examples of this mature style include Bach's Mass in B Minor and Beethoven's Mass in D.

Grand Motet This musical form is a motet for large ensembles of voices and instruments, contrasting solo voices with the larger chorus. The grand motet was originally performed in the liturgies of the court chapel of Louis XIV, and later performed as concert pieces throughout 18th-century France and Germany.

Oratorio An *oratorio* is a dramatic musical setting of a religious libretto, for solo singers, choir, and orchestra. An oratorio is like a nonsecular opera, but without the scenery or costumes; oratorios are typically performed in concert halls or churches. The oratorio originated in plays given in the Oratory of St. Philip Neri in 16th-century Rome; the musical form developed ca. 1600. Emilio del Cavalieri's (ca. 1550–1602) *La rappresentazione di anima e di corpo* (The Representation of Soul and Body) is generally recognized as the first oratorio. Later oratorios were written by A. Scarlatti, Schütz, Haydn, Beethoven, Mendelssohn, and Handel; Handel's *Messiah* is perhaps the most recognized of all oratorios.

Some secular works, such as Handel's *Semele* and Stravinsky's *Oedipus Rex*, are also considered oratorios—or, in some cases, *opera-oratorios*. Certain biblical oratorios, such as Shütz's *The Christmas History*, are called *historia*.

Plainsong *Plainsong*, also known as *plainchant*, is the large body of traditional ritual melody of the Western Christian Church. A plainsong is a chant composed of a single line of vocal melody, typically unaccompanied and performed in a free rhythm. The rhythm of plainsong is the free rhythm of speech. Plainsong developed during the early centuries of Christianity. The form matured during the sixth century, at the request of Pope Gregory I, and was subsequently known as *Gregorian chant*.

Plainsong has its own system of notation, using a four-line staff (in contrast to the modern five-line staff) and no bar lines. There are two primary types of plain-song: *responsorial* (developed from the recitation of psalms) and *antiphonal* (developed as pure melody).

Other religions, including the Greek Orthodox and Jewish churches, have similar types of ritual songs, although they are not included in the definition of plainsong.

Voluntary A *voluntary* is an organ piece played before or after a service of the Anglican Church. The voluntary is often, but not always, extemporized.

Vocal Music

Western vocal music evolved from both sacred forms and secular folk songs. Vocal forms can incorporate either solo vocals (either *a cappella* or with instrumental accompaniment) or group (choral) vocals.

Aria As developed in Italy during the 18th century, an *aria* is a lengthy and involved solo vocal piece in A-B-A form. The aria is an integral part of the operatic form.

There are eight primary types of arias: *aria cantabile*, slow and smooth; *aria di portamento*, dignified in a legato style; *aria di mezzo carattere*, passionate and with elaborate orchestral accompaniment; *aria parlante*, declamatory; *aria di bravura*, requiring great vocal control; *aria all'unisono*, with accompaniment in unison or octaves with the vocal part; *aria d'imitazione*, imitative of bird songs or other natural sounds; and *aria concertata*, with elaborate instrumental accompaniment.

Arietta The *arietta* is a shorter and simpler aria, typically without the middle (B) section.

Caccia The *caccia* is a 14th-century Italian form in which two vocalists "chase" each other in strict canon. The word *caccia* means "chase" or "hunt" in Italian, and the text often deals with hunting.

Cantata The term *cantata* has described different musical forms over the centuries. The earliest form, as practiced in the 17th century, referred to a dramatic madrigal sung by a solo vocalist or vocalists, accompanied by lute or basso continuo. There were two variations of this cantata form, the secular *cantata da camera* ("chamber cantata") and nonsecular *cantata da chiesa* ("church cantata").

Scarlatti was one of the chief proponents of this form, writing more than 600 pieces.

During the 18th century the cantata became longer and more complex, typically containing recitatives and arias—much like a short, unstaged opera. This type of cantata typically was written for soloist with organ or orchestral accompaniment. Composers in this style included Bach (who wrote close to 300 church cantatas), Handel, Schütz, and Telemann. Representative cantatas of this period include Bach's *Coffee Cantata* and *Peasant Cantata*.

By the 19th century the cantata evolved into a form resembling a short oratorio, on both sacred and secular themes. In the 20th century the term defines vocal music of various forms, although still loosely defined as vocal solo with instrumental accompaniment.

Canzona The *canzona* is a song form, similar to the madrigal, originally practiced by troubadours of the 16th century. The canzona evolved from a literal transcription of French chanson into Italian, and has a characteristic A-A-B form.

In the late 16th and 17th centuries, the vocal canzona was translated into lute and keyboard compositions that foreshadowed the later sonata and fugue forms. Primary practitioners of the keyboard canzona included J. S. Bach, Girolamo Frescobaldi (1583–1643), and Andrea Gabrieli (1510–86).

Concert Aria The *concert aria* is a virtuoso solo song, with accompaniment, based on the Italian operatic aria.

Lieder The word *lieder* is the plural of *lied*—German for "song." In popular usage, lieder refer to a distinctive type of German vocal composition of the Romantic period. The traditional lieder is a nonoperatic art song with lyrics based on a dramatic poem; in performance, the vocal and the piano accompaniment are of equal importance.

There are two types of lieder. *Strophic song* is similar to a hymn, with each stanza receiving the same melody; *through-composed* song provides different music for every stanza. Brahms, Schubert, Schumann, Mahler, and Strauss were all noted for their lieder; representative examples include Schubert's "Gretchen am Spinnrade" and Brahms's extended cycle of solo songs, the *Magelone* Romances, Op. 33.

Madrigal The *madrigal* is a secular vocal composition that originated in Italy during the 13th century. The typical madrigal is a polyphonic composition for four to six voices, typically unaccompanied, based on a poem or other secular text. Early composers in the madrigal form included Lassus, Palestrina, and A. Gabrieli; chief among the later Italian madrigal composers was Monteverdi, who created several madrigals based on sacred text.

The madrigal was introduced to England in the late 16th century, most notably by Nicholas Yonge's (d. 1619) 1588 publication of *Musica Transalpina*, a collection of Italian madrigals with English words. Several English composers embraced the madrigal form, notably Morley, William Byrd (1543–1623), and Thomas Weelkes (ca. 1576–1623).

The madrigal survived another hundred years, but was superseded by the cantata by the early 17th century.

Ode An ode is a ceremonial vocal work, typically with orchestral accompaniment. Examples include Purcell's *Ode for St. Cecilia's Day* and Sir Edward Elgar's (1857–1934) *Coronation Ode*.

Serenata A *serenata* is a type of serenade performed outdoors in the evening.

Instrumental Music

Instrumental music developed later than vocal music, as it was dependent on the evolving musical instrument technology over the ages. Many instrumental forms are based on types of local dance; others evolved from earlier sacred and vocal forms.

Allemande As derived from German and Swiss peasant dance, the *allemande* is a dance in 4/4 or duple time, popular in the 17th and early 18th centuries. The allemande was often the first movement of a suite, or the first movement after the prelude. It has a serious character and moderate tempo.

Chaconne A *chaconne*, also known as a *passacaglia*, is a dance in triple time with a repeating bass line (known as *ground bass*). Many operas of the Baroque era—by Lully, Rameau, and others—ended with a chaconne movement. Some of the best-known chaconnes include the solo violin section at the end of Bach's 2nd Partita in D Minor; Purcell's aria *"When I am laid in earth,"* from *Dido and Aeneas*; Beethoven's 21 Variations in C minor for piano; and the finale of Brahms's Symphony no. 4.

Chamber Music *Chamber music* is music for a small group of solo instruments, originally designed for performance in houses and small halls—not intended for the church, theater, or large concert hall.

Chamber music is easiest understood as what it is not;

it is not music for a vocal or instrumental soloist, nor is it music for an orchestra or chorus. Instead, most chamber music is written for two (duet), three (trio), four (quartet), five (quintet), six (sextet), seven (septet), or eight (octet) instruments, with all the parts being relatively equal in importance—that is, the music is not intended for a soloist with accompaniment.

Chamber music can be written for string or wind instruments. Perhaps the most popular form is the *string quartet*, composed of two violins, one viola, and one cello.

Haydn could be considered the father of modern chamber music. Before Haydn, most music of this type was supplied with a figured bass, extemporized on harpsichord. Haydn introduced the concept of four (or more) equal parts, precisely arranged without room for extemporization. Subsequently, most major composers have contributed in some way to the modern chamber music repertory.

Choral Symphony A *choral symphony* is a symphony that incorporates a choir. The most notable example of this form is Beethoven's Symphony no. 9 in D Minor, in which the choir joins the orchestra in the final movement, an adaptation of Schiller's *Ode to Joy*.

Chorale Prelude The *chorale prelude* (also known as the *choral prelude*) is a solo keyboard piece that grew out of the custom of playing organ preludes and interludes to the vocal chorale in the services of the Protestant Church. There are two types of chorale preludes. The first is based on an imaginative treatment of the chorale melody, often with elaborate counterpoint; the second suggests rather than reproduces the chorale melody, by means of elaboration on the first few notes of the theme.

Composers who helped to developed the form included Jan Pieterszoon Sweelinck (1562–1621), Samuel Scheidt (1587–1654), and Johann Pachelbel (1653–1706). Chief among the practitioners of the mature form were J. S. Bach and Henry Purcell.

Concertino As developed in the 19th century, a *concertino* is a short concerto for orchestra and one or more soloists. (The term *concertino* can also refer to a small instrumental ensemble within a larger orchestra.)

Concerto A *concerto* is an instrumental work in which one or more solo instruments are contrasted with a larger orchestra. While the first known concertos date back to the late 16th century, the form came to prominence in the late Baroque era with Vivaldi's violin concertos (notably his programmatic "Four Seasons"), Handel's organ concertos, and Bach's harpsichord concertos; also notable are Bach's orchestral "Brandenburg" Concertos.

The modern concerto was established by Mozart, who composed nearly 50 works for various combinations of instruments. Most modern concertos are in three movements. While early concertos featured a *cadenza* where the soloist would display his virtuoso skills via improvisation, modern composers are more likely to write out the cadenza beforehand, dispensing with the improvisation.

Many different types of concertos were composed during the Baroque era. A concerto designed for performance in a secular venue was called *concerto da camera*, or chamber concerto. A concerto designed for performance in church was called *concerto da chiesa*, or church concerto. A concerto with a small group of soloists (called a *concertino*), in addition to the traditional orchestra or string ensemble, was called *concerto grosso*, or great concerto.

In the 20th century the term *concerto for orchestra* was used to describe a concerto-like work that did not have a specific soloist (although individual members of the orchestra might be called upon to perform solo passages). Composers in this form include Bartók, Zoltán Kodály (1882–1967), and Sir Michael Tippett (1905–98).

Courante The *courante* is a French dance in rapid time, popular in the 17th century. Some variations combine simple triple time with compound duple rhythms; Bach, especially, favored this variation, representing the conflicting rhythms in the right and left hands of his keyboard pieces. The courante was typically the second movement of the suite.

Divertimento A *divertimento* is an 18th-century Italian suite of light entertaining music, typically written for a small number of instruments. Mozart wrote 25 of these pieces; they are sometimes referred to as serenades or cassations. The French version of divertimento is *divertissement*; these are sometimes inserted into ballet, opera, or other stage spectacles.

Fantasia A *fantasia* is an instrumental composition that avoids conventional forms and structures; form is of secondary importance. As developed in 16th century Italy, early fantasias strictly imitated vocal motets; early English fantasias (called *fancy*) were primarily contrapuntal in construction and in several sections with a common theme, thus representing an early version of theme and variation. Later organ fantasias by Sweelinck and Bach suggested more of an improvisational character and the play of free fancy.

In the 19th century several composers used the term *fantasia* to describe their short mood pieces; most notable of these pieces is Schumann's *Fantasie-stücke*. The term can also describe a composition comprising a string of tunes from an opera. The English equivalent of the fantasia is the *fancy*; the French is *fantaisie*; and the German, *fantasie*.

Fugue The *fugue* is a particularly strict type of contrapuntal composition, usually for instruments but occasionally for choir. In a fugue, the first "voice" states a short melody or phrase (known as the *subject*); additional voices enter successively in imitation. Bach wrote a number of organ and other instrumental fugues. Also notable is Beethoven's *Grosse fuge* for string quartet, op. 133. A shortened type of fugue is sometimes called a *fughetta*. A passage in fugal style from another musical form is called *fugato*.

Gavotte The *gavotte* is a French dance in common time, popularized in the court of Louis XIV by Lully and other composers.

Intermezzo As originally conceived in the 16th century, an *intermezzo* was an instrumental piece played between sections of more serious fare. In this context, an intermezzo might be a song or madrigal performed between the acts of a play.

In the early 18th century, the concept of the intermezzo had evolved to describe the separate plots introduced by secondary, comic characters recently introduced into opera seria. (This development eventually became the new form called opera buffa.) By the 19th century, the word *intermezzo* was applied to any short instrumental interlude inserted into an opera to denote a passage of time. The word *intermezzo* also describes a short piano piece with no set form, such as Brahms's eight *Klavierstücke*, Op. 76.

Miniature As established in the Romantic period, a *miniature* is a short piano piece based on a single musical idea. Several different types of works carry this classification, including the *ballade, etude, impromptu,* and *nocturne.* Frédéric Chopin's (1810–49) *Ballade in G Minor* is an example of a ballade miniature.

Minuet A *minuet* is a dance in triple time, originally as practiced by the court of the 17th century. The minuet originated and was adapted from French rustic dance, and is so-called because of its characteristic small steps. Lully and other Baroque-era composers embraced the form, and it soon became one of the optional movements of the instrumental suite. Bach and Handel incorporated the minuet into their overtures, and in the 18th century the minuet was integrated into symphonies (as the standard third movement) by Haydn, Mozart, and others.

A typical minuet is in A-B-A form. The B section is often a contrasting minuet called the *trio*. (The name comes from the practice of some French composers who wrote this middle section in three-part harmony.)

Overture Not to be confused with the piece of instrumental music played before an opera, oratorio, or play, this type of *overture* (sometimes called a *concert overture*) is an independent single-movement instrumental work, typically used to open a concert. Some overtures are written in sonata form; others are more like symphonic poems. A good example of the later style is Mendelssohn's *The Hebrides*.

Prelude Strictly defined, a *prelude* is a piece of music that precedes something else. Examples would be the first movement of a suite, or an orchestral introduction to an opera. The word *prelude* is also used to describe a short piece for solo piano. Composers contributing to the prelude repertory include Debussy, Chopin, and Rachmaninov.

Programme Music As originally described by Liszt, *programme music* is instrumental music that tells a story, illustrates a literary idea, or evolves a pictorial scene. Primary contributors to the form included Liszt, Berlioz, Tchaikovsky, Strauss, and Modest Petrovich Mussorgsky (1839–81). Notable works include Berlioz' *Symphonie Fantastique*, Strauss's *Also sprach Zarathustra*, and Mussorgsky's *Pictures at an Exhibition*.

Ricercare The *ricercare* was initially a transcription of a vocal work for keyboard or instrumental ensemble; in the 16th and 17th centuries it evolved into an independent instrumental work. There are two types of ricercare: homophonic (with a single melody line) and contrapuntal (with two or more contrasting melody lines). The last style is more common, typically with elaborate fugal or canonic stylings, as witnessed in Bach's *Das musikalische Opfer*.

Sarabande The *sarabande* is a dance form that originated in Latin America. It appeared in Spain in the early 16th century, and traveled to France and England in the early 17th century. The Spanish sarabonde was in a lively triple time, but the French and English preferred a more stately version of the form. It became a standard version of the instrumental suite, as practiced by Purcell, Bach, Handel, and others.

Sonata A *sonata* is a composition for solo piano or another instrument with piano accompaniment; sonatas typically have no more than two performers.

The sonata originated in the 16th century as any piece that was played rather than sung. During the 17th century the term was used to describe instrumental compositions divided into five or more contrasting sections. The Baroque sonata, as practiced by A. Scarlatti, C. P. E. Bach, and others, had from three to six movements, like a suite. During the Classical period, Haydn, Mozart, and Beethoven established the sonata as having three movements, allegro-andante-allegro; this format, dubbed *sonata form*, is also used in other musical forms.

Baroque-era sonatas designed for performance in secular venues are called *sonata da camera* or chamber sonata. Sonatas from the same era designed for performance in church are called *sonata da chiesa* or church sonata. The *trio sonata* is a Baroque-era sonata for voice, violin, and cello, and the *sonatina* ("little sonata") is a short sonata, typically lighter and easier to perform than a regular sonata.

String Quartet The *string quartet* is a particular form of chamber music written for two violins, viola, and cello. In terms of importance, the string quartet is to chamber music as the symphony is to orchestral music; most major composers have contributed to the string quartet repertory.

The first string quartets were written at the beginning of the 18th century, during the closing years of the Baroque era. Early composers for the string quartet included A. Scarlatti and Guiseppe Tartini (1692–1770), but the form reached its zenith with the works of Haydn, Mozart, Beethoven, and Schubert.

Suite As established in the Baroque period, a *suite* is a piece of instrumental music in several movements, usually in dance style. The form was most important in the 17th and 18th centuries.

A typical suite of the Baroque period might commence with an overture and include the following movements: allemande, courante, sarabande, and gigue, all typically in the same key. Additional movements might include bourrée, gavotte, minuet, musette, passepied, and rigaudon. Examples of Baroque-era suites include Handel's *Fireworks Music* and Bach's six cello and four orchestral suites.

In later eras the term was used to describe assemblages of movements from ballet or opera scores, as well as original multimovement compositions. Popular instrumental suites include Ravel's *Daphnis et Chloé*, Tchaikovsky's *Nutcracker Suite*, and Gustav Holst's (1874–1934) *Planets Suite*.

Symphony The *symphony* (in Italian, *sinfonia*) evolved from the overture to late 17th-century operas, as first practiced by A. Scarlatti, and came to prominence in the 18th century. The modern symphony is a large-scale instrumental composition, much like a sonata for orchestra, usually in four movements (although this varies). In the Classical and Romantic periods, the typical symphony opened with an allegro movement, followed by a slow movement, then a minuet or scherzo, ending with an allegro or rondo movement; in some instances the slow movement is moved to the third or fourth position.

Symphonic Poem As developed by Liszt, *the symphonic poem*—also called the tone poem—is a single-movement orchestral work on a symphonic scale. The symphonic poem is a type of programme music; Liszt composed 13 symphonic poems that dealt with subjects taken from classical mythology, Romantic literature, and imaginative fantasy, including *Prometheus* and *Les Préludes*. Other proponents of the form include Tchaikovsky, Bedrich Smetana (1824–84), and Camille Saint-Saëns (1835–1921). Richard Strauss composed symphonic poems that he dubbed *Tondichtungen*, or "tone-poems."

Toccata The *toccata* is a short keyboard piece, originally a movement (often a prelude) within a longer instrumental work but later a self-contained solo work. The foremost composer for the toccata form was J. S. Bach, who wrote several toccatas and fugues, as well as harpsichord toccatas in multiple movements.

Structure of the Symphony Orchestra

The modern symphony orchestra consists of approximately 100 musicians organized into sections, or choirs, according to the sound produced by each family of instruments. Each section is led by a "principal", or "first chair" whose role is to play the solos written for their instrument in an orchestral piece. The principal first violinist is called the "concertmaster" who has the additional responsibility of selecting the bowing strokes to be used in the string section, thus ensuring that all the bows will move in the same direction.

Strings
Violin (divided into first and second violin sections)
Viola
Cello
Bass (also called double bass or contra bass)

Woodwinds

Flute	Bass clarinet
Piccolo	Bassoon
English Horn	Double Bassoon
Oboe	Saxophone (not always included in an
Clarinet	orchestra, but considered a wind instrument)

Brass
Trumpet
French Horn
Trombone
Tuba

Percussion

Timpani (also called kettle drum)	Chimes
Snare Drum	Bells
Bass Drum	Glockenspiel
Cymbals	Celesta
Triangle	Xylophone
Gong (also called tam tam)	Woodblock
Castanets	
Tambourine	

What Does a Conductor Do? The symphony conductor is the most important musician in an orchestra although he or she doesn't play an instrument during the performance. The conductor's role is to indicate and control the tempo of the music, the dynamics (loud vs. quiet) of each section of instruments, and how the music is played and interpreted. In a sense, the conductor turns a group of individual musicians into a single, beautiful instrument. Conductors have their own artistic sense and style which is why the same piece of music may sound different in each recording or live performance.

History of American Popular Music

Music from The Civil War to World War I

The original settlers of the American continent brought their popular musics with them. Prior to the Civil War, much of America's popular music was directly influenced by these sources; fiddle tunes and dance music, mostly derived from British and French roots, along with a rich tradition of folk balladry and songs, were the staples of the popular music repertoire. The first truly "American" songs were topical ones, addressing political campaigns, the hard life faced by the settlers, and military/patriotic songs.

Minstrel Music   In the period just prior to the Civil War, a new American musical hybrid came to the fore: the minstrel song. Minstrels were white performers who performed in black face, supposedly presenting "authentic" versions of African-American dance tunes and songs. By the early 1840's minstrel troupes gained popularity, beginning with the famous Virginia Minstrels, featuring Dan Emmett (1815–1904). These troupes toured Europe as well as the United States.

Initial minstrel hits included such perennials as "Old Zip Coon" (later known as "Turkey in the Straw"). The Civil War inspired countless new songs, including Emmett's "Dixie" (which became the official anthem of the Confederacy) and its Northern counterpart, "The Battle Hymn of the Republic." Abolitionist and pro-slavery forces alike developed songs to promote their causes.

Stephen Foster   The first great American songwriter was undoubtedly Stephen Foster (1826–64). Foster made his name with minstrel songs, many of which he sold to Edward Christy, leader of Christy Minstrels. His early hits include "Oh! Susanna" from 1848, "De Camptown Races," (1850) "Old Folks at Home" (1851; also known as "Swanee River"), and 1853's "Old Kentucky Home." Later in his career, Foster turned to writing sentimental ballads, most famously "Jeannie With the Light Brown Hair" (1854) and the posthumously published "Beautiful Dreamer."

African-American Composers   African-American composers also began to receive recognition during this period. Most notable was James Bland (1854–1911), a per-former and songwriter best remembered for his major hits, "Carry Me Back to Ole Virginny" (1873), "In the Evening by the Moonlight," and "Oh, Dem Golden Slippers" (1879). Other prominent African-American composers of the era include Will Marion Cook, Bert Williams (the famous comic performer), and the Johnson Brothers.

Brass Bands   The late 19th century was the heyday of the brass band movement and the instrumental march. Perhaps the best-known bandleader/composer of the era was John Philip Sousa (1854–1932), who led the U.S. Marine Band from 1880 to 1892 before forming his own famous outfit. His numerous hits included such classics as "The Washington Post" (1889), "The Liberty Bell" (1893), and "The Stars and Stripes Forever" (1896), among many others.

Ragtime   The march form became the format for a new piano instrumental style called ragtime. Scott Joplin (1868–1917) had composed marches himself before syncopating its oom-pah beat to form the "classic" piano rag. Joplin's 1899 "Maple Leaf Rag" was the first instrumental sheet music publication to sell over a million copies, and became the classic model for Joplin's later works and rags by other prominent composers.

Joplin was a master creator of memorable melodies, from the bouncing "The Entertainer" (used as the theme for the 1973 film, *The Sting*) to the lyrical "Wall Street Rag." Joplin influenced many other composers, including James Scott, Arthur Marshall, and white pianist Joseph Lamb.

The great popularity of ragtime spread from rural areas to the major cities, first St. Louis, then Chicago and New York. More than 1,000 rags were published during the genre's heyday from 1900 to 1925.

The Growth of the Music Publishing Industry

During the final three decades of the 19th century, the American music industry continued to grow. Smaller publishing houses became "farm teams" for the bigger ones, so that a local hit would eventually be purchased for republication by a larger house, gaining it national exposure. Popular song was basically divided into two main streams: minstrel or "coon" songs, written in a pseudo-African-American style, usually on comic themes; and sentimental or "parlor" ballads, aimed at young ladies to perform at home, usually on themes of romantic love (or loss). Topical songs also continued to enjoy popularity.

Prominent among the hit makers of the final decades

of the 19th century was Charles K. Harris (1867–1930), who wrote the classic "After the Ball" in 1893, which eventually sold more than 5 million.

American Popular Song

The classic American popular song has a characteristic sound and feel. Most songs have a similar four-part structure: two verses, a chorus, and a repeat of the verse, typically called the AABA form. Each of the verses typically have different lyrics, and sometimes the chorus is repeated at the end of the song, with the same lyrics.

More important than this structural consistency is the way the melodies of these songs are written, so that they can be sung by a person with no more than an average vocal range. These melodies are typically harmonized with chords that fit within the underlying musical scale, with few, if any, nonscale notes or chord tones. This results in music that is pleasing to the ear, with few unexpected harmonies or dissonant notes.

In the first half of the 20th century, most popular music incorporated a light swing beat and jazz rhythms, often with a slight emphasis on the first and third beats of the measure. This changed in the rock, soul, and country music of the second half of the century, all of which typically used straight eighth-note rhythms instead of a swing beat, as well as a heavily accented "backbeat" on the second and fourth beats of the measure.

Despite these rhythmic differences, the American popular songbook—as well as popular music from other countries that influenced the American genre—is an interconnected and evolving body of work, from the Tin Pan Alley tunes of the 1920's to the highly engineered pop music of today.

The Great American Songbook The story of American popular music in the 20th century is written, in large part, by the professional songwriter. Professional songwriters apply their craft to the three-minute song, writing memorable words and melodies for other musicians to perform.

The first half of the 20th century was a prolific era for popular songwriters. The approximately 300,000 compositions copyrighted between 1900 and 1950 make up what aficionados call the Great American Songbook—a collection of some of the most memorable songs ever put to paper.

Tin Pan Alley During the first part of the 20th century, professional songwriting in America was concentrated in the area of New York City on West 28th Street, between Broadway and Sixth Avenue, commonly called Tin Pan Alley. (The name came from writer Monroe Rosenfeld, who likened the cacophony of so many songwriters pounding on so many pianos to the sound of beating on tin pans.) Songwriters, together and in teams, churned out their compositions in factory-like style; the best of these songs were sold to music publishing companies, and were then issued as sheet music (before the explosion of the record business) or picked up by one of the major singers of the day. Sometimes these Tin Pan Alley tunes ended up in vaudeville productions, Broadway plays, or Hollywood movies. The best of the best endured, and became classics.

The most talented songwriters of a generation filtered through Tin Pan Alley. Irving Berlin, Cole Porter, George and Ira Gershwin, and their contemporaries were all professional songwriters for hire. Their songs were sung by the top singers of the day—Fred Astaire, Bing Crosby, Frank Sinatra, Mel Tormé, Ella Fitzgerald, Tony Bennett, Nat "King" Cole, and the like. These songwriters contributed the bulk of the Great American Songbook—compositions filled with pretty melodies, sophisticated chord progressions, and mature, often witty, lyrics.

George M. Cohan The century's first great popular songwriter was a legendary vaudeville and Broadway song-and-dance man, playwright, actor, and producer. George M. Cohan (1878–1942) is considered the father of American musical comedy; along with partner Sam H. Harris (1872–1941), Cohan produced more than three dozen Broadway shows between 1906 and 1926.

For these and other plays, Cohan wrote more than 1,500 original songs. Cohan's songs are noted for their hummable melodies, clever lyrics, and, during the World War I era, patriotic themes. His songs include "Forty-Five Minutes from Broadway," "Give My Regards to Broadway," "Harrigan," "Mary's a Grand Old Name," "Over There," "So Long, Mary," "Yankee Doodle Dandy," and "You're a Grand Old Flag."

Jerome Kern (1885–1945) was the first true master of 20th century musical theater, writing from the turn of the last century through the 1940's. A composer, Kern wrote with various lyricists, including Dorothy Fields, Ira Gershwin, and Oscar Hammerstein II. During the course of his career, Kern wrote more than 700 songs and 100 scores for plays and films, including the groundbreaking 1927 musical, *Show Boat* (lyrics by Hammerstein) which includes the song "Make Believe."

Kern's songs were harmonically rich, which made them ideal for improvisation by jazz performers. His most notable songs include "A Fine Romance," "Lovely to Look At," "Never Gonna Dance," "Pick Yourself Up," and "The Way You Look Tonight" (with Fields); "All the Things You Are," "Can't Help Lovin' Dat Man," "The Folks Who Live on the Hill," and "Ol' Man River" (with Hammerstein); "Smoke Gets In Your Eyes" and "Yesterdays" (with Otto Harbach); "Look for the Silver Lining" (with Buddy G. DeSylva); and "Till the Clouds Roll By" (with Guy Bolton and P.G. Wodehouse).

Irving Berlin (1888–1989) was a gifted, prolific, and extremely versatile songwriter who epitomized the Tin Pan Alley experience. Over his long career, Berlin rode the crest of several fads in the music world–he popularized the idea of syncopated rhythms in his 1911 hit "Alexander's Ragtime Band"; in the 1920's and 1930's, he incorporated jazzy swing rhythms, as typified in his score for the Fred Astaire-Ginger Rogers film *Top Hat* (1935); in 1938 he captured a growing sense of American patriotism in "God Bless America" (actually written during World War I); and in 1940 penned the perennial holiday favorite, "White Christmas."

Berlin wrote music and lyrics for more than 3,000 songs; he also composed the scores for 21 films and 17 Broadway shows. His songs are among America's best-loved and include "Always," "Anything You Can Do I Can Do Better," "Cheek to Cheek," "Easter Parade," "How Deep Is the Ocean," "I'm Putting All My Eggs in One Basket," "Isn't This a Lovely Day (to Be Caught in the Rain)," "Let Yourself Go," "Let's Face the Music and Dance", "A Pretty Girl is Like a Melody," "Puttin' on the Ritz," "There's No Business Like Show Business," and "What'll I Do?"

George and Ira Gershwin George Gershwin (1898--1937) was arguably the most gifted composer of the 20th century. His innovative work ranged from pop songs (many incorporating jazz-influenced rhythms and harmonies) to classical pieces, such as "Rhapsody in Blue" and "An American in Paris." George's brother, Ira (1896–1983), collaborated on lyrics; his clever rhymes perfectly matched his brother's sophisticated music.

Together, the Gershwins composed music for more than a dozen Broadway shows and the 1935 jazz opera *Porgy and Bess*. Their most famous songs include "Bidin'

My Time," "But Not for Me," "Embraceable You," "Fascinating Rhythm," "A Foggy Day," "I Got Rhythm," "Let's Call the Whole Thing Off," "Love Is Here to Stay," "Nice Work If You Can Get It," "'S Wonderful," "Shall We Dance," "Someone to Watch Over Me," "Summertime," "The Man I Love," "They All Laughed," and "They Can't Take That Away from Me."

Cole Porter (1891–1964), a contemporary of the Gershwins and Irving Berlin, blended complex melodies and harmonies with witty, sophisticated lyrics and clever rhymes. His lyrics often caught the attention of censors of the day; he could be both highly romantic and slightly ribald, taking on the subject of love with cynicism and double entendres.

Porter composed music for numerous Broadway and Hollywood musicals, including *Gay Divorce*, *Anything Goes*, *Red Hot and Blue*, *Silk Stockings*, and *Kiss Me, Kate*. His vast songbook includes "All of You," "All Through the Night," "Anything Goes," "Begin the Beguine," "Ev'ry Time We Say Good-bye," "I Get a Kick Out of You," "I've Got You Under My Skin," "In the Still of the Night," "It's Bad for Me," "It's De-Lovely," "Just One of Those Things," "Love for Sale," "Night and Day," "So in Love," "What Is This Thing Called Love," and "You're the Top."

Harold Arlen Several years younger than the Berlin/Gershwin/Porter generation, Harold Arlen (1905–1986) was a popular songwriter for both Broadway and Hollywood musicals, most notably The Wizard of Oz. He also wrote music for various dance bands of the era.

Arlen wrote his first song in 1929, later forming successful partnerships with lyricists Ted Koehler (1894–1973), E.Y. "Yip" Harburg (1896–1981), and Johnny Mercer (1909–1976). Arlen's songs include "Accentuate the Positive," "Blues in the Night," "Come Rain or Come Shine," "One for My Baby," and "That Old Black Magic" (with Mercer); "Last Night When We Were Young" and "Over the Rainbow" (with Harburg); "It's Only a Paper Moon" (with Harburg and Billy Rose); "I've Got the World on a String" and "Stormy Weather" (with Koehler); "Brother, Can You Spare a Dime?" (with Jay Gorney); and "The Man That Got Away" (with Ira Gershwin).

Hoagy Carmichael (1899–1981) was a talented songwriter in the Tin Pan Alley tradition, even if he didn't live or write in New York City. Carmichael hailed from Bloomington, Indiana, home of Indiana University, where he began his songwriting career.

Carmichael's easygoing compositions reflect his love of the jazz music of the 1920's. He wrote with a number of the era's best lyricists, including Frank Loesser (1910–1969), Mitchell Parish (1900–1993), and Johnny Mercer. Carmichael's most famous songs include "In the Cool Cool Cool of the Evening" and "Lazybones" (with Mercer); "Two Sleepy People" (with Loesser); "Star Dust" (with Parrish); "Georgia on My Mind" (with Stuart Gorrell); "I Get Along Without You Very Well" (with Jane Brown Thompson); "Lazy River" (with Sidney Arodin); "The Nearness of You" (with Ned Washington); and "Ole Buttermilk Sky" (with Jack Brooks).

Richard Rodgers (1902–1979) was not a Tin Pan Alley writer, although his songs became staples of the Great American Songbook. Rodgers was the dean of 20th century musical theater; he created more than 40 Broadway musicals, including *Oklahoma!* (1943), *Carousel* (1945), *South Pacific* (1949), *The King and I* (1951), and *The Sound of Music* (1959).

Working originally with lyricist Lorenz Hart (1895–1943) and later with Oscar Hammerstein II (1895–1960), Rodgers's compositions were known for their consistent inventiveness and sophistication. His songbook with Hart includes "Bewitched, Bothered and Bewildered," "Blue Moon," "Isn't It Romantic?," The Lady Is a Tramp," "Manhattan," "Mountain Greenery," "My Funny Valentine," "My Romance," "Spring is Here," and "Thou Swell"; and with Hammerstein, "Climb Every Mountain," "Hello, Young Lovers," "If I Loved You," "It Might As Well Be Spring," "My Favorite Things," "Oh, What a Beautiful Mornin'!'," "People Will Say We're in Love," "Shall We Dance?," "Some Enchanted Evening," and "You'll Never Walk Alone."

Other Tin Pan Alley Songwriters
Dorothy Fields, lyricist (1905–1974): "Don't Blame Me," "I Can't Give You Anything but Love," and "On the Sunny Side of the Street" (with Jimmy McHugh); and "Big Spender" and "The Rhythm of Life" (with Cy Coleman).

Irving Caesar, lyricist (1895–1996): "Crazy Rhythm" (with Joseph Meyer and Roger Wolfe Kahn); "Tea for Two" (with Vincent Youmans); and "Swanee" (with George Gershwin).

Walter Donaldson, composer (1893–1947): "Love Me or Leave Me," "Makin' Whoopee," and "Yes, Sir! That's My Baby" (with Gus Kahn); and "My Mammy" (with James Lewis and Joe Young).

The trio team of Buddy DeSylva (1895–1950), Lew Brown (1893–1958), and Ray Henderson (1896–1970): "The Best Things in Life are Free," "Black Bottom," "Button Up Your Overcoat," "Sonny Boy," and "You're the Cream in My Coffee."

The American Musical

Before the advent of the phonograph and movies, before radio and television, people went out to theaters and music halls for live entertainment, or they stayed at home and sang around the piano.

The American musical grew from roots in English and European operetta, vaudeville, and minstrel shows. Initially, lightly plotted musical comedies featured popular songs by Tin Pan Alley songwriters. Many of the songs became stand-alone hits on radio and recordings, as well as part of the Great American Songbook. Then, during a "golden age" of the 1950's and 60's, more serious musical plays with character-driven songs integrated into the plots took the stage. More recent developments include "concept" musicals, faux-opera musicals, rock musicals, Disney spectaculars, and "jukebox" musicals.

Beginning in 1871, the 14 comic operettas of the British team W.S. Gilbert and Arthur Sullivan featured slyly simple plots with fiercely clever lyrics and very singable melodies. Their first great success, *H.M.S. Pinafore*, opened in London in 1878 and was playing in unauthorized versions in American cities the same year. In order to secure copyright protection, their next show, *The Pirates of Penzance*, premiered in New York. These two operettas, and their masterpiece, *The Mikado*, continue as U.S. musical favorites, as do *Iolanthe*, *Princess Ido*, and *The Gondoliers*.

In 1878, the American team of Harrigan and Hart began a series of popular, vaudeville-like musical shows that featured sometimes rowdy songs and sketches about immigrant and tenement life in New York, centering on the Irish. Now forgotten titles include *The Mulligan Guards* and *McSorley's Inflation*, shows that hinted at modern musical comedy.

In the new century much creative talent came to the American musical. Beginning in 1904 with *Little Johnny Jones*, the "Yankee-Doodle" composer/actor/director George M. Cohan had a string of hits that included *Forty-Five Minutes From Broadway* and *Little Nellie Kelly*. From 1911 to 1931, the *Ziegfeld Follies* revues or variety shows brought lavish spectacle to the stage, often with songs by such first-rate composers as Irving Berlin and Jerome Kern. Kern also composed a series of charming musical comedies for the intimate Princess Theatre on Broadway, including *Very Good Eddie* (1915) and *Leave It to Jane* (1917).

1920's and 1930's *Show Boat* (1927) and *Porgy and Bess* (1935) revolutionized the American musical. Both works went beyond musical comedy by telling serious stories of believable characters whose emotional lives are illuminated by song. Jerome Kern and Oscar Hammerstein's *Show Boat* (1927), considered the first modern musical, tells a generational story of miscegenation and redemption. George and Ira Gershwin's *Porgy and Bess* (1935), its jazz and folk elements equally at home on musical and opera stages, treats the joy, sorrow, and yearning of African-American life on Catfish Row.

The Hungarian-born composer Sigmund Romberg brought many successful romantic operettas to Broadway, some in collaboration with Oscar Hammerstein, including *The Desert Song* (1926) and *The New Moon* (1927).

The team of Richard Rodgers and Lorenz Hart began in 1925 with *The Garrick Gaieties*, and ended in 1940 with *Pal Joey*. *On Your Toes* (1936) featured choreography by George Balanchine, foreshadowing the importance of dance in future musicals. *I'd Rather Be Right* (1937) brought political satire to musicals and featured George M. Cohan playing F.D.R. *The Boys From Syracuse* (1938) was an adaptation of Shakespeare's *Comedy of Errors*, and paved the way for later shows such as *Kiss Me Kate* (1948) and *West Side Story* (1957).

Two other musicals of the 1930's are notable, and Ethel Merman sang gorgeously loud in both of them: the Gershwins' *Girl Crazy* (1930) and Cole Porter's *Anything Goes* (1934), the often-revived and possibly classic musical comedy. Irving Berlin had some success with *Face the Music* (1932) and the revue *As Thousands Cheer* (1933), but his biggest hit came in a later decade.

1940's and 1950's   Richard Rodgers and Oscar Hammerstein were hardly newcomers to the American musical, but together they took the *Show Boat* model of integrated song and story and made it their own, beginning with *Oklahoma!* (1943). The show also brought the musical back "on its toes" with a psychological "dream ballet" by Agnes de Mille. Then came a series of critical and popular hits, including their masterpiece, *Carousel*

(1945), as well as *South Pacific* (1949), *The King and I* (1951), *Flower Drum Song* (1958), and *The Sound of Music* (1959).

Irving Berlin and Cole Porter were one-man teams; they wrote both words and music. The Russian-born Berlin, perhaps best known for "God Bless America," had more success on Tin Pan Alley and in movies than with book musicals. However, *Annie Get Your Gun* (1946) and *Call Me Madam* (1950) were hits, both starring Ethel Merman. The Midwesterner Cole Porter showed new sophistication with *Kiss Me Kate* (1948), his clever backstage adaptation of *The Taming of the Shrew*, and a musical often revived.

The team of Alan Jay Lerner and Frederick Loewe took the musical somewhat back to its operetta roots with *My Fair Lady* (1956), an enormous hit, and the less successful but memorable *Camelot* (1960). Another team, Richard Adler and Jerry Ross, created two sprightly musical comedies: *The Pajama Game* (1954) and *Damn Yankees* (1955).

The classical composer and conductor of the New York Philharmonic Leonard Bernstein also wrote an operetta-style musical in *Candide* (1956), a cult favorite at home on the opera stage, though initially a flop. Earlier, Bernstein had teamed up with Betty Comden and Adolph Green for two popular musical comedies: *On the Town* (1944) and *Wonderful Town* (1953). Then came the blockbuster *West Side Story* (1957), bringing *Romeo and Juliet* to New York's mean streets with lyrics by young Stephen Sondheim and vibrant choreography by Jerome Robbins. Interestingly, the Tony Award for best musical went to the more homespun *The Music Man* by Meredith Willson.

Another classical composer, the German-born Kurt Weill, had some success on Broadway with *Lady in the Dark* (1941) and *One Touch of Venus* (1943). Then in 1954, a Greenwich Village revival of his *Threepenny Opera* (1928) ran for more than 2,600 performances and helped create Off Broadway. Later, a charmingly simple show, *The Fantasticks* (1960), by Harvey Schmidt and Tom Jones, began a run of 31 years, firmly establishing Off Broadway as part of New York theater.

Frank Loesser and Jule Styne both came to Broadway from Tin Pan Alley. Loesser's first show was *Where's Charley?* (1948), followed by *Guys and Dolls* (1950), for many the classic musical comedy, the operatic *Most Happy Fella* (1956), and *How to Succeed...* (1961). Styne wrote the scores for such pleasant shows as *High Button Shoes* (1947),

Longest-Running Broadway Musicals

Show	Years open	Number of Performances
1. **Phantom of the Opera**	**1988—present**	9,699
2. Cats	1982—2000	7,485
3. Les Misérables	1987—2003	6,680
4. A Chorus Line	1975—90	6,137
5. **Chicago** (**revival**)	**1996—present**	6,027
6. Oh! Calcutta! (revival)	1976—89	5,959
7. **The Lion King**	**1997—present**	5,613
8. Beauty and the Beast	1994—2007	5,461
9. Rent	1996—2008	5,123
10. Miss Saigon	1991—2001	4,097
11. **Mamma Mia!**	**2001—present**	3,976
12. 42nd Street	1980—89	3,486
13. Grease	1972—80	3,388
14. Fiddler on the Roof	1964—72	3,242
15. **Wicked**	**2003—present**	3,134
16. Hello, Dolly!	1964—70	2,844
17. My Fair Lady	1956—62	2,717
18. Hairspray	2002—09	2,642
19. Avenue Q	2003—09	2,534
20. The Producers	2001—07	2,502
21. Cabaret (revival)	1998—2004	2,377
21. Annie	1977—83	2,377
23. Man of La Mancha	1965—71	2,328
24. **Jersey Boys**	**2005—present**	2,289
25. Oklahoma!	1943—48	2,212
26. Smokey Joe's Café	1995—2000	2,036
27. Pippin	1972—77	1,944
28. South Pacific	1949—54	1,925
29. The Magic Show	1974—78	1,920
30. **Mary Poppins**	**2006—present**	1,883
31. Aida	2000—04	1,852
32. Dancin'	1978—82	1,774
33. La Cage Aux Folles	1983—87	1,761
34. Hair	1968—72	1,750
35. The Wiz	1975—79	1,672
36. Crazy for You	1992—96	1,622
37. Ain't Misbehavin	1978—82	1,604
38. The Best Little Whorehouse in Texas	1978—82	1,584
39. Spamalot	2005—09	1,575
40. Evita	1979—83	1,567
41. Jekyll & Hyde	1997—01	1,543
42. 42nd Street (revival)	2001—05	1,524
43. Dreamgirls	1981—85	1,521
44. Mame	1966—70	1,508
45. Grease (revival)	1994—98	1,501
46. The Sound of Music	1959—63	1,443
47. Me and My Girl	1986—89	1,420
48. How to Succeed in Business Without Really Trying	1961—65	1,417
49. Hellzapoppin	1938—41	1,404
50. The Music Man	1957—61	1,375

Note: Titles in bold indicate shows currently in runs, as of May 22, 2011.

Gentlemen Prefer Blondes (1949), and *Bells Are Ringing* (1956). But in collaboration with Stephen Sondheim and Arthur Laurents, he created a quintessential musical theater piece in *Gypsy* (1959), with Ethel Merman center stage, a show that is still frequently revived.

Harold Arlen is perhaps best known for movie songs such as "Over the Rainbow," but he did have some success on Broadway with *Bloomer Girl* (1944), *St. Louis Woman* (1946), and *House of Flowers* (1954).

1960's and Beyond The composer/lyricist Jerry Herman had great success with *Hello, Dolly!* (1964) and *Mame* (1966), and later with *La Cage aux Folles* (1983), but *Mack and Mabel* (1974), though not a hit, deserves another look.

Two other collaborations are notable. John Kander and Fred Ebb brought stylish cynicism to the musical stage with *Cabaret* (1966) and *Chicago* (1975), the latter with the distinctively dark choreography of Bob Fosse. Jerry Bock and Sheldon Harnick had hits with *Fiorello!* (1959), *She Loves Me* (1963), and the long-running *Fiddler on the Roof* (1964).

Stephen Sondheim came into his own as a composer/lyricist with the uproarious *A Funny Thing Happened on the Way to the Forum* (1962), but he hit his sophisticated stride with *Company* (1970), considered a "concept" musical, one with a psychological rather than a narrative arc. Its choreographer was Michael Bennett, whose production of *A Chorus Line* (1975) took the concept musical further, to long-running success. Sondheim's later works are a virtual showcase of musical styles, including *Follies* (1971), *A Little Night Music* (1973), *Sweeney Todd* (1979), *Into the Woods* (1987), and *Passion* (1994).

The London-born composer/lyricist Andrew Lloyd Webber introduced a faux-opera style to musicals, including *Jesus Christ Superstar* (1971), *Evita* (1979), and the all-time record-breaking champ *The Phantom of the Opera* (1988); *Cats* (1981) harked back to vaudeville, ironically with lyrics from T. S. Eliot. The French team of Claude-Michel Schönberg and Alan Boublil also brought a sung-through operatic style to Broadway with *Les Misérables* (1984) and *Miss Saigon* (1991).

Rock music began to shake up the American musical with the "Summer of Love" *Hair* (1968) and the 1950's nostalgic *Grease* (1972); both shows had opened downtown but quickly moved to long runs on Broadway, as did Jonathan Larson's *Rent* (1996), with a rock score and a story adapted from opera's *La Bohème* set in New York's Lower East Side.

The Disney Company came to Broadway and helped clean up Times Square, while cleaning up profits as well. The Disney musical favors production values over traditional words and music in popular shows such as *Beauty and the Beast* (1994), as well as the still-running (as of 2011) *The Lion King* (1997) and *Mary Poppins* (2007).

The latest evolution of the American musical is the "jukebox" musical, which takes the songs of a popular music group and arranges them around a loose narrative, something of a return of the American musical to its vaudeville roots. Recent examples include the still-running shows (as of 2011) *Mamma Mia!* (ABBA), *Jersey Boys* (Frankie Valli and the Four Seasons), and *Rain* (Beatles).

The Brill Building Era

By the 1950's, Tin Pan Alley and the New York music business had moved uptown—to the stretch of Broadway between 49th and 53rd streets. The hub of this activity was the Brill Building, located at 1619 Broadway, along with a neighboring building at 1650 Broadway. The Brill Building was built in 1931, and some of its first tenants were music publishers, including Famous Music, Mills Music, and Southern Music. By 1962 the building was home to more than 150 music companies, and this concentration of companies made the Brill Building (and its across-the-street companion) a kind of "one stop shop" for aspiring musicians.

In the Brill Building era, the entire music process was contained in a single building. A musician could write a song on one floor, sell it to a publisher on another floor, have an arrangement written on another, and cut a demo disk on another. If musicians were needed for a demo, there were plenty available; if a publisher or a singer was shopping for a song, all the person had to do was wait around a few minutes and someone would be knocking at the door.

1650 Broadway and Aldon Music While the Brill was the nexus of the Broadway music complex, some of the biggest hits came out of 1650 Broadway. This building housed Aldon Music, a music publishing company run by Don Kirshner (b. 1934) and Al Nevins (1916–1965). Aldon Music signed the best of that generation's songwriting teams, and soon became the most successful of all the Brill Building publishing companies.

By 1962 Aldon had 18 songwriters on staff, none older than 26. The list of songwriters who were signed to Aldon Music is startling, and includes the teams of Neil Sedaka and Howard Greenfield, Doc Pomus and Mort Shuman, Gerry Goffin and Carole King, Barry Mann and Cynthia Weil, Ellie Greenwich and Jeff Barry, and Tommy Boyce and Bobby Hart.

Brill Building Pop While so-called Brill Building pop was every bit as well crafted as Tin Pan Alley pop, the Brill Building songwriters were writing to a completely different audience–the then-new teen market. The 1950's marked the first time that teenagers were identified separately from their parents, and they craved their own clothing, movies, and music. Brill Building songwriters targeted the teen market and wrote songs with which that era's teenagers could identify.

From the late 1950's to the mid 1960's, Brill Building songwriters sent one song after another to the top of the pop charts. Brill Building songs fueled the careers of many teen idols and helped create the Girl Group craze of the early 1960's. They were also influential in inspiring the compositions of John Lennon and Paul McCartney, as well as the sound and the songs of the Motown label.

Jerry Leiber and Mike Stoller One of the earliest Brill Building songwriting teams was that of Jerry Leiber (b. 1933) and Mike Stoller (b. 1933). Leiber and Stoller brought "uptown" sophistication to "downtown" R&B, writing and producing a long string of hit songs for artists such as the Coasters, the Drifters, Ben. E. King, and Elvis Presley. Their best-known songs include "Along Came Jones," "Charlie Brown," "Hound Dog," "Jailhouse Rock," "Love Potion No. 9," "Poison Ivy," "Ruby Baby," "Searchin'," "Spanish Harlem," "Stand By Me" (with King), and "Yakety Yak."

As successful as Leiber and Stoller were as songwriters, they had an even bigger influence as producers. They produced almost all their New York records in the Brill Building studios and introduced numerous new techniques in pop music production. In particular, they added strings and more sophisticated production to a standard R&B beat— sound that influenced both Phil Spector (who studied under the pair) and Barry Gordy's Motown sound.

Doc Pomus and Mort Shuman During the late-50's/early-60's, the songwriting team of Doc Pomus (born Jerome Solon Felder, 1925–91) and Mort Shuman (1936–91) were second only to Leiber and Stoller in terms of number of hits. Before meeting Mort Shuman, Doc

Pomus had achieved moderate success as a writer, composing "Lonely Avenue" for Ray Charles and teaming up with Leiber and Stoller for the Coasters' "Young-blood." Pomus partnered with Mort Shuman in 1958; Pomus wrote the lyrics, while Shuman handled the music. They soon took up residence in the Brill Building and later signed with Aldon Music.

For the next several years, Pomus and Shuman wrote some of the most poetic, soulful tunes of the Brill Building era, for artists such as Dion & the Belmonts, the Drifters, and Elvis Presley. They composed more than 500 songs between 1958 and 1965, including "A Teenager in Love," "Can't Get Used to Losing You," "His Latest Flame," "Hushabye," "I Count the Tears," "Little Sister," "Save the Last Dance for Me," "Suspicion," "Sweets for My Sweet," "This Magic Moment," "Turn Me Loose," and "Viva Las Vegas."

Neil Sedaka and Howard Greenfield Neil Sedaka (b. 1939) was a 13-year-old classical music student when he first met 16-year-old neighbor Howie Greenfield (1936–86). Several years later, Sedaka and Greenfield were the first songwriters signed by Aldon Music—literally as Kirshner and Nevins were unpacking their furniture. Soon the duo was writing tunes for performers such as Connie Francis and Clyde McPhatter; Sedaka also forged a career as a performer of his own songs.

The Sedaka-Greenfield team wrote catchy pop tunes for white teenagers. Sedaka wrote the simple yet classically influenced music while Greenfield contributed lyrics, typically about the joy and angst of teen love. Their songs include "Breaking Up Is Hard to Do," "Calendar Girl," "Everybody's Somebody's Fool," "Frankie," "Happy Birthday, Sweet Sixteen," "Love Will Keep Us Together," "Oh! Carol," "Stairway to Heaven," "Stupid Cupid," and "Where the Boys Are." Sedaka enjoyed a brief comeback as a writer and performer after he broke with Greenfield in the early 1970's, with songs such as "Bad Blood," "Laughter in the Rain," and "Solitaire," all written with lyricist Phil Cody.

Gerry Goffin and Carole King Gerry Goffin (b. 1939) and Carole King (b. 1942) met in 1958, married in 1960, and shortly after signed with Aldon Music. Goffin wrote the words and King the music; their best efforts melded keen observations on the human condition with sophisticated harmonies, creating a body of work that shaped the sound of early 1960's pop music.

Goffin and King wrote songs for artists as diverse as Blood Sweat & Tears, the Drifters, Aretha Franklin, the

Monkees, the Shirelles, and Dusty Springfield. Their songs include "Chains," "Hey Girl," "I'm Into Something Good," "It Might as Well Rain Until September," "The Loco-Motion," "No Easy Way Down," "Oh No Not My Baby," "One Fine Day," "Pleasant Valley Sunday," "So Much Love," "Up on the Roof," "Will You Love Me Tomorrow," and "(You Make Me Feel Like A) Natural Woman." After divorcing Goffin in 1968, King had unparalleled success as the progenitor of the 1970's singer/songwriter movement; her 1971 album, *Tapestry*, sold more than 20 million copies and won a Grammy for Record of the Year.

Barry Mann and Cynthia Weil Barry Mann (b. 1939) started writing songs in 1958, and had two dozen tunes published by the time he signed with Aldon Music in 1961. It was at Aldon that Mann met lyricist Cynthia Weil (b. 1941), an aspiring actress who had worked previously for famed composer Frank Loesser; Mann and Weil married in August, 1961. They ably navigated the changing pop music trends of the 1960's; their compositions run the gamut from light pop to straight-ahead rock, with the common thread being Weil's socially conscious lyrics. Their best-known song is also the most-played pop tune in the 20th century; according to performing rights organization BMI, "You've Lost That Lovin' Feelin'," (co-written with Phil Spector), has been performed more than 8 million times.

The songwriting duo's songs have been recorded by a variety of artists, including the Animals, the Crystals, the Drifters, Edie Gormé, Jay and the Americans, the Righteous Brothers, and the Ronettes. Their Brill-era songs include "Blame It On the Bossa Nova," "Kicks," "On Broadway," "Only in America," "Uptown," "Walking in the Rain," "We Gotta Get Out of This Place," "You, Baby," and "(You're My) Soul and Inspiration." At the dawn of the 21st century, Mann and Weil are still together, and still writing; their later songs include "Here You Come Again," "I Just Can't Help Believing," "Sometimes When We Touch," and "Somewhere Out There," from the film *An American Tail*.

Ellie Greenwich and Jeff Barry Songwriters Ellie Greenwich (b. 1940) and Jeff Barry (b. 1939) first met in 1960, and married in 1963. Greenwich and Barry provided the fuel to the musical fire known as the Girl Group sound. These "girl groups" were groups of teenage girls who sang songs about puppy love, problems in school, and other topics relevant to the youth of the day. Many of these groups were formed spontaneously by the girls

themselves, and then were discovered and promoted through an independent label owner or producer.

Compared to other Brill Building songwriters, Greenwich and Barry's compositions were lighter-weight trifles with nonsense lyrics—but with terrific melodic hooks. They wrote dozens of top 10 hits in the early 1960's, including "Baby I Love You," "Be My Baby" "Chapel of Love," "Da Doo Ron Ron," "Do Wah Diddy Diddy," "Leader of the Pack," and "Then He Kissed Me." Their songs were performed by artists such as the Crystals, the Dixie Cups, the Ronettes, and the Shagri-Las. After divorcing Greenwich in 1965, Barry went on to co-write songs for the cartoon group the Archies ("Sugar, Sugar" and "Jingle Jangle"), as well as several well-known television show themes (*The Jeffersons, One Day at a Time*, and *Family Ties*).

Greenwich and Barry were also favored songwriters for Phil Spector's Wall of Sound productions. Spector hoped to create what he called "teenaged symphonies"—recordings that employed a large stable of professional Los Angeles studio musicians (known collectively as the "Wrecking Crew") to create a dense sonic style that became known as the Wall of Sound. To create this, Spector used multiple guitars, drums, strings, and vocalists, all packed together and playing live in a small, reverb-soaked recording studio. He used this production technique for recording many of the most popular girl groups of the time, including the Ronettes and the Crystals, and also performers such as the Righteous Brothers, and Ike and Tina Turner.

Burt Bacharach and Hal David Burt Bacharach (b. 1928) and Hal David (b. 1921) are the least Brill-like of all the Brill Building artists. In reality, the duo's time at the Brill Building was only a brief part of their careers; they started writing well before the height of the Brill Building era, and quickly moved beyond typical Brill Building work for hire. Somewhat older than their Brill-era colleagues, Bacharach and David were arguably the most sophisticated and mature songwriting team of the 1960's. Their songs incorporate complex harmonies, meters, and structure, along with unusually adult lyrics.

Bacharach and David created a remarkable series of sophisticated pop songs, including "Alfie," "Do You Know the Way to San José," "I Just Don't Know What to Do With Myself," "I Say a Little Prayer," "I'll Never Fall in Love Again," "The Look of Love," "Make It Easy on Yourself," "One Less Bell to Answer," "Raindrops Keep Fallin' on My Head," "(They Long to Be) Close to You,"

"This Guy's in Love with You," "Walk on By," and "What the World Needs Now is Love." Their songs have been recorded by a variety of artists, including Herb Albert, the Carpenters, Jackie DeShannon, the Fifth Dimension, Tom Jones, Gene Pitney, Dusty Springfield, the Stylistics, and their favored singer, Dionne Warwick. In 1968 Bacharach and David teamed up for a Tony-nominated Broadway musical, *Promises, Promises*. Bacharach also composed the music for several films, including *Butch Cassidy and the Sundance Kid*, *Casino Royale*, and *What's New, Pussycat?*.

Other Brill-Era Songwriters The Brill Building might have been the East Coast nexus of the professional songwriting world, but there were other professional songwriters operating in the 1960's, out of many other locations.

For example, there was a West Coast equivalent of the Brill Building combine in Los Angeles. The two driving forces of this West Coast sound were the local office of Aldon Music, headed by Lou Adler, and Metric Music, the California extension of New York's Liberty Music. The songwriters working for Aldon and Metric included Jackie DeShannon (b. 1944), David Gates (b. 1940), and Randy Newman (b. 1943).

Another songwriting nexus was located in Detroit, as Barry Gordy employed a raft of songwriters and songwriting teams for his Motown label. The Motown composers are legend, and include Marvin Gaye (1939–1984),

Smokey Robinson (b. 1940), Norman Whitfield (b. 1943), and the team of Brian Holland (b. 1941), Lamont Dozier (b. 1941), and Edward Holland, Jr. (b. 1939).

Not all professional songwriters of the era were American. In England, the center of professional songwriting activity was London's Denmark Street. Successful British songwriters of the period included Tony Hatch (b. 1939), Tony Macaulay (b. 1944), Les Reed (b. 1935), and Geoff Stephens (b. 1934), and the team of Roger Cook (b. 1940) and Roger Greenaway (b. 1938).

The End of An Era

The golden age of Tin Pan Alley ended after World War II, when the movie and stage musical went into decline and rock 'n' roll began to dominate the charts. Short-playing 45 RPM records ("singles") became the major means of selling songs, and individual performers became more important than the songwriters. During the late 1950's and particularly the 1960's, these factors contributed to a decline in sheet music sales, and it became less common for music publishers to hire their own stables of songwriters. Composers started to perform their own songs, and singers started to write their own music. Despite the demise of Tin Pan Alley as a place, the Great American Songbook remains fixed in the musical firmament. These are songs that will live forever in our memory and on the lips of talented singers of all generations.

Blues to Jazz: The Origins of Modern Popular Music

African-American culture contributed significantly to the American musical landscape of the 20th century. Beginning with the rural blues, black music evolved into a variety of musical styles, from jazz and blues to rhythm & blues to hip hop. To no small degree, rock 'n' roll resulted from a collision between the black and white musical worlds. From the dawn of the recording era to well after World War II, the music industry was highly segregated; records by black artists were marketed separately from those by whites and typically labeled as "race records." Despite this early separation, the history of African-American music in America is just as influential to the development of popular music as Tin Pan Alley and the Brill Building. The roots of African-American music date back even farther.

Blues The style commonly called "the blues" is actually an entire family of musical styles, all sharing similar roots although each having a unique development. The blues style dates back at least to the post-Civil War period, when the guitar was introduced to rural black culture. Black guitarists shaped a unique accompaniment style that enabled them to sing songs using many flattened notes (called "blue notes"), vocal slides, and syncopated rhythms. Blues guitarists were able to "bend" notes when they played the guitar by pushing against the strings with the fingers of their fretting hand; this allowed them to play many quarter and half tones that lie between the notes of the scale.

The classic blues structure is called the twelve-bar blues. This form is comprised of three melodic phrases, each four bars long. Another distinguishing feature of the blues is its narrowly defined chord progression. The blues scale is different from the normal major scale, using the scale tones 1-b3-4-b5-5-b7.

A Generation's Vanity as Heard Through Lyrics

By JON PARELES

After a computer analysis of three decades of hit songs, Dr. Nathan DeWall and other psychologists report finding a statistically significant trend toward narcissism and hostility in popular music. As they hypothesized, the words "I" and "me" appear more frequently along with anger-related words, while there's been a corresponding decline in "we" and "us" and the expression of positive emotions.

"Late adolescents and college students love themselves more today than ever before," Dr. DeWall, a psychologist at the University of Kentucky, says. His study covered song lyrics from 1980 to 2007 and controlled for genre to prevent the results from being skewed by the growing popularity of, say, rap and hip-hop.

Defining the personality of a generation with song lyrics may seem a bit of a reach, but Dr. DeWall points to research done by his co-authors that showed people of the same age scoring higher in measures of narcissism on some personality tests. The new study of song lyrics certainly won't end the debate, but it does offer another way to gauge self-absorption: the *Billboard* Hot 100 chart. The researchers find that hit songs in the 1980s were more likely to emphasize happy togetherness, like the racial harmony sought by Paul McCartney and Stevie Wonder in "Ebony and Ivory" and the group exuberance promoted by Kool & the Gang: "Let's all celebrate and have a good time." Diana Ross and Lionel Richie sang of "two hearts that beat as one," and John Lennon's "(Just Like) Starting Over" emphasized the preciousness of "our life together."

Today's songs, according to the researchers' linguistic analysis, are more likely to be about one very special person: the singer. "I'm bringing sexy back," Justin Timberlake proclaimed in 2006. The year before, Beyoncé exulted in how hot she looked while dancing—"It's blazin', you watch me in amazement." And Fergie, who boasted about her "humps" while singing with the Black Eyed Peas, subsequently released a solo album in which she told her lover that she needed quality time alone: "It's personal, myself and I."

Two of Dr. DeWall's co-authors, W. Keith Campbell and Jean M. Twenge, published a book in 2009 titled *The Narcissism Epidemic*, which argued that narcissism is increasingly prevalent among young people—and possibly middle-aged people, too, although it's hard for anyone to know because most of the available data comes from college students. For several decades, students have filled out a questionnaire called the Narcissism Personality Inventory, in which they've had to choose between two statements like "I try not to be a show-off" and "I will usually show off if I get the chance." The level of narcissism measured by these questionnaires has been rising since the early 1980s, according to an analysis of campus data by Dr. Twenge and Dr. Campbell.

During this period, there have also been reports of higher levels of loneliness and depression—which may be no coincidence. These researchers note that narcissism has been linked to heightened anger and problems maintaining relationships. Their song-lyrics analysis shows a decline in words related to social connections and positive emotions (like "love" or "sweet") and an increase in words related to anger and antisocial behavior (like "hate" or "kill").

Some psychologists are skeptical that basic personality traits can change much from one generation to the next (or from one culture to another). Even if students are scoring higher on the narcissism questionnaire, these skeptics says, it may just be because today's students are more willing to admit to feelings that were always there.

The song-lyrics analysis, published in the journal *Psychology of Aesthetics*, "Creativity and the Arts", goes up to 2007, which makes it fairly up-to-date by scientific standards. But by popular music standards, 2007 is an eon ago. Could narcissism have declined since then? It would take a computerized linguistic analysis to be sure, but there are reasons to doubt it. In 2008, the same year as Weezer's "Greatest Man That Ever Lived," Little Jackie had a popular song titled "The World Should Revolve Around Me." The current *Billboard* chart includes the Cee-Lo Green comic ode to hostility with its unprintable refrain (for the Grammy television audience, he changed it to "Forget you") as well as Keri Hilson's paean to her own beauty: "All eyes on me when I walk in, no question that this girl's a 10." Regardless of whether the singers really mean it, there's obviously a market for these sentiments.

Blues music is important not only in its own right, but also because it is incorporated into so many other musical genres. Many jazz tunes are based on the blues progression, and many jazz soloists lean heavily on the blues scale. Much of rock is also blues-based, and many lead guitarists rely on a large repertoire of blues licks.

Delta Blues The Mississippi Delta area produced an intense, highly charged style of blues performance. Delta blues guitarists played mostly slow blues tunes, letting the guitar take the place of the vocalist and "sing," and using a metal or glass slide and special tunings to play the melodies. Famous Delta bluesmen include Charley Patton (1887–1934), Robert Johnson (c. 1912–37), and Son House (Edgar James House Jr., 1902–ca. 75).

Ragtime-Blues In the middle South, a more lighthearted blues was performed. This is sometimes called ragtime-blues, because of its syncopated melodies. The guitarists picked the strings with their fingers, the thumb establishing a regular bass on the lower strings and the second and third fingers picking a melody that emphasized the offbeats. Famous ragtime blues performers include Blind Boy Fuller (Fulton Allen, 1908–41) and Blind Blake (ca. 1890–ca. 1933).

Religious Blues Another popular blues form joined words about religious experiences with a blues guitar accompaniment. These religious blues were related to the spirituals and ring shouts that came before them. The singer often shouted the lyrics, to express his or her deep conviction. Noted religious blues singers include Blind Willie Johnson (1902–49) and Reverend Gary Davis (1894–1972).

Urban Blues The country blues were brought to new audiences as blacks migrated from the country to the city. At the turn of the last century, the song "The Memphis Blues" was a hit, and it made composer W. (William) C. (Christopher) Handy (1873–1958) famous. Handy, a trained musician, made the blues attractive to a city audience by smoothing out its irregularities, and adapting the blues to the dance band format.

Many city blues singers were female, beginning with the great Ma Rainey (Gertrude Malissa Nix Pridgett, 1866–1939), the first blues singer to achieve a major hit recording. She was followed by perhaps the best known of all blues performers, Bessie Smith (1895–1937), known as "The Empress of the Blues." Smith began recording in 1923, and often was accompanied by the great jazz players of the day, including Louis Armstrong. Her use of blue notes, syncopated delivery, rasping vocals, and occasional gospel shouts all became standard jazz techniques, and she inspired many great jazz singers, including Billie Holiday.

Electric Blues After World War II, a new development transformed the blues from a solo guitar tradition. The introduction of the electric guitar enabled bluesmen to perform in noisy bars. A large number of blacks in urban areas, particularly in Chicago, made up a ready audience for this music. The result was city or electric blues. Famous city bluesmen include Muddy Waters (McKinley Morganfield, 1915–80), Howlin' Wolf (Chester Arthur Burnett, 1910–76), and B.B. King (b. Riley B. King, 1925).

Rhythm & Blues (R&B)

From the early days of sound recording, recordings by black artists had been marketed separately from those by whites. World War II pop music was breaking down into distinct categories, reflected by Billboard's new charts for mainstream pop, country, and a new genre that was called Rhythm & Blues (quickly shortened to R&B). R&B has its roots in the ensembles of the late 1940's and early 1950's, most notable of which was the band led by saxophonist Louis Jordan. Jordan's music, dubbed "jump blues" or "jump jazz," blended jazz, blues, a shuffle beat, and lighthearted lyrics. The music proved as popular among whites as blacks, opening the door for other black artists with similar crossover appeal.

Ray Charles By the mid-1950's, performers such as Ray Charles (1930–2004) and Ruth Brown broke through with their own combination of jazz, blues, and pop. Signing with Atlantic Records in 1955, Charles had his first major R&B hit, "I Got a Woman." Charles's intense vocals—showing the influence of gospel—set the pattern for later hits, notably his 1958 pop crossover, "What'd I Say."

Sam Cooke Charles's main competition among male singers in the later 50's was Sam Cooke (1931–64) who came out of a gospel background. Cooke's first hit, 1956's "You Send Me," showed a mix of gospel-tinged pleading in the vocal similar to Charles's "I Got a Woman," but had more of a pop accompaniment. Cooke continued to cut classic R&B songs such as "Chain Gang," but increasingly sought a broad audience with more pop material and lusher accompaniments.

The distinction between R&B and rock 'n' roll was quickly blurred despite the segregation practiced by the music industry. Many black artists succeeded in the early years of rock 'n' roll, paving the way for the black-influenced developments in mainstream pop music.

The first of these artists was Fats Domino, who combined a relaxed New Orleans backbeat with pop-flavored material on songs like "Ain't That a Shame" and "Blueberry Hill." Also from New Orleans was Little Richard, a manic performer who combined gospel fervor with piano-pounding theatrics in his mid-1950s hits "Tutti Frutti," "Long Tall Sally," and "Good Golly Miss Molly."

Arguably the most influential black musician during the formative years of rock 'n' roll, however, was Chuck Berry. Berry defined rock's instrumental voice, in particular its guitar sound and the straight-ahead 4/4 rock beat. He was also a key shaper of the rock 'n' roll song form and a sharp lyricist. Berry was able to craft songs that addressed classic topics from a teenage perspective in the teenage vernacular. His key recordings were made between 1955 and 1965, including "Maybellene," "Roll Over Beethoven," "Rock 'n' Roll Music," "School Days," "Sweet Little Sixteen," "Johnny B. Goode," "Memphis, Tennessee," and "No Particular Place to Go."

Motown

By the 1960's R&B as a genre began to break down into distinct streams: Motown picked up the teen-pop end of the spectrum, while soul took up the gospel intensity and high energy of the best R&B performers.

The Motown label and sound is rooted in the vision of two men: Berry Gordy (b. 1929) a onetime boxing promoter and would-be songwriter, and Smokey Robinson, a songwriter, singer, and Gordy's right-hand man through most of the 1960's. Thanks to a talented staff of studio musicians, Motown's recordings had a distinctive sound that set them apart. The label developed a stable of female (Supremes, Martha and the Vandellas) and male (Miracles, Four Tops, Temptations) groups, along with numerous solo stars. The success of Motown showed the potential for black music to cross over onto the traditionally white pop charts, which would have a profound impact on the development of all forms of popular music.

In the early 1970's several Motown artists rebelled against Gordy's formula and were able to achieve independence while still maintaining popular success. Most noteworthy among these was Stevie Wonder (b. 1950), with a string of critically acclaimed early 1970's albums (culminating in the multi-disc set, *Songs in the Key of Life*),

and Marvin Gaye (1939–84), whose landmark 1971 album, *What's Going On*, provided a black perspective on current events.

Funk and Soul

James Brown (b. 1933–2006) created a high-energy, rhythmic style called funk that propelled him to great success in the mid-to-late 60's. In songs like "Papa's Got a Brand New Bag" and "I Got You (I Feel Good)" (1965), "Cold Sweat" (1967), and the anthemic "Say It Loud—I'm Black and I'm Proud (Part 1)" (1968), Brown combined stripped-down harmonies, driving rhythms, and his high-energy vocals to create a compelling musical mix. Brown's message of black pride resonated during the upheavals of the Civil Rights movement.

If Brown was the King of Funk, Aretha Franklin (b. 1942) was Queen of Soul. Franklin had begun her career singing jazz and gospel; producer Jerry Wexler recognized her potential, and sent her to Muscle Shoals's studio to produce her great 1960's hits, including "Respect," "A Natural Woman," and "Chain of Fools," all from 1967.

Jazz

Jazz is America's home-grown classical music. Derived from the blues, it is one of this country's truly indigenous musical styles. For a time, jazz was the country's popular music; as the genre evolved, it became more improvisational and experimental, encouraging group interplay and musical virtuosity.

New Orleans/Dixieland Jazz   The style of jazz that developed in the New Orleans region from about 1885 through 1915 is known as *New Orleans, Dixieland,* or just *classic jazz.* New Orleans bands of that era usually had five to seven pieces, led by cornet, clarinet, and trombone on melody, with tuba or string bass, piano, banjo or guitar, and drums on accompaniment. Initially, there were no soloists; the group played all at once, with the melody instruments improvising around one another's parts. The rhythmic accompaniment emphasized a regular, four-beat accent, as a basis for the melodic syncopation.

Buddy Bolden and King Oliver   Cornetist Buddy Bolden (b. Charles Joseph Bolden, 1877–1931) is generally considered to be among the first great jazz cornetists. Contemporaries reported that he played with a loud, piercing tone that could be heard over considerable distances. He was said to be a particularly expressive player of the blues.

Bolden served as a model for the next generation of players, beginning with cornet player Joseph "King" Oliver (1885–1938). Oliver was only eight years younger than Bolden, but he nonetheless took Bolden's style to a new level, first in New Orleans, and then on the road in Chicago and Los Angeles. Like Bolden, Oliver specialized in playing slow blues, using a growling style that would influence the "jungle" style of Duke Ellington. In 1919 Oliver took his band to Chicago, where it made its first recordings in April 1923. These records, including "Chime Blues" and "Dippermouth Blues," are considered the first classic New Orleans jazz recordings.

Louis Armstrong One name towers over all others in the history of early jazz: trumpeter and vocalist Louis Armstrong (1901–71). His small ensemble recordings of the mid-1920's, famously known as the Hot Fives and Hot Sevens, revolutionized jazz music and introduced the era of the virtuosic leader/soloist. Armstrong was the "star," and his solo breaks, comic vocals, and overall musical personality dominated. He also greatly expanded the typical band repertory, introducing popular and comic novelty songs, his own compositions, and more contemporary dance numbers through his recordings.

Armstrong's classic recordings of this period include the oft-praised "West End Blues," which features a stunning solo that showed Armstrong's incredible range, power, and imagination as a trumpeter. More breezy vocal numbers such as "You Rascal You" displayed the playful side of Armstrong's performing personality.

Jelly Roll Morton and Jazz Piano Besides small-band jazz, New Orleans was a center for the development of jazz piano. Its famous Storyville district—a legal center for bars and houses of prostitution—created a great demand for pianists who could attract customers. These pianists were called on to accompany the energetic show dances and more sensuous slow drags that the prostitutes performed to bewitch their customers, as well as to provide general entertainment and accompany songs.

The greatest of the New Orleans jazz pianists—and the most influential—was Jelly Roll Morton (b. Ferdinand Joseph La Menthe, or Lamothe, 1890–1941). Morton's piano style melded blues, Spanish dance rhythms, ragtime, and folk and classical influences. Morton's flamboyant originality made his compositions, such as "King Porter Stomp," "The Pearls," and "Milenberg Joys," stand out; melodic, with dramatic contrasts in timbre, rhythm, and volume, they were perhaps the most thoughtfully composed of early jazz compositions.

Swing and Big Band Jazz By the mid-1920's, the center of jazz development had moved from New Orleans to major urban centers, notably Chicago and New York. New Orleans jazz evolved into *swing*, and most jazz groups grew into *big bands*. Big band swing was the popular music of its day, featuring a combination of complex arrangements, innovative improvisation, and smooth vocals by the likes of Bing Crosby and Frank Sinatra.

The swing style marked a basic change in approach to jazz's basic rhythm. The New Orleans jazz bands inherited from ragtime an oom-pah beat, with the heavy emphasis falling on the first and third beats of the four-beat measure. In swing, the emphasis was evened out so that all four beats were lightly accented, making for a much less mechanical feel.

Birth of the Big Band While there had been large bands active since the teens, these early dance bands primarily played in a lightly syncopated manner, and were not true jazz ensembles. The innovation that brought jazz to a larger band format is generally credited to arranger Don Redman, who worked for Fletcher Henderson's orchestra from 1923 to 1927. Redman came up with the idea of dividing the band into two primary voices, the brasses (trumpets, trombones) and the reeds (saxes, clarinets), which would trade riffs back and forth in a call-and-response format. These parts were relatively fixed; improvisation was introduced through the featured soloists, who were brought forward to play one or two choruses.

During the big band era, the bands were further divided by jazz fans into two camps: "hot" versus "sweet" bands. The "sweet" bands focused on moody ballads and lightly syncopated dance music. The "hot" bands emphasized syncopation and improvised solos over playing popular melodies.

Count Basie The Count Basie (b. William Basien, 1904–84) Orchestra is generally credited as one of the first great swing bands, with its famous rhythm section of piano, guitar, bass, and drums. Basie's light piano accompaniment also helped keep the music flowing and eliminated some of the four-square feeling that a more regular piano accompaniment gave earlier bands. Previously, jazz drummers had kept a steady beat by hitting the bass drum, making a heavy, thudding sound; Basie's drummer, Jo Jones, keep the steady beat on the ride cymbal, creating a lighter, more airy accompaniment.

Benny Goodman Benny Goodman's (1909–86) band was important not only as the first major popularizer of swing music but also for its many great band members. Jazz critic and producer John Hammond took Goodman under his wing early in the clarinetist's career and was responsible for introducing Goodman to Don Redman's innovative new arrangements. He also encouraged him to hire black musicians to create the first integrated jazz band, including pianist Teddy Wilson, vibraphone player Lionel Hampton, and the innovative electric guitarist Charlie Christian.

Duke Ellington One of the most original big bands was led by pianist/composer/arranger Duke Ellington (b. Edward Kennedy Ellington, 1899–1974). Ellington's band predated the official swing era, coming into being in the late 1920's as the house band at New York's Cotton Club. Ellington was an unusually gifted and perceptive arranger, and the long tenure of many of the musicians who played in his band allowed him a unique opportunity to craft his music to reflect their individual personalities.

Ellington's band originally was known for its "jungle" style, featuring often campy effects such as growling trumpets and wailing clarinets, aimed to be immediate audience pleasers. However, by the mid-1930's, Ellington had matured into a unusually sensitive composer, writing a number of classic jazz compositions, ranging from 1932's "It Don't Mean a Thing (If It Ain't Got that Swing)" and "Sophisticated Lady" to 1935's "In a Sentimental Mood" and 1942's "Don't Get Around Much Anymore." Aided by his second-in-command, arranger/composer Billy Strayhorn (who joined the band in 1939), Ellington extended considerably the palette of jazz composition.

Big Band Vocalists With the exception of very popular vocalists such as Bing Crosby (b. Harry Lillis Crosby, 1903–77), nearly every jazz singer of the era was associated with one of the leading bands, sometimes moving from band to band. Artie Shaw broke the color line when he took singer Billie Holiday (b. Eleanora Fagan, 1915–59) on the road with his band, although this arrangement didn't last long due to the difficulties that they encountered. Frank Sinatra (1915–98) began his career singing for the Dorsey Brothers and Harry James bands; Ella Fitzgerald (1917–96) sang with Chick Webb's band (and became the band's de facto leader after Webb's death). It wasn't until after World War II that singers like Sinatra achieved enough personal success that they could strike out on their own.

Bebop Bebop was a new style of jazz music that developed in New York City during the early to mid-1940's, reaching its height immediately after World War II. The typical bebop ensemble was much smaller than the big bands that it replaced. Taking a new approach to melody, rhythm, and harmony, the bop musicians revolutionized jazz, transforming it from a commercial, popular music into a serious art form.

Bebop's story centers on the lives and music of two seminal jazzmen: saxophone player Charlie "Bird" Parker (1920–55) and trumpeter John Birks "Dizzy" Gillespie (1917–93), who began jamming together at after-hours clubs like Minton's in Harlem. Using the basic chord structures of well-known pop songs, the musicians experimented with new melodies, harmonies, and rhythms, often taken at breakneck speed. The bebop musicians emphasized instrumental virtuosity. While jazzmen had always used flatted notes (or "blue notes") and seventh chords, bebop musicians used more unusual chord harmonies, either by "altering" standard chords (by lowering one or two notes in the chord to purposely disrupt the usual harmony), extending chords (by using ninths, elevenths, or thirteenths as harmony notes), or by substituting related chords. The results may have sounded dissonant, but in fact were stretching the boundaries of chord harmony.

The role of the accompanying instruments radically changed in bop. The pianist mostly "comped" in the accompaniment, playing disjointed, fragmentary chords behind the soloist; Thelonious Monk (1917–82) and Bud (Earl) Powell (1924–66) are the two pianists credited with creating this new style. Bebop drummers, led by Kenny Clarke (1914–85) and Max Roach (b. 1925–2007), also were innovators, eliminating the traditional use of the bass drum and snare as timekeepers; instead they kept time lightly on the high-hat cymbal, dropping the occasional "bomb" on the bass.

Cool Jazz On the other side of the spectrum from the high-powered and energetic bebop style was "cool jazz," which came into popularity in the early 1950's. Cool jazz artists took a purposely intellectual approach to jazz, trying to wed white classical music to black soul. There were two branches of cool players, one based on the West Coast and the other in the East; the dominance of the West Coast musicians led to cool sometimes being referred to as "West Coast" jazz. Cool jazz ensembles included the sweetly classical Modern Jazz Quartet, led by pianist John Lewis and vibes player Milt Jackson; the very popular Dave Brubeck Quartet, featuring Brubeck on piano and Paul Desmond on alto sax; and the ultimate cool ensemble, Miles Davis' mid-1950's group that featured John Coltrane or Sonny Rollins on sax and Davis on trumpet. There were even cool soloists, such as the cerebral jazz pianist Bill Evans.

Hard Bop

Hard bop was a reaction to both bebop and cool jazz. Bebop certainly had power and energy, but it seemed to lack the deep emotions and the kind of interaction between musicians and audience found in black gospel music. Similarly, jazz didn't need to get closer to white classical music, the hard boppers argued, but rather to its roots in black folk forms. To that end, hard bop was out to infuse bebop's power with the intensity of soul.

A prime mover in hard bop was pianist/group leader Horace Silver (b. 1928), whose familiarity with gospel piano and organ led him to introduce gospel-shaded harmonies and melodic riffs borrowed from gospel song. Another key figure in the growth of hard bop was drummer/bandleader Art Blakey (1919–90), whose group the Jazz Messengers focused on accessible music with a tight, propulsive drive. Also associated with the beginnings of hard bop were tenor saxophone player Sonny Rollins (b. 1929) and alto sax player Nat "Cannonball" Adderly (1928–75).

Soul Jazz

Hard bop eventually mutated into a more R&B-oriented form called soul jazz, which became one of the most popular types of jazz in the 1960's. Soul jazz incorporates a more contemporary rock/soul beat, complete with a funky bass line, with hard bop and bebop-type chord progressions. Popular soul jazz musicians include pianists Horace Silver and Ramsey Lewis, organist Jimmy Smith, and saxophonists Eddie Harris and Stanley Turrentine.

Free Jazz

Free jazz musicians, led by sax player Ornette Coleman (b. 1930) and pianist/composer Cecil Taylor (b. 1929), felt they should be free to explore all of the tones and textures of their instruments, without adhering to traditional harmonic demands. For this reason, many people associate free jazz with dissonant squawks and squeals produced by frenzied and self-absorbed musicians. In fact, free jazz was based on musicians listening carefully and reacting to one another's playing; the point was to extend the soloist's capabilities, and not be hampered by chord changes and melodic clichés.

Jazz/Rock Fusion

By the mid-1960's rock 'n' roll was dominating the airwaves and record charts. The adventuresome avant-garde of jazz was appealing to its own specialized but limited audience. Older jazz figures, such as Miles Davis, were still respected, but their record sales were minuscule compared with rock. It appeared that jazz was going to fizzle out without much public notice—when a group of pioneering musicians decided to blend the rock and jazz idioms in a new jazz/rock, or fusion style.

In reality, the two musics discovered each other. Many progressive rockers were playing improvised melodic parts, and looked to the great jazz players for inspiration. Still others—such as Chicago and Blood, Sweat, and Tears—introduced brass instruments into the rock format and borrowed classic jazz tunes for their hits. Jazz players, meanwhile, were fascinated with the possibilities that electric instruments offered and the special effects that could be generated by wiring acoustic ones for amplification. Many of the young sidemen in jazz sympathized with the rock revolution.

Miles Davis   Several tentative jazz/rock outfits cropped up in the mid-1960's, but it took Miles Davis (1926–91) to popularize the style. Tentatively edging toward a more rock-oriented sound, Davis released a series of records that featured steadier, rocklike drumming, occasional electric piano, and funkier melodies. Davis's two major thrusts into rock and roll were the 1969 recordings, *In a Silent Way* and *Bitches Brew*. On these albums, Davis borrowed rock instrumentation, supplemented the drums with exotic percussion instruments, and amplified his own trumpet playing with special effects. Davis also changed his style of playing to fit in with the more aggressive arrangements. No longer coolly laid back as it had been in the 1950's, his playing was now emotional and angry. Although he still played slow ballads, he was usually fiery and outgoing, playing throughout the entire range of the instrument, including the ultra-high register—a legacy of free jazz.

Mahavishnu Orchestra   Many of the musicians who played with Davis's first fusion bands would become leaders in the new movement. British jazz/rock guitarist John McLaughlin (b. 1942) played with Davis and then formed his own Mahavishnu Orchestra, which gained rock-level popularity in the early 1970's. McLaughlin's music is an interesting amalgam of the energy of jazz with many of the techniques of rock, often played over complicated odd-time signatures.

Weather Report   Perhaps the most successful of all the fusion groups was Weather Report, founded by Austrian pianist/composer Joe Zawinul (b. 1932–2007). Previously,

Zawinul had composed "In a Silent Way," the title track of Davis's first jazz-rock album, and also served as arranger for *Bitches Brew*. In 1971 he assembled a group featuring Davis alumnus Wayne Shorter (b. 1933) on saxophone, Miroslav Vitous on bass, and drummer Alphonse Moreira. Zawinul took an orchestral approach in his compositions, using each instrument as an individual voice to construct a coherent and complex whole. The hiring of bassist Jaco Pastorius (1951–87) in 1976 considerably beefed up the Weather Report sound; Pastorius always contributed a virtuoso bass solo to the group's live performances.

Other Fusion Innovators The creative and financial success of these bands led many older, more seasoned hands to embrace fusion music. Some of these musicians, such as Herbie Hancock (b. 1940) and Chick Corea (b. Armando Anthony Corea, 1941), achieved significant popularity with their fusion bands, but also managed to work in the "pure jazz" idiom. For many, the sharp demarcation line between jazz and rock was an artificial one; they failed to see any reason to limit their music. In fact, the 1970's and 1980's saw much more dialogue between jazz and all other types of music, as well as an increased acceptance of jazz as an art form.

Post Bop In the 1980's and 1990's, there was a resurgence of more traditional jazz, incorporating hard bop harmonies with a variety of swing, rock, and funk beats. This fresh approach to the jazz genre, which incorporates a variety of musical influences, is alternately known as *post bop*, *contemporary*, or *modern mainstream*—terms that describe virtually all serious jazz being played today. The most notable post bop players include saxophonists Kenny Garrett, Joshua Redman, and Wayne Shorter; trumpeter Freddie Hubbard; guitarists Pat Metheny, and John Scofield; and pianists Ahmad Jamal and Keith Jarrett.

Smooth Jazz While post bop appeals to jazz traditionalists, the most popular form of jazz today is a controversial genre known as *smooth jazz*. Purists deride the genre's slick arrangements and play-it-safe improvisations; fans say that it's a particularly melodic and listenable form of jazz. Mood music or not, smooth jazz *does* feature jazz-inspired improvised solos, and many of its adherents are veterans of the 1970's/1980's fusion scene. And even critics admit that smooth jazz has become the most commercially viable form of jazz since the 1940's, with popular artists such as pianist David Benoit; guitarists George Benson, Larry Carlton, and Lee Ritenour; saxophonist David Sanborn; and the groups Fourplay, Spyro Gyra, and the Yellowjackets.

Modern American Popular Music

There is considerable controversy over exactly when rock 'n' roll was born and who can lay claim to being the first artist to record a rock record. Suffice to say, rock developed gradually after World War II out of a convergence of a number of different styles, artists, and influences, crystallizing in the popular imagination around 1954 in recordings by Bill Haley (1925–81) and Elvis Presley (1935–77). Record producer Sam Phillips famously described Elvis as a "white man who sounds black." And, indeed, Elvis's first release in 1954 paired an R&B hit ("That's Alright, Mama," originally recorded by Big Mama Thornton) with a country song ("Blue Moon of Kentucky," by Bill Monroe).

As the musician most responsible for popularizing rock 'n' roll on an international level, Elvis was one of the most important figures in 20th-century popular music. A country boy from Tupelo, Mississippi, Elvis got his first guitar at age nine. His family moved to Memphis two years later, where Elvis started playing with other musicians, as well as singing gospel in his church choir. He grew up listening to a mix of "hillbilly" music on the radio and blues music performed live in Memphis clubs.

Elvis made his first recording in 1953, at the age of 18, as a present for his mother. That recording was made at the now-famous Sun Records studio in Memphis, and it caught the ear of Sun's boss, Sam Phillips. Phillips, who was already in the business of recording Memphis blues artists such as Howlin' Wolf, was on the lookout for a crossover artist to deliver black music to a white audience. Elvis fit the bill.

Presley was the first performer to fuse country and blues music into the style known as rockabilly, and he also was the first rock artist to inspire a mania among his fans, thanks to his sneering good looks and hip-swiveling style. His records sold millions of copies and almost single-handedly established rock 'n' roll as a viable musical form.

Elvis's most important early recordings include

"Heartbreak Hotel," "Hound Dog," and "Love Me Tender," all in 1956, as well as the later "All Shook Up" and "Little Sister." After a stint in the army and as an actor, Elvis had a late-1960s resurgence with the 1969 hits "Suspicious Minds," "In the Ghetto," "Kentucky Rain," and "Burning Love." In his final years, Elvis was almost a parody of his former self, giving lethargic and often shortened performances. He died of apparent drug misuse in 1977.

Rockabilly Sun Records, the small Memphis label where Elvis first recorded, became the center of a variant of the basic rock style known as rockabilly. A more country-flavored music than mainstream rock, it was one strand of Elvis's initial style, and was built on by several Sun artists, most notably Carl Perkins (1932–98) a talented guitarist and songwriter ("Blue Suede Shoes"). Johnny Cash (1932–2003) initially began his career in the rockabilly mold, although he always had a hard-country edge, which soon became predominant in his music. Jerry Lee Lewis (b. 1935) was the closest to Little Richard-styled R&B in piano playing and performance style; his music was country on overdrive. Texan Buddy Holly (1936–59) created a unique rockabilly sound in hits like "Peggy Sue" (1957), "Oh Boy" (1957), and "That'll Be The Day" (1958).

The Day the Music Died

The classic era of rock 'n' roll is generally defined as lasting from about 1954 through 1959. At the turn of the decade, Elvis Presley was drafted into the army, Chuck Berry was imprisoned for transporting an underage woman across state lines for "illicit purposes," and on February 3, 1959, Texas rocker Buddy Holly died in a plane crash in Iowa that also killed performers Ritchie Valens and J. P. "The Big Bopper" Richardson. But the music industry carried on by following the path carved out by the earlier promotion of a young Frank Sinatra, i.e. presenting young, attractive vocalists whose songs appealed to teenagers because of their lyrics about young love and the dramatic change the rhythm and blues sound brought to dancing.

The most successful purveyor of the new teen pop was businessman, promoter, and TV host Dick Clark. Clark's enormously popular *American Bandstand* television program became a launching pad for numerous teen singers, including several native to the program's hometown of Philadelphia. Clark had ties with several local record labels, who in turn released the recordings of his latest "discoveries." This led to the brief careers of a number of cookie-cutter teen idols, such as Paul Anka, Frankie

Avalon, and Bobby Vee.

Surf Music and the Beach Boys

Also popular in the early 1960s was surf music: guitar-based rock songs about girls, cars, surfing, and other California-based youth activities. The primary purveyors of the surf sound were Dick Dale, "The King of Surf Guitar" and the Beach Boys, led by composer/singer Brian Wilson.

Wilson, an untrained but naturally brilliant composer and arranger, was a flawed genius who expanded rock's vocabulary to include complex harmonies, sophisticated chord progressions, and an overriding spirituality. While Wilson's early tunes were simple three-chord constructions extolling the joys of surfing and hot rods, his later compositions with the lyricists Tony Asher and Van Dyke Parks explored more adult themes and were more musically complex.

Wilson's crowning achievement was the 1966 album *Pet Sounds*, considered among the greatest rock albums of all time. Wilson's innovative arrangements and production techniques (learned at the knee of Phil Spector), influenced and inspired John Lennon and Paul McCartney in their expanding body of work. Wilson's most memorable tunes from this period include "In My Room," "Surfer Girl," "Don't Worry Baby," "The Little Girl I Once Knew," "Caroline No," "God Only Knows," "Good Vibrations," "Heroes and Villains," and "Wouldn't It Be Nice."

The Beatles and the British Invasion

American popular music in the early 1960s was considered tame. That all changed in 1964, when the British group the Beatles arrived on American shores. The "Fab Four," as they were known, livened up the music scene with their perky blend of American country, R&B, and early rock 'n' roll. It also didn't hurt that they were smart, funny, and terribly photogenic.

The Beatles had the good fortune to be fronted by two Brill Building–caliber songwriters, John Lennon and Paul McCartney. Unlike the previous generation, Lennon and McCartney were skilled songwriters who performed their own songs, leading subsequent popular performers to likewise eschew outside songwriting. To be "like the Beatles" was to be both songwriters and performers, even if an artist had little or no formal musical training.

From the start, the Beatles had a unique sound, understanding that the recording of a song was at least as important as the composition itself. Their compositions progressed over the course of the 1960s from simple melodic constructions to more harmonically complex experiments, all the while maintaining a keen sense of melody. By the mid-1960s, the group began experimenting further in the studio, producing unique effects using backwards tape loops, double and triple tracking, experiments with vocal processing, and feedback. They also pioneered the "concept album" with 1967's *Sgt. Pepper's Lonely Hearts Club Band*. This creation of a "group within the group" was also a first and would influence future artists to create musical alter egos. Later groundbreaking tracks such as "The Inner Light" and the musique concréte–inspired "Revolution 9" helped pave the way for avant-garde, postmodern experiments of the 1970's and '80's in pop music.

The Beatles' success led to a "British Invasion" of similar-sounding groups riding on the Fab Four's coattails. Though most of these groups were "one-hit wonders," one group that did have lasting success was the Rolling Stones. In contrast to the teen-friendly Beatles, the Stones were cleverly marketed as the "bad boys" of rock 'n' roll. Originally a blues band playing covers of American material, band members Mick Jagger and Keith Richards eventually started to write their own material. The Stones' more aggressive sound and lyrics, in songs such as "(I Can't Get No) Satisfaction," "Paint It Black," and "Let's Spend the Night Together," influenced other British bands, including the Animals, the Kinks, and the Who.

Rock

The term *rock* has become somewhat generic, referring to a wide range of music popular in the second half of the 20th century. Everything from Chuck Berry's pounding, three-chord rockers to the sweet harmonies of the Beatles to the angry white noise of Sonic Youth has been categorized as rock—and correctly so.

In all its forms, rock is defined by its energy, its driving beat, its simple melodies and catchy hooks, and, above all else, its attitude. From Brill Building pop to heavy metal, from disco to grunge, rock is about youth and rebellion.

From Rock 'n' Roll to Just Rock
In the mid-to-late 1960's, rock 'n' roll matured into "rock," which combined influences from folk, country, jazz, pop, and other musical styles. Many of the best-known rock groups came out of the Haight-Ashbury district of San Francisco, where low rents, good weather, and a sympathetic culture attracted many would-be musicians and hangers-on.

The longest-lasting of these groups was the Grateful Dead, which began its life as a communal group living together in a rented house in the neighborhood. The Dead combined elements of blues, jazz, bluegrass, avant-garde classical, and pop into a musical stew that appealed to the burgeoning community of hippies.

Psychedelic Rock
Psychedelic rock—an attempt to capture the drug experience by performing music of a looser, more improvisational style—had a brief but powerful influence in this period. It involved experiments with new sounds, created through amplification (particularly feedback), special sound manipulators (the wah-wah pedal for the guitar), and changes in recording techniques (using tape montage, backwards tape, multiple-tracking, and other devices).

Jimi Hendrix (1942–70) was perhaps the greatest live performer in this style, as he was able to create numerous effects on the guitar through creative use of amplification, distortion, and feedback. Going beyond the live performance aspect of the music, groups such as Pink Floyd developed as pure recording bands, creating soundscapes that could not be reproduced live.

Woodstock and Altamont: The End of an Era
The 1960's came to a close with two major festivals, each emblematic of its era. Woodstock was the ultimate hippie dream; a three-day gathering of peace, love, and heavy rain and mud in August 1969, it epitomized the belief that people could live together freely sharing love, drugs, and music. The fact that a half million people gathered peacefully on Max Yasgur's farm in upstate New York was a testament to the appeal of the hippie movement in its heyday, and there was much memorable music created over the three days that summed up the major movements in rock. The film of Woodstock enabled millions more to participate (vicariously) in the free love and good feelings of the festival.

In December 1969, the Altamont festival, featuring the Rolling Stones, represented the dark underbelly of the 1960's. Held at a desolate race track in Southern California, the festival's "security force" was the notorious Hell's Angels. When a scuffle broke out during the Stones' set, one listener was savagely beaten to death while a horrified crowd witnessed the event. Remarkably, the event was captured on film and even more remarkably the Stones allowed the film to be released; this film had a more sobering impact than the Woodstock documentary.

Pop/Rock in the 1970's Once the innocence of the 1960's was shattered, rock itself could no longer be a unified force. The 1970's were a time of regrouping, of developing new musical strategies. The musical possibilities hinted at by the major 1960's creators—the Beatles, Stones, Bob Dylan—were all extended, parodied, and explored further over the coming decade. And these 1970's styles in turn would form the basis for the following decades of rock's explorations.

Country-Rock In the 1960's many rock acts rediscovered the joys of real country music. Probably the first and most important country-rock LP was the Byrds' 1968 release, *Sweetheart of the Rodeo*, which featured country standards along with compositions by Bob Dylan and new member Gram Parsons, performed by the band along with some of the better, younger Nashville session men. A year later, Bob Dylan gave the movement added legitimacy by releasing *Nashville Skyline*.

In the early 1970's Gram Parsons and Byrds bassman Chris Hillman formed the most influential country-rock band, the Flying Burrito Brothers. Their first two LPs are considered classics today, combining traditional country subject matter and sounds with a decidedly new outlook.

Singer/Songwriters The 1960's-era folk and country rock movements naturally evolved into the singer/songwriter movement of the early 1970's. Artists such as James Taylor, Carly Simon, Carole King, and Joni Mitchell all took the notion of writing their own material away from social protest, and toward self-exploration and autobiography. King's 1971 album, *Tapestry*, was among the decade's most successful; in it she explored her personal growth as a woman of the 1960's. Joni Mitchell became one of the most articulate voices for both the liberation and confusion felt by young women as sexual roles shifted. Even Bob Dylan turned inward, chronicling the collapse of his marriage in the classic album *Blood on the Tracks* (1974).

Other influential singer/songwriters include Paul Simon (b. 1941), known for his lyrically complex and introspective songs which often incorporate multicultural rhythms; and Jimmy Webb (b. 1946), one of the most musically literate and harmonically sophisticated composers of his generation, whose songs rival those of Burt Bacharach's for use of complex chord progressions and extended harmonies.

Heavy Metal At the opposite end of the spectrum from the singer/songwriters, heavy metal emphasized rock's raw power. Heavy metal is loudly aggressive rock, appealing primarily to a male, adolescent audience.

British bands Led Zeppelin and Black Sabbath (with lead singer Ozzy Osbourne b. 1948) are generally cited as among the first metal bands in the early 1970's, taking the earlier blues-rock style and exaggerating its aggressive, loud guitar parts, playing repetitive riffs accompanied by pounding bass and drums. The style first came to America in the work of Alice Cooper, who brought a heightened theatricality to the form, and then in the band Kiss, which combined glam-rock makeup with the metal style.

Metal evolved somewhat in the later 1970's, when newer bands (such as Judas Priest and Iron Maiden) emerged who played more aggressively, faster, and louder than the earlier generation of bands. However, as metal became increasingly popular, a return-to-roots movement was inevitable; new American bands of the 1980's, such as Metallica and Megadeath, pioneered the subgenre of thrash-metal, returning metal to its roots in noise and speed.

Progressive Rock Progressive rock—also known as "prog" or art rock—was popular from the late 1960's through the mid-1970's and featured more ambitious instrumentation, extended compositions, and lyrics influenced by myth, science fiction, and other literary sources. Although there had been some hints of the progressive movement, it was King Crimson's 1969 debut album, *In the Court of the Crimson King*, that is generally viewed as the first great prog-rock album. Through the mid-1970's, several bands carried the progressive-rock banner, including Emerson, Lake and Palmer, Genesis, and Pink Floyd.

Glam-Rock Glam-rock is a gender-bending, highly theatrical form of rock that developed in Britain in the early 1970's. The British group T. Rex, led by flamboyant lead singer Marc Bolan (1948–77), is the epitome of pure glam-rock; the entire focus is on Bolan's unabashed showmanship, with the music taking a secondary role. However, more ambitious musicians were also drawn to glam, notably David Bowie (b. 1947) during his Ziggy Stardust/Spiders from Mars period.

Disco Disco is a mid-1970's dance style emphasizing a heavy, repeated beat, melodic riffs, and simple lyrics. As it developed in the gay dance clubs of New York, the disco style was pioneered by deejays who took to creating remixes of popular songs, particularly soul and funk tracks that emphasized a repetitive beat. By sequencing songs with the same basic rhythm and tempo, they could extend a dance session up to 30 minutes.

Early disco groups, such as KC & the Sunshine Band and Niles Rodgers's (b. 1952) Chic, evolved out of funk bands. Other artists quickly evolved to cater to this new musical style, some with an overtly gay image (such as the Village People), others exploiting heterosexuality (Donna Summer, b. 1948). The disco craze reached its greatest mainstream acceptance thanks to the 1977 film *Saturday Night Fever*, which featured the Bee Gees playing such songs as "Stayin' Alive."

Punk Punk rock was a "back to basics" movement that occurred in the mid-1970's, in reaction to the increasing commercialism and aging of the previous generation of rock stars. Most punk songs were simple to play, as a reaction to the increasing complexity of the music of progressive rock. Punk also tackled topics from homosexuality to radical politics that were not usually addressed by rock songs.

In England, the punk rockers Sex Pistols were purposely poor musicians, emphasizing outrageous clothes and hair styles and an aggressive, in-your-face stage presence; their single "God Save the Queen" was banned on British radio. However, the greatest politically oriented punk band was undoubtedly the Clash, whose 1978 album *London Calling* is recognized as one of the great rock albums of all time.

In New York City, the punk movement centered on a small club in New York's Bowery district, CBGB's. New York punk artists ranged from the Ramones, who specialized in ultra-short, purposely simple, and aggressively loud songs performed at breakneck speeds, to poet Patti Smith (b. 1946).

California Rock One of the most successful groups of the late 1970's-early 1980's was the Eagles, a group that began its life as a country-rock band but developed into a mainstream pop act. Combining a Southern Californian singer/songwriter sensibility, sweet vocal harmonies, and a powerful twin-guitar lead sound, the group had many top ten hits.

Another group that combined confessional songwriting with a rock beat was Fleetwood Mac, which in its 1970's/mid-1980's lineup combined the British rhythm section of John McVie and Mick Fleetwood with the romantic themes of the group's three singer/songwriters, Stevie Nicks, Lindsey Buckingham, and Christine McVie. The soap opera couplings and uncouplings among the group's members also helped sell their records.

Pop/Rock in the Modern Era While the 1970's saw a splintering of rock's main line into many subgenres, the 1980's and 1990's saw a gradually decreasing presence of rock as a mainstream pop music. It was a time of nostalgic retrenchment, when older groups such as the Who and Rolling Stones were able to sell out major stadiums, but few new groups arose with equal drawing power.

MTV The year 1981 was a watershed year for pop music, thanks to the launch of MTV, the first cable network devoted solely to music. MTV's combination of music videos, youthful video jockeys (VJs), irreverent commentary, and music news resulted in immediate and widespread popularity among youthful viewers. More important, MTV's music videos helped to define the sound—and the look—of popular music throughout the 1980's.

The early format of the network was modeled after Top 40 radio, with popular videos played in heavy rotation. A large number of pop stars were made household names by MTV; artists such as Duran Duran and Madonna gained widespread success based primarily on the popularity of their music videos.

New Wave The New Wave movement of the early 1980's came out of punk, but had a far more commercial edge. Groups such as the Police combined punk attitude with a pure pop sound. Talking Heads began as an art-punk band propelled by the off-center sensibility of lead singer/songwriter David Byrne (b. 1952), but developed into a band that combined elements of commercial pop with world beat and contemporary classical music. And singer/songwriter Elvis Costello (b. Declan MacManus, 1954) adopted some of punk's back-to-basics ethos but wed it to far more sophisticated lyrics and arrangements.

Bruce Springsteen Straight-ahead rock 'n' roll music in the post-punk world was defined by Bruce Springsteen (b. 1949). Springsteen combined in his music elements of Bob Dylan's word-strewn folk-rock; a love for classic 1960's rock styles, from Motown to Stax to garage-rock; and his own Wagnerian sensibilities, enhanced by his primal backup group, the E Street Band. Springsteen's 1985 album, *Born in the USA*, represented his greatest commercial success, producing multiple hit singles and a long-running, financially rewarding world tour of stadiums.

Pop-Rock Pop-rock music in the early 1980's was dominated by the dance-oriented music of Michael Jackson (b. 1958–2009) and Madonna (b. Madonna Louise Ciccone, 1958). Twenty-five-year-old Jackson, former lead singer of the Motown group the Jackson Five, released *Thriller* in 1982; the album became the biggest-selling pop record of all time. Madonna was one of MTV's first video stars; she continuously redefined her sound and image over the course of two decades, beginning with a "boy toy" teen pop phase and then maturing into a plethora of fashion looks and musical styles.

Grunge The early 1990's saw the birth of a new hybrid of punk and heavy metal music, dubbed *grunge*, that was a back-to-basics response to the synthesized pop music of the 1980's. Born out of the Seattle music scene, the first wave of grunge bands—including Green River, Mudhoney, and Soundgarden—played music that blended angst-ridden, introspective lyrics with distorted guitars and pounding drums. Grunge's second wave, led by Nirvana and Pearl Jam, achieved widespread popularity with a slightly more melodic sound.

Grunge was history by the mid-1990's, but the grunge sound lived on in more mainstream post-grunge bands, including the Foo Fighters and Queens of the Stone Age. These bands applied grunge instrumentation and production to more radio-friendly lyrics and melodies.

Teen Pop The late 1990's were notable for its many "manufactured" teen pop artists, from Britain's Spice Girls to America's Backstreet Boys and 'N SYNC boy bands to pop Lolitas (and ex-Mouseketeers) Britney Spears (b. 1982) and Christina Aguilera (b. 1980). These artists distinguished themselves more as entertainers than musicians, although their mixture of sugary-sweet pop melodies with heavy hip hop beats proved especially popular among the pre-teen audience.

The pop music world continues to use professional songwriters to provide material for solo singers and "manufactured" boy and girl bands. One of the most prolific such songwriters is Swedish producer Max Martin (b. 1971), who, along with partner Rami Yacoub, was the creative force for such 1990's pop acts as Britney Spears and the Backstreet Boys.

Martin's songs have been performed by artists such as Bryan Adams, Ace of Base, Bon Jovi, Kelly Clarkson, Celene Dion, and 'N SYNC. His most popular songs include "Baby One More Time," "Behind These Hazel Eyes," "Cloud No. 9," "Oops! I Did It Again," "I Want It That Way," "It's My Life," "Lucky," "Never Gonna Say I'm Sorry," "Quit Playing Games," "Shape of My Heart," "Since U Been Gone," and "That's the Way It Is."

At the dawn of the 21st century, what was considered pop music was more a blend of several modern styles than its own unique category. Radio stations that call themselves "pop" play as much alternative rock as they do bubblegum pop. Artists such as Lady Gaga (b. Stefani

Germanotta, 1986), who blends electronic beats with pop hooks, and Gwen Stefani (b. 1969), who incorporates R&B, electronica, disco and ska into her albums, have helped to blur this distinction.

Modern Songwriting In the last decades of the 20th century, due to the profusion of artists who wrote their own songs, professional songwriting became a dying art—with a handful of exceptions. Professional songwriters are still used to compose songs for movie soundtracks. Many movies today include one or more big songs from contemporary artists, in order to boost the appeal of both the movie and the movie's soundtrack album.

While many soundtrack artists provide their own material, professional songwriters such as Diane Warren (b. 1956) are often employed to come up with a "blockbuster" track to play over the movie's closing credits. Warren's songs have been heard in more than 60 films; she received Academy Award nominations for her songs "Because You Loved Me" (*Up Close and Personal*), "How Do I Live" (*Con Air*), "I Don't Want to Miss a Thing" (*Armageddon*), "Music of the Heart" (*Music of My Heart*), "Nothing's Gonna Stop Us Now" (*Mannequin*), and "There You'll Be" (*Pearl Harbor*).

Rap and Hip Hop

Urban Contemporary In the 1980's and 1990's, the style of soft soul crooning became known as *urban contemporary*. Many urban contemporary artists, such as Whitney Houston, Luther Vandross, and Kenneth "Babyface" Edmonds, were able to cross over into the pop charts. Other artists, such as Janet Jackson and En Vogue, blended urban contemporary with elements of hip hop. In the late 20th and early 21st century, this style was no longer specific to African-American performers, but heard in popular music across the charts.

Rap/Hip Hop Rap music as a genre is over a quarter-century old, and has gone through many changes in its history. Rap is the general term for the musical expression; it is a part of a broader movement, known as *hip hop*, that includes dance, graffiti art, fashion, and political expression. Nonetheless, the two terms are used somewhat interchangeably to refer to a variety of musical styles.

First Generation The first generation of rappers developed alongside the mobile deejay movement, which was first seen in Jamaica and then came to urban neighborhoods in New York and Los Angeles. Deejays outfitted trucks with powerful sound systems that they set up in a local park or playground. They would spin their records, while improvising boasts over the music. Eventually, the role of rapper and deejay separated, with the rapper taking on the job of drawing the crowds, while the deejay focused on manipulating the turntables.

The first commercially successful rap group was New York's Sugarhill Gang, with their 1979 release, "Rapper's Delight." Other important early rappers include Kurtis Blow, with his 1981 single, "The Breaks"; Afrika Bambaataa, with his 1982 recording, "Planet Rock"; and Grandmaster Flash and The Furious Five, who issued 1982's powerful "The Message," one of the first rap songs to deal with contemporary urban issues.

Second Generation The first second-generation rap group was Run D.M.C., who began issuing records in 1983. The group wed heavy metal rhythms to a tough, urban sensibility, epitomized by their cover of Aerosmith's "Walk This Way" from 1986, the first rap recording to cross over to popularity among traditional rock fans. Following Run-D.M.C. were more popularly oriented rap groups, including the humorous Fat Boys, and the more romantic material popularized by L. L. Cool J.

Gangsta Rap The next innovation in rap came with the so-called *gangsta* style, originating on the West Coast. Rapper Ice-T's 1986 release "6 'N the Mornin'" is considered among the first gangsta rap recordings, but it was N.W.A.'s 1988 album, *Straight Outta Compton*, that was the most influential and controversial work in the new style. The group's violent imagery was deplored by the mainstream press, making them all the more attractive to their core listeners. The group's members included Dr. Dre, Eazy-E, and Ice Cube, all of whom went on to have solo careers.

Later gangsta rappers became so embroiled in the genre's mythology of violence that they fell victim (literally) to their own success. Rappers Tupac Shakur and the Notorious B.I.G. died within six months of each other, each murdered by unknown assailants. This brought more bad publicity to the music, and led some major record labels to disassociate themselves with their rap subsidiaries.

Female Rappers Rap also had its noteworthy female stars, who could be just as macho as their male counterparts. Queen Latifah (b. Dana Owens, 1970) was among the first and most feminist in her message, beginning with her 1989 single, "Ladies First." Salt-n-Pepa were the first all-female crew, and broke through to great popularity in the late 1980's and early 1990's with their mix of frank lyrics and brassy stage presentation.

Other important female rappers include Lil' Kim, Missy "Misdemeanor" Elliott, and Lauryn Hill, who combined rap with R&B, soul, and gospel influences.

Rap Becomes Mainstream As the 1990's wore on, rap became less political and more mainstream. Sean Combs (aka Puff Daddy; P. Diddy; Diddy) was the major entrepreneur of rap in the later 1990's, as both performer and producer. Elements of rap were heard in all styles of music, and rap stars were regularly featured on MTV and at the top of the pop charts.

In 2003 a controversial white rapper named Eminem (b. Marshall Bruce Mathers III, 1972) made history when his song "Lose Yourself" from the movie *8 Mile*—in which he starred—won the Oscar for Best Original Song, making him the first hip hop artist to win an Oscar. The group Three 6 Mafia became the first hip hop artists to perform at the Academy Awards when they performed "It's Hard Out Here for a Pimp"—from the movie *Hustle and Flow*—in 2006. The song won the Oscar for Best Original Song, making the group the second hip hop act to win the award, and further cementing the genre's place in popular music.

Country

Country music is, like the blues, a traditionally simple musical form that lends itself to endless variation. Even though many country songs are built around three chords and a simple melody, these songs can be interpreted in a variety of styles, from the gritty sounds of honky-tonk to the smooth stylings of country pop.

Traditional Country Country music grew out of southern American folk music, including Appalachian folk and rural blues forms. Old-time country music was simple and folksy, often performed with just guitars and fiddles.

First Recordings The first popular country recording, "Turkey in the Straw," was made in 1922, by Texas fiddlers Eck Robinson and Henry Gilliland. The following year, Okeh Records released "The Little Log Cabin in the Lane," by Fiddlin' John Carson, which sold an impressive number of copies. In 1927 Victor Records spent two weeks recording acts in Bristol, Tennessee; included in these legendary "Bristol Sessions" were the first recorded performances of Jimmie Rodgers and the Carter Family.

Jimmie Rodgers Rodgers (1897–1933) brought rural country music to national popularity by streamlining the music and lyrics, thus making the genre a viable commercial property. Known as the "Singing Brakeman," he cut 110 records in just six years, singing in a bluesy style with a trademark high-pitched yodel.

The Grand Ole Opry Country music was the staple of local radio for the mid-20's. One of the most popular of all these programs was the "Grand Ole Opry," a weekly radio broadcast that defined the world of country music in the 1930's and 1940's.

Western Swing Western Swing is a unique combination of string band music with jazz styles. It was born in the Texas-Oklahoma region in the late 20's. The band credited with creating the Western Swing sound was The Lightcrust Doughboys. This band, popular in 1931–32, featured fiddler Bob Wills and vocalist Milton Brown, who soon formed their own bands. A second wave of Western Swing came in the late 1940's in Southern California, where many Western musicians had settled after the war.

The 1950's and 1960's were lean times for Western Swing, but in the early 1970's new young bands, such as Asleep at the Wheel, began introducing a new generation to the sound. Country superstar Merle Haggard recorded an album in homage to Wills's music, and then brought the star out of retirement for his famous last session in 1973.

Bluegrass Developing at the end of World War II, bluegrass music drew on the earlier string band music and melded it with influences from Western Swing, cowboy, and honky tonk. A typical bluegrass band consists of mandolin, banjo, fiddle, guitar, and bass, with a lead vocalist often complemented on the chorus by tenor and bass singers.

Traditional Bluegrass Bill Monroe (1911–96) is generally called the "father of bluegrass music." His group, the Blue Grass Boys, was named for his home state of Kentucky. In 1946, vocalist/guitarist Lester Flatt and 19-year-old North Carolina-born banjo player Earl Scruggs joined the band and it quickly became the model for others, beginning with Flatt and Scruggs themselves, who left to form their own band in 1948. Virginia's Stanley Brothers were another group to pick up the bluegrass mantle.

Contemporary Bluegrass During the 1950's and 1960's bluegrass's popularity began to spread to several urban centers, with groups like the Country Gentlemen, the Greenbriar Boys, and the Charles River Valley Boys. By the 1970's, jazz, folk, and world music influences all became part of the bluegrass style, as evidenced by eclectic

mandolinist David Grisman. The 1980's saw a return to traditional bluegrass styles among younger musicians, and by the mid-1990's, Nashville took a renewed interest in bluegrass music.

Singer/fiddler Alison Krauss was the first new bluegrass artist to break onto the country charts, followed by her protégés, the band Nickel Creek. Ricky Skaggs, whose mainstream country career had slowed in the later 1980's and early 1990's, returned to playing bluegrass, and his band, Kentucky Thunder, brought him renewed popularity. Established country singers, including Dolly Parton, Patty Loveless, and the Dixie Chicks, all recorded bluegrass albums.

Honky-Tonk Music Following World War II, the honky-tonk—a small bar often located on the outskirts of town—became a center of musical creation. In the period from about 1948 to 1955, honky-tonk music—with lyrics about drifting husbands and the subsequent lyin', cheatin', and heartbreak—became the predominant country form.

The foremost honky-tonk performer was Hank Williams (1923–53), whose backup combo of crying steel guitar and scratchy fiddle became the model for thousands of honky-tonk bands. The honky-tonk style reached its apex in Hank Thompson's 1952 recording of "The Wild Side of Life," which inspired the wonderful answer song, "It Wasn't God that Made Honky Tonk Angels," that made a major star out of Kitty Wells.

Country-Pop Following the emergence of rock and roll, country music began to incorporate more pop oriented production techniques, resulting in a smoother sound than was typical with traditional country.

The Nashville Sound In the 1950's RCA Records producer/guitarist Chet Atkins and Owen Bradley combined country and pop music in what became known as the *Nashville Sound*. Atkins surrounded country's traditionally simple melodies and song structures with polished pop-oriented arrangements, creating a lush sound that blended rural sensibility with urban sophistication. The result was increased popularity for the country genre, and a number of pop crossover hits for artists such as Jim Reeves and Patsy Cline.

Countrypolitan By the late 1960's the Nashville Sound had metamorphosed into *countrypolitan*, with an even heavier emphasis on pop production flourishes; most countrypolitan recordings featured multiple layers of keyboards, guitars, strings, and vocals. Producer Billy Sherrill was especially noted for this style which produced numerous crossover hits for George Jones, Tammy Wynette, Charlie Rich, Conway Twitty, and other artists.

Progressive and Alternative Country

Progressive country developed in the late 1960's as a reaction to the increasingly polished sound of mainstream country music. This was a songwriter-based genre inspired in parts by the of classic honky-tonk, the hard-driving beat of rock 'n' roll, and the introspective writing of Bob Dylan and other contemporary folk musicians.

Very much anti-Nashville in its sentiments, progressive country was both rootsier and more intellectual than the country-pop of its day. The top progressive artists—including Kris Kristofferson, Willie Nelson, Tom T. Hall, and Jimmie Dale Gilmore—were better known for their songwriting than for their singing skills, and wrote distinctive, individual songs that pushed the boundaries of the country genre. In the 1980's progressive country evolved into *alternative country*, as popularized by Emmylou Harris, Lyle Lovett, k.d. lang, and similar artists.

Country-Folk and Americana

During the 1980's and 1990's, several artists blurred the lines between country and folk music, creating a subgenre alternately known as *country-folk* and *Americana*. The most popular country-folk and Americana artists also fall under the singer/songwriter umbrella. The most prominent of these artists include Mary Chapin Carpenter, Steve Earl, Nanci Griffith, John Hiatt, Shelby Lynne, Kathy Mattea, and Lucinda Williams.

Contemporary Country

By the late 1980's a new breed of country-pop evolved that was significantly influenced by pop/rock sensibilities, spawning crossover superstars such as Garth Brooks and Billy Ray Cyrus. A wave of male singers—dubbed "hat acts," after their ubiquitous cowboy headwear—dominated the country charts with songs that sounded more like rock than traditional country.

A decade later, the emphasis had shifted to female vocalists, typically bathed in glossy pop productions. These vocalists—most notably Shania Twain, LeAnn Rimes, and Faith Hill—deemphasized traditional country twang and found massive success with a mainstream audience.

Folk Music

American folk music describes everyday events and common people, often in mythic terms. Modern folk music stands alone as its own independent genre, yet also informs many other styles, including rock and country.

Traditional Folk

Although there had been collections of dance music, songs, and spirituals through the 19th century, folk music itself was not really prized until the early years of the 20th century. The first music collection to have a major impact was Texas song collector John Lomax's *Cowboy Songs and Other Frontier Ballads*, published in 1910. In 1928 the Library of Congress established its Archive of American Folk Song, to preserve and promote America's traditional music.

Lead Belly In 1933, with the support of the Archive of American Folk Song, John Lomax and his son, Alan, made a collecting trip to southern prisons. There they discovered a 12-string guitar player/singer nicknamed Lead Belly (b. Huddie Ledbetter, 1888–1949) by his fellow prisoners because of his unusual strength and physical stamina. The Lomaxes brought Lead Belly north to perform for urban audiences, where he recorded for various labels through the later 1930's and until his death in 1949.

Woody Guthrie Another important Lomax "discovery" was Woody Guthrie (1912–67). Born in Oklahoma, Guthrie was an itinerant sign painter and guitarist who gained fame as a member of the New York folk community in the 1930's. A banjo player named Pete Seeger (b. 1915) became a close friend, and the two often performed together at union rallies and labor meetings. Guthrie was a prolific songwriter, churning out dozens of songs, including the classics "Pastures of Plenty," "Roll On, Columbia," and "This Land Is Your Land." He continued to record and perform until the early 1950's, when an inherited disease, Huntington's chorea, began to affect his motor skills. He died in 1967.

The Weavers Pete Seeger was also a member of the influential group The Weavers. In the late 1940's and early 1950's, the group enjoyed mainstream pop hits with Lead Belly's "Irene Goodnight," the African "Wimoweh," and the Israeli "Tzena, Tzena." The Weavers were the model for many of the popular folk groups of the late 1950's and early 1960's, including The Kingston Trio and the Chad Mitchell Trio; after the group's breakup, Seeger continued as a solo perfomer.

1960's Folk Revival A second generation of folk music fans formed the seedbed for the next great folk performers of the late 1950's and early 1960's. Some were oriented toward strict re-creation of earlier folk styles, such as the old-time country stringband The New Lost City Ramblers; others were influenced by Woody Guthrie to take up topical songwriting.

Bob Dylan Perhaps the best and most creative of the Guthrie acolytes was a young Minnesotan who came to New York to visit Guthrie in his hospital room. Taking the name of Bob Dylan (b. Robert Zimmerman, 1940), the young singer soon established the social-protest genre, penning such folk classics as "Blowin' in the Wind" and "The Times They Are A-Changin'." Others who wrote in this style included Phil Ochs, Tom Paxton, Malvina Reynolds, and Buffy Sainte-Marie.

Folk-Pop Although Dylan was a talented performer, his songs were initially popularized by more polished musicians, notably the popular folk trio of Peter, Paul and Mary. They topped the charts with compositions by Dylan and the other "folkniks."

Another important early champion of Dylan's songwriting was Joan Baez (b. 1941), the sweet-voiced singer who began her career covering old ballads and folksongs but soon took on social causes including the Civil Rights and anti-Vietnam War movements.

Contemporary Folk The folk movement of the 1960's splintered into many smaller, more focused movements in the 1970's and 1980's, such as the bluegrass and old-time music revivals; the beginnings of interest in world music; and New Age and "new acoustic" music. Meanwhile, many folk performers had already crossed over into performing either folk-rock or country-rock.

Several new singer/songwriters were promoted as "New Dylans," beginning with Chicago's Steve Goodman (writer of "The City of New Orleans") and the wry Loudon Wainwright. Female singer/songwriters were very successful, ranging from the melancholy Joni Mitchell to the more playful songs of the Canadian sisters Kate and Anna McGarrigle. The Texas "outlaw" movement spawned several talented songwriters, ranging from country's Willie Nelson to the category-bending work of Jerry Jeff Walker ("Mr. Bojangles"), Townes Van Zandt ("Poncho and Lefty"), and Joe Ely.

In the mid-1980's, social conscience songwriting returned in the hands of songwriters such as Suzanne Vega ("Luka") and Tracey Chapman ("Fast Car"). Even rock performers such as Bruce Springsteen and John Cougar Mellencamp showed an interest in folk song; Springsteen consciously emulated Woody Guthrie in the sparse songs he wrote for his albums *Nebraska* (1982) and *The Ghost of Tom Joad* (1995), and Mellencamp put together an all-acoustic band for his 1987 album, *Lonesome Jubilee*.

Rock and Roll Hall of Fame

1986

Buddy Holly, "That'll Be the Day," "Peggy Sue," "It's So Easy."

Chuck Berry, "Rock and Roll Music," "Roll Over Beethoven," "Sweet Little Sixteen."

Elvis Presley, "Love Me Tender," "All Shook Up," "Hound Dog," "Blue Suede Shoes," "Can't Help Falling in Love."

Fats Domino, "Blueberry Hill," "Ain't That a Shame," "Let the Four Winds Blow."

James Brown, "I Got You (I Feel Good)," "Papa's Got a Brand New Bag," "Black and I'm Proud."

Jerry Lee Lewis, "Whole Lotta Shakin' Going On," "Great Balls of Fire."

Little Richard, "Good Golly Miss Molly," "Long Tall Sally," "Tutti-Frutti."

Ray Charles, "I Got a Woman," "Georgia On My Mind," "Hit the Road, Jack."

Sam Cooke, "Another Saturday Night," "Wonderful World," "Chain Gang."

The Everly Brothers, "Wake Up Little Susie," "All I Have to Do Is Dream," "Cathy's Clown."

1987

Aretha Franklin, "Respect," "I Never Loved a Man (The Way I Love You)," "Chain of Fools."

B.B. King, "The Thrill Is Gone," "Rock Me Baby," "Every Day I Have the Blues."

Big Joe Turner, "Shake, Rattle and Roll," "Corrina, Corrina."

Bill Haley, "Rock Around the Clock," "Shake, Rattle and Roll," "See You Later, Alligator."

Bo Diddley, "I'm a Man," "Mona," "Who Do You Love?" "Hey, Bo Diddley."

Carl Perkins, "Blue Suede Shoes," "Everybody's Trying to Be My Baby," "Matchbox."

Clyde McPhatter, "A Lover's Question," "Little Bitty Pretty One," "The Treasure of Love."

Eddie Cochran, "Summertime Blues," "Something Else," "C'mon Everybody."

Jackie Wilson, "(Your Love Keeps Lifting Me) Higher and Higher," "Lonely Teardrops," "You Better Know It."

Marvin Gaye, "What's Going On?" "I Heard It Through the Grapevine," "Sexual Healing."

Muddy Waters, "Long Distance Call," "She's Nineteen Years Old," "Hoochie Coochie Man."

Ricky Nelson, "Poor Little Fool," "Hello Mary Lou, "Travelin' Man."

Roy Orbison, "Oh! Pretty Woman," "Running Scared," "Only the Lonely."

Smokey Robinson, "You've Really Got a Hold on Me," "The Tracks of My Tears," "Shop Around."

The Coasters, "Poison Ivy," "Charlie Brown," "Smokey Joe's Café."

1988

Bob Dylan, "Blowin' in the Wind," "A Hard Rain's A-Gonna Fall," "Like a Rolling Stone."

The Beach Boys, "Surfin' Safari," "California Girls," "Good Vibrations," "Wouldn't It Be Nice."

The Beatles, "I Want to Hold Your Hand," "Can't Buy Me Love," "Sgt. Pepper's Lonely Hearts Club Band," "Revolution," "Let It Be."

The Drifters, "Save the Last Dance for Me," "Stand By Me," "Under the Boardwalk."

The Supremes, ""Back in My Arms Again," "Baby Love," "Stop! In the Name of Love."

1989

Dion, "A Teenager in Love," "Runaround Sue," "The Wanderer."

Otis Redding, "(Sittin' On) The Dock of the Bay," "Mr. Pitiful."

Stevie Wonder, "Superstition," "I Just Called to Say I Love You," "Sir Duke."

The Rolling Stones, "(I Can't Get No) Satisfaction," "Honky Tonk Women," "Under My Thumb," "Can't Always Get What You Want," "Let's Spend the Night Together."

The Temptations, "My Girl," "Ain't Too Proud to Beg," "The Way You Do the Things You Do."

1990

Bobby Darin, "Splish Splash," "Mack the Knife," "Dream Lover."

Hank Ballard, "Work With Me, Annie," "Annie Had a Baby," "Annie's Aunt Fannie."

Simon and Garfunkel, "Mrs. Robinson," "The Sounds of Silence," "Bridge Over Troubled Water."

The Four Seasons, "Sherry," "Big Girls Don't Cry," "Walk Like A Man," "Rag Doll."

The Four Tops, "Baby I Need Your Loving," "It's the Same Old Song," "I Can't Help Myself."

The Kinks, "You Really Got Me," "All Day and All of the Night," "Pressure."

The Platters, "The Great Pretender," "Smoke Gets in Your Eyes," "Only You."

The Who, "Baba O'Riley (Teenage Wasteland)," "My Generation," "Pinball Wizard," "Who Are You."

1991

Ike and Tina Turner, "A Fool in Love," "It's Gonna Work Out Fine," "Proud Mary."

Jimmy Reed, "Big Boss Man," "Bright Lights, Big City," "Ain't That Lovin' You Baby."

John Lee Hooker, "Boogie Chillen," "Boom Boom," "Crawling Kingsnake."

LaVern Baker, "Tweedle Dee," "Jim Dandy," "See See Rider."

The Byrds, "Mr. Tambourine Man," "Turn! Turn! Turn!," "Eight Miles High."

The Impressions, "People Get Ready," "Keep On Pushing," "We're a Winner."

Wilson Pickett, "Land of 1,000 Dances," "Mustang Sally," "Funky Broadway."

1992

Bobby "Blue" Bland, "I Pity the Fool," "That's the Way Love Is," "Turn On Your Love Light."

Booker T. and the M.G.'s, "Green Onions," "Hang 'Em High," "Time Is Tight."

Johnny Cash, "Ring of Fire," "I Walk the Line," "A Boy Named Sue."

Sam and Dave, "Soul Man," "You Don't Know Like I Know," "I Thank You."

The Isley Brothers, "Twist and Shout," "Love the One You're With," "Fight the Power."

The Jimi Hendrix Experience, "Little Wing," "Purple Haze," "All Along the Watchtower," "Voodoo Child."

The Yardbirds, "For Your Love," "Heart Full of Soul," "Shapes of Things."

1993

Cream, "Sunshine Of Your Love," "Tales of Brave Ulysses," "I'm So Glad."

Creedence Clearwater Revivial, "Bad Moon Rising," "Suzie Q," "Who'll Stop the Rain."

Etta James, "Good Rockin' Daddy," "All I Could Do Was Cry," "Tell Mama." Frankie Lymon and the Teenagers, "Why Do Fools Fall in Love," "I Want You to Be My Girl," "Who Can Explain?"

Ruth Brown, "5-10-15 Hours," "(Mama) He Treats Your Daughter Mean," "So Long."

Sly and the Family Stone, "I Want to Take You Higher," "Everyday People," "Family Affair."

The Doors, "Light My Fire," "Love Her Madly," "Riders On the Storm," "The End."

Van Morrison, "Brown Eyed Girl," "Wild Night," "Gloria."

1994

Bob Marley, "No Woman No Cry," "Three Little Birds," "Redemption Song."

Duane Eddy, "Cannonball," "Rebel Rouser," "Forty Miles of Bad Road."

Elton John, "Bennie and the Jets," "Goodbye Yellow Brick Road," "Tiny Dancer."

John Lennon, "Imagine," "Give Peace a Chance," "Whatever Gets You Thru the Night," "Watching the Wheels."

Rod Stewart, "Maggie May," "Tonight's the Night," "Da Ya Think I'm Sexy."

The Animals, "House of the Rising Sun," "It's My Life," "We Gotta Get Out of This Place."

The Band, "I Shall Be Released," "They Night They Drove Old Dixie Down," "The Last Waltz."

The Grateful Dead, "Stealin," "The Other One," "Touch of Grey."

1995

Al Green, "Let's Stay Together," "I'm Still in Love With You," "Here I Am (Come and Take Me)."

Frank Zappa, "Brown Shoes Don't Make It," "Cosmik Debris," "Valley Girl."

Janis Joplin, "Me and Bobby McGee," "Get It While You Can," "Cry Baby," "Try (Just a Little Bit Harder)."

Led Zeppelin, "Stairway to Heaven," "Black Dog," "Whole Lotta Love," "Kashmir."

Martha and the Vandellas, "Dancing in the Street," "(Love Is Like a) Heat Wave," "Nowhere to Run."

Neil Young, "Broken Arrow," "Down by the River," "Cinnamon Girl."

The Allman Brothers Band, "Ramblin' Man," "Midnight Rider," "Whipping Post."

1996

David Bowie, "Space Oddity," "China Girl," "Modern Love."

Gladys Knighs and the Pips, "Every Beat of My Heart," "If I Were Your Woman," "Neither One of Us (Wants to Be the First to Say Goodbye."

Jefferson Airplane, "White Rabbit," "Somebody to Love," "Plastic Fantastic Lover."

Little Willie John, "Fever," "Take My Love (I Want to Give It All to You)," "All Around the World."

Pink Floyd, "Another Brick In The Wall," "Money," "Comfortably Numb," "Dark Side of Moon."

The Shirelles, "I Met Him on a Sunday," "Will You Love Me Tomorrow," "Soldier Boy."

The Velvet Underground, "I'm Waiting for the Man," "Heroin," "Venus in Furs."

1997

Buffalo Springfield, "For What It's Worth."

Crosby Stills and Nash, "Suite: Judy Blue Eyes," "Ohio," "Just a Song Before I Go."

Joni Mitchell, "Day by Day," "Big Yellow Taxi," "The Circle Game," "River."

Parliament-Funkadelic, "(I Wanna) Testify," "Flash Light," "One Nation Under a Groove."

The (Young) Rascals, "Good Lovin'," "You Better Run," "I've Been Lonely Too Long."

The Bee Gees, "To Love Somebody," "Jive Talkin'," "Stayin' Alive," "Night Fever."

The Jackson Five, "I Want You Back," "ABC," "I'll Be There."

1998

Fleetwood Mac, "Landslide," "Black Magic Woman," "Over My Head," "Rhiannon."

Gene Vincent, "Be-Bop-A-Lula," "That's All Right (Mama)," "Summertime Blues."

Lloyd Price, "Personality," "Lawdy Miss Clawdy," "Stagger Lee."

Santana, "Oye Como Va," "Jingo," "Maria, Maria."

The Eagles, "Take It Easy," "The Best of My Love," "Tequila Sunrise," "Hotel California."

The Mamas and the Papas, "California Dreamin'," "Dedicated to the One I Love," "Monday Monday," "I Saw Her Again."

1999

Billy Joel, "Piano Man," "Captain Jack," "New York State of Mind," "Movin' Out (Anthony's Song)."

Bruce Springsteen, "Born to Run," "Thunder Road," "Blinded by the Light," "Born in the USA."

Curtis Mayfield, "Freddie's Dead," "Superfly," "Don't Worry (If There's a Hell Below We're All Going to Go)."

Del Shannon, "Runaway," "Hats Off to Larry," "Do You Wanna Dance."

Dusty Springfield, "You Don't Have to Say You Love Me," "Wishin' and Hopin'," "I Only Want to Be With You."

Paul McCartney, "Jet," "Uncle Albert/Admiral Halsey," "Mull of Kintyre."

The Staple Singers, "I'll Take You There," "Let's Do It Again," "Uncloudy Day."

2000

Bonnie Raitt, "Runaway," "Something to Talk About."

Earth, Wind & Fire, "Shining Star," "Serpentine Fire," "Getaway."

Eric Clapton, "Layla," "Cocaine," "Lay Down Sally," "Change the World."

James Taylor, "You've Got a Friend," "Country Road," "Fire and Rain," "Sweet Baby James."

Lovin' Spoonful, "Do You Believe in Magic," "Good Time Music," "Summer in the City."

The Moonglows, "Sincerely," "Most of All," "See Saw."

2001

Aerosmith, "Dream On," "Walk This Way," "Janie's Got a Gun," "Crazy."

Michael Jackson, "Thriller," "Billie Jean," "Beat It," "Heal the World."

Paul Simon, "Still Crazy After All These Years," "50 Ways to Leave Your Lover," "Kodachrome," "Corona."

Queen, "Bohemian Rhapsody," "Fat Bottom Girls," "We Are the Champions," "Another One Bites the Dust," "Crazy Little Thing Called Love."

Ritchie Valens, "La Bamba," "Come On, Let's go," "Donna."

Solomon Burke, "Cry to Me," "Just Out of Reach (Of My Two Open Arms)," "Got to Get You Off of My Mind."

Steely Dan, "Reelin' in the Years," "Do It Again," "Rikki Don't Lose That Number."

The Flamingos, "Golden Teardrops," "I'll Be Home," "I Only Have Eyes For You."

2002

Brenda Lee, "Sweet Nothin's," "I Just Want to Be Wanted," "Rockin' Around the Christmas Tree."

Gene Pitney, "It Hurts to Be In Love," "She's a Heartbreaker," "I'm Gonna Be Strong."

Isaac Hayes, "Theme from 'Shaft'," "Walk on By," "By the Time I Get to Phoenix."

Ramones, "I Wanna Be Sedated," "Sheena Is a Punk Rocker," "Rock 'n' Roll High School."

Talking Heads, "Psycho Killer," "Uh-Oh, Love Comes to Town," "Take Me to the River."

Tom Petty and the Heartbreakers, "Free Fallin'," "Mary Jane's Last Dance," "Breakdown," "American Girl."

2003

AC/DC, "You Shook Me All Night Long," "Back in Black," "Highway to Hell," "Hells Bells."

Elvis Costello & the Attractions, Alison," ""(The Angels Wanna Wear My) Red Shoes," "Watching the Detectives."

Righteous Brothers, "Unchained Melody," "(You're My) Soul and Inspiration," "You've Lost That Lovin' Feelin'."

The Clash, "London's Burning," "White Riot," "Safe European Home," "Stay Free."

The Police, "Every Breath You Take," "Roxanne," "Message in a Bottle."

2004

Bob Seger, "Heavy Music," "Ramblin' Gamblin' Man," "Night Moves."

George Harrison, "My Sweet Lord," "Crackerbox Palace," "Give Me Love (Give Me Peace On Earth)," "All Those Years Ago."

Jackson Browne, "Somebody's Baby," "Boulevard," "Shadow Dream Song."

Prince, "Let's Go Crazy," "When Doves Cry," "1999," "Purple Rain."

The Dells, "Oh, What a Night," "Stay in My Corner."

Traffic, "I'm a Man," "Somebody Help Me," "Gimme Some Lovin'."

ZZ Top, "Francene," "Cheap Sunglasses," "Legs."

2005

Buddy Guy, "Stone Crazy," "When My Left Eye Jumps."

Percy Sledge, "Warm and Tender Love, "It Tears Me Up," "Take Time to Know Her."

The O'Jays, "Use Ta Be My Girl," "Back Stabbers," "Love Train."

The Pretenders, "Tattooed Love Boys," "Message of Love," "Back on the Chain Gang."

U2, "I Will Follow," "Sunday Bloody Sunday," "New Year's Day," "Pride (In the Name of Love," "With or Without You," "I Still Haven't Found What I'm Looking For."

2006

Black Sabbath, "Crazy Train," "Black Sabbath," "Iron Man," "War Pigs," "Solitude."

Blondie, "Heart of Glass," "Call Me," "The Tide Is High," "Rapture."

Lynyrd Skynyrd, "Sweet Home Alabama," "Simple Man," "Freebird."

Miles Davis, "All Blues," "He Loved Him Madly," "My Funny Valentine," "So What."

Sex Pistols, "Anarchy in the U.K.," "God Save the Queen," "Pretty Vacant."

2007

Grandmaster Flash and the Furious Five, "White Lines (Don't Don't Do It)," "New York, New York," "Beat Street Breakdown- Part 1."

Patti Smith, "Gloria," "Gone Again," "People Have the Power," "Birdland."

R.E.M., "Losing My Religion," "It's the End of the World As We Know It (And I Feel Fine)," "What's the Frequency, Kenneth?"

The Ronettes, "Be My Baby," "(The Best Part of) Breaking Up," "Walking in the Rain."

Van Halen, "Running With the Devil," "Jump," "Hot for Teacher."

2008

Leonard Cohen, "Bird on a Wire," "Famous Blue Raincoat," "Chelsea Hotel No. 2."

The Dave Clark Five, "Glad All Over," "Any Way You Want It," "Please Tell Me Why."

Madonna, "Like a Virgin," "Papa Don't Preach," "Holiday."

John Mellencamp, "Pink Houses," "Small Town," "Jack & Diane."

The Ventures, "Walk—Don't Run," "Hawaii Five-0."

2009

Jeff Beck, "I'm a Man," "Escape," "Plan B."

Little Anthony and the Imperials, "Tears on My Pillow," "Shimmy, Shimmy, Ko-Ko Bop," "Goin' Out of My Head."

Metallica, "Enter Sandman," "One," "The Unforgiven."

Run-D.M.C., "It's Tricky," "My Adidas," "Walk This Way."

Bobby Womack, "Harry Hippie," "If You Think You're Lonely Now," "I Wish He Didn't Trust Me So Much."

2010

ABBA, "Dancing Queen," "Take a Chance on Me," "Waterloo."

Jimmy Cliff, "You Can Get It if You Really Want," "The Harder They Come," "Many Rivers to Cross."

Genesis, "I Know What I Like(In Your Wardrobe)," "Invisible Touch," "Throwing it All Away."

The Hollies, "Stop Stop Stop," "I Can't Let Go," "On A Carousel," "Carrie-Anne."

The Stooges, "Search and Destroy," "1969," "No Fun," "I Wanna Be Your Dog."

2011

Alice Cooper, "School's Out," "I'm Eighteen," "Be My Lover."

Neil Diamond, "Cracklin' Rosie," "Sweet Caroline," "Hello Again," "America."

Dr. John, "Right Place, Wrong Time," "Such a Night," "Iko Iko."

Darlene Love, "He's a Rebel," "(Today I Met) The Boy I'm Gonna Marry," "Wait Til My Bobby Gets Home."

Tom Waits, "Time," "Downtown Train," "Tom Traubert's Blues," "16 Shells from a Thirty-Ought-Six."

Source: www.rockhall.com

Country Music Hall of Fame

Alabama, b. (Jeffrey Cook) Fort Payne, Ala., 1949. b. (Teddy Gentry) Fort Payne, Ala., 1952. b. (Mark Herndon) Springfield, Mass., 1955. b. (Randy Owen) Fort Payne, Ala., 1949. "Song of the South," "Mountain Music."

Arthur E. Satherley, b. Bristol, England, 1889; d. 1986. Producer, talent scout, salesman, "recording genius for Columbia Records."

Barbara Mandrell, b. Houston, Tex., 1948. "(If Loving You is Wrong) I Don't Want to Be Right," "I Was Country When Country Wasn't Cool," "Sleeping Single in a Double Bed."

Bill Anderson, b. Columbia, S. Carolina, 1937. "Mama Sang a Song," "Still."

Bill Carlisle, b. Wakefield, Ken., 1908; d. 2003. "Rainbow at Midnight," "Rattlesnake Daddy."

Bill Monroe, b. Rosine, Ken., 1911; d. 1996. "Uncle Pen, "Raw Hide."

Billy Sherrill, b. Phil Campbell, Ala., 1936. Record producer and arranger; architect of countrypolitan sound.

Bob Willis, b. Kosse, Tex., 1905; d. 1975. "Take Me Back to Tulsa," "San Antonio Rose."

Bobby Braddock, b. Lakeland, Fl., 1940. Songwriter ("D-I-V-O-R-C-E," "Golden Ring," "Texas Tornado," "Time Marches On.")

Brenda Lee, b. Atlanta, Ga., 1944. "I Want to be Wanted," "Fool."

Bryant, Boudleaux and Felice, b. (Boudleaux) Shellman, Ga., 1920; d. 1987. b. (Felice) Milwaukee, Wis., 1925; d. 2003. Husband-wife songwriting team, "Country Boy," "Hole in My Pocket."

Buck Owens, b. Sherman, Tex., 1929; d. 2006. "Act Naturally," "My Heart Skips a Beat."

Carl Smith, b. Maynardville, Tenn., 1927. "Let Old Mother Nature Have Her Way," "Are You Teasing Me."

Carter Family, b. (A.P.) Maces Spring, Va., 1891; d. 1960. b. (Sara Dougherty) Flat Woods, Va., 1989; d. 1979. b. (Maybelle Addington) Nicklesville, Va., 1909; d. 1978. "Keep on the Sunny Side," "Worried Man Blues."

Charley Pride, b. Sledge, Miss., 1938. "Is Anybody Goin' to San Antone," "Kiss an Angel Good Mornin'."

Charlie McCoy, b. Oak Hill, West Va., 1941. "Blue Christmas," "I'm So Lonesome I Could Cry."

Chet Atkins, b. Luttrell, Tenn., 1924; d. 2001. "Classical Gas," "Guitar Blues."

Cindy Walker, b. Mart, Tex., 1918. Composer, "Cherokee Maiden," "You Don't Know Me."

Cliffie Stone, b. Stockton, Calif., 1917; d. 1998. "Silver Stars, Purple Sage, Eyes of Blue," "Peepin' Through the Keyhole."

Connie B. Gay, b. Lizard Lick, N. Carolina, 1914; d. 1989. Media liaison, one of first to coin term 'country music.'

Conway Twitty, b. Friars Point, Miss., 1933; d. 1993. "It's Only Make Believe," "What Am I Living For."

DeFord Bailey, b. Smith County, Tenn., 1899; d. 1982. "Fox Chase," "Pan American Blues."

Delmore Brothers, b. (Alton) Elkmont, Ala., 1908; d. 1964. b. (Rabon) Elkmont, Ala., 1916; d. 1952. "Brown's Ferry Blues," "Gonna Lay Down My Old Guitar."

Dolly Parton, b. Locust Ridge, Tenn., "Jolene," "I Will Always Love You."

Don Gibson, b. Shelby, N. Carolina 1928; d. 2003. "(I'd Be) A Legend in My Time," "I Can't Stop Loving You."

Don Law, b. London, England, 1902; d. 1982. Head of Columbia Records' country music division through 1950s and 60s.

Don Williams, b. Floydada, Tex., 1939. "Tulsa Time," "I Wouldn't Want to Live if You Didn't Love Me."

Eddy Arnold, b. Henderson, Tenn., 1918. "Fade to Blue," "Somebody Like Me."

Elvis Presley, b. Tupelo, Miss., 1935; d. 1977. 'The King of Rock & Roll,' "Hound Dog," "Jailhouse Rock."

Emmylou Harris, b. Birmingham, Ala., 1947. "Beneath Still Waters," "To Know Him is to Love Him."

Ernest Tubb, b. near Crisp, Tex., 1914; d. 1984. "I'll Get Along Somehow," "Walking the Floor Over You."

Ernest V. "Pop" Stoneman, b. Monarat, Va., 1893; d. 1968. "The Titanic," "The Fatal Wedding," "Two Little Orphans."

E.W. Wendell, b. Akron, Ohio, 1927. Manager of the Grand Ole Opry, later president and CEO of companies that owned the Opry and Opryland.

Faron Young, b. Shreveport, La., 1932; d. 1996. "If You Ain't Lovin' (You Ain't Livin'," "Live Fast, Love Hard, Die Young."

Ferlin Husky, b. Cantwell, Mo., 1926; d. 2011. "A Dear John Letter," "Forgive Me John," "Little Tom."

Flatt, Scruggs, and the Foggy Mountain Boys, b. (Lester Raymond Flatt) Duncan's Chapel, Tenn.,

1914; d. 1979. b. (Earl Eugene Scruggs) Flint Hill, N. Carolina, 1924. "The Ballad of Jed Clampett," "Foggy Mountain Breakdown."

Floyd Cramer, b. Shreveport, La., 1933; d. 1997. Studio pianist, "Last Date."

Floyd Tillman, b. Ryan, Okl., 1914; d. 2003. Pioneering songwriter, "It Makes No Difference Now," "I Love You So Much It Hurts."

Frances Preston, b. Nashville, Tenn., 1934. Opened a Broadcast Music, Inc. regional office in Nashville.

Fred Rose, b. Evansville, Ind., 1989; d. 1954. Songwriter, producer, music publisher, and talent scout.

Gene Autry, b. Tioga, Tex., 1907; d. 1998. "Back in the Saddle Again," "Tumbling Tumbleweeds."

George D. Hay, b. Attica, Ind., 1895; d. 1968. Founder of radio station WSM's Grand Old Opry

George Jones, b. Saratoga, Tex., 1931. "White Lightning," "Why, Baby, Why."

George Morgan, b. Waverly, Tenn. 1924; d. 1975. "Candy Kisses," "Rainbow in My Heart."

George Strait, b. Poteet, Tex., 1952. "Love Without End, Amen," "Carrying Your Love With Me."

Glen Campbell, b. near Delight, Ark., 1936. Star of CBS series "The Glen Campbell Good-Time Hour," "Rhinestone Cowboy."

Grandpa Jones, b. Niagra, Ken., 1931; d. 1998. "Rattler," "Mountain Dew."

Grant Turner, Baird, Tex., 1912; d. 1991. Grand Ole Opry announcer/ disc jockey.

Hank Snow, b. Brooklyn, Nova Scotia, Canada 1914; d. 1999. "I'm Moving On," "Rhumba Boogie."

Hank Thompson, b. Waco, Tex., 1925. "Green Light," "Whoa Sailor."

Hank Williams, b. Mount Olive, Ala., 1923; d. 1953. "Long Gone Lonesome Blues," "Jambalaya," "Hey Good Lookin'."

Harlan Howard, b. Detroit, 1927; d. 2002. "I Fall to Pieces," "Blame It on Your Heart."

Harold Bradley, b. Nashville, Tenn., 1926. "Chattanoogie Shoe Shine Boy," Guitarist and bassist for many country hits.

Homer and Jethro, b. (Homer Haynes) Knoxville, Tenn., 1920; d. 1971. b. (Jethro Burns) Conasauga, Tenn., 1920; d. 1989. Musical comedy team, "(How Much Is) That Hound Dog in the Window."

Hubert Long, b. Poteet, Tex., 1923; d. 1972. Promoter and publisher.

Jack Stapp, b. Nashville, Tenn., 1912; d. 1980. Program director of Nashville radio station WSM; Founder of music publishing firm Tree Publishing Company.

Jean Shepard, b. Pauls Valley, Okl. 1933., "Satisfied Mind," "A Dear John Letter," "Forgive Me John."

Jimmie Davis, b. Beech Springs, La., 1899; d. 2000. "Nobody's Darling But Mine," "You Are My Sunshine."

Jim Denny, b. Buffalo Valley, Tenn., 1911; d. 1963. Manager of Grand Ole Opry Artists Service, promoter.

Jim Foglesong, b. Lundale, W. Virginia, 1922. Producer, label executive.

Jimmie Rodgers, b. Meridian, Miss. 1897; d. 1933. "Blue Yodel (T for Texas)," "Treasures Untold."

Jim Reeves, b. Panola County, Tex., 1923; d. 1964. "He'll Have to Go," "Four Walls."

Jimmy Dean, b. Olton, Tex., 1928; d. 2010. "Big Bad John," "The Cajun Queen," "I.O.U."

J.L. Frank, b. Limestone County, Ala., 1900; d. 1952. First major promoter and manager.

Johnny Bond, b. Enville, Ok., 1915; d. 1978. "Cimarron," "10 Little Bottles."

Johnny Cash, b. Kingsland, Ark., 1932; d. 2003. "Ring of Fire," "Walk the Line."

Jo Walker-Meador, b. Orlinda, Tenn., 1924. Executive Director of the Country Music Association from 1962-1991.

Ken Nelson, b. Caledonia, Minne., 1911. A&R man in charge of Capitol Record's country division.

Kitty Wells, b. Nashville, Tenn. 1919. "It Wasn't God Who Made Honky Tonk Angels," "Release Me."

Kris Kristofferson, b. Brownsville, Tex., 1936. Songwriter, "Me and Bobby McGee," "For the Good Times."

Lefty Frizzell, b. Corsicana, Tex., 1928; d. 1975. "I Love You a Thousand Ways," "If You've Got the Money I've Got the Time."

Little Jimmy Dickens, b. Bolt, W. Virginia, 1920; d. 1983. "Take an Old Cold Tater (And Wait)," "Country Boy."

Loretta Lynn, b. Butcher Holler, Ken., 1935. "Coal Miner's Daughter," "You Ain't Woman Enough."

Marty Robbins, b. near Glendale, Az., 1925; d. 1982. "El Paso," "A White Sport Coat (and a Pink Carnation)."

Mel Tillis, b. Tampa, Fl., 1932. "I Ain't Never," "Good Woman Blues," "Coca-Cola Cowboy."

Merle Haggard, b. Bakersfield, Calif., 1937. "Today I Started Loving You Again," "Workin' Man Blues."

Merle Travis, b. Rosewood, Kent., 1917; d. 1983. "So Round, So Firm, So Fully Packed," "Divorce Me C.O.D."

Minnie Pearl, b. Centerville, Tenn., 1912; d. 1996. "Giddyup Go-Answer," Grand Old Opry comedian.

Owen Bradley, b. Westmoreland, Tenn., 1915; d. 1998. "Night Train to Memphis," "Zeb's Mountain Boogie."

Patsy Cline, b. Winchester, Va., 1932; d. 1963. "Crazy," "Walkin' After Midnight."

Patsy Montana, b. Hope, Ark., 1908; d. 1996. "I Wanna Be a Cowboy's Sweetheart," "Swing Time Cowgirl."

Paul Cohen, b. 1908; d. 1970. Record Producer- Decca, Todd Records, Kapp Records, ABC Nashville.

Pee Wee King, b. Milwaukee, Wis., 1914; d. 2000. "Slow Poke," "Tennessee Waltz."

Porter Wagoner, b. Howell County, Mo., 1927. "A Satisfied Man," "Misery Loves Company."

Ralph Emery, b. McEwen, Tenn., 1933. Disc jockey and television host of *Pop! Goes the Country* and *Nashville Now.*

Ralph S. Peer, b. Kansas City, Mo., 1892; d. 1960. Early pioneer in country and popular recording, publishing and artist management.

Ray Price, b. Perryville, Tex., 1926. "Crazy Arms," "For the Good Times."

Reba McEntire, b. McAlester, Okl., 1966. "How Blue," "Somebody Should Leave," "Can't Even Get the Blues."

Red Foley, b. Blue Lick, Ken., 1910; d. 1968. "Old Shep," "Chattanoogie Shoe Shine Boy."

Rod Brasfield, b. Smithville, Miss., 1910; d. 1958. Grand Ole Opry comedian

Roger Miller, b. Fort Worth, Tex., 1936; d. 1992. "Dang Me," "King of the Road."

Roy Acuff, b. Maynardville, Tenn., 1903; d. 1992. "Back in the Country," "Old Time Sunshine Song."

Roy Clark, b. Meherrin, Va., 1933. Country musician and host of *Hee Haw*; helped popularize the genre.

Roy Horton, b. near Broad Top, Penn., 1914; d. 2003. "Mockin' Bird Hill," "Sugarfoot Rag."

Roy Rogers, b. Cincinnati, Ohio, 1911; d. 1998. (with The Pioneer Trio) "Cool Water," "Tumbling Tumbleweeds."

Sam Phillips, b. Florence, Ala., 1923; d. 2003. Founder of Sun Records (Elvis Presley, Johnny Cash, B.B. King, Roy Orbison, Jerry Lee Lewis.)

Sonny James, b. Hackleburg, Ala. 1929. "Need You," "Here Comes Honey Again."

Sons of the Pioneers, b. (Roy Rogers) Cincinnati, Ohio, 1911; d. 1998. b. (Bob Nolan) New Brunswick, Canada, 1908; d. 1980. b. (Lloyd Wilson Perryman) Ruth, Ark., 1917; d. 1977. b. (Vernon Tim Spencer), Webb City, Mo., 1908; d. 1974. b. (Thomas Hubert Farr) Llano, Tex., 1903; d. 1980. b. (Karl Marx Farr) Rochelle Tex., 1909; d. 1961. "Cool Water," "Blue Prairie," "A Cowboy Has to Sing."

Stephen H. Sholes, b. Washington, D.C., 1911; d. 1968. Record executive who signed Elvis Presley.

Tammy Wynette, b. Itawamba County, Miss., 1942; d. 1998. "I Don't Wanna Play House," "D-I-V-O-R-C-E."

Tennessee Ernie Ford, b. Bristol, Tenn., 1919; d. 1990. "Sixteen Tons," "What a Friend We Have in Jesus."

Tex Ritter, b. Panola County, Tex. 1905; d. 1974. "I Dreamed of Hillbilly Heaven," "I'm Wastin' My Tears on You."

The Duke of Paducah, b. DeSoto, Miss., 1901; d. 1986. Country comedian.

The Everly Brothers, b. (Isaac Donald) Brownie, Ken., 1937. b. (Philip) Chicago, Ill., 1939. "Wake Up, Little Susie," "All I Have to Do Is Dream."

The Jordanaires, 13 members, b. 1923-1943. Known for background harmonies and gospel tunes.

The Louvin Brothers, b. (Ira Lonnie) Section, Ala., 1924; d. 1965. b. (Charlie Elzer) Section, Ala., 1927. "When I Stop Dreaming," "Hoping That You're Hoping."

The Statler Brothers, b. (Harold Reid) Augusta County, Va., 1939. b. (Phil Balsley) Staunton, Va., 1939. b. (Lew DeWitt) Roanoke, Va., 1938; d. 1990. b. (Don Reid) Staunton Va., 1945. b. (Jimmy Fortune) Williamsburg, Va. 1955. "Flowers on the Wall," "Bed of Roses."

Tom T. Hall, b. Olive Hill, Ken., 1936. Songwriter and singer "Harper Valley PTA," "I Love," "A Week in a Country Jail."

Uncle Dave Macon, b. Smart Station, Tenn., 1870; d. 1952. First star of the Grand Ole Opry, "Keep My Skillet Good and Greasy," "Hill Billie Blues."

Vernon Dalhart, b. Jefferson, Tex., 1883; d. 1948. "The Prisoner's Song," "Farm Relief Song."

Vince Gill, b. Norman, Okl., 1957. "When I Call Your Name," " Go Rest High on That Mountain," "Look at Us."

Waylon Jennings, b. Littlefield, Tex., 1937; d. 2002. "The Chokin' Kind," "Only Daddy That'll Walk the Line."

Webb Pierce, b. West Monroe, La., 1921; d. 1991. "Wondering," "That Heart Belongs to Me."

Wesley Rose, b. Chicago, 1918; d. 1990. Music publishing executive.

Willie Nelson, b. Abbott, Tex., 1933. "Good Hearted Woman," "Blue Eyes Crying in the Rain."

Source: www.countrymusichalloffame.com

World Music

To Western audiences, the term *world music* refers to music that doesn't fall into the North American and Western European pop tradition. World music is indigenous music from a variety of countries, often combined with Western pop sensibilities.

African Music There is no single "African" musical style; as expected of a continent covering more than 50 independent nations, African music varies, evolving out of a multiplicity of cultures and histories. Most African music incorporates complex rhythms, exotic instruments, and call and response singing, as exemplified by the *mbube*, an a cappella choral music of the South African Zulus.

Caribbean Music The Caribbean is primarily known for two indigenous musical forms, *reggae* and *calypso*. Reggae comes from Jamaica, where it evolved from the rhythmic *ska* style that was the island's interpretation of early R&B. Reggae, as interpreted by Bob Marley (1945–81) and other local musicians, has a slower beat with a heavier emphasis on the upbeat. Calypso comes from the island of Trinidad, and incorporates a traditional rhythm section with steel drums and horns. It is typically built around a syncopated bass guitar line and an infectious uptempo dance beat.

Celtic Music Celtic music encompasses the folk music of Ireland and Scotland—both traditional and contemporary. Instrumentation typically includes stringed instruments, fiddles, and pipes; contemporary Celtic music often adds New Age spirituality and production.

Central and Eastern European Music Central European music includes traditional Greek music, as well as gypsy music characterized by exotic rhythms and folk dances. Eastern European music is also home to gypsy music, as well as folk dances such as *polka* and the *mazurka*. The music of Eastern European Jews, known as *klezmer*, has enjoyed a revival since the mid-1970's.

Indian Music Indian music is rhythmically and harmonically complex, compared with popular Western music. Classical Indian compositions are called *ragas*, and are typically played on tabla, sitar, and other native instruments.

Latin Music Latin music describes a number of diverse styles from different regions and countries in Latin America. The best known of these styles include *bossa nova*, a laid-back jazz-influenced dance music; *mambo*, an Afro-Cuban dance with a characteristic quadruple meter rhythmic pattern; *mariachi*, a traditional Mexican music built around an ensemble of trumpets, violins, guitar, and bass guitar; *rumba*, an Afro-Cuban dance in duple or quadruple time; *salsa*, a lively Brazilian dance music; *samba*, a dance built around a pulsating bass drum rhythm; and *Tejano*, a form of contemporary Latin pop.

Middle Eastern Music Middle Eastern music shows the influence of Arabic culture and the Muslim religion. Traditional music from this area is overwhelmingly vocal, often without any instrumental accompaniment. More popular forms include Turkish *Sufi* and Algerian *rai* music, both representative of the high-energy, melismatic fervor of their Muslim heritage.

Worldbeat The term *worldbeat* refers not to a style of music, but rather to the fusion of musical styles in a multicultural approach designed to expose ethnic music to a world audience. This often takes the form of traditional folk music set to a Western dance beat, or Western melodies set to native rhythms. Western proponents include Paul Simon (*Graceland*), Peter Gabriel, and David Byrne.

Selected World Music Styles

bolero Spanish dance in triple time.

bossa nova (1) Brazilian dance, similar to the samba. (2) Brazilian jazz.

fandango lively Spanish dance, believed to be of South American origin, in triple or compound duple time.

gagaku traditional court music of Japan.

gamelan musical ensemble of Java or Bali, comprised of gongs, chimes, drums, and other instruments.

habanera Cuban dance in moderate duple meter.

jarabe traditional Mexican dance form, with multiple sections in contrasting meters and tempos.

jota spanish dance song in a quick triple meter, typically with guitar and castanet accompaniment.

jig vigorous dance in compound meter, developed in Britain and Ireland.

mazurka Polish folk dance in triple meter.

mbube a cappella choral singing style of the South African Zulus, featuring call-and-response patterns and close-knit harmonies.

polka lively Bohemian dance.

polonaise national Polish dance, in triple time and of moderate tempo.

raga Indian melodic pattern. There are various raga "systems" that describe different series of pitches, patterns, and ornamentation.

reel dance in rapid quadruple time for two or more couples; popular in Scotland, Ireland, and parts of England.

tango Argentinean dance at a slow walking pace in duple time.

tarantella Neapolitan dance in 6/8 time.

Musical Instruments

String Family

The string family of instruments consists of those that are primarily played with a bow, and those that are primarily plucked with fingers or a pick. Sound is created by the vibration of thin strings of wire or gut, typically amplified by a hollow resonating chamber within the body of the instrument.

Bowed   These instruments can be either bowed or plucked, although bowing is more typical of orchestral use. Primary bowed instruments include: Violin, Viola, Cello, Double bass.

Plucked   These instruments are either plucked one string at a time, or strummed to sound multiple strings simultaneously. Primary plucked instruments include: Harp, Lute, Guitar, Banjo, Mandolin, Ukulele.

Brass Family

The brass family consists of wind instruments made of brass or other similar metals. (It does not include instruments formerly made of wood but now sometimes made of metal, such as the flute, or metal instruments with reed mouthpieces, such as the saxophone.) All brass instruments include a cup- or funnel-shaped mouthpiece, which is pressed against the player's lips and then vibrates to produce a tone. The tone is amplified through a long metal tubing, intricately coiled around itself, which culminates in a flared bell. Different pitches are produced by varying the vibration of the lips and by pressing (in most instruments) a series of valves. The notable exception is the trombone, which uses a slide to change the length of the brass tubing, changing the pitch accordingly. Primary brass instruments include: Trumpet, Piccolo trumpet, Flugelhorn, Bugle, Trombone, French horn, Baritone horn, Tuba.

Woodwind Family

The woodwind family of instruments consists of wind instruments originally and usually made of wood, either blown directly by mouth or by means of a thin wooden reed. Many woodwind instruments are available in different sizes to produce differing pitch ranges; for example, the clarinet family consists of alto, bass, and contrabass instruments.

Single Reed   Single reed instruments incorporate a mouthpiece with a wide and flat single reed. Sound is generated by blowing against the reed, causing it to vibrate. Primary single-reed instruments include: Clarinet (alto, bass, contrabass), Saxophone (soprano, alto, tenor, baritone, bass, contrabass).

Double Reed   Double-reed instruments incorporate a mouthpiece with two thin and narrow reeds. Sound is reproduced by blowing air between the two reeds, causing them to vibrate against each other. Primary double-reed instruments include: Oboe, Bassoon, Contrabassoon, English horn.

Direct Blown   Direct-blown woodwind instruments reproduce sound when air is blown across (flute, piccolo) or into (recorder) a small round mouth-hole at one end of the instrument. Different pitches are reproduced by opening and closing a series of finger holes aligned along the length of the instrument. Primary direct-blown woodwind instruments include: Flute, Piccolo, Recorder.

Percussion Family

Percussion instruments are those that are played (generally) by striking a resonating surface with the hand, a stick or mallet, or a pedal. Other percussion instruments, such as the tambourine and maracas, are played by shaking or rattling the instrument.

There are two general types of percussion instruments: those that generate a definite pitch, and those that do not.

Definite-Pitched   Percussion instruments that reproduce definite pitches include: Glockenspiel, Xylophone, Marimba, Vibraphone, Chimes (tubular bells), Timpani.

Indefinite-Pitched   Percussion instruments that do not generate a definite pitch include: Drum, Bongo, Conga, Timbale, Cymbal, Triangle, Tambourine, Maracas.

Keyboard Instruments

Keyboard instruments are those in which specific pitches are determined by depressing one of a number of keys, typically presented in a continuous sequential arrangement. The actual sound of the keyboard instrument is generated by a related apparatus; for example, the piano generates sound by hitting a string with a small mallet, whereas the organ generates sound by blowing air through a reed or large pipe.

Some experts classify keyboard instruments as part of the string family, even though they are played percussively. Primary keyboard instruments include: Piano (pianoforte), Harpsichord, Clavier, Organ.

Electronic Instruments

The late 20th century saw the invention of a new class of instruments called electrophones. These instruments generate sound via any number of nonphysical methods, such as oscillation, electromagnetic, or electrostatic means. (The family of electronic instruments does not include those that simply amplify acoustically generated sounds electronically, such as the electric guitar or electric piano.) Primary electronic instruments include: Synthesizer, Sequencer.

Glossary of Musical Terms

a cappella vocal music without instrumental accompaniment.

accent a note played louder or with more emphasis than regular notes.

accompaniment a background performance, typically instrumental, subservient to the main performer.

air (1) a melody. (2) melodious composition.

alto that female voice below the soprano, in much choral music the lowest primary female voice.

antiphonal a singing style characterized by two parts of a choir singing alternately, one answering another.

aria a lengthy and involved solo vocal piece which is an integral part of the operatic form.

atonal having no tonal center, and no underlying key. In pure atonal music, the notes of the chromatic scale are used impartially and independently, with no home degree or tonic.

ballad (1) A song to be danced to. (2) Self-contained narrative song, such as Schubert's *Erlkönig*.

ballade a type of piano miniature, typically dramatic or heroic in nature.

ballata a poetic form of secular song in 14th and early 15th century Italy.

band a body of instrumental players. Sometimes defined by the primary instrumental grouping or function, as in "brass band" or "dance band."

baritone a male voice category between bass and tenor voices; not present in all choral music. Sometimes called bass-baritone.

bass (1) the lowest male voice. (2) the lowest pitch of a chord (not necessarily the root).

basso low male bass voice.

basso continuo continuous bass; a bass line in music of the 17th and 18th centuries, played by the organist.

beat any pulsing unit of musical time.

bel canto literally, "beautiful singing," a type of Italian opera with complex and ornate melodies.

blend (1) the combination of voices in group singing so that individual performers are indistinguishable. (2) Smooth transitions between the registers of the singing voice.

blue note (1) the flatted third, fifth, or seventh tone of the scale, common in blues and jazz. (2) a slight drop of pitch on the third, fifth, or seventh tones; also known as bent pitch.

bourrée lively French dance in duple meter, popular in the Baroque period.

break in jazz, a short improvised solo without accompaniment that "breaks" an ensemble passage or introduces an extended solo.

bridge a short section that links two important sections of a piece of music.

cadenza (1) in opera, a flourish of difficult, fast, high notes sung at the end of an aria, designed to demonstrate the vocal ability of the singer. (2) a virtuosic unaccompanied improvisation, typically free of key or meter.

call and response (1) melodic technique where a phrase is stated in the first part of the melody, and then answered in the second part. (2) performance style with a singing leader who is imitated by a chorus of followers; also called responsorial singing, and commonly heard in spiritual or gospel music.

canon strictest form of contrapuntal imitation. Simple forms of choral canon include the catch and the round.

strict canon canon in which the intervals of the imitating voice are exactly the same as the voice being imitated.

choir a group of singers who perform together, usually in parts, with several singers on each part; often associated with church singing.

chorale a singing group.

chord progression a series of chords over a number of measures.

chorus (1) fairly large group of singers who perform together, usually with several on each part. (2) a choral movement of a large-scale work. (3) in jazz, a single statement of the melodic-harmonic pattern. (4) in popular music, the part of the song (typically following the verse) that recurs at intervals; also known as the B section of a song.

chromatic pitches outside the underlying key or scale. The opposite of diatonic.

chromaticism (1) the use of chromatic intervals, chords, and scales. (2) a style of composing that employs chromatic harmony.

coloratura soprano the highest, and perhaps most "agile" female voice. Comfortable in the highest register and able to perform rapid, dazzling passages.

contrapuntal see *counterpoint*.

counterpoint two or more simultaneous, independent lines or voices in a piece of music. The art of counterpoint developed in the ninth century, and reached its zenith in the late 16th and early 17th centuries; some music theorists apply strict rules to the creation of contrapuntal lines.

country blues early guitar-driven blues form, performed primarily on acoustic instruments, complete with elaborate fingerpicking and slide playing. Notable country blues musicians include Lonnie Johnson, Josh White, and Scrapper Blackwell.

cover a performance or recording that remakes a previously recorded song.

crossover a recording or artist that appeals primarily to one audience but also becomes popular with another.

dissonance a combination of tones that sounds discordant and unstable, in need of resolution to a more pleasing and stable harmony. The opposite of consonance.

double indicates that a second voice or instrument is to duplicate a particular line of music, either in unison or an octave above or below.

duet a musical composition for two performers.

electronic music music that employs computers, synthesizers, and other electronic equipment to generate, modify, and combine all manner of sounds.

ensemble literally, "together;" a group of performers singing or playing together at the same time.

entr'acte a musical composition played between acts or scenes of an opera.

exposition (1) in the sonata form, the first section of the composition, in which the principal themes are first presented. (2) in a fugue, the first statement of the subject by all the voices in turn.

falsetto vocal technique whereby men can sing above their normal range, producing a lighter, higher sound.

finale the last song of an act, or the last movement of a multiple-movement work.

folk music (1) traditional songs, generally local or regional in origin. (2) traditional American music, typically consisting of vocals accompanied by guitars and other acoustic instruments.

form the structure or shape of a musical work, based on repetition, contrast, and variation; the organizing principle in music.

frequency a scientific measurement of how fast molecules of air are vibrating; the faster the vibrations, the higher the pitch. Frequency is measured in vibrations per second, or Hertz (Hz).

funk see *groove*.

gigue (1) English Baroque dance type in lively compound meter. (2) A standard movement of the Baroque suite.

gospel 20th century sacred music style associated with the Protestant African-American church.

groove (1) a specific beat. (2) indicating that a song was played at just the right tempo and feel, as in "in the groove." (3) a dance-oriented type of jazz, derived from soul jazz in the late 1970s, with a deep bass line and blues-oriented chord progressions.

ground bass a repeating bass line, typically a short motif over which other parts play changing harmonies.

harmonic interval two notes sounded simultaneously.

harmonization the choice of chords to accompany a melodic line.

harmony (1) the sound of tones in combination. (2) accompanying parts behind the main melody.

head register a vocal adjustment producing light, flute-like tones, conducive to soft and high singing. Also called head tone or head voice.

homophony music composed of melody and accompanying harmony, as distinct from polyphony or monophony.

hook a piece of melody designed to deliberately grab the attention of the listener.

hymn song in praise of God.

improvisation spontaneous creation of a musical composition while it is being performed; a musical performance without a written score.

intonation the act of singing or playing in tune. Intonation can be "good" (in tune) or "bad" (out of tune).

introduction the beginning of a piece of music.

isorhythmic the art of repeating a rhythmic idea over and over, typically in multiple voices.

libretto the text of an opera or oratorio. (Literally, "little book.")

lieder a German art song, based on poetry.

madrigal comedy short drama set to music, as a series of secular vocal pieces.

march a musical style incorporating characteristics of military music, including strongly accented duple meter in simple, repetitive rhythmic patterns.

melisma a group of notes sung to a single syllable, typically including both a primary note and ornamentation.

melodic improvisation the art of creating a continuous new melodic line using a song's existing chords—not just playing chord- or scale-based patterns.

melody the combination of tone and rhythm in a logical sequence.

mezzo-soprano a soprano voice with more power in the lower range.

modulation a change of key. For example, when a piece of music changes from the key of C to the key of G midway through, that piece of music has modulated.

motif a brief melodic or rhythmic idea within a piece of music. Sometimes called a figure or motive.

movement self-contained part within a larger musical work.

new age music musical style characterized by soothing timbres and repetitive forms. First popular in the 1980's.

nocturne a type of piano miniature, of romantic character.

opera buffa a type of comic opera popular in the 18th century.

opera seria the serious operatic form that dominated the 17th and 18th centuries.

operetta literally, a "little opera." A type of light opera or musical comedy.

opus (1) a single work or composition. (2) when followed by a number, e.g. Opus 12, used for the numbering of a composer's works.

ornamentation notes that embellish and decorate a melody.

passepied french Baroque court dance; a faster version of the minuet.

pedal point a note sustained below changing harmonies.

phrase within a piece of music, a segment that is unified by rhythms, melodies, or harmonies and that comes to some sort of closure; typically composed in groups of 2, 4, 8, 16, or 32 measures.

pitch the highness or lowness of a tone.

placement a technique of singing guided by sensations of vibrations in the face, behind the teeth, in the nose, etc.; i.e., "forward placement".

portamento a smooth movement from one note to the next.

quarter tone an interval half the distance of a Western half-step; difficult to notate, and impossible to play on a traditional keyboard instrument.

range the distance between the lowest and highest tones of a melody, instrument, or voice. This span is typically described as narrow, medium, or wide.

register (1) the specific area in the range of a voice or an instrument. (2) a series of tones that are produced by similar vocal fold vibration and placement, resulting in similar tone quality (i.e., chest register or head register).

repetition a technique that involves repeating all or part of a motif; typically used in conjunction with variation.

rhapsody a composition, in a single continuous movement, based on popular, national, or folk melodies.

riff a short melodic or rhythmic pattern.

rondeau Medieval and Renaissance fixed poetic form; type of chanson.

rondo a type of instrumental composition in which one section intermittently recurs; the usual form for the last movement of a concerto or sontata.

sacred music religious or spiritual music, for church or devotional use. Also called non-secular music.

score (1) the written depiction of all the individual parts played by each of the instruments in an ensemble. (2) to orchestrate a composition.

shuffle a rhythmic feel based on triplets or a dotted eighth note/sixteenth note pattern.

solo a vocal or instrumental piece or passage performed by one performer, with or without accompaniment.

song short vocal composition.

soprano the highest female voice.

spiritual American folk-hymn, typically of the African-American church tradition.

stanza see *verse.*

string band musical style from the early 1900's that precurses modern bluegrass and country music, characterized by guitars, mandolins, fiddles, and other stringed instruments.

style a characteristic manner of presentation of musical elements such as melody, harmony, rhythm, or dynamics.

subject a motif, phrase, or melody that is a basic element in a musical composition.

syncopation an accent on an unexpected beat, or the lack of an accent on an expected beat.

synthesizer electronic instrument, typically activated via a keyboard, that reproduces a wide variety of sounds via the use of sound generators and modifiers.

tenor the highest male voice.

theme a recurring melodic or rhythmic pattern.

theme and variations musical technique involving the statement of a theme and then the varying of that theme, either in pitch or rhythm. See *variation.*

timbre tone quality or tone color. (Pronounced "tambor.")

tonality the organization of musical notes around a tonic, or home pitch, based on a major or minor scale or mode.

tune (1) melody (2) as a verb, to establish correct intonation of an instrument.

unison (1) two notes of the same pitch. (2) voices or instruments all singing or playing the same pitch.

valve mechanism that alters the pitch of a brass instrument by opening or closing the metal tube, thus increasing or decreasing the length of the tube.

variation a technique in which some aspects of the music are altered but the original is still recognizable. Typically used in conjunction with repetition. See also *theme and variations.*

verismo an opera of the late Romantic period in which violent or sordid events are realistically portrayed in contemporary settings.

verse (1) a short division of a musical composition. (2) in popular music, the first or A section of a song, preceding the chorus.

virtuoso performer of extraordinary technical ability.

vocalize to exercise the voice.

voice melodic or harmonic line.

Music Notation

Notation

enharmonic different notations of the same pitch. For example, F♯ and G♭ are enharmonic notes.

half step the smallest distance between notes in the Western chromatic scale.

interval the distance between two pitches. Typically measured in half-step or whole steps, or expressed numerically (second, third, fourth, etc.).

ledger lines short lines above or below a musical staff, indicating notes too high or low to appear on the staff itself.

notation the art of writing musical notes on paper.

semitone the interval of a half-step.

staff an assemblage of horizontal lines and spaces that represent different pitches. Also called a stave.

whole step an interval equal to two half steps.

Tempo

backbeat in 4/4 time, beats two and four; in popular music, the backbeat is typically played by the drummer on the snare drum.

bar line vertical line placed on the staff between measures.

bar see *measure*.

coda (1) ending section of a piece of music. (2) a specific music symbol indicating the ending section of a piece of music.

common time the 4/4 time signature. Also known as quadruple meter.

compound time or compound meter time signature in which each beat in a measure consists of a dotted note or its equivalent. For example, 9/8 time can be treated as compound time, by playing three dotted eighth-note beats per measure.

downbeat the major beats in a measure; in 4/4 time, the downbeats are 1, 2, 3, and 4.

measure a group of beats, indicated by the placement of bar lines on the staff.

meter the organization of beats and their divisions.

odd time any non-4/4 time signature, such as 3/4, 5/4, or 9/8.

simple time meter in which each beat has a simple note value. For example, 3/4 and 4/4 are both simple time signatures. Compare to compound time, where each beat has the value of a dotted note.

staccato an articulation that indicates a note is to be played short and clipped.

tie a curved line over or under two or more notes that "ties" the two notes together into one.

time fundamental rhythmical patterns of music.

triple meter metrical pattern with three beats to a measure.

triple time any time signature with three beats per measure. For example, both 3/8 and 3/4 are triple time.

triplet a group of three notes performed in the space of two.

upbeat (1) the last beat of a measure as conducted; a weak beat which anticipates the downbeat (the first beat of the next measure). (2) the eighth-note "and" after the downbeat.

Scales

chromatic scale a scale containing 12 equal divisions of the octave—all the white keys and black keys within an octave.

diatonic notes or chords that are contained in the underlying key or scale. For example, in the key of C Major, the diatonic notes are C, D, E, F, G, A, and B; all other notes are chromatic.

major scale the most common scale, consisting of the following intervals: whole-whole-half-whole-whole-whole-half.

minor scale one of three scales, each with a flatted third of the scale. The natural minor scale is identical to the Aeolian mode. The harmonic minor scale is the same as the natural minor scale, but with a raised seventh. The melodic minor scale used in jazz and popular music is the same as the harmonic minor scale, but with a raised sixth as well; in classical music, this scale contains the raised sixth and seventh when ascending, but when descending lowers the sixth and seventh (making it identical to the natural minor scale).

relative keys keys that share the same key signature, but not the same root. For example, A minor and C Major are relative keys.

scale a sequence of related pitches, arranged in ascending or descending order.

tonic (1) the primary note in a scale or key; the "Do" in Solfeggio. (2) The chord built on a scale's first degree.

whole tone scale a seven-note scale (including the octave) with each degree a whole step part. For example, the C whole tone scale includes the notes C-D-E-F♯-G♯-A♯-C.

Intervals

interval the distance between two pitches. Typically measured in half-step or whole steps, or expressed numerically (second, third, fourth, etc.).

major interval in the major scale, the distances between the tonic and the second, third, sixth, and seventh scale degrees. For example, in the C Major scale, the distance between C and E is a major third interval.

minor interval any major interval lowered by a half step. For example, a minor third interval from the note C is the note E♭.

Chords

chord three or more notes played simultaneously.

major chord a chord with a major third (1-3-5). For example, the C Major chord contains the notes C-E-G.

minor chord a chord with a minor third (1-♭3-5). For example, the C minor chord contains the notes C-E♭-G.

Modes

Aeolian mode a mode starting on the sixth degree of the corresponding major scale, equivalent to the natural minor scale.

Dorian mode a mode starting on the second degree of the corresponding major scale.

Ionian mode a mode starting on the first degree of the corresponding major scale, equivalent to the major scale.

Locrian mode a mode starting on the seventh degree of the corresponding major scale.

Lydian mode a mode starting on the fourth degree of the corresponding major scale.

Mixolydian mode a mode starting on the fifth degree of the corresponding major scale. Also known as the dominant scale.

mode a set of scales, based on centuries-old church music, that preceded today's major and minor scales. The modes are based on and named for the note of the major scale on which they start and stop; these include the Dorian, Phrygian, Lydian, Mixolydian, Ionian, Locrian, and Aeolian modes.

Phrygian mode a mode starting on the third degree of the corresponding major scale.

Embellishments

embellishment melodic decoration, either improvised or indicated through ornamentation signs in the music.

trill melodic ornament consisting of the rapid alternation between one tone and the next above it.

turn a five-note melodic ornament, starting on the original note, then up one scale step, back down to the original note, down one scale step, and then up to the original note again.

Expression

a tempo return to the previous tempo after some sort of deviation; literally, "in time."

accelerando gradually speed up. (Abbreviated as accel.)

adagio (1) tempo marking for moderately slow. (2) A slow movement in a larger work of music.

adante tempo marking for a moderate, walking pace.

agitato agitated or restless.

allegro (1) tempo marking for a fast, cheerful tempo. (2) A fast movement in a larger work of music.

andante slow.

cantabile singable or singingly, typically with the melody smoothly articulated. In Italian, "in a singing style."

con amore with love; tenderly.

con fuoco with fire.

con passione with passion.

crescendo gradually louder.

da capo an indication to return to the beginning of a piece. Abbreviated D.C. See *D.C. al Coda* and *D.C. al Fine*.

decrescendo gradually softer.

doice sweetly.

dolente sad; weeping.

doppio movimento play twice as fast.

espressivo expressively.

fin end.

forte loud. (Abbreviated as f.)

fortissimo very loud. (Abbreviated as ff.)

gioioso joyous.

grave tempo marking for a very slow or solemn pace.

lamentoso like a lament.

largo tempo marking for slow and dignified.

legato notes sung or played smoothly together, for the full rhythmic value of each note. (From the Italian, meaning "bound" or "tied.")

lento tempo marking for slow.

maestoso majestic.

meno less.

mesto sad.

mezza voce Italian for "medium voice," an indication to lower the singing volume.

mezzo forte medium loud. (Abbreviated as mf.)

mezzo piano medium soft. (Abbreviated as mp.)

misterioso mysteriously.

moderato tempo marking for a moderate pace.

molto very. For example, allegro molto indicates that a piece is to be played very quickly.

non troppo not too much.

obbligato indispensable; an instrumental or vocal part where the part is obligatory, and often special or unusual in effect.

pianissimo very soft. (Abbreviated as pp.)

piano (1) soft. (Abbreviated as p.)

pizzicato notes on a string instrument that are plucked rather than bowed.

poco a little; used to modify tempo and other markings. For example, poco lento means "a little slow."

prestissimo tempo marking for an extremely fast tempo, faster than presto.

presto tempo marking for a very fast tempo.

rallentando gradually slow down. (Abbreviated as rall.)

ritardando gradually slow down. (Abbreviated as rit. or ritard.)

ritenuto hold back the tempo. (Abbreviated as rit. or riten.)

rubato "borrowed time," common in Romantic music, where the performer either hesitates or rushes through certain notes, imparting flexibility to the written note values.

sforzando a sudden stress or accent on a single note or chord.

sostenuto sustained singing; long, rather slow phrases that the singer is capable of singing on one breath. Considered one of the hallmarks of bel canto singing.

sotto voce in a soft voice.

subito suddenly.

tempo a piacere performer designates tempo; "please yourself" as to speed.

tempo comodo play at a convenient or moderate speed.

tempo di ballo play at a dance tempo.

tempo di gavotte at gavotte speed.

tempo giusto in exact time; play at the tempo the music demands.

tempo minore moderate speed.

tempo ordinario play in ordinary time; moderate speed.

tempo primo return to the tempo designated at the beginning of a piece. In German, tempo wie vorher.

tempo rubato see *rubato*.

tempo the rate of speed at which beats are played in a song. For example, a tempo of presto is very fast; a tempo of largo is slow. Sometimes expressed in precise beats per minute. Plural is tempi.

tenendo sustaining.

tenero tender.

tutti "all," the opposite of solo.

vivace tempo marking for a lively tempo.

FILM

History of Film

As popular entertainment, the origins of cinema lie in the magic lantern and shadow puppet shows that were around as early as the 17th century. Scientifically, its history begins with Joseph Plateau's (1801–83) theories of the persistence of vision (1829) and the stroboscopic effect (1836), which he demonstrated with a device he called a Phenakistoscope, an illustrated wheel that when spun gave the illusion of motion. A similar device, the Zoetrope ("Wheel of Life") was invented by William George Horner (1786–1837) in 1834. By the 1870's Eadweard Muybridge (1830–1904) was using banks of as many as 40 still cameras to photograph motion studies of animals. In 1880 he exhibited some of these photographic series with a sort of projecting Phenakistoscope that he called a Zoopraxiscope.

The Dawn of Film (1888–1908)

Although several inventors from America, Britain, France, and Germany were working on the idea simultaneously, credit for the invention of the motion picture camera is most often given to the Thomas Edison laboratories. By 1889, Edison's assistant, William Kennedy Laurie Dickson (1860–1937), had synthesized Edison's ideas into a workable motion picture camera, which he called a Kinetograph. He followed the Kinetograph with a device for viewing his short films called the Kinetoscope, a peep-show box with a scope on top. One person at a time looked into the scope to watch the films, which were looped through the machine in 50-foot strips. Powered by a huge electric motor, the kinetograph was large, bulky, and therefore stationary. Many celebrities such as boxer "Gentleman" Jim Corbett and vaudeville performer Annabella the Serpentine Dancer made the journey to the Edison labs in New Jersey to be photographed in a 30-second film.

The Lumières and Film Projection Edison did not believe motion pictures would grow beyond a parlor amusement, so he did not bother to pay the extra $150 for an international patent to prevent European inventors from developing their own versions of the Kinetograph or Kinetoscope. Two such entrepreneurs were the Lumière brothers, Auguste (1862–1954) and Louis (1864–1948), from Lyons, France, who invented their own version of the motion picture camera around 1895. Instead of being powered by electricity, the Lumières' Cinématographe was hand-cranked and weighed only 16 pounds. It was not only a camera; it was also a printer and a projector all in one machine. On December 28, 1895, they held the first paid public showing of projected motion pictures in the Salon Indien in the basement of the Grand Café in Paris. Projection quickly became the format of choice for commercial showings of motion pictures around the world; the obvious advantage was that many viewers could watch the same films at the same time.

The portability of the Cinématographe broadened the content of the Lumière films. They recorded the happenings of life—workers at their jobs, parades in the park, children at play—using simple titles that telegraphed the subject of their 30-second films, such as *Workers Leaving the Lumière Factory*, *Baby's Lunch*, or *Train Arriving at a Station*.

Storytelling on Film Like Dickson, the Lumières simply recorded whatever unfolded in front of the camera, without attempting to tell a story. That step was taken by Georges Méliès (1861–1938), who was already in show business when he began making motion pictures in 1896 in a suburb of Paris. He owned the Théatre Robert-Houdin, which specialized in showcasing magicians and mounting plays with supernatural or fantastic narratives. Méliès—ever the showman—discovered simple visual effects such as dissolves, superimpositions, fast and slow motion, and stop-motion animation, then constructed increasingly complicated stories to exploit them. Most of his films were fairy tales or fantasy stories, such as his 1902 adventure *A Trip to the Moon*, in which a group of stuffy scientists journey to the moon. In expanding the storytelling possibilities of the new medium, Méliès gradually increased the average length of a film to one reel—a little less than 1,000 feet, or 12–14 minutes at 16 feet per second (fps)—the standard length until the mid-1910's.

The movies soon outgrew vaudeville houses and one-night traveling shows. The first permanent movie theater in America was Thomas H. Tally's Electric Theater, which opened in Los Angeles in 1902. The Nickelodeon, whose name became generic for these early storefront theaters, opened in Pittsburgh in 1905. The first important American director was Edwin S. Porter (1870–1941), who, while working for the Edison Company, stumbled across the fundamentals of editing when he made *Life of an American Fireman* in 1903. He combined stock footage of a fire engine racing to a fire with staged shots of a mother and child trapped in a burning house, cutting back and forth between the two scenes in such a way as to suggest they were happening simultaneously, a technique later called parallel editing. Later that year, Porter made his masterwork, *The Great Train Robbery*, which contained simple but effective cinematic techniques, including cutting on motion, moving the camera to keep the action centered in the frame, and using diagonal compositions to exploit the depth that only the cinema offers.

D.W. Griffith and the Language of Film (1908–15)

David Wark Griffith (1875–1948) was introduced to filmmaking in 1907, when he acted in Porter's *Rescued from an Eagle's Nest*. He soon left the Edison Company for Biograph, for whom he acted and supplied story ideas. In 1908 he directed his first film, *The Adventures of Dollie*. Between 1908 and 1913, Griffith made hundreds of one-reelers for Biograph in which he developed and mastered the techniques that became the language of film. While Griffith did not invent many of these techniques, he had an instinct for exploiting them to advance the narrative, create drama, and evoke emotion in the viewer.

Innovations in Editing Griffith varied his shots in terms of distance from the camera, carefully dividing his scenes into long, medium, and close-up shots. Each type of shot had a specific function, with close-ups carrying the most emotional weight because they could suggest what a character was thinking or feeling. In addition, Griffith added a deliberate rhythm to the editing of his shots, increasing or decreasing the pacing depending on the content of the scene. Although Porter had been the first to use parallel editing, Griffith became such a master at using it to add excitement to his conclusions that the technique became known as "the Griffith last-minute rescue." He also used a range of optical effects for transitions between

shots, including the cut, the dissolve, the fade, and the iris, and he gave each effect a consistently specific function. Ably assisted by the first great cameraman, Billy Bitzer (1872–1944), Griffith innovated techniques and practices still in use today. Collectively, the techniques that Griffith pioneered are known as the classic narrative style, or the classical style.

New Acting Styles Moving the camera closer to the actors necessitated a more realistic style of acting than what was found in most one-reelers at the time. Together with his stable of actors at Biograph, including Dorothy and Lillian Gish, Henry B. Walthall, Lionel Barrymore, and Mary Pickford, Griffith developed a style of acting for film that was more natural and less broad than stage acting.

The Feature-Length Film Inspired by the spectacular historical epics of early Italian directors, including *Quo Vadis* (Enrico Guazzoni, 1912) and *Cabiria* (Giovanni Pastrone, 1914), Griffith began pushing Biograph to let him direct longer films with complex and meaningful stories. When Biograph resisted, he left and joined the Mutual Film Company in Hollywood. In 1915 he directed *The Birth of a Nation*, a three-hour historical epic about the Civil War and Reconstruction that was the culmination of his innovations in film. It was an exciting, artistic use of his techniques, representing his complete control of the medium on a grand scale. Unfortunately, the script was an adaptation of two racist pieces of literature by Thomas Dixon. Griffith's film offered indefensible stereotypes of African Americans while depicting the Ku Klux Klan as the heroic saviors of a defeated South.

The Rise of the American Film Industry (1915–30)

Hollywood European moviemaking was severely curtailed by World War I, and the American film industry soon dominated the world market. The first commercial production companies, such as American Biograph, Vitagraph, and Selig, had been established in New York, New Jersey, and Chicago. Led by Edison, who by now was putting as much energy into patent litigation as he used to put into laboratory experiments, the nine most powerful of these companies attempted to monopolize the production, distribution, and exhibition of motion pictures by forming a trust, the Motion Picture Patents Company (M.P.P.C.), in 1909. To escape the M.P.P.C.'s oppressive business tactics, independent filmmakers moved west as early as 1911. Most of them settled in a sleepy community just outside Los Angeles called Hollywood.

The Studio System　The move coincided with the development of more organized business practices, including the studio system, which was started by independent producer Thomas Ince (1882–1924) in 1912. Ince's studio, dubbed "Inceville," was much larger than the production companies based in New York and included administrative offices, shooting stages, permanent outdoor sets, photo labs, and wardrobe warehouses—a method of operation that facilitated the efficient mass production of movies. Instead of writing, directing, and editing himself, Ince hired others who were talented in these areas to execute these tasks. He then oversaw the production of their films, retaining financial and creative control. He also instituted the practices of shooting out of sequence to save time and adhering to strict budgets and schedules. These practices were soon adopted by other independents who established their own studios and became powerful figures by the end of World War I, including Carl Laemmle at Universal Studios and Adolph Zukor at Famous Players-Lasky (later Paramount).

New Genres, New Directors　Many genres emerged in this period, including the western, the action-adventure film, the romantic melodrama, and the historical/biblical epic. These genres share a sense of scale, larger-than-life romance, and fantasy that were well suited to the silent film—an art form dependent on images, action, and imagination. From these, the western can be singled out because of its cultural significance as America's foundation myth, but also because of its rapid evolution during the silent era. Launched by *The Great Train Robbery* in 1903, the genre at first consisted of cheap shorts shown primarily in small-town theaters. But during the teen years, cowboy star William S. Hart appeared in a series of gritty, serious films that added prestige to the genre. In western epics such as *The Iron Horse* (1924), directed by John Ford, and *The Covered Wagon* (1925), directed by James Cruze, the western developed during the 1920's with mature and substantive narratives.

Mack Sennett (1880–1960), head of the Keystone Studio and producer-director of hundreds of slapstick comedies, developed a style of physical humor that was fast-paced and action-oriented but also character-driven, establishing a tradition of American screen comedy that still survives. Directly or indirectly, he passed this style on

to a pantheon of comedians who epitomize the best of the silent era, including Fatty Arbuckle, Harold Lloyd, and Harry Langdon, as well as two others who must be counted among the greatest film artists of all time—Charles Chaplin (1889–1977) and Buster Keaton (1895–1966).

Though specific directors are associated with certain genres, such as Ford with the western, Cecil B. DeMille with the biblical epic, and Erich von Stroheim with the historical drama, many directors were adept in any genre, including Allan Dwan (1885–1981) and King Vidor (1894–1982). Many survived the coming of sound, becoming the veterans who helped the industry bridge the gap between the two eras.

The Star System　Despite the great directors of the silent era, films were rarely promoted based on who was behind the camera. Instead, they were sold based on the personalities who appeared in them, an industry practice known as the star system, which had begun in 1909, when the "Biograph Girl" was publicized under her real name, Florence Lawrence. A star's image was a consistent persona or archetype that an actor played repeatedly until the audience associated the actor with it. The stars were under contract to the studios, who used publicity and promotion to showcase the actors' images to attract audiences to their films. Stars provided a way to differentiate films for audiences and a way to boost sales for studios. The star system became so successful that often a film's narrative, camerawork, lighting, and editing were designed around its stars. The great stars of the 1920's included swashbuckling adventurer Douglas Fairbanks, Sr.; Latin lover Rudolph Valentino; America's sweetheart, Mary Pickford; and sophisticated lady Gloria Swanson.

Censorship and the Hays Office　Civic and religious pressure groups attempted to censor the movies as far back as the 1890's, when some of the vaudeville acts recorded by W.K.L. Dickson featured women in skin-baring costumes. Through the early 1920's, local and state authorities attempted to protect their individual jurisdictions, using censorship systems that were inconsistent, haphazard, and often unworkable. As the film industry grew larger and movies became more popular, religious and civic pressure groups called for governmental censorship at the federal level. Fearful of federal interference of any kind, the film industry embraced self-regulation. The major studio heads established the Motion Picture Producers and Distributors of America (M.P.P.D.A.) in 1922, and made former postmaster-general Will H. Hays (1879–1954) its president. Hays proved to be an artful speaker and a persuasive public relations man; because of his high profile, the censorship arm of the MPPDA was nicknamed the "Hays Office." He temporarily appeased the pressure groups with the Purity Code (1927), known as the "Don'ts and Be Carefuls," for filmmakers to follow.

In 1930 Hays adopted a strict, extensive set of guidelines to regulate onscreen content—the Motion Picture Production Code, coauthored by Father Daniel Lord, a Jesuit priest, and Martin Quigley, a prominent Catholic layman. The code detailed specific suggestions and prohibitions for such topics as crime, sex, profanity, religion, and race. At first, following the code was voluntary for studios, but in 1934, at Hays's urging and under increased pressure from the Catholic Church and other watchdog groups, the M.P.P.D.A. voted to make the code mandatory for all films from all studios. Hays created the Production Code Administration (P.C.A.), to be headed by Joseph Breen (1890–1965), whose sole purpose was to administer the code.

The Academy of Motion Picture Arts and Sciences

As a trade organization, the MPPDA worked behind the scenes to support and aid the film industry, but the Academy of Motion Pictures Arts and Sciences (A.M.P.A.S.) chose a more public profile with its stated goal of advancing the cultural, educational, and technical standards of American movies. Initially organized in 1927 to combat the rise of trade unions in Hollywood, the Academy soon settled into its main function, which was the annual presentation of awards for distinguished film achievement. Presented in 1929, the first Academy Awards (also called "Oscars") went to *Wings* (William Wyler) as outstanding picture, and *Sunrise* (F. W. Murnau) as best artistic achievement. Emil Jannings was the first to win the best actor award, while Janet Gaynor was named best actress.

Oscar Micheaux and Independent Black Cinema

The history of Hollywood is not necessarily the history of the entire American cinema. Movies produced and directed by African-Americans during the silent era provided an alternative to the limited and often racist portrayal of blacks in Hollywood films. Using all-black casts, these films were exhibited through a small circuit of theaters across the South and northern industrial centers that catered specifically to African-Americans. These films and filmmakers operated outside the production, distribution, and exhibition outlets of Hollywood, making them pio-

neers in the arena of independent filmmaking.

The most enduring independent African-American filmmaker was Oscar Micheaux (1884–1951). His films explored issues of concern to black audiences, including lynching, interracial marriage, and the effects of racism on the black community. Of the 30 or so films attributed to Micheaux, *Within Our Gates* (1920), which featured controversial rape and lynching scenes, and *Body and Soul* (1924), which starred Paul Robeson, are the most acclaimed. While most black-operated production companies folded because of the coming of sound, Micheaux managed to come back from bankruptcy to make *The Exile* (1931), the first synch sound film directed by an African-American.

The Coming of Sound (1927–1934)

The Hollywood industry was the first to successfully add synchronized sound to film. Warner Brothers studio produced several synch-sound musical shorts in the mid-1920's before adding a soundtrack to a feature-length film titled *Don Juan* in 1926, consisting of sound effects and orchestrated music but no spoken dialogue. The next step taken by Warner Brothers was to add musical performances to a feature film, which they did for *The Jazz Singer* (1927), starring Al Jolson. For the studio, the focus was on the six songs performed by Jolson; the rest of the film was shot in the silent format. However, for the audience, the attraction was the few hundred unscripted words ad-libbed by Jolson during a scene in which his character jokes with his mother. It was soon apparent that silent films and sound films could not coexist; audiences were simply riveted by spoken dialogue. By 1930, Hollywood was producing only sound movies. Chaplin alone successfully resisted; *City Lights* (1931) and *Modern Times* (1936) contain synchronized sound effects but no dialogue. When Chaplin finally did speak, it was to ridicule Hitler in *The Great Dictator* (1940).

The change from silent to sound films was not easy to accomplish. The expense of changing equipment for the studios and for the theaters was enormous, but other short-term problems also existed: few Hollywood personnel were trained to make sound films; each studio had a backlog of silent movies rendered obsolete by sound; some silent stars with heavy accents could not make the adjustment to talking films; and some foreign markets were lost because they were not interested in films in which the characters spoke English. The biggest problem proved to be the limitations imposed by the poor and cumbersome synch-sound equipment, resulting in talky, static-looking films.

By the early 1930's, these problems were resolved, but the coming of sound had permanently changed production practices from the scriptwriting stage through post-production. Production moved inside the studio for the majority of films, the method and manner of directing actors on the set changed, and dialogue necessitated a different style of acting. No longer entirely dependent on visual techniques to depict the narrative, sound films generally used fewer close-ups and required less editing. While some critics mourned the loss of visual artistry, sound brought an immediacy and spontaneity to the movies that made them more exciting and appealing for audiences.

The Golden Age of Hollywood (1934–1948)

The Studio Era   After the problems related to the introduction of sound were resolved, eight studios emerged to dominate the Hollywood film industry. The key to their domination was the vertical control the studios had over the industry, meaning they controlled the means of production, distribution, and exhibition. The five major studios, Paramount, MGM, Warner Brothers, RKO, and Twentieth Century Fox, not only owned their own production facility but also a distribution company and a chain of theaters in the large urban centers. Universal, Columbia, and United Artists, known as the minors, did not own any theaters, but they did produce and distribute their films. Together, these eight studios produced around 80 percent of the feature films released during the 1930's and 1940's, and they took in roughly 85 percent of the total rental income. Each studio produced about 50 feature films per year, a rate of production possible only because of the effectiveness of the studio system.

Producers, Directors, Stars   During this period, the average moviegoer was more likely to identify the style of a film with its studio than with its director or even its star. A studio head, such as Louis B. Mayer (1884–1957) of MGM or Harry Cohn (1891–1958) of Columbia, had ultimate creative and financial control of all films, but the day-to-day management of filmmaking was in the hands of producers. Producers answered directly to the studio head for the slate of films under their control. In general, they oversaw the writing of scripts, assigned directors and stars to films, supervised editing, and kept the process on schedule and under budget. This industrial, hierarchal organization gave each studio its own standardized, corporate identity. MGM, for whom Irving Thalberg (1899–1936) produced such films as *The Crowd* (1928), *Mutiny on the Bounty* (1935), and *The Good Earth* (1937), was known for prestige, glamour, and "more stars than there are in Heaven." Later on, Arthur Freed (1894–1973) produced MGM's glossy Technicolor musicals, including *On the Town* (1949), *An American in Paris* (1951), and *Singin' in the Rain* (1952), all starring Gene Kelly. Val Lewton (1904–51) of RKO oversaw a series of low-budget but acclaimed horror films in the 1940's, including *Cat People* (1942) and *The Body Snatcher* (1945). Warner Brothers was known for gangster films starring James Cagney and Edward G. Robinson, as well as social problem films such as *I Am a Fugitive from a Chain Gang* (1932), while Universal was famous for horror films starring Boris Karloff and Bela Lugosi.

In this producer-dominated system, several directors adapted well enough to the studio system to add distinctive touches to their films, making their work identifiable as their own. John Ford (1895–1973) shaped the conventions of the western into a personal chronicle of American history (*Stagecoach*, 1939); Frank Capra (1897–1991) encapsulated the virtue of the common man and idealized small-town values in his social comedies (*Mr. Smith Goes to Washington*, 1939); Alfred Hitchcock (1899–1980) depicted moral ambiguity in his sharply crafted mystery thrillers (*Notorious*, 1946). Other important directors of the period included Howard Hawks (1896–1977), Preston Sturges (1898–1959), Joseph Von Sternberg (1894–1969), and Dorothy Arzner (1897–1979).

The star system reached its zenith during the studio era, and some stars became icons of the era: John Wayne (1907–79) was the ultimate cowboy hero; James Cagney (1899–1986) the urban gangster; Jean Harlow (1911–37) the blonde bombshell; James Stewart (1908–97) the morally upright everyman; Humphrey Bogart (1899–1957) the hard-boiled private eye; Katharine Hepburn (1907–2003) the independent woman.

Despite the dependence on systems, standards, conventions, and formulas—and perhaps because of them—this period produced a variety of genres. Such diverse films as *It Happened One Night* (1934), *Gone With the Wind* (1939), *The Philadelphia Story* (1940), and *Casablanca* (1942) epitomize the glamour, craft, and appeal of Hollywood. Unfortunately, the system that perfected generic formulae discouraged formal experimentation. An exception is *Citizen Kane* (1941), cowritten (with Herman J. Mankiewicz) and directed by the iconoclastic Orson Welles (1915–85).

With its deep-focus photography (by Gregg Toland), chiaroscuro lighting, and expressive camera angles, *Citizen Kane* looked decidedly unlike any other film. Eschewing the linear plot, Welles offered a dark, complex fable of American capitalism and enterprise that featured no big stars and no happy ending. The film failed at the box office and garnered little support from the industry, save an Academy Award for best original screenplay. The very reasons for its failure—not following the systems and practices of the era—are now part of the reason for its reputation as arguably the greatest American film ever made.

Hollywood in Transition (1948–1962)

Fall of the Studio System In 1948 the Supreme Court ruled that certain business practices favorable to the eight major studios, including vertical control and block booking, violated American antitrust laws. Often referred to as the Paramount decree or the antitrust decree, the Court's ruling forced the studios to sell their theaters and to halt block booking (a practice in which the distributor coerced exhibitors into renting additional films in order to get the desired hits). The ruling made filmmaking riskier for the major studios, because they no longer had a guaranteed outlet for every film. As a result, studios began making fewer films and cutting costs.

They stopped financing expensive publicity tours or extensive buildups for new starlets and leading men, dropped many stars from their contracts, and reduced the average length of a contract from seven years to three years. Some stars, such as Burt Lancaster, Kirk Douglas, and Marilyn Monroe, took control of their own images and careers by forming their own production companies.

The Independent Production System The studios also let go of directors and producers, some of whom formed independent production companies, which were not under long-term contract to a studio nor directly involved with distribution. An independent producer or director found a book, play, or story to turn into a script, and then looked for interested stars, thereby putting the project and star together into one deal. He then took the deal to a major studio, which partially financed the film and distributed it after completion. This package-unit system, or independent production system, dominated Hollywood production by the mid-1950's, replacing the studio system of the Golden Age. The major studios were still a force in the industry, but their role became that of financiers and distributors rather than producers.

Freed from the contractual binds of the studios, several producers and directors took advantage of the package-unit system to make their best films. Though visually conventional, the films of Stanley Kramer (1913–2003) are notable for their social content, particularly because the major studios had shied away from controversial topics. *The Defiant Ones* (1958) offered a portrait of race relations while cementing the stardom of African-American actor Sidney Poitier (b. 1927). Poitier's Academy Award nomination as best actor paved the way for other black actors and actresses to secure roles that broke free from the hideous stereotypes of the Golden Age. The dark comic genius of Billy Wilder (1906–2001) peaked during this era in *Sunset Boulevard* (1950), with its masterly written script (by Wilder and Charles Brackett), and in *The Seven Year Itch* (1955) and *Some Like It Hot* (1959), two sex farces starring Marilyn Monroe.

The Impact of Television The television industry expanded rapidly after World War II, and by 1949 the film industry began to lose a large percentage of its audience to television. That year theater attendance dropped to 70 million, down from 90 million the year before. The decline would continue throughout the 1950's, accelerated by the suburbanization of America. Young couples and families began moving to the outskirts of urban centers, where the dominant leisure activities were television, listening to recorded music, children's sports, and bowling. By 1957 the film industry's profits had dropped 74 percent. The film industry eventually made peace with television. Some studios established subsidiaries to produce filmed programming for television; others rented their backlots to television production companies and sold or rented their libraries of film titles to television.

New Film and Projection Technology Color (in the form of hand-tinted prints) and wide-screen technologies, such as the three-screen-wide presentation of Abel Gance's *Napoleon* (1927), had been around since the silent era, but were mainly used for experiments, curiosities, and blockbusters like *Gone With the Wind* and *The Wizard of Oz* (both 1939). Now, in order to draw spectators back into the theaters, Hollywood embraced technology that offered visual experiences audiences could not get on the small black-and-white television screens. For example, color filmmaking increased rapidly at this time, particularly after the introduction of film stocks that were cheaper and easier to use than the standard three-strip Technicolor process. In the Golden Age, 20 percent of films were in color; during the 1950's, 50 percent were in color.

Screen size became larger and changed shape between 1952 and 1955, when wide-screen processes were adopted by the studios. Cinerama, a wide-screen system that required three electronically synchronized cameras, was introduced in 1952 with the novelty film *This Is Cinerama*. Over the next decade, a handful of feature films were made in Cinerama, but its multicamera setup for production and three-projector system for exhibition proved too expensive and too cumbersome for widespread use. CinemaScope, introduced in 1953 with *The Robe*, became the wide-screen process of choice because it used conventional 35mm film and required only a change in lens. The anamorphic lens squeezed the image onto 35mm film stock during production; then a special projector lens widened the image during projection. Panavision, another anamorphic process, replaced CinemaScope in the early 1960's. Most wide-screen films were recorded in stereo, so the increase in image size was complemented by sound with depth. Although wide-screen is still the norm, most films today are composed with everything happening in the center of the frame, so that the image can fit easily onto a standard TV screen.

Color, wide-screen, and stereo became permanent changes to the film image, but the studios tinkered with a few technological wonders that were not successful in the long term. A stereoscopic, or 3-D, projection system was introduced in 1952 in *Bwana Devil*, but by mid-1954 the public's interest in 3-D had greatly diminished, largely because the process had been reduced to a gimmick. Also, the awkward glasses that patrons had to wear to make the illusion work were a nuisance and gave some people headaches.

The New Movie Audience　Television and suburbanization altered the nature of the movie audience, at least indirectly. Because families and mature adults routinely spent their leisure time at home or in their communities, young adults and teens became the most consistent audience for movies in theaters. In 1956 young adults and teens bought seven-eighths of all movie tickets. For the first time, the industry began to seriously target the youth market, instead of focusing all of their attention on the mainstream market. In the landmark *Burstyn vs. Wilson* case of 1952, the Supreme Court ruled that films were protected by the First Amendment. This decision, along with the demise of the old studio heads, severely weakened the authority of the industry's self-regulated censorship system. In addition, producers and directors no longer under contract to the studios were far less concerned with following the rigid guidelines of the old Production Code, while exhibitors were no longer obligated to show only films with a code seal. As for the new youth audience, if they noticed a subtle change in the content of films during this period, they did not seem to mind.

Hollywood in the 1960's and 1970's

During the 1960's movie attendance continued to decline, and studios released fewer films per year. Senior producers in the studios floundered in the changing industry, and some of them steered their studios toward big-budget, large-scale ventures that seemed out of date compared to the modern styles of European films. By the end of the decade, every studio faced financial difficulties. Many were absorbed by larger, healthier conglomerates, leading the industry to accept and even embrace a corporate mentality. Universal was acquired by MCA in 1962, Paramount was absorbed into Gulf and Western in 1966, and Warner Brothers was bought by Seven Arts in 1967. The studios no longer had a system to foster new talent, increasing the uncertainty over their future.

The American "New Wave"　As it turned out, the next generation of writers and directors came from unexpected sources: some, such as Francis Ford Coppola, Martin Scorsese, Brian DePalma, Steven Spielberg, and George Lucas, had attended university film programs; others, such as Robert Altman, Woody Allen, Mel Brooks, Sidney Lumet, and Arthur Penn, had learned how to write or direct by working in live television during the 1950's; and, a few, such as Peter Bogdanovich and Paul Schrader, had written film criticism. Many had been exposed to the new waves and new directions that were part of European and Asian film.

The unique training, artistic predilections, and exposure to world cinema gave this generation a kind of media literacy. They were well versed in the history of film, understood the techniques of the medium, and realized the impact of those techniques on the audience in ways the old studio directors had not. At first dubbed the "New Hollywood," and then disparagingly called "the movie brats," this group of directors has since been labeled the "Film School Generation."

Hollywood's dire financial situation made it open to new ideas, particularly after the release of three films in 1967: *Bonnie and Clyde*, *The Graduate*, and *Cool Hand Luke*. The critical and financial success of these films signaled the arrival of a "new wave" of American filmmakers. In *Bonnie and Clyde*, director Arthur Penn (1922–2010) used several editing techniques generally not associated with continuity editing. His combination of slow-motion photography and montage editing in the climactic shoot-out became a standard technique for the depiction of onscreen violence. In *The Graduate*, director Mike Nichols (b. 1931) used pop songs by Simon and Garfunkel played over wordless scenes to comment on the state of mind of the main character, a use of music that became a staple for this generation of directors. Finally, *Cool Hand Luke*, directed by Stuart Rosenberg (1927–2007), showcased Paul Newman in the title role as a rebel who is alienated from the social institutions and common goals of mainstream society.

End of the Production Code   By the 1960's, enforcement of the Motion Picture Production Code was impractical, and many directors paid little attention to it. Jack Valenti (1921–2007), who became head of the Motion Pictures Association of America in 1966, replaced the code with a letter-ratings system two years later. The ratings system used a series of letters to represent the degree of graphic or adult content in films: G (suggested for general audiences); M (suggested for mature audiences); R (children under 17 not admitted without adult guardian); and X (children under 17 not admitted). The system was designed to alert viewers to the nature of a film's content, rather than prevent them from seeing certain types of material. In theory, the system freed directors to pursue explicit imagery and adult ideas.

New American Classics   The Film School Generation produced many outstanding films, such as *In the Heat of the Night* (1967), *Easy Rider* (1969), *The Godfather* (1972), *Dog Day Afternoon*, *One Flew Over the Cuckoo's Nest* (both 1975), *Taxi Driver* (1976), and *Days of Heaven* (1978). They were innovative, entertaining, and daring in form and/or content. Most directors experienced minimal interference from the studios when making their films. They approved the mixing of the soundtracks, inserted all optical effects, determined that all necessary shots and scenes had been included, and approved the final sound mix.

The era of the Film School Generation came to an end because the business side of Hollywood could not endure chaos indefinitely. By the close of the 1970's, many filmmakers were guilty of self-indulgence, driving the budgets of their films higher and higher in pursuit of their artistic visions. Initially, these directors had gained creative control and power because of the large returns on their low-budget films, but their later films followed the inverse equation, prompting the studios to step in. In 1980 the budget overruns on the western *Heaven's Gate* almost destroyed United Artists, and the industry blamed the situation on the excesses of director Michael Cimino. The film was a financial flop; consequently, executives at all studios became more closely involved with creative decisions. The policy of allowing directors substantial creative control quickly fell out of favor.

The Blockbuster Era (1975–)

Birth of the Blockbuster   Many of the industry practices that define the contemporary cinema began with *Jaws* (1975), directed by Steven Spielberg (b. 1946), and were cemented with *Star Wars* (1977), directed by George Lucas (b. 1944). Both films were action-driven narratives fueled by mechanical and special effects, which became blockbusters that attracted youth audiences and set box-office records. Released in July, *Jaws* established summer as the season of action blockbusters. Both *Jaws* and *Star Wars* benefitted from product tie-ins, including T-shirts, mugs and cups, and action figures.

Contemporary Hollywood   In the 1980's and 1990's the studios reclaimed their control over the industry. While the studios continued to solicit films from small production companies and produce films in conjunction with them, they exerted more creative control over script preparation, casting, and editing. Studios continued to be absorbed into large corporations: Columbia Pictures was purchased by Sony Corporation; Universal became part of Seagram. Only the Disney Company remained a freestanding, independent entity, though their other holdings (amusement parts, television networks) turned them into a corporate giant as well.

A corporate mentality, in which films are dubbed "products" and series of films are called "franchises," pervades contemporary Hollywood. Unlike the movie moguls of the Golden Age, who had experienced firsthand the many facets of the movie business, contemporary studio executives are recruited from talent agencies, the television industry, or business and marketing programs. They prefer the familiar stories of formulaic genres or projects that showcase popular stars, because those films appeal to mass audiences and inspire repeated viewings. The studios have moved the commercial Hollywood cinema away from the artistic inclinations of the Film School Generation as a way to secure box-office success.

The costs for producing films rapidly increased during this period, due to the high salaries and participation percentages of stars and emphasis on special effects and computer-generated imagery. The marketing and promotion of major studio films also expanded, with marketing costs sometimes equaling and even exceeding the film's initial budget. To handle the costs of large-scale films that are heavy on action and dependent on special effects, the big studios sometimes cofinance with companies related to the industry, or seek product tie-in deals with toy and fast-food companies.

The blockbuster did not fade away, however, and since 2000 a good number of films have drawn enormous audiences, espcially in the younger demographic. The eight *Harry Potter* movies, the *Lord of the Rings* trilogy, superheroes of all types and aliens from space, several movies about vampires, and many about young men and women trying to have sex and/or getting drunk and feeling cool about themselves, all made substantial profits. The younger set were fed a steady diet of animated films, and some like the *Toy Story* group were considered first-rate.

In 2009, the release of *Avatar*, the first serious 3-D film in over 40 years was a huge success. The 3-D films that followed, however, were not of the same quality and Hollywood's hopes for a new profit center seemed to have fizzled out by 2011.

Independent Filmmakers   The emergence of a large independent filmmaking community has become the main source of artistically driven films in the United States. Independent filmmakers generally find the funding for their low-budget, no-frills productions on their own to avoid studio interference. After the film is completed, it is showcased at large and small film festivals in the hopes that a studio or distributor will pick it up for release. Film festivals such as those at Telluride, Colorado, and the Sundance Institute in Utah, which was established by actor Robert Redford, and have become important outlets for new talent. Though truly independent film continued to thrive, the beginning of the 21st century saw studio productions mimicking independent style as it moved into the mainstream.

The success of some independent filmmakers has allowed them to straddle both worlds. Some talented directors, such as Quentin Tarantino (*Pulp Fiction*, 1994; *Kill Bill*, 2003; *Inglourious Basterds*, 2009), the Coen Brothers (*Fargo*, 1996; *No Country for Old Men*, 2008), Spike Lee (*Do the Right Thing*, 1989; *Inside Man*, 2006) and Steven Soderbergh (*Traffic*, 2000; *The Informant*, 2009), began as independents and then gradually moved to big Hollywood studios, where they enjoy more creative control than most directors. Others, including John Sayles (*Lone Star*, 1996) and Jim Jarmusch (*Ghost Dog*, 2000), prefer to make their films completely outside the studios.

International Film

France

Following the pioneering efforts of Méliès and the Lumières, France took the lead in film production during the years before World War I. The stage-bound *Films d'art* were popular around the world. The most important figure in early French film was Louis Feuillade, whose crime serials (*Les Vampires*, 1915) were admired by the Surrealists and the New Wave cineastes for their naturalistic surfaces, dreamlike logic, and subtle eroticism.

During the 1920's, Surrealist and Dadaist artists such as Man Ray and Salvador Dali experimented with the possibilities of film to manipulate time and space or to depict dream states (as in the 1929 Surrealist masterpiece, Luis Buñuel's *Un Chien Andalou*). Simultaneously, a loosely knit group of avant-garde filmmakers gathered around author-editor Louis Delluc (1890–1924) to expand upon the ideas of the various artistic movements centered in Paris. Known as the Impressionists, these filmmakers—Germaine Dulac, Jean Epstein, Marcel L'Herbier, and Abel Gance—were seeking a poetic cinema in which content or story were subordinate to the imagery, or an expressive cinema in which visual techniques were used to depict interior states.

Their work influenced subsequent filmmakers such as Jean Cocteau, René Clair, Jean Vigo, and Marcel Carné to be expressive and distinctive in their styles and themes. Cocteau (1889–1963), for example, was an artist, poet, playwright, and filmmaker who knew some of the surrealist artists and writers. That he was heavily influenced by them is evident in most of his films—from the personal symbolism of *Le Sang d'un Poète* (1930) to the imaginative set design of *La Belle et la Bête* (1946).

Though various artistic movements inspired specific French filmmakers, the style known as poetic realism defined French film of the 1930's. The term implied a skill-ful integration of two seemingly contradictory ideas—the settings and characters of everyday life combined with a lyrical, expressive visual style designed to evoke a heavy atmosphere of fate and longing. The darkest of the poetic realists was Marcel Carné (1909–96), who collaborated with the surrealist poet Jacques Prévert (1900–77) to pro-duce the most haunting films of the era, *Quai des Brumes* (1938) and *Le Jour se Lève* (1939). Both films showcase leg-endary French screen star Jean Gabin (1904–76) as a decent man irreversibly trapped by fate, and both favor the low-key lighting and emphasis on mise-en-scène associ-ated with poetic realism.

Jean Renoir (1874–1979), the son of the famous Im-pressionist painter, became the most celebrated director to emerge from the era. Marginally connected to poetic real-ism because of the social commentary in his films, Renoir preferred stories that examined class differences or skew-ered the lifestyle of the bourgeois, as in *Boudu Sauve des Eaux* (1932). As Renoir's commitment to social causes grew, themes involving class issues and politics pervaded his work, including his two masterpieces, *La Grande Illusion* (1937) and *La Règle du Jeu* (*The Rules of the Game*, 1939). During the war, he worked in Hollywood on several films, most notably *The Southerner* (1945). He returned to France in 1954 to experiment with color and motion in his later films. A filmmaker with a strong personal vision and lengthy career, Renoir represented a pinnacle of French filmmaking in the era between the wars.

The French New Wave   In the mid-1950's, the direc-tors who made up the new generation of French filmmak-ers began as film critics, protégés of the great critic André Bazin, and centered on the film journal *Cahiers du cinema*. The group taught themselves world cinema by viewing the whole of its history at Henri Langlois's Cinémathèque Français. In their writings, they tended to attack the French film establishment while championing the films of older master directors such as Renoir and Cocteau. They also appreciated and admired mainstream Hollywood films, singling out films by directors who transcended the constraints of the studio system to forge their own style or vision. By the end of the decade, the Cahiers group had begun to make their own films. They released three award-winning films in 1959: *Les Quatre Cents Coups* (*The 400 Blows*) by François Truffaut won the director's award at the Cannes International Film Festival; *Hiroshima, Mon Amour* by Alain Resnais won the critics' prize at Cannes; and *A Bout de Souffle* (*Breathless*) by Jean-Luc Godard won the director's award at the Berlin International Film Festival. The acclaim bestowed on these young directors focused attention on them as a group, prompting the press to dub them *la nouvelle vague* (the New Wave).

Visually, the New Wave sought to achieve the opposite effect of the seamless and invisible classic narrative style. Their films often looked rough, casual, even sloppy. They were shot on location with hand-held cameras, using nat-ural lighting and direct sound. They purposefully played with the possibilities of editing, camera movement, sound, and mise-en-scène. The characteristic most associ-ated with the New Wave was the use of *hommage*, or "quot-ing" from the films and directors that influenced them. Other important New Wave directors include Claude Chabrol, Jacques Rivette, Eric Rohmer, Jacques Demy, Agnès Varda, and Louis Malle.

More recent French film has seen a return to more con-ventional narratives and production values, while retain-ing youthful themes and expressive techniques of the New Wave. Andre Téchiné, Claude Sautet, Claire Denis, Léos Carax, and Olivier Assayas have all managed to impress a personal style onto their provocative films.

Germany

German Expressionism   While Hollywood edged closer to a domination of the international motion picture market after World War I, Germany pushed film to a high-er level of artistry. The German filmmakers offered a more sophisticated use of mise-en-scène while pursuing a dark subject matter with psychological undertones.

Three types of film dominated German production during the 1920's. Historical/mythological films, such as Ernst Lubitsch's *Passion Madame du Barry* (1919) and Fritz Lang's *Die Niebelungen* (1924), used stylized archi-tectural settings, elaborate costuming, and the calculat-ed blocking of massive crowds to portray history and mythology in spectacular fashion. The opposite of the historical/mythological films, at least in scope, were the "street films," which were intimate studies of work-ing-class life, often set in an entertainment or under-world milieu. Concerned primarily with the personal disintegration of individuals, street films depicted the dark psychological states of the characters. More signifi-cant, they made a fuller use of the moving camera. *The Last Laugh* (1924), directed by F.W. Murnau and photographed by Karl Freund, used the moving camera as a narrative tool to introduce the setting and to scrutinize the central character.

Best known were the Expressionist films, which dealt with fantastic or supernatural subjects rendered in low-key and high-contrast lighting styles, obtuse camera angles, and fantastic set designs. A part of the art movement known as German Expressionism, these films attempted to visually depict inner feelings or states of mind. *The Cabinet of Dr. Caligari* (1919), directed by Robert Weine, presents an exaggerated, distorted mise-en-scène to represent the tortured mind of its insane protagonist. *Metropolis* (1924), directed by Fritz Lang, is a futuristic tale of the oppressed working class that uses low-key lighting to create an atmosphere of despair and massive sets to suggest the subjugation of the masses.

Many great German directors, actors, and cameramen were lured to Hollywood, either by money or to escape the increasing control of the Nazis. Expressionist techniques, such as distorted lighting styles and camerawork, were easily absorbed into the classic narrative style. Nowhere is the Expressionist influence more realized than in the American horror genre, which was born at Universal Studios in the early 1930's, just after the arrival of the German émigrés.

Aside from the horribly effective propaganda films of Leni Riefenstahl, Nazi Germany produced no notable cinema. In fact, it took more than 20 years for the German film industry to recover from the war. In the 1970's a new generation of iconoclastic directors turned on the conformism and bad faith of the Adenauer years with a vengeance. R. W. Fassbinder, Wim Wenders, and Werner Herzog made intense, formally inventive films about wanderers, drug addicts, and seemingly every kind of physical and mental defective. Herzog's *Aguirre, the Wrath of God* (1972), about Spanish conquistadors in the Amazon, ends with the title character, alone, dreaming of fathering a new race of supermen with his daughter, while his corpse-covered raft is overrun by marmosets.

Great Britain

At the turn of the 20th century, the filmmakers of the "Brighton School" drew upon the work of the French while in some ways anticipating Porter and Griffith. Cecil Hepworth's *Rescued by Rover* (1905), presented entirely without titles, showed how to keep an audience oriented to a swiftly moving narrative by carefully repeating sets and shots.

Britain's finest achievements in film prior to World War II were in documentaries. John Grierson (1898–1972) launched a documentary movement in the late 1920's that produced films related to public needs and national interest. *Drifters* (1929) detailed the hard work of the Scottish herring fisherman; *Night Mail* (1936) told the story of the dedicated mail train that transported letters and packages across the British Empire.

When war began in 1939, a series of semi-documentary films were released that drew on Grierson's ideas about the capacity for documentary to fulfill a public service. The narratives were fictional but the subject matter and characters were authentic. *Target For Tonight* (1941), directed by Harry Watt, followed the activities of Royal Air Force (R.A.F.) fliers on a fictional bombing mission over Germany. Starring actual R.A.F. pilots, the film informed the public about the R.A.F., while rallying support and bolstering national confidence.

Although the semi-documentary film disappeared after the war, Grierson's documentary tradition exerted a strong influence over feature filmmaking in Great Britain. The Ealing Studios hired several of the documentarians to direct their feature films, including a series known as the Ealing comedies. Postwar bureaucratic entanglements were tackled in Henry Cornelius's *Passport to Pimlico* (1949); the hostilities of the Scottish for the British were exposed in Alexander MacKendrick's *Whiskey Galore* (aka, *Tight Little Island*, 1949); and the eccentricities of the British middle class were showcased in Charles Crichton's *The Lavender Hill Mob* (1951). These films introduced the world to the comic genius of the likes of Alec Guinness and Peter Sellers.

The three greatest British filmmakers were Alfred Hitchcock, David Lean, and Carol Reed. Hitchcock and Lean would achieve great fame in America but not before learning their craft in England, Hitchcock with *The Man Who Knew Too Much* (1934), *The 39 Steps* (1935), and *The Lady Vanishes* (1938); Lean with *In Which We Serve* (1942), *Brief Encounter* (1945), *Great Expectations* (1946), and *The Sound Barrier* (1952). Carol Reed (1906–76) also made movies in the U.S. and won an Oscar for *Oliver* (1968), but his best work was done in England, especially two films based on stories by Graham Greene: *The Fallen Idol* (1948) and *The Third Man* (1949).

In the late 1950's the British documentary tradition was revived and reworked in the films of the Free Cinema movement. According to filmmakers Lindsay Anderson, Karel Reisz, and Tony Richardson, "free" meant free from serving a sponsor's purpose and free from pandering to the tastes of the box office. Their documentaries, such as Anderson's *O Dreamland* (1954) and Reisz's *Momma Don't Allow* (1955), revealed a class consciousness and a social commitment. The themes and rough style of Free Cinema fit the working-class narratives of the Angry Young Men, giving birth to a social realist type of filmmaking in Jack Clayton's *Room at the Top* and Richardson's *Look Back in Anger* (both 1959). In the 1960's Lindsay Anderson startled audiences with his unvarnished portrayal of class in England, first in *This Sporting Life* (1963), which used rugby as a metaphor for working-class struggles. His look at upper-class angst in a posh prep school in *If* (1968), won the Palme d'Or at Cannes, and caused a great stir.

Aside from the Free Cinema, British cinema has been, like British art in general, more of a collection of eccentric individual talents than a series of movements or schools. That is especially true today, when Ken Russell's hysterical expressionism, Mike Leigh's proletarian comedies, Ken Loach's politically committed tales, Peter Greenaway's super-baroque art films, and the eloquent lunacy of Monty Python all remain resolutely sui generis.

The Soviet Union

Silent Filmmakers   Unlike the capitalist-based film industries of the United States and Europe, the Soviet film industry was rooted in socialist economics. Film production had existed in Russia prior to 1917, but the Bolshevik Revolution of that year sparked a full-fledged industry financially supported by the state and characterized by formal experimentation. The Bolsheviks, led by V.I. Lenin (1870–1924), believed film to be the most effective means to indoctrinate the masses to their new form of government.

The newsreels of Dziga Vertov (b. Denis Kaufman, 1896–1954) explored the possibilities of editing through the specific juxtaposition of images in order to create a meaning. In 1922 he launched a monthly newsreel called *Kino Pravda*, the ultimate goal of which was to support the tenets of the revolution. For instance, when Vertov combined one shot of the former czar sternly reviewing his troops with another of Lenin with a group of workers, he made an effective and persuasive political statement.

Theory of Montage   Instrumental in advancing the art of editing was teacher-theorist-director Lev Kuleshov (1899–1970), who conducted editing experiments in his capacity as an instructor at the Vsesoyuznyi Gosudarstvenyi Institut Kinematografia (VGIK), Moscow's state film school. His experiments ultimately concluded that each shot in a film acquired meaning from its immediate context, which is the shot that comes before it and the shot that follows it. This discovery became the foundation of montage editing, which focuses on the impact created by the juxtaposition of one or more shots. Russian montage is dynamic and often discontinuous in comparison to Hollywood's continuity editing, which offers the illusion of continuous action from shot to shot.

Sergei Eisenstein (1898–1948) used what is called "intellectual montage," which is the juxtaposition of two or more shots to create a metaphor or idea not inherent in any one of the shots themselves. In *Battleship Potemkin* (1925), about a real-life mutiny in the Russian Navy in 1905, Eisenstein juxtaposes a close-up of an officer's sword with a close-up of a priest's cross to suggest that both are instruments of oppression to keep the masses in their place. In addition to intellectual montage, *Potemkin* uses other editing tactics, including the juxtaposition of opposing shots, such as light shots with dark ones, static shots with movement, and close-ups with long shots.

Not all Russian directors held the same views regarding editing. Vsevolod I. Pudovkin (1893–1953) was the most conventional of the Russian filmmakers of the 1920's, preferring a less radical style of editing and a more traditional approach to filmmaking. To Pudovkin, editing had to work in conjunction with a message-driven story and credible acting in order to produce a powerful film, such as his heart-wrenching drama *Mother* (1926). Alexander Dovzhenko (1894–1956) stood apart from those experimenting with editing and form. A regionalist, Dovzhenko celebrated the agricultural lifestyle of his native Ukraine in such poetic films as *Earth*, which stressed imagery over form and mood over pacing.

The era of the great Russian silent filmmakers drew to a close with the consolidation of the Soviet government under Josef Stalin during the early 1930's and the coming of sound. Stalin, who was as provincial as Lenin had been intellectual, disliked the esoteric nature of montage-driven films and demanded Soviet movies be simple stories readily understandable to all audiences. The 50's and 60's saw brief glimmers of hope for a resurgence of Soviet cinema in the regional films of Sergei Paradjanov and the literary adaptations of Grigori Kozintsev. The U.S.S.R. finally gave the world one last cinematic artist, Andrei Tarkovsky, just before its collapse in the 1990's.

Eastern Europe

The film industries of the Soviet Union and satellite countries of Czechoslovakia, Poland, Yugoslavia, and Hungary were under the supervision of the Communist Party until the fall of Soviet-style communism in 1989. The Party favored socialist realism, which consisted of simple, uplifting stories of communist heroes whose lives had meaning for the revolution, or ideologically correct stories in which everyday people enacted or embodied the tenets of communism. National film schools trained directors, actors, and technicians who went on to work for studios controlled and funded by the state. Despite this rigid control, a few great films and filmmakers emerged from Eastern Europe.

After Josef Stalin died in 1953, the Eastern bloc film industries enjoyed a relaxation of internal controls and a growing expression of national sentiment known as the Great Thaw. In Poland in 1956, the Poznan uprising protested Soviet control, which resulted in loosened censorship over the arts. Director Andrzej Wajda (b. 1926) led a resurgence of Polish production in the late 1950's, which included his films *Kanal* (1956) and *Ashes and Diamonds* (1958). Combined with an earlier work, *A Generation* (1954), the films explored Poland's sad history during the German occupation of World War II.

Agnieszka Holland (b. 1948) was part of Poland's "cinema of moral concern," also known as the "cinema of moral unrest." Most of this generation of film directors had attended the film school in Lodz, Poland, during the 1970's, and were united by an interest in personal moral issues, or in the struggles of the individual to do what's right in a corrupt system. In addition to Holland, the group included Krysztof Zanussi (b. 1939) and Krysztof Kieslowski (1941–96).

In Czechoslovakia the political climate loosened sufficiently during the 1960's to allow a greater degree of experimentation in the arts, including film. A young generation of filmmakers educated at FAMU, the national film academy in Prague, produced a cinema of wry social commentary, acutely observed comedy, and formal experimentation. Dubbed the "Czech New Wave," these directors include Milos Forman, Vera Chytilova, Jan Nemec, Ivan Passer, Jiri Menzel, and Jaromil Jires. Milos Forman's (b. 1932) award-winning Czech films, *Black Peter* (1964), *Loves of a Blonde* (1965), and *The Fireman's Ball* (1967), are characterized by an acute observation of ordinary people, a documentary-like visual style influenced by the French New Wave, and excellent performances by nonprofessionals. The most unconventional filmmaker of the Czech New Wave is Vera Chytilova (b. 1929), whose formal experimentation and surreal imagery in her best-known feature, *Daisies* (1966), tested the patience of the political tastemakers. Like Forman, Ivan Passer (b. 1933) and Jiri Menzel (b. 1938) directed films in which close observations of ordinary people produced wry comedies about contemporary life. Menzel's best-known film is the Academy Award–winning *Closely Watched Trains* (1966), a coming-of-age story about a shy train station attendant. Passer, who cowrote Forman's *Fireman's Ball*, directed *Intimate Lighting* (1966), about the reunion of two old musicians whose lives have gone in different directions.

Important filmmakers have also come from other countries behind the Iron Curtain. Hungary gave filmgoers the swooping camera and intricate compositions of Miklos Janczo and the historical dramas of Istvan Szabo. Before it disintegrated into civil war, Yugoslavia produced the anarchic comedies of Dusan Makevejev. Since the fall of communism, the former Eastern bloc countries have struggled to keep their film industries afloat in a free-enterprise system. With the distribution of Hollywood films in Eastern Europe, fewer and fewer native filmmakers find their films on the big screens.

Italy

After World War I, the Italian film industry that had produced the great silent superspectacles quickly declined into mediocrity. Despite the construction of the massive state-funded Cinecittà studio complex, fascist Italy produced nothing more notable than "white telephone" movies, named after the instruments into which the characters in these films were seen interminably speaking.

Italian Neorealism   Perhaps the most influential postwar movement, Italian neorealism strove to capture the dignity of ordinary people in everyday life in a stripped-down documentary style. Neorealism actually began while the war was still raging. *Ossessione*, directed by Luchino Visconti (1906–76), considered to be the blueprint for neorealism, was released in 1943, and *Open City*, directed by Roberto Rossellini (1906–77), the first neorealist film to reach other countries, was shot in 1944 and released the following year. *Open City* was a loosely structured story based on actual events that occurred just as the

Allies were approaching Rome. It used documentary-like techniques that became associated with the movement, including on-location shooting, the use of nonprofessional actors, a focus on the daily lives of ordinary people, and references to recent history. *The Bicycle Thief* (1949), directed by Vittorio de Sica (1902–74), is considered the undisputed masterpiece of the movement.

Neorealism as a movement ended during the early 1950's, but it remained a strong influence on Italian filmmaking for many decades. The postwar generation of Italian directors, such as Federico Fellini and Michelangelo Antonioni, adopted such neorealistic characteristics as location shooting, long shots in long takes, and nonprofessional actors, but they used them to shape their own individual styles.

Italian filmmakers of the 1960's, dubbed the New Italian Cinema, returned to films with sociopolitical content and themes. Bernardo Bertolucci and Ermanno Olmi mixed their neorealist roots with a pronounced French New Wave influence.

Spain

Thanks to the Franco regime, Spain's greatest filmmaker, Luis Buñuel (1900–83), made very few films in Spain. After a few odd jobs in the United States, he divided his directorial career between Mexico and France, where he applied Surrealist poetics and antifascist politics to narratives a shade more conventional than *Un Chien Andalou*. After the death of Franco, a national cinema finally emerged, led by Carlos Saura and Victor Erice, while the work of Pedro Almodovar happily walks back and forth across the line that separates art from camp.

Scandinavia

In the 1910's and 1920's Denmark boasted the directorial talents of Holger Madsen, Carl-Theodor Dreyer, and Benjamin Christensen, while Danish superstar Asta Nielsen enjoyed international popularity. In Sweden Charles Magnusson guided the Svensk Filmindustri into a leading force in film production, while directors Victor Sjostrom and Mauritz Stiller achieved a unique national expression. Because Sweden remained neutral during World War I, their film industry continued to thrive into the 1920's. Thereafter, the Swedish film industry often teetered financially, but it managed to retain its national identity. After World War II, Ingmar Bergman (1918–2007) emerged to become an eminent filmmaker around the world. Bergman began his directorial career in 1945, but *Smiles of a Summer Night* (1955), *The Seventh Seal* (1957), and *Wild Strawberries* (1957) announced him as an international force.

The Danish film industry struggled to continue after World War II. Its recovery has been steady but slow. From the 1960's through the 1980's, the films of such directors as Henning Carlson and Bille August turned attention toward Denmark periodically, while the simplified practices and stripped-down style of iconoclast Lars Von Trier (*Zentropa*) grabbed the spotlight in the 1990's. Other noteworthy contemporary Scandinavian filmmakers include Jan Troell (*Hamsun*), the unclassifiable Aki Kaurismaki, and Lucas Moodysson (*Togetherness*).

India

In 1956 at the Cannes International Film festival, director Satyajit Ray's *Pather Panchali* garnered critical acclaim as well as a jury prize for being "the best human document." Ray (1921–93) followed *Pather Panchali* with *Aparajito* (1956) and *The World of Apu* (1958); together, these films form a trilogy about the lives of a Bengali family in the 1920's and 1930's. Strongly influenced by Italian neorealism, Ray's films are humanist and naturalist, focusing on small subjects, scenes of everyday life, and ordinary people. His other major films included *The Music Room* (1963) and *Distant Thunder* (1973).

Ray's films stood apart from most of the Indian film industry, a highly commercial enterprise that still produces more films per year than any other film industry. The center of production for the popular Hindi cinema is Bombay, nicknamed "Bollywood" because of its focus on producing slick, big-budget genre films for the masses.

Ray made films outside the styles and confines of Bollywood, and his work influenced other politically minded directors. Around 1969 the New Indian Cinema, or Parallel Cinema, was founded by directors Ritwak Ghatak and Mrinal Sen and financed in part by the government. Ghatak and Sen, both Marxists, made films about social problems and serious issues. Sen's biggest success was *Bhuvan Shome* (1969), about a railroad executive who is transformed by a trip to rural India. Perhaps the best known member of the New Cinema is Shyam Benegal (b. 1934), whose critically acclaimed and widely successful films include *Manthan* (1976) and *Bhumika* (1977).

During the late 1980's and 1990's, several Indian directors gained attention by directing for the film industries of other countries. Mira Nair, whose films include *Salaam Bombay!* (1988) and *Mississippi Masala* (1991), moved to Hollywood; Deepa Mehta, who directed *Fire* (1996), is based in Canada. After scoring an international success with *The Bandit Queen* (1994), Shakhar Kapur relocated to Great Britain to direct *Elizabeth* (1999), before ending up in Hollywood to make *The Four Feathers* (2001).

China

The history of filmmaking in China is a tale of three cinemas—those of the People's Republic of China, Hong Kong, and Taiwan.

The film industry in the People's Republic, or mainland China, produced films primarily for indoctrination until 1978, when constraints on the state-supported studios were lifted by the government. At that point, the studios began to make films for entertainment. Most of the filmmakers who initially rose to prominence had graduated from the Beijing Film Academy, which prompted critics to group them together, referring to them as the "Fifth Generation." Success at high-profile film festivals brought this group of directors international attention, beginning in the mid-1980's with Chen Kaige and his beautifully photographed *Yellow Earth* (1984). While each director of the Fifth Generation worked toward a personal style, they all shared a sophisticated pictorial sense. Most celebrated is Zhang Yimou (b. 1951), who had been the cinematographer on *Yellow Earth*. When he turned to directing in 1988, his films became renowned for their stunning visuals, radiant color, and precise compositions. Thematically, Yimou's films, including *Ju Dou* (1990), *Raise the Red Lantern* (1991), and *Shanghai Triad* (1996), are notable for their focus on the oppression of women.

Hong Kong has always benefitted from a capitalist-based film industry, in which films are produced fast and furiously. In the 1970's its movies were known for choppy editing, laughably out-of-synch overdubbing, and the Kung Fu legend of Bruce Lee. Even after Hong Kong was returned to China in 1997, the film industry was left alone to operate as it always had. Unlike the artistic aspirations of mainland China's film industry, Hong Kong prefers the formulaic narratives of popular genres—gangster films, martial-arts films, and comedies. Characterized by a dynamic editing style, energetic camerawork, elaborate stunts, and stylized violence, Hong Kong films appealed to American audiences, prompting Hollywood to lure away such major directors and actors as John Woo, Chow Yun-Fat, and Jackie Chan.

Filmmaking in Taiwan became possible after martial law ended in 1987. Taiwanese films are less known than those of mainland China or Hong Kong, probably because they emphasize the country's history and traditional Chinese formal techniques, making them less accessible to Western audiences. Taiwan's first internationally acclaimed feature was *City of Sadness* (1988), which launched director Hou Hsiao-hsien's career (b. 1947). Hou's films, including *The Puppetmaster* (1993) and *Flowers of Shanghai* (1995), are contemplative essays on his country's history and culture. His work contrasts with that of fellow Taiwanese director Ang Lee (b. 1954), whose films (*The Wedding Banquet*, 1993) have been influenced by the West. In the late 1990's, Lee was absorbed into the Hollywood system, where he has worked on large-scale commercial films for the major studios, including *Sense and Sensibility* (1995) and *The Hulk* (2003). In 2000 he directed an award-winning independent feature, *Crouching Tiger, Hidden Dragon*, a martial-arts fairy tale designed to appeal to Western audiences.

Japan

The Japanese film industry was launched in 1904–05, when the first film studios were constructed. Similar to Hollywood, the industry was dominated by a handful of studios, which also controlled distribution and exhibition. Most Japanese films fell into two central types: the *jidai-geki*, which were period dramas set in the in past, and the *gendai-geki*, modern-era stories set in urban centers.

In 1951 Japanese film was internationally celebrated for the first time when *Rashomon*, directed by Akira Kurosawa (1910–98), won the Golden Lion at the Venice Film Festival. *Rashomon's* fragmented, nonlinear narrative structure established Kurosawa as a master filmmaker. His loose adaptations of Shakespeare's plays and his action-filled samurai films, including *Yojimbo* (1961) and *Sanjuro* (1962), made his work accessible to Western audiences. Kurosawa's films set in the contemporary era, such as *Ikiru* (1952), eschewed the action and sensory appeal of his samurai films to focus on subtle, complex characters, and modern social problems. Kurosawa's key collaborator in his films was actor Toshiro Mifune (1920–97), who interpreted the director's central characters with charisma and intensity.

Other Japanese directors who drew attention to Japanese cinema during this period were Kenji Mizoguchi (1898–1956) and Yasujiro Ozu (1903–63). Mizoguchi, whose style and subjects were more traditionally Japanese than Kurosawa's, favored historical films that focused on the plight of women. *Street of Shame* (1956) and *Women of the Night* (1957) dealt with prostitution; *Princess Yang Kwei Fei* (1955) focused on the false importance placed on the appearance of women. His masterpiece, *Ugetsu Monogatari* (1953), dealt with the effect of war on humanity. The films of Ozu are unique in their austerity: most take place in interiors, feature little camera movement, and consist largely of conversations. The most recognizable stylistic characteristic of Ozu's films is the position of his camera, which generally presents the point of view of a person seated on a tatami mat. The rigid formal style seemed appropriate for his key theme, which contrasted traditional Japanese ways with contemporary changes, best exemplified in *Tokyo Story* (1953). His best-known films, *Late Autumn* (1960), *Early Summer* (1951), and *Late Spring* (1949), have titles that recall the cyclical nature of life.

In the 1960's a group of young Japanese directors began their careers with the help of the Arts Theater Guild, which financed and showcased more daring films than the studios were willing to support. Shohei Imamura (*The Pornographers*, 1966), Nagisa Oshima (*In the Realm of the Senses*, 1976), and Masahiro Shinoda (*Pale Flower*, 1964) made films that were more modernist than their predecessors, resulting in the label "Japanese New Wave."

By the mid-1970's, the golden age of Japanese cinema had ended. In 1972 the continued decline of the Japanese cinema induced the government to create a fund for quality productions. In the 1980's and 1990's a new generation of filmmakers, including Yoshimitsu Morita and Juzo Itami, emerged to breathe life into the Japanese industry.

Latin America

The films of many Latin American directors feature strong sociopolitical content, reflecting the backlash against the various military regimes, ruling elites, and colonialist policies that have dominated this part of the world. Their work attempts to raise social awareness in the hopes of improving conditions, especially among the peasantry and urban poor. Added to the political commitment are influences from the traditions and aesthetics of Latin American painting, music, and literature, including a predilection for allegory, vivid color, and powerful music, a style generally referred to as "tropicalism."

Cuba's modern film industry began in 1959, when the new revolutionary government centralized the film industry to regulate all production, distribution, and exhibition. At first, newsreels and documentaries were produced to meet the needs of the people as determined by the new government. Narrative filmmaking often captured the immediacy and naturalism of documentary, while focusing on content involving the issues and problems of the new revolutionary culture. Tomas Gutierrez Alea (1928–96) became the best-known Cuban director when his *Memories of Underdevelopment* (1968) garnered international recognition. Alea continued to explore problems in Cuban society till the end of his life when he directed *Strawberry and Chocolate* (1993), an exploration of gay sexuality in a machismo-based culture.

Elsewhere in Latin America, filmmakers struggled to find funding for indigenous films. In some countries cooperatives were formed, which united filmmakers economically and politically. In Brazil directors Ruy Guerra, Glauber Rocha, and Nelson Pereira dos Santos formed the Cinema Novo cooperative and secured funding from a state-supported agency. Cinema Novo was dedicated to films that focused on the impoverished and the disenfranchised. In these films serious political allegories were depicted in a tropicalist style. Rocha led Cinema Novo, becoming an internationally known director with *Black God, White Devil* (1964) and *Antonio das Mortes* (1969). The generation after Cinema Novo, led by Hector Babenco (*Kiss of the Spider Woman*, 1985) has been more prolific, producing both political and commercial films.

A group of political directors in Argentina also established a cooperative to facilitate filmmaking in their country. The Grupo Cine Liberacion (GCL) were more politically driven than Cinema Novo, advocating filmmaking that was, according to their manifesto, "militant in politics and experimental in language." To the GCL, part of the filmic experience should be active audience involvement in the form of political discussion and debate inspired by the films. Their most inspired achievement to that end was Fernando Solanas and Octavio Getino's *The Hour of the Furnaces* (1968), a three-part documentary in which the second and third sections were developed from audience reaction to the first section. More recent Argentinean directors who have used film for sociopolitical criticism include Eliseo Subiola (*Man Facing Southeast*, 1986) and Maria Luisa Bemberg (*Camila*, 1984).

Africa

While indigenous filmmaking in Africa has been limited, largely due to poverty and the ever-changing political scene, some important directors have emerged since the 1970's. Because distribution is controlled through American, European, and East Indian systems, African filmmakers experience difficulty obtaining funding and getting exposure and recognition. The type of films associated with Africa are frequently described as belonging to traditions of folklore, particularly those of oral storytelling. Political criticism and anticolonial sentiment are sometimes intertwined with folkloric structures to form powerful narratives, as in the films of novelist and filmmaker Ousmane Sembene (b. 1923–2007) of Senegal. Sembene burst onto the international scene in 1966 with his first film, *Black Girl*, an attack on the racism endured by blacks at the hands of French colonists. Dedicated if not prolific, Sembene continued to make films into the millennium (*Faat Kine*, 2000), earning his nickname as the father of black African film. Other important African directors include Souleymane Cissé (b. 1940), of Mali (*Yeelen*, 1987) and Idrissa Ouedraogo (b. 1954) from Burkina Faso (*Yaaba*, 1989).

Glossary of Film Terms

angle *normal angle* (or eye level) is the standard camera position in which the camera is placed straight on to the subject at approximate eye level. When the camera deviates from that position, a connotation or idea is suggested. In a *high-angle* shot, the camera is placed above the subject, suggesting the subject is weak or vulnerable. In a *low-angle* shot, the camera is placed below the subject to suggest importance or power. In a *bird's-eye view*, or *God's-eye view*, the camera is in an extremely high angle to suggest fate or God looking down upon the subject. A *dutch*, or *oblique*, angle occurs when the camera is tilted, suggesting that something about the subject is wrong or off-kilter.

classic narrative style standard style used by the Hollywood industry to depict a story on film. Also called the classical style or the invisible style, it strives for a subtlety or unobtrusiveness so that the audience is unaware of its impact on them. It consists of a consistent approach to camera work, editing, and lighting and a consistent depiction of plot and character.

continuity editing standard style of editing by the Hollywood industry. It offers the illusion of continuous action from shot to shot by moving the action forward in time in a smooth, fluid, and logical way.

cut editing transition accomplished by splicing one shot to another shot. It suggests an instantaneous passage of time. Also called an edit.

dissolve editing transition accomplished by the slow fading out of one shot and the gradual fading in of the next shot. At one point, both images are superimposed. It suggests the slow passage of time.

fade editing transition in which the image gradually appears from an all-black screen, or gradually disappears to an all-black screen. Fades *from* black are used to open a film, while fades *to* black conclude a film. When used within the body of a film, fades suggest a complete break in time or place.

freeze frame shot frozen on screen for a desired length of time to resemble a still photograph.

genre type or category of story, such as westerns, horror films, or musicals.

hand-held camera work footage shot by a cameraman who is holding the camera instead of using a tripod or dolly. The resulting footage appears shaky or unsteady, suggesting the action is unfolding instantaneously and spontaneously as though the viewer is there witnessing it.

lighting Most films utilize *high-key lighting*, in which the lighting is bright and even, with few discernible shadows. To deviate from high-key adds a suggestion or connotation to a shot or scene. *Low-key lighting*, which implies that something is hidden, mysterious, or evil, consists of an overall dark look, with dark, diffused shadows dominating the set. *High-contrast lighting*, which tends to intensify mood or emotion, consists of harsh contrast between light and dark in the same shot.

intertitles titles between shots in a silent film to help explain the action or provide dialogue or commentary for the scene.

iris transition to open a scene in which the image is brought into view by starting with a circle at center screen and expanding the circle until the entire image is on screen, or to close a scene by gradually shrinking the image in circular form until the screen is black. A partial iris occurs when the screen closes in on a character or object via a circular shape, leaving the rest of the screen black.

jump cut edit between two shots that are so similar that a jarring or abrupt effect is created. In continuity editing, jump cuts are errors because they disrupt the smooth flow of images, but the French New Wave used them deliberately to disorient and disturb the viewer.

mise-en-scène all of the visual elements that go into composing a shot, including camera angle, lighting style, set design, props, position of the character in the frame, and costumes and makeup.

montage style of editing developed by the Russian filmmakers of the 1920's in which a collection of shots are edited together to form an impression, emotion, or idea. The impression or effect is created through the accumulation, frequency, and the juxtaposition of shots. *Intellectual montage* is a specific technique of montage in which two unrelated shots are edited together to suggest a metaphor or concept not inherent in either shot by itself.

package-unit system system of organization for the production of films in the Hollywood industry begun after the decline of the studios in the 1950's. In this system independent production companies or producers find a book, play, or story to turn into a script, and then seek interested stars, putting the project and star together into one deal. The deal is taken to a major studio, which partially finances the film and distributes it after completion. Also called the *independent production system*.

pan rotation of the camera around its vertical axis, creating a panoramic effect.

parallel editing cutting back and forth between two or more scenes to create the illusion of simultaneous action.

persistence of vision theory on which the motion picture camera was developed. It involves the capacity of the eye to maintain an image on the retina for a brief instant after the image disappears, thus giving continuity to a succession of still images and creating the illusion of movement.

production phase of filmmaking in which the shooting occurs and the raw footage is produced. The action is shot, the principal sound recorded, and the entire crew is put to full use. This phase comes after preproduction, in which the script is written and prepared, the actors hired, and the director does required preparation. It comes before postproduction, in which the film is edited, the sound is assembled in its final form, and special effects are added.

scene segment of film consisting of related shots.

shot basic unit of film construction. A single piece of film without any breaks in the action; an unedited, uncut strip of film. Different types of shots have different functions in a scene. The purpose of a *close-up*, in which the camera is closest to the subject, is to show the emotion of the character or elicit emotion from the audience. A *medium shot* best shows the interrelationship among characters, and the *long shot*, in which the camera is farthest from the subject, establishes the setting. In a *zoom shot*, the magnification of objects by the camera's lenses is increased (zoom in) or decreased (zoom out/back). A *two-shot* is a medium close-up shot of two subjects, usually framed from the chest up. A *point of view shot* (or *POV*) is a brief shot from the perspective of a specific character so the viewer sees what that character sees from his or her angle of vision. (see also *angle, subjective camera movement*)

shot sequence segment of film composed of related scenes, leading to a climax or resolution of some sort.

star system method or manner of exploiting movie stars to market films and lure audiences into the theater.

studio system system for organizing the major studios in the Hollywood industry that began in the 1910's and lasted until the 1950's. In the studio system, the head of the studio had creative and financial control, which he delegated through his producers. They in turn oversaw the work of the writers, directors, actors, and editors, who were all under contract to the studio and were assigned to films by the producers.

subjective camera movement shot in which the camera takes on the viewpoint of a specific character for a deliberate amount of time, so that the camera moves about the set as though it were that character. The viewer sees what that character sees from his or her angle of vision.

synchronized sound sound that seems to emanate directly from its source on the screen, as when spoken dialogue is heard at the exact moment it is seen being spoken.

tilt rotation of the camera around its horizontal axis.

tracking moving the camera alongside, above, beneath, behind, or ahead of the subject, generally following the movement of the subject. Movement is accomplished via a wheeled support, such as a dolly on a small track.

vertical control term applied to the major studios' ownership of production, distribution, and exhibition during the silent era and the Golden Age.

wide-screen any film employing an aspect ratio wider

than 4:3 or 1.33:1, giving the screen a rectangular shape. Wide-screen processes were adopted by the industry during the 1950's to combat the popularity of television. From the silent era to the 1950's the screen had been standardized at a ratio of 1.33:1, which was almost square.

wipe transition device in which the image moves diagonally across the screen to reveal the next image. A wipe signifies a complete change in time and/or locale. (see also *iris*)

The Production Crew

art director person responsible for the design of the film's sets or locations; also responsible for their construction.

best boy assistant to the gaffer; sometimes the assistant to the head grip.

cinematographer (director of photography) person responsible for photographing the images for the film. Cinematography involves technical knowledge about cameras, lenses, film stock, and lighting in addition to an aesthetic sense involving camera placement, angle, the interplay of light and shadow, and movement.

director person responsible for translating the script, which is the written word, into a film, which is a visual and performance-based medium.

editor person responsible for assembling the film's footage into its final form.

foley artist specialist in sound effects that are dubbed onto the visuals.

gaffer chief electrician in a film production, responsible for lighting the set.

grip jack-of-all-trades responsible for a variety of tasks on the set, including the transportation and movement of equipment and scenery, laying down dolly track, and pushing the dolly along the track. The *key grip* is the person in charge of a group of grips.

producer person in charge of the financial and administrative duties for a film, including securing the rights to a book, story, or script, monitoring scriptwriting, and keeping the film on schedule and on budget. Sometimes the producer is involved in casting, raising finances for the film, and monitoring the editing. The *executive producer* usually deals with business and legal affairs.

screenwriter person who writes the script, either adapting it from another source or creating an original story. Often, several scriptwriters are employed to create and polish a single script.

American Film Institute
100 Best American Movies

The American Film Institute was established in 1967 to preserve the quickly fading heritage of American film. Below is their "100 Years... 100 Movies—10th Anniversary Edition" list that was compiled in 2007 to celebrate American cinema, 1896–2006. Films produced after 2006 are not included.

1. Citizen Kane, 1941. Directed by Orson Welles. Written by Herman J. Mankiewicz and Orson Welles. Starring Joseph Cotton, Dorothy Comingore, Agnes Moorehead, Ray Collins.

2. The Godfather, 1972. Directed by Francis Ford Coppola. Based upon the novel Mario Puzo; Screenplay by Mario Puzo and Francis Ford Coppola. Starring Marlon Brando, Al Pacino, James Caan, Robert Duvall, Talia Shire.

3. Casablanca, 1942. Directed by Michael Curtiz. Based upon the play *Everybody Comes to Rick's* by Murray Burnett and Joan Alison; Screenplay by Julius J. & Philip G. Epstein, Howard Koch. Starring Humphrey Bogart, Ingrid Bergman, Paul Henreid, Claude Rains.

4. Raging Bull, 1980. Directed by Martin Scorsese. Based upon the novel by Jake La Motta, Joseph Carter and Peter Savage; Screenplay by Paul Schrader and Mardik Martin. Starring Robert De Niro, Cathy Moriarty, Joe Pesci, Frank Vincent, Nicholas Colasanto.

5. Singin' in the Rain, 1952. Directed by Stanley Donen and Gene Kelly. Written by Adolph Green and Betty Comden. Starring Gene Kelly, Donald O'Connor, Debbie Reynolds, Jean Hagen, Millard Mitchell.

6. Gone With the Wind, 1939. Directed by Victor Fleming. Based upon the novel by Margaret Mitchell; Screenplay by Sidney Howard. Starring Clark Gable, Vivien Leigh, Leslie Howard, Olivia deHavilland, Thomas Mitchell.

7. Lawrence of Arabia, 1962. Directed by David Lean. Based upon the writings of T.E. Lawrence; Screenplay by Robert Bolt and Michael Wilson. Starring Peter

O'Toole, Alec Guinness, Anthony Quinn, Jack Hawkins, Omar Sharif.

8. Schindler's List, 1993.   Directed by Steven Spielberg. Based upon the novel by Thomas Keneally; Screenplay by Steven Zaillian. Starring Liam Neeson, Ben Kingsley, Ralph Fiennes, Caroline Goodall.

9. Vertigo, 1958.   Directed by Alfred Hitchcock. Based upon the novel *...d'Entre les Morts* by Pierre Boileau and Thomas Narcejac; Screenplay by Alec Coppel and Samuel A. Taylor. Starring James Stewart, Kim Novak, Barbara Bel Geddes, Tom Helmore, Henry Jones.

10. The Wizard of Oz, 1939.   Directed by Victor Fleming. Based upon the novel *The Wonderful Wizard of Oz* by Frank L. Baum; Screenplay by Noel Langley. Starring Judy Garland, Frank Morgan, Ray Bolger, Bert Lahr, Jack Haley, Billie Burke.

11. City Lights, 1931.   Directed by Charles Chaplin. Written by Charles Chaplin. Starring Virginia Cherrill, Florence Lee, Harry Myers, Al Ernest Garcia, Hank Mann, Charles Chaplin.

12. The Searchers, 1956.   Directed by John Ford. Based upon the novel by Alan Le May; Screenplay by Frank S. Nugent. Starring John Wayne, Jeffrey Hunter, Vera Miles, Ward Bond, Natalie Wood, John Qualen, Olive Carey.

13. Star Wars, 1977.   Directed by George Lucas. Written by George Lucas. Starring Mark Hamill, Harrison Ford, Carrie Fisher, Peter Cushing, Alec Guinness, David Prowse.

14. Psycho, 1960.   Directed by Alfred Hitchcock. Based on the novel by Robert Bloch; Screenplay by Joseph Stefano. Starring Anthony Perkins, Janet Leigh, Vera Miles, John Gavin, Martin Balsam.

15. 2001: A Space Odyssey, 1968.   Directed by Stanley Kubrick. Written by Stanley Kubrick and Arthur C. Clarke. Starring Keir Dullea, Gary Lockwood, William Sylvester, Daniel Richter, Leonard Rossiter, Margaret Tyzack.

16. Sunset Boulevard, 1950.   Directed by Billy Wilder. Written by Charles Brackett and Billy Wilder. Starring William Holden, Gloria Swanson, Erich von Stroheim, Nancy Olson, Fred Clark.

17. The Graduate, 1967.   Directed by Mike Nichols. Based upon the novel by Charles Webb; Screenplay by Calder Willingham and Buck Henry. Starring Anne Bancroft, Dustin Hoffman, Katharine Ross, William Daniels, Murray Hamilton.

18. The General, 1927. Directed by Clyde Bruckman and Buster Keaton. Adapted from the memoir *The Great Locomotive Chase* by William Pittenger; Screenplay by Buster Keaton and Clyde Bruckman.   Starring Buster Keaton and Marion Mack.

19. On the Waterfront, 1954.   Directed by Elia Kazan. Written by Malcolm Johnson and Budd Schulberg. Starring Marlon Brando, Karl Malden, Lee J. Cobb, Rod Steiger.

20. It's a Wonderful Life, 1946.   Directed by Frank Capra. Based on the story "The Greatest Gift" by Philip Van Doren Stern; Screenplay by Frances Goodrich and Frank Capra. Starring James Stewart, Donna Reed, Lionel Barrymore, Thomas Mitchell, Henry Travers.

21. Chinatown, 1974.   Directed by Roman Polanski. Written by Robert Towne. Starring Jack Nicholson, Faye Dunaway, John Huston, Perry Lopez, John Hillerman, Diane Ladd.

22. Some Like It Hot, 1959.   Directed by Billy Wilder. Based on a story by Robert Thoeren and Michael Logan; Screenplay by Billy Wilder and I.A.L. Diamond. Starring Marilyn Monroe, Tony Curtis, Jack Lemmon, George Raft, Pat O'Brien.

23. The Grapes of Wrath, 1940.   Directed by John Ford. Based upon the novel by John Steinbeck; Screenplay by Nunnally Johnson. Starring Henry Fonda, Jane Darwell, John Carradine, Charley Grapewin, Dorris Bowdon.

24. E.T. The Extra Terrestrial, 1982.   Directed by Steven Spielberg. Written by Melissa Mathison. Starring Henry Thomas, Dee Wallace, Robert MacNaughton, Drew Barrymore, Peter Coyote.

25. To Kill a Mockingbird, 1962.   Directed by Robert Mullian. Based upon the novel by Harper Lee; Screenplay by Horton Foote. Starring Gregory Peck, John Megna, Frank Overton, Rosemary Murphy, Ruth White.

26. Mr. Smith Goes to Washington, 1939.   Directed by Frank Capra. Based on a story by Lewis R. Foster; Screenplay by Sidney Buchman. Starring Jean Arthur, James Stewart, Claude Rains, Edward Arnold, Guy Kibbee.

27. High Noon, 1952.   Directed by Fred Zinnemann. Based on a story by John W. Cunningham; Screenplay by

Carl Foreman. Starring Gary Cooper, Thomas Mitchell, Lloyd Bridges, Katy Jurado, Grace Kelly.

28. All About Eve, 1950.   Directed by Joseph L. Mankiewicz. Written by Joseph L. Mankiewicz; Based on a story "The Wisdom of Eve" by Mary Orr (uncredited). Starring Bette Davis, Anne Baxter, George Sanders, Celeste Holm, Gary Merrill.

29. Double Indemnity, 1944.   Directed by Billy Wilder. Based upon the novel *Double Indemnity in Three of a Kind* by James M. Cain; Screenplay by Billy Wilder and Raymond Chandler. Starring Fred MacMurray, Barbara Stanwyck, Edward G. Robinson, Porter Hall, Jean Heather, Tom Powers, Byron Barr.

30. Apocalypse Now, 1979.   Directed by Francis Ford Coppola. Written by John Milius and Francis Ford Coppola. Starring Marlon Brando, Martin Sheen, Robert Duvall, Sam Bottoms, Laurence Fishburne.

31. The Maltese Falcon, 1941.   Directed by John Huston. Based upon the novel by Dashiell Hammett; Screenplay by John Huston. Starring Humphrey Bogart, Mary Astor, Gladys George, Peter Lorre, Barton MacLane, Lee Patrick.

32. The Godfather Part II, 1974.   Directed by Francis Ford Coppola. Based upon the novel by Mario Puzo; Screenplay by Mario Puzo and Francis Ford Coppola. Starring Al Pacino, Robert Duvall, Diane Keaton, Robert De Niro, John Cazale, Talia Shire.

33. One Flew Over the Cuckoo's Nest, 1975.   Directed by Milos Forman. Based upon the novel by Ken Kesey; Screenplay by Bo Goldman. Starring Jack Nicholson, Louise Fletcher, William Redfield, Michael Berryman, Peter Brocco.

34. Snow White and the Seven Dwarfs, 1937.   Walt Disney's first full-length animated feature. Based upon the story by Jacob & Wilhelm Grimm. Starring (voice) Roy Atwell, Stuart Buchanan, Adriana Caselotti, Eddie Collins, Pinto Colvig, Lucille La Verne.

35. Annie Hall, 1977.   Directed by Woody Allen. Written by Woody Allen and Marshall Brickman. Starring Woody Allen, Diane Keaton, Tony Roberts, Carol Kane, Paul Simon.

36. The Bridge on the River Kwai, 1957.   Directed by David Lean. Based upon the novel *Le pont de la rivière Kwai* by Pierre Boulle; Screenplay by Michael Wilson and Carl Foreman. Starring William Holden, Jack Hawkins, Alec Guinness, Sessue Hayakawa, James Donald.

37. The Best Years of Our Lives, 1946.   Directed by William Wyler. Based upon the novel by MacKinlay Kantor; Screenplay by Robert E. Sherwood. Starring Myrna Loy, Fredric March, Dana Andrews, Teresa Wright, Virginia Mayo.

38. The Treasure of the Sierra Madre, 1948.   Directed by John Huston. Based upon the novel by B. Traven; Screenplay by John Huston. Starring Humphrey Bogart, Walter Huston, Tim Holt, Bruce Bennett, Barton MacLane.

39. Dr. Strangelove or: How I Learned to Stop Worrying and Love the Bomb, 1964.   Directed by Stanley Kubrick. Based upon the novel *Red Alert aka Two Hours to Doom* by Peter George; Screenplay by Stanley Kubrick, Terry Southern, Peter George. Starring Peter Sellers, George C. Scott, Sterling Hayden, Keenan Wynn, Slim Pickens, James Earl Jones.

40. The Sound of Music, 1965.   Directed by Robert Wise. Based upon the novel *The Trapp Family Singers* by Maria von Trapp; Book by Howard Lindsay and Russel Crouse; Screenplay by Ernest Lehman; Music by Rogers and Hammerstein. Starring Julie Andrews, Christopher Plummer, Richard Haydn, Peggy Wood, Nicholas Hammond, Angela Cartwright.

41. King Kong, 1933.   Directed by Merian C. Cooper and Ernest B. Schoedsack. Written by James Ashmore Creelman and Ruth Rose. Starring Fay Wray, Robert Armstrong, Bruce Cabot, Frank Reicher, Sam Hardy, Noble Johnson, Steve Clemente.

42. Bonnie and Clyde, 1967.   Directed by Arthur Penn. Written by David Newman and Robert Benton. Starring Warren Beatty, Faye Dunaway, Michael J. Pollard, Gene Hackman.

43. Midnight Cowboy, 1969.   Directed by John Schlesinger. Based upon the novel by James Leo Herlihy; Screenplay by Waldo Salt. Starring Dustin Hoffman, Jon Voight.

44. The Philadelphia Story, 1940.   Directed by George Cukor. Based upon the play by Philip Barry; Screenplay by Donald Ogden Stewart. Starring Cary Grant, Katharine Kepburn, James Stewart, Ruth Hussey, John Howard, Roland Young, Mary Nash.

45. Shane, 1953.   Directed by George Stevens. Based upon the novel by Jack Schaefer; Screenplay by A.B. Guthrie Jr. Starring Alan Ladd, Jean Arthur, Van Heflin, Brandon De Wilde, Jack Palance, Ben Johnson.

46. It Happened One Night, 1934. Directed by Frank Capra. Based upon the story by Samuel Hopkins Adams; Screenplay by Robert Riskin. Starring Clark Gable, Claudette Colbert, Walter Connolly, Roscoe Karns.

47. A Streetcar Named Desire, 1951. Directed by Elia Kazan. Based upon the play by Tennessee Williams; Adaptation by Oscar Saul; Screenplay by Tennessee Williams. Starring Vivien Leigh, Marlon Brando, Kim Hunter, Karl Malden, Rudy Bond, Nick Dennis.

48. Rear Window, 1954. Directed by Alfred Hitchcock. Based upon the story by Cornell Woolrich; Screenplay by John Michael Hayes. Starring James Stewart, Grace Kelly, Wendell Corey, Thelma Ritter, Raymond Burr, Judith Evelyn.

49. Intolerance, 1916. Directed by D.W. Griffith. Written by D.W. Griffith. Starring Lillian Gish, Robert Harron, Mae Marsh, Constance Talmadge, Bessie Love.

50. The Lord of the Rings: The Fellowship of the Ring, 2001. Directed by Peter Jackson. Based on the novel by J.R.R. Tolkien; screenplay by Fran Walsh, Philippa Boyens, and Peter Jackson. Starring Elijah Wood, Viggo Mortensen, Sean Astin, Ian McKellen, Christopher Lee, Andy Serkis

51. West Side Story, 1961. Directed by Jerome Robbins and Robert Wise. Concept written by Jerome Robbins; Play written by Arthur Laurents; Adapted for the screen by Ernest Lehman. Starring Natalie Wood, Richard Beymer, Russ Tamblyn, Rita Moreno, George Chakiris.

52. Taxi Driver, 1976. Directed by Martin Scorsese. Written by Paul Schrader. Starring Robert De Niro, Cybill Shepherd, Peter Boyle, Jodie Foster, Harvey Keitel.

53. The Deer Hunter, 1978. Directed by Michael Cimino. Written by Deric Washburn. Starring Robert De Niro, John Cazale, John Savage, Christopher Walken, Meryl Streep, George Dzundza.

54. M*A*S*H, 1970. Directed by Robert Altman. Based upon the novel by Richard Hooker; Screenplay by Ring Lardner Jr. Starring Donald Sutherland, Elliott Gould, Tom Skerritt, Robert Duvall, Sally Kellerman.

55. North by Northwest, 1959. Directed by Alfred Hitchcock. Written by Ernest Lehman. Starring Cary Grant, Eva Marie Saint, James Mason, Jessie Royce Landis, Leo G. Carroll, Josephine Hutchinson, Philip Ober.

56. Jaws, 1975. Directed by Steven Spielberg. Based upon the novel by Peter Benchley; Screenplay by Peter Benchley and Carl Gottlieb. Starring Roy Scheider, Robert Shaw, Richard Dreyfuss, Lorraine Gary, Murray Hamilton, Carl Gottlieb.

57. Rocky, 1976. Directed by John G. Avildsen. Written by Sylvester Stallone. Starring Sylvester Stallone, Talia Shire, Burt Young, Carl Weathers, Burgess Meredith.

58. The Gold Rush, 1925. Directed by Charles Chaplin. Written by Charles Chaplin. Starring Charles Chaplin, Mack Swain, Tom Murray, Henry Bergman.

59. Nashville, 1975. Directed by Robert Altman. Written by Joan Tewkesbury. Starring Keith Carradine, Ned Beatty, Karen Black, Lily Tomlin.

60. Duck Soup, 1933. Directed by Leo McCarey. Based on a story by Bert Kalmar and Harry Ruby. Starring Groucho Marx, Harpo Marx, Chico Marx, Zeppo Marx.

61. Sullivan's Travels, 1941. Directed by Preston Sturges. Written by Preston Sturges. Starring Joel McCrea and Veronica Lake.

62. American Graffiti, 1973. Directed by George Lucas. Written by George Lucas, Gloria Katz, and Willard Huyck. Starring Richard Dreyfuss, Ron Howard, Paul Le Mat, Charles Martin Smith, Cindy Williams, Candy Clark, Mackenzie Phillips.

63. Cabaret, 1972. Directed by Bob Fosse. Adapted from *The Berlin Stories* by Christopher Isherwood; screenplay by Jay Presson Allen. Starring Liza Minnelli, Michael York, Joel Grey.

64. Network, 1976. Directed by Sidney Lumet. Written by Paddy Chayefsky. Starring Faye Dunaway, William Holden, Peter Finch, Robert Duvall, Wesley Addy.

65. The African Queen, 1951. Directed by John Huston. Based upon the novel by C.S. Forester; Screenplay by James Agee. Starring Humphrey Bogart, Katharine Hepburn, Robert Morley, Peter Bull.

66. Raiders of the Lost Ark, 1981. Directed by Steven Spielberg. Based on a story by George Lucas, Philip Kaufman; Screenplay by Lawrence Kasdan. Starring Harrison Ford, Karen Allen, Paul Freeman, Ronald Lacey, John Rhys-Davies.

67. Who's Afraid of Virginia Woolf?, 1966. Directed by Mike Nichols. Adapted from the play by Edward Albee; screenplay by Ernest Lehman. Starring Elizabeth Taylor, Richard Burton, George Segal, Sandy Dennis.

68. Unforgiven, 1992. Directed by Clint Eastwood. Written by David Webb Peoples. Starring Clint Eastwood, Gene Hackman, Morgan Freeman, Richard Harris.

69. Tootsie, 1982. Directed by Sydney Pollack. Based on a story by Larry Gelbart and Don McGuire; Screenplay by Larry Gelbart and Murray Schisgal. Starring Dustin Hoffman, Jessica Lange, Teri Garr, Dabney Coleman, Bill Murray, Sydney Pollack, Geena Davis, Charles Durning.

70. A Clockwork Orange, 1971. Directed by Stanley Kubrick. Based upon the novel by Anthony Burgess; Screenplay by Stanley Kubrick. Starring Malcolm McDowell, Patrick Magee, Michael Bates, Warren Clarke, John Clive, Adrienne Corri.

71. Saving Private Ryan, 1998. Directed by Steven Spielberg. Written by Robert Rodat. Starring Tom Hanks, Tom Sizemore, Matt Damon.

72. The Shawshank Redemption, 1994. Directed by Frank Darabont. Adapted from the novella *Rita Hayworth and Shawshank Redemption* by Stephen King; screenplay by Frank Darabont. Starring Tim Robbins and Morgan Freeman.

73. Butch Cassidy and the Sundance Kid, 1969. Directed by George Roy Hill. Written by William Goldman. Starring Paul Newman, Robert Redford, Katharine Ross, Strother Martin, Jeff Corey, Cloris Leachman.

74. The Silence of the Lambs, 1991. Directed by Jonathan Demme. Based upon the novel by Thomas Harris; Screenplay by Ted Tally. Starring Jodie Foster, Anthony Hopkins, Scott Glenn, Anthony Heald, Ted Levine.

75. In The Heat of The Night, 1967. Directed by Norman Jewison. Based on the novel by John Ball; screenplay by Stirling Silliphant. Starring Sidney Poitier, Rod Steiger, Lee Grant.

76. Forrest Gump, 1994. Directed by Robert Zemeckis. Based upon the novel by Winston Groom; Screenplay by Eric Roth. Starring Tom Hanks, Robin Wright Penn, Gary Sinise, Mykelti Williamson, Sally Field.

77. All the President's Men, 1976. Directed by Alan J. Pakula. Based on the non-fiction book by Bob Woodward and Carl Bernstein; screenplay by William Goldman. Starring Dustin Hoffman, Robert Redford, Jason Robards.

78. Modern Times, 1936. Directed by Charles Chaplin. Written by Charles Chaplin. Starring Charles Chaplin, Paulette Goddard, Henry Bergman, Tiny Sandford, Chester Conklin, Hank Mann, Stanley Blystone.

79. The Wild Bunch, 1969. Directed by Sam Peckinpah. Based on a story by Walon Green and Roy N. Sickner; Screenplay by Walon Green and Sam Peckinpah. Starring William Holden, Ernest Borgnine, Robert Ryan, Edmond O'Brien, Warren Oates.

80. The Apartment, 1960. Directed by Billy Wilder. Written by Billy Wilder and I.A.L. Diamond. Starring Jack Lemmon, Shirley MacLaine, Fred MacMurray, Ray Walston, Jack Kruschen, David Lewis, Hope Holiday.

81. Spartacus, 1960. Directed by Stanley Kubrick. Based on the novel by Howard Fast; screenplay by Dalton Trumbo. Starring Kirk Douglas, Laurence Olivier, Peter Ustinov.

82. Sunrise, 1927. Directed by F.W. Murnau. Adapted from the short story "Die Reise nach Tilsit" by Hermann Sudermann; screenplay by Carl Mayer. Starring George O'Brien and Janet Gaynor.

83. Titanic, 1997. Directed by James Cameron. Written by James Cameron. Starring Leonardo DiCaprio, Kate Winslet, Kathy Bates, Billy Zane.

84. Easy Rider, 1969. Directed by Dennis Hopper. Written by Peter Fonda, Dennis Hopper, and Terry Southern. Starring Peter Fonda, Dennis Hopper, Antonio Mendoza, Phil Spector, Mac Mashourian, Warren Finnerty.

85. A Night at the Opera, 1935. Directed by Sam Wood. Written by George S. Kaufman, James Kevin McGuinness, Morrie Ryskind. Starring Groucho, Chico, Harpo Marx, Kitty Carlisle.

86. Platoon, 1986. Directed by Oliver Stone. Written by Oliver Stone. Starring Tom Berenger, Willem Dafoe, Charlie Sheen, Forest Whitaker, Francesco Quinn.

87. 12 Angry Men, 1957. Directed by Sidney Lumet. Adapted from a teleplay by Reginald Rose; screenplay by Reginald Rose. Starring Henry Fonda, Lee J. Cobb, Ed Begley.

88. Bringing Up Baby, 1938. Directed by Howard Hawks. Based on a story by Hagar Wilde; Screenplay by Dudley Nichols and Hagar Wilde. Starring Katharine Hepburn, Cary Grant, Charles Ruggles, Walter Catlett, Barry Fitzgerald, May Robson.

89. The Sixth Sense, 1999. Directed by M. Night Shyamalan. Written by M. Night Shyamalan. Starring Bruce Willis, Haley Joel Osment, Toni Collette.

90. Swing Time, 1936. Directed by George Stevens. Written by Howard Lindsay, Allan Scott, Erwin Gelsey. Starring Fred Astaire and Ginger Rogers.

91. Sophie's Choice, 1982. Directed by Alan J. Pakula. Based on the novel by William Styron; screenplay by Alan J. Pakula. Starring Meryl Streep, Kevin Kline, Peter MacNicol.

92. Goodfellas, 1990. Directed by Martin Scorsese. Based upon the novel *Wise Guy* by Nicholas Pileggi; Screenplay by Nicholas Pileggi. Starring Robert De Niro, Ray Liotta, Joe Pesci, Lorraine Bracco, Paul Sorvino, Chuck Low, Frank DiLeo, Frank Sivero, Tony Darrow.

93. The French Connection, 1971. Directed by William Friedkin. Based upon the novel by Robin Moore; Screenplay by Ernest Tidyman. Starring Gene Hackman, Fernando Rey, Roy Scheider, Tony Lo Bianco.

94. Pulp Fiction, 1994. Directed by Quentin Tarantino. Based on stories by Quentin Tarantino and Roger Avary; Screenplay by Quentin Tarantino. Starring Tim Roth, John Travolta, Samuel L. Jackson, Amanda Plummer, Bruce Willis, Uma Thurman.

95. The Last Picture Show, 1971. Directed by Peter Bogdanovich. Adapted from a semi-autobiographical novel by Larry McMurtry; screenplay by Peter Bogdanovich and Larry McMurtry. Starring Jeff Bridges, Cybill Shepherd, Ben Johnson.

96. Do the Right Thing, 1989. Directed by Spike Lee. Written by Spike Lee. Starring Danny Aiello, Spike Lee, John Turturro.

97. Blade Runner, 1982. Directed by Ridley Scott. Based on the novel *Do Androids Dream of Electric Sheep?* By Philip K. Dick; screenplay by Hampton Fancher. Starring Harrison Ford, Rutger Hauer, Sean Young, Edward James Olmos.

98. Yankee Doodle Dandy, 1942. Directed by Michael Curtiz. Written by Robert Buckner and Edmund Joseph. Starring James Cagney, Joan Leslie, Walter Huston, Richard Whorf, Irene Manning, Rosemary DeCamp.

99. Toy Story, 1995. Directed by John Lasseter. Written by Joss Whedon, Andrew Stanton, Joel Cohen, Alec Sokolow. Starring Tom Hanks, Tim Allen, Don Rickles, Annie Potts (voices).

100. Ben-Hur, 1959. Directed by William Wyler. Based upon the novel by Lew Wallace; Screenplay by Karl Tunberg. Starring Charlton Heston, Jack Hawkins, Haya Harareet, Stephen Boyd, Hugh Griffith, Martha Scott.

Note: Reprinted by permission of The American Film Institute.

Great American Film Directors

In 1968, the film critic Andrew Sarris published *American Cinema: Directors and Directions*, in which he put forth what earlier French critics called the *auteur* theory. The central idea behind the theory was that the director was the single most important person in the making of a film. Essentially it was the director's vision that stood behind the making of those films we have come to regard as essential, classic, brilliant. Several film historians have shown the flaws in this argument (notably Thomas Schatz in *The Genius of the System*, 1989) and demonstrated that the studios produced fine films, often under the guidance of the producer, and that some highly regarded directors worked very well under the studio system's restrictions. After all, *Gone With the Wind, The Wizard of Oz, Casablanca, All About Eve* and many others were produced by the studios and have achieved iconic status in the history of American film.

Still, the *auteur* theory has helped serious moviegoers understand that a director's body of work, when taken as a whole, can reveal a personal style and sensibility that accounts for their long-term success and the high standing of their films. Below is a short list (in alphabetical order) of directors with their best-known films highlighted. Anyone who takes the time to see these pictures will have a solid introduction to the most important aspects of American film.

Frank Capra Born in Sicily in 1897 and raised in California, Capra started working in movies after serving in World War I. He started directing in 1926 and made dozens of movies over the next decade. In 1934, the cheeky comedy *It Happened One Night* made stars of Clark Gable and Claudette Colbert, and won an Oscar for them as well as Capra. Capra would soon produce and direct a string of idealistic stories that featured the common man (played either by Gary Cooper or Jimmy Stewart) as hero and dupe to the rich and powerful, including *Mr. Deeds Goes to Town* (Oscar for Best Director, 1936); *You Can't Take it With You* (Oscar for Best Picture and Best Director, 1938); *Mr. Smith Goes to Washington* (1939); *Meet John Doe* (1941), and *It's a Wonderful Life* (1946). In these films Capra stood up for the traditional values of honesty, loyalty and patriotism that some regard as corny, but which won the public's attention and affection. During World War II, he made a series of powerful propaganda films for the government, *Why We Fight* (1942, 1943).

Francis Ford Coppola Born in 1939, he attended film school at U.C.L.A. in the mid-1960's. Coppola started as a screenwriter and by the time he was in his early 30's he had written or collaborated on more than a dozen screenplays including the smash hit *Patton* (1970). In 1972 he directed the first of three films based on the novel *The Godfather*, about Italian mafia families in New York. The first two won multiple Oscars and gave Coppola the clout to make his most ambitious film, *Apocalypse Now* (1979), a Vietnam war story based on Joseph Conrad's novel *Heart of Darkness*. A controversial film from the outset, it has attained a large following over the years because of Coppola's outstanding storytelling ability.

John Ford Born Sean Aloysius O'Fearna to Irish immigrants in Maine in 1895, he went to Hollywood when he was 19 and three years later, in 1917, became a contract director at Universal Studios making westerns. At the age of 29 he directed his first western epic, *The Iron Horse* (1924). During the Depression years he made several comedies but won his first Oscar for *The Informer* (1935), a bitter story of betrayal set in Ireland; a second Oscar followed in 1940 for *The Grapes of Wrath*, based on the bestselling novel by John Steinbeck. His third Oscar-winning film was also set in Ireland, *The Quiet Man* (1952).

Ford is best known for the westerns he made beginning with *Stagecoach* (1939) which featured John Wayne. After World War II, he directed a string of extraordinary films that together forged a history of American expansion and the civilizing of the western frontier: *My Darling Clementine* (1946), *She Wore a Yellow Ribbon* (1949), *Wagonmaster* (1950), *The Searchers* (1956), and *The Man Who Shot Liberty Valance* (1962).

Elia Kazan A Greek immigrant from Turkey, he arrived in New York in 1913 at the age of four. Kazan was well-educated at Williams College and Yale Drama School and in the 1940's became an established stage director of major American plays by such writers as Arthur Miller and Tennessee Williams. Hollywood soon lured him west where he directed several powerful films including the first to deal with anti-Semitism, *Gentlemen's Agreement* (1947), which won Academy Awards for Best Picture and Best Director, and *Pinky* (1949), a realistic view of race and racial prejudice in America that still resonates with audiences today.

In April 1952, Kazan testified before the U.S. House Committee on Un-American Activities and admitted being a member of the Communist Party in the 1930's, but he also named others as members. He was now a hated man in Hollywood, but he responded by making one of the great films of all time, *On the Waterfront* (1954), the story of union corruption on the Brooklyn docks, and how a former boxer, played by Marlon Brando, broke the union's power by testifying against them. It won six Academy Awards, including Best Picture and Best Director.

Kazan followed up with a string of highly regarded films, including *East of Eden* (1955), based on John Steinbeck's novel and starring a young James Dean; *Baby Doll* (1956); *A Face in the Crowd* (1957), and *Splendor in the Grass* (1961), which marked the film debut of Warren Beatty.

George Stevens California born and bred, Stevens was 17 when he started in film as a cameraman. He joined RKO in 1934 and the following year directed a young Katharine Hepburn in the highly successful *Alice Adams*, a painful story about the cruelties of class relations, a theme Stevens would revive later in two of his famous works, *A Place in the Sun* (1951) and *Giant* (1956), both of which won him the Academy Award for Best Director.

Stevens directed films in a wide range of categories including the Astaire-Rogers musical, *Swing Time* (1936), the war film, *Gunga Din* (1939), the sophisticated comedy of the first Tracy-Hepburn movie, *Woman of the Year* (1942), the classic western drama, *Shane* (1953), the tragic *The Diary of Anne Frank* (1959), and the biblical epic, *The Greatest Story Ever Told* (1965). All together Stevens made 40 feature films, 15 in the silent era.

Billy Wilder Born Samuel Wilder in Vienna in 1906, he graduated from law school and in 1929 drifted into screenwriting for several German filmmakers. In 1933 he went to Hollywood and together with Charles Brackett forged a successful screenwriting career over the next decade. Their most well-known script was *Ninotchka* (1939), starring Greta Garbo. By 1942 his long career as a director began but he always continued working as a screenwriter.

By 1950 he had written and directed seven films, three of them considered classics today: *Double Indemnity* (1944), a bitter and cynical story of infidelity, lust, greed, and murder; *The Lost Weekend* (1945), which chronicles the painful descent into alcoholism of a struggling writer, won Oscars for Best Picture, Best Director, Best Screenplay and Best Actor (Ray Milland); and *Sunset Boulevard* (1950), a hard-bitten look at the movie business and its forgotten older stars and ambitious young men.

During the 1950's Wilder wrote, directed and occasionally produced a string of major films that showed his extraordinary creative talent, but now in sophisticated comedies: *Stalag 17* (1953); *Sabrina* (1954); *The Seven Year Itch* (1955); and *Some Like It Hot* (1959). In 1960, Wilder won the Academy Award for *The Apartment*, a typical Wilder film that included elements of love, sex, and money, all mingled together with humor and a healthy dollop of cynicism about the human species. This was followed by four more films, including two highly regarded comedies, *Irma La Douce* (1963) and *The Fortune Cookie* (1966).

Over his long career Wilder was nominated eight times for the Academy Award for directing, but also 12 times for screenwriting (he won three: *The Lost Weekend, Sunset Boulevard*, and *The Apartment*). In 1986 he received a Lifetime Achievement Award from the American Film Institute.

William Wyler Like several other famous American directors, Wyler was born in Germany and came to the United States to work in the movie business. In Wyler's case it was his mother's cousin, Carl Laemmle, head of Universal Studios, who convinced the 18-year-old Wyler to start in the publicity department in New York in 1920. In 1925 he was given a chance to direct low-budget westerns and when sound arrived he began a stellar career that would last until 1970.

Over 40 years Wyler would be nominated for an Academy Award 11 times and would win three times: *Mrs. Miniver* (1942), which tells the story of an English family's struggles during World War II; *The Best Years of Our Lives* (1946), the moving account of three G.I.s returning from the war and the emotional upheaval they experience; and *Ben-Hur* (1959), the epic story of how a Jewish nobleman is persecuted by the Romans and finds hope and salvation in the Christian message. Ben-Hur won 11 Academy Awards.

Other well-known and critically acclaimed films were several based on famous literary works including the Brontë classic, *Wuthering Heights* (1939), Lillian Hellman's *The Little Foxes* (1941), and *The Heiress* (1949), based on a play derived from a novel by Henry James. Wyler was awarded the American Film Institute's Lifetime Achievement Award in 1976.

Fred Zinnemann Another Viennese-born (1907) giant of American film, he studied law but became very interested in movies and left for the United States to study film. By the early 1940's he had learned enough to direct several nondescript feature films. Over the next 40 years he would direct 20 more features, almost all of them highly regarded no matter what genre they represented: musical (*Oklahoma!*, 1955), drama (*The Nun's Story*, 1959), thriller (*The Day of the Jackal*, 1973).

Zinnemann's most famous film is undoubtedly *High Noon* (1952), a western starring Gary Cooper and Grace Kelly. It tells the story of a town threatened by a violent gang and defended only by a sheriff who believes his duty requires that he fight them. Famous for its attempt to tell the entire story in real time (about 80 minutes), *High Noon* was among the first 25 films chosen for the National Film Registry in 1989.

Two of Zinnemann's films would win both Best Picture and Best Director, *From Here to Eternity* (1953), a story about illicit love, adulterous love, loyalty and friendship on the eve of the attack on Pearl Harbor; and *A Man for All Seasons* (1966), based on the play about St. Thomas More, whose refusal to violate his beliefs cost him his life at the hands of Henry VIII.

DANCE

Dance is one of humankind's earliest forms of expression. It existed long before written language, and like all the arts, reflects the culture and time period in which it was created. Early dance was associated with religious ritual, and we also know that the Greeks and Romans included dance in their theatrical presentations. World dance is a vast subject, covering everything from theatrical traditions to "folk" dances of various cultures. This overview will focus on the history of dance performance from the 18th century to today.

Ballet

Webster's Dictionary defines ballet as "an artistic dance form based on an elaborate formal technique, characterized by gestures and movements of grace, precision, and fluidity." Ballet dates back to the 16th-century French courts. In 1581 Catherine de Medici brought a group of Italian dancers to the court to provide entertainment for a wedding; the spectacle was called *Le Ballet Comique de la Reine* (The Comic Ballet of the Queen). Based on the kind of performances given in Italy since the Renaissance, ballet caught on as a favorite court entertainment in France. For its first 100 years ballet was performed by male courtiers as an amateur entertainment.

In 1661 French king Louis XIV, an accomplished dancer who earned the nickname the "Sun King" from his role as Apollo—god of the sun—in "Le Ballet de la Nuit" (Ballet of the Night, 1653), established an Académie Royale de Danse to train professional ballet dancers. Pierre Beauchamp was named the "superintendent of the king's ballets" and is credited both with developing the French ballet terminology (still in use today) and the five positions of the feet, which remain the basis for ballet instruction throughout the world. In 1669 Louis established the Académie Royale de Musique, which was run by Jean-Baptiste Lully, (1632–87) who created a dance academy within the school. This dance company survives today as the Paris Opera, the oldest continuously running ballet company in the world. In 1789 choreographer Jean Dauberval created *La Fille Mal Gardée*, the first ballet with a plot drawn from "peasant" life, and the oldest ballet still in the repertoire.

Meanwhile, news of the development was spreading through Europe. After making a tour of Europe in the late 17th century, Czar Peter the Great returned to Russia and began a process of introducing the contemporary arts to his homeland. French ballet teacher Jean Baptiste Lande came to Russia, and in 1738 established the first school there, the Imperial Theatre School in St. Petersburg. Several French masters followed in his wake, and the seeds of the great age of Russian ballet were planted.

The nascent United States did not miss out on the craze for ballet. As early as 1735, ballet troupes performed in the American colonies. The first ballet produced in the U.S. was staged by Alexander Placide and his wife in Charleston, South Carolina, in 1791, followed a year later by an entire season presented by them in New York. The first American professional dancer, John Durang, said to be George Washington's favorite, appeared in this production.

The 19th century was the heyday of the Romantic ballet. Dance technique had matured to the point where truly expressive, plot-driven works could be created. These techniques were summarized in Carlo Blasis's landmark 1820 work, *An Elementary Treatise Upon the Theory and Practice of the Art of Dancing*, which was published in Milan. Blasis taught in Italy, France, and England, spreading the technique. In 1832 Italian choreographer/dancer Fillipo Taglioni's ballet *La Sylphide* appeared, generally accepted as the first Romantic ballet. It featured his daughter, Marie, in the lead, establishing the importance of the prima ballerina as the "star." Marie popularized dancing on pointe (some credit her as the originator of the technique), and by the 1860's, ballet shoes were reinforced to facilitate this skill. *La Sylphide* was followed by a second great Romantic work, *Giselle*, in 1841, starring another great Italian ballerina, Carlotta Grissi.

The Romantic ballet dancer Fanny Elssler spread the new style far and wide. In 1840 she toured the United States, making the bold (for the time) choice of partnering with an American dancer, George Washington Smith; the tour helped build an audience for dance in America. Eight years later, she traveled to Russia with dancer Jules Perrot, and they were an immediate sensation. Perrot remained in Russia, where he would head the Maryinsky Ballet for a decade. He was succeeded by another Frenchman, Arthur Saint-Leon, who remained in Russia from 1858 to 1870, and then returned to France, where he created the last great Romantic ballet, *Coppélia*. In 1847, the young French dancer Marius Petipa performed at the Imperial Theater in St. Petersburg, and 20 years later became the chief ballet master. Petipa dominated the ballet scene until his retirement in 1903 and ushered in a golden age of ballet, creating 77 works, including *Don Quixote* (1869) and *La Bayadère* (1877). His most beloved and widely performed ballets are those with scores by Pyotr Ilyich Tchaikovsky: *The Sleeping Beauty* (1890), *The Nutcracker* (1892), perhaps the most popular ballet in the world today, and *Swan Lake* (1895).

By the early 20th century, the great patrons of the Romantic ballet—the courts of France, Russia, and Italy—were no longer able to sponsor lavish productions and the associated schools. Meanwhile, changes in the art world were bringing new ideas to dance makers, who were rejecting the artifice of the 19th-century plots and the highly stylized dancing that accompanied them. Key to the new movement was a Russian ballet producer named Sergei Diaghilev (1872–1929). In 1911, he brought his company, Les Ballets Russes, to Paris, and a revolutionary new style was born. Diaghilev sought out the greatest modern artists to create sets and costumes for his dances—including Leon Bakst, Pablo Picasso, and Henri Matisse—and contemporary musicians—Igor Stravinsky, Sergei Prokofiev, Maurice Ravel, Claude Debussy, and Erik Satie—to create dynamic new scores. He also nurtured the careers of great dancers and choreographers, whose imprints remain on ballet today. Mikhail Fokine revolutionized ballet by eliminating the use of mime to tell the story and instead using dance movement to reveal emotion and move the story forward. His best-known works were created for Vaslav Nijinsky, who drew huge crowds in Europe with his spectacular leaps and dramatic presence. Among these were *Schéhérazade* (music by Nicolai Rimsky-Korsakov, 1910), *Firebird* (music by Igor Stravinsky, 1910) and *Petrouchka* (music by Igor Stravinsky, 1911). In 1912 Nijinsky replaced Fokine as the primary choreographer for

Les Ballets Russes, creating works that foreshadowed the development of modern dance. Audiences were shocked by the sensuality of *Afternoon of a Faun* (music by Claude Debussy, 1912), and a year later, *Rite of Spring* (music by Igor Stravinsky, 1913), the story of an ancient fertility ritual in which the chosen virgin is forced to dance herself to death, famously inspired riots at its premiere in Paris.

Another of Diaghilev's notable protégés was George Balanchine, a Russian dancer and choreographer who studied at the Imperial School of Ballet at the Mariinsky Theatre. Balanchine left the Soviet Union in 1923 to join Les Ballets Russes where he created 10 new works, including *Apollo* (music by Igor Stravinsky, 1928) and *Prodigal Son* (music by Sergei Prokofiev, 1929), but his greatest influence was on the growth of ballet in the United States.

Modern ballet in America has its roots in the vision and persistence of one man: dance critic and promoter Lincoln Kirstein (1907–96). While still a student at Harvard in the early 1930's, Kirstein began dreaming of creating an American ballet company. In 1933 he first engaged Balanchine to open the School of American Ballet, followed a year later by establishing a related company. After several false starts, Kirstein and Balanchine established the New York City Ballet in 1948, still one of the world's great ballet companies. Balanchine created more than 150 works for the company, including a full-length version of *The Nutcracker*, but his preference was for programs that included several short ballets with simple sets and costumes that enhanced the movements of the dancers.

Others had similar ideas, and new companies sprang up through this period, notably in San Francisco (in 1933), Chicago (The Littlefield Ballet, a year later), and New York (American Ballet Theatre, in 1937). The Joffrey Ballet, founded in 1956 by Robert Joffrey (1930–1988) a visionary teacher, and Gerald Arpino (1923–2008), a noted choreographer is another notable American ballet company. The Joffrey began as a touring company that performed original ballets and contemporary renderings of classical ballets, and had homes in New York and Los Angeles before settling permanently in Chicago. Among its "firsts," the company was the first to perform in the White House, at the invitation of Jacqueline Kennedy, and the first American ballet company to tour the Soviet Union.

In 1969, Arthur Mitchell, an African-American dancer retired from the New York City Ballet, opened the Dance

Balanchine: The Radical in Classical Garb

by ANNA KISSELGOFF

"I don't want my ballets laughed at 50 years from now." So said George Balanchine when I asked him if he wanted his works to survive him.

What did he mean? That over time ballets are distorted or modified by dancers and choreographers when their creators are gone? Yes, but more certainly he meant that tastes change, that dancing changes and that, since he choreographed for his time, even if his ballets were preserved in amber, they would not speak to another age.

Very likely Balanchine will be proved wrong. It has been 20 years since he died, and his ballets are performed more widely than ever. Balanchine was one of the greatest choreographers in the history of ballet and one of the 20th century's most innovative artists. To know Balanchine in depth is to know him through his work. His monumental achievement remains relevant for all time.

Moving past Serge Diaghilev's definition of ballet as a synthesis of painting, music and dance, Balanchine insisted that dance was primary. Like an abstract painter concerned with paint, he created nonillusionist art. It was art focused on its own essence. In a typical Balanchine ballet, the material of dance is dance.

To anyone familiar with Balanchine, such concepts are basic truths. More than anyone, he raised choreography in ballet to an independent art. He introduced speed, energy, attack and startling compositional patterns that pushed dance into the space age.

When *Agon*, the milestone Balanchine-Stravinsky collaboration, had its premiere in 1957, the choreographer and Lincoln Kirstein, City Ballet's founders, compared the work in a program note to an I.B.M. computer. (How many people in 1957 knew what a computer was?) Yet in the seminal *Agon* Balanchine also remained loyal to the 350-year-old idiom of classical ballet. He transformed it and extended it into a contemporary language but respected it as a grammar of movement. Unlike Isadora Duncan, Martha Graham, and Merce Cunningham, he rejected the idea of a personalized dance idiom.

Tradition was the springboard for his innovation. That he used toe shoes and a centuries-old vocabulary did not make him old fashioned. Even today his focus on pure dance, steps and structure, is too rigorous for those who demand dance-drama or movement that expresses specific emotion.

It is worth repeating the significant statement Balanchine made upon his arrival in New York in 1933. "Classicism is enduring because it is impersonal." The dance idiom he chose was classical (codified) and impersonal. If Balanchine will indeed remain relevant in other times, it is precisely because he uses this classical vocabulary as both form and content. It is, in fact, enduring.

Can anyone date two of his signature works by looking at them? *Concerto Barocco*, created in 1941 to Bach's Double Violin Concerto, has undergone a series of costume changes. Now stripped of its overdone designs and danced in white tunics for the women and black tights for its sole male dancer, it is arguably Balanchine's greatest and most spiritual work. Streamlined in its clear design but complex in its interplay between music and dance, between soloists and ensemble, it looks freshly choreographed. By contrast *Symphony in C* is a grand tutu ballet. But its partnering and technique are contemporary. It is not, as might seem, one of Balanchine's tributes to the Russian Imperial Ballet.

Balanchine became Balanchine as we know him today in the 1940's. That is, he arrived at his signature style after initial, more rebellious experiments. Tradition, however, was in his training. His family encouraged him to study both music and dance in the Russian academies. After entering the school of the Maryinsky Ballet in St. Petersburg, he was virtually abandoned, when his parents, brother and sister moved to Tbilisi in 1918.

The myth is that Balanchine, as a Maryinsky student, was part of the czar's household. The reality is that his formative years were spent in the maelstrom following the czar's overthrow in 1917. Life was hard but exciting. He lived through the artistic ferment of Russia in the 1920's and choreographed ballets for Diaghilev, for the Royal Danish Ballet, and for English music halls. He had been asked to be ballet master at the Paris Opera Ballet. But in New York he was initially treated as a talented unknown by all but his patron, Lincoln Kirstein. When Balanchine said, "Classicism is enduring," most in the dance audience didn't know what he was talking about in 1933. Now they do.

Theatre of Harlem, which began as a school run out of a garage in Harlem. The school became the nucleus of a professional company which debuted in 1971.

At the same time that ballet companies were being formed throughout the United States, choreographers and dancers were introducing the form to theater and movie audiences. George Balanchine created a new style of theatrical dance by incorporating elements from tap and ballet in *Slaughter on Tenth Avenue* (1936), choreographed for the Broadway musical *On Your Toes*. In Hollywood, it was Fred Astaire who began to integrate dances into movie musicals. Considered the greatest popular music dancer of all time, Astaire took his inspiration from tap, classical ballet, and ballroom dancing. In his iconic partnership with Ginger Rogers, he created memorable moments in such musical films as *Top Hat* (1935) and *Swing Time* (1936). Legendary Russian ballet star Mikhail Baryshnikov called Astaire "a genius...a classical dancer like I never saw in my life."

Gene Kelly, a versatile dancer/choreographer, combined an athletic, masculine dance style with classical ballet technique. As a dancer, he is best remembered for his soft-shoe in *Singin' in the Rain* (1952), but as a choreographer, the 13-minute ballet at the conclusion of *An American in Paris* (1951) is considered his masterpiece.

Agnes de Mille (1905–93), an American dancer and choreographer, took this new theatrical dance style forward. In addition to *Rodeo* (1942) created for Les Ballet Russe de Monte Carlo, and *Fall River Legend* (1948), which had its premiere at the American Ballet Theatre, de Mille's undisputed classic work is the *Dream Ballet* from *Oklahoma!* (1943) which was followed by *Carousel* (1945). In both musicals, the dance sequences were an important element of the overall stories.

Jerome Robbins (1918–98) was inspired by Agnes de Mille and is undoubtedly the most successful and prolif-ic choreographer to move between Broadway and ballet. He joined the New York City Ballet as assistant artistic director in 1948, choreographing an array of plotless, yet moving ballets, including *Dances at a Gathering* (music by Frédéric Chopin, 1969) in which the piano is onstage and the dancers interact with the pianist. At the same time, he choreographed such landmark musicals as *West Side Story* (1957), *Gypsy* (1959) and *Fiddler on the Roof* (1964). His two worlds came together in *I'm Old Fashioned*, choreographed for the New York City Ballet in 1983, in which a pair of dancers on stage parallel the Fred Astaire–Rita Hayworth dance sequence from the musical, *You Were Never Lovelier*, which appears on screen.

By the end of the 20th and beginning of the 21st centuries, ballet was facing new challenges and absorbing new techniques. Most notably, ballet and modern dance—after a century of being pitted against each other as rivals—were moving closer together, in both spirit and actual productions. Among the notable young choreographers working today, Christopher Wheeldon stands out, having created more than 40 works for numerous ballet companies, as well as pieces for the movie *Center Stage* and the Broadway production of *The Sweet Smell of Success*. His first ballet, *Polyphonia* (music by Gyorgy Ligeti) premiered in 2001 and he choreographed his own version of *Swan Lake* for the Pennsylvania Ballet in 2004.

Alexei Ratmansky, born in Leningrad in 1968, resigned his post as director of the Bolshoi Ballet to become artist-in-residence at the American Ballet Theatre. His full-length ballet, *The Bright Stream*, (music by Dmitri Shostakovich, 2003) won a Critic's Circle National Dance Award. In 2009 he choreographed new dances for the Metropolitan Opera's *Aida*, and his first commission for American Ballet Theatre, *On the Dnieper* (music by Sergei Prokofiev), premiered that same year.

Modern Dance

In the early years of the 20th century, in a reaction to the sentimental plots and exaggerated movement style of ballet, a few dancers, primarily in America and Germany, began experimenting with more "natural" movement styles. In America, one of the leaders of this new movement was Isadora Duncan (1877–1927), a Californian who championed a return to a pseudo-classical dance style, featuring free-flowing tunics, bare feet, and movements based on what she imagined Greco-Roman dance to have been. Like Duncan, Ruth St. Denis created exotic dances based on world dance styles—notably Egyptian dance in her famous solo, "Incense." A third dancer, Loie Fuller, experimented with oversized costumes, bathing herself in dramatic stage lighting. She became a favorite among French audiences in the teens and 20's, inspiring Art Deco artists to create "Loie Fuller lamps" and other objects.

In Germany choreographer-dancer Mary Wigman (1886–1973) pioneered a dance style that mirrored the Expressionist movement in theater and the arts. Her angular, dramatic poses expressed deep-seated emotions. The powerful theatricality of her style would be passed on by her students, most notably Hanya Holm, who became a leading choreographer in the 1930's after she moved to the United States

Ruth St. Denis (1877–1968) had the longest-lasting impact on modern dance because, along with dancer/husband Ted Shawn (1891–1972), she formed a dance company and school, known as Denishawn, in 1914. Shawn eventually established the famous Jacob's Pillow Dance School in Massachusetts. Two of their most talented students became the leading choreographers of the next generation: Martha Graham (1894–1991) and Doris Humphrey (1895–1958). Graham is better remembered today, but both Graham and Humphrey were leaders in the modern dance world in the late 20's and 30's. Graham was a dramatic dancer who absorbed the psychological interests of Wigman in dances like her "Primitive Mysteries" (1935), featuring a set by sculptor Isamu Noguchi. Her 1944 work "Appalachian Spring" (with music by Aaron Copland) is recognized as one of the masterpieces of modern dance. Graham choreographed 181 works over the course of 60 years and formed the Martha Graham Company, an incubator for many formidable talents, including Merce Cunningham, Alvin Ailey, and Paul Taylor, all of whom went on to form their own major companies. Humphrey, with her dance partner Charles Weidman, explored everything from movements drawn from nature ("Life of a Bee") to the dangers of fascism ("With My Red Fires").

Humphrey's legacy was continued after World War II by her student José Limón (1908–72), one of the leading dancers in her company. Limón established his own company after World War II, creating works built around aspects of the human character. His first major work, "The Moor's Pavane" (music by Henry Purcell, 1949) expressed the jealousy and remorse of Shakespeare's Othello. The José Limón Dance Company was the first modern dance company to tour South America. Carrying on the legacy of Hanya Holm was Alwin Nikolais (1910–93), who began staging his artfully theatrical dancers—featuring music scores, costumes (often with elaborate masks and body extensions), and sets by the choreographer—in the 1950's. Of this generation, it was Merce Cunningham

(1919–2009) who had the greatest impact on successive generations of dancers. He was interested in movement for its own sake, and many of his pieces were performed in silence. He had a long collaboration with his life-partner, composer John Cage, and worked with an array of visual artists and designers. Many of Cunningham's early works featured costumes, lighting and sets by the abstract artist Robert Rauschenberg, notably "Xover" (Crossover), which included the last designs completed before the artist's death.

Paul Taylor (b. 1930) was a soloist with Martha Graham's company, and he also performed several Balanchine ballet roles with the New York City ballet. Taylor is known for pieces that convey the human experience, incorporating everyday gestures, and often juxtaposing humor and tragedy for effect. Among his most influential pieces are "Three Epitaphs" (featuring early New Orleans jazz music, 1956), "Duet" (music by John Cage, 1957), and "Airs" (music by George Frideric Handel, 1978). Still choreographing and teaching today, his works are much in demand by ballet and modern dance companies around the world.

Alvin Ailey studied dance with Martha Graham and acting with Stella Adler. He formed his own company— Alvin Ailey Dance Theater—in 1958, featuring primarily African-American performers. This highly successful touring company performs the work of many pioneering choreographers of modern dance, as well as works by Ailey himself. Their signature piece is "Revelations" (1960), danced to the music of African-American spirituals.

In the early 1960's, a group of dancers in New York, primarily working out of the Judson Church, carried Cunningham's vision further to encompass even freer, more naturalistic movement. The best-known of these young choreographer/dancers is Twyla Tharp (b. 1941), whose work embodies the intertwining of ballet and modern dance, and is characterized by technically precise, offbeat movements. Tharp frequently collaborated with Mikhail Baryshnikov, and her popular ballet "Push Comes to Shove" (music by Johann Sebastian Bach, 1976) is a result of that association. Like Jerome Robbins, Twyla Tharp has created dances for film (*Hair*, 1978; *White Nights*, 1985) and Broadway, including the Tony award-winning *Movin' Out* (2003), set to the music of Billy Joel.

Other new dance forms began to emerge in the

1960's, leading to the postmodern dance movement, which was less technique-oriented than the work of the earlier period, and more reflective of the cultural interests of Americans at that time. In addition to creating works based on serious social issues, postmodern choreographers used dancers of varied body types and choreographed in a unisex style, so there are no traditional masculine or feminine roles.

Trisha Brown is one of the notable choreographers of this movement, known for moving dance out of the theater and into natural and urban settings, and for exploring alternative ways of moving, such as walking in harnesses. Her piece, *Set and Reset* (music by Laurie Anderson, 1983), about the choreographic process, is considered a postmodern classic.

Beginning in the mid-70's, ballet and modern dance began moving closer together. George Balanchine shared many of the same concerns as the modern choreographers, and the divisions that seemed to exist between the two techniques began to fade. Twyla Tharp began choreographing for American Ballet Theatre, and that same company also staged some of Cunningham's landmark

works, notably "Summerspace." Mark Morris (b. 1956) is an influential dancer/choreographer whose work straddles several dance forms. As a dancer, he performed with the companies of Eliot Feld, Lar Lubovitch, and Laura Dean, and he formed his own company in 1980. In 1988 he became the resident choreographer of the Théâtre de la Monnaie in Brussels, where he created some of his finest work, including *Dido and Aeneas* (music by Henry Purcell, 1989). He returned to the United States in 1991 and began a collaboration with Mikhail Baryshnikov, known as the White Oak Dance Project. His best-loved work from this period is *The Hard Nut* (1991) his own retelling of the Nutcracker story, in which both men and women dance on pointe and in tutus. At the same time, Morris created classical ballets for the American Ballet Theatre and the San Francisco Ballet, as well as other international companies. Once called the "bad boy of modern dance," Morris is now considered a leading member of the dance establishment.

Dance is a living art, and movement styles are constantly changing as each generation experiments with new ideas.

Social Dance

Social dance in America goes back to the square dances, jigs, and reels that were imported by the European colonists. In the mid-19th century, French quadrilles became popular—elaborate series of dances that were always performed in a fixed order. Similarly, the craze for Eastern European polkas and waltzes was imported to America beginning in the mid-19th century through succeeding generations of immigrants.

However, truly indigenous American dance styles—like most great American art forms—were mainly derived through the wedding of European and African-American traditions. The first true American dance style was probably clog dancing, which evolved from Irish step dancing. By the minstrel era of the 1850's, dances like the buck-and-wing were adopted by blackface performers, probably based largely on dances performed by slaves. Later in the 1880's and 90's, the craze for the cakewalk—based on plantation dances by slaves imitating (and satirizing) the dances of their European masters—was another unique American style born of this cross-cultural interchange.

However, like many originally African-American art

forms, it took a pair of white dancers—British-born Vernon Castle and his American-born wife, Irene—to popularize African-flavored dances in the early 20th century among white audiences. The Castles developed a dance called the fox trot, with music provided by their (African-American) bandleader, James Reese Europe, which launched the craze for "animal" dances in the later teens and 1920's: the turkey trot, bunny hug, and countless others. The Charleston, with its syncopated 4/4 rhythm, became the most popular dance craze of the Jazz Age.

Meanwhile, black vaudevillians had developed clog dancing into a new style, which became tap dancing. In the teens and 1920's, virtuosic dance teams developed many elaborate forms of tap, each trying to top the moves of the others. Perhaps most famous and inventive were the Nicholas Brothers, who developed a highly athletic dance style featuring incredible splits, leaps, and slides. Bill "Bojangles" Robinson (1878–1949) was the other leading tap dancer of the day. White tap dancers—most notably Fred Astaire—brought the style to Broadway and eventually to films.

Popular dance reached a height of athleticism in the 30's with the craze for big band jazz and the development

Is Ballet Dying? Sure, It's Died Many Times

by ALASTAIR MACAULAY

Each ballet dies with the fall of the curtain. Will it return to real life when next danced? Nobody can be sure. Some dances need occasional periods in cold storage; others—having forever passed their sell-by dates—carry on in some macabre afterlife onstage that feels spectral. For those of us who adored a work in its youth, which alternative is grimmer: never to see it again or to watch it acquire the lines of age and then become one of the dance dead or, worse, undead?

The famous Shades scene in Marius Petipa's 1877 *Bayadère* is just one example. I loved this in many performances by the Royal Ballet in the 1970's and the Kirov Ballet in the 1980's. In the last 20 years, though, it has grown pale and gray as danced by those companies and others. I can applaud its general look, but the details that made it matter have been blurred out of recognition.

One of the keenest debates in dance right now has been about something larger: is ballet itself dead or dying? This we owe to the epilogue that Jennifer Homans, dance critic for The New Republic, has placed at the end of *Apollo's Angels*, her welcome new history of ballet. (I am thanked in her acknowledgments, but I do not deserve it. Over five years ago, before we met, she sent me part of her chapter on British ballet for my comments, which were not, as I recall, generally complimentary.) "After years of trying to convince myself otherwise," Ms. Homans writes, "I now feel sure that ballet is dying."

When ballet makers retire or die, their whole repertories become endangered species. By 1992, George Balanchine's "Divertimento No. 15"—a ballet that had been the apogee of his purest classicism—seemed so trivial and small at City Ballet that I found it hard to recall what had moved me so greatly.

I have written this before, but it bears saying again: Ballet has died again and again over the centuries. The dances that Louis XIV and Voltaire and Pushkin cherished did not survive. We can smile at that now, because we know how ballet, phoenixlike, rose again

from its ashes; how, protean, it changed its nature with each new era. But I did not smile when writing that 20 years ago. The deaths of Balanchine (1983) and Frederick Ashton (1988) gave my generation too much cause for mourning. Ballet had a beginning (in the Renaissance); it may well therefore have an end.

Yes, in the period after Balanchine, Ashton and other great choreographers, we are living through an often dark era of ballet. There were times in the 1990's when I too felt the art form was essentially dead. But since I began this job almost four years ago, I've seen performances of Balanchine's "Divertimento No. 15" at City Ballet, San Francisco Ballet and (best of all) Miami City Ballet that confounded the misery I had felt about that work in 1992.

Ashton told me in 1988 that his "Symphonic Variations" was "dead," a view with which I concurred. But he added that "the right dancer" might bring it back to life: this has happened in more than one company, but above all in recent performances at Covent Garden by Alina Cojocaru. I know New Yorkers who attended City Ballet in Balanchine's lifetime for whom the young ballerina Sara Mearns exerts a compelling fascination they have not felt since Suzanne Farrell and Kyra Nichols. David Hallberg at American Ballet Theater seems to be taking male classical dancing to fresh peaks. And many, many people who lived through the Balanchine-Ashton era feel that Mr. Ratmansky's choreography gives cause for more than hope.

Perhaps a later history will view all these as the final gutterings of a spent flame. This is no golden age, and several of its ballets are indeed dead. My own main alarm about ballet—not one that troubles Ms. Homans—is that its dependence on pointwork for women and partnering by men proposes a dichotomizing view of the sexes that is at best outmoded and at worst repellently sexist. Nevertheless, this balletgoer testifies that the scene feels brighter than it did 10, 15 or 20 years ago.

of swing dancing, notably the Lindy Hop (named for Charles Lindbergh). Large ballrooms catering to dance enthusiasts sprang up in major cities, and the competition was intense for couples to develop the most intricate movements. The Lindy Hop and Jitterbug incorporated precision moves between the male and female performers, demanding a high level of skill.

Latin or Latin-flavored dances were also extremely popular from the early 20th century on. The Argentinian tango was among the first to inspire a wide following, originally in Paris and then—thanks again to Vernon and Irene Castle—in the U.S. in the teens and 20's. Movie star Rudolf Valentino got his start performing his own version of the dance, which established him as a major sex symbol. In the 30's the tango was supplanted by the Cuban rumba, propelled by several popular Cuban-American performers, as well as the popularity of Havana as a playground for the American elite. The 40's brought the samba, popularized by film star (and fruit-behatted) Carmen Miranda.

During the post-World War II era, a new generation of dancers arose. While the older dancers continued to perform the social dances of their youth, albeit in more sedate versions, teenagers—influenced by the growth of rock 'n' roll—adapted more free-form versions of dance expression. Notable dance crazes spawned by the rock revolution included Chubby Checker's landmark "Twist" (with its many variants) in the late 50's and early 60's; followed by a number of even less structured dances, including the frug, watusi, swim, and dozens more. The message was that anyone could dance, and that—on the dance floor—anything goes.

In the 1970's the rise of disco led to the development of flashy styles of dance. Dances like the hustle showed strong influence from the ballroom styles of the 50's and 60's, notably the Latin mambo and cha-cha (an American adaptation incorporating several Latin-flavored moves). Arising in the black and gay communities, disco demanded precision movement, athletic capability, and intense dedication. It was also a return to couples-dancing, which had diminished in the post-Woodstock music era. Disco dancing moved into the mainstream thanks to choreographer Lester Wilson (1942–93), whose choreograpy for John Travolta in the landmark film *Saturday Night Fever* (1977) was a catalyst for the disco craze that swept the country.

Meanwhile, urban Latino and African-American youth moved on to an even higher and more expressive level of precision dancing, in the many styles that began to blossom with the growth of hip hop music. Mobile DJs had their own "crews," including "b-boys" who danced during the musical breaks, giving the new style its name, breakdancing. Breakdance moves draw from a cross-cultural mx of influences: Nigerian and other African dance styles, boogaloo, funk and soul dancing, and the spinning and rocking movements from Brazilian capoeira. Some dancers developed incredible body control, and highly athletic moves—such as performing head spins and "pop locking," in which joints and muscles are manipulated in unnatural ways—became part of the necessary skills for breakdancers.

The rise of MTV in the 1980's made dancing an important aspect of a hit video, and many pop stars made slick moves an integral part of their appeal. The "King of Pop" Michael Jackson (1958–2009) used his considerable dancing and choreographing skills to great effect in the videos for "Thriller" and "Billie Jean," which introduced the world to his trademark Moonwalk. Nearly every video produced for his albums *Thriller* (1983) and *Bad* (1987) included extravagant dance numbers, studiously copied by adoring fans. Michael's sister Janet Jackson (b. 1966) capitalized on top-notch choreography by then-unknown Paula Abdul (b. 1962) to propel her videos from the *Control* (1986) album. Paula Abdul went on to leverage her dancing and choreography talents to create her own hit albums. Madonna (b. Madonna Ciccone, 1958) took various club dance styles of the 80's and helped popularize them, notably "voguing" drawn from the gay drag ball scene, in which dancers "strike a pose" emulating the exaggerated stances of fashion models. Other musicians, including MC Hammer, Salt 'n' Pepa, Wham!, The Smiths, and many others became known for particular styles of dance emulated by their fans.

While synchronized dance numbers have declined somewhat in music videos since the 1980's, they remained essential parts of large stage shows for pop musicians. Dance-oriented groups, such as the Backstreet Boys, Menudo, Bel Biv Devoe, N 'SYNC, the Spice Girls, Destiny's Child, and TLC, as well as solo acts such as Beyonce and Lady Gaga, made choreographed moves an essential part of their image.

DRAMA

History of Western Drama

Greek Drama (ca. Fifth Century B.C.)

Western drama originated in ancient Greece when, legend has it, one member of the chorus, Thespis, stepped aside and conversed with the rest—hence the term *thespian*. More than entertainment, drama for the Greeks was a vital part of the community's cultural life. It was derived from the dithyramb, a choral hymn and dance performed in honor of Dionysus, god of fertility and wine. Tragic and, later, comic playwriting competitions dating from 534 B.C. were held in Athens (and later in other cities) during the City Dionysia, an annual festival in honor of Dionysus.

Greek Festivals and Theaters The City Dionysia was a five-day festival that began with two days of pageantry in the name of Dionysus and ended with three days of drama. Three competing playwrights were each given a day on which to present their tetralogies, sets of four plays consisting of three tragedies and a brief satiric play called a satyr play. The tragedies almost always drew on familiar stories of the gods and heroes of Greek culture, often from stories found in the *Iliad* and the *Odyssey*. The productions consisted of two actors (later three actors) and a chorus. The satyr plays were bawdy, comic looks at mythology featuring choruses costumed to resemble satyrs, the half-man, half-goat minions of Dionysus.

Beyond writing the plays, the competing playwrights were responsible for creating the music, scenery, and costumes. They were also responsible for the directing and choreography, and in most cases acted in the productions as well. Each play interspersed narrative or dialogue elements, or both, with dance-songs performed by a chorus. All of the participants in the plays wore elaborate masks and costumes, allowing actors to assume the roles of the different characters.

Greek theaters were semicircular stone structures built into slopes of hills. Each theater had a central area called an *orchestra*, or dance space, where the chorus performed. At the back of the orchestra was the *skene*, a structure believed to have been used first as a storage area, later as a scenic background for plays, and finally as a raised stage. The area where the audience sat was called the *theatron*, or "seeing place." The theaters typically held between 14,000 and 19,000 audience members, though some held even more (the theater at Epidaurus held 25,000 audience members).

Tragic Playwrights Although there were many tragic playwrights, the work of only three survives from the fifth century B.C.: that of Aeschylus (ca. 523–456 B.C.), Sophocles (ca. 496–406 B.C.), and Euripides (ca. 480–406 B.C.). Each is credited with an innovation that changed the form of theater. Aeschylus is said to have introduced a second actor to the stage, and was instrumental in the transition from the early dithyramb form to the tragic form. He is thought to have written some 90 plays, of which 70 fragments still exist. His *Oresteia* follows Orestes as he avenges his father's murder by his mother, and exemplifies Aeschylus's concerns with issues of vengeance and justice. The *Oresteia* is the only trilogy that survives intact. Sophocles introduced a third actor and increased the size of the chorus from 12 to 15 members. He is thought to have written some 123 plays, of which only seven have survived. Euripides is credited with having introduced realistic characterization and dialogue. He has 19 surviving plays, including *The Trojan Women* and *Medea*.

Comic Playwrights The comic playwrights Aristophanes (ca. 450–388 B.C.) and Menander (ca. 342–292 B.C.) show a division in comic styles. Their work is categorized as Old Comedy (Aristophanes) and New Comedy (Menander). Old Comedy, typified in Aristophanes's masterpiece, *The Frogs*—which satirizes Aeschylus and Euripides and puts them onstage as characters—showed the world in chaos. In *Lysistrata* he creates an anti-war play in which the women of Athens refuse to have sex with their husbands until there is peace. New

Comedy introduced stock characters, and in this way provided a direct link to the comedies of Rome and later the stock characters of the Italian commedia dell'arte.

Drama and Aristotle's Poetics
After the fifth century B.C., with the defeat of Athens in the Peloponnesian War, the golden age of the Greek tragedy faded. In writing on fifth-century drama in his *Poetics*, considered the most important tract on Western drama ever written, Aristotle (384–322 B.C.) defined the elements of drama. He introduced the term *catharsis*—the purging of spectators' emotions through pity and fear—and the concept of the unities of time, place, and action—that the action of a play should take place within no more than 24 hours, have but one location, and have only one main plot. His work would inform Western drama for centuries to come.

Roman Drama

The theater of the Roman Empire was, to a large degree, a transfer of Greek theater into a Roman vernacular. Plays, though performed at Roman festivals, were set in Greece; actors wore costumes similar to those worn in Greek theater; and most of the surviving Roman plays are adaptations of Greek plays. However, whereas drama in ancient Greece was intrinsically tied to religious experience, drama in the Roman Empire increasingly found value as entertainment. Farce, typified in the works of Plautus (ca. 254–184 B.C.) and Terence (ca. 195–159 B.C.), was a popular form, and the chorus of Greek theater diminished in importance.

Spectacle in Roman Drama
Whereas in Greek theater action took place offstage, in Roman theater, which relied heavily on spectacle, action took place directly onstage. In Seneca's (ca. 4 B.C.–A.D. 65) *Medea*, for example, Medea kills her children onstage. Euripides' Medea, in contrast, kills her children offstage; the audience hears the events taking place offstage but does not see them.

With the fall of Rome in the fifth century, theater fell into a void for nearly 800 years. The rise of Christianity saw the festivals of Rome become incorporated in the Christian liturgical calendar, giving birth to what would be the liturgical drama of the late Middle Ages.

Medieval Drama (ca. 500–1500)

As the Christian church rose to power during the Middle Ages, a new style of drama that celebrated the life of Christ and Christian principles emerged. By the late Middle Ages (ca. 1300–1500), with the rise in the importance of craft and trade guilds and of universities, these plays began to be performed outside of churches, often outdoors at festivals where they were produced and performed by the guilds in the towns in which they were presented.

Mystery Plays
Mystery plays, also called liturgical plays or cycle plays, had their roots in Christian liturgy and in the church calendar. They enacted moments from the life of Christ, and were performed in cycles. The most popular mystery plays were connected to Easter and depicted events involved in Christ's resurrection. Also popular were plays performed during the Christmas season, depicting scenes about the birth of Christ. Special stages were erected for the plays, and the festivals at which they were performed began with processions through the town.

Morality Plays
Morality plays dramatized Christian morals by portraying scenes in which actors personified allegorical characters. One actor might take the role of Goods or Fellowship, while another might enact the role of Sloth. The best known of these plays, *Everyman* (ca. 1500), shows the character of Everyman summoned by Death and accompanied on his journey by actors personifying the material elements of his earthly life, such as Kindred and Fellowship. By the time Everyman reaches Death, only Good Deeds remains as his companion. Morality plays, though first performed by guild members, eventually were performed by professional actors who traveled from town to town.

Theater of the Italian Renaissance (ca. 1300–1600)

During the Italian Renaissance theater developed along two lines: the courtly theater in which the scenic arts flourished and for which new theaters were built; and the improvisational theater of commedia dell'arte. Within the courtly theater there were few playwrights of significance. Among them were Ludovico Ariosto (1474–1533) and Niccolò Machiavelli (1469–1527), both of whom modeled their work after that of the Romans. Plays were often performed at court with amateur performers who were usually courtiers. Although there are few memorable plays from this period, a number of innovations were made in terms of scenic design that influenced theater throughout Europe for centuries to come, including scenes painted on backdrops and the proscenium arch, a frame at the very front of the stage that hid the mechanisms for moving scenery. The proscenium has remained in place in theaters through modern times.

Commedia dell'Arte

Commedia dell'arte was exuberant, largely improvisational theater, dependent on actors rather than on playwrights. It was performed by touring acting troupes throughout Italy, and later throughout Europe. The productions were generally farces, and, while dialogue was improvised, the plots were standardized. Many of the standard plots were laid out in Flaminio Scala's *Teatro delle favole rappresentative* (*The theater of stage plots*). Each plot had a main story, usually involving a pair of youthful lovers, and a comic subplot that was moved along by the characters of comic servants, or *zanni*. Performances relied on visual humor and set comic bits called *lazzi*. With the exception of the young lovers, all actors wore masks. Actors had some scripted speeches that they could draw upon and insert where appropriate, but because of the improvisational dialogue, every performance was different. Music, dance, and acrobatics were often incorporated into the action.

Commedia dell'arte troupes were made up of between eight and 12 members and included women as well as men. Each performer took on the role of a commedia character, often playing the same role throughout his or her career. The roles were the same throughout all troupes—among them were the middle-aged Pantalone; the maid, Colombina; and the servant, Arlecchino (Harlequin).

By the late 16th century, commedia dell'arte troupes had begun to tour throughout Europe. Commedia reached the peak of its popularity by the mid-17th century, though it continued to be performed until the mid-18th century. Commedia's influence was far-reaching and can be seen in the work of, among others, Molière and Shakespeare.

Elizabethan and Jacobean Drama (1558–1642)

In the early part of the 16th century English drama was still beholden to the conventions and practices of the medieval stage. Performances were given by companies that were under the patronage of wealthy gentlemen and were presented both to the court and to the general public. The performances combined elements of popular entertainment with a wide range of source material including biblical stories, romantic tales, classical myths, and English folklore. They often took place on temporary stages consisting of a simple platform, or on pageant wagons that could travel from town to town. In 1559, however, Queen Elizabeth I prohibited plays that dealt with political or religious subjects, forbade the presentation of the medieval cycle plays, and made local authorities responsible for the performances that took place in their area. In addition, she passed a number of laws that were designed to keep the growing number of theatrical companies under close supervision. It was with these developments that the first professional companies appeared, and with them, the need for playwrights and permanent theaters.

Elizabethan Playwrights

In the 1580's the University Wits, a group of highly educated playwrights influenced by an interest in the classical ideal of ancient Greece and Rome that was common throughout Renaissance Europe, appeared in London. They elevated the English language and introduced Senecan devices such as the use of soliloquies, ghosts, and confidantes. The best-known of these playwrights were Christopher Marlowe (ca. 1564–1593), a great innovator in the use of iambic pentameter; and Ben Jonson (1572–1637) who, like Shakespeare, did not have a university education, but was perhaps the most ardent of the period's playwrights in following the classical ideal.

Elizabethan Theaters

The late 16th- and early 17th-century theaters were generally divided into two categories: public (open-aired; outdoor) and private (closed roof; indoor). By the middle of the 1600's, professional companies performed in both. James Burbage built the first permanent public theater (the Theatre) in 1576, and by the start of the English Civil War in 1642 there were as many as nine others competing for business. These theaters included, among others, the Globe, the Swan, the Rose, and the Fortune. The layout of the public theaters is still a matter of speculation, but it is generally thought that they consisted of a raised platform stage that could be surrounded on three sides by standing spectators. Surrounding the standing audience were two galleries of seated spectators. To the rear of the stage was a wall with doors leading to a backstage area. Above the doors was a gallery used for musicians, and above that a tower contained stage machinery. Covering the stage was a painted canopy that was supported by columns and referred to as the "heavens." The private, or indoor, theaters were the venue of choice for the more classically-minded playwrights such as Ben Jonson. The best-known of these theaters was the Blackfriars Playhouse.

Theater Companies Although Elizabethan and Jacobean theater companies operated under the patronage of noble or wealthy gentlemen, most still relied on the public for support. These companies, like the Italian commedia dell'arte troupes, generally operated according to a profit-sharing system. Most company members had multiple responsibilities within the company, such as playwriting, business management, costuming, or acting. Some companies owned their own theaters. Women were not allowed to perform; female roles were played by male actors. A high level of competition existed among the various companies, making it necessary for companies to perform often and maintain a large repertory of plays. Commissioned plays became the property of the company once the playwright's fee was paid. Plays were tightly guarded and rarely published. Rather, the actors would be given the lines for their individual parts alone, and the play would come together as a whole only during its presentation.

William Shakespeare Although much speculation and debate surround the identity of William Shakespeare, official documents and literary references lend valid evidence of his existence.

In 1564 William Shakespeare was born to John and Mary Arden Shakespeare on April 23, as scholars infer from his christening date, April 26. As Shakespeare grew up and attended school in Stratford, his father worked at a number of local government jobs to support the family and became one of the town's most noted citizens. At age 18, William married Anne Hathaway, another citizen of Stratford, and in 1585 they had a twin son and daughter, Hamnet and Judith. One year after the birth of his first two children, Shakespeare left his family in Stratford and traveled to London to pursue his career as an actor and playwright.

In London, between 1589 and 1591, Shakespeare wrote his first plays, a trilogy chronicling the reign of King Henry VI. But in 1592 the plague that swept through the city, killing thousands and forcing all theaters closed by official decree until 1594, compelled Shakespeare to retreat to the outer areas of London.

As his career advanced, a friendly competition arose between Shakespeare and his contemporary Christopher Marlowe, author of *The Jew of Malta* (published posthu-mously in 1633), *The Tragical History of Dr. Faustus* (1588), and other plays, as both playwrights attempted to win the favor of English audiences. Despite the rarity of theatrical performances during the time of the plague, Shakespeare continued to write plays and, ultimately, 154 sonnets.

In 1593, one year before London's theaters reopened, Christopher Marlowe was killed in a bar fight, leaving Shakespeare as the preeminent playwright of the era. When the theaters did reopen, acting troupes returned to business, and the troupe with which Shakespeare worked as an actor and writer of plays for the rest of his career, the Lord Chamberlain's Men, came together. In 1599 the Globe Theatre—the theater most regularly used for Shakespeare's performances—opened for exclusive use by the Lord Chamberlain's Men. In 1601, the year of John Shakespeare's death, and the year William Shakespeare wrote *Hamlet*, his history *Richard II* played at the Globe Theatre. At about the same time, the earl of Essex attempted a rebellion against Queen Elizabeth. Because of the content of *Richard II*, many felt that Essex's party had instigated this performance as an incentive to rebellion, thus implicating Shakespeare as a sympathizer to the earl of Essex and his cause. After the failed rebellion an investigation into Shakespeare's actions disclosed no irregularities, and ultimately the authorities brought no charges against him.

Queen Elizabeth died in 1603, leading to accession of James I (James VI of Scotland) and ushering in the Jacobean period in England. King James was a great supporter of the theater, and after he saw a performance of Shakespeare's comedy *As You Like It*, he issued a royal order to change the name of the Lord Chamberlain's Men to the King's Men.

Shakespeare's artistic production was astounding, not only in number but in quality: the 38 plays and the poems and sonnets are a trove of both astounding insights into human character and arguably the most magnificent poetry ever written in the English language.

Shakespeare died on April 23, 1616. It seems an unlikely coincidence that his death took place on his 52nd birthday. Yet, since we can infer the date from the date of his burial (April 25) and from an inscription on a statue carved in his honor a few years after he died, scholars have more or less agreed on April 23 as the correct date of his death.

Timeline for Shakespeare's Writings

Year Written	Play and Publication Date
1590–1591	*2 Henry VI* (pub. 1594), *3 Henry VI* (pub. 1594)
1591–1592	*1 Henry VI* (pub. 1623)
1592–1593	*Richard III* (pub. 1597), *Venus and Adonis* (pub. 1593)
1592–1593	*The Comedy of Errors* (pub. 1623), *The Rape of Lucrece* (pub. 1594), *Titus Andronicus* (pub. 1594), *The Taming of the Shrew* (pub. 1623)
1594	*Two Gentlemen of Verona* (pub. 1623)
1594–1595	*Love's Labour's Lost* (pub. 1598), *Romeo and Juliet*
1595–1596	*Richard II* (pub. 1597)
1595–1596	*A Midsummer Night's Dream* (pub. 1600)
1596–1597	*King John* (pub. 1623)
1596–1597	*The Merchant of Venice* (pub. 1600)
1597–1598	*1 Henry IV* (pub. 1598)
1598	*2 Henry IV* (pub. 1600)
1598–1599	*Much Ado about Nothing* (pub. 1600)
1598–1599	*Henry V* (pub. 1600), *Julius Caesar* (pub. 1623), *As You Like It* (pub. 1623)
1596–1600	
1599–1600	*Twelfth Night* (pub. 1623)
1600–1601	*The Merry Wives of Windsor* (pub. 1602)
1600–1601	*Hamlet* (pub. 1603)
1601–1602	*Troilus and Cressida* (pub. 1609)
1602–1603	*All's Well That Ends Well* (pub. 1623)
1604–1605	*Measure for Measure* (pub. 1623), *Othello* (pub. 1622)
1605–1606	*King Lear* (pub. 1608), *Macbeth* (pub. 1623)
1606–1607	*Antony and Cleopatra* (pub. 1623)
1607–1608	*Coriolanus* (pub. 1623), *Timon of Athens* (pub. 1623)
1608–1609	*Pericles* (pub. 1609)
1609–1610	*Cymbeline* (pub. 1623)
1610–1611	*The Winter's Tale* (pub. 1623)
1611–1612	*The Tempest* (pub. 1623)
1612–1613	*Henry VIII* (pub. 1623)
1613	*The Two Noble Kinsmen* (pub. 1634)

Shakespeare's Major Plays

Tragedies

Romeo and Juliet   This is a tragedy of young—indeed, very young—love, doomed from the start; the hero and heroine are introduced in the prologue as "star-crossed lovers."

Act I A street-brawl erupts between servants of the feuding Montague and Capulet families, then spreads to involve members of the families. The absence of Romeo Montague is noted, and he is found by his cousin Benvolio to have been brooding with love-sickness. They disguise themselves and attend a ball at which Romeo's beloved is to be present. There, however, he and Juliet, a Capulet who is to marry Count Paris, fall in love. Tybalt, a Capulet, recognizes Romeo and predicts a bitter meeting ahead.

Act II In the celebrated balcony scene, Romeo and Juliet eloquently express their love and agree to marry secretly. Friar Laurence, entreated by Romeo, agrees to officiate, hoping to bring peace to the families. The lovers go to him in stealth.

Act III After the ceremony, Tybalt chances to meet Romeo and challenges him. Romeo demurs, but Mercutio engages Tybalt and is killed; when Tybalt returns, he is slain by Romeo, who is then exiled by the Prince of Verona. The lovers steal one night together, as the Capulets arrange for Juliet and Paris to marry very soon. Informed of this, the daughter spurns her parents.

Act IV Friar Laurence proposes that Juliet fake her death with a potion he will provide, and then be rescued by the banished Romeo. However, her father moves up the marriage by one day, so Juliet takes the arranged potion immediately. The next morning her nurse finds her body and presumes her to be dead.

Act V By mischance, Juliet's death is reported to Romeo, and he plans to poison himself at her tomb. There he finds Paris, who challenges him and is killed. Romeo takes the poison. Juliet awakes, finds him dead, and kills herself with his dagger. Capulet, Montague, and others arrive, learn of events from Friar Laurence, and, moved by them, end their feud.

This early Shakespearean tragedy presents literature's most famous lovers. Filled with action that brings out the danger of their rashness, the language presents a major enrichment in the beauty of Shakespeare's poetry.

Julius Caesar The fear of a power-hungry Caesar leads to betrayal and self-sacrifice in 44 B.C.

Act I Cassius and Brutus, Caesar's friend and ally, agree that Caesar has grown arrogant and ambitious, and that his rule has left many unhappy in Rome. Caesar meets a soothsayer, who tells him to beware the Ides (the 15th) of March. Mark Antony three times offers Caesar the crown, which he declines to great cheers from the crowds. Cassius plans to lure Brutus to conspire against Caesar by forging letters that show support from other nobles.

Act II Brutus resolves to join the conspiracy for the general good of Rome. Caesar's wife describes a dream she had of Romans' dipping their hands in Caesar's blood. Caesar resolves reluctantly to go to the Capitol on March 15.

Act III Caesar once again rejects warnings from the soothsayer. The co-conspirators assassinate Caesar, who as he dies cannot believe that Brutus is one of the murderers. They dip their hands in his blood, fulfilling the dream. Mark Antony asks to speak after Brutus at Caesar's funeral. Brutus and Cassius justify to the crowds their killing of Caesar, but Mark Antony sways the citizens to fury, forcing Brutus and Cassius to flee.

Act IV Mark Antony, Lepidus, and Octavius form the Second Triumvirate, discuss which conspirators should live and die, and plan the attack on Brutus and Cassius's armies. When Brutus and Cassius meet again, they argue heatedly over mutual grievances, then reconcile. A servant reports that the enemy approaches and that Brutus's wife, Portia (Cassius's sister), has killed herself. Mark Antony convinces distraught Cassius to bring his armies to Octavius and Antony. That night, Brutus sees Caesar's ghost, which foretells that they will meet again in Philippi.

Act V Brutus and Cassius exchange insults with Mark Antony and Octavius. On the battlefield Brutus's men defeat Octavius, but Cassius's men retreat. Cassius sends Titinius to assess battle progress. When he believes that Titinius has fallen into enemy hands, Cassius kills himself on Pindarus's sword. But Titinius returns to report Brutus's success; when he finds Cassius dead, Titinius kills himself. Brutus finds the dead bodies of Cassius and Titinius then returns to battle. As his army is cornered, Brutus asks the remaining men to kill him. They refuse; he runs into his own sword and dies. When Octavius and Mark Antony find Brutus's body, they declare Brutus the noblest of the conspirators because he believed he was doing good for Rome and not seeking personal gain.

Hamlet, Prince of Denmark The first of Shakespeare's greatest tragedies is a drama of revenge and is considered by many Shakespeare's most psychologically complex play.

Act I Set in Denmark in the royal castle at Elsinore sometime during the late Middle Ages, the play begins with a question—"Who's there?"—establishing a theme of mystery and a motif of searching. King Hamlet of Denmark has inexplicably died, and Prince Hamlet, his son, has returned from university for the funeral. He is suspicious about the hasty marriage of his mother, Gertrude, to his uncle Claudius, who is now king. Informed that his father's ghost has been appearing on the castle battlements, Hamlet arranges to encounter it. The ghost tells him that Claudius had poisoned him and directs Hamlet to avenge him.

Act II Hamlet feigns madness in a confrontation with Ophelia, once his lover, and the daughter of the king's counsellor, Polonius. King and counsellor secretly listen to the exchange and deem Hamlet mad. Two schoolmates of Hamlet are employed to spy on him. Hamlet, in turn, employs a troupe of "players" to enact before Claudius a scene simulating King Hamlet's murder, and so determine the king's guilt by his reaction.

Act III The "play within the play" is performed, and Claudius flees the room in distress. Hamlet judges his uncle guilty. Gertrude calls Hamlet to her room, and, on his way, he spies Claudius alone, but passes up this opportunity for revenge because the king is praying, and, if killed, would go to heaven. While mother and son converse, Polonius hides behind a curtain. When Gertrude, frightened by Hamlet, calls for help, Polonius cries out, and Hamlet, mistaking him for Claudius, stabs and kills the hidden figure.

Act IV Hamlet, with his school friends, leaves for England, where Claudius has sent him to be executed. Ophelia goes mad and dies, and Laertes, her brother, seeks revenge for the death of his sister and his father, Polonius. Hamlet has escaped and returned to Denmark, and Claudius plans a duel between him and Laertes, allowing Laertes to use a poisoned sword, backed up by a poisoned chalice.

Act V Hamlet confronts Laertes when Laertes jumps into his sister's grave at her funeral, but Claudius comes between them and arranges a duel, at which the swords get exchanged and both are fatally wounded. Gertrude mistakenly drinks from the poisoned chalice, then confesses her and the king's guilt. Hamlet stabs and kills Claudius. King Fortinbras of Norway arrives and claims the throne of Denmark.

The complex and uncertain motives, moods, emotions, actions—and inaction—of a hero burdened with duty, grief, and conscience, inform one of the towering works of literature, a compelling story that searches deep into the mystery of being human.

Othello, the Moor of Venice   Its action unfolding with descending force over a few days, this is the most compactly structured of Shakespeare's mature tragedies. Indicative of its concentration and unity, at least one of the three main characters appears in each scene. It is Othello's tragedy, but its most vivid, psychologically intriguing character may be Iago, one of literature's greatest villains.

Act I Iago, ensign to Othello, the black-skinned Moor who is military commander of Venice, is violently jealous that Cassio has been promoted over him to be Othello's lieutenant. He declares his diabolically cunning revenge on his leader, beginning with the revelation of Othello's secret marriage to Desdemona, daughter of Senator Brabantio. Outraged, Brabantio has Othello brought before the Duke. Othello, with his wife's support, defends himself, and matters are let stand as the Duke orders his general to Cyprus, where he will be joined by Desdemona, to oppose a Turkish force. Iago plots to make Othello suspect an affair between Desdemona and Cassio, and he enlists Roderigo as his aide.

Act II Iago seeks to bring down Cassio, whom he now suspects is involved with Emilia, Iago's wife and Desdemona's attendant. He gets Cassio drunk and instructs Roderigo to provoke him into a fight. Cassio strikes both Roderigo and the Cyprus official Montano, and, as a result, Othello demotes him. Iago counsels Cassio to appeal to Desdemona and hints to Othello that she supports Cassio because she loves him.

Act III Othello and Iago secretly observe a conversation between Desdemona and Cassio, then Iago finds an opportunity to deepen his leader's suspicion when Emilia picks up Desdemona's dropped handkerchief, a gift from Othello. Iago hides it in Cassio's rooms and tells Othello that he has seen Cassio carrying it. Othello asks his wife for the handkerchief and is told she has lost it.

Act IV Othello sees Cassio's companion, Bianca, with the handkerchief, and he now believes that Desdemona is unfaithful. He resolves to kill her. He berates his dumbfounded wife and directs Iago to kill Cassio, who deputizes the job to Roderigo.

Act V Roderigo's assault fails, and Cassio wounds him. Iago appears and wounds Cassio, then kills Roderigo to silence him. In the next scene, after a speech in which he reveals his enduring love and a painful dialogue in which she protests her innocence, Othello smothers Desdemona in their bed. Emilia enters and rails against the Moor. When Iago arrives, she realizes his plot and her role in it. Othello lunges at Iago, who stabs Emilia. The eloquently remorseful Othello stabs himself and dies. A Venetian official sentences Iago to be tortured.

King Lear   Commonly considered one of Shakespeare's greatest plays, this tragedy is set in an unknown period of ancient Britain.

Act I Aging King Lear resigns his authority by dividing his kingdom among his daughters Goneril, Regan, and Cordelia, the youngest, who is unable to match her sisters' insincere declarations of love, and so is disinherited. When the Earl of Kent objects, he is banished, but will later return in disguise to attend the king. The King of France resolves to marry Cordelia, while Goneril and Regan conspire with their husbands to deprive Lear of all majesty. When he visits Goneril, she offends him, and he goes to Regan.

A subplot is revealed when the bastard Edmund attempts to convince his father, the Earl of Gloucester, that his legitimate son, Edgar, is planning for the two sons to usurp the father's authority.

Act II Edmund feigns to his father that Edgar has wounded him, as Regan and her husband, Cornwall, avoiding Lear, arrive at Gloucester's castle. Kent attacks Goneril's messenger, Oswald, and is placed in the stocks. Lear arrives at Gloucester's, attended by his "all-licens'd Fool," who nags the king for his own folly. After Goneril and her husband, Albany, appear, Lear becomes aware of his daughters' treachery. They protest that he is no longer entitled to his attendance of knights, and, raging, he departs, with Kent and the Fool, into the storm-threatened night.

Act III As Cornwall and Albany contend with each other, France and Cordelia arrive with an army at Dover to campaign for Lear, who has gone mad amid the blasting storm. Gloucester supports Lear, and Edmund betrays him to Cornwall, while Edgar, in retreat and pretending madness, seeks shelter in a hovel with Lear and his companions. Cornwall arrests Gloucester and tears out his eyes. His own servant attacks and fatally wounds him, and is slain in turn by Regan. Gloucester learns the truth about his sons.

Act IV Edgar, unrecognized by his blind father, escorts him to Dover, where Lear also has headed. Still distracted, Lear goes to sleep, and wakes to recognize Cordelia beside him. With Cornwall dead and "milk-livered" Albany denounced, Regan and Goneril have both fallen for Edmund. Oswald has been employed by both sisters to take love messages to Edmund, and, by Regan, to kill Gloucester. But Edgar kills Oswald when he threatens Gloucester; then he discovers Goneril's letter.

Act V As France and Britain prepare for battle, Edgar reveals Goneril and Edmund's liaison to Albany, and Edmund condemns Lear and Cordelia to death. Edgar, supporting Albany, engages and mortally wounds his brother. Goneril poisons Regan and stabs herself; the dying Edmund suggests that Cordelia can still be saved. But she has been hanged, and her father enters carrying her body, opening a powerful scene in which he briefly hopes that she lives, grieves for her, then himself dies. The last words and, apparently, the fate of Britain, are left to Edgar.

This profound, thematically dense, painfully sad drama searches without illusion into evil, yet balances, in part with its own beauty, the diabolical and angelic capacities of humanity.

Macbeth   Set in Scotland and England during the 11th century, this tragedy explores the role of destiny and an overpowering ambition to influence it.

Act I Three witches on a Scottish countryside scheme about Macbeth's future. King Duncan declares Macbeth the new Thane of Cawdor after Macbeth has defeated his enemy. Macbeth and Banquo encounter the three witches, who tell Macbeth that he will be "king hereafter" and that Banquo's descendants will be kings. Macbeth considers whether to usurp Duncan; when Duncan visits Dunsinane, Macbeth's castle, Macbeth wavers. Lady Macbeth calls him a coward and pushes him to action through her own steely resolve.

Act II Macbeth murders Duncan; Lady Macbeth plants the bloody dagger on Duncan's guards. Noblemen Lennox and Macduff arrive expecting to see Duncan, and Macbeth leads them to Duncan's quarters to find him brutally murdered. Macbeth kills the guards, accusing them of being the assassins. Duncan's sons, Malcolm and Donalbain, escape, implicating them in their father's death. Macbeth becomes king.

Act III Macbeth orders the murders of Banquo and his son, Fleance. Fleance escapes. At a banquet celebrating his kingship, Macbeth sees Banquo's ghost. Malcolm gains the support both of the King of England and Macduff.

Act IV Macbeth returns to the witches, who show him three apparitions: an armed head warning of Macduff's return to overthrow Macbeth, a bloody child saying that no man born of a woman can harm him, and a child wearing a crown and holding a tree who predicts that Macbeth's demise will come only when the Burnham woods outside Dunsinane move against him. Macbeth has Lady Macduff and her son murdered. Macduff meets Malcolm, who tests Macduff's loyalty. Macduff's wife's and son's death enrage Macduff; Malcolm leverages Macduff's anger against Macbeth.

Act V Lady Macbeth grows mad. She sleepwalks, imagining blood on her hands. Macbeth prepares for battle; he fears no man born from woman and is certain that woods cannot move. However, Malcolm orders his men to camouflage themselves with tree branches as they attack Dunsinane. Macbeth learns that his wife has killed herself and that the woods are moving toward the castle. Macduff admits that he was "untimely ripped" from his mother's womb, therefore not "born" in the conventional sense. He kills Macbeth. Macduff takes Macbeth's head to Malcolm's army and hails Malcolm as the new King of Scotland.

Comedies

A Midsummer Night's Dream   Although set in and around ancient Athens, this early Shakespearean romantic comedy owes its fantastic quality to the English conceit that strange, dreamlike events are likely to occur on Midsummer night, June 23rd.

Act I As the marriage of Theseus, Duke of Athens, and Hippolyta approaches, the duke is forced to judge on the fate of other lovers. Egeus has promised his daughter, Hermia, to Demetrius, but she loves Lysander. When Theseus rules that she must marry Demetrius, Hermia and Lysander run off into a local wood. When they reveal their plan to Helena, she determines to tell Demetrius, whom she loves.

A group of laborers—the "rude mechanicals"—meet in the same wood to rehearse a playlet to be performed at the Duke's wedding celebration.

Act II The wood's inhabitants, the Fairies, appear, as Queen Titania quarrels with King Oberon and refuses to give up the changeling boy she has seized. In his wrath, Oberon assigns his jester, Puck, to bring him a flower whose juice, when rubbed on the eyelids of the sleeping queen, will cause her to fall in love with the first being she sees when she awakes. When he hears Demetrius, who has entered the wood to search for Hermia, harshly rejecting Helena, Oberon decides also to apply the love potion to Demetrius. Puck, however, mistakenly sprinkles it on Lysander, while Oberon anoints Titania. Helena discovers Lysander and wakes him. Stricken with love, he follows her.

Act III The mischievous Puck, coming across the mechanicals, turns Bottom the Weaver's head into a donkey's, and this hybrid creature is the first living thing that the waking Titania spies. Hermia, looking for Lysander, meets Demetrius and accuses him of murdering Lysander. Oberon and Puck, realizing their error, apply the juice to Demetrius and arrange for Helena to be present when he awakes. Both youths now love Helena, and prepare to battle, but Oberon and Puck and make them fall asleep, and plan to anoint Lysander with an antidote to the love potion.

Act IV When Oberon finds Titania clinging to Bottom, he applies the antidote to her. Meanwhile Theseus, Hippolyta, and Egeus enter the wood in a hunting party and discover the four young lovers asleep. Egeus appeals to Theseus to enforce the marriage of Hermia and Demetrius, but when Demetrius protests that he now loves Helena, the duke permits the new pairings.

Act V A triple wedding feast follows at Theseus' palace, and the mechanicals present their version of Ovid's "Pyramus and Thisbe," which is followed by a dance of the Fairies.

One of Shakespeare's most attractive, delightful, and humorous plays, what this "Dream" may lack in depth is compensated for by its consummate artistry.

The Merchant of Venice

The Merchant of Venice Shakespeare's dark comedy pits love against usury and revenge in 16th-century Venice.

Act I A sad Antonio listens as his friend Bassanio requests more loan money to woo and marry Belmont heiress Portia. Antonio's money is tied up in his ships at sea, but he puts up his own property to borrow from Shylock, a Jewish moneylender, in order to help Bassanio.

Shylock hates Antonio because the Christian merchant loathes Shylock's usury; Shylock will provide the money, but if Antonio does not repay the debt in three months Shylock will extract a pound of Antonio's flesh. Meanwhile, Portia, who remembers Bassanio fondly, carries out her father's wishes by making anyone who wants to marry her solve a riddle and choose from a gold, silver, or lead box to find her portrait.

Act II Ashamed of her father, Jessica, Shylock's daughter, vows to marry Bassanio's friend Lorenzo; when Lorenzo comes for her, she steals her father's gold and jewels and escapes disguised as a boy. The Prince of Morocco takes his chance at Portia's riddle; he chooses incorrectly, as does the Prince of Aragon. Shylock mourns the loss of his daughter and part of his fortune and blames Antonio.

Act III Bassanio solves the riddle and accepts a ring from Portia, which he swears will be removed only at his death. Bassanio's friend Gratiano marries Portia's woman-in-waiting, Nerissa. Antonio's fortunes apparently have failed, and Shylock will take his pound of flesh. Portia and Nerissa insist that Bassanio and Gratiano help Antonio; the women disguise themselves as men to witness the encounter with Shylock.

Act IV Shylock refuses appeals to spare Antonio. Portia, here named Balthazar, presides over the case. She rules in favor of Shylock, but under penalty of death to the usurer, she invokes the "quality of mercy" and tells him that he must take exactly one pound of flesh, with not a drop of blood. Further, since Shylock conspired to kill a Venetian, he must give half his fortune to Jessica and must convert to Christianity. Bassanio stops Balthazar (Portia in disguise) to thank him. Testing Bassanio's loyalty to his wife, Balthazar demands the wedding ring; after refusing, Bassanio then sends it to Balthazar. Nerissa resolves to play the same trick on Gratiano.

Act V Portia and Nerissa arrive home and feign anger when Bassanio and Gratiano cannot produce their wedding rings. The women scold their husbands for giving away the important symbols of their love and faithfulness. Then the women present the rings to their husbands and reveal their involvement in the judgment against Shylock.

As You Like It

As You Like It Composed alternately in verse and prose, this is one of Shakespeare's finest mature comedies.

Act I In a troubled, unnamed duchy, from which the rightful Duke Senior has been banished to the Forest of

Arden by his brother, Frederick, Oliver de Boys plots against his own brother, Orlando, arranging for the wrestler Charles to attack him. Orlando, however, defeats Charles. Rosalind, Duke Senior's daughter, observes the battle and falls in love with Orlando. Frederick banishes Rosalind to Arden, accompanied by Frederick's daughter, Celia.

Act II When he learns that Oliver intends to murder him, Orlando flees to the forest, where Rosalind and Celia have disguised themselves as the boy Ganymede and his sister, Aliena, and plan to live as shepherds. Orlando, searching for food, discovers the duke in the company of his cynical courtier, Jaques, who speaks of the "seven ages" of man, and the clown Touchstone. Orlando approaches the duke's domain, brandishing a sword, but the duke recognizes and welcomes him.

Act III Frederick demands that Oliver find Orlando, under threat of losing his estates. In the forest, Orlando seeks Rosalind by hanging love poems on trees. She greets him as Ganymede and proposes that Ganymede pose as Rosalind so that Orlando can practice courting her. Before this occurs, Ganymede speaks disapprovingly to the shepherdess Phebe about her scornful treatment of her lover, Silvius—and Phebe falls in love with Ganymede.

Act IV After Orlando practices his lovemaking, a changed Oliver encounters Rosalind as Ganymede, and tells her that Orlando has saved him from an attack by a lion and has been wounded. He shows her a cloth stained with Orlando's blood, and she faints.

Act V Oliver reveals to Orlando, who is well, that he loves and will marry "Aliena." "Ganymede" then talks to Orlando about his love for the still-missing Rosalind. He tells Orlando that he has the power to arrange his marriage to Rosalind, as well as the reconciliation of Phebe and Silvius. Rosalind reveals herself, and Hymen bestows wedding blessings on Rosalind and Orlando, Celia and Oliver, and Phebe and Silvius. The duke appears, reveals that he has found religion, and restores the dukedom to Frederick.

Although sportive and magical, this play, moving meaningfully back and forth from city to forest, is an earnest exploration of love and society, cruelty and redemption.

Twelfth Night Given by its author the alternative title *What You Will*, this gay comedy is named for the twelfth night of Christmas, January 6th, when it may have first been performed.

Act I Duke Orsino of Illyria seeks the hand of Olivia, but, mourning for her brother, she rejects him. Viola and a ship's captain are survivors of a wreck off Illyria, and she, believing her brother Sebastian is also lost, disguises herself as "Cesario" to seek Orsino's aid. She falls in love with the duke, but agrees to help him woo Olivia.

In Olivia's household, the characters of a subplot appear: her glum, "ill-willed" steward, Malvolio, her able maid, Maria, her bibulous uncle, Sir Toby Belch, and the idiotic Sir Andrew Aguecheek, from whom Toby takes money to help him conquer Olivia. When Viola-as-Cesario arrives, Olivia is smitten by "him," and, when he has left, sends him her ring, pretending that she has found it and presumes it to be his.

Act II "Cesario," seeing the ring, realizes unhappily that Viola loves "him." Toby and Andrew become raucously drunk, and Maria bids them to calm down. Malvolio then reproves all three, and Toby and Andrew plot revenge. They send him a love-note supposed to be from Olivia, bidding him to come to her in yellow hose and "cross-gartered." The presumed-dead Sebastian appears in the company of Antonio.

Act III Olivia professes her love to Cesario, while Malvolio, dressed ridiculously and smirking constantly, follows his false instructions and is locked up as insane. Toby stokes Andrew's jealousy of Cesario, and a duel is arranged, which Antonio, thinking that Cesario is Sebastian, prevents. Confusion thickens when Antonio asks "Cesario" for his (Antonio's) purse, and is naturally denied. At length, Viola-Cesario, who has heard the name "Sebastian," senses that her brother is alive.

Act IV Andrew challenges the "cowardly" Cesario, but finds himself confronting Sebastian. Olivia arrives to head off a fight. Olivia asks Sebastian, who she thinks is Cesario, to solemnize their betrothal, and he agrees.

Act V Antonio, in the duke's presence, confronts Cesario, still believing him to be Sebastian. The duke is upset when Olivia addresses Cesario as her beloved, and grows angrier still when a priest reveals that he has married them. Andrew and Toby appear, wounded after a battle with Sebastian, whom they had assumed to be the weak Cesario. The puzzlement dissolves when Sebastian enters. Duke Orsino then proposes to Viola, and it is revealed that Toby has married Maria. Only the gulled Malvolio remains unhappy, and swears revenge "on the whole pack of you."

So ends one of Shakespeare's most delightfully plotted, amusing, and popular plays.

The Tempest   This Shakespearean "romance" is the author's last complete play.

Act I   Antonio, Duke of Milan, and his party, returning by sea to Italy from a wedding celebration, are driven by a storm to the island where Prospero, the former duke, deposed and set adrift by Antonio, his brother, has settled with his daughter, Miranda. Prospero, a magician, has usurped the witch Sycorax, freeing the spirit Ariel, whom Sycorax has imprisoned in a tree, and subordinating the witch's brutish son, Caliban. Prospero's "art" has caused the tempest and, through Ariel, manipulates the shipmates, separating the crew from the courtly passengers. The innocent Miranda falls immediately in love with one of the latter, Ferdinand, who represents to her a "brave new world," but Prospero consigns Ferdinand to be his wood-carrier.

Act II   Ferdinand's father, Alonso, King of Naples, mourns for his lost son as he, Antonio, Sebastian, and Gonzalo wander about. When Ariel causes the former two to sleep, the others plan to kill Alonso. Elsewhere, the drunken seamen Trinculo and Stephano discover Caliban, who considers their liquor "celestial" and kneels in homage to Stephano.

Act III   Ferdinand proposes to Miranda, and Caliban enlists his new friends to murder Prospero. Ariel performs tormenting tricks on the noble companions and reminds them of their crime against Prospero, in which all took part. Repentant Alonso believes Ferdinand's death to be his punishment.

Act IV   Prospero employs spirits and nymphs to create a masque to celebrate the betrothal of Miranda and Ferdinand. Ariel reports to his master that he has charmed the would-be assailants and driven them into a "filthy pool." When they arrive, soaked, at Prospero's cell, the spirit beguiles the sailors with glittering garments, and a phantasmal pack of hounds drives off all three.

Act V   Prospero discloses himself to the four noblemen when they in turn are led to his cell. He reclaims his dukedom and the plot against Alonso, pardons his offenders, and reveals Ferdinand, in Miranda's company, to his joyful father. Ariel brings the ship's boatswain to report that it is ready to sail. Caliban rues his admiration for Stephano and Trinculo. Prospero directs Ariel to provide smooth sailing for the travelers, then sets him free. In an epilogue he renounces his "charms" and begs the audience to release him from the island—and the play.

This play, an adventure into enchantment, music, and fancy, moves playfully through darkness to establish the mood of forgiveness and theme of restoration that distinguishes Shakespeare's late romances, while it also expresses the author's farewell to his own incomparable poetic art.

History

King Henry IV, Part I   Set in about the year 1400, this "history play" focuses both on the reign of Henry IV and the transition of his son, the Prince of Wales, from wild youth to noble heir apparent.

Act I   King Henry IV, who has usurped the crown of Richard II, faces continued civil war. His general, Mortimer, has been defeated and captured by Glendower of Wales, and Mortimer's brother-in-law, the fiery Hotspur, has defeated Douglas of Scotland. The king, suspecting that Mortimer is in league with Glendower, will not ransom him, and Hotspur, in turn, will not yield his prisoners. Henry, who had favorably compared Hotspur to his own dissipated son, threatens him, and Hotspur, his father, Northumberland, and uncle, Worcester, join with Mortimer, Glendower, and Douglas in rebellion against the king.

Prince Hal appears in the company of the much older, rotund Sir John Falstaff, who plans a highway raid with his companions. Hal's soliloquy declares his intention to break off soon with the frivolous life of his youth.

Act II   Hal and Poins foil the raid by robbing the robbers, an event that Sir John distorts to his advantage at the Boar's Head Tavern before Hal and Poins reveal their role. In an extraordinary scene, Hal and Falstaff conduct a dialogue in which they alternately play the king and the prince.

Act III   The rebels propose their partition of Britain, while the king reproves his son. Hal promises to compensate for his wanton ways by taking revenge on Hotspur. Before leaving for the battlefield, however, he returns to the Boar's Head, where he enlists Falstaff in the war.

Act IV   Hotspur finds himself deprived of support, but, ever vainglorious, relishes the challenge. Falstaff, ever corruptible, accepts money to release soldiers, then joins the prince. The king sends a messenger to arrange a meeting with the rebels.

Act V A peace is arranged, but the emissaries, Worcester and Vernon, fearing that the rebels will nonetheless be punished, report the opposite to Hotspur, and the battle begins. Falstaff, for whom "the better part of valor is discretion," drinks sack (sherry) and feigns death amid the fighting, while Hal routs Douglas, who has confronted King Henry, and, in an inevitable encounter, slays Hotspur. Henry condemns Worcester and Vernon to death, and prepares to continue the war on two fronts—king and prince will fight together in Wales.

So gripping are the events in this play, so brilliantly realized the characters—particularly Hotspur and the universally appealing Falstaff—so deft the balance of humor and high seriousness, that some believe its sequel, *Henry IV, Part II*, was staged in response to popular demand.

The Shakespeare Controversy Some people actually believe that Shakespeare was not a real person, but the pseudonym of another author of the Elizabethan era. Others believe that because the works are so brilliant they cannot possibly be the work of one man, and therefore bear the mark of many writers. The controversy endures today as the Calvin Hoffman Prize, worth almost 1 million British pounds, is still offered as an incentive for researchers to investigate and uncover a concrete answer to the question of Shakespeare's identity.

Some people have suggested that Francis Bacon wrote much of what we attribute to Shakespeare, since Bacon possessed the range of cultural knowledge exhibited in Shakespeare's works and was often seen in the royal court. Another popular choice for the real identity of Shakespeare is the 17th earl of Oxford, Edward de Vere, whose life seems to be reflected in a number of Shakespeare's works.

Many people prefer a more obvious choice for Shakespeare's identity, the playwright, poet, and translator Christopher Marlowe, Shakespeare's rival. Marlowe and Shakespeare always competed with each other to turn out popular plays, all of which followed a similar poetic style—a blank verse version of iambic pentameter.

The abundant theories notwithstanding, several local government and church documents from Stratford-upon-Avon in the 16th century mention John Shakespeare and his various business and government dealings in addition to the births of his children. Nevertheless, the search continues for the identity of the author of William Shakespeare's works. Today virtually every serious scholar of Shakespeare believes that Shakespeare—who is also called simply the Bard or the Poet (to attest to his supreme standing in the world of poetry)—did exist and wrote all of his own dramatic and poetic works.

Jacobean Theater Shortly after the ascension of James I (1566–1625) to the throne in 1603, a new kind of dramatist emerged in England. The work of these technically skilled playwrights was highly polished but lacked the profundity of the work of their Elizabethan predecessors. The Jacobean playwrights were more interested in sensation and thrills than in illuminating universal truths. The work of this period is often described as decadent. John Ford (ca. 1586–1639), in *'Tis Pity She's a Whore* (1629), treats themes of incestuous love sympathetically. Other writers of note were John Fletcher (ca. 1579–1625), Francis Beaumont (ca. 1585–1616), and John Webster (ca. 1580–ca. 1632), whose plays *The White Devil* (1609) and *The Duchess of Malfi* (1613) are still often produced.

In general, the theater in England began to decline after Shakespeare's death in 1616, and when civil war broke out in 1642 the theaters were effectively closed. By the time theatrical activity reemerged in 1660, the great theater culture that had marked the Elizabethan and Jacobean stages and the genius of Shakespeare had vanished, and English theater was forced to begin anew.

French Neoclassical Theater and Molière (1500–1700)

The neoclassical movement encouraged imitation of classical works and adherence to classical literary rules, and eventually led to French plays written in the classical manner. By 1550, plays by Sophocles, Euripides, Aristophanes, Terence, and Seneca, as well as critical works by Horace and Aristotle, including Aristotle's *Poetics*, had been translated into French. During this time the Pleiade, a group of French intellectuals, formalized rules of French grammar and poetry with the goal of developing the French language into a vehicle for classical works and defining the neoclassical ideal.

The Neoclassical Ideal Realized By the 17th century, a group of highly learned and technically proficient playwrights led the neoclassical movement. Chief among them was Pierre Corneille (1606–1684). In *Le Cid* (1636), Corneille adapted a sprawling Spanish play, compressing the original into the neoclassical five-act structure. In addition, he attempted to adhere to the unities by reducing the original play's many locations to four settings in a single town, and the original play's many years into the course of a single day. Despite Corneille's efforts, *Le Cid* was still criticized for not adhering closely enough to the three unities and for lacking verisimilitude. Jean Racine (1639–99) was later credited with perfecting the neoclassical tragedy with *Phedra* (1677).

Molière   Jean-Baptiste Poquelin (1622–73), who took the name Molière, was an actor, manager, and dramatist who combined the exuberance of the touring acting companies with the ideas of the neoclassicists. He was considered the greatest comic playwright of France and perhaps all of Europe, and his work (together with the tragedies of Racine) marks the high point in French neoclassical theater. Molière was highly educated, but he abandoned a promising career at court in 1643 to join the acting company Théâtre Illustre. He eventually became the head of the company and soon began to write its plays. Among Molière's numerous plays are the comedies *Tartuffe* (1664), *The Misanthrope* (1666), *The Miser* (1668), *The Learned Ladies* (1672), and *The Imaginary Invalid* (1673). His work was often controversial, both reflecting and commenting on the social and religious hypocrisies of his day. His full-length plays, often written in verse, adhered to the five-act structure and the three unities espoused by the neoclassicists. Molière worked in the theater until his death, directing and often performing the leading role in his plays himself.

Restoration Drama (1660–1700)

In 1660 the restoration of Charles II to the English throne after his exile in continental Europe paved the way for the reopening of theaters and the reestablishment of English drama. For the first time, women were allowed to perform on the British stages. New theaters were built using innovations, such as the proscenium arch, from the Italian theaters. The new theaters were opened only with a mandate from the king. Audiences, mostly from the upper class, were more sophisticated than in earlier times. Plays often made allusions to gossip of the day, so that to a large degree Restoration theater was an insider's theater.

Restoration Comedy   Plays of the Elizabethan and Jacobean periods were performed in the Restoration period but were often rewritten versions. Even many of Shakespeare's tragedies were reworked with happy endings. Restoration comedies reflected the worldly-wise sensibility of the period. These comedies of manners

were set in London, not in the country or in the courts where dramas of earlier periods had been set. They often involved sexual intrigue among characters who were members of the upper class. For the first time, characters spoke in a conversational style, displaying sparkling wit and jaded sensibilities. Two playwrights of note during the Restoration period were the poet John Dryden (1631–1700) and William Congreve (1670–1729), whose *Love for Love* (1695) and *The Way of the World* (1695) are considered masterpieces of the form.

18th-Century Drama

In the 18th century the identity of each of London's theaters was strongly shaped by actor-managers. In 1747 the actor David Garrick (1717–79) became manager, with John Lacy, of the Drury Lane Theatre. Garrick, considered the greatest actor of his day, was instrumental in bringing spectacle to the stage. His style of acting, much admired throughout Europe, included the use of pauses in action to heighten dramatic tension, and elaborate costumes (such as, famously, a trick wig with hair that stood on end at the moment when Hamlet sees his father's ghost). In 1728 *The Beggar's Opera* by John Gay (1685–1732) opened at the Lincoln's Inn Fields Theatre, launching a new dramatic form, the ballad opera, which combined social and political satire with popular song. Comedies that rejected sentimentality and drew on the Restoration form were also popular. *The School for Scandal* by Richard Brinsley Sheridan (1751–1816) was first performed in 1771. *She Stoops to Conquer* by Oliver Goldsmith (1730–1774) was first performed in 1773.

Melodrama   The 19th century saw the height of the melodramatic form, as well as various technological innovations in theatrical effects (particularly in lighting), and the rise of the English music hall. In melodrama every aspect of a production—including costuming, sets, lighting, and acting—served the purpose of expressing dramatic content. Now the stage setting of a dark night or a lonely forest became symbolic of a character's emotional state. Plot took precedence over characterization, with virtuous heroes or heroines beset by disasters and under attack by sinister villains. Limelight, originally used to create atmosphere and later as a focused spotlight, was first used in the mid-19th century.

English Music Hall   Music halls at first were eating or drinking establishments that catered to a lower- or middle-class clientele and that also provided entertainment. But as they attracted larger audiences, halls were built specifically for the purpose of entertainment. The performances at music halls consisted of separate acts such as jugglers, dancers, magicians, and singers. Music halls, more affordable than the theater and aimed at a less sophisticated audience, soon rivaled theater in popularity. In America vaudeville was the equivalent of English music hall entertainment.

19th-Century American Drama

Vaudeville, the Minstrel Show, and the Musical Revue   During the 19th century, drama in the United States evolved in a manner similar to that in England. Stylish comedies imported from England were produced in theaters in urban centers throughout the country, as were ballad operas and melodramas. By the mid-19th century, vaudeville, the American counterpart to music hall entertainment, had developed into a genre of its own. It reached its height in the late 19th century, then declined in popularity in the 1920's with the advent of talking films.

Vaudeville bills, like those in music halls, comprised separate acts that usually included singers, dancers, and comedians, as well as jugglers, musicians, or magicians. Like music hall entertainment, vaudeville grew out of a need for a popular form of entertainment for working-class audiences—often audiences made up of frontier workers in the American West. The minstrel show, at first a part of vaudeville and later an event unto itself, consisted of songs, comic bits, skits, and stories depicting caricatures of slaves. Minstrel shows were first staged by white performers wearing blackface; later there were some African-American minstrel troupes as well. The first minstrel show was performed by T. D. Rice (1806–60), who first sang and danced his "Jim Crow" act in 1828. Burlesque—shows that featured satirical or slapstick humor and striptease acts—was also popular during the 19th century. Musical revues such as the Ziegfeld Follies, which included music, dancing, and spectacle, became popular in the early 20th century.

Modern Drama in Europe

European Modern Drama (1880–1920)   This period was marked by revolutionary, idea-driven styles sparked first by playwrights and then by the directors and institutions that interpreted and presented the writers' works. During the modern period, European theatrical movements were no longer localized within any given country; they were broadened to include or correspond with movements throughout Europe. Among the movements were realism, naturalism, symbolism, and expressionism.

Henrik Ibsen and Psychological Realism   The Norwegian Henrik Ibsen (1828–1906) is considered the first modern playwright. His later plays, most notably *A Doll's House* (1879), were revolutionary: realistic, written in colloquial prose, set in the domestic world, and displaying an until then unseen concern with psychology. Because of the realistic nature of the dialogue, the emotionally intimate content, and the domestic settings, actors could no longer rely on the presentational styles popular in the mainstream 18th- and 19th-century theater. Sets no longer were designed for a painterly effect, but rather reproduced in a detailed way the interiors where scenes took place. The idea of the fourth wall—audiences viewed action onstage as though a fourth wall had become invisible, thereby giving them a window onto private action—was adopted.

In several plays Ibsen set out to show how the rigid mores of a modern society were hypocritical especially regarding marriage, sex, and family life. In addition to *A Doll's House*, his major works (*Ghosts*, 1881, *An Enemy of the People*, 1882, and *The Wild Duck*, 1884) were not completely accepted by audiences. In *Hedda Gabler* (1890) he returned to the idea of a strong woman struggling to find happiness in a repressive society.

Theaters of the Modern Era   Venues for the new realistic theater sprang up throughout Europe. In Paris the Théâtre Libre opened under the direction of André Antoine. In Berlin the Freie Bühne opened under the direction of Otto Brahm (1856–1912). In Russia the Moscow Art Theater, under the direction of Konstantin Stanislavski (1856–1938), presented the new acting style necessitated by the work of Anton Chekhov (1860–1904). In London the Independent Theater presented work by, among others, George Bernard Shaw (1856–1950). Shaw's career as a comic and satirical dramatist spanned nearly two decades from *Mrs. Warren's Profession* (1893) and *Candide* (1896) to *Pygmalion* (1913) and *Heartbreak House* (1917). In Copenhagen the Scandinavian Experimental Theater opened under the direction of the Swedish playwright August Strindberg (1849–1912).

August Strindberg's best-known early play, *Miss Julie*, was a work in the naturalistic style. In it a wealthy girl seduces her father's servant. Strindberg used the play to examine the schism between the old and the new eras, and its form mirrored the radicalism of its content—the play is written without acts and calls for a sparsely furnished stage. *Miss Julie* was considered so controversial that its opening in Stockholm was canceled and it was instead first produced in 1893 at the Theâtré Libre in Paris. Strindberg's later plays *The Ghost Sonata* and *The Dream Play* rejected realism, relying heavily instead on symbols in an attempt to portray internal reality on the stage.

Anton Chekhov, like Ibsen, used the stage to explore the psychology of his characters. His dialogue was subtle and often understated, helping to make his plays compelling to actors and directors even today. His characters were simply drawn, their lives limited by circumstances, their tragedies based on the meaningless nature of everyday life. When first presented in the traditional 19th-century acting style in St. Petersburg, his play *The Seagull* (1896) had met with failure. It was only when *The Seagull* was produced at the Moscow Art Theater in 1898 under the direction of Stanislavski, whose method called upon actors to identify with the characters they played in a search for emotional truth, that it met with success. Three powerful works for the stage followed: *Uncle Vanya* (1896), *The Three Sisters* (1901), and *The Cherry Orchard* (1904), all stalwarts of the repertory.

Symbolism, Expressionism, and the Birth of the Avant-Garde   The playwright Maurice Maeterlinck (1862–1949) came to epitomize the Symbolist movement, whereby experience and ideas were evoked through the use of images, with his play *Pelléas and Mélisande*. Franz Wedekind (1864–1918) sparked the expressionist movement, which distorted action and images in order to stress the subjectivity of experience, with his play *Spring Awakening*. Alfred Jarry (1873–1907), whose play *Ubu roi* was first produced in 1896, is considered the forefather of such avant-garde theatrical movements as surrealism and theater of the absurd, although it was not until more than a generation after *Ubu roi* was first produced that these movements would find their names.

European Modern Drama (1920–1960)   During the period between World War I and World War II, theater increasingly became a venue for social and political protest. In Russia agitprop drama (propaganda-driven theater) developed. First in Switzerland and later in Germany the Dada movement found its way to theater. It aimed to promote social change through acts of simultaneity and spontaneity, in which public displays, such as the disruption of a parliamentary debate, became theater. Such displays necessitated audience participation, breaking down further what theater could be or mean. At the same time theater itself became a subject for drama. Luigi Pirandello (1867–1936) wrote *Six Characters in Search of an Author* (1921), in which six characters interrupt the rehearsal of a play; it became an instant classic. As the 20th century progressed, theater became increasingly influenced by theory.

Bertolt Brecht and Epic Theater   Bertolt Brecht (1898–1956), influenced by agitprop, saw theater as a force for social change. He created epic theater, which consciously rejected Aristotle's classical vision of catharsis. For Brecht, theater, the importance of which lay in its social relevance, was a forum for making the spectator not only feel but think as well. To this end he employed the alienation effect, devised to remind audiences that they were watching a theatrical production. His productions called attention to the mechanics of theater: signs gave scene information, scene changes were fully visible to the audience, and his company (the Berliner Ensemble) practiced a non-naturalistic style of acting. Among Brecht's plays were *The Caucasian Chalk Circle*, *Mother Courage and Her Children*, and *The Good Person of Setzuan*. Brecht, in collaboration with the composer Kurt Weill (1900–50), updated John Gay's 18th-century ballad opera *The Beggar's Opera* for their *Threepenny Opera*.

Antonin Artaud and the Avant-Garde   In France, Dada evolved into surrealism in the work of, among others, Jean Cocteau (1889–1963). Theater of cruelty was a term first employed by Antonin Artaud (1896–1949) in his collection of essays *The Theater and Its Double* (1938), considered the most important work of theater criticism since Aristotle's *Poetics*. In *The Theater and Its Double* Artaud called for theater that would completely involve the audience. To witness theater meant to participate in it, and by participating, the audience was forced to confront itself. Artaud sought to move not through logic but through invoking "communicative delirium," a collective, almost religious, fervor in the audience. *The Theater and Its Double* became the manifesto of the next generation of avant-garde playwrights, including the absurdists Eugène Ionesco (1909–94), best known for *The Lesson* (1951), *Exit the King* (1962) and *The Rhinoceros* (1958) and Jean Genet (1910–86), whose radical plays about sex and power included *The Maids* (1947), *The Balcony* (1957), and *The Blacks* (1959), which also ran in New York for more than 1400 performances in 1961.

Samuel Beckett After World War II drama began to reflect an even more fractured view of the world. *Waiting for Godot*, by the Irish playwright Samuel Beckett (1906–89), was first produced in 1953. In the play two tramps, Vladimir and Estragon, are trapped on a road, waiting for the arrival of Godot. In this vacant world they are forced to repeat the same patterns over and over. Though the play did not meet with immediate success, it went on to become the seminal work of the second half of the 20th century. Other strange and startling works by Beckett have found permanent place on the repertory, especially *Endgame* (1957), *Krapp's Last Tape* (1959), and *Happy Days* (1961).

The Angry Young Men In England the drama of the mid-20th century evolved with less obvious experimentation than it did in the rest of Europe. Its experimentation at first lay in content rather than in style. *Look Back in Anger* by John Osborne (1929–1994), was first produced in 1956. This stylistically realistic play, which followed the struggles of its main character, Jimmy Porter, raised highly charged questions about class and social roles. It gave rise to the generation of so-called "angry young men"—playwrights such as John Arden (b. 1930) and Arnold Wesker (b. 1932), whose work called into question the accepted political and social norms of the times.

Modern American Drama

Modern drama in America was formed by many of the same forces that influenced modern European drama. However, because American theater developed in a country where the two world wars had not been fought, it allowed for a coherence in theatrical traditions uninterrupted by war. American modern theater was as subversive as its European counterpart, but not so extreme in its expression.

Eugene O'Neill, Thornton Wilder, and Tennessee Williams Eugene O'Neill (1888–1953) was the most important playwright in bringing new European ideas of theater to America. Although his primary influence was expressionism, O'Neill's work is marked by an interest in psychology and virtuosity in a variety of styles. *The Emperor Jones* (1920) employs Symbolist techniques; *The Hairy Ape* (1922) employs expressionist techniques; *Long Day's Journey into Night* (1943), which was not produced until 1956, three years after O'Neill's death, uses realism paired with psychological symbols to paint a brutally honest portrait of a family.

Thornton Wilder's (1897–1975) best-known plays are *Our Town* (1938) and the highly theatrical *The Skin of Our Teeth* (1942). Tennessee Williams (1911–83), also influenced by expressionism, paired realism with psychological symbols to comment on American culture, the nature of memory, and the vulnerability of the artist in the modern world. During the 1940's and 50's, he wrote several emotionally wrenching plays that were enormously popular and critically acclaimed, starting with *The Glass Menagerie* (1944), and followed by his most famous work *A Streetcar Named Desire* (1948) that launched Marlon Brando's career. In quick succession came *The Rose Tattoo* (1951), *Camino Real* (1953) and *Cat on a Hot Tin Roof* (1955), solidifying his very high place in American theater history.

The Group Theatre and Method Acting In the 1920's experimental theater in New York was localized in Greenwich Village. Eugene O'Neill's company, the Provincetown Players, was originally part of the Washington Square Players (later known as the Theatre Guild). The Neighborhood Playhouse became a venue not only for plays but also for dance and avant-garde performances. The Group Theatre, founded in 1931, had a social and political agenda, reacting to the enormous unemployment and extreme working conditions of the times. The work of Clifford Odets (1906–63) reflects this agenda. Odets's most famous play, *Waiting for Lefty* (1935), draws on agitprop techniques to dramatize the concerns of union workers.

The Group Theatre employed an Americanized version of Stanislavski's approach to acting which became known simply as the Method. Method acting used emotional recall—in which actors drew on their own experiences to imbue a character with life—to create genuine emotion and highly realistic performances. The Group

Theatre disbanded in 1941, but its influence continues to this day.

British and American Theater since 1960

British Theater   In the 1960's the social concerns and experimentation of the earlier generation gave rise to an explosion of new playwrights. In England Harold Pinter (1930–2008), whose plays combine the fractured worldview of Samuel Beckett with a kind of realism akin to that of the "angry young men," rose to prominence with such plays as *The Birthday Party* (1959), *The Caretaker* (1959), and *The Homecoming* (1964). Pinter's plays, imbued with a sense of menace, often take place in a vague world where naturalistic dialogue is paired with an unexplained or mysterious situation. The comic playwright Joe Orton (1933–67) used sex farce as a tool to satirize the social norms of the times in such plays as *Entertaining Mr. Sloane* (1964) and *What the Butler Saw* (1969). Tom Stoppard (b. Zlin, Czechoslovakia, 1937) combines high theatricality with dazzling linguistic invention to explore philosophical matters such as the nature of reality in *Rosencrantz and Guildenstern are Dead* (1967), *Jumpers* (1972), *The Real Thing* (1982), *Arcadia* (1993), and the trilogy *The Coast of Utopia* (2002).

American Theater   Arthur Miller (1915–2005), whose plays comment on societal injustices, rose to prominence when his play *All My Sons* was produced in 1947. Other plays include *The Crucible* (1953), which used the Salem witch hunts to comment on McCarthyism; and *Death of a Salesman* (1949), which introduced the tragic everyman, Willy Loman.

A profusion of new types of theater arose during the 1960's. Happenings, whose roots can be traced to the Dadaist spontaneous theater of Europe in the 1930's, gave birth to performance art, in which experimental theater companies such as the Living Theater, the Open Theatre, Mabou Mines, the Wooster Group, and Richard Foreman's Ontological-Hysteric Theatre expanded the boundaries of what were considered theatrical events. The playwrights best able to navigate a path between the experimental and popular theater of the 1960's and 1970's are Sam Shepard (b. 1943), who in plays such as *Buried Child* (1978) and *True West* (1980) combines a surreal, poetic style with a realistic setting to explore concern for American identity and mythology; Edward Albee (b. 1928), who rose to prominence in the 1960's and for over four decades has produced such masterpieces as *The Zoo Story* (1959), *Who's Afraid of Virginia Woolf?* (1962), *A Delicate Balance* (1966), and *Three Tall Women* (1991); and David Mamet (b. 1947), who in signature work such as *American Buffalo* (1976) and *Glengarry Glen Ross* (1983) uses vernacular patterns and rhythms to create recognizable characters and an emblematic American speech. Contemporary American theater exhibits a globalization of styles, drawing upon theater forms from the world over.

World Theater

Although countless forms of theater are found throughout the world, the traditions that have most influenced Western drama are found in India, China, and Japan. Two of South India's classical dance forms, *bharata natyam* (performed by women) and *khatakali* (performed by men) combine systems of movements and gestures to create characters and tell stories. In China, Peking opera, in existence since the late 18th century, uses male and female actors, elaborate costumes and makeup, mime, stylized gestures, and acrobatics to tell stories set in China's past.

Three traditional Japanese theater forms, *noh*, *bunraku*, and *kabuki*, are very different in style and origins. *Noh*, dating from the 14th century and originally performed only for the samurai class, exhibits the austerity and restraint of Zen Buddhism. Its goal is to inspire an emotional state through meditating on a related event from the past. Movement and song within *noh* plays are more important than spoken text, and every movement has a codified meaning. Actors wear masks and brightly colored, stylized costumes. The less esoteric *bunraku* and *kabuki* both date from the 17th century. *Banruku*, a form of puppet theater, operates according to strict conventions. Puppets are manipulated by black-clothed puppeteers. The story is told by a narrator and is accompanied by music. Puppets vary in size and complexity according to their importance in the story. *Kabuki* was originally performed for the lower classes, although it became popular among the samurai class as well. The characters in *kabuki* are made up of types—villains, courageous heroes, etc. The stories often involve erotic subjects or heroic exploits, and many are drawn from *bunraku* plays. Actors wear elaborate makeup, and each character has a traditional costume. Acrobatics and stylized gestures are employed.

SCIENCE & TECHNOLOGY

ASTRONOMY

History of Astronomy

Ancient Astronomy

The roots of astronomy extend to before written records, but it is clear that humans have always observed the sky. The earliest known records of astronomical observations come from the Sumerian and Babylonian cultures (in what is modern-day Iraq) and date from as far back as 3000 B.C. Careful observations by court-sponsored astronomers led to the first known star maps, the zodiac, and many of the other constellations still referred to today, as well as the sexigesimal (base-60) counting system on which our angular measures are based. Babylonian astronomers knew the length of the year to high precision. These measurements were probably used for political and agricultural purposes. During the same epoch, a number of astronomical monuments, including Stonehenge, were being constructed as calendar devices around what is now Great Britain. Egyptian astronomers undertook similar cataloging and mapping work, using stars as references in alignment of construction projects like the Great Pyramids.

Greek philosophers were the first to speculate on the structure of the universe, but were constrained by philosophical traditions relying on pure geometrical forms. Aristotle (ca. 350 B.C.), established a model of the universe described as nested spheres with the Earth at the center, while the Sun, Moon, planets and stars moved around the Earth in constant motion each with its own rate.

Some Greek "natural philosophers," though, did make more detailed measurements and surmises about the structure of space. For instance, Pythagoras (ca. 500 B.C.) and Plato (ca. 400 B.C.) made strong arguments, based on the shape of the Earth's shadow during lunar eclipses and the changing view of the sky as one traveled north or south, that the Earth was a sphere. Eratosthenes (ca. 200 B.C.) estimated the diameter of the Earth to high precision based on the angle of sunlight observed at different locations. Aristarchus (ca. 280 B.C.) is the first person known to have proposed that the Earth orbits the Sun. One of the outstanding problems noted by Greek

astronomers was the motions of the planets. The culmination of ancient astronomical endeavors was the work of Ptolemy (ca. A.D. 140), whose great work *Syntaxis* was an attempt to match the complicated motions of the planets about the Earth. In his model, Ptolemy proposed that the Sun, Moon, planets, and stars moved around the stationary Earth on circular orbits onto which were placed smaller circles that carried the planets eastward, then briefly westward ("retrograde"), then eastward again relative to the fixed stars. In melding the tradition of Aristotle with an attempt to match what was actually observed, Ptolemy ensured his place in astronomical history.

The Middle Ages

The decline of Greek and Roman influence throughout the ancient Middle East spelled the end of real astronomical progress for the following 13 centuries. In the Mediterranean basin, the religious customs of Islam, which relied on precise astronomical calculations, fostered scientific collaboration. As a result, Islamic astronomers made precise catalogs of stellar brightness and developed trigonometric tools. Much of the work revolved around refining Ptolemy's system of planetary motion. Many of the names given to stars descend either directly from or as modified versions of the names given them by Islamic scholars during this time.

At the same time, other cultures were making measurements of astronomical phenomena. Several cultures in the Americas constructed astronomical monuments similar to those found in Europe. In China, courts noted the appearance of comets and supernovas.

Renaissance Astronomy:
The Copernican Revolution

A complete revision of thinking about the universe began with the speculative work of the Polish cleric Nicolaus Copernicus in the early 16th century. Copernicus was the first modern astronomer to propose that the Sun was the center of the universe, and that the Earth orbited the Sun like the other planets. He correctly attributed the daily motions of the Sun and stars to the rotation of the Earth, annual changes in the appearance of the sky to the orbital motion of the Earth about the Sun, and retrograde motion to the relative speeds of planets as they orbited the Sun. But his model still relied on the perfect circular orbits preferred by Aristotle, and as a result his predictions, published in 1543 in *De Revolutionibus* as he lay dying, were no more accurate at predicting planetary positions than the 1,300-year-old geocentric model of Ptolemy. Nonetheless, he laid the groundwork for the revolutionary changes that were to occur in the understanding of the cosmos over the following 200 years.

The great Danish astronomer Tycho Brahe was concerned that both the Ptolemaic and Copernican models failed to accurately reproduce careful observations. During the last 30 years of the 16th century, Tycho undertook the most accurate observations of planetary and stellar positions that had ever been made, in an attempt to prove his own model of the universe in which the Earth lay stationary at the center while the other planets orbited the Sun. When Tycho died suddenly in 1601, the data came into the possession of the talented German mathematician Johannes Kepler. Based on his analysis of Tycho's data, Kepler was able to show that planets orbit Sun on elliptical paths (rather than circular paths as had been assumed for nearly two millennia), that planets moved faster along their orbits when closer to the Sun, and that there was a precise mathematical relation between a planet's distance from the Sun and the time to complete at orbit. These results, published in 1609 and 1619, are known as Kepler's laws of planetary motion. So precisely could Kepler's results predict the locations of planets that they lent great support to Copernicus's Sun-centered universe.

In 1608, as Kepler labored to interpret Tycho's data, a usable telescope design was invented by the Dutch lens maker Hans Lippershey. The following year, the Italian empirical scientist Galileo built his own version of the device and made the first careful observations of astronomical objects with a telescope. With the telescope, he observed the Moon's physical geologic features, sunspots, the changing illumination of Venus as it orbited the Sun, and moons of Jupiter in orbit around that planet. These provided strong evidence in support of a Sun-centered universe. In 1633 Galileo was famously tried and exiled for flouting Catholic doctrine; which relied heavily on the Earth-centered universe, but his work stands today as a crucial moment in scientific history, when observation became paramount to belief.

Post-Renaissance Astronomy: The 17th and 18th Centuries

In the aftermath of the Copernican revolution, astronomy flourished. The most important developments came from the work of Isaac Newton, the brilliant, eccentric, and moody English physicist and mathematician. Newton established his laws of motion, which described both the motions of objects on Earth and the motions of planets around the Sun. He constructed the law of universal gravitation, which described precisely the forces that held the planets in orbit about the Sun. While developing these laws, he also invented calculus, which would turn out to be an invaluable tool for making predictions of the motions of astronomical bodies. His work was published in 1687 as the *Philosphiae Naturalis Principia Mathematica* (usually referred to as the *Principia*) . Newton also applied his talents to optics and invented the reflecting telescope, a design still used in modified form today.

Newton's law of gravity was put to use by his friend Edmund Halley even before the *Principia* was published. Halley had collected observations of comets made in previous centuries. Using Newton's methods, he argued that a number of comet observations were actually of the same comet, and in 1705 he predicted the comet's return would occur in 1758. For the success of this prediction, the comet is now known as Halley's Comet.

Despite the successes of Kepler's and Newton's laws, both were able to predict only the relative distances from each planet to the Sun, not the absolute distances. The distance from the Earth to the Sun was referred to as an astronomical unit, and both sets of laws could show for instance that Mars orbited the Sun at an average distance of one-and-a-half astronomical units, but the absolute number of miles or meters in an astronomical unit remained unknown. In 1672 the Italian astronomer Giovanni Cassini made the first accurate attempt at determining this scale when he and an assistant measured the projected position of Mars against distant background stars from two different locations on Earth. Their result, about 87 million miles for one astronomical unit, agrees closely with the modern number value of about 93 million miles. (Using this number and comparing observed and predicted appearances of Jupiter's moons, the Danish astronomer Ole Roemer made the first accurate estimate of the speed of light in 1676.) In 1716, Halley showed that a more accurate measure of the astronomical unit could be made if observers in different locations on Earth recorded the passage of the planet Venus across the face of the Sun, an event that would occur twice in the 18th century, first in 1761 and again in 1769. Halley did not live to see these events, but several hundred astronomers positioned around the Earth did.

In 1781 the German-English astronomer William Herschel discovered the planet Uranus, the first planet found since antiquity. In several following years, Herschel applied himself to measuring the dimensions of the Milky Way, the large grouping of stars to which the Sun belongs. Herschel demonstrated that the Sun lay in the plane of a flattened disklike structure that was substantially thinner than it was wide, but he incorrectly concluded that the Sun lay at the center of the Milky Way.

19th- and Early 20th-Century Astronomy: The Birth of Astrophysics

The 19th century continued much of the empirical study of the 18th century. In 1801 the Italian astronomer Giuseppe Piazzi discovered the first asteroid, a rocky object smaller than a planet orbiting the Sun in the gap between Mars and Jupiter. In 1838 the German mathematician and astronomer Freidrich Bessel made the first successful observation of the distance to another star by measuring the tiny apparent shift in the star's position when observed from different sides of the Earth's orbit. And in a great triumph for Newton's law of gravity, the planet Neptune was discovered independently by German and French astronomers in 1846 based on small perturbations in the orbit of Uranus.

The most important developments in astronomy during this time were those that occurred outside of traditional astronomical observations. In 1800 Herschel discovered that the Sun produced light outside the range of colors detectable with the human eye. In 1814 the German Joseph Fraunhofer split sunlight into its constituent colors with a prism and identified the element sodium in the Sun, the first time that the chemical composition of an astronomical object was made. In 1842 the Austrian Christian Doppler showed that the motion of an object could be inferred from a shift in the wavelengths of light received from that object. In 1865 the Scottish physicist James Clerk Maxwell showed formally that visible light was a subset of the wavelike phenomenon by which charged particles interact, known as electromagnetic radiation. In the 1880's the Austrian physicists Josef Stefan and Ludwig Boltzmann showed that the energy output of an object was directly related to that object's temperature. In 1893 the German physicist Wilhelm Wien showed that the temperature of an object could be determined by determining the color that an object emitted most intensely. And many developments in quantum mechanics, beginning with the work of Danish physicist Neils Bohr in 1913, showed that details of an object's spectrum could be used to deduce it's chemical composition. Although seemingly peripheral to astronomy, these developments allowed astronomers for the first time to interpret the light they collected from astronomical objects and marked the birth of modern astrophysics.

Techniques of Astronomy

As in other sciences, progress in astronomy comes from the comparison between the predictions of physical theories and the results of observations. Astronomy is nearly unique, however, in that most of the objects under study are not directly accessible, mainly because of the huge distances separating the Earth and even nearby astronomical objects.

Direct Sampling and Spacecraft Reconnaissance

Some samples of the solar system enter the Earth's atmosphere as meteors; intact meteorites have been recovered, most are samples of asteroids but some include samples of the Moon and Mars. High-altitude aircraft and Earth-orbiting spacecraft have collected smaller samples of solar system dust.

Even for objects in the solar system, the vast majority of study has been done from Earth-based observatories or by spacecraft using remote sensing techniques. The same techniques used for reconnaissance of the Earth, including imaging of geological features, tracking of weather patterns, radar study of surface features, and spectroscopic measurements of temperature and atmospheric composition, have been used to study planets, moons, comets, and asteroids.

Direct sampling has occurred only within the solar system, and thus far has been limited to: surface measurements (pre-Apollo) and sample returns from the Moon (approximately 1,000 pounds of rock returned by the U.S. Apollo missions); planetary surface and atmospheric measurements by U.S. and Soviet spacecraft that have landed on Mars and Venus; atmospheric sampling by a single probe descending into Jupiter's upper atmosphere; and several spacecraft encounters with smaller objects in the solar system such as Halley's Comet and the asteroid Eros. Missions to sample Titan (the largest of Saturn's moons) and to return comet material from Comet Wild-2 are currently under way.

Indirect Sampling

For all practical purposes, astronomical objects beyond the solar system are out of reach and all information about them is gleaned from the collection, analysis, and interpretation of *electromagnetic radiation*, the energy given off by all objects in the universe. The electromagnetic spectrum is broken up into six bands: radio, infrared, visible, ultraviolet, X-ray, and gamma-ray. Successive bands probe progressively hotter or more energetic phenomena (with a few exceptions).

Radio–Infrared–Visible–Ultraviolet–X-ray–Gamma-ray
Low Energy ⟵⟶ High Energy
Long Wavelength ⟵⟶ Short Wavelength

Radio radiation is the lowest-energy electromagnetic radiation. It is emitted by cold gas and the early universe. Radio radiation passes freely through the Earth's atmosphere and is detectable from ground-based observatories.

Infrared radiation is emitted by planets, cool stars, stars that are forming, dust and gas in star-forming regions, and the cores of active galaxies. It is blocked by water and carbon dioxide in the Earth's atmosphere, so infrared observatories must be placed on high mountains, in aircraft, or in orbit.

Visible radiation ("light") is emitted by stars and reflected by planets. It passes freely through the Earth's atmosphere and is detectable from ground-based observatories.

Ultraviolet radiation is emitted by hot stars and gas. Ozone in the upper atmosphere prevents it from penetrating to ground level, so ultraviolet observatories must be located in orbit.

X radiation is emitted by the remnants of hot stars, the Sun's corona, and galaxy clusters. Atoms in the upper atmosphere block these emissions, so X-ray observatories must be placed in orbit.

Gamma radiation is emitted when stellar collisions occur, from the regions around black holes, and in supernova explosions. It is blocked by the upper atmosphere, so gamma ray observatories must be placed in orbit.

Collection of radiation is done through the use of a telescope. A telescope consists of one or more optical elements serving to collect as much electromagnetic radiation as possible. Performance of a telescope is determined by the size of the main radiation-collecting element (usually a mirror or lens). The larger the size, the more radiation is collected. Larger telescopes can be used to detect fainter objects than smaller telescopes. In addition to this collecting ability, the size of the telescope also determines the level of detail that can be discerned in an observation: the larger the main optical element, the finer the detail. The Earth's atmosphere tends to smear out this detail through the bending of light ("twinkling"), though advanced engineering techniques have been developed to counter atmospheric effects. Telescopes in space are not affected by the Earth's atmosphere; thus the Hubble space telescope is able to produce images with stunning detail despite being much smaller than many modern ground-based telescopes.

The radiation collected with a telescope is then fed through telescope optics to a detector. The ability to detect an astronomical source depends on the efficiency of the detector at collecting radiation as well as the inherent random signal in a detector ("noise"). The human eye, for example, is about 1 percent efficient at detecting visible light (99 percent is not detected); it has no sensitivity outside the visible part of the electromagnetic spectrum; and it has no ability to accumulate light over time. Astronomers used photographic film as a detector throughout much of the 20th century; film can be made to detect about 10 percent of the visible or infrared radiation striking it, and long exposures could be made in order to collect as much light as possible from a faint source. For the past 25 years, astronomers have used Charge-Coupled Devices (CCDs) as detectors of infrared, visible, and X-ray radiation. These solid-state devices have efficiencies of nearly 100 percent and produce a digital record of the detection that is especially convenient for analysis using computers. Detection of X rays and gamma rays requires specialized hardware, and detection of radio radiation requires specialized receivers. These typically have lower efficiencies than CCDs.

The collected and detected electromagnetic radiation is then used in a variety of ways. Astronomers undertake three basic types of collection and detection: Imaging involves focusing the electromagnetic radiation to create a representation of the source's physical appearance and distribution in space. Spectroscopy involves passing the collected radiation through an optical element that spreads the light out into its constituent wavelengths to determine the temperature, chemical composition, and motion of an astronomical source. Photometry is the very careful measurement of the quantity of electromagnetic radiation emitted by a source.

Examples of important telescopes studying each wavelength band are given below.

Gamma ray: Compton Gamma Ray Observatory Four specialized instruments for detecting gamma radiation, operation in Earth orbit (1991–2000)

X-ray: Chandra X-Ray Observatory 1.3 meters, operation in Earth orbit (1999–)

Ultraviolet: Lyman FUSE 0.4 meter, operation in Earth orbit (1999–)

Visible: Single—Keck I 10 meters, Mauna Kea, Hawaii, 1993–; Multiple—Very Large Telescope (VLT) 16.4 meters (4–8.2-meter mirrors), Cerro Paranal, Chile (1997–)

Infrared: SIRTF (Space Infrared Telescope Facility) 0.85 meter, Earth-trailing orbit (2003–); SOFIA (Stratospheric Observatory for Infrared Astronomy) 2.5 meters, housed in Mountain View, Calif., but operation from airplane (2005–)

Radio: Single—Arecibo 305 meters, Arecibo, Puerto Rico (1963–); Multiple—Very Long Baseline Array, 10 locations across North America/Pacific, 5,800 miles

Contents of the Universe

The contents of the universe range in size from individual gas atoms and dust grains up to enormous clusters and superclusters of galaxies. As in other sciences, astronomers develop classifications for objects, organizational boundaries that suggest common origins or physical processes. These classifications change as additional data are collected. For instance, until 1995 only the planets around the Sun were known, and the classification "planet" was suitable for objects orbiting the Sun. Over the past 20 years, more than 1800 planets have been identified orbiting stars outside the solar system, as well as some planet-mass objects that are not in orbit around stars. In 2011, Japanese astronomers announced that space is littered with hundreds of billions of planets.

Solar System Summary

The solar system comprises a single star, the Sun, and all of the objects that orbit the Sun. The largest objects that orbit the Sun are referred to as planets. These planets are grouped broadly into two categories: the terrestrial planets and the Jovian planets, named after the planet Jupiter and also known as gas giants. The terrestrial planets are the four closest to the Sun: Mercury, Venus, Earth, and Mars. These are composed primarily of silicon-based rock and metals. The Earth is the largest of the terrestrial planets, slightly more massive than Venus, 10 times as massive as Mars, and nearly 20 times the mass of Mercury. Earth has a substantial atmosphere dominated by nitrogen and oxygen; Venus and Mars have atmospheres dominated by carbon dioxide; Mercury has no appreciable atmosphere.

The Jovian planets are Jupiter, Saturn, Uranus, and Neptune. Jupiter, at more than 300 times the Earth's mass, is the largest object in the solar system besides the Sun.

Jupiter and Saturn are composed mostly of hydrogen gas. Uranus and Neptune, each approximately 15 times the mass of Earth, are composed of icy cores surrounded by substantial hydrogen atmospheres.

Beyond the orbit of Neptune (see the Kuiper Belt, below) are two dwarf planets, Pluto and Eris. These two bodies are similar in size (smaller than the Moon) and are composed primarily of ice. Their orbits are somewhat erratic.

All of the planets except Mercury and Venus have moons, or natural satellites, in orbit around them. Only three moons are known to orbit the terrestrial planets: the Moon, in orbit around the Earth; and two much smaller objects in orbit about Mars. The Jovian planets, however, are accompanied by large numbers of moons. As of this writing, Jupiter holds the record with 61 moons, ranging in size from larger than Mercury to as small as a kilometer in diameter. Saturn, Uranus, and Neptune have 31, 27, and 13 known moons, respectively.

Planet Details

Mercury (Average distance from Sun: 0.38 AU. Mass: 0.055 Earth masses. Diameter: 0.38 Earth diameters. Orbit time: 88 days. Rotation time: 59 days.)

As the planet closest to the Sun, Mercury has the shortest orbit. Its view from Earth is usually obscured by the Sun's glare, but it is sometimes visible on the horizon just after sunset, when it is called the Evening Star, or just before dawn, when it is called the Morning Star. About 14 times each century, Mercury can also be seen crossing directly in front of the Sun.

The U.S. *Mariner 10* space probe provided the first detailed pictures of Mercury's surface during flybys in 1974 and 1975. *Mariner 10* mapped about 35 percent of the

Characteristics of the Sun

Position in solar system	Center
Mean distance from Earth	92,960,000 mi. (149,600,000 km)
Distance from center of Milky Way galaxy	27,710 light-years
Period of rotation	25.45 days at 16° longitude
Inclination (relative to Earth's orbit)	7.25°
Equatorial diameter	865,000 mi. (1,392,000 km)
Diameter relative to Earth	109.2 times
Mass	2.192x10^{27} tons (1.9891x10^{30} kg)
Mass converted to energy each second	9,500 million pounds (4,300 million kg)
Surface gravity relative to Earth's	28 times
Temperature at core	28,280,000°F (15,710,000°C)
Temperature at bottom of photosphere	12,400°F (6,900°C)
Main components	Hydrogen and helium
Present age	4.6 billion years
Expected future life of hydrogen fuel supply	6.4 billion years

planet's heavily cratered, moonlike surface. No space probe has visited the planet since, though NASA sent the *Messenger* orbiter there in 2004, and the European Space Agency plans to send the Bepi-Columbo orbiter-lander mission to Mercury in 2009.

Mercury is a waterless, airless world that alternately bakes and freezes as it orbits the Sun. The high temperatures on the sunlit side mean that the planet cannot retain a substantial atmosphere. A small number of paticles in Mercury's atmosphere have been detected, though are believe to consist of atoms streaming out from the Sun as well as atoms knocked off surface rock by the fast-moving solar atoms; the total mass of these particles is thought to be less than 1,000 kilograms. Without a substantial atmosphere, temperatures are poorly regulated. On Mercury's sunlit side temperatures reach 850°F (450°C) and plummet to –300°F (–180°C) on the dark side. The extremes of temperature are largely due to Mercury's slow rate of rotation: one single rotation is two-thirds of a Mercury year, or 59 days for a rotation compared with 88 days for a revolution. Mercury's axis is almost perpendicular to its plane of rotation, so any single place on the planet sees dawn only once every 176 days—the planet must rotate three times and go through two of its "years" before a new day dawns.

Mercury's surface is scarred with hundreds of thousands of craters, formed probably during the early history of the solar system, when large numbers of asteroids and comets were slamming into planetary surfaces. Many craters have been smoothed over by ancient lava flows. The surface is also crisscrossed by huge cliffs, or *scarps*, formed probably as Mercury's surface cooled and shrank. Some of the scarps are up to 1.2 miles (1.9 kilometers) high and 932 miles (1,500 kilometers) long.

Mercury is so dense that astronomers think that its rocky outer crust is very thin and that the planet is mostly iron. It probably was once larger. During the early bombardment, it is conjectured that a large planetesimal or protoplanet (about a sixth of the size of the early planet) hit Mercury so hard that it ripped most of the rocky crust away.

Venus (Average distance from Sun: 0.72 AU. Mass: 0.82 Earth masses. Diameter: 0.95 Earth diameters. Orbit time: 224 days. Rotation time: 243 days retrograde.)

In Earth's night sky, Venus is second only to the Moon in luminosity, since it passes closer to Earth than any other planet (24,000,000 miles, or 39,000,000 kilometers). Since it orbits between Earth and the Sun, Venus, like Mercury, can be seen either just before sunrise or just after sunset.

Because of its proximity to Earth and its position between Earth and the Sun, Venus became (in 1962) the first planet beyond Earth to be studied in situ by a space probe (*Mariner 2*). The pull of the Sun's gravity makes Venus and Mercury "downhill" from the Earth; one must travel against the Sun's gravity to reach other planets. Since 1962 numerous U.S. and Soviet spacecraft have visited Venus. Soviet space probes *Venera 13* and *Venera 14* were the first to make a soft landing and send back pictures from the Venusian surface.

The Venusian atmosphere is 96.4 percent carbon dioxide and 3.4 percent nitrogen. Thick clouds shroud the planet's surface from direct view. The Venusian clouds range from about 28 to 37 miles (45 to 60 km) above the planet's surface and are differentiated into three layers. Droplets of sulfuric acid and water have been identified in the clouds.

The clouds and high level of carbon dioxide in the atmosphere have combined to trap heat in the lower atmosphere of Venus. This is an extreme form of the greenhouse effect and is responsible for high temperatures in the lower atmosphere, 870°F (460°C)—hot enough to melt lead. The atmospheric pressure at the surface is 92 times that of Earth. The atmospheric CO_2 is so efficient at trapping heat that there is little variation of temperature between night and day.

One feature of the Venusian upper atmosphere is markedly different from that of Earth. The atmosphere superrotates on Venus—that is, the atmosphere above the clouds moves 60 times faster than the planet rotates—whereas the Earth and its atmosphere rotate at the same speed. So, high winds and steady upper-atmosphere winds—100 mph (160 km/hr) or faster—are a dominant factor in Venusian weather. But at ground level, winds are calmer, with an average closer to 2 mph (3.6 km/hr).

Soviet space probes that soft-landed on Venus have provided photographs of the planet's surface. Radar maps of 99 percent of the Venusian surface, completed by the U.S. Pioneer spacecraft (from 1978 to 1993), and Magellan (from 1989 to 1994), now give a detailed picture of features as small as 350 ft. (100 m) in diameter. More than a thousand Venusian mountains, volcanoes, rifts, basins, impact craters, and other features have been identified.

About 10 percent of the surface is highland terrain, 70 percent rolling uplands, and 20 percent lowland plains. There are two major highland areas: one about half the size of Africa and located in the equatorial region and the other, about the size of Australia, located to the north. The highest mountain on Venus—Maxwell Montes—is in the northern highlands and is higher than Earth's Mt. Everest. Volcanic activity has dominated Venusian geology, as the planet is covered with volcanic domes and lava channels. It is not clear whether such volcanic activity continues at the present time.

Like Earth, Venus is thought to have an internal structure. The crust, however, is much thicker than that of Earth, perhaps twice as deep on the average, making the crust of Venus about 60 mi. (100 km) thick. Below the crust is a large layer called the mantle; below the mantle is a core thought to be molten nickel-iron, similar to Earth's outer core.

Earth (Average distance from Sun: 1 AU = 93 million miles = 150 million km. Mass: 13 trillion trillion pounds = 5.9 trillion trillion kilograms. Diameter: 7,900 miles = 12,800 km. Orbit time: 365.25 days. Rotation time: 24 hours.)

Third from the Sun, Earth is the only one in the solar system known to harbor life, the result of its distinct atmosphere and the presence of an ozone layer that, together with Earth's magnetic field, blocks deadly radiation. From space, our planet appears as a bright blue-and-white sphere—blue because some 70 percent of the surface is covered by water, and white because clouds cover about half the planet's surface. (See "Geology.")

The Moon is Earth's only natural satellite. It is more than one-quarter the size of Earth in diameter (2,160 mi. or 3,476 km). At an average distance of 238,000 mi. (380,000 km), it is the brightest object in Earth's nighttime sky. The Moon regularly changes in appearance as seen from Earth.

The Moon is slightly egg-shaped, and the same side of the satellite always faces Earth—this side being the elongated small end. As a result, the Moon's rotation and revolution are synchronized. The side we do not see is called the far side (not the dark side—all parts of the moon undergo 14 Earth days of light, followed by 14 days of darkness).

Over a decade of exploration of the Moon by space probes was capped by the landing of two U.S. astronauts on the Moon on July 20, 1969. A total of six two-man crews of American astronauts eventually landed on the Moon between 1969 and 1972, and they brought back some 842 pounds (382 kg) of samples of Moon rocks. Study of these rocks has led to a far greater understanding of the Moon's history and of the formation of the solar system. Analysis of the Moon's composition has led to the hypothesis that the Moon formed when the collision of a large protoplanet stripped material from the Earth's crust.

The world the astronauts found was airless and devoid of life. Temperatures on the Moon range from up to 273°F (134°C) on the bright side to −274°F (−170°C) on the unlighted side. A mixture of fine powder and broken rock blankets the Moon's surface. The near side also has large regions called *maria* ("seas") of solidified lava. The lunar surface is pockmarked with craters and larger impact basins, the largest about 1,300 miles (2,100 km) across, and is broken by huge mountain ranges. Some craters at the poles may contain frozen water in their depths. In 2010, NASA scientists examining crater at the Moon's south pole discvovered ice mixed in the soil in much higher concentration than had been hypothesized.

Mars (Average distance from Sun: 1.52 AU. Mass: 0.11 Earth masses. Diameter: 0.53 Earth diameters. Orbit time: 1.88 years. Rotation time: 1.03 days.)

Mars is the outermost of the four terrestrial planets and has a distinctive reddish coloring, coming from iron oxide in the Martian soil. The Romans named the planet after their god of war, and the two irregularly shaped satellites of Mars have been named after the horses—Deimos ("terror") and Phobos ("fear")—that pulled the war god's chariot. Earth lies directly between Mars and the Sun once every 780 days, though because of the eccentric shape of Mars's orbit, its closest approach to Earth (33,800,000 mi., or 54,500,000 km) comes at 15- or 17-year intervals.

The so-called canals on Mars—later found to be optical illusions—were first observed by 19th-century astronomers and led to the widespread belief that there was life on Mars. (In 1900 the French Academy offered a prize to the first person to find life on any planet except Mars, presumably because everyone knew that there was life on that planet.) The planet thus became the target of numerous space probes, both U.S. and Soviet, from the early years of interplanetary exploration.

The first successful flyby of Mars was achieved by the U.S. spacecraft *Mariner 4* in 1965. The Soviets became the first to land a probe successfully on the surface of Mars, in 1971, but the probe malfunctioned and stopped transmitting after only 20 seconds. It was not until 1976, when the U.S. *Viking 1* and *Viking 2* landers touched down on Mars, that extensive study of the planet from its surface became possible. The *Viking 1* lander continued to function until 1983. *Pathfinder* landed on Mars on July 4, 1997. Using a remote-controlled robot called Sojourner, whose travels to Martian rocks were televised, the *Pathfinder* mission reported the details of the weather and geology of Mars. In January 2004, the U.S. landed twin rover spacecraft (*Spirit* and *Opportunity*) to study Martian geology and to test for the past presence of water on the Martian surface.

The big question of whether there is (or was) life on Mars has yet to be answered with certainty. The Viking landers conducted three experiments on Martian soil to check for biological processes. Some of the tests yielded positive results, but these could also be explained by the soil chemistry. The lack of other evidence of organic molecules adds to the case against life on Mars. A British spacecraft, *Beagle II*, was set to conduct further biological experiments in 2004, but the craft failed to land safely on the Martian surface.

Orbiting satellites have mapped the entire planet down to a resolution of 500–1,000 ft. (150–300 m), and in smaller regions have imaged surface features 1.5 ft. (0.5 m) across. The planet's surface is heavily cratered, and there is extensive evidence of once-active volcanoes. There are also such spectacular features as Olympus Mons (an extinct volcano three times as high as Earth's Mt. Everest); mammoth canyons, one of which is four times deeper than the Grand Canyon and as wide as the U.S.; and a gigantic basin (larger than Alaska) in the southern hemisphere that was probably created by a single, huge asteroid. The planet has ice caps at both poles, and the ice caps advance and recede with changes in the seasons.

But the most intriguing aspect of the Martian surface is that water once flowed there in great quantities. Parts of the terrain apparently have sedimentary origins, and there are many long channels, complete with smaller tributary channels and islands, that extend for hundreds of kilometers. There are also volcanic formations similar to those found in Iceland where hot lava has run over wet ground. Scientists speculate that Mars once had a much thicker atmosphere, made up of gases vented during volcanic eruptions, which would have made it possible for liquid water to exist on the surface. Martian atmospheric pressure is now so low, however, that surface water would immediately vaporize. It is conjectured that in the past, water flowed through the channels to lowland areas and then sank into the Martian *regolith* (upper soil layer), since there is no geologic evidence that standing bodies of water ever existed. In 2002 the orbiting *Mars Odyssey* detected signs of a large amount of water ice just below soil level in the south polar region. In early 2004 the European spacecraft *Mars Express* began an orbital survey of the water content as far as 2.5 miles (4 km) below the Martian surface.

Mars is too small to sustain continual volcanic activity. Its atmosphere apparently thinned out after volcanic activity ceased. Atmospheric pressure is now just seven one-thousandths of that on Earth at sea level, and the predominant gas is carbon dioxide, which is relatively heavy. A small amount of water vapor in the atmosphere is enough to form some clouds, small patches of fog in some valleys, and occasionally even patches of frost. Surface temperatures vary from a high of about 70°F (20°C) during summer at the equator to a low of about −220°F (−140°C) during winter at the poles. By far the most pronounced feature of Martian weather is dust storms, which regularly engulf the entire planet for a period of several months.

Jupiter (Average distance from Sun: 5.20 AU. Mass: 318 Earth masses. Diameter: 11.2 Earth diameters. Orbit time: 11.9 years. Rotation time: 9 hours 56 minutes.)

The largest planet in the solar system, Jupiter has 2.5 times more mass than all the other planets of the solar system combined and is 11 times as large as Earth in diameter. Jupiter is so large that scientists believe it almost became a star: as the gases and dust contracted to form the planet, gravitational forces created tremendous pressure and temperature inside the core—as high as tens of thousands of degrees. But there was not enough mass available to create the temperatures needed to start a fusion reaction such as that of the Sun (above 27,000,000°F, or 15,000,000°C, at the Sun's core); thus Jupiter has been slowly cooling down ever since. Even so, Jupiter radiates about as much heat as it receives from the Sun.

The first object to reach Jupiter from Earth was *Pioneer 10*. It returned the first close-up pictures of the giant planet in 1973. Subsequently, the more sophisticated space probes *Voyager 1* and *Voyager 2* passed by Jupiter in 1979 and sent back images and more data on the planet. One of the most exciting discoveries by *Voyager 1* was that Jupiter has a faint but extensive ring system that extends almost 186,000 miles (300,000 km) out from the planet's surface. The *Galileo* spacecraft found another faint ring at 1 million miles (1.6 million km) in 1998. A probe released from the *Galileo* spacecraft arrived at Jupiter on December 7, 1995, finding winds of 435 mph (700 km/hr) and much less water vapor than expected. Scientists later determined that the probe had arrived in what amounts to a Jovian desert. In September 2003, *Galileo's* mission ended with a final plunge into Jupiter's atmosphere.

The most prominent features of Jupiter are its colorful cloud layers. Because the planet spins so fast (one rotation in just under 10 hours), its clouds tend to form bands that give the planet a striped appearance. Darker bands are called belts; light ones are zones. Clouds at higher altitudes are carried eastward by jet streams; those at lower levels are blown westward.

There are numerous eddies and swirls in Jupiter's atmosphere, but none can compare with the Great Red Spot, a massive hurricane (rotating counterclockwise) located in the southern hemisphere near the equator. The Great Red Spot was first observed some 300 years ago, and this storm continues unabated today. Since 1938 three smaller white ovals have been observed to the south of the Great Red Spot.

Jupiter's cloud tops are extremely cold (about −202°F, or −130°C), but temperatures increase deeper inside the atmosphere. The interior of Jupiter is largely a mystery, since no information has been gleaned from direct observations. Jupiter's density is only about one-fourth that of the terrestrial planets, indicating that it is composed of light atoms, more than 90 percent hydrogen. Although hydrogen normally is a gas on Earth, it takes on somewhat more exotic forms at the high pressures inside Jupiter. Below a gaseous cloud layer, the hydrogen is compressed into a liquid and then a liquid metal. At the very center of the planet there may be a small core of rocklike and icelike material, no more than a few times the mass of the Earth. There is nothing like a solid surface anywhere near the cloud tops. Most of Jupiter is just an unusual gaseous-liquid atmosphere. Jupiter's extremely rapid rotation, combined with its large metallic hydrogen interior, gives rise to the strongest magnetic field in the solar system.

Jupiter is now known to have 63 moons, many of them quite small (less than 6 miles in diameter). The four largest are the Galilean moons, so called because the Italian scientist Galileo first observed them. The Galilean moons are Ganymede, Callisto, Europa, and Io—after the Roman god Jupiter's cupbearer (Ganymede) and three of Jupiter's lovers. Ganymede is the largest moon in the solar system and is larger even than the planets Pluto and Mercury. It is a huge, cratered ball of ice and may have a core of solid silicate rock with liquid water between the thick ice covering and the core. Callisto, with an orbit outside that of Ganymede, is also covered with ice and is riddled with thousands of craters. Europa, which orbits inside Ganymede, is about the size of our Moon and has a smooth surface marked by networks of cracks. The most interesting of Jupiter's moons are Io, which orbits closest to Jupiter, and Europa.

Io undergoes the most intense volcanic activity known, heated it is thought by tidal energy generated by gravitational tugs from Jupiter, Europa, and Ganymede. One giant volcano may have been erupting for the past 19 years. Orange-red patches on Io's mottled surface are apparently molten sulfur beds, but most other parts of Io's surface are cold (about –229°F, or –145°C).

Europa, on the other hand, is covered in ice, but some have speculated that a liquid ocean beneath the ice could contain life. The liquid, which probably contains salts like oceans on Earth, could be heated by the same tidal forces that propel Io's volcanoes.

Saturn (Average distance from Sun: 9.54 AU. Mass: 95 Earth masses. Diameter: 9.5 Earth diameters. Orbit time: 29.4 years. Rotation time: 10 hours 40 minutes.)

Saturn is the sixth planet of the solar system and the second largest after Jupiter. The outermost of the planets that can be identified easily in Earth's nighttime sky with the unaided eye, Saturn has a pale yellowish color and is not nearly so bright as Mars. Saturn's spectacular ring system is visible through even a small telescope. Its rings are more extensive than those of any other planet.

Like Jupiter, Saturn is composed of densely compacted hydrogen, helium, and other gases. Liquid or metallic hydrogen probably exists underneath the planet's thick atmosphere, and scientists believe there is a solid core of rock about two times the size of Earth at its center. Saturn's high rotational speed makes it the most oblate (flattened) of all the planets; it is almost 6,800 miles (11,000 km) wider at the equator than on a line through the poles.

Exploration of Saturn began in 1979 with the first fly-by (*Pioneer 11*), but the *Voyager 1* (1980) and *Voyager 2* (1981) missions provided the first detailed look at the planet. Scientists have spent years sifting through the data gathered. Though there were important new findings, many questions about Saturn remain unanswered.

The *Voyagers* found a huge storm thousands of miles across on Saturn, along with a wide band of extremely high winds—up to 1,000 miles (1,600 km) per hour—at the equator. Winds in this band all travel in the direction of the planet's rotation (unlike bands of wind on Jupiter). The *Voyagers* also discovered a vast hydrogen cloud circling the planet above the equator.

The *Voyagers'* most exciting discoveries concern the planetary rings. Previously, about six different rings had been identified within the ring system, but *Voyager 1* pictures show as many as 1,000 separate rings. Narrow rings can even be seen within the Cassini Division, once thought to be an empty gap between the two major parts of the ring system. Some rings are not circular, and at least two rings are intertwined, or "braided." A strange new phenomenon was also discovered in the rings. *Voyager 1* pictures clearly show dark, radial fingers—"spokes"— moving inside the rings in the direction of rotation. Scientists speculate that they are made of ice crystals.

Voyager 2 pictures show that Saturn has far more than 1,000 rings—perhaps as many as 100,000 or more. One of the brightest rings is less than 152 meters (500 ft.) thick. *Voyager 2* also found seasonal differences between the planet's two hemispheres and photographed a storm 4,000 miles (6,500 km) wide.

Twelve of Saturn's moons were known before the arrival of the *Voyagers*, and instruments aboard the space probe helped locate five new ones in the 1980's. In 1990 an 18th moon, later named Pan, was located in images made by *Voyager 2*. The discovery of 12 small moons of Saturn, found with ground-based telescopes, was reported in 2001, and another new moon was spotted in 2003, bringing the total number of moons to 31. Most of Saturn's moons are relatively small and composed of rock and ice. All but one of the small moons are pockmarked by meteor craters, and in some cases the moons appear to have been cracked by collisions with especially large meteors. But *Voyager* pictures show that one moon, Enceladus, is smooth in large regions apparently unmarked by collisions with meteors. Scientists believe that Enceladus is being pulled and stretched by the combined gravities of a nearby moon and Saturn itself. Tidal forces have apparently heated the core of Enceladus and made its surface soft enough to smooth over any craters formed by meteor impacts.

Titan, Saturn's largest moon (3,000 mi., or 4,800 km, in diameter), is one of the few moons in the solar system known to have an atmosphere of any substance. Scientists suspect that at least some precursors of life may have formed there. For this reason *Voyager 1* was guided to within about 2,500 miles (4,000 km) of Titan during the Saturn flyby. Though Titan's surface was obscured by dense clouds, the Voyagers' sensors nevertheless returned a considerable amount of information about the moon and its atmosphere. Titan's atmosphere is composed mostly of nitrogen, like that of Earth, with only a small percentage of methane and carbon monoxide. Atmospheric pressure is at least 1.5 times that on Earth, and temperatures range around –294°F (–181°C). Titan in fact appears to be a frozen version of Earth before life evolved. The Cassini-Huygens probe landed on Titan's surface in December 2004. In 2007, images from Cassini revealed that the mass of the ring is two to three times the previous estimate.

The possibility of oceans of liquid methane (or of nitrogen or methane rain) on Titan was a matter of considerable controversy for some time after *Voyager 1* investigated the moon. But Titan is "dry," at least in the regions investigated. Pools of liquid methane might still exist in other low-lying regions, but it is unlikely that either methane or nitrogen condenses to liquid form on Titan.

Uranus (Average distance from Sun: 19.2 AU. Mass: 14.5 Earth masses. Diameter: 4.0 Earth diameters. Orbit time: 84 years. Rotation time: 17 hours 14 minutes.)

Uranus is the seventh planet in the solar system and the third of the Jovian gas giants. The planet is barely visible in Earth's nighttime sky (it looks like a faint star), and for that reason it went undiscovered until 1781.

Nearly the same size as Neptune and only about 5 percent of Jupiter's mass, Uranus is a faintly greenish color, perhaps because its atmosphere contains methane. The planet's axis of rotation is tipped over on its side. Astronomers discovered a system of nine faint rings in 1977, and *Voyager 2* found two more rings in 1986. There are thought to be 21 moons of Uranus. Among these, Caliban and Sycorax were found in 1997; a still unnamed moon was noticed in 1999 by a researcher studying a photograph taken in 1986 by *Voyager 2*. Three more discovered later in 1999 have been named Prospero, Setebos, and Stephano.

Uranus's atmosphere is very cold (−355°F, or −215°C). No clouds have been observed. Scientists speculate that, as on Jupiter and Saturn, temperatures and pressures increase dramatically down through the outer layer of atmosphere. At some point the hydrogen and helium would be sufficiently compressed to form a liquid or slushy surface "crust." Underneath this crust, they believe, is a mantle of solidified methane, ammonia, and water; and inside this mantle, a rocky core of silicon and iron about 10 times as massive as Earth. The core is thought to be hot, probably about 12,000°F (7,000°C).

Neptune (Average distance from Sun: 30.1 AU. Mass: 17.1 Earth masses. Diameter: 3.8 Earth diameters. Orbit time: 165 years. Rotation time: 16 hours 6 minutes.)

The last of the Jovian gas giants, Neptune is the eighth planet in the solar system. It was discovered in 1846 after mathematical calculations based on irregularities in the orbit of Uranus provided astronomers with the correct location of the planet. Neptune, like Uranus, has been surrounded by considerable uncertainty because of its enormous distance from Earth. The visit by *Voyager 2* in 1989 contributed greatly to improved understanding of the planet.

Neptune is a pale bluish color, but it has a clear atmosphere and is very cold at the cloud tops (about −365°F or −220°C). Scientists believe Neptune has a three-layered structure similar to that of Uranus: a crust of solidified or liquid hydrogen and helium that gradually thins outward into an atmosphere; a mantle of solidified gases and water; and a hot, rocky core (about 12,000°F or 7,000°C) some 15 times as massive as Earth. But one aspect of Neptune remains a mystery. Despite similarities with Uranus, Neptune has been found to radiate 2.7 times as much heat as it receives from the Sun (at a rate of 0.03 microwatts per ton of mass). Uranus, on the other hand, does not emit as much excess heat. As a result, Neptune is about the same temperature as Uranus, despite being 50 percent farther from the Sun.

Neptune has 11 known moons: Triton and Nereid, discovered from Earth; six others discovered by *Voyager 2*; and three more newly spotted in 2002. Triton is the largest moon and has an atmosphere. Triton is unusual in that it travels in a direction opposite that of Neptune's rotation, suggesting that it had a different origin from the planet. Triton also has volcanic activity: geysers of nitrogen rising as high as 5 miles (8 km).

Dwarf Planets

From 1930 through the end of the 20th century, the solar system was thought to contain nine planets, the ninth planet being Pluto. In recent years, however, several objects similar to Pluto were discovered in the outer solar system. This caused a rethinking of what makes a planet a planet.

On August 24, 2006, the International Astronomical Union (I.A.U.) for the first time defined the term planet. In this new definition, a planet is a celestial body that is in orbit around a star, has sufficient mass so that it assumes a nearly round shape, and has cleared its orbit of planetesimals and similar debris. The first eight planets (Mercury through Neptune) meet all three criteria, but Pluto meets only the first two.

Pluto was thus removed from the rank of major planets and reclassified as a dwarf planet. The I.A.U. classifies a dwarf planet as a celestial body that is in orbit around the sun, has sufficient mass so that it assumes a nearly round shape, has not cleared its orbit of planetesimals, and is not a satellite of another similar object. Today there are five recognized dwarf planets: Pluto, Eris, Ceres, Haumea, and Makemake.

Pluto (Average distance from Sun: 39.5 AU. Mass: 0.002 Earth masses. Diameter: 0.18 Earth diameters. Orbit time: 248 years. Rotation time: 6.4 days.)

Main components of atmosphere: methane and nitrogen (quantities unknown). A ball of frozen gases probably only about the size of Earth's moon, Pluto was discovered in 1930 as a result of an extensive search by Clyde Tombaugh. It was originally thought to be a planet, until that term was redefined by the I.A.U. in 2006. Pluto resides in the Kuiper Belt outside the orbit of Neptune; its chaotic orbit causes it at times to cross inside Neptune's orbit.

Today Pluto is about as close to the Sun as it ever gets and possesses a thin atmosphere, but it is expected to freeze solid as the planet moves away from the sun. Pluto has one known moon, Charon, discovered in 1978. Charon is about half the size of Pluto. Pluto and Charon rotate and revolve synchronously like a double planet system.

Eris (Average distance from Sun: 67.7 AU. Mass: .002 Earth masses. Diameter: 0.19 Earth diameters. Orbit time: 557 years. Rotation time: not yet known.)

Main components of atmosphere: methane and nitrogen (quantities unknown). Similar in composition and mass to Pluto, Eris was discovered in 2005 by a Mount Palomar-based team of astronomers, led by Michael Brown. Eris has one known moon, Dysnomia. Eris resides in the Kuiper Belt, and is at this time the most distant known body in the solar system; its orbit is more eccentric and tilted than that of its neighbor Pluto.

Ceres (Average distance from Sun: 2.767 AU. Mass: 0.00016 Earth masses. Diameter: .075 Earth diameters. Orbit time: 4.6 years. Rotation time: 9 hours.)

Discovered in 1801 by Giuseppe Piazzi, Ceres is the largest and most massive body in the asteroid belt between Mars and Jupiter. First thought to be a comet, then a large asteroid, Ceres has most recently been classified as a dwarf planet. Unlike other objects in the asteroid belt, Ceres is spherical; it has no discernable atmosphere.

Haumea (Average distance from Sun: 43.335 AU. Mass: 0.0007 Earth masses. Diameter: 0.195 Earth diameters. Orbit time: 281.93 years. Rotation time: 3.915 hours.)

Discovered by the Sierra Nevada Observatory in 2003, Haumea is named for the Hawaiian goddess of fertility and childbirth. Its very fast rotation is thought to have given it its odd, elongated shape. It sits among the trans-Neptunian objects, in the Kuiper Belt. Haumea has two moons, Hawai'i and Namaka. Astronomers believe it is made of rock with a coating of ice.

Makemake (Average distance from Sun: 45.791 AU. Mass: 0.00067 Earth masses. Diameter: 0.102–0.149 Earth diameters. Orbit time: 305.34 years. Rotation time: 22.48 hours.)

Discovered in 2005, Makemake is composed mainly of ice and rock and its diameter is roughly three-quarters that of Pluto. It has no moons, which makes it unique among Kuiper Belt objects. In 2008, the I.A.U. formally classified Makemake as a *plutoid*, a term for dwarf planets beyond the orbit of Neptune. It is named for the god of creation for the native people of Easter Island.

Smaller Objects in the Solar System

In addition to the eight major and three dwarf planets, a large number of smaller objects orbit the Sun.

Asteroids, small objects with compositions similar to the terrestrial planets, are found primarily in the asteroid belt, a band lying between the orbits of Mars and Jupiter. Smaller numbers are found in orbits that cross those of the terrestrial planets, including Earth's orbit, and leading or trailing several planets. The largest of the asteroids, Ceres, is nearly half the diameter of Pluto, though most are much smaller, with diameters of several kilometers. More than 200,000 asteroids are now known.

Comets are icy bodies, composed mostly of water ice and carbon dioxide ice. When far from the Sun, comets are essentially in deep freeze, but if a comet's orbit carries it closer to the Sun, significant amounts of the ice evaporate and trail away from the main body of the comet, forming the comet's distinctive tail. As the ice evaporates, small solid grainlike particles mixed in with the ice are also released. The main body of a comet may be only a few kilometers in diameter, but upon close approach to the Sun, the tail may extend for millions of kilometers. Upon leaving the inner solar system, a comet returns to deep freeze. Two different locations are recognized as sources of comets. Long-period comets, ones that take more than several hundred years to complete an orbit of the Sun, are thought to come from the Oort Cloud, a large group of as many as a million comets located 50,000 times farther from the Sun than Earth, halfway to the next nearest star. Small gravitational perturbations occasionally sling one or more of these in toward the Sun. Some end up on long, repeating elliptical orbits; others make a single pass by the Sun and are flung out of the solar system, while some

The Constellations

Name	Genitive	Abbr.	Translation	Remarks
Andromeda	Andromedae	And	Andromeda	Character in Greek myth
Antlia	Antliae	Ant	Air pump	Named by Nicolas Lacaille in 1750
Apus	Apodis	Aps	Swift, or Bird of Paradise	Named by Johann Bayer in 1603
Aquarius	Aquarii	Aqr	Water Bearer	In zodiac
Aquila	Aquilae	Aql	Eagle	Contains Altair
Ara	Arae	Ara	Altar	Part of the Centaurus group
Aries	Arietis	Ari	Ram	In zodiac
Auriga	Aurigae	Aur	Charioteer	Contains Capella
Boötes	Boötis	Boo	Herdsman	Contains Arcturus
Caelum	Caeli	Cae	Chisel	Lacaille, 1750
Camelopardalis	Camelopardalis	Cam	Giraffe	Named by Jakob Bartsch in 1661
Cancer	Cancri	Cnc	Crab	In zodiac
Canes Venatici	Canum Venaticorum	CVn	Hunting dogs	Named by Johannes Hevelius in 1687
Canis Major	Canis Majoris	CMa	Big Dog	Contains Sirius and Adhara
Canis Minor	Canis Minoris	CMi	Little Dog	Contains Procyon
Capricornus	Capricorni	Cap	Goat	In zodiac
Carina	Carinae	Car	Ship's Keel[1]	Lacaille, 1750; contains Canopus
Cassiopeia	Cassiopeiae	Cas	Cassiopeia	Character in Greek myth
Centaurus	Centauri	Cen	Centaur	Character in Greek myth; contains Rigil Kentaurus and Hadar/Agena
Cepheus	Cephei	Cep	Cepheus	Character in Greek myth
Cetus	Ceti	Cet	Whale	Sea monster slain by Perseus
Chamaeleon	Chamaeleontis	Cha	Chameleon	Bayer, 1603
Circinus	Circini	Cir	Compass	Lacaille, 1750
Columba	Columbae	Col	Dove	Bayer, 1603
Coma Berenices	Comae Berenices	Com	Berenice's Hair	Third Century B.C. Egyptian Queen
Corona Australis	Coronae Australis	CrA	Southern Crown	Also Sagittarius' crown
Corona Borealis	Coronae Borealis	CrB	Northern Crown	Also Ariadne's crown
Corvus	Corvi	Crv	Crow	Companion of Orpheus
Crater	Crateris	Crt	Cup	—
Crux[2]	Crucis	Cru	Southern Cross	Named by Augustine Royer in 1679; Contains Beta Crucis and Acrux
Cygnus	Cygni	Cyg	Swan	Contains Deneb
Delphinus	Delphini	Del	Dolphin	—
Dorado	Doradus	Dor	Goldfish	Bayer, 1603
Draco	Draconis	Dra	Dragon	Dragon slain by Hercules
Equuleus	Equulei	Equ	Little Horse	—
Eridanus	Eridani	Eri	River Eridanus	Contains Achernar
Fornax	Fornacis	For	Furnace	Lacaille, 1750
Gemini	Geminorum	Gem	Twins	In zodiac; contains Pollux
Grus	Gruis	Gru	Crane	Bayer, 1603
Hercules	Herculis	Her	Hercules	Character from Greek myth
Horologium	Horologii	Hor	Clock	Lacaille, 1750
Hydra[3]	Hydrae	Hya	Hydra	Monster from Greek myth

The Constellations (continued)

Name	Genitive	Abbr.	Translation	Remarks
Hydrus	Hydri	Hyi	Sea serpent	Bayer, 1603
Indus	Indi	Ind	Indian	Bayer, 1603
Lacerta	Lacertae	Lac	Lizard	Hevelius, 1687
Leo	Leonis	Leo	Lion	In zodiac; contains Regulus
Leo Minor	Leonis Minoris	LMi	Little Lion	Hevelius, 1687
Lepus	Leporis	Lep	Hare	Prey of Orion
Libra	Librae	Lib	Scales	In zodiac
Lupus	Lupi	Lup	Wolf	Part of Centaurus group
Lynx	Lyncis	Lyn	Lynx	Hevelius, 1687
Lyra	Lyrae	Lyr	Harp	Contains Vega
Mensa	Mensae	Men	Table (mountain)	Lacaille, 1750
Microscopium	Microscopii	Mic	Microscope	Lacaille, 1750
Monoceros	Monocerotis	Mon	Unicorn	Royer, 1679
Musca	Muscae	Mus	Fly	Bayer, 1603
Norma	Normae	Nor	Carpenter's Square	Lacaille, 1750
Octans	Octanis	Oct	Octant	Lacaille, 1750
Ophiuchus	Ophiuchi	Oph	Serpent Bearer	Character in Greek myth
Orion	Orionis	Ori	The Hunter	Character in Greek myth; contains Rigel, Betelgeuse, and Bellatrix
Pavo	Pavonis	Pav	Peacock	Bayer, 1603
Pegasus	Pegasi	Peg	Pegasus	Winged horse in Greek myth
Perseus	Persei	Per	Perseus	Character in Greek myth
Phoenix	Phoenicis	Phe	Phoenix	Bayer, 1603
Pictor	Pictoris	Pic	Easel	Lacaille, 1750
Pisces	Piscium	Psc	Fish	In zodiac
Piscis Austrinus	Piscis Austrin	PsA	Southern Fish	Contains Fomalhaut
Puppis	Puppis	Pup	Ship's Stern[1]	Lacaille, 1750
Pyxis	Pyxidis	Pyx	Ship's Compass[1]	Lacaille, 1750
Reticulum	Reticuli	Ret	Net	Lacaille, 1750
Sagitta	Sagittae	Sge	Arrow	—
Sagittarius	Sagittarii	Sgr	Archer	In zodiac
Scorpius	Scorpii	Sco	Scorpion	In zodiac; contains Antares and Shaula
Sculptor	Sculptoris	Scl	Sculptor	Lacaille, 1750
Scutum	Scuti	Sct	Shield	Hevelius, 1687
Serpens	Serpentis	Ser	Serpent	Snake held by giant Ophiuchus
Sextans	Sextantis	Sex	Sextant	Hevelius, 1687
Taurus	Tauri	Tau	Bull	In zodiac; contains Aldebran and Elnath
Telescopium	Telescopii	Tel	Telescope	Lacaille, 1750
Triangulum	Trianguli	Tri	Triangle	Contains spiral galaxy M33
Triangulum Australe	Trianguli Australis	TrA	Southern Triangle	Bayer, 1603
Tucana	Tucanae	Tuc	Toucan	Bayer, 1603
Ursa Major	Ursae Majoria	UMa	Big Bear	Big Dipper
Ursa Minor	Ursae Minoris	UMi	Little Bear	Little Dipper
Vela	Velorum	Vel	Ship's Sails[1]	Lacaille, 1750
Virgo	Virginis	Vir	Virgin	In zodiac; contains Spica
Volans	Volantis	Vol	Flying Fish	Bayer, 1603
Vulpecula	Vulpeculae	Vul	Little Fox	Hevelius, 1687

1. Formerly part of the constellation Argo Navis, the Argonauts' ship. 2. Smallest constellation. 3. Largest constellation.

crash into the Sun. Short-period comets move on elliptical orbits that take them out no farther than the orbit of Pluto. The source of short-period comets is now thought to be a recently discovered group of icy objects just outside of Neptune's orbit called the Kuiper Belt. The first Kuiper Belt object was discovered in 1992, and hundreds have now been discovered, including four with at least one-third the diameter of Pluto. In 2010, NASA's *Deep Impact* spacecraft passed within 435 miles Comet Hartley, recording highly precise images of the object in deep space.

Extrasolar Planets Astronomers have long suspected that planets were not unique to our solar system, and numerous searches for planets around other stars have been undertaken. In 1995 the first detection of an extrasolar planet around a Sun-like star was announced. The discovery was made by looking for very small shifts in the spectrum of the star 51 Pegasi as the star wobbled back and forth under the gravitational influence of a much smaller object in orbit around it. From the time it took for the star to complete one wobble, it was determined that the planet orbited much closer to 51 Pegasi than Mercury's distance from the Sun, completing an orbit in only four days. From the strength of the gravitational pull, the planet was found to have a mass about one-half that of Jupiter. Since this discovery, more than 1,200 more extrasolar planets have been found around ordinary stars. Many of the planets orbit their star at very small distances, but the search has now turned up systems similar to the solar system, with Jovian-sized planets at large distances from their stars. The techniques presently being used are not capable of finding Earth-size planets, so it is not yet possible to know whether terrestrial planets exist around other stars.

Stars and the Universe

Astronomical Distances The very large distances between stars and the even larger ones between the vast groups of stars called galaxies are usually expressed in terms of units of length that are peculiar to astronomy. The most familiar is the *light-year,* defined as the distance light travels through a vacuum in a year (approximately 3,651 / 4 days). Light travels through a vacuum at the rate of about 186,250 miles per second (exactly 299,792,458 m/s—exact because the meter is defined in terms of the speed of light in a vacuum). A light-year is approximately 5,880 trillion miles (9,460 trillion km).

Astronomers also use a measure even larger than the light-year, the parsec, equal to about 3.26 light-years, or about 19,170 trillion miles (30,840 trillion km).

A smaller unit, for measurements within the solar system, is the astronomical unit, which is the average distance between the Earth and the Sun, or about 93 million miles (150 million km).

Constellations consist of several bright stars that are treated as a group. Long ago, before recorded history, people began naming these groups. By Sumerian times (3000–2500 B.C.), stories were already being told about how particular constellations were formed. Most of our present knowledge of such stories, however, comes from the ancient Greeks.

One group of constellations has exerted a special influence on human thought, at least since 1500 B.C. As the Sun, Moon, and planets move through the sky, they pass through a group of 12 constellations, called the constellations of the zodiac. The ancient belief that the presence of the Sun in one of these constellations at a person's birth influences happenings on Earth is called astrology.

Today astronomers use constellations for mapping the sky. Each part of the sky is named by a particular constellation. These constellations, especially in the southern hemisphere, may not be traditional ones, but rather, groups of stars astronomers have named so that for reference purposes all of the sky is labeled.

Star Names While astronomers often use the traditional names of stars, most of which come to us from Latin or Arabic sources, they also use another system for naming objects in the sky that is based on constellations. Generally, the brightest star in a particular astronomical constellation is called alpha (}), the next brightest beta (ß), and so on through several letters of the Greek alphabet; then numbers are used. All astronomers' constellations are named in Latin. When astronomers refer to a star within its constellation, they use the genitive case, meaning "of the thing." Thus the constellation Big Dog is officially Canis Major, and Sirius is alpha Canis Majoris, or "alpha of Big Dog," usually abbreviated to }CMa. This means it is the brightest star in the constellation Big Dog (Sirius has long been known as the dog star). Since Sirius is a binary star (see "Binary stars"), the much brighter main star is officially }CMa A. Further along, numbers are used instead of Greek letters. Numbered stars in the news in the 1990's included 51 Pegasi and 71 Virginis.

Magnitude The brightness of a star is designated by a number called its magnitude, although the relationship between size and brightness is complicated. When the magnitude system was first developed, by the early Greek astronomers Hipparchus (c. 190–c. 120 B.C.) and Ptolemy (c. 100–c. 170), astronomers did not know the actual distances to stars, so magnitude always referred to brightness as seen from Earth. They classed the brightest stars as the first magnitude and the dimmest they could see as the sixth. These numbers were somewhat arbitrary until 1856, when George Phillips Bond (1825–65) determined that photographs of stars show magnitude in a way that is directly measurable—bright stars appear as larger spots than dim stars in photographs even though all stars appear as points to the naked eye. Astronomers could use accurate measures to compare two stars and thus measure magnitude with mathematical precision. Under Bond's system, stars with a magnitude of 1.00 are exactly 100 times as bright as those with a magnitude of 6.00. On this scale, the very brightest stars have negative magnitudes.

Roughly, each whole number difference in magnitude corresponds to 2.5 times the brightness.

By the time this system was introduced, astronomers already were able to determine the distances of some stars from Earth. Friedrich Wilhelm Bessel was the first to make such a measurement, which he announced in 1838. A closer star appears brighter than a similar star that is farther away. To better understand the relative brightness of stars as they actually are, astronomers imagine viewing all stars from the same distance away. A star's brightness from this distance, which is 10 parsecs or 32.6 light-years, is called its absolute magnitude.

If we could see it clearly, the star Cygnus OB2 #12 would be the brightest star in the Milky Way galaxy (absolute magnitude -9.9), but it is not only far from Earth but also is obscured by dust. The brightest single object known is not a star, but a quasar (see "Quasars"), BR 1202-07, with an absolute magnitude of about –33. The Sun has the brightest apparent magnitude of any star, –26.8, but its absolute magnitude is only 4.75.

The Universe

Most of the universe was greatly misunderstood until the 20th century. The most common notion from the time of the ancient Greek philosophers until the end of the Middle Ages was that a number of crystal spheres revolved about Earth, and that each of the planets, the Sun, and Earth's Moon occupied one of these spheres. All the stars occupied the farthest sphere. There were only about 6,000 stars known, those visible to the naked eye (and about half of these were south of the equator, so few Europeans had ever seen them).

In 1609 Galileo of Italy turned the first astronomical telescope on the heavens. Galileo's early telescopes were good enough to show that the Milky Way was not merely a whitish band across the sky but consisted of a vast number of stars, far more than the few thousand visible with the naked eye. His observations also disproved the old idea of crystal spheres. People began to speculate about astronomical entities beyond a simple sphere of stars. Not until 1924 were telescopes sufficiently powerful to show that many cloudy patches in the sky consisted of millions of stars far away from the Milky Way. This discovery led to the recognition of the enormous complexity and diversity of the universe.

Binary Stars Almost half the stars in the visible universe are actually pairs of stars that orbit each other. Astronomers can sometimes see both stars, but more commonly they recognize that a star is part of a binary because of the influence of the dimmer star's gravitational pull on the other star.

Black Holes When a body becomes so dense for its size that not even light can escape the powerful gravitational pull it exerts, it is called a black hole. Black holes were predicted as early as 1784 (by John Michell) and invoked later by various astronomers and physicists to explain many strange astronomical phenomena. Black holes have been observed at the center of many galaxies, including our own Milky Way. Several smaller black holes, thought to be remains of supernova explosions, have also been located.

Brown Dwarfs are bodies too small to be stars, but too large to be planets. They glow dimly as a result of energy released by gravitational contraction. A brown dwarf must be between 13 and 80 times the mass of Jupiter. The first brown dwarf to be definitely established orbits the star Gliese 229. Although about 50 times Jupiter's mass, its diameter is about the same as Jupiter's. Since then, a number of brown dwarfs have been located, including some not in orbit about other stars.

Clusters of Stars Stars often form together, forming associations of hundreds or thousands or clusters of millions of stars. Open clusters, such as the Pleiades (Seven Sisters), contain several hundred to a thousand stars gathered in an irregular region perhaps tens of light years across. There are about a thousand open clusters in the Milky Way Galaxy. Globular clusters contain millions of stars, most very old, that have formed into a sphere a 100 to 200 light-years in diameter. There are about 125 known globular clusters associated with the Milky Way.

Dark Matter and Dark Energy are thought to be the main part of the universe, with ordinary matter accounting for only 5 percent of the universe's mass. The evidence is that galaxies rotate in a way that indicates they must be embedded in a gravitational field caused by undetectable matter (*dark matter*) while all galaxies are flying apart with increasing speed caused by some unknown force that opposes gravity, called *dark energy*. There are a number of competing theories as to the nature of these entities. The dark matter, previously known as missing mass, may consist of slow-moving, unknown subatomic particles, while dark energy might be a cosmological constant inherent in the vacuum of empty space.

Dwarfs are small stars—the brightest are blue dwarfs, the dimmest red dwarfs. The Sun is a yellow dwarf; there are also white and brown dwarfs.

Expanding Universe When Albert Einstein developed his general theory of relativity, he found it predicted that the universe would either expand as if it were exploding, or else collapse. He tried to correct this prediction by inserting a term in his equations to counteract the prediction, but in the 1920s, Edwin Hubble discovered that the universe actually is expanding. It is easier to measure the speed of recession than the distance, so astronomers commonly use the speed at which something is moving away as the measure of its distance from us. Of course, it is not just moving away from us. In the expanding universe, everything is moving away from everything else.

Galaxies are systems of very many stars separated from one another by largely empty space (sometimes galaxies are called island universes). In the 18th century, William Herschel concluded that many cloudy patches of light seen among the stars were actually giant systems of billions of stars, but so far away from Earth as to look like clouds. Better telescopes proved him right in the early 20th century, and these far-off, great masses of stars became known as galaxies, after our own Milky Way, the galaxy that includes the Sun. Observation with large telescopes in the 20th century has revealed two main types of galaxies—spiral and elliptical—although some galaxies are neither (irregular).

Milky Way This is the galaxy to which the Sun and Earth belong; it contains about 100 billion stars. If you are in a place unafflicted with much light pollution, when you look at the night sky, you can see a faint band crossing it. The ancient Greeks named this the Milky Way (*galaxy* in Greek). Early in the 19th century, William Herschel determined that our Sun was a star in a vast lens-shaped star system, and that the Milky Way was the part of the star system we see from our vantage point inside it. Today, recognizing there are very many other such star systems, scientists often call it the Milky Way galaxy.

Nebulae are patches of gas and dust observable in telescopes. Before Herschel discovered that some cloudy patches seen through telescopes were vast collections of stars, all such patches were called *nebulae* (meaning clouds). Some "clouds" turned out to be galaxies, but many did not. The patches of gas emit light, often by the same mechanism that a fluorescent light does; energy from stars ionizes the gas, which gives off visible light. Some patches of dust also glow, usually reflecting the light of nearby stars. Other patches of dust are opaque or nearly so, blocking out part of the sky. Some of the most striking nebulae consist of glowing gas surrounded by opaque dust or vice versa, which gives the nebula a definite shape, such as the North America Nebula or the Horsehead Nebula. Herschel also studied a class of nebulae that looked to be giant spheres. He correctly concluded that these planetary nebulae were balls of gas produced when a star exploded.

Neutron Stars are stars that have collapsed in a violent explosion, such as a supernova, so that the force keeping electrons apart is overcome. All the neutrons and protons can touch, forming the equivalent of a giant atomic nucleus. The star is electrically neutral because of the charge of the collapsed electrons. Such a star may be only a dozen miles in diameter but may have a mass twice that of the Sun.

Novae are stars that seem to appear out of nowhere. Later, they disappear. Early peoples were surprised from time to time by the appearance of a *nova* ("new") star in the sky. Ancient Chinese astronomers called them guest stars. It is now clear that a truly new star does not appear; instead, a dim, existing star suddenly brightens. In early days, before the telescope, the dim stars could not be seen at all, so it looked as if a star came from nowhere. Today we know that there are two different types of "guest stars," and we reserve the name nova for one type and call the other a supernova (see below). The type referred to today as novae are less bright than supernovae and may appear more than once. It is thought that they occur when material from one star in a binary pair falls on the other star, causing it suddenly to flare up.

Kepler Planet Hunter Finds 1,200 Possibilities

By DENNIS OVERBYE

Astronomers have cracked the Milky Way like a piñata, and planets are now pouring out so fast that they do not know what to do with them all. In a long-awaited announcement, scientists operating NASA's Kepler planet-hunting satellite reported in February 2011 that they had identified 1,235 possible planets orbiting other stars, potentially tripling the number of known planets.

Of the new candidates, 68 are one and a quarter times the size of the Earth or smaller—smaller, that is, than any previously discovered planets outside the solar system, which are known as exoplanets. Fifty-four of the possible exoplanets are in the so-called habitable zones of stars dimmer and cooler than the Sun, where temperatures should be moderate enough for liquid water.

Astronomers said that it would take years to confirm that all of these candidates were really planets—by using ground-based telescopes to measure their masses, for example, or inspecting them to see if background stars are causing optical mischief. Many of them might never be vetted because of the dimness of their stars and the lack of telescope time and astronomers to do it all. But statistical tests of a sample suggest that 80 to 95 percent of the objects on it are real, as opposed to blips in the data.

At first glance, not one of them appears to be another Earth, the kind of cosmic Eden fit for life as we know it, but the new results represent only four months' worth of data on a three-and-a-half-year project, and have left astronomers optimistic that they will eventually find Earth-like planets. The Kepler telescope surveys only one four-hundredth of the sky. If it could see the whole sky, there would be 400,000 candidates.

Kepler, launched into orbit around the Sun in March 2009, stares at a patch of the Milky Way near the Northern Cross, measuring the brightness of 156,000 stars every 30 minutes, looking for a pattern of dips that would be caused by planets crossing in front of their suns.

The goal is to assess the frequency of Earth-like planets around Sun-like stars. But in the four months of data analyzed so far, a similar telescope looking at our own Sun would have been lucky to have seen the Earth pass even once. Three transits are required for a planet to show up in Kepler's elaborate data-processing pipeline, which means that Kepler's next scheduled data release, in June 2012, could be a moment of truth for the mission.

For dimmer and cooler stars, the habitable, or "Goldilocks," zone, would be smaller, however, and planets in it would rack up transits more quickly.

Scientists had eagerly anticipated the data release since June 2010, when Kepler scientists issued their first list of some 300 stars that were suspected of harboring planets but held back another 400 for study. In the intervening months some of those candidates had been eliminated, but hundreds more were added.

The growing number of small planets revealed by Kepler was a welcome change from the early days of exoplanet research, when most of the planets discovered were Jupiter-size giants hugging their stars in close orbits, leading theorists to speculate that smaller planets might be thrown outward from their stars by gravitational forces or dragged right into those suns.

Pulsars are neutron stars that emit electromagnetic signals from their magnetic poles in a direction that reaches Earth. All neutron stars emit signals and rotate very rapidly (at least when they are first formed; they gradually slow down). These signals form a tight beam. If the beam intersects Earth, a radio telescope observes a fast pulsing on and off. The pulses are so regular that when they were first discovered, they were thought to be the work of extraterrestrial beings.

Quasars are distant sources of great energy. The name quasar is short for Quasi-Stellar Object, and the objects are so called because they seem to be about the size and general appearance of stars, but produce far too much energy to be stars. No one knows for sure what they are, but there is some evidence that quasars are caused by black holes in the central part of distant galaxies. The stars in the galaxies cannot be seen because of the great distance, so we see only the central part, which is the quasar.

Red Giants are stars that have used their hydrogen fuel and expanded as a result. Young stars "burn" hydrogen in a nuclear fusion process that leads to helium. When a star has consumed the hydrogen in its core, new fusion reactions that start with helium begin, leading to carbon. The new reactions are hotter than the fusion of hydrogen to helium. This added energy causes the hydrogen and helium outside the core to expand. The star is red because the outer layers are relatively cool. When the Sun becomes a red giant in the distant future, it will expand almost to the orbit of Earth, completely engulfing Mercury and Venus, and charring Earth to a cinder.

Stars are bodies of gas large enough to undergo fusion reactions in their core. As a result of the energy produced by fusion, stars emit visible light, as well as electromagnetic radiation at other wavelengths. The Sun is a star. The hotter or larger a star is, the brighter it is.

Superclusters and Clusters of Galaxies are groups of galaxies associated in space. There may be just a few members of a cluster or as many as thousands. About two dozen galaxies near us form, with the Milky Way, our Local Group. The members of the Local Group also include the Andromeda galaxy and the Large and Small Magellanic Clouds. All are traveling through the universe together. The Local Group is a member of a supercluster of galaxies, called the Local Supercluster, that contains about 100 clusters. Clusters and superclusters are recognized because the average distance within a cluster or a supercluster from one galaxy or cluster to another is much less than the distance to other galaxies or clusters.

Supernovae are explosions of large stars. A supernova explosion is much more dramatic than the brightening of a nova. A supernova reported by Chinese astronomers from A.D. 1054 was visible in the daytime. The remnants of this explosion are known today as the Crab Nebula. At its heart the Crab Nebula has a pulsar, all that is left of the star that exploded.

Variable Stars Any star that periodically changes brightness is called a variable (a nova changes brightness but not at regular intervals). The period varies with the cause of the change and the individual star. Some variables are part of a binary system in which one star periodically passes in front of the other. Other kinds of variables are called Mira variables and Cepheid variables, after the first stars known of each type. It is not clear what causes the brightness to vary.

Stars

The Life Cycles of Stars Stars are spheres of gas that generate energy by nuclear fusion. Their life cycles are responsible for the rich chemical complexity of the universe and are intimately connected to the existence of life. Since soon after the beginning of the universe, stars have been forming and then producing heavy elements as a byproduct of energy generation at their cores. When their nuclear fuel is exhausted, some of these fusion products are released back into space, in the process enriching the interstellar medium, the raw materials for formation of subsequent generations of stars.

The Interstellar Medium and Star Formation
The space between stars is vast (typically tens of trillions of miles between pairs of stars), and that space is not empty. Astronomers refer to this space as interstellar space; the material distributed throughout interstellar space is referred to as the interstellar medium (ISM). The ISM is composed of thinly spread gas atoms, mostly hydrogen with a smaller amount of helium, and traces of other elements, as well as a small amount of dusty solid aterial. Conditions in the ISM are extreme: atoms are so thinly spread that a cube-shape region 500 miles on a side contains only about a gram of matter. Forming a star from such diffuse material requires compacting interstellar gas by a trillion trillion times. Most star formation occurs in denser accumulations of interstellar gas called Giant Molecular Clouds (GMCs), so called because they contain enough raw material, mostly in the form of hydrogen mol-

ecules, to make hundreds of thousands of stars. In these clouds, the gas can be thousands of times denser than average but even colder, reaching temperatures of 10 Kelvins (less than −400° F). GMCs are found in the spiral arms of our galaxy (see the Milky Way). The formation of individual stars occurs in denser clumps within GMCs, where gravity pulls together the million trillion trillion kilograms of interstellar matter necessary to make a star. This accumulated matter is known as a protostar, enough raw material to make a star but not yet producing energy through nuclear fusion. Astronomers have yet to definitively observe the initial conditions needed to form a protostar, though later stages have been seen. Observations also show that collapse is accompanied by the formation of a disk of interstellar material around the protostar's equator; this protoplanetary disk is presumably the material from which planets form.

As more material accumulates, the central temperature of the protostar reaches the millions of degrees necessary for hydrogen atoms to combine to form helium. The mass of helium produced in these reactions is smaller than the initial hydrogen; the difference is converted to energy (see Physics: $E = mc^2$). The onset of fusion marks the true birth of the star. After a period during which the star settles into its final configuration and surrounding cloud material is cleared away, the star becomes a stable main-sequence star, steadily converting hydrogen to helium in its hottest central regions. Within GMCs, stars form in groups of hundreds or thousands of stars, and a GMC may experience multiple episodes of star formation. The smallest stars have masses of about 1/12 the Sun's mass. Below this mass, the center of a hydrogen gas sphere does not reach high enough temperatures to fuse hydrogen into helium; an object below this mass is known as a brown dwarf. Stars form with masses up to about 100 times the Sun's mass. The smaller the mass, the more stars of that mass there are; stars smaller than the Sun are the most common; high-mass stars are rare.

The Main Sequence Once the structure of a star stabilizes, it steadily converts hydrogen to helium in its core. This phase in a star's life, known as the main sequence, lasts far longer than a star's formation or death. The stable structure arises from the balance between gravity, trying to compress the star; and internal pressure, generated by energy released in the nuclear reactions, pushing outward. Since the fuel for nuclear fusion is hydrogen, and since stars are made of enormous quantities of this fuel, the main-sequence stage can continue for millions or billions of years. Although high-mass stars contain more hydrogen fuel than low-mass stars, they have higher power outputs and run through the available hydrogen faster. The highest-mass stars use up their nuclear fuel in a few million years; the Sun has enough fuel to last 10 billion years; the smallest stars will take hundreds of billions of years to run through their fuel.

Post-Main Sequence Evolution and Star Death
As hydrogen is replaced by helium in a stellar core, a star enters the post-main-sequence stage. The core shrinks and becomes hotter, allowing helium fusion to begin, increasing the nuclear reaction rate and power output of the star. The star's outer layers expand to 100–1,000 times the main-sequence diameter and become cooler. This is known as the red giant phase.

In lower-mass stars like the Sun, atoms as massive as carbon and oxygen are formed at the core. The expanded outer layers begin to flow away from the core, dispersing back into interstellar space during the planetary nebula phase. The remaining stellar core, composed of carbon, oxygen, and electrons, has about the mass of the Sun but with a diameter about the same as Earth. This remnant of a low-mass star's life is a white dwarf. The large gravitational force trying to collapse the core is offset by *electron degeneracy pressure*, a quantum effect which prevents electrons from occupying the same space and as a result provides an outward force to hold up the core.

In higher-mass stars, central pressures are high enough to allow additional fusion reactions, producing heavier elements like silicon, sulfur, and iron. The resulting internal structure is onionlike, with layers of earlier fusion products lying atop the stellar core. When iron is formed in the core, no other fusion reactions can occur without removing pressure from the system, and the core rapidly collapses. If the core mass is less than three times the mass of the Sun, collapse is halted by neutron degeneracy pressure when the core is about 10 kilometers across. The resulting high-density object is a neutron star. As neutron pressure halts collapse of the core, the resulting rebound ejects the star's outer layers back into interstellar space in a supernova explosion. The interstellar medium is thereby enriched with heavy elements, including elements such as carbon, oxygen, iron, sulfur, and phosphorous, which are crucial to life on Earth. The Sun and Earth presumably formed from supernova-enriched interstellar gas.

In stars where the core mass exceeds three times the Sun's mass, even neutron pressure cannot halt the collapse once all core fuel sources have been exhausted. The core collapses to an infinitely dense mass called a black hole. The gravitational force within a few tens of kilometers of such a stellar black hole is so strong that even light cannot escape from it. The precise fate of the star's outer layers is not clear. Since high-mass stars are rare, few possible stellar black holes have been identified, and none has been observed during the collapse phase.

The Milky Way Galaxy

The Sun is one of several hundred billion stars that belong to the Milky Way galaxy (in astronomical usage known as "the Galaxy"), a vast accumulation of gravitationally associated stars, star-forming material, and other matter. The common name Milky Way dates from antiquity and refers to the white "spilled milk" appearance of the Galaxy, easily seen from dark viewing sites cutting across the nighttime sky. In the 17th century, Galileo used a telescope to show that this light band was actually made up of a large number of individual stars. Studies were made throughout the 18th and 19th centuries in attempts to measure the scale of the Galaxy, but incorrect interpretations of the data led to underestimates of the Galaxy's extent and mistakenly placed the Sun at the Galaxy center. In the early 20th century, work by American astronomers Henrietta Leavitt and Harlow Shapley showed that the Sun was located about halfway out from the center of the Galaxy's flattened disk of stars, about 24,000 light-years (144 quadrillion miles) from the Galactic Center and a similar distance from the disk's outer edge. This disk is just one of several components of the Galaxy.

The Galactic Disk The Milky Way is a spiral galaxy, distinguishable by its prominent, bright, flattened disk of stars, all orbiting about the Galactic Center in the same direction (clockwise as viewed from the North Galactic Pole). This disk contains most of the stars in the Galaxy and nearly all of the interstellar gas and dust. The thickness of the disk ranges from a few hundred light-years for the youngest stars and star-forming clouds to a few thousand light-years for the oldest disk stars. The diameter of the disk is some 100,000 light-years. The disk is thus extremely thin, with a width-to-height ratio of more than 1,000 (comparable to a sheet of letter-size paper). The

disk is the site of most star formation in the Galaxy.

To an observer outside the Galaxy, the disk would stand out because of the young, blue, massive stars that have recently formed there. These stars tend to be found along one of at least four arclike spiral arms extending outward from the center of the Galactic Disk. In these arms, star-forming material is accumulated and compressed into the Giant Molecular Clouds (GMCs) where new stars are formed. From studies of chemical composition (see "Stellar Evolution"), astronomers have identified stars with ages up to 10 billion years in the disk. Older disk stars have lower abundances of metals than the stars just emerging from molecular clouds. The Sun, with an age of approximately 5 billion years, lies in the middle of the continuum of disk star ages; presumably the Sun formed out of a molecular cloud in a galactic spiral arm some 5 billion years ago.

Despite the apparent crowding of stars along the Milky Way disk, the typical separation between stars is quite large. In the Sun's vicinity, the separation between stars is several light-years (1 light-year = 6 trillion miles), and the chance for stellar close encounters is extremely small during the lifetime of the Galaxy.

The Sun travels in a roughly circular orbit about the Galaxy at a speed of 220 km/s (about 140 miles/second). A single orbit about the Galaxy at this speed, 24,000 light-years from the center, takes approximately 240 million years. Applying Newton's law of gravity, astronomers can use the speed of the Sun at this distance to determine the Galaxy's matter content interior to the Sun's orbit. Similar observations of the motions of stars located elsewhere yield information about the matter distribution in other parts of the Galaxy. These observations indicate the presence of a thinly populated, though massive, halo of material extending well beyond the Galactic Disk (see below).

The Galactic Halo Surrounding the Galactic Disk is a diffuse Galactic Halo. The halo is roughly spherical and contains widely spaced old stars and almost no star-forming gas. Many of the halo stars are found in dense concentrations of stars called Globular Clusters. These are the oldest structures in the Galaxy, with stellar ages of approximately 15 billion years, and are thought to have formed before the Galactic Disk. By counting stars, astronomers estimate that the stellar mass of the halo is only a few percent that of the disk. However, motions of stars in the outer Galactic Disk imply the presence of large amounts of matter that does not give off light; mass estimates range up to as much as 10 times the mass of the Galactic Disk, bringing the Galaxy's mass to more than a trillion times that of the Sun. The presence of this Dark Matter Halo has prompted searches for exotic subatomic particles or a large population of compact but non-light-emitting dead stars. These searches have, thus far, been inconclusive.

The Galactic Bulge Within approximately 2,000 light-years of the Galactic Center, the shape of the Galaxy changes. A separate component, the Galactic Bulge, is the prominent feature. The bulge is about 1,000 light-years thick, nearly as thick as it is wide, shaped somewhat like a football. The bulge contains both old and young stars and also has significant amounts of star-forming gas. Stars are up to a thousand times closer together in the bulge than they are in the disk. The stellar density and presence of gas and dust in the bulge makes observations confusing, and little is known about the Galaxy on the far side of the bulge. Because dense clouds of gas and dust block visible-wavelength starlight, astronomers typically use long-wavelength infrared or radio-wavelength light to probe the bulge structure. The bulge is dynamically distinct from the disk; bulge stars move on elongated orbits about the Galactic Center, with no tendency toward the ordered motion seen in the disk.

By studying the motion of stars very near to Galactic Center, astronomers have discovered that a very large mass, several million times more massive than the Sun, lies within the inner few tenths of a light-year of the Galaxy. This information, combined with observations of powerful X-rays and gamma rays emerging from the Galactic Center, implies the presence there of a massive black hole. Studies of other galaxies seem to show that black holes are a common galaxy feature, so it is not surprising that the Milky Way should house one as well.

Other Galaxies

Considerable debate raged among astronomers during the 18th and 19th centuries about whether all of the contents of the universe lay within the Milky Way or whether the Milky Way was but one of numerous stellar swarms. In 1923 Edwin Hubble measured the distance to what is now known as the Andromeda Galaxy, showing that it lay well outside the confines of the Milky Way and establishing that the Milky Way was but one of an enormous number of galaxies. The visible universe is thought to contain perhaps hundreds of billions of galaxies.

Galaxies are classified into three types: *spiral, elliptical,* and *irregular.* A spiral galaxy has a structure similar to that of the Milky Way: a bright, flattened disk of stars, gas, and dust showing evidence of spiral arms, along with a bulge and diffuse halo. The Milky Way is at the large extreme of spiral galaxy sizes and masses—most spiral galaxies have smaller disks and fewer stars. Elliptical galaxies do not have disks. Instead, they are roughly the shape of a football or basketball, with stars orbiting the galaxy center in random directions. Elliptical galaxies contain mostly old stars, have little gas or dust, and show no evidence of ongoing star formation. The largest elliptical galaxies have masses 100 times that of the Milky Way; the smallest, dwarf spheroidals, may only have one millionth the mass of the Milky Way. Galaxies that do not fit the spiral or elliptical descriptions are classified as irregular galaxies. These tend to be smaller than spiral galaxies and have asymmetric shapes.

Some galaxies exhibit energetic activity originating near their cores, including strong outputs of high-energy X rays and enormous jets of radio radiation. These phenomena are caused by material plunging into a galaxy's central black hole. These active galaxies provide a link to an earlier phase in the evolution of galaxies. In addition to finding the distances to galaxies, Hubble found that galaxies tended to be moving away from the Milky Way and that the farther away they were the faster they were moving. This relation, now known as Hubble's law, serves as the most valuable indicator of large distances in the universe. Light from galaxies located far from the Milky Way may have left those galaxies billions of years ago, so we are seeing these galaxies as they were long ago. Some very distant galaxies can be detected only because of the energetic activity at their centers. These distant, active galaxies, known as quasars, represent an earlier time in the evolution of galaxies when more gas was available to fuel the activity associated with galactic black holes.

Typical separations between large galaxies are millions of light-years, but many galaxies are found in galaxy clusters, concentrations of tens to thousands of galaxies extending over 10 million to 20 million light-years in diameter. On scales of 100 hundred million light-years, galaxies are found in superclusters. On even larger scales, superclusters are arranged in gigantic sheets, separated by even larger voids with very small numbers of galaxies.

The Big Bang and the Origins of the Universe

Astronomy at its core tries to determine the origins of the universe, and observations have helped to constrain the conditions in the early universe. Three key observations underpin the understanding of the early universe. First, Hubble's Law (see "Galaxies") shows that all galaxies are moving away from one another. This results from the expansion of the universe and implies that the universe evolved from an earlier dense, compact point. Second, the universe is observed to be composed of roughly 75 percent hydrogen (by number) and 25 percent helium. Third, a faint glow of radio-wavelength radiation is observed coming from every direction in the universe.

Taken together, these observations make up strong evidence for the standard picture of the early universe, the Big Bang. All of the data support the idea that the universe began in a hotter, denser state than we currently find it. Cosmic expansion is the most direct by-product, as space continues to stretch outward, carrying galaxies along with it and away from one another. The abundance of hydrogen and helium is naturally explained as having formed during the first extremely hot moments after the Big Bang, when the universe was hot enough to produce matter from energy and fuse hydrogen into helium. The radio glow seen in all directions, known as *cosmic background radiation*, is the remnant of heat from the Big Bang, weakened by the stretching of space since the Big Bang.

The speeds of galaxies combined with their distances from one another gives an estimate of the time they have been receding from one another and therefore of the time since the Big Bang. Careful measurements of the recession rate and the cosmic background radiation combine to give an age of the universe of 13.7 billion years. For comparison, the Sun and solar system formed in the Milky Way 4.5 billion years ago.

The standard picture of the Big Bang does not explain several observations. For instance, the cosmic background radiation is incredibly smooth in all directions. This is a problem since there are regions of the universe that cannot have had contact with one another at the time the background radiation was produced. To explain this, a period of rapid expansion, known as inflation, has been proposed. Inflation puts all points in the universe much closer together during the earliest instants after the Big Bang, and causes them to expand more rapidly during those first fractions of a second.

Recent observations may force a revision of astronomers' understanding of the universe. The gravitational pull of galaxies on one another should have caused the cosmic expansion to slow over the past 13.7 billion years. New observations of distant galaxies seem to show that, on the largest scales, the rate with which galaxies are moving away from one another is increasing rather than decreasing. This cosmic acceleration is as yet unexplained.

Glossary of Astronomical Terms

asteroid one of many small rocky or metallic objects remaining from the formation of the solar system, most of which are found in the asteroid belt, the region between Mars and Jupiter.

Big Bang beginning of the expansion of the universe from a high-density, high-temperature state.

black hole infinitely dense remnant of a massive star that results from the inability of the star to support itself against gravity; also, similar but more massive objects often found in the centers of galaxies.

brown dwarf sphere of hydrogen gas too small to begin nuclear fusion.

charge-coupled device (CCD) sensitive solid-state detector capable of recording visible light and other types of electromagnetic radiation.

comet icy remnant of the formation of the solar system, composed primarily of water ice as well as a smaller portion of rocky material; sublimation of the ices when a comet approaches the Sun produces the distinctive cometary tail.

cosmic background radiation electromagnetic radiation resulting from the time after the Big Bang when radiation could flow freely throughout the universe.

dark matter any of a number of possible constituents of the universe evidenced by a gravitical effect on other matter but not producing any discernable radiation.

detector part of a telescope system in which light from an astronomical source is actually collected.

electromagnetic radiation energy emitted by all objects with a temperature above absolute zero.

electromagnetic spectrum all of the possible forms of electromagnetic radiation, including gamma rays, X rays, ultraviolet radiation, visible light, infrared, and radio waves.

galaxy large collection of stars and gasses, bound together by gravitational force, containing as many as hundreds of billions of stars.

gamma rays the most energetic form of electromagnetic radiation.

globular cluster group of up to millions of stars that orbit the cores of spiral galaxies out of the galactic plane.

inflation period just after the Big Bang during which the universe was thought to expand exponentially.

infrared radiation electromagnetic waves emitted by relatively cool astronomical objects, such as forming stars and planets.

interstellar medium gas and dust found in the regions between stars in a galaxy; this is the raw material from which stars form.

Jovian planet large planet composed primarily of light atoms such as hydrogen. The Jovian planets in the solar system are Jupiter, Saturn, Uranus, and Neptune; most extrasolar planet candidates are thought to be similar.

Kuiper Belt collection of small icy bodies found beyond the orbit of Neptune and thought to be the source of short-period comets.

metals in the astronomical sense, any atom heavier than helium and therefore necessarily a product of stellar fusion.

meteor object that glows brightly from frictional heating as it plunges through Earth's atmosphere; a "shooting star."

meteorite any portion of a meteor that survives intact all the way to the Earth's surface.

main sequence portion of a star's life during which hydrogen fusion is the main source of energy production; this is generally the longest stage in a star's life.

Milky Way galaxy in which the Sun and solar system reside; "the Galaxy."

molecular cloud large, dense collection of interstellar gas and dust in which stars form.

Moon Earth's only natural satellite.

moon natural satellite of a planet.

neutron star compact remnant of a star massive enough to become a supernova but not so massive that a black hole forms.

nuclear fusion production of heavy atomic nuclei from lighter atomic nuclei; the process by which hydrogen is converted to helium in the core of the Sun.

Oort Cloud large spherical swarm of comets orbiting the Sun at a distance of about 10,000 astronomical units, thought to be the source of long-period comets.

planet relatively large object that orbits a star but is incapable of producing energy by nuclear fusion.

planetary nebula escaping outer layers of a dying low-mass star.

planetesimal one of a large number of small objects present in the early solar system that collided to form the cores of planets.

protostar collection of accumulating interstellar material that will become a star but has not yet begun producing energy by nuclear fusion.

quasar high-luminosity core of an active galaxy.

radio waves the lowest-energy band of the electromagnetic spectrum.

red giant cool, large-radius star resulting from the onset of helium fusion in the core of a low-mass star.

spiral arm one of a number of extended structures in the plane of a spiral galaxy in which interstellar material is denser than average and in which young stars are found.

solar system planets and other objects that orbit the Sun.

star sphere of gas, mostly hydrogen, that produces energy by nuclear fusion.

supernova explosion resulting from the collapse and rebound of a high-mass star after nuclear fusion has completed in the stellar core.

telescope device for collecting electromagnetic radiation.

terrestrial planet small, rock- and metal-based planet, including Mercury, Venus, Earth, Mars.

ultraviolet radiation band of the electromagnetic spectrum slightly more energetic than visible light.

visible light form of electromagnetic radiation to which the human eye is sensitive.

white dwarf compact core left over after a low-mass star has shed its outer envelope as a planetary nebula.

X rays band of the electromagnetic spectrum just less energetic than gamma rays.

BIOLOGY

Biology is the study of living creatures—also called organisms. Organisms are distinguished from nonliving matter by their structure and their ability to carry out certain processes. They are composed of one or more cells that are highly organized and able to maintain a relatively constant internal environment. They can assimilate and use energy, in complex series of chemical reactions that make up metabolism. They can grow and reproduce, using information encoded in their genetic material. They can respond to their environment and adapt to changes in that environment.

These characteristics are shared by all of the more than 1.8 million known kinds of organisms present on Earth. The organisms are tremendously diverse, ranging from microscopic bacteria to giant whales and sequoia trees, from green plants to black bears, from mushrooms to manatees.

A Word about Viruses Because they are unable to accomplish life's processes by themselves, viruses are not considered living organisms. They are able to metabolize and reproduce only when they are within living cells. Thus, all viruses are parasites, and many of them cause disease.

Much smaller than the smallest bacteria, most viruses consist only of a strand or two of a nucleic acid—DNA or RNA—wrapped in a protein coat. Some also have a lipid envelope outside the coat. A virus reproduces and spreads because once its nucleic acid is inside a cell, the virus uses the cell's own DNA to produce additional copies of itself.

Numerous Disciplines Originally the study of living creatures was informal, revolving around knowledge useful for hunting, farming, and early medicine. Following the scientific revolution of the 17th century, biology was formalized and came to consist of three broad categories: *zoology* (study of animals), *botany* (study of plants), and *taxonomy* (classification of organisms). Later, additional disciplines had their beginnings, including *microbiology* (study of organisms visible only with a microscope), *genetics* (study of how traits are inherited), *molecular biology* (study of chemistry used by organisms), *ecology* (study of interactions between organisms and their environment), and *ethology* (study of animal behavior). Numerous subdisciplines also developed. Some scientists focus on specific organisms; for instance, herpetologists study reptiles and pomologists study fruits. Other scientists are concerned with structure and functions; for instance, cytologists study cells and plant pathologists study plant diseases.

In recent years the lines between disciplines have blurred, owing mainly to advances in molecular biology and the development of new technologies, such as the ability to sequence genomes (the complete complement of species' DNA). Information science has been applied to biology to create the field of bioinformatics, which is concerned with the development and maintenance of databases of biological information. Such databases help scientists compare disparate genomes, examine evolutionary relationships, predict the structure and function of newly discovered proteins, and better understand the complexity of life.

History of Biology

The systematic approach to biology started with the Greek philosophers about 2,500 years ago. Aristotle (384–322 B.C.) is considered the "father of biology" for his classification of animals and for performing the first known biology experiments, dissecting plants and animals and studying the development of the chick in its egg. His student Theophrastus (ca. 372–286 B.C.) laid the foundation of botany, describing and classifying more than 500 plants and also describing the ways plants can germinate and grow. In Roman times, Lucretius (99–55 B.C.) proposed one of the earliest theories of evolution. But other than medical knowledge, biology made little progress until after the Middle Ages.

In the 15th and 16th centuries Europeans explored the Americas and some of the Pacific islands, and regular contact between Europe and southern Africa and eastern

Asia was instituted. As a result European scholars were exposed to a great variety of plants and animals that were new to them. They responded with books describing and classifying both newfound and familiar plants and animals, starting as early as 1530. A few years later the first botanical gardens began to be established. When the scientific revolution of the 17th century began, scientists undertook more detailed experiments in biology. For example, Jan van Helmont (1579–1694) carefully measured the weight of soil in a tub as a willow grew there, establishing that the increase in mass of the willow was much greater than any diminution of mass of the soil.

Also in the 17th century, biologists began to use an important new tool, the microscope (probably invented in 1595). A previously unseen world opened, beginning with the identification and naming of capillaries (1660), cells (1665), the various tiny organs of insects (1669) and plants (1675), sperm (1667), protists (1673), and bacteria (1683). Microscopic studies contributed to increasingly sophisticated methods of classification of organisms; in 1735 these methods took the basic shape that taxonomy has retained until today, although with many refinements and improvements.

In the 19th century, biology advanced with two overarching theories that have been central to the science ever since. A number of scientists from as early as 1668 had performed experiments to show that life arises only from life and is not spontaneously generated from nonliving matter. In 1838 and 1839, Matthias Schleiden (1804–81) and Theodor Schwann (1810–82) concluded that living things are composed of cells and that reproduction always begins with cells. Since then the cell theory has been confirmed over and over, whether for single-celled bacteria or protists or for the largest organisms, giant trees and whales. About the same time, Charles Darwin (1809–82) began to formulate his theory of evolution by natural selection, published as *The Origin of Species* in 1859. Darwin's theory provides a framework in time and space that can be used to analyze almost all biological topics ranging from animal behavior to changes in the chemicals that cells employ in respiration.

A third unifying idea also began in the mid-19th century, but few knew of it at the time. Gregor Mendel (1822–84) had by 1865 discovered from experiment the basic laws of heredity, but his work was described to a local scientific society and published in its journal. In 1900, Mendel's work was rediscovered and the science of genetics began. Chromosomes were recognized as the carriers of genes (the units of heredity) as early as 1902. In 1907, Thomas Hunt Morgan (1866–1945) began a long series of experiments with fruit flies that detailed the relationship between heredity and development of traits in organisms.

Biologists also pursued the details of basic life processes (respiration, nutrition, synthesis, excretion, transport, regulation, growth, reproduction). As early as 1779, Jan Ingenhousz (1730–99) recognized the essentials of photosynthesis, which is the basis of both respiration and nutrition for nearly all forms of life; however, the chemical pathways involved were not firmly identified until 1957. The role of vitamins in nutrition began to be understood in 1901, chemical control of life processes through hormones began to be unraveled in 1902, and the chemical transmission of nerve impulses was first identified in 1920. Similarly, the chemical bases of metabolism and respiration were uncovered during the first half of the 20th century, and the details of growth and development became one of the main advances of the second half of that century.

Other 20th-century advances involved the recognition of both the study of complex interactions of organisms in particular environments, which became the science of ecology and also of animal behavior, or the science of ethology.

Biology obtained a new basis in the advances of genetics, which began with the study of heredity at the beginning of the 20th century and reached a high point when the human genome (totality of genes) was almost completely deciphered, as announced in 2003. Along the way, advances in genetics had included the recognition that genes are found in the DNA of chromosomes (1944), the discovery of the structure of DNA (1953), working out the genetic code (1961–68), the invention of genetic engineering by inserting genes from one species into another (1972–73), deciphering the genomes of viruses (1977), using DNA to unravel evolutionary relationships (1981), sequencing the genome of a bacterium (1995), and cloning the first mammal with a set of genes taken from an adult body cell (1997).

Taxonomy

In 2009, scientists announced the discovery of a bizarre species of fish that has lush tan and peach stripes and that bounces along the sea floor like a fist-sized rubber ball. It did not resemble any other known species of fish, and scientists were unsure what to call it. Scientists give all organisms both common and Latin names to describe their appearance and their taxonomical classification, but before a newly found organism can be named it must be successfully categorized, usually by appearance or structure. In this case, scientists were unsure whether they had found a completely new sort of fish. After studying the anatomy and DNA of this Indonesian fish, they concluded that it is closely related to frogfish of the genus *Histiophryne*. Because of its wild behavior and coloring, it was named *Histiophryne psychedelica*.

In naming the fish, the scientists used a system of *taxonomy* (scientific classification) invented in the 18th century by the Swedish botanist Carolus Linnaeus (1707–78). The forerunner of Linnaeus's taxonomy was developed by Aristotle, who broadly classified animals by their characteristics and first used the terms genus and species, though his work was eventually forgotten. In Linnaeus's era, researchers around the world collected more and more different types of organisms, but no uniform system for naming them existed. Some biologists gave species long, awkward names, and different biologists commonly referred to the same organism by different names. The lack of a universal naming convention became a serious hindrance to biological study.

Linnaeus organized animals and plants on the basis of natural characteristics into a hierarchy comprising (from widest to narrowest): *kingdom, phylum, class, order, family, genus*, and *species*. Each level in the hierarchy groups similar organisms by increasingly fine degrees of differentiation. The smallest unit in the system is the species, in which members are nearly identical in genetic makeup, physical structure, and behavior. Linnaeus also developed the binomial naming system, in which each organism is referred to by genus and species, e. g. the lion is referred to as *Panthera leo*.

In Linnaeus's day, all organisms were classified in either the plant or animal kingdom, but as biologists learned more about organisms, they recognized that many are neither plant nor animal. The number of kingdoms was gradually expanded, and then a top level, *domain*, was added to the taxonomy. Today, there are three domains: Prokarya, Archaea, and Eukarya.

Viruses, though generally not considered living organisms, are classified in a similar hierarchical scheme, with groups identified by the type of nucleic acid that forms their core: double-stranded DNA, single-stranded DNA, double-stranded RNA, ordinary single-stranded RNA, and negative-sense single-stranded RNA. In addition, there are two groups known as reverse-transcribing viruses because they alter the DNA of the host cell to match the viral nucleic acid, which may be either RNA or DNA. Within each group are families of viruses, a classification usually based on the type of host that the virus infects.

Basic Life Processes

All living organisms must perform certain life processes in order to survive. Some processes are common to all organisms; others are unique to certain groups.

Making or Obtaining Food   Green plants and algae are autotrophs; in the presence of light, they produce their own food in a complex series of reactions called photosynthesis. The process takes place in special cell structures, typically chloroplasts, that contain the light-absorbing pigment chlorophyll. Photosynthesis converts carbon dioxide, water, and light energy into glucose sugar and oxygen; the light energy is changed into chemical energy that holds the glucose molecule together.

Without photosynthesis, life as we know it would not exist. Animals and other heterotrophs depend, directly or indirectly, on autotrophs for their food. Herbivores, such as cows and sea urchins, are heterotrophs that feed directly on green plants and algae. Carnivores, such as lions and spiders, feed mainly on the flesh of other animals. Omnivores, including humans and bluebirds, eat both plants and animals.

Chemical Synthesis   In numerous chemical reactions, an organism makes, or synthesizes, molecules needed to maintain structure, grow, and carry out chemical processes. For instance, plant cells convert some of the glucose created during photosynthesis into cellulose, a complex carbohydrate that is the main constituent of plant cell walls. The human body takes phosphorus obtained from meat and other foodstuffs and incorporates it in nucleic acid molecules.

Major Taxons, with Representative Species

Domain Archaea   Discovered in the 20th century, archaea are one-celled organisms that look like bacteria but are genetically different. As with bacteria, the genetic material is not contained within a nucleus and there are no other membrane-bound organelles. Unlike bacteria, archaea lack the sugar-polypeptide compound peptidoglycan in the cell wall. Also, the composition and assembly of flagella (filaments that extend from the organism and that are used in propulsion) differ in the two groups. Archaea were once believed to live almost exclusively in extreme environments such as hot springs and deep-sea hydrothermal vents, but they are now recognized as being widespread.

Kingdom Euryarcheota Extreme halophiles (salt-lovers), extreme thermophiles (heat-lovers), methanogens (which metabolize methane instead of oxygen)

Kingdom Crenarcheota Extreme thermophiles, nonthermophiles

Kingdom Korarcheota Extreme thermophiles

Domain Prokarya   Discovered the 17th century, following the invention of the microscope, prokaryotes are better known by their common name, bacteria. Unlike archaea, they have peptidoglycan in the cell wall. And unlike eukaryotes, they lack a distinct nucleus and any other membrane-bound organelles. Bacteria are much more common than archaea and live in almost every type of environment (there are more bacteria in your mouth than there are people on Earth). The group, which in some classification schemes is called Monera, includes both autotrophs (which produce their own food) and heterotrophs (which depend directly or indirectly on autotrophs). The classification and naming of large taxons are in flux.

Kingdom Proteobacteria Purple bacteria, nitrifying bacteria (Nitrosomonas, Nitrobacter), nitrogen-fixing bacteria (Azotobacter), pseudomonads, enteric bacteria (Escherichia, Enterobacter), myxobacteria, rickettsia

Kingdom Gram-positive bacteria Cocci (spherical): Staphylococcus; bacilli (rod-shaped): Bacillus; Mycoplasma

Kingdom Spirochetes Long, slender, tightly coiled bacteria: Spirillum, Treponema

Kingdom Chlamydiae Parasitic: Chlamydia

Kingdom Cyanobacteria Blue-green algae-like autotrophs: Anabaena, Nostoc

Kingdom Green sulfur bacteria Photosynthetic: Chlorobium

Kingdom Green nonsulfur bacteria Thermophiles: Chloroflexus

Kingdom Flavobacteria and relatives Flavobacteria, bacteriodes

Kingdom Hyperthermophiles Extreme heat-lovers: Aquifex, Thermotoga

Domain Eukarya   First classified by the ancient Greeks, eukaryotes include unicellular, filamentous, colonial, and multicellular species—everything from amoebas to humans. The genetic material is contained within a nucleus delineated by a nuclear membrane, and cells also contain a variety of additional membrane-bound organelles.

Kingdom Protista The simplest eukaryotes. Most are one-celled, but some species are colonial or multicellular. The algae are autotrophs; other protists are heterotrophs. Protists live mainly in aquatic habitats.

    Phylum Mastigophora flagellates: Trypanosoma

    Phylum Ciliophora ciliates: Paramecium, Vorticella

    Phylum Sporozoa amoeboid parasites: Balantidium, Plasmodium

    Phylum Sarcodina amoeboids: Amoeba, foraminifera, radiolarians

    Phylum Euglenophyta flagellate algae: Euglena, Volvox

    Phylum Chrysophyta golden algae, diatoms

    Phylum Pyrrhophyta fire algae; dinoflagellates: Gonyaulax, Ceratium

    Phylum Chlorophyta green algae: sea lettuce, Spirogyra

    Phylum Phaeophyta brown algae: kelps

    Phylum Rhodophyta red algae: Porphyra

    Phylum Myxomycota acellular slime molds: Physarum

Kingdom Fungi One-celled and multicellular heterotrophs with cell walls made of chitin. They reproduce asexually by spores and sexually by conjugation.

    Phylum Zygomycota bread molds: Rhizopus

    Phylum Ascomycota sac fungi: morels, truffles, yeasts

    Phylum Basidiomycota club fungi: bracket fungi, mushrooms, puffballs, rusts

    Phylum Mycomycota fungi that appear in lichens, in symbiotic relationships with algae

Kingdom Plantae Multicellular autotrophs that carry out photosynthesis. Cells contain a large central vacuole and have walls made of cellulose. Most species live in terrestrial habitats.

    Phylum Bryophyta hornworts, liverworts, mosses

    Phylum Lycopodiophyta club mosses, quillworts, spike mosses

    Phylum Sphenophyta horsetails: Equisetum

    Phylum Filicophyta ferns

    Phylum Cycadophyta cycads

    Phylum Ginkgophyta ginkgo

    Phylum Coniferophyta conifers: cypresses, pines, redwoods, yews

    Phylum Anthophyta angiosperms: flowering plants

        Class Monocotyledoneae monocots (have a single cotyledon, or seed leaf): grasses, irises, lilies, onions, orchids, palms

        Class Dicotyledoneae dicots (two cotyledons): apples, cacti, carrots, geraniums, legumes, maples, mints, oaks, poppies, roses, sunflowers

Kingdom Animalia Multicellular heterotrophs. The cells do not have cell walls.

    Phylum Porifera sponges

    Phylum Cnidaria coelenterates

        Class Hydrozoa hydroids: Hydra

        Class Scyphozoa jellyfish: Aurelia, Cassiopaea

        Class Anthozoa corals, sea anemones

    Phylum Ctenophora comb jellies, sea gooseberries

    Phylum Platyhelminthes flatworms

        Class Turbellaria turbellarians: planarians (Dugesia)

        Class Trematoda flukes: Clonorchis, Fasciola, Schistosoma

        Class Cestoda tapeworms: Diphyllobothrium, Taenia

    Phylum Nematoda roundworms: Ascaris, Trichinella

    Phylum Rotifera rotifers: Philodina

    Phylum Bryozoa moss animals

    Phylum Brachiopoda lamp shells: Hemithyris, Lingula

    Phylum Nemertea ribbon worms: Baseodiscus, Lineus

    Phylum Phoronida horseshoe worms: Phoronis

    Phylum Annelida segmented worms

        Class Polychaeta bristleworms: Eunice, Nereis

        Class Oligochaeta earthworms: Lumbricus

        Class Hirudinea leeches: Hirudo

    Phylum Onychophora velvetworms: Peripatopsis, Peripatus

Major Taxons, with Representative Species (continued)

Phylum Mollusca mollusks; the soft body usually is enclosed in a hard shell secreted by a tissue called the mantle.

　　Class Polyplacophora chitons: Callistoplax, Chiton
　　Class Bivalvia bivalves: clams, mussels, oysters, scallops
　　Class Scaphopoda tusk shells: Cadalus, Dentalium
　　Class Gastropoda nudibranchs, slugs, snails
　　Class Cephalopoda nautiluses, octopuses, squids

Phylum Arthropoda arthropods

　　Class Merostomata horseshoe crabs: Limulus
　　Class Crustacea barnacles, crabs, lobsters, shrimps
　　Class Arachnida harvestmen, mites, scorpions, spiders, ticks
　　Class Chilopoda centipedes: Geophilus, Lithobius
　　Class Diplopoda millipedes: Glomeridesmus, Hirudisoma
　　Class Insecta insects: ants, bees, beetles, bristletails, butterflies, dragonflies, flies, grasshoppers, mayflies, silverfish, springtails, termites

Phylum Tardigrada water bears: Echiniscus

Phylum Chaetognatha arrowworms: Ferosagitta, Mesosagittia

Phylum Echinodermata echinoderms

　　Class Crinoidea feather stars, sea lilies
　　Class Asteroidea sea stars (starfish)
　　Class Ophiuroidea basket stars, brittle stars
　　Class Echinoidea heart urchins, sand dollars, sea urchins
　　Class Holothuroidea sea cucumbers

Phylum Hemichordata acorn worms

Phylum Chordata

　　Subphylum Urochordata tunicates: sea squirts
　　Subphylum Cephalochordata lancelets
　　Subphylum Vertebrata vertebrates
　　Class Agnatha jawless fish: hagfish, lampreys
　　Class Chondrichthyes cartilaginous fish: rays, sharks, skates
　　Class Osteichthyes bony fish: bass, eels, salmon, seahorses, trout, tuna
　　Class Amphibia amphibians
　　　　Order Gymnophiona caecilians
　　　　Order Caudata newts, salamanders
　　　　Order Anura frogs, toads
　　Class Reptilia reptiles
　　　　Order Chelonia tortoises, turtles
　　　　Order Crocodylia alligators, caimans, crocodiles, gavial
　　　　Order Rhynchocephalia tuataras
　　　　Order Squamata lizards, snakes
　　Class Aves birds
　　　　Order Struthioniformes ostriches
　　　　Order Rheiformes rheas
　　　　Order Casuariiformes cassowaries, emus
　　　　Order Apterygiformes kiwis
　　　　Order Tinamiformes tinamous
　　　　Order Sphenisciformes penguins
　　　　Order Gaviiformes divers, loons
　　　　Order Podicipediformes grebes
　　　　Order Procellariiformes albatrosses, fulmars, petrels, shearwaters
　　　　Order Pelecaniformes anhingas, boobies, cormorants, frigatebirds, pelicans

Order Ciconiiformes bitterns, herons, ibises, spoonbills, storks

Order Phoenicopteriformes flamingos

Order Anseriformes ducks, geese, screamers, swans

Order Falconiformes birds of prey: condors, falcons, hawks, osprey, vultures

Order Galliformes fowl: curassows, grouse, hoatzins, pheasants, quail, turkeys

Order Gruiformes bustards, coots, cranes, hemipodes, rails

Order Charadriiformes auks, gulls, jacanas, murres, plovers, puffins, stilts, terns

Order Columbiformes doves, pigeons, sandgrouse

Order Psittaciformes cockatoos, lories, parakeets, parrots

Order Cuculiformes cuckoos, roadrunners, turacos

Order Strigiformes owls

Order Caprimulgiformes goatsuckers, nighthawks, nightjars, poorwills, potoos

Order Apodiformes hummingbirds, swifts

Order Coliiformes colies, mousebirds

Order Trogoniformes quetzals, trogons

Order Coraciiformes bee-eaters, hoopoes, hornbills, kingfishers, motmots, rollers

Order Piciformes barbets, honeyguides, jacamars, puffbirds, toucans, woodpeckers

Order Passeriformes perching birds: blackbirds, chickadees, finches, jays, larks, mockingbirds, nuthatches, sparrows, swallows, thrushes, tits, warblers, wrens

Class Mammalia mammals

　　Order Monotremata echidnas, platypuses
　　Order Marsupialia marsupials: bandicoots, kangaroos, koalas, numbats, opossums, wallabies, wombats
　　Order Insectivora insectivores: moles, shrews, solenodons, tenrecs
　　Order Dermoptera flying lemurs
　　Order Chiroptera bats
　　Order Primates primates: chimpanzees, gorillas, humans, lemurs, monkeys, tarsiers
　　Order Endentata edentates: anteaters, armadillos, sloths
　　Order Pholidota pangolins
　　Order Lagomorpha hares, pikas, rabbits
　　Order Rodentia rodents: beavers, capybara, chinchillas, hamsters, mice, muskrats, porcupines, rats, prairie dogs, squirrels
　　Order Cetacea dolphins, porpoises, whales
　　Order Carnivora carnivores: bears, cats, dogs, foxes, hyenas, mongooses, otters, raccoons, skunks, weasels
　　Order Pinnipedia seals, sea lions, walruses
　　Order Tubulidentata aardvarks
　　Order Proboscidea elephants
　　Order Hyracoidea hyraxes
　　Order Sirenia dugongs, manatee
　　Order Perissodactyla odd-toed hoofed mammals: horses, rhinoceroses, zebras
　　Order Artiodactyla even-toed hoofed mammals: antelopes, buffaloes, camels, cattle, deer, giraffes, goats, hippopotamuses, pigs, sheep

Cellular Respiration Every living cell needs a continuous supply of energy to perform life processes. During a series of many reactions that make up respiration, food molecules are broken down, releasing energy in the form of adenosine triphosphate (ATP).

Excretion Metabolism produces various waste products that must be excreted, or removed, from an organism. The oxygen produced during photosynthesis is a waste product; although the organism uses some of the oxygen for respiration, most is released into the atmosphere by land plants or water by algae. In birds, the metabolism of proteins produces uric acid, an insoluble waste excreted as a thick paste.

Coordination and Regulation To maintain a stable internal environment, an organism must regulate internal processes as well as responses to changes in the external environment. In plants, for example, chemicals called auxins and gibberellins work together to elongate stems. If one side of a dahlia stem is in the shade, auxins concentrate there; the cells on the shaded side grow faster and longer, causing the stem to gradually bend toward the light. In animals, nerve cells and chemicals called hormones regulate many aspects of physiology and behavior.

Growth and Reproduction All organisms grow in size. Plants grow only at the tips of their shoots and leaves, whereas humans grow throughout their entire length. In most plants, growth goes on indefinitely, whereas humans grow only to a certain point in their development.

Reproduction is not necessary for an individual organism but is essential if a species, or type of organism, is to continue to exist. Asexual reproduction involves only one parent and results in offspring that are genetically identical to the parent. For instance, a strawberry plant can reproduce asexually by sending out a special stem that runs along the ground; a daughter plant develops at the end of the stem, developing roots and leaves and eventually producing runner stems of its own. Strawberry plants, like all plants and animals, also reproduce sexually. Sexual reproduction typically involves two parents and results in offspring that are not genetically identical to either parent. This promotes variability, which is the basis of evolution.

Cell Biology

All organisms are composed of one or more cells. A bacterium consists of a single cell, whereas an elephant is made up of trillions of cells. Almost all cells are microscopic; the largest of the few visible to the naked eye is only 0.03 inch (0.76 millimeter) in diameter.

All cells share four characteristics. First, every cell is enclosed in a thin cell membrane, which provides shape and acts as a barrier between the cell and its environment. The membrane is semipermeable, composed largely of lipids (fats, oils, and fatty substances such as cholesterol), with embedded proteins that regulate the transport of molecules into and out of the cell.

Second, all cells are filled with cytoplasm. Cytosol, the fluid portion of cytoplasm, contains nutrients, enzymes, and other dissolved materials vital for cell metabolism. Also in the cytoplasm are specialized structures called organelles, held in place by a network of protein filaments.

Third, within the cytoplasm of all cells are organelles called ribosomes, which manufacture proteins for the cell. Some of the proteins are structural components; others are enzymes that control chemical reactions in the cell.

Fourth, all cells contain chromosomes composed of genetic material, which encodes instructions for making the hundreds or even thousands of different proteins found in a cell.

Homeostasis and Enzymes

If the internal environment of a cell (or an organism as a whole) changes significantly, the cell dies. Thus, it is important that a cell maintains homeostasis: a relatively stable internal environment regardless of changes in the external environment.

Cells perform many metabolic reactions to maintain homeostasis. Proteins called enzymes act as catalysts of these reactions. Enzymes are very specific; many catalyze only a single reaction whereas others are able to catalyze a few closely related reactions. Some enzymes break compounds into smaller molecules. Others act to combine small molecules into a larger molecule. In either process, the enzymes are neither changed nor destroyed; they can be reused again and again.

If temperature, acidity, or other environmental conditions vary outside a narrow range, the rate of a catalytic reaction is affected. For instance, in humans, the optimal temperature for catalytic reactions is normal body temperature, approximately 98.6 degrees F. If body temperature gets too cold, enzymes are unable to bind to molecules quickly enough and the rate of the reaction will decrease, possibly to levels that cannot sustain life. If body temperature rises too high, the heat causes enzymes to denature and lose their catalytic ability.

Cell Transport

Cells obtain nutrients and other needed materials from their environment, and excrete wastes and other substances into the environment. These materials must move through the cell membrane, which is selectively permeable; that is, it controls the passage of materials between the cell and its environment, allowing some substances in while keeping others out. Two basic methods transport materials through the membrane.

Passive transport, including diffusion and osmosis, requires no energy. Small molecules such as oxygen, carbon dioxide, and water plus ions such as those of sodium and calcium pass freely across the membrane, from an area of higher concentration to an area of lower concentration.

Active transport moves substances from an area of low concentration to an area of high concentration. The cell must expend energy for active transport. For example, in a process called *endocytosis*, human white blood cells engulf harmful invaders, which it then destroys. In a reverse process, *exocytosis*, a cell can expel large waste molecules. Another type of active transport relies on membrane proteins called pumps. They capture molecules from one side of the membrane and release them on the other side.

Cell Division

Cells create new cells in a process known as cell division. The two basic types of cell division, which differ in their end results, are mitosis and meiosis.

Additional Specialized Cell Structures

Organelle	Description	Function
Cell wall	Rigid structure exterior to the cell membrane; found in most organisms other than animals	Protection, support
Chloroplast	Contains chlorophyll, a pigment needed for photosynthesis; present in plants and protists called algae	Site of photosynthesis
Cilium	Hairlike projection; common in archaea, bacteria, protists, and animals	Locomotion (single-celled organisms), movement of cells or materials (multicellular organisms)
Endoplasmic reticulum (ER)	Extensive network of convoluted membranes; found in protists, fungi, plants, and animals	Rough ER helps synthesize proteins and lipids; smooth ER metabolizes carbohydrates and lipids, stores calcium, and breaks down poisons
Flagellum	Whiplike projections; found in archaea, bacteria, protists, and animals	Locomotion (single-celled organisms), movement of materials (multicellular organisms)
Golgi body	Stack of flattened, membrane-bound sacs; found in most protists, fungi, plants, and animals	Modifies food molecules manufactured in the ER
Mitochondrion	Oblong, with highly folded interior; present in protists, fungi, plants, and animals	Site of cell respiration
Nucleus	Central structure surrounded by a membrane; largest organelle in a cell; present in protists, fungi, plants, and animals	Contains the genetic material DNA, which directs operations of the cell, including cell division
Vacuole	Found in some animals; common in protists, fungi, and plants.	Storage of food or water

Peering Over the Fortress That Is the Mighty Cell

By NATALIE ANGIER

J. Craig Venter announced at a news conference in May 2010 that he and his co-workers had created the first "synthetic cell." Dr. Venter, the renowned genome wrassler and president of the J. Craig Venter Institute, praised his two dozen team members and described the long years of struggle that preceded their moment of triumph. He called out important figures in the audience: his editor, his literary agent, the celebrity diet doctor Dean Ornish. And he acknowledged that none of his group's work would have been possible without a lot of help from the parents—Mother Nature and Father Time.

After all, that stalwart pair was responsible for designing and gradually refining the real cells that brought the Venter team's synthetic constructs to life. There is, as yet, no escaping the cell. Every past and present lodger on the twisted bristlecone tree of life is built of cells, every cell is a microcosm of life, and neither the Venter team nor anybody else has come close to recreating the cell from scratch. If anything, the new report underscores how dependent biologists remain on its encapsulated power.

As reported in the journal *Science* to international attention, the Venter team managed to recreate with bottled chemicals the entire genetic code of one species of bacterium and transplant that manufactured genome into the housing of a closely related species of bacterium. Once installed, the synthetic DNA began operating like the real thing, prompting its cellular surroundings to produce a protein work force appropriate to its needs rather than that of the original bacterial host, to copy the synthetic DNA, and to do what all bacteria love to do, which is divide over and over again.

The researchers now have many descendants of that founding microbial construct stored in a freezer, all of them nearly indistinguishable from what you'd get if you cultivated the "donor" bacterium naturally. Only on looking carefully at the genetic sequence in each cell would you find the researchers' distinguishing "watermarks," brief chemical messages inserted into the otherwise plagiarized string of one million-plus letters of bacterial DNA.

Bonnie L. Bassler, a microbiologist at Princeton, said, "They started with a known genome, a set of genes that nature had given us, and they had to put their genome into a live cell with all the complex goo and ingredients to make the thing go."

Dr. Venter freely admitted his indebtedness to precedence. His team, he said, was "taking advantage of three and a half billion years of evolution." Throughout those preposterous eons, nature has had a chance to perfect the splendid entity of all earthly animation that is the living cell. And though researchers have made some tentative progress in their efforts to synthesize other essential elements of the cell apart from the genome, don't expect even a cheap knockoff anytime soon. "I am always awed by nature," Dr. Bassler said, "and how it manages to work so well."

There is a reason why life is built of cells, and why most cells are too small to see without a microscope. It's easy in a small space to keep critical components squeezed together and close at hand, the better for the right enzymes to encounter the right substrates in a timely fashion and a million tiny bonfires to burn. "Cells are not like an aquarium where a fish swims by now and again," said Dr. Bassler. "They're jam-packed inside. They're teeming with stuff. They're like a house filled with necessary clutter, or New York City, or a Thanksgiving table loaded with so many dishes you don't know where you might put another plate."

Much of the cell's interior is taken up by the cytoplasm, which, as several biologists have gleefully observed, pretty much has the texture of snot. The appearance of random ooze, however, is deceptive. "There's a beautiful architecture" to the cytoplasm, Dr. Bassler said. "Everything is in the right place and bumping around, and the membrane holds them together so they can't get away from each other."

When the Venter team inserted the synthetic version of the Mycoplasma mycoides genome into the cellular housing of the Mycoplasma capricolum bacterium, the newcomer took full advantage of the resident cytoplasmic wares. It used the thousands of little biodevices called ribosomes to stitch together amino acids into new proteins. It relied on complex molecular assemblages to maintain its DNA in working order and to duplicate that DNA when it was time to divide. It thanked its lucky base pairs that a greasy lipid cell membrane and stiffer bacterial wall not only kept the inside appropriately, bioactively dense, but also kept the outside appropriately out, for an exposed cytoplasm would soon be scavenged for parts, most likely by a neighboring microbe.

Mitosis   Mitosis results in two new daughter cells that are structurally and functionally like the parent cell, with exactly the same chromosome material. In amoebas and other one-celled protists, mitosis is a form of asexual reproduction, producing new organisms and thereby increasing the population. In animals and other many-celled organisms, mitosis results in growth and in the replacement of dead and injured cells.

The cells in these organisms are diploid: that is they contain a double set of chromosomes (2n). For example, muscle, skin, and other body cells of a human contain 46 chromosomes each arranged in 23 pairs. During a series of mitotic phases, these chromosomes are duplicated (4n). The two double sets of chromosomes move to opposite sides of the parent cell and the parent cell cleaves along its center, forming two diploid (2n) cells.

Meiosis   In a series of phases somewhat different from those of mitosis, meiosis produces reproductive cells, or gametes, that are not exact copies of the parent cell. Most importantly, they are haploid (n), containing only one chromosome of each pair found in the parent cell. For example, human eggs and sperm each contain 23 chromosomes. When a sperm (n) unites with an egg (n), the result is a fertilized egg that is diploid (2n).

Types of Cells and Tissues   All cells carry on fundamental activities such as cellular respiration. However, the cells that make up a multicellular organism are specialized to perform specific functions for the whole organism. For example, in humans nerve cells are specialized for coordinating body activities whereas red blood cells are designed to carry oxygen.

Specialized cells are organized in groups called tissues, which perform a common task. Muscle cells form muscle tissue, which causes movement; nerve cells form nerve tissue, and so on.

In turn, various kinds of tissues are bound together to form a unit known as an organ, which accomplishes more complex tasks. Your stomach, for example, contains muscle tissue that helps churn food and other tissues that manufacture acids and enzymes necessary to digest the food. Organs are further organized into organ systems, such as the digestive system of an animal or the root system of a tree. Some organs function in more than one system; for example, some cells in the liver manufacture a chemical used in digestion and other cells have an excretory function. Most important, all the systems work together to maintain the organism's homeostasis.

The Human Body

Like other animals, a human begins from a single cell, the fertilized egg. By the time the human reaches adulthood, the body consists of some 100 trillion cells. Each is part of an organ system designed to perform essential life functions.

The Circulatory System

This system transports useful materials to every cell in the body and carries wastes away from the cells. It has three parts: blood, a heart, and blood vessels.

Blood   An average adult contains 5 to 6 quarts of blood, a fluid tissue that carries materials throughout the body. The blood consists of plasma, a yellowish liquid containing dissolved substances such as salts and proteins, and three types of cells or cell fragments: red blood cells, white blood cells, and platelets.

Red blood cells (RBCs), or erythrocytes, are the most numerous type of blood cell; a normal adult has about 25 billion RBCs. Produced in the bone marrow, they differ from other cells in that they do not have nuclei as adults. RBCs contain hemoglobin, a reddish protein-iron compound that binds to oxygen during circulation through the lungs, then releases the oxygen to cells elsewhere in the body.

White blood cells (WBCs), or leukocytes, also manufactured in the bone marrow, are larger than RBCs and have nuclei. They help protect the body from bacteria and other disease-causing organisms. They are an important part of the immune system, described below.

Platelets are colorless cell fragments produced in the bone marrow and involved in clotting. When a blood vessel is cut or broken, the damaged tissue sends out a chemical signal that causes platelets to aggregate at that location. The platelets secrete an enzyme that starts the clotting process. The end result is a clot that prevents blood from leaking out of the vessel. Over time, the tissue repairs itself and the clot dissolves.

The Heart   The human heart is a large muscular organ with four chambers. Two small, thin-walled chambers called atria at the top of the heart receive blood from the veins, then move the blood to the lower chambers of the heart.

These are large, thick-walled chambers called ventricles, which pump blood to the body cells through arteries. Between the atria and ventricles lie valves, flaps of tissue that maintain blood flow in one direction.

Circulation The left and right sides of the heart act independently, as two separate pumps. Blood from body cells flows through the vena cava to the right atrium. This blood is rich in carbon dioxide and deficient in oxygen. It flows into the left ventricle, which pumps it through the pulmonary artery to the lungs. Here, carbon dioxide is excreted and oxygen is absorbed into the blood.

The oxygen-rich blood flows through the pulmonary vein to the left atrium and then into the left ventricle. When the ventricle contracts, the blood is pumped through the body's largest artery, the aorta, to the rest of the body cells—including, via coronary arteries, cells that make up the heart's own muscles.

To keep blood flowing properly, the atria and ventricles must alternately contract and relax at precisely the correct time. A signal to contract originates from a group of cells in the right atrium called the sinoatrial node. The signal first reaches the atria and they contract, moving blood into the ventricles. The signal then reaches another group of cells in the right atrium called the atrioventricular node, which relays the signal to the ventricles and causes them to contract, forcing the blood out of the heart. After this wave of contractions, the heart muscles relax and blood again fills the atria.

The period when heart muscles contract is called systole; the period of relaxation is diastole. When doctors measure blood pressure, they report both values, with the pressure during systole higher than that during diastole. Normal blood pressure is 120/80.

Blood vessels The human circulatory system is a closed system, meaning that blood never leaves the network of blood vessels, which consists of arteries, veins, and capillaries.

Arteries carry blood away from the heart. Because they receive a large volume of blood from the heart under very high pressure, the arteries have thick, muscular walls that allow them to expand during systole and contract during diastole. This rhythmic expansion and contraction of arteries is a person's pulse, and can be used to measure the number of times the heart contracts each minute.

Veins carry blood toward the heart. The blood has traveled a significant distance since being pumped from the heart; therefore, pressure in the veins is much lower than in arteries. For this reason, veins have much thinner walls than arteries. However, because the pressure is low, there is a risk that blood might flow backward when the heart relaxes. To prevent such backflow, veins contain valves, similar in purpose to the valves in the heart. In addition, veins are sometimes embedded in skeletal muscle, such as the thigh, so that as the muscle contracts, it squeezes the veins and assists in moving the blood back to the heart.

As blood travels from the heart, the arteries that carry it branch from one another and get progressively smaller as they spread to all parts of the body. Eventually the smallest arteries attach to microscopic capillaries. Every cell is located in close proximity to a capillary.

Capillary walls are only one cell thick, allowing materials to diffuse into and out of the blood. Materials move from the blood into intercellular space, the space between cells, which contains intercellular fluid—the cells' aqueous environment. From this fluid, cells absorb vital gases and nutrients and deposit metabolic wastes, which are picked up by the blood. At their distal end, capillaries connect to tiny veins, which join to form progressively larger veins that return the blood to the heart.

The Immune System

This system protects the body from invaders, such as viruses and bacteria. The system includes the lymphatic system and various white blood cells (WBCs).

Lymphatic system The lymphatic system has a network of vessels that drain intracellular fluid from the intracellular space and return it to the blood. The lymph vessels are not connected to the heart and do not benefit from its contraction. They, like many veins, are embedded in skeletal muscle and rely on muscle contractions to move the lymphatic fluid (intracellular fluid inside lymph vessels). Also like veins, lymph vessels contain valves that prevent backflow. The lymph vessels deliver the fluid into large veins in the chest, where the fluid again becomes part of the blood.

Connected to lymph vessels are small masses of spongy tissue called lymph nodes, which remove contaminants such as bacteria and dead cells from lymphatic fluid. In addition, the nodes are homes for certain types of WBCs.

White blood cells A healthy human typically has 5,000 to 9,000 WBCs per milliliter of blood. When bacteria or other foreign particles are present, however, WBCs rapidly proliferate. Unlike RBCs, WBCs can move on their own; they frequently pass through the walls of blood vessels and go into intercellular space and the lymphatic system in search of invaders.

Most WBCs are granulocytes. These are phagocytes ("eating cells"), moving like amoebas to surround and engulf foreign particles. Monocytes, the smallest group of WBCs, move out of blood and into intercellular space whenever an infection develops. There they turn into phagocytic macrophages and destroy invaders. Monocytes also destroy worn-out RBCs.

Lymphocytes are WBCs more common in the lymph system than in the blood. There are two classes: T cells and B cells. Helper T cells and suppressor T cells regulate the immune response, including the activities of B cells. Killer T cells kill cells they attack, such as body cells infected with viruses. B cells produce antibodies, highly specific proteins secreted in response to foreign chemicals called antigens, such as protein molecules on the surface of bacteria. The antibodies bind to and inactivate the antigens. Some B cells, called memory cells, have learned to recognize a specific invader and patrol the body to defend against it. If the invader reappears, the memory cells trigger a massive defense. This reaction protects a person from getting certain diseases more than once, and is the basis of vaccination against disease.

The Respiratory System

This system obtains oxygen from the environment and gets rid of carbon dioxide and water vapor. Its function can be divided into two parts: breathing, which carries air into and out of the lungs; and gas exchange, during which the blood trades carbon dioxide and water vapor for oxygen.

Drawing air into the lungs from the environment—a process called inhalation—begins with a signal that travels from the respiratory center of the brain to the diaphragm, a dome-shaped muscle that lies beneath the lungs, separating the thoracic (chest) and abdominal cavities. The diaphragm contracts, pushing downward and decreasing the pressure on the lungs, allowing them to inflate. This in turn decreases pressure in the respiratory passages. Air is forced through the nasal passages and mouth and passes through the throat and trachea (windpipe) into the two bronchial tubes that lead to the lungs.

In each lung, the bronchial tube branches into smaller and smaller tubes, ending in millions of tiny air sacs surrounded by capillaries. The air sacs, or alveoli, are the site of gas exchange. Because there is a higher concentration of oxygen in the inhaled air than in the blood in the capillaries, oxygen diffuses from the alveoli into the blood, where RBCs immediately bind it to their hemoglobin molecules. Conversely, concentrations of carbon dioxide and water are higher in the blood than in the air, so these substances diffuse into the alveoli.

As gas exchange is completed, the diaphragm relaxes and moves upward. Pressure on the lungs increases, causing them to deflate and resulting in exhalation—expulsion of air out of the lungs. The air follows the same path it took during inhalation.

The Digestive System

The human digestive system is designed to take in and break down large food molecules into small molecules that can be absorbed into the blood and distributed to the cells of the body.

Organs of the digestive system   Two groups of organs are involved in digestion. One group, the gastrointestinal tract, also known as the alimentary canal, begins with the mouth and includes the esophagus, stomach, small intestine, and large intestine. Food enters through the mouth; is digested in the mouth, stomach, and small intestine and is absorbed into the blood from the intestines. Undigested material forms feces, which are expelled through the anus, the distal opening of the tract. Food is pushed down through the tract by muscles in the organ walls. By contracting and relaxing in sequence, the muscles create a wavelike movement called peristalsis. In addition to moving matter through the tract, peristalsis helps mix food with digestive juices.

The second group of digestive organs makes enzymes and other substances needed for digestion, and secretes these substances into the gastrointestinal tract. These accessory organs include the salivary glands, gastric glands, intestinal glands, liver, gallbladder, and pancreas.

The digestive process   Food undergoes both chemical and mechanical digestion. Chemical digestion uses enzymes to change the chemical properties of food so it can be absorbed into the blood. Mechanical digestion breaks food into small pieces, increasing the surface area that enzymes can work on, and thereby speeding the rate of chemical digestion.

Digestion begins in the mouth. Teeth bite, tear, crush, and grind food. Salivary glands secrete saliva into the mouth, which wets the food, making it easier to mechanically digest and swallow. Saliva also contains amylase, an enzyme that chemically breaks down complex starches into sugar molecules.

When a person swallows, food passes into the esophagus and is moved by peristalsis into the stomach. As muscles in the stomach's wall contract and relax, food is churned and broken into even smaller particles. Gastric glands embedded in the stomach walls secrete hydrochloric acid, which kills bacteria in the food; and pepsin, an enzyme that chemically breaks proteins into smaller amino acid chains.

When the proteins have been sufficiently digested, a round muscle at the base of the stomach opens, allowing the food to be pushed into the small intestine. In the duodenum, the upper portion of the small intestine, an alkaline solution secreted by the pancreas neutralizes the stomach acids, preventing damage to intestinal tissues. The pancreas also secretes the enzyme trypsin, which continues to break down protein molecules, plus enzymes that digest lipids and complex carbohydrates. Finally, glands embedded in the intestinal walls secrete enzymes that finish the digestion of proteins and carbohydrates.

In the jejunum and ileum, the middle and lower portions of the small intestine, the walls have millions of tiny fingerlike projects called villi. Fully digested sugars, lipids, and proteins are absorbed into the blood through the walls of the villi.

The large intestine, shorter in length but larger in diameter than the small intestine, serves three important functions. Beneficial bacteria that make the large intestine their home manufacture and secrete vitamins necessary for human metabolism. Vitamins, minerals, and much of the water that was mixed into the food during digestion are absorbed into the blood through the organ's walls. And undigested materials and dead bacteria are stored in the large intestine until it is ready to be excreted.

The Excretory System

As by-products of metabolism, cells create wastes. These wastes must be disposed of before they accumulate to toxic levels. Organs involved in excretion include the lungs, which, as mentioned above, excrete carbon dioxide and water vapor; and the skin, liver, and urinary system.

The skin   One waste product of metabolism is heat energy. To dissipate excess heat, the body takes advantage of the large surface area of the skin—the body's largest organ, accounting for about 12 percent of a person's weight. As blood flows through vast numbers of capillaries just under the skin's surface, heat is transferred from the blood to the skin and eventually to the environment. During periods of exertion, when more heat than normal is generated, glands in the skin produce sweat, a solution of salts and water, to expedite heat transfer. The sweat absorbs large amounts of heat energy and evaporates, releasing that heat into the environment.

The liver   The liver is the largest internal organ in the human body, weighing an average of 55 ounces (1,560 grams). In addition to other vital functions, it performs two excretory functions. It produces enzymes that detoxify the blood, breaking down alcohol and other harmful substances into inactive or less toxic compounds. The liver also breaks down excess amino acids, forming urea. These breakdown materials are carried by the blood to the kidneys for excretion.

The Urinary System

This system removes wastes from the blood and excretes them into the environment. The system's pivotal organs are the two kidneys, bean-shaped structures at the back of the upper abdomen. Each kidney has about a million nephrons, microscopic structures where water, urea, salts, and other substances diffuse out of the blood. Substances needed by the body are reabsorbed by the blood. The remaining materials form urine. The urine produced in each kidney empties into a ureter, a tube that carries the fluid to the urinary bladder. This muscular sac stores the urine until it is excreted through a tube called the urethra.

The Musculoskeletal System

Skeletal muscles and bones work together to perform functions such as support, protection, and locomotion.

Bones   The body contains 206 bones. The longest is the thighbone, or femur, which grows to an average length of 19.88 inches (50.5 centimeters). The smallest is the stapes, the innermost of three tiny bones in the middle ear, only 0.07 inch (1.8 millimeter) long. Bones give the body its shape and support and protect various organs. For example, the skull protects the brain, and the rib cage prevents lung and heart damage.

Bones are made from cells that secrete long, strong fibers of a protein called collagen. These fibers are reinforced by calcium and phosphorous deposits, which make bone hard and able to support large amounts of weight. The long bones, such as those in the arms and legs, have hollow spaces that are filled with bone marrow. Part of this bone marrow manufactures blood cells.

How Does the Brain Work?

By SANDRA BLAKESLEE

In the continuing effort to understand the human brain, the mysteries keep piling up. Consider what scientists are up against. Stretched flat, the human neocortex—the center of our higher mental functions—is about the size and thickness of a formal dinner napkin. With 100 billion cells, each with 1,000 to 10,000 synapses, the neocortex makes roughly 100 trillion connections and contains 300 million feet of wiring packed with other tissue into a one-and-a-half-quart volume in the brain.

These cells are arranged in six very similar layers, inviting confusion. Within these layers, different regions carry out vision, hearing, touch, the sense of balance, movement, emotional responses and every other feat of cognition. More mysterious yet, there are 10 times as many feedback connections—from the neocortex to lower levels of the brain—as there are feedforward or bottom-up connections.

Added to these mysteries is the lack of a good framework for understanding the brain's connectivity and electrochemistry. Researchers do not know how the six-layered cortical sheet gives rise to the sense of self. They have not been able to disentangle the role of genes and experience in shaping brains. They do not know how the firing of billions of loosely coupled neurons gives rise to coordinated, goal-directed behavior. They can see trees but no forest.

They do think they have solved one long-standing mystery, though. Most neuroscientists are convinced the mind is in no way separate from the brain. In the brain they have found a physical basis for all our thoughts, aspirations, language, sense of consciousness, moral beliefs and everything else that makes us human. All of this arises from interactions among billions of ordinary cells. Neuroscience finds no duality, no finger of God animating the human mind.

So what have neuroscientists been doing? Like a child who takes apart his father's watch, they have dissected the brain and now have almost all the pieces laid out before them. There are thousands of clues about what makes the brain tick.

But how to put it back together? How to understand something so complex by examining it piecemeal? Even harder, how to integrate the different levels of analysis? Some brain events occur in fractions of milliseconds while others, like long-term memory formation, can take days or weeks. One can study molecules, ion channels, single neurons, functional areas, circuits, oscillations and chemistry. There are neural stem cells and mechanisms of plasticity, which involve how the brain changes with experience or recovers from injury.

New research tools continue to drive progress. In the late 1970's, researchers mostly placed sharp-tipped electrodes into single cells and measured firing patterns. By the 1990's, they had machines that could take images of brain activity while people spoke, read, gambled, solved moral dilemmas or, as in a recent study, had orgasms.

Unfortunately, studies like these, while fascinating, tend to feed the fires of a huge disagreement within the brain sciences; is the brain made up of discrete modules that pass information among themselves? Or is it more loosely organized so that varied pockets of distant neurons fire together when called upon to perform a particular task? In mapping the brain, some researchers say that areas dedicated to aspects of language, arm movements or face recognition are hard-wired modules.

Other researchers say that such areas are surprisingly flexible. For example, the human face recognition area is where expert bird watchers distinguish features of closely related species or car experts decide if a 1958 or 1959 Plymouth had bigger fins.

While the two sides in this debate agree that the brain is prewired to some degree at birth, the nature of that prewiring is uncertain. What do genes expressed in the brain do? How do genes influence behavior? What is innate and what is flexible? What is the role of culture in shaping a brain?

One of the most exciting developments is the recent exploration of the frontal lobes. Located behind the forehead, the frontal lobes help create the social brain, melding emotions, cognition, error detection, the body, volition and an autobiographical sense of self. Special circuits containing spindle cells appear to broadcast messages—this feels right, this does not feel right—to the rest of the brain. Researchers are finding that emotions arise from body states as well as brain states, confirming that the supposed distinction between mind and body is illusory.

Others are delving into individual differences. What makes one person empathic, another mean or shy or articulate or musical? How do genes relate to temperament and how is a baby's brain constructed from early experience? Specialized cells called mirror neurons seem to help babies imitate the world to learn gestures, facial expressions, language and feelings.

Brain chemistry is no longer the study of neuromodulators as "juices" that make us feel good or awake. Substances like serotonin, dopamine and norepinephrine play crucial roles in learning, updating memories and neuropsychiatric disease.

The question of free will is on the table. Some of our behavior is conscious, but most of it is notoriously unconscious. So although we make choices, is free will mostly an illusion? And what is consciousness? In seeking an explanation, a new mystery has emerged. Many scientists now believe that the brain basically works by simulating reality. The sights, sounds and touches that flow into the brain are put in the framework of what the brain expects on the basis of previous experience and memory.

In the words of many neuroscientists, all these mysteries are terrific job security.

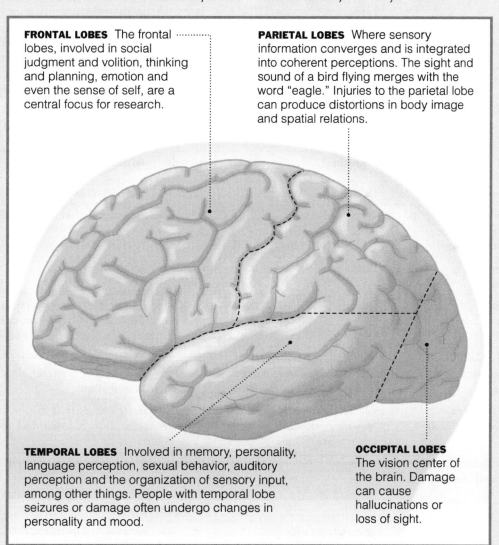

FRONTAL LOBES The frontal lobes, involved in social judgment and volition, thinking and planning, emotion and even the sense of self, are a central focus for research.

PARIETAL LOBES Where sensory information converges and is integrated into coherent perceptions. The sight and sound of a bird flying merges with the word "eagle." Injuries to the parietal lobe can produce distortions in body image and spatial relations.

TEMPORAL LOBES Involved in memory, personality, language perception, sexual behavior, auditory perception and the organization of sensory input, among other things. People with temporal lobe seizures or damage often undergo changes in personality and mood.

OCCIPITAL LOBES The vision center of the brain. Damage can cause hallucinations or loss of sight.

Endocrine Glands and Their Secretions

Gland and Its Location	Hormones	Major Effects
Pituitary Anterior lobe at the base of the brain	Growth hormone	Stimulates cell growth and division by prompting protein synthesis.
	Thyroid-stimulating hormone (TSH)	Stimulates thyroid to produce thyroxine.
	Adrenocorticotropic hormone (ACTH)	Stimulates adrenal cortex to secrete hormones.
	Follicle-stimulating hormone (FSH)	In female: stimulates follicle development in ovaries and secretion of estrogen. In male: stimulates sperm production.
	Luteinizing hormone (LH)	In female: stimulates discharge of mature egg from ovary and formation of corpus luteum. In male: stimulates secretion of testosterone.
	Prolactin	In female: stimulates mammary glands to secrete milk.
Hypothalamus Part of the brain (its hormones are stored in the pituitary until secreted into the bloodstream)	Vasopressin	Stimulates reabsorption of water in kidneys.
	Oxytocin	In female: stimulates uterine contractions during childbirth; stimulates mammary glands to produce milk.
Thyroid In neck, wrapped around the trachea	Thyroxin	Stimulates and controls metabolic rate.
	Calcitonin	Regulates blood calcium levels.
Thymus Under the breastbone just above the heart	Thymosin	Stimulates development of white blood cells.
Parathyroids Embedded in thyroid gland	Parathormone	Regulates blood calcium level.
Pancreas In abdomen, near the stomach	Insulin	Lowers blood sugar level; stimulates protein, glycogen, and lipid synthesis in certain cells.
	Glucagon	Antagonist to insulin: increases blood sugar level.
Adrenals: Medulla Innermost layers of adrenal, located atop kidneys	Adrenaline (epinephrine) and Noradrenaline (norepinepherine)	Secretions of both increase under stress; they increase blood sugar level, heart rate, blood pressure, and metabolism.
Adrenals: Cortex Outer layers of adrenals	Glucocorticoids	Stimulate glucose synthesis and storage.
	Mineralocorticoids (aldosterone)	Regulate concentrations of sodium and potassium.
Ovaries In abdomen of females	Estrogen	Stimulates development of secondary sex characteristics.
	Progesterone	Stimulates breast development; maintains uterine lining during pregnancy.
Testes In scrotum of males	Testosterone (androgens)	Stimulates maturation of sperm and development of secondary sex characteristics.

Muscles   Muscles generate movement. Skeletal muscles, numbering about 700, are considered to be voluntary muscles. Their movement requires signals from the nervous system, but the person can usually control the signals and hence the movement, whether it involves bending a leg, raising the eyebrows, or moving the fingers over the keys of a piano.

In addition to the voluntary muscles that are part of the musculoskeletal system, the body contains cardiac and visceral muscles. Cardiac muscle, found exclusively in the heart, is unique in that it does not require signals from the brain to contract and relax; it generates its own signals from cells within the heart. Visceral, or smooth, muscles are found in the stomach, diaphragm, intestines, arterial walls, and other internal organs. Like cardiac muscle, they are involuntary; however, their function is regulated by a part of the brain called the medulla oblongata.

Movement   Movement of the skeleton occurs at a joint, where two bones meet. Tough elastic connective tissue called a ligament connects the two bones. The ends of the bones are covered with pads of flexible tissue called cartilage, which acts as a cushion, preventing damage to the bones as they rub against each other during movement. A slippery fluid also is present to lubricate the joint.

Skeletal muscle is anchored to a bone by tough connective tissue called a tendon. Because skeletal muscles cause movement only when they contract, they are present in pairs that allow opposite movement. For example, the biceps muscle on the upper side of the arm pulls the forearm toward the upper arm when it contracts, making the arm bend. To straighten the arm, the triceps on the underside of the upper arm contracts.

The Nervous System

This system controls body functions, telling structures what to do and when to do it. The nervous system monitors the internal and external environment and coordinates responses to changes. Its overriding objective is to maintain the stable state called homeostasis.

Neurons   The nervous system is made up of neurons, cells that transmit electrochemical signals throughout the body. Sensory neurons receive information—changes in light, pressure on the skin, arterial blood volume, and so on—and carry the information to the brain or spinal cord. Interneurons, located in the brain and spinal cord, act as bridges, transmitting impulses from sensory neurons to motor neurons. Motor neurons carry instructions to tissues and effect change, such as causing a hand to jerk away from a hot stove or causing an eye to blink.

Although they differ greatly in shape and size, neurons typically have three main parts. The cell body contains the nucleus and carries out most metabolic processes. Branched projections called dendrites receive impulses from other cells and carry them toward the cell body. The axon conducts impulses away from the cell body.

Neurons that function in a particular area are often bundled together. These bundles are called nerves. The longest human nerve is the sciatic nerve, which extends along the back of the leg from the buttocks to the ankle; some of its branches measure more than 3.3 feet (1 meter) in length.

Signal transmission   The terminal branches of an axon do not actually touch the dendrites of another neuron. Rather, the two cells are separated by a tiny space called the synapse.

Within a neuron, a signal is transmitted electrically, through the movement of positively charged ions. At a synapse, neurons must rely on chemical rather than electrical signals. Chemicals called neurotransmitters are synthesized by a neuron and released to transmit a signal to specific receptors on the receiving cell. Several dozen substances that can act as neurotransmitters have been identified, each with different functions. For example, acetylcholine is released from the tips of motor neurons and is responsible for moving skeletal muscles. Serotonin, produced in the brain and spinal cord, is believed to play an inhibitory role in sleep.

Parts of the nervous system   The nervous system has two main parts. The central nervous system consists of the brain and spinal cord. The latter is a hollow cylinder of nerve tissue within the backbone. It is connected to muscles, glands, and other body parts by 31 pairs of spinal nerves.

The peripheral nervous system includes all neurons outside of the brain and spinal cord. It can be subdivided into the somatic nervous system, over which we have voluntary control; and the autonomic nervous system, which serves muscles—such as those of the diaphragm and bladder—that generally are not under our voluntary control. The autonomic nervous system also controls glands and their release of chemicals.

The brain   The brain weighs about 3 pounds (1.4 kilograms) and consists of two types of cells: about 100 billion neurons and ten to fifty times that many glial cells, which surround the neurons and provide support and electrical insulation. The brain has seven major regions, of which the largest are the cerebrum, cerebellum, and medulla oblongata.

The largest portion of the human brain is the cerebrum, which is separated by a long fissure into right and left hemispheres. The cerebrum interprets sensory impulses it receives from the eyes and other sense organs. It is responsible for consciousness, language, memory, thinking, and personality. It also controls the movement of voluntary muscles.

The cerebellum, located below the posterior part of the cerebrum, regulates body movements, muscle coordination, and balance. It helps us repeat learned movements such as playing a trumpet or swinging a baseball bat.

The medulla oblongata, the lowermost portion of the brain, is connected to the spinal cord. It controls involuntary activities such as breathing, heartbeat, and swallowing.

The sense organs   These structures gather information about the external environment and send the information to the central nervous system, which processes the information and determines a response. The organs include the ears, which detect sounds; the eyes, which detect light radiation; receptors in the nasal cavities of the nose, which detect smell; receptors in the skin that detect pressure; and taste buds, which detect chemicals in food. Other sense organs detect body position and temperature.

The Endocrine System

Working closely with the nervous system is the endocrine system, which is composed of glands that produce and secrete hormones, compounds that help coordinate and regulate body activities. Hormones are secreted directly into the blood. Although the blood carries them to every cell in the body, only certain cells have the appropriate receptor proteins on their outer membrane to allow the hormones to activate a change.

Some glands, such as the pituitary, serve only an endocrine function. Others, such as the pancreas, have additional functions. Also, organs such as the heart, liver, and kidneys contain tissues that secrete hormones.

Controlling secretion   Hormone secretion is primarily controlled by a feedback mechanism in which the secretion is controlled by another factor. An example is the maintenance of sugar levels in the blood. As we consume food, our blood sugar level rises. In response, the pancreas secretes insulin, which lowers the blood sugar level. As a result of the decrease, the pancreas stops secreting insulin.

A more complex feedback mechanism is involved in control of cellular metabolism. The pituitary releases thyroid-stimulating hormone (TSH) in response to decreased metabolic levels. TSH stimulates the thyroid to increase secretion of thyroxine. Thyroxine stimulates metabolism but also inhibits the pituitary from releasing TSH. As TSH levels drop, the thyroid decreases its secretion of thyroxine and the metabolic rate in cells is again altered.

Reproductive Systems

The male and female reproductive systems produce gametes, or sex cells—eggs in females, sperm in males. The male system is designed to deliver sperm into the female's system, where under proper conditions an egg and sperm unite, forming a zygote, or fertilized egg, that contains all the genetic material needed to develop into a new human being. The female's reproductive system also provides the environment in which the fertilized egg develops over a period of about nine months into an infant ready to be born.

Male reproductive system   The main organs are two testes that lie in the scrotum, a sac of skin outside the lower abdomen. Beginning during puberty, the testes produce the hormone testosterone. This initiates sperm production within the testes, in a vast network of seminiferous tubules. Testosterone also is responsible for the development of facial hair, increased muscle mass, and other secondary sex characteristics of men. Atop each testis is the epididymis, where sperm mature and are stored.

The penis is designed for delivering sperm inside the female reproductive system. It contains spongy tissue that can fill with blood, causing the penis to become erect. It also contains the urethra, a tube that carries semen—a mixture of sperm and fluids—out of the body during waves of muscle contraction called ejaculation.

During ejaculation, millions of sperm leave the epididymis through the vas deferens, tubes that carry them to the urethra. Almost simultaneously, accessory organs release fluids into the urethra. These fluids provide a medium in which the sperm can swim through the female reproductive system, plus sugar, which nourishes the sperm.

Female reproductive system   Eggs are produced in the two ovaries. Beginning at puberty the ovaries also produce the hormone estrogen, which stimulates development of breasts, growth of genital hair, and other secondary sex characteristics of women.

Each immature egg, or ovum, is contained in a separate follicle in the ovary. During the menstrual cycle, one egg matures and its follicle ruptures, releasing the egg into the fallopian, or uterine, tube. The egg travels through the tube to the uterus (sometimes called the womb), a muscular organ capable of changing shape and dilating. It is here that an embryo develops into a fetus. When fully developed, the fetus is pushed from the uterus through a muscular tube, the vagina, to the outside.

Menstrual cycle   The female reproductive system prepares itself for pregnancy on a regular cycle called the menstrual cycle. The cycle begins at puberty and continues until about age 50, when the cycle ceases, a stage called menopause.

The menstrual cycle lasts about 28 days, its stages regulated by a variety of hormones. In the first stage, the walls of the uterus thicken with blood vessels, preparing it to nourish an embryo. About a week later, a follicle in one of the ovaries bursts, releasing an egg into the fallopian tube. The egg travels toward the uterus, where the lining continues to thicken.

If the egg isn't fertilized, the uterine lining begins to break down and slough off the blood vessels constructed during earlier stages of the cycle. This tissue passes out of the body through the vagina, constituting the characteristic menstrual flow.

Fertilization and embryo development   As an egg travels through the fallopian tube, it may meet and be fertilized by a sperm. The menstrual cycle then ceases. About seven days after fertilization, the fertilized egg has divided numerous times and developed into a young embryo. The embryo implants itself in the uterine wall, where it will reside and grow until birth.

One section of the young embryo forms a network of blood vessels similar to those in the thickened uterine wall. The two sets of blood vessels—one from the embryo, the other from the mother—form the placenta, a temporary organ that allows materials such as nutrients and wastes to move from one set of vessels to the other. Basically, the placenta acts as the embryo's organs of respiration, digestion, and excretion.

After approximately two months, most major organ systems have begun to form in the embryo and it takes on a human appearance. Now called a fetus, it is about 1 inch (2.5 centimeters) long and weighs about 0.035 ounce (1 gram). Between now and birth it will grow to 14 to 21 inches (35 to 50 centimeters) in length and increase in weight to 106 to 140 ounces (3,000 to 4,000 grams).

Evolution

Evolution is the change in organisms from generation to generation. Modern evolutionary theory states that the millions of different kinds of organisms on Earth today did not come into existence in their present form but descended from earlier forms as a result of genetic change. This theory began in the mid-19th century with the work of Charles Darwin and Alfred Russel Wallace (1823–1913). Darwin's observations of fossils and living organisms during a five-year voyage around the world aboard H.M.S. *Beagle* led him to conclude that new species arose as existing species gradually changed in response to environmental conditions. Wallace, working in the Malay Archipelago, reached a similar conclusion and communicated his findings to Darwin. Darwin presented his and Wallace's theory before the Linnaean Society in London in 1858 and published the theory in 1859 as *The Origin of Species*.

Their theory states that natural selection is the main force in evolution. Organisms with the most favorable inherited traits have an advantage, making them more likely to survive, reproduce, and pass on their traits to the next generation. In species that reproduce sexually, individuals vary in size, coloration, physiology, and other characteristics. Some of these variations are acquired characteristics resulting from differences in environmental factors—as in a human who develops bulging muscles from weight lifting, for example. Such characteristics are not inherited by offspring. Other variations, however, are genetic and can be passed from one generation to the next during reproduction—differences in the proteins that regulate metabolism in muscle cells, for instance.

Evidence of Evolution

A vast body of evidence supports the theory of evolution by natural selection.

The Fossil Record   Scientists today are able to accurately date fossils, the rock-bound remains of organisms from past geologic ages. When fossils are arranged along a time line, scientists can see gradual changes from simple to more complex life forms. In some cases, evolution through various intermediate forms over millions of years can be detected and compared to the present state of an organism. For example, the earliest known species of horse lived some 60 million years ago and, according to the fossil record, was shorter than 20 inches (50 centimeters) high at the shoulders. Successive rock layers yield fossils of increasingly larger horse species, culminating in the horses of today. As size changed, so did other aspects of the horses' anatomy: teeth became adapted to eating grass, the bones of the lower leg fused, and multiple toes evolved into a single toe surrounded by a hoof.

Comparative anatomy   Organisms that are closely related, such as mammals, share similar anatomical structures. For instance, although they are used very differently, a bat's wing, a dog's foreleg, a seal's flipper, and a human's arm are composed of the same bones arranged in similar ways. All these species have a humerus bone in the upper arm, radius and ulna in the lower arm, wrist carpals, hand metacarpals, and finger phalanges. Such homologous structures, scientists believe, are explained by common ancestry. In contrast, some organisms have analogous structures that look similar externally but have different internal structures. The wings of a bat, a buzzard, and a butterfly all have the same purpose, but they are completely different in origin.

Evolutionary theory can predict which anatomical mutations might occur and which will not. For instance, because birds evolved from reptiles some 150 million years after mammals, a mutant mammal with feathers is an impossibility. However, since whales evolved from legged mammals, it is possible for a whale to be born with limbs, as does indeed occur on rare occasions.

Comparative embryology   Similarities in the earliest stages of development are also evidence of common ancestry. For example, early in their embryonic development, fish, chickens, and humans all have tails (as well as gill slits and other analogous structures). In the human embryo, most of the tail vertebrae normally disappear by the eighth week in a process called "programmed cell death." Four of the tail vertebrae remain; normally they fuse to form the irregular tapering bone called the coccyx at the distal end of the spine.

The human coccyx is an example of a vestigial organ—one that appears to serve no useful function but suggests a common ancestry with organisms in which the homologous structure is functional. The coccyx is homologous to the functional tail of other primates. Similarly, the eyes of blind cave-dwelling salamanders are homologous to those of related species that live in a world of light.

Genetics and comparative biochemistry   The strongest and most direct evidence of common descent comes from genetics, a field that did not exist in Darwin's time. All living things—from human beings to bacteria—have nucleic acids called DNA and RNA, hereditary material that directs the operation of cells. What's more, the DNA molecule has the same components in every species, and even uses the same codes to carry information. Scientists have tracked evolution at the molecular level in lab experiments with certain bacteria and viruses that reproduce and mutate rapidly, and conjecture that the same process has been at work for millennia in organisms that reproduce and mutate far more slowly.

Because organisms share the same genetic material, there's a biochemical similarity in their basic processes. For example, in all known species, proteins are built from the same 20 amino acids, even though there are about 250 naturally occurring amino acids. All aerobic (oxygen-breathing) organisms use cytochrome c, evidence that all of these different life forms descended from a common ancestor that used this compound for respiration. Additionally, the cytochrome of cows is more like ours than that of fish, suggesting that humans and cows are more closely related than are humans and fish.

Biogeography   When Darwin was in the Gálapagos he observed 13 species of finches spread out among the islands. Each population was slightly different: some had small, thin beaks and fed on small seeds; others had larger, thicker beaks that allowed them to eat the large seeds of their home island. He reasoned that populations of a species that are separated for a long period of time, when spread out among different environments, gradually evolve along different paths.

During Earth's history, the continents have slowly changed their relative positions as a result of plate tectonics (movement of pieces, or plates, of Earth's crust), but for millions of years, all the continents were joined together in a single landmass called Pangaea. Evidence of this includes fossils of a certain fern discovered in Africa, South America, Australia, and India; unless the continents were somehow joined, there is no way the fern could have spread. The fern's descendants, like other flora and fauna, either evolved to meet their changing environments or became extinct.

Human Evolution

Homo sapiens are, of course, a distinct species, with our own evolutionary past. The *sapiens* species (under the genus *Homo*) branched off from our genetic cousins, the chimpanzees, some 5 to 7 million years ago. Several different species of the *Homo* genus (including *Homo erectus* and

Homo neandrathalensis—more commonly known as Neanderthals) are thought to have evolved as well, but sapiens is now the only nonextinct species of the genus. There is not yet a consensus on which of these groups should be counted as a separate species and which as the subspecies of another. The *Homo erectus*, which lived about 70,000 to 1.8 million years ago, is considered a human ancestor; it was the first species in the *Homo* genus to walk upright, the result of adaptive traits like locking knees. The Neanderthals, on the other hand, are most likely a separate species descended from a common ancestor.

There is evidence of skull expansion and stone tool technology development in the period between 400,000 to 250,000 years ago, which mark a transition from *Homo erectus* to *Homo sapiens*. Though it is a hotly debated subject, many scientists believe that this transition occurred first in Africa, and that Homo sapiens gradually migrated from that continent and came to replace other species of the Homo genus around the globe.

Genetics

Genetic information is carried in cell structures called chromosomes. A chromosome is composed of DNA and associated proteins. (An exception is certain viruses, in which RNA is the hereditary material.)

The basic unit of inheritance is the gene. It consists of a specific segment of a DNA (or RNA) molecule. All the genes of an organism can be thought of as constituting the blueprint for the organism, determining all its anatomical and physiological characteristics.

Structure of DNA and RNA

A molecule of DNA, or deoxyribonucleic acid, consists of repeating subunits called nucleotides. Each nucleotide has three parts: a phosphate unit (phosphorus bonded to oxygen), a sugar unit, and a nitrogen base. The sugar is deoxyribose. There are four types of nitrogen bases: adenine (A), thymine (T), guanine (G), and cytosine (C). Because of their chemical properties, adenine and thymine always bond together and guanine and cytosine always bond together.

In 1953, James Watson (b. 1928) and Francis Crick (1916–2004) determined that the DNA molecule resembles a long, twisted ladder—a shape called a double helix.

The sides of the ladder are composed of alternating sugar and phosphate units. Each "rung" consists of a pair of nitrogen bases: A-T, T-A, G-C, or C-G. The two bases are held together by weak hydrogen bonds that can be readily broken by enzymes in the cell, so that the DNA molecule can unwind and duplicate itself during cell reproduction.

A molecule of RNA, or ribonucleic acid, also is a chain of nucleotides. However, it commonly is single-stranded; its sugar is ribose; and instead of thymine it contains the base uracil (U), which pairs with adenine. Also unlike DNA, RNA exists in several forms, the best known of which are three forms involved in protein synthesis: messenger RNA (mRNA), ribosomal RNA (rRNA), and transfer RNA (tRNA).

Nonchromosomal DNA   In addition to making up chromosomes, DNA can be found in other cell structures: plant chloroplasts and plant and animal mitochondria. Mitochondrial DNA is inherited from the female parent; it is passed to offspring solely via the egg cell.

Patterns of Inheritance

The scientific study of inheritance can be said to have begun in the mid-19th century with the work of Gregor Mendel. He crossbred garden pea plants and kept meticulous records of certain traits of parent plants (P generation) and of first and second offspring (filial) generations (F1 and F2 generations).

Mendel developed several theories that have since been proved and today are known as basic principles of heredity. It is important to note that Mendel's work was accomplished before scientists knew about chromosomes, genes, and DNA.

Principle of Segregation   When Mendel crossbred two parent plants from strains that always bred true to type—for example, a tall plant and a short plant—he found that the F1 generation all resembled one parent; in this case, they all were tall. However, when he allowed a plant from the F1 generation to self-pollinate, its offspring (F2 generation) had a ratio of approximately three tall plants for every one short plant.

Mendel concluded that each plant possessed two inheritance factors for height. In parent plants, the two factors were alike, but the F1 plants were hybrid. That is, the two factors for the trait were different. The factors separated (segregated) when the plant produced sex cells, and one factor from each parent was passed to the offspring.

Principle of Dominance   Today we know that a gene can exist in more than one form. A particular form is called an allele. In pea plants, there are two alleles that control height.

Mendel noted that one factor (allele) for a trait may appear to be "stronger" than another factor. He called this the dominant form, and the "weaker" factor the recessive form. In pea plants, the allele for tallness is dominant and the allele for shortness is recessive; therefore, hybrid plants will be tall.

The crosses can be described in shorthand using T for tall and t for short, with TT and tt indicating purebred plants and Tt representing hybrid plants:

TT × tt   100% Tt
Tt × Tt   25% TT + 50% Tt + 25% tt

Principle of Independent Assortment   When Mendel tracked more than one trait, he found that each trait acted in accordance with the principle of segregation; one trait did not appear to have any influence on the other trait. He concluded that each trait segregates independently of the other traits.

The Genetic Code and Protein Synthesis

Between 1961 and 1967, scientists from around the world cracked the genetic code, the sequence of nucleotides in a gene. It's a set of instructions needed by cells for protein synthesis, spelling out the sequence of amino acids in a particular protein. The basic unit of the genetic code is the codon, a sequence of three nucleotides on a DNA or mRNA molecule that codes for a specific amino acid. For example, chromosome 11 contains the code for hemoglobin: 444 DNA letters instruct cells how to make HBB (the hemoglobin gene).

The gene can be thought of as the template for the manufacture of mRNA. This process takes place in the nucleus. The mRNA leaves the nucleus and in the cytoplasm attaches to ribosomes (made partly of rRNA). Amino acids are brought to the ribosomes by tRNA. In a process called translation, the amino acids are linked together in the order coded by mRNA to form the protein.

Mutations   An alteration in an organism's genetic code is called a mutation. Such an alteration may change the order of amino acids in a protein and affect the biochemical properties of the protein. A well-known example is the replacement of A by T at the 17th nucleotide of the gene for hemoglobin, changing the codon from GAG to GTG. This single difference in the 444 DNA letters containing instructions for the hemoglobin gene wreaks havoc on the gene, resulting in the fatal blood disease sickle-cell anemia.

Non-Mendelian Inheritance Patterns   Organisms contain many traits that do not exhibit the predictable patterns discovered by Mendel. In some cases, there is incomplete dominance; neither gene is dominant over the other. A well-known example is four-o'clock flowers. When a four o'clock plant with red flowers (RR) is crossed with a plant that has white flowers (WW), the hybrid offspring have pink flowers (RW).

Additionally, some traits have multiple alleles. An example is the major human blood alleles, of which there are three: A, B, and O. Neither A nor B is dominant over the other, but both are dominant over O. Thus, a person with type A blood may have two A alleles or an A and an O allele. A person with type B blood has two B's or BO. A person with AB blood has an A and a B, and a person with type O blood has two O alleles.

Although Mendel's principle of independent assortment states that traits are inherited independently from one another, genes on the same chromosome are usually inherited together. Certain genes are carried on the sex chromosomes. In females, who have two X chromosomes, the laws of dominance apply. Males have an X chromosome inherited from the mother and a Y chromosome from the father. The two chromosomes are not alike; there are numerous genes on the X chromosome and comparatively few on the Y chromosome. One important gene on the X chromosome codes for factor VIII, a protein needed to enable blood to clot. Lack of factor VIII results in a life-threatening condition called hemophilia. Since males have only one X chromosome, they have hemophilia if that chromosome carries the abnormal gene, but females would have to have both abnormal X chromosomes to have the disease.

Genetics in Medicine

Genetic Engineering   The deliberate alteration, or engineering, of an organism's genetic material may involve changing the sequence of DNA letters, or moving DNA from one species to another. For example, when the human gene that directs production of the hormone insulin is inserted into the DNA of bacteria, the bacteria—and all their descendants—produce human insulin. This process has made it possible to manufacture large quantities of insulin, tissue plasminogen activator (for dissolving blood clots), several types of interferon (for treating hepatitis B and other diseases), and other substances.

Gene therapy is a method of correcting defective genes that cause disease. In the most common technique, a normal gene is inserted into the genome to supplant a dysfunctional gene. The first human gene therapy occurred in 1990, when a young girl received a blood transfusion containing billions of cells with copies of a gene she lacked. The gene enabled her body to make adenosine deaminase, an enzyme essential for a healthy immune system.

Genetic Diseases   Hundreds of human diseases are caused wholly or in part by genetic errors—mutations in genes that result in physical, chemical, or mental abnormalities. If an individual inherits a mutated dominant gene or two copies of a mutated recessive gene, the result may be an inherited disease or increased susceptibility to disease. For example, Tay-Sachs disease is caused by a single recessive gene; the recessive gene must be inherited from both parents for the disease to develop.

Multiple genes may be involved in any one disease. For example, scientists have identified more than 600 cancer-related genes. The normal genes are involved in numerous different activities, but when mutated they can result in the development of a malignant growth.

Some genetic diseases, termed familial, are inherited, though their pattern of inheritance is not clear. An example is familial hypercholesterolemia, which is characterized by high cholesterol levels.

Other disorders sometimes described as genetic are not caused by abnormal genes but by defects in whole chromosomes. Down syndrome is the most familiar example; the nucleus of each body cell contains 24, instead of the normal 23, pairs of chromosomes. Fragile X syndrome is another example; it results from an abnormal number of repetitions of a normal sequence that is part of the genetic code. In some cases, genetic disease occurs because an individual receives an abnormal number of chromosomes. For example, in Klinefelter syndrome, a male is born with an extra X chromosome.

The Human Genome Project

The National Center for Human Genome Research was instituted on January 3, 1989, and with the participation of both the U.S. Department of Energy and National Institutes for Health, became the Human Genome Project in 1990, with the goal of examining and identifying the more than 20,000 genes that make up the human genome. Scientists from the European Union, Japan, and China also participate, forming together the International Human Genome Sequencing Consortium.

Teams from the U.S. and Britain completed the genome of *Caenorhabditis elegans*, a nematode worm, at the end of 1998. Scientists mapped their first plant genome at the end of 2000 with a mustard, *Arabidopsis thaliana*, a common laboratory plant for botanists. In October 2001, sequencing of the genome of the Japanese puffer fish was finished, the first fish to be mapped. The first complete draft of the human genome was completed in 2003, spurring advances in genetic medicine and biotechnology. In 2007, *The New York Times* reported that the full genome of James D. Watson had been deciphered, and in 2009, *The Times* reported that numerous low-cost technologies for decoding DNA were opening the floodgates of genetic sequencing, but actual medical applications to curing specific diseases remained years away.

Pas de Deux of Sexuality is Written in the Genes

By NICHOLAS WADE

When it comes to the matter of desire, evolution leaves little to chance. Human sexual behavior is not a free-form performance, biologists are finding, but is guided at every turn by genetic programs.

Desire between the sexes is not a matter of choice. Straight men, it seems, have neural circuits that prompt them to seek out women; gay men have those prompting them to seek other men. Women's brains may be organized to select men who seem likely to provide for them and their children. The deal is sealed with other neural programs that induce a burst of romantic love, followed by long-term attachment.

So much fuss, so intricate a dance, all to achieve success on the simple scale that is all evolution cares about, that of raising the greatest number of children to adulthood. Desire may seem the core of human sexual behavior, but it is just the central act in a long drama whose script is written quite substantially in the genes.

In the womb, the body of a developing fetus is female by default and becomes male if the male-determining gene known as SRY is present. This dominant gene, the Y chromosome's proudest and almost only possession, sidetracks the reproductive tissue from its ovarian fate and switches it into becoming testes. Hormones from the testes, chiefly testosterone, mold the body into male form.

In puberty, the reproductive systems are primed for action by the brain. Amazing electrical machine that it may be, the brain can also behave like a humble gland. In the hypothalamus, at the central base of the brain, lie a cluster of about 2,000 neurons that ignite puberty when they start to secrete pulses of gonadotropin-releasing hormone, which sets off a cascade of other hormones.

The trigger that stirs these neurons is still unknown, but probably the brain monitors internal signals as to whether the body is ready to reproduce and external cues as to whether circumstances are propitious for yielding to desire.

Several advances in the last decade have underlined the bizarre fact that the brain is a full-fledged sexual organ, in that the two sexes have profoundly different versions of it. This is the handiwork of testosterone, which masculinizes the brain as thoroughly as it does the rest of the body.

It is a misconception that the differences between men's and women's brains are small or erratic or found only in a few extreme cases, Dr. Larry Cahill of the University of California, Irvine, wrote last year in *Nature Reviews Neuroscience*. Widespread regions of the cortex, the brain's outer layer that performs much of its higher-level processing, are thicker in women. The hippocampus, where initial memories are formed, occupies a larger fraction of the female brain.

Techniques for imaging the brain have begun to show that men and women use their brains in different ways even when doing the same thing. In the case of the amygdala, a pair of organs that helps prioritize memories according to their emotional strength, women use the left amygdala for this purpose but men tend to use the right.

It is no surprise that the male and female versions of the human brain operate in distinct patterns, despite the heavy influence of culture. The male brain is sexually oriented toward women as an object of desire. The most direct evidence comes from a handful of cases, some of them circumcision accidents, in which boy babies have lost their penises and been reared as female. Despite every social inducement to the opposite, they grow up desiring women as partners, not men.

Presumably the masculinization of the brain shapes some neural circuit that makes women desirable. If so, this circuitry is wired differently in gay men. In experiments in which subjects are shown photographs of desirable men or women, straight men are aroused by women, gay men by men. Such experiments do not show the same clear divide with women. Whether women describe themselves as straight or lesbian, "Their sexual arousal seems to be relatively indiscriminate—they get aroused by both male and female images. I'm not even sure females have a sexual orientation. But they have sexual preferences. Women are very picky, and most choose to have sex with men," said Dr. Michael Baily of Northwestern.

Dr. Bailey believes that the systems for sexual orientation and arousal make men go out and find people to have sex with, whereas women are more focused on accepting or rejecting those who seek sex with them.

Sexual behavior includes a lot more than sex. Helen Fisher, an anthropologist at Rutgers University, argues that three primary brain systems have evolved to direct reproductive behavior. One is the sex drive that motivates people to seek partners. A second is a program for romantic attraction that makes people fixate on specific partners. Third is a mechanism for long-term attachment that induces people to stay together long enough to complete their parental duties.

Romantic love, which in its intense early stage "can last 12–18 months," is a universal human phenomenon, Dr. Fisher wrote in *Proceedings of the Royal Society,* and is likely to be a built-in feature of the brain. Brain imaging studies show that a particular area of the brain, one associated with the reward system, is activated when subjects contemplate a photo of their lover.

Researchers have devoted considerable effort to understanding homosexuality in men and women, both for its intrinsic interest and for the light it could shed on the more usual channels of desire. Studies of twins show that homosexuality, especially among men, is quite heritable, meaning there is a genetic component to it. But since gay men have about one-fifth as many children as straight men, any gene favoring homosexuality should quickly disappear from the population.

A straightforward clue to the origin of homosexuality is the fraternal birth order effect. Two Canadian researchers, Ray Blanchard and Anthony F. Bogaert, have shown that having older brothers substantially increases the chances that a man will be gay. Older sisters don't count, nor does it matter whether the brothers are in the house when the boy is reared.

The finding suggests that male homosexuality in these cases is caused by some event in the womb, such as "a maternal immune response to succeeding male pregnancies," Dr. Bogaert wrote in the *Proceedings of the National Academy of Sciences.* Antimale antibodies could perhaps interfere with the usual masculinization of the brain that occurs before birth, though no such antibodies have yet been detected.

The fraternal birth order effect is quite substantial. Some 15 percent of gay men can attribute their homosexuality to it, based on the assumption that 1 percent to 4 percent of men are gay, and each additional older brother increases the odds of same-sex attraction by 33 percent.

The effect supports the idea that the levels of circulating testosterone before birth are critical in determining sexual orientation. But testosterone in the fetus cannot be measured, and as adults, gay and straight men have the same levels of the hormone, giving no clue to prenatal exposure. So the hypothesis, though plausible, has not been proved.

A significant recent advance in understanding the basis of sexuality and desire has been the discovery that genes may have a direct effect on the sexual differentiation of the brain. Researchers had long assumed that steroid hormones like testosterone and estrogen did all the heavy lifting of shaping the male and female brains. But Arthur Arnold of the University of California, Los Angeles, has found that male and female neurons behave somewhat differently when kept in laboratory glassware. And last year Eric Vilain, also of U.C.L.A., made the surprising finding that the SRY gene is active in certain cells of the brain, at least in mice. Its brain role is quite different from its testosterone-related activities, and women's neurons presumably perform that role by other means.

It so happens that an unusually large number of brain-related genes are situated on the X chromosome. The sudden emergence of the X and Y chromosomes in brain function has caught the attention of evolutionary biologists. Since men have only one X chromosome, natural selection can speedily promote any advantageous mutation that arises in one of the X's genes. So if those picky women should be looking for smartness in prospective male partners, that might explain why so many brain-related genes ended up on the X.

"It's popular among male academics to say that females preferred smarter guys," Dr. Arnold said. "Such genes will be quickly selected in males because new beneficial mutations will be quickly apparent."

Several profound consequences follow from the fact that men have only one copy of the many X-related brain genes and women two. One is that many neurological diseases are more common in men because women are unlikely to suffer mutations in both copies of a gene.

Another is that men, as a group, "will have more variable brain phenotypes," Dr. Arnold writes, because women's second copy of every gene dampens the effects of mutations that arise in the other.

Greater male variance means that although average IQ is identical in men and women, there are fewer average men and more at both extremes. Women's care in selecting mates, combined with the fast selection made possible by men's lack of backup copies of X-related genes, may have driven the divergence between male and female brains. The same factors could explain, some researchers believe, why the human brain has tripled in volume over just the last 2.5 million years.

Who can doubt it? It is indeed desire that makes the world go round.

Ecology

Ecology is the study of how organisms interact with their environment—both with other living things and with the air, water, and other physical aspects of their surroundings. Although it is a relatively young science, ecology is based on work done over more than 2,000 years, starting with efforts of Theophrastus (ca. 372–286 B.C.), who described relationships within communities of organisms. The term *ecology* was coined by Ernst Haeckel (German, 1834–1919), who gave its first definition in 1866. In the early part of the 20th century, plant and animal populations were studied separately until scientists realized that interrelationships among all types of living organisms are a fundamental aspect of ecology. Today, ecological studies are based on the concepts of ecosystems, a term coined in 1935 by Arthur Tansley (1871–1955).

Ecosystems, Biomes, and Habitats

An ecosystem consists of a community of organisms and the physical environment in which they live. Ecosystems vary greatly in size, ranging from small ponds to coral reefs to the vast expanse of coniferous forests. All the members of a species that live within an ecosystem constitute a population.

A group of ecosystems occupying a large area of land and having characteristic climate, soil, and mixture of plants and animals is called a biome. Major biomes include desert, chapparal, savanna, tropical rain forest, temperate grassland, temperate deciduous forest, taiga, and tundra. Biomes merge gradually with their neighbors in transition zones called ecotones. Some evidence suggests that the greatest diversity of species, long believed to exist in rain forests, may actually be present in the ecotones between rain forests and savannas.

The particular kind of surroundings in which individuals of a species normally live is their habitat. The habitat consists of both living and nonliving components, including competitors, predators, soil, water, and so on. Some organisms, such as blue whales, have habitats as large as an ocean. Others, such as butterflies and sea anemones, have habitats the size of a meadow or tide pool. Very small habitats, such as the ground beneath a rock, are called microhabitats.

Within its habitat, an organism occupies a unique position, or niche. For instance, five species of North American warblers all live in spruce forests and eat insects. But they feed in different parts of the trees—for example, Cape May warblers look for food in the uppermost parts of a tree whereas bay-breasted warblers feed mainly on somewhat lower branches. Because they occupy slightly different niches, they can coexist.

Interactions Within a Community

Interactions in a community occur between members of the same species (intraspecific) and between members of different species (interspecific). Most interactions fall into three categories: competition, predation, and symbiosis.

Competition   Competition may involve any resource needed to live, grow, or reproduce. It generally is greatest among members of the same species because all their needs are identical. An acorn eaten by one gray squirrel means one fewer acorn for other gray squirrels in the community. But it also means one fewer acorn for white-breasted nuthatches that live in the same community.

If competition for a resource is significant and one species is better adapted for acquiring the resource, it may eventually crowd out the other species. The introduction of nonindigenous species into a community is a serious issue because it often leads to loss of native species and significant change in the habitat. For example, purple loosestrife, a native of Eurasia, has crowded out native plants in many North American wetlands in part because of its reproductive edge: a single plant may produce as many as 250,000 seeds. Kudzu, a native of Asia nicknamed "the plant that ate the South," has strong, tough vines that can grow up to 60 feet (18 meters) in just one season, smothering any vegetation in its path.

Predation   Lions, snakes, and eagles are examples of predators—organisms that hunt and eat other organisms. Those that have the best techniques for obtaining food are the ones most likely to grow and reproduce. Predation affects the size of prey populations and the diversity of species within a community. One reason nonindigenous species often are a serious problem is a lack of natural predators in their new homes. Purple loosestrife is such a species, whereas in its native habitats its populations are kept in check by a leaf-eating beetle and root-eating weevil. Parasitism is a variety of predation; a parasite feeds on prey but often weakens rather than kills its host. Some parasites, such as wheat rust, have very specific host requirements. Others, such as mistletoe, parasitize a variety of species.

Symbiosis Two organisms of different species may live together in a long-term association in which neither organism is harmed and one or both may benefit.

Commensalism is a symbiotic relationship in which one species benefits while the other is neither helped nor harmed. Suckerfish (Remora) use a flat suction disk behind the head to attach to the underside of sharks and other fish. This arrangement does not affect the larger fish, but the suckerfish obtains food, feeding on material that drops from the host's mouth.

Mutualism is a relationship that benefits both species. A sea anemone attached to the back of a shell housing a hermit crab camouflages and protects the crab. In turn, as the crab moves about the sea anemone gains a larger feeding range.

Adaptations

Every organism has certain characteristics that adapt it for life in a certain environment. These include structural adaptations, based on how the organism is built; physiological adaptations, based on how the parts of the organism operate; and behavioral adaptations, based on the things an organism does. A bald eagle's structural adaptations that aid in predation include sharp eyesight to locate prey, strong feet with sharp claws to grasp prey, and a hooked bill for tearing flesh. Physiological adaptations include production of enzymes needed to digest flesh. A behavioral adaptation is the eagle's tendency to sit on a high branch overlooking a river where salmon and other prey swim. From this perch, the eagle can see fish underwater and small movements up to a mile away.

Some organisms are highly adapted to a particular niche. This adaptation makes it difficult for them to cope if their environment is altered. Many endangered species facing extinction fall into this category. Other organisms are able to thrive in a variety of niches. Norway rats are an example, living in habitats as diverse as wharves, salt marshes, garbage dumps, sewers, and many types of human dwellings.

Biodiversity

All the living organisms on Earth make up the biosphere. The variety of these organisms is called Earth's biodiversity. Biodiversity can be measured in three different but equally important ways: the variety of genes within a species, the variety of genes among all the species on Earth, and the variety of ecosystems that provide homes for these species.

Biodiversity provides the oxygen needed by most life-forms for metabolism, rich soils in which plants can grow, systems for breaking down wastes, clean water, chemicals that humans can use as pharmaceuticals, and raw materials for clothing, homes, and other human needs.

The greater the degree of biodiversity, the more stable and resilient Earth's ecology. However, with humanity's spread, increasing population, and overconsumption, biodiversity has come under attack. Introduced species, habitat degradation, overhunting, deforestation, and pollution imperil species, speed the rate of extinction, and decrease biodiversity (see "Environment").

Biochemistry

Biochemistry is the study of chemical compounds and processes that occur in living organisms. Like nonliving components of our world, organisms are composed of atoms and molecules that interact in a vast variety of chemical reactions. The sum of all the chemical reactions that occur in the cells of an organism is called metabolism. It includes both anabolic reactions, in which energy is used to build matter used for growth and repair; and catabolic reactions, in which compounds are broken down to release energy. Reactions generally occur in a sequence of steps that make up a metabolic pathway. For example, the sugar glucose is broken down in a 10-step reaction called glycolysis.

Compounds of Living Organisms

Four major groups of chemicals are found in living organisms: carbohydrates, lipids, proteins, and nucleic acids. These are called organic compounds; the term means that each molecule contains one or more carbon atoms.

Carbohydrates Carbohydrate molecules consist of carbon (C), hydrogen (H), and oxygen (O), typically with a two-to-one proportion of hydrogen atoms to oxygen atoms. For example, the simple sugar glucose has the formula $C_6H_{12}O_6$. Linking together hundreds or thousands of simple sugar molecules forms more complex carbohydrates, called polysaccharides. The main sources of energy for most organisms are the carbohydrates sugar, starch, and glycogen. The carbohydrate cellulose is the main structural component of plants. It is the most common organic compound on Earth.

Lipids Lipid molecules contain carbon, hydrogen, and oxygen, in a ratio different from that found in carbohydrates. Some lipids also contain elements such as nitrogen (N) and phosphorus (P). Fats, oils, and waxes are lipids. They are important energy-storage molecules and structural components of cells.

Proteins Proteins are large, complex molecules composed of amino acid molecules. An amino acid molecule has at least one amino group (NH2) and one carboxyl group (COOH). The molecules are linked together to form peptides; a polypeptide is a long chain of amino acids; proteins consist of one or more polypeptide chains. Soluble proteins function mainly as enzymes, which promote biological reactions, or as carriers—for instance, hemoglobin carries oxygen. Other proteins are fibrous and insoluble; they are mainly structural materials, forming cell membranes, muscles, cartilage, hair, and so on.

Nucleic acids The molecules of nucleic acids are composed of repeated units called nucleotides. Each nucleotide consists of a phosphate group, a 5-carbon sugar, and a nitrogen base. The nucleic acids, deoxyribonucleic acid (DNA) and ribonucleic acid (RNA), carry the genetic material of an organism.

Other compounds Combinations of the above are common. For instance, lipoproteins are proteins that contain lipid groups in their molecules, and glycoproteins are proteins that have sugar as part of their molecules.

Hormones are chemicals produced in minute amounts by endocrine glands. They turn on, turn off, speed up, or slow down activities. Some hormones are steroids, fatty compounds synthesized from cholesterol. Other hormones are nitrogen-containing compounds such as proteins, peptides, and amino acid derivatives.

Neurotransmitters are chemicals that transmit signals across spaces that separate one nerve cell from another. They are derived from precursor proteins.

History of Biochemistry

Biochemistry has its beginnings in the 18th century when scientists discovered that plants give off oxygen and, in the presence of light, absorb carbon dioxide. During the same period, Antoine-Laurent Lavoisier (1743–94) demonstrated that animals need oxygen and that respiration involves the oxidation of compounds. In 1828, Friedrich Wöhler (1800–82) synthesized the organic compound urea from an inorganic compound, establishing that the chemistry of living organisms was essentially the same as that of nonliving materials such as minerals.

The first amino acid, asparagine, was isolated in 1806; the first hormone, adrenaline (epinephrine), in 1897; and the first neurotransmitter, acetylcholine, in 1920. The discovery and synthesis of hundreds of biological compounds over the past two centuries have been accompanied by elucidation of the major pathways of metabolism, such as those involved in photosynthesis and respiration. It is now known that seemingly minor changes in a complex molecule may have dramatic consequences. For instance, many if not all cancers result from changes in the structure of nucleic acid molecules.

In recent years, biochemical research has increasingly been part of interdisciplinary efforts involving cell biology, molecular biology, genetics, and immunology. The synthesis of biochemical compounds such as insulin and other hormones has dramatic medical consequences. Other advances in biochemistry are critical to genetic engineering and agriculture.

BOTANY

Also known as phytology, or plant science, botany is the scientific study of plant life. Botany includes a wide range of related scientific disciplines that examine plant structure, growth, reproduction, and development, among other studies, in more than 550,000 plant species.

History of Botany

Early Studies in Botany

Human civilization depends on a knowledge of plants and their cultivation, making botany one of the oldest sciences. In many aspects, the study of botany dates to early tribal lore that was used to identify different types of plants as being poisonous, edible, or medicinal.

The taxonomy (classification) of plants—plant systematics—began in the fourth century B.C., with the publication of *Historia Plantarum (On the History of Plants)*, by the Greek philosopher Theophrastus (ca. 371–286 B.C.), a pupil of Aristotle. Written around 300 B.C., this work did not propose a formal classification theme; instead, it used a combination of groupings from folklore and the observation of growth form. Together with the companion book, *Causis Plantarum (On the Causes of Plants)*, Theophrastus's work built on his teacher's library and unpublished works, serving as an indispensable guide for the study and teaching of botany through the 17th century.

Another important early compendium was *Materia Medica* by Dioscorides, a first century A.D. Greek physician in the Roman army. This work, compiled around 65 A.D., contained more than 500 botanical descriptions and herbal remedies, and remained the single most important reference on medicinal plants for the next 16 centuries.

Modern Botany

In the early 16th century, Gaspard Bauhin (1560–1624), a Swiss botanist, began to develop a more modern classification system for plants. His *Pinax Theatri Botanica (An Illustrated Exposition of Plants)*, published in 1623, described and classified some 6,000 plant species, using traditional groups such as trees, shrubs, and herbs. At around the same time, the Italian physician

and botanist Andrea Cesalpino (1519–1603) began to classify plants according to their fruits and seeds. His *De Plantis Libri XVI*, published in 1583, helped establish classification by the organs of fructification as the foundation of the botanical system.

More detailed classification schemes were introduced during the 17th century by the English naturalist John Ray (1627–1705) and the French botanist Joseph Pitton de Tournefort (1656–1708). Ray established species as the basic unit of taxonomy and listed more than 18,000 plant species in his work *Historia Plantarum*, published in 1686. Tournefort was the first to clearly define the concept of genus for plants.

Botany as a science developed more rapidly in the 17th century, owing in part to the invention of the microscope, which enabled more detailed examination of plant life. In particular, the English scientist Robert Hooke (1635–1703) used an early microscope to discover cells in living plant tissue, as detailed in his work 1665 work *Micrographia (Small Drawings)*.

During the 17th and 18th centuries an increased understanding of plant processes moved the field ahead dramatically. Belgian scientist Jan Baptista van Helmont (1580–1644) demonstrated that plant growth had little to do with soil and identified CO_2, while the famed English chemist Joseph Priestley (1733–1804) showed that growing plants "restored" air from which the oxygen has been removed. And the Dutch physiologist Jan Ingenhousz (1730–1799) proved that light is required for plants to restore air. Combined, these and other studies formed the basis for modern plant physiology.

In the early 18th century, Swedish scientist Carolus Linnaeus (1707–78) developed a system for naming, ranking, and classifying plant and animal organisms that is still used today. Linnaeus was dubbed the father of taxonomy for his pioneering work *Systema Naturae*, published in 1735. This work moved beyond the superficial observations common at the time to provide an anatomically-based classification system of genus and species.

Plant Evolution and Genetics

In the 19th century, plant systematics was developed further through the theory of evolution, as expressed in the 1859 work, *On the Origin of Species,* by the English naturalist Charles Darwin (1809–1882). This, and the increased interest in plant anatomy, drove an effort to group plants by their phylogenetic, or evolutionary, relationships.

A further understanding of genetics was achieved by Austrian botanist Gregor Mendel (1822–84), who formulated the concept of particulate heredity factors, later called genes. Mendel worked out the basic principles of genetics by observing variations in the floral and vegetative features of garden peas. Although Mendel's work was little known at the time, its rediscovery at the turn of the 20th century prompted the foundation of the study of genetics.

Today, botanists occupy themselves with a broad range of activities. These range from basic botanical studies, such as forestry and horticulture, to related but more divergent studies, such as agronomy and pharmacology.

Fields of Botanical Study

Botany is an interconnected series of individual studies. Major botanical studies include the following:

Agricultural science a multidisciplinary field that encompasses those studies used in the practice of farming—producing food, feed, and fuel from the systematic raising of plants for human use.

Agronomy a branch of agricultural science that studies crops and the soils in which they grow.

Economic botany the study of the relationship between people and plants—in particular, the various ways in which people use plants.

Forestry the study and management of forests, plantations, and related natural resources.

Horticulture the culture or growing of garden plants, including plant breeding and genetic engineering.

Paleobotany the study of fossil plants.

Phytopathology the study of plant diseases.

Phytotomy the study of plant structure by dissection (also known as plant anatomy).

Plant ecology the study of the distribution and abundance of plants, and how that is affected by interactions between plants and their environment.

Plant genetics the study of genetic inheritance in plants.

Plant morphology the study of the external structure of plants, in particular the diversity in forms.

Plant physiology the study of the function of plants, including fundamental processes as photosynthesis, respiration, nutrition, and the like.

Plant taxonomy the description and classification of plants.

Pomology the study and cultivation of fruits.

Pteridology the study of ferns.

Practical Uses of Botany

Plants are a fundamental part of Earth's life cycle. They generate the oxygen, food, fibers, fuel, and medicine that enable higher life forms to exist. The study of plants has always been crucial to the working of human society. When society understands how plants work, it can use that knowledge to produce food, medicine, and materials that can be used to feed, clothe, and heal its population. A thorough understanding of plant science also helps us to understand changes in the environment, such as global warming.

Nutrition Humans and animals obtain virtually all their food from plants—either directly, by eating fruits and vegetables, or indirectly, by eating animals that rely on plants for their nutrition. Plants are at the base of Earth's food chain, because they convert energy from the Sun and nutrients from the soil into a form that can be consumed and used by animals. This initial level of the food chain is called the first trophic level.

By studying how plants grow and their role in the food chain, botanists can learn how to increase yields. Increasing yields through selective breeding and genetic manipulation has become integral to providing food security for the growing human population.

Medicine Throughout history, plants have been a key component of humankind's medicine chest. Many medicinal drugs come directly from plants; other drugs are derived from plant byproducts. Research is ongoing, as future cures for many existing diseases are likely to be derived from plants.

Fuels and Materials Plants provide us with many natural materials used for clothing, construction, and other uses. These materials include cotton, linen, paper, rope, and rubber. Plants are also used to create biofuels, which are likely alternatives to fossil fuels.

The Environment The study of plants also helps us to better understand Earth's environment. For example, studying plant systematics and taxonomy helps us understand species extinction and habitat destruction. Studying plant life cycles helps us understand climate change, and studying plants' responses to ultraviolet radiation helps us monitor ozone depletion. In many ways, plants can act as an early warning system, alerting us to important changes in the environment.

Life Processes Plant experimentation poses none of the ethical dilemmas of experimenting on animals, which is why scientists often use plants to study fundamental life processes, such as cell division, genetic inheritance, and protein synthesis. This research typically yields benefits beyond the subject of botany.

Plant Anatomy

The study of plant structure is called plant anatomy, or phytotomy. (This is not to be confused with plant morphology, which is the study of plants' external structure as used in the field identification of plants.) Most plants contain some or all of the following structural elements.

Flower the reproductive structure of a flowering plant. After the flower has been fertilized, portions of the flower develop into a fruit that contains seeds. The flower structure includes several subparts, including the colorful petals, the sepals (the green areas under the petals, collectively called the calyx), and the gynoecium (the female reproductive part, composed of one or more pistils).

Seed a small embryonic plant. Most plants produce multiple seeds, each encased in a seed coat that contains stored food.

Fruit a hard or fleshy structure that contains the seeds of flowering plants. The fruit is essentially the ripened ovary of a fertilized plant.

Leaf the flat and thin part of the plant responsible for photosynthesis. In most plants, leaves are also responsible for respiration, transpiration, and guttation. They can also store food and water.

Stem the structure that supports the plant's leaves and fruits and which transports liquids between the roots and other parts.

Bark the outermost layer of stems and roots of woody plants, such as trees.

Root the organ of the plant that bears no leaves and typically lies beneath the surface of the soil. (Some roots can be aerial, however.) Roots exist to anchor the plant body to the ground, absorb water and inorganic nutrients, and in some plants, to store food.

Photosynthesis

Plants are multicellular organisms that carry out photosynthesis, a term meaning to "build with light," which is how plants convert energy for their own use.

The process of photosynthesis uses the energy of sunlight to convert carbon dioxide and water into the simple sugar glucose. The glucose is then used to build leaves, flowers, fruits, and seeds.

Photosynthesis occurs in specialized cell structures found in leaves and green stems. These structures are called chloroplasts; a single plant leaf might contain 40 to 50 of these cells.

The chloroplast is an oval-shaped structure divided by membranes into numerous disk-shaped compartments, called thylakoids. The membrane of a thylakoid is embedded with hundreds of molecules of chlorophyll, a light-trapping pigment, as well as enzymes and other molecules required for photosynthesis.

There are two stages to plant photosynthesis—the light-dependent reaction, and the light-independent reaction. In the light-dependent reaction stage, the chloroplast traps energy from sunlight and converts it into chemical energy. This chemical energy is stored in two separate molecules: nicotinamide adenine dinucleotide phosphate (NADPH) and adenosine triphosphate (ATP).

In the light-independent reaction stage (formerly called the "dark reaction"), NAPDH provides the hydrogen atoms that help form glucose, while ATP provides the energy for the reactions that synthesize the glucose. This reaction requires the presence of carbon dioxide molecules, which enter the plant via pores in the leaf. During this process, the plant decomposes water into its oxygen and hydrogen atoms; the oxygen is released into the atmosphere while the hydrogen is combined with the carbon and oxygen atoms of the carbon dioxide to form a series of increasingly complex compounds. These compounds eventually evolve into glucose and water.

One important byproduct of the photosynthesis process is oxygen, which is left over when carbon dioxide molecules are rearranged to create glucose molecules during the light-independent reaction. Plants are a major source of the Earth's oxygen; without photosynthesis, the planet would not have the oxygen-rich atmosphere required for animal life. Conversely, animals are a primary source of carbon dioxide, which plants need to conduct photosynthesis.

Types of Plants

All plant life is classified as Kingdom Plantae, which is divided into 12 phyla based largely on the following characteristics:

Tissue structure non-vascular (mosses) and vascular (all other).

Seed structure naked seeds, covered seeds, and spores (reproductive cells capable of reproducing without fusion with another reproductive cell).

Stature mosses, ferns, shrubs and vines, trees, and herbs. The 12 plant phyla are more commonly organized into five major groupings—mosses, ferns, conifers, flowering dicots (two seeds), and flowering monocots (one seed).

Mosses Mosses, liverworts, and hornworts—Bryophyta, Hepatophyta, and Anthoceraphyta—are the only plants that lack a vascular structure for the internal transportation of fluids and nutrients. Instead, they rely on moisture from the surrounding environment. Most mosses are small plants that thrive in moist conditions; they reproduce by means of spores. There are approximately 24,000 species of bryophytes.

Ferns Ferns are vascular plants that transport fluids through their stem structures and reproduce by means of spores. The general category of "fern" includes several distinct phyla—Pteridophyta (ferns), Equisetophyta (horsetails), Lycopodophyta (club mosses), and Psilophyta (whisk ferns), for a total of approximately 15,000 species.

Conifers Conifers are slightly more evolved than ferns; they reproduce by means of seeds instead of spores. The seeds, however, are "naked"—not covered by an ovary. In most conifers, the seed is produced inside a cone-like structure, such as a pine cone. Conifers typically have needle- or scale-like leaves with no flowers.

Conifers are classified in the phylum Gymnospermae. Related phyla include Ginkophyta (Maidenhair Tree), Cycadophyta (cycads), and Gnetophyta (herb-like cone-bearing plants).

Flowering Dicots The vast majority of plants—some 200,000 species—are flowering dicots. This class of angiospermophytes includes most trees, shrubs, vines, flowers, fruits, vegetables, and legumes.

The plants in the phylum Angiospermophyta, class Dicotyledonae, grow their seeds inside an ovary, which is embedded in a flower. After the seed is fertilized, the flower falls away and the ovary swells to become a fruit. Dicots grow two seed leaves.

Flowering Monocots Monocotyledonae, the other class of the phylum Angiospermophyta, are flowering plants that have a single seed leaf. There are around 30,000 monocot species, including grasses, orchids, lilies, irises, and palms. Grain-producing plants are also monocots, including wheat, oats, and corn; fruits such as dates and bananas are also part of the monocot class.

Other Types of Plants

Beyond this formal classification, professional and amateur botanists have additional ways to describe various types of plants. These informal classifications include:

Annual a plant that germinates flowers and dies in a single year. In gardening, an annual is a plant grown outdoors in the spring and summer that survives for just one growing season.

Bulb a plant that grows from an underground shoot that has modified leaves. These plants, monocots all, include onions, lilies, tulips, and irises.

Fruit a culinary term (not a botanical one) for the seed covering; the means by which edible flowering plants disseminate seeds. When dealing with fruit as food, the term typically refers to those plant fruits that are sweet and fleshy, such as apples, pears, peaches, and oranges.

Grass a type of monocot plant from the family Poaceae. Most grasses are grown for pasture or lawns, or as cereals.

Herb an upright plant without woody stems. Herbs are typically employed for medicinal, culinary, or even spiritual uses.

Nut a type of simple dry fruit with a single seed. The ovary wall becomes very hard at maturity, and some nuts are edible.

Perennial a plant that lives for more than two years.

Shrub also known as a bush, defined as a short (usually less than 15 feet) perennial tree with multiple stems.

Succulent a water-retaining plant, such as the cactus, that has adapted to desert conditions. These plants store water in their leaves, stems, and roots to survive long periods without external moisture.

Tree a woody, perennial plant—typically at least 20 feet high at maturity—with secondary branches supported on a main stem (trunk).

Vegetable a culinary term for the edible part of a plant. Vegetables can include plants with edible leaves (lettuce), stems (asparagus), roots (carrots), flowers (broccoli), bulbs (garlic), and seeds (peas and beans). Generally, if a plant has seeds inside, it is considered a fruit (tomato).

Vine a type of plant that has long, flexible stems, such as the ivies and grape plants.

Water plant a type of plant, woody or not, that has adapted to living in or on aquatic environments.

Wildflower literally a flower that grows wild—that was not intentionally seeded or planted.

Plant Diseases and Disorders

The study of plant diseases is called Phytopathology. Plant diseases can be either infectious or non-infectious in nature.

Infectious Diseases

The most common infectious plant diseases include the following:

Bacteria unicellular microorganisms that are ubiquitous in every habitat. Of the approximately trillions of bacterial species, only about 100 cause disease in plants; these plant-harming bacteria are most prevalent in tropical and subtropical regions.

Fungi plant-like organisms that reproduce via spores. Of the 200,000 species of fungi, 10,000 are dangerous to plants; these include biotrophs (which feed on living plant tissue), necrotrophs (which kill plant cells and then feed on the nutrients released), and hemibiotrophs (a hybrid of biogroph and necrotroph).

Nematodes small wormlike creatures that live freely in the soil. Some nematode species in tropical and subtropical regions are parasitic.

Oomycetes also known as water molds. These are microscopic fungal-like organisms that are aggressive plant pathogens.

Parasitic plants plants, such as mistletoe and dodder, that obtain nutrition from other plants.

Viruses microscopic particles that infect the walls of a plant. Most plant viruses do not kill the plant, but only reduce its yield.

Noninfectious Disorders

Other plant disorders are caused not by external organisms, but rather by environmental factors. These physiological plant disorders are exacerbated by factors such as poor light, weather damage (frost, wind, lightning, and the like), too much or too little water, too few nutrients, and pollution. The effects of noninfectious disorders can often be reduced by altering environmental conditions.

Green, Life-Giving and Forever Young

By NATALIE ANGIER

Show somebody a painting of a verdant, botanically explicit forest with three elk grazing in the middle and ask what the picture is about, and the average viewer will answer, "Three elk grazing." Add a blue jay to the scene and the response becomes, "Three elk grazing under the watchful eye of a blue jay."

We barely notice plants, can rarely identify them and find them incomparably inert. But the antidote to plant apathy is at hand. Botanists urge everyone to venture outside and check out the world through nature's rose-colored glasses—and the daffodil, cherry blossom, dogwood and lupine ones, too. If this view doesn't move you, you're pushing up daisies.

As it happens, plants are not only alive in their own right. They are also the basis of virtually all life on earth, including ours. The core feature of planthood is autotrophy, that is, the happy ability to make one's own food. Plants essentially eat the sun, transforming solar energy into sugars and starch through the stepwise enzymatic stitchery of photosynthesis.

Moreover, because plants release oxygen as a byproduct of photosynthesis, plants also give us aerobes leave to breathe. Our atmosphere is currently about 20 percent oxygen, all of it the bounty of the planet's green-skinned autotrophs.

In addition to their caloric self-sufficiency, plants can be envied for their eternal youthfulness. A plant elongates itself through constant cell growth in two zones of its body, at the very tips of the roots, which grow down into soil or other surface to which the plant clings, and the outer tips of the shoots, from which new leaves, flowers and fruits sprout. Whereas an animal, upon reaching maturity, has almost no young cells left in its body.

A plant is also always drinking, slurping water and nutrients the only way it can, through its roots. Everything needs water to survive, but another radical difference between the faunal and floral crafts is that while we can drink water and keep it circulating through the body via the bloodstream, water moves through a plant's body in a continuous stream, entering through the roots, crawling up the stem and evaporating out through little openings, or stomata, in the leaves. In fact, the upward tug of evaporation is what pulls more water up from the soil, as the clingy water droplets follow each other skyward through the hollow capillaries of the plant's stem and leaves, shinnying as high as 300 or 400 feet above ground in the case of the giant redwoods.

No, there's no rest for the weary, especially if you're immobile. Unable to defend themselves by running away, plants have instead become crackerjack chemists, evolving a vast armamentarium of insect repellents, fungicides, microbicides, ultraviolet blockers and other defensive compounds that human chemists have just begun to tally.

Rootedness also complicates a plant's love life. Plants, like everybody else, want to spread their seed around and diversify their genetic stock through sexual reproduction, but it's hard to meet fresh faces when you don't have legs. A number of plant species like pine trees, oaks, cottonwoods and grasses rely on wind to blow their pollen around, with the hope that some of the male sperm contained therein will land on receptive female parts of their far-flung kind. Or if not the same kind, at least something in the same general group: the boundaries between plant species are far more porous than they are in animals, and different species and even genera of plants cross-hybridize with each other surprisingly often.

Nevertheless, wind sex is highly iffy and inefficient, and many species of modern plants, the angiosperms, instead manipulate members of the animal kingdom to serve as yentas in a more discriminating style. The plants offer up brilliant blossoms to entice a specific pollinating insect or bird, which gets drunk on the blossom's nectar and wants more and so seeks out other blossoms of similar shape, color or scent. And as the bee or hummingbird flits from one favored flower to the next, it incidentally delivers pollen pockets to just the right spots.

When we eat, we are parasites on the foundational labor of plants; and when we "say it with flowers," we are plagiarists, too.

ZOOLOGY

History of Zoology

Humans have always lived with animals and have long sought to understand their fellow members of the animal kingdom. As such, the study of zoology—the structure, classification, embryology, evolution, and physiology of all animals, both living and extinct—predates modern science.

The study and classification of animals dates to at least 400 B.C., as detailed in the *Hippocratic Collection*, a 60-book collection of medical knowledge. A more formal classification was realized when the Greek philosopher Aristotle (384–322 B.C.) created his *History of Animals*. This work collected all the known facts about approximately 500 animals, and included the first known classification system, based on reproduction and habitat.

A further study of the animal kingdom was given in *Naturalis Historia* by Pliny the Elder (A.D. 23–79), a Roman author and natural philosopher. This multivolume encyclopedic work collected much of the knowledge of his time and helped to define the study of natural history.

After the fall of the Roman Empire (ca. A.D. 200–300), a book called the *Physiologus* gained widespread popularity. Written in Greek by an unknown source, this work examined 49 different animals (some fictional, such as the unicorn), giving each an allegorical interpretation. The *Physiologus* gained popularity as a teaching companion for the Bible and remained in widespread use for more than a thousand years.

All of these early works presented anecdotal descriptions of the animal kingdom; associated works relied equally on folklore and superstition. As time passed, however, scholars began to record more accurate information through observation and collection.

Scientific Zoology

Zoology emerged as a science during the 12th and 13th centuries, driven by the work of the German scholar St. Albertus Magnus (ca. 1193–1280). Magnus denied many of the superstitions associated with biology and reintroduced the work of Aristotle. Later, Leonardo da Vinci (1452–1519) dissected and compared the structure of humans and animals, establishing the concept of *homology*, the similarity of corresponding parts in different kinds of animals.

In the 17th century, European scholars began to band together into academies and societies for mutual discourse in their chosen field. The first of these academies, the Academia Naturae Curiosorum was founded in 1651, dedicated to the description and illustration of the structure of plants and animals. This was followed by the charter of the Royal Society of London in 1662 and the Paris Academy of Sciences in 1666. These societies brought together museum collectors and systematizers with physicians and anatomists, leading to the further development of zoological science.

In the 18th century, Carolus Linnaeus (1707–78) developed a system for naming, ranking, and classifying organisms that is still used today. Linnaeus was dubbed the father of taxonomy for his pioneering work *Systema Naturae*, which moved beyond the superficial observations common at the time to provide an anatomically-based classification system of genus and species.

By the 19th century, modern technology began to be applied to the study of zoology. In particular, the microscope was used to study animal structure on the cellular level. In 1839, the German scientists Matthias Schleiden (1804–81) and Theodor Schwann (1810–82) proved that the cell is the common structural unit of all living things. This concept inspired Karl Ernst von Baer (1792 - 1876) to establish the field of embryology, and for Claude Bernard (1813–78) to advance the study of animal physiology.

Evolution and Heredity

The 19th century also saw the slow acceptance of the doctrine of organic evolution. Led by a small group of zoologists and botanists, including Jean-Baptiste Lamarck (1744–1829) and Erasmus Darwin (1731–1802), these scientists advanced the theory that all living organisms had developed by a slow process of transmutation over a series of generations, evolving from simple ancestors to more complex creatures.

In 1859, Erasmus Darwin's grandson, Charles Darwin (1809–82), discovered the process by which organic evolution can occur, and provided observational evidence of the process. In his groundbreaking work *On the Origin of Species*, Darwin introduced the theory of evolution by natural selection to explain the diversity of all animal and plant life, thus revolutionizing both the botanical and zoological sciences.

Coincident with Darwin's work, the Austrian monk Gregor Mendel (1822–84) formulated the concept of particulate heredity factors, later called genes. The rediscovery of his work at the turn of the 20th century prompted the foundation of the study of genetics.

Modern Studies

Modern zoology builds on the taxonomy first developed by Linnaeus and the evolutionary theories of Darwin. It is a broad-based science that is not confined to traditional concerns such as classification and anatomy. Zoology today is an interdisciplinary field that encompasses such studies as biochemistry, ecology, and genetics to better understand the many diverse types of animals existing today and in history.

Branches of Modern Zoology

Zoology today is actually an interconnected series of individual studies. There are two main areas of zoological study today: taxonomic groups and the structures and processes common to those groups.

Taxonomic Studies

Taxonomic studies focus on the classification, evolution, distribution, and life cycles of different types of animal life. The major fields of taxonomic zoology include the following:

Acarology the study of mites and ticks.

Apiology the study of bees.

Arachnology the study of spiders and related organisms, such as scorpions, harvestmen, and the like.

Cetology the study of marine mammals (whales, dolphins, and porpoises).

Cryptozoology the study of animals that are rumored to exist, but for which conclusive proof does not (yet) exist.

Entomology the study of insects.

Herpetology the study of reptiles and amphibians.

Ichthyology the study of fish.

Invertebrate zoology the study of invertebrate animals.

Malacology the study of mollusks.

Mammalogy the study of mammals.

Myrmecology the study of ants.

Ornithology the study of birds.

Paleozoology a branch of paleontology that deals with the study of fossils from multicellular animals.

Primatology the study of non-human primates.

Vertebrate zoology the study of vertebrate animals.

Process Studies

Process studies focus on animal functions, behaviors, and interactions. The major fields of process zoology include the following:

Ethology study of animal behavior.

Anthrozoology the study of human-animal interaction.

Ecology the study of how animals react with their environment.

Embryology the study of development in individual animals.

Evolutionary zoology the study of the evolutionary history of the animal groups.

Morphology the study of animal structure.

Physiology the study of function.

Evolutionary History

All animals are believed to have evolved from simple flagellate protozoa. The first animal fossils, known as the Ediacaran or Vendian biota, date from the end of the Precambrian period, around 575 million years ago. These simple organisms appear to be the precursors of modern phyla, although many paleozoologists question whether they are true representatives. More definitive examples of animal phyla appear during the Cambrian period, about 542 million years ago, a result of the so-called Cambrian explosion—a geographically brief period of biological diversity that marked the emergence of the first modern animals.

Arthropods (crustaceans, insects, arachnids, and similar animals) emerged from the sea about 500 million years ago, and began to colonize the land. They were followed by amphibians and reptiles (300 million years ago), mammals (200 million years ago), and birds (100 million years ago). The human genus developed around 2 million years ago, with the earliest modern humans arising approximately 200,000 years ago.

Animal Characteristics

The word "animal" is derived from the Latin word *anima*, meaning vital breath or soul. The biological definition of the word refers to all members of the Kingdom Animalia, which range in size from no more than a few cells to organisms that weigh many tons. The largest number of species in the Kingdom Animalia are insects, with groups such as mollusks and nematodes being similarly diverse.

Animals have several characteristics that set them apart from other living organisms. All animals are multicellular, *eukaryotic* (their cells contain a nucleus and membrane-bound organelles), *heterotrophic* (obtaining nourishment by eating other organisms or parts of organisms), *motile* (capable of self-propelled movement), and they digest food in an internal chamber.

Structure

All animals have eukaryotic cells, surrounded by an extracellular matrix of collagen and elastic glycoproteins. This matrix may calcify to form structures such as bones, shells, and spicules; during development, this matrix forms a flexible framework upon which cells can move about and be reorganized, making complex structures possible. In contrast, other non-animal multicellular organisms, such as plants and fungi, have cells held in place by cell walls, and thus develop by progressive growth.

With a few exceptions, most notably the sponges, animals have bodies made of up cells organized into tissues, with each tissue specialized to perform specific functions.

These include muscle tissue, which contracts to control locomotion, and nerve tissue, which sends and processes electronic signals. Most animals also have an internal digestive chamber with one or two openings, and are capable of complex and relatively rapid movement—especially compared with plants and other organisms.

Reproduction and Development

Almost all animals undergo some form of sexual reproduction, by means of specialized reproductive cells—eggs (ova) and sperm. These cells fuse to form a single fertilized cell, called a zygote, which then divides many times to produce the millions of cells in a fully formed individual.

A zygote initially develops into a hollow sphere, called a blastula, which undergoes rearrangement and differentiation. In most animals (sponges excluded), the blastula splits into a gastrula with digestive chamber and two separate germ layers (an internal endoderm and external ectroderm). These germ layers then differentiate to form tissues and organs that carry out specialized functions.

Unlike plants that draw energy directly from sunlight, most animals grow by indirect use of sunlight. Animals eat plants (or other animals who have eaten plants), which have previously converted the energy of sunlight into chemical energy stored in a type of sugar called glucose. When an animal eats a plant, the sugars produced by the plant are broken down by the animal, and used to either help the animal grow or provide motion. This process is known as glycolysis.

Phyla of the Kingdom Animalia

All animals are members of the Domain Eukarya and Kingdom Animalia. There are around 9 or 10 million known species within the Kingdom Animalia.

Within the Kingdom Animalia, animals are classified first into phyla, and then further subclassified into classes, orders, families, and species. The 19 phyla of Kingdom Animalia are organized by internal anatomy, patterns of development, and genetic makeup.

Porifea *Porifea* are sponges—simple multicelluar organisms that spend their lives anchored to a rock or the ocean floor. They are mostly saltwater marine animals, but some species live in fresh water. Sponges have a radial symmetry with a cylindrical, globular, or irregular body.

The body of a sponge contains an internal skeleton of minute spicules; the surface contains numerous pores that connect to canals and chambers lined by flagellated collar cells (choanocytes). Sponges are filter feeders that take in microscopic plankton by miniature currents created by the choanocytes. There are three classes of *Porifea*: *Calcarea* (chalk sponges), *Hexactinellida* (glass sponges), and *Demospongiae* (horn sponges).

Cnidaria The phylum *Cnidaria* includes jellyfishes and corals. These marine and freshwater animals have a radial symmetry with two distinct body forms: a solitary or colonial polyp and a bell-shaped, free-swimming medusa. Both types of cnidaria are typically fringed and have stinging tentacles with rows of "stinging cells" called cnidoblasts. There are three classes of *Cnidaria*: *Hydrozoa* (hydroids), *Scyphozoa* (jellyfishes), and *Anthozoa* (sea anemones and corals). Some zoologists include a fourth class, *Cubozoa*, which describe box jellyfishes.

Ctenophora *Ctenophora*, or comb jellies, are solitary marine animals with transparent, symmetrical bodies. Externally, the body contains eight plates of fused cilia that resemble long combs; the rows of comb plates are used for locomotion. With the exception of a single species, ctenophores do not have the stinging tentacles of the jellyfish. They are often bioluminescent, glowing like miniature hot-air balloons at twilight.

Platyhelminthes This phylum consists of flatworms and tapeworms—small worms with flattened and symmetrical leaflike or ribbonlike bodies. There are three classes in this phylum: *Turbellaria* (free-living flatworms), *Trematoda* (flukes), and *Cestoda* (tapeworms).

Nematoda This is a large phylum of worms, often called roundworms or threadworms. These worms live free in soil or water, or parasitically on or inside plants and animals. Examples include hookworms, pinworms, the trichinosis worm, and the giant kidney worm.

Rotifera Rotifers are microscopic aquatic animals that live in fresh water, particularly among plants and debris and sometimes in moist soil. The name derives from a Latin word meaning "wheel-bearer," which refers to rotating cilia at the anterior end of organism; the rapid movement of the cilia in some species makes them appear to whirl like a wheel. The digestive tract is complete with both a mouth and an anus.

Bryozoa Bryozoans are aquatic organisms that form coral-like colonies in both fresh and saltwater. They are often called "moss animals," due to their interconnected fan-like colonies. Each animal has a fringe of tentacles around its mouth. Over 125 species of bryozoa are known to grow on the bottom of ships, and on piers and docks. These animals are often considered nuisances, reducing the efficient travel of the affected ships and clogging water intakes.

Brachiopoda The phylum *Brachiopoda*, otherwise known as lamp shells, are marine animals that superficially resemble clams or similar mollusks. In reality, brachiopods are primitive bivalve animals that attach to rocks by a fleshy stalk; the two valves enclose the body dorsally and ventrally. Brachiopods typically live in very cold water, either in polar regions or at great ocean depths. There are about 300 known living species today, a small fraction of the 30,000 species that flourished during the Paleozoic and Mesozoic eras.

Nemertea Nemertines are also known as proboscis or ribbon worms. These are free-living marine worms with a distinctive proboscis that consists of a long, hollow tube. The worm's unsegmented body is covered with cilia, and it has a complete digestive system. There are approximately 900 known species in this phylum. Some species are up to 100 feet in length, although most are much shorter. Most nemertines are carnivorous, feeding on crustaceans and other small invertebrates.

Phoronida Phylum *Phoronida* contains only about a dozen living species. Though few in number, they are found in all oceans and seas. These so-called horseshoe worms have a gut that loops and exits the body near the mouth. They feed using a lophophore, a ciliated structure that surrounds the mouth. Phoronids are hermaphroditic and reproduce asexually.

Annelida Annelids are segmented worms, typically found in wet environments. Each segment of the worm has fine bristlelike setae, which are used for locomotion. This is a large phylum with more than 10,000 modern species, including terrestrial, marine, and freshwater species. There are three classes of *Annelida*: *Polychaeta* (clamworms), *Oligochaeta* (earthworms), and *Hirudinea* (leeches).

Onychophora Onychophorans, or velvet worms, are related to arthropods; some zoologists categorize them in a subphylum of the arthropods. Rarely seen, these worms they live in tropical and subtropical forest regions; there are about 100 known living species. These are segmented, caterpillar-like creatures, with two antennae and a pair of eyes on the first head segment, and a mouth on the second head segment. Their skin is covered with fine hair (papillae), which gives a velvety feel.

Mollusca The phylum *Mollusca* describes animals whose shell is reduced, internal, or entirely absent. All molluscs have a mantle, which is a fold of the outer skin lining the shell, as well as a muscular foot used for motion. In many molluscs, the mantle produces a calcium carbonate external shell. All species have a complete digestive tract.

There are a wide variety of species, more than 250,000 in all, including mollusks, snails, clams, mussels, squid, and octopuses. They are found in virtually all habitats, including freshwater, saltwater, and land. There are eight classes in the phylum: *Gastropoda* (univalve mollusks, including snails, slugs and limpets; over 40,000 species), *Bivalvia* or *Pelecypoda* (clams, mussels, oysters, scallops; 8,000 species), *Cephalopoda* (squid, octopuses, cuttlefish, 780 species), *Polyplacophora* (chitons; 600 species), *Scaphopoda* (tusk or tooth shells, 350 species), *Aplacophora* (deep-sea worm-like creatures; 250 species), *Caudofoveata* (deep-sea worm-like creatures; 70 species), *Monoplacophora* (deep-sea limpet-like creatures, 11 species). Of these species, the class *Gastropoda* comprises more than 80 percent of known species.

Arthropoda

Arthropoda is the phylum that includes insects, spiders, and crabs. The body of an arthropod consists of a head, thorax, and abdomen, with three or more pairs of jointed legs. There is a dorsal heart and a ventral nervous system. All body parts are covered by a hard exoskeleton; an arthropod sheds this covering when it periodically molts. All arthropods have a complete digestive system.

Arthropods are common in all environments—marine, freshwater, terrestrial, and aerial. They comprise the largest phylum of animals; more than 80 percent of all described animal species are in this phylum. There are seven major classes of arthropods: *Onychophora* (walking worms), *Crustacea* (crustaceans—shrimp, crabs, and barnacles), *Insecta* (insects), *Chilopoda* (centipedes), *Diplopoda* (millipedes), *Arachnida* (spiders and ticks), and *Merostomata* (horseshoe crabs).

Tardigrada

Tardigrades or water bears are small creatures that live on moist mosses and lichens. They have short legs with small claws, and are able to roll up into a ball to survive long periods of desiccation. A tardigrade has a body with four segments (not counting the head) and four pairs of legs. There are more than 1,000 species of tardigrades existing all over the world, from the depths of the ocean to the heights of the Himalayas.

Chaetognatha

The phylum *Chaetognatha* consists of arrow worms—small, transparent, predatory worms with bristles or hooks around the mouth. They have a distinct head, trunk, and tail, with paired fins on the main body trunk and a tail fin for locomotion. Although they have a mouth with rows of tiny teeth, compound eyes, and a nervous system, these worms have no respiratory, circulatory, or excremental systems. They are found in all marine waters, and range in size from 3 mm to 12 cm (.12 inches to 4.72 inches). There are more than 120 modern species.

Echinodermata

Echinoderms are sea stars, commonly known as starfish although they are not fish, sea cucumbers, and sea urchins—marine animals that exist at all depths. Most echinoderms have a fivefold symmetry, with arms or rays in fives or multiples of five. They possess a hydraulic water vascular system in the form of fluid-filled canals, typically forming suckered "feet" used for locomotion and feeding. They also have an open circulatory system and a complete digestive tube. Many echinoderms have remarkable powers of regeneration; a sea star cut into a number of parts as small as a single arm will regenerate into as many separate sea stars.

This is the largest phylum that lacks any freshwater or land species. There are five classes of echinoderms: *Crinoidea* (sea lilies), *Asteroidea* (sea stars), *Ophiuroidea* (brittle stars), *Echinoidea* (sea urchins and sand dollars), and *Holothuroidea* (sea cucumbers).

Hemichordata

Phylum *Hemichordata* consists of a small group of invertebrates that serve as an important link in vertebrate evolution, possessing some (but not all) characteristics of the phylum chordata—gill slits, dorsal nerve cord, and the like. Although there are only about 100 species of hemichordates, three classes exist in the phylum: *Enteropneusta* (acorn worms), *Pterobranchia* (graptolites), and *Planctosphaeroidea* (rare, known only by larval samples). Acorn worms are quite large (up to 8 feet) and burrowers; graptolites are much smaller (1 millimeter) and exist in interconnected colonies.

Chordata

Chordata is the most evolutionarily advanced phylum, containing all vertebrate species and several closely related invertebrates. Chordates are defined by the following characteristics, which are present at some point in their life (for some species, only in the embryo): pharyngeal slits (gills), dorsal nerve cord (a bundle of nerve fibers that connect the brain with the lateral muscles and other organs), notochord (spine), and post-anal tail.

The phylum Chordata is divided into three major subphyla: *Urochordata* (tunicates), *Cephalochordata* (lancets), and *Vertebrata* (vertebrates).

Vertebrate Zoology

There are two major categories within zoology, invertebrate zoology and vertebrate zoology. Invertebrate zoology deals with those creatures that lack a spinal column, including various worms, mollusks, and insects. (Of all the world's animals, 90 percent are invertebrates.) Vertebrate zoology deals with those species in the phylum chordata and subphylum *Vertebrata*—animals that have a spinal column or backbone, such as fish, birds, amphibians, reptiles, and mammals.

The subphylum *Vertebrata* is a very diverse group, ranging from lampreys to *homo sapiens*. More than 57,000 species of vertebrates have been described, the first of which evolved about 530 million years ago during the Cambrian explosion. The defining characteristics of most vertebrate species are the backbone or spinal cord, a braincase, and an internal skeleton. All vertebrates also have a separate head that contains sensory organs, such as eyes and ears.

There are eight major classes of vertebrate: *Agnatha* (jawless fishes), *Placoderms* (armored fishes), *Chondrichthyes* (cartilaginous fishes), *Osteichthyes* (bony fishes), *Amphibia* (amphibians), *Reptilia* (reptiles), *Aves* (birds), and *Mammalia* (mammals).

Agnatha This vertebrate class consists of jawless fishes. Agnatha have existed since the Cambrian era, and continue to live in modern times. Current Agnatha include lampreys and hagfish, with 100 species between them. Members of class *Agnatha* are characterized by the absence of jaws and paired fins, the presence of a notochord (flexible, rod-shaped body), and seven or more paired gill pouches. These fish have a light-sensitive pineal eye, but no identifiable stomach. Fertilization is external.

Placodermi Placoderms are prehistoric armored fishes, known from fossils dating from the late Silurian to the end of the Devonian period. The head and thorax were covered by articulated armored plates; the rest of the body was either naked or scaled. Placoderms were among the first of the jawed fish, their jaws probably evolving from their gill arches.

Chondrichthyes Class *Chondrichthyes* are cartilaginous fishes, such as sharks and rays. They are jawed fishes with paired fins, paired nostrils, two-chambered hearts, scales, and skeletons made of cartilage rather than bone. Brain development of these fishes is similar to that found in birds and mammals; brain weight relative to body size comes close to that of mammals, and is about 10 times that of bony fishes.

There are two subclasses of *Chondrichthyes*: *Elasmobranchii* (sharks, rays, and skates) and *Holocephali* (chimaera, sometimes called ghost sharks).

Osteichthyes *Osteichthyes* are bony fishes. The class is characterized by a pattern of cranial bones, rooted teeth, and mandibular muscle in the lower jaw. The head and pectoral girdles are covered with large dermal bones; even the eyeball is supported by a ring of four small bones. Osteichthyans do not have fin spines, but instead support the fin with bone fin rays (lepidotrichia). All species have a lung or swim bladder.

There are two classes of *Osteichthyes*: *Actinopterygii* (ray-finned fish) and *Sarcopterygii* (lobe-finned fish). Most bony fishes belong to the *Actinopterygii*, which consists of more than 29,000 species; there are only eight living species of lobe-finned fish, including the lungfish and coelacanths.

Amphibia The class *Amphibia* are all four-legged vertebrates that are cold-blooded, spend at least part of the time on land, and do not have amniotic eggs. Most amphibians are bound to fresh water for reproduction. Amphibian eggs hatch into larvae (tadpoles or polliwogs) that breathe with exterior gills. The larvae undergo a gradual metamorphosis into the adult, replacing the gills with lungs and developing other distinct body parts—eyelids, eardrums, and such. (And in frogs and toads, the tail of the tadpole disappears.)

Amphibians are divided into three subclasses: *Labyrinthodontia* (diverse Paleozoic and early Mesozoic group), *Lepospondyli* (small Paleozoic group), and *Lissamphibia* (modern amphibians). Of these classes, only the last includes recent species, and it is itself divided into three orders: *Anura* (frogs and toads), *Caudata* or *Urodela* (salamanders), and *Gymnophiona* or *Apoda* (caecilians). There are approximately 6,000 species of amphibians living today.

Reptilia The phylum *Reptilia* are reptiles—all of the amniotes (animals whose embryos are surrounded by an amniotic membrane) except birds and mammals. Reptiles are thick-skinned and, unlike amphibians, do not need to absorb water. Most modern species of reptiles do not generate enough heat to maintain a constant body temperature, and are thus referred to as ectothermic (cold-blooded). Instead, they rely on gathering and losing heat from the environment to regulate their internal temperature—moving between sun and shade, for example.

Except for a few species of turtles and tortoises, reptiles are covered by scales. Most species are oviparous (egg-laying) and have closed circulation via a three-chamber heart. All reptiles, even aquatic species, use lungs to breathe—although, owing to the lack of a secondary palate, they must hold their breath when swallowing.

Modern reptiles inhabit every continent except for Antarctica, although they are most common in the tropics and subtropics. There are four reptilian orders: *Crocodilia* (crocodiles, alligators, and caimans), *Squamata* (lizards, snakes, and amphisbaenids), *Testudines* (turtles and tortoises), and *Sphenodontia* (two species of tuataras from New Zealand). Of these orders, *Squamata* is the most populous, with approximately 7,900 species.

Aves The class *Aves* contains all bird species—bipedal, warm-blooded, oviparous vertebrates that have feathers, wings, and (in most) hollow bones. Common characteristics include a beak with no teeth, the laying of hard-shelled eggs, a high metabolic rate, a four-chambered heart, and (thanks to those hollow bones) a light but strong skeleton. Most, but not all, birds are capable of flight.

Some scientists believe that birds evolved from theropod dinosaurs. This theory is supported by evidence that some of these dinosaurs were capable of powered flight, and in fact were feathered.

Birds range in size from tiny hummingbirds to huge ostriches and emus. There are approximately 10,000 living bird species, making birds the most diverse class of terrestrial vertebrae. Modern birds are divided into two superorders: *Paleognathae* (flightless birds) and *Neognathae* (all other birds).

Mammalia *Mammalia* are characterized by the production of milk in females (lactation). Most mammals also have hair or fur, specialized teeth, three small bones within the ear, and a neocortex region in the brain. Mammals are also *endothermic* (warm-blooded).

Most mammals have seven bones in the neck, or cervical vertebrae. The mammalian heart has four chambers, including left and right atria (to receive blood) and ventricles (to pump blood to the lungs and body). Most mammals give birth to live young and are terrestrial in nature, although some (such as dolphins and whales) are aquatic or semi-aquatic (seals).

The first true mammals appeared in the early Jurassic period, and were egg layers. The earliest known marsupial and placental mammals date from the middle to late Cretaceous period. Today, mammals are organized into two major subclasses: *Prototheria* (monotremes, such as platypuses and echidnas) and *Theriiformes* (live-bearing mammals).

Human beings are a small subsection of the class *Mammalia*—just one of the approximately 5,800 mammalian and 10 million animal species. The full classification for human mammals is Kingdom *Animalia*: Phylum *Chordata*: Class *Mammalia*: Subclass *Therriformes*: Infraclass *Holotheria*: Supercohort *Theria*: Cohort *Placentalia*: Magnorder *Epitheria*: Grandorder *Archonta*: Order *Primates*: Suborder *Haplorrhini*: Infraorder *Simiiformes*: Parvorder *Catarrhini*: Superfamily *Hominoidea*: Family *Hominidae*: Subfamily *Homininae*: Tribe *Hominini*: Genus *Homo*: Species *Homo sapiens*. Simplified, *Homo sapiens* are vertebrate mammalian primate hominids; although we are genetically related to all other members of the animal kingdom (including the humble sponge), our closest existing relatives are other primates, such as the great apes.

Chimps Wage War and Annex Rival Territory

By NICHOLAS WADE

Every day, John Mitani or a colleague is up at sunrise to check on the action among the chimpanzees at Ngogo, in Uganda's Kibale National Park. Most days the male chimps behave a lot like frat boys, making a lot of noise or beating each other up. But once every 10 to 14 days, they do something more adult and cooperative: they wage war.

A band of males, up to 20 or so, will assemble in single file and move to the edge of their territory. They fall into unusual silence as they penetrate deep into the area controlled by the neighboring group. They tensely scan the treetops and startle at every noise. "It's quite clear that they are looking for individuals of the other community," Dr. Mitani says.

When the enemy is encountered, the patrol's reaction depends on its assessment of the opposing force. If they seem to be outnumbered, members of the patrol will break file and bolt back to home territory. But if a single chimp has wandered into their path, they will attack. Enemy males will be held down, then bitten and battered to death. Females are usually let go, but their babies will be eaten.

These killings have a purpose, but one that did not emerge until after Ngogo chimps' patrols had been tracked and cataloged for 10 years. The Ngogo group has about 150 chimps and is particularly large, about three times the usual size. And its size makes it unusually aggressive. Its males directed most of their patrols against a chimp group that lived in a region to the northeast of their territory. Last year, the Ngogo chimps stopped patrolling the region and annexed it outright, increasing their home territory by 22 percent.

The objective of the 10-year campaign was clearly to capture territory, the researchers concluded. The Ngogo males could control more fruit trees, their females would have more to eat and so would reproduce faster, and the group would grow larger, stronger and more likely to survive. The chimps' waging of war is thus "adaptive," Dr. Mitani and his colleagues concluded, meaning that natural selection has wired the behavior into the chimps' neural circuitry because it promotes their survival.

Chimpanzee warfare is of particular interest because of the possibility that both humans and chimps inherited an instinct for aggressive territoriality from their joint ancestor who lived some five million years ago. Only two previous cases of chimp warfare have been recorded, neither as clear-cut as the Ngogo case.

Dr. Mitani's team has now put a full picture together by following chimps on their patrols, witnessing 18 fatal attacks over 10 years and establishing that the warfare led to annexation of a neighbor's territory.

The benefits of chimp warfare are clear enough, at least from the perspective of human observers. Through decades of careful work, primatologists have documented the links in a long causal chain, proving for instance that females with access to more fruit trees will bear children faster.

A simpler explanation is that the chimps are just innately aggressive toward their neighbors, and that natural selection has shaped them this way because of the survival advantage that will accrue to the winner.

Warfare among human groups that still live by hunting and gathering resembles chimp warfare in several ways. Foragers emphasize raids and ambushes in which few people are killed, yet casualties can mount up with incessant skirmishes. Dr. Richard Wrangham of Harvard University argues that chimps and humans have both inherited a propensity for aggressive territoriality from a chimplike ancestor. Others argue the chimps' peaceful cousin, the bonobo, is just as plausible a model for the joint ancestor.

Dr. Wrangham's view is that since gorillas and chimps are so similar, their joint ancestor, which lived some seven million years ago, would have been chimplike and therefore so would the joint ancestor of chimps and humans when they parted ways two million years later. "So I think it's very reasonable to think this behavior goes back a long way," he said, referring to the propensity to wage war against one's own species.

Dr. Mitani, however, is reluctant to infer any genetic link between human and chimp warfare, despite the similarity of purpose, cost and tactics. "It's just not at all clear to me that these lethal raids are similar sorts of phenomena," he said. More interesting than warfare, in his view, is the cooperative behavior that makes war possible.

Why do chimps incur the risk and time costs of patrolling into enemy territory when the advantage accrues most evidently to the group? Dr. Mitani invokes the idea of group-level selection — the idea that natural selection can work on groups and favor behaviors, like altruism and cooperation, that benefit the group at the expense of the individual. Selection usually depends only on whether an individual, not a group, leaves more surviving children.

Many biologists are skeptical of group-level selection, saying it could be effective only in cases where there is intense warfare between groups, a reduced rate of selection on individuals, and little interchange of genes between groups. Chimp warfare may be constant and ferocious, fulfilling the first condition, but young females emigrate to neighboring groups to avoid inbreeding. This constant flow of genes would severely weaken any group selective process, Dr. Wrangham said.

Samuel Bowles, an economist at the Santa Fe Institute who has worked out theoretical models of group selection, said the case for it "is pretty strong for humans" but remains an open question in chimpanzees.

Chimp watching is an arduous task since researchers must first get the chimpanzees used to their presence, but without inducements like bananas, which could interfere with their natural behavior. Chimpanzees are immensely powerful, and since they can tear each other apart, they could also make short work of any researcher who incurred their animosity.

"Luckily for us, they haven't figured out that they are stronger than us," Dr. Mitani said, explaining that there was no danger in tagging along behind a file of chimps on the warpath. "What's curious is that after we do gain their trust, we sort of blend into the background and they pretty much ignore us."

Primates

Primates are a specific order within the class *Mammalia*. The primate order includes monkeys, apes, and humans. Linnaeus first established primates as an order in 1758. Virtually all primates are found in Africa and Asia except for humans.

Primate Groups There are approximately 235 species of primates, classified into two major groups: *Prosimians* and *Anthropoids*.

Prosimians are primitive primates, such as lemurs, pottos, marmosets, capuchins, monkeys, macaques, and galagos. These are small- to medium-size mammals with pointed muzzles and well-developed senses of smell and hearing. Most prosimians are nocturnal.

Anthropoids are more humanlike, and in fact include the human species, along with chimpanzees, baboons, gorillas, and apes. Most anthropoids have flat faces and a relatively poor sense of smell. With few exceptions, anthropoids are most active during the day.

Characteristics Primates evolved from tree-dwelling ancestors, and all primates share features related to this ancestry. These include arms and legs that move more freely than those of other mammals, flexible fingers and toes, forward-facing eyes, and large brains. In the higher primates—apes, gorillas, and humans—a keen visual ability, including color vision give them great advantage.

Nearly all primates have a full set of five fingers or toes on each limb. In many primates, the thumbs and big toes are opposable, permitting them to meet the other digits at the tips. This enables primates to grip branches, as well as pick up and handle small objects.

Compared with most other mammals, primates have relatively few young. The gestational period is relatively long, as is the length of time it takes for offspring to develop. Primates have a relatively long childhood—most extreme in humans—which enables complex patterns of behavior to be passed on by means of learning.

Primates have the most highly developed brains in the animal kingdom, rivaled only by those of dolphins and whales. In particular, anthropoid primates are intelligent and inquisitive, quick to learn new patterns of behavior. This increased brainpower not only helps primates move about to forage for food, but also to develop social skills. Most primate species are social animals, living in groups with a defined social order.

THE ENVIRONMENT

Environment and Civilization

The environment is the whole of the physical and biological elements that surround us, which affect humans and are in turn affected by them. In addition to what we think of as the natural environment, there is also an extensive "built" or human-created and human-managed environment of cities, suburbs, farms, fishing grounds, and protected areas. The climate in which we live today began about 10,000 years ago, at the end of the last ice age. During this period, called the Holocene, conditions have been relatively stable in the earth's physical environment, although there have been extreme events—floods, droughts, earthquakes, tidal waves—that have affected the biosphere and human life.

The relative climatic and environmental stability of the Holocene period provided the framework for the development of human civilization, beginning with the Neolithic ("new Stone Age") revolution about 8,000 years ago. This brought with it settled agriculture and domesticated animals, and in later millennia the great civilizations of Asia, the Middle East and South America, with highly developed urban areas and large irrigation systems. Since the Neolithic revolution humans have had significant effects on their own environments (although earlier effects associated with the migration of humans out of Africa also occurred). We know, for example, that the Romans' use of lead caused pollution as far north as Scandinavia. In turn, some of the natural climatic variations during the Holocene period have had a significant impact on the course of human civilization. The medieval warm period in the North Atlantic world provided conditions that made possible the expansion of the Vikings throughout Europe and as far west as North America. The Little Ice Age, from about 1400 to 1650, caused rivers in Northern Europe that are now generally ice-free, such as the Thames in Great Britain, to freeze over. Such events were not necessarily global, but were related to particular regions, reflecting the complex interactions of atmosphere, oceans and land that create climatic conditions.

Prehistoric Conditions

Earth's climate and environment have not generally been as stable as in the Holocene period. Rather, over the long history of the Earth substantial environmental change has been the norm, including great episodes of change such as the extinction event at the boundary of the Cretaceous and Tertiary geologic periods 65 million years ago. Attributed at least in part to the climatic and other consequences of a large asteroid hitting Earth, this resulted in the extinction of 70 percent of Earth's species, including the dinosaurs. Closer in time to the present, Earth's climate during about the past one million years has been characterized by a series of glacial and interglacial periods. A great deal of information on this period, and especially the last several hundred thousand years, has been deduced from "proxy variables" such as evidence in ice cores, ancient ocean sediments, and the radiometric dating of rocks. During most of this period, Earth has been considerably colder, about 9 degrees Fahrenheit (5 degrees Celsius), than it is today, and the sea level was much lower because water was locked in immense ice sheets. For example, the oceans were about 395 feet (120 meters) lower during the last ice age than they are today. The most recent period of warmth comparable to our current climate was the Eemian interglacial, about 130,000 years ago.

Glacial Periods

The cycles of glaciation are attributed in large part to changes in the amount of the Sun's energy hitting the Earth at different times. The relation of the Earth to the Sun changes over long periods owing to periodic changes in the Earth's orbit, the gradual movement of the Earth's axis of rotation (called precession), and the tilt of the axis relative to the Sun. These changes are referred to collectively as the Milankovitch cycles, after the Serbian engineer and scientist Milutin Milankovich (1879–1958), who investigated their effects. Unless there are large human-induced changes (see "Global Warming") or unexpected factors, the next cycle of cooling is expected to begin in several thousand years. The ice age cycles, although regular, have not been without surprises: some episodes of climate change within the larger pattern have come with startling rapidity. For example, 13,000 years ago there was an abrupt reversal of warming trends, leading to a drop in temperatures of about 11 degrees Fahrenheit (6 degrees Celsius), bringing renewed glacial conditions. This event ended some 1,300 years later with a period of rapid warming of 12–13 degrees Fahrenheit (7 degrees Celsius). Called the Younger Dryas, after an Arctic flower, this period of sudden change is a reminder of the potential instability of the Earth's environment.

The New World

A leading example of the changes brought about by large-scale interactions of humans and the environment is the peopling of North and South America by migrants from Asia. Because the sea level was much lower during the last ice age than it is today, North America and Asia were connected by a land bridge between Siberia and Alaska, now submerged by the higher sea level of the present. This permitted Asian peoples to migrate to the Americas, a migration that in turn brought substantial human effects on the natural environment of the New World. The extinction of many of the large mammals of North America about 10,000 years ago is thought to have been at least in part due to hunting by the new inhabitants, although it might also have resulted in part from climate shifts. The New World was far from a pristine wilderness when Europeans arrived in force midway through the second millennium of the present era; the human population of the Americas was in the tens of millions. The developed societies of the New World (and elsewhere in the ancient world) both affected the environment and were affected by it. This is illustrated by the collapse of classic Maya civilization (in Mexico's Yucatán Peninsula and nearby areas of Central America) in the years from about A.D. 760–910. This apparently resulted both from human activities—including the deforestation of hillsides for wood and cultivation, with consequent soil erosion—and climate variability, a prolonged period of drought that lasted more than a century and devastated water supplies, food production, and the Mayan population.

Environmentalism in the United States

In the United States, the dominant approach to the environment through much of the 19th century involved exploiting natural resources in a largely uncontrolled way. In the latter part of the century, two alternative approaches developed that are important today: preservation of natural areas, and "conservation," or "wise use."

Preservation of Natural Areas

With the exploration of the West, and the work of artists and photographers portraying its natural wonders to easterners, an awareness of the importance of preserving some natural environments developed. One landmark was the first national park, Yellowstone, established in 1872. Five parks were designated during the presidency of Theodore Roosevelt (1901–09), an ardent outdoorsman; his presidency also saw the Antiquities Act of 1906, which permits presidents to designate national monuments. A leading figure in the movement for preservation in this period was John Muir (1838–1914, b. Scotland), who through his travels and scientific work became convinced of the need to set aside natural areas. He founded the Sierra Club in 1892. The National Park Service was established in 1916 to administer 37 parks and monuments. The U.S. National Park System now comprises nearly 400 units covering more than 84 million acres, 3.5 percent of total U.S. area. The system has more than 275 million visitors annually, and employees more than 20,000 permanent and seasonal workers.

Conservation of Natural Resources

A dominant theory of the environment from the later 19th century was "conservation" or "wise use." According to this theory, natural resources such as forests and pasturelands should be under scientific management to ensure their long-term sustainability, primarily for economic reasons. It arose from a concern with the long-term impact of earlier exploitation of natural resources without regard to future consequences. Conservation or scientific management of natural resources for sustained production is therefore different from the desire to preserve natural areas in their original state; and its concept of sustainability differs from the modern view that sustainability is related to the whole Earth system and is for noneconomic as well as economic goals. The conservation movement is associated particularly with Gifford Pinchot (1865–1946), chief forester of the U.S. Forest Service under President Theodore Roosevelt, who was himself a supporter of conservation as well as a proponent of the National Park System.

Environmentalism

What is now called environmentalism came later. Among the pioneers were Aldo Leopold (1887–1948), with his call for a "land ethic" that transcends economics; and Rachel Carson (1907–64), whose *Silent Spring* (1962) brought issues of chemical pollution and its effects on humans and ecosystems to the fore. A significant legal framework for incorporating environmental issues into government decision-making was provided in the National Environmental Policy Act (N.E.P.A., 1969), followed by

the Clean Air (1970) and Clean Water (1972) acts, among others. Similar laws have been enacted in other countries, especially in the developed world. In the 21st century, interest in environmental issues has escalated due to the increasingly visible effects of human behavior on the environment. "Going Green" is now an international movement addressing land and water conservation, air and water pollution, solid waste disposal, global warming, and biodiversity.

Environmental issues such as energy, pollution and global warming are interrelated and affect many areas, people, and interests. Without losing sight of these interrelationships, it is helpful to discuss the principal issues under certain headings: global warming, ozone depletion, biodiversity, water, air pollution, and waste disposal.

Global Warming

Scientists now regard the warming of the Earth's climate system as unequivocal, and most scientists believe that this warming is due in large part to human activities, principally the injection of carbon dioxide into the atmosphere through the burning of fossil fuels that has accompanied industrialization. Warming during the 100 years from 1906 to 2005 totaled 1.3 degrees Fahrenheit (0.74 degrees Celsius). The International Panel on Climate Change reported that the average global tempterature for the years 2090–99 will likely be a 3.2 to 7.2 degree Fahrenheit (1.8 to 4 degrees Celsius) increase from the 1980–99 global average.

Nine of the 10 warmest years in the instrumental record (since 1850) have occurred since 2001—the exception being 1998, the third-warmest year on record. The year 2010 tied with 2005 as the warmest on record. Moreover, analyses of data such as tree rings, ice cores, growth of corals, and historical records indicate that at least in the Northern Hemisphere, the last 50 years were probably the warmest period in at least the past 1,300 years. In the 20th century, sea levels rose 6.7 inches (0.17 meters), and it is believed with high confidence that this exceeded the rate in the previous century. The continuing rise of sea levels has alarmed the scientific community, and planning for adaptive measures is underway in many coastal cities (see "Sea Level Rise").

The Greenhouse Effect

Global warming occurs because of the characteristics of the Earth's energy balance. The Earth receives solar energy at short wavelengths, and reflects energy back into space at longer infrared wavelengths. Some gases in the atmosphere have molecules that absorb energy reflected at these longer wavelengths, and they thus trap heat in the earth's atmosphere. These gases are referred to as greenhouse gases (GHGs). The analogy of the greenhouse is used because, as in the atmosphere, the sun's rays enter a greenhouse, warming the plants inside, while the glass absorbs and re-emits some of the infrared radiation from soils and plants back into the greenhouse, keeping it warm. The naturally occurring types and amounts of greenhouse gases—water vapor, carbon dioxide, and a few trace gases—keep the Earth warm enough to sustain its current ecosphere. If the atmosphere had no greenhouse gases, but only its main constituents of nitrogen and oxygen, the surface temperature of the earth would be about 36 degrees Fahrenheit (20 degrees Celsius) cooler than it is. Global warming has occurred recently because carbon dioxide and other greenhouse gases produced as a result of human—anthropogenic—activities have been increasing. This is sometimes called the enhanced greenhouse effect—i.e., beyond the natural effect. The consequences of the additional warming will be profound and could, under some scenarios, be disastrous.

Greenhouse Gases The most important anthropogenic greenhouse gas is carbon dioxide (CO_2). Other long-lived greenhouse gases are methane (CH_4), nitrous oxide (N_2O), and halocarbons (a group of gases containing fluorine, chlorine, or bromine). Increases in atmospheric carbon dioxide are due primarily to the burning of fossil fuels including oil, coal, and natural gas, as well as to deforestation. Methane has natural sources (such as wetlands); sources from human activities include agriculture, natural gas, and landfills. Nitrous oxide has anthropogenic sources in fertilizer use and high-temperature combustion of fossil fuels in power plants and engines. The CFCs, now being phased out by many countries, have been widely used in air conditioning units and in various industrial processes.

Greenhouse Gas Concentrations The total amount of carbon dioxide in the atmosphere has increased markedly since the beginning of the industrial revolution, from about 280 parts per million (ppm) to nearly 390 ppm in 2010. From 1979 to 2009, the growth rate of CO_2 averaged about 1.66 ppm per year, with the rate increasing over this period. The present concentration of CO_2 is quite high, and according to ice core data it exceeds by significant amounts the natural range over the last 650,000 years (180 to 300 ppm). Because of the total carbon dioxide in the atmosphere, this gas contributes most to warming of the anthropogenic greenhouse gases, although it is not the most effective absorber of infrared radiation on a per unit basis compared with other greenhouse gases. (It is conventional to convert the effects of all the gases into "carbon dioxide equivalents" to obtain a single index of warming substances.) Concentrations of methane (the second biggest contributor to warming) and nitrous oxide have also increased significantly since the beginning of the industrial revolution. Ozone, formed in the lower atmosphere by photochemical reactions on pollutant emissions, also contributes to warming, as do changes in surface reflectivity from changes in land use.

Aerosols and Cooling Effect Aerosols (sulphate and others) are a complicating factor in calculating the potential effects of greenhouse gases. These are liquid or solid particles, anthropogenic or natural, that, although short-lived in the atmosphere, have a direct cooling effect by reflecting incoming solar radiation, and an indirect cooling affect by increasing cloud formation. Aerosols have been an important focus of analysis in recent years and their estimated effects are now included in global climate models.

Human Contributions to Global Warming

For a time there was debate about whether the observed warming of the Earth's surface was due primarily to greenhouse gases generated by human activities or whether the warming was part of natural variation. The most authoritative studies have been those of the Intergovernmental Panel on Climate Change (I.P.C.C.), established by the United Nations Environment Programme and the World Metorological Organization and endorsed by the General Assembly of the United Nations. Over the years many thousands of scientists have contributed to the work of the I.P.C.C. In reports in 1996 and 2001 based on decades of climate science, the I.P.C.C. pointed with increasing certainty to the likelihood of anthropogenic effects on climate. In its most recent report (2007) the I.P.C.C. concluded that the evidence of global warming is now unequivocal and that most of the global average warming since the mid-20th century is very likely to be due to human activities.

Moreover, discernible human influences extend to other aspects of climate, including ocean warming, temperature extremes, and wind patterns. The effects of human-induced changes in climate will last for centuries, although change will be reduced if emissions can be stabilized. With the 2007 I.P.C.C. report, the debate on whether there is significant human influence on climate is essentially over for most scientists and policy makers, and the important issues now relate to more detailed evaluation of changes and impacts, and the development and implementation of policies toward climate change.

Future Climate Scenarios

Climate Models Scientists study the future of the Earth's climate system through complex mathematical models of the oceans, land, ice, and atmosphere called General Circulation Models or Global Climate Models (both abbreviated GCMs). These models, of which many are operated by climate research centers worldwide, have developed rapidly and have become increasingly reliable over the past decade, although uncertainties remain. In the models, the atmosphere and oceans are represented by mathematical equations embodied in three-dimensional grid systems that include millions of cells covering the entire globe. For the atmosphere, cells are typically at least

70 miles (113 kilometers) across at the equator. Simulations of future global climate conditions for periods of a century and more are made by running these models on fast computers. For the next I.P.C.C. report, GCMs (such as the Community Earth System Model of the National Center for Atmospheric Research in Boulder, Colorado) have been further developed to include more complex influences and feedbacks.

Temperature Scenarios On the basis of best-estimate results of GCM simulations and assumptions about alternative greenhouse gas emissions scenarios, the 2007 I.P.C.C. report projects that the Earth's surface is likely to warm by 3.2 to 7.2 degrees Fahrenheit (1.8 to 4 degrees Celsius) by the last decade of the 21st century, as compared with the period 1980–99. According to the U.S. National Oceanic and Atmospheric Administration (N.O.A.A.), the 2010 combined global land and ocean surface temperature was 58.12 degrees Fahrenheit, 1.12 degrees Fahrenheit (0.62 degrees Celsius) above the 20th century average.

Although global warming will cause an increase in average world temperatures, this increase is not expected to be uniform. In general, climatologists expect greater warming over land and at high northern latitudes, and least warming over the Southern Ocean and the North Atlantic. The complexity of change is suggested by the possibility that a warmer Arctic, by breaking down a wind system called the Arctic Vortex and allowing cold air to spill south, can result in more extreme winter storms in North America and Europe. Oceans are particularly sensitive to extreme temperature change—in 2010, coral reefs (among the oceans' richest ecosystems) from Thailand to Texas began reacting to heat stress by bleaching, or losing their color. This is only the second time that this is known to have happened on a global scale, the other being in 1998 when an estimated 16 percent of the world's shallow reefs died. Scientists have also found a link between higher sea-surface temperature and the decline in marine algae, or phytoplankton. Phytoplankton are an essential part of life on earth, being responsible for 50 percent of net photosynthesis.

Sea Level Increasing global temperatures will be accompanied by rising sea levels. The most recent (2007) estimates are that sea levels will rise by between 7 inches and 23 inches (.18 and .59 meters) from 1980 levels by the end

of the 21st century. (These estimates exclude future rapid changes in ice flows, which are challenging to model.) Sea levels will rise for two reasons: warming directly expands the volume of existing seawater and causes melting of land ice, which increases the total amount of water in the oceans. The effective rise in sea level in any region, given global changes, also depends on local factors such as land subsidence. Higher sea levels not only mean the loss of land and salt water intrusion into aquifers, but they also mean that flooding and damages from a storm of given intensity will increase as compared to the present because the flooding will take place from a higher base.

Precipitation, Droughts, and Storm Intensity The warming of the Earth adds energy to the hydrologic cycle, and thus affects amounts and patterns of precipitation as well as storm characteristics. The 2007 I.P.C.C. report projects increases in the amount of precipitation in higher latitudes, with decreases in many subtropical land areas. More frequent droughts will occur in some areas because of changing precipitation patterns and higher temperatures. It is also expected that intense precipitation will become more frequent, and that tropical cyclones (typhoons and hurricanes) will become more intense. Evidence of such effects has already been observed: for example, the I.P.C.C. reports that more intense precipitation events (storms) have increased over most land areas, and that more intense and longer droughts have been observed in many areas. The N.O.A.A. Geophysical Fluid Dynamics Laboratory reported in 2010 that although it's premature to conclude that human activity has already had a detectable impact on Atlantic hurricane activity, if sea surface temperature rises as predicted in the 21st century, it is likely that hurricanes globally will be more intense and have substantially higher rainfall. Some modeling studies suggest that, while the total number of Atlantic hurricanes might decrease, there could be a significant increase in very intense storms with high potential damages.

Large-scale, Low-probability Events There are several potential climatic consequences that would have large-scale negative impacts, but that do not now appear highly probable. Over millennia, the melting of the Greenland ice sheet would raise the sea level by about 23 feet (7 meters), and the melting of the west Antarctic ice sheet would raise the sea level by another 16 feet (5 meters). There is substantial uncertainty about the likely melting rates of these two large ice masses, and continued monitoring and study are required.

Another potential large-scale effect is the slowing or stopping of the deep ocean circulation pattern, the so-called thermohaline ("heat and salt") circulation, in the North Atlantic region. The thermohaline circulation (or "ocean conveyor belt") is a global phenomenon that, among other things, brings heat to the North Atlantic region and keeps it considerably warmer than regions at equal latitudes in the Pacific. Increased freshwater inflow to the northern ocean through more precipitation and more melting of glaciers and ice caps could alter the balance that produces these North Atlantic climate patterns, slowing or shutting down the thermohaline circulation. This is believed to have happened in the geologic past. If a shutdown occurs, extremely rapid cooling in the North Atlantic would result. According to the 2007 I.P.C.C. report, current climate models mostly show a slowing of the thermohaline circulation, but not a complete shutdown, over the course of the 21st century. There are many uncertainties about longer-term changes in this phenomenon.

Impacts of Global Warming

Effects of global warming and related rising sea level, precipitation, and storms have already been observed, and more are expected as the Earth continues to warm. The I.P.C.C. reports (2007) that observational evidence from all continents and most oceans shows that many natural systems are now being affected by climate change. These impacts include changes in some Arctic and Antarctic ecosystems, earlier spring peak discharge in many glacier and snow-fed rivers, warming of lakes and rivers, and shifts in plant and animal species ranges toward the poles and to higher altitudes. The I.P.C.C. organized some 29,000 observational data series from 75 studies showing significant changes in physical and biological systems, and more than 89 percent are consistent with the direction of change expected from global warming. Among the effects documented are earlier spring planting of crops, forest disturbances from fire and pests, and health effects such as heat-related mortality in Europe and allergenic pollen in high and middle latitudes in the Northern Hemisphere.

Future changes with continued warming are expected to be more dramatic. Freshwater annual average river runoff is projected to increase by 10 to 40 percent in high latitudes, and decrease by 10 to 30 percent over some dry regions at mid-latitudes and in the dry tropics (many already water-stressed). Drought-affected areas will increase in extent, and more intense precipitation events are likely to increase in frequency, with heightened risks of flooding. Ecosystems and species will be highly affected by climate change as well as by population increases and changes in land use. It is expected that 20 to 30 percent of species assessed are likely to be at increased risk of extinction if increases in global average temperature exceed 2.7 to 4.5 degrees Fahrenheit (1.5 to 2.5 degrees Celsius). In agriculture, crop productivity is expected to increase slightly in middle to high latitudes for temperature increases of 1.8 to 5.4 degrees Fahrenheit (1 to 3 degrees Celsius), depending on the crop, and then decrease with further increases in temperature in some regions. At lower latitudes, crop productivity will decrease with even small local temperature increases.

Coastal systems and low-lying areas are expected to be at risk. Continued rises in sea level will result in further loss of coastal lands, including highly productive wetlands. The Atlantic and Gulf coasts of North America are one of the more sensitive areas worldwide for wetlands loss. It is estimated that a rise in sea level toward the high end of the 2007 I.P.C.C. estimates—1.5 feet (0.5 meters)—would inundate perhaps one-third of the coastal wetlands in North America. It would also erode recreational beaches, exacerbate coastal flooding, and increase the salinity of aquifers and estuaries. It is likely that the people of an industrialized continental nation such as the United States could sustain the changes in the built environment and the population shifts that will result from a rise in sea level. However, about 40 percent of the world's population, including many extremely poor people, live within 60 miles (100 kilometers) of the sea, mostly along low-lying floodplains and estuaries, presenting difficult challenges for policy makers. In 2008, the new president of the small nation of Maldives in the Indian Ocean suggested the possibility of diverting a portion of tourist revenue into a fund for buying a new homeland; the president stated that even a small rise in sea levels would inundate a significant part of the archipelago.

The impacts of global warming will be felt unevenly throughout the world, and different regions have different capacities to adapt to these changes. One of the hardest-hit areas will be Africa (which has contributed relatively little to warming through emissions), because of multiple stresses of water shortages, decreases in crop productivity, and inundation of low-lying areas. Moreover, Africa has a relatively low capacity for adaptation to these impacts. The extent to which effects of further climate change can be avoided or confronted depends on human responses to climate change.

Responding to Climate Change

There are two broad approaches to policy with respect to climate change: mitigation and adaptation. Mitigation involves measures, such as a reduction in the use of fossil fuels, that will reduce the contribution of human activities to climate change. Adaptation involves measures, such as the construction of flood barriers, that will prevent some of the consequences of climate change. There are various strategies actually and potentially available for both mitigation and adaptation, each with its estimated cost and effectiveness.

Mitigation Mitigation strategies include legal and administrative policies and technological changes. An example of the former is the imposition of increased taxes on fuel to increase its price and thereby reduce consumption. Another example is the "cap-and-trade" system, in which emissions limits are placed on an industry or a geographical area, with rights to emissions bought and sold in a market so as to minimize the total cost of meeting the emissions cap. Such a cap-and-trade system for power plant emissions of CO_2 is the goal of the Regional Greenhouse Gas Initiative (R.G.G.I.), a successful cooperative effort by 10 Northeast and Mid-Atlantic states. (In 2011, New Jersey made a controversial decision to leave R.G.G.I., reducing the program to 9 states.) Together the R.G.G.I. states have committed to reducing their power sector CO_2 emissions 10 percent by 2018.

Many technological approaches to mitigation are also possible and are being studied, including the widespread use of more efficient versions of existing technologies, such as lower fuel consumption in internal combustion engines. Newer technologies such as fuel cells are under intensive development, and some older technologies such as the use of wind power have been refined and are being implemented. In northern Europe there are increasing numbers of high-tech wind turbines (the modern windmill), and countries such as Denmark now generate a substantial fraction of their electricity through wind power. In 2010, the first offshore wind farm lease in the United States won Federal approval; Cape Wind Associates will install 130 wind turbines to build a wind farm in

Nantucket Sound off the coast of Massachusetts. There are also attempts to increase the capacity to absorb carbon through reforestation of land areas, providing a carbon sink (a carbon reservoir in which the amount of carbon is increasing). The main potential carbon sinks are the oceans and plants and other organisms that use photosynthesis to remove carbon from the atmosphere by incorporating it into biomass.

The challenging problem for mitigation is whether it is possible for emissions to not only be reduced, but reduced enough to ensure that the low end of future climate change scenarios is attained. The international treaty aimed at stabilizing emissions is the 1992 United Nations Framework Convention on Climate Change. Article 2 of this convention declares its objective to be the stabilization of greenhouse gas concentrations at a level that avoids "dangerous anthropogenic interference" with climate. In December 1997 at a conference in Kyoto, Japan, representatives of more than 150 countries reached an agreement, the Kyoto Protocol, to reduce greenhouse gases an average of 5 percent worldwide (from 1990 levels) between 2008 and 2012. As of 2011 the Protocol had 192 signatories. The protocol divides countries into Annex I, developed countries, and Annex II, developing countries. Under the agreement, the 37 countries and the European Community that make up Annex I countries—responsible for most of the emissions leading to current warming—are required to reduce their emission of greenhouse gases by an average of 5 percent worldwide (from 1990 levels) over the five-year period 2008 to 2012. Annex II countries, which have relatively low per-capita emissions, are not required to meet targets under the protocol, although several are now substantial sources of GHGs. In 2011, though China was the world's largest emitter of greenhouse gases (having acknowledged passing the U.S. as such in late 2010), as a developing nation it was not required to reduce its emissions. In 2004, however, Beijing announced plans to generate 10 percent of the country's power from renewable resources by 2010. In 2009, the Chinese National Development and Reform Commission announced that renewable energy was expected to account for 15 percent of the nation's energy consumption by 2020.

The Kyoto Protocol was ratified by the required 55 countries, and by countries representing 55 percent of 1990 Annex I emissions, in 2004, and went into force in 2005. Annex I countries can meet their targets either through action within the country or by purchasing emissions reductions elsewhere. These include purchases from financial exchanges, from other Annex I countries, and, most notably, by financing projects that reduce emissions in non-Annex I countries. Annex I countries can purchase only reductions approved by the Clean Development Mechanism as Certified Emissions Reductions.

The Kyoto Protocol has provided an important framework for stabilizing GHG emissions, but overall progress has been slow, and a huge amount remains to be done. In the United States, which accounts for nearly a quarter of global emissions, the Kyoto target is a 7 percent reduction, but the United States has not ratified the protocol and has done little at the national level to stabilize emissions, although states, cities, and regions have been active in developing emissions stabilization initiatives. One notable initiative is the U.S. Mayors Climate Change Agreement (2005), which as of 2009 has more than 900 hundred signatories, who strive to have their cities reduce GHG emissions by amounts equal to or better than the targets in the Kyoto Protocol. International efforts to address climate change have become more coordinated than ever before, although much remains to be done. World leaders met in Copenhagen in December 2009 in an effort to reach a new agreement, which called on developed nations to take more effective action immediately; the U.S. agreed to reduce emissions by 14–17 percent below 2005 levels by 2020. As of 2010, 109 countries had signed the accord; however, the agreement has many critics because of its failure to enforce these reductions.

Adaptation   Adaptation measures include a wide variety of changes in management and infrastructure that can be utilized to avoid the worst effects of some ele-

ments of global warming. For example, to deal with the need for animals and plants to migrate to different latitudes, land corridors can be protected to provide avenues for transitional movements. To protect against the health effects of heat, more air conditioning will be required. Infrastructure on or near the sea, such the dikes of the Netherlands, can be strengthened and raised, or, like the many wastewater treatment plants in coastal areas of the United States, protected with new flood walls.

To deal with changing precipitation patterns and intensities, water supply systems can be linked and expanded. However, all these adaptive measures require resources, both financial and institutional, which will not always be available in many areas. Moreover, some adaptations themselves have adverse environmental consequences: seawalls and other coastal protection measures can prevent wetlands affected by a rising sea level from migrating landward. In some cases, there are few adaptive measures available to deal with global warming. Low-lying areas of Bangladesh are often cited in this regard: it would be prohibitively expensive to protect these, even if it were physically possible, and the prospect of moving populations at risk is daunting. For small island nations at risk, at least the movement of populations to other areas would be feasible. Adaptive measures are planned or under consideration primarily in wealthy and highly organized countries, such as the Netherlands, Great Britain, and the United States; much more remains to be done worldwide. Because of the difficulty of controlling GHG emissions in the near future, there will continue to be impacts of climate changes over many decades that must be dealt with by adaptation measures.

The Ozone Layer

The problem of stratospheric ozone depletion was one of the first truly global environmental problems to be recognized by scientists, and it is one that has been addressed by the international community. Ozone is a pollutant in the lower atmosphere, but the problem of depletion refers to the higher protective layer of ozone in the stratosphere. Stratospheric ozone absorbs harmful ultraviolet radiation from the Sun. A significant reduction of the ozone layer would lead to increases in the incidence of skin cancer in humans and a variety of potentially serious negative

effects on plants, marine plankton, and animals. Ozone depletion is related to global warming in that the chlorofluorocarbons (CFCs) and related substances that are its principal cause are greenhouse gases, but the science of the depletion of the ozone layer makes it a separate problem.

Dynamic Balance of the Ozone Layer

Complex natural forces are continually at work creating and destroying ozone in the stratosphere. The formation of ozone begins with the breaking apart of an oxygen molecule (O_2) by ultraviolet radiation from the Sun, producing two oxygen atoms. Each of these combines with an oxygen molecule to produce an ozone molecule (O_3). The production of ozone in the stratosphere is balanced by destructive chemical reactions. Ozone reacts with a wide variety of natural and human-made substances in the stratosphere. In each reaction, an ozone molecule is lost and other chemical compounds are produced. Prior to the introduction of human-made chemicals into the stratosphere, ozone production and destruction remained in balance, influenced by sunlight intensity, location in the atmosphere, temperature, and other factors.

Destruction of the Ozone Layer

In 1974, scientists first recognized that a group of chemicals known as long-lived halogen compounds, such as the CFCs, were destroying the natural stratospheric ozone balance by adding chlorine and bromine to the stratosphere. Chemically inert, nontoxic, and easily liquefied, CFCs were developed in the 1930's as an ammonia substitute for use in refrigeration, and their use became widespread in air conditioning, packaging, insulation, solvents for cleaning electronic circuit boards, and aerosol propellants.

It is the absence of chemical reactivity that makes CFCs so dangerous to the ozone layer. Unlike less inert compounds, CFCs and related gases are not destroyed or removed in the lower atmosphere by rain, oxidation, or sunlight; their atmospheric chemical lifetimes have been estimated to be up to 100 years. From the lower atmosphere they drift into the upper atmosphere, where they react with and destroy ozone molecules. A single chlorine or bromine atom can destroy hundreds of ozone molecules in a series of chemical reactions before it reacts with another gas, breaking the cycle. Because of this, a small amount of chlorine or bromine can have a large impact on the ozone layer.

The destruction of ozone in the stratosphere has been most evident in the Antarctic, where ice crystals in the air speed up chemical reactions. This produces the ozone hole, a region of extremely low levels of atmospheric ozone, over the South Polar region during the Antarctic winter. A system of cold winds called the Antarctic vortex amplifies this effect. The National Aeronautics and Space Administration (NASA) reported that the average size of the ozone hole over the period of September 21–30, 2006, was the largest on record, at 10.6 million square miles (27.5 million square kilometers). The second-largest hole on record occurred in 2008, covering roughly some 10.4

million square miles (27 million square kilometers), an area larger than North America.

Protecting the Ozone Layer

Owing in part to some fine diplomacy by the United States and other countries, the international community moved to deal with the threat to the ozone layer relatively quickly. Even before the science was altogether certain, the Vienna Convention on Protection of the Ozone Layer (1985) cited this as a source of danger to the Earth system, and in 1987 the Montreal Protocol on Substances That Deplete the Ozone Layer was signed. This landmark treaty provided for binding commitments by developed countries to reduce the production and use of ozone-depleting substances; it has been strengthened by a series of amendments. As a result the production of CFCs has completely stopped in developed countries. Some 20 years after its inception, the Montreal Protocol had phased out nearly 97 percent of 100 ozone-depleting chemicals. As these have been phased out, they have been replaced in some uses by related halocarbons. Hydrofluorocarbons (HFCs) do not contain chlorine or bromine, but are also greenhouse gases and actually have thousands of times the global warming potential of carbon dioxide. They themselves replaced even more dangerous ozone-depleting chemicals known as HCFCs—targeted for phase-out by 2040. In 2011 the U.S. together with Canada and Mexico advanced a proposal to phase down HFC consumption and production under the Montreal Protocol.

According to a 2006 report from N.O.A.A., as the overall decline in these gases continues—in response to the provisions of the Montreal Protocol—global stratospheric ozone is expected to recover, approaching or exceeding pre-1980 values. This is perhaps the most remarkable and successful human attempt to date to deal with assaults on the global environment. Although problems remain and some production of CFCs and other ozone-destroying gases continues in developing nations, progress has been good, and computer models suggest that recovery of the ozone layer will be attained around 2060–2075, although some of the gases will linger beyond that date, a reminder of the care with which substances that alter the environment should be treated. September 16, the day in 1987 on which the Montreal Protocol was signed, is now celebrated by the United Nations Environment Program as Ozone Day.

Biodiversity

Biodiversity is the variety of living things and their interactions, and it is often characterized on three levels: species, genetic, and ecosystem biodiversity. All of these interact. The number of known species—that is, those characterized by scientific analysis and description, is more than 1.7 million, ranging from nearly 1 million species of insects (mostly beetles) to about 14,000 species of amphibians and reptiles and 5,400 mammalian species. This number is thought to be only a fraction of the species living on earth; the total number is believed to be at least 10 million and possibly many more.

Species Extinction and Biodiversity

The question of biodiversity has come to the fore in recent decades because of the alarming loss of species and ecosystems that has come about through population growth, economic development, pollution, and global warming. Some species have become extinct through hunting (the passenger pigeon in the United States in the 19th century, and many other examples), but more have become extinct or are threatened through the destruction of habitat. Today's extinction rate is estimated to be many times the natural rate, and some scientists believe we are in the midst of a mass extinction. Global warming is already having an effect on the geographic distribution of species, putting further stress on species adaptation and survival. Efforts are now being made to estimate the economic value of biodiversity as a guide to public policy, but there are many who believe that the preservation of biodiversity has an ethical or moral value regardless of economic value. At the same time, in developing countries those people who are impinging on habitats are themselves often desperately poor, and it is difficult to find ways to meet their needs without pressure on fragile ecosystems.

A further issue has to do with exotic species (or invasive species)—species that are imported into ecosystems by accident or design and take over ecological niches from native species. Species have always migrated, but in modern times, with transport easier than it has ever been, exotic or invasive species have been introduced deliberately or by accident in many regions, often with a serious impact on native species and ecosystems. There are some extreme cases, such as the brown tree snakes introduced in Guam, which have driven most of the forest-dwelling native birds to extinction. In the United States, the zebra mussel has caused hundreds of millions of dollars of damage to water and power facilities in the Great Lakes and elsewhere, and it is estimated that invasive plants cover about 100 million acres (40 million hectares) in the United States, with the amount growing each year. Exotic species, once established, are difficult to eradicate, and for this reason laws are often introduced to prohibit the importation of such species. The most recent of these laws in the United States was the Asian Carp Prevention and Control Act, signed into law by President Barack Obama in 2010. According to a study of 57 countries published in 2010 by the Global Invasive Species Program, the number of documented invasive alien species is significantly underestimated. Pressure caused by invasive species is driving declines in native species diversity by altering ecosystem processes and changing community structures, and some invasive species directly harm native species classified as threatened.

Endangered Species Worldwide

In 2010, the International Union for Conservation of Nature (I.U.C.N.) issued its updated list of threatened species of animals and plants worldwide, the "Red List" (www.iucnredlist.org). Species judged as "critically endangered," (with population declines of at least 80 percent), "endangered," or "vulnerable," are regarded as threatened with extinction. The Red List contained 9,618 species of animals and 12,914 species of plants in 2010. These include 21 percent (more than one in five) of mammalian species described and 12.4 percent (one in eight) of bird species. The list includes 8,724 threatened plants, but because only about 4 percent of plant species have been evaluated for threat, the number actually endangered is believed to be much larger. Although the endangered species include plants and animals of every type, the growing list of endangered mammals (for example, the great panda, the Siberian tiger, and orangutans), has caught the attention of the general public. Overall 1,131 mammalian species, large and small, were considered threatened in 2010.

Among the most gravely affected animals are primates, man's closest relatives, which are threatened by deforestation, commercial hunting for bush meat, and the illegal animal trade; about one in four primate species and subspecies are at risk of extinction. Most threatened species are in the tropical areas of continents (South and Central America, sub-Saharan Africa, and South and Southeast

Asia), especially on mountains and islands. In 2008, the I.U.C.N. found that Indonesia had by far the most threatened species of mammals, 183; Indonesia is also the most diverse country for mammals (670 species). Mexico is the country in the Americas with the most threatened mammal species, 99. Half the top 20 countries for number of threatened mammals are in Asia. Habitat loss is the greatest global threat to threatened species, affecting over 2,000 mammal species. In 2009, the I.U.C.N. reported that a third of the world's open-ocean sharks are threatened—more than 100 million sharks are killed globally each year due to commercial and recreational fishing. From 2006 to 2010 the number of critically endangered fish increased from 253 to 317, in significant part because of long-line fisheries.

Preservation of Species

There are international efforts to stem the tide of extinctions. Among the most important is the Convention on International Trade in Endangered Species of Wild Fauna and Flora (CITES), which has been in force since 1975. It lists species for which international trade in live organisms, meat, lumber, or other parts of species is banned or restricted. As of 2011, 175 countries were Parties to CITES, which means that the Convention had entered into force in those countries. Although smugglers are thought to violate CITES restrictions regularly in what is believed to be a multibillion-dollar annual illegal trade, CITES continues to be one of the main forces in species preservation.

Supplementing bans on international trade in endangered species is the Convention on Biodiversity. Agreed to at the 1992 Earth Summit in Rio de Janeiro, this treaty commits nations to protect and preserve species and habitats within their own borders. There are now 193 parties to the treaty; the United States has signed but not ratified the convention. The Cartagena Protocol on Biosafety is a supplement to the Convention on Biodiversity that governs the movements of living organisms resulting from modern biotechnology from one country to another. This agreement was adopted in 2000 and entered into force in 2003. As of 2011, 161 countries were parties to the Protocol, but the U.S. was not among them.

In 2010, after years of discussion, most United Nation member states agreed to set significant new goals to reverse the extinction of plant and animal species. Negotiated in Nagoya, Japan, the agreement, known as the Nagoya Protocol, another supplement to the Convention on Biodiversity, sets a goal of cutting the current extinction rate by half or more by 2020. New targets include increasing the amount of protected land to 17 percent from 12.5 percent. As an important part of the protocol, it was agreed that rich and poor nations would share profits from pharmaceutical or other products derived from genetic material.

Other international treaties and organizations pertain to particular groups and species and habitat preservation. The International Whaling Commission (I.W.C.) was set up under the International Convention for the Regulation of Whaling, signed in Washington, D.C. on December 2, 1946. The commission has had some success in preserving whale species and stocks, notably with its near total ban on commercial whaling since the late 1980's. (The ban has exemptions for scientific whaling and for aboriginal hunting, which takes place in several countries including the United States.) However, the I.W.C. also has weaknesses, including exemptions and the ability of nations to opt out of decisions. Norway and Japan have each killed hundreds of whales annually since the early 1990's. In 2010, Norway set a quota of 1,286 whales; Japan's quota for 2010 was 1,280. Japan claims that its whaling is for research, exploiting a loophole in the longstanding international moratorium, whereas Norway exempted itself from the ban and regards its whaling as explicitly commercial. Quotas are not always met: of the Norwegian quota for 2009 (885), the actual number taken was 484 and the season was closed early for lack of demand.

Measures to preserve species worldwide include setting aside reserves, both terrestrial and marine; the development of ecotourism to provide revenues from species and habitat preservation; programs to provide local people with income opportunities consistent with species and habitat preservation; genetic banks to preserve wild strains of grains and other species; captive breeding and reintroduction into the wild of species; the eradication of exotic species; and the development of programs to survey wild species for valuable medical uses. However, species extinctions and habitat destruction continue at a rapid rate, and substantial challenges lie ahead if the world's biodiversity is to be protected.

Endangered Species in the United States

The United States is home to more than 200,000 species of plants and animals, of which many are thriving but many are under threat. The U.S. Fish and Wildlife service classifies species as threatened or endangered in accordance with the Endangered Species Act of 1973 (E.S.A.). However, the list of endangered species maintained by the

Department of the Interior goes back to the original Endangered Species Act of 1966. The first list, in March 1967, included 78 species.

The E.S.A. list (as of April 2011) contained 580 endangered and threatened animals and nearly 800 plants. Species listed are legally protected, and in some cases habitat critical to the species' survival can be designated and protected as well. The ultimate aim of the act is to provide for the recovery (and then delisting) of species. The E.S.A. is also the vehicle by which the United States participates in CITES. The animals and plants listed under the E.S.A. (www.ecos.fws.gov) range from the large and well-known, such as the whooping crane (Grus americana), the bighorn sheep (Ovis Canadensis) and the Florida panther (Felis concolor coryi), to small and little-known plants and animals that are nonetheless important for the maintenance of the environment. Since the listing was started in 1967, several listed species have become extinct, including the Tecopa pupfish (Cyprinodon nevadensis calidae, 1982), the blue pike (Stizostedion vitreum glaucum, 1983), the Santa Barbara song sparrow (Melospiza melodia graminea, 1983), Sampson's pearly mussel (Epioblasma = Dysnomia sampsoni, 1984), and the dusky seaside sparrow (Ammodramus = Ammospiza maritimus nigrescens, 1990).

There have also been some success stories: several species listed as either threatened or endangered have recovered sufficiently to be removed from the list, including the brown pelican (Pelecanus occidentalis, 1985), the American alligator (Alligator mississippiensis, 1987), the American peregrine falcon (Falco peregrinus anatum, 1999), and the Yellowstone grizzly bear (Ursus arctos horribilis, 2007). Perhaps the most visible success has been the recovery of bald eagle populations, which had been severely threatened by the effects of the pesticide DDT in the food chain (DDT is now banned in the United States). Other causes included loss of habitat and lead shot in waterfowl carcasses on which eagles and other birds of prey feed (the use of lead shot has been phased out in the United States). The bald eagle was delisted in 2007, due to recovery in the conterminous states, but was relisted as threatened in 2008 in the Sonoran Desert region of Arizona and New Mexico. There are hundreds of refuges in the U.S. where a bald eagle population is known to occur, and even if it is again removed from the endangered list, it will remain protected under various other statutes.

Habitats

Broadly, habitats include forests, grasslands, deserts, tundra, wetlands, and water, such as the oceans; there are many specific types of habitats within each of these categories: for example, the coral reefs of the oceans. Habitat preservation is important for many reasons, including species preservation, the preservation of economically important plants and animals, and the maintenance of habitats important in the global hydrologic and carbon cycles. Two particularly significant types of habitats are rain forests and wetlands.

Rain Forests Rain forests are among the habitats under the most pressure from humans. They are defined as forests that grow in regions that receive large amounts of rain, in turn often defined as more than 60–80 inches (1.5–2.0 meters) of rain each year. It is estimated that rain forests formerly covered about 14 percent of the Earth's land surface, but that they now cover only about 6 percent. Some rain forests are in temperate areas, such as western edges of North and South America (including southern Chile and the northwestern coast of North America), but the majority are found in the tropics. They are found in Central and South America (including the vast Amazon rain forest), equatorial Africa, Southeast Asia, and northeastern Australia. Tropical rain forests are located in areas with mean monthly temperatures of from 68 to 82 degrees Fahrenheit (20 to 28 degrees Celsius), with rains spread evenly throughout the year.

In rain forests, tall trees form a dense canopy high above the forest floor, with a few very tall ("emergent") trees reaching above the general canopy. Vines climb up the trees in search of sunlight. The understory, which receives relatively little light, contains vines, smaller trees, ferns, and palms. The floor of a rain forest is in deep shade, covered with wet leaves and plant and animal litter, with only a few shrubs and grasses. The rich plant life of rain forests supports food chains that include many of the world's most spectacular animals: harpy eagles, monkeys, tigers, slow-moving sloths, and columns of army ants, among many others. Tropical rain forests are lush habitats, filled with a greater variety of organisms than any other type of habitat. They may hold at least half of the world's species. According to one study, a patch of rain forest covering 4 square miles (10.4 square kilometers) might contain 750 species of trees, 125 species of mammals, 400 species of birds, 100 species of reptiles, and 60 species of amphibians. Although the diversity of plant life in tropical rain forests is rich, the soil generally is not. The lush plants take up so much of the nutrients in rain forests that little is left for the soil below.

Destruction of rain forests The destruction of rain forests comes about from many causes. Individuals often cut down the trees for firewood and to clear land on which to raise crops (including for biofuels), build ranches, and raise cattle. Large commercial operations deforest vast areas for lumber, paper, and other products. Development projects such as roads, hydroelectric dams, and mines also destroy large areas. In 2010, the Food and Agriculture Organization (F.A.O.) of the United Nations estimated that world deforestation, mainly the conversion of tropical forests to agricultural land, has decreased over the past ten years but continues at an alarmingly high rate in many countries. The F.A.O. said that globally, around 32 million acres (13 million hectares) of forests were converted to other uses or lost through natural causes each year between 2000 and 2010 as compared to around 39.5 million acres (16 million hectares) per year during the 1990's. In some countries most of the rain forests have been destroyed already, and forests in other countries are under heavy stress.

The formulation and implementation of policies to preserve rain forests is difficult because of the multiple causes of their destruction. Efforts include the purchase of parcels for preservation, international pressure on governments to curtail road building and economic development in forest areas, projects to encourage sustainable harvesting, and ecotourism. Despite widespread concern, current policies to protect rain forests are having only modest success, and the preservation of these biodiversity reservoirs remains a substantial challenge for the world's nations.

Wetlands Wetlands are areas where saturation with water is the dominant factor determining the nature of soil and the ecosystems in the soil and on its surface. Wetlands are found from the northern tundra to the tropics, and on every continent except Antarctica. They differ widely because of differences in soils, topography, climate, hydrology, water chemistry, vegetation, and other factors. The principal types of wetlands include marshes (tidal and non-tidal), swamps (forested and shrub), bogs, and fens.

Wetlands are among the most productive ecosystems of the world, comparable to rain forests and coral reefs. They provide enormous volumes of food that a great variety of living things use for part or all of their life cycle. The small organisms that feed on the dead leaves and stems that break down in the water are at the base of the food chain for many other species. Wetlands also play an integral part in the ecology of watersheds. They provide a natural means of flood control, absorbing water from nearby rivers and lakes during periods of high runoff to buffer the impact of storms and reduce shoreline erosion, and they have the capacity to filter out some pollutants, helping to maintain water quality. Moreover, their microbes, plants, and animals are part of global cycles for water, nitrogen, and sulfur, and they store carbon in their plant communities.

In the United States at the end of the 20th century there were about 105.5 million acres (42.7 million hectares) of wetlands in the lower 48 states, with a larger total in Alaska—170 million to 200 million acres (69 million to 81 million hectares). The states with the largest wetlands acreage after Alaska are Florida, Louisiana, Minnesota, and Texas. There have been heavy pressures on wetlands from housing, industrial, and agricultural development and pollution, but losses have decreased from the high rates of the 1950's to 1970's; between 1986 and 1997 about 58,500 acres (23,700 hectares) of wetlands were lost each year in the lower 48 states. Losses have decreased because of increased regulation, public interest in wetlands preservation, and the reduction of some incentives for drainage. According to the N.O.A.A., however, between 1998 and 2004 an estimated 361,000 acres of coastal wetlands of the eastern U.S. were lost. Wetlands restoration efforts have increased, but the extent to which such efforts produce wetlands equal in quality to those that continue to be lost is an important issue. According to the U.S. Fish and Wildlife Service, in fiscal year 2009 602,595 acres of wetland in North America were restored.

Wetlands, like rain forests, are under stress worldwide. Internationally, the Convention on Wetlands (RAMSAR), signed in Ramsar, Iran, in 1971, is an intergovernmental treaty that provides the framework for national action and international cooperation for the conservation and sustainable use of wetlands and their resources. There are 1,929 wetland sites (2011), totaling 465 million acres (188 million hectares), designated for inclusion in the RAMSAR List of Wetlands of International Importance.

Water

Freshwater is essential to human, plant, and animal life on Earth. The freshwater environment is affected by the hydrologic cycle, which is driven by solar energy. Water precipitates as rain or snow to the Earth's surface, moves into soil and surface waters, is used by plants and animals, and evaporates again to the atmosphere. About 26,300 cubic miles (110,000 cubic kilometers) of freshwater precipitates on all the continents combined each year, much of which evaporates or is absorbed by plants. About 10,300 cubic miles (43,000 cubic kilometers) flows through the world's rivers. Of this renewable freshwater, about 2,200 cubic miles (9,000 cubic kilometers) is readily available for human use. This water, in lakes, rivers, reservoirs and accessible aquifers, represents only about one-hundredth of one percent of the water on Earth. About 97.5 percent of the Earth's water is salt water in the oceans, and most of the 2.5 percent freshwater is locked in glaciers and ice caps. Most of the rest of the freshwater is found in deep underground aquifers that are inaccessible for human use, or as soil moisture. Available freshwater is thus a limited resource, subject to overuse, pollution, and potential climate change. In the first decade of the 21st century the scarcity of worldwide became a serious policy issue. Some countries with large populations, such as China, Egypt, and Pakistan, face critical water issues in the 21st century.

Water Use   The largest use of water worldwide by volume is for irrigation: it is estimated that approximately 70 percent of world freshwater withdrawals are for agriculture, 20 percent for industry, and 10 percent for direct human use. These percentages vary greatly by country and region depending on the degree of industrialization. (In 2000, for example, the United States used 41 percent of its freshwater withdrawals for agriculture, 46 percent for industry, and 13 percent for personal use; the 2000 figures for Somalia were less than 1 percent for both industry and personal use.) Some water is withdrawn, used, and returned to a stream many times. In addition, water is also used in-stream to generate hydroelectric energy, for navigation, and for recreational uses and ecosystem preservation. Many river systems have dams, diversions, or canals, and dams are estimated to impound about 14 percent of world freshwater runoff.

Water Scarcity   When large differences in the pattern of regional availability and use, pollution, the expense of developing additional supplies, and uses for ecosystem preservation are considered, there is a scarcity for human use in many freshwater systems. In many parts of the world, problems of water quantity and quality have arisen through poor management and lack of cooperation. For example, in the Rio Grande valley in the United States and Mexico, water scarcity has worsened because of uncontrolled development and lack of foresight on both sides of the river. Lake Mead, a reservoir filled 1937 that supplies roughly 30 million users in the American West, had dropped to 40 percent capacity in 2010. One 2008 study published by the Scripps Institute of Oceanography estimated that if current consumption patterns aren't altered, the reservoir has a 50 percent chance of running dry by 2021—something that would be devastating to cities such as Las Vegas, which draws about 90 percent of its supplies from Lake Mead. Water availability per capita is sometimes used to give a rough measure of water scarcity: an area is defined as water-stressed if there is less than 2,200 cubic yards (1,700 cubic meters) per capita per year or highly stressed if there is less than 1,300 cubic yards (1,000 cubic meters) per capita per year. According to Population Action International estimates, more than 2.77–3.25 billion people will live in water-scarce or water-stressed regions by 2025. However, this rough measure leaves out economic, technological, and social factors, which have important affects on the availability of water.

Water Quality   Because of stringent laws (such as the U.S. Clean Water Act of 1972 and its amendments), water quality in the United States, Europe, and some other developed areas has improved in recent decades. However, in many developing nations, water of already poor quality has continued to deteriorate. Barely controlled sources of pollution heavily contaminate freshwater resources. For example, the World Bank found that many rivers in China are so polluted that they are unsuitable for direct human contact. Although the largest uses of water by volume are in agriculture and industry, the uses most intimately involved in the daily life and health of populations are water for drinking, household uses, and sanitary sewage systems. The World Health Organization estimated that as of 2010, almost 1 billion people (15 percent of total population), lacked access to safe drinking water, and an estimated 2.6 billion people (almost 40 percent of the population of the developing world) lacked access to sanitation facilities. The World Bank and other aid agencies have substantial programs to attack problems of water supply and sanitation, but catching up with even basic needs worldwide will take decades.

Water Resources Management Population growth, economic growth, and increased urbanization will continue to increase demands on and pollution of water supplies. These demands will impose needs for enormous infrastructure investments in developing countries for safe water and sewage, and the maintenance and improvement of water systems and related ecosystems. Most experts expect that, at least for the near future, stresses on world freshwater supplies will increase. There are possibilities for the application of more efficient management techniques. On a global scale, large multinational firms, led by French and British companies, have begun to provide management services on a contract basis to municipal and private water utilities.. These types of efforts have introduced some efficiencies, especially in developed countries, but the situation has been more controversial in some developing areas. Issues of fairness to all users, the right to at least a minimum of clean water, and control over local resources have come into conflict with the financial imperatives of market-based system management by multinationals. In 2000 in Bolivia, for example, violent local protests caused the abrogation of a contract given to a multinational company to run the Cochabamba water system. In 2010, an investor-based nonprofit based in San Francisco, the Carbon Disclosure Project, began asking 302 global companies to issue detailed reports on their water use, on the grounds that enterprise water use (like carbon emissions) is an issue of concern to investors.

Water in the United States

In the United States, principal concerns about water include pollution, which affects water bodies throughout the nation; the allocation of scarce supplies in dry Western areas; increased efficiency in water use and management; the preservation of rivers for natural beauty and ecosystem values; and the removal of unneeded dams. All these problems are often highly contentious and costly, but they are generally manageable; most people are able to enjoy reasonable quantities of water of good quality.

Pollution Control Freshwater use depends on quality as well as quantity. The greater the population, industrial activity, and agriculture in a region, the worse is the pollution of freshwater systems. Scientists refer to water pollution as coming from point sources, such as a factory pipe or a sewage outlet; and from nonpoint sources, such as farmland. Among the main sources of water pollution are human and animal wastes, pesticides and fertilizers from farms, and industrial discharges of chemicals. Organic pollutants impose a biochemical oxygen demand (BOD) on a stream or lake, thus reducing the amount of oxygen available for natural ecosystems. Both surface waters (lakes and rivers) and underground waters are subject to pollution.

Clean Water Act Until 1972, the United States had a series of laws that were relatively ineffective in dealing with water pollution. The Federal Water Pollution Control Act Amendments of 1972, with its amendments of 1977, is commonly known as the Clean Water Act, and was the first strong and enforceable water pollution control act in the United States. The crucial approach in the 1972 act, which set high standards for eventual cleanup of the nation's waters, was the requirement for permits for discharges, granted only when certain prescribed levels of technology for effluent control were met. Both "conventional" pollutants and "toxic" pollutants, on which more stringent requirements are placed, are controlled. The emphasis in the current water pollution control system has been primarily on controlling effluents, although ambient standards for water quality are defined. The 1972 act also increased the federal share of the costs of municipal water treatment plants, and increased the available funding; this has greatly reduced the problem of raw sewage being dumped into the nation's waters. The control of nonpoint sources has been mainly left as a state responsibility with some federal funding, and nonpoint sources have been less effectively controlled than point sources. The Clean Water Act continues to be a driving legislative force. For example, in 2010, the E.P.A. and the U.S. Department of Justice announced a comprehensive Clean Water Act settlement with the Northeast Ohio Regional Sewer District to address the flow of untreated sewage into Cleveland area waterways and Lake Erie. The settlement will result in improved water quality and human health.

In recent years, the E.P.A. has focused on its Total Maximum Daily Load (T.D.M.L.) program, which operates under Clean Water Act regulations from 1985 and 1992. The T.D.M.L.'s are defined as the allowable loads of a pollutant from all sources that will ensure, with a margin of safety, that waters meet state water quality standards. The T.D.M.L.'s must be developed for all waters (currently more than 40 percent of assessed waters) that do not meet state standards even after point sources have installed minimum levels of pollution control technology. The E.P.A. is responsible for reviewing and approving state T.D.M.L. programs.

Safe Drinking Water Act   In addition to the Clean Water Act, the Safe Drinking Water Act of 1974 (S.D.W.A.) set stringent standards for public water systems, of which there are approximately 155,000, large and small, in the United States. Most of these are Community Water Systems (C.W.S.), defined as systems that serve a population year-round. Twenty-two percent of these systems, ranging from medium to large, serve 70 percent of the population receiving water from C.W.S. The result of this legislation and the accompanying regulations has been a substantial increase in the quality of the public water supply in the United States. The S.D.W.A. originally focused on treatment to provide safe drinking water; 1996 amendments enhanced the law by recognizing source water protection, operator training, funding for water system improvements, and public information as important components of safe drinking water. In 2010 the E.P.A. announced a Drinking Water Strategy, aimed at finding ways to strengthen public health protection from contaminants in drinking water. This ongoing program is designed to streamline decision-making, expand protection under existing laws, and promote cost-effective new technologies to meet the needs of rural, urban and other water-stressed communities.

Coastal Pollution Ratings   Despite the progress, however, much remains to be done. For example, in 2008 the E.P.A. in conjunction with other federal resource agencies issued the results of a survey of coastal waters in the United States. The overall condition of these waters was rated as fair; the waters of South Central Alaska and Hawaii were rated good; the Southeast Coast and West Coast regions, fair; the Northeast Coast, Gulf Coast, and Great Lakes regions, fair to poor; and Puerto Rico, poor.

The greatest improvement from earlier surveys was in water quality, with smaller improvements in sediment quality and benthic (bottom) conditions. Fifty-seven percent of U.S. coastal waters rated good for water quality; 34 percent fair; and 6 percent poor (3 percent had data missing). Most of the pollution of coastal waters is attributed by experts to polluted runoff from agriculture and urban sources such as street runoff, storm drains, and sewer overflows.

Wild and Scenic Rivers   In addition to pollution control measures, the United States in 1968 created the National Wild and Scenic Rivers system. This system emphasizes the visual, environmental, and cultural benefits of free-flowing rivers, and only uses compatible with the purposes of the act are permitted. In 2008, the 40th anniversary of the Act, the National System protected more than 11,000 miles of 166 rivers—less than one percent of the nation's river miles. A large percentage of designated river miles are in Alaska and the Northwest, but the system has components nationwide. By comparison, in 2008, more than 75,000 large dams had modified more than 600,000 miles, about 17 percent of American river miles. The removal of dams that have outlived their usefulness helps to restore freely flowing streams, rejuvenate ecosystem elements such as fish runs, and improve the visual attractiveness of rivers.

Water Allocation   Water allocation problems have been of great concern, especially in the relatively dry areas of the West and Southwest. One of the biggest allocation problems is that of the waters of the Colorado, governed by the Colorado River Compact of 1922 and later agreements. In these areas, which are water-short in general, the increasing urbanization of the country has put pressure on and provided incentives for farmers, who hold rights to irrigation water, to sell water to the cities. This reallocation of long-existing patterns of water use can bring substantial efficiencies, as some irrigation uses are inefficient and inappropriate for dry areas, such as growing alfalfa, a heavy water-using crop. Organized water markets have been established in several Western states to allow those with rights to water (for irrigation and other purposes) to sell them to other users, often-urban water systems, for whom the value of water is higher. As of late 2010, seven states nationwide had statewide water trading program frameworks in place, and in four more states trading frameworks were in development; there are also trading programs within states. The E.P.A. supports some water trading programs, and all must meet Clean Water Act and other legal and regulatory standards. The Department of the Interior's Bureau of Reclamation operates in the 17 Western states; it is the largest wholesaler of water in the country, bringing water to more than 31 million people, and is also the second largest producer of hydroelectric power in the West. The states it serves include some that are among the most problematic in the country for water supply. From 2008 to 2011 California was officially declared to be in drought, though the worst droughts on record in the U.S. were still in the 1930's (the "Dust Bowl" years) and the 1950's.

Efficient Water Management   In addition to concerns about water-short areas, there has been a movement toward efficient management through the increased use of conservation measures, markets, and other innovative allocation methods, and the privatization of water system management. In the well-watered Northeast, both the Boston and the New York City water systems have been successful in implementing conservation measures such as low-flow toilets and other fixtures to reduce demands. In California the large Metropolitan Water District of Southern California has arranged to store water during wet years in groundwater "water banks" for withdrawal in drought years. In the United States and Canada many water utilities, including Houston, Indianapolis, Hamilton-Wentworth (Ontario), Jersey City, and Milwaukee, have contracted with large for-profit water companies for the management of all or part of their water supply and wastewater treatment operations. Although not a panacea (Atlanta canceled its privatization agreement in 2003), privatization has the potential to introduce important efficiencies. In 2010, the U.S. Department of Agriculture's Natural Resources Conservation Service announced the availability of $61.2 million in funding for Agricultural Water Enhancement Program projects. Such projects would be designed to conserve surface and groundwater and improve water quality on agricultural land. A challenge that will become increasingly important for all water systems is global warming, which will bring rising temperatures, rising sea levels, and changing precipitation patterns. These changes will affect both demands for and supplies of water. Coastal water systems are especially at risk from saltwater intrusion in estuaries and aquifers. Adapting to the effects of global warming on water systems will require careful planning to link regional systems and to insure that new infrastructure is appropriately designed.

Ocean Pollution

A worldwide problem is the pollution of the oceans, which cover about 75 percent of the Earth's surface. Such pollution occurs from many sources on land, at sea, and in the air. Among the main sources are polluted runoff from land and rivers, including garbage, sewage, and toxic waste; polluted precipitation; coastal mining operations; bilge cleaning; and oil spills. The *Deepwater Horizon* oil spill in the Gulf of Mexico in 2010 was the largest accidental oil spill in history, gushing nearly 5 million barrels of oil over a three-month period, with damaging effects on wildlife habitats and the Gulf's tourism and fishing industries. A study published in the journal *Science* in 2010 confirmed the existence of a huge plume of dispersed oil deep in the Gulf, the lasting threat of which to area wildlife is unknown. The massive spill resulted in new U.S. regulations imposing tougher reviews on deepwater drilling.

This pollution affects ocean ecosystems, in some cases very seriously, and there is no international authority analogous to the E.P.A. in the United States to deal with the issue. Each country has its own approaches, which vary widely in strength, and there are some international agreements. The London Convention, which entered into force in 1975, prohibits the disposal of many harmful materials, including plastic wastes, which generally do not break down in the ocean. These plastic wastes can kill or maim creatures that become entangled in them, but the treaty is difficult to enforce. Plastic and other wastes can accumulate in massive floating pockets. The largest of these is known as the Great Pacific Garbage Patch, located in the North Pacific between North America and Asia. It is roughly the size of Texas, and is formed through the concentration of ocean waste by the currents of the Pacific Gyre, a large-scale feature of the Pacific Ocean. There is a less famous massive garbage patch in the Atlantic Ocean; its size in not known, but in the North-South dimension it extends roughly from Virignia to Cuba. For 22 years, students on the Sea Education Association's cruises have sampled trash in this patch, finding more than 520,000 bits of trash per square mile (200,000 per square kilometer) in some places.

In the United States, the Clean Water Act prohibits dumping of oil into navigable waters, and the Marine Protection Research and Sanctuaries Act (1972) governs discharges of waste in U.S. territorial waters and discharges by U.S. vessels anywhere. Internationally, there has been some increase in effectiveness in controlling oil spills from ships, although these are still a substantial danger. The most important international agreements include the Convention on the Prevention of Marine Pollution by Dumping of Wastes and Other Matter (1972) and the International Convention on Oil Pollution Preparedness, Response, and Cooperation (1990). However, ocean pollution is difficult to prevent and the polluters are not easy to trace, and so the problem of ocean pollution and its effects on ecosystems remains serious. These pressures are compounded by the effects of overfishing and global warming. In recognition of the many issues affecting the oceans and coastal waters, President Obama issued in 2010 an Executive Order establishing the first comprehensive National Policy for the stewardship of the ocean, U.S. coasts, and the Great Lakes and creating the interagency National Ocean Council to strengthen ocean governance.

Air Pollution

Air pollution has been an increasingly serious problem accompanying worldwide economic development. Some types of air pollution are spectacularly evident, as were London's famous pea soup fogs that resulted from heating by coal furnaces; some other kinds of pollution, such as microparticle pollution, are less obvious but also very harmful. Air pollution can sometimes be a local problem, but it is also regional and transnational. It is usually assumed that pollutants are relatively unharmful at low levels, but become harmful at higher and more concentrated levels. Thus controlling air pollution is a problem of identifying harmful levels of pollutants and their sources, controlling emissions, and dealing with nonlocal consequences. In the United States increasing concern with air pollution after World War II led to federal legislation, with the first truly effective legislation being the Clean Air Act Amendments of 1970. The E.P.A. was created in 1970 and charged with implementing this legislation. Many other countries have their own legislation and implementing agencies, and the United Nations and the World Bank have information and assistance programs dealing with air pollution. Since the implementation of the Clean Air Act Amendments of 1970, there has been a substantial improvement in air quality in the United States; this has also been the case in other developed countries that have implemented air quality standards. Air quality in developing countries, on the other hand, has generally deteriorated in recent years through lack of resources and effective policy.

Air Pollution Standards

In the United States, the E.P.A. sets ambient air standards and monitors air quality at thousands of sites for six criteria pollutants: particulate matter, sulfur dioxide, carbon monoxide, nitrogen oxides, lead, and ozone. These standards are called National Ambient Air Quality Standards (N.A.A.Q.S.). Primary standards are based on health considerations, and secondary standards relate to the effects of pollutants on other aspects of the environment, such as esthetics (visibility), vegetation, and physical objects (e.g., houses and monuments). Standards are generally defined in two ways: as a long-term average, and as a short-term peaks. These standards must be met throughout the country, although not all areas are in compliance. An area that does not meet the air quality standard for one of the criteria pollutants can be subjected to a formal rule-making process, which designates it as a nonattainment area. Non-attainment classifications can be used to specify what measures an area must adopt to reduce air pollution, and when the area must reach attainment. The development of plans to meet the standards is the responsibility of the states. Under the Clean Air Act, the E.P.A. is required to review air quality standards every five years.

Particulate Matter   Particulate matter includes dust, dirt, soot, smoke, and liquid droplets emitted directly into the air from factories, power plants, cars, construction sites, fires, and natural erosion, as well as particles formed in the atmosphere by condensation or transformation of emitted gases such as sulfur dioxide and volatile organic compounds. Particles with a diameter less than 10 micrometers tend to cause the most health problems because they can be inhaled and accumulate in the respiratory tract. Particles with diameters of less than 2.5 micrometers are called "fine" particulars; those from 2.5 to 10 micrometers are referred to as "coarse" particles. (One micrometer, or micron, is equal to one millionth of a meter.) Particulate matter is responsible for a range of adverse health effects in the lower respiratory tract. People with chronic obstructive pulmonary or cardiovascular disease or influenza, asthmatics, the elderly, and children are especially sensitive.

Sulfur Dioxide Sulfur dioxide (SO_2) is emitted primarily from stationary sources including power plants, steel mills, refineries, pulp and paper mills, and nonferrous smelters. The health hazards associated with exposure to SO2 include impaired breathing and aggravation of existing respiratory and cardiovascular disease. Those most sensitive to SO2 include asthmatics and people with bronchitis and emphysema, children, and the elderly. Sulfur dioxide also damages trees, crops, historic buildings and statues, and is an agent of acid rain.

Carbon Monoxide Carbon monoxide (CO) is a colorless, odorless, poisonous gas produced by incomplete burning of carbon in fuels. Transportation sources, primarily motor vehicles, account for about 77 percent of CO emissions nationwide. Carbon monoxide enters the bloodstream and disrupts the supply of oxygen to the body's organs and tissues. The health threat from carbon monoxide is significant for those who suffer from cardiovascular diseases. Healthy individuals are also affected, and exposure to elevated carbon monoxide levels is associated with impairment of visual perception and manual dexterity. Federal regulations have succeeded in cleaning up much of the CO pollution that plagued the U.S. in the 1980's. Between 1980 and 2009 there was an 80 percent drop in average parts per million (ppm) of carbon dioxide in 114 trend sites, from about 9 ppm to about 2 ppm.

Nitrogen Oxides (NOx) Nitrogen oxides includes NO, NO2, and other oxides of nitrogen. E.P.A.'s ambient air quality standards cover the entire group, but nitrogen dioxide is of most interest and is the indicator for the entire group. Nitrogen dioxide (NO_2) forms when another pollutant, nitrogen oxide (NO), combines with oxygen; NO is emitted from cars and trucks and sources such as power plants. Once formed, NO_2 reacts with other pollutants such as volatile organic compounds (VOCs), reactions that lead to the formation of ground-level ozone. Together with particles in the air, NO_2 can sometimes be seen as a reddish-brown layer over urban areas. Even short exposures to NO_2 can irritate the lungs and lower resistance to respiratory infections such as influenza. Prolonged exposure to higher than normal concentrations can cause pulmonary angina. Nitrogen dioxide is also an agent of acid rain. Between 1980 and 2009 there was a 48 percent decrease in average ppm of nitrogen dioxide in the air based on 81 trend sites, from just under 0.03 ppm to about 0.015 ppm. All areas in the U.S. now meet NO_2 standards.

Lead Atmospheric lead emissions are primarily from lead gasoline additives (now almost completely phased out in the United States), nonferrous smelters, and battery plants. Lead can affect almost all body organs and systems, including the nervous system (brain), kidneys, and reproductive system. Lead that is taken into the body and not excreted is ultimately stored in the bones, where it can last for a lifetime. Excessive exposure to lead may cause seizures, mental retardation, and behavioral disorders. Even at low doses, lead exposure is harmful; infants and children are especially susceptible to low doses of lead and can suffer damage to the central nervous system.

Ozone Ozone (O_3) in the upper atmosphere (see "The Ozone Layer," above) protects life against ultraviolet radiation. Ozone in the lower atmosphere, formed by nitrogen oxides (NOx) and volatile organic compounds (VOCs) reacting chemically in the presence of sunlight, is a harmful pollutant, especially in the summer, when high temperatures and long hours of sunlight provide ideal conditions for creating it. The NOx are emitted by motor vehicles, power plants, and other sources, and VOCs from motor vehicles and chemical and industrial processes. High levels of ozone affect people with an impaired respiratory system, such as asthmatics; and exposure to relatively low concentrations of ozone for only a few hours has been found to significantly reduce lung function in normal, healthy people during exercise. Ozone also causes noticeable damage to leaves in many crops and trees, responsible each year for significant domestic losses in crop yields.

Air Quality Index To provide information to the public on daily air quality, the E.P.A. has developed the air quality index (A.Q.I.), which measures the levels of the criteria pollutants (except lead) on a scale of 0–500. The higher the A.Q.I. value, the greater the level of air pollution and the greater the health concern. For example, ratings of 0–50 represent good air quality, and ratings of 301–500 represent hazardous air quality.

Emissions Control

The second part of the clean air program, in addition to the definition of ambient air quality standards, is the control of emissions. Here, E.P.A. sets emissions standards for new or renovated sources of criteria pollutants. These standards for stationary sources such as factories are complemented by standards for mobile sources, such as automobiles. The command-and-control approach on which the program is primarily based is not always as efficient in meeting given targets as more innovative market-based efforts. Hence, states are now permitted to allow trading in emission reduction credits to encourage cost-effective reductions in emissions to meet air quality standards. In 2009, President Barack Obama, in an attempt to cut greenhouse gases by 900 million metric tons, proposed rules for vehicle emissions that would require new cars and trucks to get an average 35.5 m.p.g. by 2016. After some contentious discussions with a then-ailing auto industry, the Administration issued new rules under its existing authority that will require an average vehicle emission standard of 34.1 m.p.g.

The approaches in the Clean Air Act have resulted in substantially cleaner air in the United States. From 1990 (1999 for particulate matter) to 2009, air quality has improved for each of the six criteria pollutants, and emissions have decreased. Many of these improvements are quite substantial. On the other hand, much remains to be accomplished: In 2007, 158.5 million people lived in counties that exceeded at least one national ambient air quality standard. Ground-level ozone and particulate matter still present challenges in many areas of the US. Hazardous pollutants (or "air toxics") are another class of air pollutants regulated by E.P.A. These are pollutants that pose substantial health hazards, such as benzene, which is found in gasoline; perchlorethyelene, emitted from some dry-cleaning establishments; and methylene chloride, used as a solvent and paint stripper. The E.P.A. regulates 188 pollutants of this type. In a significant expansion of E.P.A.'s regulatory mission the Supreme Court ruled (2007) that carbon dioxide and other GHGs are pollutants under the Clean Air Act, and that E.P.A. has the authority to regulate GHG emissions from new cars and trucks. The ruling was made in a suit against E.P.A. brought by Massachusetts and other states, cities and environmental groups.

Air pollution in the developing world, especially in urban areas, is a significant problem. Emissions from vehicles, large and small stationary sources, and burning vegetation contribute to serious health consequences. The World Health Organization estimates that of the more than 2 million premature deaths each year from urban outdoor air pollution and indoor pollution from burning solid fuels, more than half are in developing countries, where many cities have very high levels of air pollution. The worst air pollution is undoubtedly in Asia. Anything over 100 micrograms of particles per cubic meter of air is considered dangerous, yet in cities such as Taiyuan, China and Delhi, India, the levels routinely top 500 micrograms. Substantial resources will be needed to bring air quality in developing countries up to reasonable standards for human health.

Acid Rain

Acid rain is another air pollution problem. This term refers to acidic precipitation of all kinds, including rain, snow, and fog (wet deposition) as well as acidic dust particles (dry deposition). Acid rain has a pH value of less than about 5.0 (ordinary rain is about 5.6). Acid rain results from the emission of pollutants into the air, especially sulfur dioxide and nitrogen oxides, which are emitted primarily by the burning of fossil fuels. In the United States, about two-thirds of all SO_2 and one-fourth of all NOx come from electric power generation. These gases dissolve in atmospheric water to form sulfuric and nitric acids in rain and other forms of precipitation. An early study, the National Surface Water Survey, found that acid rain caused acidity in 75 percent of acidic lakes and 50 percent of acidic stream miles surveyed.

Acid rain has serious consequences for biosystems on land and in water. Acid rain damages leaves, hinders photosynthesis, and acidifies soils, and the acidification of water bodies makes them unable to support fish and other organisms. Because acid rain is regional and global, finding solutions is a challenge. There are, for example, hundreds of lakes in the Adirondack Mountains in New York

State that have become acidified, primarily because of pollutants emitted from coal-fired power plants in Midwestern states. In such cases, the costs of reducing sulfur dioxide emissions are imposed in one area, and the benefits to ecosystems and recreational values are felt in another. These issues are transnational as well—much of the acidification in Canada is from U.S. emissions sources, and most of the acid deposition in Norway and Sweden results from emissions from Britain, Germany, Poland, and other areas. The E.P.A. has an Acid Rain Program that has helped to reduce both SO_2 and NOx emissions. The goal for SO_2 emissions from power plants is a reduction of 10 million tons below 1980 emissions; implementation includes restrictions on utilities and a cap-and-trade emissions program. Emissions of NOx are regulated, but without a cap-and-trade program.

Waste

Worldwide, people, industry and agriculture put enormous amounts of waste materials into the environment. A portion of these wastes is regulated effectively, such as some types of air and water pollution in developed countries; and some wastes are recycled, such as organic manures in agriculture. However, most wastes are simply dumped, and these are a serious and growing problem for health and the environment throughout the world. Among the most important issues are municipal solid waste, toxic waste management and cleanup, and nuclear waste.

Municipal Solid Waste

As economic welfare increases, people buy more goods, reuse products less, and generate more waste. Many areas of the United States face serious problems in safely and effectively managing the garbage they generate. The United States in 2009 produced 243 million tons of municipal solid waste (M.S.W.), about 4.3 pounds (2.0 kilograms) per person per day. The per capita figure has remained roughly constant since 1990, but it represents a substantial increase from the 2.7 (1.2 kilograms) pounds per person per day generated in 1960. In 2009, the waste stream (before recycling) consisted of paper (28.2 percent); yard trimmings (13.7 percent); food scraps (14.1 percent); plastics (12.3 percent); metals (8.6 percent); rubber, leather, and textiles (8.3 percent); glass (4.9 percent); wood (6.5 percent); and other materials (3.0 percent). This M.S.W. stream is distinct from and in addition to other types of wastes: industrial wastes produced by factories, tailings from mines, construction and demolition waste, sludge from sewage treatment, and junked machinery.

Disposing of Solid Waste

There are four primary methods of dealing with M.S.W.: source reduction, recycling (including composting), landfills, and incineration. The first two methods prevent materials from entering, or divert them from, the waste stream; the last two are disposal methods.

Source Reduction Source reduction is the use of fewer materials in manufacturing, packaging, and transporting commodities, and the extension of the useful lives of products. Many experts believe that it is the key to solving the challenges of M.S.W. A broad variety of products and packaging that reduce waste and save money have been developed, and many are straightforward. For example, some fast-food outlets have reduced the textured design on napkins, permitting more to be shipped in a given container and thereby reducing the amounts of corrugated cardboard required for packaging and the costs of transport. Others have substituted paper wrappers for sandwiches for polystyrene plastic containers. Source reduction is the generally preferred method for dealing with solid waste, but progress depends both on financial incentives and on public pressure and continued technological development of new methods. In 2007, San Francisco became the first U.S. city to limit the use of plastic bags in grocery and drug stores. Several other cities have since passed similar ordinances, and still others are considering bag-reduction measures. Other initiatives include a New York state law that, effective January 1, 2009 requires certain retail and grocery stores to accept plastic bags for recycling.

Recycling and Composting Recycling and composting recovered 33.8 percent (82 million tons) of waste generated in 2009. Recycling involves the collection, sorting, and processing of used materials, which are then remanufactured and sold in new products. Recycling rates in 2009 reached 74.2 percent for office-type paper, 59.9 percent for yard trimmings, 50.7 percent for aluminum beer and soft drink containers, and 95.7 percent for automobile batteries. By 2005, almost 9,000 curbside recycling programs had sprouted up across the nation, and about 500 material recovery facilities had been established to process the collected materials. Recycling saves energy and raw materials, and reduces the need for landfills and combustion. In addition, recycling reduces the emission of carbon dioxide and other GHGs. Cost considerations, as well as environmental concerns, enter into recycling decisions at the municipal and personal levels; some recycling is a money-losing proposition for municipalities. One of the most successful recycling programs, for aluminum cans, depends in large part on the deposit programs run by many states. Compostable waste (yard trimmings and food scraps) make up about a quarter of all M.S.W. in the U.S. There are about 3,500 community composting programs, primarily for yard trimmings, nationwide. In 2009 about 21 million tons of M.S.W. had been recovered for composting.

Landfills In the United States over 54 percent of M.S.W. is sent to landfills. In 2008, there were 1,812 of these, compared with about 8,000 in 1988. However, although the number of landfills has decreased, the average size has increased so that the total capacity of landfills has remained relatively constant. Landfills are the cheapest method of disposing of M.S.W., but they pose a number of environmental problems, including the release of methane gas and contamination of groundwater supplies. They also contain toxic wastes, and therefore require regular monitoring. It is becoming more common for urban areas to send waste to rural landfills for reasons of cost and space, and these remote landfills bring both revenues and controversy to rural areas.

Incinerators Of the U.S. M.S.W. stream, 12 percent was incinerated in combustion facilities (with energy recovery) in 2009. Incineration used to be a more common method of disposing of M.S.W. In the 1940's there were approximately 700 municipal incinerators in the United States. Despite the efficiency with which they reduced the volume and weight of waste (up to 90 percent in volume and 75 percent in weight), they posed environmental problems that became increasingly evident, including odors, particulate

matter, and toxic gases. For these esthetic and environmental reasons, their number declined dramatically in the 1950's. Incinerator use increased in the 1980's and early 1990's as space for landfills became scarce, and as the energy produced by incineration became a valuable commodity. There are some 85 combustors in the United States with energy recovery capabilities, able to incinerate close to 99,000 tons of M.S.W. per day. Their use has been limited, however, by the need to regulate toxic emissions, including ash containing heavy metals.

Hazardous Waste

Hazardous waste is a general term for wastes that are dangerous to people and the environment. These are typically produced by large industrial facilities such as chemical manufacturers, electroplating companies, and petroleum refiners; and by more common businesses such as dry cleaners, auto repair shops, hospitals, exterminators, and photo processing centers.

In the United States, the millions of tons of hazardous waste generated each year (35 million tons in 2009) are regulated by E.P.A. under the Resource Conservation and Recovery Act of 1976 (R.C.R.A.). E.P.A.'s figures include hazardous wastes as defined and regulated by R.C.R.A. This act in principle establishes a lifecycle or cradle-to-grave regulatory system for listed hazardous wastes, including standards for shipping, handling, and disposing of these wastes. The wastes are subject to a tracking (or manifest) system, and may be delivered only to permitted hazardous waste disposal sites. The E.P.A. has studied and identified hundreds of hazardous wastes, including slags from primary metals production, wastewater and sludges from specified industrial processes, and chemicals such as polychlorinated biphenyls (PCBs) and trichloroethylene. There is international as well as national regulation of hazardous waste. The Basel Convention on the Control and Transboundary Movements of Hazardous Wastes and Their Disposal (1989) provides a framework for monitoring implementation of and compliance with rules and regulations on the generation of and movement of hazardous wastes. The United States is a signatory to this convention but has not ratified it.

Superfund The R.C.R.A. system is intended to deal with wastes that are generated during current commercial and industrial activities. However, long before the public became concerned about preserving the environment, private and public enterprises operated in a relatively uncontrolled manner that resulted in the contamination of many sites. To deal with these sites, and also with emergency situations involving hazardous wastes, Congress in 1980 enacted the Comprehensive Environmental Response, Compensation, and Liability Act (CERCLA), better known as the Superfund, a multibillion-dollar, multiyear program to clean up thousands of hazardous waste sites. The fund was renewed in 1986 by the Superfund Amendments and Reauthorization Act (SARA).

Site Evaluation The E.P.A. evaluates hazardous waste sites for their levels of soil and water contamination, the mobility of toxins, and people and sensitive environments that might be affected by the toxins. Four pathways for toxins are analyzed: groundwater, surface water, soil, and air. On the basis of these evaluations, the sites are ranked by a numerical Hazard Ranking System (H.R.S.). In 2006, the E.P.A. estimated that one in four Americans lived within four miles of a toxic waste site. The highest-ranking sites are placed on the E.P.A.'s National Priorities List (N.P.L.). The CERCLA also provides for states and territories to designate one top priority site regardless of its score. The first N.P.L. had 406 sites (1983); there were 1,279 sites on the N.P.L. pending clean up in 2011. The E.P.A. estimates that some 300 current or former N.P.L. sites are or would soon be, in productive use.

Cleanup Actions Once the E.P.A. deems a site a national priority, it can take two types of action. It can remove the hazard in an emergency action, or it can develop and oversee the implementation of a site remediation plan. A notable example of emergency action occurred with the town of Times Beach, Missouri, where high levels of dioxin were discovered. Beginning in 1983, the town was bought out, evacuated, and later demolished. The second approach represents the more typical Superfund process. Many site remediation plans have been developed and completed, but the process is challenging both technically and financially, especially as many of the original polluters are bankrupt or cannot be found when multimillion-dollar bills for cleanup are presented.

Among the criticisms of Superfund procedures are that cleanup standards may be set unrealistically high for the uses foreseen for a site, and that the strict liability provisions of the law may be unfair to those who contributed only marginally to the pollution of a site. Nevertheless, the United States and other nations continue to confront the policy challenges left over from a less environmentally conscious age.

Nuclear Waste

Nuclear waste in the United States comes from nuclear weapons production facilities, nuclear power plants, medical equipment (primarily used in radiation treatments), industrial sources of radioactivity used as a more powerful alternative to X rays, and residues from uranium mining. Nuclear waste is grouped into two categories: "low-level" and "high-level." Low-level waste is slightly radioactive, often from exposure to a high-level source. High-level waste is either civilian, mainly spent fuel from nuclear reactors; or military, wastes produced in the manufacture of nuclear weapons. In 2011 there were 104 nuclear power plants in the United States, producing about 20 percent of the nation's electricity.

Characteristics of Nuclear Waste The main problem with nuclear waste is that it is radioactive and can remain that way for long periods of time—in the case of some substances, for thousands of years. Thus the disposal of nuclear waste has consequences not only for ourselves and the next generation, but for human society over the long future. In this respect, nuclear wastes are unique. Early methods of disposal included dumping the wastes at sea and suspending them in a liquid or in cement and injecting the radioactive combination into wells. The United States was among the signatories of the London Ocean Dumping Convention (1975), which bans ocean dumping, and stopped deep-well injection in 1984.

Disposal Sites The nuclear waste disposal problem remains one for which long-lasting solutions have not yet been found. The Department of Energy now stores high-level wastes at sites in West Valley, New York; Savannah River, South Carolina; and Hanford, Washington. Nuclear wastes from power plants and other facilities often remain in "temporary" sites, including the sites where they were generated. Fuel rods used in nuclear power plants need to be replaced every three to five years. The used rods are stored underwater in pools near the plants; these pools store about 80 percent of used fuel in the U.S.

In 1998, the E.P.A. certified the Department of

Energy's Waste Isolation Pilot Plan in the Chihuahuan Desert of southern New Mexico, the nation's first deep-underground facility for disposal of transuranic waste generated from defense activities. (Transuranic wastes consist primarily of sludges, tools, rags, glassware, and protective clothing that has been contaminated with radioactive elements from weapons production.) The facility is 2,150 feet (640 meters) underground in excavated, natural salt formations that are believed to have been stable for more than 200 million years. The first shipment of transuranic waste was delivered to the facility on March 26, 1999, and the site remains in operation. Although it is expected that this use of the site will significantly reduce the number of Americans living within 50 miles of nuclear waste sites elsewhere in the country, residents of the area and others concerned with the potential hazards of waste transportation fought its implementation since the site was first proposed in 1974.

The difficulty of resolving issues of nuclear waste disposal is illustrated by the saga of Yucca Mountain, Nevada, which was approved by the President and Congress in 2002 as the nation's first long-term geologic repository for spent nuclear fuel and high-level radioactive waste. If the site survived further challenges, it could begin accepting waste in 2025, with closure and decommissioning slated to begin a century later. The cost of the program for 150 years (1983–2133) has been projected to be $96 billion. Over a tenth of this had been spent by 2011. However, the site (about 100 miles northwest of Las Vegas) has been the subject of fierce opposition not only in Nevada, but also in states along proposed transportation routes for nuclear waste, and in 2011, the Obama administration proposed to finally remove the Yucca Mountain site from consideration. These controversies reflect the fact that the true costs of waste disposal have not been factored into the costs of nuclear power plants. This will be an important element of energy decision making if nuclear power, which could replace some fossil fuel generation, is to provide a larger part of the country's energy supply.

Major Events in the History of the Environment

1775 Percivall Pott (English, 1714–88) observes that chimney sweeps develop cancer as a result of their contact with soot—the first recognition of environmental factors in cancer.

1854 John Snow (English, 1813–58) demonstrates the relationship between contaminated water and the incidence of cholera.

1864 George Perkins Marsh (American, 1801–82) publishes *Man and Nature*, the first textbook on conservation and the first detailed study of human influence on the environment.

1872 Robert Angus Smith (Scottish, 1817–84) describes acid rain.

1885 Yellowstone, world's first national park, opens.

1892 Canada establishes first national park at Banff, Alberta. John Muir (American, b. Scotland, 1838–1914) founds the Sierra Club.

1895 Svante Arrhenius (Swedish, 1859–1927) is the first person to investigate effect of increasing carbon dioxide in the atmosphere on global climate.

1905 President Theodore Roosevelt of the United States opens the first national refuge, Pelican Island in Florida, to protect nesting sites of brown pelicans. United States Forest Service established. National Audubon Society founded.

1911 Canada, Japan, Russia, and the United States sign treaty to limit the harvest of northern fur seals.

1916 National Park Service established.

1928 Boulder Canyon project (Hoover Dam) authorized to bring irrigation, electric power, and flood control system to western United States.

1933 Tennessee Valley Authority created to develop the Tennessee River for flood control, navigation, electric power, agriculture, and forestry.

1939 Paul Müller (Swiss, 1899–1965) discovers insecticidal properties of DDT.

1952 Smog blamed for 4,000 deaths in London.

1955 Link between exposure to asbestos and lung cancer established.

1957 Nuclear wastes stored by the Soviet Union in a remote mountain region of the Urals explode; radioactive contamination affects thousands of square miles; several villages permanently evacuated.

1962 *Silent Spring* by Rachel Carson (American, 1907–64) attacks pesticide use and stimulates major environmental movement.

1963 Clean Air Act allocating $95 million to local, state, and national efforts to control air pollution.

1964 Wilderness Act, setting up the National Wilderness Preservation System.

1965 Highway Beautification Act, banning many highway billboards. Water Quality Act, giving federal government power to set water standards. Solid Waste Disposal Act, first major solid waste legislation.

1966 Rare and Endangered Species Act.

1967 S. Manabe and R. T. Wetherald predict that increased amounts of carbon dioxide in the atmosphere will lead to global warming.

1968 Wild and Scenic Rivers Act, identifying areas of scenic beauty for preservation and recreation.

1970 First Earth Day celebrated on April 22. Clean Air Act Amendments of 1970. Environmental Protection Agency (E.P.A.) created.

1972 Clean Water Act, controlling discharges of pollutants into navigable waters. Oregon passes the nation's first bottle recycling law. The E.P.A. bars registration and interstate sales of DDT because of its persistence in the environment and accumulation in the food chain.

1973 Representatives of 80 nations sign the Convention of International Trade in Endangered Species of Wild Fauna and Flora (CITES), which prohibits commercial trade in 375 endangered species of wild animals.

1974 F. Sherwood Rowland and Mario Molinas warn that chlorofluorocarbons (CFCs) are destroying the ozone layer.

1976 Toxic Substances Control Act controlling hazardous industrial chemicals.

1978 Community of Love Canal, near Niagara, N.Y., evacuated after hazardous waste dumps are uncovered. The E.P.A. declares site safe in 1990.

1979 Nuclear reactor at Three Mile Island, near Harrisburg, Pa., suffers partial meltdown; radiation confined to reactor dome.

1980 Comprehensive Environmental Response, Compensation, and Liability Act (the "Superfund") to clean up hazardous waste sites.

1985 British scientists discover that a "hole" in the ozone layer develops over Antarctica each winter. The United States sets up a Conservation Reserve Program to remove environmentally sensitive farmland from agricultural use.

1986 Chernobyl nuclear reactor number 4 explodes and burns, causing 31 deaths within days, shortening the lives of thousands, and forcing the evacuation of hundreds of square miles in Soviet Ukraine.

1988 In the United States, the Ocean Dumping Ban Act mandates an end to ocean dumping of industrial waste and municipal sewage sludge.

1989 Exxon *Valdez* grounds, leaking 35,000 tons of oil into Prince William Sound, Alaska. Montreal Protocol on Substances That Deplete the Ozone Layer goes into force.

1991 Iraq dumps over 1 million tons of oil from occupied Kuwait into Persian Gulf.

1992 Representatives from 178 countries attend the first Earth Summit in Rio de Janeiro, where they sign treaties pledging to preserve the diversity of animal and plant species and to halt global warming.

1994 United States Fish and Wildlife Service recommends reducing the status of the American bald eagle from "endangered" to "threatened" in most of the United States.

1995 U.N. Working Group I of the Intergovernmental Panel on Climate Change acknowledges global warming, reporting that "the balance of evidence suggests that there is a discernible human influence on global climate."

1997 Kyoto Protocol, international agreement to reduce greenhouse gases using fixed targets, emissions trading, and other methods.

2001 Intergovernmental Panel on Climate Change (I.P.C.C.) reports that there is new and stronger evidence that most of the warming in the last half century is due to human activities.

2006 California enacts Global Warming Solutions Act, the first enforceable statewide program in the United States to cap all GHG emissions from major industries.

2007 Intergovernmental Panel on Climate Change (I.P.C.C.) Fourth Assessment Report says that evidence for global warming is unequivocal, that negative effects of warming have already been observed, and that emissions control programs must be implemented.

2009 Delegates from nearly 200 countries meet as part of the United Nations Climate Change Conference at Copenhagen as an attempt to shape an international response to climate change.

2010 The B.P. *Deepwater Horizon* drilling rig explosion results in the largest marine oil spill in history, with roughly 5 million barrels of crude oil lost in the Gulf of Mexico.

2011 The Fukushima-Daiichi nuclear plant in eastern Japan is disabled by an earthquake-caused tsunami with waves as high as 46 feet, releasing radiation into the air and ocean, and requiring evacuations of people living within a radius of 20 kilometers (12.4 miles) from the plant; people living within 20 to 30 kilometers were instructed to remain indoors.

Glossary of Environmental Terms

acid rain Acidic precipitation including rain, snow, and fog (wet deposition) as well as acidic dust particles (dry deposition). Acid rain has a pH value of less than about 5.0 (ordinary rain is about 5.6).

adaptation A policy measure dealing with the effects of global warming, such as building barriers against rising sea levels. (See "Mitigation")

biodiversity The variety of living things and their interactions, often characterized on three interacting levels: species, genetic, and ecosystem biodiversity.

chlorofluorocarbons (CFCs) Chemically inert, nontoxic, and easily liquefied man-made chemicals developed in the 1930's as an ammonia substitute for use in refrigeration. They destroy the stratospheric ozone balance by adding chlorine to the atmosphere, and are by treaty no longer produced in developed countries.

criteria pollutants Air pollutants for which the U.S. Environmental Protection Agency (E.P.A.) sets ambient air standards and monitors air quality: particulate matter, sulfur dioxide, carbon monoxide, nitrogen dioxide, lead, and ozone.

ecosystem A system formed by populations of species and the nonliving environmental elements—such as water—that surround and interact dynamically with them.

endangered species Species threatened with extinction, often by human activities. International agencies and countries keep lists of endangered species.

exotic ("invasive") species Species introduced deliberately or by accident into ecosystems in which they are not naturally found.

global climate models (GCMs, also called **general circulation models**) Large, complex computer models used to simulate and analyze linked ocean, land, air, and ice systems, which are represented in a three-dimensional grid system covering the entire globe.

greenhouse gases (GHGs) Atmospheric gases whose molecules absorb energy reflected from the earth's surface, thus trapping heat in the Earth's atmosphere and contributing to global warming. They include carbon dioxide, methane, nitrous oxide, ozone, and CFCs.

mitigation The reduction of GHG emissions through policy and technological changes. (See "Adaptation.")

ozone hole A region of extremely low levels of atmospheric ozone over the south polar region during the Antarctic winter, resulting from the depletion of the ozone layer by CFCs and other gases.

particulate matter In air pollution control, dust, dirt, soot, smoke, and liquid droplets emitted directly into the air from factories, power plants, cars, construction sites, fires, and natural erosion, as well as particles formed in the atmosphere by condensation or transformation of emitted gases such as sulfur dioxide and volatile organic compounds.

point and nonpoint sources In water pollution control, point sources are those that can be identified with a single source (such as a factory outlet pipe) and nonpoint sources are those that cannot be so identified (such as urban and agricultural runoff).

rain forest Forest (both temperate and tropical) growing in a region of heavy rain, typically defined as more than 60–80 inches (1.5–2.0 meters) of rain each year. Tropical rain forests are located in regions with mean monthly temperatures of from 68 to 82 degrees Fahrenheit (20–28 degrees Celsius), with rains spread evenly throughout the year.

species A biological classification referring to a group of organisms with similar characteristics capable of interbreeding and producing fertile offspring in the wild. There are about 1.7 million known species—those characterized by scientific description and analysis—of plants and animals, but the total number is thought to be much larger.

sustainability An objective or goal according to which human activities are conducted on the basis of maintaining a stable biosphere over the long term for humans and other species.

total maximum daily loads (T.D.M.L.) Under the Clean Water Act (U.S.), defined as the allowable loads of a pollutant from all sources that will ensure, with a margin of safety, that waters meet state water quality standards.

wetland Area where saturation with water is the dominant factor determining the nature of soil development and the ecosystems in the soil and on its surface. Wetlands include marshes (tidal and nontidal), swamps (forested and shrub), bogs, and fens.

GEOLOGY

Geology is the study of Earth, its substances, makeup, forms, processes, and history. Geology is a great unifying discipline, built on the sciences of physics, chemistry, and biology, and using everything from astronomy and climatology to mathematics. Through geology, we come to understand the life cycle of our planet and thus explore the processes that bring about other bodies in our solar system and universe.

The field breaks down into two significant areas: historical geology, which delves into the formation and physical evolution of Earth; and physical geology, which describes the state of the planet and its physical structures and systems.

Historical geology begins before Earth itself was

whole, when the processes that formed the materials of today's Earth had just begun. It introduces us to the geologic time scale, the system by which scientists measure and classify the "ages of Earth." Through this study, we can begin to glimpse the enormousness of the time scale that underlies the science of geology. We see how what we call "prehistory" in fact dwarfs the almost infinitesimally short span of human existence on Earth, only a part of which we call "history."

Physical geology studies the formation of the largest structures on earth—from the highest mountain ranges to the deepest trenches on the ocean bottom—as well as smaller-scale objects such as rocks, minerals, and crystals.

History of Geology

Speculation about the origin and composition of Earth is as old as civilization itself. Most religions contain some form of creation myth, and many hold that the natural forces governing the planet are embodied by gods and spirits. In antiquity, various philosophers propounded theories of the natural world. Anaximander (610–ca. 546 B.C.) recognized that Earth is curved, but thought it cylindrical. Pythagoras (ca. 569–ca. 480 B.C.) correctly noted that Earth is a sphere. Xenophanes (ca. 570–480 B.C.), noting seashells on mountaintops, was among the first to recognize that Earth's surface rises and falls over time. Aristotle (384–322 B.C.) offered plausible, but incorrect, theories for volcanoes, earthquakes, fossils, and other natural phenomena. Theophrastus (372–287 B.C.) classified a number of rocks and minerals, and Pytheas (fl. 300 B.C.) described the tides and noted that they are controlled by the moon. Eratosthenes (ca. 276–ca. 194 B.C.) calculated the size of Earth with reasonable precision. In China, Zhang Heng (A.D. 78–139) developed a primitive seismograph.

Before the Enlightenment of the 18th-century, most European scientists were heavily influenced by religious belief, including the biblical story of creation. Scholars

attempted to fix the age of Earth through a careful and literal reading of the Bible, concluding that creation took place about 6,000 years ago (far short of the present-day estimate of 4.6 billion years). Another biblical story with geologic import concerned Noah's great flood, which was used by many scientists at that time to explain a number of observable geologic phenomena, such as the existence of marine fossils on mountaintops. Believing that great singular events such as the flood—either natural or divine in origin—were responsible for the formation of Earth, this school of thought came to be known later as catastrophism.

In the 17th century a few scientists developed ideas that we still believe to be correct today. The French philosopher René Descartes (1596–1650) was among the first to suggest that Earth is much older than biblical chronologies indicate. The Danish scientist Nicolas Steno (1638–86) correctly explained fossils as the remains of long-dead organisms and introduced the idea that layers of rock, called strata by geologists, were deposited at different times, with older layers lying below more recent ones (1669).

In the 18th century, the French polymath Georges-Louis Leclerc, comte de Buffon (1707–88), proposed (1778) that instead of the Judeo-Christian period of six days, creation took six epochs; and Earth might be about

75,000 years old instead of 6,000 years old—privately he thought it was even older. In Scotland in 1785, an amateur geologist, James Hutton (1726–97), suggested that Earth's strata must have formed gradually. He claimed that cataclysmic events had not contributed in any significant way to the overall structure of the planet—a principle that we now call uniformitarianism. Simply stated, Earth's history is a long, gradual development that can be explained in terms of natural forces that are still observable today. This idea became a cornerstone of modern geology.

Hutton had little influence initially, but another Scot, Sir Charles Lyell (1797–1875), expanded on and popularized Hutton's ideas and work. He argued strongly that one could explain geologic history perfectly well by pointing to the geological processes—the action of wind and water, earthquakes, and volcanoes—presently at work and observable on Earth. Lyell rejected the short time line derived from the Bible and proposed a much greater period for the development and evolution of Earth. Lyell's notion of a vastly great "geologic time" had a profound effect on science well beyond the study of geology and on our very understanding of its place in the world. The length of geologic time made possible the evolutionary theory of Lyell's good friend Charles Darwin. It provided the time scale necessary for natural selection to take place.

Historical Geology

Formation of Earth

Although Hutton described Earth as having "no vestige of a beginning," that purely uniformitarian view was not accepted by most geologists. As with many ideas in earth science, one of the first to propose a scientific explanation of Earth's beginnings was Comte Buffon, who suggested in 1745 that Earth was created from material splashed from the sun when a comet struck it. Buffon's theory, however, assumed an impossibly large comet. In 1755 the German philosopher Immanuel Kant (1724–1804) proposed an idea that, with many adjustments by astronomers, became the basis of the modern theory of Earth's formation. He said that Earth and the other planets coalesced from a dust cloud around the sun.

The modern version of Kant's theory is as follows: About 4.6 billion years ago, a mass of gas and dust slowly condensed under the force of gravity into a spinning disk. This solar nebula continued to coalesce, with the sun forming at the center of the disk, and planets coming together out of the material in the outer regions. Earth and the other planets assembled as a result of countless collisions of smaller bodies, some mere microscopic specks and others as large as minor planets. The growing planet swept up and incorporated most of the debris in its path as it orbited the sun, and generated an extremely high temperature from the energy of all those impacts and explosions.

This violent infancy of bombardment and collision brought most of Earth's minerals (some continue to arrive as dust or impacts from space), while the high temperature melted the entire planet. During this period, gravity drew heavier elements into the interior of the new planet, whereas lighter ones remained near the surface. As the planet cooled, Earth took on a three-part form: a thin crust, the surface of Earth; a solid mantle that makes up the main part of the planet; and a liquid core of molten metal (high pressure also created a solid inner core within the molten outer core).

Composition of the Earth

In their study of the Earth, scientists distinguish a number of distinct layers from the inner core—the center of which is about 6,400 km (roughly 4,000 miles) below the surface—to the farthest limit of the atmosphere, about 1,000 km (600 miles) above the surface. This section describes these layers, from the innermost to the outermost.

Core   The core consists of two parts—one solid, the other liquid—both thought to be a mixture of iron and a lighter element, probably sulfur or oxygen. The solid inner core begins about 4,650 km (2,890 miles) from the surface, and the liquid outer core at about 2,900 km (1,800 miles) from the surface.

Mantle   The bulk of the Earth—roughly two-thirds of its mass—is composed of the mantle, which extends from the outer core to within about 90 km (55 miles) of the Earth's surface below the higher mountains, and to within only 5 to 8 km (3 to 5 miles) of the Earth's surface below some areas of the oceans. Silicon dioxide constitutes almost half of the mantle, and there is an abundance of magnesium oxide, some iron oxide, and smaller amounts of oxides of other metals. (Although silicon dioxide is known as quartz when found in the Earth's crust, under the heat and pressure of the mantle it may have very different properties from the form we know.) Part of the upper mantle is somewhat fluid and is known as the asthenosphere.

Lithosphere   Formerly called the crust, the lithosphere is the outermost solid layer of the Earth. Under the continents, the crust varies from 30 to 90 km (19 to 55 miles) in thickness, while under the oceans it is generally only 5 to 8 km (3 to 5 miles) thick. Continental and oceanic crust differ from each other in thickness and composition. Continental crust consists of granite and other relatively light rocks; oceanic crust is made up chiefly of basalt. The crust is separated from the mantle by the Mohorovičić discontinuity, or Moho.

Hydrosphere   Water exists on Earth in all three states—solid, liquid, and vapor—and is found on the surface, within the crust, and in the atmosphere. The overwhelming majority of Earth's water, over 97 percent, is contained in the oceans. Another 2 percent is the vast fields of polar ice and the glaciers and ice caps that exist in mountains and other high-altitude regions. The remaining portion is found in surface water—rivers, lakes, streams, etc.—and groundwater and soil water. The abundant presence of water is, of course, what distinguishes Earth from the other planets in the solar system. The unique conditions that allow so much water to exist in liquid form on Earth are the same conditions that make life possible.

Water—virtually all of it seawater—covers about 71 percent of the Earth's surface and thereby constitutes a distinct layer of the Earth. Seawater varies in composition from place to place, but on average it is about 3.5 percent salts—that is, evaporating 100 pounds of seawater would yield 3.5 pounds of salt. Sodium chloride (ordinary table salt) constitutes 2.7 percent of seawater, or 77.8 percent of total solids in seawater.

Atmosphere   The atmosphere is the gaseous layer that envelopes the Earth. The lower atmosphere consists of the troposphere and the stratosphere. The *troposphere* has an average thickness of about 11 km (7 miles), although it is only 8 km (5 miles) at the poles and as much as 16 km (10 miles) around the equator. Most clouds and weather phenomena occur in this region. The composition of dry air at sea level is: nitrogen, 78.08 percent; oxygen, 20.05 percent; argon, 0.93 percent; and carbon dioxide, 0.03 percent. There are also lesser amounts of neon, helium, krypton, and xenon. These proportions change with altitude, lighter gases being more common at higher altitudes, but they are approximately the same everywhere on Earth at the same altitude. There are also variable quantities of water vapor, dust particles, and other compounds whose proportions change from place to place at the same altitude—fewer dust particles being found over oceans, and less water vapor over deserts. Temperature decreases with altitude in the troposphere.

The *stratosphere* is found between 11 km and 50 km (7–30 miles) out from the Earth's surface. Temperatures in this region rise slightly as altitude increases, to a maximum of about 0°C (32°F). Virtually coextensive with the stratosphere is the *ozonosphere*, or ozone layer, the region in which most of the atmosphere's ozone is found. Because ozone absorbs most of the sun's ultraviolet radiation, it is vital to the continued existence of life on the planet.

Beyond the stratosphere is the upper atmosphere, or *ionosphere*, so called because it is the layer in which atmospheric gases have been ionized by solar radiation. The ionosphere reflects certain wavelengths back to the surface, making it possible to transmit radio waves around the curve of the Earth. The ionosphere is further divided into the *mesosphere*, between 50 km and 80 km (30–50 miles), in which the temperature decreases with altitude to −90°C (−130°F); and the *thermosphere*, from about 80 km to 450 km (50–280 miles), in which the molecular temperature increases to as much as 1,475°C (2,690°F). To spacecraft traveling in the atmosphere, as the space shuttle does, however, the temperature seems cold because the molecules are so widely spaced. Beyond the thermosphere is the *exosphere*, extending to about 1,000 km (600 miles). In this layer, temperature no longer has the customary meaning.

Geologic Time

The life of our planet is measured in immense blocks of time divided into eons, eras, period, and epochs. These mark the development of Earth and form the geologic time scale. The planet's origin is generally put at about 4.6 billion years ago, the age of the oldest meteorites found. To appreciate the true length of geologic time, we can think of those 4.6 billion years as represented by a single year. The oldest fossil records go back only about 40 days, and humans' presence on the planet only about two hours. Modern humans would exist for only about five minutes of that year. As Lyell and Darwin demonstrated, the vastness of geologic time makes the notion of evolution possible and comprehensible.

One of the major divisions in the history of life occurs at the beginning of the Paleozoic Era and the Cambrian Period, about 540 million years ago, when some of the main groups of invertebrats appear for the first time in the geologic record. As a result, geologists often speak of the period before this as Precambrian time (4.6 billion years ago to 542 million years ago, also known sometimes as the Precambrian Epoch). More than 88 percent of Earth's history is Precambrian. Of the remaining time, when Earth has been home to animal life as we know it, the part that includes humans and their ancestors is less than 1 percent.

During the Mesozoic Era (245 million to 65 million years ago) marine reptiles, frogs, crocodiles and turtles appeared during the Triassic Period, and dinosaurs and early birds in the Jurassic and Cretaceous periods (208 million to 65 million years ago.) The Cenozoic Era, beginning 65 million years ago is divided into two periods, the Tertiary (65 million years ago to 1.8 million years ago) and the Quaternary (1.8 million years ago to the present); these are further divided into several Epochs that include the development of many of the mammals including horses, whales, elephants, dogs, and cats. (The Paleocene, Eocene, and Oligocene Epochs ended 23 million years ago.) During the next three Epochs lasting until 11,000 years ago (Miocene, Pliocene, and Pleistocene) giraffes, bears, mammoths, apes, and early hominids appeared; during the Pleistocene early human species, including *Homo erectus*, appeared. The final Epoch is the Holocene, which covers the last 11,000 years when modern humans, as well as much of the flora and fauna we know today, came into existence.

In recent years geologists have begun to say that the Earth may have entered a new Epoch at the beginning of the 20th century when science and technology combined to cause extraordinary changes in the composition of the Earth and its atmosphere. Some are now calling it the Anthropocene, the period when humans (*anthro* is Greek for man) changed the Earth through their use of fossil fuels, artificial nitrogen fertilizer, and the breeding of enormous numbers of livestock. Moreover, soaring population growth rates have introduced an element into the equation never experienced before.

Plate Tectonics

This scientific theory describes the drifting and shifting of large parts of Earth's crust and upper mantle, called plates. These complex motions cause the formation of mountains and abysses, of volcanoes and earthquakes, and of the very location of Earth's landmasses today. The plates move at an extremely slow pace—perhaps only a few centimeters each year, and the great distances now between them further deepen our appreciation of the length of geologic time.

In 1915 the German meteorologist Alfred Wegener (1880–1930) became the first to make a convincing case for these motions, although a few earlier scientists had recognized some parts of the concept. Wegener began with two simple observations: first, that the coastlines of some continents, such as Africa and South America, appear to fit together like the pieces of a jigsaw puzzle; and second, that many land species (contemporary ones and also those found in the fossil record) of widely disparate continents bear striking resemblances to one another. Wegener postulated that the continents must have at one time been joined together. Most earlier geologists and paleontologists had explained the similarities of coastline shapes as coincidence and the similar species as the result of "land bridges" which had once existed across oceans, but which had subsequently sunk into the sea floor.

Continental Drift Wegener gradually refined his theories and described a single, great protocontinent, which he dubbed Pangaea after the Greek for "whole Earth." This massive body was surrounded by a single vast ocean, Panthalassa, or "universal sea." For reasons that he was not at that time able to determine, Pangaea broke apart and pieces drifted slowly into place around the globe. This theory is known as *continental drift*. As refined by Wegener and later geologists, the theory states that toward the end of the Carboniferous period, Pangaea broke into two main bodies. The northernmost one, encompassing modern Europe, North America, and Asia, is called Laurasia. The southern one, Gondwana-land, contained Africa, South America, the Indian subcontinent, Australia, and Antarctica.

At the time of Wegener's death, however, many remained unconvinced. After World War II the idea of continental drift gained wide acceptance, first in a modified form called seafloor spreading and later as a part of plate tectonics.

Seafloor Spreading   One of the unexplained parts of continental drift concerned the great mountain chains and deep trenches found at the bottom of the oceans. The first to be recognized was the mid-atlantic ridge, which matches in general shape both the coastlines on each side of the Atlantic Ocean. A trench runs through the crest of this ridge. Other oceans have similar features, which are connected to form a worldwide mid-Oceanic ridge and also deep, curved trenches near chains of islands, such as the Marianas trench and the Philippine trench in the Pacific. In 1962, the American oceanographer Harry Hammond Hess (1906– 69) proposed that the ocean floor is created at the mid-Oceanic ridge and then spreads, widening the oceans. Sometimes the spreading pushes continents farther apart, but in places the ocean floor away from the ridges plunges into deep trenches. In the early 1960's the record of changes over long periods of time in Earth's magnetic field, found preserved in the rock of the ocean floor and in rocks on continents, confirmed both seafloor spreading and relative changes in the positions of the continents. The best explanation was that Earth's crust is broken into giant plates that move with respect to one another, sometimes carrying continents along.

Convergence and Divergence   The action and interaction of the plates, both gradually and in occasional sudden outbursts, have created most of the familiar features of the landscape. When the leading edge of one plate meets another plate, we call it convergence, and this is largely responsible for the creation of most mountain ranges. When plates pull apart, a process called divergence, hot molten rock wells up into the void between them. This happens generally under the oceans and is how new material is commonly brought from Earth's interior to the crust or surface. Sometimes, the plates neither come together nor pull apart, but simply move past each other, rubbing together along the edges. These transforms, as they are called, constitute the great geologic faults that we tend to fear, like the San Andreas Fault. The sudden spasms of activity lead to earthquakes, volcanic eruptions, and other natural cataclysms.

Physical Geology

The lithosphere is composed overwhelmingly of rock, or fragments of rock. (The specific scientific study of rocks is called petrology.) Most rock occurs in deposits called beds, which can form in a vertical plane as well as the more common horizontal plane. Rocks, in turn, are made up of minerals, although for the most part, minerals are not rocks. A mineral is a naturally occurring element or compound that has a precise chemical formula. Geologists classify rocks in three main groups, sorted by the process of formation: igneous, sedimentary, and metamorphic.

Igneous rocks are rocks that have formed by solidifying or crystallizing from a molten state, either lava (molten rock on Earth's surface) or magma (molten rock below the surface). Igneous rocks that form from lava are generally called volcanic rocks. Igneous rocks are often subcategorized according to texture, and in addition to the fine-grained rocks such as basalt, lava can also form glassy rocks, typified by obsidian. The speed of cooling normally determines the texture of the rocks, with glasses formed by very quick cooling. Since magma cools more slowly at depth than it does on the surface, rocks that crystallize far deeper within Earth, called plutonic rocks, typically form larger mineral crystals than the fine-grained surface-cooled rocks.

Sedimentary rocks are created by accumulation of deposited materials, including particles and fragments of rocks (sand or gravel), shells of sea animals, and chemical precipitates such as salt from evaporating water. The deposits slowly cement together over long periods of time. Examples of sedimentary rocks include sandstone, shale, and limestone. Sedimentary rocks often capture and contain fossils, footprints, and other clues to evolution.

Metamorphic rocks form as the result of heat, pressure, and chemical activity on igneous or sedimentary rock. These processes are slow and complex, highlighted by the recrystallization of the minerals of the rock. Without melting, the chemical elements and compounds reorganize under the influence of intense heat and pressure. Sometimes, even new minerals can be formed. As a result, metamorphic rocks are largely characterized by a regular crystalline structure, as opposed to the more random internal structure of igneous or sedimentary rocks. The regular patterned structure is typical of rocks like mica or gneiss, which tend to shear off cleanly (a property called

U.S. 100% Reliance on Imports[1] for Selected Strategic and Non-Strategic Minerals, 2010

Mineral	Major Import Sources in Order of Importance (2006–2009)
Arsenic (trioxide)	Morocco, China, Belgium
Asbestos	Canada
Bauxite and Alumina	Jamaica, Brazil, Guinea, Australia
Cesium	Canada
Fluorspar	Mexico, China, South Africa, Mongolia
Graphite (natural)	China, Mexico, Canada, Brazil
Indium	China, Canada, Japan, Belgium
Manganese	South Africa, Gabon, China, Australia
Mica, sheet (natural)	China, Brazil, Belgium, India
Niobium (Columbium)	Brazil, Canada, Germany, Estonia
Quartz Crystal (industrial)	China, Japan, Russia
Rare Earths	China, France, Japan, Austria
Rubidium	Canada
Strontium	Mexico, Germany
Tantalum	Australia, China, Kazakhstan, Germany
Thallium	Russia, Germany, Netherlands
Thorium	United Kingdom, France, India, Canada
Yttrium	China, Japan, France

Note: 1. Import reliance is defined on a net basis: U.S. imports minus U.S. exports, adjusted for government and industry stock changes. **Source:** United States Geological Survey, *Mineral Commodity Summaries 2011.*

cleavage) when broken. These rocks typically form under the more extreme conditions of metamorphism, and their minerals are arranged in roughly parallel lines (foliation), giving the rocks something of a banded appearance.

Strategic Minerals

Minerals are naturally occurring substances with characteristic and uniform chemical compositions and physical properties. A few minerals are elements (e.g. gold, iron, silver) but most are chemical compounds. Minerals are generally obtained by mining on land, although there is some ocean mining. Minerals are conveniently divided into two types: fuel and non-fuel minerals. This section deals with non-fuel minerals, especially those that are considered strategic. Strategic minerals are those deemed essential to the functioning of an economy, particularly with respect to war or other emergency conditions. Only some non-fuel minerals are strategic; others are widely found and produced. Some common and widely used minerals are so heavy and bulky that production tends to be relatively local; these minerals include crushed stone and sand and gravel for construction. Other minerals are traded internationally; the United States is wholly dependent on imports from other countries for at least 18

non-fuel minerals, both strategic and non-strategic.

In the United States, the concept of strategic minerals dates as far back as the First World War. By the late 1930s there were seven designated strategic minerals: chromium, manganese, mercury, mica, nickel, tin and tungsten. In the pre-computer, pre-space age economy of World War II, it was a relatively simple matter to identify a small number of strategic minerals. Now, although opinions differ, some 20 or more minerals can be considered as potentially strategic, depending on the nature of threat assessments. A strategic mineral is one that has key applications in defense or the civilian economy, cannot be easily replaced by other substances, and for which there are few or no available domestic supplies. Often strategic minerals have applications in the aerospace and electronics industries, alloys and superalloys, armaments, and high technology uses such as lasers and computers. An example of a strategic mineral is niobium (also called columbium), on which the United States is 100 percent import dependent. Niobium is vital as an alloy in steels and superalloys for aircraft turbine engines and other products; the principal source of imports is Brazil. The U.S. is also 100 percent import dependent for manganese, which is essential to iron and steel production; no practical tech-

9 Strategic Minerals with 75% or More U.S. Import Reliance[1], 2010

Mineral	% Import Dependence	Principal Uses	Sources (in order of importance, 2006–2009)
Cobalt	81	Superalloys for aircraft turbine engines	Norway, Russia, China, Canada
Germanium	90	Solar cells, fiber optics, infrared military devices	Belgium, China, Russia, Germany
Indium	100	Thin-film coatings for LCDs	China, Canada, Japan, Belgium
Manganese	100	Iron and steel production	South Africa, Gabon, China, Australia
Niobium (Columbium)	100	Alloys and superalloys for aircraft turbine engines	Brazil, Canada, Germany, Estonia
Platinum	94	Catalytic converters, laboratory equipment, electrical contacts and electrodes	South Africa, Germany, United Kingdom, Canada
Rare Earths	100	Catalytic converters, armaments, electronics, magnets	China, France, Japan, Austria
Tantalum	100	Electronic components	Australia, China, Kazakhstan, Germany
Zinc	77	Galvanizing, zinc-based alloys, brass and bronze	Canada, Peru, Mexico, Ireland

Note: 1. Import reliance is defined on a net basis: U.S. imports minus U.S. exports adjusted for government and industry stock changes. **Sources:** United States Geological Survey, *Mineral Commodity Summaries 2011*, The Hague Center for Strategic Studies (HCSS) and TNO, *Rare Earth Elements and Strategic Mineral Policy*, 2010, Department of Defense, *Reconfiguration of the National Defense Stockpile: Report to Congress*, 2009, National Research Council, *Managing Materials for a Twenty-first Century Military*, 2008.

nologies exist for replacing manganese with other materials and there is little prospect of substantial domestic production. The main import sources are South Africa and Gabon. Chromium, used in stainless steel and non-ferrous alloys, has been a strategic concern since World War I; there are few domestic sources and the U.S. is currently 56 percent dependent on imports, but recycling accounts for 46 percent of demand. Other critical minerals have special properties. For example, tungsten (68 percent import dependent), which is used to make heavy metal alloys for armaments, has the highest known melting point of all metals, 61700 F (34100 C). The United States is more than 75 percent import dependent on nine strategic minerals.

Policy toward strategic minerals requires the development of stockpiles, secure sources, recycling of materials, and research on substitute materials. The United States has had a strategic minerals stockpile program since just after World War II. The Defense National Stockpile Center oversees 20 depots, where 42 minerals are stored with a market value of $1.3 billion dollars. (Minerals research and reporting are functions of the U.S. Geological Survey.) Minerals are bought, sold and warehoused; there are sales from the stockpile when materials are no longer required and market disruptions can be minimized. Holding levels vary by mineral, year, and need.

The geopolitical problem of strategic minerals is assuring supplies and lines of communication. Source countries may be friendly or unfriendly, close or distant, developed or undeveloped, diverse or concentrated. Thus in times of international tension attempts may be made to diversify supplies and to draw supplies from friendly countries. The most favorable sources from the U.S. standpoint are countries such as Canada (cobalt, columbium, indium, thallium and other minerals) and Mexico (zinc, strontium and other minerals). These are friendly countries that are geographically close and linked to the U.S. by trade agreements. An example of a strategic mineral with favorable and diverse sources is zinc, which the U.S. imports primarily from Canada, Peru, Mexico and Ireland.

However, mineral supplies are not always conveniently and securely located in friendly countries, and are not always controlled by governments that meet reasonable standards of democratic process. Such cases can pose difficult and controversial geopolitical choices. For example, South Africa is the principal U.S. source of manganese, and dealing with this regime in the days of apartheid (dismantled beginning in 1989) provoked moral and ethical debate in the U.S. Chromium is a mineral imported by the U.S. from countries that have not always been friendly with the U.S.: South Africa, Kazakhstan, Russia, and China; in addition, shipping routes from all of these sources are subject to interruption in times of conflict.

There are also important moral and geopolitical issues in

trade of some non-strategic minerals. A leading example is "conflict diamonds," diamonds mined in Africa, the proceeds from which have been used to support civil conflicts in Sierra Leone, Angola and elsewhere. The United Nations General Assembly condemned trade in these diamonds in 2000, and in an effort to halt trade in conflict diamonds, initiated the Kimberly Process, which attempts to provide a paper trial identifying diamonds that are not from conflict areas. The U.S., which imports about half (by value) of finished diamonds, has a critical role to play if this trade is to controlled. The problem of conflict diamonds is reminiscent of earlier bloody episodes in Africa in which indigenous and outside forces fought at least partly over minerals in the Congo, South Africa and elsewhere.

The international situation has changed in recent decades in ways that may reduce some concerns with strategic minerals. The collapse of the Soviet Union and the development of trading relationships with China have provided somewhat more secure sources of minerals, although China's near-monopoly on rare earths and its attempts to control trade in them have been a concern (see "Lanthanides" in "Chemistry"). Russia, the former Cold War antagonist, supplies the U.S. with chromium, quartz crystal, cobalt and other minerals, and China supplies fluorspar, manganese, rare earths, tantalum and other minerals. As a result of such international developments, sales of some critical minerals from the U.S. stockpile have been permitted. However, geopolitical conditions can change rapidly and there will be a continued need for a strategic minerals policy.

Two other favorable developments are progress in materials science and in recycling. For example, the use of natural quartz crystals (except as gemstones) has largely been replaced by cultured quartz crystals, which are produced in highly controlled laboratory conditions. Among the many minerals for which recycling is an important source is chromium, which can be obtained from recycled stainless steel. These factors, like the easing of international tensions, provide more flexibility for the United States and other developed countries in strategic materials policy.

Structural Geology

Photographs of Earth from airplanes and satellites, as well as those taken from the surface of the moon or from cameras in space, display the great landmasses and the connected world ocean. There are mountains and canyons, fertile plains and swamplands, vast barren deserts and wide inland lakes. Although hidden from sight, similar variety exists at the bottom of the ocean. The processes that gave rise to each of these features are common, yet each locality, each type, has its own unique geologic history.

Folds, Faults, and Joints

Earth's surface is often deformed by tremendous pressures and forces. The resulting structures make up a major area of study for structural geologists. Faults and folds, which exist at the meeting point between various geologic planes and beds, hold special interest, as they are often the site of ongoing seismic activity.

Folds are deformed arrangements of stratified rock. Specialized terms for measuring and describing them include *strike*, the compass direction of the line made by the leading edge of an inclined bed; and *dip*, the angle of inclination of the bed from an imaginary horizontal plane. Where the *limbs*, or two sides of a fold, angle down, away from each other and from the central axis, the fold is called an *anticline*. Where they fold up, toward each other, it is called a *syncline*. The Appalachian Mountains in the eastern United States are characterized by complex fold structures.

Joints are long cracks or fractures common to most rock beds on the surface of Earth. Some joints result from folding or other deforming processes. Others are caused by contraction during the cooling of igneous rock, or when moist earth dries. Some are vertical, while others are parallel to the topographic surface of the area. The origin of these horizontal joints is uncertain, although possibly they are produced when rocks that have formed under great pressure at depth find their way to the surface through natural uplift, where they release some of that pressure.

Faults, like joints, are also breaks in Earth's crust. The critical difference is that a joint is a stable separation, but in a fault there either is or has been movement of rock on one side of the break in relation to the other. Faults are classified according to the type of movement they exhibit—vertical, horizontal, or sideways.

The San Andreas Fault is a well-known example of a fault. This fault, which is actually a system of smaller faults, extends from the Gulf of Mexico to northern California, a distance of roughly 600 miles, and continues into the Pacific. The *fault line* represents the meeting point of two large-scale sections of the lithosphere, the Pacific and the North American plates. Most earthquakes tend to happen along fault lines, and the San Andreas Fault is very active and has been the site of some significant events, such as the great earthquakes of 1906 and 1989 in San Francisco.

Other common geologic structures are formed by the fluctuation of forces beneath the surface of Earth, acting on a crust where the material varies in density and flexibility. We see a variety of upwellings and depressions—called, variously, domes, plateaus, basins, and esplanades—that formed through these geologic processes combined with erosion by wind and water.

Mountains

Mountains occur largely in long chains called ranges and in closely located groups called clusters. Occasionally one mountain appears to be isolated from all the others. The principles of plate tectonics provided geologists with the first reasonable explanations for the sources of mountains. Mountains are formed by a variety of complex processes, and each mountain range or cluster has a unique origin.

Volcanic Mountains
Some of the least complex mountains are volcanic; these form out of accumulation of material—magma, lava, ash, and other debris—that is released from the interior of Earth during a cataclysmic fissure or other event. Some of the iconic mountains of the world—Fuji, Kilimanjaro, Etna, Rainier—are volcanic mountains. Although volcanic mountains can appear in clusters, as they do in the Pacific Northwest of America, they do not arise in great chains and ridges like other forms of mountains. Where mountains appear in clusters or along ranges, they are formed from magma created by one plate sliding under another (along the west coasts of the Americas) or by a plate moving over a rising plume of magma (a "hot spot") from deep in Earth's interior.

Folded Mountains
The collisions of Earth's plates of crust that give rise to some volcanoes are related to the activity that causes folded mountains. These occur when plates push against each other also. Most of the great ranges of our world, such as the Alps and Himalayas, are folded mountains. In each case, a long period in which sedimentary material is built up is followed by the vertical uplifting of the mountains that results from compression, thrusting, and faulting of lithospheric plates. Much of this accumulation occurs in subsidence areas (where the crust has lowered), such as geosynclines, which are long, troughlike depressions, sometimes underlying large bodies of water.

Block Mountains
The origin of block mountains (sometimes called fault-block mountains) is also caused by collision of plates. Plates or sections of the crust collide and exert pressure against each other or pull apart, causing tension. When rock sections break, the results include large differences in elevation between the sections. Such processes are responsible for many of the rift valleys in Africa and for the Basin and Range region of the American West. The midocean ridges are also caused by plates moving apart from each other.

Last, mountains and ranges can be the result of a combination of processes that may include faulting, folding, and some igneous or volcanic element. Scientists describe these as complex mountains.

Glaciers

Glaciers are vast sheets of ice and rock that advance and recede across Earth's surface. They are found throughout the world at very high elevations, as well as in the high-latitude regions approaching the poles. Although they are an uncommon feature of the current landscape, glaciers played a major role in the geology of the relatively recent past and are responsible for many of the landforms and formations we take for granted today.

In order to form, glaciers require not only consistently cold temperatures, but also a significant amount of snowfall. The snow provides the raw material that accumulates to maintain the mass of the glacier. In some regions, such as parts of Antarctica, there is no permanent snow or ice cover on the land, because even though the temperature is sufficiently low, the region is too dry.

Once snow settles on the ground, it tends to undergo a structural transformation and is recrystallized into granules of ice. It is this new ice that becomes part of a glacier. Glaciers are said to "flow" or to behave like "rivers of ice," but this flow usually occurs very slowly.

Glacial advance is tremendously slow, ranging from a few inches to several miles annually, although it is punctuated by periods of greater velocity, called surges, which are possibly attributable to the breaking up of damlike accumulations of ice and rock at the leading edge of the ice sheet. The movement of ice sheets is partly due to the instability of the ice, which creates a certain plasticity. Some motion also results from the slippage of the entire ice sheet over the surface of the bed underneath it. As with rivers or streams, the central portion of a glacier tends to advance faster than the edges.

An ice age is a period of large-scale glaciation. Ice ages have occurred regularly throughout the history of the planet. The last one, which occupied the Pleistocene epoch and is believed to have ended as recently as 11,000 years ago, saw an enormous sheet of ice advance downward from the North Pole and spread across a major percentage of the Northern Hemisphere. In North America, the ice traveled down as far as New York in the East, Wisconsin in the Midwest, and Montana and Washington in the West. In Europe, it covered Scandinavia, northern Germany, Russia, and the British Isles. The Andes of South America, as well as major Asian mountain ranges, were also overtaken.

Many geologic features of today—including the sharply cut fjords of Scandinavia, the long lateral ridges of the northeastern United States, and large inland bodies of water such as the Great Lakes—are relics of the last ice age. The Pleistocene epoch probably had numerous periods of glaciation, with periods in between when the ice sheets shrank or receded. Scientists believe that we may be in just such an interglacial period and that in the not too distant future, another ice age is likely to be upon us.

The Earth in Upheaval

The apparent solidity and constancy of the land mask continued activity and upheaval. Just as the atmosphere can produce catastrophic phenomena such as hurricanes and gales, the lithosphere is also the site of cataclysmic events, from terrible earthquakes and volcanic eruptions to more commonplace landslides and sinkholes.

There were about 1,500 active volcanoes on the Earth's surface in 2009, with approximately 50 eruptions per year. The majority of these volcanoes are found in the "Ring of Fire," an almost 25,000 mile-long, horseshoe shaped seismically active belt that outlines the length of the Pacific Rim. The ring is formed by the subductions and collisions of seismic plates. The major plates found within this region are the Juan de Fuca plate, Filipino plate, Pacific plate, Cocos plate, Nazca plate, and the Antarctic plate. About 75 percent of the world's volcanoes are located here and 90 percent of the world's earthquakes take place here.

Earthquakes

Tension and compression build up in the Earth's crust, particularly along faults, where large masses of rock or tectonic plates push against each other. When the pressure is released, it usually happens quite suddenly, and the resulting vibrations, or seismic waves, are observed as an earthquake (the word *seismic* means "shaking" and simply refers to earthquakes). Several kinds of seismic waves are produced. Surface waves—also called L waves—travel along Earth's surface. Body waves, which travel through the interior, can be either compressional waves (P waves) or shear waves (S waves), which displace material in different directions and at different speeds as they travel. P waves are back-and-forth waves, essentially the same as sound waves; but for S waves the movement of rock is perpendicular to the movement of the wave, similar to ocean waves.

There are thousands of tiny earthquakes annually. Most are gentle tremors detectable only by sensitive seismographs, but each year a few are of moderate or greater intensity. Major earthquakes are dangerous and destructive, causing buildings or rock formations to fall, often resulting in great loss of life. The point of origin of an earthquake's energy is called its focus, and the depth of the focus below the surface of Earth is the focal depth. The point on the surface directly above a quake's focus is the epicenter, and the location of an earthquake is defined by both the epicenter and the focal depth.

Major earthquakes have occurred frequently around the Pacific Rim and running through the Indian subcontinent to the Mediterranean region. Some places hit by disastrous earthquakes have been California, Alaska, Peru, El Salvador, Iran, Turkey, the islands of the southern Pacific, China, and especially Japan.

Due to its location on the meeting point of the Eurasian, Filipino, and North American plates, located along the "Ring of Fire," Japan has had over 40 major earthquakes in its recorded history. The 1730 Hokkaido Island quake killed 137,000 people while the 1923 Great Kanto earthquake killed upwards of 142,000, making it the deadliest in Japan's history. Up to 1,500 earthquakes are recorded in Japan yearly, although they vary greatly in magnitude. Earthquakes in Japan are usually accompanied by tsunamis—such as the deadly Mar. 11, 2011 Tohoku earthquake that left over 15,000 people dead, with nearly 8,000 more people missing or unaccounted for. The tsunami that followed totally destroyed towns and villages and flooded a nuclear power plant that spewed radioactive material as far away as 20 miles.

In 2010, a powerful earthquake struck the island nation of Haiti, destroying the capital city of Port-au-Prince and killing more than 200,000 people, making it one of the most destructive quakes in history. However, the United States Agency for International Development puts the death toll between 46,000 and 92,000 people.

Measuring Earthquakes The size of an earthquake is generally reported in the United States using the Richter scale, a system developed by the seismologist Charles Richter (1900–85) in 1935. The Richter scale measures the magnitude of an earthquake, that is, the size of ground waves generated by an earthquake as shown on a measuring device called a seismograph. Each whole number on the scale represents a tenfold increase (or decrease) in magnitude: a magnitude 6 earthquake produces a ground wave 10 times greater than a magnitude 5.

This does not mean, however, that a magnitude 6 earthquake has 10 times the energy as one of magnitude 5. Measuring the actual energy requires instruments placed at the site of the earthquake. Various methods have been developed for inferring energy from magnitude, and these suggest that one change in magnitude corresponds to a thirty- to sixtyfold change in energy. According to these proportions, the energy of a magnitude 8 earthquake, a very serious event, can be 1 million to 10 million times as much as that of a magnitude 4 earthquake, one that can be felt but causes almost no damage.

Richter Scale and Effects Near the Epicenter

Note: The epicenter is the point on Earth's surface above the center of the quake

Below 2.5 Not felt except by a very few.

2.5 to 3.5 Felt only by a few persons at rest, especially on upper floors of buildings.

3.5 to 4.5 At lower levels or farther from the quake, it is felt by many people, sometimes quite noticeably indoors, especially on upper floors of buildings. At somewhat higher levels or nearer to the epicenter, during the day the quake is felt indoors by many but outdoors by few. Sensation is like heavy truck striking building. At the highest level, the earth movement is felt by nearly everyone, with many awakened if the quake occurs during the night. Disturbances of trees, telephone poles, and other tall objects can sometimes be noticed.

4.5 to 6.0 Felt by all. Some heavy furniture moved; there will be a few instances of fallen plaster or damaged chimneys. Other slight local damage may occur. At higher level, however, everybody runs outdoors. At the upper level, while damage is still negligible in buildings of good design and construction, there can be moderate damage even to well-built ordinary structures; there will be considerable damage to poorly built or badly designed structures.

6.0 to 7.0 Destructive earthquake. Damage may be slight in specially designed structures, but will be considerable in ordinary buildings, often with partial collapse. Damage will be great in poorly built structures, including collapse of chimneys, factory stacks, columns, monuments, and walls. At the upper level, damage is likely to be considerable even in specially designed structures. Most ordinary buildings will be shifted off foundations. Even the ground will be cracked conspicuously.

7.0 to 8.0 Major earthquake. Worldwide, about 10 of these occur each year. Some well-built wooden structures will be destroyed. Most masonry and frame structures will be destroyed along with their foundations. Ground becomes badly cracked.

8.0 and above Great earthquakes. These occur once every five to 10 years. Few if any masonry structures remain standing. Bridges are destroyed. Broad fissures appear in ground. At the highest levels and near the epicenter, damage total. Waves seen on solid ground. Heavy objects thrown upward into air.

Major Earthquakes (50,000 deaths or more)

Date	Location	Estimated Deaths	Date	Location	Estimated Deaths
Dec. 22, 856	Iran	200,000	Feb. 4, 1783	Calabria, Italy	50,000
Mar. 23, 893	Iran	150,000	Dec. 28, 1908	Messina, Sicily	75,000
Aug. 9, 1138	Aleppo, Syria	230,000	Dec. 16, 1920	Gansu, China	200,000
1268	Silicia (Turkey)	60,000	Sept. 1, 1923	Tokyo/Yokohhama, Japan	143,000
Sept. 1290	Chihli, China	100,000	May 22, 1927	Nan-Shan, China	200,000
Jan. 23, 1556	Shansi, China	830,000	Dec. 25, 1932	Gansu, China	70,000
Nov. 1667	Shemakha, Azerbaijan	80,000	May 30, 1935	Quetta, India (Pakistan)	50,000
Jan. 11, 1693	Catania province, Sicily	60,000	Oct. 5, 1948	Ashkaban, Turkmenistan	110,000
1693	Naples, Italy	93,000	May 31, 1970	Yungay and Huaras, Peru	66,000
Nov. 18, 1727	Tabriz, Iran	77,000	July 27, 1976	Tangshan, China	655,000
Dec. 30, 1730	Hokkaido Island, Japan	137,000	June 20, 1990	Caspian Sea, Iran	50,000
Nov. 30, 1731	Beijing, China	100,000	Oct. 8, 2005	Islamabad, Pakistan	86,000
Oct. 11, 1737	Calcutta, India	300,000	May 12, 2008	Eastern Sichuan, China	69,185
Nov. 1, 1755	Lisbon, Portugal	60,000	Jan. 12, 2010	Haiti	230,000[1]

Note: 1. Reported figure from Haitian government, although U.S. government says death toll was between 46,000 and 85,000.

Tsunamis

A tsunami is a destructive wave, usually formed by an underwater earthquake, a coastal landslide or the eruption of a volcano. These events displace huge amounts of water, causing it to rush towards land with devastating results. At sea a tsunami travels up to 500 miles per hour and is mostly underwater, as a boat encountering one is likely to experience a rise in sea level of only a few feet. As the wave approaches shore the sea-bed becomes steeper and more shallow, causing the tsunami to push above the surface. Rapidly, coastal waters are sucked out to sea, only to return in a crushing wave of up to 100 feet above sea level. This rush of water undergoes several oscillations (towards land, then back to sea,) destroying virtually anything in its path.

Historians believe the first known tsunami to have taken place in 6100 B.C. in the Norwegian Sea, based on recovered sedimentary material. In the 5th century B.C., the historian Herodotus described the Persian siege of the Greek town of Potidaea and its subsequent destruction by "a great flood-tide, higher, as people of the place say, than any of the many that had been before." And in 1755 an earthquake in Lisbon, Portugal caused a tsunami in Lisbon Bay, drowning many who had come to watch the suddenly receding tides. That earthquake and tsunami helped lead scientists to begin serious study of the Earth's makeup.

To this date the most destructive tsunami was caused by the eruption of the volcano Krakatoa in Indonesia in 1883. Approximately 36,000 people were killed in the ensuing waves with whole islands and villages left submerged throughout the entire Pacific region. On December 26, 2004 a tsunami off the island of Sumatra, Indonesia killed over 200,000 people in a wide area of Asia including Sri Lanka and India. Seven hours later it caused damage at the Horn of Africa, up to 1,800 miles away. An early warning system, established by the United States after a 1946 tsunami hit Hilo, Hawaii, could have saved many lives. As a result U.N.E.S.C.O. has set a goal to establish similar warning systems for the Indian Ocean and eventually the entire world.

Japan has experienced at least twenty major tsunami events in the modern era, so not surprisingly the word tsunami ("harbor wave") originated there. The March 11, 2011 event, caused by a 9.0 magnitude earthquake off the coast of Japan, left more than 23,000 people dead or missing and caused a nuclear crisis at the Fukushima I Nuclear Power Plant. The destruction was highlighted by the fact many around the world watched on live television, as video and photos poured in from Japan.

Blindsided by Ferocity Unleashed by a Fault

By KENNETH CHANG

On a map of Japan that shows seismic hazards, the area around the prefecture of Fukushima is colored in green, signifying a fairly low risk, and yellow, denoting a fairly high one. But since Japan sits on the collision of several tectonic plates, almost all of the country lies in an earthquake-risk zone. Most scientists expected the next whopper to strike the higher-risk areas southwest of Fukushima, which are marked in orange and red.

"Compared to the rest of Japan, it looks pretty safe," said Christopher H. Scholz, a seismologist at the Lamont-Doherty Earth Observatory at Columbia University, referring to the area hit worst by the quake on March 11. "If you were going to site a nuclear reactor, you would base it on a map like this."

Records kept for the past 300 years indicated that every few decades, part of the Japan trench, an offshore fault to the east of Fukushima, would break, generating an earthquake around magnitude 7.5, perhaps up to magnitude 8.0. While earthquakes that large would be devastating in many parts of the world, the Japanese have diligently prepared for them with stringent building codes and sea walls that are meant to hold back quake-generated tsunamis.

Shinji Toda, a professor of geology at Kyoto University in Japan, said a government committee recently concluded that there was a 99 percent chance of a magnitude-7.5 earthquake in the next 30 years, and warned there was a possibility for an even larger magnitude-8.0 quake. So much for planning. Although Japan's foresight probably saved tens of thousands of lives, it could not prevent the vast destruction of a magnitude-9.0 temblor, which releases about 30 times as much energy as a magnitude-8.0 quake. It was the largest ever recorded in Japan, and tied for fourth largest in the world since 1900. Thirty-foot tsunamis washed over the sea walls and swept inland for miles. The death toll is expected to be more than 20,000, and nearly 500,000 were living in shelters.

"I was surprised," Dr. Toda said. "Nobody expected magnitude 9."

This was not the first time scientists have underestimated the ferocity of an earthquake fault. Many were also caught by surprise by the magnitude-9.1 quake in 2004 off Sumatra, which set off tsunamis radiating across the Indian Ocean, killing more than 200,000 people.

Sometimes, scientists are blindsided by earthquakes because they occur along undiscovered faults. The deadly earthquakes in New Zealand in 2011; in Haiti in 2010; in Northridge, Calif., in 1994; and in Santa Cruz, Calif., in 1989 all happened along faults that scientists were unaware of until the ground shook. That raises a worrisome question: How many major quakes are lurking in underestimated or unknown faults?

The basic dynamics of earthquakes have been understood for decades. Earth's crust is broken into pieces—tectonic plates—which slide and collide. But the sliding is not always smooth. When the plates stick together, they begin to buckle. Stress builds until the ground breaks and jumps, releasing energy in the form of vibrations: an earthquake. Not surprisingly, places close to plate boundaries are beset by earthquakes, while those far from the boundaries are not earthquake-prone.

The largest earthquakes occur in subduction zones, places where an ocean plate collides with and slides under a continental plate, particularly around the edge of the Pacific Ocean.

But some subduction zones seemed to produce more large earthquakes than others. One explanation was offered in 1980, when Hiroo Kanamori of the California Institute of Technology and Larry J. Ruff, now at the University of Michigan, published a paper that said giant earthquakes occurred more often along ocean faults where the subducting ocean plates were geologically young. The younger plates, like those off Alaska and Chile, were warmer, less dense and harder to push down into the Earth's mantle, their thinking went. Meanwhile, the older, colder and denser ocean plates like those off Java and the Marianas trench in the Pacific would sink more easily and not produce the giant catastrophic quakes.

And yet the Pacific plate off Japan is 130 million years old, one of the oldest, and it generated a magnitude-9.0 counterexample.

Most regions of the world have less historical data than Japan, making it even harder to judge the earthquake patterns. Haiti is a prime example.

Even the notion of an earthquake fault—a long crack in the earth—is not quite as certain as it once was. Near Landers, Calif., seismologists had identified three faults, each capable of a magnitude-6.5 quake. Then, in 1992, an earthquake shook along all three faults at once, at a magnitude of 7.3.

In Japan's history, there does seem to have been a precedent for the recent quake, but it took place more than a thousand years ago. A text known as *Nihon Sandai Jitsuroku*, or *The True History of Three Reigns of Japan*, described an earthquake in July 869 and a tsunami that flooded the plains of northeast Japan: "The sea soon rushed into the villages and towns, overwhelming a few hundred miles of land along the coast. There was scarcely any time for escape, though there were boats and the high ground just before them. In this way about 1,000 people were killed." These were the same plains that were submerged this month. Analysis of sediments left by the 869 tsunami led to an estimate that the earthquake had a magnitude of 8.3.

Volcanoes

A volcano is an opening, called a vent or fissure, in Earth's crust through which solid rock fragments propelled by gases and lava (molten rock) escape from Earth's interior. The term *volcano* is used to describe both the vent itself and the mountain of accumulated discharged materials that builds up around it. The solid material is usually called ash or cinders when the pieces are small, but larger rocks are called bombs. When large amounts of ash, bombs, lava, or gases escape destructively, the process is called an eruption of the volcano. Volcanic eruptions can be both beautiful and horrific. History has seen untold thousands of lives lost and entire pockets of civilization wiped out by volcanic eruptions. Names like Vesuvius, Tambora, Krakatoa, Pinatubo, and Mount St. Helens echo as reminders of Earth's inherent instability and destructive power.

An active volcano either is currently erupting or has erupted in the very recent past (that is, in recorded history) and is considered likely to do so again, as Hawaii's Kilauea is. A volcano is dormant (sleeping) if it is not currently erupting but is believed likely to erupt at some point in the future. Many of the volcanic mountains in the American Northwest are considered dormant. We say a volcano is extinct if it has not erupted in historical time, and if geologists believe it unlikely to erupt in the future, because of a lack of seismic activity or other indicators of subsurface volatility. Africa's Mount Kilimanjaro is considered extinct.

Molten rock below Earth's surface, or magma, tends to rise because liquid rock is less dense than the surrounding solid rock and because magma contains gas under pressure. It collects in pockets or reservoirs under the surface, where its heat causes more of the surrounding rock to melt. Pressure builds in these reservoirs, and the magma and gases eventually force their way up through the surface, either through existing vents or fissures or through structurally weak sections of the crust. Some eruptions seem slow, with lava seeping and flowing gently through cracks in the surface; others are more like massive detonations, spewing great plumes of ash, rock, and steam over large areas of land and into the atmosphere. Either way, volcanic eruptions invariably alter the landscape, sometimes by blasting away large peaks and structures and always by depositing quantities of new material in the form of lava and debris, which build up new land formations. The vent becomes enlarged into a hole in the Earth called a crater. Sometimes an exploded volcano forms a caldera, a large-scale crater created by the collapse of underground magma reservoirs below the volcano.

Eruptions are categorized using the names of historically notable volcanoes or volcanic regions. The quietest eruptions are called Hawaiian and involve gentle emanations of lava and the ejection of debris with some small explosions. Somewhat more dramatic are Strombolian eruptions (after Stromboli in the Mediterranean), with constant recurring explosions and a relatively mild discharge of heavy, viscous lava. Plinian eruptions (after the Roman naturalist Pliny the Elder, killed in an eruption of Vesuvius in A.D. 79 that was described in detail by his nephew, Pliny the Younger) are still more explosive. Immediately prior to these eruptions, the magmatic pressure builds up behind a plug that has naturally formed in the vent that would have been the natural channel to the surface. Eventually, the dam bursts, ejecting material and vapor with great velocity. The most violent eruptions are the Peleean (named for a destructive eruption of Mount Pelée on Martinique in 1902), in which enormous clouds of fine ash and cinder, small bits of molten lava, and superheated steam are propelled sidewise from the eruption, destroying all in the path of the blast.

As catastrophic as volcanoes can be, they are also a mechanism by which valuable elements and minerals, including iron, magnesium, and potassium, are brought from Earth's interior to the surface. Volcanic soils are tremendously rich in these materials and are therefore very fertile. In addition, the study of volcanoes, much like the study of earthquakes, has engendered a much deeper understanding of the mechanisms and processes at work in Earth's interior.

Historic Volcanic Eruptions

Mt. Vesuvius, Italy (Aug. 24–26, 79)   Despite being dormant for centuries, Mt. Vesuvius erupted, crushing the city of Herculaneum under a torrent of mud and burying the cities of Pompeii and Stabiae under 25 meters of ash. Best known for the destruction of Pompeii and its remarkably preserved ruins, rediscovered in 1748, that show how its citizens died almost instantly while going about their daily lives. An estimated 2,000 people were killed.

Mt. Tambora, Sumbawa, Indonesia (Apr. 5, 1815) The largest volcanic eruption in recorded history, the explosion could be heard over 1,200 miles away on the island of Sumatra. The following year, 1816, became known as the "Year Without a Summer" because of the ash cloud's effect on the global climate. The resulting changes in weather patterns led to poor harvests while livestock died in large numbers. This led to one of the worst famines of the 19th century. Many of the estimated 92,000 victims died of starvation and disease, with up to 12,000 being killed by the actual eruption.

Krakatoa, Indonesia (Aug. 26, 1883)   A series of four massive explosions destroyed practically the entire island and produced what is considered the loudest sound ever in modern history— heard nearly 3,000 miles away. Most of the 36,000 victims died in the ensuing tsunamis, as the island was sparsely populated. Global temperatures dropped by an average of 1.2 degrees Celsius following the eruption, with weather patterns remaining changed for up to five years afterwards.

Mt. Pelee, Martinique (May 8, 1902)   Dubbed the worst volcanic disaster of the 20th century, 15 percent of the population, or 30,000 people, were killed in the eruption. Most of the victims were in the nearby town of St. Pierre, which was completely destroyed by the pyroclastic flow—a superheated cloud of ash, gas, and rock.

Mt. St. Helens, Washington, U.S. (May 18, 1980) Following a series of earthquakes that caused a huge bulge in the side of the mountain, the north face of Mt. St Helens collapsed, causing the largest known debris avalanche in recorded history. The pyroclastic flow flattened plants and buildings over a 230 square mile area, while 3,900,000 cubic yards of material was transported to the Columbia river, a distance of 17 miles. Due to its remote location, only 57 people were killed in the eruption.

Nevado del Ruiz, Colombia (Nov. 13, 1985)   Despite being monitored by scientists, the sudden eruption occurred amidst a terrible storm, preventing authorities from evacuating the surrounding areas. The snow-covered glacier quickly melted, sending rivers of water, hot ash, and debris cascading down the mountain. Most of the 23,000 victims were killed in this debris flow, which was recorded at speeds up to 31 miles per hour and reached distances of 45 miles away.

Mt. Pinatubo, Luzon, Philippines (June 9, 1991) After two months of minor earthquakes and emissions, Mt. Pinatubo erupted, sending ten cubic meters of material into the atmosphere and making it approximately ten times larger than the eruption of Mt. St Helens. Over 800 people were killed in the eruption with the majority being crushed under buildings toppled by the weight of the huge amounts of ash. The eruption had an enormous effect on the economy of the Philippines, with the GDP falling more than 3 percent between 1990 and 1991.

Eyjafjallajokull, Iceland (Apr. 14, 2010)   The series of eruptions sent massive plumes of ash into the atmosphere, caused electrical storms and disrupted flights to Europe over a period of six days. Caused minor damage to infrastructure resulting from melting ice and mud flows, but its greatest impact was on the airline industry and the economies of Europe.

Paleontology

Paleontology is the science of prehistoric life, generally defined as organisms that lived more than 10,000 years ago, prior to the end of the most recent ice age. The science is based on the nature and distribution of fossils, the remains or traces of organisms. In addition to satisfying our curiosity about organisms that lived long ago, paleontology provides evidence to support the concepts of evolution and continental drift (the idea that the positions of the continents have changed over time as a result of plate tectonics). It also helps to support the theory that impacts of asteroids and comets have been instrumental in wiping out significant portions of Earth's life at intervals in our planet's history—so-called mass extinctions. Economically, the study of fossils is valuable in searching for deposits of oil, coal, and other minerals, and in locating limestone and other materials used for construction and building.

The science has subdisciplines, such as paleobotany, the study of ancient plants; paleozoology, the study of ancient animals; and taphonomy, the study of the biological, chemical, and physical processes that lead to an organism's fossilization or its disintegration. Paleontology also relates to other disciplines that study the Earth's past, such as paleogeography, which focuses on Earth's geography as it existed during past eras; paleoecology, which considers the relationships between fossil organisms and the environment in which they lived; and paleoclimatology, the study of ancient climates.

The History of Paleontology

Ancient peoples knew of fossils, and presented various explanations to account for them. Some cultures turned fossils into mythological creatures and described giants that once terrorized Earth. In Greece, Herodotus (ca. 484–ca. 425 B.C.) and others realized that fossil seashells found in mountains were the remains of once-living creatures; but Aristotle (ca. 384–ca. 322 B.C.) suggested that fossils were natural accidents, produced much as crystals are produced, a theory that held sway for many centuries.

The scientific study of fossils began in the 17th century. In 1667 Nicolaus Steno (1638–86) showed that fossils previously believed to be serpent tongues were shark teeth. He proposed that sediments are deposited in horizontal layers, or strata; that strata represent different ages; and that fossils are remains of living creatures from those ages.

William Smith (1769–1839) showed that each rock layer has its own distinctive mix of fossils. In 1815, Smith published the first geologic map of England, proving the value of using fossils to define the order of rock layers.

Georges Cuvier (1769–1832), often called the founder of paleontology, discovered that species become extinct, identified pterosaurs as flying reptiles, and was the first scientist to systematically compare the anatomy of fossils and living organisms.

In South America during the 1830's, Charles Darwin (1809–82) examined the fossil remains of giant sloths and other extinct animals, and found fossils of ocean life high in the Andes. His publication in 1859 of *On the Origin of Species*, which proposed that a process he called natural selection is the main force in evolution, profoundly influenced paleontologists. They began looking for ancestors of modern organisms as well as "missing links"—intermediate, transitional forms between known species. The first such link, discovered in Germany in 1861, was *Archaeopteryx*, a primitive bird with characteristics of both its flightless reptile ancestors and modern birds.

Radioactive dating, computer imaging, molecular genetics, and other technologies introduced in the 20th century greatly expanded the study of fossils. Today, new fossil finds are filling blanks in the biological record and pushing back the dawn of life.

Fossils

More than 1 million species of fossil organisms have been identified. These range from microscopic bacteria to giant dinosaurs and tree ferns. Evidence of truly ancient fossils, much of it controversial, suggests that Earth may have had simple bacteria-like life as long as 3.5 billion years ago.

Fossil Types   There are two basic types of fossils. Body fossils are either actual remains of organisms or remains in which original chemicals have been replaced by other chemicals, typically silicon dioxide and other minerals from water seeping through the buried remains. Shells, bones, teeth, and petrified wood are common body fossils. Softer tissues, such as those that compose worms, are less likely to be preserved; they often are eaten by animals or broken down by bacteria and other decomposers. Thus the abundance of a species in the fossil record does not necessarily indicate its relative abundance during the age in which it lived.

Trace fossils are marks made by the activities of ancient organisms, such as footprints, burrows, leaf imprints, chemical traces, and tooth marks on bones. They reveal much about anatomy as well as the habits and habitats of their creators. For example, footprint size and the distance between prints in a track provide clues to the size, weight, and speed of the animal that made the track. Pollen from plants preserved in bog sediments in northern Europe demonstrates that cold-adapted species once lived much closer to the equator than they do today.

Dating Fossils   The age of a fossil may be determined using relative and absolute dating methods. Relative dating methods compare the ages of various fossils, indicating their relative ages but not their actual ages. For example, stratigraphy is based on the fact that in an undisturbed sequence of rock layers, fossils in lower layers are older than those in upper layers. Amino acid racemization uses the fact that amino acids—the building blocks of proteins—exist in two mirror-image forms, L and D. Amino acids in living things are of the L-form. At death, the L-form racemizes, or changes, into the D-form at a more or less steady rate, though this rate varies from site to site depending on environmental conditions. Thus the greater the extent of racemization, the older the fossil.

The discovery of radiation and radioactive decay led in the 20th century to the development of absolute dating methods that provide specific ages for fossils. These methods are based on the fact that radioactive isotopes decay at a specific rate, called a half-life. For instance, potassium 40 (half-life approximately 1.25 billion years) decays into argon 40 and calcium 40. Potassium-argon dating is usually used to date fossils found in volcanic rock or ash deposits, which are rich in potassium. Another technique, electron spin resonance dating, uses the changes that background radiation indirectly makes, at a predictable rate, in the magnetic field of crystalline minerals. It is used to date calcium carbonate in shells, teeth, and coral.

Dinosaurs   The fossil organisms of greatest appeal to laypeople are dinosaurs, land-dwelling reptiles that evolved from reptiles called thecodonts about 225 million years ago. Scientists have named approximately 700 species of dinosaurs. The smallest was *Compsognathus longipes*, a chicken-sized dinosaur that lived about 145 million years ago. The heaviest included *Brachiosaurus*, which lived about 150 million years ago and weighed as much as 70 to 90 tons. The longest may have been *Seismosaurus*, a long-necked plant eater that lived about 150 million years ago and reached lengths of more than 130 feet (39 meters).

Dinosaurs are classified in two groups. Ornithischia, or bird-hipped dinosaurs, had pelvic bones arranged like those of a bird hip, with the pubic bone bent backward. They were plant eaters with hooflike claws. This group included the duck-billed hadrosaurs, plated stegosaurids, beaked ceratopsians, and long-snouted iguanodontids.

The second group is the Saurischia, or lizard-hipped dinosaurs. Their pelvic bones were arranged like those of a lizard hip, with the pubic bone pointing forward. There were two main subgroups. The Theropoda were fast, agile hunters; they included *Tyrannosaurus rex*, *Velociraptor*, *Allosaurus*, and the ancestors of modern birds. The Sauropodomorpha were plant eaters with massive bodies, long tails, and front legs smaller than the back legs. *Brachiosaurus* was a well-known example.

Dinosaurs became extinct around 65 million years ago during a mass extinction known as the Cretaceous-Tertiary or K/T event. It is believed that the event resulted from the collision of an asteroid with Earth, at a point on the northwest coastline of the Yucatán Peninsula in Mexico. A crater 106 miles (170 kilometers) across formed, shooting billions of tons of matter into the atmosphere, which blotted out the sun and caused global temperatures to plummet.

CHEMISTRY

Chemistry is the study of the nature of matter, the way substances can change and interact with one another, and the energy flows that result when these changes take place. Following a long period of impressive development in the 18th and 19th centuries, chemistry has become one of the great scientific disciplines, an expansive enterprise of exploration, analysis, and application. Chemical methods are essential to the working of modern economies, and chemical knowledge and processes relate the discipline to many other pure and applied sciences, including agronomy, biology, ecology, metallurgy and solid-state physics. The main branches of chemistry include *organic chemistry*, the study of carbon compounds including those essential to living beings; *inorganic chemistry*, the study of compounds other than those containing carbon; *physical chemistry*, in which the laws of physics are used to study chemical substances and processes; and *analytic chemistry*, the study of the constituents of a substance and their relative amounts. There are also many more specialized fields, such as electrochemistry, photochemistry, quantum chemistry, and others. Biochemistry, the study of the chemistry of biological processes, has developed into a separate discipline.

History of Chemistry

The early development of applied chemical processes can be dated to the Neolithic Revolution (about 6000 B.C.), which brought the spread of sedentary agriculture and a rise in population. The first metal to be extracted from ore by heating was probably copper. Both copper and lead were in use by 4000 B.C., and bronze, a combination of tin and copper produced by 3000 B.C., gave its name to the Bronze Age. Silver was produced as a by-product of smelting lead, and iron was made by about 1000 B.C. (the Iron Age). Pottery making was another early chemical process: by 3000 B.C. kilns were in use that had temperatures high enough to cause chemical changes in clays to produce durable pottery. Dyes were also made by chemical means.

Greek Science In Greece in the first millennium B.C., an atomic theory of matter was developed, but the theory that dominated chemistry for centuries was Aristotle's view that there are four elements: earth, air, fire, and water. They could be transformed one into the other, and in turn all were composed of the fundamental primary matter. In reality Aristotle's theories explained relatively little, but they held sway in the West as late as the 16th century.

Alchemy In Alexandria, Egypt, chemical practices in the early centuries A.D. were linked to alchemy (the attempt to turn base metals into gold). It was believed that the end product of the maturation of metals in the earth was gold, and that this process might be accelerated in the laboratory. The center of alchemical work later shifted to the Islamic world, and finally to Europe, where alchemical ideas held sway into the 17th century. China also had a long alchemical tradition, which contributed to the development of early forms of gunpowder. Throughout its history alchemy was bound up with a series of philosophical and mystical beliefs. Although the alchemists did not succeed in their goal, many laboratory techniques were developed in their efforts that were later used for more productive purposes.

The Scientific Revolution The beginnings of the scientific revolution in the West and the ultimate rise of scientific chemistry can be traced generally to the 16th and 17th centuries, when Nicolaus Copernicus and Galileo Galilei challenged the idea of the Earth as the center of the universe. Experimental science too hold in the 17th century and Robert Boyle (1627–91) took the lead in the study of how chemical reactions occur. Evangelista Torricelli (1608–47) demonstrated the possibility of a vacuum, formerly thought impossible. Boyle's protégé Robert Hooke (1635–1703), who improved the microscope, prepared regular experiments for the meetings of the Royal Society in London. Sir Isaac Newton (1642–1727) proposed his theory of gravity. These developments had a profound influence on the development of modern chemistry.

The Chemical Revolution

Between 1770 and 1790, the so-called chemical revolution gave birth to modern chemistry. Early in the century, the process of combustion, perhaps the most obvious of chemical reactions, was explained by the theory of phlogiston, which was believed to be a common constituent of matter but one so hard to detect that it could be noticed only when phlogiston left a burning substance and ashes remained. This view seemed to explain many chemical phenomena, but became increasingly hard to accept as new discoveries proliferated. Joseph Black (1728-99) discovered carbon dioxide in 1755; Joseph Priestley (1733–1804) discovered oxygen in 1774; and Henry Cavendish (1731–1810) discovered that water was hydrogen and oxygen in 1784 (all of these gases were known by different names at the time). However, the chemical revolution is most closely associated with the name of the great French chemist Antoine-Laurent Lavoisier (1743–94). He demonstrated the true nature of combustion and definitively overthrew the phlogiston theory, worked with others to reform chemical nomenclature from its older alchemical roots, and introduced the modern idea of an element as a substance that could not be decomposed. His famous textbook, called in English *Elements of Chemistry*, was published in 1789. The work of Lavoisier and his colleagues is the foundation of chemistry as a science.

Chemistry and Industrialization

During the 19th century there were many developments that still mark chemistry as a science. By the end of the 19th century more than 80 elements were known, as compared with some 32 at the end of the 18th. Early in the century, the chemical atomic theory held that each element had a different atom and that therefore elements could not be transmuted, as had been the goal of alchemy. Robert Bunsen (1811–99) developed his gas burner, and Bunsen and Gustav Robert Kirchhoff (1824–87) developed the atomic spectrograph, with which elements could be identified by their characteristic wavelengths. Dmitry Mendeleyev (1834–1907) developed the first satisfactory periodic table of the elements, later much revised and extended. In the latter half of the 19th century studies of molecular structure and the optical activity of molecules flourished. The nature of carbon bonds was discovered, and the organic chemical industry grew rapidly. Perhaps the most important aspect of 19th-century chemistry from the standpoint of the average person was the rise of the chemical industries and the crucial role they played in industrialization and economic modernization. The 19th century also saw the professionalization of chemistry as a discipline and career.

Modern Chemistry

The 20th century provided the chemical developments that in large part define the modern world. Building on the discovery of radioactive substances in the late 19th century, scientists studied the nature of radioactivity. The concept of the electron was elucidated by Joseph Thomson (1856–1940), and the structure of the atom, using quantum-theoretic ideas, was developed by Neils Bohr (1885–1962). The nature of the chemical bond through valence electrons was understood. This activity in chemistry (and physics) created the nuclear age. Industrial and practical chemistry continued to develop throughout the century, beginning notably with the Haber-Bosch process used to produce ammonia for fertilizers and other uses prior to World War I. Among new drugs were the sulfanilamide drugs and penicillin (first produced in quantity during World War II), which revolutionized medicine in war and peace. The chemistry of materials continued to flourish. In the postwar period there was also increased concern about the negative environmental effects of chemistry, and there is now a focus on "green chemistry" to alleviate these.

Applications of Chemistry

Enormous chemical industries underpin modern industry, commerce, and agriculture. The table on page 579 shows the top 20 industrial chemicals produced in the United States. Two of these of particular importance are described here.

Sulfuric Acid Most people know sulfuric acid (H_2SO_4) only from the high school chemistry laboratory, where it provides a lesson in the careful handling of dangerous chemicals, and from the one common consumer product that contains it, lead-acid automobile batteries. But in fact sulfuric acid is the most important industrial chemical in the world, and the most commonly used strong acid; nearly all manufactured products depend on sulfuric acid in some way. About 40 million metric tons are produced in the United States each year, far exceeding the amount of other important industrial chemicals. Sulfuric acid is used in the production of agricultural fertilizers (the largest volume use), and in metal processing and refining, electroplating, water treatment, petroleum refining, and the removal of oxides from iron and steel prior to galvanizing and electroplating.

Ammonia and Feeding the World Ammonia (NH_3) is a pungent, colorless gas that is soluble in water; it is a familiar household cleanser. But its main use is much more important: manufactured ammonia is used primarily to produce nitrogen fertilizers, which are of immense importance in feeding the world's population: it is estimated that some 40 percent of the world's protein needs are produced with nitrogen fertilizers. Fritz Haber (1868–1934), after years of experimentation, developed the first successful process (1908) to produce ammonia from the elements, a feat for which he won the Nobel Prize for Chemistry (1918). Carl Bosch (1874–1940) provided the engineering to bring the first commercial plant on line in 1913. The Haber process uses nitrogen, separated from liquid air; and hydrogen, produced usually from a hydrocarbon. An iron catalyst is used to speed up the reaction, which is undertaken at about 4,500 degrees Celsius and an air pressure equivalent to several hundred times normal atmospheric pressure. (Nitrogen-fixing bacteria perform a similar function under normal pressure and temperature conditions.) The production of ammonia is one of the most widespread applied chemical processes. There are hundreds of plants that produce ammonia in 80 countries, with an estimated production (in 2000) of 130 million metric tons. More than half of ammonia production is in developing countries, and about 85 percent of worldwide production is used to make nitrogen fertilizers; India and China together account for more than one-third of nitrogen fertilizer production. Ammonia is used for other products as well, including dyes, resins, and explosives.

Top 20 Industrial Chemicals Produced in U.S.

Rank	Chemical	Production (in 10^9 kg)
1.	Sulfuric acid	39.62
2.	Ethylene	25.15
3.	Lime	20.12
4.	Phosphoric acid	16.16
5.	Ammonia	15.03
6.	Propylene	14.45
7.	Chlorine	12.01
8.	Sodium hydroxide	10.99
9.	Sodium carbonate	10.21
10.	Ethylene chloride	9.92
11.	Nitric acid	7.99
12.	Ammonium nitrate	7.49
13.	Urea	6.96
14.	Ethylbenzene	5.97
15.	Styrene	5.41
16.	Hydrogen chloride	4.34
17.	Ethylene oxide	3.87
18.	Cumene	3.74
19.	Ammonium sulfate	2.60
20.	1,3-Butadiene	2.01

Source: *Chemical Engineering News*

The Elements

The elements are the basic building blocks of the chemical world. Elements are known by abbreviations of one to three letters, most often from their modern names but sometimes from earlier (especially Latin) names. For example, aluminum has the abbreviation Al, from its name in English, whereas gold has the abbreviation Au, from the Latin word for gold, *aurum*. An element is defined by the number of protons (positively charged particles) in its atomic nucleus. This number is the atomic number of the element. There are at present more than 100 known elements. Elements 1 through 94 are observed in nature; the elements beyond 94, not all of which have been observed, are produced in nuclear facilities and research laboratories. Elements above 83 (bismuth) decay radioactively. The highest atomic number of an element that has been observed to date is 116; elements 113 and 115 have not yet been produced.

Atomic Structure

An atoms's nucleus contains *neutrons*, which have no electric charge, as well as *protons*. Each neutron weighs approximately as much as a proton. An element's atoms all have the same number of protons, but some atoms of an element can have different numbers of neutrons. Different combinations of neutrons with the fixed number of protons that defines the element are called *isotopes* of the element. The total of protons and neutrons of an element or one of its isotopes is the *mass number* of the element. In addition to the particles in the nucleus of an atom, there are negatively charged *electrons*, which have very little mass, in orbit around the nucleus. The *atomic weight* of an element is its weight as compared with one-twelfth of the weight of the principal isotope of carbon, carbon 12, which is used as the standard atomic mass unit, or amu. The atomic weight in tables is the average atomic weight of an element's known isotopes, adjusted for the frequency with which they occur. Thus, the atomic weight of carbon, which would be 12.00 if all carbon were isotope 12, is given as 12.011 because there are small amounts of carbon 13 and carbon 14 in every sample of carbon. In 2010, the International Union of Pure and Applied Chemistry adopted new values of atomic weights for 10 elements: hydrogen, lithium, boron, carbon, nitrogen, oxygen, silicon, sulfur, chlorine and thallium, that have two or more stable (nonradioactive) isotopes. These new weights are given as ranges, rather than single values, to reflect the fact that isotopes of these elements occur in different proportions in different natural materials. (Such differences in isotopic composition can make it possible for scientists to trace samples of material to their sources.) For example, the atomic weight of carbon is now given as [12.0096–12.0116], rather than the previous single value of 12.011. The chemical activity of an element is produced by the electrons in outer orbits, called valence electrons; in chemical reactions, the nucleus is not changed. Elements are thus the building blocks of chemical reactions.

The Periodic Table

The periodic table arranges the elements in an orderly fashion that reflects their underlying atomic characteristics. The term "period" refers to the rows of the table, which group elements in such a way that elements in the columns, progressively heavier, have similar chemical characteristics. The periodic table shown here is the so-called "long form" in current use. Each entry shows the chemical symbol for the element, its name, its atomic number (which is equal to the number of protons in the nucleus), and its atomic weight. For elements that do not occur in nature, the most common known isotope is listed.

The current periodic table stems from the first successful early periodic table, compiled in 1869 by Dmitry Mendeleyev. Mendeleyev built on the considerable knowledge developed by chemists in the 18th and 19th centuries about the elements (more than 50 were known at the time) and their characteristics, including atomic weights and spectrographs.

THE PERIODIC TABLE OF THE ELEMENTS

The Modern Form of the Periodic Table   The long form of the table reflects our current knowledge of atomic structure and the many new elements found in the 20th century, including those synthesized in nuclear facilities. The table consists of seven rows of 2, 8, 8, 18, 18, 32, and 32 elements, respectively. The elements are arranged by atomic number, rather than by atomic weight. Most elements are classed as metals, i.e., substances with good electrical and heat conductivity. These are divided into groups: alkali metals, alkaline earth metals, transitional metals, and other metals. The table also includes nonmetals, toward the right-hand side, and the noble gases in the last column on the right. Two elements are classed as liquids: mercury and bromine. Elements with atomic numbers higher than uranium have been produced in nuclear facilities and laboratories; two elements with atomic numbers smaller than that of uranium that occur naturally in very small traces (technetium and promethium) are also shown here as human-created, which is how they were first identified. The lanthanide and the actinide series do not fit neatly into the column structure of the table, and are usually shown separately from the rows of which they are a part. Hydrogen and helium are placed as shown because of their special characteristics, hydrogen as a gas and helium as a noble gas.

Finding New Elements   In the first third of the 20th century, 88 elements were known, up through uranium (92), with four elements missing. The first of these, technetium (43), was produced in 1937; francium (87) was produced in 1939; astatine (85) in 1940; and promethium (61) in 1945. The extent to which new elements (the transuranic elements) can be produced beyond the elements up to 92 is limited by the basic properties of nature. These fundamental forces suggest an upper bound to the periodic table of about 125 elements. The reactions involved in nuclear synthesis are complex, and success in finding a new element requires a balancing of the production of a new element with its ability to survive long enough to be identified. In general, the heavier the new element, the more likely it is to decay by fission, and therefore the less likely are the prospects for its survival. The first transuranic element to be produced and identified was neptunium (93), by Edwin M. McMillan (1907–91) and Philip H. Abelson (1913–2004) at Berkeley, Calif., in 1940. Neptunium was produced by bombarding uranium with neutrons in the Berkeley cyclotron (neptunium also occurs naturally in minute quantities in uranium ores).

The element with the highest atomic weight thought to have been observed as of 2010 is 118. Additions to the Periodic Table are approved by the Internation Union of Pure and Applied Chemistry and the International Union Pure and Applied Physics.

The Elements

The known elements are described here in alphabetical order. Following the name of the element, the symbol is given in parentheses. The atomic number and weight of each element can be found in the periodic table. The generally accepted discoverers of the elements found in modern times are given together with the date of the discovery and the country in which it took place.

Actinium (Ac) Actinium is the first of the radioactive rare-earths, the metals 89–102, which are called collectively the *actinides* and are grouped in a separate row in the periodic table. Discovered by André Debierne (1899, France), who extracted it from uranium ore, it is a soft, silvery-white metal used in research. Actinium glows in the dark and is named from the Greek *aktinos*, or "ray."

Aluminum (Al) Aluminum, a soft workable metal, is the most abundant metal in the Earth's crust. Its name is from the Latin *alumen*, "bitter salt." It was known in ancient times in the form of alum (potassium aluminum sulfate), and has been used in medicine to stop bleeding, in papermaking, and to fix dyes in cloth making. The first metal was obtained in 1825 (Hans Christian Oersted, Denmark), but the aluminum metal industry was begun only late in the 19th century when a process was developed to extract the metal from its salts by electric current. Today, aluminum and its alloys have many uses, including metal parts for houses, cars, aircraft, and drink cans. Compounds are used in paper treatment and water purification. Aluminum is still produced with heavy input of electricity, which makes recycling this metal especially advantageous.

Americium (Am) A radioactive rare-earth element, discovered by Glenn T. Seaborg and others (1944, U.S.) and named for America. Am-241, produced by nuclear reactors, is the source of ionizing radiation in smoke detectors.

Antimony (Sb) A *metalloid*, antimony has characteristics of both metals and nonmetals. It was known in ancient times and used for vases, as a cosmetic, as a glaze, and for medicinal purposes (although it is now known to be toxic to humans). Its name is from the Greek, *antimonos* ("not alone"), and its symbol is from the Latin *stibium* for antimony sulfide.

Argon (Ar) Discovered in 1894 by William Ramsay and John Strutt (England), argon is a noble gas whose name derives from the Greek *argos*, "idle." Obtained from liquid air, argon is completely unreactive in ordinary conditions, but is important commercially as an inert atmosphere in lightbulbs and for metallurgical processes.

Arsenic (As) Arsenic (thought to be from the Greek *arsenikon*, for a yellow mineral) compounds were known in ancient times, and were used for purposes including gilding; the element itself was discovered by Albertus Magnus in the 13th century. Arsenic, which is essential in trace amounts for some animals, has a long history as a poison. Its modern uses include gallium arsenide semiconductors and specialized glasses.

Astatine (At) A member of the halogen group, astatine (after the Greek for "unstable") was discovered (1940, U.S.) by Dale R. Corson and others. Little is known about this dangerously radioactive element, whose longest-lived isotope has a half-life of eight hours.

Barium (Ba) An abundant alkaline earth element, barium was first isolated by Humphry Davy (1808, England) and named for the Greek *barys*, "heavy." Many of its compounds are toxic to humans, but barium sulfate can be ingested for X-ray medical diagnosis. Other uses are in lubricants and alloys.

Berkelium (Bk) Berkelium was first produced in 1947 by Glenn T. Seaborg and others (U.S.) at the University of California at Berkeley and named after the university. It is a radioactive, silver-colored metallic transuranic element; the 243 isotope has a half-life of five hours. There is no known use for berkelium, and it is not found in nature.

Beryllium (Be) Beryllium, discovered (1798, France) by Nicholas Louis Vauquelin, is named after one of its minerals, beryl. The element beryllium is toxic when breathed or swallowed; it is used primarily as an alloy with copper and nickel. When beryl is of high quality it is a well-known gemstone, emerald.

Bismuth (Bi) Bismuth (after the German *weisse masse*, "white mass," referring to an ore) was discovered in the Middle Ages and used to craft caskets and other objects, sometimes alloyed with lead, with which it was confused until the 18th century. Its principal current use is as a catalyst for the production of synthetic fibers ; it also yields a pearl color in cosmetics.

Bohrium (Bh) Bohrium is a radioactive transfermium metal named after Neils Bohr, the Nobel Prize–winning

Danish physicist. Credit for its discovery is shared by the Laboratory for Heavy Ion Research (1981, Germany) and Yuri Oganessian and others (1976, Russia). Uses: research.

Boron (B) Boron, from the Arabic *buraq*, "borax" (sodium borate), is essential to plants. The element was discovered independently (1808) by Louis-Joseph Gay-Lussac and Louis-Jacques Thenard (France) and Humphry Davy (England), but borax was known at least since the early Middle Ages, when it was used in metalwork and in medicine; more recently it was used as a bleaching agent in household detergents. Boron is now used in making heat-resistant glass and ceramic glazes, and as an additive to fertilizers.

Bromine (Br) Bromine, a member of the halogen group, was isolated by Antoine-Jerome Ballard (France, 1826); it is named from the Greek word for "stench," *bromos*. Bromine is highly toxic; bromides, used in 19th-century medicine, are only mildly so. Bromine is used in industry to make compounds for pharmaceuticals, pesticides such as methyl bromide, and fire extinguishers. Bromine is implicated in ozone destruction and many of its uses are being phased out; the production of methyl bromide, for example, will eventually cease by international treaty.

Cadmium (Cd) Discovered by Friedrich Strohmeyer (1817, Germany), and named after the Latin for the mineral calamine (*cadmia*), cadmium is highly toxic to humans and poses dangers from accumulation in the environment. It is used in nickel-cadmium batteries and to electroplate steel for protection from seawater; many other uses have been discontinued.

Calcium (Ca) Calcium is essential to most living things, and is the most abundant metal in the human body, primarily in bone. Elemental calcium was discovered by Humphry Davy (1808, England), and named after the Latin for "lime," *calx*. In metallic form it is soft and silvery, a member of the alkaline earth metal group. Since ancient times, calcium, as calcium oxide (lime), has been mixed with sand and water to produce mortar. Calcium is now used as lime in metallurgy, chemicals, water treatment, and the production of cement. Calcium metal is also used in metallurgy and alloys. Gypsum, a hydrated calcium sulfate, is used as plaster.

Californium (Cf) Highly radioactive rare-earth (actinide) element produced in 1950 in Berkeley, California by Stanley G. Thompson and others, and named after the university and state. It is produced in nuclear reactors and has limited uses as a neutron emitter in mineral prospecting and cancer therapy.

Carbon (C) Carbon has been known since ancient times in various forms such as coal, charcoal, peat, the soft crystal graphite, and the hard crystalline form diamond; its name is from the Latin for "charcoal," *carbo*. Carbon forms very strong bonds to itself which are resistant to chemical attack, and the resulting chains of carbon atoms form compounds that are found in all living cells. Carbon represents 23 percent of human body mass, and most of our food is made up of carbon compounds. An entire field, organic chemistry, is devoted primarily to the study of carbon compounds (of which some 20 million are known). Carbon has several isotopes, the most common of which is carbon 12, which makes up 99 percent of carbon; carbon 13 amounts to about 1 percent. (Small amounts of carbon 14 exist; this is radioactive with a half-life of 5,730 years and is used to date archeological material.) Carbon is used industrially in ironmaking, printing, as activated charcoal in water treatment, and as fibers to strengthen laminates in aerospace and in sports equipment. The most substantial industrial use of carbon is as fuel: enormous amounts of carbon are extracted from the earth in the form of fossil fuels, and the resulting increase in carbon in the atmosphere has led to global warming. In 1985 *fullerenes*, a new form of carbon, were produced. These are polyhedral (approximately spherical) structures composed of carbon 60; *nanotubes* are cylindrical forms of fullerenes.

Cerium (Ce) A soft gray reactive rare-earth metal, cerium was discovered 1803 or 1804 by Jöns Jacob Berzelius and Wilhelm Hisinger in Sweden and independently by Martin Klaproth in Germany. Widely available in mineral form, it is used in carbon-arc electrodes for floodlights, in catalytic converters, in glass as a filter for ultraviolet rays, and in self-cleaning ovens. It is named after the asteroid Ceres, which in turn was named after the Roman goddess of agriculture.

Cesium (Cs) Discovered (1860, Germany) by Robert Bunsen and Gustav Kirchhoff, and named after the Latin for "sky blue," *caesius*, for the blue rays of its atomic spectrum. Cesium from minerals has specialized industrial uses in enhancing catalytic reactions, as a glass coating, and in medical diagnosis. Cesium-137, a radioactive isotope produced in nuclear reactors, is environmentally dangerous (it was emitted at Chernobyl).

Chlorine (Cl) Chlorine is a greenish-yellow gas (C_2) that is highly reactive and dangerous; it is a member of the halogen group. As chloride (a chlorine atom with a negative electron) it is essential to many living things, including humans. It was identified as an element (1810, England) by Humphry Davy, and named after the Greek for "greenish-yellow," *chloros*. The first significant use of chlorine was as a bleach in the late 18th century (hydrochloric acid had been used earlier by alchemists). Chlorine today is used in the chemical industry, in manufacturing polyvinylchlorides (PVCs), in water purification (one of the most effective of public health measures), bleaching and other uses. The production of chlorofluorocarbons, harmful to the ozone layer, is being phased out.

Chromium (Cr) Chromium is an essential trace metal in humans and other species. Discovered (1798, France) by Nicholas Louis Vauquelin, it is named after the Greek for "color," *chroma*, for its bright compounds. Used in stainless steel and other alloys, it can also be used to coat steel for car parts ("chrome").

Cobalt (Co) Cobalt, a constituent of vitamin B12, is essential to humans, and cobalt minerals have been used since ancient times to produce a deep rich blue in glass and other materials. The element itself was isolated in 1739 (Sweden) by Georges Brandt; it is thought to be named after the German for goblin, *Kobald*, so called by miners who were fooled into thinking one of its ores was silver. Cobalt is widely used in alloys for such varied products as razor blades, jet engines, and magnets (cobalt maintains its magnetism at high temperatures). It is a blue pigment in glass, ceramics, and jewelry; a radioactive isotope, Co 60, is used in medicine and to irradiate food.

Copernium (Cn) A transfermium element produced in 1996 by Peter Armbruster and others (Germany), it is below mercury in the periodic table. Uses: research.

Copper (Cu) Copper is essential to living things, in which it forms part of important enzymes; in large amounts it can be toxic. It was known and worked in ancient times; its name and symbol derive from the Latin name for Cyprus, *Cuprum*, where copper was mined. It has been used for 10,000 years, worked from natural nuggets, and has been mined and smelted for 7,000 years and used as copper or in an alloy with tin to produce bronze. Copper is an excellent conductor of heat and electricity, and most copper is now destined for electrical equipment. Other uses are in construction and industrial machinery.

Curium (Cm) Highly radioactive rare-earth element produced in 1944 by Glenn T. Seaborg and others (U.S.). Curium 242, produced from plutonium in reactors, is used as an energy source in pacemakers, navigational buoys, and space missions. It is named after Pierre and Marie Curie.

Darmstadtium (Ds) A transfermium element produced in 1994 by Peter Armbruster and others (Germany), with earlier Russian and American claims. Uses: research.

Dubnium (Db) A radioactive transfermium element reported in 1967 by Georgy Flerov and others (Russia) and named after the city in which they worked, Dubna. Uses: research.

Dysprosium (Dy) A soft, bright silvery rare-earth metal, it has limited uses in halide lamps and as a neutron absorber in nuclear reactors. Its name (from the Greek, *dysprositos*) means "hard to get"; its discoverer, Paul-Émile Lecoq de Boisbaudran (1886, France), found it difficult to isolate.

Einsteinium (Es) Discovered from analysis of the debris of the first thermonuclear explosion at Eniwetok, 1952, by Albert Ghiorso and others (U.S.), this actinide element does not occur naturally; it is named after Albert Einstein. Uses: research.

Erbium (Er) A bright, silvery rare-earth metal. It is used in optical fibers, protective goggles, as an alloy in magnetic resonance imaging (MRI) machines, and to tint glass pink. Discovered 1843 by Carl Gustav Mosander (Sweden) and named after Ytterby, Sweden.

Europium (Eu) A soft, silvery rare-earth metal that is highly reactive with oxygen and water. It produces red emissions in TV tubes and in low-energy light bulbs provides both red and blue emissions. Isolated from a form of samarium in 1901 by Eugène-Anatole Demarçay (France).

Fermium (Fm) Discovered from analysis of the debris of the first thermonuclear explosion at Eniwetok, 1952, by Albert Ghiorso and others (U.S.), this highly radioactive actinide element does not occur naturally; it is named after the Nobel Prize–winning physicist Enrico Fermi. Uses: research.

Fluorine (F) Fluorine is a pale yellow gas (F_2) that is highly reactive and dangerous. The form found in nature, fluoride (F-), is stable and is essential for humans in small amounts. Elemental fluorine was isolated (1886, France) by Henri Moissan; it is named after the Latin *fluere* ("to flow") because its mineral fluorspar (calcium fluoride) melts when heated. Fluorspar was used in preindustrial times in metallurgy and in glass etching. Today, fluoride is best known as an additive to water and toothpaste to prevent tooth decay. It is also an element in non-stick pan coatings, and has uses in the nuclear, electrical, and chemical industries. Its use in chlorofluorocarbons, harmful to the ozone layer, is being phased out.

Francium (Fr) Discovered (1939, France) by Marguerite Perey and named after France. It is an unstable, highly radioactive element; the longest-lived isotope (223) has a half-life of only 22 minutes. Uses: research.

Gadolinium (Gd) Gadolinium is a soft, silvery rare-earth metal used in alloys in magnets and electronic components, and as a neutron regulator in nuclear reactors. Discovered in 1880 by Jean-Charles Gallissard de Marignac (Switzerland); named after an early investigator of rare-earth minerals, Johan Gadolin (Sweden).

Gallium (Ga) A soft, silver-white metal, Gallium was discovered (1875, France) by Paul-Émile Lecoq de Boisbaudran and named after the Latin for "France," *Gallia*. Especially as gallium arsenide, it has semiconductor properties and is used in light-emitting diodes (LEDs), supercomputers, and cell phones.

Germanium (Ge) A silver-white semi-metal, germanium has few uses except in specialized lenses and infrared detectors, although it was the first element to be used in transistors. Discovered (1886, Germany) by Clemens A. Winkler and named after the Latin for the country, *Germania*.

Gold (Au) Gold occurs naturally in surface waters and on land. It also occurs underground, often in quartz veins or pyrites. The most malleable of all elements, its ready availability and easy workability made it one of the first metals used in prehistoric times. The word "gold" is originally Anglo-Saxon and its symbol is from the Latin for gold, *aurum*. Gold's sparkling beauty and sunlike color have led people to attribute magical and religious properties to it, and it has from ancient times been the basis of monetary systems. In addition to its uses in jewelry and the decorative arts, gold has electronics and aerospace applications; it is relatively unreactive and a good conductor of electricity. Gold is usually mixed with other elements to harden it—pure gold is called 24 karat gold; an alloy of 75 percent gold is called 18 karat gold. Most gold produced is mined, principally in the U.S., Canada, Russia, and South Africa.

Hafnium (Hf) Discovered by George Charles de Hevesy

and Dirk Koster (1923, Denmark) and named after the Latin name for Copenhagen, *Hafnia,*hafnium is a silvery metal used for control rods in nuclear plants as a neutron absorber; it is also used for alloys and ceramics. Because of the difficulty of separating it from zirconium, to which it is chemically similar, it was one of the last non-radioactive elements to be discovered.

Hassium (Hs) A radioactive transfermium element synthesized in 1984 by Peter Armbruster and others (Germany) and named after the state of Hesse.

Helium (He) Helium, a colorless, odorless and unreactive noble gas, is the second-most abundant element in the universe, after hydrogen. It was discovered (1868, England) by Norman Lockyer and (1868, observing an eclipse in India) by Pierre J. C. Janssen, through analysis of the sun's spectrum, and is named after the Greek *helios,* "sun." It was then discovered that the element also existed on earth, in uranium minerals. The principal uses of helium are cooling low-temperature instruments, such as the magnets in magnetic resonance imaging and providing inert atmospheres for industrial processes; it is also provides the lift in lighter-than-air craft.

Holmium (Ho) A soft, bright silvery rare-earth metal. From the Latin name for Stockholm, *Holmia.* Independently discovered in 1878 by Marc Delafontaine and Louis Soret (Switzerland) and by Per Teodor Cleve (Sweden), it has limited uses in nuclear reactors as a control and in lasers.

Hydrogen (H) The first element in the periodic table and the most abundant element in the universe (80 percent), hydrogen fuels the stars, including our Sun. The lightest of gases, odorless and highly flammable, it was discovered in 1766 by Henry Cavendish (England), but its properties were recognized earlier. Hydrogen's name comes from Greek words meaning "forming water," (H_2O), *hydro* and *genes*. Hydrogen is essential to life, is found in most molecules in living cells, and is a part of DNA, the bases of which are joined by hydrogen bonds. About 10 percent of human body mass is hydrogen. Hydrogen is also a component of common acids, such as sulfuric, nitric, and hydrochloric acids. Its main industrial use is in the production of ammonia for fertilizers. Hydrogen is a constituent of atmospheric water vapor, the most potent greenhouse gas, which keeps earth more than 300 degrees C (800 degrees F) warmer than it would be otherwise. Its form in the atmosphere is generally H_2.

Indium (In) Indium is a soft, silvery metal discovered (1863, Germany) by Ferdinand Reich and Hieronymous Richter, and named for the Latin for "indigo," *indicum,* for its bright color in the atomic spectrum. Its main use is in low-melting alloys for fire-sprinkling systems.

Iodine (I) Named after the Greek for "violet" (the color of its fumes), *iodes,* the element was first identified by Bernard Courtois (1811, France). It is essential to many animal species, and iodide is added to table salt to prevent iodine deficiency in humans, especially goiter (enlarged thyroid gland). Iodine is used in pharmaceuticals (especially as a disinfectant), and in animal feed, photographic chemicals, dyes, and catalysts.

Iridium (Ir) A hard, silvery metal of the platinum group, Iridium was discovered by Smithson Tennant (1803, England) and named, for its colorful salts, after the Greek goddess of the rainbow, Iris. Modern uses include spark plug tips, electrode coatings, and aircraft engine parts.

Iron (Fe) Iron is a soft, workable metal that is the most abundant element on Earth (it makes up most of Earth's molten core). Named for the Anglo-Saxon for "iron," *iren,* its symbol is from the Latin *ferrum*. It is essential to most living things, and an iron deficiency in humans leads to anemia. Iron was known in ancient times, when it was worked from nuggets, probably from meteorites, found on the surface. About 3,500 years ago the technique of smelting from ores was discovered in the Middle East and the use of iron transformed human societies. Iron still accounts for perhaps 90 percent of refined metals, and has more uses as iron, steel (which includes carbon), stainless steel (with chromium and nickel), and other alloys than any other metal.

Krypton (Kr) Krypton, a noble (chemically inert) gas, was discovered in 1898 by William Ramsay and Morris Travers (England); its name is from the Greek for "hidden," *kryptos*. Except under very cold conditions, it reacts only with fluorine gas. Extracted from liquid air, it is used in specialized lighting such as flash lamps.

Lanthanides The lanthanides (also called lanthanoids) are the metallic elements with atomic numbers 57–70. They are named after lanthanum, element 57, and in the long form of the periodic table are shown grouped in a separate row. Lutetium, element 71, is traditionally included with the lathanides, but it is actually a member of the next grouping in the periodic table. The lanthanides, together with the chemically similar scandium and yttrium, are commonly called the rare-earth elements, but many of them are not in fact rare. They generally occur together in rare-earth minerals, and 19th century chemists had great difficulties in isolating the separate elements. (Indeed, the name of one, dysprosium, is from the Greek meaning "hard to get.")

The lanthanides, many of which are soft, silvery metals, are similar chemically because as the atomic number increases and the number of electrons increases, the extra electrons are added, not, as expected, to the outer ring but to inner orbits. Swedish chemists were active in analyzing the rare-earths, and three of them (terbium, erbium, and ytterbium) are named after Ytterby, a village near Vauxholm where, in 1787, a rock was found that led later to some of the rare-earths. (Yttrium, which is not a lanthanide, is also named after the village.) Among the many minerals in which rare-earth elements are found, the two most important sources are monazite, which is a phosphate ore, and bastnasite, a flouride carbonate ore.

Rare earths are essential to many high-tech uses in modern economies, including computers, smartphones, hybrid motors, wind turbines, and guided missiles. Until the last decade, rare earths were produced in several countries, with the United States and China the principal sources. But because of the high economic and environmental costs of rare earth extraction, more recently about 96 percent of global rare earth production has moved to China, which has low wages and weak environmental regulations. Since then, China has controlled exports to other countries with taxes and export quotas, in part to favor its own emerging industries. In 2010, following a dispute over territorial waters, China stopped exports of rare earths to Japan for two months, a crucial challenge to Japan's high-tech economy. There was also a brief halt in shipments to the U.S. and Europe.

Recognizing the economic and security risks from China's dominant supply position, developed countries have begun efforts to diversify rare earth supplies. The first large supplier to go on line is expected to be a new mine in Australia, Mount Weld, with production commencing as early as 2011; in addition, the Mountain Pass, California, mine that has been off-line for a decade is now to reopen; and production possibilities elsewhere are being explored.

Lanthanum (La) Named after the Greek *lanthanein*, "to be hidden." Discovered (1839, Sweden) by Carl Gustav Mosander. Lanthanum is a reactive, silver-white metal, the first of the lathanide group of the periodic table, it is found

in ores with other rare-earth metals. As a metal it has no commercial uses, but its alloys are used in carbon-arc electrodes and to increase the refractive index in glass.

Lawrencium (Lr) A transfermium element produced by Albert Ghiorso and others (1961, U.S.) and named after Ernest O. Lawrence, the inventor of the cyclotron. Uses: research.

Lead (Pb) Lead is a soft, ductile gray metal that has been known and used since ancient times. The name *lead* is Anglo-Saxon in origin, and its symbol is from the Latin, *plumbum*. Lead is harmful and even fatal to humans and other animals when it accumulates in the body, and for this reason many of its uses (in paints and as an additive in gasoline, for example) have been phased out. The Romans used lead extensively in water pipes and other products; and in the Middle Ages lead was added as a sweetener to wine. Current uses of lead are primarily for electrodes in vehicle storage batteries, in TV and computer screens as a shield against radiation, and in medicine as protection against X rays.

Lithium (Li) Lithium, the first of the alkali group of metals, was discovered (1817, Sweden) by Johan August Arfvedson and named for the Greek *lithos*, "stone." A soft, silvery metal, it has many uses, including the production of glass, lithium batteries, and a strong, light alloy with aluminum for airplanes. Lithium carbonate is used in the treatment of mental illness, and an unknown amount is used as lithium hydride in the production of nuclear weapons.

Lutetium (Lu) Densest of the elements grouped as rare-earths and discovered in 1907 by Georges Urbain (France), it is a transition element in the periodic table. Mostly used for research purposes, small amounts are used in magnetic bubble memories and in oil refining. From *Lutetia*, the Roman name for Paris.

Magnesium (Mg) Magnesium is an essential element for both animals and plants, in which it is part of the chlorophyll molecule. Recognized as an element by Joseph Black (1755, Scotland) and named after a district in Greece, Magnesia, its main commercial uses are as an alloy with aluminum for car and plane bodies and to remove sulfur in steel production.

Manganese (Mn) Essential to all species, including humans, manganese was identified as an element by John Gottlieb Gahn (1774, Sweden). Its name may be from the Latin for "magnet," *magnes*, as one of its minerals is slightly magnetic. It is used in steel alloys, in which it is essential for strength and wear resistance. The U.S. is 100 percent import dependent for manganese. Produced mainly in South Africa, Gabon, Russia, and Australia, manganese is also widely found in nodules on the ocean floor.

Meitnerium (Mt) Produced in 1982 by Peter Armbruster and others (Germany) and named after the Austrian physicist Lise Meitner. Uses: research.

Mendelevium (Md) A transferium element produced in 1955 by Albert Ghiorso and others (U.S.), it is named after Mendeleyev, who developed the early periodic table. Uses: research.

Mercury (Hg) A liquid, silvery metal with a melting point of −390 degrees C (−380 degrees F), Mercury was known and used in ancient times (indeed, as mercury sulfide (HgS) it was used to produce red color in cave paintings more than 30,000 years ago). It has long fascinated humans because of its silvery, liquid quality and its ability to dissolve gold to form an amalgam. Found throughout the atmosphere and ecosystem, it is ubiquitous in living things. Tolerated in small amounts, in larger amounts it is highly poisonous and has caused sickness and death through its use in medicine, commerce, and industry. These harmful uses have included its application in gilding, in making felt hats, and in making mirrors. Many uses of mercury (including thermometers) have been phased out, and it is currently used in limited quantities in electrical equipment, specialized batteries for small electronic devices, and fluorescent lights.

Molybdenum (Mo) An essential trace element for plants and animals, molybdenum was identified by Peter Jacob Hjelm (1781, Sweden). Earlier, an ore was mistaken for lead ore, and so the element inappropriately bears the Greek name for "lead," *molybdos*. It has many industrial uses, especially for alloys, such as "moly steel," which has high strength and resists wear and corrosion.

Neodymium (Nd) Isolated in 1885 by Karl Auer in Vienna, neodymium is a silver-white rare-earth metal. It is alloyed with iron and boron to make magnets used in cars and trucks, and to produce a purple tint in glass. Its name, from the Greek *neos didymos*, means "new twin," referring to its discovery with praseodymium.

Neon (Ne) Neon was discovered in 1898 by William Ramsay and Morris Travers (England); its name is from the Greek for new, *neos*. Relatively rare, it is found in the atmosphere, sea, and land. Neon is completely unreactive

with known chemicals because of its complete outer electron shell; it is one of the noble or inert gases. Uses: neon lights, low-temperature refrigerants.

Neptunium (Np) Edward McMillan and Philip Abelson (U.S.) announced the discovery of the first transuranic element in 1940. It is named after the planet Neptune, which follows Uranus in the solar system. Minute quantities are found in nature. Uses: nuclear facilities and research.

Nickel (Ni) Nickel was discovered as an element by Alex Fredrik Cronstedt (Stockholm, 1751), but nickel-tin alloys were known in ancient times. It takes its name, "Devil's copper," for a seemingly useless nickel-containing ore known to German copper miners, kupfernickel. Much of the nickel mined from the surface of the earth may have arrived in meteorites; there is also nickel in the Earth's core. Its first modern use was as a base for silver plating (19th century). Its main current use is as a component of stainless steel alloys; it is also used in a variety of other alloys with chromium, copper, and molybdenum, and it is still used in coinage in many countries.

Niobium (Nb) A steel-gray, corrosion-resistant metal, it is named after Niobe, daughter of Tantalus in Greek mythology, because of niobium's chemical similarity to tantalum. Discovered by Charles Hatchett (1801, England), most niobium now comes from Brazil; it has specialized uses as an alloy in stainless steel and other metals, and in the production of anodes. Its alloys with tin and titanium are superconducting.

Nitrogen (N) Nitrogen exists in compounds and in the form of N_2, an odorless, colorless, unreactive gas that composes 78 percent of the air we breathe. Nitrogen was identified as the main constituent of air by Daniel Rutherford (1772, Scotland); it is named after the Greek *nitron* and *genes*, for "niter" (saltpeter), which is potassium nitrate, and "forming." Nitrogen is essential for life; it is part of DNA, amino acids, and the body messenger nitric oxide. Plants require nitrogen, which must be "fixed" (combined with oxygen or hydrogen) for them by bacteria as part of the nitrogen cycle. Commercially nitrogen is produced by liquefication of air and is used to make ammonium nitrates for fertilizer and for many other chemical compounds. Nitrogen is also used as a supercoolant and an inert atmosphere.

Nobelium (No) A transfermium element named after the founder of the Nobel prizes, Alfred Nobel, it was produced by Albert Ghiorso and others, (1958, U.S.).

Osmium (Os) Osmium (from the Greek *osme*, "smell") was discovered in 1803 by Smithson Tennant (England) during investigations into platinum. A sparkling, silvery metal, osmium is the densest metal known but is hard to work. Its few uses include microscope slide stains, catalysis, and alloys. Osmium tetroxide gives off a pungent odor.

Oxygen (O) Oxygen is a colorless and odorless reactive gas that exists naturally as O_2. Oxygen was discovered as an element by Joseph Priestley (1774, England) and named for the Greek for "acid-forming," *oxy* and *genes*. Oxygen makes up one-fifth of the air; it is essential for sustaining animal life through the respiratory process, which brings oxygen to the blood, and as a constituent of many important compounds in our bodies including DNA. On Earth oxygen is formed by the photosynthesis of carbon dioxide and water by plants (it is also formed as part of the fuel cycle of stars). Oxygen used commercially is produced from liquefied air and is used primarily in steelmaking and chemical production; other uses include water purification and medicine. Ozone consists of three oxygen atoms, O_3.

Palladium (Pd) A silvery, malleable metal that is one of the platinum group, palladium was discovered by William Wollaston (1802, England) and named after the asteroid Pallas. Produced primarily as a by-product of mining other metals, it is used in jewelry, cars, electronics, dental fillings, and catalytic convertors.

Phosphorus (P) Phosphorus (Greek for "bringer of light") was isolated by Hennig Brandt (1669, Germany). In the form of phosphates, phosphorus is essential to all living cells. Most is calcium phosphate in bones, and there are also the organophosphates in key molecules such as ATP (adenosine triphosphate), which is a source of chemical energy in the body. Phosphorus itself is highly toxic. Commercial and industrial uses of phosphate include fertilizers, detergents, flameproofing, rat poison, and tracer bullets. Excess phosphates in water produce eutrophication (the growth of algae), and the use of phosphates is now regulated in many countries.

Platinum (Pt) From the Spanish for "little silver," *platina*, platinum was known and worked in some ancient New World societies but was used rarely in Old World civilization. It became widely known in Europe during the 18th century. Nuggets occur naturally, and it is also mined, obtained as a by-product from copper and nickel refining, and recycled. A bright, silvery, dense metal, it is used primarily for jewelry, with other principal uses in catalytic convertors and in the chemical and electronics industries.

Plutonium (Pu) Discovered by Glenn T. Seaborg and others (1940, U.S.) and named for the planet Pluto. Plutonium was the fissile material in the first atomic weapon tested (July, 1945) and the second used in war. Plutonium is a byproduct of nuclear reactors, and its handling and storage are a considerable environmental challenge. It is used for weapons, in research, and as a power source for pacemakers and space equipment.

Polonium (Po) Discovered in 1898 (France) by Marie Curie and named after her native country, Poland, polonium is a dangerously radioactive element. Produced in research facilities, small amounts are used as a heat source for satellites.

Potassium (K) Potassium, named after *kalium*, the Middle Latin for potash (potassium carbonate), was identified as an element by Humphry Davy (1807, England). It is a soft metal in the alkali metal group. Potassium is essential for most living things; in the human body its many functions include transmitting nerve impulses. Before the industrial era potassium salts were used for flavoring and preserving food and improving soil. Most potassium produced today goes into fertilizers, because of plants' need for the element. Other uses are in glass manufacturing, detergents, and pharmaceuticals.

Praeseodymium (Pr) Isolated in 1885 by Karl Auer in Vienna, praeseodymium is a soft silver-yellow rare-earth metal used to color glass used in protective goggles and in electrodes for carbon arc lighting. The name (from the Greek, *prasios didymos*) means "green twin" and refers both to the color of its oxide and its discovery with neodymium.

Promethium (Pm) Identified in 1945 by J. Marinsky and others (U.S.), promethium is a radioactive rare-earth metal produced in nuclear reactors; traces are also found naturally. Named for Prometheus, the mythical Greek who stole fire from the gods, it is used in luminous paint but has few other applications.

Protactinium (Pr) Discovered in 1900 by William Crookes (England), it decays to actinium. Its name, "precursor to actinium," is from the Greek *protos*, "first." Intensely radioactive, it occurs naturally in uranium ores including pitchblende. Uses: nuclear facilities and research.

Radium (Ra) Discovered by Pierre and Marie Curie (1898, France), radium is a highly radioactive alkaline earth; it causes some of the natural background radiation of Earth. In metallic form soft and silvery and named for the Latin *radius*, "ray," it was very widely used for luminous dials and medicinal purposes before its dangers to humans were understood. Uses: research.

Radon (Rn) Radon, a noble (chemically inert) gas that is highly radioactive, was discovered in 1900 by Friedrich Ernst Dorn (Germany). A decay product of uranium and other elements, it is part of natural background radiation. Accumulations in mines and basements can be a health hazard. The name is from radium with the suffix -*on* for the noble gases. Uses: research.

Rare earths, See *Lanthanides*.

Rhenium (Re) Discovered in 1925 by Walter Noddack and Ida Tacke (Germany) and named after the Latin name for the Rhine River, *Rhenus*. It is a silvery metal that is the last stable, non-radioactive, naturally-occurring element to be discovered. It is used in alloys for lamp filaments and as a catalyst in chemical processes.

Rhodium (Rh) A member of the platinum group of metals, rhodium was discovered by William Wollaston (1803, England) and named, after the Greek *rhodon*, for the rose color of rhodium chloride. A hard, silvery metal obtained as a byproduct of copper and nickel refining, almost all rhodium is used in catalytic converters for cars.

Roentgenium (Rg) A transfermium element produced in 1994 by Peter Armbruster and others (Germany), it is below gold in the periodic table. Uses: research.

Rubidium (Rb) Discovered by Robert Bunsen and Gustav Kirchhoff (1861, Germany), it is an alkali metal, named after the Latin *rubidius* for the deep red lines in its atomic spectrum. Uses: research.

Ruthenium (Ru) A silvery metal, discovered (1840, Russia) by Karl Klaus and named after the Latin for Russia. Obtained as a byproduct of nickel refining, it has specialized uses in electronics, chemicals, and as an alloy in platinum for jewelry.

Rutherfordium (Rf) Transfermium element produced by Albert Ghiorso and others (1969, U.S.) with an earlier claim by researchers in Dubna, Russia (1964). It is named after the New Zealand chemist Ernest Rutherford. Uses: research.

Samarium (Sm) A silver-white rare-earth metal discovered in 1879 by Paul-Émile Lecoq de Boisbaudran (France). Found in minerals, it is alloyed with cobalt to produce magnets and is also used in ceramics, glass, and lasers. It is named for the Russian engineer V. E. Samarsky.

Scandium (Sc) A soft, silver-white metal, scandium was discovered (1879, Sweden) by Lars Frederik Nilson and named after the Latin for Scandinavia, *Scandia*. It has specialized uses as a neutron filter in nuclear reactors, in mercury vapor lamps, and in oil refining.

Seaborgium (Sg). Produced in 1974 by teams in Dubna, Russia (Georgy Flerov and others) and Berkeley, California (Ghiorsi and others). Named after Glenn T. Seaborg (U.S.), a leading investigator of transuranium elements. Uses: research.

Selenium (Se) Selenium is an essential element for humans, although in excessive doses it is toxic. Discovered (1817, Sweden) by Jöns Jacob Berzelius, it is named after the Greek for "moon," *selene*. It exists in two forms, a silver metal and a red powder, and is used in electronics, in the glass industry, in animal feeds, and as a red pigment.

Silicon (Si) Elemental silicon was first obtained by Jöns Jacob Berzelius (1824, Sweden); its name is derived from the Latin for "flint," *silex* or *silicus*. Early humans made flint from silicon dioxide (silica), and many ancient civilizations made glass from sand. Silicon is used in many ways: as sand in construction, as pure silicon in computer chips, as quartz (silicon dioxide) with its many uses, and as a raw material for the steel and chemical industries. Opal, agate, and rhinestone are gemstones that are forms of silica.

Silver (Ag) Silver is from the Anglo-Saxon *siolfur*, and takes its symbol from the Latin *argentum*. Silver has been known and worked since ancient times in the Old and New Worlds. It is rarely found as the metal; it must be mined from ore and refined, so that although silver is more abundant than gold, it came into use later. A principal use for silver, in which it is alloyed with copper, is in jewelry and tableware. Silver salts are used in still and movie films and prints. Silver, which conducts heat and electricity very well, is widely used in the electrical industry; it also has uses as a disinfectant in medicine. It is found in the food chain in generally harmless amounts, which accumulate in humans.

Sodium (Na) Sodium is a soft, silvery metal named after the English word "soda"; its symbol is from the Latin *natrium* (soda). Sodium is essential to animals; among other functions it moves electric impulses along nerve fibers. Although discovered as an element in the 19th century (Humphry Davy, 1807, England) it has been known in its compounds sodium carbonate ("soda") and sodium chloride (table salt) since biblical times. Table salt is now iodized to prevent thyroid disease, and packets of glucose and salt are used in developing countries to prevent dehydration in young victims of diarrhea and other diseases. Sodium is also an important industrial element. Sodium compounds are widely used in glassmaking, the chemical industry, and metallurgy, and in the manufacture of fire extinguishers; sodium metal is employed in chemical manufacturing, metallurgy, and street lamps.

Strontium (Sr) An alkaline earth element, strontium was first isolated by Humphry Davy (1808, England) and named for the Scottish village of Strontian. It is a constituent of some shelled sea animals and stony corals. The isotope Strontium-90, produced by above-ground nuclear tests, is highly dangerous. Strontium has limited specialized uses in flares, glass for TV screens, and as a power source for remote navigation as well as space and weather stations.

Sulfur (S) Sulfur is essential to all living things, and in humans it is part of the essential amino acid methionine and of vitamin B1. In ancient times it was used for matches, in making wine, and in bleaching cloth; it was also a component of the "Greek fire" of Byzantium and gunpowder. Its name is derived from the Sanskrit and Latin terms *sulvere* and *sulfurium*, for sulfur. Today it is a leading industrial chemical; most of it goes into sulfuric acid, which has an enormous range of uses in phosphate fertilizers, removing rust, and producing paints, detergents, fuels, and many other commodities.

Tantalum (Ta) Discovered by Anders Ekeburgy (1802, Sweden), and named after the mythical King Tantalus; obtained by mining and as a by-product of tin production. Tantalum is easy to work and resists corrosion; it is used to coat other metals, in specialized alloys, and for surgical implants.

Technetium (Tc) Discovered by Emilio Segrè and Carlo Perrier (1937, Italy), although possibly found earlier in Germany (1925), it is a radioactive metal occurring naturally in only minute amounts. Its name is from the Greek *tekhnetos*, "artificial." It is primarily a by-product of nuclear reactors. Uses: medical diagnosis; research.

Tellurium (Te) Discovered (1783, Romania) by Franz Joseph Müller and named for the Latin for "earth," *tellus*, tellurium is a silver-white semi-metal. Uses: specialized alloys with copper, stainless steel, and lead.

Terbium (Tb) A soft, silvery rare-earth element; more costly and less common than most rare-earth elements, Terbium has limited commercial use in magnets, lasers, and lighting. Isolated in 1843 by Carl Gustav Mosander (Sweden) and named after Ytterby, Sweden.

Thallium (Tl,) Discovered (1861, England) by William Crookes, and named (from the Greek *thallos*, "green shoot") after the green line in its atomic spectrum, thallium is a soft, silver-white metal. It has a few specialized uses in lenses and photoelectric cells. Toxic to humans, its use as a pesticide is banned in many countries

Thorium (Th) Discovered by Jöns Jakob Berzelius (Sweden) in 1829, and named after Thor, the Germanic god of war. It occurs naturally in several minerals; its radioactivity was discovered in 1898. Thorium has uses in metallurgy, oil refining, and photoelectric cells.

Thulium (Tm) Isolated by Per Teodor Cleve (1874, Sweden) and named after Thule, the ancient name for Scandinavia. A soft, bright, silvery metal, it is more expensive than other chemically similar rare-earth metals and so has few practical applications.

Tin (Sn) Tin has been known since ancient times; it symbol is from the Latin, *stannum*. Its main use for millennia was to produce bronze, its alloy with copper; it was also anciently used for tinplating; modern "tin cans" are coated with a thin layer of tin. Tin is also used in a wide range of metal alloys to produce engine parts, bearings, and superconducting magnets, and in glassmaking.

Titanium (Ti) Discovered by Martin Klaproth (1795, Germany), titanium was produced as a metal only in 1910 (U.S.). Named for the Titans of Greek mythology, titanium is an unusually strong, easily worked metal that is essential to aircraft engines and frames. It has other commercial uses, such as power plant condensers and architectural sheeting, and is used for replacement parts and pins in the human body, in which it bonds with bone. Titanium dioxide is used in paints.

Transfermium Elements The transfermium elements are the elements beyond fermium (100), from 101 on up to the most recently discovered. These elements have all been produced in the course of research; they are created by bombarding isotopes of elements with subatomic particles. Many have very short half-lives of less than a second. Relatively little is known about them beyond the fact that they have been observed in experimental conditions, the atomic number, isotopes, and in a few cases something about compounds. The elements from 101 through 111 are relatively unstable; then there is a predicted "island of stability" from 112 to 118. As of 2010, the highest-numbered element to be produced is 118; all the elements up to 118 have also been produced.

A long and successful international collaboration led by scientists at the Lawrence Livermore National Laboratory in Livermore, California and the Joint Institute for Nuclear Research in Dubna, Russia, has produced six of the transfermium elements, from 113 to 118. Elements without presently agreed-on names use words representing the digits of the atomic number: ununnilium for element 110 (i.e., one, one, zero + ium, the suffix for "metal").

Tungsten (W) A silver-gray metal discovered in 1783 by the de Elhuyar brothers (Spain). It is very hard and resistant to corrosion, with the highest melting point of any metal, 61,700 degrees F (34,100 degrees C). Tungsten is used to make heavy steel alloys for armaments and has been regarded as a strategic mineral since World War I. The United States is dependent on imports for tungsten, primarily from China and Russia. Other uses of tungsten include drilling and abrasives. It is named after the Swedish *tung sten*, "heavy stone," and its abbreviation is from its alternative name, wolfram.

Ununhexium (Uuh) A transfermium element discovered in 2000 by Russian and American scientists. No formal name yet assigned. Uses: research.

Ununoctium (Uuo) A transfermium element produced in 2005 by Russian and American scientists. No formal name yet assigned. Uses: research.

Ununpentium (Uup) A transfermium element produced by Russian and American scientists in 2003. No formal name yet assigned. Uses: research.

Ununquadium (Uuq) A transfermium element discovered in 1998 by Russian and American scientists. No formal name yet assigned. Uses: research.

Ununseptium (Uus) A transfermium element announced by Russian and American scientists in 2010. No formal name yet assigned. Uses: research.

Ununtrium (Uut) A transfermium element produced in 2003 by Russian and American scientists. No formal name yet assigned. Uses: research.

Uranium (U) Uranium is a naturally radioactive rare-earth metal that was identified by Eugène Pelicot (France) in 1841 and named after the planet Uranus, which is named for the Greek god of the sky. Its radioac-tive nature was not understood until 1896 (Henri Becquerel, France). Uranium is abundant in mineral ores; it is widely mined, and the most important use is fuel for nuclear reactors. Nuclear fission occurs when the proportion of the U-235 isotope, naturally only about 1 percent, is increased. The fission of nuclear weapons (the first atomic bomb dropped in wartime was a uranium bomb) is controlled in nuclear power plants by neutron absorbers such as heavy water.

Vanadium (V) Vanadium is essential as a trace element for humans and some other animals. Discovered by Andrés del Rio (1801, Mexico), it is named after the Scandinavian goddess of beauty, Vanadis. A silvery metal, vanadium is mainly used in steel alloys to provide strength and rustproofing.

Xenon (Xe) Xenon, a noble (chemically inert) gas, was discovered in 1898 by William Ramsay and Morris Travers (England); its name is from the Greek for "stranger," *xenos*. Produced from liquid air, it is used in biocidal lamps, flash lamps, and other lighting.

Ytterbium (Yb) Named after Ytterby, Sweden, the soft, silvery-white rare-earth metal was isolated by Jean Charles Gallissard de Marignac (Switzerland) in 1878. Chemically similar to other rare-earths, it has few commercial applications.

Yttrium (Y) Isolated by Johan Gadolin (1794, Finland) and named after the village of Ytterby, Sweden, yttrium is a soft, silvery metal obtainable from ores. It is used in many metal alloys and provides the red color in TV monitors. The radioactive isotope yttrium-90 is used in cancer therapy.

Zinc (Zn) Zinc is essential for animals and plants; it is in hundreds of enzymes and in the transcription factors through which RNA is synthesized, and zinc deficiency is a risk in developing countries. As a metal, zinc has been known since ancient times; alloyed with copper, it produces brass. The modern use of zinc is mainly in galvanizing steel; other uses are in castings, in making brass, and in batteries. Zinc oxide is used in pigments, as a catalyst in rubber production, and in sunscreen.

Zirconium (Zr) Discovered by Martin Klaproth (1789, Germany), it is named after the Arabic word for "gold colored," *zargun*. It is widely found in ores, and is used for ceramics and heat resistant furnace linings; as a metal, it does not absorb neutrons and is used for tubing in nuclear reactors. Zircons are gems, known in ancient times, containing zirconium.

Glossary of Chemistry Terms

acid compound that contains hydrogen and dissociates in water, producing hydrogen ions. Among the most common *acids* is sulfuric acid (H^2SO_4). Alternative definitions: a substance that tends to release a proton (Lowry-Brønsted); a substance that accepts two electrons from a base (Lewis).

analytic chemistry the branch of chemistry in which the constituents of substances, and their relative amounts, are analyzed.

anion a negatively charged ion. In electrolysis, anions move to the anode.

atom the smallest part of an element that exists chemically. Atoms have a nucleus of protons and neutrons that is surrounded by electrons that move in orbits, or, more precisely, regions of space, around the nucleus.

atomic number the number of protons (positively charged particles) in the nucleus of an atom. Elements are defined by their atomic numbers; all atoms of an element have the same number of protons.

atomic weight weight of an element as compared with 1/12 of the weight of the principal isotope of carbon, carbon 12. Also called relative atomic mass.

atomic mass unit 1/12 of the weight of the principal isotope of carbon, carbon 12; this is the standard atomic mass unit, or amu. Symbol = u.

base compound that reacts with an acid to produce water and a salt. Alternative definitions: a substance that tends to accept a proton (Lowry-Brønsted); a substance that yields two electrons to an acid (Lewis).

boiling point the phase transition between liquid and gas.

catalyst a substance that increases the rate of a chemical reaction without undergoing any permanent chemical change.

cation a positively charged ion. In electrolysis, cations move to the cathode.

electrochemistry the study of chemical reactions and properties relating to ions in solution, including electric cells and electrolysis.

electrolysis the production of a chemical reaction by passing an electric current through an electrolyte. In electrolysis, positive ions (cations) move to the cathode, and negative ions (anions) move to the anode.

electrolyte a liquid that conducts electricity through the presence of positive or negative ions.

electron negatively charged particles in orbit around the nucleus of an atom. Electrons have very little mass compared with protons and neutrons.

element a substance that cannot be decomposed into simpler substances; it is defined by the number of protons (the atomic number) in its atoms.

free radical an atom or group of atoms with an unpaired valence electron; most free radicals are highly reactive.

freezing point phase transition between liquid and solid.

gas a state of matter in which the molecules are not held together, but move freely; a gas takes the shape of its container regardless of the quantity of molecules.

inorganic chemistry study of chemical properties and reactions in compounds not containing carbon.

ion an atom or group of atoms that has gained or lost an electron. If an electron is lost, the ion is positively charged (cation), and if an electron is gained, the ion is negatively charged (anion).

isotope an element's atoms all have the same number of protons, but some atoms of an element can have different numbers of neutrons. Different combinations of neutrons with the fixed number of protons that defines the element are called isotopes of the element.

liquid state of matter between solid and gas, in which the three-dimensional regularity of the solid is lost but the complete disorganization of the gaseous state is not reached. The phase transition between solid and gas is the melting point, and between liquid and gas the boiling point.

mass number the total of protons and neutrons in an atom of an element or one of its isotopes is the mass number of the element or the isotope.

melting point the phase transition between liquid and solid.

mole unit of the amount of a substance in the SI notation system. It is defined as the amount of a substance that contains as many elementary entities as there are atoms in 0.012 kilograms of carbon 12. The entities can be atoms, molecules, ions, electrons, etc.; and they must be specified. Abbreviation: mol.

molecule particle composed of atoms of elements that are combined in a whole-number ratio. Molecules can be composed of atoms of the same element (e.g., ozone, O_3), or, more commonly, of different elements (e.g., table salt, NaCl).

neutron an element's nucleus contains neutrons, which have no electric charge, as well as protons. Each neutron weighs approximately as much as a proton.

organic chemistry the branch of chemistry in which carbon compounds and their reactions are studied.

periodic table the periodic table arranges the elements in groups according to their atomic weights; the "periods" are the rows of elements, which group elements in such a way that elements in the columns, progressively heavier, have similar chemical properties.

pH a logarithmic scale for expressing the acidity or alkalinity of a solution, introduced in 1909 by Søren Sørensen (1868–1939). The term stands for "potential of hydrogen." A pH of 7 is neutral; acids are less than 7, and bases are greater than 7.

phase change the movement of a substance from one phase to another, e.g. from solid to liquid or liquid to gas.

photochemistry the study of chemical reactions that are caused by light.

polymer a substance that has large molecules composed of repeating structural units. There are natural polymers, such as rubber, and many synthesized polymers, such as those that make most plastics.

proton positively charged particle in the nucleus of an atom. The number of protons in an element's atoms is the atomic number of the element.

reagent a substance reacting with another substance. In the laboratory reagents are used in analysis or experiments.

salt a compound produced by the reaction of an acid and a base, in which hydrogen in the acid is replaced by metal or other positive ions.

SI system the International System of Units used in chemistry and other sciences. The initials are from the French, Système International d'Unités.

solid state of matter in which there is three-dimensional regularity of the components (which may be atoms, molecules, or ions), due to the nearness of the components and the strength of the forces between them. At the melting point, a solid turns into a liquid.

valence electron an electron in one of the outer ("valence") shells of an atom that takes part in forming chemical bonds.

PHYSICS

According to the *Oxford Dictionary of Physics*, physics is "the study of the laws that determine the structure of the universe with reference to the matter and energy of which it consists. It is concerned with the forces that exist between objects, and the interrelationship between matter and energy. Until the early 20th century, physics was divided into six diverse areas of study: heat, light, magnetism, sound, and electricity. Since then quantum mechanics and Einstein's theory of relativity have become separate fields of inquiry." Modern physics also includes other subdivisions that are useful. Matter and energy are manifest in the interactions of subatomic particles and the nuclei of atoms as well as in the materials (condensed matter) that make up solids, liquids, and other forms of matter, leading to the branches of study known respectively as particle physics, nuclear physics, and condensed-matter physics. Relativity theory also predicted the expansion of the universe, linking physics for the first time to cosmology, the study of the universe as a whole. Recently the links between physics, astronomy, and cosmology have become tighter; nuclear and particle physics are needed to explain the stars and galaxies. At the same time, physicists who study advanced concepts such as string theory, which replaces particles with strings, now look to astronomy to validate their work.

History of Physics

Physics in Antiquity and the Middle Ages

The ancient Greeks tried, sometimes successfully, to explain materials and motion on the basis of observation and reasoning. One successful explanation, advocated by Democritus of Abdera (ca. 470–380 B.C.) and others, is that all matter is composed of small particles called atoms. Their theories proposed that different atoms have different shapes and that all materials can be based on atoms of fire, air, water, and earth. Today scientists recognize that most matter is made from combinations of nearly 100 different atoms, usually joined to form larger particles called molecules. (Traditionally there are 92 elements, although only 88 or so are normally found on Earth; there is hardly any astatine, francium, or protactinium, and no promethium or technitium. Some transuranic elements are manufactured in relatively large amounts, notably plutonium, americium, and californium. Neptunium, although considered artificial, may exist in greater supply on Earth than astatine, owing to some natural creation. Other synthetic elements are not stable enough to be counted.)

Aristotle The most complete Greek theory of physics, incorporating the ideas of earlier writers as well as his own, is that of Aristotle (384–322 B.C.). Most of what Aristotle thought about physics is now recognized as incorrect. Aristotle rejected atoms because any space between atoms must be empty, but he had based his theories on the idea that a vacuum cannot exist. He thought that an object in motion requires a continuing force to keep it in motion. If an object is moving fast enough, he conjectured, air rushing to prevent a vacuum behind the object could provide the necessary force for a time, but that force would gradually diminish. So a thrown object could travel through the air, but eventually would drop to the ground. The object slows and falls, in Aristotle's view, because the natural place for material objects containing earth or water is toward the center of Earth.

Aristotle remained the main influence on physics for the next 2,000 years. Although some Chinese philosophers developed ideas of motion similar to those we use today, they were unknown in the Arab world or in Europe. Arabic scholars followed the ideas of Aristotle and other Greek philosophers, but they also advanced beyond Greek concepts in some areas of physics, notably optics (the science of light). Aristotle had believed that light travels from an object to the eye, but other influential writers of antiquity, such as Euclid (fl. ca. 300 B.C.) and Ptolemy (ca. 100–170), thought that light proceeds from the observer to the object. The decisive arguments in favor of Aristotle's view were made by Alhazen (Al-

Haytham, 965–ca. 1040) around 1020. Alhazen extended the laws of reflection from those applying to flat mirrors, which had been known to Ptolemy, to cover curved mirrors and lenses.

In the Middle Ages, physics began to free itself from some of Aristotle's inaccurate ideas about motion. The French philosopher Jean Buridan (ca. 1295–ca. 1358) was the first to propose that a body in motion contained a mysterious inner force, called impetus, that maintains motion for a time. As a body moves, the impetus dissipates, especially if some force opposes the motion, speeding dissipation.

The Scientific Revolution

Near the end of the 16th century, Galileo Galilei (1564–1642) accepted Aristotelian ideas and such modifications as impetus at first, but he soon brought a radical concept to studies of motion. Instead of trying to explain why objects move as they do, he experimented and then described exactly how they move. He also used experiment to determine how forces affect objects that do not move. Although he made some errors, his basic conclusion in 1590—that an object in motion continues to move in a straight line until stopped by a force—is still accepted. His other famous conclusion—that light bodies and heavy bodies fall through the same distance in the same amount of time—is also true. He had established it by experiment, and announced the correct mathematical law governing falling (distance increases with the square of time) in 1638.

Other scientists continued in the same vein as Galileo during the 17th century. The German astronomer Johannes Kepler (1571–1630) advanced optics and showed in 1604 that the intensity of light diminishes as the square of the distance from its source. In 1643 the Italian physicist Evangelista Torricelli (1608–47), with the invention of the barometer, showed that Aristotle had been wrong about the vacuum, since a vacuum forms above the mercury column in the original barometer. Blaise Pascal experimented with the vacuum and with fluids, establishing that in a fluid, force is transmitted in all directions and always acts perpendicular to the surface of the container (1654, published 1662). Isaac Newton experimented with breaking light into its components (1665) and reported that white light is the combination of the colored lights of the rainbow (1675).

This period when experiments began to dominate physics is known as the scientific revolution. It culminated in 1687 when Newton's *Principia* emerged. Newton improved on Galileo's laws of motion and combined them with a mathematical law of gravity. The combination was sufficient to explain not only the motions of objects on Earth, but also the motions of the heavenly bodies (see Law of Gravity and Newton's Laws of Motion). Newton (and independently Leibniz) had also invented a new mathematical tool, the calculus. Throughout the 18th century, Newtonian physics and calculus were combined to develop systematically a wide range of topics in physics, ranging from acoustics to detailed orbits of the planets. Some scientists believed that if the exact position and momentum of every point in space were known, the future of the universe could be predicted exactly as well.

Electromagnetism Although Newton's work explained how gravity functioned, it did not explain why material objects attract each other with this force. There were also other forces that were unexplained, and less was known of their rules. As early as 1600 William Gilbert applied the experimental method to two of these forces, identifying and differentiating between magnetism and static electricity. A hundred years later, scientists began to attempt to tease from nature the secrets of these forces. Weak electric charges were made by rubbing glass tubes with silk or by similar means at first. In 1729 another English experimenter, Stephen Gray (1666–1736), was the first to recognize that these weak charges could travel from one material to another through substances that were later called conductors. He soon showed that when conductors do not carry away the charge, almost anything—even a human being—could be charged with electricity. A French experimenter, Charles Du Fay (1698–1739), was the first to recognize that there are two kinds of charge and that like charges repel, whereas different charges attract, each other (1733).

The English and French experimenters and their assistants also began to build up charges strong enough to produce the first recognized shocks. In 1746 the invention of the way to store static electricity (called a Leiden jar after the site of its discovery) permitted experiments with much more powerful charges. In 1751 Benjamin Franklin connected the small shocks from Leiden jars with the powerful shock of lightning, proving his theory by flying a kite in a thunderstorm and conducting the charge down the wet string. In 1769 a Scottish scientist, John Robison (1739–1805), showed that the repulsive force caused by charge obeys an inverse-square law like the law for loss of intensity of light over distance.

A new source of electric charge began to be developed in Italy during the 1770s and 1780s when Luigi Galvani (1737–1798) investigated charge produced in the muscles of animals, which Alessando Volta (1745–1827) recognized as the result of chemical interactions. Volta in 1800 built a chemical device (similar to a modern automobile battery) that produced the first current electricity.

Meanwhile a parallel set of experiments with magnets began in 1749 when the English experimenters John Canton (1718–72) and John Michell (1724–93) developed stronger magnets than occur in nature. Michell immediately used his magnets to derive the mathematical laws of attraction and repulsion. In 1751 Benjamin Franklin showed that electric charge can produce magnetism. In 1785 the French physicist Charles Coulomb (1736–1806) carefully measured both electric and magnetic forces and also found that both obey exactly the same inverse-square laws. As early as 1807 the Danish physicist Hans Christian Oersted (1777–1851) began to search for a deeper connection between electricity and magnetism, which he found in 1820 when he observed that an electric current affects a magnetized needle. The recognition that electricity and magnetism are closely connected quickly led to the discovery of the laws governing electromagnetism (see Laws of Current Electricity) as well as to devices that combined the two forces to produce motion (electric motors), powerful electric currents (generators, or dynamos), and powerful electromagnets.

Light   At the same time as charge and magnetism were being analyzed, there were apparently unrelated studies concerning light. As early as 1678, the Dutch physicist Christiaan Huygens (1625–95) had proposed a theory of light based on waves. But in 1704 Newton published *Opticks*, which summarized his view that light consists of small particles. About a hundred years later the study of light experienced several rapid advances. In 1800 and 1801 two forms of invisible light were discovered: infrared by William Herschel and ultraviolet by Johann Ritter (1776–1810). Also in 1801, the English scientist Thomas Young (1773–1829) conducted experiments that convinced scientists everywhere that light must be a wave phenomenon, a view reinforced in 1808 when the French physicist Etienne Malus (1775–1812) discovered polarized light, a form of light in which waves are confined to a plane.

It was already known that electric charge could in some circumstances produce light (in lightning, for example). In 1839 the French physicist Edmond Becquerel (1820–91) determined that the opposite also occurs in some circumstances; light produces electric current, known as the photovoltaic effect. A few years later Michael Faraday showed that a magnetic field changes the polarization of light (1845). With these discoveries in mind James Clerk Maxwell concluded that light consists of waves incorporating both electricity and magnetism—that is, electromagnetic waves. He predicted that electromagnetic waves exist in the electromagnetic spectrum below infrared and above ultraviolet radiation. In 1873 Maxwell published a complete mathematical theory of electromagnetism.

There were still mysteries. While setting up the equipment to produce and detect radio waves (the long electromagnetic waves predicted by Maxwell) in 1887, the German physicist Heinrich Hertz (1857–94) observed that light shining on the apparatus affects the size of an electric spark. Further investigation with more energetic electromagnetic radiation revealed that the amount of charge released by the metal depends on the frequency rather than the intensity of the radiation, a finding which made no sense at first. The problem was resolved in 1905 when Albert Einstein proved that light, as Newton had proposed, behaves in this case as a particle instead of as a wave.

Heat   As early as 1724 scientists tried to explain heat and cold with the idea that heat is an unusual component of matter, similar to a liquid, which they called caloric. Caloric persisted throughout the 18th century until a decisive experiment by Benjamin Thompson (Count Rumford, 1753–1814) showed that heat is closely connected to motion. Scientists since have believed heat to be an effect of the motion of molecules in any substance (cold is simply the absence of heat, or slower molecular motions), but it was not until 1860 that James Clerk Maxwell and, independently, the Austrian physicist Ludwig Boltzmann (1844–1906) worked out the mathematical theory of such particles.

Meanwhile, physicists were discovering the general laws of heat. The French physicist Sadi Carnot (1796–1832), after studying the still new steam engines, established mathematically in 1824 that work is done as heat passed from a high temperature to a lower one and that the maximum amount of work possible depends only on the temperature. Heat was recognized as a form of energy, along with motion, electricity, light, and stored, or potential, energy. Several English and German physicists measured exactly the amount of heat produced by motion, work that led to the laws of thermodynamics ("movement of heat"). With the new understanding of heat the British physicist William Thomson (Baron Kelvin, 1824–1907) recognized in 1851 that the total absence of heat would produce a specific coldest temperature, absolute zero.

Experimentalists used various methods to lower temperatures nearly to absolute zero, liquefying air in 1878, hydrogen in 1895, and helium, the element that has the coldest known transition from a gas to a liquid, in 1908.

With liquid helium near absolute zero, strange new forms of matter could be created. One of the most important is matter that superconducts—an electric current started in a ring of a superconducting material will continue around the ring as long as the temperature is maintained at a few degrees above absolute zero. Since the Dutch physicist Heike Kamerlingh-Onnes (1853–1926) discovered the first form of superconductivity in 1911, other materials, called high-temperature superconductors, have been found (starting in 1986), although none are superconducting at temperatures above −200°F (−130°C). Liquid helium itself was found to have unusual properties similar to those of superconductors, such as superfluidity. Like some very cold gases, first produced in 1995, liquid helium is a Bose-Einstein condensate (BEC), matter in which the atoms merge into a single superatom, first predicted by Albert Einstein in 1924.

Relativity Maxwell's theory of electromagnetism (proposed in 1873) assumed that electromagnetic waves must be motions in some all-pervasive but undetectable substance, which was called ether. Various attempts were made to define the properties of ether and, in a famous failed experiment of 1888, to determine Earth's motion through the ether. The Polish-American physicist Albert Michelson (1852–1931) and the American physicist Edward Morley (1838–1923) used a sensitive device invented by Michelson to measure the speed of light in the direction of Earth's motion through space and perpendicular to that motion, but failed to find any difference, suggesting that ether was a flawed concept. When Einstein developed the special theory of relativity (1905), however, he concluded that electromagnetic waves do not need ether to explain their properties. He took as a postulate that light travels through a vacuum at the same speed under all conditions; thus you cannot determine how Earth is moving by looking for variations in the speed of light that such motion would cause. He also observed that physical laws as measured should be the same for two entities moving with respect to each other with no change

in velocity. From these ideas he concluded that the universe can be described in terms of four-dimensional space-time and that matter and energy are related by the famous equation $E = mc^2$, where E is energy, m is mass, and c is the speed of light in a vacuum. Relativity theory also showed that time can be viewed as a dimension related to the dimensions of space. A definition of modern physics, then, might be that it is the study of matter-energy in space-time.

Next Einstein considered what happens if one entity is accelerated with relation to the other. He based this theory, the general theory of relativity, on the idea that no test can determine a difference between gravitational force and the force produced by acceleration, called inertia.

The general theory of relativity, which resulted from this postulate in 1915, is a description of gravity in terms of the curvature of space-time. Einstein's theory explained previously observed, but unexplained, changes in the orbit of Mercury and in 1919 described how light from a star was bent by the sun's gravitational field. Almost as soon as the general theory was published, it became clear that the theory as originally formulated predicted an expanding universe and also predicted the existence of what we now call black holes (1917), stars that have collapsed into points with such a strong gravitational force that light cannot escape. In 1979 another effect predicted by the theory, the lensing effect caused by the gravitational force of an entire galaxy, was observed for the first time; since then, gravitational lenses have become one of the principal tools astronomers use to observe the early universe.

Einstein thought in 1917 that the universe should be static, but assumed that gravity would cause the universe to be contracting. He interpreted his original equations as showing a universe that is slowly collapsing. To resolve this, he added a "cosmological constant" to the equations for general relativity to provide a small force opposing gravity. Einstein was clearly wrong about the possibility of gravitational collapse, for the Dutch physicist Willem de Sitter (1872–1934) showed in 1919 that Einstein's equations without the cosmological constant actually predicted an expanding universe. When expansion of the universe was observed by astronomers in the 1920's, Einstein abandoned the cosmological constant. In recent years, however, astronomers have detected an acceleration of the expansion of the universe. The mysterious force that causes this expansion is called "dark energy." Some physicists think that dark energy is evidence suggesting that Einstein's cosmological constant was correct and should be reinstated.

Particles and Quantum Theory

Several Greek and Roman writers had a theory that matter is made from small, indivisible particles; this theory was revived in 1803 as atomic theory by the British chemist John Dalton (1766–1844). During the 19th century, the idea of indivisible atoms came to be accepted, but near the end of the century evidence emerged that atoms themselves are made from even smaller particles. The electron was discovered by the English physicist J. J. Thomson (1856–1940) in 1897 and measured to be smaller by far than the smallest atom. Two years later, Thomson showed that the electron is a part of the atom.

Because electrons have a negative charge, but atoms are electrically neutral, it was apparent that there must be some particle (or other entity) in the atom with a positive charge to neutralize the charge of the electron. By 1911 the New Zealand-born British physicist Ernest Rutherford (1871–1937) had established that the positive charge is carried by a particle much heavier than the electron; he named this new particle the proton. The Danish physicist Niels Bohr (1885–1962) developed the mathematical theory of hydrogen, which has the simplest atom, in 1913. He found that the theory was correct in terms of experiment only if he used the idea that electrons can travel in only a few orbits and that they must be able to change from one orbit to another instantly (giving off or absorbing light in the process).

The idea that light energy has only separate (discrete) levels had first been used in 1900 to explain the spectrum of light emitted as a body is heated. The discrete levels were called quanta by the German physicist Max Planck (1858–1947), who had developed this theory. In 1905 Einstein used the same idea to explain the phenomenon discovered by Hertz in 1887, showing that light behaves like particles (quanta of light). Bohr showed that electron orbits are also quanta. Thus the theory of particle behavior is called the quantum theory.

Quantum theory advanced rapidly in the 1920s, beginning with the idea of the French physicist Louis de Broglie (1892–1987) that particles such as the electron have a wave aspect. The following year the Pauli exclusion principle (see "Two Basic Laws of Quantum Physics") and the matrix theory of the electron were established, along with the concept of particle spin. In 1926 the German physicist Erwin Schrödinger developed the equation of the electron wave. In 1927 the Heisenberg uncertainty principle was introduced. During this period, the only known particles were the photon, electron, and proton, but in 1930 Wolfgang Pauli (1900–58) proposed the neutrino, which was followed by dozens of other particles (see Subatomic Particles). Quantum theory was cast into the more precise form called quantum electrodynamics in 1947, when several physicists developed mathematical techniques to resolve problems with the original quantum theory.

Nuclear Physics

Radioactivity, which was discovered in 1896 by the French physicist Henri Becquerel (1852–1908), was the key to discovery of the proton and the concept that each atom has a positive nucleus surrounded by negative electrons. The study of the nucleus could not advance much until the discovery, in 1932, of the neutral particle the neutron, which is part of the nucleus in all atoms but the simplest hydrogen atom. Different forms of the same element, called isotopes, have the same number of protons in the nucleus, but different numbers of neutrons.

The French wife-and-husband team Irène Joliot-Curie (1897–1956) and Frédéric Joliot-Curie (1900–58) showed in 1934 that an element can be changed to a radioactive isotope by bombarding the atoms with neutrons. In 1937 the Italian-American physicist Emilio Segrè used the same idea to produce a previously unknown artificial element, technetium. In 1940 the first artificial element with an atomic number higher than that of uranium was created and named neptunium, element 93. The following year element 94, plutonium, joined the list. Today there are artificial elements through element 116.

In 1938 the German physicist Otto Hahn (1879–1968) and the Austrian physicist Lise Meitner (1878–1968) discovered that the large uranium atom could break into pieces (fission) when stuck with a neutron, releasing additional neutrons and other forms of energy in the process. This discovery led to the atomic, or nuclear fission, bomb and nuclear power (see "Technology"). Also in 1938 two physicists, Hans Bethe and Carl von Weizsäcker, proposed that in the intense heat and pressure of the interior of a star, hydrogen nuclei combine with each other to form helium (fusion), releasing energy in the process. This process also led to the development of a fusion bomb (the hydrogen bomb, 1952).

In the last decades of the 20th century physicists developed the standard model of elementary particles. This model incorporates three of the four fundamental forces in nature: the strong and weak nuclear forces and elec-

The Large Hadron Collider and the Higgs Particle

From NYTimes.com, "Times Topics"

Call it the Hubble Telescope of Inner Space.

The Large Hadron Collider, located 300 feet underneath the French-Swiss border outside Geneva, is the world's biggest and most expensive particle accelerator. It is designed to accelerate the subatomic particles known as protons to energies of 7 trillion electron volts apiece and then smash them together to create tiny fireballs, recreating conditions that last prevailed when the universe was less than a trillionth of a second old.

Whatever forms of matter and whatever laws and forces held sway Back Then—relics not seen in this part of space since the universe cooled 14 billion years ago—will spring fleetingly to life. If all goes well, they will leave their footprints in four mountains of hardware and computer memory that international armies of physicists have erected in the cavern.

After 16 years and $10 billion, on March 30, 2010, the collider finally began its work of smashing subatomic particles. The day was a milestone—delayed a year and a half by an assortment of technical problems—and brings closer a moment of truth for CERN and for the world's physicists, who have staked their credibility and their careers, not to mention all those billions of dollars, on the conviction that they are within touching distance of fundamental discoveries about the universe. If they fail to see something new, experts agree, it could be a long time, if ever, before giant particle accelerators are built on Earth again, ringing down the curtain on at least one aspect of the age-old quest to understand what the world is made of and how it works.

"If you see nothing," said John Ellis, a theoretical physicist at CERN, "in some sense then, we theorists have been talking rubbish for the last 35 years."

Machines like CERN's new collider get their magic from Einstein's equation of mass and energy. The more energy that these machines can pack into their little fireballs, in effect the farther back in time they can go, closer and closer to the Big Bang, the smaller and smaller things they can see.

The new hadron collider, scientists say, will take physics into a realm of energy and time where the current reigning theories simply do not apply, corresponding to an era when cosmologists think that the universe was still differentiating itself, evolving from a primordial blandness and endless potential into the forces and particles that constitute modern reality.

One prime target is a mysterious particle called the *Higgs* that is thought to endow other particles with mass, according to the reigning theory of particle physics, known as the Standard Model. That theory will now face its most severe test. Other theories go beyond this model to predict new forms of matter that explain the mysterious dark matter waddling the cosmos and even new dimensions of space-time.

The guts of the collider are some 1,232 electromagnets, thick as tree trunks, long as boxcars, weighing in at 35 tons apiece, strung together like an endless train stretching around the gentle curve of the CERN tunnel.

In order to bend 7-trillion-electron-volt protons around in such a tight circle these magnets, known as dipoles, have to produce magnetic fields of 8.36 Tesla, more than 100,000 times the Earth's field, requiring in turn a current of 13,000 amperes through the magnet's coils. To make this possible the entire ring is bathed in 128 tons of liquid helium to keep it cooled to 1.9 degrees Kelvin, at which temperature the niobium-titanium cables are superconducting and pass the current without resistance.

Running through the core of this train, surrounded by magnets and cold, are two vacuum pipes, one for protons going clockwise, the other counterclockwise. Traveling in tight bunches along the twin beams, the protons will cross each other at four points around the ring, 30 million times a second. During each of these violent crossings, physicists expect that about 20 protons, or the parts thereof—quarks or gluons—will actually collide and spit fire. It is in vast caverns at those intersection points that the detectors, or "sunken cathedrals" in the words of a CERN theorist, Alvaro de Rujula, are placed to capture the holy fire.

The payoff for this investment, physicists say, could be a new understanding of one of the most fundamental of aspects of reality, namely the nature of mass. This is where the shadowy particle known as the Higgs boson, a.k.a. the God particle, comes in.

In the Standard Model, a suite of equations describing all the forces but gravity, which has held sway as the law of the cosmos for the last 35 years, elementary particles are born in the Big Bang without mass.

Some of the particles acquire their heft, so the story goes, by wading through a sort of molasses that pervades all of space. The Higgs process, named after Peter Higgs, a Scottish physicist who first showed how this could work in 1964, has been compared to a cocktail party where particles gather their masses by interaction. The more they interact, the more mass they gain.

The Higgs idea is crucial to a theory that electromagnetism and the weak force are separate manifestations of a single so-called electroweak force. It shows how the massless bits of light called photons could be long-lost brothers to the heavy W and Z bosons, which would gain large masses from such cocktail party interactions as the universe cooled.

The confirmation of the theory by the Nobel-winning work at CERN 20 years ago ignited hopes among physicists that they could eventually unite the rest of the forces of nature.

Moreover, Higgs-like fields have been proposed as the source of an enormous burst of expansion, known as inflation, early in the universe, and, possibly, as the secret of the dark energy that now seems to be speeding up the expansion of the universe. So it is important to know whether the theory works and, if not, to find out what does endow the universe with mass.

But nobody has ever seen a Higgs boson, the particle that personifies this molasses. It should be producible in particle accelerators, but nature has given confusing clues about where to look for it. Measurements of other exotic particles suggest that the Higgs's mass should be around 90 billion electron volts, the unit of choice in particle physics. But other results, from the LEP collider before it shut down in 2000, indicate that the Higgs must weigh more than 114 billion electron volts. By comparison, an electron is half a million electron volts, and a proton is about 2,000 times heavier.

The new collider was specifically designed to hunt for the Higgs particle, which is key to the Standard Model and to any greater theory that would supersede it. The Tevatron is also searching for the Higgs.

Theorists say the Higgs or something like it has to show up simply because the Standard Model breaks down and calculations using it go kerflooey at energies exceeding one trillion electron volts. If you try to predict what happens when two particles collide, it gives nonsense, explained Dr. Ellis.

tromagnetic force (the other force is gravity). The standard model has so far stod up to testing, thought the goal for scientists is to incorporate gravity into the standard model, creating a "theory of everything" (see "String Theory and Supersymmetry" and "Subatomic Particles").

Condensed Matter　Nuclear and particle physics apply to what occurs within atoms and in isolated subatomic particles but do not explain the behavior of surface interactions, of clusters of small numbers of atoms or molecules, of complex molecular structures such as colloidal solutions or foams, or of electromagnetic phenomena in solids or liquids. Physicists have come to refer to the branch of the science that is concerned with the collective behavior of many particles as "condensed matter" physics. Today condensed-matter physics is one of the most active areas of the science.

Although scientific studies of magnetism and static electricity began in 1600, the first accurate theory of the cause of magnetism was that of the French physicist André-Marie Ampère (1775–1836) in 1825. Michael Faraday (1791–1867) recognized in 1845 that there are several magnetic effects, including diamagnetism (opposition to a magnetic field), paramagnetism (which disappears when a magnetic field is removed), and ferromagnetism (the familiar "permanent" magnetism that can be induced in iron and some other metals). Another major advance occurred in 1907 when the French physicist Pierre-Ernest Weiss (1865–1940) explained ferromagnetism as the effect produced when many small regions, called domains, become aligned by a magnetic field.

Early experimenters with static electricity observed that some substances—notably metals—conduct electricity and others are insulators. But not until 1900 did the German physicist Paul Drude (1863–1906) establish that in conductors some electrons are free to move away from their atoms, carrying negative charge with them. When quantum theory was developed, the Russian-German physicist Arnold Sommerfeld (1868–1951) developed in detail the theory of how electrons behave in a conductor. But there were still mysteries unsolved, for superconductivity was not explained until 1957, and high-temperature superconductivity still lacks a satisfactory explanation.

Understanding how conductors and insulators work led to a better understanding of semiconductors. This provided the background for the development in 1947 of the transistor and for subsequent applications of semiconductors, including some types of lasers and light-emitting diodes. Today condensed-matter physicists are applying the concept of spin to produce the effective disk drives in modern computers and look forward to using the electronics of spin, called spintronics, to develop improved devices that accomplish the tasks of transistors and their variants better and faster.

Physics and Other Disciplines   Physics is a fundamental underpinning of most science other than the studies of human beings and some theories concerning living organisms, and sometimes physics becomes completely combined with parts of other sciences. Three notable examples are combinations of physics with astronomy, earth science, and biology.

Astrophysics is the study of stars, gas clouds, and other astronomical bodies, based on the application of the laws of physics, including energy production, composition, and evolution. While a broad view of astrophysics would include virtually all of astronomy, the disciple was originally concerned primarily with energy production and the development of stars from gas clouds through several stages such as red giants or white dwarfs to concluding explosions as supernovas or collapse into burned-out cinders or black holes. In recent years, the evolution of the universe as a whole (cosmology) has become a central focus of many astrophysicists; cosmology includes the development of subatomic particles in the early universe and the possible roles of subatomic particles and physical forces in such concepts as dark matter or the unknown energy that is accelerating the expansion of the universe.

Geophysics is the study of the structure of Earth based on the application of physical laws to Earth's shape, seismology, electromagnetic properties, oceans, and atmosphere. The methods of geophysics have revealed Earth's layered structure, consisting of inner and outer cores, mantle, and crust, and have provided the theoretical basis of plate tectonics. In recent years, the definition of geophysics has been stretched to include the physical properties of planets other than Earth as well as of the satellites of planets.

Biophysics is the study of such physical processes as transport of materials in living organisms, growth of such organisms, and their structural stability in terms of the laws of physics. Of particular concern are transport of ions across cell membranes and the mechanisms of protein folding along with the physics of such imaging techniques as CT, MRI, and PET scans.

String Theory and Supersymmetry   Although quantum theories of particle physics explain many phenomena and allow interactions to be calculated to a high degree of accuracy, some of the mathematics involved has been viewed as questionable. Positive and negative infinities are added in such a way that their difference nearly cancels, but leaves a tiny amount that is exactly the amount measured by experiment. Also, physicists since Einstein have hoped to develop a unified theory that would include relativity and quantum mechanics as the logical outgrowth. Several developments since 1970 have attempted to resolve the mathematics and unify the various theories. The first was string theory, which replaced the concept of particles with one-dimensional strings whose properties are mathematically tractable, but only in spaces with more than four dimensions. In 1974 this was joined with a theory that every particle has a partner—if one particle represents matter, then the other represents force, and vice versa. This symmetry, called supersymmetry, called for a wide range of new particles that had not been previously observed. Two years later the recognition that certain strings behave like the graviton, a particle predicted by general relativity theory, led to combining relativity with string theory in a theory called supergravity. By 1984 string theory and supersymmetry had also been combined to create superstring theory—strings instead of particles, very massive and unknown partners for every known string, and all in ten- or eleven-dimensional space. The dimensions above the three known dimensions of space and the dimension of time are also unobserved and thought to be curled so tightly that they are too small to observe. In 1995 the American physicist Edward Witten (b. 1951) extended the symmetric theory of supergravity to a theory in which the fundamental entities are membranes in eleven-dimensional space. Variations on this concept, known as M theory or brane theory, remain the most popular concept of the underlying reality of the universe, called the "theory of everything," for today's theoretical physicists, although these theories are hampered by the inability of experimenters to prove or disprove them.

Basic Laws of Physics

Key Terms

Mass is a measure of the amount of matter; it is proportional to weight. Near the surface of Earth it is roughly equivalent to weight.

Velocity measures how an object changes position with time.

Acceleration is how an object changes velocity with time.

Momentum is the product of mass and velocity.

Energy is the ability to do work.

Law of Gravity

The gravitational force between any two objects is proportional to the product of their masses and inversely proportional to the square of the distance between them. If F is the force, G is the number that represents the ratio (the gravitational constant), m and M are the two masses, and r is the distance between the objects:

$$F = \frac{GmM}{r^2}$$

In metric measure, the gravitational constant is 0.0000000000667390 (6.67390×10^{-11}) newton m^2/kg^2, so another way of writing the basic law of gravity is

$$F = \frac{0.000000000667390mM}{r^2}$$

This law implies that objects falling near the surface of Earth will fall with the same rate of acceleration (ignoring drag caused by air). This rate is 32.174 feet per second per second (ft/sec²), or 9.8 m/sec², and is conventionally labeled g. Applying this rate to falling objects gives the velocity, v, and distance, d, after any amount of time, t, in seconds. If the object starts at rest and 32 ft/sec² is used as an approximation for g,

$$v = 32t$$
$$d = 16t^2$$

For example, after 3 seconds, a dropped object that is still falling will have a velocity of $32 \times 3 = 96$ feet per second and will have fallen a distance of $16 \times 32 = 144$ feet.

If the object has an initial velocity v_0 and an initial height above the ground of a, the equations describing the velocity and the distance, d, above the ground (a positive velocity is up and a negative velocity is down) become

and

$$v = v_0 - 32t$$

$$d = -16t^2 + v_0 t + a$$

After 3 seconds, an object tossed in the air from a height of 6 feet with a velocity of 88 feet per second will reach a speed of $88 - 96 = -8$ feet per second, meaning that it has begun to descend, and will have a height of $(-16 \times 9) + (88 \times 3) + 6 = -144 + 264 + 6 = 126$ feet above the ground.

The maximum height, H, reached by the object with an initial velocity v_0 and initial height a is

$$H = a + \frac{v_0^2}{64}$$

For the object tossed upward at 88 feet per second from a height of 6 feet, the maximum height reached would be $6 + 88^2/64 = 6 + 121 = 127$ feet. Therefore, after 3 seconds, the object has just reached its peak and has fallen back only 1 foot.

Albert Einstein's general theory of relativity introduced laws of gravity more accurate than those just given, which were discovered by Sir Isaac Newton. Newton's gravitational theory is extremely accurate for most practical situations, however. For example, Newton's theory is used to determine how to launch satellites into proper orbits.

Newton's Laws of Motion

Newton's laws of motion apply to objects in a vacuum and are not easily observed in the real world, where forces such as friction tend to overwhelm the natural motion of objects. To obtain realistic solutions to problems, however, physicists and engineers begin with Newton's laws and then add in the various forces that also affect motion.

1. *Any object at rest tends to stay at rest.* A body in motion moves at the same velocity in a straight line unless acted upon by a force. This is also known as the law of inertia. Note that this law implies that an object will travel in a curved path only so long as a force is acting on it. When the force is released, the object will travel in a straight line. A weight on a string swung in a circle will travel in a straight line when the string is released, for the string was supplying the force that caused circular motion.

2. *The acceleration of an object is directly proportional to the force acting on it and inversely proportional to the mass of the object.* This law, for an acceleration a, a force F, and a mass m, is more commonly expressed in terms of finding the force when you know the mass and the acceleration. In this form it is written as

$$F = ma$$

The implication of this law is that a constant force will produce acceleration, which is an increase in velocity. Thus a rocket, which is propelled by a constant force as long as its fuel is burning, constantly increases in velocity. Even with an infinite supply of fuel, the rocket would eventually cease to increase in velocity, however, because Einstein's other relativity theory, the special theory of relativity, states that no object can exceed the speed of light in a vacuum (see "Conservation of Mass-Energy"). Nevertheless, even a small force, constantly applied, can cause a large mass to reach velocities near the speed of light if enough time is allowed.

3. *For every action there is an equal and opposite reaction.* (See "Conservation of Momentum.")

Conservation Laws

Many results in physics come from various conservation laws. A conservation law is a rule that a certain entity must not change in amount during a certain class of operations. All such conservation laws treat closed systems. Anything added from outside the system could affect the amount of the entity being conserved.

Conservation of Momentum In a closed system, momentum stays the same. This law is equivalent to Newton's third law of motion. Since momentum is the product of mass and velocity, if the mass of a system changes, then the velocity must change. For example, consider a person holding a heavy anchor in a stationary rowboat in the water. The momentum of the system is 0, since the masses have no velocity. Now the person in the rowboat tosses the anchor toward the shore. The momentum of the anchor is now a positive number if velocity toward the shore is measured as positive. To conserve momentum, the rowboat is accelerated in the opposite direction, away from the shore. The positive momentum of the anchor is balanced by the negative momentum of the rowboat and its cargo. In terms of two masses, m and M, and matching velocities v and V,

$$mv = MV$$

Conservation of Angular Momentum An object moving in a circle has a special kind of momentum, called angular momentum. As noted above, motion in a circle requires some force. Angular momentum combines mass and velocity with distance from the point the object is spinning around. For a body moving in a circle, the acceleration depends on both the speed of the body in its path and the radius of the circle. The product of this speed, the mass, and the square of the radius is the angular momentum of the mass.

In a closed system, angular momentum is conserved. This effect is used by skaters to change their velocity of spinning. Angular momentum is partly determined by the masses of a skater's arms combined with the rate of rotation and the square of the radius to the center of mass of each arm (the point that can represent the total mass of the arm). When skaters bring their arms close to their body, this would tend to reduce the angular momentum, because the center of mass is closer to the body. But, since angular momentum is conserved, the rate of rotation has to increase to compensate for the decreased radius. Because the rate depends on the square of the radius, the rate increases exponentially.

Conservation of Mass In a closed system, the total amount of mass appears to be conserved in all but nuclear reactions and other extreme conditions.

Conservation of Energy In a closed system, energy appears to be conserved in all but nuclear reactions and other extreme conditions. Energy comes in very many forms: mechanical, chemical, electrical, heat, and so forth. As one form is changed into another (excepting nuclear reactions and extreme conditions), this law guarantees that the total amount remains the same. Thus, when you change the chemical energy of a dry cell into electrical energy and use that to turn a motor, the total amount of energy does not change (although some becomes heat energy—see "Laws of Thermodynamics").

Conservation of Mass-Energy Einstein discovered that his special theory of relativity implies that energy and mass are related. Consequently, mass and energy by themselves are not conserved, since one can be converted into the other. Mass and energy appear to be conserved in ordinary situations because the effect of Einstein's discovery is very small most of the time. The more general law, then, is the law of conservation of mass-energy: The total amount of mass and energy must be conserved. Einstein found the following equation that links mass and energy:

$$E = mc^2$$

In this equation, E is the amount of energy, m is the mass, and c is the speed of light in a vacuum.

One instance of energy changing to mass occurs in Einstein's equation for how the mass increases with velocity. If m_O is the mass of the object when it is not moving, v is the velocity of the object in relation to an observer who is considered to be at rest, and c is the speed of light in a vacuum, then the mass, m, is given by the equation

$$m = \frac{m_O}{\sqrt{1 - \frac{v^2}{c^2}}}$$

This accounts for the rule that no object can exceed the speed of light in a vacuum. As the object approaches this speed, so much of the energy is converted to mass that it cannot continue to accelerate.

In both nuclear fission (splitting of the atomic nucleus) and nuclear fusion (the joining of atomic nuclei, producing the energy of a hydrogen bomb), mass is converted into energy.

Conservation for Particles Many properties associated with atoms and subatomic particles are also conserved. Among them are charge, spin, isospin, and a combination known as CPT: charge conjugation, parity, and time.

First and Second Laws of Thermodynamics

First Law This is the same as the law of conservation of energy. It is a law of thermodynamics, or the movement of heat, because heat must be treated as a form of energy to keep the total amount of energy constant. All bodies contain heat as energy no matter how cold they are, although there is not much heat at temperatures close to absolute zero.

Second Law Heat in a closed system can never travel from a low-temperature region to one of higher temperature in a self-sustaining process. *Self-sustaining* in this case describes a process that does not need energy from outside the system to keep it going. In a refrigerator, heat from the cold inside of the refrigerator is transferred to a warmer room, but energy from outside is required to make the transfer happen, so the process is not self-sustaining.

The second law has many implications. One of them is that no perpetual motion machine can be constructed. Another is that all energy in a closed system eventually becomes heat that is diffused equally throughout the system, so that one can no longer obtain work from the system.

The equations that describe the behavior of heat also can be applied to order and therefore to information. The word *entropy* refers to diffuse heat, disorder, or lack of information. Another form of the second law of thermodynamics is that in a closed system, entropy always increases.

Laws of Current Electricity

Key Terms When electrons flow in a conductor, the result is electric current. The amount of current is based on an amount of electric charge called the coulomb, which is the charge of about 6.25 quintillion (6.25×10^{18}) electrons. When 1 coulomb of charge moves past a point in 1 second, it creates a current of 1 ampere. Just as a stream can carry the same amount of water swiftly through a narrow channel or slowly through a broad channel, the energy of an electric current varies depending on the difference in charge between places along the conductor. This is called potential difference and is measured in volts. The voltage is affected by the nature of the conductors. Some substances conduct an electric current much more easily than others. This resistance to the current is measured in ohms. Electric power is the rate at which electricity is used.

Ohm's Law Electric current is directly proportional to the potential difference and inversely proportional to resistance. If you measure current, I, in amperes, potential difference, V, in volts, and resistance, R, in ohms, then the current is equal to the potential difference divided by the resistance.

$$I = \frac{V}{R}$$

Law of Electric Power If electric power, P, is measured in watts, then the power is equal to the product of the current measured in amperes and the potential difference measured in volts.

$$P = IV$$

Laws of Light and Electromagnetic Radiation

Key Terms Light is a part of a general form of radiation known as electromagnetic waves, or, when thought of as particles, photons. Here, electromagnetic radiation is considered as a wave phenomenon for the most part. The velocity of a wave is how fast the wave travels as a whole. The wavelength is the distance between one crest of the wave and the next crest. The frequency is how many crests pass a particular location in a unit of time. One crest passing each second is called a hertz.

Law of Electromagnetic Energy   The energy of an electromagnetic wave depends on a small number known as Planck's constant. Measured in joules per hertz (energy per frequency), Planck's constant is 6.67259×10^{-34}. The energy is equal to the product of Planck's constant and the frequency. Using E for energy, h for Planck's constant, and f for frequency,

$$E = hf$$

When thought of in terms of the particles called photons, the energy of a photon obeys the same law. The law of wave motion and the law of electromagnetic energy can be combined with the speed of light in a vacuum (c) to give

$$E = \frac{hc}{l}$$

The energy of a photon is the product of Planck's constant and the speed of light, divided by the wavelength (l) of the photon.

Inverse-Square Law   All radiation obeys an inverse-square law, which is similar to the law of gravity. The intensity of the radiation decreases as the inverse of the square of the distance from a point source of radiation.

Two Basic Laws of Quantum Physics

When one considers effects on very small masses and at very small distances, it is necessary to recognize that objects behave differently from their action at sizes and distances one can observe directly. Since these effects occur in discrete steps based upon Planck's constant times the frequency, called the quantum—which is the size by which energy changes in steps (instead of continuously)—the science of such effects is called quantum physics. Small masses act sometimes like particles and sometimes like waves. Two laws in particular that describe the behavior of small masses are basic and easily stated.

Heisenberg's Uncertainty Principle   It is impossible to specify completely the position and momentum of a particle, such as an electron, at the same time.

Pauli's Exclusion Principle   Two particles of matter cannot be in the same exact state. Particles of matter include the electron, neutron, and proton. Bosons, particles of force, do not obey Pauli's exclusion principle. (see "Subatomic Particles.")

Subatomic Particles

The idea of an atom goes back to the ancient Greek philosophers, who thought that matter was composed of tiny indivisible particles. The concept was put on a scientific basis by John Dalton (1766–1844) in 1803 and became the foundation of chemistry. Nearly a hundred years later, experiments by J. J. Thomson (1856–1940) in 1899 were the first to show that atoms are not indivisible after all. In the past hundred years, physics at almost all levels has been completely revolutionized by the study of the particles that make up atoms or that are smaller than atoms. In the last decades of the 20th century physicists developed the standard model of elementary particles. This model incorporates three of the four fundamental forces in nature: the strong and weak nuclear forces and electromagnetic force (the other force is gravity). In the model, bosons mediate the forces: gluons for the strong nuclear force, the photon for electromagnetism, and W and Z particles for the weak nuclear force. Within this model, the weak and electromagnetic forces have been combined into electroweak theory. The standard model

has thus far met all experimental challenges, but it has some gaps in addition to the omission of gravity: in particular, the strong and electroweak forces are not completely unified. Theories that attempt to unify the strong and electroweak forces are called grand unified theories (GUTs). Beyond grand unified theories, a great challenge for physicists is a "theory of everything" (TOE) that would account for all of the fundamental forces in nature. Below is a list of all the most important subatomic particles, in the chronological order of their discovery.

1897 Electron   The first subatomic particle to be identified, also by J. J. Thomson, was the electron, a low-mass particle that can be found in the outer reaches of the atom. One property of the electron is charge, the response to electric or magnetic fields. The charge of a single electron is always the same, and is identified as −1 (negative one). Each atom consists of a cloud of electrons around a center of positive charge, which is called the nucleus.

1905 Photon   The photon is the particle that carries the electromagnetic force. This concept began with Albert Einstein (1879–1955) in 1905, when he established that light acts sometimes as a particle instead of as waves. Although we usually think of the photon as the particle of light, it is also the particle form of radio waves, X rays, or gamma rays. The mass of the photon is 0.

1911 Proton   At least one proton is always found in the nucleus of every atom. The proton has a charge that is the same in size as that of the electron, but responds in the opposite direction to an electric or magnetic field. This charge is +1 (positive one). Each proton is almost 2,000 times as heavy as an electron, or about the same as the mass of a single hydrogen atom.

1924 Bosons   While matter is made from subatomic particles, the forces that act on matter are also produced by subatomic particles. The particles that create these forces are collectively called bosons because the mathematics of the behavior of this type of particle was worked out originally by Satyendranath Bose (1894–1974) in 1924, although it was put into final form by Einstein. The observed bosons are the photon, pions, gluons, W particles, and Z particles. Bosons that are predicted, but that have not been observed, include the Higgs particle and the graviton.

1925–26 Quantum Mechanics   The basic theory of subatomic particles, called quantum mechanics, was developed in two different forms, in 1925 by Werner Heisenberg (1901–76) and in 1926 by Erwin Schrödinger (1887–1961). Although the two forms appear very different, they produce the same results.

1926 Fermions   All the particles that make up matter are called fermions, as opposed to the bosons that create forces. The fermions include all the leptons and quarks as well as the particles made from quarks (see below). Fermions are named for Enrico Fermi (Italian-American, 1901–54), who first worked out the mathematics of their interactions in 1926. Fermions all obey the Pauli exclusion principle (see Basic Laws of Physics, earlier in this chapter); that is, they occupy a definite space. Two fermions cannot be in the same place at the same time.

1930 Antiparticles   When Paul A. M. Dirac (1902–84) completed his mathematical version of the theory of the electron in 1930, he observed that one solution to his equations predicted a particle that would be a mirror image of the electron, exactly the same as the electron but with a positive instead of a negative charge. The particle, discovered two years later in 1932, was named the positron. The same equations predicted mirror images for all subatomic particles. These particles are called antiparti-

cles, so another name for positron is antielectron.

1932 Neutron   The neutron is very much like a neutral proton, with just slightly more mass. Neutrons are stable when they are found in atoms, but decay into other particles when left to themselves.

1935 Muon   The muon is now recognized as a high-energy analogue to the electron with a mass about 200 times that of the electron.

1947 Pion   (Predicted in 1935.) A pion carries the strong force that holds the nucleus of atoms together, but since each pion appears and disappears almost instantly, the pions are not usually counted as part of the nucleus. In the same year that the pion was found, theoreticians were able to work out a comprehensive theory of the electron, called quantum electrodynamics (QED).

1950 Strange Particles   Starting in 1950 experimenters observed a number of previously undetected particles that did not behave as particles were expected to. Because these particles have masses greater than that of the proton and neutron, they were called hyperons. Other unexpected particles, about the size of the pion, were classed as mesons. A classification scheme for the hyperons, developed in 1961, helped physicists understand them better, but their essential difference was already labeled "strangeness."

1955 Neutrinos   Neutrinos are thought to be among the most common particles in the universe, but they interact with ordinary matter so weakly that they are very difficult to observe. Predicted in 1930, neutrinos were thought to have no rest mass, but Canadian experiments in 2001 indicate that they have a very small mass equal to less than about 10^{-7} of the mass of an electron. Different neutrinos are associated with electrons, muons, and tauons.

1964–95 Quarks   Murray Gell-Mann (b. 1928) and several other physicists determined that a way to explain the properties of protons, neutrons, mesons, and hyperons is to think of the heavy particles as made from combinations of light ones, just as the atom is made from combinations of electrons, protons, and neutrons. The smaller particles are quarks; there are six of them in all. Two quarks, known as up and down, form protons and neutrons. The top quark is the most massive—about as heavy as an atom of gold—and was the last to be detected. (First version of theory in 1964, evidence for top quark in 1995.)

1965–73 Gluons   The eight different bosons that produce a force between quarks known as the color force are called gluons. The color force is also the basis of the strong force that holds the nucleus together. Because of the color force, the study of quarks and gluons is today called quantum chromodynamics (QCD).

1974 J/psi Particle   Like the strange hyperons, the J/psi particle is a heavy particle that appears at high energies. It also is produced by a different kind of quark, the charm quark. The odd name J/psi comes from the particle's having been discovered independently by two investigators, of whom one called it J and the other named it psi.

1983 W and Z Particles   The particles that produce the weak force are called W and Z. At high energies, however, the weak force merges with the electromagnetic force, so that W and Z are to some extent analogues to the photon, although they could not be more different, since the photon has a 0 rest mass and both W particles and the single Z particle are very massive.

1995 Antiatoms   Since antiparticles have all the properties of ordinary particles except for being mirror images, it is possible to create an antiatom by combining subatomic antiparticles. This was accomplished in 1995 with the production of a few antiatoms of antihydrogen made by causing an antielectron (positron) to orbit an antiproton.

(Not Yet Observed) Graviton and Higgs Particle
A particle that produces gravitational force by its exchange between all kinds of particles is known as the graviton, but so far it is known only in theory. The Laser Interferometer Gravitational Wave Observatory (LIGO) that began operations in 2000 seeks to observe gravity waves, the wave version of the graviton. The Higgs particle is the main undetected particle of the standard model of subatomic particles. Physicists believe that the Higgs, named after Peter Higgs (b. 1919), who predicted it in 1964, confers mass on all other particles.

Glossary of Physics Terms

alternating current electric current in which an electric field flows first in one direction and then the opposite way at a constant frequency (in the United States, 60 cycles per second). It is produced by switching current back and forth at the source. Current supplied over power lines is alternating current because AC voltages can be stepped up for transmission and down for distribution to users, allowing current to travel farther with less loss.

anode positive electrode. In an electron tube the anode attracts electrons from the cathode.

atom electrically neutral particle that is the smallest part of a chemical element. Atoms are formed by a nucleus of at least one proton and, except for the hydrogen atom, one or more neutrons, surrounded by a cloud of exactly as many electrons as protons.

boiling point temperature at which the vapor pressure of a liquid equals that of the surrounding gas or vapor. At this temperature, a phase change begins, as the liquid boils and changes to a vapor (gas) state at a given pressure.

Bose-Einstein condensate phase of matter occurring at extremely low temperatures in systems consisting of large numbers of atoms in the same quantum state, so that they act like a single entity or superatom. The atoms must be bosons (particles with integral spin, which can apply to either atomic nuclei or atoms). The first Bose-Einstein condensate was created in 1995 by physicists at the Joint Institute of Laboratory Astrophysics, in Boulder, Colo.

capillary action process by which liquid in a very narrow tube rises against the pull of gravity. When the surface of a liquid is in contact with a solid, the liquid is elevated or depressed depending upon the relative attraction of the molecules of the liquid for each other or for those of the solid.

cathode negative electrode. In a vacuum tube, electrons flow from the cathode to the anode.

centripetal and centrifugal force centripetal force acts on a body to cause it to move in a circular path. A satellite circling the earth is held by the centripetal force of the Earth's gravity. Inertia tends to keep the body moving straight, and this is referred to as centrifugal force.

Cerenkov radiation any charged particle traveling faster than light moves in a liquid or solid medium produces a wake of electromagnetic radiation called Cerenkov radiation or Cerenkov light. The phenomenon was discovered in 1934 by Pavel A. Cerenkov (Russian, 1904–90).

charge property of matter that gives rise to electrical phenomena. The unit of charge is that of the proton or the electron; the proton is designated as positive (+1) and the electron as negative (−1). All other charged elementary particles have charges equal to +1 or −1, except quarks, whose charge can be 1/3 or 2/3. Every charged particle is surrounded by an electric force field so that it attracts any charge of opposite sign brought near it and repels any charge of the same sign. This force is responsible for holding protons and electrons together in atoms and for chemical bonding.

colloid combination of two materials in which one is in a gas, liquid, or solid phase (called the medium) and the other is dispersed through the first in tiny clusters of atoms or molecules or in very large molecules. A colloid in which liquid or solid particles are dispersed in a gas is also called an aerosol; one with gas in a liquid or solid is a foam; one with liquid particles in another liquid is an emulsion; and solid particles in a liquid form a sol. Gels are colloids in which both elements have a three-dimensional structure throughout the material. Examples of colloids include the aerosols fog (water in air) and smoke (soot in air); the foams whipped cream (air in milk) and Styrofoam (air in styrene); the emulsion mayonnaise (oil in egg); the gel gelatin (protein in water); and the sol ruby glass (metal in glass).

convection process in which heat is transported by the movement of a fluid. Responding to gravitational force, parts of a fluid such as air that are denser than surrounding parts sink. The sinking fluids displace hotter, less dense material and cause it to rise, transporting heat. From the point of view of someone surrounded by the fluid, as we are by air, it is more obvious that the less dense fluid is rising than that the denser fluid is sinking. Thus people say "hot air rises," although that occurs only because cold air sinks. When a fluid is heated from the bottom, the unheated fluid sinks and the heated fluid is pushed away—but then the previously unheated fluid becomes heated.

crystal solid with a regular geometric shape, with a defined internal structure, and enclosed by symmetrically arranged plane surfaces that intersect at definite and char-

acteristic angles. The particles (atoms, ions, or molecules) in a crystal have a regular three-dimensional repeating arrangement in space, called the crystal structure.

decay spontaneous disintegration of the nucleus of an atom, such as an isotope of uranium, by the emission of particles, usually with the emission of electromagnetic radiation. The half-life of a radioactive substance is the time that is required for half of the quantity of the substance to decay.

density mass of a substance per unit of volume, which can be measured in units such as pounds per cubic inch or kg/m^3. It is commonly confused with weight; lead is denser than water, not heavier. Density is often compared with that of water. Such a comparison, made with the densest water—at 39.2°F (4°C)—is called relative density (formerly specific gravity). Relative density of lead is about 11 (it is 11 times as dense as water); the lightest metal, lithium, has a relative density of about 0.5, so it floats on water.

diffraction bending or spreading of waves (such as light) when a wave encounters either an object or an opening; some of the wave near the edges of the object or opening is bent. The diffracted waves interfere with each other, producing reinforcement or weakening.

direct current electric current in which the net flow of charge is in one direction.

Doppler effect apparent change in the frequency of a wave with the relative motion between source and observer (after Christian Doppler, 1803–53). For example, sound from an approaching vehicle, such as a siren, is perceived as having a higher pitch because more sound waves per second are perceived by the human ear; the apparent pitch falls as the vehicle passes and moves away from the observer. Light from distant galaxies is affected by a related phenomenon. As the universe expands, electromagnetic waves emitted in the distant past become longer in wavelength, shifting frequencies lower, which for visible light is toward the red.

efficiency measure that applies to any transformation of energy by an engine, machine, etc., from one form to another. It is the ratio of the amount of work done to the amount of energy used to produce the work. Since work and energy are measured in the same unit (in scientific notation, the joule), this ratio is a pure number, most commonly expressed as a percent. No transformations in the real world have 100 percent efficiency.

energy measure of a system's ability to do work (measured in joules).

entropy measure of the unavailability of a system's energy to do work. In a closed system entropy tends to increase (the second law of thermodynamics), resulting in less energy available to do work. In a more general sense, all ordered systems tend to become less ordered—that is, to increase in entropy: solids crumble; liquids and gases diffuse.

field in physics a field assigns to every point in space an amount—often the size of a force—and a direction, for example the direction in which a force acts. Typical fields include gravitational, electric, and magnetic fields.

fluorescence light produced by a material that was induced by incident radiation. A fluorescent light is one in which a gas in a glass tube coated with a fluorescent substance is excited by electrons, resulting in the emission of photons of ultraviolet radiation converted to visible light by the coating in the tube.

force any push or pull; that is, a quantity that changes the motion of a body if it is free to move. Force has both magnitude and direction; the magnitude is measured in pounds or newtons. A force acting on a mass produces acceleration proportional to the force unless balanced by a force in the opposite direction. Physicists generally recognize four fundamental forces: gravity, electromagnetism, and two atomic-level forces: the strong force, which holds the atomic nucleus together; and the weak force, which is associated with beta particle emission and particle decay.

frequency number of waves per second; it is measured as hertz (Hz): 10 Hz is 10 cycles per second. Frequency is determined by wavelength and the speed at which a wave travels.

friction resistance to the movement of one object past another with which it is in contact. Friction is dependent on the size of the force holding the objects together. For an object sliding on top of another, this is the weight (or force of gravity). An increase in the weight causes an increase in resistance. Friction is also dependent to some degree on the smoothness of the surfaces; generally, rougher surfaces have more friction, i.e., require a greater force to move one object past another.

half-life time in which one-half of the original quantity of a radioactive element will decay. Radioactive elements decay atom by atom in random events. Which individual atom decays is inherently unpredictable, but statistically the change follows a specific decay function for each isotope of an element.

incandescence light emitted by heating a material to a high temperature. In the common lightbulb a tungsten filament, usually in an inert gas, is heated to a high temperature to produce light.

inertia property that causes objects to resist any change in their motion. Objects at rest tend to stay at rest unless acted upon by an external force, and objects in motion continue in motion unless acted upon by an external force. This is a statement of Newton's first law of motion.

ion atom or group of atoms that either gains one or more electrons, and thus becomes negatively charged (anion), or loses one or more electrons, becoming positively charged (cation).

isotope substance formed from atoms that each have the same number of protons and neutrons per atom. Elements usually exist in several different isotopes. The number of protons in each atom determines which element it is and most of the properties; the number of neutrons determines the specific isotope. The number that is the sum of the protons and neutrons per atom is combined with the element name to identify a specific isotope. For example, two isotopes of carbon are carbon 12, with six protons and six neutrons; and carbon 14, with six protons and eight neutrons.

kinetic energy energy of motion.

mass measure of an object's inertia, that is, its resistance to acceleration. Inertial mass is exactly equivalent to gravitational mass, measurable by the force between two bodies separated by a given distance. The international standard of mass is a 1-kg platinum-iridium cylinder.

melting point temperature, usually measured at a pressure of 1 bar, at which a solid becomes liquid. The melting point is the same temperature as the freezing point, at which liquids become solid.

noise random changes in a signal being received at a detector. A mixture of sound or electromagnetic waves of random amplitude and frequency is called white noise.

osmosis process of diffusion of a solvent such as water through a semipermeable membrane that will transmit the solvent but impede most dissolved substances. Normally the flow of solvent is from the more dilute solution to the more concentrated solution; flow will stop when the solutions are of equal concentration. Movement of water in plants and animals is determined to a large extent by osmosis.

period time that it takes for an oscillation or wave motion to repeat. Period (p) is the reciprocal of the frequency (f): $p = 1/f$. Any repeated motion, as for a pendulum or vibrating atom, similarly has a period—the amount of time for one repetition.

phase of matter traditionally matter exists in three states or phases—solid, liquid, and gas—but the modern view is that there are five phases of matter: the three traditional states plus plasma and Bose-Einstein condensates. For most elements and compounds, phases of matter change in response to heating.

phosphorescence light produced by causes other than increasing the heat of a substance that persists after the source of excitation has been removed.

photoelectric effects various electrical effects caused by light. The photoelectric (or photoemissive) effect occurs when electromagnetic waves strike a substance and liberate electrons from its surface In the photovoltaic effect a current flows across the junction of two dissimilar materials when light falls upon it. In the photoconductive effect, an increase in the electrical conductivity of a semi-conductor is caused by radiation.

piezoelectricity electric current caused by a mechanical force. When a mechanical force is applied to both sides of any of various nonconducting crystals such as quartz or Rochelle salt, positive charge builds on one face and negative charge on the opposite face, inducing a small electric current, in a circuit. The effect also works in reverse. Applying a current changes the shape of the crystal or other material as the faces repel or attract each other. These properties give rise to a variety of applications in acoustic and other devices such as microphones and quartz clocks.

pitch highness or lowness of a sound to an observer; higher pitches correspond to higher frequencies; pitch can also be affected by the loudness of a sound.

plasma one of the five phases of matter, consisting of a low-density, fully ionized gas with approximately equal numbers of positive and negative ions. Plasmas are electrically conductive and affected by magnetic fields. Interstellar gases, as well as the matter inside stars, is believed to be in the form of plasma. The study of plasma is important in the attempt to produce a controlled thermonuclear reaction as an energy source.

polarized light electromagnetic field confined to two dimensions, also called plane-polarized light. The electromagnetic field of unpolarized light vibrates in all directions perpendicular to the line of travel. One use of polarizing materials is in certain kinds of sunglasses, which absorb horizontally polarized light reflected off surfaces such as water.

potential energy energy stored in a system or body as a result of its position or shape; examples are gravitational, electrical, chemical, and nuclear energy. A rock on the edge of a cliff has potential energy because of its position in the Earth's gravitational field.

power rate at which work is done or energy transferred. It is measured scientifically in watts (joules/second). In common usage, it is sometimes measured in horsepower (1 horsepower = 745.7 watts).

radiation emission and transmission of energy through space or a material medium; also the radiated energy. Generally the term is applied to the electromagnetic spectrum, which (from longest to shortest waves) includes radio, microwave, infrared, visible light, ultraviolet, X rays, and gamma rays; or to radioactivity, which includes streams of electrons or alpha particles as well as gamma rays.

radioactivity radiation produced by decay from one element to another or by nuclear fusion or fission. The disintegration of certain atomic nuclei is accompanied by the emission of alpha particles (helium nuclei), beta particles (electrons or positrons), or gamma radiation (short-wavelength electromagnetic radiation). Natural radioactivity is the disintegration of naturally occurring radioisotopes. Radioactivity can also be induced by bombarding the nuclei of normally stable elements in a particle accelerator to produce radioactive isotopes.

refraction deflection of a ray of light as it passes obliquely from one medium to another in which its speed is different. The incoming ray is the incident ray, and the deflected ray is the refracted ray. Other electromagnetic waves and sound waves can also be refracted.

spectrum rainbow or any of various related electromagnetic displays. A rainbow is just the spectrum of visible light. The complete electromagnetic spectrum includes (from longest to shortest waves) radio, microwave, infrared, visible light, ultraviolet, X-ray, and gamma-ray emissions. The emission (or "bright line") spectrum of a body is the characteristic radiation pattern produced when the body is heated, bombarded by electrons or ions, or absorbing photons; the lines in the spectrum can be used to identify elements with the spectroscope. The absorption (dark line) spectrum is the reverse of the emissions spectrum; it is produced by white light passing through a gas not hot enough to be incandescent.

specific heat amount of heat needed to raise the temperature of 1 gram of a substance, at a given pressure, by 1°C. For water at sea level, this is 4.187 joules (1 Calorie). Different substances have different specific heats.

spin quantum characteristic of particles best described as intrinsic angular momentum that is not associated with rotation. The quantum values of spin are restricted to integer or half-integer multiples of $h/2$, where h is Planck's constant. Because of spin, particles also have their own intrinsic magnetic moments.

sublimation change of a substance directly from a solid to a gas without first becoming a liquid. This process is most familiar from frozen carbon dioxide, known as dry ice. Water ice also sublimes slowly at temperatures below 32°F (0°C).

surface tension property of liquids in which the liquid appears to be bounded by a thin elastic skin. Molecules in a liquid attract each other from all directions, but at the surface of a liquid there are attractive forces only from below. The unbalanced attraction creates the illusion of a skin at the surface.

suspension mixture in which finely divided particles of solid or liquid are suspended in a liquid or gas.

temperature measure of the average energy of motion in the atoms or molecules of a substance. As more heat is added to a system, its temperature rises. Temperature determines the direction of heat flow: heat transfers from a higher-temperature system to a lower one until the two systems are at the same temperature and thus in thermal equilibrium.

tunneling quantum-mechanical effect by which a particle can penetrate a barrier into a region of space that would be forbidden according to ordinary classic mechanics. Tunneling occurs because of the wavelike properties of particles; the wave associated with a particle can leak or decay through the barrier, and there is a finite probability of finding the particle on the other side. The theory of tunneling is the basis of the tunnel diode, used in electronic applications.

ultrasound sound beyond the range of human hearing, at frequencies greater than 20,000 cycles/second. Unlike audible sound, in which high intensity produces discomfort, ultrasound can increase in pressure (intensity) with little impact on human hearing. Ultrasound is widely used for medical and industrial imaging and testing: objects are scanned with ultrasound and the echoes recorded and analyzed.

vacuum region of space with very few atoms or other particles. A true or perfect vacuum would be a region of space that contains no matter, but in practice this is unattainable. The uncertainty principle permits subatomic particles to appear out of nothing and disappear before violating any physical laws. Thus any vacuum contains virtual particles.

viscosity property of a fluid's resistance to flow; a higher viscosity means a slower flow. The cause of viscosity is internal molecular friction.

wave disturbance in space or a medium with a periodic form, such as electromagnetic waves and sound waves. The main characteristics of waves are speed of propagation, frequency, amplitude, and wavelength.

work a force that causes an object to move produces work, which is the product of the force and the distance moved. Work is measured in joules, the same unit used to measure energy.

MATHEMATICS

History of Mathematics

The roots of mathematics can be traced to ancient Egypt, China, India, and Babylonia; the discipline owes the biggest debt, however, to the ancient Greeks. Western Europeans expanded Arabic and Latin translations of Greek mathematical texts, which were developed from mathematical discoveries that predate recorded history.

Early Arithmetic It took thousands of years for the concept of numeration to evolve. The languages of many hunter-gatherer societies exhibited a "one, two, many" logic system, in which any number larger than two was simply expressed as "many." This type of system was probably the norm for much of human history, but as civilizations grew, more sophisticated mathematical systems developed to simplify trade, facilitate construction, and regulate agriculture.

The Lebombo bone, a baboon fibula etched with 29 marks, is the oldest known mathmetical artifact, dating back to 35,000 B.C. Later, Middle Eastern traders used small pieces of hardened clay as tokens to facilitate transactions. Arithmetic began as a system of manipulating tokens to determine sums and differences.

Counting boards improved on the token system by demarcating one section of a tablet for individual units, a different section for groups of 10, and a third for groups of 100s. The abacus, developed by the Sumerians around 2700 B.C., evolved from counting boards. The Chinese adapted the abacus to their number system, forming the basis for the Hindu-Arabic numerals, which would evolve into the numbers we use today.

By 2000 B.C., the simple mathematics of counting and whole-number arithmetic led to what conceptually was algebra—although not easily recognized as such because symbols were not employed. In Mesopotamia of that era, simple quadratic equations (such as $x^2 + 2 = 3x$) could be solved.

Measurement and Geometry Standards for length and weight are known to have existed 5,000 years ago. In Egypt, methods were developed to measure property and to restore boundaries after the annual Nile flood. Construction of pyramids and temples required knowledge of how to measure angles.

Measurement soon led to a practical sort of geometry. Formulas were developed for area and volume in Egypt, Mesopotamia, and China. The Pythagorean theorem and its relation to right angles were also recognized to varying extents in these early civilizations, starting ca. 1850 B.C. By 1750 B.C. Egyptian mathematicians could calculate volumes of many figures, including a pyramid with its top removed (a truncated pyramid). In a few instances, the early mathematicians recognized that one idea followed from another—the beginnings of proof.

Proof became central to geometry in the Greek civilization starting soon after 600 B.C. By A.D. 300 it was possible for Euclid of Alexandria (ca. 325–ca. 265 B.C.) to gather all known results of geometry and arithmetic and arrange them into a logical system. Some results were proved directly from a few simple rules (called axioms and postulates) and from the definitions of geometric shapes. The mathematics of Euclid remains the basis of geometry today, although some of the reasoning behind the results has been improved by modern mathematicians.

Mathematics in the East While some ideas of Greek mathematics followed conquest and trade into India, for the most part mathematics developed independently in Asia. *The Nine Chapters of Mathematical Art*, a Chinese text that dates from 200–300 B.C., contains problems solved using geometry, algebra-like manipulations, and even more advanced algorithms. The Chinese and Hindu-Arabic number systems allowed for the incorporation of innovations such as decimals and fractions (ca. A.D. 5) and negative numbers (ca. A.D. 200). Several Chinese mathematicians calculated the ratio of the distance around a circle to the distance across, which we now call pi (π), to many decimal places, beginning as early as A.D. 263.

Indian mathematicians introduced a numerical relative of geometry, called trigonometry ("triangle measuring"). By about A.D. 800 the Indians' recognition that zero is a number, seemingly a small advance, allowed the development of the flexible system of place-value, decimal numeration used around the world today.

Beginnings of Algebra   Another Greek innovation was the use of symbols to represent very general problems. The originator of this approach, Diophantus (ca. 210–ca. 290) is often called the "father of algebra," although his book of problems is named *Arithmetica*.

In 835, the Arab mathematician Muhammad Al-Khwarizmi (ca. 780–ca. 850) wrote the work *Al-jabr wa'l muqábalah* ("restoring and simplifying"), known in the West as *Algebra*. This work introduced methods for finding the solutions to equations of the first and second degree (linear equations and quadratics, respectively).

Mathematic Renaissance   The work of 13th-century Italian mathematician Leonardo Fibonacci (c. 1170–1250) introduced the decimal system and Arabic numerals to Europe. He wrote books that helped mathematicians calculate prices and profits. He is best known today for the Fibonacci Sequence of numbers, in which each number is the sum of the two preceding numbers: 1, 1, 2, 3, 5, 8, 13, 21, 34, 55, 89 ... The progression of numbers in this sequence describes a relationship often found in nature, and Fibonacci's work still benefits scientists and mathematicians today.

European mathematics had a rebirth in the 15th century, aided by the institution of symbols for operations and relationships (such as +, −, and =). Geometry was enriched by the studies of perspective made by Renaissance painters, starting with Leon Battista Alberti (1404–72) in 1436. The need for better computation, especially for navigation, led to the invention of logarithms by John Napier (1550–1617) in 1614.

By the 17th century, algebra had reached the level taught in high school today, and mathematics was moving into new fields, such as analytic geometry. This field, which combines geometry and algebra into a single entity, was invented independently by Pierre de Fermat (1601–65) in 1636 and René Descartes (1596–1650) in 1637, and became the basis of nearly all subsequent mathematics. In 1639 the idea of perspective led to a new kind of geometry, called projective geometry, which showed that geometry did not have to depend on measurement. Another new field of mathematics, which started during the Renaissance and was revived in the 17th century, was probability, developed largely in correspondence between Fermat and Blaise Pascal (1623–62) ca. 1660.

Rise of Calculus   Ancient Greek mathematicians frequently solved problems by separating a geometric figure into tiny pieces, then recombining the pieces to find a solution. Using similar methods, mathematicians divided curved lines into a large number of small, nearly straight segments, which could then be added together to approximate the length of the curve. Such methods were used to measure all manners of irregular shapes. Analytic geometry provided a way to measure using "infinitely small" and "infinitely numerous" segments, laying the foundation for a method of problem solving now called calculus.

In 1665 and 1666, Sir Isaac Newton (1643–1727) expanded on methods of approximation developed by earlier mathematicians, creating the first version of calculus. About 10 years later, Gottfried Wilhelm von Leibniz (1646–1716) developed the same mathematical tools, using different symbols and words with somewhat different meanings. Leibniz published his first account in 1684 and Newton his first public account in 1687, although Newton had circulated manuscripts much earlier. Most of the symbolism and language used today derive from Leibniz.

Calculus allowed a degree of precision of measurement that was previously impossible. Mathematicians used calculus to model, measure, and predict velocities, volumes, and densities, as well as model physical phenomena and predict how changes in one variable affects others. The discipline became an indispensable scientific tool of the Enlightenment.

19th-Century Reform   Although many physical and mathematical problems were solved by calculus, some applications appeared to produce nonsensical or contradictory results. Furthermore, it was obvious that the logic of the term *infinitely small*, an essential calculus concept, was unclear. Throughout the 19th century, although the applications of calculus were largely successful, mathematicians sought to improve the theoretical underpinnings of the discipline. Bernard Bolzano formalized the definition of a "limit" in 1817, which replaced the "infinitely small" quantities of Newton and Leibniz with a more precisely defined quantity.

Geometry also experienced a revolution in the 19th century. *Projective geometry* produced alternative geometries as logical as Euclid's, but which followed different rules. This new non-Euclidean geometry greatly expanded mathematics, which no longer seemed to need a connection with observable reality.

Nineteenth-century mathematicians also looked for the simplest theoretical concepts that underlie arithmetic, algebra, geometry, and logic. Abstract algebra and symbolic logic are concerned with the implications of these underlying rules rather than physical entities. Despite the seemingly "imaginary" nature of some of these branches of study, surprising applications often followed theoretical discoveries. Albert Einstein's general relativity theory of 1916 showed that the true geometry of space may be non-Euclidean, and symbolic logic led to the binary operators that make modern computers possible.

By the late 19th century, mathematics became highly abstract. New disciplines such as set theory produced sometimes contradictory results that proved impossible to eliminate. After trying to resolve these contradictions, logicians surmised that not all problems are solvable by mathematics, and that reducing problems to arithmetic does not eliminate contradictions.

Crisis in Foundations Late in the 19th century, the search for a logical basis for mathematics led to inclusion of the infinitely large. Because this work generally dealt with infinite sets of points, the beginning part of this change in mathematics was called set theory.

Set theory led to contradictory results that were harder to eliminate than the contradictions that had surfaced in the early work with calculus. Several different groups of mathematicians tried to resolve the contradictions. These efforts came to a halt as logicians first proved that not all problems could be solved within mathematics; then that reducing problems to arithmetic did not eliminate contradictions, since any complete system of arithmetic will contain contradictions itself; and finally that the basis of modern mathematics is consistent with diametrically opposed statements.

Mathematics Today These results have not deterred mathematicians from solving old and new problems using all the tools developed in the long history of the subject. In the 20th century, applied methods of statistical inference ("confidence intervals" and other techniques) have been highly developed and widely applied, through computer programs, in the sciences, engineering, and social sciences. There have also been dramatic advances in the ancient science of geometry, such as the development of fractal geometry, in which patterns of smaller parts (such as a coastline seen very close up) relate in complex ways to the whole seen at a distance. These and other modern developments in mathematics and statistics mean that, while students today study some math that is thousands of years old, their lives are affected by up-to-date mathematical techniques embodied in powerful computational packages.

Branches of Mathematics

The growth of mathematics from counting, measuring, and reasoning led to the development of a discpline with many parts. As late as the 19th century, a mathematician might have been skilled in all its branches; since the field has become so complex and diverse, however, modern mathematicians specialize.

Arithmetic

The trunk from which all other branches of mathematics sprouted, arithmetic dates to before 2000 B.C. It encompasses the basic operations required to combine or divide quantities: addition, subtraction, multiplication, and division. The theoretical study of these fundamental operations is called Higher Arithmetic or Number Theory.

Algebra

Algebra concerns the writing and solving of equations, which are mathematical statements that use a letter or symbol to represent an unknown quantity (called a vari-able). For example, the equation $2 + x = 11$ states that 2, plus an unknown quantity, equals 11. To find the solution for an equation, procedures called algorithms reduce the statement to the simple form x = (an amount); for example, by subtracting 2 from 11 in the earlier example, we are left with $x = 9$.

As equations become more complex, the algorithms become more sophisticated. Many complex equations cannot be solved with general algorithms; for such equations, there are procedures for estimating solutions and refining those estimates. Computers and graphing calculators have made the study of algebra easier and rendered some of the most complex algorithms obsolete.

Modern algebraic study focuses more on analytic geometry: the study of lines and curves on a plane that are applied as mathematical models for real-world phenomena. Modern or abstract algebra, often studied at the collegiate and postgraduate level, is not concerned with solving specific equations. Instead, this discpline deals with systems where equations obey general rules. Letters no longer necessarily represent unknown numbers but are variables that may stand for anything—numbers, points, operations, and so forth.

Geometry

The Greeks, notably Euclid, established geometry as reasoning about the properties of figures, although earlier Egyptian and Mesopotamian mathematicians discovered the basic rules concerning lengths, areas, and volumes. Euclid arranged the various proofs concerning figures into a powerful axiomatic system that was the basis of geometry for the next 2,000 years. In the 1800s, mathematicians discovered a system of geometry different from Euclid's, which while orignally a purely theoretical discipline, later became valuable in the study of relativity and quantum physics.

Measurement grew from geometry into its own discipline. Measurement has been used since antiquity to find lengths and weights; current applications include everything from electric current to download speed.

Topology is another discipline that evolved from geometry. The field of topology springs from deceptively simple observations: for example, although no one would confuse a square and a circle, the shapes have important similarities (both are two-dimensional, have "inside" and "outside" regions, and so forth). Topology also studies the properties of objects that are preserved despite "deformations" like squeezing or stretching. The Möbius strip, a twisted strip that has only one surface and one edge, is a classic example of the types of figures studied in elementary topology.

Trigonometry

Trigonometry begins with the study of the interrelation between the sides and angles of right triangles. Given the measure of one angle and one side of a right triangle, it is easy to determine the lengths of the other sides, as they adhere to a fixed ratio. These ratios, called the sine, cosine, and tangent (terms coined in the 12th century A.D.), can be used to solve practical problems about distance and direction. Trigonometry was used in construction and navigation for centuries. Later, mathematicians discovered that the graphs of sine and cosine functions were infinite, oscillating waves. This discovery led to a host of new applications, from modeling circular motion to measuring the frequency and amplitude of electromagnetic waves. Trigonometry is also one of the most powerful tools for understanding complex, multidimensional curves.

Calculus

Calculus, the mathematics of change, is used to analyze quantities that change with respect to other variables, such as velocity and acceleration. Calculus can also be used to find areas or volumes of regions bounded by curves. As arithmetic is based upon numbers and algebra on variables, calculus is based on functions, which are relationships between sets of two or more variables. The relationship between velocity and displacement (as velocity increases, so does an object's displacement from its point of origin) is a simple example of a function. In its simplest form, calculus solves two kinds of problems: the rate of change problem (called the derivative) and the area problem (called the integral). These problems are actually two sides of the same coin: the algorithms to find the derivative, when applied in reverse, can be used to find the integral. These two simple concepts have surprisingly diverse applications. The derivative can be used to find marginal cost and revenue in economics, for example, and the integral can be used to analyze anything from physical forces to population densities.

Discrete Mathematics

Discrete mathematics is a blanket term for the study of noncontinuous mathematical structures. While most physical phenomena can be modeled using smooth, continuous graphs (the velocity of an automobile, for example, cannot climb from 0 to 50 without briefly reaching every velocity in between), many economic, technological, or probabilistic phenomenon cannot. In modern mathematics, discrete structures have become increasingly important; the binary language of computers is one example of a discrete phenomenon. Some subcategories of discrete mathematics are:

Probability is the study of events that occur within finite systems, and the likelihood of a certain outcome. Although employed in simple dice and coin-toss problems, probability also functions importantly in fields such as meteorology and economics.

Logic is the study of the relationship between true, false, and contradictory statements. Set theory, the study of finite groups of countable objects, is a subcategory of logic. True and false logic systems developed into binary on-off circuit logic that make computers possible. Other fields of discrete mathematics include cryptology, statistical theory, and game theory.

Chaos Theory

Beginning in the 1880's, mathematicians discovered that some systems are so complex that even tiny changes in initial conditions yielded wildly unpredictable results. Although originally these strange results were blamed on imprecision, it was later realized that this "noise" was inherent in most complex systems. Chaos theory is the study of the complexity and unpredictability of such systems.

Chaos theory has philosophical implications, as it demonstrates that some things are "unknowable" even within the structure of mathematics. Some of its concepts are part of popular culture, featured in movies such as *Jurassic Park* and *The Butterfly Effect*. While chaos theory suggests limits to the accuracy with which humans can model and predict weather patterns and economic markets, the discipline is more than the acceptance of uncertainty. Chaos theory is used to find order within seemingly disorderly systems: random phenomena such as molecular vibrations and the neurological impulses that cause epileptic seizures have been predicted using chaotic models.

Number Theory

Number theory (sometimes called "higher arithmetic") is the study of properties of natural numbers, or integers greater than zero. Studied for its own sake since the time of the Greek author Diophantus (ca. A.D. 200–299), number theory has recently had important applications in codes used for protecting information transmitted by computer. The study of prime numbers (numbers divisible by no other natural numbers besides themselves and one) falls under the number theory umbrella. Large prime numbers are essential in cryptology.

Number theory also encompasses the axiomatic approach to the study of simple arithmetic, formalizing the definitions and properties of basic operations such as addition. The Commutative Property of Addition, which states a + b = b + a, is a simple and well-known example of number theory applied to arithmetic. "New Math," a much criticized reform of American mathematics educa-

tion in the 1960's, emphasized a number theory-based approach to arithmetic instruction. While New Math was deemed impractical by most experts, the theory behind it helps connect all branches of mathematics, from simple counting through the most abstract concepts.

Network or Graph Theory

Figures called networks can be formed by connecting distinct points by line segments or arcs. Shapes and sizes do not count. The points are called the vertices of the network, and the connections are sometimes called edges, terminology inspired by networks that define polyhedrons in three-dimensional space. In a network all vertices are connected—you can travel via the edges to any vertex from any other—and edges do not intersect except at vertices. The theory can also deal with edges that are directed—a message can travel in a specific way on a specific edge. This theory has become increasingly important for dealing with problems of communication, including the Internet, but it also has many applications in understanding trade or other systems of two-way interactions.

Probability and Statistics

Probability is concerned with numbers that reflect the concept of chance. The theory is built on the idea that an event that occurs a certain number of times (called *successes*) in so many tries has a probability that is the ratio of the successes to the number of tries. Thus an event with no chance of happening has a probability of 0, and one that always happens has a probability of 1. In a coin toss where heads and tails have equal probability, the probability of heads is 1/2. The probability that any of a die's six faces will face up is 1/6.

Set Theory

Set theory studies the properties of sets, fundamental objects used to define all other concepts in mathematics. A set is determined by its elements; two sets are deemed equal if they have exactly the same elements. The language of set theory is based on the relation called membership. We say that A is a member of B, or that set B contains A as its element. In practice, one considers sets of numbers, points, functions, and so on.

Mathematical Formulas

Most formulas needed in solving everyday problems are collected below, with special emphasis on formulas relating to measurements, as these are used in everything from sewing to building a house. However, some important formulas from algebra, graphing, and trigonometry are at the end. Additional formulas can also be found in "Basic Laws of Physics."

General

The **distance** d, given the rate r and the time t:

$$d = rt$$

Length

The **perimeter (distance around)** p **of any polygon** (closed plane figure with straight sides that do not cross), given the lengths of the sides a, b, c, and so forth:

$$p = a + b + c + \ldots$$

Perimeter p **of a rectangle,** given the length l and the width w:

$$p = 2l + 2w$$

Perimeter p **of a square,** given the length of a side s:

$$p = 4s$$

Circumference (distance around) C **of a circle,** given the diameter d (distance across) or the radius r (distance from the center to the circle):

$$C = \pi d$$
$$\text{or } C = 2\pi r$$

The number π is an infinite decimal that begins 3.14159 . . . and is often approximated as either 3.14 or as 22/7.

Area

In each of the following, the area (amount of surface) is A. For three-dimensional figures, A is the total surface area.

Rectangle, given the length l and the width w:

$$A = lw$$

Square, given the length of a side s:

$$A = s^2$$

Circle, given the radius r:

$$A = \pi r^2$$

Triangle, given the base b and the height h:

$$A = \tfrac{1}{2} bh$$

Right triangle, given the lengths a and b of the two sides (legs) that form the right angle:

$$A = \tfrac{1}{2} ab$$

Parallelogram, given the base b and the height h:

$$A = bh$$

Trapezoid, given the two bases B and b and the height h:

$$A = \tfrac{1}{2} h (B + b)$$

Kite, given the lengths of the two diagonals D and d:

$$A = \tfrac{1}{2} Dd$$

Regular polygon (polygon with all sides of equal length and all angles of equal measure), given the perimeter p and the apothem a (the distance from the center of the regular polygon to one of its sides):

$$A = \tfrac{1}{2} ap$$

Equilateral triangle (all sides the same length), given the length of a side s:

$$A = \frac{s^2\sqrt{3}}{4}$$

Heron's formula Any triangle, given half the length of the perimeter (the semiperimeter) s and the lengths of the sides $a, b,$ and c:

$$A = \sqrt{s(s-a)(s-b)(s-c)}$$

Right circular cylinder (a cylinder with a circular region as its base whose sides make a right angle with the base), given the radius r of the base and the height h of the cylinder:

$$A = 2\pi r(h + r)$$

Right circular cone (a cone with a circular region as its base, whose altitude makes a right angle with the base), given the radius r of the base and the slant height l of the cone (the shortest distance from the tip of the cone to the circle of the base):

$$A = \pi r(l + r)$$

Sphere, given the radius r:

$$A = 4\pi r^2$$

Volume

In each of the following, the volume (space enclosed) is V.

Cube, given the length of an edge e:

$$V = e^3$$

Right rectangular prism (box), given the length l, the width w, and the height h:

$$V = lwh$$

Prism, given the area of the base B and the height h:

$$V = Bh$$

Right circular cylinder, given the radius r of the base and the height h:

$$V = \pi r^2 h$$

Right circular cone, given the radius r of the base and the height h:

$$V = {}^1\!/3\, \pi r^2 h$$

Pyramid, given the area of the base B and the height h:

$$V = {}^1\!/3\, Bh$$

Sphere, given the radius r:

$$V = {}^4\!/3\, \pi r^3$$

Algebra

If a, b, and x are any numbers or variables ("unknowns"):

$$(a + b)^2 = a^2 + 2ab + b^2$$
$$(a - b)^2 = a^2 - 2ab + b^2$$
$$x^2 - a^2 = (x + a)(x - a)$$
$$x^3 - a^3 = (x - a)(x^2 + ax + a^2)$$
$$x^3 + a^3 = (x + a)(x^2 - ax + a^2)$$

If a, b, c, and d are any numbers or variables except that neither b nor d can be zero:

$$a/b + c/d = (ad + bc)/bd$$
$$a/b - c/d = (ad - bc)/bd$$
$$a/b \times c/d = ac/bd$$
$$a/b \div c/d = ad/bc\ (c \neq 0)$$

Quadratic formula for the solutions of a second degree polynomial equation in one variable of the form $ax^2 + bx + c = 0$:

$$x = \frac{-b \pm \sqrt{b^2 - 4ac}}{2a}$$

Laws of exponents, given that a, b, x, and y are numbers or variables:

$$a^x a^y = a^{x+y} \qquad (a^x)^y = a^{xy}$$
$$(ab)^x = a^x b^x \qquad (a/b)^x = a^x/b^x$$
$$a^x/a^y = a^{x-y}$$
$$a^{-x} = \frac{1}{a^x}$$
$$a^0 = 1 \qquad\qquad a^1 = a.$$

Laws of logarithms, given that a, b, x, and y are positive numbers; c is any real number; and $a \neq 1$, $b \neq 1$.

$$\log_a (xy) = \log_a x + \log_a y \qquad \log_a 1/x = - \log_a x$$

$$\log_a (x/y) = \log_a x - \log_a y \qquad \log_a (x_c) = c \log_a x$$

$$\log_b x = (\log_a x)/(\log_a b) \qquad \log_a 1 = 0$$

$$\log_a a = 1 \qquad\qquad a^{\log_a x} = x$$

$$\log_a (a^c) = c$$

Graphs

In a rectangular (Cartesian) coordinate plane, where the horizontal axis is x and the vertical axis is y:

Slope of a line, m, given two particular points (x_1, y_1) and (x_2, y_2) where $x_1 \neq x_2$:

$$m = (y_2 - y_1)/(x_2 - x_1)$$

Point-slope equation of a line, given the slope m and a point on the nonvertical line (x_1, y_1):

$$y - y_1 = m(x - x_1)$$

Slope-intercept equation of a line, given the slope m and the y-intercept b (the number on the y axis where the line crosses the y axis):

$$y = mx + b$$

Distance d between any two points, (x_1, y_1) and (x_2, y_2):

$$d = \sqrt{(x_2 - x_1)^2 + (y_2 - y_1)^2}.$$

Trigonometry

In a right triangle whose two shorter sides (or legs) are a and b, opposite angles A and B respectively, and whose longest side (or hypotenuse, always the side opposite the right angle, C) is c:

Pythagorean theorem:

$$c^2 = a^2 + b^2$$

Trigonometric functions:

sine: $\sin A = a/c$ $\qquad$ cosine: $\cos A = b/c$
tangent: $\tan A = a/b$ $\qquad$ cotangent: $\cot A = b/a$
secant: $\sec A = c/b$ $\qquad$ cosecant: $\csc A = c/a$

In any triangle labeled such that side a is opposite angle A, side b is opposite angle B, and side c is opposite angle C:

Angle sum:

$$A + B + C = 180°$$

Law of sines:

$$(\sin A)/a = (\sin B)/b = (\sin C)/c$$

Law of cosines:

$$c^2 = a^2 + b^2 - 2ab \cos C$$

If x is any real number or a measure of an angle in degrees, the following statements are true.

Defining trigonometric identities:

$\tan x = \sin x/\cos x$ $\qquad$ $\csc x = 1/\sin x$
$\cot x = \cos x/\sin x$ $\qquad$ $\cot x = 1/\tan x$
$\sec x = 1/\cos x$

Trigonometric identities of symmetry:

$$\sin(-x) = -\sin x \qquad \cos(-x) = \cos x$$
$$\tan(-x) = -\tan x \qquad \cot(-x) = -\cot x$$
$$\sec(-x) = \sec x \qquad \csc(-x) = -\csc x.$$

Pythagorean identities:

$$\sin^2 x + \cos^2 x = 1$$
$$\tan^2 x + 1 = \sec^2 x$$
$$\cot^2 x + 1 = \csc^2 x$$

Sum and difference formulas: If x and y are any two real numbers or measures of angles:

$$\sin(x + y) = \sin x \cos y + \cos x \sin y$$
$$\cos(x + y) = \cos x \cos y - \sin x \sin y$$
$$\tan(x + y) = (\tan x + \tan y)/(1 - \tan x \tan y)$$
$$\sin(x - y) = \sin x \cos y - \cos x \sin y$$
$$\cos(x - y) = \cos x \cos y + \sin x \sin y$$
$$\tan(x - y) = (\tan x - \tan y)/(1 + \tan x \tan y)$$

Fractions, Decimals, and Percents

To find the equivalent of a fraction in decimal form, divide the numerator (top number) by the denominator (bottom number). To change from a decimal to a percent, multiply by 100. To change from a percent to a decimal, divide by 100.

Fraction	Decimal	Percent (%)
1/16	0.0625	6.25
1/8 (= 2/16)	0.125	12.5
3/16	0.1875	18.75
1/4 (= 2/8 = 4/16)	0.25	25.0
5/16	0.3125	31.25
1/3	0.3 . . .	33 1/3
3/8 (= 6/16)	0.375	37.5
7/16	0.4375	43.75
1/2 (= 2/4 = 4/8 = 8/16)	0.5	50.0
9/16	0.5625	56.25
5/8 (= 10/16)	0.625	62.5
2/3	0.6 . . .	66 2/3
11/16	0.6875	68.75
3/4 (= 6/8 = 12/16)	0.75	75.0
13/16	0.8125	81.25
7/8 (= 14/16)	0.875	87.5
15/16	0.9375	93.75
1 (= 2/2 = 4/4 = 8/8 = 16/16)	1.0	100.0

Large Numbers

There are two primary naming systems for large numbers. The United States and France (among others) use one system, while Germany and Great Britain use the other. (Googol and googolplex, invented by the nephew of the mathematician and author Edward Kasner, are rarely used outside the United States.)

Number of zeroes after 1	American name	British name
6	million	million
9	billion	milliard
12	trillion	billion
15	quadrillion	1,000 billion
18	quintillion	trillion
21	sextillion	1,000 trillion
24	septillion	quadrillion
27	octillion	1,000 quadrillion
30	nonillion	quintillion
33	decillion	1,000 quintillion
100	googol	googol
googol	googolplex	googolplex

Numbers and Number Systems

Counting, or Natural, Numbers

The counting numbers (1, 2, 3, 4, and so forth) are the numbers used in counting. The whole numbers are the counting numbers with 0 added to the set, or 0, 1, 2, 3, 4, . . . These distinctions are somewhat elastic; mathematicians use the term *natural numbers*, but sometimes they include 0 and sometimes not. There are two ways to define these kinds of numbers—by matching sets with the same number of members (which permits 0), and by starting with 1 and defining the numbers as 1, 1 + 1 = 2, 2 + 1 = 3, and so forth.

These numbers can be shown in order as equally spaced points on a line that extends indefinitely, which is called a number line.

0 1 2 3 4 5 6 7 8 . . .

Integers

Integers are a set of numbers consisting of the whole numbers (or natural numbers including 0) and their opposites, Two numbers at equal distances from 0 on the number line are called opposites.

Integers are also known as the positive and negative whole numbers. When the real numbers are arranged in order on a line from least to greatest, all the numbers greater than 0 (on the same side of 0 as 1) are positive numbers. All the numbers less than 0 (on the opposite side of 0 from 1) are negative numbers. The integers extend infinitely in both directions, so they can be shown as ... −3, −2, −1, 0, +1, +2, +3, ...

... -4 -3 -2 -1 0 +1 +2 +3 +4 ...

Real Numbers

A rational number is any number that can be represented as the ratio of an integer to a nonzero integer. The positive and negative fractions (with integral parts), such as 1/2 or 2/3 or 22/7, are rational numbers, but so are all the integers. If you divide the numerator of the fraction by the denominator, the answer will be the rational number expressed as a decimal fraction. As decimals, rational numbers either terminate (that is, become a string of 0s after some decimal place, such as 0.25 = 0.2500000 ...) or repeat a finite pattern over and over (such as 0.33 ... = 1/3 or 0.142857142857142857 ... = 1/7).

Greek mathematicians from ca. 400 B.C. discovered that that some numbers, such as the diagonal of a square whose sides are rational numbers, are not rational. Any real number that cannot be represented as the ratio of two integers is an irrational number. When real numbers are expressed as infinite decimals, any decimal that fails to repeat the same finite pattern of digits over and over represents an irrational number.

The totality of rational numbers and irrational numbers constitutes the real numbers. The real numbers are most easily pictured as all the numbers that can be represented as points on the number line, filling in all of the points between the integers. Another way to define the real numbers is as all numbers that can be represented by decimal fractions. Note that two different decimals can equal the same real number, as, for example, 2.0000 ... and 1.99999 ...

Complex Numbers

Multiplying a number by itself produces a square of that number. For real numbers the square is always positive; for example, not only does 3^2 = 9, but also $(-3)^2$ = 9. For a given positive number p, the square root is a number that, when multiplied by itself, has the product p. For example, the two square roots of 9 are +3 and −3.

The square roots of the negative numbers are called imaginary numbers. To avoid inconsistencies, imaginary numbers are expressed in terms of the square root of −1, known as i. Examples include $2i$, $-i$, $i/3$, and $4i\sqrt{2}$. The existence and utility of such numbers is beyond question, but the name (to contrast with real numbers) was coined when mathematicians doubted that such numbers made sense.

A complex number is the sum of a real number and an imaginary number, expressed usually as $x + iy$ where i is the square root of negative 1. All numbers are included among the complex numbers. For real numbers, y is 0; for integers, x is an integer and y is 0; and so forth.

While real numbers are shown on a number line, complex numbers require a plane. The usual y axis is replaced by an iy axis. On the plane of complex numbers, the imaginaries occupy the vertical or y axis, while the real numbers are on the horizontal or x axis. The other complex numbers form the other parts of the plane.

Probability

Probability is the measure of how likely it is that some event will occur. The simplest form of probability is based on the ratio of a selected outcome (called a success) to the total number of possibilities. For example, if you toss one die one time, only one face (from the six possible faces) can land facing up; the probability is 1/6 for a selected face to be a success. If an outcome never occurs, then its probability is 0, but if it always occurs, the ratio becomes 1.

Any result of an experiment or observation that can lead to success or failure is called an event. Events that cannot be simplified further are called simple; those that can be decomposed into simple events are compound.

For many events in ordinary life, such as weather, probability is based on analysis of past events. For example, a meteorologist might determine that a certain weather pattern has previously led to rain about 2 times in 10; this probability is expressed as a 20 percent chance of rain. For the toss of a die, chances that any one face will land up are thought to be equal for any toss, so the past history is not considered.

Probability theory is the mathematical formulation of these ideas, and requires outcomes that can be enumerated. For example, tossing a coin twice has four possible outcomes. Representing heads with H and tails with T, the only possible outcomes to that experiment (discounting the coins landing on edge) are HH, HT, TH, and

TT. These four outcomes form what is called the sample space for that experiment. Each of the simple events, such as HH, is a sample point. A compound event, such as getting one head and one tail, is represented by several sample points (in this case two, HT and TH). Thus, while the simple event of getting two heads has a probability of 1/4, the probability of the compound event of getting one head and one tail has a probability of 2/4, or 1/2.

It is possible to compute the probability of some compound events from known probabilities of other events. If two events cannot occur at the same time, they are mutually exclusive and the probability of one or the other of the events is just the sum of the probabilities of the two events. For example, when one die is tossed, the probability of getting a face up with fewer than three dots is 1/3 (since there are two successful outcomes out of six), while the probability of getting exactly five dots is 1/6. Since these two events are mutually exclusive, the probability of getting fewer than three dots or five dots is 1/3 + 1/6 = 1/2.

Often a person wants to know the probability that two events will both occur. For example, one might want to know if on a particular day it will rain and also if a friend will telephone. These events appear to be unconnected in any way, and are called independent. For these independent events, the probability that one and the other will happen is the product of the probabilities. For example, if the probability of rain is 40 percent (or 2/5—40 percent expressed as a fraction); and if your friend calls every other day on the average, for a probability of 50 percent (or 1/2); and if these are independent events, the probability that it will rain and your friend will call is 2/5 times 1/2, which is 2/10, or 1/5. (For percents, one calculates 0.4 times 0.5 = 0.20, which is the same result, since 20 percent expressed as a fraction is 1/5).

Finally, we must consider the probability of dependent events — for example, determining if on a given day it will rain and if you will wash your car. Since these events can be connected in one way or another, they are not independent. In the instance of dependent events like these, you cannot multiply the probabilities to determine if both will happen on the same day.

Glossary of Mathematical Terms

absolute value distance of a number from 0. Indicated by vertical lines, as in |−6|. Distance is always a positive number or 0, so absolute value is always nonnegative: |−6| = 6, |3/4| = 3/4, and |0| = 0.

algebra branch of mathematics that substitutes letters for numbers.

algebraic expression expression that contains at least one variable.

algorithm step-by-step procedure for solving a mathematical problem.

analytic geometry idea that graphs and equations are two different ways of expressing the same concepts.

angle union of two rays with a common end point.

arc portion of the circumference of a circle.

area number of square units covering a shape or figure.

arithmetic branch of mathematics usually concerned with the four numerical operations (adding, subtracting, multiplication, and division).

average single number that represents in some way a typical member of a collection. The arithmetic mean, usually called the mean, is commonly used as the average. The mean of n numbers is the sum of the numbers divided by n. Another number commonly used is the median. A median is the middle number for a set with an odd number of members, but if there are an even number of members there is no middle number, and the median is half the sum of the two numbers nearest the middle. Sometimes another measure of central tendency, called the mode, is used; this is the number in the set that occurs most frequently.

axiom self-evident and necessary truth.

axes vertical and horizontal lines that make up the quadrants of a coordinate plane. The vertical axis is typically referred to as the y axis, and the horizontal axis is usually referred to as the x axis.

biconditional statement "if-then" statement that is true in both directions.

binomial polynomial equation with two terms usually joined by a plus or minus sign.

bisect divide into two equal parts.

calculus branch of mathematics involving derivatives and integrals.

cardinality number of elements in a set.

circumference distance around a circle.

coefficient factor of a term.

collinear word describing points that lie in a straight line.

commutative property the order of elements in a calculation makes no difference in the outcome, i.e. $ab = ba$.

complement set of elements in the universal set that are not in the current set.

complementary angles two angles that combine for a total of 90 degrees.

conditional statement "if-then" statement. The "if" section has a condition that must be met; the "then" section results if the condition is true.

constant value that does not change.

coordinates ordered grouping of numbers that corresponds to a point on a line, a line on a plane, or a plane in space.

cosine in a right triangle, the ratio of the length of the side adjacent to an acute angle to the length of the hypotenuse.

cube and cube root multiplying a number by itself twice produces the cube of that number, which can be indicated with the exponent ^{3}; for example, $4^3 = 4 \times 4 \times 4 = 64$. For a given number, the cube root is the number that, when multiplied by itself twice, has the product that is the number. For example, the cube root of 64 is +4 and of −64 is −4.

decimal our common way of writing numbers is based on 10, and is called decimal, from the Latin word for ten. For whole numbers the digit farthest right shows ones, the next left shows tens, and so on, with each place indicating the next higher power of 10. A decimal point at the right of a whole number marks the beginning of a decimal fraction with places continuing as tenths, hundredths, thousandths, and so on. To convert a common fraction such as 3/4 to its decimal equivalent, divide the numerator ("top number") by the denominator ("bottom number"); for example, for 3/4 the decimal equivalent is 0.75.

decimal fraction fraction expressed in decimal notation. For example, 1/4 is expressed as the decimal fraction 0.25.

degree unit of measurement for an angle.

denominator bottom number of a fraction.

derivative slope of the tangent line to a curve at any instant a.

diameter length of the line that passes through the center of a circle, cutting it in half.

discontinuous function that cannot be drawn without a gap.

disjoint sets two or more sets with no elements in common.

dividend number that is being divided.

divisor number that is doing the dividing.

elements individual items or objects in a set.

empty set set with no contents, also known as a null set.

equation statement composed of two equal mathematical expressions, joined by an equals ($=$) sign.

equilateral having all sides equal.

exponent number that gives reference to the repeated multiplication required. For example, the exponent of 2^3 is $2 \times 2 \times 2$, or 8.

expression mathematical statement using numbers, variables, and operations.

factor as a noun, a factor is one of the numbers used to form a particular product. As a verb, to factor is to locate all factors of the number. For example, the factors of 12 are 1, 2, 3, 4, 6, and 12. In most cases only prime number factors are found and they are often shown as forming the product, which for 12 is $2 \times 2 \times 3$.

factorial number multiplied by every integer less than the number, down to 1. Represented by the symbol !. For example, 3! equals $3 \times 2 \times 1$, or 6.

finite not infinite.

finite set set whose cardinality is a finite number; a set whose number of elements is countable.

formula mathematical sentence that expresses the relationship between two or more variables.

fraction a *common fraction* is a type of numeral that represents division of two numbers, with the one being divided into (the numerator) above a short line and the one being divided by (the denominator) below the line. For example, the fraction 3/4 means that 3 (the numerator) is to be divided by 4 (the denominator). If the numerator is larger than the denominator, as in 5/2, the fraction is called *improper*. The same numbers can be represented as *decimal fractions* by carrying out the division: 3/4 is the same as 0.75, and 5/2 is the same as 2.5. Different fractions can show the same number; for example 2/3 and 8/12 are two different common fractions for the same number. Fractions can be added or subtracted if they have the same denominator, by adding or subtracting the numerators.

Fractions can be multiplied by multiplying their numerators and their denominators separately. For division, the fraction that is being divided into another number is replaced by its reciprocal, and then the two numbers are multiplied.

geometry branch of mathematics that studies lines, angles, shapes, and their properties.

hypotenuse longest side of a right-angled triangle.

imaginary numbers square roots of negative numbers.

infinite having no limit or end.

integer whole number, positive or negative, including zero.

intersection what is common between two sets.

interval set containing all the points between two end points.

irrational number number that cannot be expressed as the ratio of two integers.

least common denominator addition or subtraction of fractions requires that fractions have the same denominator. Calculations are simplest if that denominator is the smallest natural number that will suffice, a number called the least common denominator. For example, the least common denominator of 2/3 and 1/4 is 12, since 12 is the smallest number that can be divided evenly by both 3 and 4.

line straight infinite path joining an infinite number of points.

line segment straight path that has a beginning and an end (end points).

linear equation equation whose graph is a line.

logarithm power to which a base must be raised to produce a given number.

matrix array of numbers in columns and rows.

mean See *average*.

median See *average*.

mode See *average*.

monomial algebraic expression consisting of a single term.

natural numbers regular counting numbers.

negative number number that is less than zero.

noncollinear word describing points that do not all lie in a straight line.

null set See *empty set*.

numeral written symbol corresponding to a number.

numerator top number in a fraction.

obtuse angle angle measuring between 90 and 180 degrees.

octagon polygon with eight sides.

odd number whole number that is not divisible by 2.

operation addition, subtraction, multiplication, or division.

ordered pair set of two numbers, with the x-coordinate listed first and the y-coordinate listed second.

parallel word describing two or more lines that never intersect.

parallelogram quadrilateral that has both sets of opposite sides that are parallel.

percent numeral showing a ratio of a number to 100. For example, 35 percent denotes a ratio of 35 to 100. This can be expressed as a common fraction, 35/100, or more commonly as a decimal fraction, 0.35. The rule for rewriting a percent as a decimal is to drop the percent sign and move the decimal point two places to the left; for example, 5.6 percent becomes 0.056 as a decimal. To add, subtract, multiply, or divide ratios indicated by percents, first change all the percents to decimals. The symbol for percent is %.

perpendicular word describing two intersecting lines that form a right angle (90 degrees).

pi (π) an infinite decimal that begins 3.14159265358..., often approximated by 3.14 or by 22/7. π is the ratio of the circumference of any circle to its diameter.

plane set of points joined to form a flat surface.

polygon line segments joined to form a closed figure.

polynomial algebraic expression with more than one term.

power the power of a number is the value of a numeral indicated by an exponent, shown as a superscript numeral. For example, 8 is the third power of 2, shown as 2^3.

prime number natural number greater than 1 that has no divisors other than itself and 1. Non-prime natural numbers are called composite numbers. Thus, 2, 3, 5, 7, 11, 13, 17, 19 are the prime numbers less than 20; and 4, 6, 8, 9, 10, 12, 14, 15, 16, and 18 are composite numbers. (The number 1 is neither prime nor composite.)

probability likelihood of an event.

product sum obtained when two or more numbers are multiplied together.

proof demonstration that, given certain axioms, a certain statement is true.

proportion correct statement that two ratios are equal. A proportion can be written in fraction form, such as 3/4 = 9/12.

Pythagorean theorem theorem that relates the three sides of a right triangle, as $a^2 + b^2 = c^2$.

quadratic equation second-degree polynomial equation in one variable of the form $ax^2 + bx + c = 0$.

quotient solution to a division problem.

radical number shown with the sign √. For example √2, the positive square root of 2, can also be called radical 2. In this notation, the number 2 is said to be inside or under the radical, and such a number is called a radicand. For roots other than square roots, the same sign is used with a small numeral greater than 2 written in the V of the radical sign. The small numeral, called an index, shows which root is indicated: 3 for the cube root, 4 for the fourth root, etc. When a radical has an even index, it always means the positive root.

radius line segment from the center of a circle to any point on the circle.

range difference between the largest and smallest numbers in a set.

ratio amount of one entity with respect to another, usually expressed as a fraction. Ratios are essentially the same as rates, such as miles per gallon.

rational number number that can be expressed as the ratio of two integers.

ray straight line with one end point.

real numbers combined set of rational and irrational numbers.

reciprocal number obtained when a given number is divided into 1. For example, the reciprocal of 5 is 1 divided by 5, or 1/5. For common fractions, the reciprocal can be obtained by interchanging numerator and denominator, so the reciprocal of 3/7 is 7/3.

rectangle parallelogram with four right angles.

rhombus parallelogram with four equal sides.

right angle 90-degree angle.

scientific notation system of writing numbers as the product of a number between 1 and 10 and a power of 10. A number such as 2.398×10^9 takes less space and, if you know the system, is easier to read than 239,800,000. Negative exponents provide scientific notation for small numbers: 0.00000087 in scientific notation is 8.7×10^{-7}.

set defined collection of items or objects.

slope steepness of a line, determined from two points on the line.

solution substitution for the variable that will make the equation true.

square and square root multiplying a number by itself produces a square of that number, which can be indicated with the exponent 2. For real numbers the square is always positive; not only does $3^2 = 9$ but also $(-3)^2 = 9$. For a given positive number, the square root is a number that when multiplied by itself has the product that is the original number. Positive numbers have two square roots, one positive and one negative. For example, the two square roots of 9 are +3 and −3. Square roots of negative numbers are called imaginary.

subset set, all of whose elements are also elements of another set.

supplementary angles two angles whose sum equals 180 degrees.

tangent in a right angle, the ratio of lengths of the side opposite angle x to the side adjacent to angle x.

term See *monomial*.

trapezoid quadrilateral with exactly two parallel sides.

triangle three-sided polygon.

trigonometric function function that includes algebraic operations and any of the six trigonometric definitions (sine, cosine, tangent, cosecant, secant, cotangent).

trigonometry branch of mathematics that deals with the relationships between the sides and angles of triangles, and the calculations based on them.

trinomial algebraic equation with three terms.

union joining of two or more sets into a master set, without creating multiples of any single item.

variable symbol that represents an unknown quantity.

whole number number that does not contain a fraction.

PSYCHOLOGY

Psychology (literally, "study of the mind") is the scientific study of mental processes and behavior in humans and other animals. Psychiatry, on the other hand, is the branch of medicine that specializes in mental illness. Psychology is intimately related to the biological and social sciences.

A Brief History of Psychology

Psychology emerged as a formal discipline in the late 19th century, but its intellectual origins date back to early Greek philosophers such as Socrates, Plato, and Aristotle, who debated human perception (epistemology), motivation (ethics), and the organization of the mind (associationism). In the 17th century, the philosopher René Descartes (1596–1650) theorized that the body and mind are two separate entities (dualism); Thomas Hobbes (1588–1679) and John Locke (1632–1704) disagreed, arguing that all thoughts and sensations are physical processes occurring within the brain (monism).

Psychology also has roots in the pseudoscience of the 18th century and the early 19th century. Franz Joseph Gall (1758–1828) introduced the study of phrenology, which explored the alleged relationship between psychological traits and the bumps on a person's head. More important, Franz Anton Mesmer (1734–1815) developed the theory of mesmerism, which used magnetic fields to put patients into a trance, and was the precursor to the more legitimate science of hypnotism.

The physiological roots of modern psychology date to the late 19th century, when naturalist Charles Darwin (1809–82) and his theories of natural selection invited comparisons between humans and animals in later psychological research. Concurrently, surgeon Paul Broca (1824–80) and neurologist Carl Wernicke (1848–1904) discovered the relationship between physical damage to the brain and specific changes in behavior, while neurologist Jean-Martin Charcot (1825–93) discovered that patients with certain nervous disorders could be cured through hypnosis.

The Birth of Modern Psychology

The birth of modern psychology is often said to have occurred in 1879 at the University of Leipzig, where physiologist Wilhelm Wundt (1832–1920) established the first laboratory dedicated to the scientific study of the mind. Wundt taught thousands of students, established the first scholarly psychological journal, and introduced the scientific method to psychological studies.

Wundt's progress was mirrored in the United States by William James (1842–1910), a professor at Harvard University who in 1875 offered the first academic course in psychology. In 1890 James published *Principles of Psychology*, a groundbreaking two-volume work that solidified his position as the founder of American psychology. Like Wundt, James taught many students who made their own contributions to the burgeoning field of psychology.

James also developed one of the first schools of psychological thought, known as functionalism, which proposed that the goal of psychology is to investigate the function of consciousness—the purpose of human thought. This goal was contradicted by the proponents of structuralism, led by one of Wundt's former students, Edward Bradford Titchener (1867–1927). Structuralists believed that the goal of psychology is to identify the basic elements of consciousness, and thus define consciousness itself.

Other scholars followed Wundt and James in developing the new field of psychological study. In 1885 Hermann Ebbinghaus (1850–1909) pioneered the study of memory, using nonsense syllables to examine how humans retain information. In 1896 Lightner Witmer (1867–1956) opened the first psychological clinic; he later founded the field of clinical psychology. In 1905 Alfred Binet (1851–1911) devised the first intelligence test; this test was later revised by Stanford University psychologist Lewis Madison Terman (1877–1956), and is now known as the Stanford-Binet intelligence test. In 1912 Max Wertheimer (1880–1943) inspired the gestalt psychology movement, which theorized that people tend to perceive organized patterns that are different from the sum of isolated sensations.

Psychoanalysis

The most influential early figure was Sigmund Freud (1856–1939). A neurologist by training, Freud formulated the form of psychotherapy known as psychoanalysis, which became one of the most influential schools of thought in the 20th century.

Freud developed his theories when treating patients who appeared to suffer from certain ailments but had nothing physically wrong with them. He discovered that these patients' symptoms would often disappear through the use of hypnosis, or even just through talking. In his book *The Interpretation of Dreams* (1889), Freud proposed that people are primarily motivated by unconscious forces; by finding a suitable outlet for these unconscious motivations, a person can develop a more healthy personality.

To probe the unconscious mind, Freud developed the technique of free association. In this form of psychotherapy, patients recline on a couch and talk about their dreams or anything else that comes to mind; the analyst then interprets these thoughts to determine their psychological significance and reveal their underlying latent content.

Freud's Theory of Sexuality

In 1905 Freud published the landmark work *Drei Abhandlungen zur Sexualtheorie* (*Three Essays on the Theory of Sexuality*), in which he concluded that sexuality is the prime mover in much of human behavior. According to Freud, beginning at the youngest age, a person goes through a series of stages in which they are focused on a particular part of the body known as an erogenous zone. Freud identified the stages as oral (birth to 18 months); anal (18 months to 3 years); phallic (3 years to 7 years); latency (7 years to puberty); and genital (puberty to adulthood). Freud contended that If properly stimulated at each stage, the individual reaches sexual and psychic maturity. If not, the individual fixates on a particular stage, which when expressed openly, can result in a perversion, while the same fixation, when repressed, can produce a neurosis.

Freud's Theory of Personality

Perhaps Freud's greatest contribution to psychology is his psychoanalytic theory of personality which posits that the human personality is composed of three elements: the *id*, the *ego*, and the *superego*. The id is the only part of the personality that exists at birth. It is entirely unconscious and is the primary component of an individual's personality. The id seeks immediate gratification and is important in early life because it ensures that the needs of infants are met. However, in adulthood, it is not realistic to expect that one's desires will be satisfied immediately. The ego therefore is the component of the personality that deals with reality. The ego strives to satisfy the id's desires in a manner that is acceptable in the real world. The ego develops in toddlers when they discover that they are individuals with their own wants and needs. The superego emerges around age five and is the aspect of personality that contains the morals and ideals that are acquired from parents, teachers, and society. Simply put, it is our internalized sense of right and wrong. To Freud, a balance between id, ego, and superego is the key to a healthy personality.

Neo-Freudian Thought

Freud's theories dominated psychological thought in the early 20th century, although many of his followers (dubbed neo-Freudians) did not share Freud's emphasis on sex as the primary motivating factor for human behavior.

The most notable was Carl Jung (1875–1961), who had been one of Freud's most devoted adherents. They severed all relations when Jung published his *Psychology of the Unconscious* (1912), in which he theorized that all humans experience a collective unconscious that contains universal memories (called archetypes) from their shared past. Jung developed the concept of attitude types, in which he differentiated two classes of people: extroverted (outward-looking) and introverted (inward-looking). He also explored how any one of four functions of the mind—thinking, feeling, sensation, and intuition—can predominate in any given person. Jung made the ideas of extroversion and introversion part of all psychological discourse.

Karen Horney (1885–1992) disagreed with Freud's view of female psychology as an offshoot of male psychology, in particular the notion of penis envy; instead, she argued that male-dominated culture was the source of much female psychiatric disturbance. Alfred Adler (1870–1937) believed that people are motivated by feelings of inferiority (the inferiority complex) and are influenced by birth order in the family, sometimes leading to sibling rivalry. Other researchers, led by Hermann Rorschach (1884–1922), developed projective tests designed to uncover various aspects of the unconscious psyche. The Rorschach test—also known as the ink blot test—was created in 1921 and is designed to identify personality traits and emotional functioning by recording and analyzing individuals' perceptions of ink blots. Another important projective test used to diagnose mental illness, is the Minnesota Multiphasic Personality Inventory (MMPI), originally developed in the late 1930's by Starke Hathaway, a psychologist, and J.C. McKinley, a psychiatrist. The MMPI-2 was released in 1989.

Behaviorism

Not all psychologists accepted Freud's theories of unconscious motivation; many rejected the method of introspection and turned their attention to the direct observation of human behavior. This approach, first developed in the early 20th century, was known as behaviorism.

The Law of Effect and Classical Conditioning

In 1898 Edward Lee Thorndike (1874–1949) conducted a series of experiments on how animals learned various behaviors. This led him to propose the "law of effect," which states that behaviors that lead to a positive outcome are repeated, whereas those followed by a negative outcome are abandoned.

In 1906 Ivan Pavlov (1849–1936) expanded on Thorndike's theory when he discovered that dogs would salivate in anticipation of food, based on the ringing of a bell before being fed. He named this form of learning *classical conditioning*, in which a person or animal comes to associate one stimulus with another. Later research found that this basic process explains how people form certain fears and prejudices.

These early studies were codified in 1913, when an animal psychologist, John Watson (1878–1958), published a paper entitled "Psychology as the Behaviorist Views It," followed the next year by the book *Behaviorism: An Introduction to Comparative Psychology*. Watson redefined psychology as an objective branch of natural science with its goal the predication and control of behavior. He stressed observational technique and the use of animals in psychological research.

After Watson, the primary proponent of behaviorism was B. F. Skinner (1904–90), who coined the term *reinforcement* to describe how animal and human behavior is motivated, in a process he called *operant conditioning*. Skinner and his followers applied these theories to attempt to modify behavior in the workplace, the classroom, and other social settings; this technique became known as behavior modification.

Post-Behaviorist Psychology

By the middle of the 20th century, many psychologists found it difficult to resolve the diametrically opposed theories of psychoanalysis and behaviorism. This led to the new fields of exploration known as humanistic psychology and cognitive psychology.

Humanistic Psychology   In an attempt to bridge the gap between the dark forces of the unconscious mind and the effects of reinforcement on behavior, psychologists in the 1950's and 1960's developed the "third force" known as humanistic psychology. This new movement was aimed at a better understanding of the conscious mind, free will, and the human capacity for self-reflection and growth.

The humanistic movement was led by Carl Rogers (1902–87), who believed that all humans are born with a drive to achieve their full capacity. He developed a nondirective technique known as person-centered therapy, which helped patients clarify their sense of self to facilitate their individual healing process.

Concurrently, Abraham Maslow (1908–70) proposed a hierarchy of needs that humans are motivated to fulfill, in ascending order. At the bottom of the hierarchy are basic physiological needs, such as hunger, thirst, and sleep; ascending the hierarchy, humans attempt to fulfill the needs for safety and security, the needs for belonging and love, and the needs for status and achievement. Once these needs are met, people strive for self-actualization, the ultimate state of personal fulfillment.

Cognitive Psychology   Other psychologists moved beyond behaviorism to study cognition, the mental processes involved in acquiring, storing, and using forms of knowledge. This new field of cognitive psychology was based partially on the work of psychologist Jean Piaget (1896–1980) in the 1920's. Piaget explored how children think and reason, and theorized about a predictable series of cognitive stages. Piaget's work was supplemented in the late 1950's by the observations of the linguist Noam Chomsky (b. 1928), who theorized that the human brain is "hardwired" for language as a product of evolution.

Later researchers, influenced by the pioneering work of the computer scientist Alan Turing (1912–54), compared human thought to the information-processing abilities of computers. In 1943 Donald O. Hebb (1904–85) published *The Organization of Behavior: A Neuropsychological Theory*, which defined a consolidation theory that explained thought processes in terms of interconnected neurons and synapses. George A. Miller (b. 1920) explored the concept of short-term memory, which can hold only seven "chunks" of information at a time. While many psychologists consider themselves adherents to one specific school of thought, today it is common to take an integrated approach in studying consciousness, behavior, and social interaction. This is referred to as the biopsychosocial model, which posits that all human behavior and mental processes are the products of biological, psychological, and social influences and the interactions between them.

Areas of Psychological Research

Biopsychology examines the biological foundations of behavior and mental processes, or the interconnect between the body and the mind. Important subfields in biopsychology include behavioral genetics (the study of how various characteristics and mental illnesses are inherited), behavioral neuroscience (the study of the links between behavior and the brain and nervous system), cognitive neuroscience (the study of how activities in the brain correspond to operations of the mind), comparative psychology (the study of behavior among different animal species, including humans), ethology (the study of animal behavior in natural habitats), evolutionary psychology (the study of the origins of various human behaviors), and psychopharmacology (the study of how drugs affect mental functions and behavior).

Clinical psychology is concerned with the study, diagnosis, and treatment of mental illnesses and other behavioral and emotional disorders. This is the largest field of psychological study; the goal is to design non-drug-related treatments for all types of psychological disturbances. Clinical psychologists have developed many successful forms of therapy, including psychoanalysis and behavioral therapy.

Cognitive psychology is the scientific study of how people acquire, process, and use information. Cognitive psychologists examine how people learn, how they solve prob-

lems, and how their brains store important information.

Developmental psychology examines mental and behavioral changes as people age. Researchers compare people of different ages and track individuals over time to learn how both nature (inherited qualities) and nurture affect human development.

Social psychology is the study of how people think, feel, and behave in social situations. Social psychologists observe individuals in both laboratory and real-world social settings to determine how people interact with one another.

Types of Therapists

Therapists fall into several categories depending on what degrees they hold. Choosing a therapist can be a confusing process and requires research on the part of the individual to identify the mental health professional who will be best able to assist with a particular issue.

Psychiatrists are doctors who diagnose and treat mental or psychiatric illnesses. They are licensed to prescribe drugs and are also trained in psychotherapy.

Psychologists study human behavior and the human mind, and are trained in counseling, psychotherapy, and psychological testing. They have Ph.Ds or Psy.Ds, but do not prescribe medication.

Social workers provide services designed to help people function in their environments and to deal with relationships and personal problems. They often work in managed settings such as schools or hospitals for which a masters degree is required. Social workers in private practice must also have an MSW and complete 3,000 of supervised clinical experience.

Licensed professional counselors are required to have at least an M.A. or M.S., and 3,000 hours of supervised work experience, after which they are certified to diagnose and treal mental disorders such as depression, addiction or substance abuse.

Disorders

Mental Disorders

Researchers estimate that just over 22 percent of U.S. citizens aged 18 or older, or about 45 million adults, suffer from a diagnosable mental disorder in any given year. The acknowledged authoritative guide to the various types of

mental illnesses is the *Diagnostic and Statistical Manual of Mental Disorders*, 4th edition (DSM-IV), published by the American Psychiatric Association, which describes more than 300 different mental and addictive disorders. The DSM-V won't be released until 2013 but the first draft has been released to the public on its website (www.dsm5.org). Among the proposed changes in the "psychiatrist's bible" are new categories for behavioral addictions, such as gambling, and for addiction and related disorders including substance abuse and dependence. The DSM-V will replace the controversial term "mental retardation" with "intellectual disability."

Anxiety involves the inability to cope with excessive apprehension, worry, and fear. Symptoms are long-lasting and often socially disruptive; treatment involves systematic desensitization and training in social skills.

Acute stress is typically caused by exposure to a traumatic event that threatened death or serious injury, and typically occurs within four weeks after the event. Symptoms include a sense of numbing or detachment, a reduction in awareness of one's surroundings, depersonalization, or dissociative amnesia; the event is often reexperienced in dreams, illusions, or flashbacks. It is much more severe than common stress, in which the strains of everyday life affect our mood and behavior.

Generalized anxiety (GAD) involves constant anxiety about routine events in one's life; this is an excessive and long-lasting anxiety that is not related to any one specific event or object. Approximately 4 million Americans aged 18 to 54, or about 2.8 percent of all adults, suffer from GAD.

Obsessive-compulsive disorder (OCD) involves having upsetting and unwanted thoughts (obsessions) or feeling compelled to perform certain repetitive behaviors (compulsions). The first symptoms of OCD often begin during childhood or adolescence.

Panic disorder and resultant panic attacks are marked by a sudden, intense terror, often manifested in such physical symptoms as rapid heartbeat, shortness of breath, chest pain, dizziness, and sweating. About one in three people with panic disorder will also develop agoraphobia. (See below, Phobias.)

Post-traumatic stress disorder (PTSD) involves anxiety and stress about traumatic events in one's past. This disorder frequently occurs after violent personal assaults, such as rape, mugging, domestic violence, terrorism, natural disasters, or accidents. About a third of Vietnam veterans experienced PTSD at some point after the war.

Phobias are persistent, intense, and irrational fears and the subsequent avoidance of a specific object, activity, or situation. Common phobias include fear of closed spaces (claustrophobia), fear of heights (acrophobia), fear of snakes (orphiophobia), fear of spiders (arachnophobia),

and so on. Also common are social phobia, the fear of embarrassment; and agoraphobia, the fear of being in any place or situation where escape might be difficult or help unavailable in the event of a panic attack.

Childhood Disorders

Many psychological disorders found in children involve physiological or genetic components, although many of these disorders have no physical causes.

Attention deficit hyperactivity disorder (ADHD) is one of the most common mental disorders in children and adolescents, affecting an estimated 4.1 percent of youngsters aged nine to 17. Symptoms include difficulty in paying attention, not seeming to listen when spoken to directly, inability to follow through on tasks or finish schoolwork, persistent fidgeting, and excessive talking. Treatment is typically medication (stimulants) and behavior therapy.

Autistic spectrum disorder (ASD) is a range of disorders characterized by impaired social interaction, difficulty in communication and repetitive patterns of behavior. Autism is about four times more common in boys than in girls, although girls tend to have more severe symptoms and greater cognitive impairment. Asperger's syndrome is the mildest variant, characterized by social isolation and eccentric behavior. Autistic disorder, or classical ASD, is the most severe form of the condition. It affects a child's ability to communicate, form relationships with others, and respond appropriately to the environment. Treatment for autism along the spectrum is a combination of drug and behavioral therapy, and family counseling is also encouraged.

Conduct disorder is a repetitive and persistent pattern of behavior in which age-appropriate societal norms are violated. Children with conduct disorder frequently engage in bullying and are often cruel to other children and animals.

Oppositional defiant disorder is a pattern of hostile and defiant behavior, lasting at least six months. Children with this disorder often lose their temper, argue with adults, and refuse to comply with adults' requests or rules.

Separation anxiety is characterized by inappropriate and excessive anxiety concerning separation from home, family members, or close friends. Children with separation anxiety disorder worry about losing, or about possible harm befalling, those close to them.

Cognitive Disorders

Cognitive disorders involve a significant loss of mental functioning, typically a result of a medical condition, substance abuse, or adverse reactions to medication. The goal of treatment is to control or reverse the cause of the symptoms, which varies with the specific condition.

Delirium is excessively confused or disorganized thinking. This is often manifested in a reduced ability to maintain attention to external stimuli, and sometimes in a reduced level of consciousness.

Dementia is characterized by impaired memory and difficulties in such functions as speaking, abstract thinking, and the ability to identify familiar objects. The most common cause of dementia among people aged 65 and older is Alzheimer's disease, affecting an estimated 4 million Americans; the duration of illness, from onset of symptoms to death, averages 8-10 years.

Multi-infarct dementia (MID) occurs when blood clots block small blood vessels in the brain and destroy brain tissue. MID is a common cause of dementia in the elderly; high blood pressure and advanced age are likely risk factors. The disease can also cause migraine-like headaches, stroke, and psychiatric disturbances.

Dissociative disorders

Dissociative disorders involve a sudden, often temporary disturbance in one's consciousness, memory, and identity. Treatment is a combination of drug therapy and psychotherapy.

Depersonalization disorder is the third most common psychological symptom and frequently occurs when one is in life-threatening danger; it can also occur as a symptom in other psychiatric disorders. One has a chronic feeling of being detached from one's body or mental processes; common objects and familiar situations seem strange or foreign. Treatment is warranted only if the disorder is persistent, recurring, or especially distressing.

Dissociative amnesia is an inability to recall important personal information, a memory loss that is too extensive to be explained by normal forgetfulness. With treatment, most patients recover the missing memories and resolve their amnesia; however, some never break through the barriers to reconstruct their missing past.

Dissociative fugue is one or more episodes of amnesia in which the loss of one's identity or the formation of

a new identity coincides with sudden departure from home or work. A fugue might last from hours to weeks to months; most episodes are brief and self-limited.

Dissociative identity disorder (DID), also known as multiple personality disorder (MPD), is characterized by a person's having two or more distinct personalities that alternate in their control of his or her behavior. Drug therapy may help to manage specific symptoms; psychotherapy is a more effective treatment.

Eating Disorders

An eating disorder is a severe disturbance in eating behavior. While these disorders occur most frequently among young women in Western societies, it is currently estimated that 10 percent of the people in the U.S. suffering from eating disorders are men. Treatment typically involves a short-term intervention to restore body weight and long-term therapy (often accompanied by antidepressants) to prevent relapse.

Anorexia nervosa is characterized by a disturbed sense of body image and a morbid fear of obesity. People with anorexia nervosa often refuse to eat adequately or even to maintain a normal body weight.

Binge eating is characterized by episodes in which an individual feels a loss of control over their eating. Unlike bulimia, these episodes are not followed by purging, fasting, or excessive exercise. People suffering from this disorder, nearly half of whom are male, are often overweight or obese, and tend to be older.

Bulimia nervosa is characterized by binge eating followed by self-induced vomiting or the use of laxatives, diuretics, or other medications to prevent weight gain. Patients are overly concerned about their body shape and weight.

Factitious Disorders

People with factitious disorders intentionally fake physical or psychological symptoms in order to receive medical attention and care. Factitious disorders are not to be confused with somatoform disorders, in which one actually believes that he or she has a (nonexistent) physical illness. The most extreme and chronic factitious disorder is Munchausen syndrome, which involves the repeated and often convincing fabrication of a physical illness by a person who wanders from hospital to hospital for treatment.

Patients with this type of disorder are rarely treated successfully.

Mood Disorders

Mood disorders, also called affective disorders, are conditions in which a person regularly experiences moods that are inconsistent with events, or shifts in mood from one extreme to another. In any given year, nearly 18.8 million American adults—9.5 percent of the population aged 18 and older—have a mood disorder; nearly twice as many women as men are affected by this type of disorder. Treatment with antidepressant drugs is often effective.

Bipolar disorder, also known as manic-depressive illness, is characterized by a person's mood alternating between the extremes of mania (an overexcited, hyperactive state) and depression. There are two primary types of bipolar disorder. *Bipolar I* disorder is characterized by alternating manic and depressive episodes. *Bipolar II* disorder is characterized by depressive episodes alternating with hypomanic periods, when the patient's mood is generally brighter and the patient has less need for sleep.

Cyclothymic disorder is a less extreme type of bipolar disorder, in which mild hypomanic and mini-depressive episodes follow an irregular course. This disorder is commonly a precursor of bipolar II disorder, but it can also occur as extreme moodiness in the affected person.

Depression is by far the most common psychological disorder today, and the leading cause of emotional disability in the U.S. Symptoms of depression may include feelings of sadness, hopelessness, and worthlessness, as well as changes in appetite, sleep patterns, and energy level, all lasting for two or more weeks. Persons with major depressive disorder typically lose interest in people and activities, experience little pleasure or enjoyment from normal activities, and find that even simple tasks become difficult.

Dysthymic disorder is characterized by a chronic mild depression that persists for several years. This disorder often begins in childhood or adolescence; affected persons are typically perceived as gloomy, pessimistic, humorless, and introverted.

Postpartum Depression is an acute depression that develops within three-six months of childbirth. Feelings of inadequacy, sadness and anxiety interfere with daily activities and childcare.

Seasonal Affective Disorder (SAD) is a type of depressive disorder that follows the seasons, though it typically occurs in the winter months. Symptoms include lethargy, irritability, depression and sleep problems.

Personality Disorders

Personality disorders are enduring and inflexible behavior patterns that impair normal social functioning. People with personality disorders have a poor perception of themselves or others, which commonly manifests itself in weak impulse control, troubled social relationships, and inappropriate emotional responses. These disorders are classified by three primary clusters of personality types: odd/eccentric, dramatic/erratic, and anxious/inhibited.

Odd/Eccentric Personalities in this cluster include paranoid (cold, distant, and suspicious), schizoid (introverted, withdrawn, and prone to daydreaming), schizotypal (emotionally detached, often expressing oddities of thinking, such as clairvoyance).

Dramatic/Erratic Personalities in this cluster include antisocial (often called psychopathic or sociopathic: callously disregardful of the rights and feelings of others); borderline (unstable in self-image, relationships, and behavior); histrionic (often called hysterical: dramatically and conspicuously seeking attention); and narcissistic (possessing an exaggerated sense of superiority).

Anxious/Inhibited Personalities in this cluster include avoidant (hypersensitive to rejection, fearful of starting new relationships), dependent (surrendering responsibility for major areas of their lives to others), obsessive- compulsive (overly orderly, inflexible, and unable to adapt to change).

Other Personality Types Personality types not falling within the three major clusters include cyclothymic (alternating high spirits with gloom and pessimism), depressive (morose, worried, and self-conscious), and passive-aggressive (employing inept or passive behaviors in an attempt to avoid responsibility or to control or punish others).

Psychotic Disorders

People with psychotic disorders lose touch with reality; symptoms may include delusions and hallucinations, disorganized thinking and speech, bizarre behavior, a diminished range of emotional responses, and social withdrawal. People who suffer from psychotic disorders often experience an inability to function in one or more important areas of life.

Schizophrenia is actually a group of disorders marked by severely disturbed thinking, perception, and behavior. It significantly impairs one's ability to communicate and relate to others, and disturbs most aspects of daily functioning. Typical symptoms include disorganized thought and language, hallucinations, and muted emotional expression (called flat affect); these symptoms usually last more than six months. The major types of schizophrenic disorder include catatonic, disorganized, paranoid, residual, and undifferentiated. Treatment with neuroleptic drugs is common.

Shared psychotic disorder is typified by delusions that occur in the context of a relationship with another person who already has his or her own delusions.

Somatoform Disorders

Somatoform disorders are characterized by the presence of physical symptoms that cannot be explained by a medical condition or have no identifiable physical cause. Such symptoms typically result from psychological conflicts or distress—psychological conditions taking a physical form.

Conversion disorder, also known as hysteria, is characterized by the loss of physical functioning without any physiological reason, typically the result of emotional conflict. Symptoms appear suddenly and at times of extreme psychological stress; patients often have a lack of concern over these symptoms (known as *la belle indifférence*).

Hypochondriasis (hypochondria) involves fear that one will develop a serious disease, typically misinterpreting minor physical symptoms as evidence of a major illness. Hypochondria typically lasts at least six months and causes significant distress.

Somatization disorder is a condition in which the patient has numerous physical complaints, persisting for several years, that have no physical cause. Common complaints include chronic pain and problems with the digestive, nervous, or reproductive systems; a lifetime history of sickliness is often found, although no specific disease is ever linked to the symptoms. This disorder typically begins before the age of 30, and occurs more often in females.

Substance-Related Disorders

Substance-related disorders, often called addictions, typically result from the abuse of drugs, medications, or other toxic substances. The most common substance-related disorders include alcohol dependence, amphetamine dependence, cannibis dependence, cocaine dependence, hallucinogen dependence, inhalant dependence, nicotine dependence, opoid dependence, phencyclidine dependence, and sedative dependence.

Common Treatments

Before the dawn of modern psychology, mental illness was thought to be the result of possession by demons, and treatment ranged from trepanning (the drilling of a hole in the head) to exorcism, torture, and hanging—all designed to release evil spirits from the body. Today there are three primary forms of treatment for patients with mental disorders: organic treatments, psychotherapy, and drug therapy.

Organic Treatments

Older forms of organic treatments involve some sort of physical approach to mental illness, but have gradually fallen out of favor.

Electroconvulsive therapy (ECT) uses electrical current, passed through the patient's brain for several seconds, to deliberately induce a controlled seizure; treatments are typically repeated over a period of several weeks. This treatment is most commonly used to treat severe depressions that has not responded to other forms of treatment; it is also sometimes used to treat schizophrenia. This is a controversial treatment, with major side effects such as confusion and memory loss.

Psychosurgery is the surgical removal or destruction of sections of the brain, in order to reduce severe and chronic psychiatric symptoms. The best-known psychosurgical procedure is the lobotomy, which was widely performed in the 1940's and early 1950's. As no research has proved this technique effective, and because it can produce drastic changes in personality and behavior, psychosurgery is now rarely performed.

Psychotherapy

Psychotherapy is a nonorganic treatment that is psychodynamic in nature, focusing on the resolution of internal psychic conflict. Unlike organic treatments, psychotherapy produces no physical side effects, although it can cause psychological damage when improperly administered; it also typically takes longer to produce noticeable results.

Behavioral therapy does not focus on past experiences, but instead helps the patient change abnormal behavior by applying established principles of conditioning and learning. This type of therapy has proved effective in treating phobias, obsessive-compulsive disorder, and other behavioral disorders.

Cognitive therapy attempts to identify patterns of irrational thinking that cause a person to behave abnormally. The patient learns to perceive people, situations, and self in a more realistic way, and thus develops improved problem-solving and coping skills. Cognitive therapy is commonly used to treat depression, panic disorder, and some personality disorders.

Group therapy brings a number of people together, under the guidance of a therapist, to discuss their individual problems; by sharing their feelings and experiences with others, group members learn that their problems are not unique and receive group support. Psychodrama is a type of group therapy in which participants act out emotional conflicts.

Humanistic and existential therapy These therapies treat mental illnesses by helping the patient achieve personal growth and meaning in life. The best-known humanistic therapy is client-centered therapy, in which the therapist provides no advice, instead restating the observations of the patient in nonjudgmental terms. Existential therapy encourages the patient to confront basic questions about the meaning of his or her life, in a journey toward discovery of personal uniqueness.

Psychodynamic therapy is used to untangle the sources of unconscious conflict and subsequently restructure the patient's personality. The first psychodynamic therapy was psychoanalysis, which typically involves the patient lying on a couch and saying whatever comes to mind (free association); some therapists may use hypnosis to uncover repressed memories. This type of treatment is lengthy and expensive, with multiple sessions often taking place over a period of several years. For this reason, classical psychoanalysis is not so widely practiced today as in previous years.

Drug Therapy

Drug therapy is a newer form of organic treatment, first introduced in the mid-1950's. Psychotherapeutic drugs help relieve the symptoms of many common mental disorders, although relapse may occur when their use is discontinued.

Antianxiety drugs, typically benzodiazepines such as Valium or other minor tranquilizers, are used to treat anxiety, insomnia, and other stress-related disorders. These newer drugs replace barbiturates, the previous antianxiety drugs of choice, which produced more severe side effects and were more likely to be abused. Benzodiazepines can also be addictive, however, and can also cause drowsiness and impaired coordination.

Antidepressant drugs help relieve symptoms of depression. There are three major classes of antidepressant drugs: tricyclics and tetracyclics, monoamine oxidase (MAO) inhibitors, and selective serotonin reuptake inhibitors (SSRIs), such as Prozac. Side effects may include dizziness, blurred vision, dry mouth, difficult urination, drowsiness, and sexual dysfunction.

In 2004, the Food and Drug Administration issued a warning that children and adolescents taking antidepressants may be at an increased risk of suicidal behavior and thinking in the early stages of their treatment, and drug manufacturers were required to include this warning on their labels. Only Prozac was approved for pediatric patients. Subsequent studies have challenged this finding, indicating the importance of considering the risks and benefits when prescribing medicine for this age group.

Antimanic drugs help control the mania related to bipolar disorder. The most common antimanic drug is lithium carbonate, also known as lithium. Side effects may include nausea, vertigo, and increased thirst and urination; long-term use may result in kidney damage.

Antipsychotic drugs, also called neuroleptics, are powerful tranquilizers primarily used to treat schizophrenia; they work by diminishing symptoms such as delusions, hallucinations, and thought disorder. The most commonly prescribed antipsychotic drugs are the phenothiazines; other popular antipsychotics include thioxanthenes, butyrophenomes, and indoles. Side effects may include dry mouth, blurred vision, and tardive dyskinesia, typified by involuntary movements of the lips, mouth, and tongue.

Glossary of Psychology Terms

abnormal psychology the area of psychological study concerned with deviations of the mind and behavior.

altruism positive social behavior carried out without consideration for one's own safety or benefit.

anal retentive Freudian concept suggesting underdevelopment in anal stage (around 18 months to three years old) leads to compulsive habits of tidiness and order.

anima Jung's term for the part of the psyche that is in touch with the subconscious. Also refers to the feminine part of a personality.

animus Jung's term for the masculine side of a personality.

anxiety see "Disorders."

archetype in Jungian psychology, a primitive mental image inherited from our earliest ancestors which is present in the collective unconscious: anima, animus, persona, self, shadow (see individual entries).

association a learned correlation between two actions or elements; often referred to when dealing with stimuli and response.

attachment in child psychology, an emotional relationship between children and their regular caregiver.

behaviorism a scientific approach that limits the study of psychology to observable behavior.

biofeedback therapy a method in which a person learns to control non-conscious biological processes.

biological psychology a field of study that posits behavior can be explained by understanding human physiology.

body image the subjective view that people have of their own body. Inappropriate body image is at the root of many neuroses including bulimia and anorexia nervosa.

catharsis the relief of anxiety through the process of bringing repressed feelings to the surface.

codependence when two people are reliant on each other for survival or emotional balance.

cognitive theory looks at how the mind processes information, with an emphasis on reasoning, memory, and problem-solving.

collective unconscious in Jungian terms, the part of our unconscious that is inherited, and common to all humans.

conformity changes in behavior as the result of real or perceived group pressure.

conscious the mental state of a person who is capable of having feelings, thoughts, and sensations.

defense mechanisms the ways we protect ourselves psychologically against our anxieties and painful thoughts. The primary defense mechanisms are denial, intellectualization, projection, rationalization, reaction formation, regression, and repression.

delusion an unreasonable belief that continues regardless of any evidence or argument presented to the contrary.

denial the most common defense mechanism, in which we refuse to accept a situation or event.

depression see "Disorders."

ego in Freudian theory, the intermediary between our impulses (id) and the outside world.

ego awareness in child psychology, the emerging comprehension in a child that they are an individual and independent person.

egocentrism self-absorption to the point of being insensitive to others.

egoist/egoistic conceited, self-serving and motivated solely by self-interest.

egotistic/egotist in addition to the characteristics exhibited in egoism, these personalities also have an unrealistic and obnoxious sense of their own importance.

empathy the awareness and understanding of other people's feelings.

emotional intelligence the ability to perceive, evaluate, and express emotions appropriately, and to use this knowledge effectively in social situations.

extrovert a personality that gets gratification from the outside physical and social environment.

fixation the process in which an action becomes unalterable; an abnormal fixation is persistent behavior without rational instigation.

gestalt the theory that our minds organize the world into a meaningful whole that meets our individual needs.

guilt a state that arises when someone feels they have done wrong or violated a moral standard. It is a form of self-punishment.

hard-wired a slang term commonly used instead of "genetically preprogrammed."

hypochondria see "Disorders."

id in Freudian theory, the repository of our impulses.

inhibition the process by which the brain limits a certain behavior or tendency.

innate characteristics native to an organism, often through genetics.

introvert a personality that is focused on one's own thoughts and tends to withdraw from social contacts.

libido in Freudian theory, our life energy and urges. Freud modified his use of the term over time, to play down its sexual component.

magical thinking in child development, the normal stage when children think their thoughts and wishes cause events to happen. In adults it is usually a symptom of a psychiatric disorder.

mania a non-clinical term for erratic behavior, madness, or in extreme cases, violence.

meme term for the "genes" of cultural foundation; shared ideas or experiences specific to a culture or group.

narcissist/narcissism an exaggerated sense of self-importance that makes normal love or consideration for others impossible.

nature vs. nurture the debate about the importance of heredity in determining behavior as opposed to the importance of experience and learning.

neurosis a personality disturbance, generally benign, that is not associated with any physical dysfunction.

Oedipus complex Freud's description of a condition in which a boy has an unhealthy attraction to his mother that blossoms into a hatred for his father.

paranoia disorder characterized by delusions of oppression, envy, or eminence; usually does not impair intellectual abilities.

pathology an atypical condition that causes normal functions to be inhibited. Refers to an organic malady, not a functional one.

perception the process by which we organize and provide meaning to the sensations we receive.

persona Jung's term for the role that someone takes on in society, or how they are perceived by others.

preconscious contains our ordinary and everyday memories.

projection the act of attributing an aspect of ourselves to someone else.

psychosis a mental disorder in which a person is unable to normally stay in touch with reality. Examples are bipolar disorder, dementia and schizophrenia. (See "Disorders.")

rational-emotive therapy developed by Albert Ellis (b. 1913) this is a highly directive therapy in which the patient is told what they must do to feel better and are encouraged to act accordingly. The main goal is to change behavior, not to delve into the reasons for it.

rationalization creating an incorrect but plausible explanation for a situation or feeling.

reaction formation the process in which negative or unacceptable feelings are controlled by acting in exactly the opposite way from how we feel.

regression reverting to a childlike form of defense as a way of dealing with stress.

repression how we keep thoughts out of our consciousness.

self the compelling sense of one's existence. In Jungian theory, the self sits between consciousness and the unconscious and is the ultimate expression of our spiritual development.

self-actualization a person's continuous quest to find and develop their full potential.

shadow in Jungian theory, the animal instincts passed along in the evolutionary process; a human "alter ego" representing the negative side of personality.

sublimation the process in which unacceptable, primitive impulses are redirected and processed into socially accepted behavior.

superego in Freudian theory, our conscience which keeps our behavior in check.

transference in psychoanalysis, the process in which clients attach feelings to their therapist that they previously held toward another significant person in their life and with whom they had conflict.

type-A a personality type that is in a relentless struggle to achieve more in the least amount of time (Type B is the term for the opposite personality).

unconscious in Freudian theory, holds the memories and experiences we aren't aware of. Freud believed this is where our truest feelings reside.

variability in statistical reasoning, the extent to which scores in a sample differ from the mean; used to determine psychological import of tests.

MEDICINE

A Brief History of Medicine

The practice of medicine began long before the advent of written records. Prehistoric people in every culture had ideas on the causes of illness, often placing responsibility on gods, evil spirits, or angry ancestors. To cope with pain and disability, they tried various remedies, ranging from magical incantations to rational strategies.

More than 10,000 years ago people practiced trepanation: a hole was made in the skull bone, possibly in hopes of alleviating the effects of head injuries or symptoms of mental illness. Otzi, the Iceman, who lived some 5,300 years ago and whose mummified body was discovered in the Italian Alps in 1991, appears to have been familiar with a natural antibiotic. He was carrying the fruit of the fungus *Piptoporus betulinus*, which contains oils toxic to the parasitic whipworm *Trichuris trichiura*. An autopsy of the Iceman's body revealed that his intestine was infested with *Trichuris* eggs. The history of medicine is the story of innovation emerging from the human desire to extend life and eliminate physical suffering.

Medicine in Antiquity

Beginning around the time of the Iceman, civilizations formed in the Middle East and people started to use numbers, pictures, and words to record information. The scientific study of medicine began as slowly information was disseminated from one healer to another and from one civilization to another.

Mesopotamia Clay tables from early civilizations in Mesopotamia contain diagnostic treatises with subsections covering gynecology, pediatrics, and convulsive disorders. Skin lesions, venereal disease, and fevers were described, and some of the described treatments were similar to modern treatments for the same conditions. Surgeries were performed and the earliest known legal code, the Code of Hammurabi, composed by the ruler of Babylon around 1700 B.C., included laws pertaining to the liability of physicians who "used the knife."

Egypt Papyruses from ancient Egypt, dating from 3000 B.C. to 1200 B.C., include methods for diagnosing pregnancy and the sex of a fetus, accurate descriptions of diseases, and rational treatment of various diseases. Particularly well known are the Ebers Papyrus (ca. 1550 B.C. but possibly based on papyri dating back to 3000 B.C.), which describes a wide range of diseases plus more than 700 remedies, and the Edwin Smith Papyrus (also ca. 1550 B.C.), which details 48 surgical cases of wounds of the head and upper body, showing particularly astute knowledge of fractures.

Greece In Greece, nonmagic medicine based on empirical knowledge emerged around 500 B.C. Hippocrates (ca. 460–ca. 377 B.C.), today often referred to as the "father of medicine," is credited with establishing medicine as a scientific undertaking. He wrote the first clinical description of diphtheria, recognized that tuberculosis occurs most commonly between the ages of 18 and 35, and stated "those naturally very fat are more liable to sudden death than the thin." The Hippocratic Oath, dating from around the time of Hippocrates, pledges physicians to do their best for patients, to avoid doing harm, and to keep secret information about their patients; it continues to serve as a code of conduct for today's physicians.

Around 300 B.C., the Greek physician Herophilus (ca. 335–280 B.C.), who practiced in Alexandria, Egypt, where dissections of human corpses were permitted, founded the first school of anatomy. He differentiated between sensory and motor nerves and established that the brain is the center of the nervous system. He made important observations about organs such as the liver and ovaries, and he invented a water clock to measure the pulse of arterial blood.

Rome By the beginning of the Christian era, the Romans had created a widespread empire that included lands from Gaul (France) through Greece and as far east as Syria. But the center of their empire, Rome, was crowded, dirty, and the frequent victim of epidemics of smallpox, bubonic plague, and other diseases. The Romans adopted important public health measures, building aqueducts to bring freshwater into the city and sewers to carry away wastes. Public baths were established to encourage personal hygiene and special buildings were set aside for care of the sick. War injuries advanced surgery: Roman surgeons could surgically reduce limb fractures, tie ligatures around blood vessels, and cauterize wounds to stop bleeding.

The most influential physician of ancient Rome was a Greek, Galen of Pergamum (ca. 129–ca. 216). He used pulse readings in diagnosing problems, showed that different parts of the spinal cord control different muscles, and demonstrated that arteries contain blood, not air as had been believed. But his misconceptions were many. For instance, he stated that pores connect the two sides of the heart and the liver is the main organ of the blood system. In his 300 known writings on physiology, anatomy, disease, and drugs, over half of which have survived, Galen brought together his ideas and those of predecessors and contemporaries. For more than 1,400 years, these writings were considered infallible and were the basis of medical education in Europe.

Medicine During the Dark Ages

Following the collapse of the Roman Empire in the fifth century, medical knowledge withered in Europe. Religious teachings about the causes of disease—and about other knowledge—were paramount; questioning these teachings risked charges of heresy and blasphemy. Dissections of human corpses were forbidden and experimental investigations suppressed. The great pestilences of the period were considered the will of God. Infirmaries were founded, but they were crowded, unsanitary places where care consisted of little more than kindness to the dying.

Arabic Contributions Meanwhile, Arab physicians preserved, adopted, and expanded on the rational ideas of the ancient Greeks and Romans. Persian scholar ar-Razi (Rhazes: ca. 860–ca. 925) was the first to write a scientific paper on infectious diseases and the first to describe smallpox; he used opium as an anesthetic, plaster of Paris for casts, and animal guts for sutures. His multivolume *al-Hawi* (Comprehensive Book) included all the medical knowledge of the time, including work handed down from earlier times. Beginning in the late eighth century, hospitals providing both medical care and medical apprenticeships were opened in major cities in the Empire. Another vast encyclopedia of medical information, the *Qanum* (Canon of Medicine) was written by another Persian polymath, Ibn Sina (Avicenna, 980–1037), who recognized that tuberculosis is a contagious disease and that some diseases are spread through water or soil. In the Islamic empire, medicinal plants were avidly collected; the number of drugs used to treat illness increased greatly and pharmacy became a separate vocation.

The Renaissance Through the 18th Century

In the 12th century, the first medical school in Europe was established in Salerno, Italy, and was so influential that the Holy Roman Emperor Frederick II decreed that anyone who wanted to practice medicine had to be approved by the masters of Salerno. A revival of learning took place in Europe beginning in the early 13th century. Classical medical texts as well as works by Razi, Ibn Sina, and other Islamic scholars were translated from Arabic or Greek into Latin, and physicians such as Taddeo Alderotti (1223–95) urged their colleagues to read these texts. Major centers for the study of medicine opened in Paris and Montpellier in France and Bologna in Italy.

By the end of the 1400's the Renaissance was well under way. The invention of printing in Europe led to books on surgery and medicinal plants. Experimentation became more common, as did dissection of human corpses. Seafaring explorations also influenced medical history— for instance, a monk who accompanied Christopher Columbus described for Europeans how Native Americans smoked tobacco for medicinal purposes; sailors introduced smallpox to the Americas and brought syphilis into Europe.

Anatomy In the 16th century, as religious prohibitions against human dissection were lifted, the modern study of anatomy began, allowing scientists to distinguish between abnormal and normal anatomical features. Andreas Vesalius (1514–64), a Belgian physician, dissected human and animal cadavers, demonstrating that Galen's descriptions of human anatomy were based on the dissection of animals whose structure differs markedly from that of humans. In 1543 Vesalius published *De Humani corporis fabrica* ("On the Structure of the Human Body"), the first work to accurately illustrate human anatomy.

Gabriele Falloppio (1523–62), a student of Vesalius, described the tubes between the ovary and the uterus, now called Fallopian tubes, as well as previously unknown structures in the skull and inner ear. Bartolomeo Eustachio (1513–74) described tooth structure at different ages and the tube that connects the middle ear to the back of the nasal cavity, today known as the Eustachian tube. Hieronymus Fabricius (ca. 1533–1619) helped found embryology. He compared the anatomy of embryos of dogs, cats, horses, and humans, and was the first to describe the placenta. He also provided detailed descriptions of the semilunar valves in blood veins. This led to the discovery of blood circulation by his student William Harvey (1578–1657). Harvey's *Anatomical Study on the Movement of the Heart and Blood in Animals*, published in 1628, accurately explained that the heart pumps blood into arteries, the arteries carry the blood throughout the body, and the veins return the blood to the heart.

This new understanding of human anatomy allowed surgery to emerge as a separate discipline. Previously surgery was performed by barber-surgeons, and was considered a less dignified occupation than medicine. This perspective was changed by Ambroise Paré (1510–90) the leading surgeon in the 16th century, who served four kings and earned the reputation as the "father of modern surgery." Using the experience he gained on the battlefield, Paré pioneered the use of ligatures and dressings to stop bleeding instead of the painful practice of cautery. Paré is credited with originating the use of prostheses— artificial replacements for a missing part of the body—and popularized the use of the truss for treating hernias, which were previously often "cured" by castration.

One of the most important medical tools, helping physicians understand anatomy and identify signs of disease, was the compound microscope, invented in 1590 by Zacharius Janssen, a Dutch optician. News of this invention traveled quickly, and curious people began studying ever-tinier structures. Marcello Malpighi (1628–94) discovered blood capillaries and nephrons (structures in the kidney where urine is formed). In 1655 Robert Hooke (1635–1703) discovered cells. In the 1670's, using single-lens microscopes he made himself, Antoni van Leeuwenhoek (1632–1723) became the first person to see blood cells, sperm cells, and one-celled organisms.

Understanding normal anatomy led to the scientific study of diseased organs. This field of pathological anatomy was founded by Giovanni Morgagni (1682–1771), who carefully related his postmortem findings to detailed clinical records of patients' symptoms. Symptoms came to be viewed as "the cry of the suffering organs" and people with a technical bent looked for ways to detect organ abnormalities in living patients. In a 1761 paper, Leopold Auenbrugger (1722–1809), who recognized that the sounds of lungs full of air differ from those of lungs containing fluid, introduced percussion—tapping on a patient's chest and listening to the resulting sounds. In the early 1800's René Laënnec (1781–1826) invented the stethoscope to detect abnormal heartbeats and other chest sounds.

Study of Disease   Interest in epidemiology—the causes of disease—developed, nurtured by the epidemics of plague and other diseases that killed huge numbers of Europeans during this period. Paracelsus (Theophrastus Bombastus von Hohenheim, 1493–1541), a German-Swiss physician and alchemist, attacked the widely held belief, handed down from ancient Greece, that disease results from internal disturbances of four bodily "humors" (blood, phlegm, yellow bile, and black bile). He stated that external agents cause disease; for example, in his *On Diseases of Miners*—the earliest book on occupational diseases—he wrote that inhaling metallic dust causes silicosis ("miner's disease"). Paracelsus also pioneered the use of chemicals to fight diseases, advocating the use of specific medicines for specific diseases.

The 1546 work *De contagione et contagiosis morbis* ("On Contagion and Contagious Diseases") by Girolamo Fracastoro (1483–1553) proposed that epidemic diseases are spread by tiny particles, with contagion occurring by either direct contact, indirect contact via infected items, or without contact from a distance. Fracastoro also identified typhus and gave syphilis its name.

Physiology   Modern physiology began with Harvey's discovery of blood circulation. Also in the 17th century, men such as Thomas Wharton (1614–73) and Regnier de Graaf (1641–73) initiated the study of glands and their secretions. Around 1670 Thomas Willis (1621–75) was the first to recognize diabetes mellitus when he noted that patients whose urine has a sweet taste suffer from fatigue and other symptoms. Later, Luigi Galvani (1737–98) showed that nerves conduct electricity and that electric stimuli cause muscle contractions. Antoine Lavoisier (1743–94) studied breathing, proving that muscles need less oxygen at rest than when working.

Improved Treatment   People with a technical bent looked for ways to detect organ abnormalities in living patients. Traditionally, physicians used a collection of basic tools—to deal with patients. In the 1620's, Santorio Santorio developed the *pulsilogium*, originally conceived by Galileo, to measure the beats of a man's pulse. Later, John Floyer (1649–1734) invented a special watch for measuring the pulse. Leopold Auenbrugger (1722–1809) introduced percussion—tapping on a patient's chest and listening to the resulting sounds—as a way of determining if their lungs were filled with fluid. New medical practices also emerged. Dominique Amel (1679–1730) invented the fine-point syringe. James Lind (1716–94) discovered that ingesting lemon juice could prevent and cure scurvy, and William Withering (1741–99) discovered the value of digitalis in treating edema and heart disease.

It was in this period that one of the most far-reaching advancements in the fight against disease occurred. In 1796, Edward Jenner, an English surgeon (1749–1823), developed a vaccination against the virus that caused smallpox. Subjects were inoculated with a serum containing material from cowpox—a bovine form of the disease—and were found to be immune from smallpox when they were exposed to it later. Although it took another 50 years to find an effective method of producing this antiviral medication in volume, Jenner's early work was responsible for eradicating the disease.

In the 18th century, physicians created the foundation for modern hospitals, where treatment and restored health, rather than containment and death, were attainable goals, and the first medical school was established at the University of Pennsylvania, in what would become the United States. At the same time, Philippe Pinel (1745–1826), a French physician, pioneered the humane treatment of the mentally ill, discarding the long-held belief that mental illness was caused by demonic possession.

19th-century Contributions

Medical advances occurred on many fronts during the 19th century. Of fundamental importance was the growing effect on medicine of the scientific method: observing a phenomenon, forming a hypothesis or possible explanation of the phenomenon, designing experiments to test the hypothesis, carefully observing and studying the experimental results to determine if they support the hypothesis—and if not, why not. As a result, many long-used remedies were found worthless or too harmful and were discarded; the use of addictive opium to soothe pain and the use of poisonous mercury to cure syphilis are examples.

The connection between filth and disease was firmly established, leading to improved sanitation and other public health measures. John Snow (1813–58) traced a number of cholera cases to a specific water pump in London—the first time that water pollution was proven to cause illness. More and more communities began treating water supplies with chlorine, first used to purify water in 1800.

The *germ theory of disease*, which holds that bacteria and other microbes ("germs") cause infectious diseases, was established independently by Louis Pasteur (1822–95) and Robert Koch (1843–1910) in the 1870's. In 1879, Pasteur accidentally discovered that bacteria could be weakened, which prevents them from causing disease but still enables them to trigger immunity in infected individuals. Using weakened anthrax bacteria taken from the blood of diseased animals, Pasteur developed the first artificially produced vaccine in 1881. This soon led to isolation of the causative agents of diphtheria, gonorrhea, tuberculosis, cholera, and other scourges—and sounded the death knell for theories that ascribed disease to such factors as spontaneous generation and alien spirits.

In 1892 came the first indication that some agents of disease are smaller than bacteria—indeed, so small that they cannot be seen with light microscopes. The discovery was confirmed in 1898 by Martinus Beijerinck (1851–1931), who named the agents "filterable viruses."

Diagnostic Advances Diagnoses became more accurate as physicians applied new knowledge of human anatomy and physiology. In the 19th century scientists recognized that all organisms are composed of cells. Charles Bell (1774–1842) discovered the functions of nerves and showed that a nerve is not a single unit but a collection of filaments within a common sheath. William Beaumont (1785–1853) experimentally studied digestion in the exposed stomach of a wounded man, greatly advancing understanding of the process. Thomas Addison (1793–1860) helped found endocrinology when he reported that a form of anemia (now called pernicious anemia) was related to a fatal disease of the adrenal glands—the first time that anyone demonstrated that the adrenals are necessary for life. Jean Pierre Flourens (1794–1867) discovered the functions of the cerebellum and Paul Broca (1824–80) discovered the part of the brain that controls speech.

Claude Bernard (1813–78), often considered the founder of experimental medicine, investigated carbohydrate metabolism, discovering the ability of the liver to change glycogen to sugar and showing that blockage of the pancreatic duct prevents digestion of fats. Bernard also found that oxygen is not carried in solution in the blood but is bound to the red blood cells. He also proposed that in order to survive, a body maintains a stable internal environment even though external conditions change, a concept later termed *homeostasis*.

Numerous diseases, both acute and chronic, were carefully described for the first time: "shaking palsy" by James Parkinson (1755–1824), for whom the disease is now named; the facial paralysis now known as Bell's palsy, by Charles Bell; hemophilia, by Johann Schonlein (1793–1864); Hodgkin's disease, a cancer of the lymph nodes, by Thomas Hodgkin (1798–1866); and so on.

New Tools   New tools included the stethoscope, invented by René Laënnec (1781–1826) in 1816 and used to investigate the lungs and heart, allowing physicians to hear for the first time "the cry of the suffering organs." The invention of other influential tools soon followed, including the ophthalmoscope, invented independently by Charles Babbage (1792–1871) and Herman Helmholtz (1821–94) in mid-century and used to view the interior of the eye; and the sphygmograph, the predecessor of the modern sphygmometer, used to measure blood pressure, invented by Etienne-Jules Marey (1830–1904) in 1863. Endoscopy, or passing an instrument into a hollow organ in order to view its interior, had its beginnings in 1877 with the invention of a cystoscope to view the urinary bladder; candlelight was its source of illumination.

Until the 1860's, doctors used very long thermometers to take a patient's temperature, a process that took about 20 minutes. In 1866 Thomas Allbutt (1836–1925) introduced the short, efficient clinical thermometer. Its use was advanced by Carl Wunderlich (1815–77), who showed that fever is a symptom, not a disease.

In 1895, as the century neared its end, Wilhelm Röntgen discovered x-rays and how the radiation could be used to create a "shadow picture" revealing bone structure. Medicine diagnosis was revolutionized, for doctors could now examine a patient's insides without cutting into the body.

Modern surgery emerged in the 19th century as well. Physicians recognized the three major obstacles to successful surgery—pain, infection, and bleeding. Two American dentists, Horace Wells and William Morton, discovered anesthesia in the 1840's. By reducing the trauma of surgery for patients, anesthesia allowed doctors to take more time over their work and to apply surgery to more ailments. In 1842 Crawford Long (1815–78) painlessly removed a tumor from a patient's neck after the patient sniffed ether. James Young Simpson (1811–70) discovered the anesthetic properties of chloroform and began using the substance to relieve the pain women experienced during childbirth.

Illness and death in hospitals decreased markedly with the introduction of antiseptic practices. In 1847 Ignaz Semmelweiss (1818–65) ordered doctors to wash their hands in a chlorine solution before each examination of a patient. In the late 1860's Joseph Lister (1827–1912) introduced the use of carbolic acid on surgical instruments, wounds, and bandages, decreasing the death rate in his surgery from 49 percent to about 15 percent. Around 1890 William Halsted (1852–1922) introduced the practice of wearing sterilized rubber gloves during surgery.

By the end of the 19th century, the age-old practice of bloodletting was finally abandoned. The modern blood-type classification system, used to replenish a patient's blood through transfusions, began with the 1900 discovery of the A-B-O blood groups by Austrian scientist Karl Landsteiner.

Chewing willow bark had been a successful method of combating fever for more than 2,000 years. Starting in 1838, chemists tried to produce a safe derivative of the active ingredient. Success came in 1893, when Felix Hoffmann (1868–1946) found acetylsalicylate. His employer, the Bayer pharmaceutical company, named the new drug "aspirin" and began selling it in 1899. Other drugs in the physician's medicine cabinet included digitalis for heart ailments, amyl nitrate for angina, quinine for malaria, and sedatives such as chloral hydrate and paraldehyde.

Not all of the milestones in medicine were achieved in laboratories and operating rooms. In 1849 Elizabeth Blackwell (1821–1910) graduated from Geneva Medical College in upstate New York, earning the designation as the first woman doctor in modern times. At roughly the same time, Elizabeth Garrett (1836–1917) circumvented Britain's rigid opposition to medical training for women and received a medical degree in 1865. Blackwell and Garrett eased the way for other women, both professionals and patients, by establishing women's medical colleges, and infirmaries which specialized in obstetrics and pediatrics.

In 1889, Sir William Osler (1849–1919) a renowned Canadian physician, now revered as the "father of modern medicine," was appointed the first Physician-in-Chief at John's Hopkins Hospital in Baltimore, where he revolutionized the way the medical curriculum was taught. Osler insisted that students learn at the bedside, implementing his belief that "the good physician treats the disease; the great physician treats the patient who has the disease." Students took patient histories, conducted physical examinations, and studied laboratory results, leading to a more interactive and humane treatment of medical conditions.

Osler established the medical residency, in which doctors in training make up much of a hospital's medical staff. This system remains in place today in most teaching hospitals. In 1907, Dr. Osler invited Maude Abbott (1869–1940), a Canadian doctor, to contribute a chapter on cardiac abnormalities to his renowned work, *Systems of Modern Medicine*, which established her as the leading authority on the topic. Abbott literally wrote the book on cardiac disease, when she published *The Atlas of Congenital Heart Disease* (1936), which remained the primary source on the subject for decades.

20th-century Advances

When the 20th century began, life expectancy in the United States was 47 years. By 2000 average length of life had increased to almost 77 years. This steady improvement was due largely to a decline in deaths during childhood, the development of drugs to combat infectious diseases, improved nutrition, and better environmental sanitation. Public health measures, including pasteurization, inspection of food supplies, and fluoridation of water supplies, also were of great value.

Basic Discoveries   Enormous strides in basic biological sciences—microbiology, biochemistry, genetics, and so on—coupled with technological advances led to explosive growth of pharmaceuticals and the development of new surgical techniques. For instance, the first indication that viruses can cause disease in humans came in 1901, when Walter Reed (1851–1902) and an associate proved that a virus causes yellow fever. Development of electron microscopes in the 1930's gave scientists their first glimpse of viruses, and tissue culture techniques enabled researchers to grow viruses in the laboratory, for drug testing, preparation of vaccines, and other purposes.

Another type of disease-causing agent was first isolated in 1982 by Stanley Prusiner (b. 1942). Called *prions*, these particles consist solely of a protein. For reasons not yet understood, they can be transformed into abnormal shapes capable of destroying cells. Prions cause spongiform encephalopathies, fatal diseases characterized by the breakdown of brain tissue. These diseases include bovine spongiform encephalopathy, popularly called "mad cow disease," and Creutzfeldt-Jakob disease in humans.

In 1901 Jokichi Takamine (1854–1922) became the first scientist to isolate a hormone, adrenalin. Isolation and, subsequently, synthesis made it easier to identify the roles played by hormones in diseases and led to improved treatments. The therapeutic use of hormones began in 1921, when Frederick Banting (1891–1941) and colleagues injected insulin, a hormone produced by certain pancreatic cells, into a person with diabetes.

Perhaps the most significant contribution in the field of endocrinology came 50 years later, with the creation of the birth control pill. In the early 1950's, Gregory Pincus, an American biologist and researcher (1903–1967) discovered that injections of the hormone, progesterone, would inhibit ovulation and prevent pregnancy. Seed money for this effort was provided by Margaret Sanger, a lifelong advocate for women's rights. At the same time, working independently, Carl Djerassi (b. 1923) created an orally effective form of synthetic progesterone. It was another decade before "the Pill" received F.D.A. approval and became commercially available, ushering in both a medical and social revolution.

In the first decade of the 20th century, scientists realized that certain "accessory food factors" are essential for good health. In 1911 Casimir Funk (1884–1967) found the first of these factors, B, and in a 1912 paper proposed the factors be called *vitamins*. The discovery of vitamins A (1913), D (1922), E (1922), C (1928), and K (1934) followed; it was shown that vitamin B actually is a complex of several vitamins, and synthesis led to widespread availability of the substances.

Rise of Genetics   Nineteenth-century developments in genetics went largely unnoticed until 1900, when three botanists independently rediscovered basic laws of heredity published by Gregor Mendel (1822–84) in 1866. In 1902 Walter Sutton (1877–1916) correctly suggested that chromosomes—discovered and named in the late 19th century—carry Mendel's "hereditary units," later named genes.

By 1911 Thomas Hunt Morgan (1866–1945) had discovered that mutations could occur in the hereditary material; by the 1940's scientists had established that all organisms as well as viruses can mutate. Meanwhile, other research demonstrated that exposure to x-rays, radioactive materials, and various chemicals increases the mutation rate. Scientists began identifying the connections between genes and disease. Today it is known that many diseases are triggered by altered genes. Some of these diseases are inherited while others result from random mutations that develop in body cells during one's lifetime. Genetic abnormalities have been linked to illnesses from Alzheimer's disease to osteoporosis to Tay-Sachs disease; scientists have identified more than thirty genes that cause different types of muscular dystrophy, and nearly 400 cancer-related genes have been identified.

Genetic engineering, the deliberate alteration of an organism's genetic material, began in 1973. By inserting specific human genes into bacteria or yeast, it became possible to manufacture large quantities of important human compounds: insulin, for people who have diabetes; erythropoietin, for treating anemia; tissue plasminogen activator (TPA), for dissolving blood clots; and so on. Researchers also took the first steps in *gene therapy*, transferring normal genes into the cells of people who suffer from diseases caused by defective genes. In 1990 a 4-year-old girl became the first person to undergo gene therapy, receiving a blood transfusion containing billions of cells with copies of the gene that would enable her body to made adenosine deaminase, an enzyme essential for a healthy immune system.

New Medications   At the beginning of the 20th century, pneumonia and tuberculosis were the leading causes of death in the United States. By the century's end, thanks to modern drug development, these and most other common bacterial infections had been brought under control, at least in the United States and other developed nations. Paul Ehrlich (1854–1915) helped found modern chemotherapy (the use of chemicals to fight disease) when he synthesized Salvarsan and in 1910 successfully used it to cure syphilis. In 1932 Gerhard Domagk (1895–1964) discovered that the red textile dye Prontosil protected against deadly *Staphylococcus* and *Streptococcus* bacteria. Prontosil was the first drug that could be used against a variety of bacteria; later, more powerful drugs, called sulfonamides or sulfa drugs, were derived from Prontosil. They would eventually be largely replaced by safer and more effective antibiotics.

Medicine was revolutionized in 1928 when Alexander Fleming (1881–1955) discovered the antibiotic properties of penicillin, but he was unable to produce it in a form pure enough to use on patients. Ten years later, Howard Florey and others at Oxford University, solved this problem, and by World War II, techniques were developed in the United States for the commercial production of the drug. Its disease-fighting potential was recognized in the early years of World War II, and it saved the lives of countless wounded soldiers. Today a number of penicillins are available, including ampicillin, amoxicillin, and oxacillin, and they are among the most widely used antibiotics. Other antibiotics include cephalosporins (for example,

cephalothin), tetracyclines (tetracycline), macrolides (erythromycin), aminoglycosides (streptomycin), quinolones (ciprofloxacin), and glycopeptides (vancomycin). Unfortunately, bacteria evolve rapidly, developing strains resistant to one or more antibiotics and requiring researchers to search for new drugs to combat the "superbugs."

Other drugs added to the pharmaceutical arsenal included corticosteroids, to treat rheumatoid arthritis; antabuse, to prevent alcoholics from drinking; cyclosporine, to prevent rejection of transplanted organs; antidepressants and antipsychotics, for mental problems; and thrombolytic drugs to dissolve blood clots. Some new offerings actually were ancient drugs in new form. In 1950, for instance, reserpine was introduced for treatment of high blood pressure; the drug had long been used in India in the form of snakeroot.

Beginning in 1944, Gertrude Elion, along with her colleague, George H. Hitchings joined Burroughs Wellcome Laboratories (now GlaxoSmithKline), and using innovative new research techniques, developed an array of drugs that were effective against leukemia, autoimmune diseases, malaria, and viral herpes. They were awarded the Nobel Prize in Physiology or Medicine in 1988 for their discoveries. Elion later participated in the development of azidothymidine (AZT), the first drug used in the treatment of AIDS.

Advances in Surgery   In the early 20th century, surgeons began to specialize and new fields emerged, building on the efforts of a few extraordinary individuals. Not for the first time, the theater of war made an enormous contribution to the progress of medicine. In 1914, Harold Gillies (1882–1960) a New Zealand-born, British Red Cross doctor in World War I, saw that while soldiers could survive their battle wounds, surgeons had neither the skill nor the time to deal with their often dramatic disfigurements. Gillies devoted himself to the study and practice of plastic surgery, founding Queen's Hospital in Kent, England where more than 10,000 reconstructive surgeries were performed. The techniques he invented, including skin grafts, were adopted by surgeons around the world and ushered in the era of reconstructive and, ultimately, cosmetic surgery.

Working in some of America's finest hospitals, including John's Hopkins Hospital in Baltimore and Peter Bent Brigham Hospital in Boston, Harvey Cushing

(1869–1939) is recognized today as the first true neurosurgeon. Among his many innovations, Cushing created a way to stem the flow of blood with clamps and cuffs, allowing for a better visual field, and minimizing the possibility that the patient would bleed to death. He pioneered the use of the "electric scalpel," and demanded that his team work with masks and gloves to minimize infection. His patients were the first to receive around-the-clock nursing care after surgery, and this type of post-operative treatment was the forerunner of intensive-care units. Taken together, Cushing's contributions made brain surgery safer and more effective.

There were other surgical milestones during this period. The first successful appendectomies were performed in Davenport, Iowa in 1885 by Dr. William West Grant, and at roughly the same time by Dr. H. Hancock, in England. In 1932, American surgeon Michael E. DeBakey developed a roller pump that became an essential component of the heart-lung machine, and in 1944, Dr. Helen Taussig (1898–1980), an American cardiologist, developed an operation to correct the congenital heart defect that causes "blue baby" syndrome, an operation which has prolonged the lives of many children, and which was an important step in the development of adult open-heart surgery, successfully performed for the first time by John H. Gibbon, Jr. in 1953. In 1954, a team of physicians at Peter Bent Brigham Hospital transplanted a kidney from a young man into his identical twin.

In 1966, DeBakey implanted the first mechanical heart in a human, and other successful transplantations soon followed: liver (1963), lung (1963), pancreas (1966), intestine (1966). In 1967, Dr. Christiaan Barnard performed the first successful human heart transplant. Bone marrow transplants (in which blood-forming stem cells are used to treat certain cancers and blood disorders) began in 1964 when the first successful transplant took place, between identical twins. Today, stem cell transplants represent one of the most exciting—and controversial—frontiers in modern surgery. In 1990, the so-called laparoscopic technique was perfected, allowing surgeons to make much smaller incisions in the patient's abdomen, and remove small organs through the navel.

New Technologies

Twentieth-century technologies such as computers, electronics, fiber optics, lasers, and ultrasound were all incorporated into medicine, making diagnoses much more accurate and treatments safer and more effective. Mammography for diagnosing breast cancer was introduced in 1913, the electroencephalogram (EEG) for recording brain waves in 1929. The heart can be monitored by recording electrical activity via skin electrodes with the electrocardiography (EKG) machine, and the implantable pacemaker for regulating heartbeat was developed in 1958. The CT scan for producing three-dimensional images of internal organs was developed in 1972, balloon angioplasty for unclogging diseased arteries in 1977, and the lithotripter for breaking up kidney stones in 1980.

Great advances also occurred in the construction of artificial body parts. Aluminum, titanium, plastic resins, and three-dimensional computer modeling were used to build sophisticated limbs and joints. An artificial kidney was first used in 1943 and artificial skin was introduced in 1981. As the century neared its end, artificial blood vessels were being successfully tested in dogs.

Alternative Therapies

Modern Western medicine has not been without its critics. Patients complain about assembly-line atmospheres in doctors' offices, improper or ineffective treatments, botched operations, the debilitating side effects of many drugs, and health care costs that spiral higher and higher. In recent decades factors such as these helped fuel interest in alternative forms of medicine.

Acupuncture the insertion of needles into specific points on the body to stimulate and balance the flow of energy through the body, has been used in China for more than 2,000 years.

Ayurvedic medicine which focuses on natural diet, herbs, exercise, and such therapies as massage, has been practiced in India for at least 4,000 years.

Biofeedback learning to detect and consciously control physiological functions, developed in the mid-1900's.

Chiropractic manipulation of the spine to treat spinal and nervous disorders, began in 1895.

Herbalism the use of potions derived exclusively from plants, has been practiced in China, India, and other places for thousands of years.

Homeopathy treating a disease with minuscule doses of the natural substances that in larger amounts would bring on the disorder, was developed in the early 1800's.

New scientific evidence supported the effectiveness of some alternative therapies. For example, acupuncture was found to ease chronic back pain and arthritic pain in some patients; migraine sufferers who learned relaxation techniques had fewer migraines and needed less medication to cope with their headaches. Physicians began integrating certain alternative therapies with conventional medicine—recommending biofeedback and stress-management techniques to heart patients, offering hypnosis programs to people who wanted to quit smoking, and referring patients to chiropractors and acupuncturists.

Current and Future Developments Humans continue to face major health challenges. Many infectious diseases have been brought under control in developed countries but remain huge epidemics elsewhere. Some of these diseases, such as malaria, tuberculosis, and dengue fever, actually are increasing and spreading to new regions. AIDS, Lyme disease, and other emerging diseases discovered only in recent decades have created new medical battlefields. So, too, has the growing resistance of ever-mutating germs to antibiotics; physicians have few weapons to combat once-treatable organisms such as *Streptococcus pneumoniae*, a major cause of bacterial pneumonia and MRSA (methicillin-resistant Staphylococcus Aureus), an infection often contracted in hospitals and nursing homes.

People are living longer, resulting in a growing incidence of arthritis, Alzheimer's disease, congestive heart failure, and other diseases of the elderly. High-risk behaviors such as illicit drug use and limited access to health care are additional issues. Preventable illnesses kill many millions of people annually. Worldwide, tobacco use causes approximately 4.2 million premature deaths annually, a number expected to increase to 10 million by 2030. Obesity, a major contributor to chronic disease and disability, has also reached epidemic proportions globally, with more than 1 billion adults overweight, at least 300 million of them clinically obese. Also, more than 7 million children under age five die every year from diarrhea, pneumonia, and other preventable diseases; they could be saved if malnutrition and poor sanitary conditions were eradicated and basic medical treatments, including prenatal and neonatal care, were provided.

On a positive note, there is hope that some of the world's worst diseases are being brought under control. Under the auspices of the World Health Organization (W.H.O.) and other governmental and private organizations, elimination and eradication programs are in place for polio, measles, leprosy, guinea-worm disease (dracunculiasis), river blindness (onchoceriasis), and Chagas' disease. Results have been encouraging. After the Global Polio Eradication Initiative was launched in 1988, the number of polio cases fell by over 99 percent—from an estimated 350,000 cases in 1988 to 1,900–2,000 cases in the mid-2000's; the number of countries in which polio was endemic decreased from more than 125 to four.

Better understanding of human biology, genetics, and psychology are leading to improved preventive measures, diagnostic tools, and therapies. Genetic engineering, computerization, miniaturization, and other technological advances also will continue to improve people's health and medical care.

Medical researchers are particularly excited about the potential benefits of research on stem cells, undifferentiated cells that can develop into specialized cells. Embryonic stem cells, found only in embryos, give rise to all the different kinds of cells in the body. It appears that adult stem cells, found in children and adults, are only able to develop into a limited number of cell types; for example, adult stem cells in the skin develop into different kinds of skin cells. The best-known stem-cell therapy to date is the bone marrow transplant, in which blood-forming stem cells are used to treat certain cancers and blood disorders. Work with embryonic stem cells is still in its early stages, but many scientists believe these cells may provide entirely new treatments for heart disease, diabetes, Parkinson's disease, and other ailments. Another area that may one day benefit is the development and testing of new medicines.

Through past millennia, human life span has increased as people have learned how to prevent and treat illness. By the beginning of the 21st century, average life span had exceeded 80 years in some countries. There is much reason to believe that future medical advances will increase not only life span but also quality of life.

Disease

Disease can be defined as a disturbance or abnormality in which part of the body is not functioning properly, thereby making a person physically or mentally ill and possibly leading to death. The most common types of diseases include:

Infectious diseases, which are caused by viruses, bacteria, fungi, and other organisms, and transmitted from person to person—or from animal to person. Examples: common cold, influenza, chickenpox, measles, tuberculosis, AIDS.

Hereditary diseases, which are transferred from parent to child via the genes. Examples: Down syndrome, hemophilia, sickle cell anemia.

Degenerative diseases, which result from a general breakdown of body structures and natural aging processes. Examples: certain types of arthritis and cardiovascular disease.

Hormonal disorders, resulting from an insufficiency or excess of hormones—chemicals that act as messengers in the body. Examples: diabetes, hypoglycemia, hypothyroidism, Graves' disease.

Environmental diseases, caused by chemical and physical agents such as radiation, smoke, drugs, and poisons. Examples: allergies, asbestosis, bysinosis, lead poisoning.

Deficiency diseases, caused by the lack of vitamins or other essential nutrients. Examples: beriberi, scurvy, pellagra, rickets.

Mental and emotional illnesses, caused by chemical, genetic, and environmental factors. Examples: anxiety, bipolar disorder, dementia, schizophrenia.

The etiology (origins) of some ailments, such as chronic fatigue syndrome, fibromyalgia, and irritable bowel syndrome, has not yet been clarified. It is possible that two or more factors are responsible for each of these diseases or for its progression, as is true for many other diseases. For instance, when a person who smokes and is a heavy drinker develops throat cancer, it is probable that the cancer was caused by both tobacco and alcohol. A study in India reported in 2003 found that smokers are four times as likely as nonsmokers to die of tuberculosis.

The most common disease is cardiovascular disease. The World Health Organization (W.H.O.) estimated that 17.5 million people died from cardiovascular disease in 2005, representing approximately 20 percent of all global deaths. In the U.S., cardiovascular disease accounts for about 36 percent of all deaths.

Some diseases, such as bone cancers, tuberculosis, and stomach ulcers, have plagued humans since prehistoric times. Others are new. West Nile virus, spread by mosquitoes, was unknown in the United States prior to 1999. By

Discovery Dates and Effects of Human Pathogens

Year	Pathogen	Disease
1975	Human parvovirus B19	*Erythema infectiosum* (fifth disease), chronic hemolytic anemias
1976	Cryptosporidium parvum	Acute and chronic diarrhea
1977	Ebola virus	Ebola hemorrhagic fever
1977	Legionella pneumophilia	Legionnaire's disease
1977	Hantaan virus	Hemorrhagic fever with renal syndrome
1977	Campylobacter jejuni	Enteric diseases
1980	Human T-lymphotropic virus 1 (HTLV-1)	T-cell lymphoma-leukemia
1981	Toxin-producing strains of *Staphylococcus aureus*	Toxic shock syndrome
1982	Escherichia coli O157:H7	Hemorrhagic colitis; hemolytic uremic syndrome
1982	HTLV-II	Hairy cell leukemia
1982	Borrelia burgdorferi	Lyme disease
1983	Human immunodeficiency virus (HIV)	AIDS (acquired immune deficiency syndrome)
1983	Helicobacter pylori	Peptic ulcer disease
1988	Hepatitis E	Enterically transmitted non-A, non-B hepatitis
1992	Vibrio cholerae O139	Epidemic cholera
1992	Bartonella henselae	Cat-scratch disease (bacillary angiomatosis)
1995	Hepatitis G virus	Parenterally transmitted non-A, non-B hepatitis
1997	Avian influenza, type A (H5N1)	Influenza
2003	SARS virus	SARS (severe acute respiratory syndrome)

Leading Causes of Death, Worldwide, 2004[1]

	Number (ooo's)	Percent
World total deaths	**58,772**	**100.0%**
Communicable diseases	17,971	30.6
maternal/perinatal conditions; nutritional deficiencies		
Infectious and parasitic diseases	9,519	16.2
Diarrheal diseases	2,163	3.7
HIV/AIDS	2,040	3.5
Malaria	889	1.5
Childhood cluster diseases	847	1.4
Respiratory diseases	4,259	7.2
Respiratory infections	4,177	7.1
Noncommunicable conditions	35,017	59.6
Cardiovascular diseases	17,073	29.0
Cancers	7,424	12.6
Injuries	5,784	9.8
Intentional	1,642	2.8

Note: 1. Estimates. **Source:** World Health Organization, *The Global Burden of Disease, 2004.*

Leading Causes of Death, United States, 2009[1]

	Number	Death Rates per 100,000 Population
Deaths, all causes	**2,436,682**	**793.7**
Cardiovascular diseases	598,607	195.0
Cancer	568,668	185.2
Chronic lower respiratory disease	137,082	44.7
Cerebrovascular diseases	128,603	41.9
Accidents	117,176	38.2
Alzheimer's disease	78,889	25.7
Diabetes	68,504	22.3
Influenza and pneumonia	53,582	17.5
Kidney diseases	48,714	15.9
Suicide	36,547	11.9
Septicemia	35,587	11.6
Chronic liver diseases	30,444	9.9
Hypertension and hypertensive renal disease	25,651	8.4
Parkinson's disease	20,552	6.7
Homicide	16,591	5.4

Note: 1. Preliminary data based on estimate. **Source:** Center for Disease Control and Prevention.

2006 the virus had spread to every state except Alaska and Hawaii; it had caused 4,261 cases of disease, including 174 fatalities. An avian influenza ("bird flu") caused by the H5N1 virus was identified in 1997. It is highly contagious among birds, but usually only infects humans who have direct or close contact with infected poultry or virus-contaminated surfaces. By early 2007 there had been 291 laboratory-confirmed cases worldwide, with 172 deaths. Health officials fear that the H5N1 virus could mutate into a form that spreads easily from person to person. Should this occur, a worldwide flu pandemic, infecting and killing millions of people, could result.

In *World Health Report* 2002, W.H.O. identified the top 10 health risks in terms of the burden of disease they cause. These risks are responsible for more than one-third of all deaths worldwide. They are: underweight, unsafe sex, high blood pressure, tobacco consumption, alcohol consumption, unsafe water, sanitation and hygiene, iron deficiency, indoor smoke from solid fuels, high cholesterol, and obesity.

Common Diseases

AIDS Acquired immune deficiency disease (AIDS) is caused by human immunodeficiency virus (HIV). The disease was discovered in 1981 and the causative agent was identified in 1983. By 2009 an estimated 33.3 million people were infected worldwide and more than 25 million had died of the disease. Sub-Saharan Africa has been the region hardest hit by the HIV/AIDS pandemic; more than two-thirds of all people with HIV/AIDS are in this region. In the United States, more than 1 million people were living with HIV/AIDS, with an estimated 25 percent unaware of their infection.

HIV is spread through contact with infected body fluids such as blood and semen. Infected people may harbor the virus within their bodies for several years or even longer before developing symptoms of AIDS. Though symptomless, they can still infect others. Worldwide, most HIV transmission occurs during sexual relations between heterosexual partners. In the United States, the majority of transmission has been between homosexual partners. Transmission among drug addicts who share infected needles is another significant route of transmission in many countries.

In the body, HIV invades immune system cells called T-helper lymphocytes. The viruses reproduce in the cells and send out new viruses to attack additional T-helper lymphocytes. Eventually, the lymphocytes are destroyed, leaving the patient vulnerable to *Pneumocystis carinii* and other "opportunistic" pathogens.

No cure for AIDS is known. Researchers are working on preventative AIDS vaccines, but none are expected to be ready for market in the near future. Antiretroviral drug therapies introduced in the mid-1990's have been extremely effective in controlling AIDS progression for some patients. However, the medications are expensive; without comprehensive programs and sustained financial support, they are beyond the reach of the vast majority of the world's HIV-positive people.

Allergies   Allergies are overreactions of the immune system to foreign substances. Any substance that triggers an allergic reaction is called an allergen. Pollen, mold spores, dust mites, foods, alcohol, medications, chemicals, and animal dander are common allergens. Allergens cause the body to produce and release histamine and other "mediator" compounds. These compounds affect local tissues and organs, causing symptoms of the reaction.

Symptoms may include itchy or blistering skin, stuffy or runny nose, sneezing, shortness of breath, red or swollen eyes, headache, swelling of the lips or tongue, nausea, vomiting, or diarrhea. If the release of mediator compounds is sudden or extensive, the allergic reaction may be severe, resulting in anaphylactic shock. U.S. incidence of allergic diseases has grown dramatically in recent years. An estimated 60 million Americans suffer from allergies; more than 700 die each year due to allergies, about half of them due to drug allergies from penicillin.

Measures such as staying away from poison ivy and eliminating certain foods from the diet can prevent many problems. Medications such as antihistamines and corticosteroids are helpful in treating allergic reactions. Prompt injection of the hormone epinephrine (adrenaline) can stop anaphylactic shock, saving the person's life.

Alzheimer's disease   This progressive degenerative condition is characterized by forgetfulness in early stages and, as the disease progresses, increasingly severe debilitating symptoms that create demanding care-giving needs. As life expectancy has increased, so has the incidence of Alzheimer's disease. In the U.S., more than 5.1 million people, most of them elderly, are estimated to have the disease, and it causes about 79,000 deaths annually. These figures are expected to rise in the coming years.

The cause of Alzheimer's disease is unknown, but genetic abnormalities appear to play a role. There is a gradual degeneration of brain tissue. Areas involved with mem-ory are damaged first, then structures involved with emotion and control of behavior. No cure yet exists. Treatment consists of alleviating symptoms and providing long-term care. Death usually occurs 10 to 15 years following onset of the disease.

Amyotrophic lateral sclerosis (ALS)   ALS is a fatal disorder of the nervous system. Its cause is not known. It involves the progressive deterioration and death of the nerve cells that control the muscles. In its early stages, weakness in the limbs is the primary symptom. Gradually, cramping and twitching develop and the person has difficulty walking and carrying out everyday tasks. Weakening of muscles in the throat make speaking and swallowing difficult. When the diaphragm and chest muscles involved in breathing become affected, the person may require a ventilator. There is no cure for ALS; treatment consists of relieving symptoms and using physical therapy to slow muscle atrophy.

An estimated 30,000 Americans have ALS; about 50 percent die within three years of the first symptoms. ALS is also known as Lou Gehrig's disease because the New York Yankee star was one of its most famous victims.

Anthrax   This infectious disease is caused by the bacterium *Bacillus anthracis*. People contract it by inhaling bacterial spores, touching infected animals or animal parts (infected cattle hide, for example), or eating infected meat; the disease does not spread from one person to another.

Early symptoms vary depending on the source of infection. Anthrax bacteria that colonize the skin form a dark sore. Intestinal anthrax induces vomiting and abdominal pain. Inhaled spores are the most dangerous; they cause breathing difficulties, change into actively dividing cells, and pass quickly from the lungs into the lymph and blood. Swift diagnosis and treatment with antibiotics are critical in preventing death.

Arthritis   Arthritis is a generic term that encompasses more than 100 different diseases, all of which cause pain, stiffness, and usually swelling in the joints. According to the National Arthritis Foundation, arthritis affects nearly 46 million Americans and is the leading cause of physical disability. Although it affects people of all ages, it most commonly develops as people get older.

The causes of most types of arthritis are unknown, although certain factors—particularly excess weight and joint injuries caused by accidents or overuse—increase risk. Genetic factors can increase risk for some types of arthritis. The most common types of arthritis include osteoarthritis, rheumatoid arthritis, and gout.

Osteoarthritis is a degenerative disease that involves the breakdown of cartilage and bone, particularly in the fingers and weight-bearing joints such as the spine, hips, and knees. Treatments include regular exercise, medication, and if a joint is seriously deformed, surgery.

Rheumatoid arthritis, the most severe form of arthritis, is an *autoimmune disorder* in which the immune system attacks joint tissues, causing inflammation that can eventually lead to serious damage, including bone erosion and dislocated joints. In some cases, the heart, lungs, and eyes also are affected. Effects of the disease can be limited by regular exercise during periods of remission and by rest and anti-inflammatory medications during attacks. Juvenile rheumatoid arthritis is the most common type of arthritis in children. It often is mild, disappearing after several years, but serious cases can last a lifetime.

Gout results from an accumulation of uric acid in the blood, which leads to deposits of uric acid crystals in a joint. Typically, the first joint to be affected is the one in the big toe; other joints of the extremities—fingers, wrist, knee, and ankle—often become affected as well. Attacks, which last for days, can be extremely painful. Fortunately, gout generally can be successfully controlled. Uric acid is a waste product of the digestion of compounds called purines; avoiding alcohol, organ meats, legumes and other foods rich in purines prevents or reduces the severity of attacks. During attacks, anti-inflammatory and corticosteroid drugs counteract joint inflammation and pain.

Asthma   Some 20 million Americans are estimated to have asthma, an immune disorder that affects the muscles around the bronchial tubes leading to the lungs. In a reaction to certain stimuli, the muscles tighten, narrowing the airways and causing them to become inflamed and clogged. The person finds breathing difficult, and wheezes and coughs. In severe episodes, the person finds it almost impossible to breathe and requires immediate medical attention.

Most asthma attacks are caused by allergies to inhaled substances such as pollen, dust, and animal dander. Food allergies, infections, and emotional stress also can cause attacks. There is no cure for asthma, and proper management is essential. People with the disease can avoid substances and situations that act as triggers. They also can learn to recognize early warning signs and take medications to reduce underlying inflammation and prevent or relieve narrowing of the airways.

Autoimmune diseases   Several dozen known diseases result from immune system malfunctions that cause disease-fighting cells to attack the body's own tissues. What initiates such autoimmune diseases is usually not known. However, their incidence appears to be increasing, particularly in industrialized nations. In the United States, 14 million to 22 million people are believed to be affected. About twice as many women as men developed autoimmune diseases.

Symptoms of an autoimmune disease can vary widely, as can the disease's course. Some patients develop mild cases, while in others the disease causes severe damage and can be fatal. Mild symptoms may be treated with non-steroidal anti-inflammatory drugs (NSAIDs). Stronger anti-inflammatory compounds, including corticosteroids, are prescribed for severe symptoms. Common autoimmune diseases include:

Addison's disease Affects adrenal glands; causes a deficiency of adrenal hormones, which can be life threatening if not treated.

Crohn's disease Affects intestinal wall; causes chronic diarrhea, abdominal pain, rectal bleeding; increases risk of colon cancer.

Graves' disease Affects thyroid; most common cause of hyperthyroidism, or overactive thyroid.

Multiple sclerosis Affects brain, spinal cord; causes partial or complete paralysis and muscle tremors.

Myasthenia gravis Affects synapses between nerves and muscles, causing muscle weakness.

Psoriasis Affects skin, forming red patches covered with white scales.

Rheumatoid arthritis Affects connective tissue, joints; characterized by pain, stiffness, inflammation, swelling.

Systemic lupus erythematosus (lupus) Affects connective tissue, joints, kidneys, blood vessel walls, mucous membranes (such as those surrounding the lungs); causes joint pain, skin rashes, chest pain, enlarged lymph nodes.

Cancer   This group of diseases is characterized by the unrestrained growth of cells. Physicians describe the extent or spread of a cancer using a process called staging. This aids in determining the most appropriate treatment and in assessing the prognosis. One system widely used for many types of cancer classifies cancers into four stages. In this system, stage I is early stage cancer with no involvement of lymph nodes and no spread of the cancer from its original site (metastases); stage IV is advanced cancer, with both lymph node involvement and distant metastases.

Rise Seen in Number of Survivors of Cancer

By PAM BELLUCK

About one in every 20 adults in the United States has survived cancer, including nearly one-fifth of all people over 65, according to new federal data.

The numbers, released Thursday by the Centers for Disease Control and Prevention and the National Cancer Institute, indicated that the number of cancer survivors increased by about 20 percent in just six years, to 11.7 million in 2007, the latest year for which figures were analyzed, from 9.8 million in 2001. In 1971, the number of cancer survivors was three million.

"There's still a concept that cancer is a death sentence," said Dr. Thomas R. Frieden, director of the Centers for Disease Control. But, he said, "for many people with cancer there's a need for them and their families and caregivers to recognize that this is a stage. They can live a long and healthy life."

About 65 percent of cancer survivors have lived at least five years since receiving their diagnosis, 40 percent have lived 10 years or more, and nearly 10 percent have lived 25 years or longer.

The implications, Dr. Frieden said, are that many cancers are treatable and that it is just as important for people who have had cancer not to assume that they will necessarily die early.

"You might think, 'I've had cancer—I don't have to worry about eating right, quitting smoking, exercising,'" Dr. Frieden said. But people with cancer "need to be just as concerned about heart disease and other risks as they would otherwise," he said.

The study defined a survivor as anyone who ever received a diagnosis of cancer who was alive on Jan. 1, 2007, and it did not indicate if the person was cured, undergoing treatment, afflicted with a chronic cancer-related illness, or in the process of dying at that time.

And the numbers tell only a piece of the cancer story. Some cancers, like lung cancer, are aggressive and difficult to treat. And the death rate from cancer, an indicator that many health experts consider a more accurate measure of progress in fighting the disease, has stayed virtually the same as it was in 1950—about 200 deaths per 100,000 people a year, and about 1,000 deaths annually per 100,000 people over 65.

Dr. Frieden said the increase in cancer survivors was due to several factors, some of which varied by type of cancer. In some cases of breast cancer and colon cancer, for example, improved treatment and increased follow-up after treatment have helped increase survival. In others, like prostate cancer, an explosion in screening has identified many men with the disease, but the cancer is often so slow-growing that they would be unlikely to die from it. And other cancer diagnoses are simply the consequence of the country's aging population and improved care for other diseases—in other words, people are living long enough to develop cancer.

About a million more of the survivors were women than men, partly because women live longer than men, and partly because breast and cervical cancers are often diagnosed and treated at younger ages. About 22 percent of the survivors had breast cancer, about 19 percent had prostate cancer, and about 10 percent had colorectal cancer.

The study identified only the type of cancer first diagnosed in each person; additional tumors or cancer diagnoses were not recorded. Health authorities urged families and physicians to be aware of the health needs of cancer survivors. "Having cancer may be the first stage, really, in the rest of your life," Dr. Frieden said. "We need to continue to scale up" the services available for cancer survivors.

Cancer afflicts people of all ages and races, although about 77 percent of all cases are diagnosed at ages 55 and above. Cancers vary greatly in cause, symptoms, response to treatment, and possibility of cure.

W.H.O. estimated that there were 7.9 million cancer deaths worldwide in 2007. Deaths from cancer worldwide are projected to continue rising, with an estimated 12 million deaths in 2030. A healthy, non-smoking U.S. male has slightly less than a 1 in 2 lifetime risk of developing cancer; a female slightly more than 1 in 3.

Bladder cancer Smoking is the main risk factor for cancer of the urinary bladder; exposure to certain hazardous chemicals in the workplace also places people at risk. Warning signs include blood in the urine, pain during urination, and frequent urination. Early stage cancer can often be removed surgically. Additional treatment may include chemotherapy and radiation.

Breast cancer The most common, though not the deadliest, cancer among women is breast cancer. Risk factors include advancing age, obesity, physical inactivity, alcohol use, hormone replacement therapy, a family history of breast cancer, and inherited susceptibility genes, particularly mutated *BRCA1* or *BRCA2* genes. Early detection of the tumor—typically by breast self-examination or, more effectively, by mammography—is critical in improving a person's survival rate. Treatment options include removal of the tumor (lumpectomy) or the entire breast (mastectomy), radiation, chemotherapy, and hormone therapy.

Cervical cancer Sexually transmitted diseases (STDs), particularly genital warts, appear to be the major cause of cancer of the cervix (the lower opening of the uterus). Tobacco use and obesity also increase risk. The first noticeable symptom generally is abnormal bleeding or discharge from the vagina. Treatment may include surgical removal of the tumor, cyrotherapy (freezing the cancerous cells), radiation, and chemotherapy. A vaccine introduced in 2006 protects against four human papilloma viruses (HPV) that are a major cause of genital warts and cervical cancer. The vaccine is recommended for girls and women before they become sexually active.

Colorectal cancer Major factors that increase the risk of cancer of the rectum and colon include increasing age, inflammatory bowel disease, and familial history of colorectal cancer. Obesity, smoking, physical inactivity, alcohol consumption, and high-fat or low-fiber diets also increase risk. Symptoms include rectal bleeding, blood in the stool, and lower abdominal cramps. Because symptoms generally are not noticeable until the disease is advanced, people age 50 or more are advised to have periodic fecal occult blood tests and sigmoidoscopies or colonoscopies. Surgery is the most common treatment; chemotherapy and radiation may also be used.

Leukemia Leukemia affects bone marrow, the lymph system, and other tissues involved in forming white blood cells, resulting in excessive production of abnormal white blood cells. The cause is unknown, though exposure to viruses, radiation, and certain hazardous chemicals (benzene, for example) increase risk. Common symptoms include fatigue, fever, weight loss, swollen lymph nodes, a tendency to bleed, and pain in the bones and joint. Treatment options include chemotherapy, radiation, and bone marrow transplants.

Lung cancer The leading cause of cancer deaths in the United States and worldwide is lung cancer. The great majority of these deaths could be prevented if people did not use tobacco. Initial symptoms often are not noticeable until the lung cancer has grown for five to 10 years; they include chronic coughing, shortness of breath, wheezing, and chest or shoulder pain. Treatment may include surgical excision of part or all of the affected lung, radiation, and chemotherapy.

Lymphoma Cancers that develop in lymph tissue fall into two main categories: Hodgkin's disease and non-Hodgkin's lymphoma. Risk factors are unclear, though viruses or other infectious agents are believed to play a role in at least some cases. The first noticeable symptom of lymphoma usually is a swelling of lymph glands; fever, night sweats, itching, fatigue, and weight loss also are common symptoms. Treatment may involve chemotherapy, radiation, and, in advanced stages, bone marrow transplants.

Melanoma This is the deadliest type of skin cancer, and it may also occur in the eyes and in other areas where melanocytes (pigment-producing cells) are found. The major risk factors include certain inherited characteristics (light-colored skin, blond or red hair, blue eyes) and exposure to natural and artificial sunlight. Most often, the first noticeable sign of melanoma is a mole that has one or more ABCD characteristics: Asymmetry, Border irregularity, Color variation, and Diameter greater than that of a pencil. If caught early, before it has penetrated deeper levels of the skin or spread to other parts of the body, melanoma is very treatable. Treatment options include surgical excision of the melanoma and, if the cancer has spread, chemotherapy, radiation, and immunotherapy.

Ovarian cancer Major risk factors for cancer of the ovaries include advancing age, familial history of breast or ovarian cancer, and the use of fertility drugs and hormone replacement therapy. The most common symptom is an enlarged abdomen due to accumulation of fluid. Treatment options include surgical removal of the ovaries and other female sex organs, radiation, and chemotherapy.

Pancreatic cancer Risk factors for cancer of the pancreas include tobacco use, advancing age, and obesity; pancreatitis, diabetes, and cirrhosis may also be factors. Symptoms usually are not noticeable until the disease has metastasized. Surgery, chemotherapy, and radiation may help ease pain and prolong survival.

Prostate cancer Increasing age is a leading risk factor for cancer of the prostate gland. Other risk factors are a family history of the disease and ethnicity—African-American men have the world's highest incidence rates of prostate cancer. Noticeable symptoms generally develop after the disease has advanced, and include difficulty urinating, pain during urination, and pain in the lower back, pelvis, or upper thighs. Treatment may include surgery, hormone therapy, chemotherapy, and radiation.

Uterine cancer Cancer of the uterus (other than cervical cancer) typically begins in the lining, or endometrium. The major risk factor is exposure to the hormone estrogen; obesity, diabetes, and hypertension also increase risk. The first noticeable symptom generally is abnormal bleeding or discharge from the vagina. Treatment involves removal of the uterus and perhaps other female sex organs. If metastasis has occurred, radiation and chemotherapy may also be used.

Estimated New Cancer Cases and Deaths by Site and Sex, United States, 2010

Site	New cases			Deaths		
	Total	Male	Female	Total	Male	Female
All Sites	1,529,560	789,620	739,940	569,490	299,200	270,290
Skin[1]	74,010	42,610	31,400	11,790	7,910	3,880
Oral	36,540	25,420	11,120	7,880	5,430	2,450
Lung, bronchus, and other respiratory	222,520	116,750	105,770	157,300	86,220	71,080
Breast	209,060	1,970	207,090	40,230	390	39,840
Esophagus	16,640	13,130	3,510	14,500	11,650	2,850
Stomach	21,000	12,730	8,270	10,570	6,350	4,220
Small intestine	6,960	3,680	3,280	1,100	610	490
Colon, rectum, and anus	147,830	74,090	73,740	52,090	26,860	25,230
Liver, gall bladder, and bile passages	33,880	21,880	12,000	22,230	13,960	8,270
Pancreas	43,140	21,370	21,770	36,800	18,770	18,030
Other digestive organs	4,880	1,660	3,220	2,290	810	1,480
Urinary (bladder, kidney, etc.)	131,260	89,620	41,640	28,550	19,110	9,440
Leukemia	43,050	24,690	18,360	21,840	12,660	9,180
Lymphoma	74,030	40,050	33,980	21,530	11,450	10,080
Myeloma	20,180	11,170	9,010	10,650	5,760	4,890
Bone and joints	2,650	1,530	1,120	1,460	830	630
Endocrine system	46,930	11,890	35,040	2,570	1,140	1,430
Eye	2,480	1,240	1,240	230	120	110
Brain, other nervous system	22,020	11,980	10,040	13,140	7,420	5,720
Ovary	21,880	—	21,880	13,850	—	13,850
Uterus	55,670	—	55,670	12,160	—	12,160
Other genital, female	6,200	—	6,200	1,700	—	1,700
Prostate	217,730	217,730	—	32,050	32,050	—
Testis	8,480	8,480	—	350	350	—
Other genital, male	1,250	1,250	—	310	310	—
All other plus unspecified sites[2]	30,680	15,170	15,510	44,030	23,690	20,340

Note: Except for urinary bladder, figures for invasive cancer only. Carcinoma in situ of the female breast accounts for about 54,010 new cases annually and melanoma carcinoma in situ accounts for about 46,770 cases annually. 1. Melanoma and other nonepithelial skin cancers only; higher curable basal cell and squamous cell skin cancers account for more than one million new cases annually. 2. More deaths than cases suggest lack of specificity in recording underlying causes of death on death certificate. **Source:** American Cancer Society, *Cancer Facts & Figures* (2010).

The Hard Facts of Hypertension

By JANE E. BRODY

Over the course of their remaining lives, Americans now 55 or over face a 90 percent chance of developing high blood pressure, or hypertension, a major risk factor for heart attacks, strokes, congestive heart failure, circulatory failure, kidney disease, and loss of vision. This finding emerged from a 22-year follow-up study of 1,298 residents of Framingham, Mass., who were from 55 to 65 in 1976.

If applied to the whole population, the risk of developing hypertension represents a huge public health burden, in addition to the costs to the health of those affected. Hypertension is a primary or contributing cause of more than 10 percent of American deaths each year. Complicating the picture is more bad news: of the 50 million Americans with hypertension, only 27 percent are receiving treatment that restores blood pressure to normal.

What Is Normal? Despite three decades of efforts to educate physicians and the public, there is still profound ignorance about what is normal blood pressure. And many physicians seem reluctant to provide adequate treatment and guidance. Your blood pressure should be measured at every visit to a health professional, regardless of the reason for the visit.

In most cases, hypertension is a silent disease, producing either no symptoms or symptoms readily attributed to other causes—headaches, ringing in the ears, lightheadedness, fatigue. The only way to be sure your pressure is normal is to have it taken.

The test is fast, cheap, noninvasive and painless. A cuff is wrapped around your upper arm, inflated to temporarily stop blood flow and then slowly deflated as the examiner listens through a stethoscope to your blood flowing through an artery just above the elbow, recording the number when a pulse noise is first heard and the number when the noise stops.

The two numbers, expressed in millimeters of mercury, represent the force of blood pushing against the walls of your arteries when your heart pumps, the systolic pressure, and when your heart rests between beats, the diastolic pressure. The final reading is the systolic pressure (the higher number) over the diastolic. Hypertension is defined as a systolic blood pressure of 140 or more, a diastolic pressure of 90 or more, or both. Both numbers are important; when either is elevated, so is the risk of developing heart and blood vessel disorders. Contrary to the practice of some physicians, bringing only the diastolic pressure down to normal is not enough to protect against complications.

Further, when a person already has a disease affected by hypertension, like heart or kidney disease, current medical guidelines call for lowering blood pressure even more, well below the 140-over-90 cutoff.

Finally, Some Good News How people live can make a big difference in their risk of becoming hypertensive. Several factors have already proved effective in controlling blood pressure. Other minor influences that can help keep blood pressure under control are continually being discovered.

First, the main actors: diet, weight control and exercise. In a major collaborative study sponsored by the National Heart, Lung and Blood Institute, the so-called DASH diet rich in fruits, vegetables and low-fat dairy products and moderate in fat, saturated fat, red meat, sweets and sugar-containing drinks not only lowered blood pressure, it lowered blood levels of L.D.L. cholesterol and homocysteine, each increasing the risk of heart disease. In a second study, a reduction in dietary sodium combined with the DASH diet was even more effective in lowering blood pressure than DASH alone. The DASH diet can also help prevent another major contributor to hypertension: being overweight. The third main factor in preventing hypertension, regular physical activity, can also help control the second, being overweight. Even among those who already have hypertension, aerobic activities like brisk walking, jogging, lap-swimming and cycling at least five days a week can reduce blood pressure. If nondrug measures are not enough to bring high blood pressure under control, there are now numerous effective and safe drugs that can drastically reduce the risks associated with this condition.

For more information, see the booklet "High Blood Pressure: What You Should Know About It and What You Can Do to Help Your Doctor Treat It," available on the Web at www.hypertensionfoundation.org.

Cardiovascular disease Diseases of the heart and blood vessels kill more than 17 million people worldwide and account for 30 percent of the total number of deaths each year. Additional millions are disabled, frequently in their prime years. In the U.S., an estimated 79.4 million adults live with cardiovascular disease. Heart disease and stroke, the main cardiovascular diseases, account for one-third of all deaths in the nation.

Decades of research show that lifestyle, beginning in childhood, is the main cause of cardiovascular disease. The major risk factors are high blood pressure, tobacco use, poor dietary habits, especially the intake of saturated fat, elevated blood cholesterol, lack of physical activity, obesity, and diabetes.

Lifestyle changes are the first line of prevention and treatment of cardiovascular disease. Medical interventions range from drugs to surgery. For example, a bypass operation may be performed to reduce a person's risk of a heart attack. In this operation, a blood vessel from elsewhere in the body is used to reroute blood around a blocked coronary artery (one of two arteries that arise from the aorta and supply the tissues of the heart with blood).

Atherosclerosis This condition is characterized by the deposition of fatty material called plaque on the inner walls of the arteries. As plaque builds up, the arterial channel narrows and blood flow is reduced. Usually there are no noticeable symptoms until plaque buildup is significant. Indeed, the first symptoms may be those of a heart attack or stroke. Treatment options include lifestyle changes, drugs to lower blood pressure or cholesterol, and surgery.

Heart attack A heart attack, or coronary event, occurs when the blood supply to the heart muscles is blocked. An uncomfortable pressure, fullness, squeezing, or pain in the center of the chest that lasts for two minutes or more may be a sign of a heart attack. Sweating, dizziness, nausea, fainting, or shortness of breath may also occur.

Many people who have heart attacks go into sudden cardiac arrest, in which the heart stops beating and begins to fibrillate (quiver). Unless its rhythm is rapidly restored by a defibrillator, the patient's oxygen-starved brain will begin to die.

Heart failure In this disease, the heart's pumping power is weaker than normal. Blood moves through the heart and body sluggishly, and pressure in the heart increases. The muscles surrounding the chambers of the heart respond by stretching, which keeps the blood moving but gradually weakens the muscles. The kidneys may then cause the body to retain water and sodium, resulting in fluid buildup in arms, legs, feet, or other organs—a condition known as congestive heart failure. Important warning signs of heart failure include swollen feet and ankles, fatigue, dizziness, rapid or irregular heartbeats, and shortness of breath. Heart failure often is a progressive condition, worsening over time and ultimately fatal. Treatment options include lifestyle changes, medication, and surgery.

Hypertension The pressure of blood against the walls of arteries is recorded as two numbers—the systolic pressure (as the heart beats) over the diastolic pressure (as the heart relaxes between beats). Normal blood pressure is less than 120 milliliters of mercury systolic and less than 80 milliliters mercury diastolic.

About 74.5 million people in the United States age 20 and older have high blood pressure. If left untreated, high blood pressure can lead to strokes, heart attacks, and kidney failure. Conversely, controlling elevated blood pressure can cut strokes 35 to 40 percent and heart attacks 20 to 25 percent. Often, dietary and other lifestyle changes are sufficient to keep blood pressure controlled. If not, if may be necessary to add blood pressure medications such as diuretics, ACE inhibitors, beta blockers, or calcium channel blockers.

Stroke A stroke occurs when the blood supply to the brain is blocked, usually by a clot. The primary signal of a stroke is a sudden, temporary weakness or numbness of the face, arm, or leg on one side of the body. Other signals include temporary loss of speech, difficulty in speaking or understanding speech, temporary vision problems (particularly in one eye), unsteadiness, sudden severe headache, or unexplained dizziness.

Prompt medical attention may increase a person's chances of survival and limit the amount of disability. Treatment, involving drugs or surgery, is aimed at stopping the stroke and preventing another stroke.

Blood Pressure Guidelines for Adults*

Category	Systolic Pressure**		Diastolic Pressure**
Normal	Less than 120	and	Less than 80
Prehypertension	120 to 139	or	80 to 89
Stage 1 hypertension	140 to 159	or	90 to 99
Stage 2 hypertension	160 or greater	or	100 or greater

* Age 18 and older. **Millimeters of mercury. **Source:** National Heart, Lung and Blood Institute, 2003.

Cerebral palsy This disorder is characterized by damage to the areas of the brain that regulate movement. It results from damage to the brain before, during, or soon after birth. Poor oxygen supply to the brain, trauma, severe dehydration, and maternal infections such as rubella are among the factors that may result in cerebral palsy, but often the precise cause of the damage cannot be identified.

The most common form of the disorder is spastic cerebral palsy, in which the arm and leg muscles become stiff and weak. In the ataxic form, the sense of balance and depth perception are affected, resulting in coordination difficulties and unsteady movements. The choreoathetoid form is characterized by abrupt, jerky, spontaneous movements. Some individuals have symptoms of more than one of these forms, indicating damage to more than one area of the brain; this is called mixed cerebral palsy. The severity of cerebral palsy varies greatly. There is no cure. Drugs, surgery, and therapy are used to minimize its effects.

Cholera The bacterium *Vibrio cholerae* causes this infectious disease, which is typically spread via contaminated food and drinking water. Cholera is rare in the United States but common in Asia, Africa, and Latin America. For example, an epidemic in Latin America during the 1990's infected 1.3 million people, killing 12,000.

Symptoms include severe diarrhea and vomiting. Without treatment, the person becomes dehydrated, which can lead to kidney failure, shock, and death. Treatment consists of antibiotics and rapid replacement of fluids. Cholera vaccines are available, but they provide only limited protection; they are not available in the United States.

Common cold More than 200 different viruses, about one-third of them rhinoviruses, cause contagious respiratory illnesses known as the common cold. Generally, an infection is short-lived, lasting about a week. Symptoms include a runny nose, sore throat, sneezing, and occasional coughing. There are no proven preventative measures and no known cure; over-the-counter cold remedies may relieve symptoms.

Cold viruses often spread as infected individuals cough or sneeze, releasing virus-laden droplets in the air. People become infected by breathing in the viruses or touching contaminated items (furniture, clothing, and so on) and rubbing their contaminated hands against their mouth, nose, or eyes. Frequent hand washing and keeping one's hands away from the mouth, nose, and eyes—where the viruses thrive—help reduce one's risk of catching a cold.

Congenital problems Congenital disorders are defects or malformations that are present at birth. In many cases, the cause is unknown. However, some factors are associated with an increased chance of developing certain congenital disorders. For example, alcohol or drug abuse during pregnancy or maternal viral infection can increase the risk of congenital heart disease. Down syndrome may cause congenital malformations of the heart or gastrointestinal system.

Treatment is based on the severity of the problem. Mild problems may not require any treatment; others may be treated with medication or surgery.

Dengue fever This infectious disease is caused by four different dengue viruses and transmitted by certain *Aedes* mosquitoes. Infection with one type of virus produces immunity only to that type; a person may later become infected by another dengue type. Symptoms include fever, headache, vomiting, and severe joint and muscle pain. Symptoms typically disappear within a week, and the disease is rarely fatal. There is a form known as dengue hemorrhagic fever which is much more dangerous and causes bleeding as capillaries burst. No cure for the diseases have yet been developed; treatment is mostly palliative—making patients as comfortable as possible and encouraging them to drink large amounts of fluids.

Worldwide, an estimated 50–100 million cases of dengue fever and up to hundreds of thousands of cases of dengue hemorrhagic fever occur each year. Most cases are in tropical and subtropical regions, particularly Southeast Asia. Cases in the United States are usually brought in from other countries.

Diabetes Diabetes mellitus is a group of diseases characterized by high blood sugar levels that result from the body's inability to make or use insulin, a hormone produced by the pancreas that plays a vital role in metabolism. Symptoms include increased thirst and urination, hunger, weight loss, fatigue, and blurred vision. Diabetes can lead to debilitating and life-threatening complications including blindness, memory problems, kidney disease, heart disease, nerve damage, and amputations.

The most common type is type 2 diabetes, previously called adult-onset diabetes. It usually develops because the body fails to use insulin properly. It occurs in people, including children, who are overweight; other risk factors include high cholesterol, high blood pressure, ethnicity, and a family history of diabetes. Treatment includes a healthy diet, weight loss, and regular exercise. Many patients require daily insulin injections.

Vast Gene Study Yields Insight on Alzheimer's

By GINA KOLATA

The two largest studies of Alzheimer's disease have led to the discovery of no fewer than five genes that provide intriguing new clues to why the disease strikes and how it progresses. Researchers say the studies, which analyzed the genes of more than 50,000 people in the United States and Europe, leave little doubt that the five genes make the disease more likely in the elderly and have something important to reveal about the disease's process. They may also lead to ways to delay its onset or slow its progress. The discoveries double the number of genes known to be involved in Alzheimer's, to 10 from 5, giving scientists many new avenues to explore. The two studies were published in the journal *Nature Genetics* in April 2011.

For years, there have been unproven but persistent hints that cholesterol and inflammation are part of the disease process. People with high cholesterol are more likely to get the disease. Strokes and head injuries, which make Alzheimer's more likely, also cause brain inflammation. Now, some of the newly discovered genes appear to bolster this line of thought, because some are involved with cholesterol and others are linked to inflammation or the transport of molecules inside cells.

An estimated 5.4 million Americans have Alzheimer's disease, most of whom are elderly. According to the Alzheimer's Association, one in eight people over age 65 have the disease. Its annual cost to the nation is $183 billion.

By themselves, the genes are not nearly as important a factor as APOE, a gene discovered in 1995 that greatly increases risk for the disease: by 400 percent if a person inherits a copy from one parent, by 1,000 percent if from both parents. In contrast, each of the new genes increases risk by no more than 10 to 15 percent; for that reason, they will not be used to decide if a person is likely to develop Alzheimer's. APOE, which is involved in metabolizing cholesterol, "is in a class of its own," said Dr. Rudolph Tanzi, a neurology professor at Harvard Medical School and an author of one of the papers.

But researchers say that even a slight increase in risk helps them in understanding the disease and developing new therapies. And like APOE, some of the newly discovered genes appear to be involved with cholesterol.

Of the 10 genes now known to be associated with Alzheimer's in old age, four were found in the past few years and are confirmed by the new studies. APOE may have other roles in the disease, perhaps involved in clearing the brain of amyloids that pile up in plaques, the barnacle-like particles that dot the brain of Alzheimer's patients and are the one unique pathological feature of the disease.

It is known that one of the first signs of Alzheimer's disease is an accumulation of beta amyloid, or a-beta, a protein that forms plaques. And it is known that later in the disease, twisted and tangled proteins—tau—appear in dead and dying nerve cells. But what is not known is why a-beta starts to accrue, why the brains of people with Alzheimer's cannot get rid of its excess, or what is the link between amyloid and tau.

The American study got started about three years ago when Gerard D. Schellenberg, a pathology professor at the University of Pennsylvania, went to the National Institutes of Health with a complaint and a proposal. Individual research groups had been doing their own genome studies but not having much success, because no one center had enough subjects. So Dr. Schellenberg set out to gather all the data he could on Alzheimer's patients and on healthy people of the same ages. The idea was to compare one million positions on each person's genome to determine whether some genes were more common in those who had Alzheimer's. He got what he wanted: nearly every Alzheimer's center and Alzheimer's geneticist in the country cooperated. Dr. Schellenberg and his colleagues used the mass of genetic data to do an analysis and find the genes and then, using two different populations, to confirm that the same genes were conferring the risk. That helped assure the investigators that they were not looking at a chance association.

Type 1 diabetes, formerly called juvenile diabetes, usually develops in childhood. It is caused by the inability of the pancreas to produce insulin. Genetic predisposition combined with exposure to viruses are the main risk factors. Treatment consists of carefully monitored insulin replacement, typically via needles or a special pump.

A small percentage of pregnant women develop gestational diabetes as a result of changing hormonal levels. Blood sugars often return to normal after delivery, but almost half of the women who experience gestational diabetes develop type 2 diabetes later in life.

The World Diabetes Foundation reported in 2010 that 285 million people worldwide had diabetes, mostly Type 2, with almost 80 percent of the total in developing countries. The number is expected to grow to 438 million by 2030, nearly 8 percent of the adult population.

Diphtheria   The bacterium *Corynebacterium diphtheriae* causes this highly contagious infectious disease, which is spread mainly by coughing. Once a leading childhood disease, diphtheria is now rare in developed countries due to widespread vaccination.

Symptoms include sore throat, fever, coughing, and headache. As the disease progresses, tissues in respiratory passages may swell, making breathing difficult. The toxin produced by the bacteria may damage nerves and the heart muscle, leading to heart failure and death. Treatment consists of antibiotics to kill the bacteria and antibodies to neutralize the toxin.

Eating disorders   Several mental health disorders are characterized by insufficient or excessive consumption of foods. These disorders are much more prevalent among females, particularly teenage girls and young women, than among males, although recent evidence suggests higher incidence in males than previously realized.

People who starve themselves because of a pathological fear of weight gain suffer from anorexia nervosa. Excessive weight loss and malnutrition result, and anorectics have many symptoms associated with chronic starvation, including low blood pressure, slow heartbeat, constipation, osteoporosis, weakened immunity, and failure to menstruate. Treatment is often difficult, and death occurs in about 5 percent of cases.

Bulimia nervosa is an abnormal, rapid consumption of large amounts of food (bingeing) followed by self-induced vomiting or the use of laxatives to get rid of the food (purging). The person may experience rapid fluctuations in weight, but the weight generally remains close to normal. Other symptoms may include swollen salivary glands, erosion of tooth enamel, dehydration, and electrolyte imbalances. Treatment generally includes psychiatric counseling to break the binge-purge cycle.

Some Food-borne Bacteria That Can Cause Serious Illnesses

Bacteria	Serious illnesses that can result	Foods in which the bacteria may be found
Campylobacter	Arthritis; blood poisoning; Guillain-Barre syndrome (paralysis); chronic diarrhea; meningitis; inflammation of the heart, gallbladder, pancreas, and colon	Poultry, raw milk, meat
E. coli O157:H7	Kidney failure, neurologic disorders	Meat, especially ground beef; raw milk; produce
Listeria	Meningitis, blood poisoning, stillbirths	Soft cheese and other dairy products; meat, including poultry; seafood; fruits and vegetables
Salmonella	Arthritis, blood poisoning; inflammation of joints, heart, thyroid, pancreas, spleen, gallbladder, and colon	Meat, including poultry; eggs; dairy products; seafood; fruits and vegetables
Shigella	Kidney failure, neurologic disorders, pneumonia, blood poisoning, inflammation of the joints and spleen	Salads, milk and other dairy products, fruits and vegetables
Vibrio vulnificus	Blood poisoning	Seafood
Yersinia enterocolitica	Pneumonia; inflammation of the joints, vertebrae, lymphatic glands, liver, and spleen	Pork, dairy products

Binge eating disorder is characterized by eating abnormally large amounts of food, which leads to significant weight gain. People with this problem tend to be older than anorectics and bulimics, and their numbers are more evenly divided among men and women. Treatment consists of behavior therapy.

Emphysema This debilitating, often fatal disease is characterized by the enlargement and destruction of alveoli—the tiny air sacs that make up the lungs. This obstructs the exchange of oxygen and carbon dioxide with the blood, leading to coughing, breathing difficulties, rapid heartbeat, and—in advanced cases—mental problems. Smoking is the most important cause of emphysema. Air pollution also increases the risk.

Damage caused by emphysema cannot be reversed. However, regular exercise, medication, and giving up smoking can slow progression of the disease. A lung or heart/lung transplant may be used in certain severe cases.

Encephalitis Encephalitis is a viral inflammation of the brain. While some infections are mild, with few if any specific symptoms, others can be deadly. Early symptoms often include headaches, fever, and nausea. If the disease progresses, the person may suffer seizures, paralysis, mental confusion, and coma. Often the disease is accompanied by viral meningitis.

Mosquitoes carry some of the most dangerous types of encephalitis, including equine encephalitis, West Nile encephalitis, and St. Louis encephalitis. In other cases, encephalitis develops as a secondary complication of other viral diseases, including chickenpox, herpes, mumps, polio, and rubella. Treatment depends on the type and severity of the disease. It may include antiviral drugs and steroids to combat brain swelling.

Food-borne illnesses An estimated 76 million illnesses caused by food poisoning occur in the United States each year. Generally, the result is diarrhea and other temporary disorders of the digestive tract. But the illnesses can lead to more serious consequences, including about 325,000 hospitalizations and 5,000 deaths in the United States each year. People most at risk are pregnant women, children, those with compromised or suppressed immune systems, and the elderly.

Most food-related illnesses can be avoided—by washing fresh fruits and vegetables, cooking meat thoroughly, drinking only pasteurized milk, and common-sense hygiene.

Microbial contamination is the most common cause of food-borne illnesses. Pesticides, heavy metals, and other chemical agents that enter the food supply can also cause gastrointestinal, as well as neurologic and respiratory, symptoms.

(See also "Prion diseases" and "Worms and disease.")

Genetic diseases Hundreds of diseases are due wholly or in part to genetic errors—mutations in genes that result in physical, chemical, or mental abnormalities. Genes work in pairs; in many cases, one form of the gene is stronger, or dominant, while another form is weaker, or recessive. If an individual inherits a mutated dominant gene or two copies of a mutated recessive gene, the result may be an inherited disease or increased susceptibility to disease. For example, Tay-Sachs disease is caused by a single recessive gene; the recessive gene must be inherited from both parents for the disease to develop. Although genetic diseases usually are inherited from parents, they also can appear as a result of a new mutation in either the mother's egg or father's sperm.

Abnormal genes on the X chromosome cause x-linked diseases. A female inherits two X chromosomes, one from each parent. A male inherits an X chromosome from his mother and a Y chromosome from his father. If the male inherits an abnormal gene on the X chromosome, the gene will express itself. Hemophilia is a well-known example. The genes responsible are located on the X chromosome. A female must inherit two copies of a recessive form to develop hemophilia, but a male need inherit only one.

In some cases, genetic disease occurs because an individual receives an abnormal number of chromosomes (the structures on which genes are located). For example, in Klinefelter syndrome, a male is born with an extra X chromosome.

Often, multiple genes may be involved in any one disease. For example, scientists have identified nearly 400 cancer-related genes plus evidence that multiple genes may contribute to development of Parkinson's disease. Many disorders are believed to have a genetic component even though this has not yet been proven.

Hemorrhagic fevers These dangerous viral infections are characterized by bleeding (hemorrhaging). Each is commonly linked to a specific geographic region. For instance, outbreaks of Lassa fever have been limited to West Africa, while hantavirus pulmonary syndrome occurs mostly in the western United States. As a group, they are most common in tropical regions. The diseases spread to humans in various ways. Lassa fever and hantavirus are carried by rodents and spread in their droppings and saliva. Ebola, an exceptionally virulent African disease, is usually spread via the blood or secretions of an infected person.

The first symptoms of hemorrhagic fevers are flulike, including fever, headache, nausea, and fatigue. The symptoms may be mild and taper off after several days or become increasingly severe. Not all cases progress to hemorrhaging. Fatality rates vary with the disease. Treatment is mostly palliative; maintaining appropriate fluid balance, blood pressure, and oxygen status is often critical.

Hepatitis Inflammation of the liver, called hepatitis, can be caused by excessive alcohol use or the use of certain medications. However, hepatitis usually results from one of several unrelated viruses. In the United States, hepatitis viruses A, B, and C are most prevalent. Hepatitis E occurs mostly in tropical regions, causing large epidemics on the Indian subcontinent, in Central and Southeast Asia, in the Middle East, and in parts of Africa. Hepatitis can be acute (short-term) or chronic (long-term).

Hepatitis A is spread primarily by fecal contamination of food and water and through person-to-person contact. Inflammation lasts only a few weeks and may be asymptomatic, which makes its frequency difficult to estimate. People who have had the disease do not get it again. Vaccines can prevent the disease; since their introduction there has been an 84 percent decline in reported cases.

Hepatitis B is generally transmitted via contact with the blood of an infected person during sex, during birth, or through contaminated needles and syringes. It can cause a

Well-known Genetic Diseases

Disease	Cause	Symptoms
Cystic fibrosis	Mutated recessive gene	Glands produce abnormal secretions, resulting in lung inflammation, infection, and damage.
Down syndrome	Extra copy of chromosome 21	Physical abnormalities, mental retardation.
Fragile-X syndrome	Mutated recessive gene on X chromosome	Mental retardation.
Hemophilia	Mutated recessive gene on X chromosome	Blood does not clot properly; excessive bleeding from small wounds and increased susceptibility to bruising.
Huntington's disease	Mutated dominate gene	Deterioration of nerve cells in the brain, interfering with mental abilities and control of muscles.
Klinefelter syndrome	Extra copy of X chromosome in male	Problems with speaking and language skills.
Muscular dystrophy	Depends on the form; the two most common, Duchenne muscular dystrophy and Becker muscular dystrophy, are caused by a mutated recessive gene on the X chromosome.	Progressive weakening and deterioration of muscles.
Polycystic kidney disease	Depends on the form; the more common inherited form is caused by a mutated dominant gene.	Formation of numerous clusters of cysts on the kidneys reducing kidney function and resulting in kidney failure.
Sickle cell anemia	Mutated recessive gene	Misshapen ("sickled") red blood cells, causing insufficient oxygen delivery to cells.
Tay-Sachs disease	Mutated recessive gene	Inability to produce a vital enzyme, resulting in progressive damage to the nervous system.
Von Willebrand's disease	Mutated dominant gene	Abnormal blood clotting, with excessive bleeding from small wounds and increased susceptibility to bruising.
Wilson's disease	Mutated recessive gene	Inability to process copper, resulting in progressive damage to the liver and other organs

chronic infection leading to cirrhosis of the liver, liver cancer, liver failure, and death. A vaccine is available, and medical groups recommend that all newborns be vaccinated. W.H.O. estimates that more than 350 million people worldwide are chronically infected with hepatitis B.

Hepatitis C is spread through exposure to infected body fluids. Major risks include unprotected sex and sharing contaminated needles. No vaccine is available. W.H.O. estimates that 170 million people are chronic carriers. In the United States, hepatitis C is the leading cause of chronic liver disease and the main reason for liver transplants.

Influenza   Several types of viruses cause this highly contagious disease, commonly called the flu. The viruses are spread from one person to another via airborne droplets released during coughing and sneezing. They lodge in the lungs and breathing passages, causing fever, chills, sore throat, coughing, headache, fatigue, and weakness. Most symptoms subside in several days, but complications, particularly pneumonia, can occur. Treatment consists of bed rest and plenty of fluids; antiviral drugs may be prescribed.

Vaccination to avoid infection is strongly recommended for children age 6 months to 5 years; people age 50 and older; people with heart disease, diabetes, or immune system problems; residents of nursing homes; family members and caregivers of such individuals; and health care workers. Unfortunately, the flu vaccine only protects against certain viral strains; evolution of a new strain can result in a worldwide epidemic. One of the worst such epidemics, the 1917–18 "Spanish flu," killed some 20 million people. An even deadlier epidemic is feared if the virulent H5N1 avian influenza virus mutates into a form able to spread easily among humans.

Leprosy (Hansen's disease)   Known since ancient times, leprosy is a chronic disease caused by the bacterium *Mycobacterium leprae*. Once widespread, the number of infected people has declined rapidly since the early 1990's. According to WHO, improved diagnosis and treatment sharply reduced the number of leprosy cases in recent years, to about 212,000 at the beginning of 2010. However, as many as 2 million people were disabled due to past and present leprosy. Of the approximately 100 new cases of leprosy identified in the United States each year, the vast majority develop among immigrants who acquired the disease in their home countries.

Although infectious, leprosy is not very contagious. In most people, the immune system easily fights off the bacteria. Leprosy primarily damages the skin, peripheral nerves, eyes, and mucous membrane of the upper respiratory system, resulting in numbness, muscle weakness, blindness, and internal damage to the nose. Left untreated it can cause permanent disfigurement, especially of the face, hands, and feet, which historically cause people to fear the afflicted and expel them from society. Today, the disease is easy to treat with a combination of antibiotics.

Lyme disease   Named after Lyme, Connecticut, where it was first reported, Lyme disease is caused by the spirochete bacterium *Borrelia burgdorferi*. It is transmitted to humans through the bite of ticks, including the deer tick *Ixodes dammini*. Its symptoms often mimic those of other diseases, and may include pain, diarrhea, nausea, swollen glands, difficulty swallowing, and coughing. A rash may appear several days after infection; the hallmark of Lyme disease is a bull's-eye rash—a round ring with a central clearing. As the disease advances, it may produce a painful joint condition known as Lyme arthritis.

Prevention includes performing tick checks after walking in woods and other areas infested with ticks. Vaccines are available, but they are not completely effective. Antibiotics usually cure the illness.

Malaria   This infectious disease is caused by single-celled *Plasmodium* protists, including *P. falciparum*, *P. vivax*, *P. malariae*, and *P. ovale*. The parasites are usually transmitted from infected to noninfected people via the bite of female *Anopheles* mosquitoes; about 60 species of *Anopheles* can serve as vectors. The parasites take up residence in the victim's red blood cells.

The disease is characterized by episodes of chills and fever followed by profuse sweating; shaking and fatigue are other common symptoms. Repeated bouts can result in severe anemia, dehydration, and death. Infants, children, and pregnant women are at greatest risk of severe illness and death.

Treatment with chloroquine or other drugs that kill the *Plasmodium* has become more difficult in recent years. The parasites have become resistant to the drugs, and the *Anopheles* mosquitoes have become resistant to insecticides. Several candidate vaccines are being developed and show promise in early trials.

Malaria is most common in tropical and subtropical lands, particularly sub-Saharan Africa and Southeast Asia. It is both a cause of poverty and a result of poverty. Each year, between 350 million and 500 million acute cases are diagnosed and at least 1 million people, mostly African children younger than 5 years old, die of the disease. Almost all of the approximately 1,000 Americans who contract malaria each year get the disease while traveling abroad.

Measles (rubeola) An itchy rash consisting of small, reddish raised spots characterizes this highly contagious viral disease. Measles epidemics were once common, afflicting thousands of people, particularly young children, annually. Since the 1960's vaccination has greatly reduced its incidence, to 100 or fewer cases a year in the United States. People who contract measles develop a natural immunity to the disease.

Initial symptoms include fever, coughing, a runny nose, and red eyes. Several days later the rash begins, usually on the face and neck and then spreading to the trunk and limbs. The rash typically fades in about a week. Treatment is palliative, keeping the patient comfortable while his or her immune system combats the virus.

In some cases, secondary bacterial infections or viral encephalitis develop. As a result, measles is sometimes, though rarely, fatal.

Meningitis This is an inflammation of the membranes (called meninges) that envelop the brain and spinal cord. It can result from a broad variety of bacterial, viral, fungal, and protozoan infections, including AIDS, brucellosis, cat-scratch disease, chickenpox, herpes, Lyme disease, malaria, mumps, rubella, syphilis, toxoplasmosis, trichinosis, and tuberculosis. The viruses that cause encephalitis can also infect the meninges.

Early symptoms include headache if the meninges around the brain are infected, and back pain if the spinal cord is infected. If the disease progresses, the patient may experience fever, vomiting, confusion, paralysis, and coma. Treatment depends on the causative agent and disease severity; it may include antibiotics (bacterial meningitis) or other medications.

Meningitis can also have noninfectious causes: brain disorders (cancer, multiple sclerosis, stroke), medications (including nonsteroidal anti-inflammatory drugs such as ibuprofen and naproxen), lead poisoning, and adverse reactions to antibiotics, chemotherapy, and certain vaccines. These cases usually are mild and do not require treatment.

Mental illness Among the commonest illnesses are those characterized by impaired psychological functioning and a significantly decreased ability to cope with emotions, thinking, and other basics of everyday life. According to the National Institute of Mental Health, four of the 10 leading causes of disability in the United States and other developed countries are mental disorders: major depression, bipolar disorder, schizophrenia, and obsessive-compulsive disorder. The institute has indicated that an estimated 22 percent of Americans age 18 and older—more than 44 million people—suffer from a diagnosable mental disorder in a given year. (See also "Psychology.")

The causes of mental illness are gradually being identified. Some illnesses involve abnormal brain chemistry, such as an excess or deficiency of the neurotransmitter dopamine. Others develop after great trauma, such as that caused by child abuse, rape, or war. Genetics appears to play an important role and viruses are suspected of triggering or causing at least some problems.

Treatment generally involves medications, psychotherapy, or some combination of the two.

Anxiety disorders Excessive, chronic apprehension, tension, or uncertainty resulting from imagined or unreal threats are the hallmarks of anxiety disorders. The illnesses include general anxiety disorder, obsessive-compulsive disorder, panic disorder, phobias, and post-traumatic stress disorder.

Attention deficit/hyperactivity disorder (ADHD) ADHD, characterized by inattention and hyperactivity, is the most treated childhood-onset mental disorder in the United States, where it affects 3 to 5 percent of school-age children. Boys are two to three times more likely than girls to have ADHD. Many children with ADHD retain symptoms into adulthood. Additionally, many adults with attention-deficit disorder (ADD) probably had the illness when young but its symptoms weren't obvious or the problem wasn't correctly diagnosed.

Autism Evidence of this developmental disorder appears by the age of three. Autistic individuals have difficulty relating emotionally to other people, difficulty in communicating with others, and poor cognitive and language skills. They exhibit compulsive, ritualistic behavior and are easily upset by even slight changes in their surroundings or daily schedule.

Asperger's syndrome is a comparatively mild autistic disorder characterized by normal intelligence and language development but impaired social and non-verbal communications skills.

Depression Depression is marked by feelings of extreme sadness, hopelessness, and inadequacy. Individuals often experience disturbed sleep and weight change. Most people who commit suicide suffer from depression.

Bipolar disorder, formerly known as manic depression, is characterized by alternating periods of abnormally intense elation and depression, with episodes lasting a week or longer.

Dissociative disorders Individuals separate, or dissociate themselves from, their identity and other aspects of their personality. They may have multiple personalities, each with its own set of temperaments, responses, and even memories. Dissociation is believed to be a mechanism for coping with physical abuse or other severe trauma.

Schizophrenia A loss of contact with reality, irrational fears, delusions, hallucinations, bizarre behavior, and a restricted range of emotions characterize schizophrenia. Both genetic and environmental factors appear to be involved in causing the disorder, with severity varying significantly among individuals.

Oral diseases

A normal person's mouth harbors some 400 species of bacteria, which combine with saliva to form a sticky, colorless film called plaque. The plaque accumulates on teeth and gums, as does its hardened product, tartar. This leads to tooth decay and periodontal (gum) disease. Many of these problems can be prevented by good oral hygiene, including daily brushing and flossing as well as regular checkups in which the dentist or dental hygienist removes plaque. Proper diet and avoidance of tobacco also help keep teeth and gums healthy.

Periodontal disease is the most frequent cause of tooth loss in adults. It is progressive; the earlier it is treated, the less the damage. In its early form, called *gingivitis*, plaque builds up along the gum line; toxins released by the bacteria cause the gums to become red, swollen, and prone to bleeding. In the advanced stages of the disease, called *periodontitis*, the bacterial toxins deepen the openings between the gums and the roots of the teeth, and corrode the bone and ligament that anchor the teeth in the jaw.

In addition, periodontal disease can easily release bacteria into the bloodstream. This can exacerbate problems in other parts of the body. For instance, people with periodontal disease are more likely to suffer a stroke or fatal heart attack than those without periodontal disease.

Other common oral diseases include small sores called cankers and cold sores. Cankers, of unknown cause, form singly or in clusters and generally heal by themselves. Cold sores, caused by the *Herpes simplex* virus, are highly contagious; acyclovir ointment fights the virus and aspirin or ointment containing benzocaine may help relieve pain. Trench mouth is a painful inflammation of the gums caused by bacteria whose rapid growth is triggered by stress, poor diet, smoking, or other factors. Treatment options include careful cleaning of teeth, painkillers, and antibiotics.

Osteoporosis

This condition is characterized by a progressive decrease in bone density. The person may experience back pain, stooped posture, increased curvature of the spine, and an ever-greater likelihood of fractures. Aging, physical inactivity, poor nutrition, smoking, and genetics are major risk factors. The disease is particularly common in post-menopausal women, partly because women start out with lower bone mass. An estimated 44 million Americans have osteoporosis. Millions more have low bone mass and thus are at risk of developing the disease.

Prevention should begin in childhood, with a diet containing sufficient calcium and vitamin D, both critical for building strong bones. Weight-bearing and strength-building exercises are important throughout life. Calcium and vitamin D supplements help build and maintain bone mass. Certain medications, including alendronate and raloxifene, slow bone loss and may help increase bone density.

Parkinson's disease This degenerative disease, which usually begins between ages 45 and 65, is characterized by the gradual deterioration of brain cells that control muscles. The cells stop producing the chemical dopamine, which serves as a messenger to transmit impulses from one nerve cell to the next. As dopamine production is reduced, the person experiences tremors in a hand. Tremors may gradually appear in the other hand as well as the arms and legs. As the disease progresses, muscle stiffness, difficulty walking, stooped posture, reduced sense of smell, and decreased facial expression become noticeable. About 50 percent of the people develop dementia.

The cause of Parkinson's disease is unknown. Nor is there a known cure. Treatment is designed to slow progression and reduce the severity of tremors.

Parkinsonism is a disorder with similar characteristics except that its causes are known. These include viral encephalitis, head injury, brain tumors, use of the illicit drug MPTP, and certain medications that interfere with the action of dopamine. Treating the underlying problem may result in a cure.

Pneumonia Various bacteria, viruses, and fungi cause this inflammatory lung disease. Common symptoms include coughing that produces sputum, which may contain blood; fever; chills; and chest pain. Severity ranges from mild to life threatening. For example, so-called walking pneumonia is a mild form of bronchial pneumonia that infects a relatively small area of the bronchi. In contrast, double pneumonia involves inflammation of both lungs. More than 54,000 Americans die from pneumonia each year; worldwide it is a leading cause of death in young children.

Vaccines are available to prevent certain types of pneumonia and are recommended for people who are particularly susceptible to the disease, including individuals age 65 and older. Antibiotics are used to treat bacterial pneumonia but are not effective against viral pneumonia. Antifungal drugs are used to fight pneumonia caused by fungi.

In addition to microscopic organisms, pneumonia can be caused by inhaling food, liquids, or toxic chemicals. A common form of such aspiration pneumonia develops after a person inhales stomach acid during vomiting.

Poliomyelitis   "Polio" is an infectious disease caused by three types of polioviruses that attack the central nervous system. The great majority of people who are infected are asymptomatic or experience only mild flulike symptoms that disappear in a few days and require no medical intervention. They are, however, a potential threat for others because polioviruses are excreted in their feces.

A small percentage of people develop major polio, with weakness or paralysis developing in certain muscles. Permanent disability can result, though often may be prevented or limited through an intensive program of physical therapy, to rebuild and maintain strength and muscle tone.

Polio is highly contagious and was once widespread in the United States. Vaccines introduced beginning in 1955 eradicated polio in the United States and the rest of the Western Hemisphere and are now part of routine childhood immunizations. Since 1988 the World Health Organization has led a worldwide vaccination effort to eliminate polio completely. The number of cases has been reduced from an estimated 350,000 in 1988 to 1,300 in 2010.

Prion diseases   Misfolded proteins called prions appear to be the cause of a group of degenerative diseases of the central nervous system known as transmissible spongiform encephalopathies (TSEs). Prions are not organisms; they have no cell structure and no genetic material (DNA or RNA). They are infectious, however; prions can pass to humans and certain animals that eat the remains of infected organisms. The prions may incubate for years before beginning to destroy brain tissue, leaving parts of the brain porous and spongy and leading to dementia and loss of muscle control.

The best-known TSE is bovine spongiform encephalopathy (BSE)—so-called mad cow disease. In 1996 it was discovered that BSE can pass from infected meat to humans. The humans develop a disease similar to the TSE Creutzfeldt-Jakob disease (CJD), called variant CJD (vCJD). Other human TSEs are kuru, Gerstmann-Straussler syndrome, and fatal familiar insomnia. All are rare but fatal.

Rocky Mountain spotted fever   Caused by the bacterium *Rickettsia rickettsii* and spread by ticks, Rocky Mountain spotted fever causes high fever, headache, fatigue, and a rash that spreads across most of the body. Some 2,500 cases were reported in the United States in 2008. If treated early with antibiotics, a patient usually recovers without serious problems. But if treatment is delayed, complications may include damage to the heart, lungs, liver, and kidneys.

Rubella   Also known as German measles, rubella is a contagious viral disease that prior to the introduction of a vaccine in 1969 was very common among children. Its symptoms are mild and include low fever, swollen lymph nodes, and a rash. Treatment includes rest, fluids, and painkillers. Rubella infection poses serious problems for women in the early stages of pregnancy. The virus can pass through the placenta to the fetus, causing miscarriage, stillbirth, or permanent mental and physical disabilities in the infant.

Sexually transmitted diseases (STDs)   The United States has the highest rates of STDs in the industrialized world, some 50 to 100 times higher than in other industrial nations. An estimated 15.3 million new cases of STDs are reported each year in the United States, with roughly half of these incurable. STDs are difficult to track, in part because many infected people do not have symptoms and remain undiagnosed, though able to infect other individuals.

The most prevalent STD in the United States, infecting some 45 million people, is genital herpes, caused by a virus. It is followed by human papillomaviruses (HPV), which cause genital warts and cervical cancers; chlamydia, caused by a bacterium; trichomoniasis, caused by a protozoan; and gonorrhea, caused by a bacterium. Syphilis is another STD caused by a bacterium; the number of cases has declined significantly but the disease remains a significant problem in certain areas.

People who have STDs have a significantly increased risk of becoming infected with HIV, the virus that causes AIDS, in part because they may have open sores that provide the virus with an easy route of entry to the body.

Prevention—practicing safe sex—is of critical importance in controlling the spread of STDs. Most STD cases caused by bacteria can be treated with antibiotics, although strains of gonorrhea bacteria resistant to common antibiotics have increased greatly in recent years. There is no known cure for viral STDs but a vaccine that protects against four HPV types that together cause 70 percent of cervical cancers and 90 percent of genital warts, was introduced in 2006; it is recommended for girls and women before they become sexually active.

In addition to STDs, some other diseases can be sexually transmitted. These include amebiasis, giardiasis, hepatitis, salmonellosis, scabies, and shigellosis.

Shingles   This is a very common and intensely painful skin rash caused by the same varicella-zoster virus that causes chicken pox. After a case of chicken pox, the virus may reside in sensory nerves; it remains dormant for decades but may then emerge as shingles, usually in people age 50 or older whose immune system begins to weaken. The disease is treated with antiviral drugs such as *acyclovir*. A vaccine for shingles was introduced in 2006; in clinical trials it prevented shingles in about 50 percent of people age 60 and older.

Smallpox   This is a highly contagious, deadly disease caused by *Variola* viruses. Its symptoms include high fever, headache, muscle pain, and a rash that develops into oozing pustules that contain viruses able to infect others. People who recover have permanent scars from the pustules.

Smallpox once caused deadly epidemics. In the 20th century alone, experts estimate, it took up to a half billion lives. But by 1979, due to worldwide vaccination programs, smallpox had been eradicated in nature. By 2002 the only known stocks of *Variola* were kept in research laboratories in the United States and Russia, although there are fears that samples may have slipped into the hands of other countries or terrorists.

Tuberculosis (TB)   TB, which usually infects the lungs, is caused by the bacterium *Mycobacterium tuberculosis*. Except for young children, few people become ill soon after *M. tuberculosis* enters their body. Their immune system kills most of the bacteria. The rest of the bacteria are confined by white blood cells, not causing problems but remaining alive in a state of dormancy. In most cases, these bacteria do not cause any problems. But if a person's immune system is compromised by poor nutrition, unhealthy living conditions, aging, cancer, or certain infections, the bacteria may start to multiply; the person becomes sick and can spread the germs when he or she coughs or sneezes.

Left untreated, TB gradually destroys the lungs. Treatment consists of at least six months of daily antibiotic therapy; generally, this results in a complete cure. However, many patients stop taking the drugs after several weeks because their symptoms disappear. Not only do they risk developing active TB in the future, but they increase the likelihood that the TB they develop, and pass on to others, will be drug-resistant and difficult to treat. Since the mid-1990's, W.H.O. has recommended "directly observed treatment strategy" (DOTS), in which health care workers watch patients take their medications to ensure the antibiotics are taken as instructed.

Approximately 11,000 cases of TB are reported in the United States each year, more than half of them among foreign-born individuals. About 98 percent of the world's new TB cases occur in developing countries, and each year nearly 2 million people die from the disease. Incidence has surged in Africa, taking advantage of the vulnerability of people with HIV/AIDS.

Typhoid   Also known as enteric fever, typhoid is caused by the bacterium *Salmonella typhi*. It is spread via food or liquids contaminated with the feces and urine of infected people. The disease causes flulike symptoms, including headache, joint pain, and prolonged fever. If untreated, complications such as pneumonia and internal bleeding may occur. Treatment consists of antibiotics. Although rare in developed nations, it is estimated that each year there are 17 million typhoid cases worldwide, with 600,000 deaths. Multidrug resistant strains of *S. typhi* have been reported in parts of Asia, Latin America, and the Middle East, where the disease is common.

Vitamin-related diseases   Consuming too little or too much of a vitamin can interfere with cell building and other basic physiological processes, resulting in potentially fatal disease. For instance, a lack of biotin (a B vitamin) causes skin problems, nausea, and depression. Too much vitamin A can cause liver and nerve damage, dry skin, hair loss, blurred vision, and birth defects.

Vitamin deficiency diseases are most common in poor lands where proper nutrition is difficult to achieve. However, these diseases are not unknown in the United States and other developed countries. For instance, alcoholics are at high risk of vitamin B1 and folic acid deficiencies. Also, certain diseases such as cystic fibrosis and Crohn's disease interfere with absorption of some vitamins; this problem, like other vitamin deficiencies, can be resolved with vitamin supplements.

Worms and disease   A variety of parasitic worms can take up residence in the human body. They commonly enter through the skin or via contaminated food and water. Depending on the parasite and the number of worms present, an infected person may be asymptomatic, have mild symptoms, or experience life-threatening difficulties.

Guinea worms The worm *Dracunculus medinensis* causes guinea worm disease, or dracunculiasis. People become infected by drinking water contaminated with *Dracunculus* larvae. In the body, the worms grow to adults up to 3 feet (90 centimeters) long. The worms migrate to the surface of the body and a blister and ulceration develop on the skin where each worm emerges. The person typically experiences painful swelling, fever, nausea, and vomiting. Ulcers often become infected with bacteria, which causes disabling complications. A worm can be removed surgically or by slowly pulling it out—a process that can take months. No medication is available to prevent or treat infection.

People in poor communities in remote parts of Africa are most commonly affected by Guinea worm disease. An international effort to eradicate the disease was begun in 1986. By 2002, as a result of educating and encouraging people to make the behavioral changes necessary to stop disease transmission, the number of infected individuals was reduced by 98 percent, from 3.5 million to fewer than 3,200 reported cases in 2010.

Hookworms Almost 1 billion people who live in moist tropical and subtropical areas where sanitation is poor are infected with small roundworms of the genera *Necator* and *Ancylostoma*. Worm larvae present in the soil can penetrate the skin and travel to the intestines, where they mature; the adult worms produce huge numbers of eggs that are excreted in feces. Abdominal pain and diarrhea are common symptoms; however, many infected people are symptomless. Oral medications are available to treat the infection.

Pinworms Pinworm infection, or enterobiasis, is caused by certain roundworms that live in the intestine. Infections are common among children, who typically ingest the worms when sucking their thumbs or eating food contaminated with fecal matter. Itching in the anal or vaginal area is the most common symptom. Infections can be cured with medication, but children are often reinfected.

Schistosomiasis Also known as bilharziasis, *schistosomiasis* is caused by several species of the flatworm Schistosoma. People become infected by swimming or bathing in contaminated freshwater. Once established in a person's body, the worms produce great numbers of eggs, which elicit an immune system response. This eventually results in internal bleeding and irreversible tissue damage. Globally, an estimated 200 million people are infected, mainly in the tropics and subtropics. About 120 million show symptoms of schistosomiasis, with 20 million suffering severe consequences of the infection. Treatment consists of daily doses of an oral medication, either praziquantel or oxamniquine.

Tapeworms Several species of parasitic flatworms known as tapeworms can infect humans. The most common are the beef tapeworm, *Taenia saginata*; pork tapeworm, *Taenia solium*; and fish tapeworm, *Diphyllobothrium latum*. Infection—rare in North America but common in Asia, eastern Europe, and Latin America—can be prevented by prolonged freezing or thorough cooking of meat and fish. In the human body, the tapeworms attach themselves to the intestinal wall, where some species may attain lengths of 25 feet (7.6 meters) or more. Common symptoms include abdominal pain and diarrhea, but many infected people are symptomless. Treatment consists of praziquantel.

Trichinosis Larvae of the tiny roundworm *Trichinella spirali* live in the muscle tissue of many mammals. A person becomes infected by eating undercooked or poorly smoked meat, especially pork, from infected animals. The larvae mature into adult worms in the person's intestines. When the adult worms reproduce, new larvae move into the blood and to the muscles, where they form cysts. Swollen upper eyelids, muscle pains, fever, fatigue, and weakness are common symptoms. Treatment consists of antiparasitic medicines. The disease is rare in the United States.

Selected Vitamin-Deficiency Diseases

Disease	Cause	Major Symptoms
Beriberi	Vitamin B1 (thiamine) deficiency	Muscle cramps, nerve or heart abnormalities; in advanced cases, coma and death.
Night blindness	Vitamin A deficiency	Difficulty seeing in dim light; can cause blindness.
Pellagra	Niacin (a B vitamin) deficiency together with a deficiency of the amino acid tryptophan	Rash and other skin abnormalities, diarrhea, nausea; in advanced cases, mental problems and death.
Rickets	Vitamin D deficiency	Abnormal bone growth, weakened bones.
Scurvy	Vitamin C deficiency	Swollen gums, loose teeth, infection, irritability, bleeding, anemia.

Whipworms Whipworm infection, also known as trichuriasis, is caused by the small roundworm *Trichuris trichiura*. It is most common in subtropical and tropical regions where sanitation is poor; an estimated 800 million people are infected worldwide. Whipworm eggs are ingested orally, via contaminated food or unclean hands. The eggs develop into worms in the intestines. Most people have no noticeable symptoms but if a large number of worms are present, abdominal pain and diarrhea may occur. Treatment consists of antiparasitic medicines.

Yellow fever A virus transmitted by mosquito bites causes this infectious disease. Initial symptoms are flulike and disappear after a few days. In some cases, the fever returns, accompanied by nausea, vomiting, bleeding, jaundice, and delirium. There is no cure; treatment is palliative. However, a highly effective vaccine is available; people visiting tropical areas of Africa and Latin America where the disease is a problem should be vaccinated prior to travel.

Diagnostic Tests

Health care professionals rely on a broad variety of diagnostic tests to look for the presence of disease or injury, to pinpoint its cause, and to monitor its course. Diagnostic tests also help determine the appropriate treatment and, subsequently, the effectiveness of therapy. Some tests are invasive, requiring at least minor surgery, while others are noninvasive. Common diagnostic tests include:

Amniocentesis This common prenatal test usually performed between 15 and 20 weeks of pregnancy, involves insertion of a needle through the mother's abdomen and into the amniotic sac that surrounds the fetus. A sample of fluid, which contains fetal cells, is removed from the sac. The fetal cells are then tested for genetic defects such as Down syndrome. The procedure also can be used to identify the sex of the fetus. Chorionic villus sampling (CVS) provides similar information but can be performed earlier in the pregnancy.

Angiography In this procedure, a thin tube, or catheter, is passed through the skin into a blood vessel and a contrast dye is introduced into the bloodstream, allowing visualization of blood vessels. Angiography is commonly used to examine the coronary arteries of the heart and arteries that carry blood to the brain. It also is used to view blood vessels in the lungs, liver, kidney, spleen, and legs.

Biopsy In a biopsy, a tissue sample is extracted and examined microscopically. Depending on the site, the sample may be removed surgically or through a needle. Biopsies are performed to look for abnormal cells damaged by injury or disease. Biopsy is a standard procedure for confirming a diagnosis of cancer.

Blood tests Numerous laboratory tests can be performed on blood. Which tests are performed depends on what the physician wishes to check. For example, enzyme-linked immunosorbent assay (ELISA) looks for the presence of antibodies to HIV in the blood; positive results indicate that the person is infected with HIV, the virus that causes AIDS. For the most common blood tests, such as those for cholesterol levels and red blood cell count, laboratories establish a so-called normal result range. Typically, 95 percent of healthy patients fall within a laboratory's normal range. This means that 5 percent of healthy patients fall outside the normal range. Results may also be outside the normal range for non-illness-related factors such as age, dietary habits, physical activity, pregnancy, use of prescription and nonprescription drugs, and alcohol intake. It is therefore critical that the physician carefully evaluate results.

Bone density tests These imaging techniques are used to measure bone density—an important aid in detecting osteoporosis, a disease characterized by brittle, easily fractured bones. The best-known test is dual-energy x-ray absorptiometry (DEXA), which uses photons given off by x-rays to measure photon absorption by the bone. The more radiation absorbed, the denser the bone.

Bone scan In this imaging technique, a radioisotope (radioactive material) that concentrates in bones is injected into the patient's bloodstream. After an hour or more, during which the bones pick up the radioisotope, special equipment is used to detect radiation emissions and translate them into images. These bone scans can be used to detect abnormalities such as stress fractures, arthritis, tumors, and infection (osteomyelitis).

Colonoscopy This endoscopic procedure allows examination of the interior of the entire large intestine and sometimes the lower part of the small intestine. A thin, flexible tube is passed through the anus and into the large intestine. Colonoscopy is commonly used to screen

Common Blood Tests

Substance	Test Description	Result Indications
Blood Urea Nitrogen (BUN)	Measures the concentration of nitrogen in the form of urea in the blood; used to evaluate the rate at which blood is filtered across blood vessels in the kidney.	Elevated levels may indicate kidney dysfunction.
Cholesterol: high density lipoprotein (HDL)	Measures "good" cholesterol: HDL helps prevent cholesterol buildup in arteries.	Elevated levels may counteract the negative effects of high LDL levels.
Cholesterol: low density lipoprotein (LDL)	Measures "bad" cholesterol: LDL is the primary source of cholesterol buildup and blockage in arteries.	Elevated levels are a major risk factor for cardiovascular disease.
Cholesterol, total	Measures blood levels of cholesterol, a fatlike substance found in all cells. Total blood cholesterol is the sum of HDL and LDL.	Elevated levels suggest an increased risk of cardiovascular disease.
C-reactive protein	Measures the amount of a protein linked to artery disease.	The lower the level the better; elevated levels are associated with increased risk of heart attack or stroke.
Creatinine	Measures the amount of creatinine, a waste product of muscle breakdown that is excreted by the kidneys.	Elevated levels, especially accompanied by high BUN levels, may indicate renal failure or other kidney problems, dehydration, or hyperthyroidism.
Glucose	Measures the level of sugar in the blood.	Elevated levels are associated with diabetes, medications such as steroids, and eating before the test.
Hemoglobin (Hgb)	Measures the amount of oxygen-carrying hemoglobin contained within the red blood cells (RBCs).	Low levels suggest anemia, which can be due to a variety of causes. High Hgb may indicate lung disease or excessive production of RBCs; living at high altitudes elevates Hgb.
Iron	Measure blood levels of iron. Iron is essential for the formation of red blood cells.	Abnormal results may indicate bleeding, anemia, malabsorption, malnutrition, liver disease, cancer, infection, or other problems.
Platelets (PLT)	Estimates the number of platelets (cell fragments critical in initiating blood clotting).	Elevated levels may indicate bleeding or excessive production by the bone marrow. Low levels may result from acute blood loss, infections, bone marrow failure, or usage of certain drugs.
Potassium	Measures blood levels of potassium. Potassium regulates muscle activity, including contraction of heart muscles.	Abnormal levels may indicate kidney disease.
Prothrombin time (PT), Activated partial thromboplastin time (APTT)	Measure the time needed for a clot to form after certain reagents are added to the blood sample.	Abnormalities may indicate problems with anticoagulant drug therapy.

Common Blood Tests (continued)

Substance	Test Description	Result Indications
Sodium	Measures the amount of sodium in the blood.	Elevated levels may result from dehydration, diabetes, or excessive salt intake. Low levels may result from heart or kidney dysfunction, use of diuretic or diabetes drugs, vomiting, or diarrhea.
Thyroid hormones	Measure the blood levels of thyroxine (T4) and triiodothyronine (T3), hormones that regulate body metabolism.	Elevated levels suggest an underactive thyroid; low levels suggest an overactive thyroid.
Triglycerides	Measures triglcerides, a form of fat carried in the blood on very-low density lipoprotein (VLDL).	Elevated triglycerides, usually accompanied by low HDL cholesterol levels, may be associated with heart disease and pancreatitis.
Uric acid	Measures the blood levels of uric acid, a breakdown product of building blocks of DNA and RNA.	Elevated levels are associated with gout, kidney problems, and the use of certain diuretics.
White blood cells (WBC)	Measures the number of white blood cells in a unit of blood. A WBC differential count measures the different types of white blood cells (lymphocytes, monocytes, and so on).	A high WBC may be a sign of infection. A low WBC may indicate bone marrow disease or an enlarged spleen.

for colon cancer and to detect polyps, infectious bowel disease, and other abnormalities. (Most polyps found during colonoscopy can be completely removed during the procedure.) Colonoscopy can also be done to obtain tissue samples for biopsies or stool samples for microscopic examination. A related endoscopic procedure is **sigmoidoscopy**, in which the lower 10 to 12 inches (25–30 centimeters) of the large intestine are inspected.

CT   Computer tomography is an imaging technique that uses X rays to take pictures—tomograms or, more commonly, CAT scans—of the body. The pictures are reconfigured by a computer to produce 3-D images. CT is particularly helpful in locating tumors, organ injuries, abscesses, and fluid accumulation.

Culture   To identify bacteria or other disease-causing agents, samples of blood or other fluids or tissues are placed in laboratory dishes containing special culture media that encourage the growth of microorganisms. For example, if cholera is suspected, a stool sample or a swab from the patient's rectum is cultured. The diagnosis is confirmed by isolation of the organism *Vibrio cholerae* from the culture.

Electrocardiogram   For an ECG, small metal sensors are placed on the skin to record the electrical activity of the heart. The information is transmitted to a machine that creates a graph of the data. ECGs are used to diagnose heart attacks and other heart problems, to detect noncardiac problems such as potassium deficit, to monitor patients recovering from heart problems, to determine the effectiveness of pacemakers and certain heart medications, and in exercise stress tests to determine a person's fitness for strenuous exercise. An echocardiogram is another test used for many of the same purposes. In this test, sound waves emitted from a device placed on the chest bounce off the heart; the echoes are then converted into images.

Electromyogram   In electromyography, small needle sensors, or electrodes, are inserted into a selected muscle; they record the electrical activity of the muscle at rest and when contracting. The data are displayed on a screen or printed as a graphic record (electromyogram, or EMG) for study. Test results aid in diagnosing muscular, nerve, and neuromuscular diseases, including muscular dystrophy, amyotrophic lateral sclerosis, and myasthenia gravis.

Endoscopy An *endoscope* consists of a miniaturized camera mounted on a thin tube; the tube is inserted into the body to inspect the interior surface of a joint or other body part. High-definition technology may be used to improve clarity and visibility. Instruments may be passed through the tube to obtain fluid or tissues samples for laboratory examination. In some tests, the tube is inserted through a natural opening in the body. For instance, in a cystoscopy an endoscope called a cystoscope is passed through the urethra and into the urinary bladder. In other cases, endoscopy requires minor surgery. In arthroscopy, for example, an arthroscope is inserted through a small incision into a knee or other joint. See also *Colonoscopy*.

Fecal occult blood test In this test, samples of a person's stool (feces) are examined microscopically and chemically to detect occult blood ("hidden" blood not visible to the naked eye). The test detects bleeding in the digestive tract, which may be caused by a variety of disorders such as hemorrhoids, ulcerative colitis, inflammatory bowel disease, and cancer. It is recommended that all individuals age 50 or older have the test annually, to screen the colon and rectum for premalignant growths and cancer.

Imaging Production of an image using X rays, sound waves or other signals. These techniques enable physicians to obtain highly detailed views of internal organs without surgery. (See "Bone density tests," "Bone scan," "CT," "MRI," "Ultrasound," and "X rays.")

Mammogram Images of the internal tissues of the breasts (mammary glands) are produced by passing low-dose X rays through the breasts. Abnormalities show up as masses, shadows, and other distortions. The test is used to detect benign and malignant tumors and to monitor breast cancer patients during and following treatment. Women age 50 and older are urged to have a mammogram every year. A newer test is digital mammography, which records the X rays on digital film that can then be manipulated for more precise study of the images.

MRI Magnetic resonance imaging uses a combination of a strong magnetic field and radio waves to measure the distribution and chemical bonds of the protons in the body's hydrogen atoms. A computer translates measurements into 3-D images. MRI is frequently used to view the brain and other soft tissues.

Myelogram The spinal column can by studied by injecting a dye into the cerebrospinal fluid that surrounds the spinal cord. X rays are used to track the flow of the dye and to identify abnormalities, including tumors, arthritic bone spurs, and herniated disks.

Pap smear For a Papanicolaou (Pap) test, a small sample of cells is scraped from the female patient's cervix. The cells are examined microscopically for signs of cancer or inflammation. Women age 21 and older are urged to have regular Pap smears.

PSA test The prostate-specific antigen (PSA) test is a screening test for prostate cancer. It measures the blood level of the protein PSA, which is made by the prostate. PSA level fluctuates naturally over time, and cancer is not the sole factor that can raise the level. It is recommended that males over age 50 have the PSA test annually.

Pulmonary function tests These measure the lungs' capacity to hold air and to inhale and exhale air. The patient is asked to do certain breathing exercises while breathing through a mouthpiece. The tests help diagnose and assess the severity of breathing ailments. They also are used to determine whether a patient has restrictive lung disease, which primarily interferes with breathing in, or obstructive lung disease, which primarily inhibits breathing out.

Scratch tests These tests are used to identify allergies—sensitivities to substances in the environment, called allergens. Scratches are made on the surface of the person's skin, and a small amount of a suspected allergen is applied. If the person is allergic to the substance, the skin usually reddens and swells within about 15 minutes. Alternate techniques include pricking the skin or injecting the allergen between layers of the skin.

Spinal tap Also called a lumbar puncture, this procedure involves inserting a thin needle into the spinal canal and removing a sample of cerebrospinal fluid for analysis. The test helps diagnose disorders of the brain and spinal cord, including infections, tumors, bleeding, and multiple sclerosis. Spinal taps are also used therapeutically, to introduce medication into the cerebrospinal fluid.

Ultrasound Ultrasound imaging, or sonography, beams high-frequency sound waves at the body's organs. The echoes that bounce back are translated into computer images. Because it doesn't use X rays, sonography is recommended for use on pregnant women. It is well suited for examining soft tissue, such as the gall bladder, liver, heart, and thyroid gland. Doppler ultrasound images blood flow in blood vessels, enabling the detection of blockages and aneurysms.

Upper GI series   Sometimes referred to as the barium swallow, the upper gastrointestinal series is used to examine the esophagus, stomach, and upper part of the small intestine. It detects structural abnormalities, inflammation, tumors, hiatal hernia, and other problems. The patient swallows a liquid containing barium sulfate, a dye that coats the interior of the gastrointestinal tract. X rays are used to view the flow of the barium sulfate.

Urinalysis   The chemical, physical, and microscopic analysis of urine often is a first step in diagnosing kidney disorders, urinary bladder infections, and certain metabolic diseases. For example, the presence of bacteria such as *Escherichia coli* or *Proteus vulgaris* signals a bladder infection (cystitis). Excessive glucose is a symptom of diabetes mellitus. Bilirubin—an orange-yellow pigment formed when red blood cells are broken down, and normally excreted in bile—suggests possible liver disease.

X-rays   X-ray pictures, or radiographs, are two-dimensional images commonly used to detect bone fractures and displacements, dental problems, and tumors in certain organs. They are the most widely used diagnostic imaging technique.

Medications

Prescription drugs ease pain, combat infections, control blood pressure, relieve allergy symptoms, and play numerous other important roles in health care. They make up the fastest-growing health-care expenditure in the United States. In 1980 the nation spent $12 billion on drugs. By 2006 the nation's pharmaceutical tab had risen to $274.9 billion, as retail pharmacies filled more than 3.2 billion prescriptions. An aging population and the introduction of new therapies for chronic conditions helped fuel the increasing demand for drugs. Additionally, newer drugs tended to be much costlier than older medications.

Side effects

Every medication has possible side effects. These can range from slight nausea or temporary drowsiness to kidney failure and other deadly conditions. The side effects can vary depending on the size of the dose and on the patient's genetic makeup, body size, age, and overall health. People with one medical problem may not be able to take medication designed to treat another medical problem. For example, the cholesterol reducer simvastatin (Zocor) can lead to kidney failure in people with severe infections.

Side effects are among the most common causes of hospitalization in the United States. To avoid or limit such problems, it is important that patients know the common side effects of any medication, including over-the-counter medications, that they are taking. Medications should be taken as directed, problems should be reported promptly to the physician, and expired drugs should be discarded.

Some drugs interact with foods, causing side effects or inhibiting the effectiveness of the drugs. For example, antidepressants known as MAO inhibitors can cause severe headaches and potentially fatal increases in blood pressure in people who consume foods high in tyramine (many cheeses, yogurt, cured meats, red wine, and so on).

Additionally, drugs taken during the same time period can interact with one another, sometimes in deadly fashion. For instance, certain blood pressure medications can dangerously increase levels of lithium in people taking lithium drugs to combat manic depression. Pain relievers such as ibuprofen can reduce the effectiveness of diuretics. Alcohol consumption increases the risk of seizures among people taking the antidepressant bupropion hyudrochloride (Wellbutrin). Thus it is also important that patients inform all their doctors about all prescription and over-the-counter medications they are taking, including herbal remedies and weight loss pills.

Commonly Prescribed Medications

A medication has a chemical name that describes its molecular structure, a generic (nonproprietary) name, and a brand (proprietary) name. In the following list, which is by no means inclusive, the generic name is followed by a brand name in parentheses.

Acne therapy Substances used to treat a common skin condition characterized by pimples and pus-filled pockets on the face and upper torso. Isotretinoin (Accutane), antibiotics such as tetracycline and doxycycline.

Analgesics Substances that relieve pain. Prescription analgesics include both narcotics, such as Oxycodone (OxyContin) and hydrocodone/APAP, and non-narcotics, such as Sumatriptan succinate (Imitrex Oral) and

Tramadol (Ultram). The most widely used over-the-counter analgesics are nonsteroidal anti-inflammatory drugs (NSAIDs), such as aspirin and ibuprofen.

Antianxiety medications Substances used to treat panic, phobias, and other anxiety disorders. Alprazolam (Xanax), clonazepam (Klonopin), diazepam (Valium).

Antiarthritics Substances used to reduce symptoms of osteoarthritis. Celecoxib (Celebrex), rofecoxib (Vioxx).

Antibiotics Substances that destroy or inhibit the growth of bacteria. Amoxicillin/clavulanae (Augmentin), Azithromycin (Zithromax), Ciprofloxacin (Cipro), Levofloxacin (Levaquin).

Antidepressants Substances used to treat depression. There are three types:

Selective serotonin reuptake inhibitors (SSRIs) Fluoxetine (Prozac), paroxetine (Paxil), sertraline (Zoloft), Citalopram (Celexa).

Tricyclic antidepressants Clomipramine (Norpramin, Pertofrane), imipramine (Tofranil).

Monoamine oxidase inhibitors (MAOIs) Bupropion HCL (Wellbutrin SR), Venlafaxine (Effexor XR), Isocarboxazid (Marplan), phenelzine sulfate (Nardil).

Antihistamines Substances that interfere with the action of histamines, which play a critical role in allergic reactions. Loratadine (Claritin), fexofenadine (Allegra), cetirizine (Zyrtec).

Antihypertensives Substances used to combat high blood pressure. There are four types:

Angiotensin-converting enzyme (ACE) inhibitors Benazepril (Lotensin), captopril (Capoten), enalapril maleate (Vasotec), lisinopril (Zestril).

Beta blockers Acebutolol (Sectral), metoprolol (Lopressor), penbutolol (Levatol).

Calcium channel blockers Amlodipine (Norvasc), diltiazem (Dilacor), verapamil (Verelan).

Diuretics Thiazides such as chlorothiazide (Diuril) and chlorthalidone (Thalitone), potassium-sparing diuretics such as amiloride (Midamor) and spironolactone (Aldactone).

Antimanic medications Substances that treat bipolar disorder. Gabapentin (Neurontin), divalproex sodium (Depakote), lithium citrate (Cibalith-S).

Antiplatelet medications Substances that destroy or interfere with blood platelets, to prevent excessive blood clotting and help prevent strokes caused by blood clots.

Clopidogrel (Plavix), ticlopidine (Ticlid), aspirin.

Antipsychotic Substances that alleviate the symptoms of schizophrenia and other psychotic states. Olanzapine (Zyprexa), quetiapine (Seroquel), risperidone (Risperdal), chlorpromazine (Thorazine).

Antiulcerants Substances that prevent or treat ulcers. Omepravole (Prilosec), Lansoprazole (Prevacid), Rabeprazole (Aciphex), Ranitidine (Zantac).

Asthma therapy Substances that prevent or treat asthma. Leukotriene modifiers such as montelukast sodium (Singulair), inhaled corticosteroids such as beclomethasone (Beclovent), beta-adrenergic agonists such as albuterol (Proventil), mast cell stabilizers such as cromolyn (Gastrocrom).

Bone density therapy Substances used to treat osteoporosis. Bisphosphonates such as alendronate (Fosamax), calcium and vitamin D supplements.

Bronchodilator Substances that relax and widen respiratory passages leading to the lungs, relieving wheezing and bronchial spasms. Albuterol (Proventil), salmeterol xinafoate (Serevent).

Cholesterol reducers Substances that lower cholesterol and trigylceride levels. Statins, including lovastatin, simvastatin (Zocor), pravastatin (Pravachol), and atorvastatin (Lipitor); fibric acid derivatives such as fenofibrate (TriCor); bile acid binders such as cholestyramine (Prevalite).

Contraceptives Medications that prevent fertilization of an egg by a sperm. Ethinyl estradiol (Ortho Tri-Cyclen).

Diabetes therapy Substances that lower blood sugar levels in people with type II diabetes. Metformin (Glucophage), pioglitazone (Actos), rosiglitazone maleate (Avandia).

Erythropoietins Substances that combat anemia by stimulating the bone marrow to produce red blood cells. Epoetin alfa (Epogen, Procrit).

Hormone therapy Substances used to treat endocrine gland disorders. For example, levothyroxine (Synthroid) is used to replace thyroid hormones in people with an underactive thyroid gland.

Proton pump inhibitors Substances that reduce gastric acid production in the stomach. Omeprazole (Prilosec), lansoprazole (Prevacid, Zoton), esomeprazole (Nexium), pantoprazole (Protonix), rabeprazole (Aciphex).

Sedatives Substances that calm or tranquilize, reducing anxiety and inducing sleep. Zolpidem (Ambien), temazepam (Restoril).

Sexual function therapy Substances used to treat impotence in men. Sildenafil citrate (Viagra), vardenafil HCl (Levitra).

Steroids Substances that treat inflammation by suppressing the immune system. For example, respiratory steroids such as fluticasone propionate (Flovent, Flonase) provide relief from allergy symptoms.

Immunization

When bacteria or viruses invade the body, they trigger a counterattack, or immune response. This response includes synthesizing antibody proteins that combine with antigen molecules on the surface of the invader, destroying the invader. Secondarily, the body forms long-lived "memory cells." If again exposed to the same antigen at a later time, the memory cells immediately go into action, releasing antibodies. This is the basis for immunity to certain infectious disease and the basis for immunization programs that vaccinate against diseases.

Vaccines consist of dead or weakened bacteria or viruses. When a person is inoculated with a vaccine for a specific disease, the vaccine stimulates the production of antibodies without producing the disease. Some vaccines provide lifelong immunity. In other cases, immunity can begin to fade over time, requiring booster shots. The three most widely recommended vaccines for adults are:

Tetanus, diphtheria (Td) vaccine To combat tetanus and diphtheria. One dose booster every 10 years.

Influenza vaccine To combat the flu. One dose annually for individuals age 50 and older. For younger adults, one dose annually for those with medical or exposure indications. Medical indicators include chronic cardiovascular and pulmonary conditions, certain chronic metabolic conditions, and women who will be in the second or third trimester of pregnancy during influenza season.

Pneumococcal vaccine To combat pneumonia and other pneumococcal bacteria. For people age 65 and older; people with chronic lung (excluding asthma), heart, liver, or kidney disorders; and people with illnesses such as diabetes, sickle cell disease, alcoholism, or HIV/AIDS. For most people, one dose provides lifetime protection.

Some people may need a booster shot after 5 years.

In 1998 a British doctor and his associates published a paper asserting that their research demonstrated a strong connection between a common childhood vaccine for measles, mumps, and rubella and of autism. Parents around the world were understandably alarmed and many decided not to have their children vaccinated, leaving them vulnerable to harmful illnesses.

In 2010, the C.D.C. reported that 40 percent of American parents with young children delayed or refused one or more of the 10 required vaccines for their child. After 12 years of intense research the medical community determined not only was the research poorly done it was, in the end, fraudulent.

Childhood and Adolescent Vaccines: Recommended Immunization Schedule, 2010

Age	Vaccines
Birth	Hepatitis B
2 months	Hepatitis B, polio, rotavirus, diphtheria, tetanus, pertussis (DTaP), haemophilus B (Hib), pneumonia and other pneumococcal bacteria (PCV)
4 months	Rotavirus, Polio, DTaP, Hib, PCV
6 months	Rotavirus, DTaP, Hib, PCV
6–18 months	Hepatitis B, polio
6 months–18 years	Influenza (yearly)
12–15 months	Hib; measles, mumps, rubella (MMR#1); chicken pox, PCV
12–23 months	Hepatitis A series
15–18 months	DTaP
4–6 years	Polio, DtaP, MMR#2, chicken pox
11–12 years	DTaP, human papillomavirus (HPV, 3 doses, females only), meningococcal (MCV4)

Note: It generally takes several doses of each vaccine for full protection. In some cases, there is a range of acceptable ages for vaccination. For example, the third dose of hepatitis B vaccine may be given between 6 and 18 months of age. Children who have not been vaccinated against Hepatitis B in infancy may begin the series during any childhood visit. For additional information, contact your physician. **Sources:** American Academy of Pediatrics; American Academy of Family Physicians; and U.S. Dept. of Health and Human Services, Centers for Disease Control and Prevention.

Really?

By ANAHAD O'CONNOR

Despite or perhaps because of the enormous amount of medical information now available on the Internet, everyone knows that medical myths and old wives' tales about symptoms, treatments, etc. still hold a prominent place in everyday conversation. So every week *The New York Times* runs a small column devoted to affirming the validity of these "theories" or, more frequently, debunking them. Below are a few examples:

THE CLAIM: Lying on your left side eases heartburn.

THE FACTS For people with chronic heartburn, restful sleep is no easy feat. Fall asleep in the wrong position, and acid slips into the esophagus, a recipe for agita and insomnia.

Doctors recommend sleeping on an incline, which allows gravity to keep the stomach's contents where they belong. But sleeping on your side can also make a difference—so long as you choose the correct side. Several studies have found that sleeping on the right side aggravates heartburn; sleeping on the left tends to calm it.

The reason is not entirely clear. One hypothesis holds that right-side sleeping relaxes the lower esophageal sphincter, between the stomach and the esophagus. Another holds that left-side sleeping keeps the junction between stomach and esophagus above the level of gastric acid.

In a study in *The Journal of Clinical Gastroenterology*, scientists recruited a group of healthy subjects and fed them high-fat meals on different days to induce heartburn. Immediately after the meals, the subjects spent four hours lying on one side or the other as devices measured their esophageal acidity. Ultimately, the researchers found that "the total amount of reflux time was significantly greater" when the subjects lay on their right side.

"In addition," they wrote, "average overall acid clearance was significantly prolonged with right side down."

In another study, this one in *The American Journal of Gastroenterology*, scientists fed a group of chronic heartburn patients a high-fat dinner and a bedtime snack, then measured reflux as they slept. The right-side sleepers had greater acid levels and longer "esophageal acid clearance." Other studies have had similar results.

THE BOTTOM LINE Lying on your right side seems to aggravate heartburn.

THE CLAIM: Humming can ease sinus problems.

THE FACTS Dealing with a cold is bad enough, but when it leads to a sinus infection, the misery can double. Some researchers have proposed a surprising remedy: channeling your inner Sinatra.

Sinus infections—which afflict more than 37 million Americans every year—generally occur when the lining of the sinuses becomes inflamed, trapping air and pus and other secretions, and leading to pain, headaches and congestion. Because the inflammation is often caused by upper-respiratory infections, people with asthma and allergies are more vulnerable than others to chronic sinusitis.

Keeping the sinuses healthy and infection-free requires ventilation—keeping air flowing smoothly between the sinus and nasal cavities. And what better way to keep air moving through the sinuses and nasal cavity than by humming a tune?

In a study in *The American Journal of Respiratory and Critical Care Medicine*, researchers examined this by comparing airflow in people when they hummed and when they quietly exhaled. Specifically, they looked to see if humming led to greater levels of exhaled nitric oxide, a gas produced in the sinuses. Ultimately, nitric oxides during humming rose 15-fold.

Another study a year later in *The European Respiratory Journal* found a similar effect: humming resulted in a large increase in nasal nitric oxide, "caused by a rapid gas exchange in the paranasal sinuses." Since reduced airflow plays a major role in sinus infections, the researchers suggested that daily periods of humming might help people lower their risk of chronic problems. But further study is needed, they said.

THE BOTTOM LINE Studies show that humming helps increase airflow between the sinus and nasal cavities, which could potentially help protect against sinus infections.

THE CLAIM: To reduce snoring, try sleeping on your side.

THE FACTS Chronic snoring can be more than a noisy nuisance. Up to three-quarters of nightly snorers also have sleep apnea, which causes breathing interruptions throughout the night. Sleep apnea raises the risk of heart disease, stroke and high blood pressure.

Snorers looking for a cure are often told to sleep on their sides, not on their backs, so that the base of the tongue will not collapse into the back of the throat, narrowing the airway and obstructing breathing. But for some snorers, changing sleep position may not make much of a difference.

Scientists say there are two types of snorers: those who snore only when they sleep on their backs, and those who do it regardless of their position. After sleep researchers in Israel examined more than 2,000 sleep apnea patients, for example, they found that 54 percent were "positional," meaning they snored only when asleep on their backs. The rest were "nonpositional."

Other studies have shown that weight plays a major role. In one large study, published in 1997, patients who snored or had breathing abnormalities only while sleeping on their backs were typically thinner, while their nonpositional counterparts usually were heavier. The latter group, wrote the authors, consequently suffered worse sleep and more daytime fatigue.

But that study also found that patients who were overweight saw reductions in the severity of their apnea when they lost weight. According to the National Sleep Foundation, in people who are overweight, slimming down is generally the best way to cure sleep apnea and end snoring for good.

THE BOTTOM LINE Sleeping on your side can help reduce snoring, though in people who are overweight, it may not make much difference without weight loss.

THE CLAIM: Eating local honey cures allergies.

THE FACTS Among allergy sufferers, there is a widespread belief that locally produced honey can alleviate symptoms—the idea being that the honey acts like a vaccine. Bees that jump from one flower to the next end up covered in pollen spores, which are then transferred to their honey. Eating that honey—just a spoonful a day—can build up immunity through gradual exposure to the local allergens that can make life so miserable for allergy sufferers.

Or at least that's the thinking behind it. But when University of Connecticut Health Center researchers did a test, they found that the honey had no such effect.

In the study, published in the *Annals of Allergy, Asthma and Immunology* in 2002, the scientists followed dozens of allergy sufferers through the springtime allergy season. The subjects were randomly split into three groups. One consumed a tablespoonful daily of locally collected, unpasteurized and unfiltered honey; another ate commercial honey; and a third was given a corn syrup placebo with synthetic honey flavoring.

After tracking the subjects' symptoms for months, the scientists found that neither of the honey groups saw improvements over the placebo group.

Dr. Stanley Fineman, president-elect of the American College of Allergy, Asthma and Immunology, said he has seen a growing number of patients ask about local honey. "Seasonal allergies are usually triggered by windborne pollens, not by pollens spread by insects," he said. So it's unlikely that honey "collected from plants that do not cause allergy symptoms would provide any therapeutic benefit."

THE BOTTOM LINE There's no evidence that local honey relieves allergy symptoms.

TECHNOLOGY

The earliest technologies were practiced or developed through trial and error, and their practitioners did not necessarily understand why particular methods or materials worked better than others. For example, early potters did not know the chemistry behind ceramics and had no way of measuring the heat used in firing; but they produced excellent pots based on craft knowledge. In the past

several hundred years, especially, technology has become increasingly allied with science.

But even when a new technology appears to come directly from a scientific theory—the laser, for example—it is built on many of the technologies that preceded it, traceable back to the earliest stone tools and fire if one looks hard enough.

History of Significant Technologies

Stone Tools Ancestors of humans began to improve rocks to make better tools about 2.5 million years ago. These first tools, called Oldowan pebble tools, were medium-size rocks broken to have a sharp edge. About a million years later, other ancestors began to create specialized tool shapes. The hand ax, or biface, had sharpened edges on both sides and a characteristic teardrop form. Starting about 200,000 years ago, Neandertals and early humans developed points for spears, and stone knives and awls. Small points for arrowheads date from about 25,000 B.C. Other small stone tools, called microliths, were introduced about 18,000 B.C. Some microliths were mounted in wood.

Fire The earliest evidence that humans used fire is more than 1.5 million years old, but it is impossible to tell when people began to make fire with sparks or friction. Hearths in Africa and Israel, well-defined places used over and over again for small fires, are at least 750,000 years old and possibly older. By 40,000 B.C. fireplaces with walls were built and stone lamps made. Although wood was the main fuel, people also burned bone where wood was scarce, and early stone lamps burned animal fat. By about A.D. 300 people in China began to burn coal and later natural gas and petroleum. As forests were replaced by fields, coal became the fuel of choice in both Asia and Europe. Air pollution from coal burning has been the main impetus for replacing coal with natural gas and oil as a source of heat since the mid-twentieth century.

Baskets and Cloth It is thought that woven baskets preceded cloth and pottery and led to both (a basket lined with clay to hold a liquid may have been the earliest pot, although this theory is mostly speculation). The earliest woven cloth was made either from the flax plant (linen) or from wool. Cotton and silk fibers were introduced about 3000 B.C. In each case, short fibers needed to be spun together to make yarn. For centuries spinning was accomplished with a simple weight turned by hand as the spinner added bits of fiber to the yarn. A better method, using the spinning wheel, originated in China around A.D. 1000, reaching Europe by at least 1280. In the 18th century, the spinning jenny, a device that could spin several strands of yarn at once and that was powered by water or steam, heralded the Industrial Revolution. This was followed by power looms that wove the yarn into cloth.

In the 19th and 20th centuries, scientists developed plastics that resembled the silk spun by caterpillars and spiders—rayon, nylon, Dacron, and polyester.

Ceramics and Glass Clays heated to high temperatures permanently harden into ceramics. The earliest, dating from about 28,000 B.C., were made in Moravia (Czech Republic) and are small statues of animals. Bricks made from clay were first dried in the sun, but by 23,000 B.C. were also fired to harden them. Coatings used on ceramics, called glazes, made them shiny. About 2000 B.C. in Egypt one glaze material was melted separately and cooled to form glass. Another type of ceramic, formed when water bonds particles of powdered rock, is the basis of plaster (7000 B.C.) and concrete, the latter first made by the Romans.

Bow and Arrow The early history of bows used to propel small spears called arrows is unclear. Some evidence points to use in Spain and North Africa about 25,000 B.C., but the earliest direct evidence (preserved arrow shafts) dates from 8500 B.C. The arrow was only one of several weapons that strike at a distance—boomerangs, slings, and blowpipes are all ancient—but became the weapon of choice in most societies until the advent of firearms. Bows were improved in several steps. The Persians sometime before 500 B.C. replaced wooden bows with bows made from horn and animal tendons. Bows so powerful that unaided human strength could not draw them were developed—crossbows that were drawn with levers, pulleys, or cranks. Large versions of crossbows were an early form a catapult, the first weapon of mass destruction. A very effective crossbow, the arbalest, was developed as a weapon of war in the 14th century, but quickly lost out to firearms, which were introduced to Europe about that time.

Metals Most metals combine easily with nonmetals, so elemental metals are rare in nature. Early humans discovered the few metals that are relatively common "native" minerals—gold, copper, and silver. These are all shiny and flexible and can be used for decoration.

Copper is hard enough to form tools. The earliest evidence for copper use dates from 8000 B.C., but copper was not melted and cast until about 1,500 years later. Common copper ores break down easily with heat, releasing metallic copper. Smelting—making metal from an ore—of copper had begun by about 4500 B.C. in the Near East. A period of using copper extensively for weapons and tools lasted about 500 years from about 3500 B.C.

This brief Copper Age ended when a better metal, the alloy bronze, was introduced about 3000 B.C., starting the more familiar Bronze Age, which lasted more than 1,500 years. Bronze, usually copper alloyed with tin, is stronger and harder than copper.

The Bronze Age ended after people in Anatolia discovered how to smelt and work iron, which is even harder and stronger than bronze. Early iron had too high a melting point to be cast, so it was hammered into shape ("wrought"). The Chinese, about 300 B.C., discovered that mixing charcoal with iron reduces the melting point enough so that it can be cast. About 400 years later cast iron was rediscovered in Greece, but cast iron did not begin to replace wrought iron in the West until the 12th century.

Steel, the very strong, hard alloy of iron and carbon, was made in small amounts for most of iron's history. Inexpensive processes for making large quantities of steel were discovered only in the 19th century, the best known being the Bessemer process invented in 1856. Steel gradually replaced iron as the main metal for structural uses.

Aluminum, known since 1825, gradually became the second most common metal in use after an electrochemical extraction discovered in 1888 dramatically lowered production costs.

Boats and Ships Using rafts of logs or reeds tied together or simple dugouts, canoes made by hollowing large tree trunks, humans crossed deep water to Japan as early as 100,000 years ago. There is evidence for regular trade between the mainland and various islands by 11,500 B.C., the end of the last Ice Age. Since wood is seldom preserved, the earliest physical evidence for canoes is from 7500 B.C.; the oldest complete canoe preserved, in Paris, is from 4300 B.C.

Canoes are usually propelled by paddles, but can also use sails. The earliest use of sails has been dated to the second half of the fourth millennium B.C. in Egypt. Sails were gradually improved, from flat sails to "bags of wind," to complex arrangements of several types of sails on different masts on the same ship. Triangular sails could easily be moved to catch the wind from different directions. The wind was too fickle for warships, however, so in antiquity warships in battle used banks of oars (an oar is a paddle that pivots on a fixed point, providing the mechanical advantage of a lever).

By 3000 B.C. the technique of joining planks to form a hull was in use. This was replaced by the modern technique of building an internal framework and then planking it, a process whose evolution began about the seventh century A.D. Early sailing ships were steered with a large paddle, but the Chinese introduced a stern-mounted rudder around the start of the common era. The kind of vessel we would recognize as a "modern" sailing ship with a combination of square sails (set perpendicular to the centerline of the hull) and fore-and-aft (set parallel to the centerline) did not come into being until about 1400. The wooden sailing ship reached its peak for speed and size with the ships-of-the-line of the late seventeenth century and the merchantman in the nineteenth century.

Ships propelled by steam (as early as 1783 in France) and with steel hulls (1843 in England) gradually replaced wooden-hulled sailing ships. In their first decades, these were propelled by paddle wheels, generally mounted on either side of the hull amidships or at the stern. Although people had experimented with screw propulsion for centuries, it was not until the 1830s and 1840s that practical screw propellers were developed. In 1836, working independently, Francis Petit Smith, a British farmer; and Swedish-American inventor John Ericsson (1803–89), secured patents for ships' propellers, and the first ship built with a screw, aptly named *Archimedes*, was launched in 1838. The next major advance in marine propulsion was the development of the steam turbine engine by English designer Charles Parsons (1854–1931) in 1897. But two decades later the diesel engine began to replace steam turbines as well. Large oceangoing ships continued to use steam turbines until after World War II, but in the 1950's nearly all ships shifted to diesel power. Diesel ships are more fuel-efficient, although they emit more particulate pollution.

Submarines were first imagined during the 16th century, and occasionally built thereafter. A small, one-man, acorn-shaped submarine named *Turtle* built by David Bushnell in 1775 operated in New York Harbor during the Revolutionary War. Submarines of more familiar tube-shaped design, among them the *Alligator, Pioneer,* and *H.L. Huntley*, were built for use during the American Civil War, though their effectiveness as stealth attack craft was limited.

By the turn of the 20th century, more modern submarines were being built which incorporated diesel engines, periscopes, and double-hulled construction. The first nuclear-powered submarine launched in 1954.

Canals and Locks Canals for irrigation were built about 6000 B.C. in the Middle East soon after the "agricultural revolution." The need to transport stone from quarries to sites of temples and pyramids produced the first transportation canals in Egypt. Egyptians also built the first canal intended to connect major waterways, a canal from the Nile to the Red Sea, as early as 2000 B.C.

Canals helped unify China. The Magic Canal of 219 B.C., by linking two key rivers in the interior, made much of interior China accessible to the sea. China's Grand Canal, which links Beijing and Hangzhou, is a series of canals the genesis of which can be traced to the fifth century B.C. and which was gradually extended to reach its full length of 1,100 miles in 1293.

Although early transportation canals connected bodies of water at the same level, it soon became apparent that some canals could not be level. At places where canal levels changed, water flowed rapidly downhill. Going uphill, boats had to unload all their goods and passengers for

towing through such sections, called spillways or stanches. Boats were often lost in the process and goods stolen by people waiting on the shore for any disaster. In 983, in response to the losses at spillways, a Chinese official invented the first canal lock. Gates across the canal are closed and opened to raise or lower water levels in a small section of the canal, allowing a boat to move from one canal level to another. Similar canal locks were introduced in Europe during the 14th century.

The great age of canal building in Europe began in France in the 17th century and continued in England (18th century) and the United States (19th century). Inexpensive shipping of goods by canal was one crucial element of the Industrial Revolution, although most canals became unnecessary after the introduction of railroads and the internal combustion engine. The notable exceptions connect large bodies of water—the Panama Canal (completed 1914) between two oceans, the Suez Canal (completed 1869) between two seas, and the St. Lawrence Seaway (completed 1959) connecting the Great Lakes to the Atlantic Ocean.

Wheels Rotary motion dates from early drills used in making beads. The first wheels were potter's wheels, used to rotate the clay as it was made into a symmetrical vessel. Soon after the introduction of the potter's wheel (about 4000 B.C.), wheels replaced runners on sledges in Mesopotamia, creating the first carts. Early cart and chariot wheels were made by joining three or four wooden boards and carving the edge into a circle. A strip of wood or metal might be placed around the rim to reduce wear. By 1800 B.C. the weight of the wheel was reduced by connecting spokes to the rim, leaving open space within the wheel. The first wheels were attached to axles that rotated with the wheel. Later wheels rotated about fixed axles, with friction reduced by small rolling devices called bearings, in occasional use since the Roman Empire.

Wheels were also used for grinding grain into flour; the grain was placed under the flat face of a heavy wheel as it rotated against a fixed surface. Another application of the wheel is for transmitting rotary motion from one place to another, especially when two or more wheels are connected at their rims by projections called teeth, an arrangement called a gear. Gears of two different sizes are used to change speed of rotation and rotational force.

Papyrus, Parchment, and Paper Writing began somewhat before 3000 B.C. While people in Mesopotamia pressed cuneiform symbols into clay tables,

Egyptians painted hieroglyphs on material made by pounding stems of a reed, called papyrus. Parchment, a treated animal skin invented in Turkey about 250 B.C., gradually replaced papyrus in the Roman Empire. Meanwhile in China, paper, a material similar to papyrus, was prepared from pounded cloth fibers. At first paper was used for cleaning or as a packing material, but by A.D. 100 paper was used for writing Chinese. The secret of making paper from rags slowly spread from China, reaching the Arab world in 751 and Europe in 1150. After printing was introduced in the 15th century, the need for paper rose dramatically. An industry was built around collecting used cloth to feed paper mills. Paper was made one sheet at a time until 1798, when French inventor Nicolas-Louis Robert (1761–1828) developed the first continuous process for making paper, commercialized in 1807 by the Fourdrinier brothers. In 1850 the first attempts to produce paper from ground wood began in Germany and England; although the earliest versions were unsuccessful, improved versions of ground-wood paper are still used for newsprint and most books.

Water Mills and Windmills

In 25 B.C. the Roman architect Vitruvius (ca. 90 B.C.–ca. 20 B.C.) described the use of a wheel with paddles pushed by running water as a source of power for grinding grain. A similar wheel for operating a bellows was described in China as invented in A.D. 31. The Vitruvian water wheel had a horizontal axis and used gears to reduce speed and increase power enough to turn a millstone. The use of such mills, sometimes placed on boats—it was easier to anchor a floating mill over a fast-moving stream than to build a stationary one that projected over the water—increased throughout the Roman Empire and the Middle Ages. Toward the end of the Roman Empire, however, a more efficient water mill was invented; the water was retained in a small pond and allowed to flow over the paddles, adding the force of the water's weight to that of its movement. Thousands of such mills were built all over the world. The mills were also adapted to many purposes, including making thread and cloth, sawing wood, and forging iron. They remained the basic source of power for factories until the development of the steam engine in the 19th century.

Windmills were inspired more by sailing ships than by water mills. The first windmills, about A.D. 600 in what is now Iran, had a vertical axis from which several sails extended. By protecting the sails on one side of the axis from the wind, the wind turned the axis. European windmills, which date from the 12th century, were based on angled sails on a horizontal axis. The sails had to face the wind, but all the sails received the wind's force at once. These became the familiar Dutch windmills, used to pump water and increase the amount of dry land for farming. The fantail, which aims the windmill into the wind automatically, was added in 1745.

Hydroelectric power As electricity became common, water mills and windmills were nearly abandoned. Hydroelectric power is produced in a way similar to water mills, except that the mill pond is replaced with a giant reservoir and water wheels are replaced with turbines. In recent years, there has been a rising movement to generate electricity with windmills. The earliest, built in 1929 in France, used a rotor 66 feet in diameter and generated about 10 kW. Today windmills with aerodynamic designs are grouped together in wind farms. More than 30,000 windmills in farms located in mountain passes, at sea, or wherever winds are common generate about a million kW each year. (See also "Energy")

Clocks

In ancient Egypt and Mesopotamia sundials were used to measure the time of day by the position of a shadow, while water clocks measured the passage of time by the level of water flowing from a vessel. About A.D. 725 Chinese inventors improved the accuracy of the water clock with a device called an escapement, a gear mechanism that permits a small amount of water to flow and then briefly stops the flow (the sound of the escapement stopping and starting is the familiar tick of a clock). Shortly before 1280 an unknown European inventor recognized that an escapement could be used to slow a falling weight and make it fall at a uniform average speed. Clocks using this method are still in use. The first large town clocks, built in the 14th century, were all powered by falling weights. Hours were sounded by striking bells. Such clocks kept only approximate time, however. Dials with hour hands were added to town clocks, but the first clocks accurate enough to use a minute hand were not built until the 17th century.

Several mechanisms were added to escapements to improve accuracy, but not until the pendulum was introduced were good timekeepers developed. Leonardo da Vinci, Galileo, and others recognized that the regular swing of a pendulum could be used to regulate a clock, but the first to make accurate clocks—to within ten to fifteen seconds per day—according to this idea were Dutch scientist Christiaan Huygens (1629–95) and the Dutch clockmaker Salomon Coster, starting in 1656. An alternative to the falling weight, the watch spring, was devised by English scientist Robert Hooke (1635–1703) in 1658. This type of clock achieved great accuracy with the marine chronometer of English clockmaker John Harrison (1693–1776) in 1759.

In 1927 the quartz crystal was introduced as an electronic form of pendulum. Clocks driven by electric motors instead of falling weights or springs and modulated by quartz crystals are by far the most common today. While these are sufficiently accurate for most purposes, the atomic clock (1949), which uses the natural vibration period of an atom to regulate time (1949), is the basis of modern timekeeping. By 1993 the best atomic clocks were accurate to within one second in three million years.

Gunpowder and Guns   The first mention of gunpowder—an explosive mixture of saltpeter, charcoal, and sulfur—is in a Chinese book published about A.D. 850. For about 300 years, the primary use of gunpowder involved devices such as firecrackers used to create loud noises, but by 1150 gunpowder explosions were also used to power the first rockets. In 1221 gunpowder bombs laced with destructive shrapnel were used in war. After this application, the use of bombs and rockets spread throughout Asia and Europe, where the first forms of cannon were built early in the 14th century.

Small arms are first mentioned in 1381. The charge of gunpowder in early small arms (muskets) and cannon was ignited with a match, but about 1500 muskets incorporating a wheel-lock that strikes a spark from flint were invented. Improvements gradually led to the flintlock shortly before 1700. In 1807 Scottish clergyman Alexander Forsyth (1769-1843) developed percussion gunpowder, which explodes when struck. A small amount of this material contained in a thin metal cup is called a percussion cap. Since about 1840 nearly all firearms use percussion caps. Today the cap is part of a cartridge that also contains the gunpowder and the bullet.

Printing   About A.D. 600 the Chinese began using ink to transfer images carved in a wood block to paper or other materials. At first text was handled by carving the entire page in a mirror image onto a block. Whole books were printed by this method in the ninth century. By 1050, however, Chinese printers had begun to compose pages from individual carved characters for words, the first form of movable type. Movable type became even more useful when applied to European languages, since only the limited forms of the alphabet—twenty-six letters in the case of modern English—needed to be cast. About 1440 Johannes Gutenberg (1397–1468) created the first European books printed with cast metal movable type. Gutenberg's method, with improvements, was the main form of printing until the nineteenth century. The development of the rotary press in 1812 quadrupled the speed of printing, a rate that was quickly improved upon. In 1884, German printer Ottmar Mergenthaler (1854–99) invented the Linotype, which cast a single line of type (hence the name) at a time. Twenty years later another printing innovation made a fundamental change; in offset printing, the image is first transferred to a rubber roller and then to the page. The original type is usually pressed into a plate that might have 16 to 48 pages on it. Other 20th-century techniques changed the way type is cast and introduced photographic methods for setting type and for making the plates.

The advent of the computer made new forms of printing possible and also produced a need for versatile printers that could be used to print pages from a computer display. In 1971 printers were introduced for which a computer controlled separate elements in an array, called a dot matrix. The computer and printer select a particular set of the elements from the matrix, forming each individual letter. Four years later IBM introduced the first printer to use a laser to create images by a process similar to xerographic copying. The following year IBM developed a different computer-controlled printer, the ink jet, which uses either heat-produced bubbles or a crystal to fling tiny drops of ink onto the page in precise patterns.

Calculators   The first calculators were based on moving counters (the counting board) or moving beads on a string (the abacus) to add or subtract. Counting boards were used in Europe throughout antiquity and the abacus in Asia from at least A.D. 300. Although it is possible to multiply or divide with these tools, it is not very efficient. In the 17th century, English mathematicians developed the first effective mechanical methods for multiplying and dividing. John Napier (1550–1617) was the force behind a simple device called Napier's bones, which was based on a medieval algorithm for multiplication of whole numbers. Napier also invented logarithms, which became the basis of the slide rule (1621). A slide rule uses two logarithmic scales which can be aligned to give approximate results of any multiplication, division, or power. At essentially the same time as the slide rule, the German inventor Wilhelm Schickard (1592–1635) built what is generally recognized as the first calculating machine, a device based on Napier's bones—but only one of the Shickard machines was ever built.

Blaise Pascal (1623–62) invented the adding machine. Pascal's device used gears to accomplish mechanically the kinds of calculation done by hand with an abacus. He made and sold about 50 of the machines, starting in 1642. In 1694 Gottfried Leibniz (1646–1716) developed a calculator that could perform all four arithmetic operations and even extract square roots. Like Pascal's adding machine, it was based on gears, but it contained an additional gear for multiplication and division. Leibniz made only two working models, but his device became the basis for one of the first commercially successful desk calculators in 1820. The next improvement in design replaced the additional multiplication gear with built-in times tables (1889), followed by calculators using electric motors to turn the gears (1902, introduced commercially in the United States in 1922).

After the transistor was invented (1947), it became possible to dispense with gears completely. Logic gates in transistors translate decimal numerals into binary and back, and electric charges moving through the transistors replace the moving gears. The modern handheld calculator (1971 to the present) combines transistorized calculations with electronic displays. (See also "The History of Computing.")

Steam Engines   The power of steam to move objects was recognized in antiquity. Heron of Alexandria (ca. A.D. 10—ca. 75) built a toy that rotated as steam issued from nozzles, the prototype of the steam turbine. The first serious efforts to take advantage of the great expansion in volume as water is vaporized took place at the end of the 17th century. French-English engineer Denis Papin (1647–1712) and English inventor Thomas Savery (1650–1715) each invented pumps powered by the expansion of steam. In 1710 English entrepreneur Thomas Newcomen (1663–1729) combined Papin's concept of steam lifting a piston with Savery's pump to create the first practical steam engine, which he sold for pumping water out of mines.

Scottish engineer James Watt (1736–1819) became interested in the Newcomen engine and produced a much improved version (1776). The original Watt engine, like the Newcomen engine, moved a cylinder back and forth—reciprocating motion—but Watt developed ways to convert the output to rotary motion as well as methods for improving power and control. Watt's steam engines not only replaced water for powering mills, but also were used to power boats and vehicles, and by 1882 were being used to generate electric power.

In addition to the reciprocating steam engine, the steam turbine, a sophisticated version of Heron's toy, began to be used for powering boats and generating electricity (1884). Steam turbines replaced most reciprocating steam engines in the first half of the 20th century, but later in the century the steam turbine was often replaced by diesel engines. (See also "Energy.")

Railroads   The idea of rolling carts along fixed grooves or rails for more efficient ground transportation is of great antiquity. By the 16th century, wooden wagonways were used in mines to carry out ore or coal; donkeys or oxen could pull several linked carts because of the smooth ride on the rails. By the start of the 19th century, animal-drawn trains rode iron-covered rails to bring heavy goods to canals, where they could be loaded onto boats.

Early steam engines were too heavy to use for travel on poor 19th-century roads, but rail lines could handle the heavy locomotives, the first vehicles to power travel by rotating the wheels. Several inventors in England designed and built early locomotives, starting with Richard Trevithick (1771–1833) in 1804. By 1825 the first railroad with a regular schedule for passengers and freight was in service in England.

The first American rail tracks were laid in Boston in the early 19th century, initially to transport construction materials over very short distances. The first railroad—the 13-mile Baltimore & Ohio line—opened in 1827. Early engines and rails were modeled after designs by British engineers, but as railroads expanded outward from urban centers, engineers quickly discovered that British locomotives would not serve American terrain; to traverse mountain passes between eastern cities and interior markets, more powerful engines were developed to cope with steeper inclines and cruder track.

In 1830, only 23 miles of railroad existed in the United States, but by midcentury entrepreneurs and government officials were dreaming and planning of connecting much larger sections of the country by rail. Fueled by government subsidies, generous land grants, and widespread collusion between railroad tycoons and local municipalities, a track-building boom occurred in the decades leading up to the Civil War. By 1840, 2,800 miles of railroad had been laid, and by 1850, 9,000 miles of track were in operation, as much as existed in the rest of the world combined at the time; by 1860, 30,000 miles of railroad had been built.

In 1869, construction of the Transcontinental Railway was completed, uniting Omaha, Nebraska and Sacramento, California, with a single track.

In the 20 years between the completion of the coast-to-coast route and the start of World War I, rail travel in the United States tripled, and the amount of railroad track increased to 254,000 miles. At the end of the 19th century, 90 percent of passenger travel between cities in the United States occurred by rail, and in 1920, the peak of rail travel, there were 1.2 billion riders.

Although a few steam-powered locomotives are still in operation, most are now powered by electric (1879) or diesel (1912) engines. Starting in the 1970's, engineers in Japan and Germany began experimenting with trains using magnetic levitation (maglev) technology. Maglev trains, which float on a magnetic field above a guideway in which magnets are turned off and on to pull it forward, are capable of reaching speeds of 500 km/hr (300 mph).

Photography See "Photography" in *Fine Arts*.

Rubber Native Americans discovered that the sap of a tropical tree (latex) hardens into a substance that bounces, which they used to make balls for games. Hardened latex became known to Europeans after the second voyage of Columbus, but Europeans did not pay much attention to it. After French explorer Charles de la Condamine (1701–74) rediscovered it in 1730, however, it came to be used in making flexible hoses. The substance acquired the name rubber after British chemist Joseph Priestley (1733–1804) noticed in 1770 that it could be used as an eraser to rub out pencil marks. Other uses of rubber were slow to develop because natural rubber is unstable in both heat and cold. In 1823 the Scottish inventor Charles Macintosh (1766–1843) found a way to use rubber to waterproof cloth, resulting in the raingear called a mackintosh.

In 1839 the American inventor Charles Goodyear (1800–60) discovered a way to make a tough form of rubber that resisted environmental changes. He named the process vulcanization. Rubber bands of vulcanized rubber were introduced as early as 1845. Air-filled tires using vulcanized rubber were developed by Scottish veterinarian John Dunlop in 1887 for use on his son's tricycle, but soon Dunlop was manufacturing the tires for bicycles and carriages. The very first automobiles used rubber tires.

In 1931 the Du Pont laboratories began marketing a synthetic rubber called neoprene. As World War II restricted access to tropical sources of natural rubber, other artificial forms of rubber were created. Since 1960 more synthetic than natural rubber has been used in the world market.

Subways Originally devised to aid traffic congestion, plans for an underground railway beneath London were underway by the mid-1850's, and the first section of London's Underground opened in January 1863. London's early subway railcars were pulled by gas-powered engines. The earliest experiments in New York City utilized a more novel approach. In 1870, a small section of tunnel beneath New York city hall opened which utilize pneumatic pressure to shoot a single car down the 300-foot track. The idea was quickly scrapped.

Telegraph and Telephone The possibility of transmitting messages with electric current was recognized soon after William Sturgeon (1783–1850) invented the electromagnet in 1825. Three methods using this process, which came to be called telegraphy, were introduced in 1837—in the United States, Germany, and England. After a dramatic demonstration of the American system in 1844 by inventor Samuel F. B. Morse (1791–1872), the Morse version came to dominate rapid communication in the remainder of the 19th century. Morse's method relied on a simple binary code using short pulses (dots) and longer ones (dashes) known as Morse code.

Alexander Graham Bell (1847–1922) and other inventors attempted to use a varying electric current instead of simple pulses to transmit voice. Bell's telephone, patented in 1876, used a metal membrane that vibrated in response to changes in electromagnetic force. Within two years a commercial telephone system was in operation in New Haven, Connecticut, the beginning of a worldwide network. The microphone, invented by Emile Berliner (1851–1929), proved a more effective way to translate sound waves into electric currents, and was the first in many improvements to the telephone. By 1900, the invention of loading coils allowed for long-distance telephone service between cities.

Motion Pictures See "Film" in *Performing Arts*.

Internal Combustion Engine In a steam engine, water is boiled outside the engine itself and the steam is introduced into the engine's cylinders to propel a piston up and down. The engine used on most automobiles, small nonelectric machinery, and propeller-driven airplanes is called an internal combustion engine because an explosion of fuel inside the cylinder moves the piston. The first such engine, invented by Belgian engineer Jean-Joseph Lenoir (1822–1900), used an electric spark to explode coal gas. Because the piston movement consists of a compression stroke (which also draws fuel and air from the tank) followed by a combustion stroke (ignition from the spark plug), the Lenoir engine is the first example of a two-stroke engine.

The German inventor Nikolaus Otto (1832–91) first improved the Lenoir engine and then in 1876 developed the more complex four-stroke engine, which adds a separate intake and exhaust step to the two strokes of the Lenoir engine. Because the four-stroke engine is more fuel-efficient and easier to lubricate, improved versions of the Otto engine are used in most automobiles and larger machinery. Early Otto engines ran on coal gas, but in 1893 German inventor Wilhelm Maybach (1846–1929) developed a carburetor that mixed gasoline with air, leading to internal combustion engines that burn gasoline. Many modern engines use fuel injection just outside the cylinder instead of a carburetor.

Not all internal combustion engines run on gasoline. In 1892 the French-German engineer Rudolf Diesel (1858–1913) patented an engine in which the compression of air creates a temperature high enough to ignite less volatile oils than gasoline; some diesel engines, for example, run on cooking oil. No spark plug is needed, but air must be much more compressed than in a gasoline engine. Diesel engines can be either four-stroke (used in some automobiles and trucks) or two-stroke (used in trains and large ships). Diesel engines get more energy from their lower-cost fuel, and produce less carbon dioxide than gasoline engines, but their particulate emissions are greater than those from gasoline engines.

Sound Recording In 1877 Thomas Alva Edison recorded and played back his voice with a device that used a needle attached to a diaphragm to make a groove in waxed paper. Later that year he was able to record several minutes of speech by using a cylinder on which a much longer continuous groove could be made by the same method. In recording, the depth of the groove reflected the movements of the diaphragm that were caused by spoken words. During playback, the same needle transmitted the pattern of groove depths back to the diaphragm, which reproduced the original words. Edison called his device a phonograph and intended it to record dictation, but soon recorded music became its principal application.

Various alternatives to Edison's phonograph were invented in the 1880s, including the Dictaphone (1885, words recorded in a belt), Alexander Graham Bell's gramophone (1886, shellac cylinders with grooves that veered back and forth), and Emile Berliner's gramophone (1888, shellac discs using Bell's groove system). Berliner's discs, which could be reproduced by stamping, soon dominated the new industry. Sound quality was greatly improved after 1924 when electric microphones and amplification were introduced.

An alternative technology, recording sound as changes in magnetism, was patented in 1898 by Danish inventor Valdemar Poulsen (1869–1942). Poulsen's device used a steel wire, but in the early 1930's German engineers improved sound quality by using a coated tape instead of a wire.

Recording sound as changes in grooves or magnetism is an analog process, but the first digital system, the compact disc (CD), was introduced in 1982. A laser is used to detect tiny pits in a rapidly rotating disk, which are then transformed into analog sound for loudspeakers by an electronic system. Although CDs continue to be the main commercial medium for sound recording, much home recording today is done by copying digital files from a computer onto a magnetic disk, for example with mp3 (short for Motion Picture Experts Group, Layer 3, or MPEG-3), which was introduced in 2000.

Skyscrapers The first buildings had only one floor, but by Roman times apartment houses five stories tall were being built (ca. 100 B.C.). The first office building recognized as a skyscraper was William Le Baron Jenney's (1832–1907) Leiter Building (Chicago, eight stories) of 1879. The Leiter Building's iron frame, not its height, gives it this distinction. Tall buildings without an iron or steel skeleton had to have progressively thicker walls and fewer and smaller windows for lower floors. Another Chicago building built a decade later was twice as tall as the Leiter Building: lacking an internal frame, it had walls six feet thick and narrow slits for windows on the first floor.

By the end of the 19th century, the tallest office building had reached 30 stories. Taller buildings awaited improvement in elevators. Early elevators were effective to about 20 floors, but the modern cable elevator, introduced in 1900, had no obvious limits. Famous skyscrapers of New York, such as the Chrysler Building and the Empire State Building, were built in the early 1930's. Even taller buildings, including the twin towers of the World Trade Center (New York, 1,368 feet) and the Willis Tower

(Chicago, 1,450 feet) were built in 1972 and 1973. As of 2010 the tallest skyscraper, at 2,716 feet, is the Burj Khalifa in Dubai (finished in 2010).

Radio In 1888 Heinrich Hertz (1857–94) showed that invisible electromagnetic waves could be produced and detected at a distance. By 1894 several researchers had demonstrated that Hertz's wave could be detected over distances ranging from 30 to 180 feet. One of these researchers, Italian inventor Guglielmo Marconi (1874–1937) extended the distance and used the waves, which he named radio waves, to transmit Morse code. He demonstrated wireless telegraphy across the Atlantic in 1901. Wireless soon became an important way to transmit messages to and between ships. Inventors also recognized that the same principles behind voice transmission through the telephone could be used with radio waves. The Canadian-American physicist Reginald Fessenden (1866–1932) was the first to succeed in transmitting voice (1903), although signals were quite weak. A key improvement was the invention of the triode vacuum tube (or valve; 1907) by American inventor Lee De Forest (1873–1961) which could amplify weak signals. By 1920, the first radio station in the United States was broadcasting both voice and music. The initial development of radio was based on Fessenden's method of amplitude modulation (AM), which used changes in the intensity of waves to transmit signals. The American physicist Edwin Howard Armstrong (1890–1954), who had contributed many of the technical improvements to AM radio, developed a method that eliminated interference by transmitting signals by varying frequency (frequency modulation, or FM; patented 1933). FM radio was limited in distance by the curvature of Earth, while AM signals reflect from the ionosphere to travel much farther.

Refrigeration and Air Conditioning The first machine to cool air was the refrigerator, invented by French engineer Ferdinand Carré (1824–1900). It was based on two physical principles: as a gases expands, its temperature falls; and heat travels from warmer to cooler material. Carré used the expansion of ammonia gas to lower the temperature inside an insulated box. He pumped the cool ammonia back to a higher pressure outside the box, raising its temperature. The effect was to pump heat from inside the box to outside.

Reducing air temperature lowers the amount of water vapor that air can hold. In 1902 American engineer Willis H. Carrier (1876–1950) used this effect to reduce humidity in a printing plant so that ink would dry faster. Instead of cooling the interior of an insulated box, he forced air through the refrigerated chamber, lowering both humidity and temperature. Soon he was hired by other manufacturers to condition the air in their plants. In 1921 Carrier invented an air conditioner that used a better pump to circulate the gas through the pipes; on the basis of this invention, he formed a company to manufacturer air conditioners. In 1924 a department store in Detroit, Michigan, became the first air-conditioned public building. Motion picture theaters soon became the biggest users of air conditioning equipment. The first home units were built as early as 1928, but home air conditioning did not become common until after World War II.

Flight Although Leonardo da Vinci and others designed various forms of flying machines with wings that flapped or rotating propellers, the first actual flight by humans came in balloons. Both hot air and hydrogen balloons were introduced in 1783, the former by the Montgolfier brothers (Joseph-Michel, 1740–1810; and Jacques-Étienne, 1745–99) and the latter by French scientist Jacques Charles (1746–1823). Even after balloons that can be steered, called dirigibles, were developed in 1852, balloons failed to become a major form of transportation, although they have contributed to scientific advances and have also had occasional use in warfare.

A more promising start for human flight occurred in 1853 when a glider built by the English inventor Sir George Cayley (1773–1857) carried a full-grown human 900 feet. By the end of the 19th century, a number of inventors had recognized that a combination of a glider, a lightweight engine, and a propeller similar to that found on ships could be used for sustained flight. But the first inventions along this line failed because of poor control mechanisms.

The Wright brothers (Wilbur, 1867–1912; and Orville, 1871–1948) became the first to solve the control problem. After successful experiments with gliders, they achieved powered flight in 1903. Although their original method of control by warping the wings of the aircraft was soon replaced by a system of small flaps, their success marks the beginning of heavier-than-air flight.

Activities such as mail service and crop dusting quickly began using airplanes, but passenger air travel developed more slowly. The first commercial airline service, the St.

Petersburg–Tampa Airboat Line went into operation in 1914, shuttling a single passenger at a time across Tampa Bay, Florida. The first airplane crossing of the Atlantic took place in 1919, as U.S. Navy pilots flew from Newfoundland to London.

World War I produced many pilots, trained for reconnaissance and fighter planes. After the war, these pilots and others carried mail, demonstrated aircraft, and set new records for long-distance flight. Charles Lindbergh's solo transatlantic flight from New York to Paris in 1927 captivated the nation and made him an instant worldwide celebrity. In his plane "Spirit of St. Louis," Lindbergh made the 3,610-mile journey in 33 1/2 hours. More important, his feat set off a wave of investment in commercial flight. By 1929, investments in aviation had grown greatly, and new technologies, including gyroscopic instruments and automatic pilot, helped expand the range and safety of flying. In the 1930s, improvements to airplanes made air travel more affordable and comfortable. In 1933, the Boeing 247, often considered the first modern airliner, began flying with room for 10 passengers, and in 1935 the DC-3, which would serve the first true coast-to-coast routes, took to the air, carrying up to 32 passengers.

During World War II, the widespread strategic use of reconniasance and bombing aircraft sharply increased the demand for trained pilots, and again the end of the war left many pilots available for commercial flight. Also during World War II, commercial airline fleets were pressed into military service, and the resulting contracts with manufacturers meant a boom in business after the war. By 1949, 16.7 million people were flying each year, and by 1954 that number had reached 35.5 million.

In the postwar decades, new airplanes sped travel and increased the number of passengers per trip. In 1958, the jet-engine Boeing 707 began flying passengers across the Atlantic, cutting New York–London travel time to six hours, and prompting many airlines to quickly replace propeller-based aircraft with jet planes. In 1970, Boeing's 747, the first "jumbo jet" went into service, carrying 450 passengers. Other jumbo jets quickly followed, including the McDonnell Douglas DC-10 and Lockheed L-1011.

Another approach to flight had roots extending back to Leonardo's designs and some of Sir George Cayley's experiments—the helicopter. In the 1930's Spanish inventor Juan de La Cierva (1895–1936) established with his autogiro that a large propeller, called a rotor, can provide enough lift for a heavier-than-air craft. In 1936 German engineer Heinrich Focke developed the first successful craft to use a rotor both for lift and propulsion. His helicopter could rise nearly vertically and fly either forward or backward. But the helicopter did not become practical until the designs of Russian-American Igor Sikorsky (1889–1972) at the close of World War II.

Plastics Synthetic materials that resemble such natural materials as amber, ivory, and rubber are called plastics, from the Greek word meaning "to mould." These materials are composed of small molecular units, called monomers, linked together to form polymers. Plastics are polymers that under heat or pressure can be molded or otherwise shaped easily, producing fibers or thin films as well as solid objects. The first plastics were Celluloid (1871) and rayon (1924). Celluloid is easily shaped, but flimsy, easily melted, and flammable. It was invented by American chemist John Hyatt (1837-1920) in 1869 as a replacement for ivory in billiard balls, but soon thin films of Celluloid became the basis for photographic film.

In 1906 the Belgian-American chemist Leo Baekeland (1863–1944) discovered a synthetic material that he first used as a hard varnish. When molded and heated, however, it turned into a plastic that did not melt. He named the new material Bakelite, and by 1917 it began to replace natural materials in many applications. The plastics polystyrene and polyvinyl chloride were invented in 1930, polyethylene in 1933, nylon in 1935, and polyurethane in 1944. Some new plastics, such as Kevlar, invented by American chemist Stephanie Kwolek (b. 1923) in 1964, are tougher than any natural materials previously used in such applications as bulletproof vests or lightweight canoes.

Television Transmission of images over wires preceded broadcast television. As early as 1884 the German inventor Paul Nipkow (1860–1940) created a method based on a rotating disk that broke images into varying electrical pulses that could be reconstructed using a second disk. Several inventors used versions of the Nipkow disk for early television. The British engineer John Logie Baird (1888–1946) was most successful, transmitting still images in 1925, moving images in 1926, and images across the Atlantic in 1928. The British Broadcasting System (BBC) used Baird's method for the first wireless television. But the future of television was not with the electromechanical Nipkow disk. In 1927 American inventor Philo T. Farnsworth (1906–71) created the first all-electronic television. By 1936 the BBC was broadcasting an all-electronic version. Today television uses electronic cameras of various types to create images, which are broadcast along with sound by FM signals (or transmitted over coaxial cables or fiber cables). The images are reconstructed by various electronic means, ranging from a cathode-ray tube that produces images by directing electrons toward a phosphorescent screen to displays of all modern types.

The sales of analog TV sets crested in 2000 and quickly declined, as all-digital televisions quickly took off. The move to digital technology in television enable other advances which resulted in flatter televisions with dramatically higher resolution and larger screens. Analog televisions finally disappeared from store shelves in 2007.

By 2007, manufacturers were promoting flatscreen high-definition flatscreens TVs of ever-increasing size. By 2010, as sales of flatscreen TVs slowed, manufacturers began to heavily promote 3D technology, though it was slow to be adopted.

Radar

Radar   As early as 1900, Nikola Tesla (1856–1943) suggested using radio waves to detect objects, which is the basic principle of radar. At the time, however, there was no way to produce electromagnetic waves between the short length of infrared waves and very long radio waves. Radio waves were used to detect objects as early as 1904, but the waves were too long to locate objects precisely. By 1935, however, British physicist Robert Watson-Watt (1892–1973) and coworkers were observing airplanes from as far as 15 miles away using short-wave radio.

In 1920, American physicist Albert W. Hull (1880–1966) had developed the first vacuum tube to produce more energetic than short waves. Watson-Watt and others secretly developed improved versions of microwaves during the late 1930's and early 1940's, which were used to great effect during World War II. Radar detects aircraft, ships, and other objects by bouncing microwaves from the surface, collecting the echoes, and using the time between the initial signal and the echo to determine distance.

After World War II radar was used to measure the motion of planets. Weather prediction relies on radar to observe storms. Radar from satellites and space probes has also been used to map features on earth and other planets.

Rockets and Jet Engines

Rockets and Jet Engines   The Chinese observed that explosions of gunpowder in a container could propel the container some distance. By A.D. 1150 they had controlled the explosion enough to propel a container with a sustained burning. These first rockets were used for fireworks but soon also employed in warfare. By 1380 the use of military rockets had reached Italy, but rocket technology fell behind the development of cannon. Rockets maintained a modest role in warfare until the end of World War II, when large, liquid-fueled V-2 rockets were used by Germany against England.

By then, the basic science behind rocket propulsion was understood. Newton's third law of motion established that expelling material in one direction exerts an equal force in the opposite direction. This self-contained process does not require air or water to act against, as a propeller does; rockets work even in the vacuum of space.

World War II also brought new propulsion systems to aircraft. In Germany and England aircraft designers replaced the propeller with jet engines that expelled jets of hot gases to obtain thrust. The difference between a jet engine and a rocket is that the jet heats atmospheric air to create the fast-moving gases that propel it, while a rocket carries all its own fuel and does not need air to operate. Jet engines enabled greater speeds than could be obtained from propellers. Rocket planes were attempted by the Germans toward the end of the war, but were unsuccessful. Since then, however, experimental rocket-propelled aircraft have set all atmospheric records for speed and height. In 1947, American pilot Chuck Yeager became the first man to fly faster than the speed of sound, in the Bell X-1 experimental rocket plane. Starting in 1957, rockets were successfully used to propel artificial satellites and space probes, including spacecraft carrying people.

Microwave Ovens

Microwave Ovens   During World War II the special vacuum tubes used to produce microwaves were greatly improved for radar. The American engineer Percy L. Spencer (1894–1970) observed that an operating microwave tube melted the candy bar in his pocket. After experimenting by using microwaves to pop corn, he patented the idea of cooking with microwaves in 1945. Two years later a microwave oven the size of a home refrigerator went on sale, intended for restaurants to cook or reheat food. The first microwave oven designed for home use was marketed in 1955, but it was not until 1967 that an inexpensive home unit was available. After that, the microwave oven became a fixture in most kitchens.

Microwaves used in ovens are radio waves in the 2.5 gigahertz range, which are absorbed by molecules of water, fat, or sugar, but not by molecules of glass, plastic, or ceramics. The energy from the microwaves causes molecules that absorb it to vibrate faster, raising the temperature of the food. For most foods, the microwaves will penetrate the entire food item, so the temperature rise is nearly uniform throughout.

Space Flight   Many of the early accomplishments in space flight were spurred by Cold War competition between the United States and the Soviet Union. The space programs of the former Soviet Union and the United States both had dramatic flights by human pilots as an important component, although most of the serious scientific progress was made by satellites or probes—the general name for space vehicles that neither carry humans nor orbit Earth—that are directed internally or from Earth. The Soviets stunned the U.S. military, scientific, and political communities by being first to launch an artificial satellite, named *Sputnik 1*, into orbit on Oct. 4, 1957, inaugurating what would be called the "Space Race." The first successful U.S. satellite, *Explorer 1*, was launched the following January. The Soviets were also first to send a probe to the Moon (*Lunik 2*, launched September 12, 1959), and the first to send a human into outer space (pilot Yuri Gagarin, aboard *Vostok 1*, on April 12, 1961).

The first U.S. manned space missions were named for mythological figures: Project Mercury, which comprised 20 unmanned and 9 manned launches between 1959 and 1963, had the goal of putting humans into orbit. Project Gemini, with the goal of readying NASA to undertake a journey to the Moon, comprised 2 unmanned and 10 manned flights. Project Apollo, chartered specifically to land Americans on the Moon, ran from 1961 to 1975, and comprised 3 unmanned and 12 manned launches. The most famous of these missions was *Apollo 11*, launched on July 16, 1969 and in which Neil Armstrong became the first human to walk on the Moon on July 20. Armstrong's walk on the Moon was televised with sound to a captivated worldwide audience.

The Space Race culminated overlapping medical, scientific, engineering, and military research and was beneficiary of massive investments by the U.S. government. The space program was driven both by visionary desires to see humans in space, and also by Cold War anxiety to keep ahead of Soviet advancements in rocket, surveillance, and communications technology.

Early astronauts returned to Earth in re-entry capsules slowed in their descent by parachutes, splashlanding in the ocean. In the early 1980's, NASA's Space Shuttle program replaced single-use capsules and modules with a reusable craft that glided back to earth and could land at an airstrip. The first Space Shuttle, *Columbia*, launched on April 14, 1981, and was resued in another launch on November 11 that same year. For a time, it appeared that the shuttle progam would be long-lasting, but the dramatic explosion of the *Challenger* moments after launch on January 28, 1986, killed everyone on board and effectively stalled NASA's manned space program. No shuttle would return to space until *Discovery*, launched on July 26, 2005. The space shuttle program was discontinued in 2011.

Lasers   A laser is a device that produces an intense and focused beam of light waves that are all aligned with each other. Although Albert Einstein (1879–1955) described the science behind the laser as early as 1917, it was not until 1960 that American physicist Theodore Maiman (b. 1927) built the first working laser. In some ways the action of a laser is similar to the chain reaction that powers a nuclear reactor—one photon of light absorbed in an energized molecule releases two or more that are exactly the same as the first. By reflecting such photons back and forth, but allowing some to escape in one direction, the energy of the laser emerges as a beam of identical photons.

Maiman's laser used the molecules of a ruby to create its beam. Improvements in design started quickly and by 1965 a laser was built that could be adjusted to different wavelengths of light. In 1970 the first carbon-dioxide lasers could cut through metals or be used for welding. Applications proliferated. As early as 1962 a laser was used in eye surgery, where lasers have become a common tool. Perhaps the most common uses of lasers today are in barcode scanners, CD and DVD players, and fiber-optic communications. Special tools for farmers and carpenters use lasers as aids in leveling fields or measuring distances.

Robotics   The concept of a mechanical person or animal goes back to antiquity. Greek and Chinese inventors made clever moving statues that could duplicate the actions of a person or animal, such as playing a musical instrument or flapping wings and crowing. Such devices are called automatons. Most worked by some form of clockwork, wound with a spring or powered by flowing water.

Automatons appear lifelike, but whenever they are activated, they repeat the same motions as the time before; they do not react to their environment. A device that accomplishes tasks similar to those a human can perform and that reacts to at least some changes in the environment is called a robot. Robots may or may not be made to resemble humans, although many have parts that are similar to human arms, hands, or eyes. The first robot to be manufactured and sold (in 1962, but based on a 1954 design) was an arm that performed repetitive tasks in automobile factories. The earliest models could be programmed to perform different tasks, but lacked sensors to recognize sizes or shapes of objects. Although called robots, their capabilities were about the same as a player piano, which plays different songs when different music rolls are inserted. Soon, however, robot arms that could distinguish the objects by weight or temperature or shape became available.

Another group of useful robots began with the space program. The best examples are the various Mars rovers, such as Sojourner, Spirit, and Opportunity, which move through the landscape, detecting obstacles and compensating for them, and also sample and analyze rocks and soil. Because of the time lag for signals to reach Mars from Earth and return, the rovers had to be given robot skills.

In some companies today, robots deliver mail, following a programmed path, but also sensing obstacles and avoiding them. There are also robot vacuum cleaners, pool cleaners, and lawn mowers available. None of the working robots so far resemble humans or animals very much, but toys are another matter. Toy manufacturers have developed humanoid robots that can sense some of their environment and react, as well as robotic pets whose behavior seems similar to that of real animals.

The Internet See "The Internet.".

Nanotechnology In 1959 the American physicist Richard Feynman (1918–88) proposed that useful electronic devices could be built one atom at a time and that the smallest devices might consist of as few as seven atoms. Although Feynman did not specify exact methods for making small tools, his speech is considered the founding document of nanotechnology, the art of creating useful objects whose size is less than 100 nanometers—a single atom may be about half a nanometer in size or somewhat less, down to about 0.1 nanometer. The word *nanotechnology* was coined in 1974, but no working devices less than 100 nanometers in size were created until the 1980's.

Chemists have also contributed to nanotechnology. In the 1990's they devised chemicals that when combined would self-assemble their molecules into particular configurations. Silicon has been fabricated into dust particles that can detect chemicals or that emit tiny jolts of electricity when exposed to light, providing a power source for nanomotors. One of the most dramatic ideas in nanotechnology is based on using the DNA molecule as a computer. Experimental DNA computers can in a test tube detect enzymes produced by cancer cells and on their own release a form of chemotherapy only when the proper combination of enzymes is present.

Home Computers See "History of Computing.".

Barcodes First introduced on packs of Wrigley's gum in the 1970's, barcodes are the sequence of black lines of varying width, usually on a white background, found on the backs of most packaging and are used in routine transactions and information transference. The lines represent binary digits 0 and 1 that can be read by a laser scanner, which are then processed into information by a digital computer. Most commonly they are used to scan consumer goods at purchase to help with inventory control.

Increasingly, a new generation of barcodes called quick response (QR) codes are being used. These new barcodes are comprised of black and white boxes that can incorporate much more information than current commercial barcodes. An example: McDonalds customers in Japan can scan the barcode on hamburger wrappings with their cellphone cameras, which translates it into onscreen text that presents nutrition information about the hamburger.

Cellphones Experiments with radio phones and automobile phones began in the 1940's but what we think of as modern cellular phones—lightweight, mobile, battery-powered handsets—were first introduced in the early 1970's, as U.S. companies Motorola and Bell competed to develop effective equipment. The first steps toward establishing commercial wireless cellular phone systems began in 1977 in Chicago and Washington D.C. By 1983, those two cities had begun operating the first cellphone markets.

The first cellular phone, Motorola's DynaTac mobile telephone unit, weighed 28 ounces and stood 10 inches high (without antenna), and had one hour of talk time and eight hours of standby. Since then, each successive generation of cellular phones has grown lighter, smaller, and more powerful.

Cellphones today are more than just phones. Most current cellphones incorporate digital cameras, digital music and video playback, and include email and Internet browsing capability. The first cellular phone rightfully called a "smartphone" was IBM's Simon, released in 1993. Simon incorporated a calendar, address book, email, fax, and games. An early smartphone leader, Research In Motion's (RIM) BlackBerry device was first introduced in 1999, and used patented "push" technology to automatically send email to the device. The BlackBerry included features common to other personal digital assistant (PDA) devices, such as calendar, address book, scheduling devices, and so on, but is best known for including full keyboards on the device itself, which facilitated sending and replying to email messages.

At the end of 1983, there were just more than 340,000 wireless subscribers in the U.S. By the end of 2000, that number had grown to roughly 109 million, and at the end of 2010, over 303 million Americans were cellular subscribers. (See "Computing goes Mobile" in "History of Computing.")

Recent Developments in Technology

Digital Music Players Apple's original iPod portable music player hit the market in 2001, capable of storing either 5GB or 10GB of digital music. Capacity has increased over the years; in 2010, the largest iPods held up to 160GB of storage—as many as 40,000 songs, 25,000 photos, 200 hours of video, or any combination of the three. In 2010, Apple announced that life-to-date iPod

sales had exceeded 275 million, confirming its status as the best-selling digital audio player—and one of the fastest-selling consumer electronics products in history.

DVD DVDs are used for audio and video storage, most commonly as a medium for movies and other video programming. A dual-layer DVD can hold up to 8.5 gigabytes (GB) of data, compared to 800 megabytes (MB) of storage on an audio CD. The first commercial DVDs were released in 1995, and the format has gradually replaced the older (and now practically obsolete) VHS videotape for- mat. The current DVD format stores video programming in the standard definition format, with 480 lines of resolution.

Blu-ray disc formats were developed to store high definition video programming, with 1080 lines of resolution. Blu-ray uses standard diameter DVD discs but with much denser data storage—more than three times the storage of a standard DVD disc.

DVR Digital video recording (DVR) technology enables subscribers to record television shows for future viewing, storing programming on an internal hard disk. Since programs are recorded digitally, viewers can seamlessly fast forward, rewind, pause, or stop recorded programming. These features are also available when watching "live" programming because the current program is automatically cached to the hard disk while being viewed. Most DVRs feature a sophisticated onscreen electronic program guide (EPG) to facilitate program selection; entire television series can be set to record without having to manually enter individual stop and start times. One of the most popular DVRs is offered by TiVo (first released in 1999); most cable and satellite companies offer DVR functions in their set top boxes. By 2009, 43 percent of U.S. households had a DVR player.

Energy

Electric Power

Electricity was known in antiquity and became an important subject for scientific investigation as early as 1600 with English scientist William Gilbert's (1544–1603) studies of magnetism and electrical attraction. The electric charge then known resulted from rubbing one substance (such as amber—in Greek, "electron") with another (such

as wool). Despite extensive experiments with electricity in the 18th century, no successful applications were developed. At the end of the century, however, Italian scientists Luigi Galvani (1738–98) and Alessandro Volta (1745–1827) discovered that certain chemical reactions produce an electric charge. Volta recognized that this effect can be employed to make a continuous transfer of charge, the first known electric current. Shortly after Volta announced his first chemical battery in 1800, English chemist Humphry Davy (1778–1829) used electric current to heat metal so that it glowed and to produce visible arcs between two conductors. By 1807 Davy had shown that electric current is powerful enough to separate compounds into their components, finding half a dozen new elements by electrolysis.

A connection between electricity and magnetism had long been suspected, but was not established until 1820 when Danish scientist Hans Christian Oersted (1777–1851) reported that a magnetic compass needle responds to an electric current. Other scientists immediately began to extend Oersted's discovery, notably French physicist André-Marie Ampère (1775–1836) and English chemist Michael Faraday (1791–1867). Faraday and American physicist Joseph Henry (1797–1878) independently discovered that a moving magnetic field generates an electric current (first published by Faraday in 1831). Unlike the electric battery, which ceases operation after several hours, the generator can produce a continuous current so long as the magnet keeps moving.

The Electric Motor   The first practical application of electric current was telegraphy in 1837. By 1873 the first electric motor was demonstrated—a generator reversed so that current produced motion instead of motion producing current. In 1879 both Thomas Edison (1847–1931) and English inventor Joseph Swan (1828–1914) developed practical lights powered by electric current. Edison quickly began to build electric generating stations and power grids to capitalize on his invention. Soon electric power was available to thousands of homes.

Edison's power plants developed a form of electric current called direct current (DC) in which electrons flow through a conductor in a single direction. Another form of electric current, alternating current (AC), is produced as electrons swish back and forth in the conductor. Beginning in 1884, Croatian-American engineer Nikola Tesla (1856–1943) developed motors and other devices using AC that are now the basis of the modern electrical grid.

The first hydroelectric power plant went into operation in 1882 in Appleton, Wisconsin. The first hyroelectric plant to produce AC power went into operation in 1890 on the Williamette River in Oregon.

Electrification   Electricity spread from city to city throughout the industrialized world, bringing with it a flood of electric inventions that would quickly change both living and working conditions. The modern vacuum cleaner was invented in 1901 by the Englishman Hubert Booth, the air conditioner in 1902 (Willis Carrier, American), the residential refrigerator in 1903 (Marcel Audiffren, French), electric automobile ignition in 1911 (Charles Franklin Kettering), the television in 1925 (Philo T. Farnsworth, American), and the household toaster in 1926 (Charles Strite, American).

Electrification also brought into sharp relief the difference between industrialized city life and conditions in rural areas. Electrification was most feasible when located close to industrial centers that could supply the required capital, infrastructure, and market, and until the 1920s the ability to transmit electricity over long distances was very limited. Until the large-scale government projects of the 1930s, electrification in the U.S. was limited to urban areas; 90 percent of urban dwellers had access to electricity in the early 1930s compared to only 10 percent in rural areas.

In 1933, as a response to the Great Depression, the Tennessee Valley Authority was established to build hydroelectric dams to bring electricity to the American Midwest. In 1935, the Rural Electrification Administration, created by President Franklin Roosevelt, began an expansive program to electrify the nation's farmlands; within 15 years, electricity was available to 90 percent of farms nationwide. Also in 1935, the hydroelectric generators at the Hoover Dam went into operation, generating power for the Southwest.

By the 1950s, electrical devices were everywhere, and demand nationwide for electrical power was surging at an annual rate of 9.8 percent. Even as the U.S. population has grown, improvements in the design and efficiency of electric-powered devices has meant that power demand has slowed in growth. In the 1990s the power demand for electricity averaged 2.4 percent growth per year, and from 2000 to 2009, the growth averaged 0.9 percent per year.

Petroleum

Literally meaning "rock oil," petroleum seeps out of porous rock. Until 1857, when the first commercial oil well was drilled in Ploiesti, Romania, nearly all petroleum came from oil-saturated sand deposits called oil sands or from surface-level oil seeps. Petroleum had been known to ancient people in Asia and the Middle East, though its use as an effective engine fuel awaited 19th-century advances in chemistry. Crude petroleum burns, but not very efficiently; it must be refined and distilled to become one of several usable fuel grades, e.g. kerosene, diesel, gasoline, or jet fuel.

The first oil well in the United States was drilled in 1859 in Titusville, Pennsylvania. Early oil production focused on the distillation of kerosene, with gasoline as a discarded by-product. In 1870, the Standard Oil Company of Ohio was formed by John D. Rockefeller to refine and distribute kerosene throughout the Midwest. The company quickly grew to dominate oil production and transport throughout the country, often through aggressive competition with local companies and collusion with railroad barons who controlled distribution. By 1904, Standard Oil exerted complete dominance over U.S. oil, controlling over 90 percent of oil production (at that time oil was still drilled primarily for making kerosene), but was forced by the Supreme Court to dissolve in 1911 under the Sherman Antitrust Act. The breakup resulted in 35 regional "Standards," including Standard Oil of California (which would later become Chevron), Standard Oil of New Jersey (later Exxon) and Standard Oil of New York (later Mobil).

Foreign Oil   By the beginning of World War I, all the industrialized nations of Europe and the Americas had thriving oil markets, though the spurt of wartime industrial production caused a temporary oil shortage during 1916–17. Intense international interest in Middle East oil fields discovered in 1908 focused military and diplomatic efforts on disrupting Turkish–Ottoman control of the region and opening it to European trade and political influence.

The Sykes-Picot Agreement of 1916 and the San Remo Conference established English and French protectorates in the region, assigning parts of modern Iraq to Britain and parts of Iran and Syria to France, arranging for access to pipelines and railways.

Until 1950, the United States was thought to have the largest oil reserves of any oil-producing nation. The U.S. supplied 85 percent of Allied oil during World War II, so much in fact that the U.S. became intensely concerned that the country was depleting its oil fields too quickly, and began looking for large sources of foreign oil to import.

As France and England exerted tight control over Syria, Iran, and Iraq, American speculators looked to the unproven reserves of Saudi Arabian oil fields. Geologists were increasingly convinced that Saudi Arabia sat atop an enormous supply of oil. Today, Saudi Arabian oil fields contain an estimated 25 percent of the global oil supply.

By the close of the Second World War, U.S. domestic consumption had nearly caught up to production. The first sizable import of oil to the United States occurred in 1950, initially to supplement domestic production, though by 1958 the U.S. was consuming more energy than it produced, a development fueled by postwar prosperity and the love of automobiles. Imports made up 10 percent of U.S. oil consumption during the 1950s; a decade later it was 18 percent; in the 1970s, 35 percent. The U.S.–Saudi relationship resulted in affordable oil prices even as consumption mushroomed.

During this period, the three largest Standards (California, New York, and New Jersey), along with British-Dutch owned Royal Dutch Shell, the British-owned Anglo-Persian Oil Company (later BP), Gulf Oil, and Texaco, operated as a cartel and collectively dominated worldwide oil production and distribution, and were known as the "Seven Sisters." The initial development of the Saudi oil fields was undertaken by the Californian-Arabian Standard Oil Company (CASOC), of which Texaco was part owner. In the late 1940s, CASOC was renamed the Arabian-American Oil Company (Aramco), and gained as part owners Standard Oil Company of New Jersey and Standard Oil Company of New York. Under the wing of the Seven Sisters, Saudi Arabian oil fields increased production from 60 million barrels in 1946 to 3.1 billion barrels in 1976.

The lines connecting political, economic, and military spheres in regard to Middle Eastern oil became increasingly tangled during the Cold War. In 1960, a cartel of oil-producing nations was formed under the name OPEC (Organization of the Petroleum Exporting Countries) and originally included Iran, Iraq, Kuwait, Saudi Arabia, and Venezuela. OPEC's aim was to collectively regulate export prices and production quotas and to exert leverage against European and American pressures. By the mid-1970s, Qatar, Indonesia, Libya, the United Arab Emirates, Algeria, and Nigeria had also joined.

Meanwhile, as access to the world's largest oil supply became a strategic necessity for both the U.S. and Soviet Union, local political upheavals in the Middle East took on global ramifications. When the United States sided with Israel in the 1973 Arab–Israeli War, Arab nations, including Saudi Arabia, responded with the oil embargo of

1973–74, which sent United States prices skyward and caused shortages at pumps. Furthermore, the Saudi royals nationalized Aramco assets, ending American dominance over oil fields there.

In response, the United States in 1977 created the Strategic Petroleum Reserve, which permitted the storage of 580 million barrels of oil. By 1985, the reserve held enough oil to provide a normal level of petroleum for 115 days in the absence of any other petroleum imports. The reserve proved useful in preventing additional oil price hikes during the Iraqi invasion of Kuwait in 1990. The reserve can also be used as an emergency supply of oil in case of a disaster such as Hurricane Katrina (2005), which shut down production and refining in the Gulf of Mexico for weeks. By 2010, however, the reserve had dwindled to 75 days of oil.

Domestic oil production in the United States peaked in 1972; since then, production has fallen and leveled off, though demand has continued to grow steadily. According to the Department of Energy, in 1970 the U.S. produced 9.6 million barrels of oil per day; in 2008, 5.0 million barrels a day. In terms of consumption, in 1970 the U.S. consumed 14.7 million barrels a day; 2008, 19.5 million barrels a day. As a result, reliance on foreign oil will only grow larger over time. Imports made up 55.0 percent of oil consumption in 2001; by 2010 that number reached 58.1 percent; by 2020, it will reach 66.3 percent; by 2030, 69.6 percent. In 2010, top suppliers of exports to the U.S. were Canada (2.5 million barrels a day), Mexico (1.2 million barrels a day), Saudi Arabia (1.1 million barrels a day), Nigeria (1.0 million barrels a day), and Venezuela (1.0 million barrels a day).

With the growing reliance on foreign oil comes the increasing dependence on vicissitudes of the foreign oil market. Oil prices spiked to $28.26 per barrel in 2000, retreated to $22.95 in 2001, and rebounded to $28.50 in 2003, all dramatic swings that seemed extreme at the time. On August 30, 2005, after Hurricane Katrina hit the Gulf coast, the price of oil skyrocketed to an all-time high of $70.85 a barrel, and continued to rise thereafter, crossing the $100.00 mark in January 2008 and holding near $134.00 a barrel through summer before falling sharply in the global financial upheaval late that year.

On April 20, 2010, the explosion of a BP rig in the Gulf of Mexico caused the worst oil-related environmental disaster in history. After three months, the oil well, more than one mile below the surface, was still spewing 60,000 gallons of oil into the Gulf each day. The financial and ecological damage will be incalculable.

Nuclear Power

Between 1939 and 1945, the United States emerged as the leading nuclear power, as demonstrated with terrible force in the bombings of Hiroshima and Nagasaki in 1945. Manhattan Project scientists devised the most powerful weapons ever conceived and permanently changed global politics. Their research also led to the creation of the modern nuclear power industry, which today provides 2 percent of the world's power and 15 percent of the world's electricity.

The principal stages in the creation of both nuclear power and nuclear weapons are very similar. Both rely on chain reactions that occur when unstable atoms are bombarded with neutrons. These neutrons penetrate nearby nuclei and cause them to split, which—along with creating lighter elements—releases gamma radiation and frees more neutrons that in turn impact the nucleus of another atom, and so on. In very dense elements like uranium, the cumulative effect generates an incredible amount of heat and power. The main difference between the chain reactions in nuclear energy and weapons is that in nuclear power generation, the goal is the tightly controlled creation of intense heat to make steam, whereas in weapons the goal is a maximum explosive force. Both applications for nuclear fission rely on particularly unstable variants, or allotropes, of either uranium or plutonium.

The Atomic Energy Act of 1946 established the Atomic Energy Commission, a civilian-run organization that would oversee nuclear reactors and programs in the United States. Under the act, all nuclear reactors were government-owned and nuclear technology was a closely guarded state secret. In the decade following World War II, many of the resources in the nuclear community were devoted to the H-bomb race with the Soviet Union, and the attention of military strategists was already turning to unrest in South Korea. During this period, the commission oversaw production of experimental reactor prototypes for converting nuclear fission into electricity. However, most of the uranium being enriched was earmarked for weapons testing, and it was not until 1951 that experiments using nuclear reactions to generate electric power (at reactor EBR-1 in Arco, Idaho) would prove fruitful, though the electrical output was minimal.

The Atomic Energy Act of 1954 widened access to

previously secret data and began a period of rapid expansion of the nuclear power industry, which now had access to government reactor designs, prototypes, and technical information. President Eisenhower's Atoms For Peace plan also called for uranium stockpiles to be monitored by an international body, eventually organized in 1957 as the International Atomic Energy Agency (IAEA). In 1956, the first commercial electricity-generating nuclear plant went online in Calder Hall, England. The first operational U.S. commercial nuclear power plant was opened in 1957 in Shippingport, Pennsylvania.

By the 1970s, several factors led to the declining growth of the nuclear power industry. First, the price of competitive fuels such as oil and coal declined as U.S. imports and production grew. Second, and more important, was the growing perception that nuclear power plants were ecologically unsafe and potentially disastrous. The nuclear accident at the Three Mile Island plant in 1979 had dramatic ramifications for the industry, thrown into even sharper relief by the 2011 meltdown at Japan's Fukushima Daiichi Nuclear Power Station following a catastrophic earthquake and tsunami.

Nuclear Disasters   There have been four major nuclear disasters at commercial power plants: the 1957 Windscale fire, the 1979 Three Mile Island meltdown, the 1986 Chernobyl explosion, and the 2011 Fukushima meltdown.

Windscale fire   The Windscale reactors near Cumbria, England, were early enrichment reactors, designed for producing allotropes of plutonium and uranium, relying on graphite core rods that had to be annealed (heated slightly and cooled) periodically. On October 10, 1957, the reactor's cooling process failed, and the rods began to superheat, fueled by the intense heat given off by the radioactive reactions. The graphite core caught fire, and in the course of battling the blaze, 20,000 curies of radioactivity were released into the atmosphere in a cloud of steam and smoke. It is estimated that radioactive iodine released into the surrounding area caused 240 cases of thyroid cancer.

Three Mile Island   While the Windscale fire originated inside the nuclear core, in the Three Mile Island, Pennsylvania, meltdown, the problem began in an auxiliary system. On March 28, 1979, feed water pumps in secondary sections of the plant failed, which affected the plant's ability to cool itself. As a standard safety measure, the turbine and reactor automatically shut down.

However, during the shutdown process, a valve for coolant failed and drained the nuclear core, which began to overheat. Alarms alerted technicians to the secondary systems failures, but not to the problems in the core until it was too late. Nearly half the core melted, but fortunately the radioactive material was contained within the building. Government officials have repeatedly asserted that negligible amounts of radiation escaped the site, and that no harmful effects have been detected in people as a result.

Regardless, the Three Mile Island incident brought the U.S. nuclear power industry to a standstill. The widespread opinion that a nuclear catastrophe had only narrowly been averted fueled efforts to cast the nuclear power industry as unsafe. In addition, the falling production costs for coal and petroleum made nuclear power seem both risky and expensive. As a result, construction on nuclear power plants effectively halted, and several states enacted moratoriums on any new construction.

Chernobyl   The most famous nuclear disaster took place on April 26, 1986, at the Chernobyl Nuclear Power Plant in Pripyat, Ukraine. A power surge inside the reactor core caused it to overheat, which set off a cascade of systems failures. The superheated core caused a steam explosion that released large amounts of volatile hydrogen gas, which in turn also exploded, destroying part of the building and exposing the reactor to the outside. Once fresh air contacted the reactor core, the superheated graphite in the reactor caught fire and began to melt. The explosion and fire generated a massive cloud of radioactive smoke and steam that spread over a very wide area, including parts of nearby Belarus and Russia, and contaminated the adjacent Pripyat River, which flows toward the Ukrainian capital of Kiev.

The disastrous effects of the reactor explosion were worsened by the way the Soviet government handled the crisis. Firefighters called to battle the reactor fire were not told the smoke was radioactive, and the nearby town of Pripyat was not evacuated until the following day. The U.S. Nuclear Regulatory Commission (N.R.C.) estimates that 4,000 radiation cancer-related deaths may be traced to the Chernobyl disaster.

Fukushima Daiichi   The March 11, 2011, earthquake and resulting tsunami in northern Japan caused a number of explosions, fires, and leaks of radioactive gas in three of six reactors at the Fukushima plant. It is believed that spent radioactive rods in a storage pool at a fourth, inactive reactor were exposed to the air, releasing large

Harnessing Ocean Power

By SONIA KOLESNIKOV–JESSOP

Generating renewable energy from the ocean through Ocean Thermal Energy Conversion, known as O.T.E.C., has been studied for nearly a century but, although several demonstration plants have been built to prove that the technology works, it has never been put into commercial operation. Now, however, despite the high costs involved, several companies are working toward commercial projects.

O.T.E.C. generates electricity by exploiting the temperature differential between warm surface water and the cold ocean depths. Surface water is pumped through a heat exchanger, where it heats a fluid with a very low boiling point, such as ammonia, which expands as it vaporizes. The vaporized gas drives turbines producing electricity before being piped into a condenser, where cold deep ocean water chills it, returning it to its liquid state. The liquid is then pumped back to the warm water heat exchanger to repeat the cycle.

To work effectively, the technology requires a temperature differential of at least 20 degrees Celsius (36 Fahrenheit). This can be found in large expanses of the tropical oceans. "Every additional degree will help produce 15 percent more energy," said Philippe Dubau, general manager of Pacific Otec, a subsidiary of Pacific Petroleum, an oil product distributor in French Polynesia, New Caledonia and Vanuatu that has been moving into the renewable energy sector.

According to Kevin Joyce, a renewable energy consultant at Black & Veatch, based in Overland Park, Kansas, one of the more exciting characteristics of the technology is that, unlike most renewable energy sources, it can provide steady, reliable baseload power.

"This would generate electricity 24 hours a day in a predictable and dependable manner," Mr. Joyce said. "Other renewable technologies with this kind of resource potential, like wind and solar, are intermittent, which means that they need conventional generation to fill the gaps."

Sometimes, he said, that could mean building additional, fast-response, conventional power plants to kick in with power to the grid when the renewable sources go dark. O.T.E.C., in contrast, "has the ability to avoid those requirements and even displace some of our baseload plants."

"That means that it has more potential for CO_2 reduction than many other renewable technologies," Mr. Joyce said. It also has other advantages. "The technology is compact compared to wind and solar," he said, adding that it can be "offshore and out of sight."

Pacific Otec is working with DCNS, the French government-owned naval architect and military shipbuilder, and Xenesys, a Japanese specialist in desalination and thermal energy conversion technology, on a feasibility study for a commercial O.T.E.C. plant in Tahiti. Financial backing for the project has been provided by the French and French Polynesian governments, which are paying 50 percent and 18 percent, respectively, of the cost of the feasibility study.

The project aims to build an offshore O.T.E.C. platform, with a 10 megawatt-hour generating capacity, which will be connected to the Tahiti power grid and could produce enough electricity to cover 10 percent of the islands' needs, Mr. Dubau said.

"We are in the same situation as the people who were making the first steam engine," he said. "There is still a very long and difficult road in front of us, but if we succeed, we can bring something interesting and relevant in terms of energy and water supply to the communities, so it is worth trying."

The Tahiti project will center on an offshore O.T.E.C. plant 25 meters, or 80 feet, high and submerged 25 meters below the surface to avoid strong currents and big waves.

"Below that sea level, it's much more stable," Mr. Dubau said. "This feasibility study is not about the technology; we know it works. We also know the design of the plant is correct. But what we need to do now is to design the optimal energy system, considering local environmental data; to design the integration of the process into the chosen platform type; and, of course, study the economic feasibility of the whole project."

Engineering and design work in the yearlong study will be supervised by DCNS, with Xenesys providing the generating system technology. The feasibility phase should be followed by a contract for DCNS to build a commercial plant, he said.

The science behind ocean thermal energy conversion was first explored in France in the late 19th century and an experimental O.T.E.C. plant was built and briefly operated by a French engineer, Georges Claude, in Cuba in 1930. In the 1970s, as the first oil crisis hit, several countries started to look more seriously at the technology. A test facility was built with U.S. government funding at Keahole Point in Hawaii and another, by Tokyo Electric Power of Japan, on the island of Nauru. In the 1980s however, as oil prices slid back, attention shifted away.

"It didn't make sense at the time to go into the technology," Mr. Dubau said. "It is still extraordinarily expensive because there is a lot of innovation, not only in the process itself but also in the pipeline."

Because the technology uses large volumes of cold water from the deep ocean, it calls for an extremely long, wide-bore intake pipe. "You need special materials to build pipelines that are over three to five meters in diameter, which is extraordinarily big, and the pipeline needs to go about 1,000 meters deep, to get the cold water," Mr. Dubau said.

Michinaga Takeda, a Xenesys project engineer for the Tahiti project, said his company had also done some preliminary studies for an onshore O.T.E.C. project in Cuba that would utilize waste heat discharged from a thermal power plant to increase the temperature of the surface seawater. He said the combination of onshore construction and the use of recycled heat could result in both cost savings and higher efficiency; but the project had been stalled by the difficulty for the Cuban government of finding external sources of financing.

In the United States, Lockheed Martin's alternative energy development team is currently working on the design of a pilot plant, with a generating capacity of 5 to 10 megawatts, which could become operational in Hawaii by 2014. But while this system is the same size as Pacific Otec's feasibility project in Tahiti, Lockheed Martin's prototype will serve to validate technologies for much bigger O.T.E.C. plants with capacity of more than 100 megawatts.

Larger O.T.E.C. plants would benefit from lessons learned building and operating the pilot plant, with anticipated improvements like streamlined maintenance strategies, better monitoring and control of the thermodynamic cycle, said Ted Johnson, director of alternative energy development at Lockheed Martin. The pilot plant would also help to determine the cost and technical risks associated with scaling up to larger, utility-scale capacities of 100 megawatts or more, he said.

"I think our approach and theirs is different," Mr. Dubau said. "The U.S. is looking at the use of such plants to generate electricity for their military base in Guam and Diego Garcia, for example. We're looking at a much smaller-sized plant that would meet the needs of a small island community."

amounts of radioactivity. The immediate area of the Fukushima plant was so violently dangerous and hot that disaster responders could not effectively pump water into the damaged reactors to cool the destroyed containment and cooling systems, and ongoing efforts to cool the damaged reactors with water proved largely unsuccessful.

The exact chain of events and scope of the disaster had not become clear by the time this book went to press, due to the apparent mix of confusion and misinformation regarding the reactors' condition, as well as the extremely dangerous conditions inside the reactors. Disaster workers were allowed inside the facility for only short periods and ongoing investigations into the conditions inside the plant were conducted by remote control robots. On June 6, Japanese officials conceded that three of the reactors had probably suffered fuel meltdowns, contrary to earlier assertions. Nuclear regulatory officials have placed the Fukushima disaster on par with the Chernobyl disaster; the human and ecological toll is not yet known.

In May 2011, Japan's prime minister Naoto Kan stated that Japan would abandon further nuclear development.

Disposal Nuclear reactors generate two kinds of radioactive materials: first, anything used by reactor personnel to handle, transport, or cool reactor fuel, including clothing and tools; and second, the spent fuel itself. Compared with the spent reactor fuel, the items in the first group emit very little radioactivity, and the isotopes they contain have a relatively short half-life. For spent fuel, however, disposal requires elaborate steps. The radioactive half-life of spent uranium is more than 100,000 years; there is nowhere on the surface of the planet to store it where it will become safe. To date, the United States has no permanent repository for spent nuclear fuel, and used cores are held in various temporary locations, usually onsite at nuclear plants when possible. In the 1980s, plans began for the construction of a permanent underground disposal facility at Yucca Mountain, Nevada, though the plan has met vociferous opposition and the facility has yet to be built.

Solar Power

Nearly all energy used on Earth comes ultimately from the sun. Photosynthesis in plants provides all food and fossil fuels, winds blow from unequal solar heating, and water flows in part because solar evaporation lifts water molecules into the air. "Solar power" refers to ways to tap sunlight directly.

In 1883, a French experiment demonstrated that sunlight captured with a parabolic mirror could heat water enough to power a small steam engine. Solar water heaters were first used in the United States in the 1890's. In 1948 a house in Dover, Mass., was heated by collecting solar heat in flat plates containing water, which was then pumped into the house to warm it, but the house was not sufficiently warmed on cloudy days and the method was judged a failure. The method, called *passive solar*, has since been refined and used on many houses, most effectively in mild climates. The first passive solar office building, Albuquerque, New Mexico's Bridgers-Paxton Building, was built in 1956.

Generally when we speak of solar power, we are referring to direct conversion of sunlight into electricity. Culminating advances in *photovoltaic* (literally meaning "light current") cells, scientists at Bell labs first began producing moderately efficient silicon photovoltaic (PV) cells in 1954. These early cells were able to convert 4 percent of the sunlight hitting them into electric current. Since then, improvements in efficiency have been incremental; efficiency reached 10 percent by 1959. Other materials have since been used, improving efficiency in some instances to 32 percent by 1999.

Most uses of this form of solar power were isolated installations such as lighthouses or artificial satellites, or small appliances such as watches and calculators, although several experimental automobiles have been powered this way. More recently homes have used solar panels for power. These are usually connected to the local power grid; they sell any excess power to the grid and buy power when the sun is not shining. Larger installations based on this concept have also been connected to the power grid, starting in 1982 with Hesperia, California's 1-megawatt capacity solar array, composed of 108 solar panels. Also in 1982, the first solar-powered car, the Quiet Achiever, drove from Sydney to Perth, Australia in 20 days.

In 2001, commercial solar panels hit mainstream DIY America, as The Home Depot began selling solar power systems in stores.

Timeline of Modern Energy Developments

1901 First U.S. oil gusher near Beaumont, Texas.

1902 First building with air conditioning, Armour Building, is built in Kansas City.

1903 Charles G. Curtis and William Le Roy invent the steam turbine generator, greatly improving efficiency of steam-powered electricity creation.

1904 First self-contained mechanical refrigerator debuts at St. Louis World's Fair.

1908 Henry Ford introduces the Model T, the first low-cost, mass-produced automobile.

1908 The first solar collector is invented, which uses copper coils in an insulated box.

1910 The world's first geothermal plant begins operation in Lardello, Italy.

1913 Thermal cracking, which increases the efficiency of gasoline distillation, is first used.

1917 The first long-distance high-voltage power transmission line.

1920s First commercial residential wind-powered generators are sold to U.S. farms.

1921 Leaded gasoline is introduced.

1928 First mobile offshore drilling platform is built.

1931 First large-scale wind farms go into use in Russia.

1933 The Tennessee Valley Authority (TVA) is established with a mandate to build and manage hydroelectric power generators and dams throughout the Midwest.

1935 Hoover Dam hydroelectric generator begins operation.

1935 Rural Electrification Administration (REA) is established to bring electricity to rural Americans.

1936 Catalytic cracking, which further increases the efficiency of gasoline distillation, is first used.

1938 First mass-produced flourescent lamps.

1938 First offshore oil well begins operation near Louisiana.

1939 First fission experiments split uranium atoms, conveting mass into energy.

1939 The combustion turbine is invented.

1942 First sustained nuclear fission reaction.

1942 Construction of the Grand Coulee Dam on Washington's Columbia river, begun in 1933, is completed. The Dam's hydroelectric generators provide power throughout the Northwest.

1944 Federal Aid Highway Act establishes the U.S. Interstate system.

1945 The first magnetron experiments, which will lead to the developent of microwave ovens by the 1960's, are conducted.

1947 First far-offshore oil driling platform is built out of sight of land off the coast of Louisiana.

1951 Experimental Breeder Reactor 1 in Idaho creates first usable nuclear power.

1952 First nuclear power plant goes into operation outside Moscow, Russia.

1953 The seven-state power grid is implemented, which can redistribute power over a large area as needed.

1954 The Atomic Energy Act of 1954 allows private companies to use nuclear fuel and operate commercial power plants.

1954 First nuclear-powered submarine, the *USS Nautilus*, is launched.

1955 Nuclear reactor BORAX-III powers the entire town of Arco, Idaho with electricty.

1957 First U.S. nuclear power plant goes into operation at Shippingport, Pennsylvania.

1954 First practical photovoltaic cell.

1950's The first oil supertankers are built.

1959 The first large-scale geothermal electric plant goes into operation in New Zealand.

1962 First light-emitting diode (LED) is produced.

1965 First major U.S. power blackout affects the northeast.

1967 Very-high power transmission lines go into use in the U.S., capable of transporting 750,000 volts.

1967 The U.S.S.R. completes the Krasnoyansk Dam in Siberia, producing three times the hyroelectric power as the Grand Coulee Dam.

1973 The OPEC oil embargo creates first energy crisis, driving up gasoline prices and creating demand for more efficient automobiles.

1973 President Nixon establishes Project Independence,

meant to eliminate U.S. reliance on foreign oil by 1980.

1975 Energy Policy and Conservation Act establishes Strategic Petroleum Reserve, creates minimum fuel economy standards, and extends fuel price controls.

1977 U.S. Department of Energy is created.

1979 The Iranian revolution causes a worldwide oil shortage.

1979 Partial meltdown at nuclear power plant at Three Mile Island, Pennsylvania.

1979 President Carter creates national progam to foster solar power research.

1982 The Strategic Petroleum Reserve reaches 250 million barrels of oil.

1980's Tens of thousands of wind turbines are built in California.

1986 A meltdown occurs at Chernobyl nuclear power reactor in Ukraine.

1987 National Appliance Energy Conservation Act sets minimum energy efficiency standards for large home appliances.

1992 Energy Policy Act of 1992 creates tax credits for various commercial investments in alternative fuels.

1997 First mass-produced hybrid vehicle, the Toyota Prius, is sold.

1999 Wind Powering America program is launched to increase U.S. wind power over ten years.

2000—01 California power crisis.

2001 The U.S. and European Union agree on joint research into fusion and non-nuclear energy.

2002 The Strategic Petroleum Reserve reaches 592 million barrels of oil.

2003 New, flexible drill pipes make horizontal drilling possible, increasing the efficiency of existing coal and gas harvesting sites.

2003 The largest power blackout in U.S. history hits on August 14, affecting eight states and leaving 50 million people without electricity.

2008 First wave power plant goes into operation at Aquacadoura, Portugal.

2010 First 24-hour flight of a manned, solar-powered aircraft.

2011 An earthquake causes fires, explosions and meltdowns at Japan's Fukushima Daiichi Nuclear Power Station.

History of Computing

The early history of computing contained four distinct generations, along with a rich prehistory of mechanical computing devices. Each generation was characterized by dramatic improvements in the technology used to build computer hardware, the internal organization of computer systems, and the computers' programming languages. Since the late 1990's the major evolution in the computer industry has been the increasing ubiquity of computers and the decreased importance of large desktop machines in favor of laptops and mobile computers.

The Mechanical Era

Computers as we know them had their beginnings in the so-called computing machines of the early 17th century. These machines were like crude calculators, designed to automate complex mathematical calculations, but had no memory or data storage. In fact, these machines did not even have a way to output the results of their calculations, other than dials or indicators.

Babbage's Difference and Analytical Engines

Charles Babbage (1792–1871) is often referred to as the "father of computing," due to his development of two separate computing machines—the Difference Engine and the Analytical Engine. The initial prototype of the Difference Engine was produced in 1822, and Babbage started work on the full machine in 1823. The Difference Engine was conceived as a steam-powered, fully automatic machine, capable of printing the results of its computations on paper.

The Difference Engine was never completed; Babbage ceased work on it in 1834 because he had an idea for a better calculating machine. This new machine, to be called the Analytical Engine, was a parallel decimal computer that could operate on words of 50 decimals and was capable of storing 1,000 such numbers. The Analytical Engine included a number of built-in operations, including conditional control that enabled the machine to execute instructions in a specific order. The instructions themselves were entered into the machine on punch cards, thus introducing the input method used in computers through the 1970's.

The Birth of International Business Machines

Herman Hollerith (1860–1929) first came to prominence in 1886, when he constructed the first electromechanical adding and sorting machine. This machine, which he dubbed a "tabulator," was put to its first commercial use in 1890 for the U.S. Census Bureau. Hollerith's tabulator could read census data that had been punched into rectangular cardboard cards, later known as punch cards. The use of these punch cards significantly reduced the incidence of data entry errors and increased the speed of data entry; in addition, a stack of punch cards served as a crude form of data storage.

Based on this success, Hollerith formed the Tabulating Machine Company in 1896. In 1911 the Tabulating Machine Company merged with the International Time Recording Company and the Computing Scale Company to form the Computing-Tabulating-Recording Company (C-T-R); in 1924, the name of the company was changed to International Business Machines (I.B.M.). By the end of the 20th century I.B.M. had more than 300,000 employees and revenues exceeding $88 billion.

Early 20th-century Computers: The Dawn of the Digital Age

In spite of U.S. Patent Director Charles Duell's infamous claim in 1899 that "everything that can be invented has already been invented," new calculating and computing machines continued to be invented after the turn of the century. These new machines were the forerunners of the modern computer, electrifying formerly mechanical devices, adding storage capability (and the ability to manipulate the stored results), and developing the capability of printing the results on paper.

Zuse's Binary Computing Machines

In 1936 scientist Konrad Zuse (1910–95), with assistance from Helmut Schreyer (1912–84), began construction of the Z1, the world's first programmable binary computer. The Z1, built in Zuse's bedroom (and overflowing into his parents' living room), was controlled by perforated strips of discarded movie film. This machine (originally dubbed the V1, but retroactively renamed Z1 after World War II) was completed in 1938, and is the ancestor of all modern computers.

Perhaps the most important development of the Z1 is the adoption of the binary system—also called digital computing. Zuse went on to develop the Z2, Z3, and Z4, which further refined the processes originally incorporated into the Z1.

Stibitz's Complex Number Calculator

In 1937 George Stibitz (1914–95,) of Bell Labs constructed one of the first binary computers, a 1-bit binary adder built for demonstration purposes only. Stibitz spent the next few years improving the device, which when completed in

1939 was dubbed the Complex Number Calculator (and was later called the Bell Labs Model 1). The Complex Number Calculator used electromagnetic relays, and was the first computing machine to be used over normal telephone lines, setting the stage for the future linking of computers and communications systems.

Desch and Mumma's Electronic Accumulator

The next major leap in computing technology involved the use of vacuum tubes as on/off valves. This enabled calculations to be made electronically rather than mechanically, which resulted in a significant increase in calculating speed.

The first use of the vacuum tube in a computing device was in 1938, when Joseph Desch (1907–87) and Robert Mumma (b. 1905) built a machine they called the Electronic Accumulator. This machine primed the world for true first-generation computers, and would be the dominant switching technology for the next 20 years.

First-Generation Computers: 1940–56

The first generation of true computers used vacuum tubes and electronic circuits to replace the mechanical switches and moving parts of mechanical calculators. While these first computers were physically massive and operationally complicated, they delivered on the promise of handling increasingly large and complex calculations and were essential to deciphering secret codes in World War II and developing America's atomic energy program in the years after.

The Turing Machine   The first true computer was strictly theoretical. In 1937 the Cambridge mathematician Alan Turing (1912–54, England), in a paper on the mathematical theory of computation, conceived of the idea for a "universal machine" capable of executing any describable algorithm. This theoretical machine, dubbed the Turing Machine, formed the basis for the concept of "computability," separate from the process of calculation.

Colossus   The first fully electronic computer to actually be built was named Colossus. Commissioned to crack the secret code used by German Enigma cipher machines, Colossus was completed in December of 1943 by Thomas Flowers (1905–98) at London's Post Office Research Laboratories. Ten Colossus machines were built over the course of the war, but all were destroyed immediately after completing their work, to keep the design from falling into enemy hands.

Harvard Mark I   The Harvard Mark I, more formally known as the Automatic Sequence Controlled Calculator (ASCC), was the world's first fully programmable computer. It was an electromechanical machine that executed commands in a step-by-step fashion; instructions were fed into the machine by means of paper tape, punch cards, or switches.

The Mark I, partially financed by IBM, was developed by Howard Aiken (1900–73) and James W. Bryce (1880–1949) at Harvard University, where it occupied an entire building. The Mark I was completed in 1944, and was kept in operation for more than 15 years. During World War II it was employed by the U.S. Navy to run repetitive calculations for various mathematical tables.

ENIAC   The most famous first-generation computer was arguably the Electronic Numerical Integrator and Computer, or ENIAC. ENIAC was developed as a result of a wartime commission by the U.S. Army Ordinance Corps to design an electronic machine that could quickly compute firing and bombing tables. John W. Mauchly (1907–1980) and J. Presper Eckert, Jr. (1919–1995) of Pennsylvania's Moore School of Engineering began work on ENIAC in 1943, and the machine was completed in 1946.

Compared with today's computers, ENIAC was a monster. It was composed of 30 separate units (plus power supply and forced-air cooling); weighed over 30 tons; and contained more than 18,000 vacuum tubes, 1,500 relays, and hundreds of thousands of resistors, capacitors, and inductors.

On completion, ENIAC was put into service for calculations involved in the design of the hydrogen bomb. It served as the nation's main computational workhorse through 1952, and was finally dismantled in 1955.

UNIVAC   After the success of ENIAC, Mauchly and Eckert decided to go into business for themselves. In 1948 they began development on the Universal Automatic Computer, or UNIVAC—one of the first large computers developed for business use, not war use. In 1950 Mauchly and Eckert sold their company to Remington Rand Inc.; in 1951 the U.S. Census Bureau accepted delivery of the first UNIVAC computer.

Second-Generation Computers: 1956–63

The second generation of computers was characterized by the shrinking size and increased computing power made possible by the replacement of vacuum tubes and large electronic circuits with smaller transistors and integrated circuits. These second-generation computers were the first that were powerful enough to handle interpreted programming languages, such as FORTRAN and COBOL, and dominated information processing in the late 1950's and early 1960's.

Introducing the Transistor The transistor—short for transfer resistor—was developed at AT&T Bell Laboratories in 1947 by Walter H. Brattain (1902–87), William Shockley (1910–89), and John Bardeen (1908–91), who would be awarded the 1956 Nobel Prize in physics for their work. The transistor's small size, high yield, low heat production, and low price helped to make the next generation of computers run 1,000 times faster than the previous generation.

Transistorized Computers Building on Brattain and others' groundbreaking research, the first completely transistorized computer, TRADIC, was developed by Bell Laboratories in 1953. Another early transistorized computer was the Transistorized Experimental Computer (TX-0), developed at MIT's Lincoln Laboratories in 1956.

Introducing the Integrated Circuit (IC) Chip The integrated circuit (IC) is a single electronic circuit on a single slice of silicon. The first IC was developed by two teams of scientists, working independently of each other, at Fairchild Semiconductor and Texas Instruments. The Texas Instruments team, led by Jack St. Clair Kilby (b. 1923), developed their IC in December of 1958. The following year the Fairchild team—consisting of Jean Hoerni (1924–97), Kurt Lehovec (b. 1918), and Robert N. Noyce (1927–90)—successfully completed their IC project. The first commercial implementation of this technology hit the market in 1961.

Third-Generation Computers: 1964–71

The third generation of computing is based on the development of the integrated circuit. It was this generation of computer that gained widespread acceptance in corporate America, and led to the growth of data processing.

Moore's Law In 1965 Gordon Moore (b. 1929), then a scientist at Fairchild., in an article for the 35th anniversary issue of *Electronics* magazine, wrote what would later be dubbed "Moore's Law," which predicted that integrated circuits would double in complexity every year, while prices would stay the same. Moore's Law proved remarkably accurate in the years to come. (By the end of the 20th century, however, the rate of change had slowed down, and Moore's Law was revised to state that integrated circuits would double in complexity every 18 months while remaining at the same price.)

Computers in the Corporate World Third-generation computers were both powerful and affordable enough to be adopted by large corporations around the world. From the mid-1960's on, formerly manual tasks were automated by large mainframe computers, creating a new profession that became known as data processing. The most popular uses of these third-generation computers included inventory management, payroll management, file management, and report generation.

During this period the computer landscape was dominated by one company: IBM. IBM's dominance of the business market was even more profound outside the U.S.; at one point in the 1960's, 90 percent of the installed computers in the European market were IBM models.

Fourth-Generation Computers: 1970–Present

Fourth-generation computing is characterized by the use of the microprocessor, which is a computer processing unit (CPU) contained in an integrated circuit on a tiny piece of silicon. This generation of computers remains the longest to date, 30 years and counting at the start of the new millennium. During the fourth generation, improvements in computing have come from increases in speed and power, not from entirely new technology.

Introducing the Microprocessor The development of the microprocessor fueled a revolution in computing, and enabled the creation and popularization of the so-called personal computer. Now that the brains of the computer could be contained in a thumbnail-sized chip, computers could be made smaller and lighter than ever before and thus be used for a greater variety of practical applications.

Exactly who invented the microprocessor is open to debate. Independent engineer Gilbert Hyatt (b. 1938) filed for a patent for microprocessor technology in 1970, as did three engineers from Intel, led by Marcian E. Hoff (b. 1937). A year earlier Ray Holt (b. 1945) developed the onboard flight computer for the U.S. Navy's F-14A "Tomcat" fighter jet—a "computer on a chip" that was more powerful than Intel's first microprocessor. This controversy was similar to the one surrounding the invention of the integrated circuit; Hyatt was eventually awarded the patent in 1990.

Intel's Microprocessors

Intel Corporation was founded in 1968 by three former employees of Fairchild Semiconductor: Gordon Moore, Robert Noyce, and William Shockley. Intel would soon become one of the world's largest technology companies, and one of the three founding fathers of personal computing technology.

4-Bit Microprocessors Intel released its first microprocessor, the 4001, in October 1970. It was followed a month later by the 4002, and then the 4003, all 4-bit processors. The 4004 chip, released in November 1971, contained the equivalent of 2,300 transistors.

8-Bit Microprocessors Development of new microprocessor technology was fast and furious. Just five months after the release of the 4004 chip, in April 1972, Intel released its first 8-bit processor, the 8008, which contained the equivalent of 3,500 transistors.

Intel's next chip, the 8080, was released in January 1974. The 8080 was an 8-bit processor that was 10 times faster than the 8008, and contained the equivalent of 6,000 transistors. It was this chip that led to the development of the world's first personal computers.

IBM System/370

IBM quickly capitalized on the miniaturization enabled by the development of the microprocessor. In 1971 IBM released the System/370 family of computers, the first mainframe machines to be powered by microprocessor chips.

Personal Computing: The Early Years

Microprocessor technology enabled the construction of more powerful mainframe computers, and of smaller, lower-priced machines that came to be known as personal computers. The first personal computers were sold in kit form for the hobbyist market, but these smaller, easier-to-use computers soon gained a foothold with both business users and general consumers.

Hobby Computers

The earliest personal computers were based on Intel's 8-bit microprocessors, and were designed strictly for hobbyists. The first of these, the Mark 8, was actually a how-to project introduced in the July 1974 issue of *Radio Electronics* magazine, based on a design by Jonathan Titus.

Altair 8800: The World's First Personal Computer In 1975 a New Mexico-based company called MITS (Micro Instrumentation and Telemetry) released what is generally regarded as the world's first true personal computer, the Altair 8800. The Altair was based on Intel's 8080 microprocessor, contained 256 bytes of memory, and sold for $395 in kit form, or $498 assembled. Two thousand Altair 8800s were sold in the first year of release.

CP/M: The First Personal Computer Operating System All personal computers used a special type of program—called an operating system—that controlled the machine's most basic operations. The primary operating system for these first personal computers was called CP/M (Control Program for Microcomputers). It was developed in 1974 by Gary Kildall (1942–94) and John Torode of Digital Research specifically for the 8080 microprocessor.

Tandy Enters the Fray

As it became apparent that personal computers had mainstream appeal, many manufacturers and retailers sought to offer their own computer models for the hobbyist and home markets. One of the most successful of these early entrants was Tandy Corporation, which began selling computers through its Radio Shack retail stores in 1977.

Tandy TRS-80 Tandy's first personal computer was dubbed the TRS-80. It included a built-in keyboard, cassette storage, and 4Kb RAM. The TRS-80 was based on the Zilog Z80 chip, and sold for $599 (without a monitor); it could be hooked up to any black-and-white television set.

Tandy Color Computer In 1980 Tandy released its first color computer, named simply the Color Computer, or "coco" for short.

Commodore Sets Sail

Commodore Business Machines was a major player in the calculator and office machines market. When the personal computer market took off, it sought to complement its business machine offerings with a line of business- and home-oriented personal computers.

Commodore PET The Commodore PET was released in 1977. It was based on a 1-MHz MOS 6502 processor, had 8 Kb of RAM, and displayed monochrome text on a 9-inch monitor. Programs were loaded into the system on audiocassettes. The PET sold for $795, and was an overnight success.

Commodore VIC-20 The first of Commodore's true home computers was the VIC-20, released in 1981. It combined the computer and the keyboard in a single unit that could be connected to any color television set, contained 5Kb of RAM, and was targeted at a mass market with a price of $300. It was the industry's first million-unit seller, with production peaking at 9,000 units per day.

Commodore 64 The Commodore 64 was released in January 1982. The C-64 was built on the MOS 6502 microprocessor, contained 64Kb RAM, and sold for $595. It sold more than 17 million units over the course of its lifetime.

Other Early Players

The promise of the home market inspired many manufacturers to offer their own proprietary low-priced personal computers. The late 1970's and early 1980's saw a plethora of such machines released, although few would be considered long-term financial successes.

Apple Apple Computing was a major player from the very beginning of the personal computer era, with its Apple I (1976) and Apple II (1977) machines targeted at the business, home, and education markets.

Atari Over the course of the 1970's Atari became known for its coin-operated and home videogames. When the personal computer burst onto the scene, Atari decided to build on its success with games and migrate development to the personal computer platform. Atari ended up releasing two personal computer models in 1978. The Atari 400 and the Atari 800 were both powered by the MOS 6502 microprocessor and had more of a video game than a business feel; neither machine was fully accepted by the marketplace.

Osborne Adam Osborne (1939–2003) introduced the world's first portable computer, the Osborne I, in 1981. The Osborne I wasn't all that portable, however; it weighed more than 23 pounds and had a built-in 5-inch monochrome display, 64Kb RAM, and two floppy disk drives. It ran the CP/M operating system and sold for $1,795, and met with moderate success, ultimately losing the marketplace to IBM and IBM-compatible computers.

KayPro Like Osborne's, KayPro's main offering (the KayPro II) was a heavy portable computer. The KayPro II, released in 1982, came with a larger 9-inch monochrome display and ran the CP/M operating system. Also like the Osborne, the KayPro computer ultimately lost the format war to IBM.

Texas Instruments The TI 99/4 was Texas Instruments' initial entry into the burgeoning personal computer market. Released in 1979, it used TI's 16-bit 9940 microprocessor, but at $1,150 was significantly overpriced for the market. In 1980, TI replaced this initial unit by the more affordable TI 99/4A, which featured color graphics and a $525 price tag.

Sinclair In 1979 Sinclair Research introduced the ZX80 personal computer, based on Zilog's Z80 microprocessor. It featured 1Kb of RAM, had a membrane keyboard, and sold for $199. The low price of this model made it quite popular among the hobbyist crowd.

The IBM PC

The most important development in the history of personal computers was the entry of IBM into the marketplace. The initial IBM PC was an unparalleled success, driven by a combination of three factors—Intel's fast and affordable microprocessor chip, IBM's open architecture and marketing power, and Microsoft's operating system.

The Microprocessor: Intel The heart of the IBM PC was an Intel microprocessor chip. Over the course of the years Intel has provided many different microprocessors, supplying more power and faster speeds for new generations of personal computers.

Intel 8086/8088 Intel's 8086, released in 1978, was the first commercially successful 16-bit processor. When it was found to be too expensive to include in early personal computers, Intel developed (in 1979) an 8-bit version of the chip, dubbed the 8088. It was this chip, the 8088, that was chosen by IBM for use in the first IBM PC.

Intel 80286/80386/80486 The so-called x86 family of microprocessors, based on Intel's earlier 8086 chip, was designed to replace the 8088 in newer IBM-compatible PCs and introduced 16-bit processors to the world of personal computing. The first chip in this family was the 80186, released in 1982, although it saw little use in personal computers; it was better suited for self-contained controller devices. It was Intel's next chip, the 80286, that met with widespread acceptance among PC manufacturers. Also released in 1982, the 80286 contained the equivalent of 134,000 transistors. The 80286 was succeeded by the 80386 in 1985, and the 80486 in 1989.

The Hardware: IBM IBM, with its history of mainframe computing, legitimized the personal computing industry. IBM wasn't a fly-by-night company, and it didn't sell kits for hobbyists; it sold a ready-to-use, relatively easy-to-use, fully functioning computer through traditional retail stores—and was a name that consumers could trust.

The Original IBM PC IBM released its first personal computer—called, simply enough, the IBM PC—in August 1981. The standard model had 64Kb RAM and a single 160Kb single-sided floppy disk drive, and sold for $1,565 (without the green-on-black monochrome display). It was sold through IBM's established network of retail stores.

IBM initially hoped to sell 240,000 units in a five-year period. It received that many orders in the machine's first month of release. In fact, the IBM PC was so successful that its hardware technology and operating system became the standards for the industry; other operating systems, such as CP/M, soon disappeared from the personal computer landscape.

Compaq and Other Clones Competing computers that were functionally compatible with the IBM PC were called clones. The first of these clone computers was released by Compaq in 1982. The Compaq Portable—actually more of a "luggable"—was the size of a small suitcase and several times the weight. It included a built-in 9-inch monochrome monitor, 128Kb RAM, and a detachable keyboard. It sold for $3,590.

The Operating System: Microsoft Microsoft Corporation was founded in 1975 by Bill Gates (b. 1955) and Paul Allen (b. 1953). Their first product was a version of the BASIC programming language that they sold to MITS for use in its Altair computers, but the key to their long-lasting success was their contract with IBM to supply an operating system for the original IBM PC.

PC-DOS and MS-DOS The operating system that Microsoft supplied to IBM was called PC-DOS. (A variant of this operating system was sold to clone manufacturers as MS-DOS; PC-DOS and MS-DOS were operationally identical.) Microsoft began work on MS-DOS/PC-DOS in 1980. More accurately, that was when Microsoft acquired an operating system called QDOS (for Quick and Dirty Operating System) from a small company called Seattle Computer Products. QDOS was essentially a 16-bit version of the older CP/M operating system developed for Intel's 8086 microprocessor; Microsoft reworked the code to IBM's specs, and PC-DOS was born.

Versions of PC/MS-DOS powered IBM-compatible personal computers through the early 1990's, when it was replaced by another Microsoft operating system—Windows.

Microsoft Windows Whereas DOS was a text-based operating system, Windows was graphical—and supported the click-and-drag operation of a mouse. The first version of Windows, launched in November 1985, required more power than machines of that era could deliver, and had little impact on the market. A more fully functional version, Windows 2.0, was released in 1987. But it was version 3.0, released in 1990, that introduced true multitasking to the personal computing environment, and eventually led to the demise of PC/MS-DOS.

OS/2 OS/2 (Operating System 2) was designed as a 32-bit graphical replacement for PC-DOS, to be used on IBM's PS/2 computers. Although IBM and Microsoft jointly developed the operating system, a falling-out between the two giants resulted in IBM marketing OS/2 for its higher-end PCs, and Microsoft further developing the code into its Windows NT operating system.

Apple Computing

While the story of the personal computer is primarily a story about IBM and compatible computers, there is a secondary story—that of Apple Computing, and the company's proprietary computers.

Apple Computer, Inc., was founded in 1976 by Steven Jobs (b. 1955) and Steven Wozniak (b. 1950), two former game programmers at Atari. They built their first computer (the prototype for the Apple I) in Jobs's garage; by the mid-1980's, Apple had become the fastest-growing company in history, generating, at its peak (in 2000), almost $8 billion in revenues.

Apple I, II, and III The first computer from Apple, dubbed the Apple I, was released in 1976. It was based on the MOS 6502 microprocessor, and sold for $666.66.

Apple's second computer, the Apple II, was introduced in April 1977. Like the Apple I, the Apple II used the MOS 6502 chip, but it included an integrated keyboard and color graphics. The selling price was $1,295.

The next iteration, the Apple III, was released in 1980, but was less successful than its predecessors. This was partly due to the unit's higher price and business focus; depending on configuration, the Apple III sold for between $4,340 and $7,800.

LISA Breaking off from the Apple I/II/III line of computers, in 1983 Apple introduced the LISA computer. LISA (Largely Integrated Systems Architecture) was the first personal computer to use a graphical user interface (GUI), complete with icons and pull-down menus, and also the first to have a mouse for users' input.

Macintosh Apple released the first Macintosh computer in January 1984, supported by an attention-getting advertisement during that year's Super Bowl broadcast. Based on Motorola's 68000 microprocessor, it incorporated many features of the failed LISA project, including an icon-driven GUI and mouse input. Priced at $2,495, it was an immediate success, and in various incarnations remains the core of Apple's line of computers

Personal Computing in the 1990's and Beyond

As the personal computer industry moved into the 1990's, machines became both more affordable and more powerful, and software programs became much easier to use. The decade continued to be dominated by Intel microprocessors, IBM-compatible hardware, and Microsoft software and operating systems.

Microprocessor Power Microprocessor development in the 1990's was ruled by Moore's Law; every year saw the introduction of a new chip that was faster and lower-priced than its predecessor—and most of these chips were from Intel.

Intel Pentium Family Instead of following the 80486 chip with an 80586 model, Intel took the opportunity to introduce an entirely new family of microprocessor chips, called the Pentium, that contained the equivalent of 1.5 million transistors. The first Pentium chip was released in 1993, in both 60-Mhz and 66-MHz versions; increasingly faster versions of this chip were released throughout the 1990's.

In 1995 Intel released the next chip in the Pentium family, the Pentium Pro, which contained the equivalent of 5.5 million transistors and operated at up to 200 MHz. This was followed, in 1997, by the Pentium II, which contained the equivalent of 7.5 million transistors and operated at was capable of 300-MHz speeds.

Intel's Pentium III chip was released in 1999. The initial version of this microprocessor operated at 500 MHz, and contained the equivalent of 9.5 million transistors. Intel released the Pentium 4 in 2000; it contained the equivalent of 42 million transistors, and operated at speeds up to 1.5 Ghz.

In 2006, Intel introduced a new generation of microprocessors specifically for mobile computing. The Intel Core was a 32-bit processor that packaged two cores on a single silicon chip, resulting in faster performance with a lower power drain. This chip line was superseded in late 2006 by the Intel Core 2 processor family, which merged Intel's mobile and desktop proceessing lines and saw the retirement of the Pentium family of chips. The Core 2 series is available in Duo (twin-core), Quad (four-core), and Extreme (two- or four- core with higher speed) models, all with 64-bit processing.

AMD and Other Competitors While Intel dominated the market for microprocessor chips, it wasn't the only manufacturer out there. Intel's chief competitor, Advanced Micro Devices (AMD), was founded in 1969, and for the next 20 years produced microprocessors for proprietary devices. In 1991 AMD decided to challenge Intel in the personal computer marketplace with its AM386 microprocessor, which competed head-to-head with Intel's 80386 chip.

Another competitor in the microprocessor market was Cyrix, a division of National Semiconductor, which released chips to compete with Intel's 80486 and Pentium series. Cyrix was less successful than AMD in carving out a market niche, and in 1999 the company was acquired by Taiwanese chipset manufacturer VIA.

Hardware: Growth, Consolidation, Contraction

The market for personal computer hardware experienced significant expansion in the 1990's—and significant contraction.

PC Industry Consolidates As the 1990's started, there were dozens of PC manufacturers, including Acer, IBM, Compaq, CompuAdd, Dell, Gateway, Hewlett Packard, Northgate, and Zeos. With the market growing at annual rates in excess of 10 percent, there seemed to be room for everyone. But as the decade progressed, competition became fierce, and the industry saw a consolidation. Minor players dropped by the wayside, and even major players found reason to consolidate—one example was the acquisition of Compaq by Hewlett Packard.

Postmillennium Technology Slump The technology market was expanding continuously, and PC hardware manufacturers were benefiting from seemingly endless growth until 2000, when the bubble burst and the technology market crashed to reality. PC sales actually declined for the first time in memory. The slump continued into 2003.

Windows   Even during the darkest period of the technology slump, one company continued to log record profits. Microsoft, thanks primarily to the income from its Windows operating system, weathered the slump well, and continued to dominate the PC operating systems market—as it had all decade long.

Microsoft released a series of new Windows versions over the course of the decade, starting with Windows 3.0 in 1990 and continuing with Windows 95, Windows 98, Windows Me, and Windows XP. The company also released two versions of Windows designed for the corporate market, Windows NT and Windows 2000.

In 2007, Windows XP was replaced by Windows Vista. This latest version of Windows features a new interface, increased security against viruses and improved network capabilities.

Open Source Competition   As dominant as Microsoft was in the operating systems arena, it has never been fully without competition. In the early days of the PC era, that competition came from DOS clones such as Digital Research's DR DOS; in the late 1990's, competition came from an offshoot of the UNIX operating system called Linux.

Linux   Linux, first introduced in 1991, is an open source variant of the established UNIX operating system, which was developed by Ken Thompson (b. 1943) and Dennis Ritchie in 1975. The Linux operating system was developed by (and named for) Linus Torvalds (b. 1970), a second-year student of computer science at the University of Helsinki. Torvalds permitted his operating system to be distributed free; it subsequently gained ground as alternative to Windows on enterprise and Web servers.

The Open Source Software Movement   Concurrent with the rise of Linux, other application developers were touting the acceptance of open source software—applications whose underlying code lies in the public domain, and could be distributed free of charge. The open source movement believes that when programmers can modify and redistribute program code at no cost, the software evolves faster than it would if distributed through traditional commercial means. This movement, whose members are quite vocal in the software community, has yet to make major inroads against commercial software; the lack of central control inherent in the concept actually discourages large corporations from adopting free software of this type.

Computing Goes Mobile

The history of portable computing is one of increasingly smaller devices, enabled by the shrinking size of microprocessor chips and peripheral devices. As computing moved into the mid-1990's, users wanted to take their information with them wherever they went—they didn't want to be tied to an immovable desktop computer. The result was a profusion of portable computing devices, from notebook PCs to handheld devices.

Portable PCs   Early portable PCs—such as the Osborne 1, the KayPro II, and the Compaq Portable—were portable only in the sense that they could be picked up and carried. They were neither small nor light, and consequently did not see much portable use. Over the years portable computers gained the new designation of laptop or (for even smaller models) notebook and netbook computers. The typical laptop computer of the late 1990's featured a 14-inch LCD screen that folded over a standard-size keyboard into a 4-inch-thick package that weighed just a few pounds. This new portable PC operated on either AC or battery power, with the built-in batteries lasting for three hours or more—enough power to last through a typical plane flight.

Handheld computers, also called palmtops or personal digital assistants (PDAs), incorporated many of the essential functions of a laptop computer, but with a much smaller screen and without a keyboard. Instructions were entered by tapping the touch-sensitive screen with a pen-like stylus; most people used their PDAs to store contact and schedule information, and to send and receive e-mail.

The First Handheld Computer   The very first handheld computer, Hewlett-Packard's HP95LX, was introduced with limited success in 1991. It weighed 11 oz., and used the DOS operating system. Subsequent models, all DOS-based, were released through 1994.

Apple Newton   In 1993 Apple entered the PDA market with the Newton MessagePad. The Newton's notoriously poor handwriting recognition, however, resulted in poor marketplace acceptance; the product was finally pulled from the market in 1998.

PalmPilot   The first truly successful PDA was the PalmPilot 1000, released in 1996 from Palm Inc. (later acquired by 3Com Corp.). The first-generation PalmPilot offered simple schedule and contact management capabilities, accessed with a stylus and touchpad. Subsequent models added more advanced features, including a color display and built-in wireless modem.

Handspring and Compatibles/Competitors It wasn't long before the PalmPilot had marketplace competition. The most direct competition came from Handspring, a company founded by former Palm developers. The Handspring Visor, first released in 1999, used the Palm operating system, but offered more advanced features and met with widespread market acceptance.

Microsoft Windows CE In 1996 Microsoft introduced a version of its Windows operating system for handheld devices. Windows CE was designed for devices that included (small) built-in keyboards, and featured scaledscaled down versions of Microsoft's key desktop applications, including Word and Excel. Windows CE proved more than the consumer wanted, however, as the Windows CE devices were larger and harder to use than the competing Palm PC; they had only limited market success.

Microsoft Pocket PC Four years later, in 2000, Microsoft released a new handheld operating system, dubbed Pocket PC. The new Pocket PC devices were almost identical to Palm devices in size and functionality; they had the added benefit of being applicationand document-compatible with Microsoft's desktop applications.

Windows Mobile In 2003, Microsoft's Pocket PC platform was superseded by the Windows Mobile operating system. Windows Mobile marked the convergence of PDA, personal computer, and mobile phone functionality in a single operating system and device.

Smartphones

Blurring the lines between portable computer, cellular phone, and PDA, smartphones evolved out of multifunction cellular phones and devices such as Research in Motion's BlackBerry. BlackBerrys were used most heavily by corporate customers to provide staff with constant access to company email, meeting schedules and internet connections, and featured a QWERTY-style keyboard. The newer smartphones were defined by their complete adaptability and wide availability of desktop-style applications that transformed the device from phone to handheld video camera, to GPS, to portable gaming device, to musical instrument, and more.

iOs The most famous smartphone was Apple's touchscreen iPhone, along with its closely related cousin the iPod Touch (which carried most of the same hardware except the phone). The first version of the iPhone, released in 2007, was sold with a small collection of Apple's applications installed. Bowing to pressure from developers, Apple soon opened the device to third-party applications,

beginning a flood of compatible apps that quickly numbered in the hundreds of thousands. In the U.S., the iPhone was locked to a single carrier, AT&T, until 2011, when Apple announced the end of their exclusivity agreement and Verizon began to carry the phone.

The iPhone, iPod, and Apple's iPad tablet all ran the same iOS operating system, which was designed specifically for touchscreen devices.

Android Responding to the success of the iPhone and iOS, Google launched the Android operating system and released it as an open-source competitor to Apple's tightly controlled devices. Phones running Android were quickly developed for many wireless carriers, and the phones were poised to overtake the iPhone by the end of 2010.

Wi-Fi Thanks to steadily decreasing prices of wireless networking equipment, one can find wireless nodes on corporate networks, home networks, and public access points (called "hotspots") in various hotels, airports and cafes. The most popular wireless connection technology proved to be that bassed on the IEEE 802.11 standard, otherwise known as Wi-Fi. There are several variations of the Wi-Fi standard, including 802.11a (operating in the 5.8 GHz RF spectrum, with 54Mbps connection speeds), 802.11b (2.4GHz, 11Mbps) and 802.11g (2.4GHZ, 54 Mbps). The most recent Wi-Fi protocol, 802.11n, operates in the 2.4 GHz spectrum but with speeds exceeding 240 Mbps. Nearly all new notebook PCs and PDAs come with Wi-Fi technology built in.

Bluetooth Bluetooth is a wireless technology that both competes with and complements Wi-Fi. Designed by the portable phone manufacturer Ericsson as a cable replacement technology, Bluetooth lets devices connect over short distances at 1 Mbps, using the same 2.4-GHz RF band used by Wi-Fi. While Bluetooth's transmission speed is much less than that of Wi-Fi, Bluetooth-enabled devices also consume much less power—making the technology ideal for small, portable devices. Today, Bluetooth wireless technology is used to connect wireless headsets to cellular and traditional phones, and printers, scanners, keyboards, and mice to personal computers.

Tablets

Attempted several times since the 1980's with only meager success, the development of tablet computers finally took off in 2010 with the release of Apple's touchscreen iPad, originally advertised for casual "living room" computer use: reading e-books, watching videos, e-mailing, accessing social networking websites, and listening to music. Essentially an oversized iPod touch, the iPad immediately gained acceptance and appeared ready to open a new class of mobile computers—not quite a laptop, but easier to use than a smartphone. Other computer manufacturers, including Samsung, Asus, and Panasonic, quickly moved to ready tablets for the market, as e-reader manufacturers including Amazon (Kindle) and Barnes & Noble (Nook) wondered about whether the new tablet market would disrupt the burgeoning e-reader market.

Supercomputing

Although the personal computer was the technology story of the 1980's and 1990's, larger computers continued to evolve—into faster, more powerful machines called supercomputers. Supercomputers are used by universities, governments, and corporations to solve complex mathematics and physics problems, forecast the weather, and create sophisticated computer animation.

Cray Computers Seymour Cray (1925–96, USA) was the inventor behind the first commercial supercomputer. Finished in 1976, his Cray-1 contained 200,000 ICs and could perform at 160 million flops (floating point operations per second; a million flops is called a megaflop). Its price was approximately $8.8 million.

Throughout the 1980's and 1990's Cray delivered faster and more powerful supercomputers, including the Cray XMP (1982, 500 megaflops), the Cray-2 (1985, 1.9 gigaflops), and the Cray C90 (1991, 16 gigaflops). Cray Research merged with Silicon Graphics, Inc., in 1996.

IBM Supercomputers IBM Corporation has long been at the forefront of computer development. IBM's supercomputers include Deep Blue (1996; 1 teraflop), ASCI White (2000; 12.3 teraflops), and Blue Gene/L (2007; 478.2 teraflops).

Tianhe-1A In October 2010, the Chinese National University of Defense Technology's Tianhe-1A set the bar, utilizing more than 14,300 Intel Xeon processors and 7,100 Nvidia graphics processing units to reach 2.507 petaflops (or 2,507 teraflops). Tianhe-1A is used to create aircraft simulations and aid in petroleum exploration.

The Internet

During the 1990's, the biggest impact on personal computing came not from hardware or software of individual machines, but from a global computer-to-computer network called the Internet. The Internet changed the way computer users communicated and accessed information, and led to a new, fast-paced economy made up of companies seeking to exploit the commercial applications of the Internet space.

ARPANET

The first incarnation of the Internet was called ARPANET and was proposed in 1967 as a research project by the U.S. Department of Defense. The main aim of the project was to enable reliable communication between two computers by using packet switching, the relay of information bundled into chunks or packets. The first two nodes of this network were at UCLA and the Stanford Research Institute, then part of Stanford University. It became operable in 1969. E-mail was first conceived in 1972, and quickly became the main service provided by ARPANET. As the single main network of the day, ARPANET was seen as a communication and research tool meant for a limited number of sites; the original specification described a maximum of 256 host mainframes. The protocol TCP/IP—a standard for packet transfer, particularly how to handle smooth data flow if transfer was interrupted—was proposed and the word Internet first used in 1974. For many in the computer industry, the two things are synonymous, as the term Internet referred to the ability of TCP/IP to enable communication between separate networks, "inter-networking" them.

By 1981 more than 200 host computers were connected to ARPANET, with new hosts being added every 20 days. In 1983, ARPANET formally adopted TCP/IP as its official protocol, and the federal government began requiring that network-related contracts support TCP/IP, helping to promote it as the de facto engine of the Internet. Also that year, a new service allowed for the use of domain names, unique and meaningful identifiers for networked devices and files. Still in use, the domain name system matches up a computer's network address (a long complex number that describes its location in the network) to an arbitrary name, and is what allows users to remember a web address as www.nytimes.com, for example, instead of a seemingly meaningless string of numbers.

ARPANET was not the only network active in the

1980s; many government and private networks were begun, serving dedicated and often isolated research and academic communities, all transferring information via TCP/IP. In 1985, the National Science Foundation founded (and funded) NSFNET to serve the broader academic community regardless of discipline, with a notable caveat—no commercial activity allowed. With universities eager to take advantage of government-funded infrastructure improvements, NSFNET grew quickly while the commercial restriction had two important effects on the development of the Internet: it helped foster an environment of open collaboration, planting the idea that information should be free, and it spurred private commercial interests to develop competing infrastructural networks.

The World Wide Web

Although most people use the terms Internet and World Wide Web interchangeably, they are actually different entities. In the same way that television broadcasting is different from television programming, the Internet is the structure or medium, while the World Wide Web is the content (interconnected documents and files) that the Internet makes possible. The World Wide Web was invented in 1989 at Switzerland's CERN Particle Physics Library by Tim Berners-Lee (b. 1955). The Web applies the concept of hypertext linking, originally conceived to network citations for academic papers, to Internet documents. The concept of hypertext was very simple: every online computer and file has a unique location in the network, so any networked document can contain one or more references (called hyperlinks) to any other by simply indicating the location or URL—the address that shows the name of the server and the precise virtual location of the document on that server—of the other document. Along with the idea of finding documents by URL, a simple markup language called HTML (hypertext markup language) made creating new hyperlinked documents easy. The number of hyperlinked pages comprising the Web quickly mushroomed.

The Commercial Internet Is Born

ARPANET was decommissioned in 1990, and the NSF lifted the ban on commercial traffic in 1991, clearing the way for the commercial Internet. Still, until Netscape shocked the financial world with its 1995 IPO (first day of trading saw the stock close at $75/share, inaugurating the first Internet stock market boom), most people thought of the Internet as a purely academic curiosity, a tool for trad-

ing research papers. Most activity over the Internet was text-based, and web browsers were unfamiliar to many, mostly limited to terminals on university campuses and large libraries.

Commercial Services Connect to the Net Home computer users were unable to access high speed data networks available on campuses, and instead subscribed from a growing number of local or national internet service providers (ISPs). Features common to early ISPs were proprietary information portals and directories that subscribers would visit upon first logging on. The most famous commercial service, America Online (AOL), positioned itself as a service separate from the World Wide Web, offering cordoned-off profiles, discussion groups, and keyword searches.   AOL and others, such as CompuServ, Prodigy, and others, helped drive up the numbers of home Internet users in the U.S.

Internet Applications As the number of people going online ballooned, software makers created a whole new class of computer software for accessing the web, emailing, and chatting. The first software developed to surf the Web was Mosaic, a Web browser developed at the University of Illinois by undergraduate student Marc Andreessen (b. 1971). Mosaic was available free of charge over the Internet, but was soon supplanted by the more fully featured Netscape browser, also developed by Andreessen at his new company, Netscape Communications. Over the next few years users would be subjected to the so-called browser wars, with Netscape fending off a similar Web browser from Microsoft. Microsoft's Internet Explorer would win the 1990's browser wars, in part because Microsoft integrated the browser into its Windows operating system.

The other new kind of Internet application was the e-mail client, typified by Microsoft's Outlook. Outlook, like other e-mail programs, could also post and read messages to and from Usenet newsgroups.

The next new development was the instant messaging program. Instant messengers—such as AOL Instant Messenger, iChat, Yahoo! Messenger, and Microsoft Messenger—let users exchange private messages in real time over the Internet, and quickly supplanted the earlier Internet public chat programs.

The First Dot-com Boom

During the late 1990's the promise of Internet riches inspired an investment boom heretofore unknown in U.S.

and global markets. Each week saw IPOs from dozens of so-called dot-com companies, offering all manner of goods and services online.

Unfortunately, the vast majority of these dot-com companies had weak business models, and never turned a profit surviving, instead, on venture capital money and the paper profits realized from skyrocketing stock prices. In 2000, the dot-com bubble burst and the stock prices collapsed, forcing thousands of dot-com companies to close their doors.

The Internet Since 2000

In 1995 there were 25 million users connected to the Internet worldwide. The number of users exploded to 527 million by the end of 2001, and grew to nearly 2 billion by the end of 2010. In 2010, Asia had more than 825 million Internet users. According to the U.S. Census Bureau, 191 million American adults (85 percent) had access to the Internet in 2008, either from home or work. The rapidity of this growth can be attributed to several factors: private commercial investment in infrastructure gave incentive to companies to develop high-speed access for homes and offices; a generation of students graduated from college with expectations of chatting, e-mailing and browsing online; and businesses migrated many internal and external communications to e-mail and set up company presences online. Also, during the 1990s and 2000s, the increased power and lower prices of desktop and laptop computers encouraged people to buy them for uses beyond the office, both widening the context and environments for going online, and also providing market incentive to ISPs. For many people, access to the Internet helped to make the decision whether to buy a home computer, since an Internet connection was now a means of corresponding and socializing.

In the U.S., the most popular internet activities in April 2009 were reading and sending email (57 percent of people surveyed by the Pew Internet & American Life Project reported doing it "yesterday"), using a search engine to find information (50 percent), reading news (38 percent), checking weather forecasts (33 percent), using a social networking site (27 percent), and doing banking (24 percent).

E-commerce

By 2010, online shopping had become commonplace, and dedicated online promotional sales days—such as Cyber Monday, the Monday following Thanksgiving—had entered the American mainstream.

Despite the surging popularity of online shopping, retail did not make up the majority of online commerce (also called e-commerce). The vast majority (92 percent in 2008) of all e-commerce was conducted between businesses, as the Internet has helped cut transaction costs, locate surplus or low-cost goods, and otherwise increase efficiencies. The total value of U.S. business-to-business (B2B) online commerce, made up of manufacturing and merchant wholesale, reached $3.4 trillion in 2008. Of manufacturing transactions, the largest groups of sales were for transportation equipment and chemical products. Online business-to-consumer (B2C) business remained a small overall portion of Internet commerce. Online direct retail shopping accounted for less than 4 percent ($142 billion) of all e-commerce in 2008. Web sites such as Amazon.com and other online retailers accounted for $93 billion. Of online retail sales, the most commonly purchased goods were clothing and footwear.

Searching the Web

Yahoo! And Google   One of the most-visited early sites was a searchable directory called Yahoo! Created in 1994 by two Stanford University students, Yahoo! eventually grew into a full-fledged information and services portal. Yahoo's directory was fairly comprehensive, but its organization became limiting as the Web grew beyond any straightforward hierarchy. To be listed in its directory, webmasters were required to choose a category for their site and submit a listing to Yahoo. As businesses realized that the Web was too large and too crowded to expect that customers would find them by browsing alone, an economy related to Web advertising was born, and this helped launch an early Internet giant, Google.

Google, a search engine launched in 1998 by another pair of Stanford students, Larry Page and Sergey Brin, dispensed with the idea of a managed directory altogether. Instead, they developed their service around search, with automated programs scouring the Web link by link and indexing everything they found. Thanks to a proprietary system for ranking search results, Google was able to deliver more accurate results than its competitors. In 1999, Google handled 3 million searches a day, but by 2004 that number had risen to 200 million. In 2010, analysts estimated that more than 2 billion searches were being done on Google each day.

Google went public in 2004, raising more than $1.6

billion in an initial public offering, and today has more more than 10,000 employees. From its beginnings in search and search advertising, Google has quickly expanded and offers an evolving group of free utilities, applications, and services, all under the grandly stated company mission to organize the world's knowledge.

That mission statement, when mixed with the company's imperative to mind its bottom line, typifies both the paradoxical nature of business on the Web and also the main tension of the commercial Web itself. The complexity lies in the business requirement to make money from information and services that most people expect for free. Additionally, the copying and sharing of online content has complicated businesses' relationships to their own intellectual and commercial property. Google has run afoul of the book publishing industry repeatedly in this regard during its effort to reproduce scans of copyrighted works online as part of Google book search. That compromises have been reached thus far point to both the disruptive, game-changing nature of the Internet for traditional businesses like print publishing, and also to Google's importance to the Internet. In that sense, Google is one of the keystone online businesses that demonstrate the power of the Internet to affect industries outside of cyberspace. Along with challenges to traditional commerce models that have come from sites like ebay.com, craigslist.org, and amazon.com, Google continues to expand its reach beyond just search.

The Social Web

The rapidly evolving nature of the Web is driven in part by the word-of-mouth—so-called viral—spread of both new technology and interesting content. Online social networking is as old as the ARPANET, but a new generation of tools helped make the practice of conversing and sharing with new and old acquaintances much easier and simpler. Some of the most wildly popular Web sites of the 2000's were services that help facilitate that social interaction.

Blogging A blog is a Web site that displays journal-style entries written, at least in the early days, by mostly unknown authors seeking an audience. Justin Hall, one of the earliest bloggers, launched Justin's Links from the Underground in 1994. A student at Swarthmore College at the time, he used the site to chronicle the interesting things he found on the early Web, as well as the personal events of his own life. In 1997, Jorn Barger, creator of the

Web site Robot Wisdom, coined the term "web log" to describe his own online diary, and information architect Peter Merholz broke that word into "we blog" on his site, Peterme, in 1999. Although personal diaries represent the vast majority of the hundreds of millions of blogs in existence today, many of the most popular blogs specialize in a range of topics including politics, current events, food, sports, film, music, and sex.

At first, blogging required Web programming and remained mostly confined to those with the necessary technical skills. But with the launch of blog hosting services in the late 1990's such as Open Diary, the first to allow readers' comments, and LiveJournal, which put an emphasis on forming online communities, blogging became free and accessible to the general public.

Although blogs had entered the mainstream by 2003, it was the Iraq War that legitimized them as news sources. While members of the press were required to accept "embedded" assignments with strict controls on what they could and could not say, bloggers (some of them members of the Allied forces, others Iraqi citizens under siege in Baghdad) reported the conflict as they witnessed it, uncensored and sometimes within minutes of the events they were describing. Simultaneously, American political blogs such as Talking Points Memo and the DailyKos found a large audience by offering fresh viewpoints sometimes at odds with the editorial position of the mainstream media. Readers responded in droves, and in 2004 Merriam-Webster's Dictionary declared "blog" the word of the year.

As blog readership grew, many of the more prominent and active blogs grew to resemble online newspapers or journals. Of these, the best known is The Huffington Post, which has grown to one of the most widely read sources of political commentary.

Today, hundreds of different blogging services exist, with including TypePad (www.typepad.com), WordPress (www.wordpress.com), and Google-owned Blogger (www.blogger.com). Technorati (www.technorati.com), a blog searching and ranking site, provides a variety of services for finding and reading blogs.

In July 2008, the Pew Internet & American Life Project reported that 33 percent of internet users read blogs, and that about 12 percent of internet users had their own blog. By April 2010, the service Technorati was tracking 125 million blogs (and reported that it was arbitrarily capping its tracking service at that number), and reported that

175,000 new blogs were being created each day. In addition to individuals, nearly every major media outlet, from newspapers to television networks, offered blogs to complement its primary content, and most large corporations have experimented with using blogs to update consumers on their products and services.

Microblogs A quickly growing trend among Web users was the use of so-called microblogging to share, post, or repost images, links, short messages, and files. The most popular microblogging service of the late 2000s was Twitter, which limits posts to 140 characters. Some blogging platforms, such as Tumblr, specialize in microblogging, with built-in features allowing users to quickly "repost" interesting items with only a few clicks.

Social Networking Web sites Since 2002, hundreds of millions of people have joined a wide variety of social networking services where users generate personal profiles, connect with others based on shared interests or real-life connections, and are subsequently linked to people in an extended social network. Personal profiles typically feature photographs of the user, along with biographical information, from gender and age to favorite songs and movies, and a list of the user's connections on that network. Social networking services are used to maintain contact with existing friends, make new ones, meet potential dating partners, network for professional purposes, and promote bands, artists, and other would-be celebrities.

The popularity of online social networking continues to grow—according to the Pew Internet & American Life Project survey, the percentage of American adults using social networking sites has nearly doubled since 2008, from 26 percent to 47 percent of adults who go online. While most social networking services are generalized tools, some focus specifically on set of users, including Dogster.com, for dog owners, or on a service. For instance, Flickr.com, a photo sharing site, complements its primary function with social networking features, as do YouTube, a video sharing site, and Yahoo! Trip Planner, a travel site. In the late-2000s, a push toward simplifying the sharing of items and links across websites led to a dramatic increase in the users of social networking sites, as people were increasingly able to collect interesting tidbits and respond to conversations from many different web pages from a single home profile. Globally, several social networks emerged as leaders, each with a geographic core. For exam-

ple, in Brazil, Google's Orkut was dominant, Russia had V Kontakte, China had QQ, and Germany had Hi5. Increasingly in North America, India, Oceania, and much of Europe, the social networking giant has been Facebook, which in the U.S. held profiles for 92 percent of all social network site users in 2010.

Facebook (www.facebook.com) Founded by Mark Zuckerberg, Dustin Moskovitz, and Chris Hughes at Harvard University in February 2004, Facebook was intended for use by the university's students, faculty, and staff, but it quickly spread to other American universities and eventually expanded to include university and high school students in several other countries. In 2006, Facebook opened registration to everyone. Facebook had over 18 million users as of February 2007. In three years, the number of Facebook users mushroomed to more than 600 million worldwide. In 2010, Facebook.com surpassed Google.com as the most-visited web site, and had already generated its own search advertising business. Facebook allows users to share links and files, create discussion groups, microblog content, tag friends in photos, and play games, all within a highly interconnected network that promotes sharing what members are doing and allowing users to see what their friends are doing.

LinkedIn (www.linkedin.com) LinkedIn is a business oriented social networking site designed to help professionals make business connections and post and find jobs. The emphasis is placed firmly on connecting professionals in various fields and building social capital in the form of shared expertise and recommendations. Founded by CEO Reid Hoffman in 2003, the site claimed to have over 60 million users by February 2010.

Wikis A wiki is different from a traditional website because it is designed to allow its users to easily modify its contents. Given mainstream prominence by the success of Wikipedia, a wiki-based encyclopedia with millions of user-generated articles, the technology behind wikis was originally developed by computer programmer Ward Cunningham. In 1994, Cunningham built WikiWikiWeb, a site designed to help software engineers exchange ideas. (Cunningham named the site after the Hawaiian word for quick, wiki.)

Typically, a public wiki contains a number of articles that consist of text, images, and other media files. Users are allowed to edit any wiki page on the spot, often without registering, using a simple "markup" language. Edits might consist of anything from corrected typos to deleted passages a user considered erroneous.

Generally, all versions of a wiki page are saved chronologically, allowing users who disagree with a particular revision to "roll back" the page to an earlier one. A separate discussion area for each entry allows users to justify their changes to each other and resolve conflicts collaboratively.

Wikis, which can be viewed with any web browser, continue to grow in popularity, particularly in the corporate sector, where they have replaced static intranets for many companies. Individuals who wish to create wikis for personal use, from basic word processing to collaborative authoring, can use one of a variety of hosted wiki services.

Wikipedia continues to be the most popular public wiki on the Web. Begun in 2001 as a complement to an existing, expert-written online encyclopedia, now defunct, Wikipedia quickly took on a life of its own. It now boasts a large international community of volunteers who regularly write and edit articles, moderate existing articles, and police the Wikipedia community. The site features millions of articles, with articles in hundreds of languages. While the site has been criticized in the mainstream media for inaccuracies, biases, and uneven quality, its popularity as a source of general information continues to grow.

Online Media Thanks to the rise of high-bandwidth cable and DSL internet connections, Web-based audio and video experienced a tremendous surge in popularity. Once average home users could quickly download large files over the Internet, the demand for such content skyrocketed. Two phenomena resulting from this explosive growth were podcasting and YouTube. Podcasting Podcasting as a hobby and a viable business model took hold in 2004 as millions of people around the world, from audio amateurs to radio professionals, began recording podcasts in their homes featuring their own original audio content and distributing them to listeners via RSS (Really Simple Syndication). RSS allows users to "subscribe" to a blog, news site, or other regularly updated source of information. The RSS feed automatically delivered new content to a user's "feed reader" when it became available.

In the years prior to RSS, several online services offered regularly updated digital audio content to users, but RSS made such delivery easy and accessible for both content creators and listeners. Suddenly, anyone with a microphone and a computer could deliver new episodes of their audio content to listeners automatically.

In early 2004, the term podcasting was coined by a journalist to describe the growing trend of audio bloggers who were doing everything from deejaying their favorite underground bands to sharing events from their personal lives. Within the year, a host of podcast creating and listening applications were released, along with several podcast directories. The concurrent, meteoric rise in popularity of Apple's iPod MP3 player only increased the demand for free audio content. Whereas radio, in its efforts to attract the greatest number of listeners, had gravitated almost completely toward the repetition of Top 40 pop hits alternating with lengthy commercial breaks, podcasts found dedicated audiences by appealing to small, unserved niches, from comic books readers to fans of indie rock. Many of the most popular podcasts, like the Dawn and Drew Show, created by a married couple living in Milwaukee, Wisconsin, featured nothing but uncensored, personal banter.

In June 2005, Apple added podcast features to its iTunes music software, and established a podcast directory in its music store. Podcasts quickly entered the mainstream, hindered partially by the common misconception that podcasts could only be listened to on iPods. Today, millions of people have listened to podcasts, and nearly every major media producer releases them, ranging from re-broadcast radio episodes to commentary from the cast and crew of television shows.

YouTube Despite the increased bandwidth available to home users, online video was still notoriously difficult to distribute over the Internet. There were a variety of different formats for distribution, and the resulting video was either displayed at the size of a postage stamp or would stutter and jerk during playback. In addition, uploading and sharing video content was next to impossible for average users. All of this changed in 2005 when YouTube was launched. This website used Adobe's Flash format to distribute video. Unlike the other methods of video distribution, Flash worked equally well on Macintosh or Windows computers, downloaded quickly, displayed smoothly at a fairly large size, and worked right away without any special settings required.

Instead of using the new platform to deliver corporate media content, YouTube gave its users the tools to easily upload their own videos, effectively beginning a media revolution. Thousands of people all over the world began sharing short videos of their own, from clips of birthday parties gone awry to copyright-infringing clips of favorite movies. YouTube quickly became notorious for the viral creation of Internet celebrities.

Glossary of Computer and Internet Terms

802.11 more accurately described as IEEE 802.11, the radio frequency (RF)-based technology used for home and small business wireless networks, and for most public wireless Internet connections. There are various subsets of the 802.11 standard; the most popular is 802.11b, which uses the 2.4-GHz RF band and is more commonly known as Wi-Fi.

adware stealth software that tracks your online activity and sends that data to a marketing or advertising company.

anonymizer a Web site or service that enables anonymous Web browsing or e-mail communications.

anti-aliasing a technique used to smooth the ragged edges from electronic type or graphic images.

application a computer program designed for a specific task or use, such as word processing, accounting, or missile guidance.

artificial intelligence (AI) the capability of machines to be programmed to perform human functions. The primary AI functions are expert systems, programs that contain a body of knowledge (contributed by experts) that the machine can draw on to solve specific types of problems; natural language interfaces that make it possible for users to access a computer's database with commands entered in ordinary written or spoken language (for example, "Give me a list of countries bordering the Atlantic Ocean"); and speech recognition, speech synthesis, and optical recognition systems that enable computers to understand spoken commands, make speech, and interpret visible images (such as bar codes on retail goods).

Asynchronous Javascript and XHTML (AJAX) A technique for creating sophisticated interactions on a Web page that mimic the operations of a desktop application

attachment a file, such as a Word document or graphic image, attached to an e-mail message.

backbone a high-speed connection that forms a major pathway within a network, or over the Internet.

backup the process of creating a compressed copy of computer data that can be restored to its original location if the original data have somehow been erased or corrupted.

bandwidth the amount of data, graphics, sound, and other information that can be transmitted through cyberspace at a certain time. Bandwidth is measured in kilobits per second (kbps). Most cable modems and DSL can offer bandwidths of more than 5 megabit per second (Mbps).

beta a prerelease version of a software program, typically in the process of being tested for bugs. The process of testing software before its public release is called beta testing.

bit in the binary system, a bit (binary digit) either of the digits 0 or 1. It is the basic unit for storing data, with "off" representing 0 and "on" representing 1.

blog short for "weblog," a diarylike website, usually presenting informal writings in chronological order.

Bluetooth the specification for a wireless connection technology operating in the unlicensed 2.4-GHz radio frequency band. Originally intended to be a "wire replacement" technology for both computers and cellular phones, the Bluetooth specification has since been expanded to compete somewhat with the more powerful Wi-Fi wireless networking standard.

boot the process of turning on a computer system.

broadband a high-speed Internet connection (faster than a typical dial-up connection), accomplished via ISDN, cable, DSL, satellite, T1, or T3 lines.

browser a program that translates the hypertext mark-up language of the World Wide Web into viewable Web pages. The two most common browsers today are Microsoft's Internet Explorer and Mozilla Firefox.

buffer any memory location where data can be stored temporarily while the computer is doing something else.

bug an error in a software program or the hardware.

byte a group of eight bits that together represent one character, whether alphabetic, numeric, or other. A byte is the smallest accessible unit in a computer's memory.

C a high-level programming language, particularly popular among personal computer programmers.

C++ an object-oriented version of the C programming language.

cable modem a high-speed, broadband Internet connection via digital cable TV lines.

cache pronounced "cash," the place on a hard drive or in memory where a software program temporarily stores data. If a user needs to access that data again, it can be read from the cache rather than from its original location.

captcha a device meant to thwart automated bots from submission of web-based forms. A captcha usually involves typing the letters shown in a heavily distorted image that a human can read but a computer cannot decipher.

cascading style sheets (CSS) The list of properties that control how various parts of a Web page appear.

central processing unit (CPU) the group of circuits that directs the entire computer system by (1) interpreting and executing program instruction and (2) coordinating the interaction of input, output, and storage devices.

chat text-based real-time Internet communication, typically consisting of short one-line messages back and forth between two or more users. Users gather in chat rooms or channels.

client in a client/server relationship between two devices, the device that pushes or pulls data from the other device (the server).

client/server computing a relationship between two or more computers where one computer (the server) serves as the host for all data and applications, and all other machines (the clients) access the server for all key operations.

cloud, as in, "in the cloud." Stored on the web or on remote servers.

clustering connecting two or more computers to be-have as a single computer. Thanks to clustering, two or more computers can jointly execute a function, activity can be distributed evenly across a computer network, and systems can respond gracefully to unexpected failures.

command line the terminal prompt for typing in commands to the computer, bypassing the operating system's graphic display interface.

complimentary metal oxide semiconductor (CMOS) pronounced "see-moss," this is a small, 64-byte memory chip on the computer motherboard that stores information a PC needs in order to boot up.

computer a programmable device that can use to store, retrieve, and process data. The computer's brain is the microprocessor, which is capable of doing math, moving data around, and altering data after storing it in binary code.

computer virus a computer program or piece of program code that attaches itself to other files and then replicates itself, or causes the computer to perform some damaging or malicious act.

computer-aided design (CAD) a type of software that automates complex drafting tasks.

content management system (CMS) a type of software application for organizing and creating large or complex websites.

cookie a small file created on a hard disk by a Web site visited. Cookie files contain small pieces of information that can be read and altered by that site or other Web sites, thereby making it possible to identify users who have been to the site before.

copyleft an alternative to copyright, a permissions model that allows for freer distribution of intellectual property.

cracker an individual who maliciously breaks into another computer system. (Not to be confused with a hacker, who typically does not have malicious intent.)

creative commons a framework for describing various intellectual property allowances and ranging from full copyright protections to completely open and free permissions.

cursor the highlighted area or pointer that tracks with the movement of a mouse or arrow keys onscreen.

cyberspace an all-encompassing term for online world of the Internet and other computer networks.

data information that is convenient to move or process.

database either a program for arranging facts in the computer and retrieving them (the computer equivalent of a filing system) or a file set up by such a system.

digital a means of transmitting or storing data using "on" and "off" bits, expressed as "1" or "0."

digital subscriber line (DSL) a high-speed Internet connection that uses the ultrahigh-frequency portion of ordinary telephone lines, allowing users to send and receive voice and data on the same line at the same time.

directory an area or data structure in which information is stored regarding the location and contents of files or file structures. On the Web, a directory is a hand-assembled collection of Web pages, sorted by category; Yahoo! is currently the biggest directory on the Internet.

disk a device that stores data in magnetic or optical format. disk drive a mechanism for retrieving information stored on a magnetic disk. The drive rotates the disk at high speed and reads the data with a magnetic head similar to those used in tape recorders.

domain the identifying portion of an Internet address. In e-mail addresses, the domain name follows the @ sign; in Web site addresses, the domain name follows the www. Domain names are followed by a period and a zone that indicates the type of organization. Commercial entities end with .com; educational institutions end with .edu; govern- ment bodies end with .gov; and other organizations end with .org.

domain name system (DNS) the system used to translate Internet domain and host names to IP addresses.

driver a support file that tells a program how to interact with a specific hardware device, such as a hard disk controller or video display card.

DSL See digital subscriber line.

e-commerce electronic commerce, or business conducted over the Internet.

e-mail electronic mail, a means of corresponding to other computer users over the Internet through digital messages. Also spelled email.

e-tailer a retailer engaging in e-commerce; an online merchant.

emoticon a cluster of punctuation marks commonly used in online chat, postings, and e-mail to signify a facial expression or emotional response. For example, :) represents a smile, and :(a frown.

encryption a method of encoding files so only the recipient can read the information. Encryption is necessary for transmitting secure data like credit card numbers over computer networks.

Ethernet the most common computer networking protocol; Ethernet is used to network, or hook, computers together so they can share information.

extensible markup language (XML) a universal format for structured documents and data transmitted on the Web.

file any group of data treated as a single entity by the computer, such as a word processor document, a program, or a database.

file transfer protocol (FTP) a protocol for downloading files from the Internet, pre-Web.

firewall computer hardware or software with special security features to safeguard a network server (or individual computer connected to a network, or to the Internet) from damage by authorized or unauthorized users.

FireWire a high-speed bus used to connect digital devices, such as digital cameras and video cameras, to a computer system. Also known as iLink and IE-1394.

flame to post insulting comments in a discussion group.

Flash proprietary software created by Adobe that contains powerful animation capabilities and its own programming language. Not related to flash memory.

flash memory solid state memory that does not rely on a spinning hard disk.

GIF pronounced "jif," a common file format for image files on the Internet.

gigabyte (GB) one billion bytes. Gopher a pre-Web method of organizing material on Internet servers.

GNU General Public License (GPL) The most widely used free software license.

graphical user interface (GUI) a system that uses graphical symbols called icons to represent available functions. These icons are generally manipulated by a mouse and/or a keyboard.

groupware software that enables groups of users to work together by providing communication, workflow, and task-sharing functions.

hacker an individual who enjoys exploring the details of computer systems and programming code, typically by "hacking" into those systems and programs—but without causing any intentional damage. (Not to be confused with a cracker, who engages in intentionally malicious behavior.)

hard disk a sealed cartridge containing magnetic storage disk(s) that holds much more memory—up to more than 100 gigabytes—than floppy disks. Usually a hard disk is built into the computer, but it can be a peripheral. hardware the physical equipment, as opposed to the programs and procedures, used in computing.

hit a single request from a Web browser to view an item (typically a Web page) stored on a Web server.

home page the first or main page of a Web site.

host the computer used to run programs and store files for remote users or over a network.

hover the act of selecting an item by placing a cursor over an icon without clicking.

hub hardware used to network computers together, usually over an Ethernet connection.

hyperlink a connection between two tagged elements in a Web page, or separate sites, that makes it possible to click from one to the other.

hypertext a system of organizing information based on its relationship to other information, rather than linear or alphabetical orders. Hypertext allows users to link related Web pages and to store information in more than one place.

hypertext markup language (HTML) the scripting language used to create documents on the World Wide Web (WWW).

HTML5 The latest version of HTML, the templating language for Web pages. Not yet widely used in 2010, HTML5 allows for sophisticated creation and embedding of media, graphics and animations without the use of external tools.

hypertext transfer protocol (HTTP) the protocol used to transfer World Wide Web pages from one computer to another.

icon a graphic symbol on the display screen that represents a file, peripheral, or some other object or function.

instant messaging text-based real-time one-on-one communication over the Internet. Not to be confused with chat, which can accommodate multiple users, instant messaging (IM) typically is limited to just two users.

integrated circuit an entire electronic circuit contained on one piece of silicon. The first integrated circuit began with a single board (originally plastic), onto which strips of conducting material were sprayed; electronic components could then be inserted directly onto the board.

Internet the global "network of networks" that connects millions of computers and other devices around the world.

Internet protocol (IP) the protocol that defines how data are sent through routers to different networks, by assigning unique IP addresses to different devices.

Internet Relay Chat (IRC) an Internet-based network of chat servers and channels that facilitates real-time public chat and file exchanges.

Internet service provider (ISP) a company that provides end-user access to the Internet via its central computers and local access lines.

intranet a private network of computers, using Internet protocols, accessible only by members of the network.

iOS the name of Apple's mobile, touch-based operating system in use on iPods and iPads.

JavaScript a scripting language used to create advanced Web page functionality, such as rollovers, pull-down menus, and other special effects.

JPG/JPEG a common file format for photographic images on the Internet.

kilobyte (K) a unit of measure for data storage or transmission equivalent to 1,024 bytes; often rounded to 1,000.

ligh-emitting diode (LED) an electronic device that lights up when electricity is passed through it.

link a hypertext connection that allows a user to jump from one Internet site to another by pointing and clicking. On the World Wide Web, links are often underlined or highlighted.

Linux a Unix-like operating system that runs on many different types of computers. There are many different flavors of Linux, many of which are freely distributed under open source guidelines.

liquid crystal display (LCD) a flat-screen display where images are created by light transmitted through a layer of liquid crystals.

local area network (LAN) a system that enables users to connect PCs to one another or to minicomputers or mainframes.

macro a series of instructions in a simple coding language, used to automate procedures in a computer application, document, or template.

mainframe computer generally the largest, fastest, and most expensive kind of computer, usually costing millions of dollars and requiring special cooling. Mainframe computers can accommodate hundreds of simultaneous users and normally are run around the clock; typically they are owned by large companies.

malware "malicious software," shorthand for any virus, Trojan, or worm. megabyte (MB) one million bytes.

megahertz (MHz) a measure of microprocessing speed; 1 MHz equals 1 million electrical cycles per second.

memory temporary electronic storage for data and instructions, using electronic impulses on a chip.

microcomputer a computer based on a microprocessor chip. Also known as a personal computer.

microprocessor a complete central processing unit assembled on a single silicon chip.

MIDI (musical instrument digital interface) a file format for sound and music on the Internet.

MPEG Motion Picture Experts Group, a file format for high-quality video in small file sizes.

modem (modulator-demodulator) a device capable of converting a digital signal to an analog signal, which can be transmitted via a telephone line, reconverted, and then "read" by another computer.

monitor the display device on a computer, similar to a television screen. Mosaic the very first Web browser, developed in 1993 by the National Center for Supercomputing Applications (NCSA) at the University of Illinois.

motherboard the largest printed circuit board in a computer, housing the CPU chip and controlling circuitry.

mouse a small handheld input device connected to a computer and featuring one or more button-style switches. When moved around a desk, the mouse causes a symbol on the computer screen to make corresponding movements.

multimedia the combination, usually on a computer, of interactive text, graphics, audio, and video.

netiquette the etiquette of the Internet.

network an interconnected group of computers.

newbie inexperienced user.

node any single computer connected to a network.

open source software for which the underlying programming code is available (free) for users to make changes to it and build new versions incorporating those changes.

operating system a sequence of programming codes that instructs a computer about its various parts and peripherals and how to operate them. Operating systems, such as Windows or Linux, deal only with the workings of the hardware and are separate from software programs.

partition a division in a hard drive, allowing a user to create separate areas of memory for separate purposes.

path the collection of folders and subfolders (listed in order of hierarchy) that hold a particular file.

peer-to-peer (P2P) a communications network where two or more computers work together as equals, without the benefit of a central server.

peripheral a device connected to the computer that provides communication or auxiliary functions.

personal digital assistant (PDA) a handheld device that organizes personal information, combining computing and networking features. A typical PDA includes an address book and a to-do list.

phishing pretending to be a website to illegally gather sensitive personal information.

pixel the individual picture elements that combine to create a video image.

pixelization the stair-stepped appearance of a curved or angled line in a digital image.

Pocket PC Microsoft's handheld computer operating system and hardware platform, similar to the competing Palm OS.

podcast a digital audio or video file intended for download.

port an interface on a computer to which one can connect a device. Personal computers have various types of ports. Internally, there are several ports for connecting disk drives, display screens, and keyboards. Externally, there are ports for connecting modems, printers, mice, and other peripheral devices.

Post Office Protocol (POP) a protocol used to retrieve e-mail from a mail server.

Pretty Good Privacy (PGP) one of the most popular tools for public-key encryption.

printer the piece of computer hardware that creates hardcopy printouts of documents.

program as a noun, a prepared set of instructions for the computer, often with provisions for the operator to choose among various options. As a verb, to create such a set of instructions.

protocol an agreed-upon format for transmitting data between two devices.

public key cryptography (PKC) a means of encrypting data and messages using a combination of public and private keys.

random-access memory (RAM) a temporary storage space in which data may be held on a chip rather than stored on disk or tape. The contents of RAM may be accessed or altered at any time during a session, but will be lost when the computer is turned off.

read-only memory (ROM) a type of chip memory, the contents of which have been permanently recorded in a computer by the manufacturer and cannot be altered by the user.

reduced instruction set computing (RISC) a type of microprocessor that gains speed by using fewer instructions than the Complex Instruction Set (CISC) chip.

resolution the degree of clarity an image displays. The term is most often used to describe the sharpness of bit-mapped images on monitors, but also applies to images on printed pages, as expressed by the number of dots per inch (dpi).

root the main directory or folder on a disk.

router a piece of hardware or software that handles the connection between two or more networks.

scanner a device that converts paper documents or photos into a format that can be viewed on a computer and manipulated by the user.

scripting language an easy-to-use pseudo-programming language that enables the creation of executable scripts composed of individual commands.

search engine a Web server that indexes Web pages, then makes the index available for user searching.

serial a type of external port used to connect communication devices, such as modems, PalmPilots, etc.

server the central computer in a network, providing a service or data access to client computers on the network.

shareware a software program distributed on the honor system; providers make their programs freely accessible over the Internet, with the understanding that those who use them will send payment to the provider after using them. See also freeware.

social graph the description of the connections between members of a social network.

software the programs and procedures, as opposed to the

physical equipment, used in computing.

spam junk e-mail. As a verb, it means to send thousands of copies of a junk e-mail message.

spider a software program that follows hypertext links across multiple Web pages, but is not directly under human control. Spiders scan the Web, looking for URLs, automatically following all the hyperlinks on pages accessed. The results from a spider's search are used to create the indexes used by search engines.

spreadsheet a program that performs mathematical operations on numbers arranged in large arrays; used mainly for accounting and other record keeping.

spyware software used to surreptitiously monitor computer use (i.e., spy on other users).

static RAM (SRAM) random-access memory that retains data bits in its memory as long as power is being supplied.

stack a group of interrelated technologies that operate together to enable an application or service.

Structured Query Language (SQL) a computer language used to send queries to databases.

supercomputer the fastest (and biggest and most expensive) of the mainframe class of computers, usually used for complex scientific calculations.

Telnet an older protocol used to log in to and access data stored on an Internet server.

terabyte (TB) one trillion bytes.

terminal an application for sending typed commands, bypassing the operating system's graphic display

transistor a small piece of semiconducting material (material that conducts electricity better than, say, wood but not as well as metal). Flows of electrons within the transistor can be controlled, enabling it to act as an electronic "switching" device, recoding information in the form of an "on" or an "off" signal.

Transmission Control Protocol/Internet Protocol (TCP/IP) the protocol used for communications on the Internet; coordinates the addressing and packaging of the data packets that make up any communication.

Trojan horse a malicious program that pretends to be another, harmless program or file.

universal serial bus (USB) an external connection standard that supports data transfer rates of 12 Mbps and can connect up to 127 peripheral devices, such as keyboards, modems, and mice.

troll a repeatedly rude or unmannered member of a discussion group.

UNIX A multi-user, multitasking operating system designed to run on a wide variety of computers, from microcomputers to mainframes.

unsolicited commercial e-mail (UCE) spam.

URL (Uniform Resource Locator) the address that identifies a Web page to a browser. Also known as a Web address.

virtual private network (VPN) a network that allows offsite computer users to access company servers as if they were connected via office network.

virus a computer program segment or string of code that can attach itself to another program or file, reproduce itself, and spread from one computer to another. Viruses can destroy or change data and in other ways sabotage computer systems.

warez pronounced "wheres," this is illegally distributed software, from which normal copy protection has been cracked or removed.

Web page an HTML file, containing text, graphics, or mini-applications, viewed with a Web browser.

Web site an organized, linked collection of Web pages stored on an Internet server and read using a Web browser. The opening page of a site is called a home page.

Wide Area Information Servers (WAIS) a software program that enables the indexing of huge quantities of information across the Internet and other networks.

wide area network (WAN) a connection between two or more local area networks (LANs). Wide area networks can be made up of interconnected smaller networks spread throughout a building, a state, or the globe.

Wi-Fi the various 802.11 wireless networking standards; short for "wireless fidelity."

wiki a special website that is designed to allow its users to easily modify its contents.

Windows the generic name for all versions of Microsoft's graphical operating system.

Wireless Equivalent Privacy (WEP) the encryption and security protocol for Wi-Fi networks.

wireless LAN (WLAN) a local area network composed of wireless connections between devices.

World Wide Web (WWW) a vast network of information, mainly from business, commercial, and government resources, that uses a hypertext system for quickly transmitting graphics, sound, and video over the Internet.

worm a parasitic computer program that replicates but does not infect other files.

These Days, the Web Unmasks Everyone

By BRIAN STELTER

Not too long ago, theorists fretted that the Internet was a place where anonymity thrived.

Now, it seems, it is the place where anonymity dies.

The collective intelligence of the Internet's two billion users, and the digital fingerprints that so many users leave on Web sites, combine to make it more and more likely that every embarrassing video, every intimate photo, and every indelicate e-mail is attributed to its source, whether that source wants it to be or not. This intelligence makes the public sphere more public than ever before and sometimes forces personal lives into public view.

To some, this could conjure up comparisons to the agents of repressive governments in the Middle East who monitor online protests and exact retribution offline. But the positive effects can be numerous: criminality can be ferreted out, falsehoods can be disproved and individuals can become Internet icons.

This erosion of anonymity is a product of pervasive social media services, cheap cellphone cameras, free photo and video Web hosts, and perhaps most important of all, a change in people's views about what ought to be public and what ought to be private. Experts say that Web sites like Facebook, which require real identities and encourage the sharing of photographs and videos, have hastened this change.

"Humans want nothing more than to connect, and the companies that are connecting us electronically want to know who's saying what, where," said Susan Crawford, a professor at the Benjamin N. Cardozo School of Law. "As a result, we're more known than ever before."

This growing "publicness," as it is sometimes called, comes with significant consequences for commerce, for political speech and for ordinary people's right to privacy. There are efforts by governments and corporations to set up online identity systems. Technology will play an even greater role in the identification of once-anonymous individuals: Facebook, for instance, is already using facial recognition technology in ways that are alarming to European regulators.

After the riots in Vancouver following the 2011 Stanley Cup finals, locals needed no such facial recognition technology—they simply combed through social media sites to try to identify some of the people involved, like Nathan Kotylak, 17, a star on Canada's junior water polo team.

On Facebook, Mr. Kotylak apologized for the damage he had caused. The finger-pointing affected not only him, it affected his family: local news media reported that his father, a doctor, had seen his ranking on a medical practice review site, RateMDs.com, drop after people posted comments about his son's involvement in the riots. Other people subsequently went to the Web site to defend the doctor and improve his ranking.

Predictably, there was a backlash to the Internet-assisted identification of the people involved in the alcohol-fueled riot. Camille Cacnio, a student in Vancouver who was photographed during the riot and who admitted to theft, wrote on her blog that the "21st-century witch hunt" on the Internet was "another form of mobbing."

Half a world away, in Middle Eastern countries like Iran and Syria, activists have sometimes succeeded in identifying victims of dictatorial violence through anonymously uploaded YouTube videos.

They have also succeeded in identifying fakes: In a widely publicized case in June 2011, a blogger who claimed to be a Syrian-American lesbian and called herself "A Gay Girl in Damascus" was revealed to be an American man, Tom MacMaster.

"Publicity"—something normally associated with celebrities—"is no longer scarce," Dave Morgan, the chief executive of Simulmedia, wrote in an essay this month.

He posited that because the Internet "can't be made to forget" images and moments from the past, like an outburst on a train or a kiss during a riot, "the reality of an inescapable public world is an issue we are all going to hear a lot more about."

The History of Home Video Games

First Generation: 1972–77

In 1966 Ralph Baer (b. 1922), an employee of the defense contractor Sanders Associates, first came up with the concept of a "television gaming apparatus." Originally designed to develop the reflexes of military personal, this device included both a chase game and a video tennis game, and could be attached to a normal television set.

Magnavox licensed Baer's game and on January 27, 1972, launched the Odyssey videogame console—the world's first home video game system. Priced at $100, the Odyssey featured simple black-and-white graphics, enhanced by plastic overlays for the television screen. This pioneering game system was not a lasting success, however; it sold only 200,000 units over its three-year life.

That same year, inspired by Baer's original video tennis game, Atari released an electronic arcade game called PONG, which became a huge success. Unfazed by Odyssey's short shelf life, in 1975 Atari released a home version of PONG, under the Sears Tele-Games label. The $100 game system was Sears's best-selling item during the 1975 Christmas season, with sales of more than $40 million. Atari released its own branded PONG unit in 1976.

In August 1976 Fairchild Camera and Instrument leveraged its position as the creator of the microchip to release the first programmable home video game system, based on the 8-bit F8 processor. The Channel F Video Entertainment System sold for $169 and accepted $20 "Videocart" game cartridges; it displayed its games in 16 colors.

RCA's Studio II followed Fairchild to market in January 1977 at a price of $149. Even though the Studio II used the same 8-bit COSMAC 1802 microprocessor that was used in NASA's *Voyager* and *Galileo* spacecraft, its chunky black-and-white graphics were notably inferior to those of the Channel F, and the unit was discontinued in 1979.

Second Generation (Golden Age): 1977–82

The "golden age" of home video games was launched in October 1977, when Atari released its own programmable video game system. Priced at $199, Atari's Video Computer System (VCS), later known as the Atari 2600, was based on an 8-bit Motorola 6507 microprocessor, with 256 bytes of RAM. On the market through 1990, the Atari VCS went on to sell more than 25 million units over its product life. Over the course of its production run, 40 dif-ferent manufacturers created more than 200 different games for the system, selling more than 120 million cartridges of popular games such as Space Invaders, Asteroids, and Pac-Man.

One of Atari's first competitors in the programmable video game market was Bally, which launched the Bally Professional Arcade in 1977. Even though the Bally unit had better graphics than the Atari VCS, it sold at a higher price ($350) and failed to catch on.

Magnavox jumped into the programmable video game market with Odyssey². Launched in 1978, Odyssey² featured an integrated membrane keyboard. The Odyssey² was more popular in Europe than in the U.S., where the parent company Philips Electronics marketed it as the Videopac.

Atari faced a more serious competitor in 1980, when Mattel launched its Intellivision video game system. Intellivision featured better graphics than the VCS, and was the first video game system to use a 16-bit microprocessor—the General Instruments 1600. Intellivision became known for its proprietary sports titles, such as Major League Baseball, NFL Football, NHL Hockey, and NBA Basketball, even though the lack of third-party games contributed to its second-place showing against the Atari 2600.

Third Generation: 1982–84

The third generation of video games became known as the "dark ages," not because of any new technology, but rather because of the precipitous drop in sales that started in 1982. The crash was caused by too many derivative or poor-quality game cartridges from too many manufacturers. Many third-party game developers went out of business during this period, and even established companies lost money on unsold inventory.

The most prominent third-generation game system was Coleco's Colecovision. Launched in 1982 at a price of $199, Colecovision featured high-quality graphics and used an 8-bit Z-80A microprocessor with 8K RAM. Colecovision's main claim to fame is that it offered high-quality versions of arcade favorites: *Donkey Kong, Defender, Frogger, Joust, Spy Hunter,* and *Zaxxon.*

Atari responded to Coleco by releasing the $299 Atari 5200 SuperSystem, which was based on the graphics and audio chips found in the Atari 400 personal computer. Games for the 5200 were essentially improved releases of older 2600 (VCS) games; this lack of new games failed to excite consumers, and the 5200 was lost amid the overall market crash of 1982.

Fourth Generation: 1985–89

Following the crash of 1982–84, the home video game industry experienced a rebirth with the introduction of a new generation of game units driven by two technological innovations—less expensive memory chips and higher-power 8-bit microprocessors. These developments enabled game designers to produce home video game consoles that could successfully compete at a quality level equal to that of arcade machines.

In 1983 Nintendo had released the Famicon ("family computer") video game system to the Japanese market. The console was a hit, selling 2.5 million units in its first year, and Nintendo began negotiations with Atari to distribute the system in the United States. These talks fell through, and Nintendo decided to distribute the system itself in the U.S., under the name Nintendo Entertainment System (NES).

The $199 NES was based on an 8-bit Motorola 6502 microprocessor and shipped with a version of the hit arcade game *Super Mario Bros*. Quantities of the NES were shipped into the New York market in time for Christmas 1985, and national distribution followed early in 1986. Nintendo sold more than 3 million NES units in its first two years of release; it is estimated that, over its entire product life, more than 65 million NES consoles were sold worldwide, along with 500 million cartridges.

In 1989, Sega released its first game system in the United States, the Sega Master System (SMS). The SMS had two cartridge ports; one in a standard cartridge configuration, and a second port that accepted small credit card–shaped cartridges. The system was capable of using both ports at any given time, and Sega used this feature to produce plug-in 3-D glasses for use with certain games.

Also released in 1989 was the first programmable handheld game system, Nintendo's GameBoy. Priced at $100, GameBoy featured a black-and-white LCD screen, and came prepackaged with a Tetris cartridge. With more than 100 million units shipped in various configurations, GameBoy holds the honor of being the world's all-time best-selling video game system.

Fifth Generation: 1989–95

The fifth generation of home video game systems was ushered in by the 1989 American release of NEC's TurboGrafx-16. (The system was launched in Japan in 1988 as the PC Engine.) Although the TurboGrafx-16 was advertised as a 16-bit system, it actually used an 8-bit microprocessor, assisted by a 16-bit graphics chip and 64K RAM; it was notable as the first game console to have a CD player attachment.

More formidable was the Sega Genesis game system (sold as the Mega Drive in Japan). Released to the U.S. market in 1989, Genesis was the first true 16-bit game system, using a Motorola 68000 microprocessor. Genesis was priced at $199, and ran excellent translations of Sega arcade hits; sales received a significant boost with the 1991 release of the *Sonic the Hedgehog* game.

To compete with the Sega Genesis, Nintendo launched its own 16-bit system in 1991. The Super NES, known as the Super Famicon in Japan, sold for $199 and included the Super Mario World cartridge. The initial U.S. production run of 300,000 units sold out overnight; over the course of its product life, more than 46 million Super NES units were sold worldwide.

Sixth Generation: 1995–98

The sixth generation of home video games featured high-powered microprocessors and dedicated graphics processors that enabled extremely realistic graphics and game play. These game consoles outperformed the much higher-priced personal computer systems of the day.

The Sega Saturn, released in May of 1995, achieved its high graphics quality by using twin 32-bit microprocessors and CD-ROM-based games. The Saturn's high $399 price and lack of third-party games led to its being overshadowed by Sony's upcoming game console.

In September 1995 Sony released its first video game system, the Playstation, to the U.S. market. The Playstation was priced at $299, $100 less than the competing Sega Saturn, and incorporated a 32-bit microprocessor designed to produce polygon graphics. Backed with a massive advertising campaign, the Playstation unseated both Nintendo and Sega to become the leading home video game system; to date, it has sold more than 50 million units worldwide.

In 1996, five years after the release of the Super NES, Nintendo released its own sixth-generation game system, the Nintendo 64. The Nintendo 64 used a 64-bit microprocessor (hence the name), and was priced at just $150, significantly lower than its competition. The launch was hugely successful, with 1.7 million units sold in the first three months of release.

Next Generation: 1998–2001

As game consoles outpaced PCs in performance, Sega, Microsoft, Sony, and Nintendo all released platforms capable of playing games equal or superior to those in video arcades, and home computer gaming entered a new era.

Sega upped the video game ante in 1999 with the release of its Dreamcast system. Incorporating a 128-bit microprocessor, the Dreamcast ran on Microsoft's Windows CE platform. Dreamcast had strong sales until Sony's release of its Playstation 2; continuing financial problems led Sega to discontinue production in March 2001.

Building on the success of the first-generation Playstation, Sony released the Playstation 2 (PS2), powered by a 128-bit "Emotion Engine" microprocessor. The PS2 was an immediate success; 38.2 million units are still in use in the U.S. and it remains the dominant video game system in the market.

Microsoft entered the game console market in November 2001 with its widely anticipated Xbox system, which incorporated a 733MHz Pentium III microprocessor.

Also released in November 2001 was Nintendo's latest game system, the GameCube. Priced at $199, $100 less than Xbox, the GameCube was Nintendo's first noncartridge system, instead running small-diameter CD-ROM discs. Nintendo sold more than 500,000 GameCubes in the first week of release; total U.S sales reached 11.7 million units.

Gaming Expands: 2002–present

Since 2002, home video gaming has grown up and gone mobile as game manufacturers took advantage of new console and handheld power to make games more sophisticated, elaborate and pervasive.

In 2005, Microsoft launched the first of a new generation of consoles, the Xbox 360, which housed a Xeon processor, supported high definition video, and was available in three models: Core, Premium, and Elite. In late 2006, Sony launched the Playstation 3, which utilizes a 3.2 GHz Cell processor, and played high definition Blu-Ray discs. Opting for a lower-powered console that emphasizes a novel motion-sensitive controller, Nintendo gambled on the Wii (pronouced 'we'). By mid-2007, Nintendo's gamble appeared to have paid off; 2.5 million Wii's have sold in the U.S., outpacing the PS3 by more than a million units. Sony and Micorsoft responded with their own motion control devices, the Playstation Move and Xbox Kinect, respectively.

In handhelds, Nintendo and Sony released powerful mobile game players, and then saw their territory threatened by a new, powerful class of smartphones and multifunction devices capably of playing video games. Nintendo produced several models in its wildy popular Game Boy line: the Advance (2001); the Advance SP (2003); the DS (2004),which includes a touch sensitive dual screen; the Micro (2005); the DS lite (2006); and the 3DS (2010). Released in 2004, Sony's Playstation Portable (PSP) was capable of many functions besides mobile gaming; it also played movies and music and connected wirelessly to the Internet. In 2009, Sony launched the PSP Go model, and in 2011 announced the Sony Ericsson Xperia Play, capable of playing some Playstation-certified games.

The success of Apple's iPod Touch and iPhone as gaming platforms took the console industry largely by surprise. The number of games, many of them low-cost and so called casual games, developed for Apple's (and later Android) phones dwarfed those available on any single console or handheld gaming device, and number in the hundreds of thousands.

SOCIAL SCIENCES

HISTORY

World History

The Peopling of the World (ca. 150,000–15,000 B.C.)

Africa is the cradle of humanity. An early human species, Homo erectus ("Java Man," "Peking Man," and others) evolved in Africa and migrated to Eurasia perhaps a million years ago. These very early humans used fire, created stone weapons and tools, and were successful in occupying a wide range of habitats. Nevertheless, all non-African populations of Homo erectus eventually died out without leaving descendents. Human beings of fully modern type—members of our own species, Homo sapiens—evolved from Homo erectus through various transitional stages in the savannah lands of eastern Africa about 150 millennia ago. Homo sapiens was a highly social and adaptable species, fully capable of using complex language. Modern humans moved out from the original species homeland on the eastern plains of Africa to occupy much of eastern, northern, and southern parts of the continent; the special challenges of the rain forest environment slowed the movement of humans into the western regions of Africa.

Around 105,000 years ago, taking advantage of one of the periodic eras of warm, wet climate that can turn the deserts of northern Africa into a relatively green and pleasant landscape, modern humans migrated northward through Egypt and out of Africa via the Sinai Peninsula to the Middle East. There they apparently met and co-existed with humans of a different and older species—Neanderthals (Homo neandertalensis)—that had a simpler and less flexible culture and tool technology.

Following the coast of southern Asia, modern humans were in India and Southeast Asia by 90,000 years ago. (Ocean levels were generally much lower at the time, because a vast amount of water was locked up in the glaciers of the Ice Age; much of Southeast Asia was dry land, part of an exposed continental shelf. Any traces that these early people might have left of their coastal migrations would now be submerged off the present-day coastlines of Asia.) Sometime between 65,000 and 40,000 years ago, humans crossed miles of open ocean (probably on rafts) to reach New Guinea and Australia. No later than 50,000 years ago, other populations migrated from the Middle East across the plains of Central Asia to China and northeastern Asia, eventually making it to the islands of Japan. As Homo sapiens spread to East and Southeast Asia, remnant populations of Homo erectus, such as "Peking Man" and "Java Man," were displaced and became extinct.

Humans made their way into Europe beginning around 40,000 years ago, challenging the existing populations of Neanderthals there. Whether from superior social organization and technology, from outright human extermination of the Neanderthal competitors, or from some other cause (or combination of causes), the last Neanderthals became extinct around 30,000 years ago, and humans of our own species were in undisputed possession of the Eurasian continent. The early human occupants of Europe and northern Asia of the Paleolithic ("Old Stone Age") period, roughly 40,000 to 12,000 years ago, devised highly sophisticated means of dealing with the cold glacial environment, including the efficient hunting of large animals; the processing of hides and the creation of cut and sewn hide and fur garments; the use of fire for heating, cooking, and light; and the creation of warm shelters from the elements. The "tool kit" of these Paleolithic Homo sapiens was far more elaborate than that of earlier human species, and included not only a wide range of edged tools and projectile points, but also such important devices as spear-throwers, awls, needles, and hammers, made of carefully chosen materials (such as antler and bone) and skillfully crafted.

Using this technology, some humans moved as far as northeasternmost Eurasia, and from there across a broad plain of open land connecting Eurasia with North America (a "land bridge" where the Bering Strait now separates the two continents), introducing humans to the Americas around 15,000 years ago. The timing of human settlement of the Americas is much debated. Some scholars adhere to a conservative view that dates the event to around 13,500 years ago, with the appearance in the archaeological record of the Clovis Culture complex (originally identified in New Mexico but found widely in North America), characterized by distinctive and finely made projectile points. Others rely on apparently securely dated sites that predate the Clovis Culture by at least several thousand years, including some in South America, to argue for a considerably earlier migration.) With this migration, or series of migrations, all of the main land masses of Earth except for icebound Antarctica had become human habitats. Settlement of the Indo-Pacific archipelagos soon followed, with the ancestors of the Austronesian-speaking peoples setting out from the Fujian coast of China around 7000 B.C. to settle Taiwan, the Philippines, Indonesia, and onward to Melanesia, Micronesia, and Polynesia.

In the course of these migrations, humans became adapted to specific habitats (hot, cold, sunny, light-deprived, and so on), while widely separated populations developed in genetic isolation from one another. These two factors combined allowed the evolution of superficial traits of skin color, hair color and texture, eyelid shape, and others that are the external defining characteristics of human "races." All humans during the millennia of the great migrations also demonstrated the shared human capacity for the creation of culture and art of great diversity and refinement, from the cave paintings and ivory sculptures of prehistoric Europe to the equally ancient rock art of Australia.

All humans at that time shared the basic lifestyle of hunting and gathering. Animals, birds and fish were hunted and trapped for food, shellfish were gathered in oceans and rivers, and great numbers of plants were identified and harvested for use as food, fiber, medicine, dyes, and for other purposes. It was a potentially rich and abundant way of living, but one that depended on low population density and little population growth. The latter probably resulted from prolonged nursing of children (which suppresses maternal fertility), as well as from high infant and child mortality. Even very slow growth in population density was probably a significant spur to the great migrations that peopled the earth, as bands of out-migrants left populated areas in search of new hunting and gathering grounds.

The end of the last ice age 12,000–11,000 years ago led in some places to unprecedented population growth, which had momentous consequences for human history.

The Last Ice Age and the Neolithic Revolution (ca. 10,000 B.C.)

Beginning about 10,000 B.C., a strong global warming period in the earth's climate began to melt the huge glaciers that had covered much of northern Eurasia and

North America for thousands of years. Some results of this warming trend, which lasted for several millennia and resulted in the rapid retreat of glaciers and permafrost to far northern latitudes, included the creation of vast steppes or prairies south of the retreating glaciers that were the ideal habitat for huge herds of horses, bison, and other food animals. Further south, warmer, wetter conditions encouraged the growth of food plants and the animals (such as antelope and wild goats) that grazed on them. Humans quickly took advantage of these new food sources, and human numbers and population density began to climb as a result.

At this point, some people in crowded environments began to take a more active role in managing food resources—encouraging certain plant crops, for example, through seeding, weeding, and harvesting plants in certain locations that were well known and over which some form of ownership may have been asserted. This led to the development of a wide range of domesticated plants, including wheat and legumes in Mesopotamia and northwestern India; millet in North China, rice in South China and Southeast Asia; and corn (maize) and beans in Mesoamerica. Neolithic hunters began following, directing, managing and culling herds of horses or wild cattle, protecting them from wild predators to save them for human use. In this way, the first steps toward the domestication of plants and animals were taken. With food management came a tendency to travel less and to settle down more, to guard and enjoy the resources that were under management. Camps became villages, or at least season-long settlements. Animals that acted as scavengers at these settlements (wolves, swine, fowl) were seen to be useful, selected for docility (the fiercer ones were killed, the tamer ones tolerated), and eventually domesticated (as dogs, pigs, and chickens). A more sedentary life reduced the hunter-gatherer nomad's requirement that possessions be light and portable. Pottery was perhaps the most significant consequence of this change; too heavy to carry on nomadic migrations, it greatly improved the possibilities for storing and cooking food in a proto-village environment. Imperceptibly, the people of the post-ice-age world were inventing the Neolithic Revolution.

The full-scale Neolithic ("new stone") culture, evident in the Middle East by 8000 B.C. and found in many parts of the world over the course of time, involves agriculture, particularly the raising of grain crops, and a sharply reduced reliance on wild plants; the domestication of animals for various purposes, and a reduced reliance on wild game; settled life in villages; pottery; water management; the production and use of cloth and of a wide range of well-made stone tools; evidence of belief systems, including ceremonial burial of the dead; and a range of other adaptations to a settled lifestyle. Life for Neolithic villagers may have been harder than it had been for their hunter-gatherer ancestors. Raising, harvesting, storing, and processing grain for food took unremitting toil; so too did the work of animal husbandry. Crowding together in villages, and living in close proximity to domestic animals, exposed farmers to many more diseases than had affected hunter-gatherer bands. But the payoff, for people caught in a cycle of population growth and limited opportunities for migration to unpopulated areas, was that the same land that might support a few hundred hunter-gatherers could support several villages housing thousands of Neolithic farmers.

The Dawn of Civilization (ca. 3000–1500 B.C.)

The transition from prehistoric Neolithic culture to civilization seems to have involved in every case a combination of two things: a culture founded on settled agricultural communities and, on the basis of such settled communities, the development of urban centers with literate religious and social hierarchies whose members asserted control over such matters as irrigation and water control, ritual and religious observances, and the application of military power or legitimized violence, as well as the right to appropriate for their own use a portion of the goods produced by ordinary farmers and workers. The first condition came into being over time in a great many parts of the prehistoric world, including Mesopotamia (the "land between the rivers," i.e. the Tigris and the Euphrates); several of the large river valleys of China; parts of India and Southeast Asia; the Nile Valley and the great bend of the Niger River in Africa; the Danube Valley in Europe; parts of Central America and Mexico, the Mississippi Valley, and the Amazon Basin in the New World; and in the highlands of New Guinea and throughout the islands of the Pacific Ocean. The second condition of civilization, the urban center, eventually appeared in some, but not all, of these Neolithic cultures. It happened first in Mesopotamia in the fourth millennium B.C., but other areas, such as Egypt and the Indus Valley, soon followed. Across Eurasia, the invention and spread of the technologies of metallurgy (by the early third millennium B.C. in Mesopotamia and Egypt, but not until a thousand years later in China) gave the Bronze Age its name.

Mesopotamia The 600-mile-long plain of the Tigris and Euphrates Valleys stretching from Anatolia to the Persian Gulf is the site of the earliest known civilization, which takes its name from the city-state of Sumer. The first of a succession of Mesopotamian civilizations, Sumerian culture first blossomed about 3500 to 3000 B.C. Each of the cities within the Sumerian culture area was a sacred temple city, the realm of a god whose regent on earth was the priest-king. Sumerian culture gave rise to a number of important innovations, including a calendar, the invention of writing (cuneiform, written with a stylus on tablets of soft clay), the plow, the potter's wheel, and wheeled carts. The development of writing, in particular, was an important element in the commercial and administrative success of the Sumerian city-states.

Separate and frequently warring city-states such as Lagash, Nippur, and Ur came under the control of the more northerly Empire of Akkad, whose greatest king was Sargon (ca. 2250 B.C.). The Akkadian Empire in turn fell under the sway of the Babylonian Empire, whose king Hammurabi (ca. 1750 B.C.) conquered all of Mesopotamia and is credited with the first known Code of Laws. Shortly before 1500 B.C. this empire fell under the domination of the Kassites, northern invaders who relied on a new military shock weapon, the horse-drawn chariot.

Egypt The great valley of the Nile, which creates a slender green oasis through the Sahara, had given birth by about 3000 B.C. to a network of farming villages whose population was of urban density, though not yet to cities as such. Tradition, which may incorporate elements of legend, credits the founding of the Egyptian monarchy to Menes (fl. 3100 B.C.), whose conquest of Lower (i.e., northern) Egypt laid the foundation for the Old Kingdom (ca. 3000–2200 B.C.). Political unification, quite different from the autonomous city-states of Sumer, permitted a rapid assimilation of some aspects of Sumerian culture and technology into the indiginous culture of the Nile Valley, while the desert meant relative freedom from invasion. The pharaohs did not rule on behalf of the gods, but were divine beings themselves; the building of their colossal tombs, the pyramids, were great religious works directed by the unitary state. The most famous is the Great Pyramid of Cheops at Gizeh (ca. 2500 B.C.). The development of hieroglyphic writing in Egypt, not much later than the invention of cuneiform writing in Sumer, facilitated both the administrative and the religious roles of the Egyptian monarchy.

The older diversity of the valley reappeared during a century of dissolution and division called the First Intermediate Period, after which the traditions of Menes were revived in the Middle Kingdom (ca. 2100–1800 B.C.). Architecture and sculpture were consciously restorationist, modeled after the Old Kingdom. This period was also the "classical age" of Egyptian literature.

But this age ended with the invasion from Syria-Palestine of a warlike charioteering people known as Hyksos, who ruled during the Second Intermediate Period (ca. 1800–1600 B.C.). The Eighteenth Dynasty, with its capital at Thebes, at last managed to drive out the Hyksos and reestablish royal authority throughout the valley, initiating the New Kingdom (ca. 1600–1100 B.C.).

The Indus River Basin The Indus Basin, stretching from the Himalayas to the Arabian Sea, had become by about 3000 B.C. another locus of settled agriculture. The emerging Indus culture showed obvious signs of Sumerian influence. The great cities of Harappa and Mohenjo-Daro have been excavated, along with many small villages. Small statuary and cylinder seals demonstrate a rich religious, artistic, and commercial life. Some evidence of writing has been discovered, but it remains undeciphered. This Indian civilization flourished from about 2500 to about 1500 B.C. when it was conquered by Central Asian ("Aryan") tribesmen who used chariots and arrows.

The Eastern Mediterranean Around 2000 B.C. three centers of civilization influenced by Mesopotamia and Egypt began to develop: the Canaanites in Syria and Palestine, the Hittites in Asia Minor, and the Minoan civilization on the island of Crete. It is not clear whether Minos was a name or, like "pharaoh" a title; but the palace of Minos, called the Labyrinth, dominated the trading city of Knossos, center of a "sea empire" whose ships were in contact with Italy, Egypt, Asia Minor, and mainland Greece. Yet by about 1500 B.C. the Minoan economy was in decline, possibly because of overexploitation of the Cretan environment as well as the damage wrought by a series of earthquakes, and not long after a Greek prince was ruling at Knossos.

China In China around 1950 B.C., the millet-based agricultural villages of the North China Plain gave rise to the semi-legendary Xia Dynasty, which ushered in the Bronze Age in East Asia. The Xia were overthrown around 1550 B.C. by Tang the Victorious, who established the Shang Dynasty, which endured for 500 years. The Shang Dynasty is noted for its sophisticated bronze vessels, used in worship of the royal ancestors, and for oracle bones inscribed with an early form of Chinese script asking questions of the gods. Shang culture was enriched after around 1350 B.C. by new technologies from western Eurasia, including the chariot, the cultivation of wheat, and sheepraising. Roughly contemporary with the Shang state was the separate Bronze Age culture of the Bah or Shu people, characterized by large, highly stylized bronze human statues and masks, with sites in the Sichuan Basin near the present city of Chengdu.

From the Bronze Age to the Iron Age (ca. 1500–500 B.C.)

In the millennium from about 1500 to about 500 B.C., the area of civilized life continued to spread as the civilizations took on their classic form in the "heroic age" of the ancient world. By the mid-first millennium B.C., iron had begun to replace bronze, first for tools and later for weapons, ushering in the Iron Age of classical civilization. The impact of the chariot warriors from the Eurasian steppes, a huge area of grassland stretching from the Black Sea almost to the Pacific Ocean, altered the earliest civilizations in different ways and to different degrees—least in the Near East, most in India.

Egypt Almost immediately after the Hyksos conquerers had been expelled from Egypt proper, the pharaohs of the New Kingdom (1570–1065 B.C.) reconsolidated the monarchy and began an expansion of the empire into Syria. Thutmose I (d. 1495 B.C.) sent an invading army as far as the Euphrates River. His successor Thutmose II (r. ca. 1495–1490 B.C.) did not sustain his father's conquests, and lost power to his half-sister, queen and regent Hatshepsut (d. ca. 1468 B.C.), who maintained her control over the throne during the first twenty years of the reign of Thutmose III (ca. 1500–1436 B.C.). After the death of Hatshepsut in 1468 B.C., Thutmose III again sent armies to the east, winning a great battle at Megiddo in Palestine. The result was an Egyptian empire in Palestine and Syria in which local princes ruled their peoples while Egyptian bureaucrats and garrison commanders oversaw imperial interests, especially the tribute payments. Egyptian control southward along the Nile into the Sudan and Nubia was also reestablished.

The radical religious reforms of Pharaoh Amenhotep IV (r. ca. 1372–1354 B.C.) brought about a period of severe political disruption. The pharaoh changed his name to

Akhenaton and led a movement after 1370 B.C. to obliterate the name and memory of all the Egyptian gods save for the sun-god Aton (and his incarnation on Earth, the pharaoh). This almost-monotheistic revolution absorbed the attention of the monarchy to such an extent that it helped the empire to crumble and the dynasty to be overthrown. A rigid traditionalism accompanied the painful recovery of the empire. Akhenaton's son-in-law, Tutankhamen (r. 1361–52 B.C.), sponsored a return to older religious norms, including the return of the god Amon and the eclipse of Aton. Tutankhamen (whose famous tomb was discovered in 1922) was also known as a lawgiver, and as the sponsor of new monumental buildings in the capital at Thebes. But by 1200 B.C. a series of invasions, by Hittites and others, forced the Egyptians to abandon their empire in Palestine and Syria to defend the Nile Valley.

The Third Intermediate Period (1065–525 B.C.) saw Egypt's survival in a cultural and religious sense, with the priesthood exerting control over a series of ineffective monarchs. But the state, weakened by invasions of Libyans from the western desert and Nubians from the Upper Nile, finally fell victim to conquests by the Assyrians (671 B.C.) and the Persians (525 B.C.).

Mesopotamian Empires and the Rise of the Persian Empire

The Kassite conquest of the First Babylonian Empire shortly before 1500 B.C. did not lead to substantial changes in the empire, as the northern conquerors adopted the culture and political structure of the conquered. The Assyrians retained their own rulers, under Kassite domination; those rulers eventually took advantage of a series of incursions by other northern horsemen against the Kassites to gain their independence in the First Assyrian Empire (ca. 1150–728 B.C.). The Assyrians were fierce warriors and in the course of establishing the Second Assyrian Empire (728–612 B.C.) they launched attacks on southern Mesopotamia, on Syria and Palestine, and even, briefly, on Egypt. The great Assyrian capital of Nineveh was destroyed, however, in 612 B.C. by the cavalry of an Indo-European people called the Medes. The Medes proceeded to conquer the Assyrian territory east of the Tigris as well as Armenia and eastern Iran, forming a short-lived empire (625–559 B.C.). Assyria's fall permitted the Second Babylonian Empire (625–538 B.C.) to arise in Mesopotamia.

Both Medes and Assyrians fell victim to the Persian Empire (559–331 B.C.). Cyrus the Great (r. 550–533 B.C.) overturned his Median overlord (559 B.C.), conquered

King Croesus of Lydia in Asia Minor (546 B.C.) and overthrew King Nebuchadnezzar III of Babylon (538 B.C.). In the next generation a war of succession threatened the empire; unity was restored when Darius I (r. 521–485 B.C.), grandson of Cyrus, came to the throne. Darius brought the empire to its greatest extent, consolidating the conquest of Egypt, and expanding eastward beyond the Indus by 519 B.C. Dividing his empire into 20 "satrapies" (administrative offices), Darius improved communications by building good roads and was farsighted enough to commence the construction of a Mediterranean war fleet.

Under this Persian dynasty's patronage, the religious doctrines of Zoroaster (ca. 628–ca. 551 B.C.) spread through its immense empire. Zoroaster taught a dualist doctrine of a cosmic struggle between the god Ahuramazda, the god of light, truth and peace, and Ahriman, the god of darkness, lies, and discord. Zoroastrian doctrines influenced many later religions.

The People of Israel

Tracing their origin to the ancient city of Ur in Mesopotamia and the covenant between their patriarch, Abraham, and their god, Yahweh, the Israelites migrated to Canaan sometime after 1900 B.C. Entering Egypt, probably in the Hyksos period, they dwelt in the Egyptian delta until about 1280 B.C., when, against strong resistance from the pharaoh, Moses led the Hebrews out of Egypt into the desert of Sinai, where, according to the Old Testament, they became God's chosen people in the Sinai covenant. Shortly before 1200 B.C. they occupied parts of Canaan during the decline of Egyptian power there. (This account is based upon biblical narratives; no independent archaeological evidence has yet been discovered for Abraham, Moses, and the other patriarchs.)

The religious league of clans was transformed into the Kingdom of Israel (ca. 1020–922 B.C.) which flourished under the kings Saul (r. ca. 1028–1013 B.C.), David (r. 1013–973 B.C.), and Solomon (r. 973–933 B.C.) largely undisturbed by the neighboring great powers of Egypt and Assyria. But after the death of Solomon, the kingdom divided into Israel in the north and Judah in the south. The northern kingdom fell to the Assyrians under Sargon II (r. 722–705 B.C.) in 721 B.C. Judah held on until the Second Babylonian Empire under Nebuchadnezzar II (r. ca. 605–562 B.C.) destroyed the capital Jerusalem in 587 B.C.

With the establishment of the Persian Empire, the Jews were permitted (538 B.C.) to return to Palestine and to build the second Temple, there to live under the code of law, the Torah.

Greece The Minoan culture of Crete had been in contact with the Greek mainland before 1650 B.C. The people of Greece (called Achaeans) lived in small principalities of which Mycenae, located on the Greek mainland, was pre-eminent. Adopting the courtly style of the Minoans and the war chariots of the Hyksos, the Achaeans expanded their settlements and with Cretan decline became heirs of Minoan trade with Egypt and Syria.

About 1100 B.C., a second wave of Greek-speaking Dorians invaded from the north and the Achaeans were forced to migrate to the islands and the coast of Asia Minor. In defeat they preserved Mycenaean traditions both socially and in the Homeric epics. Through these great poems the enterprise against Troy became the living symbol of the unity of the Greeks, the mythology of Mycenae provided a common religious background for local cults, and the language of the Achaeans became the norm for the whole Greek world.

By about 750 B.C. the Greek world had recovered from the Dorian invasions. Colonies spread westward to Italy and Sicily and eastward to the northern Aegean and the Black Sea. The lyric poetry of Archilochus (ca. 700 B.C.) and Sappho (ca. 600 B.C.) testifies to a flourishing literary culture. The first philosophers (including Thales, Heraclitus, and Parmenides), later called the pre-Socratics, commenced their speculations on nature and the cosmos; the Pythagoreans taught that mathematics is the foundation of cosmic order. During this period also, the characteristic unit of Greek political life, the city-state or *polis*, developed.

The greatest of these city-states were Athens and Sparta. Sparta emerged in 716 B.C. as conqueror of about 3,200 square miles of territory; by about 610 B.C. Sparta already had the formidable military organization based on strict education for citizenship to inculcate the "savage valor" that Spartans so esteemed. And by 540 B.C. Sparta had formed the Peloponnesian League, uniting all but two of the city-states of the peninsula.

The polis of Athens was, like other Greek cities, dominated by its aristocratic families and characterized by deep inequities. Social grievances led the Athenian leaders to turn over power to Solon, a wealthy merchant and poet, descended from the old kings. Taking office in 594, he cancelled all debts, abolished debt-slavery, encouraged both agriculture and industry, and opened the assembly to all free men. But Athens remained divided among wealthy landowners, a merchant class, and poor peasants, with a large population of slaves.

The Indian Subcontinent The charioteers who invaded the civilization of the Indus Valley called themselves Aryans, a word meaning "noble" in their Sanskrit language. Those they conquered were called sudras, "slaves." The Aryans settled in villages along the Indus, organized in tribal principalities about which almost nothing is known. From about 800 B.C. to about 300 B.C. they moved south along the coast and east across the peninsula to the delta of the Ganges River. There, once the lush jungle vegetation was cleared (using the new tools of the iron age), rice could be cultivated in the rich soil, a food supply sufficient for a very dense and stable population.

The religious classics of Hinduism date to this era. The ancient Vedas, hymns to the gods, date back to about 1000 B.C.—though not written down until much later. The Brahmanas are a body of instructions for rituals, evidence of the rise of an important priestly body, composed over the years 800–600 B.C. Lastly, about 600 B.C. appeared the Upanishads with their stress on asceticism and mysticism. Embodied in this religious literature is the caste system, in which society is divided into four varnas or castes: priests (brahmans), warriors (kshatriyas), artisans (vaisyas), and peasants (originally indistinguishable from slaves: sudras). This system was later to evolve into the fundamental structure of Indian society.

China The late Shang dynasty, known for the extravagance of its royal burials, declined into misrule; the dynasty was overthrown around 1046 B.C. by the ruler of the state of Zhou, centered in the Wei River Valley, northwest of the Shang kingdom (now north-central China). The duke of Zhou served as regent (ca. 1042–1036 B.C.) for the third Zhou ruler, King Cheng (r. 1042–1006 B.C.), and established a system of rule, sometimes loosely described as "feudal," in which the territory of China was parceled out in small states governed by Zhou clansmen and supporters. These states gradually grew larger at the expense of the Zhou royal domain. Zhou authority and territorial control declined drastically after around 770 B.C., and became vestigial during the Warring States Period (ca. 480–221 B.C.), when a handful of large feudal states swallowed up their smaller neighbors.

Despite political turmoil, the Warring States Period was an era of cultural brilliance in philosophy, technology, and the arts. Confucius (ca. 551–479 B.C.), China's first known philosopher, sought a remedy for the political turmoil of his time in an attempted revival of the golden age of the duke of Zhou. Thwarted in his search for a ruler who would put his ideas into practice, Confucius became a teacher whose disciples perpetuated his prescription for good government. Confucius looked to a natural aristocracy of virtue, rather than an hereditary elite, for social leadership; this led centuries later to the Chinese innovation of government by means of a professional civil service recruited through competitive examination. The Taoists, rivals of the Confucian school, rejected government altogether in favor of individual self-cultivation. They claimed as their founder a philosopher named Laozi, who was supposed to have lived in the sixth century B.C.; nothing is known about his life, and he may be wholly legendary.

During this era, the principal states of northern China became known collectively as zhongguo, the "middle kingdoms;" isolated from the high cultures of western Eurasia and India, the Chinese imagined their culture to be at the center of the world, surrounded by zones of ever-increasing barbarism. In this view, the Chinese ruler governed "all under heaven" by authority of the Mandate of Heaven (tian ming). This theory held that a dynastic founder, because of his own virtue, attracted the cosmic force of heaven itself in his support; heaven's mandate was bequeathed to his descendants so long as they cherished the principle of virtuous rule. This political theory, which assumed that exhausted and corrupt dynasties would eventually be overthrown by righteous rebellions, was a force for both dynastic renewal and long-term institutional stability throughout Chinese history.

The Americas   The domestication of plants and the creation of Neolithic cultures began in Mexico as early as 7000 B.C., and led to settled village cultures by 2500 B.C. based on the cultivation of squash, beans, chilies, and corn (maize). The earliest civilization in the Americas was that of the Olmec, whose cities lay in the Valley of Mexico, on the coast in the vicinity of Vera Cruz, and in the highlands around Oaxaca. The Olmec cities are marked by large square step-pyramids, and by carvings of enormous stone heads. Olmec culture appears to have begun around 1200 B.C., and to have persisted for some 800 years before being supplanted by the Zapotec.

Meanwhile, to the south, the great civilization of the Maya was beginning to take form in what is known as the late Preclassic Period, beginning around 300 B.C. in the Yucatán Peninsula and adjacent areas of southern Mexico, Belize, Guatemala, and parts of Honduras and El Salvador. Some ancient Maya villages had by this time begun to evolve into cities marked by plazas flanked by pyramids, temples, and palaces.

With the late Olmec, the Zapotec, and the Preclassic Maya, all the hallmarks of Mesoamerican civilization were in place: pyramids and other monumental architecture, a 260-day and 52-year calendar, ritual ballgames, bar-and-dot numbers and hieroglyphic inscriptions, and personal blood sacrifices by members of the ruling elite, together with ritual human sacrifice to nourish the maize goddess and other deities.

The First Imperial Era (ca. 500 B.C.-A.D. 500)

The millennium after 500 B.C. was characterized by the growth of great empires in several parts of the world, including Persia, India, China, and Rome; elsewhere, other polities began to emerge on the stage of world history.

Rival Empires: Persians and Greeks   What the Greeks called the Persian Wars (499–479 B.C.) began with a failed revolt of the Greek cities of coastal Asia Minor against the Persian Empire (of which they had become a part in 546 B.C.). To punish the mainland Greek allies of the rebels, the city-states of Athens and Eretria, the Persian Empire made war on Greece, but unsuccessfully. From the Persian point of view the victories of Athens and Sparta in the "Persian Wars" were only a border issue of minor import; but to the Greeks, great battles such as Marathon (490 B.C.) and the fleet engagement at Salamis (480 B.C.) were inspiring symbols of the superiority of their ideals of liberty and free citizenship over the servitude of Eastern despotism.

Under the leadership of Pericles (ca. 495–429 B.C.) Athens transformed itself from the leading power of a naval league into an aggressive conqueror of an Athenian Empire. Athenian aggrandizement allowed Sparta to present itself as the defender of Greek liberties. Athens and Sparta, formerly allies, each at the head of a league of city-states, fought the Peloponnesian War (431–404 B.C.) in which the Spartans won a crushing victory. The history of the war was recorded by the great Greek historian, Thucydides (ca. 460–400 B.C.) Spartan hegemony in Greece lasted only until 387 B.C., when a league of Greek cities with Persian assistance imposed a settlement which made all Greek city-states autonomous (and therefore weak) except for those in Asia under Persian rule. In the midst of this political and military turmoil, Greek culture had flourished: in writing for the theater (Aeschylus, Sophocles, Euripides), philosophy (Socrates, Plato,

Aristotle), history (Herodotus, Thucydides), architecture (the Acropolis) and sculpture (Myron, Phidias).

The Empire of Alexander the Great   Immediately to the north of the disunited Greek city-states lay the small but militarily powerful kingdom of Macedon, provincial but greatly influenced by Greek civilization. Having conquered the territories of Illyria and Thrace along the northern coast of the Aegean Sea, King Philip (r. 356–330 B.C.) intervened in Greece and forced the formation of a Hellenic League which, under Macedonian influence, began war against Persia (336 B.C.). Philip was assassinated soon after the war began, and his death occasioned the revolt of the Greek cities he dominated. But his son and successor, Alexander the Great (r. 336–323 B.C.) ruthlessly crushed the revolt and then began his conquest of Asia. After winning a great victory in the battle of Issus (in what is now southeastern Turkey, 333 B.C.) over Darius III (r. 336–330 B.C.) of Persia, Alexander declared himself successor to the last Persian emperor under the title King of Asia, continuing rule through the satrapies after the final defeat of the Persians in 330 B.C. In the meantime he added Egypt to his conquests (331 B.C.) and founded the great city of Alexandria. He pushed on into Bactria (modern Uzbekistan) and then to the Indus Valley beyond which his soldiers would not go. When he died of a fever in Babylon in 323 B.C., he had assembled in a dozen years the largest empire the world had known; but his premature death meant the division of the empire among the Diodochi (Alexander's generals who claimed the succession). After half a century of warfare, the successor states became stabilized: the heirs of Antigonus ruled Macedonia, the Ptolemys ruled Egypt, and the descendants of Seleucus inherited Alexander's territories in western Asia.

Rome: From Republic to Empire   Shortly before 500 B.C., the small community of Rome broke free from its Etruscan rulers and established a republic. A century of patient expansion against neighboring tribes in central Italy suffered a setback in 390 B.C., when Celts from the Po Valley plundered and burnt the city. But the Roman expansion resumed, and within three generations they had brought under their control all of the Italian peninsula except the Greek cities (Magna Graecia) in the south. These they added by 272 B.C., just as the Diodochi were stabilizing the successor kingdoms to Alexander's empire.

Expansion into southern Italy involved Rome in a struggle with Carthage. Originally a Phoenician colony, the city of Carthage in North Africa had established commercial colonies along the eastern, southern, and northwestern coasts of the Mediterranean and on the Atlantic coasts of Spain and Morocco. In a prodigious series of struggles called the Punic Wars (264–146 B.C.), during which Rome itself narrowly escaped conquest by Hannibal (247–183 B.C.), the Romans utterly vanquished Carthage.

Meanwhile, after the Second Punic War (218–201 B.C.) Rome had become embroiled in the east as Pergamum, Rhodes, and Athens appealed for help against the Diodochi. Rome's eastward expansion began with a war against Macedonia (200–197 B.C.). By 62 B.C. Greece, Macedonia, Asia Minor, Syria, Palestine, Egypt, and the whole North African coast were under Roman rule. The Mediterranean Sea truly became what the Romans called *mare nostrum*: "our sea."

Rather than attempting further conquests in Asia, the Romans looked westward, as Julius Caesar (100–44 B.C.) and his successors embarked on the conquest of Gaul (modern France and southern Germany) and of Britain (A.D. 43–84). Eastern defense considerations led to the annexation of Armenia, Mesopotamia, and Assyria (A.D. 114–16). At its greatest extent, the Roman Empire stretched from the North Sea to the Sahara Desert, from the Scottish borderlands to the Persian Gulf.

But in winning their empire, the Romans lost their republic, in which sovereignty had been invested in an elected Senate and the power of government was exercised by magistrates. The tremendous population losses in the Second Punic War, the increase in the slave population with every conquest, the transformation of land tenure from peasant agriculture to huge latifundia (plantations), the rise of a class of financiers, the rivalry of military commanders, the involvement of the military in politics—all overwhelmed the old republican institutions. In the century and a half from 298 B.C. to 133 B.C., the rivalry for power among demagogues and generals meant endless civil war leading to the final victory of the revolutionary adventurer Octavian, who, renamed Augustus (r. 27 B.C–A.D. 14, initiated imperial rule in Rome itself. Augustus initiated the era of the Pax Romana, 200 years of peace under the aegis of the Roman Empire (27 B.C–A.D. 180).

The Roman Empire, East and West, and the Spread of Christianity   A lasting legacy of the Roman conquests was the spread of Roman civic tradition into continental Europe and western Asia. The empire became a network of administrative departments centered on cities with central power at Rome; with the external forms of civic life came economic prosperity and the intellectual culture of the Hellenized Roman civilization.

In this milieu, Jesus of Nazareth (ca. 4 B.C.–A.D. 30) was born in the Roman colony of Judea. His followers preached the "good news" (gospel) that God himself had become man and died for man's sins, a message that became the core teaching of the early Christians, as the Romans called them. Christianity soon spread beyond the Jewish world as the preaching of missionaries such as Paul, Barnabas, and Timothy expanded the Christian community through the cities of the Roman world: from Palestine to Syria, Anatolia and Greece, to Africa and Italy; in the second century to Gaul, Germany, Yugoslavia, and Spain. Although the Roman authorities were generally tolerant of all kinds of religious beliefs, the Christians were persecuted because of their secretive practices and their refusal to acknowledge the Roman civic gods; after A.D. 110, adherence to Christianity became a capital offense. Yet the church continued to spread.

When after the death of the Stoic emperor Marcus Aurelius (r. 161–180) the empire fell into civil war, economic decline, and the exhaustion of civic life through excessive taxation and centralized government control, the frontiers became unstable. After A.D. 226 a revived Persian Empire grew aggressive in the east while great confederations of tribes (Goths, Vandals, Allemani, Franks) arose on the Rhine and Danube Rivers. The emperor Diocletian (r. 284–305) attempted to stem the decline with a political and military reorganization, but it was the emperor Constantine (r. 312–37) who saw that much more was needed.

Constantine attempted to provide a new internal principal of spiritual unity to the Roman Empire through Christianity. His "new Rome" of Constantinople was a Christian city from the start; Christianity had progressed from persecution to toleration to favored position to state religion in less than a century. But the state itself was far gone in decline. Visigothic troops sacked Rome in 410 (the first time in 800 years that Rome had been pillaged) then carved out a realm in southern Gaul and Spain by 450. Vandals tore North Africa away from Rome (429–39). Franks reached the Loire by 486, and Saxons, Angles, and Jutes ended Roman rule in Britain.

Meanwhile in the Roman east, imperial control remained intact, but Christianity itself fell into disarray, as peoples in various parts of the eastern empire followed one or another of the heresies that flourished after the formal definition of Christian orthodoxy at the Council of Chalcedon (450).

India and Southeast Asia   Alexander's armies had stopped their conquest of Asia at the Indus River. The India that lay beyond was a complex welter of tribal principalities and republics, of which a certain primacy attached to the kingdom of Magadha in the Ganges Valley. In 317 B.C. Chandragupta Maurya (r. 321–297 B.C.), who had met Alexander and was married to a Macedonian princess, attacked and conquered Magadha with the aid of northwestern tribes, founding the Mauryan Empire (317–184 B.C.). Chandragupta subdued the Indus valley as well, and the legitimacy of his rule was recognized by the Diodochus, Seleucus Nicator. By the reign of his grandson Asoka (269–232 B.C.), central and most of southern India had been added to the empire, which extended north to the foothills of the Himalayas and west to the eastern reaches of Afghanistan.

Asoka was known as the Buddhist Emperor, personally devout and publicly the protector and propagator of the religion of the Buddha. Prince Siddhartha Gautama (563–483 B.C.) was a member of the Kshatriya caste; enlightenment came when he left the favored precincts of his father's palace and came face-to-face with the reality of suffering. (The title Buddha, a Sanskrit word meaning "enlightened one," was applied to Gautama after his discovery of religious truth. See "World Religions.") The Buddha's disciples lived in communities dedicated to putting into practice his "eightfold path" to holiness, and such monastic communities were fostered and supported by Asoka (ca. 273–233 B.C.).

After the death of Asoka the Mauryan Empire began to crumble into its constituent parts; the last emperor was assassinated by one of his generals in 184 B.C. One of the successor states was the Graeco-Indian kingdom in the north and northwest founded by a general of the Diodoch king of Bactria; another was the Kushan Empire of the first and second centuries A.D., which was the route by which Buddhism expanded into central Asia.

A second Chandragupta (ca. 380–ca. 415) was the founder of the last great Indian imperial regime of the ancient period, the Gupta Empire (320–535 A.D.) which at its greatest extent stretched across the subcontinent from the mouth of the Indus to the mouth of the Ganges. The source of its unity was a revived Hinduism, whose brahmans provided advisers to the emperors and drew up codes of Hindu law that articulated the structures of the caste system. It was the age also of Sanskrit as a literary language, in the drama of Kalidasa (ca. 400–455) and in the final composition (from earlier, partly oral, roots) of the epic poems Mahabharata and Ramayana. The Gupta period was the golden age of Indian science, especially astronomy and mathematics, to which we owe the decimal system and the invention of the number zero. Classic Indian civilization was spread far beyond the political borders of the Gupta realm by Hindu and Buddhist merchants and Buddhist missionaries, to Burma, Thailand, and Indo-China, to the Malay peninsula and beyond into Indonesia. The shores of the Bay of Bengal and of the South China Sea thus became a kind of "greater India."

The First Chinese Empire   In 246 B.C., the massed infantry troops, supported by cavalry and chariots, of the northwestern state of Qin, hardened by years of warfare with the nomads of the northern steppes, hurtled eastward to conquer and subjugate, one by one, all of the other feudal principalities, putting an end to the period of the Warring States. These conquests gave rise to the first Chinese Empire under the Qin Dynasty (221–206 B.C.). Qin Shihuangdi ("The First Emperor of Qin," r. 221–210 B.C.) proved more than just a conqueror: he oversaw the completion of the Great Wall along the edge of Inner Mongolia and reorganized the structure of government by dividing the land into regions of civil administration and military garrisons, governed by officials responsible to himself alone. The old nobility was weakened by land confiscations. Scholars and philosophers were persecuted or intimidated; private possession of books was banned. Although the harshness of Qin rule quickly provoked rebellions and the First Emperor's weak successor met his death by assassination (206 B.C.), the structure of imperial rule inaugurated by the Qin would endure for more than two thousand years.

A rebel leader named Liu Bang emerged victorious in the confused and bloody uprisings that brought the Qin Dynasty to an end. Liu (r. 206–195) proclaimed himself emperor of the Han Dynasty, which was to endure (with a brief interregnum, A.D. 7–25, under the usurper Wang Mang) for four centuries, until A.D. 220. The Han founder partly restored the pre-Qin system of semi-autonomous states, awarded as kingdoms to his kinsmen and allies, and partly (in the lands under direct imperial rule) retained the central bureaucratic structure of the Qin government, courting popular approval by moderating Qin's harsh punishments and lowering taxes. The neofeudal kingdoms proved troublesome and were mostly absorbed into the imperial domains by 100 B.C., by which

time a revival of Confucian principles had begun to have a notable impact on the conduct of government. The greatest Han ruler, Emperor Wu (r. 140–87 B.C.) instituted the practice of choosing officials on the basis of learning and merit. He brought the rich ricelands of the Yangtze River Valley firmly under imperial control, and also greatly extended the boundaries of the empire, conquering south to the South China Sea, southwest to the borders of Burma and Tibet, northeast to northern Korea, and westward to the deserts of Central Asia. He pacified the northern frontier, defeating the Xiongnu tribes, whose descendants, the Huns, would later invade Europe. In an early arms race, the powerful laminated compound bow and cavalry tactics of the northern nomads were countered by Chinese infantry armed with mass-produced crossbows—a refinement of a weapon of Southeast Asian origin. Trade increased along the Silk Route, a network of caravan trails that, through many intermediaries, brought Chinese silk to the Roman Empire and warhorses from Central Asia to China.

The "dynastic cycle" completed its course in the last decades of the Han period, when court corruption, peasant uprisings, and military insurrections led to the overthrow of the last Han emperor in A.D. 220. There followed the Three Kingdoms Period (220–265), when rival states tried without success to reunite the empire, and the period of the Northern and Southern Dynasties (265–589), when northern China was ruled by a succession of short-lived dynasties, often imposed by invaders from the steppes, while southern China was fragmented into short-lived and ineffectual kingdoms. During this period of disunion Buddhism, which had entered China via Central Asia in late Han times, began to establish itself as one of China's major religions. Especially successful were sects of Mahayana ("Greater Vehicle") Buddhism, which promised salvation to the faithful through the mediation of saints called bodhisattvas.

The Silk Road   "Silk Road" is a 19th-century term for an ancient network of caravan trails that linked China with India, the Middle East, and the Mediterranean world. Some long-distance trade among the early civilizations of Eurasia had taken place since prehistoric times, but regular, organized trade on the Silk Road commenced around 100 B.C. Emperor Wu of the Han Dynasty implemented a policy of trading silk cloth for war horses from the Ferghana Valley, west of the Pamir Mountains, in the late

2nd century B.C. The success of this policy ensured a regular supply of horses for China's cavalry, and helped the Chinese to deal a series of defeats to the aggressive Xiongnu tribal confederation. The establishment of official trade made the caravan routes safer for private merchants as well, leading to further increases in trade.

The network of trails began in China at Chang'an (modern Xi'an) and went northwest, soon dividing into two branches; the northern ended at the Volga River and the southern roamed through present day Afghanistan, Uzbekistan, and continued westward to Baghdad, Damascus, and the Mediterranean ports of Tyre, Sidon, and Antioch.

Goods traded by both land and sea tended to be high in value relative to their weight and bulk: from China, plain and patterned silk, dried rhubarb and other herbal medicines, and lacquerware; from Persia and the Middle East, silver and gold metalwork, glassware, and musical instruments. The maritime trade routes sent high-value goods in several directions: spices from India and Indonesia, gemstones from Burma and Sri Lanka, porcelain from China, sandalwood from India, tropical hardwoods from mainland Southeast Asia and Indonesia. By both land and sea, most trade was "down-the-line" trade—meaning that individual merchants tended to travel only for relatively short segments of the whole route, but goods traveled much further, bought and sold several times along the way.

The land and maritime routes also served as highways for the exchange of ideas and beliefs, including astronomical and mathematical techniques, paper and printing, the technology of silkworm cultivation and silk production, gunpowder, and many others. Especially noteworthy is the role of the Silk Road in the spread of religions across Asia, including (successively) Zoroastrianism, Buddhism, Nestorian Christianity, and Islam. A similar dynamic on maritime routes brought Hinduism, Buddhism, and Islam to mainland and island Southeast Asia.

The volume of trade along the Silk Road tended to wax and wane with the strength of imperial governments in China, Persia, and (after the 7th century) the Islamic world. Strong governments produced wealth, which stimulated trade; they also projected power far afield to protect trade routes and suppress banditry. Overland trade, originating on a regular basis around 100 B.C., continued to flourish during the remainder of the Han dynasty (206 B.C.–220 A.D.), waned somewhat during China's period of disunion from the 3th to the late 6th century A.D., and revived strongly during the powerful Tang dynasty (618–907). It flourished again following the 13th century Mongol conquests, when Mongol power prevailed from the Middle East to Korea, and the *Pax Mongolica* ("Mongol peace") facilitated trade across Asia; it was then that Marco Polo made his epic journey from Venice to Beijing.

Japan and Korea   Around 300 B.C., invaders from southern Manchuria had invaded Japan via the Korean peninsula. These invaders, equipped with horses, bronze weapons, and the wealth produced by rice agriculture, displaced the ancient Jomon culture of the original inhabitants of Japan. This bronze-age Yayoi civilization, which also shows evidence of influence from Austronesian culture via Taiwan and Okinawa, laid the foundations for the subsequent Japanese empire. But for several centuries Japan was divided into small states ruled by military clans, with those associated with the Shinto shrines at Izumo and Ise claiming some degree of primacy.

In Korea the decline of the Chinese colony at Lolang led to the establishment of indigenous kingdoms; three of these—Silla, Paekche, and Koguryo—predominated during the period A.D. 313–668, with Silla ultimately emerging victorious and uniting the whole Korean peninsula under its rule. Chinese cultural influence, via Korea, as well as cultural influence and waves of immigrants from Korea itself, helped to transform the Japanese petty states into a centralized kingdom by the fifth century A.D.

The Americas   The Zapotec capital city of Teotihuacán, in the Valley of Mexico, flourished from about A.D. 300 to 900. It was a rich and fertile city of irrigated fields, urban residential districts, and ceremonial pyramids, temples, and administrative buildings, and a population approaching 200,000. Zapotec trade networks extended north to what is now the southwestern United States, and south to the culture area of the Maya.

In the Yucatán and adjacent regions, the era from approximately A.D. 250 to 475 is the Early Classic Period of Mayan civilization. Great cities at Petán, Tikal, and other lowland sites demonstrate that Mayan civilization reached its full flowering near the beginning of the Early Classic period; stelae, altars, lintels, and other stone structures in these cities are replete with inscriptions celebrating the conquests and other deeds of the Mayan kings.

North of the Mexican border, the Hohokam and other cultures of the American Southwest were powerfully influenced by Zapotec civilization. These were provincial areas, with towns and villages linked by ties of trade, administration, and warfare, but they were not independent centers of civilization. In the Mississippi and Ohio Valleys, village-based agrarian centers of the Woodland Culture were sufficiently rich and well organized to construct large earthen mounds for ceremonial purposes.

In South America, the long-lived prehistoric Tiwanaku culture (c. 400 B.C.–A.D. 1000), centered on Lake Titicaca, was noted for its monumental stone structures, a tradition continued by later Peruvian cultures. The overlapping Moche culture (A.D. 100–800) in the coastal lowlands was based on irrigated agriculture, and was known for sophisticated pottery and textiles. The Moche culture was succeeded by the Chimu culture, which flourished c. 900–1470 before it was conquered by the Inca empire. East of the Andes, the prehistoric agricultural cultures of the Amazon basin are just beginning to be investigated and understood by archaeologists.

Africa　The Aksum civilization of Ethiopia, the only independent literate culture to arise in the history of Africa beyond the Nile Valley as well as one of the world's earliest Christian cultures, began to flourish during the first century A.D. and reached its zenith in the fourth and fifth centuries A.D. At its height it encompassed an area extending from the fringes of the Sahara in the west, across Ethiopia, and across the Red Sea to the Arabian Desert. The Aksumite economy was based on the cultivation of teff, a grain unique to Ethiopia and still widely cultivated there. The Aksumites built in stone, and inscribed their monuments with a script known as Ge'ez, the precursor of the script still used to write the classical languages of Ethiopia today.

Elsewhere in Africa, most people lived as hunter-gatherers, as pastoral nomads, or in communities of Neolithic farmers. The great migration of Bantu-speaking peoples, which had begun with an expansion from the Congo River Basin in the third millennium B.C., was essentially complete by around A.D. 400. From that time, most of Africa south of the Congo was settled by speakers of Bantu languages, and with earlier populations (such as Khoi-San peoples) displaced to marginal environments.

A Second Age of Empires (A.D. 500–1000)

The appearance in the seventh century of the new religion of Islam, with its militant emphasis on bringing as much of the world as possible into the "realm of submission to God," gave rise to an empire stretching from the Iberian Peninsula to the Indus Valley, but influencing events as well in places as far distant as Ghana and China. It also was a catalyst for the division of Christendom into western and eastern realms.

Under the Tang Dynasty, one of the most brilliant eras of Chinese history, Chinese culture was influenced by that of Central Asia, and spread to Korea and Japan. And in isolation from the Old World, the Mayan civilization of Central America reached its zenith.

The Late Roman Empire and Early Medieval Europe　The lapse of direct Roman rule in the West did not imply an immediate "fall" of the Roman Empire so much as a shift of Roman power elsewhere. In the city of Rome, the heir and representative of the Roman Empire was the Catholic Church. The emperor Justinian (r. 527–565) did much to revive the fortunes of the empire, but from a base in Constantinople rather than Rome itself. Maintaining a rough alliance with the Christian Franks in Gaul under their Merovingian dynasty, the emperor Justinian's armies recovered the western provinces: Vandal Africa, Ostrogothic Italy, and the Mediterranean sector of Visigothic Spain. Meanwhile, his jurists codified and preserved the whole body of Roman law that had been built up since the days of the republic. And under imperial patronage there grew up a magnificent cluster of churches whose pinnacle was Hagia Sophia in Constantinople, constructed in 537. The city of Rome itself, however, was well launched on a centuries-long period of decline, with a shrinking population and many buildings disused or in ruins.

The cost of Justinian's efforts was great, and the defense of the West was short-lived. After Justinian's death the empire had neither treasure nor troops enough to save much of Italy from new invaders, the Lombards. The city of Ravenna kept its link with Constantinople, and Rome remained the principality of the popes. Pope Gregory "the Great" (590–604) not only organized the defense of the city but oversaw the work of converting Visigothic Spain and began the restoration of Christianity in faraway Britain through the mission of St. Augustine (354–430) to Kent. In this effort Gregory relied upon the monks who followed the Rule of St. Benedict (ca. 480–547), which provided a uniform way of life for monks living as a community, including vows of poverty, chastity, and obedience, regular and frequent hours of prayer, study of the Bible, and manual work.

The Byzantine Empire　In the east lay the empire proper, in the era after Justinian usually called the

Byzantine Empire or the Eastern Roman Empire (610–1453). Its wealth and power were based in Asia Minor, its unity dependent upon three factors: Orthodox Christianity (slowly drifting away from Roman Catholicism until the final break with Rome in 1054); Hellenistic culture and the Greek language; and Roman law and administration. Missionary ventures carried Christianity and Byzantine influence to the Serbs and Croats in the Balkans, to the Moravians and Slovaks north of the Danube, and even as far as Kievan Rus, all in the ninth and 10th centuries.

The empire was "byzantine" in the common sense of that word, a world of complex politics involving a wide variety of factors: emperors who were often weak and ineffectual; self-interested palace bureaucrats; powerful generals prone to warlordism; Orthodox prelates engaged in endless struggles with schismatic and heretical clerics; and popular political factions verging on mob rule, often linked to the fortunes of chariot-racing teams in the hippodromes. Yet the empire also prospered through trade, agriculture, and artisanal production of goods. It made brilliant cultural achievements, particularly in the ecclesiastical arts, and managed to survive, in gradually attenuating form, for more than eight centuries.

The empire, which barely held on in the east against Persia, lost large areas to the conquering armies of Islam (see below). Between 636 and 642, Syria, Egypt, and Libya converted to Islam; in a second wave of Islamic expansion (696–711) the rest of North Africa and Spain became part of the world of Islam as well. The Mediterranean seemed on its way to becoming a Muslim lake, threatening both the Byzantine Empire and the emerging successor states to the old Roman Empire in the West.

Charlemagne and His Heirs   In the west there arose the Carolingian Empire (751–888). Pepin III (r. 751–768) cooperated with St. Boniface to reform the Frankish Church in close relation with Rome, deposed (with papal approval) the last Merovingian shadow-king, and was himself anointed king. Before his death, Pepin had made Frankish sovereignty felt southward to the Pyrenees and the Mediterranean. His son, Charlemagne (r. 768–814), conquered Lombardy, absorbed Bavaria, expanded into Saxony and beyond the Pyrenees, bringing under his sway an area equal in size to the old Roman Empire in the West. At the same time, to foster missionary endeavors, he ordered the creation of cathedral and monastic schools, drawing heavily for his scholars on Northumbria, the small English kingdom where Celtic and Roman monas-

tic traditions had intermingled. The monasteries, with their libraries and traditions of theological scholarship, kept learning alive during the centuries between the fall of Rome and the rise of medieval monarchies, with their cities and universities.

The pinnacle of Charlemagne's achievements came on Christmas Day in the year 800, when in the city of Rome the pope acclaimed and crowned him as Roman Emperor. But with his death his realm began to disintegrate. By 843 his grandsons divided his realm in three parts with a middle kingdom of the emperor Lothair (r. 855–869) separating the kingdoms of the East and West Franks (lands that much later would become Germany and France). One of the greatest threats to these realms was the Vikings of Scandinavia. Starting in the eighth century, Vikings descended the rivers of eastern Europe to the Caspian, Black and Mediterranean Seas, attacked all along the coast of Western Europe, ravaged the British Isles, established commercial bases between the Baltic and Byzantium, and settled Iceland and Greenland. Eastern Europe was invaded around 900 by the Magyars, who settled in what is now Hungary.

The family of the Carolingians proved unable to lead any effective resistance to the attacks of Vikings, Magyars, and Muslims; military power devolved to local nobles and petty kings. This was the origin of the pattern of decentralized authority and allegiance known as feudalism. Political and military power had become essentially the private possessions of the strong, who became richer as their agricultural land benefited from the use of new technologies (crop rotation, improved horse harness for heavy plows). Under those circumstances, feudalism provided for the grant (from monarch to lords, and from lords to knights) of rights to govern and receive the revenues from certain territories (known as "fiefs"), in return for the remission of some revenues (from knights to lords, and from lords to monarchs), and the provision of military service on demand. This system brought some degree of order to a dangerous and uncertain age. Monarchy was not dead, but the medieval kings' relationship to the nobility had become "firsts amongst equals." King Alfred the Great of Wessex (r. 871–899) defended England against the Danes. Henry the Fowler (r. 919–36) began the Saxon Dynasty of German kings while his son Otto I (r. 936–973) also assumed (962) the title of Emperor; and Hugh Capet (r. 987–996) began the Capetian Dynasty of France, which ruled into the 19th century.

On the fringe of the older Carolingian world, the Scandinavian monarchies were consolidated and converted to Christianity around 1000; an independent and Catholic Kingdom of Poland was established (966); Kievan Rus converted to Christianity (988) under St. Vladimir (r. ca. 956–1015); and in 1001 a Catholic Hungarian kingdom was founded by St. Stephen (r. 997–1038).

The Islamic World   To Rome at the height of the empire, the Arabs were not much more than a frontier annoyance; they posed no serious menace. Centuries later, the militant new religion of Islam arose in the Arabian Desert to pose a deadly threat to the heirs of the Roman world. The founder of Islam, Muhammad (or Mohammed) (570–632) was a religious prophet whose revelations came from God; these revelations form the heart of the Muslim sacred book, the Koran. The Koran clearly emerges from the biblical traditions of Abraham, and accepts Jesus as a prophet; but Muhammad is seen as the "Seal of the Prophets," beyond whom no further revelations will be given. (The word Islam means "submission to God"; a Muslim is "one who submits"; for more on Islam, see "Religion.") Muhammad was driven out of Mecca by his enemies in 622; he escaped to Yathrib (now Medina), where he and his followers formed a religious and political community. This event, the hijira, marks the Year 1 of the Muslim calendar. After eight years of desert warfare, Muhammad and his followers returned to capture Mecca (630).

Within two years of Muhammad's death the armies of Islam were marching. Islam divides the world between the Dar al-Islam ("world submissive to God") and the Dar al-Harb ("world at war with God"); conversion of the world is a religious imperative. They detached Syria, Mesopotamia, Egypt, and Libya (636–46) from the Roman Empire, and conquered Persia (637–49). A crisis over the succession to Muhammad was settled in 661, when the old tribal aristocracy triumphed over the family of the prophet and established the Umayyad Dynasty (661–750) of caliphs ("successors") ruling not from Medina but from Damascus and utilizing the old Persian and Roman bureaucracies. This question of succession led to a fundamental split in Islam, between the Shi'a Muslims who remained loyal to the family of the prophet, and who look toward the return of the "hidden Imam" to restore the rightful succession, and the Sunni Muslims who accept the legitimacy of the caliphs. For almost half a century Islam gave its attention to such internal political problems, and to the consolidation of the first wave of conquests; then, with the conversion of the Berbers, Byzantine Africa was brought into the world of Islam (696), as was Visigothic Spain (711). In the same year a Muslim commander established himself in the lower Indus Valley.

A series of revolts protesting the Arabic dominance of the Umayyads led to the establishment of a new dynasty of caliphs, the Abbasid Dynasty (750–1258), descended from a cousin of Muhammad. Arab by descent, the Abbasids nonetheless moved the capital to the new city of Baghdad in Mesopotamia. Persian culture strongly influenced Abbasid politics and literature, while the Islamic scientific and mathematical flowering drew on the scientific and mathematical discoveries of Gupta India (especially the decimal system of numeration and the use of the zero) and ancient Greece as well as on ancient Babylonian astronomy and astrology.

The Umayyads had not been totally overturned; Spain followed their rule when the rest of the empire turned to the Abbasids; after about 800 there were independent Muslim states in Morocco, Tunis, and eastern Persia; and by about 875 in Egypt and Turkistan. Before the year 1000, the caliphs had lost almost all their political power, becoming largely a focus of religious unity, relying even then on members of the ulema, experts in Islamic law and tradition (the hadith). Because Islam in principle does not recognize a distinction between the secular and the sacred, ultimate authority in many Islamic states remains with religious leaders.

India and Africa on the Fringe of Islam   After the White Huns (also known as Rajputs) overthrew the Gupta Dynasty in 535, India reverted to its older pattern of a large number of tribal principalities. The Rajputs coexisted with the Hindu princes and established a feudal state across north India east of the Indus Valley, the kingdom of Rajputana. The Sind (or lower Indus Basin) was already in Muslim hands after 711. By the ninth century Buddhism virtually disappeared from India, absorbed into Hinduism; one exception was in the state of the Pala kings, who ruled Bengal and Magadha, in the northeast, into the 12th century. Buddhism remained influential in parts of "greater India:" in the small kingdoms of Burma, in the kingdom of Dvaravati in Siam, in Sri Lanka, and in the Sumatran state of Srivijaya under its Sailendra dynasty. The Sailendra rulers built the Buddhist temple-mandala of Borobudur in central Java ca. 800; the nearby temple of Prambanan was built a century later by the Hindu rulers of the kingdom of Mataram, which succeeded Srivijaya as the dominant trading empire of the East Indies.

At the other extremity of the Muslim world, Muslim traders from Morocco were in contact with the Kingdom of Ghana by about the year 800. Camel caravans crossed the Sahara to the grasslands between the upper Niger and Senegal Rivers, bearing salt and goods from the Mediterranean basin, and returned with gold and ivory from Ghana. Extracting import and export taxes and monopolizing the gold supply, the kings of Ghana exercised an imperial control over the trading cities of the region, growing wealthy and powerful. Yet by 1076 the caliphs in Morocco were able to conquer the region.

At the opposite side of Africa, Muslim Arabs crossed the Red Sea and annexed the Somali coast (ca. 1050) from the ancient Christian kingdom of Ethiopia.

China: Tang and Song Dynasties Three centuries of disunion in China came to an end with the establishment of the Sui Dynasty in 589. The Sui was a short-lived dynasty that paved the way for a long-enduring one. Extravagant expenditures on the Grand Canal linked Hangzhou to the south with the capital at Chang'an to the west, a distance of more than 1,000 miles. This undertaking, combined with a disastrous attempt to conquer Korea and a Turkish invasion of northwestern China, doomed the Sui. It was replaced by the Tang Dynasty (618–907), one of the most glorious eras in all of Chinese history. Buddhism flourished, as did poetry and the fine arts; Tang Chang'an was the largest and most cosmopolitan city in the world by around 700. But in 751 Chinese troops on the westernmost frontier were defeated by an Arab army in the Battle of Talas, and the Tang abandoned much of Central Asia; in 755 China's greatest general at the time, An Lushan (703–757), rebelled against the throne. The rebellion was defeated, but the empire never recovered fully. An imperial persecution of Buddhism in the 840's, during which the wealth of many temples was confiscated, signaled the rise of Neo-Confucianism, reinvigorating China's oldest philosophical tradition. But with the imperial house in disarray, the Tang collapsed in 907.

After five decades of inconclusive attempts to restore central rule, the Song Dynasty was founded in 960, and endured until 1279. But the Song never had firm control of northern China. The northeast was controlled by the Liao Dynasty in the hands of the non-Chinese Khitan people (whose name gives us the word Cathay). They were replaced in the early 12th century by the Jurchen Jin Dynasty, which in 1127 conquered all of northern China, sending the Song emperors south to a new capital at Hangzhou. Although the Song were politically weak, this was nevertheless a time of cultural brilliance, when Chinese landscape painting was perfected, poetry flourished, and urban life (rich from overseas trade from the South China Sea and the Indian Ocean) attained new heights of sophistication. With the old northern aristocratic clans destroyed by the downfall of the Tang and subsequent centuries of barbarian rule, the Song state was run by a modern bureaucratic government recruited from a prosperous and well-educated rural gentry.

Annam, comprising the northern and central parts of what is now Vietnam, capped several centuries of resistance to Chinese domination by driving out the Chinese in 939 and establishing an independent monarchy, though one that in many respects continued to adhere to Chinese Confucian cultural norms.

Japan and Korea In Korea, the state of Silla in 562 put an end to Japanese attempts to carve out colonial enclaves on the peninsula, and then, with Tang support, turned its attention to defeating its rivals Paekche and Koguryo. This process was completed by 670, and Silla grew prosperous with Tang support and cultural influence. But Silla in turn was defeated in 935 by the small western state of Koryo, which established a dynasty ruling all of Korea until 1392. Relatively isolated from Song influence by the intervening states of Liao, and later Jin, the Koryo state became culturally more independent of China.

In Japan, the Yamato clan, which had gradually pressed its claim to recognition as an imperial dynasty on the Chinese model, was firmly established on the throne by the fifth century A.D. Buddhism came to Japan in the following century, along with such continental innovations as the use of Chinese script to write (phonetically) the very different Japanese language (as well as the adoption of Classical Chinese itself as a literary language). In 604 Prince Shotoku (572–622) issued a 17–article "constitution" establishing imperial support for Buddhism and enjoining all aristocrats to respect the imperial throne. The throne thereupon came under the influence of the powerful Soga clan until 645; an early 8th-century restoration movement emphasized emulation of the Chinese model of government. But the principle of appointment to office on the basis of merit never caught on in Japan, which continued to be ruled by a hereditary aristocracy.

Japan's first planned capital city was founded at Nara in 710; by 750 the city was wholly dominated by its rich and powerful Buddhist temples. In response the emperors moved the capital to the new city of Heian-kyo (now Kyoto) in 794; the emperors remained there for over a thousand years. Both Nara and Heian-kyo were built on a grid plan, modeled after the Chinese capital at Chang'an; Heian-kyo especially boasted a glittering cultural life, supported by agrarian wealth from the provinces. The powerful Fujiwara clan gained control of the country's political life through the expedient of making sure that every emperor married a Fujiwara daughter, and abdicated the throne for a life of monastic retirement shortly after producing an heir; the head of the Fujiwara clan thus was always first the regent for and then the father-in-law of one emperor and regent-to-be for the heir-apparent.

The Classic Age of Mayan Culture   The period A.D. 475–900 encompasses the Middle Classic and Late Classic periods of Mayan history. Great temple-cities arose throughout the Mayan cultural area, encompassing southern Mexico and the Yucatán, Guatemala, Belize, and parts of Honduras and El Salvador. Cities such as Palenque, Copá, and Tikal, among many others, supported an aristocracy dedicated to warfare and sacrifice to the gods, as well as a priesthood and classes of scribes and artisans. As in the Early Classic Period, the activities of the Mayan rulers were recorded in a hieroglyphic script on stone monuments. Mayan culture was supported by intensive agriculture, especially utilizing the technique of raised crop beds surrounded by irrigation channels. The total population of the Mayan cultural region during the Late Classic era may have been 8 to 10 million people. Remarkably, the Maya reached a high cultural level without the use of metal or wheeled vehicles, and with limited use of domestic animals (mainly dogs and fowl).

Around 900, or slightly before, most of the great Mayan cities suffered precipitous declines, or were abandoned altogether. Many theories have been advanced to explain the sudden decline of Mayan civilization, including prolonged drought, deforestation, excessive devotion of resources to warfare, and the encroachment of the Toltec from the north. In any case, the Post-Classical Mayan world does seem to have come under at least the loose control of the Toltec empire; Toltec and Maya alike would be conquered by the Aztec after about 1300.

Meanwhile, in the Valley of Mexico, the Zapotec civi-lization, with its cultural center at the great city of Teotihuacán, was supplanted first by the Mixtec and then (around 900) by the Toltec, who built a great capital at Tula, not far from Teotihuacán.

The World on the Eve of European Expansion (A.D. 1000–1500)

The four major centers of Old World civilization that had been established by the year 1000—European Christendom, the Islamic world, India, and China—all underwent tremendous challenges from confederations of warlike Turkish and Mongol tribes in the next 500 years. By the end of the 15th century, Europe had already commenced its expansion to the Americas, to Africa and to southern Asia.

Expansion of the Islamic World: Asia and Africa
The Abbasid dynasty of caliphs of Baghdad had long employed Turkish auxiliaries (rather as the Romans had used German tribes) in their Near Eastern armies; one such army, under their chieftain Mahmud of Ghazni (r. 997–1030), moved out of Afghanistan into the Punjab about the year 1000 and by 1030 established a Muslim dynasty there. Over the next 200 years they spread their conquests over the Rajputs eastward into the plain of the Ganges, establishing their capital at Delhi about the year 1200. Many of the rich Hindu temples were plundered and destroyed by the invaders. Under the sultan of Delhi Ala-ud-din (r. 1296–1316) most of the subcontinent was brought under one rule for the first time since Asoka.

Unable to break the caste tradition, the ruling Turks became a casteless minority of warrior-aristocrats extracting heavy taxes but relying upon the Hindu princes for administration. Though the Hindu temples had been devastated, they were rebuilt, as the Muslim Turks had to permit a practical tolerance for Hinduism. After the death of Ala-ud-din his empire dissolved into a medley of warring kingdoms ruled by Muslim generals or Hindu princes over whom the sultans at Delhi exercised greater or lesser control.

In the "greater India" of Southeast Asia, Islamic influence expanded through trade and Chinese influence through trade and warfare. In Burma, King Anawrahta (r. 1044–77) transformed the capital city Bagan (formerly Pagan) into a major center of Buddhist scholarship and pilgrimage, with hundreds of temples dotting the central plain of the Ayeyahwadi (Irawaddy) River. The complex was destroyed by the invading Mongol armies of Kublai Khan in 1287, and the land was divided into a number of small principalities. In nearby Cambodia, King Suryavarman II (r. 1113–50) built the temple of Angkor Wat, dedicated to the Hindu god Vishnu and still the largest religious building in the world. King Jayavarman VII (r. 1181–1215) defeated a Cham invasion and pursued a program of further temple building at Angkor, introducing Buddhism into the Khmer Empire. After his reign, the Khmer Empire began to lose territory and power to its Thai, Cham, and Viet neighbors. A rump kingdom of Cambodia continued to exist, but Angkor began to fall into ruins by the mid-14th century. Dvaravate Siam (briefly annexed to the Khmer Empire in the 11th century) was overrun by Thai tribesmen from southwestern China in the 13th century; by 1350 a Thai kingdom of Siam had established its capital at Ayutthaya (north of present-day Bangkok), which was to remain its capital until the end of the 18th century. Over the next century, Siam subdued the independent kingdom of Cambodia to the east and expanded against Burma as well. In the archipelago of Indonesia and curving north into the Philippines, Muslim traders and missionaries spread the Islamic faith. Over 20 Islamic states had been established through religious conversions of rulers by the year 1500, though many of the inhabitants of those states continued to follow indigenous religious beliefs. The Hindu aristocracy of Java took refuge on the island of Bali, which still preserves elements of pre-Islamic Indonesian culture and where a unique form of Hinduism is still practiced.

Muslim expansion occurred in western Africa as well. The conquest of ancient Ghana by Muslim Berbers in 1076 (who had conquered Morocco 20 years earlier) led to a series of successor states. One of these, Kangaba, had by the 13th century established another trading state of immense size, the Kingdom of Mali, which stretched, in the 14th century, from the Atlantic coast eastward beyond Gao on the Niger. Under Mansa Musa (r. ca. 1312–37) Islam spread through the western savanna, the king himself making a pilgrimage to Mecca in 1324. Farther east, the king of the Songhay people on the great bend of the Niger had already converted to Islam in the 11th century; thus, when the dominance of Mali was replaced in the 15th century by the Kingdom of Songhay, Islam dominated not only the northern coast of Africa but almost the entire belt of savanna south of the Sahara as well.

Also in this period, Bantu-speaking peoples established polities in several parts of central, east, and southern Africa. On the Zimbabwe Plateau, Great Zimbabwe, the largest of some 300 stone complexes in the area, was built between the twelfth and fifteenth centuries. A capital city and trading center of the Kingdom of Makaranga, it may have had nearly 20,000 inhabitants at its height.

Transformation of the Muslim World: The Turks and the Fall of Byzantium   Leaders of the Seljuk clan of Turks seized Afghanistan (1037) from the Turkish Muslim rulers of the Punjab, then expanded into Persia and Mesopotamia by 1055. After the battle of Manzikert (1071) the Seljuks took most of Asia Minor from Byzantium, and conquered Syria in 1084, creating an empire that stretched from Egypt to India and endured in some form until 1243. During the 12th century, in the aftermath of the First Crusade (1096–99), the Seljuk Empire dissolved in all but name, becoming a collection of small emirates ruled by princes or generals. The heirs to the Seljuks were another Turkish clan, the Ottomans. In 1326 they drove Byzantine forces entirely out of Asia Minor, thus beginning the Ottoman Empire (1326–1920). By century's end they controlled all of Asia Minor and the Balkans as far north as Bosnia. Half a century later (1453) they took Constantinople, turning Hagia Sophia into a mosque in their renamed capital of Istanbul.

The 11th century had been the apogee of the Eastern Roman Empire (Byzantium) as it conquered the Christian kingdom of Bulgaria (1018) and made Serbia a client state, while to the east Armenia and the Crimea were annexed (1022). But by mid-century the Normans, descendants of Vikings who settled in the French province of Normandy, were establishing themselves in Byzantine Italy (and Muslim Sicily). Furthermore, the battle of Manzikert, which left most of Asia Minor in the hands of the Seljuk Turks, proved a catastrophe from which the empire never recovered, losing both its granary and its military recruiting ground in a single blow. Although the first three crusades (1096–1192) were initially successful in wresting the Holy Land from Islam, the subsequent organization of the territory in the French pattern of small, squabbling and isolated feudal statelets rendered them impotent and hence of only marginal help to Byzantium.

The Fourth Crusade (1202–04) was a disaster, for the crusaders took Constantinople, establishing what is called the Latin Empire (1204–61). In 1261 Michael Palaeologus (1261–82) restored a rump Byzantine state along the shores of the Aegean, and it was against this enfeebled state that the Ottoman Turks expanded. The doom of Constantinople brought Turkish power right to the borders of Hungary, with the Balkans absorbed into the

Ottoman Empire for 450 years. In the northeast it was not the Turks but the Mongols whose arrival transformed Christendom. Hungary, Poland, and Kievian Rus were weakened by dynastic struggles from the 11th century on, yet remained independent of the Holy Roman Empire to the west and the Turkish Cumans in the east.

The Mongol Empire (1200–1500)

In Mongolia, a young orphan, Temujin (ca. 1162–1227), relied on his personal skills as a warrior, his charisma, his ruthlessness as a conqueror, and his organizational genius to create a great confederation of the Mongol tribes. He took the title Genghis Khan in 1206, and lay claim to leadership of all of the nomadic peoples of Asia—"all who live in felt tents." His confederation grew strong enough to strike at China, the Near East, and Europe at the same time, and his realm extended from Korea to the borders of Persia and Russia. The Mongol conquest of northern China (ruled at that time by Jurchen tribesmen from Manchuria) was completed by Genghis Khan's successors in 1234. The Mongols then turned their attention to Korea, which they conquered in 1231–36, and to the Chinese Song Dynasty in the Yangtze River Valley. The Song defended their territory vigorously, while the Mongols were slowed down as their horsemen learned to cope with wet rice-fields and rivers defended by heavily armed ships; but in 1271 Kublai Khan (1215–94), a grandson of Genghis Khan, proclaimed himself emperor of the Yuan Dynasty of China, and in 1279 the last Song emperor died at sea and the dynasty collapsed.

During his reign Kublai Khan tried twice (1274 and 1281) to invade Japan; his armies were defeated by Japan's samurai defenders, aided by thimely typhoons (regarded by the Japanese as *kamikaze*, "divine winds") that scattered or sank the invaders' ships. An attempt to conquer Java. 2,500 miles to the south, failed when the Mongols were betrayed and forced to withdraw. Nevertheless the expedition resulted in the decline of the Singhasari kingdom in Java and the emergence of the Majapahit Empire which dominated much of what is now Indonesia and the Malay Peninsula, including the growing spice trade, until the arrival of the Portuguese more than 200 years later.

Meanwhile, Mongol armies under another of Genghis Khan's grandsons, Batu (d. 1255), fell upon Europe (1237–40) and advanced beyond Russia into Poland and Hungary and the lands of the German knights on the Baltic. Europe was saved by the death of the Genghis Khan's son and successor, Ögödei Khan (r. 1229–41), which necessitated a khuraltai (conference) in Mongolia of all the Mongol chieftains to choose the next Great Khan. The Mongol armies withdrew from their campaigns in Europe while this conference was in progress. The outcome of the khuraltai was a division of the Mongol Empire into four sub-empires ruled by Genghis Khan's grandsons, which weakened and fragmented the great conqueror's legacy. Still, the "Golden Horde," Batu's Khanate on the lower Volga River, ruled all of south Russia and reduced the north Russian principalities to vassal status. Not until the late 15th century was the prince of Moscow powerful enough to refuse tribute money to the empire of the Golden Horde. Mongol rule in China endured until 1368, and the Ilkhanate of Persia, which converted to Islam, left its mark on Central Asia as well. The Khanate of Chagatai, in Turkestan, lasted until the mid-14th century.

Part of the Mongol Empire was reconstituted in the late 14th century by Timur Leng (ca. 1336–1405, known in Europe as Tamerlane), who claimed descent from Genghis Khan. Assembling a confederation of Turkish and Mongol tribes, Timur conquered much of Turkestan by 1369 and established his capital at Samarkand. Further campaigns brought most of Persia into Timur's empire by 1387, and in 1392 he extended his territory to include Mesopotamia and eastern Anatolia. A campaign in 1398 annexed northwestern India and put an end to the Delhi Sultanate. At his death in 1405 Timur was planning an invasion of China. His empire was divided among his sons, and though Samarkand became one of the greatest cities in the world in the early 15th century, the Timurid empire collapsed after the reign of Timur's grandson, Ulugh Beg (r. 1447–49). The last of the Timurids, Babur (1483–1530) founded the Mogul Dynasty in India.

The Rise of Western Christendom

Western Christendom slowly emerged from the ruins of the western Roman Empire and the destruction wrought by barbarian invasions. The Christian conversion of Europe was essentially completed by 1050, as Scandinavia, Poland, and Hungary became Christian kingdoms. (The penetration of Christianity into the lives of the common people did not necessarily follow immediately from the conversion of kings and nobles.) Europe remained divided into feudal kingdoms and domains; its unity, such as it was, was more religious and cultural than political.

Whether the leadership of this society should fall to the popes or the Holy Roman Emperors was settled in the 11th century in the Investiture Struggle in which the papacy emerged victorious. From Pope Gregory VII (r. 1073–85) to Boniface VIII (r. 1294–1303) the papacy gave the lead to western Christendom, often in alliance with reforming monastic leaders. In the 12th and 13th centuries the characteristic Gothic architecture and sculpture of medieval Europe (which succeeded the earlier Romanesque style) spread across Europe under church patronage while the Leagues of the Peace and the Crusades attempted to limit the warrior ethos of the feudal nobles or channel it to the Christian project of conquering the Holy Land.

In 1066 William of Normandy (ca. 1028–1087), thereafter known as the Conqueror, led an invading army to England, where he defeated the Saxon king Harold Godwinson (r. 1066) at the Battle of Hastings. England was thus transformed into a participant in the world of European monarchical power. The Domesday Book, surveying all of the territory under the control of the new rulers, was a landmark of royal administration. For two centuries the kings of England looked more to the Continent (in their continuing role as dukes of Normandy) than to the British Isles, while the French language made an indelible impact on vernacular English.

In 1215 King John (r. 1188–1216) was forced by his rebellious barons—a powerful and self-confident military aristocracy—to sign a treaty, later known as Magna Carta, that guaranteed aristocratic rights and made the king as much a subject of the law as his people. This event was part of a trend, beginning late in the 12th century in Spain and Italy, and continuing in the 13th century in Germany, England, and France and in the 14th and 15th centuries in Hungary, Poland, and Scandinavia, toward the creation of parliaments, as monarchs (often under political pressure) began to call the elected representatives of the towns to meet in formal sessions along with prelates and nobles to render advice to the throne. (This trend toward parliamentary government had been anticipated two centuries earlier in Iceland, where the Althing representative assembly had been established in 930.)

Beginning in 11th-century Italy and 12th-century Netherlands, the commune movement, in which all the inhabitants of a town bound themselves by oath to obey their magistrates, keep the peace, and defend their liberties, revived town life and created the medieval city as a confederation of self-governing guilds. Guilds were associations of craftsmen of one trade or merchants bound together for mutual aid. Fairs held regularly in the towns of Western Europe both reflected and stimulated the reestablishment

of trade, while in the Mediterranean, the Italian cities (especially Venice and Genoa) linked the West with Byzantium and the Muslim Near East. The Crusades, ironically, stimulated trade with the Muslim world, while the pax Mongolica reinvigorated trade along the Silk Route between China and Western Asia in the 13th century. (The celebrated journies to China of such missionaries, traders and geographers as William of Rubruck, Marco Polo, Odoric of Pordenone and Ibn Battuta from the mid-13th century on reflected the continued importance of this trade route.) The sea lanes from East Asia, the Spice Islands, and India brought Asian goods to the Persian Gulf and the Red Sea, thence overland to the cities of the Levant and on to Europe.

In the commercial and ecclesiastical towns of Europe, such as Paris, Bologna, Salerno, and Oxford, universities were founded where Greek and Arab learning met with the Christian traditions of the Carolingian schools. The classical philosophy of Aristotle was rethought in Christian terms and gave rise to the legal, philosophic, theological, and scientific work of scholasticism. Prominent 13th-century scholars such as Albertus Magnus, Thomas Aquinas, Bonaventure, Roger Bacon, and Duns Scotus were all members of the newly established religious orders, Franciscans (St. Francis, 1182–1226) and Dominicans (St. Dominic, 1170–1221). Committed to evangelical poverty and combating heresy, they played a role in university life as well.

The development of these social and cultural and religious institutions was accompanied by the first stirrings of European expansion. This was based in part on new economic initiatives, such as the clearing of forests and the cultivation of new farmland able to support an increased population. It also involved bringing peripheral territories firmly into the religious and political orbit of Europe, as with the reconquest of Spain from the Muslims (1085–1492), the conquest of Prussia and Livonia by the Teutonic Knights (1229–1466) and the conversion of Lithuania (1386 and after).

Poland attained its status as the largest state in Christendom with the marriage of its queen Jadwiga (r. 1384–99) to the Grand Duke Jagiello of Lithuania, who ruled as Wladislaw II (1386–1434). In the 15th century the Jagellon Dynasty (1386–1572) controlled the entire region between the Baltic and Black Seas. It was however in a precarious position, exposed to danger from the Teutonic Knights, Tatars, and Hungarians, as well as the Ottomans, Russians, and Swedes. The marriage of Ivan III "the

Great" (r. 1462–1505) to the niece of the last Byzantine emperor established the czar's claim to imperial succession as he took the title "czar" (= Caesar or emperor); his conquest of the principality of Novgorod (1478) established a large Russian state northeast of Poland.

All aspects of the political, economic, and social life of Western Europe were affected by the precipitous decline in population caused by the Black Death, an outbreak of bubonic plague that swept over Europe (1347–51), wiping out perhaps 25 million, a third of the population. The sudden demand for agricultural labor helped to do away with the old feudal structure of land use and gave rise to a tenant peasantry; new economic opportunities arose in cities and towns for those who survived the plague.

The loose unity of western Christendom began to alter in the 14th century in significant ways. First of all, the universality of the papacy was compromised when seven popes in succession (1305–78) preferred to reside at Avignon rather than Rome (the "Babylonian captivity"), in too close an association with the kings of France; then, after the return to Rome there arose a series of disputed elections to the papacy that is called the Great Schism (1378–1417); and finally, with the end of the schism, the popes became more and more involved in the politics of Renaissance Italy.

Meanwhile, while theories of sovereignty derived from the study of Roman law exalted the authorities of kings, royal powers disastrously declined due to chronic feudal violence: the "age of princes" in Germany (1273–1493), the Hundred Years' War in England and France (1337–1453), and the dynastic Wars of the Roses in England (1455–85). Out of the turmoil arose the "new monarchies" of more unified states: the Tudors in England (1485–1603), the Valois in France (1328–1529), and the Spanish branch of the Habsburgs (1504–1700).

In the Italy of the 14th and 15th centuries, increasingly at the mercy of the more powerful monarchical states to the north and west, there began the great cultural transformation known as the Renaissance. Humanists such as Petrarch (1304–74) and Boccaccio (1313–75) sought a revival of the ideals of Greek and Roman antiquity, both pagan (Cicero, Virgil, Tacitus) and Christian (Augustine and the other Church fathers), in an educational movement that sought to unite the values of Hellenism with Christianity. At the same time artists, studying Roman architecture and Hellenistic sculpture on the one hand and the new sciences of anatomy and perspective on the other, created a new visual aesthetic. Florence alone produced the genius of Botticelli and da Vinci in painting, Brunelleschi (1377–1446) in architecture, and Ghiberti (1378–1455) and Donatello (1386–1466) in sculpture; and other city-states had their own artistic geniuses to rival them.

Building on medieval foundations and new navigational discoveries (magnetic compasses, the astrolabe, the quadrant), and spurred by the 1453 Ottoman conquest of Constantinople which placed all European trade with Asia in Muslim hands, Prince Henry "the Navigator" of Portugal (1394–1460) and his successors pursued a program of exploration of the coast of Africa, which ultimately led to the discovery of a direct sea route to India, Southeast Asia, and China. The Gulf of Guinea was reached by 1470, the Cape of Good Hope by 1487, and India by 1498. The Spanish monarchs sponsored the voyage of Christopher Columbus (1451–1506) in search of a westward route to the Orient. His three ships reached the Bahamas and inaugurated uninterrupted transatlantic traffic between the "old," known world of Eurasia and Africa and the "new," unknown world of the Americas. By the end of the 15th century Europe was launched on the period of maritime exploration and expansion that would bring much of the world under European rule over the next few centuries, and spread European ideas and technology around the globe.

The Americas At the end of the 15th century, the Americas were home to two great empires, the Aztec in Mexico and the Inca in Peru, as well as smaller states, tribes and communities of hunter-gatherers and village agriculturalists spread from the northern sub-Arctic region to Tierra de Fuego, the southern tip of South America. Contrary to Europeans' initial expectations, the Americas were neither unpopulated nor a trackless wilderness.

In the three centuries after the collapse of the Late Classical Mayan civilization around 900, the Toltec empire had expanded to include most of the old Mayan lands in Mexico and northern Central America. Its capital was in the magnificent temple city of Tula, not far from the old Zapotec city of Teotihuacán. The 12th and 13th centuries saw a series of incursions by diverse tribes known collectively as Chichimecs, whose armed might destroyed the Toltec civilization. One of these tribes, of obscure origins, was known first as the Mexica and later as the Aztec. Eventually rising to a dominant position, the Aztec established a capital at Tenochtitlán (now Mexico City), in the Valley of Mexico, and from about 1360 to about 1470 conquered neighboring peoples and constructed the sanguinary Aztec Empire (ca. 1360–1520). Montezuma I (r. 1440–69) was a ruthless conqueror but a great builder who transformed the capital into a magnificent city of stone. By 1500 the Aztec had expanded south to Guatemala. For their subject peoples the Aztec were a catastrophe, constantly in need of human sacrificial victims to offer to the sun god who required human blood for his nourishment.

Stretching for more than a thousand miles along the towering Andes Mountains that parallel the west coast of South America lay the empire of the Inca with their capital at Cuzco. It was basically a highland empire, but it controlled contiguous lowland regions as well and traded with the forest peoples of the Amazon Basin to the east. The Inca Empire was a centralized bureaucratic state, assembled through military conquest and sustained by the religious vision of the Inca monarchy; it engaged in extensive road and bridge building and irrigation projects. Begun about 1200, the empire attained its greatest size under Huayna Capac (r. ca. 1493–1527).

China, Japan, and Korea (1300–1500)

In China, the Mongols of the Yuan Dynasty (1279–1368) were seen as an alien occupying power; their habit of using foreign, Persian-speaking tax-collectors made them especially hated. The successors to Kublai Khan were mediocre rulers; in 1368 a Chinese nativist rebellion led by a charismatic ex-Buddhist monk named Zhu Yuanzhang succeeded in overthrowing the Mongols and establishing the Ming Dynasty (1368–1644). The early Ming emperors were vigorous and forward-looking; they rebuilt the Great Wall, rerouted the northern section of the Grand Canal to Beijing, built a new southern capital at Nanjing, and sent maritime expeditions on missions of exploration and diplomacy throughout the South China Sea and the Indian Ocean as far as Sri Lanka, and beyond, to the Persian Gulf, the Red Sea and the east coast of Africa. These expeditions, under Admiral Zheng He (ca. 1371–ca. 1433), were however abruptly terminated in 1433, criticized by the conservative Confucian bureaucracy as a waste of money and resources. Thus, the Chinese missed by only half a century the chance to confront the Portuguese as rival maritime powers in the Indian Ocean.

In Korea, the Koryo Dynasty did not long survive their Mongol patrons. The last Koryo king in 1388 sent his best general, Yi Songgye (ca. 1335–1408), already famous for his victories over Japanese pirates, to invade China to try to overthrow the Ming Dynasty on behalf of the Mongols. General Yi instead turned back at the border, overthrew the Koryo king, and established his own dynasty, the Kingdom of Choson, which soon proclaimed its support for the Ming emperors. The third Choson (or Yi Dynasty) ruler, King Sejong (r. 1418–50), was Korea's greatest sovereign, a patron of art, science, and technology during whose reign Korean scholars and craftsmen perfected printing with moveable metal type, invented a syllabic script to write vernacular Korean, and equipped Seoul with what was, for a time, the best astronomical observatory in the world. The Choson monarchs tolerated Buddhism, promoted Confucianism, ruled through a very conservative aristocracy, and remained on the throne until 1910.

In Japan, the Fujiwara-dominated aristocrats of Heian-kyo ignored the rise of a provincial warrior aristocracy in the provinces until it was too late. The Fujiwaras were ousted by the western Taira clan in 1160; they in turn were defeated by Minamoto no Yoritomo (1147–99) at the naval battle of Dan-no-Ura in 1185. Yoritomo then took the hereditary title of shogun ("supreme general"), and established a military capital at Kamakura, leaving the emperors to reign but not rule in Heian-kyo. The Minamoto were shunted aside by their own hereditary retainers, the Hojo Clan, in 1229. Amid an imperial succession crisis (1331–33), a general named Ashikaga Takauji (1305–58), overthrew the Hojo, proclaimed himself shogun, and moved the capital to the Muromachi district of Kyoto, putting the emperors firmly in their place once again. The Muromachi shogunate endured until 1568, though with little military power; the shoguns were better known as patrons of Zen Buddhism, Noh theater, and the tea ceremony. With the waning of central authority, Japanese merchants were more free to establish domestic and overseas trade routes which fostered economic prosperity amid political instability. While the Japanese were not major players in foreign trade, by the end of the 1500's there were Japanese merchant communities in ports throughout Asia, including the Philippines, Macao, Malacca, Java, Burma and Thailand.

European Expansion: The First Phase (1500–1650)

During this period, Ottoman Turkey, Safavid Persia, Mogul India, and Ming China remained traditional Asian empires, while a new dynamism infused the emerging nation-states of Europe. Although severe religious and political divisions led to incessant warfare within Europe, the major European powers managed to dominate the sea lanes of the globe and control the coasts and islands of Africa, southern Asia, and the Americas.

The Near East: Ottoman Empire and Safavid Persia   Under their sultans Selim I the Grim (r. 1512–20) and Sulayman I the Magnificent (r. 1520–66) the Ottoman Turks added Syria and Egypt to their domains, then from their fortress at Belgrade launched an invasion of Hungary, which climaxed at the battle of Mohacs (1526). This brought three-quarters of the Hungarian Empire under Turkish rule, either directly or through Ottoman client princes of Transylvania. The Turks moved on to besiege Vienna (1529), halting the campaign because of troubles with Persia in the east. Turkish fleets added the ports of Yemen and Aden on the Persian Gulf and Tripoli, Algeria, and Tunis on the southern shores of the Mediterranean to the Ottoman domain.

Sulayman's successor was Selim II "the Sot" (r. 1566–74), the first in a series of weak sultans who came to the throne between 1566 and 1718 as a result of harem intrigues of wives and eunuchs, and of the specifically Ottoman problem, an inability to prevent the sultans' guard troops, the Janissaries, from acting as a power unto themselves. Ottoman naval power suffered a temporary setback in 1571, when the Holy League (an alliance of the Papacy, Venice, Tuscany, and Spain) triumphed over the Turkish navy in the battle of Lepanto, off the coast of Italy. But the dissolution of the league after the victory meant that Ottoman seapower in the Mediterranean was only temporarily impaired.

In Persia, the native Iranian Safavid Dynasty (1501–1736) came to power. Its founder Shah Ismail seized power from the White Sheep Turks in 1501 and successfully defended Persia from Ottoman expansion into Mesopotamia, a work continued under his son and successor, Shah Tahmasp (r. 1524–76). Shah Abbas I "the Great" (r. 1587–1629) made his capital city of Isfahan into one of the great showplaces of Islamic architecture. The dynasty weakened after his reign, and Ottoman encroachments on Mesopotamia resumed; the Turks succeeded in taking Baghdad (1638).

In the meantime, the Portuguese had established a trading presence in the Persian Gulf at Hormuz in 1507. In 1622 the Portuguese were expelled by Shah Abbas, who invited English merchants to replace them.

Mogul India and the Spice Trade   In 1526 Babur (1483–1530), a descendent of Timur Leng, who had already established himself as the ruler of Afghanistan, overthrew the Sultanate of Delhi and extended his domi-nance east of the Indus. Although Babur, like all the Timurids, was a Turk, because of the long association of his family with the Mongols, his empire came to be called the Mughal Empire (1526–1857; Mughal was a local variant pronunciation of Mongol). Babur then expanded east to the borders of Bengal. Although his son Humayun lost almost all Babur had conquered, his grandson Akbar (r. 1556–1605), contemporary of Philip II of Spain and Elizabeth of England, restored Babur's realm and expanded it further until it included all of India north of the Deccan Plateau highlands of central India. Akbar's empire was both peaceful and prosperous. Most of the Deccan region was added in the reign of his grandson Shah Jahan (r. 1628–58), who also built the Taj Mahal.

In 1497 the Portuguese navigator Vasco da Gama (ca. 1469–1524) began a voyage that took him around Africa's Cape of Good Hope and across the Indian Ocean to Calicut, a major trading entrepôt on the southwestern coast of India. The incentive for the Portuguese (and soon other European) voyages of the Age of Expansion was the trade in spices and other Asian commodities. The European appetite for spices was fueled for the obvious reason that spices make food taste better, as well as for their effectiveness as a preservative (cinnamon was used not only to flavor food, but as an embalming agent for the noble dead), but the idea that they were needed to cover up the taste of rotten food in the era before refrigeration is merely a myth. (No one rich enough to afford spices had to eat spoiled meat.) But spices, carried from the East Indies by Malay, Indian, and Arab ships to Hormuz on the Persian Gulf or Aden at the entrance to the Red Sea, and thence to Europe, became exorbitantly expensive as they passed through the hands of Levantine and Venetian middlemen; this provided ample incentive for western European monarchs to look for direct sea routes to India and the Spice Islands. East Asia became a goal of navigation as well, because the overland Silk Route trade with China had been seriously disrupted by the fall of Constantinople, one of the trade's main transshipment points, in 1453.

After da Gama's second voyage (1502), the Muslim state of Gujarat, allied with Mameluke Egypt, attempted to fend off the newcomers with military force, but at Diu, the Portuguese won a complete victory (1508). The Portuguese viceroy organized the building of a "rosary" of over a dozen forts stretching from Hormuz on the Persian Gulf through Goa to Malacca on the Malay Peninsula. Thus the Portuguese could monopolize the carrying trade in the Indian Ocean as well as divert the spice trade around Africa. From Malacca, captured in 1511, they established trading posts in the Spice Islands (Melaku), China, and Japan. This network provided the route for Christian missionaries as well.

During the 16th century the Portuguese assumed a dominant role in Europe's trade with China and Japan from their trading colony at Macao, on the southeastern coast of China, established in 1557. But Portugal's early near-monopoly on European shipping in Asia was soon challenged. The Spanish conquered the Philippines in a series of campaigns in the mid-16th century, and established a trans-Pacific trade route between Acapulco in New Spain (Mexico) and Manila. The English and the Dutch established their East India Companies in 1600 and 1602, respectively, and in the 17th century the Dutch gradually supplanted the Portuguese in Asia through a combination of war and diplomacy. By 1639 the English were at Madras (now Chennai), the first step in their long involvement with the Indian subcontinent.

East Asia: China, Korea, Japan
The late Ming emperors were great patrons of culture, but mediocre rulers. After China's abandonment of long-range ocean voyages in 1433, and the adoption of an inward-looking policy of isolationism, China gradually began a long period of decline as a great power.

Annam, which had briefly (1407–28) been reconquered by China under the vigorous third emperor of the Ming dynasty, in 1558 split into two monarchies, with the Trinh dynasty ruling the kingdom of Tonkin (northern Vietnam) from Hanoi, and the Nguyen dynasty ruling the kingdom of Annam (central Vietnam) from its capital at Hue. The Hindu kingdom of Champa, in southernmost Vietnam, was continually under pressure from the rulers of Annam but retained its independent existence until the mid-17th century, when its last vestiges were absorbed by its northern neighbor.

The danger to China from Mongolia, from where Altan Khan (r. 1543–1583) raided almost annually across the Great Wall, was kept in check by adroit Ming diplomacy, and further allayed by the Mongol acceptance of Tibetan religious authority; with the spread of Lamaism, monasteries absorbed surplus sons who might otherwise have become warriors. But in the northeast, descendants of the 12th-century Jurchen rulers of the Jin Dynasty were forming a new tribal confederation of people who would become known as Manchus. Their chieftain, Nurhachi (r. 1586–1626), took the title of emperor; his son Alatai (d.

1643, also known as Hong Taiji) brought all of Mongolia under his rule, overran Korea in 1627, and took the northeastern Ming outpost of Mukden in 1636.

Within China, a combination of rising imperial expenditures and increasing land tax evasion by the rural gentry eventually destabilized even so rich an empire as the Ming. Factionalism and eunuch intrigues in the capital weakened the dynasty further; popular rebellions broke out and were not thoroughly suppressed. In desperation, the last Ming emperor invited a Manchu army to Beijing to expel a rebel band that had seized the city. Having expelled the rebels, the Manchus refused to leave. The Ming emperor hanged himself, and the Manchus proclaimed the founding of the Qing Dynasty (1644–1911). Ming resistance in southern China was quashed by 1661; all Chinese men were required to braid their hair in a queue as a sign of submission.

During the last decades of the Ming, China began to feel the first effects of European influence. The Jesuit missionary Matteo Ricci (1552–1610) reached Macao in 1582 and Beijing in 1601. Adapting himself to local custom, he became an accomplished Confucian scholar and used that guise as a means of introducing to China such things as the astrolabe, the weight-driven clock, prisms, and the Mercator map of the world. For a brief time Christianity became a vogue among some members of the mandarin class, but imperial disapproval (exacerbated by factional disputes among the Christian missionary orders) discouraged conversions. Under Qing rule the Jesuits were prohibited from preaching, but allowed to remain in China for their technical skills in astronomy, mathematics, painting, and cannon making.

In Korea, the Choson Kingdom was badly shaken by a destructive invasion (1592–98) from Japan. The invasion was finally repelled with Chinese aid, but Korea suffered long-term economic and social damage during the six years of guerrilla warfare and occupation by Japanese and Chinese armies. Conquered by the Manchus in 1627, the Koreans had no difficulty in transferring their loyalty from the Ming to the Qing; Choson remained a loyal vassal of China, and isolated from the rest of the world, until the late 19th century.

Japan borrowed the old Chinese term "Warring States Period" to describe the century from 1467 to 1568, when Muromachi rule dissolved in a welter of mutually hostile feudal domains. Order was gradually restored after 1568 by three remarkable generals: Oda Nobunaga (1534–1582), who was the first Japanese general to use firearms extensively in battle; Toyotomi Hideyoshi

(1537–1598), a peasant who rose to rule Japan, only to squander his resources in the fruitless invasion of Korea; and Tokugawa Ieyasu (1543–1616), who defeated a coalition of enemies at the Battle of Sekigahara (near the modern city of Nagoya) in 1600 and established the Tokugawa shogunate, military rulers of Japan until 1868. The Tokugawa period is sometimes known as the Edo Period, after its capital (now Tokyo).

Japan readily absorbed European influence in the sixteenth century. The Portuguese arrived as traders in 1543; another Jesuit, Francis Xavier (1506–52) began his mission to the Japanese in 1549. By the end of the century the number of Catholic converts, including some members of the high military aristocracy, peaked at about 300,000. Thereafter Hideyoshi began to suppress Christianity as a foreign threat, banishing Portuguese missionaries in 1587. The Tokugawa shoguns persecuted Christianity even more fiercely, executing thousands after 1612 and driving the church underground after the Christian Shimabara Uprising of 1637–38 ended in an appalling slaughter. Thereafter no foreigners were allowed in Japan except for a small number of Dutch traders, who were rigorously confined to an island in Nagasaki harbor.

The European Impact on Africa, 1500–1650

The expansion of Portuguese sea power to the African coast profoundly changed Europe's relations with Africa. Earlier Portuguese traders had brought cotton goods and metal manufactures to exchange for ivory and gold as far as the delta of the Niger river. Further south, at the mouth of the Congo, a Bantu-speaking Christian state developed under Portuguese influence after 1483. These early contacts were supplanted by the rapid growth of the slave trade, as the new world of the Americas provided a large market for traffic in human beings. The Portuguese dominated the slave trade to Brazil and New Spain until the Dutch drove them out of the Gold Coast in 1642. African slavery, once an incidental result of tribal warfare, now became a cause of warfare and social dislocation throughout West Africa. First the Portuguese, then the Dutch, English and others encouraged states along the west coast to provide them with captives to be sold as slaves in the Americas.

The trading Kingdom of Songhay, which reached its greatest extent under Askia Mohammed II (r. 1531–37) and Askia Dawud (r. 1549–82), was smashed by a Moroccan invasion in 1591. The fall of Songhay brought decline farther east to the Kingdom of Kanem (Bornu) in the savanna surrounding Lake Chad after 1617. The paradoxical result was the decline of Islamic influence, for with the destruction of the Muslim towns, trade on the old caravan routes across the Sahara dwindled. Farther south, the Portuguese established themselves in southeast Africa in Mozambique (1507), and southwest Africa in Angola (1574). The Dutch established a trading colony at Capetown, at Africa's southern tip, in 1652.

The Americas: Europe's New Provinces

The Treaty of Tordesillas (1494) between Spain and Portugal divided the world by a line 370 leagues west of the Azores (approximately 45°W), establishing monopolies for Spain westward and Portugal eastward of the line. Thus Brazil, first explored separately in 1500 by Vicente Yáñez Pinzón (a veteran of Columbus's 1492 voyage) and Pedro Cabral (ca. 1467–ca. 1520), became Portuguese territory. But it was not immediately clear to Portugal and Spain what to do with their conquests in the Americas. It was increasingly obvious that the New World was not part of Asia, but rather a barrier to reaching Asia by a westbound sea route.

The picture changed entirely in the years 1519–22. In 1520, Ferdinand Magellan (ca. 1480–1521) sailed around the southern tip of South America, bringing the Spanish to the Philippines and the Moluccas across the Pacific. Then in 1521, the conquistador (conqueror) Hernando Cortés (1485–1547) conquered the Aztec Empire. When Francisco Pizarro (1476–1541) toppled the Inca Empire in 1533, Spain acquired a stupendous world empire, the wealth of whose silver mines dwarfed the riches of the Indies. The conquistadores brought with them diseases, including smallpox, mumps, and measles, to which the native peoples of the Americas had no resistance, with devastating results: by the end of the 16th century the native population had been reduced by as much as 90 percent, to a total of about five million people in the two American continents combined.

Organized into two vice-royalties, the Spanish Empire granted *encomiendas* (plantations) to the conquerors; although enslavement of the Indians was forbidden, the Spanish reduced them to serflike status and forced them to work for their new lords. Christian missions were immediately established with such success that more than 20 bishoprics had been created by the mid-16th century. Five universities were flourishing by the middle of the 17th century.

Despite the restrictions of the Treaty of Tordesillas, the new Tudor monarchy of England financed John Cabot's (ca. 1450–ca. 1499) search for a Northwest Passage to the Orient, which took him as far as Newfoundland in 1497; he disappeared on his second voyage. France also sent exploratory ventures to America led by Giovanni da Verrazano (ca. 1485–ca. 1528) in 1524 and Jacques Cartier (1491–1557) in 1534; but it was not until the 17th century that a permanent settlement was established by Samuel de Champlain (1567–1635), who founded New France (1608) with a capital at Quebec on the St. Lawrence River. Missions began in 1615, but the process of christianizing the Indians met with limited success. After 1642, Montreal grew up around the Indian village of Hochelaga, 150 miles farther up the St. Lawrence River from Quebec, and grew into a center of the fur trade on which the economy of New France was based.

Earlier the French had also begun colonizing the Lesser Antilles, on the fringe of the Spanish Empire, and by 1656 they controlled a dozen of these islands. In a scramble for Caribbean possessions, the Dutch also colonized several of the Antilles Islands, and the English in 1627 settled Barbados, soon establishing a sugar-plantation economy that became a spectacular source of wealth.

England's Queen Elizabeth (1558–1603) did not undertake any large-scale projects of exploration and colonization, but did encourage courtiers such as Sir Humphrey Gilbert (ca. 1539–83) and Sir Walter Raleigh (1554–1618) in their early, ill-fated attempts at settlement (Roanoke Island, 1585) in North America. She also authorized Sir Francis Drake (1540–96), Sir John Hawkins (1532–95), and other adventurers in their plundering Spanish ships, and she apparently gave Drake her tacit support of his circumnavigation of the globe (1577–80). The rich fisheries off the coast of New England and the Canadian maritime provinces attracted fishermen from many parts of Western Europe long before actual settlements were established. Not until the Stuart Dynasty (1603–49) did English settlement begin in earnest. Henry Hudson, backed by various patrons, made several attempts to find a northern passage from Europe to Asia in 1607–11, during which he explored much of the northern coast of North America. Through grants to commercial companies and individual proprietors, the English established colonies from the Chesapeake to Maine broken only by the Swedes on the lower Delaware River and the Dutch in the Hudson Valley; the Dutch colony of New Amsterdam was established in 1624 and seized by the English in 1664. Chesapeake Bay became the center of a thriving agricultural region based upon tobacco, while New England flourished as a haven for the English Calvinists known as Puritans.

Europe in the Age of the Reformation Throughout the 15th century, leading members of the Catholic Church had called for reform of the clergy, who often led scandalous lives amid great wealth. The sale of God's forgiveness (indulgences) to raise cash for the rebuilding of Rome as a splendid Renaissance city struck some critics as a particular outrage. But not even the powerful voices of the Dutch humanist Desiderius Erasmus (1466–1536) or the English statesman Sir Thomas More (1478–1535) had any impact.

In 1517 the call of the Augustinian monk Martin Luther (1483–1546) for a cleansing of the church swept across northern Germany; the adherence of the Scandinavian monarchies to the new faith made the Baltic almost a Lutheran lake. Luther's assertion that "the just shall live by faith alone" implied that the established priesthood of the Catholic Church and priestly administration of the sacraments were unnecessary for the salvation of believers; Luther's Reformation thus involved fundamental doctrinal issues as well as proposals for secular reform. The English king Henry VIII (1509–47), while anti-Lutheran, severed his realm from the Catholic Church after 1532. Most influential in consolidating the Reformation was John Calvin (1509–64) who, from 1541 until his death, made Geneva a theocratic state, from which Calvinism spread to France, the Low Countries, and the British Isles.

The attempts of the Holy Roman Emperor Charles V (r. 1519–56) to halt the spread of the Reformation were hampered by his need to retain the support of the Lutheran princes in the struggle against the Ottoman Turks and to maintain his dynastic territories against the kings of France, who allied with the Turks against him. Charles V was ruler of the Netherlands and Spain in addition to being the Holy Roman Emperor. At his abdication he divided his inheritance between his brother Ferdinand (r. 1558–64) who received the Holy Roman Empire along with Habsburg holdings in central Europe, and his son Philip II (r. 1556–98), who inherited Spain with its empire both in the New World and Europe, including the Netherlands, Burgundy, Milan, and Naples.

Philip faced rebellion in the Netherlands, and by the end of his reign the northern provinces had all but won their independence. His armada (1588) against England met with disaster, thereby strengthening Queen

Elizabeth's rule and the triumph of Protestantism in both England and Scotland. France was badly damaged by the Wars of Religion (1562–98) in which Philip ineffectively intervened on the Catholic side against the Calvinists. The upshot was victory for the Calvinist claimant Henry IV (1589–1610), who embraced Catholicism when he came to the throne but also issued the Edict of Nantes (1598) granting toleration to French Calvinists (Huguenots).

The Counter Reformation, with the support of Philip II, led a great renewal within the Catholic Church. Spanish religious leadership was exemplified by Ignatius Loyola (1491–1556), who in 1540 founded the Jesuit Order, a fertile source of missionaries, preachers, scholars, and schoolmasters, as well as by the great mystic theologians Theresa of Avila and John of the Cross. Institutionally, the Council of Trent (1545–63) failed to heal the breach with the Protestants but did manage to reform the most glaring abuses in the church and provide an authoritative expression of Catholic belief.

Germany and the Hapsburg Empire were devastated by the Thirty Years' War (1618–48) in which the triumph of the Catholic Habsburgs was prevented by the interventions of Lutheran Sweden, under Gustavus II Adolphus (r. 1611–32) and Catholic France, under the effective leadership of Cardinal Richelieu (Louis XIII chief minister, 1628–42). Britain was shaken by the religious struggle between Anglicans and Puritans, reflected in the political struggle between the Stuart kings and Parliament. This clash resulted in the English Civil Wars (1642–49), in which the victory of the Puritan forces led to the execution of Charles I (r. 1625–49) and the establishment of a military dictatorship under Oliver Cromwell (1649–58).

In Russia during the long reign of Ivan IV the Terrible (r. 1533–84), the entire Volga came under Russian rule and expansion began beyond the Ural Mountains. After Ivan's death the monarchy was weakened by a succession struggle, settled when the national assembly in 1613 elected as czar Michael Romanov (r. 1613–45), founder of the Romanov Dynasty (1613–1917).

In Poland, Sigismund II (r. 1548–72) halted the spread of the Reformation and joined Lithuania and Poland into a single state (1569). But Sigismund was the last of the Jagellonian dynasty and after his death the monarchy became the plaything of other great powers. From 1587 to 1648 two members of the Catholic branch of Sweden's royal family, the Vasas, ruled in Poland.

In 1543 Andreas Vesalius (1514–64) published his great work on anatomy, the first step in the creation of a modern science of medicine. Also in 1543 a Polish priest, Copernicus (1473–1543), published his heliocentric theory of the cosmos, one of the key works of the Scientific Revolution. The process of overturning the old Ptolemaic geocentric cosmology continued with the observational work of the Dane, Tycho Brahe (1546–1601) and the theoretical insights of his scientific heir, the German Johannes Kepler (1571–1630). The movement reached its first climax in the system of the Italian Galileo (1564–1642), the greatest scientist of the age.

The period between 1500 and 1650 was an age of the great flowering of the vernacular literatures of Europe, especially in epic poetry and drama: in England, Edmund Spenser (ca. 1553–99) and William Shakespeare (1564–1616); in Italy, Ludovico Ariosto (1474–1533) and Torquato Tasso (1544–95); in Spain, Miguel de Cervantes (1547–1616), Lope de Vega (1562–1635), and Rodrigo Calderón (ca. 1576–1621); in Portugal, Luíz Vaz de Camoëns (ca. 1524–80). This turbulent age also saw the magnificent flowering of the visual and plastic arts, for example in the work of the painter and sculptor Michelangelo (1475–1564), the sculptor Bernini (1598–1680), and the painters Raphael, Titian (ca. 1490–1576), El Greco (ca. 1541–1614), Velázquez (1599–1660), Rubens (1577–1640), and Rembrandt (1606–69).

Expansion of the European World Hegemony (1650–1815)

In the century and a half after the Thirty Years' War, France dominated Europe both politically and culturally. In the Americas, European colonies matured, with the British dominating North America (though challenged by the French in the St. Lawrence and Mississippi valleys) and the Spanish controlling Mexico and Central America, much of the Caribbean, and South America. In Africa and the Middle East, Western influence grew primarily through trade, an increasing proportion of which was controlled by Britain. In Eurasia, Russia and China acquired huge land empires. In South Asia, British control of India evolved slowly, while the Dutch built a colonial empire in the vast archipelago now known as Indonesia.

Europe in Enlightenment and Revolution Partly in response to the religious controversies of the previous era, there had arisen the philosophical movement known as rationalism, which sought to reconstruct philosophy on the basis of "clear and distinct ideas" (René Descartes, 1596–1650). The Scientific Revolution reached a climax in the achievement of Isaac Newton (1642–1727), whose *Principia Mathematica* (1687) expressed in precise mathematical terms such key ideas as inertia, acceleration, the conservation of energy, and the force of gravity. Newton's commitment to scientific rigor built on the work of such earlier figures as Erasmus and Francis Bacon (1541–1626), and was spurred by competition with contemporaries such as Gottfried Leibniz (1646–1716).

The three streams of political philosophy, rationalism, and scientific reasoning flowed together in the movement known as the Enlightenment, whose adherents sought to understand the world in rational terms without appeal to traditional authority, whether of the divine right of rulers or religious doctrine. The Enlightenment contended that the world could be understood in purely rational terms, and that knowledge of the universe could be put to use for the benefit of humankind; this attitude lay behind the early mechanical and scientific discoveries that led to the Industrial Revolution, first in Britain and later in continental Europe and North America. Nevertheless, the era of the Enlightenment also remained an age of class privilege, economic inequity, and wealth derived from slavery and exploitation.

Louis XIV (r. 1661–1715) was an absolute monarch whose court at Versailles became the model for sovereigns across Europe, establishing a French cultural dominance backed by significant political and military power. In a series of four wars the "Sun King" expanded France's frontiers to the Rhine and his Bourbon dynasty to the throne of Spain. It took alliances of almost all Europe, organized principally by the Dutch stadtholder William III of Orange (r. 1672–1702), to limit his gains. Louis XIV's revocation of the Edict of Nantes (1685) forced the Protestant Huguenots to leave France for Holland, Britain, and Prussia, where they became industrious businessmen and artisans; through their dominance of publishing, especially, they contributed to the spread of the Enlightenment.

In England, the largely Protestant aristocracy, never comfortable with the Catholic faith of the restored Stuarts, drove James II (r. 1685–88) from his throne and invited William III of Orange (related by marriage to English royalty) to reign in his place as William III of England. This event is known as the Glorious Revolution; and it turned England essentially into an aristocratic republic dominated by Parliament, with an unwritten "constitution" that progressively limited the powers of the British monarchy.

In eastern Europe, the age of Louis XIV saw the decline of Polish and Ottoman power and the rise to dominance of Prussia and Russia in the Baltic region and the new Habsburg Empire to the southeast. With the Spanish Habsburgs sliding toward extinction and the Holy Roman Empire virtually obsolete by the Thirty Years' War, the Austrian Habsburgs drove the Ottomans out of Croatia and Hungary (1699) and took Galicia from Poland (1772). Meanwhile, the War of the Spanish Succession (1702–13) which established the Bourbons on the throne of Spain also detached from Spain its holdings in the Spanish Netherlands (roughly modern Belgium) and northern Italy (Milan and Tuscany), awarding both to the Austrian Habsburgs. The heart of Catholic Baroque culture in art and architecture and music, Austria became in the reign of Joseph II (1765–80) the seat of an enlightened despotism as well.

Brandenburg excelled in switching alliances: Frederick William "the Great Elector" (r. 1640–88) gained sovereignty in the Duchy of Prussia from Poland (1660); thus the Hohenzollern dynasty's holdings are usually called Prussia. Under Frederick II "the Great" (r. 1740–86), friend and patron of the French writer Voltaire (1694–1778), Prussia snatched Silesia from the Habsburgs (1748). Participating in the partitions of Poland (1772, 1793, 1795) the Hohenzollerns again doubled the size of their dynastic holdings.

The Seven Years' War (1756–63) was fought on three continents. In the European theater the alliances (Great Britain and Prussia against France, Austria, and Russia) fought to a draw; the war was won by the British overseas. In North America (where it was called the French and Indian War) and India, the British drove out the French and established their hegemony over the areas that had been under French control.

Great Britain and North America   Between the crises of the Cromwellian period (1643–60) and the Glorious Revolution (1688) the Stuart kings of England fostered new proprietary grants in the Hudson Valley, in Pennsylvania, and in the Carolinas. Thereafter, the North American colonies became habituated to self-government under their elected assemblies in a period, from the late 1600's to the 1760's, when the home government paid relatively little attention to them. Legally colonies, they became something more like provinces of Great Britain overseas. The Seven Years' War in North America was hard fought, and the death in victory of General Wolfe at the Battle of the Plains of Abraham (near Quebec, 1759) became a rallying point of British colonial sentiment. The war ended with Great Britain realizing nearly all of its objectives, the most important of which was that French Canada came under British rule. When in the aftermath of the war the British government attempted to organize its vast new North American holdings (in the "new imperial system"), the old coastal colonies were provoked into rebellion. Their grievances included British efforts to limit settlement beyond the Appalachians, to tax the colonists for the costs of administering the enlarged British holdings, and British appeasement of religious and other grievances of the culturally French portions of Canada. Colonial resistance to these British policies led to rebellion.

The publication of the Declaration of Independence (July 4, 1776) initiated a war that the British found impossible to win in the face of a highly motivated colonial populace supported by French military and financial assistance. The American Revolution was primarily a war for self-government; it did not produce immediate revolutionary social changes in the former colonies, though it did result in the replacement of a monarchy by a republic. The independence of the United States of America was recognized in the Peace of Paris (1783). (For North American developments afterward, see "History of the United States.")

The French Revolution and the Napoleonic Wars

France was the most prosperous state in Europe, but the long series of wars since 1660 combined with the clergy's and the aristocracy's exemption from taxation impoverished the monarchy. As a way out of the impasse, Louis XVI resurrected the old medieval Estates General (1789) in the hope of reaching consensus on reform measures. But the representatives transformed themselves into a constitutional convention called the National Assembly. After abolishing the feudal privileges of the aristocracy, they remodeled the French state into a constitutional monarchy, inspired to some extent by the recent experience of the United States. But they also confiscated church lands, dissolved the monasteries, and attempted to make the church a department of the state, thus alienating many Catholics.

The widespread appeal of the French Revolution to people across Europe frightened the monarchs and encouraged the National Assembly to declare war on them all. The new mass armies of the French, fired by ideology

and national pride, easily outmatched the old-fashioned armies of the monarchical states. At home, the war emergency and a revolt in a pro-royalist area (the Vendée) against the newly declared republic were used to justify a Committee of Public Safety led by Georges Danton (1759–94) and Maximilien Robespierre (1758–94). This committee quickly instituted a Reign of Terror (1793–94), marked by guillotine executions of thousands of aristocrats and "enemies of the revolution," beginning with the royal family, including Louis XVI and his wife, Marie Antoinette. The rule of the Directory (1795–99) that followed was overturned by its most daring and charismatic general, the Corsican adventurer and military genius Napoleon Bonaparte (1769–1821), who established a popular and military dictatorship (1799) first in the guise of a republic, then as the French Empire (1804–15).

Several coalitions of nations were formed to stop Napoleon, but he defeated all of them. At its peak, the empire dominated all of Europe from the English Channel to the Ottoman Empire, incorporating some former states into the empire, or turning others into satellites, or enlisting them as allies. But Britain's success in maintaining dominant power on the seas, together with a popular uprising in Spain supported by Britain, and the catastrophic failure of Napoleon's invasion of Russia (1812) began the crumbling of his empire. By 1814 the anti-French nationalisms that conquest had evoked and the recovery of the monarchs' courage brought Napoleon to defeat, and he was exiled to the Mediterranean island of Elba. When he escaped and returned to France in 1815, initially to a warm welcome from much of the French populace, he resumed his military campaigns but suffered his final defeat at Waterloo (1815) at the hands of the first duke of Wellington (1769–1852). Napoleon was exiled again to the remote island of St. Helena, in the south Atlantic, for the rest of his life.

At the time of the French Revolution, a revolution in European agriculture and industry was also under way, particularly in Great Britain. Landowners were enclosing the commons (the village lands tenant farmers used to graze cattle) and developing new crops, such as the white potato (originally from South America). This produced real gains in agricultural productivity, but also serious agrarian unemployment. Surplus rural workers migrated to the burgeoning cities, where inventors were creating the machinery (the spinning jenny, the waterframe, and the steam engine) that launched the Industrial Revolution. Thus an industrial workforce was born.

Spain, Portugal, and the Americas The Spanish New World colonies, with new viceroyalties of New Granada (1717; roughly modern Venezuela, Colombia, and Ecuador) and La Plata (1776; Bolivia, Paraguay, Uruguay, and Argentina) were governed paternalistically by the king of Spain, in whose name all regulations were sent to the viceroys. After about 1650 the Indian populations of the viceroyalties recovered rapidly from the disasters of the conquest period. While rule remained in the hands of "peninsulares" from the home country and, to a lesser degree, of "creoles" (colonists of Spanish descent), in the towns, the Indians' chief contact with Spanish culture was through church missionaries and bishops who constituted a spiritual elite. Brazil prospered as a Portuguese colony and by 1800 had a population larger than that of Portugal itself.

To the viceroyalty of New Spain (Mexico) was attached the Philippines. No one was sure where in the Pacific lay the treaty line of 1494 so that while the Philippines were in fact on the Portuguese side, it was Spain that claimed them in 1565, founding Manila in 1571, which became the western terminus for the famous "Manila galleon" trade in Mexican silver and Chinese silk and porcelain. In the course of the 17th and 18th centuries, voyages of English, Dutch, and Spanish mariners discovered the islands of the South Pacific: the Carolines, the Marshalls, Tasmania, New Zealand, and Australia; but before the late 18th century, no settlements of European colonists disturbed their original inhabitants.

Europe and Africa In Africa, the slave trade continued, peaking in the 1780's but with demand dropping decade by decade thereafter. In the early years of the 19th century, Britain, Denmark, and the United States abolished the trade, Britain actively but not always effectively trying to block the trade (still carried on by several other nations) along the African coast. In west Africa, there was an Islamic revival in the savanna as the Fulbe people, over the century after 1670, spread eastward toward Lake Chad in a series of campaigns against Hausa cities.

In the late 1700's, the Zulu nation of southern Africa employed trained infantry units armed with spears to establish a small empire over their neighbors, who still relied on the hurling of javelins. Near the southern tip of the continent, at the Cape of Good Hope, with its Mediterranean climate and its sparse indigenous population of Khoikhoi hunter-gatherers, the Dutch built a Dutch-speaking, Calvinist colony that by 1815 had a population of about 80,000. The pioneering *trekboers* who founded agrarian settlements beyond the Cape found their expansion limited by the resistance of the Xhosa people, and when the colony passed from the Dutch to the British (1814), British governors attempted to halt the expansion in the name of peace. In East Africa, trade reached inland as far as Lake Victoria. This was in the hands of the Nyamwezi people of Tanzania until after 1800 when it was absorbed into the trade network of Oman, an ally of Britain.

The Russian Empire While in one aspect the development of the Russian Empire was an eastward expansion of Europe, in another it was the creation of a huge Eurasian state menacing Europe. Russian pioneers had already reached the Pacific by 1637; expansion into Central Asia brought the Russians up against Chinese expansion westward into the same region. Peace was established in 1689 by the Treaty of Nerchinsk, which set the boundary along the peaks of the Stanovoi Mountains north of the great bend of the Amur River; the Russians evacuated a fort they had constructed on the Amur. This shifted Russian interests farther to the northeast, leading eventually to Russian settlements on the west coast of North America from Alaska to California (1805–1912).

Peter the Great (1689–1725) presided over a revolution from above that autocratically imposed upon his land western modes of manufacturing, political administration, military techniques, court manners, and dress. Russia had already taken eastern Ukraine including Kiev from Poland (1667), and in 1681 they added the portion that their allies the Ottomans had won in the same war. Peter's attempts to gain Azov—the warm-water port on the Black Sea that offered access to the Mediterranean—from the Ottoman Empire proved ineffectual. But in the Great Northern War against Sweden (1700–21), he proved more successful, establishing Russia on the Baltic and founding a new capital at St. Petersburg.

Under Catherine II "the Great" (r. 1762–96), Russia fought a war with the Ottoman Empire and achieved most of the objectives that Peter the Great had attempted a century earlier. The Treaty of Kuchuk Kainarji (1774) established Russia in the Crimea along the north of the Black Sea, granted navigation rights to Russia in Turkish waters, including the Bosporus and Dardanelles Straits into the Mediterranean, and provided a legal basis for Russia to intervene to protect Orthodox Christians in the provinces of Moldavia and Walachia. Catherine also participated in the partitions of Poland (1772, 1793, 1795), which obliterated that ancient state.

In a third stage of expansion during the Napoleonic Wars, Russia took Finland (1809) from Sweden and Bessarabia (1812) from the Ottomans. After repulsing Napoleon's 1812 invasion, Czar Alexander I (r. 1801–25) participated in the great coalition that at last brought Napoleon down, and in 1815 Russian troops participated in the occupation of Paris. Under terms laid down at the Congress of Vienna, central Poland was reconstituted as a nominally independent kingdom, but in a "personal alliance" with the Russian throne and Alexander as its king.

The Ottoman Empire in Decline

The Russian ascendancy was paralleled by Ottoman decline. Of the dozen sultans who ruled between 1648 and 1839 only Selim III (r. 1789–1807) was a man of intelligence and vigor. The period began with misleading signs of strength, as the Turks took Podolia from Poland (1672) and advanced against the Habsburgs, a campaign that culminated in the siege of Vienna (1683). The failure of the siege proved the start of a long slow sag in Ottoman fortunes that made it by the 19th century "the sick man of Europe." Facing war after war against Austria and Russia (often in tandem) in the west and Persia in the east, the empire yielded territory, strained its finances, and developed a defensive mentality. Its domestic power waned as well as frontier garrisons meant for defense had to be used to suppress rebellions and endemic banditry.

The year after the siege of Vienna was lifted, the Austrians were victorious in the second Battle of Mohacs (1684), and they were victorious again in the Battle of Zenta (1697); as a result, Hungary and Croatia were detached from Ottoman control. After the Treaty of Kuchuk Kainarji, the Black Sea was no longer a Turkish lake and Russian ships sailed freely through Ottoman waters. Egypt, temporarily independent in 1769, gained its autonomy in 1805, while Serbia became the first Christian Balkan state to gain autonomy. Even Arabia, the original homeland of Islam, slipped from Ottoman rule as the Saud clan provided political and economic support for the puritanical and fundamentalist Wahhabi movement, which sought a return to the theocracy of the original Islamic vision. The Saud clan controlled most of Arabia by the end of the 18th century, but the Egyptians defeated and overthrew them in a series of military campaigns (1811–19) and they remained out of power for most of the 19th century.

The Growth of British Influence in the Middle East and India

With the Portuguese control of the Indian Ocean trade routes eclipsed by Dutch and British competitors, and the Dutch concentrating their colonial efforts on the Malay Archipelago and the Spice Islands, British commercial interests grew ascendant in India. Bombay became the headquarters of the East India Company (1661) from which Calcutta was founded (1690). But British gains in India were not uncontested: the French founded their East India Company in 1664 and established a trading post at Pondicherry in 1674. The British gains in India compensated for the declining importance of their trade interests in Safavid Persia.

In the long reign of Aurangzeb (1659–1707), the Mughal empire had reached its greatest territorial extent, principally through conquests in the Deccan plateau in south-central India. But within the empire his rule was weak as local governors grew increasingly independent. The Maratha people of west-central India, under Raja Sivadi, established an independent Hindu state against which the emperor waged inconclusive war until his death. In the Punjab, in northwestern India, the Sikhs—followers of a religion founded by Guru Nanakh (ca. 1469–1539)—became dominant under the militant leadership of Govind Singh.

After Aurangzeb's death Mogul decline became precipitous. The Maratha state became the dominant Indian power, collecting taxes in southern India from 1720 onward. Nadir Shah's invasion (1738) wrested northwestern India from the Moguls, who were unable to reassert control after Nadir Shah's death. In the turmoil the European East India companies began forming private armies of Indian troops ("sepoys") under European officers. After the War of the Austrian Succession (1746–48) French forces ruled virtually the entire south. But in the Indian theater of the Seven Years' War (1756–63), Robert Clive (1725–1774) roundly defeated the French; the Treaty of Paris left but a few holdings to the French. In the aftermath, the English East India Company gained direct control of the rich province of Bengal (1764).

During this struggle the Afghans invaded from the northwest, establishing their rule over the Maratha domains and the Punjab (1761–62). Faced with a choice between the Afghans and the British, most Indian princes gravitated toward the British. The trend toward British domination in India was not halted by Parliament's India Act (1784), which was intended to bring the company under government control and to prohibit it from interfering in Indian affairs or from engaging in war. Between 1786 and 1813, the company's governors-general began a judicial system, gained control over the foreign affairs of most southern principalities in return for British protection, and entered into treaties with Persia and Afghanistan.

The term British Empire probably exaggerates the degree to which Great Britain exercised direct control over India in the 18th and early 19th centuries. In reality, the company ruled directly only certain territories whose princes could not (at least in the judgment of the British) secure peace and order, and established treaty obligations with other princes. There were as yet no Protestant missionaries in India (although Portuguese Catholic missionaries had tended to the needs of Christian communities in Goa and other enclaves for some 300 years), nor the rule of British law. A thin layer of foreign administrators and merchants assumed an odd combination of feelings of British superiority and the trappings of Oriental wealth; Indian culture was largely ignored by the British. To the majority of Indians, meanwhile, the foreigners were outside the caste system and largely irrelevant to the concerns of daily life.

China and Japan, 1650–1800

The Manchu emperors of China, having established the Qing Dynasty, adapted themselves rapidly to the ancient Chinese system of imperial government, maintaining the examination system for the bureaucracy (though sometimes doubling officials, one Manchu, one Chinese). So serene and sensible (and nontheological) did the Manchu state appear to many European Enlightenment political thinkers that it was often held up as a kind of ideal model for the reform of European monarchy.

Taiwan was annexed in 1683 and Tibet was gradually brought under Chinese control (1705–51) with the emperor managing succession of the Dalai Lamas, who functioned as both religious and temporal rulers of Tibet. But the great expansion was into Central Asia, settled diplomatically with the Russians in 1689 to China's advantage. All this was the work of the Kangxi Emperor (1661–1722), a contemporary of Louis XIV. The papacy's finding (1715) that reverence shown toward Confucius or toward one's ancestors was incompatible with Catholic belief led China's rulers to ban proselytizing by Christian missionaries in 1720, though some Jesuits were encouraged to stay on in China as experts in astronomy, painting, architecture, and other technical fields.

Under the Qianlong Emperor (r. 1736–95), China forced Burma (1769) and Nepal (1792) to recognize Chinese overlordship. Burma had only recently been reunited (1753) with British assistance, so the relationship between Burma and China became an avenue of British influence. In Annam (Vietnam), a Confucian ruling elite adopted many features of Chinese culture and recognized China's suzerainty, but the country's rulers permitted Catholic missions, which met with surprising success, especially after Gia Long (r. 1802–20) emerged as emperor of Vietnam.

The whole period was for China one of expansion, economically as well as territorially. In agriculture new crops from the Americas (maize and sweet potatoes, as well as the Mexican chili pepper, which had become an essential element of many Asian cuisines in the 16th century) provided a larger and more diversified food supply, though by the end of the 18th century population was once again pressing up against the limits of food production. Trade with Europe, initially carried in Portuguese ships but later open to ships of all European nations through the Portuguese colony of Macao, was based upon Chinese exports of tea, silk, and porcelain, the latter increasingly produced on a mass basis in imperial and private kilns. There was also some small-scale trade with Japan, carried both by Chinese craft and the Dutch merchants authorized to trade at Nagasaki.

But China showed little interest in the outside world. European trade was restricted after the mid-18th century to the port of Canton, under onerous conditions. No substantial Chinese market for European manufactured goods developed, nor did many Chinese intellectuals show strong interest in European culture. The late 19th-century mission of the British diplomat Lord George MacCartney, which sought diplomatic relations and improved conditions of trade between China and Great Britain, was met with indifference. China, oblivious even to the superiority of European military technology, would soon suffer badly from its imperial self-satisfaction, as Britain began balancing its China trade deficit with a massive trade in opium from Bengal to Canton.

In Japan, the splendid isolation of the Tokugawa period continued. But the internal peace that they enforced left the samurai warriors functionless, increasingly dissolute and in debt to the thriving merchant class. The heyday of the latter in the Genroku Period (1688–1704) led to a flourishing of Japanese literature, including haiku poetry, especially under the master Matsuo Basho (1644–1694), plays by Chikamatsu Monzaemon and others for the Kabuki and Bunraku (puppet theater) stages, and the development of popular art in the form of woodblock prints celebrating the pleasures of urban life. In the last decades of the Tokugawa period there were signs of restiveness against the shogunate, not only from the great clans excluded from power but from the imperial court as well, both merging patriotic feeling and imperial loyalty with a revival of the Shinto religion. Informed of world affairs by the Dutch merchants, who were required to report annually to the shogun, many Japanese increasingly worried about the danger of the Westerners to Japan's isolated development.

Triumph and Tragedy of Western Hegemony (1815–1945)

With the defeat of Napoleon in 1815, Europe entered 100 years of general peace—the so-called Pax Britannica. Europe underwent reforms of land tenure and improvements in agricultural technology, the development of industrial capitalism and the spread of liberal and democratic institutions, and spread its imperial influence worldwide. But the century of peace was followed by 30 years of tumultuous upheaval. Two world wars were waged with new weapons of mass destruction; the interval between them was marked by the subjection of much of Europe to grim totalitarian domination. By 1945, Europe lay devastated, its fate and that of the world in the hands of the two atomic superpowers, liberal-democratic America and communist Russia.

Europe: The Rise of Nationalism
After a quarter-century of exhausting warfare against revolutionary France and the imperial ambitions of Napoleon, the conservative monarchs and statesmen of Britain, Austria, Prussia, and Russia made a generous peace with France at the 1815 Congress of Vienna, restoring the Bourbon dynasty but hedging France's borders with an enlarged Netherlands to the north, the Prussians on the Rhine, and the Habsburgs in northern Italy. The achievements of the Congress of Vienna owed much to the Austrian diplomat Prince Metternich (1773–1859), who brokered the establishment of the Concert of Europe, a series of international conferences (to which France was soon admitted) to regulate European affairs, initiating the longest sustained general European peace since Rome's Antonine emperors in the second century A.D. Fearing revolution as the source of war and therefore a threat to themselves, they suppressed liberal and nationalist organizations and sent troops into Italy and Spain to prop up their tottering monarchies. But Britain, supporting America's Monroe Doctrine barring

European interference in the affairs of the New World, prevented Spain from intervening effectively against the revolts in Latin America. With the slow collapse of the Ottoman Empire in the Balkans, the powers supported an independent Greece (1829) and autonomy for Serbia, Moldavia, and Walachia.

Liberal revolts in 1830 led to independence for Belgium and a change of dynasty for France; in the same year, however, Russia crushed a Polish revolt and absorbed that state into her empire. Britain, without revolution, carried out a liberal reform of her constitution (1832). Parliament was reformed by abolishing "rotten" or underpopulated boroughs and expanding the electorate by 50 percent (from a tiny base), especially in the new manufacturing centers, by extending the franchise to property-owners and lease-holders of modest means. But Parliament was still dominated by rural constituencies, and it took two more Reform Acts (1867 and 1884) to extend the franchise fairly to urban populations. Equally significant was the repeal (1846) of the Corn Laws, which for centuries had restricted the importation of staple foods into Britain; the repeal was a victory for manufacturers, who supported free trade.

The year 1848 saw liberal and nationalist revolts in many of the capitals of the German and Italian principalities and of the Habsburg realms. Yet none of the 1848 uprisings succeeded in turning monarchies into republics, as the armies remained loyal to their sovereigns. Still the uprisings of 1848 had lasting effects, as feudal restrictions on land tenure, which had locked the peasantry into an unfree status, were abolished throughout central Europe. The 1848 revolt in Paris led to the establishment of a brief Second Republic, then, in a revival of Bonapartism, a Second Empire (1852–70) under Napoleon III (Louis Napoleon Bonaparte, 1808–73).

In July 1853 Russia seized some Ottoman territories in the Crimea. This was opposed by a British-French-Sardinian coalition in support of the Ottoman Empire, leading to the Crimean War (1853–56). The inconclusive war showcased the inadequacy of traditional weapons and tactics in the face of more modern weaponry, including new-style warships, backed by telegraphic communications and rapid troop movements by railroad. The war's high death toll from disease and infected wounds led to Florence Nightingale's reforms of British military hospitals.

The years 1848–61 marked the Italian *Risorgimento* (resurgence). The key figures in the struggle for Italian

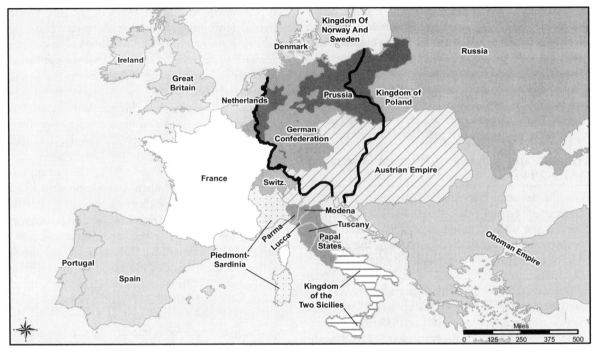

Europe in 1815

unification were the radical republican Giuseppe Mazzini (1805–72), Giuseppe Garibaldi (1807–82), who had spent his youth fighting in South America's wars of independence but who turned away from republicanism to embrace a pragmatic constitutional monarchy, and Camillo Benso di Cavour (1810–61), the supporter of the would-be Italian king. After a series of adept military and diplomatic moves, in which Louis Napoleon rendered crucial assistance to Piedmont's conquest of most of Italy, Victor Emmanuel II (1820–78) of Sardinia was crowned king of the Kingdom of Italy in 1861. Transformed from a collection of weak states and dependencies, by 1870 the Kingdom of Italy included Venice and Rome as well, and had become a player in the game of 19th-century European international relations. An incidental effect was to deprive the papacy of its secular territories, except for the tiny enclave of the Vatican in Rome.

The 1870 completion of Italian unification was accomplished with the aid of one of the 19th century's most dominant figures, Prussia's Otto von Bismarck (1815–98), the unifier of Germany. In a series of brief wars, Bismarck incorporated all of non-Habsburg Germany into the German Empire, proclaimed in 1871. In the process Bismarck forced the reform of the Austrian empire, in effect excluding Austria from German affairs and leading to the establishment in 1867 of the "Dual Monarchy" of Austria-Hungary. Another of Bismarck's wars (the Franco-Prussian War, 1870–71), took Alsace and Lorraine from France, toppled Napoleon III, and led to the formation of France's Third Republic (1871–1940).

In one decade the map of Europe had been transformed, its most powerful state the new Germany which, with rapid industrialization, became stronger still in the years that led up to World War I.

The Troubled Independence of Latin America

The impact of the Napoleonic wars upon Europe's transatlantic provinces (and the newly independent United States as well) was profound. Haiti maintained its independence, gained in 1794 as the result of a slave insurrection-turned-republican movement, against Napoleon's attempt to reconquer it. This in turn led to Napoleon's abandonment of any scheme for a New World empire; Louisiana was therefore sold to the United States. When Joseph Bonaparte (brother of Napoleon) ascended the throne of Spain (1808), Spanish America was thrown into confusion: which king to obey? Juntas loyal to the Bourbon king Ferdinand VII, led by creoles such as

Simon Bolivar (1783–1830) and José de San Martín (1778–1850), resisted French rule at first, but then turned against the absolutism of the restored Ferdinand in whose name they had first risen up. In colony after colony the juntas' armies fought for and won their independence: La Plata (Argentina, 1810), Chile (1818), New Granada (Ecuador, Colombia, Panama, and Venezuela, 1819), Peru (1821). In separate and more complicated developments, Mexican and Brazilian independence followed in 1822.

The Monroe Doctrine (1823) of the United States, which suited the interests of and was supported by Great Britain, shielded the new states from Spanish repression. But nothing could shield them from the effects of their own inexperience in politics (an effect of Spanish imperial centralization) or from boundary disputes (for New World boundaries too were purely Spanish creations) or from the internal struggles of local leaders (caudillos) seeking autonomy within the new republics. Thus independence was followed by a long period of war, civil war, insurrection, and/or coup.

When the trade links with Spain were cut, the new states found a welcome from Great Britain for their products. British investment fostered mining and industrial development; American investment entered late in the 19th century. The development in the 1880's of adequate methods of refrigeration on steamships meant that beef could join wheat and sugar and coffee as exports. The needs of the Allies in World War I for massive increases in raw materials brought a great increase in trade; large-scale postwar investment from the United States both in industry and in plantation agriculture helped continue economic growth, though this declined sharply after the start of the Great Depression in 1929.

This expansion brought social tension through the growth of both a middle class and agricultural and industrial working classes, adding new elements to the older political instability. In the 1930's governments in Mexico, Argentina, and several other Latin American states followed the "popular front" or "corporate state" models of Europe, and followed Europe's lead also in relying too much on political strongmen. In the Caribbean, the United States played a dominant role, whether as "policeman" or, as after 1934, "good neighbor."

European Empires in Africa For 60 years after the Napoleonic wars, Europeans evinced only small interest in Africa. Liberal economic thought supported free trade rather than empire. Trading forts dotted the west African coasts,

while steamboats penetrated only somewhat farther inland and missionaries began evangelization on a small scale. "Cash crop" agriculture depended on European markets for such commodities as nuts and palm products, especially oil for lighting and machine lubrication, but in this early period the plantations tended to be domestic ventures of various African kings and chiefs, who were, with the drying up of the trade in slaves, eager for new sources of revenue. In the south, the expansion of the Zulu nation after 1818 led to disruptions lasting into the 1850's while among the Boers in the Dutch colony at the Cape of Good Hope, the British ban on slavery provoked the Great Trek of some 10,000 settlers into the grassy interior plateau known as the high veld, where they came into conflict with indigenous peoples. This movement of Dutch farmers out of the old Cape Colony paved the way for the arrival of new British settlers and set the stage for later conflicts between the two main groups of Europeans in south Africa. On the east coast the sultan of Oman moved his capital to Zanzibar, the better to control his network of trade in cloves and slaves; the continuation of the slave trade brought increasing British estrangement from their protégé. Along the Mediterranean coast of North Africa, the Ottoman Empire was nominally sovereign though rule in fact was exercised by local beys and sultans whose revenues depended largely on the profits from harassing merchant ships, or accepting payments for safe passage. This provoked armed reactions first by the United States in the Tripolitan War (1801–1805) and again in 1815, by an Anglo-Dutch fleet in the latter year, and finally by the French who in 1830 occupied Algiers and a few other coastal cities.

About 1880 a group of French projects—a railways scheme at Dakar, new trading posts on the Ivory Coast and north of the Congo river—alarmed the other powers into the "scramble for Africa," which brought Britain and Portugal and later Germany into a contest to annex territory, principally to prevent the others from doing the same and gaining some unknown and unpredictable benefit. The Congress of Berlin (1885) sought to put some order into the competition, and by 1900 the entire continent had been divided between European powers, save for the colony of freed American slaves in Liberia and the ancient Christian empire of Ethiopia. Colonial theorists gained the ear of Western governments for grand schemes of great belts of territory, the French to stretch from Dakar to the Red Sea, the British from Capetown to Cairo—even though the construction of the Suez Canal (1859–69) had rendered such schemes economically pointless. One specific and concrete interest was the discovery of gold and diamond deposits in the republic of Transvaal, which led to Britain's conquest of the Boer republics in the Boer War (1889–1901) and her formation (1910) of the Union of South Africa, which through elections Boers soon governed.

The End of Imperial China and the Rise of Japan

If Africa had not yet felt the full impact of European sovereignty, Asia's experience of European rule was no illusion. British rule was established in India, Burma, and Malaya, the Netherlands' in Indonesia, America's in the islands of the Pacific (Hawaii, Samoa, and later the Philippines) and France's in Indochina. Two new provinces of Western civilization grew in Australia and New Zealand. China underwent yet another cycle of imperial decline but with the new element of the presence of the "southern barbarians" (the Europeans) and the aggressive designs of a suddenly modernized Japan.

A succession of wars and rebellions marked the decline of China's power and prestige in the 19th century. Her attempts to maintain Canton as the sole port for Western trade and to end Britain's sale of opium led to the Opium War (1839–42) and a thorough British victory. The Treaty of Nanking opened four more cities to trade and ended the "Canton system." Western nations were now accepted as China's equals rather than treated as tribute-bearing "barbarian" states. A uniform tariff of 5 percent was levied on foreign trade; in addition, Hong Kong was ceded to the United Kingdom. In the aftermath of the war, in 1844 and 1845, the United States gained the right of "extraterritoriality" (exemption from Chinese law) for its citizens, soon extended to all the Western states, and the French gained toleration for Catholic Christianity, soon extended to Protestant Christians as well.

The social and economic dislocations caused by the Opium War in south China culminated in the Taiping Rebellion (1851–64), led by Hong Xiuquan, a failed examination candidate who, having read some Christian missionary pamphlets, imagined himself to be the younger brother of Jesus Christ. A charismatic figure, he raised a huge army and seized much of southern and central China, including the city of Nanjing. To put down the rebellion the Qing emperor resorted to the very dangerous expedient of allowing provincial governors-general to raise their own military units; these were effective but would prove destabilizing in the future. Some Western military assistance helped keep the Taipings away from the trading port of Shanghai.

At the same time China experienced three other major rebellions: Muslim uprisings in the northwest and in Yunnan Province in the southwest, and the millenarian Nian Rebellion in the north-central plains. Total loss of life from all of these rebellions exceeded 20 million; the dynasty itself barely survived. In 1856, in the midst of this turmoil, the Chinese were forced to fight a second war with Europeans, when the British provoked a small affray called the Arrow War. This was settled by the Treaty of Tientsin in 1858, which resulted in the opening of yet another 11 ports, the legalization of the opium trade, and the collection of China's customs by Great Britain. When the Chinese court attempted to delay implementation of the treaty, a British expeditionary force burned the imperial Summer Palace, near Bejing, in 1860 to punish the emperor and force his compliance. With customs revenues under British control, Sir Robert Hart became, in effect, China's finance minister through the years 1863–1908.

Japan's attempt to gain concessions like those of the Western powers and to challenge Chinese control over the Manchu tributary state of Korea led to the third of the China's disastrous foreign wars. Losing the Sino-Japanese War (1894–95), China had to cede Taiwan and certain mainland territories to Japan and recognize the independence of Korea, a prelude to that kingdom's annexation as a Japanese colony in 1910. Meanwhile, in Indochina the French ignored the protests of China's Qing Dynasty and established protectorates over Annam (1883) and, right on China's border, Tonkin (1893).

After an unsuccessful attempt in 1898 to reform the imperial government, followed by the abortive, anti-Western Boxer Rebellion (1900), discontent with the feebleness of the Manchu government led to the Chinese Revolution (1911), led by Sun Yat-sen (1866–1925). Forced by Western pressure to put aside his leadership of a new China, Sun yielded the presidency of the new Chinese Republic to a Qing Dynasty general, Yuan Shikai (1859–1916). General Yuan promptly made plans to establish yet another new dynasty with himself as founding emperor, but his death permitted the republic to continue, though rent by warlordism and anarchy made more dangerous by modern weapons and mass political organizations.

Japan's rise to great power status was rooted in an extraordinary adaptability. After the American Commodore Matthew Perry forced the opening of Japan to Western trade in 1853–54, antiforeign and pro-imperial sentiment grew until in 1867 young patriots at the court of the teenage emperor Mutsuhito (r. 1867–1912) felt strong enough to end the shogunate and restore imperial control. The emperor's reigning name, Meiji, gave the movement its name: the Meiji Restoration. During his long rule, Japan embarked on a course of furious imitation of Western ways, as earlier they had sometimes imitated the Chinese. The pre-1867 isolationist slogan "revere the emperor, expel the barbarians" gave way to "enrich the state, strengthen the military," a goal realized through the energetic adoption of Western science, technology, industry, and arms. Japan's feudal class structure was abolished; some former samurai declined into poverty, while others became enthusiastic and successful entrepreneurs. The topmost layer of the old samurai class was reconstituted in 1884 as a Japanese peerage so that there might be an upper house on the British model when the Meiji Constitution (1889) established a Diet. But it was the military and industrial spheres that showed most rapid advance, providing the basis for triumphs over China (1895) and much more surprisingly Russia (1905), the takeover of some German holdings in the Pacific and in China's Shandong Province during World War I, and the incursions against China in the 1930's.

India Under the Raj

In India, the British kept up the fiction of Mughal rule but proceeded to act more and more like a sovereign power: commencing the repair of the Mogul system of canals (1818) and building roads and irrigation projects; replacing Persian as the language of law courts with English in the higher courts and local tongues in local courts; founding schools whose curriculum was European and whose language of instruction was English; and intervening more and more in matters of local custom and culture.

In the 1840's, warfare in Afghanistan, in the Sind, and against the Sikhs made Britain a true imperial power, the ruling authority in India, protecting Indian princes from subversion and aggression, and annexing territory when princely families died out. After the Great Mutiny (1857–58) of the sepoys (Indian soldiers in the British army), Britain banished the last of the Moguls. Twenty years later came the symbolic climax, the proclamation (1877) of Queen Victoria (r. 1837–1901) as empress of India.

At the same time the British were establishing executive and legislative councils with Indian representation and courts with Indian justices sitting on the bench. And in both world wars, Indian troops fought loyally and with valor on the British side. Nevertheless, the tides of nationalism and anticolonialism that swept through all of Asia in the early 20th century brought a new measure of political awareness to many Indians. The Indian National Congress, first established in 1885, came increasingly under the influence of Mahatma Gandhi (1869–1948). His campaigns of civil disobedience in 1921 and in 1930 presaged the post-war demands that would signal the end of British rule.

Australia and New Zealand

More enduring than British India or British rule in Singapore (1819) or Burma (1886) as vehicles of European influence were Australia, a convict colony founded in 1788, that was gradually transformed by generous land grants into the Commonwealth of Australia (1901), and New Zealand, where after 1840 assisted immigration and land grants brought dominion status by 1907. Both fought loyally among Britain's allies in both of the world wars. As in the Americas, in Australia and New Zealand the rights of indigenous inhabitants were ignored in the rush of European settlement; Aborigine rights (in Australia) and Maori rights (in New Zealand) are important political issues in both countries today.

The First World War, 1914–18

World War I had its roots in strains that had been accumulating in Europe since the late 19th century. One of Bismarck's political objectives was to keep France isolated. He encouraged its colonial expansion to compensate for diminished status in Europe and in the hope that imperial rivalry with Britain would keep those western states apart. He hoped for similar results from Russian and British rivalry in Persia and Afghanistan. To strengthen Germany's position in Europe, he formed the Triple Alliance of Germany, Austria-Hungary, and Italy.

However, France and Russia allied in 1894; a decade later, after settling colonial issues that had nearly brought them to war, France and Britain came to a "friendly understanding." The triangle of alliances that Bismarck had sought to prevent was completed in 1907, when Britain and Russia agreed to establish spheres of influence in Persia. Bismarck's diplomacy was undone by the aggressive foreign policy of Kaiser Wilhelm II (r. 1888–1918) and a naval arms race with Britain.

While colonial disputes generally proved amenable to diplomatic solution, in the Balkans events moved beyond any statesman's ability to control. In the disintegration of Ottoman power there, Serbia, Romania, and Montenegro became independent in 1878 and Bulgaria in 1908. The powers consistently checked Russian advances in the Balkans while the influence of Austria-Hungary grew. Struggling for territory from the Ottomans and from one another, the Balkan states fought a series of three wars in 1912, 1913, and 1914. It was the third, which began with the assassination of Austria's Archduke Franz Ferdinand (1863–1914) in Sarajevo by a Serbian nationalist, that expanded into the catastrophe of World War I.

Outside Europe fighting was slight: German holdings in the Pacific and Africa were taken by British and French imperial forces, and German concessions in China were seized by Japan; Russian and British forces engaged the Ottomans in Mesopotamia and Armenia; and Western-backed Arab revolts further weakened Ottoman strength. But in Belgium and northern France, armies fought through four years of horrifying trench warfare, and on the gigantic eastern front immense armies clashed without resolution until 1917. In February-March of that year a moderate (Menshevik) revolution led by Aleksandr F. Kerensky and others put an end to centuries of czarist autocracy; Nicholas II (r. 1894–1917) abdicated on March 15 and a Provisional Government was established. But the moderates were progressively undermined by the Bolsheviks, led by Vladimir I. Lenin (1870–1924), who seized power in a coup on November 6 (October 24 by the old calendar, hence the term "October Revolution"). Nicholas II and his family were arrested; they were executed, apparently on Lenin's orders, on July 16, 1918. Kerensky fled the country, and many moderate leaders were arrested. The Bolshevik regime took Russia out of the world war, but the country was soon plunged into a civil war between Reds (Bolsheviks and other communists) and Whites (supporters of the old regime). The effect on World War I of Russia's withdrawal from the east was offset in the west by the entry of the United States, provoked by Germany's resumption of unrestricted submarine warfare in a futile attempt to escape the noose of Britain's naval blockade. The fighting ended on November 11, 1918. (see pp. 265–68 for a history of the war.)

The Aftermath of World War I

Besides its immense cost in treasure and blood—more than 8 million died in battle and 6 million civilians perished—the war overturned the old European state system as four empires collapsed and were partitioned. Germany, under the Treaty of Versailles (1919) emerged as the Weimar Republic with small territorial losses to France and a resurrected Poland, but burdened with the war guilt clauses and the immense financial reparations they were meant to justify. Russia lost all her western gains since Peter the Great, retreating eastward to build a Leninist communist state on the founda-

tions of the 1917 revolution. Austria-Hungary disappeared utterly, two little republics maintaining only the names of those once great states. By 1923 in Asia Minor a one-party Turkish Republic emerged under Mustafa Kemal Ataturk (1818–1938), replacing the last vestiges of the Ottoman Empire.

The successor states in eastern Europe, whether republican or monarchical in form, readily adopted the parliamentary government of the victorious western Allies, which, in the years after 1848, had steadily democratized the franchise. But most contained substantial ethnic minorities whose rivalries poisoned parliamentary life; tariff barriers that arose everywhere fragmented the old common markets of the empires they replaced, protecting inefficient industries and penalizing those that were efficient; and in agriculture depression was chronic.

To the east the czarist Russian Empire was replaced by the somewhat smaller but still vast Soviet Union. With the death of Lenin in 1924 the dictatorship of the Communist Party turned increasingly into the personal dictatorship of Joseph Stalin (1879–1953), who oversaw the murderous collectivization of agriculture and the forced industrialization of the Five Year Plans, then purged the party, the army and the secret police of all but his own men. Millions died.

Western and central Europe seemed sheltered from these grim developments by the "cordon sanitaire" of the new states of east-central Europe. After a period of postwar adjustment, prosperity returned to the Western democracies, especially in Germany, whose adherence to the Locarno Treaties (1925) presaged an enduring peace. Yet in Italy, whose wartime sacrifices seemed unrewarded by territorial gains and whose economy seemed to dissolve into the chaos of socialist and anarchist and capitalist violence, there arose in 1922 the second (after Lenin) of Europe's interwar dictators, Benito Mussolini (1883–1945). His fascist movement promised a halfway house between liberal individualism and communist class war, stressing a belligerent nationalism with a corporative economy. Mussolini's personal charisma obscured the bombast and incoherence of the Fascist program.

The needs of the Allies in World War I for massive increases in raw materials brought a great increase in trade. Large-scale postwar investment from the United States both in industry and in plantation agriculture helped continue economic growth but with serious decline after 1929 in the rate of growth.

In Latin America, postindependence economic growth and expanding trade with Europe from the late 19th century onward had brought social tension through the growth of both a middle class and agricultural and industrial working classes, adding new elements to the older political instability. In the 1930's governments in Mexico, Argentina, and several other Latin American states followed the "popular front" or "corporate state" models of Europe, and followed Europe's lead also in relying too much on political strongmen. In the Caribbean, the interests of the United States predominated whether as "policeman" or, as after 1934, "good neighbor."

In China, the Nationalist Party of the revolutionary leader Dr. Sun Yat-sen (the Kuomintang, KMT; modern spelling Guomindang), came after his death in 1925 under the control of his Moscow-trained general, Chiang Kai-shek (1887–1975), whose armies gave the KMT military control of south China. Chiang's Northern Expedition (1927–29) reunited most of the country under Nationalist rule, but his decision to try to exterminate his nominal Communist Party allies beginning in Shanghai in 1927 led to a failed series of Communist uprisings and their retreat to the northwest in the Long March (1932–34). In their new stronghold of Yan'an, Mao Zedong (1893–1976) emerged as the party leader and Chiang's chief rival. Their struggle was submerged in the 1930's by the need to oppose Japanese aggression.

In Japan, the western-style parliamentary government that had been established in the late 19th century broke down in the reign of the Meiji Emperor's grandson Hirohito (always known in Japan by his reign-name, the Showa Emperor, r. 1926–89), as military cliques and gangs came to control government after government and political violence became the order of the day. Japan occupied Manchuria as a protectorate in 1931–32 and created the puppet state of Manchukuo in 1934. Japan's military leaders, alarmed by the December, 1936 declaration by China's Nationalist and Communist parties of an anti-Japanese United Front, used a minor military engagement near Beijing in July, 1937 as an excuse to invade northern China—the beginning of World War II in Asia. The invaders quickly routed China's defense forces, using such tactics as the extensive aerial bombardment of Shanghai and the "Rape of Nanjing," an orgy of atrocities against civilians in that city in November, 1937. Chiang Kai-shek's Nationalist government retreated to Chongqing where, with American aid, it survived throughout the war.

The Second World War (1939–45) In much of Europe, the collapse of the world economy after 1929 was exacerbated by the social and ethnic divisions of the successor states, their boundary grievances, and the real or imagined fear of communist revolution. Most of Europe outside the monarchies of the north and west turned to right-wing authoritarian regimes which, though often called "fascist," made little pretense of being ideologically based; they resembled Italy less than they did Latin America. Germany presented a very different and very grievous case; there, the 1933 elevation of Adolf Hitler (1889–1945) to the office of chancellor proved that thuggery, the repellent doctrines of National Socialism (including virulent anti-Semitism), and German nationalistic resentment over the post–World War I settlement were sufficient to establish the Nazi dictatorship in the heart of Europe.

The Western democracies dithered, deluded themselves, and sought peace through appeasement. Having neglected their own military capabilities while Hitler was rebuilding the German war machine, there were few realistic alternatives to appeasement in any case. Domestically, the German persecution of Jews accelerated throughout the 1930's, while Hitler, bent on overturning the Versailles settlement, successfully remilitarized the Rhineland (1936) and absorbed Austria (in a sudden campaign called the Anschluss) and the ethnically German parts of Czechoslovakia (1938), then turned the remainder of Czechoslovakia into a satellite, took the city of Memel from Lithuania, and began demands on Poland (1939). In August 1939 Germany and Russia agreed to partition Poland yet again. With Hitler's invasion of Poland in September, World War II began in Europe. (The Asian phase of World War II had begun two years earlier.)

The European war was, until 1941, an unbroken series of totalitarian triumphs; by June of 1940, when France fell, all of Europe outside Britain was neutral or an ally or satellite of Germany. But in June of 1941 Hitler invaded Russia, and in December Hitler's ally, Japan, attacked the U.S. Navy base at Pearl Harbor, Hawaii. The attack was designed to cripple the American Pacific fleet, thus giving the Japanese a free hand for the invasion of southeast Asia, which brought Japanese forces by mid-1942 to occupy the American Philippines, the Dutch East Indies, British Hong Kong, Malaya, Singapore, and Burma, while French Indochina and independent Thailand collaborated. But the American carrier fleet survived the attack on Pearl Harbor; having failed to defeat the United States in a single blow, the Japanese war effort gradually was ground down by American industrial and military might.

In Europe, German armies penetrated as far east as Leningrad, Moscow and Stalingrad before being fought to a stalemate on the Eastern Front. The grand alliance of Britain and the U.S. with the USSR forced Nazi Germany to fight a two-front war, which ultimately spelled utter defeat in May of 1945—but not before Germany killed 6 million Jews and a like number of Gypsies, homosexuals, handicapped people, Communists, and other "undesirables" during the Holocaust. In Asia, the great powers, especially America, kept up the illusion that China was a great power with Chiang as its ruler, which helped to keep Japanese troops tied down on the Asian mainland. In August 1945, atomic bomb attacks on Hiroshima and Nagasaki, major Japanese cities, hastened Japan's surrender, and World War II came to its end. The United States and the Soviet Union, with Great Britain a very junior partner, bestrode the globe. Japan itself was occupied by American forces. In China, civil war led to the establishment of a Communist state within four years of the end of the war, while Eastern Europe came under the domination of the Soviet Union. A new era in world history had begun.

The Modern World (1945–Present)

Planning the Postwar World   By the end of 1943, it had become obvious to the leaders of the Allied Powers that, barring some completely unforeseen development, Germany and Japan would be defeated in World War II. The allied leaders—Churchill, Roosevelt, and Stalin—met in a series of conferences not only to plan the later stages of the war, but to establish the outlines of the postwar world. Conferences at Cairo (1943), Casablanca (1944), and Yalta (1945) affirmed the policy of pursuing the war until Germany and Japan had surrendered unconditionally; established a four-power (U.S., U.K., France, and USSR) occupation of Germany; gave the United States responsibility for the occupation of Japan; and permitted the European colonial powers (principally Britain, France, and the Netherlands) to reestablish their empires. The Yalta Conference also had the effect of creating a Soviet sphere of influence in Eastern Europe that would soon be exploited (against the wishes of the Western powers) to install communist governments throughout the region. The Potsdam Conference (1945) recognized the division of Germany into East and West. In effect the cold war had begun before World War II had even ended.

Other wartime conferences had a lasting positive impact on the postwar world. The Dumbarton Oaks Conference (1944) laid down the basic principles of the United Nations; the U.N. Charter was written at the San Francisco Conference in the spring of 1945, signed on June 26, and ratified by the requisite number of countries in October of that year. Meanwhile, the Bretton Woods Conference (1944) established the International Monetary Fund and the International Bank for Reconstruction and Development (the World Bank), both governed by their member countries and associated with the U.N. as specialized agencies; these immediately began to play a vital role in postwar economic development and financial stabilization.

Realities of the Postwar World   The occupation of Germany quickly devolved into a hostile confrontation between the USSR and the Western Allies in a rigidly divided country. Despite earlier agreements, East Germany was cut off from contact with the west, while Berlin, an enclave under four-power occupation surrounded by East Germany, also was divided into eastern and western zones. The American occupation of Japan, designed initially to turn defeated Japan into a democratic, demilitarized, and largely deindustrialized backwater, changed course to promote greater economic reconstruction as Japan came to be seen as a potential ally in the face of communist gains in the Chinese Civil War and the establishment in North Korea of a communist government under Soviet sponsorship.

The reaffirmation of British colonial rule in India, and of French rule in northern and western Africa, and especially the reestablishment of colonial regimes in areas that had been under Japanese control during the war (French Indochina, British Malaya, Dutch Indonesia) was widely resented, and engendered armed independence movements in many of those colonies. America's speedy honoring of its pledge of independence for the Philippines (1946) had the effect of inspiring more urgent calls for decolonization elsewhere.

In Europe, wartime destruction and economic privation began to be alleviated in 1947 with the inauguration of the Marshall Plan, an American foreign-aid program aimed at the rapid rebuilding of the noncommunist countries of Europe. The signatories to the agreement (Austria, Belgium, Denmark, France, West Germany, Great Britain, Greece, Iceland, Italy, Luxembourg, the Netherlands, Norway, Sweden, Switzerland, Turkey, and the United States) formed the Organization for European Economic Cooperation (O.E.E.C.), later known as the Organization for Economic Cooperation and Development (O.E.C.D.). Meanwhile, the American president announced what was to become known as the Truman Doctrine, committing the U.S. to oppose the establishment "by force or outside influence" of dictatorships in Europe. Under this doctrine, American military and political aid helped forestall communist movements in Greece, Turkey, and Italy.

Eastern Europe, the "Iron Curtain," and the Cold War
The Soviet Union, devastated by the war, its industrial base and agricultural economy in a shambles, crippled by military and civilian casualties that probably exceeded 20 million deaths, sought to insulate itself behind a zone of friendly and submissive European neighbors so as never again to suffer the kind of invasion that Germany had mounted against the USSR. In Europe, the Soviet Union's interpretation of the wartime Yalta agreements enabled it to move rapidly to depose fledgling democratic governments in the Eastern European countries under Soviet occupation; as early as 1946 Winston Churchill warned that an "Iron Curtain" was being drawn around a Soviet zone in Eastern Europe. Soviet power was made credible with the rapid development of atomic weapons through Russian research, captured foreign scientists, and atomic secrets stolen from the United States during the war. Pro-USSR communist governments were in place in Poland, Czechoslovakia, Hungary, Yugoslavia, Bulgaria, and Romania by 1948. (Communist Yugoslavia, under Josip Broz Tito (1892–1980), pursued a tenuous independence form Soviet control, while Albania under Enver Hoxha (1908–85) broke with the Soviet Union in 1961 and allied itself with the People's Republic of China thereafter.) Austria and Finland accepted a neutral status highly deferential to the Soviet Union. A popular uprising in Hungary in 1956 was ruthlessly crushed, making clear the USSR's determination to maintain tight control of Eastern Europe.

India and the Partition; Southeast Asia
Bowing to intense pressure, in 1946 Britain pledged independence for India. But the issue of how to apportion power between the (Hindu) Congress Party and the Muslim League proved impossible to resolve, and in August 1947 British India was divided into the separate states of India and Pakistan. Communal violence in 1947–48, in which at least 500,000 people died, led to widespread displacement of Hindus from Pakistan to India, and of Muslims from India to Pakistan, the latter comprising the non-contiguous areas of West Pakistan (now Pakistan) and East Pakistan (now Bangladesh); the status of Kashmir remained unresolved. Relations between India and Pakistan have been strained throughout the postindependence period. In 1971 the awkward division of Pakistan into eastern and western halves was resolved through bitter fighting when East Pakistan broke away to become the independent state of Bangladesh.

Burma, administratively separated from India in 1935, became independent in 1947; Sri Lanka gained independence in 1948. Malaya achieved independence in 1957, after the British fought a communist insurgency there from 1948 to the the mid-1950's. In 1963, Malaya joined with Singapore and the former British colonies of Sarawak and British North Borneo (Sabah) to form a new nation, the Federation of Malaysia. Singapore withdrew from the federation in 1965 and became an independent nation thereafter. In Indonesia, a proclamation of independence in 1945 led to four years of fighting as the Dutch attempted to reimpose colonial control; they withdrew in 1949 and the Republic of Indonesia won international recognition. (In 1965 popular backlash against an attempted communist coup in Indonesia led to the slaughter of several hundred thousand people, many of them ethnic Chinese.)

The State of Israel
The Zionist movement of the late 19th century had promoted Jewish emigration to the ancient homeland of Israel, more recently known as Palestine. Palestine was part of Great Britain's League of Nations Mandate in the Middle East after World War I. British policy there was governed by the Balfour Declaration of 1917, which pledged support for a Jewish homeland in Palestine provided that the rights of the Palestinian people were protected. After World War II and the Holocaust, support for a Jewish state grew dramatically and became a cornerstone of American policy in the Middle East. The creation of the State of Israel was formally proclaimed on May 14, 1948; but allegations of forced displacement of Palestinians led to the immediate outbreak of war between Israel and its Arab neighbors. Israel's victory turned out to be only the first round in more than half a century of armed confrontation with the Arab world.

The People's Republic of China
In China, the simmering conflict between Communist and Nationalist forces in China broke out into open civil war by 1946, despite American efforts at mediation. With only grudg-

ing material support from the USSR, Chinese Communists under the leadership of Mao Zedong defeated the far larger and better equipped Nationalists, whose corruption, ineptitude, and bourgeois orientation proved no match for the simple communist slogan, "Land to the tiller." The Nationalists retreated to Taiwan in 1948–49, and Mao proclaimed the founding of the People's Republic of China in Beijing on October 1, 1949. (A break between the USSR and the People's Republic of China in the late 1950's, over both geopolitical and ideological issues, did not alter American policy assumptions of monolithic international communism. U.S.-Chinese relations were nearly nonexistent before Pres. Richard M. Nixon initiated a rapprochement in 1973.)

The Cold War Heats Up A Soviet attempt in 1948 to blockade the Western occupied zone of Berlin was met with the Berlin Airlift, which preserved a Western presence in the city. The Berlin Wall was built in 1961 to stem a tide of illegal migration from East to West Germany. (Its fall in 1989 marked the end of the cold war.) The North Atlantic Treaty Organization (NATO, 1949) was founded under American leadership as part of a strategy to contain the Soviet Union; it was countered by the organization of the Eastern-bloc Warsaw Pact (1955). The Soviet Union made a concerted effort to match the United States in production of nuclear weapons and delivery systems; the resulting arms race eventually resulted in the production of enough nuclear weapons by the two powers to obliterate the entire population of the world. The death of Joseph Stalin in 1953 made no appreciable difference in the atmosphere of hostility between the Eastern and Western blocs.

The Korean War In Korea, divided after the war into separate occupation zones roughly north and south of 38° N., the Soviet-backed government led by the veteran Communist Kim Il-sung (1912–94) rapidly took control in the north, whereas in the south an inept and ill-prepared American occupation squandered the opportunity for democratic development and eventually backed the corrupt right-wing movement of Syngman Rhee (1875–1965). When North Korean troops invaded across the demilitarized zone at the 38th parallel on June 25, 1950, the United States successfully obtained United Nations backing to rescue the south; the Korean War ensued. Hard-pressed at first when China sent troops in support of North Korea, the U.N. forces fought the war to a bloody standoff over the next three years.

Domestically, America's "loss" of China and the stale-mate of the Korean War led to purges, orchestrated by Sen. Joseph McCarthy of Wisconsin, of supposed "communist sympathizers" in the State Department. Abroad, in the cold war struggles of the 1950's and 1960's between the U.S. and the USSR for influence in the Third World, America often wound up allied with corrupt, repressive "anticommunist" governments, while the Soviet Union was able to pose as the champion of progressive anticolonial, nationalist, and antiimperial movements. Soviet- and Cuban-backed insurgencies in Latin America countries (including El Salvador, Nicaragua, Peru, Chile, Colombia, and others) drew particular attention from the United States, while repressive rightist regimes in Argentina and Chile engineered the "disappearance" of tens of thousands of political opponents and Brazil fell under military rule.

Decolonization The colonial powers of western Europe were on the whole slow to see the ill effects of trying to maintain the old order. The French effort to retain colonial Indochina led to a debilitating war culminating in a devastating defeat at Dienbienphu in 1954. The terms of the French withdrawal left Vietnam divided between a communist north and a non-communist south. In 1956, the United States blocked a proposal for internationally supervised elections that would likely have resulted in a victory in the south for the northern government of Ho Chi Minh (1890–1969), long-time leader of communist and nationalist anti-French resistance who came to power in the north after the French withdrawal. This set the stage for American involvement in the Vietnam War a few years later. Just as the French withdrew from Indochina, they faced a disaster in Algeria, where an uprising was aimed at driving out the more than 1 million ethnic French settlers there. After eight years of brutal struggle, the French withdrew in 1962.

Meanwhile, in 1956 Great Britain and France went to war with Egypt in an attempt to retain control over the Suez Canal, which had been nationalized by Egypt under its leader Gamel Abdul Nasser (1918–70). The war, opposed by the United States, was a political disaster, and hastened the collapse of British colonial rule everywhere. The outcome bolstered Nasser's socialist regime, already friendly to the USSR for aid in building the Aswan High Dam, while Iraq, Syria, and Libya became anti-Israeli Soviet clients.

The 1950's also saw the beginning of decolonization in Africa, beginning with the independence of Ghana in 1957. Within two decades nearly all of the former European colonies of Africa would be independent; but the anomalies of colonial boundaries transformed into national borders regardless of topography or ethnicity led to severe strains in many of the new states. The civil war that followed Biafra's attempted secession from Nigeria in 1960, and the 40–year civil war in the Sudan between the Arab, Islamic north and the Black, Christian/Animist south, attest to the difficuty of making nations from what had been colonies. Struggles in the Congo, Namibia, Angola, and elsewhere turned into proxy conflicts of the cold war. At the continent's southern tip, the Republic of South Africa, which gained independence from Great Britain in 1961, became an international pariah because of its policy of "apartheid" racial segregation.

The Cuban Revolution   The 1959 triumph of Fidel Castro's (b. 1926) communist revolution in Cuba was a bitter blow to the United States, which had supported the old, corrupt regime of Fulgencio Batista. With the support of the CIA, an army of Cuban exiles invaded Cuba at the Bay of Pigs in January 1961, and were immediately killed or taken prisoner by Castro's troops; the hoped-for anti-communist popular uprising failed to occur. The incident was a humiliation for the United States and its new president, John F. Kennedy. Castro thereafter remained one of the most loyal supporters of the Soviet Union and relied on Soviet economic aid to counter the effects of an American-led trade embargo on Cuba.

The Russians took advantage of this alliance in 1962 to place missiles in Cuba that were aimed directly at the United States. An American demand (ultimately successful) that they be removed led, in October 1962, to 10 days of tense confrontation. The Cuban missile crisis, as the incident was called, is generally regarded as having been the most serious single incident of the cold war and, in retrospect, the high water mark of Soviet influence internationally. Thereafter, having looked into the abyss and been daunted by what they saw, both superpowers began efforts to reduce the cold war atmosphere of confrontation. Beginning in the 1960's, a series of agreements between the U.S. and the USSR succeeded in limiting the testing and production of nuclear weapons, and reducing their numbers.

The Vietnam War   In South Vietnam, a nationalist, anticolonial, communist-allied movement (Vietminh) became increasingly transformed into a communist-led armed struggle (Vietcong) supported by North Vietnam and dedicated to the overthrow of the American-backed southern government. American military and political advisers sent to South Vietnam by President Kennedy failed to stem the communist insurgency; ground troops followed in 1963–64, in numbers that escalated for the next several years. Relying on poorly informed views of "Asian communism" and fears of a communist revolutionary "domino effect" in Southeast Asia, America found itself embroiled in a war that proved impossible to win in the field and deeply devisive at home. The Vietcong and North Vietnamese Tet offensive of February 1968 was defeated by American and South Vietnamese forces, but the victory was costly both in military terms and in its effect on American public opinion. Later in 1968 President Johnson declined to run for reelection in the face of dwindling public support for the war. American troop reductions began in 1969 as part of a "Vietnamization" program, and in 1972 a cease-fire agreement (never implemented) was signed in Paris between North Vietnam, South Vietnam, the Vietcong, and the United States. Saigon fell to communist forces on April 30, 1975; the last remaining Americans were evacuated, and Vietnam was reunited under communist rule in 1976.

Development in the Third World   The post-World War II creation of the new field of development economics was intended to assist the economic growth of the emergent countries of the Third World. The nations of Asia, Africa, and South America have acted in effect as laboratories to test different approaches to development, approaches that have had uneven results. Overemphasis on raising the gross domestic product of target countries has led in many cases to corruption, environmental damage, and extremes of wealth and poverty. This has been exacerbated in cases where exploitation of valuable natural resources, such as petroleum, has led to the squandering or embezzlement of wealth by a small ruling class (Venezuela, Nigeria, Iraq), with little benefit to the country as a whole.

A more comprehensive approach to development that combines investments in infrastructure (water resources, transportation systems, and the like), widely available public education, improved public health, and the empowerment of women, in combination with free trade (facilitated by the World Trade Organization and the General Agreement on Tariffs and Trade or GATT) and the protection of workers (through the International Labor Organization), has been a more effective recipe for rapid and reasonably equitable development. This has been evident especially in Asia, with the postwar recovery of Japan and the development of new "tiger" economies in South Korea, Taiwan, Thailand, Malaysia, and elsewhere. In contrast, client states of the Soviet Union, encouraged to pursue state ownership of industry, subsidized food and housing prices, restraints on foreign trade, and pervasive economic planning, have had far less impressive results. Much of Africa has yet to recover from quasi-socialist experiments in economic planning combined with kleptocratic government, a situation made much more difficult in some parts of the continent by the crippling prevalence of HIV/AIDS.

Social Change in the 1960's

The Vietnam War engendered a persistent and powerful antiwar movement, especially among young people, that became part of a more pervasive atmosphere of youth rebellion and social change in the 1960's. Another strong component of that impulse for change was the Civil Rights movement, which embraced both government action (school desegregation, voting rights legislation) and political action with wide public participation ("sit-ins" and "freedom marches," and the formation of groups such as the Rev. Martin Luther King's Southern Christian Leadership Council and the more radical Student National Coordinating Council [SNCC] and the Black Panthers). By the end of the decade the legal structure of segregation had been overturned, and new efforts, such as affirmative action initiatives, were implemented to try to counter the effects of past discrimination.

In the late 1960's and early 1970's, the women's movement sought to emulate the tactics and successes of the Civil Rights movement with an agenda that embraced a spectrum of issues from equal pay for equal work, to coeducation at traditionally male colleges and equal access for women students to school athletic programs, to legalization of abortion.

Abroad, the social ferment of the 1960's also found expression in China. In 1958 Mao Zedong had initiated the Great Leap Forward, an effort at rapid economic development in agriculture and industry that proved to be a costly failure, with between 20 and 30 million people dying in the resulting famine of 1958–61. The country had barely recovered before Mao launched the Great Proletarian Cultural Revolution (1966–68), a bizarre campaign to combat complacency and bureaucratism within the Communist Party and government at all levels by unleashing the revolutionary energies of youthful "Red Guards" and workers' "revolutionary committees." The Cultural Revolution (the chaotic destructiveness of which was not widely understood outside China) in turn helped to inspire student revolts in 1968 in the United States, Western Europe, Japan, and elsewhere.

Demographic and Environmental Issues

In 1950 the world's population was about 2.5 billion people; that figure doubled to 5 billion by 1985. This demographic explosion, a result of a complex of factors including improved public health, sanitation, medicine, and nutrition, produced widespread fears that world population growth would soon outstrip food supplies and other global resources. In fact, population growth began to slow in the mid-1980's, as economic growth produced a demographic transition of longer lifespans, reduced infant mortality, and lower fertility rates.

Fears of widespread food shortages were also alleviated beginning in the 1960's by the Green Revolution, involving the development of new varieties of major food plants (especially corn [maize] and rice) that, under the proper conditions, produce far higher yields than older varieties. These high yields come at an environmental price, including increased use of chemical pesticides and fertilizers. Genetically-modified (GM) crops, some of which produce their own insecticides, have also begun to increase yields in America and in parts of Asia, but have been little used in Europe and Africa in the face of popular opposition.

Economic development and population growth have produced a range of environmental effects, from human encroachment on wetlands, forests, and other ecosystems, to production of greenhouse gasses, resource depletion, and production of waste. On the other hand, lack of development also has negative environmental consequences, including deforestation, soil depletion and desertification, and overexploitation of wild species, while development can produce benefits such as substitution of energy-efficient devices for wasteful burning of fuels, and the preservation of selected environments for recreational, aesthetic, and conservation purposes.

The postwar period has seen a significant increase worldwide of national parks, U.N. World Heritage sites, wildlife refuges, and other protected areas. Environmental issues, most especially global warming and associated environmental changes, remain serious challenges for the 21st century, but the rise of environmental science and the beginnings of international cooperation on environmental issues have been major steps forward. Landmarks of this process include the Convention on International Trade in Endangered Species (CITES, 1973); the Treaty on the International Law of the Sea (1983), and an international conference in Rio de Janeiro, Brazil (1992) that produced major agreements on biodiversity and global warming.

International conferences on global warming under United Nations auspices in Kyoto (1997) and Copenhagen (2009) produced international protocols (the Kyoto treaty took effect in 2005) aimed at combating climate change; the agreements however were weakened by the refusal of the United States, China, and several other important countries to be bound by them.

The Iranian Revolution and the Rise of Islamism

The CIA-sponsored overthrow of the democratic regime of Mohammad Mossadegh (1880–1967) in 1954 led to the return to power of Mohammad Reza Shah Pahlavi (1919–80), who had been deposed the year before. In 1979 his unpopular and autocratic government fell to a fundamentalist Islamic revolution. The disheartening ordeal of dozens of Americans taken hostage at the U.S. embassy in Teheran played a major role in the defeat of President Jimmy Carter (b. 1924) by Ronald Reagan (1911–2004) in the 1980 presidential election. The subsequent Iran-Iraq war of 1980–88, which cost millions of lives but led to no clear military victory for either side, led the U.S. into the anomalous position of supporting the former Soviet client, Iraq's Saddam Hussein.

The Soviet Union in Afghanistan

In 1978 a leftist military coup overthrew the republican government of Afghanistan. A popular anticommunist revolt the next year led to a Soviet invasion to support its client regime; the USSR soon found itself in a Vietnam-style war, fighting amid a hostile population. The U.S.-funded anticommunist forces included religiously-motivated guerrilla fighters from all over the Islamic world, some of whom would later turn against the United States in militant opposition to Western values as they understood them. The Afghan war cost the USSR lives, treasure, and popular support; Soviet forces were withdrawn, under a face-saving agreement, beginning in 1988. After several years of instability, in 1995 the Taliban, a fundamentalist party, came to power and instituted what became the world's strictest and most repressive Islamic government.

Israel and Palestine

Israel emerged from wars with Egypt and Syria in 1967 and 1973, and military actions in Lebanon in 1975–76 and 1978, militarily strong and in possession of the West Bank, the Golan Heights, and the Gaza Strip, but no closer to peace with its Arab neighbors. The U.S.-brokered Camp David accords of 1979 led to a peace agreement with Egypt. Palestinian *intifada* uprisings (including the use of suicide bombers) against Israeli occupation of Gaza and the West Bank, countered by Israeli military action against various Palestinian militarized groups and their backers, have led to a continuing state of unrest in the Palestinian territories. The Oslo Agreement, providing for the withdrawal of Israeli forces from the Palestinian territories, which would have become self-governing under a Palestinian Authority, was signed in 1994 but never completely implemented. The Israeli-Palestinian conflict remains among the world's most intractable political problems.

Post-Mao China and the Limits of Reform

The death in September 1976 of Mao Zedong meant the end of the "ten terrible years" of the Cultural Revolution and its aftermath. Mao's widow and several associates (the "Gang of Four") were arrested and tried for their roles in that period of turmoil. China's new leader, Deng Xiaoping (1904–1997), in 1978 ushered in a policy of modernization of industry, education, science, and defense that led to the rapid development of a hybrid socialist-capitalist economy. A student-led democracy movement, demonstrating in Beijing's Tiananmen Square in May-June 1989, was put down with great loss of life, a signal that economic liberalization would not be accompanied by political liberalization. By the early years of the 21st century, China had become a great economic powerhouse, though still under repressive communist rule.

Glasnost, Perestroika, and the Fall of the Soviet Union

The resolutely anti-Soviet policies of Pres. Ronald Reagan in the 1980's apparently hastened the cold war's end. With a restless population and a crumbling economy, and still reeling from its disastrous adventure in Afghanistan, Russia found itself unable to sustain the military expenditures needed to keep pace with the U.S. in cold war competition around the world. With Mikahil Gorbachev's (b. 1931) glasnost ("openness") and perestroika ("restructuring") policies in the mid-80's, people in Poland, East Germany, Czechoslovakia, the Baltic states, and elsewhere in Eastern Europe, sensed the end of Russia's will to retain a Soviet empire. In rapid and largely peaceful revolutions, the people of these countries overthrew their governments and demanded the withdrawal of Soviet troops. The fall of the Berlin Wall in November 1989 meant in effect the fall of international communism, and the end of the cold war.

The Computer Revolution and the Information Age

The first digital computers, built in the 1940's, were huge, expensive, slow, and extremely limited in their capabilities, but they pointed the way to a transformed future. By the 1950's mainframe computers were processing actuarial data, handling mailing lists, and changing the way the world does business. The invention of the transistor, the integrated circuit, the memory chip, the floppy disk, and other key components made personal computers a reality by the late 1970's. (A crucial event was the introduction of the Apple II, the world's first widely popular personal computer, in 1977.) Since that time speed and memory have steadily increased, and cost has plummetted. The Internet, search engines, and online databases have made vast quantities of information available to virtually anyone, anywhere in the world; e-mail and cell phones have transformed personal communications. Of all changes in the post–World War II period, the computer revolution may prove to have been the most profound.

A remarkable example of the possibilities opened up by new computer technology and applications was the Apollo Program. On July 20, 1969, American astronaut Neil Armstrong (b. 1930) stepped onto the surface of the Moon, an event that marked a technological and propaganda triumph for the United States. Since that time, manned spaceflight has turned out to be expensive, dangerous, and lacking in clear purpose; but unmanned orbital and interplanetary vehicles, notably for broadcasting and telecommunications, military surveillance, remote imaging, and scientific research have become the basis of a multibillion-dollar industry that has contributed substantially to the development of the information age.

Globalization and Its Discontents

One consequence of the information revolution has been the increasing globalization of the world economy, with manufacturing and service industries easily relocating anywhere in the world where skilled workers can be hired at low cost. This has led to decreased costs for food, clothing, and many other basic goods for much of the world's population. At the same time, it has led to exploitation of ill-paid labor in developing countries; the "flight" of jobs overseas; controlled and subsidized markets for many agricultural goods; and other negative consequences, real and perceived. The question of how nation-states and national markets are to adjust to global manufacturing, transportation, and marketing of goods remains unresolved. Meetings of economic ministers of the world's largest economies (Seattle 1999, Genoa 2001, and others) have been met by massive demonstrations and some rioting aimed especially at what protesters considered the pro-globalization policies of the World Bank and the IMF.

In 2008, the collapse of the housing bubble in many industrialized nations together with systemic failures in the banking system led to a worldwide recession with long-lasting economic and political effects. Various stimulus programs were undertaken with varying degrees of success. In 2011 China replaced Japan as the world's second-largest economy (after the United States); its export-driven industrial sector allowed China to recover with relative ease from the Great Recession. In Europe recovery was much slower; in 2011 the Euro-zone countries continued to debate whether and how to bail out Ireland, Greece, Spain, and other nations with chronic debt and deficit problems, while in the United States, the question of limiting the national debt emerged as a key political issue.

A Single Superpower World

With the end of the cold war, the United States had to adjust to being the world's sole superpower, while Europe, China, and Russia had to adapt to finding ways to make their voices heard and their interests taken into account in the face of American military and economic might. America responded to a 1990 Iraqi invasion of Kuwait with the first gulf war (1990–91); an easy American military victory led to Iraq's withdrawal from Kuwait but no lasting change in the Iraqi government. In 1992 a major American intervention under U.N. auspices into an ongoing civil war in Somalia led to limited and short-term gains; American forces were withdrawn in March, 1994 after the downing of an American helicopter led to a deadly ambush of U.S. Marines. In 1994 neither the U.S. nor the U.N. intervened to stop the genocidal killing of ethnic Tutsis by their Hutu neighbors in Rwanda. The limits of America's power as "the world's policeman" were tested by participation in U.N. peacekeeping forces in Bosnia in 1995 and a NATO police action in 1999 designed to halt Serbian "ethnic cleansing" of Albanians in the province of Kosovo.

Undoubtedly the most difficult adjustment for U.S. policy in the new millennium has been the growth of international terrorist organizations, most notably al-Qaeda, that are privately organized and funded with few or no ties to any government or state and that have goals which do not fit into traditional categories of international relations. The destruction of New York's World Trade Center by Al-Qaeda terrorists on September 11, 2001, led to an American response against al-Qaeda bases in Afghanistan, resulting in the overthrow of the Taliban government but neither to the effective social and political rebuilding of Afghanistan nor to the capture or destruction of the Al-Qaeda leadership. The American invasion of Iraq in 2003 led to the downfall of Saddam Hussein's government, but early military success was followed by a long and difficult occupation period that did not produce any gains in America's war against terrorism.

Terrorism and War In the years following the attacks of 9/11, the U.S. and Great Britain launched an all-out assault on Islamic terrorist networks, which included the use of illegal kidnappings, secret imprisonments, and torture. Terrorist bombings in Bali (2002) and even Saudi Arabia (2003) helped gain support for what became known as the "War on Terror." The invasion of Iraq by mostly American and British troops was a turning point in this war. At first the governments said they invaded because of weapons of mass destruction, but when such weapons never materialized they began to say that Iraq was a central front in the war on terror. Terrorist bombings on a commuter train in Madrid (2004) and in the London Underground (2005) gave credence to this view for a while, but when no links could be found between Iraq and these attacks the argument was quietly dropped. Suddenly the War on Terror seemed to be located only in Iraq where thousands of foreign fighters, soon to be given arms by Iran, came to attack and kill mainly U.S. troops. But it was the unforeseen violence between the two Islamic sects, Sunnis and Shiites, that stalled any plans the U.S. had for leaving Iraq and by 2005 had devolved into a vicious civil war.

In Afghanistan, the overthrow of the fundamentalist Taliban government proved to be only a temporary victory. After they fled to Pakistan they reinforced their army and in 2006 began a series of attacks in southern Afghanistan that caused the U.S. to use troops from NATO (an organization meant to guard western Europe) to block the Taliban's forward movement. As so often happened in the past, western armies became bogged down in this region as well as in the heart of the Middle East.

In Israel, the struggle to achieve peace with the Palestinians was again thwarted by terrorist acts against Israelis and Israel's reprisals. Although Prime Minister Ariel Sharon agreed to a U.S.-backed plan to cut back on new settlements in Gaza and the West Bank only a token number were dismantled. Resentment grew worse as the Israelis built a huge barrier to wall themselves off from the Palestinians who had continually threatened their lives and safety. In early 2006, Sharon suffered a massive stroke and his successor, Ehud Olmert, proved ineffective.

After the radical group Hamas won the elections in Palestine, defeating the P.L.O.-based government, the U.S. withdrew all aid and Israel refused to deal with the new leaders. In July 2006, rockets were fired into Israel and an Israeli soldier was captured and held hostage, provoking Israel to launch a large-scale attack against Hamas in Lebanon. Within a week severe damage was inflicted on Lebanon's infrastructure, and there were many civilians killed and wounded by air and tank attacks. A cease-fire, initially resisted by the U.S. citing belief that Israel could inflict serious damage on Hamas, was eventually reached after a good deal of Lebanon lay in ruins. The "Arab Spring" popular demonstrations of 2011, which overthrew autocratic regimes in Tunisia and Egypt and destabilized Libya, Yemen, Bahrain, and Syria, added new urgency to finding a solution to the Israel-Palestinian impasse, as did a pending vote in the United Nations later in 2011 to recognize a Palestinian state. But prospects for a solution nevertheless remained remote.

In the midst of all this chaos, Iran emerged as a force to be reckoned with in the region. A new fundamentalist president asserted Iran's right to acquire nuclear technology for peaceful uses, continually defying the threat of U.N. sanctions. Iraq's Shiite government was a natural ally of Shiite-dominated Iran, and a counter weight to the Sunnis who ruled Saudi Arabia. The possibility of confrontation and conflict in the region seemed to be growing every month even after the Saudi leaders called the U.S. occupation of Iraq "illegal."

On November 26, 2008, terrorists bombed and assaulted hotels and other targets in Mumbai; evidence that the attackers had trained in Pakistan led to a worsening of already tense relations between Pakistan and India. Pakistan's toleration of terrorist cells in its northern territories, adjacent to Afghanistan, strained the nation's ties with the United States, while Pakistani popular resentment of clandestine American attacks by drone aircraft on Taliban and al-Qaeda targets there grew. On May 1, 2011, a team of U.S. Special Forces attacked an al-Qaeda compound in Abbottabad, Pakistan, and killed the movement's leader, Osama bin-Laden.

The Spread of Nuclear Weapons Although the war in Iraq dominated the news throughout 2003-2007, the disturbing revelations about the proliferation of nuclear weapons technology was for many observers the crucial development of the period. In early 2004 the Pakistani government admitted that the head of its nuclear research institute, Abdul Qadeer Khan, had secretly built a global network of nuclear equipment builders and had sold Pakistan's technology to Iran, North Korea, and Libya. When Libya decided to dismantle its nuclear weapons technology in exchange for lifting of oil sanctions and increased trade with the west, the Khan network was exposed and soon after North Korea would end negotiations to limit its nuclear programs. The C.I.A. said it was certain that North Korea had built six to eight weapons.

Although the U.S. had been diligent about trying to limit the spread of nuclear weapons for over a half-century, the Bush Administration decided in 2005 to sell some of its nuclear technology to India. The reasons were doubtless related to the emergence of China as a global power whose economic aims in Asia might eventually pose to threat to American interests.

Disasters, Natural and Man-made   Several enormous natural disasters occurred between 2004 and 2006 including earthquakes in Iran and Pakistan that killed tens of thousands of people (75,000 in Pakistan alone). The most devastating event, however, was the huge tsunami that occurred in the Indian Ocean where a 9.0 quake occurred off the coast of Sumatra on December 26, 2004. Over 200,000 people were killed, most of them in Indonesia (131,000), Sri Lanka (31,200), and India (10,700).

The roster of severe natural disasters grew, with devastating earthquakes in Sichuan province, China (May 12, 2008, more than 70,000 people killed); Sumatra, Indonesia (September 30, 2009, at least 1000 people killed); in Haiti (January 12, 2010, more than 230,00 deaths); and in Chile (February 27, 2010, centered in a relatively remote and unpopulated region but killing nearly 600 people); and in Christchurch, New Zealand (February

11, 2011; atleast 75 people killed). A strong earthquake and tsunami in northeastern Japan on March 9, 2011, killed more than 25,000 people and seriously damaged a nuclear power plant. Severe flooding from excessive monsoon rains caused widespread destruction in Pakistan in July-August 2010. Severe drought and widespread wildfires affected Russia in August, 2010. A series of unusually strong tornados caused widespread destruction in the southern United States in the spring of 2011.

In Africa, a different kind of tragedy played out in the Darfur region in western Sudan. In 2003, after years of conflict, African armies in that region rebelled against the Arab-dominated government and the government enlisted militias to strike back at them. Over the following months the Arab militias struck not at the rebel forces but at the towns and villages they came from. More than a million people were driven from their homes and tens of thousands were killed. By 2006, over 200,000 were dead, many of them young children who had starved to death. Neither the U.N. nor the African Union could establish a firm peace, although the worst violence had subsided and a worldwide humanitarian effort brought some relief to the hundreds of thousands of people who remained in refugee camps.

In other parts of Africa, peace finally came to Liberia in 2006 after 14 years of civil war, the election of an American-educated woman, Ellen Johnson-Sirleaf (the first woman to be elected head-of-state in Africa) brought hope for the future.

But the spread of AIDS throughout sub-Saharan Africa posed an enormous challenge to many governments there. Almost 6.5 percent of adults in the region have HIV, with over 2.5 million becoming newly infected each year and 2 million deaths occurring annually. The U.S. has taken the lead in providing the drugs needed to stem the death the toll and there were signs that much more would be done.

Major Wars in History

Greco-Persian Wars (500–448 B.C.)

The empire of the Persian king Darius I (r. 521–486 B.C.) stretched from modern Afghanistan to Egypt. Beginning in the early 5th century B.C., Greek cities in Ionia (modern western Turkey and several islands) and Cyprus revolted and the Persians quickly put down the revolt and then

moved into Thrace. The mainland Greek cities of Athens and Eretrea had supported the revolt so in 490 B.C. the Persians attacked Greece by sea, but their troops were defeated on the plains of Marathon by the Athenians. After the death of Darius (486 B.C.) his son Xerxes I launched a second invasion (480 B.C.) overland through Thrace and Macedonia. At first successful, the Persians destroyed a brave Spartan force defending the pass at Thermopylae and then marched to Athens. But a Greek fleet defeated the

Persian navy at Salamis in 480 B.C., and Greek heavy infantry (*hoplites*) crushed the Persian army at Plataea (479 B.C.), ending the threat to the mainland. Additional fighting followed over many years in Egypt, Asia Minor, and Cyprus. By the end of the war (traditionally 448 B.C.), the Greeks had swept Persia from the Aegean.

The Peloponnesian Wars (431 B.C.–404 B.C.)

The Peloponnesus, the peninsula in southwestern Greece connected to the mainland by the Isthmus of Corinth, was the home of ancient cities including Sparta, Corinth, Pylos and Argos. The Peloponnesian wars were fought on both land and sea between Athens and Sparta, with varying allies on both sides. Athens and Sparta had fought intermittently several decades before (460 B.C.–445 B.C.) but the major conflict broke out with an attack by a Spartan ally, Thebes, on an Athenian ally, Plataea, followed by an invasion of Attica by the Peloponnesians. At first Athens, led by Pericles, avoided direct battle with Sparta and a siege of Athens (431 B.C.) by the Spartans failed as Athens mounted naval raids on the Peloponnesus. In 430-28 B.C. plague killed Pericles and a quarter of Athens's population. Under the leadership of Cleon the Athenians began a more aggressive policy by establishing bases in the Peloponnesus, but they encountered reverses including defeat at Delium (424 B.C.). After the deaths of the Spartan and Athenian leaders Brasidas and Cleon in battle (422 B.C.), peace was won under the Athenian leader Nicias (d. 413 B.C.).

Fighting was soon renewed, however, and an anti-Spartan coalition was defeated at Mantineia (418 B.C.). Alcibiades (d. 413 B.C.) then convinced the Athenians (415 B.C.) to send a large fleet to Sicily but this venture ended in complete disaster (413 B.C.). The heavy loss of ships and personnel changed the war as Sparta began, with Persian support, to compete with the Athenians at sea. Alcibiades, who had defected to Sparta, rejoined Athens and a series of land and sea victories under his command caused the Spartans to sue for peace. Cleophon (d. 404 B.C.), the new Athenian ruler, rejected this request in 410 B.C. and another in 406 B.C. But in 405 B.C., the Spartan commander Lysander (d. 395 B.C.) destroyed the Athenian fleet at the decisive battle of Aegospotami in the Dardanelles. The Spartans sailed to Athens and blockaded the city and port. Athens, dependent on the sea for supplies, capitulated and the ensuing peace made Sparta the greatest power in Greece. Athens, bankrupt and defeated, never thereafter played a major political role in the ancient world.

The Punic Wars (264 B.C.–146 B.C.)

The three Punic Wars were fought between Rome and Carthage, which was located in northern Africa near modern Tunis. (Punic is from the Latin for Carthaginian.) In 264 B.C. Carthage was the great commercial power of the western Mediterranean while Rome was only an Italian power, not even having conquered northern Italy. By 146 B.C., however, Carthage had been destroyed and Rome dominated the Mediterranean world.

The first war (264–241 B.C.) began with the intervention of the two powers in factional conflict on Sicily, then controlled by Carthage. Fought in and around Sicily, this was primarily a naval conflict, with rowed galleys (*triremes* and *quinqueremes*) used to ram or come alongside and board opposing ships. The Romans caught up quickly with Carthaginian sea power and ultimately their fleets were victorious. Their ships had a spiked boarding ramp (the *corvus*, crow) that allowed legionaries to board enemy vessels for close combat. The war concluded with Carthage giving up her possessions in Sicily and her fleet.

The second war (218-201 B.C.) began in Spain with conflict between Roman and Carthaginian allies. Hannibal, the Carthagian commander in Spain, took the city of Sargentum and then began his audacious march from Spain to Italy, crossing the Alps with a force including war elephants. Prevailing in several key battles (notably at Lake Trasimere, 217 B.C., and Cannae, 216 B.C.), he seemed to achieve victory with many Roman colonies and allies coming over to his side. But the Romans followed the cautious policy of Fabius Maximus (d. 203 B.C.), avoiding pitched battles, maintaining key positions, and recapturing places when Hannibal's army left. Over many years in Italy, Hannibal was unable to achieve final victory. Beginning in 210, the Roman commander Scipio Africanus (236 B.C.–184/3 B.C.) was triumphant in Spain and carried the war to Africa in 204 B.C. Hannibal was recalled to defend Carthage, but was defeated at Zama (202 B.C.). In the ensuing peace, Carthage gave up its possessions in Spain and its navy, but maintained its commercial activities.

The third war (149–146 B.C.) resulted from Roman concern with Carthage's revived commercial power. Rome supported a rival kingdom in Numidia (modern Algeria); its conflict with Carthage provided an excuse for Roman intervention, which led to the final destruction of Carthage in 146 B.C. The city was razed, its inhabitants were killed or sold into slavery, and Rome took control of North Africa.

The Crusades (1095–1272)

First Crusade (1095–1099) Jerusalem had been in Islamic hands since the seventh century, but Christian pilgrimages continued, although by the 11th century there was persecution of Christians and the Holy Sepulcher (Tomb of Christ) was despoiled. In 1071 the Seljuk Turks took control of Jerusalem, and in the same year defeated the Byzantine army at Manzikert. The Byzantine Emperor requested help from Latin Christendom but it is uncertain what effect this had. The impetus for the First Crusade was the preaching of Pope Urban II at the Council of Clermont, France in 1095, urging Christians to go to war for the Holy Sepulcher. In addition to religious fervor the possibility of territorial expansion and riches contributed to the enthusiastic response. Norman designs against the Byzantines as well as the Muslims and the interest of Italian cities in increased trade with the east were also factors.

The organized crusade was preceded by a disorganized band (called "The People's Crusade") led by Walter the Penniless and another composed of followers of Peter the Hermit. Their journeys through Byzantium were not entirely peaceful, and their arrival in the Holy Land led to quick defeat. The main force was under the command of noblemen such as Godfrey of Bouillon, Bohemond I, Raymond IV of Toulouse, and Robert II of Flanders. The First Crusade was successful. The Latin Christians took Nicaea in 1097, defeated the Turks at Dorylaeum (1097), took Antioch in 1098, and Jerusalem in 1099. The latter victory was marked by the slaughter of Muslims and Jews. Godfrey of Bouillon was elected defender of the Holy Sepulcher; on his death his brother Baldwin assumed the title King of Jerusalem. Other fiefs were created at Edessa, Tripoli, and Antioch. After the First Crusade, and partly because of enmity with the Byzantines, later (and less successful) crusades were primarily dependent on sea transport rather than the overland route.

Second Crusade (1147–49) After the Turks recaptured Edessa (1144), a new Crusade was preached by St. Bernard of Clairvaux. The Holy Roman Emperor Conrad III and Louis VII of France led the Crusade, both armies pillaging in Byzantine territory en route. Conrad's force arrived first, was forced to retreat by the Turks at Dorylaeum (1147), and joined the French (1148). A joint assault on Damascus miscarried through jealousy among the leaders; Conrad returned home in 1148 and Louis in 1149, the Crusade a failure.

Third Crusade (1189–92) After the recapture of Jerusalem in 1187 by Saladin (1137/38–1193) and the defeat of the Latin princes at Hattin, Pope Gregory VIII asked for a new crusade. It was led by Richard I of England ("The Lion Heart," 1157–99), Philip II of France (1165–1223), and the Holy Roman Emperor Frederick I (1123–90). Frederick left first and encountered difficulties with the Byzantine Emperor, who had made an alliance with Saladin. He forced his way to Asia Minor but died en route and only part of his army continued on. Richard took Cyprus from the Byzantines and joining up with Philip took Acre in 1191. Philip returned home, and Richard moved his base to Jaffa. Jerusalem remained in Muslim hands, but Richard made a truce that permitted access to the city and the Holy Sepulcher.

Fourth Crusade (1202–04) Pope Innocent III (1160/61–1216) preached the Fourth Crusade, which became entirely diverted from its original purpose. The Crusaders arrived at Venice in 1202, and to help pay sea passage to the East agreed to assist the Venetians in capturing the Dalmatian city of Zara (for which they were excommunicated by the Pope). A combination of scheming by aspirants to the Byzantine throne, Venetian pressure, money, and aid for the capture of Egypt led to a plan to overthrow the Byzantine Emperor. The fleet arrived in 1203, and in 1204 the Crusaders stormed and sacked the city, dividing the spoils with the Venetians and setting up a short-lived Latin Empire of Constantinople (1204–61). From the standpoint of the church, this Crusade was a total failure: the Byzantine Empire was undermined and Western resources were diverted from the Holy Land.

After the Fourth Crusade came the sad event of the Children's Crusade in 1212. Mobs of enthusiastic children, led by a charismatic French boy, Stephen of Cloyes, took ship at Marseilles to rescue the cause in which their elders had failed. It is thought that they were sold into slavery by rapacious ship captains.

Fifth Crusade (1217–21) At the Fourth Lateran Council (1215) Pope Innocent III and his successor, Honorius III, called for a new Crusade against the center of Muslim power in Egypt. Under the leadership of John of Brienne, the papal legate Pelagius, Andrew II of Hungary, and Duke Leopold VI of Austria, Crusaders took Damietta in the Nile delta (1219), which was evacuated in 1221 after the defeat of an attempt on Cairo; the Crusaders settled for a truce.

Sixth Crusade (1228–29) The Holy Roman Emperor Frederick II (1194–1250) undertook a largely diplomatic visit to the Holy Land that resulted (1229) in a 10 year treaty that ceded Jerusalem and other holy places; he then crowned himself King of Jerusalem. After the peace expired in 1239 the conflict continued.

Seventh Crusade (1248–54) A treaty with Damascus (1244) restored Palestine to the Christians, but in 1244 the Egyptians and Turks retook Jerusalem and defeated the Christians at Gaza. The fall of Jerusalem prompted Louis IX of France (1214–70), a canonized saint, to launch a new Crusade with the support of Pope Innocent IV, aimed at Egypt. The Crusaders took Damietta in 1249, but an attack on Cairo failed and led to Louis's capture. After his ransom, Louis spent four years shoring up the defenses of the remaining Crusader states.

Eighth Crusade (1270) When Jaffa and Antioch fell to Muslims in 1268, Louis IX of France undertook a new Crusade, cut short when he succumbed to disease in Tunis in 1270.

Ninth Crusade (1271–72) Prince Edward of England, later King Edward I, arrived in North Africa too late to help the French but at Acre he negotiated a truce before returning to England.

Muslims captured Tripoli in 1289 and Acre, the last Christian stronghold, in 1291 effectively ending the Crusaders' presence in the East except for Cypus, which was captured by the Ottoman Turks in the sixteenth century. Thereafter no Crusades were directed toward the Holy Land, although Crusades continued to be preached. Crusade-like campaigns were undertaken in Europe against Muslim incursion in Europe. The most famous of these was the victory of a Christian fleet under the command of John of Austria against the Turks off Lepanto, Greece, 1571. The Crusades to the Holy Land, although ultimately a failure, led to a wide range of influences on the West through contacts with other civilizations, increased commerce, and improved geographical knowledge. They also strengthened monarchs against the Pope, who lost the power to direct these great Christian enterprises.

The Hundred Years War (1337–1453)

The origins of The Hundred Years War can be traced to 1066, when the Duke of Normandy, known as William the Conqueror, invaded and defeated England. The French-speaking Normans now maintained possessions on both sides of the English Channel. In the 14th century, kings of England held the Duchy of Guienne (also called Aquitaine) in southwest France, where they were in conflict with the French kings who were their feudal lords. The immediate causes of the war were the failure of Philip VI to restore part of Aquitaine, English attempts to control Flanders, and Philip's support of Scotland against England.

The war began in 1337, when Edward III of England took the title of King of France, even though it was still held by Philip VI. Invading through the Low Countries, Edward and his son, Edward the Black Prince, won at Crecy with his English archers (1346) and then took Calais (1347). The English captured King John II at Poitiers (1356); by the treaty of Bretigny (1360) they received Calais and Aquitaine and a ransom for the king.

The war began again in 1369 after uprisings against the English in France over taxation. By 1373, most of the lost French territory had been regained. But in 1415 Henry V of England won a great victory at Agincourt as English long bows helped to defeat heavily armored French cavalry. With help from Burgundian allies Henry gained most of France north of the Loire. In 1429, the peasant girl Joan of Arc raised the English siege of Orleans on behalf of the Dauphin, the French king's son, and brought him to Reims to be crowned king. Her execution by the English did not stop French successes, which culminated in the reconquest of Normandy by 1450 and Aquitaine by 1453. The sole English possession remaining in France (until 1558) was Calais. England became engaged in a dynastic war, the Wars of the Roses, and so undertook no further adventures in France. The immense devastation of the war in France helped destroy the power of the feudal nobility and permitted Louis XI to bring the country increasingly under royal authority.

Wars of the Roses (1455–85)

The Wars of the Roses were dynastic conflicts in England between the house of Lancaster, whose symbol was a red rose, and the Yorkists, whose symbol was a white rose. Chronicled by Shakespeare in several history plays, the wars extended intermittently over 30 years, but the amount of fighting was limited. The immediate cause of conflict was the weakness of the Lancastrian King, Henry VI, and the struggle for influence at court between the factions of the Queen, Margaret of Anjou, and Richard, Duke of York. Richard defeated the Lancastrians at St. Albans (1455) and briefly won control of king and government. He rebelled again in 1459; while the Yorkists were initially outmaneuvered, they captured the king in 1460 and Richard was declared Henry's heir. Margaret then raised an army, defeating and killing Richard at Wakefield (1460), and Henry was rescued in 1461. Richard's son Edward took up his claim and won a decisive victory at Mortimer's Cross (1461) and became king as Edward IV (1442–83). The Yorkists had prevailed, but desertions and quarrels among them led to a renewed Lancastrian offensive in 1470. Edward fled England and Henry VI was briefly restored. Edward regained power in 1471 and ruled until 1483. On his death his younger brother, taking the throne as Richard III (1452–85), imprisoned (and may have murdered) Edward's sons. Opposition to Richard provided an opening for Henry Tudor, who had a remote claim to the throne. He defeated Richard at Bosworth Field in 1485, and as Henry VII (1457–1509) founded the Tudor dynasty and brought the Wars of the Roses to an end.

Thirty Years War (1618-48)

Fought with vast destruction and loss of life primarily in Germany, the Thirty Years War, was the complex result of religious conflict, the ambitions of the Hapsburg Holy Roman Empire, and the national interests of European states including France, the Netherlands, Sweden, Denmark, Spain and the German principalities. The Peace of Augsburg (1555) had permitted each ruler to choose the religion of his state and many became Lutheran. In this context the immediate cause of the war was the appointment of the Emperor Matthias' heir apparent, the ardently Catholic Ferdinand, as King of Bohemia (who therefore also became an Elector of the Empire). He was rejected by Protestant Bohemian nobles and the Calvinist Elector of the Palatine was chosen king as Frederick V (1596–1632). The king and his allies were quickly defeated by the imperial forces at White Mountain (1620), and Ferdinand (now Holy Roman Emperor) set about imposing Catholicism in Bohemia and elsewhere. These anti-Protestant developments discomfited both Protestant states and Catholic France, which opposed the extension of Habsburg power. Denmark, with aid from England and the Netherlands,

entered the war (1625) for both religious and territorial reasons but was defeated and sued for peace (1629). The Emperor issued the Edict of Restitution (1629), by which all lands secularized since 1552 were restored to the Roman Catholic Church. The evident power of the Counter-Reformation and the Hapsburgs in Germany greatly alarmed Sweden and other Protestant states as well as France. Sweden, under King Gustavus Adolphus, entered the fray (1630) with subsidies from France and the Netherlands. After winning at Breitenfeld (1631) Gustavus was killed at the victory of Luetzen (1632).

After further fighting, the Peace of Prague (1635) seemed to end the conflict, at least for the German states (the Emperor had mostly annulled the Edict of Restitution), but neither the French nor the Spanish were content with this. The French came out openly in support of the Swedes in the last phase of the war, which then became a general European war as Spanish troops entered France from bases in the Spanish Netherlands, France entered Spain, and Portugal declared independence.

Peace negotiations began in 1644, with participation of the contending states and the German principalities, strengthening the rule of nation states in Europe. In the resulting Peace of Westphalia (1648), the independence of the Netherlands and Switzerland was confirmed; France took territories in Alsace and Lorraine; Sweden gained territory in North Germany; and the Holy Roman Empire ceased to have a significant role in international affairs. The Protestant states won a complete victory regarding annexed church lands, the Counter-Reformation was checked, and the Peace of Augsburg was expanded to include Calvinism as well as Catholicism and Lutheranism.

English Civil Wars (1642–51)

The first two Stuart kings of England, James I (1566-1625) and Charles I (1600-49), believed in the divine right of kings to rule without interference. Parliament, however, strove to assert control over taxation and royal expenditures. Charles I, fearing that Parliament would try to limit his power, ruled without it for 11 years. At the same time, Puritans were at odds with the established Anglican church, a situation complicated by the Presbyterianism and shifting alliances of the Scots. War in Scotland (1639) over attempts to institute Anglican practices forced Charles to call two parliaments in 1640 to raise money. The "Short Parliament" was quickly dismissed, and the "Long Parliament" resulted in bitter conflict with the king over constitutional and religious issues, which led to war in 1642. A first encounter between Royalists and Parliamentary forces (Edgehill, 1642), was indecisive, but Oliver Cromwell (1599-1658) and the Scots crushed the Royalists at Marston Moor (1644), and Cromwell was victorious with Parliament's New Model Army at Naseby (1645). The King fled to Scotland and the first war ended in 1646.

Charles began a second war in 1648, this time with Scottish aid; this uprising was quickly defeated, and Parliament and King began negotiations. Army leaders, who were more radical than many members of Parliament, seized power, purging Parliament of their opponents (leaving the "Rump Parliament"); the King was tried and executed (1649) and a Commonwealth instituted. In 1651 Cromwell put down a Royalist rebellion in Ireland, where he slaughtered thousands.

Charles II (1630-85), recognized as King in Scotland, was also proclaimed king of England by the Scots. His large army was defeated by Cromwell in a third war both at Dunbar (1650) and at Worcester (1651). Cromwell became Lord Protector; after his death his son Richard ruled briefly. In 1660 Charles II was restored to the throne.

War of the Spanish Succession (1701–14)

The succession of the childless Charles II of Spain caused widespread concern in Europe. England and Holland were opposed to a Bourbon and the potential union of Spanish and French power; France, England, and Holland were opposed to the Imperial candidate, re-uniting the Austrian and Spanish Habsburgs. Eventually Charles named the grandson of Louis IV as his heir—Philip V of Spain. French commercial and military moves, and the reservation of Philip's right to the French crown (1700) led to war with England, Holland and the Holy Roman Emperor. In Italy, Prince Eugene of Savoy led Imperial forces in outmaneuvering the French. In 1704, with the French menacing Vienna, John Churchill, Duke of Marlborough (1650–1722), marched to Bavaria and with Eugene won the great victory of Blenheim; victories at Ramillies (1706) Oudenard (1708) and finally Malplaquet (1709) followed. After further indecisive moves, England, Holland and France agreed to terms in the Peace of Utrecht (1713). The crowns of France and Spain would remain separate; the Protestant succession in Britain was guaranteed; the Empire received the Spanish Netherlands and Britain retained Gibraltar. France ceded Acadia, Newfoundland, and Hudson Bay—reflecting fighting in the North

American part of the conflict, Queen Anne's War—to Britain. The war had significant balance of power results: the containment of France, the eclipse of Spain in Europe, and recognition of British maritime strength.

War of the Austrian Succession (1740–48)

The Holy Roman Emperor Charles VI (1711–40) had other German princes recognize the right of his daughter, Maria Theresa (1717–80), to inherit his Austrian possessions through the Pragmatic Sanction of 1713. When he died, however, several claimants challenged Maria Theresa's rights; in particular, Frederick II, the Great, of Prussia, pressed a claim for Silesia in modern Poland. At first, the Prussians, together with their French, Spanish, Bavarians and Saxons allies, were successful, but Austria managed to detach Prussia and Saxony from the alliance and Austrian armies, aided by the British and Hanoverians forces under the leadership of King George II, ruler of both states, began to enjoy success. The French, after being driven to the west bank of the Rhine began a drive on the Austrian Netherlands, modern Belgium, that was largely successful. Prussia reentered the war against Austria and, despite being politically isolated, the Prussians were able to repel successive Imperial armies. By the Treaty of Aix-la-Chapelle (1748), Prussia was confirmed in control of Silesia, but otherwise, Maria Theresa's rights under the Pragmatic Sanction were recognized, as well as the election of Maria Theresa's husband, Francis I (1708–65), as Holy Roman Emperor.

The war in Europe spread to India and North America. In America, where the war was known as King George's War, a joint British and colonial force managed to capture the heavily fortified French stronghold of Louisbourg on Cape Breton and the French captured the important British trading post of Madras in southern India. At war's end, both captures were exchanged, leaving Britain and France in a position to pursue their ambitions in both places in the future.

The Seven Years War (1756–63)

This war embodied both the conflict between Prussia and Austria for supremacy in Germany, and the worldwide engagement between Britain and France. In Germany, Frederick the Great preempted an anticipated attack by the Austrians and their allies, France and Russia (and later Sweden), and entered Saxony in 1756 and then Bohemia.

At first successful, reverses put the Prussians in difficulties redeemed by victories at Rossbach and Leuthen (1757). Defeat at Rossbach led to a reduction in France's commitment to the European conflict. Britain, under the government of William Pitt the Elder (1758-61) provided heavy subsidies to Prussia, but even with these and his eventual mastery of the Austrians, Frederick was only spared defeat at the hands of the Russians (who briefly occupied Berlin) by the death of his enemy Empress Elizabeth and the accession of the pro-Prussian Peter III. Russia and Sweden made peace with the Prussians in 1762 and the treaty of Hubertusburg (February 1763) between Prussia, Austria and Saxony restored the central European territorial status quo.

In British-French conflict on the continent, the French started with victories but were soon decisively defeated at Krefeld in 1758 and Minden in 1759, ending the French threat to Hanover in Germany. British superiority at sea brought victories off Lagos (Portugal) and Quiberon Bay (Brittany) in 1759. In Portugal, the British helped to repel an invasion from Spain, which had joined France in a Bourbon alliance.

In North America (The French and Indian War), the British seized French Canada with victories at Louisbourg (1758), Quebec (1759) and Montreal (1760). In the Caribbean, the British took Guadaloupe and Martinique from France and Cuba from Spain (and also, in the Pacific, the Philippines). In India, Robert Clive (1725-74) defeated the French at Plessey (1757) and secured Bengal for the East India Company. British victories at Wandiwash (1760) and Pondicherry (1761) weakened the French position in the Carnatic coast (southeast India).

The results of the Seven Years War decisively established Britain as the leading colonial and sea power of the age. According to the Treaty of Paris (1763), the French abandoned their claims to North America and India. Other provisions of the treaty provided for the return of Guadaloupe and Martinique to France, and Cuba and the Philippines to the Spanish; Spain ceded Florida to Britain and received Louisiana from the French.

The American Revolution (1775-83)

1775　Tensions between England and the Colonies had been steadily growing worse since 1773 as colonists—especially in Boston—took drastic actions to protest British taxation problems. On March 20, 1775, a member of the House of Burgesses in Virginia, Patrick Henry (1736-99), delivered a stirring speech. He concluded by saying: "I know not what course others may take, but as for me—give me liberty, or give me death." In Boston, General Thomas Gage decided to move against radical leaders. Troops moved out of the city towards Concord on the night of April 18. Paul Revere and William Dawes, two local patriots, rode out of Boston to warn of the British move. When troops arrived in Lexington in the early morning hours of April 19, a skirmish broke out between the British and armed citizens known as "minutemen." The British then moved on to Concord, where more militia awaited them. After furious fighting, the British retreated back to Boston, where they were surrounded by patriot militia gathered in the hills overlooking the city. The seige of Boston had begun.

On May 10, patriot troops under the joint command of Ethan Allen and Benedict Arnold seized the British strongpoint of Fort Ticonderoga. That same day, the Second Contintental Congress convened in Philadelphia. John Hancock was elected president of the Congress on May 24. The Congress, on June 15, appointed George Washington as commander in chief of a fledgling American army. But on June 17, British forces assaulted patriot positions on Breed's Hill and Bunker Hill and after a furious battle, the patriots retreated. The cost to the British was horrendous, however, as their casualty rate was nearly 50 percent. Washington arrived in Boston on July 2 and took command of a hodge-podge of colonial militia with a troop strength of about 14,000. On August 23 King George III proclaimed America to be in a state of rebellion. As the seige outside Boston continued through summer, an American force led by General Richard Montgomery set out from Fort Ticonderoga on August 28, bound for Canada with the hope of drawing Canada into the war. On September 12, Washington sent Benedict Arnold north to join the invasion. The British countered the American moves by bombarding and burning Falmouth, now called Portland, Maine on October 18. American troops under Generals Montgomery and Arnold begin a seige of Quebec on December 8. On New Year's Eve, 1775, Montgomery launched an attack to break the siege. The assault failed, and Montgomery was killed. The battered Americans were forced to retreat.

1776　On January 1, the enlistments of thousands of militiamen outside Boston expired, and many went home. George Washington had hoped to have 20,000 men in army in a new Continental Army by this date, but only about 10,000 men volunteered. Washington called up other militia units to fill in gaps in the patriot line until new recruits could be found. Washington could not have asked for better recruiting propaganda than a pamphlet published on January 9 in Philedelphia. Entitled *Common Sense*, it was written by a self-educated Englishman newly arrived in America, Thomas Paine. He assailed the monarchy and advocated complete separation between America and Great Britain.

The war moved south on January 20, when the new British commander in Boston, General William Howe, sent infantry units to North Carolina, where they were to operate with militia units loyal to Britain. Washington convened a council of war at his headquarters in Cambridge, Mass., on Feburary 16 and proposed an assault on Boston to break the siege. His fellow generals, however, were opposed, and the plan was dropped. But on March 4, Washington ordered American troops to fortify Dorchester Heights, which overlooks Boston from the south. Artillery brought from Fort Ticonderoga by Henry Knox (1750–1806) was put in place, allowing the Americans to bombard the British garrison. The British briefly considered an assault on the heights, but weather prevented the action. The last British soldiers evacuated the city on March 17. The Americans took possession of the city later that day.

The war then moved to New York. Anticipating a British assault on the city, Washington's army began marching south on April 13 to set up a defense of Long Island. On April 17 the American warship Lexington, under the command of Capt. John Barry, defeated the British warship HMS Edward off the Virginia coast. Barry was later called the founder of the American Navy. An American adventure in Canada, however, was not as successful. A battle at Trois Rivieres on June 8 ended with a devastating American defeat, bringing the Canadian invasion to an end. On July 3, British General Howe and nearly 10,000 British troops sailed into New York harbor to begin preparations for an attack on the city. The following day, in Philadelphia, the Second Continental Congress accepted the final draft of a Declaration of Independence. The vote, by state, was unanimous, although New York abstained.

British forces began their attack on the American army in what is now Brooklyn on the night of August 26. After suffering high casualties, the Americans withdrew across the East River on the night of August 29, and subsequent-ly withdrew from lower Manhattan in early September. On September 29, a mysterious fire consumed huge swaths of the city. On November 16, the last American outpost in Manhattan fell when Fort Washington and its garrison of 3,000 soldiers surrendered. The bedraggled Americans withdrew through New Jersey and into Pennsylvania, with the British hard on their heels. But on the morning after Christmas, December 26, the Americans launched a successful surprise attack on German mercenaries in Trenton.

1777 As the main British force hurried to Trenton, Washington followed up his victory with another surprise attack, this one on January 4 in Princeton. The armies, following the custom of the day, then retired to winter quarters. Washington camped in Morristown, N.J.

In the summer the British launched an offensive from Canada into upper New York. Troops under General Burgoyne captured Fort Ticonderoga without a fight on July 6. On August 16 the Americans responded, when troops under the command of Brigadier General John Stark defeated an enemy detachment in Bennington, Vt. With General Howe now threatening Philadelphia, Washington moved south and paraded his troops through the city on August 24. But on September 11, the British defeated Washington at the Battle of Brandywine, outside Philadelphia, and members of Congress began to flee the city. The British captured the capital on September 23, and on October 4 defeated Washington again at the Battle of Germantown near Philadelphia.

Meanwhile, in northern New York, American troops under Horatio Gates inflicted huge casualties on Burgoyne on September 19 at Bemis Heights. A new American assault on October 7 led to Burgoyne's surrender in Saratoga on October 17. Gates's victory led to a movement in Congress to appoint him as the army's new commander. And on December 6, the French government revived talks about a prospective alliance with the American rebels. Washington's battered army established winter quarters in Valley Forge, Pa., on December 19.

1778 The French government recognized American independence on January 6 but throughout the harsh winter American soldiers lived in desperate conditions in snowy Valley Forge, where a breakdown in supplies led to terrible suffering among the troops. On April 24 Captain John Paul Jones (1747–92) of the American navy, in command of the warship *Ranger*, defeated the HMS *Drake* in

British waters. Both armies prepared for a new campaign, but the British suddenly began withdrawing from Philadelphia on June 16. The Americans reoccupied the city on June 19 and General Benedict Arnold was named military governor. As the British marched from Philadelphia to New York, Washington attacked on June 28 at Monmouth Court House. The battle was a draw, but it proved the Americans were still strong enough to fight. The British withdrawal continued. The Battle of Monmouth was the last major engagement of the war in the north. The French Navy arrived off Newport, R.I., on July 29, but a planned Franco-American offensive fizzled.

1779 An expedition in the west under the command of George Rogers Clark led to an attack on Fort Sackville near Vincennes in the Illinois Territory. The British garrison surrendered a day later. In the south, a new British strategy to move the war to the Carolinas and Georgia showed promise when the American force was defeated on June 20 at Stono Ferry, S.C. John Paul Jones, commanding the warship *Bonhomme Richard*, won a brutal, costly victory over HMS *Serapis* off the coast of England on September 23. On October 9 American and French forces were mauled in an attack on Savannah, Ga.

1780 On May 12 the Americans suffered their worst defeat of the war and Charleston, S.C. surrendered. The British captured nearly 5,000 prisoners, but on June 23 a small British advance in New Jersey was checked, when Americans under the command of Nathanael Greene won the Battle of Springfield. Congress ordered Horatio Gates to rally the Americans in the South, but on August 16 Gates was defeated when he tried to attack Camden, S.C. For the second time in less than four months, an American force was crushed. More terrible news followed when on September 25, Washington discovered that Benedict Arnold had betrayed the cause and tried to hand over the garrison at West Point to the British. Congress approved Washington's selection of Nathanael Greene to reorganize the American army in the South on October 7. That same day, American militia defeated Loyalist American troops at the battle of Kings Mountain, S.C.

1781 Greene, now in the South, divided his army as he prepared to confront British Lord Cornwallis. The detachment under Daniel Morgan stunned the British at the Battle of Cowpens, S.C., on January 17. Greene and Morgan rejoined forces and retreated into Virginia.

Greene returned to North Carolina after gathering militia reinforcements, and on March 15, he fought Cornwallis at the Battle of Guilford Courthouse. Though technically a British victory, Cornwallis suffered high casualties. He eventually withdrew, and on April 24, he left Wilmington, N.C. and marched to Virginia. He settled into camp in Yorktown, Va., on August 5. Sensing an opportunity to attack by land and sea, Washington and his French allies marched and sailed from the north. Pinched between the Franco-American armies and the French Navy, the British surrendered on October 19. Though hostilities continued, in essence the war ended with the surrender of Yorktown.

1783 The final peace treaties were signed on September 3 in Paris. The British evacuated New York, their last outpost, on November 25, and Washington bade farewell to his officers in Fraunces Tavern on December 4.

The Wars of the French Revolution (1792–1802)

These wars arose out of the tumultuous changes of the French Revolution (1789) and its impact on the rest of Europe. The Wars of the French Revolution (1792-1802) began as attempts to defend the revolution and then extended into wars of conquest. The peace of 1801-2 is usually taken as the dividing line with the Napoleonic Wars (1803-1815). Napoleon fought as a brilliant commander in the first series of wars and as the absolute ruler of France in the second.

The European powers, fearful of revolutionary ideas, pressed France to restore Louis XVI. But France declared war on Austria in April, 1792; at first falling back before the allied forces, the French won at Valmy (Sept. 1792) and advanced in the Austrian Netherlands and on the Rhine. The execution of Louis XVI (Jan. 1793) and other actions brought the First Coalition (Britain, Holland, Spain, Austria, and Prussia) into being, . The allies pushed into France, but with the aid of a mass military draft, the French expelled them by the end of 1793; Prussia, Holland, and Spain made peace quickly. Fighting continued, with an Austrian offensive (1796), rapid victories of Napoleon in Italy, and the defeat of the French fleet by Admiral Horatio Nelson (1758–1805) at Aboukir (1798) during Napoleon's invasion of Egypt.

The Second Coalition (Russia, Britain, Turkey, Portugal and Naples) was created in 1798 under Russian leadership. The Allies were victorious in north Italy and Switzerland.

Returning from Egypt, Napoleon crushed the Austrians at Marengo (1800) and Moreau won at Hohenlinden (1800). Austria was forced out of the war, and Great Britain, victorious still at sea but war-weary, made peace in 1802 (Treaty of Amiens). In France, Napoleon had become First Consul (1799), First Consul for Life (1802), and then Emperor (1804).

The Napoleonic Wars (1806–15)

Napoleon then faced a new so-called Third Coalition (1805) but he crushed the Austrians at Ulm, scored a brilliant victory over the Russians and Austrians at Austerlitz, and defeated Prussia at Jena (1806), entering Berlin in triumph. After defeating Russia at Friedland (1807) he became master of the continent. Napoleon reorganized the map of Europe, with new kings, including his brothers, other family members, allies and some of his officers, placed on new and existing thrones. Britain remained master of the sea, however, with a decisive victory over the French at Trafalgar (1805), again led by Nelson. Napoleon resolved to beat Britain with an economic blockade, the Continental System.

Austria attempted to reopen the war and was beaten at Wagram (1809), but Napoleon faced continuing problems in the Peninsular War in Spain and Portugal, where (1808–14) he was frustrated and his marshals ultimately defeated by the British under Wellington and Spanish and Portuguese regulars and guerrillas. The Russian Czar's rejection of the economically ruinous Continental System was the impetus for the turning point in Napoleon's fortunes. He crossed into Russia with an army of 500,000 in June, 1812 but in September he failed to achieve a decisive victory at Borodino and entered a devastated and burning Moscow, set ablaze by the Russians. Now he had no winter quarters, long supply lines, and few sources of local supply. He began a disastrous retreat and after the crossing of the Berezina River (November) his decimated army was in complete rout. Napoleon abandoned his forces to return to Paris to regroup. A new anti-French coalition was formed, and at Leipzig (Oct. 1813) Napoleon was forced to retreat; he was offered terms (France to return to borders of Rhine and Alps) and refused; the Allies entered Paris in March, 1814. Napoleon abdicated, was exiled to the island of Elba and replaced by Louis XVIII. In March 1815 he escaped and landed at Cannes. Thus began the Hundred Days, when the Allies finally destroyed Napoleon's army at Waterloo, under the Duke of Wellington (1769–1852) and von Blücher (1742–1819). Napoleon died in 1821 in exile on the desolate island of Saint Helena.

Crimean War (1853–56)

Claiming the right to protect Orthodox Christians within the Ottoman Empire, the Russian Czar Nicholas I (1796-1855), sent troops into Moldavia and Wallachia (Romania today), and defeated a Turkish fleet at Sinop on the Black Sea (1853). The British and French, fearing Russian ambitions in the Balkans and the Near East, supported Turkey and declared war on Russia (March, 1854). In September 1854 British, French, Sardinian and Turkish troops landed on the Crimean peninsula (Black Sea) for a bloody yearlong siege of the Russian naval base at Sevastopol. The appalling condition of sick and wounded Allied troops was given prominence by Florence Nightingale (1820–1910), leading to important reforms in nursing care. The allies were victorious at Balaklava (immortalized in Tennyson's poem "The Charge of the Light Brigade") and Inkerman. After the capture of strong points overlooking the city, the allies secured Sevastopol in 1855. (The Crimean War also involved fighting in the Caucasus and the Baltic.) Alexander II (1818-1881), Nicholas's son and successor, sued for peace. The Treaty of Paris (1856) provided for the territorial integrity of the Ottoman Empire, the neutralization of the Black Sea, and Russian renunciation of its claim of protection of Orthodox Christians under Turkish rule.

The American Civil War (1861–65)

1861 The Civil War began when the first shots were fired at Fort Sumter on April 12, 1861. Determined to maintain a symbolic presence of federal authority in the heart of the Confederacy, newly installed President Abraham Lincoln informed the South Carolina government of his intention to send a ship with supplies to Fort Sumter, a garrison in Charleston harbor still in federal hands. Confederates responded by demanding surrender of the fort and when he refused began an artillery assault and the garrison surrendered the next day. On April 15 Lincoln declared the lower South to be in state of "insurrection" and called for 75,000 men to enlist for the purposed of putting down the rebellion. Immediately, four more southern states seceded, and the nation prepared for war.

Despite their lack of training and equipment, the Confederate and Union armies met at the Battle of Bull Run (The First Battle of Manassas) in Virginia on July 21, 1861. After the Union Army under nearly drove the Confederates from the field, the latter rallied and staged a furious counter assault. Exhausted and undisciplined, Union soldiers panicked and began a chaotic retreat to Washington. The loss was deeply embarrassing to the Lincoln administration and greatly boosted morale in the Confederacy.

1862 While the Union Army in Virginia (soon to named the Army of the Potomac), now under the leadership of Gen. George B. McClellan (1826–85), regrouped, the war in the west heated up. Union victory depended on the army controlling the Mississippi River (thereby splitting the Confederacy in two) and seizing the key rail lines vital to the southern economy.

In February 1862 Union troops, led by a virtual unknown named Gen. Ulysses S. Grant (1822–85), seized Forts Henry and Donelson on the Tennessee River. The twin victories gave the Union control of vital communication and transportation routes on the Tennessee and Cumberland Rivers and drove the Confederates out of Kentucky and most of Tennessee.

An extraordinary naval clash occurred on March 8, 1862 when the *Virginia* (Confederate) and *Monitor* (Union) met off Hampton Roads, Virginia. The ensuing battle—the first ever between ironclad vessels—ended in a draw and left both ships badly damaged. The Virginia retreated up the James River where it did no damage, but did prevent McClellan from using the river in his upcoming campaign.

Less than three weeks later, Confederate fortunes in the west suffered another setback. The far west, including California, was secured from Confederate seizure after Union forces triumphed at the Battle of Glorieta Pass (March 26–28, 1862) in New Mexico. Further east, Grant withstood a surprise Confederate attack near Shiloh Church, Tennessee (April 6) and then counter-attacked to drive the Confederates off in retreat. Grant's victory left the Union Army in control of the Mississippi River south to Memphis, Tennessee. Working at the other end of the Mississippi, Union Navy Captain David G. Farragut (1801–1870) captured New Orleans (May 1), dealing a devastating blow to Confederate hopes as it closed the mouth of the Mississippi and put under Union control the South's largest city and most important commercial center.

In the spring of 1862, after lengthy delays (despite Lincoln's constant urging to move on the Confederate capital at Richmond, Va.), McClellan finally commenced his Peninsular Campaign. When the campaign became bogged down with delays, a Confederate force under General Thomas "Stonewall" Jackson (1824–63) went north and threatened an attack on Washington, D.C., prompting Lincoln to withhold 30,000 troops from McClellan to protect the capital.

It was late May before McClellan finally moved on Richmond. The Confederates attacked McClellan's slow moving force of 110,000 in the Battle of Fair Oaks (also called Seven Pines) on May 31–June 1, 1862. Although technically a Union victory the battle proved inconclusive. Yet it was an important turning point in that the Confederate general was severely injured and replaced by Robert E. Lee (1807–70).

Lee recalled Jackson from the Shenandoah Valley and led an offensive against McClellan to separate the Army of the Potomac from its York River base and destroy it. The Seven Days Battle (June 25–July 1, 1862) was bloody but inconclusive as both armies remained in the field. McClellan's army lay just 25 miles from Richmond, but he refused to move on Lee's weakened army, claiming he had inadequate amounts of intelligence, men and supplies.

Thoroughly frustrated, Lincoln ordered McClellan to abandon the Peninsular Campaign and remove the Army of Potomac to northern Virginia to unite with other forces for a traditional overland assault on Richmond. But Lee moved north and defeated those troops (August 29–30, 1862) in the Second Battle of Bull Run (Second Manassas) before McClellan could join him.

In September McClellan attacked Lee's army which had moved north into Maryland. The Battle of Antietam (Sharpsburg) claimed a total of 6,000 lives and left 17,000 wounded, making it the bloodiest single day of the war. The next day Lee took his tattered army back into Virginia, handing McClellan, who opted not to pursue, a technical victory.

Lincoln issued a preliminary Emancipation Proclamation that declared unless the seceded states returned to the Union by January 1, 1863, their slaves "shall be then, thenceforward, and forever free." Emancipation struck a blow at the foundation of southern society and all but eliminated the possibility that England would intervene in the conflict.

On Nov. 7, after McClellan refused to move against Lee, claiming as always that he lacked sufficient troops and supplies, an exasperated Lincoln relieved him of command and replaced him with General Ambrose E. Burnside (1824–81) who immediately formulated plans for an offensive against Richmond. Yet Burnside's impulsiveness proved almost as ruinous as McClellan's timidity for at the Battle of Fredericksburg (December 13, 1862) he ordered repeated attacks on fortified Confederate positions with disastrous results (nearly 13,000 casualties compared to Lee's 5,300).

Not all the news from the Union battlefields in late 1862 was negative. Union troops turned back an attempt by Confederates, to regain western Tennessee and Kentucky. After months of inconclusive maneuvering, the two forces finally clashed on December 31 in Tennessee in the Battle of Murfreesboro (Stone's River). When the Confederates retreated on January 2, 1863, the west was firmly in the hands of the Union Army for the rest of the war.

1863 The Emancipation Proclamation took effect on January 1, 1863, but it would be no more than a lofty declaration if the Union lost the war. In April 1863, 120,000 soldiers of the Army of the Potomac, now under Gen. Joseph Hooker (1814–79), once again set out to defeat Lee and take Richmond. At Chancellorsville (May 2, 1863) Lee divided his army and led one half in frontal assault against Hooker's center, while "Stonewall" Jackson attacked Hooker's right flank. After three days of bloody fighting the Army of the Potomac was nearly destroyed, and Hooker barely managed to retreat.

But Lee's stunning victory at Chancellorsville came at a very high price as he lost more than 20 percent of his men, including the man he had come to count on most, "Stonewall" Jackson, killed accidentally by his own men.

Despite these losses, Lee took the offensive and plunged into Union territory, crossing through Maryland into Pennsylvania. It was a risky move, but one he hoped would cause such alarm in the North as to force Grant to pull back from the west. Victory on northern soil would demoralize the Lincoln administration and strengthen the hand of "Peace Democrats" who were calling for a negotiated settlement with the Confederacy.

Although slow to react, the Army of the Potomac, now under Gen. George C. Meade, eventually confronted Lee at Gettysburg, a small town at the junction of several major

roads. For two days, the two armies clashed in the bloodiest fighting yet. On numerous occasions, each side seemed about to gain the upper hand, only to be turned back. On the third and decisive day, Lee threw caution to the wind and ordered on all-out assault on the heavily fortified Union center. "Pickett's Charge" as it became known, proved gallant, but suicidal as Union forces devastated Gen. George Pickett's 15,000 men as they tried to cross one mile of open field and ascend Cemetery Ridge. The next day, July 4, having lost one-third of his men (28,000 killed, wounded, or missing), Lee removed his tattered army back toward Virginia. Gettysburg was a major Union victory that ensured the Confederate Army would never again threaten the North.

On the day of Lee's retreat, Grant accepted the surrender of Vicksburg where he had been laying siege since mid-May. Vicksburg was the Confederacy's last stronghold on the Mississippi and the victory severed the South in two, leaving the Union in control of the entire Mississippi River.

Ten days later rioting broke out in New York City and lasted for four days before federal troops quelled the violence. Mobs of poor workers, many of them immigrants, took to the streets to protest the imposition of a draft instituted by the Lincoln administration to replenish the dwindling ranks of the Union Army. The riots did millions of dollars in damage and left 119 dead, including more than a dozen blacks blamed by the mob for the war and draft.

Even as rioters in New York blamed African Americans for the bloody war, 54th Massachusetts regiment, a unit made up of free blacks, became one of the first African American units given a chance to fight. Their nighttime assault on Fort Wagner (July 18, 1863), a key Confederate outpost that guarded the harbor in Charleston, S.C., like all others before it, was repulsed with extremely high casualties. But the courage exhibited by the soldiers under fire won them universal praise and did much to undermine the racist belief that blacks would not stand and fight. Eventually, some 180,000 blacks served in the Army (ten percent of the total Union Army), 38,000 of whom died.

In November, Grant and the general he increasingly counted on, William T. Sherman (1820–91), attacked the Confederate army in Tennesee and drove his army back into Georgia. Victory in the Battle of Chattanooga (Nov. 23–25, 1863) boosted northern morale and put most of eastern Tennessee and the vital Tennessee River in Union hands. Already cut in two after the fall of Vicksburg, the Confederacy now faced the prospect of being sliced into thirds.

1864 In the beginning of 1864 Lincoln named Grant commander of all Union armies. He recognized in Grant a commander who understood the key to victory in modern warfare—seek out and destroy the enemy's army rather than seize territory. Grant planned a two-pronged attack to finish off the Confederacy. He sent the 120,000 men of the Army of the Potomac south to destroy Lee's army of 66,000 and to take Richmond. Sherman, a man who shared Grant's understanding of modern warfare, took an army of 90,000 from Tennessee and pushed east to destroy the Confederate force of 60,000 and to seize Atlanta.

In the first clash, known as the Battle of the Wilderness, Grant hurled his army against Lee's for two days (May 5-6). Aided by the rough, wooded terrain and sluggish Union leadership, the Confederates successfully survived Grant's offensive and withdrew. Both sides lost huge numbers of men (18,000 federals to 12,000 Confederates). Unlike his predecessors who customarily opted for rest and recouperation after a major engagement, Grant ordered his army to pursue Lee the very next day. On May 8 the two armies clashed again 10 miles closer to Richmond in the Battle of Spotsylvania Court House, an epic struggle that played out for days and left another 30,000 casualties between the two armies. Lee's army was weakened but remained intact.

Grant continued southward, trying to draw Lee out for a final, decisive battle. Lee worked to keep his army between Grant and Richmond, playing for time and avoiding total defeat. A third major engagement occurred on June 3 at Cold Harbor. Grant again ordered a massive assault against Lee's smaller but heavily entrenched force. The result was the greatest loss of life since Fredericksburg in December 1862. More than 7,000 federals fell compared to fewer than 1,500 Confederates.

After the disaster at Cold Harbor, Grant changed his strategy. He moved his army south past Richmond and seized the vital railroad junction at Petersburg. If he took the town, he would cut Richmond off from the rest of the Confederacy. But Lee kept his exhausted army on the move and managed to dig in around Petersburg before Grant arrived. By now Grant recognized the futility of staging frontal assaults against entrenched troops and settled down for a prolonged siege.

General Sherman faced less resistance. His opponent tried to avoid a direct fight. But Sherman, like Grant, refused to stop in his drive toward Atlanta and took the city on September 2. It was a crushing blow that all but doomed the Confederacy to collapse. Further adding to their woes was the fact that the victory boosted northern morale and helped re-elect Lincoln in November, thereby killing the hope that a war-weary Democrat would win and open peace negations with the Confederacy.

Shortly after seizing Atlanta, Sherman's army embarked on an epic journey across the state of Georgia to deprive the Confederate Army of badly needed supplies and to demoralize the southern people. Six weeks after Lincoln won re-election, as Sherman moved into Georgia, he sent a detachment of troops which all but destroyed the Confederate force at the Battle of Nashville (December 15-16, 1864). Less than a week later, Sherman's army took Savannah. Known as the "March to the Sea," Sherman's 285-mile campaign left a 60-mile wide swath of destruction in its wake. More than $100 million in property was seized or destroyed and the Confederate army had lost a major source of supplies.

1865 With Georgia now in ashes, the stage was set for the final phase of Grant's plan—the crushing of Lee's army between his and Sherman's forces. On February 1, Sherman left Savannah and headed north into South Carolina. He faced almost no opposition and took the city of Columbia, South Carolina on February 17th then continued north into North Carolina where the meager opposition provided by General Joseph E. Johnston's force slowed him only slightly.

By now Grant's nearly nine-month long siege of Lee's army at Petersburg began to take its toll. Cut off from supplies, Lee's men were starving. Thousands had deserted. On April 1, in the Battle of Five Forks, General Philip Sheridan's (1831–88) cavalry and a large force of infantry attacked Lee's right flank and cut off the only remaining railroad line into Petersburg. When Grant attacked all along the Confederate line the next day, he forced Lee to retreat from both Richmond and Petersburg. Lee's one remaining hope was to somehow slip his ragged army west and south to join forces with Johnston in North Carolina. To prevent this, Grant dispatched Sheridan's cavalry which headed them off at a place called Appomattox Courthouse, Virginia. On April 8 Lee made one last attempt to break out, but failed. The next day, April 9, 1865, Lee surrendered. Almost four years to the day that the first shots were fired at Fort Sumter, the Civil War was over.

The Franco-Prussian War (1870-71)

Otto von Bismarck (1815–98), the Prussian Chancellor, believing that a victorious war with France would encourage independent south German states to join with the Prussian-led North German Confederation, goaded the French into declaring war (July 15, 1870) over an attempt to place a German prince on the Spanish throne. A Prussian-led invasion of France under Marshall Helmuth von Moltke (1800–91) resulted in an overwhelming victory at the Battle of Sedan (September 1, 1870) in which 80,000 prisoners were taken, including Napoleon III; the fortress of Metz surrendered October 27, 1870. A provisional French government deposed Napoleon III (1808–73) and declared the Third Republic. Paris was surrounded in September and capitulated on January 28, 1871. The Treaty of Frankfurt (May 10, 1871) resulted in France's loss of most of Alsace and Lorraine and the payment of a heavy indemnity. At Versailles, William I of Prussia (1797–1888) was declared Emperor of Germany. The war transformed Germany, changed the balance of power, and prefigured the First World War.

World War I

On June 28, 1914, a Serb nationalist assassinated the Austrian Archduke Francis Ferdinand, the heir to the Austrian throne, in Sarajevo. This was the flashpoint that led to war, but the causes ran much deeper. The war followed decades of imperialist, economic, and territorial rivalries among the great powers, accompanied by an armaments race empowered by new technology and industrial development. Serbia rejected an ultimatum by Austria-Hungary, which declared war on July 28. Russia mobilized, and was answered by a German declaration of war (August 1). The Germans, believing France was about to attack, declared war on France (August 3) and sent troops through Belgium and Luxembourg. Britain joined the war in response to the German invasion and violation of the treaty of Belgian neutrality. The two sides in the war were the Central Powers (Germany and Austria-Hungary, later joined by Turkey and Bulgaria) and the Allies (France, Great Britain, Russia the Triple Entente countries, Serbia and Belgium, later joined by the U.S. and many other countries). Italy declined to fight with the Central Powers and later joined the Allies.

1914

The Western Front   Following mobilization, the Germans and the French acted in accordance with their pre-war battle plans. The German commander Helmuth von Moltke (1848–1916), nephew of the 19th century Prussian commander, carried out the Schlieffen plan, named for its author, a former chief of the German general staff, and launched an invasion of Belgium. During the initial weeks of the war, the Germans were able to keep to their plan's timetable. Despite a setback delivered by the British at Mons, the Germans occupied almost all of Belgium and were soon deep in France. In the course of their occupation, German soldiers were accused of committing atrocities, which were used by the Allies to turn neutral opinion against the Central Powers.

The German plan was formulated on the assumption that the French would stay on the defensive behind a line of fortresses. Since the Germans did not wish to mount a direct assault on the French fortresses, the invasion through Belgium was a way to outflank them. The French, however, in their final pre-war plan, Plan XVII, proposed a massive frontal attack against the German border, leaving the northern border with Belgium largely undefended. The resulting offensive, known as the Battle of the Frontiers, squandered countless French lives against superior German firepower. Meanwhile, the main German force continued to push south towards Paris, although their plan had originally called for a sweep west of Paris. The French and British attacked the German right flank and forced the Germans back at the First Battle of the Marne. The Germans , however, were able to retreat to easily defended positions within France. As the Germans began to fortify their new positions, there began the "Race to the Sea." The initial French retreat had left the northern coast undefended. The French sent troops north to insure that they, and not the Germans, controlled the coast, representing as it did a vital link to Britain. The Germans too moved to seize the coast, culminating in the First Battle of Ypres in which the Germans suffered heavy casualties. As 1914 ended, the Western Front had assumed the shape, from the sea to the Swiss border, that it would retain until the autumn of 1918. This front was the scene of innumerable casualties on both sides in seemingly unending trench warfare.

The Eastern Front   A small German army had been left to guard the Prussian heartland against a larger

Russian force. To relieve pressure on the French, the Russians moved swiftly against the Germans. Command in the East was turned over to Paul von Hindenburg (1847–1934) and his chief of staff, Erich Ludendorff (1865–1937). The Russians were forced to split their armies and the numerically inferior Germans were able to defeat them at the Battle of Tannenberg and at the Masurian Lakes. Elsewhere in the east the Central Powers were less successful. A divided Austrian army was unable to defeat Serbia in the south and was itself defeated in Galicia, Austrian Poland.

War Outside Europe   The Allies quickly seized Germany's overseas possessions with the exception of German East Africa (modern Tanzania), where resistance continued up to 1918. On the borders of the Ottoman Empire there were three major areas of combat. After years of stalemate, British and Commonwealth troops, aided by Arab rebels, overwhelmed Turkish troops in Palestine and by war's end, the Allies had seized Damascus in Syria. Anglo-Indian troops invaded Mesopotamia (modern Iraq) early in the war to protect British oil interests in the Persian Gulf. After initial successes, an invading army was forced to surrender at Kut al-Amara in 1916 and by war's end the Allies had failed to make a breakthrough on this front. The Turkish war effort was primarily directed against the Russian Trans-Caucasus provinces. The Russians repulsed these attacks and pushed into Turkey. Local support for the invaders triggered massacres of Armenians in the Ottoman Empire. After the outbreak of the Russian Revolution, the Caucasus front collapsed and by war's end German and Turkish troops had invaded the Trans-Caucasus region and Russian Central Asia.

1915

The Western Front   As 1915 began, the combatants began to realize that, notwithstanding pre-war predictions, the war would be long. The British in particular realized that they could not rely only on their navy to conduct the war and began to raise and equip a large continental army. The stalemate on the Western Front continued, despite the second battle of Ypres, in which the Germans used poison gas for the first time in the West. Allied offensives—the French in Artois and Champagne, and the British toward Lens and Loos, failed to effect breakthroughs.

The Eastern Front   Although denied additional troops from the west, von Hindenburg and Ludendorff finally got permission to mount an offensive against the

Russians in conjunction with the Austrians. This offensive proved successful and the Russians were driven from Poland, but the Russian army remained intact. Serbia and Montenegro were overrun by Bulgarian and Austro-Hungarian troops.

Winston Churchill (1871–1974), the British First Lord of the Admiralty, and others had begun to question direct assaults on the Western Front early on. Churchill, a firm believer in sea power, began to lobby for the opening of another front; he proposed a naval attack on the Dardanelles opening the way to Constantinople. Such an attack, it was argued, would drive the Turks out of the war and relieve pressure on the Russians. Although Allied military commanders were reluctant to spare troops from the Western Front a force was collected and dispatched to aid the naval operations. After the navy proved unable to clear the Dardanelles itself, these troops were landed on the European shore of Turkey near the town of Gallipoli. Despite substantial casualties on both sides, the Turks remained in possession of the heights and late in 1915 it was decided to abandon the attack.

The Naval War   The British, with substantial naval supremacy, relied on an ever tightening blockade of the Central Powers to drive their enemies to sue for peace. In 1914 a series of engagements designed to eliminate German naval and commercial presence outside Europe had moderate success. Despite a setback at the Battle of Coronel off Chile, this goal was largely accomplished by year's end. Germany feared to risk its battle fleet in a single great battle, and was content to launch a series of raids on British North Sea ports. Finally, in 1916, the Germans steamed out to meet the British high seas fleet at the Battle of Jutland (May 31). The battle was a draw but because the Germans needed to break the blockade, it was essentially a German loss. Mounting German frustration with the British blockade led eventually to unrestricted submarine warfare, which would lead to the United States' entry into the war. Although Allied commerce was disrupted by this warfare, the Germans never possessed sufficient submarines to inflict a serious blow on the Allied cause.

1916

The Western Front   In an attempt to weaken the French the German Chief of Staff Erich von Falkenhayn (1861–1922) decided to attack the French fortress town of Verdun, which the French would have to defend, if they chose, at heavy cost. The town was of little strategic importance but the French rose to the bait and resolved to hold the position at all costs. As time passed, however, the Germans lost sight of their original objective and became obsessed with taking the town without regard to their own casualties. In the end, both sides came to invest the battle with an importance far beyond its strategic significance. By the end of 1916 the French had recaptured lost ground and the position was approximately what it was before the attack, at the cost of an estimated 300,000 casualties on both sides. Von Falkenhayn was dismissed.

In order to take pressure off of the French at Verdun the British in June launched a campaign of five months duration known as the Battle of the Somme. The British used tanks for the first time, and after months of deadly attritional warfare the British could claim, in November, small territorial gains and the imposition of heavy casualties on the German field army. But at the end of the year stalemate continued in the West and an estimated 1.2 million men lost their lives, perhaps 650,000 Germans, 400,000 British, and 200,000 French.

The Eastern Front The Russians launched an offensive against the Austrians in southern Poland, but after driving them back a considerable distance, the offensive stalled and there was no general reversal of the Russian losses of 1915. The offensive did, however, prompt Romania, which had been neutral from to declare for the Allies. This proved disastrous. Bulgaria, which had joined the Central Powers, served as a staging ground for a Bulgarian-Turkish invasion of Romania, while German and Austrian troops stopped a Romanian invasion of Hungary and went on the offensive. In a matter of weeks, all of Romania had fallen to the Central Powers, except for a portion close to Russia. Anglo-French troops in Salonika in Greece attempted to put pressure on Bulgaria by marching north, but a small force of Bulgarians and Germans was able to stop them.

The Italian Front Italy joined the Allies in 1916. The Italians launched a series of battles on the Isonzo River. The strategic goal was to breach the Alps and drive on to Vienna. However, those Alps were among the most rugged in Europe and the Austrian position was easily defensible. The Austrians attacked from Trentino, crossing the border and driving on Venice, only to be stopped by resolute defense at Monte Ciova.

1917

The Western Front The French commander since the beginning of the war, Marshall Joseph Joffre (1852– 1931), lost the confidence of the government and was replaced in late 1916 by Robert Nivelle (1856–1924), who had convinced his political superiors that he had a formula for breaking the stalemate in the west. His offensive in early 1917 proved a disaster. The offensive in Champagne resulted in little gain, but stretched the morale of the French army to the breaking point, resulting in widespread mutinies. Nivelle was replaced by Philippe Petain (1856–1951), who quickly dealt with soldiers' grievances instituting a policy of rest and retraining that effectively took the French army out of the war for the rest of 1917. The British responded to requests to take pressure off the French by planning a summer offensive in Flanders. This offensive, the Third Battle of Ypres, consisted of a series of engagements, among them the battle for Passchendaele ridge, that resulted in horrific British and Commonwealth losses for little gain. On April 6, the United States declared war on Germany, but needed time to mobilize troops.

The Eastern Front Having crushed Romania, the Central Powers turned on Serbia. Austrian, German, and Bulgarian troops launched an offensive, Amid great hardships, the Serbian army managed to escape and was eventually ferried to Salonika. In March of 1917, revolution broke out in St. Petersburg and within a short period of time, the Tsar abdicated. Power was assumed by Alexander Kerensky (1881–1970), a Socialist committed to continuing the war against the Central Powers. Kerensky's policy was undermined by the Bolsheviks under V.I. Lenin (1870–1924) and Leon Trotsky (1879–1940), who seized power in November. The Bolsheviks offered the Central Powers a truce and in March 1918, the Treaty of Brest-Litovsk was signed, effectively ending the war against the Central Powers in the east, although civil war continued in Russia for years.

The Italian Front The Austrians, re-enforced by Germans, decisively defeated the Italian army at the Battle of Caporetto, driving it back to the River Piave. Timely re-enforcement by British and French troops stabilized the line, but at the cost of weakening the Western Front.

1918 The collapse of Russia in 1917 meant that soldiers were available for a last German offensive in the west. In March of 1918, the Germans attacked the British army near Amiens in an attempt to separate it from the French. After enjoying initial success, the German advance slowed and eventually stalled. Having failed to break the British army, Ludendorff turned against the French army in Champagne, culminating in the Second Battle of the Marne, in which the Germans were stopped short of Paris

(July-August). In August, the Allies began a counter offensive that made steady progress at high cost. For the first time in the war American troops distinguished themselves in such battles as St. Mihiel, Chateau Thierry, and the Argonne Forest. The German army was not routed but increasing numbers of German troops surrendered, in part because the Americans represented an accession of power to the Allies that more than offset Russia and in part because of Germany's deteriorating political and military position. Internal opposition to the war grew resulting in strikes and other disturbances in German cities. Finally, the government was forced to ask for an armistice based on principles set forth earlier by U.S. President Woodrow Wilson (1856–1924). Austria, Bulgaria and Turkey sued for peace and the German fleet mutinied at its home port of Kiel. Wilhelm II (1859–1941) left Berlin and went into exile in the Netherlands for the rest of his life. The armistice ending the war was signed by an interim government on November 11, 1918.

Aftermath A peace conference was held in Paris that resulted in 1919 in signing of the Treaty of Versailles ending the war with Germany. (Other treaties were signed with Austria, Hungary, Bulgaria, and Turkey.) The Treaty of Versailles placed the responsibility for the war on Germany and its allies, imposed reparations and military sanctions on Germany, returned Alsace and Lorraine to France, demilitarized the Rhineland, and made other territorial arrangements including several crucial ones in the Middle East that gave Great Britain and France a firm foothold in the oil-rich region. The United States Senate refused to ratify the Treaty of Versailles and with it the League of Nations, simply declaring in 1921 that the war with Germany was over. The treaties that concluded the war in the end satisfied neither victors nor vanquished, and hope for permanent collective security through creation of the League of Nations, which had some successes, ultimately proved ephemeral.

World War II

1939 On September 1, Germany invaded Poland from the west. Britain and France declared war on Germany on September 3. The United States had declared its neutrality on May 1, 1937, when Roosevelt signed the Permanent Neutrality Bill into law, and on September 5 he invoked that law. On September 8, however, President Roosevelt authorized a military buildup. The Soviets invaded Poland from the east on September 17. Warsaw surrendered on September 27, and the Germans and Soviets partitioned Poland on September 29. The Soviets then invaded Finland on November 30. In mid-December, the Royal Navy battled the German warship *Graf Spee* off the South American (Montevideo) coast. The ship's captain scuttled the *Graf Spee* on December 17, giving the British a morale boost.

1940 With little action on the main front, the Germans occupied Denmark and invaded Norway on April 9. The so-called "phony war" in Europe came to an end on May 10 with a massive German invasion of Belgium, the Netherlands, and Luxembourg. British Prime Minister Neville Chamberlain (1869–1940) resigned and was replaced by the First Lord of the Admiralty, Winston Churchill. On May 13, Churchill told Britain and the world that he had "nothing to offer but blood, toil, tears and sweat." German troops crossed into France that same day. On May 26, with the battle in France lost, the British began evacuating their expeditionary force from the port of Dunkirk.

Norway surrendered on June 9; France, on June 22. With Hitler triumphant in Europe, Roosevelt declared a national emergency in the United States on June 27. In preparation for a planned invasion of Britain, the German air force (Luftwaffe) attacked Royal Air Force bases on August 15. The onslaught was massive, but the R.A.F. prevailed. Not long after this pivotal battle, the Germans changed their strategy and began bombing cities. The R.A.F. bombed Berlin on August 25 and 26.

On September 16, President Roosevelt signed the Selective Service Bill, authorizing the draft of Americans between the ages of 21 and 35. With a cross-channel invasion scheduled for September 21, the Germans launched their largest air raid on Britain on September 15, hoping to destroy the R.A.F. The effort failed, and the invasion was postponed. The Luftwaffe continued to bomb England, leading to a massive raid on Coventry on November 14.

1941 British forces in Libya routed the Italians, capturing Tobruk on January 22. The Australians and British followed up with a victory in Benghazi on February 6. On that day, Erwin Rommel (1891–1944) was given command of Germany's Afrika Korps, which was sent to Libya to assist the beleaguered Italians. On March 11, the U.S. Senate passed the Lend-Lease Act, which authorized Roosevelt to send arms and equipment to Britain and other countries opposing the Axis (50 destroyers had already been exchanged in September 1940).

On April 6 German troops invaded Yugoslavia and Greece. Rudolf Hess, the third most-powerful man in Nazi Germany, parachuted into Britain on May 10 on a bizarre, unauthorized mission to broker peace between Germany and the British. The Royal Navy sank the German battle-ship Bismarck on May 27.

In a move that stunned a world already familiar with the unthinkable, Germany invaded the Soviet Union on June 22. Hitler's huge commitment of men and material to the Eastern Front meant that Britain was safe from invasion. It also changed the war's dynamics. On July 31, the head of the Luftwaffe, Hermann Göring, used the phrase "final solution" in discussing what was to be done with Europe's Jews.

Winston Churchill and President Roosevelt met face to face in Newfoundland on August 9-12 to create an eight-point program of war aims, subsequently named the Atlantic Charter. After Nazi U-boats attacked numerous American ships, Roosevelt issued the order on September 11 to "shoot at sight" any German or Italian ship encoun-tered by American ships or planes.

Germany ordered Jews to wear a Star of David begin-ning September 13. The following day, more than a half-million Russians surrendered near Kiev. In Asia, Japan's War Minister, Hideki Tojo (1884–1948), was named Prime Minister on October 16, signaling a more aggres-sive policy toward the United States. On December 6, the new Soviet commander of Moscow, General Georgi Zhukov (1896–1974), launched a massive counter-attack against German forces.

On December 7 Japanese warplanes attacked the U.S. naval base of Pearl Harbor in Hawaii. The United States declared war on Japan the following day. Germany and Italy declared war on the U.S. on December 11.

1942 The German SS, the elite military units of the Nazis, officially adopted a policy of genocide against the Jews on January 20. The Japanese captured the British garrison of Singapore, thought to be impregnable, on February 15. On March 11 U.S. General Douglas MacArthur left the Philippines, soon to fall to the Japanese. He told the Filipinos: "I shall return." The Japanese overran an American garrison on Bataan on April 9. Nearly 75,000 American and Filipino prisoners were captured, and many died during the Bataan Death March. American morale improved on April 18 when General James Doolittle, fly-ing from the carrier USS Hornet, led an air raid on Tokyo. Less than a month later, from May 4–8, U.S. carriers and

planes clashed with Japanese forces in the Battle of the Coral Sea. On May 6 American ground forces on Corregidor surrendered.

More than a thousand British aircraft bombed the German city of Cologne during the night of May 30. Thanks to intercepts of Japanese communications, the American fleet won the Battle of Midway on June 4–6. Japan lost four carriers, and America would now go on the offensive in the Pacific. In North Africa, Rommel overran the British garrison of Tobruk in Libya on June 21.

America's 1st Marine Division invaded Guadalcanal on August 7. British forces under the command of General Bernard Montgomery (1887–1976) launched the battle of El Alamein on October 24, beginning the Allied recon-quest of North Africa. American and British troops invad-ed Algeria and Morocco on November 8. Code-named Operation Torch, it was the beginning of major Anglo-American operations against the Germans. In Russia, the Red Army began a major offensive to relieve Stalingrad on November 19.

1943 The Battle of Stalingrad ended with a stunning German surrender on January 31, a turning point of the war in Europe. In the Pacific theater, the Japanese evacuat-ed Guadalcanal on February 9. And in North Africa, the leader of Germany's famed Afrika Korps, Rommel, left the region on March 9 after a string of defeats. Polish Jews in Warsaw launched an uprising on April 19. It would end on May 16, with few survivors.

The Anglo-American conquest of North Africa was completed on May 12 with the surrender of remaining Axis troops. The victorious Allies then invaded Sicily on July 10. Fifteen days later, on July 25, the Italian dictator Benito Mussolini (1883–1945) was overthrown and placed under arrest. Italy ended hostilities with the Allies on September 3, and the American army invaded Salerno on September 9 to fight German forces in Italy. German troops rescued Mussolini from his captors on September 12. The Soviets continued their dramatic westward push, recapturing Kiev on November 6.

U.S. Marines landed on Tarawa in the Gilbert Islands on November 20. Roosevelt, Churchill and Stalin met together for the first time in Tehran, Iran, from November 28 to December 1. The leaders discussed preparations for an invasion of Nazi-held France. Rommel was named to oversee German defenses in France on December 12. Dwight Eisenhower was appointed supreme commander of the Mediterranean unified command on December 24.

1944 Allied troops landed in Anzio on January 22. The Red Army relieved Leningrad on January 27 after a 900-day siege. A million or more civilians most likely died.

American troops entered Rome on June 4 after weeks of bitter fighting. On June 6, American, British and Canadian troops landed in Normandy as part of the long-expected invasion of Hitler's Fortress Europe. Five thousand ships, the largest armada in history, took part in the D-Day invasion, Operation Overlord. Some 150,000 troops were put ashore on five beaches.

U.S. Marines, moving closer to the Japanese home islands, invaded Saipan on June 15. American naval forces sank two Japanese carriers during the Battle of the Philippine Sea on June 19–20. Tojo was ousted as the civilian and military leader of Japan in July.

With the Allies pressing on both the western and eastern fronts, a group of dissident German officers attempted to kill Adolf Hitler on July 20. The plot failed. Among those implicated was Field Marshal Erwin Rommel, who was allowed to commit suicide. American and Free French troops invaded southern France on August 15 in what became known as the "Champagne Campaign." The Russians moved into Poland in late July and into Romania on August 20. The liberation of Paris took place on August 25, with the Free French army leading the way. A new German offensive from the air began on September 8, when a V-2 rocket landed in Britain.

U.S. Marines landed on Peleliu Island in the Pacific on September 15. In a daring but vain move, the Allies tried to get behind German lines by landing paratroops near Arnhem in Holland on September 17 (Operation Market-Garden). Survivors later were evacuated.

On October 2 German troops put down a two-month civilian uprising in Warsaw that was encouraged but not supported by the Soviets. General MacArthur made good on his promise to return to the Philippine Islands as Americans landed there on October 20. A huge naval engagement between American and Japanese warships, the Battle of Leyte Gulf, followed on October 23 to October 26. The Japanese lost 34 ships.

After retreating through France since D-Day, the German army counterattacked through the Ardennes Forest on December 16. The fight which ensued became known as the Battle of the Bulge. On December 22 the commander of the besieged American garrison, General Anthony McAuliffe, gave a one-word answer when Germans demanded his surrender: "Nuts." The siege ended on December 26.

1945 More than a million Soviet troops under Zhukov launched an attack against German troops in Poland on January 12. Stalin, Roosevelt and Churchill met in Yalta from February 4–11 to discuss postwar plans. Royal Air Force and U.S. airplanes firebombed Dresden February 13–15, killing some 50,000 civilians. U.S. Marines landed on Iwo Jima on February 19. On March 7, American troops crossed the Rhine River at Remagen.

The American air force firebombed Tokyo and other Japanese cities on March 9, killing more than 80,000 civilians. On April 1 American forces invaded Okinawa. The Buchenwald concentration camp was liberated on April 11. The following day, President Roosevelt died in Warm Springs, Georgia. Harry Truman succeeded him. Soviet troops reached Berlin on April 23, and on April 25, American and Soviet forces linked up on the Elbe River.

The former dictator of Italy, Benito Mussolini, was captured and killed by Italian irregulars on April 28. Hitler committed suicide on April 30 as Russian troops closed in on his bunker. Germany surrendered on May 7. The allies designated May 8 as V-E Day—Victory in Europe. In his victory speech, Churchill reminded his nation that Japan remained unconquered. Nevertheless, he would be turned out of office on July 26 when British voters chose the Labor Party to lead them.

The atomic bomb was tested successfully in New Mexico on July 16. On August 6, the American warplane *Enola Gay* dropped the bomb on the Japanese city of Hiroshima. Another atomic bomb fell on Nagasaki on August 9. The Japanese surrendered on August 14, and August 15 was designated as V-J Day.

The Changing Face of War

The atomic bombs dropped on two Japanese cities were at first welcomed around the world because they brought an immediate end to the most devastating war in history. But within a decade the power of these weapons was increased exponentially and their numbers increased to frightening levels. Like so many military "advancements" in human history, atomic weapons had been developed in self-defense.

In 1939, physicist Leo Szilard met with his former teacher Albert Einstein on Long Island, New York, to discuss two startling developments taking place in Europe. Two German physicists had published their discovery of

War Evolves With Drones, Some Tiny as Bugs

By ELISABETH BUMILLER
and THOM SHANKER

Two miles from the cow pasture where the Wright Brothers learned to fly the first airplanes, military researchers are at work on another revolution in the air: shrinking unmanned drones, the kind that fire missiles into Pakistan and spy on insurgents in Afghanistan, to the size of insects and birds.

Half a world away in Afghanistan, Marines marvel at one of the new blimplike spy balloons that float from a tether 15,000 feet above one of the bloodiest outposts of the war, Sangin in Helmand Province. The balloon, called an aerostat, can transmit live video—from as far as 20 miles away—of insurgents planting homemade bombs.

From blimps to bugs, an explosion in aerial drones is transforming the way America fights and thinks about its wars. Predator drones, the Cessna-sized workhorses that have dominated unmanned flight since the Sept. 11, 2001, attacks, are by now a brand name, known and feared around the world. But far less known is the sheer size, variety and audaciousness of a rapidly expanding drone universe, along with the dilemmas that come with it.

The Pentagon now has some 7,000 aerial drones, compared with fewer than 50 a decade ago. Within the next decade the Air Force anticipates a decrease in manned aircraft but expects its number of "multirole" aerial drones like the Reaper—the ones that spy as well as strike—to nearly quadruple, to 536. Already the Air Force is training more remote pilots, 350 this year alone, than fighter and bomber pilots combined.

The Pentagon has asked Congress for nearly $5 billion for drones in 2012, and by 2030 envisions ever more stuff of science fiction: "spy flies" equipped with sensors and microcameras to detect enemies, nuclear weapons or victims in rubble. Peter W. Singer, a scholar at the Brookings Institution and the author of "Wired for War," a book about military robotics, calls them "bugs with bugs."

In recent months drones have been more crucial than ever in fighting wars and terrorism. The Central Intelligence Agency spied on Osama bin Laden's compound in Pakistan by video transmitted from a new bat-winged stealth drone, the RQ-170 Sentinel, otherwise known as the "Beast of Kandahar," named after it was first spotted on a runway in Afghanistan. One of Pakistan's most wanted militants, Ilyas Kashmiri, was reported dead this month in a C.I.A. drone strike, part of an aggressive drone campaign that administration officials say has helped paralyze Al Qaeda in the region — and has become a possible rationale for an accelerated withdrawal of American forces from Afghanistan. More than 1,900 insurgents in Pakistan's tribal areas have been killed by American drones since 2006, according to the Web site www.longwarjournal.com.

Large or small, drones raise questions about the growing disconnect between the American public and its wars. Military ethicists concede that drones can turn war into a videogame, inflict civilian casualties and, with no Americans directly at risk, more easily draw the United States into conflicts. Drones have also created a crisis of information for analysts on the end of a daily video deluge. Within the military, no one disputes that drones save American lives. Many see them as advanced versions of "stand-off weapons systems," like tanks or bombs dropped from aircraft, that the United States has used for decades. "There's a kind of nostalgia for the way wars used to be," said Deane-Peter Baker, an ethics professor at the United States Naval Academy, referring to noble notions of knight-on-knight conflict. Drones are part of a post-heroic age, he said, and in his view it is not a always a problem if they lower the threshold for war. "It is a bad thing if we didn't have a just cause in the first place," Mr. Baker said. "But if we did have a just cause, we should celebrate anything that allows us to pursue that just cause."

To Mr. Singer of Brookings, the debate over drones is like debating the merits of computers in 1979: They are they here to stay, and the boom has barely begun. "We are at the Wright Brothers Flier stage of this," he said.

Mimicking Insect Flight   A tiny helicopter is buzzing menacingly as it prepares to lift off in the Wright-Patterson aviary, a warehouse-like room lined with 60 motion-capture cameras to track the little drone's every move. The helicopter, a footlong hobbyists' model, has been programmed by a computer to fly itself. Soon it is up in the air making purposeful figure eights. The push right now is developing "flapping wing" technology, or recreating the physics of natural flight, but with a focus on insects rather than birds. Birds have complex muscles that move their wings, making it difficult to copy their aerodynamics. Designing a an insect is hard, too, but their wing motions are simpler. In 2011, researchers unveiled a hummingbird drone, built by the firm AeroVironment for the secretive Defense Advanced Research Projects Agency, which can fly at 11 miles per hour and perch on a windowsill. But it is still a prototype. One of the smallest drones in use on the battlefield is the three-foot-long Raven, which troops in Afghanistan toss by hand like a model airplane to peer over the next hill.

There are some 4,800 Ravens in operation in the Army, although plenty get lost. One American service member in Germany recalled how five soldiers and officers spent six hours tramping through a dark Bavarian forest—and then sent a helicopter—on a fruitless search for a Raven that failed to return home from a training exercise.

In the midsize range: The Predator, the larger Reaper and the smaller Shadow, all flown by remote pilots using joysticks and computer screens, many from military bases in the United States. A Navy entry is the X-47B, a prototype designed to take off and land from aircraft carriers automatically and, when commanded, drop bombs. A larger drone is the Global Hawk, which is used for keeping an eye on North Korea's nuclear weapons activities. In March 2011, the Pentagon sent a Global Hawk over the stricken Fukushima Daiichi nuclear plant in Japan to assess the damage.

A Tsunami of Data   The future world of drones is here inside the Air Force headquarters at Joint Base Langley-Eustis, Va., where hundreds of flat-screen TVs hang from industrial metal skeletons in a cavernous room, a scene vaguely reminiscent of a rave club. In fact this is one of the most sensitive installations for processing, exploiting and disseminating a tsunami of information from a global network of flying sensors.

The numbers are overwhelming: Since the Sept. 11, 2001 attacks, the hours the Air Force devotes to flying missions for intelligence, surveillance and reconnaissance have gone up 3,100 percent, most of that from increased operations of drones. Every day, the Air Force must process almost 1,500 hours of full-motion video and another 1,500 still images, much of it from Predators and Reapers on around-the-clock combat air patrols.

The pressures on humans will only increase as the military moves from the limited "soda straw" views of today's sensors to new "Gorgon Stare" technology that can capture live video of an entire city — but requires 2,000 analysts to process the data feeds from a single drone, compared with 19 analysts per drone today.

nuclear fission. Moreover, the German military had seized uranium mines in Czechoslovakia and halted the sale of uranium ore. It was obvious to Szilard that the Germans had discovered both the process and the fuel to make a nuclear weapon. He convinced Einstein to write to President Franklin D. Roosevelt to inform him of the threat.

In response to Einstein's letter, President Roosevelt set about formulating and implementing a massive, secret program to develop nuclear technology, and in less than six years nuclear weapons went from obscure theory to dreadful reality. In the United States, the project to develop a nuclear bomb was called the Manhattan Project and was staffed by hundreds of scientists in 30 secret locations, the most famous of which was the laboratory complex at Los Alamos, New Mexico. The Manhattan Project was headed by J. Robert Oppenheimer, often called the "father of the bomb."

By the time the first prototypes of the bomb were being readied in the end of June 1945, Hitler had already committed suicide, the Germans had surrendered, and the Allied powers were busy dividing the country. Meanwhile, nuclear tests at Los Alamos continued. The first bomb test on July 16, 1945, code-named Trinity, released 20 kilotons of force, the equivalent of 20,000 tons of TNT. The following day, 70 Los Alamos scientists signed a petition urging President Harry S. Truman not to use the bomb on Japanese targets unless Japan first had been given the chance to surrender. Ten days later, Truman issued an ultimatum to Japan, which was ignored. Meanwhile, two bombs were readied for deployment.

"Little Boy," the 15-kiloton uranium bomb dropped on Hiroshima, Japan, on August 6, 1945, was detonated in the air over the city at a height that would maximize the explosion's reach. It released a fireball 1,200 feet in diameter of unimaginable heat—7,200 degrees Fahrenheit. The bomb instantly vaporized thousands of people and sent out a shockwave that shredded much of the city. What was left caught fire. More than 80,000 people were killed immediately. Radiation poisoning killed some of the survivors and debilitated more. In all, as many as 140,000 people were killed by the Hiroshima bomb. "Fat Man," with improved design and more volatile plutonium fuel, was dropped three days later on Nagasaki and released 21 kilotons, though, as Nagasaki sits in a protected valley, killed fewer—40,000. Japan surrendered six days later.

The debate over Truman's decision to unleash such a devastating attack on civilian populations has not abated even today. Supporters argue that the lives of hundreds of thousands of soldiers were saved by avoiding an invasion of Japan. Opponents contend that the first bomb should have been dropped on an unpopulated area.

Nuclear Weapons after Hiroshima The speed and urgency of wartime development of the theoretical physics, experimental know-how, and military infrastructure needed to make the United States a nuclear power reflected the widely held belief that first Germany and then the Soviet Union were developing a nuclear weapon. Subsequent historical research, however, casts doubt on any of these powers as early innovators in the area; paradoxically, most of the early innovations in the Soviet nuclear weapons program could be traced to stolen secrets delivered by Klaus Fuchs, a Los Alamos scientist who delivered intelligence to Soviet agents between 1944 and 1946.

Even before World War II ended, the U.S. had become wary of Stalin's U.S.S.R. and knew that the Soviet scientists were racing to develop comparable nuclear technology. It was only a matter of time before the Soviet Union would "have the bomb," even though it did not become clear until later how much Soviet progress was due to espionage.

The U.S.S.R.'s first successful A-bomb test had taken place in 1949, much sooner than U.S. predictions, and citing the seemingly inevitable Soviet discovery of the new weapon, work on the H-bomb continued. U.S. scientists conducted tests of increasingly refined and destructive bombs, magnifying their yield from kilotons to megatons, while suspecting that Soviet work was close behind. In the 1950's, most U.S. nuclear weapons tests were performed

either at U.S.-controlled Pacific islands or in Nevada testing facilities. According to the Department of Energy, a total of 106 tests were conducted on or near Bikini, Christmas, Johnston, and Enewetak Islands, before the dangers and extent of fallout radiation were well understood. (Those islands remain radioactively "hot" today.) The first successful two-stage thermonuclear weapon test, code-named "Mike," was off Enewetak Island in the South Pacific on November 1, 1952. It released 10.4 megatons of force, nearly 1,000 times the explosive yield of "Little Boy," and completely destroyed the island it was on, leaving only a crater in the ocean floor. The first Soviet thermonuclear detonation took place the following year, on August 12, 1953.

Rocket technology was improving, and nuclear-armed rockets began testing in the early 1950's, but rocket range was limited. Military strategy of the time relied on the assumption that an enemy's weapons would have to be housed in silos or carried by large planes. In the early 1950's, the reasoning behind military nuclear strategy was to prepare a large, overwhelming force that could eliminate an enemy's weapons with a single, indefensible "first strike."

When newly elected President John F. Kennedy appointed Robert McNamara as secretary of defense in 1961, U.S. military strategy underwent a dramatic shift. McNamara was a proponent of the doctrine of "mutually assured destruction," which stated that the best way to deter an enemy was to stockpile such an overabundance of weapons and keep them readied in such a variety of places that a retaliatory "second strike" would be unpreventable. To this end in 1961, the Air Force's Strategic Air Command began mission Looking Glass, in which one of a fleet of modified, nuclear-armed Boeing EC-135Cs remained in the air continuously for over 29 years, to provide an airborne base of military command in the case of a large-scale attack on ground posts. During the 1960's, the U.S. successfully developed nuclear delivery systems for submarines and other naval vessels. The global nuclear picture now looked complicated and precarious, as the two superpowers tried to locate ever-increasing numbers of weapons in locations all over the planet.

The nuclear arms race reached its crisis point in 1962, when a Soviet missile base was discovered under construction in Cuba, prompting what was to be called the "Cuban missile crisis." The U.S. Navy quarantined Cuba, prompting a duel between President Kennedy and Prime

Minister Nikita Khrushchev that put the world at the precarious edge of a nuclear conflict. In the end, Khrushchev agreed to remove the weapons, and Kennedy secretly ordered U.S. missiles removed from Turkey.

In the wake of the near-cataclysm, both the U.S. and U.S.S.R. began a period of nuclear détente, gradually limiting the scope of nuclear weapons testing. In 1963, the U.S. and U.S.S.R. agreed to halt all aboveground and airborne nuclear tests. (Since 1963, all U.S. tests have been underground, and almost all have taken place in Nevada testing facilities.) Strategic Arms Limitation Talks (SALT) held between the U.S. and U.S.S.R. between 1969 and 1972 resulted in the Anti-Ballistic Missile Treaty, which limited the number of ballistic missiles in either nation's stockpile. In 1976, the U.S. and U.S.S.R. agreed to limit tests to fewer than 150 kilotons. SALT II talks, held between 1972 and 1979, resulted in agreements to limit the total number of strategic weapons for either nation, though the treaty was never ratified by the United States and President Reagan withdrew from SALT II in 1986.

Arms reduction after the Cold War   At the end of the Cold War, the U.S. and U.S.S.R. had a combined stockpile of more than 40,000 nuclear warheads, down from the Cold War peak of 70,000. Building on détente-based agreements from the 1970s, two international agreements in 1995 and 1996 banned further nuclear weapons testing outright; the 1995 Nuclear Nonproliferation Treaty was a U.N. initiative to limit nuclear weapons to those states that had them already, and the 1996 Comprehensive Nuclear Test Ban Treaty prohibited any nuclear testing by any state. In 2002, the Strategic Offensive Reductions Treaty (SORT, also known as the Moscow Treaty) was signed between the U.S. and Russia; it contained agreements to reduce the number of active warheads to between 1,700 and 2,200 by 2012.

In the United States, there is a publicly known process for dismantling old nuclear weapons, but in the case of the old Soviet stockpile, the process is much less regulated, and there is widespread international concern regarding the state of the Russian/Soviet stockpile amid speculation of nuclear weapons smuggling and theft in Eurasia. Although Russian officials deny that any nuclear materials have been stolen, fairly numerous anecdotal accounts, including those from former military, black marketeers, and smugglers, suggest otherwise.

New nuclear powers   The various treaties and agreements aimed at reducing the number of thermonuclear weapons worldwide have not prevented other nations from researching nuclear weapons production. When the Nuclear Nonproliferation Treaty was signed in 1995, three nations declined to sign and a fourth acceded and then violated the treaty. Perhaps unsurprisingly, those nations—India, Israel, Pakistan, and North Korea respectively—all subsequently became nuclear weapons powers. The current list of nuclear weapons states contains these four plus the United States, Russia, the United Kingdom, France, and China. In addition, current international scrutiny focuses on Iran's suspected nuclear weapons program.

The emergence of two rogue groups—the global Islamic terrorism network and the global arms black market—complicates the picture considerably. Much of the suspected resources of these two groups is thought to originate in stolen Russian or Soviet materials (referred to as "loose nukes"). Moreover, due to the affinity between Islamic terrorist groups and radical Islamic factions inside Iran, there is great concern about Iran's potential participation (willing or not) in augmenting the striking capabilities of rogue groups.

Key Battles in World History

The Ancient World

Marathon (490 B.C.) This was the first battle fought on the Greek mainland during the Persian Wars. Persia's ruler, Darius I, sought to impose his rule over the divided and rebellious city-states of Greece. The Persian expeditionary force consisted of 25,000 professional troops,

dispatched across the Aegean Sea by a formidable fleet of 600 ships. After attacking the city of Eritria, the Persians divided their forces. About 15,000 landed near the Plain of Marathon on the Charadra River, about 25 miles from Athens. Some 10,000 Athenian citizen soldiers and about 1,000 of their Plataean allies gathered to oppose the invaders. After a standoff of several days, the Greeks attacked the invading force, taking advantage of their superior speed and knowledge of the terrain. The Persians suffered more than 5,000 casualties before being driven back to their ships. The Greeks lost fewer than 200 soldiers. The battle earned Athens respect even from its rival, Sparta, and checked Persia's imperial ambitions in the Aegean.

Salamis (480 B.C.) The Persian assault on Greece was fought at sea as well as on land. Greek and Persian warships gathered off the coast of Salamis, and on September 23, 480 B.C., the Persian fleet began its attack. About 200 ships maneuvered off Salamis to prevent the Greek fleet from withdrawing. Then the main fleet, 800 strong, rowed into a narrow channel, where the Greek fleet waited. The Greek ships were larger and heavier than the swifter Persian fleet, but in the channel, speed was less important. The Greeks surrounded, trapped and rammed the Persian vessels with merciless efficiency. Half the Persian fleet was destroyed in a day's fighting. The Athenian navy took its place alongside the city-state's army as a force to be reckoned with in the Mediterranean world.

Plataea (479 B.C.) The Persians remained intent on expanding their rule beyond the Aegean, so King Darius I put plans in motion for another invasion of Greece. He died before those plans reached fruition, but his son, Xerxes, harbored similar ambitions for expansion, and led a second invasion in 480 B.C. Sparta and Athens joined in a common defense against the renewed invasion. The Spartans tried unsuccessfully to check the Persian advance at Thermopylae, where a vain but courageous stand taken by 300 members of King Leonidas's bodyguard became part of military legend. But as a Persian force pressed ahead, they were met by Athenians and Spartans fighting together at Plataea in central Greece. The Persians were routed and forced to withdraw. Plataea marked an end to Persia's ambitions in Greece.

Syracuse (415–413 B.C.) Athens and its allies fought a series of inconclusive battles against Sparta and its allies between 460 and 445 B.C., and again between 431 and 421 B.C. After a six-year peace, a charismatic general and orator named Alcibiades (ca. 450 B.C.–404 B.C.) persuaded Athens to send an invasion force to conquer the Sicilian city-state of Syracuse. The invasion was part of a larger plan to extend Athens' influence westward in preparation for yet another war with Sparta. Athens sent some 27,000 troops to Sicily under the command of Alcibiades, but before the invaders reached Syracuse, Alcibiades was accused of religious heresy and ordered to return to Athens. He escaped en-route and informed Sparta of the Athenian plan, leading the Spartans to send help to

Syracuse. Meanwhile, the Athenians became bogged down in an ineffective siege outside the city. A second invasion force landed in July, 413 B.C., prompting Athens to launch an offensive. The Spartans, under their leader Gylippus, defeated them at Euryalus. For Athens, escape from the Sicilian quagmire became impossible when a Spartan fleet inflicted crippling losses on Athenian ships in Little Harbor off Syracuse. The Athenian force surrendered in 413—more than 40,000 troops were killed or taken prisoner and sold into slavery. Athens' defeat at Syracuse helped set the stage for Sparta's victory in the second Peloponnesian War.

Leuctra (371 B.C.) Sparta replaced Athens as the dominant power in Greece after Athens surrendered in 404 B.C., ending the second Peloponnesian War. But Athens and its allies, resentful of Spartan discipline and its harsh domination, continued to harass their conquerors. Persia, too, resisted Sparta's expansion, defeating a Spartan fleet in 394 B.C. The city-state of Thebes, an occasional ally of Athens and a leader of the Boeotian League, walked out of a peace conference brokered by Sparta, an act of defiance which the powerful city-state could not abide. Sparta sent 10,000 troops towards Thebes. Under the command of King Epaminondas, Thebes marshaled a force of about 6,000 foot soldiers and more than 1,000 cavalry. Numbers were not in Thebes' favor, so Epaminondas devised a brilliant new tactic. Rather than fight head-on in a phalanx, he strengthened his left flank and used it to attack the Spartan right. The Theban right would hold rather than advance while the left move forward. Combined with effective cavalry, the Theban left phalanx, some 50 soldiers deep, overwhelmed the Spartans at little cost to King Epaminondas. The Theban tactic became a standard in classical warfare, and Sparta's influence began to diminish.

Gaugamela (331 B.C.) Alexander the Great, king of Macedonia, had defeated Persian forces in Syria and Egypt not long after inheriting the throne from his murdered father, King Philip II. Persia's king, Darius III, offered his antagonist a bribe if only he would cease his attacks on Persia, but Alexander refused, hoping to draw the Persians into battle. The Persian king had a force of perhaps as many as 250,000 troops at his disposal. Alexander's army consisted of about 50,000. The two sides met in Gaugamela in today's Iraq, the battlefield chosen by Darius himself because it was flat and so seemed amenable to Persian chariots. As Alexander approached,

Darius ordered his chariots, armed with scythes, to cut through the Macedonian infantry. Alexander's men were prepared for the tactic, unleashing a barrage of javelins and spears to foil the assault. With the two armies engaged, Alexander himself aimed a javelin at Darius. He missed, but he hit a chariot driver near the king. Persian troops heard that their king was dead and began to fall back. The retreat quickly turned into a rout. About 35,000 Persians were killed, while Alexander lost only about 300 troops. The victory added to Alexander's legend, and to his burgeoning empire.

Cannae (216 B.C.) The center of imperial rivalry moved west after Alexander's conquests. With Athens and Sparta in decline, Rome and the African city-state of Carthage engaged in a bitter duel for control of the Mediterranean world. Rome defeated Carthage in the first Punic War (264-241 B.C.), winning control of the strategic island of Sicily, save for Syracuse. Hannibal, the son of a prominent Carthaginian general, sought to avenge his city's defeat, raising an army and recruiting allies in Spain to prepare for an invasion of Italy. In 218 B.C., Hannibal and his 90,000 troops and 80 elephants set out on what has become one of history's most-famous marches, taking them through the Alps. Hannibal established himself on the Adriatic coast in southeastern Italy at Cannae, a strategic point on Rome's supply line. Rome dispatched a force of 80,000 foot soldiers and 6,000 cavalry. The Roman infantry attacked Hannibal's center, which fell back in a planned, orderly retreat. Hannibal's cavalry, which were dispatched to attack the Roman flanks, were now behind the surging Roman infantry. The cavalry wheeled and turned on the inexperienced legions, which were hacked to pieces. Rome lost 50,000 troops to 6,000 for Carthage and its allies. Hannibal's tactics at Cannae have influenced military commanders ever since.

Zama (202 B.C.) After Cannae, Hannibal believed Rome would ask for terms. He was mistaken, and while he remained in Italy for more than a dozen years after his decisive victory, he never did conquer Rome. The Carthaginians were forced to withdraw north, towards Hannibal's position. The Romans did not give chase, instead, they formed an alliance with leaders in Numidia (today's Tunisia) in North Africa. Scipio dispatched 30,000 men across the Mediterranean to bring the war home to Carthage. Hannibal and his brother Mago were recalled from Italy as the Carthaginians were forced on the defensive. On a field about five miles outside of Carthage,

Hannibal, his elephants and some 50,000 troops faced Scipio's 35,000 infantry and 9,000 cavalry. Hannibal's assault failed when his elephants became confused and frightened, and the infantry action quickly turned in Rome's favor. When Roman and Numidian cavalry attacked from the rear, the rout was on. Hannibal fled, but 20,000 of his troops were killed. The second Punic War ended as the first one did, in a Roman victory. Rome was now more than an ambitious city-state. It was an international power, intent on expansion.

Pharsalus (48 B.C.) As Rome's influence and power grew, so did the ambitions of those who sought to rule the great empire. Two great military commanders began to see each other as obstacles to their respective paths to power. Gnaeus Pompeius, or Pompey, led Roman forces in Spain, while a onetime ally turned rival, Julius Caesar, ruled the Roman province of Gaul. Pompey was an accomplished political conspirator in addition to being an effective military commander, and in 52 B.C., he won election as the government's single consul, becoming the most-powerful man in the republic. The Senate ordered Caesar to surrender control of his army if he wished another term as consul for Gaul. Caesar refused the Senate's order, and, with an army of loyalists, he crossed the Rubicon River—an illegal act—to march towards Rome itself. Pompey fled, Caesar defeated forces loyal to his rival, and in 49 B.C., the Senate declared him dictator. But Pompey still posed a threat, and in 48 B.C., the two rivals and their armies met in Pharsalus, across the Adriatic Sea from Italy. Though badly outnumbered, Caesar's battlefield tactics, especially his use of reserves, carried the day. Pompey fled to Egypt, where he was murdered. Caesar's ambitions were fulfilled. He was declared dictator for life in 44 B.C., but was assassinated a month later.

Philippi (42 B.C.) Caesar's murder plunged the Roman world into another civil war. The chief conspirators in the assassination plot, Marcus Junius Brutus and Gaius Cassius, formed an army to oppose the three men named by the Senate to rule in Caesar's place: Caesar's grandnephew Octavian, later called Augustus, Mark Antony and Marcus Lepidus. Brutus and Cassius, viewing themselves as the keepers of Rome's republican ideals, prepared to take on a force led by Antony and Octavian in northern Greece. In the first engagement between the two armies, Brutus defeated Octavian's forces, but Antony routed the republican army under the command of Cassius, who committed suicide. After a lull of about three weeks,

Brutus went on the offensive but was repulsed with heavy losses, and he, too, fell on his sword in defeat and disgrace. Rome's republican spirit died with its champions in Philippi. The main victor at Philippi was Antony, whose performance on the battlefield outshone that of Octavian. Eventually, however, Octavian's reputation as a strong but fair leader grew, and he went on to rule as Augustus Caesar while Rome solidified its transition from republic to empire.

Actium (31 B.C.) The alliance between Mark Antony and Octavian was short-lived. Antony, who emerged from Philippi with a strong military reputation, was dispatched to the East to look after the empire's interests, and while doing so fell in love with the ruler of Egypt, Queen Cleopatra. Antony was married to Octavian's sister at the time, so when news made its way to Rome that Antony had married Cleopatra, Caesar's successor had many reasons to be displeased. Antony and Cleopatra went about building their own alliances in a direct challenge to Roman authority. War soon followed. The decisive battle took place at sea, off Actium. On September 2, Octavian's fleet faced the combined navies of Antony and Cleopatra. After nearly a full day of inconclusive fighting, a gap in Antony's line developed and Octavian's ships took advantage. Cleopatra chose to retreat rather than come to Antony's assistance, and Antony soon followed. Although they escaped, the romantic couple were dead within a year, by their own hand, as Octavian's land and sea forces closed in on them. Egypt and its granaries and wealth came under Roman rule.

The Teutoburg Forest (A.D. 9) Beyond Roman-controlled Gaul, across the Rhine River, lived Germanic tribes who lived an almost nomadic life, with none of the great cities that were emblematic of Roman civilization. Augustus saw the tribes as a potential threat to Gaul and viewed Germany as ripe for Roman expansion. He ordered an armed force to cross the river and establish a Roman military presence east of the Rhine. In A.D. 9, Quinctilius Varus was appointed military governor of the Roman-held territories in Germany. Varus earned the enmity of the locals with his insistence that they pay taxes to their Roman overlords. Among the Germans he alienated was a young man named Arminius, who also served on Varus' staff as an officer and a citizen of Rome. Arminius began to plot against the Romans even as he appeared to be the model of loyalty to the empire, marrying the daughter of a German noble who also served the Roman occu-

piers. In late summer, A.D. 9, a series of well-planned revolts against Roman rule broke out near the Rhine. Still trusted, Arminius suggested that Varus move three legions through a heavily wooded area to put down the revolt. In the Teutoburg Forest, Arminius slipped away and took command of the Germans. The Romans came under attack as they hacked their way through the woods. Three days of fighting left 20,000 Romans dead, including Varus, who died by his own hand. The battle marked the end of Rome's initial hopes to expand east of the Rhine and Augustus took immediate action to strengthen Rome's borders.

Milvian Bridge (A.D. 312) In A.D. 311, two strong-willed men vied for control of the western portion of the Empire: Constantine, based in Gaul, and Maxentius in Italy. The latter was not content to share power and in 312, began preparations to end the arrangement. Constantine heard of his antagonist's plans and countered with his own: He and 40,000 troops moved from Gaul into northern Italy, stealing the initiative from Maxentius. Constantine's force marched south relentlessly towards Rome, defeating several armies. Maxentius moved out from Rome to oppose the invaders, setting up a defensive position with the River Tiber at his back. Legend has it that on the eve of battle, Constantine said he saw a flaming cross in the sky, and on the cross, the words *en tutoi nika*, a Greek phrase meaning "in this sign conquer." He promised to convert to Christianity if he won the battle, which he did, and he did convert. Maxentius' overwhelmed forces were cut down as they tried to flee over the Milvian Bridge, their only escape route. Maxentius himself died in an attempt to swim across the river. After Constantine's victory, Christianity become the official religion of an empire which once martyred Christians. The Christian-ization of Europe followed, and the Latin translation of "in this sign conquer"—in hoc signo (HIS)—became a commonplace symbol, as it is today.

Adrianople (378) Valentinian became Roman emperor in 364, and named his brother, Valens, to rule as co-emperor in Constantinople, a title he kept after Valentinian died. When the Visigoths asked for permission to settle within the eastern empire's boundaries, Valens demanded that they first surrender their weapons and then turn over their military-age sons. When Valens went off to fight the Persians in 377, his stand-ins further exploited the Visigoths, and refused to allow another

Gothic tribe, the Ostrogoths, or Eastern Goths, refuge from the rampaging Huns. The eastern Goths moved in despite the opposition of Valens' subordinates. Tired of paying bribes to Byzantine officials, the Goths joined forces under Fritigern and demanded an end to imperial exploitation. Valens' subordinates attempt to murder Fitigern failed, and the Gothic tribes sought vengeance, defeating a Byzantine army at Marianopolis and forcing Valens to return from his Persian adventure. The two sides faced each other at Adrianople on August 9, 378. Valens was outnumbered by almost 2 to 1, but he was convinced that the Goths were poor soldiers. The battle began amid confusion, but when it was over, the Ostrogoth cavalry proved to be the deciding factor. The Gothic victory was a crushing blow for the Empire, and it illustrated the growing importance of cavalry. The Ostrogoth assault influenced European strategy and tactics for the next thousand years.

Chalons (451) The Huns originated in Asia, and began their first moves towards Europe in the fourth century, when they crossed into today's Russia. They soon made their presence felt farther west and north, forcing the eastern Goths, the Ostrogoths, to seek the sanctuary of the Byzantine empire. Under the leadership of Attila, who shared power with his brother, Bleda, until he had Bleda murdered, the Huns attacked Constantinople and, by 451, they were rampaging through the very heart of Europe, besieging Orleans in the Loire Valley of France. The Roman leader, Aetius, and the leader of the Visigoths, Theoderic, made common cause, putting aside past enmity in the face of Attila's challenge. As the combined Roman-Visigoth force approached Orleans in the spring of 451, Attila withdrew and regrouped his army after suffering the loss of his entire rearguard of 15,000. Attila's entire force is estimated to have been about 100,000 strong. The Huns took up a position near Chalons-sur-Marne in what is today the Champagne region of southern France, placing his Ostrogoth allies on his left flank. The Visigoths, fighting with Rome, were deployed to face their fellow Goths. When the two armies came to grips, the Visigoths on the Roman right overwhelmed the Ostrogoths, allowing them to turn and perhaps envelop Attila and his Huns. Attila ordered a retreat, which led to a siege by the Roman-Visigoth army. The Huns eventually slipped away after the Visigoths returned home. Attila's rampages were not finished, but his aura of invincibility had been shattered.

The Middle Ages

Tours/Poitiers (732) In the seventh century, the prophet Mohammed set in motion events and ideologies that will sound familiar to readers in the 21st century. Within decades of the prophet's death, the religion he founded, Islam, was spreading well beyond the land of his birth. Even before Muslim armies attempted, in vain, to capture Constantinople in 718, Islamic influence had entered Europe through the back door of North Africa into Spain. The Muslim advance received the unwitting assistance of the dominant local population, the Franks, who were weak and divided. In 732, a Muslim army commanded by Abd-ar-Rahman marched towards Tours, his troops enriching themselves with the spoils of war as they made their way north. The Frankish King, Charles Martel, formed a hasty alliance with an old enemy, Eudo of Aquitaine, and prepared to challenge the Muslim incursion in the early fall of 732. After a week-long standoff between the towns of Tours and Poitiers, the Muslims attacked but the disciplined Franks held their position. Sensing defeat, some of ar-Rahman's men retreated, perhaps to collect the loot they had accumulated. After ar-Rahman was killed, the retreat became a rout which drove Muslims from Spain, and Islamic influence in Western Europe would never spread further.

Hastings (1066) After the death of King Edward the Confessor of England in 1066, a body of prominent Anglo-Saxons named the late king's brother-in-law, Harold Godwinson, Earl of Essex, as his successor. This came as a surprise to the ambitious Duke William of Normandy, who insisted that Edward had named him to be his successor years earlier. Before taking the throne in England, Edward the Confessor had spent decades in Normandy, so William's claim was not implausible. What's more, he was prepared to fight for it. He enlisted Pope Alexander II to his cause, persuading the pontiff that he had the true claim to the throne. Alexander's approval helped William's recruiting efforts. While Harold was forced to fight off another claimant to the throne, his own brother, Tostig, William prepared an invasion force on the Normandy coast. The Normans and their allies crossed the Channel in the fall of 1066 and marched towards Hastings. Harold's army made its stand on Senlac Hill. The two forces met on October 14, 1066, in a bitter battle that finally tilted in William's favor when English troops were ambushed as they pursued a feigned Norman retreat.

Harold was killed in a fusillade of arrows, and William marched to London to assume the throne. The Norman conquest was the last successful invasion of Britain, and it changed the character of Saxon-dominated England.

Manzikert (1071) In the middle of the 11th century, Byzantium faced a new Muslim threat in Alp-Arslan (1030-1072), leader of the Seljuk Turks. The Seljuks were originally from central Asia, but they converted to Islam as they moved west and conquered Baghdad and Persia. In Constantinople, Romanus IV Diogenes came to power in 1068 thanks to a timely marriage to the widow of Emperor Constantine X Doukas. Romanus immediately rose to the Seljuk Turk challenge after Alp-Arslan conquered the capital of resource-rich Armenia. Romanus won several early battles, but in 1071, Alp-Arslan captured Manzikert in eastern Turkey and then marched back to Persia, and then to Syria. Romanus recaptured the city in short order, but after marching out of the city, soon was face to face with Alp-Arslan's main army. But Romanus had more than one enemy with which to contend; his wife, determined that her son with Emperor Constantine succeed to the throne, was conspiring against him with other military commanders. Romanus had the advantage after a day of fighting Alp-Arslan's troops, but when the Seljuks regrouped, many of the Byzantine troops continued to retreat towards their camp rather than stand and fight. Romanus was captured, and the region of Anatolia—the Asian portion of Turkey—was turned into a vast foraging area for Seljuk horses. Deprived of a region from which it recruited its finest soldiers, Byzantine grew weaker. Less than 30 years after Manzikert, Constantinople asked for military assistance from Pope Urban II, who proclaimed the first Crusade to capture the holy sites of the Middle East for Christianity.

Hattin (1187) Europeans established a foothold in the Holy Land after the first Crusade in 1099, but their rule did little to recommend Christianity to the local population. Muslims and Jews alike were slaughtered indiscriminately, while the Europeans themselves feuded with each other. Taking advantage of European disunity, Muslims under the command of Nur ed-Din captured Syria and the city of Edessa in 1144. One of Nur ed-Din's top subordinates was the great Muslim military leader, Saladin, who won control of Egypt and Syria by 1176, prompting the Europeans to agree to a truce in 1180. Six years later, however, the Crusader, Reynald of Chatillon, attacked a Muslim caravan in violation of the truce. The Crusader King of Jerusalem, Guy de Lusignan, refused to intervene. Saladin marched to Tiberius, a Crusader city on the coast of Sea of Galilee. Guy responded to the threat, but his water supplies ran dry in the hot July sun near the town of Hattin. Saladin's troops fired barrages of arrows into the Crusader lines, prompting a cavalry charge that failed to break the enemy line. The Crusaders were forced to surrender not only themselves, but a relic they believed to be the True Cross on which Christ was crucified. Christian control of the Holy Land was lost.

Bouvines (1214) After the papacy brought Europe's nobles together in a common cause during the Crusades, it proceeded to take sides in the internecine rivalries which divided the continent in the 13th century. Pope Innocent III, who took office in 1198, used his position and influence to carve out a dominant political role in Europe's affairs. In 1209, Innocent III announced his approval of Otto IV of Germany to lead the Holy Roman Empire, leading to an alliance between the empire and Otto's uncle, King John of England. Caught between the two allies was King Phillip Augustus of France, whom John viewed as an obstacle to his plan to rule all of France. To Philip's east, Otto IV went to war in Italy to head off a challenge from Henry VI, the young son of the previous emperor and a threat to Otto's legitimacy as Holy Roman Emperor. Innocent III disapproved, excommunicated Otto and gave his crown to Henry. Philip supported the Pope's move, leading to war with Otto, who had John's financial support. Philip's army of 22,000 met Otto's 24,000 near Bouvines on July 27, 1214. The Germans gave way when Otto fled the field. Philip's victory solidified his control over northern France. Meanwhile, in England, King John's demands for money to support foreign intrigue led to an uprising by nobles, who forced him to sign the Magna Carta in 1215.

Bannockburn (1314) The English had been warring with the Scots to the north of their kingdom since the late 13th century. English rule over the Gaelic tribes in Scotland seemed inevitable after several victories in the early 1300's. But when Robert the Bruce (1274–1329) murdered a rival to the throne of Scotland in 1306, the balance shifted in favor of the Scots. Bruce seemed to be an unlikely champion of the Scots, for he had been aligned with the English King Edward I for a time. Then again, he also had been an ally of Scotland's great champion, William

Wallace, whose death in 1305 gave Bruce the chance to seize control of the throne. A Scots force under Bruce's brother, Edward, surrounded a key English castle near a creek called Bannockburn, not far from the River Forth. The new English King, Edward II, sent a huge force north to crush this act of defiance. King Robert Bruce rode to the scene to take personal command of his Scots. After a vicious two-day battle beginning on June 23, 1314, the English were forced to concede. Years of fighting would follow, but the Scots finally won independence in 1328.

Crécy (1346) When King Charles IV of France died in 1327, the most-direct heir to the throne was King Edward III of England. Edward, however, supported the choice of France's nobles, who was crowned as Philip VI. It was a decision Edward came to regret, and, as the English and French began fighting what became known as The Hundred Years War, he decided to enforce his claim to be King of France. Philip decided to hit Edward where it was bound to hurt—in English-controlled Aquitaine, a province in southwest France. French forces put the English on the defensive, forcing Edward to send a fleet across the Channel to Normandy. Philip was caught off guard, but quickly put together an army to challenge Edward in Crecy, north of Paris. The French attacked on August 26, 1346, The French put great hope in their cavalry, but the English had the longbow, a weapon they used with fearsome efficiency. Firing quickly and mercilessly, the English archers mowed down the French horses and Philip was forced to retreat. The war, however, dragged on for decades, but at Crécy, the English established themselves as an important power, and the longbow announced the end of cavalry's dominance.

Agincourt (1415) Today, this battle is best remembered as the setting for Henry V's remarkable speech on Saint Crispin's Day, inspiring England's band of brothers to defeat a larger French army in Normandy. Of course, Henry's speech was delivered not on the battlefield, but on the stage, and the soaring phrases were uttered not by the king, but by actors playing him in William Shakespeare's historical drama, Henry V. But there was good reason for Shakespeare to focus on Henry's leadership in this important battle, which was the last English victory in the Hundred Years War against France. The English were heavily outnumbered, perhaps by more than two to one. Nevertheless, as both armies jockeyed for position all day on October 25, 1415, Henry ordered his men to advance

rather than maintain their strong defensive line. The move caught the French off guard, but they recovered well enough. The fight was bitter and desperate, with the English King fighting in the midst of his troops. Once again, English archers and their longbow made a critical difference, but so did the King's personal leadership in the field. The French suffered perhaps as many as 6,500 casualties, while the English lost fewer than 500. Henry's victory allowed him to consolidate control of Normandy, but when the Hundred Years War finally ended in 1463, the English were forced to withdraw.

Constantinople (1453) The Byzantine Empire, the last remnant of the late Roman empire, was but a shell of its former self by the 15th century. It had been fighting the advance of Islam, in both its religious and political manifestations, since the seventh century. By the middle of the 15th century, Constantinople was beyond help and without allies, for other European powers were engaged in wars with each other and so were too busy to help defend the capital of Christian Orthodoxy from Muslim expansionists. Sultan Mohammed II, sensing Byzantine's weakness and isolation, prepared to assail the aging empire's capital, Constantinople, with 90,000 Turks in 1452. But even in its decaying state, Constantinople was not defenseless. A fortified wall protected the city from assault by seaborne troops, and the city's harbor was well-defended as well. Mohammed, however, had artillery. The cannons opened fire in April, 1453, creating breaches in the city's wall. The Turks brought in siege towers, and after weeks of fighting, The Byzantine ruler, Constantine XI, and his exhausted troops were wiped out in a last desperate attempt to check the Turk advance. The fall of Constantinople stunned Christian Europe, and announced the arrival of the Ottoman Turks who would rule their own Muslim empire for centuries.

Hakata Bay (1281) Towards the end of the 13th century, Kublai Khan, grandson of Genghis Khan, hoped to extend his rule to Japan after having taken control of most of China and of Korea. He believed he might be able to intimidate Japan's ruler, 18-year-old Hojo Tokimune, with a stern ultimatum: accept the Khan's rule over Japan, or suffer the consequences. The young ruler did not back down, but instead prepared his forces for an inevitable invasion. His expectations were realized on November 18, 1274, when a Mongol fleet carrying as many as 40,000 troops sailed across the Korean Strait into Hakata Bay in northern Japan. They were attacked by an outnumbered force of samurai, and suffered significant casualties. The invaders withdrew to their transports to regroup, but that night, a storm ripped apart the fleet. The Mongols were forced to withdraw. But they returned in 1281, to the same place, and with similarly disastrous results. The Japanese were better prepared than they were in 1274—small Japanese vessels launched surprise nighttime attacks on the Mongols' transports, forcing some to sail to the island of Tsushima in the Korean Strait. But the killing blow came, once again, from the weather. A huge storm on August 15, 1281, wiped out the invaders' fleet, killing as many as 75 to 80 percent of the invasion force. The victory ensured that Japan would remain unconquered by the Mongols, and the Japanese would guard their independence fiercely for hundreds of years.

Bosworth Field (1485) Richard III, another English monarch destined to win fame and notoriety thanks to the pen of William Shakespeare, became king in 1483. His ascension was not popular, and he soon was forced to defend his throne against an insurgency led by Henry Tudor, who had been living in France, dreaming of a chance to secure the monarchy through his mother's lineage. Henry launched his campaign in August, 1485, but while he was able to attract troops who were not happy with Richard, the king himself summoned an army of about 10,000. Henry had about half that number. Henry landed on the west coast of Wales, and marched northeast to Bosworth in Leicestershire. He and Richard fought for the throne on August 22. As the two armies battled, Richard himself led a charge against Henry and his bodyguards. As he neared his enemy, Richard was thrown from his horse by Sir William Stanley. The king continued to fight on foot, even as his forces melted away. His brave defiance did him no good, and he was killed by Henry's men, ending the War of the Roses. Henry won the throne and took the name Henry VII, establishing the Tudor dynasty and signifying a new era of expansion for England.

Tenochtitlán (1521) As European power and influence spread across the Atlantic Ocean after the voyage of Christopher Columbus in 1492, conflict with the indigenous peoples in the Americas was inevitable. The Spanish, who financed Columbus' expeditions, were quick to militarize this new world as they searched for riches and sought to create a trans-Atlantic empire. They soon confronted the empire of the Aztecs, who had built a magnificent capital city called Tenochtitlán in today's Mexico. Under Montezuma, who became their ruler in 1502, the Aztecs ruled between five to six million people from other tribes in today's Central America. The Aztecs were constantly at war, but not necessarily for riches. Believers in human sacrifice, the Aztecs slaughtered prisoners and offered them to the sun god. This was the civilization which the Spanish explorer Hernan Cortes (1485–1547) and several hundred troops encountered in 1519. Montezuma invited Cortes to enter Tenochtitlán peacefully, but hostilities broke out between the Spanish and the Aztecs in 1520. The Aztec leader was killed in the fighting, but the Aztecs had many more men than Cortes. Beginning in May, 1521, the Spanish made alliances with local tribes and prepared to besiege the Aztec capital. On August 13, the Spanish and their allies launched a huge assault that finally defeated the Aztec defenders marking the end of the Aztec empire and its civilization. War and disease wiped out the population, while Spain became the richest and most powerful nation in Europe.

Vienna (1529) With the fall of the Byzantine Empire, Islam and the Ottoman Turks were at the doors of Europe. The European powers themselves were bitterly divided as they competed for riches across the Atlantic and in Asia. Adding to the discord was a deep schism in Christianity, as Protestant reformers challenged the power and prestige of the Papacy. By the early 16th century, Sultan Suleiman, ruler of the Ottoman Empire, was eager to take advantage of Europe's disarray. With fearsome artillery and zealous troops, he conquered parts of today's Eastern Europe, in what is now Hungary and Romania. And in April, 1529, his troops left Constantinople on a mission to bring Europe into the Islamic fold. Their target was Vienna, a gateway to Europe. The Archduke Ferdinand tried to piece together enough troops to defend the city and its ancient walls—a critical advantage for Ferdinand's men. The Ottoman invading force numbered about 250,000 troops. Ferdinand had about 16,000. The Turks reached Vienna in late September after an extremely wet summer in Europe, which hindered the invading army and its train of artillery. The Turks were frustrated by Vienna's walls, and after several attempts to attack the city, they simply marched away. Never again would the Ottomans come so close to extending Islamic rule in Western Europe.

The Spanish Armada (1588) Catholic Spain was the dominant nation in Europe in the middle of the 16th century, thanks to its aggressive pursuit of riches in the New World and its powerful navy. Protestant England was far behind Spain in the race for American possessions, and was beset by internal strife thanks in part to Henry VIII's break with Roman Catholicism and his vain effort to produce a male heir. But when Henry's daughter, Elizabeth I, gained the throne in 1558, England set out to challenge Spain. The queen's aggressive effort to promote Protestantism and her tacit approval of piracy on the high seas—most of it directed at Spain's lucrative trans-Atlantic trade routes—infuriated the Spanish King Philip II, a devout Catholic. When, in 1587, Elizabeth executed her cousin, Mary, a Catholic and a rival for the throne, Philip decided to confront England. A huge fleet of 130 ships set sail from Spain on May 20, 1588. The Armada sailed into the English Channel on July 19, but lighter, quicker English ships forced the Spanish to head for cover in northern France. An English counter-attack on July 29 devastated the Armada, prompting an inglorious retreat around Scotland. Bad weather then took over, and by the time the Armada returned home, it had lost half its vessels. The Armada's defeat did not mark the end of Spanish power, but Spain's influence was diminished. England did not immediately dominate the Atlantic, but its victory was a turning point in its attempt to become a global power.

Sekigahara (1600) There were two centers of power in 16th century Japan: The emperor, and the shogun. The shogun commanded Japan's military sources, and his control over troops was absolute. While the shogun technically served at the pleasure of the emperor, his power over the military—and his own ambitions—created separate alliances and arrangements independent of the throne. At the end of the 16th century, years of civil strife and rivalries among the nobility exploded during a succession crisis. Two ambitious men, Tokugawa Ieyasu and Ishida Mitsunari, surrounded themselves with allies in hopes of seizing power, Tokugawa by becoming shogun, Ishida by supporting the five-year-old heir to the throne. Most of Japan's nobles, the daimyo, sided with Ishida, who put together an army of about 120,000. Tokugawa's force, called the Eastern Army (as opposed to Ishida's Western Army), numbered about 75,000. The two armies met on October 21 at Sekigahara in southern Japan, between Osaka and Tokyo. At a critical moment in the battle, one of Ishida's top commanders betrayed him and sided with

Tokugawa. The battle turned in the Eastern Army's favor. With the victory, Tokugawa consolidated political and military power, and during his reign and that of his heirs, Japan remained an island unto itself, with limited commercial contacts with the outside world until the middle of the 19th century.

Naseby (1645) Less than a century after England's milestone triumph over the Spanish Armada, the country was torn apart in a civil war pitting King against Parliament. King Charles I, like his father James I, found it increasingly difficult to pay for military expeditions against rivals Holland and Spain. Without absolute power, the King of England was forced to consult and work with Parliament on issues such as taxation and finance. An uprising in Scotland made matters worse, and in 1642, all-out war broke out between the King's allies and Parliament and its allies. Oliver Cromwell took command of Parliamentary forces in 1645, forming a professional, well-trained organization that became known as the New Model Army. Some 14,000 New Model troops, almost half of them cavalry, met the Royal army near Naseby, a town in central England. The Royalists were outnumbered by about 2 to 1, but might have prevailed had Charles deployed his reserves to counter Cromwell's attempt to outflank him. Instead, the king hesitated, the Royalists were surrounded, and the day was Cromwell's. Charles returned to the throne but was executed in 1649. Cromwell rose to become Lord Protector—virtual dictator—of England from 1653 to his death in 1658. Attitudes towards the monarchy and Parliament dating from this period greatly affected Englishmen and Scots who left the British Isles for America in the 17th century.

The Modern Period

Blenheim (1704) As Spain's influence in Europe decreased during the 17th century, France under the brilliant leadership of Louis XIV, became the dominant power on the Continent. The inevitable rivalry with England came to a head when Louis' grandson, Philip of Anjou, was named king of Spain. Other European powers regarded this as a power grab by Louis. The remnant of the Holy Roman Empire, based in Vienna, joined forces with Britain's King William III to oppose France, which responded in turn by supporting the Catholic King of Scotland, James III, in his jockeying against the Protestant William. In 1702, England sent troops under the command of John Churchill, the First Duke of Marlborough, across the Channel to face French occupiers of the Netherlands. After several campaigns, Marlborough marched towards the Danube River and linked with an ally, Eugene of Savoy, in Bavaria. French and Bavarian troops took up positions on high ground above the town of Blenheim in today's Germany. Marlborough and his allies attacked the Franco-Bavarian flanks on August 13, 1704. As the battle raged, Marlborough hit the center hard with infantry and artillery, tipping the battle in his favor. England handed Louis his first military defeat, weakening the French monarchy and establishing Marlborough's image as a great field commander.

Poltava (1709)

Under a succession of capable and ambitious kings, especially Gustavus Adolphus, Sweden emerged as a leading military power in northern Europe during the 17th century. In 1655, King Charles X defeated Denmark and Poland, making Sweden the unchallenged master of the Baltic region. In 1700, however, Poland, Denmark and Russia formed an alliance to oppose Swedish influence. Under the young king, Charles XII, Swedish forces struck quickly, overrunning Denmark in the late summer of 1700. Charles continued to press his advantage, marching on and defeating Poland in 1704. The Russian leader, Czar Peter I the Great, quickly rebuilt his army to face the inevitable Swedish assault. It came in January, 1708, with Swedes invading Russia from Poland, intent on capturing Moscow with Charles's Cossack allies. The Russian winter took its toll on the Swedes, who lost nearly half of their 40,000 men before spring. More than a year later, on June 28, 1709, the depleted Swedish-Cossack army was defeated by a much larger Russian force after a long siege outside the town of Poltava. Czar Peter's victory allowed Russia to replace Sweden as the region's dominant military power, and marked the end of Sweden's expansion in central and northern Europe.

Culloden (1746)

As was so often the case in wars fought in Great Britain and Ireland, religion was very much part of the Battle of Culloden. Catholic descendents of the deposed Stuart king, James II, considered themselves the rightful heirs to the British throne. English Protestants, however, installed the Protestant Hanovers from Germany on the throne in 1714, explicitly rejecting the Stuart claims. Prince Charles, who would become known to history as Bonnie Prince Charlie, decided to press his claim with the support of his French hosts. In 1745, with the European powers at war, Charles landed in Scotland and put together an army of several thousand troops. After capturing Edinburgh, Charles invaded England, prompting a distracted London to send the Duke of Cumberland to oppose the rebel army. Charles, thinking he was vastly outnumbered, withdrew to the Highlands, The Duke of Cumberland followed, and on April 16, 1746, the Scots who followed Bonnie Prince Charlie faced an army that consisted not only of Englishmen, but of Scots who rejected the Stuart claim. The Battle of Culloden was short and decisive, lasting only 40 minutes. The Scots had little artillery; the English had a great deal. When the Scots charged with their great broadswords, the English cut them down. After the Scots were beaten, the English took their revenge, expropriating Highland property, banning the Scots language, and forcing many into exile, some to a land that became known as Nova Scotia (New Scotland). Culloden solidified the Hanover claim to the throne and ended the Stuart threat.

Plassey (1757)

Commercial and political rivalry between the English and the French affected people all around the globe in the 18th century. Both nations cast covetous eyes on India, forming alliances with an assortment of tribal leaders who served as surrogates for the Anglo-Franco rivalry on the subcontinent. But not all the local rulers were willing to play the European's game. The *nawab* (local prince) of Bengal, Siraj-ud-Dawlah, was determined to oust the British from Calcutta and elsewhere, and in 1756, his army of 50,000 attacked a few hundred British troops in the city. Some fled, but 146 were captured and thrown into a small prison cell. All but about two dozen died in a matter of 24 hours. An official with the East India Company, Robert Clive (1725-1774), was sent to Calcutta to exact revenge. After a brief battle, Clive and the Bengal leader agreed to a treaty, but peace was short-lived. Siraj-ud-Dawlah led an army that included French allies towards Calcutta, where Clive awaited. The British were vastly outnumbered, but Clive decided to fight, emboldened by reports that one of his enemy's commanders would switch sides at a critical moment. He took up a position near the town of Plassey along the Hooghli River. As Clive hoped, treachery won the day as one of Siraj-ud-Dawlah's allies and his 45,000 men did not fight. Clive prevailed, strengthening the position of the East India Company and paving the way for creation of the British Raj in India.

Quebec (1759) Hostilities between the French and English broke out in 1755 across the Atlantic as the two rivals engaged in what came to be known as the Seven Years War. In the new world of North America, the conflict was called the French and Indian War. The French and their Indian allies sought to halt expansion of English settlements to the west of the Appalachian Mountains in North America, which threatened French claims in the Ohio Valley and Indian sovereignty. Responding to French provocations, English General Edward Braddock failed to rout the French from Fort Duquesne near present-day Pittsburgh in 1755. Years of inconclusive fighting followed, until the British took the offensive in 1759, launching a campaign against the French stronghold of Quebec. The British, under the command of General James Wolfe, achieved tactical surprise with a nighttime attack on September 12-13. The French, commanded by the Marquis de Montcalm, left the walled city and attacked the British on the Plains of Abraham. Both young commanders were killed in the fighting, and on September 15, the British entered Quebec and assumed command of the St. Lawrence River. When the war ended in 1763, the British gained control of Canada and of French claims in the Ohio Valley, greatly expanding their North American empire while dismantling their rival's. The cost to the British treasury was great, leading politicians in London to demand that North American colonists pay for their own defense through new taxes.

Saratoga (1777) Britain's American colonies erupted in revolt in 1775, and declared their independence in July, 1776. A series of disasters followed. A huge British army routed the Americans from New York and forced them to retreat through New Jersey and into Pennsylvania. But on Christmas night, 1776, the American commander, George Washington, led his troops on a surprise attack against Trenton, followed by another successful action in Princeton. Hoping to capitalize on French memories of their defeat in the Seven Years War, American diplomats sought recognition, and assistance, from Paris. The French were skeptical, and watched as the British launched a plan to end the rebellion by seizing control of the Hudson River. A large British army under General John Burgoyne invaded New York from Canada, intending to march south towards British-held New York. Burgoyne, however, was stymied by the terrain in upstate New York. On October 17, 1777, an American force of about 5,000 regulars and 12,000 militia fought a brilliant battle against

Burgoyne's 7,000 troops, with the Americans cutting off the British line of retreat and supply line. On October 17, Burgoyne surrendered to his counterpart, Horatio Gates. The collapse of Burgoyne's campaign meant that the strategic Hudson River was denied to the British. More important, the French were persuaded to join the fight, giving the Americans the powerful navy they lacked.

Valmy (1792) Revolutionary thoughts and actions spread across the Atlantic Ocean from the new United States of America to France, where enraged citizens stormed the Bastille in 1789. The French Revolution was more radical, and more violent, than the successful rebellion in America. The monarchy was overthrown, leading many of the country's aristocrats to flee for their safety. Among the exiles were thousands of officers in the French army. In their new homes, they spread fear of the radical new order taking shape in France, a republican revolution that threatened the power of Europe's crowned heads and nobility. A movement arose to crush the revolution from the outside. William II, ruler of Prussia, and Leopold II of Austria combined forces, and with the support of other monarchs, they marched towards France to overthrow the revolutionaries in early 1792. The French army, they believed, would be a rabble without its elite officer corps. In August, more than 30,000 Austrian and Prussian troops invaded France. After several successes, however, the allies were confronted by nearly 60,000 Frenchmen fighting on their native soil in the town of Valmy, near the Auve River. The French citizen-soldiers did not buckle in the face of an artillery barrage on September 20, forcing the Austro-Prussian infantry to cross open ground to assail the French position. The French continued to stand fast. The assault was called off, and soon the invaders left France. While neither side suffered large casualties, the battle demonstrated that the new French army could defend the revolution. Not long afterwards, King Louis XVI was sent to the guillotine.

Trafalgar (1805) The French threat to Europe's established order changed from an idea, radical republicanism, to a single individual, Napoleon Bonaparte, a brilliant military leader committed to the expansion of French power. Napoleon seized power in from the Directory in 1800 and immediately he set his sights across the English Channel towards Great Britain, symbol of the status-quo and his nation's traditional rival. In 1804, French warships under Admiral Pierre de Villeneuve sailed into the Atlantic to

Is War Our Biological Destiny?

By NATALIE ANGIER

In these days of hidebound militarism and round-robin carnage, when even that beloved ambassador of peace, the Dalai Lama, says it may be necessary to counter terrorism with violence, it's fair to ask: Is humanity doomed? Are we born for the battlefield—congenitally, hormonally incapable of putting war behind us? Is there no alternative to the bullet-riddled trapdoor, short of mass sedation or a Marshall Plan for our DNA?

Was Plato right that "only the dead have seen the end of war"? In the opinion of a number of researchers who study warfare, blood lust and the desire to wage war are by no means innate. To the contrary, recent studies in the field of game theory show just how readily human beings establish cooperative networks with one another, and how quickly a cooperative strategy reaches a point of so-called fixation. Researchers argue that one can plausibly imagine a human future in which war is rare and universally condemned.

The incentive to make war anachronistic is enormous, say the researchers, though they worry that it may take the dropping of another nuclear bomb in the middle of a battlefield before everybody gets the message.

Archaeologists and anthropologists have found evidence of militarism in perhaps 95 percent of the cultures they have examined or unearthed. Time and again groups initially lauded as gentle and peace-loving—the Mayas, the !Kung of the Kalahari, Margaret Mead's Samoans—eventually were outed as being no less bestial than the rest of us.

Warriors have often been the most esteemed of their group, the most coveted mates. Geneticists have found evidence that Genghis Khan, the 13th century Mongol emperor, fathered so many offspring as he slashed through Asia that 16 million men, or half a percent of the world's male population, could be his descendants.

Wars are romanticized, subjects of an endless, cross-temporal, transcultural spool of poems, songs, plays, paintings, novels, films. The battlefield is mythologized as the furnace in which character and nobility are forged. "The rush of battle is a potent and often lethal addiction," writes Chris Hedges, a reporter for *The New York Times*. Even with its destruction and carnage, he adds, war "can give us what we long for in life."

Chimpanzees, which share about 98 percent of their genes with humans, also wage war: gangs of neighboring males meet at the borderline of their territories with the express purpose of exterminating their opponents.

And yet Dr. Frans de Waal, a primatologist and professor of psychology at Emory University, points out that a different species of chimpanzee, the bonobo, chooses love over war, using sex to resolve any social problems that arise. Serious bonobo combat is rare. Bonobos are as closely related to humans as are common chimpanzees, so either might offer insight into the primal "roots" of human behavior.

Even the ubiquitousness of warfare in human history doesn't impress researchers. Indeed, national temperaments seem capable of rapid, radical change. The Vikings slaughtered and plundered; their descendants in Sweden haven't fought a war in nearly 200 years. The tribes of highland New Guinea were famous for small-scale warfare, said Dr. Peter J. Richerson, an expert in cultural evolution at the University of California at Davis. "But when, after World War II, the Australian police patrols went around and told people they couldn't fight anymore, the New Guineans thought that was wonderful," Dr. Richerson said.

Dr. Wilson cites the results of game theory experiments: participants can adopt a cheating strategy to try to earn more for themselves, but at the risk of everybody's losing, or a cooperative strategy with all earning a smaller but more reliable reward. In laboratories around the world, researchers have found that participants implement the mutually beneficial strategy, in which cooperators are rewarded and noncooperators are punished.

As Dr. de Waal and many others see it, the way to foment peace is to encourage interdependency among nations, as in the European Union. "It's not as if Euro-peans all love each other," Dr. de Waal said. "But you're not promoting love, you're promoting economic calculations."

skirmish with the Royal Navy in preparation for a planned cross-Channel invasion of southern England. They were joined by 15 Spanish warships. British Admiral Horatio Nelson joined his fleet off the coast of Spain, and on October 21, 1805, the two navies met off of Cape Trafalgar in the Atlantic. Nelson's ships attacked in two columns, rather than simply sailing parallel to the enemy and launching a broadside. The British tactic succeeded, leaving the French and their Spanish allies utterly confused. During the battle, however, Nelson was mortally wounded and died aboard his flagship, Victory. He was one of Britain's few casualties. The outcome was so decisive in Britain's favor that Napoleon abandoned his invasion plans, and Britannia ruled the waves for the next 150 years.

Leipzig (1813)   The specter of Napoleon continued to haunt Europe, even after France's defeats at Trafalgar and its disastrous retreat from Moscow in 1812. French losses during its long march from Russia were so appalling that few of Europe's generals believed they would have to contend with Napoleon any time soon. They underestimated the resiliency of their foe. He recruited yet another army, this one of inexperienced and very young troops, and by 1813 he was preparing to march again. Austria, Sweden, Russia and Prussia came together under the prodding of the Austrian diplomat, Karl von Metternich, to form a coalition to oppose the Frenchman. Napoleon unleashed his new army in May, 1813, and soon reached Dresden. By June, three allied armies were marching towards Dresden. Diplomacy now played its part, with all sides agreeing on a truce and Metternich himself offering peace if Napoleon agreed to give up land he had captured in his new campaign. He refused. By mid-August, hundreds of thousands of troops were prepared for a climactic battle as the truce expired. Weeks of fighting forced Napoleon to fall back to Leipzig. On October 16, more than 320,000 allied troops attacked Napoleon's 185,000. The first day of fighting was not conclusive, but on October 18, Napoleon ordered a retreat. Sixty thousand young French soldiers died; tens of thousands deserted during the retreat to France. Napoleon abdicated as emperor of France in April, 1814, and was sent into exile on the island of Elba.

Waterloo (1815)   Napoleon's successor as France's ruler was Louis XVIII, installed on the throne by France's victorious enemies and wildly unpopular with the French themselves. Napoleon saw his opportunity and took it. He

escaped from Elba and returned to France in March, 1815. The King's troops were more than happy to defect to Napoleon and Louis fled to England. Napoleon was restored to power on March 19, 1815, and by the summer he was on the march again, hoping to take advantage of the allies' widely scattered forces. He captured the Belgian town of Charleroi in June, and prepared to take on British and allied forces under the command of the Duke of Wellington. The allies retreated in the face of Napoleon's advance to a position near the town of Waterloo. Hampered by faulty intelligence and fooled by Wellington's deployment, Napoleon underestimated the number of troops, (more than 65,000) arrayed against him. At the battle's climactic moment, Wellington called on reserves hidden from Napoleon's view. Their entrance on the field turned the tide. Napoleon suffered a shattering defeat, losing some 30,000 men. Finally, the threat of Napoleonic expansion was over. He was dispatched to St. Helena in the Atlantic. Meanwhile, the Congress of Viennna (1815) redrew the map of Europe and ushered in several decades of peace on the continent.

Antietam (1862)   The American union dissolved in war in 1861 after the election of Abraham Lincoln, who opposed slavery. Southern states, dependent on the cotton trade and the slaves who worked the fields, seceded and formed their own government. Lincoln sent troops to the South to restore the union, but despite the North's numerical and industrial advantages, the Confederates stubbornly and sometimes spectacularly defended their slave-based society and government. After successfully defeating Union troops at the Second Battle of Bull Run on August 29 and 30, 1862, Confederate general Robert E. Lee (1807–70) continued to push north into Maryland, with the intention of capturing the Federal capital of Washington. On September 17, Lee's troops were engaged by Union forces under the command of General George B. McClellan (1826–85) in Sharpsburg, Maryland near Antietam Creek, from which the battle took its name. McClellan blocked Lee's advance by organizing three major assaults on his left flank and one on his right, but he didn't move quickly enough to destroy Lee's army, which was able to retreat to Virginia. The 12 hour battle of Antietam has the distinction of being the bloodiest one-day battle in American history, with each side losing close to 13,000 troops. Although McClellan was widely criticized for his tactics, which ultimately resulted in his dismissal from command, he nonetheless put an end to Lee's first invasion of the North which provided Abraham Lincoln with the opportunity to issue his preliminary Emancipation Proclamation.

Gettysburg (1863)

The famed Confederate commander, Robert E. Lee, decided in 1863 to bring the war to the North in an attempt to impress would-be Confederate allies in Europe and perhaps embolden critics of the war in Washington. Lee led his army north into Maryland and then to Pennsylvania in June, 1863. The Union's Army of the Potomac, under the command of General George Meade, met the threat head-on in the small Pennsylvania town of Gettysburg. The battle opened on July 1 and raged through the day and into the next. On the night of July 2, Lee decided to assail the center of the Union position in broad daylight. The attacking force, under the command of General James Longstreet, had to cross an open field to attack Union troops massed on a ridge. Amazingly, some troops made it to the ridge, but the assault was turned back. Lee retreated, and never again would a Confederate force carry the war to the north. Lee's reputation as an invincible commander suffered a serious blow, and the war's skeptics in the North were denied a platform to denounce Lincoln's strategy.

Sedan (1870)

After the Napoleonic wars in the early 19th century, the Prussian army eventually emerged as Europe's most-powerful military force. With military strength came political genius in the form of Chancellor Otto von Bismarck, who came to power in 1862 and pledged to unify the disparate, independent entities of Germany. Bismarck's ambitions began to collide with those of Napoleon III of France, who hoped to re-create a new French empire. Tensions were raised during a bitter dispute over a Prussian plan to install a member of the Prussian royal family as king of Spain. France opposed the move, fearing encirclement. Attempts to resolve the dispute through diplomacy failed and Prussia mobilized quickly. France did not. War broke out in July, 1870, and within just a few weeks, the French were in retreat. In late August, French forces under Field Marshal Maurice MacMahon established a defensive position in Sedan, near the border with Belgium. But the Prussians, led by Helmuth von Moltke, quickly surrounded the town and the French were forced to surrender on September 1. On September 4th, a popular uprising in Paris caused Napoleon III to flee, toppling the government of the Second Empire and leading to the formation of a provi-

sional republic. The victorious Prussians demanded that France turn over the Alsace and Lorraine region, a bitter blow for the French. Bismarck was now in position to make good on his dream to create a unified German state, which came into being in 1871. The Franco-Prussian war so enraged the French that they drew closer to their former enemy, Great Britain.

Tsushima (1905)

Japan had been a closed society for over two centuries, until an American fleet under the command of Commodore Matthew Perry sailed into Tokyo Bay in 1854. By the late 19th century, Japan was both an economic and military power, thanks to its victory over China in 1895. The spoils of war included Korea and Port Arthur on the Liaotung Peninsula. The European imperial powers, however, persuaded Japan to give up its conquest. When it did so, Russia moved in, taking Port Arthur for its fleet and for the terminus of its trans-Siberian railroad. Russia also blocked Japan from a share of Manchuria's vast resources. Japanese resentment led to war with Russia in 1904. Japanese troops invaded Manchuria, and its fleet inflicted heavy losses on Russia's Pacific-based warships. In response, Russia dispatched its Baltic fleet to the Pacific. Waiting for it was a Japanese force under the command of Heihachiro Togo. On May 27, the Japanese fleet successfully outmaneuvered the Russians off the island of Tsushima in the Korea Strait. The Russians lost eight battleships (six were sunk, two captured), four cruisers, all nine of their destroyers and 10,000 men. The Japanese lost three torpedo boats. The one-sided victory marked the Japanese as a first-class naval power and pointed to Russia's fading prominence. In the United States, fear of Japanese expansion fueled anti-Japanese sentiment, especially on the West Coast.

Marne (1914)

The rivalries, resentments, petty jealousies, ethnic hatreds and romantic illusions of the European powers reached their logical, and terrible, conclusion in the late summer of 1914. Shots rang out in the Balkan city of Sarajevo, the archduke of the Austro-Hungarian Empire and his wife were killed, and men by the millions were mobilized in the great empires and cities of Europe. Alliances fell into place: Great Britain, France, Russia and their allies on one side, with Germany, Austro-Hungary and, soon after war broke out, the Ottoman Empire on the other. The Germans took the offensive immediately, launching a huge invasion of France through Belgium in early August in hope of knocking the French out of the war right away. The French countered by attacking Germany through the Alsace region. The German push was swifter and more powerful, and within weeks the Germans were threatening Paris. The French military pressed all able-bodied men into service, putting many of them in taxicabs, and sending them to the front, east of the city along the Marne River. During September 5–10, French and newly arrived British troops halted the German attack, foiling the German plan to a quick march into Paris. The Western Front soon settled into the long, murderous grind of trench warfare.

Tannenberg (1914)   Even as the German army rolled its way toward Paris, France's Russian ally was mobilizing more quickly than the Germans had anticipated. The German strategy was aimed at avoiding a huge, two-front war by knocking out France and fighting a holding action in the east until troops could be moved from the French to the Russian front. Even before the Marne, however, the strategy went awry when the Russians took the offensive to help take pressure off their embattled allies in France. After the Russians invaded East Prussia, the Germans replaced their commanders in the east with Paul von Hindenburg and Erich Ludendorff. The two commanders decided to throw the bulk of their forces against Russia's Second Army near Tannenberg, south of the Russian First Army's position. The German counter-attack and encirclement of the Second Army began on August 25. The German move severed communications between the two Russian armies, creating chaos. The Russian Second Army was overwhelmed, losing 30,000 dead, with more than 130,000 taken prisoner. The Second Army's commander, Alexander Samsonov, committed suicide. The German victory not only reduced the threat of invasion from the east, but contributed to the ensuing stalemate. Had the Germans lost at the Marne and at Tannenberg, the war would most likely have ended quickly. The split decision ensured that the war would continue, at a cost of millions of lives.

Jutland (1916)   Germany's pre-war buildup was designed not only to win battles on land, but on the sea as well. In the years leading up to the war, Germany explicitly challenged Great Britain's mastery of the seas. As an island nation dependent on shipping, Britain regarded such a challenge as a threat to its very existence. When war broke out in August, 1914, the German fleet remained inferior to Britain in sheer numbers, but some of Germany's capital ships were better-built. The first engagements between

the two navies were disasters for Germany. However, under the command of Reinhard Scheer, the German navy began challenging British shipping again in early 1916. The biggest challenge came in late May, when a German fleet steamed into the North Sea along the coast of Denmark. British warships, based in Scotland, sailed east to meet the challenge. During the ensuing battle off Jutland, which began on May 31, the Germans twice outmaneuvered the British, allowing them to fire broadsides at a column of British ships. (The maneuver is called "crossing the T.") The Germans inflicted heavy damage on the British and considered Jutland a tactical victory. But the Germans did not drive the Royal Navy out of the North Sea. As a result, the Germans decided to change their strategy to emphasize U-boats rather than surface ships.

Poland (1939)   World War I had ended abruptly and badly for the Germans, who were forced to accept humiliating terms dictated by the French and British. The postwar economy crashed, the government was unstable, and in 1933, a veteran of the western front, Adolf Hitler, came to power as Germany's Chancellor. He disowned the Treaty of Versailles, which ended World War I, and embarked on a program of re-arming Germany. His bellicose rhetoric cowed Britain and France, emotionally scarred by their horrendous losses in Verdun, the Somme and elsewhere. Hitler annexed Austria into his new order, the Third Reich, and demanded, and received, German-speaking parts of Czechoslovakia. He then turned his attention to Poland, and after weeks of threats, he unleashed his army and air force on Sept. 1, 1939. The rebuilt German army struck with incredible speed and agility—their tactics were called a blitzkrieg, or lightning war. With close integration between air power and armor, the Germans wiped out the Polish army in a month. The battle not only was the start of World War II, destined to be even bloodier than World War I, but introduced new concepts of maneuver, especially by tanks. Static war, exemplified by the trenches of World War I, was now consigned to history.

Britain (1940)   After the German invasion of Poland, Great Britain and France—ancient enemies, now firm allies—declared war. There was little they could do for Poland, so they prepared for the inevitable invasion of France. After the Germans moved against Denmark and Norway in April, 1940, they launched a massive attack on France through Belgium—again—on May 10, 1940. As was the case in Poland, the German blitzkrieg overwhelmed more-traditional deployments. Britain's entire expeditionary force found itself trapped between the Germans and the English Channel. Miraculously, the bulk of the BEF escaped the trap, leaping aboard a hastily put together rescue flotilla that brought the troops home, beaten but not vanquished. France surrendered, leaving Britain to fight alone. Like Napoleon, Hitler dreamed of crossing the channel, but first he sought to soften the island nation with air power. Beginning in July, 1940, waves of bombers with their escorts of fighter planes attacked Britain's military infrastructure. Outnumbered, but with the help of newly developed radar, the Royal Air Force's fighter pilots fought brilliantly through the summer. Denied command of the air, and unable to break Britain's morale thanks to Winston Churchill's stirring speeches, Hitler shelved his plans to attack Britain. He turned his attention to the east, to Russia. But with Britain unconquered, Hitler's western flank remained vulnerable even as the bulk of his army marched toward Moscow.

Moscow (1941) The Soviet Union and the Third Reich had signed a non-aggression pact before Germany's invasion of Poland. The agreement not only shored up Hitler's eastern flank, at least for the moment, but also divided Poland between the two dictatorships. As the Germans launched their blitzkrieg from the west, the Soviets moved in from the east, squeezing the Poles out of existence as an independent nation. But the pact between Hitler and Soviet dictator Josef Stalin was not designed to last. It was more of a holding action while Hitler pursued his ambitions in the west. With his armies touching the English Channel and across the Baltic Sea, Hitler decided the time was right to move on Russia. The Germans invaded on June 22, 1941, and in a repeat of their previous invasions, the Germans struck quickly and with great success. The difference between previous campaigns and Russia was, of course, space. The Poles, the French, the Norwegians and Danes could retreat only so far. The Red Army could retreat, and retreat, and retreat even more. And so they did, even as they took massive casualties. The Germans pushed on, and by late September, were near Moscow. Some 750,000 troops moved against the city beginning September 30. A million Red Army soldiers opposed them. Weather, Russia's most-dependable ally, rallied to the cause, with rain and then cold stalling even the lightning-quick Germans. When the Germans pulled back in early December, the Red Army launched a counter-attack. The Germans were forced to abandon Moscow, and

Hitler's goal of leveling the Soviet capital went the way of Napoleon's dreams of conquest.

Midway (1942) In 1932, Japan invaded China, and by the 1940's, its imperial gaze moved south and east, towards Europe's resource-rich Pacific colonies. But the United States Pacific fleet, based in Pearl Harbor in Hawaii, posed a potential obstacle to Japanese hegemony. Japan's surprise attack on Pearl Harbor on December 7, 1941, nearly succeeded in knocking out the U.S. fleet in one brilliant stroke. The attack sent six battleships to the bottom and damaged three others. But naval warfare had changed dramatically and aircraft carriers, not battleships, were about to become the bulwarks of a powerful navy, and the U.S. lost none of its carriers on December 7. So, despite the disaster at Pearl Harbor, the U.S. was hardly crippled. In the spring of 1942, the U.S. cracked the Japanese secret code, and knew that Admiral Isoroku Yamamoto had put together a four-carrier strike force to gain control of Midway Island, a strategic speck of real estate in the central Pacific. From Midway, the Japanese could attack Hawaii and force the U.S. to retreat to the west coast. The U.S. deployed two task forces with three carriers, Yorktown, Enterprise and Hornet, between them. Carrier-based U.S. planes attacked the Japanese force from June 4 to June 6, sinking all four Japanese carriers, among other scores. Yamamoto called off the invasion of Midway, and, a mere six months after Pearl Harbor, the United States had turned the tide of the Pacific war.

Stalingrad (1942–43) Despite the German setback outside Moscow, Hitler refused to give up his dream of conquering the Soviet Union, overthrowing its communist leadership and acquiring the vast resources of Russia, Georgia and the Ukraine. The center of German strategy shifted from Moscow to Stalingrad, a gateway to the resources of the Caucasus region. The battle for Stalingrad began in September, 1942. The man for whom the city was named, dictator Josef Stalin, ordered that there would be no retreat from the city. The Soviets would defend it, or die in the process. The Red Army defenders were put under the command of the Soviets' best general, Georgi Zhukov. In late November, as the Russian winter approached, Zhukov ordered a massive assault against Romanian troops deployed north of Stalingrad, guarding the flanks of their Nazi allies. The main German force was threatened with encirclement, but Hitler ordered it to stand and fight. The fight for Stalingrad continued through

December and into January. The Germans supply line broke down, and troops became desperately ill. The battle ended in early February, at a cost to Germany of more than 250,000 killed or captured. The Red Army lost almost a half-million dead and even more wounded or ill. The battle was a cataclysm for both sides, but for the Germans, it was especially bitter. They lost the initiative on the eastern front. From now on, the Soviets had the upper hand.

Normandy (1944) Since the entry of the United States into the war after Pearl Harbor, British and American generals prepared for an inevitable cross-Channel invasion of Nazi-held northern France. American officers believed the sooner the invasion took place, the better. The English, with fresh memories of World War I's slaughter and the loss of a generation of young Britons, were more cautious. The Anglo-American joint command decided to continue to build up an invasion force in Britain, but also launched a successful invasion of North Africa, followed by an offensive in Sicily and then the Italian mainland. All these assaults were amphibious operations, as any invasion of France would be as well. Finally, in early June, 1944, all was ready. Hundreds of thousands of American, British, Canadian, Polish and Free French troops left their training grounds and boarded troops ships to take them across the Channel to Normandy. The invasion's target was a brilliantly kept secret; through a clever campaign involving radio transmissions from non-existent armies. The Anglo-Americans led Hitler to believe the invasion would come in Calais, just across from Dover, but the 5,000-vessel armada appeared off the coast of Normandy on June 6, 1944.

The Allies landed on five beaches; one, code-named Omaha Beach, saw the fiercest German resistance and was the key to the invasion's success. Allied command of the air was critical, and by day's end, the Allies had won a foothold in France.

Okinawa (1945) The war in Europe ended in May, 1945, In the Pacific, however, bitter fighting continued as U.S. forces moved ever closer to the Japanese homeland. A bloody U.S. victory on Iwo Jima in early 1945 was followed up by an invasion of Okinawa, close to the main islands of Japan. The American invasion force landed on April 1 and encountered almost no resistance. The Japanese defenders were dug in, waiting for the invaders to move inland, where they would be caught in well-planned crossfire. Once the Japanese defense began, the Americans were forced to fight for every yard of ground. With the Japanese fighting in caves, the Americans called on flamethrowers to rout the defenders. Some Japanese were buried alive when American bulldozers sealed up their positions. Civilians killed their children and committed suicide rather than submit to American occupation. Offshore, the Japanese air force unleashed kamikaze attacks against U.S. warships. About 112,000 of the 119,000 Japanese defenders died. Some 150,000 civilians also died, while the Americans lost about 13,000. The appalling cost of Okinawa helped persuade U.S. President Harry Truman to drop atomic bombs on Hiroshima and Nagaski as a way to avoid a full scale invasion of the main Japanese islands. Japan surrendered in August, 1945, ending World War II.

History of the United States

Prior to the arrival of European colonists, the area now constituting Canada and the United States was inhabited by as many as 1.5 million indigenous peoples, mistakenly called Indians by Europeans who initially believed they had landed in the East Indies. Descendants of migratory peoples who came from Asia (theoretically via a land bridge across the present-day Bering Sea) some 20,000 to 35,000 years earlier, native Americans lived in virtually every region of North America, grouped into countless tribes and bands. Lifestyle and culture varied by region, as did fishing, hunting, gathering, and farming techniques.

By the time of Columbus's arrival, many of these peoples had developed sophisticated tools, pottery, and architecture, as well as knowledge of irrigation, agriculture, and medicine.

The Age of Exploration

European explorers probably arrived in North America long before Columbus's famed voyage of 1492. Viking explorer Leif Ericson explored the east coast of North America ca. A.D. 1000, making his way as far south as Newfoundland in present-day Canada, where he established a small settlement. Vikings appear to have traveled as far south as the coast of present-day New England. Centuries later, in 1452 Portuguese explorers Pedro Vásquez and Diogo de Teive were blown off course from the Azores and sent on a voyage that may have taken them to Newfoundland.

These episodic encounters made no discernible impact on North America and its inhabitants. The same cannot be said of the voyages of Christopher Columbus, an Italian in the service of the Spanish crown who came ashore in the Bahamas on October 12, 1492. Columbus's discovery of the New World unleashed a frantic effort by other European powers to establish colonies. The steady influx of migrants bearing European technology, language, religion, culture, and disease brought profound and in some cases catastrophic changes for the indigenous inhabitants of the New World.

Subsequent explorers of note include John Cabot (Giovanni Caboto, 1450–99), who sailed to Newfoundland and Maine in 1497 and claimed the area in the name of King Henry VII of England, and Juan Ponce de León, who in 1513 explored Florida on behalf of the Spanish monarchy. Giovanni de Verrazano (1485–1528), sponsored by Francis I of France, arrived at the Carolinas in 1524 and explored northward to Nova Scotia. Hernando de Soto (1496/97–1542) landed in Florida in 1539 with 600 Spanish soldiers and proceeded to explore as far north as the Carolinas and then west to Oklahoma. The following year fellow Spaniard Francisco Vásquez de Coronado (1510–54) explored New Mexico and Arizona (becoming the first European to see the Grand Canyon), and then northward as far as Kansas. In 1542 Juan Rodríguez Cabrillo (d. 1543) explored the west coast and claimed California for the Spanish crown.

After many failed efforts to establish permanent settlements in these areas, Pedro Ménendez de Avilés of Spain succeeded in establishing St. Augustine in Florida in 1565. Sir Walter Raleigh explored the Carolinas and Virginia in 1584 and returned the following year to establish an English settlement on Roanoke Island. Three years later, in 1587, an expedition bearing additional settlers arrived to find the colony wiped out, presumably by local Indians. These settlers, including Virginia Dare, the first English child born in America, also had vanished by the time a supply ship arrived in 1590.

The First European Colonies

The first successful English settlement was Jamestown, established in Virginia in 1607 by a group of investors called the Virginia Company. The early years were marked by great suffering, sickness, and starvation—many of the original colonists were adventurers intent on making fortunes by finding gold rather than through hard work. A lack of adequate supplies and Indian attacks nearly caused the colony to fail, but effective leadership by Captain John Smith (baptized 1580–1631), land policy reform, and the successful cultivation of tobacco in 1612 led to a gradual improvement in conditions, profits, and the number of English settlers willing to migrate. In 1619 a new charter created the House of Burgesses, the first European-style representative government in North America. That same year, however, slavery was introduced in Virginia with the arrival of 20 Africans.

In 1620 religious dissenters (Separatists), who were suffering persecution under the Church of England, founded a second English colony at Plymouth in Massachusetts. They created a form of self-government called the Mayflower Compact and quickly set about establishing a flourishing colony. In contrast to their fellow colonizers in Jamestown, Plymouth residents benefited from a healthier climate and a sense of religious mission. Settlers also included many families and people dedicated to building a functioning settlement rather than fortune-seeking. The colony was debt-free and self-supporting by 1627.

Farther to the south settlers brought by the Dutch West India Company in 1624 established the colony of New Netherland with a principal town known as New Amsterdam (present-day New York City). It prospered with the development of a booming fur trade with the Iroquois Indians. In 1664 the colony was seized by the English and renamed New York, after the Duke of York, the king's son.

The Massachusetts Bay Colony was established by English Puritans (dissenters who sought to "purify" the Church of England by ridding it of "popish" practices). The first 1,000 emigrants arrived in 1630 and the settlement quickly flourished for the same reasons that marked the rise of nearby Plymouth. Word of its success enticed some 25,000 Puritans to migrate between 1630 and 1640, leading to rapid expansion and the establishment of several new towns outside Boston. When quarrels over religious doctrine led Puritan leaders to expel Roger Williams (1603?–83) and Anne Hutchinson (baptized 1591–1643) for their unorthodox beliefs, the two established new settlements in present-day Rhode Island (1636). Similar circumstances led to new settlements in Connecticut, beginning with Hartford in 1636.

Lord Baltimore (1578/79–1632) founded Maryland in 1632 as a haven for English Catholics, the first of whom arrived in 1634. Like nearby Virginia, the colony quickly established a flourishing economy based on tobacco.

Pennsylvania, too, was founded as a religious haven, in this case for Quakers. William Penn (1644–1718), a wealthy member of the sect, received a massive land grant from the English king, Charles II, in 1661. Penn's colony was unique both for its firmly established principle of religious toleration and relatively benign treatment of Indians. Residents, who numbered 12,000 by 1689, also enjoyed democratic government in the form of an elected legislature.

The last major colony established in the 17th century was Carolina in 1653 (North and South Carolina were not created until 1729). Lacking a major cash crop like tobacco, the colony struggled until the 1690's, when a thriving fur trade and rice cultivation were developed.

Georgia was the last of the 13 original colonies to be settled. Georgia's first settlers, mostly debtors led by James Oglethorpe, arrived in 1733, but the colony struggled and grew slowly as a result of low migration and frequent conflict with Spanish Florida to the south.

Although each colony developed its own distinct character in the 17th century, several common trends emerged. All the colonies experienced conflicts with Indians, who naturally resisted European seizure of their lands. In some cases, attacks by Indians nearly destroyed colonies, as in the case of a war in 1622 that left 357 Virginia colonists dead. But the colonists' technological superiority in military affairs and the devastating effects of European diseases led to the steady decline of the Indian population.

Slavery also took hold in all the colonies, but to a far greater extent in the south, where labor intensive agriculture (tobacco and rice) flourished. By 1700 some 20,500 slaves had been brought to the colonies, a number destined to rise dramatically in the decades to come.

Finally, as the examples of Roger Williams and Anne Hutchinson indicate, the colonies were frequently beset by social conflict. Virginia experienced an uprising of poor farmers in 1676 known as Bacon's Rebellion, while several colonial governments were toppled in the wake of England's "Glorious Revolution" of 1688, when the Stuart dynasty was overthrown. In Salem, Mass., for reasons that still baffle historians, hysteria over witchcraft in 1692 spiraled out of control and led to the executions of 21 accused witches.

The Colonies in the 18th Century

Economy   The tumultuous politics of 17th century England (the execution of Charles I, the civil war) left the American colonies substantially unregulated in many matters, especially economic affairs. The stability that followed the accession of William III to the throne in 1689 led to an effort by Crown officials to impose strict regulations on the colonies regarding manufacturing and trade. Guiding these decisions was the theory of mercantilism, which argued that the colonies ought to provide England with raw materials such as timber, tobacco, fur, and fish and a market for sale of finished goods such as clothes, tools, books, and luxury goods. In other words, the colonies were to serve the economic interests of England.

In 1696 the English government established the Board of Trade (1696–1776) to oversee the administration of colonial policy. One of its main purposes was to enforce a series of Navigation Acts regulating colonial trade, the first of which were passed in 1660, 1663, and 1673. They required that all goods sent from the colonies to England be carried on English ships (or ships built in English colonies), that all European goods bound for the colonies must pass through England, and that certain "enumerated articles" produced in the colonies (tobacco, sugar, cotton, indigo, etc.) must be sold only to England.

Despite passage of these laws, England adopted a policy of "salutary neglect" for the decades leading up to the 1760's, allowing the colonies tremendous freedom in economic matters. Colonists developed a thriving "Triangular Trade" in food (fish, grain, meat), slaves, and sugar with north Africa and the West Indies. Shipbuilding also emerged as a major industry in response to the requirement that all goods must travel in British ships.

Population   The population of colonial America not only increased dramatically in the 18th century, it also grew increasingly diverse. Some 250,000 Palatine Germans arrived after 1700, settling mainly on the Pennsylvania and Virginia frontiers and in an area outside of Philadelphia that soon became known as Germantown. Immigrants from northern Ireland, the so-called Scotch Irish, totaled more than 200,000 by 1776. Like their German counterparts, they also settled primarily on the frontier. Smaller numbers of settlers from Portugal, Spain, France, Sweden, and many other European nations could be found in the major port cities such as Boston and New York.

During the 18th century there was a sharp increase in the number of slaves imported from Africa and, as was more common, the West Indies. Most of the estimated 500,000 who arrived in this period were sent to the southern colonies.

Religion Beginning in the 1720's, the English colonies experienced an intense revival of religious fervor known as the Great Awakening. It began with revivals in New Jersey and Pennsylvania and eventually spread to New England and the South. Ministers such as Jonathan Edwards (1703–58) preached an evangelical and highly emotional form of Christianity that stressed a person's sinfulness and need for a closer relationship with God. The movement's power diminished by 1745, but not before dramatically increasing church membership and causing lasting splits in several denominations.

England Defeats France The British faced several European rivals in the contest for control of North America. The Spanish controlled Florida and vast areas of the Southwest. The French settlement of New France covered a huge triangle of territory stretching from Nova Scotia to New Orleans to Montana. For much of the 18th century France loomed as the biggest threat to English colonial ambitions, especially in matters related to trade, resulting in three protracted wars between 1689–97, 1701–13, and 1744–48, with much of the action taking place in upper New York, New England, and Canada.

The decisive Anglo-French conflict, called the French and Indian War in America (see "The Seven Years' War" in World History), began in 1754. The fight resulted from a struggle for control of the Ohio River Valley and the rich trade opportunities therein. The French allied themselves with several powerful Indian tribes and enjoyed the upper hand in the early years of warfare. But the British reorganized and proved victorious by 1763. Under the Treaty of Paris (1763) France was forced to cede all of Canada to the English.

The Road to Revolution With peace restored in 1763, English government authorities decided to end the period of "salutary neglect" and reassert control over the American colonies. They were particularly eager to gain control over colonial trade as a means of raising badly needed revenue to pay for the huge cost of the French and Indian War and the anticipated expense of defending the now vastly enlarged colonial frontier. British leaders believed the colonists ought

to pay for their own defense, because they stood to gain the most from it. Colonists came to reject this interpretation, arguing that taxation by a government in which they were not represented was unjust. They also resisted taxation because of a severe economic recession that afflicted the colonies through much of the 1760's.

Nevertheless, the English Parliament passed a series of laws that stirred fierce opposition in the colonies. The first was the Proclamation Act of 1763, which prohibited English settlement beyond the Appalachian Mountains. Designed to ensure peace with Indians on the frontier, it angered many colonists eager to acquire western lands. The Sugar Act of 1764 (an extension of the never-enforced Molasses Act of 1733) imposed a duty on foreign molasses, sugar, and other products imported into the colonies. The Currency Act of the same year prohibited the issuance of paper money by colonial governments. Opposition to these measures first emerged in Massachusetts, where leaders denounced "taxation without representation" and organized the first boycott, or nonimportation movement, against English goods. Communication with leaders in other colonies caused the movement to spread.

Colonial opposition to British policy exploded in 1765 with the passage of the Stamp Act, which imposed a tax on a wide range of products, including newspapers, almanacs, legal documents, licenses, and even playing cards. Outraged over this first instance of an "internal" tax on the colonies, colonists formed secret organizations known as the Sons of Liberty, which staged several riots against the agents in charge of collecting the taxes and marking the articles with a special stamp. In October representatives of nine colonies gathered for a Stamp Act Congress in New York, where they drew up resolutions stating their reasons for opposing the act and sent them to England. Hundreds of merchants throughout the colonies joined in a renewed nonimportation effort to put economic pressure on the government. Parliament repealed the Stamp Act in March 1766.

Still determined to rein in the rebellious colonies and generate revenue, Parliament passed the Townshend Acts in 1767, which imposed duties on lead, glass, paint, paper, and tea. It immediately sparked resistance in the form of a renewed nonimportation movement that severely reduced the importation of British goods. Deeply concerned about the loss of trade, Parliament in 1770 limited the duties imposed by the Townshend Acts to tea. Calm returned to the colonies and nonimportation was ended on all goods except tea.

Tensions remained high in places where large contingents of British soldiers were stationed. A serious clash in New York between the Sons of Liberty and soldiers in January 1770 was followed by the "Boston Massacre" on March 5, 1770. Panicky British soldiers opened fire on a jeering crowd, killing five. In spite of the outrage among colonists, tension between England and the colonies diminished substantially over the next few years.

Passage of the Tea Act in 1773 sparked renewed agitation because it granted a monopoly on sales of tea to the British East India Company, a move interpreted as harmful to American merchants and the ongoing effort to boycott tea. In protest, a group of colonial protestors dressed as Indians boarded a merchant ship in Boston Harbor on the night of Dec. 16, 1773, and dumped hundreds of chests of British tea into the harbor, an event known thereafter as the "Boston Tea Party." Parliament reacted by passing the Coercive Acts (called the "Intolerable Acts" in the colonies) in 1774. The legislation closed the port of Boston, drastically altered the colonial charter of Massachusetts, and suppressed town meetings.

In response, 10 of the 11 colonies sent delegates to a Continental Congress, which met in Philadelphia on September 5, 1774. The body issued a "Declaration of Rights and Grievances" that pledged obedience to the king but denied the right of Parliament to tax the colonies. It also renewed the nonimportation effort.

In Massachusetts resistance to the Coercive Acts increased, most notably with the mobilization of the colonial militia in anticipation of a clash with British troops. On April 19, 1775, General Thomas Gage, the colony's military governor, led a force of British troops to Concord, Mass., to seize a large cache of arms and ammunition stored there by the militia. They were attacked by a force of so-called Minute Men and driven back to Boston in two clashes known as the Battles of Lexington and Concord.

The Second Continental Congress convened on May 10, 1775, with many delegates recommending a declaration of independence from Britain. Instead, the body established an army and named George Washington as its commander.

The American Revolution (1775–83)   See "Major Wars in History."

The Articles of Confederation   After the war began the Continental Congress urged the former colonies to establish state governments. Eleven of the 13 states drafted constitutions that established representative governments (elected by limited suffrage) with bicameral legislatures and a bill of rights. A national government based on the Articles of Confederation was devised during the war and approved by the Continental Congress on November 15, 1777. Fearing centralized power, the architects of the Articles created a weak national government (in the form of a unicameral Congress) that left most power with the individual states. These included the power to tax and to regulate the economy.

The new Confederation government was ratified by the states in March 1781 but soon proved ineffective. At the end of the Revolution, the new nation was beset by severe economic problems, much of it brought on by the war but also by the chaos of having 13 different trade, tariff, and tax policies established by the individual states. The suffering led to protests like Shay's Rebellion (1786) in Massachusetts by debtors who faced foreclosure on their farms. Moreover, major threats loomed from foreign powers such as Spain, which still controlled Florida and the lower Mississippi. Concerned leaders convened at the Annapolis Conference in 1786, where they approved a resolution calling upon the states to send representatives to a convention to discuss changes to the Confederation government.

The Constitution and New Government   The Constitutional Convention gathered in Philadelphia in May 1787 and considered several revisions before agreeing in September to adopt an entirely new form of government. The Constitution of the United States created a strong national government consisting of an executive (president), legislature (Senate and House of Representatives), and judiciary (federal courts, including the Supreme Court). The required nine states ratified the Constitution by June 1788 and the new government took effect in the spring of 1789. Concerns over states' rights and civil liberties led Congress to approve 12 amendments to the Constitution. The states ratified 10 of them, known collectively as the Bill of Rights. (See "The Constiution of the United States.")

The Federalist Era

George Washington was inaugurated as the nation's first president on April 30, 1789. The most important figure in his administration was Treasury Secretary Alexander Hamilton, whose successful effort to fund the national debt, assume individual state debts, and establish a Bank of the United States did much to restore economic growth, especially in the long term. His decision to impose a tax on whiskey, however, led to a revolt by Pennsylvania farmers known as the Whiskey Rebellion (1794) which ended only after Washington sent federal troops to quell the uprising.

By the mid-1790's opponents of Hamilton's policies united behind Thomas Jefferson, marking the beginning of the first political parties. The Hamilton faction took the name Federalists, while the Jeffersonians tried several names before settling on Republicans (also known as Jeffersonian Republicans, and the forerunner of the modern Democratic party).

Washington's administration faced many challenges, especially in the realm of foreign affairs. Warfare with Indians raged on the frontier, while relations with Spain were strained over boundary disputes in the southeast. Worse was the turmoil caused by the French Revolution and the subsequent war between England and France (1793). Despite a declaration of neutrality, England seized some 150 American ships for trading with the French, an outrage the weak American nation was powerless to stop until ratification of the Jay Treaty in 1795, although England never actually abandoned the practice.

Federalist John Adams was elected president in 1796 after George Washington decided to retire. In 1797 a diplomatic crisis (the XYZ Affair, in which French officials tried to elicit bribes from U.S. diplomats) had many Americans demanding war with France. Adams resisted, but the U.S. was soon embroiled in an undeclared war on the high seas with France (1798–1800). Irritated by criticism from his Jeffersonian adversaries and leery of the influence of radical French émigrés on U.S. politics, Adams signed the Alien and Sedition Acts, a series of constitutionally questionable measures (including making criticism of the government a crime) vigorously challenged by Jefferson and James Madison in their Kentucky and Virginia Resolutions.

Jeffersonian Democracy   After a bitter election campaign in 1800, Thomas Jefferson was elected president over John Adams. The peaceful transfer of power from one party (Federalists) to another (Jeffersonian Republicans) marked a major moment in American democracy. Jefferson emphasized a strict interpretation of the Constitution that argued the federal government possessed very limited powers relative to the states. Jefferson ignored this principle, however, when in 1803

cash-strapped France offered to sell the Louisiana Territory to the United States for $15 million. The acquisition of 828,000 square miles (the Louisiana Purchase) doubled the size of the nation and prompted Jefferson to dispatch the Merriwether Lewis and William Clark expedition (1804–06) to explore it. That same year the Supreme Court issued its decision in *Marbury v. Madison*, the first time the Court declared an act of Congress unconstitutional.

With the resumption of the Napoleonic Wars in 1803, U.S. shipping again faced hostility from the French and British, both of whom sought to deny the other access to American trade. The British posed the biggest threat, seizing hundreds of American ships and forcing many crewmen into the British navy. When treaty negotiations failed, Congress, at Jefferson's urging, imposed an embargo (1807) on virtually all foreign commerce. It proved a very controversial measure, as it inflicted heavy damage on the fragile U.S. economy, especially in Federalist-dominated states in the northeast.

The War of 1812   James Madison won the presidency in the election of 1808 and inherited from Jefferson the foreign policy crisis with England. Matters eventually deteriorated to such a point that the U.S. declared war on England on June 18, 1812.

The war represented America's participation in the global Napoleonic Wars that had arisen from the French Revolution of 1789. Both Britain and France had attacked American commerce, but Britain, the dominant naval power, was responsible for more injuries. In particular, the British did not recognize the right of a person to change nationality and so claimed the right to impress into their navy American sailors whom they claimed were still British subjects.

James Madison had been reelected President in 1812 under the slogan, "Free men, free trade, free ships" and he led a deeply divided country into war. A U.S. attack on Montreal failed, but in the West, U.S. forces were generally successful. Captain Oliver Perry defeated the British fleet on Lake Erie; Detroit, which had fallen to the British, was retaken; and General William Henry Harrison, a future president, defeated the British and an Indian confederacy under Tecumseh at the Battle of the Thames in Canada. Despite these U.S. victories, however, the British were largely successful in blockading American ports.

In 1814, in the wake of Napoleon's defeat in Europe, the British took to the offensive, but were generally unsuccessful. An invasion of New York from Canada was stopped at Plattsburgh; and while an invading army succeeded in taking and burning Washington, D.C., it was repulsed at Baltimore. Finally, a British attack on New Orleans was crushed by another future American president, Andrew Jackson, who became a national hero. The American victory occurred two weeks after a peace treaty had been signed in Ghent, Belgium, in December of 1814. By its terms, Britain finally accepted U.S. independence.

Even as peace negotiations progressed, disgruntled Federalists from New England sent representatives to the Hartford Convention (1814). Embracing a states' rights doctrine, they adopted several resolutions that would have seriously undercut the war effort if Congress had approved them. News of the peace treaty and Jackson's victory deeply embarrassed the convention and brought lasting discredit upon the Federalist Party.

The Early National Period (1815–40)

Peace in 1815 ushered in an era of national pride, westward expansion, and economic growth. To facilitate the latter, Madison won reauthorization of the Bank of the United States in 1816 and signed into a law a high protective tariff. Many states and private companies spurred economic development and westward expansion by building networks of roads and canals, while the development of steamboats after 1811 greatly expanded transportation on rivers. James Monroe, the last of the "Virginia Dynasty" presidents, won the presidency in 1816. Soon after his inauguration in early 1817 he embarked on a national tour that took him through New England and westward to Detroit. The outpouring of enthusiasm and national pride, even in Federalist strongholds in the northeast, led some to dub Monroe's eight years in office as "The Era of Good Feelings." But beneath the surface of this exuberant nationalism lay several divisive issues that call into question the accuracy of the phrase.

Warfare broke out in Spanish Florida in 1818 as a U.S. force invaded, ostensibly in response to threats by Seminole Indians and escaped slaves to the state of Georgia. Led by Andrew Jackson, the force seized most of Florida, forcing the Spanish to cede it to the U.S. in subsequent treaty negotiations. Financial distress set in with the Panic of 1819 and lasted until 1821. Controversy over slavery erupted in 1819 when Missouri applied for statehood, with many northerners opposed to the extension

of slavery into the western territories. The resulting Missouri Compromise (or the Compromise of 1820) admitted Missouri as a slave state, but offset it with the admission of Maine as a free state, thus retaining the balance of power between slave and free states in Congress. It also adopted a provision barring slavery from the former Louisiana Territory above the latitude 36′30″, the southern boundary of Missouri.

To ensure American security, Monroe issued the Monroe Doctrine in 1823. It announced that America would not tolerate intervention by European powers into the affairs of recently liberated Latin American nations. In addition, he pledged that America would not intervene in any European wars.

Economic Expansion   The 1820's and 1830's witnessed a dramatic transformation of the economy, politics, population, and values of the United States. By the end of the 1820's, the granting of the vote to virtually all white men through the abolition of property requirements made politics far more democratic. Major advances were made in transportation technology with the spread of canals—most notably the Erie Canal in upstate New York (completed 1825)—steamboats, and the first railroads. Similarly, the movement of information was dramatically accelerated with the invention and subsequent spread of the telegraph. Industrial manufacturing achieved prominence with the construction of the first factory town in Lowell, Massachusetts. The onset of mass immigration in the 1830's (especially Irish, Germans, and Scandinavians) added greatly to the nation's demographic diversity and spurred rapid urbanization.

Jacksonian Democracy   The election of Andrew Jackson as President in 1828 inaugurated a new era in American democracy. He was the first president elected after expansion of the franchise, and he pledged to represent the interests of the "common man" against the forces of elitism, wealth, and privilege. During his term, the Democratic Party also evolved from the earlier Jeffersonian Republicans and other political factions.

Indian Removal   Jackson's two terms as President were marked by several major controversies. The first began in 1830 with Jackson's decision to forcibly remove Indian tribes from the southeast United States to remote settlements in the west. He carried out this program despite a Supreme Court ruling in 1832 that upheld the rights of the tribes. Thousands of Cherokee Indians died during the harsh journey to Oklahoma, an experience that came to be called "The Trail of Tears."

The Nullification Crisis Congress passed a new tariff in 1828 that pleased northern manufacturing interests and angered southern planters. Vice-President and later Senator John C. Calhoun (1782–1850) of South Carolina led the outcry against the tariff and issued a decree that states possessed the right to "nullify" any act of Congress they deemed unjust or unconstitutional. Jackson threatened to use force if South Carolina continued its resistance. Eventually the matter was settled when a new tariff was adopted in 1833.

The Bank War Because he viewed banks as undemocratic institutions that favored the rich over the common man, Jackson decided to destroy the Bank of the United States. The charter for the bank, created in 1792 by Alexander Hamilton, was due to expire in 1836. Congress passed a bill authorizing a new charter in 1832 but Jackson vetoed it. When Congress was unable to override the veto, the Bank ceased operations in 1836.

The Texas Republic Thousands of Americans had moved to northern Mexico in the 1820's at the invitation of the Mexican government. But the abolition of slavery in Mexico in 1829, a ban on further American settlement in 1830, and the assumption of dictatorial powers by Mexican president General Santa Ana in 1835 prompted American settlers to revolt. They set up a provincial government, declared Texas an independent republic, and raised an army. Santa Ana defeated the Americans at the Battle of the Alamo in March 1836 but suffered a crushing defeat at the Battle of San Jacinto a month later. Texans celebrated their independence but hoped for annexation by the United States.

The Abolitionists

Expansion of plantations and slave labor into the fertile regions of Georgia, Alabama, Mississippi, Arkansas, Louisiana, and Texas led to a boom in the output of cash crops like tobacco, sugar, rice, and especially cotton. Production of cotton jumped from 1.35 million bales in 1840 to an incredible 4.8 million bales by 1860. Southern cotton by this time accounted for three-fifths of American exports and three-quarters of the world supply of cotton, leading many southerners to boast that "Cotton is King."

The growth of the southern economy, much of it based on the forced labor of slaves, alarmed many north-erners who had hoped that slavery in the South would wither away as it had in the North. Beginning in the early 1830's, they formed a movement dedicated to the abolition of slavery. The most notable of them was William Lloyd Garrison (1805–79), who in 1831 founded *The Liberator*, an influential abolitionist newspaper, and in 1833 started the American Anti-Slavery Society. Abolitionists collected thousands of signatures in support of abolition and forwarded them to Congress. Southern congressmen became so exasperated at this mounting attack on slavery that they passed the so-called "Gag Rule" that prohibited the reading of these anti-slavery petitions in Congress. They also denounced abolition as an unconstitutional attack on property rights and an effort to encourage slave uprisings, a sentiment that gained widespread support in 1831 when a slave named Nat Turner (1800-31) led a bloody insurrection in Virginia, killing more than 50 white people.

The Second Great Awakening

Abolition was only one of many reform movements that swept antebellum America. Much of this support for reform emanated from the enthusiasm generated by a religious revival known as the Second Great Awakening. Beginning in the 1820's evangelical ministers such as Charles Grandison Finney traveled the country preaching a new doctrine of Christianity that urged individuals to eradicate sinful practices both in their personal lives and in society at large.

Temperance

Many people inspired by this upsurge in religious enthusiasm came to see slavery as an evil and joined the abolitionist movement. Many also joined a growing crusade against alcohol. Led by the American Society for the Promotion of Temperance, founded in 1826, they delivered speeches and published tracts urging their fellow Americans to abstain from drinking. The first law banning alcohol outright was passed in Maine in 1846, followed by 12 more states by 1860.

Women's Rights

Some of the most committed reformers in this era were women. Their involvement in abolition and temperance led many to demand greater rights for women. Few states in this era recognized a woman's right to own property, execute contracts, sue for divorce, or vote. In 1848 more than 100 men and women gathered at the first Women's Rights Convention in Seneca Falls, N.Y. and issued a stirring call for an end to laws and customs that kept women subordinate to men.

Manifest Destiny In the mid-1840's many Americans began to see westward expansion and development as the key to the nation's rise to greatness. The construction of canals, railroads, and roads enticed thousands to head west to establish farms or small businesses in trading centers like St. Louis and Cincinnati. Enthusiastic supporters of expansion declared that it was America's "manifest destiny" to become a continental power reaching all the way to the Pacific. That much of this territory was part of Mexico, or controlled by Great Britain, or occupied by Native American tribes did not trouble them. In keeping with this spirit, Congress annexed the Texas republic in 1845 and settled a longstanding border dispute between the U.S. and Great Britain in the Pacific northwest in 1846.

The Mexican War American annexation of the Texas Republic in 1845 triggered war with Mexico. At issue was the border between Mexico and Texas, the Rio Grande or the more northerly Nueces River. Mexican troops attacked American forces under a future American president, Zachary Taylor, in the disputed area, and President James K. Polk asked Congress for a declaration of war. General Taylor's army defeated Santa Ana at Buena Vista. Other American forces seized Santa Fe in present day New Mexico and proceeded to California, where American settlers had already seized power in the name of a separate Great Bear Republic. General Winfield Scott landed at the Mexican port of Santa Cruz and, in a series of battles culminating in the Battle of Chapultepec, commemorated in the Marine Corps Hymn as the "Halls of Montezuma," Scott took Mexico City. Mexico capitulated in the Treaty of Guadalupe Hidalgo (1848), ceding to the United States the territories of Texas, California, and what would become Arizona, Utah, Colorado, and Nevada. The U.S. agreed to pay Mexico about $18 million.

The California Gold Rush Gold was discovered in January 1848 along the American River in northern California. By August stories of California gold reached the East. Any lingering skepticism was swept aside in December when more than 300 ounces of pure gold arrived in Washington, D.C. Tens of thousands of Americans caught "gold fever" and left farms and workshops for San Francisco. California's population exploded, rising from just 14,000 at the start of 1849 to more than 100,000 by year's end and 220,000 by 1852.

Slavery and the Road to Civil War

In 1849 California's application to be admitted to the Union touched off another political crisis over the issue of slavery. Most northerners were willing to leave slavery alone where it currently existed, but demanded that it be prevented from the new territories. They cited moral opposition to human bondage and the fact that Mexico had abolished slavery in 1829. Most southerners demanded with equal firmness that slaveholders had every right to bring slaves into the west and vehemently opposed any attempt to limit the spread of what was called the "peculiar institution."

The struggle to reach a compromise in the coming months set the stage for the final performances of three legislative giants—westerner Henry Clay of Kentucky, northerner Daniel Webster of Massachusetts, and southerner John Calhoun of South Carolina. As he had done so in the Missouri Compromise in 1820 and the Nullification Crisis of 1832-33, Clay ("the great compromiser") endeavored to broker a deal acceptable to the various factions, sections, and interests by granting each part of what they demanded. Accordingly he drafted an omnibus bill that gave northerners and southerners a portion of their wishes: California admitted as a free state, New Mexico organized into two territories with slavery determined by popular sovereignty, the Texas border adjusted in exchange for federal assumption of its debt, the slave trade banned in Washington D.C., and a stronger federal fugitive slave law.

The debate over Clay's proposed compromise inspired some of the most renowned speeches in the history of Congress. But the views expressed in them illustrated a hardening of positions on the issue of slavery. On March 4 Calhoun, speaking for southern hardliners, rejected Clay's proposal and demanded that the North accord the South equal rights in the territories, enforce the fugitive slave laws, cease attacking slavery, and accept a constitutional amendment creating two presidents, one northern and one southern, each possessing a veto. Three days later Webster delivered his famous "Seventh of March Address" in which he chastised both southern nationalists and northern abolitionists and spoke passionately on behalf of compromise as a rational course and a patriotic duty. William Seward of New York then delivered an address invoking the authority of "a higher law than the Constitution" (the law of God) to denounce slavery.

The dispute was settled by Illinois Senator Stephen A. Douglas's Compromise of 1850, parts of which appealed to proslavery southerners and others to antislavery northerners. California was admitted as a free state. To offset this concession to slavery's opponents, a second bill organized the southwest as the New Mexico and Utah territories and left the question of slavery to be decided by popular sovereignty when each applied for statehood. Left unexplained was the status of slavery in the years leading to statehood. The most important concession to the South was a new, more stringent Fugitive Slave Act to replace the original one passed in 1793.

Vowing to resist the Fugitive Slave Act, abolitionists formed so-called vigilance committees throughout the North. Some of the earliest and most memorable incidents occurred in Boston, the unofficial headquarters of the abolitionist movement. In early 1851 when word spread that an escaped slave named Shadrach Minkins had been arrested, an incensed black mob broke into the courthouse, overpowered the marshals, and whisked him off to Montreal. When another escaped slave, Thomas Sims, was apprehended in Boston two months later, President Millard Fillmore sent 250 soldiers to guard the courthouse and escort the captive to a ship bound for Georgia. Similar incidents by abolitionist mobs occurred in New York City, Philadelphia, Detroit, Syracuse and many smaller towns.

Sentiment against slavery also was fueled by the publication of the novel *Uncle Tom's Cabin* in 1852. Written by Harriet Beecher Stowe, a member of a prominent abolitionist family, it sold an astonishing 300,000 copies in one year, making it the best-selling book of the era. Its account of slavery's brutality moved the hearts and minds of millions of northerners.

The Kansas-Nebraska Act of 1854 created the Kansas Territory west of Missouri and the Nebraska Territory west of Iowa. The issue of whether slavery would be permitted in these territories would be determined by popular sovereignty. This last provision, intended to placate both North and South by allowing the eventual establishment of Kansas as a slave state (since its soil and climate were similar to neighboring Missouri) and Nebraska as a free state, required the repeal of the Missouri Compromise of 1820 that had barred slavery above 36'30". The bitter fight over this bill intensified sectional animosities.

The political impact of the Kansas-Nebraska controversy became clear in the 1854 midterm elections. Free Soilers, ex-Whigs, and antislavery Democrats in the North formed dozens of local parties under names like the Anti-Nebraska or the People's Party. By far the most popular name, and the one under which they would eventually unite, was Republican Party. Despite their varied names, they shared an overriding commitment to opposing further concessions to southern slave interests.

Antipathy toward slavery in the North competed with rising anti-immigrant sentiment. The latter reached a fever pitch in 1854 with the emergence of a political party whose core constituents were members of secret anti-immigrant societies. Referred to as "Know Nothings," they called for legislation restricting office holding to native-born citizens, barring the use of public funds for parochial schools, and raising the period of naturalization for citizenship from 5 to 21 years. With the Whig party in decline and the Democrats closely associated with the immigrant vote, Know Nothings achieved stunning success in the 1854 elections in Massachusetts, Delaware, and Pennsylvania and polled well in most other northeast and border states.

The controversy over slavery erupted once again in the Kansas Territory in 1855-56. Pro-slavery and anti-slavery settlers flocked to the territory in advance of a vote that would determine the fate of slavery there. Armed conflict between the two sides broke out all across "Bleeding Kansas," resulting in hundreds of deaths. The violence even reached Congress when, in 1857, South Carolina Representative Preston Brooks attacked Senator Charles Sumner of Massachusetts with a cane after the latter delivered a spirited speech denouncing the South for its "crimes against Kansas."

The Dred Scott Decision   Passions were further inflamed when the Supreme Court issued its decision in the Dred Scott case. Scott, a slave, had sued for his freedom, arguing that the years he spent with his owner in Illinois and the Wisconsin Territory (where the Missouri Compromise barred slavery) had made him a free man. The southern-dominated Supreme Court, led by Chief Justice Roger B. Taney of Maryland, a slave state, rejected Scott's claim, arguing that slaves were property, not people, and as such, they were not citizens and therefore lacked standing in a court of law. The Court went further and declared that Congress had no authority to regulate slavery in the territories. Many northerners denounced the Court's decision, seeing it as an example of southern dominance of the federal government.

Slavery emerged as a dominant theme in an election for U.S. Senate from Illinois in 1858, when a former congressman named Abraham Lincoln challenged two-term incumbent Stephen Douglas. In accepting the Senate nomination, Lincoln famously warned that "a house divided against itself cannot stand." The two candidates agreed to a series of debates around the state, during which Lincoln, running as the candidate of the new Republican Party, articulated his opposition to the extension of slavery into new territories. Douglas was one of the foremost champions of popular sovereignty. Douglas went on to win the election, but Lincoln emerged as a candidate for national office.

In the fall of 1859 a band of white and black abolitionists led by John Brown (1800–59) staged a raid on a federal arsenal at Harper's Ferry, Va. Their plan had been to move on to the South, arming slaves as they went and touching off a wave of rebellion across the South. But militia and U.S. Marines arrived and stormed their stronghold, killing 10 and taking Brown and the rest as prisoners. All were summarily tried, convicted, and executed. Southerners were enraged by what they perceived as an increasingly aggressive abolitionist movement, while many in the North hailed Brown as a martyr.

The Election of 1860

The breaking point came in the election of 1860. Four candidates vied for the presidency in a contest dominated by the slavery question. Abraham Lincoln, nominee of the Republican Party, won the election. But the details of the results foreshadowed a crisis. Lincoln swept most northern states, but received virtually no support in the South, where the Republican Party was condemned as the party of abolition.

Southerners had threatened secession as far back as the Constitutional Convention, but had always accepted compromise in the end. Not so in 1860, for secessionist-minded southerners now declared that they would not live under a Republican administration. On December 20, 1860, South Carolina declared that the bond between their state and the United States of America "is hereby dissolved." Six more slave states—Florida, Alabama, Georgia, Mississippi, Louisiana, and Texas—quickly followed. Within months Virginia, North Carolina, Tennessee, and Arkansas joined with them to form a new nation, the Confederate States of America. All efforts at compromise failed and war began in April 1861 when the newly elected president, Lincoln, attempted to resupply Fort Sumter, a federally held garrison in Charleston, South Carolina.

The Civil War (1861-65)   See "Major Wars in History."

Transformation of the Union   While war raged, Republicans took advantage of their dominant position in Congress to enact legislation which had long been opposed by Southerners. Most of these were policies designed to promote westward settlement, industrialization, and a modern financial system. In 1862 Congress passed the Homestead Act, which granted 160 acres of land to any settler who agreed to live on it for five years and improve it. The Morrill Act that same year gave thousands of acres of land to individual states. The money raised from its sale was designated to fund public education, especially to what became known as land grant colleges. To protect Northern manufacturers from foreign competition, Congress raised the tariff on imported goods to its highest level ever. Deeming a transcontinental railroad a national necessity, Congress created two federally chartered railroads, the Union Pacific and the Central Pacific, and provided them with vast tracts of free land and inexpensive loans to finance the project, which was completed in 1869. Finally, the National Bank Acts of 1863 and 1864 established a national banking system whereby member banks could issue treasury notes, or "greenbacks," as currency.

Reconstructing the Union

After critical Northern victories in 1863, Lincoln began to outline a moderate plan for restoring the Southern states to the Union. That December his Proclamation of Amnesty and Reconstruction proposed that all Southerners (except for high-ranking military officers and Confederate officials) who took an oath pledging loyalty to the Union and support for emancipation would be pardoned. As soon as 10 percent of a state's voters took this oath, they could call a convention, establish a new state government and apply for Congressional recognition.

Under Lincoln's leadership, Congress passed the 13th

Amendment abolishing slavery in late January 1865. In March 1865 Congress established the Bureau of Refugees, Freedmen and Abandoned Lands. Known simply as the Freedmen's Bureau, it was to serve as an all-purpose relief agency in the war-ravaged South, providing emergency services, building schools, and managing confiscated lands.

The relief that followed the end of the Civil War quickly changed to despair. On the night of April 14, 1865, just five days after Lee's surrender, Lincoln was shot at close range by Confederate sympathizer John Wilkes Booth. Lincoln died the following day. News of the tragedy elicited an enormous outpouring of grief for the martyred president among citizens of the North and freed slaves in the South.

Lincoln's successor, Andrew Johnson, also promoted a very lenient policy toward the South with an eye toward rapidly restoring the Union. In late May 1865 he issued two proclamations outlining his policy. One offered "amnesty and pardon," including the return of all property, to southerners who took an oath of allegiance to the Constitution and Union. Former Confederate leaders and wealthy planters worth more than $20,000, however, would have to apply to him personally for a pardon. The second set forth extremely lenient terms for ex-Confederate states to gain readmission to the Union. With Congress out of session, Johnson's plan faced little formal opposition. In December 1865, with all 11 former Confederate states having established new governments under his terms, he announced the Union was restored and that reconstruction was "over."

Radical Reconstruction Johnson's actions outraged many northern Republicans who viewed them as far too easy on the South. They noted that in the supposedly "reconstructed" South voters elected to office dozens of ex-Confederate officials and army officers, among them Alexander Stephens, former vice president of the Confederacy. Republicans also observed that new southern state governments, beginning in late 1865 with Mississippi and South Carolina, passed laws or "Black Codes" that limited the civil and economic rights of the former slaves. So-called "Radical Republicans" in Congress repudiated Johnson's Reconstruction plan and refused to recognize the new southern state governments. They then set out to pass a much more aggressive and vindictive plan for reconstructing the South.

The 14th Amendment In June 1866 Radical and moderate Republicans passed the 14th Amendment to the Constitution. A long and complex amendment, it contained five main provisions. First, it defined freedmen (all persons born or naturalized in the United States) as national citizens. Second, all citizens were entitled to "equal protection of the laws" of the states where they lived. Third, all high-ranking former Confederates were prohibited from holding public office, unless pardoned by act of Congress. Fourth, African-American men were granted the right to vote. Fifth, it repudiated the Confederate debt (thus punishing those who lent money to the Confederacy) and denied all claims for compensation by ex-slave owners. The 14th Amendment represented a radical redefining of the role of the federal government as the definer and guarantor of individual civil rights.

The Reconstruction Acts In March 1867 Republicans in Congress passed several Reconstruction Acts and divided the South (except Tennessee) into five military districts, each governed by a military commander empowered with wide authority to keep order and protect individuals, especially freedmen. As soon as order was established, the ex-Confederate states could begin a new, stricter readmission process. Voters, including African-American men but excluding former Confederates, would elect delegates to state conventions. The new state constitutions drawn up by these conventions had to allow universal male suffrage, regardless of race. If a state's voters approved the new constitution, the state could hold elections to fill government office. Finally, if Congress approved the state's constitution and the state legislature ratified the 14th Amendment, the state would be readmitted to the Union.

The Impeachment of Andrew Johnson Radical Republicans came to despise Johnson for his attempts to obstruct their reconstruction plans and began looking for a way to remove him from office. They passed a law (the Tenure of Office Act) requiring the president to seek Congressional approval before removing a cabinet official. When Johnson fired Secretary of War Edwin Stanton, his enemies in Congress voted to impeach him. The trial began in March 1868 and included two months of heated debate and accusation. In the end the Senate failed—by one vote—to convict Johnson and remove him from office.

The 15th Amendment

With southern resistance on the rise in 1867–68, many Republicans in Congress argued that an additional amendment was necessary to guarantee unequivocally the right of African-Americans to vote. Consequently they drafted the 15th Amendment. In succinct language it stated "The right of citizens of the United States shall not be denied or abridged by the United States or by any state on account of race, color, or previous condition of servitude." It was passed by Congress in February 1869 and ratified in 1870.

By the early 1870's the northern effort to reshape southern society and protect the rights of the ex-slaves began to lose support. Many northerners had grown tired of the endless debates in Washington over Reconstruction policy. By the end of the decade white Southerners had succeeded in reacquiring political power and using it to deprive the former slaves of their rights.

The Age of Industry

America experienced an industrial boom during the Civil War that continued after the war ended. New technology such as improved steam power generation and sophisticated manufacturing machinery led to an explosion in industrial output. New industries such as steel and oil transformed the economy and added thousands of new jobs.

One of the driving forces behind the industrial revolution was what many termed the "inventive spirit" of the age. Inventiveness was driven by dreams of profit and led to constant improvements in existing products and the creation of whole new industries. Christopher Sholes, for example, was one of dozens of men working on a machine that eventually bore the name "typewriter." Sholes sold his design to the Remington Company and the typewriter soon became a standard piece of equipment found in every office and eventually many homes. Other inventors of note include George Eastman (Kodak camera), William S. Burroughs (adding machine), Isaac Singer (sewing machine), Alexander Graham Bell (telephone), and Thomas Edison (incandescent lightbulb, phonograph, motion picture camera, mimeograph machine, and more). Between 1860 and 1900 American inventors registered nearly 700,000 patents with the U.S. Patent Office, prompting its commissioner to boast in 1892 "America has become known the world around as the home of invention."

Captains of Industry

The new industrial economy witnessed the emergence of immensely rich and powerful men such as Andrew Carnegie (steel), John D. Rockefeller (oil), Jay Gould (railroads), J.P. Morgan (finance), and Philip Armour (meatpacking). They were alternately praised for their business genius and success and condemned for their questionable practices and exploitation of workers. Many Americans also grew concerned over the power wielded by these men and the huge corporations and trusts they headed.

Conflict and Crisis

Industrialization generated enormous wealth for successful entrepreneurs and investors and raised the standard of living for the average worker. It also brought new freedoms, comforts, styles, and forms of entertainment. But these benefits were accompanied by disturbing trends. Many workers suffered from long hours, dangerous conditions, monotonous work, and low pay.

Farmers likewise complained about the exploitation they suffered at the hands of banks, suppliers, and railroads. The new industrial economy was also marked by instability that produced several recessions and two severe depressions (1873–77 and 1893–97). Political leaders held fast to a laissez-faire policy toward business, with the exception of the Interstate Commerce Act (1887) and Sherman Antitrust Act (1890), both of which proved ineffective.

Labor Movement

Wage earners responded to these challenges by engaging in record numbers of boycotts and strikes. The latter frequently turned violent when police or militia confronted strikers. The great railroad strike of 1877 shut down much of the national rail system from Baltimore to Chicago and saw scores of workers killed and millions of dollar of property destroyed. Workers also formed unions to help them achieve shorter hours and better pay. In the 1880's the Knights of Labor, a national industrial organization with hundreds of local union affiliates, emerged as a major force in labor's struggle. Membership soared to 700,000 in 1886 before the organization went into decline and was replaced by the American Federation of Labor.

American farmers likewise turned to organization to address their grievances. Thousands joined the Grange, or Patrons of Husbandry (founded 1867), a fraternal and educational association that became a political force in the Midwest by the mid-1870's. Grange-supported candidates took control of state legislatures and passed several laws regulating railroads. It faded in the 1880's but its spirit was revived in the People's Party in the 1890's.

Westward Expansion   The end of the Civil War unleashed a flood of westward migration and settlement. Thousands of Americans and recent immigrants, attracted by cheap land and the perception of widespread opportunity, crossed the Mississippi River to settle on the Great Plains and beyond. Ranching and mining developed, along with farming, as the primary elements of the western economy. Economic development was hastened by the rapid expansion of the railroad system, most notably with the completion of the Transcontinental Railroad in 1869.

Conflict with Native Americans   Westward settlement brought increased conflict with Native American tribes who believed they had a right to the lands where they had lived for generations. This was especially true of the eastern tribes that had agreed before 1860 to relocate to so-called "Indian Country," lands west of the Mississippi. Beginning in the 1850's, however, the U.S. government pursued a policy of confining Indian tribes to specific tracts of land known as reservations and in 1867 it established two huge Indian Territories in Oklahoma and the Dakotas. Units of veteran Union Army soldiers were sent west after the Civil War to enforce this policy. Wars broke out repeatedly on the Great Plains and elsewhere as white settlers encroached on Indian land and tribes resisted confinement to reservations. Native Americans lacked the firepower and unity to withstand the army, but nonetheless put up fierce resistance. In the most notable incident, a band of 2,000 Sioux and Cheyenne warriors in June 1876 wiped out a small force under the command of Gen. George A. Custer (1839–76) at the Battle of Little Big Horn in Montana.

Continued conflict led Congress to pass the Dawes Act in 1887. Declaring reservations a failure, it aimed to break up Indian communities and encourage assimilation into white culture by distributing allotments of reservation land to individual Indians who in turn would become farmers. This and subsequent acts led to the reduction of Indian lands from 156 million acres in 1881 to 53 million by 1934 when the policy was ended.

The End of Armed Resistance   Large-scale Native American resistance waned in the late 1880's with the surrender of the Apache warrior-chief Geronimo in 1886, and in 1890 the massacre at Wounded Knee, South Dakota. In the latter incident, soldiers opened fire on hundreds of Sioux who had recently fled their reservation, killing nearly 200 men, women, and children. Thereafter, Indians resisted white authority by working to preserve their culture and traditions.

Mass Immigration   Immigration soared in the last third of the 19th century to record levels. After 1880 the majority of the newcomers came from southern and eastern Europe, the largest groups being Italian and Jews from the Russian empire. Significant numbers of Chinese immigrants arrived in California. Most newcomers settled in urban areas where they often formed ethnic enclaves known to outsiders as Little Italy or Little Russia. They provided a huge source of cheap labor for the economy and made lasting contributions to American culture.

Just as it did in the antebellum era, mass migration produced hostility among native-born Americans who feared the newcomers as competition for jobs and bearers of strange habits. In 1882 Congress passed the Chinese Exclusion Act and in 1890, the Federal Immigration Act. The latter established guidelines for admitting immigrants and authorized construction of screening centers, the most famous of which was Ellis Island (1892) in New York Harbor. Still, record numbers of immigrants continued to arrive, hitting a peak of 1,004,756 in 1907.

The Turbulent 1890's

Many of the nation's most pressing social problems came to a head in the 1890's. Two landmark strikes in Homestead, Pa. (1892) and Pullman, Ill. (1894) highlighted the grievances of American workers and the immense power of big business as workers lost both strikes. Frustrated farmers and industrial workers threw their support to a new third party, the Peoples Party (Populist), which garnered 1 million votes in the 1892 presidential election.

Over the next few years national politics was dominated by debate over currency reform and the gold standard. Republicans, conservatives, and industrialists defended the policy of tying American currency to the gold standard. Such a policy benefited businesses and banks by restricting the money supply and keeping inflation low. Democrats, led by a flamboyant congressman from Nebraska, William Jennings Bryan (1860–1925), demanded the un-limited coinage of silver which would benefit farmers and other debtors by increasing the money supply and inflation. Bryan's impassioned "Cross of

Gold" speech at the Democratic national convention in 1896 won him the party's presidential nomination. Republican William McKinley won the election handily, but Bryan succeeded in reshaping the ideology of the Democratic party to support activist and interventionist government. Bryan earned his party's nomination again in 1900 and 1908 but lost both elections.

Jim Crow   Southerners successfully stripped away most of the civil, political, and economic rights of African Americans. Voting rights were suppressed through tactics such as literacy tests, poll taxes, and the infamous grandfather clause, requiring proof that your grandfather had voted. Segregation received sanction in several decisions by a conservative Supreme Court, most egregiously in *Plessy v. Ferguson* (1896). To discourage resistance, vigilante groups like the Ku Klux Klan waged a campaign of terror that included arson, beatings, and lynchings. Nonetheless African Americans and sympathetic whites founded the National Association for the Advancement of Colored People in 1905 to oppose the oppression.

The Spanish American War   America's rise as an industrial power convinced many that it should take a more active role in world affairs—if only to protect national interests overseas. Congress authorized a massive ex-pansion of the navy and promoted a more vigorous foreign policy, especially in matters pertaining to Latin America and the Caribbean.

Encouraged by a jingoistic press, Americans increasingly took an interest in the efforts of Cubans to free themselves from Spanish colonial rule. In addition, many American businesses had substantial investments in Cuba. The American government pressured Spain to end its repression, but resisted calls for military intervention, even after the naval vessel U.S.S. *Maine* exploded and sank in Havana harbor (February 15, 1898), killing 260. But the U.S. press insisted on blaming the Spanish and diplomatic relations rapidly deteriorated. At the request of President McKinley, Congress declared war on April 17, 1898. A weak Spain was no match for the U.S. forces.

The U.S. Pacific fleet under Commodore George Dewey proceeded to the Philippines, where it defeated its larger Spanish counterpart at the Battle of Manila Bay, capturing the island of Guam on the way. American troops later landed, and together with Filipino insurgents, secured control of the Philippines. In the Atlantic, the U.S. fleet blockaded its Spanish opponent at Santiago de Cuba. American troops, led by (among others) future U.S. president Theodore Roosevelt, stormed the heights overlooking Santiago de Cuba at the Battle of San Juan Hill. With the heights in U.S. possession, the Spanish fleet was forced to give battle and was destroyed. By the Treaty of Paris of December, 10, 1898, the Spanish yielded sovereignty to Cuba and gave the U.S. possession of Puerto Rico, Guam, and the Philippines. With some reluctance, and subject to numerous conditions, the United States conceded Cuban independence but decided to retain control of the Philippines and there became embroiled in an insurrection with its former allies, the local insurgents under Emilio Aguinaldo. The insurrection continued at substantial costs to both sides until 1902.

After more than a century of steadfast isolationism, the U.S. was now a global power. The coming years would see repeated military intervention in countries like Haiti (1915–34), the Dominican Republic (1916–24), Nicaragua (1909–10, 1912–25, 1926–33), and Colombia (1904), the latter as a prelude to building the Panama Canal, which opened in 1914.

The Progressive Era (1900–17)

The Progressive Spirit   The immense social and economic change brought on by the industrial revolution produced, at the turn of the century, a growing popular demand for reform over a wide range of issues. Americans of all walks of life became concerned over the enormous and unchecked power wielded by large corporations. Equally disturbing was the growing gap between rich and poor, a trend exemplified by the rise of industrial elites such as the Rockefellers, Carnegies, Morgans, and Whitneys and masses of impoverished, slum-dwelling workers. Many Americans likewise decried the corruption and undemocratic aspects of the political system at all levels of government.

Much of this rising concern and demand for reform was generated by the writings of investigative journalists, or "muckrakers," who penned exposes of corporate and political wrongdoing. Ida Tarbell (1857–1944), for example, wrote a scathing exposé of John D. Rockefeller and the corrupt practices of Standard Oil. Upton Sinclair (1878–1968) shocked the nation with his novel, *The Jungle* (1906), which exposed the horrors of Chicago's meatpacking industry. Lincoln Steffens's (1866–1936) book, *Shame of the Cities* (1906), attacked corrupt political machines. Jacob Riis (1849–1914) shed light on the urban poor in *How the Other Half Lives* (1890).

Progressive-era reformers came from widely divergent backgrounds and supported a diverse array of causes, from child labor legislation to prohibition. Some drew their inspiration from religion, others from feminism and socialism. Yet they shared one fundamental belief: that government ought to be used to eradicate social ills and promote equality and the common good.

Political Reform

Movements for reform of state government led to the adoption of the initiative and referendum in dozens of states. These forms of direct democracy were intended to allow the people to gain passage of reforms over the opposition of corrupt or out-of-touch legislatures. Similarly, the wide adoption of the recall put pressure on legislators to heed the needs of their constituents, rather than lobbyists and special interests.

Reforms of municipal government saw the adoption of measures designed to undercut the power of corrupt political machines. These included the introduction of nonpartisan elections, direct primaries, the secret ballot, and city manager and city commission forms of government, as well as the expansion of civil service.

On the national level reformers gained adoption of the 17th Amendment to the Constitution (ratified in 1913), which required popular election of U.S. Senators, and the 19th Amendment (ratified in 1920) granting women the right to vote.

Economic Reform

Vice President Theodore Roosevelt became president following the assassination of William McKinley in 1901, and he immediately launched an effort to curb the power of large trusts. The Justice Department (under the Sherman Antitrust Act) initiated 44 lawsuits against trusts it charged engaged in unlawful practices. The most famous case resulted in the breakup of the Northern Securities Trust (1904), a massive railroad combination. Roosevelt signed the Elkins Act (1903) and Hepburn Act (1906), which greatly enhanced the power of the Interstate Commerce Commission to regulate the railroad industry. The administration of Roosevelt's successor, William Howard Taft, initiated 90 lawsuits against trusts.

The cause of consumer protection was advanced with the signing of the Pure Food and Drug Act (1906), which prohibited the use of harmful drugs or chemicals in food. The Meat Inspection Act (1906) increased the regulation of the meat industry to prevent the sale of tainted meat.

American workers saw many important gains in this era, mainly in the form of state laws. By 1917 more than two-thirds of the states had adopted laws prohibiting child labor and mandating workmen's compensation. At the federal level, the Roosevelt administration created the Department of Commerce and Labor (1903).

Conservation

Concerned over the loss of wilderness lands to the timber, mining, and ranching industries, conservationists called upon the government to take action. An avid outdoorsman, Roosevelt used his presidential authority to set aside 238 million acres of federal lands to protect them from development. He also established wildlife preserves, expanded the national park system, and created the National Conservation Commission (1909). The 1902 Newlands Reclamation Act provided federal funds for dams and large-scale irrigation projects in semiarid regions of the U.S.

In 1909 President Taft fired Gifford Pinchot, head of the forestry service, when Pinchot accused Secretary of the Interior Richard A. Ballinger of failing to protect forests and other natural resources. The so-called Ballinger-Pinchot controversy caused a major political upheaval and gave many Americans the impression Taft was undermining Roosevelt's conservation achievements.

The Wilson Administration

Woodrow Wilson won the 1912 presidential election, a contest that saw Roosevelt mount an insurgent campaign as the candidate of the Progressive Party (Bull Moose Party), while Eugene Debs garnered nearly 1 million votes as candidate for the Socialist Party. Taft finished third (behind Roosevelt) in his bid for re-election.

Wilson added to earlier progressive economic reforms by signing into law several landmark pieces of legislation. The Federal Reserve Act (1913) created a national banking system designed to bring greater stability to banking and the money supply. The Clayton Antitrust Act (1914) supplemented and strengthened the Sherman Act of 1890 by defining a series of specific "unfair methods of competition," making corporate officers liable for illegal actions, and exempting labor unions from antitrust lawsuits. The Federal Trade Commission (FTC) was established to enforce these antitrust measures.

The 16th Amendment to the Constitution (ratified 1913) authorized Congress to impose an income tax, a measure designed to make the wealthy pay a greater share of the nation's tax burden and to eliminate the reliance on tariff revenue to fund government operations.

The War in Europe   When World War I broke out in Europe in the summer of 1914, America declared its neutrality, a position Wilson hoped would allow the U.S. to play the role of peacemaker between the Triple Entente (England, France, and Russia) and the Central Powers (Germany and Austria-Hungary). He resisted pressure to declare war on Germany after the sinking of the *Lusitania* (1915) and won re-election in 1916 on the slogan "He Kept Us Out Of War." But Germany's decision to resume unrestricted submarine warfare (January 31, 1917) against all ships trading with the Allies and the interception of the Zimmerman Telegram, in which Germany encouraged Mexico to wage war against the U.S., prompted Congress to declare war (April 6, 1917).

World War I   See "Major Wars in History."

Radicalism and Reaction   The end of World War I (November 11, 1918) touched off months of domestic unrest, including the biggest strike wave in U.S. history as 4 million workers walked off the job in 1919. Most were angry about attempts by employers to revoke wartime policies that had reduced hours, boosted wages, and recognized unions. The scale of the work stoppages and violence that attended many of them caused widespread alarm and eventually a campaign of repression known as the "Red Scare." Leftist newspapers were closed, union leaders arrested, and hundreds of radicals deported. This conservative mood also led to the ratification (1919) of the 18th Amendment banning the manufacture, sale, or transportation of alcoholic beverages and the rejection of the Versailles Treaty (1920) and U.S. membership in the new League of Nations.

The Roaring Twenties and The New Deal

Republican Warren G. Harding won the election of 1920 on a pledge to restore "normalcy." A poor leader, his administration was rocked by corruption, most notably the Teapot Dome Scandal. Harding died in office (1923) and was succeeded by his vice-president, Calvin Coolidge.

After a sharp recession in 1920-21, the American economy roared until late 1929. Industrial output boomed, and the automobile industry put nearly 27 million cars on the road by 1929. Per capita income rose for nearly everyone except farmers. Rising stock prices on Wall Street enticed millions to invest and to borrow money to do so.

The 1920's also witnessed profound social and cultural changes. The American music form known as jazz became wildly popular, as did the dance called the Charleston, professional boxing, silent movies, and radio. Many women shocked their contemporaries by taking on the so-called "flapper" look, with short hair, short dresses, and subdued bustlines.

Many Americans, especially those not living in urban areas, condemned the ebullient spirit of the era. A revived Ku Klux Klan saw its membership top 5 million by 1926. Congressed passed the National Origins Act in 1924, sharply curtailing immigration for the first time. And in Tennessee, John Scopes was convicted for teaching evolution in science class in the so-called "Monkey Trial" in 1925.

The Crash   The stock market crash that began on October 29, 1929 announced the arrival of the Great Depression. After nearly a decade of overheated economic growth, excessive borrowing, and widespread crisis among farmers, the economy slowly but inexorably collapsed. President Herbert Hoover resisted calls for government relief and instead urged Americans to be patient. Hoover eventually signed several relief bills by 1932 but they did little to ease the suffering and boost the economy.

The Great Depression was an economic catastrophe for the United States. Unemployment quickly reached 25 percent—five million people were out of work in 1930, but by 1932, that figure had risen to 13 million. People thrown out of their homes set up makeshift residences called Hoovervilles, a derisive reference to the President who seemed overwhelmed by events. Families waited in long lines for bread. Rural workers left the Dust Bowl of the Plains and headed west in search of work. Mighty companies like General Motors and U.S. Steel saw their stock prices collapse. Banks around the nation failed, causing a run on those institutions by customers who stood to lose their life's savings if their bank closed. In 1929, before the crash, about 600 banks failed. In 1931, nearly 3,000 did. More than 100,000 businesses went under from 1929 to 1932. The despair of the period would sear its way into the souls of all those who lived through it. In 1932, voters turned Hoover out of office, replacing him with a man with a sunny disposition and a determination to change the nation's social contract, Franklin D. Roosevelt of New York.

The New Deal Promising a "new deal" during the campaign, Roosevelt and his advisors entered office committed to a program of bold experimentation to end the Depression. Over the next eight years Roosevelt signed into law some of the most far-reaching legislation in American history. In general, the initiatives fell into three broad categories: relief, recovery and reform.

Relief To relieve suffering, hunger, and homelessness, the New Deal included jobs programs such as the Public Works Administration, which spent $4.3 billion on 34,000 public projects. Related programs included the Civilian Conservation Corps (C.C.C.), National Youth Administration (N.Y.A.), and Works Progress Administration (W.P.A.).

Recovery To stimulate economic recovery, the government spent billions on jobs programs and public projects like the Tennessee Valley Authority (1933), a massive water control and hydroelectric project that constructed 16 dams, and Boulder Dam, finished in 1935 and later renamed Hoover Dam, in Nevada. The National Recovery Administration was established to set price, wage, and production codes for business. The Agricultural Adjustment Act aimed to limit farm production and boost farmer income.

Reform The most profound achievements of the New Deal were those that took advantage of the crisis to enact major social and economic legislation. To bring stability to the economy and prevent future crashes, Congress passed the Glass-Steagall Act (which separated banking and investing) and created the Securities and Exchange Commission to regulate dangerous speculative practices on Wall Street. The Wagner Act aimed to improve labor-employer relations by guaranteeing a wide range of rights to workers and unions. Most significant of all was the Social Security Act of 1935 which established pensions for the aged and infirm as well as a system of unemployment insurance.

Though the New Deal did not achieve all of its goals, it changed the nation's political dynamics and built a coalition that would define the nation's politics until the 1970s. Roosevelt and his administration aggressively sought a larger role for government in regulating the nation's economy. Government expanded rapidly under Roosevelt's tenure as new agencies were given unprece-

dented powers over private industry. In addition, innovations like the Social Security Act led the construction of a social safety net for the unemployed, the young and the disabled. Many of the reforms Roosevelt instituted on a national level had been tried successfully in New York state when Alfred E. Smith was governor in the 1920's.

Franklin D. Roosevelt easily won re-election in 1936. Yet the ultimate goal of the New Deal—ending the Depression—remained elusive as unemployment still hovered at 14 percent as late as 1940. The nation's economy would not recover until America entered World War II.

Neutrality As the threat of war loomed in Europe, Americans supported a policy of strict neutrality. Congress passed three Neutrality Acts in the late 1930's designed to prevent the President from lending money or selling arms to any combatants.

But soon after hostilities broke out in Europe in September 1939, Congress took steps to prepare the U.S. for war, including a massive naval build-up and the institution of a draft in 1940. The Neutrality Act of 1939 allowed the U.S. to sell arms to the Allies. In 1941 Congress passed the Lend-Lease Act to allow Britain to acquire U.S. arms and ships without payment.

The hope that the U.S. could stay out of the war ended with the surprise attack by Japan on the U.S. naval base at Pearl Harbor (December 7, 1941). Congress declared war on December 8. Three days later, Japan's allies Germany and Italy declared war on the U.S.

World War II See "Major Wars in History."

Post-War America

Post-War Boom As with the end of the First World War, the end of World War II inaugurated a period of strife. Millions of Americans went on strike in 1946. In response, Republicans, who gained control of Congress in 1946, passed the Taft-Hartley Act (1947) curbing some of organized labor's powers gained under the Wagner Act.

The conversion of the national economy from wartime to peacetime production by 1947 touched off an unprecedented period of prosperity and economic growth. The wartime economy had put billions of dollars into the pockets of American families which they now spent on consumer goods such as cars, radios, and refrigerators, items they could not afford during the Depression and were unavailable during the war. The G.I. Bill and other legislation also stimulated a movement to the suburbs and sent tens of thousands of former soldiers off for a college education.

The election of 1948 featured one of the greatest political upsets in U.S. political history. Virtually every poll showed Republican challenger Thomas E. Dewey defeating President Harry S. Truman. But Truman won and immediately proposed a major domestic legislative agenda called the "Fair Deal," much of which was blocked by Republicans in Congress.

The Cold War   Although the Soviet Union and U.S. were allies during World War II, they became bitter adversaries afterward in a geopolitical rivalry that came to be known as the Cold War. Tension first emerged over the Soviet occupation of Eastern Europe, the struggle over the future of Germany, and Soviet backing of communist insurgencies in Greece and Turkey.

The Truman Doctrine   To counter the perceived Soviet threat, Truman announced in early 1947 that the U.S. was committed to the "containment" of communist expansion anywhere in the world. As part of this effort, the administration adopted the Marshall Plan, which provided $12 billion to rebuild nations ravaged by the war. In 1949 the U.S. joined with Great Britain, France, Canada and other European nations to form the North Atlantic Treaty Organization (NATO). Under the terms of the alliance, signatory nations pledged to come to the aid of any member that was attacked.

Fear of the Soviet Union rose sharply with the Soviet blockade of East Berlin (1948-49), the Soviet announcement that they had detonated their first atomic bomb (1949), the arrest of several people accused of spying for the Soviets (1948-50), the overthrow of the pro-U.S. Chinese government by communist revolutionaries (1949), and news that communist North Korea had invaded non-communist South Korea (June 1950). The latter event prompted Truman to intervene militarily.

At the end of World War II, Korea was divided, for administrative purposes, at the 38th parallel between the United States and the Soviet Union, which created separate governments in their zones of occupation. On June, 25, 1950, the northern Communists invaded the south without warning and, within two months, they had driven South Korean and U.S. forces to the southeastern tip

of the Korean Peninsula, the Pusan Perimeter. The United Nations supported the south and U.N. forces were placed under the command of U.S. general Douglas MacArthur. MacArthur launched an amphibious assault at Inchon on the western coast of Korea that successfully drove the North Koreans back to the Yalu River, the border between North Korea and China. On November, 26, 1950, however, a large Communist Chinese army counterattacked and drove the U.N. forces back south. By 1951, the front had stabilized along the 38th parallel, the original dividing line between the two Koreas. Negotiations dragged on as fighting continued without material gain to either side. During the negotiations, General MacArthur favored bombing China and was removed for insubordination by Truman in 1951. An armistice was signed on July 27, 1953, but no peace treaty has ever concluded the war.

This atmosphere of fear led to the emergence of Wisconsin Senator Joseph McCarthy (1908–57) in 1950 as the nation's leading anti-communist. His accusations that the U.S. government was riddled with communists earned him wide public support. He held hearings and continued his accusations before being censured by the U.S. Senate in 1954.

Despite the Cold War, the 1950's and early 1960's was a period of unprecedented prosperity. Per capita income rose steadily as did levels of education and homeownership. The latter was most evident in the explosion of suburban housing. Seventy percent of American homes had a television by 1960, with dramatic implications for pop culture, politics, social mores and consumer habits.

Peace and prosperity gave rise to a spirit of optimism and confidence that was reflected in the election of John F. Kennedy as president in 1960. The youngest man ever elected to the office (age 43) and the first Roman Catholic, he brought youth, charisma, and energy to national politics. While much of his administration was dominated by cold war events (a failed invasion in Cuba, the Berlin Wall Crisis, Cuban Missile Crisis, and Vietnam), Kennedy pushed for the space program, civil rights legislation, and efforts to eradicate poverty. His assassination on November 22, 1963 stunned the nation.

The Civil Rights Movement   Not all Americans shared in the prosperity and optimism of the post-war period. By the mid-1950's African-Americans in the South began to demand civil rights and an end to state-sponsored discrimination. In 1954 the Supreme Court issued *Brown v. Board of Education*, a landmark decision that declared segregation in schools unconstitutional. One year later the African-American residents of Montgomery, Ala., initiated a boycott of the city's bus lines to protest segregation. In 1957 local resistance to a plan to desegregate the public schools of Little Rock, Ark., led President Dwight Eisenhower to send in federal troops to keep order and protect nine African American students enrolled in the formerly all-white Central High School. As a result of these incidents, Congress passed the Civil Rights Act of 1957, which created a Commission for Civil Rights and strengthened federal protection of voting rights.

The civil rights movement increased its profile and appeal in the early 1960's. Hundreds of African-American college students in places like Greensboro, N.C., staged sit-ins at segregated lunch counters (1960). Civil rights activists also organized Freedom Rides on buses in 1961 to challenge segregated bus stations across the South. In 1962 federal troops were sent to protect James Meredith as he became the first African-American to enroll in the University of Mississippi. The following year Rev. Martin Luther King Jr. of the Southern Christian Leadership Council began leading protest marches in Alabama demanding the right to vote. When a brutal police assault on a march in Birmingham was broadcast on television, it caused a national outcry and eventually led President Kennedy to call for a new Civil Rights Act. In August 1963 King delivered his famous "I Have A Dream" speech during a march on Washington.

Lyndon Johnson became president following Kennedy's assassination. He immediately made passage of a Civil Rights Act a priority and signed it into law on July 2, 1964. The act prohibited segregation of public facilities, created an Equal Employment Opportunity Commission to combat racial discrimination in the workplace, and added protections to voting rights. The following year Johnson signed the Voting Rights Act which led to a dramatic rise in African American voting.

While many rejoiced at these achievements, a more radical faction of the civil rights movement emerged. Preaching a doctrine of separatism and Black Power and rejecting non-violence, they gained significant support among young African-Americans, especially in northern cities. Their frustration led to major riots in Los Angeles, New York, and Detroit. Rioting broke out in more than 100 cities following the assassination of Rev. Martin

Luther King, Jr. (April 4, 1968).

The Johnson administration also launched a massive initiative dubbed the War on Poverty. It included expanded welfare and healthcare benefits, education and job training programs, early childhood development initiatives (Head Start), public housing construction, and economic development programs for inner-city communities.

The War in Vietnam American involvement in Vietnam marked the second phase of a war that began in 1946. In the first, the French, who had ruled Indo-China since the 19th century, were defeated by the Vietnamese under Ho Chi Minh. Vietnam was divided at the 17th parallel into the nominally democratic Republic of Vietnam (South Vietnam) and the communist Democratic Republic of Vietnam (North Vietnam). In 1956, an insurgency broke out in the south; the insurgents, the Viet Cong, were supported by the government of North Vietnam. The United States provided aid, including advisors, to the south and, in 1961, the advisors were authorized to fight with South Vietnamese troops. In 1964, in response to purported attacks on U.S. naval vessels, Congress passed, at President Johnson's request, the Gulf of Tonkin Resolution, authorizing the use of force to repel any armed attack on U.S. troops. U.S. troops were dispatched to South Vietnam and bombing missions commenced there, eventually extending to North Vietnam and Cambodia.

At the beginning of 1968, the Viet Cong launched the Tet Offensive (named for the lunar new year during which it occurred). Although U.S. troops crushed the offensive and largely destroyed the Viet Cong, whose place was largely taken by North Vietnamese regulars, sentiment in America turned steadily against the war and, in July of 1968, the United States announced a policy of substituting Vietnamese troops for U.S. soldiers. In 1972, peace talks, which had been going on sporadically since 1968, broke down and President Richard Nixon ordered an intensive bombing campaign against the north. A cease fire agreement was signed in January of 1973, but fighting continued as American troops were withdrawn. A final North Vietnamese offensive in January of 1975 led to a collapse of South Vietnam by April of that year.

Politics and Protest Johnson's accomplishments in the areas of civil rights and poverty eradication were eventually overshadowed by his decision to escalate the war in Vietnam. Isolated protests in 1965 gave way to massive demonstrations in 1967 and 1968 as initial support for the war crumbled in the face of soaring U.S. casualties.

When Johnson nearly lost the New Hampshire primary to anti-war challenger Eugene McCarthy in early 1968, he withdrew his bid for re-election. Senator Robert F. Kennedy, brother of the slain president, then entered the race but was himself assassinated (June 5, 1968) after winning the California primary. Clashes between police and anti-war demonstrators broke out at the Democratic National Convention in Chicago. In November Nixon defeated Democrat Hubert H. Humphrey on a campaign that stressed a return to law and order at home and a dignified solution to the conflict in Vietnam.

The Counterculture   Many young Americans grew disillusioned with their society, condemning it as hopelessly materialistic, racist, militaristic, and repressed. They called themselves "hippies" and turned to a counterculture of rock music, radical politics, sexual liberation, and experimentation with drugs.

Years of Crisis (1970–80)

The anti-war movement receded in 1969-70 as Nixon began a sustained removal of American troops from South Vietnam while pressing the North Vietnamese to enter peace talks by launching massive airstrikes against North Vietnamese cities. Protests resumed in May 1970 when U.S. troops entered Cambodia, suggesting a re-escalation of the conflict. Four students were killed at Kent State University in Ohio when panicky National Guardsmen opened fire on an anti-war rally. The so-called "Pentagon Papers" leaked to the press in June 1971 added to anti-war sentiment by revealing how poorly the war was going and the extent to which the government had covered it up. Nonetheless, on January 27, 1973, North Vietnam and the U.S. announced a truce. In truth, it was merely a temporary stoppage to allow U.S. forces to pull out. North Vietnam soon renewed its offensive and toppled the pro-U.S. government of South Vietnam in April 1975.

The 1970's brought additional foreign policy crises. In the wake of the Arab-Israeli War of 1973, Arab nations cut off oil shipments to the U.S., causing fuel prices to soar and plunging the economy into a period of sustained inflation. In 1979 Islamic nationalists toppled the pro-U.S. government in Iran and seized 58 Americans in the U.S. embassy. That same year Cold War tensions spiked when the Soviet Union invaded neighboring Afghanistan.

Watergate   President Nixon had won a landslide reelection victory in 1972, but soon found himself embroiled in a major political scandal. It began when men connected with his re-election campaign were arrested for breaking into Democratic campaign headquarters at the Watergate Hotel in Washington, D.C. During congressional hearings attention eventually shifted to Nixon's role in a cover-up attempt and he resigned from office in August 1974. His vice president, Gerald Ford, became president and subsequently issued a controversial pardon to Nixon.

Economic Crisis   The oil embargo and ensuing inflation were not the only troubling economic developments. U.S. manufacturers faced increasing competition from abroad and thousands of factory jobs were lost. The unemployment rate soared while economic growth stagnated. Interest rates rose to a staggering 21 percent, crippling the housing market and discouraging investment. The economic malaise was felt across the country, but most intensely in major cities, leading to an era of budget crises, labor unrest, high crime, and infrastructure deterioration.

Women's Rights   The seventies saw record numbers of women enter college and the workplace. Congress passed the Equal Rights Amendment in 1972 and by 1974 it had been ratified by 33 of the needed 38 states. Conservative opposition to the amendment, however, successfully stymied any additional ratifications. Many women also hailed the 1973 Supreme Court decision *Roe v. Wade* that legalized abortion. In 1976 Democrat Jimmy Carter defeated Ford, promising he would never lie to the American people. Carter's presidency was dogged by a poor economy and the Iran hostage crisis. But he also emphasized human rights around the world and tried to broker peace in the Middle East.

The Rise of the Conservative Movement

The Reagan "Revolution"   In the election of 1980, former California Governor Ronald W. Reagan defeated Carter, a victory that signaled the emergence of a strong conservative political movement that would exert great influence in the coming decades. The new conservatism combined antagonism toward government regulation and taxes, support for an aggressive foreign policy toward the Soviet Union, and promotion of so-called family values based on Christian morality.

Reagan pursued an economic policy ("Reaganomics") of tax cuts and deregulation. When the disastrous economy of the late 1970's entered a period of record expansion after 1982, Reagan's popularity soared. His tough rhetorical stance against the Soviet Union and massive defense build-up likewise earned him support not only from conservatives, but many disaffected middle-class voters who traditionally had voted Democratic. In 1984 he won re-election in a landslide.

Though many found Reagan charming, his presidency was controversial. Annual budget deficits reached record levels in the 1980's, pushing the national debt to nearly $3 trillion by 1988. Conservative zeal for prosecuting the Cold War also led to the administration's greatest crisis, the Iran-Contra scandal, an illegal scheme that involved arms sales to Iran to secretly fund anti-communist rebels in Nicaragua. A number of Reagan administration officials were convicted for their role in the scheme, but Reagan avoided prosecution. He also later admitted that his administration had traded arms for hostages with Iran.

The election of 1988 brought Reagan's vice president, George H. W. Bush, to the White House. His presidency was largely a continuation of Reagan's conservatism, with some notable exceptions including enactment of the Americans with Disabilities Act and a significant increase in taxes (despite Bush's campaign promise of "no new taxes").

The most significant event during this period was the end of the Cold War, an event occasioned by the tearing down of the Berlin Wall in 1989 and subsequent collapse of the Soviet Union. Bush's popularity soared in 1991 when he successfully organized an international force to fight Iraq after that nation attacked Kuwait. But Bush lost his bid for re-election in 1992 to Democrat William J. Clinton in large measure because voters believed his administration poorly handled a severe economic recession in the early 1990's.

The Clinton Years President Clinton's administration got off to a rocky start when it attempted to craft a plan for universal healthcare coverage. Intense opposition from Republicans and special interests combined to kill the proposal. In 1994, under the leadership of Newt Gingrich, the Republicans took complete control of Congress for the first time in 40 years. The Clinton administration pursued politically moderate policies, many of them supported by Republicans. It ignored concerns of environmentalists and organized labor by signing the North American Free Trade Agreement which lowered tariffs among the United States, Canada, and Mexico. In 1995 Clinton signed the Welfare Reform Act that dramatically reshaped the nation's welfare system, setting time limits for benefits and requiring recipients to work. This popular political strategy, plus a booming economy and rising sense of security engendered by the end of the Cold War, was more than enough to gain Clinton re-election in 1996.

During these years, however, the U.S. economy grew quite strongly and the stock market boomed because of the rise of the Internet and the hundreds of businesses created around it. Clinton also was able to raise taxes on upper-level incomes and by 2000 the U.S. Treasury showed a surplus for the first time in over 40 years. But Clinton also accepted the premise that unregulated financial markets worked best for the nation so he championed, and Congress passed a cancellation of the New Deal measure that kept limitations on the banks that wanted to participate in investing in stocks and bonds.

In foreign policy Clinton took an aggressive stance against Iraq by continuously enforcing a no-fly zone there. He personally visited China and made a positive impression while urging membership for China in the World Trade Organization. But in the end his failure to recognize the nature of the terrorism threat to the U.S. remains a serious deficiency in his record. In 1993 the World Trade Center was bombed; the U.S. military barracks in Saudi Arabia were bombed in 1996; two U.S. embassies in Africa were blown up in 1998, and a navy ship, the *USS Cole* was seriously damaged in Yemen in October, 2000. Why these attacks did not lead to strong military action against the group called al-Qaeda remains a serious question.

Clinton's second term was marred by scandal after revelations of an extra-marital affair between Clinton and Monica Lewinsky, a White House intern. The cover-up of the scandal and Clinton's lying to a grand jury led to him becoming only the second President to be impeached and tried by the Senate, a process that ended in acquittal.

George W. Bush   The election of 2000 pitted Democrat Albert Gore, the sitting Vice-President, versus Republican George W. Bush, governor of Texas and son of former President Bush. The result was one of the closest and most controversial presidential elections in U.S. history. Gore won the popular vote by 500,000 votes, but the electoral vote tally—the vote that determines the victor—was left unclear because of questions regarding the vote count in Florida. After 36 days of intense debate, vote recounts, and legal maneuvering, the Supreme Court, in the unprecedented *Bush v. Gore* decision, ruled (5–4) against a request for a continuing recount of ballots in Florida, upholding Bush's victory in the state and awarding him the electoral votes that gave him the presidency.

Elected on a conservative platform, Bush pushed for and signed into law a steep cut in taxes, a plan to allow federal funds to be used by religiously-affiliated charities, and a large increase in defense spending. But the event that defined his first term and left a lasting impact on American society and world affairs was the terrorist strike on September 11, 2001. The attack against the Pentagon in Virginia and the World Trade Center in New York City claimed the lives of some 3,000 people and led the U.S. to invade Afghanistan, the nation that harbored the radical Islamic terrorist organization responsible for the plot.

Bush announced that this was but the first phase of a global war on terrorism and soon began making the case for international action against Iraq for violations of the terms of the ceasefire signed at the end of the Gulf War of 1991. The most serious charge was that the government of Saddam Hussein had built an arsenal of weapons of mass destruction and thus posed a threat to regional stability and world peace. Although the United Nations and many European governments questioned these claims and urged restraint, Bush ordered an invasion in March 2003. Joined by forces from Great Britain, the U.S. quickly toppled the government of Saddam Hussein and then commenced a very difficult occupation in an effort to establish a representative Iraqi government. The failure to find evidence of weapons of mass destruction led many to question the wisdom of the decision to invade Iraq.

Soon it would be revealed that the Bush Administration's assertions that Iraq posed an imminent threat to America's security, and that the war was connected to the events of 9/11, proved to be based on questionable evidence at best.

Over the next four years, the ineptitude of the civilian and military leadership caused the occupation of Iraq to fail almost completely, as a long and vicious insurgency against the U.S. devolved into a civil war between Shiites, who make up the vast majority of Iraqis, and Sunnis who had power during Saddam Hussein's rule. Despite successful national elections and the formation of a central government, revelations of torture by U.S. soldiers at Abu Ghraib prison in Iraq, and the killing of thousands of Iraqi civilians, though mostly inadvertent, by the U.S. military, turned Iraqi public opinion against the U.S. and tens of thousands of refugees fled the country. Moreover, the establishment of a camp for detainees accused of terrorism by the C.I.A. or the military at the U.S. base at Guantanamo Bay, Cuba brought international condemnation since no evidence of guilt was ever offered nor at first were the prisoners to have access to lawyers. The Administration's position that detainees were not protected by the Geneva Convention and so had essentially no legal rights was overturned by the Supreme Court but the Republican controlled Congress quickly passed a bill supporting the Administration's position.

By 2006, with more than 3,000 U.S. troops killed and more than 20,000 wounded, the nation began to question the way the war was being conducted and Bush's approval ratings began to plummet. Soon they were below 35 percent. It was not just the war, however. In August 2005, a Category 5 hurricane named Katrina formed in the Gulf of Mexico and devastated the city of New Orleans as levees broke, causing massive floods and driving hundreds of thousands from their homes. The federal government's late and weak response to this tragedy was seen as an example of the results of cronyism and lack of planning in the Administration.

Corruption, too, played a role in the sinking fortunes of the president and the Republican party. In 2005 the House majority leader, Tom DeLay of Texas, was indicted for violating election laws in his home state. By January he was forced to resign his position and eventually left congress. In 2006 Randy (Duke) Cunningham, a long-serving congressman from southern California, admitted to taking $2.4 million in bribes from defense contractors and was sent to prison. But it was a much larger scandal involving Jack Abramoff, a high-powered lobbyist who admitted to making millions of dollars by selling access to Republicans in congress and in federal agencies, that made headlines for weeks since Abramoff had ties to the

White House and even to the president.

Despite all this negative publicity, Bush was able to create a conservative legacy by getting to nominate two new Supreme Court justices, including a Chief Justice and a new jusice after the death of William Rehnquist and the retirement of Sandra Day O'Connor. The new Chief Justice, young, personable John Roberts, and the new justice, Samuel Alito, while both on record as opposing *Roe v. Wade*, and supporting the death penalty, were confirmed with relative ease. The balance on the court of conservatives and liberals was now a more delicate situation than in the last 30 years.

The mid-term congressional election revealed just how poorly the nation regarded the conduct of the war in Iraq and the lack of leadership at home as the Democrats gained control of both houses of congress. They immediately began to challenge President Bush by using their Constitutional power to fund the war, a war the president insisted would continue for years after he left office.

On the domestic front, the Bush Administration failed to solve or adddress in any serious way the grave problems facing the future of Social Security and Medicare. Despite the conservative label the Republicans embraced, President Bush pushed through a Medicare Prescription Drug Bill at the end of 2003 that added nearly $800 billion to the nation's already strained resources. Every Democrat voted against it. The president then stated a year later that Medicare was "unsustainable" in its present state.

As the administration entered its lame-duck phase in mid-2007, its vaunted plan to reform immigration laws collapsed utterly, mainly through Republican opposition. Bush's approval ratings barely surpassed 30 percent as the nation grew weary of his tenure in office.

Toward the end of Bush's final year in office weariness turned to frustration and anger as the president and his economic advisors proclaimed a national emergency caused by the near-collapse of the financial system. Mired deeply in debt, the nation's largest banks and investment firms teetered on the edge of insolvency as credit, the crucial element of capitalist institutions, simply seized up. The stock market tumbled downward for weeks and banks and businesses began to fail at a rapid pace. The government stepped in to provide enormous loans to help established banks such as Citigroup, Chase, Goldman Sachs, Morgan Stanley and Wells Fargo. The once-powerful Bear Stearns collapsed and was sold off to Chase for pennies on the dollar. In September 2008 the venerable banking firm, Lehman Brothers, was inexplicably allowed to fail sending shock waves across the world. (See "Finance.")

Barack Obama Unsurprisingly the presidential election of 2008 resulted in a victory for Senator Barack Obama, a Democrat from Illinois and the first African-American to attain the nation's highest office. The Democrats also took control of the House and Senate with strong majorities giving the new president a clear path to press for the agenda he campaigned for in the months before the election: Closing the prison at Guantánamo Bay, pressing for repeal of the military policy of "don't ask, don't tell" for gay Americans, passing a healthcare reform bill, and reaching out to Muslim nations to help end the rancor between them and the United States.

Much of this would be achieved but the economic dislocation caused by the financial crisis soon led to massive layoffs and a surging unemployment rate. In addition, the dismal management performance of the leading American carmakers and the precipitous decline in auto sales put GM, Ford, and Chrysler on the edge of bankruptcy. Faced with the loss of more than 300,000 jobs the Obama administration took the unpopular step of providing loans to these failed companies but forcing several senior executives to resign.

During Obama's first year in office his economic advisors, several of whom had strong ties to the financial industry, pressed for a strong financial stimulus to counter the effects of the private sector's retreat from the economic battlefield. A housing crisis was at the center of the financial collapse so the government rescued its own institutions, Fannie Mae and Freddie Mac, buying up a trillion dollars of failed mortgage-based securities based on subprime loans. A stimulus package of $700 billion meant to create public sector jobs and to fix failing infrastructure had a positive but limited effect.

The result of these policies led to a swelling of the federal deficit and the national debt and provided the Republicans with a strong issue which they used successfully to rally their members against government spending. Across the country, small so-called Tea Party groups sprung up seemingly overnight to challenge what they called big government and the growing debt. Several Republican state attorneys-general launched several lawsuits to have the healthcare reform act declared unconstitutional. Obama and his inner circle fought back but without the passion to match their opponents and in the 2010 elections, the Republicans took back the House of Representatives and significantly narrowed the Democrats' lead in the Senate.

The Republicans immediately mounted strong attacks on the federal deficit that had piled up over the Bush years and the first two years of the Obama presidency. With unemployment remaining at or above 9 percent the president's popularity began to sag noticeably and his decision to extend the Bush tax cuts for the wealthiest Americans caused dismay among his strongest supporters. But to others that compromise enabled him to obtain Republican support for a nuclear weapons reduction treaty with Russia.

Further disappointment for many Democrats grew from the Obama administration's decision to expand the war in Afghanistan by sending 50,000 more troops to the region in the hope that Taliban insurgents could be halted in their attempt to rule the country through Islamic law. Obama continued the use of imprisonment without charges for large numbers of Afghanis in the Bagram prison. At the end of his second year as president Obama was forced to admit that the Guantánamo prison could not be shut down since Congress had voted not to fund an alternative and later voted that no terrorist trials could be held in the U.S. As a result the 170 prisoners remaining (out of more than 600) would be tried in military courts. The president also said that there were prisoners who would not be released even if they were not convicted.

On April 20, 2010 a huge explosion on the Deepwater Horizon, a BP oil rig in the Gulf of Mexico killed 11 workers and set off the largest oil spill in U.S. history. Obama appeared to take control of the situation to avoid any comparisons with the Bush White House inaction during and after Hurricane Katrina, which decimated New Orleans. But the spill was so enormous, spewing 4.1 million barrels of oil into the Gulf that the oil was not fully contained for 86 days.

As the nation prepared for the 2012 elections its people were pessimistic about the future and seriously divided on many vital issues including taxes, Social Security, Medicare and Medicaid, the wars in Iraq and Afghanistan, and most importantly on the role of government in their lives. The Supreme Court continued to reflect this division in 5–4 decisions, none more telling than the 2010 *Citizens United v. Federal Election Commission* that struck down nearly a century of laws by ruling that corporations and unions may spend as much as they wish on elections.

It could be argued that nothing divided the American people more than the ever-increasing income inequality which had begun in the 1980's but revealed itself most obviously in the years following the financial crisis. Over 14 percent of the population had fallen below the poverty line bringing the total to 44 million people, the highest number since 1994. In 2010 over 41 million were receiving food stamps and the number of Americans without health insurance grew to 51 million. But for most of the wealthiest citizens prosperity returned quickly as seen in the recovery of the stock market as the Dow and NASDAQ rose by 30–40 percent by 2011. U.S. corporations were still refusing to hire back workers in 2010 but executive compensation returned to pre-recession levels. So too did the incomes of Wall Street bankers and the managers of hedge funds who also spent tens of millions of dollars lobbying Congress to make changes to the Dodd-Frank financial reform bill designed to bring stricter rules to the trading of stocks, bonds, and most of all to the opaque derivatives market.

By mid-2011, the Republicans had made clear that deficit and debt reduction would be the centerpiece of their election campaign, despite the fact that they had been responsible for a large part of the problem during the Bush years. Their demands for drastic cuts in spending but no increase in taxes for the wealthiest Americans put them on a collision course with Democrats over spending on social welfare programs, Medicare and Medicaid.

The question is how all of these divisions will play out in the 2012 election. Over the years the U.S. has often been a nation at the proverbial crossroads and more often than not compromise has carried the day. Only the tragedy of the Civil War stands as a reminder of the results of failing to reach an accommodation with political opponents. No one expects anything remotely similar but it would be foolish not to recognize that the stakes today are so high because future generations will or will not live in a nation bitterly divided by income, education, and status.

GEOGRAPHY

Geography, in the broadest sense, is the systematic study of the Earth, its physical makeup (oceans, rivers, continents, islands, climate, etc.), and how those elements affect the way humans organize their societies and live productive lives. More specifically geographers examine human populations and population distribution by region and by urban and rural segmentation; political systems; and economic structures such as agriculture, trade, industry, and transportation.

This section focuses on physical geography, which is the study of those parts of the Earth that have the greatest impact on human life: the atmosphere (the air, and in particular climate and weather); the hydrosphere (oceans, lakes, and rivers); the lithosphere (the Earth's crust, the surface of which is the land and the ocean floor); and the biosphere (that part of the atmosphere, lithosphere, and hydrosphere inhabited by living things).

First-order features of the Earth's geography are the continents and the oceans. Second-order continental features include mountain ranges, valleys, plains, and deserts. Third-order features include mountains and valleys.

The boundaries of continents and oceans are affected by long-term global changes such as glaciation. During an ice age, much of the globe's water is frozen in ice on land, and sea levels drop accordingly. During the last ice age, which ended about 11,500 years ago, the oceans were about 100 meters (328 ft.) lower than they are today. At that time, the now submerged Bering land bridge connected Asia and North America.

Climate and Weather

Climate is generally defined as the characteristic condition of the atmosphere near the Earth's surface in a particular place or region. It includes patterns of temperature, wind, precipitation, cloud cover, and other variables. Earth's climate is ultimately dependent on solar radiation, its distance from the sun (which varies by about 6 million kilometers/3.5 million miles over the course of a year), the orientation of the Earth's axis of spin away from or toward the sun, and other factors. Climate varies from region to region depending on such things as latitude, the topography of the land, ocean water currents and temperature, and atmospheric pressure and wind. It is predictable in terms of the average and variation of temperature, precipitation, and other variables, but it is subject to change due to the long-term cycle of ice ages and human activities.

Winds The world's major wind systems are determined by variations in atmospheric pressure. Broadly speaking, the Earth is covered by seven belts of atmospheric pressure, alternately low and high, starting with a low at the equator and working toward highs at the poles. These pressure systems are themselves regions of relatively light and variable winds: *the equatorial low* (or *intertropical convergence zone*), which strad-

dles the equator between about 10°S and 10°N; *the subtropical highs*, or *horse latitudes*, between 30° and 40°S, and 30° and 40°N; and the *subpolar lows* at about 50°-60°S and 50°-60°N. The poles are capped by *polar high pressure zones*.

The major wind systems are found between these zones of low and high pressure. North and south of the equatorial trough, the *northeast* and *southeast trade winds* blow toward the equator and west in bands about 1,200 miles wide. (Winds are named for the direction *from which they come.*) Between the horse latitudes and the subpolar lows, the winds blow away from the equator and toward the east. In the northern hemisphere, the *westerlies* cross the Atlantic, Eurasia, the Pacific, and North America. The strong westerlies of the Southern Ocean, almost uninterrupted by land, are called the *roaring forties* and *furious fifties*, depending on latitude. Between the subpolar lows and the polar high are the *polar easterlies*.

The *trade winds* do not prevail in the northern Indian Ocean (the Arabian Sea and Bay of Bengal) or the northwest Pacific, including the South China Sea and waters around Japan. Here the general pattern is modified by the seasonal warming and cooling of adjacent land masses that creates areas of low and high pressure respectively. The resulting wind system is called the monsoon (from the Arabic *mawsim*, or season). The *northeast*, or dry, *monsoon* (during which the wind blows from the northeast to the southwest) is strongest between November and March, when the land is cooler than the ocean. (In the Pacific, the northeast monsoon lasts from about September to April.)

Weather is the climate at a place at a particular time. It is predictable in detail over short periods of time (several days), and over somewhat longer periods of time (months) for some purposes. Climatologists have defined climate zones in term of climate variables such as temperature and precipitation; the best-known system is the Köppen-Geiger system, which has five basic categories: tropical rainy climates, dry climates, mild humid climates, snowy-forest climates, and polar climates. These are defined in terms of temperature, except for dry climates, which are defined in terms of ratios of precipitation to evaporation. Geographers have more recently attempted to characterize areas by adding characteristics relating to ecosystems.

Global interrelationships of climate
In recent decades there has been sharply increased scientific and popular awareness of the extent to which climate in one part of the world, especially the Pacific, affects climate elsewhere.

El Niño and La Niña The *El Niño* and *La Niña* phenomena in the Pacific, and the associated changes of air pressure in the region (the "Southern Oscillation") are known jointly as the *El Niño-Southern Oscillation (ENSO)*. The principal element of El Niño is the presence of large amounts of warm water in the eastern Pacific every three to eight years, and the associated lower barometric pressure over the eastern Pacific and higher pressures over the Western Pacific (Indonesia and Australia). Cold water in the eastern Pacific, and the associated reversal of air pressure, is known as La Niña.

The sheer size and breadth of the Pacific allow El Niños and La Niñas time to develop and to have widespread effects. During La Niñas, tropical ocean temperatures become colder in the eastern and central Pacific regions and warmer in the west; tradewinds are stronger and normally wet regions become drier. During El Niños the shift is exactly the opposite: weaker tradewinds, colder tropical water in the west and warmer water in the east off the coast of South America, and much more rain in dry areas—and more frequent and more intense hurricanes in the eastern Pacific. These systemic changes also noticeably affect winters in the continental U.S.: La Niñas bring warmer than normal winters to the

Southeast and colder than normal to the Northwest, while El Niños generally cause warmer winters in the North Central states and colder winters in the Southeast and Southwest.

Fishermen off the coasts of Peru, Ecuador and Colombia first noticed and named El Niño for the tendency of its very warm waters to arrive around Christmastime. Before the 1982–83 El Niño, scientists had no ability to forecast these massive weather changes, and, despite great advances in the field, still missed the rapid onset, the great magnitude and sudden demise of the 1997–98 El Niño. Yet once forecasters had some of the data, they were able to predict six months in advance the unusual 1997–98 winter in the U.S. season and government, business and individuals were better prepared for disaster. La Niñas often (but not always) occur after El Niños. Typically, La Niñas occur less frequently than El Niños, which occur irregularly every 2–7 years (1976–77, 1982–83, 1986–87, 1991–94, 1997–98) and last 12–18 months. In between these extremes is "normal" weather.

Enough is known about ENSO and its effects that some practical forecasts are attainable. For example, it is possible to forecast ENSO effects months in advance to provide guidance to farmers in East Africa on what crops to plant, and when. It was recognized in the early 20th century that the strength of the Asian monsoon was related to atmospheric pressure in the Pacific, but it has been the great increase in data and analytic capability in recent decades that has permitted the analysis of global climate impacts such as that of ENSO.

So far, researchers have been unable to link El Niños-La Niñas to sunspots or volcanic eruptions. Scientists are studying the compelling question of whether there is a relationship between El Niños-La Niñas and the greenhouse effect. And there is still considerable disagreement and contending theories about exactly what constitutes these phenomena, what their effects are and what role they play in Earth's complex climate and ecology.

Deserts are generally defined as areas with less than 10" (25 cm) of precipitation. (Semiarid land is defined as land with annual precipitation of 10" to 20" [25 to 51 cm].) Deserts are located in many latitudes, and their lack of precipitation can be caused by their locations with respect to mountain ranges, wind patterns, air pressure, and temperature. Some deserts are sandy, but others have land surfaces of rocks, pebbles and even mountains. The largest desert in the world is the Sahara in Africa; the second-largest is the desert area of central and western Australia. The Gobi desert in China and Mongolia is a large mid-latitude desert. Other significant desert areas lie in the region from northwestern India through Pakistan, Afghanistan, Iran, Iraq, and Arabia. The United States has deserts in the Southwest; the largest is the Chihuahuan Desert that stretches from Texas, Arizona, and New Mexico into Mexico; the Death Valley Desert in California and Nevada includes the lowest point in the Western Hemisphere (282 feet/86m below sea level).

In addition to areas normally thought of a desert, the lands at the poles are in effect desert, because of low precipitation caused by high air temperatures; these are called "cold" or polar deserts. Warm deserts cover about 1/5 of the Earth's land surface (1/3 if semi-arid lands are included), and "cold deserts" cover about 1/6 of the land surface. Europe is the only continent without deserts, but there is semiarid land by the Black and Caspian seas and in parts of Ukraine and the north Caucasus.

Glossary of Weather Words

air mass a large body of air that, at a given elevation, has about the same temperature and humidity throughout.

barometric pressure the weight of a column of air at a particular place is determined by measuring the height of a column of mercury under a vacuum. The instrument for making such a measurement is called a barometer. At sea level, the standard barometric pressure is 29.92 inches (76 cm). In the International System, air pressure is measured in bars or in kiloPascals. A bar is slightly less than the standard air pressure at sea level, and a kiloPascal is one-hundredth of a bar. At any location, however, barometric pressure is affected by changes in temperature, humidity, or elevation. When the barometric pressure is falling, the air pressure is decreasing, usually a sign of a storm. When the barometer is rising, fairer weather is on its way.

climate general weather conditions over a long period of time.

cold front the place where cold air that is advancing meets warm air that is retreating before it. This kind of weather not only lowers temperature as it passes but also causes high winds and may cause thunderstorms.

cyclone a region of low atmospheric pressure (see *depression*). Severe cyclones are known as hurricanes, tropical cyclones, and typhoons.

degree-days a degree-day is one degree of deviation of the daily mean temperature from a given norm, usually 65°F. Cooling degree-days are the number of degrees Fahrenheit by which the mean temperature exceeds 65°F, while heating degree-days are the number of degrees the mean temperature is below 65°F. During a year, keeping track of the total number of degree days for each day is used to keep track of cooling or heating needs. For example, oil companies use heating degree-days to estimate how much oil their customers have used and when they might need a refill.

depression any region of low air pressure. In temperate regions over land, the typical depression is a low. The often more powerful depression occurring over tropical waters is called a tropical depression. If the air pressure in a tropical depression continues to fall, it becomes a tropical storm, or, lower still, a hurricane.

dew point the temperature at which dew (drops of water) begins to form as air cools. Air can hold only a certain amount of water vapor at a given temperature. When the temperature falls, excess water vapor must turn into a liquid.

front the boundary between two different air masses.

high an air mass characterized by higher-than-normal air pressure; usually this is a fair-weather system. Some highs are typically found in the same place each year, such as the one that occurs over Bermuda in most summers.

hurricane a huge tropical rainstorm with winds that swirl rapidly around a calm, dry central "eye." To be classified a hurricane, a tropical storm must have wind speeds of more than 74 mph (119 km/hr). The average hurricane is 375 miles (600 km) in diameter and extends up 40,000 feet (12,000 m) above the surface of the ocean. The eye averages 12.5 miles (20 km) in diameter. When a hurricane hits land, its fierce winds and floods can do great damage. On average five hurricanes each year threaten the eastern and southern United States.

jet stream a strong river or two of high winds in the

upper atmosphere (but below the stratosphere) that travels from west to east at between 75 and 150 mph (120-240 km/hr), most often in the middle latitudes. Discovered by American bomber pilots in World War II, it is now known to have significant effects on weather.

low an air mass characterized by lower-than-normal air pressure; usually this is the heart of a storm system. Some lows are found in the same region most of the year, such as the low in the Pacific just off the coast of Alaska.

mean temperature technically, this should be the average of all temperatures during the day. Sometimes it is the average of 24 temperatures taken once each hour, but most often the mean temperature is simply the average of the high and low for the day.

monsoon a wind system in which the prevailing direction of the wind reverses itself from season to season. Southeast Asia is the most typical monsoon region. The summer (southwest) monsoon, characterized by hot, moist air and heavy rains lasts from April to September. The winter (northeast) monsoon lasts from October to March and is characterized by cool, dry air.

occluded front when a cold front overtakes a warm front, the denser cold air flows under the less dense warm air.

prevailing winds throughout the world, winds follow regular patterns. In some places winds are so light and infrequent as to scarcely exist, such as in the doldrums along the equator and in the horse latitudes near latitude 30° N and S. In other places the winds tend to come from a particular direction and are called prevailing winds.

rain shadow an area on the leeward side of a mountain range that receives little rainfall.

relative humidity the amount of moisture (water vapor) in the air compared with the total amount it can hold expressed as a percent. Warm air can hold more water vapor than cold air, so a relative humidity of 75 percent on a warm summer day is moister than a relative humidity of 75 percent on a cool winter day. However, because evaporation is greater on warm days, the relative humidity is generally higher in summer than in winter.

secondary cold front a cold front that sometimes forms behind another cold front and that is often even colder than the first front.

secondary depression a low that forms to the south or east of a low that is a storm center.

squall line a line of instability that often precedes a cold front, marked by wind gusts and often by heavy rain.

stationary front a front that stays in the same place.

storm surge the rise in water levels in the ocean or a large lake that comes from a combination of wind and low pressure during a storm, especially pronounced during a hurricane.

temperature-humidity index a number derived from a formula relating temperature and humidity to discomfort. When it is 75, many are uncomfortable, while at 80 or above, almost everybody is uncomfortable. Temperatures are less comfortable at high humidities because cooling by sweating is less efficient.

temperature inversion a layer of warm air on top a layer of cooler surface air. Such layering, usually occurring at night, can prevent air pollutants near the surface from rising into the upper air. A long-lasting inversion, especially in industrial areas, can cause an excessive concentration of pollutants to accumulate in the surrounding air.

tornado a small and short-lived but very severe windstorm. Tornadoes are whirling columns of air that reach down from a cloud, and they often accompany thunderstorms, rain, and hail. With wind speeds up to 300 mph (480 km/hr), tornadoes can do tremendous damage. The diameter of the average tornado is between 500 and 2,000 feet (150–600 m). The average tornado moves along the ground at 28 mph (45 km/hr) and has a "path" that is 16 miles (26 km) long. In the United States, some 750 tornadoes are reported every year, most frequently between April and June.

tropical storm a storm that forms over the ocean in the tropics and often moves onto land, where it loses strength. Technically, a storm is designated a tropical storm only when winds are between 39 and 73 miles per hour. If winds become greater, a tropical storm becomes a hurricane.

trough a low that is long, rather than nearly circular.

typhoon a hurricane formed in the western Pacific Ocean.

warm front the boundary of a moving warm air mass.

weather the condition of the atmosphere—temperature, rain, and wind, for example—in a particular place. A climate is defined by weather conditions over a long period.

Determining Wind-Chill Factor

Wind speed

Actual Temperature	5 mph	10 mph	15 mph	20 mph	25 mph	30 mph	35 mph	40 mph	45 mph
35°F	31°F	27°F	25°F	24°F	23°F	22°F	21°F	20°F	19°F
30°F	25	21	19	17	16	15	14	13	12
25°F	19	15	13	11	9	8	7	6	5
20°F	13	9	6	4	3	1	0	−1	−2
15°F	7	3	0	−2	−4	−5	−7	−8	−9
10°F	1	−4	−7	−9	−11	−12	−14	−15	−16
5°F	−5	−10	−13	−15	−17	−19	−21	−22	−23
0°F	−11	−16	−19	−22	−24	−26	−27	−29	−30
−5°F	−16	−22	−26	−29	−31	−33	−34	−36	−37
−10°F	−22	−28	−32	−35	−37	−39	−41	−43	−44
−15°F	−28	−35	−39	−42	−44	−46	−48	−50	−51
−20°F	−34	−41	−45	−48	−51	−53	−55	−57	−58
−25°F	−40	−47	−51	−55	−58	−60	−62	−64	−65
−30°F	−46	−53	−58	−61	−64	−67	−69	−71	−72
−35°F	−52	−59	−64	−68	−71	−73	−76	−78	−79
−40°F	−57	−66	−71	−74	−78	−80	−82	−84	−86
−45°F	−63	−72	−77	−81	−84	−87	−89	−91	−93

wind any current of air, measured on land in miles per hour, and at sea in knots. The direction of a given wind is determined from the point of the compass from which it blows (e.g., northeast, south). In various regions of the world, names are given to seasonal winds of particular quality. Among these are the **bora**, a cold usually dry north/northeast wind along the eastern Adriatic; **brickfielder**, a hot north wind of southeastern Australia; **buran**, a cold, violent north/northeast wind of Siberia and Central Asia, common in winter; **chinook**, a dry winter or spring wind which blows down the eastern slopes of the Rocky Mountains often warm enough to melt the snow; **harmattan**, a hot, dry north wind in West Africa which cools as it evaporates the moist air of the coast; **mistral**, a cold, strong north/northwest wind of the western Mediterranean with a surface strength of 60 km/hour, frequent in winter; **pampero**, a sudden, cold south or west wind in Argentina and Uruguay frequent in summer; **Santa Ana** a hot, dry wind that blows from the north or east in Southern California; **sirocco**, a hot south wind of North Africa and southern Italy;

southerly burster, a cold, violent south wind of southeastern Australia; **williwaw**, a violent squall that blows in the Strait of Magellan (South America); and **zonda**, a hot, dry north wind of Argentina and Uruguay.

Determining the Wind-Chill Factor

Sometimes called a wind-chill index, this is a measure of the cooling power of air movement and low temperature on the human body. Because heat passes directly from a warm body to the cooler air surrounding it—a process known as convection—wind produces a continuing source of cooler air and a chilling effect that is equivalent to a lower temperature. The effect on a warm day is pleasant, but as temperatures approach freezing, wind chill is not only unpleasant, but can be dangerous. As the table below shows, a temperature of 5°F combined with a breeze of 20 mph produces a wind-chill temperature of −15°F, a temperature at which frostbite occurs much sooner than at 5°F. Wind speeds above 45 mph have little additional cooling effect.

The Continents

Africa

Physical features Africa is the second-largest continent, between Asia and North America, with a land area of 30,065,000 square kilometers (11,608,156 square miles). On the north, the continent is bounded by the Mediterranean Sea, on the west and south by the Atlantic Ocean, and on the east and south by the Indian Ocean. The greatest east-west dimension, in the north, is about 7,400 kilometers (4,600 miles); the greatest north-south dimension is about 8,050 kilometers (5,000 miles.) from Tunisia to Cape Agulhas, South Africa. Africa is connected with Asia across the Sinai Peninsula.

The main islands and island groups around Africa include the Madeiras, the Canary Islands, the Cape Verde Islands, São Tomé and Príncipe, in the Atlantic Ocean, and Socotra, Zanzibar, the Seychelles, the Comoros, and Madagascar in the Indian Ocean.

One of Africa's largest and most dramatic topographical features is the East African Rift System, an extension of a rift system that begins in Jordan in the north and includes the Red Sea, the Danakil Depression of Eritrea and Ethiopia, the East African lake system, and ends on the coast of northern Mozambique—a total distance of about 6,400 kilometers (4,000 miles). Lake Assal, in Djibouti, is the continent's lowest point, 156 meters (512 feet) below sea level. The Danakil Depression is the hottest place on Earth, with an average annual temperature of 35 degrees C (95 degrees F); the world's highest temperature was 58 degrees C (136 degrees F) recorded at Al-'Aziziyah, near Tripoli, Libya, in 1922.

The East African lakes include Victoria (headwaters of the Nile and the world's second-largest freshwater lake), Tanganyika, at 1,435 meters (4,710 feet), the world's deepest, and Nyasa. The East African Rift is bounded on the west by the Ethiopian Highlands, which rise to more than 4,570 meters (15,000 feet) and the Ruwenzori Mountains of Uganda and Congo, more than 4,880 meters high (16,000 feet), and on the east by Mts. Kenya and Kilimanjaro—at 5,895 meters (19,340 feet), the highest on the continent. Other important mountains are the Drakensberg Range in South Africa, the Atlas Mountains of Morocco and Algeria (highest peak 4,167 meters (13,671 feet), the Egypt's Red Sea Mountains, the Nimba Mountains of Guinea, Liberia, and Côte d'Ivoire.

Africa's single-largest geographic feature is the Sahara,

the largest desert on Earth and seven times larger than the Gobi Desert, the next biggest. Covering 9,065,000 square kilometers (3.5 million square miles, slightly less than the total area of the United States), the Sahara is bounded on the north by the Atlas Mountains of Morocco and Algeria, and the Mediterranean, on the east by the Red Sea, and on the south by the Nuba Mountains of western Sudan, Lake Chad and its tributaries, and the Niger River. Lake Chad, which borders Chad, Niger, Cameroon, and Nigeria, is one of the world's shallowest, with a maximum depth of only seven meters. The main deserts of southern Africa are the Kalahari of southern Africa (which ranks fifth), and the Namib Desert of coastal Namibia (16th).

Africa has relatively few major rivers that offer navigable access to the interior because they flow through regions of uneven terrain and are characterized by stretches of rapids, cataracts (as on the Nile), and waterfalls (such as Victoria Falls). The world's longest river is the 6,673-kilometer-long Nile, sources of which are in the Ethiopian Highlands (the Blue Nile) and Lake Victoria (the White Nile) and which flows north through Sudan and Egypt to the Mediterranean. Other major rivers include the Senegal, Volta, Niger, Congo (with its tributary the Kasai), and Orange, which flow into the Atlantic, and the Zambezi and Limpopo, which empty into the Indian Ocean. The Okavango River rises in Angola and flows through Namibia before emptying into the wildlife rich Okavango Delta north of the Kalahari Desert.

Climate Africa is the most tropical of the continents, stretching from 37 degrees N to almost 35 degrees S; the climate of its northern and southern halves is broadly symmetrical. The equatorial center of the continent is characterized by lush tropical and subtropical rain forests that extend from the East African lakes region in the east to the Atlantic coast and along the southern coast of West Africa as far as Guinea. There are also rain forests in the southeast (coastal Mozambique and South Africa) and the eastern half of Madagascar.

To the north, east, and south is a zone of savannah and other grasslands, including the semi-arid Sahel region, which borders the Sahara to the north. This zone reaches from the Atlantic to the Horn of Africa in the north, encompasses much of the East African Rift, and south of the equator extends from the Indian Ocean and the Atlantic. A large area of central southern Africa—mostly Zambia and Angola—is characterized by dry forest.

By far the largest uninterrupted climate zone is desert or dry steppe, including the Sahara from the Atlantic to

World Land Area and Population by Selected Region, 2000

Region	Land Area			Population			
	Square miles	Square kilometers	Percent of world total	Total ('000s)	Percent of total	Per square mile	Per square kilometer
World total[1]	57,308,738	148,429,000	100.0%	6,068,511	100.0%	99.5	38.4
Africa	11,608,156	30,065,000	20.3	805,243	13.3	69.4	40.9
Antarctica	5,404,000	14,000,000	9.4	(2)	(2)	(2)	(2)
Asia	17,212,041	44,579,000	30.0	3,688,072	60.8	214.3	82.7
Australia	2,967,966	7,687,000	5.2	19,164	0.3	6.5	2.5
Europe	3,837,082	9,938,000	6.7	728,981	12.0	190.0	73.4
North America	9,365,290	24,256,000	16.3	480,545	8.0	51.3	19.8
South America	6,879,952	17,819,000	12.0	346,504	5.7	50.4	19.4

Notes: 1. Land only. Includes small islands not shown separately. 2. Antarctica has no indigenous population.

the Red Sea and south in a narrow band along the coast of the Horn of Africa to just below the equator. Another band of desert stretches along the Atlantic coast from central Angola, across Namibia, and into western South Africa.

After Australia, Africa is the driest inhabited continent. Africa has 22 percent of the world's land area, 15 percent of the world's population, but less than 10 percent of the world's renewable water resources. Less than a fifth of the continent experiences sufficient annual moisture for plant growth throughout the whole year.

People Africa is the second-largest continent in population, between Asia and Europe; the estimated 2000 population is 805,243,000. The continent is sparsely populated; however there are many large urban areas, including Lagos, Nigeria (eighth-largest in the world, 13.4 million), and Cairo, Egypt (19th, 10.6 million).

Africa includes 53 nations and some 1,000 linguistic and cultural groups. There are six major language groups: Hamito-Semitic (or Afro-Asiatic, including Arabic), north of a line drawn from southern Somalia to southern Mauritania; Nilo-Saharan, spoken in a broad area around the headwaters of the Nile and northwest of Lake Chad; Niger-Congo, spoken throughout west, central, and southeast Africa; Khoisan, spoken in remote areas of Namibia and Botswana; Indo-European (English and Afrikaans, derived from Dutch), spoken in South Africa south of the Orange River; and Malayo-Polynesian, spoken in Madagascar.

The continent's colonial past is reflected in the fact that 50 nations use Arabic or a European language as an official language. French and English are official languages in 18 countries (in some cases they are both official), Portuguese in five, and Spanish in one. Eighteen countries have two or more official languages, and South Africa has 11—five more than the number of working languages at the United Nations. Nonetheless, indigenous languages are spoken throughout the continent, and in many countries only a minority of the people speaks the official language.

Economy The U.N. classifies 31 countries in Africa as "least developed countries," and all 53 countries on the continent are members of the "Group of 77" developing countries. Of the 26 countries with the lowest per capita income worldwide, all but three are in Africa. Not one of the world's 25 leading merchandise exporters or importers is in Africa, and not one of the world's 50 largest banks or 100 largest industrial companies is headquartered in an African nation.

Although industrial production in Africa is low, the continent has an abundance of mineral wealth. Among the principal mineral resources are iron ore, ferro-alloy metals (chrome, chromite, and manganese), copper, bauxite (aluminum ore), cobalt, gold, petroleum, and diamonds. Leading producers of primary energy include South Africa, which ranks sixth for production of coal, Algeria, eighth-largest producer of liquid natural gas, and Nigeria, 11th-largest producer of crude oil. Other oil producers include Angola, Equatorial Guinea, Chad, Gabon, Congo, Cameroon, Democratic Republic of Congo, and Cote d'Ivoire; plentiful reserves have also been found in São Tomé.

The most important regional alliances include: the Organization of African Unity (53 members); the Common Market for Eastern and Southern Africa (20); the Economic Community of West Africa States (16); and the Southern African Development Community (13). Algeria, Libya, and Nigeria are members of OPEC. The 14 countries of the African Financial Community share a common currency, the CFA franc, created in 1945. There are two versions, one used by Benin, Burkina Faso, Côte d'Ivoire, Guinea-Bissau, Mali, Niger, Senegal, and Togo, the other by Cameroon, Central African Republic, Chad, Republic of Congo, Equatorial Guinea, and Gabon.

Africa accounts for only about 10 percent of world exports and 5 percent of world imports, and in consequence has relatively few major ports. The most important include Durban (which ranks 23rd in the world) and Richard's Bay, South Africa; Lagos, Nigeria; and Alexandria, Egypt. One reason for the relatively low volume of trade and industrial development is that imperial administrators tended to build transportation corridors between colonies in the interior and a seaport but to neglect intercolonial transportation networks. Seven percent of the world's seaborne trade transits the Suez Canal.

The extensive, if diminishing, reserves of big game—including elephants, lions, antelopes, zebras, rhinoceros, and hippopotamus, as well as great apes—are an increasingly important part of the tourist economy in eastern and southern Africa.

Antarctica

Physical features   Antarctica is the fifth-largest continent with an area of 14,000,000 square kilometers (5,404,000 square miles). Apart from the tip of the Antarctic Peninsula, the continent lies entirely within the Antarctic Circle (latitude 66°30'S). West Antarctica is a mountainous region that includes the Antarctic Peninsula and is separated from East Antarctica by the Transantarctic Mountains. The continent is covered by an ice sheet with an average thickness of about 2,160 meters—at its thickest the ice is 4,776 meters—which makes Antarctica the world's highest continent. The highest point on the continent is the top of the Vinson Massif (5,140 meters) in the Sentinel Range near the base of the Antarctic Peninsula.

There are two large coastal indentations: the Weddell Sea (about 45°W) faces the Atlantic Ocean, and the Ross Sea (175°W) faces the Pacific. In each of these areas, there are large ice shelves, the Filchner-Ronne ice shelf and the Ross ice shelf, respectively. Fed by glaciers and snow accumulations, they move steadily outward and large bergs break off at the seaward margins. Smaller ice shelves are found around the coast, and the continent is surrounded by the Southern Ocean, a continuous band of ocean in which the strong prevailing winds of the "Roaring Forties" and "Furious Fifties" blow from west to east.

In 2002 the Larsen B ice shelf on the Antarctic Peninsula collapsed due to a regional rise in temperature. The ice shelf was relatively small—3,250 square kilometers and approximately 200 meters thick.

Climate   The climate of Antarctica is characterized by extreme cold and high winds. According to some estimates, the conversion of all of Antarctica's ice to water would raise global sea levels by 45 to 60 meters (150–200 feet). Although the ice sheet contains approximately 70 percent of the world's fresh water in a frozen state, because cold air holds little water vapor for precipitation, Antarctica is the driest continent on the planet. The enormous accumulations of snow and ice have taken place over long periods, and most blizzards consist mainly of existing snow blown by high winds. Although some snow falls around the warmer margins of the continent, the average precipitation over interior Antarctica is about 50 millimeters. High altitude, high latitude, and the absence of sunlight in winter combine to make the interior of Antarctica the coldest place on Earth, with mean temperatures around of −57°C (−70°F). The lowest temperature ever recorded on Earth was −88.3°C (−126.9°F) at Vostok, a Russian scientific station located at 78°S, 106°E.

People   Antarctica has no indigenous population; the only humans are at research stations, and there are no large land animals. The few species of plant life adapted to the Antarctic environment include mosses, lichens, and algae. On the Antarctic Peninsula there are several species of flowering plants. The birds and seals that spend part of their time on coastal lands depend on the sea for food; Antarctic waters are rich in plankton that is eaten by krill, small shrimplike crustaceans that are the principal food of some species of whales, seals, penguins, and fish.

Although geographers had long postulated the existence of a southern continent, James Cook (England, 1728–79) was the first navigator to cross the Antarctic Circle (1768). Antarctica was first sighted in January 1820, first by the Russian Fabian Gottlieb von Bellingshausen, and independently by the British sealer William Smith sailing as pilot of a Royal Navy ship. Sealers and whalers continued to visit Antarctic waters through the century, but no one stepped foot on the continent until 1895, the same year that the Sixth International Geographical Congress pronounced Antarctica "the greatest piece of geographical exploration still to be undertaken." A Norwegian team of five men led by Roald Amundsen (1872–1928) was the first to reach the South Pole, on December 14, 1911.

Many countries have established research stations on the continent. During the International Geophysical Year (1957–58), 12 nations maintained 65 research stations and operational facilities in Antarctica. The Antarctic Treaty of 1959 prohibited military operations, nuclear explosions, and the disposal of radioactive waste in Antarctica and provides for cooperation in scientific research. A 1991 protocol to the treaty barred for 50 years the exploration of Antarctica for oil or minerals, and contained additional provisions covering wildlife protection, waste disposal, and marine pollution.

Asia

Physical features   Asia is the world's largest continent, with a land area of 44,579,000 square kilometers (17,212,041 square miles). Asia is the larger part of the Eurasian land mass, which it shares with Europe. By convention, the boundary between the two continents is defined by the Ural Mountains, the Ural River, the Caspian Sea, and the Caucasus Mountains.

Asia is bounded on the north by the Arctic Ocean and its marginal seas (the Kara, Laptev, and East Siberian Seas), on the east by the Pacific Ocean (the Sea of Japan, East China Sea, and South China Sea), on the south by the Indian Ocean (the Bay of Bengal, the Arabian Sea, the Gulf of Aden, and the Red Sea), and on the east by the Mediterranean, Aegean, and Black Seas and Europe. Asia is connected to Africa by the Sinai Peninsula (the Suez Canal is an artificial divider), and is separated in the extreme northeast from North America by the 90-kilometer (55-mile)-wide Bering Strait. Major islands and island groups include Sakhalin, the Japanese Islands, the Philippines, the islands of Indonesia and Malaysia in the east, the Andaman and Nicobars, the Maldives, and Laccadives in the south, and in the Arctic the Northern Land (Severnaya Zemlya) and New Siberian Islands (Novosibirskiye Ostrova).

Mountains stretch from Asia Minor across northern Southwest Asia and the Caucasus, through Iran and Afghanistan. The Himalayas divide the flat Gangetic Plain of northern India from the Tibetan Highlands, which have an elevation of about 4,570 meters (15,000 feet). Mount Everest is the world's tallest, 8,856 meters (29,035 feet), and all of the world's 50 tallest mountains are in Asia. To the east and southeast, the Himalayas and Tibetan Plateau give way to the Szechuan Basin, South China highlands, and the highlands of mainland Southeast Asia. To the west of the Tibetan Plateau are the Pamir Mountains, and to the north the Taklimakan Desert, beyond Tien Shan and Altai Mountains. The world's lowest point is the Dead Sea, between Jordan and Israel, 408 meters (1,339 feet) below sea level.

In the north are the lowlands of the West Siberian Plain, the Central Siberian Plateau, the Chersky Range, and the mountainous Kamchatka Peninsula. Eastern China is dominated by the North China Plain, south of Beijing. A sequence of plateaus and uplands runs northeast from the Caspian Sea toward Siberia. In India, the Indo-Gangetic Plain runs in a broad crescent from the Arabian Sea, northeast to the base of the Himalayas, and then southwest toward the Bay of Bengal. To the south are the Deccan Plateau and a number of smaller mountain ranges. The principal island groups of Asia also contain mountainous regions, including Sri Lanka, Malaysia, Indonesia, and Japan.

Eighteen of the world's 50 largest rivers are found in Asia, which helps account for the enormous concentrations of people found on the continent. These rivers generally have their sources in the high plateau region and flow through mountain ranges toward broad alluvial lowlands and the sea. The great rivers of ancient civilization included the Tigris and Euphrates of Mesopotamia, which rise in Turkey and flow through Iraq to the Persian Gulf; the Indus River, which descends from the Himalayas through Pakistan to the Arabian Sea; and the Huang Ho (Yellow) River of north China, which enters the East China Sea near Shanghai.

Of equal or greater importance since antiquity are the Ganges (sacred to Hindus), and Brahmaputra, which flow southeast from the Himalayas to the Bay of Bengal; the Mekong, which rises in the Himalayas and flows through Southeast Asia to the South China Sea; and the Yangtze, which rises in the Kunlun Mountains and flows into the East China Sea. Other important rivers of southern Asia are the Salween and Irriwaddy, which enter the Bay of Bengal and the Honghe (Red) River of northern Vietnam. Many of the rivers of northern Asia flow toward the Arctic Sea, among them the Yenisei-Angara, the Ob-Irtysh, the

Lena, and the Kolyma in Siberia.

Other water resources of particular importance are the large lakes of northern Asia, including the saltwater Caspian Sea (at 371 million square kilometers, the world's largest lake), the Aral Sea (fourth) and Lake Balkash. Russia's Lake Baikal is the largest freshwater lake in Asia and the eighth largest in the world. Central Asia has large areas of interior drainage, where watercourses form interior lakes or disappear into the ground.

Six of the world's largest deserts are found in Asia: the Gobi (second), Great Arabian Desert, including much of Saudi Arabia, and part of Jordan, Syria, and Iraq (fourth), China's Taklimakan (sixth), Turkmenistan's Kara Kum (eighth), the Thar in India and Pakistan (ninth) and Uzbekistan's Kyzyl Kum (10th).

Climate   Asia has a vast range of climate conditions. In the north there is arctic cold. In some areas of northern India and central China there are moderate climates, and in the southeast there are the rains and heat of the monsoon climate. The wettest place on Earth is Mawsynram, Assam, India, with an annual rainfall of 11.9 meters (38.9 feet). There are arid areas with little precipitation, such as parts of the Gobi Desert that receive 50–100 millimeters (2–8 inches) per year.

The Asian landmass also accounts for one of the world's most dramatic climatic features, the monsoons. As the warm air over Asia rises during the summer, it draws cooler air off the water to create the southwest monsoon, which is characterized by hot, moist air with heavy rains and lasts from April to September. In winter, the process is reversed, as the relatively warm air over the ocean draws off the colder and dryer northeast monsoon, which lasts from October to March. The pattern of monsoon winds, which varies in duration, intensity, and direction depending on one's location on the coast of Asia, accounts for the widespread dissemination of trade and culture from East Africa to East Asia over the past 3,000 years.

People   Asia accounts for about 30 percent of the world's landmass, but contains 60 percent of the world's population. All or part of 50 countries are in Asia, including six of the 10 most populous nations: China (first, with 1.3 billion people), India (second; 1.1 billion), Indonesia (fourth, 220 million), Pakistan (sixth), Bangladesh (seventh), and Japan (ninth). (Russia ranks eighth, but more than three-quarters of its people live in European Russia. Part of Turkey is also in Europe, and most of Egypt is in

Africa.) The nations of Asia are often grouped into regions. The definitions are inexact, but one grouping is as follows: Asia Minor and the South Caucasus (Turkey, Armenia, Azerbaijian, and Georgia); Southwest Asia, also known as the Middle East or Near East (the countries of the Arabian Peninsula, Jordan, Israel, Palestine, Syria, Iraq, and Iran); South Asia (Pakistan, India, Bangladesh, the countries of the Himalayas, Sri Lanka, and the Maldives); Central Asia (Afghanistan, Kazakhstan, Kyrgyzstan, Tajikistan, Turkmenistan, and Uzbekistan); Southeast Asia (Burma, Thailand, Malaysia, Laos, Cambodia, and Vietnam on the mainland) and the islands (chiefly Indonesia, the Philippines, and Singapore); and East Asia (Asiatic Russia, Mongolia, China, the Koreas, and Japan).

Some areas in northern and Central Asia are sparsely populated, but the bulk of Asia's population is distributed in areas of adequate rainfall and fertile soils in the east, southeast, and south. Areas such as the North China Plain, the valley of the Yangzte in China, and the Gangetic Plain of India have especially dense populations. Fourteen of the world's 25 largest urban areas are found in the densely settled areas of the east, southeast, and south: in Japan, Tokyo (first, with 26.4 million people) and Osaka (fourteenth, 11 million); in India, Mumbai (Bombay, third, 18.1 million), Calcutta (ninth, 12.9 million), Delhi (13th, 11.7 million), and Hyderabad (22nd, ca. 9 million); in China, Shanghai (seventh, 12.9 million) and Beijing (15th, 10.8 million) and Tianjin (21st, ca. 9 million); Dhaka, Bangladesh (11th, 12.3 million); Karachi, Pakistan (12th, 11.8 million); Jakarta, Indonesia (16th, 11.0 million); Manila, the Philippines (17th, 10.9 million); and Bangkok, Thailand (23rd, 7.2 million).

More than 30 languages have official status in Asia, and there are scores of other languages in common use. By far the languages with the greatest number of speakers are Chinese (various dialects in China, Taiwan, and Singapore, where it is one of four official languages), Hindi, Malay (various dialects in Indonesia, Malaysia, Singapore, and Brunei), Japanese, and Bengali. Arabic is the official language in most of the countries of Southwest Asia.

Asia is also the most religiously diverse continent, as well as the birthplace of all the world's major religions: Judaism, Christianity, Islam, Hinduism, and Buddhism.

Economy   Asia is a continent of great but uneven economic potential. Japan has the second-largest economy in the world, but only four other countries in Asia are considered to have advanced economies: Israel, Singapore,

South Korea, and Taiwan. Nine of the countries in the top 25 merchandise exporters and seven of the exporters are in Asia. Six of the world's largest 50 banks are based in Asia—all of them in Japan. Of the world's top 100 industrial companies, 23 are based in Asia, all but three of them in Japan; two are South Korean and one is Chinese. Thirty-seven of the "Group of 77" developing nations are in Asia. The Asian countries of the former Soviet Union are considered transitional economies, while eight Asian states rank among the world's "least developed." Tajikistan, Nepal, Cambodia, and Kyrgyzstan rank in the bottom 25 by per capita income.

The major Asian alliances are the Asia Pacific Economic Cooperation, the Association of South East Asian Nations (ASEAN), the Arab League (22 members, 13 in Asia and 11 in Africa), and the Commonwealth of Independent States (nine Asian members, and three European). Seven of the 11 members of OPEC are located in Asia.

Oil and gas are the pillars of the economy of Southwest Asia, where Saudi Arabia, Iran, and Iraq rank first, fourth, and ninth in crude oil production; Russia and China are the second-and-fifth biggest producers, respectively. Indonesia, and Southwest and Central Asia also have large reserves of natural gas. Five of the world's largest producers of coal are also in Asia: China (first), India (fourth), Russia (fifth), North Korea (ninth), and Indonesia (10th). Among the more important non-fossil-fuel mineral resources include antimony, boron, copper, fluorspar, gemstones, gold, iodine, lead, magnesite, manganese, molybdenum, nickel, rare earths, tin, titanium, tungsten, and zinc.

The "little tigers" (South Korea, Taiwan, Singapore, and Hong Kong) experienced rapid economic growth starting in the 1970's and 1980's, as did Malaysia and Indonesia. More recently, China and India have emerged as engines of economic growth. India has developed a high-tech industry of software production and other services. Asian agriculture is very intensive, especially rice growing; because of the dense populations of many Asian countries, much agricultural production is for the home market. Some areas have developed hydroelectric energy, and the Three Gorges project on the Yangtze in China will be the world's largest.

Transportation networks have not fully kept up with other economic developments. Nonetheless, Asia is home to 15 of the world's 25 largest ports, including Singapore (the world's busiest), Hong Kong, China (second), Kaohsiung, Taiwan (fourth), Busan, South Korea (sixth),

and Nagoya, Japan (10th).

Australia

Physical features   Australia is the smallest continent, 7,687,000 square kilometers (2,967,966 square miles). It is the only continent that constitutes a single country, and it is the most southerly of the inhabited continents. Lying between the Indian and Pacific Oceans, Australia measures about 3,860 kilometers (2,400 miles) east to west and about 3,220 kilometers (2,000 miles) north to south. It is surrounded by the Indian Ocean to the northwest and west, the Southern Ocean to the south, the Tasman Sea and Coral Sea to the east, and the Gulf of Carpentaria, Arafura Sea, and Timor Sea to the north. Its closest land neighbor is Papua New Guinea, from which the Cape York Peninsula is separated by the 80-mile wide Torres Strait.

Australia is a geologically inert continent. Its highest elevation, Mt. Koskiusko in New South Wales, only 2,228 meters (7,310 feet)—lower than any other continent—and its lowest point, Lake Eyre, in South Australia, is 16 meters (52 feet) below sea level—higher than any other continent. From the narrow western coastal plain the land rises to a rough plateau that occupies the western half of the continent. There is a small area of fertile soil and moist climate in the southwest, but most of the state of Western Australia, which comprises about half the country, is arid. At 1,554,000 square kilometers, the Australian Desert (including the Great Sandy, Gibson, Great Victoria, and Simpson Deserts) is the third-largest in the world. In the north there are areas with tropical temperatures and a winter dry season. On the eastern side of the continent are the mountains of the Great Dividing Range, which parallels the coast from northern Queensland to Melbourne, and the temperate areas of the south and east, the center of settlement in Australia. The longest Australian river system, the Murray River and its tributaries, drains the southern part of the interior basin that lies between the mountains and the great plateau.

The major offshore islands include Tasmania and Kangeroo Island on the south, the Torres Strait Islands on the north, and on the northeast, the Great Barrier Reef, a 2,000-kilometer-long maze of coral reefs and islands that make up the world's largest coral reef along the northeast coast of the continent.

Australia has a number of large, shallow lakes whose surface area varies considerably with the season, including

Lake Eyre (maximum depth one meter), Torrens (0.2 meters), and Gairdner (0.2 meters); Eyre and Gairdner are saltwater lakes.

Climate   Australia is the driest of the six inhabited continents. Eighty percent of the continent has annual rainfall of less than 600 mm, and this rainfall has high variability. The low rainfall combined with high evaporation, especially in the inland areas, results in low surface water flow. The plant life of the interior areas is adapted to dry conditions, and responds rapidly when rainfall occurs. Temperatures in coastal areas are moderate year-round, but there are occasional frosts inland. Because of its isolation from other continents in recent geologic time, Australia has developed unique ecosystems with many forms of plant and animal life not found elsewhere. Most distinctive are the marsupials such as kangaroos, koalas, wombats, and Tasmanian devils, and the world's only egg-laying mammals, the duck-billed platypus and echidna.

People   Humans have populated Australia for some 40,000 years, arriving from Asia, and there are today close to 400,000 descendants of the original indigenous population, now referred to as Aborigines (from the Latin *ab origine* meaning "from the beginning"). The continent may also have been visited by various peoples of the Pacific islands, though without permanent settlement. The first Europeans to visit the continent were the Dutch, who landed in 1606. Captain James Cook claimed the east coast for Britain in 1770, and eight years later the British established a convict settlement at Port Jackson near modern Sydney. Between 1901 (when it gained independence) and 1973, Australia had a "whites only" immigration policy, which meant that the majority of its nonaboriginal population was of European origin or descent. More open immigration has led to a rapid rise in Asian immigration.

Despite its considerable size, Australia has only about 20,000,000 people, who make up one of the most urban populations in the world. More than 90 percent of the people live in cities. Brisbane (1.4 million), Sydney (3.7 million), Melbourne (3.2 million), and Adelaide (1.1 million) in the east and southeast are the principal industrial and commercial cities; the capital, Canberra (325,000), is also in the southeast. Perth (1.2 million), the principal city of Western Australia, is considered one of the most remote urban areas on the planet; the closest city is Adelaide, 2,200 kilometers to the east across the Nullarbor (Latin for "no tree") Plain. Darwin, the largest city in the north, has a population of about 104,000.

Most Australians speak English. In the 20th century there were approximately 260 Australian Aboriginal languages. Of these, many are now extinct and only about 20 have a sufficient number of speakers to ensure survival.

Economy   Australia has a highly developed economy and ranks 20th in the world in terms of per capita income, and 25th among the world's exporters. The most important exports are from mining—bauxite, copper, gold, iron ore, lead, nickel, silver, titanium, uranium, and zinc—and agriculture, including wool, beef (of which Australia is the world's largest exporter), and mutton, and industrial products. The National Australia Bank ranks 48th worldwide. Australia's major seaports include Melbourne, Sydney, Brisbane, Fremantle, and Newcastle, the largest coal port in the world. Long oriented to British and other western markets, the Australian economy is increasingly dependent on economic ties with Asia and the Pacific Rim.

Europe

Physical features   Europe is the sixth-largest continent, between Antarctica and Australia, with an area of 9,938,000 square kilometers (3,837,082 square miles). Europe is not a geographically distinct continent, but rather a large peninsula of Eurasia. By convention, the boundary between Europe and Asia is defined by the Ural Mountains, the Ural River, the Caspian Sea, and the Caucasus Mountains. Europe is bounded on the south by the Black Sea and Mediterranean, including the Aegean and Adriatic Seas, to the west by the Atlantic Ocean, and North Sea, and to the north by the Arctic Ocean.

The British Isles are separated from continent by the 20-mile-wide English Channel, and northern Europe is indented by the Baltic Sea, including the Gulf of Bothnia and Gulf of Finland. Other large islands include Iceland and the Faeroes in the Atlantic, and Spitzbergen, Franz Josef Land, and Novaya Zemlya in the Arctic Ocean.

In the south, along the coast of the Mediterranean, Europe is mountainous and heavily indented. The principal mountain chains are the Pyrenees, between Spain and France, the Alps (France, Switzerland, Italy, Germany, and Austria), the Apennines in Italy, the Julian and Dinaric Alps in the Balkans, and the Pindus Mountains in Greece, and the Carpathians in Ukraine and Romania. To the north is a broad plain that runs from the Atlantic coast of France across Germany and into Russia, where it widens to the north and south before reaching the Urals. Much of this plain, which includes hills and low mountains, is highly fertile. Toward the east are the steppe and forest regions. The long peninsula occupied by Norway and Sweden is mountainous in the west. The highest points are Mt. Elbrus 5,633 meters (18,481 feet) in the Russian Caucasus and Mont Blanc 4,807 meters (15,771 feet) in the French Alps. Europe's lowest point is 28 meters (92 feet) below sea level, on the surface of the Caspian Sea.

Europe is especially favored with a number of long navigable rivers that provide good communication between the coasts and the interior. On the Atlantic and North Sea coasts are the Tagus, Garonne, Loire, Rhine, and Elbe, and in England the Thames. The Baltic receives the Oder, the Vistula; the Danube, Dnieper, and Don (via the Sea of Azov) flow into the Black Sea; and the Volga into the Caspian Sea. The Rhone is the only major river to enter the Mediterranean. In 1992–93, the last section of the Rhine-Main-Canal was opened, making it possible to ship goods by water diagonally across Europe from the North Sea to the Black Sea.

Climate   The climate of Europe varies from warm subtropical climates to polar conditions in the far north. The Mediterranean climate of the south is dry and warm. The western and northwestern parts have a mild, generally humid climate. In central and eastern Europe the climate is more continental, with cooler summers. The deep ocean thermohaline ("heat and salt") circulation of the Gulf Stream brings heat to Europe's North Atlantic coast, which makes northwest Europe considerably warmer than places at the same latitude on the east coasts of North America or Asia. There are no significant desert areas in Europe, although there is concern that areas of European Russia, Portugal, Spain, Italy, and Greece are now threatened with desertification.

People   With an estimated 728,981,000 inhabitants, Europe ranks third among the continents in terms of population, between Africa and North America. Except for areas in northern Scandinavia and a few other regions, Europe is the most densely populated of the world's highly developed areas. Two of the continent's cities rank among the world's 25 largest urban areas: Paris is 24th (9.6 million people) and Moscow 25th (9.3 million); London ranks 26th (7.3 million people). However, there are many other major urban areas throughout the continent.

Europe is home to all or part of some 46 countries (Russia and Turkey are partly in Asia). European nations range from large and influential countries such as Germany, the United Kingdom, and France, to small independent principalities such as Andorra and San Marino. Since World War II, the political situation has been characterized by two broad phases. The cold war division pitted the Western capitalist democracies against the communist countries of Eastern Europe. The collapse of the Soviet Union and related political institutions in the early 1990's was followed by the expansion of Western alliances. Formerly eastern bloc countries Czech Republic, Hungary, and Poland were admitted to NATO (the North Atlantic Treaty Organization, founded in 1949 to maintain European security in the face of perceived Soviet expansion).

With the exception of Finno-Ugric (Finnish and Hungarian) and a few language isolates such as Basque, most European languages are part of the Indo-European language family. These include the Romance, Germanic, Balto-Slavic, and Greek languages, as well as Albanian and Celtic. There are almost as many national languages as there are nations in Europe, and the 27-member European Union has 23 working languages: Bulgarian, Czech, Danish, Dutch, English, Estonian, Finnish, French, German, Greek, Hungarian, Irish, Italian, Latvian, Lithuanian, Maltese, Polish, Portuguese, Romanian, Slovak, Slovene, Spanish, and Swedish.

Economy   Western Europe as a whole is highly developed in the west but less so in the east. The largest economies are Germany, France, the United Kingdom, and Italy. However, the U.N. describes the 14 Eastern European nations that were formerly part of the Soviet Union, members of the Warsaw Pact, part of Yugoslavia, and Albania, as having transitional economies. Only four European nations are members of the "Group of 77" developing nations: Bosnia and Herzegovina, Cyprus, Malta, and Romania.

Among the areas in which Western economies are strong are financial services, heavy industry (including cars, aircraft, and ships), and engineering: 35 of the world's 50 largest banks, and 39 of the top 100 industrial corporations are headquartered in Europe. Tourism is an important industry in many countries. There is also extensive agriculture, much of it heavily subsidized; forestry industries in the far north; and fishing. Mineral resources include coal, copper, mercury, potash, tin, and zinc, and oil and gas in the North Sea and in Eastern Europe. Europe also relies heavily on both hydroelectric and nuclear power genera-tion; 214 of the world's 439 nuclear power plants are locat-ed there.

Europe's transportation infrastructure is highly devel-oped, and there are extensive rail, road, water, and air net-works. Twelve of the world's 25 biggest importing nations and 12 of the exporting nations are in Europe. Not sur-prisingly, the continent boasts some of the world's busiest seaports, notably Rotterdam, the Netherlands (third in the world), Antwerp (ninth), Le Havre, France (14th), and Hamburg, Germany (17th).

The European Union has 27 member states. By 2011, the euro was the official currency of 17 countries: Austria, Belgium, Cypress, Estonia, France, Germany, Finland, Greece, Ireland, Italy, Luxembourg, Malta, the Nether-lands, Portugal, Slovakia, Slovenia, and Spain.

North America

Physical features   North America is the third-largest continent, between Africa and South America, with a land area of 24,256,000 square kilometers (9,365,290 square miles). North America includes all of the mainland and related offshore islands lying north of the Isthmus of Panama, which connects it with South America, and the Caribbean islands. The continent is bounded on the west by the Pacific Ocean and the Bering Sea, on the north by the Arctic Ocean, and on the east by the Atlantic Ocean and the Gulf of Mexico, and on the south by South America. Geographically, North America stretches from about 9°N to 83°N south to north (Panama to the tip of Ellesmere Island), and about 166°E to 50°W east to west (from the end of the Aleutian Islands to Greenland).

Geographers divide North America into 13 physio-graphic regions. The northernmost are the narrow Arctic plain of Alaska and northwest Canada, the Canadian or Laurentian Shield, which includes much of Ontario and Nunavut, as well as the island of Greenland, and the islands of the Canadian Arctic Archipelago. The western half of the continent is dominated by mountain ranges: the Western Cordillera, which stretches from the Aleutians and southern Alaska along the west coast as far south as Baja California and the adjacent coast of Mexico. Roughly parallel to this, from west to east, are the Intermontaine Plateaus, the Eastern Cordillera, and the Great Plains, all three of which end at about the U.S.-Mexico border.

The large, irregularly shaped Interior Lowlands domi-nate the center of the United States and part of south cen-tral Canada, and the Appalachian Mountains stretch from Georgia northeast through the Canadian Maritimes and Newfoundland. The Coastal Plains run from the Yucatán Peninsula around the Gulf of Mexico and up the Atlantic coast as far as Long Island, New York.

Central Mexico is dominated by the Mexican Highlands, which run into the Central American Ranges. The Caribbean islands comprise a region known as the Antilles Arc, including a ring of volcanic islands that stretches from Puerto Rico to South America. The highest peak in North America is Denali or Mt. McKinley, 6,194 meters (20,320 feet), in the Alaska Range.

The dominant river system of North America compris-es the Missouri-Mississippi River and their tributaries, which drain an area of 3.2 square kilometers (1.2 million square miles). The fifth-largest drainage system in the world includes all or part of 31 of the United States and two Canadian provinces from the Rocky Mountains in the west to the Appalachians in the east, and flows into the Gulf of Mexico in a broad delta below Baton Rouge, Louisiana. From the Gulf to its headwaters in Lake Itasca, Minnesota, the Mississippi measures 3,780 kilometers (2,348 miles). However, a case can be made that the lower Mississippi is an extension of the Missouri River, which meets the upper Mississippi just above St. Louis.

The Missouri River is formed by the confluence of three smaller rivers in Three Forks, Montana, from which it is 3,969 kilometers (2,466 miles) to the Gulf. Other major tributaries of the Mississippi include the Illinois, Ohio, Cumberland, Tennessee, and Yazoo to the east, and the Arkansas and Ouachita to the west. Up until the 1940s, the Red River also flowed into the Mississippi, but it was captured by the Atchafalaya 50 miles above Baton Rouge, Louisiana. Recognizing that without intervention, the Atchafalaya would also capture the Mississippi, the U.S. Army Corps of Engineers created the Old River Control Project to keep this from happening. Were the Mississippi to shift its channel, the current river channel would become a saltwater estuary past Baton Rouge while the Atchafalaya—which now receives 30 percent of the river's flow—would overflow its banks. Such an event would change the geographic, demographic, and econom-ic landscape of southern Louisiana beyond recognition.

Other large or economically important North American rivers include, on the Atlantic seaboard, the St. Lawrence (which forms part of the U.S.-Canada border), Hudson (connected to the Great Lakes via the Erie Canal), and Delaware; the Rio Grande, which forms part of the U.S.-Mexico border and flows into the Gulf of Mexico; the Colorado, which flows into the Gulf of California; the San Joaquin, Sacramento, and Columbia, which flow into the Pacific; the Yukon, which flows from Canada through Alaska to the Bering Sea; the Mackenzie, which flows north into the Arctic Sea, and the Nelson, which flows into Hudson Bay. There are no major rivers in Central America or the Caribbean islands.

Another notable characteristic of North America's hydrographic landscape is the abundance of lakes, including the five interconnected Great Lakes of the United States and Canada, the largest of which is Lake Superior, at 82,414 square kilometers (31,820 square miles), the second largest lake in the world; the others are Huron (fifth), Michigan (sixth), Erie (12th), and Ontario (14th). In addition to these, 10 of the world's 50 largest lakes are found in Canada. The only other large North American lakes south of the Canadian border are the Great Salt Lake (43rd) in Utah, and Lake Nicaragua, or Cocibolca (22nd), which is home to the only freshwater sharks in the world.

Major deserts in North America include the Chihuahan (the world's sixth largest, which covers parts of Mexico, Texas, New Mexico, and Arizona), the Sonoran (Mexico, California, and Arizona), the Mojave (California and Arizona), the Painted Desert (Arizona), and Death Valley (California and Nevada). Death Valley is also the lowest point on the continent, 86 meters (282 feet) below sea level.

The North American mainland is also surrounded by large islands, including Greenland (the world's largest), the Canadian Arctic (which includes four of the world's 25 largest islands); on the Atlantic Ocean, Newfoundland, Long Island, the Outer Banks, and the West Indies, including Cuba (which ranks 14th) and Hispaniola (23rd); and on the Pacific Canada's Queen Charlotte Islands and the Aleutians, which extend 2,700 kilometers almost to Asia. The largest marginal seas around North America are the Caribbean Sea, the Gulf of Mexico, the Gulf of California, the Bering Sea, and Hudson Bay.

Climate   North America extends across 74° of latitude, from 9°N to 83°N, and every major climatic type is found there, from permanent ice cap in central Greenland to tropical rain forest in parts of southern Central America. The northernmost reaches of Alaska and Canada have an Arctic and sub-Arctic climate with tundra and, in central

Greenland, ice cap. Farther south the climate is mostly temperate—continental in the north, subtropical in the south—with adequate rainfall for a wide variety of crops. West of the Mississippi River, the climate is semi-arid, becoming arid in the desert areas of the southwest and northern Mexico. The climate of southern Florida, the Caribbean islands, southern Mexico, and Central America is tropical.

People   The fourth-largest continent in population, between Europe and South America, North America is home to 480,545,000 people. The United States (third) and Mexico (11th) are the only two countries in the North America that rank in the top 20 by population. Although Canada is the second-largest country in the world by area, its population is only about 10 percent larger than that of California. There are very sparsely populated areas in North America, especially in northern Canada, Alaska, and the western mountains and plains of the United States and Canada. The majority of people in United States and Canada live in urban areas, while Mexico and the countries of Central America and the Caribbean are more rural. North America includes three of the world's 25 largest urban areas: Mexico City (second largest, 2000 urban population 18.1 million); New York (fifth, 16.6 million), and Los Angeles (sixth, 13.1 million).

The major cultural regions include Central America, the island nations of the Caribbean, Mexico, the United States, and Canada. The population of Arctic and sub-Arctic regions of Alaska, Canada, and Greenland also make up a unique cultural zone.

There are 23 independent countries in North America, as well as overseas territories of France, Great Britain, the Netherlands, and the United Kingdom. There are a number of international trade organizations, including the North American Free Trade Agreement (NAFTA), composed of the United States, Canada, and Mexico), the Caribbean Community, and the Central American Common Market. In addition, all countries are members of the Organization of American States, together with the nations of South America.

The dominant languages are English (the United States, Canada, Belize, and several Caribbean nations and territories) and Spanish (Mexico, Costa Rica, El Salvador, Guatemala, Honduras, Nicaragua, and Panama, and in the Caribbean, Cuba and the Dominican Republic). About 20 million people in the United States consider Spanish their first language. French is one of two official languages in

Canada (with English) and Haiti (Creole). It is estimated that about 300,000 people still speak one of the roughly 200 Native-American languages still extant in North America as far south as Mexico and parts of Central America, and from Greenland in the east to the Aleutian Islands to the west. There are thought to be about 5 million speakers of the 70 Meso-American languages— chiefly Mayan, Uto-Aztecan, and Oto-Manguean—still in use in Central America.

Economy The United States has the world's largest and most diversified economy, and it is a leader in many fields of information technology, industry, and defense technology, although agriculture is an also important part of the economy. Canada mirrors the U.S., though on a smaller scale. The U.S. and Canada rank fifth and eighteenth, respectively, in per capita income. Together, the U.S., Canada, and Mexico produce about a third of the world's measured G.N.P., and all three number among the world's leading importing nations and exporting nations. (The U.S. ranks first in both categories.).

The five largest ports in North America are Los Angeles/Long Beach, California (fifth in the world), New Orleans (seventh), Houston (eighth), Port of New York and New Jersey (12th), and San Francisco (13th).

The United States, Canada, and Mexico are leading producers of primary energy. Canada produces more energy from hydroelectric power than any other country, while the U.S. ranks fourth, and the U.S. ranks first in production of nuclear-generated electricity, and Canada ranks eighth. North America's abundant mineral wealth includes silver, lead, zinc, aluminum, nickel, and gold. Jamaica accounts for nine percent of the world's bauxite production.

North America has extensive and productive agricultural lands. The continent produces much of the world's corn, meat, cotton, soybeans, and wheat. Farm employment in Mexico, Central America, and the Caribbean is higher than in the U.S. or Canada. Tourism is of particular importance for the countries of the Caribbean.

South America

Physical features South America is the fourth-largest continent, between North America and Antarctica, with an area of 17,819,000 square kilometers (6,880,000 square miles), and the fifth in terms of population

(346,500,000), between North America and Australia. The continent extends about 7,640 kilometers (4,750 miles) from Punta Gallinas, Colombia, south to Cape Horn, Chile, in the south. At its broadest point south of the equator, the continent extends 5,300 kilometers (3,300 miles) from east to west. South America is connected to North America by the Isthmus of Panama. It is bordered by the Caribbean Sea to the north, the Atlantic Ocean to the east, the Drake Strait of the Southern Ocean to the south, and the Pacific Ocean to the west.

The principal physical features of the continent include the South American cordillera of the Andes, a high, seismically active mountain range that extends nearly the whole length of the continent on its western side. At 7,265 meters (23,834 feet), Argentina's Aconcagua is the highest point in the Western Hemisphere. There are two main highland areas, the Guiana Highlands to the north and the Brazilian Highlands to the south of the Amazon basin. The only substantial desert is the Atacama Desert, on the Pacific Coast of northern Chile. Roughly 150 kilometers from east to west and about 1,000 kilometers from north to south, the Atacama is the driest place on Earth; in some parts, no rain has ever been recorded.

The continent's three main river systems include Orinoco, which flows north from the Guinea Highlands to the Caribbean; the Amazon, the world's largest river by volume and second-largest by length, which rises in the Peruvian Andes and flows some 6,440 kilometers (4,000 miles) to the Atlantic. Its drainage basin includes the world's largest rain forest. Farther south is the La Plata system, including the Paraguay, Paraná and Uruguay Rivers, which flow out of the Brazilian highlands to the Atlantic. Other major rivers include the Madeira and Purus, which are tributaries of the Andes, and Brazil's São Francisco and Para-Tocatins, which flow into the Atlantic. The three largest lakes are Maracaibo (18th), Patos (19th), and Titicaca (21st). The former two are lagoons, while Titicaca, on the border of Bolivia and Peru, is the highest major lake in the world, at an elevation of 3,810 meters (12,500 feet).

Climate The climate of South America is largely tropical especially in the vast region east of the Andes and extending from the Caribbean to the Tropic of Capricorn, an area dominated by the tropical rain forests of the Amazon and Orinoco drainage basins, and along the coast as far south as Ecuador. The climate of the Andean regions is characterized by cooler highland climate. The narrow lowland along the west coast tends to be dryer, the extreme being found in the Atacama Desert of northern Chile, the driest place on Earth. The south coast of Chile is characterized by a cooler, moister climate. The climate of Paraguay, Uruguay, southern Brazil, and northern Argentina is warm and moist. The climate of southern Argentina becomes drier as one moves south and west.

People   South America has 12 independent countries—Argentina, Bolivia, Brazil, Chile, Colombia, Ecuador, Guyana, Paraguay, Peru, Suriname, Uruguay, and Venezuela—while French Guiana is an overseas department of France, and the Falkland Islands (Islas Malvinas) are a dependency of the United Kingdom contested by Argentina. The ethnic composition of South American countries varies widely and reflects the degree to which Europeans and Africans assimilated with or in some cases replaced native populations. At one extreme, the people of Argentina, Chile, and Uruguay are overwhelmingly of European origin. Bolivia's population is 55 percent Indian, 30 percent mestizo, and 15 percent Indian, while Peru's population is 45 percent Indian and 37 percent mestizo, and 95 percent of Paraguayans are classified as mestizo. East Indians comprise half the population of Guyana and nearly a third that of Suriname, where another 15 percent are classified as Javanese. Slightly more than half of Brazilians are white, 38 percent mestizo, and 6 percent black, proportions that belie the heavy influence of African culture on the country.

Although there is substantial rural subsistence farming and many interior areas with few inhabitants, South America is also a heavily urbanized continent. Three of the 25 largest urban areas in the world are São Paulo, Brazil (fourth, 17.8 million), Buenos Aires, Argentina (10th, 14.1 million), and Rio de Janeiro, Brazil (18th, 11.9 million). These and other urban areas combine modern business and cultural districts with outlying districts of immigrants, usually characterized by poverty, high unemployment, and inadequate services such as water, policing, and sewage.

The primary languages of South America are Spanish (Argentina, Bolivia, Chile, Colombia, Ecuador, Paraguay, Peru, Uruguay, Venezuela) and Portuguese (Brazil). American Indian languages are official in Bolivia (Quechua and Aymara), Peru (Quechua), and Paraguay (Guarani). English is the official language of Guyana, and Dutch of Suriname, where Sranang Tongo (Surinamese or Taki-Taki), Hindustani, and Javanese are also widely spoken. An estimated 15 million people still speak the 400 or so indigenous languages still used in South America. Probably three-quarters of these speakers live in the central Andean highlands of Peru, Bolivia, and Ecuador, where the most widely spoken languages are those of the Quechumaran group, including the various Quechuan and Aymaran languages.

Economy   The economy of South America is highly varied. There are still hunter-gatherer tribes in the interior, and agriculture ranges from widespread subsistence farming to commercial farming and ranching in Argentina, Uruguay, Brazil, and elsewhere. Brazil has a significant industrial sector, and its economy has grown rapidly over the last decade, so much so that it is now one of the top 20 economies in the world. Venezuela, the only member of OPEC in the Americas, is the world's fifth largest exporter of oil and the eighth largest exporter of liquid natural gas; Argentina ranks seventh in the production of dry natural gas. South America's other mineral resources include copper, tin, iron, silver, bauxite, zinc, and gold. Brazil ranks second, after Canada, in the production of hydroelectricity. Major ports include Santos (the biggest in South America) and Rio de Janeiro, Brazil; Buenos Aires, Argentina; Cartagena, Colombia; Callao, Peru; and Curaçao, Venezuela.

The United States

The United States shares the North American continent with Canada, Mexico, and the Central American nations. (See "North America.") It is the third-largest country in the world in land area (3,717,797 sq. mi/6,629,091 km², after Russia and Canada) and the third-largest country in population (after China and India). The United States is by far the world's largest and most advanced economy, a leader in many fields of information technology, industry, and defense technology. The 48 conterminous states are bordered on the north by Canada, on the South by Mexico and the Gulf of Mexico, on the east by the Atlantic, and on the West by the Pacific. Alaska is bordered on the east by Canada, on the north by the Arctic Ocean, and on the west by the Pacific. The Hawaiian Islands lie approximately 2,400 southwest of California.

U.S. Census Geographic Divisions The United States Bureau of the Census groups the states into four geographic divisions, with nine subdivisions. These are used to define, group, and present demographic and other information.

Northeast The Northeast region includes two subdivisions: New England (Maine, New Hampshire, Vermont, Massachusetts, Rhode Island, Connecticut) and Middle Atlantic (New York, New Jersey, Pennsylvania).

Midwest The Midwest region includes two subdivisions: East North Central (Ohio, Indiana, Illinois, Michigan, Wisconsin) and West North Central (Minnesota, Iowa, Missouri, North Dakota, South Dakota, Nebraska, Kansas).

South The South region includes three divisions: South Atlantic (Delaware, Maryland, District of Columbia, Virginia, West Virginia, North Carolina, South Carolina, Georgia, Florida); East South Central (Kentucky, Tennessee, Alabama, Mississippi); and West South Central (Arkansas, Louisiana, Oklahoma, Texas).

Pacific The Pacific region includes two subdivisions: Mountain (Montana, Idaho, Wyoming, Colorado, New Mexico, Arizona, Utah, Nevada) and Pacific (Washington, Oregon, California, Alaska, Hawaii).

Geographic Distribution of Population The 2010 United States population of 308,745,538 was distributed among the four main census regions as shown in the table on the following page, which also includes total and regional population for 1980, 1990, and 2000. This table illustrates the gradual long-term geographic shift of population toward the south and west of the United States.

Urban areas and urbanization Although the parks and great open landscapes of the United States are tourist destinations, and although there are areas in the north central and western U.S. that are uninhabited or very lightly populated, the United States population is largely urban, located mostly in densely settled urban areas or suburban areas. U.S. Census definitions of urban have changed in recent censuses, so that comparison are inexact, but by 1980 the urban population was 73.7 percent of the total, by 1990 75.2 percent.

In 2000, more than 80 percent of the population lived in metropolitan areas, defined as urban counties surrounding a city with a population of at least 50,000. Remote sensing images of the United States paint a clear picture of the urban nature of the country, with dense urban belts in the Northeast Corridor, around Dallas-Fort Worth, Houston, Chicago, Phoenix, Los Angeles, and other areas, and smaller urban areas throughout much of the eastern half of the country, in settled areas in the mountain west, and along the West Coast. The fastest growing urban areas are in the west and southwest.

Geography and Physiographic Regions of the United States The broad geographic outlines of the United States begin with the beaches and lowlands of the Eastern coastal plains and the large cities of the East dating to colonial times. Further inland are the ranges of the Appalachians, important in the nation's history, in industrial development (coal) and for recreation. To the north are the Great Lakes, a key shipping route shared with Canada. The rivers flowing into the Ohio are the eastern boundary of the great Mississippi basin, which includes the fertile interior plains and the Great Plains, with a drainage area stretching all the way to the Rocky Mountains. Beyond the Rockies is the intermountain West reaching to the coastal ranges of the West Coast and the long Pacific coastline of Washington, Oregon, and California. In the Southwest are the arid areas of Arizona, New Mexico, and eastern California. Underlying this broad outline are the seven physiographic regions—the main geological features and landforms—into which the United States is divided.

Atlantic and Gulf Coast Plains These extend from the islands of southern New England, Cape Cod, and Long Island through New Jersey, Delaware, Maryland, Virginia, North Carolina, South Carolina, Georgia, Florida, Alabama, Mississippi, Louisiana, and Texas; it also includes lower Mississippi Valley in Arkansas, Missouri, and Tennessee. The Atlantic plain is narrower in the north and widens toward the south where it meets the Gulf plain.

Appalachian System The Appalachians, a system of old weathered mountains, are divided into five parts:

New England White Mountains (New Hampshire), Green Mountains (Vermont), Champlain Lowland and Hudson Valley (Vermont, New York), Catskill Mountains (New York).

The Piedmont Pennsylvania, Virginia, North Carolina, South Carolina, Georgia, Alabama.

Great Smoky and Blue Ridge Mountains Pennsylvania (Poconos), Virginia, North Carolina, Georgia.

Ridge and Valley Pennsylvania, West Virginia,

Regional populations and percentages, United States 1980–2010

Region	1980 pop.	% total	1990 pop.	% total	2000 pop.	% total	2010 pop.	% total
Northeast	49,135,283	22	50,809,299	21	53,594,378	19	55,317,240	18
Midwest	58,865,670	26	59,668,632	24	64,392,776	23	66,927,001	22
South	75,372,362	33	85,445,930	34	100,236,820	36	114,555,744	37
West	43,172,490	19	52,786,082	21	63,197,932	22	71,945,553	23
Total	**226,545,805**	**100**	**248,709,873**	**100**	**281,421,906**	**100**	**308,745,538**	**100**

Virginia, Kentucky, Tennessee, Alabama.

Appalachian Plateau Pennsylvania, Ohio, West Virginia, Kentucky, Tennessee, Alabama.

Canadian (or Laurentian) Shield This region covers much of eastern Canada and extends into the U.S. in two places: the Adirondack Mountains in New York, and Superior Upland in Upper Michigan, Wisconsin, and Minnesota.

Central Lowland The Central Lowland includes most of the U.S. interior. This area was earlier in geologic time covered by a large inland sea. The Central Lowland is divided into four parts:

Interior Lowlands Ohio, Kentucky, Tennessee.

Mississippi Great Lakes Basin Ohio, Indiana, Illinois, Michigan, Wisconsin, Iowa, North Dakota, South Dakota.

Interior Highlands Ozark Mountains (Missouri, Arkansas, Oklahoma); Ouachita Mountains (Arkansas, Oklahoma).

Great Plains North Dakota, South Dakota, Nebraska, Kansas, Oklahoma, Texas, Montana, Wyoming, Colorado, New Mexico.

Cordilleran Province This province includes the Rocky Mountain states of New Mexico, Colorado, Wyoming, and Montana. The Rocky Mountains are a geologically young range.

Intermontane Region This generally arid area of mountains, river basins, and plateaus is divided into four sections:

Colorado Plateau Colorado, Utah, New Mexico, Arizona (including Grand Canyon).

Basin and Range Plateau Nevada, Utah (including Wasatch Range).

Desert Basin and Range California (including Death Valley), Arizona.

Snake and Columbia River Basins Idaho, Washington, Oregon.

Pacific Coastlands This region is divided into four sections, three oriented north-south, the other east-west:

Cascade Mountains and Sierra Nevada: Washington, Oregon, California, Nevada.

Puget Sound, Willamette Valley, and Central Valley Washington, Oregon, California.

Coast Ranges Washington, Oregon, and California.

Los Angeles Extension Tehachapi Mountains (east west), San Gabriel Mountains, and San Bernardino Mountains.

The National Park System One of the most striking aspects of the physical and bio-geography of the United States is the extensive National Park System. This had its origin in 1872 with the establishment of the Yellowstone National Park in the Territories of Montana and Wyoming, "as a public park or pleasuring-ground for the benefit and enjoyment of the people." This is believed to be the first area in the world designated as a National Park, and it was placed under the secretary of the interior in part because no state governments were in place in the area of the park. Among the other early parks created by Congress were Sequoia, Yosemite, Mount Rainier, Crater Lake, and Glacier.

President Woodrow Wilson created the National Park Service as a bureau within the Department of the Interior in 1916, and charged it with protecting the 35 national parks and monuments then in existence. Through the 1920's the national park system was essentially a western park system, with only Acadia National Park in Maine east of the Mississippi. In 1926 Congress authorized Shenandoah, Great Smoky Mountains, and Mammoth Cave national parks, and in later decades many smaller historical sites in the east became part of the system. The U.S. National Park System now includes nearly comprises 385 areas covering more than 79 million acres (three percent of total U.S. area) in 49 states (there are no areas in Delaware), the District of Columbia, Guam, Puerto Rico, Saipan, and the Virgin

Islands. Additions to the National Park System are generally made through acts of Congress, and national parks can be created only through such acts. But under the Antiquities Act of 1906, the president has authority to proclaim national monuments on lands already under federal jurisdiction.

The diversity of the parks managed by the National Park Service (N.P.S.) is reflected in the variety of titles given to them. Although the system is best known for its scenic National Parks, more than half the areas of the National Park System preserve places, and commemorate persons, events, and activities important in the nation's history. The types of holdings in the system include at least 16 categories, from National Battlefield to Wild and Scenic River.

World Population

By early 2011, world population had reached 6.9 billion, of which more than 1.2 billion were in more developed regions and more than 5.6 billion were in less developed regions. The United Nations Population Fund (U.N.F.P.A.) estimates that world population will reach 9.3 billion by 2050.

World population grew by 76 million in 2010. That's a growth rate of 1.1 percent, down significantly from the all-time high of around 2 percent. Almost all of the increase in world population (95 percent) came in less developed regions. Six countries were responsible for half of the increase: India (21 percent), China (12 percent), Pakistan (5 percent), Bangladesh (4 percent), Nigeria (4 percent) and the United States (4 percent).

China and India both have more than a billion people (China has 1.330 billion people; India has 1.175 billion). The United States has the third-largest population with more than 308 million people, followed by Indonesia with 238 million, and Brazil with 191 million people.

By 2016, the U.N. estimates that India will have a population of 1.38 billion, which will be larger than all the more developed countries combined, that is, all the countries of Europe, including Russia, Australia, New Zealand, Japan, Canada, and the United States. It is projected that India will have a larger population than China by 2045, with a total of 1.63 billion people (compared to China's 1.43 billion).

Urbanization

The United Nations reported that in 2009 slightly more than half the world's population lived in urban areas, 3.42 billion people compared to 3.41 billion in rural areas. It was estimated that 75 percent of people in developed countries lived in urban areas compared to 45 percent in developing regions that were urban dwellers. Globally the level of urbanization is projected to increase from 50 percent urban in 2009 to 69 percent urban in 2050. At this time the world's urban population is expected reach 6.3 billion people and to comprise 86 percent of the more developed areas and 66 percent in less developed countries. Urban populations are distributed unevenly among cities in different sizes. Over half of the 3.42 billion urban dwellers (51 percent) lived in cities or towns with fewer than 500,000 people. It is projected that between 2009 and 2050 these small cities will account for 45 percent of urban growth.

Cities with fewer than 100,000 people accounted for one third of the world urban population or 1.5 billion people in 2009. Cities with 100,000 to 500,000 people had an additional 629 million people, or 18 percent of the world urban population. All cities having fewer than 500,000 people accounted for 51.9 percent of urban population. In 2009, there were 21 megacities, each having at least 10 million inhabitants and accounted for 9.4 percent of world urban population. The number of megacities is forecast to increase to 29 by 2025 when they will hold 10.3 percent of world urban dwellers. In 2009 about one in every 20 people on earth lived in a megacity. In 1975 there were just three megacities, New York, Tokyo and Mexico City. Today Asia has 11 megacities, Latin America has four, and Africa, Europe and Northern America have two each.

Currently, Tokyo is the largest urban agglomeration with 36.5 million people in 2009, which is more people than 196 countries or areas. Tokyo, the megacity, actually comprises Tokyo and 87 surrounding cities and towns. Delhi, India with 22 million is the next largest urban agglomeration, followed by São Paulo and Bombay, each with 20 million, and Mexico City and New York-Newark with 19 million each.

The number of rural dwellers, 3.41 billion in mid-2009, is expected to reach its maximum of 3.5 billion in 2020, and to then slowly decline to 2.9 billion in 2050. Declining populations will also create a decline in urban dwellers in a number of countries, with the largest decreases between 2009 and 2025 projected to be in

World's Largest Countries, by Population, 2009–20

2009 Rank, Country	Population	Percent of Total	2020 Rank, Country	Population	Percent of Total
1. China	1,345,751,000	19.71%	1. China	1,431,155,000	18.65%
2. India	1,198,003,000	17.54	2. India	1,367,225,000	17.81
3. United States	314,659,000	4.61	3. United States	346,153,000	4.51
4. Indonesia	229,965,000	3.37	4. Indonesia	254,218,000	3.31
5. Brazil	193,734,000	2.84	5. Pakistan	226,187,000	2.95
6. Pakistan	180,808,000	2.65	6. Brazil	209,051,000	2.72
7. Bangladesh	162,221,000	2.38	7. Nigeria	193,252,000	2.52
8. Nigeria	154,729,000	2.27	8. Bangladesh	185,552,000	2.42
9. Russia	140,874,000	2.06	9. Russia	135,406,000	1.76
10. Japan	127,156,000	1.86	10. Japan	123,664,000	1.61
11. Mexico	109,610,000	1.60	11. Mexico	119,682,000	1.56
12. Philippines	91,983,000	1.35	12. Philippines	109,683,000	1.43
13. Vietnam	88,069,000	1.29	13. Ethiopia	107,964,000	1.41
14. Egypt	82,999,000	1.22	14. Egypt	98,638,000	1.29
15. Ethiopia	82,825,000	1.21	15. Vietnam	98,011,000	1.28
16. Germany	82,167,000	1.20	16. Congo, Dem. Rep.	87,640,000	1.14
17. Turkey	74,816,000	1.10	17. Turkey	83,873,000	1.09
18. Iran	74,196,000	1.09	18. Iran	83,740,000	1.09
19. Thailand	68,000,000	0.99	19. Germany	80,422,308	1.04
20. Congo, Dem Rep	66,020,000	0.97	20. Thailand	71,443,041	0.93

Source: United Nations, Department of Economic and Social Affairs, Population Division. *World Population Prospects: The 2008 Revision extract from DEMOBASE*, July 2009.

Russia with a decrease of three million and Ukraine with a decrease of 700,000 urban dwellers.

1950–2050: Trends

In 1798 Thomas Malthus (England, 1766–1834) presented his famous theory of population: that the human population grows geometrically, but food supply only arithmetically. Therefore, Malthus held, population will inevitably outstrip food supply and would be kept in check by war, famine, disease, human vice, and the preventive influence of "moral restraint." But the rapid growth of the human species over the last two centuries suggests that Malthus's theory greatly underestimated the effects of technological change, increases in food production, and advances in health in providing for an enormous growth in world population. Although prospects are for a still larger population by the mid-21st century, changing human aspirations and control over fertility have resulted in steadily decreasing rates of population growth, and a relatively stable (or even declining) future population is possible.

Population and Projections   Expectations about world population growth during the period since World War II have changed dramatically several times. After the war, world population projections underestimated growth: one respected 1949 projection was for a world total population of 3.48 billion in 1990; the actual figure was 5.3 billion. These underestimates resulted from the way the demographic transition unfolded. The demographic transition has four stages: 1) high death and birth rates; 2) a drop in death rates; 3) a subsequent drop in birth rates; and 4) death and birth rates at low (and balanced) levels. After World War II, death rates fell more rapidly than expected from widespread improvements in public health measures such as vaccinations and sanitary facilities, but birth rates took a longer time to decline. Thus rates of population growth increased.

The population growth rate peaked between 1965 and 1970 at about 2 percent per year; at that rate, the 1970 population of 3.7 billion would have grown to 7.7 billion in 2007, instead of the actual 6.7 billion—1 billion people less than predicted. Population forecasts made in the late 1960's and early 1970's reflected this peak world population growth rate. Some observers foresaw hundreds of millions of deaths from population growth combined with food shortages, a Malthusian disaster. But these worries were overstated: fertility rates (the average number of children per woman aged 15 to 44) and population growth rates began to decline between 1965 and 1970, a turning point in modern history, and the "Green Revolution" in agriculture—dramatic increases in grain yields in developing nations from genetically-improved plant varieties—exerted its full effect. So although the "population bomb" was not as large as feared in the late 1960's and early 1970's, the total expected increase in world population before the completion of the demographic transition will still place enormous burdens on world resources and the environment. (See "Global Food Supply.")

Births and Deaths Underlying the modern trends in population growth is the relationship between birth and death rates. Demographic figures for the last half of the 20th century show a decline in the global birth rate from about 36 per thousand in 1955–59 to about 19.3 per thousand in 2010, and a decline in the death rate from 19 per thousand annually in 1955–59 to about 8.2 per thousand in 2010. Thus, population continues to increase as a function of a positive reproductive change (birth rate exceeding death rate), aided by dramatic declines in infant mortality, but the rate of increase has fallen with a narrowing of the gap between rates.

The last half of the 20th century witnessed global slowdowns in death rate, birth rate, fertility, and infant mortality, largely due to changes in the world's less developed countries.

Decreases for those regions outstripped those for the industrial world in every statistical category, albeit from higher starting levels. The global declines are expected continue for at least the next half-century, with the less developed nations continuing to drive the trend.

Factors Affecting Birth and Death Rates. The main factors affecting birth rates in modern times are individual choices, economic development, technology, and public policy. The widespread reduction in desired family size has been a product of the education and empowerment of women, the increasingly attainable possibility of an economically rewarding life for parents and children alike, and the availability of birth control information and technology.

Aggressive public policy has also been an important variable in many countries. There has been a substantial range of programs, both locally- and externally-sponsored, to provide for women's and children's health and contraceptives. Such programs have contributed to long-run declines in fertility as people have chosen fewer but healthier children. In a few cases, notably China, public policy has not just made the technology of birth control available, but has been highly coercive in limiting births, including forced abortions. A negative consequence of individual attitudes and public policy in some countries, such as India and China, has been "missing girls:" gender-selective abortion and even infanticide have resulted in a deficit of girls compared to boys.

Death rates, which are expected to continue to decline overall, are reduced by better nutrition and public health programs, but can be increased by economic, agricultural and military disasters and epidemics. For example, droughts, poor harvests, and policy failures have resulted in deaths from starvation in some regions, including North Korea and Ethiopia. The AIDS epidemic, which in the early years of the 21st century hit hardest in Africa, has increased death rates in many areas enough to affect populations both now and for decades to come.

Reflecting the net effect of all of these influences on birth and death rates, the general trend in both population growth rates and population forecasts over the last years of the 20th century has been downward. For example, the U.N.'s 1992 medium forecast for world population in 2050 was 10.0 billion; the 2000 forecast for 2050 was 9.3 billion; and the most recent medium forecast, made in 2009, is for 2050 world population of 9.3 billion. This forecast reflects further drops in fertility rates in the developing world as well as high impacts from the AIDS epidemic.

Infant Mortality Dramatic changes in the world's vital statistics include the decline in infant mortality and increase in life expectancy—both a function of medical progress and the spread of public health facilities. For the world as a whole, infant mortality fell from an estimated 148 per thousand births in 1955 to 47 per thousand in 2005–10. A further drop, to about 23.4 deaths per thousand, is projected for the period 2045–50.

The ongoing decline in infant mortality has contributed to a remarkable extension of the average human lifetime. In the last half-century alone, life expectancy at birth for the world's population has risen nearly 20

The World's Largest Urban Areas, 1950–2015

2010 Rank, Urban area	Population (millions)						Rank	
	1950	1970	1990	2000	2010	2015	1950	2015
1. Tokyo, Japan	11.3	23.3	32.5	34.5	36.7	36.2	2	1
2. Delhi, India	N.A.	3.5	8.2	12.4	22.2	20.9	N.A.	3
3. São Paolo, Brazil	2.3	7.6	14.8	17.1	20.3	20.0	27	5
4. Mumbai (Bombay), India	3.0	6.2	12.3	16.1	20.0	22.6	17	2
5. Mexico City, Mexico	3.0	8.8	15.3	18.1	19.5	20.6	20	4
6. New York–Newark, U.S.	12.3	16.2	16.1	17.8	19.4	19.7	1	6
7. Shanghai, China	5.3	11.2	13.3	12.9	16.6	12.7	6	15
8. Calcutta, India	4.4	6.9	10.9	13.1	15.6	16.8	10	10
9. Dhaka, Bangladesh	N.A.	N.A.	6.5	10.2	14.7	17.9	N.A.	7
10. Karachi, Pakistan	N.A.	3.9	7.1	10.0	13.1	16.2	N.A.	11
11. Buenos, Aires, Argentina	5.0	8.4	11.2	12.6	13.0	14.6	8	12
12. Los Angeles–Long Beach, U.S.	4.0	8.4	10.9	11.8	12.8	12.9	12	14
13. Metro Manila, Philippines	N.A.	3.5	8.0	9.9	12.6	12.6	N.A.	16
14. Beijing, China	3.9	8.1	10.8	10.8	12.4	11.1	13	20
15. Rio de Janeiro, Brazil	3.0	6.6	9.6	10.4	12.0	12.4	18	17
16. Osaka–Kobe, Japan	4.1	9.4	11.0	11.2	11.3	11.4	11	18
17. Cairo, Egypt	2.4	5.6	9.1	10.4	11.0	13.1	24	13
18. Lagos, Nigeria	N.A.	N.A.	N.A.	8.7	10.6	17.0	N.A.	9
19. Moscow, Russia	5.4	7.1	9.1	10.9	10.6	10.9	5	21
20. Istanbul, Turkey	N.A.	N.A.	6.6	8.7	10.5	11.3	N.A.	19
21. Paris, France	5.4	8.4	9.3	9.7	10.5	10.0	4	22
22. Seoul, South Korea	N.A.	5.3	10.5	9.9	9.8	9.2	N.A.	26
23. Tianjin, China	2.4	5.2	8.8	9.2	9.4	11.3	26	19
24. Jakarta, Indonesia	N.A.	3.9	7.7	11.0	9.2	17.5	N.A.	8
25. Chicago, U.S.	5.0	7.1	7.4	8.3	9.2	9.4	9	24

Note: An urban area is a central city or central cities, and the surrounding urbanized areas, also called a metropolitan area. 1. Projected. **Source:** United Nations Population Division, *World Urbanization Prospects: The 2009 Revision* (2009).

World Births, Deaths and Population Growth, 2010

Characteristic	World	Developed	Developing
Population	6,853,019,414	1,231,105,689	5,621,913,725
Births	132,397,533	13,482,444	111,915,090
Deaths	56,167,829	12,820,127	43,347,702
Natural increase	76,229,704	662,316	75,567,388
Births per 1,000 population	19.3	11.0	21.2
Deaths per 1,000 population	8.2	10.4	7.7
Rate of natural increase (percent)	1.1%	0.05%	1.3%

Source: U.S. Bureau of the Census, International Data Base (2010).

years—from about 48 in 1955 to an estimated 68 in 2005–10. By the year 2050, according to U.N. forecasts, another 10 years will be added to the average life span. Life expectancy in less developed regions lags that in more developed regions, but the gap is closing. Women generally outlive men by 3–7 years.

The Aging Population Among the most prominent trends in contemporary demography is the aging of the world's population. The rapid increase in life expectancy and a spike in fertility among developed nations in the two decades after World War II—the "Baby Boom"— yielded an overall rise in the median age from 23.9 to 29.1 between 1950 and 2010. From the middle to the end of the 20th century, the percentage of the world's population aged 60 or over climbed from 8 percent to 10 percent. Demographers expect the aging trend to become even more pronounced during the first half of the 21st century, as the rate of population growth slows and the statistical "bubble" of previous decades moves through higher age categories—and as life expectancy continues to increase. By 2050, the median age is projected to jump nearly ten years, reaching 38.4. The percentage of people aged 60 and over, meanwhile, is expected to double from 2005 to 2050, from 11.6 percent to 22 percent. These changes in age structure are expected to be especially striking, and to have important economic and social consequences, in countries like China, which has had strict birth control policies. In 2050, the U.N. projects that 31 percent of the population of China will be 60 and over, and only 15.3 percent 14 years and under.

HIV/AIDS A conspicuous exception to the projected increase in life expectancy is the HIV/AIDS pandemic. The U.N. estimates that the annual number of "excess deaths" (beyond those due to non-HIV/AIDS causes) will peak between 2020 and 2025 at nearly 8 million globally. The countries of sub-Saharan Africa have been the hardest-hit by the disease. In 2007, sub-Saharan Africa, which has just over 10 percent of world population, had about 67 percent of the world's people living with HIV. In much of the area a substantial fraction of the population—ranging up to more than 20 percent in a few countries—is infected by the virus. During 2007, an estimated 2.7 million people were newly infected with HIV (370,000 were children) and 2 million people died from AIDS (490,000 were children).

Developed and Less Developed Nations Comparative statistics show that the population of less developed countries is growing much faster than that of more developed nations—216 percent vs. 50 percent from 1950 to 2007, and a projected 46 percent vs. 2 percent from 2007 to 2050. As a result, the proportion of total world population represented by less developed countries rose from 68 percent in 1950 to 82 percent in 2007, and is expected to reach 86 percent by 2050. At the same time, however, the rate of growth in less developed countries is falling more rapidly than in the industrialized world, contributing more substantially to the global deceleration. Technology has come later to the developing world; the decline phase in its growth rate is catching up with that of the industrialized world, which peaked many decades earlier.

Oceans

The water of the world's oceans covers more than 70 percent of the world's surface. While for most of the 20th century the so-called World Ocean was divided into the Pacific, Atlantic, Indian, and Arctic Oceans, a decision by the International Hydrographic Organization in 2000 delimited a fifth ocean, the Southern Ocean, extending from 60 degrees south latitude to the coast of Antarctica.

Arctic Ocean northern polar sea between North America, Asia, and Europe; fifth-largest ocean.

Atlantic Ocean second-largest ocean, between South America, North America, Europe, and Africa.

Indian Ocean third-largest ocean, between Africa, Asia, and Australia.

Pacific Ocean largest ocean, between Australia, Asia, North America, and South America.

Southern Ocean fourth-largest ocean, south of the Antarctic Circle (66°30'S); completely encircles Antarctica.

U.N. Forecasts 10.1 Billion People by Century's End

By JUSTIN GILLIS and CELIA W. DUGGER

The population of the world, long expected to stabilize just above 9 billion in the middle of the century, will instead keep growing and may hit 10.1 billion by the year 2100. The projections were made by the United Nations population division, which has a track record of fairly accurate forecasts. In the new report, the division raised its forecast for the year 2050, estimating that the world would most likely have 9.3 billion people then, an increase of 156 million over the previous estimate for that year, published in 2008.

Among the factors behind the upward revisions is that fertility is not declining as rapidly as expected in some poor countries, and has shown a slight increase in many wealthier countries, including the United States, Britain and Denmark. Growth in Africa remains so high that the population there could more than triple in this century, rising from today's one billion to 3.6 billion, the report said—a sobering forecast for a continent already struggling to provide food and water for its people.

The new report comes just ahead of a demographic milestone, with the world population expected to pass 7 billion in late 2011, only a dozen years after it surpassed 6 billion. Demographers called the new projections a reminder that a problem that helped define global politics in the 20th century, the population explosion, is far from solved in the 21st.

The director of the United Nations population division, Hania Zlotnik, said the world's fastest-growing countries, and the wealthy Western nations that help finance their development, face a choice about whether to renew their emphasis on programs that encourage family planning.

Though they were a major focus of development policy in the 1970's and 1980's, such programs have stagnated in many countries, caught up in ideological battles over abortion, sex education and the role of women in society. Conservatives have attacked such programs as government meddling in private decisions, and in some countries, Catholic groups fought widespread availability of birth control. And some feminists called for less focus on population control and more on empowering women.

Over the past decade, foreign aid to pay for contraceptives—$238 million in 2009—has barely budged, according to United Nations estimates. The United States has long been the biggest donor, but the budget compromise in Congress cut international family planning programs by 5 percent.

In Nigeria, the most populous country in Africa, the report projects that population will rise from today's 162 million to 730 million by 2100. Malawi, a country of 15 million today, could grow to 129 million, the report projected.

The implicit, and possibly questionable, assumption behind these numbers is that food and water will be available for the billions yet unborn, and that potential catastrophes including climate change, wars or epidemics will not serve as a brake on population growth.

One message from the new report is that the AIDS epidemic, devastating as it has been, has not been the demographic disaster that was once predicted. Prevalence estimates and projections for the human immunodeficiency virus in Africa in the 1990's turned out to be too high, and in many populations, treatment with new drug regimens has cut the death rate from the disease.

But the survival of millions of people with AIDS who would have died without treatment, and falling rates of infant and child mortality—both heartening trends—also mean that fertility rates for women need to fall faster to curb population growth, demographers said.

Other factors have slowed change in Africa, experts said, including women's lack of power in their relationships with men, traditions like early marriage and polygamy, and a dearth of political leadership. While about three-quarters of married American women use a modern contraceptive, the comparable proportions are a quarter of women in East Africa, one in 10 in West Africa, and a mere 7 percent in Central Africa, according to United Nations statistics.

The new report suggests that China, which has for decades enforced restrictive population policies, could soon enter the ranks of countries with declining populations, peaking at 1.4 billion in the next couple of decades, then falling to 941 million by 2100.

The United States is growing faster than many rich countries, largely because of high immigration and higher fertility among Hispanic immigrants. The new report projects that the United States population will rise from today's 311 million to 478 million by 2100.

The Oceans of the World

Ocean	Area	Coastline	Deepest Pt.
Arctic	14.056 mil sq km 5.427 mil sq miles *slightly less than 1.5x the size of U.S.*	45,389 km 28,203 miles	4,665 m (Fram Basin) 15,305 ft
Atlantic	76.762 mil sq km 29.638 mil sq miles *slightly less than 6.5x the size of U.S.*	111,866 km 69,510 miles	8,605 m (Milwakee Deep, Puerto Rico Trench) 28,232 ft
Indian	68.556 mil sq km 26.47 mil sq miles *about 5.5x the size of U.S.*	66,526 km 41,337 miles	7,258 m (Java Trench) 23,812 ft
Pacific	155.557 mil sq km 60.061 mil sq miles *about 15x the size of U.S.; covers roughly 28 percent of global surface; larger than total land area of the planet*	135,663 km 84,297 miles	10,924 m (Challenger Deep in the Mariana Trench) 35,840 ft
Southern	20.327 mil sq km 7.848 mil sq miles *slightly more than 2x the size of U.S.*	17,968 km 11,165 miles	7,235 m (S. end of South Sandwich Trench) 23,737 ft

Note: Conversions to miles and feet have been rounded. **Source:** *The CIA World Factbook, 2007*

Second-order submarine features of the oceans include *continental shelves, abyssal plains, mid-ocean ridges,* and *trenches.* Continental shelves generally slope gently away from the shore to a depth of about 600 feet (183 meters). The seafloor then turns sharply down a continental slope to the abyssal plain, or sea floor. In the middle of the oceans there are typically mid-ocean ridges, which occur where the ocean crust is slowly separating and molten magma seeps to the surface and hardens. The global mid-ocean ridge runs north to south through the Arctic and Atlantic Oceans, the Indian Ocean, the South Pacific, and north to North America. In the Pacific, the western part of the ocean floor includes mountain arcs that rise above sea level as island groups (such as the Solomons and New Zealand). Ocean trenches, the deepest of which are at the outer margins of the western Pacific continental shelf, form where tectonic plates meet and one edge is driven under the other. (For information on ocean pollution, see "The Environment.")

Major Seas, Gulfs, and Straits of the World

Other large bodies of water such as the Caribbean Sea, the Gulf of Mexico, Hudson Bay, the Mediterranean and Black Seas, and the South China Sea are termed marginal seas. The International Hydrographic Organization identifies 66 seas, gulfs, bays, bights, straits, channels, and passages, many of which are further subdivided. For instance, the Mediterranean Sea is divided into western and eastern basins, and the western basin is subdivided into the Strait of Gibraltar, Aboran Sea, Balearic Sea, Ligurian Sea, Tyrrhenian Sea, Ionian Sea, Adriatic Sea, and Aegean Sea.

Aden, Gulf of arm of western Indian Ocean between Yemen and Somalia.

Adriatic Sea arm of Mediterranean between Italy, Croatia, Bosnia and Herzegovina, Serbia and Montenegro, and Albania.

Aegean Sea arm of Mediterranean between Greece and Turkey.

Alaska, Gulf of arm of Pacific off southeast coast of Alaska.

Albemarle Sound inlet of Atlantic between North Carolina and Outer Banks.

Amundsen Sea part of Southern Ocean off Marie Byrd Land, Antarctica.

Anadyrskiy Zaliv (Anadyr Gulf) arm of Bering Sea off northeast Russia.

Andaman Sea arm of Indian Ocean between Andaman Islands, Myanmar, Malaysia, and Indonesia.

Aqaba, Gulf of arm of the Red Sea between Egypt, Israel, Jordan, and Saudi Arabia.

Arabian Sea arm of Indian Ocean between Oman, Iran, Pakistan, and India.

Arafura Sea arm of Indian Ocean between East Timor, Indonesia, New Guinea, and Australia.

Aral Sea landlocked Asian sea between Kazakhstan and Uzbekistan.

Azov, Sea of small sea north of Black Sea between Ukraine and Russia.

Bab el Mandeb passage from Red Sea to Indian Ocean (Gulf of Aden) between Djibouti and Yemen.

Baffin Bay arm of Arctic Ocean between Baffin Is. and Greenland.

Bali Sea Indonesian sea between Java and Bali.

Baltic Sea nearly enclosed European sea between Denmark, Sweden, Finland, Russia, Estonia, Latvia, Lithuania, Poland, and Germany.

Banda Sea Indonesian sea between Timor, Celebes, and Seram Islands.

Barents Sea arm of Arctic Ocean between Norway, Spitsbergen, Novaya Zemlya, and Russia.

Bass Strait passage from Indian Ocean to Tasman Sea between Australia and Tasmania.

Beaufort Sea arm of Arctic Ocean off coast of Alaska and Canada.

Belle Isle, Strait of passage from Atlantic to Gulf of St. Lawrence between Labrador and Newfoundland.

Bellingshausen Sea part of Southern Ocean west of Antarctic Peninsula.

Bengal, Bay of arm of Indian Ocean between by India, Bangladesh, Myanmar, and Sri Lanka.

Berau, Gulf of arm of Seram Sea in western New Guinea.

Bering Sea arm of Pacific Ocean between Russia, Alaska, and Aleutian Is.

Bering Strait passage from Pacific to Bering Sea between Russia and Alaska.

Biscay, Bay of arm of Atlantic between Spain and France.

Bismarck Sea arm of Pacific between Bismarck Archipelago, and New Guinea.

Black Sea nearly enclosed sea between Turkey, Bulgaria, Romania, Ukraine, Russia, and Georgia, with outlet to Aegean via Bosporus.

Bo Hai (Gulf of Chihli) arm of Yellow Sea between Shandong and Liadong Peninsulas.

Bosporus Turkish strait from Black Sea and Sea of Marmara.

Bothnia, Gulf of arm of Baltic Sea between Sweden and Finland.

Bristol Channel arm of Celtic Sea in southwest England between England and Wales.

Cabot Strait passage from Atlantic to Gulf of St. Lawrence between Nova Scotia and Newfoundland.

California, Gulf of arm of Pacific in northwest Mexico.

Campeche, Bay of southwest arm of Gulf of Mexico on Mexican coast.

Canso, Strait of passage from Atlantic to Gulf of St. Lawrence between mainland Nova Scotia and Cape Breton Is.

Cape Cod Bay arm of Massachusetts Bay.

Caribbean Sea arm of Atlantic Ocean between Panama, Costa Rica, Nicaragua, Honduras, Guatemala, Mexico, West Indies, Venezuela, and Colombia.

Carpentaria, Gulf of Australian arm of Indian Ocean between Arnhem Land and Cape York Peninsula.

Caspian Sea central Asian sea between Azerbaijan, Russia, Kazakhstan, Turkmenistan, and Iran.

Celebes (Sulawesi) Sea Indonesian sea between Celebes, Kalimantan (Borneo), and Philippines.

Celtic Sea arm of Atlantic south of Ireland and England.

Chesapeake Bay inlet of Atlantic between Maryland and Virginia.

Chukchi Sea arm of Arctic Ocean between Siberia and Alaska.

Cook Strait passage from Pacific to Tasman Sea between North and South Is. of New Zealand.

Coral Sea arm of Pacific between Australia, Papua New Guinea, Solomon Islands, Vanuatu, and New Caledonia.

Dardanelles Turkish strait from Aegean to Sea of Marmara.

Davis Strait passage from Labrador Sea to Baffin Bay between Baffin Is. and Greenland.

Delaware Bay inlet of Atlantic between New Jersey and Delaware.

Denmark Strait passage from Atlantic to Norwegian Sea between Greenland and Iceland.

Dover, Strait of passage from English Channel to North Sea between Great Britain and France.

Drake Passage broad passage from Atlantic to Pacific south of South America.

East China Sea (Dong Hai) arm of Pacific between Taiwan, China, South Korea, and Japan.

East Sea (Sea of Japan) sea between South and North Korea, China, Russia, and Japan.

East Siberian Sea arm of Arctic Ocean between Siberia and New Siberian Islands.

English Channel arm of Atlantic between England and France

Finland, Gulf of arm of Baltic between Finland, Russia, Lithuania, Latvia, and Estonia.

Flores Sea Indonesian sea between Flores and Celebes.

Florida, Straits of passage from Gulf of Mexico to Atlantic between Florida and Cuba.

Foxe Basin arm of Hudson Bay between Nunavut and Baffin Is.

Fundy, Bay of arm of Atlantic between Maine, New Brunswick, and Nova Scotia; has greatest tidal ranges (16 m/53 ft.) in the world.

Galveston Bay inlet of Gulf of Mexico on coast of Texas.

Gibraltar, Strait of passage from Atlantic to Mediterranean between Morocco and Spain.

Great Australian Bight arm of Indian Ocean, off south coast of Western Australia.

Greenland Sea arm of Arctic Ocean between Greenland and Spitsbergen.

Guayaquil, Gulf of arm of Pacific off coast of Ecuador.

Guinea, Gulf of arm of Atlantic between Ghana, Togo, Benin, Nigeria, Cameroon, Equatorial Guinea, and Gabon.

Hecate Strait passage between Queen Charlotte Is. and British Columbia.

Hormuz, Strait of passage from Persian Gulf to Gulf of Oman between Oman and Iran.

Huang Hai (Yellow Sea) arm of East China Sea between China and Korean Peninsula.

Hudson Bay Canadian Bay between Ontario, Manitoba, Nunavut, and Quebec.

Hudson Strait passage from Labrador Sea to Hudson Bay.

Inland Sea (Seto Naikai) Japanese sea between Kyushu, Honshu, and Shikoku Is.

Ionian Sea arm of Mediterranean between Italy and Greece.

Irish Sea arm of Atlantic between Ireland and England.

James Bay arm of Hudson Bay between Ontario and Quebec.

Japan, Sea of see *East Sea*.

Java Sea arm of South China Sea between Sumatra, Borneo, and Java.

Juan de Fuca Strait passage from Pacific to Puget Sound between Washington and Vancouver Is.

Kara Sea arm of Arctic Ocean between Russia, Novaya Zemlya, and Severnaya Zemlya.

Kattegat passage from Skagerak and Baltic to Denmark and Sweden.

Korea Strait (Strait of Tsushima) passage from East China to East Seas between South Korea and Japan.

La Perouse Strait passage from Sea of Okhotsk to East Sea between Hokkaido and Sakhalin Is.

Labrador Sea arm of Atlantic between Labrador, Baffin Island, and Greenland.

Laguna Madre inlet of Gulf of Mexico between Texas and Padre Is.

Laptev Sea arm of Arctic Ocean west of Novosibirskiye Ostrova (New Siberian Is.).

Leyte Gulf Philippines gulf between Samar and Leyte.

Liaodong Wan (Gulf) arm of Bo Hai.

Ligurian Sea arm of Mediterranean between Corsica, France, and Italy.

Lincoln Sea arm of Arctic Ocean between Ellesmere Is. and Greenland.

Lion, Gulf of arm of Mediterranean off southern France.

Lombok Strait passage from Indian Ocean to Java Sea between Bali and Lombok Is.

Long Island Sound passage from Atlantic to New York Harbor between Connecticut, Rhode Island, and Long Is.

Luzon Strait broad passage from Pacific to South China Sea between Taiwan and Philippines.

Magellan, Strait of passage from Atlantic to Pacific

between Chile and Tierra del Fuego.

Maine, Gulf of arm of Atlantic between Massachusetts, New Hampshire, Maine, New Brunswick, and Nova Scotia.

Makassar Strait Indonesian strait between Java and Celebes Seas between Kalimantan (Borneo) and Celebes.

Malacca, Strait of main passage from Indian Ocean to South China Sea between Indonesia (Sumatra), Malaysia, and Singapore.

Mannar, Gulf of arm of Indian Ocean between India and Sri Lanka.

Marmara, Sea of nearly enclosed Turkish sea, with outlets to Aegean via Dardanelles and Black Sea via Bosporus.

Massachusetts Bay arm of Atlantic off Massachusetts.

Matagorda Bay inlet of Gulf of Mexico on Texas coast.

Mediterranean Sea marginal sea of the Atlantic between Africa, Europe and Asia, with outlets to Atlantic via Strait of Gibraltar, Black Sea via Bosporus, and Red Sea via Suez Canal.

Melaku (Halmahera) Sea Indonesian arm of Pacific between Celebes and Halmahera.

Mexico, Gulf of arm of Atlantic Ocean between Mexico, Texas, Louisiana, Mississippi, Alabama, Florida, and Cuba.

Mobile Bay inlet of Gulf of Mexico in Alabama.

Mona Passage passage from Atlantic to Caribbean between Puerto Rico and Dominican Republic.

Mozambique Channel Indian Ocean passage between Mozambique, Comoros, and Madagascar.

Nantucket Sound arm of Atlantic between Nantucket, Martha's Vineyard, and Cape Cod.

Nares Strait Arctic passage from Baffin Bay and Lincoln Sea.

New Georgia Sound Solomon Is. arm of the Pacific west of Guadalcanal; also known as "The Slot" and "Ironbottom Sound."

North Sea arm of the Atlantic between Great Britain, Norway, Denmark, Germany, Netherland, and Belgium.

Northern Sea Route east-west Arctic passage between Atlantic and Pacific across top of Norway and Russia; first west-east transit, 1878–79.

Northumberland Strait Gulf of St. Lawrence Passage from Nova Scotia and Prince Edward Is.

Northwest Passage east-west Arctic passage between Atlantic to Pacific across top of Canada and U.S.; first east-west transit 1904–06; first west-east transit, 1941–42.

Norwegian Sea arm of Atlantic and Arctic Oceans between Norway and Iceland.

Okhotsk, Sea of arm of northwest Pacific between Sakhalin Is., Siberia, Kamchatka Peninsula, and Kurile Is.

Oman, Gulf of arm of Indian Ocean bordered by Oman, United Arab Emirates, and Iran.

Oresund passage from Kattegat to Baltic between Denmark and Sweden.

Palk Strait passage from Bay of Bengal to Gulf of Mannar between India and Sri Lanka; maximum draft is 4 meters.

Pamlico Sound inlet of Atlantic between North Carolina and Outer Banks.

Panama, Gulf of arm of Pacific on south coast of Panama.

Persian Gulf arm of Indian Ocean between United Arab Emirates, Saudi Arabia, Qatar, Bahrain, Kuwait, Iraq, and Iran.

Philippine Sea arm of Pacific between Philippines, Northern Marianas, Micronesia (Caroline Islands), and Palau.

Plata, Rio de la arm of the Atlantic between Argentina and Uruguay.

Red Sea arm of Indian Ocean between Djibouti, Eritrea, Sudan, Egypt, Israel, Jordan, Saudi Arabia, and Yemen.

Ross Sea arm of Southern Ocean off Ross Ice Shelf, Antarctica.

St. Georges Channel passage from Celtic Sea and Irish Sea.

St. Lawrence, Gulf of Canadian arm of the Atlantic between New Brunswick, Quebec, Newfoundland, Nova Scotia, and Prince Edward Is.

Sakhalinskiy Zaliv arm of Sea of Okhotsk between Russia and Sakhalin Is.

San Bernardino Strait Philippines passage between Luzon and Samar.

San Jorge, Golfo arm of Atlantic off southern Argentina.

San Matias, Golfo arm of Atlantic off southern Argentina.

Savu Sea (Sawu Sea) Indonesian sea between Sumba, Flores, and Timor.

Scotia Sea arm of Southern Ocean east of Drake Passage between South Georgia, South Sandwich, and South Orkney Is.

Seram (Ceram) Sea Indonesian sea between Seram, Halmahera, and New Guinea.

Shelikhova, Zaliv (Shelikhova Bay) arm of Sea of Okhotsk between Siberia and Kamchatka Peninsula.

Sibuyan Sea Philippine sea between Panay, Mindoro, and Luzon.

Sicily, Strait of east-west Mediterranean passage between Sicily and Tunisia.

Singapore Strait passage from Malacca Strait to South China Sea between Malay Peninsula and Singapore.

Skaggerak strait between North and Baltic Seas between Denmark and Norway.

Solomon Sea arm of Pacific between Papua New Guinea and Solomon Islands.

South China Sea (Nan Hai) arm of Pacific between China, Philippines, Malaysia, Brunei, Indonesia, Singapore, Thailand, Cambodia, and Vietnam.

Spencer Gulf inlet of Indian Ocean between South Australia and Kangaroo Is.

Suez Canal Egyptian canal between Mediterranean Sea and Red Sea.

Suez, Gulf of arm of Red Sea bounded entirely by Egypt, with access to Mediterranean via Suez Canal.

Sulu Sea nearly enclosed sea between Borneo (Malaysia) and Philippine islands of Palawan, Panay, Negros, Mindanao, and Sulu Archipelago.

Sunda Strait passage from Indian Ocean to Java Sea between Sumatra and Java.

Surigao Strait Philippines passage from Pacific to Sulu Sea between Leyte and Mindanao.

Taiwan (Formosa) Strait passage from South China to East China Sea between China and Taiwan.

Tasman Sea arm of Pacific between Australia and New Zealand.

Tatarskiy Proliv (Tatar Strait) passage from East Sea to Sea of Okhotsk between Russia and Sakhalin Is.

Teluk Bone (Gulf of Bone) arm of Banda Sea in southern Celebes.

Teluk Tomini (Gulf of Tomini) arm of Melaku Sea in northern Celebes.

Thailand, Gulf of arm of South China Sea between Thailand and Cambodia.

Timor Sea arm of Indian Ocean between East Timor and Australia.

Tongking, Gulf of arm of South China Sea between Vietnam and Hainan Island, China.

Torres Strait passage from Pacific Ocean to Arafura Sea between Papua New Guinea and Australia.

Tsushima, Strait of see *Korea Strait*.

Tyrrhenian Sea part of Mediterranean between Sardinia, Corsica, Italy, and Sicily.

Venezuela, Gulf of arm of Caribbean in western Venezuela.

Weddell Sea part of Southern Ocean east of Antarctic Peninsula.

White Sea arm of Arctic Ocean in northwest Russia.

Windward Passage passage from Atlantic to Caribbean between Cuba and Haiti.

Yellow Sea see *Huang Hai*.

Yucatán Channel passage from Caribbean to Gulf of Mexico between Mexico and Cuba.

Rivers and Canals of the World

Amazon 4,007 mi. (6,448 km). World's largest river by volume and second-largest in length rises in Peruvian Andes as Marañón River and flows through Brazil to Atlantic.

Amu Darya (Oxus) 1,578 mi. (2,541 km). Rises in Tajikistan and flows through or borders Afghanistan, Turkmenistan, and Uzbekistan to Aral Sea.

Amur (Heilong Jiang) 2,705 mi. (4,355 km). Formed by confluence of Silka and Argun Rivers on Chinese-Russian border, flows through Russia to the Tatar Strait.

Apalachicola 90 mi. (145 km). Flows from Lake Seminole through Florida to Gulf of Mexico.

Arkansas 1,450 mi. (2,335 km). Rises in the Colorado Rockies and flows through Kansas, Oklahoma, and Arkansas (Little Rock) to Mississippi. McClellan-Kerr Arkansas River System (455 mi./733 km) is a combination of natural and artificial waterways—including sections of Verdigris, Arkansas and White Rivers—from Catoosa, Okla. (near Tulsa) and junction of White and Mississippi Rivers.

Major Rivers of the World, by Length

River	Length Miles	km	Source	Outflow
Nile	4,145	6,673	Tributaries of Lake Victoria, E. Africa	Mediterranean Sea
Amazon	4,000	6,440	Andes Mts., Peru	Atlantic Ocean
Mississippi–Missouri	3,740[1]	6,021[1]	Confluence of Jefferson, Madison, and Galatin R., Montana	Gulf of Mexico
Changjiang (Yangtze)	3,720	5,989	Kunlun Mts., China	China Sea
Yenisei–Angara	3,650[2]	5,877[2]	Lake Baikal, Russia	Kara Sea (Arctic Ocean)
Amur–Argun	3,590[2]	5,780[2]	Khingan Mts., China	Tatar Strait
Ob–Irtysh	3,360[2]	5,410[2]	Altai Mts., China	Gulf of Ob (Arctic Ocean)
Plata–Parana	3,030[2]	4,878[2]	Confluence of the Paranaiba and Grande rivers, Brazil	Atlantic Ocean
Huang He (Yellow)	2,903	4,674	Kunlun Mts., China	Gulf of Chihli (Yellow Sea)
Congo (Zaire)	2,900	4,669	Confluence of the Luapula and Lualaba rivers, Zaire	Atlantic Ocean
Lena	2,730	4,395	Baikal Mts., Russia	Laptev Sea (Arctic Ocean)
MacKenzie	2,635[2]	4,242[2]	Headwaters of Finlay Rivers, British Columbia, Canada	Beaufort Sea (Arctic Ocean)
Mekong	2,600	4,186	T'ang-ku-la Mts., Tibet	South China Sea
Niger	2,600	4,186	Guinea	Gulf of Guinea
Missouri	2,315	3,725	Confluence of Jefferson, Madison, and Montana Galatin rivers, Montana	Mississippi River
Mississippi	2,348[3]	3,780[3]	Lake Itasca, northwestern Minnesota	Gulf of Mexico
Murray–Darling	2,330	3,751	Great Dividing Range, Australia	Indian Ocean
Volga	2,290	3,687	Valdai Hills, Russia	Caspian Sea
Madeira	2,013	3,241	Confluence of the Mamore and Beni rivers, Bolivia/Brazil	Amazon River
São Francisco	1,988	3,201	Minas Gerais State, Brazil	Atlantic Ocean
Yukon	1,979	3,186	Confluence of Lewes and Pelly rivers, Yukon Territory, Canada	Bering Sea
Rio Grande	1,885	3,035	San Juan Mts., southwestern Colorado	Gulf of Mexico
Purus	1,860	2,995	Andes Mts., Peru	Amazon River
Tunguska, Lower	1,860	2,995	North of Lake Baikal, Russia	Yenesei River
Indus	1,800	2,898	Himalayas, Tibet	Arabian Sea
Danube	1,776	2,859	Confluence of Breg and Brigach rivers, Germany	Black Sea
Brahmaputra	1,770	2,850	Himalayas, Tibet	Ganges River
Salween	1,750	2,818	Tibetan Plateau, Tibet	Bay of Bengal
Para–Tocantins	1,710[2]	2,753[2]	Goias State, Brazil	Atlantic Ocean
Zambezi	1,700	2,737	Northwestern Zambia	Mozambique Channel
Paraguay	1,610	2,592	Mato Grosso State, Brazil	Parana River
Kolyma	1,320	2,130	Kolyma Mts., Russia	Arctic Ocean
Nelson–Saskatchewan	1,600	2,576	Rocky Mts., Canada	Hudson Bay
Orinoco	1,600	2,576	Sierra Parima Mts., Venezuela	Atlantic Ocean
Amu Darya	1,578	2,541	Pamir Mts., Uzbekistan/ Turkmenistan	Aral Sea
Ural	1,575	2,536	Ural Mountains, Russia	Caspian Sea

Major Rivers of the World, by Length (continued)

River	Length Miles	km	Source	Outflow
Ganges	1,560	2,512	Himalayas, India	Bay of Bengal
Euphrates	1,510	2,431	Confluence of the Murat Nehri and Kara Su rivers, Turkey	Shatt-al-Arab
Arkansas	1,450	2,335	Central Colorado	Mississippi River
Colorado	1,450	2,335	Northern Colorado	Gulf of California
Dneiper	1,420	2,286	Valdai Hills, Russia	Black Sea
Atchafalaya–Red	1,400	2,254	Eastern New Mexico	Gulf of Mexico
Syr Darya	1,370	2,206	Tien Shan, China/Kyrghyzstan	Aral Sea
Kasai	1,338	2,154	Central Angola	Congo (Zaire) River
Irrawaddy	1,300	2,093	Confluence of Mali and Nmai rivers, Myanmar	Bay of Bengal
Ohio–Allegheny	1,300	2,093	Pennsylvania	Mississippi River
Orange	1,300	2,093	Lesotho	Atlantic Ocean
Columbia	1,243	2,001	Columbia Lake, British Columbia, Canada	Pacific Ocean
Tigris	1,180	1,900	Eastern Turkey	Shatt-al-Arab
Rhine	820	1,320	Confluence of Hinterrhein and Vorderrhein rivers, Switzerland	North Sea
St. Lawrence	800	1,288	Lake Ontario	Gulf of St. Lawrence

Notes: 1. From the mouth of the Mississippi, up the Missouri to the Red Rock River in Montana. 2. Includes the length of tributaries that are part of the main trunk stream. 3. From the mouth of the Mississippi, up to its source in Minnesota.
Source: U.S. Dept. of Commerce, National Oceanic and Atmospheric Administration.

Arno 150 mi. (242 km). Rises in Apennines and flows via Florence to Ligurian Sea.

Atchafalaya 220 mi. (354 km). Flows from confluence of Mississippi and Red Rivers through Louisiana via Morgan City to Gulf of Mexico.

Baltic-White Sea Canal 141 mi. (227 km). Complex of natural and manmade Russian waterways connecting Baltic and White Seas.

Black Warrior 217 mi. (350 km). Rises in Alabama and flows into the Tombigbee.

Brahmaputra 1,770 mi. (2,850 km). Rises in Tibet and flows through China, India and Bangladesh (Dhaka) to the Ganges-Brahmaputra Delta and Bay of Bengal.

Cape Cod Canal 17 mi. (27 km). Canal between Massachusetts Bay and Buzzards Bay built in 1914.

Cape Fear 202 mi. (325 km). Rises in North Carolina and flows to Atlantic.

Chao Phraya (Me Nam) 227 mi. (365 km). Rises in Thailand and flows via Bangkok to Gulf of Thailand.

Chattahoochee 436 mi. (702 km). Rises in Georgia. Dammed to create Lake Seminole (on Alabama border) from which flows the Apalachicola.

Chesapeake and Delaware Canal 14 mi. (23 km). Canal between Delaware Bay (Delaware) and Chesapeake Bay (Maryland) built in 1824–29.

Colorado 1,450 mi. (2,335 km). Rises in Colorado Rockies, flows through Utah, Arizona (Grand Canyon), Nevada, California, Baja California Norte, and Sonora to the Gulf of California.

Columbia 1,243 mi. (2,001 km). Rises in British Columbia and flows through Washington and Oregon (Portland) to the Pacific.

Congo (Zaire) 2,900 mi. (4,669 km). Rises in Zaire and flows along border with Congo via Kinshasa and Brazzaville to Atlantic.

Connecticut 407 mi. (655 km). Rises in New Hampshire and flows through Vermont, Massachusetts, and Connecticut (Hartford) to Long Island Sound.

Cumberland 694 mi. (1,117 km). Rises in Kentucky and flows through Tennessee to the Ohio.

Danube (Donau) 1,776 mi. (2,859 km). Rises in Germany and flows through and/or forms border of Austria (Vienna), Hungary (Budapest), Croatia, Yugoslavia (Belgrade), Bulgaria, Ukraine and Romania, where it enters Black Sea. Part of Rhine-Main-Danube Waterway.

Delaware 367 mi. (590 km). Rises in New York and borders New York, New Jersey (Trenton), Pennsylvania (Philadelphia), and Delaware (Wilmington) en route to Delaware Bay.

Dnieper 1,420 mi. (2,286 km). Rises in Russia and flows through Belarus and Ukraine (Kiev and Dnepropetrovsk) to Black Sea.

Dniester 877 mi. (1,412 km). Rises in Ukraine and flows along Moldova border to Black Sea.

Don (Tanais) 1,224 mi. (1,970 km). Russian river that flows to Black Sea via Voronezh and Rostov.

Douro (Duero) 556 mi. (895 km). Rises in Spain and flows through Portugal (Oporto) to Atlantic.

Elbe 724 mi. (1,165 km). Rises in Czech Republic and flows through Germany (Hamburg) to North Sea.

Erie Canal 363 mi. (584 km). Main artery of New York State Barge Canal, built 1817–25 between Hudson River (Albany) and Lake Erie (Buffalo).

Euphrates 1,510 mi. (2,431 km). Rises in Turkey and flows through Syria and Iraq to join the Tigris and form the Shatt-al-Arab.

Ganges (Ganga) 1,560 mi. (2,512 km). Rises in India and flows through Bangladesh to the Ganges-Brahmaputra Delta and Bay of Bengal.

Garonne 357 mi. (575 km). French river that forms, with the Dordogne, Gironde Estuary on the Atlantic below Bordeaux.

Grand Canal (Da Yunhe) 1,114 mi. (1,795 km). Inland canal in China between Beijing and Hangzhou. First stage between Yangtze River (Chiang Jiang) and Yellow River (Huang He) built in 5th century B.C.; extended south to Hangzhou on East China Sea, A.D. 618, and north to Beijing, 1292.

Green 360 mi. (580 km). Rises in Kentucky and flows into Ohio River.

Guadalquivir 408 mi. (657 km). Spanish river that flows via Córdoba and Seville to Atlantic.

Houston Ship Channel 57 mi. (92 km). Waterway cut through Buffalo Bayou between Houston and Galveston, Texas, in 1914.

Hudson 306 mi. (493 km). New York river that flows via Albany and New York City to Atlantic.

Illinois Waterway 327 mi. (526 km). Natural and man-made waterways connecting Lake Michigan and Mississippi and comprising Chicago River, Chicago Sanitary and Ship Canal (1900), Des Plaines River, and Illinois River.

Indus 1,800 mi. (2,898 km). Rises in Tibet and flows through China, Jammu & Kashmir and Pakistan to Arabian Sea.

Intracoastal Waterway Improved channels, both natural and man-made, authorized by U.S. Congress in 1919 to provide sheltered navigation from Massachusetts to Texas. A trans-Florida section was never built, and it is divided into the Atlantic Intracoastal Waterway (1,800 mi./2,900 km) from Cape Cod to Miami, and the Gulf Intracoastal Waterway (1,100 mi./1,770 km) from Apalachee Bay, Fla., to Brownsville, Tex.

Irrawaddy 1,300 mi. (2,093 km). Rises in Myanmar and flows into Bay of Bengal

Irtysh River 2,760 mi. (4,444 km). Rises in China and flows through Kazakhstan and Russia (Novosibirsk) to Ob. Combined length of Lower Ob and Irtysh is 3,360 mi./5,410 km.

James 340 mi. (547 km). Rises in Virginia and flows via Richmond and Hampton Roads to Chesapeake Bay.

Jordan 200 mi. (322 km). Rises in Syria and flows through or borders Lebanon, Israel, and Jordan to the Dead Sea via Sea of Galilee.

Kanawha 97 mi. (156 km). Rises in West Virginia and flows into Ohio River.

Kasai 1,338 mi. (2,154 km). Rises in Angola and flows through Zaire and Congo to the Congo.

Kentucky 259 mi. (417 km). Rises in Kentucky and flows into the Ohio.

Kiel Canal (Nord-Ostsee Kanal) 53 mi. (86 km). German canal built in 1887–95 between Baltic (Kiel) and North Sea (mouth of the Elbe).

Kwai (Khwae) Noi Western Thailand river across which infamous railway "bridge on the River Kwai" at Kanchanaburi was built during World War II, at the cost of more than 60,000 lives.

Lena 2,730 mi. (4,395 km). Russian river that flows via Yakutsk to Laptev Sea.

Liffey 50 mi. (80 km). Irish River that flows into Irish Sea at Dublin.

Limpopo (Crocodile) 1,600 mi. (2,575 km). Rises in South Africa and borders and/or flows through Botswana, Zimbabwe and Mozambique to Indian Ocean.

Loire 634 mi. (1,020 km). French river that flows via Orléans and St. Nazaire to Bay of Biscay.

Mackenzie 2,635 mi. (4,242 km). Rises in British Columbia and flows through Alberta and Northwest Terr. to Beaufort Sea. Length includes Peace River above Great Slave Lake, and Finlay River above Williston Lake.

Madeira 2,013 mi. (3,241 km). Formed by confluence of Mamoré and Beni Rivers at Bolivian border and flows through Brazil to the Amazon.

Marne 326 mi. (525 km). French river that flows to the Seine.

Mekong 2,600 mi. (4,186 km). Rises in China and flows through or borders Laos (Vientiane), Myanmar, Thailand, Cambodia (Phnom Penh), and Vietnam to South China Sea.

Mississippi 2,348 mi. (3,780). Rises in Minnesota (Minneapolis/St. Paul) and forms all or part of eastern border of Iowa, Missouri (St. Louis), Arkansas and Louisiana, and western border of Wisconsin, Illinois, Kentucky, Tennessee (Memphis) and Mississippi; flows through Louisiana (Baton Rouge and New Orleans) to Gulf of Mexico. Measured from head of the Missouri, total length is 3,740 mi./6,021 km (not including Upper Mississippi).

Missouri 2,315 mi. (3,725 km). Rises in Montana and flows through and/or borders North Dakota (Bismarck), South Dakota (Pierre), Iowa (Sioux City), Nebraska (Omaha), Kansas and Missouri (Kansas City), en route to the Mississippi.

Mobile 45 mi. (72 km). Alabama river that flows via Mobile to Mobile Bay.

Monongahela 129 mi. (208 km). Rises in West Virginia and flows through Pennsylvania to the Ohio.

Moscow Canal 80 mi. (129 km). Canal built in 1937 to link Russian capital to the Volga.

Murray-Darling 2,330 mi. (3,751 km). Rises in the Great Dividing Range and flows to Indian Ocean.

Nelson 1,600 mi. (2,576 km). Rises in Alberta and flows through Saskatchewan and Manitoba to Hudson Bay; length includes Saskatchewan River above Lake Winnipeg and Bow River near Calgary.

New York State Barge Canal 353 mi. (568 km). Network of waterways between Hudson River and Lake Erie including Erie Canal, Champlain Canal (to Lake Champlain), and Oswego Canal (to Lake Ontario).

Niagara 35 mi. (56 km). Forms border between New York and Ontario and flows from Lake Erie to Ontario; unnavigable because of the 170-ft. high (52m) Niagara Falls. See *Welland Canal*.

Niger 2,600 mi. (4,186 km). Rises in Guinea and flows through Mali (Bamako and Tombouctou), Niger (Niamey), Benin and Nigeria to Gulf of Guinea.

Nile 4,145 mi. (6,673 km). World's longest river rises in Uganda and flows through Sudan (Khartoum) and Egypt (Cairo, Alexandria, and Rosetta) to Mediterranean. Passes through Lakes Victoria, Kyoga, and Albert. Known as White Nile in Sudan; at Khartoum merges with Blue Nile (850 mi./1,370 km), which rises in Ethiopia.

Ob River 2,287 mi. (3,682 km). Russian river that flows via Tobolsk to Gulf of Ob (Kara Sea). With Irtysh River, 3,360 mi. (5,410 km).

Oder 567 mi. (912 km). Rises in Czech Republic and flows through Poland via German border and Szczecin to Baltic.

Ohio 981 mi. (1,580 km). Formed by confluence of the Monongahela and Allegheny at Pittsburgh, Pennsylvania, and flows through Ohio (Cincinnati), West Virginia, Indiana, Kentucky, and Illinois to the Mississippi.

Orange 1,300 mi. (2,093 km). Rises in Lesotho and flows through South Africa and along Namibian border to Atlantic.

Orinoco 1,600 mi. (2,576 km). Rises in Venezuela and flows to Caribbean; forms part of border with Colombia.

Ouachita 605 mi. (974 km). Rises in Arkansas, and flows through Louisiana to the Mississippi. Lower 57 mi. (92 km) known as Black River.

Panama Canal 50 mi. (80 km). Panamanian waterway built 1904–14 between Atlantic (Colón) and Pacific (Panamá).

Paraguay 1,610 mi. (2,592 km). Rises in Brazil and flows through Paraguay (Asunción) and Argentina to the Paraná.

Paraná 1,827 mi. (2,941 km). Rises in Brazil and flows through and/or borders Paraguay and Argentina en route to La Plata.

Pará-Tocantins 1,710 mi. (2,753 km). Brazilian river that flows to the Amazon via Pará. The Pará River is southern branch of the Amazon at its mouth.

Plata (Plate) 123 mi. (198 km). Estuary of Paraná and Uruguay Rivers that flows to Atlantic and washes Buenos Aires and Montevideo.

Po 405 mi. (652 km). Italian river that flows via Turin to Adriatic.

Potomac 287 mi. (462 km). Rises in West Virginia and flows through and/or borders Maryland, Virginia, and Washington, D.C., to Chesapeake Bay.

Purus 1,860 mi. (2,995 km). Rises in Peru and flows through Brazil to the Amazon above Manaus.

Red 1,018 mi. (1,639 km). Rises in New Mexico and flows through and/or borders Texas, Oklahoma, Arkansas, and Louisiana (Shreveport) to Mississippi.

Rhine 820 mi. (1,320 km). Rises in Switzerland (Basel) and flows through and/or borders Liechtenstein, Austria, Germany (Köln), France (Strasbourg), and the Netherlands (Rotterdam) to North Sea.

Rhine-Main-Danube Waterway 2,173 mi. (3,505 km) Trans-Europe canal linking North and Black Seas: Rhine River from North Sea to Mainz (334 mi./539 km); Main River to Bamberg (238 mi./384 km); Main-Danube Canal (106 mi./171 km); Danube River to Black Sea (1,495 mi./2,411 km). Waterway completed in 1992—1,199 years after Charlemagne first attempted to link Rhine and Danube.

Rhone 300 mi. (485 km). Rises in Switzerland and France and flows via Marseilles to Mediterranean.

Rio Grande (Río Bravo, Río Bravo del Norte) 1,885 mi. (3,035 km). Rises in New Mexico and forms border between Texas (El Paso, Brownsville) and Mexican states of Chihuahua (Ciudad Juarez), Coahuila, Nuevo León, and Tamaulipas (Matamoros) to Gulf of Mexico.

Roanoke 410 mi. (660 km). Rises in Virginia and flows through North Carolina to Albemarle Sound.

Sacramento 374 mi. (602 km). California river that flows via Sacramento to San Francisco Bay.

Saint Johns 285 mi. (459 km). Florida river that flows via Jacksonville to Atlantic.

St. Lawrence 800 mi. (1,288 km). Rises in Ontario and flows through Quebec (Montreal and Quebec) and New York to Gulf of St. Lawrence. The St. Lawrence Seaway—2,340 mi. (3,766 km)—is a U.S./Canadian navigational project (1954–59) that allows ocean-going ships to ascend St. Lawrence and cross the Great Lakes to Duluth, Minn., and includes Welland Canal and Sault Ste. Marie Canals.

Salween 1,750 mi. (2,818 km). Rises in China, flows through Myanmar, forms part of border with Thailand, and enters Bay of Bengal at Moulmein, Myanmar.

San Joaquin 340 mi. (547 km). California river that flows to the Sacramento.

São Francisco 1,988 mi. (3,201 km). Brazilian river that flows to Atlantic Ocean.

Sault Ste. Marie (Soo) Canals 1.6 mi. (2.6 km). Built to overcome 12 ft. (3.7 m) drop between Lakes Superior and Huron; first built 1895. Part of St. Lawrence Seaway.

Savannah 314 mi. (506 km). Rises in South Carolina and flows through Georgia (Savannah) to the Atlantic.

Seine 482 mi. (776 km). French river that flows via Paris and Le Havre to English Channel.

Shannon 270 mi. (370 km). Irish river that flows via Limerick to Atlantic.

Shatt-al-Arab 120 mi. (193 km). Waterway between confluence of Tigris and Euphrates and the Persian Gulf; forms part of Iran/Iraq border. Major cities include Basra, Abadan, and Khorramshar.

Snake 1,083 mi. (1,744 km). Rises in Wyoming and flows through Idaho, Oregon, and Washington to the Columbia.

Somme 152 mi. (245 km). French river that flows via Amiens to English Channel. Scene of World War I battle, July–November 1916.

Suez Canal 101 mi. (163 km). Egyptian canal, built 1859–69, between Mediterranean (Port Said) and Red Sea (Suez).

Syr Darya 1,370 mi. (2,206 km). Rises in Uzbekistan and flows through Kazakhstan to Aral Sea.

Tagus 675 mi. (1,007 km). Rises in Spain and flows through Portugal to Atlantic at Lisbon.

Tennessee 652 mi. (1,050 km). Rises in Tennessee (Chattanooga) and flows through Alabama, Mississippi, and Kentucky to the Ohio.

Tennessee-Tombigbee Waterway 253 mi. (407 km). Manmade waterway, completed 1985, between the Tennessee in Mississippi and the Tombigbee in Alabama.

Thames 210 mi. (338 km). English river that flows via London to North Sea.

Tiber 252 mi. (406 km). Italian river that flows via Rome to Tyrrhenian Sea.

Tigris 1,180 mi. (1,900 km). Rises in Turkey and flows through Iraq (Mosul, Baghdad) and joins the Euphrates to form the Shatt-al-Arab above Persian Gulf.

Tombigbee 362 mi. (583 km). Rises in Mississippi and flows through Alabama to the Mobile.

Tunguska, Lower 1,860 mi. (2,995 km). Russian river that flows to the Yenisei.

Ural 1,575 mi. (2,536 km). Rises in Russia and flows through Kazakhstan to Caspian Sea.

Vistula 675 mi. (1086 km). Polish river that flows via Warsaw and Gdansk to Baltic Sea.

Volga 2,290 mi. (3,687 km). Russian river that flows via Gorki and Volgograd (Stalingrad) to Caspian Sea. Longest river in Europe.

Volga-Baltic Canal 685 mi. (1,110 km). Network of canals and improved waterways connecting the Volga with Baltic Sea near St. Petersburg.

Volga-Don Canal (Lenin Canal) 62 mi. (100 km). Last link in Russian waterway system that connects the Baltic, Black, White, and Caspian Seas, and the Sea of Azov; opened in 1952.

Welland Canal 27 mi. (43 km). Canal (first built 1824–29) to overcome 327 ft. (100 m) drop from Lake Ontario to Erie; current canal built 1913–32. Part of St. Lawrence Seaway.

Willamette 294 mi. (473 km). Oregon river that flows to the Columbia at Portland.

Yangtze (Chang Jiang) 3,720 mi. (5,989 km). Chinese river that flows via Wuhan, Nanjing, and Shanghai to East China Sea.

Yazoo 169 mi. (272 km). River in Mississippi that flows to the Mississippi.

Yellow (Huang He) 2,903 mi. (4,674 km). Chinese river that flows to Bo Hai (Yellow Sea).

Yenisei 2,566 mi. (4,131 km) Russian river that flows to Kara Sea. Combined length with Angara (Upper Tunguska) River is 3,650 mi. (5,877 km).

Yukon 1,979 mi. (3,186 km). Rises in Yukon Territory and flows through Alaska to Bering Sea.

Zambezi 1,700 mi. (2,737 km). Rises in Zambia and flows through Angola, Namibia, Zambia, Zimbabwe, and Mozambique to Mozambique Channel.

Islands and Archipelagos of the World

Åland Is. (Ahvenanmaa) 60°N, 20°E. Finnish archipelago of more than 6,000 islands between Finland and Sweden.

Aleutian Is. 51°-55°N, 163°W-166°E. Chain between Pacific Ocean and Bering Sea stretching 2,700 km: Unimak, Fox Is., Andreanof Is., Rat Is. and Near Is. (Alaska) and Komandorskiye Ostrova (Russia).

Andaman and Nicobar Is. 12°N, 93°E. Union Territory of India comprising some 300 islands in two major archipelagos stretching 725 km north-south in the Bay of Bengal off the coast of Myanmar.

Anticosti 50°N, 63°W. Canadian island in Gulf of St. Lawrence.

Antigua and Barbuda 17°N, 62°W. Two-island Caribbean country.

Antilles' name for the Caribbean islands from Cuba to Trinidad and Tobago, but not including the Bahamas.

Greater Antilles: Cuba, Jamaica, Hispaniola, and Puerto Rico. Lesser Antilles: Leeward Is. Virgin Is., Antigua and Barbuda, and Dominica) and Windward Is. (Martinique, St. Lucia, St. Vincent, Grenada, Barbados, Trinidad and Tobago, and Aruba).

Aran Is. 53°N, 10°W. Three islands—Inishmore, Inishmaan, and Inisheer—off western Ireland.

Aruba 12°N, 70°W. Dutch Caribbean island 30 km north of Venezuela.

Ascension 7°S, 14°W. Island of the British Crown Colony of St. Helena about 1,100 km northwest of St. Helena, 2,250 kilometers east of Brazil and 2,500 km west of Africa.

Auckland Is. 51°S, 166°E. Group about 300 km south of New Zealand.

Azores/Açores 37°-40°N, 25°-31°W. Portuguese Atlantic group 1,400 km west of Portugal; first settled in 1430's.

Baffin 68°N, 70°W. Largest Canadian Arctic island, on Davis Strait opposite Greenland.

Bahamas 21°-27°N, 71°-79°W. Chain of 2,700 islands and cays stretching 800 km southeast of Florida; shared by Bahamas and Turks and Caicos (British); Columbus's first American landfall in 1492.

Balearic Is. 39°N, 3°E. Sixteen Spanish Mediterranean 16 islands: Majorca, Minorca and Ibiza.

Bali 9°S, 115°E. Predominantly Hindu Indonesian island east of Java.

Banks 73°N, 121°W. Westernmost large Canadian Arctic island, on Beaufort Sea.

Barbados 13°N, 60°W. Island nation about 150 km east of southern Antilles.

Bermuda 32°N, 65°W. British dependency of 138 coral islands, 20 inhabited, 900 km east of North Carolina.

Bismarck Archipelago 5°S, 150°E. Papua New Guinea archipelago: Admiralty Is., New Britain, and New Ireland; formerly a German colony.

Block 41°N, 72°W. Island between Long Island Sound and Atlantic Ocean, 15 km off Rhode Island.

Borneo 0°N/S, 114°E. Large equatorial Southeast Asian island shared by Indonesia, Malaya and Brunei.

Canary Is. 28°N, 16°W. Spanish archipelago of seven islands 100 km west of Morocco. Inhabited since antiquity (Latin: Fortunatae Insulae); colonized by the Spanish in 1400's.

Cape Verde Is. 15°-17°N, 23°-25°W. 10-island nation 500 km west of Senegal. Settled by Portuguese in mid-1400's.

Capri 41°N, 14°E. Italian island in Bay of Naples.

Caroline Is. 5°-10°N, 130°-166°E. Micronesian group of more than 600 islands: Belau (Palau), Kusaie, Ponape, Satawal, Truk, and Yap.

Cayman Is. 20°N, 81°W. British dependency of three main islands 240 km south of Cuba.

Chagos Archipelago 6°S, 72°E. Part of the British Indian Ocean Territory 600 km south of the Maldives. Diego Garcia has been a UK/U.S. military base since the 1970's when its 1,500 inhabitants—the descendents of slaves—were deported.

Channel/Santa Barbara Is. 34°N, 120°W. Eight-island group off Los Angeles.

Channel Is. 49°N, 2°W. Group in English Channel near France: Jersey, Guernsey, Alderney, and Sark. They are dependent territories of the English Crown, as successor to William the Conqueror, duke of Normandy, but not part of the UK.

Chatham Is. 44°S, 176°W. Polynesian group 860 km east of New Zealand from where they were settled around 1500.

Chincha Is. 14°S, 76°W. Group of three Peruvian islands; important source of guano before synthetic fertilizers.

Christmas 10°S, 106°E. Australian dependency 360 km south of Java.

Cocos/Keeling Is. 12°S, 97°E. Australian archipelago of 27 coral atolls 2,800 km northwest of Perth, settled in 19th century.

Comoros 12°S, 44°E. Indian Ocean nation of three islands about 325 km east of Mozambique.

Cook Is. 8°-23°S, 156°-167°W. Group of 15 islands 3,200 km northeast of New Zealand: Rarotonga.

Corsica 42°N, 9°E. French Mediterranean island.

Cuba 21°N, 80°W. Northernmost Caribbean island, 1,250 km east-west; largest of 1,200 islands in Cuban archipelago.

Cyclades/Kikládhes 37°N, 25°E. Greek Aegean archipelago of about 220 islands; so-called because they encircle sacred island of Delos.

Devil's 5°N, 52°W. Island off French Guiana; used as penal colony until 1938.

Dodecanese/Sporádhes 36°N, 27°E. Greek Aegean archipelago of 12 islands, including Samos, Kos, and Ródhos.

Dominica 16°N, 61°W. Caribbean island nation.

Easter Island/Isla de Pascua/Rapa Nui 27°07′S, 109°22′W. The most remote island on Earth, Rapa Nui is the eastern tip of Polynesia, about 3,700 km west of Chile, which administers it, and 1,600 km east of Pitcairn Island. Settled by Marquesans around the fourth century, it is famous for its thousand carved statues, some 10 meters tall.

Elba 43°N, 10°E. Italian island where Napoleon was briefly exiled.

Ellesmere Island, Nunavut Territory 79°N, 82°W. Cape Columbia (83°08′N) is the northernmost point in Canada.

Faeroe Is. 62°N, 7°W. Group of 18 islands about 118 km north-south, 320 km north of the Shetlands and halfway between Norway and Iceland; settled in seventh century they are an autonomous part of Denmark.

Falkland Is./Islas Malvinas 51°-53°S, 57°- 62°W. British Crown Colony of 340 islands about 600 km east of Argentina. Claimed by French sailors from St. Mâlo (hence Malvinas), contested by Spanish, settled by

English. An Argentine invasion in 1982 failed.

Faylakah 29°N, 48°E. Persian Gulf island off Kuwait.

Fernando de Noronha 4°S, 32°W. Atlantic island about 500 km east of Brazil.

Fernando Po 3°S, 9°E. Former name for Bioko, Equatorial Guinea.

Fiji Is. 16°–19°S, 178°W–177°E. Pacific country of about 330 islands, a third inhabited, about 1,770 km north of New Zealand.

Florida Keys 24°–25°N, 80°–82°W. Chain of coral islands running 240 km west from tip of Florida: Key Largo, Islamorada, Key West, and Dry Tortugas.

Frisian Is. 53°–55°N, 5°–8°E. Chain of North Sea islands, 18 inhabited, off the Netherlands, Germany, and Denmark: Rømø, Sylt, Terschelling, Vlieland and Texel.

Galápagos 1°S, 91°W. Archipelago of 60 volcanic islands about 430 km across and 1,000 km west of Ecuador; known for its diverse flora and fauna and Charles Darwin's research there in 1835.

Gotland 57°N, 18°E. Swedish Baltic island, thought to be the homeland of the Goths.

Hainan 19°N, 109°E. Chinese island between South China Sea and Gulf of Tonkin.

Hawaiian Is. 19°–28°N, 155°–178°W. Polynesian chain comprising eight large and 124 smaller islands stretching 2,400 km from Hawaii to Midway and Kure. Settled in eighth century from the Marquesas. U.S. state: Hawaii, Maui, Lauai, Molokai, Oahu, Kaui, and Nihau.

Hebrides/Western Isles 57°N, 7°W. Islands off the west coast of Scotland. Inner Hebrides: Skye, Mull, and Islay; 210-km-long Outer Hebrides: Lewis, North Uist, and South Uist.

Hispaniola 19°N, 71°W. Caribbean island divided between Haiti and Dominican Republic.

Hokkaido 43°N, 143°E. Northernmost of main Japanese islands.

Hong Kong 22°N, 114°E. Chinese island at mouth of Pearl River, 145 km southeast of Guangzhou (Canton).

Honshu 36°N, 136°E. Largest of main Japanese islands; cities include Tokyo.

Indonesia From the Greek meaning "Indian islands," the name applies to the archipelagic nation of 18,108 islands: Sumatra, Java, Sulawesi, Bali, Malaku Is., and parts of Borneo, Timor, and New Guinea.

Ionian Is. 39°N, 21°E. Greek Adriatic archipelago of seven islands: Kerkira (Corfu), Kefallinia, Zákinthos, and Odysseus's Itháki.

Jamaica 18°N, 75°W. Caribbean island nation about 175 km south of Cuba.

Jan Mayen 71°N, 8°W. Norwegian island 400 km east of Greenland.

Java 7°S, 110°E. Indonesian island east of Sumatra.

Juan Fernandez Is. 33°S, 80°W. Three-island group 650 km west of Chile. Alexander Selkirk, model for Daniel Defoe's Robinson Crusoe, was marooned on Más a Tierra 1705–09.

Kerguelen/Desolation Is. 49°–50°S, 69°–71°E. French Indian Ocean territory of 300 islands and islets, including Crozet Is., about 4,500 km southeast of South Africa.

Komandorskiye Ostrova 55°N, 167°E. Russian group at western tip of Aleutians.

Krakatoa 6°S, 105°E. Volcanic Indonesian island west of Java.

Kuril Is. 44°–51°N, 146°–155°E. Chain of some 56 islands stretching about 1,200 km between Japan and Russia.

Kyushu 33°N, 131°E. Southernmost of main Japanese islands.

Lakshadweep/Laccadive Is. 8°–12°N, 71°–74°E. Indian archipelago of 12 atolls about 250 km west of India.

Leeward Is. see *Antilles*.

Line Is. 6°N–11°S, 162°–152°W. Group of islands straddling the Equator (Line) south of Hawaii and belonging variously to the U.S., Great Britain and Kiribati.

Lofoten Is. 69°N, 15°E. Northern Norwegian archipelago.

Long Island 41°N, 73°W. New York island, 190 km long, between Atlantic Ocean and Long Island Sound.

Madeira 33°N, 17°W. Portuguese Atlantic archipelago of four main islands about 500 km west of Morocco: discovered in 1400's.

Madeleine, Iles de la 47°N, 61°W. Canadian group in Gulf of St. Lawrence.

Maldive Is. 7°N–1°S, 73°E. Country of 26 archipelagos stretching 823 km north-south about 670 km southwest of Sri Lanka.

Malta 36°N, 14°E. Strategic island nation in central Mediterranean south of Sicily.

Maluku (Moluccas)/Spice Is. 2°N–8°S, 124°–131°E: Indonesian archipelago; in the 16th century, sole source of cloves, nutmeg, and mace, and a major goal of European merchants.

Man, Isle of 54°N, 4°W. Irish Sea crown dependency of Great Britain.

Manhattan 41°N, 74°W. New York island at confluence of Hudson River/Long Island Sound.

Manitoulin 46°N, 83°W. Canadian island in Lake Huron.

Mariana Is. 13°–20°N, 146°E. Micronesian archipelago 2,400 km east of the Philippines comprising Commonwealth of the Northern Mariana Is. (Saipan, 15°N, 146°E), and Guam (13°N, 144°E).

Marquesas Is. 7°–10°S, 138°–141°W. French Polynesian archipelago of 12 islands about 1,200 km northeast of Tahiti.

Marshall Is. 5°–15°N, 161°–172°E. Micronesian group of 34 atolls and islands including Ratak and Ralik chains. Bikini was a nuclear test site in the 1940–50's.

Martha's Vineyard 41°N, 71°W. Massachusetts island south of Cape Cod.

Martinique 15°N, 61°W. French Caribbean island.

Matsu (26°N, 120°E) and **Quemoy** (24°N, 118°E) Chinese coastal islands about 250 km apart; administered and garrisoned by Taiwan since 1950.

Mauritius 20°S, 58°E. Indian Ocean island 800 km east of Madagascar. Part of Mascarene Archipelago, with Réunion.

Melanesia from the Greek meaning "black islands;" Pacific islands south of Micronesia and west of Polynesia—including New Guinea, the Solomons, New Hebrides, and Fiji.

Micronesia from the Greek meaning "small islands;" Pacific islands north of the equator between Hawaii and the Philippines.

Nantucket 41°N, 70°W. Massachusetts island south of Cape Cod. Major 19th-century whaling port.

Nauru 1°S, 167°E. Island nation 2,300 km northeast of Sydney, Australia.

New Caledonia 18°–22°S, 163°–168°E. Pacific island that forms, with Loyalty Is., French overseas territory.

Newfoundland 48°N, 56°W. Large Canadian Atlantic island south of Labrador.

Novaya Zemlya 74°N, 57°E. New Land; Russian archi-pelago comprising two main islands, 960 km long, between Barents and Kara Seas.

Novosibirskiye Ostrova 75°N, 142°E. New Siberian Is.; Russian group between Laptev and East Siberian Seas.

Orkney Is. 59°N, 3°W. Group of more than 20 islands, 85 km north-south, 10 km north of Scotland.

Outer Banks, North Carolina 35°N, 76°W. Barrier islands—Roanoke, Pea, Bodie, Hatteras, Ocracoke, and Portsmouth—stretching 145 km north-south off North Carolina between the Atlantic Ocean and Albemarle and Pamlico Sounds.

Ouessant, Ile d' (Ushant) 48°N, 5°W. Atlantic island off northwest France at entrance to English Channel.

Paracel Is. 17°N, 112°E. South China Sea group about 400 km east of Vietnam; also claimed by China and Taiwan.

Philippines Southeast Asian nation of more than 7,000 islands: Luzon, Samar, Palawan, Mindanao, Sulu Archipelago, Zamboanga.

Pitcairn 25°S, 130°W. British colony (with Ducie, Henderson and Oeno Is.) halfway between Tahiti and Easter Island. HMS Bounty mutineers arrived in 1790.

Polynesia from the Greek meaning "many islands;" Pacific islands within a triangle drawn between Hawaii, New Zealand and Easter Island.

Pribilof Is. 57°N, 170°W. Alaskan Bering Sea group.

Prince Edward 46°N, 63°W. Canadian island province in Gulf of St. Lawrence and connected to Nova Scotia by bridge.

Puerto Rico 18°N, 66°W. Easternmost and fourth largest of Greater Antilles.

Qeshm 26°N, 56°E. Iranian island in Strait of Hormuz at the mouth of the Persian Gulf.

Queen Charlotte Is. 51°N, 129°W. Canadian group off British Columbia.

Queen Elizabeth Is. 74°–82°N, 60°–125°W. Northern-most Canadian Arctic archipelago: Ellesmere Is., Parry Group and Sverdrup Group.

Réunion 21°S, 56°E. French Indian Ocean island 690 km east of Madagscar; part of Mascarene Archipelago, with Mauritius.

Ryukyu Is. 24°–31°N, 123°–131°E. Japanese chain stretch-ing 1,000 km between Taiwan and Kyushu. Okinawa was a major World War II battleground.

St. Helena 15°S, 6°W. British Atlantic island where Napoleon was exiled and died.

St. Lawrence Is. 64°N, 171°W. Alaskan Bering Sea island south of Bering Strait.

St. Lucia 14°N, 61°W: Second largest of Windward Is.

St. Pierre & Miquelon 47°N, 56°W. French Atlantic islands southwest of Newfoundland, Canada.

Sakhalin 51°N, 143°E. Russian island, 950 km long, between Sea of Japan and Sea of Okhostk.

Samoa Is. 13°–14°S, 168°–173°W. Pacific group divided between Western Samoa and American Samoa.

Sardinia 40°N, 9°E. Italian island in western Mediterranean.

Severnaya Zemlya 80°N, 98°E. Russian group (four main islands) discovered in 1913, between Kara and Laptev Seas.

Seychelles 4°-5°S, 56°E. Indian Ocean republic of 115 islands extending 1,200 km northeast-southwest about 1,600 km east of Kenya.

Shetland Is. 61°N, 1°W. British group of about 100 islands 80 km northeast of the Orkneys.

Shikoku 33°N, 133°E. Smallest of four main Japanese islands.

Sicily 37°N, 14°E. Italian island in central Mediterranean.

Singapore 1°N, 104°E. Island nation off tip of Malay Peninsula at east end of Strait of Malacca.

Society Is. 16°–18°S, 148°–154°W. French Polynesian archipelago, 750-km long, including Tahiti; settled around 500 B.C.

Socotra 13°N, 54°E. Yemeni Indian Ocean island about 250 km northeast of Somalia.

Solomon Is. 156°–171°E, 5°–13°S. Melanesian archipelago of about 1,000 islands stretching 1,400 km southeast from New Guinea. Guadalcanal was major World War II battleground.

South Georgia Is. 54°S, 37°W; and South Sandwich Is.: 56°S, 26°W. British dependent territory 1,500 km east of the Falklands.

South Orkney Is. 61°S, 44°–46°W. British group about 1,440 km southeast of South America.

South Shetland Is. 61°–64°S, 54°–63°W. Four-group chain, 540-km long, about 120 km north of the Antarctic Peninsula.

Spitsbergen 79°N, 20°E: Norwegian Atlantic island; forms, with Bear Island (74°N, 19°E), dependency of Svalbard.

Spratly Is. 9°N, 112°E. South China Sea archipelago about 500 km southeast of Vietnam; also claimed by China, Taiwan, Malaysia, and the Philippines.

Sulawesi (Celebes) 2°S, 121°E. Indonesian island between Borneo and Maluku Is.

Sulu Archipelago 5°–7°N, 120°–122°E. Philippine archipelago of about 900 islands between Celebes and Sulu Seas.

Sumatra 0°, 100°E. Largest and westernmost island in Indonesia.

Tierra del Fuego 54°S, 69°W. Island shared by Chile and Argentina between the Atlantic and Pacific Oceans; separated from South America by Strait of Magellan, and north of Cape Horn (55°59'S, 67°16'W).

Tongan (Friendly) Is. 15°–23°S, 173°–177°W. Polynesian country of 171 islands (36 inhabited) stretching 1,000 km north-south about 2,000 km northeast of New Zealand.

Trinidad, Isla 39°S, 62°W. Brazilian island 1,200 east of Brazil.

Trinidad and Tobago 10°N, 61°W. Caribbean nation group off Venezuela.

Tristan da Cunha 37°S, 12°W. British Atlantic group about 2,800 km east southeast of South Africa.

Tsushima 34°N, 129°E. Japanese island in Korean (or Tsushima) Strait.

Tuamotu Archipelago 14°–23°S, 134°–149°W. French Polynesian chain of 80 islands, 1,700 km long, east of Tahiti.

Vancouver 50°N, 126°W. Largest island on west coast of Canada; part of British Columbia.

Vanuatu (New Hebrides) 13°–20°S, 166°–170°E. Melanesian island nation, 900 km long.

Victoria 71°N, 114°W. Canadian Arctic island.

Volcano Is. (Kazan-Retto) 25°N, 141°E. Japanese group of three islands 1,100 km southwest of Tokyo. Iwo Jima was a major World War II battleground.

Wake Is. 19°N, 177°E. U.S. Pacific atoll, 1,900 km west of Midway: Wilkes, Wake and Peale Islands.

Wight, Isle of 51°N, 1°W. British English Channel island off Portsmouth and Southampton.

Windward Is. see *Antilles*.

Wrangel Island (Ostrov Vrangelia) 71°N, 180°E/W. Russian island in East Siberian Sea.

Mountain Ranges

Adirondacks New York. Mt. Marcy, 1,629m (5,344′).

Altai Shan China, Kazakhstan, Mongolia, and Russia. Gora Belukha (Russia, Kazakhstan) 4,506m (14,784′).

Ahaggar (Hoggar) Mts. SE Algeria. Tahat, 2,918m (9,573′).

Alaska Range S Alaska. Denali (Mt. McKinley) 6,194m (20,320′); highest point in North America.

Aleutian Range SW Alaska. Mt. Katmai, 2,047m (6,715′).

Alps European range that runs in a 660-mi. arc from France through Italy, Switzerland, Germany, Liechtenstein, Austria, Slovenia, Croatia, and Bosnia and Herzegovina. Ranges include Maritime, Ligurian, Cottian, Graian, Dauphiné, Savoy, Pennine, Lepontine, Rhaetian, Bernese, Noric, Hohe Tauern, Carnic, Dolomites, Julian, Karawanken, and Dinaric Alps. Mont Blanc (France), 4,807m (15,711′).

Andes South American range (cordillera) divided into 12 smaller ranges that run 7,240 km (4,500 mi.) through Argentina, Chile, Bolivia, Peru, Ecuador, Colombia, and Venezuela. Ranges include Cordillera Apalobamba, Cordillera Real, Cordillera Blanca, Cordillera Huayhuash, Cordillera Central, Cordillera Occidental, Cordillera Oriental, Sierra Nevada del Cocuy, Sierra Nevada de Santa Marta, Sierra Nevada de Merida, and Central Highlands of Venezuela. Aconcagua (Argentina), 6,962m (22,385′); highest point in South America.

Apennines Italy. Corno Grande, 2,912m (9,554′).

Appalachians North American chain divided into Blue Ridge, Allegheny, Berkshire Hills, Taconic, Green, White, Longfellow, Notre Dame Mts. Mt. Mitchell (N.C.), 2,037m (6,684′).

Ararat (Agri Dagi) mountain in E Turkey upon which Noah's Ark is said to have landed. 5,165m (16,945′).

Athos, Mt. Greece. 2,033m (6,667′).

Atlas Mts. 1,900-km.-long (1,200-mi.) North African range in Morocco, Algeria, and Tunisia. Toubkal (Morocco), 4,165m (13,665′).

Balkan Mountains Bulgaria. Botev Peak, 2,375m (7,793′).

Barisan Mts. Indonesia (Sumatra). Kerintji, 3,807m (12,483′).

Black Hills South Dakota, Wyoming. Harney Peak (S.Dak.), 2,207m (7,242′).

Brooks Range N. Alaska. Mount Isto, 2,762m (9,060′).

Cantabrian Mts. Spain. Torre de Cerredo, 2,648m (8,688′).

Carpathian Mts. range, including Transylvanian Alps, in Poland, Slovakia, Ukraine, and Romania. Gerlachovka (Slovakia), 2,655m (8,711′).

Cascade Range Range between Sierra Nevada and Coast Mountains in California, Oregon, and Washington. Mt. Rainier, 4,392m (14,410′).

Caucasus Mts. Range between Black and Caspian Seas in Azerbaijan, Armenia, Georgia, and Russia. Mt. Elbrus (Russia, Georgia), 5,633m (18,481′).

Cerro Chirripo Costa Rica; highest mountain in Central America, 3,820m (12,533′).

Cévennes France. Mt. Mezenc, 1,754m (5,755′).

Coast Mts. British Columbia. Extension of U.S. Cascade Range. Mt. Waddington, 4,016m (13,177′).

Coast Ranges mountains in California, Oregon, Washington, British Columbia, Yukon Terr., and Alaska. Includes San Jacinto Mts., Olympic Range, Vancouver Is., Queen Charlotte Is., Alexander Archipelago, and St. Elias and Chugach Mts. Mt. Logan (Yukon Terr.), 5,959m (19,550′); highest point in Canada.

Daxue Shan Central China. Minya Konka (Gonggashan), 7,590m (24,900′).

Drakensberg Range South Africa, Lesotho. Thabana Ntlenyana (Lesotho), 3,482m (11,425′).

Elburz (Alborz)Mts. N Iran. Damavand, 5,670m (18,602′).

Ellsworth Mts. Antarctic range, including Heritage and Sentinel Ranges. Vinson Massif, 4,897m (16,066′); highest point in Antarctica.

Fujiyama (Mt. Fuji) tallest mountain in Japan; 3,776m (12,389′).

Ghats, Western range in SW India. Anai Mudi, 2,695m (8,841′). Separated from Eastern Ghats, Mahendra Giri, 1,501m (4,924′) by the Deccan.

Great Dividing Range E Australia. Mt. Kosciuszko, 2,228m (7,310′), highest point in Australia.

Guiana Highlands Venezuela, Guyana and Brazil. Mt. Roraima (Venezuela), 2,772m (9,094′). Site of world's highest waterfalls; Angel Falls, 980m (3,212′).

Harz Mts. Germany. Brocken, 1,143m (3,747′).

Himalayas Asian range that runs in a 2,414-km (1,500-mi.) arc in Pakistan, India, Tibet, Nepal, Sikkim, and

Bhutan. Mt. Everest, 8,850m (29,035'); highest point on Earth.

Hindu Kush Afghanistan, Pakistan. Tirich Mir (Pakistan), 7,695m (25,230').

Jotunheimen Norway. Galdhopiggen, 2,469m (8,098').

Jura Mts. France, Switzerland. Mt. Neige (France), 1,723m (5,652').

Karakoram India, Pakistan. K2 (Mt. Godwin-Austin; Chogori), 8,611m (28,250'). K2 is so called after a 19th-century surveyor's identification; it was the second mountain listed in the Karakoram (K). Balti porters in the region now call it Ketu.

Kenya (Kirinyaga) mountain in central Kenya. 5,199m (17,058').

Kilimanjaro mountain rising on the border between Tanzania (where the peak is) and Kenya. 5,895m (19,340'); highest point in Africa.

Kunlun Shan China. Includes Altun Shan and Qiliang Shan (Nan Shan) ranges. Kongur (Kung-ko-erh), 7,719m (25,326').

Laurentian Mts. Quebec. Mt. Tremblant, 1,190m (3,905').

Mackenzie Mts. Yukon Territory and Northwest Territories. Mt. Sir James McBrien, 2,758m (9,049').

Mauna Kea highest mountain in Hawaii. 4,205m (13,796'). If measured from its base on the on the floor of the Pacific, it is 9,698m (31,796')—taller than Mt. Everest.

Mauna Loa Hawaii. 4,169 m (13,677').

Olympus, Mt. highest mountain in Greece and home of the gods of Greek myth; 2,917m (9,570').

Ouachita Mts. Arkansas and Oklahoma. Magazine Mt., 840m (2,753').

Ozarks Arkansas, Missouri, and Oklahoma. Hare Mt., 726m (2,380').

Pamirs (Pamir Knot) Afghanistan, China, Tajikistan. Pik Samani (Communism Peak), Tajikistan, 7,495m (24,590'). Surrounded by Tian Shan, Kunlun Shan, Himalayas, Karakoram, and Hindu Kush.

Parnassus, Mt. Greece, at south end of Pindus Mts.; sacred to the god Apollo and the Muses. 2,457m (8,062').

Pegunungan Maoke New Guinea. Puncak Jaya (Irian Jaya, Indonesia), 5,030m (16,502').

Pennines England. Cross Fell, 893m (2,930').

Pikes Peak Colorado. "America's Mountain," in Rockies.

4,300m (14,109').

Pindus Mts. Albania and Greece. Smólikas Oros (Greece), 2,637m (8,652').

Pisgah (Nebo), Mt. Jordan. 806m (2,644').

Pontic Mts. N Turkey. Kaçkar, 3,942m (12,933').

Pyrenees range between Atlantic and Mediterranean on border between France, Spain, and Andorra. Pico de Aneto, 3,404m (11,168').

Queen Maud Mts. Ross Dependency, Antarctica. Mt. Kirkpatrick, 4,529m (14,860').

Rhodope Mts. Bulgaria and Greece. Musala (Bulgaria), 2,925m (9,596').

Rocky Mts. 6,500-km-long (4,000-mi.) North American chain running from Alaska through Yukon Territory, British Columbia, Alberta, Idaho, Montana, Wyoming, Utah, Colorado, New Mexico, and Arizona. Divided into Arctic Rockies (Brooks Range and Mackenzie Mts.), Northern Rockies (Purcell, Selkirk, and Cariboo Mts.), Middle Rockies (Bighorn and Uinta Mts., Wind River, Absaroka, Wasatch, and Teton Ranges), and Southern Rockies (Front Range, Sangre de Cristo, San Juan, and Sawatch Mts.). Mt. Elbert (Colorado, Sawatch Range, 4,399m (14,433').

Ruwenzori (Mountains of the Moon) Uganda, Zaire. Mt. Stanley (Zaire), 5,109m (16,763').

San Bernardino Mts. S California. San Gorgonio Mt., 3,508m (11,502').

San Gabriel Mts. S California. San Antonio Peak, 3,074m (10,080').

Sayan Mts. Russia. Munku-Sardyk, 3,490m (11,451').

Sierra Madre Occidental 1,125-km (700 mi.) range in Mexico. Nevada de Colima, 4,340m (14,239'). Sierra Madre Oriental runs along the east coast of Mexico.

Sierra Madre del Sur Mexico, Guatemala. Volcan Tacan, 4,092m (13,425').

Sierra Maestra Cuba. Pico Turquino, 1,993m (6,540').

Sierra Nevada 645-km (400-mi.) range in eastern California. Mt. Whitney, 4,418m (14,494').

Sierra Nevada Spain. Mulhacen, 3,477m (11,408').

Sinai (Horeb), Mt. mountain in the Gebel Musa of Egypt's Sinai Peninsula, where Moses is said to have received the Ten Commandments. 2,287m (7,497').

Soback-san South Korea. Ch'eonwhang-bong, 1,915m (6,283').

Southern Alps New Zealand. Mt. Cook, 3,754m (12,316').

Sulaiman Range Pakistan. Takht-i-Sulaiman ("Throne of Solomon"), 3,443m (11,295′).

Taeback-san South Korea. Sorak-san, 1,708m (5,604′).

Taurus Mts. Turkey. Erciyas Dag, 3,916m (12848′).

Tian Shan China, Kyrgyzstan. Includes Dzungarian, Kungei, Täläss, Terskei, and Trans-Ili ranges (ala-tau). Pobeda Peak, 7,439m (24,407′).

Tibesti Mts. Chad. Emi Koussi, 3,415m (11,204′).

Transantarctic Mts. Antarctica. Mt. Markham, 4,354m (14,275′).

Ural Mts. 2,640-km-long (1,640-mi.) chain in Russia and Kazakhstan that forms boundary between Europe and Asia. Narodnaya (Russia), 1,895m (6,215′).

Virunga Mts. volcanic chain in Rwanda, Uganda, and Zaire. Karisimbi (Rwanda, Zaire), 4,507m (14,787′).

Vosges Mts. France. Mt. Guebwiller, 1,424m (4,672′).

Washington, Mt. in New Hampshire's White Mts.; peak is the windiest place on Earth. 1,917m (6,288′).

Wind River Range Wyoming. Gannett Peak, 4,207m (13,804′).

Wrangell Mts. S Alaska. Mt. Bona, 5,005m (16,421′).

Zagros Mts. Iran. Zardeh Kuh, 4,550m (14,021′).

Glossary of Geographical Terms

abyssal plain a relatively flat area in the deepest part of the ocean with an average depth of 3.1 miles.

Antarctic Circle a parallel of latitude at 66°32′S, south of which the sun does not rise on the southern winter solstice (about June 22), and does not set on the southern summer solstice (about December 22). The phenomenon is due to the angle of the Earth's inclination toward the sun.

archipelago a group of islands.

Arctic Circle a parallel of latitude at 66°32′N, a point on the Earth's surface north of which the sun does not set on the northern summer solstice (about June 22), and does not rise on the northern winter solstice (about December 22). The phenomenon is due to the angle of the Earth's inclination toward the sun.

atoll a coral island in the shape of a ring around a central lagoon.

basin a natural depression in the land.

bay a curved indentation of a sea or lake into the land. In practice, bays are considered to be bigger than coves and smaller than gulfs.

bight a bay formed by a bend in the coastline.

canyon a deep valley in the Earth's surface formed by a stream or river.

coastal plain a gently sloping lowland bordering the sea.

continent the largest continuous landmasses on the Earth's surface.

continental divide The ridgeline on a continent (as in the Americas) on one side all water flows into the Pacific, and all water on the other side flows into the Atlantic.

continental shelf a gently sloping (ca. 1°) underwater plain extending out from the land to the edge of a continental slope; often a continuation of a coastal plain.

continental slope a more sharply inclined (2°–5°) area of the seafloor that plunges toward the abyssal plain.

delta a triangular-shaped piece of land formed by sediment at the mouth of a river.

desert a location where the rate of evaporation exceeds the rate or precipitation.

dune a hill or ridge of sand deposited by wind.

equator a parallel on the Earth's surface midway between the North and South Poles. Parallels of latitude are measured in degrees north or south of the equatorial parallel, 0°.

estuary an area in which freshwater from a river meets salt water from the sea.

fjord a long, narrow inlet of the ocean with steeply sloping sides.

floodplain flat, low-lying land along either side of a river that is subject to flooding.

glacier a large mass of ice moving, often imperceptibly, down a valley or slope.

gorge an especially narrow and steep-walled canyon.

gulf a curved indentation of a sea or lake into the land. In general, gulfs are bigger than bays and cut more deeply into the land.

hemisphere one half of the Earth's surface, however it is divided. For example, the Northern Hemisphere lies north of the equator; the Southern Hemisphere, south of the equator.

international date line an artificial line along roughly 180° meridian, with some deviations. Crossing the date line from east to west, a day is lost; crossing from west to east, a day is gained.

island a piece of land surrounded entirely by water.

isthmus a narrow strip of land that joins two larger land masses and is surrounded by water on two sides.

lagoon a shallow pool or pond completely or almost completely separated from the sea.

lake an enclosed body of water. Most lakes contain freshwater although there are notable exceptions, including the Great Salt Lake, the Caspian Sea, Aral Sea, and Dead Sea.

latitude the angular distance between a point on the surface of the Earth and the equatorial plane running through the middle of the Earth. Latitude is measured in degrees, minutes, and tenths of minutes or (more rarely) seconds (up to 90°) north or south of the equator. A circle connecting all the points of the same latitude is known as a parallel of latitude.

leeward the direction or side sheltered from the wind. (See *windward.*)

longitude the angular distance between a point on the surface of the Earth and a plane running vertically through the Earth and intersecting the north and south poles. By convention, the prime meridian (0°) runs through Greenwich, England. Longitude is measured in degrees, minutes and tenths of minutes or (more rarely) seconds (up to 180°) east or west of the prime meridian. A line connecting all the points of the same longitude from pole to pole is called a meridian.

magnetic pole poles toward (North) and away from (South) which a magnetized compass needle points; not the same as true north, the location of the North Pole.

mountain a natural rise in the land characterized by a sharp vertical rise from the surrounding land and a summit much smaller in area than the base.

ocean the largest continuous bodies of salt water on the Earth's surface, which collectively cover 70 percent of the Earth's surface. By convention, the world ocean is divided into five smaller oceans: Atlantic, Arctic, Indian, Pacific, and Southern.

peninsula a piece of land connected to a larger landmass and surrounded on three sides by water.

plain an area of the Earth's surface characterized by uninterrupted flat or gently rolling terrain.

plateau an area of flat or nearly flat terrain generally separated from the surrounding land by a steep slope.

prairie level or rolling land generally covered with grasses, with few trees.

rain forest a forest that receives more than 1.8 meters (70 inches) of rain per year.

range a single line of connected mountains. A chain is usually regarded as a series of parallel ranges.

reef a line of rock, coral, or sand in the sea usually exposed at low tide and covered at high tide.

ridge a relatively long stretch of elevated land, or the line that connects the summits of a mountain range.

rise a raised area of the abyssal plain.

river a continuous stream of water that flows into a lake, sea, enclosed depression, or another river.

savanna a portion of land in the Tropics or subtropics with only scattered trees but whose grasses can survive with scant rainfall.

sea a large body of salt water, smaller than an ocean but larger than a gulf.

sound a body of water that separates an island from the mainland or that connects two oceans, seas, or other bodies of water. Sounds are generally long and narrow.

steppe a portion of land with little rainfall, extreme temperature variations, and drought-resistant vegetation.

strait a narrow body of water that connects two large bodies of water.

tide the rise and fall of the surface of the ocean and of bays, gulfs, and other bodies of water connected to the ocean. Tides are caused by the gravitational pull of the moon, which passes over the same meridian of the Earth about once every 24 hours and 50 minutes. The length of time between successive high (or low) tides is about 12 hours and 25 minutes.

trench a depression in the abyssal plain formed at the junction of two tectonic plates, the bases of which are often very deep below the surface of the water.

Tropic of Cancer a parallel of latitude at 23°30'N, a point on the Earth's surface where the sun's rays strike the Earth perpendicularly on the northern summer solstice (about June 22). This marks the northern limit of the Tropics.

Tropic of Capricorn a parallel of latitude at 23°30'S, a point on the Earth's surface where the sun's rays strike the Earth perpendicularly on the southern summer solstice (about December 22). This marks the southern limit of the Tropics.

tsunami a wave generated by an undersea earthquake. Generally unnoticed at sea, these waves can reach great heights and wreak enormous destruction.

tundra an area of treeless plain near or above the Arctic Circle. Tundra subsoil is permanently frozen, but the soil thaws enough to support the growth of mosses, etc.

valley a long depression in the land, usually open at one end.

wetland a location in which the soil is saturated with water for much or all of the year. Different types of wetlands include bogs, marshes, swamps, and tidal flats.

windward the direction or side facing the wind.

Languages of the World

Human beings are unique in their use of language. Many other animals communicate by vocal and visual signals; in some (apes, whales, parrots) communication is highly developed. But only humans have the innate, hard-wired ability to employ a large vocabulary of words with a complex grammar to create language itself. Fully developed language is thought to have been an evolutionary innovation of Homo sapiens, separating us from all ancestral human and hominid species and facilitating the spread of our species around the globe.

Languages themselves are highly changeable, in vocabulary, pronunciation, and (more slowly) grammar. Words fall into disuse; others are coined or borrowed; pronunciations change both over time and geographically, as populations disperse. If a population of speakers of a given language becomes divided geographically and the two new populations have little or no contact with each other, in just a few tens of generations their speech will have diverged so widely that it will no longer be mutually intelligible: one language will have become two. The relatedness of the two languages will still be apparent, however.

Language Families

Languages that are related by descent from a common ancestor are said to belong to the same language family. The study of language families began in the late 18th century, when an official of the British East India Company, Sir William Jones (1746–94), noticed that Sanskrit, Greek, and Latin have many similarities in vocabulary and grammar. Jones proposed that all three (and thus all other languages descended from them as well) were derived from an extinct ancestral language, now known as proto-Indo-European. All languages descended from proto-Indo-European are members of the Indo-European language family. As study of the historical development of languages progressed, many other language families were discovered. Scholars recognized that language families come into existence as populations migrate and become geographically separated, so that their original language splits into new but related languages, which themselves evolve separately and can split and resplit again.

Traces of linguistic relatedness disappear over long periods of time. Few or perhaps none of the language families known at present can be dated back further than the end of the last ice age, some 12,000 years ago. Attempts by some linguists to discover much older "superfamilies" of languages remain highly controversial. The most significant of these hypotheses is the Nostratic hypothesis, first proposed in 1903. It puts forth the idea that Indo-European, Uralic, Altaic, and Afro-Asiatic languages are part of one broad category. New research in the 1990s refined and eliminated many doubtful parts of the theory, and though it is still controversial, the Nostratic theory is among the most promising concerning linguistic classification. Linguists vary in how they classify languages. Some tend to lump languages together, in part on the basis of common grammar; others, insisting on commonly evolved vocabulary as the criterion for relatedness, tend to split languages into smaller families.

The physical distribution of languages within language families (supplemented now by genetic DNA studies, which generally confirm the linguistic evidence) can be used to trace the movement of populations over the past several thousand years. Examples include the spread of Indo-Europeans from somewhere near the Black Sea to India, Europe, and beyond; the spread of Austronesians from southeastern China to Indonesia, and from there eastward to the islands of the Pacific and westward to Madagascar; and the spread of Turks from eastern Central Asia westward to Anatolia and beyond.

Most languages can be can be classified as members of a language family or subfamily. A few (Basque is the most famous example) are linguistic isolates; there are also a number of hybrid forms (pidgins and creoles) that cross linguistic boundaries.

Eurasia

Indo-European embraces about 150 languages spoken by some 3 billion people worldwide; it is the most widely distributed language family, evidence of a persistent Indo-European drive for territorial expansion throughout history. It comprises several subfamilies, including *Indo-Iranian* (Sanskrit, Hindi, Bengali, Sinhalese, Pashto, Farsi, and others); *Italic* or *Romance* (Latin, Italian, French, Spanish, Portuguese, Catalan, Romanian, and others); *Germanic* (Gothic, German, Dutch, English, Swedish, Icelandic, and others); *Celtic* (Gaelic, Welsh, Breton, and others); *Baltic* (Latvian, Lituanian, and others); *Slavic* (Slavonic, Russian, Polish, Czech, Serbo-Croation, and others); and Albanian, Greek, and Armenian.

Other language families of Eurasia include *Caucasian* (Georgian, Circassian, Chechen, the several languages of the *Kartavelian* subfamily, and many others) and *Uralic* (Finnish, Estonian, Hungarian, and Saami). *Turkic* (Turkish, Uzbek, Uighur, and others), *Mongolic* (such as Mongolian, Buryat, and Kalmyk), and *Tungusic* (Manchu and others) are grouped together by some linguists as the *Altaic* language family, and the Uralic and Altaic families are sometimes combined as the *Uralic-Altaic* language family; but those amalgamations are not accepted by all authorities. Korean and Japanese are sometimes also described as Altaic languages; this identification is highly controversial. Despite obvious similarities and many years of research, no organic link between Korean and Japanese has been proven; some authorities conclude that Korean is linguistically isolated, and Japanese is part of the small *Koguryoic* language family (along with Okinawan and several extinct languages of Korea and northeastern China). The smallest of the world's language families is *Chukchi-Kamchatkan* (also known as *Paleo-Siberian*), comprising five languages spoken by fewer than 25,000 people in northeastern Siberia.

Elamo-Dravidian includes Tamil, Malayalam, Kannada, and other languages of South India. *Sinitic* includes all dialects of Chinese (Mandarin, Guangdong (Cantonese), Min, Wu, Hakka, and others). These are more like independent languages than dialects of a single language, except that they can all be written mutually intelligibly with Chinese characters, which are not closely tied to par-

ticular pronunciations. Some authorities combine the Sinitic languages with the *Tibeto-Burman* language family to form *Sino-Tibetan*.

Austroasiatic contains some 250 languages spoken in mainland Southeast Asia, including Vietnamese, Khmer (Cambodian), Mon, and Thai. (Some linguists, however, propose that Thai and closely related languages, such as Lao, belong instead in the Sino-Tibetan family.)

Southeast Asia and the Pacific Islands

Austronesian (also called *Malayo-Polynesian*) family includes several hundred languages spoken in Southeast Asia and the islands of the Indian and Pacific Oceans, ranging from Malagasy (spoken in Madagascar, off the coast of Africa) to Hawai'ian and Maori in the Pacific, and reflecting a strong seafaring heritage. The family is divided into two groups, *Western Austronesian* and *Eastern Austronesian*. Western Austronesian (including Malay, Indonesian, Javanese, Tagalog, and many others) languages are spoken by more than 300 million people. The Eastern Austronesian subfamily is further divided into *Micronesian* and *Polynesian* languages.

Papuan language family of New Guinea (and also nearby island groups of the Moluccas and Melanesia) includes several hundred languages divided into at least six subfamilies. The *Australian* languages of the aboriginal peoples of Australia, isolated from external contact for perhaps 40,000 years, are divided into several families and subfamilies.

Africa

The languages of Africa (and the adjacent Middle East) are divided into four families. *Afro-Asiatic* includes Berber, Coptic, Hausa, and the languages of the *Semitic* subfamily (Hebrew, Arabic, Aramaic, and Amharic). The *Nilo-Saharan* family, found in northeastern, eastern, and central Africa, includes (among many others) Turkana, Masai, Dinka, Mangbetu, Efe, and the numerous languages of the *Eastern Sudanic* (including Nubian) and *Central Sudanic* subfamilies. The *Niger-Kordofanic* family is found widely in west, central, and southern Africa. It has two main branches, *Kordofanic* and *Niger-Congo*; the latter includes the subfamilies *West Atlantic* (Wolof, Fulani), *Gur* (or *Voltaic*), *Mande*, *Kwa* (Ewe, Yoruba, Igbo, Ashanti), *Benue-Congo*, and *Adamawa*. The Benue-Congo group includes hundreds of languages of the *Bantu* subfamily (Swahili, Zulu,

Xhosa, Sotho, Setsuana), reflecting a historic expansion of the Bantu peoples southward and eastward from an original homeland in the Congo basin. Finally, Africa is home to the *Khoisan* family, ancient languages (San and others) spoken by peoples largely displaced by the Bantu expansion; these languages are known for their distinctive "click" sounds.

The Americas

The language families of the Americas include *Eskimo-Aleut* (including Inuktatut, the language of the Inuit, as well as Aleut); *Na-Dene* (Athabascan and Navajo); and, according to the controversial theory of the late Joseph Greenberg, *Amerind*, which includes all other Native American languages. Other authorities divide these languages into numerous families (which Greenberg regarded as subfamilies), including, in North America and Mexico, *Algonquian-Wakashian* (eastern and northern woodlands and Pacific Northwest, including Algonquin, Delaware, Cheyenne, Cree, Salish, Nootka, and Kwakiutl); *Penutian* (central and coastal California into Mexico and Central America; includes the widespread Mayan languages); *Hokan-Siouan* (widely distributed, including Choktaw, Seminole, the Iroquois languages, Cherokee, Lakota, and many others); and *Aztec-Tanoan* (southwestern North America and Mexico, including Paiute, Shoshone, Comanche, Hopi, Nahuatl, and many others). The languages of Central America, the Caribbean, and South America are, according to many bewildering and contradictory schemes, divided into dozens of proposed families and subfamilies, the most prominent of which include *Mixtecan* and *Toltecan* (Mexico and Central America); *Cariban* and *Arawakan* (Caribbean); and *Chibchan, Ge, Quechua, Aymara, Araukanian*, and *Tupi-Guarani* (South America).

Isolates, Pidgins, and Creoles

A few languages are classified as *isolates*, unrelated to others; examples include Basque or Euskara (a survival from the time before the Indo-Europeans expanded into Europe); the extinct Etruscan language of Italy; Korean; Burushaski, spoken in Kashmir; Gilyak, spoken on the island of Sakhalin off the eastern coast of Siberia, and a dozen or so others.

Pidgins are simplified languages often used for trading purposes between peoples with no common language (the word *pidgin* itself derives from the English word *business*); South China Coast Pidgin is a well-known example.

Pidgins can evolve into creoles, independent languages that combine features of two or more parent languages; examples include Jamaican (with English and West African roots), Haitian (French and West African), and Hawai'ian Creole (combining Hawai'ian and English with Japanese, Tagalog, and other Asian languages).

Major Languages of the World Today

According to UNESCO there were approximately 6,000 living languages in the world in 2010, most of which are spoken only by a small number of people. The eight most commons languages—Mandarin Chinese, English, Hindi (with Urdu), Spanish, Russian, Arabic, Bengali, and Portuguese—are spoken by half the world's population. It is estimated that more than 3,000 languages are spoken by less than 10,000 people. These 3,000 are considered "endangered languages," categorized as such when 30 percent of children in the community are no longer taught it. Africa currently has the highest number of languages in danger of extinction; of the continent's 1,400 languages approximately 250 are threatened with imminent disappearance.

Chinese is the native language of more than 1.2 billion people, principally in China, but also in ethnic Chinese communities worldwide. All dialects of Chinese are written in essentially the same way, using Chinese characters (hanzi), which are not closely tied to particular pronunciations. Major dialects include Mandarin, also known as *guoyu* ("national language") or *putonghua* ("ordinary speech"); Guangdong (Cantonese, widely spoken in southern and southeastern China, and in many Chinese communities overseas); Min (Fujian Province, Taiwan, and in Southeast Asia overseas Chinese communities); Wu (Shanghai and nearby regions); and Hakka (southeastern China and Southeast Asian overseas Chinese communities). Chinese is also an official language of the United Nations.

Hindi one of 16 official languages of India, is spoken by an estimated 474 million people in India alone. This number increases if lumped together with the similar Urdu (an official language of Pakistan). Collectively these and other closely related lanugages are known as Hindustani. Hindustani is also spoken in Malaysia, Singapore, Trinidad, Guayana, South Africa, Mauritius, and other countries with large expatriate Indo-Pakistani communities.

English is the native language of an estimated 450 million people in the British Isles, the United States, Canada, Australia, South Africa, Philippines, India, Nigeria, Oceania, many Caribbean countries, and others. English is used as a second language to some degree by another 1.5 billion people; it is an official language of 55 countries and the United Nations. English is also the most common language used on the Internet; nearly 28 percent of all Internet users in the world.

Spanish is the official language of 23 countries, including Spain, Mexico, Colombia, Argentina, and many other nations of Central and South America and the Caribbean; native speakers total about 350 million, including about 40 million in the United States. Over 15 percent of Americans speak Spanish as a first language. Spanish is also an official language of the United Nations.

Malay and Indonesian Malay is spoken as a first language by some 40 million people in Malaysia and on the Indonesian island of Sumatra. Indonesian, closely similar to Malay, is the official language of Indonesia but the second language of most people who speak it—who might be native speakers of Javanese, Sundanese, Balinese, or any of 700 or more other languages spoken in Indonesia. About 230 million people regularly use Malay or Indonesian as a first or second language.

Bengali is the official language of Bangladesh, and also widely spoken in the Indian state of West Bengal. There are significant Bengali-speaking communities in Great Britain and the United States. Native speakers total about 230 million.

Arabic is the native language of some 280 million people worldwide, and, as the language of the Koran is studied throughout the Islamic world. There are approximately 250 million non-native Arabic speakers in the world. It is an official language of the United Nations and of 25 countries worldwide.

Portuguese is spoken by only 10 million people in Portugal, but by about 160 million more in eight additional countries and territories where it is an official language: Brazil; Angola and four other countries in Africa; East Timor, an island Southeast Asia; and the special administrative region of Macau, on the southeastern coast of China. There are roughly 210 million native Portuguese speakers worldwide and 240 million non-native speakers.

Russian is the native language of about 160 million people. It is the official language of Russia and Belarus (together 130 million native speakers), and widely used also in Ukraine (17 million) and Kazakhstan (8 million), as well as Uzbekistan, Kyrgyzstan, and Moldova. Approximately 114 million speak Russian as a second language. It is an official language of the United Nations.

Japanese is the official language of only two countries (Japan and Palau), but is spoken by more than 130 million people. Significant Japanese-speaking populations are also found in Brazil and the United States.

German is an official language of six European countries (Germany, Austria, Switzerland, Luxembourg, Liechtenstein, and Belgium); there are sizable German-speaking populations in Poland, Russia, Brazil, and the United States. Native speakers total nearly 120 million.

Turkish Standard (Anatolian) Turkish, plus closely related dialects and languages including Azeri, Kyrgyz, Kazakh, Türkmen, Tartar, Uighur, and Uzbek, have approximately 120 million native speakers. Turkish languages are spoken across a huge span of central Eurasia, including Turkey, Azerbaijan, Kazakhstan, Kyrgyzstan, Turkmenistan, Uzbekistan, and the province of Xinjiang in northwestern China. There are significant Turkish-speaking populations in Iran, Russia, Germany, and the United States.

French has fewer than 150 million native speakers, but its significance stems from the fact that it is an official language of 29 countries—more than any other language except English—including France, Switzerland, Belgium, Canada, Ivory Coast, Congo, Cameroon, Madagascar, and in French overseas territories and possessions from Martinique to New Caledonia. It is widely used as a second language, especially in West Africa. French is an official language of the United Nations.

Vietnamese is spoken primarily in Vietnam, with sizable Vietnamese-speaking populations in the neighboring countries of Cambodia and Laos, as well as in the United States. Native speakers total about 80 million people.

Korean is spoken primarily in North and South Korea, with significant Korean-speaking populations in Japan, Russia, China, and the United States. Native speakers total about 70 million people.

Tamil is the principal language of the province of Tamil Nadu, in southeastern India; it is also spoken by a large minority population of Sri Lanka, concentrated in the northern and eastern parts of that country. There are about 66 million native speakers of Tamil.

Persian includes Farsi, the official language of Iran, plus the closely related languages of Tajik (Tajikistan and parts of Afghanistan) and Dari (spoken by nearly half the population of Afghanistan). There are about 55 million native speakers of various dialects of Persian.

The English Language Today

Although English ranks only third among the world's most spoken languages, it is on its way to becoming the first truly global language—used throughout the world as the language of commerce, diplomacy, and science. English is the mother tongue for some 450 million people, and a further 1.5 billion people use it as a second language to some degree. Beginning in the 17th century, the language spread throughout the British Empire to the Americas, Africa, India, and Oceana. Today 70 countries designate English as an official language (although it does not have that status in the United States), and it is an official language of the United Nations, the European Union, Nafta, NATO, and the Organization of American States.

A Brief History of the English Language English belongs to the Germanic branch of the Indo-European family of languages, and is related to most languages spoken in Europe, Scandinavia, India, and western Asia. The story of English begins with the arrival of the Jutes, Angles, and Saxons, Germanic peoples who invaded Britain in the fifth century and divided the island nation among themselves. In Common Germanic, the Angles were called Angli, which later mutated to Engle, and *Engla land* soon became the name of the nation these tribes now occupied. Old English (Anglo-Saxon), which is dated from the first written documents of this period to 1066, was an amalgamation of Germanic dialects, Latin, which persisted from the time of the Roman occupation, and Norse, which was brought by the Viking invaders who arrived in force in 865. Literacy came to England when the Anglo-Saxons converted to Christianity in the ninth century.

Middle English emerged following the Norman Conquest in 1066, which brought a distinctive French influence to the language. The Normans not only introduced new vocabulary, but changed the style of writing, from a clear, easily readable hand to the more ornate Carolingian script that was used on the Continent. Norman scribes began to change the spelling of Old English as well, introducing many of the conventions that remain in the language today. For example, the Old English *cw* became *qu*, giving us *queen*, instead of *cwen*.

As Anglo-Saxon rulers were replaced by the Norman conquerors, Norman-French became the language of government and high society, and the Norman influence on the English language is still apparent, notably in the abundance of words related to the law and government, e.g. *jury*, *court*, and *parliament*.

The Chancery Standard (CS) was developed during the reign of King Henry V (1413–1422), who ordered his government officials to use English instead of Norman-French in the course of business. CS was based on the dialects of London and the Midlands, which were the largest population centers at the time. By mid-century, CS was used in all official transactions, except by the church, which continued to use Latin, and its spread throughout the country was aided by the introduction of the printing press by William Caxton in the late 1470's.

The transition to Modern English began in the 15th century, with what is known as the "Great Vowel Shift"—a term coined in the 20th century by the Danish linguist Otto Jespersen. It refers to a major change in pronunciation that took place between 1450 and 1750. The exact cause of the shift remains a mystery, and some linguistic scholars are skeptical about its existence. One theory is that it was the result of a dramatic social change in the wake of the Black Death, which ravaged Europe from 1347 to 1351. In England, this caused a massive migration of people to the south of England, and an unprecedented mixing of social classes, who began to modify their regional vowel sounds into a standard pronunciation. Many of the peculiarities of English spelling persist from this period.

English in America The playwright and public intellectual George Bernard Shaw famously observed at the beginning of the 20th century that the United States and the United Kingdom are "two countries divided by a common language." American English came into existence as soon as the first settlers arrived on the continent, bringing with them traditional English speech, leavened with their distinctive regional dialects. To this, they quickly added words from the local Indian languages, particularly those describing plants and animals that they had not seen before (*raccoon, moose, squash*). Within 100 years, the original English settlers were joined by the Irish, Dutch, Scandinavians, and other European colonists who built settlements in the South and Midwest, while Spanish and Mexican settlers populated the Southwest and West. The American lexicon overflows with loanwords from these languages, including *adobe*, *barbecue*, and *rodeo* from the Spanish; *cookie*, *freight*, and *dock* from the Dutch.

With time and distance, the differences between British English and American English became more profound, and in 1806, Noah Webster set out to establish American English as a distinctive voice, quite apart from the British standard, with the publication of *A Compendious Dictionary of the English Language*, which defined 37,000 words. His more famous *American Dictionary of the English Language*, published in 1828, was a two-volume dictionary, included 65,000 words, and was based on the principles that spelling should be practical, and that grammar should reflect the way that language was actually spoken, not according to the rules set down by "experts." The dictionary was not a commercial success, but was highly influential, and the name "Webster" has become synonymous with American dictionaries.

Americans continued to coin new words to reflect their evolving economic, political and social realities. *Ballpark*, *supermarket*, *gerrymander*, *gasoline* all entered the language in the 19th and 20th centuries, and in the same period, a new influx of German and Jewish immigrants taught us to *schmooze* and to eat *hamburgers*.

In 1877, Henry Sweet, an English philologist, predicted that within 100 years, American, British, and Australian English would be mutually unintelligible, but in the 21st century, because of globalization and advances in communications technology, regional variations are understood around the world.

New Words Dictionary publishers are always on the lookout for new words in an effort to keep the English language corpus up to date. Yet there is no formal mechanism for adding words to the English language. Neologisms—newly coined words that have not yet entered mainstream language—become popular mainly through the mass media and word of mouth. Thousands of words are coined each year, while only a few hundred achieve any kind of permanency in our vocabulary. Lexicographers often follow the use of a word for years before determining whether it deserves inclusion in a dictionary, and publishers retain panels of experts to consider the words being created within their areas of expertise. Ultimately, there are as many opinions about the legitimacy of a word as there are publishers and lexicographers.

New words most often come from the worlds of science, popular culture, business, and now, from advances in the digital world. In 1955, Vladimir Nabokov coined the word *nymphet*, in the novel *Lolita*; in 1960, the word *laser* (from *light amplification by stimulated emission of radiation*) entered the language; in 1984, *cyberspace* appeared for the first time in William Gibson's novel *Neuromancer*. New words that have made their way into dictionaries since 2000 include:

business: *big-box; insourcing; rightsizing*
food: *chai; locavore; olestra; turducken*
military: *waterboarding; weaponize; WMD*
popular culture/lifestyle: *chill pill; emo; grunge; metrosexual; plus-one; puh-leeze; supersize; unibrow*
technology: *biodiesel; digerati; google (as a verb); podcast; ringtone; USB port*

Since 1991, the American Dialect Society has designated a Word of the Year (WOTY), and the major English-language dictionary publishers followed suit. The winning words are not necessarily new, but may have taken on a new meaning or usage beyond the original, such as the 1992 selection *Not!*, meaning "just kidding." Some words are assimilated into the language so quickly that it seems they have always existed. The winning words in 2009 were: *unfriend*, which beat out *hashtag*, and *sexting* (from the *New Oxford American Dictionary*); *tweet*, which won over *birther*, and *shovel-ready* (from the American Dialect Society), while *Webster's New World College Dictionary* selected *distracted driving*.

Some experts argue that it takes two generations to know whether a word will have durability.

Phonetic Clues Hint Language Is Africa-Born

By NICHOLAS WADE

Language is at least 50,000 years old, the date that modern humans dispersed from Africa, and some experts say it is at least 100,000 years old. Now, a researcher analyzing the sounds in languages spoken around the world has detected an ancient signal that points to southern Africa as the place where modern human language originated. The finding fits well with the evidence from fossil skulls and DNA that modern humans originated in Africa. It also implies, though does not prove, that modern language originated only once, an issue of considerable controversy among linguists.

The detection of such an ancient signal in language is surprising. Because words change so rapidly, many linguists think that languages cannot be traced very far back in time. The oldest language tree so far reconstructed, that of the Indo-European family, which includes English, goes back 9,000 years at most.

Quentin D. Atkinson, a biologist at the University of Auckland in New Zealand, has shattered this time barrier, if his claim is correct, by looking not at words but at phonemes—the consonants, vowels and tones that are the simplest elements of language. Dr. Atkinson, an expert at applying mathematical methods to linguistics, has found a simple but striking pattern in some 500 languages spoken throughout the world: A language area uses fewer phonemes the farther that early humans had to travel from Africa to reach it.

Some of the click-using languages of Africa have more than 100 phonemes, whereas Hawaiian, toward the far end of the human migration route out of Africa, has only 13. English has about 45 phonemes.

This pattern of decreasing diversity with distance, similar to the well-established decrease in genetic diversity with distance from Africa, implies that the origin of modern human language is in the region of southwestern Africa, Dr. Atkinson says in an article published in the journal *Science*.

Dr. Atkinson's finding fits with other evidence about the origins of language. The Bushmen of the Kalahari Desert belong to one of the earliest branches of the genetic tree based on human mitochondrial DNA. Their languages belong to a family known as Khoisan and include many click sounds, which seem to be a very ancient feature of language. And they live in southern Africa, which Dr. Atkinson's calculations point to as the origin of language. But whether Khoisan is closest to some ancestral form of language "is not something my method can speak to," Dr. Atkinson said.

His study was prompted by a recent finding that the number of phonemes in a language increases with the number of people who speak it. This gave him the idea that phoneme diversity would increase as a population grew, but would fall again when a small group split off and migrated away from the parent group.

Such a continual budding process, which is the way the first modern humans expanded around the world, is known to produce what biologists call a serial founder effect. Each time a smaller group moves away, there is a reduction in its genetic diversity. The reduction in phonemic diversity over increasing distances from Africa, as seen by Dr. Atkinson, parallels the reduction in genetic diversity already recorded by biologists.

For either kind of reduction in diversity to occur, the population budding process must be rapid, or diversity will build up again. This implies that the human expansion out of Africa was very rapid at each stage. The acquisition of modern language, or the technology it made possible, may have prompted the expansion, Dr. Atkinson said.

"What's so remarkable about this work is that it shows language doesn't change all that fast—it retains a signal of its ancestry over tens of thousands of years," said Mark Pagel, a biologist at the University of Reading in England who advised Dr. Atkinson.

"Language was our secret weapon, and as soon as we got language we became a really dangerous species," he said.

In the wake of modern human expansion, archaic human species like the Neanderthals were wiped out and large species of game, fossil evidence shows, fell into extinction on every continent shortly after the arrival of modern humans.

GOVERNMENT

Origins of Government

In the earliest reaches of history, as soon as humans came to live together in large settlements, they were faced with the need to organize complex economic activities and protect themselves from outside attack. From this need arose the first forms of government. Whether despotic in nature or formally delineated by a constitution, governments exist to direct, control, and regulate the actions and affairs of a people or a state.

Ancient civilizations provided the basic origins of modern government. Beginning with the Mesopotamian city-states of Sumeria, it is possible to trace the development of governmental institutions through the Kingdom of Egypt, China, and the Persian Empire, and then onto the more modern "republican-style" governments of Greece and Rome.

Mesopotamia (ca. 3500–539 B.C.)

Often called "the cradle of civilization," Mesopotamia stretched along a 600-mile-long plain of the Tigris and Euphrates valleys reaching to the Persian Gulf (an area that encompasses the present-day Nile Valley, parts of Syria, Iraq, and Palestine). The Sumerians, residents of southern Mesopotamia, not only developed writing and early mathematics, but also created a sophisticated form of government. In early Sumeria, the first city-state, a priest-king ruled as a representative of the city's god together with an assembly of elders or citizens. As the kingdom of Sumeria grew, each new city had its own governor who ruled for the king.

As agricultural activity intensified along the banks of the Nile River, the need for water grew. The area was suitable for agriculture, but there was often a shortage of water during growing seasons. The Sumerians needed a mechanism for harnessing the rivers and allocating resources to ensure that farmers could irrigate their crops. The entity that developed for regulating water use eventually came to rule the people in other aspects of their lives.

Each of the Nile Valley city-states was a sacred temple city, and its ruler was believed to be a representative of god. The vast majority of the population consisted of peasants, while the monarch surrounded himself with a small cadre of court officials, scribes, and priests. The monarch was the supreme intermediary, or the "vicar of the gods" for the common people; religion fortified and reinforced social conformity in every way. The skills of writing and mathematics were the exclusive province of the bureaucrats who maintained power for the monarch. Each monarch oversaw the building of temples, the maintenance of a priestly order, and the organization of an army to defend his kingdom. Acting as a steward of the gods, he organized and controlled the economy, which included building dikes and canals, maintaining the city-state's structure, and developing and enforcing a code of law.

King Hammurabi, the ruler of Babylonia, one of the most important states in southern Mesopotamia, developed a comprehensive legal system. Archaeologist were fortunate to discover well-preserved documents spelling out the Code of Hammurabi (created ca. 1780 B.C.), one of the earliest and most sophisticated set of laws ever found from the ancient world.

The Sumerian city-states lasted for about 800 years. A series of military defeats combined with economic stagnation sent this once-great civilization into decline.

The Kingdom of Egypt (ca. 3000–1100 B.C.)

Around 3000 B.C., the Kingdom of Egypt emerged when Upper and Lower Egypt were joined under one monarch, called Menes. There is evidence to suggest contact with Sumeria just prior to this consolidation, as several of Sumeria's innovations appear in the Kingdom of Egypt. The earliest kings are credited with commanding allegiance by devising the concept of divine kingship. The Sumerians believed that their kings were appointed by the gods, but the Egyptians believed that their kings were gods.

The Old Kingdom (ca. 3000–2200 B.C.) The Egyptians established political unity of the Nile Valley and the Delta. Unlike the discrete Sumerian city-states, the Egyptians were organized as a "country-state," with multiple villages held together to form one large economy. Their kings, called pharaohs, were autocrats—considered to be living gods, not just agents of the gods—and they wielded religious authority that influenced all institutions of government and society. Just below the king stood a multi-layered bureaucracy of scribes; this tiny elite of nobles, scribes, and priests controlled a massive illiterate peasantry.

The divinity of the king meant that the pharaoh was the highest authority in the land. He was not bound by a code of law; in fact, he was the supreme arbiter of all legal decisions. He appointed all ministers, and he decided on war or peace. His religious duties included not only taking care of state business, but also building and maintaining the famous pyramids, or temples to the dead.

Egypt at this time was around 750 miles long and very, very slender; most travel in the kingdom was done by water. To govern this far-flung empire, the kings set up a system of provinces run by governors. The central administration was run by a chief executive, who oversaw a number of specialized departments. The state controlled the economy, and used the monies from foreign trade and taxes to build monuments and support the lavish royal lifestyle.

The New Kingdom (ca. 1600–1100 B.C.) This state was a perfect autocracy and totally centralized, controlling all human and natural resources in its realm, including the entire economy. Like their predecessors in the Old Kingdom, the pharaoh was considered divine. The pharaohs of this period enjoyed spectacular wealth and power, dictating all aspects of life in the kingdom. The central government controlled a cast of lesser officials who oversaw the provinces, ruling a population of four million through a sophisticated system of taxation. Egypt fielded a well-equipped army that was totally devoted to the pharaoh. Very little is known about the judiciary of the New Kingdom except that in a criminal trial, evidence and interrogation techniques were used.

Ancient China

The Xia Dynasty (ca. 2070–1600 B.C.) Scholars generally divide Chinese history into a series of dynasties (successive rulers from the same families). The first was the Xia dynasty, led by the legendary king Yu, who began China's long history of family or clan control. Although there are few records of this dynasty, scholars feel that this society produced some governmental innovations: the first benign civilian government, harsh punishment for criminal legal transactions, and a Chinese legal code.

The Shang Dynasty (ca. 1600–1040 B.C.) When a rebel leader overthrew the last ruler of the Xia dynasty, the Shang dynasty came into existence in the Yellow River Valley. Shang China was situated in the North China Plain

and extended as far north as modern Shandong province and westward through present Henan province.

The kings of the Shang dynasty are believed to have fought frequent wars with neighboring settlements. They occupied several capitals one after another, but appear to have settled at Anyang in the 14th century B.C. The king appointed local governors, and there was an established class of nobles elevated above the masses of peasants. In this largely agricultural society, the king issued pronouncements as to when to plant crops. Elaborate court rituals were developed to appease spirits: in addition to his secular position, the king was the head of the ancestor- and spirit-worship cult. During this period Chinese writing began to develop and a calendar system with 12 months of 30 days each was created.

The Persian Empire (ca. 550–330 B.C.)

The Persian Empire was actually a long series of historical empires that ruled over what is now modern-day Iran. Perhaps the greatest of these was the Achaemenid Empire (550–330 B.C.), which encompassed parts of Egypt and much of the Middle East, extending well into Central Asia and the Caucasus. This massive empire, the largest the ancient world had ever seen, sprawled over nearly 2.5 million square miles. It ruled over some 50 million people with diverse ethnicities, religions, and customs. The empire's administrative capital lay roughly equally between Macedonia and Ghandara, 1,600 miles from each.

Below the Persian monarchs stood a complex class of powerful, enormously wealthy territorial nobles. There was no all-pervasive religion to buttress state power. The king, known as the Shah of Shahs, ruled supreme, but his empire was actually administered by local satraps, or provincial governors who worked for the king's nobles. The king gave his orders through his noblemen, from whom he demanded loyalty. To govern this massive territory, the king exercised a loose administrative authority over the entire land, demanding tribute and obedience while delegating most local matters to regional officials.

Ancient Greece (2000–334 B.C.)

From the beginning of recorded history, ancient civilizations were monarchies that ruled through priests or noblemen. But Greece dispensed with the notion of kings and gods, creating an entirely new model of governance. Its subjects were organized for the first time as citizens who participated in a *polis*.

The Greek word polis is often translated as "city-state,"

but Aristotle defined it as an "association of citizens." The concept of citizenship was a true innovation, implying the right for people to participate in running their own government. (It is worth noting, however, that only adult males could be considered citizens; women, slaves, and foreigners were excluded.)

Ancient Greece was a relatively small area defined by mountains and sea. From about 800 B.C., Greece was divided into many discrete self-governing communities, most isolated by their location. When the population outgrew this limited territory, the Greeks began to colonize other far-flung regions. By the sixth century B.C., Greeks both at home and abroad had organized themselves into independent communities and the city-state had become the fundamental unit of Greek government.

The basic political structure, the polis, included an executive (the *basileus*), a council of elders (the *gerontes*), and a meeting of all warriors (the *agora*). A polis had several fundamental characteristics including independence, political unity, identification with a cult, and a surrounding rural area forming an extension of its identity. Most importantly, there was no monarchy.

Athens The Greek city-state of Athens was the first "direct" democracy, meaning its citizens cast their own votes on legislation rather than relying on elected representatives to act as intermediaries. All posts—executive, legislative, and judiciary—were open to all citizens for a one-year term, and candidates worked to muster support among the citizens. This was *demokratia*, meaning "rule of the people," or "government by the people" in its earliest form.

Cleisthenes (570–508 B.C.) assumed power around 507 B.C. and was responsible for implementing many reforms that came to define Athenian democracy. He eliminated the four traditional Athenian tribes, which curtailed the power of families and reorganized Athenian society into 10 new tribes based on their area of residence (each was named after an Athenian hero). The 10 tribes regularly provided men to serve in the various parts of Athenian government: the Assembly, the Council, the administration, and the judiciary. By design, each tribe contained men from the city, the coast, and the plain. Cleisthenes also devised legislative bodies with leaders chosen by lot rather than by heredity or kinship. He reorganized the council into a 500-member body made up of 50 representatives from each tribe. The council proposed laws to the Assembly, an open gathering of citizens who convened to vote at least 40 times a year. Cleisthenes also set up a court

system with hundreds of new jurors chosen every day.

The Assembly was open to all Athenian citizens, and it is thought to have met at least 10 times a year in the main marketplace, giving each of the 10 tribes a chance to organize and preside over the Assembly on a rotating basis. An agenda was published four days in advance. The Council, as well as citizens, could put forth proposals or amendments. Votes were taken by a show of hands. No quorum was required for most voting, with a few exceptions that required at least 6,000 citizens to be present.

The powerful Assembly had jurisdiction over matters of war and peace, the army, finances and currency, political alliances, taxation, and offenses against the state. It controlled all magistrates, who had to appear before the Assembly 10 times a year.

Though subordinate to the Assembly, the Council was the central organ of executive power. From 507 B.C. on, it consisted of 500 members who served one-year terms (they could only be re-elected once). The men on the Council had to be at least 30 years old and hail from one of the 10 tribes. There were few candidates because the responsibilities were onerous, the expenses high, and the daily stipend very small—factors that discouraged the poor from serving. The Council met every day, and its sessions were public and open to citizen participation.

The "presiding committees" were the 50 men from the 10 tribes. The foreman, appointed to serve as president of the Athenian Republic for one day, held the keys to the temples and presided over the Council (and the Assembly if it met that day). The Council tightly controlled the Assembly's agenda. The latter could discuss nothing that had not already been discussed in the Council and had been pronounced it as a resolution. It was also the only body that could coordinate and control a multitude of 10-man boards, all of equal standing and mutually independent, which carried on the day-to-day administration. Its judicial duties were challenging claims to citizenship, ruling on the validity of candidates for the Council and other government posts, and determining entitlement to public assistance.

Magistrates, elected to one-year terms, were the executive agents of the Council and the Assembly. Most served on commissions made up of 10 members, one from each tribe. There were three levels of administrator: the political, the administrative, and the subordinate staff of freedman or slaves who worked as clerks. Their areas of concern included sacrifices, the calendars, family law, protection of property, and general law. The Commission for Public

Contracts collected taxes.

The Athenian judicial system had two parts: the magistracies and the courts. The magistracies processed and administered actions, and the courts judged on them. All citizens had the right to be a juror in the popular courts.

The Roman Republic (509–27 B.C.)

The Romans contributed many ideas, innovations, and institutions to the modern world, including many of the foundations of modern governance. Their methods enabled the Romans to successfully homogenize and incorporate diverse populations into a unified community and to enjoy continuous military dominance. Most notably they created the concept of checks and balances in government, a mechanism that remains vital today.

In the beginning, Rome was a tiny city of just six by eight miles, governed by a king. A Council of Elders advised him and an Assembly of Warriors voted on matters of war and peace. But in 509 B.C., following the overthrow of Lucius Tarquinius Superbus, the last of Rome's seven kings, the monarchy was replaced by several separate magistrates, called consuls, who took on the royal functions. The Council was renamed the Senate and was composed of ex-magistrates with life tenure; it was dominated by noble clans and families. The Assembly of Warriors evolved into various popular Assemblies. With the creation of the Senate in 509 B.C., the Roman Republic came into being. The word Republic comes from the Latin *res publica*, which means "public matters" or "matters of state."

Like the Greek polis, the Roman Republic was a city-state—a community of citizens with a similar tripartite structure of magistrates, Council, and Assembly. But from the beginning, Roman society was dominated by wealthy families. There were four classes of people in Rome, and the distinctions were all-important. A census divided the population according to how much property they owned. The slaves were the lowest class. The plebeians, who were free, came next. The equestrians, or "knights," who were fairly rich, were called to serve in the army; they made up the second-highest class. The upper echelon was occupied by the nobles, or "patricians."

The system, with magistrates rotating annually, was actually more complex than it sounds. The Assemblies were restricted from taking action unless it was initiated by a magistrate, and they were restricted to simple yes-no votes. In addition, the magistrates could veto one another's actions, and some officers, known as tribunes, could stop all business or initiate legislation.

In 451 B.C. Rome set out its first written legal code, inscribed upon 12 bronze tablets and publicly displayed in the Forum. Its provisions concerned such matters as legal procedure, debt foreclosure, paternal authority over children, property rights, inheritance, and funerary regulations. This so-called "Law of the 12 Tables" later formed the basis of all subsequent Roman private law.

Roman society was imperialist by nature, and over time, Rome grew to tremendous scale as it conquered other nations through its enormous military might. The newly acquired lands, inhabited by diverse peoples, presented a huge challenge of governance. In addition to stationing troops in these regions to maintain their occupation, the Romans organized the conquered peoples into provinces, appointing governors who wielded absolute power over all non-Roman citizens.

In 134 B.C. Rome issued a formal constitution to codify the role of each body of government. The constitution called for 22 magistrates (two were military consuls, two censors who maintained the census, and others who were charged with maintaining justice, the treasury, and public works). There were also 10 elected officers known as tribunes, who could veto and halt any action in any of the agencies (the magistrates, the Senate, or the Assemblies).

The Senate was now an advisory body consisting of ex-magistrates, who were nominated for life by the two censors. The Senate met only when it was convened by a magistrate; in those cases the Senators would listen to the matter at hand, issue an opinion, and be finished. Each of the Assemblies was made up of popular citizens. The Centuriat Assembly was the citizen-army, organized into voting blocs known as centuries. They were classified into five census categories, and their votes were weighted accordingly. The Centuriat elected the magistrates, who ruled the Republic for one year. The Tribal Assembly was made up of exactly the same citizens, but they were organized into 35 different groups, or tribes, and their votes were not weighted. The Tribute Assembly voted on peace and war, and passed legislation.

Government Systems

Throughout history, the power structures responsible for providing internal and external security, order, and justice have varied greatly from country to country. In most cases, a constitution lays out the framework and basic rules of government. The underlying principles may be implied in various laws, institutions, and customs, or contained in one fundamental written document. In some cases, the constitution is largely unwritten, as in Great Britain. As modern governments have moved into areas such as providing welfare services, regulating the economy, guarding civil liberties, and setting up educational systems, contemporary leaders frequently find it necessary to amend their original framework.

Democracy

A democracy is a system of government in which citizens participate in the decision-making process, either by voting directly or by electing representatives in periodic, free elections. In this system, the majority rules, usually through representation, and all votes count equally.

A direct democracy refers to the form of government in which the entire body of citizens has the right to make political decisions through the power of majority. This kind of democracy works well on a small scale, such as a charity board or a school. As the number of people to be governed grows larger and more complex, it becomes necessary for the people to elect representatives who will serve their interests. This is known as a representative democracy. A constitutional democracy, which is usually representative in nature, operates within the boundaries of a constitution that is designed to guarantee certain basic rights.

The normal pre-conditions for democracy are a constitutional government; free elections for legislatures and the executive; more than one political party; checks and balances between the various branches of government; an independent judiciary; the protection of each citizen's personal liberties; and stability of government.

Presidential Democracy A presidential democracy, sometimes called a liberal democracy, typically features a freely elected president who presides over the executive branch and acts as head of state. He or she works in concert with the legislative branch, an independent judiciary, a constitution, and some degree of participation by political parties. The president cannot, in normal circumstances, dissolve the legislature, although in some presidential democracies, the president can veto bills. The president serves for a fixed term, and generally there are procedures for removing him from office if need be. The president can appoint a cabinet and nominate judges, but legislative approval is usually needed for these appointments.

Examples of presidential democracies include the United States, Indonesia, the Philippines, Mexico, South Korea, and most South American countries, as well as much of Africa and Central Asia.

Parliamentary Democracy The features of a parliamentary democracy normally include popular representation, a legislature (unicameral or bicameral), and a cabinet or ministry. This type of democracy typically makes a distinction between the head of state and the head of government. The president is often a figurehead and not an active political participant; the constitutional duties of the head of government fall to the prime minister. The figurehead presidents tend to be appointed by the legislature rather than elected, although there are exceptions. Normally, a parliamentary democracy features an executive branch of government that depends on the support of the parliament, which is often expressed through a vote of confidence or no confidence. As a general rule, constitutional monarchies are often parliamentary. This system normally includes a constitution, but in some cases, as with the United Kingdom, there are instead "constitutional conventions" instead of one formal written document.

The British style of parliamentary democracy spread throughout its colonies and continues to hold sway in many countries. Finland, Greece, Israel, and many of the newly formed states of Eastern Europe feature unicameral parliamentary democracies. Australia, Canada, India, and Spain are bicameral parliamentary democracies.

Monarchy

A monarchy is a form or government that is headed by a king or queen, the monarch. In a constitutional monarchy, such as Great Britain, Denmark or Sweden, the prime minister is the active head of the executive branch of government and also head of the legislature. The head of state is the monarch, who only exercises power with the consent of the government, the people, or their representatives. In a semi-constitutional monarchy, such as Kuwait or Liechtenstein, the prime minister heads the executive branch, but the monarch has a great deal of political power that can be used as he or she sees fit. In an absolute monarchy, such as Saudi Arabia or Tonga, the monarch is the active head of the executive branch and can exercise complete power in government.

Theocracy

A theocracy is a form of government predicated on the elevation of one officially sanctioned state religion. The head of state is selected by some form of religious hierarchy, and may be considered to represent divine power on earth. Laws are crafted to enforce the principles of the one chosen religious. In many but not all cases, theocracies are non-democratic governments. Examples of theocracies are Iran and the Vatican.

Socialism

Socialism, in theory, envisages a socio-economic system in which wealth and property are distributed equally and are controlled by the people. In the mid-19th century, Karl Marx helped establish the modern socialist movement with his writings, in which he called for abolishing money, markets, and capital, and the use of people's labor as a commodity. For Marxists, socialism was the transitional stage between capitalism and communism, in which the state would take control of the means of production. Once private property was abolished, the state would wither away and people would move on to a higher stage of communism.

The most famous example of socialism was the system put into practice by Vladimir Lenin in 1917, when the Communist Party of the Soviet Union (CPSU) took over Russia. The CPSU sought to "build socialism" by bringing all of the means of production (except agriculture) under state control, and creating a mechanism of central planning for the entire economy. This proved to be very difficult to implement, and unworkable as envisaged; gradually the Soviet Union developed into a bureaucratic authoritarian state, while continuing to maintain publicly that their socialism was on the path to communism.

Communism

Communism is an ideology that seeks to establish a classless society based on common ownership of property and the means of production. A communist government has a one-party system with an allegiance to Marxism-Leninism (as in the old Soviet Union and Eastern Europe) or Marxism-Leninism–Mao Zedong Thought (as in China). The Communist Party is the only legal political party. Most communist states feature centrally planned economies. There are few individual rights for citizens, no genuinely free elections, and no independent judiciary.

Fascism

Fascism is a set of authoritarian ideologies that focus on state control of individuals in the interest of forging national unity, usually based on ethnic, religious, or cultural considerations. It emphasizes conformity to forge a mobilized national polity. Mussolini's Italy is generally thought to be the first fascist government, and Mussolini himself defined fascism as the merging of corporate interests with the state. Fascist nationalism was hostile to both socialism and feminism, and attempted to create a new elite acting in the name of the people. This form of government tends to be headed by a charismatic leader and focused on glorifying the military. Fascist regimes have included Nazi Germany under Hitler and Spain under Franco.

Authoritarian Governments

Authoritarian governments are intent on maintaining social control; their citizens are subject to state authority in many aspects of their lives. This type of government normally demands strict obedience—and may obtain that obedience through oppressive measures.

Like a democracy, an authoritarian regime can be a very stable system that adheres to a constitution. But normally an authoritarian government does not allow free elections; more than one political party; checks and balances between the executive, legislative, and judicial branches; an independent judiciary; or civil liberties.

Dictatorship A dictatorship is an autocratic form of government ruled by a dictator who has no legal, constitutional, social, or political restrictions on his power. Dictators often head military governments, a situation that has occurred in some Latin American, Asian, and African nations.

Totalitarianism A totalitarian system is one in which the state regulates almost all aspects of private and public behavior. This type of government attempts to mobilize the entire population toward an official state ideology. A totalitarian regime typically outlaws activities that are not sanctioned by the state, and it often uses repression or state control of all activities. Citizens have been persecuted in totalitarian states for reasons of religion and ethnicity, as well as belonging to trade unions or political parties. Authoritarian regimes often maintain power through the use of a secret police force, heavy propaganda distributed through state-controlled media, restricted speech, a tightly controlled judiciary, single-party politics, and mass sur-veillance and terror tactics. Often totalitarian govern-ments feature a personality cult revolving around the leader. The former Soviet Union is a prime example of a totalitarian state, as is North Korea.

American Government

The United States is a federal republic consisting of 50 states and the District of Columbia. As mandated by the U.S. Constitution, each state has considerable powers of self-government. A liberal democracy, the United States has a formal Constitution; free elections; clear separation of powers between the executive, legislative and judicial branches; an independent judiciary; and protection of civil liberties.

In May 1787, the Founding Fathers held a Constitutional Convention in Philadelphia to create a government that would have checks and balances. After four months of ran-corous deliberations, they devised a system that would give the government power while protecting the rights of citizens. In a solution known as the "Virginia Plan," the con-ventioneers called for three branches of government: the legislative body; the executive, led by a president who would run the country; and the judiciary, entrusted with the power to enforce laws and punish those who do not obey them. The first three articles of the U.S. Constitution clearly set forth the fundamental workings of each branch.

At the Constitutional Congress, there was also much debate about how to give each state fair representation, since some of the states were large and some very small. In what came to be known as the "Great Compromise," the delegates created a bicameral system, dividing the con-gress into two chambers (the Senate and the House of Representatives). Each state, regardless of size, sends two elected officials to the Senate. (Senators serve six-year terms, and in any given cycle, one-third of the Senate faces re-election.) Conversely, the states send differing numbers to the House of Representatives, with their allotment based on population. Congressional representatives serve two-year terms; the entire House is up for re-election every two years. (For a complete description of the U.S. Constitution see "Law.")

The Legislative Branch

The legislature, or congress, is charged with making laws.

Many of the bills considered by congress are produced by specialized committees drawn from its membership. Under the Constitution, only congress has the power to declare war.

The Senate is most often thought of as the more powerful body, because it approves key federal appointments and rati-fies foreign treaties, and it is generally a more deliberative chamber than the House of Representatives. Although impeachment cases brought against federal officials must originate in the House of Representatives, the Senate hears the formal trial of impeachment cases, with a two-thirds majority vote required for conviction.

The House of Representatives has a large role in the fiscal area, since all spending bills originate in this chamber. The House Budget and Finance Committee is therefore the most powerful of all the legislative committees.

Both houses of congress are involved in ratifying amend-ments to the Constitution. This requires two-thirds majori-ties from both chambers, and three-fourths of all state legislatures across the nation. Alternatively, a Constitutional amendment may be initiated by two-thirds of state legisla-tures, which can call for a special National Constitutional Convention.

How a Bill Becomes a Law

Every law starts out as a bill that is introduced by a member of the House or Senate. The bill is assigned to an appropriate committee or subcommittee in the chamber where it origi-nated; there the bill is examined and debated, and hearings may be held. In "mark up," the committee in charge can change, add, or take away provisions of the proposed bill. Once that process is finished, the bill is placed on the calen-dar for debate and a vote. When the members meet to vote on the proposed bill, it is either approved, sometimes with changes, or it is killed.

If the members vote to pass the bill, it is then introduced into the other chamber of congress for debate and enhance-ment. If the bill passes through both chambers, it is sent to the president for signature. If the House and Senate pass dif-fering versions of the same bill, the proposals go to "confer-ence committee," where both sides must hammer out their differences.

The president has 10 days to sign a bill into law. If he does not sign it in 10 days, and congress is in session, the bill automatically becomes law. If he turns it down (issuing a "veto"), he may send it back to the congress with his suggestions for changes, and the process starts again in the chamber where the bill originated. At this point, the House and Senate can attempt to override the president's veto, a move that requires a two-thirds majority vote. If the veto is overridden in both chambers, it becomes law. If the president does not act on a bill and congress adjourns before the end of the 10-day period, the legislation is dead. This is called a "pocket veto."

The Executive Branch

The executive's main job is to carry out the laws of the country. Article 2 of the U.S. Constitution states that the president can conduct foreign affairs and act as commander-in-chief of the U.S. military. He can also appoint a cabinet to advise him on specialized subjects.

The cabinet includes the vice president and the heads (or "secretaries") of 15 executive departments: Agriculture, Commerce, Defense, Education, Energy, Health and Human Services, Homeland Security, Housing and Urban Development, Interior, Justice (the head of this department is the Attorney General), Labor, State, Transportation, Treasury, and Veterans Affairs. Under President George W. Bush, cabinet-level rank also has been accorded to the administrator of the Environmental Protection Agency; the director of the Office of Management and Budget; the director of National Drug Control Policy; and the U.S. Trade Representative.

The president and vice president run for election every four years. Article 2 specifies that these elections are actually decided by indirect voting; the citizens cast their votes for candidates, but in reality, they are voting for a slate of "electors" pledged to those candidates. These electors ratify the final result in the Electoral College, in a process that is further outlined in the 12th Amendment. (See "The Constitution") Most states have a winner-take-all rule that awards all of their electors to the candidates who win the popular vote, no matter how slim their margin of victory may be.

The Constitution also requires that the president must be born in the United States, that he or she must be at least 35 years old, and he or she must have lived in the United States for 14 years. Once elected, the president serves as the head of state, commander-in-chief of the armed forces, and head of the civil service. The 22nd Amendment limits the president to two terms in office.

In the event that a president becomes disabled, power is transferred according to procedures outlined in the 20th Amendment, the 25th Amendment, and the Presidential

Succession Law of 1947. The 20th and 25th Amendments establish the method for the vice president to assume the duties and powers of the presidency in the case of a permanent or temporary disabling of the president. The 25th Amendment also provides a method for filling a vacated office of the vice president. The president must nominate a new vice president, who must be confirmed by a majority vote of both houses of Congress. The Presidential Succession Law of 1947 addressed the simultaneous disability of both the president and vice president.

Presidential Order of Succession

Vice President of the United States
Speaker of the House
President Pro Tempore of the Senate
Secretary of State
Secretary of the Treasury
Secretary of Defense
Attorney General
Secretary of the Interior
Secretary of Agriculture
Secretary of Commerce
Secretary of Labor
Secretary of Health & Human Services
Secretary of Housing & Urban Development
Secretary of Transportation
Secretary of Energy
Secretary of Education
Secretary of Veterans Affairs
Secretary of Homeland Security

The Judicial Branch

Article 3 of the U.S. Constitution provides for the judicial branch, consisting of a Supreme Court and lower federal courts. The U.S. Supreme Court consists of nine justices who are appointed by the president and confirmed by the Senate. The justices serve lifetime terms—a system that was designed to insulate the Court from the political pressures of the moment. A justice can only be removed by impeachment.

Directly under the Supreme Court are the appellate courts, including 10 Regional Circuit Courts of Appeals and one U.S. Court of Appeals for the Federal Circuit. These courts hear appeals of cases that have already been decided by lower courts. The trial courts, or the U.S. District Courts, are made up of 94 judicial districts across the nation.

The Supreme Court is the "court of last resort." Each year some 7,000 requests for Supreme Court judgments arrive for review, and are placed on a docket. The Court cannot hear all of these cases, and chooses to rule on about 100 of them, and to write opinions on about 80. The Supreme Court may also determine whether or not a law passed by Congress violates the U.S. Constitution.

State Governments

The 10th Amendment to the U.S. Constitution states that, "The powers not delegated to the United States by the Constitution, nor prohibited by it to the States, are reserved to the States respectively, or to the people." State powers have evolved over time to include jurisdiction over the rules pertaining to internal communications, property, industry, business, and public utilities. Each state also has its own criminal code and regulations regarding working conditions.

Article 5, Section 4 of the U.S. Constitution further mandates that each state will implement a republican form of government. The Founders envisioned state governments that would mirror the structure of the federal government, complete with checks and balances. Each state has its own constitution, which specifies the workings of a legislature, an executive (the governor), and a state-level judiciary.

Almost every state has a bicameral legislature. (Nebraska is the lone exception, with a unicameral legislature called the Senate.) Because each state has its own constitution, the various legislative bodies may go by different names. But these are differences in name only, for no matter its name, each state legislature contains elected officials who represent the populace. Each state has a chamber of state senators and a chamber of state representatives.

Just like the U.S. Congress, these state legislatures pass laws and create a budget to pay for state-run programs. Because the United States is such a large and varied country, each state can create the government that best suits its needs. While state laws cannot contradict or violate federal law or the U.S. Constitution, there are times when interests of the state and federal governments intersect. These usually have to do with matters of health, education, welfare, transportation, and housing and urban development. In these cases, state and the federal governments cooperate.

Each state's executive branch, like its federal counterpart, carries out state laws. A popularly elected governor is the chief executive, and most states also have a lieutenant governor. Most governors serve four-year terms, although in Vermont and New Hampshire, the term is two years. The governor oversees all the state agencies and departments.

Each state's judiciary is set up to mirror the hierarchy of the federal judiciary. There is a state Supreme Court, which hears appeals from the lower state courts. The state's constitution or legislation governs the methods by which judges are elected or appointed in each state.

Speakers of the House of Representatives

Speaker	State	Date Elected	Speaker	State	Date Elected
Frederick A.C. Muhlenberg	Pennsylvania	Apr. 1, 1789	John W. Taylor	New York	Dec. 5, 1825
Jonathan Trumbull	Connecticut	Oct. 24, 1791	Andrew Stevenson	Virginia	Dec. 3, 1827
Frederick A.C. Muhlenberg	Pennsylvania	Dec. 2, 1793	Andrew Stevenson	Virginia	Dec. 7, 1829
			Andrew Stevenson	Virginia	Dec. 5, 1831
Jonathan Dayton	New Jersey	Dec. 7, 1795	John Bell	Tennessee	June 2, 1834
Jonathan Dayton	New Jersey	May 15, 1797	James K. Polk	Tennessee	Dec. 7, 1835
Theodore Sedgwick	Massachusetts	Dec. 2, 1799	James K. Polk	Tennessee	Sept. 4, 1837
Nathaniel Macon	North Carolina	Dec. 7, 1801	Robert M.T. Hunter	Virginia	Dec. 16, 1839
Nathaniel Macon	North Carolina	Oct. 17, 1803	John White	Kentucky	May 31, 1841
Nathaniel Macon	North Carolina	Dec. 2, 1805	John W. Jones	Virginia	Dec. 4, 1843
Joseph B. Varnum	Massachusetts	Oct. 26, 1807	John W. Davis	Indiana	Dec. 1, 1845
Joseph B. Varnum	Massachusetts	May 22, 1809	Robert C. Winthrop	Massachusetts	Dec. 6, 1847
Henry Clay	Kentucky	Nov. 4, 1811	Howell Cobb	Georgia	Dec. 22, 1849
Henry Clay [1]	Kentucky	May 24, 1813	Linn Boyd	Kentucky	Dec. 1, 1851
Langdon Cheves	South Carolina	Jan. 19, 1814	Linn Boyd	Kentucky	Dec. 5, 1853
Henry Clay	Kentucky	Dec. 4, 1815	Nathaniel P. Banks	Massachusetts	Feb. 2, 1856
Henry Clay	Kentucky	Dec. 1, 1817	James L. Orr	South Carolina	Dec. 7, 1857
Henry Clay [2]	Kentucky	Dec. 6, 1819	William Pennington	New Jersey	Feb. 1, 1860
John W. Taylor	New York	Nov. 15, 1820	Galusha A. Grow	Pennsylvania	July 4, 1861
Philip P. Barbour	Virginia	Dec. 4, 1821	Schuyler Colfax	Indiana	Dec. 7, 1863
Henry Clay [3]	Kentucky	Dec. 1, 1823	Schuyler Colfax	Indiana	Dec. 4, 1865
			Schuyler Colfax	Indiana	Mar. 4, 1867

Speakers of the House of Representatives (continued)

Speaker	State	Date Elected	Speaker	State	Date Elected
Theodore M. Pomeroy[4]	New York	Mar. 3, 1869	William B. Bankhead	Alabama	Jan. 5, 1937
James G. Blaine	Maine	Mar. 4, 1869	William B. Bankhead[8]	Alabama	Jan. 3, 1939
James G. Blaine	Maine	Mar. 4, 1871	Sam Rayburn	Texas	Sept. 16, 1940
James G. Blaine	Maine	Dec. 1, 1873	Sam Rayburn	Texas	Jan. 3, 1941
Michael C. Kerr[5]	Indiana	Dec. 6, 1875	Sam Rayburn	Texas	Jan. 6, 1943
Samuel J. Randall	Pennsylvania	Dec. 4, 1876	Sam Rayburn	Texas	Jan. 3, 1945
Samuel J. Randall	Pennsylvania	Dec. 4, 1876	Joseph W. Martin, Jr.	Massachusetts	Jan. 3, 1947
Samuel J. Randall	Pennsylvania	Mar. 18, 1879	Sam Rayburn	Texas	Jan. 3, 1949
J. Warren Keifer	Ohio	Dec. 5, 1881	Sam Rayburn	Texas	Jan. 3, 1951
John G. Carlisle	Kentucky	Dec. 3, 1883	Joseph W. Martin, Jr.	Massachusetts	Jan. 3, 1953
John G. Carlisle	Kentucky	Dec. 7, 1885	Sam Rayburn	Texas	Jan. 5, 1955
John G. Carlisle	Kentucky	Dec. 5, 1887	Sam Rayburn	Texas	Jan. 3, 1957
Thomas B. Reed	Maine	Dec. 2, 1889	Sam Rayburn	Texas	Jan. 7, 1959
Charles F. Crisp	Georgia	Dec. 8, 1891	Sam Rayburn[9]	Texas	Jan. 3, 1961
Charles F. Crisp	Georgia	Aug. 7, 1893	John W. McCormack	Massachusetts	Jan. 10, 1962
Thomas B. Reed	Maine	Dec. 2, 1895	John W. McCormack	Massachusetts	Jan. 9, 1963
Thomas B. Reed	Maine	Mar. 15, 1897	John W. McCormack	Massachusetts	Jan. 4, 1965
David B. Henderson	Iowa	Dec. 4, 1899	John W. McCormack	Massachusetts	Jan. 10, 1967
David B. Henderson	Iowa	Dec. 2, 1901	John W. McCormack	Massachusetts	Jan. 3, 1969
Joseph G. Cannon	Illinois	Nov. 9, 1903	Carl B. Albert	Oklahoma	Jan. 21, 1971
Joseph G. Cannon	Illinois	Dec. 4, 1905	Carl B. Albert	Oklahoma	Jan. 3, 1973
Joseph G. Cannon	Illinois	Dec. 2, 1907	Carl B. Albert	Oklahoma	Jan. 14, 1975
Joseph G. Cannon	Illinois	Mar. 15, 1909	Thomas P. O'Neill, Jr.	Massachusetts	Jan. 4, 1977
James Beauchamp Clark	Missouri	Apr. 4, 1911	Thomas P. O'Neill, Jr.	Massachusetts	Jan. 15, 1979
			Thomas P. O'Neill, Jr.	Massachusetts	Jan. 5, 1981
James Beauchamp Clark	Missouri	Apr. 7, 1913	Thomas P. O'Neill, Jr.	Massachusetts	Jan. 3, 1983
			Thomas P. O'Neill, Jr.	Massachusetts	Jan. 3, 1985
James Beauchamp Clark	Missouri	Dec. 6, 1915	James C. Wright, Jr.	Texas	Jan. 6, 1987
			James C. Wright, Jr.[10]	Texas	Jan. 3, 1989
James Beauchamp Clark	Missouri	Apr. 2, 1917	Thomas S. Foley	Washington	Jun. 6, 1989
			Thomas S. Foley	Washington	Jan. 3, 1991
Frederick H. Gillett	Massachusetts	May 19, 1919	Thomas S. Foley	Washington	Jan. 5, 1993
Frederick H. Gillett	Massachusetts	Apr. 11, 1921	Newt Gingrich	Georgia	Jan. 4, 1995
Frederick H. Gillett	Massachusetts	Dec. 3, 1923	Newt Gingrich	Georgia	Jan. 7, 1997
Nicholas Longworth	Ohio	Dec. 7, 1925	J. Dennis Hastert	Illinois	Jan. 6, 1999
Nicholas Longworth	Ohio	Dec. 5, 1927	J. Dennis Hastert	Illinois	Jan. 3, 2001
Nicholas Longworth	Ohio	Apr. 15, 1929	J. Dennis Hastert	Illinois	Jan. 7, 2003
John N. Garner	Texas	Dec. 7, 1931	J. Dennis Hastert	Illinois	Jan. 4, 2005
Henry T. Rainey[6]	Illinois	Mar. 9, 1933	Nancy Pelosi	California	Jan. 4, 2007
Joseph W. Byrns[7]	Tennessee	Jan. 3, 1935	John Boehner	Ohio	Jan. 5, 2011
William B. Bankhead	Alabama	Jun. 4, 1936			

Source: *Biographical Directory of the U.S. Congress*, Congressional Research Service **Notes:** 1. Resigned from the House of Representatives, January 19, 1814. 2. Resigned on October 28, 1820. 3. Resigned from the House of Representatives, March 6, 1825. 4. Elected Speaker, March 3, 1869, and served one day. 5. Died in office, August 19, 1876. 6. Died in office, August 19, 1934. 7. Died in office June 4, 1936. 8. Died in office, September 15, 1940. 9. Died November 16, 1961. 10. Resigned from the House of Representatives, June 6, 1989.

LAW

A Brief History of Law

The roots of the American legal system lie in Great Britain and the English common law. However, English law itself borrowed concepts and rules from the legal systems of the ancient world, including early Babylonia, ancient Greece, and Rome. Whether the Roman concept of "criminal intent" that still underlies the entire modern U.S. criminal law, or the more ancient concept of strict liability of an "eye for an eye" found in the Code of Hammurabi and the Old Testament, early law casts an illuminating light on choices we have made in our current system.

Code of Hammurabi

The earliest known figure of great legal importance is Hammurabi (1792–50 B.C.), the king of Bablyonia and creator of one of the most comprehensive early codes of laws. The code, engraved on an eight-foot-tall black stone monument, is well known for its thoroughness and complexity, addressing commercial, family, labor, property, and personal injury law. But it is also known for the harsh dictum, "an eye for an eye," a literal legal punishment. Many other crimes that would seem relatively minor today incurred capital punishment. Rather than attempting any of the more modern aims of the law, such as rehabilitation, Hammurabi's Code mandated simple retribution.

Ancient Greece

Law began to emerge as an instrument of a more humanitarian impulse in Greece during the rule of Solon (ca. 639–ca. 559 B.C.), the Athenian general and statesman who helped lay the groundwork for democracy in Athens. Prior to Solon, the harsh laws of Draco, promulgated in 621 B.C., were in force. Under Draco's laws, most crimes, even idleness, were punishable by death. After his election in 594 B.C., Solon instituted a milder legal regime, in which punishments were calibrated to the seriousness of the crime. Courts also took on a more powerful role under Solon's law. The Roman historian Plutarch suggested that Solon intentionally wrote laws with a measure of ambiguity in order to increase the power of the courts through interpretation—a step that foreshadowed the U.S. law-

makers' proclivity to let the courts decide the application of the general provisions of statutes to specific situations. Finally, Athenian law became more democratic, as Solon reformed the existing social, economic, and political systems in Athens. Solon gave his reforms popular appeal by, among other measures, annulling all mortgages and debts, limiting the amount of land any single citizen could hold, and forbidding all borrowing that could cause a debtor to lose personal liberty.

Rome

Early Roman law, as stated in the Twelve Tables (ca. 450 B.C.), formed the basis for the legal systems that would later influence those of Europe and through Europe the entire world. While some of the rules contained in the Twelve Tables are nearly identical to those of the modern world, such as requiring the accused to appear before a magistrate in the initial stages of a criminal proceeding, others were rooted in their time, such as the prohibition of marriages between plebeians and patricians. Law was made more sophisticated as a method of stabilizing society by Lucius Cornelius Sulla (138–78 B.C.), a Roman general and dictator whose usurpation of power paved the way for the fall of the republic. His *leges corneliae* provided specific punishments for homicide, arson, the intention of killing or stealing, poisoning, and the manufacture and possession of poison. However, his rule was also marked by efforts to check the populist branches of Roman government. For example, Sulla protected the power of the Senate from populist incursions by giving it control of the courts and new measures against the tribunes.

Law continued to be developed during the reign of Augustus (63 B.C.–A.D. 14), who took power in 29 B.C. Augustus established legal principles that would influence Western law, including clear procedures for formalizing contracts, strengthening personal property law, and the presumption that defendants were innocent until proven guilty. Augustus's legal reforms were extensive but were rooted in Roman tradition. Rome technically remained a republic governed by the Senate, but with Augustus as leading man or *princeps*. The term *emperor* derives from the Latin *imperator*, meaning victorious general.

Roman law underwent some of its most important developments under Emperor Justinian I (A.D. 483–565). Previously disparate Roman legal decisions and laws were now systematized and codified as the *Corpus Juris Civilis* (body of civil law). What was important about Justinian's Code was not necessarily what was new in it, but rather the influence that this systematic restatement of law would have on the development of future legal systems worldwide.

Medieval Law

In the early medieval period, the Germanic tribes' invasion of the Roman Empire resulted in a complex coexistence of Roman and German legal systems. In general, Roman subjects of barbarian kings remained subject to Roman law, while their Germanic neighbors were subject to traditional Germanic laws and customs. A key difference between the two systems was that Roman law retained a notion of the *rei publicae* or common good, whereas Germanic law tended to reduce every good, even justice, to a private right.

During the seventh, eighth, and ninth centuries, the Germanic tribes codified their customary law. The influence of Roman law grew enormously after Charlemagne's establishment of the Holy Roman Empire in A.D. 800 because the Roman Catholic church used Roman law in its tribunals, giving them a uniform system of justice throughout the West. The collapse of the Carolingian empire in the 10th century led to the emergence of feudalism, placing many disputes in the hands of the local lord whose control of the land was seen as giving him the concurrent right to administer justice. Property law, especially in the Anglo-American legal systems, remains influenced by concepts of ownership derived from the Middle Ages. However, modern law has moved away from the medieval treatment of crime, under which harsh punishments were meted out for minor offenses (a thief, for example, might be hanged or have his eyes gouged out).

Legal procedures in the early Middle Ages were heavily influenced by Germanic customs. An accused criminal was often subjected to an "ordeal," such as being bound and thrown into water, to determine guilt or innocence. Over time, largely through the church's influence, judicial procedures on the Continent came to conform to Roman practices, including the use of torture to extract evidence in certain situations. In the 11th century, the founding of the University of Bologna in Italy, which specialized in the teaching of law using Justinian's Code as the basis of instruction, contributed to a revival of Roman law. This revival was aided by the efforts of both stronger monarchies and the church to suppress the jurisdiction of local feudal courts and to replace them with royal and ecclesiastical courts, often administered by clerics and others who had been specifically trained in Roman law.

Anglo-American Law

Anglo-American jurisdictions are said to be "common law" systems rather than "civil law" systems as found on the continent of Europe (see "Civil Law," below). After William the Conqueror invaded England in 1066, he introduced feudal concepts that had taken hold in France, and embarked on what would become a centuries-long struggle to centralize control over justice and taxation. One result was his order to prepare the Domesday Book, an inventory of all the property in his new realm. Subsequent rulers, with greater or lesser success, sought to maintain the supremacy of the royal courts, introducing new ones and modifying old ones as new situations arose. Most significant was the development of "equity jurisdiction" under a series of lord chancellors. Equity filled the gaps in the common-law system and gave faster and more efficient justice than traditional royal courts, which had particularly inflexible procedural rules that often seemed to impede rather than facilitate justice. By the late 15th century, the supremacy of the royal courts was established, but how the different court systems were related to one another was unclear. In the early 17th century, Charles I began to collect taxes without the consent of Parliament, and soon the role of the courts became crucial as the king attempted to use them as the means of collecting taxes. In general, the traditional courts supported Parliament; and with the triumph of Parliament in the English civil wars, the supremacy of the traditional courts with their customary, non-Roman procedures was ensured.

The Common Law   Common law stands in contrast to European civil law, which governs society through extensive and specific codes, devised at once by a legislature. Common law evolves as scores of decentralized judges independently make legal decisions on cases. Over time, operative legal principles in cases become clear. Thus legal rules emerge from "case law."

The common law yields a flexible and organic legal system at the cost of precision and clarity. Generations of American and British law students have bemoaned the process of unthreading legal rules from dense cases. The common law does not always hold sway, however. Legislatures are free to overrule judge-made law with statutes, and so there is a balance between statutory and case law on many legal matters. Some scholars have predicted a decline in common-law rules of property, tort, contract, and family law as legislators grow more bold in these areas. Yet basic common-law principles that emerged centuries ago in England are still quite powerful in most U.S. jurisdictions. American common law continues to be made every day by plaintiffs, defendants, lawyers, and judges, and to be amended by statutes passed by citizens and legislators.

The common law borrows its basic foundation from English constitutionalism. While Great Britain has never had a written constitution, it has, for several centuries, relied strongly on laws and judges rather than rules handed down by divine authority. The beginnings of English constitutionalism lie in Magna Carta, the document that English barons and church elders forced King John I to sign in 1215. Magna Carta required King John to refrain from encroaching on feudal rights and to abandon the practice of waging expensive, unsuccessful wars and auctioning off church offices. Between the lines of the charter's 63 brief clauses lay a recognition of individual and communal rights inviolable by any authority. These new rights helped to form the basis of the emerging British constitution.

The common law evolved as a coherent system under a series of jurists. Sir Edward Coke (1552–1634), a chief justice of the King's Bench, helped cement the common law, rather than royal prerogative, as the default law of England. Sir Matthew Hale (1609–76), the lord chief justice under Charles II, helped synthesize the common law into a field of careful study. And Sir William Blackstone (1723–80), a professor of law at Oxford, wrote the four-volume *Commentaries on the Laws of England*, which conclusively demonstrated that English law was comparable to the two other grand legal systems—Roman law and the civil law of Europe.

A century later, the development of common law under the control of British and American judges was chronicled by Oliver Wendell Holmes (1841–1935). In his lectures and book *The Common Law*, Holmes argued provocatively that the common law developed in accordance with social reality and collective desires, rather than clear moral or philosophical precepts. "The life of the law is not logic, but experience," he wrote. Holmes's approach formed the foundation for the early 20th-century legal realist movement, which understood judicial reasoning not as an abstract logical process but instead as a reflection of judges' own personal and political lives and the society of which they are a part.

The Enlightenment

Although the form and process of American law came from the British common law model, dating to the late Middle Ages, many of the ideas underpinning America's legal and political choices came from a more modern period, the Enlightenment. In the 17th and 18th centuries, philosophers began arguing for the power of rational, equality-focused, and humanistic reasoning over the inherited authority of the church and other traditional sources of law. The Enlightenment's impact on the law was therefore deep and lasting. The law now evolved to fit societies that were learning to value rational ideas and the value of individual rights, rather than the divine right of kings or the rigidity of traditional institutions. The law itself became more enlightened, more logical, more systematic, and more humane.

The familiar American rights to "life, liberty, and the pursuit of happiness," included by Thomas Jefferson in the Declaration of Independence, may be traced directly to John Locke (1632–1704), whose *Treatises on Government* helped shape the American notion of a government dedicated to protecting private property and individual liberties. Locke's political and legal theories directly contradicted those of Thomas Hobbes (1588–1679), who believed that life for men in a state of nature was "solitary, poor, nasty, brutish, and short," driving the need for a strong collective state to protect men from themselves. Locke avoided such a dark view, arguing instead that life in the state of nature was fundamentally felicitous, and that the state was necessary only because certain people would never recognize the rights of others to "life, health, liberty, or possessions." The American dedication to natural rights and a government dedicated to protecting them borrows directly from these ideas.

In France, *Spirit of the Laws* (1748), by Charles Louis Montesquieu (1689–1755), contained the basic notion of separation of powers to guarantee the freedom of the individual. The Founding Fathers of the United States emphasized balancing the executive, legislative, and judicial branches, an approach that can be traced directly to Montesquieu, as can their thoughtful approach to avoiding the fate of the Roman republic (the subject of a study by Montesquieu in 1734).

The American legal idea of popular sovereignty can be traced to the work of another French philosopher, Jean-Jacques Rousseau (1712–78). Rousseau's political theory, found in *Of the Social Contract* (1762), was that people were intrinsically good prior to their involvement in a state. They traded their original sovereignty to the state in exchange for protection and social progress, so the state must recognize and obey the collective desires—the people's "general will"—on issues of political and legal significance. Such ideas stood in stark contrast to traditional monarchical or aristocratic theories of the state. They also led the Founding Fathers to base American law on the consent of the people, the limitations of the state, and the embrace of individual rights.

The American Constitutional System

The United States possesses a highly unusual, innovative legal system as complex as it is elegant. The American legal system has several interlocking elements that depend on federalism, which ensures that state legal systems will always have some independent authority to balance against the strength of the federal system. The two interdependent systems share a number of elements. First, each state has explicitly incorporated the British common law as the default set of rules on matters of torts, contracts, and other basic areas of the law. Second, each state as well as the federal government has a constitution, which not only gives citizens individual rights not found in the common law but also governs the operations of the various branches of government. Third, both the states and the federal government have complex and ever-growing bodies of statutory law: rules passed by the legislature which often supplant the common law. The growth of federal statutes (regarding labor, the environment, and consumer protection, among other matters) was one of the principal legal stories of the 20th century. In sum, it is an enormous system with many moving parts, designed for stability rather than agility.

The basic American constitutional system required interpretation and molding before it could take its present form. A strong hand was provided by John Marshall (1755–1835), chief justice of the United States for three decades. Marshall's extraordinary opinion in *Marbury v. Madison* (1803) established the doctrine of "judicial review," which essentially gave the Supreme Court and lower courts final power to consider and reject actions by the legislative and executive branches of government. His decision in *McCulloch v. Maryland* (1819), rejecting the argument that states could trump federal statutes and establishing congressional enactments (in this case, to launch a bank) as the law of the land, had a similar structural impact on the constitutional system.

In contrast with the common law, constitutional law stems exclusively from the U.S. Constitution and the constitutions of the states. In federal constitutional law, two separate documents are at work: the seven articles of the original Constitution, and the amendments subsequently added to the Constitution (including the original ten, the Bill of Rights). The articles deal primarily with the organization and powers of the national government: interstate commerce, claims of the states against the federal government, qualifications for public office, and the checks and balances within the government. The Bill of Rights, on the other hand, focuses on civil liberties, the concepts popularly associated with constitutional law: freedom of speech, religion, and assembly; the right to bear arms; the right against self-incrimination and improper search and seizure; and a variety of other claims individuals may hold against a potentially oppressive government.

The Bill of Rights

The Bill of Rights was not incorporated in the original Constitution, which was a document designed mainly to ensure the stability of the national government. But many of the states had adopted bills of rights, and opponents of ratification of the Constitution insisted on its eventual inclusion.

Freedom of Speech and the Press   Today perhaps the paramount constitutional right for Americans, freedom of speech (which includes the broader idea of freedom of expression), has had a fascinating career since the early days of the republic. Despite the explicit guarantee in the First Amendment, it was only nine years before passage of the Alien and Sedition Acts (1798), designed to silence criticism of the Federalist-controlled government by the Jefferson-led Republican Party. The free speech clause was seldom invoked until government repression during World War I led to a flurry of cases. Through the first half of the 20th century, a variety of cases allowed the government to suppress political speech under flexible doctrines such as the "clear and present danger test." In *Dennis v. United States* (1951), for example, defendants were convicted simply of organizing the Communist Party, which was conspiring to overthrow the federal government, without any proof that they had encouraged any direct or immediate acts of violence. This expansive doctrine was abandoned in *Brandenburg v. Ohio* (1969), which allowed the suppression only of speech which incited "imminent lawless action." The only speech that is constitutionally unprotected today is obscenity, criminal speech (such as yelling "Fire!" in a crowded theater when there is no fire), defamatory speech (such as libel), and words that incite violence.

Freedom of Religion

Some have speculated that the Founding Fathers intended the "establishment" clause ("Congress shall make no laws respecting the establishment of religion") to protect only active religious dissenters, while still protecting Protestantism as the de facto state religion of the United States. Whatever the original intent, the establishment clause has been interpreted by the Supreme Court as barring almost any state involvement, explicit or implicit, with religion. The three-pronged test announced in *Lemon v. Kurtzman* (1971) required government action to have a secular purpose, to have a neutral effect on religion, and to avoid entanglement between government and religion. The Supreme Court has interpreted the clause, to ban school prayer, government funding of Christmas trees, and aid to religious schools. In recent years, the Rehnquist court has been somewhat less hostile toward government actions that are religion-neutral on the surface, for example by allowing the state prejudicial treatment of Native Americans for smoking peyote at religious ceremonies, and ratifying a state-based school voucher system that would support parochial schools with state money.

Search and Seizure Law

Contained in the Fourth Amendment of the Bill of Rights, search and seizure law represents perhaps the most substantial constraint on the everyday exercise of the power of the police. The text of the amendment states, "The right of the people to be secure in their persons, houses, papers and effects, against unreasonable searches and seizures, shall not be violated, and no warrants shall issue, but upon probable cause." The amendment has generated scores of cases on precise questions, such as whether a car's glove compartment or trunk is protected from a search, and exactly what may constitute "probable cause" for a wiretap, a strip search, or a drug test. This area of the law speaks to the Founding Fathers' deep fear of a government and police force that could operate with no controls whatsoever. It embodies a respect for individual rights that would rather allow a person to break the law than be searched without due protections.

The protection against improper searches is strengthened by the *exclusionary rule*, which requires the courts to discard evidence if it has been obtained through constitutionally improper procedures. Examples range from an officer's failure to read a witness a Miranda warning or a detective's failure to obtain a warrant before searching a property. In both cases, unless acceptable extenuating circumstances applied, any evidence found would be inadmissible in court as the "fruit of the poisonous tree." The rule exists primarily to discourage abuses of police power, but it occasionally allows demonstrably guilty defendants to go free. Critics say more efficacious, less costly methods—such as police review boards or a new tort describing police misconduct—could discourage misconduct while saving valuable evidence for trials.

Race and the Civil War Amendments

No issue has been more vexatious or more profound in the development of American law than race. The original Constitution considered a slave (no slaves were white), for the purposes of congressional represenation, "three-fifths" of a person. Three constitutional amendments (the 13th, 14th, and 15th) were directly tied to both freeing slaves and ensuring their civil rights. A century of case law then followed, interpreting the rights guaranteed by those amendments. At first, southern Reconstruction denied African Americans the rights supposedly protected by the 14th Amendment's guarantee of equal protection and due process of the law. The Supreme Court's decision in *Plessy v. Ferguson* (1896) that the "separate but equal" doctrine underlying segregation was constitutional effectively rescinded the 14th Amendment for blacks. As the 20th century wore on, a consensus gradually developed that segregation was wrong. The Supreme Court's antisegregation decision in *Brown v. Board of Education* (1954), while a lightning bolt from the court, failed to effect much change over the southern white establishment's policy of "massive resistance." Not until the Civil Rights Act of 1964 did federal action succeed in substantially reversing segregation.

Although blacks were denied the protections of the amendments designed to protect them, two clauses of the 14th amendment became crucial to the development of American law. The "due process" clause gradually was used by the Supreme Court to "incorporate" almost all of the freedoms of the Bill of Rights against the states. The "equal protection" clause has been used to help not only African Americans, but also women, the young, the old, the disabled, and various other demographic, ethnic, and religious groups.

Criminal Law and Civil Law

Citizens may appear in court under two different legal umbrellas: criminal or civil law. In criminal law, the state prosecutes a crime, with the legal result of the dispute, whether imprisonment, a fine, public service, probation, or any other of a variety of punishments, administered directly by the government. In civil law, an individual citizen sues another, often for money damages.

Criminal Law

Criminal law, the field of law that aims to protect society in general, focuses on acts such as murder, rape, theft, and battery, as well as "white-collar" crimes such as fraud and embezzlement. As crimes threaten society rather than just an individual, the prosecution of these crimes is left up to the state and is placed in the hands of prosecutors, who are state employees.

Criminal law leans heavily on the notion of voluntariness. Conviction for many crimes involves a finding of *mens rea*, Latin for "state of mind," as well as *actus reus*, Latin for the "actual act." Hence, for example, the distinction between murder (intentional killing) and manslaughter (killing with lesser degrees of intentionality—by someone who was drunk or someone who meant only to harm, not kill). A prosecution can be derailed by attacks on evidence or on witnesses, or with inventive tools such as the insanity defense, which argues that the defendant lacked the requisite *mens rea*. While widely criticized, such developments are generally consistent with the early framework of criminal law. American criminal law rests considerably on the goal of retribution, answering crimes with simple punishment. From time to time critics have argued for a greater emphasis on improving criminals themselves through rehabilitation, but their success has been modest at best.

Civil Law

Civil law is broader than criminal law, incorporating a variety of different areas of human interaction that may occasion private lawsuits—contracts, injuries, real and personal property, and family relations.

Contract Law Contract law provides for the enforcement and regulation of private agreements, including informal contacts between individuals and complex agreements between large corporations. Because contract law focuses on agreement, contracting parties have substantial latitude to make whatever agreements they want on whatever terms they want, and the law will provide a remedy if the promises made are not kept. Increasingly, contracts are made through the use of standard forms with boilerplate language, such as the terms of agreement one must accept when purchasing a product over the Internet; this practice has produced much controversy about what it means to "agree" to terms which may not be available, read, or understood at the time of contracting.

Tort Law The term *tort* derives from Latin for "twisted" or "turned aside" and applies to any act that "twists away" from reasonable actions, resulting in harm to others. Torts are as diverse as the injuries they cause. A tort can be the placement of a dangerous ladder on a public sidewalk or the sale of a dangerous drug. Tort law includes intentional torts (in which the defendant intended to injure the victim), negligence (in which the defendant has failed to act with reasonable care), and strict liability (in which the defendant is liable for harm caused even in the absence of intent to injure or negligence). Damages in tort cases include both *compensatory damages* such as medical bills and lost wages, and *punitive damages* to deter wrongdoers from potentially dangerous conduct. Tort reformers believe that the field recklessly delivers enormous awards that too lavishly punish corporations, raising insurance rates and prices for everyone. Defenders cite a generation of consumer protections and unprecedented increases in safety, all generated by more vigorous enforcement of tort law.

Property Law Stemming from medieval feudal law, in which landowning lords granted privileges to renting knights and vassals, property law still mediates conflicts between owners, renters, and borrowers. But the subject has branched out to cover, among other mattters, intellectual property (products of the mind, whether novels or computer programs, protected as property); tenants' rights (landlords are now required to provide tenants with not just land, but also certain services, including habitable and safe conditions); and zoning restrictions (local boards are allowed to control property rights for the sake of community standards). Property law becomes especially important in matters of marriage, life, and death, when divorces, wills, trusts, and estates are administered in accordance with centuries of procedures and modern reforms.

Family Law   A critical area of the law is the regulation and distribution of legal rights within the private realm of the family. The "hot-button" areas of family law are, sadly, most familiar to those who have experience in troubled homes: divorce, alimony, custody, child support, domestic violence. Other areas help structure some of the more felicitous circumstances of private life, such as marriage and adoption. Like most other areas of the civil and criminal law, family law is almost wholly contained within individual states, and the states' systems of family law vary dramatically. Regarding the division of marital property after a divorce, for instance, the states fall into two categories: "community property" states, in which spouses are entitled to an equal share of much of each other's property; and "equitable distribution" states, where a judge attempts to divide the economic products of the marriage fairly, taking account of the contribution and needs of each spouse. Today the most controversial issue in family law is what constitutes a marriage: whether same-sex marriage or a substitute like civil union should be recognized.

The Court System

Federal Courts   Federal courts hear cases involving federal law and significant disputes between citizens of different states. The federal court system has three levels: district courts, circuit courts, and the Supreme Court. Federal district courts have jurisdiction in both civil and criminal matters. Circuit courts of appeals hear cases on appeal from district judges' decisions. The 50 states are organized into 11 circuits, and there are separate appeals courts for the District of Columbia and for such specialties as federal patent issues. A circuit court will hear a case in one of two ways: a panel, usually of three judges, may decide a case; or an *en banc* ruling may be issued by the entire court. A panel decision may be appealed for a full *en banc* hearing. Both district judges and circuit court judges are "Article Three" judges, so called because they are for-

mally chartered by Article Three of the Constitution and are appointed by the president and confirmed by the Senate for life terms. The third and final level is the Supreme Court, which hears most of its cases on a discretionary appeal known as a "writ of certiorari." The Supreme Court receives several thousand writs a year, and accepts only about 150 for review, usually on issues of great legal, social, or political significance.

How a Case Comes Before the Supreme Court
In order for a case to be heard by the Supreme Court, at least four justices have to agree that the legal questions posed by the case merit the Supreme Court's attention. They may decide to take a case because a state supreme court or a federal appeals court has ruled on a question of federal law that the Supreme Court needs to review, or they may feel compelled to act because a lower court ruling conflicts with previous Supreme Court decisions. They may aim to provide clarity when an important point of law has been decided in conflicting ways, or to step in and rectify the situation when a lower court seriously violates the judicial process.

Once the Supreme Court has decided to hear a case, the Court solicits briefs from the two opposing sides in the form of oral and written arguments. Briefs may come from the parties involved in the case, or from federal or state governments and any persons who have an interest in the case's outcome. After all the briefs are filed, the Court hears the oral arguments, which are limited to one hour. A lawyer for each side gets a half hour, and while he or she is presenting, the Justices are allowed to interrupt for questions or clarifications. These proceedings are open to the public.

State Courts   Most state court systems roughly parallel the federal system, with three levels: courts of general jurisdiction, which hear all kinds of cases; intermediate appeals courts; and a state supreme court. State court systems also have courts of limited jurisdiction, which hear only certain matters, such as small claims issues. In many states, judges are popularly elected rather than appointed by the legislature or the governor.

Civil Procedure

If a civil lawsuit is initiated, parties will enter the "private law"—the legal processes that occur when one citizen, rather than the government, confronts another. Examples of civil lawsuit include contract disputes, personal injury claims, and divorces.

Chief Justices of the United States

Chief Justice	Tenure[1]	Appointed by
John Jay	1789–1795	George Washington
John Rutledge[3]	1795	George Washington
Oliver Ellsworth	1796–1800	George Washington
John Marshall[4]	1801–35	John Adams
Roger B. Taney	1836–64	Andrew Jackson
Salmon P. Chase	1864–73	Abraham Lincoln
Morrison R. Waite	1874–88	Ulysses S. Grant
Melville W. Fuller	1888–1910	Grover Cleveland
Edward D. White	1910–21	William Howard Taft
William Howard Taft[5]	1921–30	Warren G. Harding
Charles Evans Hughes[2]	1930–41	Herbert Hoover
Harlan F. Stone[2]	1941–46	Franklin D. Roosevelt
Fred M. Vinson	1946–53	Harry S Truman
Earl Warren	1953–69	Dwight D. Eisenhower
Warren E. Burger	1969–86	Richard M. Nixon
William H. Rehnquist[2]	1986–2005	Ronald Reagan
John G. Roberts, Jr.	2005–	George W. Bush

Notes: 1. Dates are for tenure as Chief Justice. For complete tenure on Supreme Court, see "Supreme Court Justices." 2. Served as Associate Justice prior to appointment as Chief Justice. 3. Served one term, but appointment not confirmed by Senate. 4. Longest tenure as Chief Justice. 5. Formerly served as 27th president of the United States.

Getting a Lawyer   The first step is to secure legal representation from a lawyer, though it is possible for litigants to file *pro se* lawsuits, in which they represent themselves. In all the American states and the District of Columbia, lawyers are admitted to practice under rules promulgated by the courts, typically requiring graduation from an accredited law school, passing a bar examination, and screening for character and fitness.

Jurisdiction   A confusing but important second step is to choose the jurisdiction in which the dispute will be filed and settled. For jurisdiction to be proper, a court must have both subject matter jurisdiction and personal jurisdiction over an issue. Subject matter jurisdiction means the court is chartered to hear the type of issue being raised (federal district courts, for example, can hear only those cases authorized by statute). Personal jurisdiction exists if the event in question occurs in the court's jurisdiction, if one or both of the parties are residents of the juris-

diction, or if a corporation's headquarters are in a jurisdiction. A complaint that would otherwise be in state court may end up in federal court if diversity jurisdiction exists—if the parties are from two different states, for instance.

Filing a Complaint   A plaintiff's complaint frames the upcoming litigation. It lays out the parties, describes the facts of the circumstance occasioning the lawsuit, outlines the allegations of the legal issues (the "cause of action"), and makes a demand. A complaint usually is written by a lawyer, and then filed with the court and "served" on the defendant.

The Defendant's Response   The defendant does not have to accept the complaint on its face. Often, a defendant (or one's lawyer) files a motion to dismiss, formally requesting that the court dismiss the complaint before litigation even gets under way. There can be several grounds for such a motion, including that the court lacks proper jurisdiction, or that there is no proper legal basis for the claim. Otherwise, the defendant "answers," denying the allegations in the plaintiff's complaint. Defendants can also "counterclaim" against the plaintiff, introducing a new claim of their own related to the original complaint.

Discovery   If the court does not dismiss the original complaint, the case goes into the next phase of litigation: the "discovery" of all the evidence relevant to the litigation. This process involves several stages. Potential witnesses are identified and required to provide relevant facts through their written response to interrogatories, or their oral testimony in a deposition. Depositions are made under oath and are usually conducted with lawyers from both parties in the room, with one lawyer questioning the witness in an adversarial fashion. Opposing parties also may subpoena relevant documents. The purpose of discovery is to disclose as much relevant evidence as possible in advance of trial.

During the discovery period, parties have the option to make a motion for summary judgment. Such a motion asks the court to rule that, on the basis of evidence, there is no "genuine issue of material fact," and so no reason to go to court. Summary judgment is intended to allow courts to weed out undeserving cases prior to trial.

Alternative Dispute Resolution   In an attempt to avoid unnecessary and expensive litigation, parties may arbitrate or mediate their disputes in advance of trial. Some states require alternative dispute resolution before going to trial, and parties may choose on their own to submit to the process. In mediation, a mediator assists the parties in the effort to find a compromise solution to their dispute. In arbitration, one arbitrator or an arbitration panel decides the case; depending on the path to arbitration and the agreement to arbitrate, the arbitrators' decision may be binding or the dissatisfied party may proceed to trial.

Trial   Many people are familiar with the basic elements of trials from countless courtroom dramas on television and in films. However, trials can vary a great deal. Not all have juries, for instance; parties may elect to have a "bench trial" in which only the judge sits. Furthermore, certain trials are very short, such as minor slip-and-fall cases; other trials, such as those between large corporations, can go on for months, with various hearings on certain motions causing the entire trial to take years.

The basic elements of all trials are the same, however. The plaintiff's attorney makes an opening statement, and the defense attorney does the same. The counsel then introduces the first witness and performs a direct examination of him or her. The defense counsel then has an opportunity for a cross-examination, with the plaintiff's counsel having the option of a redirect. This process continues until all the plaintiff's witnesses have been heard. The defense counsel then introduces witnesses, with the same steps being followed in reverse order. After all witnesses have been heard and all the evidence has been introduced, plaintiff and defense make closing arguments, after which the plaintiff has an opportunity for a rebuttal. The jury (or the judge) then removes to consider the case and make a decision. After trial, the losing party may appeal, claiming errors of law in the conduct of the trial or a verdict that is so unreasonable it should not stand.

Criminal Procedure

Criminal procedure shares many elements of civil procedures. However, this critical area of "public law" has some important differences, most stemming from the government's involvement not just as a mediator but as the initiator of the procedures themselves, raising constitutional and ethical issues.

Jurisdiction   Most criminal law is state-based, so most criminal trials occur in state courts. However, the growing body of federal criminal law, on issues ranging from racketeering to securities fraud, ensures that federal courts also hear criminal cases.

The Arrest   A person is arrested if an officer determines that this person broke the law. Arrest may occur on the spot, if the officer witnesses the instance of lawbreaking, or it may occur after a criminal investigation. In either case, the person becomes an arrestee. After the case of *Miranda v. Arizona* (1966), officers today must always advise arrestees of their constitutional rights, including the right to remain silent and to have an attorney.

The Complaint   A high-ranking police officer or a prosecutor, or both, will make a decision to charge the arrestee with a crime. The complaint sets forth the legal grounds for the arrest, as well as any other laws that the arrestee may have broken. The arrestee formally becomes a defendant after the filing of the complaint.

Preliminary Hearings   Defendants are first brought before a judge or magistrate, to be informed of the charges against them and advised of their basic rights. Bail is also set, sometimes at a separate bail hearing. This is the amount of money the defendant must pay to be released from jail while the case is tried; the intent of bail is to reduce the chance that a defendant will flee the jurisdiction. If the court determines a high likelihood of flight, bail can be denied altogether. In cases involving crimes of a certain level, a preliminary hearing may also be held, at which the basic elements of the crime are outlined by the prosecutor, and the defendant's lawyer has a chance to cross-examine witnesses. The judge then determines whether or not probable cause exists to charge the defendant. In felony cases, a grand jury of citizens drawn from the jurisdiction decides whether to issue an indictment of the defendant; only the prosecutor appears before the grand jury, whose proceedings are secret. The defendant is then arraigned before the court, where the charges are announced and the trial date is set.

The Trial   If the defendant pleads not guilty, the case may go to trial. Frequently, the prosecutor and the defense attorney plea-bargain: the defendant can plead guilty in exchange for a lower charge or lesser punishment. At trial, the defendant can be defended by a public defender or by a private attorney of the defendant's choosing. In criminal trials involving felonies or certain serious misdemeanors, all states provide the constitutionally required trial by a jury of one's peers, which may be waived for a bench trial with only the judge presiding. As in civil proceedings, the prosecutor and defense attorney each make opening statements, present witnesses for direct and cross-examinations, introduce evidence, and make closing statements. If an unfavorable verdict is delivered, a right to appeal exists.

Other Legal Systems

While the common law is naturally most familiar to Americans, several other legal systems exist, which are organized quite differently and which can take different attitudes toward the principles Americans hold most dear, such as individual rights and the authority of judges to make the law.

Civil Law

Best understood in contrast with Anglo-American common law, civil law is the umbrella term for the code-driven legal systems that exist in countries on the European continent or their former colonies. The origin of civil law was Roman law, particularly Justinian's *Corpus Juris Civilis* of the sixth century. Whereas the common law induces legal rules from the decentralized decisions of judges, civil law instead deduces its principles and conclusions from a pre-fabricated, systematic code. The Napoleonic Code of 1804 is perhaps the most famous modern example. All of the former English colonies, as well as all of the American states (with the exception of formerly French-ruled Louisiana, and with some modifications in states with vestiges of Spanish rule, such as California), follow the common law instead.

Shariah Law

The law of Islam, Shariah law functions in countries that have made Islam the official state religion and works both as a religious and as an ordinary legal code. Shariah legal rules stem from four sources: the Koran's legislative segments; the stories of Muhammad, as related through the *hadith*; the general agreement of Muslims (as reflected in Muhammad's saying, "My nation cannot agree on an error"); and principles arrived at by analogy to other rules. Legal rules themselves are prescriptive and fall into five categories: obligatory, meritorious, permissible, reprehensible, and forbidden. Best understood in contrast with a more passive and decentralized system such as the common law, Shariah law makes an active and ambitious attempt to shape the behavior of Muslim citizens.

Canon Law

Canon law is the body of law that governs in the Roman Catholic Church. Although canon law may generally be traced back to centuries of legal rules in the church courts, its formal embodiment took place in 1917, with the *Codex juris canonici*, which was itself superseded by the Code of Canon Law for the Latin Church, published in 1983. Canon law contains rules for the governance and regulation of both clergy and the church, covering issues such as the qualifications and responsibilities of clergy, rules for marriage, and holy orders. While it does not compare in size with state-based legal systems such as the common or civil law, canon law has had wide influence in countries where the Roman Catholic Church was the state church, and still governs today in the Vatican.

International Law

Several sources are cited for international law in Article 38 of the Statute of the International Court of Justice (1945). First, international conventions such as treaties hold sway over agreements and obligations between different states or political actors. Second, customary law, the general practice of states and intergovernmental organizations, is generally legally binding and recognized by states. Third, general principles of law are seen to be the source of universally applicable rules in any disputes or agreements. Fourth, the judicial decisions and teachings of highly qualified jurists in individual nations are relied upon to inform international law. Taken together, this web of information constitutes international law.

Some scholars have suggested that international law is weaker than might otherwise be supposed. This view stems from the prevailing "realist" school of international relations, which holds that international legal relationships reflect and wholly depend upon underlying power relations. In other words, international law exists at the whim of superpowers; if they choose, international law can be broken, with barely any consequences. Momentum is gaining, however, for the liberal view that international law does exist and does matter. Liberal scholars observe that the United Nations, the International Monetary Fund, the World Bank, the North Atlantic Treaty Organization, and the North American Free Trade Agreement all have rule-making authority. Taken together, these institutions contain many courts where even the powerful United States can be brought up on charges and will, on occasion, comply, lending legitimacy to the independent strength of international law.

Important Supreme Court Decisions

***Marbury v. Madison* (1803)** The Court struck down a law "repugnant to the constitution" for the first time and set the precedent for judicial review of acts of Congress. In a politically ingenious ruling on the Judiciary Act of 1789, Chief Justice John Marshall asserted the Supreme Court's power "to say what the law is," while avoiding a confrontation with President Thomas Jefferson. Not until the *Dred Scott* case of 1857 would another federal law be ruled unconstitutional.

***Fletcher v. Peck* (1810)** The Court ruled that Georgia could not deprive land speculators of their title, even though the previous owners had obtained the land from the state through fraud and bribery. Arising from the infamous Yazoo land frauds of 1795, this decision followed the Constitution's obligation of contracts clause and was the first time the Court invalidated a state law.

***Dartmouth College v. Woodward* (1819)** The Court encouraged business investment with this decision by treating corporate charters as fully protected contracts. Not even the state legislatures that originally granted them could tamper with charters to private corporations, unless the legislature retained the power to do so. Dartmouth College remained a private institution despite New Hampshire's attempt to take it over. This decision, which opened the way for abuse of corporate privileges, would later be modified in the *Charles River Bridge* (1837) and *Munn v. Illinois* (1877) cases.

***McCulloch v. Maryland* (1819)** "Broad," as opposed to "strict," construction of the Constitution received high court approval in Chief Justice John Marshall's opinion upholding the constitutionality of the national bank against a challenge by Maryland. This ruling enhanced federal governmental authority by liberally interpreting the power of Congress to make laws "necessary and proper" for its specified powers. At a time when states were trying to tax the Bank of the United States out of existence, this decision also forbade such state interference with the federal government. "The power to tax," Marshall wrote, "involves the power to destroy."

***Cohens v. Virginia* (1821)** With this ruling, the Court reiterated its power to hear appeals from state courts, and affirmed the national supremacy of federal judicial power. Virginia's conviction of the Cohens for selling lottery tickets in violation of state law was upheld, but so too was the Cohens' right to appeal to the Court, which Virginia had challenged. Critics of judicial "consolidationalism" were reminded of the Court's comprehensive powers as the ultimate appellate court for all Americans.

***Gibbons v. Ogden* (1824)** In a dispute arising from a ferry monopoly in New York, the Court ruled that states could not restrain interstate commerce in any way, and that congressional power to regulate interstate commerce "does not stop at the jurisdictional lines of the several states." The decision helped prevent interstate trade wars, quite common under the Articles of Confederation, from breaking out under the Constitution. Chief Justice Marshall's opinion also confirmed the broad potential power of the Constitution's commerce clause.

***Charles River Bridge v. Warren Bridge* (1837)** A key decision for economic development, this case arose when state-chartered proprietors of a toll bridge in Boston objected that a new state-chartered bridge across the Charles River would put them out of business. Chief Justice Roger B. Taney, in his first constitutional ruling, held that state charters implied no vested rights and that ambiguities must be construed in favor of the public, which would benefit from the new toll-free bridge. This decision balanced private property rights against the public welfare.

***Dred Scott v. Sanford* (1857)** Dred Scott, a Missouri slave, sued for his liberty after his owner took him into free territory. The Court ruled that Congress could not bar slavery in the territories. Scott remained a slave because the Missouri Compromise of 1820, prohibiting slavery from part of the Louisiana Purchase, violated the Fifth Amendment by depriving slave owners of their right to enjoy property without due process of law. Scott himself could not even sue, for he was held to be property, not a citizen. This decision sharpened sectional conflict by sweeping away legal barriers to the expansion of slavery.

***Ex Parte Milligan* (1866)** President Abraham Lincoln's suspension of some civil liberties during the Civil War was attacked in this decision, which upheld the right of *habeas corpus*. The Court ruled that the president could not hold military tribunals in areas remote from battle and where civil courts were open and functioning. Milligan's conviction by such a Civil War tribunal in Indianapolis was overturned. The Constitution, admonished the Court, applies "at all times, and under all circumstances."

Slaughter-House Cases (1873) In its first ruling on the Fourteenth Amendment, the Court held that Louisiana's grant of a butcher monopoly did not violate the privileges and immunities of competitors, or deny them equal protection of the laws, or deprive them of property without due process. Only a few rights deriving from "federal citizenship" were subject to federal protection; states still protected most civil and property rights. Federal protection of civil rights, even for former slaves, was very narrowly interpreted in this ruling. But this decision broadly upheld business regulation by states until *Santa Clara Co. v. Southern Pacific Railroad Co.* (1886) applied the Fourteenth Amendment to defense of corporate property rights.

Munn v. Illinois (1877) This decision enabled states to regulate private property in the public interest when the public had an interest in that property. The Court held that laws in Illinois setting maximum rates for grain storage did not violate the Fourteenth Amendment's ban on deprivation of property without due process of law, and did not restrain interstate commerce.

Civil Rights Cases (1883) Racial equality was postponed 80 years by this decision, which struck down the Civil Rights Act of 1875 and allowed for private segregation. The Fourteenth Amendment's guarantee of equal protection, the Court ruled, applied against state action— but not against private individuals, whose discrimination unaided by the states was beyond federal control. Segregation of public facilities was approved soon afterward in *Plessy v. Ferguson* (1896).

United States v. E. C. Knight Co. (1895) The first ruling on the Sherman Antitrust Act of 1890, this decision curtailed federal regulation of monopolies by placing national manufacturers beyond the reach of the Constitution's commerce clause. Only the actual interstate commerce of monopolies, not their production activities, was subject to federal control. The Court's distinction between production and commerce impeded federal regulation of manufacturing until *National Labor Relations Board v. Jones & Laughlin Steel Corp.* (1937).

Plessy v. Ferguson (1896) The "separate but equal" doctrine supporting public segregation by law was affirmed in this ruling, which originated with segregated railroad cars in Louisiana. The Court held that as long as equal accommodations were provided, segregation was not discrimination and did not deprive blacks of equal protection of the laws under the Fourteenth Amendment. This decision was overturned in *Brown v. Board of Education* (1954).

Lochner v. New York (1905) This decision struck down a law in New York placing limits on maximum working hours for bakers. The law violated the Fourteenth Amendment by restricting individual "freedom of contract" to buy and sell labor, and was an excessive use of state police power, the Court held. The ruling was soon modified in *Muller v. Oregon* (1908), which approved state-regulated limits on women's labor after the Court used sociological and economic data to consider the health and morals of women workers.

Standard Oil Co. of New Jersey v. United States (1911) Federal efforts to break up monopolies under the Sherman Antitrust Act had to follow the "rule of reason," according to this ruling. Only those combinations in restraint of trade that were contrary to the public interest, and therefore unreasonable, were illegal. Although the Taft administration's prosecution of Standard Oil was upheld, breaking up one of the nation's leading monopolies, further antitrust suits were impaired by this decision, which facilitated the merger movement of the 1920's.

Schenk v. United States (1919) The Court unanimously held that limits on freedom of speech during World War I did not violate the First Amendment—if the speech in question represented a "clear and present danger." That famous doctrine of Justice Oliver Wendell Holmes, which approved the arrest of a draft resister for handing out pamphlets to soldiers in wartime, became an important standard for interpreting the First Amendment. But in subsequent cases of this period, the Court added that the mere "bad tendency" of speech to cause danger could be grounds for censorship.

National Labor Relations Board v. Jones & Laughlin Steel Corp. (1937) Under pressure from the public and President Franklin D. Roosevelt, the Court abruptly reversed itself and began approving New Deal legislation. In this case, laws protecting unions and barring "unfair labor practices" were upheld by the "stream of commerce" doctrine that employers who sold their goods and obtained their raw materials through interstate commerce were subject to federal regulation. This ruling overturned *United States v. E. C. Knight Co.* (1895) and became the basis for an expansive understanding of the commerce clause.

Erie Railroad Co. v. Tompkins (1938) The Court held that there could be no federal common law, but rather that federal courts must turn to the law of the state in which they sit when ruling on substantive issues. The case overruled *Swift v. Tyson* (1842), in which Justice Story had argued strongly for a federal common law, in part because of his opinion that federal judges had an almost divine ability to channel the correct rulings, in contrast to more clumsy state courts. *Erie* rejected that view, reestablished state-based federalism at the heart of jurisdiction, attempted to discourage forum-shopping, all while sapping federal judges of their ability to create much law.

West Virginia Board of Education v. Barnette

(1943) The Court reversed its earlier ruling in *Minersville School District v. Gobitis* (1940), which had required Jehovah's Witnesses to salute the flag in school. In this case, also brought against a Jehovah's Witness, the Court recognized that refusing to salute the flag did not violate anyone's rights, and that the First Amendment protected the "right of silence" as well as freedom of speech.

Korematsu v. United States (1944) President

Franklin D. Roosevelt's executive order No. 9066, which approved the evacuation and internment of 120,000 Japanese-Americans on the West Coast during World War II, was upheld on the grounds of "military necessity" in this ruling. The Court was reluctant to interfere with executive authority in time of national emergency. But in *Ex parte Endo* (1944), the Court held that persons of proven loyalty should not be interned. In August 1988, Congress made a formal apology to former internees and appropriated $1.25 billion in compensation for the 60,000 survivors.

McCollum v. Board of Education (1948) In 1940,

the Champaign, Illinois schools created a program to teach religion in the elementary grades. Vashti McCollum and her husband, a college professor, withheld their fourth-grade son because they believed religion did not belong in the public schools. After losing battles in the lower courts, the Supreme Court ruled 8–1 in their favor, thereby applying the principle of separation of church and state in the public schools.

Dennis v. United States (1951) At the height of the

postwar "red scare," the Court upheld the conviction of 11 American Communist leaders under the Smith Act of 1940, which made it a crime to belong to organizations teaching or advocating the violent overthrow of the government. The "clear and present danger" doctrine could be disregarded, the Court held, if "the gravity of the 'evil,' discounted by its improbability, justifies such invasion of free speech as is necessary to avoid the evil." More than 100 Communists were indicted as a result, effectively destroying the Communist Party as a political force.

Youngstown Sheet and Tube Co. v. Sawyer

(1952) During the Korean War, when President Harry S Truman seized steel plants to keep them operating despite a strike, the Court held that his action was an unconstitutional usurpation of legislative authority. Only an act of Congress, not the president's inherent executive powers or military powers as commander-in-chief, could justify such a sizable confiscation of property, despite the wartime emergency.

Brown v. Board of Education of Topeka (1954)

Chief Justice Earl Warren led the Court to decide unanimously that segregated schools violated the equal protection clause of the Fourteenth Amendment. The "separate but equal" doctrine of *Plessy v. Ferguson* (1896) was overruled after a series of cases dating back to *Missouri ex. rel. Gaines v. Canada* (1938) had already limited it. "Separate educational facilities are inherently unequal," held the Court. Efforts to desegregate southern schools after the *Brown* decision met with massive resistance for many years.

Baker v. Carr (1962) Overrepresentation of rural dis-

tricts in state legislatures, which effectively disfranchised millions of voters, led the Court to abandon its traditional noninterference in drawing legislative boundaries. Citizens in Tennessee deprived of full representation by "arbitrary and capricious" malapportionment were denied equal protection under the Fourteenth Amendment, ruled the Court. All states eventually reapportioned their legislatures in conformance with the "one man, one vote" doctrine of *Reynolds v. Sims* (1964).

Gideon v. Wainwright (1963) Reversing an earlier

ruling in *Betts v. Brady* (1942), the Court held that the Sixth Amendment guaranteed access to qualified counsel, which was "fundamental to a fair trial." Gideon was entitled to a retrial because Florida failed to provide him with an attorney. After this decision, states were required to furnish public defenders for indigent defendants in felony cases. In *Argersinger v. Hamlin* (1972), the ruling was extended to all cases that might result in imprisonment.

Heart of Atlanta Motel, Inc. v. United States

(1964) The Court upheld Title II of the Civil Rights Act of 1964, outlawing private discrimination in public accommodations, as a legitimate exertion of federal power over interstate commerce. Congress had "ample power" to forbid racial discrimination in facilities that affected commerce by serving interstate travelers. The Heart of Atlanta

Motel was located on two interstate highways, so the Court could sidestep the *Civil Rights Cases* (1883) protection of private discrimination to overrule it.

New York Times Co. v. Sullivan (1964) Rejecting a civil action for libel filed by a city commissioner of Montgomery, Ala., the Court created a wide berth for the press to criticize public figures. In a unanimous opinion written by Justice William J. Brennan, the Court found that even false statements must be protected "if the freedoms of expression are to have the 'breathing space' that they 'need to survive.'" The Court announced a new standard for libel of public figures: actual malice, combined with actual knowledge that such statements are false or reckless disregard of whether they are true or not.

Griswold v. Connecticut (1965) In striking down a Connecticut law of 1879 against the use of contraceptives, the Court established a "right to privacy" that was implied by, though not specifically enumerated in, the First, Third, Fourth, Fifth, Ninth, and Fourteenth Amendments. The case is most notable for laying the groundwork for other legal challenges invoking this newfound right to privacy. Foremost among them is the decision in *Roe v. Wade* (1973) allowing women to choose abortion.

South Carolina v. Katzenbach (1966) South Carolina sued the attorney general, contending that the Voting Rights Act of 1965 encroached on the reserved powers of the states, treated the states unequally, and violated separation of powers. Chief Justice Warren ruled that the Fifteenth Amendment gave Congress broad powers to "use any rational means to effectuate the constitutional prohibition of racial discrimination in voting."

Miranda v. Arizona (1966) Expanding upon *Gideon v. Wainwright* (1963) and *Escobedo v. Illinois* (1964), the Court set forth stringent interrogation procedures for criminal suspects to protect their Fifth Amendment freedom from self-incrimination. Miranda's confession to kidnapping and rape was obtained without counsel and without his having been advised of his right to silence, so it was ruled inadmissible as evidence. This decision obliged police to advise suspects of their rights upon taking them into custody.

Loving v. Virginia (1967) Loving was a white man who had married a black woman and had been convicted under Virginia's law prohibiting interracial marriage. In a unanimous opinion Chief Justice Warren struck down the law as an invidious racial classification prohibited by the Fourteenth Amendment's equal protection clause.

The ruling continued the Court's commitment to equality under the law signaled in *Brown v. Board of Education* (1954).

New York Times Co. v. United States (1971) When the *New York Times* and the *Washington Post* published the top-secret Pentagon Papers in 1971, revealing government duplicity in the Vietnam War, the Nixon administration obtained an injunction against the *Times* on grounds of national security. But in a brief *per curiam* opinion, the Court observed that in this case, the government had not met the "heavy burden of showing justification" for "prior restraint" on freedom of the press.

Roe v. Wade (1973) In a controversial ruling, the Court held that state laws restricting abortion were an unconstitutional invasion of a woman's right to privacy. Only in the last trimester of pregnancy, when the fetus achieved viability outside the womb, might states regulate abortion—except when the life or health of the mother was at stake. In *Planned Parenthood of Central Missouri v. Danforth* (1976), the Court added that wives did not need their husbands' consent to obtain abortions.

United States v. Nixon (1974) In a unanimous ruling, the Court held that the secret White House recordings of President Richard M. Nixon's conversations with aides were subject to subpoena in the Watergate cover-up trial. Nixon's claim to "executive privilege" was rejected as invalid because military and national security issues were not at stake, and Chief Justice Warren Burger cited *Marbury v. Madison* (1803) to assert the Court's primacy in constitutional issues. Once the tapes were released, documenting Nixon's obstruction of justice, the president resigned to avoid impeachment.

University of California Regents v. Bakke (1978) Twice refused admission to medical school, Bakke sued the University of California for giving "affirmative action" preference to less-qualified black applicants. In an ambiguous 5-4 ruling, the Court agreed that Bakke's right to equal protection had been denied, that he should be admitted, and that affirmative action quotas should be discarded. But at the same time, the Court recognized race as "a factor" in admissions and hiring decisions. Affirmative action could continue so long as rigid quotas did not constitute, in effect, "reverse discrimination."

Immigration and Naturalization Service v. Chadha (1983) The legislative veto, contained in hundreds of federal statutes since 1932, was disallowed in this decision. Congress exceeded its constitutional powers when it blocked the attorney general's suspension of a deportation order for Jagdish Rai Chadha, a Kenyan student who had overstayed his visa. The Court held that the Immigration and Nationality Act's legislative veto provision violated the constitutional separation of powers. Chief Justice Burger recognized that Congress would prefer to delegate authority to the executive branch and reserve the right to veto administrative regulations, but "we have not found a better way to preserve freedom" than the separation of powers.

United States v. Lopez (1995) The Court struck down an act of Congress for the first time in 60 years and in so doing sparked the federalism revolution for which the Rehnquist court will be known in the future. Congress had passed the Drug Free School Zones Act under its traditional loose grant of power under the Constitution's "commerce clause," allowing regulation of interstate commerce. In a strongly worded opinion, Chief Justice Rehnquist observed that no obviously commercial activity was involved in the act. Assailed by critics for attempting a return to a retrograde era of state-based federalism, the ruling struck a blow against the "living Constitution" argument, holding instead that anything Congress does must be explicitly authorized by the text.

Bush v. Gore (2000) For the first time in the nation's history, the Court found itself in the position of deciding a presidential election. With Florida's decisive 25 electoral votes hanging in the balance, Vice President Al Gore filed suit in state court to begin a recount of ballots in several counties where machines were unable to determine the voters' selection. Governor George W. Bush of Texas appealed the decision to the Supreme Court, which ruled that because there were no uniform standards for how to conduct a recount, doing so would violate the Fourteenth Amendment's guarantee of equal protection. The highly controversial 5–4 decision ended the recount 36 days after Election Day, and with it, Gore's chance of winning the presidency.

Lawrence v. Texas (2003) The Court struck down a statute in Texas that made it criminal for two persons of the same sex to engage in sexual acts. In a controversial case, *Bowers v. Hardwick* (1986), the Court had ruled that the constitutional right to privacy does not protect homosexual relations, even between consenting adults in the privacy of their home. In *Lawrence*, the Court overruled *Bowers*, relying on a different view of the history of sodomy statutes and the changes in law and social mores since *Bowers*.

Hamdi v. Rumsfeld (2004) In a case that maintained judicial authority over a wartime executive, the Court ruled that the president could not deny defendants access to American courts simply by labeling them "enemy combatants." Declaring that "a state of war is not a blank check for the president," the Court said the government had deprived Yaser Esam Hamdi, an American citizen seized in Afghanistan, of his due process rights. In two companion cases, the Court ruled that non-citizens seized during military operations could not be held without access to U.S. courts.

Kelo v. City of New London (2005) This eminent domain case was brought against New London, Connecticut by its residents. The city planned to turn a faded residential neighborhood into a multi-use complex, but the owners of 15 of the houses scheduled for demolition rejected the city's compensation offer and filed suit. Taking private property for "public use" traditionally referred to highway projects and utility right-of-ways, but the Court ruled that "public use" should be understood as "public purpose," and that the city's plan for economic rejuvenation fell under that heading. The 5–4 decision upholding the plan was met with strenuous objections from politicians and the public.

Hamdan v. Rumsfeld (2006) In a 5–3 decision, the Court blocked President Bush's plan to try Guantanamo Bay detainees before the military commission he established without Congressional approval in 2001. Salim Ahmed Hamdan, a Yemini detainee captured in Afghanistan in 2001, brought to Guantanamo in 2002, and charged with conspiracy to commit terrorism in 2004, would have been the first tried before the commission. The Court ruled that the commission's procedures violated the Uniform Code of Military Justice and the Geneva Conventions by permitting a defendant to be barred from his trial and denied access to evidence presented against him.

Massachusetts v. Environmental Protection Agency (2007) Twelve states, two cities and several interest groups filed suit against the Environmental Protection Agency (E.P.A.) in an attempt to force the agency to regulate carbon dioxide emissions, which the Bush Administration had declined to do, citing a lack of regulatory authority. This 5–4 decision found that the Clean Air Act gives the agency that authority and obligation and the court ordered the E.P.A. to either implement such regulations or justify its refusal to do so. The most significant aspect of the decision may be the court's conclusion that sovereign states have "standing to sue" the federal government.

***Parents Involved in Community Schools v. Seattle School District No. 1* (2007)** Combining two affirmative action cases, the court invalidated school integration plans adopted by Seattle and Louisville, Ky. school systems, finding that they violated the 14th Amendment guarantee of equal protection. While the plans differed, both were similar to those in hundreds of school districts around the country that seek to maintain school diversity by using race as a deciding factor in granting school assignment or transfer requests. Although the minority found that such plans were consistent with *Brown v. Board of Education*, Chief Justice Roberts, writing for the 5–4 majority, said, "The way to stop discrimination on the basis of race is to stop discriminating on the basis of race."

***Boumediene v. Bush* (2008)** In 2004, the Court ruled (*Rasul v. Bush*) that foreign detainees who were being held without charges outside U.S. territory were entitled to challenge their detentions through habeas corpus. Lakhdar Boumediene, an Algerian held since 2001 on suspicion of planning an attack on the U.S. embassy in Bosnia, and 36 other Guantanamo Bay detainees then filed a joint habeas corpus petition. But, in 2005, Congress passed the Detainee Treatment Act, which stripped federal courts of the power to hear such cases, and instead gave the D.C. Court of Appeals sole jurisdiction to review decisions of the military tribunals overseeing such detainees. In a 5–4 decision that brought strong words from the minority and politicians, the court majority declared these provisions unconstitutional, holding that habeas corpus does apply to aliens imprisoned at Guantanamo and that a military tribunal with only a limited appeal is not an adequate substitution for a writ in a federal court.

***Citizens United v. Federal Election Commission* (2010)** In a 5–4 decision, the Court ruled that the federal government may not limit political spending by corporations and unions in elections. While the majority held that the decision upheld the First Amendment freedom of speech clause, the dissenters warned that corporate money would corrupt the political process. The decision overturned two recent decisions that restricted corporate and union election spending.

Glossary of Legal Terms

accessory person who helps another person plan, commit, or attempt to escape the consequences of a crime.

acquittal judgment that a person is not guilty of the crime of which he or she has been charged.

actus reus wrongful act, regardless of the intentions behind the act; see *mens rea*.

adjudication final judgment in a legal proceeding; see also *judgment*.

affidavit written statement confirmed by oath or affirmation, for use as evidence in court.

amicus curiae Latin, "friend of the court." a party who joins a case voluntarily in order to present evidence and arguments to the court.

appeal application to a higher court for a decision of a lower court to be reversed, or for a new trial to be granted.

arbitration use of an independent person or body officially appointed to settle a dispute, as an alternative to going to court.

arraignment call to bring someone before a court to answer a criminal charge.

arrest to seize someone by legal authority and take that person into custody.

assault attempted or actual attack on a person that has the potential to result in palpable harm. Aggravated assault involves the use of a weapon; battery results when an attacker makes physical contact with the victim.

attachment court writ authorizing the seizure of property or income in order to obtain payment of damages resulting from a judgment in a legal proceeding.

attorney-client privilege rule that keeps communications between an attorney and his or her client confidential and bars them from being used as evidence in a trial, or even being seen by the opposing party during discovery.

bail amount of money left in the custody of a court by a defendant who has been allowed to remain free while awaiting trial, to ensure that he or she will not flee the jurisdiction.

bar the legal profession; lawyers collectively. Traditionally a partition (actual or symbolic) in a courtroom beyond which most persons may not pass and at which an accused person stands.

bench office of judge or magistrate; a judge's seat in a court of law; judges or magistrates collectively ("the bench").

bench trial in which only a judge, as opposed to a jury of the defendant's peers, presides.

breaking and entering entering a building with criminal intent; the charge does not require actual damage to the building's doors, windows, or locks.

brief formal written document in which a lawyer presents arguments and case law in support of a client in court.

burden of proof obligation to prove a case. A basic principle of U.S. law is that the state (in a criminal action) or the plaintiff (in a civil action) must prove its case; the defendant is considered not guilty (or not liable) until proven guilty (or liable) and does not need to prove his or her innocence.

burglary unlawful presence in a building for the purpose of committing a crime (usuallly theft).

case law law as established by the outcome of former cases. See *common law*.

certiorari writ or order from a higher court consenting to review a decision of a lower court.

circumstantial evidence evidence in a court of law that points indirectly toward someone's guilt but does not conclusively prove it.

civil law system of law concerned with private relations between members of a community rather than criminal, military, or religious affairs; as opposed to criminal law. Also, the reliance on codified statute law typical of European legal systems, contrasted with Anglo-American common law.

class-action suit lawsuit filed or defended by an individual or small group acting on behalf of a larger group of similar individuals—e.g., all persons injured by a particular defective product. All members of the group share in any judgment or settlement.

commerce clause Article 1, section 8 of the U.S. Constitution is commonly referred to as the commerce clause; it gives wide fiscal powers to the federal government.

common law part of law that is derived from long-standing custom and judicial precedent, in contrast to statute law. Common law is the foundation of the Anglo-American legal system.

compensatory damages money awarded in tort law in an attempt to compensate the injured plaintiff for any loss suffered at the hands of the defendant.

complaint initial statement of facts in a civil case, or initial accusation in a criminal case.

consent agreement to do or to refrain from doing some action. Informed consent means that the person understands the consequences of his or her consent.

consent decree court order ratifying an agreement between two or more parties in settlement of a legal case.

conspiracy agreement by two or more persons to break the law.

constitutional law branch of law dealing specifically with questions of whether statutes, regulations, and court rulings conform to the provisions of state constitutions and the federal Constitution.

contract legally binding agreement between two or more parties, enforceable by law.

copyright legal right of the creator of written, visual, or musical material to publish, reproduce, distribute, or perform the material, or authorize others to do so, for a fixed period of time. See also *intellectual property*.

corpus delicti Latin, "body of offense"; the physical evidence that a crime has taken place. Possibly, but not necessarily, a human corpse; a vandalized automobile can be a corpus delicti, for example.

court order directive issued by a court of law, ordering a person to do something or to refrain from doing something; see also *injunction*.

covenant *n.* contract drawn up by deed; a clause in a contract. *v.* to agree, especially by lease, deed, or other legal contract.

criminal intent See *intent*; *mens rea*.

criminal procedure criminal case in court; also, the rules governing the presentation and evaluation of evidence in a criminal case.

cross-examination questioning of a witness designed to cast doubt upon or discredit testimony the witness has already given in court.

damages sum of money claimed or awarded in compensation for a loss or an injury. See also *compensatory damages*; *punitive damages*.

defamation act of damaging another person's reputation in writing or in speech. See also *libel*; *slander*.

defendant person against whom charges or actions are brought in a criminal or civil case.

degree in criminal law, the level of severity of a crime (e.g., murder in the first degree, assault in the third degree), established by statute and specifying particular circumstances for one degree of the crime or another.

deposition pretrial examination of a witness. A witness so examined is said to be "deposed."

discovery pretrial process in which attorneys for both sides in a civil or criminal action assemble their evidence and disclose that evidence to the other party.

double jeopardy prosecution of a person twice for the same offense; prohibited in American law.

due diligence reasonable steps taken by a person to satisfy a legal requirement.

due process fair treatment through the normal judicial system; guaranteed by the Fifth and 14th Amendments to the U.S. Constitution.

eminent domain right of a government or its agent to expropriate private property for public use, with payment of compensation.

equal protection phrase used in section 1 of the 14th Amendment to the U.S. Constitution. Ratified on July 9, 1868, it says in part: "No State shall make or enforce any law which shall abridge the privileges or immunities of citizens of the United States; nor shall any State deprive any person of life, liberty, or property, without due process of law; nor deny to any person within its jurisdiction the equal protection of the laws."

evidence testimony, documents, and objects used to prove questions of fact in a trial.

exclusionary rule rule requiring U.S. courts to discard evidence if it has been obtained through constitutionally improper procedures.

ex parte Latin, "from one party"; refers to a legal action in which only one party to a lawsuit appears to argue a case.

ex rel(atione) Latin, "on the relation of"; refers to a legal action based not on firsthand information but on behalf of another person.

family court court established to deal exclusively with matters of family law, and often operating under strong rules of confidentiality.

felony any serious crime, such as murder, assault, or the theft of property of substantial value, usually punishable by imprisonment. See also *misdemeanor.*

fraud conduct intended to cheat someone by lying, by repeating information known to be wrong, or by concealing

relevant information.

grand jury jury, typically of 23 jurors, empaneled by the state to examine whether the evidence supporting a criminal accusation is sufficient for prosecution to proceed.

habeas corpus, writ of Latin, "produce the body"; a writ requiring a person under custody to be brought before a judge or into court.

hearing act of listening to evidence or arguments in a court of law or before an official.

hearsay testimony attributing statements to another person who is not present in court to give testimony or be cross-examined; generally, hearsay is not admissable as evidence.

homicide killing of a person by another person. Not necessarily in itself a crime, but prerequisite to a charge of murder or manslaughter.

indictment formal charge or accusation of a crime, presented by a prosecutor to a grand jury. If the grand jury ratifies the indictment, it becomes a true bill.

intellectual property creative work, invention, or similar intangible good to which rights of ownership can be asserted through copyright or patent.

immunity grant of exemption from prosecution for some crime, thus making irrelevant to that person the constitutional protection against self-incrimination; the person granted immunity can then be compelled to testify against others involved in the case.

injunction court order requiring a person to behave in a specified way. A "cease and desist" order requires the person to stop doing something and refrain from doing it in the future.

intent purpose or intention. A crime committed "with intent" is committed with purpose and forethought.

judgment a court's final ruling in a case; based on, but subsequent to, the verdict of a judge or jury.

judicial review review by a court, especially a state high court or the federal Supreme Court, of the constitutionality of a law, regulation, or legal decision.

jurisdiction legal right of a court to try or adjudicate a case; the jurisdiction of a particular court is usually limited to a specific locality.

jury group of people, representing the public at large, chosen to determine issues of fact at a trial. Also called a petty jury or petit jury. See also *grand jury.*

larceny taking of money or other property by overtly unlawful means. See also *theft*.

liability state of being legally responsible for an act or an omission that causes or leads to loss, damage, injury, or death to another.

libel published false statement that is or may be damaging to a person's reputation. See also *defamation*; *slander*.

lien right to take or keep possession of property belonging to another person until a debt owed by that person is discharged.

litigation process of taking a civil case to court for adjudication. Parties to or subjects of a lawsuit are *litigants*; *to litigate* means to try a civil case at law.

malice aforethought mental state characterized by willingness to do harm to a person through recklessness or violence.

malpractice improper, illegal, or negligent professional treatment or activity, especially by a medical practitioner, lawyer, or public official.

manslaughter killing of a person without prior intent. Manslaughter may be voluntary (such as the consequence of a fight in which someone meant to harm, but not kill, the victim) or involuntary (resulting from negligence, for example by an intoxicated driver).

mens rea Latin, "state of mind"; under common law, a key to whether or not a defendant can be tried for a crime. Insane or severely mentally handicapped people, for example, cannot form criminal intent because they have diminished capacity to understand the consequences of their behavior.

Miranda warning result of the Supreme Court case *Miranda v. Arizona* (1966) stating that the police must inform persons taken into custody of their right to legal counsel and to remain silent under questioning.

misdemeanor lesser crime, usually punishable by a fine, community service, or brief incarceration.

motion request to a trial judge to make a ruling (for example, on the admissability of evidence).

murder intentional killing of a person, with or without premeditation.

negligence failure to use reasonable care, resulting in damage or injury to another.

nolo contendere Latin, "I do not wish to contest"; a plea in which a person does not challenge the charges against him or her but also does not admit guilt or liability.

patent government grant of authority to a person of the sole right, for a limited period of time, to use, manufacture, license, or sell something, usually an invention. See also *intellectual property*.

per curiam Latin, "by the court"; an opinion of a court in which the author of the decision is not identified.

perjury knowingly giving false testimony while under oath.

plaintiff person who files a lawsuit against another person in a civil case.

plea person's answer to a criminal charge: usually "guilty" or "not guilty." See also *nolo contendere*.

plea bargain deal between a prosecutor and a person accused of a crime, whereby the person pleads guilty to a lesser crime, or to the original crime in a lesser degree, to avoid trial and conviction on the original complaint.

power of attorney authority, which may be limited or unlimited, to act for another person in legal or financial matters; a legal document giving such authority to someone.

precedent See *case law*.

preponderance greater or weightier part; civil cases must normally be proved with a preponderance of the evidence, but not necessarily beyond reasonable doubt (as in criminal cases).

probable cause requirement that the police must have a reasonable belief that a person has committed a crime before the person may be arrested, or that a piece of evidence is physically present in a place before the place may be searched and the evidence seized.

probate official proving (verification) of a will. Probate results in the issuing of a verified copy of a will to the executors of an estate. Matters relating to the proving of wills are handled in probate court.

pro bono Latin, "for the [public] good"; services provided without charge (for example, legal services performed without charge on behalf of the indigent).

prosecutor elected or appointed public official responsible for pursuing criminal charges against accused persons in court.

punitive damages damages awarded to a plaintiff with the sole purpose of punishing the defendant for doing wrong.

rape forced sexual intercourse with another person, especially through the use or threat of violence, or intercourse with a person without that person's consent. Statutory rape defines as rape any sexual intercourse with a person below a certain age.

reasonable doubt doubt as to the guilt of a defendant

such as might be entertained by a reasonable person in light of all the available evidence. The state is obliged to prove criminal charges beyond a reasonable doubt.

restraining order court order temporarily preventing someone from taking some action, until the validity or permissability of the action can be adjudicated in court.

robbery theft accomplished by means of violence or intimidation. Distinct from burglary. See also *larceny*.

search and seizure law Fourth Amendment to the U.S. Constitution, guaranteeing that "the right of the people to be secure in their persons, houses, papers and effects, against unreasonable searches and seizures, shall not be violated, and no warrants shall issue, but upon probable cause."

self-defense possible defense against charges of violence against another; self-defense is justified if an attack is unprovoked and seems likely to cause actual harm, and safe retreat is impossible.

self-incrimination act of answering questions or offering testimony that might lead to one's own prosecution for a crime. The Fifth Amendment to the U.S. Constitution prohibits the state from forcing a person to testify against himself.

slander spoken false statement that is or may be damaging to a person's reputation. See also *defamation*; *libel*.

small claims court special court, often with simplified procedures, for civil proceedings involving sums of money below a specified low threshold.

statute of limitations statute prescribing a period of time beyond which certain kinds of legal action (e.g., prosecution for a crime) may no longer be undertaken.

statutory law body of principles and rules written down and pased by a legislative body; statutes often supplant, supplement, or clarify the common law.

subpoena writ ordering a person to attend a court; to summon (someone) with a subpoena or to require (a document or other evidence) to be submitted to a court of law.

summary judgment court ruling that, on the basis of the evidence, there is no "genuine issue of material fact," and thus no reason to proceed with a case.

testimony sworn statements given by a witness in court as evidence in a case.

tort act under civil law whereby one person causes injury to another, or to another's property; tort law deals specifically with torts and damages arising from them.

verdict judge's or jury's finding of the facts of a case.

voir dire French, "to speak the truth"; a preliminary examination of a witness or a potential juror by a judge or a lawyer.

warrant court order directing a public official to do something—for example, to make an arrest, or to search some premises for evidence.

writ legal directive from a court directing some person or some entity to act or refrain from acting in a certain specified way.

The Constitution of the United States of America
An Annotated Guide

On May 25, 1787, 55 delegates from 12 states convened in Philadelphia to attempt the writing of a new constitution to replace the woefully inadequate Articles of Confederation. On September 17th, after 17 weeks of wrangling, compromising, and deal-making, the 42 remaining delegates signed the new document and presented it to the states for ratification. On June 21, 1788, New Hampshire became the ninth state to accept the Constitution and it became the law of the land.

Below is the text of the Constitution and all of the amendments added over two centuries and more.

Interspersed between articles and sections are brief explanatory remarks by Stanley I. Kutler, professor emeritus of constitutional history at the University of Wisconsin. The commentary is from *Your Constitution: What It Says, What It Means* (copyright © 1987 by G&H Soho Inc. and reprinted with permission).

Preamble

WE, THE PEOPLE of the United States, in order to form a more perfect union, establish justice, insure domestic tranquillity, provide for the common defense, promote the general welfare, and secure the blessings of liberty to ourselves and our posterity, do ordain and establish this Constitution for the United States of America.

The Preamble embodies long-standing English and

colonial beliefs in the social contract or covenant, a notion that society is bound together through the common agreement of the people—the ultimate sovereign. People created governments as part of the social contract to establish political order for the better protection of their liberties. The purposes set forth here reflected the needs of 1787 and also the enduring demands for an ordered, civilized society.

Article I

Section 1 All legislative powers herein granted shall be vested in a Congress of the United States, which shall consist of a Senate and House of Representatives.

At the outset, the Constitution established the concept of separation of powers, providing that the two houses of Congress would exercise "all" legislative powers. English political theory and practice had emphasized that legislative power could not be delegated. In the United States, however, Congress can delegate and has delegated significant power. For example, it has given power to presidents to allow them to respond to national security matters or the need for adjusting tariffs, and to regulatory agencies, such as the Federal Trade Commission or the Federal Communications Commission, that have the expertise to deal with specialized and complex problems.

Section 2 [1] The House of Representatives shall be composed of members chosen every second year by the people of the several States, and the electors in each State shall have the qualifications requisite for electors of the most numerous branch of the State legislature.

The "Great Compromise" resolved the basic division at the Constitutional Convention in 1787. Delegates had split over the apportionment of legislative power for the various states, largely between larger and smaller states. The compromise provided for two separate houses of Congress. The House of Representatives is determined by population and is subject to reelection every two years. The Senate is based on the idea of state equality, with each state having two senators, and its members serve six-year terms (see "section 3(1)"). This section also clearly provided for state control over voting qualifications, but subsequent amendments (15, 19, and 24) and legislation (Voting Rights Act of 1965) have permitted significant federal involvement in this area.

[2] No person shall be a Representative who shall not have attained to the age of twenty-five years, and been seven years a citizen of the United States, and who shall not, when elected, be an inhabitant of that State in which he shall be chosen.

The American Constitution contains state residency requirements for members of Congress, unlike the English system, where members of Parliament typically are not residents of the constituencies they represent.

[3] Representatives and direct taxes shall be apportioned among the several States which may be included within this Union, according to their respective numbers, which shall be determined by adding to the whole number of free persons, including those bound to service for a term of years, and excluding Indians not taxed, three-fifths of all other persons. The actual enumeration shall be made within three years after the first meeting of the Congress of the United States, and within every subsequent term of ten years, in such manner as they shall by law direct. The number of Representatives shall not exceed one for every thirty thousand, but each State shall have at least one Representative; and until such enumeration shall be made, the State of New Hampshire shall be entitled to choose three; Massachusetts, eight; Rhode Island and Providence Plantations, one; Connecticut, five; New York, six; New Jersey, four; Pennsylvania, eight; Delaware, one; Maryland, six; Virginia, ten; North Carolina, five; South Carolina, five; and Georgia, three.

Sharp sectional differences occurred at the Constitutional Convention, particularly about slavery. Northern delegates agreed to several forms of protection for what the Constitution labels "all other persons." The concessions included arrangements to facilitate the recapture of fugitive slaves, the denial of congressional authority to prohibit the slave trade until 1808, and the above clause, popularly known as the "3/5ths Compromise." It provided that each slave would count as 3/5ths "of all other persons" for purposes of determining the number of representatives for each state and the amount of direct taxation. Following the abolition of slavery, the Fourteenth Amendment, Section 2, superseded this clause.

This section also mandates a federal census every 10 years. Some delegates feared that new sections of the nation would gain influence and power greater than the original states. As such, they favored congressional determination of national apportionment. But the inclusion of the census requirement reflected the framers' faith in republican principles, ensuring support for the idea that representation would be determined by persons, and not property or other interests.

[4] When vacancies happen in the representation from any State, the executive authority thereof shall issue writs of election to fill such vacancies.

The requirement that state governors arrange for the filling of congressional vacancies again indicates the framers' desire to give states control over the election of representatives and senators.

[5] The House of Representatives shall choose their Speaker and other officers, and shall have the sole power of impeachment.

The House impeaches civil officers; the Senate tries them. The analogy is somewhat similar to the idea of a grand jury that indicts, leaving the determination of guilt to another panel. But the analogy is limited. Until the Clinton impeachment in 1998–99 the House only considered impeachment when it believed the evidence would result in conviction.

Section 3 [1] The Senate of the United States shall be composed of two Senators from each State, chosen by the legislature thereof for six years; and each Senator shall have one vote.

The original Constitution provided that state legislatures would choose senators, again recognizing the necessity for some state influence in the affairs of the national government. The method of indirect election presumably would help create a more conservative body, yet this provision is at odds with the framers' supposed fear of state legislatures. The Seventeenth Amendment, which was ratified in 1913, eventually provided for the direct election of senators.

[2] Immediately after they shall be assembled in consequence of the first election, they shall be divided as equally as may be into three classes. The seats of the Senators of the first class shall be vacated at the expiration of the second year, of the second class at the expiration of the fourth year, and of the third class at the expiration of the sixth year, so that one-third may be chosen every second year; and if vacancies happen by resignation or otherwise

during the recess of the legislature of any State, the executive thereof may make temporary appointments until the next meeting of the legislature, which shall then fill such vacancies.

[3] No person shall be a Senator who shall not have attained to the age of thirty years, and been nine years a citizen of the United States, and who shall not, when elected, be an inhabitant of that State for which he shall be chosen.

The Senate is a continuing body, unlike the House of Representatives, which assembles a new group every two years. Only one-third of the Senate stands for election every two years. This practice again reflected the framers' belief that the Senate would be the more conservative body, providing stability and continuity in government. The same interpretation can explain the differing age requirement for a senator as opposed to a representative.

[4] The Vice-President of the United States shall be President of the Senate, but shall have no vote, unless they be equally divided.

Every newly elected president seems to promise a greater role and enhanced powers for the vice president. In fact, this clause provides the only constitutional power for that officer: to preside over the Senate and to cast a vote to break a tie vote of the body.

[5] The Senate shall choose their other officers and also a President pro tempore in the absence of the Vice-President, or when he shall exercise the office of President of the United States.

The stipulation that the Senate chooses its own officers gives that body a degree of independence, presumably from the executive. The Twenty-fifth Amendment provided for the selection of a successor in the event the elected vice president succeeded to the presidency. The Senate nevertheless elects a president pro tempore, but largely for honorific reasons.

[6] The Senate shall have the sole power to try all impeachments. When sitting for that purpose, they shall be on oath or affirmation. When the President of the United States is tried, the Chief Justice shall preside; and no person shall be convicted without the concurrence of two-thirds of the members present.

The House of Representatives votes impeachment articles; the Senate tries the issues. House action requires only a majority vote. The requirement of a two-thirds vote for conviction by the Senate offers another example of checks and balances in the Constitution, for a two-thirds vote is not easily gained. The difference in voting requirements indicates that the framers believed that impeachment hearings—inquests into the behavior of public officials—served the public interest. Conviction, however, was not to be achieved as readily. The requirement that the chief justice preside in a presidential impeachment trial provided another check and balance by including the authority of the third branch of government.

[7] Judgment in cases of impeachment shall not extend further than to removal from office, and disqualification to hold and enjoy any office of honor, trust, or profit under the United States; but the party convicted shall, nevertheless, be liable and subject to indictment, trial, judgment, and punishment, according to law.

Impeached officers are subject to subsequent indictment and trial for their alleged crimes. This clause is the basis of the argument that impeachment is not meant to be confined to criminal acts, as ordinary legal procedures could punish such violations adequately.

Section 4 [1] The times, places, and manner of holding elections for Senators and Representatives shall be prescribed in each State by the legislature thereof; but the Congress may at any time by law make or alter such regulations, except as to the places of choosing Senators.

This provision again shows a willingness to give the states a significant measure of control over elections. Congress, as this clause provides, may make exceptions, but the states still largely determine the time, place, and manner of holding elections.

[2] The Congress shall assemble at least once in every year, and such meeting shall be on the first Monday in December, unless they shall by law appoint a different day.

The Twentieth Amendment superseded this section, reflecting modern improvements in transportation and communications.

Section 5 [1] Each House shall be the judge of the elections, returns, and qualification of its own members, and a majority of each shall constitute a quorum to do business; but a smaller number may adjourn from day to day, and may be authorized to compel the attendance of absent members, in such manner, and under such penalties, as each House may provide.

[2] Each House may determine the rules of its proceedings, punish its members for disorderly behavior, and with the concurrence of two-thirds, expel a member.

[3] Each House shall keep a journal of its proceedings, and from time to time publish the same, excepting such parts as may in their judgment require secrecy, and the yeas and nays of the members of either House on any question shall, at the desire of one-fifth of those present, be entered on the journal.

[4] Neither House, during the session of Congress, shall, without the consent of the other, adjourn for more than three days, nor to any other place than that in which the two Houses shall be sitting.

The clauses in this section reinforce the independence of the legislative branch and guarantee each house the right to determine its internal rules. They can be traced back to the English Parliament's long struggle for independence from the Crown; as such, they are basic components of the American doctrine of separation of powers. During the controversy over Reconstruction following the Civil War, Congress's authority to determine its own membership gave that body enormous leverage in determining when the ex-Confederate states could be readmitted to the Union. The courts generally have given Congress almost absolute control over these matters, but in 1968, the Supreme Court held that Congress had no "authority to exclude any person, duly elected by his constituency who meets all the requirements for membership expressly prescribed" in the Constitution. Congress polices the internal behavior of its members and thus may censure, criticize, or change assignments of its members. The Congressional Record offers a public record of the congressional debates and votes.

Section 6 [1] The Senators and Representatives shall receive a compensation for their services, to be ascertained by law and paid out of the Treasury of the United States. They shall, in all cases except treason, felony, and breach of the peace, be privileged from arrest during their attendance at the session of their respective Houses, and in going to and returning from the same; and for any speech or debate in either House they shall not be questioned in any other place.

Under the Articles of Confederation, the states paid the salaries of congressional representatives, thus diminishing legislators' loyalties to the national government. This clause, like similar ones for the executive and judiciary, strengthens the independence of the three branches of government.

The second sentence refers to hard-won privileges and prerogatives secured by Parliament during its lengthy struggles with the English monarchy in the 16th and 17th centuries. Essentially, they provide immunity for what legislators say in Congress and immunity from arrest while they are attending legislative sessions, except if charged with a felony. The "speech and debate" clause has been extended to provide immunity for congressman from libel suits for remarks made in a press release.

[2] **No Senator or Representative shall, during the time for which he was elected, be appointed to any civil office under the authority of the United States, which shall have been created, or the emoluments whereof shall have been increased during such time; and no person holding any office under the United States shall be a member of either House during his continuance in office.**

The English parliamentary system allows members of the legislature to become ministers of the Crown, or cabinet officers. This clause underlines the principle of separation of powers, for it ensures that no one may simultaneously be a member of Congress and hold a federal civil office.

Section 7 [1] All bills for raising revenue shall originate in the House of Representatives; but the Senate may propose or concur with amendments as on other bills.

The framers of the Constitution to some extent saw the House of Representatives as analogous to the English House of Commons, which traditionally had the exclusive power for originating revenue measures. In practice, the Senate has equal power in revenue matters because of its ability to amend bills.

[2] **Every bill which shall have passed the House of Representatives and the Senate shall, before it becomes a law, be presented to the President of the United States; if he approves he shall sign it, but if not he shall return it, with his objections, to that House in which it shall have originated, who shall enter the objections at large on their journal and proceed to reconsider it. If after such reconsideration two-thirds of that House shall agree to pass the bill, it shall be sent, together with the objections, to the other House, by which it shall likewise be reconsid-**

ered, and if approved by two-thirds of that House it shall become a law. But in all such cases the vote of both Houses shall be determined by yeas and nays, and the names of the persons voting for and against the bill shall be entered on the journal of each House respectively. If any bill shall not be returned by the President within ten days (Sundays excepted) after it shall have been presented to him, the same shall be a law, in like manner as if he had signed it, unless the Congress by their adjournment prevent its return, in which case it shall not be a law.

This lengthy section involves the president's veto power and his role in legislation. The requirement that two-thirds of each house vote to override presidential objections usually is difficult to secure, thus giving the president a significant role in the lawmaking process. The last part of this section describes what is known as the "pocket veto," which is the president's practice of withholding his signature as Congress adjourns, thereby preventing Congress from overriding his action.

[3] **Every order, resolution or vote to which the concurrence of the Senate and House of Representatives may be necessary (except on a question of adjournment) shall be presented to the President of the United States; and before the same shall take effect shall be approved by him, or being disapproved by him, shall be repassed by two-thirds of the Senate and House of Representatives, according to the rules and limitations prescribed in the case of a bill.**

In recent times, Congress has used the concurrent resolution to prohibit or recall presidential authority delegated by Congress, which in effect subjects presidential actions to a legislative veto. At times, Congress has provided that the veto of one house is adequate to reject or repudiate an executive action. The Supreme Court ruled in 1983 that such action violated constitutional requirements for bicameralism and for presidential involvement in the legislative process.

Section 8 [1] The Congress shall have power to lay and collect taxes, duties, imposts and excises, to pay the debts and provide for the common defense and general welfare of the United States; but all duties, imposts and excises shall be uniform throughout the United States;

Section 8 enumerates the major powers of Congress. The first grant of power remedied one of the great defects of the government under the Articles of Confederation, namely, the inability of the national government to raise its own sources of revenue. The aims of taxation are broadly stated:

to pay the nation's debts, and to provide for the common defense and general welfare. The latter clause in particular has been liberally construed to give Congress great latitude in determining its scope. For example, it has been used to authorize the Social Security system, which is financed by payroll taxes. James Madison believed that the power to tax and spend was limited to the enumerated objects of congressional authority; Alexander Hamilton, however, advanced a broad construction and maintained that the power existed apart from others granted to the national government. History and constitutional law clearly have sustained Hamilton's view.

[2] To borrow money on the credit of the United States;

This clause enables the United States government to utilize deficit financing. Many state constitutions specifically prohibit such practice. This authority, along with the preceding one, and clauses 5 and 6 below, constitute the national government's fiscal powers.

[3] To regulate commerce with foreign nations, and among the several States, and with the Indian tribes;

The "commerce clause" fulfilled one of the basic aims of the Constitutional Convention: to reduce state economic rivalries and establish the national government as arbiter of the national economy and market. Chief Justice John Marshall in *Gibbons v. Ogden* (1824) ruled that "Commerce undoubtedly is traffic, but it is something more—it is intercourse." That statement has been the basis for using the commerce clause as the primary vehicle for expanding the regulatory powers of the national government over the national marketplace. These expanded powers include, for example, rate regulations of various means of transportation, the regulation of stock markets and commodities exchanges, the limitations on monopoly powers, minimum wage and maximum hours laws, the prohibition of child labor products, quality control of food products and medicines, the policing of water and air pollution, and the guarantee of equal access to public accommodations.

[4] To establish an uniform rule of naturalization, and uniform laws on the subject of bankruptcies throughout the United States;

Throughout our history, Congress has regulated aliens and immigrants in a variety of ways, even to the point of exclusion. As early as 1798, responding to charges that aliens represented a subversive threat, Congress imposed severe restrictions on their entry, activities, and ability to acquire citizenship. In the 1880's, Congress responded to west coast political pressures and barred Asians from citizenship. During World War II, Congress amended the law to enable Chinese to acquire citizenship, and then, in 1952, provided that neither race nor sex could be a barrier to naturalization. The Constitution lacked a definition of citizenship until the Fourteenth Amendment stipulated that all persons born or naturalized in the United States were citizens.

The bankruptcy provision again shows the framers' desire that commercial relations be as uniform as possible. But it was not until the post–Civil War period that Congress finally overcame state and sectional concerns and developed effective national bankruptcy legislation.

[5] To coin money, regulate the value thereof, and of foreign coin, and fix the standard of weights and measures;
[6] To provide for the punishment of counterfeiting the securities and current coin of the United States;
[7] To establish post offices and post roads;

The national government derives its power to handle and protect mail service from clause 7. The provision regarding post roads offered an opening wedge for Congress's role in providing for "internal improvements," such as roads, bridges, and, eventually, railroads. The clause also comprehends a "police power," enabling the federal government to exclude "harmful" items from the mails, such as circulars relating to fraudulent schemes. But the Supreme Court has ruled that Congress may not authorize the Postal Service to prevent or detain the mailing of "political propaganda."

[8] To promote the progress of science and useful arts by securing for limited times to authors and inventors the exclusive right to their respective writings and discoveries;

This clause is the basis for federal patent and copyright laws.

[9] To constitute tribunals inferior to the Supreme Court;

The Constitution does not require any federal courts other than the Supreme Court. The First Congress in 1789 seriously considered using the existing state judiciaries to conduct federal business, with an appeal to the national Supreme Court. Anti-Federalists and those suspicious of expanding the national government vigorously opposed creating a lower federal court system. But the Judiciary Act of 1789 created both federal district courts and intermediate courts of appeal.

[10] **To define and punish piracies and felonies committed on the high seas and offenses against the law of nations.**

[11] **To declare war, grant letters of marque and reprisal, and make rules concerning captures on land and water;**

[12] **To raise and support armies, but no appropriation of money to that use shall be for a longer term than two years;**

[13] **To provide and maintain a navy;**

[14] **To make rules for the government and regulation of the land and naval forces;**

[15] **To provide for calling forth the militia to execute the laws of the Union, suppress insurrections, and repel invasions;**

[16] **To provide for organizing, arming and disciplining the militia, and for governing such part of them as may be employed in the service of the United States, reserving to the States respectively the appointment of the officers, and the authority of training the militia according to the discipline prescribed by Congress;**

Clauses 10 through 16 form the so-called war powers. These statements underline civilian control over the military, as they empower Congress to provide for the maintenance and governance of military forces. Military appropriations may not be for a period of longer than two years, thus requiring military officials to submit to regular congressional scrutiny.

Chief Justice John Marshall once referred to Congress's power to "declare and conduct a war," thus indicating a notion of resultant and implied powers. The war powers in general have been used to create and sanction extensive authority for the national government in wartime. Much of this authority inevitably has flowed to the president in his capacity as commander in chief under Article II, Section 2. Thus during World War II, President Roosevelt issued an executive order directing the forced evacuation and internment of Japanese-Americans from the West Coast. In more recent times, presidents have on numerous occasions committed American soldiers to combat situations without formal congressional action, claiming that the realities of the moment required prompt action by the nation. The Vietnam War resulted in the War Powers Act of 1973, which requires the president to consult with Congress before committing troops, or to withdraw those troops if directed by congressional resolution.

Clause 15 has significant scope aside from its contribu-

tion to the war powers. This clause provided the power necessary to cure what James Madison believed to be a fundamental defect of the Articles of Confederation, that is, the "want of power" to enforce the granted powers of government. In 1795 Congress gave President Washington the authority to decide whether to use military force to quash potential insurrection. That law largely survives today and has been used by various presidents, such as Eisenhower, Kennedy, and Johnson, to maintain order or to ensure the enforcement of federal court orders.

[17] **To exercise exclusive legislation in all cases whatsoever over such district (not exceeding ten miles square) as may, by cession of particular States and the acceptance of Congress, become the seat of the Government of the United States, and to exercise like authority over all places purchased by the consent of the legislature of the State in which the same shall be, for the erection of forts, magazines, arsenals, dockyards, and other needful buildings;**

This section provides for the establishment of a separate district as the site of the national government. The District of Columbia was formed from land cessions by Virginia and Maryland, and Congress has had a primary responsibility for governing the area. In recent years, however, the District has elected its own mayor and city council and has gained more control over its local affairs. The District does not have a voting representative in Congress, but the Twenty-third Amendment enabled residents to vote in presidential elections.

[18] **To make all laws which shall be necessary and proper for carrying into execution the foregoing powers, and all other powers vested by this Constitution in the Government of the United States, or in any department or officer thereof.**

This is the "necessary and proper" clause, sometimes known as the "elastic clause" in that it provides for an interpretation of congressional powers beyond the simple enumeration of those listed in Section 8. Chief Justice Marshall established the time-honored interpretation of the clause in 1819: "Let the end be legitimate, let it be within the scope of the Constitution, and all means which are appropriate, which are plainly adapted to that end, which are not prohibited, but consistent with the letter and spirit of the Constitution, are constitutional." Marshall's view responded to those who opposed the development of national power beyond those items specifically laid down in the Constitution. Marshall insisted that the Constitution had a vitality that enabled it "to be adapted to the various crises of human affairs." Clearly, Marshall did not intend his words as license for Congress to do whatever it wishes. The formula he enunciated, as well as his published essays at the time, carefully reinforced the notion that the Constitution not only granted power but also prescribed limitations of power, such as those that follow in the next section.

Section 9 [1] **The migration or importation of such persons as any of the States now existing shall think proper to admit shall not be prohibited by the Congress prior to the year one thousand eight hundred and eight, but a tax or duty may be imposed on such importation, not exceeding ten dollars for each person.**

This clause refers to the importation of slaves, although here, as throughout the document, the framers carefully avoided mentioning slavery. The constitutional stipulation that the slave trade could not be prohibited for 20 years represented another sectional compromise.

[2] **The privilege of the writ of habeas corpus shall not be suspended, unless when in cases of rebellion or invasion the public safety may require it.**

The writ of habeas corpus is a fundamental guarantee of Anglo-American justice, providing that a person may seek a judicial inquiry into the cause of his detention by authorities. During the Civil War, Lincoln temporarily suspended the writ in Maryland, and Congress eventually approved the action retroactively. The result left unresolved the constitutional issue of which branch had the power to suspend the writ.

[3] **No bill of attainder or ex post facto law shall be passed.**

A bill of attainder is a legislative judgment that imposes punishment without proper judicial proceedings. The prohibition of attainder reinforces the separation of powers doctrine as it denies Congress any judicial role, except for the Senate's role in impeachment proceedings. Following the Civil War, the Supreme Court ruled that Congress could not impose loyalty oaths as a precondition for the practice in the federal courts. The prohibition against attainders, the Court said, voided any act "which inflicts punishment without a judicial trial." Ex post facto laws retroactively impose penalties; thus all legislation must be prospective in effect.

[4] **No capitation or other direct tax shall be laid, unless in proportion to the census or enumeration herein before directed to be taken.**

This clause protected the institution of slavery , as it ensured that no form of direct tax would be imposed, except under the three-fifths compromise arrangement.

[5] **No tax or duty shall be laid on articles exported from any State.**

The inference here is that Congress may never tax exports, a clear reservation to the otherwise broad scope of the federal tax and commerce powers. Southern delegates at the Constitutional Convention feared the possibility of an export tax on cotton. But in general, the provision reflected the framers' desire to encourage economic development and enterprise.

[6] **No preference shall be given by any regulation of commerce or revenue to the ports of one State over those of another; nor shall vessels bound to or from one State be obliged to enter, clear or pay duties in another.**

Several of these clauses reflect the framers' concern for the development of a national common market that would be unimpeded by artificial state constraints or barriers. This particular section offers a corollary to congressional control over interstate commerce.

[7] **No money shall be drawn from the Treasury but in consequence of appropriations made by law; and a regular statement and account of the receipts and expenditures of all public money shall be published from time to time.**

Here again, the Constitution reflects the framers' awareness of the long struggle between the Crown and Parliament in England. This provision is designed to prevent unauthorized expenditures by the president, ensuring congressional control of the "purse." There have been exceptions to public accounting of expenditures in recent years. The Central Intelligence Agency's budget and those of other security agencies, for example, are not fully published.

[8] **No title of nobility shall be granted by the United States; and no person holding any office of profit or trust under them shall, without the consent of the Congress, accept of any present, emolument, office, or title of any kind whatever from any king, prince, or foreign state.**

Since American presidents have become world figures in the 20th century, they have received numerous presents from foreign states. The executive branch and Congress have worked out appropriate rules for the disposition of these gifts.

Section 10 **[1] No State shall enter into any treaty, alliance, or confederation; grant letters of marque and reprisal; coin money; emit bills of credit; make anything but gold and silver coin a tender in payment of debts; pass any bill of attainder, ex post facto law or law impairing the obligation of contracts, or grant any title of nobility.**

This section clearly repudiates any notion of state sovereignty, for everything denied to the states represents traditional attributes of sovereign power. Historically, the most important clause has been that prohibiting the state from "impairing the obligation of contracts." That language reveals the framers' fears that ever-changing popular majorities would repudiate and overturn contracts and property titles. The original intention seemed to confine the restraint to any interference in private contracts, but John Marshall later extended it to public grants and charters. The contract clause, perhaps as much as any part of the Constitution, fortified the framers' concern for the protection of private property rights.

[2] No State shall, without the consent of the Congress, lay any imposts or duties on imports or exports, except what may be absolutely necessary for executing its inspection laws; and the net produce of all duties and imposts, laid by any State on imports or exports, shall be for the use of the Treasury of the United States; and all such laws shall be subject to the revision and control of the Congress.

[3] No State shall, without the consent of Congress, lay any duty of tonnage, keep troops and ships of war in time of peace, enter into any agreement or compact with another State or with a foreign power, or engage in war, unless actually invaded or in such imminent danger as will not admit of delay.

Clauses 2 and 3 again restrict state power and reject any notions of state sovereignty. States are restrained from interfering with the flow of the national market. Their relations with other states and foreign powers, aside from normal commercial dealings, are subject to congressional control.

Article II

Section 1 **[1] The executive power shall be vested in a President of the United States of America. He shall hold his office during the term of four years, and together with the Vice-President, chosen for the same term, be elected, as follows.**

Executive power as vested in Article II generally has been interpreted in a broad, expansive manner. Theodore Roosevelt believed that the president could do "anything that the needs of the Nation demanded unless such action was forbidden by the Constitution and the laws." The 20th-century developments that spurred national consolidation, the growth and complexity of the national market, and the dramatic increase of involvement in world affairs have all resulted in greater activity and responsibility by the chief executive. Basically, the nation has accepted the steadily expanding notion of presidential power and authority; many attempts to limit presidential power in foreign and military affairs have been unsuccessful. Yet political realities and the restraining influences of other branches periodically have served as both informal and formal checks and balances on presidential power. Presidents need congressional appropriations of funds to conduct foreign policy. Also, the Supreme Court in recent times has rejected broad claims of "inherent powers" and "executive privilege" by Presidents Truman, Nixon, and George W. Bush.

The framers specified a four-year presidential term, but they deliberately left open the question of reeligibility. Thomas Jefferson periodically expressed fears that incumbents would serve for life, but until 1940, all presidents followed George Washington's two-term precedent. Franklin D. Roosevelt broke the tradition and was elected for third and fourth terms. In large measure, the Twenty-Second Amendment, limiting presidents to two elected terms, represented a reaction against Roosevelt.

[2] Each State shall appoint, in such manner as the legislature thereof may direct, a number of Electors, equal to the whole number of Senators and Representatives to which the State may be entitled in the Congress; but no Senator or Representative, or person holding an office of trust or profit under the United States shall be appointed an Elector.

[3] The Electors shall meet in their respective States and vote by ballot for two persons, of whom one at least shall not be an inhabitant of the same State with themselves. And they shall make a list of all the persons voted for, and

of the number of votes for each; which list they shall sign and certify, and transmit sealed to the seat of government of the United States, directed to the President of the Senate. The President of the Senate shall, in the presence of the Senate and House of Representatives, open all the certificates, and the votes shall then be counted. The person having the greatest number of votes shall be the President, if such number be a majority of the whole number of Electors appointed; and if there be more than one who have such majority, and have an equal number of votes, then the House of Representatives shall immediately choose by ballot one of them for President; and if no person have a majority, then from the five highest on the list the said House shall in like manner choose the President. But in choosing the President the votes shall be taken by States, the representation from each State having one vote; a quorum for this purpose shall consist of a member or members from two-thirds of the States, and a majority of all the States shall be necessary to a choice. In every case, after the choice of the President, the person having the greatest number of votes of the Electors shall be the Vice-President. But if there should remain two or more who have equal votes, the Senate shall choose from them by ballot the Vice-President.

[4] The Congress may determine the time of choosing the Electors and the day on which they shall give their votes, which day shall be the same throughout the United States.

The second, third, and fourth paragraphs in this section established the "Electoral College." The framers' apparent intention was to create an independent body of electors, but in fact, the electors have traditionally followed the election results in their individual states. Each state has electors equal to its delegation of representatives and senators; the "electoral" votes are cast by those representing the victorious candidate. Presidents Abraham Lincoln and Woodrow Wilson received less than a majority of the popular votes because of significant third-party candidacies, but they had decisive margins in the Electoral College. Presidents Rutherford B. Hayes, Benjamin Harrison, and George W. Bush gained electoral college victories, yet they finished second in the popular balloting; none of those elections had a substantial third-party vote. Periodic efforts to abolish the Electoral College have failed, despite serious concerns in recent years of the possibility of a popular choice failing to attain an electoral majority.

The third paragraph resulted in the complex stalemate between Thomas Jefferson and Aaron Burr in 1800–01. Jefferson clearly had been his party's choice for president and Burr for vice president. When party electors met, however, they failed to divert one vote from Burr. The result was a tie, and the House of Representatives finally had to choose between the two. The Twelfth Amendment subsequently was designed to prevent that situation, requiring electors to ballot separately for president and vice president.

[5] No person except a natural-born citizen, or citizen of the United States at the time of the adoption of this Constitution, shall be eligible to the office of President; neither shall any person be eligible to that office who shall not have attained to the age of thirty-five years, and been fourteen years a resident within the United States.

This section has never been litigated. Some candidates for the presidency were born abroad of American parents, but they have generally been regarded as American citizens. Herbert Hoover had not lived in the United States for 14 years prior to his election in 1928, but he had maintained a legal residence.

[6] In case of the removal of the President from office, or of his death, resignation, or inability to discharge the powers and duties of the said office, the same shall devolve on the Vice-President, and the Congress may by law provide for the case of removal, death, resignation, or inability, both of the President and Vice-President, declaring what officer shall then act as President, and such officer shall act accordingly until the disability be removed or a President shall be elected.

Congress has periodically altered the manner of presidential succession beyond the vice president. We have had legislation that variously established the president pro tempore of the Senate, the secretary of state, or the Speaker of the House of Representatives as next in line in the event that the vice president succeeded to the presidency. The problem of determining presidential disability has been difficult. Mindful of intruding on executive independence, Congress historically had been reluctant to find a legislative solution. Finally, Congress devised a formula and proposed it in the form of the Twenty-fifth Amendment, which was ratified in 1967.

[7] The President shall, at stated times, receive for his services a compensation, which shall neither be increased nor diminished during the period for which he

shall have been elected, and he shall not receive within that period any other emolument from the United States or any of them.

This clause is essential for the separation of powers and the independence of the executive. Congress may not punish the president by reducing his salary during his elected term; similarly, a Congress composed of the president's friends and allies may not increase his salary in that same period.

[8] **Before he enter on the execution of his office he shall take the following oath or affirmation:**

"I do solemnly swear (or affirm) that I will faithfully execute the office of President of the United States, and will to the best of my ability preserve, protect, and defend the Constitution of the United States."

This oath binds the president to the Constitution, as it does all civil officers in the United States (see Article VI, Section 3), thus reinforcing the supremacy of the Constitution. When the House of Representatives impeached Andrew Johnson in 1868 and Bill Clinton in 1998, and when the House Judiciary Committee voted impeachment articles against Richard Nixon in 1974, they did so, in part, on the grounds that the presidents had violated their oath.

Section 2 [1] The President shall be Commander in Chief of the Army and Navy of the United States, and of the militia of the several States when called into the actual service of the United States; he may require the opinion, in writing, of the principal officer in each of the executive departments, upon any subject relating to the duties of their respective offices, and he shall have power to grant reprieves and pardons for offenses against the United States, except in cases of impeachment.

The president as commander in chief again asserts the idea of civilian supremacy over the military. Presidents have claimed, and exercised, the prerogative of conducting military policies in their capacity as overall commander. President Abraham Lincoln issued direct orders to his army commanders; President Harry Truman directly ordered the dropping of the atomic bomb; and Presidents Lyndon Johnson and Richard Nixon supervised and directed military attacks on North Vietnam. In 1951 Truman removed General Douglas MacArthur as military commander in Japan and Korea on the grounds that the general had been insubordinate to the president.

Largely for practical reasons, the president has been the beneficiary of a widened scope of national power resulting from the war powers enumerated in Article I, Section 8. Those powers, combined with the president's assumption of wartime leadership sanctioned by this section, have resulted in presidential exercises of power that involve nonmilitary matters. President Truman, for example, justified his seizure of the steel mills as necessary to prevent a strike and maintain essential steel production. The Supreme Court rejected his argument and restored the mills to private owners.

This section also refers to the advisory capacity of the heads of the executive departments—that is, the cabinet. That body, however, has no authority except for what individual presidents may bestow on it.

The president's pardoning power is absolute, and it may be granted even before an individual has been convicted, such as when President Gerald Ford pardoned former President Richard Nixon in 1974.

[2] **He shall have power, by and with the advice and consent of the Senate, to make treaties, provided two-thirds of the Senators present concur; and he shall nominate, and, by and with the advice and consent of the Senate, shall appoint ambassadors, other public ministers and consuls, judges of the Supreme Court, and all other officers of the United States whose appointments are not herein otherwise provided for, and which shall be established by law; but the Congress may by law vest the appointment of such inferior officers, as they think proper, in the President alone, in the courts of law, or in the heads of departments.**

The president's treaty-making power, together with his ability to send and receive foreign ambassadors, provides the foundation for his authority to conduct the foreign policy of the United States. The stipulation that two-thirds of the Senate must consent to the ratification of a treaty indicates that the Senate, at least, was given some share in the making of such policy. Treaties, according to Article VI, Section 2, are part of the "supreme law of the land"; as such, the framers established a rigorous standard for their incorporation into the fundamental law. The Senate's role in providing "advice" in the formulation of foreign policy is largely dependent upon the president's wishes. President Wilson's failure to consult with the Senate during the formulation of the Treaty of Versailles, establishing the League of Nations, often is cited as a leading cause for the Senate's rejection of the treaty. Since then, presidential consultation with Congress is considered politically imperative.

The Senate also shares power in the appointment of executive and judicial officers, since it must consent to their nomination by the president. As it establishes various offices, Congress may determine what levels of executive officers the Senate must confirm. When the First Congress created the original executive departments, congressmen debated at length whether the president required Senate consent to remove any officers that the Senate had confirmed. By indirection, Congress provided that removal was a matter of presidential discretion.

[3] The President shall have power to fill up all vacancies that may happen during the recess of the Senate, by granting commissions which shall expire at the end of their next session.

This paragraph provides for "recess" appointments; that is, the president may appoint an executive officer, a judge, or an ambassador without consent while the Senate is not in session. Such appointments are rare as they are considered offensive to Congress.

Section 3 He shall from time to time give to the Congress information of the state of the Union, and recommend to their consideration such measures as he shall judge necessary and expedient; he may, on extraordinary occasions, convene both Houses, or either of them, and in case of disagreement between them with respect to the time of adjournment, he may adjourn them to such time as he shall think proper; he shall receive ambassadors and other public ministers; he shall take care that the laws be faithfully executed, and shall commission all the officers of the United States.

Presidents are expected to provide a "State of the Union" message to Congress. The tradition has been that the information is given annually. Washington and John Adams appeared in person, but Jefferson began a practice of submitting written messages, one that continued until Woodrow Wilson's first message in 1913. Today, the president uses the State of the Union report in large measure as a vehicle to communicate with the nation. Earlier, presidents provided a review of the year's important national events and developments; in the 20th century, the message has been a device for articulating the president's agenda.

The requirement that the president "take care that the laws be faithfully executed" basically supplements the oath of office and offers a reference for accountability in the event Congress seeks to impeach and remove the presi-

dent. This section also has been used by various presidents to justify armed intervention in the case of strikes or defiance of court orders. President William McKinley ordered federal troops to break the Pullman strike in 1894; Dwight D. Eisenhower and John F. Kennedy dispatched soldiers and federal marshals to enforce court-ordered desegregation in the 1950's and 1960's; and Lyndon Johnson did the same to quell urban disorders in 1967.

Section 4 The President, Vice-President and all civil officers of the United States shall be removed from office on impeachment for and conviction of treason, bribery, or other high crimes and misdemeanors.

Andrew Johnson, the 17th president of the United States, was impeached in 1868, but acquitted by one vote in the Senate. In 1974 the House Judiciary Committee voted three articles of impeachment against Richard Nixon, but Nixon resigned before the full House could act. In 1998–99 Bill Clinton was impeached for three alleged offenses but the Senate could not muster even a majority for any of them.

Article III

Section 1 The judicial power of the United States shall be vested in one Supreme Court, and in such inferior courts as the Congress may from time to time ordain and establish. The judges, both of the Supreme and inferior courts, shall hold their offices during good behavior, and shall, at stated times, receive for their services a compensation which shall not be diminished during their continuance in office.

The opening statement of this section is similar to ones in the previous articles for the legislative and executive branches. Judicial power is vested in the courts, meaning that power is separate and distinct and cannot be exercised by other branches. Except for an impeachment trial, Congress has no judicial authority. The Constitution does not mandate the size of the Supreme Court. There is an earlier reference to the Chief Justice of the United States, but that is the only judicial officer specified. Congress has varied the number of justices from five to ten, but since 1869, it has kept the membership at nine. When Franklin D. Roosevelt proposed increasing the Court from nine to 15 members in 1937, public opinion polls reported a widespread belief that his action was "unconstitutional." It was not; no number is mandated in the Constitution.

In 1789 Congress established a lower court system, and

it has regularly increased the number of such courts as federal court business has warranted. Federal judges hold their offices for life, dependent on their "good behavior." They may be removed through the impeachment process. The stipulation regarding compensation prevents legislative or executive reprisals against judges who might deliver unpopular opinions.

Section 2 [1] The judicial power shall extend to all cases, in law and equity, arising under this Constitution, the laws of the United States, and treaties made, or which shall be made, under their authority; to all cases affecting ambassadors, other public ministers, and consuls; to all cases of admiralty and maritime jurisdiction; to controversies to which the United States shall be a party; to controversies between two or more States; between a State and citizens of another State; between citizens of different States; between citizens of the same State claiming lands under grants of different States, and between a State, or the citizens thereof, and foreign states, citizens, or subjects.

This section establishes the scope of judicial power, giving to the federal judiciary the right to rule in cases that involve the Constitution, federal laws, or treaties. In addition, the Constitution sets forth a number of other contingencies for federal judicial authority. This section provides an opening for the exercise of judicial review, that is, the power of the judiciary to declare laws unconstitutional. Contemporary comments at the time of the Constitutional Convention generally acknowledged that interpreting laws was the "proper and peculiar province of the courts," including resolving the superiority of the fundamental law over acts of legislative bodies. Chief Justice John Marshall's decision in *Marbury v. Madison* (1803) reinforced this view and since then, judicial review has been an acknowledged fact of American constitutional practice. Marshall rationalized judicial review as resulting from general principles of constitutional government. He declared that the Constitution was the nation's "fundamental" law and that the judiciary had the particular duty "to say what the law is."

[2] In all cases affecting ambassadors, other public ministers and consuls, and those in which a State shall be party, the Supreme Court shall have original jurisdiction. In all the other cases before mentioned the Supreme Court shall have appellate jurisdiction, both as to law and fact, with such exceptions and under such regulations as the Congress shall make.

The Supreme Court has original jurisdiction—that is, it is the court of first instance—in only a few areas. Its jurisdiction is essentially appellate. But Congress determines that jurisdiction, offering one of the few checks on judicial power. Congress may even revoke jurisdiction previously conferred, as it did shortly after the Civil War, although that action had no real consequence at the time.

[3] The trial of all crimes, except in cases of impeachment, shall be by jury; and such trial shall be held in the State where the said crimes shall have been committed; but when not committed within any State, the trial shall be at such place or places as the Congress may by law have directed.

The Sixth Amendment has a similar provision on jury trials. Such trials may be waived by the accused.

Section 3 [1] Treason against the United States shall consist only in levying war against them, or in adhering to their enemies, giving them aid and comfort. No person shall be convicted of treason unless on the testimony of two witnesses to the same overt act, or on confession in open court.

This is the only crime that is specifically defined in the Constitution and is borrowed literally from the English Treason Act of 1694. The narrow, strict definition of treason serves to restrain public officials from bringing treason charges against political opponents, such as had been the practice of English monarchs. In that sense, the treason clause serves to legitimate political opposition.

[2] The Congress shall have power to declare the punishment of treason, but no attainder of treason shall work corruption of blood or forfeiture except during the life of the person attained.

Quite simply, a conviction of treason shall not bring punishment on the children or heirs of those convicted.

Article IV

Section 1 Full faith and credit shall be given in each State to the public acts, records, and judicial proceedings of every other State. And the Congress may by general laws prescribe the manner in which such acts, records, and proceedings shall be proved, and the effect thereof.

This section is borrowed from the international law concept of comity. The Constitution requires that states honor one another's laws and judicial decrees. Much of the litigation of the full faith and credit clause has involved the validity of divorce decrees in states other than that in which they have been granted.

Section 2 [1] The citizens of each State shall be entitled to all privileges and immunities of citizens in the several States.

The privileges and immunities provision has been interpreted in a variety of ways, but mostly it has been understood as a restraint on state action. States may not discriminate against citizens of other states in favor of their own. But in certain cases, if the so-called discrimination is uniform, states may have different requirements for outsiders. They may, for example, have a reasonable residency requirement for voting or practicing law, and they may require lower fees for college tuition or less expensive licenses for hunting and fishing.

[2] A person charged in any State with treason, felony, or other crime, who shall flee from justice, and be found in another State, shall, on demand of the executive authority of the State from which he fled, be delivered up, to be removed to the State having jurisdiction of the crime.

The requirement of extradition of criminally accused or convicted persons marked another attempt to cement the union of states. But extradition is not mandatory, as governors have some discretionary power to deny another state's request.

[3] No person held to service or labor in one State, under the laws thereof, escaping into another, shall, in consequence of any law or regulation therein, be discharged from such service or labor, but shall be delivered up on claim to the party to whom such service or labor may be due.

This section applied to escaped slaves or indentured servants. Together with the "three-fifths" arrangement in Article I, it represented a crucial element in the sectional compromise that produced the Constitution. Congress enacted a fugitive slave law in 1793, and reinforced it with subsequent laws through the 1850's. Many northern states and officials supported abolitionist efforts to aid fugitive slaves and refused to comply with the various laws providing for recapture, thus sharpening the sectional controversy.

Section 3 [1] New States may be admitted by the Congress into this Union; but no new State shall be formed or erected within the jurisdiction of any other State; nor any State be formed by the junction of two or more States or parts of States, without the consent of the legislatures of the States concerned as well as of the Congress.

This section has been interpreted by the Supreme Court as guaranteeing the admission of new states as equal members of the Union.

[2] The Congress shall have power to dispose of and make all needful rules and regulations respecting the territory or other property belonging to the United States; and nothing in this Constitution shall be so construed as to prejudice any claims of the United States or of any particular State.

The section originally applied to governing territories of the United States. But it also has been used to sustain the inherent power of the nation to acquire new territory, such as was done with the Louisiana Purchase in 1803. As the United States expanded across the continent in the 19th century, Congress regularly provided territorial laws and constitutions prior to the granting of statehood. During the long controversy over slavery, much attention focused on whether Congress could prohibit slavery in the territories. Antislavery forces relied on this paragraph, but supporters of slavery contended that such prohibition interfered with one's property rights, in violation of the Fifth Amendment.

Section 4 The United States shall guarantee to every State in this Union a republican form of government, and shall protect each of them against invasion, and on application of the legislature, or of the executive (when the legislature cannot be convened), against domestic violence.

Protecting the states from domestic violence or the threat of foreign invasion certainly was one of the great objects of the Constitution. The fear of domestic insurrection and the possibility of anarchy generated the drive for a constitutional convention in 1786–87. This section supplements other sections of the Constitution that give the national government authority to defend public order. The phrase, "republican form of government," has had no satisfactory, conclusive definition other than that it repudiates any monarchial or totalitarian form of government.

Article V

The Congress, whenever two-thirds of both Houses shall deem it necessary, shall propose amendments to this Constitution, or, on the application of the legislatures of two-thirds of the several States, shall call a convention for proposing amendments, which in either case shall be valid to all intents and purposes as part of this Constitution, when ratified by the legislatures of three-fourths of the several States, or by conventions in three-fourths thereof, as the one or the other mode of ratification may be proposed by the Congress; provided that no amendment which may be made prior to the year one thousand eight hundred and eight shall in any manner affect the first and fourth clauses in the Ninth Section of the First Article; and that no State, without its consent, shall be deprived of its equal suffrage in the Senate.

The Articles of Confederation required unanimous consent of the states for any amendment. The process is made easier in the Constitution; still, the requirement for a two-thirds vote of both houses, or the application of two-thirds of the states, plus the ratification of three-fourths of the states, usually ensures great difficulty for the passage of an amendment. No constitutional amendment has ever been successfully proposed by the states. The amending process is, like the Electoral College, an important vestige of state power. The three-fourths requirement for ratification does not necessarily reflect majoritarianism, for that number of states may represent less than half the population. Similarly, one-fourth plus one of the states that might block an amendment can represent a population number far less than one-fourth.

Article VI

[1] All debts contracted and engagements entered into, before the adoption of this Constitution, shall be as valid against the United States under this Constitution as under the Confederation.

This section was designed to maintain the continuity of the United States and announced that the government under the new Constitution would honor whatever public debts had been incurred since 1776. In this manner, the framers of the new government hoped to establish public credit, both at home and abroad.

[2] This Constitution, and the laws of the United States which shall be made in pursuance thereof, and all treaties made, or which shall be made, under the authority of the United States, shall be the supreme law of the land; and the judges in every State shall be bound thereby, anything in the Constitution or laws of any State to the contrary notwithstanding.

The "supremacy clause" emphasizes the paramount authority of the Constitution, national laws, and treaties over state laws, and it has been called "the linchpin" of the constitutional system. The clause has been the basis for national preemption of authority over the states in a variety of matters. The provision for judicial enforcement, in part, supported arguments on behalf of the judiciary's special role in interpreting the Constitution.

[3] The Senators and Representatives before mentioned and the members of the several State legislatures, and all executive and judicial officers both of the United States and of the several States, shall be bound by oath or affirmation to support this Constitution; but no religious test shall ever be required as a qualification to any office or public trust under the United States.

Again, the framers sought to bind the nation to the Constitution as fundamental law. Alexander Hamilton wrote in *The Federalist Papers* that all governmental officers were "incorporated into the operations of the national government as far as its just and constitutional authority extends, and will be rendered auxiliary to the enforcement of its laws." Thus state officials are as responsible for maintaining the integrity of national laws as national officials. The proviso that no religious tests could be imposed as a qualification to office-holding underlined the framers' strong sentiments against any kind of religious establishment. In 1962 the Supreme Court struck down a long-standing Maryland law requiring notary publics to declare their belief in God in order to secure a state license.

Article VII

The ratification of the conventions of nine States shall be sufficient for the establishment of this Constitution between the States so ratifying the same.

The stipulation that only nine states needed to ratify the Constitution in order to make it effective again marked a reaction against the requirement for unanimity to amend the Articles of Confederation. Practically speaking, however, the original union needed the participation of key states such as New York and Virginia, which were among the last to ratify. After those states ratified, the Constitution went into effect in 1788, although North Carolina and Rhode Island stayed out of the Union for several more years. The requirement of conventions stemmed from a belief that the Constitution needed the consent of the "sovereign people," thus rationalizing a bypass of the state legislatures.

The Bill of Rights

During the process of ratification from 1787 to 1789, proponents of the new Constitution found it necessary to promise that they would support a Bill of Rights as the first order of business for the new government. Nearly everyone agreed that the national government was restricted to the powers delegated by the Constitution; as such, many supporters of the Constitution believed that a Bill of Rights was superfluous and unnecessary. Still, James Madison, the leading architect of the Constitution, considered it politically expedient to provide such amendments to counter fears of the new government and to discredit a budding movement for a new convention that might impose added restrictions on national powers. Congress submitted 12 amendments to the states in September 1789, and two years later, the requisite number of states ratified 10.

Unquestionably, the Bill of Rights originally applied only against action by the federal government. Madison and others failed in their attempt to ensure similar guarantees against state action. Chief Justice John Marshall confirmed that the amendments referred only to the national government. But since 1925 the Supreme Court has steadily expanded the doctrine that the Fourteenth Amendment "incorporated" the Bill of Rights and has applied the restrictions of the Bill of Rights against the states. In that year, the Court declared: "[W]e may and do assume that freedom of speech and of the press—which are protected by the First Amendment from abridgment by Congress—are among the fundamental personal rights and 'liberties' protected by the due process clause of the Fourteenth Amendment from impairment by the states." That incorporation subsequently extended to the religion guarantees and various rights of the criminally accused.

Amendments to the Constitution

The first 10 amendments, known collectively as the Bill of Rights, were adopted in 1791.

Amendment I

Congress shall make no law respecting an establishment of religion, or prohibiting the free exercise thereof; or abridging the freedom of speech or of the press; or the right of the people peaceably to assemble, and to petition the government for a redress of grievances.

The religion clauses of the First Amendment reflected widespread antagonism toward official support for religion. As colonists, Americans had resented compulsory taxes levied on behalf of the Church of England, despite the fact that the settlers belonged to a variety of sects. Following the Revolution, many states repealed the taxes and incorporated provisions against the establishment of religion in their new state constitutions. In many states, and certainly in the minds of James Madison and other framers of the Constitution, the nonestablishment of religion meant opposition to any nonpreferential aid to religion as well. Constitutional interpretation of the establishment clause has varied. Traditionally, we have accepted tax exemption for religious groups, as well as the maintenance of chaplains for the military and various legislatures. Yet direct aids such as tuition grants for parochial schools or government support for religious activity, including public school prayers, have been held to violate the establishment clause. Since 1971 the Court has tried to invoke a three-pronged test for determining when governmental action does not violate the establishment clause. Such a statute, the Court said, "must have a secular legislative purpose; second, its principal or primary effect must be one that neither advances nor inhibits religion; finally, the statute must not foster 'an excessive government entanglement with religion.'"

The free exercise clause offers a historical lesson on the need for tolerance in a diverse, pluralistic society. Religious expression is protected by the Constitution; as such, a state cannot compel children to attend high school and thereby defy their parents' religious beliefs. But the courts have held that the free exercise clause cannot justify actions that violate "social duties or [are] subversive of good order." Accordingly, the Supreme Court upheld a congressional act prohibiting polygamy in the territories of the United States.

Few constitutional clauses have been subjected to as many doctrinal theories and abstract formulas as the free speech clause of the First Amendment. The best evidence indicates that the framers intended to prohibit any "prior restraints" on political speech. As understood at the time, the common law of "seditious libel" allowed government officials to prosecute political dissenters, yet the government could not formally restrict such activity in advance. After a number of prosecutions under the Sedition Act of 1798, however, prosecutions for seditious libel became discredited, and generally, there was an understanding that political dissent had a legitimate place in the American political order.

The diverse political world of the 20th century, aided by improved communications, often made the First Amendment a key battleground for the assertion of constitutional rights and privileges. The courts have responded with varied doctrines on the permissibility of speech, including "tests" to determine whether particular speeches or writings offer a "clear and present danger," whether they represent a "bad tendency" or a "clear and probable danger," whether there is an absolute prohibition against any governmental restraint upon expression of opinion, or whether the competing demands of individual rights and the security needs of the state must be "balanced" on a case-by-case basis. The net result has been inconsistency, and decisions have been reached depending on the facts of individual cases, the climate of opinion at a given moment, and the different values of the judges.

Speech is understood to be more than verbal and more than political. Courts have protected "symbolic speech," such as the wearing of protest badges or carrying picketing signs. For some judges, however, such activity is "conduct," and not speech, and thus not protected by the First Amendment. In recent years, "commercial speech" has found protection in the First Amendment as courts have ruled that states may not prohibit advertising of prescription drugs or legal services.

The right of assembly and petition clause of this amendment largely has been understood as "cognate to those of free speech and free press and is equally fundamental." Still, there are restrictions. An assemblage can be subject to requirements of a peaceful social order, such as the unimpeded flow of traffic. "The constitutional guarantee of liberty," the Supreme Court held in 1965, "implies the existence of an organized society maintaining public order, without which liberty itself would be lost in the excesses of anarchy."

Amendment II

A well-regulated militia being necessary to the security of a free State, the right of the people to keep and bear arms shall not be infringed.

The historical record is somewhat ambiguous as to whether the framers intended that the "right to bear arms" be considered separate from the concerns for the maintenance of a militia. Many of the political figures of the period regarded a "people's militia" as an alternative to a standing army. In any event, courts have sustained a variety of regulations regarding the registration and concealment of firearms and the prohibition of some weapons.

Amendment III

No soldier shall, in time of peace, be quartered in any house without the consent of the owner, nor in time of war, but in a manner to be prescribed by law.

This amendment reflected colonial and revolutionary era problems, when the British Crown required Americans to quarter troops and pay for the soldiers' maintenance. In some cases, the British insisted on quartering soldiers in private dwellings, thus violating the ancient maxim that a "man's house is his castle." The amendment also demonstrated again the framers' concern for civilian control of the military.

Amendment IV

The right of the people to be secure in their persons, houses, papers, and effects, against unreasonable searches and seizures, shall not be violated, and no warrants shall issue but upon probable cause, supported by oath or affirmation, and particularly describing the place to be searched, and the persons or things to be seized.

This amendment also had its roots in British imperial practices. The Crown often would issue general warrants, or writs of assistance, allowing for indiscriminate searches and seizures as officials sought to suppress smuggling or illegal trade. In the past century, the courts have applied this amendment with the self-incrimination clause of the Fifth Amendment to exclude the unreasonable seizure of evidence from being introduced as evidence against a defendant. But court decisions have varied on the meaning of "unreasonable," and, in fact, courts have ruled that there can be permissible arrest and searches and seizure of evidence without a warrant. Common sense, for example, dictates that airline passengers submit themselves and their baggage to some examination before boarding. Wiretapping and other forms of electronic surveillance have presented modern challenges for the Constitution. President Richard Nixon's attorney general contended that the government had "inherent power" to maintain electronic surveillance of alleged political subversives and need not apply to the courts for a proper warrant. The Supreme Court responded by asserting that neither the Constitution nor any statute justified such an extravagant doctrine. The requirement of a warrant, the Court concluded, "is justified in a free society to protect constitutional values" and would reassure the public "that indiscriminate wiretapping and bugging of law-abiding citizens cannot occur."

All of this changed in 2001 with passage of the Patriot Act only 45 days after the 9/11 attacks. Congress authorized government agencies to search any individual's financial and medical records, Internet searches, and travel patterns without a warrant, nor do they have to show cause.

Amendment V

No person shall be held to answer for a capital, or otherwise infamous crime, unless on a presentment or indictment of a grand jury, except in cases arising in the land or naval forces, or in the militia, when in actual service in time of war or public danger; nor shall any person be subject for the same offense to be twice put in jeopardy of life or limb; nor shall be compelled in any criminal case to be a witness against himself, nor be deprived of life, liberty or property, without due process of law; nor shall private property be taken for public use without just compensation.

The Fifth Amendment is at the heart of procedural guarantees for accused persons. It is a summary of English and colonial legal developments, most notably with the due process of law clause that stems directly from Magna Carta of 1215. The double jeopardy prohibition provides a barrier to the massed resources of the state, which may not, the Supreme Court has ruled, subject a person to "repeated attempts to convict [him], ... thereby subjecting him to embarrassment, expense and ordeal and compelling him to live in a continuing state of anxiety and insecurity, as well as enhancing the possibility that even though innocent he may be found guilty."

The provision against self-incrimination developed as part of the accusatorial rather than inquisitional system of criminal justice. It reflects a reaction against torture or oth-

er inhumane means of gaining information from the accused. In recent years, the Supreme Court has asserted that the provision dictates "a fair state-individual balance by requiring the government to leave the individual alone until good cause is shown for disturbing him and by requiring the government in its contest with the individual to shoulder the entire load." Individuals, however, can be compelled to testify in exchange for immunity from prosecution.

Due process of law originally applied in a general way to procedures, including proper notice and hearing in civil cases, and as a supplement to the specific provisions of the Fourth and Sixth Amendments for criminal cases. But the due process clause also developed a substantive content to serve, the Supreme Court has said, as a "bulwark also against arbitrary legislation." Courts have invoked the due process clause against legislation, which "given even the fairest possible procedure in application to individuals, [might] nevertheless destroy the enjoyment of" life, liberty, or property.

The Fifth Amendment specifically protects an individual's right to hold and enjoy lawful property. The last clause explicitly guarantees that private property cannot be appropriated for public use without fair compensation.

Amendment VI

In all criminal prosecutions, the accused shall enjoy the right to a speedy and public trial, by an impartial jury of the State and district wherein the crime shall have been committed, which district shall have been previously ascertained by law, and to be informed of the nature and cause of the accusation; to be confronted with the witnesses against him; to have compulsory process for obtaining witnesses in his favor, and to have the assistance of counsel for his defense.

The provision for a speedy and public trial represented a reaction to the arbitrary forms of justice practiced in royal prerogative courts in England. A speedy public trial affects both the defendant and the society, giving the former a hearing in reasonable time and also providing the society with a trial before evidence grows cold and witnesses die or disappear. The defendant's right to know the charges, to be confronted with witnesses, and to challenge witnesses and evidence with his own, again formed a reaction against arbitrary justice in England and extended the concepts of due process of law. Prosecutors, for example, cannot offer anonymous reports of undercover agents as evidence of criminal behavior; the witness must be produced for cross-examination. In 2004 the Supreme Court ruled (*Hamdi v. Rumsfeld*) that U.S. citizens detained as "enemy combatants" in the Bush administration's war on terror have the right to a lawyer; to learn of the evidence against them; and to confront their accusers in a court of law.

Amendment VII

In suits at common law, where the value in controversy shall exceed twenty dollars, the right of trial by jury shall be preserved, and no fact tried by a jury shall be otherwise reexamined in any court of the United States, than according to the rules of the common law.

Critics of the Constitution during the ratification process pointed to the omission of a guarantee of a jury trial in civil matters. The amendment also provides some limits to judicial power, for it stipulates that the courts cannot reconsider the facts of a case on appeal.

Amendment VIII

Excessive bail shall not be required, nor excessive fines imposed, nor cruel and unusual punishments inflicted.

The provision against excessive bail again involves the procedural rights of the criminally accused. It has been interpreted as part of the presumption of innocence and as sometimes necessary to enable an accused to prepare an adequate defense. The cruel and unusual punishments clause has served (with other constitutional provisions) to challenge the death penalty. Judicial rulings in this area often have been contradictory, but by the mid-1970's, the Supreme Court had held that the death sentence "for the crime of murder" was not unconstitutional under the Eighth Amendment.

Amendment IX

The enumeration in the Constitution of certain rights shall not be construed to deny or disparage others retained by the people.

This amendment was designed to allay fears that the partial listing of individual rights might be inadequate to protect all the rights of the people. In recent years, some Supreme Court justices have used the amendment to advance a right of individual privacy.

Amendment X

The powers not delegated to the United States by the Constitution, nor prohibited by it to the States, are reserved to the States respectively, or to the people.

The Tenth Amendment was intended to summarize the Bill of Rights as a series of statements restricting Congress to the powers granted to it by the Constitution. But as Chief Justice Marshall noted in 1819, the amendment does not confine Congress to powers "expressly delegated," as it did in the Articles of Confederation. In fact, opponents of the new Constitution lobbied hard to confine the national government to "expressly" enumerated powers. But James Madison insisted that some powers had to be "admitted by implication." That omission served Marshall's doctrine of "broad construction" of the Constitution when he interpreted the meaning of the "necessary and proper" clause (Article I, Section 8, Clause 18).

Many decisions over the last 20 years, however, offer ample testimony to the persistent vitality of federalism and the recognition of state authority, without unduly hindering the need for national action and uniformity.

Later Amendments

Amendment XI [Adopted Jan. 8, 1798]

The judicial power of the United States shall not be construed to extend to any suit in law or equity, commenced or prosecuted against one of the United States by citizens of another State, or by citizens or subjects of any foreign state.

The Supreme Court ruled in 1793 that it had jurisdiction to hear a suit against Georgia by a citizen of another state. That decision provoked violent reaction protests and actions in various states and Congress promptly responded with this amendment. The amendment established sovereign immunity for the states; nevertheless, other rulings have permitted a variety of suits, particularly against state officials. Since 1824, the Supreme Court has held that governmental officers can claim no immunity when acting in alleged violation of a constitutional right.

Amendment XII [Adopted Sept. 25, 1804]

[1] The Electors shall meet in their respective States and vote by ballot for President and Vice-President, one of whom, at least, shall not be an inhabitant of the same State with themselves; they shall name in their ballots the person voted for as President, and in distinct ballots the person voted for as Vice-President, and they shall make distinct lists of all persons voted for as President and of all persons voted for as Vice-President, and of the number of votes for each; which lists they shall sign and certify, and transmit sealed to the seat of the government of the United States, directed to the President of the Senate. The President of the Senate shall, in the presence of the Senate and House of Representatives, open all the certificates and the votes shall then be counted. The person having the greatest number of votes for President shall be the President, if such number be a majority of the whole number of Electors appointed; and if no person have such majority, then from the persons having the highest numbers not exceeding three on the list of those voted for as President, the House of Representatives shall choose immediately, by ballot, the President. But in choosing the President the votes shall be taken by States, the representation from each State having one vote; a quorum for this purpose shall consist of a member or members from two-thirds of the States, and a majority of all the States shall be necessary to a choice. And if the House of Representatives shall not choose a President whenever the right of choice shall devolve upon them, before the fourth day of March next following, then the Vice-President shall act as President, as in the case of the death or other constitutional disability of the President.

[2] The person having the greatest number of votes as Vice-President shall be the Vice-President, if such number be a majority of the whole number of Electors appointed; and if no person have a majority, then from the two highest numbers on the list the Senate shall choose the Vice-President; a quorum for the purpose shall consist of two-thirds of the whole number of Senators, and a majority of the whole number shall be necessary to a choice. But no person constitutionally ineligible to the office of President shall be eligible to that of Vice-President of the United States.

This amendment resulted from the electoral tie between Thomas Jefferson and Aaron Burr in the election of 1800. The electors clearly intended Jefferson to be President, but they inadvertently all cast their ballots for the "ticket," thus creating a tie. The Twelfth Amendment superseded Article II, Section 1, and provides that electors vote separately for president and vice president. If no candidate receives a majority of the electoral vote, the House of Representatives chooses between the three leading candidates (as opposed to five in Article II), but the balloting is by states, with each having only one vote.

Amendment XIII [Adopted Dec. 18, 1865]

Section 1 Neither slavery nor involuntary servitude, except as a punishment for crime whereof the party shall have been duly convicted, shall exist within the United States, or any place subject to their jurisdiction.

Section 2 Congress shall have power to enforce this article by appropriate legislation.

Congress proposed a Thirteenth Amendment to the states early in 1861, providing that no future amendment would authorize the abolition of slavery. Only three states ratified this amendment before the Civil War erupted in April 1861. The amendment eventually adopted in 1865 was a radical act, for it abolished all slavery—which was, of course, private property—without compensation. In subsequent years, the amendment was interpreted to prohibit peonage, which is compulsory service for payment of debts. The second section provided Congress with substantive enforcement powers. Consequently, Congress enacted the Civil Rights Act of 1866 to ensure equality of treatment for newly freed slaves.

Amendment XIV [Adopted July 28, 1868]

Section 1 All persons born or naturalized in the United States, and subject to the jurisdiction thereof, are citizens of the United States and of the State wherein they reside. No State shall make or enforce any law which shall abridge the privileges or immunities of citizens of the United States; nor shall any State deprive any person of life, liberty or property, without due process of law; nor deny to any person within its jurisdiction the equal protection of the laws.

Section 2 Representatives shall be apportioned among the several States according to their respective numbers, counting the whole number of persons in each State, excluding Indians not taxed. But when the right to vote at any election for the choice of Electors for President and Vice-President of the United States, Representatives in

Congress, the executive and judicial officers of a State, or the members of the legislature thereof, is denied to any of the male inhabitants of such State, being twenty-one years of age, and citizens of the United States, or in any way abridged except for participation in rebellion or other crime, the basis of representation therein shall be reduced in the proportion which the number of such male citizens shall bear to the whole number of male citizens twenty-one years of age in such State.

Section 3 No person shall be a Senator or Representative in Congress, or elector of President and Vice-President, or hold any office, civil or military, under the United States or under any State, who, having previously taken an oath as a member of Congress, or as an officer of the United States, or as a member of any State legislature, or as an executive or judicial officer of any State, to support the Constitution of the United States, shall have engaged in insurrection or rebellion against the same, or given aid or comfort to the enemies thereof. But Congress may, by a vote of two-thirds of each House, remove such disability.

Section 4 The validity of the public debt of the United States, authorized by law, including debts incurred for payment of pensions and bounties for services in suppressing insurrection or rebellion, shall not be questioned. But neither the United States nor any State shall assume or pay any debt or obligation incurred in aid of insurrection or rebellion against the United States, or any claim for the loss or emancipation of any slave; but all such debts, obligations, and claims shall be held illegal and void.

Section 5 The Congress shall have power to enforce, by appropriate legislation, the provisions of this article.

The Fourteenth Amendment represents the most substantial and fundamental change in the Constitution since the ratification of the first 10 amendments. A great majority of the nation's constitutional history of the past century can be viewed from the perspective and interpretation of this amendment.

When written, the Fourteenth Amendment was understood to be the centerpiece of efforts to reconstruct the nation following the Civil War. At that time, attention focused on Sections 2, 3, and 4, dealing with postwar loyalty and claims matters. Section 2 repealed the infamous "three-fifths compromise" (Article I, Section 2), but it also provided for the reduction of congressional representation for those states

that racially discriminated against the voting rights of its citizens. This clearly was designed to guarantee suffrage for the freedmen; but Congress never has reduced any state's representation in accordance with this provision.

Section 1 has had enduring relevance and meaning for American constitutional development. The first sentence defined citizenship—one of the notable omissions of the original Constitution—and was designed specifically to settle the status of the newly freed slaves. National citizenship is given primacy, and state citizenship derives from it. The scope is generous. Children born of foreign nationals, even those only temporarily living in the United States, are citizens of the nation. So although the United States denied citizenship to Japanese immigrants in the late 19th and early 20th centuries, their children born here automatically become citizens.

The privileges and immunities and due process clauses are designed to prevent violations of those guarantees, in the same manner as citizens are protected against federal intrusions in these areas. Since 1925, the Supreme Court consistently has ruled that the Fourteenth Amendment incorporates most of the Bill of Rights—for example, free speech, free press, no establishment of religion, and right to counsel—and secures those rights against state action.

The "equal protection of the laws" clause might well be the most vital part of the amendment during the last century. It has been used to strike down discriminatory racial, gender, and age practices and laws, residency requirements, discrepancies in criminal proceedings and sentences, and the apportionment of voting districts.

Amendment XV [Adopted Mar. 30, 1870]

Section 1 The right of citizens of the United States to vote shall not be denied or abridged by the United States or by any State on account of race, color, or previous condition of servitude.

Section 2 The Congress shall have power to enforce this article by appropriate legislation.

The last of the trio of post–Civil War amendments supplemented Section 2 of the Fourteenth Amendment in its attempt to extend suffrage to the freedmen. But in 1876, the Supreme Court ruled that the Fifteenth Amendment did "not confer the right [to vote] . . . upon anyone." Instead, the justices held that the amendment merely prohibited discrimination on the grounds of race. As a result, for nearly 80 years, southern states devised a series of literacy and educational requirements that were stringently applied against blacks as a means of denying them suffrage. Through much of that period, the Court ignored the reality of such practices or only partially prohibited them. Post–World War II demands for the political rights of blacks resulted in several congressional acts to ensure the franchise. The climax came in the Voting Rights Act of 1965, when Congress, under authority of Section 2, granted federal authorities the right to suspend state discriminatory practices and provided federal registrars and poll-watchers to secure suffrage rights. The legislation and the use of the Fifteenth Amendment represented a significant reversal of the traditional constitutional recognition of state supervision of voting rights.

Amendment XVI [Adopted Feb. 25, 1913]

The Congress shall have power to lay and collect taxes on incomes, from whatever source derived, without apportionment among the several States, and without regard to any census or enumeration.

This amendment resulted from the Supreme Court's conflicting views on the constitutionality of an income tax. In 1895, the Court held income taxes unconstitutional as they were direct taxes, and thus violated provisions in Article I stipulating that direct taxes be apportioned among the states according to population. However, the national government's expanded role and responsibilities in the early 20th century required expanded sources of income. The progressive income tax promised to be the most lucrative and equitable and there was widespread support for an amendment.

Amendment XVII [Adopted May 31, 1913]

Section 1 The Senate of the United States shall be composed of two Senators from each State, elected by the people thereof, for six years; and each Senator shall have one vote. The electors in each State shall have the qualifications requisite for electors of the most numerous branch of the State legislatures.

Section 2 When vacancies happen in the representation of any State in the Senate, the executive authority of such State shall issue writs of election to fill such vacancies: Provided that the legislature of any State may empower the executive thereof to make temporary appointments until the people fill the vacancies by election as the legislature may direct.

Section 3 This amendment shall not be so construed as to affect the election or term of any Senator chosen before it becomes valid as part of the Constitution.

This amendment provided for the direct election of senators and superseded the provisions in Article I, Section 3, directing that state legislatures choose senators. The amendment reflected one of the reform drives of the Progressive Movement in the early 20th century.

Amendment XVIII [Adopted Jan. 29, 1919]

Section 1 After one year from the ratification of this article the manufacture, sale, or transportation of intoxicating liquors within, the importation thereof into, or the exportation thereof from the United States and all territory subject to the jurisdiction thereof, for beverage purposes, is hereby prohibited.

Section 2 The Congress and the several States shall have concurrent power to enforce this article by appropriate legislation.

Section 3 This article shall be inoperative unless it shall have been ratified as an amendment to the Constitution by the legislatures of the several States, as provided in the Constitution, within seven years from the date of the submission hereof to the States by the Congress.

The prohibition amendment resulted in a first-time challenge to the constitutionality of a constitutional amendment. One of the nonratifying states contended that the amendment invaded state sovereignty and that it was really a legislative act, not a constitutional amendment relating to the nature of governmental power. The Supreme Court rejected the argument, and in subsequent cases upheld the amendment against challenges that its enforcement violated aspects of other constitutional guarantees, such as those in the Fourth and Fifth Amendments.

The Eighteenth Amendment marked the first time that Congress stipulated that the proposed amendment must be ratified within seven years. Such a provision is discretionary for Congress.

Amendment XIX [Adopted Aug. 26, 1920]

Section 1 The right of citizens of the United States to vote shall not be denied or abridged by the United States or by any State on account of sex.

Section 2 Congress shall have power to enforce this article by appropriate legislation.

The woman's suffrage amendment can be grouped with the three preceding ones as reflecting some of the key reform drives of the Progressive Era. By that time, a number of states, particularly western ones, had granted women the right to vote. The amendment became effective in time for the 1920 presidential election.

Amendment XX [Adopted Feb. 6, 1933]

Section 1 The terms of the President and Vice-President shall end at noon on the 20th day of January, and the terms of Senators and Representatives at noon on the 3d day of January, of the years in which such terms would have ended if this article had not been ratified; and the terms of their successors shall then begin.

Section 2 The Congress shall assemble at least once in every year, and such meeting shall begin at noon on the 3d day of January, unless they shall by law appoint a different day.

Section 3 If, at the time fixed for the beginning of the term of the President, the President-elect shall have died, the Vice-President-elect shall become President. If a President shall not have been chosen before the time fixed for the beginning of his term or if the President-elect shall have failed to qualify, then the Vice-President-elect shall act as President until a President shall have qualified; and the Congress may by law provide for the case wherein neither a President-elect nor a Vice-President-elect shall have qualified, declaring who shall then act as President, or the manner in which one who is to act shall be selected, and such person shall act accordingly until a President or Vice-President shall have qualified.

Section 4 The Congress may by law provide for the case of the death of any of the persons from whom the House of Representatives may choose a President whenever the right of choice shall have devolved upon them, and for the case of death of any of the persons from whom the Senate may choose a Vice-President whenever the right of choice shall have devolved upon them.

Section 5 Sections 1 and 2 shall take effect on the 15th day of October following the ratification of this article.

Section 6 This article shall be inoperative unless it shall have been ratified as an amendment to the Constitution by the legislatures of three-fourths of the several States within seven years from the date of its submission.

This amendment, reflecting improved transportation and communications facilities, reduced the gap between the November elections and the inauguration of the president and the beginning of a new Congress. It thereby eliminated the "lame-duck" session of Congress that regularly occurred between the November elections and the expiration of the old Congress the following March.

Section 3 reinforced Congress's right to determine the presidential succession in the absence of both a president and a vice president. For much of the 19th century, the president pro tempore of the Senate stood next in succession. In the 1880's, Congress determined that the secretary of state would be the successor. But in 1947, Congress again changed the law, providing for the speaker of the House to assume office in such a contingency. The theory was that it would be best to have an elected official, rather than an appointed one, succeed to the presidency.

Amendment XXI [Adopted Dec. 5, 1933]

Section 1 The eighteenth article of amendment to the Constitution of the United States is hereby repealed.

Section 2 The transportation or importation into any State, territory, or possession of the United States for delivery or use therein of intoxicating liquors, in violation of the laws thereof, is hereby prohibited.

Section 3 This article shall be inoperative unless it shall have been ratified as an amendment to the Constitution by conventions in the several States, as provided in the Constitution, within seven years from the date of the submission hereof to the States by the Congress.

The Twenty-First Amendment not only marked the first repeal of a constitutional amendment, but for the first time, Congress required ratification by conventions rather than by state legislatures. The courts have sustained Section 2 by requiring passenger trains to honor state prohibition laws.

Amendment XXII [Adopted Feb. 26, 1951]

Section 1 No person shall be elected to the office of President more than twice, and no person who has held the office of President, or acted as President, for more than two years of a term to which some other person was elected President shall be elected to the office of President more than once. But this Article shall not apply to any person holding the office of President when this Article was proposed by the

Congress, and shall not prevent any person who may be holding the office of President, or acting as President, during the term within which this Article becomes operative from holding the office of President or acting as President during the remainder of such term.

Section 2 This article shall be inoperative unless it shall have been ratified as an amendment to the Constitution by the legislatures of three-fourths of the several States within seven years from the date of its submission to the States by the Congress.

This amendment resulted from a combination of resentment and concern after Franklin D. Roosevelt shattered the two-term tradition and was reelected to third and fourth terms. It did not become effective until Dwight D. Eisenhower's term. There was periodic talk of its repeal then, and again in the 1980's, but such efforts have made little headway. Nevertheless, many commentators view the amendment as in effect creating a "lame duck" and greatly weakened presidency during the second term.

Amendment XXIII [Adopted Apr. 3, 1961]

Section 1 The District constituting the seat of Government of the United States shall appoint in such manner as the Congress may direct:

A number of electors of President and Vice President equal to the whole number of Senators and Representatives in Congress to which the District would be entitled if it were a State, but in no event more than the least populous State; they shall be in addition to those appointed by the States, but they shall be considered, for the purposes of the election of President and Vice-President, to be electors appointed by a State; and they shall meet in the District and perform such duties as provided by the twelfth article of amendment.

Section 2 The Congress shall have power to enforce this article by appropriate legislation.

The amendment grants residents of the District of Columbia the right to vote in presidential elections. Together with the Twenty-Fourth Amendment, it fulfilled the demands of the 1950's and 1960's for making suffrage as democratic and broad as possible.

Amendment XXIV [Adopted Jan. 23, 1964]

Section 1 The right of citizens of the United States to vote in any primary or other election for President or Vice-President, for electors for President or Vice-President, or for Senator or Representative in Congress, shall not be denied or abridged by the United States or any State by reason of failure to pay any poll tax or other tax.

Section 2 The Congress shall have power to enforce this article by appropriate legislation.

Congress in this amendment sought to eliminate another barrier to black voters in southern states. States-rights' arguments had defeated previous legislative attempts to abolish the poll tax dating back to 1939. Two years after the adoption of this amendment, the Supreme Court invoked the equal protection clause of the Fourteenth Amendment to invalidate the requirement of a poll tax in state elections.

Amendment XXV [Adopted Feb. 10, 1967]

Section 1 In case of the removal of the President from office or of his death or resignation, the Vice-President shall become President.

Section 2 Whenever there is a vacancy in the office of the Vice-President, the President shall nominate a Vice-President who shall take office upon confirmation by a majority vote of both Houses of Congress.

Section 3 Whenever the President transmits to the President pro tempore of the Senate and the Speaker of the House of Representatives his written declaration that he is unable to discharge the powers and duties of his office, and until he transmits to them a written declaration to the contrary, such powers and duties shall be discharged by the Vice-President as Acting President.

Section 4 Whenever the Vice-President and a majority of either the principal officers of the executive departments or of such other body as Congress may by law provide, transmit to the President pro tempore of the Senate and the Speaker of the House of Representatives their written declaration that the President is unable to discharge the powers and duties of his office, the Vice-President shall immediately assume the powers and duties of the office as Acting President.

Thereafter, when the President transmits to the

President pro tempore of the Senate and the Speaker of the House of Representatives his written declaration that no inability exists, he shall resume the powers and duties of his office unless the Vice-President and a majority of either the principal officers of the executive department or of such other body as Congress may by law provide, transmit within four days to the President pro tempore of the Senate and the Speaker of the House of Representatives their written declaration that the President is unable to discharge the powers and duties of his office. Thereupon Congress shall decide the issue, assembling within forty-eight hours for that purpose if not in session. If the Congress, within twenty-one days after receipt of the latter written declaration, or, if Congress is not in session, within twenty-one days after Congress is required to assemble, determines by two-thirds vote of both Houses that the President is unable to discharge the powers and duties of his office, the Vice-President shall continue to discharge the same as Acting President; otherwise the President shall resume the powers and duties of his office.

This amendment was designed to deal with the problem of presidential disability and succession. In 1973 criminal charges forced Vice President Spiro Agnew to resign. President Richard Nixon invoked this amendment to nominate Gerald Ford as Agnew's successor, and Congress confirmed his selection. Less than a year later, following Nixon's resignation, Ford followed the amendment to nominate Nelson Rockefeller as vice president.

Before this amendment established a procedure for determining disability, Presidents Eisenhower, Kennedy, and Johnson had informal arrangements with their vice presidents in the event they were incapacitated. When President Ronald Reagan was hospitalized for a few days in 1985, he publicly transferred power to his vice president. The subject of presidential disability, obviously, is a very sensitive one, opening the possibility that a politically protagonistic Congress might deal unfairly with a president only marginally disabled. Presumably, the requirement for a two-thirds vote is designed to safeguard against that contingency. In 1918 President Woodrow Wilson suffered a stroke, and serious questions were raised about his ability to conduct the nation's affairs. This amendment would have provided a procedure for inquiring into the president's effectiveness in such a case.

Amendment XXVI [Adopted June 30, 1971]

Section 1 The right of citizens of the United States, who are eighteen years of age or older, to vote shall not be denied or abridged by the United States or by any State on account of age.

Section 2 The Congress shall have power to enforce this article by appropriate legislation.

In 1970 Congress passed a voting rights act lowering the voting age to 18 in both federal and state elections. But the Supreme Court quickly ruled that Congress lacked legislative authority to determine requirements for state elections. Congress responded with this amendment to eliminate confusion. The unusually quick ratification by the states resulted from pressures generated by the Vietnam War, especially the growing belief that if young people could serve in the military they should be entitled to all the rights and privileges of adults.

Amendment XXVII [Adopted May 18, 1992]

No law, varying the compensation for the services of the Senators and Representatives, shall take effect until an election of Representatives shall have intervened.

First proposed as an amendment in 1789 along with the first ten amendments but ratified by only six states. In 1982 Gregory Watson, a University of Texas student, began a campaign to have it submitted to the states again and it was finally approved in 1992.

ANTHROPOLOGY

Anthropology is the science of humankind, the study of the evolution and biology of humans and the social, cultural, and linguistic characteristics that distinguish different groups of humans. Anthropology uses methods from the sciences, the social sciences, and the humanities. At the broadest level, the field is divided into physical and cultural anthropology with an important subfield in linguistic anthropology.

Branches of Anthropology

Physical anthropology Physical anthropology deals with the animal origins of humans, the evolution and biology of humankind, the classification of physical differences among human groups, and the differences between humans and other primates. This branch of anthropology developed in the first half of the 19th century partly as an attempt to find a physical basis for perceived differences among races, and subsequently was influenced by Darwin's concept of evolution as well as by 19th-century archeological discoveries. As practiced in the modern era it draws upon a wide range of scientific disciplines and techniques such as genetics, chemistry, and electron microscopy.

Cultural anthropology Cultural anthropology is the study of human culture in all its aspects. It uses a wide variety of methods from the social sciences, humanities, linguistics, and archaeology to describe human groups and the details and meaning of their culture and cultural practices. Originally focused on "primitive" societies, cultural anthropology now studies contemporary societies and subgroups as well. Cultural anthropology includes the study of material culture, asking how and under what circumstances textiles and clothing, articles of adornment, tools and weapons, ceremonial articles, and other material goods are made and used, and what they signify. Within this broad field, psychological anthropology examines the mind and subjective existence of individuals in whom a given culture is embodied. This focus on the experience of individuals provides an important complement to the often schematic approach of traditional cultural anthropology. Other subfields of cultural anthropology include medical anthropology, the anthropology of music and dance, and the anthropology of gender.

Linguistic anthropology Linguistic anthropology is an important and influential subfield of anthropology. It deals with the development of and relationships among languages and the relationship of language to culture. Key questions include the ancient roots of languages and their relationship to human migrations, and the extent to which language shapes understanding in cultural groups, for example in distinguishing the characteristics of oral and literate societies. Linguistic anthropology draws upon the fields of descriptive, historical, and comparative linguistics but is not itself generally considered a subfield of linguistics.

Although the two broad subdivisions of anthropology, as well as linguistic anthropology, cover the range of interests of anthropologists, the subject is often divided into many diverse subfields, which include differing institutional arrangements in teaching and research in the United States and abroad. For example, cultural anthropology is sometimes referred to as "sociocultural" or "cultural and social" anthropology, and is sometimes divided into separate disciplines of cultural and social anthropology. Social anthropology as a separate field is associated particularly with the British tradition of anthropology; it focuses on social institutions, structures, and values, such as the structures and role of kinship in society. Some work in cultural anthropology is referred to as ethnology, the study and comparison of human societies.

The branch of physical anthropology dealing with human prehistory from the study of fossil hominid remains is sometimes called paleoanthropology. Moreover, much of anthropology is linked to and draws from archaeology, which uses the recovery and study of material and physical remains to examine past human societies and their environments. Archaeology as a discipline is distinct from anthropology; in the institutional arrangements of modern universities, archaeology sometimes shares a department with anthropology but often is housed in other departments such as classics or art history or, less commonly, forms a separate department in its own right.

History of Anthropology

Anthropology has its roots in the experience of Europeans in the Age of Exploration who, as they navigated the world's oceans and explored overland through interior regions of Eurasia and the Americas, encountered many groups of people whose languages, appearance, dress, customs, and other characteristics were radically different from their own. Anthropology as a distinct discipline began to coalesce in the 19th century, with developments in science, archaeology, history, and linguistics supporting efforts to understand non-European and supposedly "primitive" peoples throughout the world. Although early anthropological work was often independent of or only indirectly linked to the European imperial enterprise, such involvement as early anthropologists had in promoting commerce, religious conversion, and colonialism would cause much soul-searching for later scholars in the discipline.

Anthropology in the 19th Century

The roots of physical anthropology were intertwined with 19th-century beliefs that physical characteristics of individuals were directly predictive of intellectual and personality traits. Such pseudosciences as phrenology (the study of shape and surface features of the skull as indicators of personality; Franz Joseph Gall, German, 1758–1828), craniometry (the analysis of racial "types" and the prediction of intelligence and other traits from skull shape and brain size; Paul Broca, French, 1824–80), and anthropological criminology (the prediction of criminal behavior from facial features; Cesare Lambroso, Italian, 1835–1909) were closely related to the now discredited ideas of eugenics and "scientific racism."

Physical anthropology began to find firmer footing with the discovery of fossil remains of early hominids that provided physical evidence of the complexity of the human family tree. The first recognized and typed Neanderthal (German for "Neander Valley") remains were found near Düsseldorf, Germany, in 1856, the year to which the establishment of the field of paleoanthropology is conventionally dated. Neanderthals were at first thought to be a human ancestor, but are now widely regarded as a subspecies driven to extinction by a combi-

nation of climate change and anatomically modern humans. Scholars began to recognize that the material remains of ancient human ancestors and their societies were found in geological strata that could be dated. Remains of the extinct species *Homo erectus* (extant from about 1.6 million to 250,000 years ago) were found in Java in 1891 ("Java Man") and in China ("Peking Man") in the late 1920's. The discovery, beginning in the late 19th century, of elaborate Paleolithic era (ca. 35,000–20,000 B.C.) cave art at Lascaux and other sites in southwestern France and northern Spain led to the understanding that prehistoric cultures were more ancient and more complex than had previously been believed.

Just three years after the discovery of the first Neanderthals, Charles Darwin's (English, 1809–82) *On the Origin of Species* (1859) described the principles of evolution, and his *Descent of Man* (1871) posited a common ancestor for apes and men. Darwin's work provided a revolutionary impetus for the study of the prehistory of humans, which was recognized as stretching back hundreds of thousands of years. A further important scientific advance that provided significant perspectives for anthropology was the discovery of the basis of genetics by Gregor Mendel (Austrian, 1822–84).

Earlier, in 1786 Sir William Jones (English, 1746–94) had observed that Latin, Greek and Sanskrit and many other Western languages had a common source; later systematic work by Franz Bopp (German, 1791–1867) supported this hypothesis. From this work emerged the understanding that nearly all languages can be classified into language families, an insight that provided anthropologists with an important tool for understanding human migrations and the historical interactions of societies.

One by-product of colonialism was widespread collection of ethnographic information and artifacts (often by amateurs, missionaries, and colonial officials) that served to broaden the field of anthropological analysis. Some of these materials were housed in newly-established museums or museum departments, such as the ethnographic collections of the British Museum (London), the American Museum of Natural History (New York), and the Smithsonian Institution (Washington, D.C.) as well as the Musée de l'Homme ("Museum of Man," Paris) and the Tropenmuseum ("Museum of the Tropics," Amsterdam), providing scholars with a wealth of material for analysis. The professionalization of the field was marked by the founding of the Royal Anthropological Institute of Great Britain and Ireland in 1871; the American Anthropological Association in 1902, and the German Anthropological Association (Deutsche Gesellschaft für Völkerkunde) in the 1920's.

Cultural anthropology also became more respected during the last part of the 19th century, as the social theories of August Comte (1798–1857), Karl Marx, and Emile Durkheim (1858–1917) helped establish the study of western societies in a rational and scientific manner. In addition, James George Frazer's two-volume book, *The Golden Bough* (1890), about religious and mythological beliefs throughout the world, attained great notoriety for its assertion that all religions are rooted in ancient magical practices and rituals. By 1915, Frazer's study had expanded to 12 volumes and had become one of the most influential works, not only in anthropology but in literature and art as well.

Theories of Social Development

During the latter part of the 19th century the prevailing idea in cultural anthropology, particularly in the Anglo-American world, was that, by analogy with Darwin's theory, human societies progressed in stages from the primitive to the highly civilized. The widely shared view that civilization was essentially a Western phenomenon was associated with debates on the concept of diffusionism. Some scholars held that the essential characteristics of civilization had originated in the ancient Near East and spread (or had yet to spread) to other parts of the world; others theorized about a small number of "culture circles" from which advanced traits radiated to peripheral peoples; still others, primarily in the German-speaking countries, emphasized the particular environmental and other conditions in which cultures developed. This view held that societies might change unpredictably, through borrowing and migrations, rather than following a fixed series of changes.

The latter approach was brought to the United States most notably by Franz Boas (American, b. Germany, 1858–1942); who became the first professor of anthropology at Columbia University and inspired a generation of younger scholars. Boas argued strongly against the Eurocentric bias of many anthropologists. His own studies included work among the Inuit and the Native Americans of British Columbia, and the analysis of Native American languages.

Fieldwork and Theories in the 20th century

The first professionally trained anthropologists to undertake fieldwork on their own went into the field early in the 20th century. The results of their efforts provided much of the framework for theoretical developments. The most notable early intensive fieldwork was by Bronislaw Malinowski (English b. Poland, 1884–1942) between 1915 and 1918 in the Trobriand (now Kiriwina) Islands in the South Pacific. This work represented a movement away from simply listing traditions and customs to close observation of individuals and groups in every day life. The fieldwork of Malinowski and other like-minded contemporaries contributed to the further development of anthropological reasoning away from an attempt to find and explain the primitive origins of civilization and toward the concept of assessing the purposes served by elements of culture such as institutions and beliefs. A substantial literature developed in the 1930s and later classifying and assessing social structures, kinship relations, and belief systems. Malinowski, along with Alfred Radcliffe-Brown (English, 1881–1955), is associated with the theory of structural functionalism, which argues that social and cultural traits evolve to promote overall cohesion within a society. That theory was in turn criticized by other anthropologists as excessively reductionist.

Ruth Benedict (American, 1887–1948), a student and later colleague of Boas, did fieldwork among Native Americans and also studied contemporary Asian and European cultures. She focused on national character and the role of culture in the development of individual personalities. Her best-known work is *The Chrysanthemum and the Sword* (1946), a study of Japanese culture undertaken during World War II. Margaret Mead (American, 1901–78), perhaps the best known anthropologist to the general public in the United States, completed her graduate work at Columbia during Boas's tenure. She did extensive fieldwork among Pacific islanders, and became known for books, such as *Coming of Age in Samoa* (1928), that focused on personality, sexuality, child rearing and culture.

Claude Lévi-Strauss (French, b. Belgium, 1908–2009) carried out fieldwork in Brazil, 1935–39, taught in the United States 1942–45, and, returning to Europe, became the most distinguished anthropologist. Lévi-Strauss founded structural anthropology, which considers culture as a system of communication and looks to patterns of ideas and beliefs that lead to practical activity. His major works include *The Elemetary Structure of Kinship* (1949), *The Savage Mind* (1962), and his four-volume

Mythologies (1964–71); the first volume, *The Raw and the Cooked*, would become the most well-known.

Clifford Geertz (American, 1926–2006) was a cultural anthropologist who did fieldwork in Java, Bali, and Morocco. He is perhaps best known for his seminal essay "Deep Play: Notes on the Balinese Cockfight" (1973). He argued for "thick description," the recording of great detail in fieldwork. Exploring the methodologies of anthropology, he argued that cultures should be interpreted in all their detail as texts. His most influential essays are collected in *The Interpretation of Cultures* (1973, 2000). Victor Turner (American, b. Scotland, 1920–83), who spent most of his professional career at the University of Chicago, emphasized the importance of rituals, and especially rites of passage, in human social behavior.

Joseph Campbell (American, 1904–87), though more of a popularizer than an original researcher, did much through his publications and media appearances to acquaint the general public with the anthropological study of mythology and comparative religion, especially in his books *The Hero With a Thousand Faces* (1949) and *The Power of Myth* (1988), which was based on interviews for a television series.

Human Origins in Africa

The fields of paleoanthropology and physical anthropology were greatly advanced by the African work of Louis Leakey (Kenyan, 1903–72) and Mary Leakey (Kenyan, b. England, 1913–96), and their many successors, who showed decisively that human ancestors originated in Africa. Such investigations were facilitated by the scientific research of Willard Libby (American, 1908–80) whose discovery of radiocarbon dating in 1949 provided an important tool for anthropology (and archeology) that permitted the dating of organic remains up to about 60,000 years old. This led to the development of further methods of dating materials of much greater antiquity. Paleoanthropological work in Africa has given rise to the "out of Africa" theory of human origins, which holds that modern humans (Homo sapiens) evolved uniquely in Africa and radiated throughout the world in a series of migrations. Earlier theories, positing an Asian origin or multiple origins, have largely been abandoned, though Milford H. Wolpoff (American, b. 1942) continues to defend his "multiregional hypothesis."

Modern Developments and Controversies

The cultural upheavals that rocked the academic world in the late 1960's and 1970's had a particularly profound impact on anthropology, which was criticized from both within and outside the profession as Eurocentric, racist, sexist, essentialist, colonialist, and more. This was perhaps to be expected in a field in which there is a very wide range of subject matter, professional skills and perspectives, with often limited evidence and a complex history. However, the radicalism and vehemence of the critique plunged the profession into a crisis from which it was slow to recover. Individual scholars came in for heavy criticism, including Carleton Coon (American, 1904–81), perhaps the last major scholar to take race seriously as an anthropological category, and Margaret Mead, whose work in Samoa was attacked as naive, exoticizing, and methodologically flawed. Some critics suggested that societies under study, rather than the anthropologists studying them, had the right to control how they were presented in the professional literature, and certain subjects regarded as derogatory towards non-Western peoples became effectively taboo as research topics. The latter point was dramatically demonstrated in the case of the noted American physical anthropologist Christy G. Turner II, who was strongly criticized for suggesting in his book, *Man Corn* (1998), with Jacqueline A. Turner (1934–96), that the ancient Anasazi of the American Southwest practiced cannibalism in times of famine.

On the other hand, many scholars agree in retrospect that the radical critiques of anthropology had the salutary effect of making scholars aware of ways in which the profession had been appropriative of or condescending toward people studied by anthropologists, and of opening new and unexpected areas of research. Many anthropologists now have turned from the traditional study of isolated non-Western peoples to explore such new fields as corporate culture, ethnic subcultures in urban settings, and sports culture.

In the late 20th and early 21st centuries, anthropology had grown as a field, with important new analytic tools from science and technology. Aerial photography, satellite observations, and other remote sensing techniques have enabled the discovery of valuable sites for archaeological excavation and anthropological study. DNA analyses have improved the ability to evaluate human genetic relationships and migration patterns. Electron microscopy has made possible the detailed study of such things as fossilized pollen and diet-related abrasions on prehistoric teeth. At the same time, there have been many controversies about anthropological studies and issues, both enduring and new.

Issues in Modern Anthropology

How culture structures the worldviews of societies, and how to interpret those worldviews. This issue was at the root of a celebrated, protracted, and unresolved debate between Marshall Sahlins (American, b. 1930) and Gananath Obeyesekere (American, b. Sri Lanka, 1920) about how to interpret the death of Captain Cook at the hands of Hawaiian islanders in 1779. Adopting a postcolonial, culturally relativistic stance, Sahlins argued that Cook's death could only be understood in the context of Hawaiian religious beliefs. Cook was first taken to be a god but was subsequently killed when the ritual context in which he was seen by the Hawaiians changed. Obeyesekere criticized Sahlins for presuming to speak for "natives," and put forward a more universalistic and rationalistic explanation of events. The positions of the two scholars, roughly representing postmodernism and traditionalism, were complex and difficult to disentangle; as one observer noted, the vituperativeness of the dispute "almost engulf[ed] the important intellectual questions" involved. But the issue of the interpretation of cultural worldviews remains the source of much controversy within anthropology.

The grouping and interrelationships of languages. This continues to be a controversial field, with implications for migration patterns, relationships of human groups, and culture. The preeminent figure in this field was Joseph H. Greenberg (American, 1915–2001), an anthropologist and linguist who classified African languages into four broad groups. He also classified Native American languages into three groups: Eskimo-Aleut, Na-Dene, and Amerind. His methods generated controversy because of the need to review large numbers of languages and the possibility of source errors, but he is still regarded as an important pioneer in the field. Greenberg's work has been extended by Luca Cavalli-Sforza (American, b. Italy, 1922), who has pioneered the coordinated use of genetic and linguistic data to track ancient migrations. One of the pioneers of linguistic anthropology was Edward Sapir (American, 1884–1939), founder of the field of structural linguistics and co-formulator of the Sapir-Whorf Hypothesis, which posits that the grammatical structure of the language spoken by any group of people plays a key role in shaping their worldview.

The date and circumstances of the peopling of the Americas. The standard paradigm has been that humans migrated to the Americas via the Bering Strait land bridge about 11,000 years ago, and that the first Paleo-Indians were the Clovis people whose culture was characterized by stone implements specialized for hunting big game. This view has been challenged by evidence for much older human settlements in the Americas, notably Monte Verde, Chile, dating to about 12,500 years ago, as well as (controversial) other sites that may be more ancient still, and the view that there may have been multiple inland and coastal routes for migration of the early peoples.

The role of women in early human societies, including:

The existence or non-existence of an early, matriarchal "goddess culture" in Paleolithic Eurasia, a position strongly argued by Marija Gimbutas (American, b. Lithuania, 1921–1994) but disputed by many other scholars.

The role of mothering and maternal instincts in primate and human societies, a field associated especially with Sarah Blaffer Hrdy (American, b. 1946).

Women's work in paleolithic society, notably the role of textiles and clothing production in early societies, a field pioneered by Elizabeth Wayland Barber (American, b. 1940).

Art, numeracy, paleoastronomy, and the use of symbolic systems in prehistoric societies. Alexander Marshak (American, 1918–2004) and André Leroi-Gourhan (French, 1911–86) were among the pioneers of the study of ancient technology and symbolic systems, a field that continues to grow with the discovery and interpretation of new evidence. Marshak held that lines on ancient bones were markings reflecting astronomical observations. Since the 1980's, for example, great strides have been taken in understanding the written language, art, and other symbolic systems of the Mayan cultures of ancient Mesoamerica.

Gender Studies. The burgeoning of gay, lesbian, and transgender studies in all fields of cultural inquiry has had a strong influence on anthropology, which has seen a flowering of research on sexual identity and sex roles in sociocultural systems.

PHILOSOPHY, RELIGION & MYTHOLOGY

PHILOSOPHY

Philosophy (Greek, "love of wisdom") attempts to understand basic questions of the human condition rationally, without resorting to superstition or myth. Some of those questions are: What is the world? Does God exist? What is truth? What is knowledge? What is the best form of government? What gives life meaning?

These questions have never been settled to widespread satisfaction. As a result, many people have the impression that philosophical inquiry is futile. Yet the study of philosophy has deeply affected most people, even those who are not themselves philosophers. Most branches of knowledge (such as physics, biology, and the social sciences) are highly specialized studies of questions that were originally discussed by philosophers. Today, philosophers continue to debate the basic assumptions that make these specialized studies possible. Philosophy also considers how different branches of knowledge ought to relate to a question, when they seem to overlap and conflict with one another. For example, *bioethics* (a branch of philosophy) asks whether a problem, such as euthanasia, should be a matter of medical science, of individual rights, or of government.

Branches of Philosophy

Philosophical inquiry may be directed at practically any field of study. There is, for example, *political philosophy* (the philosophy of politics) and *natural philosophy* (the philosophy of nature, or science). As a more general field of study, philosophy is traditionally broken down into four major branches:

Metaphysics (Greek, "after physics") seeks to describe the ultimate nature of reality. It asks questions that go beyond physics; it considers the ultimate nature of spiritual or nonphysical entities, such as ideas and emotions. It also debates fundamental questions about existence that are often accepted as self-evident by the hard sciences.

Epistemology, or theory of knowledge, is closely associated with metaphysics, and considers how people come to know what they know. It is the study of the nature, source, and limits of understanding.

Logic is the branch of philosophy devoted to understanding and expressing the rules of reasoning and inference. Logic originated with Aristotle, who introduced the use of variables as a tool for describing logical argument in general terms.

Ethics is the study of principles for proper human behavior. It is primarily concerned with establishing moral guidelines and debating their usefulness.

Aesthetics is sometimes counted as a fifth branch of philosophy. It is concerned with the nature and benefits of art, beauty, and other sensual experiences.

History of Western Philosophy

Pre-Socratic Philosophers of Ancient Greece

Although their surviving written work is fragmentary, ancient Greek thinkers of the seventh to fifth centuries B.C. are usually credited with founding Western philosophy. Most of their work is known to us only through references made by other writers, especially Aristotle.

The pre-Socratics sought explanations over and above those offered by mythology. Most of these philosophers believed they could find rational explanations for the behavior of natural phenomena. The most common object of their inquiries was the nature of matter. These musings were thus the beginning of both *ontology* (the search for a rational explanation of the nature of existence) and science. Some pre-Socratics also made major advances in the early development of mathematics and ethics.

Although the word *pre-Socratic* appears to slight the achievements of Greek philosophers preceding Socrates, it also implies that Socrates' achievements did not arise out of a vacuum. His thinking was heavily influenced by those who came before him.

The Milesian School: The First Greek Philosophers
The work of Thales of Miletus (ca. 625–ca. 545 B.C.), renowned as an astronomer and statesman as well as a

metaphysician, is traditionally regarded as the starting point of Western philosophy. He and his disciples Anaximander (ca. 610–ca. 540 B.C.) and Anaximenes (fl. ca. 545) suggested that everything in the world derives from a single "original principle." Thales argued that the source of all things is water, presumably because it was believed that Earth floated on water. Also, water is known to assume various forms as solid, liquid, and gas.

Although no philosopher after Thales agreed that all things come from water, Thales successfully proposed a problem that intrigued all who came later. Perhaps the world works according to definite rational principles, and perhaps the nature of those principles could be discovered through observation of the natural world.

Anaximander argued that the source of all things could not itself be a material. Instead he proposed that it is something called "the boundless." Anaximenes, by contrast, argued that the source of all things is air, of which all other substances (such as fog, water, earth, metal) are condensed forms.

Pythagoreanism

In Croton (now Crotona), on the Italian peninsula, Pythagoras (ca. 570–ca. 495 B.C.) founded a school of philosophy which survived through the fourth century B.C. It is now impossible to distinguish the achievements of Pythagoras himself from those of the school named after him. The Pythagoreans are credited with discovering the famous geometrical theorem defining the relative lengths of the sides of a right triangle. They also discovered the mathematical basis of musical pitch, which is the foundation of our understanding of harmony. Socrates and Plato were influenced by the Pythagorean belief that mathematics should be a model for true human understanding.

Heraclitus

(late fifth century B.C.) lived in Ephesus, not far from Miletus; he appeared to be interested in taking up the problems proposed by the Milesians. He proposed that the source of all things is fire. This belief was probably metaphorical, because Heraclitus loved paradox: fire needs to consume in order to exist. Heraclitus appeared to believe that existence is by nature paradoxical; the definition of anything seems to depend on its opposite: hot depends on cold, up depends on down, and so on. He is credited with the often-quoted line, "You can never step in the same river twice, for fresh waters are ever flowing in."

The Eleatic School and the Nature of Being

Philosophers of the Eleatic school were the first Westerners to articulate a problem that has occupied philosophers ever since: the notion that there is a marked difference between the "real" world, accessible only through reason, and the mundane world that humans normally perceive and experience, accessible through the senses.

Parmenides (b. ca. 515 B.C.) argued that the concepts of "being" and "not-being" are so exclusive that nothing can be understood about not-being. In other words: nothing can come out of nothing. It then follows that any change is impossible, because change implies that something previously nonexistent has come into being. Motion is also logically impossible, because motion can happen only if change is possible. The real world must be thus one in which change and motion exist only as illusions.

Zeno of Elea (ca. 490–ca. 430 B.C.), Parmenides's most famous pupil, came up with a series of paradoxes that illustrate the theory of an unchanging universe. These paradoxes seek to prove that motion is impossible because time and space can be divided into an infinite series of parts. For example, in order for an arrow to reach its target, it must first cover half the distance to the target, then half of the remaining distance, then half of that distance, and so on. Since time is infinitely divisible, the arrow will always have a little more distance to travel before it reaches its target. Hence, the arrow will never reach its target.

Advances in Natural Philosophy

Despite the largely impractical theories of the Eleatic school, natural philosophers continued to pursue the investigation of matter, basing their theories (at least in part) on observation and experience. Some of the theories developed were remarkably sophisticated and useful.

Empedocles (ca. 495–ca. 435 B.C.) proposed four natural sources of existence (earth, fire, water, and air) which reside in different proportions in all things and are transformed by the forces of harmony and discord. In response to Parmenides's theories, Empedocles also proposed that the four elements exist in constant and unchanging quantities in the universe—an early statement of the conservation of matter, a principle of Newtonian physics.

Anaxagoras (ca. 500–ca. 428 B.C.) further expanded the list of elements, proposing that they are infinite in number. The universe was originally a homogeneous mixture of all the elements, until they were set into motion and order by "mind." This mind is characterized as being capable not only of acting on matter; it could also mix itself into matter, being the distinguishing feature of animate matter, or living organisms.

Leucippus (late fifth century B.C.) posited that the world consists of nothing but empty space containing indivisible atoms. His pupil Democritus (ca. 460–ca. 370 B.C.) developed a more complete system to explain the entire physical universe through atomic structure. Atoms, in his view, have various shapes and sizes accounting for the visual characteristics of, and interactions between, objects, as well as the emotions and ethical character of men.

The Sophists   In the fifth century B.C., Greek learning expanded in almost every direction. It became more and more difficult for learned men to keep up with new developments and to educate the next generation. Also, the ability to influence others through the use of rational argument was increasingly prized, mostly for arguing legal cases, but also for advancing one's political agenda in the more democratic city-states. In this environment, teachers called Sophists began to travel from town to town in the Greek-speaking world. Usually they made their living by charging fees for giving instructional speeches on rhetoric, logic, and ethics.

The teachings of the Sophists varied widely; there was no "school" of sophistry. But in general, Sophists tended to use skilled argument and logic to expound on the political and ethical issues of the day. The Sophists were less concerned with natural philosophy. Some found the more paradoxical teachings of Heraclitus and the Eleatics very useful for confusing opponents in a debate.

Of the Sophists, Protagoras (ca. 490–ca. 420 B.C.) was the most well known. His famous dictum that "Man is the measure of all things" emphasized the relativity of truth. Since each person is a judge of truth, the relative "correctness" of any argument depends entirely on the speaker's ability to persuade. Protagoras professed to be able to teach people, through rhetorical skill, how to transform the weaker argument into the stronger, whether or not the weaker argument is true.

Socrates

It would be difficult to overestimate the influence of Socrates of Athens (469–399 B.C.) on the development of Western philosophy—particularly in the fields of ethics and epistemology. Nearly every major philosopher interested in these fields has addressed the basic questions formulated by Socrates.

Most Athenians of his time regarded Socrates as one of the Sophists, but Socrates was not a traveling lecturer and accepted no fees for instruction. He was preoccupied by philosophical questions that he debated freely and frequently in public gathering places. He also attracted a following of bright young men, which his enemies found threatening. At the age of 70, Socrates was convicted by the Athenian assembly on charges that he was impious, introduced false gods, and corrupted the youth. These crimes brought the penalty of death. Rather than escape and live in exile, as his friends had arranged and urged, Socrates chose to accept the sentence of the assembly and drink poison hemlock about one month after his conviction.

Socrates' philosophical beliefs are known primarily through the dialogues written by his disciple Plato. Although Socrates is featured as a character in most of Plato's dialogues, there is general agreement among philosophers (beginning with Aristotle) that not all of Plato's dialogues reflect the beliefs of Socrates alone. The dialogues, especially those written later in Plato's life, more closely reflect Plato's own philosophy. Perhaps only the early dialogues reflect the thinking of Socrates without much Platonic embellishment.

In the early Platonic dialogues Socrates is usually looking for the definition of a virtue such as "piety" (in the *Euthypro*) or "courage" (in the *Laches*). Professing ignorance of the matter, Socrates asks his querent to supply a definition. Then through a round of questioning Socrates tests the definition, and all participants find it wanting. The querent is then urged to alter the definition, and the new definition is tested. This usually goes on for a couple of rounds until the querent professes to be in a state of *aporia*, or helplessness. None of his definitions avoids self-contradiction. The dialogue ends with no definition holding up under this *Socratic method* of questioning. But the actual exercise of creating and dismissing the definitions may have been in some way enlightening for all participants.

Although the exact nature of Socrates' underlying assumptions is a matter of debate, it is possible to make some general observations about Socratic principles that are not controversial. Socrates loathed the title Sophist, mostly because some of the Sophists, such as Protagoras, were relativists. They felt that truth could be claimed by the argument that swayed the most people. Socrates did not accept the notion that truth can be relative or changeable. Since a mathematician knows with certainty that a good geometric proof admits no contradiction, Socrates believed that important ethical ideas should aspire to a similar standard of certainty.

Additionally, Socrates frequently characterized virtue as a form of knowledge that should be learned. He believed that anyone who goes through a process of self-scrutiny and ultimately discovers the true nature of virtue, *must act virtuously*. In a sense, he believed that bad behavior is a form of ignorance.

Finally, the Socratic method itself appears to arise from an assumption that an individual cannot understand virtue without going through this process of rigorous self-examination. Socrates himself stated before the Athenian assembly, in his self-defense, that life without self-examination "is not worth living."

Plato

Plato's (427–347 B.C.) primary contribution to philosophy is a series of about 24 pieces of writing that have come to be known as Platonic dialogues. These dialogues are neither plays nor philosophical treatises. Instead, they are a peculiar literary form designed to reflect the importance of the Socratic method of teaching: discussing and answering probing questions. As such, these dialogues contain no explicit message; readers are left to form their own opinion based on the arguments presented. Because of this method of presentation, Plato's actual philosophy and its differences from Socratic thought are both subjects of debate among scholars.

The most well-known passage in Plato's written work, and also the most debated, is the "Allegory of the Cave" section of the *Republic*. In the allegory, normal human perception is depicted as analogous to the perception of slaves chained since birth in a position where they are facing the wall of a cave. On the wall, shadow play is enacted by puppets paraded in front of a fire, but the slaves' chains don't permit them to look backward and see the source of the shadow play or the firelight. Supposing one of the slaves were freed from his chains and looked backward, he would come to understand that the shadows have no existence of their own that does not derive from the firelight and the puppets. This freed slave might later even travel out of the cave to witness daylight and look upon the world illuminated by the sun. Yet if he went back into the cave and tried to convince his fellow slaves that they perceived only illusions, they would be angry with him and perhaps kill him for disrupting their

illusion. (This is a clear allusion to the life and death of Socrates.)

The point of the allegory is to describe how reality might be quite different from normal perception. Theories of existence (*ontology*) that argue that reality is different from normal perception are known as *realism*. To this day, the Allegory of the Cave remains the best known justification of a realist ontology.

Several of Plato's dialogues present a theory of *forms*. According to this theory, there are ideal and unchanging versions of the things we know; Plato calls these unchanging ideals "forms." For example, there is a form for "table" that is an ideal table which never changes. More important, there are forms for virtues, such as piety, justice, and courage, all of which add up to the highest form (the sun in the allegory) of "the good." According to Plato, these forms should be the object of a philosopher's study.

Aristotle

Plato's other lasting contribution to the development of philosophy was the founding of the Academy (387 B.C.), a school dedicated to philosophical and political learning. The school lasted nine centuries, until Emperor Justinian closed it and every other remnant of the Greek philosophical schools in A.D. 529. The most famous and influential product of the Academy, Aristotle (384–322 B.C.), set up a rival school, the Lyceum, in 335 B.C.

Aristotle produced a massive body of work on widely divergent topics. His writings shaped philosophical and scientific inquiry for centuries. Unlike Socrates and Plato, who were both focused on finding unifying principles through abstract reason, Aristotle was much more open to contemplating and understanding the complexities of nature as perceived by the senses. Aristotle traveled widely, collecting biological data wherever he went, and he took an interest in the pre-Socratics' work on the nature of matter.

He opposed Plato's theory of forms, suggesting that they are not fixed and absolute. The highest form, or "the good," means different things for different creatures. Virtue and happiness both derive from realizing one's individual nature, and thus for humans, who are highly social and adaptable, this can mean many different things. Some of the most realized humans are those who develop humanity's peculiar gift for thought and contemplation, but it would be ridiculous to expect the same virtue from a turtle. Consequently, Aristotle's ethics stresses discovering *how* to achieve personal happiness, rather than defining *what* correct behavior is for everyone.

Another of Aristotle's contributions to the development of philosophy was his structured analysis of logic. He defined a *syllogism* as a logical argument consisting of a major premise, a minor premise, and a conclusion: all men are mortal; Socrates is a man; therefore, Socrates is mortal.

Perhaps Aristotle's most widely-read work is his esoteric treatise on aesthetics, the *Poetics*. According to his analysis of tragic poetry (a section on comedy was either lost or never completed), the theatrical audience experiences *katharsis* ("purgation") of the heightened emotions of pity and fear as the tragic hero, a basically good but flawed aristocrat, is brought down by his own "error of judgment."

Hellenistic and Roman Philosophy

After Aristotle, philosophy spread out from the domain of cultured aristocrats in Athens and entered the imagination of a wider audience, one that seemed eager for a supplement to pagan religious beliefs in more troubled times. The popular philosophies of the Hellenistic and Roman periods were often less intellectually rigorous than Athenian philosophy, but far more influential on the culture and history of the period. Still, the figure of Socrates remained highly influential, not so much because of his reasoning, but because of his exemplary life.

Skepticism   All Hellenistic philosophies took an interest in epistemology and tended to question the basis of knowledge. The Skeptics were most extreme in this regard, denying even the possibility of knowledge.

Pyrrho of Elis (ca. 360–ca. 275 B.C.) was the most influential of the Skeptics. According to one source he traveled to India with Alexander's army, and there he encountered philosophies that denied the existence of the physical world. Pyrrho believed that existence is impossible to prove, and happiness is possible only through emotional indifference to events in the apparent world. After Pyrrho, Skepticism was widely adopted by the scholars in the Academy of Athens founded earlier by Plato.

Epicureanism   Named for Epicurus of Samos (341–270 B.C.), Epicureanism was essentially agnostic, professing no knowledge of any world outside of the physical one. Given the lack of a divine directive for human behavior, the Epicureans turned to personal pleasure as a source of happiness.

Many have since misinterpreted the Epicurean attitude toward pleasure as a ruling principle. The original Epicureans were not hedonistic. They believed that pleasure consisted in removing pain from life, resulting in tranquility. This would be best achieved by satisfying only a limited number of desires, the ones that would cause pain if not satisfied.

Stoicism   Although Stoicism is often described as inferior to the great philosophies of the Athenian period, Stoic thinkers are the source of many lasting and influential ideas, such as beliefs in the fundamental equality of all persons (universal brotherhood) and the concept of natural rights. The Stoics also admired Socrates because he remained focused on universal, timeless principles despite personal hardship and eventual martyrdom. Similar ideas were later widely accepted by, and considered characteristic of, Christianity.

Zeno of Citium (334–262 B.C.) founded Stoicism, teaching in the porticos (or *stoa*) of Athens. He was influenced by the teachings of Pyrrho, but stopped short of Pyrrho's radically negative theory of knowledge. Zeno's ideas were furthered by many who came later, including Chrysippus (ca. 280–207 B.C.), and the Romans Seneca (3 B.C.–A.D. 65), Epictetus (ca. A.D. 55–ca. 135), and Emperor Marcus Aurelius (A.D. 121–180).

The Stoics believed that people are alone among all beings in that they possess the ability to understand and react to the reason (*logos*) that orders the universe. People cannot control the world, but they can seek to understand and live by the principles that govern the world. Like the Skeptics, the Stoics sought to develop an emotional indifference to their environment, because it signaled an acceptance of the order of things.

Medieval Philosophy

Medieval philosophy covers a vast time period: from the fall of the Roman Empire in the fourth and fifth centuries to the dawn of the Renaissance in the 15th century. During most of that time the climate in Europe was not hospitable to philosophical ideas, mostly due to Christian hostility to pagan beliefs. Major Christian thinkers were often inspired by Greek philosophy, but they were checked by a faith that subordinated reason to divine revelation as a source of knowledge. As time went on, most manuscripts of Greek philosophy were either destroyed or allowed to disintegrate. It was not until the 12th century that scholars regained access to copies of Greek manuscripts preserved in the Islamic world.

The predominant philosophical debate throughout this period was, in fact, related to the predominant debate of the Hellenistic and Roman periods: to what extent should one trust philosophical reason as a source of knowledge? Before the rise of Christianity, this debate was purely epistemological: is knowledge possible? But Christianity supplied a challenge to reason that was quite different from that of Skepticism. Christians professed profound certainty of some forms of knowledge, knowledge based on divine revelation through faith, not based on reason. But from time to time Christian thinkers emerged making various claims about the usefulness of reason along with faith.

Early Medieval Philosophical Theology   Saint Augustine of Hippo (354–430) was perhaps the first significant Christian philosopher. His interest in non-Christian philosophy emboldened other educated Christians to read philosophy as well. His thinking drew heavily from Plotinus (205–71), whose mixture of Platonic, Aristotelian, and Stoic beliefs came to be known as *Neoplatonism*. Plotinus believed that the order (*logos*) of the universe emanated from a single spiritual entity, and Augustine, in his major work, *The City of God*, identified these features with the Christian godhead.

Saint Anselm of Canterbury (1033–1109) promoted reason as an important and valuable counterpart to revelation, a position that helped to pave the way for later Scholasticism. Anselm used Aristotelian logic to produce three proofs of the existence of God. One of those proofs, known as the "ontological argument for the existence of God," was remarkably original. It deduced God's existence from humanity's ability to understand God as a being so great that it is impossible to conceive of one greater. According to the argument, people would not have the capacity to understand this concept if God did not exist.

Scholasticism   In the 12th century, an increase in urban development led to major changes in the centers of learning, which were evolving from religious institutions into universities. The universities of Paris and Oxford were founded in 1150 and 1168 respectively, and their curricula began to place greater emphasis on disciplines that had come down from the Greek philosophers, such as logic, dialectic, and the natural sciences.

Aristotle was the most influential ancient philosopher during the high Middle Ages, thanks to the appearance of new translations of and commentaries on his work from the Arab Islamic world. Chief among the Arab scholars were Ibn Sina, known as Avicenna (980–1037), and later, Ibn Rushd, known as Averroës (1126–98).

Saint Thomas Aquinas (1225–74) was a Dominican monk whose interest in Aristotle caused him to write a complete systematic Christian theology, the *Summa Theologica*, based on Aristotelian principles. He constructed five arguments proving the existence of God, all based on reason. He also argued that, ultimately, both reason and revelation were viable and parallel pathways to knowledge of God. The former is accessible only to a few, but the latter is available to all.

The Divergence of Philosophy and Theology   Late in the medieval period more philosophers at the leading universities began to suggest that reason might be more important than revelation, and that scholarship should pursue reason even if it diverged from accepted theology. A group at the University of Paris known as the Latin Averroists (for their adherence to principles articulated in Averroës's commentaries on Aristotle), led by Siger de Brabant (ca. 1240–84), were among the most vocal proponents of this position. Augustinians and other churchmen cited this development as proof that pagan and Islamic influences were leading to the disintegration of the Christian faith.

William of Ockham (ca. 1285–1347), was a Franciscan monk whose interpretations of Aristotle introduced the possibility of greater conflict between scholars and the church. His logical principle, known as *Ockham's razor*, maintains that when choosing between possible explanations of a phenomenon, the simplest explanation is best. Following his principle (and Aristotle), Ockham dismissed the notion that categories of thought, universals, or ideals were real things. He asserted that they were instead only intellectual constructs. (By contrast, Augustine and Aquinas had seen universals as an important bridge between spiritual reality and reason.) Ockham's position became known as *nominalism*, because he believed these categories of thought were only names (*nomoi*) and had no existence, spiritual or otherwise.

Early Modern Philosophy

Whereas medieval philosophy was overwhelmingly associated with and influenced by the Christian church, philosophical inquiry in the 15th and 16th centuries took quite a different direction, due to social and technological changes. As secular state power displaced the power of the church in Europe, many philosophers focused anew on political and social theory. Rapid advances in technology and geographical exploration went hand in hand with new leaps in natural philosophy; and the invention of the printing press allowed more people to read and participate in the major philosophical debates of the time.

Renaissance Political Theorists

As the power of the Christian church waned, many philosophers turned from theology to the study of social morality and political power. Among the most prominent of political thinkers was Niccolò Machiavelli (1469–1527), whose examinations of political power echoed those of the Sophists. Machiavelli suggested that the power and authority of the state was often more important than individual morality or liberty, and that life could be improved only through the effective application of power. Others, like Thomas Hobbes (1588–1679) saw government and the rule of law as an antidote to the natural state of man, a war of all against all in which life was "nasty, brutish, and short."

Renaissance Humanism

One of the defining movements of the Renaissance, Humanism was not strictly a philosophical school. Rather, it represented a broad worldview that placed humanity and reason at the center of the universe. It gave humans pride of place in the natural world by virtue of their superior faculties of reason. New translations of the complete works of Plato played a role in the new focus on Humanism, as did renewed appreciation for the works of the Stoics and Skeptics. Humanism prompted a resurgence of the dialogue form of philosophical writing, which was a style more in keeping with the broadly artistic and literary nature of the movement.

Early Empiricism

Until at least the early 18th century, philosophy still encompassed the fields of inquiry that would later splinter off into mathematics, physics, and other sciences. The medieval image of a God-driven universe was challenged by new scientific discoveries and philosophical descriptions of a world that obeyed only mechanical and mathematical rules.

This changing view of the world was also reflected in epistemology. Sir Francis Bacon (1561–1626) was one of the first proponents of Empiricism, a philosophic school that stressed sensory experience and rigorous observation as the true path to knowledge. He was extremely skeptical of any claim to knowledge based on any other authority. In his view, only "bodies" (material objects) exist and these must conform only to natural laws, or "forms."

Like Bacon, René Descartes (1596–1650) sought to establish a system of knowledge that rejected the authority of the church and all previous philosophy. But Descartes did not place his greatest trust in information obtained through the senses. In his *Meditations on First Philosophy* (1641) his skepticism extended to refute naive empiricism. He maintained that the senses must be doubted, because when we dream we think we are taking in sensory information, when, in fact, we are not. Also, Descartes invented an additional reason to be skeptical of almost all knowledge. Suppose there is an omnipotent evil demon with the power to deceive people at every turn; how could one know that any information is not being skewed by such a demon?

Descartes's response gave rise to one of the most famous phrases found in the history of philosophy. He reasoned that even in the case of an evil demon's deception, the demon could not have the power to make Descartes doubt his own existence, as long as he remains a thinking being. The thinker knows his thoughts are the thoughts of a being with existence: "I think; therefore I am" (Latin: *cogito ergo sum*). On this foundation Descartes proceeded to build a rational philosophy, i.e. a philosophy based on reason rather than experience.

Despite the apparent primacy of reason in Descartes's thinking, most would agree that the philosophical system he subsequently built contained vestiges of medieval Christian thinking. Most heavily criticized is Descartes's view of humans as exceptional beings, the only ones possessing minds composed of a substance wholly different from matter. This view is commonly characterized as mind-body dualism, and it appears to reflect Christian beliefs more than either reason or science. It fails to explain the mutual dependence of mind and body and their coincidence in space and time.

Baruch Spinoza's (1632–77) earliest writings were expositions of Descartes. Like his mentor's philosophy, Spinoza's thinking was firmly entrenched in the rationalist school. But unlike Descartes, Spinoza was Jewish (and at odds with orthodox Jewish beliefs). Consequently, he was far less influenced by medieval Christian patterns of thinking about God and the world. As a result, Spinoza's highly original philosophy was much more true to the spirit of a hyperrational age.

Spinoza resolved a host of philosophical difficulties by defining God as one and the same as nature and all existing matter. This view is often characterized as *pantheism*, a belief that all things are divine. Accordingly, the question of God's existence is settled, since everything that exists is itself God by definition. Matter may appear in different forms, but the differences are not substantial. Instead, they are characterized as local and finite extensions of God that differ in various "attributes," and God's attributes are infinite. Many of Spinoza's contemporaries were uncomfortable with his theology, and they interpreted his views as atheism in disguise.

Spinoza's philosophy resolves the issue of mind-body dualism by characterizing mind as only the "idea" form of the body. Body and mind are simply parallel extensions of two attributes of God. In essence they are one and the same thing, looked at from two different perspectives.

The Enlightenment

Isaac Newton's (1642–1727) mathematical analysis of the natural world seemed to validate human reason as the key to understanding all existence. Having confirmed the power of empirical research for understanding the world, intellectuals renewed their interest in using empirical methods to understand reason itself—to describe the origin of the force that had laid bare the secrets of nature. The interest in empiricism was strong in Britain, despite the scientific credentials of many rationalist philosophers such as Descartes and Gottfried Wilhelm Leibniz (1646–1716). In the philosophies of Locke, Berkeley, and Hume, British Empiricism would have stood as the quintessential philosophical movement of the Enlightenment—were it not for the monumental achievement of Immanuel Kant, who later attempted to resolve many of the debates between rationalists and empiricists.

The Enlightenment also brought a shift in the major themes of political philosophy, responding to the dawn of new democratic governments. Philosophers moved away from the analysis and defense of state power and focused instead on individual morality and the role of ordinary citizens.

British Empiricism   The school of British Empiricism inquired into the process by which humans came to possess knowledge about the world. John Locke (1632–1704), an acquaintance of both Newton and Robert Boyle, pre-sented his theory of knowledge in *Essay Concerning Human Understanding* (1689). He asserted that there are no innate ideas or knowledge independent of interaction with the world. Knowledge begins when human sense organs are influenced by entities in the world mechanically, producing mental impressions of reality upon which humans reflect. The mind, on which the impressions are imprinted, was characterized by Locke as a blank slate (Latin: *tabula rasa*) at birth.

Locke's *Second Treatise of Government* was a highly influential account of liberal political theory. It detailed both the rights and responsibilities of citizens to their government on the basis of a "social contract," motivated by the desire for civilization rather than the "state of nature." Government by mutual consent is necessary to protect life, liberty, and property, and as long as the government fulfills its side of the agreement, citizens owe their allegiance and obedience in return. Locke's version of the social contract was later contested by Jean-Jacques Rousseau (1712–78), who stated that the common man was attracted to such an agreement only to find himself later in chains. According to Rousseau, the "state of nature" was superior to subjection to modern governments.

Irish philosopher and Anglican bishop George Berkeley (1685–1753) took Locke's theory of knowledge to an interesting metaphysical conclusion. If one accepts the assertion that there are no innate ideas independent of interaction with the senses, then it is also impossible to assert that matter exists. If knowledge of existence depends on perception, and that perception is an idea in the mind, then the only thing that must exist is the idea. Without perception matter does not exist, because we cannot know that it exists.

The third major British Empiricist was the Scotsman David Hume (1711–76), who pushed the empirical theories of Locke and Berkeley to their extreme limits, provoking the interest of both Immanuel Kant and Adam Smith. Hume was ultimately skeptical that any knowledge is possible. Since everything we know depends on the experience of perceptions, we can make only educated deductions about how the world behaves. But these deductions are not knowledge. They do not carry the certainty of an irrefutable proof. For example, we can believe wholeheartedly that the sun will rise tomorrow, but there is no way we can know that it will, just because it has always done so before. Certainty is beyond our grasp.

Kant For many, the work of German thinker Immanuel Kant (1724–1804) is synonymous with Enlightenment philosophy. After reading David Hume, Kant began to work on *Critique of Pure Reason* (1781, revised 1787), the foundation of Kant's theory of knowledge. Kant was troubled by empiricism and extreme skepticism primarily because they fail to explain how the achievements of mathematics are possible. Also, empiricism does not explain why almost all people share the experiences of space and time without significant differences in their understanding of them.

Kant observed that there is a difference between the temporal priority of experience and the logical priority of experience. In other words, Kant agrees that knowledge depends on experience, but he does not believe that this dependence prevents us from understanding certain features of thought that must have preceded experience in order for learning to take place. These features of mind can be deduced *after* knowledge is gained, even though they are not detected by the senses beforehand. They cannot be observed independently of experience, but their existence cannot be denied. Such features are the common human experience of space and time, and the logical truths of mathematics. They are an integral part of the way people think. Their logical necessity is due not to coincidence, but to the way human thought works. Hence they will always behave the same way for everybody. Kant's resolution of the main difficulties between the rationalists and the empiricists is often characterized as *idealism*, because it retains the notion that ideal metaphysical realities, such as time and space, can be known, even in a world where knowledge depends on experience.

Similarly, Kant's moral philosophy sought to resolve the contradiction between free will and determinism. Kant reasoned that the individual will is necessarily determined; that is, it must be subject to some force that gives it direction. People may think that they are free to make individual choices, but that is an illusion, usually at the service of some passion of the senses. It is only when one conditions the will to follow some "ideal," or rationally determined duty, that one can know freedom. The best solution is to search for the best ideal and dedicate yourself to the service of that ideal. Kant's formulation of this ideal, known as the "categorical imperative," states that one's actions should be governed by "maxims," and those maxims should be such that everyone follows them. In other words, rules that would serve everyone are the best rules to govern individual behavior, and training yourself to live by such rules is the key to freedom.

19th-Century Philosophy

The greatest commonality among the various philosophical movements of the 19th century was their operation under the broad shadow of Kant. The first wave of Kantians, known as Idealists, sought to broaden metaphysics beyond Kant's very modest list of structures (such as space, time, and mathematical deductions) that guide human understanding. Growing disillusion with the hopes of the Enlightenment, coupled with the growing extravagance of the claims of the Idealists, prompted a reaction against Idealism, and against philosophy itself, in intellectual circles. By the end of the century, especially in continental Europe, philosophy became a weapon for attacking the notion that people are rational beings. Instead, according to such thinkers as Nietzsche and Freud, people merely use the guise of rationality to achieve irrationally motivated ends.

German Idealism By opening up a new space for philosophy to discuss the metaphysics of mind, Kantianism gave rise to a series of more mystical speculations about the ultimate nature of humankind and anything else that might be universal about the human experience. Georg Wilhelm Hegel (1770–1831) extended this discussion to the point that mind is characterized as a universal and *evolving* entity. Just as Kant deduced the structure of the human mind after the fact of knowledge, Hegel sought to determine the course of universal mind by analyzing the course of history. He concluded that universal mind is on an inexorable course toward self-awareness, although the path from ignorance to pure self-awareness is not marked by a straight line. Instead, the course of history has been a series of social upheavals marked by philosophical confusions that must be resolved before the next historical epoch can begin.

Hegel often coined new phrases in service to his philosophy, prompting a great deal of debate—about both his intended meaning and its value. To this day there is very little agreement among philosophers about either, yet there is no doubt that Hegelian speculation had a strong impact on some of the great minds of the 19th century, including Schopenhauer, Marx, Kierkegaard, Darwin, Nietzsche, and Freud.

Reaction to Idealism: Søren Kierkegaard and Karl Marx Both the Danish philosopher Søren Kierkegaard (1813–55) and Karl Marx (1818–83) attended Friedrich Schelling's (1775–1854) lectures in Berlin propounding his distinctive version of German Idealism. Both reacted against Idealism in highly individual yet influential directions.

Although he was not a pastor, Kierkegaard was a Lutheran theologian. As such, he was mostly interested in the individual's relationship to God, which he viewed as parallel to the Idealists' characterization of the relationship between the individual and the universal. Kierkegaard saw the various claims of the Idealists as extravagant, and he gravitated to a more skeptical view in which universals are beyond the reach of human knowledge. Likewise, he saw God as an entity that humans cannot really know. Rather than languish in despair, however, Kierkegaard saw this gap in human understanding as an opportunity for faith. Kierkegaard maintained that faith is an extremely important concept undervalued in philosophical circles. In fact, it is only through faith that people can meet the various challenges they face in an irrational life filled with uncertainties.

Karl Marx accepted much of Hegel's characterization of history, but Marx sought to change the story from its "fairy tale" version into a real account of actual historical forces struggling to liberate people from the chains of oppression. Marx called his version of Idealism "historical materialism" to highlight the differences. For Marx the key to materialism was understanding the economic forces that determine human interest. The ultimate hope for human liberation depends on the common working people understanding their economic interests and taking control of their destiny through collective action.

Friedrich Nietzsche (1844–1900)
As Kierkegaard had done earlier, intellectuals in continental Europe at the end of the century (such as Sigmund Freud) were taking a greater interest in the exploration of the irrational mind. Building on the thought of Arthur Schopenhauer (1788-1866), Friedrich Nietzsche characterized philosophy as part of a grand deception designed to prevent people from recognizing the truth about human nature.

According to Nietzsche, Western Judeo-Christian values were invented to subvert a prior and more important moral order. In the world of nature, strength wins out and weakness is eliminated. Yet Judaism and Christianity conspire to assure people that weakness has its own strengths and morality is rewarded in a future life that is, in fact, nonexistent. Almost all of philosophy (with the exception of Schopenhauer) has conspired with this inverted value system to justify Judeo-Christian morality.

Metaphysics is merely the creation of a false world that proceeds according to rules people prefer, rather than according to the rule of nature. In response, intellectual thought should be primarily negative and antimetaphysical. Philosophical critique should strip away false metaphysics and expose the real, physical world in all of its naked brutality.

20th-Century Philosophy

Independent Visions of Philosophy   Philosophy in the 20th century was dominated by what is commonly called analytic philosophy (Anglo-American) and continental philosophy (European), but a number of individual voices, not associated strongly with any particular school, also made significant contributions. At the turn of the century, Henri Bergson (1859–1941) developed a philosophy that distinguished between the intellect, which uses reason and analysis to know the world, and intuition, which enables man to identify with entities in the world and which provides a basis for metaphysical knowledge. Bergson shared this metaphysical inclination with Alfred North Whitehead (1861–1947), who promoted a "speculative philosophy" whose primary goal was the definition of universal ideas that would explain the general nature of reality.

John Dewey (1859–1952), the dominant American philosopher of the early 20th century, came from the school of Pragmatism, a descendant of Positivism and other anti-Idealistic schools of thought. Dewey and his followers adopted the position that reality and human responses to it were constantly evolving; in light of that state of change, philosophy's primary task should be to find practical solutions to human problems. Dewey's pursuit of this goal made him an influential figure in the philosophy of education in the 20th century.

Analytic Philosophy   The first major branch of analytic philosophy was *Logical Positivism*, which emerged at the University of Vienna in 1923. This branch was influenced heavily by the work of David Hume and the new logical system of Bertrand Russell (1872–1970) and A. N. Whitehead. The Logical Positivists argued for a strictly scientific approach to philosophy, which was newly redefined by Ludwig Wittgenstein (1889–1951) as "the logical clarification of thoughts," and focused in particular on the structure and use of human language. The Positivists claimed that unverifiable statements were meaningless, and thus practically all metaphysical inquiry had no value due to its purely speculative nature.

Later, however, Logical Positivists such as Wittgenstein and G. E. Moore (1873–1958) contributed to the development of *Linguistic Analysis*, which focused on the language people used in daily existence instead of the rarefied and artificial language of Logical Positivism. Wittgenstein asserted that the ambiguous and highly contextual nature of language is what produces most philosophical problems—thus, the ultimate question of philosophy is to ask why a person uses a particular word or expression in a given situation.

Another important attack on Positivism came in the 1950's from J.L. Austin (1911-1960), who pointed out that certain sentences, such as promises, are unverifiable but still carry meaning. He called such sentences "speech acts" and criticized Positivists for ignoring the truthful aspects of "ordinary" language. W.V. Quine (1908-2000) attacked the "analytic-synthetic" distinction, a concept crucial to Positivism, in his 1951 paper "Two Dogmas of Empiricism."

By the 1960's, Ordinary Language had usurped Positivism as the dominant trend in analytic philosophy. However, Ernest Gellner (1925-1995), with the support of Bertrand Russell and others, accused the new movement of trivializing philosophy. Ordinary Language fell from prominence, but had permanently altered the intellectual landscape. Rather than striving to prove one monolithic idea, analytic philosophy became much more eclectic and branched into numerous sub-disciplines.

Political Philosophy   Positivists had mostly neglected questions of politics and ethics. In 1971, the landmark publication of *A Theory of Justice* by John Rawls (1921–2002) reintroduced formal systems to political thought. Rawls created an idealized political framework with the aim of inspiring and legitimizing modern liberal democracy. He revived Rousseau's social contract theory and Kant's moral imperatives, combining them with his own concepts of fairness, liberty, and provision for the least-advantaged. Rawls made use of a thought experiment called "original position": an idealized state in which individuals must determine the best system of government without having awareness of power inequalities. His work spawned responses and critiques from many different political positions.

Epistemology   For centuries, most philosophers followed Plato's definition of knowledge as "justified true belief," but a single three-page paper published in 1963 by Edmund Gettier (b. 1927) reopened epistemology for

debate. Gettier described situations where a belief could be both justified and true, but could not intuitively be considered knowledge. His "Gettier cases" prompted widespread debate over how to redefine the concept of knowledge.

Metaphysics   In the 1960's, P.F. Strawson (1919–2006) revived metaphysics, then out of fashion in analytic philosophy, as a respectable topic of inquiry. He studied the relationships between words and concepts and created a system to describe Ordinary Language philosophy called *descriptive metaphysics*.

Most of the metaphysics that followed in the analytic tradition were concerned with science, logic, and mathematics. W.V. Quine outlined a metaphysics of science known as *scientific holism*. He claimed that ontological answers could only be sketched from the most current scientific theories and that the limited role of the philosopher is to translate these into logic.

In the 1960's, Saul Kripke (b. 1940) invented a system of logic now called *Kripkean Semantics*. This system introduced logic to *modality*, or qualities of possibility, probability, and necessity. To resolve logical paradoxes, Kripke introduced the notion of *possible worlds*, different from the actual world but still logically valid. In 1986, David Lewis (1941–2001) took this idea further with the concept of *modal realism*, which controversially argues that possible worlds concretely exist in reality. Lewis stressed that possible worlds are logically and philosophically useful and that similar mathematical concepts are assumed to exist without controversy.

Philosophy of Mind   With the end of Positivism, the mind-body problem once again became an issue and proved to be a rich area of philosophical debate. The core conflict was between Dualism, the Cartesian proposal that the mind is somehow of a different substance than the physical world, and Monist Materialism, which argues that both mind and body are physical matter. Debate amongst Monists dominated the 20th century, with most of the argument about how to best show that mental phenomena are explainable by science.

Positivists such as Rudolf Carnap (1891–1970) avoided the problem with *Logical Behaviorism*, which explained mental phenomena only in verifiable terms, such as an organism's observed behavior. This view was challenged in 1949 by the Ordinary Language philosopher Gilbert Ryle (1900–76). Ryle accused Behaviorists of committing a "category error" by conflating the language of mental phenomena with the language of the physical world.

In the wake of Ryle's attack, philosophers tried to clarify the role that science had to play in explaining mental phenomena. *Type Identity Physicalism,* promoted in the 1950's by J.J.C. Smart (b. 1920) and D.M. Armstrong (b. 1926), suggested that the mental states are necessarily identical to physical-chemical brain states, using the analogy that lightning is necessarily the same as an electrical discharge.

Hilary Putnam (b. 1926) criticized Smart and Armstrong with the argument of "multiple realizability." Putnam pointed out that identical mental states could intuitively occur between beings with different physical properties. In the 1960's, Putnam and Jerry Fodor (b. 1935) developed the theory of *Functionalism,* which proposes that something is a mental state by virtue of how it functions within a system. Functionalism was attacked by John Searle (b. 1932) who in 1980 devised a thought experiment called the "Chinese Room," which showed that it is possible for a system to perform all the functions of mental state without intuitively being conscious. Searle's system, *Biological Naturalism,* poses that consciousness is a state of the brain caused by neurobiological processes.

Anomalous Monism, put forth in 1970 by Donald Davidson (1917–2003), is a revision of Type Identity Physicalism. Davidson made use of the "type-token distinction." A "type" is an abstract concept, while a "token" is a specific instance of an abstract concept. For Davidson, token mental events are identical to token physical events. However, mental event types and physical event types are not identical and cannot be connected by strict laws.

David Chalmers (b. 1966) argued in the 1990's that Physicalism and Monism ultimately fail to answer the "hard problem" of consciousness: how and why there are subjective phenomenal experiences, or *qualia.* He revived Cartesian concepts and placed them in a modern context to reach an alternative philosophy: *naturalistic dualism.* Chalmers believes that qualia are independent of physical laws and governed by contingent but as-yet unknown laws of nature.

Daniel Dennett (b. 1942) denied the "hard problem" of consciousness and regarded the concept of *qualia* as incoherent. He proposed the "Multiple Drafts Model" cognitive theory of consciousness. Dennett held that many different processes occur in the brain and that the content regarded as "conscious" is a very small part of a larger system.

Richard Rorty (1931–2007), deeply influenced by Quine and Wittgenstein, resurrected the pragmatism of Dewey and created the philosophy of *neopragmatism.* Rorty critiqued the "foundationalist" attempts of analytic philosophy to represent knowledge and was skeptical of the privileged role of philosophy in general. He also accused continental philosophers like Derrida and Foucault of inadvertently creating a negative and pessimistic version of philosophical order. Rorty envisioned a "post-philosophical" culture, and his later work explored liberal ethics and the role of literature.

Continental Philosophy While the analytic philosophers turned their attention to language as a tool and construct of human reason, philosophers of the continental school retained a more metaphysical orientation. Elucidating on Kant's proposition that only phenomena, not things-in-themselves, are perceivable, Edmund Husserl (1859– 1939) developed the phenomenological method. His method, and the whole school of *Phenomenology,* attempted to describe phenomena through intuition in the immediate moment of experience, divorced from metaphysical and scientific presumptions. Martin Heidegger (1889–1976), who worked with Husserl at Freiburg University, discussed phenomenology as a method of access to being. His early works did much to influence philosophers in not only phenomenology, but many other fields, including existentialism (e.g. Sartre), and postmodernism (e.g. Foucault).

Existentialism, the last major development in 20th-century philosophy, owed a direct debt to Kierkegaard's studies of human anxiety and despair. Karl Jaspers (1883– 1969) rejected the existentialist label but nonetheless worked within its boundaries, exploring the question of individual Being. In his view, one's Being was revealed most clearly in extreme situations or states of mind, such as despair and suffering—occasions when the individual was confronted with the temporal nature of his or her own existence. Jean-Paul Sartre (1905–80), on the other hand, embraced the existentialist label, and his literary and philosophical works are perhaps more closely associated with Existentialism than any other individual. Sartre denied the existence of God, and thus the existence of any essential or preexisting human nature; people, therefore, exist in a state of total freedom and are responsible only to themselves. In most people, said Sartre, recognition of this fact leads not to a feeling of liberation, but rather to a state of overwhelming indecision and anxiety, and subsequently to a perverse immersion in behaviors and institutions that negate that freedom and responsibility.

Structuralism   Along with the enduring influence of Nietzsche, Hegel, and Marx, continental thought can trace its roots to the linguist Ferdinand de Saussure (1857–1913). De Saussure pioneered the field of semiotics with his concept of the *sign*. The sign is the relationship between the "signifier" (a written word or utterance) and the "signified" (a mental concept). Importantly, a sign alone has no inherent meaning; the sign acquires meaning only through contrast with other signs within a wider system. Most linguists abandoned de Saussure's theories in the 1950's after Noam Chomsky (b. 1928) developed his theory of transformational grammar that said humans have an innate ability to learn language. However, the relativistic nature of the sign opened up new areas of inquiry based on language, systems, and symbols,

In the 1940's and 1950's, Claude Lévi-Strauss (1908–2009) applied the theories of de Saussure to the field of anthropology. Lévi-Strauss theorized social systems to explain primitive customs of alliance, marriage, and taboo. His use of semiotics in the social sciences became the foundation for *structuralism*, a mostly French intellectual movement in the 1960's that examined how human behavior and experience is governed by social structures.

The psychoanalyst Jacques Lacan (1901–81) updated Freudian theory under the influence of de Saussure, Hegel, and Heidegger. Lacan created an abstract structure of psychology composed of three orders: the Imaginary, The Symbolic, and the Real. He introduced the concept of the "mirror stage," in which self-awareness emerges once a child's ego discovers itself as an object. Lacan found the source of mental illness in symbolic "castration": when the child first realizes they cannot fulfill the desires of the mother.

Post-Structuralism   Michel Foucault (1926–84) used Nietzsche's technique of *genealogy* to critique the power relations that govern modern society. Foucault's writings on crime, madness, punishment, and sexuality often took the perspective of marginalized groups such as criminals, the mentally ill, and sexual deviants. He critically explored the origins of science, the order of modern life, and the restrictions that society puts on freedom.

Jacques Derrida (1930–2004) is famously credited for the technique of *deconstruction*: a complex interweaving of textual interpretation and philosophical critique. His larger project was to dismantle the legacy of Platonism, representational thinking, and metaphysics, which he saw as violently dominating modern existence. Derrida's method was to reverse value assumptions, reveal and explore paradoxes, and to show the possibilities of variation in art, literature, and philosophy.

The critical approach and complex methods of Foucault and Derrida are sometimes called the beginning of *post-structuralism*, although both philosophers were uncomfortable with the label.

The Frankfurt School   The Frankfurt School was a multi-disciplinary movement that sought to critique modern capitalism using Marxist social theory. It began as a college called the Institute for Social Research in Frankfurt, founded by Felix Weil (1898–1978) and directed by philosopher-sociologist Max Horkheimer (1895–1973). Theodor Adorno (1903–69), a student of Horkheimer, was deeply affected by the Holocaust and lost his faith in the idea of modern progress. Adorno developed a system of negative dialectics, which inverted the ideas of Kant, Hegel, and Heidegger. Adorno found possibilities of salvation from capitalist culture in the idea of the "nonidentical."

Walter Benjamin (1892–1940), a close friend of Adorno, was an art critic, historian, and philosopher whose wide-ranging thought influenced many continental philosophers. He sought to understand the uniqueness of the modern age through the lens of Marx, Hegel, and Nietzsche. Benjamin rejected Romantic art criticism and demanded that art be understood in relation to history. He critiqued traditional historical narrative in his unfinished opus, *The Arcades Project*, a vast and unique study of Parisian landmarks, philosophy, and literary figures. As a philosopher, he envisioned a messianic Marxist future that arrives by recognizing the past in the present moment.

Herbert Marcuse (1898–1979) united the ideas of Marx and Freud in his book *Eros and Civilization* (1955). Marcuse used the Marxist concepts of objectivation and alienation to argue that modern people define themselves through their relationships with commodity objects. In *One Dimensional Man* (1964), he attacked industrial society in both the U.S. and the Soviet Union for fostering consumerism as a means of social control.

Jürgen Habermas (b. 1929) became the second director of the Institute for Social Research in 1964. He led the Frankfurt school away from its strict alliance to Marxism and explored other intellectual possibilities. Habermas created the concept of "communicative rationality," which combines elements of liberal ethics, analytic philosophy, and the linguistic thought of Wittgenstein. Habermas's analysis of late capitalism and defense of modernity influenced many political philosophers.

Glossary of Philosophy Terms

aesthetics the study of beauty, or that which the senses find pleasurable. Also, theories of taste with respect to criticism of the arts.

analytic philosophy the currently dominant form of philosophy in the English-speaking world. Analytic philosophy asserts that analysis is the best method for solving philosophical problems; it assumes that problems in philosophy lie in broad conceptualizing and can be solved by analyzing concepts and identifying their simple constituents. The focus of analytics eventually landed on language, in the hopes of clarifying long-standing semantic confusions. Analytic philosophy is often called linguistic philosophy.

atomism the materialistic theory that asserts that the existence is comprised exclusively of atoms and the space in which they move. Different things and events are explained by the speed of atomic movement at different times and spaces. Initially a Greek proposition, it has found proponents in the modern era amongst scientific hypothesizers.

Cartesianism also known as dualism, it's a philosophy drawn from French philosopher Rene Descartes's (1596–1650) proposed a theory of mind and body. In this theory it is possible to conceive consciousness wholly separate from the physical world; mental phenomena are non-physical. Descartes's famous phrase, "I think, therefore I am," negated the possibility of nothingness; he concluded that as long as man has the capacity to conceive of himself as something, it was impossible for him to be nothing. This made the mental life and one's experience of it (as opposed to bodily functions and physical surroundings) the focus of philosophical argument.

conceptualism proposes that universal concepts exist only in the mind, apart from external reality. Kant argued that such universals concepts are a priori mental functions.

cosmology the quantitative study of the universe. Cosmology deals with the proposed a priori aspects the universe, such as space and time as well as its origin and structure.

critical philosophy a movement that sees the primary task of philosophy to be criticism rather than the justification of knowledge. Also known as Kantian philosophy, characterized by Kant's ideas in the Critical Period of his work. Critical philosophy questions where the boundaries of reason lie and what the possibilities of knowledge might be.

cynicism a view that self-interest is the primary motive of human behavior. The Cynics were ancient Greek philosophers who believed that nothing could be known and rejected the morals of the time. The ultimate goal of their indifference to society was greater personal freedom and self-reliance. The Cynics stood for a lifestyle more than a fully realized philosophy; many of their ideas carried over into Stoicism.

deconstruction a form of textual analysis whose aim is to reveal and prevail over hidden conceptual or theoretical privileges. Deconstruction assumes that concepts used in various texts (philosophical, literary, legal, theological, etc.) suppress a presupposed opposite concept. The concept being directly expressed is seen as dominant and privileged. For every directly expressed concept deconstruction presupposes an opposite concept that is suppressed and consequently marginalized. This presupposed marginalized, suppressed concept brings new meaning to the dominant concept, which deconstructionists posit is meaningless without an equal opposite. In literary theory, deconstruction seeks to disassemble texts in order to explicate hidden agendas that work against and destabilize the meaning of the text.

deduction deductive reasoning is where the conclusion is reached from previously known facts or premises. If a premise is true, it is deduced that the conclusion must also be true.

deontology also known as deontological ethics, the theory of duty or moral obligation. Coined by philosopher Jeremy Bentham (1748–1832), this term refers to his ideas on the "science of morality" and the whole of his larger ethical theories.

dialectic originating in Ancient Greece, dialectic was an exercise much like a lawyer's cross examination of a witness at a trial, where a series of questions are put to a party who must answer "yes" or "no." The purpose of the dialectics is to either affirm or deny the truth of a proposition, and dialectics were a central part of the arguments of Plato and Aristotle. Kant and Hegel later adopted dialectics to their own philosophies.

emotivism a theory stating there are no ethical facts or knowledge; ethical statements are neither true nor false but only express the emotionally charged agendas of the speaker.

empiricism the belief that all knowledge arises through

and is confirmed by personal experience. The difficulty inherent in empiricism is that some knowledge and cognitive processes are hardwired and empiricism struggles theoretically to resolve this fact.

Epicureanism a philosophy founded on the ideas of Epicurus (341–271 B.C.), an ancient Greek hedonist whose ethics were based solely on the pursuit of individual pleasure and personal satisfaction. Epicurus also held atomistic ideas about physics that were subsequently revived in the seventeenth century. Around the same time, Epicurus's moral ideas underwent a revival of their own; Epicurean morality was considered the provenance of free thinkers who wished to find freedom from piety-induced anxieties of the day.

epiphenomenalism a theory asserting that there is a physical basis for every mental event; mental states are side-effects, or epiphenomena, of physical states of the world. In this theory, mental events occur in the brain only and have no bearing on physical events outside the individual. Mental phenomena are seen as derivatives of physical cause and effect with no causal power of their own to impact the physical world.

epistemology a branch of philosophy that inquires into the nature, limits and possibilities of knowledge. Included in its realm of inquiry are perception, memory, proof, and justified belief. Epistemological inquiry began with Plato; different theories of what constitutes knowledge have been proposed over the years, from the factual (i.e., the ability to provide a correct answer on a test) to the epistemological ideas of Bertrand Russell (1872–1970), who differentiated between knowledge of higher truths and knowledge of simple facts.

ethics the study of values and customs; derived from the Greek, "ethos," which means habit or custom. There are many branches of ethics, which can broadly be understood as the study of what is good or bad or right or wrong in conduct, which should be accepted and agreed upon as good and bad conduct by a group. The group could be all of humankind, or a more narrowly defined group such as a professional or political body.

existentialism a philosophical movement that claims human beings have full responsibility for creating the meanings of their own lives. Danish philosopher Søren Kierkegaard first articulated Existentialism, though the movement was named in the mid-twentieth century by Jean-Paul Sarte. Existentialists are individualists and as such their ideas differ greatly from one another, but they are brought together by their attitudes about modern society. Primarily, their concern for the individual within society and his resistance to forces exerted by inherently distrusted groups are what bind them. Kierkegaard, Nietzsche, Sarte, Heidegger, and Camus all wrestled with the ramifications of individualism in modern life such as freedom of choice, will, and personal responsibility.

humanism a Renaissance movement that stressed individual development over the religiosity of the time. This new concept for humanity's potential resulted in advancements in secular studies like languages and literature. A neo-humanist movement followed in 18th century Germany that included the great writers Goethe and Schiller. The thread that runs across humanist thinking is a non-religious worldview that states man has boundless capacity to improve his condition and ultimately determines his own destiny.

idealism expressed originally by Plato in his theory of forms, which stated that ideas alone are the realm of true reality. Idealists view existence as a product of the mind; there is no material world outside the mind, only the mental representation of the world produced by it. In the more popular sense it means a higher or refined form of an idea that guides one's actions and shapes personal belief.

induction inductive reasoning is the forming of a broad conclusion from a certain set of particular cases; the premises are believed to support the conclusion, but do not ensure it. If one were to observe snow falling for the first time and saw that it was white, and then saw white snow fall again, one could induce that the next time snow falls it will be white, and that more generally that all snow is white. This is a plausible conclusion, but since the conclusion (that all snow is white) goes beyond the factual information supplied by the premise (that white snow has fallen on two occasions), the truth of inductive reasoning cannot be assured. This is opposed to deductive reasoning, where the truth of the premise assures that of the conclusion.

inference the drawing of a conclusion from evidence or knowledge.

logic an inquiry that utilizes the principles of proper reasoning. Currently, this is most often applies to deductive reasoning, but logic has had many meanings and applications over the centuries, including epistemology and the scientific methodology. Colloquial usage refers to the process of how one has come to a certain conclusion, a broad usage that is actively avoided by philosophers.

logical positivism (See below, positivism) a twentieth century manifestation of positivism that has focused on empirical evidence and science as they pertained to the rejection of metaphysics. This is in contrast to the larger, earlier positivism movement, which was more politically charged, socially radical, and concerned with the rejection of religiosity and the status quo.

Marxism the central ideas in Marx's philosophy were that labor is an essential activity for man, and that private property represents the product of man's labor in the form of things. During production, labor is alienated from itself through process of making commodities. The end of this alienation requires the abolishment of private property and wage labor. Marx cast history as a drama of class struggle; as new, progressive classes form, they wrestle with the old over means of production. The new ruling classes win power as society progresses and maintain their rule over the lower classes (the proletariat) through property and wages. This concept of history as struggle between classes over the means of production is also called historical materialism.

metaethics the philosophical analysis of morality. Includes the semantic study of moral terminology, logical arguments about the validity of morality, ontological questions about moral facts, and epistemological questions about moral knowledge.

metaphysics the branch of philosophy concerned with explaining the nature of reality, beauty, and the world. The term is derived from Aristotle, whose work was initially edited such that his writings on the "First Philosophy" were presented after his work on physics; or literally, "after physics." Metaphysics inquires into an ultimate reality lying beyond sensory perception. This transcendent realm is beyond the material world and can only be accessed through rational analysis. Concepts in metaphysical inquiry include reality, existence, and substance.

monism any doctrine with a unique, singular subject that has but one fundamental principle or value. In metaphysics, monism states that there is exactly one reality; in the late 19th century it came to mean that there is only one truth. Monism was then also associated with secularist movements that aimed to reform traditional religious philosophy.

naturalism a view in modern metaphysics asserting that all objects and events are a part of nature, space, and time. Rejects superstitions and other systems beyond the purview of science and states that knowledge does not exist a priori but is only a part of empirical science.

Neoplatonism from the third century A.D. forward, there have been periodic revivals of Plato's influence. Generally aimed at reaching an understanding of higher realities and perfect forms, Plato's ideas were subsequently applied to theology, metaphysics, and logic by philosophers in the centuries to come. Each group of later followers of Plato believed they were developing his ideas more fully. Beginning in the eighteenth century and continuing through Hegel, philosophers thought Neoplatonism to be a degraded form of classical Greek thought and distinctions were then drawn between Neoplatonism and Platonism.

objectivism developed by novelist and philosopher Ayn Rand (1905–82), this philosophical system states that truth is independent of the subjective tastes and preferences of a specific place and time. Rand praised rational self-interest and free market capitalism as the highest moral aims of the individual and society.

ontology a more specific branch of metaphysical inquiry that studies being and the nature of reality; ontology attempts to establish what is. In analytical philosophy, ontology is the general theory of what is, including the possibility of abstract, unreal and impossible entities.

phenomenalism an empiricist theory of knowledge first articulated by George Berkeley (1685–1753) and later John Stuart Mill (1806–73), according to which all knowledge of our external world is conveyed to us by experience. According to contemporary phenomenalism, everything we know about the reality can be reduced to statements about sensory input; physical objects do not exist as things in themselves, but only as perceptual phenomena.

physicalism also known as materialism, a view held by some logical positivists that the language of science must relate only to material things. They also asserted that all meaningful language must be rendered in terms of the physical, including that which pertains to mental and cultural phenomena. Physicalists since the 1970's continue to assert that all things existent are solely physical and material but have dropped the necessity for all meaningful language to be reduced as such, conceding that this isn't always possible.

Platonism the idea that there exists such things as abstract objects, called universals. Plato (ca. 428–ca. 348 B.C.) posited the existence of abstract objects and a theory of ideal forms that are separate from what we experience in reality. These forms and abstractions are ultimately real and this idea of ultimate reality has found application over time in Christianity and among other secular thinkers who adopted Plato's ideas.

positivism positivism is a worldview shaped by modern science, which rejects all areas of inquiry outside the bounds of scientific investigation (including superstition, religion, and metaphysics) as ideas that will become increasingly superfluous as scientific inquiry progresses. Positivists define knowledge by empirical experience, sensory input, and the explanation of facts.

pragmatism a philosophy that believes the truth value of a proposition lies in its practicality or advantageousness. The intention of the pragmatists was to formulate a philosophy that produced successful outcomes for the philosopher. Critics claimed the pragmatists confuse the pursuit of truth with the pursuit of their own satisfaction.

rationalism denotes a knowledge theory where knowledge stems from rational processes, as opposed to sensory experiences; contrasted with Empiricism. Since the 19th century, rationalism comprises an emphasis on reason as the highest authority to which man can appeal, as opposed to any divinity or human authority.

realism realists state that the world exists separately from the interior mental life of human beings; things exist apart from what emotions we have towards them, or what we might think about them.

relativism reflects a growing sense of a lack of clarity and objectivity with respect to knowledge, culture, ethics, and truth. Relativism states that what is true or ethical for one social system or conceptual scheme is only necessarily true or ethical with respect to that person or thing's subjective perspective.

scholasticism a medieval term for the academic philosophy emanating from universities, as opposed to the monastic philosophy of the church. More recently, scholasticism has become an expression that refers to unnecessary obfuscation in the realm of philosophy.

skepticism the proposition that knowledge has limits, and that knowledge can be obtained via systematic doubt and testing. Dating back to ancient Greece, skeptics asserted that nothing can be known with certainty; at best there are competing opinions, some more probably correct than others, regarding a particular subject. Over time there have been revivals of skepticism, including doubts about Christian religious dogma and the absolute certainty of Descartes's philosophy. Contemporary usage has come to pertain more to intellectual rejection rather than doubt.

solipsism an ontological and epistemological view that nothing exists or can be known but one's own self and the contents of one's consciousness. Solipsism is similar to egoism, asserting that nothing is valuable but one's own interests and pleasure.

sophistry the art of making a deliberately false argument in the hope of deceiving someone. The Sophists were ancient Greek traveling rhetoric teachers. Plato took umbrage with the fact that they charged students for their services. Also, they taught how to make the weaker argument in a debate appear to be the stronger through persuasion, regardless of whether the position they were arguing was fair or meritorious.

stoicism the belief that self-control and detachment, sometimes interpreted as an indifference to pleasure or pain, enables one to argue in an unbiased fashion. Named for the place where its founder, Zeno of Citium (ca. 335–ca. 263 B.C.), lectured, the stoics distrusted senses and perception and asserted that the only way to truly grasp the external world was through logic. They developed a materialistic physics and an ethics that accorded virtue with logic, advocating the passionless state of mind that the popular contemporary understanding of the word reflects.

subjectivism questions whether knowledge of the external world is possible and posits that man can know nothing but his own mind. Morally, subjectivism conflates pleasure and fear with notions of good and bad; subjective experience is the ultimate measure of things, and things exist only in the individual's awareness of them.

teleology a system of describing things according to their purpose.

Thomism philosophy based on the works of St. Thomas Aquinas (1225–74), especially his very influential *Summa Theologica*. It can be broadly described as Aristotelianism applied to Christian theology.

utilitarianism a moral theory that asserts an action is right if it maximizes pleasure or happiness, or minimizes discomfort or unhappiness more so than any other action outcome. Individual welfare and optimal social outcome has sometimes been substituted for pleasure/discomfort when applying utilitarianism to morality.

RELIGION

Judaism

Judaism is the oldest of the world's three major monotheistic religions and a forerunner of Christianity and Islam. Modern Judaism evolved from the ancient religion of the Hebrews, whose law, culture, and religious practices were influenced in turn by Mesopotamian and Babylonian culture.

Scripture

The Bible The Hebrew Bible consists of 24 books. These include the five books of the Torah, or Law (also known by the Greek *Pentateuch*, five books); the eight books of the Former and Latter Prophets (*Nevi'im*); and the eleven books of Writings (*Ketuvim*) (see Books of the Bible). Composed between the 10th and second centuries B.C. and based in part on oral traditions, the various books of the Hebrew Bible include the creation story, the laws and the history of the Jewish people, prophecies about the fate of God's chosen people depending on their acceptance of God and his law, and stories, poems, and proverbs. (See below for a full description of the Bible.)

The Talmud The Talmud ("learning") is a collection of rabbinical commentaries dating to about A.D. 200, when written scholarship began to replace or supplement oral rabbinical teachings. It consists of two main parts, the *Mishna* ("repeated studies"), a compendium of debates and opinions concerning oral law, and *Gemara* ("completion"), elaborations on the Mishna that often concern the legal basis for Jewish practices in daily life. The subjects considered in the Talmud are arranged under 63 headings in six categories, and include not only commentaries on the law (*Halakha*) but also explanations of Biblical incidents and stories, legends and parables that teach religious lessons, exegetical treatises concerning astronomy, geography, and the calendar, and a wide range of other subjects. The Talmud is second only to the Hebrew Bible as the basis for Jewish law, scholarship, and religious practice

Kabbalah Also of note is a body of Jewish mystical literature known as the *Kabbalah* ("tradition"). The Kabbalah movement arose in 11th-century France; it is, among other things, an esoteric system for understanding the Scriptures, based on the conviction that words, letters, and numbers in the Scriptures contain mysteries interpretable by the adept.

Belief and Practice

God Jews believe in a single, all-powerful God; in the Hebrew Bible he is referred to by the four-letter name YHWH (reconstructed as the modern name *Yahweh*). Because pronouncing this name aloud was considered taboo, in Scripture God is more frequently addressed as *Adonai* ("my great lord") or referred to by generic names for God such as *Elohim*. Central to Jewish belief is the idea that the Hebrew people have a unique and privileged relationship with God, as demonstrated by God's covenant with them, his law, and his direct intervention on numerous occasions in the history of the Jewish people.

Law Judaism is distinctive for its body of law, which offers an extensive system of guidance and regulation of religious practice as well as daily social conduct. Jews believe that although God guides human destiny, the humanity of mankind is defined by the ability of individuals to make ethical choices in keeping with God's law. The failure to act according to God's law is sin, and a basic tenet of Jewish faith is that sin is a willful act; so, too, is turning, or returning, to God. At the core of Jewish law are the Ten Commandments, given directly to Moses by God, and the large body of law contained in the Torah itself; these are supplemented by the teachings of the prophets as well as the centuries of oral law and biblical commentary codified in the Talmud.

Dietary Restrictions Devout Jews observe a detailed set of dietary rules and restrictions. The rules for *kosher* ("ritually correct") food preparation and consumption include prohibitions against eating specific animals (including pork and shellfish); guidelines for the slaughter, butchering, and inspection of meat; and a prohibition against mixing meat and dairy products. Some scholars speculate that thousands of years ago many of these rules may have served a practical hygienic purpose, but their true significance may lie in the obligation of God's chosen people to obey him in all things, however seemingly unimportant. Today the observance of dietary laws varies widely within the Jewish community. The ultra-Orthodox observe the restrictions with meticulous care; many Conservative Jews keep kosher but not always with strict attention to every detail. Reform Judaism regards the dietary laws as being mainly of symbolic significance and many Reform Jews observe the laws only in part or not at all.

Prayer and Worship   Devout Jews generally pray at dawn, noon, and dusk; some also pray at bedtime. Among the more traditional sects of Judaism, individuals (mostly males) also make use of special objects and clothing in prayer. These include *tefillin*, small boxes containing handwritten passages of Scripture, which are strapped to the forehead and the upper left arm; *talit*, or prayer shawls, which cover the head and upper body during prayer to show humility before God; and *kippah* (more commonly known by the Yiddish term *yarmulke*), or skullcaps. The Jewish Sabbath (day of rest) is observed from sunset Friday to sunset Saturday; many religious Jews worship in a synagogue (Greek, "assembly"), where a *rabbi* (teacher or master) leads them in readings from Scripture, prayer, and singing.

Rites of Passage   Jewish males are traditionally circumcised eight days after birth; the ceremony also marks the occasion at which they receive their name. At age 13, their official coming-of-age is marked with a ceremony known as a *bar mitzvah* ("son of the commandment"). Some branches of Judaism hold a similar ceremony for women, called a *bat mitzvah*, celebrated between age 12 and 18.

Schools and Sects

Orthodox Judaism   is the most rigorous, and smallest branch of Judaism, with an estimated 1.8 million adherents worldwide (900,000 to 1 million in Israel, 550–650,000 in the United States). Orthodox Jews may keep entirely separate kitchens for milk and meat, refuse to operate electric and mechanical devices on the Sabbath, and often attend temple services or hold prayer sessions every day. Orthodox services are generally conducted entirely in Hebrew; men and women are required to pray separately, even when not in temple. Many orthodox (or so-called

ultra-orthodox) communities, especially self-contained communities such as those of the Hasidic Jews (located in large numbers in New York and in Israel), impose strict dress codes. Hasidism emerged in late 18th-century Poland and Lithuania. The Hasidim ("the pious") are strict observers of Jewish religious laws. Today there are several sects, all of which stress prayer and direct mystical experience of God.

Reform Judaism   traces its origins to the 18th century; it was strongly influenced by the writings of Moses Mendelssohn (1729–86), who advocated a movement to integrate Judaism with mainstream European culture. Reform Judaism has a liberal interpretation of Jewish doctrine and ritual, and is especially prevalent in the United States. Men and women may worship together, and many worship services are conducted in local vernacular languages. Dietary and other laws (such as wearing tefillin or talit during prayer) are often not observed. Women can become rabbis in Reform Judaism.

Conservative Judaism   combines elements of doctrinal reform with more traditional observance. Conservative Judaism rose in Europe and the United States in the late 19th century in response to the Reform movement, and sought to preserve more of the ancient observances of the old orthodoxy, but without losing touch with modern culture and behavior. Conservative Jews have been slower to question tradition than Reform Jews, but over time have come to accept many of the same changes, including the ordination of female rabbis. About one-third of affiliated Jews in the U.S. belong to Conservative institutions.

History

The Bible recounts the story of the Jewish people from the creation. (There is, however, relatively little archaeological and independent textual evidence corroborating the earliest history of the Jewish people, so that the historical reliability of the biblical account is uncertain.) In the historical narrative, the foundation of Jewish faith began with the exodus from Egypt and the transmission of the Ten Commandments (the Decalogue) from God to his people through Moses, probably sometime between 1450 and 1290 B.C. The people of Israel conquered and settled in Canaan—the promised land—and were governed by a succession of judges. The monarchical period under David and Solomon dates to the 11th and 10th centuries B.C. Then Israel (the Northern Kingdom) and Judah (the

Southern Kingdom) continued under separate rulers until the fall of Israel in 722 B.C. Judah was conquered by Babylonians, and the First Temple of Solomon in Jerusalem destroyed in 586 B.C. The Babylonian captivity marks the start of the Jewish Diaspora, or dispersal. Exile lasted until 538 B.C., and the Second Temple was dedicated in 516 B.C. Under Seleucid rule, the Maccabees successfully resisted efforts to suppress Judaism (168–142 B.C.). Under Roman rule (63 B.C.–A.D. 135), there were several revolts, the first of which resulted in the destruction of the Second Temple (A.D. 70). With the loss of the land and especially the temple, which had formerly been the center of Judaism, the Jewish religion was reconstructed and continued by the rabbinate.

The early Middle Ages saw the flourishing of the Talmudic tradition. Following the rise of Islam, Judaism evolved into two distinct strains, the Sephardim, centered in Spain, and the Ashkenazim, a term that applied to Jews from Northern France through Germany, Poland, and Russia. The long history of persecution of Jews in Europe includes expulsion from France (1306) and Spain (1492) and the pogroms of the 19th century in eastern Europe, culminating in the Nazi regime's attempt to eradicate all Jews during the Holocaust.

Zionism was a European Jewish political movement of the late 19th century, expounded in works such as Theodor Herzl's *The Jewish State*. A response to the Diaspora, the rise of European nationalism, and the growing problem of anti-Semitism, the Zionist search for a Jewish homeland led eventually to the birth of the state of Israel in 1948. Though Israel is a secular republic, religious parties play an active role in politics, and the Orthodox rabbinate has a role in defining civil status, such as marriage.

Holidays

The Jewish calendar is lunar, so the dates of Jewish holidays vary in relation to the standard solar calendar each year. Rosh Hashanah, the Jewish New Year, is celebrated on the first two days of the seventh lunar month. Ten days later is Yom Kippur, the Day of Atonement, which is celebrated with fasting and prayers seeking God's forgiveness. These two holidays are together referred to as the High Holy Days.

The festival of Sukkot, a celebration of the harvest, is celebrated from the 15th through the 22nd days of the seventh lunar month. Hanukkah is celebrated over an eight-day period in the ninth lunar month; it commemorates the rededication of the Second Temple in 165 B.C. Purim, celebrated in the 12th lunar month, just before the beginning of spring, recalls events from the book of Esther (a Persian queen of Jewish origin who saved the Hebrews). Passover (*Pesach*) is celebrated for an entire week in the first lunar month; it commemorates the flight of the Hebrews from Egypt. Central to the Passover celebration is a meal called the *Seder* ("order"), which consists of a number of symbolic foods, and to which many Jews often invite non-Jews.

Geography and Numbers

There are an estimated 14 million Jews in 134 countries, the overwhelming majority of whom live in the United States (6.5 million) and Israel (5.6 million). There are an estimated 1.5 million Jews in Europe.

Christianity

Christianity was founded by followers of Jesus of Nazareth, who was born a Jew in Bethlehem ca. 4 B.C. Details of his life before about A.D. 26–28 are obscure. According to the four Gospels of the New Testament, Jesus was baptized by John the Baptist, who recognized Jesus as the Messiah (Hebrew *Mashiah*, "anointed one"). Jesus' ministry of teaching, healing and miracles, which lasted only a few years, was conducted primarily in Galilee in northwest Palestine. After a fateful journey to Jerusalem, he was tried and executed by the Roman authorities, who together with members of Jewish priestly circles were concerned with the civil and religious consequences of Jesus' preaching of the Kingdom of God. According to Christian belief, Jesus rose from the dead on the third day after his crucifixion, appeared to the disciples at various places, and then ascended bodily to heaven on the fortieth day after his resurrection. Christians believe that Jesus, the Son of God, died on the cross as an offering and sacrifice for the salvation of humankind, and that this sacrifice makes salvation available to all who believe in him.

Scripture

Christian Bibles consist of two parts: the Old Testament and the New Testament. The Protestant Old Testament includes the text of the Hebrew Bible, with some books renamed and in a different order (see Books of the Bible); Roman Catholic and other Christian religions add some additional books from the *Septuagint*, the Greek translation of the Hebrew Bible (third century B.C.). The New Testament of 27 books is accepted by both the Roman Catholic and Protestant churches. (See "The New Testament.")

Belief and Practice

Although Christian churches and sects vary greatly in structure, practice, and certain points of faith, a few core beliefs and rituals are common to most.

The Trinity This fundamental Christian doctrine states that God has three natures, or exists equally in three persons: God the Father, God the Son (Jesus), and God the Holy Spirit. God the Father is the all-powerful creator of the world, who continues to govern his creation and judge mankind. Jesus, also called Christ (Greek for "anointed one"), is God in the flesh; Christians believe his crucifixion removed the stain of Adam's original sin from mankind. The Holy Spirit is generally viewed as a distinct part or aspect of God that provides strength and guidance to followers of Christianity.

Each of these is properly viewed as only one aspect of a singular God. However, this concept is difficult to grasp even for many Christians, among whom it may be accepted as a mystery beyond human understanding; and some adherents of other religions view the doctrine of the Holy Trinity as evidence of polytheism in Christianity. The doctrine of the Trinity poses special difficulties for the rigorously monotheistic adherents of the other two religions of the tradition of Abraham—Judaism and Islam.

The Sacraments Central to the practice of most Christians are seven sacraments: baptism, the washing or immersion of persons in water (often soon after birth) to symbolically cleanse them of sin and welcome them to the Christian church; confirmation, the sacrament by which an adult Christian confirms the sacrament of baptism and enters into full church membership; marriage; ordination, or entry into the clergy; the sacrament of the sick, the anointing and absolution of the sick and dying; the confession of sins; and communion, or the ceremonial sharing of bread and wine in memory of Jesus' Last Supper with his disciples.

The Afterlife Christians believe that each human possesses an eternal soul, which after the death of the body is judged by God and then rewarded (in heaven) or punished (in hell) according to that individual's actions in life. Many Christians (particularly Roman Catholics and some Eastern Orthodox believers, but not most Protestants) also believe in purgatory, an intermediate state in which some less-pure souls are prepared for entry into heaven.

Schools and Sects

Roman Catholic Church The Roman Catholic Church is the largest Christian denomination in the world, claiming more than 17 percent of the total world population. Worldwide, there are more than 1 billion Roman Catholics; in the U.S. there are 63.7 million, or 22 percent of the U.S. population

Early Christians based the organization of their church on the political structure of the Roman Empire and accepted the bishop of Rome (later known as the pope, from the Latin *papa*, "father") as the leader of the worldwide Christian community. Christianity was granted legal toleration within the Roman Empire under the emperor Constantine (ruled 312–27), and was proclaimed the official religion of the empire in 380. The church flourished in the fourth and fifth centuries amid the political decline of Rome, and also found fertile ground in the empire's new eastern capital, Constantinople. After the fall of the Roman Empire the church continued to embody its language, architecture and other cultural features.

The pope continues to lead the Catholic Church from Vatican City in Rome. Bishops (and, at a higher level of organization, archbishops) administer church affairs in a given region; certain bishops are elevated to the College of Cardinals, which advises the pope and comes together after his death to choose a successor. Priests are male and (except in a few splinter organizations within the Catholic Church that have rejected the authority of Rome) must be and remain unmarried. Orders of nuns and monks, most of whom take lifelong vows of charity, chastity, poverty, and obedience, provide educational and charitable services. Local churches operate parochial elementary schools, and regional bodies and religious orders operate high schools and administer seminaries and church-related colleges.

Eastern Catholicism The various churches of Eastern Catholicism hold doctrinal beliefs and liturgical practices that are generally similar to those of the Roman Catholic Church, but they regard themselves as co-equal with what they call the "Roman Rite" church, and do not recognize the primacy of the Roman church and its pope.

In general, Eastern Catholic Churches exist in areas where Eastern Orthodox Churches are dominant; the Eastern Catholic churches in those countries and regions have chosen Roman forms of belief and practice without uniting with the Roman Church.

There are 22 Eastern Catholic Churches, divided into several broad categories, as follows: Byzantine Rite Churches: Albanian, Bulgarian, Belarussian, Croatian, Georgian, Greek, Hungarian, Italo-Albanian, Melkite, Romanian, Russian, Ruthenian, Slovak, and Ukrainian; Armenian Rite Church; Alexandrian Rite Churches: Coptic and Ethiopic; Antiochene Rite Churches: Maronite, Syrian, Syro-Malankar; Chaldean Rite Churches: Chaldean, Syro-Malabar. The Maronite Church (which recognizes the primacy of the Roman pope) is centered in Lebanon, and has played an important political and social role in that country in the 20th century. The Chaldean Rite churches have historical roots in common with the Nestorian Church (see below); there is a large community of Chaldean Catholics (mostly of Iraqi origin) in the United States, particularly in the Detroit area.

With the resurgence of the Orthodox Church in Russia, Ukraine, and other areas following the fall of the Soviet Union, leaders of the Eastern Catholic Churches have complained of interference and repression at the hands of Orthodox authorities.

Roman Rite Churches The term *Roman Rite Church* is used by Eastern Catholic Churches to refer to Rome as one of (in their view) many co-equal Catholic Churches, each with its own rites and traditions. In modern parlance, however, the term is also used to denote former Roman Catholic Churches that have broken with the Vatican but still adhere to Roman Catholic rites and practices. Some of these split with Rome over doctrinal and political issues in the 19th century (for example, the Polish Roman Rite Church, established in Scranton, Pennsylvania, in the 1890's by church leaders of Polish descent). Other Roman Rite churches broke with Rome over objections to the reforms and modernizations decreed by the Vatican II Council (1962–65); these churches tend to adhere to the Latin Mass rather than using vernacular language at worship.

Eastern Orthodox Church In 1054, the bishops of Rome (representing the Western church) and Constantinople (representing the Eastern church) excommunicated each other, creating a major schism that remains to this day. The word *orthodox* means "correct

belief" and is applied to the Eastern church because it has attempted to keep its beliefs and practices unchanged. Monasticism is of great importance in the Orthodox tradition; monasteries serve as focal points of Orthodox spirituality and as centers for the study and preservation of ancient beliefs, rituals, and practices.

Orthodox Churches are organized hierarchically, in a manner similar to the Roman Catholic churches, although the Orthodox community rejects the supreme authority of the Catholic pope and subscribes to a decentralized model of decision making in important church matters; archbishops and bishops possess special spiritual authority and administer church affairs. There are 15 independent churches within the Orthodox community. Four of them —those of Constantinople, Alexandria, Antioch, and Jerusalem—occupy a position of primacy because of their antiquity. They are ruled by patriarchs, of whom the patriarch of Constantinople (known as the Ecumenical Patriarch) is recognized as senior, though without any powers comparable to those of the pope in the Roman Catholic Church. The churches of Bulgaria, Georgia, Romania, Russia, and Serbia are also headed by patriarchs; the heads of the churches in Albania, Cyprus, Greece, Poland, Slovakia, and the U.S. are known as metropolitans.

Orthodox religious observances tend to be solemn and elaborate, and ancient liturgies have been carefully preserved in their original languages such as Greek, Slavonic, Armenian, and Georgian. The display and veneration of religious images known as icons is a distinctive feature of Orthodox Churches. Orthodox clergy are male, and in most churches they are allowed to marry. Because Orthodox churches continue to use the Julian calendar, and also because of differences in the methods for calculating feast days, Christmas, Easter, and other feasts often occur on different dates in the Orthodox Church than in Western churches.

In the U.S., many Orthodox Churches have served as cultural centers for immigrants seeking to preserve their own ethnic heritage. At the same time, however, many denominations are active members of ecumenical groups such as the National Council of Churches. The two largest Orthodox Churches in the U.S. today are Greek and Russian, respectively. The next largest represent Armenians and Syrians.

The Coptic Church The Coptic Church is the indigenous and independent Christian church of Egypt. It broke from the Orthodox Church in A.D. 450 after theological disputes over how to define the human and divine natures in Christ; the Coptic Monophysite position rejects the idea of the duality of Christ's nature. The Coptic Church thereafter was headed by its own leader, known as the pope of Alexandria and patriarch of the See of St. Mark, rivaled by the Orthodox patriarch of Alexandria (who continued to lead those Egyptian Christians who remained within the Orthodox community).

The Coptic Church uses the Coptic language (descended from the ancient language of Pharonic Egypt) in its liturgies, but has tended increasingly to employ vernacular Arabic in other church activities. As in Orthodox Christianity, monasticism plays an important role in church life; monks must be celibate, but married men may be ordained to the clergy (though single clergymen may not marry). Coptic Christians make up 9.4 percent of the population of Egypt, and have suffered persecution in the late 20th century at the hands of Islamic militants. There is also a Coptic community among Egyptian immigrants in the United States.

The Ethiopian Orthodox Church

Despite its name, the Ethiopian Orthodox Church is affiliated, not with the Orthodox community, but with the Coptic Church of Egypt. The ancient Ethiopian kingdom of Aksum converted to Christianity in the fourth century and sided with the Coptic Church at Alexandria in the disputes over Monophysitism in the mid-fifth century. The Ethiopian Church is independent, but is similar in beliefs and practices to the Coptic Church. Its liturgical language is Amharic. About half the population of Ethiopia is Christian, the overwhelming majority of them adherents of the Ethiopian Orthodox Church; church members are also a presence in Ethiopian overseas communities in Europe and the United States.

The Nestorian Church

Nestorianism takes its name from Nestorius (d. A.D. 451), an influential monk and bishop of Constantinople who denied that Mary could be the "mother of God" (as she had become popularly known) because the complete Trinity had always existed. He was condemned as a heretic in 431; some communities of Syrian Christians rejected his condemnation and followed his teachings. The Nestorian Church, which used Syriac as its liturgical language, was the most prominent form of Christianity in Central Asia between the sixth and 14th centuries, with communities as far east as Mongolia and China. However, it lost ground to Islam thereafter and declined to relative insignificance, with remnant communities surviving into modern times in India, Iraq, and the United States. Since the 16th century some Nestorian Churches, such as the one in Malabar in southwest India, have reunited with the Syro-Malabar Eastern Catholic Church.

Protestant Churches Protestant denominations number in the hundreds. There is no single governing authority for all of them, and they vary widely in organization and in forms of worship. Most, however, teach that Christian belief and worship should follow the simple model outlined in the New Testament, without the pageantry and ritual added by later generations. The term *protestant* is now commonly understood as referring to the churches that developed from the objections of Martin Luther and other reformers to Catholic practices; the specific early use of the term (1529) referred to protests against an edict of the Holy Roman Empire prohibiting cities and principalities from choosing their own religion. The belief in Scripture as the sole definitive source of Christian wisdom and guidance (rather than the creeds and doctrines of the Catholic Church) is often referred to as the Protestant Principle. Martin Luther's expansion of the New Testament injunction that "the just shall live by faith" (to which Luther added, "alone") implies the rejection of a separate priesthood in favor of "the priesthood of all believers." Most Protestant denominations also stress the singular importance of Jesus as a connection between man and God, and reject or downplay the veneration of Mary and the saints. Some Protestant denominations are described as evangelical, meaning that they emphasize Scriptural authority, the responsibility of believers for the personal acknowledgment of sin and the experience of salvation, and the obligation of believers to spread the message of Christian salvation to others.

Adventist Churches sprang up in the U.S. in the 1840's, a time of fervent religious revival and widespread prophecies of the end of the world. Adventists anticipate and prepare for the world's end and the second coming of Jesus Christ. The largest Adventist group, the Seventh-day Adventists, is one of the most dynamic religious groups in the world today, claiming a worldwide membership of 12 million. As their name suggests, they worship on Saturday rather than Sunday. They operate parochial schools, colleges, medical schools, and hospitals.

Anabaptist Churches Anabaptist, which means "rebaptizers," refers to a group of radical churches and sects that arose during the Reformation and embraced the doctrine of adult baptism for believers. The first group was the Swiss Brethren (1525); other well-known groups include the Mennonites (followers of Menno Simons, 1496–1561, the Netherlands); the Hutterites (followers of Jacob Hutter, d. 1536, Moravia); and Melchiorites (followers of Melchior Hoffman ca. 1500–ca. 1543, Germany); the Amish originated (late 17th century) as a sect of the Swiss Brethren. Beliefs include the need to separate from civil authority, and pacifism; hence members would not swear oaths and would not bear arms in the service of temporal leaders. These groups were persecuted in Europe by both Protestants and Catholics, and many believers emigrated to North America, especially to Pennsylvania and the Great Plains of the U.S. and Canada; there are also groups in other countries. The groups differ in some matters of doctrine and the extent to which they interact with the larger community. In the United States the Old Order Amish in Pennsylvania, for example, remain deeply committed to traditional ways, including the use of horses and buggies and distinctive plain dress.

Baptist Churches are collectively the largest Protestant denomination in the United States. Baptists trace their theological roots back to radical reformers in Europe in the 1500's, but the number of Baptists in the world was tiny until the 1800's, when Baptist faith and practice became predominant in the American South (both for whites and for African Americans). Baptists are still most heavily represented in the southern and border states.

Local Baptist congregations have great independence, determining many of their own policies. At the same time, these churches share many practices. They agree that the rite of baptism should be administered only to those who have reached an age of independent judgment. Consequently, Baptist children are not included in membership totals until after baptism (which usually occurs no earlier than age six or seven).

Most Baptists take a strong stand on the authority of the Bible, and many (though not all) believe that it should be interpreted literally. Baptists have traditionally been strong supporters of separation of church and state; and Baptist denominations have mounted energetic international missionary campaigns.

The Southern Baptist Convention, a predominantly white church, is the largest Protestant denomination in the United States. Three similarly-named rival organizations, the National Baptist Convention of America, the National Baptist Convention USA, and the Progressive National Baptist Convention, are predominately African-American churches. Together they account for the religious affiliation of more African Americans than any other family of churches.

Christian Churches and Churches of Christ trace their origins to a great religious awakening in 1800 on the Pennsylvania and Kentucky frontiers. Discouraged by sectarian competition among Methodists, Presbyterians, and others, leaders of the revival did not seek to form a denomination but to reestablish a single nondenominational Christian Church. In time they became a denomination themselves. In the 1870's the Churches of Christ and the Christian Church (Disciples) split over questions of using musical instruments in worship and over the issue of centralizing some church functions. The Churches of Christ opposed both instrumental music and national organization. The Disciples allowed instrumental music and established a central missionary board to coordinate mission work; they also have a long history of cooperation and discussion with other denominations. A third group, the Christian Churches and Churches of Christ, split from the Disciples in the 1920's–30's. They allow instrumental music but are theologically more conservative than the Disciples.

Church of Christ, Scientist Christian Scientists, as adherents are often known, follow the teaching of Mary Baker Eddy (1821–1910), who founded the church in 1879 in Boston and wrote *Science and Health with a Key to the Scriptures*, which remains a major source of the church's basic doctrines. Christian Science asserts that sickness and other adversities exist only in the mind and that disciplined spiritual thinking can correct them. Thus, Christian Scientists refuse most or all medical treatment. Christian Science practitioners help adherents deal with illness but do not serve as clergy. The church publishes the influential newspaper *The Christian Science Monitor* (which has been Web-based, rather than printed, since 2009), and operates many reading rooms open to the public. Christian Science has had declining membership since the 1970's.

Episcopal Churches are descendants of the Church of England, which was established as a separate church by King Henry VIII in 1534. Churches descending from the English church make up the worldwide Anglican Communion. The American church takes its name from the Latin *episcopus*, bishop; this suggests its hierarchical organization. In colonial times the Church of England was established in the southern colonies and had some influence in the middle colonies, but was less welcome in New England, where Reformed churches were predominant. During the American Revolution, many Church of England members and clergy remained loyal to England, and thousands migrated to Canada. Those who remained were under suspicion, and some were persecuted. After the Revolution, a small group of Anglicans loyal to the United States gradually revived the church, and it gained considerable influence—in eastern cities, many families of wealth and power were Episcopalian. The Episcopal Church accommodates a wide spectrum of belief and practice. It shares much with Protestant denominations, yet its worship services retain strong elements of pre-Reformation Catholic tradition, especially in the "high church" wing of the denomination.

The Religious Society of Friends was established by the English mystic George Fox (1624–91) in the mid-1600's. Known popularly as Quakers, Friends were persecuted in England for refusing to take oaths or to serve as combatants in war, but under the protection of William Penn (1644–1718), many settled in Pennsylvania. According to Fox, they were called Quakers because they were admonished to "tremble at the word of the Lord." In Pennsylvania the Quakers set themselves apart, dressing plainly and avoiding worldly amusements. In Philadelphia many became influential businesspeople, known for "doing well by doing good."

The most distinctive doctrine of the Friends is that of the Inner Light, the spark of God in each individual. Traditionally the Friends have had no church buildings (services are held in Meeting Houses) and no clergy; leadership is granted to certain individuals by common consent. Worship meetings are characterized by silent meditation, which might be interrupted from time to time by spontaneous statements by any member of the group who feels "moved by the Spirit" to speak. Some Quaker groups in America have moved away from this original austerity, and have adopted clergy, sermons, and singing at worship services. Friends have organized remarkable world relief and peace organizations, by which they are perhaps best known to outsiders.

Holiness Churches grew from a religious revival in the late 1800's, primarily in Methodist congregations. The originators of the movement objected to the excessive bureaucracy of established denominations and sought to refocus attention on the need for deep personal change. They placed great emphasis on the teachings of Methodism's founder, John Wesley, that those who are saved may aspire to the gift of complete sanctification, or holiness. Around 1900, groups of especially intense Holiness worshipers began experiencing further "gifts of the Spirit." From these experiences grew the first Pentecostal Churches with their emphasis on speaking in tongues. Many who began as adherents of Holiness Churches became Pentacostalists, but the Holiness Churches rejected Pentecostal worship as extremist.

Jehovah's Witnesses are an active sect whose members are under a strong obligation to undertake personal missionary activities. Jehovah's Witnesses displaying the magazine *The Watchtower* on street corners, or speading their message through door-to-door encounters, have made the sect a familiar part of American life. They have no clergy (all members are considered ministers and missionaries), and meet not in churches but in plain buildings that always are called Kingdom Hall. They were founded by Charles Taze Russell (1852–1916) in western Pennsylvania in the 1870's. The Witnesses preach a slightly unorthodox form of the Christian message, holding that events of Armageddon and the Second Coming of Christ have already begun, and that the end of the world (which they regard as imminent) will bring one final opportunity for believers to be saved. They refuse blood transfusions and some other forms of medicine on biblical grounds, and, considering human government to be illegitimate, refuse to perform military service, pledge alliegance to the flag, or take oaths; these positions have often resulted in the sect's persecution. They claim more than 6 million members worldwide, of whom about a quarter live in the U.S.

Lutheran Churches trace their churches back to the German reformer Martin Luther (1483–1546), who sought to reform the doctrine and practice of the Roman Christian Church in Europe. In a set of 95 theses that he nailed to the door of the church at Wittenberg in 1517, he detailed his complaints against the Roman Church and his proposals for addressing them. He stressed a Scripture-based faith and a redemptive Christ; he complained about corruption among the clergy and advocated worship in the language of the people rather than in Latin. He also came to favor a married, rather than a celibate, clergy. The Church of Rome considered Luther disloyal and eventually drove him out; he then helped establish independent churches in northern Germany.

Immigrants from Germany and Scandinavia brought the Lutheran faith to North America, concentrating first in Pennsylvania. Later immigrants settled in the upper Midwest. Most Lutheran churches retain the altar and vest-ments of the Roman Church, and emphasize preaching and congregational participation in worship services.

Methodist Churches trace their origins to John Wesley (1703–91), a minister in the Church of England who sought to bring a new sense of warmth and commitment to individuals' religious life. He urged his followers to set aside regular times to study the Bible and pray together, earning his followers the then-pejorative title "Methodists" because of their discipline and seriousness. Wesley himself remained in the Church of England his whole life, but his followers began to develop independent organizations both in England and the United States. On the American frontier, Methodist "circuit riders" traveled from settlement to settlement, ministering to pioneer families. By 1820 Methodism was the largest religious denomination in the United States, and it remained the largest Protestant church until the 1920's.

The United Methodist Church accounts for nearly two-thirds of the Methodists in America. This denomination is made up of not only traditional Methodists but also several churches of German origin whose beliefs and spirit accorded well with Methodism. The two "African" churches (the African Methodist Episcopal Church and the African Methodist Episcopal Zion Church) and the Christian Methodist Church are predominantly African-American churches, and they account for nearly all of the remaining third of the Methodist group.

Pentecostal Churches share a belief that God grants believers special spiritual gifts—especially the experience called "speaking in tongues," a common feature of Pentecostal services. ("Speaking in tongues" refers to speaking words, not necessarily of any known language, under direct divine inspiration.) Pentecostal Churches trace their origin to the day of Pentecost (from the Greek meaning "50th day," i.e. the seventh Sunday after Easter), described in the New Testament book, Acts of the Apostles, when early Christians received ecstatic or mystical powers. Modern Pentecostalism began in the early 1900's, when members of some Holiness churches received the gift of tongues (see "Holiness Churches").

Pentecostal congregations tend to be small, yet the Pentecostal faith experienced rapid growth in the later decades of the 20th century, and Pentecostal beliefs had an impact on Roman Catholic, Lutheran, Episcopal, and other denominations, who reported a growth among adherents of "charismatic renewal," a movement based on spiritual gifts. The two Churches of God in Christ and the United Pentecostal Church are predominantly African-American

denominations. The Assemblies of God is the largest predominantly white denomination. Many Pentecostal organizations are regional or purely local. Because of this loose organization, there are likely to be many thousands of Pentecostal believers not included in national membership counts because their local congregations are not affiliated with a regional or national group.

Reformed Churches, including the closely related Congregational and Presbyterian Churches, trace their descent to the French-born reformer John Calvin (1509–64). Differences among denominations within this group reflect primarily national origins rather than doctrinal differences; the various Reformed denominations share many points of belief and practice.

Central to Calvinist theology is the idea of *predestination*: because all things past, present and future already exist in the mind of God, those who will be saved—the *elect*—have already been saved. Salvation cannot be earned, but comes entirely from God's grace. However, it is assumed that only the godly are among the elect, and so, unsure of one's standing in the sight of god, it is imperative to live a godly life.

Calvin established a Christian theocracy in Geneva in the early 16th century, populated mainly by Huguenots (French Protestants). Other Calvinist churches took root in various European countries. The Pilgrims and Puritans who settled in New England established there the Congregational Church (today the major component of the United Church of Christ), reflecting the English Reformed tradition in which congregations are largely self-governing. Dutch settlers of New Amsterdam (later New York) brought with them the Dutch Reformed Church, now (after several schisms and amalgamations, and the incorporation of the Huguenot Reformed Church) the Reformed Church in America. The German Reformed Church and the Evangelical Reformed Church are both largely of German descent. Scottish and Scots-Irish settlers established the Presbyterian Church. The Presbyterian Church, established in Scotland by John Knox (1510–72), takes its name from its form of church governance by assemblies of delegates (*presbyters*). The Presbyterian Church (U.S.) unites several Presbyterian bodies that had been separated by regional and minor doctrinal differences.

Reformed Church buildings are generally simple and sparsely adorned. Similarly, worship in these churches tends to be austere and simple. Reformed churches have traditionally valued a highly-educated clergy and have been instrumental in the founding of numerous colleges and universities, including Harvard, Yale, and Princeton.

The Presbyterian Church (U.S.) is the result of several mergers between smaller churches that had been separated by regional and doctrinal differences. The United Church of Christ includes, in addition to Congregational Churches, descendants of German Reformed Churches and of the Evangelical and Reformed Church (also of German descent). The Reformed Church in America and the Christian Reformed Church are both of Dutch descent.

The Salvation Army, a religious and charitable organization founded in England in 1865 by William and Catherine Booth (and took the name Salvation Army in 1878), shares the core beliefs of other evangelical churches. It is most familiar to outsiders through its work among the homeless and the poor and its fundraising on the streets, especially before Christmas. As its name suggests, the Salvation Army is organized on military lines (symbolizing the organization's "warfare against evil"). Full-time uniformed personnel, organized in military ranks, are expected to devote their lives to its service and to accept a regime of poverty, austerity, and chastity (or marital fidelity; the organization encourages marriage within its ranks). The religious services do not follow a set form, although music and singing are often emphasized.

Unitarian Universalist Association Unitarianism was an outgrowth of New England Congregationalism in the late 1700's and early 1800's. Unitarians assert God's unity and repudiate the doctrine of the Trinity. They also interpret other Christian beliefs in a liberal, figurative manner. Universalism was a separate movement emphasizing the availability of God's care to all people, not only to a small chosen group. In 1961 Unitarian and Universalist organizations merged. Many traditional Christians do not acknowledge Unitarian Universalists as Christians, and many adherents would agree with that judgment.

Other Christian Churches

Among other denominations there is a wide variety of religious belief and practice. Some are large, such as the Mormons (below), and others are very small, perhaps a single local congregation that reports as a separate and independent church body. Many groups do not recognize any organizational or doctrinal authority beyond the individual congregation, thereby making it difficult to generalize about them. Some groups are heterodox offshoots from the Pentecostal family. (See also "Folk Religions" and "New Religions," below.)

The Church of Jesus Christ of Latter-day Saints, known popularly as the Mormon Church, was "established anew," according to Mormon doctrine, on April 6, 1830, by a 19th-century American prophet named Joseph Smith (1805–44). Smith, who grew up in western New York State, reported direct revelations from God. The Book of Mormon, which Smith said was given to him as a set of golden tablets by the Angel Moroni, and which he translated, tells of a visit by the resurrected Jesus Christ to pre-Columbian America. Smith assembled a community of believers that settled first in western New York and later in Ohio, Missouri, and Illinois. Wherever they went, the Mormons aroused the antagonism of neighboring non-Mormons, in part because Mormons allowed men to take more than one wife. Persecution peaked with the murder of Smith himself in 1844.

The next great leader of the church was Brigham Young (1801–77), who led the majority of Mormons westward to settle in the then-uninhabited basin by the Great Salt Lake. There the church grew and prospered. To this day, the majority of religiously affiliated people in Utah are Mormons. There are also many adherents in surrounding states, especially Colorado and Idaho.

About half of the church's 12.8 million members live in the United States, but the Mormons' missionary work goes on around the globe. Since about 1900, the church has encouraged converts to stay in their own countries and organize congregations there. The Community of Christ, formerly the Reorganized Church of Jesus Christ of Latter-day Saints, is the largest of the groups that did not make the trek to the Great Salt Lake. Its headquarters are in Independence, Missouri, which Smith had designated as the site of a great future temple. Members of Community of Christ (Reorganized Church) recognize their organizational and spiritual descent from the Church of Jesus Christ of Latter-day Saints but do not consider themselves Mormons.

History

At the time of his death, Jesus had a small handful of followers among Jews, but his teachings were not widely accepted among the larger Jewish community. Christianity began to outgrow its origins as a Jewish sect when the disciples of Jesus, particularly under the leadership of the Apostle Paul, preached to non-Jewish gentiles throughout the Roman Empire. Jesus' teachings were remembered in oral tradition and recorded and amplified in many writings. The 27 books recognized as the canonical New Testament were written in Greek from about A.D. 50 to the early second century A.D. (see "Books of the Bible.") The New Testament includes the four gospels, the Acts of the Apostles, the letters of Paul and others, and Revelations.

Christians were widely persecuted by Roman authorities, because they refused to accept either the secular authority or the civic religion of the empire, until the emperor Constantine legalized the religion in 313; in 380 Christianity became the official religion of the Roman Empire by proclamation of the Emperor Theodosius. Christianity also spread beyond the Roman Empire to parts of Central Asia, India, and northern Ethiopia.

Disputes over theological issues such as the nature of the Trinity and the person of Christ were resolved at a series of Ecumenical ("universal") Councils, convened by the pope and attended by bishops of most or all of the leading Christian communities. The first four of these councils—at Nicaea (325), Constantinople (381), Ephesus (431), and Chalcedon (451) were of particular importance in establishing certain Christian beliefs as orthodox and casting out others as heretical. The consolidation of Christian doctrine is reflected in the Athanasian Creed, an extended statement of faith formerly widely used in western churches (fourth or fifth century A.D., after the time of St. Athanasius himself); and in the Nicene Creed, widely used today in liturgies (it was known in the fifth century, i.e. later than the Council of Nicaea).

In 1054 the Eastern and Western churches split over differences of theology, politics, geography, and language. The issues ranged from debates over the nature and form of the sacrament of the Eucharist (the Christian sacrificial ceremony of bread and wine) and debates about clerical celibacy to the pope's objections to the patriarch of Constantinople taking the title Ecumenical Patriarch and the patriarch's objections to the crowning of emperors of the Holy Roman Empire by the pope, in contradistinction to the Roman emperor at Constantinople. The division between Catholic and Orthodox grew steadily in complexity, bitterness, and intransigence, and only recently have leaders on both sides shown a sustained willingness to enter into dialogue to heal the breach.

Meanwhile, the papacy in Rome acquired the nature of a civil authority; and within the Western church ascetic and spiritual traditions competed with secular ones. In the 16th century, papal authority was challenged by such reform-minded priests as Martin Luther and John Calvin, abetted by England's King Henry VIII, who transferred authority over the church in England from the pope to himself. Sectarian wars engulfed Europe for more than a century as Catholics and Protestants vied for temporal and spiritual power.

European explorers and colonists spread Christianity to the Americas, as well as to Asia and Africa. (In some places in both Asia and Africa, the Europeans encountered well-established indigenous Christian communities adhering to older rites such as Nestorianism or Syrian Orthodoxy.) The Spanish and Portuguese brought Catholicism to Latin America, while North America became a haven for Protestant denominations from northern Europe. Since the mid-1800's, Protestant and Catholic evangelists have carried out energetic missionary programs to Africa and East Asia.

Geography and Numbers

Christianity is the most populous and most widespread religion in the world, with more than 2 billion adherents in 260 countries. Europe is home to more than 530 million Christians (70 percent of the region's population), but Latin America has proportionally the highest number of Christian adherents—93 percent of the population. The fastest growing Christian population is in Africa, increasing 2.4 percent from 380 million in 2000 to 389 million in 2005.

Islam

The precepts of Islam were revealed through the prophet Muhammad, who was born ca. 570 at Mecca in western Saudi Arabia and died in 632 in the city of Medina. Muslims trace their descent from Abraham; but unlike Jews, who trace their descent through Isaac, the son of Abraham's wife, Sarah, Muslims trace their decent through Ishmael, Abraham's son by his servant Hagar. The word *Islam*, Arabic "surrender" or "submission," suggests an adherent's (known as a Muslim) total obedience to the will of God.

Scripture

The Koran (Arabic Qur'an, "recitation") is the sacred scripture of Islam, understood by believers to be the authentic and verbatim word of God spoken to the Prophet Muhammad by the Angel Gabriel in a series of revelations beginning in A.D. 610 and continuing throughout the Prophet's lifetime. They were recited by Muhammad to his companions, preserved in writing during or soon after the Prophet's death in 632 (year 10 of the Islamic calendar), and subsequently collected. The Koran in its present form contains 114 chapters or sections called *suras*.

The Koran is the ultimate source of authority in Islam. Other sources of authority exist, such as hadith (traditions concerning the Prophet), ijma (consensus of Muslim jurists), and qiyas (analogy, e.g. the banning of intoxicating drugs by analogy with the Koranic ban on alcohol); but nothing can be held to be true that conflicts with or contradicts the Koran.

The Koran is considered to be the fountainhead of Arabic and Islamic scholarship; it is said that there does not exist anything in the world that is outside its purview. As its title suggests, the Koran was revealed to Muhammad by oral recitation, and it is still regarded primarily as a recited rather than a read text. (In its written form the Koran is often referred to as al-Kitab, "the Book.") All Muslims memorize at least parts of the Koran for use in daily prayers. Memorization of the entire work is a prerequisite to further training as a Muslim religious scholar or jurist. Many special fields of Koranic scholarship investigate not only its meaning but also its grammar, punctuation, rhymes, and metrical structure. Recitation of the Koran is not only a religious duty but an art, and there are a number of different schools or styles of recitation. The Koran has been translated into many different languages, but because it is considered, word-for-word, the actual and authentic word of God recited by the Angel Gabriel to Muhammad in Arabic, no translation of the Koran may be considered to possess religious authority. It is widely held in the Islamic world that the Koran may properly be read and recited only in Arabic.

The standard account of the Koran's compilation holds that shortly after the death of the Prophet the first Caliph, Abu Bakr, fearing that the individuals who had heard the recitation of the Koran directly from Muhammad would soon grow old and pass away, ordered that the *suras* be written down and arranged in the order that had already been revealed to the Prophet. (Except for Sura 1, a brief invocation, the *suras* are arranged approximately, but not strictly, by order of length, longest to shortest.) Several years later the third Caliph, 'Uthman, ordered copies of this Koran to be made and distributed throughout the Islamic world to ensure its preservation. Because there is no highly devel-

oped scholarly tradition in the Islamic world equivalent to the "Biblical Criticism" movement of the Christian world, which challenged received ideas about the age, composition, and authenticity of the Scriptures, the traditional account of the Koran's compilation has persisted generally without challenge or critical enquiry within the Muslim world. Some modern scholars, both within and from outside the Muslim community, have suggested that the true picture may have been more complicated than the traditional account suggests, and that the Koran may have been compiled in stages over several decades after the death of the Prophet, reaching final form only in the late 7th century (or, in the view of some scholars, even later than that).

The Contents of the Koran The Arab people regard themselves as descendants of the Biblical patriarch Abraham, through Ishmael, Abraham's son with his servant Hagar. The Koran is very much a work in the Abrahamic tradition. It includes versions of episodes from the Hebrew and Christian Bibles, including the stories of Adam and Eve, Abraham, Moses, and David, and assumes that these stories will be familiar to the hearer. But the Koran focuses on the significance of these events rather than on their historical details. It recounts the virgin birth of Jesus, but does not portray him as the son of God. In light of the common origins of the Abrahamic religions in the tradition of Biblical monotheism, Islam accords to Jews and Christians a special status as *dhimmi* or "people of the Book," a status explicitly and repeatedly confirmed in the Koran.

Generally speaking the focus of the Koran is on the life of the Islamic community, with its commitment to justice, equality of believers before God, humility, and piety. Many *suras* refer to specific instances or circumstances in the life of Muhammad as he struggled to make his prophesy understood and accepted by his community; for example, Sura 8, "Battle Gains," refers at length to the great Muslim victory in the Battle of Badr (year 2/624); Sura 48, "Triumph," relates to an agreement reached between the Prophet and his Meccan opponents about access to Mecca for believers. Muhammad's mission is to warn the people of God's plan for the salvation of believers and assure the people that disbelievers will be condemned to eternal punishment on the day of judgement. Many *suras* emphasize the torments of hell that await those who do evil or deny God. God is merciful; but those who hear his word and do not believe will be condemned. The emphasis of God's warning, delivered by Muhammad, is on disbelievers rather than unbelievers—those who hear and reject the word of

God, rather than those who have not heard the revelations. In the *suras* God provides Muhammad with arguments to use to reassure believers and to persuade disbelievers to change their minds; and Muhammad himself is often counseled to be patient in delivering his message, and not to lose heart.

Each *sura* (except, for reasons that are unclear, Sura 9) begins with the formula, "In the name of God, the Lord of Mercy, the Giver of Mercy." The titles of the *suras* reinforce the Koran's status as primarily an oral document for recitation rather than a written book for silent reading. They are more mnemonic devices than descriptions of the contents of the *sura*. For example, the title of *Sura 2*, "The Cow," is not *about* cows; the title serves as a brief reminder to the reader that this is the *sura* that makes a reference to a cow. Many *suras* are rather diverse in content, and brief summaries can give only a general idea of what each *sura* is about.

The 114 Suras

1. The Opening This is a brief summary of the entire content of the Koran, memorized in Arabic by Muslims and recited as part of the obligatory daily prayers. It reads, in its entirety (in the translation of M. A. S. Abdel Haleem, 2004):

"In the name of God, the Lord of Mercy, the Giver of Mercy! Praise belongs to God, Lord of the Worlds, the Lord of Mercy, the Giver of Mercy, Master of the Day of Judgement. It is You we worship; it is You we ask for help. Guide us to the straight path: the path of those You have blessed, those who incur no anger and who have not gone astray."

2. The Cow By a significant margin the longest of the *suras*, "The Cow" speaks of the fates of believers, disbelievers, and hypocrites. The *sura* recapitulates many Biblical stories of Adam, Moses, Abraham, and Jesus and Mary, including God's commandment given through Moses to the Israelites that they sacrifice a cow. It also tells of Iblis, an angel who refused to obey God's commandments and became the enemy of God. Muslims, Jews, Christians, and other monotheistic followers of the Abrahamic tradition, who believe in God, in the day of judgement, and who do good, will all be rewarded by God. But Jews and Christians should not dispute with each other, nor claim that they exclusively are God's chosen people.

This *sura* reaffirms the validity of the received Scriptures; gives assurance of the truth of the revelations granted to Muhammad which completed the process of divine revelation; and specifies many rules (such as rules for prayer, dietary laws, principles governing ritual cleanliness, marital laws, and prohibition of intoxicants and gambling) for the conduct of believers.

3. The Family of 'Imran This *sura* asserts firmly that believers will be saved and disbelievers condemned. It recounts stories of the prophet Zachariah, and Mary and the birth of Jesus. People of the Book who deny God's final revelations are condemned. It draws lessons from the Battles of Badr and Uhud: those who reject or disobey the Prophet will be defeated, but People of the Book who accept God's revelations will be saved.

4. Women This *sura* defines the role of women in Islam, with emphasis on their protection by inheritance and marital laws, and discusses many specific rules relating to women. It enjoins Muslims to defend the weak and to restrain themselves from fighting. It describes tensions between Muslims and People of the Book, and warns the latter not to oppose the revelations given by God to Muhammad.

5. The Feast Here we find a detailed discussion of dietary laws and laws governing cleanliness. Muslims are prohibited only from eating carrion, blood, pork, or meat over which the name of a false god has been invoked. The *sura* reaffirms the Hebrew scriptures and the teachings of Jesus, but asserts that Jesus did not claim to be God.

6. Livestock The principal subject of this *sura* is a refutation of idolatry and a warning against the worship of false gods. God alone has created the universe, controls it, and is omniscient and omnipotent.

7. The Heights This *sura* reaffirms to Muhammad the validity of the revelations made to him and his obligation to recite them. It warns disbelievers of their fate, and of the barrier that will separate believers and disbelievers on the day of judgement.

8. Battle Gains Muslims are reminded in this *sura* that their victory at Badr (year 2/624) against overwhelming odds was due to God alone. It denounces hypocrites and disbelievers, and urges mutual loyalty and support among believers.

9. Repentance This *sura* opens with a condemnation of idolaters who repeatedly broke faith with the Muslims; believers are enjoined to kill them for their treachery. The *sura* then describes the preparations and recruitment of troops for Muhammad's expedition to Tabuk in year 9/631; hypocrites who claimed to support the Prophet but lent no help to the expedition are criticized. This is the only *sura* that does not begin with the invocation "In the Name of God, the Lord of Mercy, the Giver of Mercy," leading some scholars to believe that Sura 9 should be considered a continuation of Sura 8.

10. Jonah This contains a powerful reaffirmation of the truth of God's revelations to Muhammad, and of God's anger at those who reject those revelations; all those who hear and disobey will be condemned on the day of judgement. But Muhammad is counseled to be patient: No one can be forced to accept the truth.

11. Hud Muhammad has been sent both to warn of God's anger with disbelievers and to give the good news of his revelation. God watches everywhere and sees everything. The revelations granted to Muhammad follow in a long line of prophetic tradition; Muhammad is asked to take heart from the stories of prophets past.

12. Joseph This *sura* retells the Biblical story of Joseph and his brothers, and again affirms that Muhammad is heir to a long tradition of prophesy.

13. Thunder This *sura* evokes the power and majesty of God; even the thunder praises Him. Like the earlier prophets, Muhammad's only role is to convey God's message to his people. On the day of judgement God will hold every person accountable for his or her actions.

14. Abraham The Biblical patriarch Abraham asks that the city (Mecca) be made safe for believers, and that his descendants be protected against idolatry. Muhammad is addressed directly by God, who assures him that He is all-powerful; believers will be saved, and disbelievers condemned.

15. Al-Hijr The *sura* takes its name from a town of disbelievers destroyed by God. It warns against the power of Satan to deceive, and reminds the prophets to be patient: all disbelievers surely will be punished in a time of God's choosing, and believers will have their reward.

16. The Bee God sends down all good things, such as the fruit and flowers from which bees make honey; why do the disbelievers reject God's gifts? God through Muhammad has sent his message to the people; Muslims should follow the example of Abraham in submitting to God's will.

17. The Night Journey This *sura* alludes briefly to Muhammad's night journey across the sky from Mecca to Jerusalem, from whence he ascended to Heaven before returning to Mecca again. But the *sura's* main subject is the nature of the Koran and the meaning of prophecy: Muhammad's task is to convey God's message to the world; he is not a seer or a miracle-worker. The *sura* also gives a

series of commandments, not unlike the Ten Commandments: Avoid idolatry; honor your parents; be generous to the needy; avoid adultery; do not kill; do not be arrogant; have no other god but God.

18. The Cave A *sura* of parables, including a story about how God aided a group of young men who sought refuge in a cave by putting them to sleep for two years until they were out of danger. God will protect his people; but evildoers will be cast into a fire.

19. Mary This *sura* affirms the story of Mary and the virgin birth of Jesus, but denies that Jesus was the son of God; rather God ordained his birth and it was so. Mary and Jesus are both in the lineage of the prophets. The *sura* also tells stories from the lives of Abraham and Moses. It reiterates that God has no children, neither Jesus nor the pagan gods of Mecca nor the angels.

20. Ta Ha The title of the *sura* consists of two letters of the Arabic alphabet, of uncertain significance. The *sura* itself speaks of the Koran and Muhammad's role in transmitting it to the people; he should take encouragement from the example of Moses. Disbelievers will be destroyed.

21. The Prophets This *sura* locates Muhammad in the long line of prophets from Abraham and Moses to Job and Zachariah. Muhammad's mission is to warn of the unity and omnipotence of God; disbelievers will be destroyed on the final day of judgement.

22. The Pilgrimage Affirms that the site of the Holy Mosque was revealed to Abraham himself, and that pilgrimage is a duty of believers. Warns that disbelievers and idolaters will suffer torments after the final judgement, and reassures the faithful that they will be rewarded. Repeats dietary laws relating to cattle and camels and other religious laws.

23. The Believers Assures believers that they will be rewarded and disbelievers and idolaters will be destroyed; affirms the unity and power of God, and the reality of resurrection for believers.

24. Light God's light is likened to a lamp glowing as brightly as a star. Believers walk in light, disbelievers in darkness. Rules for the conduct of the faithful, especially relating to the status and chastity of women, are reiterated and clarified.

25. The Differentiator Idolaters and polytheists are contrasted with believers, and warned to abandon their stubbornness and ignorance. Believers are faithful, honest, dignified, and enjoy the favor of God.

26. The Poets The Holy Koran is not poetry, nor magic, but the true revelation of God's will. Examples are given of prophets throughout history whose message was not heeded by the people, who then suffered the fate of disbelievers.

27. The Ants Tells the story of King Solomon, who in his wisdom had authority even over animals and birds, and the Queen of Sheba, who through Solomon's influence submitted to God. Invites the people of the Torah to accept the Koran as God's joyful final revelation.

28. The Story Recounts the story of Moses and Pharaoh, and reiterates the destruction that awaits disbelievers and those who reject God's word. Muhammad is comforted in his struggles against the disbelievers of Mecca, and advised to be patient.

29. The Spider Those who put their trust in false gods are like spiders, building flimsy shelters for themselves. But things are not easy for believers, whose faith will be tested by the arguments of disbelievers; they must remain steadfast and remember the examples of the prophets of old who did not waver even when they were rejected by the people.

30. The Byzantines Takes note of the Persian victory over the Byzantine Empire in 613-14 and predicts that Byzantium will defeat the Persians in a year to come. God brings life to the desert and blessings to believers; but on the day of judgement idolaters and evildoers will have no excuse.

31. Luqman Luqman the Wise counsels his son against ascribing partners to God, and teaches him that God is all-powerful. Those who would lead believers away from the truth are warned of the destruction that awaits them. Believers should be patient; God alone knows when the day of judgment will come.

32. Bowing Down in Worship The Koran is God's true revelation; believers bow down to worship him. Muhammad is assured that he is in the true line of prophesy; he should ignore those who reject God's revelations. Their fate awaits them on the day of judgement.

33. The Joint Forces This *sura* describes the Battle of the Trench in year 5/627, at which an army of disbelievers unsuccessfully tried to capture Medina from the Muslims. The *sura* goes on to emphasize God's protection of believers, and to reiterate various points relating to family law, including an injunction to women to dress modestly.

34. Sheba The people of Sheba were blessed, but ungrateful for their blessings; they suffered God's punishment. Muhammad should take courage from the examples of David and Solomon. Those who reject him or, worse, accuse him of being mad, will be punished by God.

35. The Creator God alone created the world; God has no partners and is all-powerful. Disbelievers and idolaters are warned of the fate that awaits them; Muhammad is comforted that older prophets too were rejected by some of the people. Believers will be richly rewarded.

36. Ya Sin This *sura* takes its name from two letters of the Arabic alphabet, of unclear significance. The Koran is affirmed to be God's true revelation, not poetry composed by a man. God truly created the world; He truly will reward believers on the day of resurrection.

37. Arrayed in Rows God is one, and has no partners and no children; the angels are not his daughters and must not be worshipped. The life hereafter is real, and awaits believers; the line of prophesy ending with Muhammad is true.

38. Sad As with Ta Ha (*sura* 20) and Ya Sin (*sura* 36), this *sura* takes its name from a letter of the Arabic alphabet. It praises the truth and beauty of the Koran, assures Muhammad that he is in the true line of prophesy, and likens disbelievers to Iblis, an angel who rebelled against God.

39. The Throngs God gives people a choice: to believe or not to believe. Those who believe will be blessed; idolaters and polytheists who ascribe partners to God will be condemned. On the day of judgement throngs of disbelievers will be sent to Hell.

40. The Forgiver God forgives those who turn to Him, but is severe in punishment of disbelievers, as shown in God's favor toward Moses and his punishment of Pharaoh. Muhammad should take heart and pay no attention to the arguments of disbelievers.

41. Verses Made Distinct The message of the Koran is clear and available to all, but disbelievers close off their senses and reject the truth. They will be condemned on the day of judgement by their own testimony; but the Koran is true, God is One, and believers will be raised from the dead on the last day.

42. Consultation Harmony and consensus should characterize the community of believers. But religion is often a cause for strife because people reject the clear message of God's unity and power. God reminds Muhammad that no one can be compelled to believe; but believers will hear God's message and be judged according to their acceptance of the truth.

43. Ornaments of Gold God rewards his prophets not with mere riches, but with an assured place in the life hereafter. God is One. God has no partners; neither angels nor Jesus are children of God. Jesus himself understood that he was a prophet of God.

44. Smoke The smoke of the day of judgement will envelop the world; then it will be too late to repent. God will punish disbelievers and idolaters as he punished Pharaoh. The Koran's message is one of mercy, but those who reject it will be condemned.

45. Kneeling All will kneel before God on the day of judgement. The visible signs of his greatness should be sufficient to convince doubters and disbelievers, but they who persist in unbelief will be condemned by their own arrogance.

46. The Sand Dunes Sand dunes mark the former dwelling-place of the tribe of 'Ad, destroyed when they rejected the prophesy granted to them. Similar destruction awaits even the most powerful of those who deny the truth of the word of God, and of the resurrection.

47. Muhammad This *sura* describes some of the military and political conflicts that Muhammad faced dealing with the people of Mecca. It condemns those who expelled the Prophet from the city, along with all those who would obstruct others from accepting the word of God. Muslims should submit to God in all things; their reward is certain.

48. Triumph This *sura* refers to political events in Muhammad's relations with Mecca after he had been expelled from the city. A ten-year truce enabled the Muslims to consolidate their gains, and their return to Mecca is depicted as a certainty; God will reward believers.

49. The Private Rooms Believers should deal respectfully with Muhammad in his private quarters, and generously and with mutual regard toward one another; it is God's will that people live in the harmony brought about by submission to Him.

50. Qaf The title is a syllable of the Arabic alphabet. God created the world; he no less will bring believers back to life on the day of judgement. The Koran gives true warning to disbelievers.

51. Scattering Winds As the winds come from the sky, so will the day of judgement surely come. Abraham and Moses are invoked to encourage Muhammad to persevere in warning the people: God created people so that they would worship Him.

52. The Mountain Muhammad warns disbelievers: The day of judgement will surely come, as God has promised; the bliss of paradise awaits believers, but disbelievers will suffer the torments of hell.

53. The Star The truth of Muhammad's Night Journey is reaffirmed: who can doubt what the Prophet experienced with his own senses? This *sura* gives one of the Koran's most succinct summaries of Islamic teachings: God is the lord of Creation, and the source of all benefits for those who believe.

54. The Moon Demonstrates that God has punished those in the past who rebelled against his will: the people of Noah, of 'Ad, of Thamud, of Lot, of Pharaoh, and others. On the day of judgement believers will receive their reward of bliss, but disbelievers will be punished.

55. The Lord of Mercy This *sura* portrays God as having created both humans and spirits (jinn) and given them endless benefits; as each blessing, on earth or in paradise, is described the *sura* adds a refrain: "Which then of your Lord's blessings do you both [men and spirits] deny?" The world is divided into the best of believers, ordinary believers, and disbelievers; blessings await the former, but the disbelievers will suffer everlasting punishment.

56. That Which is Coming A promise of bliss for believers and punishment for disbelievers; the day of judgement is surely coming.

57. Iron God is all-powerful and all-knowing. Those who aid God's work, like the prophets of old, such as Abraham, Noah, and Jesus, are like iron. People of the Book (Jews and Christians) are urged to submit to God's true revelation.

58. The Dispute This *sura* repudiates an unjust pre-Islamic form of divorce, and reaffirms Islam's commitment to fair treatment of women. Those who repudiate God and oppose his will shall surely perish, while those on the side of God will be rewarded.

59. The Gathering of Forces This *sura* describes a victory over those who have warred with Islam; it is taken as a reference to the Jewish clan of the Banu al-Nadir, who repeatedly broke promises to Muhammad and his allies, and eventually were expelled from Medina. The victory belongs to God, not to any human agency.

60. Women Tested On the day of judgement everyone will be judged on his own merits; neither kin nor clan will matter. Wives of unbelievers who join the Muslims, if their faith is genuine, are divorced from their husbands and not sent back to them, but the bride-price must be repaid to the ex-husband by any believer who then marries such a woman. If the wife of a Muslim deserts to the unbelievers she is divorced and her assets paid over to her ex-husband.

61. Solid Lines Both Moses and Jesus were prophets; Jesus predicted that God's messenger, Muhammad, would follow him. But their communities were divided: some rebelled against God, while some followed God.

62. The Day of Congregation God has given the people a true revelation, but some reject it. The Jews err in saying that they alone of all people are friends of God; God will judge them. Believers should be faithful in gathering for Friday prayers.

63. The Hypocrites Hypocrites profess to believe but do not; God will not forgive them. They refuse the obligation of charity; true believers therefore must strive to give even more.

64. Mutual Neglect God has punished disbelievers in the past and will do so again on the day of judgement. Those who deny the day of judgement are deeply in error. Muslims must take care not to be influenced by doubters even in their own families, but also must pardon their faults and encourage them. God is merciful.

65. Divorce This *sura* lays down laws for divorce, and specifically for the waiting period before a divorce can take effect; women who are being divorced must be treated fairly and with dignity.

66. Prohibition Two of the Prophet's wives are criticized for betraying a confidence. Believers must guard themselves against wrongdoing. But God will forgive those who repent. The wives of Noah and Lot are examples of bad wives; Pharaoh's righteous wife, and Mary, are examples of devout and pious women.

67. Control God has total control over the world and everything in it. Disbelievers and those who deny God will regret their errors on the day of judgement, but it will be too late.

68. The Pen The angels record everything. Some people claim that Muhammad is not the messenger of God, but a madman; some feel secure in their worldly wealth and power and do not need God. Muhammad is urged to be steadfast; mockers and disbelievers will perish.

69. The Inevitable Hour God in the past has punished those who rejected or disobeyed Him; how much more will he do so on the day of judgement! The righteous will be rewarded by a life of bliss in a pleasant garden; disbelievers will burn in hell. The Koran is in every respect a true revelation of the word of God.

70. Ways of Ascent Mockers challenge God to punish them now rather than in the hereafter; they will receive their punishment on the terrible day of judgement, but the faithful will be richly rewarded.

71. Noah Noah was a prophet who told the people to ask forgiveness of God, but they rejected his word; they all perished in the great flood.

72. The Jinn A group of jinn heard the recitation of the Koran and submitted to God. God is all-powerful, and Muhammad's role is to deliver his revelation. Those who reject it will themselves be rejected on the day of judgement.

73. Enfolded Muhammad, enfolded in his cloak, pursued a regimen of austerity to prepare for his work as a prophet, and later was relieved of his austerities by God so that he could more effectively reach the people. As God punished Pharaoh in this life, so will he punish disbelievers on the day of judgement.

74. Wrapped in His Cloak After receiving God's first message as revealed by the angel Gabriel, Muhammad returned home and tried to conceal himself in his cloak. But God calls him to his duty to warn the world: disbelievers will be cast into hell on the day of judgement.

75. The Resurrection God has infinite power; he surely will raise the dead and restore them to their natural form. Muhammad should be patient so as to deliver God's entire revelation to the people. People are warned to think, not of this life, but of the next.

76. Man Man is created to worship and serve God, and will be tested on the day of judgement; believers will live blissfully in the garden, but disbelievers will suffer the torments of hell.

77. The Day of Decision On the day of judgement all will be sorted into groups according to their deeds. Horrible torments of fire await the disbelievers.

78. The Announcement Many refuse to believe in the reality of the coming day of judgement. Its inevitability is affirmed, along with the fates awaiting believers and disbelievers.

79. The Forceful Chargers The day of judgement will come like chargers rushing to battle. Moses warned Pharaoh; Pharaoh paid no heed and was destroyed; likewise disbelievers will be punished when the dead are brought back to life on the day of judgement.

80. He Frowned Muhammad is reproached by God for frowning at a blind man who sought wisdom, when Muhammad was distracted by disputation with disbelievers. He is told to ignore the disbelievers. The world of God is precious, and the Koran must be written down by men who are pure and holy; but mankind is ungrateful and too many forget the grace and mercy of God.

81. Shrouded in Darkness When the sun is shrouded in darkness on the last day, all will be judged according to their deeds.

82. Torn Apart The sky will be torn apart on the day of judgement; then it will be too late for the disbelievers.

83. Those Who Give Short Measure The practice of commercial cheating is strongly condemned. Those who cheat others will be punished on the last day, but those whose names are on the list of the righteous will enjoy paradise.

84. Ripped Apart When the sky is ripped apart all will be judged. Heaven and Earth obey God's will; but humans who disobey or disbelieve will perish.

85. The Towering Constellations The sky with its constellations will witness that those who persecuted believers will suffer the wrath of God.

86. The Night-Comer As man originates in a drop of semen, as a baby comes from the womb, as plants grow from the earth, so will all humans rise again on the day of resurrection.

87. The Most High Muhammad is encouraged to persist in his mission to teach the revelations of the Koran. The world lasts only a short time; the day of judgement is coming.

88. The Overwhelming Event Muhammad cannot control what happens to people; his only mission is to warn them. The day of judgement will surely come, for disbelievers and believers alike.

89. Daybreak God promises that tyrants and disbelievers in the present time will be dealt with as he dealt in the past with those who rejected the prophets; wealth and power will avail them nothing.

90. The City Man's life on earth is one of toil and hardship, and all will be judged on the last day; it is best to do good works and avoid evil.

91. The Sun Sun and moon, day and night, witness that to purify the soul leads to life, to corrupt it leads to death, as God punished the wicked people of Thamud.

92. The Night Some people choose a path of goodness, some one of evil. God guides and warns them: the pious will be spared, the wicked will burn.

93. The Morning Brightness God reassures Muhammad about his mission, and tells him not to feel forsaken.

94. Relief Muhammad should persevere through hardships; God will guide him. He should turn to the Lord for everything.

95. The Fig God has given man a world rich with good things; those who believe in God and are faithful will be richly rewarded. How can the day of judgement be denied?

96. The Clinging Form The first paragraph of this *sura* was the first revelation entrusted to Muhammad, in the Cave of Hira near Mecca. After the ritual invocation of Allah, Muhammad receives the command: "Read." The *sura* then states that God made man from a clump of matter in the womb. The second paragraph warns humans not to think themselves self-sufficient and thus turn away from God.

97. The Night of Glory This short *sura* celebrates the Night of Glory when Muhammad received his first revelation.

98. Clear Evidence Disbelievers demand clear evidence of God before they will believe; but true believers sincerely devote themselves to God through faith. They will be rewarded.

99. The Earthquake On the day of judgement the earth will shake as the good and the evil are separated into groups on the evidence of their own deeds.

100. The Charging Steeds Those who take too much pleasure in wealth are ungrateful to God, from whom all blessings come. The hearts of those who reject God will be revealed on the last day.

101. The Crashing Blow The day of judgement will fall like a crashing blow on those whose evil deeds outweigh the good; they will be cast down into hell.

102. Striving for More Striving for wealth distracts people until they die, when it is too late for them to do good. They doubted God; now their punishment is certain.

103. The Declining Day All are lost except those who believe, who do good, who help the community of the faithful.

104. The Backbiter Backbiters, motivated by greed, prepare themselves to be crushed by the fires of hell.

105. The Elephant Refers to an incident in 570, when a Christian king of Yemen tried to capture and destroy Mecca; he was defeated by God, who sent birds to confuse and panic the Yemeni war elephants.

106. Quraysh The Quraysh tribe (keepers of the Holy Ka'ba at Mecca) enjoyed God's protection after the battle referred to in *sura* 105. With that protection they can accompany their trading caravans without fear of being attacked.

107. Common Kindnesses Those who reject God are evident from their lack of common kindness toward others, especially the poor and needy.

108. Abundance God tells Muhammad that he has been blessed with abundance (although he has no surviving direct heir); those who doubt will see their lineages cut off.

109. The Disbelievers A repudiation of disbelievers and all they stand for, but also an affirmation of religious toleration. The Muslim tells disbelievers: You have your religion, and I have mine.

110. Help Praise God and repent; he is always ready to forgive.

111. Palm Fiber A curse on Muhammad's fierce opponent

Abu Lahab, and his wife: may she wear a halter of palm-fiber rope.

112 Purity of Faith A formula of faith: "He is God the One, God the eternal. He begot no one nor was he begotten. No one is comparable to Him."

113. Daybreak A formula to ward off evil and seek refuge in the Lord.

114. People A formula against doubt, seeking refuge in the Lord.

Belief and Practice

Allah The very definition of a Muslim is one who submits to God. God is referred to as Allah, although this word—a contraction of *al* (the) and *ilah* (God)—merely means "the God." It is not the name of God, who is often said to have "99 names," such as The Merciful, The Just, and The Compassionate. Muhammad viewed himself and was seen by his followers not as a divine figure, but as the last in a line of prophets, following Abraham, Moses, and Jesus.

Five Pillars of Islam A Muslim's relations with God are regulated by the Five Pillars of Islam:

Profession of Faith (*Shahadah*) This is a single sentence that essentially makes a person a Muslim: "There is no God but Allah, and Muhammad is his messenger." These are the first words spoken to a newborn Muslim, and they are recited daily throughout a person's life.

Prayer (*Salat*) Most Muslims pray five times daily: before dawn, midday, midafternoon, sunset, and night-time; some Shiite Muslims combine these into three prayers. Prayers are announced by a *muezzin* who calls from the top of a minaret. The call begins with "Allahu akbar" ("God is supreme") and continues, "I witness that there is no God but God; I witness that Muhammad is the messenger of God; hasten to prayer." Muslims are expected to perform ritual purification before prayer, washing their hands, arms, face, neck, and feet. Prayer is performed facing *qiblah*, the direction of Mecca; inside a mosque this is indicated by an arched niche known as a *mihrab*. Prayer typically consists of passages from the Koran recited in Arabic from memory, in standing, bowing, prostrate, and sitting postures. Friday is a day of public prayer, but not necessarily a day of rest, and services in a mosque will usually include a sermon by religious leader.

Charity (*Zakat*) Devout Muslims are obligated to give a portion of their wealth to the poor. The actual percentage varies, but is usually about 2.5 percent yearly—and this is based on all of a Muslim's possessions, not only their annual income. They are also expected to provide other forms of charity whenever the opportunity arises.

Fasting during Ramadan (*Sawm*) Muslims are required to abstain from food, liquid, tobacco, and sex between dawn and dusk during the ninth month of the Muslim calendar, Ramadan, in remembrance of the time of Muhammad's first revelations. Due to the lunar Muslim calendar, the month begins 11 days earlier each year.

Pilgrimage to Mecca (*Hajj*) Every Muslim is expected to visit Mecca once in his or her lifetime, unless prevented by poverty or illness, and only Muslims may enter the city. About 2 million people make the journey each year: either the "lesser pilgrimage," which is simply a visit to Mecca to worship in the great mosque and visit nearby holy sites, or a "greater pilgrimage" which involves several ritual visits to the Kabah (below) over a period of several days, interspersed with reenactments of events from the lives of Abraham, Hagar, and Muhammad. Completing the pilgrimage gives a Muslim the status of *hajji* or *hajjiyah* (male or female pilgrim).

Schools and Sects

Sunni Islam The Islamic world is divided into two main sects (each with several sub-sects), Sunni and Shiite. *Sunnah* means "tradition" and refers to the Sunni reliance on the Koran and the supplementary sayings attributed to Muhammad (*Hadiths*) as the source of all legitimate knowledge. There are four major sub-sects of Sunni Islam, differing in particulars of interpretation of the texts.

The split between Sunni and Shiite Islam initially involved a dispute about the succession to Muhammad. Sunnis believe that succession passed through a series of *caliphs* ("successors") beginning with Abu Bakr, of which the fourth was Ali, the son-in-law of Muhammad. Shiites hold that Ali was the first legitimate successor, the first in a series of divinely appointed *imams* ("guides") descended from the Prophet himself. The succession dispute, marked by the assassination of Ali and then of his son and successor Husayn, led to a civil war within Islam and the cementing of the Sunni-Shiite split. Subsequently these two main branches of Islam have developed a number of differences in beliefs, practices, holidays, and other features.

The overwhelming majority of Muslims are Sunnis (83 percent, or nearly 1 billion people), spread widely throughout the Islamic world but a minority in both Iraq and Iran.

Saudi Arabia and Egypt are the main power centers in the Sunni world.

Shiite Islam   "Shiite" means "partisans," emphasizing Shiite loyalty to Ali and his descendants as the legitimate successors to Muhammad. Shiites accept hadiths attributed to Ali and his eleven successors—the first twelve imams—as religiously authoritative. Shiite Islam is divided into three main sub-sects, the most prominent of which holds that the twelfth imam did not die but is "hidden" and will return to guide the world in anticipation of the Last Judgment. The Ismaili branch, led by the Agha Khan, follows a different interpretation of the succession of imams. Shiism, as compared to Sunni Islam, places greater emphasis on acts of piety and personal faith; on a personal level, many Shiites venerate one of a number of Islamic saints.

Shiites comprise about 16 percent of Muslims (about 180 million people). Iran is the center of Shiite power, but there are significant Shiite communities in parts of Iraq, Syria, and non-Arab countries such as Pakistan and India.

Sufism   Sufism is essentially Islamic mysticism, a branch of the religion that promotes a simple existence and seeks a direct experience of God. It emerged in response to a perceived "worldliness" overtaking Islam in its early years of development. A traditional Sufi disciple (*fakir* in Arabic, *darwish* in Persian) pursues spiritual studies with a Sufi leader, or *shaykh*. Throughout their history, Sufi orders (*tariqah*) have incorporated a variety of techniques to produce a mystical state of *sana* ("extinction" or loss of self), including breathing techniques, counting on rosaries, playing music, and spinning or dancing (the English phrase *whirling dervish* comes from the circular dance of the Mawlawiya order). Because many orthodox Muslims view Sufism as a folk religion, on a lower order than "true" Islam, it is not practiced openly in many parts of the world.

Islamism   refers to a highly politicized version of Islam that arose in various parts of the Middle East in the postcolonial era. Islamism stresses that Islam is a political system as well as a religion. The goals of individual Islamists vary, but they may include adopting Islam as the defining characteristic of personal identity; defending Islam against enemies (real or imagined); the restoration of the caliphate to unify the Islamic world; the return to Islam of areas once part of the Islamic world (e.g., Israel and Spain); the adoption of *sharia* religious law in Muslim countries; severe restrictions on women's dress and public activities; and the

importance of personal and collective *jihad* ("struggle"). Islamism is sometimes associated with, but is not identical to, Islamic political terrorism; many Islamists, though espousing ideals regarded as extreme in the non-Muslim world, reject the use of indiscriminate violence in pursuit of their goals.

History

Muhammad, the founder and first prophet of Islam, was born ca. A.D. 570 in Mecca. The city was already a holy place for a variety of local religious practices, and the home of the Kabah ("cube"), which housed hundreds of images of tribal gods, as well as a black meteorite believed to have been sent by heaven (and still the central focus of a Muslim's pilgrimage to the city). Muhammad was raised by his uncle and became a trader, traveling throughout the Arabian Peninsula and gaining exposure to a variety of religions, including Judaism, Christianity, and Zoroastrianism. At the age of 25 he married his employer, the widow Khadija.

At age 40, in a cave at Mount Hira, Muhammad claimed he received his first visitation from the angel Gabriel, who ordered him to recite the word of God to others. The first people Muhammad shared these messages with were his wife, his cousin Ali, and his friend Abu Bakr, known now as the first Muslims. Most of Muhammad's "recitations" promoted compassion, kindness, honesty, and charity. Others, however, promoting monotheism, prohibiting statues and images, and railing against unfair contracts and usury, provoked resistance from powerful businesspeople in Mecca. In 615 some of Muhammad's followers fled to Ethiopia; in 619 Khadija died, and a year later Muhammad experienced the Night Journey (or Night of Ascent), a vision of being guided by Gabriel through Heaven into the presence of God.

In 622 Muhammad and his followers were invited by the city of Yathrib (now Medina; in Arabic, *madinat an-nabi*, "city of the prophet") to leave Mecca. Their journey is called the *Hegira* ("flight" or "migration") and marks year 1 in the Muslim calendar. In Yathrib, Muhammad fought against and ultimately banished or executed his Jewish opponents and their political allies, took control of Yathrib, and built the first Islamic mosque (*masjid*). In 624 citizens of Yathrib defeated opponents from Mecca at Badr, and Muhammad returned to Mecca to rule. His followers destroyed the images of tribal gods in the Kabah and marketplace, and began the institutionalization of

Islam. Muhammad continued to extend Islamic control in Arabia until his death in Yathrib in 632.

Under a succession of secular and theocratic caliphates, Islam swept east and west from Arabia. Muslims reached the Indus River in 713, and most of North Africa was Muslim by the end of the seventh century. Islam's advance in France was stopped in 733 at the Battle of Tours; Muslims remained in Spain until 1492. Islamic armies captured the Byzantine capital of Constantinople in 1453, and controlled much of southeastern Europe until the 19th century. In the east, Muslims swept through India at the end of the 10th century and reached the East Indies in the 15th century.

The arts, architecture, and technology flourished in the golden age of Islam and Islamic learning and culture was responsible for the transmission of much of classical philosophy and science to the West. From the 18th to 20th centuries, many traditionally Islamic countries came under Western cultural and political influence. In the 20th century, some traditionally Islamic countries such as Turkey opted for a secular state; others such as Saudi Arabia and Iran came under strict fundamentalist rule.

Holidays

Id al-Adha (Day of Sacrifice) recalls Abraham's sacrifice of a ram in place of his son; celebrated during 12th lunar month, the month of the Hajj. Id al-Fitr (Day of Breaking the Fast) is observed after the end of Ramadan. Muharram (first month of Muslim year) commemorates Muhammad's migration to Yathrib (Medina); in the Shiite branch, it also commemorates of death of Husayn, son of Muhammad's son-in-law Ali. Muhammad's birthday is celebrated on the 12th day of the third month of the year.

Geography and Numbers

With 1.1 billion adherents in 184 countries, Islam is the second-largest religion in the world. It is the dominant religion throughout the Middle East, North Africa, Central Asia, Afghanistan, Pakistan, and Indonesia, the country with the largest number of adherents (172 million people). There are 104 million Muslims in India—11 percent of that country's population.

Hinduism

Modern Hinduism evolved over the course of many centuries from ancient Vedism, a religion of Indo-European origin dating from the second millennium B.C. if not earlier. The term Hinduism, however, is of relatively recent origin, having been introduced by British scholars in the early 19th century as a way of providing a conceptual framework for thinking about the widely diverse indigenous religious beliefs and practices of India. The term is now widely accepted in India itself to describe India's complex polytheistic religion and philosophy during approximately the past 2000 years. The term also informs the ideology of Hindutva, a modern political concept that regards Hinduism as wholly indigenous to India, and as India's only valid religion and culture.

Scripture

The earliest sacred books of Hinduism are the *Vedas*, which preserve in written form the chants of the priestly class of the *Aryan* ("noble") people, who, in the view of most scholars, brought Vedism to the Indian subcontinent some 4,000 years ago. The *Vedas*, which date to about 1500 B.C., are revered by Hindus as the authoritative source of religious truth, even though they are not widely read by practitioners and are not a common source of guidance in daily life or in religious practice. The four central texts are: the *Rig Veda* ("hymn knowledge"), the oldest and most important of the *Vedas*, consisting of chants to the *Aryan* gods; the *Yajur Veda* ("ceremonial knowledge"), chants to be performed in conjunction with religious ceremonies and sacrifices; the *Sama Veda* ("chant knowledge"), musical elaborations of chants; and the *Atharva Veda* ("knowledge from Atharva," a Vedic teacher), practical and protective charms and chants. In addition to the four core texts, the collective term *Vedas* also commonly encompasses the *Brahmanas* and *Aranyakas*, ceremonial rules appended in later centuries to each of the earlier collections.

Separate from the *Vedas* are the *Upanishads*, a collection of approximately 100 works in prose and poetry written over hundreds of years during the first millennium B.C. Most of the *Upanishads* are in dialogue form and constitute an exploration of basic Hindu philosophical and spiritual concepts, such as *karma* and *samsara*. In contrast to the oldest Vedic texts, which were traditionally restricted to the priestly class, the *Upanishads* insist that spiritual mastery is not limited by hereditary caste status, but is available to all who practice sufficient discipline and meditation. Hinduism evolved from Vedism largely through the influence of the *Upanishads*, which also provided some of the inspiration for the emergence at around the same time of other religions (such as Jainism and Buddhism) with Vedic roots.

Other key Hindu texts include epic mythological poems such as the *Ramayana* (ca. 300 B.C.) and the *Mahabharata* (ca. 200 B.C.). The *Bhagavad Gita*, probably originally an independent text, was incorporated into the *Mahabharata* at an early date, but it is of such great importance it is often printed and studied on its own. Written in dialogue form, it is a key source of teachings on the important questions of action and duty in accordance with one's station in life.

Belief and Practice

Hindu worship is largely an individual or family matter, stressing individual devotions rather than collective worship (except for festivals, in which tens of thousands of people might participate). There are striking regional differences in the relative importance of Hindu gods, the ways in which they are worshipped, and in various other Hindu practices. Still, some basic concepts are common to most Hindu schools and sects, many of which are articulated in the *Upanishads*:

Atman and **Brahman** are often defined as "soul" and "divine spirit," but in the *Upanishads* they carry deeper meanings. *Brahman* is both the source and substance of all existence. Manifested as the individually differentiated "self" of a living being, *brahman* is referred to as *atman*. The ultimate spiritual goal of Hinduism is understanding and experiencing that there is no difference between *atman* and *brahman*, between one's self and the rest of the universe.

Maya is frequently used to describe nature of the world in the *Upanishads*. It is commonly translated as "illusion," but, being derived from a root with the dual connotation of "magic" and "matter," the word's meaning is more complex. The connotation of *maya* is that the world is real and substantial, but that the apparent separation of substance into individual things is illusory. *Maya* implies that the world is of a singular spiritual nature in a constant state of fluctuation and change.

Karma refers to the moral consequences of every act done by an individual in life. *Karma* as such is not inherently good or bad, but on an individual level the experience of the consequences of *karma* might be perceived as good or bad.

Samsara is the Hindu cycle of birth and rebirth in life; a person's path through and rebirth into this cycle is determined by their *karma*.

Dharma refers to one's duty as determined by life circumstances (such as caste status, wealth, and power), and the actions that proceed from that duty. A person's *dharma* might also include devotion to a particular manifestation of a god, or to a particular religious goal. The concept of dharma forms the core teaching of the *Bhagavad Gita*, expressed in a dialogue between Prince Arjuna and his charioteer/adviser, Krishna, on the battlefield of a civil war. Arjuna is reluctant to fight against his rebellious cousins, who are threatening his family's rule. Krishna reveals himself as an incarnation of the god Vishnu and advises Arjuna to act in accordance with his princely role and fight; the dialogue teaches that acting in accordance with one's station in society is a form of worship, and a path to oneness with the universe.

Puja Many Hindus make daily offerings (*puja*, "reverence," "worship") to the gods particularly venerated by the family. A home *puja* typically involves an offering, in front of the home shrine, of lamp- or candle-light, water, incense, and fruit. The word *puja* also refers to more elaborate offerings made at temples, or on special occasions such as beginning a new business venture.

Moksha means "freedom" or "liberation"; breaking free of the endless cycle of *samsara*. One achieves *moksha* by freeing oneself from such selfish traits as egotism and anger, and even losing all sense of one's individuality. *moksha* is the ultimate goal of Hindu practice, achieving the recognition that ones self is inseparable and indistinguishable from *brahman*.

In addition to the spiritual goal of *moksha*, Hindus also believe in the pursuit of worldly goals, including *dharma*, or social and religious duty; *arrha*, or economic security and power; and *kama*, or pleasure.

Caste The traditional Hindu caste system provides a framework for the unfolding of one's *dharma*. The system divides society into four primary, and hundreds of subsidiary, castes defined by occupation and social standing: *brahmins* are the highest, priestly class; *kshatnyas* are warrior-aristocrats who serve as protectors of society; *vaishyas* are merchants, landowners, moneylenders, and some artisans; and *shudras* are laborers. Beyond the caste system are the *dalit*, untouchables or outcasts. India's modern constitution prohibits discrimination on the basis of caste and has abolished the concept of untouchability. This legal disestablishment of the caste system, together with modern trends such as urbanization and social mobility, has accelerated the intermingling and intermarriage of castes. Nevertheless the system is still of great importance in Indian society (for example, many arranged marriages are based in part on considerations of caste) and is particularly important in rural areas and the conservative southern parts of India.

Yoga A *yoga* is an active path to spiritual perfection. The appropriateness of a *yoga* for any individual depends upon life circumstances, including caste and personality type. A *yoga* may also be referred to as a *marga* ("way"). Three are spoken of in the *Upanishads*: *jnana yoga* ("knowledge yoga"), meditation and systematic study of Hindu texts and the teaching of gurus; *karma yoga* ("action yoga"), the unselfish performance of social duties; and *bhakti yoga* ("devotion yoga"), devotion to an external entity, which may be a god, a guru, or even (more rarely) a spouse or parent. A vast number of other yogic traditions have been developed over the centuries, among them *hatha Yoga* ("force yoga") and its many schools, which utilize stretching, breathing, and balancing exercises to achieve spiritual perfection.

Hindu Deities Hinduism has three primary theistic traditions revolving around the cults of anthropomorphic gods. Vishnu is the god embodying the force of preservation; Shiva is the god of destruction; and Brahma represents the creative force. These three are often linked together in the *trimurti*, or "triple form." Hindus also pay tribute to different incarnations of the gods, such as Rama or Krishna, both incarnations of Vishnu. Many (mostly male) Hindu gods also have animal companions and female consorts who represent different forces and may be worshipped in their own right.

Hinduism teaches a deep respect for all living things. Hindu spiritual life includes honoring many animals as manifestations of particular deities, and many Hindus are vegetarians, avoiding the consumption of all meat and meat products. The most revered animal is the cow. The fact that Islam permits the slaughter and eating of cows is often cited as one of the reasons (or at least as providing the occasion) for conflict between Hindus and Muslims. Today, however, many Hindus also eat beef as part of a modern lifestyle.

Schools and Sects

Hinduism comprises myriad religious cults and various schools of philosophy, with no central authoritative body or hierarchy. Schools are differentiated by their adherence to different practices (such as types of *yoga*), or in the case of the devotional Hinduism practiced by the majority of Hindus, by the god or gods to which they pay primary respect. In India today various Hindu nationalist parties and the Hindutva movement are often intolerant of other religions. Many individual Hindus, however, adhere to a principle of religious toleration, not only of the various

forms of Hindu religious practice but for other religions as well. In that view, Christianity, Islam, and other religions can offer alternative paths to the same goal of spiritual cultivation, and at worst they are simply inadequate, rather than wrong or evil.

History

The oldest Hindu writings are Vedic texts associated with a group of invaders (probably from southeastern Europe or somewhere in the region between the Black and Caspian Seas) known as the Aryans, who conquered much of India early in the second millennium B.C. (Hindu fundamentalists associated with the Hindutva movement regard Vedic civilization as wholly indigenous to India, and deny that any invasion took place, despite significant archaeological and linguistic evidence to the contrary.) The invaders also brought with them the caste system, the Sanskrit language, and a family of gods with obvious ties to other European deities (the Aryan father of the gods, Dyaus Pitr, was clearly the same figure as the Roman Jupiter or the Greek Zeus). Over many centuries, the Vedic religion assimilated local customs and folk religions, including the ideas of karma and reincarnation.

The mid- to late first millennium B.C.—the time when many of the *Upanishads*, along with the *Ramayana*, the *Mahabharata*, and the *Bhagavad Gita* were composed—marked a major transformation in Vedism, as ascetics challenged the religion and the power of the priests. Prominent among these reformers were Vardhamana, the founder of Jainism, and Siddhartha Gautama, later known as the Buddha. During this volatile period some Brahman priests propounded the doctrine that there is a *dharma* (duty) for each stage of a person's life. This was an argument, in effect, for social responsibility; among other things it inveighed against the increasingly widespread phenomenon of men abandoning society for a life of religious rigor and austerity. *Eremitism*, in this view, was contrary to *dharma* unless the person had reached an "appropriate" stage of life.

Between the second century B.C. and the fourth century A.D., the classic epics (probably initially composed for oral performance) became stabilized and standardized in written form; cults of Vishnu and Shiva grew in power; and Hinduism spread to southeast Asia. From the fourth to the ninth century, devotional (*bhakti*) Hinduism grew rapidly in popularity as religious leaders adapted their practices to vernacular languages, such as Tamil, rather than the traditional Sanskrit. Beginning with the establishment of the Delhi Sultanate in 1206, a succession of Muslim regimes dominated northern India, and many Hindus in areas that are now Pakistan, Bangladesh, and Kashmir, as well as in northern India itself, willingly or forcibly converted to Islam. Christianity, which had existed in India since the early centuries A.D., became more widespread in the subcontinent in the 19th century, especially under the influence of the British East India Company.

The 19th and 20th centuries also brought the struggle for Indian independence. Many major new leaders and reformers linked the struggle for independence to a revival of Hindu religion and culture. The best known of these leaders was Mohandas Gandhi, the founder of modern India, who brought the Hindu ascetic tradition and the principle of passive resistance (*satyagraha*) to bear on the social and political reform movement in India.

After Independence and the separation of Pakistan from India in 1947, the gulf between the Hindu majority and the large Muslim minority in India widened. Violent clashes continued into the 21st century, especially in the disputed territory of Kashmir. In India, two contradictory trends exist at the same time. On the one hand, Hindu nationalism, inspired in part by fear of and opposition to Islam, has emphasized the links between Hinduism and Indian identity. On the other hand, secularization and urbanization have led to the decline (though by no means the disappearance) of many traditional Hindu practices, and a diminution in the importance of the traditionally privileged priestly class.

Holidays

Because of the vast number of Hindu gods and the variety of schools and practices, there are few holidays common to all Hindus. Some of the more important and widely celebrated festival days include Dipavali, "festival of lights," sacred to Lakshmi, goddess of prosperity; Holi, a spring festival; and Dashara, a harvest festival.

Geography and Numbers

Hinduism has more than 850 million adherents worldwide. With deep roots in India, and lacking a missionary tradition and any widely recognized means of converting from another religion to Hinduism, it is found almost nowhere outside of India and neighboring countries except in expatriate Indian communities.

Buddhism

The central tenets of Buddhism were developed by Siddhartha Gautama, who was born into a royal Hindu family in present-day Nepal around 563 B.C. After observing the suffering of ordinary people in the world, he left home and embarked on a long period of travel, study, and meditation; he eventually experienced enlightenment, earning the name *Buddha*, or "awakened one." He founded an order of monks and taught a philosophy of escape from life's endless cycle of suffering through nonviolence, compassion, and moderate living, until his death in 483 B.C.

Scripture

Of primary importance to all Buddhists is the *Tripitaka*, the "three baskets" or collections of Buddhist thought. These are often treated as the exact words of the Buddha, although most of the texts were not written down by his companions until years after his death. The first "basket" is the *sutras*, teachings of the Buddha in the form of sermons or dialogues; the second is the *vinaya*, or rules of monastic life; and the third is the *abhidharma*, a more systematic presentation of the lessons of the randomly organized sutras. Some schools of Buddhism make use of additional texts: the Mahayana school utilizes new sutras written centuries after the Buddha's death (though maintaining at least the pretense that these sutras represent "recovered" teachings of the Buddha), and Vajrayana Buddhism makes use of Tantric texts as well as the *Tenjur*, a collection of commentaries on a wide range of subjects such as medicine and grammar.

Belief and Practice

Because Buddhism emerged in the midst of Hindu culture, the two religions share many beliefs and concepts, such as ahimsa, or nonviolence, and samsara, the endless cycle of birth and rebirth. The Buddhist nirvana is roughly equivalent to the Hindu *moksha*, a break or escape from samsara (contrary to popular Western usage, it does not represent a spiritual or otherworldly paradise). A key difference between the religions is the Buddhist insistence that nothing is permanent, not even the universal spirit (*Brahman*) and self (*Atman*) of Hindu belief. The key Buddhist concept meaning "no permanent identity" is expressed in Sanskrit as *anatman*, or "no-Atman." The Buddha taught that the universe is constantly changing, and all things will eventually decay and disappear; therefore desire is infinite and insatiable, because nothing can be held on to forever; as a result, peace and enlightenment are only possible through renouncing desire and accepting the impermanence of existence.

In further contrast to the overwhelming complexity and multiplicity of Hindu gods and beliefs, the central truths and teachings of Buddhism—those held in common by practically all schools and sects—are summarized quite simply in the Three Jewels, the Four Noble Truths, and the Noble Eightfold Path:

The Three Jewels   Three things constitute the essential heart of Buddhism: the Buddha, the ideal model to which humans should aspire; the Dharma, or the overall Buddhist worldview and way of life; and the Sangha, or the Buddhist community of monks and nuns.

The Four Noble Truths   The Buddhist worldview is summarized in four simple statements: (1) All life entails suffering; (2) Suffering is caused by desire; (3) Desire can be overcome; and (4) The means for overcoming desire is the Noble Eightfold Path.

The Noble Eightfold Path   These eight steps are meant to be practiced simultaneously rather than consecutively, and together they constitute a systematic method for understanding the universe, living compassionately, and achieving peace and enlightenment. They are: right views, right intentions, right speech, right conduct, right work, right effort, right meditation, and right contemplation. The term *right* may also be interpreted as "true" or "correct" and implies a distinction between the teachings of the Buddha and those of other religions and philosophies.

A hallmark of Buddhist practice has always been the monastic order, although the importance of monastic life—and even the proper interaction of monks with society at large—differs substantially between schools and sects. Buddhist temples are primarily for individual meditation and other forms of individual prayer and worship. Collective rituals play a smaller part in the lives of most Buddhists than they do in the lives of Jews, Christians, Muslims, or Hindus, though the importance of collective rituals in Buddhism varies in different sects.

Schools and Sects

Theravada Buddhism   This form of Buddhism (the name means "Doctrine of the Elders") predominates today in Sri Lanka, Myanmar, Thailand, Laos, and Cambodia and claims to adhere most closely to the tenets of the early Buddhist sects. Special importance is attached to monastic life, and followers maintain a conservative view of the Buddha's teachings. The Theravada ideal is the arhat, a person who has achieved perfect enlightenment and cessation of desire, and so will enter nirvana upon his death. Theravada Buddhism thus places great emphasis on individual religious cultivation within the supportive environment of the monastic community. Theravada monks retain characteristics of Hindu sannyasins, or wandering ascetics, including their characteristic orange or burgundy robes. Because the monks must beg for food, their monasteries are often located in the center of towns instead of remote locations. Theraveda Buddhism is also called Hinayana, "Lesser Vehicle."

Mahayana Buddhism   A defining characteristic of the Mahayana ("Greater Vehicle") school is its focus on compassion for others rather than personal progress toward enlightenment. This is expressed most clearly by the Mahayana ideal of the bodhisattva, or "enlightenment being," a person who, though having attained perfection of enlightenment and cessation of desire, consciously postpones entry into nirvana in order to help others. Mahayana Buddhism is also more liberal than Theravada in its approach to religious practice, which (much as in Hinduism) may include meditation, ritual, sacred objects, or even devotion to a deity, according to one's personality and station in life. This school's many sects account for the majority of Buddhists worldwide. It has been highly influential in China, Korea, and Japan. Many Mahayana schools were first developed in China, and some of those became dominant in the spectrum of Japanese Buddhism.

Among the more significant Mahayana schools to achieve particular prominence in Japan are Shingon (Chinese *zhen'yan*, "true word"), which emphasizes chanted mantras; Jodo (Chinese *qingtu*, "pure land"), a devotional Buddhism for laypeople that offers rebirth into the Western Paradise of Amitabha Buddha, a Bodhisattva of pure compassion; and the Nichiren School, named for its 13th-century founder, which focuses on the creation of a peaceful society on earth and which takes as its fundamental scripture the Lotus Sutra, a Mahayana scripture that predicts the eventual salvation of all sentient beings. Nichiren Buddhism is the basis for the New Religion (see below) known as Soka Gakkai which has succeeded in winning many converts in the West. Zen Buddhism is one of the most widely recognized Mahayana schools; it takes its name from the Japanese pronunciation of the Chinese word *chan* ("meditation," itself a transcription of the Sanskrit word *dhyana*), denoting the seventh step of the Noble Eightfold Path. Zen emphasizes meditation techniques as the most important path to satori, or enlightened experience.

Vajrayana Buddhism   This school, also referred to as Tantric Buddhism, is regularly treated as the third major school of Buddhism, though it shares many features of Mahayana Buddhism and may also be considered a form of Mahayana. Vajrayana Buddhism places great emphasis on ritual, including the use of prayer wheels, mantras (chants), mudras (hand gestures), and mandalas (visible icons of the universe). Music and dance are also often included in Vajrayana ceremonies. Tibetan or Lamaistic Buddhism is a major, and probably the best-known, school of Vajrayana Buddhism; its most important sect is led by the Dalai Lama, who is believed to be the spiritual emanation of Avalokteshvara, the bodhisattva of compassion.

History

In its first few centuries of development, Buddhism benefited greatly from the support of rulers in northeast India, particularly King Asoka the Great of the Maurya dynasty (ruled 269–232 B.C.), who saw the new religion as a way to weaken the powerful Hindu priestly caste. From the second century B.C. to the seventh century A.D., however, Buddhism steadily declined in India as bhakti (devotional) Hinduism grew in popularity; in some cases Hinduism even assimilated Buddhism by portraying the Buddha as an incarnation of the Hindu god Vishnu. Meanwhile Buddhism, particularly in its Theravada form, had spread to Burma and Sri Lanka, and remains the dominant religion in those countries, as well as in Thailand, Laos, and Cambodia.

Buddhism entered China in the first century A.D. and spread to Korea no later than the fourth century, achieving great prominence under the Unified Kingdom of Silla (668–935) and reaching its peak in the Koryo Dynasty (A.D. 918–1392). From Korea Buddhism spread to Japan in the mid-sixth century. Buddhist temples dominated the Japanese capital during the Nara Period (710–785), and Buddhism (augmented from time to time by new sects borrowed from China) became thoroughly assimilated to Japanese life in the ensuing Heian Period (795–1185); it remains an influential part of Japanese culture. In India, Mahayana Buddhism experienced a tremendous revival under the Pala Kings (eighth to 12th century A.D.) but subsequently collapsed along with that dynasty; meanwhile it had spread under Pala influence to Sumatra and Java. Since 1900, however, there has been a resurgence of Buddhism in India, thanks to its adoption by many Indian intellectuals, an influx of displaced Tibetan Buddhists and the mass conversion of hundreds of thousands of Hindu untouchables.

Geography and Numbers

There are an estimated 375 million people in nearly 100 countries who adhere to Buddhist beliefs and practices. Mahayana Buddhists account for about 56 percent of all Buddhists (200 million), mostly in Japan, Korea, and China; Theravada Buddhists account for 38 percent (140 million), in Southeast Asia and Sri Lanka. Lamaist Buddhists account for about 6 percent (20 million) in Tibet and Mongolia. Buddhist practice in Tibet is under threat from the Chinese government.

Other World Religions

Baha'i

Baha'i was founded in Iran in the mid-19th century by Husayn Ali (1817–92), known by followers as *Baha'u'llah* ("Glory of God"), a divine messenger prophesied by the earlier religion of Babism.

Husayn Ali was a devoted follower of Babism, an Iranian religion led by Siyyid Ali Muhammad (1819–50), also known as Bab (meaning "gate" or "door"). Bab claimed to be the last Imam, or hereditary successor of the prophet Muhammad's son Ali; Muslim leaders considered this to be heresy and ultimately executed Bab and persecuted his followers. Husayn Ali was imprisoned and later exiled from Iran, but declared himself in 1863 to be a divine messenger whose coming was foretold by Bab. Baha'i was spread to Europe and North America by Baha'u'llah's son, and expanded rapidly worldwide beginning in the 1960's. Baha'i is still treated as a heretical sect by many Muslims, and persecution of its followers continues in Iran and elsewhere.

A central doctrine of Baha'i is that all of the religions of the world are in agreement and that their respective prophet-founders revealed the will of God in forms appropriate to their particular time and place in history. Baha'i believers advocate a single world government and are staunch supporters of organizations such as the United Nations. There is no priesthood in Baha'i, and worship is often performed at followers' homes; however, there are organized Baha'i assemblies as well as large houses of prayer in several countries. The headquarters is in Haifa, Israel, Baha'u'llah's home in the final years of his life.

Unique Baha'i scriptures include many collections of writings by Baha'u'llah, including the *Kitab-i-Iqan* ("Book of Certainty"), *Kitab-I-Aqdas* ("Book of Holiness"), and *The Hidden Worlds*, a collection of ethical teachings. In addition, Baha'i followers also read from the scriptures of other religions in their worship services.

The Baha'i calendar is unique, comprising 19 months of 19 days each (plus four extra days). The last month of the year is a period of fasting similar to Islam's Ramadan (although it occurs at a fixed time each year, from March 2 through March 20). There are approximately 7 million members of the Baha'i faith in more than 200 countries.

Confucianism

Confucianism takes its name from the sixth-century B.C. scholar and civil servant Kong Qiu or Kongzi ("Master Kong"; sometimes written as Kung Fu-Tzu and Latinized as "Confucius" by 17th-century Jesuit missionaries in China), but he is not the "founder" of Confucianism in the same sense that the Buddha was the founder of Buddhism. Rather, Confucius was responsible for systematizing and teaching a scholarly tradition and code of ethical conduct that had roots hundreds of years in the past, particularly in China's ancient cult of ancestor worship. The teachings of Confucius, as recorded in the *Analects* (the collected teachings of Confucius, written down by disciples over a long period after the Master's death) advocate a humanitarian ethical system focused on five values: *ren* (reciprocal human-feeling); *yi* (righteousness); *li* (propriety, including ritually correct behavior); *zhi* (knowledge); and *xin* (trustworthiness). Collectively these values contribute to the paramount Confucian virtues *xiao* (filial piety); and *wen* (culture or civilization; also civil as opposed to military power).

Confucianism remained primarily a philosophical school of thought and a political ideology for many centuries, but began to develop into more of a religious system (complete with ceremonies, festivals, and temples) in the first century A.D., partially in response to the growing influence of Buddhism in China. Today it is widely viewed in China as an equal part of a religious triad with Buddhism and Taoism (below); Confucius is often portrayed in religious images next to Laozi and the Buddha. There are about 6.3 million self-identified Confucianists in various countries around the world, but in a sense anyone who is culturally Chinese is to some degree a Confucianist.

The Analects of Confucius The *Analects* is one of the 13 works that forms the Confucian canon of classical Chinese literature and philosophy. The Chinese title, *Lunyü*, can be translated as "Discussions and Conversations" or "Assessments and Conversations." The term "Analects" (from the Greek, meaning "literary gleanings") is now conventional; it was first used by Jesuit missionaries in China in the 17th century.

The 20 chapters of the *Analects* purport to record the conversations of the teacher and philosopher Confucius (Kongzi, 551–479 B.C.) with his disciples. Traditionally it was thought that these conversations and teachings were written down from memory by a group of disciples shortly after Confucius's death. Recent scholarship has shown that the chapters are so diverse in both language and doctrine that they cannot have been composed in a short period of time by a small group of collaborators. The current view is that the chapters were composed over a period of more than two centuries, approximately 479–250 B.C., and that the present order of the chapters within the book does not reflect the order in which they were written.

The chapters of the *Analects* can be considered in groups, reflecting their approximate date of composition.

Chapters 4, 5, and 6 These are the work of Confucius' original disciples, dating to about 479–460 B.C. They emphasize the cardinal virtue of *ren* ("reciprocal human feeling"), the *dao* (the "Way," the natural order of things), the concept of the gentleman (*junzi* or "son of a prince," but in Confucius's radical reformulation, defined by conduct rather than by aristocratic birth), and the importance of putting one's cultivation of virtue into practice by holding public office. These chapters begin to define Confucianism as a coherent "school" of teachings.

Chapters 7, 8, and 9 These derive from the disciples' disciples, and date to the last half of the fifth century B.C. They continue to define the school's doctrines and portray Confucius as a "transmitter, not an innovator," guided by the enlightened example of the sage-rulers of antiquity and emphasizing the internalization of values and virtuous conduct.

Chapters 2, 3, 10, 11, 12, and 13 The mid-fourth century (roughly 380–320 B.C.) chapters introduce ritual (*li*, a word covering meanings from the correct conduct of religious rituals to ordinary social etiquette) as a key Confucian virtue, and speak, as the earlier chapters do not, about Heaven and the realm of spirits. Individual passages specifically engage in debate with other philosophical schools of the time.

Chapters 1, 14, 15, 16, 17, 18, 19, and 20 Dating to the late fourth to mid- third century B.C., these final chapters reflect a world of escalating warfare in which the *Analects* struggles to define the role of the public official. By the mid-third century B.C. it appeared that the Confucian school had been soundly defeated; but not much more than a century later, early in the early imperial era, Confucianism made a decisive recovery, becoming the basis for China's official ideology for the next two millennia.

Druze Community

The Druze community (also called Muwahhiddun, "unitarians") originated in Egypt in 1017, when Hamza ibn Ali, leader of a heretical sect of Ismaili Shiite Muslims, declared that the present Caliph, al-Hakim, was the sole, ubiquitous and timeless incarnation of God. After al-Hakim's death Hamza developed the main doctrinal lines of the Druze faith in a series of letters to the community. Hamza also moved the main center of the community to Greater Syria and entrusted it to a series of five leaders ("missionaries") who were considered embodiments of cosmic principles. The Druze believe in human reincarnation and in the return of al-Hakim in human form some time in the future, an event that will bring to a close the present age and inaugurate a new messianic era.

The Druze community remains a vital presence in Lebanon, Syria, Jordan, and Israel, but in modern times its adherents have been subject to occasional persecution by both Muslims and Maronite Christians.

Jainism

Jainism is a polytheistic religion established in India by Nataputta Vardhamana (known as Mahavira, or "great man") in the sixth century B.C. Jainism shares many features of Buddhism, including the principle of ahimsa (nonviolence), although its practitioners are generally committed to a more austere way of living than Buddhists. Important practices include devotional acts toward Jainist saints (*tirthankaras*), fasting, and pilgrimages to various temples. There are four major Jainist branches, each of which adheres to a different set of scriptures. Almost all of the world's 4.2 million Jainists live in India.

Native American Religions

The Native American religions of North America have deep historical roots, with a wide range of beliefs about the natural and spirit worlds and highly developed ceremonial practices. Native American tribal religions practiced today include those of the Navajo, with chant complexes; the Lakota, with seven sacred ceremonies; the Iroquis Longhouse religion; and many others. Some beliefs and practices, such as the Sun Dances of the Great Plains, are shared by more than one tribe. The largest organized inter-tribal religion is the Native American Church ("peyote church"), dating to the 19th century. In Saturday all-night rituals incorporating prayer, singing and contemplation around an earth altar and fire, the psychoactive peyote cactus is used sacramentally; this religion includes both tribal and Christian elements. While many ancient Native American religious practices continue today, the lack of careful recording in the early days of European exploration means that the pre-contact forms of most Native American religions are difficult to retrieve completely.

Shintoism

Shinto (literally "way of the gods") evolved from ancient Japanese religious traditions that focused on the worship of kami, spirits who created the world and continue to inhabit the islands of Japan. Many kami are identified with forces of nature, such as wind or fire, or with specific individual trees, mountains, lakes, and other natural features. Deceased people also become minor kami, and are venerated by their descendants. Although some Shinto texts date from the eighth century, none is considered authoritative; Shinto is largely a religion of practice rather than doctrine or scripture, and places particular emphasis on worshipping the gods in a state of physical and ritual purity. Shinto underlies many Japanese folk festivals, and is the spiritual basis of the national sport of sumo wrestling. Shintoism became a state religion during the reign of the Meiji emperor in the 19th century, and the emphasis of state Shinto on the divinity of the Japanese emperor contributed to the country's destructive imperialist nationalism before and during World War II. State Shinto was repudiated (along with the emperor's claim to divine status) in the postwar period, but remains controversial in such manifestations as official visits to Tokyo's Yasukuni Shrine, where the spirits of Japan's war dead are venerated. Today Shrine Shinto is the dominant strain of Shinto practice in Japan, while Folk Shinto remains locally important in rural areas. There are also many sects and offshoots of Shinto, some of which are considered to fall within the family of New Religions (see below). Because Shinto is intimately associated with the Japanese nation itself, and contains no provisions for missionary activity or conversion, virtually all Shinto believers are Japanese, and almost all of them live in Japan.

Sikhism

The Sikh ("learner") religion was founded by Guru Nanak in the early 16th century. A monotheistic religion that draws on both Hindu and Islamic beliefs, it advocates a search for eternal truth and, while believing in reincarnation, rejects the notion of divine incarnation. It was led by a succession of 10 gurus, the last of whom declared himself the last human guru. Sikhs now follow the sacred text known as *Guru Granth Singh*, or Collection of Sacred Wisdom. There are nearly 24 million Sikhs in the world; most of them live in the Punjab region of India, but there are significant Sikh immigrant communities in the United States, Canada, and Great Britain.

Taoism

The legendary founder of Taoism (also spelled Daoism) is Laozi (old spelling Lao Tzu; probably a wholly mythical figure but traditionally dated ca. 600 B.C.), whose name means "old master." According to tradition, he is the sole author of the core Taoist text, the *Daodejing* (old spelling *Tao Te Ching* "The Way and its Power"). Modern scholarship has established, however, that the book is a work of anonymous, and probably multiple, authorship from the late fourth century B.C. The *Daodejing*, also known as the *Book of Laozi*, is a collection of 81 brief, poetic chapters that discuss, often through challenging paradoxes, the nature of the Dao (Tao), the source and essence of all being. An eponymous collection of writings by Zhuangzi (old spelling Chuang Tzu; ca. 300 B.C.) is another important Taoist text. From the beginning, Taoism included elements of both religion and philosophy. It advocated a political ideal of simplicity and austerity, with the state being ruled by a sage-king empowered by his complete oneness with the Dao itself to act with wu-wei, or nonintentionality: effortlessly effecting his actions while seeming to do nothing. Self-cultivation was central to early Daoist practice, with sagehood and immortality its religious goals.

Beginning in the third century A.D., undoubtedly under the influence of Buddhism, Taoism took on more of the overt trappings of organized religion and gave rise to various sects through divine revelations granted to their founders. The two most important sects, the Heavenly Masters Sect and the Highest Clarity Sect, organized networks of temples, ordained clergy and were governed by hereditary leaders. These sects remain a vital part of religious life in Taiwan and in many overseas Chinese communities, and are experiencing a dramatic revival in post-Mao China, and have thousands of active priests serving hundreds of temples.

Folk Religions

Worldwide, hundreds of millions of people believe in and participate in the rituals of what are known as "folk religions." While the term is a loose and elastic one, it generally implies a faith that draws selectively on disparate traditions, has little or no formal organization beyond the level of individual communities or congregations, and lacks a highly developed written canon or formal theology. Some splinter groups of mainstream religions (such as Pentecostal snake-handling congregations) can be considered to fall into the category of folk religions.

Chinese folk religions consist of a blend of ancient ancestor worship with elements of Buddhism, Confucianism, and Taoism and the worship of particular deities. One of the most important of these folk religions, widespread in the coastal provinces of southeastern China as well as on Taiwan and in overseas Chinese communities in Southeast Asia, involves the worship of the Queen of Heaven (Tian Hou, also known as Mazu, "Mother Ancestor"), venerated as the protector goddess of mariners. There are many other Chinese folk religions, often devoted to a single deity or a particular type of religious practice; these sects range in size from single temples with a few hundred believers to large denominations with hundreds of temples and tens of thousands of believers. The vast majority of believers in Chinese folk religions live in China, the rest in scattered Chinese communities around the world.

New World folk religions African religious beliefs, especially those of the Yoruba people who now live in West Africa in Nigeria and Benin, were brought to the New World with the slave trade. These traditions mixed with Catholicism in various Caribbean and South American countries to produce new syncretic religions. Among these are Voodoo, developed in Haiti, which blends beliefs from Dahomey, the Yoruba people, and the Bakongo with French Catholicism; Santeria, developed in Cuba, synthesizing Yoruba traditions and Spanish Catholicism, and Candomblé, found in Brazil, melding Yoruba beliefs, Portuguese Catholicism, and native Brazilian religious elements.

New Religions

The term *new religion* applies to a variety of more or less organized religious systems that grew up in the 19th and 20th centuries. New religions are distinguished from folk religions in that they usually have a known founder and a written body of scripture. These religions are also often characterized by a synthesis of various Asian traditions (Hinduism, Buddhism, Confucianism, and Taoism) with modern Western religion, philosophy, mysticism, and spirituality. The number of adherents of new religions worldwide is unknown, but probably rises into the hundreds of millions. Some of the most widely known of these religions include:

Cao Dai Founded by Ngo Van Chieu (1878–1926) in Vietnam, Cao Dai followers believe that all religions teach essentially the same path to spiritual perfection, but that Cao Dai offers the clearest revelation of God's truth. Cao Dai borrows many features from Buddhism (vegetarianism, avoidance of alcohol and drugs) and Confucianism (self-cultivation and learning), but also has a rigid power structure based on Catholicism, complete with a pope, cardinals, and a headquarters called the Holy See, located near Ho Chi Minh City. It is also unusual in that it includes Winston Churchill, Victor Hugo, and the Chinese leader Sun Yat-sen among its pantheon of saints.

Falun Gong Founded by Li Hongzhi (b. China 1951), and based on Qigong, exercises derived from Chinese martial arts, and meditation, it is part of a continuum of generally similar religious movements stretching back to the Yellow Turban and Five Pecks of Rice movements in the Latter Han Dynasty (second century A.D.) and the White Lotus sect that surfaced as an ideology of peasant rebellion from the 14th to the 19th centuries. The name means "law-wheel energy" and refers to the *falun*, a spiritual wheel in the abdomen that, when spinning in one direction, absorbs energy from the universe; when spinning in other direction, it releases energy to the practitioner and others. Li Hongzhi moved to the U.S. in 1996; Falun Gong is now practiced worldwide but is banned in China.

International Society for Krishna Consciousness ("Hari Krishnas") A neo-Hindu religion founded in the United States in 1965 by the Indian Hindu missionary (itself an anomalous concept within Hinduism) Abhay Charan De (1896–1977). It has succeeded in winning many converts among young people in America and Europe; Hari Krishnas in their pink robes have become a familiar sight in public places throughout the Western world, drumming, dancing, and chanting in praise of Lord Krishna.

Neo-Paganism Refers to a variety of practices based on nature-based religions of early European cultures. One of the best-known is Wicca. Both male and female practitioners may refer to themselves as witches, but contrary to popular misconceptions, Wicca is not Satan worship. Other Neo-Pagan groups include the Druids, whose beliefs and practices represent a supposed revival of Celtic religion practiced in the British Isles and France two thousand years ago, and Goddess Worship, which attempts to revive the religion of the Mother Goddess of prehistoric times (exemplified by paleolithic so-called Venus statues). The cult of the Goddess aims at recovering an era of matriarchy prior to the development of aggressive, patriarchal societies.

Rastafarianism Refers to a group of related movements taking their name from Ethiopian nobleman Ras Tafari (1891–1975), later known as that country's Emperor Haile Selassie and worshipped as a divine being. Rastafarians believe the Bible carries special messages for people of African descent, and encourages them to free themselves from any form of oppression. Because of its focus on the Bible, Rastafarian belief and practice shares many features of Christianity and Judaism: the Rastafarian God is known as Jah (related to Yahweh and Jehovah); the practice of allowing one's hair to grow in dreadlocks is related to the biblical prohibition, followed by Orthodox Jews, against the cutting of hair on the side of a male's head; and many Rastafarians follow dietary restrictions based on Hebrew law, including the avoidance of pork and shellfish. A unique component of Rastafarianism is the use of *ganja* (marijuana) as a sacramental herb.

Soka Gakkai "Value Creation Society" founded by Makiguchi Tsunesaburo as an organization to enhance the role of Buddhist values in Japanese society and associated from the beginning with the Nichiren School of Japanese Buddhism, it became an independent religious group in 1937. In Japan it became highly influential in the post–World War II period through its political arm, the Komeito ("Clean Government Party"). Under the leadership of Ikeda Daisaku (b. 1928), Soka Gakkai became an international movement, gaining converts in the United States, Europe, and elsewhere. Its principal devotional practice is chanting the mantra *namu myoho renge kyo* ("praise to the wonderful law of the lotus").

Theosophy   This ancient Greek Christian term ("divine wisdom") was revived in the 19th century by Mme. Helena Blavatsky (1831–91) and others for a new religion (the Theosophical Society, 1875) based on mysticism, spiritualism, and an eclectic mix of philosophies. Theosophy teaches that established religions exemplify the enduring truths of Theosophy, but in attenuated form; that there is an enduring spiritual realm beyond the manifest world , which can with appropriate practices be called upon directly; and that it is possible for practitioners to attain extraordinary spiritual gifts. Theosophy in the 20th century became increasingly associated with Indian philosophy, religious beliefs, and practices such as yoga.

Unification Church (Korean *Tongilgyo*) is a new religion founded in Korea by the Reverend Sun-myung Moon (b. 1920). Unification Church is largely based on Christianity, but modified by new interpretations of the Bible divinely revealed to Rev. Moon. Members of the Unification Church are expected to live highly disciplined lives within the organization and to be obedient in all things to the founder and members of the church hierarchy; mass weddings of couples selected for each other by the church are perhaps the most conspicuous practice of the sect in the eyes of the outside world. The Unification Church's cultlike aspects have given rise to the derisive nickname "Moonies" for its adherents.

Atheism

An estimated 85 percent of the world's population claims to be adherents of an organized religion. Of the remaining 15 percent, about 12 percent (816 million people) are either agnostic—i.e. they are not sure God exists—or are simply indifferent to religion, while 156 million people (2.3 percent of the world population) are declared atheists who do not believe in God or gods. In the United States roughly 16 percent of adults either profess no religion or directly claim that they are atheists.

Throughout history anyone making a public declaration that they do not believe God or the gods exist have been treated harshly and often violently. Even today in most Western countries, but especially in the United States, anyone interested in running for public office who claims to be an atheist will never gain any meaningful support. And yet the Western intellectual traditions that question the existence of powerful gods who interject themselves into earthly activities and even the fates of men and women date back some 2,500 years to ancient Greece. In the 6th century B.C. the pre-Socratic philosophers, including Thales and Anaximander, viewed the natural world, our world, as the only basis for examining everything from the properties of water to how the heavens change. This approach to learning and understanding the world is known as *rationalism* which is based on inductive reasoning, or reaching conclusions from observation of nature or of human behavior.

In the 5th century B.C., Thucydides, a prominent military commander in the Peloponnesian War, wrote a history of that war in which he specifically denied the gods any power over the men and events during that conflict. This approach was so radically different from the work of Herodotus that a new form of history based on reason as opposed to myth was created, one that would eventually become the norm. In the 4th century B.C. Plato described how his mentor, Socrates, denied that our understanding of what is good or moral depended on the gods, that humans in fact know what is moral behavior from their own experiences. Epicurus would follow later in the century and over his long life develop a thoroughly materialistic view of the world that would become highly influential in both the Hellenistic period and later during the Roman Empire. Although he never publicly denied the existence of the gods he raised questions about the fears they caused humans, producing anxiety about death. He was also among the first to raise the question of evil in the world despite the existence of gods. He concluded that the gods might exist but surely they had no concern for human affairs.

Although the Greek tradition of learning and thinking would remain influential during the long rule of the Roman Empire, paying homage to the gods was periodically demanded, especially as Christianity grew popular. More than a thousand years would pass from the time of Plato and Aristotle until a rebirth in learning led to the beginning of a reason-based scientific revolution in the 16th and 17th centuries. During the Middle Ages the rise of the Roman Catholic Church to absolute control over what constituted acceptable religious belief stymied western initiatives in both philosophy and scientific inquiry. Ironically the first serious challenge to orthodox religious teaching about the nature of the heavens came from Copernicus, a Polish cleric and scholar who claimed that the Sun was the center of our universe, not the Earth. His treatise was dedicated to the pope but not published until he was on his deathbed in 1543, at the height of the Protestant revolt against the Roman Church. This work had a profound influence on the three founders of modern astronomy, Tycho Brahe, Johannes Kepler, and most of all Galileo Galilei. In 1610 Galileo's newly invented telescope allowed him to confirm the Copernican view of a heliocentric universe and he enthusiastically published his findings. But Galileo was silenced by Church authorities in 1633 and forced to recant his views, at least in public.

Nevertheless the scientific method of inquiry was now firmly established and no religious prohibition could stop the forward movement toward greater knowledge of the universe, the Earth, and human life itself. The influence of the Protestant Reformation in this development cannot be overestimated since during the 16th and 17th centuries the intellectual struggle between faith and reason became more clearly defined. England's renowned scholar Sir Francis Bacon argued for *empiricism*—learning by observation of the world. The French mathematician René Descartes, countered that since our senses often deceive us it was necessary to start from within ourselves to discover truth. His famous dictum, "Cogito, ergo sum" ("I think, therefore I am") became the basis for the Cartesian school of philosophy which would be influential for over two centuries. Descartes's rigorous arguments to prove that God exists have remained critical for intellectual believers even today.

From the end of the 17th century and beyond, however, the secular challenges to religion as a source of knowledge never ceased. Isaac Newton, a devout Christian believer, brought a vastly deeper understanding of how the universe functions while the Scots philosopher David Hume studied human knowledge from a distinctly rational viewpoint and in England, Thomas Hobbes and John Locke did the same for human behavior under a variety of government structures. In France the 18th century movement we call The Enlightenment was also rooted in rationalist thinking. In Paris a group of intellectuals led by Voltaire and Denis Diderot produced the first encyclopedia which they claimed was based on rational and secular values. The *Encyclopédie* consisting at first of 28 volumes was published in 1772 and was an immediate success. Many of these *philosophes* were atheists, although not all of them professed their non-belief in public; some were deists who believed a supreme being existed but took no part in human affairs.

Toward the end of the French Revolution the negative influence of the *philosophes* would be seen in the establishment of atheism as a principle all citizens were forced to embrace. During the so-called "Terror" phase when thou-

sands of innocent people were executed, the denial of God's existence was seen as a cause of the slaughter. A half-century later the famous Russian novelist Fyodor Dostoevsky would have one of the Karamazov brothers declare that "without God anything is permitted." This argument for God's existence remains prominent even today as the atrocities committed under godless Nazism can never be erased. Non-believers, however, respond that the many wars fought by Christians, Muslims, and Hindus over 2,000 years or more indicate that religious people are capable of bringing death and destruction to the world.

With the coming of the Industrial Revolution in the 19th century the patterns of everyday life were transformed in a matter of decades. As people left farms and villages and started working in factories and mines their lives became totally dependent on the owners, the people with abundant financial resources. Ethereal arguments such as Kant's about the nature of morality or of Hegel's study of Mind soon became irrelevant to a wide circle of thinkers whose focus was firmly on how people were forced to live under the new emerging economic system. Radicals such as the French anarchist Pierre-Joseph Proudhon, who famously wrote in 1840 that "Property is theft," and the German Ludwig Feuerbach, had far greater influence during their lifetimes than Kant, Hegel, or Kierkegaard.

The young Karl Marx was strongly influenced by Feuerbach's idea that civilization was crippled by religion, especially Christianity. As he developed his own beliefs about the material nature of life, Marx claimed that organized religion's concept of God was an "opiate" that kept ordinary people from facing the hard facts about their lives. Of course Marx would go on to construct a philosophy of history and a penetrating analysis of how the capitalist system works that would have worldwide influence.. At the core of his thinking, however, was the denial of the existence of any outside divine power that shaped history and human lives. Marx was not alone in this viewpoint and soon gathered thousands of followers who worked to achieve worker solidarity against what they regarded as capitalist oppression.

Less militant but still extremely influential, John Stuart Mill wrote several works that are read more today than at any other time. In both *On Liberty* (1859) and *The Subjection of Women* (1869) he argued for a freer more equitable society based on the utilitarian view that human actions should aim to foster happiness. This empirical view of the world was revealed after his death when his *Three Essays on Religion* was published. Here he criticized religion for promulgating the idea that God is benevolent and all-powerful when the evidence of human suffering is so manifest in the world. He also proposed a new religion, "The Religion of Humanity."

By the end of the 19th century, philosophical thinking had clearly moved strongly into the empiricist's camp. The many successful scientists of this period, whose basic method of inquiry was empiricism, could not avoid being dragged into the debate over God's existence. The most famous of them was Charles Darwin whose theory of evolution (first published in 1859) presented a formidable challenge to the teachings of the Bible concerning the creation of human life and the age of planet Earth. Darwin himself was a devout Christian schooled in the traditions of biblical scholarship but he eventually claimed not to believe in the divinity of Christ. In his later life he called himself an agnostic, not an atheist.

The immediate impact of Darwin's book, *On the Origins of Species*, put religious belief on the defensive forcing believers to scrutinize the evidence that made their faith in the Bible seem preposterous. The long-term consequence was the emergence of empiricism as the dominant mode of inquiry, a position it has not relinquished.

Friederich Nietzsche's proclamation that "God is Dead" reverberated throughout the 20th century since his death in 1900. A continuous critic of Christianity, his declaration was meant to be about the death of belief and its consequences. Nietzsche's atheism was partly based on his conviction that people wanted power and riches and not the humble good citizens' religion taught as the model. He urged people to seek new beginnings and to use their will to achieve their goals. Although his influence was widespread at the turn of the century, much of his thought was easily seized on by the Nazis 30 years after his death and for decades thereafter his work was either ignored or misconstrued.

In the early 20th century, however, Sigmund Freud and the great mathematician, Bertrand Russell, acknowledged their debt to Nietzsche and both publicly declared their disbelief in God: according to Russell, "Religion is something left over from the infancy of our intelligence, it will fade away as we adopt reason and science as our guidelines;" Freud called religion "the universal obsessional neurosis of humanity." They would be joined in later years by famous writers, philosophers and scientists including Virginia Woolf, Albert Camus, John Paul Sartre, and Richard Feynman.

In recent years the staying power of the conflict between believers and atheists has been demonstrated numerous times. In the United States several school boards have outlawed the teaching of evolution in public schools or promulgated the "intelligent design" theory and the statements in the Bible that God created the world in seven days about 10,000 years ago. More dramatically, the famous writer, Salman Rushdie was condemned for expressing his atheism by the religious leaders of Iran who issued a *fatwa* allowing any Muslim to kill him. And the mastermind of the 9/11 attacks, Osama bin Laden declared war on atheism and its primary home, the United States.

Despite such violent threats the intellectual underpinnings of atheism continued to develop. Several well-known and respected scientists have written attacks on religion that have sold extremely well, including Richard Dawkins (*The God Delusion*, 2006), Daniel C. Dennett (*Breaking the Spell*, 2006), and Sam Harris (*The End of Faith*, 2005; and *Letter to a Christian Nation*, 2006). The polemicist, Christopher Hitchens, led the attack from a humanist perspective in *God Is Not Great* (2007) in which he argues in part that the unspeakable violence committed by forces of religion in the name of God reveals the hollowness of belief.

Glossary of Religious Terms

adhan call to prayer (Isl.)

agnosticism belief that the existence of God can be neither proved nor disproved

ahimsa nonviolence to living things (Hind., Bud., Jain.)

animism belief that animals and other common objects possess souls, or are inhabited by other supernatural entities

Annatta/Anatman "no-Atman" (see Hinduism); the nonexistence of an individual soul (Bud.)

arhat "perfect being," or one who has attained nirvana (Bud.)

ashram religious retreat (Hind.)

atheism absence of belief in God

Atman divine spirit common to all living things (Hind., Bud.)

avatar earthly manifestation of Hindu deity (Hind.)

Ayatollah leader of Shiite sect; teacher and judge (Isl.)

baptism immersion in water to symbolize cleansing of sins, admission into church (Chr.)

bhakti acts of devotion (esp. to deity) (Hind.)

bodhi enlightenment (Bud.)

Brahman source and substance of universe (Hind.)

bushido spiritual code of samurai class

caliph literally, "successor"; a religious and political leader claiming succession from Muhammad (Isl.)

canon religious doctrine; authoritative religious texts

caste social and religious division of hindu society (Hind.)

dharma spiritual and social obligations (Hind., Bud.)

dhyana meditation (Hind., Bud.)

ecumenical pertaining to Christian church as a whole

Eucharist Holy Communion, the Christian ceremony of sharing bread and wine, variously understood as representing, or as being transformed into, the body and blood of Christ

fatwa an authoritative judgement in Islamic law (Isl.)

hadith an authoritative "recollection" of Muhammad's teachings (Isl.)

hajj pilgrimage to Mecca (Isl.)

Imam leader of the Muslim community; may also be used as honorary title for prayer leader in mosque (Isl.)

jihad "struggle," both as a personal struggle to lead a faithful and pure life, and the collective struggle to defend and expand the world of Islam. (Isl.)

karma law of moral cause-and-effect, determining one's path through cycle of rebirth (Hind., Bud.)

koan mysterious or paradoxical story or question intended to spark enlightened thought by disrupting flow of everyday, logical thought (Bud.)

kosher "ritually correct," pertaining to dietary laws of Judaism (Jud.)

Lama monk or priest (Bud.)

mandala complex, ritually powerful design used in temples and other Buddhist art (Bud.)

mantra word or sound used to facilitate meditation (Hind., Bud.)

midrash nonliteral explanation of Jewish scripture

moksha "liberation" or release from cycle of rebirth and everyday suffering (Hind.)

muezzin person who calls Muslims to prayer (Isl.)

Mullah title for teacher of religious law (Isl.)

nirvana escape from cycle of rebirth (Bud.)

pantheism worship of all gods; belief that God exists in all things in the universe

polytheism worship of more than one god

sacrament religious rite that confers divine grace on the practitioner

samadhi transcendental union of individual with the object of their meditation (Bud.)

samsara cycle of birth and rebirth (Hind., Bud.)

sangha worldwide community of Buddhists; also monastic order founded by the Buddha (Bud.)

satori enlightenment (Bud.)

shari'ah Koranic law and regulations (Isl.)

Shiite smaller of two branches of Islam; defining belief is that succession of Islamic leaders should descend from Ali, son-in-law of the prophet Muhammad (Isl.)

Sunni larger of the two main branches of Islam; invests the Koran and the hadiths with exclusive religious authority (Isl.)

sura a chapter of the Koran (Isl.)

Tao the "Way" of spiritual awareness and enlightenment

Ummah the entire community of believers in Islam

Yin and Yang two opposite but complementary forms of cosmic energy, present in different proportions in all things

yoga spiritual practice or discipline, involving any number of different techniques (physical, philosophical, or devotional) to achieve higher awareness (Hind.)

The Bible

The Bible (Greek *biblia*, books) contains the fundamental texts of the Jewish and Christian religions. The product of a long history of oral and written tradition reaching back to the second millennium B.C., the Bible has been one of the most influential books in history, shaping the religion, literature, and politics of much of the world for two millennia. It has been translated into numerous languages and has been a source of history, religion, and guidance for hundreds of millions of people.

Since the rise of Christianity in the early first millennium A.D., the Bible has been divided into two parts to reflect the Christian belief that humankind's relationship to God was changed by Jesus Christ. The Old Testament, which contains the Jewish scriptures, tells the story of the creation of the world and how the first man and woman disobeyed God and were cast out of the Garden of Eden; it describes the history of the Hebrew people and their relation to God over more than a thousand years. The New Testament includes narratives of the life, ministry, death, and resurrection of Jesus, stories about his followers, and letters to young churches. It emphasizes Jesus' message of justice and love, and asserts his divinity as the Son of God.

The Hebrew Bible The Hebrew Bible dates, in its earliest parts, to before 1000 B.C. and includes material composed as late as the second century B.C. It contains the holy writings of the Jewish people, who developed a monotheistic religion in which they are the chosen people of God who has made a covenant with them. The Hebrew Bible consists of 24 books divided into three sections: the Law (Torah), the first 5 books; the Prophets (Nevi'im); and Writings (Ketuvim). (See *World Religions*.) In their present form the scriptures are believed to have passed through a long history of oral tradition before being written down in Hebrew with a few passages in Aramaic. The standard Hebrew Bible is called the Masoretic or "transmitted," text (MT).

The Septuagint Beginning in the third century B.C., the Hebrew Bible was translated into Greek to serve the extensive communities of Greek-speaking Jews in the Eastern Mediterranean. Known as the Septuagint, Greek for "seventy," a reference to the number of writers said to have been engaged in its translation, it is referred to by the Latin number seventy, LXX. Differing from the standard Hebrew bible, it includes additional books and sections of books and is partly based on alternative textual sources.

The Old Testament The Septuagint was not only the bible of Greek-speaking Jews, it was also the bible used in the early Christian church. After the Hebrew Bible became standardized about 100 A.D., Jews turned away from the Septuagint; its preservation in various versions resulted largely from its use by the Christian church. The Septuagint was translated into Latin and other languages and it is often the text to which the New Testament writers refer in connecting the story of Jesus' life to earlier events. The Old Testament of the Roman Catholic Church is based on its books and their order. The Septuagint was first referred to as the Old Testament (by contrast with the New Testament) by Tertullian (ca. 160–230 A.D.) and Origen (ca. 185–254 A.D.) The books in the Septuagint not included in the standard Hebrew Bible are referred to as the Apocrypha (Greek, "hidden") or as the deuterocanonical books, i.e. those added secondarily, or later, to the canon.

At the time of the Reformation, Martin Luther, John Calvin, and others decided that the proper Old Testament was not the entire book derived from the Septuagint, but rather the shorter and older Hebrew Bible. The Protestant Old Testament now contains, in translation, the text of the Hebrew Bible, but the order of the books is that of the Septuagint. The deuterocanonical books and parts of books in the Roman Catholic Old Testament were dropped from the Protestant

Old Testament; these are reprinted in many (but not all) Protestant Bibles as the Apocrypha. The Apocrypha are deemed by many Protestants to be worthy of consideration, but of less authority than the books in the Hebrew Bible.

The New Testament The New Testament consists of 27 books, all written in Greek in the first and second centuries (even though Jesus and his early followers spoke Aramaic); the books were first listed as the New Testament by Bishop Athanasius of Alexandria in A.D. 367. The canonical order of the books is that of the Council of Carthage, A.D. 397. Both Protestant and Roman Catholic churches accept the same books of the New Testament, although Martin Luther and others held some of the New Testament books to be less authoritative. The four Gospels (meaning "good news"), each attributed to one of Christ's earliest followers, tell stories of Jesus' birth, baptism, teaching, death, and resurrection. The story of the spread of Christianity in the first century is told in the Acts of the Apostles and the epistles (letters) of St. Paul and other followers of Jesus. These writings also present early statements of Christian belief.

English Translations of the Bible The Bible has been the subject of numerous translations into English and many other languages. In the late fourth and early fifth centuries A.D. St. Jerome, translating the Old Testament from the Hebrew, provided a standard Latin text of the Bible called the Vulgate or "common text." The earliest complete English Bible was that of John Wycliffe (1324–1384) in 1382. In 1526 the New Testament of William Tyndale (1484–1536) was published. (Both Wycliffe and Tyndale were executed for their efforts to make the Bible available to the common people.) The most famous of English Bibles is the King James Version. In 1604 James I of England approved a new translation of the Bible to replace two others in use, the Geneva Bible and the Bishops' Bible. Fifty-four translators were organized into six groups: three for the Old Testament, two for the New Testament, and one for the Apocrypha. Rules were drawn up to guide the work, and the entire new translation was ready in 1611; for the New Testament especially it draws heavily on Tyndale's translation. The King James Version, noted for its powerful language, has remained in use, although replaced in many churches by newer versions, since its publication.

In modern times, many new translations have appeared. A revision of the King James Version was published in England in 1885, with an American version in

1901. The Revised Standard Version was published 1946–1957. The New English Bible, a new translation rather than a revision of previous translations, was published 1970. The first Roman Catholic Bible in English completely translated from original Hebrew and Greek sources, the New American Bible, was published in 1970. The Good News Bible (American Bible Society) appeared in 1970, the New Revised Standard Version in 1990, and the evangelical New Living Translation in 1996. It can be expected that new translations will continue to appear because of the availability of new early manuscripts, because of the changing English language, and for doctrinal reasons.

The Bibles used today have elements to ease their use that are not in older Bibles and original manuscripts. The present chapter divisions are attributed to Cardinal Hugo de San Caro, 1248; verse divisions in the New Testament are attributed to Robert Estienne (Stephanus), 1551. Most of the punctuation and some paragraphing is modern.

The Bible as it is known today represents only a small proportion of the religious literature produced during Old and New Testament times. There is a vast sea of extra-canonical writings and different versions of canonical books, some known for centuries, some discovered more recently, such as the Dead Sea Scrolls (discovered 1947–1956 and shedding light on Judaism, the languages of Palestine and the transmission of Old Testament texts), and no doubt others yet to be discovered. For the New Testament there are noncanonical (apocryphal) writings of many types, generally of a later date then the New Testament books, such as gospels (The Gospels of Judas, Mary, Paul, Peter, Philip, and others), acts (The Acts of Andrew and others), letters, and apocalypses. Among the manuscripts studied extensively that provide information on the piety and practices of early Christians is the Gospel of Thomas, found at Nag Hammadi, Egypt, in 1945; this is a collection of 114 sayings attributed to Jesus.

Some texts contain apcryphal stories of Jesus' childhood. In one tale, the young Jesus is playing with other children on a rooftop, when one boy falls from the roof and dies. Jesus raises his playmate from the dead. In another story, Jesus makes clay sculptures of birds. He speaks to them, and the the birds become alive and fly away.

The Books of the Bible

Old Testament The Old Testament includes narrative histories, law, prayers, proverbs, poems, and wisdom literature. Some of this probably dates to before 1000 B.C. in written form; the latest material, part of Daniel, dates from the second century B.C. Much of the Old Testament is based on oral traditions, which takes the timeline even further back. Most of the books are of uncertain authorship, although they are by tradition attributed to Moses, the prophets, kings and other authors. The books went through a long series of redactions and often date in their canonical forms from long after the times of their presumed authors. Moreover, there is relatively little archaeological and independent textual evidence corroborating the historical narratives in the Old Testament for the earliest times, so that the historical reliability of these is uncertain. Nonetheless, the Old Testament has for Jewish, Christian, and many other readers, even those who do not accept it as the literal word of God, an essential religious unity

Genesis The Bible's first book describes God's creation of the world and its creatures in six days; on the seventh day God rests. He sees the disobedience of Adam and Eve in the Garden of Eden and the downward spiral of human events, and provides a new beginning with a destructive flood and the salvation of Noah. The second part of the book tells the stories of Abraham and Sarah, blessed by God and sent to find a new land, and the generations that follow: Isaac, Jacob, and Joseph in Egypt.

Exodus Tells the story of the Israelites' escape from slavery in Egypt. Moses is saved from Pharaoh's edict to kill Jewish male infants; his mother sets him afloat in the Nile and he is discovered and adopted by a princess. God commands Moses to ask Pharaoh for the Jews' freedom, but Pharaoh refuses; God sends plagues upon Egypt, ending with the slaughter of the first-born. (Passover was instituted to celebrate God's passing over the houses of the Israelites during this event.) The Israelites leave Egypt and are saved from pursuing Egyptians by the miraculous parting of the Red Sea. At Mt. Sinai Moses receives God's ten commandments, laws for society and civil life, and ceremonial laws. There God and Israel enter into a covenant: God promises to protect Israel and the Israelites promise to obey God's laws. At God's command a tabernacle is built to accompany the Israelites.

Leviticus Sets out detailed rules to govern Israelite life: the forms of sacrifices; the laws of purity (such as which animals may be eaten); the Day of Atonement; and the code of holiness, including teachings on sexual relations, festivals, ritual objects, and social matters. All of these laws were given to Moses by God. Leviticus explains the woes that have befallen Israel as a result of the people's sins, and stresses atonement.

Numbers Describes Moses' census of the Israelites; laws and cultic matters, including the priestly and temple duties of the Aaronites and Levites; travel from Sinai to Kadesh (south of Canaan); an abortive rebellion against Moses' leadership; travel from Kadesh to the plains of Moab east of the Jordan; and the preparations for conquest of Canaan, including a second census, the appointment of Joshua as leader, and detailed laws for the promised land.

Deuteronomy Composed of discourses or sermons of Moses. The first is a summary of events at Sinai and the camp at Moab, with a call for faithfulness: the people should live their lives in relation to the one true God revealed to them. The second tells of the Ten Commandments and gives an explanation of the first commandment; urges Israel to remain faithful, and presents detailed instructions for communal life. A third section recapitulates the first two, calls for faithfulness (equated to goodness and life) and warns of disobedience (equated to wickedness and death). Deuteronomy concludes with the final words and instructions of Moses linking the people to God, their past, and their future in the new land.

Joshua The Lord appointed Joshua to lead the Israelites across the Jordan; Joshua relays God's commands to the people. In a long series of battles the Israelites conquer Jericho, other cities, and much but not all of the land of Canaan that had been promised to them. The land is divided among the tribes, including tribes east of the Jordan, and cities of refuge and cities for the Levites are designated. Joshua's farewell address, prior to his death in old age, implores the Israelites to follow God.

Judges Describes the history of the Jewish people from the conquests of Joshua to the time of Samuel and the beginning of the monarchy (late 11th century B.C.) The most important judges were military leaders as well as administrators. The Israelites lived among pagan peoples in the parts of Canaan that they had conquered. In a repetitive historical pattern, the Israelites were idolatrous and worshiped the gods of their neighbors; God oppressed them with defeats and slavery but then sent a judge to save the penitent and bring peace. The thankless Israelites would then fall back into their faithless ways. Ultimately the land became completely lawless; the disasters concluded with a civil war against the Benjaminites.

Ruth Naomi and her husband leave Bethlehem during a famine for the Moabite country, where their two sons marry. After the deaths of her husband and sons, Naomi vows to return to her own land. Ruth, one of her Moabite daughters-in-law, demonstrates her loyalty and love by returning with Naomi to Judah. There, she marries her kinsman Boaz, to whom she bears a son, Obed, the grandfather of David.

1 Samuel and 2 Samuel Samuel, dedicated from birth to God's service, was the last person to rule in Israel before the monarchy. At the request of the people for a king, Samuel first anointed Saul. He, however, was disobedient to God, and so Samuel secretly anointed David, a young shepherd; the life and kingship of David, the ideal ruler, are the focus of the books. The events recounted include the combat with Goliath; David's rise to power in conflict with Saul and his family (in which his innocence of wrongdoing is stressed); various battles and revolts; David's conquest of Jerusalem, the city in which God has chosen to be worshiped by his people; the prophecy of perpetual rule for David's line; and his infidelity with Bathsheba.

1 Kings and 2 Kings These two books relate the history of the 400 years of the Jewish monarchy, beginning with the death of David and the start of the reign of Solomon (about 965 B.C.). The narrative also describes the period of the dual monarchy (Israel and Judah) and ends with the destruction of Jerusalem and the Babylonian captivity in 586 B.C. The faithfulness of each of the kings to the law of God as given to Moses is judged. Most of the kings (and all of those of Israel, which broke away from the House of David) fall short, and their repeated failures to keep the covenant of God are used to explain such disasters as the fall of Jerusalem.

1 Chronicles and 2 Chronicles 1 and 2 Chronicles cover genealogies from Adam to Saul; the reign of David, including his preparations for building the temple; the reign of Solomon (the beginning of 2 Chronicles), including the building and dedication of the temple; and the Davidic kings ending with the Babylonian conquest and exile. The main focus is on David as the founder of worship at the temple, and Solomon as its builder; the later kings of the southern kingdom are evaluated primarily on their loyalty to the temple and temple worship.

Ezra The first part of Ezra deals with the rebuilding of Jerusalem and the temple according to the decree of the Persian ruler Cyrus (late 6th century B.C.), by which Jews were permitted to return from exile. There is local opposition to reconstruction, but after confirmation from the later Persian ruler Darius the rebuilding is completed with the encouragement of Haggai and Zechariah. The second part of the book concerns Ezra's mission from Babylon to Jerusalem in the mid fifth (or early fourth) century B.C. He goes to renew and reform the temple and its rites. The Jews had been guilty of idolatry and had mixed with the local population and taken foreign wives, a practice forbidden by Ezra. The books of Ezra and Nehemiah were originally one in the Hebrew bible.

Nehemiah Nehemiah, a cupbearer to Persian King Artaxerxes, asks permission to return to Jerusalem to rebuild the walls (ca. 455 B.C.). He is allowed to go with other Jews; arriving in Jerusalem, he surveys the walls and plans their reconstruction, succeeding brilliantly in the face of opposition from neighboring communities and even from within Jerusalem. The covenant is renewed; Nehemiah institutes legal and religious reforms and remains as governor for many years, later returning for a second term.

Esther Tells the story of Esther, the foster-child of Mordecai, who becomes Queen to Ahasuerus, King of Persia. Through her beauty and courage, she foils a plot of the courtier Haman to kill all the Jews, her people, in the Kingdom. Instead, Haman is executed, the Jews are saved and avenge themselves on their enemies, and Mordecai becomes great at court. The days of salvation are to be celebrated always as the feast of Purim.

Job Examines the questions of God's nature and his relationship to humans. In particular, Job raises the question of why the righteous should suffer; he has been visited by dreadful calamities which imply that he is wicked. Yet according to the covenant calculation of righteousness equals salvation, this should not be, since he is a righteous man. So perhaps God is not a benevolent creator after all, although Job continues to engage with him. The book contains Job's laments, dialogues with friends, God's direct speeches to Job from the tempest (whirlwind) and Job's response, in which he says that he is comforted and has reached a new understanding.

Psalms The Psalms are a varied collection of songs and prayers that have long played an important liturgical role in synagogues and churches. The Psalter, as the book is called, was well known in medieval times. The psalms are of various types: some are spoken or sung by individuals, and some by groups; some celebrate and praise God, and others are petitions for divine help. The psalter includes some discernible subcollections, as indicated by the repetition of some psalms (e.g. 14 and 53) and the titles of certain psalms. Until the 19th century the psalms were taken to be personal lyrics of King David, but it is now known that they were composed over a long period.

Proverbs Traditionally called the Proverbs of Solomon although their collection dates to no earlier than the sixth century B.C. It is a compilation of collections of poems and sayings such as "Sayings of the Wise" and "The Words of King Lemuel" offering advice on an enormous range of matters, usually with a moral point, relevant to the ancient world. There is also a poem about the capable (or virtuous) wife. A key theme of Proverbs is the virtue of wisdom, personified by a woman (equated with righteousness), as opposed to folly (equated to evil).

Ecclesiastes The "Speaker," who describes himself as king (perhaps administrator) over Jerusalem, seeks to grasp the elusive meaning of human existence, and expresses his lifelong search of wisdom in a series of insightful maxims.

Song of Solomon The "Song of Songs," attributed to Solomon, but probably compiled after mid-sixth century B.C., is a book of love poems between a man and a woman, with a chorus of daughters of Jerusalem; the poems are filled with powerful erotic imagery. The book is traditionally interpreted as an allegory of the relation of God to his people.

Isaiah This book is usually regarded as three distinct but related works: First Isaiah deals with the period of Isaiah's prophecies in Judah in the second half of the eighth century B.C. (chs. 1–39); Second Isaiah (chs. 40–55), deals with the sixth to fifth centuries B.C.; and Third Isaiah (chs. 56–66) with the period after the exile. First Isaiah is concerned with the political and military developments in the world of Judah. Isaiah interprets events concerning Jerusalem and the continuity of the House of David in terms of sin, and military defeat as the form of God's punishments. But punishments are not final: justice can be restored and the people purified. Second Isaiah's author is concerned with the Babylonian captivity and exiles' feeling that God is neglectful or absent; Isaiah gives hope for the future. The victories of Cyrus the Persian, who permitted the exiles to return to Jerusalem and rebuild the temple, are seen as ordained by God. Third Isaiah, reflecting conditions in the Holy Land after the return from exile, deals with ritual matters, repentance, and promises of final salvation.

Jeremiah Born about 645–640 B.C., Jeremiah is one of the greatest prophets. His book contains long personal confessions and laments, prophecies against the nations, and restoration prophecies; the core message includes a sternly moral call to true repentance: outward ceremonies and confessions are inadequate in God's sight. After the rise of Babylon Jeremiah prophesied accommodation rather than revolt but his message went unheeded and Jerusalem was destroyed; the prophet at first remained in Jerusalem but was later taken to Egypt. Jeremiah made enemies throughout his career with his harsh prophecies;

he was imprisoned and efforts were made to kill him.

Lamentations Attributed to the prophet Jeremiah but of uncertain authorship, Lamentations contains five elegies for Jerusalem and the temple, destroyed by the Babylonians 586 B.C. The fall of the city and the extreme suffering of the people are attributed to the Israelites' failure to be true to God, but the book expresses the ultimate hope of regaining God's favor. In poetic form, four of the book's chapters have 22 verses (three are acrostics with lines beginning with each of the letters of the Hebrew alphabet).

Ezekiel Ezekiel (sixth century B.C.) was taken to Babylon after the capture of Jerusalem (597 B.C.) by Nebuchadnezzar; in exile he felt the call to prophesy. His book has three parts. The first includes oracles of judgment against Jerusalem and Judah before the final destruction of Jerusalem in 586 B.C. In the second part, there are oracles against foreign nations, including Judah's neighbors, Egypt and Tyre. But the God who acts in history gives salvation as well as judgment; his desire is to bring the nations to righteousness. In the third part, after the destruction of Jerusalem and the fulfillment of his oracles, Ezekiel's prophecies, such as the story of the valley of dry bones coming to life, focus on restoration and redemption: the return of Israel to the promised land. Ezekiel also has visions of the restoration of the temple, its regulations, the priestly order, and the distribution of land.

Daniel The first section includes narratives set in the Babylonian and Persian courts, the best known of which is Daniel in the lions' den, thrown in by the ahistorical Darius the Mede for his piety but saved by an angel of the lord. The second part is an apocalypse, in which God's visions to Daniel, interpreted by an angel, provide a prophecy of history and offer comfort: the pious martyrs will shine in the resurrection. The "son of man" who appears in one vision is used in the New Testament as a title for Jesus.

The Minor Prophets ("The Twelve")

Hosea Active from middle eighth century B.C. to the fall of the Northern Kingdom (721 B.C.), Hosea describes symbolically and historically the relationship of God to his faithless people, who are idolatrous sinners. The awful punishment of God is prophesied, but God will forgive the repentant.

Joel Describes the devastation of a locust plague, characterizing the locusts as an army; there is also drought. But for a repentant Israel the Lord will reverse this agricultural devastation and in the ideal future time will redeem Israel and defeat all its enemies.

Amos A herdsman of Tekoa in Judah, Amos was the earliest of the prophets (ca. 750 B.C.) whose words were collected and later written down. Proclaiming God's judgment on Israel and its neighbors for grievous religious and social sins, he foresees God's punishment of Israel with drought, plagues, military defeat and exile.

Obadiah Obadiah prophesies the total and final destruction of Edom for its participation in the Babylonian destruction of Jerusalem: the Edomites, held to be the descendants of Jacob's brother Esau, are kin who betrayed Judah. The book, the shortest in the Old Testament (21 verses), is in poetry except for the final three verses.

Jonah God tells Jonah to go to the Assyrian capital, Nineveh, and denounce its wickedness. Instead Jonah sails to Tarshish; en route the ship is threatened by a God-sent storm. As propitiation, Jonah is thrown into the water and swallowed by a great fish. Freed by God, he goes to Nineveh, where he preaches with success but protests God's forgiveness of the repentant Ninevites; God instructs him on the need for mercy.

Micah Punishments for evil-doing in the cities of Samaria and Jerusalem (capitals of Israel and Judah) are prophesied and a future reign of God's peace centered on Mt. Zion in Jerusalem is foreseen. The rupture between God and his people because of their wickedness is described; it will be followed by ultimate reconciliation.

Nahum Describes the wrath and power of God and vividly prophesies the destruction of Nineveh. Its aim may have been to encourage the Judean king to join in revolt against Assyria through faith in God's purpose to destroy it.

Habakkuk Laments the success of the wicked and God's use of the Babylonians to wreak punishments; but God assures him that the righteous will triumph. The book concludes with a prayer, perhaps used liturgically in the temple, depicting God as a powerful warrior.

Zephaniah Zephaniah (seventh century B.C.) prophesies against idolatry and other sins of Judah and Jerusalem; the Israelites and foreign peoples will all be laid waste by God on the awful Day of the Lord. Only repentance can save; God will leave a small remnant of the humble and righteous in Jerusalem and he will establish his kingdom over the earth.

Haggai The Lord, through his prophet Haggai, tells the leaders of Judah of his wrath because the temple has not been rebuilt. In his anger God damages Israel's harvests, but once the people begin rebuilding the temple, they have God's blessing and his temple will again be glorious.

Zechariah Zechariah reports the word of the Lord in seven visions, said to have occured in 519 B.C., that represent the Jewish community and a rebuilt temple. God is angry with his people for their failures, but is ready to forgive the repentant builders. The two last sections of Zechariah, oracles of Judah's triumph and the Day of the Lord, are later additions.

Malachi Attacks inferior and inadequate sacrifices, faithlessness, and marrying foreign wives. A "messenger of the covenant" (also identified as Elijah) will come to clear a path for the Lord who will cast down evildoers while the righteous will rejoice; this prophecy in the last book of the Old Testament greatly influenced later Jewish and Christian messianic thought.

New Testament

The New Testament includes 27 books: four gospels, the Acts of the Apostles, 21 letters (epistles), and Revelation; these are accepted as canonical by the Roman Catholic and Protestant churches, although some scholars and a few churches argue for a smaller canon. The New Testament books were written in Greek during the years from about A.D. 50 to the first half of the second century A.D. The arrangement of the books, adopted in the fourth century A.D., is roughly in chronological order of subject, rather than date of writing: the story of Jesus (gospels), the beginning of the church (Acts), advice to churches and the beginnings of Christian theology (letters), and the future vision of hope (Revelation). Aside from the genuine letters of Paul, little is known about the actual authors of the New Testament books; the traditional attributions result from the custom of writers assigning works to revered predecessors or from later decisions by church fathers.

The Gospels

The earliest gospel ("good news") is that of Mark, about A.D. 70 (the time of the destruction of the Second Temple in Jerusalem by the Romans); Luke wrote about A.D. 80–85, Matthew, about A.D. 90 , and John during the late first century A.D. Mark gathered sayings of Jesus and stories of his life and ministry from the oral traditions of the early church. Later, Matthew and Luke wrote their gospels using Mark and a collection of Jesus' sayings as sources. The first three gospels, similar in contents and in order, are called the synoptic ("seen together") gospels. John, by contrast, may not have known of the synoptics when he wrote; in any event his gospel is different in tone and focus from the other three. The four canonical gospels were collected about the mid-second century A.D., and the Acts of the Apostles, originally part of Luke, was treated as a distinct work.

The unique authority of the four gospels emerged during this period, based on liturgical usage in regional churches and the arguments of church authorities such as Irenaeus of Lyons (c. 185 A.D.). However, it was not until the late 4th century A.D. that the canonicity of these gospels and the rest of the New Testament as it is known today was recognized by the Catholic Church in the West. Much later, in response to the challenges of the Reformation, the Council of Trent (mid-16th century A.D.) declared the entire Catholic Bible, including the Old Testament apocrypha and all of the books of the New Testament, to be canonical.

Matthew Begins by saying that Jesus, descended from Abraham, is the Messiah. The story of his birth in Bethlehem is described: the adoration of the Magi, the wrath of Herod, and the flight of Mary, Joseph, and Jesus to Egypt. Jesus' baptism by John is followed by his ministry: the Sermon on the Mount, miracles, and the recognition of Jesus as the Messiah by his disciples. His journey to Jerusalem and conflict with the priestly elite is followed by his death, resurrection, and appearance to the disciples. Matthew contrasts the Old Testament time of prophecy with the era of God's fulfillment in Jesus; the believer needs to receive Jesus to be part of God's eternal kingdom.

Mark Starts with John's baptism of Jesus, then tells of Jesus' ministry: his preaching, teaching, and healing, and the activities of his disciples. The miracles of calming the waters, of feeding the multitudes with loaves and fishes, and others are described. Mark then focuses on Jesus' journey to Jerusalem, death, and resurrection. In Mark's rendering, those who hear Jesus, even his disciples, do not fully understand who he is; it is only with the crucifixion that Jesus and his mission are fully understood and he is recognized as the son of God.

Luke Luke begins with the birth of John the Baptist and continues with the story of Jesus' birth, including the annunciation, the manger, and the shepherds. Jesus' ministry begins after his baptism by John. Luke describes the conflicts with the Pharisees (an observant Jewish group), the journey to Jerusalem, Jesus' death, resurrection and appearances to the disciples, and his ascension. Luke emphasizes Jesus' concern with the poor and the duties of the rich to the poor. Several gospel incidents and parables are found only in Luke, such as the boy Jesus in the temple, the appearance to two disciples on the road to Emmaus, and the stories of the Good Samaritan and the prodigal son.

John John starts with the assertion that the eternal Word is embodied in Jesus. The focus is not on the everyday moral and religious implications of Jesus' teaching, but rather on his claims to be the Messiah, the Light of the World, the Son of God. While including miracles and healing, John omits parables, the Sermon on the Mount, the instruction to pray the Lord's Prayer, and the institution of the Last Supper. The gospel emphasizes the conflict of Jesus with the Pharisees, and more broadly Jesus versus the Jews, a focus that may reflect the writer's era, when clearer distinctions between Jews and Christians had developed. The gospel ends with Jesus' death, resurrection, and appearances to the disciples, including his appearance by the Sea of Galilee to Peter and others.

Acts of the Apostles   Written about A.D. 80–85, Acts is by the same author as Luke. It begins where Luke ends, with the Ascension of Jesus, and recalls his words that the disciples will bear witness in Jerusalem, to Judah and Samaria, and thence to the "ends of the earth." The book describes the earliest years of the church: its rapid growth among the Jews, the conversion of Paul, outreach to the Gentiles, and doctrinal controversies. Paul's missions in Asia Minor and Greece, and his trials in Jerusalem and Caesarea are detailed; the book ends with his final preaching and imprisonment in Rome.

Letters   Letters are the dominant form of literature in the New Testament: they provide early statements of Christian theology as well as advice and counsel to churches and individuals. Collections of Pauline letters were circulated among congregations by about A.D. 100. Of the 21 letters, 13 attributed to Paul are listed first: nine to churches (ordered by descending length), and four to individuals. Then come Hebrews and the seven "general" or "catholic" letters, either written to general audiences or to unidentified individuals. Today only nine letters are widely regarded as genuinely Paul's: Romans, 1 & 2 Corinthians, Galatians, Philippians, 1 Thessalonians, and Philemon. The "pastorals" (1 & 2 Timothy and Titus) are usually regarded as non-Pauline; opinions vary on 2 Thessalonians, Ephesians, and Colossians.

Romans   Written to the church in Rome probably between A.D. 55 and 58. Paul defends his gospel to the Gentiles, answering questions and challenges raised by Jewish Christians in Rome. He writes that Jesus' obedience benefits all groups, not just Jews: through the first Adam all became sinners, through the last Adam (Jesus) all were granted grace. The law that God gave to the Israelites was not wrong; rather the lack was in sinful humans, whose sin is forgiven by God's grace that now supersedes the law. Gentiles can become righteous, and in the end Jews and Gentiles will be one. Those with gifts should use them to the benefit of the church, and all should respect the state for preserving order and providing a frame for witness. In closing, Paul tells the Roman congregation that he will visit them on his way to a projected (unrealized) mission to Spain.

1 Corinthians   Paul founded the congregation at Corinth, on the isthmus between mainland Greece and the Peloponnesus, about A.D. 50/51; he wrote them at least five letters. This second letter (the first is lost) was written about A.D. 54 from Ephesus. Paul gives advice on problems that were endangering the congregation's communal life. Some people claimed special status because of supposed religious wisdom; a man had an incestuous relationship; there were disorders at the Lord's Supper; and Paul has received an inquiry from the congregation about his ideas on sexuality and marriage. Paul responds that God's revealed wisdom sets aside individual claims to status. Worldly matters are transient, but not unimportant, and Christians must behave in a worthy manner; he says that whatever is done should be done in love, with an awareness of the grace bestowed on Christians by their faith both in the present and for eternity.

2 Corinthians   This letter is thought to be a composite of at least two letters by Paul to the church in Corinth, one (chs. 1–9) written in A.D. 55, and a second (chs. 10–13) about a year later. Paul first refers to a "tearful letter," now lost, assailing the congregation for not disciplining a member with whom Paul had been in conflict. But Paul assures the Corinthians of his care and devotion, and writes of the Christian message and the Christian ministry, including his own struggles, and the need for generosity in supporting other congregations. He attacks rival missionaries and their false claims, asserts the truth of the faith he preached, and promises the Corinthians another visit.

Galatians   Written by Paul between A.D. 50 and 55 to the churches in Galatia (central or southern Anatolia). Paul admonishes these Christians not to stray from the gospel of faith in favor of a return to circumcision and the Mosaic law advocated by competing Jewish-Christian missionaries. Paul says that the new faith in Jesus Christ completely supersedes the old covenant: it is by faith that Christians are saved, not by the law. In this argument Paul provides the earliest statement of gentile Christian theology as distinct from Judaism.

Ephesians   Probably written by a disciple of Paul intent on continuing his teaching, in A.D. 80–90, the destination is traditionally regarded as Ephesus, a port city in western Asia Minor where Paul had lived and preached. The author writes that God's plan from eternity will be accomplished through Christ, who is Lord not only of humanity but the whole universe. Within the church members must behave in godly fashion, speak the truth, love one another, and stand firm against the superhuman powers of evil. Some elements of this book may have been used in early liturgies.

Philippians Written by Paul from prison (probably in Ephesus, about A.D. 55). Paul rejoices in the faith of the congregation at Philippi (a city in northeastern Greece), urges on them conduct worthy of the gospel, and thanks them for their generosity. The letter as it now exists may be a composite (probably edited before A.D. 90) of several of Paul's letters to the Christians at Philippi.

Colossians Probably written by a follower of Paul to the church at Colossae (in Asia Minor), this letter gives thanks for the faith of the Colossians, reminds them that Christ embodies all wisdom, urges them therefore to reject concerns with planets, stars, and dietary laws, and commands them to embody Christian virtues.

1 Thessalonians This letter of Paul to the church in Thessalonica (present-day Thessaloniki in northeastern Greece) was composed about A.D. 50 ; it is the earliest book in the New Testament. Writing probably from Corinth, Paul and his colleagues Timothy and Sylvanus assure the church in Thessalonica, where Paul had earlier preached, of their affection and urge the members to be steadfast in faith, love, and hope. Paul emphasizes final (eschatological) things, and affirms that Christians who die prior to the Second Coming of Christ, as well as those who are then alive, will share in the new life in Christ.

2 Thessalonians Christians at Thessalonica are told that those who cause them to suffer will be punished at the last day and the faithful will rest; that the coming of Christ is not necessarily imminent—the wicked one whom Jesus will destroy must come first; and that Christians must not be idle, but should work in order to eat.

1 Timothy, 2 Timothy, and Titus These three letters deal with similar congregational matters and are often grouped as the "pastoral letters." Sharply admonitory in tone, they urge godly church officers and leaders to demonstrate exemplary moral and religious purity, as compared to the unacceptable social, religious, and sexual behavior of heretics; they instruct congregants, men and women, old and young, on their duties. The unknown author, writing perhaps early second century A.D., attempts to convey the continuity of Paul's teachings and message, thereby stabilizing and strengthening the church in the generations following the fervor of the apostolic age.

Philemon Paul's letter to Philemon (probably in Colossae) is the shortest (25 verses) of his letters. Paul writes on behalf of Philemon's slave Onesimus (Greek, "useful"), who fled to Paul after wronging his master in some way. Paul, in his imprisonment in Ephesus about A.D. 55, converts Onesimus and appeals to Philemon to receive him as a member of the new fellowship of Jesus.

Hebrews This anonymous work, in the form of a sermon rather than a letter, was apparently aimed at encouraging Christians after the first generation. It presents a carefully developed series of comparisons between the Old Testament and Christianity to show the nature and purpose of the new faith. The author says that before, God spoke through the prophets, but now he has spoken through his son; the old faith had an earthly temple and sacrifices; the new is transcendent and eternal, with a single sacrifice for the world. Christians must be firm in their hope, and confident of their salvation.

James Traditionally ascribed to James the brother of Jesus, this general ("catholic") letter is intended for the guidance of the whole church. James emphasizes keeping the commandment to love one's neighbor, which entails especially caring for the poor and the oppressed; warns the rich; and emphasizes the importance of works as well as faith.

1 Peter Attributed to Peter but probably written late first century A.D. by another author, this letter affirms the truth of the faith and proclaims a new birth into a living hope through the resurrection. Christians may suffer from the loss of old attachments, but all, including the marginalized, are full members of the new community of believers and should aspire to live worthily in the faith.

2 Peter Ascribed to Peter but probably written by another author early second century A.D. Christians are exhorted to behave rightly, avoiding the sins of scoffers, evildoers and false prophets, in order to prepare for the Day of the Lord. Then judgment will be rendered and a new heaven and earth will be instituted. The Day has not yet come because God in his patience wishes all to repent.

John, the Letters of These three letters may have been written toward the end of the first century A.D. The first and longest asserts Jesus' role as the son of God who became man, the source and beginning of Christianity, and the bringer of eternal life; those who believe in him are the children of God and should not behave as sinners do. 2 John is a very brief letter addressed to "the Lady chosen by God and her children" (possibly a symbolic reference to churches) that emphasizes the importance of obeying the command to love one another, and to acknowledge that Jesus has come in human form. 3 John, also brief, is addressed to a Gaius: it commends him for his kindness and hospitality to fellow Christians, and criticizes a church leader who has not received others appropriately.

Jude Traditionally ascribed to Jude, a brother of Jesus; exhorts the faithful to be steadfast against heretics and false prophets in their midst. With their manifold personal and religious sins they are condemned, as were the false prophets of the Old Testament. The date of this short letter is unknown; it refers to remembering the words of the apostles, suggesting post-apostolic times.

Revelation Written about A.D. 95, John's revelations of visions from Christ were accepted as prophetic by the early church; this John is not the same as the author of the Gospel or the letters. The book describes allegorically the struggle between good and evil, reflecting the actual conflict between Christians and the Roman Empire. The vivid images include angels, the scroll with seven seals, savage beasts and plagues, the battle of Armageddon, and John's final vision of a new heaven and earth: a New Jerusalem, the rule of God, and the salvation of his faithful people.

Apocrypha The Apocrypha, originally scriptures of the Septuagint, were part of the early Christian Bible. They remain part of the Roman Catholic Old Testament and, with some additional books, of Orthodox Old Testaments, but are noncanonical (although of historical interest) in Protestant churches. Of Jewish origin, they were written in Hebrew, Aramaic, and Greek during the period 300 B.C. to A.D. 100, and mostly from about 200 B.C. to A.D. 70 (the date of the destruction of the Second Temple by the Romans). They do not form part of the standard Hebrew Bible, which under rabbinic influence after A.D. 70 was standardized on the principle that revelation, beginning with Moses, ended with Ezra. The Apocrypha are listed here with the names and in the order used when they are printed in a separate section in Protestant Bibles.

The First Book of Esdras Focuses on the temple and temple worship, including a Passover celebration after Josiah's religious reforms (ca. 620 B.C.); the restoration of the temple (520–516 B.C.); and, years later, Ezra's preaching against mingling with the heathen local population and taking non-Jewish wives. An alternative version of part of 2 Chronicles, all of Ezra, and part of Nehemiah, probably dating to the late second century B.C.

The Second Book of Esdras A Jewish apocalypse written under the name of Ezra after the Roman destruction of Jerusalem (A.D. 70). Its seven visions (the beginning and ending parts of the book are Christian additions) deal in allegorical form with the suffering of God's chosen people, his slowness in bringing justice, Ezra's dictation of the Hebrew holy books destroyed in Jerusalem, and the last times: the messianic age, resurrection, and final judgment.

Tobit Concerns the sufferings of Jews in the diaspora. God hears the prayers of the pious blind Tobit and his relative Sarah, beset with a demon. The angel Raphael, in disguise, helps Tobit's son Tobias, who marries Sarah, to defeat the demon and restore Tobit's sight. Thus God helps the righteous, and Jews will one day reunite in Jerusalem. Probably in written in Aramaic before the second century B.C.; the setting in eighth century B.C. Nineveh is anachronistic.

Judith A message of faith in God's deliverance of oppressed Jews. A beautiful and pious widow, Judith goes to the camp of Holofernes, the Assyrian general besieging Bethulia, arranges to be alone with him and decapitates him. The Assyrians retreat, Judith is honored, and celebrations and offerings are made at the temple. Possibly written in the Maccabean era (second to first century B.C.).

The Rest of the Chapters of the Book of Esther These additions provide religious content to Esther's story, which in the original Hebrew does not mention God. The additions include a dream of Mordecai and prayers of Mordecai and Esther. God responds to Esther's piety and saves his people from the destruction planned by Haman.

The Wisdom of Solomon Praises wisdom and righteousness and warns against the evils of injustice and idolatry. The wicked may prosper in this life, but they face condemnation at the heavenly judgment, of which they are unaware, and at which they will witness the final salvation of the righteous and oppressed. Other themes are the role of wisdom in governance and in history, and the origins of idolatry. Written in Greek, possibly first century A.D., probably to support Jews in a time of persecution.

Ecclesiasticus, or the Wisdom of Jesus Son of Sirach. A lengthy treatise on morals and behavior written by a tutor to the wealthy in Jerusalem about 180 B.C., it provides a picture of Palestinian Jewish society prior to the Maccabean revolt. Its primary purpose is to give advice on a huge range of matters great and small, from the fear of the Lord to good table manners. Jewish heroes are described in a section beginning "Let us now praise famous men."

Baruch From Babylonia Baruch sends the temple vessels back to the high priest in Jerusalem, along with the people's funds for sacrifices. There is a prayer of confession and repentance for the people's falling away from God; a hymn to wisdom, personified as a woman and identified with the Torah; and a psalm of comfort for those in exile. Possibly second century B.C. and anachronistically ascribed to Baruch, the scribe of Jeremiah.

Jeremiah, A Letter of A diatribe against idols: they are constructed by Gentiles of metal, wood and stone and thus, human-created, could not be gods; Jews must avoid them and believe instead in the true God of Israel.

Thou Shalt Not Be Colloquial: Why the King James Bible Endures

By CHARLES McGRATH

The King James Bible, which was first published 400 years ago, may be the single best thing ever accomplished by a committee. The Bible was the work of 54 scholars and clergymen who met over seven years in six nine-man subcommittees, called "companies." In a preface to the new Bible, Miles Smith, one of the translators and a man so impatient that he once walked out of a boring sermon and went to the pub, wrote that anything new inevitably "endured many a storm of gainsaying, or opposition." So there must have been disputes—shouting; table pounding; high-ruffed, black-gowned clergymen folding their arms and stomping out of the room—but there is no record of them. And the finished text shows none of the PowerPoint insipidness we associate with committee-speak or with later group translations like the 1961 New English Bible, which T.S. Eliot said did not even rise to "dignified mediocrity." Far from bland, the King James Bible is one of the great masterpieces of English prose.

The issue of how, or even whether, to translate sacred texts was a fraught one in those days, often with political as well as religious overtones, and it still is. The Roman Catholic Church, for instance, recently decided to retranslate the missal used at Mass to make it more formal and less conversational. Critics have complained that the new text is awkward and archaic, while its defenders (some of whom probably still prefer the Mass in Latin) insist that's just the point—that language a little out of the ordinary is more devotional and inspiring. No one would ever say that the King James Bible is an easy read. And yet its very oddness is part of its power.

From the start, the King James Bible was intended to be not a literary creation but rather a political and theological compromise between the established church and the growing Puritan movement. What the king cared about was clarity, simplicity, doctrinal orthodoxy. The translators worked hard on that, going back to the original Hebrew, Greek and Aramaic, and yet they also spent a lot of time tweaking the English text in the interest of euphony and musicality. Time

and again the language seems to slip almost unconsciously into iambic pentameter—this was the age of Shakespeare, commentators are always reminding us—and right from the beginning the translators embraced the principles of repetition and the dramatic pause: "In the beginning God created the Heauen, and the Earth. And the earth was without forme, and voyd, and darkenesse was vpon the face of the deepe: and the Spirit of God mooued vpon the face of the waters."

The influence of the King James Bible is so great that the list of idioms from it that have slipped into everyday speech, taking such deep root that we use them all the time without any awareness of their biblical origin, is practically endless: sour grapes; fatted calf; salt of the earth; drop in a bucket; skin of one's teeth; apple of one's eye; girded loins; feet of clay; whited sepulchers; filthy lucre; pearls before swine; fly in the ointment; fight the good fight; eat, drink and be merry.

But what we also love about this Bible is its strangeness—its weird punctuation, odd pronouns (as in "Our Father, which art in heaven"), all those verbs that end in "eth": "In the morning it flourisheth, and groweth vp; in the euening it is cut downe, and withereth." As Robert Alter has demonstrated in his startling and revealing translations of the Psalms and the Pentateuch, the Hebrew Bible is even stranger, and in ways that the King James translators may not have entirely comprehended, and yet their text performs the great trick of being at once recognizably English and also a little bit foreign. You can hear its distinctive cadences in the speeches of Lincoln, the poetry of Whitman, the novels of Cormac McCarthy.

Even in its time, the King James Bible was deliberately archaic in grammar and phraseology: an expression like "yea, verily," for example, had gone out of fashion some 50 years before. The translators didn't want their Bible to sound contemporary, because they knew that contemporaneity quickly goes out of fashion. In his very useful guide, *God's Secretaries: The Making of the King James Bible*, Adam Nicolson points out that when the Victorians came to revise the King

James Bible in 1885, they embraced this principle wholeheartedly, and like those people who whack and scratch old furniture to make it look even more ancient, they threw in a lot of extra Jacobeanisms, like "howbeit," "peradventure," "holden" and "behooved."

This is the opposite, of course, of the procedure followed by most new translations, starting with Good News for Modern Man, a paperback Bible published by the American Bible Society in 1966, whose goal was to reflect not the language of the Bible but its ideas, rendering them into current terms, so that Ezekiel 23:20, for example ("For she doted vpon their paramours, whose flesh is as the flesh of asses, and whose issue is like the issue of horses") becomes "She was filled with lust for oversexed men who had all the lustfulness of donkeys or stallions."

There are countless new Bibles available now, many of them specialized: a Bible for couples, for gays and lesbians, for recovering addicts, for surfers, for skaters and skateboarders, not to mention a superheroes Bible for children. They are all "accessible," but most are a little tone-deaf, lacking in grandeur and

majesty, replacing "through a glasse, darkly," for instance, with something along the lines of "like a dim image in a mirror." But what this modernizing ignores is that the most powerful religious language is often a little elevated and incantatory, even ambiguous or just plain hard to understand. The new Catholic missal, for instance, does not seem to fear the forbidding phrase, replacing the statement that Jesus is "one in being with the Father" with the more complicated idea that he is "consubstantial with the Father."

Not everyone prefers a God who talks like a pal or a guidance counselor. Even some of us who are nonbelievers want a God who speaketh like—well, God. The great achievement of the King James translators is to have arrived at a language that is both ordinary and heightened, that rings in the ear and lingers in the mind. And that all 54 of them were able to agree on every phrase, every comma, without sounding as gassy and evasive as the Financial Crisis Inquiry Commission, is little short of amazing, in itself proof of something like divine inspiration.

Probably fourth century B.C., possibly in Babylonia but attributed to the prophet Jeremiah, late seventh to early sixth century B.C.

The Song of the Three Includes a prayer for forgiveness and salvation, brief narrative material, and a hymn sung by three youths as they survive the fiery furnace. Probably added to the earlier versions of Daniel between the Maccabean revolt (167–164 B.C.) and the publication of the LXX translation of Daniel (100 B.C.).

Daniel and Susanna The beautiful Susanna is falsely accused of adultery by two lecherous elders who covet her. Condemned to death, Susanna calls on God in her innocence; Daniel intervenes to save her by confronting the elders and exposing their lies. An addition to Daniel, probably second century B.C.

Daniel, Bel, and the Snake Daniel, a valued counselor, proves to the Babylonian king that the idol Bel is not a god; sacrifices are actually secretly eaten by the priests. He also shows that a living snake is not a god by killing it with cakes of pitch. But for worshiping Israel's God he is thrown into the lion's den; he survives with God's protection. Probably added to the earlier versions

of Daniel between the Maccabean revolt (167–164 B.C.) and the publication of the LXX translation of Daniel (100 B.C.).

Manasseh, the Prayer of This short prayer of repentance asserts God's majesty and compassion and asks forgiveness for the supplicant's transgressions.

The First Book of the Maccabees Details the history of the Jewish revolt against Antiochus IV Epiphanes, Seleucid King of Syria, whose reign began in 175 B.C. and who repressed Judaism and instituted Hellenistic cults. The family of the Maccabees took the lead in winning Judean freedom, and this book, with many references to Jewish history, attributes the revolt's success to their leadership and faith in God. Written between 104 B.C. and the beginning of Roman rule in 63 B.C.

The Second Book of the Maccabees 2 Maccabees focuses on the defilement of the temple, for which Jewish Hellenizers are held responsible. God sends punishments upon his people for these sins; but repentance brings redemption in the revolt led by Judas Maccabeus. This book promises the resurrection of the righteous dead, a theological idea of late Judaism.

MYTHOLOGY

"Mythology" refers to stories that convey the beliefs of a particular culture at a particular time. Myths, which usually refer to the actions of divinities, can be distinguished from legends (which tell of heroic deeds and historical events, real or imagined) and folktales (stories, often humorous or exaggerated, involving ordinary people). Mythologies usually originated in preliterate oral traditions, at a remote but indeterminate time period. At some point they are written down and become systematized, though because of their oral roots variant and sometimes contradictory versions persist.

This section presents an overview of four traditions of mythology: those of the Classical world (Greece and Rome); Mesopotamia (the ancient Middle East); Egypt; and the Norse world of northernmost Europe. All four have had an influence on subsequent European religion, literature, art, and cultural life.

Classical Mythology

The prehistoric Indo-European settlers of the Greek peninsula and the Aegean islands brought some myths with them from their original homeland in western Central Asia, and borrowed others from their Mediterranean neighbors. With the development of literacy in Greece in the Archaic Period (ca. 800–480 B.C.), the myths began to be written down. Early sources for Greek mythology include the *Iliad* and the *Odyssey*, attributed to Homer (8th century B.C.); Hesiod's *Theogony* (ca. 700 B.C.); the so-called *Homeric Hymns* (7th–6th century B.C.); and the surviving great works of ancient Greek theater, which often involve the interactions of humans and gods.

Greek trade and the establishment of Greek colonies in Sicily and elsewhere spread Greek myths throughout the Mediterranean world; the conquests of Alexander the Great (d. 323 B.C.) carried Greek culture far into Asia. When the Romans conquered Greece and the Hellenic world during the second and first centuries B.C., they absorbed much of Greek culture; they equated many of the Greek deities, and stories of their deeds, to figures in their own pantheon. The two most important Roman sources for classical mythology and legends are Virgil's *Aeneid* (unfinished; from ca. 30 B.C.) and Ovid's *Metamorphoses* (completed A.D. 8).

In what follows, deities and legendary figures are listed by their Greek (or, in a few cases, customary English) names, followed by their Roman names in parentheses. Entries for figures that appear only in Roman myth are italicized in boldface.

Olympian Gods of Classical Mythology

Aphrodite (Venus) Goddess of love, beauty, and sensuality; patron of courtesans. Aphrodite is the daughter of Zeus and Dione in one account; in another she is born out of the foam created when Cronus castrates Uranus and throws his genitals into the sea. Aphrodite is the wife of Hephaestus but has numerous lovers, including Adonis, Anchises, with whom she has a son, Aeneas, and Ares, with whom she has Eros (Cupid) and three other children (see *Ares*).

Apollo (Apollo) God of healing, oracles, the sun, poetry, and music; son of Zeus and Leto; twin brother of Artemis. Apollo is one of the most prominent gods in Greek myth with many roles and attributes and a multitude of children and lovers, most notably Asclepius by Coronis. Apollo symbolizes order and the rational as opposed to the irrational world of Dionysus.

Ares (Mars) God of war; son of Zeus and Hera. Unmarried Ares' most famous of many lovers is Aphrodite, with whom he sires Phobus (Panic), Deimos (Fear), Harmonia (Harmony), and Eros (Cupid). Ares is often accompanied by Enyo (Horror) and Eris (Strife).

Artemis (Diana) Virgin goddess of the hunt, wild animals, and animal and human young; daughter of Zeus and Leto; twin sister of Apollo. Artemis is usually accompanied by a group of nymphs and often appears with a bow and arrow.

Athena (Minerva) Virgin goddess of wisdom, war, crafts, and city life; protector of Athens. The daughter of Zeus and Metis (see *Metis* for birth), Athena springs from the head of Zeus in full armor with a helmet and spear. Athena gives the olive tree as a gift to Athens. She also gives mankind the loom, the plough, and the flute. (See also *Nike*.)

Demeter (Ceres) Goddess of the harvest, grain, earth, and fertility; daughter of Cronus and Rhea; mother of Persephone. During the third of the year when Persephone is held by Hades in the underworld (see *Persephone*), Demeter will not allow anything to grow.

Dionysus (Bacchus, Liber) God of the vine, wine, and fertility; closely associated with theater, particularly tragedy; son of Zeus and Semele; husband of Ariadne. Dionysus's followers are maenads (also Bacchae), a drunk, frenzied, ecstatic mob of women, and satyrs, mythical creatures that are half man and half goat.

Hephaestus (Vulcan) God of fire, smiths, and crafts; son of Zeus and Hera or of Hera alone in some accounts; cuckolded husband of Aphrodite. Born lame, Hephaestus is ejected from Olympus, once by Hera and again by Zeus. Hephaestus is responsible for fashioning some of the most important objects in myth, including the chains that held Prometheus and armor for Achilles, Heracles, and Aeneas. He also crafts the first woman, Pandora.

Hera (Juno) Goddess of marriage and family; daughter of Cronus and Rhea; mother of Ares (by Zeus) and Heph-aestus (by Zeus in some accounts and alone in others). Hera is often seen in myth as the vengeful wife of the adulterous Zeus, causing havoc for his lovers and illegitimate children, most famously Heracles (Hercules).

Hermes (Mercury) Trickster god; messenger god; god of commerce; patron of travelers and thieves; son of Zeus and Maia. Hermes is often seen in myth wearing a winged helmet and winged sandals, and carrying a caduceus, a herald's staff entwined with snakes.

Hestia (Vesta) Virgin goddess of fire and the hearth; daughter of Cronus and Rhea. Hestia is the protector of the home, the household and the hearth.

Poseidon (Neptune) God of the sea and earthquakes; son of Cronus and Rhea; husband of the nymph Amphi-trite. Poseidon is closely associated with horses and classically seen carrying a trident. He is one of the less benevolent gods, responsible for unpredictable and destructive forces.

Zeus (Jupiter, Jove) Chief Olympian god; son of Cronus and Rhea. Zeus ousts Cronus and the other Titans from Olympus and takes control as the supreme sky god while his brothers Poseidon and Hades take over the sea and underworld, respectively. Zeus often appears in myth having affairs (see *Danae, Europa, Io, Leda, Semele*), much to the dismay of his typically jealous wife, Hera.

Other Figures in Classical Myth and Legend

Achilles Hero of the Trojan War in Homer's *Iliad*; son of Thetis (sea nymph) and Peleus (mortal). Thetis dips Achilles in the river Styx at birth making him invulnerable except for the heel by which he is held. Fighting for the Greeks at Troy, Achilles kills Hector and is killed by Paris, who shoots an arrow into his heel.

Adonis Lover of Aphrodite. Adonis is a young man so beautiful that both Aphrodite and Persephone want to have him. When he is killed by a boar, a compromise allows him to live in the celestial world with Aphrodite for half the year and in the underworld with Persephone the other half.

Aegisthus See *Clytemnestra* and *Orestes*.

Aeneas Legendary Trojan warrior; son of Aphrodite and Anchises; lover of Dido. Aeneas is the hero of Virgil's *Aeneid*, in which he is depicted as the father of the Roman people.

Aeolus God of the winds. In Homer's *Odyssey*, Aeolus gives Odysseus a bag of wind and warns him not to open it. Odysseus's men untie the bag, releasing dangerous winds that cause a great setback in the journey home.

Agamemnon King of Mycenae and leader of the Greeks in the Trojan War; son of Atreus; husband of Clytemnestra; father of Orestes, Electra, and Iphigeneia; brother of Menelaus. (See also *Clytemnestra, Iphigeneia*, and *Orestes*.)

Agave Daughter of Cadmus and Harmonia. In Euripides' *Bacchantes*, Agave's son Pentheus disrespects Dionysus. The god drives Agave insane, compelling her and her sisters to tear Pentheus to pieces.

Ajax Hero of the Trojan War in Homer's *Iliad*; son of Telemon. Ajax kills himself when the prize of Achilles' armor goes to Odysseus instead of him.

Amphitrite Goddess of the sea; a Nereid (sea nymph); wife of Poseidon.

Anchises Trojan prince. Anchises is a lover of Aphrodite, with whom he has a son, Aeneas. Hearing of the affair, Zeus cripples Anchises with a thunderbolt.

Andromeda Daughter of Cepheus and Cassiopeia; wife of Perseus. When Cassiopeia boasts that her daughter is more beautiful than the Nereids, an oracle demands that Andromeda be sacrificed to defuse the wrath of Poseidon. She is about to be killed by a sea monster, when Perseus, flying past on his winged sandals, rescues her and gains her hand in marriage.

Antigone Daughter of Oedipus and Jocasta; sister of Eteocles, Ismene, and Polynices. In a fight for power, Eteocles and Polynices kill each other. In Sophocles' *Antigone*, Antigone performs funeral rites for Polynices against the orders of her uncle Creon, the new king. He sentences her to be buried alive in a cave, where she hangs herself. When Haemon, Creon's son and Antigone's fiancé, finds out, he kills himself, causing Creon's wife to kill herself.

Antiope (Hippolyta) Queen of the Amazons; mother of Hippolytus by Theseus. Theseus abducts Antiope and takes her to Athens, causing the Amazons to invade in retaliation.

Arachne A young woman who challenges Athena to a weaving contest. When Athena finds no flaw in Arachne's work, she tears it up and beats her. Arachne kills herself; Athena then turns her into a spider.

Argus 1) Hundred-eyed monster that Hera sends to guard Io to whom Zeus has taken a liking. 2) Odysseus's faithful dog, which drops dead upon seeing him after his 20-year absence.

Ariadne Daughter of King Minos of Crete. After she shows Theseus how to overcome the Minotaur, the two run away together. In one version of the story, Theseus then abandons her; in another she dies, and in another she becomes the mistress of Dionysus.

Asclepius (Aesculapius) God of medicine; deified son of Apollo and Coronis (mortal). The centaur Chiron was his mentor, and he is usually seen carrying a staff entwined by a snake.

Atalanta Beautiful girl who could outrun men. Atalanta says that she will only marry the suitor who can beat her in a foot race; losers will be killed. Hippomenes, distracting her by dropping golden apples from Aphrodite, wins her hand.

Atlas A Titan in some accounts and a giant in others; brother of Prometheus. Atlas sides with the Titans in their battle with Zeus. When Zeus emerges the victor, he condemns Atlas to bear the weight of the world on his shoulders.

Bellerophon Slayer of the Chimera (see *Chimera*). With a golden bridle from Athena, Bellerophon mounts Pegasus and slays the monster. Bellerophon remains the master of Pegasus until he tries to ride the winged horse up Mount Olympus and is punished by Zeus.

Bellona Roman goddess of war. Bellona is the wife of Mars in some accounts, his sister in others.

Cadmus Legendary founder of Thebes; father of Agave, Autonoe, Ino, Polydorus, and Semele. With his wife, Harmonia, Cadmus begins an ill-fated bloodline whose woes are popular subjects of myth.

Calydonian boar Legendary boar hunted by heroes, including Theseus, Jason, Castor, and Pollux (the Dioscuri) and Nestor.

Calypso Sea nymph. A marooned Odysseus spends seven years living on an island with her. She offers him immortality to stay, but he chooses to return home.

Cassandra Daughter of Priam and Hecuba, king and queen of Troy. Cassandra promises to marry Apollo if he gives her the gift of prophesy. When she backs out of the deal, Apollo gives her the ability but makes it so that no one will believe her. She is taken by Agamemnon at the end of the Trojan War. (See also *Clytemnestra*.)

Cassiopeia See *Andromeda*.

Castor Son of Leda and Tyndareus; mortal brother of the immortal Pollux (together known as the Dioscuri), Helen, and Clytemnestra (see *Leda*). Popular subjects of myth, the brothers figure in the story of Jason and the Argonauts and Theseus's abduction of their sister Helen. When Castor dies, Pollux splits his immortality with him so that they can remain together alternating days in the world and the underworld.

Centaur Mythical creature with the head and torso of a man and the body of a horse. Centaurs are mountain and forest dwellers often seen harassing nymphs and maidens passing through the woods.

Cephalus Husband of Procris. Eos (Dawn) falls in love with him and tries in vain to lure him away. Another story tells how jealous Procris, having heard that Cephalus was unfaithful, went to spy on him hunting in the woods. Cephalus hears a noise and hurls his javelin, accidentally killing his wife.

Cerberus Three-headed dog guarding the gates of Hades; offspring of Typhon and Echidna. Heracles captures the beast in the last of his labors.

Chaos The void from which Gaea (Earth) and all things in the universe came. This creation story is most famously told in Hesiod's *Theogony*.

Charon Ferryman of the dead. For the price of an obol, Charon steers the boat that carries the dead across the rivers Acheron or Styx in the underworld.

Charybdis Dangerous whirlpool mentioned in the *Odyssey* positioned near Scylla in the Strait of Messina.

Chimera Mythical creature with the head of a lion, the body of a goat and a snake for a tail; offspring of Typhon and Echidna. The hero Bellerophon, riding his steed Pegasus, slays the Chimera, who is ravaging the city of Lycia.

Chiron Centaur son of Cronus. Chiron was Asclepius's mentor in the art of healing and reared Achilles and Theseus. When Heracles accidentally shoots him with an arrow, Chiron decides to relinquish his immortality to Prometheus.

Chloris (Flora) Goddess of flowers and fertility; personification of spring and the wife of Zephyrus, the west wind.

Circe Daughter of Helios (Sun). Circe turns Odysseus's men into swine when they land on her island. Swearing to do Odysseus no harm, she sleeps with him and releases his men from the spell. They remain on her island for a year.

Clytemnestra Daughter of Leda and Tyndareus; wife of Agamemnon; sister of Castor and half sister of Helen and Pollux (see *Leda*). In the first play of Aeschylus's *Oresteia*, she and her lover, Aegisthus, murder Agamemnon and his mistress, Cassandra, upon their return from Troy. She and Aegisthus are killed by her son Orestes, who plots with her daughter Electra in the second play of the trilogy.

Creon See *Antigone*.

Cronus (Saturn) Son of Uranus and Gaea; leader of the Titans; husband of Rhea; father of Zeus, Hera, Demeter, Poseidon, Hestia, and Hades. After Cronus ousts his father from the heavens, he swallows all his children to prevent them from ousting him. Rhea saves Zeus, who grows up to battle his father, release his siblings and hurl Cronus and his Titan allies into the underworld.

Cumaean Sibyl seer loved by Apollo. She agrees to sleep with Apollo in exchange for long life. When she refuses to follow through, Apollo grants her long life but not extended youth. She shrivels to the size of an insect.

Cyclopes One-eyed giants; children of Uranus and Gaea. Imprisoned by Uranus and then freed by Zeus, the Cyclopes become the blacksmiths of the gods, assisting Hephaestus. (See also *Polyphemus*.)

Daedalus Legendary inventor and architect who builds the Labyrinth to hold the Minotaur on Crete. When the hero Theseus slays the Minotaur and runs off with King Minos's daughter, the king imprisons Daedalus and his son, Icarus, in the Labyrinth. Daedalus builds wings so they can escape. Icarus flies too close to sun and his wings, held together by wax, melt, sending him plummeting to his death in the sea below. (See also *Pasiphae*.)

Danae Mother of Perseus; lover of Zeus. Zeus comes to Danae as a shower of gold and impregnates her. A proph-esy warned her father, Acrisius, of Danae's offspring. When he discovers the baby Perseus, he locks them both in a chest and sets it adrift at sea. They are retrieved by a fisherman's net near the island of Seriphus.

Daphne A nymph loved by Apollo. When Daphne refuses Apollo's advances, he tries to rape her. She begs her father, the river god Peneus, to save her. He turns her into a laurel tree. The laurel becomes a symbol of Apollo.

Deianeira Wife of Heracles. Heracles battles the river god Achelous for Deianeira's hand in marriage. The Centaur Nessus tricks her into poisoning her husband. Heracles dies and she hangs herself.

Dido Queen of Carthage. In Virgil's *Aeneid*, Dido falls in love with Aeneas. When he sails away without her, she throws herself on a funeral pyre.

Echidna Monster with the head of a nymph and the body of a serpent; mate of Typhon. Mother of many creatures involved in the labors of legendary heroes, including Cerberus, Chimera, Hydra, the Nemean Lion, and the Sphinx.

Echo Mountain nymph. When Echo tries to run interference for the unfaithful Zeus, Hera condemns her to say nothing more than a repetition of the last words she hears. She falls in love with Narcissus. When he rejects her, she shrivels up until only her voice remains.

Electra See *Clytemnestra*.

Enyo Goddess of war and violence. Enyo, meaning "horror," is often a companion of Ares, having varying familial relationships to him in different accounts.

Eos (Aurora) Goddess of the dawn; daughter of Titans Theia and Hyperion; sister of Helios (Sun) and Selene (Moon); mother of the winds Boreas, Eurus, Zephyrus, and Notus. Pictured as "rosy-fingered" and beautiful, Eos has many lovers including Ares and Orion. (See also *Cephalus*.)

Erinyes, Eumenides (Furiae) The Furies, tormentors of the guilty. The Furies are a trio of female spirits born out of the spilled blood of Uranus when he is castrated by Cronus.

Eris (Discordia) Goddess of strife; sister and companion of Ares. The causes of the Trojan War can be traced back to Eris's handiwork at the wedding of Peleus and Thetis when she throws the golden apple of discord into the mix.

Eros (Cupid, Amor) God of sexual love. Eros is the son of Ares and Aphrodite in some accounts; in others, the god was among the first to come out of Chaos along with

Gaea. A mischievous winged boy in many stories, Eros usually carries a bow and arrow with which he inspires love or indifference in his victims.

Europa Daughter of King Agenor of Phoenicia; mother of Minos, Rhadamanthus, and Sarpedon by Zeus. Zeus comes to Europa in the form of a white bull and carries her off to Crete, where he keeps her as his mistress. She later marries King Asterius of Crete.

Eurydice See *Orpheus*.

Fates (Greek, Moirae: Clotho, Atropos, Lachesis; Roman, Parcae: Decuma, Nona, Morta) Daughters of Zeus and Themis (Law). Often depicted spinning thread, the three goddesses are responsible for the destinies of all.

Gaea Earth goddess; among the principal deities to come out of Chaos. Gaea is the mother of Uranus (Sky) and Pontus (Sea) and, from her coupling with Uranus, the Titans.

Graces (Greek, Charites; Roman, Gratiae) Daughters of Zeus and Eurynome (an Oceanid). Aglaia, Euphrosyne, and Thalia, usually seen together, represent splendor, joy, and blossoming, respectively.

Hades, Pluto (Orcus, Pluto) God of the dead; son of Cronus and Rhea; husband of Persephone. When Zeus overthrows Cronus, he divides control of the universe with his two brothers leaving Poseidon to lord over the sea and Hades the underworld.

Harmonia Daughter of Ares and Aphrodite. (See *Cadmus*.)

Harpies Malevolent female spirits depicted as birds with human heads. Meaning "snatchers," the Harpies are associated with Hades's taking of bodies. (See also *Phineus*).

Hebe (Juventas) Goddess of youth and cupbearer of the gods; daughter of Zeus and Hera. Hebe marries the deified hero Heracles.

Hecate Goddess of night, darkness, and crossroads. Hecate is often associated with witchcraft and malevolence, but she can also be a benevolent force, as in the case of Persephone, whom she saves from Hades. She is closely associated with both Artemis and Selene.

Hector Legendary Trojan prince; son of Priam and Hecuba; husband of Andromache; father of Astyanax; brother of Paris. When Hector kills Patroclus in Homer's *Iliad*, Achilles kills Hector and drags his body from the back of a chariot until Priam convinces Achilles to let him give Hector a proper burial.

Hecuba Wife of King Priam of Troy; mother of Hector and Paris.

Helen Daughter of Zeus and Leda; sister of Pollux and half sister of Castor and Clytemnestra (see *Leda*). Helen, known for her amazing beauty, was first abducted by Theseus and rescued by her brothers, Castor and Pollux. She marries Menelaus, king of Sparta, and has a daughter, Hermione. Paris, prince of Troy, abducts her (or she willingly goes with him), and so begins the Trojan War.

Helios (Sol) Sun god; son of Titans Hyperion and Theia; brother of Selene (Moon) and Eos (Dawn); father of Circe and Pasiphae, among others. Helios drives the chariot of the sun across the sky. In a story told by Ovid, he lets his son Phaethon drive the chariot. Phaethon loses control, nearly crashes and scorches vast areas of the earth.

Heracles (Hercules) Deified hero; son of Zeus and Alcmene. Constantly persecuted by jealous Hera, Heracles is driven mad and kills his wife, Megara, and their children. An oracle orders him to perform 12 labors to redeem himself: in order, the Nemean lion, Lernaean hydra, Ceryneian hind, Erymanthian boar, Augean stables, Stymphalian birds, Cretan bull, horses of Diomedes, girdle of Hippolyta, cattle of Geryon, apples of the Hesperides and Cerberus. He succeeds and marries Deianeira, who, fooled by Nessus, accidentally poisons and kills him. After death Heracles is made immortal and marries the goddess Hebe. (See also *Cerberus, Chiron, Hydra, Jason,* and *Prometheus*.)

Hermaphroditus Beautiful son of Hermes and Aphrodite. In Ovid a nymph, Salmacis, falls in love with Hermaphroditus and, clinging to him, prays that they never be separated. Her wish is granted, and they become one being, half male and half female.

Hippolytus Son of Theseus and Antiope (Hippolyta), queen of the Amazons. Theseus leaves Antiope for Phaedra. In Euripides' *Hippolytus*, Phaedra falls in love with Hippolytus. When he rejects Phaedra's advances, she tells Theseus that he raped her and then kills herself. Theseus orders the death of his son only to find out too late that he was innocent.

Horae (Eunomia, Dike, Irene; in another version, Thallo, Auxo and Carpo) The seasons; daughters of Zeus and Themis. The Horae are goddesses of agriculture and universal order.

Hydra Nine-headed monster; offspring of Typhon and Echidna. Eight of its heads are mortal but will grow back as two when cut off; the ninth is immortal. In Heracles' second labor, he kills the Hydra by burning the stumps of the eight mortal heads so they cannot grow back and burying the immortal one.

Hypnos (Somnus) God of sleep; son of Nyx (Night) and Erebus (Darkness); brother of Thanatos (Death).

Icarus See *Daedalus*.

Ino Daughter of Cadmus and Harmonia; wife of King Athamas of Orchomenus. Ino raises the god Dionysus, offspring of her sister Semele and Zeus. Jealous Hera drives Ino and her husband insane, and they kill their children. She jumps into the sea to commit suicide and is turned into Leucothea, a sea goddess.

Io Lover of Zeus. Zeus turns Io into a heifer to spare her from Hera's wrath. Suspicious Hera places the heifer under the guard of the hundred-eyed Argus. Io is freed by Hermes, but Hera sends a gadfly to torment her. After a long journey, she regains her normal form and has a son by Zeus, Epaphus, an ancestor of Heracles.

Iphigeneia Daughter of Agamemnon and Clytemnestra. Agamemnon is ordered to sacrifice his daughter so the Greek ships can make it safely to Troy. Hearing that her husband has sacrificed Iphigeneia, Clytemnestra murders Agamemnon upon his return from Troy.

Iris Messenger goddess, particularly for Zeus and Hera; goddess of the rainbow.

Janus Roman god of the gate. Janus is depicted with two faces looking in opposite directions from gateways and doorways. Representing beginnings and endings, Janus presides over agricultural cycles, the onset and conclusion of battle, births and marriages.

Jason Son of Aeson; raised by Chiron. King Pelias of Iolcus sends Jason on a seemingly impossible quest for the Golden Fleece because it is prophesized that Jason will kill him. Along with heroes such as Heracles, Orpheus, Castor, and Pollux, Jason sets out on the ship *Argo*. With the help of the sorceress Medea, Jason takes the fleece and returns with Medea to Iolcus, where Jason kills King Pelias. They are banished from the city and move to Corinth, where after a few years Jason tries to leave Medea and marry another. In Euripides' *Medea*, Medea kills their children and flees to Athens. (See also *Calydonian boar*.)

Jocasta See *Oedipus*.

Laertes Father of Odysseus.

Laius See *Oedipus*.

Lares Roman household gods protecting the home, family and the hearth; patron spirits of travelers and crossroads. The Lares are usually seen in the plural, often as a pair of spirits. (See also *Penates*.)

Leda Lover of Zeus; wife of Tyndareus. Zeus comes to Leda in the form of a swan and impregnates her right around a time when she has also been with her mortal husband. She gives birth to four children, Pollux and Helen by Zeus (from an egg, in some accounts) and Castor and Clytemnestra by Tyndareus. (See also *Helen*, *Castor*, and *Clytemnestra*.)

Leto Daughter of Titans Coeus and Phoebe; mother of Artemis and Apollo. When Zeus falls in love with Leto and she becomes pregnant, Hera chases her away until she finally lands on Delos, where she gives birth to the divine twins, Artemis and Apollo.

Medea Daughter of King Aeetes of Colchis. A sorceress and lover of Jason, Medea uses her power to aid Jason in his quest for the Golden Fleece. (See also *Jason*.)

Medusa The only mortal of the three Gorgons, winged creatures with snakes for hair that turn anyone who looks at them into stone. When legendary hero Perseus beheads Medusa, the winged horse, Pegasus, and the giant Chrysaor spring from her neck.

Menelaus Legendary king of Sparta; son of Atreus; husband of Helen; brother of Agamemnon. When the Trojan prince Paris abducts his wife, Helen, Menelaus enlists Agamemnon to lead the Greek forces in a war against Troy.

Metis Goddess of wisdom; mother of Athena. When Metis becomes pregnant by Zeus, he swallows Metis to protect his offspring and Athena is born from his head.

Midas King of Phrygia. Granted one wish by Dionysus, Midas asks that everything he touches turn to gold. Unable to eat or drink, he realizes his folly and has the wish reversed.

Minos King of Crete; son of Zeus and Europa; husband of Pasiphae; father of Ariadne, Phaedra, and others. Minos is a main player in many of the legends of Crete (see *Ariadne, Daedalus, Minotaur, Pasiphae*). The great king and lawmaker becomes a judge of the dead after his death.

Minotaur Mythical creature with the body of a man and the head of a bull kept by King Minos of Crete in the Labyrinth; offspring of Pasiphae and a bull (see *Pasiphae* for birth). The Minotaur is killed by the Athenian hero Theseus.

Muses Nine daughters of Zeus and Mnemosyne (Memory) that serve as inspiration for the arts and sciences. Each muse is assigned a particular art: Calliope, epic poetry; Clio, history; Erato, love poetry; Euterpe, lyric poetry; Melpomene, tragedy; Polyhymnia, music and song; Terpsichore, dance; Thalia, comedy; and Urania, astronomy.

Narcissus Beautiful son of Liriope (nymph) and Cephisus (river god). When Narcissus rejects the advances of a nymph, the goddess of love, Aphrodite, damns him to fall in love with his own reflection. (See also *Echo*.)

Nemesis Goddess of vengeance, justice, and retribution; daughter of Nyx (Night).

Nereids Sea nymphs; daughters of Nereus and Doris (an Oceanid). Often numbered at 50, many Nereids have roles in Classical mythology, most notably Thetis, mother of Achilles, and Amphitrite, wife of Poseidon.

Nereus Sea god; son of Pontus and Gaea; husband of Doris (an Oceanid), father of the Nereids.

Nestor King of Pylos and hero of the Trojan War. In Homer's *Iliad* Nestor is portrayed as the voice of wisdom for the Greeks.

Nike (Victoria) Goddess of victory. She is usually winged and often seen as an aspect of Athena.

Niobe Wife of Amphion. Niobe boasts that she is better than Leto because she has seven sons and seven daughters while Leto only has two. Unfortunately, Leto's two children are Artemis and Apollo who avenge Niobe's hubris by killing all of her children.

Nyx (Nox) Personification of night; mother of Hypnos (Sleep), Thanatos (Death), and Nemesis (Vengeance), among others. Nyx is one of the principal entities to arise out of Chaos.

Oceanids Sea nymphs; daughters of the Titans Oceanos and Tethys. The most famous Oceanids in myth include Metis, mother of Athena, and Doris, mother of the Nereids.

Oceanos Sea god; Titan son of Uranus and Gaea; husband of Tethys; father of the Oceanids.

Odysseus King of Ithaca and hero of the Trojan War; son of Laertes; husband of Penelope; father of Tele-machus. In Homer's *Iliad* Odysseus is the most clever of the Greeks. His lengthy return home from the war is the subject of Homer's *Odyssey*. (See *Aeolus, Argus, Calypso, Charybdis, Circe, Penelope, Polyphemus, Scylla, Sirens,* and *Telemachus.*)

Oedipus Legendary king of Thebes; son of Laius and Jocasta, king and queen of Thebes; father of Antigone, Eteocles, Ismene, and Polynices. In Sophocles' *Oedipus the King*, Oedipus was abandoned as a child and raised in Corinth. As an adult he returns to Thebes and unwittingly kills his father and marries his own mother after solving the riddle of the Sphinx. When the truth is revealed, he blinds himself and goes into exile.

Orestes Son of Agamemnon and Clytemnestra. In Aeschylus's trilogy, the *Oresteia*, Orestes avenges his father's death by killing Clytemnestra and her lover, Aegisthus, who plotted Agamemnon's murder. Orestes is tormented by the Furies for the murders but is eventually released from their persecution by a jury in a court presided over by Athena.

Orion Son of Poseidon. Orion is a giant and a great hunter with whom Eos falls in love. In one version, Artemis disapproves of the union and kills Orion. He is made into a constellation.

Orpheus Great musician and poet; son of the muse Calliope and Apollo (in some versions); husband of Eurydice. Having been bitten by a snake, Eurydice dies on their wedding day. Orpheus convinces Hades with his beautiful music to let him escort her out of Hades on the condition that he does not look back at her until they have left the underworld. He turns around accidentally and Eurydice is sent back to Hades permanently. Orpheus is later ripped to pieces by a group of maenads, followers of Dionysus.

Pan (Faunus, Inuus) God of flocks, the forest, and fertility. He is depicted in myth as a satyr (see *Satyr*) and sexual aggressor, often seen chasing nymphs in the woods.

Pandora The first woman. Zeus enlists Hephaestus to create Pandora. When Prometheus steals fire from Olympus and gives it to man, Zeus sends Pandora to Prometheus's brother Epimetheus along with a jar that she is ordered not to open. Curiosity gets the better of her, and she opens the jar, releasing evil and misery into the world. The only thing remaining in the jar when she closes the lid is hope.

Paris Prince of Troy; son of Priam and Hecuba; brother of Hector. Paris's kidnapping of Helen causes the Trojan War. In Homer's *Iliad* he kills Achilles by shooting an arrow into the Greek warrior's weak heel.

Pasiphae Wife of King Minos of Crete; mother of Ariadne, Phaedra, and others. When Minos insults Poseidon, the god inspires Pasiphae to yearn for a bull. She enlists Daedalus to construct a wooden cow that she hides in to mate with the animal. The offspring of this union is the Minotaur. (See also *Daedalus, Minos,* and the *Minotaur*.)

Patroclus Greek hero of the Trojan War. Patroclus is the constant companion of Achilles. When Hector kills Patroclus, Achilles reenters the fighting, killing Hector and many others in a spree of vengeance.

Pegasus Winged horse; offspring of the gorgon Medusa and Poseidon. Along with the giant Chrysaor, Pegasus springs from Medusa's neck when Perseus decapitates her. (See also *Bellerophon*.)

Peleus Father of Achilles; husband of Thetis. Attended by the gods, the wedding of Peleus and Thetis is a popular theme in myth.

Penates Roman household gods; protectors of home, family, and hearth. Always seen in the plural, the Penates are often worshipped along with the Lares (see *Lares*).

Penelope Wife of Odysseus. Besieged by suitors throughout Odysseus's 10-year absence after the Trojan War, she remains faithful. She tells the suitors that she cannot remarry until she has finished weaving a shroud, but every night she unravels the work she has done, thus never finishing.

Persephone (Proserpina) See *Demeter*.

Perseus Son of Zeus and Danae (see *Danae* for birth). Challenged by King Polydectes, who is trying to get rid of him, Perseus sets out with various magical items from the gods (winged sandals, a special sword, and others) to slay the gorgon Medusa. When he returns with the gorgon's head to find Polydectes pursuing his mother, Perseus holds up the head and turns the king and his men into stone. (See also *Andromeda* and *Medusa*.)

Phaedra Daughter of Minos and Pasiphae. See *Hippolytus*.

Phaethon See *Helios*.

Phineus Legendary king of Salmydessus. Apollo gives Phineus the gift of prophesy but forbids him to reveal what he sees. When Phineus discloses details about the future, Zeus blinds him and sends the Harpies to snatch away anything he tries to eat. Jason and the Argonauts thwart the Harpies in exchange for information about the future of their journey.

Pollux (Greek, Polydeuces) See *Castor*.

Polynices See *Antigone*.

Polyphemus Cyclops encountered by Odysseus in the *Odyssey*. Odysseus and his men escape the cave of Polyphemus by blinding the one-eyed giant and hiding under his sheep as they go out to pasture.

Priam King of Troy; husband of Hecuba; father of Hector and Paris.

Priapus God of gardens, vines, flocks, and fertility. Statues of Priapus with an exaggerated phallus were often placed in Greek and Roman gardens.

Procris See *Cephalus*.

Prometheus Creator of man; son of the Titan Iapetus. Having fashioned man out of earth and water, Prometheus steals fire from Olympus and gives it to mortals. As punishment Zeus chains Prometheus to a rock with a bird incessantly pecking at his immortal liver. He is eventually freed by Heracles. Prometheus is also responsible for providing man with crafts, medicine, writing, and many other gifts.

Psyche Personification of the soul. Eros falls in love with Psyche, a beautiful nymph. Aphrodite forbids the affair, so Eros will only come to her in the dark when she cannot see who he is. Curious Psyche tries to get a look at him, but a drop of oil from her lamp falls and wakes him. He leaves her, but they are eventually reunited.

Pygmalion Sculptor in myth. Pygmalion creates a statue of a beautiful woman, which he calls Galatea. He falls in love with it and prays to Aphrodite that he find a wife like the statue. Aphrodite, impressed with his work, makes Galatea real.

Pyramus The Romeo and Juliet of Ovid's *Metamorphoses*, Pyramus and Thisbe grow up next door to each other and fall in love. Their parents forbid them to marry, so they elope. Thisbe encounters a lioness, bloody from the hunt, at the meeting spot and runs away, leaving behind her veil. When Pyramus sees the veil and the lioness, he assumes Thisbe has been killed and stabs himself. When Thisbe sees Pyramus dying, she stabs herself and they die in each other's arms.

Remus See *Romulus*.

Rhea See *Cronus*.

Romulus Legendary founder of Rome; son of Mars and Rhea Silvia (priestess); twin brother of Remus. Abandoned as infants, the twins Romulus and Remus are nursed by a she-wolf and eventually found and raised by a shepherd. They grow up to co-found a city, but a power struggle leads to Romulus killing Remus. The new city is thus called Rome after its sole leader. Romulus is deified as Quirinus after his death. (See also *Sabines*.)

Sabines When Romulus founds Rome, bandits and other riffraff populate the city, but they have no women to marry. At a festival Romulus abducts all the young Sabine women from a nearby community to couple with the Roman men.

Satyr Creature with the head and torso of a man and the horns, tail, legs, and hooves of a goat. Satyrs are the lascivious and gluttonous followers of Dionysus, often seen in the woods pursuing nymphs.

Scylla Sea monster situated across from Charybdis in the Strait of Messina. In the *Odyssey* six of Scylla's 12 dog heads snatch and devour six of Odysseus's men as they sail by.

Selene (Luna) Moon goddess; daughter of Titans Hyperion and Theia; sister of Helios and Eos. Selene is often associated with magic.

Semele Daughter of Cadmus and Harmonia; mother of Dionysus by Zeus. When Zeus displays his divine form to Semele, she is scorched by the splendor and dies. Zeus saves the unborn Dionysus and sews him into his thigh.

Sirens Nymphs with the heads and torsos of women and the wings and lower bodies of birds whose song lures passing sailors to their destruction on nearby rocks. Odysseus escapes unharmed by plugging his crew's ears with wax. He decides to be tied to the mast so he can hear the beautiful music but pass safely.

Sisyphus Underworld figure. As punishment for wronging the gods, Sisyphus is damned to eternally push a boulder up a hill only to have it roll back down once it reaches the top.

Tantalus Underworld figure; father of Niobe; ancestor of the doomed house of Atreus (see *Agamemnon, Clytemnestra,* and *Orestes*). As punishment for trying to trick the gods into eating his son Pelops, Tantalus is damned to spend eternity surrounded by plentiful food and water that he can see but cannot reach.

Tartarus The lowest level of the underworld. Tartarus is one of the principal entities to arise from Chaos. Wrongdoers, most notably the Titans after being defeated by Zeus, are banished to Tartarus.

Telemachus Son of Odysseus and Penelope. Telemachus helps Odysseus slay his mother's suitors in the *Odyssey*.

Terminus Roman god of boundaries and borders.

Tethys Titan; daughter of Uranus and Gaea; wife of Oceanos; mother of the Oceanids.

Thanatos Personification of death; son of Nyx (Night); brother of Hypnos (Sleep).

Themis Titan goddess of justice; daughter of Uranus and Gaea; mother of the Horae (Seasons) and the Moirae (Fates) by Zeus.

Theseus Legendary Athenian hero; son of Aegus (a mortal) and Poseidon with Aethra, who was impregnated by both on the same night. The stories of Theseus are similar to other heroes such as his cousin Heracles. Theseus is sent away as an infant, returns to find glory and performs a collection of labors. His most notable feat is the slaying of the Minotaur. (See also *Antiope, Ariadne, Calydonian boar, Castor, Chiron, Daedalus, Helen, Hippolytus,* and the *Minotaur*.)

Thetis See *Achilles*.

Thisbe See *Pyramus*.

Tiresias Prophet of myth. Blinded by the gods (either Athena or Hera in different versions) but given the gift of prophesy, Tiresias plays a role in many myths, particularly in the story of Oedipus.

Titans 12 children of Uranus and Gaea who make up the second generation of gods. The daughters are Eurybia, Phoebe, Rhea, Tethys, Theia, and Themis. The sons are Coeus, Crius, Cronus, Hyperion, Iapetus, and Oceanus. They form several pairings, the most notable being Cronus and Rhea, who beget Zeus and other Olympians. The Titans are defeated by Zeus and his allies and banished to Tartarus.

Triton Sea god; son of Poseidon and Amphitrite. In the plural Tritons are the half-man half-fish companions of the sea nymphs, the Nereids.

Tyche (Fortuna) Goddess of fortune, fate, and chance; daughter of Zeus in one version and Tethys and Oceanus in another. She is depicted with a wheel of fortune.

Uranus God of the sky; son and husband of Gaea (Earth); father of the Titans with Gaea. When the Titan Cronus castrates Uranus, Aphrodite is born from his blood.

Mesopotamian Mythology

Mesopotamia, the land "between the rivers" in the Tigris and Euphrates valleys (now Iraq and adjacent areas), was home to the world's earliest civilizations. The Sumerians, whose cities date back to around 4000 B.C., had a well-developed agricultural and mercantile economy and a rich religious life. A succession of other peoples, both Indo-European and Semitic, including the Hittites, Akkadians, Babylonians, and Assyrians, absorbed and added to the basic elements of Sumerian culture. There are many points of similarity between Mesopotamian mythology and events recorded in the Hebrew Bible, notably an account of a great world-engulfing flood.

The Sumerians and later Mesopotamian peoples recorded their myths (and much other information besides) in cuneiform writing inscribed on clay tablets. The main surviving sources of this mythology are the creation myth and cosmogony (account of the origin of the universe) in the Babylonian *Enuma Elish* (ca. 1000 B.C.), and the epic of *Gilgamesh*, a legendary king, known in its most complete form from tablets dating to the seventh century B.C. The myths in these sources have deep oral roots, and exist in several different and often inconsistent versions.

In the material below, deities are listed by their Sumerian names, with Akkadian, Babylonian, or Assyrian counterparts in parentheses.

Major Figures in Mesopotamian Myth and Legend

An (Anu) Personification of sky; husband of Ki (Earth); father of Enlil. An is a pivotal figure in creation myths but plays a much smaller role in later myths.

Apsu Personification of sweet water. In the Sumerian cosmogony, Apsu (masculine) and Tiamat (feminine) are the first entities to arise from the primordial oceans. From their union comes An and Enki. Apsu is killed by Enki.

Dumuzi (Tammuz) Shepherd god; god of vegetation; husband of Inanna. Inanna banishes him to the underworld, but he is given new life one day a year. This story is similar to those of the Egyptian Osiris and several Greek figures such as Persephone and Adonis.

Enki (Ea) God of the earth, groundwater, fecundity, and magic. Enki is crafty and the trickster among the gods but well disposed toward humans, to whom he gives the arts.

Enkidu Companion of Gilgamesh. Enkidu is a wild man molded from clay and sent by the gods to temper Gilgamesh, who had become a tyrannical king. They become best friends and share many adventures. Enkidu falls ill and dies after angering the gods.

Enlil Supreme sky god controlling storms and the destinies of men; son of An. Enlil is the equivalent of the Greek Zeus, king of the gods, who can be both a friendly and destructive force in human affairs.

Ereshkigal Goddess of death; sister of Inanna. Ereshkigal rules Kur, the underworld.

Gilgamesh King of Uruk; most popular legendary hero of Mesopotamian myth. Gilgamesh has many adventures, including slaying Humbaba, guardian of the forest; slaying the bull of heaven sent by Anu (An) at the request of Ishtar (Inanna), angry because Gilgamesh rejects her advances; and in a quest for eternal life, visiting the immortal Utnapishtim (Ziusudra).

Humbaba In the story of Gilgamesh, guardian of the forest in the domain of Shamash (Utu). Gilgamesh kills Humbaba, angering Enlil.

Inanna (Ishtar) Sumerian goddess of love and war; daughter of An; sister of Ereshkigal. Known for having a multitude of lovers, most notably Dumuzi (Tammuz), and for attempting to take control of the underworld from Ereshkigal.

Ki (Ninhursag) Supreme earth goddess; personification of Mother Earth; wife of An (Sky).

Kingu Second husband of Tiamat after Apsu. Tiamat intends to make Kingu the supreme deity, giving him the tablets of destiny, but they are both defeated by Marduk.

Marduk Son of Ea (Enki); protector of Babylon. A powerful figure in later Mesopotamian myth, Marduk defeats Tiamat and Kingu, becoming the supreme deity responsible for the arrangement of the universe in its current form.

Siduri Goddess of the vine. Gilgamesh comes to her in his quest for eternal life, and she tells him to eat, drink, enjoy life, and accept his mortality.

Tiamat Personification of salt water. See *Apsu*.

Urshanabi Ferryman of Utnapishtim (Ziusudra). Urshanabi helps Gilgamesh across perilous waters to the land where Utnapishtim lives in immortal bliss.

Utu (Shamash) Sun god responsible for justice among gods and men.

Ziusudra (Utnapishtim, Atrahasis) The Mesopotamian Noah, the only mortal spared from the universal flood. In his quest for eternal life, Gilgamesh goes to Utnapishtim (Ziusudra), who was made immortal, to find out how to overcome death; he tells Gilgamesh that he cannot.

Egyptian Mythology

The two most important Egyptian cosmogonies are identified with two principal pharonic cities, Heliopolis and Hermopolis. In the Heliopolitan cosmogony, the primordial waters give birth to Atum (the Sun). From his mucus (or semen) comes Shu (Air) and Tefnut (Moisture). Shu and Tefnut beget Geb (Earth) and Nut (Sky), who beget two gods, Osiris and Seth, and two goddesses, Isis and Nephthys. These nine deities are the core pantheon, joined by other gods such as Horus, son of Isis and Osiris. The Hermopolitan cosmogony features four god-goddess pairs: Kuk and Kauket (darkness), Huh and Hauhet (limitlessness), Amon and Amaunet (invisibility), and Nun and Naunet (primordial waters).

When the pharaoh Menes (also called Narmer) united Upper and Lower Egypt to found the Old Kingdom (ca. 2575–2130 B.C.), he joined together the two pantheons; in his system, Ptah spoke the eight Hermopolitan gods into existence, and then engendered the nine Heliopolitan deities.

Major Figures in Egyptian Mythology

Amon Sun and wind god. With his female counterpart, Amaunet, Amon represented the principle of invisibility in the Hermopolitan cosmogony. As Amon-Ra he became a very powerful deity in later dynasties.

Anubis Jackal-headed god of mummification.

Apis A great bull that was identified with Ptah.

Aten Personification of the sun disk. The pharaoh Amenhotep IV, who renamed himself Akhenaten, declared Aten the sole higher power. After Akhenaten's death (1350 B.C.), the cult of Aten declined.

Atum Sun god, particularly of the setting sun; chief deity and creator god. In the Heliopolitan cosmogony, Atum comes from Nun, the primordial waters, and creates Shu (Air) and Tefnut (Moisture).

Bastet Cat goddess; goddess of vengeance; daughter of Ra; consort of Ptah. The cult of Bastet did not arise until around 1000 B.C.

Hapi Personification of the annual flooding of the Nile.

Hathor Goddess of love and fertility; daughter of Ra. Hathor is depicted as a cow and thought to be present at births. Many pharaohs deemed themselves the son of Hathor.

Horus Sky god; god of horizons; son of Isis and Osiris. Horus, often depicted as a falcon, was the most popular and powerful deity at times, with many pharaohs claiming to be an incarnation of the god.

Isis Goddess of love; wife and sister of Osiris; mother of Horus.

Khnum Ram-headed god of the Nile's rising water. In older accounts Khnum creates the gods and mankind on his potter's wheel.

Ma'at Goddess of truth and justice. Her symbol is a feather that is weighed against the heart of the dead to decide the fate of the soul.

Mut Vulture goddess; consort of Amon. Mummies wore a Mut amulet.

Nephthys Daughter of Geb and Nut; sister of Isis, Osiris, and Seth. Nephthys is depicted as the companion of the dead as they make their journey to be judged in the afterlife.

Nut Personification of sky; wife of Geb (Earth); mother of Isis, Osiris, Seth, and Nephthys. **Osiris** God of the underworld and judge of the dead; son of Geb and Nut. Osiris's brother Seth cuts him into pieces, and he is reconstituted and resurrected by his sister Isis, with whom he fathers the god Horus. Osiris is also a fertility god associated with the flooding of the Nile.

Ptah Earth god. Ptah is the primordial hill that appears out of water and speaks the rest of the gods into existence in the Memphite theology. In another account he creates the gods and universe from mud.

Ra Sun god, particularly the midday sun. In the Heliopolitan cosmogony, Ra (along with his other two aspects, Atum and Khepri) emerges out of Nun, the primordial waters, and creates Shu (Air) and Tefnut (Moisture). In later dynasties Ra takes on the form Amon-Ra and becomes a very powerful deity. (See also *Sekhmet*.)

Sekhmet Personification of feminine power; goddess of war and vengeance. Sekhmet, depicted as a lioness, is created from the eye of Ra to destroy mankind. Ra changes his mind and stops her before she has completely ravaged the earth.

Seth Malevolent god of storms, foreign lands, and destructive forces; son of Geb and Nut. Seth was the patron of the desert land of Upper Egypt and was at times the chief god, while Horus ruled at other times. Seth is often seen engaged in a power struggle with Horus in myth. (See also *Osiris*.)

Thoth God of wisdom, writing, and the moon. Worshipped in Hermopolis, he was depicted as a baboon. Some accounts make Thoth the son of Ra.

ECONOMICS & BUSINESS

ECONOMICS

Economics (from the Greek, meaning "management of a household") is the study of how human beings coordinate their wants by the efficient production and distribution of goods and services. The four central issues addressed by economics are (1) what to produce; (2) how much to produce; (3) how to produce it; and (4) for whom to produce it.

Economics today deals not only with individuals and households but with cities, regions, nations, and worldwide trade. The principal concerns of economics are markets for goods and services, but there are many other aspects of economics—including the distribution of income, labor relations, the welfare of citizens, and the environment.

There are two main branches of economics: *microeconom-ics*, which deals with individual choices; and *macroeconomics*, which deals with large-scale or general economic factors, usually of nations. Additional specializations include *development economics*, the study of improving the economies of underdeveloped countries; *international economics*, the study of economic issues on a global scale; *labor economics*, the study of wages, workers, and unions; *econometrics*, the application of statistical methods to estimate economic relationships; *urban economics*, the study of cities, infrastructure, and urban populations; *Soviet economics*, the assessment of the command economy of the former Soviet Union; and *environmental economics*, the analysis of environmental costs and benefits.

Economic History

The Ancient World

Our modern economic structure based on a highly integrated system of manufacturing, services, finance, and trade, began only about 300 years ago. Human activity, however, dates back about 20,000 years so how we live today is quite a recent development. Over the last century or so history and archaeology have combined to reveal to us how the past unfolded and how many current endeavors have their origins in the ancient world.

About 12,000 years ago as the Ice Age was ending the Earth grew warmer and wetter. Archaeologists speculate that this resulted in an abundance of wild plants and grains including wheat and barley in the Middle East around the area known as the Fertile Crescent bordered by the Nile River and the Tigris and Euphrates Rivers in Mesopotamia. Over the course of several centuries humans figured out how to use seeds from the wild plants to grow as much wheat and other grains as they needed. This led to the end of foraging for food and the establishment of permanent settlements. In China around 8000 B.C., the cultivation of rice made it the key source of food for millions.

By the time written records of human activities in Mesopotamia appeared about 3500 B.C., sophisticated agricultural methods had become well-established and social organization highly structured. This is clearly demonstrated in the history of Egypt, where the annual Nile River floods produced the most fertile soil in the entire region so that as early as 3000 B.C. the brilliant civilization of the pharaohs was already in place. Egypt's ability to create large, powerful armies to conquer all of the surrounding areas was based on a reliable food supply as well as on slave labor. Egypt remained the indomitable power in the Middle East for about 1,500 years and during that time they created a complex trading system based on both land and sea routes down the Nile, and across the Mediterranean as far west as Spain and western Africa, and east to Anatolia (modern Turkey) and the Horn of Africa. So although agriculture would remain the principal occupation of the great majority of people down to the 20th century A.D., the economies of many early civilizations would be greatly affected by the development of trade routes, some of which exist today.

During the 2,000 years before the Christian era, trading activity was growing throughout the world. We now know that burgeoning civilizations in Asia, as well as Europe, had learned the intrinsic economic value of trade during this period. The Chinese were making sea voyages to Korea, Vietnam, and Japan. In the Mediterranean region, the Phoenicians and the Greeks expanded maritime exploration and trade and as early as 500 B.C. travelled freely across the Mediterranean carrying their wine and olive oil to Sicily and to the Middle East.

As the Roman republic gradually evolved into the most powerful empire in history its people were mainly farmers and land ownership was the only important sign of wealth. But by 400 B.C. sea power had become essential and Rome would conform to that necessity but in its own time. Early on the Romans were reluctant to become a maritime nation, preferring to have others carry on their trade for them and to rely on their own vaunted legions for military protection and expansion. The rise of Carthage, a north African city-state, as an aggressive naval power pursuing conquest as well as trade in Sicily and southern Italy forced a change in strategy. Between 250 B.C. and 50 B.C. the Roman navy gained total mastery over the Mediterranean, which they now called Mare Nostrum ("our sea"). In the middle of the first century B.C., when Julius Caesar was solidifying his empire, he conquered Egypt so that the Romans would have ready access to its graineries to help feed the people at home. An imperial navy designed to protect and to transport essential items to the home nation would become the standard for many future empires.

The Middle Ages and the Renaissance

In medieval Europe from the ninth to the 15th centuries, the dominant system of political and economic organization was *feudalism*, which defined the relationship between people of different social statuses. Most numerous were the peasants, who were entitled to farm their lord's land in exchange for rendering homage and service—including a portion of what they grew. In return, lords were obligated to render protection to their vassals. The feudal order was not limited to the relationship between tenants and lords: minor nobles, nobles, and kings stood in a comparable relationship to one another. Feudalism ended as a result of many factors, though the most crucial was the Black Death, which diminished the workforce to such an extent that laborers could demand better terms for their service and migrate to cities.

During the Renaissance (14th–16th centuries), banking systems were developed in Florence and other Italian cities. Venice and Genoa emerged as important trading powers with large navies and great wealth. The major states of Portugal, Spain, England, and France began to explore the world across the Atlantic Ocean, finding enormous wealth in gold and silver. They founded colonies in North and South America that in short order became sources of continuous revenue.

Joint-stock companies were formed in the 16th and 17th centuries in England and the Netherlands. From the 16th century to the 19th, European economies followed the system of *mercantilism*. The theory underlying mercantilism was that economic prosperity depended on the acquisition of gold and silver (bullion), which could be secured only by maintaining a positive balance of trade. Mercantilism encouraged foreign trade and the opening of new markets, the encouragement of domestic industry and agriculture to produce goods or crops for sale in those markets, trading companies to control the trade, and protectionist policies to protect domestic markets from competition and to minimize imports. Colonies were desirable both as sources of raw materials and as export markets, and naval power was essential to protecting sea trade and colonies. Mercantilism eventually gave way to more liberal free-trade policies based on more flexible concepts of wealth and economic prosperity.

Capitalism and the Industrial Revolution

About 1750 the Industrial Revolution began in Great Britain, initially in the textile industry, with key technologies such as the steam engine. Industrial development followed in other countries in the 19th century, including France, Germany, and the United States, and led to the rise of the economic system known as *capitalism*.

As the tools of industrial manufacturing were created, a person with money to invest could seek out the latest leading-edge inventions and develop a more efficient factory, thus stealing market share from now outdated rivals. Instead of slowly amassing wealth over a lifetime, there was now a systematic way to amass wealth relatively quickly. This new method of amassing wealth through investment in capital was called capitalism; a capitalist invests money in an enterprise with the objective of receiving more in return than what was initially invested.

The Industrial Revolution and the growth of capitalism brought unparalleled growth in economic output and in population, but also substantial dislocation of agricultural populations, destruction of natural environments, and very often harsh conditions for workers.

The First Economists

The Industrial Revolution got underway in a serious way in England, where an abundance of coal and iron, combined with a large, mobile population and a banking and investing structure that raised capital efficiently, produced the first modern economic system. So it is no surprise that the first important books about capitalism were written by two Englishmen and one Scot. Several of their insights into how this new economic system worked remain relevant today.

Adam Smith (1723–90), a Scot, was the first great exponent of capitalism and the free market system. In his most famous book, *The Wealth of Nations* (1776), Smith argued that if individuals are left to pursue their self-interest without government interference, they will act, in

Smith's famous words, as if "led by an invisible hand," which allocates goods and services to make the economy work to the benefit of society as a whole. Smith contended that competitive markets, where individuals pursue their own interests, could promote their freedoms and achieve the objectives of efficient production and economic growth. The ability of the market to correct itself through competition would provide protection from harmful actions of the selfish and the greedy. Often overlooked, however, is Smith's insistence, based on strong religious convictions, that society must care for the poor and needy. He favored higher wages for workers so they would not live in poverty, and he thought greater competition would bring those higher wages about. In the early part of the 19th century, however, economic liberalism came to be seen primarily as serving business interests.

This change in perspective was reflected in the writings of the English economists Thomas Malthus and David Ricardo, who elaborated upon Smith's application of scientific rules in the economy, with powerful implications for the working poor and the condition of laborers. Malthus is best known for the theory of population he presented in his *Essay on Population*, first published in 1798. According to Malthus, population increases geometrically while the food supply increases arithmetically. In other words, population always outgrows the supply of food, meaning that poverty and social unrest were inevitable. (See "The Global Food Supply.") War, famine, and disease therefore were useful hindrances to unwanted population growth. The Malthusian viewpoint grew increasingly controversial over the next century, but was very influential in the early years of classical economics. Ricardo built upon Malthus's thesis in his major work, *The Principles of Political Economy and Taxation* (1817), in which he argued that the pressure of population would keep wages from rising higher than subsistence level. This "iron law of wages," as he called it, was based on the fact that when wage rates rise above subsistence levels, the number of workers quickly increases, thereby putting downward pressure on wages.

The implication of these arguments was that economics is governed by scientific laws that are unalterable; consequently, poverty is inevitable, and government policies intended to help the working poor or improve their prospects to make a good living are pointless, perhaps even injurious to the smooth functioning of the economy. Ricardo is highly regarded today more because of his theory of "comparative advantage" that encouraged free trade among nations who produced different commodities more efficiently.

The Rise of Socialism

Capitalist approaches to business soon revealed a darker reality for the many people working under its rules. Dangerous working conditions, unsafe machines, and extensive use of child labor were the rule, not the exception, and by the 1830's the resulting misery brought thousands of workers together to form the first organized trade unions. These organizations, however, represented only skilled craft workers so that a division in the labor movement left the unskilled to fend for themselves.

By the 1840's, some educated men began to speak out against the treatment of human beings as mere cogs in the machinery of capitalism. The movements for workers' rights and social justice that we call "socialism" and "communism" had their origins during this time.

The principal historical figure in the history of socialism is Karl Marx (1818–83), who, along with Friedrich Engels (1820–95), conceived the theory and tactics of revolutionary proletarian socialism, which became known as Marxism. Marx was primarily concerned with the dynamics of capitalism and the historical laws he believed would cause its replacement, rather than with the structure of a socialist system. His most famous work, co-written with Engels in 1848, was the *Communist Manifesto*, which outlined a theory of class struggle and the revolutionary role of the proletariat that would force the "overthrow of all existing social conditions." At the conclusion, they urged, "Workers of the world unite!" His greatest work, however, was *Das Kapital*, published in three volumes (1867, 1885, 1894). Based on years of study in economics and history, *Kapital* contains all of Marx's best-known theories, including the "labor theory of value" and "surplus value" that in a sense turned capitalism on its head by making the worker the actual creator of capital that further enriched the capitalist, who then had more power to lower the worker's wages.

In the end Marx was wrong about many things, as virtually all influential thinkers are. But his influence has been, as the philosopher Peter Singer notes, on the order of the great religious leaders in world history. Even in societies where his communist ideas and vision of violent revolution were rejected, the political organizations that evolved over the years brought serious reform to a system based on "unfettered capitalism." The German Social Democratic Party, founded in the mid-1860's, became the largest working-class party in the world, and in France, an uprising in 1871 established the Paris Commune, hailed by Marx and Engels as the first "dictatorship of the proletariat," though it was brutally suppressed within three months. Eight years later, the creation of the Federation of the Socialist Workers of France revived the movement there, and three years after that the French Workers' Party was founded. The Fabian Society in England, founded in 1883, argued that all the programs for changing society were in place and would eventually bring about harmonious relations between workers and capitalists. This movement would evolve into the modern-day Labour Party. One could argue that all of the social welfare programs in place today had their origins in Marx's ideas.

Ironically, one of the central tenets Marx and Engels included in *The Communist Manifesto* was their belief that the uprising of the proletariat and the creation of a communist state could take place only in an advanced capitalist economy such as Germany, France, or Great Britain. But the two most successful leaders of communist revolutions, V. I. Lenin and Mao Zedong, applied Marxist ideas in nations swarming with peasants and without an urban proletariat. In the end, they and their successors twisted Marx's ideas and created violent dictatorships that caused the death of millions of people who opposed them. In time, the term *communist* became totally repugnant to most people.

The Great Depression

Capitalism continued as the world's primary economic system, and increased trading between countries in the early 20th century helped to create a more connected global economy. The business cycles of local economies began to have worldwide effects, and when the U.S. stock market boom of the 1920's turned bust on October 29, 1929 ("Black Tuesday"), it helped to throw the fragile global economy that was still recovering from World War I into a deep worldwide depression.

At the depths of what came to be called the Great Depression, in 1931, world industrial production was 38 percent less than what it had been in June 1929, and there were an estimated 30 million unemployed people worldwide. This single year saw countries descend into mass unemployment and hunger, the breakdown of international exchange, and the failure of great financial institutions.

The recovery that began in 1932 brought the world economy back to life by 1937, thanks to increased governmental deficit spending and the country-by-country abandonment of the gold standard. But the global economic downturn had lasting effects on all it touched, and helped to sow the seeds of World War II in Europe.

Social Welfare

Partly in response to the mass unemployment of the Great Depression, most advanced nations today have market systems with some form of social safety net. Markets are generally subject to standards of openness and disclosure to ensure competition, and there are prohibitions against unfair labor practices and environmental damage.

Government-funded social welfare programs date back at least to Germany in the 19th century; in the United States today these programs include unemployment benefits, Social Security, Medicare, and Medicaid. The developed European countries almost all have substantially larger social welfare programs than the United States. In addition, many developed economies have government-subsidized agricultural sectors, and some have subsidized banking and industrial enterprises; there is continuing pressure to improve productivity by eliminating such subsidies.

Microeconomics

Microeconomics is a bottom-up view of the economy, focusing on individual households and firms and the allocation of economic resources through supply and demand. It provides answers to the essential questions of which goods and services to produce, how, in what quantities, and for whom.

The economist Alfred Marshall (1842–1924), of Cambridge, developed many of the basic tools of microeconomics, such as the *demand curve*. In 1938 the American economist Abram Bergson (1914–2003) showed mathematically that, with certain assumptions, markets yield an optimal allocation of resources. At the same time, the conceptual foundations of economic analysis were further developed by the Nobel prize-winning economist Paul Samuelson (1915–2009).

The Microeconomic System

In the competitive system central to microeconomics, consumers and producers meet in markets in which, through the self-interested actions of many consumers and producers, the prices and amounts produced of each good and service are determined.

Consumers   In microeconomic theory, consumers are people who maximize their happiness through the pursuit of their most desired bundle of goods. This is the concept of what is called *economic man*, someone whose concerns are solely devoted to economic values.

Consumers can be individuals or groups of individuals united in a household; the desires of consumers guide the allocation of resources. Each individual or household begins with its income and its preferences for goods and services, and allocates its resources in the present and future among the choices that are available. Individuals compare their budgets and the prices of each alternative good, examining the utility to them of an extra hamburger versus an extra soda; this helps them decide on the final market basket of goods and services they will purchase.

Consumers' bids for goods and services give rise to the *demand curve*. This is a relationship that shows how many units of a good or service will be demanded at each given price point. There is a demand curve for each product by each consumer, and an aggregate demand curve for the market for each good and service.

Producers   Producers are responsible for the production of goods and services. They may be individuals or groups of individuals organized as companies. Many or most producers are also consumers, but in microeconomic theory their actions as producers are analyzed separately from their expenditures as consumers. Producers attempt to maximize the profits from their work; left to their own devices, they have an incentive to dominate markets for their own benefit. It is the existence of competition which keeps small groups of producers from taking control of a market, and which helps to ensure that prices will be at free-market levels and that profits will be at competitive rather than monopolistic levels.

Producers act within the constraints that every society faces: fixed supplies of labor, capital, land, and technology. Although these supplies are fixed at any moment, they are changeable over time (labor may increase or decrease, technology improves) and producers adapt to such changes. By bidding for resources in competitive markets and then combining them in production processes, individuals and companies supply products and services.

Generally speaking, increasing the supply of a good at a point in time can be accomplished only with increas-

ing costs (e.g., using more expensive overtime labor). This yields the *supply curve*, which is the relationship describing the amount that will be supplied by producers at each possible price point. In some circumstances larger production can be accomplished at lower unit costs; this is the phenomenon called *increasing returns to scale*, where production is more efficient as the total amount produced increases.

Markets, Pricing, and the Allocation of Resources
The key to the allocation of goods and services in the market is the interplay between demand curves and supply curves. These two curves determine the market price of each good, and thus the amounts of each good produced and the quantity that each consumer receives.

An equilibrium of price and quantity in a market is determined by the decentralized actions of many consumers and producers each acting in his or her own interest; this is the "invisible hand" of Adam Smith. If markets function correctly, they provide an allocation mechanism that does not require any central guidance. The operation of the markets for both inputs and outputs in a society as a whole is the *market system*. Given the distribution of income and skills in a society, if the markets operate fairly and without instances of "market failure," the allocation of resources is the right one.

Natural Monopolies   occur when a service is provided most efficiently by a single supplier. Utilities and transportation systems typically have elements of natural monopoly.

For example, having more than one set of railroad tracks between two points might yield an element of competition; but a single shared set of tracks may be most efficient in terms of resource use. The owners of single sets of tracks, left to their own devices, will tend to maximize their own profits, charging higher prices and providing less transportation than would be supplied in a freely competitive market. The government intervenes by regulating the natural monopoly to ensure that consumers are charged a fair price, similar to what would be achieved in a free market. Government intervention in utilities and transportation has been common, but such intervention carries its own problems of administrative efficiency.

Public Goods   are products that benefit everyone, even those who do not pay for them; a standard example is a defense system. If an antimissile system is installed to protect a whole country, no one person has an incentive to pay for it individually, since each person is protected whether or not each pays. A public good is therefore unlike a standard good, such as a hamburger, which we cannot consume unless we pay for it. As a practical matter, then, society as a whole must pay for these public goods by the imposition of taxes.

Tools for Social Policy

To forward these and other noneconomic goals, a society can wield three primary microeconomic tools: regulation, deregulation, and price incentives. These tools can be applied by local or federal governments, or by industrial trade organizations.

Regulation involves government control of pricing, production, or practices in an entire industry. A primary example of microeconomic manipulation by regulation can be found in the agricultural markets. Agricultural policies in the United States and many other countries have been designed to regulate free markets to support the agricultural sector and the ideals of small-family farms and rural life. These policies go back many decades and have taken various forms, all of which interfere with the market equilibrium of demand and supply by such methods as supporting prices (and storing, donating, or selling surplus crops overseas); reducing the amount supplied by paying farmers not to produce; and providing subsidized loans to farmers.

Unfortunately, regulation often has unintended side effects. In the example of agricultural regulation, many of these market interventions have proved costly for the government and consumers as a whole, and have tended to benefit mostly large producers rather than small farms. Moreover, subsidized sales to developing countries, by the U.S. and especially by European countries, have had drastic effects on low-income farmers in the developing countries. As the costs of such market interventions become more widely known (it has been estimated that the average European cow enjoys a subsidy of $2 per day), pressures for deregulation of agriculture are likely to increase; such deregulation increases production and lowers prices for consumers, but could also hurt those farmers who have benefited by controlled markets.

Deregulation is the replacement of a government-regulated market with a free market. A good example of deregulation is the U.S. air transport market. Before 1978, the U.S. Civil Aeronautics Board regulated many aspects of air transport, including routes, fares, and schedules, and chose airlines to serve particular routes. This system, designed for the objective of building an efficient national air transport system, became highly cumbersome and was challenged by free-market advocates.

Air transport in the United States was deregulated in 1978, and competition resulted in lower fares, the development of new airline companies, the creation of the hub-and-spoke system of service, and newly differentiated service levels. There have also been some negative effects, such as the loss of air service to some small markets and difficult economic conditions for large traditional airlines (which have high-cost structures compared with low-cost startups). However, the deregulation of air transport is generally regarded as a successful use of microeconomic policy making, and has been copied in Europe and elsewhere.

Price incentives are generally regarded by economists as more efficient than regulation. For example, the long-standing beverage container deposit rewards those who collect and return aluminum, plastic, and glass containers for recycling, thus forwarding a pro-environmental agenda and helping to reduce pollution.

Perhaps the most innovative market method for pollution control, however, has been emissions trading. In this approach, a company that reduces its emission of pollutants below the permitted level can sell a "permit to emit" to another company. The social benefit of this is that the second company can avoid the high costs of controlling its excess emissions, but the total emissions stay within the prescribed limits. It is estimated that billions of dollars have been saved in the United States through trading in air-quality emissions permits, with thousands of transactions among companies. This approach has been approved for international trading in emissions under the Kyoto Protocol to reduce greenhouse gas emissions, and also has been used in other sectors in the United States, such as trading in water use reduction permits in California.

Macroeconomics

Macroeconomics is the top-down study of the economy as a whole: output, employment, price levels, and rate of growth. It provides ways to analyze such issues as levels of output, business cycles, inflation and deflation, short- and long-term unemployment, exports, and economic development.

The Development of Modern Macroeconomics

Economists have long been concerned with financial crises and business cycles, but prior to the 1930's there was no satisfactory understanding of the determinants of an economy's output, employment, and price levels. A common view was that economies naturally tended toward full employment with flexible prices and wages, and that crises tended to be caused by events such as financial panics.

However, the idea of "natural" full employment was hard to accept during the Great Depression of the 1930's. It was during that depression that the modern subject of macroeconomics was born. John Maynard Keynes (1883–1946), in his widely influential book *The General Theory of Employment, Interest, and Money* (1936), was the first to develop an effective theory of employment, output, and interest rates, and to explain how monetary and fiscal policies could be used to achieve full employment. His policy recommendations reversed the received wisdom; at the start of the Great Depression, the U.S. government thought that the best course of action was to reduce expenditures, but in fact the opposite was true—bringing an economy out of depression required an increase in government spending to increase aggregate demand for goods and services.

Measuring a Nation's Economic Output

To measure a nation's economic output more accurately, economists developed the system of *national accounts*. These accounts, the work of Simon Kuznets (1901–85) and other economists, focus on the output of an economy over a given time period.

Gross Domestic Product   The most comprehensive and widely used measure of an economy's output is the *Gross Domestic Product* (G.D.P.), defined as the sum of consumption of goods and services, gross investment, government purchases of good and services, and net exports produced within a given country in a specified time period (usually one calendar year).

Economists and government policy planners have come to focus more on G.D.P. than an earlier measurement, *Gross National Product* (G.N.P.). G.N.P., in addition to measuring production within a nation's boundaries, also measured net property income flows from overseas.

G.D.P. measures goods and services that are sold to final purchasers. Intermediate goods, such as the metal, plastic, and composites that are used to make an automobile, are not counted separately—their value is included in the final price of the car. Intermediate goods are tracked in another form of economic analysis, the *input-output* system, developed by Wassily Leontief (1905–99).

G.D.P. and other national income aggregates can be measured in current dollars, or the dollars can be made comparable for different years ("constant dollars") by accounting for the effects of year-to-year price changes. In the U.S. economy, the consumption sector of G.D.P. is by far the largest, followed by government and gross investment (which are similar in magnitude), and net exports, which have been negative in recent years.

National Income   The output side of the national income accounts, as measured by G.D.P., is matched by an income side. All output flows result in costs and profits, and outputs will be equal to incomes because of the balancing effect of profits (which can be positive or negative).

There are two primary measures of this income—*national income* (N.I.) and *disposable income* (D.I.). N.I., the total income for factors of production, is equal to G.D.P. minus depreciation and indirect taxes. D.I., the total amount available to households for expenditure, is equal to N.I. minus direct taxes (such as income taxes) and net business savings (the amount of business income not distributed to consumers), plus transfer payments from government (such as Social Security).

These national income accounts are not comprehensive, primarily because some outputs, while important, are difficult to measure. For example, the value of homemaking, which is large, is omitted from all calculations. Another issue is gross investment; ideally, net investment would be used, but figures for depreciation are difficult to estimate and so gross investment (before depreciation) is used instead. In any case, the national income accounts provide a reasonable measure of economic output, and are key determinants of social well-being.

Macroeconomic Issues

Macroeconomics is concerned with the level of economic output as expressed in the national accounts systems, the level of employment, price stability, business cycles, trade, and long-term economic development, and how each one of these issues affects economic and social welfare. Various fiscal and monetary policies are used to make an impact on these objectives, and to deal with a variety of common issues.

Output and Employment

In the macroeconomic system, consumers, investors, the government, and international trading partners all strive to achieve short- and long-term goals. The interaction of these efforts determines levels of output, employment, and prices.

A key insight of macroeconomics is that there is no automatic equilibrating mechanism to ensure that aggregate demand equals full employment output (i.e., total purchases of goods and services do not always equal total output of goods and services at full employment). To understand this, consider the relationships of disposable income, consumption, saving, and investment. Some earlier economists believed that all income was spent as either consumption or investment, and that there was therefore a tendency toward full employment mediated through flexible prices and wages. However, desired savings and investment are not necessarily equal; the people who save are not the same group as the people who invest, and the decisions of the two groups are made on different grounds. Consumers make decisions that result in the consumption component of G.D.P., and businesses make decisions responsible for the gross investment component. If the saved portion of consumers' disposable income that is available to businesses for investment, when the economy is at full employment, exceeds full-employment investment by businesses, their output will exceed aggregate demand, full employment output will not be sold, profits will drop, and production and employment will fall.

Most macroeconomists also believe that the problem of employment is exacerbated by rigidity (resistance to change) in wages and prices, many of which are set under administered conditions (e.g., labor contracts) rather than free-market conditions. Thus the classical assumption of price and wage flexibility cannot be counted on to ensure full employment.

Employment usually tracks the movement of output fairly consistently: "Okun's Law," named after Arthur M. Okun (1928–80), suggests that for every two percent decline in G.N.P., the unemployment rate rises by about one percentage point. Unemployment estimates are derived from careful random sampling of tens of thousands of households each month. The labor force is considered to be composed of those working and those

actively looking for work; those who are not looking for work are considered not to be in the labor force.

The Labor Force   The *Labor Force Participation Rate* (L.F.P.R.), often referred to simply as the labor force, is the proportion of the population that is either employed or actively seeking employment. It represents the supply of labor available to the economy. The L.F.P.R. is lower for young people because many are in school, and for older people because many have retired. It is highest for married men and for women who are heads of households. In the first half of 2011, 64.2 percent of the U.S. population was in the labor force (197 million people), down from 66 percent in 2002. The decrease, in part, is the result of a rapidly aging work force.

Unemployment rate   One of the most closely watched labor force statistics is the unemployment rate. In 1997 the unemployment rate fell below 5 percent for the first time in 30 years. It dropped all the way to 3.9 percent in April 2000, before climbing slowly back to slightly over 5 percent in September 2001. After the attacks on 9/11, unemployment increased but not for long and soon settled at just below 5 percent in the following years. In 2010, U.S. unemployment rates skyrocketed as a result of the global recession, averaging 9.3 percent, passing the previous record in April, 1983 when it reached 9.9 percent. The Congressional Budget Office forecasts figures to remain around 9 percent through 2011, and suggests that by 2016 rates will return to the normal 5 percent range.

Contrary to popular opinion, the unemployment rate is only an indirect measure of the people without jobs, since it measures only the number of active (within the last four weeks) job seekers as a proportion of the total labor force. So the unemployment rate may rise as new job seekers enter the labor force. Every spring, for example, it rises slightly as school graduates enter the labor force and look for jobs. The relatively high periods of unemployment beginning in the mid-1970's are in part due to the expansion of the labor force as the baby boom generation left school and began looking for work. It may also fall as workers retire or otherwise leave the labor force. And when the economy is in a prolonged recession, the unemployment rate may actually drop slightly because some of the job seekers may give up trying to find a job and withdraw from the labor force. Unemployment rates for women have paralleled those for men since 1990.

Productivity measures how much output an economy or organization can generate from a given amount of input.

Higher levels of productivity suggest greater efficiency—doing more with the same amount of resources, just as an efficient or economical car goes farther on a gallon of gasoline. Increases in productivity, as the result of better tools or improved methods, provide the main mechanism for increasing output in an economy and ultimately for raising standards of living. Productivity is usually measured in terms of labor—output per worker or per hour of labor—not only because labor is the most important resource but also because it is one of the easiest to measure.

Wages vary not only among the different professions but also between sexes and regions of the country. For example, women in year-round, full-time executive, administrative, and managerial positions have a median yearly income of only 61 percent of the median income for men in the same occupation group. This percentage is higher in the field of laborers, precision production, craft, and repair; but for all major occupation groups reported by the U.S. Bureau of the Census, women receive only a fraction of what is received by their male counterparts. This may be due, in part, to the fact that women enter and leave the workforce more times throughout their lives than men do and spend a smaller percentage of their lives economically active.

Another factor influencing the discrepancy between men's and women's wages is the concentration of women in occupations that pay less. Women made up 98 percent of child care workers and 97 percent of receptionists, two low-paying positions.

The first minimum wage in the nation was enacted by the state of Massachusetts in 1912; it covered only women, and was designed to shorten hours and raise pay in the covered industries. The nationwide minimum wage was established in 1938, and since then has grown in both dollar value and the types of employees it covers. Some states may establish minimum wages higher than the federal minimum.

Prices and Inflation Over time, prices in general can rise, fall, or remain stable. An increase in price levels is known as *inflation*, and a decrease is known as *deflation*; the latter has been uncommon in the U.S. for many decades. Stable prices enable businesses and households to make informed decisions, and prevent the unfairness and hardship that occur when, for example, inflation erodes the value of savings.

Price levels are estimated by means of prices indexes, which are average prices over time of a selected mix of goods and services. Two of the most commonly used in the United States are the *Consumer Price Index* (C.P.I.),

based on the average prices paid for goods and services bought by consumers, and the G.D.P. *deflator*. The C.P.I., often referred to as the the cost-of-living index, is published by the Bureau of Labor Statistics, a unit of the U.S. Department of Labor that began to sample and calculate price changes in 1913. Subsequently the B.L.S established a base year of 1967 with an index of 100 and later published indexes were based on that year. The present indexes are based on the 36-month period 1982–84 set to an index of 100. In 1998 the indexes based on 1967 were discontinued. An example of inflation measured by the C.P.I. reveals that the average consumer good that was purchased for $1.00 in 1984 costs $2.26 in constant dollars in 2011. In effect, the buying power of the consumer dollar is less than half of what it was in 1984. Looking more closely at specific products calculated separately in the C.P.I., the same kind of automobile that cost $15,000 in 1984 costs $21,400 in 2011; a dozen eggs that might have cost $1.00 in 1984 costs $2.23 in 2011.

A broader measure of inflation in the national economy is the G.D.P. *deflator* (that includes consumer goods, investment goods, and government purchases of goods). It is calculated by the Bureau of Economic Analysis, an agency of the U.S. Department of Commerce.

In general, inflation hurts lenders and helps borrowers. Someone who borrows money at today's purchasing power pays it back when it purchases less because of inflation. Lenders can hedge against inflation by increasing the interest rate at which they lend but borrowers may balk at too high a rate. Investors in bonds are vulnerable to loss when inflation drives interest rates higher and lowers the price of the bonds they hold. Investors in stocks consider them a hedge against inflation as the prices of stocks often rise with inflation and the prices of bonds decline.

Following the economic crisis that began in 2007 the U.S. Federal Reserve—long seen as a bastion against inflation—lowered interest rates to near zero even though in the past that might have ignited inflation. But the slow rate of economic recovery has kept inflation in check.

The dynamics of inflation depend on a number of factors, especially the employment rate. When an economy is nearing full employment, there are pressures on price levels. Some economists posit a functional relationship between full employment and inflation, such that society must make a choice between accepting some unemployment or accepting some inflation. The best-known version of this idea is the Phillips curve, as espoused by the economist A.W. Phillips (1914–75), a graph believed to represent a trade-off that can be modified by long-term developments such as technological change, which can increase productivity without affecting unemployment. Some economists question the long-term accuracy of the Phillips curve and urge caution in its use as a guide to setting monetary and fiscal policy to control inflation.

Business Cycles and Forecasts In looking toward the future, economists make forecasts based on *econometric* methods, statistically derived estimated relationships that are used to project changes in macroeconomic variables over time. Although the future is unknowable, such econometric methods give forecasts that, in retrospect, are considerably better than "naïve " forecasts based on simple rules such as "G.D.P. will grow next year by the same percentage that it grew this year."

One use of forecasts is to anticipate the rise and fall of G.D.P. and employment. Business cycles have a long history of analysis in economic literature; there have been many theories of business cycles, including financial panics, external shocks, and internal dynamics of boom and bust. At present, while it is generally accepted that the economy will move up and down over time, there is no single accepted business cycle theory. It is believed that many elements enter into business cycles, including changes in consumer demand, business investment (including inventory) decisions, and various overseas events.

International Trade A *closed economy* is one without international trade; conversely, an *open economy* is one with such trade. Open economies have imports and exports that create the net export component of G.D.P. In open economies, considerations of macroeconomic fiscal and monetary policy must be extended to include international repercussions. For example, an increase in government spending (fiscal policy) will have a smaller effect if there are imports than if there are no imports, since part of the new spending will be for imports rather than domestically produced goods. Of course, the better off other economies are, the more they will import from the United States.

Long-Term Growth Long-term economic growth is a key objective of most societies, because it provides higher living standards for individuals (see "Development Economics"). The four basic inputs to long-term growth are human resources, natural resources, capital, and technology; the first three were traditionally labeled labor, land, and capital. Whereas earlier economists tended to emphasize the growth of the first three components, in recent decades, thanks in part to the work of Robert Solow (b. 1924) of MIT, much more

attention has been paid to the effects of technological change, education, and research on long-term growth.

Fiscal Policy

To address these macroeconomic issues, governments can use either *fiscal* or *monetary* policies. Fiscal policy is typically used to manage output, employment, and prices, and has two main instruments: changes in taxes and changes in government expenditure. It uses the relationships in the economy first analyzed by Keynes, and uses the information developed in the national income accounts as inputs to policy making.

Disposable Income A fundamental element in fiscal policy is the behavioral relationship that governs the use of disposable income. Consumers spend some of their income and save another part. When a consumer receives an extra dollar of income, the amount that the consumer will spend, and not save, is called the *marginal propensity to consume*. This measurement helps to determine the impact of fiscal policy.

Multipliers and Accelerators When the government, as part of fiscal policy, either spends more money or reduces taxes, this increases the disposable personal income of individuals. Individuals expend more on goods and services according to their marginal propensities to consume. But this new consumption adds to other people's personal incomes, and this new personal income again gives rise to consumption.

This chain of events is called the *multiplier*, because the initial increase in income from fiscal policy has a multiplied effect on total consumption (and thus production). The multiplier is greater from government expenditure than from tax reduction; government expenditure is an addition to income, but a tax reduction produces more consumption and partly more savings. Textbooks give simple formulas for the multiplier, but in fact the actual effects in a given time period are complex.

In addition, when consumption goes up, businesses tend to invest more in inventories, plant, and equipment. This increase is the *accelerator* theory of investment, i.e., generation of investment by new consumption.

Government Expenditures versus Tax Policy

While government expenditure can increase total demand through the multiplier, in practice it is difficult to time government spending to manipulate employment and output. This is because of the time required to design programs, and the complex process of congressional approval that is required. Tax policy is also effective, but tax changes can also take a long time to implement.

In both cases, there are questions of who should get the spending or the tax decrease in order to have the biggest impact on aggregate demand. There are also issues of fairness in the distribution of spending and tax decreases. It would be possible to make fiscal policy more flexible by giving the government standby authority to change tax rates within strictly defined limits; this approach is not used in the United States, and has the disadvantage that a government could use its flexibility for purposes other than countercyclical fiscal policy.

Another issue with fiscal policy is that financing government spending or tax cuts can require a substantial increase in government indebtedness. This causes distortions of investment in later time periods, because of its upward impact on interest rates. A result of these considerations is that though government occasionally uses fiscal measures, they are not routinely used in the United States for countercyclical purposes.

Monetary Policy

Monetary policy, the other principal part of macroeconomic policy, is designed to influence investment, products, employment, and prices by means of planned changes in the money supply and interest rates. Monetary policy is the primary countercyclical macroeconomic policy in the United States; it is loosened when the economy falters, and tightened when inflation threatens.

Federal Reserve System   Monetary policy is implemented through the banking system. In the United States the banking system operates through the Federal Reserve System (the "Fed"), a group of 12 regional banks chartered in 1913. It is governed by a seven-member board of governors, appointed by the president with the consent of the Senate. Because of the importance of monetary policy, the chairman of the board of governors is one of the most important economic officials in the country.

Although legally a corporation owned by the commercial banks that are members of the system, in fact the Fed operates as an independent public agency in the United States. It issues currency, against which it holds interest-bearing government securities, is one of the regulators of the banking system, and controls monetary policy.

Fractional Reserves and the Money Supply   The banking system in the United States is a fractional reserve system. Banks are not required to hold all their deposits as reserves; the Fed requires only that banks hold a certain proportion of their obligations as reserves, and the rest can be lent out at interest. For example, if a bank has $100

in deposits and the reserve requirement is 10 percent, then the bank is required to hold only $10 in cash; the remaining $90 can be lent out. The total money supply in the system is defined as the checking accounts in banks plus the currency issued by the Fed.

Open Market Transactions   There are three primary types of monetary policy: open market transactions, discount rate, and reserve requirements. These operate within the institutional context of the Fed, the fractional reserve system, and also the public's demand for money as opposed to interest-bearing assets.

Open market transactions, the most important part of monetary policy, are the sale or purchase of government securities by the Fed. The Federal Open Market Committee (F.O.M.C.) is composed of the seven governors and five of the regional bank presidents. At its regular meetings the F.O.M.C. decides whether economic activity should be restrained or promoted. If the F.O.M.C. decides that restraint is called for, it orders the Fed to sell securities; these sales are paid for by funds drawn from banks, which causes the banking system to lose reserves. Because the system is a fractional reserve system, total deposits in the banking system fall by a multiple of the amount of securities sales. This contraction of the money supply raises interest rates, and thus acts to restrain interest-sensitive economic activity such as investment and housing starts. The result is to reduce aggregate demand, and thus reduce inflationary pressure on prices.

Discount Rate Changes   In discount rate changes, the Fed raises or lowers the interest rate it charges for short-term loans to member banks (to cover temporary shortfalls in their reserves). This has a direct effect on commercial and consumer interest rates. When the Fed lowers its interest rate, consumer interest rates fall; when the Fed raises its interest rate, consumer interest rates rise. Another tool of the Fed is the *federal funds rate*, the interest rate at which banks borrow from one another, usually overnight, to maintain required reserves. The Fed does not set the federal funds rate—which is a floating rate—but it can set target rates and manage the rate by buying and selling securities. The discount rate and federal funds rate are powerful tools the Fed uses as a part of controlling interest rates generally.

Reserve Requirements   The third instrument, changes in reserve ratios (within legally set limits), is rarely used. The intended results can be accomplished by open market policy with much less disruption than would be caused by an abrupt change in reserve ratios.

Why Currency Exchange Rates Matter

By HAL R. VARIAN

Imagine living in a world where you had to have yen to buy a TV, renminbi to buy toys, and dollars to buy food. Surprise. That's the world we live in.

Most TV's we buy are manufactured in Japan, most toys come from China, and most of our food is produced in the United States. And by and large, the workers who produce those goods want to be paid in their domestic currency.

When you buy an imported TV with dollars, these dollars are exchanged—by currency traders—for yen, somewhere along the way, to pay the Japanese workers who built the TV.

The basic force determining the exchange rate is supply and demand. If the demand for yen exceeds the supply at the current exchange rate, the cost of yen in terms of dollars will rise; and if supply exceeds demand, it will fall.

If the only reason to buy foreign currency was to use it to purchase foreign goods, international exchange would be quite simple. But people also want to acquire foreign currency to make investments. If America's interest rates are higher than Japan's, Japanese investors will want to buy our bonds to take advantage of those higher rates. To do so, they must first sell yen and buy dollars. This is where things get tricky.

Eventually, those Japanese investors will want to end up with yen. So their expected return, denominated in yen, involves both the rate of interest and the likely movement of exchange rates in the future. This means that the demand for yen will depend not only on the current exchange rate, but also on anticipations of future exchange rates.

The demand for currency to support international trade is fairly predictable, since the short-term trade patterns are reasonably predictable. It's the speculative demand that causes most short-term fluctuations; foreign exchange traders have to make guesses—continually being revised—about the future.

Central banks also intervene in foreign exchange markets, for quite different reasons. The Bank of Japan might decide to sell yen on the foreign exchange market. This would push down the value of yen, making Japanese goods cheaper in dollar terms.

This translates into cheaper TV's and Toyotas, which means Americans keep buying those products, and Japanese factories—and employment—keep humming along.

In recent years the United States has had abnormally low interest rates. As a result, demand for dollars has weakened, making yen more costly, thereby raising the price and reducing sales of those imported TV's.

But to avoid increasing domestic unemployment, the Bank of Japan sold yen, keeping the currency lower than it otherwise would have been. The dollars received in exchange were used to buy Treasury bonds, with the Japanese accumulating $577 billion as of the end of January 2004.

Taiwan and China also bought United States Treasury bonds, trying to keep their currencies from appreciating against the dollar.

But the Japanese economy seems to be recovering, and the Chinese economy is overheating. This suggests that these two financial powerhouses will cut back on their purchases of dollars, pushing the value of the dollar down relative to their own currencies.

On the other hand, American interest rates are also increasing. As the economy recovers, the Fed will push rates up, making United States bonds more attractive, which will tend to push the value of the dollar up.

So will the dollar go up or down?

Many experts think the foreign exchange interventions of the last several years have maintained the dollar's value at an unnaturally high level.

Maybe. But by how much? And if it is overvalued, how rapidly will it fall? In one scenario, the dollar has a steady decline against the renminbi and the yen; the Chinese economy has a soft landing; the Japanese recovery persists; and the American economy has a healthy recovery.

In a less rosy scenario, the dollar drops precipitously; prices of imported goods shoot up here, rekindling inflation; the Japanese economy falters; and unemployed Chinese workers riot.

Keep your eye on those exchange rates. They have a lot to do with America's recovery and the health of the world economy.

Monetarism   Another approach to monetary policy is called *monetarism*. Monetarists, such as Milton Friedman (1912–2006), believe that the best way to ensure long-run growth is to have a constant, steady increase in the money supply—rather than to try to implement monetary policy in a countercyclical manner through open market transactions or changes in discount rates. This approach depends on the relative constancy of the turnover of money (the *velocity of money*), which has become much less stable then before; for this reason, there has been a steady move away from monetarism.

Rational Expectations   Still another perspective on monetary policy is the idea of rational expectations. This view is that if people make unbiased full-information forecasts about the future, they can anticipate policy—and thereby make it less effective. The empirical relevance of this view remains uncertain.

Challenges in the New World Economy

In an increasingly linked world, macroeconomic policy faces new and more complex challenges of stability, employment, balance of trade, and international equity.

The trend is for economies to become more and more open, with the continuous reduction of trade barriers. As a result, domestic fiscal and monetary policy in each country must take into account impacts from outside the national economy. The ramifications of these interconnections are not fully understood; thus there is an additional degree of uncertainty in national economic management. In some cases, notably the European Union, there is an attempt to have multinational, coordinated monetary and fiscal policy.

The new international economy poses particular issues for developing countries. As trade barriers fall, especially with respect to primary products, and as farm subsidies drop, as they will over the long term, there are greater opportunities for developing countries to export. To take full advantage of the new willingness of companies in developed countries to outsource work to developing countries (e.g., software development in India, and call centers in many countries), these developing countries will have to achieve more economic and political stability, and better legal systems to protect investments.

International Economics

Most contemporary analyses of the global economy begin with the assumption that the nations of the world are divided into two basic categories, developed and developing. The developed ones are those with the highest G.N.P. figures, and are characterized by high per capita income and low rates of population growth and illiteracy, as well as having a low proportion of their labor force in agriculture or mining or both.

These wealthy nations are at the center of the global economy and are responsible for promoting international trade, helping to finance development in the poorer countries, and maintaining a stable economic world. They attempt to do this through several multilateral and bilateral institutions that promote trade and give development advice and assistance to poorer nations.

Economic Development

Toward the end of World War II, the leaders of the victorious western powers believed that in the peaceful world of the future the possibility for an integrated global economy would benefit rich and poor nations alike. In 1945, under the auspices of the new United Nations, they created the World Bank to lend money for development projects and the International Monetary Fund (I.M.F.) to help poorer nations with debt-related financial problems.

In response to the oil shocks of the 1970's, the I.M.F. created the Trust Fund to provide financing to the world's poorest countries to help offset the balance of payment difficulties confronting many of them. Increasing interest rates led to an international debt crisis, and when problems broke out in Mexico in 1982, the I.M.F. coordinated an international response. Its measures helped calm the international crisis and allowed for the institution of harsh reforms in the debtor countries.

When the Soviet Union collapsed in 1991, many of the newly formed countries looked to shift from central-planning-oriented to market-driven economies. Working closely with the I.M.F., the former Soviet bloc benefitted from the financial support and policy advice offered. Although there was much difficulty, most of these economies had made the transition by the end of the decade, with many joining the European Union in 2004. When a string of financial crises hit the East Asian region in the late 1990's, the I.M.F. again stepped in with financial assistance and helped reform failed economic policies.

Seeking to lighten the debt burden on poor countries, the I.M.F. teamed up with the World Bank in the 1990's and launched the Initiative for Heavily Indebted Poor Countries (H.I.P.C.). Tied in with the U.N. Millenium Development Goals and supplemented by the Multilateral Debt Relief Initiative, the H.I.P.C. initiative has "the aim of ensuring that no poor country faces a debt burden it cannot manage."

The financial crises of 2007–08 led to a flood of requests for financial and policy support, making the I.M.F. more important than ever. Its lending capacity was tripled to $750 billion and its policies overhauled, allowing for faster distribution of funds to needy countries.

International Trade

International trade takes place because some nations have an advantage in producing certain kinds of products, because they have either a comparative wealth of resources (capital, labor, natural resources) or more efficient production techniques. Even an economy with the most efficient technology has a limit on its resources, and rather than using them to produce a wide variety of products, it tends to concentrate its resources on what it makes most efficiently. It then trades those particular goods for other commodities, importing those that it produces least efficiently. As a result, all countries are better off with this type of international trade; specialization results in the expansion of the total supply of goods, and the cost of acquiring them then falls.

Balance of Trade   When a country imports goods from another country worth more than the value of its exports to that country, there is said to be a deficit in the balance of trade between the countries. The balance of trade is an important issue because it indicates something about how a nation's economy is changing and, ultimately, about its competitiveness vis-à-vis other countries. A rising balance-of-trade deficit indicates that an economy is not able to sell its goods abroad and that consumers are favoring imports over domestically produced goods.

In the 1990's, when the global economy grew increasingly robust, the U.S. trade deficit climbed from $95 billion in 1995 to $716 billion in 2005. By 2010, the deficit had decreased to around $500 billion. Services had a small surplus of $145 billion but the entire U.S. trade deficit is traditionally in the manufactured goods sector, which ran a deficit of $645 bilion. Its exports of goods have not kept up with imports, in part because the strength of the dollar makes its goods more expensive for foreign nations to buy, while people in the U.S. have more money to spend on cheaper imports.

Tariffs and Quotas   One way to protect a country's own producers, especially when they are inefficient compared with the international competition, is with import tariffs—taxes on goods that are produced abroad. Import tariffs raise the price of imports relative to domestic alternatives and discourage demand for the former. If one country is the sole importer or even the main importer of another's exports, it is possible that an import tariff will simply force the exporter to cut its selling price (in order to keep the price to consumers—including the tariff—from rising sharply and cutting off demand). If, on the other hand, the importer badly needs the import and there are few substitutes, raising the tariff simply raises the costs to one's own consumers.

Import quotas attempt to achieve a restriction on imports without the price rises associated with tariffs, by setting direct limits on the number of items imported. So-called trade wars start when one country imposes a tariff on imports from a second country, and the latter responds with tariffs of its own against the first country.

Free Trade   The arguments about the benefits of trade have led to efforts to restrict the use of tariffs and maintain free trade, i.e., trade without any restrictions. Economists argue that unrestricted trade will always promote economic growth by forcing domestic prices to reflect world prices, thereby encouraging the efficient allocation of resources.

Over the last 60 years—since the end of World War II—many of the leading nations have made a strong and continuous effort to lower or eliminate tariffs, first regionally, then around the world. The most successful regional organization has been the European Union, which has encouraged the formation of many other such alliances in all parts of the world, including the North American Free Trade Association (NAFTA) that includes Canada, Mexico and the United States. Chief among these alliances are the General Agreement on Tariffs and Trade (GATT) and its successor organization, the World Trade Organization (W.T.O.).

GATT and the W.T.O.   The General Agreement on Tariffs and Trade was first established in 1948, in an attempt to regulate world trade. The representatives of 23 leading nations agreed to find ways to lower tariffs, lower quotas, and make free trade their final goal. Over a period of almost 50 years the most important trading nations met regularly to discuss specific trade matters and to continue to remove restrictions from trade; each series of negotiations (called a "round") lasted several years.

By 1975 tariffs on manufactured goods had been reduced from 40 percent to 10 percent and world trade more than tripled. By the 1980's, however, the nature of world trade had changed. In 1986 the so-called Uruguay Round of GATT (now with 92 nations repre-sented) addressed these and other issues over a period of eight years. The results—lowering of tariffs of all kinds, banning quotas, and protecting copyrights and patents—have been projected to add $500 billion annually to the global economy.

The most important accomplishment of the GATT Agreement in 1994 was the establishment of the World Trade Organization (W.T.O.), a permanent institution with real power to oversee trade agreements, enforce trade rules, and settle disputes. When it was approved by the U.S. Congress on January 1, 1995, the organization became a reality, with 110 members. By 2011 there were 153 members, including China. The basic principles of the W.T.O. are the encouragement of fair competition and increased access to markets.

The European Union

In 2007, the 50th year of its founding, the European Union had achieved success beyond the wildest dreams of its founders. It had become an enormous economic super-power, a gigantic market of over 490 million people in 27 nations with even more nations eager to join. During the previous decade its leaders had succeeded, despite dire predictions, in introducing almost seamlessly a new common currency called the *euro* which quickly took root throughout Europe and in world markets. Finally the E.U. had integrated many of the countries of post-Communist east-central Europe.

However, during the deep recession caused by the financial collapse of 2008, the E.U. experienced enormous challenges as several key members faced huge budget deficits that threatened the stability of the euro.

History

Out of the wreckage of World War II, with generous American Marshall Plan aid after 1948, western Europe commenced reconstruction; by 1954, several "economic miracles" occurred. Yet without economic integration, the recoveries of the separate nations involved duplications, inefficiencies, diminished competition, and the threats of local gluts and shortages. A small sign of what might be achieved was Benelux, the customs union between Belgium, the Netherlands and Luxembourg, constructed even before war's end in 1944 and a going concern by 1948 despite the very unequal status of the three economies.

On May 9, 1950, France's foreign minister, Robert Schuman, proposed that German and French coal and steel production (the so-called sinews of war) be placed under a supra-national, not inter-governmental, "high authority;" the West German chancellor, Konrad Adenauer, responded positively that very evening. By May 1952, ratification of the six-nation European Coal and Steel Community (often called "the Six") was complete, with Italy and the Benelux countries joining the French and Germans.

The dramatic successes of the E.C.S.C. led the six toward broader integration, with negotiations culminating in the March 1957 Treaties of Rome which established the European Economic Community (E.E.C.) and the European Atomic Energy Commission (Euratom). The E.E.C. was designed to reduce and eventually abolish all tariffs among the Six; to establish a single external tariff for the Community; and to foster the free movement of not only goods but of labor and capital as well. Euratom was intended for the common peaceful development of nuclear power, though common action proved subsequently difficult to agree on.

Soon thereafter, French president Charles de Gaulle began pushing for agricultural integration to match the E.E.C.'s industrial unity: the huge German market beckoned for France's chronic farm surpluses, yet Germany hesitated to sacrifice her own farmers in return for cheaper food. In fact, a serious crisis impended since each of the Six had its own system of protectionist duties, farm subsidies and crop controls. But the Dutch ("Mansholt") proposals met with relatively easy and rapid agreement. The Common Agricultural Policy of 1962 eventually established a highly bureaucratized, centrally-financed common market with managed prices, common duties upon imports, and subsidies for exports.

The European Community (E.C.)

With agricultural integration, the stage was set for the Brussels treaty of 1965 (often called the "The Second Treaty of Rome"), which founded the European Community. The earlier three communities (E.C.S.C., E.E.C. and Euratom) were merged into one and were provided with a four-part structure of Commission, Council, Parliament and Court.

It was this "refounded" E.C. that the United Kingdom was at last permitted to join in 1973 (after another Gaullist veto in 1967). As in its earlier attempts, it was accompanied by Ireland, Denmark and Norway (though Norwegian voters subsequently rejected admission in a referendum). The Nine subsequently became the Twelve with the admission of Greece (1981), Spain and Portugal (1986).

Twenty years after the Brussels Treaty, with the accession of Jacques Delors as president of the European Commission, the E.C. received new impetus toward what the Treaty of Rome had envisioned: a single market free of all barriers to the free movement of goods, services, capital and labor. The first result was the Single European Act of 1987, an unwieldy compendium of almost 300 rules and directives to bring about by 1992 a "Europe without frontiers." Over the next decade, tax and interest rates fell, and new regional ties developed. The abolition of capital controls in 1990 proved decisive in the movement toward monetary union.

The European Union (E.U.)

In December 1991, the E.C. approved its third foundational treaty, the Treaty of Maastricht. Following the simple idea that a single market requires a single currency, the Maastricht Treaty established a three-stage (1991, 1994, 1997) creation of the European Monetary Union (E.M.U.). During the first two stages, the E.U. members were to converge according to five criteria: inflation rates, interest rates, currency exchange, rate stability (variation within 2.25 percent), budget deficits (less than 3 percent of G.D.P.), and public indebtedness (a debt-to-G.D.P. ratio of less than 60 percent). During the second stage the transition from central bank financing of government spending to creation of the European Central Bank was to take place. In the third stage, the European Central Bank would propose and carry out the E.U.'s monetary policies and the *euro* would circulate as "bank money"—all preparatory to the actual introduction of the monetary union.

The European Monetary Union

On Jan. 1, 1999, the E.U. introduced the euro. Initially well-received in world financial markets, the euro sagged over the next six months, losing almost 20 percent of its value against the dollar. One reason for the flop was the E.U.'s decision to permit Italy's budget deficit to substantially exceed the target 2 percent of G.D.P.; one member's excessive spending was dragging the whole currency down. By September, it had lost about 27 percent of its value against the dollar, prompting voters in Denmark to reject the new currency and instead keep their *krone*.

On Jan. 1, 2002, 50 billion new euro coins and 14.5 billion euro notes went into circulation in the 12 member countries, and on Feb. 28, 2002, all other currencies were

The European Union

Year admitted	Member countries
1957	Belgium, France, Germany, Italy, Luxembourg, Netherlands
1973	Denmark, Ireland, United Kingdom
1981	Greece
1986	Portugal, Spain
1995	Austria, Finland, Sweden
2004	Cyprus, Czech Republic, Estonia, Hungary, Latvia, Lithuania, Malta, Poland, Slovakia, Slovenia
2007	Bulgaria, Romania
Candidates	Croatia, Iceland, Macedonia, Montenegro, Turkey

withdrawn from circulation in the member nations. The two-month overlap period caused more than a little bit of confusion throughout Europe, but it bolstered the value of the euro to about even with the U.S. dollar. Since then, the euro has outpaced the dollar by as much as 25 percent. After the start of the Iraq War, the dollar fluctuated negatively. The euro was around $1.30–$1.35 during the first quarter of 2007 and, as with other currencies, has fluctuated continuously since.

Expansion and Constitution   In 2004 the E.U. expanded southward and eastward to include (the Greek part of) Cyprus, the Czech Republic, Estonia, Hungary, Latvia, Lithuania, Malta, Poland, Slovakia and Slovenia. In 2007, Bulgaria and Romania were accepted. The 12 additional countries made the E.U. truly "One Europe," some 490 million people with an economy about the size of that of the U.S. While the average G.D.P. of the new states was less that half that of the earlier 15, their rate of growth was noticeably higher, not least because their corporate income tax rates were, on average, one-third lower, which encouraged capital flow eastward.

On June 17–18, 2004, The Heads of State and Government adopted the Treaty establishing a Constitution for Europe, which would replace all existing treaties with a single document. Among its notable innovations are: 1) a written bill of rights; 2) a single foreign minister; 3) introduction of majority voting in many policy areas such as energy, agriculture and immigration (while maintaining unanimity in such areas as taxation and foreign policy); 4) a Council presidency elected by heads of state for a term of up to five years; 5) streamlining the Commission by abolishing each state's right to at least one member; and 6) creation of zones of E.U. criminal law to deal with terrorism, corruption and fraud.

The Constitution will not take effect until all 27 member states have ratified it, either by Parliamentary vote or by referendum. As of 2007, 18 countries had approved the Constitution: Austria, Belgium, Bulgaria, Cyprus, Estonia, Finland, Germany, Greece, Hungary, Italy, Latvia, Lithu-ania, Luxembourg, Malta, Romania, Slovakia, Slovenia, and Spain. But both France and the Netherlands rejected the new Constitution, causing several nations to postpone their decisions until after further discussion.

The Fiscal Crisis of 2008–Present   By the early autumn of 2008, the collapse of several very large financial institutions in the United States—including the venerable Lehman Brothers—sent shock waves throughout the highly-integrated world economy. Investors in Europe were especially hard hit since so many institutions and individuals had put their money into America's mortgage bonds and other risky instruments through these institutions, as well as many others. As time went on the effects of the credit freeze spread to almost every European nation, causing severe budget deficits even for well-run economies. For those already with large deficits, the impact was catastrophic. In 2009, Greece's deficit doubled to 12 percent for the year, meaning its debt was 120 percent of its G.D.P. The I.M.F. and the E.U. agreed to provide a bailout, but only if the Greek government agreed to draconian budget cuts. This only heightened the level of fear, as Spain, Ireland, and Portugal faced similar debt problems. The value of the euro plummeted and markets declined, especially in Europe and the U.S. Some worried that the monetary union could not survive. By the middle of 2011, the core problem of debt remained a serious one, but Germany and France appeared determined to support the euro and prevent any government in the E.U. from default.

Additional information about the European Union (in 11 languages) can be found at the E.U. website. www.europa.eu.

Glossary of Economic Terms

accelerator relationship between a change in demand and the subsequent change in investment.

advanced economies as defined by the International Monetary Fund, the seven largest countries by G.D.P., all the other members of the European Union, the four "tigers" of Asia (Singapore, South Korea, Hong Kong, and Taiwan), Australia, New Zealand, and Israel.

aggregate demand total demand for goods and services from consumers, business, government, and international trade in a given time period.

aggregate supply total amount of goods and services that producers willingly produce in a given time period.

business cycles upward and downward movements of an economy's output, incomes, and employment over a period of time, usually several years.

capitalism method of amassing wealth by investment in capital; a capitalist invests money in an enterprise with the objective of receiving more in return than what was initially invested.

cartel combination of producers designed to raise prices and control a market.

closed economy economy without international trade.

command economy economy in which decisions about production and distribution are made by government rather than by markets.

competition the existence of many consumers and producers in a given market, so that no one consumer or producer is able to substantially affect prices.

Consumer Price Index (C.P.I.) estimator of the change in overall prices of goods purchased by consumers; it is an index of price changes for a selected market basket of goods.

deflation sustained drop in the general price level in the economy.

demand and supply the two sides of a market, representing desires to purchase and willingness to supply goods and services, that determine the prices and quantities of goods and services.

demand curve relationship that shows the amount of a good or service demanded at each price.

developing countries as defined by the International Monetary Fund, the burgeoning economies of China, India, Brazil, and Chile, as well as the poorest nations of sub-Saharan Africa (Mozambique, Ethiopia, and Niger, for example) and Asia (Bangladesh, Cambodia, Vietnam).

diminishing returns in productivity concept that increasing investment results in smaller increases in output.

disposable income (D.I.) national income (N.I.) minus direct taxes (such as income taxes) and net business savings, plus transfer payments from government.

duopoly market in which there are only two suppliers.

Employment Cost Index (E.C.I.) measures the rate of change in total employee compensation (wages, salaries, employer cost for employee benefits) in nonfarm private industry and in state and local governments. Provided quarterly by the Bureau of Labor Statistics, the E.C.I. has become one of the most closely watched indexes because any significant rise could signal an inflationary trend.

exchange rate ratio at which two currencies can be exchanged, or the price of one currency in terms of the other. For example, if the exchange rate between the British pound and the U.S. dollar is $1.50, then one British pound can be purchased at that price.

externalities effects of the actions of consumers and producers that affect others outside of, or external to, markets.

factor prices prices for inputs in the production of a good or service, such as land, labor, and capital.

factors of production inputs to the production process, including land, labor, and capital.

fiscal policy use of government expenditure and taxes to influence output and employment.

foreign direct investment (F.D.I.) investment by private companies of one nation in the territory of another nation. The investment can be in an existing enterprise of the host nation or the building of new facilities for the investing foreign company (which would then be known as a multinational enterprise).

free trade trade between two or more countries unhindered by any governmental restrictions, such as tariffs or quotas.

G.D.P. deflator price index used to convert G.D.P. from different years into constant dollars. Also called the *implicit price deflator*.

General Agreement on Tariffs and Trade (GATT) as first established in 1948, an attempt to regulate the world's trade by lowering tariffs and quotas, with the goal of establishing global free trade.

gross investment total investment in an economy, not adjusted for depreciation. It is a component of G.D.P. and G.N.P.

Gross Domestic Product (G.D.P.) measure of the output of production attributable to all factors of production (labor and property) physically located within a country. G.D.P. excludes net property income from abroad (such as the earnings of U.S. nationals working overseas), which is included in the G.N.P.

Gross National Product (G.N.P.) total national output of goods and services valued at market prices. G.N.P. measures the output attributable to the factors of production—labor and property—supplied by a country's residents, with allowances for depreciation and for indirect business taxes (sales and property taxes).

Group of Eight (G-8) loosely knit group of the largest economic powers whose representatives meet once a year to discuss policy in what has become a well-publicized media event. Members include Canada, France, Germany, Italy, Japan, Russia, the U.K., and the United States. Originally the Group of Seven (G-7), without Russia.

inflation sustained rise in the general price level in the economy.

input-output table comprehensive system for tracking flows of intermediate and final goods in an economy during a given time period.

International Monetary Fund (I.M.F.) a specialized agency of the United Nations charged with making loans to nations having trouble with debt.

joint stock company company in which investors pool their money and receive profits or dividends in proportion to their investments. Often are limited-liability in that investors are liable only for any debts in the amount of their original investments.

leading economic indicators composite of 10 economic statistics, published by the U.S. Department of Commerce, Bureau of Economic Analysis, that are said to "lead" economic trends because their numbers change months in advance of a change in the general level of economic activity.

liquidity extent to which an asset can be converted quickly to cash, with little loss in value.

M1 the Fed's original and most commonly reported measure of the money supply, which embraces currency and coins, demand deposits, traveler's checks, and other checkable deposits.

M2 as measured by the Fed, M1 plus money-market accounts, and savings and small time-deposits.

M3 as measured by the Fed, M2 plus money-market mutual-fund balances held by financial institutions, term repurchase agreements and term Eurodollars, and large time-deposits.

macroeconomics study of large-scale or general economic factors; a country's total economic activity.

marginal analysis approach, characteristic of microeconomics, of examining the costs and benefits of purchasing and producing increments of inputs and outputs to reach decisions about production and consumption.

marginal propensity to consume the fraction of a dollar of additional income that consumers will spend.

market system economic system in which markets determine the allocation of resources and the goods and services produced.

Marxism economic theory based on the work of Karl Marx that postulated class struggle, the eventual decline of capitalism, and its replacement by rule of the proletariat through a centrally planned economy.

mercantilism economic system prevalent in medieval and early modern times, the result of a concerted effort to establish a centralized economic unity and political control that included protectionism of a nation's businesses.

microeconomics study of economic factors affecting individual consumers and firms.

monetarism doctrine that the best way to ensure long-run economic growth is to have a continual, steady increase in the money supply, rather than to try to implement monetary policy in a countercyclical manner.

monetary policy policy undertaken by the central bank to influence interest rates, investment, and output through open market operations, changes in the discount rate, and changes in reserve requirements.

money income income received before payments for such things as personal income taxes, Social Security, union dues, and Medicare. Money income does not include income in the form of noncash benefits such as food stamps, health benefits, and subsidized housing.

monopoly market in which there is only one supplier.

multiplier total amount by which a given change in government expenditure or taxes will raise or lower total income.

neoclassical economics movement in the late 19th century and early 20th century that relates prices to the allocation of resources and uses advanced mathematics to derive models.

national income (N.I.) G.D.P. minus depreciation and indirect taxes.

national income accounts system of accounts that measures total output and its components per time period.

natural monopoly market condition resulting when a service is provided most efficiently by a single supplier.

net exports difference between total exports and total imports; a component of G.D.P.

North American Free Trade Agreement (NAFTA) as enacted in 1994, an agreement to remove all barriers to trade among the three signatory nations (Canada, Mexico, and the United States).

oligopoly market in which there are only a few suppliers, less than the number required to ensure competition.

open economy economy that engages in trade with other countries.

open market operations purchases and sales of Treasury obligations to influence the money supply and thus interest rates and investment.

personal income current income received by persons from all sources minus their personal contributions for social insurance.

Phillips curve curve showing the relationship be-tween percentage unemployment and percentage rate of inflation.

portfolio investment investing in the stocks and bonds of foreign nations.

poverty level estimate of the income necessary to purchase what society defines as a minimally acceptable standard of living; classification is based on the poverty index originated by the Social Security Administration in 1964 (revised in 1969 and 1980). In 2011 a family of four with income less than $22,350 lived below the poverty level.

present value the value today of an asset; determined by applying an interest (discount) rate to future streams of income and costs to calculate their value at present.

Producer Price Index (P.P.I.) measurement of average changes in prices received by producers of all commodities, at all stages of processing, produced in the United States.

producer's surplus difference between the costs of production of a quantity of a good or service, and the amount actually received in a competitive market by the producer.

production function relationship between combinations of factor inputs and varying levels of output.

socialism economic system that focuses on government or collective ownership of the means of production.

supply curve function showing the amount of a good or service that producers are willing to supply at each price.

trade deficit occurs when a country imports goods from another country worth more than the value of its exports to that other country.

velocity of money speed with which money circulates, defined as G.N.P. in current dollars divided by the supply of money.

World Bank agency of the United Nations charged with encouraging and funding long-term growth and development among poorer nations.

BUSINESS

A Brief History of Business

Most histories of business start out with the premise that business began with the advent of money and the end of the barter system. Many ancient civilizations therefore had a primitive business model with goods and services being sold for what we would call cash. Trade among various cultures was also a feature of the ancient world, dating back as far as the third millennium B.C. in Egypt. The Phoenecians, Greeks, and Carthaginians all created wealthy and powerful trading states during the first millennium B.C.; the Roman Empire built much of its dominance of the Mediterranean world on its continuous contact with other cultures and used its armies to help enforce good trading terms with client states.

With the decline of the empire in the fifth and sixth centuries, barter returned throughout much of Europe until the 12th and 13th centuries, when the city-states of Italy (Venice and Genoa among others) brought about a tremendous resurgence of trade on the Mediterranean. By the time the great age of exploration arrived in the late 15th century, the business of foreign trade, whether founded by monarchies or pools of investors, had been well established.

The seven northern provinces that formed the Dutch Republic were flexible enough to respond to these international market conditions; by the middle of the 17th century the Dutch were the supreme economic power, and Amsterdam was the world's leading financial and commercial center. This balance of power shifted by the beginning of the 18th century, when Britain led the world into an industrial revolution; this is the point when the history of modern business can be truly said to have begun.

The Industrial Revolution

In the late 17th and 18th centuries, economic power grew fastest in Great Britain. It arose from a proliferation of inventions, the availability of capital, a relatively fluid social order, a rising and mobile population, a responsive legal system, a government with power divided between the king and parliament, and an entrepreneurial spirit that was shared by all of the social classes. These factors—collectively called the Industrial Revolution—produced a profound change in the nature of commerce and business.

Inventions   Beginning in the 18th century, the pace of invention began to quicken as industrialization created unprecedented opportunities for wealth—and a powerful incentive for invention. The invention of the process of invention during the period of industrialization has been called the most important invention of all.

One of the inventions that drove the Industrial Revolution was the steam engine. Before the 17th century, there were essentially four means of applying power to do work: humans (pushing, lifting, carrying), animals (pulling plows, transporting people), wind (powering sailing ships and windmills), and water (turning water wheels). The steam engine changed all this, providing a reliable source of power that could be used in many of the new industries that were being developed at the time.

The first commercially successful steam engine was developed by Thomas Newcomen (1663–1729) and first used in 1712. Newcomen's primitive engine was improved upon by James Watt (1736–1819), who produced a more efficient engine using rotary mechanics. Thanks to Watt's steam engine, factories were liberated from water wheels and built closer to their sources of supply; ships could move in all directions, no longer dependent on the direction of the wind or the currents. The steam engine also made possible a critical new mode of transportation—the railroad.

Transportation   The invention of the steam engine also made possible steam-powered ships that could travel to their destination more directly than sailing ships, reducing the time and costs of voyages. Now goods that moved along the railroads to port cities moved overseas on steamships, creating a vast flow of commerce between trading nations.

One of the reasons that Britain's industrialization moved at the pace it did was the availability of cheap transportation. From the 17th to the 19th centuries, Parliament passed a number of acts that facilitated the construction of roads, canals, and railroads.

In 1829 George Stephenson (1781–1848) and his son Robert (1803–59) successfully demonstrated a steam locomotive that traveled on iron rails. In 1830 it was adopted by the Liverpool and Manchester Railway and immediately put Britain ahead of the rest of the world in a form of transportation that was even cheaper than shipping by canals. Thereafter no country that aspired to industrialization could succeed without a network of railroads to carry the goods.

The Factory System

The first important industry to undergo profound changes during the Industrial Revolution was the textile industry, which was transformed by a series of inventions. Prior to 1700, most of the processes used to turn raw cotton or wool into fabrics were performed by hand, often by people working at home. During the 18th century, machines replaced human beings in all of the essential processes. This caused the cost of production to drop over time; merchants were able to sell fabric at lower prices, thus finding a mass market for their products.

The change from small groups of widely dispersed workers to mechanized processes performed under one roof signaled the birth of the modern factory. Factories provided employment to hundreds of thousands of workers who otherwise would have found no employment or means of survival, although conditions in the factories and settlements where the workers lived were often deplorable. And although Britain had a social system based on class, it did not prevent entrepreneurs of the lower classes from rising to become factory supervisors, managers, and owners.

Industrialization Spreads to Europe

As Britain was expanding under industrialization, it not only traded with European countries but also was a party—sometimes reluctantly—to the transfer of technologies and ideas to the continent. European countries paid British engineers to help them establish new industrial enterprises; they hired British workers to come and work for them, and—as they imported the goods of British industry—they learned how the goods were manufactured. They even were the beneficiaries of British investment in some of their enterprises. Investors thus had an incentive to transfer ideas and technologies to receptive European countries. The more forward-looking of the continental countries made full use of these advantages.

Germany   In 1850 Germany was a politically diverse group of rural and agrarian states. Though it was slow to industrialize, Germany eventually enabled its nobility to engage in commerce, abolished the guilds and other obstacles to industry, and provided trained workers from schools that were the first modern educational system. As Germany's states unified, they formed a tariff union (*Zollverein*) that eliminated tolls and customs and allowed trade to flow freely within its borders. To tie these areas

together, the country built a network of railroads similar to the one that played such an important role in Britain's industrialization.

The country was also rich in resources, especially coal; it was also aggressive in developing its iron production capability. Germany was quick to adopt the new refining methods being used elsewhere, and by 1895 its steel output surpassed Britain's. Germany ultimately excelled in industries that were fostered by its many fine universities. It came to dominate the field of chemistry and it made important advances in the production and applications of electricity.

France   As early as the late 18th century, France realized that industrialization would play a leading role in economic growth. In 1794, the country established the first institution of higher learning devoted to science and technology, the École Polytechnique. In 1829, a private applied engineering school, École Centrale des Arts et Manufactures, was established. French engineers developed sophisticated weaving machines, notably the Jacquard loom, named for its developer, J. M. Jacquard (1752–1834).

Measured by industrial output against population, France was close to Britain and Germany. But in absolute growth, it lagged behind and never caught up, owing in part to slow population growth, slow urbanization, a succession of wars, a reliance on water power, the small size of its enterprises, and the scarcity of coal. France's weak industrial capability was obvious during World War I.

Industrialization in the United States

In 1800 the United States was a new nation struggling to define itself; by 1900 it had the largest economy in the world and was the world's leading industrial nation. America's extraordinary economic growth during the 19th century is probably the most important business story in history.

The country, even before westward expansion, was vast in comparison with its population. There was abundant fertile land on which to grow food and other useful crops such as cotton. Natural resources were also abundant, in the form of wood, coal, iron and copper ores, and oil.

But America's greatest resource was its people. A high birth rate provided most, but not all, of the rapidly growing population. Added to this were waves of immigrants who were ambitious, energetic, skilled, and entrepreneurial, eager to put their talents to work in the opportunities that the new country afforded. The first United States census in 1790 enumerated fewer than 4 million inhabitants; by 1870 there were almost 40 million inhabitants.

This rapidly growing population not only supplied labor to industry but was also a growing pool of customers for the products of that industry. But even with this rapid population growth, there was a constant shortage of workers; agriculture and industry simply grew faster than the population.

The country's chronic labor shortage had two salutary effects on the growth of business and commerce. The first was that wages rose, attracting both native workers and ambitious and talented immigrants. The other was that agriculture and industry compensated for scarce workers by adopting and developing new technologies to increase productivity. By 1830—a surprisingly early date—productivity in the United States exceeded that of Great Britain.

Transportation Constructing roads, canals, and railroads to connect the vast expanses of the North American continent required vast amounts of capital. The federal government did not have the financial resources to pay for transportation projects as public works, so it was up to the states and the private sector—including investors from abroad—to find most of the money. This created opportunities for visionaries to build the arteries of commerce—and, at the same time, create great wealth for themselves.

Canals During the 18th century and the early 19th, water transportation was less expensive than land transportation—especially after the introduction of steam power. The existing rivers were soon supplemented and connected by systems of canals. The longest of these canals, and the one that inspired a wave of imitators, was the Erie Canal. The governor of New York state, DeWitt Clinton (1769–1828), understood the potential of connecting the Eastern seaboard with what was then the interior of the country. He pushed through the state legislature an authorization for $7 million to build a canal from Albany on the upper Hudson River to Buffalo on Lake Erie—a distance of 363 miles. It was one of the great engineering and construction projects of the century. After overcoming many obstacles, the canal opened in 1825 to great success. Soon many states and localities had built their own canals and created a web of water transportation.

Railroads America's canals were soon displaced by an even more economical means of transportation—the railroad. The building of the nation's railroad system required enormous amounts of capital. Fortunes were made by entrepreneurs who could combine building with financing—although it was sometimes difficult to distinguish between the builders and scoundrels. The first great railroad entrepreneur was Cornelius Vanderbilt (1794–1877). He began to invest in the stock of eastern railroad companies in the 1840's; by the time of his death he controlled railroads that stretched from New York City to Chicago.

The watershed achievement of railroad building in the 19th century was the completion of the first transcontinental railroad. As the nation expanded westward it clearly needed a rail connection to California. In 1862, President Abraham Lincoln signed the Pacific Railway Act that authorized the Union Pacific to build west from Omaha and the Central Pacific to build east from Sacramento until they met at a still undetermined location. On May 10, 1869, the two lines celebrated their linking-up in Promontory Point, Utah, northwest of Salt Lake City.

Although Thomas Clark Durant (1820–85) was president of the Union Pacific, Oakes Ames (1804–73) received much of the credit for building the Union Pacific Railroad to meet the Central Pacific. It was Ames and his brother Oliver who invested their money to fund construction of the Union Pacific part of the transcontinental railroad.

On the opposite coast, the Central Pacific was a joint enterprise operated by men who became known as "the Big Four," outsize personalities who collaborated to build the western half of the transcontinental railroad. The key figure was Collis Potter Huntington (1821–1900), who, along with Mark Hopkins (1813–78), Charles Crocker (1822–88) and Leland Stanford (1824–93), incorporated the Central Pacific Railroad. Their construction company was later investigated by the government when it was revealed that it had been paid approximately twice as much as its part of the construction should have cost.

Following that first meeting of the tracks at Promontory Point, several other transcontinental lines were laid, as well as many other trunk and feeder lines. As early as 1840 the total mileage of American railroads was 4,510—exceeding the total mileage of Britain and continental Europe combined.

Inventors Inventions and innovations had been essential to industrialization in Britain and Europe—and it was the same in the United States.

Textiles American manufacturers were eager to learn about advances in technologies in their industries, and offered bounties, high pay, and advancement as inducements to ambitious Europeans willing to emigrate. One of the most influential of these immigrant inventors was Samuel Slater (1768–1835), who had apprenticed in Britain with Jedediah Strutt (1726–97), developer of the first water-powered spinning machine. In 1789 Slater immigrated to the United States, where he engaged in a series of ventures to build water-driven spinning machines. He continued to develop textile manufacturing technology and was a major innovator in the development of the American factory system.

Steamships A number of inventors contributed to the development of a reliable steam-powered shipping industry. The most important was Robert Fulton (1765–1815); in August 1807 his boat, the *Clermont*, made a test run from New York to Albany. Fulton proved the practicality of steamboat travel the following year when his rebuilt boat began weekly trips between the two cities.

The "American System" of Manufacturing A number of inventors working in different industries developed manufacturing processes that, taken together, were more important than the products they manufactured. This came to be known as the "American System"—special-purpose machines and standardized work processes that resulted in repetitive tasks that could be performed rapidly by relatively unskilled workers. This system gave American industry a competitive edge in the growing world economy.

Eli Whitney (1765–1825) is best known for inventing the cotton gin, the machine that separated cotton seeds from cotton fiber. It revolutionized textile production, but it was widely pirated, and Whitney never realized the wealth that should have been his. He also developed a precision process to make uniform parts that could be assembled interchangeably into finished guns—an achievement that was arguably as important as the cotton gin.

Another important contributor to the "American System" was Cyrus Hall McCormick (1809–84), who developed the grain reaper. This invention not only increased agricultural productivity—releasing surplus farm workers for growing industry—but also refined the efficiency of the manufacturing processes.

Thomas Edison The most prolific inventor of all was Thomas Alva Edison (1847–1931), who differed from earlier inventors by using a sustained and organized invention process. In 1876, he combined his research laboratory with his manufacturing facility. From then until his death in 1931, he worked tirelessly to produce a steady flood of commercially viable products.

General Electric The model for institutionalizing innovation was established by Charles Proteus Steinmetz (1865–1923), who fled Germany for New York in 1889, and obtained employment with an electrical equipment company. He soon founded his own laboratory, which in 1892 was acquired by the General Electric Co.. In 1900 General Electric organized the first modern industrial research laboratory, and the following year it promoted Steinmetz to chief consulting engineer.

Other companies, including DuPont, Corning Glass, Parke-Davis pharmaceuticals, and Eastman Kodak, soon had their own research laboratories, which would be the source of countless new products and processes over the coming years.

Communications If commerce were to flourish in a county as large as the United States, there needed to be not only a large and efficient transportation system but also a way to speed communication between far-flung areas. Initially, mail was conveyed by railroad; the Railway Mail Service was established in 1869 as a separate branch of the Post Office Department. But faster communications were needed—and, during the first half of the 19th century, a number of inventors in Europe and the United States worked on the problem of transmitting messages by means of electricity.

The Telegraph Samuel Finley Breese Morse (1791–1872) believed that the flow of electricity could be made visible and that "intelligence" could be transmitted by wires across distances. He and other experts constructed a machine that transmitted electrical impulses through a wire that then drove another device at the other end to inscribe a series of dots and dashes on a moving strip of paper. Morse devised a code of dots and dashes for the letters of the alphabet. The system thus permitted messages to be sent almost instantaneously between two points.

On May 24, 1844, the message, "What hath God wrought," flashed from the nation's capital to Baltimore and then back again. This was the beginning of the telegraph system and the coding that became known as "Morse Code." Morse's company, the Morse Electromagnetic Telegraphy Co., licensed his patent; the Western Union Telegraph Co. ultimately came to dominate long-distance telegraphic communications.

The Telephone If words could be transmitted by code, inventors soon realized that the voice itself might be transmitted as well. Alexander Graham Bell (1847–1922) developed a system that converted sound waves to a varying current of electricity. His father-in-law, Gardner Greene Hubbard (1822–1897), submitted Bell's patent application on February 14, 1876. It was granted on March 7, 1876; some have called it the single most valuable patent in history. In 1877 Hubbard headed a group that formed the Bell Telephone Company (later renamed American Bell), although Bell ultimately lost interest in further developing the technology.

The Telephone System In 1880 Theodore Newton Vail (1845–1920) was hired to be the first general manager of American Bell. Vail envisioned linking all of the phones in the United States into one system. He started by persuading a potential competitor, Western Union, not to enter the telephone business, and he then acquired a controlling interest in Western Electric to provide technology and equipment for his countrywide network.

In 1907 as head of American Telephone and Telegraph (a wholly owned subsidiary of American Bell), Vail successfully fought and bought out most of his competitors. He realized, however, that the monopoly he was creating would be vulnerable to government antitrust action. To forestall such action, he proposed a regulatory commission to monitor AT&T's business, ceased acquiring competitors, and agreed to connect his long-distance lines with any local independent operator that wanted to be a part of the system. In return, the government agreed not to bring antitrust actions against the company.

The agreement lasted until 1974, when the U.S. Justice Department filed an antitrust suit against AT&T—"Ma Bell"—which was then the world's largest company. The company split itself into pieces, separating its long-distance and regional phone operations. The breakup launched competition within the telephone industry, and eventually the telecommunications revolution.

Entrepreneurs and Financiers   Industrialization and the growth of the American economy in the 19th century created opportunities for many ambitious and talented entrepreneurs to become extraordinarily wealthy. Along with their wealth came power—the power to shape industries, and even the power to affect government.

John Pierpont Morgan (1837–1913) played a central role in shaping the course of American industrialization. He established his own investment bank, J. P. Morgan & Co., in 1861. The railroad boom was on, and railroads required huge amounts of capital that Morgan began to provide. Morgan's investment reach also extended to other industries; he underwrote Edison's incandescent light, invested in Edison's power generation and distribution plants, and in 1892 financed the creation of General Electric. His greatest achievement in industrial finance was the creation of the United Steel Corp., the largest industrial company in the world.

Andrew Carnegie (1835–1919) began investing at the age of 22, and established an iron works company in 1864. He used these early investments to create an empire of iron and steel. He relentlessly sought ways to reduce the costs of production by gaining control of the entire process from mining the ore, transporting it to the plants, buying the coke to convert the ore, and then processing it with the latest technology. At the same time, he bought out competitors and combined them into an ever-larger empire.

In early 1901 Carnegie sold his company to J. P. Morgan for the then unheard-of price of $480 million. Morgan combined Carnegie's company with his own to form the United States Steel Co.

John Davison Rockefeller (1839–1937) entered the refining business in 1863—four years after the first oil well was drilled at Titusville, Pennsylvania, giving birth to the American petroleum industry. Cleveland soon became a major refining center, but Rockefeller disliked the disorderly and fragmented industry and moved to bring order to it. In 1870 he organized the Standard Oil Company; his strategy was to buy smaller companies and combine them into a company large enough to exert control over the market. By the end of 1872 Standard Oil had bought 34 competitors and controlled almost all of the refining companies in Cleveland; by 1879 the company controlled 90 percent of America's refining capacity

In its search for a way of legally organizing its large and diverse business, the company tried a number of organizational structures. In 1882 it created the first modern trust in American history, the Standard Oil Trust in Ohio. But the Ohio attorney general brought suit against the trust, and in 1892 the Ohio Supreme Court annulled the charter. The company then moved the trust to New Jersey and renamed itself Standard Oil (New Jersey). By this time the company owned an estimated three-fourths of all of the petroleum business in the United States.

The passage of the Sherman Antitrust Act of 1890 intensified attention on the giant company, and it was constantly fighting efforts to break it up and limit its power. Court battles with the company continued until a Supreme Court antitrust decision of May 15, 1911, dissolved Standard Oil Trust and reorganized it into 38 companies.

The Birth of Marketing

Industrialization not only created opportunities for mass production, but also led to the development of mass markets. Mass marketing soon followed by utilizing the power of newspapers, magazines, and the U.S. Postal Service.

Mass Marketing   Before the Industrial Revolution, products were mostly handcrafted and sold on a one-to-one basis to customers. The mass production of consumer goods enabled retailers to sell quantities of similar products to a larger base of customers. Selling to mass markets required companies to communicate to all of their potential customers. Advertising, a small and scattered industry, began transforming itself into a sophisticated group of comparatively large companies.

Retail Merchandisers The 19th century brought the ascendancy of merchandisers that combined distribution with mass marketing. The growing urban population provided a concentrated market for John Wanamaker (1838–1922), who saw an opportunity to create a new kind of store—the department store—that offered a wide variety of wares under a single roof.

Wanamaker opened his first store in 1861. From the beginning he worked to build customer loyalty, and in 1868 he opened a second store and renamed the company John Wanamaker & Co. He wrote and bought advertising that proclaimed his policies: a full guarantee on all merchandise, one price for all, payment in cash, and a cash refund if the customer was not satisfied. The primary brand image was the store, and customers flocked to a store with a name they had come to trust.

A different segment of the market beckoned to Frank Winfield Woolworth (1852–1919). In 1878, Woolworth was working in a store in Watertown, N.Y., when he helped to create a new five-cent counter. He grasped the potential of the idea of eliminating skilled, expensive clerks and replacing them with low-paid women clerks. The following year, 1879, Woolworth tested his idea with his first store in Utica, N.Y., but it failed because of a poor location. That same year he opened a similar store in Lancaster, Pa., that was an immediate success.

Despite early setbacks, Woolworth persevered and continued to expand. Selling many low-priced products, he relentlessly looked for low-cost merchandise, including toys, ornaments, and glass goods from Europe. In 1900 he began to build a strong brand identity by creating a uniform design for his 59 existing stores, and by 1919 there were 1,081 Woolworth stores in the United States and Canada—with even more in Britain, where he had extended his chain in 1909.

Mail Order Merchandisers During a selling trip to small towns in the Midwest, Aaron Montgomery Ward (1844–1913) realized that many rural folks were suspicious of local stores and disliked patronizing them. He saw an opportunity and began a business in 1872 to sell directly to customers through the mail, developing proprietary systems for buying, warehousing, advertising, processing orders, and shipping goods to his rural customers.

Ward's catalogs, promising "satisfaction guaranteed—or your money back," were known as "dream books," and enticed farmers to join urban dwellers in the growing consumer culture that mass production had made possible.

What Ward had begun, Richard Warren Sears (1863–1914) improved. In 1891 Sears formed a mail order partnership with Alvah Curtis Roebuck (1864–1948) that became Sears, Roebuck and Company. Sears was a born salesman and risk taker who produced catalogs that promised thousands of items at low prices. Roebuck sold his interest to Sears in 1895, and Sears then had the good fortune to add two new partners, one of whom was Julius Rosenwald (1862–1932), who ran the business side while Sears managed the marketing. Sears offered rebates and sweepstakes, and even offered farmers the opportunity to examine goods before paying for them, with the promise "Send no money." With Sears's marketing flair and Rosenwald's business discipline, the company grew rapidly; by 1900 it had $10 million in sales, surpassing Montgomery Ward.

Product Innovation Industrialization made mass production of traditional products possible, and also led to the development of new kinds of products.

Packaged foods Willie Keith (W. K.) Kellogg (1860–1951) began experimenting with foods based on nuts and grains while he was at his brother's Seventh Day Adventist sanitarium in 1880. The brothers built machinery to produce wheat flakes, and in 1984 created cornflakes and sought to build a national market for W. K.'s packaged breakfast foods. W. K. left his brother's employ in 1902, and in 1906 incorporated the Battle Creek Toasted Corn Flake Co., later changed to the W. K. Kellogg Co. From the beginning W. K. spent heavily on advertising, and by 1909 company sales surpassed 1 million cases.

In 1891 Charles William Post (1854–1914), plagued by stomach ailments, came to Kellogg's sanitarium, hoping for a cure. When he failed to regain his health, he was treated by a local Christian Scientist and soon recovered. Convinced that part of his recovery was the result of a healthy diet, Post began experimenting with a coffee substitute made of wheat, bran, and molasses. In 1895 he launched this product as Postum, a cereal beverage, and in 1896 he incorporated the Postum Cereal Co. The next year Post brought out Grape-Nuts cereal, and in 1904 he began to compete directly with Kellogg in the corn flake cereal market with a product he eventually called Post Toasties. Post, like Kellogg, realized that advertising was the key to success, and by 1899 he was spending $400,000 annually to promote his packaged foods.

Coca-Cola Health claims were also important to the beginnings of another product that is now consumed worldwide. Coca-Cola was concocted in 1886 by a druggist in Atlanta, Dr. John S. Pemberton (1831–88), and touted as a nerve and brain tonic. The drink was not a success, and the druggist sold his ownership in pieces, with one share going to Asa Griggs Candler (1851–1929) in 1888. In 1891 Candler became the sole owner of the product, its formula, and its trademark. Candler was a marketing innovator, and before the end of the 19th century, Coca-Cola was sold in soda fountains in all of the 48 states.

It was a further innovation, however, that multiplied the company's growth. In 1899 two attorneys in Chattanooga, Tennessee, negotiated a contract with Candler for exclusive bottling rights in most of the United States, thus separating the bottling businesses from Candler's company. By the end of the 1920's bottled Coke outsold fountain Coke, and soon the company's trademark was one of the best-known in the world.

Disposable Razors When King Camp Gillette (1855–1932) took a sales job in 1891 with a company making crimped bottle caps, the president advised him to invent a similarly disposable product. Gillette enthusiastically took up the challenge, and in 1895 he conceived of a razor made up of thin disposable blades clamped in a device to hold them rigid while men shaved. He engaged an MIT graduate who developed machinery to sharpen steel ribbons into blades. By 1903, Gillette's small Boston firm was able to produce his new razors and, like other entrepreneurs with a vision, he invested in heavy advertising. By 1908 the company sold 300,000 holders and 14 million blades—and established a legacy of product innovation.

Brand Management The idea that a product or company name could become a marketing focus was not new at the end of the 19th century. Many producers and manufacturers had promoted an awareness among customers of their company or product names as a way of distinguishing them from competitors. The art of "brand management," however, was not perfected until the 20th century.

Procter and Gamble The Procter and Gamble Company, founded in 1837, introduced a cake of white soap that floated on water, taking out its first advertisement for the product in 1881. The company named this product Ivory Soap. Though Procter and Gamble advertised it widely, the company did not establish a clear and consistent theme about its virtues; nevertheless, the soap was very successful and alerted the company—and its competitors—to the possibilities of promoting products to a national market in a coordinated and carefully planned fashion.

When Procter and Gamble launched its next important product in 1912, a vegetable shortening called Crisco, it had its strategy in place. Under its president William Cooper Procter (1862–1934), son of the co-founder, the company had tested and refined the product with women cooks, secured testimonials from scientists and home economists, and persuaded one railroad to use the shortening exclusively in its dining cars. The company tested a variety of different marketing campaigns in different cities, researched how consumers used shortening, and studied how competitors' products were selling and used. Crisco was a huge success—and established the model for brands that were specifically created and marketed. Procter and Gamble became the leader in building a portfolio of branded products; the brand names, not the company name, became king.

Lever Brothers In Britain a similar company was founded in 1885 by William Hesketh Lever (1851–1925) and his brother. Lever Brothers' first product was a packaged soap that they named Sunlight—the world's first packaged and branded laundry soap. Made mostly from vegetable oil, the soap rapidly caught on with the pubic, and by 1911 the company was producing one-third of the soap sold in Britain.

Lever expanded the soap line through acquisitions, and in 1917 he diversified into foods. By 1924 the company had grown to be the largest commercial company of its kind in the world. In 1930 Lever merged the company with a Dutch margarine producer, Margarine Unie, and changed its name to Unilever.

The Growth of the Automobile Industry

Industrialization in the first half of the 20th century produced the largest industry of all, the automobile industry. Most consider Karl Benz (1844–1929) and Gottlieb Daimler (1834–1900), who in 1885 invented the internal combustion engine, the founders of this important new industry—although the industry soon revolved around a few key American automotive companies.

Ford Motor Company Henry Ford (1863–1947) wanted to produce cars he could sell at a low price, and he saw the assembly line as the means of vastly increasing the productivity of his workers—thereby lowering the cost of producing each car. He also saw that the more individual components he could produce internally—instead of buying them from outside suppliers—the more he could control the cost of the completed car. Finally, by paying his workers the unheard-of wage of $5 a day, Ford guaranteed his company a loyal and productive workforce.

Ford's great success, the Model T, was first shipped to dealers in October 1908, after two years of design and development. By the time the last Model T was produced in May 1927, 15 million cars had been sold. Ford had managed to reduce the price of the coupe to $290, and the car had made the American family mobile. It had forced governments to pave dirt roads and to create highways for long-distance travel. It had spawned a host of roadside businesses, including gas stations, restaurants, hotels, and a new kind of lodging, the "motel."

General Motors Ford's primary competitor was General Motors, which was founded by William C. Durant (1861–1947). Durant, however, was an erratic manager, and he gained and lost control of the company several times. By 1920 General Motors was again in financial trouble, and Pierre S. du Pont (1870–1954), whose family company was the second largest shareholder, forced Durant to resign. Whatever Durant's failings as a manager, his vision of mass-marketed cars, along with models of differing styles and prices, was the basis of General Motors' growth. It became the largest auto manufacturer in the United States—and, by 1928, the largest and most profitable industrial company in the world.

The man who realized Durant's vision, Alfred Pritchard Sloan, Jr. (1875–1966), had come into the organization when Durant bought the Hyatt Roller Bearing Company in 1916. From 1920 to 1923, when he became president of General Motors (GM), Sloan began an organizational transformation that was to become the model for several generations of chief executives in widely differing industries.

Under Sloan, GM offered more comfortable cars, more stylishly designed, at every price range, and with a choice of colors. He also understood that buyers at different income levels wanted different kinds of cars; this led him to organize the GM product line by income level corresponding to car price. These lines evolved into Chevrolet at the lowest price level (competing with Ford's Model T), followed in increasing price ranges by Pontiac, Oldsmobile, Buick, and Cadillac. GM also introduced the annual model change, small but noticeable changes in the styling of the cars each year to create a steady demand for new models. Chevrolet remained the auto sales leader for most of the next five decades.

Chrysler Corporation The third large U.S. automobile manufacturer, Chrysler, was created in the early 1920's by Walter P. Chrysler (1875–1940). Chrysler moved through a number of executive positions in different automobile companies, and from 1923 to 1924 he and a team of engineers at Maxwell Motors, where he was president, designed a new moderately priced car with advanced engineering features, which he named the Chrysler. It was an immediate success, and in 1925 Chrysler renamed the company the Chrysler Corp.

In 1928 Chrysler launched the Plymouth, which incorporated advanced engineering features not available on similarly priced cars. The car was an instant success, even though it cost half again as much as comparable Fords and Chevrolets. By increasing manufacturing capacity and reducing costs, Chrysler was able to reduce the price of the Plymouth and move it almost to reasonable price parity with Ford and Chevrolet. Chrysler's basic strategy of producing well-engineered cars at a slightly higher price than competitors proved successful over a long period of time.

Organizing the Corporation

The larger these new companies grew, the more problems executives encountered in managing them. It was not until the 20th century that top executives devised new organizational solutions to the increasing problems of size.

E.I. Du Pont The company that had the widest and longest-lasting influence on corporate structures was E. I. du Pont de Nemours & Company, which in 1900 was a loose collection of companies producing different kinds of explosives, owned and managed by various groups of family members. When the elders of the family considering selling the company in 1902, Pierre S. du Pont and two cousins bought them out to preserve the business within the family. The three cousins organized the firm into a centrally controlled structure with clear lines of responsibility for functional areas. Sales and profits grew faster than they had grown before the changes.

Until the end of World War I, the centralized structure of the firm served the business well. When the war ended, the company expanded into paints, chemicals, and dyestuffs. The company had been accustomed to selling explosives by the ton to a small number of customers; now it had products like paint that were sold in small quantities to innumerable customers through retail outlets. The company's centralized structure did not lend itself to a diverse product line, and in 1921 the board of directors approved a restructuring plan that created autonomous divisions.

These divisions produced and marketed distinct product lines, run by general managers who were responsible and accountable for the performance of their own division. Coordination was through an executive committee that included the president and other senior executives, but none of the operating general managers. Thus a balance was struck between the relative autonomy of the divisions and a central coordinating entity.

General Motors

During GM's crisis of 1920, Pierre S. du Pont gave Alfred P. Sloan the opportunity to put into practice his evolving ideas about organization.

The organizational challenge facing Sloan was the opposite of that facing du Pont at that time. Whereas du Pont needed to find an organizing structure to manage its new diversified product lines, GM was a loosely federated group of entities that needed some kind of stronger centralized control. In December 1920 the GM board approved Sloan's plan to create a structure with autonomous divisions under a central office with coordinating control.

Subject only to the executive control of the president and the executive committee, the general manager of each division was expected to know the demands of the market for his product line and to develop it to its fullest potential. He was held responsible for his division's success or failure.

The central coordinating group of the firm was the executive committee, consisting nearly entirely of senior officers who did not have operating responsibilities. Together with the president, the committee governed the firm by setting broad strategic policies and approving major initiatives to accomplish these policies. The finance committee oversaw the company's financial performance.

Word of the GM model's success spread rapidly to other firms that were grappling with many of the same problems of diversification. Sears Roebuck adopted a similar multidivisional structure after it realized that the United States was becoming increasingly urbanized and that its traditional catalog business would fail to capture customers who now lived in cities. The company's divisions, as eventually structured, were geographic regions rather than product lines. This was Sears' early advantage that its competitor Montgomery Ward was never able to overcome.

Oil companies, led by Standard Oil (New Jersey), responded to the need for vertical integration and crude oil sources spread increasingly all over the world by creating similar regional divisions. As they began to develop new markets for petrochemicals they also created divisions along product lines.

Management Theorists

With industrialization and the advent of the factory system, large groups of workers were brought together for the first time to produce goods using machines. Factory owners pushed workers for maximum productivity and this policy resulted in long hours at low pay, frequent injuries from dangerous machines, the use of child labor, and appalling living conditions in factory towns. The idea that treating workers well and organizing their work with careful planning would result in productivity increases was virtually unknown. That would change gradually over more than a century until the new field of "management" was born and its applications spread beyond factories to all kinds of organizations.

Robert Owen The first important thinker to address the question of how to manage factory workers was Robert Owen (1771–1858). Owen's major contribution to management came in 1800, when he and his partners bought the large cotton mills at New Lanark near Glasgow. His past experience in mill management had convinced him that if he treated workers decently and with respect, their productivity would significantly increase. He stopped employing children under the age of 10, built schools for infants and older children, and shortened the working day. He improved workers' housing, paved the streets, and opened a company store with low prices. Owen's reforms enabled the mill to prosper, and its schools became widely known.

Frederick W. Taylor The concept that both owners and workers can prosper under the right conditions was carried forward by Frederick Winslow Taylor (1856–1915), arguably the most influential management thinker in the first half of the 20th century.

As a management consultant, Taylor experimented with ways of speeding up the production of the workers, including the introduction of piecework and the use of a stopwatch to find the best way to coordinate the actions of the workers and their machines. He believed that "there is always one method and one implement which is quicker and better than any of the rest." In 1911 he published the most widely read business book of the first half of the century, *The Principles of Scientific Management*, which helped to spread the gospel of "Taylorism."

George Elton Mayo In 1927 AT&T invited a Harvard business professor, George Elton Mayo (1880–1949), to study workers at the Hawthorne Works of Western Electric in Chicago. AT&T was interested in knowing if the level of illumination in the plant had any effect on workers' productivity—a classic instance of the Taylor approach. Mayo and his team studied a room where five young women were assembling electromagnetic relay switches; over the period of 1928 to 1932 the team varied the working conditions in the room—not only illumination, but rates of pay, periods of rest, and other factors—and collected reams of data on performance. The results at first baffled them. It seemed as if everything they did improved productivity. When they introduced piecework, added rest periods, provided a free meal, and shortened the workday, output increased. But when they took all these elements away and returned the room to its original conditions, output increased to the highest level ever.

Mayo's team realized that the workers had become a dynamic social group and had responded to the attention the researchers were paying them. They concluded that the very fact of their interest in the workers had motivated the women to show the researchers how well they could work—what became known as the "Hawthorne effect." Mayo's theories, which were the beginning of the human relations approach to management, became increasingly important in the second half of the 20th century, eventually displacing the practice of Taylorism.

Chester I. Barnard   It took a working executive to fully understand and articulate the realities of managing people in large organizations. Chester Irving Barnard (1886–1961) held a succession of management positions at AT&T, Pennsylvania Bell, and New Jersey Bell, where he was responsible for consolidating a number of smaller companies into each of the larger companies. The lessons he learned in dealing with the human dimension of integrating many diverse personalities into a new whole shaped his thinking on how organizations function, what motivates workers, and how authority flows from top to bottom.

Barnard delivered a series of lectures at the Lowell Institute in Cambridge, Mass., that became a classic of management thought when they were published under the title *The Functions of the Executive* in 1938. He argued that the harmony and cooperation necessary for carrying out the purpose of the organization are achieved only when workers sense that their interests and aspirations are aligned with the organization's goals. Top management achieves this by the exercise of its authority, but workers will accept that authority only if they understand the task at hand, believe the request is consistent with the organization's goals, believe the request is compatible with their own interests, and are able mentally and physically to carry out the task.

Postwar Recovery

At the end of the 1920's a worldwide depression brought widespread business failures and a decade of struggle for the survivors. With the coming of World War II, businesses turned to the challenge of meeting the needs of wartime economies. The end of the war in 1945 created an unprecedented economic boom in the United States, as pent-up consumer demand was finally unleashed. Consumers who were deprived of many goods during the war had bought war bonds and had accumulated money to spend. Young G.I.'s returned home eager to start their lives, so they married and had children right away, helping to create the greatest baby boom in history. They also began a mass exodus out of the nation's cities to the new so-called suburbs.

The late 1940's saw an audacious bet on the future by William Jaird Levitt (1907–94) and his father and brother. They believed that they could profitably build and sell low-priced small houses in suburban areas by using mass production techniques they had learned building civilian and military housing during the war. Their first project, Levittown, was begun in 1947. Levittown consisted of 17,500 two-bedroom Cape Cod houses on Long Island, N.Y. Veteran loans helped new families to pay for the houses, and by 1951 the company began a second Levittown in Bucks County, Pa., comprising 16,000 houses. Later Levittowns appeared in New Jersey and Florida.

The Automobile Market   Suburban living demanded flexible transportation, and nothing provided it better than the automobile.

The government had brought Henry Ford II (1917–87) back from military service and installed him at Ford in 1943, fearing that his aging grandfather, Henry Ford, could not manage the company's wartime production. He led the company through several decades of successful new models, to become a strong second to General Motors.

Alfred P. Sloan retired as CEO of General Motors in 1946 and as chairman in 1956. His successors continued his management structure, which proved to be robust as the company continued to lead the U.S. automobile industry.

After some initial postwar success, the Chrysler Corporation had difficulty in finding the right product mix. Although the company pioneered the popular minivan in the 1980's, it remained third behind GM and Ford and merged with the German company Daimler-Benz in 1998.

In the late 1940's, an odd-looking car built in Germany began to appear on European streets and roads. It was noisy, with a rear-mounted, air-cooled engine and a rounded shape that looked like a giant bug. The car had been conceived and designed in the late 1930's by Ferdinand Porsche (1875–1951) to be a low-priced "people's car," or Volkswagen. The "beetle," as it was dubbed by *The New York Times*, eventually became the largest-selling car in history.

Plans to manufacture the car were interrupted by World War II, but following the war production began in Germany under the enlightened leadership of Heinz Nordhoff (1899–1968). He focused on building high-quality cars and creating a large international dealer and service organization.

In 1972 Volkswagen produced the 15,007,034th beetle and announced that it had surpassed the production of Ford's Model T. Customers—often young families—discovered that an inexpensive car could be as well-made as a luxury car. This discovery was to reverberate throughout the automobile market, as Japanese makers began to offer small, inexpensive cars of high quality in the years following. A generation of young buyers became converts to foreign cars before American manufacturers awoke to the consequences of global competition.

The oil shocks of the 1970's accelerated a major shift in the world automobile market. The Organization of Petroleum Exporting Countries (OPEC) created crises in the availability of the world's supply of oil. The steep rise in the price of gasoline that followed made smaller, fuel-efficient cars more desirable than they had been when gas was cheap and plentiful.

Unfortunately, Detroit had left the small car market to foreign producers, most of them Japanese. These foreign cars began to sell as never before, and owners discovered what earlier buyers of the Volkswagen beetle had discovered—the cars were made to high quality standards, were reliable, and were supported by strong dealer and service organizations.

The Quality Movement Prior to World War II, Japan had been known for the poor quality of its export goods. After the war both the government and industry realized that its economic recovery would depend first on its domestic market and later on exports. To compete effectively, Japanese industries had to produce goods of the highest quality. They found inspiration and methods in a surprising source—two Americans, William Edwards Deming (1900–93) and Joseph Moses Juran (1904–2008). Deming and Juran developed a range of quality concepts that found only a limited audience in the United States, but after they were invited to deliver lectures on quality control in Japan, Japanese manufacturers eagerly adopted their ideas.

The basic concept of quality control can be summarized as "Build it right the first time." Conventional mass production relied on a stage at the end of the assembly line to correct any defects that had been built into a product. But it was less expensive not to have built defects into the product as it was being manufactured. That would require an extra effort by production workers to ensure that what they did was free of defects. Japanese manufacturers developed management protocols to achieve this commitment from every worker.

The Toyota Production System Quality became the most important management movement since the end of World War II—the most notable example being the production system of Japan's Toyota Motor Company, which combined mass production and individual craft methods.

Under Kiichiro Toyoda (1894–1952), the company instituted a just-in-time (JIT) inventory system that delivered parts to the assembly line at the time they were needed—creating a more flexible manufacturing system than Fordism enabled. This was just the start of Toyota's much-vaunted production system. In 1950 a young Toyota engineer, Eiji Toyoda (b. 1913), who in 1967 became president of the company, visited Ford's vast Rouge plant to study its production methods. After three months he wrote to headquarters that he "thought there were some possibilities to improve the production system." Under its innovative production engineer, Taiichi Ohno (1912–90), Toyota instituted statistical quality control and continuous improvement (*kaizen*), and further developed its system of just-in-time inventory control (*kanban*). The company worked with its supplier companies to make them a part of its production system. Toyota also adopted its "total quality management" (T.Q.M.) system, which became the most visible aspect of its production system.

Japanese Cars on the World Market In the 1970's and 1980's, responding partly to limitations of domestic capacity, Toyota and other Japanese manufacturers opened plants in North America and successfully transplanted their production systems to American workers. They also began to produce larger cars, first family sedans and later luxury cars. Their reputation for high-quality small cars carried over to the larger cars, and now Detroit faced direct competition in its core markets.

In 1989 the Honda Accord family sedan outsold Ford's popular Taurus; Toyota's Camry took over this lead position in 1997. Internationally, by the end of the 1990's, Toyota had sold over 29 million of its compact Corollas—making it the best-selling automobile in history. In addition, Japanese cars forced European manufacturers to confront the challenge of the evolving global marketplace and to examine the source of Japan's success.

Consumer Electronics   Cars were not the only consumer products at which Japanese companies excelled. In 1957 a Japanese company—later renamed Sony—cofounded by Akio Morita (1921–99) released the TR-63, the first commercially successful pocket-sized transistor radio. The success of the TR-63 in world markets was the beginning of a shift of consumer electronics production outside the United States, mainly to Japan. Japanese manufacturers quickly learned the technology of miniaturization and applied it to a number of other products, including television sets, videotape recorders, hand-held calculators, portable cassette tape players, CD and DVD players, and cellular telephones. By combining a creative approach to new product design with high-quality manufacturing, Japanese manufacturers captured the world market for many consumer electronics products.

Business in the Information Age

As the end of the 20th century neared, businesses in Europe, Japan, and the United States began to shift from a primarily manufacturing base to technology- and information-driven organizations. Advances in communications and the spread of capitalism led to globalization, the opening of markets worldwide to competition. The industrial age was at an end, replaced by the new information age. Advances in communications and the spread of capitalism led to globalization, the opening of markets worldwide to competition.

Information Technology   In the post-World War II boom, as companies grew in size and the number of transactions multiplied, they sought economies in converting repetitive tasks requiring increasing numbers of workers into automated processes employing far fewer workers. These economies were realized by the development of the digital computer.

IBM and the Digital Computer   The first computers (See "Computers") were large mainframe machines that automated the billing process and related accounting functions. In 1964 I.B.M., under its CEO Thomas J. Watson, Jr. (1914–93), introduced its System 360 machines—a family of computers graded in size with interchangeable software and peripherals. These relatively smaller, relatively less expensive machines led to the accelerating adoption of computers by major companies, and IBM became the dominant computer manufacturer through the 1970's.

Computer Networks   Improved computer technology in the 1960's made possible interconnected computers and greater flexibility for users outside the data

processing department. One of the most successful adaptations of networked computers was American Airlines' SABRE computer reservation system. Developed in the early 1960's as a way of keeping track of one airline's sales of seats, SABRE was extended to travel agents' desks in 1976, presenting a choice of seats on many competing airlines. Eventually the system was augmented to include hotel, car, rail, and entertainment reservations; the system ultimately became more profitable for American Airlines than its passenger flights.

The Personal Computer   During the 1970's and 1980's the mainframe computer was downsized, and the so-called personal computer (PC) was born. The first inexpensive general-purpose PC was the Altair, introduced by Micro Instrumentation Telementry Systems. The PC enabled workers to run a range of application software—including word processing, spreadsheets, databases, and graphic presentations—on their desktops. It also served as the terminal for access to management information originating in remote server computers.

The Software Industry   In the early 1970's, a student at Harvard University, Bill Gates (b. 1955), wrote a version of the computer language BASIC for the Altair. In 1975, along with Paul Allen (b. 1953), he founded Microsoft to sell software products for the new PCs. Microsoft came to dominate the computer industry through its ubiquitous operating system, Windows, which ran on an estimated 95 percent of computers worldwide. Microsoft also successfully sold products ranging from computer games to word processing software. Its aggressive sales tactics and size made it a continual target of competitors' lawsuits and antitrust regulators. At the turn of the century Bill Gates was the world's richest man.

Networked computers developed in the 1960's and 1970's enabled information systems that encompassed all the workings of an organization. The German firm SAP offered company-wide software systems to integrate all aspects of a business, giving workers access to real-time management information. By the beginning of the 21st century SAP was one of the world's largest independent software companies, and an example of the globalization of the marketplace in a software industry long dominated by the United States.

The Internet   In the 1990's, the growth of the Internet, a network that linked computers all over the world, created new marketing opportunities for business. Companies opened Web sites from which they marketed their products and services, and used electronic mail (e-mail) to communicate within the office and with other offices around the world.

One of the fastest-growing businesses spawned by the Internet was that of providing Internet access to PC users. The most successful Internet service provider (ISP) was America Online (AOL), founded by Stephen M. Case (b. 1958) in 1985. During the 1990's AOL added subscribers at a much faster rate than competitors, and its market value soared so high that it was able to acquire the Time Warner media conglomerate in 2000. The merger resulted in little real business benefit. The failure of the combination was made evident when AOL was spun off from Time Warner and reverted to life as an independent firm in 2009.

The Internet also created a new kind of business, dubbed e-business, in which entrepreneurs hoped to eliminate the need for "bricks and mortar" stores and sell directly to customers. One of the most successful e-businesses was Amazon.com, founded by Jeffrey P. Bezos (b. 1954) in 1995 as an online bookseller. Amazon.com's revenues have grown steadily over succeeding years—aided by the addition of new product lines.

The most successful large Internet firm was eBay, launched in 1995 by Pierre Omidyar (b. 1968). An Internet auction house that brings sellers and buyers together in cyberspace, eBay adapted the auction concept to the Internet and has experienced rapid revenue and profit growth. In the process, it created a trading economy of $20 billion a year.

In what has been called the "dot-com boom" of the 1990's, thousands of entrepreneurs opened Web sites offering a staggering array of goods and services; significant venture capital flowed into these companies, and their stock prices climbed to astronomical heights. Then came the "dot-com bust." The stock prices of most Internet companies collapsed in 2000, as it became apparent to investors that most of the dot-com companies had few actual sales. (See "The Internet.")

Telecommunications Information technology created vast amounts of data; and transmitting these data to the growing world of computer networks required a comparable increase in the means of communication. Local phone companies and long-distance carriers rushed to add capacity and created a boom in business for suppliers of fiber-optic cable and sophisticated switching and routing systems. The added capacity far outstripped demand, however, and many companies, large and small, were caught with heavy capital investments in transmission capacity but no revenues to pay for them. The result, in 2000–01, was a series of severe downsizings of many major companies and bankruptcies at others. The largest casualty was the long-distance giant MCI, which emerged from bankruptcy in 2004 after a two-year reorganization.

Big-Box Retail   The continuing suburban expansion of the late 20th century gave retailers a new opportunity to change the basic nature of shopping. With large tracts of land available for building they created "big-box" stores, which earned their profits not through price markups but by sales volume. Big-box stores came to dominate many retail categories, including bookselling (Barnes & Noble), hardware (Home Depot), and electronic goods (Best Buy). They put many traditional mom-and-pop stores out of business and relegated others to niche positions.

Wal-Mart, a low-priced department store, became the biggest big-box chain. Founded in 1962 by Sam Walton (1918–92), Wal-Mart was guided by one overriding principle: efficiency. By simplifying store layout, pressuring suppliers to design products to its specifications, and hastening the pace at which its distributors operated, it squeezed costs out of the retail supply chain and passed on the price savings to customers. At the turn of the century Wal-Mart was the largest private employer in the United States and the world's largest company, with sales of $405 billion in 2010. Its influence was felt throughout the retail economy, as many of its competitors were forced to adopt the same high-speed, low-overhead tactics that Wal-Mart used. Wal-Mart's huge size and market power made it a target for critics who accused it of ruining downtowns across the country and depressing retail wages and benefits industry-wide.

The Biotechnology Industry   In 1973 two young biologists, Herbert Wayne Boyer (b. 1936) and Stanley Norman Cohen (b. 1935), genetically engineered molecules in foreign cells to produce predetermined patterns of DNA—called recombinant DNA—and began the modern biotechnology industry.

Genentech   In 1976 Herbert Boyer, along with the venture capitalist Robert Arthur Swanson (1947–99), founded the pioneer biotechnology company Genentech. Within the first three years the fledgling company cloned the first human protein in a microorganism, cloned human insulin, and cloned human growth hormone. In 1982 it marketed the first recombinant DNA drug, human insulin, which it licensed to Eli Lilly and Company. The same year Genentech marketed a growth hormone for children with a growth hormone deficiency, becoming the first biotechnology company to manufacture and market its own recombinant pharmaceutical product.

The Growth of Biotechnology   Today's biotechnology industry operates in medicine, agriculture, and the environment and is made up of two kinds of firms. The first group is start-up firms like Genentech, usually begun by scientists with specific products to commercialize. The other is large pharmaceutical firms that have entered the field either by acquisitions (Roche acquired Genentech in 2009) or their own research and development efforts. The former need abundant capital to grow and many have to scramble to find it—especially the smallest firms. The latter also need capital but can either generate it from their operations or can borrow it on favorable terms.

The industry grew rapidly from 2000 to 2007 when the worldwide financial crises began, but slowed considerably after that. Amgen, the world's largest independent biotechnology company rose from $3.2 billion in sales in 2000 to $15 billion in 2008, but has remained at about that level through 2010. The financial crisis was an important factor, but not the only one. The industry as a whole continues to face strong headwinds. The high cost of research and development with uncertain successes, expiring patents on major drugs, too few promising drugs in the research and development pipeline, increasing competition from larger firms, health care reform that threatens pricing in the marketplace, and the sluggish recovery from the global financial crisis have slowed the growth of the industry.

Biotechnology also raises many contentious issues. Food crops genetically engineered in the United States have been banned in Europe. Genetically "improved" livestock are feared by some as possibly harmful and decried by others as destructive of animal rights. Stem cell research looking for cures for Alzheimer's disease and diabetes, among other diseases, is limited by political pressure from some religious groups. There is little doubt that biotechnology will play an increasingly important role in medicine, agriculture, and the environment. But progress is likely to be slower than anticipated at the beginning of the 21st century.

Enron and Corporate Corruption

In the first decade of the 21st century, it began to be revealed that much of the economic boom of the 1990's was built on shady accounting practices at some of the country's largest corporations. The poster child of this wave of corporate corruption was Enron, once a Houston-based oil company that faked its way into becoming the seventh-largest corporation in America but ultimately became synonymous with corporate malfeasance.

Under a management team headed by Kenneth L. Lay, Jeffrey K. Skilling, and Andrew S. Fastow, Enron utilized a controversial but legal system of partnerships called structured finance, which allowed the company to raise billions of dollars without incurring any debt on its books. But by the end of 2001, an errant partnership caused the entire scheme to start unraveling, and all that debt was suddenly due. Within just a few weeks, Enron was bankrupt and its leadership was under criminal investigation. All three men were convicted; Mr. Lay died before he was sentenced.

A casualty of the Enron scandal was Arthur Andersen, formerly the nation's most respected accounting firm. For years, Andersen's cozy relationships with many of its clients flew beneath the radar of federal investigators. But when the Securities and Exchange Commission started looking into Enron (whose books Andersen had helped cook), the firm's partners started shredding documents that could implicate the company. On June 15, 2002, Andersen was convicted of obstruction of justice, a felony, and by law was forbidden from auditing public companies. Although the conviction was ultimately overturned, Andersen lost almost all of its clients and became the target of hundreds of civil suits. The conviction also shed light on improper accounting by other Andersen clients which in July, 2002, eclipsed Enron as the world's largest bankruptcy filing after having misstated more than $7 billion.

Other white collar crimes by executives at Tyco, Qwest, Global Crossing, Merrill Lynch, and Salomon Brothers turned 2002 into the year of the corporate scandal, and forced Congress to react with unusual muscle. Less than a week before the WorldCom bankruptcy filing, both houses overwhelmingly passed a reform bill known as Sarbanes-Oxley, and President George W. Bush signed it two weeks later, promising "no more easy money for corporate criminals, just hard time."

The legislation established a regulatory board to oversee corporate governance and the accounting industry, empowering the body to investigate and to punish corrupt auditors. It also created protections for corporate whistleblowers and mandated long prison terms for executives who deliberately defraud investors.

The hue and cry over corporate scandals dissipated with the passage of Sarbanes-Oxley, especially as the country turned its attention to a confrontation with Iraq. As a result, issues like exorbitant executive compensation and mismanagement of corporate pension funds and 401 (k) accounts went unaddressed. Indeed, by 2003, WorldCom had renamed itself M.C.I., moved its headquarters to Dulles, Va., just outside Washington D.C., and received a $45 million no-bid contract from the Pentagon to build a wireless phone network in Iraq. (Bernard Ebbers, WorldCom's former C.E.O was sentenced to 25 years in jail on July 13, 2005. M.C.I. was acquired by Verizon for $8.4 billion in January, 2006).

Business in the 21st Century

The globalization of the marketplace continued into the first decade of the 21st century. But the rapid growth of the world economy was interrupted by the financial crisis that began in 2007. On balance, however, it was the very fact of the globalized market that mitigated the effect of the crisis on certain industries and companies within those industries.

The U.S Automotive Industry in Crisis   Long before the financial crisis of 2007 the U.S. automobile industry was in a state of turmoil. The challenge of well-made foreign cars and union contracts—including restrictive work rules and the heavy costs of health care and pensions for retired workers—added costs to each car produced. Additionally the inattentiveness of top management to the growing demand of customers for high quality and reliable vehicles resulted in a decreasing market share for American manufacturers. The financial crisis only made matters worse.

General Motors and Chrysler both filed for bankruptcy protection under Chapter 11 of the Bankruptcy Code in 2009. Of the Big Three, only Ford, which had mortgaged virtually all its assets, including its iconic blue oval logo, for a cash hoard, avoided the bankruptcy court. To save GM and Chrysler from possible liquidation—apparently considering them "too big to fail"—the government invested $50 billion in GM and $7 billion in Chrysler. Bankruptcy court allowed GM to shed health and pension obligations and pare its brands to Chevrolet, Buick, Cadillac, and GMC. In 2010 the Treasury Department sold $13.5 billion of its shares in the company and by the end of the year had recovered about $23 billion of its bailout investment, but there was wide-spread belief that the U.S. would never recover its full investment. Near term, GM is concentrating on marketing in developing countries and in 2010 for the first time it sold more cars in China than in the U.S. But GM's future lies with new models due in 2012 and 2013.

Chrysler has passed through several owners since 1998 when it was bought by Daimler-Benz, the German car company that builds Mercedes-Benz cars. Looking to expand its market share in the U.S. by selling mid-priced cars, Daimler also hoped to realize economies of scale by sharing engineering departments. It did not work out and Daimler sold 80 percent of Chrysler to a private equity fund in 2007. In the bankruptcy proceedings of 2009 the U.S. Government pressured Chrysler to enter into a global strategic alliance with Italian car maker Fiat that was eager to re-enter the U.S. market. The test of this alliance will come as Fiat introduces a new version of its low priced Fiat 500 to U.S. car buyers. Its success is not assured and Chrysler's future is uncertain.

Meanwhile, Ford seemed to be spending its cash on well received new cars and models. It swung from a loss of $14.5 billion in 2009 to a profit of $3 billion in 2010. It even pushed heretofore fast-growing Toyota into third place in the U.S market behind GM and Ford.

Foreign Carmakers Jockey for Position   Toyota grew impressively from a 9 percent market share in the U.S. in 2000 to 16.7 percent in 2009. Then quality problems and increasingly larger recalls in 2009 and 2010 checked its growth in 2010 to a market share of 15 percent. Its reputation for quality and reliability was compromised and may take several years to restore.

Honda still trails Toyota with a 10.5 percent market share in the U.S. in 2010, mostly unchanged since 2008. Nissan trails Honda with 7.7 percent but is slowly increasing its market share. In the intensely competitive U.S. market, Korean carmaker Hyundai and its sister company Kia have increased their share from almost nothing in 2000 to a total of 7.6 percent in 2010 by paying close attention to detail and quality and under-pricing similar-size cars from the U.S. and Japan.

All carmakers are eyeing the markets in China, India, and Latin America as the areas where future growth is expected. Globalization is now more than moving production to low-wage countries. Increasingly car makers are moving production to countries where their future customers are, cutting transportation costs and building local brand identity. Long term automakers will have to judge how the volatile oil market will impact gas prices at the pump and how that should guide their transition to hybrid and all electric vehicles.

The Commercial Airliner Industry   The world's airlines buy their largest planes mostly from two companies, Boeing and Airbus. The former is a U.S corporation and the latter is a division of a European consortium, European Aeronautic and Space Company (E.A.D.S.). Both have responded to the need of commercial airlines for aircraft that are fuel efficient, as the cost of jet fuel has

increased and cut into profits. Boeing launched its innovative new mid-sized 787, called the Dreamliner, built of light weight composite materials by a widely scattered system of suppliers and assembled in the U.S. It has received more orders for the plane that any in its history. Airbus took a different route. It produced the huge A380, capable of carrying as many as 800 people in a one-class configuration. But the challenges of constructing such complex aircraft delayed both programs and it is likely to be years before either is profitable. Looming in the near future is China that is not only a rapidly growing market for commercial aircraft but is also putting together a company to produce large airliners in competition with the Big Two.

Heavy Equipment   The financial crisis that began in 2007, and caught most companies by surprise, did not affect all companies or countries equally. Many firms assessed the damage and repositioned themselves to grow in a global marketplace. No industry was better able to accomplish this than heavy equipment. They had the advantage of building on their existing global expertise.

Caterpillar, a manufacturer of earth moving equipment, engines, and financial products, saw sales and profits drop significantly in 2009 as a result of the crisis. But in 2010 sales and profits rebounded as developing countries enjoyed economic growth, with 68 percent of its sales revenue coming from outside the U.S.—a figure that has remained relatively steady since 2007. Approximately half of Caterpillar employees are based in Europe, Latin America, and in the Asia Pacific region to serve global customers.

John Deere was also set back by the economic crisis but rebounded in 2010. Deere positioned itself to benefit from the growth potential of its core products, farm and construction equipment, in the world marketplace. The company forecasts that 70 percent of the world's population will live in cities in the next 40 years, demanding considerable building of new infrastructure. In addition it expects that farm output will have to double by mid-century to feed the world's population. The company has focused its products and marketing to meet these demands.

Unions in American History

The story of business in the United States would be incomplete without some mention of the union movement. Since businesses are forced to make profits for its owners or its shareholders, every cost diminishes the size of their profit. Labor costs have always been a significant

factor—often the most significant—and so the struggle for owners and managers even today is how to pay workers enough to keep them working, but not so much that profits are reduced to an unsatisfactory level.

The first national labor organization was the Knights of Labor, founded in 1869 as a secret society. After a large railway strike in 1877 membership grew rapidly and in 1879 the Knights dropped the secrecy element. By 1886 membership totaled 700,000, many of them participants in the more than 1,600 strikes that took place that year. Some strikes resulted in deadly violence, including the famous Haymarket Affair in Chicago that began with the police firing into a crowd of striking workers at the McCormick Reaper Works, killing and wounding several men. At a workers' rally the next day, a bomb was thrown into a group of policemen, followed by shots being fired by workers and police. No one knows how many workers were wounded or killed but seven police officers died. Seven workers were convicted of murder on flimsy evidence and were hanged.

The union movement and the Knights of Labor in particular suffered mass defections as a result and soon disappeared. The five-year-old American Federation of Labor (A.F.L.) replaced the Knights as the dominant union but its membership was mainly made up of skilled workers. Each of the 100 national and international chapters represented a craft and each maintained power to represent its own workers. The A.F.L. avoided taking political positions and concentrated on increasing wages, reducing the number of hours members had to work, and improving working conditions. In 1900 only 5 percent of all workers were in a union.

In 1905 the International Workers of the World (I.W.W.), commonly known as the "Wobblies," was formed to oppose the A.F.L. because of its refusal to include unskilled workers in the union. "Big Bill" Haywood of the Western Federation of Miners became the spokesman for the I.W.W. and led it to hold increasingly radical positions that included more power to the workers over production. Although the original founders quickly disagreed about policy matters and several groups left the organization, Haywood expanded the I.W.W. membership by accepting immigrants, African-Americans, and women, and by organizing agricultural workers, dock workers, lumbermen, textile, and mine workers.

The I.W.W.'s aggressive tactics and outspoken attacks on capitalism created many enemies among both business and government leaders. When the U.S. declared war on Germany in 1917 the Wobblies became the object of government scrutiny under the new Espionage Act. More than 150 I.W.W. leaders were arrested that year for allegedly interfering with the draft and encouraging desertion. All were convicted and sent to prison. Although the union still exists today it never regained its power among American workers after 1917.

The Great Depression of the 1930's that led to President Franklin Roosevelt's New Deal dramatically changed American business and the federal government's role in it. In 1935 Congress passed the National Labor Relations Act (also called the Wagner Act) which guaranteed workers in private industry the right to form unions that were authorized to engage in collective bargaining and to call strikes.

In that same year the continuing problem of unions divided by craft and industry was resolved when eight unions in the A.F.L. formed the Committee for Industrial Organization (C.I.O.) and quickly organized workers in the auto, rubber, and steel industries. In 1939, under the leadership of John L. Lewis (1880–1969), the C.I.O. organized the first successful strike against General Motors and U.S. Steel. Lewis, who made his name as head of the United Mine Workers, was elected president of the C.I.O. (now known as the Congress of Industrial Organizations) the following year.

Big business did not always settle with the unions and strikes often turned violent during the Depression. In the late 1930's or early 1940's, a young outspoken socialist named Walter Reuther (1907–70) led several strikes against Ford and General Motors in Detroit. In 1937 Ford security guards savagely attacked Reuther and his union associates while they were planning to hand out leaflets to workers. Reuther was hospitalized and the membership in the United Auto Workers (U.A.W.) quickly grew. Other bloody strikes would follow but once the war broke out Reuther became a staunch supporter of the effort to defeat Germany and Japan. At the end of the war over 35 percent of the workforce was in a union.

After the war Reuther had such great success in negotiating excellent wage and benefit packages for the U.A.W. members that he became president of the C.I.O. in 1952 and brought about a merger with the A.F.L. in 1955. This was the last period of the union movement's greatest strength, when more than 25 percent of the workforce belonged to a union. In 1947 the Taft-Hartley Act had, however, blunted much of the union movement's effectiveness by preventing boycotts and hampering one union from supporting another union's strike.

Union membership steadily declined over the next 30 years as right-to-work laws and anti-union propaganda increased. Mob influence and revelations of union corruption greatly aided the growing negative image of unions as did the perception that the higher pay rates and superior benefits were hurting the nation's economy.

During the 1980's and 90's several large industries, including steel and textiles, essentially abandoned the United States for places around the world where labor costs were far less and unions did not exist. The outsourcing of traditional American jobs continued unabated for the next two decades as manufacturing declined precipitously and service industries (healthcare, finance, education, etc.) grew continuously and now make up 68 percent of the national G.D.P. In 2011, a mere 12 percent of U.S. workers were in a union and only 8 percent of private industry workers were. Workers in public sector unions make up the rest. Despite these numbers, unions remain powerful in the political arena because of their ability to organize millions of people and to raise large amounts of money for candidates who support their cause. In recent years there has been a slight increase in union membership as the service industries and government employees have made efforts to organize workers throughout the country.

Glossary of Business Terms

after-sales service service provided to buyers after a sale; often tied to warranty contracts; in some industries it is more profitable than the sale; maintains contact with the buyer and can increase the probability of repeat sales.

agile manufacturing ability of manufacturing processes to respond to individual customer demands to deliver a semi-customized product without sacrificing quality; its main object is customer satisfaction.

authority power vested in managers to direct the activities of their subordinates; accepted by subordinates because they perceive the legitimacy of that authority.

B2B commerce conducted between two or more businesses by electronic means, usually the Internet; distinguished from business conducted electronically between businesses and individual customers.

brand equity quality of a branded product or service that is recognized by customers favorably; can allow brand owners to charge a premium price over competing products or services.

brand management approach to management that focuses on the successful introduction of new brands and the continuing marketing management of the brand during its commercial life; the intention is to establish the brand in the consumer's mind and to ensure that it achieves as long a commercial life as possible.

centralized management organization of *line management* and *staff management* functions in a central location; distinguished from a *multidivisional organization*.

Chapter 11 chapter of the 1978 Bankruptcy Act that permits debtors to retain control of their businesses; debtors and creditors are given flexibility in working out a plan to keep the business operating while paying off some or all of their debt.

chief executive officer (C.E.O.) most senior executive of a firm, or other organization, who has ultimate responsibility for the whole organization; reports to a board of directors.

chief operating officer (C.O.O.) senior executive who is responsible for the day-to-day operation of the firm or organization; usually reports to the chief executive officer.

cloud computing The storing on outside computer servers of applications and data instead of on a user's computer; this can reduce the cost of computing for users but it carries the risk that the data may be more easily collected by third parties than if it were stored on the user's computer.

conglomerate corporation composed of several companies operating in different industries; in theory, different companies prosper in different market conditions, leveling the performance of the whole; conglomerates have generally fallen out of favor, as many were not able to effectively manage their diverse activities.

continuous improvement (*kaizen***)** production process in which workers continually improve their working practices; introduced by the Japanese and a factor in the high quality of Japanese products.

corporate brand reputation a company develops that distinguishes it from its competitors; distinguished from product brand; see *brand equity*.

corporate culture values, beliefs, ethics, and ways of doing things, within an organization; often communicated informally among workers; can be an important adjunct to management but can also be an impediment to change.

corporate governance control of private corporations by top management and boards of directors; can contribute to improving business performance and preventing mismanagement and fraud.

corporate strategy identification of a corporation's long-term goal for success and the organization of its resources to achieve that goal.

corporation business organization legally chartered by a state or the federal government, having its own rights, privileges, and liabilities, and distinct from its owners. Investors own shares and, in *limited liability*, their potential loss in case the business fails is limited to the amount of their investments; see *partnership*.

data collection The monitoring of data from mobile devices and desktop computers by organizations that may be unknown to users; this can include websites that install tracking technologies that collect information on visitors that can be sold to marketers; it can also include tracking the location of mobile devices; the privacy issues raised by data collection have prompted Congress to introduce several bills that require trackers to inform users when they are being tracked.

deindustrialization flight of industry from a region that results from a change in technologies or the economy; frequently caused by foreign competition.

delayering removal of layers of management deemed unnecessary; intended to increase the speed of decision making and improve responsiveness to customers.

diversification strategy that increases the company's number of products or services in order to achieve growth or to lessen the market risk of individual products or services.

e-business commerce conducted electronically between sellers and buyers, usually over the Internet.

economies of scale cost of producing a product or service declines as a firm grows in size; associated unit costs decrease when more products and services are produced.

first mover (advantage) company that first introduces a product or service; can be an advantage in some instances; some companies specialize successfully in being second movers.

Fordism production of inexpensive goods by assembly-line methods; named for Henry Ford's assembly lines that produced the Model T; see *mass production*.

general manager executive of an organization who is vested with the authority and responsibility for all aspects of the organization; in a *multidivisional organization* the general manager may be one of several, each of whom is responsible for a separate division.

globalization opening up of markets in many countries of the world to competition; companies have access to new markets but also face new competitors.

Hawthorne effect often favorable effect that supervisors can have on workers' performance when they pay special attention to the workers; named for the studies conducted by George Elton Mayo (1880–1949) at the Western Electric Hawthorne plant in Chicago from 1928 to 1932; interpretations differ on exactly what the studies showed, but the prevailing view is that the very act of the researchers' closely studying the workers motivated the latter to improve their performance.

horizontal organization organization that has minimized the layers of management between top management and the production process (of goods or services); intended to speed up decision making and responsiveness to customers; often includes reorganizing the management of process flow; see *delayering*.

human capital skills and knowledge acquired by people that improve their productive capacity; results from investment in education, health care, and training.

human resource management (HRM) approach to

management that emphasizes the value of individuals and their differences; distinguished from management that applies a single approach to everyone; see *scientific management*.

information technology systems of computers, software, and telecommunications that generate and analyze data from the operation of a firm and communicate it to decision makers.

intellectual capital/property concepts, ideas, computer programs, patents, and other creative products that are definable, measurable, and proprietary; distinguished from tangible assets such as factories and real estate.

just-in-time (*kanban*) production process in which the components of a product are produced and delivered during the final assembly; requires that manufacturers and suppliers coordinate their production schedules; minimizes the cost of idle inventory.

kanban See *just-in-time*.

kaizen See *continuous improvement*.

keiretsu network of Japanese firms linked by mutual obligations; consists of complementary firms that can include banks, manufacturers, suppliers, distributors; allows for sharing of information and resources, coordination of activities, and mutual support.

knowledge industry industry in which the principle asset is the knowledge (education, training, skills, and experience) of those who work in it; distinguished from an industry in which the principal assets are tangible; increasingly firms are realizing that almost any industry depends on the assets of the knowledge of its workers.

lean production system of production introduced by Toyota that combines *total quality management* (TQM); a highly motivated and committed workforce organized in teams; a manufacturing process so flexible that it allows different models of the same car to be built at the same time on the same assembly line in response to shifting market demand; a cooperative supplier network system that delivers high-quality components at exactly the moment they are needed during assembly; and an innumerable number of refinements in work-flow, eliminating all tasks that do not contribute value to the end result.

limited liability principle that investors in a business organization are limited in their potential loss to the amount of their investments in the event that the business fails.

line management managers who have direct responsibility for the production of products or services which generate the firm's revenues; distinguished from *staff management*.

mass customization production process in which the methods of mass production have been modified to allow for limited variation, often based on demand, of individual products; allows low pricing of customized products; see *agile manufacturing*.

mass market market that includes large numbers of consumers.

mass production production of large numbers of a single product; unit costs are minimized allowing competitive pricing.

middle management managers in an organization who are below senior management and above junior management; many organizations have eliminated layers of middle managers deemed unnecessary, in an effort to increase efficiency and responsiveness to customers.

multidivisional organization organization in which a central corporate office administers and coordinates the activities of autonomous divisions responsible for producing products for different markets, or divisions that operate in different geographical areas.

outsourcing procurement of products, or services, outside an organization; in some organizations outsourcing is limited to peripheral items or services; in others it can encompass a wide range of items; see *just-in-time* and *virtual organization*.

partnership nonincorporated business arrangement of two or more investors who agree to share profits and debts; individuals are responsible for the debts of the company if it fails; see *unlimited liability*.

postindustrial society concept that the principal source of value and wealth will come from workers' information and knowledge; argues that the traditional sources of value and wealth, labor and capital, are comparatively less important to society.

price war competition between two or more companies in which each lowers prices to increase market share; can drive some competitors out of business (which may have been the strategy of one or more of the others).

principal agent (problem) relationship between the owners of a firm and the firm's managers (agents); sometimes characterized by a conflict between the interests of shareholders and the managers who run the firm.

productivity measure of the output of goods or services compared with the input required to produce them; higher productivity results in greater profits if prices are stable; also allows for lower pricing if competition requires it.

product placement The display of products, or advertisements for products, in entertainment contexts such as TV shows and movies; such placements are an additional source of revenue for entertainment producers.

putting-out gainful small-scale manufacturing work done in the home; a widespread means of production before the age of industrialization.

quality control process of reducing the number of defects in the products and services being produced.

reindustrialization process of restoring a former industrial area; often requires initial government assistance; allows for the introduction of new technologies that can enhance competitiveness; Japan and Germany are examples of successful reindustrialization following World War II.

research and development (R&D) systematic development of new ideas, products, and processes, that can be applied to the benefit of a business organization; grew out of the requirements of industrialization for technological innovation; modeled on early laboratories, including those of Thomas Edison and General Electric.

scientific management comprehensive system of management advocated by Frederick Winslow Taylor (1856–1915). It included detailed cost accounting; meticulous production scheduling; coordinated purchasing, inventory, storage, and maintenance procedures; time studies of workers; and an incentive wage based on piecework; sometimes mistakenly thought to consist only of time and motion studies of workers.

shareholder one who owns equity securities issued by a limited corporation; the shareholder is entitled to attend annual meetings, vote on officers and initiatives presented to shareholders, and receive dividends if the corporation pays them; the shareholder is limited in liability to the amount of the shareholder's investment in the event that the corporation fails; see *limited liability*.

six sigma measure of quality that requires fewer than 3.4 defects per million operations; popularized by General Electric.

skunkworks group, generally outside the main organization, charged with developing a new product or service in a short period of time; the emphasis is on total commitment of members to rapid innovation; term coined at

Lockheed during World War II to designate groups charged with developing advanced aircraft, including the P-38 fighter; term derives from the comic strip "Li'l Abner."

smart phone A mobile phone with applications beyond voice communications; users have a wide choice of applications that include still photography, video, GPS, web browsing, e-mail, social networking, and games.

staff management executives and workers who advise but do not direct other managers and who are not directly responsible for the production of products or services which generate revenues; distinguished from *line management*.

strategic alliance agreement between two companies to cooperate on a specific business activity; the intention is to combine complementary strengths to the advantage of each; the combination often has a limited life span.

supplier chain A system of companies that produce components of a product assembled by an end manufacturer; the chain can begin with small companies producing basic components that are supplied to intermediate firms that produce sub-assemblies that are in turn sent to end producers for final assembly; supplier chains are often considered part of the end producer's strategic advantage; Toyota was a pioneer in perfecting this system.

synergy value that accrues when two or more companies combine, through merger or acquisition, in excess of their total values before combining; complementary strengths reinforce each other when synergy is achieved. This has proved difficult to achieve in practice.

systems analysis application of the concepts of systems to organizations and processes; systems are conceived as elements working together to achieve a common end in which the operation of each element affects one or more of the other elements; no element can be understood apart from its effect on at least one other element, and often on more than one other element.

Taylorism See *scientific management*.

team designated, usually small, group of workers who are charged with a specific task; they are given considerable latitude in they way that they carry out their task.

technology application of science to practical products or processes, especially in industry; technologies before the age of industrialization were mainly mechanical and were invented by trial and error.

total quality management (TQM) approach to management that empowers everyone in an organization to deliver a high-quality product or service to the customer; the customer can be the next stage within the organization or the end buyer; the object is to achieve maximum customer satisfaction at the lowest cost.

unlimited liability organization in which the principals are all responsible for debts should the organization fail; as distinguished from *limited liability*.

virtual organization organization comprising a network of independent groups that cooperate and coordinate their activities to produce a product or service; uses information technologies to manage the process; requires new management methods to achieve the required coordination and cooperation.

zero defects approach to management in which an organization sets a goal to deliver products or services that are 100 percent free of defects; an important component of *total quality management*.

FINANCE

Finance is the management of money and other assets—often in very large amounts. It includes mainly public finance (the disposition of revenues by government) and corporate finance (the capital required to start and maintain a business).

Ever since the invention of money in the ancient world it has been a medium of exchange for goods and services and a means of storing value over time. Without the medium of money, and its management, it is not an exaggeration to say that the economic growth of the world would not have been possible. The major means by which money is managed are banking systems and stock, bond, and commodity markets. The following examines the history of those institutions and describes how they operate today.

A Brief History of Finance

The earliest examples of finance are short-term loans made in civilizations in the Middle East, North America, Asia, and Africa, in cities where money first emerged. The first banks were formed in Europe during the Renaissance, after legal and accounting systems had been designed that could track money. Banks allowed people to pool their money for large-scale transactions. By the 17th century, the first stock markets gave businesses and governments the chance to raise money by selling equity rather than borrowing money. The modern era of finance has been marked by the development of ever more sophisticated and technological vehicles for managing money. Globalization has spread this Western style of finance around the world.

Money

Money was developed by traders who understood the serious shortcomings of barter, which is the exchange of goods or services. In the barter system, a laborer might keep a share of the crop he helped harvest, or a farm wife could exchange eggs and butter for an ax. Barter works only if each party has goods or services that the other wants. Values have to be renegotiated for every transaction, keeping records is difficult, and proper accounting is impossible.

The use of money brought three big improvements to barter. First, money gives goods and services a stable value, allowing exchanges to occur more efficiently. Stability also allows record keeping and, in advanced economic systems, accounting.

Money also stores value. When goods or services are exchanged for money, the value is stored for long after the goods have been consumed or the work has been done. Over time, value stored in money can build up and become surplus wealth. Surplus wealth, especially when pooled, is called capital, and can be lent to fund the large projects on which cities and nations are built.

Finally, money provides a scale of value. A scale of value makes it possible to compare unlike objects: $10 could buy a book or a shirt; $100,000 could buy a fancy car or a modest house.

Earliest Coins

Anywhere that cities arose, money emerged. Precious metals valued by weight became the basis for money in the earliest Mesopotamian civilizations, before 2000 B.C. Gold and silver were ideal because they were rare enough to be valuable, but common enough to be accepted. Precious stones have also served as money, as have cacao seeds in South America, and cowrie shells in Africa, India, and China.

The earliest coins were beads of electrum, an alloy of gold and silver. They were developed in the trading kingdom of Lydia in southwestern Anatolia, today's Turkey. Though little more than nuggets, they were stamped with symbols to show their weight and origin. The electrum beads varied widely in ratio of gold to silver, and were soon replaced with flat, round, all-silver coins. Because the coins were certified by an authority and did not have to be weighed for each transaction, they made trade easier.

Lydian society reached its peak of affluence around 550 B.C. under King Croesus. The vitality of Lydian trade made its merchants and rulers wealthy and widely known. The expression "rich as Croesus" survives to this day.

Inflation In the fifth century B.C., Athens had ample supplies of silver, and city leaders issued more money to foster commerce. They discovered that when the amount of currency in circulation exceeded the needs of trade, the value of money decreased, an effect called inflation. Athenians also discovered that their coins, drachmae, had a higher value than the content because of their convenience and reliability. That premium, now called seigniorage, discouraged leaders from debasing the currency. It also encouraged them to use taxes to pay for public works, the arts, and defense, rather than causing inflation by issuing too much money.

Rome adopted Greek monetary principles, and a basic silver coin, which was called the denarius. To this day several countries' currency is the "dinar," and "dinero" means money in several languages. As the Roman Empire grew rich through conquest rather than productivity, however, corruption and dissipation undermined the economy. The empire's infrastructure and bureaucracy were expensive, but Roman politicians knew that raising taxes was unpopular. They preferred to issue more money. The government put more gold and silver put into circulation, and adulterated coins by making them smaller or adding base metals. Inflation was a chronic problem for Roman emperors and bureaucrats.

With the rise of Islam after A.D. 622, the newly affluent societies at first copied classical coins—the Roman-derived dinar in Africa and the Near East, the Greek-derived dirham in Persia and central Asia—and then developed their own currencies.

China By about A.D. 50 Chinese money had adopted its classic form: round coins symbolizing heaven and square holes representing Earth. Paper money was first used by the Chinese about A.D. 1000. By the 13th century, the powerful Yuan dynasty had established a successful paper currency. Eventually, most societies adopted paper currency, as the need for capital to wage war outstripped supplies of hard currency.

The Renaissance

After the fall of Rome, most of Western Europe reverted to the barter system. Some Celtic and Germanic cultures used denominated coins, but most precious-metal transactions were by weight of bullion. Money re-entered most societies in Europe during the late Middle Ages. In Florence, trade was powered with gold from Africa, and by the mid-13th century, the gold florin was issued, and then the gold ducat.

Large silver deposits were discovered in Tyrolia, in Saxony, and in 1512 in Joachimsthal, Bohemia. The large silver Joachimsthaler coin soon supplanted the florin and the ducat, and the shortened name, thaler, or dollar, became generic. In the 1540's, huge new supplies of gold and silver from sub-Saharan Africa and the New World began to flow into Europe. Large copper deposits entered production in Sweden, making smaller-denomination coins available. At that point even daily transactions began to leave the barter system.

Banking Many of the functions of today's banks developed during the Renaissance as pawnbrokers, goldsmiths, and money changers began to lend at interest and to issue letters of credit. City and state governments in Italy and elsewhere in Europe began raising funds for large civic projects by issuing public debt—borrowing at interest from willing individuals rather than raising compulsory taxes.

Formal banks started when wealthy individuals or small groups put surplus wealth, capital, to use by making loans, building public works, or backing ambitious ventures. What made this possible were legal and accounting systems to record who had the money and where it went. Ironically, it is this "fixing" of the assets that frees the capital. In countries where the legal and accounting systems are weak, people are forced to keep physical ownership of their money, or buy and hoard nonperishable goods. Even a wealthy economy withers when capital is scarce.

First banks In 1609 the Wisselbank opened in Amsterdam to provide credit for local and regional governments and for the Dutch trading empire. Its notes—a bank's promises to pay a specific sum to the bearer—circulated widely, and it is considered the first bank in the modern sense. In 1683 it was allowed to do business with individuals.

Sweden's first bank arose out of the country's use of copper, rather than gold or silver, for its currency. For Swedish coins to have value comparable to other nations' coins, the coins had to be big. That was inconvenient, so in 1661 the Stockholm Banco, founded by Johan Palmstruch about five years earlier, got a charter to issue paper money. The temptation to print notes in excess of metal reserves was too great. By 1667 the notes were worthless.

The Bank of England was the first lasting and effective central bank, although it was not founded as one. The "Old Woman of Threadneedle Street" was proposed by William Paterson (1658–1719) as a joint-stock company, in which the capital of several people was pooled. The bank issued the first national notes in 1694. They were backed by a loan of 1.2 million pounds sterling to King William III, formerly William of Orange, who had brought familiarity with banking and paper money from his native Holland.

The notes were accepted readily, and the new liquidity stimulated commerce. Historians credit England's ability to raise capital and spread risk as a primary factor in the small country's rise to empire.

A Financial History of the United States

The first paper currency in North America was issued in 1690 by the Massachusetts Bay Colony to pay soldiers for an expedition against Quebec. Over time, most American colonies issued fiduciary paper money backed by taxes. Though rich in resources, they lacked precious metals that would have enabled them to issue large amounts of hard currency.

American business was conducted in colonial pounds, shillings, and pence. Those were worth about three-quarters of the same denominations in England. However, hardly any British currency circulated in the colonies. The balance of trade favored the mother country, and by law coins could not leave Britain or be minted in the colonies. Instead, Spanish eight-real dollars, or pieces of eight, were the most common coins. A quarter dollar was two reales, or two bits—and is so called even today.

The legacy of the Spanish eight-bit silver coin remained part of the U.S. economy for more than 300 years. Stocks on the New York Stock Exchange traded in halves, quarters, and eighths of dollars until 2000, when the NYSE shifted from fractional prices to decimal trading, thus erasing this vestige of the colonial Spanish eight-bit silver coin upon which the U.S. dollar was originally based.

American Revolution   As other wars had done, the American Revolution created a great need for fast money. Congress met the liquidity crisis with several issues of paper currency, collectively called continentals. They were so-called fiat money, backed by nothing but their status as legal tender, they were disdained from the start. First issued in 1775, continentals fell to half their face value by the end of that year, and to a low of $200 paper to $1 in gold by the end of the Revolution in 1783.

Under the Articles of Confederation, the federal government had no taxing authority; it could only ask the states for money. The result was economic chaos. Merchants and urban dwellers were hardest hit, while the countryside fell back on barter and self-sufficiency. The crisis came when a former officer, Daniel Shays, led other Massachusetts farmers in a tax revolt in 1786. The next year each state sent delegates to a Constitutional Convention in Philadelphia.

After leading the effort to have the Constitution adopted, Alexander Hamilton of New York, the first secretary of the treasury, proposed that Congress assume the states' outstanding war debt, redeem the debased currency at the rate of 100 continentals to one new dollar, and issue new federal notes. Opposition, led by the Virginians Thomas Jefferson and James Madison, was fierce. Many former soldiers and farmers, paid in continentals, had sold them to speculators at around the prevailing rate, 200:1. Many people thought it was grossly unfair for the speculators to be rewarded at the expense of those who had borne the brunt of the conflict. Hamilton argued they had made the best deal they could at the time, and that it would be impossible to trace the notes to their original owners. Ironically, the demand stimulated by the speculators brought the value of the continentals up to the proposed rate of 100:1 within a few months.

More ominously, states that had paid off their debt, mostly in the south, objected to a plan that would relieve other states, mostly in the north, from their debts. In April 1790 Hamilton struck a bargain over dinner with Jefferson and Madison. In return for Jefferson's support of assumption and a Bank of the United States, Hamilton would support legislation moving the U.S. capital from New York to a spot on the Potomac River that would become Washington, D.C.

The Bank of the United States   The first Bank of the United States received a 20-year charter in 1791. Hamilton's assumption and new currency plan went so well that English banks accumulated most of the new U.S. bonds originally bought by the French and Dutch. In effect Hamilton got the British to pay for the Revolution. But by 1811, when the Bank's charter came up for renewal, sentiment had turned against Europe and hard-money backers in the U.S. Creditors, especially bankers and financiers, favor tight, or hard, money linked to bullion, and low inflation. Borrowers, especially farmers, favor soft money, easy credit, and some inflation, which allows debts to be paid in dollars worth a little less down the road. Agricultural interests from southern and western states opposed the bank's hard-money policies, and the bank was not rechartered.

In 1812 a second war with England broke out. When it ended in 1815, U.S. finances were again a shambles. By 1816 a second Bank of the United States was given a 20-year charter, and again brought financial stability. When that was due for renewal, the same southern and western interests again opposed recharter. The bill passed in 1832, but was vetoed by the populist president Andrew Jackson. This left local banknotes and the meager output from the U.S. Mint, plus foreign coins, as the only currency. Most banks issued sound notes, but many—primarily in the south and west— were undercapitalized and some were simply fraudulent. The period from 1836, when the Bank closed, to 1863, when Abraham Lincoln's administration issued new federal notes, is called the "thirty years in the wilderness."

Greenbacks

The Gold Rush of 1849 allowed the banks of Sutters Mill, Calif., to provide liquidity in the decade and a half before the Civil War. For the first time in U.S. history, sufficient hard currency was circulating in most of the nation. However, the gold wasn't enough to finance the Civil War, and in 1862 Congress authorized $450 million in fiat money. In contrast to the colorful and artistic local banknotes of the time, the government printed drab bills, black on the front and green on the back. The greenbacks lost value, as the continentals had, but not nearly as much: They trade at about 70 percent of face value after a Union victory, and as low as 30 percent of face value after a Confederate victory.

The greenbacks were merely an expedient; by the next year, the federal government had come up with a way to get more federal notes into circulation. The National Bank Act of 1863, and amendments the next year, gave the government new taxing powers, including the first income tax, and a 10 percent tax on local banknotes. The tax drove the local banknotes out of circulation. Banks that wanted to issue notes had to get a federal charter requiring them to invest at least a third of their capital in federal bonds. They could then issue federal banknotes, up to the value of 90 percent of their bond holdings.

The Gold Standard

After the Civil War, a dispute over whether to use gold or silver to back paper money

intensified. Bankers favored gold because it better limited inflation. Debtors, including the recently returned soldiers of the North and South, favored silver to spur growth; vast new mines in the West promised plenty of material.

The country had been operating with a system of bimetallism. Unlimited coinage of silver and gold was authorized. The government bought any bullion brought to it; this policy meant that paper money was backed by gold and silver. When notes were redeemed, the metal entered circulation as coins. The only problem was that the ratio of silver to gold was set at 15:1, which put too much value on silver. Under Gresham's law—bad money drives out good—people hoarded gold and spent silver.

Between 1837 and 1893 four contradictory laws were passed to tinker with the system, generally favoring gold and, thereby, lenders and businesses over borrowers and farmers. Saying to eastern plutocrats, "you shall not crucify mankind upon a cross of gold," William Jennings Bryan (1860–1925) ran for president in 1896 on a populist platform of free coinage of silver. He lost to William McKinley, who signed the Gold Standard Act in 1900.

The U.S. remained on the gold standard for three-quarters of a century, with the exception of a period during Franklin Roosevelt's administration. In 1971 President Richard Nixon took the U.S. off the gold standard for good, because the country's foreign-exchange debt exceeded the country's gold reserves. All U.S. currency, and virtually all money worldwide, is now fiat money.

J. P. Morgan and the Panic of 1907

The American economy emerged after the Civil War as an irresistible force. The transcontinental railroad was completed in 1869, and soon a sprawling network of rails brought the outputs of mines, farms, and grazing lands to eastern cities recently swelled by immigrants. The wealth created by unbridled capitalism led Mark Twain to title his novel of the era *The Gilded Age*.

It was the age of the great industrialists—Vanderbilt, Rockefeller, and others (See "Business")—but the most powerful of all was John Pierpont Morgan (1837–1913), who established his own stock brokerage in 1862 and emerged after the Civil War as the most powerful financier in the country. His acquisitions consolidated many industries, especially railroads and steel mills. He reorganized General Electric, and his formation of U.S. Steel in 1901 created the first billion-dollar corporation in history.

Morgan put his fortune and prestige on the line to end the Panic of 1907. After several large corporations and stock brokerages went bankrupt, stock prices fell, causing traders to withdraw money from banks to cover their losses. Bank failures and a nationwide recession seemed likely. Morgan, however, assembled a team of businessmen who shored up weak banks and invested in corporations that were sound, but needed help. The strategy worked, and the crisis passed. The bank and brokerage house that bears J. P. Morgan's name merged with the Chase Manhattan Corporation in 2000. Now known as J.P.Morgan Chase & Co., it is still one of the largest financial firms in the world.

The Federal Reserve   The grim reality that the federal government had to call upon a private citizen to solve a national financial crisis led to the passage of the Federal Reserve Act in 1913. It created the Federal Reserve Board, which later became the Federal Reserve System, commonly called the Fed. The system, which is one of the most powerful institutions in America, consists of a board of governors and 12 regional reserve banks. The Fed regulates the money supply by buying and selling federal notes. It also sets the discount rate, the interest rate at which it lends money to its commercial bank customers. The discount rate helps decide interest rates that the banks, in turn, charge their customers. Finally, the Fed also helps regulate commercial banks.

The Great Depression   While the European landscape and economy were in ruins after World War I, the U.S. emerged from the conflict relatively unscathed. The postwar strength produced the roaring twenties, a decade in which social exuberance was matched by wild speculations in the credit and stock markets. The optimism was fueled by low interest rates and a prevailing belief that the Fed had firm control of the economy.

Few within the Fed saw the trouble that was coming. One exception was Benjamin Strong (1872–1928), head of the Federal Reserve Bank of New York. He raised interest rates in his district to try to slow the economy, but without the support of other board members, he had only a limited effect. On October 29, 1929, "Black Tuesday," the stock market crashed.

A recession after such a crash was almost inevitable. Three factors turned it into the Great Depression. First, interest rates were left high even after the bubble burst, making it difficult for surviving companies to borrow. Then the administration of Herbert Hoover pushed through a massive tax increase to boost sagging federal revenues. Worst of all, Congress bowed to special interests and passed the protectionist Smoot-Hawley Tariff.

Other countries quickly retaliated, and global trade slowed to a trickle. Similar mismanagement in other countries turned the recession into a global depression. The 1930's were the most traumatic times in U.S. financial history, as industrial output fell to half, unemployment reached 25 percent, and hundreds of banks failed, wiping out family savings across the country.

The New Deal and Reform   Soon after taking office, President Franklin Roosevelt declared a bank holiday to give solvent institutions time to recover. Senator Carter Glass of Virginia (1858–1946) and Representative Henry B. Steagall of Alabama (1873–1943) sponsored the most sweeping banking reform in the country since the days of Hamilton. The Banking Act of 1933 created the Federal Deposit Insurance Corp., ending bank runs at a stroke by establishing an insurance system for depositors' money. The act also separated banking and brokerage. Commercial banks were prohibited from underwriting stocks and bonds; investment banking firms were prohibited from taking deposits. Savings and industrial banks were allowed to join the Fed, and branch banking was allowed.

Under Franklin Roosevelt's "New Deal," massive relief efforts and huge public works projects kept the country from anarchy, but another recession struck in 1937, driven mostly by the failure of cotton crops in the South and the Dust Bowl in the West.

World War II helped to salvage the U.S. economy. All of the major corporations had mobilized to fight the war, and productivity soared. Unemployment declined dramatically and tens of millions of American workers were earning more money than ever before. Wartime restrictions, however, made consumer goods scarce or nonexistent (no new cars, for example, were built in 1942–46). When the war was won, the combination of the capacity and the pent-up demand produced the biggest boom ever. It was stoked by $200 billion in maturing war bonds and an upwardly mobile, college-educated workforce created by the G.I. Bill.

Stagflation   The decade of the 1970's was marked by the unprecedented combination of rising prices and slow economic growth. Economists coined a new term for the global phenomenon: stagflation. The factors that led to this malaise included the end of the gold standard in 1971, the Arab oil embargo of 1973, expanded social programs, and the war in Vietnam, which necessitated higher taxes. Inflation was 5–10 percent during every year of the 1970's, reaching a peak of 13.5 percent in 1980.

President Jimmy Carter (b. 1924) got most of the blame for stagflation, but decades of fiscal policy had set the stage. It took harsh treatment to get the economy moving again. Federal Reserve Chairman Paul Volcker (b. 1927) reduced the supply of money in circulation by selling federal bonds. The contraction produced a sharp recession in the early 1980's, but it ended stagflation.

Banking in the United States Today Globalization and the drive for profits during the economic boom of the 1990's pushed the largest banks to consider acquisitions of insurance companies and brokerage houses, both extremely profitable kinds of businesses. In 1998, Travelers Insurance, one of the largest insurance underwriters, was set to merge with Citigroup, one of the largest banks. Such a deal was prohibited under the Glass-Steagall Act, but banking overhauls had been rattling around congress for many years. On cue, legislators passed the Financial Services Modernization Act of 1999, called Gramm-Leach-Bliley after its sponsors. Banks, brokerages, and insurance firms were allowed to compete with and buy each other, and to do business across state lines.

Today there are about 6,500 commercial banks in the United States (down from 10,000 in 2007), divided into three groups: small local banks, which are rapidly being acquired by larger banks; larger regional banks with networks that cover one or more states; and huge national banks. The largest banks, Citigroup, J. P. Morgan Chase & Co., and Bank of America, compete internationally with similarly huge Japanese, German, and British banks.

Investment banks including Goldman Sachs and Morgan Stanley distribute, underwrite, and originate new securities for governments, corporations and individuals. This raises needed capital for the clients while the bank profits by dividing the securities purchased into smaller units with higher prices. Other services include mergers and acquisitions, trading of derivatives and commodities and general investment advice for institutions, pension funds, and wealthy individuals. Investment banks do not accept individual deposits.

Stock Markets

Stock markets are systems for raising capital and spreading risk. From the beginnings of civilization until the Renaissance rulers and wealthy families sponsored public works and ambitious ventures. Early in the Renaissance, joint-stock companies were developed under which individuals, families, villages, and trade guilds could pool their capital to underwrite new companies or trading expeditions. Trade guilds, in particular, became very powerful because of their strong organizations and ability to raise large amounts of money relatively quickly.

First Stock Market

Once ownership of a company or the right to the bounty of a trading expedition was in multiple hands, the shares became another valuable commodity that could be sold or traded. The world's first stock market began informal business in 1602 on Damrak Street in Amsterdam, trading shares of the world's first large multinational venture, the Verenidge Oost-Indische Companie (United East-India Co.). The oldest surviving stock certificates, just handwritten notes, are of the VOC from 1606.

Within a year or two futures and options on shares had been developed in Amsterdam. A futures contract represents immediate payment for future delivery of a security or commodity. An option is even more malleable; it is the right to buy or sell a commodity or security at a given price within a specific period. Once a futures contract is agreed upon, the commodity or security will be delivered. An option, however, can be left to expire unexercised.

Other Early Exchanges

The Frankfurt Stock Exchange traces its ancestry to 1585, but what existed then was a currency exchange. Bonds were added 100 years later, and stocks were not added until 1820. The London Stock Exchange traces its history to informal trading in shares in 1698 at Jonathan's Coffee-House, where trading had been going on for some time. Meanwhile, the English physician, surveyor, and economist Sir William Petty (1623–87) was posted to Ireland, where he quantified an ancient concept that the fair market value of any land is equal to its production—from crops, timber, minerals, or livestock—over 20 years. In essence Petty around 1650 had formalized the most fundamental measure of any commodity or security, its price-to-earnings ratio, an essential value indicator to this day.

Speculators and Bubbles

An investor buys and sells securities for their inherent value. Speculators buy and sell because they want to bet that securities will rise or decline in value. A little speculation helps keeps markets active and provides capital for new ventures.

When speculation runs out of control, uninformed people flock to the markets in hopes of a quick profit. The results are invariably a crash and widespread economic distress.

Tulipmania   The technology-stock bubble of the late 1990's was the latest in a long line of financial crises dating back to tulipmania, which hit Holland in the 1630's. The normally sober and industrious Netherlanders were overcome by a speculative fever. Fortunes were exchanged for rare tulip bulbs; the few clearheaded critics were ignored. Bubbles always burst when enough people lose their euphoria, and want to sell. The panic buying turns in a moment into panic selling. The tulip bubble burst in 1637, ruining many and bringing on a severe recession.

The South Sea Bubble   Less than a hundred years later it all happened again, this time in England. The South Sea Co. was founded in 1711 as a legitimate trading firm. But when granted a monopoly from Parliament, the founders proposed to retire the national debt in exchange for company stock. Stories were planted about fabulous wealth; 50:1 returns were promised. Huge dividends were paid with the money pouring in, turning the company into a pyramid scheme. The house of cards tumbled in 1720, and even some members of Parliament were ruined.

Mississippi Co.   Madness also prevailed in France. The Scotsman John Law (1671–1729), a brilliant scoundrel, got a royal charter from the regent of Louis XV to open a bank in 1716. His well-backed notes traded at a premium. He then chartered the Company of the West, commonly called the Mississippi Co., to operate the Louisiana colony. He further offered to sell shares for deeply discounted national paper money. Preposterous dividends were promised, just as for the South Sea Co. Overnight wealth gave birth to the term "millionaire," and inflation soared. The Mississippi Bubble burst about the same time as the South Sea Bubble. The Bourbon dynasty was irreparably damaged, many nobles were ruined, land and tax reforms were abandoned, and the economy was in tatters.

The Industrial Revolution   With the advent of the Industrial Revolution the European economic system rapidly acquired a strong need for capital aggregation to support the numerous new businesses being formed. Stock markets grew rapidly in all the major European cities led by London, Paris, and Amsterdam and over the course of the 19th century investors provided for the financing of factories, mines, railroads, ships, and the many technolog-

ical advances made during this period.

Unfortunately this market-based system was also subject to fiscal crises, panics, recessions, and depressions that had severe negative consequences not only for investors, but for the masses of people now dependent on wages for survival. During the 19th century these crises occurred just about every 10 years between 1816 and 1866, but they fell off with serious downturns in 1873, 1907, 1921, and 1929 when the world wide depression brought every economy in the world to its knees and forced governments to take serious action to regulate financial markets.

The U.S. Stock Market

The first stock exchange in North America opened in 1790 in Philadelphia, the second-largest city in the British Empire at the time of the Revolution. Markets hate uncertainty, so it is significant that the Philadelphia Bourse opened seven years after the end of the Revolution, the same year the federal government issued $80 million in Treasury bonds to pay off the debts from the Revolution.

NYSE   The New York Stock Exchange (NYSE) was created on May 17, 1792, when 24 stockbrokers and merchants convened under a buttonwood tree on Wall Street. According to a two-sentence contract signed that day, known as the Buttonwood Agreement, the men would trade stocks and bonds only among themselves, fix commissions (at "one quarter per cent of specie value"), and participate in no auctions other than their own.

Market activity took a quantum leap after the War of 1812, as government debt again sparked heavy trading in federal certificates. In addition, scores of new banks and insurance companies were established in the next few years and were listed on the exchange by 1815; the sale of securities generated much of the venture capital necessary to fund these new enterprises. In March 1817 the original exchange passed a formal constitution with rules of conduct, adopted the name New York Stock & Exchange Board—shortened to NYSE in 1863—and moved into a rented room at 40 Wall Street.

AMEX   Meanwhile, smaller exchanges in New York and elsewhere competed for business. Among the largest New York rivals was a group known as the Curbstone Brokers, which conducted its trade outdoors, rain or shine, beginning in the early 1800's. Later known as the New York Curb Exchange, the group finally moved indoors at 86 Trinity

Place, just west of Wall Street, in 1921. Renamed the American Stock Exchange (AMEX) in 1953, it merged with NASDAQ from 1998–2004, when ownership again returned to private hands. In 2008 the parent company of the New York Stock Exchange, NYSE Euronext, acquired the exchange and renamed it NYSE Amex equities. It's currently the third-largest stock exchange by trading volume in the United States, mostly dealing in small-cap stocks, exchange-traded funds and derivatives.

NASDAQ Opened to trading in 1971, the National Association of Securities Dealers Automatic Quotations (NASDAQ) was the world's first electronic stock market. Initially a computer bulletin board system, with no contact between buyers and sellers, it gradually expanded to include trade and volume reporting, automated trading systems and was the first U.S. stock market to allow online trading. It merged with the London Stock Exchange in 1992, forming the first intercontinental partnership of securities markets. In 1998 it merged with AMEX, forming the second-largest U.S. stock exchange, although that partnership lasted only six years. NASDAQ Stock Market, Inc. was formed as a public company in 2000. NASDAQ is known for specializing in technology based stocks, although virtually every industry is listed.

Stock Indexes

By the end of the 19th century, the NYSE had grown so large and had so many investors that it needed an easy-to-understand measurement of how the market was doing. As the stock market grew even more after World War II, the need for more and more information became obvious.

Today there are many stock indexes each measuring a specific part of the market. The NASDAQ Composite is an index of all of the common stocks and similar securities that are listed on the NASDAQ stock market, over 3,000 companies. The S&P 500, maintained by Standard & Poor's, is a free-float capitalization-weighted index of the prices of 500 large common stocks traded in the United States. These stocks are chosen by committee in order to form a representative slice of the industries of the United States economy. Many investors consider it the best overall measurement of American stock market performance. Another index, the Russell 3000, measures the performance of the largest 3,000 U.S. companies, representing approximately 98 percent of the investable U.S. equity market. The Russell 1000 measures the perform-

ance of the large-cap segment of the U.S. industry and contains approximately 1,000 of the largest securities, based on a combination of their market cap and current index measurement. The most well-known index is the Dow Jones Industrial Average.

Dow Jones Industrial Average Strictly speaking, the Dow is an index, not an average. To arrive at the index, the combined stock price of the component companies is divided, not by the number of stocks, but by a number which is adjusted to account for stock splits, mergers, and historical activity.

Although the Dow Jones Industrial Average included only a dozen industrial stocks when it was first published in 1896 in *The Wall Street Journal* (Dow was the founder and editor), it has since grown to 30 and now reflects a variety of sectors outside heavy industry. Of the original twelve stocks, General Electric is the only one currently in the Dow. The index is selected from among blue chip stocks by editors of *The Wall Street Journal* and is seldom revised; the last revision was in 2006. Also called the Dow, DJIA, or Dow 30, it is the oldest index and remains a key indicator of the overall robustness of the U.S. stock market.

Boom and Bust Cycles

Rapid economic growth and westward expansion in the first half of the 19th century brought dramatic increases in trading volume and the number and value of available stocks. Average daily volume on the NYSE hit 8,500 shares in 1830, representing a 50-fold increase in only seven years. The number of publicly traded companies rose from 20 in 1800 to more than 120 by 1835. After the first railroad stock was issued in 1830, the acceleration of track construction caused market growth in the ensuing decades. Railroads remained the nation's largest and most powerful companies throughout the 19th century, with mining, farm equipment, steel, and other manufacturing companies prominent on the exchange by the 1870's.

The financial markets proved volatile. Wall Street's first major "panic" began in 1836, amid wild speculation in federal land and commodity imports. The government responded by issuing a "specie circular" for the purchase of public land (requiring payment in gold or silver), which led to a collapse in prices and the failure of thousands of banks and businesses. Production and employment fell off rapidly, and the nation suffered a six-year depression.

Overinvestment in land and railroads produced another wave of panic selling in 1857–58. Gold prices, run up during the attempt of the financiers Jay Gould (1836–92) and James Fisk (1834–72) to corner the supply, dropped precipitously when the federal government released its own gold into the market—causing a financial debacle on September 24, 1869, known as "Black Friday."

The boom that powered the U.S. economy after the Civil War was no bar to instability. The worst financial crisis of the 19th century began in 1873, when heavy speculation in securities and the failure of Jay Cooke's banking house toppled business after business, forced the NYSE to close for 10 days, and triggered a six-year depression. In 1893, a series of railroad bankruptcies caused hundreds of banks to fail, thousands of companies to shut down, and widespread unemployment to persist for the next four years.

Securities Regulation   Amid the boom-and-bust cycles, a host of innovations brought tighter regulation and improved efficiency to the securities markets. In 1853 the NYSE began requiring listed companies to file complete statements of outstanding shares and capital resources. In 1868 memberships on the exchange were put up for sale, rather than reserved for life. And the following year, to keep companies from issuing too many stocks ("watering"), the NYSE began requiring them to register shares at a bank or another appropriate institution. Also in 1868, the first ticker tapes were introduced on the trading floor.

The year 1871 began an era of change for the NYSE, as the traditional "call market" (in which an auctioneer called out the name of each stock and brokers shouted their offers to sell or buy) was replaced by today's continuous auction market. By 1899 all listed companies provided regular financial statements both to the NYSE and to stockholders (in 1910 the exchange discontinued trading in unlisted securities).

The Crash and the New Deal   The NYSE relocated to its current location at 11 Wall Street in 1922, and the move was soon followed by a historic bull run. Beginning in 1923, stock prices and trading volume surged, virtually unchecked, for more than six years. In 1928, single-day share volume on the NYSE broke the 5 million level. The crash of October 29, 1929 ("Black Tuesday") produced a record volume of more than 16 million shares—most of them sales. The Dow Jones average dropped 11 percent in one day.

The Dow hit bottom, down 89 percent from its 1929 peak, in July 1932. The New Deal brought some relief and much reform: the Securities Act of 1933 required full disclosure to investors and prohibited fraud in the sale of securities; the Securities Exchange Act of 1934 established the Securities and Exchange Commission (SEC) to oversee the markets and protect investors against malpractice.

Modern Era

Industrial mobilization during World War II restored the economy, and the postwar period brought sustained financial growth. A bull run that began in 1949 was the longest to date, with stock prices rising almost without interruption for the next eight years. The Dow shot past the 500 mark in 1956.

Old-line brokers and investment bankers opposed the reforms of the mid-1930's as government interference in private enterprise, but some saw a new horizon opening. In the 1940's Charles E. Merrill (1885–1956) hired hundreds of investment advisers, paid them a salary, and had them solicit business from the burgeoning middle class. Until then most brokers worked largely on commission, and only wealthy clients were worth these brokers' time. Merrill also began to advertise in 1948. By 1960 Merrill Lynch had more than half a million clients and was four times the size of the next-largest brokerage.

Mutual funds also became prominent after the war. The first, the Massachusetts Investors Trust, was launched in 1924. But mutual funds first began to be popular in the 1950's. People of modest means were not willing to invest their small savings until the regulatory reforms of the 1930's took hold and the "mass affluent" had begun to respond to the enticements of Merrill Lynch and its competitors.

With people and money pouring into the market and manufacturing running at capacity, stocks broke the pre-crash levels in 1954, and soared higher. The NYSE had its first billion-share day in 1959. The boom rolled on, but by the late 1960's several factors began to drag at equities. Technology failed to keep up with volume, and markets became victims of their own success. Inflation, domestic unrest, and international troubles also took their toll.

The incorporation of the NYSE and the creation of an interdealer, over-the-counter (OTC) market—NAS-DAQ—both in 1971, opened the modern era in U.S. securities trading. NASDAQ, the first stock exchange to rely on sophisticated computer and telecommunications systems, traded and monitored millions of securities across the globe in real time.

Dow Jones Industrial Average Timeline

Jan. 19, 1906	Dow closes at 101.55, first time over 100.
July 31 -Dec. 15, 1914	Stock exchange closes during the opening months of World War I
Dec. 12, 1914	Largest one-day percentage loss: −24.3 percent
Dec. 12, 1927	Dow closes at 200.93, first time over 200
Sept. 03, 1929	Dow closes at high of 381.27, and will not surpass this mark until 1954
Oct. 24, 1929	Black Thursday, beginning of "Black Days" that mark the end of 1920's bull market.
Nov. 1929	Stock market crash marks beginning of the Great Depression
Oct. 6, 1931	Largest one-day percentage gain: 14.87 percent
July 8, 1932	Dow closes at 41.22, lowest point during the Great Depression
Dec. 1, 1954	Dow closes at 400.97, first time over 400
March 1, 1956	Dow closes at 500.24, first time over 500
Feb. 1, 1959	Dow closes at 602.21, first time over 600
May 1, 1961	Dow closes at 705.52, first time over 700
Feb. 1, 1964	Dow closes at 800.14, first time over 800
Jan. 1, 1965	Dow closes at 900.95, first time over 900
Nov. 1, 1972	Dow closes at 1003.16, first time over 1000
1974	Dow drops nearly 400 points from beginning to end of 1974
Dec. 1, 1983	Dow closes at 1511.7, first time over 1,500
Jan. 8, 1987	Dow closes at 2002.25, first time over 2,000
Oct. 1987	Dow drops 800 points during 1987 crash
Oct. 19, 1987	Black Monday, second largest one-day percentage drop in Dow, −22.61%
Apr. 17, 1991	Dow closes at 3004.96, first time over 3,000
Feb. 23, 1995	Dow closes at 4003.33, first time over 4,000
Nov. 21, 1995	Dow closes at 5023.55, first time over 5,000
Oct. 14, 1996	Dow closes at 6010, first time over 6,000
Feb. 13, 1997	Dow closes at 7022.44, first time over 7,000
July 16, 1997	Dow closes at 8038.88, first time over 8,000
Apr. 16, 1998	Dow closes at 9033.23, first time over 9,000
Mar. 29, 1999	Dow closes at 10,006.78, first time over 10,000
May 3, 1999	Dow closes at 11,014.69, first time over 11,000
Mar. 16, 2000	Largest one-day point gain: 499.19
July-Oct. 2001	Dow drops 2000 points during slump exacerbated by terrorist attacks.
Sept. 17, 2001	Largest one-day point loss: −684.81
Oct. 19, 2006	Dow closes at 12,011.73, first time over 12,000
Apr. 25, 2007	Dow closes at 13,089.89, first time over 13,000
July 19, 2007	Dow closes at 14,000.41, first time over 14,000
2008	Dow drops 8,776 points (33.84percent) making it the third worst year in Dow history
Sept. 29, 2008	Largest one-day point loss: −777.68
Oct. 13, 2008	Largest one-day point gain: 936.42
Oct. 15, 2008	2nd largest one-day point loss: −733.08
Oct. 28, 2008	2nd largest one-day point gain: 889.35
Mar. 2009	Dow drops to under 7,000 points for the first time since April 1997
Apr. 12, 2010	Dow closes above 11,000 for first time since September 2008
May 6, 2010	Dow plunges 998.5 points before recovering almost immediately. Known as the "Flash Crash," it was the largest intra-day fall ever
Feb. 1, 2011	Dow closes over 12,000 for the first time since June 2008

Source: www.djindexes.com

In the 1970's and 1980's, the spread of regulated, high-tech exchanges in Europe and Asia contributed to an expanding financial base. The abolition of fixed commissions (1975), the popularization of mutual funds and pension funds, and the advent of online brokerage brought tens of millions of new U.S. investors into the market. Single-day share volume on the NYSE hit 100 million in 1982; the Dow passed 1,000 in 1972 and 2,000 in 1987.

Unsurprisingly, given the history of financial markets, such exuberance was soon accompanied by shady deals, manias, and bubbles.

Leveraged buyouts In most bull markets there is some new wrinkle, and in the 1980's it was leveraged buyouts. Corporate raiders borrowed against the stock of the company they were planning to acquire. They also raised huge sums with unsecured or "junk" bonds. In October 1987 markets experienced one of the worst one-day falls.

However, the expected recession never occurred; the Fed cut interest rates and increased cash in the system, so individual investors did not panic. The market recovered quickly, leaving investors and money managers alike with the mistaken idea that the Fed could prevent any market fall.

S & L crisis A change in the regulatory structure in the 1980's allowed savings and loan associations to sell their consumer and commercial loans and Wall Street immediately stepped in. These large banks bought multiple loans and bundled them together as bonds backed by government institutions such as Fannie Mae and Freddie Mac. The S&L's would then buy back these bonds, paying huge transaction fees, holding $150 billion worth by 1986. When customers began to default and go into bankruptcy, these institutions were crippled. The Federal Savings and Loan Insurance Corporation stepped in and closed or resolved 296 institutions with assets up to $125 billion by 1989. With the government formation of the Resolution Trust Corporation, 747 more S&L's were closed by 1995. The United States government ultimately spent $124.6 billion to resolve this crisis.

Long-Term Capital Management Founded in 1994 by a group of wealthy investors, this hedge fund was managed by several very successful financiers including Robert C. Morton, a Nobel Prize winner in Economics in 1997. Although it had a very high ratio of debt to capital based on an initial loan of $125 billion, the fund's initial success induced several large banks to lend them more and more money. In 1998 when an enormous investment in emerging market bonds went sour the fund faced bankruptcy. But as a sign of things to come, the U.S. government intervened because of fear that the fund's collapse would ripple through the system and cause untold damage. The government convinced the large banks to rescue Long-Term Capital and take ownership of it. "Too big to fail" had been born.

Dot-com bubble In place of the LBOs of the 1980's, the new fad of the 1990's was the initial public offering (IPO). Tiny technology companies had their initial public offerings and saw their share prices reach the stratosphere on the first day of trading. The Dow soared from 5,000 in 1995 to 11,000 in 1999 before plummeting to below 9,000 in 2001. "Dot-com" companies, which sold goods and services over the Internet, led the technology boom.

As the frenzy built, some executives took to manipulating their company's financial results to sustain their stock prices. Many big accounting firms were now consultants to the same firms they audited, but denied that there was a conflict of interest. A little shuffling of costs and revenue soon gave way to wholesale fraud at some firms, aided and abetted by their erstwhile auditors. When the bubble burst, and the profits were found to be fake, huge firms, including Enron, went bankrupt and some of their executives were brought to trial.

The Bernie Madoff Ponzi scheme On December 11, 2008, Bernie Madoff, founder of the firm Bernard L. Madoff Investment Securities LLC, was arrested as his decades long Ponzi scheme began to unravel. Thousands of institutions and wealthy individuals gave billions of dollars to Madoff who in classic Ponzi scheme style took the money and paid it to the previous investors as well as to himself and his family. When the financial crisis hit he quickly ran out of money. The former chairman of NASDAQ, Madoff was able to fool individuals and large international banks into believing his high-performing fund's profits, often of 20 percent, were legitimate. Despite many red flags and several S.E.C. investigations, the massive fraud was not discovered. Many investors lost life savings and banks such as HSBC in England and BNP Paribas in France suffered massive losses. Although the exact amount of losses will never be known estimates range as high as $65 billion. Several fund managers that had invested with Madoff have since committed suicide, as did his son Mark in 2010. In 2009 he pleaded guilty and was sentenced to the maximum of 150 years in prison.

The great financial collapse of 2008 The collapse of the world financial system in the last half of 2008 was at its heart a fiscal crisis brought on by an exponential increase in the amount of debt held by hundreds of thousands of institutions, including banks, hedge funds, pension funds, states, cities, foreign entities, and individuals. The crisis began in the United States as the stock market rebounded from the dot-com bubble, and access to money through relaxed standards of lending by banks and credit card companies rapidly drove the economy into an upward spiral. Within a few years the ratio of debt to disposable income in the U.S. rose from 90 percent in the 1990's (a high figure itself) to a dangerously high 133 percent by 2008. From 2000 to 2008 consumer debt rose by 20 percent to $2.5 trillion.

During this period the nation's largest commercial banks (such as Citibank, JPMorgan Chase, Bank America, Washington Mutual) and the largest investment banks (Goldman Sachs, Morgan Stanley, Lehman Brothers, for example) also took on large amounts of debt, much of it in arcane financial instruments called derivatives, including a form of insurance against risk called credit default swaps. Moreover, according to economic historian Niall Ferguson, the 2004 rule change by the Securities and Exchange Commission allowing these banks to exceed the debt-to-capital ratio of 12:1 was instrumental in bringing ever more debt into the system. As a result of the relaxation of rules regarding debt, more and more money began to pour into the U.S. financial system, a great deal of it from Europe and Asia, all of it searching for the highest returns.

A large, complex, and very efficient system already existed to handle this surge in liquid capital including thousands of banks, brokerage houses, hedge funds, and mortgage brokers. The latter would play a key role in triggering the implosion that took down the U.S. and much of the world economy. Aided and abetted by the reckless and aggressive behavior of the two giant government guarantors of mortgage loans—Fannie Mae and Freddie Mac—mortgage brokers throughout the U.S. wrote millions of mortgage loans for people who could not afford them. The banks issuing these loans did not actually assume all of the risk because those mortgages were soon bundled with hundreds of thousands of other mortgages into bonds that were sold and traded just like other bonds. Unfortunately the leading rating agencies—Standard & Poor's and Moody's—gave a very large number of these so-called "collateralized mortgage obligations" (C.M.O.s) a triple A rating, even though they were packed with subprime mortgages.

The predictable results of all this easy money to help

achieve the "American Dream" of home ownership was the creation of yet another bubble, as home sales soared and with it rapid price increases that resulted in those prices doubling and tripling in value in only a few years. That bubble began to lose air by 2007 but no one predicted just how quickly everything would fall apart and how devastating the long-term effects would be.

In the summer of 2008 the first signs of disaster appeared when three powerful Wall Street institutions essentially went bankrupt. Debt-ridden Merrill Lynch and Bear Stearns were in such distress that with the federal government's help they were sold off to banks for pennies on the dollar. But the huge and highly respected investment bank, Lehman Brothers, simply went into bankruptcy, leaving its investors with losses totaling billions of dollars. Because of Lehman's enormous size and long reach across the globe a financial bubble suddenly turned into a serious crisis as the interconnected nature of the system revealed its inherent weakness. Major commercial and investment banks were forced to absorb huge losses as were the high flying hedge funds, many of whom collapsed.

Before the Bush administration left office in early 2009, the Treasury and the Federal Reserve gave over $700 billion of taxpayer money to banks across the nation to help stabilize the financial system. This approach did stop the death spiral, but then much of the economy collapsed as employers immediately began to lay off millions of workers. Consumers who still had a job stopped spending out of fear and the credit markets simply stopped functioning. In less than a year the Dow Jones Average declined by 39 percent from 14,164 to 8,579.

During the first two years of the Obama administration the federal government continued to support the general economy by providing $787 billion in stimulus funds which in the end proved to be too small to have a meaningful effect. The long-mismanaged U.S. auto industry was saved by a financial bailout to help preserve hundreds of thousands of jobs in large part because unemployment had risen above 10 percent. In addition, literally millions of homes soon fell into foreclosure as the bubble-inflated prices quickly tumbled by over 30 or 40 percent in Florida, Arizona, Las Vegas, and parts of California. By 2011 there were few signs that the economy was recovering as unemployment appeared to be mired at just over 9 percent and home values continued to decline. Oddly enough, however, the stock market had rebounded, the Dow rose to over 12,000, and banks and investment houses posted enormous profits.

On the New York Stock Exchange the average daily volume of shares traded jumped from 1.6 billion in 2005 to 2.4 billion in 2010. In 2010 congress had passed the Dodd-Frank Wall Street Reform and Consumer Protection Act designed to end some of the less attractive practices that had helped create the crisis. A year later not very much had happened as hordes of lobbyists descended on House and Senate members to show why reform would be counterproductive. As of 2011, it seemed that not even the $600 trillion derivatives market, so central to the collapse, would not be subject to scrutiny.

Many informed people have expressed serious concern about these developments but the financial community has won the battle over regulation in the past. And the ever-improving efficiencies brought about by the Internet have pushed the financial system into a new realm but not every part of it is beneficial. Computer servers with unprecedented power enable stock, bond, and commodity trades to be made in milliseconds anywhere on the globe. This has fostered much more trading as opposed to long-term investing. The fact that these trades are frequently initiated by the computers, not the people, is proof of that. Very often the profit per share in such trades is very small but when multiplied by millions of shares the result can be very positive. Yet so-called flash trading-caused problems in the financial system— including a 1,000 point drop in the Dow in May 2010— that are attributed to a large trade are most likely made inadvertently.

Mutual Funds

Mutual funds date back to the 1800's in England and Scotland, but did not become available in the United States until 1924. Their popularity surged in the 1980's, when many companies dropped their traditional pension plans and more Americans became responsible for planning for their own retirement incomes. When the Investment Company Institute, the trade organization of the mutual fund industry, was created in 1940, its members included 68 funds worth a total of $2.1 billion. In 2010, the ICI counted approximately 8,500 funds, representing more than 90 million shareholders, and with total assets of more than $11 trillion.

A mutual fund is a type of investment in which investors pool their money and then collectively invest that money in a variety of stocks, bonds, or other money instruments. Every mutual fund has a particular strategy that determines how much to allocate to each type of investment. For example, a fund seeking higher rewards might invest only in stocks, while a fund seeking very low risk might invest in a variety of bonds. Each mutual fund's strategy, as well its fees and information about how to buy and sell shares, is outlined in the fund prospectus.

The strategy of each mutual fund is determined by the fund manager. The fund manager is a professional investor who monitors the financial markets and continually reallocates the fund's assets to reap the best return. Mutual funds allow investors to diversify their portfolios by making a wide range of investments. Diversification reduces the risk of losing a large amount of money at one time. Like individual securities investments, mutual funds are not guaranteed by the Federal Deposit Insurance Corp. the way bank accounts are, and may lose money.

Kinds of Mutual Funds   The earliest mutual funds invested almost entirely in equities, or shares of stock in publicly traded corporations. Today, mutual funds invest in the entire spectrum of money instruments. Broadly speaking, there are four different kinds of mutual funds. Within the four categories are thousands of mutual funds, each with its own goal and strategies for achieving that goal.

Stock funds, or equity funds, are by far the most common type of mutual funds, representing more than half of all funds. These mutual funds are invested entirely in stocks. The similarities among the various kinds of stock funds end here. *Aggressive growth funds* invest in small companies poised for growth. *Growth funds* invest primarily in large well-established companies. *Sector funds* invest only in companies in a certain segment of the economy, for example, health care. *Growth and income funds* invest in large companies with growth potential and a strong record of dividend payouts. *Income-equity funds* are even more concerned with dividend income, and are less interested in growth potential. *Emerging market funds* invest in companies in developing nations. *Regional equity funds* invest only in companies in a certain part of the world. *Global equity funds* invest in equity securities traded internationally, including those of U.S. companies.

Index funds are stock funds whose portfolio mirrors the performance of various stock market indexes, such as

Standard and Poor's 500 or the Dow Jones industrial average. Because a computer, rather than a person, manages this portfolio, the management costs of index funds are usually lower than other funds.

Bond funds invest in government- and corporate-issued long-term bonds. They are generally more conservative than stock funds but promise a steadier return. This category of funds can be divided into two subcategories: taxable bond funds and tax-free or municipal bond funds.

Hybrid funds invest in a mix of stocks and bonds. Some hybrid funds have fixed percentages allotted to each type of security; other funds allow the fund manager to change the percentages depending on market conditions.

Money market funds are often called short-term funds because they invest in short-term securities (with an average maturity of 90 days or less), such as Treasury bills, CDs, and commercial paper. Within this category are both taxable funds and tax-exempt funds. Because they are free from federal taxes (and in some cases state and local taxes as well), tax-exempt funds usually provide a lower rate of return than taxable funds.

Exchange-traded funds (ETFs) first appeared in 1990 but only became popular in 2004. They are not mutual funds but act like an index fund by making a basket of assets, often in commodities but also in stockmarket indexes. Unlike mutual funds they can be bought and sold every trading day. In 2010, American ETFs had assets of $992 billion, an increase of 137 percent since 2006.

Key Terms for Mutual Funds

closed-end funds most mutual funds are considered "open-end" funds because they offer new shares to the public at all times, and will buy back shares from shareholders at any time. A closed-end fund has a fixed number of shares, which usually trade on a major stock exchange.

expense ratio cost of managing a mutual fund. The ratio is the total amount that the fund manager charges as a percentage of the fund's total assets. The costs include the fund manager's salary and the administrative costs for keeping records and mailing statements. The average mutual fund has an expense ratio of about 1.5 percent. Index funds have an expense ratio of about 0.25 percent.

load fee or sales charge for purchasing shares of a mutual fund, similar to a commission for purchasing stocks. Mutual funds are generally divided into load funds (those that charge a fee) and no-load funds (those that don't).

net asset value share price for a mutual fund. It is equal to the market value of all the fund's securities (minus expenses), divided by the total number of shares.

Hedge Funds

Like mutual funds, hedge funds are investment vehicles that pool money from corporations, syndicates and individuals, and invest it on a collective basis. But hedge funds are exempt from many federal securities regulations, including registration with the Securities and Exchange Commission. They are free to use sophisticated and aggressive investment strategies, such as derivatives, short selling, swaps, currency trading, and arbitrage.

In recent years, hedge funds have grown tremendously in size and influence. Hedge Fund Research, a tracking firm, estimates that $55.5 billion flowed into hedge funds in 2010 making it the highest annual total since 2007, but almost two-third less than the 2006 total; the total assets managed by hedge funds rose to $1.9 trillion.

Hedge funds have traditionally been limited to wealthy investors, though more recently pensions and foundations have also begun to invest heavily in them. Some types of hedge funds are restricted by law to a maximum of 100 investors. The minimum investment is extremely high, ranging from $250,000 to more than $1 million.

The speculative investments favored by many hedge funds can generate enormous profits, but they also entail huge risks. In 1998, the Federal Reserve averted a panic in world markets by engineering a bailout for Long-Term Capital Management; the fund had borrowed heavily and lost billions on a huge position in currency and Treasury markets. The crisis was averted, and Long-Term Capital eventually folded in 2000, but the episode illustrated the risks that accompany this huge and unregulated field. In late 2006, the Amaranth Advisors fund imploded after losing some $6.5 billion in a month's time by betting incorrectly on the demand for natural gas, but its losses did not have implications for the broader market.

Hedge funds charge a management fee while also collecting a percentage of the profits (typically 20 percent). This fee structure has lead to enormous paydays for fund managers. According to *AR Magazine*, each of the top 25 earners took home an average of $880 million in 2010 (down 13 percent in one year.) John Paulson, the most highly-compensated manager, made $4.9 billion in 2010.

"Funds of hedge funds" have emerged as a popular variation on this investment vehicle, allowing investors to diversify their holdings by buying shares in a basket of hedge funds. Many of these funds have lower minimum investment requirements.

Derivatives

The sudden popularity of hedge funds has also drastically increased the use of derivatives as a means of reducing risk. Derivatives are contracts between two parties that allow investors to minimize or shift risk. The value of a derivative is based on (i.e. derived from) an underlying asset such as a commodity, a security, a stock index, or a currency. For example, a derivative could be based on the future price of copper (i.e. a future), or whether it will be cold enough in Colorado to make artificial snow. Investors use derivatives to hedge their bets against loss. Broadly speaking, there are two kinds of derivatives.

Exchange-traded derivatives are publicly traded, standardized transactions that are regulated either by the Securities and Exchange Commission or the Commodity Futures Trading Commission. The two major kinds of exchange-traded derivatives are: *options*, which are the right to buy or sell something for a predetermined price at some point in the future, and *futures*, which are the obligation to buy something at that price. The total number of futures and options traded around the world has skyrocketed from 113 million in 1980 to 22.3 billion in 2010, according to the Futures Industry Association. For the first time Asia-Pacific had the largest share of global volume traded (8.86 billion contracts), an increase of 42.8 percent from the previous year.

Over-the-counter derivatives, or *swaps*, are privately negotiated arrangements, and are not regulated. Their terms are not standardized. The most popular are *credit-default swaps* used to protect investors in corporate bonds from the possibility that a company will not honor its debt and but will "default." According to the International Swaps and Derivatives Association, more than $466.8 trillion of derivatives were traded through June of 2010. That's double the number from 2005, and 20 times the amount from 1995. By comparison, the gross domestic product of the United States, the European Union, Canada, Japan and China combined is about $45 trillion.

Globalization of Finance

The seeds of globalization were planted at the end of World War II. In 1944, at a summit in Bretton Woods, N.H., a dollar-dominated global economic system was designed. The agreement created the International Monetary Fund to mitigate international currency crises by making short-term loans to countries facing a credit or liquidity crunch. It also created the International Bank for Reconstruction and Development, commonly called the World Bank, to provide long-term credit to poor and underdeveloped countries. The International Monetary Fund and the World Bank provided a measure of global financial stability that made it easier for companies to do business internationally.

By the late 1980's, advances in communications were opening up seemingly endless new opportunities for businesses. The current interaction among rich and poor economies—aided greatly by the technological revolution—has set in motion an unprecedented global movement of capital from the wealthiest nations to developing ones. Because holders of capital always seek greater returns on their investments, they will put their money in economies that show potential growth; if they own or run corporations, they will look for ways to reduce the costs of manufacturing, especially labor costs, so that they realize a greater profit. When they invest in foreign companies or establish their businesses in foreign nations, the power of capital can rapidly transform the economies of poorer nations while rearranging the patterns of daily life for millions. In 1950 there were stock markets in 49 countries. Today 116 countries are home to 215 stock and commodity exchanges.

With the rapid development of the Internet, financial transactions could be made around the world in a matter of seconds. The flow of money among nations increased enormously in the form of foreign direct investment in another nation's businesses and portfolio investment i.e. investing in stocks and bonds of foreign businesses or government debt. In 2006, foreign direct investment totaled $1.5 trillion but by 2007 it had reached $2.3 trillion. Most of these investments were in fully developed economies such as the United States, France, Germany, and Great Britain. But ever-increasing amounts were being targeted to developing nations, especially China, and also Russia, India, Brazil, Chile, and Mexico. The total investments rose from $165 billion in 2000 to $583 billion in 2008, which was actually a decrease, as all foreign investment rapidly declined during 2008–09 due to the world financial crisis.

Sovereign Wealth Funds   In recent years national governments as well as several state governments in the United States have started investment funds from revenues from their cash reserves. Known as *sovereign wealth funds*, their purpose is to increase the income from their sources of wealth—usually natural resources, natural gas, minerals and oil. Many of the largest funds are run by oil-producing states including the U.A.E., Saudi Arabia, Kuwait, Libya, and Norway. There are approximately 40 nations with sovereign wealth funds today with a total estimated value of over $4 trillion in 2011. China and the U.A.E have four or more funds.

Exchange Rates   Because countries have their own currencies, trade between them also involves exchanging or trading currencies. The exchange rate between currencies represents the ratio at which they can be exchanged or the price of one currency in terms of the other. For example, if the exchange rate between the British pound and the U.S. dollar is $1.50, then one British pound can be purchased at that price.

Before World War I, exchange rates for world currencies were artificially fixed by tying them to a certain amount of gold. Central banks would then buy and sell gold in order to equalize supply and demand for the currencies and maintain the fixed exchange rates. For this reason, the central banks maintained enormous gold stockpiles, like the one the United States had at Fort Knox. Long-term changes in trading relationships and in the demand for various currencies eventually made the fixed exchange rates of the gold standard impossible to support; in 1944 the Bretton Woods agreement established the U.S. dollar as the world standard.

Today, the exchange rate of a currency rises or appreciates when the demand for it rises or the supply falls, or both. This may happen because foreign buyers want to buy more of a nation's goods or because consumers within the country decide to buy fewer imports. It may also happen because the country reduces its money supply. In addition, the central banks of countries can manipulate their exchange rates slightly by buying and selling their own and other currencies.

The Insurance Industry

Insurance is the pooling of assets by a group of individuals to protect each member against loss. Each contributor to the pool pays a relatively small sum so as to receive a much larger sum in the event of a catastrophe. The notion of insurance can be traced all the way back to Babylonian times. But the modern insurance business has its roots in maritime commerce, where protection against fire, shipwreck, piracy, and other disasters was vital. As early as 1688, merchants, shipowners, and underwriters transacted business at Lloyd's Coffee House in London. Today, the global insurance industry is a $4 trillion business; nearly one-third of that business is generated in the United States. The U.S. insurance industry includes more than 184,000 companies, employing nearly 2.4 million people, with a payroll of $153 billion in 2007, according to the U.S. Census Bureau.

There are two major categories of insurance: life and nonlife. In the U.S. (and only in the U.S.,) these designations are more commonly referred to as life/health and property/casualty. (Because health insurance has become so complex, it is often regarded as its own segment of the industry).According to the Insurance Information Institute, premiums for all major forms of insurance totaled $582 billion in 2010.

These huge sums make the U.S. insurance industry a major player in the world's financial markets. Good, safe investments have given them enormous total assets. The great majority of the property/casualty insurance industry's assets ($886 billion, or 68 percent) were invested in credit market investments in 2009. Another $369 billion (or 28 percent of the total) were invested in municipal securities and loans. Similarly, of the life insurance industry's $3 trillion in assets in 2009, $2.2 trillion, or 74 percent, was invested in bonds (mostly corporate bonds), while $72 billion (2.4 percent) was in stocks (primarily common stocks).

Life Insurance

Life insurance is a contract between an individual and an underwriter based on the statistical likelihood of when the individual will die. The individual pays an annual premium, and the underwriter pays a death benefit in the unlikely event of the individual's death. There are two basic kinds of life insurance: term life and permanent life.

Term life and permanent life   Term life insurance is the simplest and least expensive form of life insurance. Coverage ends the minute the individual stops paying the premiums. Term life insurance grows more expensive as individuals age and become, statistically speaking, more likely to die. Permanent life insurance is often called cash value insurance because the policy has a cash value even if the individual stops paying the premiums. Permanent life insurance is much more expensive than term life insurance, but after the individual pays premiums for a certain number of years, the death benefit is guaranteed. Whole life, universal life, and variable universal life are all forms of permanent life insurance.

Annuities are the opposite of life insurance. They are a contract based on the statistical likelihood that an individual will live. In an annuity, the individual invests an amount of money and the underwriter returns an agreed-upon portion of that money (plus interest) every year until the individual's death. As Americans have begun living longer, there has been a dramatic increase in the amount of money invested in annuities. In 2010, annuities ($221 billion) accounted for slightly more than twice as much income as life insurance premiums ($101 billion), according to the Insurance Information Institute.

Property and Casualty Insurance

Property and casualty insurance protects individuals against loss of property or against liability. Private automobile insurance is the most popular form of property and casualty insurance, constituting more than one–third of all premiums written, according to the Insurance Information Institute. Homeowner's insurance, is the second-most common form, accounting for more than 12 percent of premiums in 2005. Other forms of property and casualty insurance include commercial auto (6.3 percent of premiums), workers' compensation (to protect against loss due to an employee's injury; 9.3 percent of premiums), and medical malpractice (to protect doctors against liability; 2.3 percent of premiums).

Health Insurance

Like other forms of insurance, health insurance allows individuals to defray the cost of expensive medical procedures by paying a fixed amount of money each month. Healthy individuals subsidize sick people. Approximately 253.6 million Americans are covered by some form of health insurance; another 50.7 million lacked health coverage of any kind in 2009.

Most health insurance plans are administered through groups, usually an employer, a union, or the federal government (See "Government health insurance"). The larger the group, the more healthy people there are to offset medical costs of any one person. In some cases, individuals may purchase private health insurance, but the price is usually very high. There are numerous kinds of health insurance, but most fall into one of the following categories:

Fee-for-service Individuals choose any doctor and insurance covers a portion of the cost. This is the most expensive type of health insurance.

Managed care Patients receive health care services at a lower cost as long as they stay within a network of participating doctors, hospitals, and other medical providers. There are several kinds of managed care.

Preferred Provider Organizations (PPOs) are similar to fee-for-service plans. Costs are lower (usually requiring just a $15 or $20 co-payment for an office visit to a participating provider), but also offer the flexibility to see doctors outside the network (though coverage is lower).

Health Maintenance Organizations (HMOs) are much less expensive but require patients to stay within the network except in case of emergency. Most HMOs require a co-payment for office visits, but have much lower out-of-pocket costs than other plans.

Point of Service (POS) plans are a hybrid of PPO and HMO plans. Primary care physicians in the network (sometimes called gatekeepers) make referrals to specialists and other providers. Members can go outside of the plan, but insurance will only cover a portion of the cost.

Government health insurance The Federal government funds health insurance programs for the needy (Medicaid) and for people over 65 (Medicare). Medicare also covers certain people under 65 with long-term disabilities. The State Children's Health Insurance Program (SCHIP) is a separate government health insurance plan funded at the state level for low-income children whose parents do not qualify for Medicaid.

Glossary of Finance Terms

American Stock Exchange (ASE) one of the major American stock exchanges; emphasizes lower-priced stocks and younger, growing companies; see *New York Stock Exchange*.

auction market sale in which an item is offered to bidders by an auctioneer who sells the item to the highest bidder.

barter exchange of goods or services of one kind for another without the use of money.

bear market stock market in which traders expect prices to fall; traders sell stocks, driving down prices and fulfilling their expectations; see *bull market*.

Black Tuesday October 29, 1929, the day the stock market produced a record volume of more than 16 million shares—most of them sales—and the Dow Jones industrial average dropped 11 percent in one day; began a prolonged decline in the stock market that was a contributor to the Great Depression.

bond security issued by government or public company promising to repay borrowed money at a set interest rate in a specified period of time; see *junk bond*.

bubble market in which the price of an asset continues to rise because speculators believe it will continue to rise even further, until prices reach a level that is not sustainable; panic selling begins and the price falls precipitously.

bull market stock market in which traders expect prices to rise; traders buy stocks, driving up prices and fulfilling their expectations; see *bear market*.

business cycle tendency for the economy to expand and contract; different theories attribute the cause to government policies, economic shocks (e.g., the rate of technological progress), lags in timing of economic decisionmaking, or a combination of these and other factors.

call see *option*.

central bank A bank that controls the money supply and monetary policy in a country; see *Bank of England* and *Federal Reserve System*.

closed-end fund A mutual fund that has a fixed number of shares which usually trade on a major stock exchange; see open-end fund.

collateralized mortgage obligation (CMO) a security, backed by a pool of mortgages, structured so that there are several classes of bondholders with varying maturities called tranches. The principal payments from the underlying pool of pass-through securities are used to retire the bonds on a priority basis as specified in the prospectus. Also known as mortgage pass-through security.

commercial bank bank that deals with the general public; it accepts interest-paying deposits and lends to a wide variety of households and small businesses; see *investment bank*.

commercial paper short-term unsecured promissory notes issued by a corporation. The maturity of commercial paper is typically less than nine months; the most common maturity range is 30 to 50 days or less.

credit default swaps a form of insurance that protects lenders in case of loan defaults. The buyer receives credit protection while the seller guarantees the credit worthiness of the product.

decimal trading trading in securities priced in hundredths of a unit of money; in the United States decimal trading began at the New York Stock Exchange in 2000; see *fractional trading*.

debenture any debt obligation backed strictly by the borrower's integrity, e.g., an unsecured bond.

debt money borrowed.

debt service interest payments plus repayments of principal to creditors. Investors pay close attention to whether or not a company is making enough money to service its debt.

derivative financial contract whose value is based on, or "derived" from, a traditional security such as a stock or bond, commodity, or market index.

discount rate interest rate charged by the U.S. Federal Reserve for short-term borrowing by member banks.

diversification in investing, holding a variety of assets in order to minimize the risk of losses in any single asset.

dividend portion of a company's profit paid to holders of its common and preferred stocks. A stock selling for $20 with an annual dividend of $1 a share yields the investor a 5 percent dividend.

Dow Jones industrial average An index based on the prices of 30 widely traded United States industrial stocks; often considered a gauge of overall stock market performance.

earnings before interest, taxes, depreciation, and amortization (EBITDA) financial measure defined as revenues less cost of goods sold and selling, general, and administrative expenses. In other words, a company's profit before the deduction of interest, income taxes, depreciation, and amortization expenses. EBITDA became popular in the 1980's when corporate raiders tried to assess what a company's operation generated, not counting interest, taxes, or noncash expenses such as depreciation and amortization that reflect diminished values of a company's assets.

equity ownership interest in a firm or asset. In real estate, dollar difference between what a property could be sold for and debts claimed against it, such as a mortgage. In a brokerage account, equity equals the value of the account's securities minus any money borrowed from a brokerage firm in a margin account. "Equities" is another name for stocks or company shares.

euro (€) unit of currency of the European Union; adopted in 1999, it replaced the currencies of all of the E.U. countries except the United Kingdom.

Federal Deposit Insurance Corporation (F.D.I.C.) U.S. regulatory body formed by the Banking Act of 1933, it charters banks and insures the deposits (up to a maximum of $100,000 per depositor) in member banks; financed by charges paid by member banks.

federal funds rate interest rate that banks with excess reserves at a Federal Reserve district bank charge other banks that need overnight loans. The fed-funds rate, as it is called, often points to the direction of U.S. interest rates because it is set daily by the market, unlike the prime rate and the discount rate. The Federal Reserve does not have a target for the fed-funds rate, which it moves periodically.

Federal Reserve System created in 1913 by the Federal Reserve Act, it is the U.S. central bank system. It consists of a board of governors and 12 district reserve banks; they fix bank reserve and margin requirements, the discount rate, and manage the federal funds rate; the board manages monetary policy with the intention of minimizing the fluctuations of business cycles.

fiat money money that circulates by command of the state; originally money was coined of valuable metals that corresponded to their face value; but when money was coined of base metals, and paper currency came into use, its value had to be established by the power of the state; modern money is fiat money.

fiduciary money money that is backed by real assets and owes it acceptability to pubic trust and confidence.

fractional trading trading in securities priced in halves, quarters, and eighths of a dollar; in 2000 the New York Stock Exchange converted to decimal trading.

futures market market in which contracts commit two parties to buy and sell commodities, securities, or curren-cies on a date in the future at a price fixed when the contact is made; if the market price at the time the contract matures is higher than the contract price, the buyer profits; if the market price is lower, the seller profits.

gold standard system of fixing exchange rates to the price of gold in order to facilitate trade between nations.

Gresham's law tendency for people to spend money of low intrinsic value (coins of base metal and paper currency) and hoard money of higher intrinsic value (coins of precious metals) when these forms of money circulate concurrently; often stated as "bad money drives out good"; first articulated by Sir Thomas Gresham (ca. 1519–79), an adviser to Queen Elizabeth I.

hard money money which can be converted into other money or whose price compared with other money is expected to remain stable or to rise; see *soft money*.

hedge fund investment strategy that employs a variety of techniques to enhance returns, such as both buying and shorting stocks.

inflation condition in which prices and wages increase as measured by changes in an appropriate price index such as the Consumer Price Index.

initial public offering (IPO) stock issued for the first time by a public company.

investment bank bank dealing with other firms rather than the general public; see *commercial bank*.

investor buyer and seller of securities who considers their inherent value; see *speculator*.

joint-stock company company in which investors pool their money and receive profits or dividends in proportion to their investments; often are limited liability companies in that investors are liable only for any debts in the amount of their original investments.

junk bond bond issued by companies with low credit ratings that compensate for high risk by paying high interest rates; also called a "high yield bond."

legal tender form of money that a creditor is legally obligated to accept in payment of a debt.

letter of credit letter issued by a bank authorizing the bearer to withdraw a stated amount of money from the issuing bank or its branches and agencies.

leveraged buyout purchase of the equity of a company financed mostly by borrowing against the stock of the target company; during the heyday of leveraged buyouts in the 1980's corporate raiders also raised large sums with unsecured junk bonds.

limited liability company (LLC) company in which investors' potential loss is limited to the amount of their investments in the event that the business fails.

liquid assets assets that can be converted into money rapidly and at a reasonably predictable rate.

liquidity property of assets that allows them to be converted into money rapidly and at a reasonably predictable rate; in a company, having assets that are liquid.

margin the difference between the market value of a stock and the loan a broker makes; allows investors to buy securities by borrowing money from a broker.

money medium of exchange in goods and services and a means of storing value over time.

money market fund pooled fund that invests in short-term loans.

NASDAQ (National Association of Securities Dealers and Automated Quotation system) opened in 1971, NASDAQ was the first stock exchange to rely on sophisticated computer and telecommunications systems to trade and monitor millions of securities on a daily basis. Trading was no longer limited to a single location; millions of dealers across the globe were connected by an electronic network to execute trades and deliver data in real time.

New York Stock Exchange (NYSE) largest U.S. market for trading stocks and bonds based on the specialist system.

price-to-earnings ratio (P/E) ratio obtained by dividing the current market price of a stock by the most recently published earnings for equity per share.

put see *option*.

pyramid scheme illegal, fraudulent scheme in which a con artist persuades victims to invest by promising an extraordinary return; he or she embezzles the funds while using the minimum necessary to pay off any investors who insist on terminating their investment.

ROI (return on investment) generally, income as a proportion of a company's net book value. Also known as profitability ratio.

savings and loan institution (S&L) financial institution that accepts deposits from the public and lends its funds primarily as home mortgages.

Securities and Exchange Commission (SEC) created by the Securities Exchange Act of 1934, it monitors and regulates the sale of corporate securities in the U.S.

seigniorage originally the profit made by a ruler who issues money with a face value exceeding the cost of production; today it refers to the ability of governments to issue new money to pay for goods and services.

selling short (short selling) sale of a stock that is not actually owned. If an investor thinks the price of a stock is going down, the investor borrows the stock from a broker and sells it.

soft money money which cannot be converted into other money or whose price compared with other money is expected to fall; see *hard money*.

speculator buyer and seller of securities betting that they will rise or decline in value; see *investor*.

specialist individual on the floor of a stock exchange who is employed by a specialist firm to match buyers and sellers of stocks of specific companies; obligated to "make a market" in a stock by buying shares when there are no other buyers and to sell shares from the firm's inventory when there are no other sellers.

specie money in the form of coins, not paper currency.

stock capital that a company raises by selling shares that entitle the owner to dividends and other rights of ownership.

stock exchange place where stocks, bonds, and other financial instruments are bought and sold.

stock market stock exchange; also can refer to the overall performance of the prices of stocks and bonds, as in, "The stock market rose today."

tight money money that is difficult to borrow because of high interest rates or limited availability.

traders individuals who take positions in securities and their derivatives with the objective of making profits.

trading buying and selling securities.

Treasury bill (T-bill) debt obligation of the U.S. Treasury that has maturity of one year or less. Maturities for T-bills are usually 91 days, 182 days, or 52 weeks.

Treasury bond debt obligation of the U.S. Treasury that has maturity of two years or more.

venture capital capital invested in new or small businesses, with comparatively high risk, in the hope of making a substantial profit if the businesses prosper.

yield percentage rate of return paid on a stock in the form of dividends, or the effective rate of interest paid on a bond or note.

The New Speed of Money, Reshaping Markets

By GRAHAM BOWLEY

A substantial part of all stock trading in the United States takes place in a warehouse in a nondescript business park just off the New Jersey Turnpike. Few humans are present in this vast technological sanctum, known as New York Four. Instead, the building, nearly the size of three football fields, is filled with long avenues of computer servers illuminated by energy-efficient blue phosphorescent light. Countless metal cages contain racks of computers that perform all kinds of trades for Wall Street banks, hedge funds, brokerage firms and other institutions. And within just one of these cages— a tight space measuring 40 feet by 45 feet and festooned with blue and white wires—is an array of servers that together form the mechanized heart of one of the top four stock exchanges in the United States. The exchange is called Direct Edge, hardly a household name. But as the lights pulse on its servers, you can almost see the holdings in your 401(k) zip by.

In many of the world's markets, nearly all stock trading is now conducted by computers talking to other computers at high speeds. As the machines have taken over, trading has been migrating from raucous, populated trading floors like those of the New York Stock Exchange to dozens of separate, rival electronic exchanges. They rely on data centers like this one, many in the suburbs of northern New Jersey.

While this "Tron" landscape is dominated by the titans of Wall Street, it affects nearly everyone who owns shares of stock or mutual funds, or who has a stake in a pension fund or works for a public company. For better or for worse, part of your wealth, your livelihood, is throbbing through these wires. The advantages of this new technological order are clear. Trading costs have plummeted, and anyone can buy stocks from anywhere in seconds with the simple click of a mouse or a tap on a smartphone's screen.

But some experts wonder whether the technology is getting dangerously out of control. Even apart from the huge amounts of energy the megacomputers consume, and the dangers of putting so much of the economy's plumbing in one place, they wonder whether the new world is a fairer one—and whether traders with access to the fastest machines win at the expense of ordinary investors.

It also seems to be a much more hair-trigger market. The so-called flash crash in the market May 2010—when stock prices plunged hundreds of points before recovering—showed how unpredictable the new systems could be. No one knows whether this is a better world, and that includes the regulators, who are struggling to keep up with the pace of innovation in the great technological arms race that the stock market has become.

Direct Edge's office demonstrates that it doesn't take many people to become a major outfit in today's electronic market. The firm, whose motto is "Everybody needs some edge," has only 90 employees, most of them on this building's sixth floor. There are lines of cubicles for programmers and a small operations room where two men watch a wall of screens, checking that market-order traffic moves smoothly and, of course, quickly. Direct Edge receives up to 10,000 orders a second.

Computer-driven trading began in earnest when the S.E.C. forced the New York Stock Exchange and Nasdaq to post orders electronically and execute them immediately, at the best price available in the United States— suddenly giving an advantage to start-up operations that were faster and cheaper. The N.Y.S.E. and Nasdaq fought back, buying up smaller rivals. And to give itself greater firepower, the N.Y.S.E., which had been member-owned, became a public, for-profit company.

Brokerage firms and traders came to fear that a Nasdaq-N.Y.S.E. duopoly was asserting itself, one that would charge them heavily for the right to trade, so they created their own exchanges. One was Direct Edge, which formally became an exchange in late 2010. Another, the BATS Exchange, is located in another unlikely capital of stock market trading: Kansas City, Mo.

Direct Edge now trails the N.Y.S.E. and Nasdaq in size; it vies with BATS for third place. Direct Edge is backed by a powerful roster of financial players: Goldman Sachs, Knight Capital, Citadel Securities and the International Securities Exchange, its largest shareholder. JPMorgan also holds a stake.

The exchange now accounts for about 10 percent of stock market trading in the United States, according to the exchange and the TABB Group, a specialist on the markets. Of the 8.5 billion shares traded daily in the United States, about 833 million are bought and sold on the Direct Edge platforms.

As it has grown, Direct Edge and other new venues have sucked volumes away from the Big Board and Nasdaq. The N.Y.S.E. accounted for more than 70 percent of trading in N.Y.S.E.-listed stocks in 2006. Now, the Big Board handles only 36 percent of those trades itself. The remaining market share is divided among about 12 other public exchanges, several electronic trading platforms and vast so-called unlit markets, including those known as dark pools.

The Big Board is embracing the new warp-speed world. Although it maintains a Wall Street trading floor, even that is mostly electronic. The exchange also has its own, separate electronic arm, Arca, and opened a new data center in 2010 for its computers in Mahwah, N.J.

In this high-tech stock market, Direct Edge and the other exchanges are sprinting for advantage. All the exchanges have pushed down their latencies—the fancy word for the less-than-a-blink-of-an-eye that it takes them to complete a trade. Almost each week, it seems, one exchange or another claims a new record: Nasdaq, for example, says its time for an average order "round trip" is 98 microseconds — a mind-numbing speed equal to 98 millionths of a second. The exchanges have gone warp speed because traders have demanded it. Even mainstream banks and old-fashioned mutual funds have embraced the change.

Even the savings of many long-term mutual fund investors are swept up in this maelstrom, when fund managers make changes in their holdings. But the exchanges are catering mostly to a different market breed—to high-frequency traders who have turned speed into a new art form. They use algorithms to zip in and out of markets, often changing orders and strategies within seconds. They make a living by being the first to react to events, dashing past slower investors—a category that includes most investors— to take advantage of mispricing between stocks, for example, or differences in prices quoted across exchanges.

One new strategy is to use powerful computers to speed-read news reports—even Twitter messages— automatically, then to let their machines interpret and trade on them. By using such techniques, traders may make only the tiniest fraction of a cent on each trade. But multiplied many times a second over an entire day, those fractions add up to real money. According to the TABB Group, high-frequency traders now account for 56 percent of total stock market trading. A measure of their importance is that rather than charging them commissions, some exchanges now even pay high-frequency traders to bring orders to their machines.

The exchange is making its investment because derivatives as well as stocks are being swept up in the high-frequency revolution. The Commodity Futures Trading Commission estimates that high-frequency traders now account for about one-third of all volume on domestic futures exchanges.

The "flash crash," the harrowing plunge in share prices that shook the stock market during the afternoon of May 6, 2010, crystallized the fears of some in the industry that technology was getting ahead of the regulators. In their investigation into the plunge, the S.E.C. and Commodity Futures Trading Commission found that the drop was precipitated not by a rogue high-frequency firm, but by the sale of a single $4.1 billion block of E-Mini Standard & Poor's 500 futures contracts on the Chicago Mercantile Exchange by a mutual fund company.

Since the flash crash, the S.E.C. and the exchanges have introduced marketwide circuit breakers on individual stocks to halt trading if a price falls 10 percent within a five-minute period. But some analysts fear that some aspects of the flash crash may portend dangers greater than mere mechanical failure. They say some wild swings in prices may suggest that a small group of high-frequency traders could manipulate the market. Since May 2010, there have been regular mini-flash crashes in individual stocks for which, some say, there are still no satisfactory explanations. Some experts say these drops in individual stocks could herald a future cataclysm.

Some analysts question whether everyone benefits from this technological upending. "It is a technological arms race in financial markets and the regulators are a bit caught unaware of how quickly the technology has evolved," says Andrew Lo, director of the Laboratory for Financial Engineering at M.I.T. "Sometimes, too much technology without the ability to manage it effectively can yield some unintended consequences. We need to ask the hard questions about how much of this do we really need. It is the Wild, Wild West in trading."

MEDIA

PRINT MEDIA

Newspapers

The origins of news writing date back to China and the Roman Empire before the birth of Christ. In China's Han dynasty (206 B.C. to A.D. 220), sheets called *tipao* were passed among government officials, while in the Forum of Rome, daily reports called *acta diurna* were posted, relating noteworthy events both local and throughout the Empire.

The chief limitation to a regular news service was, of course, the difficulty in production. Every sheet had to be hand-written, a laborious, time-consuming process that greatly restricted the dissemination of news. That problem, and many others, was solved by the invention of the printing press in 1436 by a German named Johannes Gutenberg (d. 1468). The printing press, arguably the most influential invention in human history, enabled production of news sheets much more easily, and at much lower cost.

However, news was not disseminated on a regular basis. Instead it was reserved for occasional postings about single, noteworthy events. Many of these one-time reports, often in pamphlet form, were printed throughout the 16th and 17th centuries. The first regular news sheet appeared in Venice, a major sea power at the time, with a trade network that required frequently updated reports. These sheets, called *gazette* or *avisi*—*gazette* comes from *gazetta*, a Venetian coin—were disseminated weekly as early as 1566, and were borne on merchant vessels to many ports in the Mediterranean and beyond.

The oldest surviving printed weekly newspaper appeared in Strasbourg, Germany, in 1609. Printed weeklies caught on quickly, popping up in Frankfurt and Vienna in 1615, Hamburg in 1616, Berlin in 1617, and Amsterdam in 1618. The first English newspaper was published in 1621, followed over the next two decades by papers in France, Italy, and Spain. The first daily newspaper, *Einkommende Zeirungen* ("Incoming News"), appeared in Leipzig in 1650; the first English daily, *The Daily Courant*, was published in London from 1702–35.

These early papers were mostly assembled from letters sent from other cities, so the news was not particularly timely. Most were printed with government permission, so their news reports focused on events outside their nation or community rather than risk offending the powers that be.

The first society to practice what might be termed freedom of the press was in England in the 1640's, in the years leading to that nation's Civil War. The conflict between Parliament and King Charles I, which seemed to weaken the king's stature, encouraged several publications to turn their focus from foreign shores to the conflict at home. Following the execution of the king, however, the Protectorate of Cromwell greatly limited the press once again.

Newspapers in Colonial America

The sense that the press could criticize government was borne across the Atlantic to the American colonies, but the theory often withered before reality. In fact, the first issue of America's first newspaper was also the last. *Public Occurrences, Both FORREIGN and DOMESTICK*, printed in Boston on Sept. 25, 1690, made several impolitic statements and was suppressed.

Fourteen years later came America's second printed paper, the *Boston News-Letter*, which survived from its first printing in 1704 until 1776. It was followed in 1719 by the *Boston Gazette* and the *American Weekly Mercury*, printed in Philadelphia. Benjamin Franklin printed the *Pennsylvania Gazette* (also in Philadelphia) starting in 1729. Other papers appeared in Maryland and Virginia in the following decade, and by 1765 all 13 colonies except for Delaware and New Jersey had weekly papers. Boston had four of its own, and New York, three.

News in these pages was scant, with most weeklies four pages long and featuring reprocessed news from Europe. Criticism of colonial administration was rare. Yet one printer dared to criticize, and John Peter Zenger's *New York Weekly Journal*, first printed in 1733, was to have a significant effect on the history of the United States.

After arguing against some of the governor's policies, Zenger was arrested in November 1734 under the charge of seditious libel. During the trial the following August, the judge instructed the jury that, according to the definition of seditious libel, truth afforded no protection against libel of the government. Zenger's attorney, however, made a stirring argument, defending "the liberty both of exposing and opposing arbitrary power... by speaking and writing truth." The jury decided that Zenger was innocent.

Zenger's acquittal was a major victory for freedom of the press in the colonies; without it, many other papers that were critical of the colonial administration over the next four decades might have been silenced. Newspapers played a major part in fueling the fires of revolution. For example, the home of Benjamin Edes, editor of the *Boston Gazette*, served as the center of organization for the Boston Tea Party in 1773.

Following the Revolution, freedom of the press, along with other freedoms, was guaranteed in the First Amendment of the Constitution, ratified in 1787. Still, partisan conflict between the major political parties of the period led to the passage of the Sedition Act in 1798, the most dire threat to freedom of the press in American history. Passed under the presidency of Federalist John Adams, it threatened to punish "any false, scandalous and malicious writing" against the government, including the Congress and the president. During the act's short life, 25 people were arrested and 10 convicted. When Thomas Jefferson ascended to the presidency following the 1800 election, the Sedition Act was allowed to lapse.

The Penny Press

Technological advances in the early Industrial Revolution affected the business of newspapers along with the rest of society. In September 1833 a small paper in New York called the *Sun* went on sale for a penny. The cheap price enabled the lower classes to buy and read the news. By 1835 the *Sun*, printed on a new steam press, was selling 15,000 copies a day, substantially higher than the circulation of other papers in New York.

Within a few years, several cities—including Boston, Philadelphia, and Baltimore—added penny papers. No longer was the common man priced out of ready daily information. Instead, thanks to the low price of printing allowed by better technology, papers could be made more cheaply and quickly. Publishers could reach more customers and sell more advertising. Newspapers became successful businesses.

Content changed as well—sensationalism crept into newspapers. Accounts from police court were common, especially among the penny press, and eventually some publishers improved their content by hiring employees to report and write news stories. This practice had been seen

in England before, but it was in the mid-19th century that the practice became common in America. The *New York Herald*, for example, employed dozens of reporters to cover the Civil War.

Another technological innovation that aided reporting and news-gathering was the invention of the telegraph by Samuel Morse in 1844, which enabled news to travel long distances almost instantly, permitting next-day coverage of faraway events. With the completion of the trans-Atlantic cable in 1866, newspapers had similar access to news from Europe.

The Rise of the Modern Newspaper

During the second half of the 19th century new technology and a better-educated public led to tremendous growth in the number of newspapers. Approximately 3,000 papers existed in the U.S. in 1860; 20 years later, the total had reached about 7,000. During this time the modern "pyramid" style of news writing was also devised. This style discarded the earlier form—a narrative and frequently unfocused account—and instead placed the most important facts near the story's beginning. Thus, the first sentence of a news story, called the "lead," contains the essential facts for the reader. Additional facts and details follow, with the least important information placed at the end.

The late 19th century was the most colorful period of American journalism. In many cities, newspapers competed using tough tactics. Nowhere was this more evident than in New York, where two newspaper barons, Joseph Pulitzer (1847–1911) and William Randolph Hearst (1863–1951), vied for the lucrative market.

Pulitzer, a native of the Austro-Hungarian Empire, emigrated to America during the Civil War and eventually started work as a reporter at a German-language paper in St. Louis. In 1878 he bought a small paper at a fire sale price, which he combined with another paper to form the *St. Louis Post-Dispatch*. The new paper prospered, but Pulitzer wanted other challenges, so he purchased the *New York World* in 1883. The *World* quickly differentiated itself from its competitors with stories that focused on lively human interest, gossip and scandal, with a healthy dose of stunts. In 1889 a *World* reporter named Nellie Bly—whose real name was Elizabeth Cochran—set out to circumnavigate the world in less than 80 days, the time required by Phileas Fogg, the protagonist of Jules Verne's novel *Around the World in Eighty Days*. Bly succeeded, returning to New York 72 days after her departure to considerable *World*-sponsored fanfare.

WikiLeaks

from NYTIMES.COM, "Times Topics"

WikiLeaks is a whistle-blowing Web site that became the focus of a global debate over its role in the release of thousands of confidential messages about the wars in Iraq and Afghanistan and the conduct of American diplomacy around the world. The once-fringe Web site, which aims to bring to light secret information about governments and corporations, was founded in 2006 by Julian Assange, an Australian activist and journalist, along with a group of like-minded activists and computer experts.

WikiLeaks made its initial reputation by publishing material as diverse as documents about toxic dumping in Africa, protocols from Guantánamo Bay, e-mail messages from Sarah Palin's personal account, and 9/11 pager messages. When it published tens of thousands of confidential military field reports about the two wars in July 2010, it was denounced by American officials for endangering the lives of soldiers and civilians. The release in late December 2010 of some of a trove of 250,000 diplomatic cables led to anger and criticism from officials worldwide.

Documents released in February 2011 involved Saudi Arabia's oil capacity. In confidential cables written between 2007 and 2009, American diplomats in Riyadh warned that the country's ability to boost oil production much above current levels was questionable and the country's overall crude reserves might have been overstated by up to 40 percent.

In April 2011, documents relating to intelligence gathered about detainees in the United States military prison at Guantánamo emerged. Files leaked to WikiLeaks and made available to *The New York Times* show why closing the prison has been so difficult, by laying bare the patchwork and contradictory evidence about prisoner's guilt that in many cases would never have stood up in criminal court or a military tribunal.

WikiLeaks has a core group of five full-time volunteers and there are 800 to 1,000 people whom the group can call on for expertise in areas like encryption, programming, and writing news releases.

Mr. Assange used years of computer hacking and what friends call a near-genius I.Q. to establish WikiLeaks in 2006, redefining whistle-blowing by gathering secrets in bulk, storing them beyond the reach of governments and others determined to retrieve them, then releasing them instantly, and globally.

WikiLeaks publishes its material on its own site, which is housed on a few dozen servers around the globe, including places like Sweden, Belgium, and the United States, which the organization considers friendly to journalists and document leakers.

By being everywhere, yet in no exact place, WikiLeaks is, in effect, out of grasp of any institution or government that hopes to silence it.

WikiLeaks has grown increasingly controversial as it has published more material. (The United States Army called it a threat to its operations in a report in March 2010.) Many have tried to silence the site; in Britain, WikiLeaks has been used a number of times to evade injunctions on publication by courts that ruled that the material would violate the privacy of the people involved. The courts reversed themselves when they discovered how ineffectual their rulings were.

In early 2011, some of Mr. Assange's closest associates in WikiLeaks abandoned him, calling him autocratic and capricious and accusing him of reneging on WikiLeaks' original pledge of impartiality to launch a concerted attack on the United States.

Attorney General Eric H. Holder Jr. has said that American officials were conducting "a very serious, active, ongoing investigation that is criminal in nature" into the WikiLeaks releases, a position the Obama administration has held for months, since WikiLeaks began releasing secret Pentagon documents on the Afghan and Iraq wars in summer.

An early attempt to shut down the WikiLeaks site involved a United States District Court judge in California. In 2008, Judge Jeffrey S. White ordered the American version of the site shut down after it published confidential documents concerning a subsidiary of a Swiss bank. Two weeks later he reversed himself, in part recognizing that the order had little effect because the same material could be accessed on a number of other "mirror sites."

This new style of journalism was much admired by William Randolph Hearst. The California native began his newspaper empire with the *San Francisco Examiner*, which was owned by his father. Hearst acquired the *New York Journal* in 1895, by which time Pulitzer had headed the *New York World* for 12 years. Almost immediately after Hearst's entry into the market, the two papers engaged in a circulation war in which each owner sought to out-sensationalize the other. Hearst hired away several of the *World's* star reporters, and both papers cut prices to a penny. Their stories and stunts were a significant cause of the furor that led the U.S. into the Spanish-American War in 1898.

This style of rabid sensationalism was dubbed "yellow journalism," a term derived from a comic strip called "The Yellow Kid" that, naturally, both papers believed was their sole right to publish. Still, such journalism sold, and both newspapers regularly sold more than 1 million copies per day. (Only four contemporary newspapers—*USA Today, The Wall Street Journal, The New York Times*, and the *Los Angeles Times*—exceed or approach that mark.) Some newspapers, such as *The New York Times*, disdained "yellow" tactics, and eventually Pulitzer tired of them as well.

Consolidation

The first half of the 20th century saw a steep decline in the number of American newspapers, a trend caused by attrition and by the development of corporations that owned papers in many cities. Scripps-Howard, another media behemoth, boasted 25 newspapers by 1929. Hearst eventually accrued 20 daily newspapers in the U.S., plus some Sunday editions, as well as magazines, a newsreel operation, and other interests.

Consolidation may have been good for the owners of the media outlets, but not necessarily for the readers. This limitation of viewpoints prompted New Yorker columnist A.J. Liebling to famously quip, in 1961, "Freedom of the press is guaranteed only to those who own one."

In the second half of the 20th century, newspapers's adversarial role with the government became more controversial. *The New York Times* won a Supreme Court battle to publish the Pentagon Papers, top secret government documents, in 1971. The next year, *Washington Post* reporters Robert Woodward and Carl Bernstein wrote a series on the Watergate scandal that is credited with leading to the resignation of President Richard Nixon. About the same time, in an effort to attract more readers, many newspapers expanded beyond hard news, adding sections to cover fashion, food, science, home design, real estate,

Top 10 Newspapers by Reported Circulation
(Monday–Friday only, 2010 average)

Paper	Owner	Circulation
1. *Wall Street Journal*	News Corporation	2,061,142
2. *USA Today*	Gannett Company Inc.	1,830,029
3. *New York Times*	New York Times Co.	876,638
4. *Los Angeles Times*	Tribune Company	600,449
5. *The Washington Post*	Washington Post Co.	545,345
6. *New York Daily News*	Mortimer Zuckerman	512,520
7. *New York Post*	News Corporation	501,501
8. *San Jose Mercury News*	MediaNews Group	477,592
9. *Chicago Tribune*	Tribune Company	441,508
10. *The Houston Chronicle*	Hearst Corporation	343,952

Source: Audit Bureau of Circulations

Newspaper Advertising Expenditures
(including national, retail and classifieds)

Year	Amount
1950	$2.0 billion
1960	$3.6 billion
1970	$5.7 billion
1980	$14.8 billion
1990	$32.3 billion
2000	$48.7 billion
2010	$22.7 billion

Source: Newspaper Association of America

and other lifestyle topics.

In recent years, the growth of television and the rise of the Internet have reduced both the number of papers and their circulation. In 1984 there were 1,688 daily newspapers in the U.S., with a circulation of 63.3 million. By 2008, those numbers had dwindled to 1,408 daily papers with a circulation of 48.6 million. Newspapers still attract a well-educated, affluent customer—about 50 percent of daily readers are college educated and 60 percent earn more than $50,000. But they are having a hard time reaching new, younger readers who get their news for free on the Internet. Online newspaper readership increased steadily during the first decade of the 2000's. Sixty percent of respondents under the age of 30 said they viewed most of their news online. According to Nielsen Online, in January 2009 online readership had reached almost 75 million U.S. readers and 3.7 billion page views. In an effort to attract the 18–34 year old crowd, some newspapers have started publishing special editions aimed at the MTV generation. In Chicago, Dallas, Boston, and New York, free daily newspapers with snazzy graphics, pretty pictures and nuggets of news are distributed on the street. Sections with weather reports, gossip columns, sports scores, and consumer advice have all been beefed up.

As circulation declined newspapers became more and more dependent on advertising for their revenues, particularly from local sources.

Today, both national and regional daily newspapers are owned by large media conglomerates. Such entities as Gannett, Knight Ridder, Tribune Co. and The New York Times Company own a number of the top newspapers in the U.S. The Tribune Co., for example, owns the *Los Angeles Times* and the *Chicago Tribune*, plus other papers. News Corporation, the parent of Fox Entertainment Group, publishes numerous English-language newspapers, including *The Wall Street Journal* and the *New York Post*.

Television and the Internet are largely responsible for the endangered state of modern print journalism. The number of Americans who read a daily newspaper dropped below 50 percent in 2007, and in 2009 the Pew Research Center found that for the first time the Internet topped newspapers as the leading news source.

The Internet has forced publications to find new ways to stay profitable. Newspapers today compete with well-funded Web sites such as Politico, Slate, and Salon, as well as blogs such as The Huffington Post, which by 2007 outranked all but six online newspapers in visitor counts even though the site itself creates little of its own content. Also in 2007, the Talking Points Memo became the first web-only publication to win a major journalism prize—the George Polk Award. Most major papers had free online versions as late as 2011, but the era of the subscription fee has arrived. In March 2011, visitors to *The New York Times* website could view up to 20 articles a month for free, but any additional access would cost between $15 and $35 per month. *The Wall Street Journal* offers an online version for $2 per week but when bundled with the print version, costs as little as 40 cents per week. *The New York Times*, *The Financial Times*, and *The Times of London* have also imple-

mented subscription fees, as the industry is rapidly moving towards this model.

In 2007, six companies accounted for nearly half of all newspaper circulation. There were massive job cuts in the print industry throughout 2008 and 2009, and papers across the country slashed original content, filed for bankruptcy, and in some cases printed their final editions. Print advertising revenue dropped by about 25 percent in 2007 and 2008, and in 2010 dropped to $22.8 billion, a decrease of 8.2 percent compared with 2009. Classifieds revenue, battered by Craigslist and other websites, declined 8.6 percent to $5.6 billion—a far cry from the $19.6 billion earned in 2000. The one bright spot for newspaper advertising revenue is in the online realm. Following declines in revenue in 2008 and 2009, online advertising rose in 2010 by 10.9 percent, bringing in $3 billion for the industry. This online growth, coupled with a slower decline in print revenue, is encouraging to publishers.

As print media wanes, online news continues to attract new readers. For the six-month period ending in October 2010, average weekly circulation for U.S. dailies dropped 5 percent and circulation for Sunday papers was down 4.5 percent from the previous year. Three of the nation's 25 largest papers reported declines of at least 10 percent. Among the sharpest drop in circulation was *Newsday's* (New York) 12 percent drop and the *San Francisco Chronicle's* 11 percent decrease. According to Nielsen Online, by 2009 print circulation of newspapers had dropped from a peak of 62 million a few decades ago to just 49 million. Online readership, however, has grown at an even faster rate, reaching almost 75 million American readers and 3.7 billion page views in January 2009. By the end of 2009, Amazon's Kindle offered nearly 100 papers, and in 2010 more versatile tablets—such as Apple's iPad—were introduced. In February 2011, News Corporation launched *The Daily*, an iPad-only newspaper available for purchase in app form. At 99 cents per week and $40 a year, *The Daily* is a much cheaper and constantly-updated alternative to traditional newspapers. *The Wall Street Journal*, *The New Yorker*, and *The Economist* also offer subscriptions for tablet versions of their papers, with many more expected by the end of 2011. In the words of the *Times*, "industry executives who once scoffed at the idea of an Internet-only product now concede that they are probably heading in that direction."

Magazines

The first magazines, single sheets covered front and back with opinion, gossip, and shipping news, circulated in the coffeehouses of early 18th-century London. Such literary giants as Daniel Defoe (*The Review*, 1704–13) and Samuel Johnson (*The Rambler*, 1750–52) wrote and edited some of these publications. The most successful practitioners of the trade were Joseph Addison (1672–1719) and Sir Richard Steele (1672–1729), who collaborated on *The Tatler* (1709–11) and *The Spectator* (1711–14). Most of the copy for these early periodicals was written by the editors themselves.

Inspired by their linguistic cousins across the Atlantic, colonial Americans started their own magazines. Benjamin Franklin's *General Magazine* published poetry and political articles, among other things, but ended its run in 1741 after only six issues.

The 19th Century

Only in the mid-19th century did magazines take on their modern form. These magazines presented more opinion and culturally focused content than newspapers, and they also targeted the wealthy, literate class. Among the more noteworthy magazines were *The Knickerbocker*, which ran from 1833 to 1865, and *Harper's Magazine*, which debuted in 1850. Harper's serialized stories and novels from prominent authors including Charles Dickens and William Makepeace Thackeray. *The Atlantic Monthly*, launched in 1857, was notable for commissioning short stories by Mark Twain and Bret Harte. Both the *Atlantic Monthly* and *Harper's* are still published today.

The advances in technology brought about by the Industrial Revolution greatly affected the magazine trade. Improved machinery and more efficient production allowed publishers to print their magazines at a lower cost. This meant magazines could be sold for lower prices and attract more readers. With more readers came more advertising, and magazines turned from organs of commentary for the upper class to periodicals of interest for the masses.

Other famous magazines of the late 19th century included *McClure's* and *Munsey's Magazine*, which were among the first to target the general public in earnest. Soon after its launch in 1893, *McClure's* published works by authors such as Sir Arthur Conan Doyle and Rudyard

Top 10 Magazines in Paid Circulation, 2009

Magazine	Subscriptions
1. *AARP The Magazine*	24,463,228
2. *AARP Bulletin*	24,174,159
3. *Reader's Digest*	7,629,105
4. *Better Homes and Gardens*	7,627,992
5. *Good Housekeeping*	4,641,651
6. *National Geographic*	4,602,119
7. *Woman's Day*	3,949,248
8. *Family Circle*	3,874,240
9. *Ladies' Home Journal*	3,850,782
10. *AAA Westways*	3,831,215

Source: Magazine Publishers of America (2010).

Top 10 Magazines by Advertising Revenue, 2008–09

Magazine	Advertising Revenues
1. *People*	$ 933,135,770
2. *Better Homes and Gardens*	811,825,109
3. *Sports Illustrated*	560,365,030
4. *Good Housekeeping*	508,230,819
5. *Family Circle*	442,686,001
6. *Time*	404,079,647
7. *Woman's Day*	398,037,552
8. *Cosmopolitan*	344,916,730
9. *In Style*	326,414,678
10. *Ladies' Home Journal*	321,071,844

Source: Magazine Publishers of America (2010).

Kipling. The magazine later distinguished itself through its muckraking articles. Muckraking was the turn-of-the-century term for a journalistic crusade, particularly against large corporations. Ida Tarbell wrote several stories in *McClure's* in the early 1900's that painstakingly exposed the questionable practices of John D. Rockefeller's monopolistic Standard Oil Company, becoming one of the creators of modern investigative journalism. *McClure's* folded in 1929.

Stylistically, magazines of this time were rather gray, with few pictures and lots of text. As artistic techniques improved, illustrations began to break the visual monotony. Cartoons provided one of the chief methods of magazine illustration. Thomas Nast, the founding father of political cartoons, doodled for *Harper's* in the late 19th century. Nast was also responsible for connecting American political parties with animals, and for the image of Uncle Sam, the gray-bearded figure who is symbolic of America. The rise of photography near the end of the century provided a startling innovation that made magazines more eye-catching—an improvement not lost on advertisers.

The 20th Century

One group of prominent contemporary magazines trace their history to the early 20th century. Henry Luce and Briton Hadden founded a weekly magazine called *Time* in 1923; they followed this successful venture with a business-focused magazine named *Fortune* in 1930. Six years later came an illustrated magazine called *Life*, and these three publications formed the cornerstone of what is now Time-Warner, one of the world's most powerful media organizations. The company added *Sports Illustrated*, one of today's top-circulating magazines, in 1954.

The New Yorker is another contemporary magazine that dates from the 1920's (the first issue was published on February 21, 1925). Upon foundation the magazine's object was to concentrate coverage on New York City, but the *New Yorker* soon broadened its scope to include short stories, poetry, cartoons, and news in its content.

In the 1960's magazines also served as a laboratory for experimental styles of journalism. Several writers, including Norman Mailer, Tom Wolfe, Gay Talese, and Hunter S. Thompson, practiced an innovative form of writing and reportage that came to be called "New Journalism." It broke away from the patterns of conventional journalism because it applied the narrative techniques of novels to nonfiction articles. These techniques included a focus on capturing dialogue and the author becoming a participant, rather than an observer, in the story.

Magazines Today

High-quality color and photography may be the most obvious differences between today's magazines and their predecessors of a century ago, but the layouts of magazines have adapted to the behavior of modern readers in other ways as well; stories jump across pages, eye-catching sidebars break out related content, and numerous quickly-read items are packed together at the front. Advertising takes up substantial portions of magazines, not least because advertising accounts for a substantial portion of magazine revenues. At the end of the first decade of the 21st century, magazine advertising declined dramatically, as the number of ad pages sold in 2009 dropped a whopping 25.6 percent from 2008. In 2010 the decline in sales

began to level off, with less than a 1 percent drop in pages sold. In fact, seven of the 12 categories that the Publishers Information Bureau tracks had a rise in ad pages sold, with a 16.9 percent increase in automotive advertising from the previous year. Circulation in 2010 was down a slight 1.5 percent, an improvement over the previous year's 2.2 percent drop. Single copy (non-subscription) purchases, however, declined more than 8 percent. One positive industry trend, according to *MediaFinder*, is that the number of magazines that folded in 2010 was 176, far fewer than the 596 magazines that went under in 2009.

The emergence of a younger readership accustomed to immediate information gratification, coupled with the rise of Internet news sources, has had a crippling effect on weekly news magazines. In December 2010, *U.S. News & World Report* stopped printing altogether and went entirely digital. *Newsweek*, after losing a third of its revenue between 2007 and 2009, was sold for the paltry sum of $1. *Time*, the last mass-market news weekly, saw a 20.3 percent drop in single copy sales. Not every publication fared so poorly. Niche news magazines such as *The New Yorker*, *The Economist*, *The Atlantic*, and *The Week* all saw gains in circulation in 2010.

The contemporary magazine industry is remarkable for the number of niche publications that seek a very specific audience. In 2008 the U.S. was served by more than 20,000 magazine titles, according to the American Society of Magazine Editors. While a magazine such as *Time* targets a large general audience, thousands of smaller publications aim for a niche audience with titles ranging from *Luxury Pools*, to *Redneck World*, to *Budget Travel*. There are also hundreds of trade magazines for every industry from media to machinery that concern themselves with a particular business.

Like newspapers, the emergence of tablet computers, led by the Apple iPad, has opened up a whole new world to magazine publishers. Many major magazines such as *Vanity Fair*, *GQ*, *Sports Illustrated* and *Time* offer apps for tablet computers. Unlike newspapers however, the magazine industry has yet to develop a subscription model. This forces the consumer to buy each magazine individually, costing them much more than the old paper subscriptions. In spite of this early hiccup, magazines are expected to thrive on this platform. Its clear crisp picture and ability to add multimedia and interactive advertising makes the tablet computer a natural future for the magazine industry.

Books

Writing and Printing

The development of writing can be considered a landmark of human history, the main catalyst of most human progress since its appearance about 6,000 years ago. But it would take more than 5,000 years for easy and rapid transmission of written thought and ideas to develop in the form of the printing press, the source of yet another revolution.

In Mesopotamia, traders in the thriving Sumerian culture were among the first in the world to see a practical use for writing and, by about 4000 B.C., professional scribes were recording business transactions and legal rulings by cutting pictographs and numerals in horizontal rows on round, handheld clay tablets. The scribe developed a stylus, a small triangle-tipped tool that allowed them to approximate the necessary symbols with a few quick stamps rather than more tedious drawing. Known today as "cuneiform" (from Latin for "wedge-shaped") writing, this Sumerian innovation spread throughout the Middle East between 2900 and 2600 B.C.

Meanwhile in Egypt, starting around 3000 B.C., a complex system of pictograms was combined with more traditional representational artwork to tell narrative stories about events or people. Many of the pictograms were painted or carved on temples, tombs, or items with religious importance; these characters were later call "hieroglyphics" (from Greek for "priestly-writing"). Egyptian scribes also used ink and brushes to write less formal (often historical and legal) documents in cursive script called "hieratic" on scrolls made from papyrus, a lightweight sheet made from the stem of a water plant from the Nile.

The Alphabet

Egyptian hieroglyphics and Sumerian cuneiform writing were familiar to the well-traveled traders of Phoenicia, and by 1500 B.C. Phoenician writers had borrowed elements of both systems to create their own written alphabet. The Phoenicians did not use pictograms to represent objects, but instead developed a series of 22 written letters that corresponded to each of their consonant sounds. While other phonetic alphabets existed, including one with 30 symbols used in Ugarit in Northern Syria, the Phoenician system spread to almost every culture that encountered it.

Across the Mediterranean, the Greeks adopted the Phoenician alphabet around 1300 B.C., although they modified some of the letter-forms and added vowels. (The word *alphabet* comes from the first two letters—alpha and beta—of the Greek lettering system.) The Greeks wrote with reed pens on papyrus and with styluses on tablets from right to left. They later began writing in both directions, creating a flow of letters back and forth. By the fifth century B.C., however, they had standardized their writing in rows of left to right and oriented all of their letters accordingly.

In Italy the Etruscans used the Greek alphabet and writing style as a model for their own and, by 700 B.C., Roman writers had borrowed and further modified the Greek and Etruscan alphabets to create the Latinate alphabet now in use throughout most of Europe and the Western world.

The Book

Egyptian, Greek, and Roman societies all developed literary cultures that used writing not just for commercial record keeping but to preserve histories, poems, plays, songs, and legends. Rulers and wealthy citizens built libraries for storing vast collections of books, almost all of which were written on papyrus or parchment scrolls. To stock these libraries, scribes were hired or enslaved to copy scrolls by hand. Since books could then be accessed by common people, censorship soon occurred, and individual scrolls or whole libraries were burned in order to suppress new ideas or punish enemies.

Around 250 B.C., the Romans began using parchment, a thin writing material made from animal skin, which was easier to write on and less expensive than the papyrus imported from Egypt. Instead of forming the parchment into long scrolls, some parchment makers cut the sheets into rectangular leaves, which they folded in half along the left edge to form a folio of four pages. Four leaves folded together formed a quarto, and longer manuscripts of several quartos were stacked and bound into a book form, known as a codex.

By the second century A.D., the codex form had been adopted by early Christians seeking to spread their new religion because it was easier to use and store than a scroll. The written Gospels proved very useful in acquiring and teaching new converts and, by the fourth century A.D., the Roman Catholic Church had created scriptoriums in monasteries where literate monks could copy Bibles and other works for use in devotional and missionary work.

The collapse of the Roman Empire slowed the spread of literacy, and many libraries were destroyed during the violence of the early medieval period. But book-copying centers in Constantinople and in religious centers across Europe still produced thousands of manuscripts. The high cost of parchment sometimes forced copyists to wash the ink off older texts and reuse the material for new works, and in order to further conserve parchment, many scribes slowly altered the large capital letters of Roman script to smaller forms. Each scriptorium developed a distinctive style of script. Celtic monks, for example, commonly added a larger, ornately decorated letter at the beginning of each paragraph.

In A.D. 780, Charlemagne, King of the Franks and future Holy Roman Emperor, charged the English scholar Alcuin with oversight of clerical education, which included a massive production of new books. In order to standardize the much altered Roman alphabet across the Empire, Alcuin devised the Carolingian script, which for the first time formally distinguished between capital (majuscule) and lowercase (miniscule) letters. Monastery scribes then spread the new script throughout Europe between 800 and 1200.

Paper and Printing

While writers and scribes in Europe wrote primarily on parchment or higher quality vellum (also made from fine animal skin), by A.D. 100 the Chinese had invented paper, an excellent and inexpensive writing material made from scraps of cloth and fiber. Paper was first introduced in Europe when Arabian merchants brought it to Italy in 1150. Italian manufacturers learned the technique and began making paper in the 13th century, and over the next two centuries it was adopted throughout Europe for use in books and letters.

During the Renaissance, the low cost of paper combined with a rising interest in learning created an unprecedented demand for books. Newly founded schools and universities required textbooks and literary works, and booksellers hired copyists to produce thousands of manuscripts. These professional scribes further altered the elegant but labor intensive Carolingian script to form several regional versions of the more efficient black letter or Gothic script.

In the early 14th century, European artisans imported the Chinese method of using carved wooden blocks and pigmented ink to print multiple copies of an image—including words—onto paper. The carving was laborious and the blocks wore out quickly, so block printing was generally restricted to short books, pamphlets, and playing cards.

The Printing Press

Johannes Gensfleisch was born about 1397 in Mainz, Germany, and later adopted the name of his family's ancestral city, Gutenberg. He trained as a goldsmith and extended his metalworking knowledge to printing. However, instead of *xylography*, using single woodblocks to print each page, he began experimenting with the idea of *typography*, using moveable blocks for each letter of text.

By 1444, Gutenberg was finally able to produce calendars and other small works. In 1450, the financier Johann Fust loaned Gutenberg additional money, and Gutenberg soon perfected his combination of moveable cast metal type, oil-based ink, and a lever-operated printing press. Between 1452 and 1455, Gutenberg produced the first major printed book in history, a massive two-volume Latin Bible of over 1,280 pages with 42 lines of type and two columns per page. He printed 200 copies, with lettering designed after the Gothic script then used for manuscripts and hired an illustrator to hand-decorate them.

By the time Gutenberg died in 1468, his inventions had been copied by dozens of other entrepreneurs. Many books were still hand-copied or block-printed, and some book collectors shunned the new machine-produced texts, but the technology spread swiftly. In 1461, Albrecht Pfister published *Der Edelstein*, the first illustrated printed book, and by 1500 printing presses had been established in 282 cities and 20 countries throughout Europe. Between 8 and 24 million individual books were in print, representing more than 30,000 titles.

Books printed in the 15th century are known as the *incunabula* (from the Latin for "swaddling clothes," indicating something in its infancy), and they include Chaucer's *Canterbury Tales*, produced by William Caxton, the first English printer, as well as many Bibles and the *Peregrinatino in terrum sanctum*, the first illustrated travel-book, produced in 1486 in Mainz by Erhard Reuwich, a Dutch artist and printer. The incunabula varied widely as printers chose texts likely to appeal to their nearby constituents and designed typefaces based on local writing styles.

The Power of Print

The power of the written word grew exponentially with the printing press. In 1517, supporters of Martin Luther used the new technology to print and distribute copies of his "95 Theses" against the Catholic Church, and within weeks Luther's radical ideas had reached beyond Germany to help spur the Protestant Reformation.

This new power, however, revived old methods of censorship. Following the publication of Luther's German-language "September Bible" in 1522, William Tyndale printed 3,000 copies of his own English translation of the New Testament in 1526, but Catholic authorities seized and burned almost all of the books as soon as they arrived in London. Although Tyndale himself was later executed as a heretic, his translations served as the basis for English Bibles published under the reign of King Henry VIII.

The rapid and inexpensive production of printed matter promoted secular thought as well, and the ideas of 17th-century writers such as René Descartes and Thomas Hobbes reached far more people more quickly than had those of earlier philosophers. The proliferation of books fueled scientific discoveries, literary creation, and political upheavals.

In the New World, printing presses were established almost as soon as the colonists arrived. Benjamin Franklin began his printing career at age 12, founded America's first circulating library in 1731, and built his reputation with *Poor Richard's Almanack*, which spread Franklin's thrift-promoting adages throughout the colonies. Thomas Paine used the press to an even more dramatic purpose with *Common Sense*, a short essay that greatly influenced the Declaration of Independence and stoked enthusiasm for the American Revolution.

Throughout history, book burning and censorship has been a common tool wielded by authorities to crush and stifle dissenting views on politics and religion. During the Spanish Inquisition, copies of the Koran, the Muslim holy book, were burned while their owners were forced to convert, flee, or accept death. In Europe and in the American-English colonies, government continuously prohibited political dissent, as well as books with explicit sexual content. In the 20th century the Nazis staged huge rallies in Germany where they burned thousands of books, many by Jewish authors and about Jewish culture.

Governments aren't the only obstacles to censorship-free books. Readers object to material so often that the American Library Association keeps a list of the most challenged books. A "challenge" is defined as an attempt to remove or restrict materials, based upon the objections of a person or group. The last book banned by the United States was John Cleland's *Fanny Hill* or *Memoirs of a Woman of Pleasure* (1749). Originally banned in 1821 for obscenity, it was republished in 1963 under a modified name and promptly banned again. This led all the way to the Supreme Court where *Memoirs v. Massachusetts* (1966) decided that the ban was improper. Today many books are banned from schools and libraries when citizens complain about their content. Among the most recently-challenged books are *And Tango Makes Three*, the story of two homosexual penguins, and the *Twilight* and *ttyl* series for young adults. Also included are the literary classics *Catcher in the Rye* and *To Kill a Mockingbird*, which are among the most challenged books in American history.

Technological Advances in Printing

In the first three centuries following the invention of the printing press, the design and durability of moveable type was improved by new metal formulation and casting techniques. Typeface design became a minor art form, but the press itself was changed only modestly. Then, in rapid succession, several innovations of the Industrial Revolution broadened the ease and accessibility of printing.

In 1796, Alois Senefelder invented the technique of lithography, which uses prepared etched plates rather than individual moveable type. The lithographic process proved ideal for full-color printing and remains a popular publishing method for high-quality text, illustrated books, and magazines.

The steam press came along in 1801, operating like a standard press but much faster, making 1,100 impressions per hour. In 1843, the American Richard March Hoe replaced the flatbed printing plate of the steam press with a revolving print cylinder that could produce millions of pages a day.

These changes and later developments, such as offset lithography (invented in 1903) and the digital printing popularized in the late 20th century, have all increased the speed of printing and publication since Gutenberg's day.

Dictionaries

As languages and words began to develop, the need arose to catalog the meanings and spellings of these words. The earliest-known examples of dictionaries date back to Sumeria in 2300 B.C. These cuneiform tablets contained wordlists in both the Sumerian and Akkadian languages, as all early dictionaries were bilingual. Some of the earliest dictionaries known to the modern world were written in Sanskrit, Chinese, and Japanese. Arabic dictionaries between the 8th and 14th centuries were the first to organize words in alphabetical order by the first letter instead of by topic.

Modern European dictionaries were originally bilingual and early English dictionaries were simply glossaries of foreign words with the accompanying English definition. *Elementarie*, written by Richard Mulcaster in 1592 was a non-alphabetical list of 8,000 English words. *A Tale Alphabeticall*, written by Robert Cawdrey in 1604, was the first purely English alphabetical dictionary, although it was widely viewed as incomplete and unreliable. The state of the English dictionary remained this way for 150 years until Samuel Johnson's *A Dictionary of the English Language* was printed in 1755. *A Dictionary of the English Language* was the first comprehensive, reliable English dictionary, and in testament to its lasting value, many people believe today it was the first English dictionary published. It remained the standard for over 150 years until the *Oxford English Dictionary* was released in 1928. This 12-volume edition remains the most trusted and comprehensive dictionary to this day, with revisions added every three months.

In 1828, American spelling reformer Noah Webster completed *An American Dictionary of the English Language*. Believing that English spelling rules were unnecessarily complex, Webster introduced Americanized spellings, replacing words like favourite, colour, and programme with the simplified versions: favorite, color, and program. He also added American words that didn't appear in English dictionaries such as "skunk" and "squash."

As dictionaries became more common, they also became more specialized. *Black's Law Dictionary* was first published in 1891 and is currently in its ninth edition. *Stedman's Medical Dictionary* debuted in 1911 and remains widely used. The market for niche publications remains strong; a quick look at Amazon.com will turn up the *Dictionary of Food Ingredients*, *The Little Dictionary of Fashion* and *The Complete Nautical Dictionary*, to name just a few.

Dictionaries have started to move into the digital age. The website Dictionary.com reports 50 million monthly users and 3.6 billion words searched annually. Many publishers offer e-book versions of their dictionaries as well as the standard large book format. With the rise of devices like the iPad and Kindle, that include built in dictionary software, the future of the large hard cover dictionary remains in question.

Books Today

In the year 2000 there were approximately 122,000 new books and editions published. By 2009 that number had skyrocketed to over 1.3 million, and by 2010 it had reached 3 million. In 2010 Fiction led the way with 47,392 new titles, followed by Juvenile with 32,638. Sociology / Economics, Science, and Religion rounded out the top five categories. The largest annual percentage increases were in the categories of Computers (51 percent), Science (37 percent), and Technology (35 percent).

Ironically the computer, predicted by many to be the book industry's death knell, has been responsible for the overall increase in book production since 1990. An array of computer programs reduce the cost of production for publishers, and the use of print-on-demand capabilities for small and major publishers continues to flourish. This means that books can be produced economically in small numbers. The Bowker Industry Study projects that 2.7 million titles were produced in 2010 that fall outside the definition of "traditional publishing," including both print-on-demand and self-published titles, and electronic editions, an increase of over 1.7 million from the previous year.

According to the Association of American Publishers, 2010 book sales in the U.S. increased by 3.6 percent from 2009 to $11.6 billion. Much of this rise was due to the increasing popularity of e-books; adult hardcover, paperback, and mass market sales were down 34 percent and the children's and young adult categories declined 16.1 percent.

The trend away from traditional books toward e-books has also had an enormous effect on bookstores. Borders, one of the nation's largest brick and mortar bookstores, filed for bankruptcy in 2011 and announced it would close more than half of its stores.

Barnes & Noble has shifted a large portion of its sales to their website, and now offers over 2 million e-books. Barnes & Noble also released its own e-book reader, the NOOK, at the end of 2009.

Several major authors have begun to bypass traditional publishers altogether. Seth Godin, a best-selling marketing author, is offering print-on-demand options as well as various electronic formats through his blog. Popular author Stephen King has been offering self-published online books since 2000. Traditional publishers aren't going to go out of business overnight, but for an industry undergoing rapid changes and grappling with advances in technology, the future promises to be very different.

Google Books

In 2002 Google began scanning and uploading digitized copies of books that were commonly found in libraries. To take advantage of this information, Google Book Search was launched in 2004. Users could view abstracts of copyrighted books and download and view full copies of books that were in the public domain. Almost immediately, the Association of American Publishers and the Author's Guild filed lawsuits. They accused Google of copyright infringement because they were creating digital copies of copyrighted works.

The opposing sides began to work out a settlement in 2006 and finally hammered out an agreement in 2008. Google would pay out $125 million, a portion of which goes to aggrieved rights-holders. Another portion would create a Book Rights Registry to monitor all future rights payments. After a 2009 amendment, the agreement came before Judge Denny Chin of the United States Court of Appeals 2nd Circuit who roundly rejected it, saying the plan violated federal copyright laws.

The case is an important moment in the world of electronic publishing. As sales of e-books continue to grow, so do the opportunities for piracy. Carefully maintaining copyrights is one way to avoid the fate of the recording industry, which saw millions of dollars in profits vanish with the arrival of MP3s and digital music.

Electronic Books

E-books have been around in primitive formats since the early 1970's. Most were technical manuals, because access to computers was limited to certain professions. With the emergence of the Internet, transferring electronic files became greatly simplified, which allowed various e-book formats to grow. With the development of dedicated e-readers, the market began to flourish.

Although several e-readers had already been released, the 2007 debut of the Amazon Kindle changed the market completely. The Kindle sold out within five hours of its release and remained out of stock for five months. The ink-based graphics and anti-glare screen kept much of the feel of reading a regular book, a sharp contrast with earlier models. Soon, dozens of e-readers appeared on the scene, such as Sony's PRS-500.

The explosion of e-readers had an immediate impact on electronic book sales. In June 2008, e-book sales reached $4,900,000, an annual increase of 87.4 percent. By the third quarter of 2010 revenues had skyrocketed to nearly $120 million dollars.

In the second quarter of 2010, Amazon.com reported for the first time that sales of e-books had surpassed the number of hardcover sales, at 140 e-books for every 100 hardcover books. By 2011, e-books had surpassed paperback sales on the site, although paperback sales are still much higher in the general U.S. market. According to the American Association of Publishers, as of 2011 electronic books commanded an estimated 17 percent of the market, up from 8.5 percent in 2010. Some estimates state that this share will rise to as much as 25 percent by 2012.

The arrival of Apple's iPad in early 2010 revealed the true potential of the e-book market, tapping into more than 125 million iTunes customers. According to the Book Industry Study Group, 25 percent of people who bought e-books in 2010 said they bought fewer print books than before. Fifteen percent reported they buy no print books at all.

Radio

The Evolution of Broadcasting

Early Uses of Radio The earliest practical applications of wireless technology involved communication between ships and land-based stations to coordinate information about cargo pickup schedules, shipping routes, and weather conditions. Wireless technology made its most dramatic impact by saving lives in several well-publicized maritime disasters. The most famous of these occurred in April 1912 when the ocean liner *Titanic* struck an iceberg while on its maiden voyage across the Atlantic. Most of the passengers and crew perished, but a ship that had picked up the *Titanic's* distress signal from 50 miles away rescued nearly 700 survivors.

In the years leading up to World War I, such events led hobbyists to purchase radio equipment and build their own transmitters and receivers. Thousands of these amateurs, eager to communicate with fellow radio enthusiasts, began experimental broadcasts, first using Morse code, then venturing into the transmission of voice and music. Radio corporations that had been formed to promote and capitalize on point-to-point communication began to glimpse the commercial potential of broadcasting to American homes. David Sarnoff (1891–1971), the future chairman of RCA, began his career as commercial manager of American Marconi, where he was credited with writing a 1916 memo that first recommended "a plan of development which would make radio a 'household utility' in the same sense as the piano or phonograph." As he observed the rapidly expanding market for household goods, Sarnoff proposed manufacturing a receiver that could take its place in the home as a "Radio Music Box," transforming radio from an instrument of two-way communication into a source of domestic amusement for the American family.

With the explosion of interest in radio, the U.S. Congress passed the Radio Act of 1912, establishing public policy and standards of operation in an attempt to impose order on the airwaves. This legislation gave the government priority and control over radio communication, including the licensing of transmitters. The government exercised its control upon the country's entry into World War I. There were more than 8,500 licensed amateurs in 1917 when the government ordered all amateur transmissions to cease and the navy assumed operational control of all radio stations for the duration of the war. To promote research and innovation, the government also untangled the welter of competing patents by suspending proprietary license agreements and creating a patents pool that gathered together the many patents held by individuals and corporations that were necessary for the operation of radio.

The Business of Broadcasting, 1919–1926

The Creation of RCA At the end of World War I the question of whether or not radio in the U.S. should be defined as a matter of public service or of private enterprise caused a serious debate in business and government circles. In the war's aftermath, with radio essentially operating under government control, some thought American radio might follow the model of the postal service and continue as a business operated solely by the federal government. European countries had begun to adopt this model by establishing radio as a state monopoly. On the other hand, the prospect of a government monopoly in the U.S. provoked strenuous opposition from amateur radio operators, manufacturers, and those companies that had stations seized by the government during the war.

But if radio was not to be operated as a government monopoly, how would American companies be able to compete against British Marconi, the world's leading radio corporation? British Marconi held key patents and dominated manufacturing and sales in the United States through its subsidiary, American Marconi. Public opinion strongly opposed foreign ownership of American radio, so placing radio in the hands of American owners became a national priority. Without a government monopoly to coordinate the development of radio, however, the marketplace had produced a tangled mess of competing patents and proprietary license agreements that stalled technological advances.

General Electric, a titan of the electric industry, solved the problem by engineering an American radio monopoly when it founded a new company that would soon become the industry leader. With the federal government still in control of American Marconi stations seized during the war and spurred by a growing sentiment against foreign ownership, British Marconi sold its holdings in American Marconi to GE in 1919. In October 1919 GE established the Radio Corporation of America as a subsidiary and transferred all tangible assets of American Marconi to the new company. Through this arrangement, GE planned to manufacture equipment, while RCA would sell receivers and operate the company's radio stations.

The chief obstacle to manufacturing quality radio receivers was that AT&T controlled key patents to De Forest's Audion tube. This problem was solved in 1920 when GE, RCA, and AT&T signed a patents pooling agreement that provided for the cross licensing of each company's patents. United Fruit, which controlled several radio patents because of its shipping interests, joined the pool in 1921. Westinghouse, GE's chief competitor and the last major company that might have competed with this growing alliance, joined the pool and acquired a stake in RCA in 1921.

By 1922 all the pieces of an American radio monopoly had been assembled. The companies in the patents pool became the majority shareholders in RCA. GE was the largest shareholder with 25.8 percent of the company's stock, followed by Westinghouse with 20.6 percent, and AT&T and United Fruit, both of which owned roughly four percent. With control of nearly 2,000 patents necessary for the manufacture of radio transmitters and receivers, the companies in the patents pool carved up the radio industry for themselves. GE and Westinghouse manufactured radio receivers, which were sold exclusively by RCA. AT&T, through its Western Electric subsidiary, manufactured and sold transmitters. From this intricate set of alliances a viable radio industry was born.

Broadcasting Booms Quickly   Once the patents pool had established a viable industry structure for radio manufacturing, factory-assembled receivers began to arrive in the marketplace. Designed to compete with phonographs as a domestic amusement and to complement household furnishings, the new receivers brought radio out of father's workshop and into the family parlor, where it began the transition from an astonishing gadget into a medium for the masses.

Westinghouse became the first manufacturer to move into broadcasting when it established regularly scheduled evening broadcasts from 100-watt station KDKA in Pittsburgh. The first broadcast reported the returns on elec-

tion night, November 2, 1920. By offering a regular program service, Westinghouse hoped to sell receivers and to promote the company's brand name. Soon the radio craze was sweeping the nation. In 1921 there were only 30 stations conducting regular broadcasts; by the end of 1922 there were 600. Radio manufacturers and dealers offered programs in order to tempt people into buying radio sets. Universities, churches, and newspapers began broadcasting in order to extend their service to their communities. In 1921 one in every 500 American households had a radio set; by 1926 there was one radio for every six households.

Advertising Comes to Radio   As stations expanded their programming they faced the inescapable question of how a program service should be financed. In European countries the answer was to subsidize program service through taxes or license fees paid by owners of receivers. In the U.S. the answer had to be found in the marketplace. By applying insights from the telephone industry, AT&T introduced two concepts—commercial sponsorship and networks—that transformed the radio business. In 1922 AT&T opened radio station WEAF in New York City, where it introduced the concept of *toll broadcasting*. In the telephone business, AT&T charged customers a toll for the length of time they used its long-distance telephone wires. AT&T proposed the same model for radio, offering to sell time by the minute to anyone who wanted to use its station. The first commercial—a 10-minute sales pitch for an apartment complex in Queens—appeared on WEAF during the evening of August 28, 1922. By 1923 Gimbels department store and other New York businesses were taking a less direct route to consumers, forgoing the extended sales pitch and instead sponsoring entertainment programs.

The next step for AT&T was to use its telephone wires in order to interconnect individual stations. This network (or "chain," as it was then called) gave sponsors access to a larger audience and allowed AT&T to charge higher rates for advertising. By 1924, WEAF had become the flagship of a 20-station network operating as far west as Chicago.

AT&T's innovations were not without controversy. Many Americans were alarmed by the rise of radio advertising and distrusted the expansion of networks. Much early advertising was *institutional*; companies hoped that a listener's gratitude for a particular program would translate into goodwill for the company and its products. Critics and politicians argued that it would be inappropriate for radio to bring *direct* advertising, in which a sponsor blatantly promoted its products, into American homes, but direct advertising soon appeared. Others argued that broadcasting was an inherently local phenomenon and that networks would inevitably undermine radio's local character. AT&T grew tired of the controversy and of the competition in the radio industry. In 1926 the telephone company sold station WEAF to RCA and withdrew from the patents pool. In the years to follow, AT&T's innovative use of advertising and networking would serve as the essential financial structure of broadcasting.

The Need for Regulation   Radio grew so quickly that by 1925 listeners in many cities complained that signal interference had begun to dim the appeal of listening. Some of this was caused by the equipment of the day—transmitters drifted from their intended frequency, receivers were hard to tune—but the most pressing problem was that too many stations shared a narrow band of the spectrum. Most transmitters of the era were not terribly powerful; at 100–500 watts, they could send a reliable signal 20–50 miles. As more ambitious stations began to transmit with ratings as high as 5,000 watts, however, they overpowered weaker signals even at a distance.

Washington recognized the need for new legislation, but broadcasting presented both technical and social challenges that changed with each new innovation. Secretary of Commerce Herbert Hoover held four annual conferences between 1922 and 1925, but no clear consensus emerged. Congress wasn't able to pass a comprehensive new radio bill until February 1927.

The Radio Act of 1927 left many questions unanswered, but it created the Federal Radio Commission (F.R.C.), a temporary agency charged with bringing order to the airwaves. In order to operate, radio stations needed a license from the F.R.C., which was responsible for assigning transmission frequencies, determining the location and power of a station's transmitter, and setting up signal coverage areas. The Radio Act also stipulated that licensees bear a responsibility to society, but refrained from specifying those obligations. Because there were vastly more applicants than available channel frequencies, those fortunate enough to be selected for a broadcast license would be expected to operate in the "public interest, convenience, and/or necessity." These vague and virtually unenforceable expectations became the cornerstone of broadcasting policy in America. By imposing order on the airwaves while limiting the public obligations of broadcasters, the legislation cleared the ground for the expansion of commercial radio and the rise of networks.

The Era of Network Radio, 1927–47

The Rise of National Networks   Broadcasting began as a local event. Each station operated independently and devised its own solution to the challenges of addressing an audience, providing a program service, and financing its operations. Radio listeners heard voices from their own communities, voices that sounded like their own, and music they recognized from church or the local dance hall. This changed with the emergence of NBC and CBS as national networks in the late 1920's. By making news and entertainment available simultaneously to listeners across the nation, networks transformed radio into the central cultural medium of American society.

NBC   The era of network radio began in September 1926 when RCA, led by chairman David Sarnoff, formed the National Broadcasting Company (NBC), with ownership held by RCA (50 percent), GE (30 percent), and Westinghouse (20 percent). The first network broadcast took place on November 15, 1926, originating from RCA's New York station, WEAF. The four-hour program, featuring singers, orchestras, and comedians, was broadcast live from the Grand Ballroom of the Waldorf-Astoria Hotel in New York over a network of 21 affiliate stations stretching as far west as Kansas City. In January 1927, NBC added a second network originating from its other New York station, WJZ, and the two networks were designated as NBC-Red and NBC-Blue. By the end of 1928, as NBC added affiliates and programs, both networks offered full-time coast-to-coast programming.

Backed by the financial resources of its wealthy corporate patrons, NBC entered the radio business with overwhelming advantages. NBC directly owned and operated 10 stations that formed the core of its networks. The majority of these were powerful stations, broadcasting on exclusive, clear-channel frequencies at 50,000 watts with signals that could be heard for hundreds of miles. Independently owned stations joined the network as affiliates. NBC supplied these stations with live programs that no independent station could afford to produce on its own. By coordinating stations around the country, NBC was able to accumulate listeners and then sell access to this newly created mass audience to advertisers. For the evening hours, when more people listened to radio, NBC supplied programs sponsored by national advertisers. The network paid affiliates a fee to broadcast the programs and charged the advertisers a much larger fee for access to a national audience. Because these stations needed to fill many hours each day, NBC also produced "sustaining" programs that affiliates could purchase in order to sell time to local advertisers. By 1933, the two NBC networks had 52 full-time and 36 part-time affiliates, or 15 percent of all the stations in the country.

CBS Unlike NBC, which was the favored child of America's largest companies, the Columbia Broadcasting System (CBS) was an orphan when William S. Paley (1901–90) purchased a controlling interest in September 1928. Paley courted new affiliates by offering more generous contracts than those being dangled by NBC. Instead of requiring affiliates to purchase sustaining programs, CBS gave away this basic program service free of charge. In exchange, CBS asked for "option time," a guaranteed number of hours in the affiliate's evening schedule. An NBC affiliate might choose not to air some of the network's programs, but CBS could guarantee sponsors that their advertisements would reach a national audience. During Paley's first year CBS had only 17 affiliates, but by 1933 it had surpassed NBC with 91 affiliates, or 16 percent of all stations.

NBC and CBS defined the successful radio network: a central corporate structure based in New York, live production from New York studios, a stable of powerful stations owned and operated by the network, affiliate contracts with the strongest stations in the largest remaining markets, and exclusive original programming that appealed to listeners. By the early 1930's, any station that wanted to compete in its local market felt it necessary to affiliate with either NBC or CBS.

The Federal Communications Commission

When Franklin D. Roosevelt became president in 1933, he appointed a commission that proposed streamlining the federal regulation of radio by creating a permanent Federal Communications Commission (F.C.C.) with responsibility for the regulation of radio and television, along with interstate telephone and telegraph use. As a result, Congress passed the Communications Act of 1934, which would govern American communications policy for the next six decades. This milestone legislation called for the F.C.C. to administer a national communications policy capable of inspiring confidence among industry leaders and the general public by establishing technical standards and operational protocols.

Virtually all of the F.C.C.'s power over the radio and television industries resided in its authority for granting broadcast licenses to local stations. Rather than support a highly centralized form of broadcasting like the national public service networks being established in European countries, American communications policy celebrated the fundamental principle of "localism," convinced that American democracy would be served best by independent local stations operating without excessive government supervision. The agency's power of enforcement came from its ability to revoke, or refuse to renew, the license of a local station—something that has happened rarely.

The Communications Act of 1934 recognized that broadcasting takes place over frequencies of the electromagnetic spectrum that constitute a rare public resource. In exchange for granting a license to use these scarce frequencies, the F.C.C. has a right to make certain demands of broadcasters. Moreover, since radio and television signals bring the public world directly into the home, broadcasters should bear a social responsibility that isn't demanded of publishers or theater owners. This responsibility was articulated as a demand that stations operate in the "public interest, convenience and necessity." In practice, this meant that stations added a few noncommercial, public service programs—religious or community information programs—usually tucked away in early morning or late evening hours that were undesirable to advertisers. With the public interest fulfilled by these programs, stations were free to pursue commercial interests.

By the late 1930's, members of Congress had begun to pressure the F.C.C. to investigate the monopolistic practices of the networks. Local stations complained about the increasingly restrictive terms of network affiliation contracts, which had tilted heavily in favor of the networks as network programming gained popularity and NBC and CBS acquired leverage as a result. Spurred by Congress, the F.C.C. conducted hearings on the structure and practices of network radio, which were known at the time as "chain broadcasting." The three-year investigation resulted in the 1941 publication of the F.C.C.'s *Report on Chain Broadcasting*. A report that might have questioned the very legitimacy of commercial networks essentially left the network system intact, choosing instead to concentrate criticism on RCA's undue influence in operating two networks. The report called for the separation of the two NBC networks, a decision that RCA vigorously appealed. In October 1943, NBC reluctantly sold its Blue network for $8 million to Life Savers candy tycoon Edward J. Noble (1884–1961). In 1944 Noble christened this new network the American Broadcasting Company (ABC), and it would eventually become a viable third network.

Network Radio Programming

National radio networks didn't conquer American radio overnight. Many local stations created popular programs starring local celebrities, and some of these lasted for decades. Independent stations with powerful signals introduced programs that appealed to regional tastes, and radio made a particularly strong impression on once-isolated rural listeners. In the 1920's these listeners embraced country-and-Western music when Chicago station WLS began broadcasting the "National Barn Dance" and Nashville station WSM debuted the "Grand Ole Opry." The signals from these 50,000-watt clear-channel stations could be heard throughout the Midwest and South.

Most local stations were on the air for 12–18 hours each day and couldn't afford to create original programs day-in and day-out. They filled many of those hours with recordings—musical phonograph records or wax-disc "transcriptions" of speeches and talk—but embraced the networks because only the networks had the financial resources to supply new, live programs on a daily basis. As these local stations relayed the network signal, network radio helped listeners negotiate local, regional, and national identities by addressing them as members of a mass audience—a national audience for news, entertainment, and, of course, brand-name goods.

Broadcast News Beginning in 1933, President Roosevelt used radio to speak directly to Americans in a series of "Fireside Chats." Roosevelt's informal speaking style and naturalistic approach to radio introduced a more intimate style of political communication that departed significantly from the grand traditions of political oratory. Radio also brought a new intimacy to the coverage of news events, as demonstrated by the emotions stirred up by radio coverage of the 1935 trial of Bruno Hauptmann, the man convicted of kidnapping the baby of aviation hero Charles Lindbergh.

Radio not only presented the news, but also brought immediacy to the coverage of world events by enabling reporters to report directly from the scene. As reporters bore witness to current events, they brought a distant world closer to radio listeners. Nowhere was this more evident than in the period 1939–41, when reporters for CBS and NBC covered the war in Europe, using short wave radio to send live reports across the Atlantic ocean. Standing on a rooftop during the nightly bombardments of the London blitz, CBS's Edward R. Murrow (1908–65) brought the war to American radio listeners, sharing not

only his personal impressions and encounters with Londoners, but also the sounds of air-raid sirens, police whistles, and explosions—a city under siege in the very moment of its distress.

Entertainment and Advertising In learning to entertain a national audience, the radio networks introduced virtually every genre that has subsequently appeared on television. The networks deserve little credit for actually inventing these genres, because advertising agencies handled the production of nearly all entertainment programs during the era of network radio, when each program had only a single sponsor. Agencies wanted programs to be compatible with their clients' marketing goals, while networks wanted to minimize operating expenses and thus saw themselves primarily as conduits for advertisers to reach consumers. The agencies hired performers and staff, supervised writing and rehearsals, contracted for studio facilities, and presented the finished product with the sponsor's commercials integrated into the flow of the program. The line separating entertainment and advertising was seldom apparent to radio listeners, who grew accustomed to a fictional character's casual mention of a product, or a star's complete identification with a sponsor. Many programs bore the name of the sponsor, and many stars represented a single brand for years at a time. One of radio's most popular performers gleefully introduced himself each week as Bob "Pepsodent" Hope. His movie partner, Bing Crosby, hosted *Kraft Music Hall* for a decade (1936–46).

Daytime Programs In order to advertise products to women, agencies invented programs for the daytime schedule, when the listening audience was composed largely of housewives. These programs were designed to encourage audience loyalty, while accommodating a preoccupied listener who might be doing housework or taking care of children. The origins of the morning talk show can be found in programs that intended to be the radio equivalent of *Good Housekeeping* magazine. Hosted by cheerful men and women who spoke directly to homemakers, these programs offered genial conversation, recipes, health information, and household advice. Hosts like Mary Margaret McBride (1899–1976) became celebrities and established long careers with these broadcasts.

The *soap opera*, as its name suggests, was invented to serve the needs of companies like Procter and Gamble that intended to sell household cleaning supplies to women consumers. Inspired by the structure of serialized fiction in newspapers and magazines, soap operas wove characters into dense emotional entanglements that continued from one daily 15-minute installment to the next. Irna Phillips (1901–73) is credited with creating the first daytime soap opera, *Painted Dreams*, which debuted in 1930. In a long career, Phillips produced many of the most enduring soap operas on radio and television—including *Guiding Light*, which aired for five decades—and trained more than one generation of soap opera writers and producers. The husband-and-wife team of Frank and Anne Hummert were the most prolific producers of radio soap operas. In order to meet the overwhelming demand for daily dramas during the era of network radio, they employed a staff of more than 30 writers.

Prime Time Radio   The networks and advertisers referred to the evening hours as *prime time* because the largest audiences tuned in during the evening, so networks could charge the highest rates for advertising during this period. In developing prime time, the networks essentially created a new cultural experience for Americans, who learned to gather around the radio in the evening hours in order to share a central cultural experience with their own families and a nation of fellow listeners. The most popular prime time programs became cultural institutions and their stars the icons of American entertainment.

The *musical-variety* genre was transplanted almost directly from vaudeville and often featured vaudeville performers or popular singers as hosts. Rudy Vallee, Ed Wynn, Eddie Cantor, and Fred Allen were among the most successful early stars; Jack Benny, George Burns and Gracie Allen, Bob Hope, and Bing Crosby had the greatest success. Many of the era's big band orchestras—led by Benny Goodman, Glenn Miller, the Dorsey Brothers, Duke Ellington, and others—appeared in their own programs or were featured on others.

Alongside professional entertainers and musicians, listeners also enjoyed hearing people like themselves—average Americans—appear on network radio. Listeners flocked to "amateur hour" programs that gave aspiring performers a shot at fame and fortune. The most celebrated of these was *Major Bowes and His Original Amateur Hour*, which premiered in 1934 and introduced, among others, a young singer from New Jersey named Frank Sinatra. The quiz or game show was another innovative genre that allowed nonprofessionals to appear on radio. It is not surprising that many of these programs—including *Stop the Music!*, *Quiz Kids*, and *Truth or Consequences*—were transplanted directly to television. In a celebrity-obsessed culture, talent competitions and quiz shows have allowed anonymous Americans to grasp fame, if only temporarily.

Broadcasting's most enduring entertainment genre—the *situation comedy*—also has roots in the comic routines of vaudeville, but came to stand by itself as writers and performers crossed vaudeville's comic sketches with the ongoing storylines of serialized fiction. The most popular and influential of all the programs in the first decade of network radio—and the progenitor of the situation comedy—was *Amos 'n' Andy*. Created and performed by Freeman Gosden (1899–1982) and Charles Correll (1890–1972), *Amos 'n' Andy* centered on the lives of two African-American friends who had migrated from the South to an all-black neighborhood in a northern city (originally the south side of Chicago, later changed to Harlem), where they operate the Fresh Air Taxi Company. It was no secret to radio listeners that Gosden and Correll were white men speaking in comic black dialect.

By the end of 1929, *Amos 'n' Andy* (broadcast in 15-minute installments six evenings a week) had become the most important program in radio, the inspiration for many people to purchase their first radio set. Because of its success in building a loyal following of 40 million listeners, many elements of *Amos 'n' Andy* came to define the situation comedy: a familiar setting; central characters surrounded by a recurring cast of comic characters; and an episodic structure that introduces and resolves a new comic incident each time. This format gave rise to a few sitcoms set in a workplace or a public setting, such as *Duffy's Tavern*, and inspired an endless series of situation comedies revolving around the experiences of a family. This pattern began with *The Rise of the Goldbergs* (later known as *The Goldbergs*), the *Fibber McGee and Molly Show*, *Easy Aces*, *The Aldrich Family*, and *The Adventures of Ozzie and Harriet*, and to this day shows no sign of ending. Many of the most popular comedies of the era—*The Jack Benny Program*, *The George Burns and Gracie Allen Show*, *The Edgar Bergen and Charlie McCarthy Show*—featured celebrity performers playing themselves in comic episodes.

Prime time network radio relied on two dramatic formats: dramatic series and anthology dramas. A dramatic series presented the adventures of a hero or a tale of mystery in 30-minute episodes; these series were most directly influenced by pulp fiction and comic strips—westerns (*The Lone Ranger*, *The Cisco Kid*, *Gunsmoke*), detective shows (*The Shadow*), police series (*Dragnet*), and tales of suspense and the supernatural (*Light's Out, Inner Sanctum, Suspense*). Many of these series either moved directly to television or served as the unacknowledged influence of subsequent television programs.

Anthology dramas were more prestigious. They often had a famous host who introduced each week's performance and a 60-minute slot in the network schedule. The stories generally consisted of adaptations of famous novels, Broadway plays, or Hollywood movies; performers often were stars of Hollywood or the New York theater. *Lux Radio Theatre*, hosted by Cecil B. DeMille, featured movie adaptations performed by movie stars, who spoke to DeMille about their latest theatrical releases. The best of these drama series was the *Mercury Theater of the Air*, a program created by Orson Welles and John Houseman using members of their New York theater troupe. The *Mercury Theater* featured many skillful adaptations of novels and plays, designed to take advantage of the storytelling opportunities offered by radio, but is best remembered for a notorious dramatization of H. G. Wells's *War of the Worlds* on October 30, 1938. By expertly mimicking a typical network broadcast interrupted repeatedly by news accounts of a Martian invasion, the broadcast panicked many listeners and made a national celebrity out of Welles.

With such an array of programs, radio listeners began to organize their daily routines around the broadcast schedule. Soon ratings services, such as Hooperatings and A.C. Nielsen, came forward to provide networks and advertisers with information about the nature and size of audiences, using modern social scientific research techniques to shed light on the habits of listeners.

The creation of national networks was an unprecedented achievement in American history. For the first time, Americans scattered throughout the country, who until recently had been isolated by geography and regional differences, experienced the same events at exactly the same moment, and this clearly changed the way people felt about what it meant to be an American. As radio entwined individual listeners into a national civic culture, it also introduced them to other forms of national culture—a culture of popular entertainment created by Hollywood movies and radio programs and a culture of consumption created by advertising and mass-produced goods.

Radio After Television The cultural role of radio changed dramatically with the full-scale launch of network television in 1948. Following a period of transition, mass-

market advertisers began to shift their national advertising budgets to television, and the networks followed by eliminating popular radio programs during the early 1950's. Radio stations adapted to the loss by introducing the disk jockey—record-spinners whose personalities gave a station its identity. In place of individual programs, radio stations began to offer "formats" aimed at fans of particular musical genres. The format with the broadest appeal came to be known as Top 40. By concentrating on the best-selling records of the day, the Top 40 format established a powerful link between the radio and recording industries and helped fuel the explosive growth of rock 'n' roll, as affluent teenagers became radio's most lucrative audience in the 1950's.

The invention of the transistor in 1947 played a significant role in the transformation of radio by allowing manufacturers to make smaller, more portable radio receivers and to improve the reception and tuning of radios in automobiles. After decades as a piece of furniture, the radio receiver cast off its mooring and floated into the public world. Inexpensive, lightweight, battery-operated transistor radios, made affordable by competition from Japanese manufacturers beginning in the early 1960's, brought radios directly into the hands of millions of listeners, including children and teenagers who made their own program choices. The automobile radio, which had been seen as a luxury before World War II, gradually became standard in the postwar years.

By the early 1960's, Americans used radio differently than ever before. The possibilities for "out-of-home" listening gave radio a new cultural role as the mobile accompaniment for everyday life. Radio advertisers began to target listeners during "drive time," the hours spent commuting to and from work with only the automobile radio for company. As radio receivers became more mobile, the medium of radio reclaimed its local roots. Local news, weather, and traffic reports—continuously updated throughout the day—made the radio station a secure anchor for listeners in motion, the only source for authoritative, real-time reports on local conditions (symbolized by the traffic helicopter's "eye-in-the-sky" surveillance). The immediacy of local radio has made it an indispensable source of information during emergencies and natural disasters.

The 1970's gave birth to the "FM revolution" in which new stations transmitting hi-fidelity stereo signals on the FM band of the spectrum presented a fresh alternative to AM stations that had drifted into repetitive commercial formulas. In the early 1960's, there were fewer than 1,000

FM stations on the air; by 1976 there were nearly 4,000. Listeners familiar with the rich sound of hi-fi stereos and drawn to the more ambitious rock albums of the late 1960's and 1970's welcomed stations that dispensed with the hit-driven Top 40 format and played obscure tracks from albums or entire albums by artistically ambitious musicians.

As FM stations became the preferred choice for listening to music, many AM stations struggling to find a new identity reinvented themselves in the late 1980's by shifting to all-news and talk formats. In the early 1980's there were fewer than 200 AM stations devoted entirely to news and talk; by 2011 there were nearly 1,300. While much of the programming at these stations features local hosts speaking to local audiences, the rise of talk radio has created national celebrities like Howard Stern, Don Imus, Dr. Laura Schlesinger, and Rush Limbaugh, whose programs are syndicated to hundreds of stations.

In the 21st century, the prospects for noncommercial radio are stronger than ever, even as commercial radio becomes increasingly homogenized. National Public Radio, with its extensive network of affiliated stations, has grown over the past quarter-century to play a vital role in the national media. Local community access stations, using low-power transmitters and operated by dedicated volunteers, have introduced a distinctly local voice to the airwaves in many communities and kept alive the free-form programming abandoned by commercial FM stations.

Meanwhile, as a result of government deregulation over the past two decades, local commercial stations have been absorbed into massive chains. Following the Telecommunications Act of 1996, which removed long-standing limits on the number of radio stations that may be owned by a single corporation, Clear Channel Communications, a Texas-based media company with a portfolio concentrated on radio and TV stations and outdoor advertising, set the pace of consolidation in the radio industry by acquiring more than a thousand local stations in all fifty states. The larger station groups that arose in the late 1990's brought industrial efficiency to local radio stations through centralized coordination of advertising sales, restrictions on decision-making at the local level, and tightly formatted music play-lists designed according to market research. Using a system known as digital voice-tracking, entire programs—including the banter of on-air DJs—could be engineered and packaged in remote studios and transmitted to local stations. Critics of media consolidation, who see autonomous local media as essential to civic participation in a democratic society, have protested this concentration of the radio industry. Still, even media titans aren't impervious to changes in the media environment. In 2007, Clear Channel announced it would sell its entire television group and over 150 of its radio stations, and in 2008 the company was sold to a private equity firm in a leveraged buyout. By 2011, however, Clear Channel Radio was the leading radio company in the U.S., with more than 850 radio stations in operation and a reach of 237 million monthly listeners. With 750 stations streaming online, more than 20 million people visit Clear Channel Radio Online every month.

Satellite Radio In the 21st century, new digital systems for transmitting radio have bypassed local stations altogether. Introduced in 2001, satellite radio transmits digital programs directly from satellites to individual receivers. The rival services—XM Satellite Radio and Sirius Satellite Radio—require consumers to purchase a special receiver and pay a monthly subscription fee, but they provide a wide range of commercial-free programming that contrasts sharply with the homogenized content and aggressive commercialism of local radio. Proponents of satellite radio hoped that the turning point for the new medium had arrived when iconic morning radio host Howard Stern abandoned regular radio for Sirius Satellite Radio in early 2006. Stern's blockbuster deal signaled that Sirius intended to challenge XM's lead in the field. By mid-2008, however, Sirius and XM had announced a merger that created a single satellite radio network in the U.S. The $13 billion merger was controversial because in 1997, when the F.C.C. approved licenses for XM and Sirius, it was on the condition that the two companies never merge. The F.C.C., in a blatant rule reversal, supported the merger in exchange for certain concessions, including an agreement from the companies to turn 24 channels over to noncommercial and minority programming. Once the merger was complete, the newly formed SiriusXM was broadcasting more than 300 channels, including exclusive broadcasts from Stern, in addition to personalities such as Oprah and Martha Stewart. Though Stern and his agent sued SiriusXM in 2011 for failure to pay stock awards, the satellite giant reported continued growth through 2010. There were a record 20.2 million subscribers to SiriusXM at the end of 2010—1.4 million more than in 2009. Revenue hit a whopping $2.82 billion, up 14 percent from the previous year. In 2010, 62 percent of vehicles sold in the U.S. market had SiriusXM capabilities factory-installed. Additionally, SiriusXM had fully penetrated the mobile device market, having developed apps for the iPhone, iPad, iPod touch, Blackberry, and Android platforms.

Internet Radio Another digital challenge to the radio industry has emerged in the numerous forms of radio broadcasting made possible by the Internet. Online radio began in 1993 when Carl Malamud launched his Internet Talk Radio, a non-streaming program on which a different computer expert was interviewed each week. In 1994, the Rolling Stones gave the first "cyber concert," and WXYC in Chapel Hill, N.C., became the first traditional radio station to announce plans to broadcast online. Today, streaming radio, downloadable podcasts, and audio blogs have allowed individuals and small groups essentially to create their own idiosyncratic radio stations, using the Internet to bypass traditional radio while transmitting programs on a global scale. By 2011, most major radio stations offered programs to stream online free of cost. Some stations, such as National Public Radio (NPR) offer free podcasts of cheap downloads of popular programs. The real growth of Internet radio, however, has been in Internet music stations. According to AccuStream Research, Internet music audio ads grossed $84 million in 2008, a 212.3 percent increase from $26.9 million in 2006. Listening hours topped 6.6 billion in 2008, having averaged 404.2 million hours per month in 2007. In 2008, AOL's Shoutcast remained the most popular Internet music station, followed by Clear Channel Online, Yahoo Music, AOL Radio Networks, and Pandora.

Television

Inventing Television, 1927–47

On the foggy morning of September 7, 1927, in a small house at 202 Green Street in San Francisco, an obscure young inventor named Philo T. Farnsworth (1906–71) transmitted the image of a triangle across a crowded laboratory, where it appeared on a receiver placed behind a partition on the far side of the room. Farnsworth's invention, registered with the U.S. Patent Office in January 1927 as an "Image Dissector" tube, scanned the image electronically, using a focused electron beam, and sent the signal through the air to the awaiting receiver. Farnsworth had invented electronic television.

Beginning with his distinctive name, Philo T. Farnsworth seems to have been conjured from fiction for his role as the quintessential American inventor. He grew up on a remote farm in Utah, and it was there as a teenage radio enthusiast tilling his family's fields that he first conceived of a method for scanning an image electronically in order to send pictures along radio waves. In the great tradition of American inventors, he began as an amateur, with no formal scientific training. He wasn't a scientist; he was a brilliant and eccentric tinkerer consumed by a singular ambition. With a small financial stake from a few California businessmen and the aid of a tiny staff—his young wife, Pem, her brother Cliff, and two engineers—he achieved at the age of 21 what had eluded scientists at America's greatest corporations. When it came time to demonstrate his electronic television to his investors, Farnsworth answered their eternal question—"When are we going to see some dollars in this gadget?"—by making the image of a dollar sign appear before their eyes on a small television screen.

RCA and Television From a wood-paneled office in a New York skyscraper 3,000 miles away, RCA commercial manager David Sarnoff also saw dollar signs, in his mind's eye, when he thought about television. He brought Russian-born scientist Vladimir Zworykin (1889–1982) from Westinghouse in 1929 to supervise television research at RCA. Starting with an annual budget of more than $100,000, Zworykin and his staff worked feverishly to develop a proprietary television system for which RCA would control all underlying patents. Zworykin soon introduced an electronic television receiver, which he called a Kinescope. Even with this breakthrough, RCA trailed Farnsworth, because Zworykin had not succeeded in creating an electronic television camera. Like all previous television systems, the RCA camera relied upon a mechanical device for scanning images. In the end RCA resorted to infringing on Farnsworth's patents and was forced to pay a licensing fee after a protracted lawsuit. But RCA would win in the end.

The key to establishing RCA's dominance depended on providing a program service through the NBC network. NBC had conducted experimental broadcasts from the Empire State Building as early as 1932. On April 30, 1939 NBC became the first network to launch regular television service with its inaugural telecast of the opening day ceremonies at the New York World's Fair. The following day

RCA television sets went on sale in New York department stores; a set with a seven-by-ten-inch screen sold for $1,000. NBC followed its debut with daily broadcasts and highly promoted live events beamed to a few thousand receivers in the New York area. A Columbia-Princeton baseball game in May and a Giants-Dodgers game from Ebbets Field in June are considered to be the first sports telecasts in America.

Televised events had few viewers but captured public attention through accounts in newspapers and magazines or displays of television sets at trade shows and department stores. The goal was to sell TV sets by stimulating curiosity about the new medium. These broadcasts—and similar ones by CBS and independent stations—were still experimental. There were no industry-wide technical standards for television broadcasting. A TV set purchased one day could be obsolete the next. This problem was solved by the F.C.C. in April 1941, but the onset of the war stalled production of new electronic equipment.

Postwar Developments The F.C.C. was anxious to pave the way for a quick launch of television once the war ended. During 1944–45 the commission conducted hearings to establish a policy for the allocation of television channels. Many historians believe that these hearings were the single most important event in determining the eventual structure of the television industry. The critical issue at stake was whether television broadcasting should remain in the VHF (Very High Frequency) band of the spectrum, where there were only 13 available channels, or should move to the UHF (Ultra High Frequency) band, which had a much greater channel capacity. These hearings offered the last opportunity to shift U.S. television to the UHF band without disrupting manufacturers, station owners, and consumers.

In May 1945 the F.C.C. approved a system of 13-channel VHF broadcasting and reserved UHF for experimental broadcasts. By selecting a system that restricted the number of available channels, the F.C.C. created an artificial scarcity that guaranteed fierce competition for channel slots. High demand for a limited number of channels essentially eliminated the possibility of exploring alternative forms of television such as theater television, subscription-based television, or noncommercial broadcasting. The channel allocation decision ensured that television would adopt the model of network radio—commercially supported programs broadcast to home receivers by stations linked to a few national networks.

Despite the intense expectations for television in the 1940's, commercial television was slow to develop after the war. The F.C.C. had received 116 station applications from 50 cities by the end of 1945, but two years later there were still only 16 stations on the air and fewer than 200,000 TV sets in the country. The electronics industry needed time to retool for consumer markets, and lingering uncertainty over technical standards made manufacturers and consumers wary about moving forward.

The Rise of Commercial Television, 1948–59

It is difficult to comprehend the speed with which television swept across the American landscape during the 1950's. The television networks had introduced regular prime time schedules in the fall of 1948, and by the end of 1949, a million American households, or just 2 percent of the population, had a television set. By 1954, however, more than half of all Americans had TV sets in their homes, as the number of households with television jumped to 26 million. By 1959 the television set was as common as a refrigerator in American homes; 44 million households, or 86 percent of the population, had TV sets and the average household had one switched on for nearly six hours a day.

As a technology and a cultural medium, television was almost ideally suited to capitalize on the social changes taking place in the United States after World War II. The postwar baby boom led to an explosion in the number of young families with children. Many of these families took advantage of low-cost government loans to purchase homes in the fast-growing suburbs. Rising wages enabled these families to participate in an expanding economy that gave Americans access to consumer goods that had seemed like unattainable luxuries before the war—a brave new world of automobiles and appliances. Innovations in marketing and more efficient transportation meant that Americans participated in a national culture of consumption, with nationally advertised brand-name goods replacing local products, and retail chains popping up alongside local businesses.

Early TV Programming In the beginning much of network television was broadcast live. Videotape wasn't invented until 1956 and didn't come into widespread use by broadcasters until the 1960's. Some programs were produced on film, but CBS and NBC initially discouraged the practice in order to promote the value of the network program service. Any station with an antenna could buy a B western and slap it on the air, but only the networks could afford to deliver live programs on a regular basis.

Over the course of the 1950's the networks gradually shifted from programs produced live in New York to those shot on film in Hollywood, but a unique appeal of television during the 1950's was the experience of immediacy offered by live broadcasts. Many of the live program formats of the early 1950's were imported directly from radio, including soap operas, quiz programs, talent contests, and talk shows. The reputation of the early 1950's as the "Golden Age" of American television rests upon fading memories of programs produced live in the era before videotape, shows that disappeared into the ether, never to be seen again.

The *comedy-variety* format represented by television's first breakout hit, *The Texaco Star Theater* (1948), starring Milton Berle (1908–2002), kept the traditions of vaudeville alive into the television era. The raucous comic sketches and musical numbers, the performances of acrobats, magicians, pantomimes, and plate-spinners on *Texaco Star Theater* (1948), *The Colgate Comedy Hour* (1950), *The Red Skelton Show* (1951), and the critically acclaimed, *Your Show of Shows* (1950), starring Sid Caesar (b. 1922) and Imogene Coca (1908–2001), made few concessions to the new medium of television. Comedian Jackie Gleason (1916–87) is best remembered as Ralph Kramden from the situation comedy *The Honeymooners* (1955), but he became a star playing a range of hilarious characters on his comedy-variety series, *The Jackie Gleason Show* (1952). The most durable of these series began in 1948 as *Toast of the Town* and, after taking on the name of its host in 1955, continued until 1971 as *The Ed Sullivan Show*.

Early television's most prestigious entertainment programs were the *live dramas* broadcast on CBS and NBC. Programs such as *Kraft Television Theatre* (1947), *Studio One* (1948), *Philco TV Playhouse* (1948), and *Playhouse 90* (1956) presented plays written for television and performed live. A playwright fortunate enough to see his work produced on a live network drama literally could become an overnight sensation. Writers like Paddy Chayefsky (author of *Marty*), Reginald Rose (author of *Twelve Angry Men*), Rod Serling (author of *Requiem for a Heavyweight*), and Horton Foote (author of *A Trip to Bountiful*) launched their careers in these early TV dramas.

The most influential television series of the early 1950's was *I Love Lucy*, which debuted on CBS in October 1951 and spent four of its six seasons as the highest-rated series on television. The remarkable popularity of *I Love Lucy*—in its initial network broadcasts and countless reruns—established the *family sitcom* as television's essential genre for decades to come. Veterans of movies, radio, and nightclubs, the married team of Lucille Ball (1911–89) and Desi Arnaz (1917–86) came to television as Lucy and Ricky Ricardo, a young married couple living in a converted brownstone in Manhattan. In each episode Ricky pursued his career as an entertainer, while Lucy wreaked havoc simply by resisting her confinement in the straightjacket of wifely duties. *I Love Lucy* placed an indelible stamp on the situation comedy. In a medium experienced primarily by families in their homes, marriage and family life became the wellspring of television comedy. A definitive moment in the early history of network television came in January 1953 when 44 million viewers tuned in to witness the birth of the Ricardo's baby, Little Ricky. That was 15 million more viewers than had watched President Eisenhower's inauguration the day before.

A Three-Network Universe The chief beneficiaries of television's explosive growth during the 1950's were the networks, which expanded by turning virtually every new television station into a network outlet. As with radio, local stations joined the national TV networks to get access to network programs and to share in the income from national advertising.

Four networks introduced regular prime time schedules in 1948, but an F.C.C. decision ensured that NBC and CBS would hold an insurmountable lead over the smaller networks, ABC and Du Mont. In spite of the many deliberations that preceded the resumption of commercial television after World War II, a significant question still hadn't been answered: how many miles apart should stations be located when assigned to the same or adjacent channels? Stations in the more crowded urban areas along the East Coast discovered that their signals frequently interfered with one another.

Faced with this serious problem, the F.C.C. froze the licensing of new stations beginning in September 1948 for four years, until the commission delivered its historic *Sixth Report and Order* in May 1952. Although there were no new licenses distributed during the years of the freeze, American television was hardly frozen. Stations licensed prior to the freeze went on the air, and advertisers and the public were drawn to the new medium. The number of stations rose from 50 in 1948 to 108 in 1952, and the number of TV sets in the U.S. increased from 1.2 million to 15 million.

During the period of the freeze, NBC and CBS effectively seized control of the television industry by establishing owned-and-operated stations in major cities (the F.C.C. allowed each network to own five) and by signing affiliate contracts with the vast majority of these early TV stations. By solidifying their positions in local markets during a period of limited competition, the former radio networks built an insurmountable advantage over their weaker rivals. In attempting to limit station interference, the F.C.C. created another form of artificial scarcity by determining that most American cities could support no more than three stations. In effect, this ruling meant that there would be only three viable television networks in the United States. As a result of its inability to sign affiliates, the fourth network, Du Mont, left the air in 1955.

NBC Leads the Way

NBC's prime time schedule was heavily oriented toward live programs, including the drama and comedy-variety series described above. In spite of its reliance on these familiar formats, NBC also introduced several key programming innovations.

Sylvester "Pat" Weaver (1908–2002) served as NBC's chief programmer from 1949 to 1953 and as president from 1953 to 1955. His programming strategies expanded the network schedule outside of prime time, into the "fringe" time periods of early morning and late night, by introducing *Today* and *Tonight* (later *The Tonight Show*). These innovative and influential programs played upon the medium's intimacy by blending information, news, advice, and conversation in an informal setting. At the same time, they allowed NBC to claim even more time in the daily schedules of its affiliate stations.

Weaver is also credited with promoting the "magazine concept" of television advertising, in which advertisers pay to have individual commercials placed within a program—as ads appear in a magazine—instead of serving as a program's sole sponsor. Following the pattern established in radio, advertisers had dominated early television production by purchasing broadcast time from the networks and hiring advertising agencies to produce the programs that filled these slots. Since TV networks served mainly as conduits for programs produced by advertisers, the networks exercised surprisingly little control over the structure and content of most television programming. By limiting advertisers to individual commercials in programs produced by the network, Weaver began to shift the balance of power toward the networks.

Weaver departed from another tradition imported from radio when he argued that regularly scheduled series succeeded in creating a viewing habit, but also threatened "to reduce the importance of network service in the lives of the people." He championed special event programs which he called "spectaculars"—prestigious live programs modeled after Broadway dramas, musicals, and variety revues. By raising the cost of production beyond the reach of most individual sponsors, these productions also supported Weaver's goal of reducing sponsor influence. NBC's most celebrated "spectacular" was the 1955 broadcast of *Peter Pan*, starring Mary Martin. Aired just days after the play had completed its Broadway run, the program drew a record audience of 65 million viewers.

ABC Finds Hollywood

ABC entered television as a distant third-place network, lagging far behind NBC and CBS in affiliates and earnings. In 1951 United Paramount Theaters—the theater chain once owned by Paramount Pictures—offered to purchase the network; the F.C.C. approved the merger in 1953. At the time, ABC had only 40 affiliates among the 354 stations in the country. Led by chairman Leonard Goldenson (1905–99), who had come of age in the movie business, ABC turned to Hollywood in order to compete with the more established networks, which had a firm grip on TV's big stars and corporate sponsors.

Goldenson and the other United Paramount executives had long-established relationships with executives at the Hollywood studios, so it made sense for ABC to cultivate the movie industry as a neglected source of television programming. ABC gambled first on independent producer Walt Disney, whose *Disneyland* television series premiered in October 1954. *Disneyland* was an immediate hit, launching a top-10 song and a craze for coonskin caps with its chronicle of the legendary Davy Crockett, and creating fanatical interest in the Disneyland theme park, which was shown under construction in several episodes. In 1956 ABC established its most profitable Hollywood alliance with Warner Brothers. The venerable Hollywood studio delivered ABC's first hit drama, the western, *Cheyenne*, and followed with a string of hits: westerns, such as *Maverick*, *Bronco*, *Sugarfoot*, and detective series such as *77 Sunset Strip*.

ABC now stocked its schedule with filmed, hour-long action-adventure series produced in Hollywood, and by the late 1950's its profits were growing by more than 20 percent per year. ABC's clear success with filmed series convinced the other networks to follow suit. In 1953, 80 percent of prime time programs were produced and broadcast live, most originating in New York. By 1958, 80 percent of prime time belonged to filmed programs made in Hollywood. In pursuit of higher ratings, the three networks began to copy each other's hits and take fewer risks. A popular genre, such as the western in the wake of *Gunsmoke* (1955), would be replicated until viewers became exhausted and moved on to something else. In 1958 more than 25 westerns filled prime time each week. The networks had settled on the staples of the network schedule: family sitcoms and dramas with cowboys and cops (later to include doctors and lawyers).

The Era of Network Television, 1955–1983

The Network Monopoly By 1960, American television had become synonymous with network television. Of the 515 television stations licensed by the F.C.C. to serve the "public interest" of its community, 96 percent were affiliated with a national network. Federal communications policy espoused a principle of "localism," but local stations were unable to resist the financial incentives to join a network. With the exception of a few independent stations in the largest cities, television viewers had no alternative to the networks. Over the next two decades, on any given evening, nearly 95 percent of those watching television were tuned into one of the three networks.

By monopolizing television in America, the networks set the terms that governed virtually every aspect of the television industry. In order to join the networks, stations signed increasingly restrictive affiliate contracts requiring them to hand over the most valuable portions of their schedules to the networks. In creating a national audience for commercial broadcasting, the networks controlled the largest advertising market in history. This allowed them to charge higher and higher rates to national brand-name advertisers for access to that market. For studios and independent producers, the networks were the only game in town. In exchange for scheduling a television series in prime time, networks began demanding an ownership stake, a percentage of any money earned by program-related merchandise or subsequent sales of the series for "off-network" reruns in domestic and foreign markets.

Many Americans watched the growing network monopoly with alarm. The airwaves were supposed to be a public domain, licensed by the F.C.C. on behalf of the American people, but they had become nothing more than an advertising medium. Politicians and intellectuals raised a litany of complaints about network programs and practices: broadcasters had failed to live up to their public service obligations; in pursuing the highest possible ratings, the networks settled for the lowest common denominator in entertainment; the range of programs had narrowed alarmingly; there was too much violence on television; the networks lacked socially responsible programs—news and current affairs, or educational programs for children. CBS journalist Edward R. Murrow summed up the protests when he complained that this powerful medium was being used simply "to distract, delude, amuse, and insulate us."

Scandals Such criticism never caused the public to question the fundamental legitimacy of a profit-driven television system sponsored entirely by advertising. The greatest threat came as a result of the "quiz show scandals" of the late 1950's. Beginning in 1955, several high-stakes quiz shows—including *The $64,000 Question*, *The $64,000 Challenge*, and *Twenty-One*—became popular hits in prime time. In the third season, disgruntled contestants began to claim that producers often rigged the programs to favor contestants who seemed to appeal to viewers. The scandals eventually led to a grand jury investigation and a full-blown congressional hearing. But the howls of outrage gradually subsided and nothing much happened. Since the quiz shows were among the last network programs still produced by advertising agencies, the scandal actually served to strengthen the networks, by giving them the leverage needed to remove sponsors once and for all from the production process.

The F.C.C. Challenge The F.C.C. had sanctioned the system of commercial broadcasting and allowed the networks to monopolize television. Under the Kennedy administration, the F.C.C. began to look seriously at the criticisms of the television networks.

F.C.C. Chairman Newton Minow (b. 1926) addressed the National Association of Broadcasters convention in May 1961, just months after taking office. Minow condemned the entire output of the American television industry, referring to American television, in his famous phrase, as a "vast wasteland." Minow admonished station owners and network executives to recall what had been lost in the rush to win the highest ratings: "Your obligations are not satisfied if you look only to popularity as the test of what to broadcast. You are not only in show business... It is not enough to cater to the nation's whims—you must also serve the nation's needs."

Network News   In commercial terms, the network news divisions were a "loss leader"—not a source of income, but one of prestige and network identity, an effort to serve the public service mandate. Edward R. Murrow at CBS was the most celebrated figure in television news, host of the groundbreaking documentary series, *See It Now*, and the interview show, *Person to Person*. Murrow's thorough critique of Senator Joseph McCarthy on *See It Now* in March 1954 is credited with turning the tide of public opinion against the senator's destructive anti-Communist investigations. The debates between Richard Nixon and John F. Kennedy during the 1960 presidential campaign were a milestone, giving television a central role in the electoral process that would continue to develop in convention coverage and political advertising.

The regular evening news programs didn't play a truly prominent role at the networks until they were expanded from 15 to 30 minutes in 1963. *The CBS Evening News* with Walter Cronkite and NBC's *The Huntley-Brinkley Report* with Chet Huntley and David Brinkley became flagship programs for their networks. Network news coverage of desegregation efforts in the South and the war in Vietnam provided unexpected momentum to the civil rights and antiwar movements during the 1960's by bringing shocking or emotionally charged pictures of these events into American homes.

The networks and their news divisions achieved new public stature in the aftermath of the Kennedy assassination on November 22, 1963. For the next three days, the networks suspended their regular programming and devoted themselves to coverage of the breaking news, followed by the memorial service and funeral. Americans huddled around their television sets in search of information and comfort. The promise of television as a national medium was fulfilled, at least for a moment, as it united a nation in a form of public ceremony that would have been unimaginable a generation earlier. Television has returned to this ceremonial function occasionally over the years—in moments of national celebration, like the moon landing in 1969, or mourning, like the space shuttle Challenger explosion in 1986 or the terrorist attacks of September 11, 2001—allowing the entire nation to experience a single event.

Public Broadcasting   The few gems of news and current affairs programs nearly always faded, however, beneath the shadow of entertainment programs designed to generate advertising revenue. Activists and politicians argued that the United States must have an alternative to commercial television. A 1967 report funded by the Carnegie Commission recommended establishing a fourth network, a noncommercial public network built upon the educational stations already in operation around the country. With President Johnson's support, Congress passed the Public Broadcasting Act in 1967, creating a Corporation for Public Broadcasting to coordinate the country's loosely organized public radio and television stations. But Congress did not work out an adequate system of funding for public broadcasting, which has survived by cobbling together government allocations, corporate underwriting, grants, and direct contributions from viewers. As a result, public broadcasting in the U.S. has been directed toward a middle-class audience likely to make contributions, and has had difficulty serving a more diverse public.

New Regulations   By the end of the 1960's, a political consensus had emerged—the networks had to be reined in. Along with the steady drumbeat of criticism from advocacy groups, Congress heard the complaints of station owners, advertisers, and producers who protested the networks' stranglehold over American television. As a result, the F.C.C. and Congress took a number of steps in the early 1970's that restricted network practices for the first time in history. The Prime-Time Access Rule set limits on the number of hours in which a network could require its affiliates to air network programs. As a result, stations gained control over 10 additional hours of their weekly schedules, which meant advertising revenue lost to the networks would be regained by the stations. The Financial Interest and Syndication Rules prohibited networks from demanding ownership in the programs they broadcast. At the same time, the F.C.C. ruled that a network could produce no more than two hours of its weekly prime time schedule. Networks would have to seek programs from outside producers, and producers no longer would feel pressure to share their profits with a network. Finally, Congress passed a law banning cigarette advertising on television, which went into effect January 2, 1971 (giving the networks one final windfall from cigarette ads during the New Year's Day football games). This was a significant blow to the bottom line at the networks, which received 20 percent of their advertising revenue from cigarette manufacturers.

Television Programming in the Network Era 1960–83

In an age before VCRs and remote controls, the experience of television was beyond the control of individual viewers, who had no choice but to build their lives around the network schedule. If you wanted to watch a program, you had to make plans to be in front of a TV when it aired. As a result, one of the defining achievements of this period was the ability to create a mass audience on a scale that had never been achieved before.

When the Beatles first appeared on *The Ed Sullivan Show* in February 1964, the event drew 73 million viewers, more than 40 percent of the total population. It's an astonishing figure—and a good measure of the band's popularity—but it's less astonishing when weighed against the fact that a routine episode of *The Beverly Hillbillies* aired two weeks earlier drew 70 million viewers. With a national audience divided among just three networks, the typical audience for a long-running hit series always numbered tens of millions of people. Still, television during this period achieved several milestones of "event" television, producing audiences that are likely never to be equaled. Some of these events were ceremonial—the Kennedy assassination coverage or the moon landing—and attracted a nearly universal audience because the networks temporarily suspended regular programming. Some, such as the Super Bowl starting in the 1970's, were transformed into national events by television.

Some entertainment programs in which there was intense viewer involvement in the story and characters could have a single episode of a series turn into a national event. The first of these involved the final episode of *The Fugitive*, which aired in August 1967 and was viewed by 51 million people, or 27 percent of the population. A decade later, 69 million people (32 percent of the population), tuned in for the final episode of the miniseries *Roots* (1977), and in 1980, 83 million people (38 percent of the population) watched the episode of *Dallas* that answered the previous season's cliffhanger question, "Who Shot J.R.?"

Although the networks competed with one another for ratings, they otherwise faced virtually no competition and perceived little incentive for innovation. In a world of limited choice, they reasoned, viewers don't watch particular programs; they simply watch television. Ratings revealed that every day at the same time the number of television sets turned on is remarkably constant—regardless of what is on the air. So the networks operated according to a theory of "Least Objectionable Programming." Under these conditions, network programmers worried less about creating exceptional programs to attract viewers than about supplying the least objectionable program on the air at any given moment.

With the F.C.C. scrutinizing network television in the 1960's for its failure to achieve its utopian promise, much of the blame fell on ABC, which came under attack as the network most responsible for the shift to filmed comedies and formulaic action series. In spite of its influence, however, ABC fell into a distant third place during the 1960's, losing money every year between 1963 and 1971. Television settled back into a two-network race between NBC and CBS.

NBC and Movies   Robert Kintner (1909–80) took over programming at NBC in 1956 and served as network president from 1958 to 1965. Kintner supervised the expansion of NBC news and the shift to color broadcasting (completed in 1965). Programming under Kintner followed the network's traditional reliance on dramas and comedy-variety. NBC formed a strong alliance with the production company MCA-Universal, whose drama series came to dominate the network's schedule well into the 1970's. NBC also took the lead in bringing feature films to prime time. In 1960 the Screen Actors Guild agreed to a collective bargaining agreement that allowed movies made after 1948 to be shown on television for the first time. NBC introduced recent Hollywood movies to prime time in September 1961 with the premiere of *NBC Saturday Night at the Movies*. Hollywood movies became an increasingly important component of prime time schedules; each network scheduled movies at least two nights a week in the 1960's.

When the Hollywood studios began to license their recent feature films for television in the early 1960's, they set off a bidding war that raised the cost of all programming. In 1965 the average price for network rights to a feature film reached $400,000; in three years that figure had doubled. As an alternative to movies, NBC joined with MCA-Universal to develop several long-form program formats, including the 90-minute episodic series (*The Virginian*), the made-for-TV movie, and the movie series (*The NBC Mystery Movie* in 1971, which initially featured a rotation of *Columbo*, *McCloud*, and *McMillan and Wife*).

CBS Holds the Lead   The ratings leader throughout the 1960's, however, was CBS, which owed its success largely to the programming philosophy of James T. Aubrey (1918–94), who served as president from 1959–65. The

Aubrey philosophy was simple: count on situation comedies first, last, and always. The most popular CBS situation comedies offered a reassuring depiction of the contemporary family (*The Dick Van Dyke Show, The Andy Griffith Show, Family Affair, My Three Sons*) or a revival of rural vernacular humor (*The Beverly Hillbillies, Green Acres, Petticoat Junction, Mr. Ed, Gomer Pyle U.S.M.C.*). To maintain audience loyalty, Aubrey also showed great faith in long-term hits, many of which dated back, in one incarnation or another, to television's earliest days: *Gunsmoke, The Red Skelton Hour, The Ed Sullivan Show, The Lucy Show.*

Viewed in retrospect, what is striking about this list is how little it says about the many social upheavals of the decade—movements for civil rights and women's rights, for consumer rights and environmental protection, youth culture and antiwar protest. Faced with these changes in society, television entertainment offered escapist fantasy. The family sitcoms of the 1950's were replaced by the fantasy sitcoms of the 1960's: *Bewitched, I Dream of Jeannie, The Addams Family, The Munsters, Mr. Ed.* As the nation found itself tangled in the Vietnam war, television offered military service comedies that wouldn't have looked out of place in World War II: *McHale's Navy, Gomer Pyle,* and *Hogan's Heroes.* CBS made a modest effort to catch up to the revolution taking place in youth culture by signing the comic duo of Tom and Dick Smothers in 1967 for *The Smothers Brothers Comedy Hour,* but the decision eventually backfired on the network. When the stars became more vocal in their opposition to the Vietnam war and the Nixon administration, CBS abruptly cancelled the series in 1970.

Nielsen and the Changing Audience For nearly two decades Nielsen based its ratings on the number of households viewing a given program. This emphasis on bulk ratings—the sheer number of viewers watching a program—helped to reinforce a lowest common denominator approach to programming, because it ignored distinctions in the viewing audience. In the late 1960's, however, Nielsen began to register demographic differences among viewers, particularly differences in age and income. Some network executives reasoned that they could charge higher advertising rates for programs that attract viewers who were more likely to be active consumers. Instead of relying on habitual viewing patterns to attract the largest quantity of viewers, networks for the first time recognized the value of creating distinctive programs in order to attract young, urban viewers, who tended to have more disposable income.

CBS President Robert Wood (1925–86) and vice president of programming Fred Silverman (b. 1937) decided to reposition CBS as a network for the young, urban viewer. In a period of two years, 1969–71, they swept aside nearly a dozen successful programs that appealed largely to the network's older viewers—*The Jackie Gleason Show, The Red Skelton Hour, Petticoat Junction,* and others. In the 1970–71 season, CBS introduced *The Mary Tyler Moore Show* and *All In The Family,* iconoclastic series that took the sitcom genre in new directions.

As the character Mary Richards, a single woman working as a producer in a Minneapolis television station, Mary Tyler Moore infused the spirit of the women's movement into a comedy of the workplace. In structure and style, *All in the Family* was more familiar—a family sitcom with jokes and punch lines, built around an outrageous lead character, Archie Bunker, played emphatically by Carroll O'Connor. But producer Norman Lear introduced a raw, confrontational edge to the family comedy. In confrontations between the working-class bigot, Archie, and his liberal daughter and son-in-law, Lear addressed the most controversial political and social issues of the day.

Striking a chord with television viewers, *All in the Family* became television's top-rated program between 1971 and 1975. In 1972 CBS added the antiwar comedy, *M*A*S*H,* to its roster. Within a few years, CBS had exchanged its rural sitcoms for a schedule that appealed to younger viewers: *Maude, Good Times, The Jeffersons, Rhoda,* and *The Bob Newhart Show.* Led by these comedies, CBS dominated the ratings until the last-place network, ABC, engineered an improbable revival in the late 1970's.

ABC Revived When Fred Pierce (b. 1933) was named ABC president in 1974, he presided over a perennial third-place network that had grown accustomed to haphazard imitation of its network rivals. Under his leadership, however, ABC rode an unprecedented wave of popular success that carried the network to first place in just three years.

In 1975 Pierce convinced Fred Silverman to leave CBS and take over programming at ABC. Soon ABC's programming was aimed squarely at younger viewers and families: warm family comedy (*Eight is Enough, Happy Days*), wacky farce (*Laverne and Shirley, Three's Company, Soap*), high-concept action (*Charlie's Angels, The Six Million Dollar Man*), and escapist fantasy (*The Love Boat, Fantasy Island*). Through an ineffable blend of intuition, audience research, and accident, ABC's program choices seemed almost perfectly attuned to popular taste for several years in the late

1970's—the final years before cable and home video began to disperse the vast network audience. As they had in the 1950's, critics labeled ABC programs crass and formulaic, but those easy criticisms still don't explain ABC's complete dominance of the ratings; in 1979, 14 of the top 20 programs on television belonged to ABC.

Sports and news played a central role in ABC's reemergence during the 1970's—particularly by attracting new affiliates and contributing to the network's profile as a national institution—and Roone Arledge (1931–2002) is the central figure in the history of both. As president of ABC Sports beginning in 1968, he was the person most responsible for creating *Monday Night Football* in 1970 and for shaping ABC's stellar Olympics coverage over the years. Arledge revolutionized television sports coverage, moving sports to the center of American culture by making sports competition meaningful for the non-sports-fan. He gave each game a storyline and developed ABC's trademark "up close and personal" style to bring out the character and personality of athletes. He was also a showman, unafraid to burnish the spectacle of sports television with multiple camera angles and flashy graphics or to use outlandish personalities, like Howard Cosell (1918–95), who often overshadowed the sports they covered. He brought these traits to ABC News when he was appointed president in 1977. He presided over the creation of *World News Tonight* in 1978 and *Nightline* in 1979 and eventually transformed ABC News into the most respected network news organization.

The Miniseries ABC's most innovative and influential programming achievement in the 1970's was the development of the miniseries. The first miniseries, *Rich Man, Poor Man* (1976), became a sensation. The 12-episode adaptation of Irwin Shaw's 1970 best seller told a sweeping story unlike anything seen before on American television. Its dark romance ranged over decades, with a story measured out in weekly cliffhangers that kept viewers dangling in suspense, waiting anxiously for the story to resume. The milestone in the miniseries format was ABC's broadcast of *Roots*, the powerful adaptation of Alex Haley's multigenerational saga of an African-American family's historical journey from slavery to freedom. Because miniseries have a clear beginning and end, they lend themselves to innovative forms of scheduling. This was the case with *Roots*, a 12-hour series that Fred Silverman chose to show on eight consecutive frigid nights in January 1977.

Prime Time Soaps While each of the networks added miniseries to their schedules, they also recognized that the format's central appeal rested in addictive, ongoing storylines—which the networks had perfected in their daytime soap operas. The answer was to bring the qualities of the daytime soaps into prime time. CBS led the way with *Dallas*, *Knot's Landing*, and *Falcon Crest*. ABC countered with *Dynasty*. These prime-time soap operas, which introduced the strategy of the season-ending cliffhanger that leaves viewers in eager anticipation, became the most popular television dramas of the late 1970's and early 1980's.

End of an Era In retrospect, the predominance of continuous, open-ended storylines in television series of the late 1970's and 1980's looks like a characteristic of a lost age. Open-ended storylines require a high degree of viewer involvement, so networks today fear that a viewer who misses one or two episodes may never return. The strategy of scheduling prime-time soap operas and miniseries developed when the networks could take their audiences for granted. Both formats survived into the 1980's, but they have largely disappeared from television because networks consider them to be too risky in an age when viewers have choices beyond the three networks.

On February 28, 1983, a record 106 million people—47 percent of all Americans—watched the final episode of *M*A*S*H*, which concluded its 10-year run on CBS. At the time, the average American home received 14 television channels; the same home today has more than 50. The *M*A*S*H* finale represents the end of the era of network monopoly, because for the last time almost half of all Americans gathered to watch a single television program.

The Cable Era

The first three decades of network television in America represent a period of remarkable stability for the television industry. Once the basic structure of the television industry had been established, the television seasons rolled past with comforting familiarity. The networks constructed their schedules around regular weekly series that seemed best suited for the purposes of delivering a predictable number of viewers to the advertisers. New series debuted each fall. Some found an audience and survived; most were cancelled. And the cycle started all over again. The three networks battled one another for ratings supremacy, because each ratings point translated into millions of dollars in advertising revenue, but little happened to challenge the fundamental logic of the television business. Under these conditions, the networks were among the country's most stable corporations. In the six decades since NBC and CBS were founded, they had never changed owners; ABC hadn't changed since 1953. And then suddenly, in the period of six months in 1985, all three networks changed ownership. By the end of the 1990's, ABC and CBS had changed owners yet again. Owned by Disney since 1996, ABC experienced a comeback in the late 2000's despite the devastating writer's strike of 2007–08. CBS, however, had split in 2005 from parent company Viacom, though both the newly formed CBS Corporation and Viacom were both still owned by National Amusements.

Cable Television Cable television began in the 1940's and 1950's as community antenna television (CATV), a solution to reception problems in geographically isolated towns where people had trouble receiving television signals with a home antenna. The answer was to erect a large antenna tower in a high location and distribute the signal to subscribers using coaxial cable. Before cable, the networks had benefited from the fact that the stronger VHF signals tended to belong to network affiliates, while newer independent channels got stuck with the weaker UHF channels. (UHF channels were even segregated onto a separate tuner knob on TV sets of the era). Because a large community antenna could receive distant signals and amplify the weaker UHF channels, it created a situation in which cable viewers received more channels than those typically available over the air, and each channel arrived with a strong, clear signal. By adding a satellite dish to the master antenna, cable system operators had the potential to liberate television viewers from all geographical constraints inherent in over-the-air broadcasting.

HBO, Turner, et al. The turning point for cable television came during the 1970's when several corporations began to distribute program services by satellite, making it possible to reach audiences on a national, and eventually international, scale without the need for local affiliate stations. Time, Inc. was the first to launch a satellite-based service when it premiered Home Box Office (HBO) in 1975. The service began on a small scale, with only a few hundred viewers for its initial broadcast, but demonstrated that subscription service of movies and special events could be a viable economic alternative to commercial broadcasting. By the end of the decade, other subscrip-

tion-based movie channels, including Showtime, The Movie Channel, and HBO's own spin-off network, Cinemax, had followed suit.

In 1976 Ted Turner (b. 1938) transformed a modest Atlanta independent station, WTCG, into the first cable-era "superstation," WTBS, by distributing its signal across the country via satellite. Turner's station later was joined by other satellite-distributed independent stations, including WGN from Chicago and WWOR from New York.

The next five years saw the birth of many networks created expressly for cable that were not burdened by the requirement to broadcast from a specific location or to fulfill a public service expectation. If the major networks were department stores, stocking a wide assortment of programs for a variety of customers, the new cable networks were boutiques, created to provide a distinct product to a discerning customer. Following decades of *broadcasting*, the cable networks introduced *narrowcasting* to the television industry.

Narrowcasting Networks Between 1976 and 1981 several cable networks emerged to offer an alternative to the major networks. Some networks provided a program service or addressed an audience that had been neglected by the broadcast networks. C-Span (introduced 1979) provided commercial-free coverage of the U.S. Congress. The Christian Broadcasting Network (CBN) was the most successful of many networks devoted to religious programming. Black Entertainment Television (BET) aimed at young, African-American viewers who had rarely been served well by the broadcast networks. Other cable networks selected a particular element of Big Three programming as the basis for an entire network; the goal was to capture the segment of the mass audience drawn to a particular element of the network schedule. ESPN attracted an audience of adult males by delivering a steady stream of sporting events and sports news. Nickelodeon offered programs for children. The Weather Channel actually introduced a new way to watch television. Instead of tuning in for a program, viewers paused in the midst of other television viewing to monitor weather conditions.

CNN Launched in 1980 by Ted Turner, who was emerging as the iconoclastic leader of the cable network revolution, Cable News Network (CNN) directly challenged the broadcast networks by delivering national and international news on a round-the-clock basis. As the commercial value of network time had soared over the years, the networks had come to devote less time to news programs and had grown reluctant to preempt regular programs for ongoing coverage of news events. In place of the networks' condensed and packaged newscasts, CNN used lightweight video equipment and satellite hook-ups to present live coverage of events in real time. As a result, CNN became the viewer's choice for breaking news and ongoing coverage of criminal trials and government hearings. CNN's coverage of the 1991 Gulf War proved to be a milestone for the network. By 2010, however, competing networks had surpassed CNN in ratings. In 2010, CNN lost 29 percent of its total viewership and 34 percent of its primetime viewers from 2009. Even compelling news events such as the 2010 earthquake in Haiti couldn't recover declining ratings for the hard-news station. At the end of 2010, CNN announced it would fire its U.S. network boss, and that heavy-hitter Larry King would be replaced in the primetime lineup after a quarter century by British tabloid guru Piers Morgan. Network executives, however, insisted that the station would not engage in politically slanted coverage like competing news stations. In early 2011 network viewership was boosted during the Egyptian political crisis, though the Fox News Channel remained the steady ratings leader in cable news.

Fox Broadcasting Company Origins of the Fox Broadcasting Company date back to 1915, when theatre proprietor William Fox formed the Fox Film Corporation. After merging with Twentieth Century Pictures in 1935, 20th Century Fox went on to release some of the best-known films of the Golden Age, culminating in the 1977 release of *Star Wars*, the highest-grossing movie of its time. By the mid-1980's, half of the film studio had been acquired by News Corporation, run by Australian mogul Rupert Murdoch (b. 1931). In 1985, after becoming an American citizen, Murdoch gained FCC approval for the Fox Inc. purchase of all Metromedia television holdings. One year later, Fox Broadcasting Company took to the air with 79 affiliate stations reaching 80 percent of American homes. By the early 1990's, Fox was a major competitor to the Big Three, with massively successful hits such as *Married...with Children*, *The Simpsons*, *Beverly Hills, 90210*, *Party of Five*, and *Ally McBeal*. Narrowcasting divisions were established, including Fox Sports, Fox Kids, and Fox Family, though the latter two were sold to the Walt Disney Company in 2002. After another sweeping success with *American Idol*, which premiered in 2002, Fox launched the Fox Reality Channel in 2005. According to

Nielsen Media Research, in 2009 *American Idol* was still the highest rated program on television.

Perhaps the most polarizing of Fox subsidiaries is the Fox News Channel, a satellite and cable news network launched in 1996. Though the station's slogan is "Fair & Balanced," Fox News is known for its conservative slant, with dominant personalities hosting opinion news shows such as Glenn Beck and Bill O'Reilly. *The Glenn Beck Show* was taken off the air in 2011, but for the 27 months it ran, the program dominated all cable news competitors, with the exception of O'Reilly. In 2010, Fox News was the highest Nielsen-rated cable news channel on air for the ninth year in a row, with more primetime viewers than CNN, Headline News, and MSNBC combined.

MTV The premiere of MTV in 1981 was a godsend for the music, advertising, and cable television industries. Created by Warner Communications, the first of the movie and television companies to operate cable delivery systems, MTV introduced a new approach to television by adopting the programming model that radio had developed following the decline of the radio networks. After the shift to all-music formats, radio listeners no longer tuned in to a station to hear a particular program, but to locate a type of music that suited their tastes. MTV adapted this approach to television—with affable young hosts who served as "veejays" and music videos featuring popular musicians. The early influence of MTV on music and style is nearly impossible to exaggerate. The network sparked a recovery in the slumping music industry, while creating countless new stars. MTV was also a boon to the advertising industry, because television never before had been an effective medium for advertising to teenagers. MTV essentially created a new audience where the Big Three had failed. With its distinctive logo and promotions, its programming and personalities, MTV was more than a television network; it was a brand, an identity for its young viewers and, therefore, an ideal vehicle for advertising.

In essence, everything on MTV during its early days was an advertisement. Music videos were supplied to the network by the music industry, which saw an unprecedented opportunity to promote record sales. Music videos blurred the distinction between advertising and programming—and no one seemed to mind. By 2011, most of MTV's programming had moved away from music and videos. The distinction between advertising and programming remained intact, however, with blockbuster reality shows such as *Teen Mom* and *Jersey Shore*.

HSN The introduction of Home Shopping Network in 1985 and its competitor, QVC, in 1986, showed that cable networks could eliminate programs and commercials entirely by selling directly to customers. Home shopping networks have been among the most profitable networks in the television industry. Along with the other cable networks of this period, they introduced a new operational model to the television business. To remain relevant in the age of online shopping, however, by 2011 both HSN and QVC maintained websites in addition to broadcasts.

The Power of the MSOs The cable systems that brought these networks into American homes became a new force in the television industry. Companies that operated cable systems in several cities around the county, such as Time Warner Cable, Cablevision, Comcast, and RCN, became known as *multiple system operators* (MSOs). These companies started by controlling the hardware of cable distribution—the network of cables that connected the master antenna or satellite receiver to individual households. The costs of wiring cities for cable were enormous, and many of these companies took on huge debts to finance the installation process. While raking in the steady income from cable subscribers, MSOs used their growing control over distribution to exercise new leverage in the television industry. By deciding which networks to carry on their systems, MSOs transformed themselves into the gatekeepers of cable television. An entrepreneur might launch a network, but it was doomed to failure unless the MSOs elected to carry it. Many of these MSOs used this leverage to invest directly in cable networks.

The Impact of Cable Before the 1980's, regulatory concerns hampered the widespread adoption of cable TV in America. But in 1984 Congress passed the Cable Communications Policy Act, which lifted most federal regulatory restraints from the cable industry, with the exception of "must-carry" provisions that required cable operators to have local stations on their systems. Cable service soon expanded rapidly. In 1978 only 17 percent of American households had cable; by 1989 cable penetration had reached 57 percent.

Television viewers subscribed to cable in part because cable offered a solution to the problem of program scarcity associated with the era of network monopoly. Given the choice of dozens of new networks, viewers began drifting away from the broadcast networks. In 1984 the Big Three still claimed 80 percent of the nation's TV audience, but that was already a sharp drop from the days when they could count on more than 90 percent of the audience. As competition has increased, the broadcast networks' share of the total audience has spiraled downward each year. By 2011, Nielsen Media Research was separating ratings according to broadcast and cable seasons. Fox joined NBC, CBS, and ABC as part of the "Big Four."

New Technologies During the era of network monopoly, viewers not only had a limited choice of programs, they also had no control over the flow of television programming or the schedule imposed by the networks. New technologies—inexpensive television sets, videocassette recorders (VCRs), and remote control devices—gave viewers a measure of autonomy from television programmers, and control over the way television could be experienced.

Multiple TV Sets In 1981, for the first time a majority of American households contained more than one television set. The availability of multiple sets in the home changes the dynamic of television viewing by freeing family members to make choices based on their individual tastes, rather than the need to conform to a common taste or, more likely, to the taste of the person who controls the TV. This created an incentive for networks to provide programs for children and teenagers, who were able to make their own choices about what to watch. In 2010, over 30 percent of American households owned four or more TVs, and the average American watched more than 35 hours of TV each week.

VCRs Videocassette recorders became a common feature in American homes during the 1980's. Home video recorders awaited the development of the videocassette by Sony in the 1970's. The consumer market for home VCRs developed slowly at first in part due to a lawsuit filed in 1976 by Disney and Universal against Sony for copyright infringement. The issue was settled in Sony's favor by a 1984 Supreme Court decision, and the consumer market for VCRs exploded. In 1982, 4 percent of households owned a VCR; by 1988 60 percent of American households did. That figure had risen to 94 percent in 2002, but with the advent of DVDs and DVD players—which quickly took over the videocassette market share—that number dropped rapidly. In 2010, only 65 percent of American households owned VCRs, compared with more than 90 percent of households that owned DVD players. In 2009, 55 percent of American households owned two or more DVD players.

The Remote The remote control device became popular during the 1980's, and it has had a significant impact on the manner in which people experience television. Industry researchers quickly began to observe new viewing patterns that they described as "grazing." Many viewers used the remote control to avoid watching commercials, while others learned to scan restlessly through the channels, not watching entire programs, but looking for an arresting image or sound that enticed them to stop on a particular channel. As a result, many cable networks crafted a signature visual style, using distinctive logos, graphic designs, and other techniques, that made the network immediately identifiable to the restless, remote-control-enhanced television viewer.

Home Video Other video technologies introduced during the 1980's also helped to alter the relationship of people to television, creating a growing awareness of a distinction between television and video. Camcorders have made people aware that video can be a technology for recording one's own experiences, creating an archive of personal memories. Video games, introduced during the 1980's and achieving their full impact in the 1990's, have initiated people into a new relationship with the video screen: a participatory mode of engagement. This interactive relationship with the screen was reinforced by the spread of the home computer during the 1980's. Each of these technologies would have a much greater impact in the years to come, but from the beginning they changed the way that people used their television sets. They broke the link that had made television seem like the natural use for video technology, revealing that television is just an effective way for certain industries to capitalize on the technology. This relationship was further changed by the Internet and the advent of sites such as YouTube, where users can post and broadcast their own home videos.

Deregulation During the 1980's, the most dramatic changes in the television industry were the result of a new approach and philosophy in the federal government's approach to the regulation of communication industries. Under the Reagan administration the F.C.C. pursued a policy to reduce the federal oversight of broadcasting and allow market forces to govern the conduct of media corporations. From a regulatory perspective, Reagan-era F.C.C. chairman Mark Fowler (b. 1941) famously asserted that television is no different from a toaster or any other household appliance. Under his administration the F.C.C. relaxed or removed many of the long-standing rules that

governed the broadcasting industries, including the public service obligations.

The old rules that had created stability in the broadcast industries by preventing stations from being easily bought and sold were relaxed. License terms were extended in 1981 from three to five years. The license renewal process was simplified and scrutiny of licensees (which had never been particularly stringent) became virtually nonexistent; a station could renew its license by sending in a postcard. For years station owners were restricted by the "5-5-5 rule" that limited any single entity to owning no more than five AM radio stations, five FM stations, and five TV stations. After first increasing the limit to seven, in 1985 the F.C.C. raised the limit to 12 television stations. The cap for radio stations was eventually raised to 40. The changes in license procedures and ownership limits created a seller's market for station licenses—a speculative market in licenses that led to a rapid turnover in stations—and encouraged consolidation in the broadcasting industries as large media corporations accumulated more and more stations.

These changes also produced a sharp increase in the number of television stations, as corporations invested in station chains. At the time of the F.C.C.'s actions to limit the power of networks in 1970, there were 862 stations in the country, only 82 of which operated independently of the three networks. By 1995, there were 1,532 stations, and 450 of these were independent of the three networks. One result of this growth in stations was the development of a first-run syndication market—a market for programs sold directly to stations, bypassing the networks. The first-run syndication market led to the proliferation of game shows (*Wheel of Fortune, Jeopardy!*) and talk shows (among which the most celebrated is *The Oprah Winfrey Show*, which entered national syndication in 1986).

As regulatory changes heated up the broadcasting business, a general trend of mergers and acquisitions swept through the industry, aided by the use of leveraged buyouts and relaxed enforcement of antitrust laws by the Reagan-era Justice Department. This climate gave rise to the series of mergers and acquisitions that saw the three major networks change hands in 1985–86, as well as the ascent of Fox.

The networks lobbied for an end to the financial-interest-and-syndication rules that had kept them out of the studio business and the lucrative syndication market since the early 1970's. They pointed to the loophole that Fox had squeezed through in order to produce its own programs and argued that increased competition in the television industry, particularly from foreign-owned companies that were not governed by such restrictions, placed them at a competitive disadvantage.

The financial-interest-and-syndication rules were gradually repealed between 1991 and 1995. The policy change not only gave networks the opportunity to produce many of their own programs, but also provided an incentive for further integration of the media industries by encouraging studio-network mergers. Two new broadcast networks debuted in 1995: Time-Warner's WB network and Viacom's United Paramount Network (UPN). As with Fox, these networks began with stations owned by the studios and then recruited affiliates from among the many stations not affiliated with the three major networks. Like Fox, these networks created programs to siphon off viewers from the dominant networks, with schedules aimed heavily at younger viewers and African-Americans.

The Telecommunications Act of 1996 eliminated most of the remaining barriers to consolidation in the media and communication industries. It also eliminated all ownership limits on radio stations, which has paved the way for a radical consolidation of the radio industry. Another significant policy change that encouraged consolidation was the F.C.C.'s 1999 decision to approve "duopolies," or the owning of more than one television station in a single market. The F.C.C. still limits an individual company to owning stations that cover no more than 35 percent of the nation's households—but some companies, such as Fox, regularly exceed the cap without penalty.

In 2003 the F.C.C. voted 3–2 to raise the national audience cap to 45 percent, to allow companies to own more than two television stations in the same market, and to eliminate the rules prohibiting cross-ownership of a newspaper and a broadcast station in the same market (a rule which already had been waived in several instances). The ruling provoked one of the few bipartisan political revolts of the past decade; the F.C.C. was inundated with complaints from opponents of media consolidation from both sides of the political spectrum. Outraged members of both parties in Congress intervened to roll back the changes, and a federal appeals court decision ultimately sent the rules back to the agency for reconsideration. In 2010, the F.C.C. again began reviewing regulations on media ownership, but as of May 2011, the review had not yet been completed and no decisions regarding ownership regulation had been made.

The Three Major Networks Today

NBC   NBC entered the 1980's mired in third place, at the depths of its fortunes as a television network. In 1981 Grant Tinker (b. 1926) became NBC chairman and together with programming chief Brandon Tartikoff (1949–97) led NBC on a three-year journey back to respectability by continuing the commitment to quality programming, including such acclaimed series as *Hill Street Blues*, *Cheers*, *St. Elsewhere*, *Family Ties*, and *Miami Vice*. The turning point for NBC came in 1984, when Tartikoff convinced comedian Bill Cosby (b. 1937) to return to series television with *The Cosby Show*. Network profits climbed from $48 million in 1981 to $333 million in 1985.

General Electric purchased RCA—and with it NBC—in 1985 for $6.3 billion. GE chairman Jack Welch (b. 1935) named Robert Wright (b. 1943) to replace Tinker as network chairman. Many observers of the media industries were dubious about GE's ability to operate a television network. General Electric was a vast conglomerate based in Fairfield, Conn., a manufacturer of medical equipment, power turbines, airplane engines, and appliances that had diversified into such businesses as the financing of commercial and consumer loans. Little in GE's recent history foretold success in programming a television network. Nearly two decades later much has changed in the television business, but Robert Wright is still chairman, and NBC has been the dominant network in the United States for much of the past two decades, a model of stability in an otherwise turbulent business.

NBC has consistently led all networks in attracting the 18- to 49-year-old adults most coveted by advertisers—winning this demographic in seven of the eight years from 1995 to 2003—and has helped to reorient the entire broadcasting industry toward the pursuit of this segment of the audience. Led by a Thursday night lineup that has launched such hits as *The Cosby Show*, *Cheers*, and *L.A. Law* in the 1980's, and *Seinfeld*, *Friends*, and *E.R.* in the 1990's, NBC had the highest advertising rates of any broadcast network. Though ad revenue dropped in the first decade of the 2000's due to competition from other networks such as Fox, by 2010 NBC had made a comeback with Emmy-winning comedic sitcoms such as *The Office* and *30 Rock*. NBC also dominated the television schedule because of self-produced entertainment and news programs that led the ratings throughout the 1990's and early 2000's: *The Today Show* and *Meet the Press* in the mornings, *NBC Nightly News* among evening newscasts, *The Tonight Show* and *Saturday Night Live* in late night.

In 2010, NBC received some negative publicity amid a shuffle that saw Jay Leno move to primetime, struggle to find an audience, then return to his old job on the *Tonight Show*, bumping Conan O'Brien from the coveted *Tonight Show* hosting chair. The conflict ended with O'Brien leaving NBC after 17 years, eventually moving his show to cable network TBS. NBC has also found success in reality TV; notable unscripted series include the hits *The Biggest Loser*, *Celebrity Apprentice*, and *America's Got Talent*.

In May 2004 GE merged with Vivendi Universal Entertainment in a deal valued at $14 billion. The new company, NBC Universal, gave GE control of the Universal movie studio, the USA Network and other cable channels, a television production unit responsible for the network's lucrative *Law and Order* franchise, and Vivendi's interest in the Universal Studios theme parks.

Most likely due to its ever-expanding number of cable networks, GE's NBC was able to weather the recession of 2008 better than many of its competitors. Operating profits fell a mere 6 percent that year, compared with double-digit declines in profits for Disney (ABC), Viacom (CBS), and News Corporation (Fox). Despite this, in late 2009 Comcast, the nation's largest cable operator, announced an agreement to acquire NBC Universal from the General Electric Company. The deal valued NBC Universal at about $30 billion. It wasn't until early 2011, however, that the F.C.C. approved the deal. The merger represents the first time that a cable company will control a major broadcast network—and the F.C.C. approval came with significant conditions.

The NBC Television Network broadcasts roughly 5,000 hours of programming each year, transmitting to more than 200 affiliate stations in the U.S. that reach an estimated 99 percent of American homes. The NBC Local Media Division owns and operates 10 local stations that reach 27 percent of U.S. households, primarily in large cities such as New York, Los Angeles, Chicago, and Washington. Like other media companies, NBC has diversified well beyond its original base in broadcasting in order to reach more viewers. In 2002, NBC purchased Telemundo, a U.S. Spanish-language broadcast network. By the time of the Comcast takeover, Telemundo reached 94 percent of U.S. Hispanic viewers through 14 owned-and-operated stations and 1,000 cable affiliates. Additionally, NBC Universal owns a trove of lucrative cable channels including USA, Bravo, SyFy, CNBC, and MSNBC. By some estimates these channels—combined with the channels Comcast brought to the table—account for 82 percent of NBC Universal's profits.

ABC The new era of corporate mergers and acquisitions dawned at ABC when Capital Cities Communications acquired the network in 1985 for $3.5 billion. This was a big leap for Capital Cities, a media corporation with interests in local television stations and magazine and newspaper publishing, and annual revenues of slightly more than $1 billion. Following the merger, severe cost-cutting measures were instituted throughout the network, but most of the network management remained in place. Capital Cities also made far-sighted investments in the cable networks A&E, The History Channel, Lifetime, and ESPN (which ABC had purchased in 1984).

The Capital Cities team placed Robert Iger (b. 1951) in charge of network programming in 1989. Iger's four years at the head of ABC Entertainment kicked off the network's last great period of ratings dominance. Iger inherited *thirtysomething* and *Roseanne* and added several other series that became hits: *Doogie Howser*, *NYPD Blue*, *Family Matters*, *Full House*, *America's Funniest Home Videos*, and *Home Improvement*. In the target market of 18- to 49-year-old adults, ABC won the prime-time ratings race three times during Iger's tenure.

ABC came under the control of the Walt Disney Co. in August 1995, when Disney acquired the network's parent company, Capital Cities/ABC, for $19 billion. Disney's merger of a major studio with a broadcast network figured to be the model for the television industry of the future, as companies jockeyed for position following the end of the F.C.C.'s financial-interest-and-syndication rules. The enticement of media synergy drove Disney to acquire ABC, and the Disney-ABC alliance has served as a model for the subsequent consolidation of networks and studios throughout the television industry.

As a result of its absorption into the Disney empire, ABC is now a highly diversified corporation with extensive U.S. and international interests in broadcasting and cable. Launched in 2004, the Disney/ABC Television Group is composed of the ABC Television Network, ABC Owned Television Stations Group, ABC Studios, Disney Channels Worldwide, ABC Family, Disney/ABC Domestic Television, Disney Media Distribution, the Radio Disney network, and Hyperion publishing. As of 2011, the Disney/ABC Television Group owned 10 broadcast stations and a television network with more than 200 affiliate stations. The ABC Cable Networks group oversees a number of cable networks that are either wholly or partially owned by Disney: ABC Family, A&E Television Networks (which include A&E, Biography, and the History Channel), ESPN Networks (including ESPN

International, which reaches television sets in more than 200 countries), Lifetime and Lifetime Movies, the Soap Network, Toon Disney, and the Disney Channel. In addition to its own sports and news production, ABC now oversees all network and syndicated television production at Disney.

The goal of the Disney-ABC alliance was to create the conditions for mutually beneficial cooperation among the company's separate divisions. Disney now has the ability to distribute its movies and television programs through a range of television networks that provide opportunities for the "repurposing" of content (as the industry refers to the practice of recycling content from one network or medium to another) and targeted access to different types of viewers—the Disney Channel for children, Lifetime for women, ESPN for men. When synergy works, as it does for ABC's sports and children's programming, it allows for convenient cross-promotion of Disney products and more efficient use of resources. ABC has stocked its Saturday morning schedule with children's programs originally produced for Disney's premium cable channel. These programs are then distributed to the international Disney channels and sold on home video. ESPN and ABC Sports have combined to purchase broadcast rights to NBA basketball and NFL football and now share production facilities and personnel. ESPN has become the world's most valuable cable network, generating more than $5 billion per year and establishing a brand name that Disney has successfully exploited by creating additional ESPN cable channels, an ESPN magazine, and ESPN Zone restaurants.

The Achilles' heel of synergy in the television business is that success still depends on having a strong broadcast network at the core. Because a broadcast network develops an enormous amount of original content and provides matchless public exposure, it must be able to create programs with enough appeal to set in motion the forces of synergy. ABC was the first-place network at the time of the Disney merger, but its ratings soon began a downward slide. In just two seasons, ABC fell from first to third in the ratings, losing 23 percent of its target 18- to 49-year-old adult viewers, 35 percent of teens, and 45 percent of children ages 2–11. Operating income dropped from $400 million to $100 million in the first two years of Disney ownership, and the network has posted significant losses in subsequent years. Except for the improbable success of 1999–2000, when *Who Wants To Be a Millionaire?* (aired as many as four times a week) carried the network into first place, ABC's prime-time ratings did not recover—in part

because the network failed to use opportunities like the fluke success of *Millionaire* to develop new hits.

The wheel of fortune finally turned in ABC's favor with the 2004–05 season and the debut of *Lost, Desperate Housewives*, and *Grey's Anatomy*. ABC's president of entertainment, Stephen McPherson, deserves the credit for shepherding these refreshing new dramas into the Nielsen Top Twenty. In the midst of these rising fortunes at ABC, longtime network chief Robert Iger succeeded Michael Eisner as the chief of the entire Disney corporation, and seized the moment to chart a new direction for network television by making ABC the first network to allow its episodes to be purchased as downloadable files on Apple's iTunes Web site. In 2010, 15 years after the Disney merger, Nielsen regularly ranked ABC programming in the top 10 weekly broadcasts, with shows such as *Dancing With The Stars, Body of Proof*, and *Modern Family*.

CBS During the 1980's, CBS was still controlled by the aging patriarch William S. Paley, who had founded the network six decades earlier. In the competitive business environment of the 1980's, CBS found itself under continuous threat of a corporate takeover, including one launched by cable mogul Ted Turner. To defend itself, the CBS board recruited Lawrence Tisch (1923–2003), the president of CBS's largest shareholder, Loew's Inc., to become president and CEO in 1986. Tisch immediately set about doing exactly what a corporate raider would have done: he slashed budgets—including that of the network's venerable news division—reduced personnel, and sold off assets like CBS Records.

CBS, which had been near the top of the network ratings for the entire history of television, found itself drifting into unfamiliar last-place territory during the late 1980's. The network's identity with older viewers began with its most prominent program, the news magazine *60 Minutes*, which has been on the air since 1968. A top-10 hit for much of its network run, *60 Minutes* rose to number one during the years 1991–94, and helped to carry the network back to the top, accompanied by such dramas as *Murder, She Wrote; Dr. Quinn, Medicine Woman; Walker, Texas Ranger*, and the situation comedies *Murphy Brown* and *Designing Women*—all of which appealed to older viewers.

For a decade after the Tisch takeover, CBS continued to operate as an independent corporation, the last network to resist becoming a subsidiary of a larger conglomerate. That ended in November 1995, when Westinghouse purchased the network for $5.4 billion. Like General Electric, its former partner in the alliance that had created the radio industry so many years before, Westinghouse was a highly diversified company with a long history in broadcasting as the owner of a large group of radio and TV stations. CBS was a Westinghouse subsidiary for four mostly undistinguished years before the media conglomerate Viacom acquired Westinghouse's media properties in a September 1999 deal valued at $50 billion.

By adding the CBS network to Paramount Communications, which it had acquired in 1994, Viacom created a fully integrated media conglomerate in order to keep pace with its chief competitors at Disney, News Corporation, and Time-Warner. Viacom led one of the major developments in television during the cable era—the transformation of cable networks into consumer brands. By creating a clearly identifiable identity and a loyal fan base for such channels as Nickelodeon and MTV, Viacom has succeeded in manufacturing new brand names that can be used to market movies, music, books, magazines, and merchandise. Viacom is dedicated to achieving the same results with the other cable networks that it has acquired or developed over the years: VH1, Comedy Central, Country Music Television (CMT), TV Land, Spike, and Black Entertainment Television (BET).

By 2000, Viacom had become the only media conglomerate with two broadcast networks—CBS and the United Paramount Network (UPN). While CBS targeted a general audience skewed toward a slightly older demographic, UPN targeted the young, African-American audience that had been neglected by the traditional broadcast networks. In 2004, Viacom merged CBS Broadcast International with Paramount International Television, and programming was produced under the banner of CBS Paramount International Television. In addition to Paramount, Viacom's other holdings included the subscription cable channels Showtime, The Movie Channel, Flix, and the Sundance Channel; Viacom Outdoor, the largest billboard company in America; Blockbuster, then the leading home video retail chain; and the publisher Simon & Schuster—all while continuing operation of 39 television stations in 15 of the top 20 television markets.

A funny thing happened in the history of media conglomerates in 2005. Viacom's CEO Sumner Redstone decided that his corporate behemoth would be more valuable if split into two separate companies. One company would retain the Viacom name and would control the cable networks and Paramount studios. The other company would be named CBS and would control the CBS and UPN broadcasting networks, the TV stations, Infinity

Broadcasting (the outdoor advertising business), and a few other companies. The companies would operate independently, with separate boards of directors and executives—except for Redstone, who would sit atop both companies. Paramount fell under the auspices of the "new" Viacom and the rights for CBS to use the Paramount name in television production expired in 2009. CBS Corporation currently owns and operates Showtime, Simon & Schuster, and the re-named CBS Outdoor—still the largest billboard company in the country. In 2008, CBS acquired the newest addition to its portfolio, EcoMedia, a leader in environmental media that partners with communities and advertisers in "green" projects and initiatives such as solar power.

Former president of Warner Bros. Television and president and CEO of CBS since 1998, Leslie Moonves (b. 1949) was brought on as president and CEO of the newly independent CBS Corporation in 2006. At Warner Bros. he had been the head of the studio that produced such hits as *Friends* and *E.R.* In 2000 he introduced the first reality-genre sensation, *Survivor*, and *C.S.I.: Crime Scene Investigation*. *C.S.I.* has spawned two highly rated spin-off series, *C.S.I.: Miami* and *C.S.I.: New York*, and essentially established the pattern for the network's remarkably popular lineup of procedural crime dramas. In 2006, Moonves's first major move as head of the CBS Corporation was to sell UPN to The WB. The WB shut down two days later, and The CW Network was formed as a joint venture between Warner Brothers Entertainment and CBS that same year. While CBS continues to target a general audience skewed toward a slightly older demographic, the CW is the only broadcast network targeting women 18–34. Its primetime schedule includes popular series such as *America's Next Top Model*, *Gossip Girl*, and *One Tree Hill*.

Television in the Digital Era

Just as the introduction of cable and home video compelled the television industry to change over the past two decades, the proliferation of digital technologies promises to transform American television in the years to come. For nearly 20 years before most Americans ever saw a television broadcast, they heard that television was just around the corner, and the same was true for fabled Internet television. Programming first became available online for free via Peer-to-Peer sharing services and illegal downloads in the early 2000's. It wasn't until News Corporation and NBC Universal decided to partner in 2007 and launch a free, legal, ad-supported online television site—meant to be the "YouTube killer"—that Internet television began to become a reality. Hulu debuted in private beta later that year, and in early 2008 Hulu.com was open to the public, offering free streams of hit TV shows, movies, and clips. At the end of 2008 Hulu increased its number of show titles to over 1,000, and was named fourth in *Time* magazine's 50 best inventions of the year. Hulu became a household word after its 2009 Super Bowl ad—which received an Emmy nomination—and in April 2009 it was announced that Disney would join NBC, News Corporation, and Providence Equity Partners as an equity owner of the site. At the end of 2010, Hulu launched its subscription service that included broadcasts in HD, hundreds of classic movies, and a vast arsenal of popular shows.

Broadcasting v. Narrowcasting

The broadcast networks still attract the largest audiences of any mass medium in America. The leading networks—currently Fox and CBS—average nearly 15 million viewers in prime time, and a top 10 series can draw more than 25 million viewers each week. A splashy, well-publicized event still can assemble an audience of unparalleled size; the final episode of *Seinfeld* attracted 76 million viewers in May 1998. According to the Nielsen Company, Americans watched more television than ever in 2010, and total viewing of broadcast networks and basic cable channels rose about 1 percent for the year. Cable hits such as MTV's *Jersey Shore* were media darlings, but the most popular new show was CBS's *Hawaii Five-0*, a revival of a 40-year-old drama. The biggest gainer on the broadcast ledger, however, was Spanish-language company Univision. The finale of *Soy Tu Dueña* (*I'm Your Owner*) averaged 4 million viewers in that demographic.

No single competitor threatens the viability of the broadcast networks, but their audiences are gradually slipping away with each passing year, and television as a cultural medium is being changed in the process. In place of broadcasting, the television and advertising industries have supported a shift to narrowcasting—the segmentation of the mass audience into smaller demographic categories. For many advertisers selling goods and services to a mass market, it is still efficient to reach the large concentrations of viewers made available by a top-rated prime time series. But even mass-market companies like McDonald's and Coca-Cola often find it more effective to target specific consumers with advertising messages designed for them. In other words, it's more efficient for advertisers to speak to consumers who are interested in what they have to say. As a result, it is virtually impossible

to make any generalized assumptions about the television audience. The Nielsen ratings reveal that African-American and white households typically prefer different programs, but at times there is virtually no overlap between the 10 highest-rated programs for the two races.

Unlike the broadcast networks, the cable networks cannot afford a full schedule of original programs. Cable networks rely on network reruns, but also have begun to concentrate their efforts on developing one or two signature programs that create an identity for the entire network—such as *Covert Affairs* on USA, or the police drama *Rizzoli & Isles* on TNT. Another strategy is for a cable network to concentrate marketing and promotion budgets to raise the profile of a single series in order to create a phenomenon that attracts media attention and, prompted by media coverage, draws viewers to the network. Such programs include Bravo's *Project Runway*, and CW's *America's Next Top Model*.

Since the 1990's, the broadcast networks have seen their status as the source of quality programs eroded by HBO, which has developed a reputation for creating the most innovative television series: *The Larry Sanders Show, Sex and the City, Curb Your Enthusiasm, The Sopranos, Six Feet Under, The Wire,* and *Deadwood*. As a subscription service, HBO doesn't have to provide a full program service or to attract an audience for advertisers; it simply has to give people a reason to pay the cost of subscribing. This leads HBO to focus on creating a few series that attract inordinate attention from critics and the media, and frees HBO from the scheduling constraints of the broadcast networks. HBO doesn't have to premiere all of its series at one time in the fall or commission 22 episodes per season. The network also allows its producers to concentrate on making 12 high-quality episodes, instead of struggling to provide 22. Most worrisome for the broadcast networks, HBO's acclaimed series siphon off the viewers most prized by advertisers—upscale 18- to 49-year-olds.

The Fate of the Broadcast Networks

When ABC's prime time ratings collapsed and the network floundered, the larger ABC organization achieved notable success in other areas. The owned-and-operated TV and radio stations are profitable for ABC, as they are for all broadcast networks. Corporate synergy has worked in sports and children's programming. The most obvious successes are in Disney's cable television group. While broadcast networks have only a single source of revenue—advertising sales—cable networks earn money from advertising and from charging transmission fees to cable and satellite delivery systems, which are passed along to viewers as higher service rates. For the most successful networks, such as Disney's ESPN, these transmission fees can be raised by as much as 20 percent annually.

Even as ABC struggled, several of Disney's cable networks, including ESPN, the Disney Channel, A&E, and Lifetime have seen steady growth in revenues and profits. The many cable networks owned by Viacom provide advertisers with the ability to target television viewers from cradle to grave: Nick Jr. for preschoolers; Nickelodeon for preteens; MTV for teens; Comedy Central, VH1, and Spike for young adults, and TV Land for aging baby-boomers.

A diversified portfolio of broadcast and cable networks allows the parent companies of ABC, NBC, CBS, and Fox to reconstitute much of the audience lost to the traditional broadcast networks over the past two decades. Although the audience for the broadcast networks continues to shrink, the six companies that control the broadcast networks still reach more than 80 percent of viewers in prime time when counting the ratings for their combined broadcast and cable networks. This explains why half of the top fifty cable networks have changed hands since 1990 and why most are now controlled by the six companies that already own broadcast networks.

Cable networks also allow companies to spread operating costs and extend their global reach. NBC has achieved greater efficiency and reach for CNBC by expanding CNBC Europe and CNBC Asia Pacific (both of which are jointly owned with Dow Jones) through a range of localized services using the resources of partners in Japan, Australia, Singapore, Hong Kong, Sweden, and several other countries. The 24-hour news network, MSNBC, uses the resources of NBC News to provide programming for both cable and the Internet. Viacom's MTV, with several unique regional services, reaches more than 400 million subscribers in more than 160 countries and territories. Cable networks also lend themselves to the establishment of brand identities and to cross-promotional opportunities, as networks like ESPN, MTV, and Nickelodeon have proven for NBC's competitors.

The competition in prime time has increased over the past several years, as the audience has continued to shrink, the advertising market has flattened, programming costs have risen, new program formats have been introduced, and new networks compete for viewers. There are now seven large broadcast networks and dozens of cable channels competing for the attention of viewers. Because viewers are more dispersed, the net-

works have relied on programs that are easily promoted, such as the reality formats that offer a low-cost, highly marketable alternative to episodic series. The success of unscripted series like ABC's *Dancing with the Stars* and *The Bachelor*, CBS's *Survivor* and *The Amazing Race*, Fox's *American Idol*, and NBC's *Deal or No Deal* have demonstrated the value of these less expensive alternatives to scripted series. The focus has shifted from building long-term audience commitment to series, as they once did, to going after big ratings—even if they're temporary and can't be repeated with regularity. In a telling sign of things to come, NBC was the first network to announce that it will attempt to reduce program costs in the future by scheduling unscripted series in the first hour of prime-time. Consider the economics: while NBC's emerging hit, *Heroes*, cost $2.7 million per episode even without recognizable stars in the cast, an episode of the game show *Deal or No Deal* costs only $1 million.

The average U.S. television household now receives more than 100 channels. Because viewers are widely dispersed across these channels, it has become difficult to introduce a new conventional scripted series. NBC did not have a breakout hit since the debut of *Will and Grace* in 1998 until the airing of *The Office* in 2005 and *Heroes* in 2006. As a result of the difficulty in launching new series, the cost of holding together a prime-time schedule has increased dramatically over the past several years. As it becomes more difficult than ever to turn a scripted series into a hit, producers of existing series find themselves with considerable bargaining leverage. When *E.R.* came up for renewal in 2000, NBC paid Warner Bros. Television a record $13 million per episode. In order to lure *Friends* back for a final season in 2003–04, NBC paid Warner Bros. $10 million per episode and reduced its order to just 18 episodes.

Over the past decade there has been a return to dramas in which each week's episode is neatly concluded, such as the *Law and Order* and *C.S.I.* franchises. The surprising success of a few open-ended series, such as *Desperate Housewives, 24,* and *Lost,* tempted the networks to offer a number of ambitious, open-ended dramas in the fall of 2006, but this proved to be a catastrophe; with viewers unwilling to commit to so many ongoing narratives, nearly all were cancelled by mid-season. By 2011, most broadcast networks were finding their scripted successes with sitcoms in the tradition of *I Love Lucy*—comedic family situation shows that didn't rely on continuous viewing to follow.

While the three *Law and Order* series or the three *C.S.I.*

series may not attract as many viewers in the 18- to 49-year-old demographic as *30 Rock* or *American Idol,* they "repeat well"and draw large numbers of viewers even in reruns. Early in the decade NBC used repeats of the *Law and Order* franchise to plug holes in its schedule, even filling entire nights with back-to-back episodes. Despite a decade of solid popularity, even *Law and Order* experienced significant ratings decline as viewers opted for cable programming over that from a major broadcast network. At the end of 2010, however, Nielsen numbers showed that while the generation-long shift to cable from broadcast continued, the smallest of the Big Four broadcast networks, NBC, still retained more than twice as many viewers a the largest basic cable channel, USA.

The Digital Future

Transition from Analog to Digital Television The Federal Communications Commission approved a digital television standard for the United States in December 1996, but the transition to a fully digital television system has occurred more slowly than anyone at the time could have predicted. After several postponements, the F.C.C. in 2006 ruled that all television broadcasting in the United States must switch from analog to digital transmission by February 17, 2009. In addition, any new television set sold after March 1, 2007 must include a tuner capable of receiving digital signals. As of June 2009, all full-power television stations in the country were broadcasting exclusively in a digital format. Analog TV sets weren't entirely obsolete, though analog set users had to connect their set to a digital-to-analog box to watch programming.

One benefit of the transition from conventional analog to digital television was the new standard of technical quality made possible by high-definition television (HDTV), which achieves photo-quality images due to a scan rate of up to 1,080 lines (the NTSC standard for conventional TV has been 525 lines). Even with a limited selection of high-definition programming available through satellite and cable, consumers have begun to switch to HDTV sets. According to a 2010 report from the Consumer Electronics Association, 65 percent of American homes owned at least one HDTV set in 2010, up 13 percent from 2009. Instead of providing HDTV-quality signals, however, broadcasters may decide that consumers will be satisfied with less than HDTV quality. Broadcasters may instead choose to use the increased bandwidth allotted for digital transmission, along with

techniques of digital compression, to transmit several standard-definition channels or to provide additional information services that may be more marketable. By 2011, most major channels offered HD programming online in addition to its regular broadcast.

In 1996, when the F.C.C. laid the groundwork for the transition from analog to digital television, the media landscape for most consumers was entirely different than it is today. There were no DVDs or digital video recorders; mobile telephones were uncommon and wireless computer networks unimaginable; videogames were still the province of teenage boys; and the World Wide Web had only recently entered the public imagination. The only comfort that traditional broadcasters may take as they look across this media landscape toward the future is that Americans are still devoted to television. According to Nielsen Media Research, the average American in 2010 watched 35 hours of TV each week, and two hours of timeshifted TV via a DVR. These numbers vary depending on age demographic; for example, those age 25–34 watched nearly three hours a week of timeshifted TV, while those 65 and older watched just over an hour. The estimated number of people using TV and Internet simultaneously rose 4.6 percent from 2008 to 2009, meaning that the rising prevalence of the Internet doesn't necessarily deter people from traditional television. In fact, the numbers show that in 2010 Americans were watching more TV than ever before. In a Bureau of Labor Statistics Time-Use Survey released in 2010, watching TV was the leisure activity that occupied the most time—accounting for about half of leisure time on average—for those age 15 and over.

Do-It-Yourself Television Networks While the big media and computer companies jockeyed for position in anticipation of television's digital future, a pair of Internet entrepreneurs, Steve Chen and Chad Hurley, quietly launched a Web site called YouTube in 2005. The site made it simple for anyone to upload video clips to the Internet, which then became immediately viewable around the globe. As the name of the site so brilliantly anticipated, this was a do-it-yourself global television network programmed by individual users according to their own unique tastes. Television is the only medium in history that has never really been open to amateurs. In every country in the world, television has been regulated by governments and monopolized by powerful institutions.

With the exception of the all-but-invisible public-access channels on cable TV, American television has been closed to non-professionals since the beginning. With user-generated content and program selections made by each individual user, YouTube accomplished nothing less than the reinvention of the television network. Even if YouTube itself fails to survive the inevitable shakeout that will occur as the big media and computer companies adapt to the conditions of broadband Internet video distribution, this is an historic achievement.

In an attempt to avoid the copyright-infringement lawsuits that crippled the file-sharing service Napster a few years earlier, YouTube limited the videos on its site to brief clips of no more than nine minutes. Of course, fans posted clips from their favorite TV programs and movies, but thousands upon thousands of people posted original videos shot with inexpensive camcorders and cell phones—with as many as 65,000 clips added to the site each day. Following the site's motto "Broadcast Yourself," within six months, users were viewing 10 million clips a day; by the end of the first year the number had risen to 50 million. By 2010, according to YouTube, the site was exceeding 2 billion views a day, and 24 hours of video was being uploaded every minute. Some of the video on YouTube may seem almost comically trivial—one clip of a baby's infectious laughter has been viewed over 15 million times—but it would be a mistake to dismiss the site as simply the latest iteration of *America's Funniest Home Videos*. In more than one instance, video distributed on the site has shredded the veil of public relations that protects American political candidates; other videos have revealed images from Iraq that remain unseen on conventional TV networks. YouTube had become so prevalent and on par with traditional TV networks that in early 2010 President Obama gave an exclusive interview to the website, answering questions submitted online by ordinary citizens. In October 2006, after less than 18 months in existence, YouTube was acquired for $1.6 billion by Google. With a stock market valuation of $172.4 billion, Google may have as much influence in determining the future of television as any of the old-guard media companies. In 2009 it was announced that YouTube and Universal Music Group planned to launch Vevo, a premium music video site that would act as a type of "Hulu for music videos" that would play copyrighted, high-quality videos. Google and Universal said they would share advertising revenue from both Vevo and YouTube and by the end of

2009, all major music labels had shared content on the channel.

The Importance of Advertising Television advertising is a $65 billion annual market that essentially underwrites the system of television that has existed in this country for more than half a century. Despite the growth of ad spending on the Internet (an increase of 13.9 percent from 2009 to 2010, a total of nearly $26 billion), television is still the richest media segment, commanding 39.1 percent of all advertising spending. According to *Advertising Age*, the amount spent on television advertising will continue to rise, to an estimated $68 billion in 2015, compared to an estimated $44.5 billion on the Internet in the same year. Television networks are sites for bringing consumers together and then providing advertisers with access to them. It is startling, therefore, to consider that this massive market rests upon the Nielsen ratings system, which can tell advertisers how many people watch a program, but cannot say how many actually watch the commercials. The inefficiency of the Nielsen ratings has been laid bare by the public's adoption of the digital video recorder (DVR) and by the introduction of targeted, relevant advertising on the Internet.

Introduced to the market in 1999 by companies like TiVo, digital video recorders are essentially computers capable of selecting television programs and recording them as digital files. Unlike conventional VCRs, a viewer doesn't need to program a digital recorder to record a certain program at a certain time. A viewer simply selects a title and the digital video recorder finds the program and records it from any channel at any time—whether it's prime time or the middle of the night. This feature ends the tyranny of the program schedule once and for all, allowing the DVR user to make all the programming decisions about what to watch and when to watch it. As DVRs are integrated into the set-top boxes of cable and satellite subscribers, they have become increasingly widespread. DVRs were used in approximately 36.7 million American homes (31 percent) in 2010, up 12 percent since 2007. According to *Advertising Age*, however, DVR penetration is slowing. The percentage of American homes with DVRs is only supposed to reach 40 percent by 2015.

From the perspective of the television industry, the most threatening feature of the digital video recorder is its ability to skip commercials by fast-forwarding at 200 times normal speed—not to scan through a commercial as VCR users learned to do, but to avoid commercials entirely. Early research has indicated that as many as 87 percent of DVR users skip commercials. By making it so easy to avoid commercials, the DVR has simply thrown a bright light on the fact that advertisers long have paid for viewers who may be ignoring their commercials. Advertisers have demanded a more precise accounting of ratings for the commercials themselves, instead of the programs, and Nielsen agreed to make commercial ratings available for the first time beginning in 2007. According to *Advertising Age*, however, by 2010 data showed that not as many people were skipping commercials as previously thought. By one rough estimate, no more than 13 percent of primetime commercials will be fast-forwarded through in the foreseeable future. Nonetheless, as advertisers shift their attention from program ratings to the measurement of viewer engagement with TV commercials, we are likely to witness significant changes in the relationship between programs and commercials.

The future of media advertising is greatly affected by the emergence of online TV sites like Hulu, but also by the prevalence of social networking, which exploded around 2005. Sites like Facebook and Twitter, where users gather online to make social connections and share experiences, now affect every media company. In fact, by 2011, Facebook had a whopping 500 million active users globally, significantly more than the U.S. population, and these users were spending more than 700 billion minutes per month on the site. According to eMarketer, Facebook commanded $1.86 billion in advertising revenue in 2010. Traditional television networks have attempted to turn their own Web sites into social networking sites, using their exclusive programs to bring users together, much as they bring viewers together through conventional television. Google has approached the challenge differently. After beginning as a Web search engine, Google has become the dominant model of Internet advertising by selling inconspicuous advertisements related to a user's search. Unlike traditional networks, Google doesn't want to control distribution of exclusive content, but to organize all the content of the Internet and then to guide users toward relevant content and targeted advertising. If the $65 billion television advertising market begins to shift toward search-based Internet video, television will be redefined in the process.

As Americans integrate digital technologies into their lives, television will not be able to exist as it has for the past fifty years. Peter Chernin (b. 1951), chairman and CEO of Fox Entertainment, expressed the sentiments of everyone in the media business when he described this as "the most revolutionary period in the history of mass media." Will television continue as an advertiser-supported medium? What will happen to television programming? Will networks continue to provide a full schedule of programs, or will that tradition be too costly to continue? How will networks manage the transition to video on demand? Will television come to resemble the publishing or recording industry, in which an array of products is made available for the selection of consumers? Is it possible to imagine television audiences dispersing so much that the cultural experience of television looks more like the experience of books and music—in which people pursue their own narrowly defined tastes and seldom come together as a mass audience for anything but the Super Bowl? Throughout its history, television has never been anything but a mass medium. Perhaps that will change in the years to come.

ADVERTISING

History of Advertising

Although rudimentary advertising existed in medieval Europe, it was the advent of the printing press in the 15th century that enabled information to be disseminated quickly and cheaply. Previously, shop owners advertised their products by displaying a pictorial sign—essential in a largely illiterate society—or hand-lettered posters to gain attention.

The first printed advertisement in English—announcing a prayer book for sale—appeared in 1477. Other early advertisements included printed handbills that shop owners passed to their customers or citizens in the street. As the newspaper became commonplace in Europe, advertising quickly became a standard feature. In the 17th century and the early 18th, British newspapers carried small, straightforward items that resemble the classified advertisements of modern newspapers. The *Tatler*, an early 18th-century London periodical, sold advertisement space at a discount to clients who promised to run a specified number of ads in a particular period. This was the first instance of the "frequency rate," a practice still in use in modern advertising.

In American cities in the 18th century, newspapers consisted mostly of advertisements, usually for a shop or a service provider. The technological changes of the Industrial Revolution set the stage for the explosive growth of manufacturing on both sides of the Atlantic, allowing for the mass production of goods at low costs. Improvements in newspaper and magazine production allowed for larger issues that cost less. Manufacturers, with an abundance of goods to sell, needed to build demand for their products by reaching a mass market, and newspapers and magazines could help them do it.

While the advertisements may not have been sophisticated, manufacturers discovered that buying display space in publications was a complicated business. The burgeoning business required a middleman, and hence the advertising agent was born. The earliest known advertising agent in the United States was Volney Palmer of Philadelphia, who operated in the early 1840's. Palmer represented several newspapers and business clients, and when a firm purchased space in a paper, he would pass along the written copy and receive a percentage of the advertisement's revenue. Other advertising agents purchased blocks of space from newspapers at a discount and then broke the space into sections for smaller, slightly marked up advertisements. By the onset of the Civil War, approximately 30 of these primitive agencies existed in the United States, most of them in New York.

The agencies brought standard business practices to advertising, including a transparent "open contract" that told advertisers exactly what their costs were and that the agency would take a 15 percent commission. This system was started in 1869 by the N. W. Ayer Agency and is still the basis for most of today's advertising transactions. As publishers realized the significance of advertising revenues, newspapers and magazines relaxed their advertising guidelines, so that advertisements could be larger and more sophisticated. Illustrations began to appear in advertisements, particularly for those selling typewriters, sewing machines, and patent medicines.

The growth of advertising fueled the demand for many products that originated in the 19th century. Consumers seeing frequent advertising messages began to connect the advertiser with a sense of quality. In 1868 James Walter Thompson (1847–1928) joined a small New York advertising agency. He knew that the popular ladies' magazines and prestige literary magazines were read and reread, and that their prestige would rub off on products advertised within. He demonstrated the power of his idea when he placed ads for asbestos roofing in the women's magazines *Godey's* and *Peterson's*; these ads sold more roofing than the company had ever sold before. Thompson went on to monopolize magazine advertising, buying out the agency's owner in 1878 and renaming the firm for himself. Thompson also pioneered the creation of the account executive position—the liaison between agency and client.

Advertising Agencies By the end of the 19th century, advertising had become an integral part of the business world. Advertising agencies grew in number and enhanced their role in the game of printed salesmanship. They no longer served merely as the middlemen between the client and the media; they now created advertisements on the client's behalf. Around the turn of the century, advertising writers developed new ways to appeal to consumers. One style of advertising, dubbed the "reason-why" style, used extensive logical arguments several paragraphs in length about why a product was better than its competitors. The Chicago-based agency Lord & Thomas was a prominent practicioner of this style in the early 20th century. An executive at Lord & Thomas, Albert Lasker, and the copywriter Claude Hopkins utilized the "reason-why" approach in illustrated, wordy ads for products like Sunkist oranges or Schlitz beer. In its advertisements for Palmolive soap, Lord & Thomas displayed alongside the text a larger slogan—"Keep That Schoolgirl Complexion"—that the agency created to increase sales to married women. Hopkins called this "salesmanship-on-paper," and he and Lasker went on to create numerous successful advertising campaigns, most notably for Lucky Strike cigarettes with a strategy to convince women that smoking was sophisticated.

Radio and Television With the emergence of radio as a popular source of public entertainment in the 1920's and 1930's, advertising moved into uncharted territory. Initially, the radio program was sponsored by a corporation, and the corporation's advertising agency took on the responsibility for producing the content. Batten Barton Durstine & Osborn (BBDO) coordinated the *Du Pont Cavalcade of America,* and Blackett-Sample-Hummert developed the daytime "soap opera" as showcases for various home products from their clients. (See also "Radio" in *Media.*)

The widespread introduction of television following World War II offered advertisers a powerful opportunity, and advertisers fell all over themselves for the chance to present their products simultaneously through visual and aural methods. In television's infancy, as with radio, advertising agencies produced shows on behalf of their clients. The Kudner Agency created a hit with its *Texaco Star Theater,* hosted by Milton Berle, and J. Walter Thompson (JWT) produced *Kraft Television Theater.*

The costs of producing content for television soon became too exorbitant for sponsors to handle. The television networks saw an opportunity to build their business by creating their own content and opening the airwaves to

Advertising Expenditures in the U.S., 1776–2015 (millions)

Year	Amount	Year	Amount	Year	Amount
1776	$0.2	1900	$450	1990	$128,640
1800	1	1909	1,000	1995	160,930
1820	3	1915	1,100	2000	243,680
1840	7	1940	2,110	2002	236,880
1850	12	1950	5,700	2004	263,766
1860	22	1960	11,960	2005	271,074
1867	40	1970	19,550	2009	147,200
1880	175	1980	54,780	2011[1]	154,600
1890	300	1985	94,750	2015[1]	173,600

Note: 1. Projected. **Source:** *Advertising Age.* These are estimated figures of the monies spent on placing advertising in all media; the costs of producing the advertising are not included.

Top 10 U.S. Advertising Categories, 2010

Category	Expenditures (millions of dollars)	% Change from 2009
Automotive	$ 13,026	19.8%
Telecom	8,751.5	4.0
Local services	7,991.7	6.9
Miscellaneous retail[1]	7,708.8	9.3
Financial services	7,689.7	6.0
Food & candy	6,672.3	7.1
Personal care products	6,161.0	11.7
Direct response	6,143.5	−5.8
Restaurants	5,652.8	2.3
Pharmaceuticals	4,327.8	−8.2
Total[2]	**$74,125.1**	**6.5**

Notes: 1. Does not include these segments: Department Stores, Home Furnishing / Building Supply Stores. 2. Sum of individual categories may differ from total due to rounding. **Source:** Kantar Media.

many more advertisers. By 1959 the networks had taken creative control of programming.

With the combination of print, radio, and television available to spread advertising through several media, advertising grew rapidly in the 1950's. Overall industry expenditures for media placements, not including the cost of producing the ads, doubled from $5.7 billion in 1950 to $12.0 billion in 1960. Film actors, baseball players, and socialites became spokespeople in ads and became associated with the products they pitched. Famous advertising characters were born as well, including such icons as the Jolly Green Giant, the Pillsbury Doughboy, and the Marlboro Man, all created by the famous Leo Burnett agency of Chicago.

In the 1960's the creative departments of advertising agencies released a torrent of ads that reflected the counterculture elements of contemporary society. William Bernbach of Doyle Dane Bernbach (DDB), a New York agency, launched several notable campaigns during this period, including a series of clever print and television spots for the Volkswagen Beetle and Avis Rent-a-Car ("We're Number 2—We Try Harder"). Both print and television advertisements gained sophistication during the period, with print ads prefering photography over illustrations and the copious text copy of earlier times. Boosted by the improvement of editing techniques, the television commercial also came of age.

Mergers and Explosive Growth But the creative eruption of the 1960's gave way in the 1970's to a series of industry mergers that formed gigantic advertising agencies. Interpublic, a holding company formed by Marion Harper of the ad agency McCann-Erickson, added several other advertising agencies to its portfolio, each operating as a separate division.

The wave of mergers continued into the 1980's, with the addition of the decade's infamous and characteristic feature—the hostile takeover. In 1987 the WPP Group, headed by Martin Sorrell, purchased the J. Walter Thompson Company for $566 million. Two years later WPP acquired the Ogilvy Group for $864 million. The holding company Omnicom was formed in 1987 in a move that combined Doyle Dane Bernbach with another agency and also added BBDO. Companies went international, as well, with offices in Europe and elsewhere.

The 1980's were a decade of explosive growth in the American advertising industry. In 1980, domestic expenditures for advertising totaled $54.8 billion. In 1990 advertisers spent approximately $130 billion on advertisements in the United States. Television commercials became famous for their pitches, such as "Where's the beef?"—spoken by an elderly woman in a commercial for the fast-food chain Wendy's—or the pink bunny that pounded a drum in more than 100 spots for Energizer, a household battery.

Advertising Today In the early 21st century, advertising continues to spur the American economy, largely based on mass consumption of mass-produced goods. Advertising dollars also provide the financial underpinnings of every major media outlet. According to industry projections, advertisers spent approximately $450 billion on worldwide advertising buys in 2010, with roughly 33 percent of that in the United States alone. Not surprisingly, Europe was the next largest media spending region, commanding more than 29 percent of worldwide ad spending in 2010. However, broken down into statistics by country, Japan followed the U.S. in top advertising spending in 2009. The trend of massive amounts of money spent on advertising shows no sign of stopping. In 2011, advertisers were forking over $3 million for a 30-second ad to air during the Super Bowl, the championship game of the National Football League. In 2011, however, the Super Bowl drew a whopping 111 million viewers, 5 million more viewers than in 2010 and the most-watched single broadcast in history.

The growth of cable television has weakened the powerful advertising position of network television. The preponderance of channels aiming at various demographic categories—such as the youth market served by MTV—was a marketing dream for advertising agencies and clients, who can now theoretically reach a more interested audience for much lower rates.

Internet Advertising Expenditures for Internet advertising still fall behind newspapers and television, but 2010, according to the Internet Advertising Board, set a new record for total Internet advertising revenue, with a 15 percent annual increase to $26 billion. The Internet offers marketers a variety of formats including text or video ads; keyword search ads that appear on a search engine page (usually on the right side of the computer screen) are by far the most common type and account for 46 percent of all Internet ads. Display ads (like video ads or sponsorship banner ads) are second in revenue, and continue to increase. In 2010 display-related advertising totaled $10 billion, an increase of 24 percent from 2009. An estimated total revenue from advertising tailored for mobile devices was released for the first time in 2010, between $550 and $650 million. With services like Google AdSense that pair ads with sites and monitor visitor traffic, anyone with a website can earn advertising revenue.

SPORTS

BASEBALL

History

Origins

Although no scholar has pinpointed the exact origins of baseball in America, most agree that it began to evolve in the early 17th century out of a family of English folk games including rounders, stoolball, and cricket. American historian David Hackett Fischer believes that bittle-battle, a game popular in southeastern England, is perhaps the most direct ancestor of the sport today regarded as America's pastime. Played with four bases, a pitcher, and a batter in the Massachusetts Bay Colony in the early 1600's, within a century bittle-battle became known as the Massachusetts Game. As early as 1791, as evidenced by the recently unearthed "Pittsfield Prohibition," the game was common enough to be a nuisance to town elders, who were forced to issue a bylaw for "the Preservation of the Windows in the New Meeting House in said Town." Because the sport was unorganized and only played informally, several versions of the game existed.

In the 19th century a somewhat different game was being played in New York City: batters hit from a corner of the diamond, for example, rather than midway between bases, and runners could not be put out by being plunked (or "soaked") with the ball. In 1845 the New York game was codified by a young bank clerk named Alexander Cartwright, who proposed 20 rules of play that covered everything from punctuality to distance between bases ("42 paces") to a balk rule and the institution of foul lines. His own club, the Knickerbocker Base Ball club, adopted these rules, which proved very popular. The club issued a challenge to any other club willing to abide by their rules. The New York Nine accepted the challenge, and on June 19, 1846, the first base ball contest was played at Elysian Field in Hoboken, N.J. With Cartwright, his team's best player, serving as umpire, the Knickerbockers succumbed by a score of 23-1. Umpire Cartwright's most memorable decision was fining a player six cents for swearing.

Professionalization: 1850–1900

Base-ball, as it was known in the 19th century, spread from the Northeast, where it had achieved craze status among English, Irish, and German immigrants, to the South and West, thanks to the enthusiasm of Union soldiers in the Civil War period and the burgeoning era of railroad expansion.

In 1869 the first professional club was formed in Cincinnati. In 1876 an eight-team league—the National League of Professional Baseball Clubs—was founded at a meeting held at the Grand Central Hotel in New York City. A 70-game schedule was announced. The first game took place in Philadelphia; the gloveless defenders committed 19 errors, but baseball was on its way. Players like first basemen Cap Anson and Dan Brouthers, the indefatigable pitcher Hoss Radbourn, and the matinee idol outfielder Mike "King" Kelly became the game's early superstars, while the game continued to tinker with its rules—initially eight balls constituted a walk, then seven, then six, then four. The league settled on three strikes as an out and permitted pitchers to deliver the ball overhand.

The game's popularity made it an attractive business venture. The National League owners fought off several competing leagues and maintained strict control over the players. But in 1901 one competing circuit, the American League, offered players greater freedom of movement among the other clubs, and grew into a rival that the National League could not vanquish. So a settlement was worked out whereby owners in both leagues agreed not to raid each other's talent and to honor the reserve clause, which bound players to teams in perpetuity. By 1903 the first World Series between the two leagues was played.

In 1908 a commission was formed to determine the true origins of baseball and a myth was born: that Abner Doubleday of Cooperstown, N.Y., drew up the rules and dimensions of play on a sandlot in that town. The apocryphal story made baseball a totally American game, quite in contrast to its international roots.

Dead Ball and Scandal: 1901–1920

With the two eight-team leagues in agreement, baseball flourished. New stars emerged—Ty Cobb as a base-thief and expert hitter, Cy Young and Christy Mathewson as scintillating pitchers, Nap Lajoie and Eddie Collins as hard-hitting second basemen. The use of gloves brought defensive stars to the fore, like Boston's third baseman

Jimmy Collins. Colorful owners and managers, from the White Sox's penny-pinching Charles Comiskey to Philadelphia's austere Connie Mack to the swaggering New York Giant John McGraw, gave the game great character and provided theater and vituperation for hungry sportswriters. The appearance of box scores in daily newspapers helped spread the excitement across the land, as fans could track more easily how their teams were doing.

The game, however, seemed to belong to the pitchers, as fewer and fewer runs were scored. The owners began to fear that the public would lose interest; the ball was livened in 1912; the spitball, a pitch made deceptive by the pitcher's saliva, was outlawed in 1920, after Cleveland shortstop Ray Chapman was hit in the temple and killed by a pitch from New York Yankee Carl Mays.

But what nearly derailed baseball was not low run production or a fatal injury but a betting scandal that rocked the country. In 1919 eight members of the Chicago White Sox (forever known as "The Black Sox") were involved in a scheme concocted by a New York gambler named Arnold Rothstein to throw the World Series to the underdog Cincinnati Reds. In the end, the baseball owners, worried about the integrity of the game, hired a commissioner, Judge Kenesaw Mountain Landis. His first action was to banish from the game, for life, all eight of the Chicago players, one of whom, Shoeless Joe Jackson, was one of the greatest players of all time.

Baseball was back on safe moral ground, and a young slugger named George Herman "Babe" Ruth revitalized and revolutionized the sport with his prodigious home runs and huge personality. After leading his Boston Red Sox to a World Series victory in 1918 on the strength of both his pitching and hitting, Ruth was sold to the rival Yankees for cash and a line of credit by Red Sox owner Harry Frazee. In his first year as a Yankee, Ruth reached theretofore unimaginable heights, knocking 54 home runs, more than any other team in the league that year and 35 more than runner-up George Sisler. Ruth gave up pitching, and the Yankees built a house for him—Yankee Stadium. Radio broadcasts—the first of which was heard on Pittsburgh's KDKA radio in 1922—helped baseball capitalize on the game's newfound integrity and its larger-than-life superhero. In 1927 Ruth hit 60 home runs, a record that would stand for 34 years.

War, Growth, and Stability: 1920–1960

Baseball remained the same for decades, with the same 16 teams divided into two leagues.

American League: Boston Red Sox, Chicago White Sox, Cleveland Indians, Detroit Tigers, New York Yankees, Philadelphia Athletics, St. Louis Browns, Washington Senators.

National League: Boston Braves, Brooklyn Dodgers, Chicago Cubs, Cincinnati Reds, New York Giants, Philadelphia Phillies, Pittsburgh Pirates, St. Louis Cardinals.

The New York Yankees dominated baseball through this era, producing a succession of great players—Ruth, Lou Gehrig, Joe DiMaggio, Mickey Mantle. The game weathered the Depression in the 1930's and in 1939 the National Baseball Hall of Fame was founded in the game's mythical birthplace, Cooperstown, N.Y. Inducted in the first class were Ty Cobb, Honus Wagner, Walter Johnson, Babe Ruth, and Christy Mathewson. In 1941 DiMaggio mesmerized the country with a 56-game hitting streak; by season's end, the era's other great hitter, Boston's Ted Williams, finished the year with a .406 batting average, connecting for four hits on the last day of the season. Williams remains the last player to hit over .400 over a full season.

Many players left the sport to serve in the military during World War II. In 1942 President Roosevelt specifically approved baseball's continuance during the war in a "green light" letter to Commissioner Landis. So weakened was the league, however, that the lowly St. Louis Browns made their only World Series appearance (a loss) in 1944. When the war was over, the economy began to boom, the stars came back, and baseball returned to its pinnacle.

With President Truman having desegregated the armed forces toward the end of the war, it was only a matter of time before baseball also ended its exclusionary racial policy. In 1947 Jackie Robinson, a college-educated four-star athlete from California, broke the color barrier by taking the field for the Brooklyn Dodgers. Robinson was followed by other black stars, including Larry Doby, Don Newcombe, Roy Campanella, and one of the greatest players of all time, Willie Mays. Soon after, the game opened to Latin American players as well, further broadening the appeal of baseball.

One victim of the racial integration of baseball, however, was what were known then as the "Negro Leagues," which operated in more than two dozen cities from around 1920 to about 1950. The Kansas City Monarchs, the Chicago American Giants, and the Detroit Stars were among the most successful teams, and the exploits of many players—Josh Gibson, Buck Leonard, Oscar Charleston, Cool Papa Bell, and Ray Dandridge—earned them induction into the Hall of Fame. But attendance slumped badly when young Negro League stars, such as the Birmingham Black Barons's Willie Mays, began signing major league contracts.

Baseball was becoming America's game. Television began to appear in many American homes in the 1950's, and baseball looked for ways to either protect itself from the new technology or profit by it. Television as well as air travel made the country smaller, and baseball, which since its inception had never been played professionally west of St. Louis, expanded in 1958, when the Dodgers and the New York Giants moved to California. The Yankees continued their dominance on the field, racking up 25 American League pennants and 18 World Series titles between 1921 and 1960.

Expansion and Labor Unrest: 1961–1980

The 16-team major leagues expanded to 18 for the 1961 season with the addition of the Los Angeles Angels and the new Washington Senators (who replaced the old Senators, who had moved to Minnesota to become the Twins). As a result, the regular season was extended from 154 to 162 games. Roger Maris of the Yankees hit his 61st home run on the last day of the 1961 season to break Ruth's record, a feat that earned Maris a place in the record book with an asterisk (since removed) explaining the longer season. Two more teams—the New York Mets and the Houston Colt .45s—joined the majors in 1962. That year the Mets, under legendary manager Casey Stengel, who earlier steered the Yankees to 10 pennants in 12 years, set a new record for futility by going 40-120 in their debut season. Seven years later, with the crosstown Yankees falling on hard times, the "Miracle" Mets won the World Series in an upset of the powerful Baltimore Orioles.

In the 1970's two mini-dynasties emerged, one in each league. The brash, young Oakland A's, with slugger Reggie Jackson, pitchers Catfish Hunter, Blue Moon Odom, and Vida Blue, won three consecutive World Series early in the decade, and were followed by Cincinnati's Big Red Machine, led by catcher Johnny Bench and second baseman Joe Morgan. In 1973 the American League, in an effort to boost attendance, instituted the designated hitter rule, which allowed another person to hit in the pitcher's place.

End of the Reserve Clause It was also a period of player unrest. Because of the reserve clause, players had no freedom to seek a more profitable position with another team. An outfielder named Curt Flood, frustrated by an unwanted trade from St. Louis to Philadelphia, filed suit against baseball in 1970, alleging that baseball violated antitrust laws. The courts sided with management, but the victory was short-lived. A's pitcher Jim "Catfish" Hunter, after a falling-out with owner Charlie Finley, became baseball's first free agent, so declared by an independent arbitrator. The nascent player's union watched intently as a player at the peak of his abilities offered his services to the highest bidder, something that had been prohibited previously by the reserve clause. Hunter signed with the Yankees (headed by new owner George Steinbrenner) for five years and $3.75 million. The next year, 1976, the same arbitrator ruled in favor of two more players, Dave McNally and Andy Messersmith. These steps opened the way for free agency to be negotiated as a part of the collective bargaining agreement. Salaries for players began to skyrocket.

Free Agency, Records, and Internationalization: 1980–2004

With free agency came increases in salaries and hard-fought labor battles between owners and players, with strikes or lockouts marking the end of almost every collective bargaining agreement. The movement of free agents to the highest bidder raised the issue of competitive imbalance. The "large market" teams that could afford more, better players were in danger of overwhelming the "small market" teams.

Because of labor strife, the last seven weeks of the 1994 season and post-season was cancelled. It was the first year without a World Series since 1904. As the influx of money from television and licensing rights continued, baseball expanded. Following the addition of teams in 1994 and 1998, there are currently 30 major league teams. As the talent spread more thinly, records began to fall, and in 1998 Mark McGwire of the St. Louis Cardinals broke Roger Maris's record by slugging 70 home runs. San Francisco Giants outfielder Barry Bonds hit 73 home runs three years later.

The Yankees returned to dominance in the late 1990's under the managerial hand of Joe Torre and a stable of quality pitchers. In the National League, the Atlanta Braves won 14 straight division titles but only one World Series. In the late 1990's the game's popularity abroad began to register in the States—accomplished Japanese players Hideo Nomo, Ichiro Suzuki, and Hideki Matsui signed lucrative contracts to play for American teams. Regular season games were played in Mexico, Japan, and Puerto Rico as ownership began to market the sport more aggressively. In 2002 a long-dreaded contract negotiation was worked out between the owners and the players' union with no stoppage of play. In the 2003 season, Barry Bonds won an unprecedented sixth Most Valuable Player award.

With the issues of competitive imbalance still being debated, baseball entered the 2004 season with several franchises in deep financial trouble—Milwaukee and Montreal among them. Concerns were also growing that performance-enhancing drugs and nutritional supplements were harming the game's integrity and possibly the health of its participants.

Major League Baseball Today

In 2005, the first major relocation of a Major League Baseball team since 1972 occurred when the Montreal Expos franchise was moved to Washington D.C. and renamed the Nationals. (Coincidently, the 1972 move saw another Washington team, the Senators, move to Texas and become the Rangers.) Performance-enhancing drugs continued to cast a pall over the league, perhaps nowhere more evident than in the failure of Mark McGwire—number seven on the all-time list with 583 career home runs—to be elected to the Hall of Fame.

Late in the decade the effects of MLB's crackdown on steroids and performance enhancing drugs began to show, as a resurgence of pitching dominated the headlines. There were 12 no-hitters and 3 perfect games from 2007 to May 2011, including the first no-hitter in postseason play since Don Larsen's perfect game in the 1956 World Series. Armando Galarraga was denied the fourth perfect game in this stretch when umpire Jim Joyce incorrectly ruled the runner safe at first on what would have been the 27th out. This egregious error has led to calls for the expanded use of instant replay. 50 home runs in a season was re-established as a benchmark, as only one player has reached that plateau since the 2007 season. A recent priority of MLB is to reduce the length of games, which has ballooned to a regular season average of 2:52 minutes compared to the 1970 average of 2:30 minutes. The average postseason game was 3:30 minutes in 2009. The longest contests were the annual Yankees-Red Sox battles which averaged a whopping 3:38 minutes in 2010. Several small rule changes dictating batter and pitcher behavior were enacted to combat this trend. Recently, talks of expanding the playoffs to include two more wild card teams has picked up steam. The two wild cards from each league would play each other to determine who advances to play the division winners. While some resistance has materialized, this progression seems inevitable.

And while Major League Baseball has shown an increasingly international face for decades, in past years this has been largely due to the success and even dominance of Latin American players. In the early 21st century, however, the league has looked increasingly to the East for new talent. The success of Seattle's Ichiro, the recent signing of Japanese hurler Daisuke Matsuzaka by the Boston Red Sox, and South Korea's gold medal at the 2008 Summer Olympics all point to this as a trend that will no doubt continue.

Rules of the Game

Although bookshelves groan with the weight of volumes analyzing baseball strategy, *The Official Baseball Rules*, in paragraphs 1.01-1.03, define the game and its objectives plainly:

1.01. Baseball is a game between two teams of nine players each, under the direction of a manager, played on an enclosed field under jurisdiction of one or more umpires.

1.02. The objective of each team is to win by scoring more runs than the opponent.

1.03. The winner of the game shall be that team which shall have scored the greater number of runs at the conclusion of a regulation game.

The Playing Field   The infield is a 90-foot square and the outfield is the area formed by extending two foul lines radiating left and right from one corner of the square, which is home base. The other bases, first, second, and third, occupy the three other corners of the square (called a "diamond") and they are ordered counterclockwise. Batters at home plate attempt to hit the offering of the opposing pitcher, who stands 60 feet six inches away and throws the ball in an attempt to make the batter swing and miss or hit the ball to one of the pitcher's eight supporting defenders, including his catcher, who is positioned behind home plate to receive the pitches. Home plate is a five-sided white rubber surface set flush to the ground 17 inches wide and 17 inches long, with the two back corners removed so that the plate comes to a point. The defensive positions, in addition to the pitcher and catcher, are four infielders (at first, second, and third bases, and one between second and third base, called a shortstop) and three outfielders, usually spaced equally apart in what are called left, center, and right fields.

Balls, Strikes, Outs   Pitches that the umpire deems have passed over home plate and at a height between the batter's knees and upper chest are considered hittable and will be called a strike if the batter does not swing. Three strikes, whether called so by the umpire or swung at and missed or fouled off by the batter, constitute an out. Four pitches out of the strike zone and not swung at are called balls, and earn the batter a free pass to first base. Balls hit into the air and caught before hitting the ground are outs, as are balls hit on the ground that are relayed to a base before the batter/runner arrives. Three outs per team per try (or half inning), and the teams switch sides for the completion of the inning.

Running the Bases   Runs are scored when a player progresses safely from home to first, second, and third and back to home. Runners trying to get to first base can be called out if the ball reaches a defensive player who is touching the base before they arrive. At second, third, and at home plate, runners have to be tagged out by the defender with the ball or a glove with the ball in it, unless there are runners on all the bases behind the lead runner, in which case a forceout is applicable—merely touching the base before the runner's arrival will suffice. A regulation game is nine innings; if the score is tied, extra innings will be played until one team has the advantage in runs. In the event of inclement weather, a minimum of five innings can constitute a complete game.

On the Field Today   In today's game, there are usually four umpires, and team rosters consist of 25 players, including, on average, 10 pitchers. The nine players who start a game assume one of the aforementioned nine defensive positions and, on offense, bat in a specified order. In the American League, since 1973, the pitcher does not bat, but is replaced in the lineup by a designated hitter, who does not play the field.

Since 2003, the winner of the All-Star game receives home-field advantage in the World Series and as of 2007 the DH is used regardless of All-Star location. Limited use of instant replay (home run, fair/foul & fan interference) has been in effect since 2008.

Glossary of Baseball Terms

all-star a player chosen, either by fan vote or by a manager, to play on a roster representing his league against the opposing league in an exhibition game played at the mid-season break in July.

backstop a screen behind home plate that protects spectators from being hit by errant pitches or foul balls; also a synonym for the catcher.

balk a motion by the pitcher deemed by an umpire to be an illegal attempt to deceive a baserunner; when a balk is called, the ball is dead and all base runners advance to the next base.

box the rectangle in which the batter stands (batter's box) or the area fielded by the pitcher, as when a pitch is hit "back to the box," a term that dates to the 19th century, when the pitcher threw from a boxed area rather than from a mound.

breaking ball an all-inconclusive term used to describe any of a family of pitches intended to swerve in some fashion—a curve ball, slider, screwball, sinker, forkball.

bunt a batted ball that is intentionally hit softly and to a short distance so as either to allow the batter to reach first base safely or to advance another runner while the bunter is retired at first base.

change-up a pitch thrown intentionally at a slower speed than preceding pitches so as to disrupt the batter's timing.

cleanup the fourth hitter in the lineup who, if all three runners reach base before him, is then set to "clean up" all the bases by virtue of a homerun; this position is usually reserved for the team's most powerful hitter.

closer the pitcher who comes in to pitch toward the end of the game to preserve a lead.

curve a pitch thrown with a downward snap of the wrist, intended to impart a spin to the ball that will force it to curve as it approaches the plate.

cycle a batter's feat that requires the hitting of a single, double, triple, and home run in the same game—"hitting for the cycle."

designated hitter (or DH) a position created in 1973 in the American League (and still in practice only there), whereby one player is designated to play offense only, batting for the pitcher, who plays defense only.

double a hit that results in the batter reaching second base safely without fielder error.

doubleheader when two teams play twice in succession on the same day.

double play when one pitched ball results in the making of two outs, either by virtue of a strikeout and a base runner being thrown out, or when a batter hits the ball and two runners are called out on the bases.

error a defensive mistake, deemed avoidable by an official scorer, that results in either a batter reaching base safely or having his at bat extended.

fastball a pitch thrown for maximum speed.

foul ball the result of a pitched ball hitting a bat but going into foul territory; it is a strike until there are two strikes, in which case it does not count as a strike.

grand slam a home run with runners on all three bases, resulting in four runs.

ground-rule double a hit that, because of a mutually agreed-upon rule particular to the ball park the game is being played in, results in the batter being awarded second base; e.g., when a ball hit fairly bounces into the stands and out of play.

grounder a batted ball that bounces one or more times in the infield.

hit-and-run a play usually ordered by the manager whereby a base runner runs for the next base when the pitch is made and the hitter tries to hit the ball into play in an attempt to advance the runner two bases or avoid a double play by virtue of the base runner's head start toward the next base.

home run when a batter either hits the ball out of the field of play in fair territory or when the batter is able to advance all around the bases to score before the defense can retrieve the batted ball and get him out on the base paths.

hot corner third base, so-called because of the hard hits often directed to that part of the field.

infield fly rule a ball hit high in the air above the infield with runners on first or first and second with less than two out, at which time an umpire calls the batter automatically out so that fielders cannot intentionally let the ball drop safely and then try to turn a double play; runners advance at their own risk once the infield fly rule is invoked by the umpire.

inning one of nine units that constitute a regular-length game, consisting of one turn on offense by each team for a duration necessary for them to make three outs. If the game is tied after the ninth inning, the game continues in extra innings until a winner is decided.

K the official scorer's shorthand for a strikeout; a backwards K denotes that the batter struck out without swinging at the third strike.

knuckleball a pitch gripped by only the finger tips or in some cases the knuckles, meant to put as little spin on the ball as possible, resulting, ideally, in the ball fluttering slowly and unpredictably toward the plate.

line drive a ball hit sharply with very little elevation (sometimes called "a rope").

mound a packed dome of dirt, 60 feet six inches from the back of home plate and no more than 10 inches high at its apex, from which a pitcher throws the ball; in the center of the mound is a rectangular slab of rubber that the pitcher uses to push himself toward the plate (using the power of his leg) when throwing the ball.

no-hitter a game in which a pitcher or pitchers for one team do not allow a base hit by the opposition.

out play in which a batter or a runner is retired.

perfect game a nine-inning (or greater) complete game victory by one pitcher who does not allow a single runner to reach first base safely by any means.

pick-off when a pitcher or catcher throws behind a runner on base, resulting in that runner being tagged out before returning to his base.

pinch-hit to take a turn at bat in place of another player, who is then removed from the game.

relief pitcher any pitcher who enters the game after the starting pitcher has been removed, usually because of ineffectiveness, injury, or fatigue, but sometimes for strategic purposes.

sacrifice when a batter intentionally makes an out in order to advance a base runner or when an out leads to the advantageous advance of a runner; a sacrifice does not count as an official at bat.

slider a pitch that is nearly as fast as a fastball and which breaks nearly as much as a curve, ideally confusing the batter as to whether it is a fastball or a curve that is being thrown, confounding his timing.

stolen base when a base runner advances from one base to the next by running at the moment of the pitch and, if the pitch is not hit, makes it to the next base before the catcher can make a throw to a fielder covering that base.

strikeout when a batter gets his third strike, either swinging and missing or judged by the umpire to be hittable and in the strike zone.

Texas Leaguer a batted ball that loops over the infielders and drops safely in front of the outfielders, so named because of one (perhaps apocryphal) player's knack for making such hits while playing in a league in Texas.

triple when a batter hits the ball safely in such a way as to enable him to make it to third base.

triple play when a ball in play leads to three base runners being called out.

umpires the official arbiters of a game, usually four in number, positioned behind home plate, and at first, second, and third base.

walk when a batter receives, in one at bat, four pitches that are deemed out of the strike zone by the umpire, and at which the batter does not swing, in which instance he is awarded first base with no official at bat charged. Also called "base on balls."

warning track usually a cinder path in front of the outfield wall that when stepped on will alert an outfielder that he is approaching the boundary of the playing field.

Baseball Hall of Fame

Player/Position/Year Inducted	Games	At Bats	HRs	Avg.	Hits	RBIs
Aaron, Henry (Hank) OF 1982	3,298	12,364	755	.305	3,771	2,297
All-time leader in home runs and RBIs						
Alomar, Roberto 2B 2011	2,379	9,073	210	.300	2,724	1134
Career .300 hitter, 10 gold gloves, 11 consecutive All-Star games						
Anson, Adrian (Cap) 1B 1939	2,523	10,278	97	.333	3,418	2,076
Managed 20 years, 1879-98, winning five pennants						
Aparicio, Luis SS 1984	2,599	10,230	83	.262	2,677	791
Led AL in stolen bases nine years in a row (1955-64)						
Appling, Luke SS 1964	2,422	8,857	45	.310	2,749	1,116
Batted .388 in 1936						
Ashburn, Richie OF 1995	2,189	8,365	29	.308	2,574	586
Hit .300 or more nine times						
Averill, Earl OF 1975	1,669	6,358	238	.318	2,020	1,165
232 hits in 1936						
Baker, Frank (Home Run) 3B 1955	1,575	5,985	96	.307	1,838	1,013
Batted .363 in six World Series						
Bancroft, Dave SS 1971	1,913	7,182	32	.279	2,004	591
Handled 984 chances in 1922						
Banks, Ernie SS, 1B 1977	2,528	9,421	512	.274	2,583	1,636
Consecutive M.V.P. awards, 1958-59						
Beckley, Jake 1B 1971	2,386	9,527	88	.308	2,931	1,575
244 career triples, mostly in 19th century						
Bench, Johnny C 1989	2,158	7,658	389	.267	2,048	1,376
Hit .529 in 1976 World Series; NL M.V.P. 1970, 1972						
Berra, Lawrence (Yogi) C, OF 1972	2,120	7,555	358	.285	2,150	1,430
Three M.V.P. awards, 1951, 1954, 1955						
Boggs, Wade 3B 2005	2,439	9,180	118	.328	3,010	1,014
12-time All-Star						
Bottomley, Jim 1B 1974	1,991	7,471	219	.310	2,313	1,422
12 RBIs in one game, 1924						

Player/Position/Year Inducted	Games	At Bats	HRs	Avg.	Hits	RBIs
Boudreau, Lou SS 1970	1,646	6,030	68	.295	1,779	789
M.V.P. in 1948; managed 16 years						
Bresnahan, Roger C, OF 1945	1,430	4,478	26	.279	1,251	530
212 stolen bases; first catcher elected to Hall of Fame						
Brett, George 3B, 1B 1999	2,707	10,349	317	.305	3,154	1,595
Hit .300 11 years; 13-time All-Star; hit .390 in 1980						
Brock, Lou OF 1985	2,616	10,332	149	.293	3,023	900
938 stolen bases; batted .391 in three World Series						
Brouthers, Dan 1B 1945	1,673	6,711	106	.342	2,296	1,296
Seven slugging and five batting titles during 19th century						
Burkett, Jesse OF 1946	2,072	8,430	75	.341	2,873	952
Led NL in batting three times and in hits four times						
Campanella, Roy C 1969	1,215	4,205	242	.276	1,161	856
Three M.V.P. awards, 1951, 1953, 1955						
Carew, Rod 2B 1991	2,469	9,315	92	.328	3,053	1,015
18-time All-Star, AL MVP 1977, AL Rookie of the Year 1967						
Carey, Max OF 1961	2,476	9,363	70	.285	2,665	800
738 stolen bases						
Carter, Gary C 2003	2,296	7,971	324	.262	2,092	1,225
11-time All-Star (1975, 1979-88); won three gold gloves						
Cepeda, Orlando 1B 1999	2,124	7,927	379	.297	2,351	1,365
Seven-time All-Star; NL M.V.P. 1967; .499 career slugging percentage						
Chance, Frank 1B 1946	1,286	4,295	20	.297	1,274	596
Managed Chicago (NL) to four pennants in five years, 1906–10						
Clarke, Fred OF 1945	2,245	8,588	67	.315	2,708	1,015
223 career triples, hit .300 or better 11 years						
Clemente, Roberto OF 1973	2,433	9,454	240	.317	3,000	1,305
Career average of over 18 outfield assists per season						
Cobb, Ty OF 1936	3,035	11,429	117	.367	4,191	1,938
Batted .320 or better in 23 straight years						
Cochrane, Mickey C 1947	1,482	5,169	119	.320	1,652	832
Two M.V.P. awards, 1928 and 1934						
Collins, Eddie 2B 1939	2,826	9,949	47	.333	3,315	1,300
Hit .340 or better 10 years; led AL in fielding nine times						
Collins, Jimmy 3B 1945	1,728	6,796	64	.294	1,997	982
Led NL in home runs, 1898						
Combs, Earle OF 1970	1,454	5,748	58	.325	1,866	629
Averaged 127 runs scored per season						
Connor, Roger 1B 1976	1,998	7,798	136	.318	2,480	1,078
Held all-time HR record before Babe Ruth						
Crawford, Sam OF 1957	2,517	9,580	97	.309	2,964	1,525
312 triples, most ever						
Cronin, Joe SS 1956	2,124	7,579	170	.301	2,285	1,424
M.V.P. in 1930; managed 1933–47						
Cuyler, Hazen (Kiki) OF 1968	1,879	7,161	127	.321	2,299	1,065
Led NL in runs scored twice, stolen bases four times						
Davis, George SS 1998	2,376	9,035	73	.295	2,665	1,435
Hit over .300 nine years in a row (1893–1901)						

Player/Position/Year Inducted	Games	At Bats	HRs	Avg.	Hits	RBIs
Dawson, Andre OF 2010	2,627	9,927	438	.279	2,774	1,591
NL Rookie of the Year in 1977 and the NL M.V.P. in 1988						
Delahanty, Ed IF, OF 1945	1,835	7,505	101	.346	2,596	1,464
Batted .410 in 1899						
Dickey, Bill C 1954	1,789	6,300	202	.313	1,969	1,209
Catcher on eight AL-pennant-winning teams						
DiMaggio, Joe OF 1955	1,736	6,821	361	.325	2,214	1,537
56 game hitting streak in 1941						
Doby, Larry, OF 1998	1,533	5,348	253	.283	1,515	969
Led AL in HR twice; seven-time All-Star (1949–55); first black man to play in AL						
Doerr, Bobby 2B 1986	1,865	7,093	223	.288	2,042	1,247
Led AL in slugging 1944						
Duffy, Hugh OF 1945	1,736	7,062	103	.328	2,314	1,299
Batted .438 in 1894						
Evers, Johnny 2B 1946	1,783	6,134	12	.270	1,658	538
NL M.V.P. in 1914						
Ewing, Buck C, IF, OF 1939	1,315	5,363	70	.303	1,625	733
Regarded as the greatest player of the 19th century						
Ferrell, Rick C 1984	1,884	6,028	28	.281	1,692	734
Led AL catchers at times in putouts, assists, fielding average, and double plays						
Fisk, Carlton C 2000	2,499	8,756	376	.269	2,356	1,330
Hit 20 or more home runs 8 seasons						
Flick, Elmer OF 1963	1,484	5,603	47	.315	1,767	756
Led AL in triples 1905-07						
Fox, Nellie 2B 1997	2,367	9,232	35	.288	2,663	790
Led AL in putouts, 1951-60						
Foxx, Jimmie 1B, 3B 1951	2,317	8,134	534	.325	2,646	1,921
Slugged over .700 three seasons						
Frisch, Frank 2B, 3B 1947	2,311	9,112	105	.316	2,880	1,244
Hit .300 or better 11 years in a row (1921–31)						
Gehrig, Lou 1B 1939	2,164	8,001	493	.340	2,721	1,990
Played in 2,130 consecutive games; first player to hit 4 HRs in one game						
Gehringer, Charlie 2B 1949	2,323	8,860	184	.320	2,839	1,427
60 doubles in 1936						
Gordon, Joe 2B 2009	1,566	5,707	253	.268	1,530	975
Nine-time All-Star; AL M.V.P. 1942						
Goslin, Leon (Goose) OF 1968	2,287	8,655	248	.316	2,735	1,609
100+ RBI 11 years						
Greenberg, Hank 1B 1956	1,394	5,193	331	.313	1,628	1,276
58 home runs in 1938; 63 doubles in 1934						
Gwynn, Tony OF 2007	2,440	9,288	135	.338	3,141	1,138
Won eight batting titles						
Hafey, Charles (Chick) OF 1971	1,283	4,625	164	.317	1,466	833
NL batting title (.349) in 1931						
Hamilton, Billy OF 1961	1,591	6,269	40	.344	2,159	739
Scored 196 runs in 1894, with a .509 on-base average and 99 stolen bases						
Hartnett, Charles (Gabby) C 1955	1,990	6,432	236	.297	1,912	1,179
Played on four NL pennant winners, managed one						

Player/Position/Year Inducted	Games	At Bats	HRs	Avg.	Hits	RBIs
Heilmann, Harry OF, 1B 1952	2,147	7,787	183	.342	2,660	1,539
Batted .403 in 1923						
Henderson, Rickey LF 2009	3,081	10,961	297	.279	3,055	1,115
All-time leader for stolen bases (1,406) and runs scored (2,295); 10-time All-Star, AL M.V.P. 1990						
Herman, Billy 2B 1975	1,922	7,707	47	.304	2,345	839
57 doubles in 1935						
Hooper, Harry OF 1971	2,308	8,785	75	.281	2,466	817
375 career stolen bases						
Hornsby, Rogers 2B, IF 1942	2,259	8,173	301	.358	2,930	1,584
Batted .424 in 1924; nine slugging titles						
Jackson, Reggie 1993	2,820	9,864	563	.262	2,584	1,702
Played in 5 World Series and 11 divisional playoffs in 21 years; World Series M.V.P. 1977						
Jackson, Travis SS 1982	1,656	6,086	135	.291	1,768	929
Batted over .300 six times in 1920's and 1930's						
Jennings, Hugh SS 1945	1,285	4,905	18	.312	1,531	840
Batted .398 in 1896						
Kaline, Al OF 1980	2,834	10,116	399	.297	3,007	1,583
3,007 career hits						
Keeler, Willie OF 1939	2,123	8,591	33	.341	2,932	810
Batted .424 in 1897; 495 career stolen bases						
Kell, George 3B 1983	1,795	6,702	78	.306	2,054	870
AL batting champ (.343) in 1949						
Kelley, Joe OF 1971	1,845	7,018	65	.319	2,242	1,193
Averaged 151 runs scored, 1894–96						
Kelly, George 1B 1973	1,622	5,993	148	.297	1,778	1,020
Led NL in RBI, 1920 and 1925						
Kelly, Mike (King) OF, C 1945	1,463	5,923	69	.307	1,820	794
Two batting titles, 1884 and 1886; 315 career stolen bases						
Killebrew, Harmon 1B, 3B, OF 1984	2,435	8,147	573	.256	2,086	1,584
40+ home runs eight years						
Kiner, Ralph OF 1975	1,472	5,205	369	.279	1,451	1,015
Second highest home run per at bat ratio of all-time						
Klein, Chuck OF 1980	1,753	6,486	300	.320	2,076	1,201
44 outfield assists in 1930						
Lajoie, Napoleon 2B 1937	2,480	9,589	82	.338	3,242	1,599
Batted .422 in 1901						
Lazerri, Tony IF 1991	1,740	6,297	178	.292	1,840	1,191
Batted .300 or better five times; clutch hitter in World Series						
Lindstrom, Fred 3B, OF 1976	1,438	5,611	103	.311	1,747	779
231 hits in 1928						
Lombardi, Ernie C 1986	1,853	5,855	190	.306	1,792	990
Two NL batting titles, 1938 and 1942						
Mantle, Mickey OF 1974	2,401	8,102	536	.298	2,415	1,509
52 home runs in 1956, 54 in 1961						
Manush, Heinie OF 1964	2,009	7,653	110	.330	2,524	1,173
Hit .378 in 1926						
Maranville, Rabbit SS, 2B 1954	2,670	10,078	28	.258	2,605	884
23-year career; hit .308 in two World Series						

Player/Position/Year Inducted	Games	At Bats	HRs	Avg.	Hits	RBIs
Mathews, Eddie 3B 1978	2,388	8,537	512	.271	2,315	1,453
1,444 career walks						
Mays, Willie OF 1979	2,992	10,881	660	.302	3,283	1,903
Slugged over .600 six seasons						
Mazeroski, Bill 2B 2001	2,163	7,775	138	.260	2,016	853
Eight-time gold glove winner. Turned a record 1,706 double plays						
McCarthy, Tommy OF 1946	1,275	5,128	44	.292	1,496	666
Averaged 122 runs scored, 1888-94						
McCovey, Willie 1B, OF 1986	2,588	8,197	521	.270	2,211	1,555
Hit 18 career grand slams						
McPhee, Bid 2B 2000	2,135	8,291	53	.279	2,250	727
Considered greatest second baseman of the 19th century, though he played without a glove						
Medwick, Joe OF 1968	1,984	7,635	205	.324	2,471	1,383
Won NL triple crown in 1937						
Mize, Johnny 1B 1981	1,884	6,443	359	.312	2,011	1,337
Four-time NL home run champ						
Molitor, Paul DH 2004	2,683	10,835	234	.306	3,319	1,307
Seven-time All-Star; 1993 World Series M.V.P.						
Morgan, Joe 2B 1990	2,649	9,277	268	.271	2,517	1,133
Won back-to-back M.V.P. Awards (1975–76)						
Murray, Eddie 1B 2003	3,026	11,336	504	.287	3,255	1,917
Third player ever with 3,000 hits and 500 HRs						
Musial, Stan OF, 1B 1969	3,026	10,972	475	.331	3,630	1,951
725 doubles and 177 triples						
O'Rourke, Jim OF 1945	1,774	7,435	51	.310	2,304	830
Batted .300+ 11 times in the 19th century						
Ott, Mel OF 1951	2,732	9,456	511	.304	2,876	1,860
Averaged 121 RBIs 1929-38						
Perez, Tony 1B 2000	2,777	9,778	379	.279	2,732	1,652
His 1,652 RBIs are the most ever by a Latin player						
Puckett, Kirby OF 2001	1,783	7,244	207	.318	2,304	1,085
Led Minnesota Twins to World Series wins in 1987 and 1991						
Reese, Harold (Pee Wee) SS 1984	2,166	8,058	126	.269	2,170	885
Finished in the top ten of M.V.P. balloting nine times						
Rice, Jim OF 2009	2,089	8,225	382	.298	2,452	1,451
Led AL in HR and RBIs during career; hit over .300 in 7 seasons						
Rice, Sam OF 1963	2,404	9,269	34	.322	2,987	1,078
Only 18 strikeouts per 154 games						
Ripken Jr., Cal SS 2007	3,001	11,551	431	.276	3,184	1,695
Played in record 2,632 games						
Rizzuto, Phil SS 1994	1,661	5,816	38	.273	1,588	563
AL M.V.P. in 1950; Played in 9 World Series						
Robinson, Brooks 3B 1983	2,896	10,654	268	.267	2,848	1357
16 consecutive Gold Gloves, 1960-75						
Robinson, Frank OF 1982	2,808	10,006	586	.294	2,943	1812
M.V.P. in both leagues; AL triple crown in 1966						
Robinson, Jackie 2B 1962	1,382	4,877	137	.311	1,518	734
First black player in MLB; Rookie of the Year 1947; M.V.P. and batting champ, 1949						

Player/Position/Year Inducted	Games	At Bats	HRs	Avg.	Hits	RBIs
Roush, Edd OF 1962	1,967	7,363	68	.323	2,376	981
Two NL batting titles, 1917 and 1919						
Ruth, George (Babe) OF, P 1936	2,503	8,399	714	.342	2,873	2211
Slugged .847 1920-21						
Sandberg, Ryne 2B 2005	2,164	8,385	282	.285	2,386	1,061
10-time All-Star, winner of nine Gold Glove awards						
Schalk, Ray C 1955	1,760	5,306	12	.253	1,345	594
176 stolen bases						
Schmidt, Mike 3B 1995	2,404	8,352	548	.267	2,234	1,595
Led NL in homers 8 seasons; won 10 Gold Gloves						
Schoendienst, Albert (Red) 2B 1989	2,216	8,479	84	.289	2,449	773
Managed Cardinals to two pennants and 1967 World Series crown						
Sewell, Joe SS, 3B 1977	1,902	7,132	49	.312	2,226	1,051
Only 22 strikeouts in his last 2,500 at bats, 1929–33						
Simmons, Al OF 1953	2,215	8,761	307	.334	2,927	1,827
Drove in over 100 runs in each of his first 11 years, 1924–34						
Sisler, George 1B 1939	2,055	8,267	100	.340	2,812	1,175
Batted .400 1920-22						
Slaughter, Enos OF 1985	2,380	7,946	169	.300	2,383	1,304
52 doubles in 1939						
Smith, Ozzie SS 2002	2,573	9,396	28	.262	2,460	793
Won 13 Gold Gloves; 15-time All-Star						
Snider, Edwin (Duke) OF 1980	2,143	7,161	407	.295	2,116	1,333
Averaged 41 home runs, 1953-57						
Speaker, Tris OF 1937	2,789	10,195	117	.345	3,514	1,529
Led AL in doubles eight times						
Stargell, Willie OF, 1B 1988	2,360	7,927	475	.282	2,232	1,540
National League M.V.P. in 1979						
Terry, Bill 1B 1954	1,721	6,428	154	.341	2,193	1,078
Hit .401 in 1930						
Thompson, Sam OF 1974	1,410	6,005	128	.331	1,986	1,299
166 RBI in 1887, 165 in 1895						
Tinker, Joe SS 1946	1,805	6,441	31	.263	1,695	782
Played in four World Series with Chicago Cubs						
Traynor, Pie 3B 1948	1,941	7,559	58	.320	2,416	1,273
100+ RBIs seven years						
Vaughan, Joseph (Arky) SS 1985	1,817	6,622	96	.318	2,103	926
Hit .385 in 1935						
Wagner, Honus SS 1936	2786	10,427	101	.329	3,430	1,732
Eight batting titles, four in a row 1906–09						
Wallace, Bobby SS 1953	2,386	8,652	35	.267	2,314	1,121
Handled 6.1 chances per game at shortstop						
Waner, Lloyd OF 1967	1,992	7,772	28	.316	2,459	598
234 hits in 1929						
Waner, Paul OF 1952	2,549	9,459	112	.333	3,152	1,309
62 doubles in 1932						
Wheat, Zack OF 1959	2,410	9,106	132	.317	2,884	1,261
Batted .375 at age 36 in 1924						

Williams, Billy OF 1987	2,488	9,350	426	.290	2,711	1,475
30+ home runs in five seasons						
Williams, Ted OF 1966	2,292	7,706	521	.344	2,654	1,839
Last .400 hitter in majors, .406 in 1941						
Wilson, Lewis (Hack) OF 1979	1,348	4,760	244	.307	1,461	1,062
56 home runs and 190 RBI in 1930						
Winfield, Dave OF 2001	2,973	11,003	465	.283	3,110	1,833
Member of both the 3,000-hit and 400-home run club						
Yastrzemski, Carl (Yaz) OF, 1B 1989	3,308	11,988	452	.285	3,419	1,844
Won Triple Crown in 1967; won batting titles in 1963, 1967, and 1968						
Youngs, Ross OF 1972	1,211	4,627	42	.322	1,491	592
Killed at age 30; .398 on-base average in four World Series, 1921–24						
Yount, Robin SS, OF 1999	2,856	11,008	251	.285	3,142	1,406
The only player ever to win AL M.V.P. awards at shortstop (1982) and center field (1989)						

Hall of Fame Pitchers

Player/Year Inducted	W	L	ERA	Games	Innings	Strikeouts
Alexander, Grover Cleveland 1938	373	208	2.56	696	5,190	2,198
Won 30 games three years; led NL in ERA five times						
Bender, Charles (Chief) 1953	210	127	2.46	459	3,017	1,711
Led AL in winning percentage three seasons						
Blyleven, Rik Albert (Bert) 2011	287	250	3.31	692	4,970	3,701
3,701 career strikeouts; 242 complete games						
Brown, Mordecai (Three-Finger) 1949	239	130	2.06	481	3,172	1,375
1.04 ERA in 1906						
Bunning, Jim 1996	224	184	3.27	591	3,760	2,855
Struck out 1,000 batters in each league						
Carlton, Steve (Lefty) 1994	329	244	3.22	741	5,217	4,136
Four-time Cy Young Award winner (1972, 1977, 1980, 1982)						
Chesbro, Jack 1946	198	132	2.68	392	2,897	1,265
41 wins in 1904						
Clarkson, John 1963	326	177	2.81	531	4,536	2,015
53 wins in 1885, with 623 innings pitched						
Coveleski, Stan 1969	215	142	2.88	450	3,093	981
Led AL in ERA in 1925, 2.84						
Cummings, Williams (Candy) 1939	21	22	2.78	43	372	37
Inventor of the curveball						
Dean, Jay (Dizzy) 1953	150	83	3.03	317	1,966	1,155
30 wins in 1934						
Drysdale, Don 1984	209	166	2.95	518	3,432	2,486
56 2/3 consecutive scoreless innings, 1968						
Eckersley, Dennis 2004	197	171	3.50	1,071	3,286	2,401
Only pitcher with 100 complete games and 100 saves						
Faber, Urban (Red) 1964	254	212	3.15	669	4,088	1,471
Led AL in ERA in 1921 and 1922						
Feller, Bob 1962	266	162	3.25	570	3,827	2,581
Led AL in wins six seasons, in shutouts seven seasons						
Fingers, Rollie 1992	114	118	2.90	944	1,701	1,299
341 saves over 17 years; AL M.V.P. in 1981						
Ford, Edward (Whitey) 1974	236	106	2.75	498	3,170	1,956
25–4 in 1961, 24–7 in 1963						

Player/Year Inducted	W	L	ERA	Games	Innings	Strikeouts
Galvin, James (Pud) 1965	365	310	2.85	705	6,003	1,807
46 wins in 1883 and 1884						
Gibson, Bob 1981	251	174	2.91	528	3,885	3,117
1.12 ERA in 1968, seven straight wins in World Series play						
Gomez, Vernon (Lefty) 1972	189	102	3.34	368	2,503	1,468
Led AL in shutouts three years						
Gossage, Richard (Goose) 2008	124	107	3.01	1,002	1,809	1,502
310 career saves; 9-time All-Star						
Grimes, Burleigh 1964	270	212	3.53	617	4,180	1,512
Last legal spitball pitcher, he won 20+ games five seasons						
Grove, Robert (Lefty) 1947	300	141	3.06	616	3,941	2,266
Led AL in ERA nine seasons, in strikeouts seven seasons						
Haines, Jesse 1970	210	158	3.64	555	3,209	981
Twice led NL in shutouts, 1921 and 1927						
Hoyt, Waite 1969	237	182	3.59	674	3,763	1,206
1.83 in 84 World Series innings						
Hubbell, Carl 1947	253	154	2.97	535	3,589	1,678
26–6 in 1936; 1.66 ERA in 1933						
Hunter, Jim (Catfish) 1987	224	166	3.26	500	3,448	2,012
21 or more wins, 1971–75						
Jenkins, Ferguson 1991	284	226	3.34	664	4,499	3,192
Cy Young Award winner in 1971; three-time All-Star						
Johnson, Walter 1936	417	279	2.17	802	5,914	3,508
36-7, 1.14 ERA in 1913						
Joss, Addie 1978	160	97	1.89	286	2,327	920
Averaged 21–11, 1.66 ERA in years 1904–08						
Keefe, Tim 1964	342	225	2.62	600	5,049	2,564
Averaged 37 wins 1883–85						
Koufax, Sandy 1972	165	87	2.76	397	2,324	2,396
95–27, 1.85 ERA for seasons 1963-66						
Lemon, Bob 1976	207	128	3.23	460	2,850	1,277
Won 20 or more seven times						
Lyons, Ted 1955	260	230	3.67	594	4,161	1,073
Pitched 27 shutouts, but never won 20 games						
Marichal, Juan 1983	243	142	2.89	471	3,509	2,303
Only 1.8 walks per nine innings over career						
Marquard, Richard (Rube) 1971	201	177	3.08	536	3,307	1,593
73–23 in years 1911–13						
Mathewson, Christy 1936	373	188	2.13	635	4,780	2,502
79 career shutouts						
McGinnity, Joe 1946	247	144	2.64	466	3,459	1,068
35–8 in 1904, with an ERA of 1.61						
Newhouser, Hal 1992	207	150	3.06	488	2,993	1,796
Led AL in victories three years in a row (1944–46)						
Nichols, Charles (Kid) 1949	361	208	2.95	620	5,056	1,873
Won 30 or more games seven seasons, 1891-94, 1896-98						
Niekro, Phil 1997	318	274	3.35	864	5,404	3,342
Knuckleballer pitched until age 48; five-time All-Star						
Palmer, Jim 1990	268	152	2.86	558	3,948	2,212
Won Cy Young Award 1973, 1975, 1976						
Pennock, Herb 1948	240	162	3.61	617	3,558	1,227
162–90 as a New York Yankee, 1923–33						

Player/Year Inducted	W	L	ERA	Games	Innings	Strikeouts
Perry, Gaylord 1991	314	265	3.10	777	5,352	3,534
Won Cy Young Award in both leagues						
Plank, Eddie 1946	326	194	2.35	623	4,496	2,246
1.32 ERA in seven World Series games						
Radbourn, Charles (Old Hoss) 1939	309	195	2.67	528	4,535	1,830
60–12 in 1884, with 679 innings pitched						
Rixey, Eppa 1963	266	251	3.15	692	4,495	1,350
Won 25 games in 1922						
Roberts, Robin 1976	286	245	3.41	676	4,689	2,357
28–7 in 1952; five-time NL leader in complete games						
Ruffing, Charles (Red) 1967	273	225	3.80	624	4,344	1,987
.645 winning percentage as a New York Yankee						
Rusie, Amos 1977	243	160	3.07	462	3,770	1,957
Won 30+ games three years						
Ryan, Nolan 1999	324	292	3.19	807	5,386	5,714
Threw seven no-hitters; struck out 300 or more six times; struck out 200 or more 15 times						
Seaver, Tom 1992	311	205	2.86	656	4,782	3,640
Won 20 or more games five times; won Cy Young Award 1969, 1973, 1975						
Spahn, Warren 1973	363	245	3.09	750	5,244	2,583
Won 20 or more games 13 times, including 23 at age 42						
Sutter, Bruce 2006	68	71	2.83	661	1,042	861
300 career saves						
Sutton, Don 1998	324	256	3.26	774	5,280	3,574
Won 15 or more games eight years in a row (1969–76)						
Vance, Clarence (Dazzy) 1955	197	140	3.24	442	2,697	2,045
60–15 over two years—1924, 1925						
Waddell, George (Rube) 1946	193	143	2.16	407	2,961	2,316
349 strikeouts in 1904						
Walsh, Ed 1946	195	126	1.82	430	2,964	1,736
40–15 in 1908 with 11 shutouts; all-time ERA leader						
Ward, Monte 1964	161	101	2.10	291	2,462	920
47 wins in 1879; 40 wins in 1880; played 1,825 games as a hitter						
Welch, Mickey 1973	307	210	2.71	565	4,802	1,850
44–11 in 1885						
Wilhelm, Hoyt 1985	143	122	2.52	1,070	2,254	1,610
227 career saves; first relief pitcher elected to Hall of Fame						
Willis, Vic 1995	249	205	2.63	513	3,996	1,651
Won 20 games eight times; 45 complete games in 1902						
Wynn, Early 1972	300	244	3.54	691	4,564	2,334
Led AL in shutouts at age 40 in 1960						
Young, Cy 1937	511	313	2.63	906	7,359	2,799
All-time leader in wins, losses, complete games, and innings pitched.						

Major League Baseball All-Time Career Leaders

Hits (3,000 or more)

1. Pete Rose	4,256
2. Ty Cobb	4,191
3. Hank Aaron	3,771
4. Stan Musial	3,630
5. Tris Speaker	3,514
6. Carl Yastrzemski	3,419
7. Cap Anson	3,418
8. Honus Wagner	3,415
9. Paul Molitor	3,319
10. Eddie Collins	3,315
11. Willie Mays	3,283
12. Eddie Murray	3,255
13. Nap Lajoie	3,242
14. Cal Ripken Jr.	3,184
15. George Brett	3,154
16. Paul Waner	3,152
17. Robin Yount	3,142
18. Tony Gwynn	3,141
19. Dave Winfield	3,110
20. Craig Biggio	3,060
21. Rickey Henderson	3,055
22. Rod Carew	3,053
23. Lou Brock	3,023
24. Rafael Palmeiro	3,020
25. Wade Boggs	3,010

Home Runs

1. Barry Bonds	762
2. Hank Aaron	755
3. Babe Ruth	714
4. Willie Mays	660
5. Ken Griffey, Jr.[1]	630
6. Alex Rodriguez[1]	613
7. Sammy Sosa	609
8. Jim Thome[1]	589
9. Frank Robinson	586
10. Mark McGwire	583
11. Harmon Killebrew	573
12. Rafael Palmeiro	569
13. Reggie Jackson	563
14. Manny Ramirez[1]	555
15. Mike Schmidt	548
16. Mickey Mantle	536
17. Jimmie Foxx	534
18. Willie McCovey	521
18. Ted Williams	521
18. Frank Thomas	521
21. Ernie Banks	512
21. Eddie Mathews	512
23. Mel Ott	511
24. Gary Sheffield	509
25. Eddie Murray	504

Runs Batted In

1. Hank Aaron	2,297
2. Babe Ruth	2,213
3. Cap Anson	2,076
4. Barry Bonds	1,996
5. Lou Gehrig	1,995
6. Stan Musial	1,951
7. Ty Cobb	1,938
8. Jimmie Foxx	1,922
9. Eddie Murray	1,917
10. Willie Mays	1,903

Runs

1. Rickey Henderson	2,295
2. Ty Cobb	2,245
3. Barry Bonds	2,227
4. Babe Ruth	2,174
4. Hank Aaron	2,174
6. Pete Rose	2,165
7. Willie Mays	2,062
8. Cap Anson	1,996
9. Stan Musial	1,949
10. Lou Gehrig	1,888

Average (minimum 5,000 at bats)

1. Ty Cobb	.367
2. Rogers Hornsby	.358
3. Joe Jackson	.356
4. Ed Delahanty	.346
5. Tris Speaker	.345
6. Ted Williams	.344
6. Billy Hamilton	.344
8. Babe Ruth	.342
8. Dan Brouthers	.342
8. Willie Keeler	.342

Stolen Bases

1. Rickey Henderson	1,406
2. Lou Brock	938
3. Billy Hamilton	912
4. Ty Cobb	892
5. Tim Raines	808
6. Vince Coleman	752
7. Eddie Collins	745
8. Arlie Latham	739
9. Max Carey	738
10. Honus Wagner	722

Total Bases

1. Hank Aaron	6,856
2. Stan Musial	6,134
3. Willie Mays	6,066
4. Barry Bonds	5,976
5. Ty Cobb	5,859
6. Babe Ruth	5,793
7. Pete Rose	5,752
8. Carl Yastrzemski	5,539
9. Eddie Murray	5,397
10. Rafael Palmero	5,388

Slugging Percentage[2]

1. Babe Ruth	.690
2. Ted Williams	.634
3. Lou Gehrig	.632
4. Albert Pujols[1]	.624
5. Jimmie Foxx	.609
5. Barry Bonds	.607
7. Hank Greenberg	.605
8. Mark McGwire	.588
9. Manny Ramirez[1]	.586
10. Joe DiMaggio	.579

Extra Base Hits

1. Hank Aaron	1,477
2. Barry Bonds	1,440
3. Stan Musial	1,377
4. Babe Ruth	1,356
5. Willie Mays	1,323
6. Ken Griffey, Jr.[1]	1,192
6. Rafael Palmeiro	1,192
8. Lou Gehrig	1,190
9. Frank Robinson	1,186
10. Carl Yastrzemski	1,157

Games Played

1. Pete Rose	3,562
2. Carl Yastrzemski	3,308
3. Hank Aaron	3,298

4. Rickey Henderson	3,081	20. Mickey Welch	307			
5. Ty Cobb	3,035	21. Tom Glavine	305			
6. Eddie Murray	3,026	22. Randy Johnson	303			
6. Stan Musial	3,026					
8. Cal Ripken	3,001					

Innings Pitched

1. Cy Young	7,356
2. Pud Galvin	6,003
3. Walter Johnson	5,914
4. Phil Niekro	5,404
5. Nolan Ryan	5,386
6. Gaylord Perry	5,350
7. Don Sutton	5,282
8. Warren Spahn	5,244
9. Steve Carlton	5,217
10. Grover Cleveland Alexander	5,190

9. Willie Mays	2,992		
10. Barry Bonds	2,986		

Strikeouts

1. Nolan Ryan	5,714
2. Randy Johnson	4,875
3. Roger Clemens	4,672
4. Steve Carlton	4,136
5. Bert Blyleven	3,701
6. Tom Seaver	3,640
7. Don Sutton	3,574
8. Gaylord Perry	3,534
9. Walter Johnson	3,508
10. Phil Niekro	3,342

Pitching-Wins

1. Cy Young	511
2. Walter Johnson	417
3. Christy Mathewson	373
3. Grover Alexander	373
5. Pud Galvin	365
6. Warren Spahn	363
7. Kid Nichols	361
8. Greg Maddux	355
9. Roger Clemens	354
10. Tim Keefe	342
11. Steve Carlton	329
12. John Clarkson	328
13. Eddie Plank	326
14. Nolan Ryan	324
14. Don Sutton	324
16. Phil Niekro	318
17. Gaylord Perry	314
18. Tom Seaver	311
19. Charles Radbourn	309

Shutouts

1. Walter Johnson	110
2. Grover Cleveland Alexander	90
3. Christy Mathewson	80
4. Cy Young	76
5. Eddie Plank	69
6. Warren Spahn	63
7. Nolan Ryan	61
7. Tom Seaver	61
9. Bert Blyleven	60
10. Don Sutton	58

Earned Run Average

1. Ed Walsh	1.82
2. Addie Joss	1.89
3. Al Spalding	2.04
4. Mordecai "Three Finger" Brown	2.06
5. John Ward	2.10
6. Christy Mathewson	2.13
7. Tommy Bond	2.14
8. Rube Waddell	2.16
9. Walter Johnson	2.17
10. Ed Reulbach	2.28

Note: As of October 2010. 1. Active during the 2010 season. 2. Total bases divided by minimum 400 at-bats.
Source: Major League Baseball.

The World Series

From 1882–90, the winners of the National League and American Association played each other in a championship series. After the A.A. folded, the top two NL clubs played for the "Temple Cup", but the idea never really caught on. The American League began operations in 1901, setting off bidding wars with the National League for the services of star players. Peace was established in 1903; toward the end of that season, the owners of the winning franchises in each league agreed to hold a "World Series" in October. Many were surprised that Boston, from the newer American League, won the title.

There was no agreement to play such a series every year, however, and in 1904 the New York Giants refused to meet the Boston club, probably due to John McGraw's dis-like of American League President Ban Johnson. But the baseball public wanted a championship series, and by 1905 Giants owner John Brush proposed rules governing a mandatory series to be played every year. With minute changes, those rules stand to this day.

1903 Boston (A) over Pittsburgh (N), 5–3. The upstart American league emerged victorious in the first World Series, a best of nine affair. The "Pilgrims" (Red Sox) staged one of the greatest comebacks in history by sweeping the final four games. Bill Dineen won three and Cy Young won two for Boston, and held Pirate immortal Honus Wagner to a .222 average.

1904 No series. New York Giant owner John T. Brush and manager John McGraw refused to play the World Champion Boston club, dismissing them as representative of an "inferior league."

1905 New York (N) over Philadelphia (A), 4–1. Every game was a shutout, with Christy Mathewson throwing three for the Giants. In 27 innings, he allowed 14 hits, struck out 18 and walked one. The Athletics committed five errors in the pivotal Game 3.

1906 Chicago (A) over Chicago (N), 4–2. The first "subway series" was a stunning upset. The "Hitless Wonders" White Sox had batted .230 with 7 home runs during the season, while the Cubs won 116 games, still the all-time record. Utilityman George Rohe hit two game-winning triples for the Sox and Ed Walsh pitched two of their wins.

1907 Chicago (N) over Detroit (A), 4–0. The Cubs shut down Ty Cobb, Sam Crawford et al., behind a superb four-man pitching performance, and the hitting of Harry Steinfeldt (.471) and Johnny Evers (.350).

1908 Chicago (N) over Detroit (A), 4–1. Johnny Evers repeated his .350 average of 1907, player-manager Frank Chance hit .421, and outfielder Wildfire Schulte batted .389 in the Cub attack. Ty Cobb led Detroit (.368), to no avail.

1909 Pittsburgh (N) over Detroit (A), 4–3. The Tigers lost their third straight series, as Honus Wagner bested Ty Cobb. The Pirate shortstop hit .333 with six RBI and six stolen bases. Babe Adams pitched three complete game victories.

1910 Philadelphia (A) over Chicago (N), 4–1. Connie Mack's infielders combined to bat .364 as the A's rolled to an easy title. Jack Coombs pitched three wins and hit .385.

1911 Philadelphia (A) over New York (N), 4–2. The Athletics beat a strong New York club featuring Christy Mathewson and Rube Marquard. Frank "Home Run" Baker got his nickname from game-winning blasts in Games 2 and 3.

1912 Boston (A) over New York (N), 4–3. This thrill-a-minute series featured an 11-inning tie in Game 2. Errors by Giants Fred Merkle and Fred Snodgrass enabled Boston to score two runs in the bottom of the 10th inning of the final contest.

1913 Philadelphia (A) over New York (N), 4–1. Home Run Baker again hammered Giant pitching, batting .450 with seven RBI. Eddie Collins also starred for the A's, hitting .421 with three stolen bases.

1914 Boston (N) over Philadelphia (A), 4–0. The red-hot "Miracle Braves" swept the heavily favored Athletics, who scored only six runs in the four games. Catcher Hank Gowdy (.545) and second baseman Johnny Evers (.438) led the Boston offense.

1915 Boston (A) over Philadelphia (N), 4–1. The famous Red Sox outfield of Speaker, Lewis, and Hooper combined to bat .364 while Rube Foster pitched two complete game wins. Foster also batted .500 and drove in the winning run in Game 2.

1916 Boston (A) over Brooklyn (N), 4–1. After three one-run games, Boston took charge with 6–2 and 4–1 victories. A young lefthander named Babe Ruth twirled a 14-inning six hitter in Game Two.

1917 Chicago (A) over New York (N), 4–2. The pitching of Red Faber (3-1, 2.33) and the hitting of Eddie Collins, Buck Weaver, and Joe Jackson were too much for the Giants in a sloppy (23 errors) series.

1918 Boston (A) over Chicago (N), 4–2. Every game was a pitchers' duel. The losing Cubs posted a 1.04 ERA over the six games. The Boston staff allowed only nine runs in the series, led by Babe Ruth who extended his consecutive scoreless inning streak to 29 2/3.

1919 Cincinnati (N) over Chicago (A), 5–3. The results of this surprising World Series were declared invalid after eight members of the "Black Sox," including Shoeless Joe Jackson, were accused of throwing games for money. A court later found the Chicago players not guilty (most of them never even received the money from the gamblers with whom they conspired), but commissioner Kenesaw Mountain Landis nonetheless banned them from baseball forever.

1920 Cleveland (A) over Brooklyn (N), 5–2. Game 5 was surely the most freakish in series history. It featured a) the first World Series grand slam (Indian rightfielder Elmer Smith), b) the first World Series home run by a pitcher (Indian Jim Bagby), and c) the first and only unassisted triple play in series action (Indians second baseman Billy Wambsganss).

1921 New York (N) over New York (A), 5–3. Six Giants batted over .300, and their pitchers held Babe Ruth to a .500 slugging average. Giant hurler Jesse Barnes won two games and batted .444.

1922 New York (N) over New York (A), 4–0. The result was said to be final proof that "brains beat brawn." Giant pitching shut down Babe Ruth, allowing only 11 runs in the five contests (one tie).

1923 New York (A) over New York (N), 4–2. The Yankees took the last three to break the spell of their cross-river rivals, behind Babe Ruth's three homers and .368 average. Casey Stengel hit two home runs for the losers.

1924 Washington (A) over New York (N), 4–3. A 12-innning Game 7, won by Walter Johnson in relief, capped an exciting affair. Player-manager Bucky Harris starred for the Senators (.333, 7 RBIs), as did outfielder Goose Goslin (.344, 7 RBIs).

1925 Pittsburgh (N) over Washington (A), 4–3. Pirate centerfielder Max Carey had 11 hits and three stolen bases, as Pittsburgh became the first team since 1903 to come back from a three games to one deficit.

1926 St. Louis (N) over New York (A), 4–3. Babe Ruth hit three homers in Game 4, but in the seventh inning of Game 7, Grover Cleveland Alexander struck out Tony Lazzeri with the bases loaded, saving the game and the series for the Cardinals.

1927 New York (A) over Pittsburgh (N), 4–0. Generally regarded as the greatest team of all time, the "Murderer's Row" Yankees disposed of the Pirates behind two Babe Ruth homers, plus the pitching of Wilcy Moore, Herb Pennock, and George Pipgrass.

1928 New York (A) over St. Louis (N), 4–0. Another Yankee sweep. Ruth and Lou Gehrig combined to bat .593, with seven home runs and 13 RBI. Waite Hoyt pitched two complete game victories.

1929 Philadelphia (A) over Chicago (N), 4–1. Trailing 8-0 in Game 4, the A's roared back to score 10 runs in the seventh inning. In the next contest, the Mackmen took the series with a three-run ninth inning.

1930 Philadelphia (A) over St. Louis (N), 4–2. Lefty Grove and George Earnshaw pitched well, while Al Simmons, Jimmie Foxx, and Mickey Cochrane combined for 11 extra-base hits. Cardinal regulars batted only .185 in the six games.

1931 St. Louis (N) over Philadelphia (A), 4–3. Cardinal centerfielder Pepper Martin set a record that stood for 33 years with his 12 hits. Martin also stole five bases and hit a home run. Bill Hallahan and Burleigh Grimes combined for a 4–0, 1.25 ERA.

1932 New York (A) over Chicago (N), 4–0. The Yankees completed a streak of 12 straight World Series victories in sweeping the Cubs. Babe Ruth and Lou Gehrig combined to bat .438, with five homers and 14 RBI.

1933 New York (N) over Washington (A), 4–1. Bill Terry's Giants defeated Joe Cronin's Senators in a battle of player-managers. Carl Hubbell won two for New York and did not allow an earned run.

1934 St. Louis (N) over Detroit (A), 4–3. Dizzy and Paul Dean hurled the Cardinals to the title, winning all four Redbird victories. A bad defensive series, with 27 errors and 13 unearned runs.

1935 Detroit (A) over Chicago (N), 4–2. The Cubs won 21 straight games in September, but came up short against Mickey Cochrane's Tigers. Charlie Gehringer and Tommy Bridges starred for Detroit, while Lou Warneke (2–0, 0.54) was superb for the losers.

1936 New York (A) over New York (N), 4–2. Joe McCarthy's "Windowbreakers" hammered Giant pitching for a record 18 runs in Game 2 and 43 runs for the series. Tony Lazzeri and Bill Dickey each drove in five runs in Game 2.

1937 New York (A) over New York (N), 4–1. Lefty Gomez pitched two of the Yankee wins and drove in the winning run with a single in the final game. The Yanks scored seven runs in the sixth inning of Game 1, then coasted to an easy championship.

1938 New York (A) over Chicago (N), 4–0. In a replay of 1932, the Bronx Bombers blew out an overmatched Cubs squad. Cubs fans are still waiting for their team's first series victory over the Yankees.

1939 New York (A) over Cincinnati (N), 4–0. New York won its fourth straight World Championship the same way they won the first three—easily. Charlie Keller batted .438 with three homers, and scored as many runs as the entire Reds team, eight.

1940 Cincinnati (N) over Detroit (A), 4–3. The Reds repeated as NL champs, then beat the Tigers when Paul Derringer beat Bobo Newsome 2–1 in Game 7. Derringer and Bucky Walters each won two games.

1941 New York (A) over Brooklyn (N), 4–1. With two outs in the ninth inning of Game Four, Dodger catcher Mickey Owen dropped a third strike on Tommy Henrich, allowing him to reach first base. The Yankees then scored four times to win the ballgame, and finished Brooklyn off the next day.

1942 St. Louis (N) over New York (A), 4–1. The Cardinals, winners of 106 games during the regular season, lost Game 1 with the tying run at bat. They then swept four in a row, behind the pitching of Johnny Beazley (2–0, 2.50) and Ernie White's shutout in Game 3.

1943 New York (A) over St. Louis (N), 4–1. In this rematch of the 1942 series, the Yanks held St. Louis to nine runs in the five games. Joe Gordon and Bill Dickey homered, while third baseman Billy Johnson drove in three runs for New York.

1944 St Louis (N) over St. Louis (A), 4–2. In their lone World Series appearance, the Browns struggled valiantly before falling short against a strong Cardinal club left relatively intact by World War II. Ten Browns errors gave the Redbirds seven unearned runs.

1945 Detroit (A) over Chicago (N), 4–3. Tiger ace Hal Newhouser was hit hard in Game 1, but he bounced back to win Games 5 and 7. Doc Cramer (.379) and Hank Greenberg (2 HR, 7 RBIs) led the Detroit offense.

1946 St. Louis (N) over Boston (A), 4–3. Enos

Slaughter scored from first on a base-hit by Harry Walker in the eighth inning of Game 7, giving St. Louis its third title in five years. Harry Brecheen won three games for the Cardinals, allowing only one run.

1947 New York (A) over Brooklyn (N), 4–3. Yankee pitcher Bill Bevens had a no-hitter for 8 2/3 innings in Game 4, but lost the game on a double by Cookie Lavagetto. Tommy Henrich (.323) had the game winning RBI in Games 1, 2, and 7.

1948 Cleveland (A) over Boston (N), 4–2. The series featured fine pitching on both sides, including Game 1, when Boston's Johnny Sain beat Bob Feller 1–0. Cleveland's Gene Beardon pitched 10 2/3 scoreless innings.

1949 New York (A) over Brooklyn (N), 4–1. Game 1 was 0–0 until Tommy Henrich led off the bottom of the ninth with a home run off Don Newcombe. Bobby Brown batted .500 with five RBIs.

1950 New York (A) over Philadelphia (N), 4–0. New York struggled to win the first three contests by scores of 1–0, 2–1, and 3–2, in a series that was closer than it looks. The "Whiz Kid" Phillies held the Yanks to a .222 batting average, but managed to hit only .203 themselves.

1951 New York (A) over New York (N), 4–2. A tired Giant pitching staff held the Yankees in check for three games, but the AL champs broke out to score 23 runs in the final three. Eddie Lopat (2–0, 0.50) starred for the Yankees.

1952 New York (A) over Brooklyn (N), 4–3. Allie Reynolds and Vic Raschi each won two games, combining for a 1.69 ERA. Johnny Mize hit three homers, and Mickey Mantle and Yogi Berra each hit two. Duke Snider batted .345 with four homers in a losing cause.

1953 New York (A) over Brooklyn (N), 4–2. The Yankees won their fifth straight World Championship as second baseman Billy Martin tied a record with 12 hits. Martin slugged .958 and drove in eight runs.

1954 New York (N) over Cleveland (A), 4–0. The Indians won 111 games during the season. But the Giants, sparked by a spectacular Willie Mays catch in Game 1, went on to beat Cleveland easily. Dusty Rhodes drove in seven runs on two homers and two singles in six at bats.

1955 Brooklyn (N) over New York (A), 4–3. The Dodgers finally won a World Series in their eighth try, behind the pitching of series M.V.P. Johnny Podres (2–0, 1.00). Duke Snider hit four homers in a series for the second time, and Dodger leftfielder Sandy Amoros made a game-saving catch in Game 7.

1956 New York (A) over Brooklyn (N), 4–3. Yankee righthander and series M.V.P. Don Larsen pitched a perfect game in the fifth contest, while Mickey Mantle and Yogi Berra each hit three homers for New York.

1957 Milwaukee (N) over New York (A), 4–3. Lew Burdette won three games for the Braves, allowing but two runs in 27 innings and won the M.V.P.. Milwaukee's hitting was led by Hank Aaron (.393, 3 HR, 7 RBIs).

1958 New York (A) over Milwaukee (N), 4–3. Hank Bauer and Moose Skowron combined for six homers and 15 RBI, as the Bronx Bombers came back from a 3–1 deficit. Yankee pitcher "Bullet" Bob Turley earned M.V.P. honors.

1959 Los Angeles (N) over Chicago (A), 4–2. Los Angeles enjoyed its first World Championship as the transplanted Dodgers prevailed. M.V.P. Larry Sherry had two wins and two saves; Ted Kluszewski of the "Go-Go" Sox hit .391, with three homers and 10 RBI.

1960 Pittsburgh (N) over New York (A), 4–3. Pirate second baseman Bill Mazeroski's home run in the bottom of the ninth capped Game 7. Ten of the runs in the 10–9 ballgame were scored in the last two innings. Yankee second baseman Bobby Richardson, a hitting star throughout the series, was named M.V.P..

1961 New York (A) over Cincinnati (N), 4–1. Whitey Ford tossed two shutouts in winning the M.V.P., and the Yankee offense pounded out 16 extra-base hits in the five games. Bobby Richardson (.391) and John Blanchard (.400, 2 HR) starred for New York.

1962 New York (A) over San Francisco (N), 4–3. Ralph Terry's four-hit shutout won the seesaw affair for the Yanks, and earned him the M.V.P.. Whitey Ford completed his series record 33 2/3 consecutive scoreless innings in the first game. Chuck Hiller hit the first National League series grand slam in Game 4.

1963 Los Angeles (N) over New York (A), 4–0. Dodger pitchers held New York to four runs, led by Sandy Koufax's two wins and 23 strikeouts, including a record-breaking 15 in the first game. Koufax was the runaway choice for M.V.P.

1964 St. Louis (N) over New York (A), 4–3. Ten Yankee home runs were not enough to beat the Cardinals. Bob Gibson was the series M.V.P., and Tim McCarver (.478) also starred. Highlights included Ken Boyer's game-winning grand slam in Game 4, and Bobby Richardson's record 13 hits.

1965 Los Angeles (N) over Minnesota (A), 4–3. As in 1963, M.V.P. Sandy Koufax again excelled for the Dodgers, allowing only two runs in 24 innings, striking out 29. Jim "Mudcat" Grant won two games and hit a three-run homer for the Twins.

1966 Baltimore (A) over Los Angeles (N), 4–0. The Orioles shone in their first World Series appearance, as their young pitchers did not allow a run after the third inning of Game 1. Slugger Frank Robinson capped a great year with the series M.V.P. award.

1967 St. Louis (N) over Boston (A), 4–3. Bob Gibson pitched three complete game victories, added a home run in Game 7, and was named M.V.P. Lou Brock batted .414 and stole seven bases, tying Eddie Collins' record and pacing the Cards.

1968 Detroit (A) over St. Louis (N), 4–3. The Cardinals were rolling behind Bob Gibson's record 17 strikeouts in Game 1 and his record seventh straight series win in Game 4. Again Lou Brock joined him in the record books with 13 hits and seven stolen bases. But their feats couldn't stop the Tigers, led by the M.V.P. pitching of Mickey Lolich (3–0, 1.67).

1969 New York (N) over Baltimore (A), 4–1. The Amazin' Mets stunned the baseball world by winning four in a row after dropping Game 1. Their young pitchers held the Orioles to nine runs, aided by great outfield catches by Ron Swoboda and Tommy Agee. Series M.V.P. Donn Clendenon (.357, 3 HR) and Al Weis (.455, 1 HR) led the Met attack.

1970 Baltimore (A) over Cincinnati (N), 4–1. M.V.P. Brooks Robinson almost singlehandedly beat the Reds with spectacular defense at third base and a .429 average with two homers and two doubles. Also chipping in for the Orioles were Paul Blair (.474), Frank Robinson, and Boog Powell (two homers each).

1971 Pittsburgh (N) over Baltimore (A), 4–3. Roberto Clemente played in 14 World Series games and hit safely in every one. Here he batted .414, slugged .759, and won M.V.P. honors. Steve Blass, Nelson Briles, and Bruce Kison won all the Pirate victories with a combined ERA of 0.54.

1972 Oakland (A) over Cincinnati (N), 4–3. A's backup catcher Gene Tenace hit home runs in his first two series at bats, then went on to hit two more, becoming the surprise star. M.V.P. Rollie Fingers relieved in six contests, winning one and saving two.

1973 Oakland (A) over New York (N), 4–3. The Mets had the worst record of any pennant winner ever (82–79), but they lasted till the Game 7 in a sloppy (19 errors) affair. Darold Knowles pitched in all seven games for the A's, saving two. Reggie Jackson slugged his way to his first series M.V.P. award.

1974 Oakland (A) over Los Angeles (N), 4–1. The A's won their third straight Championship behind the two saves and one win of M.V.P. Rollie Fingers and the hitting of Joe Rudi (.333) and Bert Campaneris (.353).

1975 Cincinnati (N) over Boston (A), 4–3. Five games were decided by one run, including Game 6, a memorable 12-inning contest decided by Carlton Fisk's famous home run. Pete Rose, the heart and soul of the Big Red Machine, hustled his way to M.V.P. honors.

1976 Cincinnati (N) over New York (A), 4–0. The Big Red Machine drove over the Yankees, slugging .522 as a team. Seven Reds hitters batted over .300, led by M.V.P. Johnny Bench's .533 (1.133 slugging average).

1977 New York (A) over Los Angeles (N), 4–2. Reggie Jackson hit five homers, including three in the final game, to equal records set by Babe Ruth and win his second M.V.P. award. Mike Torrez won two for the Yanks.

1978 New York (A) over Los Angeles (N), 4–2. Shortstop Bucky Dent and backup infielder Brian Doyle batted .417 and .438 respectively, pacing New York in its second straight six-game triumph. Dent was named M.V.P. In the last four contests, the Yankees outscored L.A. 28–8.

1979 Pittsburgh (N) over Baltimore (A), 4–3. The Pirates overcame a three games to one deficit as Earl Weaver's Orioles waited for three-run homers that never came. Led by Willie "Pops" Stargell (.400, 3 HR) and Phil Garner (.500), Pittsburgh batted .323 as a team. Stargell's leadership of the Pirates' "family" on and off the field earned him M.V.P. honors.

1980 Philadelphia (N) over Kansas City (A), 4–2. The two teams batted .292 in a series decided largely by the relief pitching of Tug McGraw (1–1, 2 saves) vs. Dan Quisenberry (1–2, 1 save). Mike Schmidt took M.V.P. honors with a .381 average and seven RBI.

1981 Los Angeles (N) over New York (A), 4–2. Many observers called this sloppy series a fitting end to this strike-stricken 1981 season. Even the M.V.P. award proved impossible to settle, as Pedro Guerrero, Steve Yeager, and Ron Cey shared the honor.

1982 St. Louis (N) over Milwaukee (A), 4–3. Joaquin Andujar won two games for the Cardinals, and Willie McGee had perhaps the greatest single series game by a rookie, with two homers and two great catches in Game 3. St. Louis' Darrell Porter won M.V.P. honors for his clutch hitting and 5 RBI.

1983 Baltimore (A) over Philadelphia (N), 4–1. The Phillies couldn't hit Orioles' pitching, scoring but nine runs in the five games. Catcher Rick Dempsey hit four doubles and a home run, held the Phils to one stolen base, and was named M.V.P.

1984 Detroit (A) over San Diego (N), 4–1. The Tigers belted seven homers and backed them up with the pitching of Jack Morris (2–0, 2.00). Sparky Anderson became the first manager to win World Championships in both leagues. Alan Trammell, the Tigers' shortstop, hit two home runs to earn M.V.P. honors.

1985 Kansas City (A) over St. Louis (N), 4–3. The Cards were one inning away from the title, but a disputed call at first base opened the door for the Royals in Game 6. They won that contest, then blew St. Louis away 11–0 in the finale. Bret Saberhagen won two for Kansas City, and the M.V.P. award.

1986 New York (N) over Boston (A), 4–3. The Red Sox were one out away from winning it all, when Bob Stanley's wild pitch let in the tying run, and Mookie Wilson's grounder slipped between Bill Buckner's legs to score the winning run in Game 6. M.V.P. Ray Knight hit a tie-breaking homer in Game 7 to send Boston to its fourth straight seven-game defeat.

1987 Minnesota (A) over St. Louis (N), 4–3. The Twins won their first championship by taking all four games at the Metrodome. Cardinal pitching held Minnesota to five runs in the three games in St. Louis, but in Minnesota, the Twins could not be contained, scoring 33 times. Frank Viola (2–1, 3.72) was the M.V.P.

1988 Los Angeles (N) over Oakland (A), 4–1. Series M.V.P. Orel Hershiser (2–0, 17 K's) dazzled the powerful A's. Injured Dodger Kirk Gibson's dramatic two-out home run in the bottom of the ninth in Game 1 set the tone for the unexpected L.A. triumph.

1989 Oakland (A) over San Francisco (N), 4–0. The A's thoroughly dominated a weak Giants' pitching staff, pounding out 32 runs, 44 hits (including nine home runs) in only four games. Series M.V.P. Dave Stewart and reliever Dennis Eckersley led the Oakland staff. This series will be long remembered for the major earthquake that struck the Bay area just before Game 3 and delayed the contest for 12 days.

1990 Cincinnati (N) over Oakland (A), 4–0. The Reds hit .317 as a team, while their pitchers, led by M.V.P. José Rijo, held Oakland's vaunted offense to a mere .207 series average. Billy Hatcher broke Babe Ruth's World Series record by hitting .750, with seven consecutive hits and four doubles.

1991 Minnesota (A) over Atlanta (N), 4–3. No team in baseball had ever gone from worst to first. In 1991, it happened twice; both the Twins and Braves had finished last the year before. Five games were decided by one run, three went into extra innings, and four were decided on the last at bat. Best of all was Game 7, a scoreless affair until the 10th inning, when the Twins finally scored. Jack Morris pitched all 10 innings for Minnesota and earned M.V.P. honors.

1992 Toronto (A) over Atlanta (N), 4–2. The Blue Jays became the first non-American team to win (or play in)

the World Series. Braves closer Jeff Reardon gave up the winning hits in games 2 and 3, and Bobby Cox was loath to use him again. Dave Winfield's double in the 11th-inning of Game 6 sent the Braves to their second straight World Series defeat. Toronto catcher Pat Borders was the M.V.P. with a .450 average.

1993 Toronto (A) over Philadelphia (N), 4–2. The Blue Jays became the first team since the 1977–78 Yankees to repeat as champions, battering the Phillies for 45 runs (despite a Game 5 shutout). Joe Carter's homer in Game 6 marked only the second time the World Series had ended on a home run (Bill Mazeroski hit the other in 1960). DH Paul Molitor went 12 for 24 with six extra-base hits to win M.V.P. honors.

1994 World Series canceled. The longest work stoppage in professional sports history, a 232-day dispute over a cap on player salaries, forced the first-ever cancellation of the World Series and playoffs.

1995 Atlanta (N) over Cleveland (A), 4–2. Good pitching beat good hitting in this dramatic series. Baseball's best pitching staff (the Braves) held the game's most explosive offense (the Indians) to a .179 average and 19 runs. Five games were decided by one run, including the clincher: a dazzling 1–0 one-hitter by Atlanta's Tom Glavine, the series M.V.P.

1996 New York (A) over Atlanta (N), 4–2. The Braves shellacked the Yankees 12–1 and 4–0 in the first two games. But the Yankees struck back and won the next four. The turning point was in Game 4, when New York rallied from a 6–0 deficit to win 8–6 in 10 innings. Jim Leyritz provided the crushing blow: a three-run homer off Mark Wohlers to tie the game at 6–6. Yankee closer John Wetteland saved all four wins and was the M.V.P.

1997 Florida (N) over Cleveland (A), 4–3. This sloppy series was marked by porous defense and poor relief pitching. Game 3 alone involved 17 walks and 6 errors. Cleveland was two outs away from winning it all in Game 7, when Craig Counsell's sacrifice fly tied the game at 2–2. In the 11th, Edgar Renteria singled home the winning run. Florida rookie Liván Hernández, winner of Games 1 and 5, was the M.V.P.

1998 New York (A) over San Diego (N), 4–0. The Yankees completed one of the greatest seasons in baseball history with a sweep that gave them a combined record of 125–50 and a .714 winning percentage. Homers by Chuck Knoblauch and Tino Martínez helped the Yankees come from behind in Game 1. Scott Brosius's three-run homer in Game 3 helped him win the M.V.P. award.

1999 New York (A) over Atlanta (N), 4–0. The Yankees' World Series winning streak increased to 12 games with their second straight sweep. Atlanta errors opened the door to big innings for New York in Games 1 and 2; the Yankees hit four homers in Game 3 to turn a 5-1 deficit into a 10-inning, 6-5 win. Mariano Rivera saved Games 1 and 4, won Game 3 in relief, and took M.V.P. honors.

2000 New York (A) over New York (N), 4-1. Every game of the first Subway Series in 45 years was decided by one or two runs. The Yankees rallied to tie Game 1 in the ninth inning, and won it in the 12th. Derek Jeter hit the first pitch of Game 4 over the center field fence and the Yankees never trailed again. Jeter batted .409 with two homers, and was the M.V.P.

2001 Arizona (N) over New York (A), 4-3. Curt Schilling and Randy Johnson powered Arizona to a 2-0 lead, but the Yankees came back with three straight one-run victories in New York. In both Game 4 and Game 5, the Yankees rallied with game-tying homers against closer Byung-Hyun Kim. Arizona had the last laugh in Game 7; the Diamondbacks entered the ninth inning trailing 2-1, but they rallied for two runs against Mariano Rivera to win. Schilling and Johnson were co-M.V.P.s.

2002 Anaheim (A) over San Francisco (N), 4-3. Anaheim pitched carefully to Barry Bonds, and although he hit .471 with four homers and 13 walks, the batters before and after him hit .276 and .231 respectively, limiting the damage Bonds was able to inflict. The Angels batted .310 as a team, led by M.V.P. third baseman Troy Glaus, who hit .385 with 3 homers and 8 RBIs. With the Giants six outs away from winning it all in Game 6, Glaus's eighth-inning double turned a 5-4 deficit into a 6-5 Anaheim victory.

2003 Florida (N) over New York (A), 4-2. New York's two victories were by both by 6-1 margins, while Florida's wins were by one or two runs. Alex González's walk-off homer in the 12th inning of Game 4 turned the tide for Florida. Brad Penny was 2-0 for the Marlins, but he was eclipsed for M.V.P. honors by Josh Beckett, who came back on two days' rest to pitch a Game 6 shutout that clinched it for the Marlins, who have not lost a postseason series in their short history.

2004 Boston (A) over St. Louis (N), 4-0. After being down three games to none against the Yankees in the League Championship, the Red Sox won four straight, a feat never before achieved in baseball. The Sox then swept the powerful Cardinals behind the hitting of M.V.P. Manny Ramirez (.412 average) and the pitching of Curt Schilling, Derek Lowe, and Pedro Martinez.

2005 Chicago (A) over Houston (N), 4-0. The Chicago White Sox used timely hitting and stellar pitching to win the club's first World Series title since 1917. It

was Chicago's first appearance in the World Series since 1959, and Houston had never participated in more than four decades of existence. Chicago outscored Houston by only six runs over the four games. In the crucial Game 3, the longest game in World Series history, the White Sox beat the Astros 7-5 in 14 innings.

2006 St. Louis (N) over Detroit (A), 4-1. The Cards' 83 regular-season wins were the fewest ever by a World Series champion. Tiger pitchers made five errors, one in each game, a World Series record. St. Louis was bolstered by the timely hitting of Series M.V.P. David Eckstein (.365, 3 runs, 4 RBI), unheralded catcher Yadier Molina (.412), sore-shouldered Scott Rolen (.421), and the inspired pitching of starters Anthony Reyes, Chris Carpenter and Jeff Weaver.

2007 Boston (A) over Colorado (N), 4—0 The wild-card Rockies entered the series having won 21 of their previous 22 games, sweeping both the Phillies and Diamondbacks in the Division Series and NLCS en route. The Red Sox greeted them in the Fall Classic with a 13-1 thumping in Fenway Park, and it was never a contest after that. Boston ultimately did dome sweeping of their own, eliminating Colorado in four games to claim their second title in four years.

2008 Philadelphia (N) over Tampa Bay (A), 4—1 The Phillies entered the World Series undefeated at home in the post season. In a World Series first, game 5 was suspended for 46 hours due to heavy rain, tied 2—2 in the middle of the sixth. The Phils had to wait two extra days to claim their second championship in 125 years. Brad Lidge sealed a perfect season by throwing his 48th save in as many games.

2009 New York (A) over Philadelphia (N), 4—2 The defending champion Phillies and ace Cliff Lee shut down the Yankees bats to win Game 1 but the Yankees rallied to win the next three contests. Again in Game 5 Cliff Lee dominated the Yankee offense, but in Game 6 the Yankees jumped out to a 7—1 lead behind a second inning two-run blast from series M.V.P. Hideki Matsui en route to their 27th World Series title.

2010 San Francisco (N) over Texas (A), 4—1 In the Rangers first Series appearance, the Game 1 pitching duel between former Cy Young winners Cliff Lee and Tim Lincecum never materialized as the Giants won 11—7. A Game 3 Texas win was sandwiched between two San Francisco shut-outs, while the pitching duel expected earlier in the series finally arrived in Game 5 as Tim Lincecum bested Cliff Lee for the second time this series, 3—1. It was the franchise's first World Series since 1954 when they were still the New York Giants.

BASKETBALL

Unlike most modern sports, which evolved from other games (as football did from rugby), basketball can be attributed to a single inventor. Dr. James Naismith, a physical education instructor at the Young Men's Christian Association (YMCA) Training School—now Springfield College—in Springfield, Mass., devised the game in December 1891 as an indoor athletic option for the winter months. Naismith's invention was a noncontact sport in which two teams of players attempted to toss a soccer ball into peach baskets hung from the railings at opposite ends of the gymnasium. Because the railings were 10 feet high the basket has been forever set at that height.

Basketball was an immediate success, catching on at other YMCAs and schools in the East. Today it is one of the most popular team sports in the United States and throughout the world. Young men and women compete at every level, including playground, youth, scholastic, collegiate, and professional leagues. Spectators throng to arenas to enjoy the game's fast-paced action and competitive drama.

Rules and Conduct of Play

The rules created by Dr. Naismith are basic to basketball today, though there have been major refinements and notable improvements in the equipment. His original 13 rules included a prohibition against running with the ball. Most formal competition is still held indoors on a wooden floor. Outdoors, the surface is typically made of asphalt or concrete. The court, which varies in size depending on the level of competition, measures up to 94 feet (28.7 meters) long and 50 feet (15.2 meters) wide. It is divided into offensive and defensive halves by a midcourt line. The baskets are metal hoops, or rims, measuring 18 inches (45.7 centimeters) in diameter and set 10 feet (3.05 meters) above the floor. The rims are attached to wood or fiberglass backboards, supported by a post or stanchion, at opposites ends of the court. An open cord net hangs from each rim. An official basketball is 30 inches (76 centimeters) in circumference—slightly smaller for women—inflated with air, and made of leather or rubber.

A basketball team consists of five players plus substitutes and coaches. Each team defends the goal, or basket, at its back. Players advance the ball toward the opposite goal by passing it to a teammate or dribbling it while in motion. Members of the opposing team try to prevent them from scoring a basket. A successful shot at the basket, called a field goal, is generally counted as two points. If attempted from behind a line marked on the floor (the distance varying by level of competition), a successful shot is worth three points. If a shot is missed, usually bouncing off the rim or backboard, a defensive player may catch the rebound and, with teammates, advance the ball toward the opposite basket. An offensive player who captures a rebound may simply shoot again, pass to a teammate, or dribble away. After each basket, possession of the ball goes to the opposing team.

Pushing, holding, and other forms of physical contact are limited. Excessive contact may be called a foul by the referees. If the fouled player was touched while attempting a shot, he is awarded two uncontested attempts at the basket, called foul shots or free throws, from a distance of 15 feet (4.6 meters). Each successful foul shot is worth one point. If a team collectively commits a certain number of fouls in a period of time (five fouls in a professional quarter, seven fouls in a collegiate half), then the other team takes foul shots for every additional infraction.

A pro basketball game has four 12-minute quarters. There are limits on the amount of time a team may take to advance the ball past the midcourt line (8 seconds) and to make an attempt at the basket (24 seconds).

History of Basketball

The introduction of metal rims, backboards, nets, and a larger ball—all in the mid-1890's—fueled enthusiasm for Dr. Naismith's invention. The new game of basketball was especially popular with young women, and in 1896 the first women's intercollegiate game was held between Stanford and California. The first men's college game was contested in 1897, the same year in which five-player teams became standard. A rule change allowing players to dribble was adopted in 1900 (before which players could advance the ball only by passing), adding speed, excitement, and more scoring to the game.

Men's College Basketball

The sport quickly spread in popularity and early college games had various numbers of players on each side. By 1900 five-a-side was standard. At the 1904 Olympic Games in St. Louis, a number of schools played the first "College Basket Ball Championship"—won by Hiram College of Ohio—and soon this became an annual event sponsored by various groups, eventually evolving in the 1930's into the annual N.C.A.A. (National Collegiate Athletic Association) men's basketball tournament, and the N.I.T. (National Invitational Tournament), initially a more prestigious event than the N.C.A.A. title.

The growth of college basketball paralleled that of college football: the sport began as a student-centered and -operated activity, and became at many schools a semi-professional enterprise with paid coaches running the squads. During the first three decades of the 20th century, the most successful coaches were Joseph Raycroft of the University of Chicago, Walter "Doc" Meanwell of the University of Wisconsin, George Keogan of the University of Notre Dame, and Ward "Piggy" Lambert of Purdue University. Among the outstanding players were John Schommer (Chicago), Charles "Stretch" Murphy and John Wooden (Purdue), and Hank Luisetti (Stanford). In addition, Dr. James Naismith continued to coach for many years at the University of Kansas, and a number of his players became famous coaches: Forrest "Phog" Allen at Kansas and Adolph Rupp at the University of Kentucky.

During its first two decades, college basketball remained a campus sport played mainly in school facilities. In the 1930's, however, with the popularity of double-header games at city arenas, college basketball gained many new fans as well as media attention. Schools in urban areas began to produce some of the best teams: City College of New York (C.C.N.Y.), New York University (N.Y.U.), Long Island University (L.I.U.), and DePaul University in Chicago. The urban influence on college basketball was complex. City schools often had African-American youngsters on their teams and helped integrate the sport, (Jackie Robinson, in fact, played basketball at U.C.L.A. from 1939 to 1941.), but city arenas also attracted large numbers of gamblers and fans betting on games.

The 1940's should have been college basketball's best era to date—the sport had become more exciting because of talented big men like George Mikan of DePaul, as well as the increased use of the jump shot and the fast break—but gambling scandals overwhelmed it. Law enforcement agencies discovered that many players on the late-1940's and early-1950's championship teams of C.C.N.Y. and Kentucky, and on many other nationally ranked squads, took bribes from gamblers to fix the outcomes of games. Moreover, the players had engaged in fixing games for a number of years, and their coaches, among the most famous in the sport—Clair Bee (L.I.U.), Nat Holman (C.C.N.Y.), and Adolph Rupp (Kentucky)—probably knew about their players' malfeasance and chose not to report it to the authorities.

Despite the scandals and their repercussions—some players went to prison and some schools deemphasized the sport—college basketball remained popular in the 1950's, particularly on college campuses in the Midwest and on the West Coast. Outstanding players such as Wilt Chamberlain (Kansas), Oscar Robertson (Cincinnati), and Jerry West (West Virginia) emerged, and such superb teams as the University of San Francisco Dons, led by Bill Russell and K.C. Jones, won N.C.A.A. championships. Toward the end of the 1950's, John Wooden, the coach at U.C.L.A., began to build excellent squads. Because his school had a history of integration and because he was the first college coach to recruit outstanding players from all regions of the country, his teams came to dominate their conference and then the N.C.A.A. tournament, winning nine out of 10 national titles from 1964 to 1973. Led by such players as Lew Alcindor (later known as Kareem Abdul-Jabbar), Bill Walton, Walt Hazzard, and Lucius Allen, U.C.L.A. dominated college basketball longer than any school has ever done.

U.C.L.A.'s reign was interrupted in 1966 by Texas Western (now the University of Texas at El Paso). In the N.C.A.A. final game, Texas Western's all-black starting five easily beat the all-white Kentucky lineup and, symbolically, ended segregation in college basketball. In 1969 an event with far-reaching consequences occurred when University of Detroit basketball star Spencer Haywood challenged the rule forbidding players from leaving school to play in the N.B.A. before their class graduated. Haywood won his case and changed the future of college basketball; from the 1970's to the present, increasing numbers of players, including a majority of stars, depart school early for the pros. By the late 1990's, players were jumping directly from high school to the professional game, bypassing college completely.

The most memorable on-court event of the 1970's took place in the N.C.A.A. final game of 1979. The Michigan State Spartans, led by Earvin "Magic" Johnson, played the Indiana State Sycamores, featuring Larry Bird. The contest, won by Michigan State, drew the highest TV ratings of any game in college basketball history. It also helped elevate the N.C.A.A. men's basketball tournament to national event status, now nicknamed "March Madness."

In the early 1980's, ESPN began televising a multitude of college basketball games, and this greatly increased the popularity of the sport. The network also prompted the creation of new conferences of universities seeking air time for their teams. The alliance between ESPN and the Big East was particularly fruitful and in the 1980's helped promote the basketball programs of schools such as Georgetown and Villanova, which won N.C.A.A. titles in 1984 and 1985, respectively. By the end of the decade, the N.C.A.A. signed its first $1 billion-plus contract with a TV network (CBS) to televise the men's and women's basketball tournaments. The current contract, a multiyear deal, is worth more than $6 billion.

By 1990, college basketball was awash in money but also in corruption. A shadowy world of "street agents" and under-the-table payments came to exist which continues to the present. Some of the best teams and players participated in the corruption. The University of Michigan's "Fab Five," led by Chris Webber, were involved in six-figure under-the-table payments; other schools and players had other problems. Some scandals, such as at the University of Minnesota, involved academic fraud.

Yet, through all the scandals, the fans, especially the students at prominent basketball schools, loved the sport and their teams, and followed them avidly. As a result, many universities built new and grandiose arenas and spent millions on their basketball programs. All of this

was far from the game's modest origins in Springfield, Mass.

On the court, college basketball is similar to the professional game but with several major differences. First is the element of time: a college game stretches over two 20-minute halves, rather than the four 12-minute quarters in its professional version. Furthermore, the shot clock lasts 35 seconds in college rules, compared to 24 seconds in the pros. The longer shot clock and the shorter game mean that college basketball features less scoring than its professional cousin, but in the eyes of many observers, the emphasis on rapid passing and player movement in the collegiate game make for better viewing.

Women's College Basketball

Women's college basketball is almost as old as the men's game; in fact, its earliest proponent, Maude Sherman, married Dr. James Naismith, the sport's inventor. Unfortunately, because of the Victorian conventions, the rules of women's basketball were different from the evolving men's game. Until the 1970's, most women played what was termed "girl ball": six players per team, three confined to each half the court, with restrictions on dribbling and ball-handling. Nevertheless, the game thrived in various regions of the country, particularly in high schools and colleges in Iowa and some adjacent states.

In the early 1970's, the associations in charge of women's sports sanctioned the use of the five-a-side, full-court game, along with a 30-second shot clock. Then, in 1973, the passage of Title IX, which mandated equal opportunities in college sports for all students, began the transformation of women's basketball into a major intercollegiate sport. The Association of Intercollegiate Athletics for Women (A.I.A.W.) organized regional tournaments and a national championship; outstanding teams from Delta State University (Mississippi) and Immaculata College (Pennsylvania) emerged, along with stars such as Ann Meyers (U.C.L.A.), Nancy Lieberman (Old Dominion University), and Lynette Woodward (Kansas).

In the early 1980's the N.C.A.A. pushed the A.I.A.W. aside and took over the sport, promoting the championship tournament on television, and mirroring women's teams to the men's squads of their universities (while still permitting underfunding of the women's teams). From the late 1980's to the present, those schools willing to fund their women's teams at a high level have amassed the best records and the most N.C.A.A. titles: the University of Tennessee, the University of Connecticut, and Stanford have all won multiple crowns.

Professional Basketball

Professional basketball was born in 1898, as several teams began barnstorming the eastern states to compete for pay against local squads. The first collegiate association, the Eastern Intercollegiate League, was formed in 1902. Basketball was introduced as an Olympic demonstration sport in the Summer Games of 1904, spreading interest to Europe and Asia.

Other notable innovations in the early years included a limit of five personal fouls per player per game (1908–09) and a change in the penalty for walking or double-dribbling from foul shots to loss of ball possession (1923). The results were a reduction in rough play and shorter breaks in the action. More changes in the early 1930's, including the 10-second rule (for advancing the ball past midcourt) and a 3-second rule (prohibiting a player from remaining inside the foul lane), further contributed to the evolution of the game.

1920's and 1930's   By the 1920's, basketball tournaments were being held in high schools and colleges across the country. Company teams and touring professionals built grassroots followings. Among the top pro teams of the era were the Original Celtics, featuring such stars as Nat Holman and Joe Lapchick (both of whom would become prominent coaches), and the Harlem Globetrotters, a talented and flamboyant all-black team founded in 1927 by promoter Abe Saperstein. Before the integration of the National Basketball Association later in the century, the Globetrotters frequently beat top teams in invitational events. Later, after the growth and integration of the N.B.A. took away their best players and talent base, the Globetrotters turned into a traveling basketball carnival, and they have entertained audiences in more than 100 countries with their on-court stunts and clowning routines.

It was not until the mid-1930's, however, with developments at the college level, that basketball began to emerge as a major spectator sport. In 1934 a sportswriter named Ned Irish promoted a college doubleheader at New York's Madison Square Garden that drew a large crowd. College basketball became a regular event at the Garden and elsewhere, prompting many universities to build arenas or launch programs.

Another turning point came in 1936, when the team from Stanford University traveled east to compete at Madison Square Garden and stunned the basketball establishment with its fast-paced, freewheeling style of play. Stanford featured the dynamic Hank Luisetti, whose running one-handed shot revolutionized offensive play (replacing the standard two-hand set shot) and delighted spectators. With the 1937–38 season came elimination of the jump ball after each field goal, further accelerating the pace of the game.

In 1938 Madison Square Garden held the first major postseason intercollegiate playoff, the National Invitation Tournament (N.I.T.), and the National Collegiate Athletic Association (N.C.A.A.) organized its own championship the following year. The N.I.T. is still held at the end of every season, but the winner of the N.C.A.A. tournament is recognized as the official collegiate champion.

The 1930's also witnessed the birth of organized competition at the international level. An official governing body, the International Amateur Basketball Federation (FIBA), was established in 1932 in Geneva, Switzerland (later moved to Munich, Germany). In 1936 basketball became a full medal sport for men at the Olympic Games in Berlin, with teams from 22 nations taking part.

1940's and 1950's   The National Basketball League (N.B.L.), founded in 1937 and based in the Midwest, was the most successful of several early professional leagues. Interest in the pro game lagged until 1946, however, when the new Basketball Association of America (B.A.A.) was launched. With franchises in 11 major cites, including Toronto, the B.A.A. attracted fans eager to see former college players compete. Four N.B.L. franchises jumped to the B.A.A. in 1948, and the expansion was completed in 1949—thereby creating the National Basketball Association. The N.B.A. dates its foundation to the creation of the B.A.A., in 1946. The original N.B.A. included 17 franchises in three divisions. George Mikan of the Minneapolis Lakers, at 6'10" the game's first great "big man," was a major gate attraction who helped ensure the success of the league. Mikan dominated the pro game until his retirement in 1956, leading his team to five N.B.A. championships.

Several developments in the early 1950's—combined with the ever-improving skills of the players—contributed to the growth of the N.B.A. The first black players were drafted into the N.B.A. in 1950. Before the 1954–55 season, the N.B.A. introduced the 24-second rule to eliminate stalling; with more shots came more excitement. The arrival of professional basketball was perhaps most clearly symbolized by the election of the first members of the Basketball Hall of Fame in 1959, a list appropriately headed by Naismith. (The original Hall of Fame building, located on the campus of Springfield College, did not open until 1968.)

Aside from Mikan's Minneapolis Lakers (later to become the Los Angeles Lakers), top N.B.A. teams of the 1950's included the Boston Celtics (champions in 1957 and 1959), Syracuse Nationals (1955), Philadelphia Warriors (1956), St. Louis Hawks (1958), and perennial powers New York Knickerbockers and Fort Wayne Pistons.

The title of the game's top center passed from Mikan to Bill Russell in the latter part of the decade. After leading the University of San Francisco to N.C.A.A. titles in 1955 and 1956, Russell teamed with passing wizard Bob Cousy and other members of the Boston Celtics in winning the first two of many N.B.A. championships. Other outstanding players of the decade included Bob Pettit, Cliff Hagan, Dolph Schayes, Clyde Lovellette, and "Easy" Ed Macauley.

1960's   By the early 1960's, the N.B.A. had 10 franchises across the United States, with annual attendance reaching several million. The print and broadcast media expanded coverage, and the game's top players became highly paid celebrities. As players also increased in height and athletic ability, the style and tempo of play also evolved. The dunk shot, or simply dunk, in which a player leaps high off the floor, extends the ball over the basket, and jams it through the hoop, became a common and crowd-thrilling part of the game. The fast break, featuring skilled dribbling and deft passing at top speed, became another trademark of modern pro basketball.

A new league, the American Basketball Association (ABA), was founded in 1967 with 11 teams. The ABA gained a following by luring graduating college stars or established pros and by introducing such innovations as the three-point shot and a red-white-and-blue ball. The league continued operations until after the 1975–76 season, when its strongest franchises were absorbed into the N.B.A.

The Boston Celtics dominated the N.B.A. in the 1960's, establishing one of the great dynasties in professional sports by capturing nine titles in 10 years. Coached by Red Auerbach and led by Russell, Cousy, John Havlicek, and a host of other future Hall of Famers, the Celtics demonstrated that smart, unselfish team play wins championships.

Russell's supremacy at the center position was challenged by a bigger, stronger new talent, the 7'1" Wilt Chamberlain. Once scoring an astonishing 100 points in a game, Chamberlain was an almost unstoppable scoring threat for the Philadelphia 76ers and later the Los Angeles

Lakers. Among the other N.B.A. greats of the 1960's were Jerry West, Elgin Baylor, and Oscar Robertson.

1970's   The decade of the 1970's marked a period of expansion, realignment, and competitive parity for the N.B.A. In 1970 the league expanded from 14 teams in two divisions to 17 teams in four divisions (two divisions each in Eastern and Western conferences). Then in 1976, with the merger of former ABA franchises, the total increased to 22. With growth came a new balance of power. The Celtic dynasty still thrived, winning championships in 1974 and 1976, but no team won consecutive N.B.A. crowns through the course of the decade. The New York Knicks were the only other team to capture two titles (1970 and 1973).

Center Kareem Abdul-Jabbar was the preeminent player of the decade, earning league M.V.P. honors six times; he would go on to become the leading scorer in N.B.A. history, retiring with 38,387 points in 1989. Other Hall of Famers from the 1970's included Bill Walton, Julius "Dr. J" Erving, Willis Reed, Walt Frazier, Rick Barry, Nate "Tiny" Archibald, Dave Cowens, Pete Maravich, Calvin Murphy, and Bob McAdoo.

1980's   Although the N.B.A. continued its expansion in the 1980's, reaching 27 teams by the 1989–90 season, the league faced declining game attendance and television ratings as the decade commenced. At least two factors contributed to a rebound in fan interest by mid-decade. One was the adoption of the three-point field goal before the 1979-80 season, which added an exciting dimension to the game. More important, perhaps, was the compelling rivalry that developed between the Los Angeles Lakers, led by Magic Johnson and Abdul-Jabbar, and the Boston Celtics, with Larry Bird. The Lakers won five championships during the 1980's, the Celtics three. Johnson and Bird each captured three M.V.P. awards. Marquee players of the decade also included Erving and Moses Malone of the Philadelphia 76ers (champions in 1983), Isiah Thomas of the Detroit Pistons (champions in 1989 and 1990), Dominique Wilkins of the Atlanta Hawks, and a young Michael Jordan.

1990's–Present   By 1991, a century after its birth, basketball had attained a following that James Naismith could hardly have imagined. The professional game was an entertainment and merchandising industry. Standout players hailed from far-flung parts of the globe.

No individual better symbolized the success of professional basketball than Michael Jordan, an international media celebrity, endorser of consumer products, millionaire many times over, and perhaps the sport's greatest-ever player. The 6'6" Jordan, a shooting guard, carried the Chicago Bulls to six N.B.A. championships during the 1990's, won the league scoring title 10 times, and was named M.V.P. five times. As Jordan's career waned, younger stars—Shaquille O'Neal and Kobe Bryant—restored the Lakers to preeminence with three consecutive league crowns (2000–02).

The 21st century promised increasing globalization at virtual every level of play. Already N.B.A. rosters were filled with talented foreign players. Olympic and international amateur tournaments were closely contested. And Naismith's game was being played in schools and playgrounds around the world.

In 2007, referee Tim Donaghy, under pressure from an FBI investigation, resigned and admitted his role in a betting scandal. Donaghy bet on the NBA over a two-year period, including games he officiated, and admitted to affecting the point spread. Recently, Lakers vs. Celtics, the league's most historic matchup, had some luster restored as the teams met for the championship two times over a three-year period, with each franchise winning one title. Today in the NBA, the current trend is for marquee players to leave their small market teams in favor of the exposure and glamour associated with the large markets such as Chicago, New York, and Miami. This movement coupled with mis-management caused 17 of the 31 franchises to lose money in 2010.

In 2004 the Charlotte Bobcats joined the league (Charlotte's earlier franchise, the Hornets, had moved to New Orleans in 2002), bringing the N.B.A. total to 30 teams. In 2008, the Seattle Supersonics franchise moved, changing their name to the Oklahoma City Thunder. There are N.B.A. teams in the United States and Canada, organized in two conferences (Eastern and Western), with three divisions in each. The season runs from October to June, with each team playing 82 regular-season games. The top 16 teams compete in four rounds of post-season playoffs, culminating in a best-of-seven championship series.

The current collective bargaining agreement expires at the end of the 2011 season and the owners hope to install a hard salary cap in the new agreement, helping to offset their losses. This proposal has been met with harsh resistance from the players and the two sides remain far apart. At this point a lockout is likely and there is a strong possibility the entire 2011-2012 will be lost.

Women's Professional Basketball   The development of women's basketball at the college level and in the summer Olympics prompted the creation of two women's leagues in the late 1990's. The American Basketball League (A.B.L.) began operations in 1996 and was followed a year later by the W.N.B.A., a women's league operated under the auspices of the N.B.A.. The W.N.B.A.'s marketing clout proved to be a decisive edge, and the ABL folded in 1999. The W.N.B.A. plays a spring/summer schedule from May through August that fits in well with the N.B.A. off-season. In the 2010 season, the W.N.B.A. had 10 teams divided between two conferences.

Glossary of Basketball Terms

assist a pass that directly leads to a field goal by a teammate. Assists are an individual statistic.

blocked shot when a defensive player interferes with an opponent's shot attempt by swatting or tipping the ball out of its desired trajectory.

double-dribble a violation in which a player dribbles the ball with two hands or stops dribbling and then resumes; the ball is awarded to the opposing team.

dribbling repetitive bouncing of the ball with one hand, while the player is in motion or standing still.

field goal a successful shot at the basket during the normal course of play; generally worth two points, or three points if shot from beyond a designated distance (the three-point line).

foul an infraction for improper physical play that is determined by the game officials. There are several types of fouls, including reaching in, blocking, charging, and over the back, among others. If a player commits six fouls in the course of the game, he is said to have fouled out, and must leave the court for the remainder of the contest. If a foul is committed on an offensive player in the act of shooting, the shooter is normally entitled to two foul shots, the exceptions being a single foul shot if the player's original attempt was successful, or three foul shots if the shooter was fouled beyond the three-point line.

foul lane the painted area under the basket, bordered by the end line and the foul line; players must stand outside the area during foul shots and may not spend more than three consecutive seconds inside it during active play.

foul shot an uncontested attempt at the basket, taken from the foul line at a distance of 15 feet; one or two shots may be awarded for a personal foul (three if a player is fouled while attempting a three-point shot).

free throw another name for a foul shot.

goaltending when a defensive player touches a shot attempt after the ball has reached the height of its arc. As a result of a goaltending infraction, the shooting team is awarded the value of the shot attempt. Goaltending is also called when a player slaps the backboard or if the ball is touched directly above the goal, even by an offensive player.

jump ball method of putting the ball into play in which a referee tosses the ball in the air and two opposing players attempt to tap it to a teammate and gain possession.

man-to-man defense a strategy in which each defensive player is responsible for guarding a single offensive opponent.

officials in the N.B.A. there are three officials who enforce the rules of the game.

position the role performed by a player. Each team has five players on the court at any time, and any combination may be employed based on the game situation. Standard starting lineups include two guards, two forwards, and a center. Each of these is occasionally referred to by a number one through five that indicates the player's role.

point guard (1) the primary ballhandler on offense. The point guard brings the ball up the court and seeks to pass the ball to other players for scoring opportunities. Their most important statistic is assists, though good shooting is also helpful. Quickness, vision, and passing ability, not height, are premium requisites.

shooting guard (2) along with the small forward, one of the primary scoring positions. The shooting guard's job is to score points, either by jump shots or by driving to the basket. Usually taller than point guards, but still quick and good shooters.

small forward (3) another of the main scoring positions, slightly taller than the shooting guard, but equally capable of scoring from inside or outside. A player who combines speed and agility with some size.

power forward (4) a player who is a main scoring threat close to the basket, and concentrates on rebounding on the defensive and offensive ends of the floor. These players are tall and strong.

center (5) the tallest players on the court. Primary duty is on defense and rebounding, and most scoring is accomplished near the basket. A dominant center displays an uncommon mix of size, agility, and skill.

rebound recovering the ball after a missed shot. Also an individual statistic.

roster a list of all of the players on a team. N.B.A. teams have 12 players.

shot clock the device that tracks the time the offensive team has to attempt a shot. This 24-second period commences with the offense's gaining possession of the ball. The clock is reset by such things as offensive rebounds, among others. If the offense does not shoot the ball before the 24 seconds elapses, the team suffers a shot clock violation, and the defending team takes possession.

steal when a defender intercepts or grabs the ball from the opposing team; a defensive statistic.

technical foul a violation called for a procedural violation or, at the discretion of the referee, misconduct; penalized by one foul shot and possession of the ball for the nonoffending team.

three-point play a two-point field goal followed by a successful foul shot; made possible by the commission of a defensive foul as the offensive player is making a successful field goal attempt.

three-point shot a field goal worth three points because the shooter released the ball from behind the three-point line.

traveling a violation in which a player advances the ball by taking three steps without dribbling; possession is awarded to the opposing team; also known as walking.

turnover when the offensive team loses possession of the ball through a variety of methods, including passing the ball out of bounds, traveling, or double dribbling; a negative statistic, as a team that commits many turnovers will attempt fewer shots.

zone defense a strategy in which each defensive player is assigned a specific area of the court and must guard any opponent who enters that area; the zone configuration may take any of several forms, such as a 2-1-2, 1-3-1, or 2-3. In the N.B.A., zone defenses were only recently permitted by the rules.

Naismith Memorial Basketball Hall of Fame

The Basketball Hall of Fame elected its first members (including Dr. James Naismith, the game's originator) in 1959, but it did not have a physical home until February 17, 1968. In 1985 the Hall of Fame moved to larger quarters in Springfield, Mass. The Basketball Hall of Fame includes players from all basketball levels, including college, women's, and foreign leagues. Career statistics are given only for players who played some portion of their career in the N.B.A.

Player (Year Elected)	Games	Points	FG%	FT%	Rebs.	Assts.
Archibald, Nate (Tiny) (1991)	876	16,481	.467	.810	2,046	6,476
Averaged 18.8 ppg over 13 seasons; six-time All-Star						
Arizin, Paul J. (1977)	713	16,266	.421	.810	6,129	1,665
N.B.A. scoring leader in 1952 (25.4 ppg) and 1957 (25.6 ppg)						
Barry, Rick (1987)	794	18,395	.449	.900	5,168	4,017
(A.B.A. Statistics)	226	6,884	.477	.880	1,695	935
N.B.A. all-time free-throw percentage leader						
Barkley, Charles (2006)	1,073	23,757	.541	.735	12,546	4,215
N.B.A. 50th Anniversary All-Time Team						
Baylor, Elgin (1976)	846	23,149	.431	.780	11,463	3,650
Named to N.B.A. All-Star First Team 10 times						
Bellamy, Walt (1993)	1,043	20,941	.516	.632	14,241	2,544
N.B.A. Rookie of the Year in 1962						
Bing, Dave (1990)	901	18,327	.441	.775	3,420	5,397
N.B.A. Rookie of the Year 1967, M.V.P. 1976						
Bird, Larry (1998)	897	21,791	.496	.886	8,974	5,695
N.B.A. Rookie of the Year 1980. N.B.A. M.V.P. 1984, 1985, and 1986. 12-time All-Star						
Bradley, Bill (1982)	742	9,217	.448	.840	2,533	2,363
Averaged 30.2 ppg in 83 games at Princeton University						
Chamberlain, Wilt (1978)	1045	31,419	.540	.511	23,924	4,643
Holds N.B.A. single-game records for points (100) and rebounds (55); led league in scoring 1959-66						
Cervi, Al (1984)	202	1,591	.359	.839	261	648
NBL MVP, 1947; NBL Coach of the Year, 1494						
Cousy, Bob (1970)	924	16,960	.375	.803	4,786	6,955
Led N.B.A. in assists eight consecutive seasons (1953-60)						
Cowens, Dave (1991)	766	13,516	.460	.783	10,444	2,950
Seven-time All-Star; three-time All-defensive team						
Cunningham, Billy (1986)	654	13,626	.446	.720	6,638	2,625
(A.B.A. Statistics)	116	2,684	.483	.791	1,343	680
Coached Philadelphia 76ers to 454-196 record in eight years						
Dantley, Adrian (2008)	955	23,177	.540	.818	5,455	2,830
Six-time All-Star, averaged better than 30 points per game 1981–84						
Davies, Bob (1969)	462	6,594	.378	.759	9801	2,050
N.B.L. M.V.P., 1947						
DeBusschere, Dave (1982)	875	14,053	.432	.699	9,618	2,497
N.B.A. All-Defensive team six consecutive seasons (1969-74)						
Drexler, Clyde (2004)	1,086	22,195	.472	.788	6,677	6,125
Nine-time All-Star; led Houston Cougars to Final Four in 1982 and 1983						
Dumars, Joe (2006)	1,018	16,401	.460	.843	2,203	4,612
Six-time All-Star						
English, Alex (1997)	1,193	25,613	.507	.832	6,538	4,351
Eight-time All-Star; Averaged 21.5 points per game over 15 seasons						

Player (Year Elected)	Games	Points	FG%	FT%	Rebs.	Assts.
Erving, Julius (Dr. J) (1993)	836	18,364	.507	.777	5,601	3,224
(A.B.A. Statistics)	407	11,662	.504	.778	4,924	1,952
A.B.A. M.V.P. 1974-76; N.B.A. M.V.P., 1981						
Ewing, Patrick (2008)	1,183	24,815	.504	.740	11,607	2,215
Two-time gold-medal-winning Olympian; 11-time All-Star						
Frazier, Walt (Clyde) (1987)	825	15,581	.490	.786	4,830	5,040
N.B.A. All-Defensive team seven consecutive seasons (1969-75)						
Fulks, Joe (1977)	489	8,003	.302	.766	1,3821	587
B.A.A. scoring leader in 1947 (23.2 ppg)						
Gallatin, Harry (1991)	682	8,843	.398	.773	6,684	1,208
Seven-time All-Star						
Gervin, George (Iceman) (1996)	791	20,708	.511	.844	3,607	2,214
(A.B.A. Statistics)	269	5,887	.480	.831	1,995	584
All-N.B.A. team five years in a row (1978-82)						
Gola, Tom (1975)	698	7,871	.431	.760	5,605	2,953
One of only two major-college players with over 2,000 points and 2,000 rebounds in career						
Goodrich, Gail (1996)	1,031	19,181	.456	.807	3,279	4,805
Scored 42 points in 1965 N.C.A.A. Final; averaged 18.6 points per game over 14 years in N.B.A.						
Greer, Harold (Hal) (1981)	1,122	21,586	.452	.801	5,665	4,540
Scored 19 points in one quarter of 1968 All-Star game						
Hagan, Cliff (1977)	746	13,447	.450	.798	5,019	2,236
(A.B.A. Statistics)	94	1,423	.496	.807	436	398
Helped St. Louis to 1958 championship with 27.7 ppg in playoffs						
Havlicek, John J. (Hondo) (1983)	1,270	26,395	.439	.815	8,007	6,114
Averaged 20.8 ppg; member of 8 N.B.A. championship teams						
Hawkins, Connie (1992)	499	8,233	.467	.785	3,971	2,052
(A.B.A. Statistics)	117	3,295	.515	.765	1,479	504
Four-time All-Star; ABA M.V.P. 1969						
Hayes, Elvin (1990)	1,303	27,313	.452	.670	16,279	2,398
Led league in scoring (1969) and rebounds per game (1970,1974)						
Heinsohn, Tom (1986)	654	12,194	.405	.790	5,749	1,318
Played for eight N.B.A. championship teams and coached two others						
Houbregs, Robert J. (1987)	281	2,611	.404	.721	1,552	500
N.C.A.A. Player of the Year, 1953						
Issel, Dan (1993)	718	14,659	.506	.797	5,707	1,804
(A.B.A. Statistics)	500	12,823	.488	.786	5,426	1,103
Averaged 33.7 points per game in senior year at Kentucky, 1969-70						
Jabbar, Kareem Abdul (1995)	1,560	38,387	.559	.721	17,440	5,660
Six-time N.B.A. M.V.P. All-time N.B.A. leader in scoring, games, minutes, field goals						
Jeannette, Buddy (1994) (B.A.A.-N.B.A.)	139	997	.341	.781	N.A.	287
Won N.B.L. M.V.P. three times						
Johnson, Earvin (Magic) (2002)	906	17,707	.520	.848	6,559	10,141
Led Lakers to five N.B.A. championships; 3-time N.B.A. M.V.P. (1987, 1989, 1990); 12-time All-Star						
Johnson, Gus (2010)	581	9,944	.440	.699	7,379	1,541
Five-time N.B.A. All-Star, two-time member of N.B.A. All-Defensive Team						
Johnston, Neil (1990)	516	10,023	.444	.768	5,856	1,269
Named to four straight all-N.B.A. First Teams (1953-56)						
Jones, K.C. (1989)	676	5,011	.387	.647	2,399	2,908
High scorer in 1955 N.C.A.A. finals (24 pts); held Tom Gola scoreless for 21 mins						

Player (Year Elected)	Games	Points	FG%	FT%	Rebs.	Assts.
Jones, Sam (1983)	871	15,411	.456	.803	4,305	2,209
Member of 10 N.B.A. championship teams						
Jordan, Michael (2009)	1,072	32,292	.497	.835	6,672	5,633
Five-time N.B.A. M.V.P.; 14-time All-Star; one of the most recognized people in the world						
Lanier, Bob (1992)	959	19,248	.514	.767	9,698	3,007
Eight-time All-Star; N.B.A. M.V.P., 1974						
Lloyd, Earl (2003)	560	4,682	.356	.750	3,609	810
First African-American to play in a N.B.A. game, 1950						
Lovellette, Clyde (1988)	704	11,947	.443	.756	6,663	1,165
Three-time All-American at University of Kansas (1950-52)						
Lucas, Jerry Ray (Luke) (1979)	829	14,053	.499	.783	12,942	2,730
N.B.A. Rookie of the Year and field-goal percentage leader (.527) in 1964						
Macauley, Edward (Easy Ed) (1960)	641	11,234	.436	.761	2,079	1,667
N.B.A. All-Star Game M.V.P., 1951						
Malone, Karl (2010)	1,476	36,928	.516	.742	14,968	5,248
Two-time N.B.A. M.V.P., second on the NBA's all-time scoring list						
Malone, Moses (2001)	1,329	27,409	.491	.769	16,212	1,796
Three-time M.V.P., 12-time All-Star. Averaged 20 points per game 11 straight seasons						
Maravich, Pete (Pistol) (1987)	658	15,948	.441	.820	2,747	3,563
N.C.A.A. career record holder for points scored (3667) and scoring avg. (44.2 ppg)						
Martin, Slater (1981)	745	7,337	.364	.762	2,3021	3,160
Played in seven straight All-Star Games, 1953-59						
McAdoo, Bob (2000)	852	18,787	.503	.754	8,048	1,951
N.B.A. Rookie of the Year (1973); led league in scoring 1974, 1975, and 1976						
McGuire, Dick (1993)	738	5,921	.389	.644	2,784	4,205
Averaged 8.0 ppg						
McHale, Kevin (1999)	971	17,335	.554	.798	7,122	1,670
Seven-time All-Star; won Sixth Man Award twice; won 3 N.B.A. Championships: 1981, 1984, 1986						
Mikan, George L. (1959)	439	10,156	.404	.782	4,1671	1,245
Three-time N.B.A. scoring leader (1949, 1950, 1952)						
Mikkelson, Vern (1995)	699	10,063	.403	.766	5,9401	1,515
Six-time N.B.A. All-Star; won 4 N.B.A. Championships: 1950, 1952, 1953, & 1954						
Monroe, Earl (The Pearl) (1990)	926	17,454	.464	.807	2,796	3,594
N.B.A. Rookie of the Year, 1968						
Murphy, Calvin (1993)	1,002	17,949	.482	.892	2,103	4,402
Set single-season free throw percentage record with .958 in 1980-81						
Olajuwon, Hakeem (2008)	1,238	26,946	.512	.712	13,748	3,058
3,000+ blocked shots, 2,000+ steals; back to back Finals M.V.P., 1994–95						
Parish, Robert (2003)	1,611	23,334	.537	.721	14,715	2,180
Nine-time N.B.A. All-Star (1981-87, 1990-91). Won 3 N.B.A. Championships (1981, 1984, & 1986)						
Petrovic, Drazen (2002)	290	4,461	.506	.841	669	701
Averaged 15.4 ppg and 43.7% from 3-pt range over 4 years before being killed in auto accident						
Pettit, Bob (1970)	792	20,880	.436	.761	12,849	2,369
Led N.B.A. in scoring (25.7 ppg) and rebounds (1164) in 1956						
Phillip, Andy (1961)	701	6,384	.368	.695	2,3951	3,759
Led N.B.A. in assists, 1951 and 1952						
Pippen, Scottie (2010)	1,178	18,940	.473	.704	7,494	6,135
Six-time N.B.A. champion; three-time All-N.B.A. first team honoree						

Player (Year Elected)	Games	Points	FG%	FT%	Rebs.	Assts.
Pollard, Jim (1977)	438	5,762	.360	.750	2,487[1]	1,417
Started four N.B.A. All-Star Games						
Ramsey, Frank (1981)	623	8,378	.402	.804	3,410	1,136
Member of seven N.B.A. championship teams						
Reed, Willis (1981)	650	12,183	.476	.747	8,414	1,186
1970 N.B.A. Most Valuable Player, All-Star Game M.V.P. and Playoff M.V.P.						
Risen, Arnie (1998)	637	7,633	.381	.699	5,011	1,058
Three-time N.B.A. All-Star (1953, 1954, and 1955)						
Robertson, Oscar (1979)	1,040	26,710	.485	.838	7,804	9,887
N.B.A. M.V.P. 1964; Member of All-N.B.A. First team, 1961–69						
Robinson, David (2009)	987	20,790	.518	.736	10,497	2,441
Rookie of the Year, 1990; 10-time All-Star						
Russell, Bill (1974)	963	14,522	.440	.561	21,620	4,100
Five-time N.B.A. Most Valuable Player; 32 rebounds in one half vs. Philadelphia, 1957						
Schayes, Adolph (Dolph) (1972)	996	18,438	.380	.849	11,256[1]	3,072
N.B.A. Coach of the Year (1966)						
Sharman, Bill (1974)	711	12,665	.426	.883	2,779	2,101
Led N.B.A. in free-throw percentage seven seasons						
Stokes, Maurice (2004)	202	3,315	.351	.698	3,492	1,062
Rookie of the Year (1955–56); hurt badly in freak accident after three N.B.A. seasons						
Thomas, Isiah, (2000)	979	18,822	.452	.759	3,478	9,061
N.B.A. Rookie of the Year (1982); 12-time All-Star; M.V.P. of the 1990 Final						
Thompson, David (1996)	509	11,264	.504	.778	1,921	1,631
(ABA Statistics)	83	2,158	.515	.794	525	308
N.C.A.A. player of the year 1974 and 1975; ABA Rookie of the Year, 1976						
Thurmond, Nate (1984)	964	14,437	.421	.667	14,464	2,575
1,000+ rebounds 1964-69, 1970-73						
Twyman, Jack (1982)	823	15,840	.450	.778	5,421	1,969
Led N.B.A. in field-goal percentage, 1958 (.452)						
Unseld, Wes (1988)	984	10,624	.509	.633	13,769	3,822
Named N.B.A. Most Valuable Player and Rookie of the Year in same year (1969)						
Walton, Bill (1993)	468	6,215	.521	.660	4,923	1,590
N.B.A. M.V.P. in 1976						
Wanzer, Robert (1987)	502	5,891	.388	.800	1,652[1]	1,575
Free-throw percentage leader, 1952 (.904)						
West, Jerry Alan (1979)	932	25,192	.474	.814	5,376	6,238
N.B.A. M.V.P. in 1970; .805 free throw percentage in 13 years in the playoffs						
Wilkens, Lenny (1989)	1,077	17,772	.432	.774	5,030	7,211
600+ assists 6 consecutive seasons						
Wilkins, Dominique (2006)	1,074	26,668	.461	.811	7,169	2,677
Nine-time All-Star; winner of two slam-dunk contests						
Worthy, James (2003)	926	16,320	.521	.769	4,707	2,791
M.V.P. of 1988 N.B.A. Finals						
Yardley, George (1996)	472	9,063	.422	.780	4,220	815
First player in N.B.A. history to score 2,000 points in a season						

Note: List is valid through 2010. All statistics for N.B.A. career unless otherwise noted. NBL = National Basketball League. ABA = American Basketball Association. N.C.A.A. (National Collegiate Athletic Association) 1. Does not include seasons played prior to 1950-51 when the N.B.A. first began keeping statistics for rebounds. 2. The National Basketball League did not keep statistics for field-goal percentage, rebounds, or assists.

Hall of Fame Coaches

Anderson, W. Harold, 1984
Auerbach, Arnold J. "Red," 1968
Auriemma, Geno, 2006
Barry, Justin "Sam," 1978
Blood, Ernest A., 1960
Boeheim, Jim, 2005
Brown, Hubert "Hubie," 2005
Brown, Larry, 2002
Calhoun, Jim, 2006
Cann, Howard G., 1967
Carlson, Dr. H. Clifford, 1959
Carnesecca, Lou, 1992
Carnevale, Ben, 1969
Carril, Pete, 1997
Case, Everett, 1981
Chancellor, Van 2007
Chaney, John, 2001
Conradt, Jody, 1998
Crum, Denny, 1994
Daly, Chuck, 1994
Dean, Everett S., 1966
Diddle, Edgar A., 1971
Drake, Bruce, 1972
Ferrandiz, Pedro, 2007
Gaines, Clarence, 1981
Gamba, Sandro, 2006

Gardner, James H. "Jack," 1983
Gill, Amory T. "Slats," 1967
Hannum, Alex, 1998
Harshman, Marv, 1984
Haskins, Don, 1997
Hickey, Edgar S., 1978
Hobson, Howard A., 1965
Holzman, William "Red," 1985-86
Hurley Sr., Robert "Bob," 2010
Iba, Henry P. "Hank," 1968
Jackson, Phil, 2007
Julian, Alvin "Doggie," 1967
Keaney, Frank W., 1960
Keogan, George E., 1961
Knight, Bob, 1991
Krzyzewski, Mike, 2001
Kundla, John, 1995
Lambert, Ward L., 1960
Litwack, Harry, 1975
Loeffler, Kenneth D., 1964
Lonborg, Arthur C., 1972
McCutchan, Arad A., 1980
McGuire, Al, 1992
McGuire, Frank J., 1976
Meanwell, Dr. Walter E., 1959
Meyer, Raymond J., 1978

Miller, Ralph, 1987
Moore, Billie, 1999
Nikolic, Aleksandar, 1998
Novosel, Mirko, 2007
Olson, Lute, 2002
Ramsay, Jack, 1992
Riley, Pat, 2008
Rupp, Adolph F., 1968
Rush, Cathy, 2008
Sachs, Leonard D., 1961
Sharman, Bill, 2004
Shelton, Everett F., 1979
Sloan, Jerry 2009
Smith, Dean, 1982
Stringer, Vivian, 2009
Summitt, Pat, 2000
Taylor, Fred R., 1985-86
Teague, Bertha, 1984
Thompson, John, 1999
Wade, L. Margaret, 1984
Watts, Stanley H., 1985-86
Wilkens, Lenny, 1998
Wooden, John R., 1972
Woolpert, Phil, 1992
Wootten, Morgan, 2000

FOOTBALL

Football, or American football, as it is known in the rest of the world, evolved from soccer and rugby in the late 19th century. On November 6, 1869, Rutgers and Princeton played a soccer-like game that would eventually evolve into modern football. During the next seven years, rugby gained popularity at eastern colleges, while soccer fell from favor. In 1876 the rules of American football became different enough from rugby that they were codified. At that time, a field goal and a touchdown were each worth four points.

Since then, American football has continued to diverge from its international cousins. Today there are hundreds of rules that differentiate American football from the version played around the world, the most ironic being that very little of the American game uses the feet.

With periodic breaks in the action, football is uniquely suited for television. Football's symbiotic relationship with television has fueled its rise to the most popular sport in the United States and one of the most popular forms of entertainment in the world.

Rules and Conduct of Play

Although football's myriad rules have evolved substantially in the sport's first century, the differences among the high school, college, and professional games are few. A football field, itself now commonly regarded in the United States as a unit of measurement, is 100 yards long, demarcated every five yards by white stripes that run the width of the field (160 feet). At either end of the 100 yards are 10-yard-long end zones. At the center of the rear boundary of each end zone is a U-shaped goalpost with a crossbar 10 feet high and two uprights 18 1/2 feet apart. The surface is grass or synthetic grass. The middle of the field is the 50-yard line; numbers decrease on either side of the center stripe until they reach the 0-yard line, or the goal line.

The object of the game is to move the football into the end zone (a touchdown), or to get close enough so as to kick the ball between the uprights (a field goal). A touchdown is worth six points and carries with it the right to attempt an extra point (kicking the ball between the uprights from the 2 1/2 yard line) or a two-point conversion (moving the ball across the goal line again from the 2 1/2 yard line). A field goal is always worth three points. The defense can score by pushing an offensive player backward into his own end zone. This uncommon method of scoring is called a safety, and is worth two points.

Each team has 11 players on the field at once. The offensive team tries to advance the ball, and the defensive team seeks to stop them by tackling the player with the ball before he can advance down the field. The offensive team has four chances (or downs) to advance the ball 10 yards (a first down). If they achieve this goal, they are rewarded with four more downs to advance another 10 yards. If they fail, they must give the ball to the other team. At any time, the offensive team has the option of punting (i.e. kicking) the ball to the defensive team. Most teams do this on fourth down when it seems unlikely that they will get a first down.

The defense may also take possession by catching a pass intended for an offensive player (an interception), or by picking up the ball after it has been dropped by an offensive player (a fumble). Any player on either team may pick up a fumbled football.

The game is played in four 15-minute quarters, with a break for halftime. The teams switch ends of the field between the first and second quarters and the third and fourth quarters. The game commences with one team kicking the ball to the other team (the kickoff). After every touchdown and field goal, the team that scores kicks off again. At the game's conclusion, the team with the most points wins.

Positions

The *quarterback* is the player who runs the offense on the field. He signals the start of play and either hands the ball to a running back or he retreats several steps into a pocket formed by the offensive line and attempts to throw the ball to an eligible receiver. Alternatively, he can run with the ball himself. Quarterbacks are usually tall with a strong arm.

The *running backs* carry the ball most frequently on running plays. Often divided into two roles: the fullback, a player who specializes in blocking, and the tailback or halfback, who will run the ball most often. These players normally align behind the quarterback and offensive line.

The primary duty of the *wide receivers* is to catch passes. They align outside—often 10 to 12 yards—the offensive line, and are almost always the swiftest players on the offense. They try to run well-designed pass routes or patterns to separate themselves from defenders.

The *offensive line* is a set of five players whose responsibility is to protect the quarterback and block defenders to clear lanes for the running backs. The *center* initiates each play by snapping the ball to the quarterback. The center is flanked by two players called *guards*, and outside the guards are two *tackles*.

The defensive team is divided into three different units. The defensive players on the line of scrimmage are known as the defensive line. They are often separated into nose tackles (who align directly over or near the offensive center), tackles, and ends.

Linebackers are a group of defenders who usually begin each play immediately behind the defensive linemen or outside the linemen on the line of scrimmage. They are responsible for stopping running plays, covering short pass routes, and rushing the quarterback.

The *defensive backs*, known collectively as the secondary, have the primary responsibility of preventing the offense from progressing by the pass. In standard situations, the secondary numbers four players: two *cornerbacks*, a *strong safety*, and a *free safety*. In likely passing plays, defenses may choose a package of players called the "nickel" (an extra defensive back) or even the "dime" (two extras) at the expense of linebackers or linemen.

College Football

Origins

American football originated in the second half of the 19th century, evolving out of the British games of soccer and rugby. During the 1870's, teams played various versions of the game, the home squad often dictating the rules. Early contests included Princeton against Rutgers in 1871 and Princeton versus Yale in 1873. The student captain was in charge of the team on and off the field. At Yale, Walter Camp proved to be a brilliant captain and, after his graduation in 1881, he stayed in New Haven and continued to run the squad as the "graduate manager."

Camp, often called the "Father of Football," worked to codify the on-field rules and to institute daily practice routines and game strategies. Because, above all, he wanted his teams to win, sometimes he enlisted athletes who were paid for playing football at Yale. Yale's rivals, as well as other schools taking up the game, also wanted to win, and soon many rosters featured "ringers" (non-students) and "tramp athletes" (ringers who sold their services to more than one school during a season and/or over a number of seasons).

By the 1890's, football moved off-campus and grew in popularity with the sporting press and the general public. The annual Thanksgiving Day contests in New York City,

usually featuring Yale and Princeton, attracted significant media attention and large crowds. From this popularity came the first football stadium at Harvard in 1903. Unfortunately the on-field game, featuring the "flying wedge" formation where the offensive team linked arms and tried to trample their opponents, resulted in many injuries and some deaths. In 1906, President Theodore Roosevelt invited the college presidents of the major Ivy League schools to the White House and insisted that they change the rules to eliminate violent play. Later that year, representatives of 28 schools with football teams met in New York City and formed the group that evolved into the National Collegiate Athletic Association (N.C.A.A.). After 1906 the rules became more uniform and outlawed fighting and open brutality; the new rules also allowed a limited version of the forward pass but kept the rugby-sized ball. Fullback plunges into the line became the main offensive weapon.

Early Success

During the first two decades of the 20th century, college football increased in popularity in the Northeast, but even more so in the Midwest. The largest schools in the Midwest—Michigan, Minnesota, Wisconsin, Illinois, Purdue, Chicago, and Northwestern—formed a conference (the forerunner of the Big Ten) in 1895, and these universities began to produce some of the best football teams in the country. Directing the on-field game were the graduate managers, who at many schools had become full-time, well-paid coaches and athletic directors. The media promoted the teams and focused public attention on the most successful and famous coaches and the best players.

From 1899 to 1924, Amos Alonzo Stagg won seven Big Ten championships for the University of Chicago with his "Monsters of the Midway"; Glenn "Pop" Warner invented the single wing and, from 1907 to 1914, won at Carlisle Institute (where few of his players were college students); and Fielding Yost had great success at the University of Michigan during the first decades of the century. The greatest player of the era was the Native American athlete Jim Thorpe, who played at Carlisle from 1908 to 1911. College football—unlike other organized sports, notably major and minor league baseball—was open to all minority groups, including African-Americans. In the mid-1910's Paul Robeson at Rutgers and Fritz Pollard at Brown were football stars, their schools amenable to their playing and attending as long as they helped their teams win.

The Roaring Twenties and Great Depression

In the 1920's, a decade of economic prosperity, college football expanded dramatically. Many schools, particularly in urban areas and in the South and Southwest, started or enlarged their teams, while many of the established football powers built huge stadiums and began organizing student and alumni activities around the games, particularly the new phenomenon of Homecoming.

The sporting press loved the hoopla of college football, and national sportswriters such as Grantland Rice turned the era's stars into national heroes. Before ever seeing him play, Rice called Harold "Red" Grange, an outstanding running back at the University of Illinois, "The Galloping Ghost of the Illini." But Rice's greatest creation was "The Four Horsemen of Notre Dame," a swift but small backfield for the decade's most popular team, the Fighting Irish of the University of Notre Dame. Their innovative and entrepreneurial coach, Knute Rockne, aided by the media, turned the teams of a small Catholic school in northern Indiana into a national phenomenon. The more games and championships that Rockne's teams won, the greater their popularity among regular fans. The Fighting Irish also made college football fans of millions of people, particularly working-class Catholics who previously had no interest in football or college. A decade later, Warner Brothers made a saccharine movie about this team and

its coach, *Knute Rockne—All-American*, with future president Ronald Reagan portraying Rockne's greatest player, George Gipp.

The Great Depression of the 1930's erased some small college football programs, but the big ones persevered and, thanks to the new medium of radio, became even more popular. Notre Dame, West Point, and the Naval Academy allowed free broadcasts of their games and developed huge national followings, but even the schools that charged the broadcasters reached large local and regional audiences. In the mid-1930's tourism promoters in a number of warm weather cities started the Sugar, Cotton, and Orange Bowls (the Rose Bowl, the "Grand-Daddy of the Bowls," had begun in 1903). The bowl promoters invited the most successful teams to participate in this extra game that took place after the regular season. This system remains in place in the modern college game. Another continuing tradition is the Heisman Trophy. In 1934 the Downtown Athletic Club of New York City created the annual trophy to honor the year's best college player. During these years, the Southeastern and Southwestern conferences, in an attempt to lure athletes from the football-rich high schools of the north, offered the first athletic scholarships.

In 1934 the rules committee of the coaches association shrank the size of the football, and the forward pass started to become a major offensive weapon, particularly in the Southwest Conference, featuring passers such as "Slinging" Sammy Baugh and Davey O'Brien of Texas Christian University. Yet, in the North, running backs and fierce linemen still dominated the game, producing national champions at the University of Minnesota under coach Bernie Bierman, a.k.a. "Hammer of the North," and outstanding teams at Fordham University, led by their "Seven Blocks of Granite" line.

World War II and Its Aftermath

During World War II, many schools curtailed their football programs, but various armed forces training camps fielded teams to play the college squads still operating. In addition, through the cooperation of draft boards around the country, West Point and the Naval Academy produced the best teams of the war era. Coach Earl "Red" Blaik's Black Knights of the Hudson, with Heisman Trophy winners Felix "Doc" Blanchard and Glenn Davis leading the running attack, captured national championships in 1944 and 1945.

After the war, college football exploded in popularity.

Hundreds of schools entered or re-entered the sport, and more than 50 new bowl games began. Atop this chaotic situation stood the traditional powers, particularly teams from Big Ten and Pacific Coast Conference universities. Cheating was rampant, with coaches often employing professional athletes and not pretending that their players were students. Ruthless buccaneers like Paul "Bear" Bryant emerged, winning at every stop—in Bryant's case at Maryland, Kentucky, Texas A & M, and eventually his alma mater, Alabama. Among the great players of the era—Heisman winners and runners-up—were Notre Dame quarterback Johnny Lujack and end Leon Hart; Southern Methodist running backs Doak Walker and Kyle Rote; Georgia's Charley Trippi; and North Carolina's Charlie "Choo-Choo" Justice.

In the 1950's, for the first time, the N.C.A.A. permitted all of its members to award athletic scholarships, bringing them in line with the conferences already allowing them. However, the Ivy League schools, terming athletic scholarships as pay-for-play, refused to grant them and dropped out of big-time football. In 1952 tailback Dick Kazmaier of Princeton was the last Heisman Trophy winner from the league that had invented American college football.

In this decade, the N.C.A.A. also gained control of all televising of college football games and parceled them out to schools across the country—but did not allow the most popular teams, like Notre Dame, to appear more than a few times a season. Coach Bud Wilkinson's Oklahoma Sooners dominated their conference, but Big Ten teams, notably coach Woody Hayes's Ohio State Buckeyes and Clarence "Biggie" Munn's Michigan State Spartans challenged Oklahoma for the top spot in the national ranking. Ohio State players Vic Janowicz and Howard "Hopalong" Cassidy won Heismans, as did Billy Vessels of Oklahoma. In addition, many black players entered big-time college football at this time; because southern and southwestern schools still excluded them, Big Ten universities were able to bring many excellent African-American players north to suit up for their teams.

The Full Integration of College Football

In 1961 Ernie Davis of Syracuse was the first black athlete to win the Heisman. A few years before, the great Jim Brown of Syracuse had finished far from the top spot because of the prejudiced voting of southern sportswriters. In the 1960's, as civil rights issues became more important politically, so did black athletes at major schools: the University of Southern California won cham-

pionships with Mike Garrett and O.J. Simpson (both Heisman winners). At the end of the decade, schools below the Mason-Dixon Line began to recruit black players—Jerry Levias at Southern Methodist was the first African-American to play in the Southwest Conference. Black athletes accelerated the integration of many colleges in the South and Southwest and, equally important, helped the fans of those teams accept integration. For most football fans, winning trumped racism, and if black players could bring championships, the fans wanted them on their teams. "Bear" Bryant of Alabama, after losing a game to a U.S.C. squad led by black running back Sam Cunningham, integrated the Crimson Tide in the early 1970's, and Alabama fans cheered as the team added more national championships to its list.

In this era, TV coverage of intercollegiate football changed. Roone Arledge began producing telecasts for ABC-TV, and he portrayed college football as a spectacle, not just a contest on a field. He employed many more cameras than had been used before, and his crews frequently focused on coaches and cheerleaders on the sidelines, fans in the crowd, as well the on-field action. Arledge wanted the TV audience to stay tuned to the game—and the ads—whether the score was lopsided or not; he wanted the spectacle to transcend the sport. His approach came to dominate television coverage of college sports, as did the increasing intrusion of commercial sponsors.

The Final Decades of the Century

In 1973 the N.C.A.A. changed athletic scholarships from a guaranteed four-year grant to a one-year contract renewed at the behest of the athlete's coach, in effect making a football player an employee of his athletic department and under the strict control of his coach. The new system rewarded martinets like Ohio State's Woody Hayes, who put his players through long, grueling practices and demanded absolute obedience. In the 1970's his Buckeyes won Big Ten titles and played in Rose Bowls, and his running back Archie Griffin garnered two Heisman Trophies (and remains the only multiple Heisman winner). But Hayes's career ended in 1978 when he ran onto the field during a bowl game between Ohio State and Clemson and punched a player on the opposing squad. Other outstanding Heisman winners of the 1970's and their national championship teams were Tony Dorsett at Pitt, Johnny Rodgers at Nebraska, and Charles White at U.S.C.

In 1976 61 of the major football schools formed the College Football Association. Dissatisfied with the

N.C.A.A.'s control of the sport, they sought more autonomy over and revenue from their football programs. Two C.F.A. schools, the universities of Georgia and Oklahoma, challenged the N.C.A.A.'s monopoly on telecasts of college football games in court. In a series of verdicts, ending with an almost unanimous 1984 Supreme Court decision, the C.F.A. schools prevailed, and the N.C.A.A. lost control of televising college football. As a result, many national and local networks began broadcasting the games, and many schools, seeking better payouts, moved the scheduling of contests from the traditional Saturday afternoon spot to night games, then games on other days and nights of the week.

In the 1980's the University of Miami Hurricanes, with such excellent quarterbacks as Bernie Kosar and Vinny Testaverde, rose to the top of the polls, and won national titles in 1983, 1987, and 1989. Other excellent teams of the decade were coach Barry Switzer's Oklahoma Sooners and coach Joe Paterno's Penn State Nittany Lions. The articulate Paterno, a graduate of Brown University, was often pointed to as an exemplary coach; he accepted the acclaim and also criticized the increasing corruption in his sport. Many critics and two major reform groups, the Knight Commission and the N.C.A.A. Presidents' Commission, suggested reforms; however, they could never convince powerful coaches and athletic directors to agree to any meaningful changes in the college sports system.

The Contemporary Era

In the 1990's the on-field game came to resemble a version of professional football, and an increasing number of coaches shuttled back and forth between college and N.F.L. teams. Many players considered themselves in minor league training for the N.F.L. and, as a result, the graduation rates of the best teams were often very low. Coach Bobby Bowden's Florida State Seminoles won conference titles, bowl games, and two national championships in the 1990's, and also featured many players who did not graduate and some who acquired criminal records while in college.

At the end of the century, the division between the have and have-not teams in college football increased, and the rich schools and conferences took the lion's share of revenue from television and the bowl games. The haves codified their status when they endorsed the Bowl Championship Series (B.C.S.) in 1992 and convinced the N.C.A.A. to give them semi-autonomous status a few years later. This situation contributed to the demise of the Southwest Conference in 1996 and major shifts in other leagues. In 2003 the Big East football conference, only formed in 1990, lost two important members, Miami and Virginia Tech, to the Atlantic Coast Conference, and this started a domino effect with stronger conferences considering raids on weaker ones to replace departed schools.

These changes had a profound effect on college football as 23 teams changed conferences. Even more defections occurred over the next few years as Colorado and Nebraska left the Big 12 for the Pac-10 and Big Ten respectively. Consequently, the Big-12 now has 10 teams while the Big Ten and Pac-10 have 12. Proponents of a playoff system have increased in recent years as several small conference teams have gone undefeated, being left out of the title game in favor of one- or two-loss teams from major conferences by the B.C.S. computers. This has led to calls for a college football playoff system from Congress and even the White House. Because of the large amount of money tied up in the B.C.S. system, it is highly unlikely that any changes will take place in the near future. In June 2011, the B.C.S. stripped U.S.C. of its 2004 National Championship, after the N.C.A.A. ruled that Reggie Bush had improperly accepted benefits, making him ineligible to play and thus voiding their title.

One thing that seems not to change is the coach at Penn State. In 2011, Joe Paterno will be entering his 62nd season on the coaching staff and 45th as head coach of the Nittany Lions. Because power and greed seem to motivate the men and women running the major conferences and schools, many more changes in college football likely will occur in the first decades of the 21st century. And the game will become increasingly commercial and professional, with more coaches earning more than $1 million a year, and their players detached from regular student life. Yet fans will continue to love college football, attend games and watch them on TV, and the sport will remain an important part of their lives. No other higher education system in the world has produced such an unusual institution as American intercollegiate football.

Professional Football

From its roots in rugby and soccer, American football began its own history in 1876, with the first set of rules. By 1902 the sport had already seen its first professional player (William "Pudge" Heffelfinger, in 1892), its first all professional team (the Allegheny Athletic Association, in 1896), and its first night game (1902, Elmira, N.Y.). But interest in the pro game was largely limited to the Great Lakes states.

Backward passes, or laterals, were always a part of the game, remnants of the sport's rugby ancestry. It wasn't until 1906 that the forward pass was legalized. However, until 1933, the forward pass had to be thrown from five yards behind the line of scrimmage. Other notable rule changes over time included reducing the value of a field goal from four points to three. The value of a touchdown was raised from four points to five in 1898 and raised again to six points in 1909. Though there have been literally hundreds of changes to the rules and equipment since then, today's game has much in common with its ancestor.

1920's and 1930's

The American Professional Football League was formed in 1920, and adopted a constitution a year later for its 22 franchises. In 1922 the association changed its name to the National Football League. Two extant N.F.L. franchises predate the league's existence: the Arizona (formerly St. Louis, formerly Chicago) Cardinals (1899), and the Green Bay Packers (1919). The number of franchises fluctuated as high as 23 clubs in 1925 and as low as eight teams in 1932, as the Depression took its toll on the league.

The sport first attracted national attention in 1925, when All-America quarterback Red Grange, from the University of Illinois, signed a contract with the Chicago Bears. A then-record crowd of 36,000 people watched the "Galloping Ghost" play his first pro game at Wrigley Field. The Bears then went on a barnstorming tour across the country that brought crowds of 73,000 to the Polo Grounds for a game against the New York Giants and 75,000 to the Los Angeles Coliseum for an exhibition against the L.A. Tigers.

The N.F.L. changed the forward pass rule in 1933, so that the ball could be thrown from anywhere behind the line of scrimmage. The rule change increased the importance of the quarterback position, giving rise to passers like "Slingin'" Sammy Baugh. In 1935 the N.F.L. adopted a draft, with teams choosing players from college's game in inverse order of finish; a year later, the Philadelphia

Eagles chose Heisman Trophy winner Jay Berwanger, a University of Chicago running back, with the first pick.

N.F.L. attendance topped 1 million for the first time in 1939. Also that year, the league's first game was televised, a game between the Eagles and the Brooklyn Dodgers. Fewer than one thousand people owned television sets at the time, but this paved the way for football to become a fixture in American living rooms.

1940's and 1950's

World War II decimated several franchises, forcing some teams to merge with each other for a season or longer. In 1943, the era of specialization began when the league adopted free substitution. Amended in 1946, it was restored in 1950, allowing players to play only offense or defense, and to go out of the game for a play or longer and then return. The league also approved a 10-game schedule and made helmets mandatory. Five years later, the Los Angeles Rams painted horns on their helmets, becoming the first team to add emblems to their headgear.

The rival All-America Football Conference started play in 1946 with eight teams, three of which (Cleveland Browns, Baltimore Colts, and San Francisco 49ers) were welcomed into the N.F.L. in 1949. This began the N.F.L.'s hegemony over competitive leagues by appropriating their strongest assets. The A.A.F.C. folded in 1950, and its players were allocated to N.F.L. franchises through a special draft.

That same year, the Los Angeles Rams, and later the Washington Redskins, negotiated deals to have all their games televised. In 1951 the Rams televised only road games in an attempt to increase attendance. Later that year, the DuMont Network paid $75,000 to televise the N.F.L. Championship game coast to coast. NBC paid $100,000 for the 1955 title game, and in 1956 CBS began broadcasting regular season games on Sunday afternoons.

On December 28, 1958, the Baltimore Colts and New York Giants played for the N.F.L. title in what many still deem the greatest football game ever played. The game went into overtime (a first for the title game) before Colts fullback Alan Ameche scored the winning touchdown.

1960's and 1970's

The N.F.L. was at a crossroads in 1960. After longtime Commissioner Bert Bell died of a heart attack, league owners could not agree on a successor. Finally, on the 23rd ballot, they settled on Rams general manager Pete Rozelle. Over the next three decades, Rozelle would guide the league through unprecedented growth, surpassing even baseball, the national pastime, as America's favorite sport.

The N.F.L. faced competition from another upstart league, the American Football League, which was scheduled to launch in the fall of 1960. But the N.F.L. eviscerated its would-be rival, awarding N.F.L. franchises to Minnesota (which then withdrew from the A.F.L.) and to Dallas (home of A.F.L. president Lamar Hunt's Dallas Texans).

Even though the A.F.L.'s two-year-long antitrust suit against the N.F.L. failed in 1962, the new league's high-scoring offenses attracted fans and television money. ABC signed a five-year deal in 1960, and NBC took over A.F.L. broadcasts in 1965 for $36 million over the next five years. In 1965 the A.F.L.'s New York Jets signed Alabama quarterback Joe Namath to a three-year, $427,000 deal, a record salary for any football player. The deal sparked a bidding war between the two leagues as they spent a combined $7 million on their 1966 draft choices.

The champions of each league squared off in the first A.F.L.-N.F.L. World Championship game in 1967. The contest wouldn't be dubbed "Super Bowl" for another year, and the game wasn't a sellout. In the first title game, the Green Bay Packers defeated the Kansas City Chiefs 35-10. Bart Starr led the Packers to a second championship a year later over the Oakland Raiders. In 1969 Namath roiled the football world again by predicting the Jets would defeat the heavily favored Baltimore Colts in Super Bowl III. His prediction was correct, and the shocking upset brought credibility to the younger league.

Unable to vanquish its newest competitor, the N.F.L. consumed it in a merger of the two leagues. In 1970 Baltimore, Cleveland, and Pittsburgh joined the 10 A.F.L. teams to form the American Football Conference. The remaining 13 teams made up the National Football Conference. From 1972 to 1980, the former A.F.L. teams dominated. The Miami Dolphins completed football's only undefeated season in 1972 and repeated as champions in 1973. They were succeeded by the Pittsburgh Steelers, whose "Steel Curtain" defense won four championships (1974, 1975, 1978, and 1979), and the Oakland Raiders (1976 and 1980).

The N.F.L.'s relationship with television changed forever because of what came to be known as the "Heidi" game. On November 17, 1968, NBC cut away in the last minute of the Jets-Raiders game so the beloved children's movie could start on time. The Raiders scored two touchdowns in the last 42 seconds for a come-from-behind 43–32 win. Since then, any time a football game has run past its scheduled ending time, the networks have delayed the programming that follows it until the contest's completion.

Football also conquered prime-time television with the advent of Monday Night Football in 1970. It would become the longest-running prime-time series in the network's history. Meanwhile, the Super Bowl began its rise from curiosity to the most-watched event in world history. By 1971 the TV audience of 24 million homes was the largest ever for a one-day sports event. Two years later, a record 75 million people tuned in. In 1978 the Super Bowl audience topped 102 million.

Another rival league, the World Football League, started operation in 1974, with franchises concentrated in the Sun Belt and Canada. The W.F.L. scored a coup by signing three Miami Dolphins stars to lucrative contracts, but the league folded after only two seasons.

The N.F.L. extended its season from 14 to 16 games in 1978 and added a second wildcard team in each conference to the playoff structure. The two wildcard teams played each other, with the winner advancing to the eight-team playoffs. Additional rule changes outlawed the head slap and allowed defenders to make contact with receivers only once; wide receivers were prohibited from blocking a defender in the back.

1980's to the Present

In 1982 an astounding 73 percent of American homes tuned in to the Super Bowl, making it the highest-rated sports event in history. The 1986 Super Bowl drew a record 127 million viewers, a greater overall number of people, but a slightly lower percentage. Although competition from more networks and channels has fractured the TV audience since then, the Super Bowl is routinely the most-watched television program of the year.

Other off-the-field developments played pivotal roles in the N.F.L.'s recent history. Players' strikes in 1982 and 1987 shortened those seasons to nine and 15 games respectively; in 1987 the owners hired replacement players for three games before the regulars returned. Those strikes resulted in increased free agency for players, but allowed clubs some leeway to retain "franchise players."

The new labor agreements maintained the N.F.L.'s system of revenue-sharing, ballyhooed as the saving grace for small market teams like Green Bay and Cincinnati. But they did nothing to stop the trend of owners hijacking franchises and moving them to the city with the most favorable deal. The Raiders moved from Oakland to Los

Angeles in 1982, and returned to Oakland in 1995. Los Angeles, the nation's second-largest media market, was left without a team, as that same year, the Rams departed for St. Louis, which had been ditched in 1987 by the Cardinals, who had fled to Phoenix.

Baltimore Colts owner Robert Irsay surreptitiously packed his team into moving vans in the middle of the night of January 14, 1984, and opened shop the next day in Indianapolis. Recognizing Baltimore's hunger for Sunday afternoon entertainment, Cleveland Browns owner Art Modell moved his team there in 1996 and renamed it the Ravens. The N.F.L. responded by awarding an expansion franchise, also called the Browns, to Cleveland to begin play in 1999. The Houston Oilers relocated to Nashville in 1998, and changed their name to the Titans the year after. In 2002 jilted Houston received an expansion franchise, bringing the total number of N.F.L. teams to 32.

To accommodate all the moving and expanding, the league realigned each conference from three divisions to four in 2002, preserving traditional rivalries while imposing some geographic order. Because the number of division champions increased from six to eight, the number of play-off wildcard teams, which had been increased to six in 1990, was reduced to four, keeping the total number of playoff teams at 12.

Two other rival leagues came and went quickly: the U.S.F.L., which won an antitrust suit against the N.F.L. in 1986, but was awarded damages of only $1, and soon went out of business; and the X.F.L., a joint venture of NBC and pro wrestling impresario Vince McMahon. The first week of the 2001 X.F.L. season drew large crowds and ratings, but the poor quality of play could not sustain that level of interest, and the league folded after its first year.

Meanwhile, the N.F.L. spread its influence across the globe. After exhibition games in London (1986), Tokyo (1989), Berlin (1990), and Montreal (1990) drew sizable crowds, the league launched the World League of American Football in 1990, scuttled it in 1993, reintroduced it in 1995 with six European franchises, and renamed it N.F.L. Europe in 1998.

All the while, the television money kept rolling in, with networks paying record sums for broadcast rights. The latest contracts were worth $20.4 billion dollars, with the rights for Sunday's games going to Fox, CBS, and NBC (Sunday Night Football) through 2011 and Monday Night Football making its home at ESPN until 2013. Looking to squeeze even more money out of its loyal fans, the N.F.L Network was created in 2006. In order to make

their venture more attractive, the league added eight Thursday or Saturday night games to their lineup starting in Week 10. Due to problems with cable distribution and the limited reach of the network, many fans were left unable to see the games, caught in a struggle for money and power between giant corporations.

There were also developments on the field. Miami's Dan Marino rewrote the record book for quarterbacks, only to have it rewritten again a few years down the line by Brett Favre, the highlight of which was his 297 consecutive regular season games started streak. San Francisco's Jerry Rice became the all-time leader in receptions and receiving yards in 1995, then continued to play past his 40th birthday for the Raiders. Chicago Bear running back Walter Payton broke Jim Brown's record for career rushing yards in 1987, and Emmitt Smith of the Cowboys surpassed Payton's record in 2002.

The NFC returned to dominance, winning 13 straight Super Bowls from the 1984 to the 1996 seasons, most of them in blowouts. Quarterback Joe Montana orchestrated Bill Walsh's pass-first West Coast offense to perfection to lead the San Francisco 49ers to four Super Bowls.

The N.F.L.'s desire for parity has kept more teams in the playoff hunt late into the season, but critics say it has led to an overall mediocrity. A total of 14 different teams appeared in the 2000–2007 Super Bowls, with six different winners.

Stung by a series of off-the-field violent incidents including shootings, DUI manslaughter and the death of a few players, new commissioner Roger Goodell has made his mark by being a strong disciplinarian. Looking to remove some tarnish from the league, Mr. Goodell has handed out yearlong suspensions on more than one occasion. During the 2010 season the N.F.L. started cracking down on violent hits, handing out hundreds of thousands of dollars worth of fines, although no players were suspended. This action has come under fire from many current and former players who feel the commissioners office is being overprotective of its marquee offensive stars, thus making the game less exciting. However, the latest medical research supports the N.F.L.'s view, showing a strong correlation between concussions in N.F.L. players and future bouts of depression and Alzheimer's disease.

After the 2010 season, the collective bargaining agreement between the league owners and the N.F.L. Player's Association was allowed to expire. The owners claimed they were losing money and asked for a reduction in player salaries. The players demanded the teams open their books and prove this was the case or they would accept no such concessions. The N.F.L. owners refused and set March 3rd as the date they would lockout the players if no deal had been reached. Talks soon broke down and the players union voted to decertify and the owners officially began the lockout. On April 25, 2011, U.S. District Court Judge Susan Nelson sided with the players and invalidated the lockout. This ruling caught the owners off-guard as they were unprepared for the return of their players. Chaos reigned for days as players across the league showed up for work, only to be denied entry to weight and locker rooms, with some players locked out of the facilities entirely. Four days after the ruling the first round of the NFL draft was held. Due to the current labor situation teams were unable to trade players during the draft and couldn't contact undrafted players after the draft had finished. On April 29th the Eighth Circuit Court of Appeals granted the league a temporary stay of Judge Nelson's ruling, and on May 16th a permanent stay was granted. The N.F.L. owners and players signed a new 10-year agreement on July 25th, salvaging the 2011 season.

Professional Football Hall of Fame

Herb Adderley (1980) CB, Packers, Cowboys.
Troy Aikman (2006) QB, Cowboys.
George Allen (2002) Coach, Rams, Redskins.
Marcus Allen (2003) RB, Raiders, Chiefs.
Lance Alworth (1978) WR, Chargers, Cowboys.
Doug Atkins (1982) DE, Browns, Bears, Saints.
Morris (Red) Badgro (1981) E, Yankees, Giants, Dodgers.
Lem Barney (1992) CB, Lions.
Cliff Battles (1968) RB, QB, Braves, Redskins.
Sammy Baugh (1963) QB, Redskins.
Chuck Bednarik (1967) C, LB, Eagles.
Bert Bell (1963 Charter) Commissioner, N.F.L. Founder/coach, Eagles, Steelers.
Bobby Bell (1983) LB, DE, Chiefs.
Raymond Berry (1973) E, Colts.
Elvin Bethea (2003) DE, Oilers.
Charles W. Bidwill, Sr. (1967) Owner/president, Cardinals.
Fred Biletnikoff (1988) WR, Raiders.
George Blanda (1981) QB, PK, Bears, Colts, Oilers, Raiders.
Mel Blount (1989) CB, Steelers.
Terry Bradshaw (1989) QB, Steelers.
Bob Brown (2004) T, Eagles, Rams, Raiders.
Jim Brown (1971) FB, Browns.
Paul E. Brown (1967) Coach and GM, Browns, Bengals.
Roosevelt Brown (1975) OT, Giants.
Willie Brown (1984) CB, Broncos, Raiders.
Buck Buchanan (1990) DT, Chiefs.
Nick Buoniconti (2001) LB, Patriots, Dolphins.
Dick Butkus (1979) LB, Bears.
Earl Campbell (1991) RB, Oilers, Saints.
Tony Canadeo (1974) RB, Packers.
Joe Carr (1963) N.F.L. President.
Harry Carson (2006) LB, Giants.
Dave Casper (2002) TE, Raiders, Oilers, Vikings.
Guy Chamberlin (1965) E, Bulldogs, Staleys, Yellowjackets, Cardinals. Coach, Bulldogs,

Yellowjackets, Cardinals.
Jack Christiansen (1970) DB, Spartans, Lions.
Earl (Dutch) Clark (1970) DB, Spartans, Lions, Rams.
George Connor (1975) OT, DT, LB, Bears.
Jimmy Conzelman (1964) QB, Staleys, Independents, Badgers, Panthers. Owner, Steamrollers, Cardinals.
Lou Creekmur, (1996) OL, Lions.
Larry Csonka (1987) RB, Dolphins, Giants.
Al Davis (1992) President, Owner, General Manager, Coach, Raiders. Commissioner, A.F.L.
Willie Davis (1981) DE, Browns, Packers.
Len Dawson (1987) QB, Steelers, Browns, Texans, Chiefs.
Fred Dean (2008) DE, Chargers, Raiders.
Joe DeLamielleure (2003) G, Bills, Browns.
Richard Dent (2011) DE, Bears, 49ers, Colts, Eagles.
Eric Dickerson (1999) RB, Rams, Colts, Raiders, Falcons.
Dan Dierdorf (1996) OT, Cardinals.
Mike Ditka (1988) TE, Bears, Eagles, Cowboys.
Art Donovan (1968) DT, Colts, Yankees, Texans.
Tony Dorsett (1994) RB, Cowboys, Broncos.
John (Paddy) Driscoll (1965) QB, Pros, Staleys, Cardinals, Bears.
Bill Dudley (1966) RB, Steelers, Lions, Redskins.
Albert Glen (Turk) Edwards (1969) OT, Braves, Redskins.
Carl Eller (2004) DE, Vikings, Seahawks.
John Elway (2004) QB, Broncos.
Weeb Ewbank (1978) Coach, Colts, Jets.
Marshall Faulk (2011) RB, Colts, Rams.
Tom Fears (1970) E, Rams.
Jim Finks (1995) President, Vikings, Bears, Saints.
Ray Flaherty (1976) Coach, Redskins, Yankees.
Len Ford (1976) DE, E, Dons, Browns, Packers.
Dan Fortmann (1965) G, Bears.
Dan Fouts (1993) QB, Chargers.
Benny Friedman (2005) QB, Bulldogs, Wolverines, Giants, Dodgers.
Frank Gatski (1985) C, Browns, Lions.
Bill George (1974) LB, Bears, Rams.

Joe Gibbs (1996) Coach, Chargers, Redskins.
Frank Gifford (1977) RB, Giants.
Sid Gillman (1983) Coach, Rams, Chargers, Oilers.
Otto Graham (1965) QB, Browns.
Harold (Red) Grange (1963 Charter) RB, Bears, Yankees.
Bud Grant (1994) Coach, Vikings.
Darrell Green (2008) CB, Redskins.
(Mean) Joe Greene (1987) DT, Steelers.
Forrest Gregg (1977) OL, Packers, Cowboys.
Bob Griese (1990) QB, Dolphins.
Russ Grimm (2010) G, Redskins.
Lou Groza (1974) OT, PK, Browns.
Joe Guyon (1966) RB, Bulldogs, Indians, Independents, Cowboys, Giants.
George Halas (1963) Founder, Coach, player, Staleys. President, Coach, player, Bears.
Jack Ham (1988) LB, Steelers.
Dan Hampton (2002) DE/DT, Bears.
Chris Hanburger (2011) LB, Redskins.
John Hannah (1991) G, Patriots.
Franco Harris (1990) RB, Steelers, Seahawks.
Bob Hayes (2009) WR, Cowboys, 49ers.
Mike Haynes (1997) CB, Patriots, Raiders.
Ed Healey (1964) OT, Independents, Bears.
Mel Hein (1963) C, Giants.
Ted Hendricks (1990) LB, Colts, Packers, Raiders.
Wilbur (Pete) Henry (1963) OT, Bulldogs, Giants, Maroons.
Arnie Herber (1966) QB, Packers, Giants.
Bill Hewitt (1971) E, Bears, Eagles.
Gene Hickerson (2007) G, Browns.
Clarke Hinkle (1964) RB, Packers.
Elroy (Crazylegs) Hirsch (1968) HB, E, Rockets, Rams.
Paul Hornung (1986) HB, Packers.
Ken Houston (1986) S, Oilers, Redskins.
Cal Hubbard (1963) OT, Giants, Packers, Pirates.
Sam Huff (1982) LB, Giants, Redskins.
Lamar Hunt (1972) Founder, AFL; Owner Texans, Chiefs.
Don Hutson (1963) E, Packers.
Michael Irvin (2007) WR, Cowboys.
Ricky Jackson (2010) LB, Saints, 49ers.
Jimmy Johnson (1994) CB, 49ers.
John Henry Johnson (1987) RB, 49ers, Lions, Steelers, Oilers.
Charlie Joiner (1996), WR, Oilers, Bengals, Chargers.
Deacon Jones (1980) DE, Rams, Chargers, Redskins.
Stan Jones (1991) G, DT, Bears, Redskins.
Henry Jordan (1995) DT, Packers.
Sonny Jurgensen (1983) QB, Eagles, Redskins.
Jim Kelly (2002) QB, Bills.
Leroy Kelly (1994) RB, Browns.
Walt Kiesling (1966) G, Eskimos, Maroons, Cardinals, Bears, Packers, Pirates. Coach, Pirates, Steelers.

Frank (Bruiser) Kinard (1971) OT, Dodgers, Yankees.
Paul Krause (1998) S, Vikings, Redskins.
Early (Curly) Lambeau (1963) Founder, Packers. Coach, Packers, Cardinals, Redskins.
Jack Lambert (1990) LB, Steelers.
Tom Landry (1990) Coach, Cowboys.
Dick (Night Train) Lane (1974) DB, Rams, Cardinals, Lions.
Jim Langer (1987) C, Dolphins, Vikings.
Willie Lanier (1986) LB, Chiefs.
Steve Largent (1995) WR, Seahawks.
Yale Lary (1979) DB, Lions.
Dante Lavelli (1975) E, Browns.
Bobby Layne (1967) QB, Bears, Bulldogs, Lions, Steelers.
Dick LeBeau (2010) CB, Lions.
Alphonse (Tuffy) Leemans (1978) RB, Giants.
Marv Levy (2001) Coach, Chiefs, Bills.
Bob Lilly (1980) DT, Cowboys.
Floyd Little (2010) RB, Broncos.
Larry Little (1993) G, Chargers, Dolphins.
James Lofton (2003) WR, Packers, Raiders, Bills, Rams.
Vince Lombardi (1971) Coach, GM, Packers, Redskins.
Howie Long (2000) DL, Raiders.
Ronnie Lott (2000) DB, 49ers, Raiders, Jets.
Sid Luckman (1965) QB, Bears.
William Roy (Link) Lyman (1964) T, Bulldogs, Yellowjackets, Bears.
Tom Mack (1999) OG, Rams.
John Mackey (1992) TE, Colts, Chargers.
John Madden (2006) Coach, Raiders.
Tim Mara (1963) Founder, President, Giants.
Wellington Mara (1997) Owner, Giants.
Gino Marchetti (1972) DE, Texans, Colts.
Dan Marino (2005) QB, Dolphins.
George Preston Marshall (1963) Founder, President, Braves (Redskins).
Bruce Matthews (2007) G/T/ C, Oilers, Titans.
Ollie Matson (1972) RB, Cardinals, Rams, Lions, Eagles.
Don Maynard (1987) WR, Giants, Titans, Jets, Cardinals.
George McAfee (1966) RB, Bears.
Mike McCormack (1984) OT, Yankees, Browns.
Tommy McDonald (1998) WR, Eagles, Cowboys, Rams.
Hugh McElhenny (1970) RB, 49ers Vikings, Giants, Lions.
John (Blood) McNally (1963) RB, Badgers, Eskimos, Maroons, Packers, Pirates, Packers.
Mike Michalske (1964) G, Yankees, Packers.
Wayne Millner (1968) E, Redskins. Coach, Eagles.
Bobby Mitchell (1983) WR/RB Browns, Redskins.
Ron Mix (1979) OT, Chargers, Raiders.
Art Monk (2008) WR, Redskins, Jets, Eagles.
Joe Montana (2000) QB, 49ers, Chiefs.
Warren Moon (2006) QB, Oilers, Vikings, Seahawks, Chiefs.
Lenny Moore (1975) WR, RB, Colts.

Marion Motley (1968) RB, Browns, Steelers.
Mike Munchak (2001) G, Oilers.
Anthony Muñoz (1998) T, Bengals.
George Musso (1982) OT, G, Bears.
Bronko Nagurski (1963) RB, Bears.
Joe Namath (1985) QB, Jets, Rams.
Earle (Greasy) Neale (1969) Coach, Eagles.
Ozzie Newsome (1999) TE, Browns.
Ernie Nevers (1963) RB, Eskimos, Cardinals.
Ray Nitschke (1978) LB, Packers.
Chuck Noll (1993) Coach, Steelers.
Leo Nomellini (1969) DT, 49ers.
Merlin Olsen (1982) DT, Rams.
Jim Otto (1980) C, Raiders.
Steve Owen (1966) T, Cowboys, Giants. Coach, Giants.
Alan Page (1988) DT, Vikings, Bears.
Clarence (Ace) Parker (1972) QB, Dodgers, Yankees.
Jim Parker (1973) OL, Colts.
Walter Payton (1993) RB, Bears.
Joe Perry (1969) RB, 49ers, Colts.
Pete Pihos (1970) E, Eagles.
Fritz Pollard (2005) HB, Coach, Pros/Indians, Badgers, Cadamounts, Steam Roller.
John Randle (2010) DT, Vikings, Seahawks.
Hugh (Shorty) Ray (1966) Supervisor of Officials.
Dan Reeves (1967) Owner, Rams.
Mel Renfro (1996), CB, Cowboys.
Jerry Rice (2010) WR, 49ers, Raiders, Seahawks.
Les Richter (2011) LB, Rams.
John Riggins (1992) RB, Jets, Redskins.
Jim Ringo (1981) C, Packers, Eagles.
Andy Robustelli (1971) DE, Rams, Giants.
Art Rooney (1964) Founder, President, Pirates, Steelers.
Dan Rooney (2000) President, Steelers.
Pete Rozelle (1985) Commissioner, N.F.L.
Bob St. Clair (1990) OT, 49ers.
Ed Sabol (2011) Founder of NFL Films.
Barry Sanders (2004) RB, Lions.
Charlie Sanders (2007) TE, Lions.
Deion Sanders (2011) CB, KR, PR, Falcons, 49ers, Cowboys, Redskins, Ravens.
Gale Sayers (1977) RB, Bears.
Joe Schmidt (1973) LB, Lions. Coach, Lions.
Tex Schramm (1991) GM, Cowboys.
Lee Roy Selmon (1995) DE, Buccaneers.
Shannon Sharpe (2011) TE, Broncos, Ravens.
Billy Shaw (1999) OG, Bills.
Art Shell (1989) OT, Raiders.
Don Shula (1997) Coach, Colts, Dolphins.
O.J. Simpson (1985) RB, Bills, 49ers.
Mike Singletary (1998) LB, Bears.
Jackie Slater (2001) OT, Rams.

Bruce Smith (2009) DE, Bills, Redskins.
Jackie Smith (1994) TE, Cardinals, Cowboys.
John Stallworth (2002) WR, Steelers.
Bart Starr (1977) QB, Packers.
Roger Staubach, (1985) QB, Cowboys.
Ernie Stautner (1969) DT, Steelers.
Jan Stenerud (1991) PK, Chiefs, Packers, Vikings.
Dwight Stephenson (1998) C, Dolphins.
Hank Stram (2003) Coach, Texans, Chiefs, Saints.
Ken Strong (1967) RB, Stapletons, Giants, Yankees.
Joe Stydahar (1967) OT, Bears.
Lynn Swann (2001) WR, Steelers.
Fran Tarkenton (1986) QB, Giants, Vikings.
Charley Taylor (1984) WR, RB, Redskins.
Jim Taylor (1976) RB, Packers, Saints.
Lawrence Taylor (1999) LB, Giants.
Derrick Thomas (2009) LB, Chiefs.
Thurman Thomas (2007) RB, Bills.
Jim Thorpe (1963) RB, Bulldogs, Indians, Maroons, Independents, Giants, Bulldogs, Cardinals.
Andre Tippett (2008) LB, Patriots.
Y.A. Tittle (1971) QB, Colts, 49ers, Giants.
George Trafton (1964) C, Staleys, Bears.
Charley Trippi (1968) RB, QB, Cardinals.
Emlen Tunnell (1967) DB, Giants, Packers.
Clyde (Bulldog) Turner (1966) C, LB, Bears.
Johnny Unitas (1979) QB, Colts, Chargers.
Gene Upshaw (1987) G, Raiders.
Norm Van Brocklin (1971) QB, Rams, Eagles.
Steve Van Buren (1965) RB, Eagles.
Doak Walker (1986) RB, Lions.
Bill Walsh (1993) Coach, 49ers.
Paul Warfield (1983) WR, Browns, Dolphins.
Bob Waterfield (1965) QB, Coach, Rams.
Mike Webster (1997) C, Steelers.
Roger Wehrli (2007) CB, Cardinals.
Arnie Weinmeister, (1984) DT, Yankees, Giants.
Randy White (1994) DT, Cowboys.
Reggie White (2006) DE, DT, Eagles, Packers, Panthers.
Dave Wilcox (2000) LB, 49ers.
Bill Willis (1977) G, MG, Browns.
Larry Wilson (1978) DB, Cardinals.
Ralph Wilson Jr. (2009) Co-founder AFC, Owner, Bills.
Kellen Winslow (1995) TE, Chargers.
Alex Wojciechowicz (1968) C, LB, Lions, Eagles.
Willie Wood (1989) S, Packers.
Rod Woodson (2009) CB, S, Raiders, Steelers, 49ers.
Rayfield Wright (2006) T, Cowboys.
Ron Yary (2001) OT, Vikings.
Steve Young (2005) QB, Buccaneers, 49ers.
Jack Youngblood (2001) DE, Rams.
Gary Zimmerman (2009) T, Vikings, Broncos.

Super Bowl Results

Super Bowl	Location	Winning Team	Losing Team
I	Jan. 15, 1967, Memorial Coliseum, Los Angeles, California	Green Bay Packers 35	Kansas City Chiefs 10
II	Jan. 14, 1968, Orange Bowl, Miami, Florida	Green Bay Packers 33	Oakland Raiders 14
III	Jan. 12, 1969, Orange Bowl, Miami, Florida	New York Jets 16	Baltimore Colts 7
IV	Jan. 11, 1970, Tulane Stadium, New Orleans, Louisiana	Kansas City Chiefs 23	Minnesota Vikings 7
V	Jan. 17, 1971, Orange Bowl, Miami, Florida	Baltimore Colts 16	Dallas Cowboys 13
VI	Jan. 16, 1972, Tulane Stadium, New Orleans, Louisiana	Dallas Cowboys 24	Miami Dolphins 3
VII	Jan. 14, 1973, Memorial Coliseum, Los Angeles, California	Miami Dolphins 14	Washington Redskins 7
VIII	Jan. 13, 1974, Rice Stadium, Houston, Texas	Miami Dolphins 24	Minnesota Vikings 7
IX	Jan. 12, 1975, Tulane Stadium, New Orleans, Louisiana	Pittsburgh Steelers 16	Minnesota Vikings 6
X	Jan. 18, 1976, Orange Bowl, Miami, Florida	Pittsburgh Steelers 21	Dallas Cowboys 17
XI	Jan. 9, 1977, Rose Bowl, Pasadena, California	Oakland Raiders 32	Minnesota Vikings 14
XII	Jan. 15, 1978, Louisiana Superdome, New Orleans	Dallas Cowboys 27	Denver Broncos 10
XIII	Jan. 21, 1979, Orange Bowl, Miami, Florida	Pittsburgh Steelers 35	Dallas Cowboys 31
XIV	Jan. 20, 1980, Rose Bowl, Pasadena, California	Pittsburgh Steelers 31	Los Angeles Rams 19
XV	Jan. 25, 1981, Louisiana Superdome, New Orleans	Oakland Raiders 27	Philadelphia Eagles 10
XVI	Jan. 24, 1982, Pontiac Silverdome, Pontiac, Michigan	San Francisco 49ers 26	Cincinnati Bengals 21
XVII	Jan. 30, 1983, Rose Bowl, Pasadena, California	Washington Redskins 27	Miami Dolphins 17
XVIII	Jan. 22, 1984, Tampa Stadium, Tampa, Florida	Los Angeles Raiders 38	Washington Redskins 9
XIX	Jan. 20, 1985, Stanford Stadium, Stanford, California	San Francisco 49ers 38	Miami Dolphins 16
XX	Jan. 26, 1986, Louisiana Superdome, New Orleans	Chicago Bears 46	New England Patriots 10
XXI	Jan. 25, 1987, Rose Bowl, Pasadena, California	New York Giants 39	Denver Broncos 20
XXII	Jan. 31, 1988, Jack Murphy Stadium, San Diego, California	Washington Redskins 42	Denver Broncos 10
XXIII	Jan. 22, 1989, Joe Robbie Stadium, Miami, Florida	San Francisco 49ers 20	Cincinnati Bengals 16
XXIV	Jan. 28, 1990, Louisiana Superdome, New Orleans, Louisiana	San Francisco 49ers 55	Denver Broncos 10
XXV	Jan. 27, 1991, Tampa Stadium, Tampa, Florida	New York Giants 20	Buffalo Bills 19
XXVI	Jan. 26, 1992, Hubert Humphrey Metrodome, Minneapolis	Washington Redskins 37	Buffalo Bills 24
XXVII	Jan. 31, 1993, Rose Bowl, Pasadena, California	Dallas Cowboys 52	Buffalo Bills 17
XXVIII	Jan. 30, 1994, Georgia Dome, Atlanta, Georgia	Dallas Cowboys 30	Buffalo Bills 13
XXIX	Jan. 29, 1995, Joe Robbie Stadium, Miami, Florida	San Francisco 49ers 49	San Diego Chargers 26
XXX	Jan. 28, 1996, Sun Devil Stadium, Tempe, Arizona	Dallas Cowboys 27	Pittsburgh Steelers 17
XXXI	Jan. 26, 1997, Louisiana Superdome, New Orleans	Green Bay Packers 35	New England Patriots 21
XXXII	Jan. 25, 1998, Qualcomm Stadium, San Diego, Calif.	Denver Broncos 31	Green Bay Packers 24
XXXIII	Jan. 31, 1999, Pro Player Stadium, Miami, Florida	Denver Broncos 34	Atlanta Falcons 19
XXXIV	Jan. 30, 2000, Georgia Dome, Atlanta, Georgia	St. Louis Rams 23	Tennessee Titans 16
XXXV	Jan. 28, 2001, Raymond James Stadium, Tampa, Florida	Baltimore Ravens 34	New York Giants 7
XXXVI	Feb. 3, 2002, Louisiana Superdome, New Orleans	New England Patriots 20	St. Louis Rams 17
XXXVII	Jan. 26, 2003, Qualcomm Stadium, San Diego, Calif.	Tampa Bay Buccaneers 48	Oakland Raiders 21
XXXVIII	Feb. 1, 2004, Reliant Stadium, Houston, Texas	New England Patriots 32	Carolina Panthers 29
XXXIX	Feb. 6, 2005, Alltel Stadium, Jacksonville, Florida	New England Patriots 24	Philadelphia Eagles 21
XL	Feb. 5, 2006, Ford Field, Detroit, Michigan	Pittsburgh Steelers 21	Seattle Seahawks 10
XLI	Feb. 4, 2007, Dolphin Stadium, Miami Gardens, Florida	Indianapolis Colts 29	Chicago Bears 17
XLII	Feb. 3, 2008, U. of Phoenix Stadium, Glendale, Arizona	New York Giants 17	New England Patriots 14
XLIII	Feb. 1, 2009, Raymond James Stadium, Tampa, Florida	Pittsburgh Steelers 27	Arizona Cardinals 23
XLIV	Feb. 7, 2010, Sun Life Stadium, Miami Gardens, Florida	New Orleans Saints 31	Indianapolis Colts 17
XLV	Feb. 6, 2011, Cowboys Stadium, Arlington, Texas	Green Bay Packers 31	Pittsburgh Steelers 25

ICE HOCKEY

History

Ice hockey evolved from the summertime sports of field hockey and Irish hurling, but the name "hockey" comes from the French word *hoquet*, which means "bent stick," or "shepherd's crook." The original game was brought by British soldiers to North America, where it was revised in the 1870's to use a flat puck instead of a ball. As the century progressed, the sport moved from the summertime fields to wintertime ice.

By the late 19th century, hockey was very popular in Canada. In 1892 the governor general of Canada, Lord Stanley, for a price of less than $50, purchased a silver cup lined with gold and declared that it should be awarded each year to the best amateur hockey team. This cup soon came to be called the Stanley Cup, and the trophy continues to be given to the champion of the National Hockey League (N.H.L.), the world's preeminent hockey league.

In the late 19th and early 20th centuries teams from all over Canada fought (often literally) for the Stanley Cup. As there was no overall league, any team could compete for the Cup. In its infancy, teams from 17 different leagues challenged for the Cup before the National Hockey Association (predecessor of the N.H.L.) took possession of the trophy in 1910. Since 1926, only N.H.L. teams have competed for the Stanley Cup.

The early days of hockey are filled with colorful stories. One club, the Dawson City Klondikers from the Yukon, traveled on dogsleds, bicycles, stagecoaches, and a boat just to reach a train to take them on a 23-day journey to vie for the Stanley Cup. Their travels came to an end against the legendary Ottawa Silver Seven, led by Frank McGee. In the second game of the series, McGee scored 14 goals—a record that still stands. Ottawa, as might be expected, won the series.

Hockey had a number of stars in the years prior to the N.H.L. Fred "Cyclone" Taylor, one of the first players to realize the financial potential of his talent, barnstormed through packed exhibitions in the United States. Taylor was a member of the famous Renfrew Millionaires, the best team money could buy in 1910. (Money couldn't buy victory, however, for the Millionaires never won the Stanley Cup.)

By the time the N.H.L. was born in 1917, hockey games were wild events in Canada, replete with rowdiness, fights, and airborne fruit in barnlike arenas. At first, the N.H.L. was just another league trying to attract players and spectators to make money on the growing popularity of the fast and brutal game. But by 1926 the N.H.L. took full control of the Stanley Cup and expanded to a collection of 10 teams, including the New York Rangers, the Chicago Black Hawks, and the Detroit Cougars.

Through the years, teams dropped out of the league until, by 1938, there were six teams remaining. The same six teams made up the N.H.L. for nearly three decades, until 1967, when the league expanded to 12 clubs. The six members of the N.H.L. before 1967 are known as the Original Six: the Boston Bruins, Chicago Black Hawks (now Blackhawks), Detroit Cougars (now Red Wings), New York Rangers, Montreal Canadiens, and Toronto Maple Leafs.

Of the Original Six, the Montreal Canadiens were the most dominant club, chiefly drawing their talent from the French Canadian players of the province of Quebec. Maurice "Rocket" Richard, the first player to score 50 goals in a season, won eight Stanley Cups with the Canadiens. The Canadiens are hockey's most honored club, having captured the Stanley Cup 23 times since the foundation of the N.H.L.

As hockey matured into the middle of the century, the N.H.L. became a glamour sport in cities where players were heroes on ice. Gordie Howe of the Detroit Red Wings was a tough, dominating competitor who played until he was 52 years old. When he retired, he held the records for career goals, assists, and points.

On November 1, 1959, goalie Jacques Plante of the Canadiens, after being hit in the face by the puck in an earlier game, donned a fiberglass mask for protection. This innovation, scoffed at by his contemporaries, soon became standard equipment for goalies. In the modern N.H.L., goalies wear helmets remarkable both for their protective and decorative qualities.

Other stars of this era are the "Golden Jet" Bobby Hull, a fast skater and powerful shooter who played for Chicago, and Boston's Bobby Orr, a superbly fluid defenseman whose attacking prowess revolutionized the sport.

In 1967 the N.H.L. doubled in size, adding franchises in Los Angeles, Oakland, Minnesota, Philadelphia, Pittsburgh, and St. Louis. In 1970 the league again expanded, to Buffalo and Vancouver, and then in 1972 two more teams were introduced in Atlanta and Long Island, New York.

In 1972 a new league was founded to compete with the N.H.L.—the World Hockey Association (the W.H.A.). By offering huge salaries to superstars such as Bobby Hull and Bruins goaltender Gerry Cheevers, the league gained instant credibility. Still, the W.H.A. only lasted until 1980, at which time four teams—Edmonton, Hartford, Quebec, and Winnipeg—joined the N.H.L. One of those teams, the Edmonton Oilers, featured a young player named Wayne Gretzky, who, on the way to shattering nearly every scoring record, deservedly acquired the moniker the "Great One." In the 1981–82 season, Gretzky scored 92 goals (still a record) and had 120 assists for a total of 212 points. In the 1985–86 season, Gretzky notched 52 goals and 163 assists for a combined 215 points, a record that may never be broken. During the 1980's, the Oilers won five Stanley Cups, four under Gretzky's leadership.

Yet the most memorable hockey achievement of the 1980's, at least to American eyes, was the gold medal team at the 1980 Winter Olympics in Lake Placid. The unheralded American squad, formed almost entirely of collegians, shocked the formidable and experienced Soviet Union in the semifinals and beat Finland to win the gold medal.

As the N.H.L. developed its own brand of hockey on smaller rinks, foreign players learned a different style of play on the larger rinks common in Europe. By the 1990's, many European players entered the N.H.L. from nations such as Russia, Finland, Sweden, and the Czech Republic, and the influx of talent transformed the league. But the biggest star was Canada's Mario Lemieux, who became the league's premier player as Gretzky entered the latter stages of his career. Lemieux's Pittsburgh Penguins won consecutive Stanley Cups in the early 1990's.

In 2004, the N.H.L. gained the dubious distinction of being the only major sports league to lose an entire season to a labor dispute. While there had been two shorter strikes in the previous decade, when the existing contract between league and players expired on September 15, 2004, commissioner Gary Bettman announced a lockout that shut down the league for 310 days. Both players and league officials feared that this unprecedented work stoppage would diminish fan interest in the sport; when play finished after the 2005–2006 season, however, the league had posted record attendance figures, with all six Canadian teams playing to 98 percent capacity or better for home games. There are now 30 teams in the N.H.L. spread out over two conferences of three divisions each.

On January 1, 2008 the first N.H.L. Winter Classic was played outdoors at Ralph Wilson Stadium in Buffalo, NY. With snow falling and game-time temperatures hovering just above freezing, 71,217 fans braved the weather to be a part of an N.H.L. record crowd. Building on the success of the first game, the 2009 N.H.L. Winter Classic was held at Wrigley Field in Chicago and featured the Detroit Red Wings and the Chicago Blackhawks, two of the "Original Six" teams. With the highest television ratings for a game in 33 years, the N.H.L. decided to make it a permanent part of their schedule. In 2009, the N.H.L. enjoyed record highs in attendance, sponsorships, and television audiences, perhaps boosted by the success of the Winter Classic.

In recent years the N.H.L. has experimented with different models for its All-Star Game. From 1998–2003 the game broke down the players into North American All-Stars vs. World All-Stars, a format that was widely criticized. The 2003–04 game was lost to the lockout and the 04–05 game was also cancelled due to the league shutting down during the Winter Olympics as per the new collective bargaining agreement. For the next three years the Eastern vs. Western Conference matchup was reinstated. Starting in the 2011 season the NHL introduced a revolutionary new All-Star format. The regular fan balloting was used to select six players while the NHL Operations department added the remaining stars. The All-Star players then elected two captains per team, after which a fantasy-style draft filled out the rosters, with the captains choosing the teams.

Equipment, Rules, and Field of Play

In hockey, two teams use hooked sticks to propel a vulcanized rubber puck in opposite directions. The idea is for each team to shoot the puck into a net, called a goal. The net for each team is at opposite ends of the ice playing surface, also called a rink.

The puck is one inch thick and three inches in diameter, and it weighs between 5 1/2 to 6 ounces. For all N.H.L. games, the pucks, supplied by the home team, must be frozen.

In the N.H.L., sticks cannot measure longer than 63 inches from heel to end of the shaft. The blade length cannot measure more than 12 1/2 inches. The blade must be between two and three inches wide, and the curve of the blade cannot be more than a half inch.

Each team of five players plus a goaltender tries to send the puck into a net (called a goal) defended by the other team. Every time the puck goes into the net, the attacking team scores a goal. The game is 60 minutes long, divided into three 20-minute periods. (In lower levels, games can be shorter—divided into 15-, 12-, 10-minute or shorter periods.) At the end of the game, whichever team has the most goals wins.

The goal is a rectangle framed by red metal posts and backed by a white net. It measures six feet wide by four feet high and is defended by the goaltender, a player with a stick and a glove who wears thick padding all over his body. If the puck passes completely over the goal line (usually, but not always, hitting the net) a goal is scored. It cannot be deliberately batted in with any part of the body or skate. It can get deflected in.

Hockey was first played on frozen ponds and lakes, but now the sport is contested in cozy arenas with smooth ice surfaces that are not at the mercy of the elements. During the intermissions between periods, the ice is resurfaced by a tractorlike machine called a Zamboni, which scrapes away the old chipped ice and lays down a light layer of water that immediately freezes smooth.

Through the years and across the world, ice surfaces have come in many different sizes. The official rink now in the N.H.L. is 200 feet long by 85 feet wide, with rounded corners. In the old days of the N.H.L., some surfaces were smaller; the rink at the venerable Boston Garden was 191 feet by 83 feet. European rinks (and those used in the Olympics) are larger—200 feet by 100 feet—making skating skills even more important.

The rules of hockey encourage skill; the rules do not permit the puck to fly back and forth across the ice without anyone touching it. The concept of hockey is to create an exciting game that thrives on quick, slick passing, hard hitting, and precise movement. Through the use of lines painted onto the ice, the playing surface requires that the puck move from player to player without long passes. These painted lines are covered with thin layers of ice.

The Red Line is a one-foot-wide line that dissects the surface from side to side, dividing the rink into two equal halves.

There are two one-foot-wide Blue Lines—60 feet from each goal, running the width of the ice, from board to board.

There is another two-inch-wide red line that serves as the goal line, running the width of the ice, from board to board.

The Red Line and the two Blue Lines are on the ice to prevent a team, or players, from moving forward or ahead of the play too fast (too far in front of the puck carrier).

An infraction is called in two cases:

If an offensive player crosses the attacking Blue Line before the puck, it is offsides. Both of the player's skates have to be completely over the line for offsides to be called by a linesman, an official situated on the Blue Line who closely watches for such infractions.

Offsides is also called for a two-line pass. A two-line pass occurs when the puck in a team's defensive zone is passed over both the defensive blue line and the attacking blue line before being touched by another offensive player. Since 2005, the red line is no longer considered in the N.H.L.'s blue line rule.

When offsides occurs, play is suspended by the game officials and there is a face-off, in which a puck is dropped between two opposing players.

Icing is called when a player is behind the Red Line and he sends the puck all the way into the offensive zone, beyond the goal line, and the first person to touch it is a player other than the goalie on the other team. As soon as the puck is touched by such a player, play is stopped. If the goalie touches the puck or the puck passes through the crease in front of the goal, the icing is waved off, or not called. The linesman is the one who will wave off an icing. When icing is called, the puck is returned for a face-off to the defensive zone of the team that iced it.

The area inside the Blue Line back to the rounded end of the rink is considered one team's defensive zone. Alternatively, it is called the others team's attacking zone. The area between the blue lines is called the neutral zone.

There is a semicircular crease in front of each goal, which most goalies consider their sacred territory. An offensive player may skate through the crease if he causes no contact with anyone.

There are five red circles on the ice where most of the face-offs will occur. A face-off restarts play following a penalty, an infraction such as offsides, or a puck that flies over the Plexiglas that surrounds the rink. The chosen method is dropping the puck between two opposing players; frequently, the face-off is won by the player who reacts quickest. When the infraction occurs (or a puck is lost) near a face-off circle, the puck is dropped in that circle. At the game's start, the beginning of each period, or after a goal, the play commences with a face-off in the center circle, in the middle of the rink.

Hockey is unique among the major sports in that teams frequently play without the same number of players. (In soccer, expulsions occur but are relatively rare.) Penalties are given for various physical infractions that go beyond the sport's permissive rules of contact. Penalties include high-sticking, roughing, and cross-checking, among others. Such penalties result in a stint in an isolated area called the penalty box, during which time the offender's team must operate a player short. The ensuing period, when teams have different numbers of players, is called a power play, and provides an excellent scoring opportunity to the larger team. Combinations of penalties may cause strange game situations such as four-on-four and even three-on-three (not counting the goalie). During a power play, the short-handed team may ice the puck without penalty (i.e. play the puck in such a way that would normally cause icing in an even-strength situation).

Starting in the 2005–06 season, games ending in a tie at the end of overtime went to a shootout format. Three players per team take shots on the opposing goalie and the team with the most goals out of those shots wins. If the teams remain tied, the shootout moves to sudden death where the first team to score and stop the opposing team from scoring wins. The winning team receives two points while the loser gains one point. In order to create more room on the ice and to increase scoring in overtime, the N.H.L. also decreased the number of players on the ice in the extra period to four per team. These rules are only in effect during the regular season, switching back to five players per side and sudden death for the playoffs.

Glossary of Ice Hockey Terms

assist a pass that leads to a goal by a teammate. Although usually assists are passes, they are also given for unintentional deflections. Up to two assists can be awarded: one for the final pass and another for the preceding pass.

Blue Lines the blue lines located 60 feet from each goal, running the width of the ice, from board to board.

center one of three players on a forward line, the center is flanked by two wingers. The center is frequently the most skilled offensive player.

check to collide with an opponent in an attempt to knock him off balance or into the boards.

defensemen the two players whose main responsibility is to prevent scoring opportunities for the other team. Defensemen usually take their shifts in set pairs.

face-off how play begins each period or in a restart after an infraction or penalty. The puck is dropped between two opposing players who battle for control of it with their sticks.

five-hole the space between a goaltender's legs. So named because the other primary scoring areas are in the upper left, upper right, lower left, and lower right corners of the goal. Many goals are scored because a goalie does not close this gap quickly enough.

forwards the primary offensive players, divided into centers and wingers. Some forwards are known for their defensive abilities and are employed against the opposing team's most skilled attackers. Normally a unit of three players who take their shifts together.

goal the only scoring play in hockey, given when the puck completely crosses an imaginary plane formed by the goal line, the posts, and the crossbar. In situations when the play happens too quickly, a goal judge (who sits behind each goal) and instant replay may be consulted to determine whether a goal was scored.

goal line the narrow red line that stretches from side to side across the ice near the end of the rink. This line is used to determine icing and goals.

icing sending the puck the length of the ice without it being touched. Icing is called when a player behind the Red Line hits the puck through the offensive zone and past the goal line and the first person to touch the puck is a defender other than the goaltender. When icing is whistled, the puck is returned for a face-off to the defensive zone of the team that iced it.

line change to switch the team's on-ice personnel during a stoppage in play or during the game. Because of the speed of hockey, players tire quickly, and line changes must be made frequently so that a team is not caught with exhausted, ineffective players.

linesmen the two game officials whose primary job is to determine offsides and icing calls. Normally found hovering about the Blue Lines.

offsides a violation called if an offensive player crosses the attacking Blue Line before the puck. When this occurs, the play is stopped and there is a face-off outside the zone.

one-timer to immediately redirect the puck with the stick without first controlling it. Although applied to passes, the term is most often used in relation to such shots. The chief benefit of a one-time shot is that the quick release allows the goalie little preparation.

overtime the period of play following a game that ends in a tie after three periods. In the regular season, the teams play one five-minute overtime. If still scoreless after five minutes, the game is tied. In the playoffs, the game continues in 20-minute periods until a goal is scored.

penalties a group of infractions that normally incur a two-minute stay in the penalty box for the offender. For severe penalties, called majors, the sentence may last four minutes. Penalties include boarding, charging, holding, cross-checking, and roughing, among others.

penalty shot a one-on-one attempt against the goalkeeper, given after the referee decides an attacker with an otherwise clear breakaway is victimized by a defender's penalty. In such cases, the referee awards a penalty shot instead of a penalty (and possible power play).

point 1) for an individual player, points are assists plus goals. 2) in team standings during the regular season, two points are awarded for a win, one for a tie or overtime loss, and nothing for a loss in regulation.

power play the period of time when one team has more players than the other, due to one or more penalties. Most frequently power plays are on 5-on-4, not counting the goalies, but other situations also occur. Power plays end if a goal is scored by the advantaged team, unless the penalty that caused the power play was determined to be a major

rather than minor.

plus/minus a statistic unique to hockey, the plus/minus rating is an indication of a individual player's offensive and defensive value. A point is added for every goal scored for his team when the player is on the ice (power play goals excepted) and, similarly, a point is subtracted for every goal scored against.

puck a flat, frozen disk of vulcanized rubber.

Red Line a one-foot-wide line, running the width of the ice from board to board, that divides the ice surface into halves. This is also called "center ice."

referee the game officials with the power to judge penalties and otherwise guide the action. Recently the N.H.L. switched to employing two referees per game instead of one.

save when a goaltender prevents the puck from entering his goal, either by catching the puck in a glove or stopping or deflecting it with part of his body or his stick.

shift the length of a player's turn on the ice before a line change; usually no more than 90 seconds.

shorthanded when a team has fewer players on the ice than the opposing team because of one or more penalties. When a team with fewer players manages to score a goal, it is called a shorthanded goal.

slap shot the hardest kind of shot in hockey, when a player draws back his stick well off the ice to fiercely strike the puck. The fastest shots are often more than 90 miles per hour.

tie the result if the score is equal after regulation and five minutes of overtime. Both teams receive one point in the standings.

wingers two of the three forwards on a line (along with the center). The two types are right and left wing.

wrist shot a type of shot so named because the impetus is provided by the player's hands alone. In other words, the player does not lift his stick to strike the puck. An accurate, quickly released shot is very useful near the goal.

Zamboni a large tractorlike machine that treats the ice surface between periods. It scrapes off chipped ice and lays down a thin layer of water that immediately freezes smooth.

The Stanley Cup, 1917–2011

Season	Champion	Season	Champion	Season	Champion
1917–18	Toronto Arenas	1949–50	Detroit Red Wings	1981–82	New York Islanders
1918–19	No decision	1950–51	Toronto Maple Leafs	1982–83	New York Islanders
1919–20	Ottawa Senators	1951–52	Detroit Red Wings	1983–84	Edmonton Oilers
1920–21	Ottawa Senators	1952–53	Montreal Canadiens	1984–85	Edmonton Oilers
1921–22	Toronto St. Pats	1953–54	Detroit Red Wings	1985–86	Montreal Canadiens
1922–23	Ottawa Senators	1954–55	Detroit Red Wings	1986–87	Edmonton Oilers
1923–24	Montreal Canadiens	1955–56	Montreal Canadiens	1987–88	Edmonton Oilers
1924–25	Victoria Cougars	1956–57	Montreal Canadiens	1988–89	Calgary Flames
1925–26	Montreal Maroons	1957–58	Montreal Canadiens	1989–90	Edmonton Oilers
1926–27	Ottawa Senators	1958–59	Montreal Canadiens	1990–91	Pittsburgh Penguins
1927–28	New York Rangers	1959–60	Montreal Canadiens	1991–92	Pittsburgh Penguins
1928–29	Boston Bruins	1960–61	Chicago Black Hawks[1]	1992–93	Montreal Canadiens
1929–30	Montreal Canadiens	1961–62	Toronto Maple Leafs	1993–94	New York Rangers
1930–31	Montreal Canadiens	1962–63	Toronto Maple Leafs	1994–95	New Jersey Devils
1931–32	Toronto Maple Leafs	1963–64	Toronto Maple Leafs	1995–96	Colorado Avalanche
1932–33	New York Rangers	1964–65	Montreal Canadiens	1996–97	Detroit Red Wings
1933–34	Chicago Black Hawks[1]	1965–66	Montreal Canadiens	1997–98	Detroit Red Wings
1934–35	Montreal Maroons	1966–67	Toronto Maple Leafs	1998–99	Dallas Stars
1935–36	Detroit Red Wings	1967–68	Montreal Canadiens	1999–00	New Jersey Devils
1936–37	Detroit Red Wings	1968–69	Montreal Canadiens	2000–01	Colorado Avalanche
1937–38	Chicago Black Hawks[1]	1969–70	Boston Bruins	2001–02	Detroit Red Wings
1938–39	Boston Bruins	1970–71	Montreal Canadiens	2002–03	New Jersey Devils
1939–40	New York Rangers	1971–72	Boston Bruins	2003–04	Tampa Bay Lightning
1940–41	Boston Bruins	1972–73	Montreal Canadiens	2004–05	No winner due to strike
1941–42	Toronto Maple Leafs	1973–74	Philadelphia Flyers	2005–06	Carolina Hurricanes
1942–43	Detroit Red Wings	1974–75	Philadelphia Flyers	2006–07	Anaheim Ducks
1943–44	Montreal Canadiens	1975–76	Montreal Canadiens	2007–08	Detroit Red Wings
1944–45	Toronto Maple Leafs	1976–77	Montreal Canadiens	2008–09	Pittsburgh Penguins
1945–46	Montreal Canadiens	1977–78	Montreal Canadiens	2009–10	Chicago Blackhawks
1946–47	Toronto Maple Leafs	1978–79	Montreal Canadiens	2010–11	Boston Bruins
1947–48	Toronto Maple Leafs	1979–80	New York Islanders		
1948–49	Toronto Maple Leafs	1980–81	New York Islanders		

Note: 1. Before 1986, Chicago spelled Blackhawks as two words.

GOLF

History

Golf's physical requirements are modest. Players come in all shapes, sizes, and ages, and golf's mix of challenge, and the consequent rewards and punishments, has made it one of the most ubiquitous individual sports. Golf has gained such popularity, in fact, that its most famous shots weren't even hit on this planet.

It is also a sport of wealth. A golf outing costs substantially more than most other sports, and private clubs demand steep membership fees for the right to enjoy their courses. This is particularly true in the United States, but in places such as Scotland, the home of golf, the sport is more egalitarian. At the professional level, elite players compete for considerable prize money on a number of circuits, or tours, under the watchful eye of an international television audience.

However, despite the million-dollar purses at the professional level and a worldwide explosion in popularity, the sport's beginnings were anything but glamorous. Golf originated in Scotland, the northern part of the island of Great Britain, during the 15th century. In its primitive incarnation, golfers struck a rock around a primitive course with an equally primitive stick or club.

Facing invasion from his English neighbors to the south, in 1457 Scotland's King James II prohibited his subjects from playing golf so they could concentrate on more martial pursuits such as archery. Setting a trend that would continue until the present, the golfers played on, and the ban was finally lifted in 1502 with the ascension of King James VI (known to history as James I) to the throne of both England and Scotland. With royal patronage, the sport prospered.

The first golf club was formed near Edinburgh in 1744, and the members named themselves The Gentlemen Golfers of Leith. Setting another trend, the club codified a list of 13 rules, including stipulations about how golfers should deal with water hazards and lost balls. Revisions were made and two more rules added in 1775.

St. Andrews, a picturesque town on the North Sea, has the cachet of being the most important center of golf. The St. Andrews Society of Golfers, founded in 1754, was and still is among the most prestigious clubs in the sport. The course at St. Andrews, with its 18 holes, inspired the modern standard, and the club received the designation of "Royal & Ancient" in 1834 from King William IV. In 1897 the Royal & Ancient Golf Club of St. Andrews, or the R&A, created a Rules of Golf Committee to write the official Rules of Golf.

Early courses were almost always by the sea, with windswept dunes and junglelike rough that devoured wayward shots. The term still applied to such seaside courses is links, or linksland, yet the word *links* is often used now (incorrectly) to describe any golf course. Equipment of golf's early era seems ancient compared to the technological marvels of modernity. Balls were constructed from a horsehide sphere filled with compacted feathers, and clubs were usually manufactured from a variety of materials, including persimmon, hickory, beech, and iron. Later advances of the Industrial Revolution made metal club heads more common, and balls were fabricated from gutta percha, a rubberlike material produced by an Asian tree.

Not until 1766 was a golf club formed outside Scotland, and the first outside of Britain, borne by the tide of imperialism, was created in Bangalore, India, in 1820. During the 19th century, clubs sprang up in Australia, Canada, South Africa, Hong Kong, India, France, Ireland, and the United States.

The first significant tournament was the British Open, first contested in 1860. Old Tom Morris won the Open in 1862, 1864, and 1867, but his feats were were surpassed by his son—Young Tom, of course—who captured four straight tournaments starting in 1869. With the sparse number of paying tournaments, professional players frequently bet with their opponents or worked at golf-related jobs such as making clubs.

During the first years of the 20th century there was a marked improvement in equipment, including one-piece rubber balls, dimpled balls, steel-shafted clubs, and groove-faced irons. By then, golf had been firmly established in the United States. In 1894 the United States Golf Association (USGA) was created. American courses, normally distant from the coastlines distinctive to British golf, were instead carved from the countryside. The differences between British and American golf were not limited to the style: a 30-year dispute between the R&A and the USGA—about a number of rules and the standard golf ball—lasted until 1951. Modern golf is jointly supervised by the two organizations.

With the increasing number of tournaments, the Professional Golfers Association (P.G.A.) of America was organized in 1916. Initially, the association played a series of contests only in the winter months, but by 1944 the tour had expanded to include 22 events. The growth of the professional tour fueled the rise of several notable golfers, first and foremost American Bobby Jones, who won the Grand Slam in 1931. (At that time, the Grand Slam—winning all four major tournaments in a calendar year—consisted of the U.S. and British Amateurs and the U.S. and British Opens.) Other great players include Walter Hagen and Sir Henry Cotton.

Eventually, four tournaments acquired more importance than the others, and these became known as the majors. They are the U.S. and British Opens, the P.G.A. Championship, and the Masters. The Masters is unique among the majors in that it is the only tournament played at the same club—Augusta National in Augusta, Ga.—every year.

Although the P.G.A. tour attracted most early interest in golf, women also became well-known players. The first U.S. women's amateur championship was held in 1895. In the first half of the 20th century, England's Joyce Wethered, and Americans Glenna Collett Vare and Babe Didrikson Zaharias were the most successful players. (In the 1932 Summer Olympics, Zaharias, the premier female athlete of the age, won gold medals in the javelin and hurdles and a silver medal in the high jump.) The Ladies Professional Golf Association (L.P.G.A.) was formed in 1950.

Three dominant players emerged in the 1960's back on the P.G.A. tour: Americans Arnold Palmer and Jack Nicklaus, and South Africa's Gary Player. The three men won a combined 34 professional majors in their careers. Palmer won seven, and Player captured nine, but Nicklaus's

18 majors remains the standard for all future golfers. Their reign lasted from Palmer's Masters breakthrough in 1958 until Nicklaus's stunning Masters victory in 1986, when he was 46 years old.

For all of these three men's success on the lush courses of earth, the most famous golf shots in history were taken on the moon. During the Apollo 14 mission in 1971, astronaut Alan Shepherd took two swings with an improvised 6-iron formed with a club head he smuggled onto the spacecraft.

Although many good golfers had moments to shine after Nicklaus's run concluded, there were no truly exceptional players until the arrival of Eldrick "Tiger" Woods in the late 1990's. Woods, three-time U.S. amateur champion, won the Masters in 1997 at the age of 21 and has since added 13 more majors to his resumé. His total of 14 brings him to second on the all-time list. Combining superior athleticism and a keen competitive mind, Woods is a threat to surpass Nicklaus's record 18 majors.

All of that changed on Thanksgiving night 2009, when Woods crashed his car into a fire hydrant while being chased by his golf club-wielding wife. Details of the night in question were murky, but allegations that another woman played a role in the crash were rampant. In the subsequent weeks, a seemingly never-ending string of women came forward to allege they had affairs with Tiger, eventually leading to the break-up of his marriage. After taking 20 weeks off, Tiger returned for the 2010 Masters and finished a respectable fourth. Woods finished the season without a win for the first time in his career. The fall of Tiger Woods opened the door for others to take the spotlight for the first time in years. Phil Mickelson now has four major championships and is beloved by the fans. With his laid-back, jovial personality, Mickelson is viewed by many as the anti-Tiger. Pádraig Harrington and Ángel Cabrera have won multiple majors in the last four years and seven players won their first major championship in the last three years. Parity has once again returned to a sport that had been dominated for the better part of a decade by one player.

Rules of the Game

Golf is contested on a course, usually consisting of 18 holes, though some smaller courses have only nine holes. To finish the hole, the golfer, with the aid of an implement

called a club, must guide a small, spherical ball into a round opening (the hole) several hundred yards away. The goal of golf is to complete each hole in as few strokes as possible, and a stroke is counted whenever the golfer contacts with the ball with a club. (There are several types of clubs, each with a particular form and function.) Scores are tracked by the hole, and the player's overall score is an addition of all the strokes for all the holes. A player who needs 73 strokes to complete an 18-hole course has done better than someone who required 76 strokes.

For each hole, there is a number called par against which players must test themselves. Par measures the standard number of strokes necessary to finish the hole. The longest holes are par 5, the shortest holes are par 3, and the most common holes are par 4. To determine the total par for the course, the figures are added for each hole. A course with a par of 72, for example, sets a standard of 72 shots to complete all 18 holes. Par varies with the length of the course, but usually ranges from 70 to 72. A par 72 course could, for example, have 14 par 4 holes, two par 5 holes, and two par 3 holes.

Play on each hole begins from what is called a tee box, where a golfer sets the ball on a small, raised peg called a tee. On most par 4 and par 5 holes, the first shot is called a drive, and players seek to hit the ball into the center of a clear lane of grass called the fairway. With the second shot, players want to hit the ball onto a close-cut, amorphous area called the green, which is where the hole is located. On tee shots on par 3's, players aim for the green from the start. Once on the green, players use a club called a putter to direct the ball into the hole. When the ball drops into the hole, the hole is complete. Typically, par 3 holes are 250 yards or less in distance from the tee box to the green, while par 4 holes range up to around 475 yards, with longer holes being par 5.

Certain terms are assigned to a particular score on each hole. On a par 4 hole, for example, if the hole is finished in only three strokes, the player has made a "birdie," that is, scored a stroke below par.

Golf is not as simple as it sounds. The act of consistently swinging a club to strike a stationary round ball so that it flies where you want befuddles even the best golfers. Furthermore, courses are designed to offer tricky obstacles: there are bunkers, low pits filled with sand that can trap poor shots, and there is rough—thick grass—to punish any misses of the fairway and green. Other hazards, such as creeks and lakes, also abound.

Glossary of Golf Terms

ace a hole in one; when a player's tee shot drops into the hole, a rare event.

away a term that describes the golfer who will play first following the tee shot. The player whose ball is farthest from the hole plays first.

ball the small spherical object that players must guide around the golf course with the aid of their clubs. Balls can weigh no less than 1.62 ounces and must be at least 1.68 inches in diameter.

birdie to complete a hole in one stroke less than the par, e.g. needing three strokes to finish a par 4. A good thing.

bogey to complete a hole in one stroke more than the par, e.g. needing five strokes to finish a par 4. A bad thing. Each additional stroke above par merits an appellation, such as "double bogey" or even "quadruple bogey."

bunker the low areas filled with sand that line the fairways and surround the greens. Bunkers, also called sand traps, present various difficulties to the player because of their depth, positioning, or sand quality.

caddy the assistant who carries the player's clubs and is allowed to dispense advice.

club one of the implements with which a player strikes the ball. Clubs consist of the grip, the shaft, and the club face, the part of the club that contacts with the ball. Players may carry only 14 clubs in their bag during a round.

clubhouse the building that serves the main nonplaying functions, such as changing rooms and dining, of a golf club and course. The clubhouse is where a round begins (at the nearby 1st tee) and ends (after the 18th hole). On many courses, the hole layout returns to the clubhouse area between the 9th and the 10th holes.

course the layout of holes, usually 18, that players must progress through to complete a round.

cut the separation of the contending golfers from the rest after the second round of a tournament. Normally, slightly less than half of the players after two rounds of play are allowed to compete in the final two rounds of a four-round tournament, and the rest are cut and eliminated from the tournament.

draw a shot made with sidespin that causes the ball to drift from right to left when hit by a right-handed golfer.

Often an intentional shot used to circumvent obstacles. Its opposite is a fade.

driver the longest hitting club, normally used for the tee shot or drive.

eagle completing a hole in two strokes less than par, such as finishing a par 5 in three strokes. A double eagle, also known as an "albatross," is three strokes below par.

fade to strike a ball with spin so that, when hit by a right-handed golfer, the ball drifts from left to right. Normally an intentional shot. Its opposite is the draw.

fairway the long, sometimes narrow lane of short grass that is the target of most tee shots and drives. Although mounds and slopes may affect the player's lie, usually the fairway is a better place from which to take the second shot than the rough.

flag the brightly colored banner atop the flagstick that marks the hole, removed or tended once players have steered their balls onto the green.

front and back nine a phrase that divides the course into its first nine holes (the front) and its last nine holes (the back).

Grand Slam to win all four of golf's major tournaments in the same calendar year. No golfer has ever won the modern Grand Slam, which consists of the Masters, the U.S. Open, the British Open, and the P.G.A. Championship.

green the close-cut area of grass, often with small mounds and subtle curves, where the hole is placed. Once the players have reached the green, they try to putt the ball into the hole.

handicap a measure of a player's skill level as compared to par. A player who averages 78 strokes on a par 72 course is said to have a 6 handicap, while a player who averages par is said to be a "scratch" golfer. Handicaps are also adjusted by course difficulty.

hole a single portion of a golf course. Typically there are 18 holes on a course, although smaller courses may have only nine. Also, the hole is the round space on the green, 4 1/4 inches in diameter and at least 4 inches deep, into which the ball must drop to complete one hole. A flag marks the hole so that it can be seen from a distance.

hook an errant shot that, when made by a right-handed golfer, will force the ball to drastically fly from right to left, not straight, because of poor club contact. Its opposite is a slice.

iron a series of clubs with metal faces of varying angles. Irons range from the 1-iron to the 9-iron, with the higher numbers indicating a higher loft to the club. A 9-iron will send the ball higher and a much shorter distance than a 1-iron. Irons are used on some tee shots (such as on a par 3) and until the players reach the green.

lie the positioning of a ball on the ground with respect to the ease with which a player will take the next shot. With a good lie, for example, the ball may rest on flat area, while with a bad lie, the ball may be buried in thick rough.

links a generic word often used incorrectly to describe any golf course. Specifically, the word applies to a seaside course, particularly in Britain, with sandy soil.

match play a type of contest, different from the stroke play seen in most professional tournaments, in which players compete by the hole, not by the shot. If one player scores better on a hole than his opponent, that player wins the hole. Whoever wins the most holes wins the match.

out and back a phrase used to describe courses that reach their farthest point from the start at the end of the 9th hole and do not return to the clubhouse until the 18th hole.

par the standard number of strokes to complete the hole or the course. Par also means to finish a hole in the standard number of strokes.

penalty a punishment, usually a number of strokes added to the players score, assessed if the player loses a ball or hits the ball into a water hazard, among other infractions.

putter the flat-faced club golfers use to strike, or putt, the ball into the hole once on the green.

rough the thick, grassy areas that border the fairway and the greens, and ordinarily a bad place to discover your ball.

round the completion of the course, whether it be nine or 18 holes. A player who needs 79 strokes to finish an 18 hole course is said to have played a round of 79.

rules the laws that legislate how golf must be played.

score the number of strokes necessary to complete a hole or a round. To total a score for a round, add up the number of strokes for each hole.

scorecard the record sheet on which a player tracks his or her score.

short game a term that describes the skills of golf near and on the greens, mainly chipping, escaping bunkers, and putting.

slice a bad shot that, because of the club's facing when meeting the ball, makes a right-handed golfer's shot curve drastically from left to right instead of going straight.

stroke a single contact of the ball with any club.

stroke play a type of competition in which the number of strokes, not the number of holes (as in match play), determines the winner. The player with the lowest number of strokes wins. This is the most common method of scoring in tournament play.

swing the physical process of striking the ball, and one of the most analyzed movements in human history. Despite years of practice, even top professionals have troublesome moments with their swings.

tee shot the shot that begins the hole, taken from an area called the tee box. On a tee shot, the ball is placed upon a small raised peg, made of wood or plastic, called a tee. The player who scored better on the previous hole plays first.

tour a series of tournaments in which players compete, usually based on their relative skills or regions. The most prestigious tours are the P.G.A. Tour, in the United States, and the European P.G.A. Tour.

tournament a competition of golfers. On the P.G.A. tour, a tournament consists of four rounds, with one round a day from Thursday to Sunday. After the first two rounds, many players are eliminated at the cut. To determine the champion, the scores for all four rounds are added together and the player with the fewest strokes wins. The scoring system is similar for tournaments on other tours, though such tours as the Seniors and the L.P.G.A. may not play four rounds.

water hazards areas on the golf course covered by water. When a shot falls into the water, the player can play it as it lies if found, but if the ball is lost, the player incurs a one-stroke penalty and must shoot again.

wedge the most lofted clubs, used to produce high short shots. The pitching wedge has the least loft, followed by the sand wedge, and then comes the lob wedge. The sand wedge has a flange that makes it useful for blasting the ball out of a bunker.

woods a set of clubs used on the tee or for long shots from the fairway to the green. The driver is considered the 1-wood, and other common woods include the 3-wood and the 5-wood. In the past, these were made from wood, but now are formed from metal.

yardage a measurement of distance from the tee, or one's current position on a hole, to the flag. The yardage of each hole varies by the position of the tee box: men's tees are farther back than the women's tees. To determine the complete course yardage, the yardage for each hole is added, with a total usually around 6,500 to 7,000 yards (give or take a few hundred).

The Masters

Year	Winner	Year	Winner	Year	Winner
1934	Horton Smith	1961	Gary Player	1988	Sandy Lyle
1935	Gene Sarazen	1962	Arnold Palmer	1989	Nick Faldo
1936	Horton Smith	1963	Jack Nicklaus	1990	Nick Faldo
1937	Byron Nelson	1964	Arnold Palmer	1991	Ian Woosnam
1938	Henry Picard	1965	Jack Nicklaus	1992	Fred Couples
1939	Ralph Guldahl	1966	Jack Nicklaus	1993	Bernhard Langer
1940	Jimmy Demaret	1967	Gay Brewer Jr.	1994	José María Olazábal
1941	Craig Wood	1968	Bob Goalby	1995	Ben Crenshaw
1942	Byron Nelson	1969	George Archer	1996	Nick Faldo
1943	Not held	1970	Billy Casper	1997	Tiger Woods
1944	Not held	1971	Charles Coody	1998	Mark O'Meara
1945	Not held	1972	Jack Nicklaus	1999	José María Olazábal
1946	Herman Keiser	1973	Tommy Aaron	2000	Vijay Singh
1947	Jimmy Demaret	1974	Gary Player	2001	Tiger Woods
1948	Claude Harman	1975	Jack Nicklaus	2002	Tiger Woods
1949	Sam Snead	1976	Ray Floyd	2003	Mike Weir
1950	Jimmy Demaret	1977	Tom Watson	2004	Phil Mickelson
1951	Ben Hogan	1978	Gary Player	2005	Tiger Woods
1952	Sam Snead	1979	Fuzzy Zoeller	2006	Phil Mickelson
1953	Ben Hogan	1980	Seve Ballesteros	2007	Zach Johnson
1954	Sam Snead	1981	Tom Watson	2008	Trevor Immelman
1955	Cary Middlecoff	1982	Craig Stadler	2009	Ángel Cabrera
1956	Jack Burke Jr.	1983	Seve Ballesteros	2010	Phil Mickelson
1957	Doug Ford	1984	Ben Crenshaw	2011	Charl Schwartzel
1958	Arnold Palmer	1985	Bernhard Langer		
1959	Art Wall Jr.	1986	Jack Nicklaus		
1960	Arnold Palmer	1987	Larry Mize		

P.G.A. Championship

Year	Winner	Year	Winner	Year	Winner	Year	Winner
1916	James M. Barnes	1935	Johnny Revolta	1954	Chick Harbert	1973	Jack Nicklaus
1917	Not held	1936	Denny Shute	1955	Doug Ford	1974	Lee Trevino
1918	Not held	1937	Denny Shute	1956	Jack Burke	1975	Jack Nicklaus
1919	James M. Barnes	1938	Paul Runyan	1957	Lionel Hebert	1976	Dave Stockton
1920	Jock Hutchison	1939	Henry Picard	1958	Dow Finsterwald	1977	Lanny Wadkins
1921	Walter Hagen	1940	Byron Nelson	1959	Bob Rosburg	1978	John Mahaffey
1922	Gene Sarazen	1941	Vic Ghezzi	1960	Jay Hebert	1979	David Graham
1923	Gene Sarazen	1942	Sam Snead	1961	Jerry Barber	1980	Jack Nicklaus
1924	Walter Hagen	1943	Not held	1962	Gary Player	1981	Larry Nelson
1925	Walter Hagen	1944	Bob Hamilton	1963	Jack Nicklaus	1982	Raymond Floyd
1926	Walter Hagen	1945	Byron Nelson	1964	Bobby Nichols	1983	Hal Sutton
1927	Walter Hagen	1946	Ben Hogan	1965	Dave Marr	1984	Lee Trevino
1928	Leo Diegel	1947	Jim Ferrier	1966	Al Geiberger	1985	Hubert Green
1929	Leo Diegel	1948	Ben Hogan	1967	Don January	1986	Bob Tway
1930	Tommy Armour	1949	Sam Snead	1968	Julius Boros	1987	Larry Nelson
1931	Tom Creavy	1950	Chandler Harper	1969	Ray Floyd	1988	Jeff Sluman
1932	Olin Dutra	1951	Sam Snead	1970	Dave Stockton	1989	Payne Stewart
1933	Gene Sarazen	1952	Jim Turnesa	1971	Jack Nicklaus	1990	Wayne Grady
1934	Paul Runyan	1953	Walter Burkemo	1972	Gary Player	1991	John Daly

P.G.A. Championship (con't)

Year	Winner	Year	Winner	Year	Winner	Year	Winner
1992	Nick Price	1997	Davis Love III	2002	Rich Beem	2007	Tiger Woods
1993	Paul Azinger	1998	Vijay Singh	2003	Shaun Micheel	2008	Pádraig Harrington
1994	Nick Price	1999	Tiger Woods	2004	Vijay Singh	2009	Yang Yong-eun
1995	Steve Elkington	2000	Tiger Woods	2005	Phil Mickelson	2010	Martin Kaymer
1996	Mark Brooks	2001	David Toms	2006	Tiger Woods		

The British Open

Year	Winner	Year	Winner	Year	Winner	Year	Winner
1860	Willie Park	1898	Harry Vardon	1937	Henry Cotton	1975	Tom Watson
1861	Tom Morris Sr.	1899	Harry Vardon	1938	R.A. Whitcombe	1976	Johnny Miller
1862	Tom Morris Sr.	1900	John H. Taylor	1939	Richard Burton	1977	Tom Watson
1863	Willie Park	1901	James Braid	1940	Not held	1978	Jack Nicklaus
1864	Tom Morris Sr.	1902	Alexander Herd	1941	Not held	1979	Seve Ballesteros
1865	Andrew Strath	1903	Harry Vardon	1942	Not held	1980	Tom Watson
1866	Willie Park	1904	Jack White	1943	Not held	1981	Bill Rogers
1867	Tom Morris Sr.	1905	James Braid	1944	Not held	1982	Tom Watson
1868	Tom Morris Jr.	1906	James Braid	1945	Not held	1983	Tom Watson
1869	Tom Morris Jr.	1907	Arnaud Massy	1946	Sam Snead	1984	Seve Ballesteros
1870	Tom Morris Jr.	1908	James Braid	1947	Fred Daly	1985	Sandy Lyle
1871	Not held	1909	John H. Taylor	1948	Henry Cotton	1986	Greg Norman
1872	Tom Morris Jr.	1910	James Braid	1949	Bobby Locke	1987	Nick Faldo
1873	Tom Kidd	1911	Harry Vardon	1950	Bobby Locke	1988	Seve Ballesteros
1874	Mungo Park	1912	Edward (Ted) Ray	1951	Max Faulkner	1989	Mark
1875	Willie Park	1913	John H. Taylor	1952	Bobby Locke		Calcavecchia
1876	Bob Martin	1914	Harry Vardon	1953	Ben Hogan	1990	Nick Faldo
1877	Jamie Anderson	1915	Not held	1954	Peter Thomson	1991	Ian Baker-Finch
1878	Jamie Anderson	1916	Not held	1955	Peter Thomson	1992	Nick Faldo
1879	Jamie Anderson	1917	Not held	1956	Peter Thomson	1993	Greg Norman
1880	Robert Ferguson	1918	Not held	1957	Bobby Locke	1994	Nick Price
1881	Robert Ferguson	1919	Not held	1958	Peter Thomson	1995	John Daly
1882	Robert Ferguson	1920	George Duncan	1959	Gary Player	1996	Tom Lehman
1883	Willie Fernie	1921	Jock Hutchison	1960	Kel Nagle	1997	Justin Leonard
1884	Jack Simpson	1922	Walter Hagen	1961	Arnold Palmer	1998	Mark O'Meara
1885	Bob Martin	1923	Arthur G. Havers	1962	Arnold Palmer	1999	Paul Lawrie
1886	David Brown	1924	Walter Hagen	1963	Bob Charles	2000	Tiger Woods
1887	Willie Park Jr.	1925	James M. Barnes	1964	Tony Lema	2001	David Duval
1888	Jack Burns	1926	Robert T. Jones Jr.	1965	Peter Thomson	2002	Ernie Els
1889	Willie Park Jr.	1927	Robert T. Jones Jr.	1966	Jack Nicklaus	2003	Ben Curtis
1890	John Ball	1928	Walter Hagen	1967	Roberto	2004	Todd Hamilton
1891	Hugh Kirkaldy	1929	Walter Hagen		DeVicenzo	2005	Tiger Woods
1892	Harold H. Hilton1	1930	Robert T. Jones Jr.	1968	Gary Player	2006	Tiger Woods
1893	William	1931	Tommy D. Armour	1969	Tony Jacklin	2007	Pádraig Harrington
	Auchterlonie	1932	Gene Sarazen	1970	Jack Nicklaus	2008	Pádraig Harrington
1894	John H. Taylor	1933	Denny Shute	1971	Lee Trevino	2009	Stewart Cink
1895	John H. Taylor	1934	Henry Cotton	1972	Lee Trevino	2010	Louis Oosthuizen
1896	Harry Vardon	1935	Alfred Perry	1973	Tom Weiskopf	2011	Darren Clarke
1897	Harold H. Hilton	1936	Alfred Padgham	1974	Gary Player		

The U.S. Open Championship

Year	Winner	Year	Winner	Year	Winner	Year	Winner
1895	Horace Rawlins	1925	W. MacFarlane	1955	Jack Fleck	1985	Andy North
1896	James Foulis	1926	Robert T. Jones Jr.	1956	Cary Middlecoff	1986	Ray Floyd
1897	Joe Lloyd	1927	Tommy Armour	1957	Dick Mayer	1987	Scott Simpson
1898	Fred Herd	1928	Johnny Farrell	1958	Tommy Bolt	1988	Curtis Strange
1899	Willie Smith	1929	Robert T. Jones Jr.	1959	Billy Casper	1989	Curtis Strange
1900	Harry Vardon	1930	Robert T. Jones Jr.	1960	Arnold Palmer	1990	Hale Irwin
1901	Willie Anderson	1931	Billy Burke	1961	Gene Littler	1991	Payne Stewart
1902	Laurie Auchterlonie	1932	Gene Sarazen	1962	Jack Nicklaus	1992	Tom Kite
1903	Willie Anderson	1933	Johnny Goodman	1963	Julius Boros	1993	Lee Janzen
1904	Willie Anderson	1934	Olin Dutra	1964	Ken Venturi	1994	Ernie Els
1905	Willie Anderson	1935	Sam Parks, Jr.	1965	Gary Player	1995	Corey Pavin
1906	Alex Smith	1936	Tony Manero	1966	Billy Casper	1996	Steve Jones
1907	Alex Ross	1937	Ralph Guldahl	1967	Jack Nicklaus	1997	Ernie Els
1908	Fred McLeod	1938	Ralph Guldahl	1968	Lee Trevino	1998	Lee Janzen
1909	George Sargent	1939	Byron Nelson	1969	Orville Moody	1999	Payne Stewart
1910	Alex Smith	1940	Lawson Little	1970	Tony Jacklin	2000	Tiger Woods
1911	John McDermott	1941	Craig Wood	1971	Lee Trevino	2001	Retief Goosen
1912	John McDermott	1942	Not held	1972	Jack Nicklaus	2002	Tiger Woods
1913	Francis Ouimet	1943	Not held	1973	Johnny Miller	2003	Jim Furyk
1914	Walter Hagen	1944	Not held	1974	Hale Irwin	2004	Retief Goosen
1915	Jerome Travers	1945	Not held	1975	Lou Graham	2005	Michael Campbell
1916	Charles Evans Jr.	1946	Lloyd Mangrum	1976	Jerry Pate	2006	Geoff Ogilvy
1917	Not held	1947	Lew Worsham	1977	Hubert Green	2007	Ángel Cabrera
1918	Not held	1948	Ben Hogan	1978	Andy North	2008	Tiger Woods
1919	Walter Hagen	1949	Cary Middlecoff	1979	Hale Irwin	2009	Lucas Glover
1920	Edward Ray	1950	Ben Hogan	1980	Jack Nicklaus	2010	Graeme McDowell
1921	James M. Barnes	1951	Ben Hogan	1981	David Graham	2011	Rory McIlroy
1922	Gene Sarazen	1952	Julius Boros	1982	Tom Watson		
1923	Robert T. Jones Jr.	1953	Ben Hogan	1983	Larry Nelson		
1924	Cyril Walker	1954	Ed Furgol	1984	Fuzzy Zoeller		

U.S. Women's Open Champions, 1946-71

Year	Champion	Year	Champion	Year	Champion	Year	Champion
1946	Patty Berg	1953	Betsy Rawls	1958	Mickey Wright	1964	Mickey Wright
1947	Betty Jameson	1954	Babe Zaharias	1961	Mickey Wright	1965	Carol Mann
1948	Babe Zaharias	1955	Fay Crocker	1962	Murle Breer	1969	Donna Caponi
1949	Louise Suggs	1956	Kathy Cornelius	1963	Mary Mills	1970	Donna Caponi
1950	Babe Zaharias	1957	Betsy Rawls	1966	Sandra Spuzich	1971	JoAnne Carner
1951	Betsy Rawls	1959	Mickey Wright	1967	Catherine LaCoste		
1952	Louise Suggs	1960	Betsy Rawls	1968	Susie Berning		

U.S. Women's Grand Slam Champions, 1972–2011

Year	Nabisco Championship	L.P.G.A. Championship	U.S. Women's Open	du Maurier Classic/ Women's British Open[1]
1972		Kathy Ahern	Susie Berning	
1973		Mary Mills	Susie Berning	
1974		Sandra Haynie	Sandra Haynie	
1975		Kathy Whitworth	Sandra Palmer	
1976		Betty Burfeindt	JoAnne Carner	
1977		Chako Higuchi	Hollis Stacy	
1978		Nancy Lopez	Hollis Stacy	
1979		Donna Caponi	Jerilyn Britz	Amy Alcott
1980		Sally Little	Amy Alcott	Pat Bradley
1981		Donna Caponi	Pat Bradley	Jan Stephenson
1982		Jan Stephenson	Janet Anderson	Sandra Haynie
1983	Amy Alcott	Patty Sheehan	Jan Stephenson	Hollis Stacy
1984	Juli Inkster	Patty Sheehan	Hollis Stacy	Juli Inkster
1985	Alice Miller	Nancy Lopez	Kathy Baker	Pat Bradley
1986	Pat Bradley	Pat Bradley	Jane Geddes	Pat Bradley
1987	Betsy King	Jane Geddes	Laura Davies	Jody Rosenthal
1988	Amy Alcott	Sherri Turner	Liselotte Neumann	Sally Little
1989	Juli Inkster	Nancy Lopez	Betsy King	Tammie Green
1990	Betsy King	Beth Daniel	Betsy King	Cathy Johnston
1991	Amy Alcott	Meg Mallon	Meg Mallon	Nancy Scranton
1992	Dottie Pepper	Betsy King	Patty Sheehan	Sherri Steinhauer
1993	Helen Alfredsson	Patty Sheehan	Lauri Merten	Brandie Burton
1994	Donna Andrews	Laura Davies	Patty Sheehan	Martha Nause
1995	Nanci Bowen	Kelly Robbins	Annika Sorenstam	Jenny Lidback
1996	Patty Sheehan	Laura Davies	Annika Sorenstam	Laura Davies
1997	Betsy King	Chris Johnson	Alison Nicholas	Colleen Walker
1998	Pat Hurst	Se Ri Pak	Se Ri Pak	Brandie Burton
1999	Dottie Pepper	Juli Inkster	Juli Inkster	Karrie Webb
2000	Karrie Webb	Juli Inkster	Karrie Webb	Meg Mallon
2001	Annika Sorenstam	Karrie Webb	Karrie Webb	Se Ri Pak
2002	Annika Sorenstam	Se Ri Pak	Juli Inkster	Karrie Webb
2003	Patricia Meunier-Lebouc	Annika Sorenstam	Hilary Lunke	Annika Sorenstam
2004	Grace Park	Annika Sorenstam	Meg Mallon	Karen Stupples
2005	Annika Sorenstam	Annika Sorenstam	Birdie Kim	Jeong Jang
2006	Karrie Webb	Se Ri Pak	Annika Sorenstam	Sherri Steinhauer
2007	Morgan Pressel	Suzann Pettersen	Cristie Kerr	Lorena Ochoa
2008	Lorena Ochoa	Yani Tseng	Inbee Park	Ji-Yai Shin
2009	Brittany Lincicome	Anna Nordqvist	Eun-Hee Ji	Catriona Matthew
2010	Yani Tseng	Cristie Kerr	Paula Creamer	Yani Tseng
2011	Stacy Lewis	Yani Tseng	So Yeon Ryu	

Note: 1. The Women's British Open replaced the duMaurier Classic as the fourth major in 2001. Source: LPGA

TENNIS

"I had one thought," said the famed tennis player, "and that was to put the ball across the net."

The statement is attributed not to a young man of the modern day, but to Helen Wills Moody, an American woman who won 19 Grand Slam singles titles between 1923 and 1938 while bearing an impassive expression that earned her the nickname "Little Miss Poker Face." The quote reveals the essence of tennis: At root, the sport, often derided as a pursuit for the country club set, demands of its practicioners incredible determination and focus. For in its most glamorous incarnation, singles play, tennis pits two opponents against each other, with no teammates, no clock, and (usually) no excuses. It is no wonder that the sport's champions, whether long ago or recent, have demonstrated a prodigious will along with their more obvious ability to hit like hammers and run like rabbits.

History of Tennis

The history of tennis is shrouded, like many sports, in an uncertain past. Some speculate that predecessors of tennis were played in ancient Egypt, Greece, and Rome. Yet the first concrete evidence of the sport's origins dates to medieval times, when the sport was played in walled courtyards by French monks. Those monastic players apparently divided their quadrangles with a rope, the forerunner of the modern net. This early form of the game was often called "jeu de paume," paume meaning the hand, which indicates the hands were used to strike the ball. Later, however, players employed gloves and short bats or paddles. Despite initial royal and even ecclesiastical obstacles to the sport, it is said that in the 13th century more than 1,800 courts existed in France. Tennis jumped across the Channel to England, where it was popular among the royalty.

The assemblage of terms that are particular to tennis may have their roots in this time. The truth is, no one knows for sure how words like *love* or *deuce*, not to mention the curious scoring system, came about. It is believed that the word *tennis* itself stems from the French *tenez*, or "take this," which was apparently shouted before the serve. The word *love* may be derived from *l'oeuf*, the French for egg, or from the Dutch/Flemish *lof*, or honor. The term *deuce* likely stems from the French a *deux du jeu*, or two points away from game. It is also not clear where the 15, 30, and 40 stem from, but theories assert score was kept on a clock face (with "45" being gradually shortened to "40") or a way to keep track of money while gambling on the match.

By 1500 the paddle used to hit the ball now included a head strung with animal intestines, and the game reached an early peak not long after. Despite innovations, the game then became less popular, so that by 1800 the game barely existed in France.

Yet tennis made a resurgence in the 19th century. In 1874 Major Walter Wingfield of the British army developed a new version of tennis with modified rules. He chose to patent the game under the unfortunate name of "sphairisitke," from the Greek for "ball game." Wingfield's version was not only played outdoors, without walls, but on a court shaped like an hourglass, narrow in the middle and wider on either end.

Neither Wingfield's obscure name for the sport nor his hourglass court left much of an imprint on history. In 1877 the All-England Croquet Club at Wimbledon contested its first lawn tennis championships, played according to a newly codified standard of rules that abandoned the hourglass court. The chosen dimensions, 78 feet long and 27 feet wide, and the created rules have stood almost untouched since that time. This initial competition was the predecessor to the modern Grand Slam tournament of Wimbledon held every summer.

Like other sports invented in Europe, tennis quickly spread to other nations. The U.S. Lawn Tennis Association, predecessor to the modern U.S. Tennis Association, was formed in 1881, while the British Lawn Tennis Association was created in 1888. An international body, the International Tennis Federation, was founded in 1913.

The newfangled sport of lawn tennis quickly surpassed its old ancestor, although its form indoor tennis, variously called Real Tennis or Court Tennis, is still played in places.

Yet it pales in comparison to its offspring. In the early 20th century, regular international competitions had begun, and the sport was even included in the program of the 1896 Olympic Games.

Modern Tennis

At the beginning of the 20th century, tennis was a preserve for the wealthy. The few tournaments that existed were contested by rich amateurs. The divide between amateur and professional would last, in fact, for nearly seven more decades. Only in 1968 were the top tournaments—the Australian, the French, Wimbledon, and the U.S. championships—made open to professionals. This period following 1968 is called the Open Era. Before that time, professional players could not compete in the most prestigious competitions of their sport, although many won the events while still amateurs.

Early stars of the pre-Open Era include Bill Tilden and Don Budge, who, in 1938, was the first person to win all four majors in the same year (the Grand Slam). Among women, Suzanne Lenglen and Helen Wills Moody rose to prominence. Yet star players could not earn a living playing amateur-only tournaments. So the professionals gave up such events and earned their wages with more unusual methods. As an example, Tilden won seven U.S. singles championships and three Wimbledons before turning pro in 1931. He conducted barnstorming tours, racing from match to match, often overnight, and played until he neared 50 years of age.

In mid-century, top players included Bobby Riggs, Jack Kramer, and Pancho Gonzales, plus several Australians, among them Roy Emerson and the great Rod Laver. Laver won the Grand Slam—all four major tournaments in a calendar year—in 1962.

Then came 1968, and the beginning of the Open Era. There is no better indication of the massive changes wrought by the coming of the Open Era than the U.S. Open champion in 1968: Arthur Ashe, an African American in a sport that had been historically almost exclusive to whites. After the Open Era, the game of tennis became more popular, freed from its image of being only for those rich, white, and amateur. It became a sport of the middle class.

With the added popularity of professional tennis came more tournaments and prize money. Four tournaments have historically held, in one form or another, more importance than the rest, and these are called the Grand Slams, or Slams, though winning the Grand Slam means winning all four of these in a single calendar year. There are

differences in surfaces among the Slams, differences that affect how the tennis is played. In the calendar year, the first is the Australian Open, played on hardcourts in Melbourne during January, the Australian summer. Next is the French Open, played on clay, the slowest surface, in Paris in early June, and it is followed a few weeks later by Wimbledon, contested at the club's London location on the fastest surface, grass. Finally, around Labor Day comes the U.S. Open, played on the hardcourts at the U.S. Tennis Center in New York City.

In international competition, there is the Davis Cup, first contested in 1900, in which countries compete against one another's teams in both singles and doubles. Tennis is also featured in the Olympic Games.

Following the advent of the Open Era, a stable of superb players sprang to worldwide attention. First among the great men's stars was an old one, Laver, who won a second Grand Slam in 1969 (still the last man to win the Grand Slam). Laver has a claim to being the best male player in history. Other male stars included Jimmy Connors (eight Slams, including five U.S. Opens), Bjorn Borg (11 Slams, including five straight Wimbledon titles and six French Opens), and John McEnroe (seven Slams).

Two early female stars, Billie Jean King (12 Slams) and Australia's Margaret Court (a record 24 Slams, including the Grand Slam in 1970) dominated the early post–Open Era years. King was a driving force behind the formation of the Women's Tennis Association (WTA) in 1970. They were soon followed by two more superlative players, Chris Evert (18 Slams) and Martina Navratilova (also 18 Slams), a Czech who became a naturalized American.

Although the Open Era brought many changes to the game, the rules have been essentially unchanged for more than a century. The court is the same size as that prescribed by the All-England Croquet Club in 1877. Also remaining is the quirky scoring system. The only substantial rule change was the introduction of the tiebreaker in the 1970's.

Although the rules are almost the same, modern competitors are essentially playing a different sport than that seen immediately after the coming of the Open Era. Technology has revolutionized tennis in the last 25 years, not always for the better in the eyes of some critics. As recently as 1980, Sweden's Bjorn Borg won his last Wimbledon title with a wooden racket. Not long after, new materials were used to manufacture the rackets. High-tech composites permitted larger faces and lighter weights. The result has been a dramatic surge in the speed of the sport, as more athletic players zip shots back and forth over the net. In modern tennis, the rewarding virtues are shot power and quickness, which is necessary to pursue the blistering shots. Men regularly serve at around 130 miles per hour, while women customarily climb above 100 mph.

The last years of the 20th century saw dominant players arise in both the men's and women's game. Germany's Steffi Graf won 22 Slams in her career, second only to Court, and she enjoyed the most decorated year in tennis history in 1988, when she not only won the Grand Slam, but added a gold medal at the Summer Olympics in Seoul. Her nickname, "Fraulein Forehand," bestowed due to her punishing forehand stroke, symbolized the power and speed of the new game. Among men, American Pete Sampras won a record 14 Slams, including seven Wimbledons, his last Slam being a surprising U.S. Open title in 2002. (However, he never won the French Open.)

Although Margaret Court won more Slams than Graf, Graf faced stiffer competition throughout her career. Sampras's total haul of 14 Slams surpasses that of Emerson (who won 12) and Laver's 11, but Sampras did not miss six years of Grand Slam competition because he was a professional, as did Laver. Other great players of the late 80's and 90's include Boris Becker, Ivan Lendl, Andre Agassi, Monica Seles, and Martina Hingis.

Contemporary men's tennis is governed by two associations, the ITF and the ATP, while the women's game is run by the WTA. These tours host regular events around the world, each with its own schedule, and come together at the majors.

As the 21st century began, a new group of players emerged. American sisters Venus and Serena Williams combined for 20 Grand Slam titles in their distinguished careers and Kim Clijsters returned from motherhood and a two-year hiatus to add three additional Grand Slams to her resume. On the men's side, Roger Federer's dominance of the early parts of the decade has given way to a genuine rivalry with Rafael Nadal. Federer started off strong—in a three year span the Swiss star captured eight Grand Slam titles including three-peats in both Wimbledon and the U.S. Open on his way to a record 16 Men's Grand Slam titles. Nadal was a wizard on clay, winning the French Open four times in a row and five out of six times, but struggled to beat Federer on other surfaces. Finally in 2008, Rafael Nadal bested Roger Federer at Wimbledon and perhaps for the first time tipped the scales in his direction. Nadal continued his winning ways, capturing three Grand Slam titles in 2010 to Federer's one.

Rules of the Game

A tennis match is contested either by single opponents (singles) or by two players per side (doubles). A coin toss determines who will begin the match with the serve.

Singles tennis is played on a court measuring 78 feet long and 27 feet wide, with a number of lines that have attached rules. A three-foot-high net stretches across the center of the court, dividing the surface into two equal halves. The only items of equipment necessary to play are a round ball, usually yellow, and a hand-held device called a racket, which has a web of taut strings. A tennis ball is a hollow rubber sphere covered with a synthetic felt fabric. It usually weighs about 2 ounces and has a diameter of just over 2 1/2 inches. Tennis rackets generally measure from 27 to 32 inches in length and weigh between 10 and 11 ounces. The frames, once made of wood, are now typically made of graphite and fiberglass with nylon strings.

The basic action of tennis is relatively simple. With the racket, players hit the ball over the net and the ball is similarly returned by the opponent. The ball can bounce only once and always on the receiving side of the court, and it must land within the boundaries. However, players can hit the ball while they, or the ball, is above a portion of the playing surface that is not legal. Players want to avoid hitting the ball outside of the legal surface or into the net.

The essential unit of scoring is the point. If a player makes a shot that the opponent cannot return (either by not reaching the ball at all or allowing it to bounce twice), the player wins the point. If the player makes a mistake, such as hitting the ball outside of the legal area ("out") or into, and not over, the net, the player loses the point. A ball that hits the net and still drops over into the opponent's half of the court is a legal shot. This legal area is either half of the court, including the lines. If the ball bounces on one of the lines, it is considered "in" and the opponent must return the ball or lose the point.

One addition to this is the serve, the action that commences each point. On the serve, one player strikes the ball, usually overhead, with the racket. On the serve alone the ball must land in a smaller box—the service box—outlined by small lines on the opponent's side of the court. If a player misses this box or hits the ball into the net, it is said to be a "fault." The player may serve again, but if the second serve is also in error, the player incurs a "double fault" and loses the point.

Following the serve, play continues in the specified manner until a player makes a mistake or hits a shot the opponent cannot return, and the point is awarded.

Scoring is one of the more confusing elements of tennis. To win a game, players must capture a certain number of points. If no points have been taken, the player has "0," or "love," a term specific to tennis. The first point is considered to be "15," the second "30," and the third "40." (The source of these terms is a matter of some debate, but they harken back to medieval times.) As an example, a player who has won two points in a particular game will have "30." The fourth point, although unnamed, will win the game but for one notable exception.

At any time, the score of the game is usually read as a combination of numbers, such as 30-40, with the first number indicating the score of the person with the serve, and the second the person receiving the serve. In the case of 30-40, the player with the serve has won two points, and the player receiving has won three.

To win a game, a player has to win by at least two points. This is a problem if the players are tied at 40, in which case a mechanism called "deuce" begins. Following deuce, the game continues until one player has captured two more points than the other. If, at deuce, a player wins the next point, he/she is said to have the advantage. If, at advantage, that player wins another point, he/she wins the game. If the opponent wins the point, the game returns to deuce, and the process begins again.

For the next game, the serve goes to the other player. After every two games, players switch sides on the court.

The outcome of a match, however, is not determined by who wins the most games, but by who wins the majority of sets. In men's singles, the player who wins three out of a maximum five sets wins the match, while in women's singles, the victor takes two out of a maximum three sets.

Players win sets by winning games. To take a set, the player must capture six games while winning the set by at least two games. If the players are tied at six games in any set except the last set of the match (fifth set if men's, third if women's), then they proceed to a tiebreaker, which, of course, must be won by two points. In the final set of a match, there is no tiebreaker, and players continue to compete in games until one has captured two more games than the other. (This can take a long time.) When a player has won a majority of the possible sets, he/she wins the match.

Doubles tennis is played in almost precisely the same manner, but with two players a side. The major change is the inclusion of alleys on either flank of the court, which add nine feet to the legal width, making the court 78 feet by 36 feet.

While electronic line judging had been around in some capacity since the early 70's, it was not until the invention of the Hawk-Eye system in 2001 that the technology really caught on. Originally designed for cricket matches, the International Tennis Federation began testing and approved the use of the Hawk-Eye device for professional use in 2005. The 2006 US Open was the first Grand Slam tournament to implement a challenge system based on the new technology. If a player disagreed with the umpire's decision, they could challenge the call using the Hawk-Eye technology, depending on the rules of the individual tournament. In 2008 a uniform set of rules regarding challenges were implemented with three unsuccessful challenges per set, and an additional challenge if the set entered a tie-break situation.

Glossary of Tennis Terms

ace a legal serve that is not touched by the opponent. The server wins the point.

backhand one of the two common strokes in tennis, along with the forehand. In a backhand, the player faces the net with the shoulder of the racket-holding arm and swings the racket across the body to strike the ball.

baseline the lines on opposite ends of the court that serve as the far boundaries; usually four inches thick.

break when the player with the serve loses the game.

chair umpire a courtside official who sits in a high chair overlooking the net and presides over the match.

deuce when a game is tied at 40. The player who wins the next point is said to have the advantage, and wins the game if he or she also scores the next point. The player without the advantage can return the game to deuce by scoring the following, point, however. The system arises because, by the rules of tennis, a player can only win a game by at least two points.

double fault if both the first and second serves result in faults, giving the opponent the point.

doubles when teams of two players compete against each

other. In doubles, the alleys on either side of the court come into play, widening the legal surface by nine feet, to 36 feet.

drop shot a light shot hit with significant spin that, because of its positioning, forces the opponent to come toward the net.

fault an errant serve, called if the ball hits the net or misses the service box. A serve that strikes the top of the net and lands in the service box results in a let.

foot fault when the foot of the server enters the court before the serve is finished.

forehand one of the two main shots in tennis, executed with the shoulder of the arm without the racket facing the net, and swinging the racket forward to strike the ball. Normally a player's strongest, most powerful stroke.

gallery the name for the area where the crowd sits; also used to describe the crowd itself.

game the incremental unit of scoring to determine the progress of a set. To win a game, a player must win at least two more points than the opponent. Scores begin at 0, or love, and progress to 15, 30, and then 40. A point won at 40 will win the game, unless the game is at deuce.

in when a struck ball lands inside the legal boundaries of the court. If the ball hits the lines, it is considered "in."

let when the served ball hits the net and lands in the service box. The server is allowed to serve again without a fault.

line the white stripes that delineate the legal portions of the court. The outer lines are thicker to ease identification of whether the ball is in or out.

line judge the officials who determine whether balls land inside or outside the court. The baseline judges, service line judges, and sideline judges are all line judges.

love a term unique to tennis that means zero points in the context of a game or in a set. Perhaps based on the French term for egg, *l'oeuf*, but no one really knows.

match a singles or doubles contest with an outcome determined by the number of sets won. In women's tennis, the winner is the player who wins two out of a maximum three sets, while in men's competition, the victor will win at least three of five sets.

match point the point where if a player wins, he or she wins the whole match. The terms game point and set point are also used to describe points where a player can win a game or set respectively.

out when a ball lands outside the legal boundaries of the court.

passing shot when a player returns the ball past an opponent who is rushing to the net.

point the smallest unit of scoring in tennis, the accumulation of which determine the result of games. Players win points thusly: hitting the ball into the opposing player's court without it being returned by the opponent; if the opponent hits a ball out of the court or into the net; if the opponent double faults.

serve the action that begins every point. A player tosses the ball in the air and strikes the ball at high velocity into the diagonally opposite service box, a space. If the first serve results in a fault, the second serve is normally slower, as the server will want to avoid a double fault.

set the units that determine the outcome of a match. To take the set, a player must win two more games than opponent and at least six games in total. If tied at six games, there is a tiebreaker to determine the set winner, with the exception if it is the last and decisive set of the match, in which case the players must continue to play until one has won two more games than the other.

singles when one player plays against another player. In these games, the court is 27 feet wide.

smash a powerful overhead shot used to return a poor, high soft shot by the opponent.

tiebreaker the mechanism to determine the winner of a set tied at six games apiece. The first player to win seven points in the tiebreaker wins the game and the set, but the tiebreaker must be won by two points, and therefore may be extended until a winner is determined.

topspin when a ball is struck with spin so that it dips toward the court after being hit. This permits the ball to be hit with more power, as the ball is more likely to dive down and remain in play.

underspin when the ball is hit with spin back toward the striking player; also called a slice. The underspin causes the ball to lose speed and bounce softly.

unforced error a shot that does not enter the opponent's court, either hitting the net or landing outside the boundaries.

volley a shot made before the ball bounces in a player's court, usually hit when close to the net. A half-volley is a shot made immediately after the ball bounces.

Men's Grand Slam Champions

Year	Australian Champion	French Champion	Wimbledon Champion	U.S. Champion
1920	Pat O'Hara Wood	—	Bill Tilden	Bill Tilden
1921	Rhys H. Gemmell	—	Bill Tilden	Bill Tilden
1922	Pat O'Hara Wood	—	Gerald L. Patterson	Bill Tilden
1923	Pat O'Hara Wood	—	William M. Johnston	Bill Tilden
1924	James Anderson	—	Jean Borotra	Bill Tilden
1925	James Anderson	René Lacoste	René Lacoste	Bill Tilden
1926	John Hawkes	Henri Cochet	Jean Borotra	René Lacoste
1927	Gerald Patterson	René Lacoste	Henri Cochet	RenéLacoste
1928	Jean Borotra	Henri Cochet	René Lacoste	Henri Cochet
1929	John C. Gregory	René Lacoste	Henri Cochet	Bill Tilden
1930	Gar Moon	Henri Cochet	Bill Tilden	John H. Doeg
1931	Jack Crawford	Jean Borotra	Sidney B.Wood Jr.	H. Ellsworth Vines
1932	Jack Crawford	Henri Cochet	Ellsworth Vines	H. Ellsworth Vines
1933	Jack Crawford	John H. Crawford	Jack Crawford	Fred Perry
1934	Fred J. Perry	Gottfried von Cramm	Fred Perry	Fred Perry
1935	Jack Crawford	Fred J. Perry	Fred Perry	Wilmer L. Allison
1936	Adrian Quist	Gottfried von Cramm	Fred Perry	Fred Perry
1937	Vivian B. McGrath	Henner Henkel	Don Budge	Don Budge
1938[1]	Don Budge	Don Budge	Don Budge	Don Budge
1939	John Bromwich	W. Donald McNeill	Bobby Riggs	Bobby Riggs
1940	Adrian Quist	No competition	Not Held	Donald McNeill
1941	Foreigners excluded	Bernard Destremau	Not Held	Bobby Riggs
1942	Foreigners excluded	Bernard Destremau	Not Held	Frederick Schroeder
1943	Foreigners excluded	Yvon Petra	Not Held	Joseph R. Hunt
1944	Foreigners excluded	Yvon Petra	Not Held	Frank Parker
1945	Foreigners excluded	Yvon Petra	Not Held	Frank Parker
1946	John Bromwich	Marcel Bernard	Yvon Petra	Jack Kramer
1947	Dinny Pails	Joseph Asboth	Jack Kramer	Jack Kramer
1948	Adrian Quist	Frank Parker	Bob Falkenburg	Pancho Gonzales
1949	Frank Sedgman	Frank Parker	Ted Schroeder	Pancho Gonzales
1950	Frank Sedgman	Budge Patty	Budge Patty	Arthur Larsen
1951	Richard Savitt	Jaroslav Drobny	Dick Savitt	Frank Sedgman
1952	Ken McGregor	Jaroslav Drobny	Frank Sedgman	Frank Sedgman
1953	Ken Rosewall	Ken Rosewall	Vic Seixas	Tony Trabert
1954	Mervyn Rose	Tony Trabert	Jaroslav Drobny	E. Victor Seixas Jr.
1955	Ken Rosewall	Tony Trabert	Tony Trabert	Tony Trabert
1956	Lew Hoad	Lew Hoad	Lew Hoad	Ken Rosewall
1957	Ashley Cooper	Sven Davidson	Lew Hoad	Malcolm Anderson
1958	Ashley Cooper	Mervyn Rose	Ashley Cooper	Ashley J. Cooper
1959	Alex Olmedo	Nicola Pietrangeli	Alex Olmedo	Neale Fraser
1960	Rod Laver	Nicola Pietrangeli	Neale Fraser	Neale Fraser
1961	Roy Emerson	Manuel Santana	Rod Laver	Roy Emerson
1962[1]	Rod Laver	Rod Laver	Rod Laver	Rod Laver
1963	Roy Emerson	Roy Emerson	Chuck McKinley	Rafael Osuna
1964	Roy Emerson	Manuel Santana	Roy Emerson	Roy Emerson
1965	Roy Emerson	Fred Stolle	Roy Emerson	Manuel Santana
1966	Roy Emerson	Tony Roche	Manuel Santana	Fred Stolle

Men's Grand Slam Champions (cont'd)

Year	Australian Champion	French Champion	Wimbledon Champion	U.S. Champion
1967	Roy Emerson	Roy Emerson	John Newcombe	John Newcombe
1968	Bill Bowrey	Ken Rosewall	Rod Laver	Arthur Ashe
1969[1]	Rod Laver	Rod Laver	Rod Laver	Rod Laver
1970	Arthur Ashe	Jan Kodes	John Newcombe	Ken Rosewall
1971	Ken Rosewall	Jan Kodes	John Newcombe	Stan Smith
1972	Ken Rosewall	Andres Gimeno	Stan Smith	Ilie Nastase
1973	John Newcombe	Ilie Nastase	Jan Kodes	John Newcombe
1974	Jimmy Connors	Bjorn Borg	Jimmy Connors	Jimmy Connors
1975	John Newcombe	Bjorn Borg	Arthur Ashe	Manuel Orantes
1976	Mark Edmondson	Adriano Panatta	Bjorn Borg	Jimmy Connors
1977	Roscoe Tanner[2] Vitas Gerulaitis[2]	Guillermo Vilas	Bjorn Borg	Guillermo Vilas
1978	Guillermo Vilas	Bjorn Borg	Bjorn Borg	Jimmy Connors
1979	Guillermo Vilas	Bjorn Borg	Bjorn Borg	John McEnroe
1980	Brian Teacher	Bjorn Borg	Bjorn Borg	John McEnroe
1981	Johan Kriek	Bjorn Borg	John McEnroe	John McEnroe
1982	Johan Kriek	Mats Wilander	Jimmy Connors	Jimmy Connors
1983	Mats Wilander	Yannick Noah	John McEnroe	Jimmy Connors
1984	Mats Wilander	Ivan Lendl	John McEnroe	John McEnroe
1985	Stefan Edberg	Mats Wilander	Boris Becker	Ivan Lendl
1986	Moved to Jan. 1987	Ivan Lendl	Boris Becker	Ivan Lendl
1987	Stefan Edberg	Ivan Lendl	Pat Cash	Ivan Lendl
1988	Mats Wilander	Mats Wilander	Stefan Edberg	Mats Wilander
1989	Ivan Lendl	Michael Chang	Boris Becker	Boris Becker
1990	Ivan Lendl	Andrés Gomez	Stefan Edberg	Pete Sampras
1991	Boris Becker	Jim Courier	Michael Stich	Stefan Edberg
1992	Jim Courier	Jim Courier	Andre Agassi	Stefan Edberg
1993	Jim Courier	Sergi Bruguera	Pete Sampras	Pete Sampras
1994	Pete Sampras	Sergi Bruguera	Pete Sampras	Andre Agassi
1995	Andre Agassi	Thomas Muster	Pete Sampras	Pete Sampras
1996	Boris Becker	Yevgeny Kafelnikov	Richard Krajicek	Pete Sampras
1997	Pete Sampras	Gustavo Kuerten	Pete Sampras	Patrick Rafter
1998	Petr Korda	Carlos Moya	Pete Sampras	Patrick Rafter
1999	Yevgeny Kafelnikov	Andre Agassi	Pete Sampras	Andre Agassi
2000	Andre Agassi	Gustavo Kuerten	Pete Sampras	Marat Safin
2001	Andre Agassi	Gustavo Kuerten	Goran Ivanisevic	Lleyton Hewitt
2002	Thomas Johansson	Albert Costa	Lleyton Hewitt	Pete Sampras
2003	Andre Agassi	Juan Carlos Ferrero	Roger Federer	Andy Roddick
2004	Roger Federer	Gaston Gaudio	Roger Federer	Roger Federer
2005	Marat Safin	Rafael Nadal	Roger Federer	Roger Federer
2006	Roger Federer	Rafael Nadal	Roger Federer	Roger Federer
2007	Roger Federer	Rafael Nadal	Roger Federer	Roger Federer
2008	Novak Djokovic	Rafael Nadal	Rafael Nadal	Roger Federer
2009	Rafael Nadal	Roger Federer	Roger Federer	Juan Martin del Potro
2010	Roger Federer	Rafael Nadal	Rafael Nadal	Rafael Nadal
2011	Novak Djokovic	Rafael Nadal	Novak Djokovic	

Notes: 1. Grand Slam winner. 2. Two tournaments were held in 1977, the first in January, the second in December.

Women's Grand Slam Champions

Year	Australian Champion	French Champion	Wimbledon Champion	U.S. Champion
1920	Not held	Suzanne Lenglen	Suzanne Lenglen	Molla Bjurstedt Mallory
1921	Not held	Suzanne Lenglen	Suzanne Lenglen	Molla Bjurstedt Mallory
1922	Margaret Molesworth	Suzanne Lenglen	Suzanne Lenglen	Molla Bjurstedt Mallory
1923	Margaret Molesworth	Suzanne Lenglen	Suzanne Lenglen	Helen Wills
1924	Sylvia Lance	Diddie Vlasto	Kathleen McKane	Helen Wills
1925	Daphne Akhurst	Suzanne Lenglen	Suzanne Lenglen	Helen Wills
1926	Daphne Akhurst	Suzanne Lenglen	Kathleen McKane Godfree	Molla Bjurstedt Mallory
1927	Edna Boyd	Kea Bouman	Helen Wills	Helen Wills
1928	Daphne Akhurst	Helen Wills	Helen Wills	Helen Wills
1929	Daphne Akhurst	Helen Wills	Helen Wills	Helen Wills
1930	Daphne Akhurst	Helen Wills Moody	Helen Wills Moody	Betty Nuthall
1931	Coral Buttsworth	Cilly Aussem	Cilly Aussem	Helen Wills Moody
1932	Coral Buttsworth	Helen Wills Moody	Helen Wills Moody	Helen Jacobs
1933	Joan Hartigan	Margaret Scriven	Helen Wills Moody	Helen Jacobs
1934	Joan Hartigan	Margaret Scriven	Dorothy Round	Helen Jacobs
1935	Dorothy Round	Hilde Sperling	Helen Wills Moody	Helen Jacobs
1936	Joan Hartigan	Hilde Sperling	Helen Jacobs	Alice Marble
1937	Nancye Wynne Bolton	Hilde Sperling	Dorothy Round	Anita Lizane
1938	Dorothy Bundy	Simone Mathieu	Helen Wills Moody	Alice Marble
1939	Emily Westacott	Simone Mathieu	Alice Marble	Alice Marble
1940	Nancye Wynne Bolton	Not Held	Not Held	Alice Marble
1941	Not Held	Not Held	Not Held	Sarah Palfrey Cooke
1942	Not Held	Not Held	Not Held	Pauline Betz
1943	Not Held	Not Held	Not Held	Pauline Betz
1944	Not Held	Not Held	Not Held	Pauline Betz Cooke
1945	Not Held	Not Held	Not Held	Sarah Palfrey Cooke
1946	Nancye Wynne Bolton	Margaret Osborne	Pauline Betz	Pauline Betz
1947	Nancye Wynne Bolton	Patricia Todd	Margaret Osborne	Louise Brough
1948	Nancye Wynne Bolton	Nelly Landry	Louise Brough	Margaret Osborne duPont
1949	Doris Hart	Margaret Osborne duPont	Louise Brough	Margaret Osborne duPont
1950	Louise Brough	Doris Hart	Louise Brough	Margaret Osborne duPont
1951	Nancye Wynne Bolton	Shirley Fry	Doris Hart	Maureen Connolly
1952	Thelma Long	Doris Hart	Maureen Connolly	Maureen Connolly
1953[1]	Maureen Connolly	Maureen Connolly	Maureen Connolly	Maureen Connolly
1954	Thelma Long	Maureen Connolly	Maureen Connolly	Doris Hart
1955	Beryl Penrose	Angela Mortimer	Louise Brough	Doris Hart
1956	Mary Carter	Althea Gibson	Shirley Fry	Shirley Fry
1957	Shirley Fry	Shirley Bloomer	Althea Gibson	Althea Gibson
1958	Angela Mortimer	Zsuzsi Kormoczy	Althea Gibson	Althea Gibson
1959	Mary Carter Reitano	Christine Truman	Maria Bueno	Maria Bueno
1960	Margaret Smith	Darlene Hard	Maria Bueno	Darlene Hard
1961	Margaret Smith	Ann Haydon	Angela Mortimer	Darlene Hard
1962	Margaret Smith	Margaret Smith	Karen Hantze Susman	Margaret Smith
1963	Margaret Smith	Lesley Turner	Margaret Smith	Maria Bueno
1964	Margaret Smith	Margaret Smith	Maria Bueno	Maria Bueno
1965	Margaret Smith	Lesley Turner	Margaret Smith	Margaret Smith
1966	Margaret Smith	Ann Jones	Billie Jean King	Maria Bueno

Women's Grand Slam Champions (cont'd)

Year	Australian Champion	French Champion	Wimbledon Champion	U.S. Champion
1967	Nancy Richey	Francoise Durr	Billie Jean King	Billie Jean King
1968	Billie Jean King	Nancy Richey	Billie Jean King	Virginia Wade
1969	Margaret Smith Court	Margaret Smith Court	Ann Jones	Margaret Smith Court
1970[1]	Margaret Smith Court	Margaret Smith Court	Margaret Smith Court	Margaret Smith Court
1971	Margaret Smith Court	Evonne Goolagong	Evonne Goolagong	Billie Jean King
1972	Virginia Wade	Billie Jean King	Billie Jean King	Billie Jean King
1973	Margaret Smith Court	Margaret Smith Court	Billie Jean King	Margaret Smith Court
1974	Evonne Goolagong	Chris Evert	Chris Evert	Billie Jean King
1975	Evonne Goolagong	Chris Evert	Billie Jean King	Chris Evert
1976	Evonne Goolagong Cawley	Sue Barker	Chris Evert	Chris Evert
1977	Kerry Melville Reid[2] Evonne Goolagong Cawley[2]	Mima Jasuovec	Virginia Wade	Chris Evert
1978	Chris O'Neil	Virginia Ruzici	Martina Navratilova	Chris Evert
1979	Barbara Jordan	Chris Evert Lloyd	Martina Navratilova	Tracy Austin
1980	Hana Mandlikova	Chris Evert Lloyd	Evonne Goolagong Cawley	Chris Evert Lloyd
1981	Martina Navratilova	Hana Mandlikova	Chris Evert Lloyd	Tracy Austin
1982	Chris Evert Lloyd	Martina Navratilova	Martina Navratilova	Chris Evert Lloyd
1983	Martina Navratilova	Chris Evert Lloyd	Martina Navratilova	Martina Navratilova
1984	Chris Evert Lloyd	Martina Navratilova	Martina Navratilova	Martina Navratilova
1985	Martina Navratilova	Chris Evert Lloyd	Martina Navratilova	Hana Mandlikova
1986	Moved to Jan. 1987	Chris Evert Lloyd	Martina Navratilova	Martina Navratilova
1987	Hana Mandlikova	Steffi Graf	Martina Navratilova	Martina Navratilova
1988[1]	Steffi Graf	Steffi Graf	Steffi Graf	Steffi Graf
1989	Steffi Graf	Arantxa Sanchez	Steffi Graf	Steffi Graf
1990	Steffi Graf	Monica Seles	Martina Navratilova	Gabriela Sabatini
1991	Monica Seles	Monica Seles	Steffi Graf	Monica Seles
1992	Monica Seles	Monica Seles	Steffi Graf	Monica Seles
1993	Monica Seles	Steffi Graf	Steffi Graf	Steffi Graf
1994	Steffi Graf	Arantxa Sánchez Vicario	Conchita Martinez	Arantxa Sánchez Vicario
1995	Mary Pierce	Steffi Graf	Steffi Graf	Steffi Graf
1996	Monica Seles	Steffi Graf	Steffi Graf	Steffi Graf
1997	Martina Hingis	Iva Majoli	Martina Hingis	Martina Hingis
1998	Martina Hingis	Arantxa Sánchez Vicario	Jana Novotna	Lindsay Davenport
1999	Martina Hingis	Steffi Graf	Lindsay Davenport	Serena Williams
2000	Lindsay Davenport	Mary Pierce	Venus Williams	Venus Williams
2001	Jennifer Capriati	Jennifer Capriati	Venus Williams	Venus Williams
2002	Jennifer Capriati	Serena Williams	Serena Williams	Serena Williams
2003	Serena Williams	Justine Henin-Hardenne	Serena Williams	Justine Henin-Hardenne
2004	Justine Henin-Hardenne	Anastasia Myskina	Maria Sharapova	Svetlana Kuznetsova
2005	Serena Williams	Justine Henin-Hardenne	Venus Williams	Kim Clijsters
2006	Amelie Mauresmo	Justine Henin-Hardenne	Amelie Mauresmo	Maria Sharapova
2007	Serena Williams	Justine Henin	Venus Williams	Justine Henin
2008	Maria Sharapova	Ana Ivanovic	Venus Williams	Serena Williams
2009	Serena Williams	Svetlana Kuznetsova	Serena Williams	Kim Clijsters
2010	Serena Williams	Francesca Schiavone	Serena Williams	Kim Clijsters
2011	Kim Clijsters	Li Na	Petra Kvitova	

Notes: 1. Grand Slam winner. 2. Two tournaments were held in 1977, the first in January, the second in December.

SOCCER

History

Commonly known as "football" outside North America, soccer is the world's most popular sport. The word *soccer* is derived from "association football," the traditional name for the game in the British Commonwealth countries. Although ball-kicking games can be traced at least as far back as ancient Greece and China, modern soccer originated in 19th-century England. The Football Association laid down the first set of rules in 1863, and the first organized league was established in 1888. Carried outside Britain by sailors and expatriates, the game quickly caught on in the rest of Europe, South America, and Asia. The Fédération Internationale de Football Association (FIFA), the world's official governing body for the sport, was founded in 1904, with headquarters in Paris (later moved to Zurich). Soccer became a medal sport in the Olympic Games of 1908. In 1930 FIFA organized the World Cup, a tournament contested every four years to determine international soccer supremacy.

The World Cup is the most coveted prize in soccer. The month-long quadrennial tournament culminates more than two years of qualifying play in six world regions. A record total of 204 national teams entered competition for the 2010 World Cup, of which 32 qualified for the final tournament. More than 700 million television viewers were estimated to have watched the 2010 final, in which Spain defeated Netherlands to capture their first title.

World Cup competition for women began in 1991, with tournaments also held every four years. The United States and Germany have won twice.

Rules of the Game

Soccer is played according to the same basic rules almost everywhere. The field, or "pitch," is rectangular in shape, measuring 100–130 yards (91-119 meters) long and at least 50 yard (46 meters) wide. Each team consists of 11 players, including a goalkeeper. The goalkeeper is the only player who may touch the ball with the hands or arms, and only within a designated area. The other players attempt to advance the ball by kicking, or sometimes heading, it to a teammate. The object is to force the ball into the opponent's goal—24 feet (7.3 meters) wide and 8 feet (2.4 meters) high—at the far end of the field. In high-level competition, a match lasts 90 minutes and is played in 45-minute halves.

Combining speed, skill, and chesslike strategy, soccer attracts numerous players and spectators throughout the world. Professional clubs play in domestic leagues before passionate crowds. Concurrent with league play, top clubs may compete in annual continent-wide tournaments, such as the European Cup and South America's Copa Libertadores (Liberator's Cup).

In the United States, the growth of soccer has taken place largely at the amateur level—community youth leagues, high schools, and colleges—since the 1960's. U.S. professional leagues (mostly notably the North American Soccer League, 1966–84 and the present Major League Soccer) have had passing success.

Club Soccer

Although the World Cup is considered the premier event in soccer, it is a competition that is held only once every four years. Most daily interest in the game is devoted to club soccer. Every year, clubs all over the world compete in domestic leagues, domestic cups, and in regional cup competitions. At the elite levels, these leagues and clubs command hundreds of millions of dollars in television fees, attendance revenues, and salaries.

Domestic leagues are typically organized in a fashion similar to American baseball: a top division, in which the best clubs and players are concentrated, with lower tiers underneath. However, clubs in the lower leagues are not affiliated with the top-level teams, as in the minor leagues of American baseball. Furthermore, teams move up and down in these divisions through a system of promotion and relegation. For example, Italy's highest division is called Serie A, and underneath are Serie B and Serie C. At the end of every season, the worst four teams in Serie A are relegated to Serie B for the following year, while the top four teams in Serie B are promoted to Serie A.

Another differentiating feature between American sports and international club soccer is the form of player movement. Players customarily change teams through payment of a transfer fee between clubs, although switching via a trade or free agency is also possible. For the best players, transfer fees can be exorbitant: in the summer of 2002, Spain's Real Madrid purchased Brazilian forward Ronaldo, fresh off a dominating (and victorious) performance in the 2002 World Cup, from Italy's Inter Milan in a package that totaled more than $40 million.

Perhaps the most significant aspect of club soccer is that, unlike American sports leagues, where the goal is a single championship, international soccer clubs pursue several trophies, of varying worth, in a single year.

Domestic leagues typically involve a home-and-away round robin, which in a league of 20 teams, such as Spain's La Liga, consists of 38 games. Three points are awarded for a win and one for a draw, and the club with the most points at the end of the season is the champion.

In most countries there is also a knockout cup competition similar to the collegiate basketball tournaments in the United States, but without a seeding system. In some nations, these have a long and significant history: England's Football Association Cup, for example, has been played since 1872, and participants include top-notch clubs such as London's Tottenham Hotspur, teams from several lower professional divisions, and amateur squads. While such cup titles add to the trophy case, they are not as coveted as the league titles.

The elite clubs also compete across international borders in regional competitions. The European Champions Cup is contested by the best teams from all members of UEFA, the European soccer federation. In South America top clubs fight for the Copa Libertadores. These are the most prestigious trophies a club can win in their respective regions.

In the United States, Major League Soccer entered its 16th year of competition in 2011. In 2007, MLS changed its rules in order to make it easier for teams to sign international players. Soon, David Beckham joined the Los Angeles Galaxy from Real Madrid and opened the door for other famous international players such as Cuauhtemoc Blanco, Juan Pablo Angel, Freddie Ljungberg, and Guillermo Barros Schelotto. Young American stars Jozy Altidore and Clint Dempsey were loaned to higher caliber European clubs in what would become a model for the MLS. Developing American stars would go overseas to gain experience in the big leagues while veteran international players came to the US to entertain the fans. This model has great potential for the future of American soccer, especially the World Cup squads. Also, the WUSA, a women's league, began play in 2001, but folded after the 2003 season.

Glossary of Soccer Terms

arc the D-shaped line at the top of the penalty area. The line demarcates a circular distance of 10 yards from the penalty spot.

cap an appearance for a country's national team, so named because, in the past, players were awarded with celebratory headwear.

card a disciplinary system available to the referee. The yellow card is given for overly tough fouls or for persistent fouling by a single player. On violent fouls, such as a lunging tackle from behind, the referee may choose to show a red card, thereby expelling the offending player from the game. Two yellow cards incurred by the same player during the course of a match equals a red card.

corner kick a free kick taken from either corner of the field by the attacking team, awarded when the ball crosses the end line after being last touched by a defender. As with any free kick, the defending team must be at least 10 yards from the spot of the kick.

cross an attacking pass from either side of the field into the penalty area. Frequently aimed at the heads of forwards.

defenders the group of players whose primary duty is to prevent the opposition's attackers from scoring goals. Customarily defenders come in several flavors, including center backs, right or left backs, and sweepers.

draw when the match is tied at game's end. In league play both teams will receive one point in the standings.

extra time an added 30-minute period of play, used only in some tournaments (such as the knockout stage of the World Cup) if the contest is tied after regulation. If there is no score after 30 minutes, the game is usually decided by a penalty shootout.

formation a team's alignment of players on the field. This is described with a set of three numbers, representative of the defenders, midfielders, and forwards, that add up to 10. (The goalkeeper is not considered.) In a 4-4-2 formation, for example, there will be four defenders, four midfielders and two forwards. There is no restriction on a team's formation, and these change based on the game situation.

forwards the players who operate closest to the opposing goal, forwards are the most frequent goalscorers and playmakers; sometimes called strikers.

foul an infraction decided by the referee; usually given for body contact that does not touch the ball first. The fouled team is awarded a free kick. (see *card*)

free kick the action that returns the ball to play after a foul. The victimized team is allowed a 10-yard circle free of enemy defenders. Near the opposing goal, free kicks offer good shooting opportunities. A penalty kick is a free kick taken from the penalty spot.

friendly an exhibition match.

goal the only kind of scoring play in soccer, worth one unit each. The entire ball must cross the goal line—the line underneath the crossbar that links the goalposts—to be counted as a goal. The goal itself is a rectangle 24 feet wide and eight feet high.

goal area a box set within the larger penalty area, from which goal kicks are taken by the defending team. The goal area extends six yards into the field of play.

goalkeeper the player responsible for stopping or blocking shots at his team's goal. The goalkeeper is also the only player allowed to use the hands, but this ability is limited to the penalty area. A keeper who touches the ball with the hands while outside the area risks a yellow or even a red card.

goal kick the kick that restarts play after the attacking team knocks the ball over the end line. This kick is usually taken by the goalkeeper.

goal line the line that marks either end of the field. If the ball exits the field over the goal line, the result is either a corner kick (if last touched by the defending team) or a goal kick. If the entire ball crosses the goal line in the area surrounded by the goal structure, a goal is awarded. Outside of the goal, the goal line is often called simply the end line.

halfway line the line that divides the field in half across the center.

handball intentionally touching the ball with one's hand; strictly forbidden in soccer, the exception being the goal-keeper while in the penalty area. If the balls hits the hand, and the referee determines the player did not touch the ball intentionally, then the referee often lets play continue. Otherwise, if the referee judges a handball, the result is a free kick for the other team.

midfielders the set of players who are equally responsible for defense and attack. Primary duties include winning the ball from the opposing team and creating scoring chances for their own team. The generic term covers a set of varying roles, including wingers, attacking midfielders, and defensive midfielders, among others.

offside an infraction at the moment the ball is passed by a teammate, and the offensive player does not have two opposing defenders (usually counting the goalkeeper as one) between him or her and the goal line. The attacker is considered offside, and this infraction awards a free kick to the defending team. This is the much misunderstood offside rule. Defenses often try to catch attackers in offside situations via a maneuver called the offside trap, in which several defending players simultaneously move away from their own goal. Of course, there are instances when an attacker, timing movement carefully, is said to beat the offside trap, usually obtaining a one-on-one chance against the goalkeeper.

penalty a serious infraction, decided by the referee, who determines that a defender handled the ball or fouled an attacking player in the penalty area. The victimized team is given a free kick from the penalty spot with only the goalkeeper to beat.

penalty area a box that begins 18 yards outside either goalpost, at right angles to the goal line, and extends 18 yards into the field of play. The penalty area has two rules attached. A goalkeeper may touch the ball only with the hands while inside the box, and a foul on the attacking team inside the penalty area results in a penalty.

penalty spot a small circle 12 yards from the goal line, at the center of the box or penalty area, from which penalties are taken.

referee the official who judges and enforces the rules of the game. He or she is aided by two assistants whose primary responsibility is to determine offside infractions. A fourth official, on the sideline, supervises substitutions.

shootout the act of taking alternating penalty kicks to decide a game. Each team receives five attempts (or more if the tie persists) from the penalty spot.

stoppage time the period of time at the end of either half to account for substitutions, injuries, and time-wasting.

substitutions in most league play, three substitutions per game. The player removed cannot return to the match. In friendly matches, usually only five substitutions are permitted, though this limit may be raised with the agreement of both teams.

tackle a defender's attempt to take the ball from an offensive player.

through ball a pass that splits the opposing defense to an onrushing attacker; often used to describe passes that beat the offside trap.

throw in the action that restarts play after the ball goes over the touchline. The player grasps the ball with two hands and throws it back onto the field.

time game time of two 45-minute halves, usually counting up from zero, with stoppage time added at the end of each half. Goals are tracked only by the minute of their scoring, i.e. the 65th minute, not 64:22.

touchline the boundary that borders either side of the field. If the entire ball goes over the touchline, the team that did not touch the ball last is awarded a throw in.

World Cup (women)

Year	Host Country	Championship Game
1991	China	United States 2, Norway 1
1995	Sweden	Norway 2, Germany 0
1999	U.S.	United States 0 (5), China 0 (4) (ET)
2003	U.S.	Germany 2, Sweden 1 (ET)
2007	China	Germany 2, Brazil 0
2011	Germany	Japan 2 (3), United States 2(1) (ET)

World Cup (men)

Year	Host Country	Final Score, Championship Game	Leading Scorer, Country (goals)
1930	Uruguay	Uruguay 4, Argentina 2	Guillermo Stábile, Arg. (8)

Thirteen nations (only 4 from Europe) participate in the first World Cup. The host country, celebrating the centennial of national independence, wins the final before 95,000 spectators.

1934	Italy	Italy 2, Czechoslovakia 1 (ET)	Three Players with 4 Goals[1]

The World Cup comes to Europe; defending champion Uruguay does not attend. A qualifying round reduces the field from 31 teams to 16. Giuseppe Meazza leads Italy to the title.

1938	France	Italy 4, Hungary 2	Leonidas, Brazil (7)

Italy, behind the great Meazza, successfully defends its crown. Leonidas, a preeminent center-forward of the prewar era, carries Brazil to a third-place finish.

1950	Brazil	Uruguay 2, Brazil 1[2]	Ademir, Brazil (9)

After cancellations in 1942 and 1946 due to World War II, 33 nations participate in qualifying play—15 in the tournament. Uruguay, led by Juan Schiaffino and Obdulio Varela, stuns the home crowd in the final match in Rio de Janeiro's Maracana stadium.

1954	Switzerland	West Germany 3, Hungary 2	Sandor Kocsis, Hun. (11)

Hungary, featuring Kocsis and Ferenc Puskas, dominates the tournament, but West Germany scores the winning goal with six minutes to play in one of the most dramatic finals ever.

1958	Sweden	Brazil 5, Sweden 2	Just Fontaine, France (13)

The first internationally televised Cup sees the emergence of Brazil's Pelé, only 17, as a major star. He scores three goals in the semifinal and two more in the final against the host country.

1962	Chile	Brazil 3, Czechoslovakia 1	Six Players with 4 Goals[3]

Brazil successfully defends its title behind goal scorers Garrincha and Vava (four each for the tournament). Pelé is injured in an early match and sees little action.

1966	England	England 4, West Germany 2 (ET)	Eusébio, Port. (9)

The host team—with Bobby Charlton, captain Bobby Moore, Geoff Hurst, and goalkeeper Gordon Banks—thrills its fans with an extra time victory in the final; Hurst scores a hat trick.

Year	Host Country	Final Score, Championship Game	Leading Scorer, Country (goals)
1970	Mexico	Brazil 4, Italy 1	Gerd Müller, W. Ger. (10)

Standouts include Pelé and Jairzinho of Brazil, Cubillas of Peru, and German Gerd Müller, the tourney's leading scorer. Brazil keeps the Jules Rimet Trophy (named for the World Cup's founder) after winning for the third time.

| 1974 | West Germany | West Germany 2, Netherlands 1 | Grzegorz Lato, Pol. (7) |

The host country, led by sweeper Franz Beckenbauer and goal-scorer Paul Breitner, defeats Holland, featuring Johan Cruyff and an innovative team style known as "Total Football."

| 1978 | Argentina | Argentina 3, Netherlands 1 (ET) | Mario Kempes, Arg. (6) |

More than 100 nations participate in qualifying play, but the host wins again. Kempes (two goals in final), and Daniel Passarella power the blue-and-white.

| 1982 | Spain | Italy 3, West Germany 1 | Paolo Rossi, Italy (6) |

The number of final-round qualifiers is increased from 16 to 24, divided into six groups. Behind Rossi and goalkeeper/captain Dino Zoff, Italy wins its third World Cup.

| 1986 | Mexico | Argentina 3, West Germany 2 | Gary Lineker, Eng. (6) |

Argentina's Diego Maradona (5 goals, 5 assists) emerges as the king of world soccer, dominating the tournament. The final between Argentina and West Germany, with three goals in the last 20 minutes, is one of the most exciting ever.

| 1990 | Italy | West Germany 1, Argentina 0 | Salvatore Schillaci, Italy (6) |

Midfielder Lothar Matthäus and striker Jürgen Klinsmann lead a powerful German squad, which wins the Cup on a penalty with only five minutes to play against the defending champions.

| 1994 | United States | Brazil 0 (3), Italy 0 (2) (ET) | Hristo Stoitchkov, Bulgaria, Oleg Salenko, Russia (6) |

In the first World Cup hosted by the United States, Romario propels Brazil to its fourth Cup. The title match against Italy, led by Roberto Baggio, is decided by penalty kicks after a scoreless tie in regulation and 30 minutes of extra time.

| 1998 | France | France 3, Brazil 0 | Davor Suker, Croatia (6) |

The field expands to 32 teams in eight groups. The host country, surprisingly, wins for the sixth time. Midfielder Zinedine Zidane, who scores twice in the final, is France's inspirational player.

| 2002 | So. Korea/Japan | Brazil 2, Germany 0 | Ronaldo, Brazil (8) |

The men's tournament is held in Asia for the first time. Ronaldo scores twice in the second half of the final—the first-ever World Cup meeting between the soccer powers—as Brazil beats Germany for its fifth title.

| 2006 | Germany | Italy 1, France 1 (Italy wins 5–3 PK) | Miroslav Klose, Germany (5) |

To some, the much-anticipated 2006 World Cup final between Italy and France was ultimately an anticlimax of sorts. While the teams played to a nerve-wracking 1-1 tie during regulation, French star Zinedine Zidane's head-butt of Marco Materazzi late in the contest—and his subsequent ejection—marred what had been beautiful football. In the end the Cup was decided on penalty kicks, with Italy winning 5-3. Host Germany defeated Portugal 3-1 to finish third.

| 2010 | South Africa | Spain 1, Netherlands 0 (ET) | Diego Forlan, Uruguay, Thomas Muller, Germany, David Villa, Spain, Wesley Sneijder, Netherlands (5) |

In the first Cup ever held in Africa, Spain rebounded from an opening match loss to win their first World Cup and become the first European country to win outside of their home continent. The final game was marred by fouls as the referee handed out a record 14 yellow cards, but was ultimately won in the 116th minute on a goal from Spain's Andres Iniesta, the latest time a goal was scored in a World Cup Final.

Notes: (ET) = Extra Time, two 15-minute periods played if the game is tied after regulation. Both periods must be played. 1. Conen (Germany), Schiavio (Italy), and Nejedly (Czechoslovakia) 2. Uruguay's upset of Brazil in the 1950 World Cup was the decisive final match of a four-team round robin group, not a single championship game. 3. Albert (Hungary), Garrincha (Brazil), V. Ivanov (Soviet Union), Jerkovic (Yugoslavia), L. Sánchez (Chile), Vavá (Brazil).

HORSE RACING

Origins

The sport of thoroughbred horse racing has a worldwide appeal that is second only to soccer. Racing can be found across five continents, with particular interest in England and France and their former colonies, especially Australia, South Africa, and Hong Kong. Japan, too, has developed a flourishing horse racing industry. In the United States there are more than 100 tracks and in 2002 $15.1 billion was wagered in America alone.

It is an ancient sport as well, tracing back to the time of the domestication of the horse. Humans may have raced horses as early as 4500 B.C. The Olympic Games first featured racing (with both chariots and riders) in the seventh century B.C. One of the key moments in "modern" racing occurred in the 12th century, when English knights returned from the crusades with Arabian horses. These faster horses became popular, and over time many more were imported from their native lands and bred to stouter English mares.

During the 16th and 17th centuries, the royalty of Europe improved the speed and stamina of their horses by importing stallions from more distant regions. England's Charles II formalized the rules of racing in the mid-17th century. In the last decade of the 17th century and the early part of the 18th century, three stallions of Arabian blood achieved prominence: the Byerly Turk, the Darley Arabian, and the Godolphin Arabian (aka the Godolphin Barb).

The Basics

An average thoroughbred weighs about 1,000 pounds and is a little more than five feet tall. Many races are restricted by age. Horses' ages are determined by the year in which they were born, i.e. every horse in the Northern Hemisphere officially has January 1 as his/her birthday. Males are called colts until they turn five, after which they are called horses. Similarly, females are known as fillies until they turn five, then later as mares. A castrated male horse is called a gelding. Horses generally begin racing at two or three years of age.

Types of Races

Races can be run on either dirt courses or grass courses, called turf. They are run at short distances (called sprints) or longer distances (known as routes). Any race of at least a mile is considered a route. Steeplechase is a closely related sport that features thoroughbreds running longer distances over hurdles. They are sometimes run at the same tracks but more often are run at "hunt meets" around the country.

Races fall into four categories:

Maiden races are races for horses who have yet to win a race. A horse who wins his first race "breaks his maiden."

Claiming races are races in which each horse is for sale for a certain predetermined price before the race takes place. This brings together horses of similar ability.

In allowance races, the horses are not for sale but they do have to meet certain conditions to enter. (For example, they have not won two races in their career.) These are the races in which very good horses usually compete once they have broken their maidens but are not ready (or good enough) to compete in stakes.

Stakes races are the cream of the crop. They offer the highest purses (prize money paid by the track), and they feature the best horses. The Kentucky Derby and the Breeders' Cup races are the most prestigious stakes races in America.

Breeding

The industry of breeding racehorses is a huge business worldwide. More than 35,000 foals were registered in the United States in 2003. Successful sires can command tens of thousands of dollars in stud fees for getting mares in foal. Currently, the stud fee for the great sire, Storm Cat, is $500,000 for a live foal. The offspring can be sold for up to millions, particularly at the famous horse sales at Keeneland in Lexington, Ky., and Saratoga Springs, N.Y. The most expensive yearling ever sold at auction was Seattle Dancer in 1985 for $13.1 million. Breeding today is conducted with serious scientific knowledge with every aspect of a horse's lineage being evaluated.

Betting

There is betting on nearly all the thoroughbred racing in America. Bets include win (horse must finish first), place (horse must finish first or second), or show (horse must run first, second, or third). Also very popular are wagers like the double (pick the winners of two consecutive races) and the exacta (pick the first and second place horses in a given race). There are many other exotic wagers to choose from. A certain percentage of each dollar bet (called the takeout) goes to the racetrack. The rest of the pool of money on each wager is divided up among the winners. This is called parimutuel wagering.

History

1890's–1930

These years were a transitional time for racing as the sport moved from stamina intensive heats covering long distances for older horses to one focused on younger horses running much shorter distances for faster times.

A dominant sprinter called Domino became one of the first great modern champions when he broke the all-time earnings record as a two-year-old in 1893. His best son was Colin, who was undefeated in 15 starts; for 80 years he was the only major thoroughbred to retire undefeated.

Regret was the first filly to win the Kentucky Derby in 1915, going wire-to-wire as the favorite.

In 1919 a maiden named Sir Barton became the first horse to win the Kentucky Derby, the Preakness, and the Belmont Stakes. There was no "Triple Crown" at the time, however, as that distinction didn't exist until later. The honor was awarded to Sir Barton retroactively.

That same year also saw a big red colt named Man O' War race for the first time. Before he was done, he would win 19 of his 20 races and own track records at five different distances. By the middle of his career, few horses would even show up to face him. Man O' War's lone loss, at Saratoga, was so shocking that it forever changed the parlance of sports: his victor was a horse named Upset. The last race of Man O' War's career was a match race thrashing of Sir Barton. Many consider Man O' War the best horse to ever don two pairs of shoes.

1930's

The Depression was a boom time for racing, as many states opened racetracks to help attract money to empty coffers. Famous tracks such as Santa Anita, Del Mar, Keeneland, Hialeah, and Gulfstream Park opened during the decade.

In 1930 Gallant Fox, trained by Sunny Jim Fitzsimmons, won the Derby, Preakness, and Belmont (the Preakness came first at that point) and the achievement was dubbed as the Triple Crown. Gallant Fox continued the tradition of great horses, losing at Saratoga when he lost to a 100-1 shot named Jim Dandy in that year's Travers Stakes.

Five years later, Gallant Fox's son Omaha, also trained by Fitzsimmons, became the third horse to win the Triple Crown. Gallant Fox remains the only Triple Crown winner to sire a Triple Crown winner.

The best rivalry of the decade pitted War Admiral against Seabiscuit. War Admiral was a regally bred son of Man O' War who won the Triple Crown in 1937. Many thought War Admiral to be the best horse since his sire. Seabiscuit was a grandson of Man O' War, and his career had modest beginnings, as he was beaten in claiming races as a two-year-old and did nothing to distinguish himself in the first half of his third year. However, he blossomed under the care of Silent Tom Smith and set nine track records. He beat War Admiral in their famous match race in the fall of 1938 and closed out his career by returning from injury to win the Santa Anita Handicap, a prize that had eluded him until then.

1940's

The 1940's saw the emergence of four more Triple Crown winners, two of whom carried the devil's red and blue silks of Kentucky's Calumet Farm. Whirlaway, trained by Ben Jones, was first in 1941, and he went on to pass Seabiscuit's all-time earnings mark in 1942, when he captured Horse of the Year for the second time.

The temperamental Count Fleet, the 1943 Triple Crown winner, never finished off the board in 21 career starts.

Assault suffered from a series of physical ailments, but none prevented him from earning the decade's third Triple Crown in 1946. His rivalry with the extremely popular former claimer Stymie was among the best of the decade, with Assault winning five of their eight meetings, though it was Stymie who ended the decade as the all-time money earner.

Stymie's record didn't last long. Calumet Farm's Citation, trained by Jimmy Jones and usually piloted by Eddie Arcaro, won the Triple Crown in 1948 as part of his famous 16-race winning streak. He set the earnings record and became the first horse to earn more than $1 million with victory in the Hollywood Gold Cup in 1951.

1950's

Alfred Vanderbilt's Native Dancer, known as the Gray Ghost, would have retired a perfect 22 for 22 had he not encountered bad luck in the 1953 Kentucky Derby, which he lost by a head to Dark Star. He was named Horse of the Year as both a two-year-old and a four-year-old.

Tom Fool won the honor in the year between, 1953. He was a perfect 10 for 10 as a four- and five-year-old.

Nashua and Swaps fought one of the great rivalries in racing's storied history. Nashua was the two-year-old champion of 1954 but Swaps upset him in the 1955 Derby. They hooked up for a match race in 1956, and Nashua achieved his revenge, winning by more than six lengths.

Many consider the 1957 Kentucky Derby the greatest ever. Gallant Man appeared the winner, but jockey Bill Shoemaker misjudged the finish line, allowing Iron Liege to pass him. Bold Ruler and Round Table were also in the field. Bold Ruler went on to win the Preakness and was named top horse in 1957. Round Table won 43 of 66 races on both turf and dirt during his career and was Horse of the Year in 1958.

1960's

The late-blooming gelding Kelso, trained by Carl Hanford and owned by Mrs. Richard C. duPont, dominated racing in the early part of the decade, winning Horse of the Year five years in a row from 1960 through 1964. He retired as the all-time money earner with nearly $2 million in combined purses.

The Canadian-bred Northern Dancer won the Kentucky Derby in a record time of two minutes flat but was denied the Triple Crown when he lost the 1964 Belmont to Quadrangle. Overall, he would win 14 of 18 races and later become one of the most influential stallions of the century. Ogden Phipps's Buckpasser was another horse that earned more than $1 million. He missed the Triple Crown in 1966 but was Horse of the Year anyway and won 25 of 31 races overall.

One of the greatest races of the decade saw Buckpasser take on Dr. Fager and Damascus in the 1967 Woodward Stakes. Damascus won that day and would win Horse of the Year. In 1968 it was Dr. Fager's turn to win the honor as he proved himself one of the most versatile and talented horses of the decade.

1970's

The advent of Off-Track Betting facilities as well as the growing popularity of state lotteries and other forms of legalized gambling started to erode the numbers of people who would go see live racing. However, wager amounts only kept increasing.

In 1970 Bill Shoemaker broke Johnny Longden's record for most wins by a jockey (6,032). Shoe's record of 8,833 stood until 1999, when Laffit Pincay Jr. surpassed him.

Secretariat, believed by many to be the greatest horse in history, won the Triple Crown in 1973. A big red colt by Bold Ruler, Secretariat had been a champion two-year-old and was wildly popular during his Triple Crown run. He set a track record that still stands in winning the Kentucky Derby in 1:59 2/5, and in the Belmont he beat the second place horse by 31 lengths. When ESPN named its 50 greatest athletes of the century nearly three decades later, Secretariat was the only nonhuman on the list.

Ruffian was a beautiful black filly who was undefeated in 10 career starts and had never seen the tail of another horse during a race. She took on Derby winner Foolish Pleasure in a match race in 1975. In one of the sport's darkest moments, she broke down during the running, and she is buried near the finish line at Belmont Park.

Seattle Slew was another undefeated two-year-old, who went on to win the Triple Crown in 1977.

The great rivalry of the 70's pitted Harbor View Farm's Affirmed against Calumet Farm's Alydar. As two-year-olds, Affirmed beat Alydar in four of six races. At three years, Affirmed also got the best of his rival, winning each of the Triple Crown races with Alydar in second each time. Alydar did achieve a measure of revenge over Affirmed in a controversial win by disqualification in the Travers.

In the 1979 Jockey Club Gold Cup, Affirmed took on Spectacular Bid, who had won both the Derby and Preakness. Affirmed won by three-quarters of a length in the last race of his career. He would retire as the all-time money earner with $2.3 million, a record soon to be broken by Spectacular Bid, who never lost another race after that and won 26 of 30 races with nearly $2.8 million in earnings.

1980's

No filly had won the Kentucky Derby since Regret, but two horses accomplished the feat in the 80's: Genuine Risk in 1980 and D. Wayne Lukas's Winning Colors in 1988.

A six-year-old gelding named John Henry made quite a splash in 1981, winning stakes races on both coasts on both turf and dirt. The temperamental and beloved star raced through age nine, banking nearly $6.6 million in the process.

The biggest story of the decade though, was the advent of the Breeders' Cup, a series of high-purse championship races to be held in one day toward the end of the year at a rotating site. The inaugural event took place in 1984 and was an instant success.

John Henry's earnings record was surpassed a few years later by Alysheba. The latter's bid for the Triple Crown was denied by his rival Bet Twice, but he raced again as a four-year-old and was Horse of the Year. In his final start, Alysheba won the Breeders' Cup Classic, a race he was denied by a nose as a three-year-old. He finished with almost $6.7 million in earnings.

One of the most exciting races in the history of the Breeders' Cup occurred earlier that day. Ogden Phipps's bay filly Personal Ensign, trained by Shug McGaughey, became the first horse since Colin to retire undefeated, a perfect 10 for 10, including a victory over the boys in the Whitney. She barely beat Winning Colors in the Distaff.

The decade went out with a bang with a great rivalry between California-bred Sunday Silence and New York-bred Easy Goer. Easy Goer was a champion as a two-year-old and he denied Sunday Silence the Triple Crown but in the end, it was Sunday Silence who owned a 3-1 record over his adversary, with wins in the Derby, Preakness, and the Breeders' Cup.

1990's Through Present

Allen Paulson's Cigar, trained by Bill Mott and ridden by Jerry Bailey, was the horse of the 90's. He was Horse of the Year twice, equaled the great Citation's win streak of 16 races in a row and won just a hair under $10 million.

Skip Away fell just short of Cigar's earnings record but was a star from ages three through six, winning Horse of the Year in 1998.

Serena's Song set a record for money won by a filly or mare by earning just under $3.3 million and beating males twice in the process.

In recent years, several horses have gone into the Belmont with a chance to become the first Triple Crown winner since Affirmed. All have seen their bids fall short. They include Silver Charm in '97, Real Quiet in '98, Charismatic '99, War Emblem in '02, Funny Cide in '03, and Smarty Jones in '04.

Barbaro easily won the Kentucky Derby in 2006, and was a huge favorite among fans and bettors to win the Triple Crown, but he stumbled and broke his right leg at the start of the Preakness. A series of highly publicized surgeries on the leg was successful, but eventually laminitis set in and Barbaro was euthanized in January, 2007.

The Triple Crown

Much of the interest in American racing is centered on the Triple Crown, a series of three races in the spring for three-year-olds. It consists of the Kentucky Derby, run at 1 1/4 miles at Churchill Downs on the first Saturday in May; the Preakness, contested two weeks after at 1 3/16 miles at Pimlico in Baltimore; and the Belmont Stakes, held three weeks after that at 1 1/2 miles at New York's Belmont Park. Only 11 horses have won all three Triple Crown races:

1919—Sir Barton
1930—Gallant Fox
1935—Omaha
1937—War Admiral
1941—Whirlaway
1943—Count Fleet
1946—Assault
1948—Citation
1973—Secretariat
1977—Seattle Slew
1978—Affirmed

Kentucky Derby Winners

1875	Aristides	1910	Donau	1945	Hoop, Jr.	1980	Genuine Risk
1876	Vagrant	1911	Meridan	1946	Assault	1981	Pleasant Colony
1877	Baden Baden	1912	Worth	1947	Jet Pilot	1982	Gato del Sol
1878	Day Star	1913	Donerail	1948	Citation	1983	Sunny's Halo
1879	Lord Murphy	1914	Old Rosebud	1949	Ponder	1984	Swale
1880	Fonso	1915	Regret	1950	Middleground	1985	Spend A Buck
1881	Hindoo	1916	George Smith	1951	Count Turf	1986	Ferdinand
1882	Apollo	1917	Omar Khayyam	1952	Hill Gail	1987	Alysheba
1883	Leonatus	1918	Exterminator	1953	Dark Star	1988	Winning Colors
1884	Buchanan	1919	Sir Barton	1954	Determine	1989	Sunday Silence
1885	Joe Cotton	1920	Paul Jones	1955	Swaps	1990	Unbridled
1886	Ben Ali	1921	Behave Yourself	1956	Needles	1991	Strike the Gold
1887	Montrose	1922	Morvich	1957	Iron Liege	1992	Lil E. Tee
1888	MacBeth II	1923	Zev	1958	Tim Tam	1993	Sea Hero
1889	Spokane	1924	Black Gold	1959	Tomy Lee	1994	Go For Gin
1890	Riley	1925	Flying Ebony	1960	Venetian Way	1995	Thunder Gulch
1891	Kingman	1926	Bubbling Over	1961	Carry Back	1996	Grindstone
1892	Azra	1927	Whiskery	1962	Decidedly	1997	Silver Charm
1893	Lookout	1928	Reigh Count	1963	Chateaugay	1998	Real Quiet
1894	Chant	1929	Clyde Van Dusen	1964	Northern Dancer	1999	Charismatic
1895	Halma	1930	Gallant Fox	1965	Lucky Debonair	2000	Fusaichi Pegasus
1896	Ben Brush	1931	Twenty Grand	1966	Kauai King	2001	Monarchos
1897	Typhoon II	1932	Burgoo King	1967	Proud Clarion	2002	War Emblem
1898	Plaudit	1933	Brokers Tip	1968	Forward Pass	2003	Funny Cide
1899	Manuel	1934	Cavalcade	1969	Majestic Prince	2004	Smarty Jones
1900	Lieut. Gibson	1935	Omaha	1970	Dust Commander	2005	Giacomo
1901	His Eminence	1936	Bold Venture	1971	Canonero II	2006	Barbaro
1902	Alan-a-Dale	1937	War Admiral	1972	Riva Ridge	2007	Street Sense
1903	Judge Himes	1938	Lawrin	1973	Secretariat	2008	Big Brown
1904	Elwood	1939	Johnstown	1974	Cannonade	2009	Mine That Bird
1905	Agile	1940	Gallahadion	1975	Foolish Pleasure	2010	Super Saver
1906	Sir Huon	1941	Whirlaway	1976	Bold Forbes	2011	Animal Kingdom
1907	Pink Star	1942	Shut Out	1977	Seattle Slew		
1908	Stone Street	1943	Count Fleet	1978	Affirmed		
1909	Wintergreen	1944	Pensive	1979	Spectacular Bid		

OLYMPIC GAMES

The Olympic Games are held every four years—in summer and winter—at a different site. Athletes from nearly every country compete for personal and national honor in a variety of sports. Television broadcasts show the Games in every corner of the globe, with recent audiences estimated to exceed 3 billion people.

The Olympics originated in ancient Greece, beginning in 776 B.C., as a festival to honor Zeus. They are named for the town of Olympia, a sacred site in the western Peloponnesus where athletes converged from far-flung city-states for a month-long festival of religious rites and athletic competition. The Olympics were revived in 1896, when athletes from 14 nations gathered in Athens, Greece, for the first modern Games. With exceptions for World War I (1916) and World War II (1940 and 1944), the modern Summer Games have been held every four years since 1896. The Olympic Winter Games, featuring competition in skiing, skating, ice hockey, and other cold-weather sports, commenced in 1924. The Winter and Summer Games followed the same quadrennial cycle through 1992, after which a staggered two-year interval was instituted.

Like their ancient predecessors, the modern Olympics were conceived as a celebration of peace, international cooperation, and pure love of sport. These ideals have often proved elusive, however, as political rancor—to the point of boycott and terrorist violence—has marred several Games. The original restriction that only amateur athletes could compete, rigorously enforced by the modern founders, has also been relaxed. Although Olympic athletes today receive no direct remuneration for taking part, highly paid professionals now are allowed to compete in most sports. Whereas ancient Olympic champions were crowned with olive wreaths, hailed as heroes, and enshrined in a sacred grove, modern Olympic champions are awarded gold medals—silver for runners-up and bronze for third-place finishers—and some earn lucrative commercial endorsements after the Games. Still, the athletes compete for national pride as much as for individual honor, and the ranking of nations by number of medals won (while not an official statistic) is closely watched. The rivalry among countries is often intense, yet most participants enjoy the spirit of celebration, friendly competition, and shared love of sport that prevails at most Games.

The International Olympic Committee (I.O.C.), based in Lausanne, Switzerland, is the governing authority of the Summer and Winter Games. In addition to establishing and administering the Olympic rules, the I.O.C. selects the host cities every four years, accepts or rejects new sports and events on the Olympic program, and oversees the efforts of various other bodies. These include the National Olympic Committee (N.O.C.) for each participating country, the Olympic Organizing Committee (O.O.C.) for each host city, and the International Federation (IF) governing competition in each sport. Each N.O.C., such as the United States Olympic Committee, is responsible for the representation of its respective country, including all necessary arrangements when it hosts the Games. The O.O.C., in conjunction with the N.O.C., raises funds, constructs venues, and oversees the myriad logistical details involved with the two-and-a- half weeks of competition, such as living quarters, dining, transportation, and communication. Federations for the individual sports establish the rules of play, monitor venue construction, supervise competition, and are responsible for officiating or judging. They also lobby the I.O.C. for the addition of new events to the Olympic program.

History

Ancient Games

The Olympics were sacred to the ancient Greeks, and nothing was allowed to interfere with them—not even war. A truce was called and trade ceased during the month-long festival; no one bearing arms could enter Olympia. According to historians, competition in the first 13 Olympics consisted of only one footrace—called the stade—of about 200 yards (183 meters), or the length of the stadium. The first known Olympic champion was a cook named Coroebus from the nearby city of Elis.

The Games were held at four-year intervals, called "Olympiads," which later Greeks began numbering from the first Panhellenic festival in 776 B.C. Over the centuries, other events were added to the program, including the double-stade and longer footraces; wrestling; the five-event pentathlon (jumping, javelin, sprinting, discus, and wrestling); boxing; chariot and horse races; and the pancration (a brutal combination of wrestling and boxing). Only men were allowed to compete, and in the nude. The Games attracted as many as 40,000 spectators, but women were not allowed to attend. In addition to athletic events, the Olympic festivals included contests in music, poetry, and oratory. (Exhibitions and performances in the arts remain an official, if often overlooked, part of the modern Olympic program.)

By the fifth century B.C., Olympia was the holiest site in Greece, and the ceremonial Games reached their peak. In 146 B.C., after Greece became part of the Roman empire, the Olympics were moved to Rome, and the original purpose was largely forgotten. The Games finally were banned in A.D. 393 by the Roman emperor Theodosius I, a convert to Christianity, who deemed them pagan.

Modern Games

A modern version of the Olympics was the idea of a French aristocrat named Pierre de Coubertin in the 1880's. Coubertin had advanced educational programs in France according to the Greek ideal of physical and mental training. Excavations at ancient Olympia fired Courbertin's imagination, and he began pursuing the idea of an Olympic revival. By 1894 he had won the support of an international athletic congress and succeeded in creating the I.O.C., of which he became the first secretary-general. The first modern Olympic Games were held in 1896 in Athens, and moved to other cities every four years.

Summer Games, 1896–2016

Year	Olympiad	Host City, Country	Nations Represented	Athletes Men	Women	Events
1896	I	**Athens, Greece**	14	245	—	43

King George I of Greece opens the first modern Games on April 6, before a crowd of 80,000. James Connolly of the U.S. becomes the first Olympic champion in more than 1,500 years with his victory in the triple jump. Spyridon Louis, a Greek shepherd, is hailed as a national hero for winning the marathon. The United States takes 11 of 43 events; the host country wins 10.

Year	Olympiad	Host City, Country	Nations Represented	Athletes Men	Women	Events
1900	II	**Paris, France**	24	1,206	19	87

Coinciding with the Paris World's Fair, the competition is spread out over five months. The Paris Games gain wider international acceptance than the Athens revival—a thousand more athletes participated—but the public takes scant notice. Women make their first appearance: the first female champion is Britain's Charlotte Cooper in tennis. Alvin Kraenzlein of the United States wins four track-and-field competitions. France leads all countries with 25 victories in 87 events.

Year	Olympiad	Host City, Country	Nations Represented	Athletes Men	Women	Events
1904	III	**St. Louis, U.S.A.**	13	681	8	89

The first Olympics held in the United States, the St. Louis Games are overshadowed by another World's Fair. Again the events are spread out over months, and again the public lacks interest. The cost and time of travel also limit participation. Americans dominate competition, earning 70 gold medals (awarded for the first time); Archie Hahn wins three sprint races, Ray Ewry repeats as champion in three jumping events, and Thomas Hicks captures the marathon.

Year	Olympiad	Host City, Country	Nations Represented	Athletes Men	Women	Events
1908	IV	**London, England**	22	1,999	36	109

After an interim Games (later declared unofficial) at Athens in 1906, the Olympics open a new chapter in London. Without the distraction of a world exhibition, the 1908 Games entertain an avid public at specially constructed venues. Held from April to October, they include the first official Opening Ceremony. The host country again wins the most events, 56. In a dramatic marathon, Italy's Dorando Pietri collapses near the finish line, is helped across it by officials, and then disqualified; John Joseph Hayes of the United States is declared the winner.

Year	Olympiad	Host City, Country	Nations Represented	Athletes Men	Women	Events
1912	V	**Stockholm, Sweden**	29	2,490	57	102

A model of efficiency and organization, these Games feature the best facilities yet and attract large crowds. For the first time, athletes from every continent participate. The standout is Native American Jim Thorpe, winner of both the pentathlon and decathlon. The I.O.C. strips Thorpe of his medals a year later for alleged violation of the rules of amateurism—only to restore them posthumously in 1982. Sweden and the United States lead all nations with 24 gold medals each.

Year	Olympiad	Host City, Country	Nations Represented	Athletes		Events
				Men	Women	
1916	VI	**Berlin, Germany**	—————————Canceled due to war—————————-			

Germany, unanimously selected to host the VI Olympics, believes that any war will be short and proceeds with preparations. But the prolonged Great War forces cancellation.

| 1920 | VII | **Antwerp, Belgium** | 29 | 2,591 | 78 | 154 |

War-weary Belgium revives the Olympic spirit. The Central Powers (Germany, Austria, Turkey, Bulgaria, and Hungary) are excluded, and an atmosphere of peace prevails. The Olympic flag and Athletes' Oath are introduced. The Finnish distance runner Paavo Nurmi takes three gold medals and one bronze; Italy's Nedo Nadi wins five golds in fencing; and France's tennis star Suzanne Lenglen takes two golds and a bronze. U.S. athletes claim 41 first-place finishes.

| 1924 | VIII | **Paris, France** | 44 | 2,956 | 136 | 126 |

Growing acceptance of the Games is reflected by increases in the number of nations, athletes, spectators, and journalists who attend. "Firsts" in Paris include an Olympic Village to house the athletes, live radio broadcasts, and introduction of the Olympic motto. Nurmi, "the Flying Finn," is the star with five gold medals; American swimmer Johnny Weissmuller claims three. The United States again leads all nations by winning 45 events.

| 1928 | IX | **Amsterdam, Holland** | 46 | 2,724 | 290 | 109 |

The Olympic flame is lit during the Opening Ceremony for the first time. Track-and-field and gymnastics events for women are added to the program. Athletes from a record 28 countries, including the first from Asia, win gold medals. The United States tops the list with 22; Germany, reinstated after 16 years, finishes second with 10. Nurmi and Weissmuller add to their medal totals and legends.

| 1932 | X | **Los Angeles, U.S.A.** | 37 | 1,281 | 127 | 116 |

Worldwide depression and the cost of travel keep many countries away, but the facilities—including the 100,000-seat Los Angeles Coliseum—are top-notch. Innovations include the three-level podium for medal ceremonies and automatic timing for track events. Mildred "Babe" Didrikson, perhaps the greatest female athlete of the century, wins two gold medals and one silver in track and field. Americans continue their domination, winning 44 events.

| 1936 | XI | **Berlin, Germany** | 49 | 3,738 | 328 | 129 |

The first torch relay belies the spirit of the so-called Nazi Olympics. Hitler stages a lavish Games as a giant propaganda event, seeking to prove Aryan supremacy. The undisputed star, however, is Jesse Owens, an African American whose record four gold medals in track and field embarrass the German leader. The host country nevertheless wins the most events, 33.

| 1940 | XII | **Tokyo, Japan** | —————————Canceled due to war—————————- | | | |

The IOC feels that holding the Games in Asia will enhance the Olympic movement, but Japan resigns as host after the outbreak of war with the U.S.S.R. in 1937. Helsinki is chosen as the new site, but World War II forces cancellation.

| 1944 | XIII | **London, England** | —————————Canceled due to war—————————- | | | |

London is designated as the site of the 1944 Games, but continued fighting in Europe and Asia make the event impossible.

| 1948 | XIV | **London, England** | 59 | 3,714 | 385 | 136 |

Facilities are modest as London recovers from war, but attendance and enthusiasm run high. Japan and Germany are barred, and the U.S.S.R. refuses to take part. The 1948 Games are the first to be broadcast on home television. Fanny Blankers-Koen of the Netherlands wins four gold medals in sprints and hurdles. American Bob Mathias, 17, becomes the youngest male to win an athletic event, taking the first of his two decathlon titles. The United States wins 38 gold medals.

| 1952 | XV | **Helsinki, Finland** | 69 | 4,407 | 518 | 149 |

The atmosphere in Helsinki makes the 1952 Games one of the most memorable, even though the Soviet bloc nations insist on separate quarters. The most impressive achievement belongs to Czech distance runner Emil Zátopek, who wins the 5,000 meters, 10,000 meters, and the marathon. U.S. sprinter and hurdler Harrison Dillard repeats his double-gold performance of 1948; Soviet gymnast Viktor Chukarin wins four gold medals and two silvers. U.S. athletes earn 40 golds.

| 1956 | XVI | **Melbourne, Australia** | 67 | 2,813 | 371 | 145 |

The first Olympics in the Southern Hemisphere, the 1956 Games are held in November-December (Australian summer) and present training problems for some athletes. Several countries withdraw over the Soviet invasion of Hungary, the Suez

Year	Olympiad	Host City, Country	Nations Represented	Athletes Men	Women	Events

crisis, and other world events. Soviet gymnast Larissa Latynina wins four of her country's 37 gold medals, plus a silver and bronze. American discus thrower Al Oerter wins the first of his four straight Olympic golds.

Year	Olympiad	Host City, Country	Nations Represented	Men	Women	Events
1960	XVII	Rome, Italy	83	4,738	610	150

The Olympics return to the city where the ancient Games ended; satellite TV broadcasts begin. More countries win medals (44) than at any previous Games; the U.S.S.R. tops the list with 43 golds and 103 medals in all. Standouts include the barefoot Ethiopian marathoner Abebe Bikila; Soviet gymnasts Latynina and Boris Shakhlin; and sprinter Wilma Rudolph, decathlete Rafer Johnson, and light-heavyweight boxer Cassius Clay (later Muhammad Ali), all of the United States.

1964	XVIII	Tokyo, Japan	93	4,457	683	163

The Olympics come to Asia, and a resurgent Japan spends heavily on new sports facilities and city infrastructure. World and Olympic records are broken almost daily. Don Schollander of the United States becomes the first swimmer to earn four gold medals in one Games. Abebe Bikila, this time running in shoes, becomes the first to repeat as marathon champion. Latynina boosts her career medal count to a record 18, including 9 gold. U.S. athletes win 90 medals, 36 gold.

1968	XIX	Mexico City, Mexico	112	4,750	780	172

Political and social unrest—in the host country, the United States, and elsewhere—intrude as never before. Two African-American track stars give the black power salute at the medal ceremony. Mexico City's high altitude is the bane of distance runners but contributes to a total of 34 world and 38 Olympic records. Most astounding is Bob Beamon's mark (29'-2 1/2") in the long jump. Debbie Meyer, also of the United States, becomes the first swimmer to win three individual events. Czech gymnast Vera Cáslavská earns six medals, four of them gold.

1972	XX	Munich, West Germany	122	6,659	1,171	195

The Olympic spirit is shattered in an assault by Palestinian terrorists that leaves 11 Israeli athletes, one policeman, and the five terrorists dead. Under a pall, the Games continue two days later. Two swimmers stand out: Mark Spitz of the United States wins a record seven gold medals, and Australian Shane Gould takes three golds (and five medals in all). Soviet gymnast Olga Korbut is the darling of the Games, and the U.S.S.R. stuns the U.S. in men's basketball. Soviet athletes take home 50 gold medals.

1976	XXI	Montreal, Canada	92	4,781	1,247	198

Twenty-four African nations boycott because of the participation of New Zealand, whose rugby team had played a match in racially segregated South Africa. Security is heavy and some facilities unfinished, but the XXI Olympics go smoothly. Romanian gymnast Nadia Comaneci, only 14, dazzles judges and charms audiences. Soviet athletes garner 125 medals, 49 gold. For the first time, a host country fails to win a gold medal.

1980	XXII	Moscow, U.S.S.R.	80	4,093	1,124	203

Political controversy again mars the Games, the first held in a communist country. The United States leads a large-scale boycott over Soviet military action in Afghanistan, reducing the number of participating nations to the lowest total since 1956. Aleksandr Dityanin continues the Soviet tradition of excellence in gymnastics with a record eight medals. Heavyweight boxer Teófilo Stevenson of Cuba wins his third straight gold. The U.S.S.R. hauls 197 medals, the most ever.

1984	XXIII	Los Angeles, U.S.A.	140	5,230	1,567	221

Supported by some 30 commercial sponsors, the L.A. Games are the first privately funded Olympics in history. The Soviet Union leads a retaliatory boycott, but participation is wider than ever. American Carl Lewis equals Jesse Owens's feat of four gold medals in track and field. Britain's Daley Thompson repeats as decathlon champion. Joan Benoit of the U.S. wins the inaugural women's marathon. The U.S. leads all nations with 174 medals.

1988	XXIV	Seoul, South Korea	159	6,279	2,186	237

Returning to Asia, the Games are restored to near-full participation by I.O.C. member nations; only Cuba and Ethiopia stay away. Ben Johnson of Canada is stripped of his gold medal for the 100 meters after testing positive for banned substances. America's Florence Griffith-Joyner dominates the women's sprints, swimmer Matt Biondi wins five golds, and Greg Louganis repeats as champion in both diving events. U.S. athletes earn 132 medals in all.

Year	Olympiad	Host City, Country	Nations Represented	Athletes Men	Athletes Women	Events
1992	XXV	Barcelona, Spain	169	6,659	2708	257

For the first time in 20 years, every country with an N.O.C. is represented. Among them are a united Germany, four Balkan states, and a "Unified Team" (EUN) representing former Soviet republics. EUN athletes take 112 medals, 45 gold. Gymnast Vitaly Scherbo accounts for six of the golds. Men's basketball is open to professionals, and the American "Dream Team" dominates. Splendid facilities and cultural events contribute to one of the best Games ever.

1996	XXVI	Atlanta, U.S.A.	197	6,797	3,523	271

The centennial modern Games are disrupted by a bomb explosion in the Olympic complex that kills one person and injures 110 others. In competition, a record 79 countries earn medals and 53 win gold; the United States tops the list with 101 in all, 44 gold. Runners Michael Johnson of the U.S. and Marie-José Pérec of France both achieve a difficult double, winning the 200 meters and the 400 meters. U.S. women gymnasts are surprise winners in the team event.

2000	XXVII	Sydney, Australia	199	6,582	4,069	300

Upbeat, positive, and bigger than ever, the Sydney Games go off without a hitch. North and South Korea march together in the Opening Ceremony. The percentage of women competitors (38 percent) is the highest ever. Cathy Freeman, an Australian Aborigine, lights the Olympic torch and becomes a national hero with a victory in the 400 meters. Russian gymnast Aleksei Nemov wins six medals. Sprinter Marion Jones takes three gold and two bronze, contributing to the U.S. total of 97.

2004	XXVIII	Athens, Greece	202	6,296	4,329	301

Despite fears of terrorism and the rush to finish the infrastructure before the games began, Athens 2004 saw the largest participation in Olympic history, both in terms of nations (202) and athletes (10,625).

2008	XXIX	Beijing, China	205	10,500(men/women)		302

The lead-up to the games was dominated by concerns over China's human rights record and the oppressive air pollution that hung over the country. By the conclusion of the games those ideas were replaced by the blinding speed of Jamaica's Usain Bolt, world records in 100m and 200m dash, and the fluid motion of the United States Michael Phelps, a record eight swimming gold medals.

2012	XXX	London, England				
2016	XXXI	Rio de Janeiro, Brazil				

Winter Games, 1924–2014

Year	Olympiad	Host City, Country	Nations Represented	Athletes Men	Athletes Women	Events
1924	I	Chamonix, France	16	245	13	16

Originally called International Winter Sports Week, the festival is officially sanctioned as the first Olympic Winter Games by the I.O.C. in 1925. U.S. speed skater Charles Jewtraw wins the first gold; Finland's Clas Thunberg medals in all five speed skating events. Norway and Finland combine for 28 of the 48 medals.

1928	II	St. Moritz, Switzerland	25	438	26	14

The original idea that one nation should host the Summer and Winter Games in the same year is abandoned. Inclement weather disrupts a number of events. Norway's Sonja Henie, 15, wins the first of three straight singles figure skating competitions; Thunberg adds two more gold medals. Norway claims 15 medals in all, six gold.

1932	III	Lake Placid, U.S.A.	17	231	21	14

The Games go on despite worldwide depression, but participation is down and more than half of all competitors are American or Canadian. Americans John Shea and Irving Jaffee sweep the speed skating events with two golds each, and the host country wins six of the 14 events.

Year	Olympiad	Host City, Country	Nations Represented	Athletes Men	Women	Events
1936	IV	Garmisch-Partenkirchen, Germany	28	588	80	17

Adolf Hitler declares open the first of two Olympic festivals on German soil in 1936. Alpine skiing events are added to the program. Norway's Ivar Ballangrud wins three gold medals and one silver in the four speed skating events, and Henie skates to her third title. The Norwegians garner 15 medals in all.

1940	—————————————————Canceled due to war———————————————————

1944	—————————————————Canceled due to war———————————————————

1948	V	St. Moritz, Switzerland	28	592	77	22

Neutral Switzerland is awarded the Games; St. Moritz, with facilities intact, is again the host. Germany and Japan are barred. Slalom and downhill events for men and women are added. France's Henri Oreiller wins two golds and a bronze in Alpine skiing. Norway and Sweden tie with four gold medals and 10 in all.

1952	VI	Oslo, Norway	30	585	109	22

The first held in a Scandinavian country, the 1952 Games attract large, enthusiastic crowds. Speed skater Hjallis Andersen of the home team captures three gold medals. Andrea Mead of the U.S. wins the slalom and giant slalom. American Dick Button repeats as men's figure skating champion. Norway tops all nations with 16 medals, seven gold.

1956	VII	Cortina D'Ampezzo, Italy	32	688	132	24

The first Winter Games to be telecast live, the Cortina Olympics also feature the debut of the U.S.S.R.—which immediately wins more medals (seven gold, 16 in all) than any other country. The individual star is Austria's Toni Sailer, who wins all three men's Alpine skiing events.

1960	VIII	Squaw Valley, U.S.A.	30	522	143	27

The Winter Games come to California, and Walt Disney produces the opening and closing ceremonies. Biathlon and women's speed skating are added to the program. The U.S. hockey team upsets the U.S.S.R. to win gold, but the Soviets lead all nations with 21 medals.

1964	IX	Innsbruck, Austria	36	891	200	34

Mild weather threatens competition, and Austrian troops haul in snow from higher elevations. East and West Germany compete as a combined team. The U.S.S.R. again heads the medals list, with 25 (11 gold); Lydia Skoblikova wins all four women's speed skating events.

1968	X	Grenoble, France	37	947	211	35

An unlikely host, the industrial city of Grenoble stages events in widespread locations. Jean-Claude Killy of the host country sweeps men's Alpine skiing. The Soviet pairs figure skating team of Beloussova and Protopopov repeats as champions. Women's figure skater Peggy Fleming wins the only U.S. gold. Norway earns 14 medals.

1972	XI	Sapporo, Japan	35	800	206	35

The first held outside Europe or the United States, the Sapporo Games are the most extravagant to date. Austrian skiing star Karl Schranz is barred for violating the I.O.C.'s rules of amateurism. Dutch speed skater Ard Schenk is the outstanding male athlete with three golds. The U.S.S.R. wins the medals race with 16 in all, eight gold.

1976	XII	Innsbruck, Austria	37	892	231	37

The Games return to Innsbruck after voters in Denver, the IOC's initial choice, reject plans. West Germany's Rosi Mittermaier takes two golds and a silver in women's Alpine skiing; Austrian daredevil Franz Klammer thrills spectators in the men's downhill. Dorothy Hamill of the United States earns gold in figure skating. Soviet athletes win 27 medals, 13 gold.

Year	Olympiad	Host City, Country	Nations Represented	Athletes Men	Women	Events
1980	XIII	**Lake Placid, U.S.A.**	37	839	233	38

Outstanding performances overshadow transportation problems. America's Eric Heiden wins all five men's speed skating events. Ingemar Stenmark of Sweden and Hanni Wenzel of tiny Liechtenstein win the slalom and giant slalom for men and women. The U.S. hockey team stuns the U.S.S.R. and later wins gold against Finland. Soviet athletes capture 22 medals in all.

Year	Olympiad	Host City, Country	Nations Represented	Men	Women	Events
1984	XIV	**Sarajevo, Yugoslavia**	49	1,000	274	39

The city will be decimated by civil war in following years, but the 1984 Games are remembered for a spirit of friendliness and goodwill. Standouts include Finland's Marja-Liisa Hämäläinen in Nordic skiing, East Germany's Katarina Witt and America's Scott Hamilton in figure skating, and the British ice dancing team of Torvill and Dean. East Germany leads all with nine gold medals.

Year	Olympiad	Host City, Country	Nations Represented	Men	Women	Events
1988	XV	**Calgary, Canada**	57	1,110	313	46

The Games are expanded from 12 to 16 days, new skiing events are added, and demonstration sports are included for the first time. Finnish ski jumper Matti Nykänen soars to three golds, Italy's charismatic Alberto Tomba takes two Alpine events, and Katarina Witt repeats in figure skating. The U.S.S.R. tallies 29 medals, 11 gold.

Year	Olympiad	Host City, Country	Nations Represented	Men	Women	Events	Nations
1992	XVI	**Albertville, France**	64	1,313	488	57	

Most former Soviet republics participate as the "Unified Team" (EUN), but several compete under their own flags. The two Germanys are reunited and top all nations with 26 medals. Norwegians win every men's cross-country skiing race. Bonnie Blair of the United States and Gunda Niemann of Germany win two golds each in women's speed skating.

Year	Olympiad	Host City, Country	Nations Represented	Men	Women	Events
1994	XVII	**Lillehammer, Norway**	67	1,217	522	61

The two-year interval between Winter and Summer Games is instituted, and the atmosphere is festive. Newly independent Soviet republics compete as separate teams. Still, Russia tops the medals list with 23, 11 of them gold; Lyubov Yegorova wins three golds in women's cross-country skiing. Norway's Johann Koss triples in speed skating.

Year	Olympiad	Host City, Country	Nations Represented	Men	Women	Events
1998	XVIII	**Nagano, Japan**	72	1,488	814	68

Snowboarding, curling, and women's hockey are added to the program. Norway's Bjørn Dählie wins three gold medals in Nordic skiing, bringing his career total to a record eight, plus four silver. At 15, American figure skater Tara Lipinski becomes the youngest to win an individual event. German athletes take home 29 medals, 12 gold.

Year	Olympiad	Host City, Country	Nations Represented	Men	Women	Events
2002	XIX	**Salt Lake City, U.S.A.**	77	1,513	886	78

With nearly 2,400 athletes, the 2002 Winter Games are the largest yet. A record 18 countries win gold medals; Germany heads the list with 12 (35 medals overall). A judging scandal mars the pairs figure skating competition, and two sets of gold medals are awarded. Croatia's Janica Kostelic wins three gold medals and one silver in women's Alpine skiing.

Year	Olympiad	Host City, Country	Nations Represented	Men	Women	Events
2006	XX	**Turin, Italy**	80	1,598	960	84

With 2,508 athletes participating, the Turin Olympics were the largest in history. Once again, Germany headed the medal count with 29, followed by the United States with 25 and Austria with 23. The athlete winning the most individual medals was Canada's speed skater Cindy Klassen (five total; one gold, two silver, two bronze).

Year	Olympiad	Host City, Country	Nations Represented	Men	Women	Events
2010	XXI	**Vancouver, Canada**	82	2,629(men/women)		86

A heat wave in Canada forced organizers to truck in snow from the surrounding mountains, not a great omen. Alexandre Bilodeau captured the men's mogul championship, winning host Canada its first gold medal at home in three attempts. The Canadian men's hockey team defeated the United States in an overtime thriller to win the gold medal. The United States set a Winter Olympic record with 37 total medals.

Year	Olympiad	Host City, Country	Nations Represented	Men	Women	Events
2014	XXII	**Sochi, Russia**				

When the Games Began: Olympic Archaeology

By JOHN NOBLE WILFORD

Opening day of the ancient Greek games was a spectacle to behold, a celebration of the vigor and supercharged competitiveness that infused the creative spirit of one of antiquity's most transforming civilizations.

People by the thousands from every corner of the land swarmed the sacred grounds, where altars and columned temples stood in homage to their gods. They came from cities that were often bitter rivals but shared a religion, a language and an enthusiasm for organized athletics.

A closer study of ancient texts, art and artifacts, and deeper archaeological excavations are giving scholars new insights into the early games and just how integral athletics was to ancient Greek life.

Organized athletics were so popular that nothing was allowed to stand in the way. When it was time for the games, armies of rival cities usually laid down their weapons in a "sacred truce."

In athletics, scholars are finding, the ancient Greeks expressed one of their defining attributes: the pursuit of excellence through public competition. "Of all the cultural legacies left by the ancient Greeks," Dr. Edith Hall of the University of Durham in England has written, "the three which have had the most obvious impact on modern Western life are athletics, democracy and drama."

Dr. Donald G. Kyle, a professor of ancient history at the University of Texas in Arlington, said that long before the Greeks, others engaged in competitive sports like running and boxing. Contemporaries of the Greeks in Egypt and Mesopotamia put on lavish entertainments at court, with acrobats and athletes performing, and also promoted some sports as part of military training.

But the Greeks took athletics out to the wider public and to regularly scheduled competitions. They spread their games as they colonized Sicily and southern Italy and Alexander the Great conquered Eastern lands. "The Greeks linked their games to recurring religious festivals," Dr. Kyle said, "and this regularized and institutionalized athletics."

Dr. Stephen G. Miller of Berkeley has sifted through literature, art; and recent archaeology to compile a comprehensive history of sports in ancient Greece and their relationship with social and political life. Dr. Miller dates the origin of Greek organized athletics to the beginning of the eighth century B.C.

Much of the new research draws heavily on texts of ancient writers, inscriptions on stadium walls and statue bases, and artifacts excavated from ruins at the sites of the contests, including the stones of starting lines and turning points for races. Vase paintings often depict the pentathlon, five competitions that a single winner had to excel in. Archaeologists have also recovered the jumping weights and discuses of athletes and jars that held the olive oil they rubbed on their bodies.

Fans of the modern Olympics would find striking differences at the original games. There were no team sports and no second-place prizes. Fouls were punished by flogging. The athletes were allowed to accept cash and valuable gifts before and after competing.

Women were prohibited from watching or taking part in the games, except as owners in the horse races. In later years, though, some separate contests were staged for women in honor of Hera, the wife of Zeus. Unmarried girls ran a footrace wearing the Greek equivalent of a gym tunic that left the right breast bare.

The most obvious difference in the early games was the nudity of the young men. Some scholars have suggested that ancient Greece was a highly body-conscious society, in which the robust nudity of young men was itself an aspect of competitiveness.

By the fourth century A.D., with the spread of Christianity and the waning of belief in the ancient Greek gods, Dr. Miller wrote, the games "ceased completely to play any meaningful role in society."

It was not until 1896 that they were revived in their modern, international form, a tribute to the competitive spirit of ancient Greece. The 2004 Olympic games in Athens are a reminder of exuberance and pageantry of the original Greek games and the land where it all began.

TRACK AND FIELD

Track and Field consists of running, jumping, and throwing events. Often there is an outdoor 400-meter track made of synthetic materials that encloses an area called the field where many of the jumping and throwing events take place. There are also smaller indoor tracks where events take place. More than 200 nations have track and field teams, making it one of the most popular sports in the world. Track and Field meets are also very popular at the high school, college, and amateur levels. The first university meet took place in 1864 between Oxford and Cambridge. The New York Athletic Club hosted the first amateur meet in the U.S. in 1868.

Track Events   Races at various distances between 50 and 10,000 meters are run. Cross-country races and road races are held outside the main track. Additionally, there are hurdle events, where runners leap over fences and steeplechase races, which are run over longer distances and contain water jumps in addition to hurdles. There are also walking races, where competitors must use a strict walking technique, and relay races. In the latter, four runners each run a section of a race, passing a baton to a teammate as they finish their portion.

Marathons, while not a standard part of track meets, are also very popular. The concept of the marathon was born in 490 B.C., when a Greek messenger named Phillippides ran from Marathon to Athens to deliver good news about a battle against the Persians. After the hilly run (about 40 km, or 25 miles), Phillippides shouted "Nike" (victory) then collapsed and died. When the Olympics were born again in 1896 in Athens, a race from Marathon to Athens was included to commemorate Phillippides' run. In 1924 the distance of the race was standardized at 26 miles, 385 yards.

Jumping Events   There are four main jumping events. In the long jump, competitors have a running start to make a leap into a sand-filled area. The triple jump consists of three continuous jumps, the first two of which occur on the runway and the third of which lands in the sand. In these events, the athlete who travels farthest wins.

In the high jump and pole vault, the idea is to jump as high as possible, over a crossbar. High jumpers jump with one foot on the ground, pole vaulters use a fiberglass pole to help propel themselves over the bar.

Throwing Events   There are four events where an athlete attempts to throw an object as far as possible. The *discus* is a frisbee-shaped object that weighs at least 4.4 lbs. for men and 2.2 lbs. for women. The *hammer* is a steel wire that connects a metal ball and a handle. It weighs 16 lbs. In the *shot-put*, a metal ball (called the shot) that weighs 16 lbs. for men and 8 lbs., 13 ounces for women is thrown. In these three events, competitors start from an area called the cage and throw as far as they can into a certain area. The *javelin* is the only throwing event that uses a runway. The javelin can be made out of metal or wood and is at least 8 1/2 feet for men and 7 feet, 3 inches for women.

Combined Events   In addition to the individual events, there are also combined competitions, where an individual competes in different events over a day or two and gets points based on each. In the ancient Olympic games, the *pentathlon* was a main event. It included the long jump, discus and javelin throwing, running and wrestling. Today, the two most important combined events are the *decathlon* for men, consisting of 10 events, and the *heptathlon* for women, a seven-event competition.

On the first day of the decathlon, athletes do a 100-meter run, long jump, shot-put, high jump, and 400-meter run. Day two consists of the high hurdles, discus, pole vault, javelin and an 800-meter run.

The heptathlon's first day events are the high hurdles, high jump, shot put, and 200 meter run. Day two includes the long jump, the javelin throw and an 800-meter run.

The Olympics

In many ways, the history of track and field is the history of the Olympics.

1896 Athens Americans won gold medals in nine of the 12 track and field events. Americans Thomas Burke, Ellery Clark, and Robert Garrett each won two gold medals. American Robert Garrett won the shot with a throw of 36'9-3/4". Burke won the 100-meter race with a time of 12.0.

1900 Paris American Alvin Kraenzlein won four gold medals, in the 60-meter dash, the 100-meter, and 200-meter hurdles, and the long jump. American Ray Ewry won three gold medals for the high jump, standing long jump, and standing triple jump. Through subsequent Olympics Ewry finished his career with a total of eight gold medals. American Francis Jarvis won the 100-meter race with a time of 11.0.

1904 St. Louis American Archie Hahn won the 60-meter, 100-meter, and 200-meter dash. American Ray Ewry also won three gold medals, as did American Harry Hillman. Hahn won the 100-meter dash with a time of 11.0.

1908 London American Melvin Sheppard won three gold medals for the 800-meter race, the 1500-meter, and for a relay. American Ray Ewry won gold medals in the standing high jump and the long jump. American Ralph Rose won the shot put, as he had in 1904 in St. Louis. In the marathon Italian Dorando Pietri fell four times on his final lap inside the stadium. Officials helped him across the finish line to the cheers of the crowd but he was disqualified because of the help. Reginald Walker of South Africa won the 100-meter dash with a time of 10.8.

1912 Stockholm American Jim Thorpe won the pentathlon and decathlon but was stripped of his gold medals a year later when it was revealed he had earlier been paid for playing baseball. Hannes Kolehmainen of Finland won three gold medals. American Ralph Cook Craig won the 100-meter race with a time of 10.8.

1920 Antwerp Tug-of-war made its final appearance as an Olympic event, and was won by the British. Athletes from Finland won three of the four throwing events, only American Patrick Ryan, by winning the hammer throw, was able to upset the Finns. American Charles Paddock won the 100-meter race with a time of 10.8.

1924 Paris Finnish runner Paavo Nurmi won five gold medals, including the 5,000-meter race only an hour after winning the 1,500. American Matthew McGrath was 45 years old when he won the silver in the hammer throw. Harold Abrahams of Great Britain won the 100-meter race with a time of 10.6.

1928 Amsterdam Women participated in track and field events for the first time. American Elizabeth Robinson won the 100-meter race with a time of 12.2. American John Kuck won the shot put. Canadian Percy Williams won gold medals in the 200-meter and the 100-meter race. He won the 100-meter race with a time of 10.8.

1932 Los Angeles Mildred "Babe" Didrikson, won two gold medals, in the 80-meter hurdles and the javelin, and a silver medal for the javelin. Stanislawa Walasiewicz won the women's 100-meter race with a time of 11.9. In the men's competition, athletes ran an extra lap in the 3,000-meter steeplechase because of a mistake by the lap counter. This caused American Joseph Mcluskey to fall from second to third. Eddie Tolan, 5'5", won the 100-meter and the 200-meter race. Tolan's win in the 100-meter race was decided by a photograph, as both Tolan and silver medal winner Ralph Metcalfe had a time of 10.38.

1936 Berlin Jesse Owens won four gold medals, including a friendly rivalry in the long jump with German Luz Long. The Germans dominated the throwing events except for the discus, which was won by American Kenneth Carpenter. Hans Woellke of Germany won the shot with a throw of 53'1-3/4". American Helen Stephens won the women's 100-meter race with a time of 11.5. Owens won the men's 100-meter race with a time of 10.3.

1948 London Fanny Blankers-Koen of the Netherlands won four gold medals. Micheline Ostermeyer won two gold medals, in the women's shot and discus events. Blankers-Koen won the women's 100-meter race with a time of 11.9. American Harrison Dillard won the men's 100-meter race with a time of 10.3.

1952 Helsinki Emil Zatopek of Czechoslovakia won gold medals in the 5,000-meters, the 10-meters and the marathon. Past Olympic star Fanny Blankers-Koen fell over a hurdle in the 80-meters hurdles and left the track in tears. She never competed again. Australian Marjorie Jackson won two gold medals, in the 200-meter and 100-meter race. In the 100-meter race, Jackson had a world record time of 11.5. American Lindy Remigino won the men's 100-meter race with a time of 10.4.

1956 Melbourne Australian Betty Cuthbert won two individual gold medals and a third as a member of a relay team. Cuthbert won the women's 100-meter race with a time of 11.5. Soviet Vladimer Kuts won the men's 5,000-meter and 10,000-meter events. American Robert Morrow won two gold medals including the men's 100-meter race with a time of 10.5.

1960 Rome American Wilma Rudolph, who suffered from polio as a child, won two individual gold medals in sprints and a third as a member of a relay. Rudolph won the women's 100-meter race with a time of 11.0. Ethiopian runner Abebe Bikila won the marathon barefoot. Don Thompson of Great Britain set an Olympic record winning the 50-kilometer walk in 4:25.30. American Rafer Johnson won the decathlon. Armin Hary of Germany won the men's 100-meter race with a time of 10.2.

1964 Tokyo Tamara Press of the Soviet Union won two gold medals, in the women's shot-put and the discus. Australia's Betty Cuthbert, who won three gold medals in 1956, won the first ever women's 400-meter race. Peter Snell of New Zealand won two gold medals, in the men's 800-meter and 1,500-meter race. American Wyomia Tyus won the women's 100-meter race with a time of 11.4. Bob Hayes, who later went on to star for the Dallas Cowboys in the N.F.L., won the men's 100-meter race with a time of 10.0.

1968 Mexico City American Dick Fosbury unveiled a new approach to high jumping by going over shoulders first. This new technique, dubbed the Fosbury Flop, helped him win the gold medal. American Al Oerter became the first athlete to win the same event four Olympics in a row when he won the discus. In the medal ceremony for the 200-meter race, won by American Tommie Smith, Smith and bronze medalist John Carlos raised black gloved fists as a demonstration for civil rights. American Wyomia Tyus won the women's 100-meter race with a time of 11.0. American Jim Hines won the men's 100-meter race with a time of 9.9.

1972 Munich Lasse Viren of Finland won the 5,000-meter and 10,000-meter race. American Frank Shorter won the marathon by more than two minutes. Renate Stecher of East Germany won the women's 200-meter and 100-meter races. She won the 100-meter race with a time of 11.07. Valeriy Borsov won the men's 200-meter and 100-meter races. He won the 100-meter race with a time of 10.14.

1976 Montreal American Bruce Jenner set a world record while winning the decathlon. Cuban Alberto Juantorena won the 400-meter and 800-meter race. Tatyana Kazankina of the Soviet Union won the women's 800-meter and 1,500-meter race. Annegret Richter of West Germany won the women's 100-meter race with a time of 11.08. Hasely Crawford of Trinidad and Tobago won the men's 100-meter race with a time of 10.06.

1980 Moscow Wladyslaw Kosakiewicz won the pole vault with a world record jump of 18'11-1/2". Ludmilla Kondratyeva of the Soviet Union won the women's 100-meter race with a time of 11.06. Miruts Yifter of Ethiopia won two gold medals, in the 5,000-meter and 10,000-meter race. Allan Wells of Great Britain won the men's 100-meter run with a time of 10.25.

1984 Los Angeles American Carl Lewis won four gold medals, three individual medals and one as a member of a relay. Sebastian Coe of Great Britain won the men's 1,500-meter race for the second straight Olympics, having won in Moscow. American Edwin Moses, won the 400-meter hurdles. American Valerie Brisco-Hooks won two gold medals, in the 200-meter and 400-meter race. American Evelyn Ashford won the women's 100-meter race with a time of 10.97. Lewis won the men's race with a time of 9.99.

1988 Seoul American Florence Griffith-Joyner won three gold medals and a silver. American Jackie Joyner-Kersee won two gold medals, in the long jump and the heptathlon. Griffith-Joyner won the women's 100-meter race with a time of 10.54. In the men's race Canadian Ben Johnson, the apparent winner, was disqualified for taking performance-enhancing drugs. American Carl Lewis won the men's 100-meter race with a time of 9.92.

1992 Barcelona The 10,000-meter men's final featured a controversial finish in which one Moroccan runner who had been lapped obstructed Kenyan Richard Chelimo, who was then passed by Khalid Skah, also of Morocco. Skah was first disqualified but then given the gold medal. Michael Stulce won the men's shot-put with a throw of 71'2". American Gail Devers won the women's 100-meter race with a time of 10.82. Linford Christie of Great Britain won the men's 100-meter race with a time of 9.96.

1996 Atlanta The track program was altered to allow American Michael Johnson to run the 200-meter and 400-meter race. He won both events, setting a world record for the 200-meter race. American Carl Lewis won the ninth gold medal of his Olympic career by wining the long jump. Jose-Marie Perek won the women's 200-meter and 400-meter race. American Gail Devers won the women's 100-meter race with a time of 10.94. Canadian Donovan Bailey won the men's 100-meter race with a time of 9.84.

2000 Sydney American Marion Jones won three gold medals and two bronze, and performed spectacularly in the third leg of the 4x400 relay, giving the American team an insurmountable lead. Romanian Mihaela Melinte, the women's hammer throw world record holder, was escorted away from the competition after testing positive for steroids. Jones won the women's 100-meter race with a time of 10.75. Maurice Green won the men's 100-meter race with a time of 9.87.

2004 Athens While the Americans were upset in the 4x100m relay by Great Britain (won by .01 seconds), the U.S. team dominated the sprinting events, nearly sweeping all the medals for the 100m, 200m, and 400m runs (only 100 meter silver was lost). Justin Gatlin won the 100m with a time of 9.85, Shawn Crawford led the three U.S. medal winners in the 200m with a 19.79 time, and Jeremy Wariner finished first in the American sweep of the 400m in 44 seconds flat. The 4x400 relay was won by the U.S. team of Otis Harris, Derrick Brew, Jeremy Wariner, and Darold Williamson in a time of 2:55.91. Britain's Kelly Holmes, ravaged by injury for much of her career, posted a double win by besting the field in both the 800m and 1500m races.

2008 Beijing Jamaica's Usain Bolt shattered the world record in both the 100-meter (9.69 sec.) and the 200-meter (19.3 sec.) races and was part of the world record-setting 4x100 relay team (37.1 sec.). The U.S. easily won the medal count with 23, sweeping the men's 400-meter and 400-meter hurdles and winning gold in both the men's and women's 4x400 relays. The Jamaican women dominated the sprints, sweeping the 100-meter race and earning three more medals in the 200-meter and 400-meter races.

SWIMMING

History

In relics from the ancient world, there are a number of references to swimming. An Egyptian hieroglyphic depicting a swimmer dates to 2500 B.C. and mosaics in early Middle Eastern civilizations and in Pompeii depict men doing the dog paddle stroke, which they presumably learned from watching animals move about in the water.

In the first century A.D. swimming gained popularity in Britain and competitive races were introduced in Japan. But swimming fell out of favor, particularly in Europe, with the rise of the plagues of the Middle Ages.

In time, swimming regained its popularity. In 1837 swim competitions were held in London. The English swam with their heads over the water and their arms under the water, coordinating both hands to pull the water at the same time while using a frog kick. This evolved into the modern breaststroke.

In 1844, in a 130-foot pool in London, two American Indians, Flying Gull and Tobacco, demonstrated an overhand stroke that enabled them to cover the distance in an amazing 30 seconds. The swimming style was described at the time as "totally un-European."

Frederick Cavill, a well-known swimmer in England, moved to Australia in 1878 and a few years later took a trip to the South Seas. On an island in the South Seas, Cavill noticed swimmers using an overhand stroke with an up-and-down kicking motion. Back in Australia, Cavill taught his sons the new stroke, and they soon were setting swimming records. One of the Cavill boys described the style as "like crawling through the water." This stroke became known as the Australian crawl.

Competitive swimming became important after it was included as part of the first modern Olympics in 1896. In the early 1900's, American Johnny Weissmuller invented a slightly modified version of the Australian crawl. This is the front crawl that is accepted as the fastest stroke in the world.

The Sport of Swimming

There are five events in competitive swimming: butterfly, backstroke, breaststroke, freestyle and medley. Although official rules allow for any stroke to be swum in freestyle races, it is rare for a swimmer to choose any stroke but the front crawl, and "freestyle" is used to describe both the race and the stroke. The medley consists of equal distances of (in this order) butterfly, backstroke, breaststroke and freestyle. Races in each event are swum by individual swimmers and also by relay teams of four. Racing distances vary, between 50m/yd and 1,500 m/yd for stroke races and between 200 and 800 m/yd for medley and relay races. Open water races are held in rivers, lakes and seas in distances of 2 kilometers or more.

There are three different sizes of pools used in competitive swimming: long course meters, short course meters and short course yards. Long course meters pools, commonly referred to as Olympic size, are 50 meters long, and are the norm for most large international meets. Short course meters pools are 25 meters long and are common throughout the world; short course yards pools (a normal size for U.S. swim meets) are 25 yards long.

In 2010, FINA (Federation Internationale de Natation), the sport's international regulatory body, banned full-length racing suits, which had become increasingly controversial due to their hi-tech buoyancy and water-shedding properties.

Basic strokes

The four competitive strokes are grouped into two pairs—the long-axis and short-axis strokes—based on each stroke's major axis of symmetry. The spine is the major axis in long-axis strokes (freestyle and backstroke) and the shoulders and hips define the short-axis strokes (butterfly and breaststroke). Although swimmers usually specialize in a single stroke, they tend to also be strong in that stroke's pair, since the mechanics and correct form in the pair are somewhat similar. Fast, strong swimming of the long-axis strokes—freestyle and backstroke—involves rotating smoothly left and right along the spine as swimmers pull themselves through the water. In the short-axis strokes, swimmers explode through short, quick bursts, maximizing powerful hip motions—abducting and adducting in breaststroke and thrusting in butterfly—and simultaneous sweeps and pulls with the arms.

The Olympics

1896 Athens Four freestyle events are held with competitors either swimming breast stroke or Trudgen stroke. Alfred Hajos of Hungary wins the 100-meter freestyle with a time of 1:22.2.

1900 Paris Swimming competition is held in the Seine River. Two events were held—underwater swimming and the 200-meter obstacle race—that are no longer held. Backstroke was added as an event. In 1900 there was no 100-meter freestyle race. Frederick Lane of Australia wins the 200-meter freestyle with a time of 2:25.2.

1904 St. Louis American Charles Daniels wins three gold medals, two individual medals, and one as a member of a relay team. Most swimmers are swimming the crawl in freestyle events, so breaststroke is added as an event. Zoltan Halmay of Hungary wins the 100-yard freestyle with a time of 1:02.8. This is the only year that the Olympics swim races are measured in yards.

1908 London British swimmer Henry Taylor wins three gold medals, two individual medals, and one as a member of a relay team. American Charles Daniels wins the 100-meter freestyle with a time of 1:05.6.

1912 Stockholm Women compete in Olympic swimming for the first time. Australian Fanny Durack wins the women's 100-meter freestyle with a time of 1:22.2. American Duke Kahanamoku, a self-taught Hawaiian who brought the classic six-beat swimming style into prominence, wins the men's 100-meter freestyle. The six-beat style includes six flutter kicks during each cycle of the arms. Kahanamoku wins the 100-meter freestyle with a time of 1:03.4

1920 Antwerp American Ethelda Bleibtrey wins the women's 100-meter freestyle with a time of 1:13.6. American Duke Kahanamoku wins the men's 100-meter freestyle with a time of 1:01.4

1924 Paris American Johnny Weissmuller wins three gold medals. Weissmuller goes on to a legendary career setting world records in 67 different events. Later Weissmuller starred as Tarzan in many movies. American Ethel Lackie won the women's 100-meter freestyle with a time of 1:12.4. Weissmuller won the 100-meter freestyle with a time of 59.0.

1928 Amsterdam Hilde Schrader of Germany wins the women's 200-meter breaststroke, setting a world record. American Albina Osipowich wins the women's 100-meter freestyle with a time of 1:11.0. American Johnny Weissmuller won the men's 100-meter freestyle with a time of 58.6.

1932 Los Angeles American Helene Madison wins the two gold medals including the women's 100-meter freestyle with a time of 1:06.8. In the 100-meter race, she has a time of 1:06.8. Clarence "Buster" Crabbe wins the 400-meter freestyle and used his fame to land in the movies. Japan's Yasuji Miyazaki won the men's 100-meter freestyle with a time of 58.2.

1936 Berlin Japan and the United States dominates the men's swimming events, winning all but three of the medals in the men's individual events. Hendrika Mastenbroek of Holland wins the women's 100-meter freestyle with a time of 1:05.9.

1948 London Denmark's Greta Andersen wins the women's 100-meter freestyle with a time of 1:06.3. In the 400-meter freestyle race, however, Andersen faints and has to be rescued. Walter Ris of the United States wins the 100-meter freestyle with a time of 57.3.

1952 Helsinki Hungary's Katalin Szoke wins the women's 100-meter freestyle with a time of 1:06.8. American Clark Scholes wins the men's 100-meter freestyle with a time of 57.4.

1956 Melbourne This Olympics marks the introduction of the butterfly stroke as a separate event. Developed in the 1930's, the butterfly double-overhand arm stroke was combined with a frog kick and used to compete in and dominate breaststroke races. A dolphin kick—keeping the legs together and using a hip through toes double kick—was added to the stroke to make it more efficient. In 1953 breaststroke and butterfly were made into separate competitions. Dawn Fraser of Australia wins the women's 100-meter freestyle with a time of 1:02.0. Murray Rose of Australia becomes the first man to win two individual gold medals in swimming since Johnny Weissmuller in 1924. Australia's John Henricks wins the men's 100-meter freestyle with a time of 55.4.

1960 Rome Medley relay events are added for this Olympics. A medley is a race in which all four strokes—butterfly, backstroke, breaststroke, and freestyle—are each swum. In a relay race, each swimmer swims a different stroke. Australian Dawn Fraser wins the women's 100-meter freestyle with a time of 1:01.2. Australia's John Devitt wins the men's 100-meter freestyle with a time of 55.2.

1964 Tokyo Individual medley races are added. An individual medley is a race in which one swimmer swims each of the four strokes. American Don Schollander wins four gold medals two in individual events and two in relays. Australian Dawn Fraser wins the women's 100-meter freestyle with a time of 59.5. Schollander wins the men's 100-meter freestyle with a time of 53.4.

1968 Mexico City American Debbie Meyer wins three individual gold medals for the 200-meter freestyle, 400-meter freestyle, and 800-meter freestyle. American Jan Henne wins the women's 100-meter freestyle with a time of 1:00.0. Australian Michael Wenden wins the men's 100-meter freestyle with a time of 52.2.

1972 Munich American Mark Spitz puts in the most dominant performance in Olympic history, winning gold medals in four individual events while setting world records. He wins three more gold medals as a member of three relay teams. Australian Shane Gould wins three gold medals, a silver medal, and a bronze in the women's events. American Sandra Neilson wins the women's 100-meter freestyle with a time of 58.59. Spitz wins the men's 100-meter freestyle with a time of 51.22.

1976 Montreal The United States and East Germany dominate the swimming events. Only the 200-meter breaststroke in both the men's and women's events are won by a competitor who wasn't German or American. American John Naber wins two individual gold medals and two as a member of a relay team. He also wins a silver medal. Naber breaks the two-minute barrier for 200 backstroke by swimming it in 1:59.19. Kornelia Ender of East Germany wins four gold medals and a silver medal. Ender wins the women's 100-meter freestyle with a time of 55.65.

1980 Moscow East German Rica Reinisch won three gold medals in women's events. Barbara Krause of East Germany wins the 100-meter freestyle with a time of 54.79. Jorg Woithe of East Germany wins the men's 100-meter freestyle with a time of 50.40.

1984 Los Angeles American Mary T. Meagher wins two individual gold medals and a third as a member of a relay team. West German Michael Gross wins the 100-meter butterfly and the 200-meter butterfly, setting world records in both. Canadian Alex Baumann sets world records in two events, winning the 200-meter medley and the 400-meter medley. American Carrie Steinseifer wins the women's 100-meter freestyle with a time of 55.92. American Ambrose Gaines wins the men's 100-meter freestyle with a time of 49.80.

1988 Seoul A short sprint—the 50-meter freestyle—is added. Kristin Otto of East Germany wins six gold medals; four individual gold medals and two as a member of a relay team. American Matt Biondi wins five gold medals, silver, and a bronze. Otto won the wins 100-meter freestyle with a time of 54.93. Biondi wins the men's 100-meter freestyle with a time of 48.63.

1992 Barcelona Yevgeniy Sadovyi of the Unified Team wins three gold medals in the men's competition and Hungarian Krisztina Egerzegy wins three gold medals in the women's competition. Yong Zhuang of China wins the women's 100-meter freestyle with a time of 54.64. Alexander Popov of the Unified Team wins the men's 100-meter freestyle with a time of 49.02.

1996 Atlanta American women are dominant, winning seven of 16 gold medals, and five silver medals. American Amy van Dyken wins four gold medals, two in individual events and two as a member of a relay team. Michelle Smith of Ireland wins three gold medals and a bronze. American Gary Hall Jr. wins two gold medals on relay teams and two individual silver medals. Le Jingyi of China wins the women's 100-meter freestyle with a time of 54.50. Alexander Popov wins the men's 100-meter freestyle with a time of 48.74.

2000 Sydney High-tech body suits were worn by many swimmers and 15 world records are broken or tied. The Americans are dominant winning 14 gold medals. American Lenny Krayzelburg wins three gold medals in backstroke events. Inge de Bruijn won the women's 100-meter freestyle with a time of 54.33. Pieter van den Hoogenband of the Netherlands wins the men's 100-meter freestyle with a time of 48.30.

2004 Athens At times, the swimming in Athens almost seemed a contest between two nations, the U.S. and Australia—and two athletes, American Michael Phelps and Australian Ian Thorpe. The U.S. took 28 total medals, 12 of them gold, while Australia totaled 15, with seven top finishes. Thorpe collected two gold medals, four medals in total; Phelps won six medals, all but one of them gold. In women's swimming, the U.S. team took the 4x200m freestyle relay, but were runners up to Australia in both 4x100m freestyle and the 4X100m medley. Three world records were set: the U.S. men's team in the 4x100m medley (3:30.68); the Australian women's team in the 4x100m medley (3:57.32); and Australian Grant Hackett in the men's 1500m freestyle (14:43.40).

2008 Beijing American Michael Phelps became one of the most decorated Olympians of all time, and the most dominant swimmer ever, winning eight gold medals in Beijing to bring his personal total to 16 medals (14 gold and two bronze). In the process he set three team and four individual world records, including the 200m butterfly (1:52.03), freestyle (1:42.96), and medly (1:54.23), and 400m medley (4:03.84). One of Phelps' three team golds was for the .08 second victory over the favored French team in the 4x100m freestyle relay, in which anchor Jason Lezak surged from behind to overtake France's Alain Bernard in the final 10m of the race (3:08.24).

AUTO RACING

The sport of automobile racing is almost as old as automobiles themselves, dating back to the 1890's. There are many types of racing, differentiated by the characteristics of the vehicles involved. The stock cars seen in NASCAR, for example, outwardly resemble something that might be found in any garage in America. Formula One and Indy car circuits are designed for low-slung cars seen nowhere else but a race track. There are vehicles built for extreme speed called dragsters that can reach speeds of more than 300 miles per hour for a few seconds. One of the world's most famous races, the 24 Hours of Le Mans held annually in Le Mans, France, is an endurance race. But the three styles of racing that attract the most attention are Formula One, NASCAR, and Indy cars.

Because of the tremendous cost involved in building and maintaining a team of cars, almost all professional racing teams have corporate sponsors who support them in exchange for displaying logos on the cars. All three of these racing circuits award a championship, for both teams and individuals, based on points accumulated through high-place finishes. Some drivers have had success in more than one of the three types of racing.

Formula One

The world's most popular form of auto racing is Formula One (F1). Formula One cars are designed according to specifications of the sport's governing body, the Federation Internationale de l'Automobile (FIA). The FIA was established in 1904 and supervised its first major event (called a Grand Prix) in 1906 near Le Mans, France. The first Grand Prix series was held in 1920. The circuit now covers 18 events in locations as diverse as Malaysia, Monaco, Germany, and the United States, with races usually ranging from 150 to 200 miles. Although Formula One cars can reach high speeds on straightaways, courses have frequent turns that require vehicles to be nimble as well as fast.

Drivers belong to teams that provide and outfit the cars. Twelve teams—each with multiple cars and drivers—will compete in the 2011 Formula One season, with Austria's Red Bull Racing the reigning Constructors Champions. This year's race schedule will expand to twenty rounds, the longest in the sports sixty-year history.

Some of the sport's biggest stars include the Argentinian Juan Manuel Fangio, who raced in the 1950's, Scotland's Jackie Stewart, a star of the 1960's and 1970's, Brazil's Ayrton Senna, a brilliant driver who died in a crash during the 1994 San Marino Grand Prix, and Germany's Michael Schumacher, who established himself in the 1990's and 2000's as one of the great Formula One drivers of all time.

NASCAR

While the National Association for Stock Car Automobile Racing ranks among the fastest-growing of all sports in terms of popularity with the public, the sport originated with a very specific activity. Stock car racing grew out of the bootlegging communities of the South, where the quest to transport illegal moonshine past the authorities led naturally to the development of fast cars. Competing bootleggers who bragged about having fast cars would race against one another. One account says the first race was contested in the mid-1930's in a town near Atlanta, Georgia.

By the 1940's, thousands of spectators attended these races. In 1947 Bill France, who promoted a race in Daytona Beach, Fla., gathered racing promoters throughout the region to organize a racing circuit that became NASCAR. In 1949 the first race in the Strictly Stock Division series was held at the 116-mile Beach & Road Course at Daytona Beach. Red Byron won in an Oldsmobile.

In the first two years of NASCAR, modified older cars were used, but in 1949 the organization began racing the same kinds of vehicles sold in automobile showrooms. Nine models of cars—Buick, Cadillac, Chrysler, Ford, Hudson, Kaiser, Lincoln, Mercury, and Oldsmobile—competed in the first Strictly Stock Division race. As manufacturers realized that victories helped sell cars, they began upgrading their stock cars for the public. Hudson drivers won 22 of 37 races in 1953 after Hudson introduced its "Twin H" carburetor setup. Then in 1955 Chevrolet introduced the legendary 355 "small block" V8 engine still employed by General Motors racing teams. Over time,

NASCAR loosened rules so that stock cars became something different from the cars sold on showroom floors.

In 1958 the final beach road race was held in Daytona Beach. The Daytona International Speedway opened in 1959, and three other major racetracks—in Hanford, Calif.; Concord, N.H., and Hampton, Ga.—opened within the next year. Racing in the early 1960's was marked by the "engine wars," as Ford, Chevrolet, and others spent millions of dollars on research and development. In 1964 Richard Petty used a Plymouth hemispherical combustion engine, or a "hemi," to win the Daytona 500.

In 1951 the name of the circuit changed to the NASCAR Grand National Series and that title remained until RJ Reynolds began sponsoring the series in 1972. For more than three decades, the NASCAR circuit was also known as the Winston Cup Series, after an RJ Reynolds cigarette brand. In a change symbolic of NASCAR's broadening appeal, cellular phone company Nextel took over the titular sponsorship of the circuit in 2004. For 10-year naming rights to the NASCAR Nextel Cup series, the company paid $700 million.

The first race of the NASCAR season is also the biggest, the Daytona 500, which is held in mid-February. The series ends with the Ford 400 in Homestead, Fla. in mid-November, with almost weekly races throughout the season.

Starting in 2004 NASCAR introduced a new format to determine its champion. Drivers gain points throughout the season with the top ten finishers qualifying for "The Chase for the Sprint Cup." "The Chase" is a ten race tournament with points awarded to drivers based on their finishing position. The driver with the highest point total after all ten races is declared champion.

Contemporary NASCAR engines are restricted to 358 cubic inches and require a restrictor plate that limits the flow of air to the engine. This decrease in air flow restricts the car to 450 horsepower. Cars weigh a minimum of 3,400 pounds and employ a steering system on oval left-turn tracks that forces them to turn right in order to go straight. This modification makes turning left easier.

Notable NASCAR Drivers

Dale Earnhardt won seven series championships and is considered by many as the most talented driver in NASCAR history. Earnhardt's aggressive style earned him the nickname, "The Intimidator." He died in a crash in the last lap of the 2001 Daytona 500.

Jeff Gordon won three cup series (in 1995, 1997, 1998) and the Daytona 500 twice.

Jimmy Johnson won the Daytona 500 in 2006 and is the only driver to win five consecutive cup championships (2006, 2007, 2008, 2009, 2010).

Junior Johnson was one of the most famous of the bootleg racers. He was arrested at his father's still in 1956 and spent two years in jail. Johnson won 50 races between 1953 and 1966, and later became a prominent car owner.

Lee Petty won 54 races. His son Richard, who went on to become the greatest NASCAR driver, was in Lee Petty's pit crew.

Richard Petty, known to racing fans as "The King," won 200 NASCAR races, seven cup series championships, and seven victories in the Daytona 500. In 1967 Petty won 27 of 48 races, including 10 in a row.

Edward Glenn "Fireball" Roberts, considered the greatest driver never to win the cup series, won the Daytona 500 in 1962. He died in a racing accident in 1964.

Darrell Waltrip won three cup championships, in 1977, 1981, 1982. He is the only five-time winner of the Coca Cola 600 at the Charlotte (N.C.) Motor Speedway.

Joe Weatherly won two cup championships, in 1962 and 1963. He was also an accomplished motorcycle racer. He died in a crash in 1964.

Cale Yarborough won three consecutive championships (1976–78), and won the Daytona 500 four times.

Indy Car

Indy car racing is the fastest multimile automobile racing in the world. Like Formula One cars, Indy cars have an open cockpit, one seat, and an engine in the rear. Each year racers compete in more than two dozen races, from oval tracks to closed-off city streets. The Indianapolis 500 is the premier event, held each Memorial Day weekend in Indiana.

In 1906 Carl Fisher, frustrated at the unreliability of automobiles, decided to build a racetrack in Indianapolis to entice car manufacturers to make better vehicles. His creation, built on a 300-acre plot of land, was the Indianapolis Motor Speedway. The original 2.5-mile track was surfaced with bricks. Of this original surface, only a yard-wide strip remains to serve as the finish line. Because of this unusual feature, the track is also known as the Brickyard.

The first race at Indianapolis was held in August 1909. In 1911 the Indianapolis Motor Speedway hosted a 500-mile race, the first Indianapolis 500. Ray Haroun, with an average speed of 74.59 miles per hour, won the race. The contest proved popular with the public, and new grandstands were added as the event grew in prestige.

In 1916, during World War I, only 21 cars competed in a race that was reduced to only 300 miles. After America entered the war, during the next two years the track was closed and served as an aviation repair depot and landing field for planes flying coast to coast through the Midwest.

Following the conflict, racing returned in earnest. The 1919 race was won by Howdy Wilcox, who was the first to drive more than 100 miles per hour. He won $50,000 in that race, in which three drivers died. The 1920 race was won by Gaston Chevrolet, driving a Monroe. In 1925 Pete DePaolo won by averaging more than 100 mph for the first time. In 1927 Fisher sold the speedway to World War I flying ace Eddie Rickenbacker for $750,000.

Racing, like everything else, suffered during the Great Depression, and the speedway was again closed during the World War II. In 1946, as the grandstands stood in disrepair and the track was overgrown with weeds, Rickenbacker sold it to Tony Hulman, who supervised the Indianapolis 500 for 30 years. Hulman spent millions of dollars to renovate the track, and the race took on renewed significance.

In 1955 Bill Vukovich, the winner of the two previous races, died while leading the race in the 57th lap. In 1956 an eight-story control tower was added, as were new seats, tunnels, and safer pit areas. And in 1957 a 15-car accident killed driver Pat O'Connor. After that, rollbars were required in all cars, and drivers were mandated to wear fireproof uniforms. In the 1960's the circuit mandated that methanol be used instead of gasoline because it is much less flammable.

Early Indy cars were made of heavy sheet metal. Modern cars are fabricated from aluminum and carbon fiber. Since drivers had trouble keeping these lighter cars on the track, wings were added to both the front and rear of the vehicle. These have the opposite effect of airplane wings—rather than giving lift, they produce downward force that keeps the car on the ground.

The two major models of race cars are Penskes and Lolas. The British-built Cosworth-Ford engine was the standard Indy car engine but the Ilmor-Ford engine has also become popular in recent years.

A. J. Foyt was among the biggest names in the sport in the 1960's and 1970's, winning four Indianapolis 500's — in 1961, 1964, 1967, 1977. A few racing families have achieved a high profile in the sport, including the Unsers. Al and Bobby Unser won the race seven times between them, and Al Unser Jr. won the race in 1992 and 1994.

A feud between two competing groups in the 1990's diminished the importance of the Indianapolis 500 for several years. The Championship Auto Racing Team (CART) was formed in 1978 after a dispute with the United States Auto Racing Club, which was operating Indy car racing. Court cases and rejected entries marked the feud, which took new meaning in 1994, when the Indy Racing League (IRL) was formed by Tony George, president of the Indianapolis Motor Speedway. By 1996 the feud deepened and CART planned the U.S. 500 for the Michigan Motor Speedway on the same day as the Indianapolis 500.

For four years, the U.S. 500 was held the same day, but in 2000 CART cleared its schedule for two weeks, and CART drivers are again participating in the Indianapolis 500. In 2009 Helio Castroneves of CART won his third Indy 500 in under ten years while 2010 winner Dario Franchitti of IndyCar Series picked up his second victory.

Le Mans

Auto racing originated as a way of testing the new vehicles for speed and endurance. In 1923 the Automobile Club of the Sarthe, which had established the first French Grand Prix, decided to organize a race that would test not only around-the-clock endurance but also auto headlights, which were still in their infancy. The result was the first 24 Hours of Le Mans race, originally called the Grand Prix of Endurance. The first race began at 4 p.m. May 26, 1923, during a tempestuous rain storm accompanied by bursts of hail. Thirty-five cars from 18 different manufacturers entered that race. When it ended at 4 p.m. the following day, the winner was a Chenard and Walcker "Sport" driven by Andre Lagache and Rene Leonard. The car covered 2,209.536 kilometers at an average speed of 92.064 kilometers per hour, about 57.2 miles an hour.

The 24 Hours of Le Mans is still a major test of the endurance of an auto, driven continuously at high speeds. Teams originally included only two drivers. Since 1977, a team has been allowed, but not required, to have three drivers. Prequalifying sessions take place in early May, with qualifying rounds a month later and the race itself on a weekend in mid-June.

Indianapolis 500 Winners

Year	Winner	Time	MPH	Year	Winner	Time	MPH
Under AAA Sanction				1963	Parnelli Jones	3:29:35	143.137
1911	Ray Harroun	6:42.08	74.602	1964	A.J. Foyt, Jr.	3:23:35	147.350
1912	Joe Dawson	6:21.06	78.719	1965	Jim Clark	3:19:05	150.686
1913	Juses Goux	6:35:05	75.933	1966	Graham Hill	3:27:52	144.317
1914	Rene Thomas	6:03:45	82.474	1967	A.J. Foyt, Jr.	3:18:14	151.207
1915	Ralph DePalma	5:33:55	89.840	1968	Bobby Unser	3:16:13	152.882
1916	Dario Resta	3:34:17[1]	84.001	1969	Mario Andretti	3:11:14	156.867
1919	Howard Wilcox	5:40:42	88.050	1970	Al Unser	3:12:37	155.749
1920	Gaston Chevrolet	5:38:32	88.618	1971	Al Unser	3:10:11	157.735
1921	Tommy Milton	5:34:34	89.621	1972	Mark Donohue	3:04:05	162.962
1922	Jimmy Murphy	5:17:30	94.484	1973	Gordon Johncock	2:05:26[4]	159.036
1923	Tommy Milton	5:29:50	90.954	1974	Johnny Rutherford	3:09:10	158.589
1924	L.L. Corum, Joe Boyer	5:05:23	98.234	1975	Bobby Unser	2:54:55[5]	149.213
1925	Peter DePaolo	4:56:39	101.127	1976	Johnny Rutherford	1:42:52[6]	148.725
1926	Peter Lockhart	4:10:14[2]	95.904	1977	A.J. Foyt, Jr.	3:05:57	161.331
1927	George Souders	5:07:33	97.545	1978	Al Unser	3:05:54	161.363
1928	Louis Meyer	5:01:33	99.482	1979	Rick Mears	3:08:47	158.899
1929	Ray Keech	5:07:25	97.585	1980	Johnny Rutherford	3:29:59	142.862
1930	Billy Arnold	4:58:39	100.448	1981	Bobby Unser	3:35:41	139.084
1931	Louis Schneider	5:10:27	96.629	1982	Gordon Johncock	3:05:09	162.029
1932	Fred Frame	4:48:03	104.144	1983	Tom Sneva	3:05:03	162.117
1933	Louis Meyer	4:48:00	104.162	1984	Rick Mears	3:30:21	163.612
1934	William Cummings	4:46:05	104.863	1985	Danny Sullivan	3:16:06	152.982
1935	Kelly Petillo	4:42:22	106.240	1986	Bobby Rahal	2:55:43	170.722
1936	Louis Meyer	4:35:03	109.069	1987	Al Unser	3:04:59	162.175
1937	Wilbur Shaw	4:24:07	113.580	1988	Rick Mears	3:27:10	144.809
1938	Floyd Roberts	4:15:58	117.200	1989	Emerson Fittipaldi	2:59:01	167.581
1939	Wilbur Shaw	4:20:47	115.035	1990	Arie Luyendyk	2:41:18	185.984[7]
1940	Wilbur Shaw	4:22:31	114.277	1991	Rick Mears	2:50:01	176.457
1941	Floyd Davis, Mauri Rose	4:20:36	115.117	1992	Al Unser, Jr.	3:43:05	134.477
1946	George Robson	4:21:16	114.820	1993	Emerson Fittipaldi	3:10:50	157.207
1947	Mauri Rose	4:17:52	116.338	1994	Al Unser, Jr.	3:06:29	160.872
1948	Mauri Rose	4:10:23	119.814	1995	Jacques Villeneuve	3:15:18	153.616
1949	Bill Holland	4:07:15	121.327	1996	Buddy Lazier	3:22:46	147.956
1950	Johnnie Parsons	2:46:55[3]	124.002	1997	Arie Luyendyk	3:25:43	145.827
1951	Lee Wallard	3:57:38	126.244	1998	Eddie Cheever	3:26:40	145.155
1952	Troy Tuttman	3:52:41	128.922	1999	Kenny Brack	3:15:51	153.176
1953	Bill Vukovich	3:53:01	128.740	2000	Juan Montoya	2:58.59	167.607
1954	Bill Vukovich	3:49:17	130.840	2001	Helio Castroneves	3:31.54	141.574
1955	Bob Sweikert	3:53:59	128.209	2002	Helio Castroneves	3:00:11	166.499
Under USAC Sanction				2003	Gil de Ferran	3:11:57	156.291
1956	Pat Flaherty	3:53.28	128.490	2004	Buddy Rice	3:14:55[8]	138.518
1957	Sam Hanks	3:41.14	135.601	2005	Dan Wheldon	3:10:21	157.603
1958	Jim Bryan	3:44:13	133.791	2006	Sam Hornish, Jr.	3:10:59	157.085
1959	Rodger Ward	3:40:49	135.857	2007	Dario Franchitti	2:44:03[9]	151.774
1960	Jim Rathmann	3:36:11	138.767	2008	Scott Dixon	3:28:57	143.567
1961	A.J. Foyt, Jr.	3:35:37	139.131	2009	Helio Castroneves	3:19:34	150.318
1962	Roger Ward	3:33:50	140.293	2010	Dario Franchitti	3:05:37	161.623
				2011	Dan Wheldon	2:56:11	170.265

1. 300 miles (scheduled). 2. 400 miles (rain). 3. 345 miles (rain). 4. 332.5 miles (rain). 5. 435 miles (rain). 6. 255 miles (rain). 7. Track record. 8. 450 miles (rain). 9. 415 miles (rain). **Source:** Indianapolis Motor Speedway Hall of Fame and Museum.

FOOD

THE GLOBAL FOOD SYSTEM

Archaeological records show that the domestication of plants for human consumption dates back to 14,000 B.C. The development of agriculture was the catalyst for the transition from nomadic tribes to civilization as we know it. As productivity of local resources improved, villages sprung up, but it wasn't until after the establishment of the Roman Empire in the first century B.C. that trade between communities was common. Trade routes developed, and areas no longer had to rely solely on goods that were able to be grown locally. By roughly 350 A.D., the Roman Empire was facing a food crisis, as wealthy merchants capitalized on an opportunity to hoard food supplies and resell it at higher prices. The difficulties of supply and demand, heavily influenced by political motivation and a growing population, had been born.

More than 1,000 years later, in 1798, English economist Thomas Malthus proposed a theory to explain this relationship, in his *Essay on the Principle of Population*. In it he argues that while population increases geometrically, the food supply increases arithmetically. In other words, population always surpasses the food supply, and therefore poverty and social unrest are inevitable. The Malthusian viewpoint grew increasingly controversial over the next century, though it was very influential in the early years of classical economics, when death rates from famines, disease and war were significantly higher than today. Malthusian projections went out of favor in the 20th century, as medicine and public health cut down the number of deaths and technology helped improve living standards and life expectancies.

Despite this, Malthusian ideas still resonate. As recent history shows, however, it's less that population absolutely surpasses food supply, and more that supply is distributed unevenly. The 20th century saw several large-scale famines that occurred as a direct result of food shortages in one region while overall global production was flourishing. In the 1930's, an estimated 7.5 million people died in Ukraine, a period known as the *Holodomor*, which some scholars regard a genocide inititated by Joseph Stalin. Mao Zedong's "Great Leap Forward" resulted in a massive Chinese famine from 1958 to 1962, in which as many as 45 million people died. Nearly a million people died in North Korea in the 1990's due to a food crisis there.

In recent years, food shortages have occurred in several regions around the world leading to riots and disorder. The Food and Agriculture Organization (F.A.O.) of the United Nations, however, estimates that there is enough food produced to meet the caloric requirements of the global population. The number of calories available has, in fact, increased continuously since 1970 and is on track to do so until at least 2050. It's the uneven distribution of these calories that is responsible for the unprecedented crisis that the food industry faces in the 21st century. An estimated 30 to 50 percent of food produced globally rots away uneaten. One reason for this excess, perhaps, is the Green Revolution, a period of intense research and development of new technological tools meant to increase agricultural yield that began in the 1960's.

The Green Revolution

The goal of the Green Revolution was to produce more food through energy-intensive farming. This involved the increased use of pesticides, synthetic fertilizers, and the use of hybridized seeds. The most notable hybrid strains that took root were maize and grain sorghum, while crossbreeding resulted in the increased production of rice and wheat.

Norman E. Borlaug (1914–2009), an American plant scientist and recipient of the 1970 Nobel Peace Prize, is generally considered the father of the Green Revolution—a title he called "a miserable term." Borlaug led the experimentation of breeding high-yield crop varieties, working primarily in developing countries that were food deficient.

The new seeds developed by Borlaug and his colleagues were engineered to absorb more fertilizer and water. By the late 1940's, researchers had learned that yield could be increased with the use of nitrogen-rich fertilizer. Borlaug's genitically modified (GM) seeds, when given large amounts of this fertilizer, produced enormous heads of grain. Wheat output could be tripled or even quadrupled on the same amount of land. Mexico adopted the breeding program whole-heartedly, and by the mid-1960's India, which had been importing the majority of its grain, began ordering shiploads of Borlaug's seeds from Mexico. Between 1961 and 1990 wheat yields rose at nearly 3 percent per year, enabling these countries to become major players in the global agricultural market.

A Warming Planet Struggles to Feed Itself

By JUSTIN GILLIS

The rapid growth in farm output that defined the late 20th century has slowed to the point that it is failing to keep up with the demand for food, driven by population increases and rising affluence in once-poor countries.

Consumption of the four staples that supply most human calories—wheat, rice, corn and soybeans—has outstripped production for much of the past decade, drawing once-large stockpiles down to worrisome levels. The imbalance between supply and demand has resulted in two huge spikes in international grain prices since 2007, with some grains more than doubling in cost.

Those price jumps, though felt only moderately in the West, have worsened hunger for tens of millions of poor people, destabilizing politics in scores of countries, from Mexico to Uzbekistan to Yemen. The Haitian government was ousted in 2008 amid food riots, and anger over high prices has played a role in the recent Arab uprisings.

Now, the latest scientific research suggests that a previously discounted factor is helping to destabilize the food system: climate change.

Many of the failed harvests of the past decade were a consequence of weather disasters, like floods in the United States, drought in Australia, and blistering heat waves in Europe and Russia. Temperatures are rising rapidly during the growing season in some of the most important agricultural countries, and a paper published several weeks ago found that this had shaved several percentage points off potential yields, adding to the price gyrations.

Experts say that in coming decades, farmers need to withstand whatever climate shocks come their way while roughly doubling the amount of food they produce to meet rising demand. And they need to do it while reducing the considerable environmental damage caused by the business of agriculture.

Agronomists emphasize that the situation is far from hopeless. Examples are already available, from the deserts of Mexico to the rice paddies of India, to show that it may be possible to make agriculture more productive and more resilient in the face of climate change. Farmers have achieved huge gains in output in the past, and rising prices are a powerful incentive to do so again.

But new crop varieties and new techniques are required, far beyond those available now, scientists said. Despite the urgent need, they added, promised financing has been slow to materialize, much of the necessary work has yet to begin and, once it does, it is likely to take decades to bear results.

When Norman E. Borlaug, a young American agronomist, began working in Mexico the 1940's under the sponsorship of the Rockefeller Foundation, the Yaqui Valley farmers embraced him. His successes as a breeder helped farmers raise Mexico's wheat output sixfold. In the 1960's, Dr. Borlaug spread his approach to India and Pakistan, where mass starvation was feared. Output soared there, too.

Other countries joined the Green Revolution, and food production outstripped population growth through the latter half of the 20th century. In the late 1980's, food production seemed under control. Governments and foundations began to cut back on agricultural research, or to redirect money into the problems created by intensive farming, like environmental damage. Over a 20-year period, Western aid for agricultural development in poor countries fell by almost half, with some of the world's most important research centers suffering mass layoffs.

Output continued to rise, but because fewer innovations were reaching farmers, the growth rate slowed. That lull occurred just as food and feed demand was starting to take off, thanks in part to rising affluence across much of Asia. Millions of people added meat and dairy products to their diets, requiring considerable grain to produce. Other factors contributed to demand, including a policy of converting much of the American corn crop into ethanol.

In 2007 and 2008, with grain stockpiles low, prices doubled and in some cases tripled. Whole countries began hoarding food, and panic buying ensued in some markets, notably for rice. Food riots broke out in more than 30 countries.

Forty years ago, a third of the population in the developing world was undernourished. By the tail end of the Green Revolution, in the mid-1990's, the share had fallen below 20 percent, and the absolute number of hungry people dipped below 800 million for the first time in modern history.

But the recent price spikes have helped cause the largest increases in world hunger in decades. The Food and Agriculture Organization of the United Nations estimated the number of hungry people at 925 million last year, and the number is expected to be higher when a fresh estimate is completed this year. The World Bank says the figure could be as high as 940 million.

Dr. Borlaug's latest successor, Hans-Joachim Braun, recently outlined the challenges facing the world's farmers. On top of the weather disasters, he said, booming cities are chewing up agricultural land and competing with farmers for water. In some of the world's breadbaskets, farmers have achieved high output only by pumping groundwater much faster than nature can replenish it.

The positive effects Borlaug's seeds had on the developing world cannot be understated, though the effects were not all positive. The farming systems that were developed during the Green Revolution require heavy irrigation, and aren't as effective in regions with water shortages. During the 1960's, local strains were abandoned as farmers opted for GM seeds, and agricultural biodiversity was considerably lessened as a result. According to the U.N., genetic diversity in food crops was diminished by 75 percent in the 20th century. Because GM seeds required massive amounts of fertilizers and pesticides, demand and prices rose accordingly, and by 2010 the price of fertilizer was higher than the price of wheat.

According to a 2010 report released by the Service for the Acquisition of Agri-biotech Applications, 81 percent of all soybeans, 64 percent of all cotton, and 29 percent of all corn produced globally was grown from GM seeds. At the beginning of the 21st century, concerns about of the harmful nutritional and environmental effects of fertilizers and pesticides necessary to GM seeds had begun to mount.

One response to the growing prevalence of modified foods has been the nascent organic foods movement, in which no artificial pesticides or chemicals are used in the production of foods or in feeding livestock. While the popularity of organic agricultural products continues to increase in developed nations—in the U.S. sales of organic food increased 7.7 percent from 2009 to 2010 alone—scientists are still uncertain whether organic agriculture and traditional methods can meet global food needs.

Growing Population

World population has been growing steadily since the Industrial Revolution, with higher standards of living and advances in technology and medicine that eradicated diseases and allowed people to live longer. World population increased more rapidly than ever before in the second half of the 20th century. In 1999, global population reached 6 billion, and in 2011 the U.N. released a report that projected global population would soon pass 7 billion. The same report predicted that population would surpass 9 billion by mid-century, and 10 billion by 2100. If there's going to be enough food to feed all 9 billion by 2050, according to the F.A.O., net investments of $83 billion must be made in agriculture each year—an increase of 50 percent from current global agricultural spending. This is further complicated by the increasing demand for agricultural resources for bioenergy, the declining amount of rural land as developing nations move toward industrialization, and the yet-to-be-determined effects of climate change.

Global Food Supply Today

Corn, wheat, rice, and soybeans amount to 75 percent of global food production, and total global agricultural exports rose nearly 200 percent from 1990 to 2008. In 2009, India led global production of rice, with 29 percent of all rice farmed, followed by Indonesia, Bangladesh, and Vietnam. China led global production of wheat, at 17 percent, followed by India, Russia, and the U.S. The U.S. is the world's largest producer of corn, amounting to 41 percent of global output, followed by China, Brazil, and Mexico. The U.S. also produces approximately 40 percent of world's soybeans. Small-scale political or environmental change in these countries, then, can have large-scale effects on the global food supply, especially in countries where small amounts of these commodities are produced locally. This was seen in 2008, when India stockpiled its rice supply by instituting a ban on export, triggering a global rice crisis, or in 2010 when Russia instituted a ban on wheat exports. Some researchers predict that commodity prices could fall by as much as 57 percent if all countries were more open to trade.

One important factor affecting the global food supply in recent years is the increasing demand for biofuels, primarily corn-based ethanol. In 2008, the E.U. passed a regulation requiring cars in all 27 member states to use at least a 10 percent ethanol blend gasoline. China had a similar goal of 15 percent. In 2005, President Bush announced the amount of ethanol used in motor fuels would be doubled to 7.5 billion gallons by 2012. With gas prices high, a 10 percent ethanol dilution comes as a bit of a relief. Yet some believe that the costs of ethanol production outweigh the benefits; in 2007, corn prices were 50 percent higher than in the previous year. The rising cost of corn for animal feed also results in the higher cost of meat and dairy. In 2011, amid mounting political and economic pressure for spending cuts, the U.S. Congress voted to end tax cuts and trade protection that benefit the corn-based ethanol industry.

Another major factor in the changing global food supply is livestock production, which since the 1980's has far outstripped that of cereals. In 1961, the world's total meat supply was 71 million tons. By 2007, it had reached nearly 285 million tons, and per capita consumption had more than doubled. Meat consumption rose twice as fast in the developing world; in China, for example, meat consumption more than doubled between 1980 and 2005. Americans eat roughly eight ounces of meat a day per capita, roughly twice the global average. To meet this increasing demand, in the second half of the 20th century, traditional methods of livestock production were abandoned in favor of "factory farms." In terms of efficiency, these assembly-line meat and dairy factories far exceed traditional methods. Yet industry experts in developed countries have begun to question the cost of factory-farming livestock, given the enormous amounts of energy (including feed grain) required, concerns of animal welfare, and the increased pollution of water supplies, and greenhouse gas emissions. According to the F.A.O., livestock production generates 20 percent of global greenhouse gas emissions, more than transportation.

Global Hunger Today

In 2010 the Food and Agriculture Organization (F.A.O.) of the United Nations estimated that there were 925 million undernourished people in the world—16 percent of the population of developing nations. "Undernourished" or "chronically hungry" is defined by the U.N. as anyone who regularly goes without the 1,800 calories per day, considered the minimum average energy intake. In 2009 there were more than 1 billion undernourished people.

Most of the decrease was in Asia (with 80 million fewer people hungry), and in sub-Saharan Africa (with 12 million fewer). Despite the modest decline, the actual number of undernourished or hungry people in the world was higher in 2010 than it was before the recession of 2008–09. In 2010 the U.N. reported that 22 nations were facing a protracted food crises—classified as such if a country reports a food crisis for at least eight years, and receives more than 10 percent of its foreign assistance in the form of humanitarian relief. These countries, including Afghanistan, Haiti, Iraq, Tajikistan, North Korea, and 17 African countries, require targeted assistance but also longer-term tools such as school meals and food-for-work programs.

The United Nations World Food Programme (W.F.P.) is the world's largest humanitarian agency fighting hunger worldwide. It was initiated in 1961, about the same time as the Green Revolution took hold. In 2011 the agency intended to reach more than 90 million people with food assistance in more than 70 countries. The W.F.P. also works toward emergency preparation and in rebuilding efforts with the goal of countries maintaining agricultural independence even in the face of disaster. In 2009 the W.F.P. was able to provide food and nutrition assistance for nearly 102 million people affected by conflict, financial crises, storms, droughts, and displacement. Much of this assistance is in the form of micronutrient powders or high-energy bars that enhance other food available regionally. The number of children under five, nursing mothers, and pregnant women who received fortified food rations doubled from 2008 to 2009. In 2008 the W.F.P. launched the Purchase for Progress program, through which the agency purchases staple crops directly from farmers' organizations in developing nations.

DICTIONARY OF FOOD

Cereals and Grains

Humans began to raise cereal crops, plants belonging to the family of grasses, at the dawn of civilization. Indeed, theory has it that grain-growing was at least partly responsible for civilization itself; the labor of growing and tending a crop was too great for a lone individual, but the harvest could support expanding populations. Wild grain fields sprang up around 8000 B.C. in the Middle East, where people aggregated to exploit them. Over the millennia that followed, barley, wheat, and rice came under cultivation in Europe and Asia, maize in the Americas. Cereals are first in importance in the human diet, as an efficient source of carbohydrate energy. In terms of their protein profile, they generally lack only one amino acid, lysine, which can be found in legumes or in meat. So suited to sustaining life are cereals that they can compose from 25 percent to 90 percent of a balanced diet (with the remainder supplying vital trace minerals and vitamins, as well as the missing protein).

The term *cereal* itself deserves a closer look; its supermarket definition as a cold breakfast food (rather than its botanical definition as a grass-family plant) is very recent in origin. Eating "cereal" (typically processed oats, wheat, corn, or rice) for breakfast was an American fashion popularized in the late 19th century. Before that, breakfast—at least for those who could afford it—revolved primarily around eggs and meat. Food reformists such as Sylvester Graham, C. W. Post, and John Henry Kellogg believed that a grain-based diet was physically and even spiritually nourishing. Post's Grape Nuts (1897) and Kellogg's Corn Flakes (1898) were early entrants in what is today a $7 billion-a-year industry.

Barley (*Hordeum vulgare*) is among the most ancient of cereals, possibly preceding even rice. Barley grew wild throughout Mesopotamia; Neolithic peoples discovered that barley malt—dried, roasted grain—could be soaked and fermented to make beer. Though never a primary crop, it was important enough to be featured on coins in Greco-Roman times. Today, it is primarily used for animal feed and beer distillation.

Maize/corn (*Zea mays*) In most countries the crop is called maize; in the United States it is known simply as corn (Other English-speaking countries describe their primary grains—be they wheat, rye, or barley—as corn.) The descendant of a wild grass called teosinte, corn originated in Mexico as early as 5500 B.C. The protective husk that surrounds the kernels prevents it from self-sowing, and thus wherever corn is grown, it is grown by human stewardship. Corn is likely to have arrived in the Old World on Columbus's return voyages, although there are other theories. It was being cultivated widely in Europe and Africa by the late 16th century; indeed, its success in Africa led to a population explosion that sustained the slave trade for years.

Economies that depend on maize as a primary staple crop run the risk of epidemics of pellagra, or niacin deficiency. But the historical Mayan preparation of maize soaked in lime renders niacin available; this process is called *nixtamalization*.

Today a number of species of corn are cultivated: dent corn for cattle, flint corn, popcorn, and the familiar sweet corn. Cornmeal and cornstarch and any number of other industrial products are derived from the plant.

Oats (*Avena sativa*) came into cultivation relatively recently—about 1000 B.C. in Europe. Like rye, oats thrive in cool climates. Though highly nutritious (with all the protein of, and more fat than, wheat), they are poor in gluten and make poor bread. When not used for animal fodder, oats are commonly ground into oatmeal, which can them be boiled for a porridge or baked into oatcakes; Scotland, Ireland, and Russia all have a long history of cooking with oats in this manner. In the United States, "rolled oats"—processed and flattened to cook more quickly—were developed by the Quaker Company during the late 19th-century cereal craze, and continue to be a popular breakfast option.

Rice (*Oryza*) Rice, which grows in innumerable varieties, has been cultivated in Asia since at least 2500 B.C. It is the "staff of life" of the Eastern hemisphere just as wheat and corn are in the West; after wheat, it is the second most cultivated grain in the world. The labor-intensive rice crop played a major role in the formation of early human settlements and civilization, since constructing its terraces and irrigation channels required extensive cooperation. Rice underpins many subsistence economies, so crop failure can result in disaster. During the green revolution of the 1960's, the International Rice Research Institute concentrated on producing a number of high-yield rice hybrids, called "miracle rices." These had the effect of erasing famine for some years in developing economies; on the other hand the high-input practices associated with the hybrids often damaged the native ecological balance. Like wheat, rice has a number of derivative products that are important throughout the world, such as rice vinegar, rice wine, and rice noodles. Specialty rices important in international cuisine include basmati, jasmine, japonica, and arborio. North American wild rice (*ZizAnia aquatica*), an aquatic grain, is unrelated to Eastern rice .

Rye (*Secale cereale*) Much hardier than its relative, wheat, rye flourished throughout the Middle East and Europe in soils too poor or cold for wheat (it has been called "the wheat of Allah"—a divinely-sent crop for hard conditions). Rye spreads like a weed wherever wheat and barley are grown; mixed crops of wheat and rye (called maslin) were common in the Middle Ages. As a cold-climate crop, rye traditionally has predominated in Russia (in traditional black bread), Germany (in pumpernickel), and Scandinavia. In the United States, the rye bread (commonly flavored with caraway) of Eastern Europe came to be a staple of Jewish delicatessens.

Wheat (*Triticum*) Wheat, a descendant of wild grains, was domesticated as early as 7000 B.C. in the Middle East, and over time became the dominant cereal crop of Western cultures. As with rice, its cultivation played a vital role in persuading humans to forgo a nomadic hunting lifestyle for a settled, agricultural one. Wheat is highly nutritious and a good source of protein (it contains nearly all the essential amino acids), though somewhat laborious to harvest. The wealthy prized its relatively light-colored flour ("wheat" has the same roots as "white"), a prejudice that persists today in the bleaching and refinement of all-purpose flours. Just as fertility and harvest rites from ancient Mesopotamia to medieval Europe centered on the success of the wheat crop, bread too serves as a near-universal symbol of sustenance. In times of hardship only aristocrats could afford wheaten bread (others relied on "lesser" grains like rye and barley).

Triticum aestivum is the most commonly cultivated wheat; cultivars are divided into hard and soft wheats. Hard refers to high-protein wheat, good for forming gluten, the strands of protein that create the texture of well-made bread. (The high protein content of wheat makes it superior among grains for leavened bread.) Soft refers to wheat low in protein, more suitable for cakes and pastries. A particularly hard type of wheat, durum, is essential for milled pastas.

Wheat arrived in the New World with the Spanish explorers and quickly took to the fertile farmlands of North and South America. Today, the United States and Canada are among the world's largest wheat producers. Wheat is the largest grain crop in the world; close to 2 billion metric tons are harvested annually.

Fruit

The term *fruit* can be confusing. Botanically speaking, a "fruit" is the structure that develops from a plant's ovary, providing nutrition and shelter for its seeds. By this definition, eggplants and tomatoes are fruits, just as apples and oranges are. But when speaking of fruit, we tend to mean sweet, succulent, often aromatic fruits suitable for dessert. Fruits have always held a special allure for humans, dating from prehistory when they may have been the only dietary source of sugar available. Nutritionally speaking, fresh fruits and vegetables are abundant in vitamins and minerals and absolutely essential for vitamin C. Two great families of fruit—the *Rutaceae* (including all citrus fruits) and *Rosaceae* (including apples, peaches, plums, etc.)—predominate heavily in a typical modern Western diet.

Apple (*Malus*) Surely the most storied of fruits, from their fabled role in the garden of Eden to the golden apples that started the Trojan war, apples originated in the forests of Alma-Ata ("father of apples") in Kazakhstan. They were known to humans as early as 6000 B.C., were later prized by Egyptians, were cultivated in the Greco-Roman empire (which perfected grafting techniques), and are now grown in temperate zones throughout the world.

Apples must be cross-pollinated by different varieties to bear fruit; as a result the seeds of each apple are genetically different. Should these seeds be planted, no two trees would bear the same fruit. Early orchardists therefore learned to propagate their trees by grafting apple branches onto selected rootstocks, essentially the same practice used today. American apples, however, enjoyed a biodiversity boom, thanks to John Chapman (1774–1845), "Johnny Appleseed," who scattered apple seeds across the Ohio Valley in the 19th century, allowing the wild forms to crossbreed and produce new varieties.

Apple varieties are divided into "dessert apples" and "cider apples." Cider apples may be bitter or sour, but their complexity benefits the resulting alcoholic or nonalcoholic beverage. (What Americans call hard cider is simply called "cider" by everyone else; what Americans call cider, others call juice.) Hundreds of varieties of dessert, or "eating," apples exist, though aggressive marketing has elevated the Red Delicious, Granny Smith, and McIntosh to supremacy in the U.S.

Bananas and plantains (*Musa*) are members of the same species. The term *bananas* refers to the sweet dessert fruit, *plantains* to the starchy, only faintly sweet fruit used extensively in cooking. Bananas—and particularly plantains—are ancient tropical staples, referred to in origin myths across the Pacific. Once they were introduced to the islands of the Caribbean by Spanish explorers, they established themselves so quickly that subsequent generations of newcomers mistook them for native plants. Consumption of bananas in North America began in the mid-19th century, and bananas became extremely popular when the United Fruit Company began to import them from Jamaica in 1885, later spinning off the internationally recognized brand Chiquita.

Blueberries and cranberries are heath shrubs belonging to the *vaccinium* family, native to the Americas. They were gathered wild by Native Americans across the present-day United States. They were not brought into commercial cultivation until around 1910, when a New Jersey botanist developed a variety with plump and almost seedless fruits. Highbush blueberries (*V. corymbosum*) have a somewhat larger fruit; lowbush blueberries (*V. angustifolium*) have more in common with small wild blueberries. Blueberries have received considerable attention in recent years for their antioxidant properties; they are also an excellent source of vitamin C.

Different species of cranberries existed in the New World and the Old, among them the Swedish lingonberry. Native North Americans gathered the American cranberry (*V. macrocarpon*), and used it and other berries in the jerky-like, long-storing food called pemmican. The pilgrims who crossed the North Atlantic in the 17th century found the American cranberry to be much larger than its European counterparts, and benefited from its high vitamin C content. The roast turkey of an American Thanksgiving is invariably served with cranberry sauce or relish, commemorating the discovery of this important native food. Cranberries, which favor highly acidic, boggy conditions, have been grown commercially in the United States, especially in Massachusetts, since the mid-19th century.

Cherry Cultivated cherries are of two types, the sour (*Prunus cerasus*) and the sweet (*Prunus avium*); both originated in western Asia. They made their way across the Mediterranean, arriving in Europe about the first century A.D. Combined, there are over 1000 varieties. Their uses are distinct: sweet cherries most often are eaten fresh or in desserts; sour cherries become preserves or liqueurs (though there are some uses for the sour cherry as dessert fruits as well). The most popular sweet cherry is the Bing cherry, named by an Oregon orchardist for his Chinese foreman.

Even more so than the plum blossom in China, the cherry blossom is a central symbol in Japan, where it is cultivated ornamentally rather than for fruit.

Dates (*Phoenix dactylifera*) The dates borne by desert date palms are among the earliest domesticated fruits. The wild palms came under human cultivation in the Indus Valley by 4000 B.C. Sugars account for up to 54 percent by weight of a fresh date's nutritional content; consumed with milk for protein, the date constitutes an important staple food. Most dates are imported from the Middle East and North Africa. Though commonly enjoyed fresh where they are grown, most dates are matured and dried for shipping worldwide.

Figs (*Ficus carica*) The cultivation of figs may have begun in Egypt; figs appear in the Sumerian epic *Gilgamesh* (3000 B.C.), and by Greco-Roman times were certainly well established. Each fig is made up of about 1,500 minuscule fruits or "drupelets" that form the fleshy interior of the fig. Pollenization in a majority of varieties depends on a tiny insect, the fig wasp, which lives inside the fruit and travels between trees in the course of its own life cycle. Figs, which grow in warm (but not tropical) regions worldwide, are sold fresh, dried, and canned.

Grapefruit (*Citrus paradisi*) resulted from the refinement of the pomelo (*Citrus grandis*), brought to the Americas in the 1700's by an English sea captain. Grapefruit became a popular breakfast item during the 19th century, eventually making its way to Europe in the 20th century. Ruby red grapefruit developed from a freak mutation in Texas around 1929; tangelos resulted from a cross between grapefruit and orange. A compound present in grapefruits is medically unusual: it affects the uptake of certain drugs by inhibiting a human digestive enzyme, with the result that grapefruit juice is counterindicated in some prescriptions.

Grapes (*Vitis*) Wild grapes abounded in the Black Sea region long before human civilization. By 3000 B.C. they were being cultivated by Sumerians. *Vitis vinifera* was cultivated throughout antiquity for table grapes and especially for wine. In the 16th century wine grapes traveled to the New World, where they joined the native Concord grape, *V. labrusca*, which was mostly eaten fresh or preserved (grape jelly is still made from Concord grapes). American table grapes are dominated by the mild-flavored Thompson seedless variety. Dried grapes are called raisins or, in the case of the Zante variety, currants (confusingly, as fresh currants belong to a completely different family).

Lemon (*Citrus limon*) The lemon was first cultivated in India. Like the orange, it traveled on the heels of Arab exploration, reaching Europe around the ninth century (though some accounts argue it was known to the Roman empire as early as the first century A.D.). Lemons certainly traveled with Columbus and his successors, and were well established in the Americas by 1700. Lemons have an exalted place in the history of scurvy; the age of discovery was nearly over before seamen were finally persuaded that lemons, with their high vitamin C content, were the cure for a disease that plagued every sustained maritime voyage. The British navy required ships to carry lemon juice rations for its sailors around 1800 (the juice was often added to rum rations), and scurvy essentially vanished. The spread of lemons to California was prompted by the Gold Rush of 1849, as miners lured to new territories scarce in food combated scurvy problems of their own.

Although its juice is too acid to appeal as a beverage, the lemon has practically innumerable culinary uses, ranging from marinades and dressings to lemonade, baked desserts, and complementing fish. Meyer lemons (a cross between a lemon and a tangerine) are milder and sweeter, and popular with confectioners.

Lime Limes accompanied lemons and oranges in their spread from Indochina first to Europe and later to the New World. The original lime (*Citrus aurantifolia*) is the small, astringent fruit called key lime in the U.S.; key limes are little cultivated here except in the Florida Keys, for the dessert called key lime pie (made with ordinary limes elsewhere).

The lime more commonly seen in the supermarket is the Persian lime (*Citrus latifolia*) a cross between the key lime and the citron, which was developed in Europe about 1920. Limes, which would ripen to yellow, are typically picked green to avoid confusion with lemons.

In the mid-19th century, limes replaced lemons in the conquest of scurvy (although they are less potent a source of vitamin C than lemons), gaining British seamen a new sobriquet: limeys.

Orange (*Citrus sinensis*) Oranges were first grown either in the Indus Valley or in China, and were of two varieties, the sweet and the sour. The sour orange (*Citrus aurantium*) traveled farthest first, accompanying Arab conquests; it was introduced in Sicily around the eighth or ninth century. The sweet (*Citrus sinensis*) did not follow until as late as the 15th century. But within a hundred years, citrus trees were being widely planted in the Spanish New World, and they have flourished in the Americas since. Today, Seville or bitter oranges are grown mainly in Spain for marmalade, which Britain imports in great quantities. The sweet orange, once an expensive rarity found in European Christmas stockings, became a common treat once refrigerated railcars made it more accessible to the public in the 19th century. Today, the orange enjoys global popularity and is the most important fruit worldwide for juice. The method of producing orange juice from frozen concentrate was perfected in the United States in 1945.

A number of United States relatives of the orange are popular as dessert fruits: blood oranges, navel oranges, tangerines, clementines, and mandarin oranges among them.

Papaya (*Carica papaya*) The papaya is native to the Pacific islands, where inhabitants introduced it to European explorers in the 1800's. It now grows in tropical regions worldwide. Aside from the fruit's sweet and faintly scented flesh (often eaten with lime for acidity), papaya plants contain a digestive enzyme, papain, which tenderizes meat and is used in industrial food processing.

Peach (*Prunus persica*) Peaches are an Asiatic fruit, cultivated in China from 2000 B.C. on. They arrived in Europe with the Greeks and Romans, and in America with the 16th-century Spanish explorers. Varieties are divided into freestone (softer flesh, pit removed easily) and clingstone types (pit closely adhering to firmer flesh, especially suited for canning). Nectarines are a smooth-skinned variant of the peach, and apricots (*Prunus armenica*) are a close relative with a very similar history. Apricots, nectarines, and peaches require very particular growing conditions; most U.S. varieties are grown in California. Apricots are particularly versatile, and are widely sold as a dried fruit as well as in preserves and jellies.

Pear (*Pyrus communis*) originated near the Caucasus, like apples, and rapidly spread east and west. At first pears were prized above apples, both in China and in the Greco-Roman empire. Like the apple, pears left to propagate by seed produce wildly different offspring; this is just what happened in colonial America, where pear seeds were planted and developed into a multitude of varieties. Today, commonly marketed pears include the Bosc, Anjou, Seckel, and Bartlett. The round, crisp Asian pear, a close relative, is also becoming popular.

Pineapple (*Ananas comosus*) Despite its striking success as a Hawaiian commodity, the pineapple is not native to the Pacific islands. It originated in Brazil, where Columbian-age explorers were introduced to it and in turn brought it to Europe. Like the papaya, pineapple contains a tenderizing enzyme, bromelin.

Plum (*Prunus domesticus*) Plums are the hardiest and most widespread of the stone-fruit trees, and thrive on every continent except Antarctica. Though the most common plums here are the red to blue-violet Burbank plums, thousands of varieties—especially European, Asian, and native American in origin—exist. Sloes, damsons, and greengages are among them. In China, the plum blossom is one of four sacred flowers (lotus, chrysanthemum, and peony are the others).

Dried plums are called prunes, and are so laxative in effect that prune juice is often prescribed medicinally.

Raspberries (*Rubus idaeus*) and blackberries (*Rubus ulmifolius*) are fruit-bearing brambles native to the cooler regions of Asia, North America, and Europe. They have been cultivated since at least the first century B.C. Raspberries were particularly dear to the Greeks (they were said to take their color from the blood of the nymph Ida, who pricked herself while feeding them to the infant Zeus). Red raspberry leaf tea has been used as a strengthening tonic by pregnant women for centuries. Raspberries occur in colors ranging from yellow to red, purple, and black; the last appear similar to blackberries but are structurally different. American hybrids developed from the raspberry include loganberries (1881) and boysenberries (1920's).

Strawberry (*Fragaria*) Before human cultivation, strawberries grew wild in both Eurasia and the Americas. In early modern Europe, they were considered a symbol of the Virgin Mary. Most of the original Old World strawberries are small, and some are intensely sweet. The modern supermarket strawberry (*F. ananassa*) descended from two American varieties, *F. virginiana* and the Chilean pineapple strawberry (*F. chiloensis*), which occurred on opposite coasts of North America. They were brought together by chance in 18th-century France, and the popular resulting hybrid dominated the market thereafter (though gourmands still hunt out the tiny *fraises de bois*). Strawberry fruits are exceedingly susceptible to disease, which growers try to discourage by placing clean straw beneath the vines (hence the name).

Tomato (*Lycopersicon esculentum*) Tomatoes may have been grown in Mexico as early as 1500 B.C., and remained there until the time of Columbus. Upon their arrival in Europe, they were at first treated as a botanical curiosity, unlike any other vegetable or fruit. And as members of the deadly nightshade family (like potatoes), tomatoes had to overcome intense suspicion before they were considered generally edible. But once they were finally adopted into the cuisines of Spain, Portugal, Italy, and, to a lesser extent, France, they became a new staple crop; and they have not been abandoned, since they are a valuable source of vitamins A and C.

Vegetables

Vegetables have been crucial to the human diet longer than any other food—from before the cultivation of cereal crops, even before the refinement of hunting techniques. Vegetables tend to be the stems, leaves, or roots of plants. Different systems of classification apply; in the supermarket, we tend to speak of "root vegetables" and "leafy greens." Growers classify vegetables by their families: the Brassicas (broccoli, cauliflower), the Solanaceae or nightshades (tomato, potato, eggplant), the Cucurbits (melons and squashes), the Alliums (onion, garlic, shallots). Many consider legumes (such as peas and beans) separate entirely, as they are distinct in their protein-rich nutritional value and broad application both dried and fresh; they are included here for ease of reference.

Avocado (*Persea americana*) Avocados are native to Latin America and the Caribbean. Though known to other cultures since the Spanish conquest, they first gained com-

mercial popularity in the 19th century; now they are cultivated in regions as far flung as Israel and Australia, as well
as in the Americas. Unlike any other tree fruit, they ripen
only off the branch (the tree itself chemically inhibits
ripening). They contain more fat than any other vegetable
or fruit and are the principal ingredient in guacamole.

Beans (*Phaseolus*) The term *beans* loosely refers to plants
cultivated for their edible seeds or pods, most commonly
members of the *Phaseolus* or *Vigna* families. The green or
haricot bean and its varietals (*Phaseolus vulgaris*) are the most
commonly eaten fresh beans.

The only cultivated bean in Europe prior to the age of
discovery was the broad bean, the fava bean (*Vicius faba*),
which was widely cultivated throughout the ancient
Middle East and the Greco-Roman empire, despite the
fact that a small minority of people are lethally allergic to
favas.

Perhaps the predominant cultivated bean worldwide is
the soybean (*Glycine max*). Widespread throughout Asia,
the soybean has been a major staple crop since the third
millennium B.C. Nutritionally, soybeans are even more
impressive than wheat and rice; they contain 35 percent
protein and a complete complement of amino acids. The
diversity of derivative soy products—ranging from soy oil,
soy sauce, and miso to bean curd, tempeh, and black
beans—is probably rivaled only by that of corn.

Beets (*Beta vulgaris*) Beets evolved from a wild root
found on Eurasian seashores. The beet was originally
grown only for its greens, but beetroot began to find favor
in the first century A.D. (although it wasn't until the 17th
century that the familiar red beet was developed). Today
the leaves and especially the root are used throughout
Europe and North America; beetroot is the principal
ingredient in borscht, the beet soup of eastern Europe.
Sugar beets, a subspecies of beet, are the second most
important source of sugar (after sugarcane) in the world.
Swiss chard is a member of the beet family whose leaves
strongly resemble beet greens, though they tend to be
used more like *Brassica* greens in cooking.

Cabbage (*Brassica oleracea*) Cabbage is the oldest of the
cultivated *brassicas*; some accounts place its origins in the
Mediterranean, but others report that it was cultivated in
China during the Zhou dynasty (500 B.C.). Cabbage
thrives in cooler climates; it has been a Russian staple, for
example, for at least three centuries. Its cooking odor
emanates from an unusually high quantity of sulfurous

compounds (as well as the isothiocyanates, or mustard
oils, present in varieties like mustard greens). Common
varieties include the hardheaded white or green and the
red cabbage, as well as the sweet, wrinkle-leaved savoy
cabbage. Cabbage's relatives are legion; they include broccoli, cauliflower, and brussels sprouts.

This extended family of *brassicas* are also known as cru-
ciferous vegetables, after the small flower in the shape of a
Greek cross that they bear.

Carrots (*Daucus carota*) originated in Afghanistan, but
were common in both East and West. They traveled to the
Americas with the Spanish conquest. They belong to a
family of plants (*Umbelliferae*) better known for its herbs—
dill, parsley, cilantro, caraway. The familiar yellow-orange
variety developed in 17th-century Holland but did not
become popular in the United States until after World
War I, when servicemen became familiar with its uses in
European cookery. A wild version (*Daucus glochidiatus*)
grows in Australia and is used extensively in aboriginal
cooking. Carrots are high in beta carotene, the vitamin A
precursor.

Chili peppers (*Capsicum*) All the pepper species—
sweet or hot—were cultivated in South America from earliest recorded history. The confusion between the hot or
sweet pepper fruits (*Capsicum* species) and the peppercorns used for black pepper (*Piper nigrum*) dates from the
spice-obsessed Columbus, who hoped his sponsors
would consider the new "peppers" as valuable as the old. A
global trade in peppers quickly ensued; Spaniards brought
them to East Asia via the Philippines, while the
Portuguese brought them to India and Southeast Asia. By
the end of the 16th century, peppers were being cultivated
wherever the climate was warm enough, from equatorial
Africa to the South China Sea. Though they quickly
became staples of some cuisines, like those of India and
China (especially the Szechuan region), Europe was slower to adopt them. Ottoman Turks brought the red pepper
to Hungary, where its dried and powdered form became
the popular condiment paprika.

The heat of chili peppers derives from the alkaloid
known as capsaicin, and is measured in Scoville units. A
sweet red pepper registers 0; a jalapeño 2,500–5,000;
and a Scotch bonnet or habañero 80,000–300,000
Scoville units.

Eggplant (*Solanum melongena*), known as aubergine in

England, is a native of tropical Asia, and gradually traveled the Silk Road to reach western Europe around the 15th century. Some eggplants actually look very like eggs—white and ovoid—though the most familiar supermarket variety, the globe eggplant, has glossy purple-black skin.

The seeds of mature eggplants are somewhat bitter; salting before cooking is thought to draw out the eggplant's native alkaloids and reduce its bitterness. Eggplants, sometimes called "poor man's caviar," have little flavor of their own (or nutritive value), but their creamy flesh readily absorbs oil, which helps saturate the eggplant with the flavor of other ingredients.

Garlic See "Onions."

Ginger (*Zingiber officinalis*) Gingerroot is a tropical rhizome that has been used for thousands of years and probably originates in Southeast Asia. It can be used fresh, dried, powdered, or candied, and has powerful preservative and antiscorbutic properties. Like black pepper, it was a valuable cash commodity in the medieval spice trade. Portuguese explorers brought ginger to the New World in the 15th century, and it became the first spice to be grown successfully in New World. Jamaican ginger is considered particularly fine in flavor. Though ginger is primarily used fresh in Eastern cuisines, in Europe and the Americas its dried form predominates as a baking ingredient (and as a legacy of medieval spice habits). Ginger beer, ginger ale, and candied ginger are also popular ginger products.

Lettuces (*Lactuca*) Lettuces were known in ancient Egypt and grew wild in the Mediterranean, but were probably first cultivated by the Greeks; the Romans were inveterate salad eaters. They were long considered cooling and medicinal; the milky fluid or latex at their cores had narcotic properties which were later largely bred out. Like so many other crops, lettuce came to the Americas with the Spaniards. Although lettuces are sometimes shredded and cooked in Asian cuisines, they are almost invariably served raw, as salads, in the West. There are hundreds of varieties: Loose leaf, oak leaf, red, and green lettuces; "butterhead" lettuces like Bibb and Boston; "crisphead" lettuce (Iceberg); and "cos" lettuce (Romaine).

Melons (*Cucumis melo*) probably originated in the wild in the Middle East or West Africa, and were not extensively cultivated until late in the first millennium A.D. The sweet melons familiar today were probably developed in medieval Europe. While cantaloupes or muskmelons,

honeydews, and watermelons are popular in the United States (and watermelons are an important source of portable water for African desert farmers), a number of nonsweet melons and gourds are eaten in Asia; e.g., the Chinese bitter melon, winter melon, and fuzzy gourd. Cucumbers are also members of the genus *Cucumis*, and thrive in similar conditions of abundant light and heat.

Olives (*Olea europaea*) are among the most ancient of food crops; wild olive trees were frequented by humans as much as 10,000 years ago. Olive trees traditionally signify peace, and in Greco-Roman times were said to have been a gift of the goddess Athena. The trees, which can live for hundreds of years, thrive in all the temperate regions of the Mediterranean, as well as in California (where they are mainly cultivated for table olives rather than oil). Olives (which are berries rather than fruits) have an unusually high fat content and have been prized for their oil for millennia. Olive oil is sold in a variety of grades: virgin or extra-virgin oil comes from the first pressing of the olives (extra-virgin denotes a lower acid content). "Cold-pressing" means that the oil has been pressed at a temperature lower than 100 degrees F. More heat yields more oil, but of an inferior quality. The lowest grade of oil was once called "pure olive oil," but now simply is referred to as "olive oil."

Table olives. Raw olives contain bitter glucosides, which are removed by curing (for table olives) or pressing (for oil). Table olives can be brine-cured or lye-cured (the most common methods), dry-cured, or sun-cured; they may or may not be fermented afterward.

Onions (*Allium* genus, *Allium cepa*). The term *onion* can be used generally, to refer to the edible Allium genus (garlic, shallots, chives, etc.), or specifically, to refer to the common yellow or white globe onion, *Allium cepa*. Originating in Central Asia, onions were esteemed in ancient Egypt (they were a staple food for pyramid laborers in 3000 B.C.) and widely eaten in Greece and Rome, and later throughout Asia; for some sects in India, they were considered too sacred to eat. Columbus brought them to the Americas in 1493; today they are grown worldwide.

Most *alliums* release volatile disulfides to greater or lesser degrees, when cut. Cut onions release allicin, which causes eyes to tear, although chilling them or rinsing them reduces the effect (and the substance is neutralized entirely in cooking).

The pungency of garlic (*Allium sativum*) comes from another disulfide. Garlic itself is integral to any number of world cuisines, and has important antifungal and antimicrobial properties; but no one can know whether its health-bestowing effects or its powerful odor gave rise to its reputation as a shield against evil spirits.

Other common cultivars are leeks (*Allium porrum*), shallots (*Allium ascalonicum*), and chives (*Allium schoenophasum*). All onions belong to the same family as the ornamental lily.

Peas (*Pisum sativum*) and **lentils** (*Lens culinaris*) are among the oldest of cultivated plants, dating back as far as 8000 B.C. in Mesopotamia. Until the modern era, peas were mainly used in their dry form, as a long-storing, valuable source of protein and carbohydrate. (They are still primarily used this way in India, for example, where few meals are complete without a serving of dahl.) Dried peas were a staple food in medieval Europe (as in "pease porridge hot, pease porridge cold"). Eating fresh green, immature peas came into vogue only in the 18th century, and today even the pods of many popular peas are eaten, e.g., sugar snaps and snow peas.

Potato (*Solanum tuberosum*) Grown in Peru since 3000 B.C., the many species of potato remained in the New World till the arrival of Spanish explorers in the 15th and 16th centuries. Once brought back to Europe, they were stigmatized as a possibly toxic food for the poor. But frequent famines soon made this easily grown staple crop more attractive; heavy promotion by argiculturalists such as Antoine Parmentier (who had witnessed potatoes eaten in Prussia with no ill effects) and the French aristocracy also helped. By the early 19th century Irish farmers had learned that a single acre of potatoes could feed a family of five; with milk, it made for a nutritionally complete meal. A population explosion ensued, which made the potato famines of 1846 and 1848 especially disastrous and prompted mass emigration.

Spinach (*Spinacia oleracea*) originated in Nepal and spread eastward to China and westward to the Middle East before arriving in Europe in the 11th century. The early 20th-century cartoon character Popeye propagated the notion that spinach is a good source of iron. But spinach contains a high quantity of oxalic acid, which inactivates iron; in fact, spinach is not as rich an iron source as comparable greens like kale. Still, its tender texture, brilliant green color, and delicate flavor make it a popular ingredient for salads, sautées, and soufflés.

Squash (*Cucurbita*) Varieties are commonly divided into "summer" squash and "winter" squash. Summer squashes, like crooknecks and zucchini, have thin skins and light-colored flesh. Winter squash, like butternut, acorn, delicata, and all pumpkins, have thick rinds and generally deeper orange flesh. The cucurbits are native to the Americas, where they were grown for human consumption since at least 10,000 B.C. Native Americans learned to grow them in tandem with ecologically complementary beans and corn (the "three sisters"). They arrived in the Old World with the returning Spanish explorers.

Sweet potato (*Ipomoea batatis*) **and Yam** (*Dioscorea*) Frequently confused, the sweet potato and yam are two entirely different species, though both are starchy tubers. The true yam is very ancient; it could have originated in the Jurassic period, before Asia and America split. It can be found throughout both continents. Starchy and bland, the yam is valued more for its hardiness and storage properties than its delectability; West African and Caribbean cuisines make use of it (as well as the sweet potato, confusingly). The South American sweet potato, on the other hand, was embraced by Spanish explorers for its superior flavor, and brought back to Europe for cultivation. They also brought it west to the Philippines, whence it spread to East Asia. Unlike the yam, the sweet potato does not store particularly well.

Most "yams" sold in U.S. supermarkets are actually sweet potatoes. Boiled, mashed, candied, spiced with nutmeg or cinnamon, or even baked in pies, they are among the more popular root vegetables.

Taro (*Colocasia*) Like the sweet potato, taro is a starchy root crop grown in all of the world's tropical regions. Though relatively insignificant in the North American diet, it is a staple in island nations from the West Indies to Japan and Hawaii. Lighter in texture than a potato, the taro root is low in protein and slightly sweet; it is used to make the paste known as *poi* in the South Pacific, as well as being useful for food starch (like arrowroot and cornstarch), mashes, and chips.

Turnips (*Brassica rapa*) **and Rutabagas or Swedes** (*Brassica napobrassica*) were originally Central European root crops; the swedes are milder and larger than the turnips. Since turnips and their kin grow even in poor soil, they often served as a subsistence crop (during the potato famine, many Irish suffered bloating and malnutrition from subsisting on a turnip-only diet). The root and especially the greens are pickled in the Middle East and East Asia.

Herbs

Generally speaking, herbs are the dried leaves of food plants used for flavoring. The two great families of culinary herbs are the loosely termed carrot family (*Umbelliferae*) and the mint family (*Labiatae*).

Carrot-family members, or umbellifers, are easily distinguished by their feathery leaves and umbrella-shaped crowns of seeds. The ones most commonly used are parsley (*Petroselinum crispum*), cilantro (*Coriandrum sativum*), dill (*Anethum graveolens*), fennel (*Foeniculum vulgare*), lovage (*Levisticum officinale*), and chervil (*Anthriscus cerefolium*).

Mint-family members tend to have squarish stems and distinctive two-lipped flowers; many have strongly scented leaves. Among them are the many species of mint (*Mentha* spp.), especially peppermint and spearmint; oregano (*Origanum vulgare*), marjoram (*Origanum marjorana*), rosemary (*Rosmarinum officinale*), basil (*Ocimum basilicum*), savory (*Satureja hortensis*), winter savory (*Statureja montana*), thyme (*Thymus vulgaris*), lavender (*Lavandula vera*), and sage (*Salvia officinalis*).

Two notable herbs not belonging to either family are tarragon (*Artemisia dracunculus*) and sorrel (*Rumex scutatus*).

Herbs have a long history of medicinal use, which could be said to have peaked in medieval Europe. They had any number of uses, ranging from mild sedative effects (e.g., (chamomile and hops) and sore-throat cures (hyssop) to drawing out fevers (feverfew) and strengthening nerves (rosemary). Today, though the scientific establishment tends to decry them, herbs are still used freely (and with varying effectiveness) as medicines—in Latin American botanicas, in Chinese pharmacies, and on the herbal supplement shelf of many ordinary supermarkets, where anyone can find echinacea or St. John's Wort. Others are simply enjoyed as herbal teas, such as lemon balm (*Melissa officinalis*) and lemon verbena (*Aloysia citriodora*)

Spices

Spices are any part of a plant other than the leaves used for flavoring—seeds, berries, hulls, roots—usually dried for storage and sometimes ground to a powder. For centuries, pepper, cinnamon, clove, and nutmeg-mace were grown only on the so-called Spice Islands of Southeast Asia. Via the Silk Road, Arab traders brought them to Europe and the Middle East, where they became valuable commodities (black pepper was even used as currency). A collapse in Silk Road trading led to the great European sea voyages of the 15th–16th centuries, bound for routes to the Spice Isles. Da Gama found his way around Africa, securing a spice monopoly for the Portuguese. The Dutch East India Company assumed control, followed by the British East India Company, whose trade first in spices and later in tea would support an empire.

Black pepper, called the "king of spices," has without question always been the fulcrum of the trade (red peppercorns and white peppercorns are merely the unfermented and hulled forms of the same berry), especially when it centered in the Spice Islands. A number of spices—cumin, caraway, juniper, bay, mustardseed—grew closer to home, from the European perspective. Allspice was discovered in the Americas, as was the tropical orchid vanilla.

Saffron, native to West Asia, is the most expensive of spices, as hours of labor are required to strip millions of saffron crocuses of their three tiny central stigmata that make up the coveted spice.

Salt

Humans cannot live without salt (sodium chloride), a vital nutrient. Fortunately, salt deposits are abundant (sodium is the sixth most common element on Earth). Prehistoric evidence shows that humans first followed animal trails to salt licks, before learning to mine rock salt and evaporate it from brine; even the earliest civilizations knew that salt could be used to preserve food and improve its flavor. In Greco-Roman times, salt's value was so universally recognized that it was commonly used for money (hence *salary*, from Latin *salarium*, salt). Because its purity linked it with the divine, salt took its place in innumerable religious practices—whether it is used to "kosher" a chicken or to bind a newlywed couple together. Today, salt comes in many forms, from common table salt and sea salt to gourmet varieties like fleur de sel, black lava salt, and Maldon crystals.

Fungi

The two most familiar edible classes of fungi are yeasts and mushrooms. Yeasts, microorganisms that inhabit the air everywhere, have been used—knowingly or not—to ferment beverages, leaven breads, and age cheeses since as early as 3500 B.C.

Mushroom reproduction is famously complex. The few species that can be commercially cultivated, are, and in copious numbers—especially button mushrooms and shiitakes. Others (such as the chanterelle, the hen of the woods, the blewit, the puffball, and the black trumpet) are gathered in the wild by amateur mycophiles for whom the uncertainty of the hunt only adds to its allure. The risk of a lethally toxic misidentification is small—but real enough that most mushroom foragers place a high value on experience, information, and reasonable caution.

Mushrooms (and "toadstools," their poisonous equivalents) grow everywhere, though especially in the Northern hemisphere. The first agriculturalists were slow to embrace mushrooms. Lacking chlorophyll, leaves, and roots, parasitic mushrooms feed off dead or living matter. Their mysteriously rapid appearance after rains and their occasionally fatal toxicity were additional deterrents, and they did not become a commonly accepted food until around 900 B.C. in China. Their nutritional value (high in potassium and protein) and exceptional range of flavors ultimately made them an irresistible food source, and today mushrooms form a prized part of cuisines the world over. A few species are especially notable.

Button mushrooms The white common button mushroom (*Agaricus bisporus*) accounts for more than 80 percent of mushroom sales in the United States (where per capita mushroom consumption in 2009 totaled 3.7 pounds). A brown-skinned variation of *A. bisporus*, the cremini, and its mature version, the portobello, are increasing in popularity. Also widely popular is the closely related but more flavorful *A. campestris*, or field mushroom, also known as champignon de Paris.

Ceps, cèpes, or porcini mushroom (*Boletus edulis*) are among the most sought-after mushrooms of all, the boletes. Dried, fresh, or pickled, boletes are hunted furiously in Europe during their brief summer season.

Morels (*Morchella*) Succulent, veined, and hollow, morels range from yellow to gray to black and are generally the first mushrooms be found in the spring, especially around neglected orchards.

Truffles Prized since Greco-Roman times, truffles are generally the costliest of fungi, commanding prices that average out at about $100 per ounce—a little less for the white truffle (*Tuber magnatum*) than the black truffle (*Tuber melanosporum*). Buried deep beneath the roots of oaks and nut trees, truffles are famously difficult to find and virtually impossible to propagate; truffle hunters use specially trained dogs in place of the pigs who traditionally hunted truffles. The costly whole truffles are typically shaved onto a prepared dish. Truffle shavings and truffle oil (oil in which truffle has been steeped) are more economically accessible ways to enjoy it.

Shiitakes (*Lentinus edodes*) Shiitakes, or black mushrooms, are the fungus most widely used in Asia, as both medicine and food. Shiitakes are thought to confer a number of health benefits, from bolstering the immune system to lowering cholesterol. Sold fresh or dried, they have become one of the most widely available "wild" mushrooms in recent years, as cultivation has grown more reliable.

Fish

Whether eaten raw, cooked, cured, or smoked, pickled, or fermented, the 20,000 species of fish in the world's oceans provide about 15 percent of the protein in the world's diet. Ninety million metric tons of fish were captured in 2009, and about 55 million tons were farmed (China leads in both categories).

Fish have been eaten by humans for at least 100,000 years. Preservation techniques—drying, smoking, salting—have been used since at least the Mesolithic era.

For thousands of years the basic techniques—spear, line and hook, and net—remained the same, changing mainly in scope with the modern era. The most ancient, dedicated fish-eating cultures included Egypt, Japan, and China; in Polynesian and Pacific island culture fish was the principal protein. Around the second millennium B.C., Cretan civilization was based on the sea, but it later abandoned fish consumption; Greeks probably started fishing again around 500 B.C. and became leaders in the craft. Romans, who inherited the tradition, kept live fish in great enclosed *vivaria*; Roman cuisine depended heavily on garum and liquamen, fermented fish-based sauces.

Around the third century A.D., fish came to be viewed as a symbol of Christ for mainly acronymic reasons: the Greek word for fish, *ichthys*, corresponded to the first letters of the inscription "Jesus Christ, Son of God, Savior" in Greek.

Medieval religious tradition, with its complex system of feast and fast (or meatless) days, promoted more extensive fish consumption in Europe, especially during Lent. (To this day, the custom of fish on Fridays prevails in Christian nations too numerous to mention.) Herring—salted, pickled, or marinated—dominated the fish market.

Fish farming, or aquaculture, has been practiced since at least 1000 B.C., though it has never approached the scale at which it is pursued now. While aquaculture relieves some of the burden of overfishing of wild species, concerns about pollution, the use of antibiotics, and the possible escape of genetically engineered species surround large-scale hatchery operations.

Fish species are often divided between freshwater and saltwater: common freshwater fish found in rivers and streams include bass, trout, and catfish; common American ocean fish are cod, bluefish, swordfish, and grouper. Some species are anadromous (spawning and breeding in freshwater, but growing to maturity in salt). The best known of these is the salmon; others are shad and sturgeon.

Overfishing is a common problem and has endangered a number of species. The most notable recent cases have been swordfish, "Chilean sea bass" (Patagonian toothfish), and sturgeon (the source of caviar). The top 10 species of fish consumed in the United States in 2002 were shrimp, canned tuna, salmon, pollock, tilapia, catfish, crab, cod, clams, and pangasius.

Cod (*Gadus*) Prolific, easy to catch, and wide-ranging, the cod has played a large role in human history. Dried cod supplied Viking voyages to North America. Basques fished for cod off the legendary Grand Banks of Newfoundland from 1000 to 1500. Later competition between English explorers, the German-based Hanseatic League, and the Basques ended in the Cod Wars of the 1530's.

The English colonies developed a close relationship with the cod, especially in Massachusetts, where it was very abundant, and where colonists grew so rich from it that an honorary cod sculpture was hung by the statehouse. Dried or salted, cod can be stored practically indefinitely, has good flavor, and provides an invaluable source of protein for many poor economies. In the 19th century, cod preserved by refrigeration gave birth to a whole new industry: the fish-and-chips shop. By the mid-20th century Europeans were so voracious for cod that a second set of Cod Wars began; it had to be brokered by NATO to provide a solution to the overfishing. Taken in sum, cod is probably the most important fish food in modern history. Small cod are called scrod. Cod-liver oil is a rich source of vitamin D.

Pollock (*Pollachius virens*). Also called saithe or Boston bluefish, the cheap and abundant pollock is commonly used for frozen or fried fish (though rarely labeled as pollock in those applications). Its bland white flesh is a fair substitute for cod, though grayer and not as fine.

Salmon The Atlantic Salmon (*Salmo salar*) and Pacific salmon (*Oxyrhyncus* spp.) are separate species, though both are anadromous (ocean fish that travel to freshwater to spawn). The wild Atlantic salmon in particular has suffered serious population decline owing to habitat loss, and to the extent that farmed fish account for the majority of Atlantic salmon on the market. Aquaculture has made salmon an affordable luxury for thousands of households, but has been the target of especially intense criticism in recent years because of the use of pesticides, concentrations of waste, and pollution hazards of some salmon farms. A number of fisheries, notably in Alaska, have taken steps to adopt sustainable cultural practices. Fresh and smoked salmon command the largest part of the salmon market, with canned salmon placing a distant third.

Tuna (*Thunnus*) Although tuna is found almost everywhere, it is most popular in North America (in canned form) and Japan (as sashimi). Tuna is a warm-blooded fish that swims constantly to replenish its oxygen stores; it can reach speeds of up to 55 miles per hour, and eats one-tenth its own weight daily. The most important type of tuna is albacore or longfin tuna, which has a lighter-colored meat than other tuna and is the most prized for canning (though yellowfin tuna was successfully popularized when albacore stocks began to diminish in 1926). Bluefin tuna is most popular eaten fresh.

Dolphin-safe is a term commonly heard in the tuna industry. Dolphins run with yellowfin tuna (less so with albacore), and in the mid-1950's tuna boats, alerted to the presence of tuna by the dolphins on the surface, began to catch tuna using encircling nets. Millions of dolphins were killed in the process; in the 1980's consumers protested with a tuna boycott. A U.S. law enacted in 1990 helped to reduce the death rate of dolphins, permitting the term *dolphin-safe* to be used only by companies that eschewed the nets and embraced a set of "dolphin-safe" fishing standards.

Shellfish The term *shellfish* is generally understood to include any aquatic animal with a shell. Crustaceans, which have a hard outer skeleton, include lobster, crab, and shrimp. Hinged and two-shelled bivalves include oysters, scallops, clams, and mussels; they are one class of the soft-bodied mollusks (the cephalopods, squid, and octopus are shell-less mollusks.) Shellfish, a good source of protein and readily available on most seacoasts, have been eaten since prehistoric times. Shrimp ranks high among the top sea foods eaten globally, whether fresh, dried, or as a paste.

Shellfish—especially bivalves—act as natural filters and can be frighteningly efficient disease vectors in contaminated waters, for organisms like the lethal *Vibrio* bacterium or sewage-borne coliform bacteria. Algae bloom—natural, but toxic to humans—occurs each year during the so-called red tides, at which time it is also unsafe to eat shellfish. (The dictum about eating oysters only in months including the letter "R," however, has to do with the oyster's breeding season rather than tide-borne plagues).

Shellfish cultivation has met with increasing success, particularly in the case of freshwater mussels. Oysters have been cultivated since Roman times.

Animal Foods

Hunting for food, one of the first recognizable human skills, predated even the use of tools. By 75,000 B.C., Neanderthals had established successful hunting techniques. For millennia human omnivores foraged for plant foods, and fished and hunted for whatever animal prey was sufficiently slow, small, or easy to outwit. Wild cattle and pigs began to appear around 10,000 B.C., and the first goats were domesticated. Following the dawn of agriculture, the domestication of animals by humans took off rapidly.

Chicken The origins of *Gallus domesticus* are obscure, but chickens were probably domesticated for their meat and eggs in Southeast Asia by 4500 B.C. Easy to raise, mild-flavored, and invaluable for their eggs, chickens have historically been accepted in nearly every meat-eating culture. Most species of chickens were spring-hatching, making "spring chicken" a seasonal luxury. In the mid-19th century, breeds that laid eggs year-round were popularized in the West.

In the 1950's medical advances introduced a drug to defeat coccidiosis, a disease afflicting large flocks of chickens. The battery system of cages was invented, and soon chicken became less expensive than beef. Today, typical commercial chickens reach maturity in 42 days.

Present-day concerns about poultry are those typical of the livestock industry: the use of hormones and antibiotics, confined living conditions, contaminated feed. Hence the abundance of alternatively raised birds and eggs on the market: "organic," "cage-free," "free-range," "raised without antibiotics." However, not all of these terms are legally defined.

The most common poultry disease is salmonella, which can flourish in imperfect processing environments but is killed at cooking temperatures exceeding 165 degrees F.

The latest news-making poultry threat is avian flu, a highly contagious disease which can be contained only by slaughtering whole flocks and which during 2004 ravaged the poultry industry in Asia.

Historically, ducks (*Anas platyrhynchos*) and geese (*Anser anser*) enjoyed some of the popularity of chickens as small family livestock, though they were never as reliable egg producers, and more difficult to feed. Sales of goose and turkey in particular tend to peak during the holiday season.

Turkey (*Melleagris gallopavo*) Wild turkeys originated in the Americas—they were certainly bred by the Aztec—and they were brought back to Spain in the 15th century with Columbus. They gained instant popularity in Europe, were widely bred, and came back to the Americas with the English colonists who settled Virginia (presumably unaware that turkeys were already there). Although turkey probably was eaten, as the legend has it, in Massachusetts at the first Thanksgiving in 1621, roast turkey didn't become a Thanksgiving tradition until the mid-18th century.

Today's commercial turkey is typically of the breed known as "broad-breasted white"—with white plumage rather than the colored feathers of folk tradition, and a breast so enormous that a mature turkey can scarcely walk; breeders rely on artifical insemination. However, some small producers are responding to consumer's demand for wild or heritage-breed turkeys.

Beef and Veal Today's cattle are descended from two strains, *Bos taurus* and *Bos indicus*, of the Middle East's ancient wild auroch. Humans prized the auroch from at least 6500 B.C. for its meat, milk, hide, and draft power. Oxen, castrated cattle, were pulling primitive plows by 4000 B.C. *Bos taurus* and the plow disseminated westward across Europe, developing countless breeds. *Bos indicus*, the humped zebu, radiated across Asia.

The "sacred cow" is no mere idiom; bovines were associated with deities from the earliest times, when their horns were thought to reflect the curve of the crescent moon. The earliest religious prohibitions against eating beef probably arose around 600 B.C.

Each wave of New World colonization starting with Columbus brought European cattle. Semiferal Spanish cattle populated Mexico and traveled north. Docile northern European dairy cattle arrived in the cold Northeast and traveled west. By the early 19th century, huge herds of mixed wild cattle—notably the Texas longhorn—were roaming the plains, and soon dominated the entire frontier economy. In the 1870's, refrigeration turned the beef industry into a nationwide, year-round industry centered in Kansas City and Chicago.

Game   generally refers to any fish, bird, or animal that is hunted rather than farmed or cultivated (in a sense, all animals eaten by humans were once "game"). Common game animals eaten today are likely to be deer (venison), rabbit, and pheasant. The wild boar, once popular prey, has largely been supplanted by readily available pork products. Some traditional "game" birds or meats—like duck, or less commonly ostrich or bison—now are bred on farms.

Goat   (*Capra hircus*) The goat was almost certainly the first animal to be domesticated by humans, in the Middle East around 9000 B.C. Goats, like the sheep that soon followed them, could forage on poor land unsuitable for cattle. They came to the Americas with Columbus and became popular herding animals throughout Latin America and the Caribbean.

Today, goat meat remains particularly popular in regions where grazing land is scarce, as in parts of Africa and Asia. In North America and Europe, goats are tended mainly for their milk, which is used to make a number of notable yogurts and cheeses.

Lamb and Mutton   (*Ovis aries*) Like goats, sheep thrive on nonarable land, and were domesticated early in the Middle East. They were useful for wool, for meat, and for sacrifice (as is evidenced widely throughout the Judeo-Christian tradition). Mutton and lamb are the principal source of protein in the Middle East and North Africa, much as beef is in North America. In Australia and the Americas, wool is more important than meat in the sheep industry. But sheep are valued worldwide for their milk, yogurt, and cheese (notably Roquefort).

Pork   (*Sus scrofa*) Wild hogs may first have roamed the Middle East or Southeast Asia; in any case, pigs were being raised for food in China by 4300 B.C. In many ways, the pig is the ideal barnyard animal for meat: it breeds fast (producing litters of 10 after four months of gestation), it grows fast (reaching maturity at six months), it has a sweet and mild-tasting flesh, and it is famously unfussy about what it eats.

This last trait may have to do with some of the strong prejudices against the pig. In a number of societies, garbage-eating pigs were an early sanitation measure;

some early civilizations even used them to dispose of human waste. Judaism and Islam both have strong, specific injunctions against the eating of pork that date from the seventh century B.C.

Cultures that embrace the pig as food, on the other hand, embrace it wholly, from snout to hoof. It would be hard to imagine European cuisine without its cured pork products, from Westphalian ham to prosciutto and soppressata. Dependency on the pig has historically been even greater in China, where the word for "meat" and "pork" is the same.

The major health hazard associated with eating swine is trichinosis, caused by the trichinella worm. This is generally avoided by cooking pork to an internal temperature of 140 degrees F, which kills the organism.

Dairy Foods

Sometime between the domestication of sheep and goats (10,000 B.C.) and the domestication of cattle (6500 B.C.), Sumerians discovered the art of dairying. The technique of cheese making was probably honed on goat and sheep milk, and transferred to cows once they had been reliably doemsticated.

Whether a culture was more likely to drink fluid milk or eat solid cheese could well have had something to do with climate. In the warm Mediterranean, perishable milk could not have been stored for long; cheese would have been one feasible means of storage. Greeks and Romans enjoyed a wide variety of cheeses, but considered milk the drink of "barbarians" to the north. By 1000 B.C., dairy products were known throughout Asia.

Climate may have encouraged a sharp division between milk-drinking and non-milk-drinking peoples, but the split was also biologically enforced. Most humans lose the ability to digest milk sugar (lactose) after toddlerhood. Northern Europeans, however, somehow avoided lactose intolerance; they could and did continue to drink milk into adulthood. Where the Europeans went, milk drinking followed; thus it is easy to forget, in a former colony like the United States, that milk-drinking is actually a minority practice around the world. Outside of Europe, yogurt and cheese tended to prevail in dairying regions; lactose breaks down in the fermentation process that produces these foods, making them more stable.

Today, the most popular bovine breed for dairying is the Holstein, followed distantly by Jerseys, Guernseys, Brown Swiss, and a few others. Other dairy animals used worldwide include goat, sheep, and yaks.

Butter Butter could be called a cream product, rather than a milk product. Churning cream drives out water, milk sugar, and some protein (these products are the "buttermilk"); the resulting solid mass, which is at least 80 percent fat, is butter. Some butters are inoculated with specific bacteria to enhance the butter's flavor. These "cultured" butters are popular throughout continental Europe. Most butter sold in American supermarkets is uncultured, or "sweet cream" butter. Both types of butter may be sold salted or unsalted. "Clarified" butter, like the ghee used throughout India, is pure butterfat that has been melted and drawn off from whole butter; clarified butter has a higher smoking point and a much longer shelf life than ordinary butter.

Cheese Cheese is a prehistoric product, thought to have been discovered by humans transporting milk in pouches fashioned from animal stomachs. The enzyme in the stomach linings, rennet, would have curdled the milk, eventually turning it into cheese. Modern cheese manufacturing depends on the same principle: controlled curdling, assisted by the introduction of select bacteria for flavor, followed by forming and aging.

Various livestock other than cows provide milk for cheese, if not for fluid consumption. Goats produce the various types of chèvre (which is merely French for "goat"); sheep produce Pecorino and Roquefort; water buffalo produce mozzarella.

"Raw milk" cheeses are not heated after the curds have formed; soft raw milk cheeses include Camembert, and Brie. Hard raw milk cheeses include Emmental, Parmesan, and Gruyère. U.S.D.A. regulations do not allow the importation of raw-milk cheeses aged less than 60 days, owing to health concerns. Artisanal cheese farms have also sprung up in the United States to try and circumvent the import ban.

Milk Milk is a whole food, completely capable of sustaining infant life on its own; it is also a perfect haven for bacterial pathogens. Thus, finding a way to preserve fluid milk (other than transforming it into butter, cheese, or yogurt) has been a priority wherever it is drunk. The earliest methods involved drying milk to a powder and rehydrating it. The industrial revolution introduced refrigeration, which helped expand milk into a national industry. Today, most milk found at the supermarket has been subjected to the heat treatment known as pasteurization. A temperature of at least 144 degrees F kills most of the bacteria in milk and extends its shelf life. The "shelf stable" or UHT (ultra high temperature) milks sold in unrefrigerated cartons have been heated even further; they can be stored unopened at room temperature, though their flavor is somewhat affected.

Because it is expensive to produce, bulky to transport, and highly perishable, fluid milk has always been a challenging commodity to produce and regulate in the United States; its price is highly volatile. For this reason, political controversies over milk price-supports versus free trade have characterized the industry for decades. Market intervention has gradually fallen out of favor, and the last 20 years have seen an increasing concentration in the milk industry (as elsewhere in food) in favor of larger producers. Small dairy farmers have struggled to survive by forming cooperatives and producing value-added commodities like cheese, yogurt, and ice cream; others have simply shut down.

The other major controversy in the milk industry is the use of rBST or rBGH (recombinant bovine somatotropin or bovine growth hormone), a hormone that increases milk production up to 15 percent. Many in the industry embrace the increased yields; in fact, as many as 30 percent of U.S. dairy cattle receive the injections. But public advocates contend that rBST is dangerous and cruel for animals, which suffer reduced life expectancy, lameness, mastitis, and other health problems. They also argue that rBST, which profoundly affects the bovine endocrine system, makes milk unsafe for human consumption.

Yogurt After cheese, yogurt is probably the world's most important fermented milk product. *Lactobacillus* bacteria convert milk sugars into lactic acid, which gives yogurt its tangy or sour taste. This makes it more digestible for the lactose-intolerant, and extends its shelf life. For long an exclusively Asian product, yogurt enjoyed a sudden rise to popularity in the West in the 20th century, as the health benefits of its live cultures began to be recognized. In 2009, U.S. yogurt consumption was about 11.5 pounds per capita, compared to six times that level in Western Europe.

Chocolate, Coffee and Tea

Chocolate The tropical cacao plant (*Theobroma cacao*) is native to Central America (though it may have grown wild in the Amazon) and may have been cultivated there as early as 1000 B.C. Cacao beans served as currency; the chocolate drink made from cacao was bitter, and important in ceremonial rites. The fall of the Aztec to Cortés introduced Spaniards, and later the rest of Europe, to chocolate, which was consumed copiously as a sweetened beverage. Not until the early 19th century were the complex processes that result in cocoa powder and bar chocolate perfected in Europe. Today, U.S. per capita chocolate consumption averages a bit over four pounds per year.

Coffee (*Coffea arabica*). Coffee is said to have been discovered in the ninth century A.D. by a goatherd from Abyssinia (present-day Ethiopia) who observed his goats dancing after eating the berries. Quickly recognized as a stimulant and an aid to thought and conversation, coffee was popularized and cultivated throughout the Middle East for centuries. In Arabic cultures, it became the social beverage of choice, since alcohol is prohibited to Muslims. In the 17th century, it arrived in Europe and soon enjoyed wide acceptance.

Coffeehouses have always seemed to be hotbeds for intellectual theorizing and political unrest. The 16th-century Turkish government banned the sale of coffee, and 18th-century European monarchs monopolized or taxed it beyond the reach of common people. Enlightenment thinkers would not do without it, and the French and American revolutions are reputed to have had their starts in coffeehouse brainstorming. The most recent surge in coffeeshop activity began in the 1990's, when Starbucks led the nation into a specialty-coffee craze. Although the frenzied pace of expansion appeared to have deflated with the tech bubble economy, the stores and their specialized drinks remain popular.

Despite the rise in coffee drinking, the cost of coffee has been kept so low that independent growers have scarcely been able to survive in recent years. The "fair trade" movement has been especially active in trying to ensure that coffee growing remains an economically viable profession for small farmers. Other terms used in the industry are *shade grown* and *organic*, which indicate that growers have used ecologically sustainable methods in the production of coffee.

Tea Though it had been known for centuries, tea first became popular around A.D. 600 in China and Japan. Tea slowly made its way west with the Turks, but not until the mid-1700's was it introduced into the new coffeehouses of Europe. It rapidly became an obsession in Britain and Russia. The British East India Company amassed a global fortune in the tea trade, and, during its heyday, tea became a symbol of British colonialism. (The Boston Tea Party of 1773 was an open revolt that helped set the stage for the American Revolution.) The company's efforts to force China to trade tea for opium led to the ill-fated Opium Wars of the mid-1800's—and the company's dissolution.

Nuts

We tend to think of nuts as shelled tree seeds, even though the peanut, for example, is a legume and the pine nut a naked seed. All nuts are a valuable source of energy: high in protein and fat, and some carbohydrate. The earliest *Homo sapiens* stored nuts, supplementing hunting and fishing, by 38,000 B.C. Today, nuts are generally viewed as a snack or "dessert" food rather than a primary source of nutrition; nevertheless, their popularity is such that in the United States alone, consumption reached 3.04 pounds per capita in 2002–03 (not including peanuts).

A number of nuts commonly eaten today arose in the New World; the best-known "nut," perhaps, being the peanut of South America. Originating in Brazil, the peanut (*Arachis hypogaea*) has become the most popular nut in the United States, at least partly because of its popularity in the form of peanut butter. (Americans alone eat about eight pounds of peanuts a year). Other South American native nut trees are the cashew (*Anacardium occidentale*) and the brazil nut (*Bertholettia excelsa*); walnuts (*Juglans regia*) and pecans (*Carya pecan*) are North American in origin.

Among the oldest Old World nut trees are almonds (*Prunus dulcis*) and pistachios (*pistacia vera*). With their starchy interiors suitable as a flour substitute, chestnuts (*Castanea sativa*) were once a staple food in the Mediterranean. Other important Mediterranean nuts are hazelnuts or filberts (*Corylus*) and pine nuts or pignoli, which help give pesto its distinctive taste and texture.

The best-known tropical nut is the macadamia (*Macadamia integrifolia*), which originated in Australia. Transplanted to Hawaii in the late 19th century, macadamias throve to the extent that they are now the state's third most important crop. Candlenuts (*Aleurites moluccana*), similar in flavor to macadamias, are widely used in Southeast Asia.

WINE

A Brief History of Wine

"The peoples of the Mediterranean began to emerge from barbarism when they learned to cultivate the olive and the vine." So wrote the Greek historian Thucydides in the fifth century B.C., and indeed, wine-making is as old as civilization itself. Just as society finds its roots in ancient Mesopotamia, the earliest evidence we have for the cultivation of grapes and the supervised fermentation of their juices dates back to 6000 B.C. in the ancient Middle East. The Egyptians recorded the harvest of grapes on the walls of their tombs; bottles of wine were even buried with pharaohs in order that they might entertain guests in the afterlife. Wine was also considered a drink of the elite in ancient Greece, and it was a centerpiece of the famous symposia, immortalized by Plato and the poets of the period. But it was during the Roman era that wine became popular throughout society. In Roman cities wine bars were set up on almost every street, and the Romans exported wine and wine-making to the rest of Europe. Soon, production and quality of wine in other regions rivaled that of Rome herself: in A.D. 92, Emperor Domitian decreed that all of the vines in the Cahors region (near Bordeaux) be pulled out, ostensibly in favor of the wheat cultivation the empire so desperately needed, but possibly also to quell the competition with Italian wine exports.

After the fall of Rome, wine continued to be produced in the Byzantine Empire in the eastern Mediterranean. It spread eastward to Central Asia along the Silk Road; grape wine was known in China by the eighth century. But the spread of Islam largely extinguished the wine industry in North Africa and the Middle East. Throughout Europe, wine-making was primarily the business of monasteries, because of the need for wine in the Christian sacraments.

During this period stronger, more full-bodied wines replaced their sweeter ancient predecessors (which usually were mixed with water before drinking). During the Renaissance, the virtues of various wine regions were appreciated by the increasingly sophisticated wine drinkers, and by the 18th century the wine trade soared, especially in France, where Bordeaux became the preeminent producer of fine wines. The development of distinctive strains of wine grapes led to the production of regional wines with easily recognizable characteristics.

In the New World, the first successful wine-making occurred in the 19th century. Ohio was the first region in America to successfully cultivate grapes for wine, but it was soon eclipsed by wine production in California. About this time grape cultivation first began in earnest in Australia. In the Old World, Champagne was establishing itself as a favorite luxury beverage; and fortified wines such as ports and sherries were becoming increasingly popular, especially in Britain. But despite the growing success of the industry, there was also a catastrophe: late in the century, the phylloxera (louse) epidemic destroyed many old European vines, which was caused by import into Europe of insect-bearing specimens from North America, and affected wine-making for decades. The plague was overcome by grafting cuttings of European varietal vines onto more resistant American rootstock.

Today wine-making is a global industry, with most of the countries of the world producing wine. Machines that can harvest huge areas by day or night have increased production, and modern viticultural science has ensured that the resulting product meets uniform standards, though sometimes at the expense of quality and flavor. Recently, there has been a trend toward more traditional methods of wine-making, such as unfiltered wines, that preserve more of the grapes' true character.

Regions

France French wines, despite recent challenges from upstart New World producers, remain the standard by which all others are judged. Indeed, many of the most suc-cessful varietals in the world—such as Cabernet Sauvignon and Chardonnay—find their origins in France. Wine-making regions, such as Burgundy, Bordeaux, Chablis, and Champagne, have become synonymous with fine wine, even lending their names to styles of wine produced in other countries. France produces more fine wine than any oth-

Wines of France

Region	Location	Principal varetials
Burgundy (Bourgogne)	Central	*Red:* Pinot Noir, Gamay *White:* Chardonnay, Aligote
Chablis	North-central	*White:* Chardonnay
Bordeaux	Southwest	*Red:* Cabernet Sauvignon, Cabernet Franc, Merlot *White:* Semillon
Rhone	South-central	*Red:* Grenache, Mourvedre, Syrah *White:* Roussanne, Marsanne, Viognier
Loire	West	*Red:* Pinot Noir, Cabernet Franc *White:* Sauvignon Blanc, Pinot Gris, Chenin Blanc
Beaujolais	Central	*Red:* Gamay *White:* Chardonnay
Provence	South	*Red:* Cinsault, Grenache, Tibouren, Carignan *White:* Rolle, Ugnin Blanc, Clairette, Bourboulenc

Region	Location	Principal varetials
Languedoc	Southwest	*Red:* Carignan, Cinsaut, Grenache, Mourvedre, Syrah *White:* Aramon Roussillon
Champagne	North	Pinot Noir, Pinot Meunier, Chardonnay
Alsace	East	*White:* Riesling, Gerwurztraminer, Pinot Gris, Muscat, Sylvaner, Chasselas, Pinot Blanc
Jura	East-central	*White:* Savagnin, Chardonnay *Red:* Poulsard, Trousseau, Pinot Noir, Gamay
Savoie	East-central	*White:* Altesse, Jacquere, Bergeron (Roussanne), Molette, Chardonnay *Red:* Mondeuse, Gamay, Douce Noir (Dolcetto)
Corsica	South	*Red:* Nielluccio, Sciaccarello, Carignan, Grenache, Cinsault, Alicante *White:* Vermentino, Muscat

er nation, and wine-making takes place in a number of clearly defined regions.

French winemakers rely as much on traditional methods as on science. The great wines of France are most often aged in wooden casks, and this "French oak" is so renowned that one of the first major investments of most up-and-coming wineries is French barrels. The fact that so many wine terms are French in origin, and that so many wines produced abroad carry the names of French varietals, indicates France's importance to the global wine-making industry.

Italy   Wine-making is as thoroughly entrenched in Italy as it is in France, and the annual volume of wine produced in Italy is second only to that of France. The entire peninsula is planted with vines of wide variety, and Italy exports more wine than any other country.

In addition, French varietals such as cabernet sauvignon, chardonnay, merlot, and sauvignon blanc have been successfully cultivated in Italy, especially in the northern and central regions. The advent of the "Super Tuscans"—Bordeaux-style blends of Cabernet Sauvignon and Merlot—ushered in a revolution in Italian wine-making in the early 1970's.

While France has largely adhered to traditional wine-making technology, Italy's vineyards are among the most modern on the continent. Steel tanks have largely replaced the wooden and cement fermentation vats of the past, and high-tech advancements such as temperature control, filters, and centrifuges are widely accepted. Together with traditional standards for high quality, these modern techniques have helped place Italian wines among the very best in the world.

Spain   The wine-making industry in Spain is as ancient and established as that of France. More land is devoted to the cultivations of the grape in Spain than in any other nation, though it is third in the world in total wine production. While Spain, like Italy, has vineyards throughout the country, the annual yields are lower owing to a less favorable climate and persistent droughts.

Spain plants more than 600 grape varieties, though 80 percent of the land is devoted to just 20 varietals. And while Spain has benefited from the relatively recent modernization of its wine-making industry, its wines are still marked by the distinct regional and cultural differences in the country. Spain, it would seem, has a wine for every taste and occasion, from the dry white wines of Galacia to

Wines of Italy

Region	Location	Principal varetials
Friuli	Northeast	*White:* Tocai, Pinot Grigio, Pinot Bianco, Ribolla Gialla, Picolit, Verduzzo, Schiopettino, Sauvignon *Red:* Refosco, Pignolo, Tazzelenghe
Veneto	Northeast	*White:* Garganega, Trebbiano, Prosecco, Vespaiola, Red: Corvina, Rondinella, Molinara (Valpolicella, Bardolino, Soave, Prosecco)
Piedmont	Northwest	*Red:* Nebbiolo, Barbera, Dolcetto, Brachetto *White:* Arneis, Cortese, Erbaluce, Moscato (Barolo, Barbaresco, Ghemme, Gattinara, Dolcetto d'Alba, Gavi, Moscato d'Asti)
Liguria	Northwest	*White:* Bosco, Vermentino, Pigato, Albarola *Red:* Ormeasco (Dolcetto), Rossese, Sangiovese, Ciliegiolo (Cinqueterre, Ligure di Ponente, Dolceacqua, Golfo di Tigullio, Colli di Luni)
Emilia-Romagna	Central	Lambrusco, Sangiovese di Romagna
Umbria	Central	*Red:* Sangiovese, Sagrantino *White:* Trebbiano, Grechetto, (Orvieto Classico, Sagrantino di Montefalco, Rosso di Montefalco, Rosso Orvietano)

Region	Location	Principal varetials
Tuscany	Central	*Red:* Sangiovese, Canaiolo *White:* Trebbiano, Vermentino, Vernaccia, Grechetto, Malvasia (Chianti, Brunello di Montalcino, Rosso di Montalcino, Vino Nobile di Montepulciano, Carmignano, Rufina, Vin Santo, Vernaccia di San Gimignano)
Le Marche (The Marches)	East-central	*Red:* Lacrima, Montepulciano, Sangiovese *White:* Verdicchio, Trebbiano (Rosso Cornero, Verdicchio)
Campania	Southwest	*Red:* Aglianico, Sangiovese, Piedirosso *White:* Falanghina, Fiano, Greco, Coda di Volpe (Greco di Tufo, Taurasi)
Puglia	Southeast	*Red:* Primitivo, Negroamaro, Malvasia Nera, Uva di Troia *White:* Bombino Bianco, Verdeca
Calabria	South	*White:* Greco, Montonico *Red:* Gaglioppo, Magliocco (Ciro Rosso, Crio Bianco) (Locorotondo, Martina Franca, Salice Salentino)
Sicily	South	*White:* Inzolia, Catarratto, Grillo, Grecanico, Malvasia, Zibibbo *Red:* Nero d'Avola, Frappato, Nerello Mascalese
Sardinia	West	*White:* Vermentino, Nuragus, Vernaccia, Mscato, Malvasia *Red:* Monica, Cannonau, Carignano

the big reds of Ribera del Duero to the world famous sherries of Jerez.

Other European Nations France, Italy, and Spain dominate European wine production, but many distinctive styles of wine are produced throughout Europe. The better German wines tend to be clean and fruity, with more than 80 percent of German vineyards devoted to white grapes. The image of German wines has suffered in part because of the dominance of exports such as the notoriously dull Liebfraumilch, but the Rieslings produced in the vineyards of Mosel-Saar-Ruwer and Rheingau can easily compete with their French counterparts. Austrian wines are becoming more and more popular, and the country's wineries are increasingly important on the international stage. While the wide variety of grapes cultivated might be expected in a country surrounded by notable national traditions of wine-making, the most popular varietal is a grape indigenous to Austria, the Gruner Veltliner, which, at its best, offers a perfume and taste reminiscent of the wines of Alsace, and represents about half of the white wine production in the country. Greece enjoys one of the richest historical traditions of

Wines of Spain

Region	Location	Principal varietals
La Rioja	North	Albarino, Tempranillo, Garnacha, Malvasia, Macabeo
Castile and Leon	North-central	Tinto Fino, Albillo, Mencia
Galicia	North-west	Albarino, Treixadura, Torrontes, Mencia
Levante	East	Bobal, Monastrell
Catalonia Coast	North-east	Tempranillo, Monastrell, Garnacha
Valdepenas	South-central	Airen, Cencibel (Tempranillo)
Andalucia	South	Palomino, Pedro Ximenez

wine-making, and many of the varietals still popular have ancient roots. The industry has modernized to a large extent over the last 40 years, and with some notable results. Portugal is known for its fortified port wines, for the eponymous wines of the island of Madeira, and as the preeminent producer of corks. Portuguese vintners have resisted the international trend toward importing grapes and standardizing wine-making practices, preferring to cultivate and blend their own indigenous varietals.

United States After France, Italy, and Spain, the U.S. is the world's fourth-largest producer of wine. Although European vines were introduced to Mexico and California under Spanish rule, the English colonies of the Atlantic coast produced little wine, and the quality of domestic wines was poor. There were no indigenous noble vines; the ubiquitous Concord grape is much better suited for grape juice than for wine. Today, however, after more than a century of cultivating grapes imported from Europe, the United States produces some of the world's best wines. All 50 states boast wineries, and wine-making is an important and successful industry in California, New York, Washington, and Oregon.

California produces 90 percent of American wine. Wine grapes were planted in the 18th century by the Spanish missionary-priest Junipero Serra, and the first commercial winery in the Napa Valley was established in 1861. California's viticultural areas are found in about two-thirds of the state, from the high-desert region of Temecula near the Mexican border to Lake County along the northern coast. The most important regions are Napa, Sonoma, Santa Barbara, Monterey, San Luis Obispo, Mendocino, and Lake County. Most of the European varietals cultivated here have flourished, with

Cabernet Sauvignon, Chardonnay, Pinot Noir, Merlot, Sauvignon Blanc, Syrah, Viognier, Sangiovese, Riesling, and Gerwurztraminer being the most successful and important. Zinfandel, long considered an indigenous grape, is the most commonly planted red wine grape in the state. It has been conclusively shown in recent years (thanks to vine DNA comparisons) to be a direct descendant of the Primitivo grape of southern Italy; however, nowhere else has this grape produced the often interesting and even complex wines that are made in California.

For the last 30 years, California wines have consistently matched or bested their Old World competition in terms of quality, and the best of the state's Cabernet Sauvignons and Chardonnays command prices often in excess of those from estates in Bordeaux and Burgundy. Famously, a Cabernet from the Stag's Leap winery won a 1974 comparative tasting in Paris, an event that marked the arrival of California wines on the international scene. Over the last 15 to 20 years there has been a growing interest in Rhone-style wines, Italian wines based on the Sangiovese grape, and Alsatian whites.

New York is second only to California in U.S. wine production, and there are four major wine-producing regions. Long Island, specifically the North Fork and Hamptons peninsulas, enjoys a maritime climate that its adherents like to compare to that of Bordeaux. This allows the region a longer growing season, and Merlot, Cabernet Franc, and Sauvingnon Blanc do especially well there. The Hudson River, Finger Lakes, and Lake Erie regions in upstate New York and produce successful varietals of Riesling, Gerwurztraminer, Chardonnay, and Pinot Noir wines.

Washington Most of the important Washington wineries are located in the eastern part of the state, where the climate is dry. The principal growing region is the Columbia Valley. Most varietals do well, and white grapes take up the most acreage. Notable successes have been with Riesling, Semillon, Sauvignon Blanc, Cabernet Sauvig-non, and Merlot, the latter arguably the most important varietal in the state. The Austrian Limberger grape has enjoyed a somewhat surprising success as well.

Oregon The cool climate of Oregon has allowed grapes that suffer from excessive heat to flourish, and the state has become best known for its production of high quality Pinot Noirs. Gamay Noir also does well, and the region is known for ice wines made from Riesling and Gerwurztraminer. The principal regions are the

Willamette Valley, Umpqua Valley, Rogue River, Illinois Valley, and Applegate Valley.

Australia and New Zealand More than 1,000 wineries dot the Australian continent, spreading through every state and growing every variety of wine, from dry whites to fortified Port-style wines. Australia is now among the top 10 producers of wine in the world and is especially known for its success with Shiraz (Syrah) and Cabernet Sauvignon. The other predominant varietals grown are Grenache, Mourvedre, Muscat, Semillon, Pinot Noir, Grenache, Riesling, Chardonnay, and Sauvignon Blanc. Australia's sophisticated, pioneering viticulturalists have had a profound influence on wine and wine-making around the world, an influence that grows with each passing year.

New Zealand wines, like their neighbors in Australia, are gaining more and more recognition internationally, and the Sauvignon Blancs produced there are now among the most acclaimed in the world. Because the wine-producing regions are spread over a distance of about 1,000 miles, grapes are grown in a wide variety of climates and soil types, and distinctive styles have been achieved with Chardonnay, Pinot Noir, Cabernet Sauvignon, Merlot, and Reisling varietals. Thanks to New Zealand's prevailing maritime climate, grapes are afforded a long, slow ripening period that allows the varietals to retain their distinctive flavors.

South Africa Although the first vineyards in South Africa were created by French Huguenots in the late 17th century, it wasn't until the establishment of a major wine cooperative (KWV) near the end of World War I that wine-making in South Africa became a viable industry. Today South Africa has 15 classified wine-growing regions, and the industry benefits from a climate very similar to that of the Mediterranean. Most popular varietals have thrived here—Cabernet Sauvignon, Pinot Noir, Chardonnay, Sauvignon Blanc, and Muscat in particular—but a notable contribution to the international wine market is Pinotage, a clone of Pinot Noir and Cinsault grapes developed in South Africa. Also of note is Hanepoot, a white varietal grown only in South Africa, used to produce fortified wines.

South America After Europe, South America is the world's second most important wine-producing continent. While most South American nations make some wine, Argentina and Chile are the most important producers in the region.

Argentina, which annually produces about four times the quantity of wine that Chile does, has eight distinct wine-growing regions, of which Mendoza is the most important. Thanks to a rich history of Italian immigration, many of the more important reds wines are produced from varietals such as Barbera, Sangiovese, Nebbiolo, Dolcetto, and Lambrusco. Cabernet Sauvignon has also done well, but the most important grape in Argentina is the French Malbec, which produces wine of world-class status. Because of its international popularity, Chardonnay is also a widely planted varietal.

Chile, with dry summers, enjoys a climate similar to that of the Napa Valley, and produces fruity and exceptionally ripe wines. Chile is especially known on the international stage for well-produced and well-priced—if somewhat uncomplicated—red wines, with those made from Cabernet Sauvignon heading the list. But without a truly unique style of wine-making, Chile's most important contribution to the world of wine is perhaps its wine made from Carmenere (also known as Grand Vidure), a Bordeaux varietal that is especially promising. Other important Chilean varietals are Merlot, Syrah, Chardonnay, and Sauvignon Blanc.

A Glossary of Wine Words

acidity when mentioned on a label, a measure of the total acid present in the wine. Excessive acidity can cause wines to taste sharp or tart, sometimes to an unpleasant extent. But too little acidity can cause wines to be flat and uninteresting. The typical acidity of a balanced table wine usually falls within the range of 0.6 percent and 0.75 percent of the total volume. Generally speaking, for proper balance the sweeter the wine the higher the total acidity should be.

alcohol by volume law requires that labels clearly show the level of alcohol in the wine. Table wines usually fall within the range of 11.5 percent and 14 percent; dessert wines range from 17 percent to 21 percent.

aperitif most often used to describe any wine that is usually consumed before a meal, but it also signifies a legal classification for wines having a level of 15 percent or more alcohol by volume.

appellation system defines the area where a wine's grapes were grown. Regulations vary from country to country.

astringent descriptive of wines with a harsh, puckery taste that leaves a sensation of dryness in the mouth. Usually caused by excessive tannins in wine.

auslese German dessert wine. *Auslese* is the German word for "selection," here used to describe specially selected, perfectly ripened bunches of grapes that are hand-picked and then pressed separately from other grapes. One of the six categories in the Qualitatswein mit Pradikat (QmP) classification system for fine German wines.

balance subjective term describing wines whose various elements are in harmony, with no single feature dominant. A wine in which the tastes of acid, sugar, tannin, alcohol, and flavor are in accord is said to be "balanced."

blend unless the label identifies a wine as derived completely from a single varietal, wines, generally blended from different lots or barrels. Tradition and regional laws dictate what grape varieties may be blended together to make a certain wine. Varietals, vintages, and barrel varieties can all be blended to create a distinctive wine.

bottled by indicates only that the winery played a very small part in the wine's production, most likely having purchased and bottled wine made somewhere else. However, if the label reads "Estate-Bottled" or "Château-Bottled," the wine was grown in the winery's own vineyards.

bouquet smell or fragrance that has its origins in the wine production or aging methods (as opposed to the fruit itself). *Bouquet* refers to the smell that develops after a wine is bottled; *aroma* is usually the more appropriate term for describing a wine's overall smell.

breathe, breathing process of aeration. When wine is poured into a wineglass, or decanter, the introduction of air releases aromas that become more pronounced as time passes.

brut term exclusively used for champagne describing the driest—or least sweet—wine. Confusion arises over the term *extra dry*, which actually denotes the sweetest of champagnes.

buttery describes the creamy taste of better white wines, particularly Chardonnay. It can also be used to describe the golden color of these wines.

claret old British synonym for Bordeaux wines, increasingly used today as a general reference to light red wines. Even though *claret* sometimes appears on labels, it has no legal definition.

corked term describing wine that has interacted with a defective or moldy cork. Wines spoiled in this manner taste dank or musty, and, unfortunately, since defective corks look the same as good ones at the time of bottling, there is no way to determine if a wine has been affected in this way without actually tasting the wine.

cru, grand cru the French word for growth, *cru* refers to a vineyard of especially high quality, such as a classified growth. *Grand cru* describes an even higher quality of vineyard, and *grand cru classé* is the designation for the most superb wines that originate in the Bordeaux region. *Cru bourgeois* is a category for the châteaux of the Médoc that ranks just below *cru classé*.

cuvée usually refers to a given lot or batch of wine held in a single tank or large cask. Generally the term indicates a specific blend of wines. It is often used on Champagne labels in lieu of a vintage date.

dessert wines wines served after meals, traditionally of two varieties: fortified wine, such as port or sherry, to which alcohol is added in the form of brandy or neutral spirits; and sweet or very sweet wines of any alcohol level, such as muscat or sauternes.

dry term describing the absence of any taste of sugar in wine. *Dry* usually indicates wines with sugars totaling no more than 0.5 percent, though the term is used rather loosely on wine labels.

eau de vie French term meaning "water of life." Describes any colorless, potent brandy or other spirit distilled from fermented fruit juice.

eiswein German word meaning "ice wine." Eiswein is made from late-harvested grapes allowed to freeze on the vine, concentrating the sugars. While it originated in Germany, eiswein is now produced in many countries with cool climates; the English term *ice wine* is often used.

enology (oenology) study of wine and wine-making.

estate-bottled label phrase meaning that the wine was produced and bottled at the winery from grapes owned and farmed by the vineyard owners.

ethyl acetate vinegary smell that indicates the presence of acetic acid in wine. While it can enhance the aroma and taste of some wines—particularly sweet ones—noticeable ethyl acetate is usually considered a flaw.

fermentation chemical process by which yeasts transform the grapes' sugar into alcohol and carbon dioxide. Most of the other elements of the original grape juice are essentially unchanged by the process.

filtering clarifying process in which yeast cells and other impurities are removed after fermentation. Unless indicated as unfiltered on the label, most wines are filtered for clarity and stability.

finish last impressions of flavor left in the mouth after the wine is swallowed.

first growth, second growth, etc. system of classification instituted in 1855 for Bordeaux wines, ranking vineyards according to price from first growths (*premier crus*) through fifth growths (*cinqième crus*). Price was seen as a directly indication of quality, and the system is still respected and in use today, though there are some obvious omissions. For example, the great wines of Pomerol were never classified according to this system.

fruity describes a wine in which fruit flavors dominate the aroma and taste. These wines are usually light in body and easy to drink.

haut French word meaning "high" or "upper." Generally used in a geographical sense, as in Haut-Médoc which is north of the Médoc region in Bordeaux. *Haut* does not mean that the quality of the wine is higher.

hock British term referring to wine from the Rhine regions of Germany.

kabinett first and lowest of the six subcategories of the QmP German wine classification system. These wines are usually the driest and least expensive in this category.

kir aperitif made of white wine that is flavored with a touch of crème de cassis, a black currant-flavored liqueur. When made with Champagne, it is called a kir royale.

late harvest indicates the condition of the fruit rather than a specific calendar date. Grapes harvested late from the vine are higher in sugars. For white wines this usually indicates a sweeter wine; for reds it may indicate a higher alcohol level as well as additional sweetness.

length almost a synonym for "finish," this term indicates how long the flavor lasts in the back of the throat after swallowing.

limited bottling rather nebulous term referring to everything from small lots of special wine to entire vintages of wines from top producers. This is not a legally defined term in the wine industry.

lot number differentiates wines of the same vintage and type bottled at different times, or wines blending vintages or growing regions.

nose character of a wine as determined through the olfactory senses, including the aroma and bouquet.

nouveau French word meaning "new," generally applied

to some Beaujolais-type wines. *Nouveau* describes a wine that is young, fresh, fruity, and simple. Nouveau wines are designed not for long aging but for immediate consumption.

old vines term used especially in California to designate wines produced from vines planted in the pre-Prohibition era. Lacking a legal definition, the term implies quality. It is commonly used to describe the higher-quality (and more expensive) zinfandels.

reserve term used liberally by winemakers (and hence of little value), ostensibly to indicate superior wines. When used to describe Champagne it refers to wine reserved for future blending.

sec French term meaning "dry," though on Champagne labels it means that the wine is sweet. *Demi-sec* is a term exclusively for Champagne indicating that the wine is medium-sweet.

spätlese German for "late picking," refers to grapes that are selectively picked at least a week after the main harvest starts for that specific variety. Because these grapes contain more sugar, the resulting wines are rich and sweet. Another QmP category for German wines.

structure interplay of elements creating a tactile impression in the mouth—such as tannin, acid, alcohol, and body.

sur lie French term meaning "on the lees." Lees is the coarse sediment that accumulates during fermentation. *Sur lie* indicates that a white wine has been kept in contact with yeast lees longer than usual in aging and processing. The hoped-for result is a more complex wine with a toasty, roasted-grain flavor.

sweet term describing the sensation of a sugar taste in wine. The intense flavor of fruit or overripe grapes is often described as sweet. The nonsugary sweetness perceived in wine is often the result of varying levels of alcohol, tannin, and acid. Alcohol in a totally dry wine often gives the wine a sweetish taste, as if sugar had been added.

tannin substance in red wines (and some whites) that imparts a bitter or astringent taste. Tannins are derived from grape skins, stems, and seeds, as well as from wood, if the wine is aged in natural casks. Many powerful young red wines have high levels of tannin that take years of aging to soften. Tannins give many big reds their heady character, though if not kept in balance they can leave an unpleasantly bitter aftertaste.

unfiltered indicates that the wine was clarified and stabilized without the filtration process. Unfiltered wines have achieved a trendy status in recent years.

varietal wine named after the single or predominant grape

BEER

A Brief History

On April 23, 1516, Duke Wilhelm IV and Duke Ludwig X of Bavaria issued a ducal decree that specified the exact ingredients that could legally be added to a beer intended for commercial sale: "We wish to emphasize that in future in all cities, markets and in the country, the only ingredients used for the brewing of beer must be Barley, Hops and Water."

By doing so, they protected bread bakeries from price competition over wheat and rye, and prevented brewers from adding cheap adjuncts to their mashes. In drafting this *Reinheitsgebot*, or beer purity law, they also created one of the oldest know food safety regulations.

Nearly 500 years later, those three ingredients, along with yeast, remain the essence of a drink that has enjoyed popularity among numerous civilizations since at least 3500 B.C. Originating in Mesopotamia, beer gradually made its way west to Egypt, where honey and ginger were added as flavorings. Greek merchants then brought a version of the fermented drink to Europe and introduced it to the Romans. Their preference for wine however, meant the eventual migration of beer across the continent would come from Germanic tribes who occupied territory that lent itself to grain cultivation rather than grape growing. The discovery of ale residue in a ceramic vessel near Kulbach, Germany dating to 800 B.C., attests to this country's long history of brewing, a tradition that endures to this day.

Beer Styles and Brewing Nations

Until the nineteenth century, yeast was an overlooked, or at best misunderstood ingredient, most often considered a by-product of fermentation. As such, wild, naturally-occurring strains of this micro-organism were responsible for converting ancient malted beverages into alcohol. On a basic level, beer can be divided into two categories, ale and lager. These categories are determined in large part by brewing methods and the yeast variety used, and not color, bitterness, or alcohol content alone. Ale yeasts ferment at warmer temperatures (60–75 degrees F) and rise to the top of the fermentation vessel during brewing while lager yeasts sink to the bottom of the vessel and require cooler temperatures (46–59 degrees F) to covert fermentable sugars into alcohol, carbon dioxide, flavors and aroma. Ales commonly rely on a greater variety of hops and malt than lagers, and might contain larger amounts of each in their recipes.

Ale and lager can be further divided into numerous styles, many of which are attributed to five principal brewing nations: Belgium, the Czech Republic, Germany, Great Britain, and the United States. While many types of beer from sour lambics to citrusy saisons are brewed within its borders, Belgium is perhaps most famous for its strong ales, complex drinks that frequently possess a fruity, spicy character. Candi sugar, the name for sugar that has been heated with citric acid, is typically added to boost alcohol levels and to enhance drinkability. Beer connoisseurs may especially appreciate the bold ales of Belgium, but internationally, pale or golden lagers are the most popular styles. Among these, the pilsener (also spelled *pilsner*) is the style that has been most imitated around the world. Originally from the city of Pilsen in what is now the Czech Republic, this crisp, clean lager has historically relied on the Saaz hop for bittering, and is also called a Bohemian Pilsener.

German brewers quickly learned to produce a similar lager of their own, and added it to their dozens of regional styles. Bavaria, in the southern part of the country, is known for its Weissbier or "white beer," an effervescent and refreshing wheat ale that can be clear or cloudy, pale or amber in color. Hefeweizen or Hefeweissbier, has flavors and aromas that are banana-like, clove-like, or even akin to bubblegum, while the darker Weizenbock or Weissbock tends to have a bready malt flavor and a caramel sweetness. Both are mildly hopped. To the north, in Rhineland, Cologne is recognized as the birthplace of Kölsch, a delicate, lightly dry pale ale, just as Franconia is associated with Kellerbier, or cellar beer, a hazy, mildly-carbonated, unfiltered lager. Other well-known styles include the bitter, copper-colored Düsseldorf Altbier, and the dark, smoky Rauchbiers of Bamberg.

Great Britain meanwhile, developed its own range of styles that are now common across much of the globe. Heavily hopped India Pale Ale for example, was designed to survive the lengthy ocean voyage to India. Malty, coffee-like, and full-bodied Russian Imperial Stout on the other hand, was crafted by for export to the Imperial court at St. Petersburg. Nutty brown ale, light-bodied English bitter, malty Scotch Ale, and Irish Dry Stout are just a few of the other beer varieties that have emerged from the United Kingdom since the Middle Ages.

The Rise of Craft Beer

In the United States, beer has been a part of the country's history since the first settlers landed in New England in the seventeenth century. Before the passage of the Volstead Act in 1920, the U.S. had thousands of small breweries, many of which had been started by European immigrants. By 1933, however, when the 21st Amendment repealed Prohibition, the number of American breweries had fallen to well under 800. Volume increased with modernization of brewing techniques, but over the course of the next 50 years, that figure continued to drop until fewer than 100 breweries existed nationwide. And yet even as the number of commercial breweries shrunk, homebrewing as a hobby was taking off. In 1974 the Maltose Falcons, one of the earliest homebrew clubs, began meeting in Los Angeles. Within four years the Falcons, as well as a number of similar clubs across the country, had successfully campaigned for the passage of H.R. 1337, a bill legalizing the practice from coast to coast.

Meanwhile, a few entrepreneurs decided to challenge convention by opening microbreweries at a time when the market was dominated by light lagers made by brewing giants such as Anheuser-Busch, Schlitz, Miller, and Pabst. First a young Fritz Maytag rescued the struggling Anchor Brewing Company from extinction in San Francisco, and then roughly a decade later, Jack McAuliffe founded the New Albion Brewery in Sonoma. These two men in particular, along with a handful of others including Ken Grossman of Sierra Nevada Brewing company, are widely regarded as pioneers in the craft brewing movement, and are often credited with sparking the craft beer revival in the United States. Today American brewers continue to experiment with classic European beer styles to create a growing number of unique, sometimes aggressively hopped ales and specialty beers.

According to the Brewer's Association, a professional organization in the United States, craft brewers are businesses that annually produce 6 million barrels of beer or less, own at least 75 percent of the company, and continue to brew all-malt beers.

The malt, or sprouted and kilned grain, that a brewer chooses to use in a given ale or lager, helps to determine that beer's density, color, and palate. All-malt beers differ from many of the products made by the largest, non-craft breweries, which rely heavily on unmalted adjuncts such as corn, rice, and wheat. These commercial beers tend to be lighter and less expensive.

The craft segment of the greater beer industry has grown at a rapid pace in the last decade and for the first time in more than a century, the total number of breweries in the U.S. now exceeds 1,700. In 2010, the three largest craft brewing companies by sales volume were Boston Beer Company of Boston, Massachusetts, Sierra Nevada Brewing Company of Chico, California, and New Belgium Brewing Company of Fort Collins, Colorado. Although California has the most breweries in total (255), Vermont alone can claim the most breweries per capita with 21 currently serving a population of 626,000 people.

FOOD AND NUTRITION

Food and Nutrition

The adage "you are what you eat" neatly summarizes many truths about human health and well-being. Food is the raw material from which the body obtains the substances it needs to grow, reproduce, repair itself, and fight disease. A diet composed of good food choices gives the body the chemical compounds it needs. A diet deficient in essential molecules inhibits or skews basic physiological mechanisms, preventing the body from functioning properly.

Nutrients

Essential nutrients are substances needed by the body to grow and remain healthy. Macronutrients are needed in large amounts; they include proteins, carbohydrates and fats. Micronutrients are needed in very small quantities; they include vitamins and minerals. Two other critical components of a healthy diet are fiber and water.

Proteins   The body needs twenty essential amino acids to assemble approximately 10,000 different kinds of proteins. These proteins include enzymes, antibodies, hemoglobin, components of cell membranes and bone, and so on.

Meat, poultry, seafood, legumes, dairy products, nuts, and seeds are rich sources of proteins. Most Americans eat far more protein than necessary, though protein-deficiency diseases are common in some poor countries. Excess dietary protein is broken down and either used as an energy source or converted into fat.

Carbohydrates   Carbohydrates—sugar and starches—are the body's primary source of energy. During a complex series of chemical reactions within cells, carbohydrate molecules are broken down to release the energy needed for everything from maintaining body temperature and heartbeat to moving limbs and eyelids. Most excess dietary carbohydrates are converted into fat.

Fats   The category of nutrients known as lipids include solid fats, liquid fats (oils), and cholesterol. These substances provide insulation, protect internal organs, main-

tain healthy skin, and play important roles in vision, hormone production, and the formation of cell membranes. However, excess dietary fat increases the risk of heart disease, diabetes, cancer, and other health problems.

There are two types of dietary fats: saturated and unsaturated. Saturated fats are the so-called "bad" fats. They are found in red meat, lard, dairy products, coconut and palm oil, and egg yolks. Within the body, they raise total blood cholesterol and low-density lipoproteins (LDL), the main source of cholesterol buildup and blockage of arteries. Unsaturated fats, the so-called "good" fats, include polyunsaturated fats and monounsaturated fats. Most come from plant sources. They lower LDL and raise high-density lipoproteins (HDL), which help prevent cholesterol from building up in arteries.

Trans fatty acids (trans fat) are components of unsaturated fats that have been hydrogenated to make them solid at room temperature. They are found in margarines, peanut butter, and commercially baked goods and fried

Cholesterol and Triglyceride Levels

Blood Level (mg/dL)*	Significance
Total Cholesterol	
Less than 200	Desirable
200-239	Borderline high
240 or higher	High
LDL	
Less than 100	Optimal
100-129	Near optimal
130-159	Borderline high
160-189	High
190 or higher	Very high
HDL	
Less than 40	Low
40-59	Acceptable
60 or higher	Optimal
Triglycerides	
Less than 150	Acceptable
150-199	Borderline high
200 or higher	High

* Milligrams per deciliter of blood.
Source: Lung, and Blood Institute

foods. They raise total cholesterol and LDL and may lower HDL.

Cholesterol is an essential component of cell membranes and needed for the production of sex hormones and other important compounds. However, high levels of blood cholesterol increase people's risk for heart disease. Generally, foods high in saturated fats are also high in cholesterol.

Another form of lipids in the blood is triglycerides— fat molecules consisting of three fatty acids joined to a glycerol molecule. They are important in helping to transfer energy from food into body cells, but excessive levels increase heart disease risk.

Vitamins and Minerals   These micronutrients are involved in numerous body processes, from building blood cells to transmitting chemical signals and regulating body temperature. A deficiency can result in illness. For example, insufficient intake of the B-vitamin niacin can lead to pellagra, a disease marked by diarrhea, dermatitis, dementia, and if untreated, death; a deficiency of dietary calcium can result in osteoporosis, a disease characterized by brittle, easily broken bones. Excessive doses of vitamins and minerals can also be dangerous. Too much vitamin A can cause nerve damage, hair loss, blurred vision, and birth defects; excessive zinc can cause a copper deficiency by competing with copper at absorption sites in the intestine.

Since the 1940's, the National Academy of Sciences has provided Recommended Daily Allowances (RDAs) for vitamins and minerals. An RDA indicates the amount of a vitamin or mineral that meets the nutrient needs of about 98 percent of all the healthy individuals in a specified gender and age group.

Vitamin and mineral needs change markedly during life. Gender, tobacco use, and whether a woman is pregnant or lactating also affect needs. For instance, a typical teenage female needs about 1200 mg of calcium daily; after age 25, about 800 mg of calcium are considered sufficient. A 7-year-old child needs 13 mg of niacin daily; a 15-year-old boy should have 20 mg daily and a 60-year-old man about 15 mg daily.

Fiber   Dietary fiber is a complex mixture of plant materials that are resistant to digestion by the human digestive system. There are two major types: insoluble (cellulose, hemicellulose, lignin) and soluble (gums, mucilages, pectins). Insoluble fiber is found mainly in vegetables, wheat bran, and whole grains. Foods high in soluble fibers include oats, dry beans and peas, and fruits such as apples, oranges, and strawberries.

Fiber provides bulk for the formation of feces, thus hastening the passage of feces through the lower digestive system and helping to prevent constipation and the formation of diverticula (small pouches in the walls of the large intestine). It provides a feeling of fullness, helping to satisfy appetite. Studies also indicate that adequate dietary fiber helps reduce the risk of heart disease and diabetes and may help prevent colon cancer.

Water   The human body is one-half to four-fifths water, with water composing about 70 percent of lean muscle, more than 75 percent of the brain, and about 80 percent of the blood. Water carries nutrients and oxygen to cells, cushions joints, helps regulate body temperature, removes wastes, and helps prevent constipation. Some research indicates sufficient water intake reduces the risks of colon cancer, bladder cancer, fatal heart attacks, and kidney stone formation. Insufficient water intake can result in dehydration.

On average, an adult loses about 10 cups of fluid a day—in urine, feces, perspiration, and exhaled breath. Most of this fluid needs to be replaced by drinking water or other non-alcoholic beverages; the rest is obtained from solid foods. Fluid intake should be increased when engaged in intense physical activities or working in warm environments.

Diet and Dieting

Daily nutritional needs vary from one person to the next, and change as a person moves through life's stages. Genetics, chronic diseases, activity levels, and pregnancy can impact nutritional needs; allergies, availability of food, and cultural and religious beliefs can influence which foods are chosen to meet these needs. Nonetheless, certain basic principles should be followed to assure good health, maintain an ideal weight, and reduce the risk of heart disease, cancer, diabetes, and other diseases:

—Eat a variety of foods.

—Do not overeat; keep portions small or moderate-sized.

—Eat plenty of fruits, vegetables, and whole grains.

—Limit intake of sugar, salt, saturated fat, and cholesterol.

—Drink plenty of water.

—Exercise daily.

The Value of Vitamins

Vitamin Adult RDA*	Major Functions	Significant Food Sources
A M: 900mcg (3000 IU) F: 700 mcg (2330 IU)	Helps form skin, bones, and mucous membranes; promotes healthy eyes	Dairy products, fish oil, fruits and vegetables rich in beta-carotene (carrots, mangos, cantaloupe, sweet potatoes, tomatoes, broccoli, spinach)
B1 (thiamine) M: 1.2 mg F: 1.1 mg	Helps cells convert carbohydrates into energy; promotes healthy brain and nerve cells	Whole grains, wheat germ, soybeans, meat, fish, nuts, brewer's yeast
B2 (riboflavin) M: 1.3 mg F: 1.1 mg	Helps cells convert carbohydrates into energy; necessary for growth and production of red blood cells; promotes healthy skin and eyes	Organ meats (liver, tongue, etc.), meats, fish, milk, bread products, fortified cereals, almonds, egg yolks
B3 (niacin) M: 16 mg F: 14 mg	Helps convert food into energy; promotes healthy skin, nerves, and digestive system	Lean meats, poultry, fish, peanuts, wheat germ, dairy products, brewer's yeast
B5 (pantothenic acid) M, F: no RDA; 5 mg is recommended upper limit	Essential for food metabolism and production of hormones	Organ meats, beans, egg yolk, brewer's yeast, whole grains
B6 (pyridoxine) M (19–50): 1.3 mg M (51+): 1.7 mg F (19–50): 1.3 mg F (51+): 1.5 mg	Essential for protein metabolism; involved in synthesis of hemoglobin and neurotransmitters; aids functioning of nervous and immune systems	Fortified cereals, beans, meats, poultry, fish, bananas, green leafy vegetables, nuts
B12 M, F: 2.4 mcg	Essential for red blood cell production, maintains normal functioning of nervous system	Liver, meats, poultry, eggs, dairy products, fortified cereals, fortified soy products
Biotin (a B vitamin) M, F: no RDA; some experts suggest 30 to 100 mcg	Aids in food metabolism and in production of proteins and fatty acids	Liver, cheese, egg yolks, brewer's yeast, peanuts, cauliflower, bananas, tomatoes, whole grains
Choline (a B vitamin) M, F: 425 mg	Promotes fetal brain development, learning, and memory	Liver, egg yolks, wheat germ
Folate (a B vitamin; folic acid is the synthetic form) M, F: 400 mcg	Aids in new cell formation, protein metabolism, and synthesis of DNA and neurotransmitters	Liver, leafy green vegetables (spinach, turnip greens), asparagus, citrus fruits and juices, fortified cereals, beans and peas, peanuts, whole grains
Inositol (a B vitamin) M, F: no RDA available	Aids in transmission of chemical signals, fat and cholesterol use, and cell membrane formation	Whole grains, nuts, liver, vegetables; can be manufactured by the body
C M: 90 mg** F: 75 mg**	Promotes healthy gums and teeth; aids in production of collagen and hormones; helps in healing wounds and absorption of iron; as an antioxidant, combats adverse effects of free radicals	Fresh fruits (especially citrus; also cantaloupe, strawberries, kiwis), green vegetables, tomatoes, potatoes, cauliflower, brussels sprouts

Vitamin Adult RDA*	Major Functions	Significant Food Sources
D* M, F (19–50): 5 mcg/200 IU M, F (51–69): 10 mcg/400 IU M, F (70+): 15 mcg/600 IU	Maintains normal blood levels of calcium and phosphorus; promotes strong bones and teeth	Cod liver oil, fish (salmon, mackerel, sardines), fortified dairy products; however, most vitamin D used by the body is made therein following exposure to the sun
E M, F: 15 mg	Aids in production of red blood cells; as an antioxidant, combats adverse effects of free radicals	Vegetable oils, whole grains, wheat germ, nuts, leafy green vegetables
K M: 80 mcg F: 65 mcg	Essential for blood clotting; helps build and maintain bones	Dark green vegetables (spinach, broccoli), soybean oil, eggs; intestinal bacteria produce some of the vitamin K needed by the body

Mg = milligrams; mcg = micrograms. * Unless otherwise specified, RDAs provided herein apply to males age 19 and older and females age 19 and older who are neither pregnant nor lactating. ** Smokers need an additional 35 mg. *** Insufficient evidence exists to establish RDAs for vitamin D. Instead, an Adequate Intake (AI) level is provided.
Sources: U.S. Department of Agriculture, National Institutes of Health.

The Value of Minerals

Mineral Adult RDA*	Major Functions	Major Food Sources
calcium M, F: 800 mg	Essential for formation of bones and teeth and for muscle growth and contraction; aids in production of androgen, estrogen, and cortisone; helps in blood blood clotting, heart rhythm, nerve transmission, cell membrane permeability	Leafy green vegetables, watercress, legumes, milk and dairy products, liver, nuts, seafood (salmon, sardines, shellfish)
chromium M, F: 50-200 mcg	Controls blood sugar level	Whole grains, egg yolks
copper M, F: 1.5-3 mg	Facilitates production of enzymes	Oysters, nuts, seeds, whole grains
fluoride M, F: 3.1 mg	Prevents tooth decay	Found naturally in some community water systems; added to water in other areas
iodine M, F: 150 mcg	Aids in production of thyroid hormones	Iodized salt, marine fish, dairy products
iron M: 8 mg F (19–50): 18 mg F (51+): 8 mg	Important in oxygen transport and metabolism	Liver, lean meats, poultry, shellfish (oysters, clams), beans, spinach, fortified cereals and breads
magnesium M (19–30): 400 mg M (31+): 420 mg F (19–30): 310 mg F (31+): 320 mg	Regulates body temperature; helps maintain normal muscle and nerve function; keeps heart rhythm steady; aids in protein synthesis	Leafy green vegetables, avocados, nuts, whole grains, meats, poultry, fish, dried fruit.

The Value of Minerals (continued)

Mineral Adult RDA*	Major Functions	Major Food Sources
manganese M, F: 2-5 mg	Aids in bone formation, needed for synthesis of proteins and fatty acids	Legumes, nuts, rice
phosphorus M, F: 800 mg	Aids in bone and soft tissue growth	Dairy products, meats
potassium M, F: 3500 mg	Maintains fluid balance and proper functioning of muscles and nerves; needed for protein and carbohydrate metabolism	Spinach and other cooked greens, potatoes, beans, fruits, milk
selenium M, F: 55 mcg	Protects cells against the effects of free radicals produced during metabolism; essential for normal functioning of the immune system and thyroid gland	Tuna, cod, liver, Brazil nuts, enriched breads and cereals
zinc M: 11 mg F: 8 mg	Helps maintain the immune response, reproductive functions, and enzyme activity	Oysters, fortified cereals, meats, nuts, seeds

Mg = milligrams; mcg = micrograms. * Unless otherwise specified, RDAs provided herein apply to males age 19 and older and females age 19 and older who are neither pregnant nor lactating. Sources: U.S. Department of Agriculture, National Institutes of Health.

How Long Does It Take to Burn Off Calories?

Food	Calories Supplied	Minutes of Activity Needed* (based on person weighing 154 pounds)				
		Reclining (1.3 calories per minute)	Walking (5.2)	Bike riding (8.2)	Swimming (11.2)	Running (19.6)
Breakfast biscuit with egg and sausage	581	447	112	71	52	30
Fast food hamburger, double patty with condiments	576	443	111	70	51	29
Chicken pot pie, frozen entrée, small pie	484	372	93	59	43	25
Pecan pie, commercially prepared, 1 piece	452	348	87	55	40	23
Tuna salad, 1 cup	383	295	74	47	34	20
Pork spareribs, 3 oz.	337	259	65	41	30	17
Turkey, roasted, 1 cup	238	183	46	29	21	12
Beef stew, canned, 1 cup	218	168	42	27	19	11
Rice, white, cooked, 1 cup	205	158	39	25	18	10
Salmon, cooked, 3 oz.	184	142	35	22	16	9
Pizza with cheese, 1 slice	140	108	27	17	12	7
Ice cream, vanilla, 1/2 cup	133	102	26	16	12	7
Cheese, cheddar, 1 oz.	114	88	22	14	10	6
Banana	105	81	20	13	9	5
Apple, raw, with skin	72	55	14	9	6	4

* Approximate. Varies according to rate of activity. For example, the faster a person walks, the greater the number of calories burned per minute.

Food Guidelines   For years, healthy eating plans were most often illustrated in the shape of pyramids that outline what to eat each day. Food meant to be consumed in large quantities comprised the base of the pyramid, while sugars and fats were the tip. The most familiar example was the Food Guide Pyramid, established by the U.S. Department of Agriculture and Department. Even the most recent of these, called MyPyramid, introduced in 2005, was criticized as being too complicated at a time when more than one-third of American adults are obese.

In 2011, the Department of Agriculture, First Lady Michelle Obama, and the Surgeon General introduced MyPlate, a new food guide diagram that looks like a divided dinner plate. It illustrates, for example, that half of a meal should consist of vegetables and fruits, and that low-fat dairy should be consumed only on the side. MyPlate not only recommends portions, but also specifics such that whole grains should be eaten over refined grains. The accompanying website is meant to help Americans learn how to stretch their dollar while purchasing fresh produce over packaged commodities.

Calories   Calories measure the potential energy in the food we eat. Foods vary widely in caloric content, particularly when factors such as processing and condiments are taken into consideration. For instance, one cup of raw strawberries contains 53 calories; one cup of frozen, sweetened, sliced strawberries has 245 calories. Similarly, 1 cup of air-popped popcorn has 31 calories; a similar amount of caramel-coated popcorn has 152 calories.

The number of calories a person burns up during a typical day depends on age, sex, size, and activity level. Teenage boys, many active men, and some very active women consume about 2,800 calories a day. Most children, teenage girls, active women, and many sedentary men burn about 2,200 calories a day. Many sedentary women and some older adults burn about 1,600 calories a day.

If a person takes in more calories than are burned up, the excess is stored as fat. In general, an excess deposit of 3,500 calories equals one pound of fat. To get rid of this pound of fat, the person must burn up the 3,500 calories.

Weight-Loss Diets   To lose weight, a person must eat fewer calories than he or she burns. How one attempts to do this varies tremendously. Some people use the slow and steady approach of dietary and lifestyle modifications—basically, eating less and exercising more. Others try fasting and other rapid-fire approaches, or one of the many weight-loss diets described in books or offered commercially. Some of the most popular weight-loss diets include:

The Atkins diet A high-fat, low-carbohydrate diet with few limits of the amount of food that can be eaten. In the first two weeks, carbohydrates are severely restricted. Without carbohydrates, the body burns stored body fat and goes into a state called ketosis, which tends to decrease appetite. After two weeks, fiber-rich carbohydrates are gradually added to the diet—but no refined sugar, milk, white rice, white potatoes, or products made with white flour.

Weight Watchers A diet in which each food is assigned a point value based on its caloric, fat, and dietary fiber content. For example: one cup of broccoli has 0 points, one slice of bread 2 points, one ounce of chocolate 4 points, and a 6-ounce steak 8 points. No foods are prohibited but the person is expected to eat only a certain number of points each day, based on body weight, with extra points earned by exercising. Weekly meetings in which dieters receive support from one another are an important part of the program.

The Ornish Diet A high-fiber, low-fat vegetarian diet that consists mainly of grains, beans, vegetables, and fruits. Nonfat or very low-fat dairy products may be eaten in moderation; eating meat, oils, nuts and seeds, sugar, and most dairy products is discouraged. The quantity of calories is

---

What Counts as a Serving?

Grains Group
  1 slice of bread
  1 cup of ready-to-eat cereal
  1/2 cup of cooked cereal, rice, or pasta
Vegetable Group
  1 cup of raw leafy vegetables
  1/2 cup of other vegetables cooked or raw
  3/4 cup of vegetable juice
Fruit Group
  1 medium apple, banana, orange, pear
  1/2 cup of chopped, cooked, or canned fruit
  3/4 cup of fruit juice
Milk Group
  1 cup of milk or yogurt
  1 1/2 ounces of natural cheese, such as Cheddar
  2 ounces of processed cheese, such as American
Meat and Beans Group
  2 to 3 ounces of cooked lean meat, poultry or fish
  1/2 cup of cooked dry beans or 1/2 cup of tofu counts as 1
    ounce of lean meat
  2 1/2-ounce soyburger or 1 egg counts as 1 ounce of lean
    meat
  2 tablespoons of peanut butter or 1/3 cup of nuts counts
    as 1 ounce of meat

Source: U.S. Department of Agriculture.

not considered critical but less than 10 percent should come from fats.

The Zone diet Somewhat higher in fats and proteins than traditional diets. An individual on the Zone obtains 40 percent of daily calories from carbohydrates such as beans and vegetables, 30 percent from low-fat proteins, and 30 percent from unsaturated fats. Saturated fats and carbohydrates that release glucose quickly (grains, bread, pasta, rice, etc.) are restricted.

South Beach diet A three-phase diet in which Phase 1 is to eliminate cravings for sugars and starches; Phase 2 is to induce long-term weight-loss; and Phase 3 is meant to maintain the healthy weight achieved. The diet plan doesn't cut food groups out—devotees know it as the "food lover's diet"—but instead focuses on eating the "right" carbs and fats. The emphasis is on vegetables and fruits that are fiber-rich and nutrient-dense. Arthur Agatston, the cardiologist credited with developing the plan, recommends at least 20 minutes of exercise daily to achieve desired results.

Diet Pills

Weight-loss drugs, whether prescribed or bought over-the-counter, were developed to help persons with obesity or obesity-related conditions such as high blood pressure or obesity. Though some drug companies claim that their pills will enable a person to shed pounds without much work, in order for diet pills to be truly effec-tive, they must be taken in combination with physical activity and healthy eating. There are two main types of weight-loss pills: appetite suppressants and fat absorp-tion inhibitors. Appetite suppressants can be bought at most drug stores, and work by increasing serotonin or cat-echolamine to fool the body into believing it is full. Fat absorption inhibitors prevent the body from breaking down fat. Xenical is the only fat absorption inhibitor approved for use in the U.S., sold over the counter as Alli.

There are no studies that conclusively report that any of these diet pills are effective over the long term, and tak-ing them comes with several risks. People can develop tol-erances, become addicted, or may experience side effects ranging from an increased heart rate or blood pressure to constipation, anxiety, headaches, insomnia, and excessive thirst.

Weight Guidelines

One of the most accurate ways to determine the correlation between weight and health risks is body mass index (BMI). A BMI of less than 18.5 is gener-ally considered a signal that an adult is underweight. A healthy BMI for most adults is between 18.5 and 24.9. A BMI of 25 to 29.9 is considered overweight; one of 30 or more is considered obese. The higher the BMI, the greater the risk of cardiovascular disease, diabetes, cancer, prema-ture death, and other health problems.

Body Mass Index

BMI	19	20	21	22	23	24	25	26	27	28	29	30	31	32	33	34	35
Height (in.)							Body Weight (pounds)*										
58	91	96	100	105	110	115	119	124	129	134	138	143	148	153	158	162	167
59	94	99	104	109	114	119	124	128	133	138	143	148	153	158	163	168	173
60	97	102	107	112	118	123	128	133	138	143	148	153	158	163	168	174	179
61	100	106	111	116	122	127	132	137	143	148	153	158	164	169	174	180	185
62	104	109	115	120	126	131	136	142	147	153	158	164	169	175	180	186	191
63	107	113	118	124	130	135	141	146	152	158	163	169	175	180	186	191	197
64	110	116	122	128	134	140	145	151	157	163	169	174	180	186	192	197	204
65	114	120	126	132	138	144	150	156	162	168	174	180	186	192	198	204	210
66	118	124	130	136	142	148	155	161	167	173	179	186	192	198	204	210	216
67	121	127	134	140	146	153	159	166	172	178	185	191	198	204	211	217	223
68	125	131	138	144	151	158	164	171	177	184	190	197	203	210	216	223	230
69	128	135	142	149	155	162	169	176	182	189	196	203	209	216	223	230	236
70	132	139	146	153	160	167	174	181	188	195	202	209	216	222	229	236	243
71	136	143	150	157	165	172	179	186	193	200	208	215	222	229	236	243	250
72	140	147	154	162	169	177	184	191	199	206	213	221	228	235	242	250	258
73	144	151	159	166	174	182	189	197	204	212	219	227	235	242	250	257	265
74	148	155	163	171	179	186	194	202	210	218	225	233	241	249	256	264	272
75	152	160	168	176	184	192	200	208	216	224	232	240	248	256	264	272	279
76	156	164	172	180	189	197	205	213	221	230	238	246	254	263	271	279	287

* Pounds are rounded off. Source: National Heart, Lung, and Blood Institute.

REFERENCE LIBRARY

A WRITER'S GUIDE

The Eight Parts of Speech

Sentence elements consist primarily of a subject and predicate. Grammarians classify the words in each element as parts of speech. The eight parts of speech are *nouns, verbs, pronouns, adjectives, adverbs, conjunctions, prepositions,* and *interjections.* We classify words as one or another part of speech according to the role they play in a sentence.

Nouns

Nouns are the names for people, places, animals, things, ideas, actions, states of existence, colors and so forth. In sentences, nouns serve as *subjects, objects* and *complements.*

Nouns may also be *appositives*; that is, they can identify another noun or pronoun, usually by naming it again in different words. In the following sentence bold indicates the appositive (or noun in apposition):

*My mother, a **police lieutenant**, works late every night.*

Common nouns name ordinary things: *ability, democracy, justice, rope, baseball, desks, library, beauty.*

Proper nouns are the names of persons, places, and things. Always capitalize proper nouns: *Amtrak, Germany, Donald A. Stone, Greek Orthodox, State Department, General Dynamics, the Rolling Stones, New York.*

Compound nouns consist of two or more words that function as a unit. They include such common nouns as *heartache, mother-in-law, father-in-law, great-grandmother,* and *worldview.* Compound nouns also may be proper nouns— *International Business Machines, Federal Bureau of Investigation, Suez Canal* and *Sacramento, California.*

Verbs

Verbs report action, condition, or state of being. Verbs are the controlling words in predicates, but verbs themselves are controlled by subjects.

Number and person The *number* of the subject determines the form of its verb. If a subject is only one thing, it is *singular.* If it is more than one, it is *plural: dog* is singular; the plural form is *dogs.* Verbs reflect these differences in subjects by taking a singular or a plural form.

In the *first-person singular,* I speak or write of myself. In the *first-person plural,* we speak or write of ourselves. In the

second-person singular and plural (the forms are the same), you are addressed. In the *third-person singular,* someone speaks or writes about somebody or something who is not being addressed. In the *third-person plural,* someone speaks or writes about more than one person or object.

	Singular	**Plural**
First person	I	we
Second person	you	you
Third person	she	they

In the present tense the only change that takes place is in the third person singular; a final *–s* is added to the common form of the verb. Most but not all verbs will add this *–s* in the third person singular.

	Singular	**Plural**
First person	I build.	We build.
Second person	You build.	You build
Third person	He builds.	They build.

Helping verbs or auxiliary verbs enable a single verb to express a meaning that it could not express by itself. A verb phrase is the helping verb plus the main verb. The final word in a verb phrase, the main verb, carries the primary meaning of the verb phrase. Sometimes more than one helping verb accompanies the main verb. In the following sentences, the verb phrases are bold; HV appears over each helping verb, and MV appears over each main verb.

  HV MV

*He **is biking** to Vermont from Boston.*

  HV MV

*They **will arrive** in time for the game.*

    HV   HV MV

*Cy Young **has** always **been considered** one of the best pitchers in baseball history.*

Notice that sometimes words not part of the verb phrase come between the helping verb and the main verb.

Typical helping verbs include: *be, being, been, is, am, are, was, were, do, did, does, has, have, had, must, may, can, shall, will, might, could, would, should.*

Particles are short words that never change their form no matter how the main verb changes. They sometimes look like other parts of speech, but they always go with the verb to add a meaning that the verb does not have by itself.

*Harry made **up** with Gloria.*

*She filled **out** her application.*

Tenses Verbs show whether the action of the sentence is taking place now, took place in the past, or will take place in the future. English has three simple tenses—present, past, and future.

Present: *She **works** every day.*

Past: *She **worked** yesterday.*

Future: *She **will work** tomorrow.*

Irregular verbs form the simple past tense by changing a part of the verb other than the ending.

Present: *We **grow** tomatoes every year on our kitchen window shelf.*

*I **run** four miles every day.*

*I **go** to the grocery store every Saturday morning.*

Past: *We **grew** corn back in Iowa.*

*In 1981 Coe **ran** the mile in three minutes and forty-six seconds.*

*I **went** to the grocery store last Saturday.*

Form the future tense of verbs by adding *will* or *shall* to the common form of the present.

Present: *I often **read** in bed.*

Future: *I **shall read** you a story before bedtime.*

*She **will read** you the ending tomorrow morning.*

Pronouns

A pronoun takes the place of a noun and can serve as subject, object, and complement in sentences. Sentences must always make clear what nouns the pronouns stand for. A pronoun that lacks a clear antecedent (the word for which the pronoun substitutes) causes confusion.

Personal pronouns refer to one or more persons: *I, you, he, she, it, we, they.*

Indefinite pronouns indicate a member of a group without naming which one we mean: *all, any, anyone, each, everybody, everyone, few, nobody, someone.*

Reflexive pronouns refer to the noun or pronoun that is the subject of the sentence; they always end in *–self* or *–selves: myself, himself, herself, yourself, ourselves.*

*She allowed **herself** no rest.*

*He loved **himself** more than he loved anyone else.*

Intensive pronouns have the same form as reflexive pronouns; they add special emphasis to nouns and other pronouns.

*I **myself** have often made that mistake.*

*President Harding **himself** played poker and drank whiskey in the White House during Prohibition.*

Demonstrative pronouns point out nouns or other pronouns that come after them: *this, that, these, those.*

***That** is the book I want.*

*Are **those** the books you bought?*

Relative pronouns join word groups containing a subject and verb to nouns or pronouns that the word groups describe: *who, whom, that, which.*

*Ian McEwan is the writer **who** won the award for his novel* Atonement.

*The tools **that** I lost in the lake cost me a fortune to replace.*

*The doctor **whom** you recommended has left town.*

Possessive pronouns show possession or special relations: *my, his, her, your, our, their, its.* Unlike possessive nouns, possessive pronouns have no apostrophes.

***Their** cat sets off **my** allergies.*

*The fault was **ours**, and the worst mistake was **mine**.*

Interrogative pronouns introduce questions: *who, which, what.*

***What** courses are you taking?*

***Who** kept score?*

***Which** of the glasses is mine?*

Like nouns, pronouns can be singular or plural, depending on the noun form they replace.

Adjectives

Adjectives modify nouns and pronouns. That is, they help describe nouns and pronouns in a sentence by answering questions such as *which one, what kind, how many, what size, what color, what condition, whose.* Adjectives appear in boldface in the sentences below.

*The **bright yellow** sun shone through the **gloomy** clouds.*

***Six** camels trudged across a **vast white** desert **one scorching** afternoon.*

Adjectives usually come immediately before, but sometimes immediately after, the words they modify.

*The **tired, thirsty, impatient** horse threw its rider.*

*The horse, **tired, thirsty, and impatient**, threw its rider.*

Subject complements An adjective modifying the subject of a sentence sometimes appears on the opposite side of a linking verb from the subject.

*The horse looked **tired, thirsty,** and **impatient.***

*My friend was **ill,** and I was **worried.***

In these examples, the adjectives are subject complements.

Articles The articles *a, an,* and *the* function as adjectives.

*He sent me **the** card in **an** old envelope.*

A and *an* are indefinite and singular. The article *a* appears before words that begin with a consonant sound; *an* appears before words that begin with a vowel sound.

a dish, a year, an apple, an entreaty, a European, a historian, an enemy, a friend, an umbrella, a union, an understanding, an hour

Degree In comparisons, adjectives show degree or intensity by the addition of an *–er* or *–est* ending or by the use of *more* or *most* or *less* or *least.*

Present and past participles of verbs often serve as adjectives:

*The trip was both **exhausting** and **rewarding.***

*The **gathering** night was filled with stars.*

***Tired** and **discouraged,** she dropped out of the marathon.*

A noun can serve as an adjective.

***Cigarette** smoking harms our lungs.*

*People who drive gas guzzlers worsen the **energy** crisis.*

Adjectives can also serve as nouns. All the words in boldface in the sentence below are normally adjectives, but here they clearly modify an implicit noun, *people* or *persons.* The words therefore assume the function of the implicit noun and become nouns themselves.

*The **unemployed** are not always the **lazy** and **inept.***

Avoid adjectives when the sentence requires adverbs Common speech sometimes accepts adjectival forms in an adverbial way; avoid this colloquial usage in writing.

Nonstandard: *He hit that one **real good.***

Revised: *He hit that one **really well.***

Nonstandard: *She **sure** made me work hard for my grade.*

Revised: *She **certainly** made me work hard for my grade.*

Adverbs

Adverbs usually modify verbs, adjectives, and other adverbs, but they sometimes modify prepositions, phrases, clauses, and even whole sentences.

Adverbs answer questions such as *how, how often, to what degree (how much), where,* and *when.*

Wearily** he drifted **away.

*She did **not** speak **much today.***

Adverbs may modify by affirmation or negation. *Not* is always an adverb.

*He will **surely** call home before he leaves.*

*They shall **not** pass.*

*We will **never** see anyone like her again.*

Many adverbs end in *–ly,* and you can make adverbs of most adjectives simply by adding *–ly* to the adjective form.

Adjective	Adverb
large	largely
crude	crudely
beautiful	beautifully

However, a great many adverbs do not end in *–ly:*

often, sometimes, then, when, anywhere, anyplace, somewhere, somehow, somewhat, yesterday, Sunday, before, behind, ahead, seldom

Note also that many adjectives already end in *–ly.*

costly, stately, lowly, homely, measly, manly, womanly, terribly, honestly

Conjunctive adverbs such as *accordingly, consequently, hence, however, indeed, meanwhile, moreover, nevertheless, on the other hand,* and *therefore* connect ideas logically between clauses.

*Descartes said, "I think, **therefore** I am."*

*He opposed her before she won the primary election; **however,** he supported her afterward in her campaign.*

*Swimming exercises the heart and muscles; **on the other hand,** swimming does not control weight as well as jogging and biking do.*

Degree Adverbs, like adjectives, show degrees by the addition of an *–er* or *–est* ending or by the use of *more* or *most* or *less* or *least.* Whether modifying an adjective or another adverb, the words *more, most, less,* and *least* are themselves adverbs.

Conjunctions

Conjunctions join words or groups of words like clauses or phrases.

Coordinating conjunctions (coordinators) join elements of equal weight or function. The common coordinating conjunctions are *and, but, or, for,* and *nor.* Some writers now include *yet* and *so.*

*She was tired **and** happy.*

*The town was small **but** pretty.*

*They must be tired, **for** they have climbed all day long.*

*You may take the green **or** the red.*

*He would not leave the table, **nor** would he stop insulting his host.*

Correlative conjunctions are conjunctions used in pairs. They also connect sentence elements of equal value. The familiar correlatives are *both...and, either...or, neither... nor,* and *not only...but also.*

> ***Neither** the doctor **nor** the police believed his story.*

> *Henry Yip **not only** baked the brownies **but also** ate every last one of them.*

Subordinating conjunctions (**subordinators**) join dependent or subordinate sections of a sentence to independent sections or to other dependent sections. The common subordinating conjunctions are *after, although, as, because, if, rather than, since, that, unless, until, when, whenever, where, wherever* and *while.*

> ***Although** the desert may look barren and dead, vigorous life goes on there.*

> *He always wore a hat **when** he went out in the sun.*

Prepositions

Prepositions are words that, with nouns or pronouns, form prepositional phrases and work as modifiers, often specifying place or time. The noun or pronoun is the *object* of the preposition. In the following sentence the prepositions are bold and their objects are underlined.

> *Suburban yards **throughout** <u>America</u> now provide homes **for** <u>wildlife</u> that once lived only **in** the <u>country</u>.*

The preposition, its noun, and any modifiers attached to the noun make up a *prepositional phrase*, which acts as adjective or adverb. Prepositions allow the nouns or pronouns that follow them to modify other words in the sentence. Common prepositions include:

about, below, including, under, above, beneath, inside, underneath, across, beside, into, until, after, beyond, like, up, against, by, near, upon, along, despite, of, via, amid, during, on, with, among, except, over, within, as, excluding, since, without, at, following, throughout, before, from, to, behind, in, toward

Some prepositions consist of more than one word.

according to, except for, instead of, along with, in addition to, on account of, apart from, in case of, up to, as to, in front of, with respect to, because of, in place of, with reference to, by means of, in regard to, by way of, in spite of

Prepositions usually come before their objects. But sometimes, especially in questions, they do not. Grammarians debate whether prepositions should end a sentence. Most writers favoring an informal style will now and then use a preposition to end a sentence.

Formal: *In what state do you live?*

Informal: *What state do you live in?*

Interjections

Interjections are forceful expressions, usually written with an exclamation point, though mild ones may be set off with commas. They are not used often in formal writing except in dialogue.

Hooray! Ouch! Oh, no! Wow!

"Wow!" Davis said. "Are you telling me that there's a former presidential adviser who hasn't written a book?"

How Words Act as Different Parts of Speech

A word that acts as one part of speech in one sentence may act as other parts of speech in other sentences or in other parts of the same sentence. The way the word is used will determine what part of speech it is.

*The **light** glowed at the end of the pier.* (noun)

*As you **light** the candle, say a prayer.* (verb)

*The **light** drizzle foretold heavy rain.* (adjective)

Basic Sentence Grammar

Sentence Structure

The *subject* is the part of the sentence that names what the sentence is about. The *predicate* is the part of the sentence that makes a statement or asks a question about the subject. Every sentence contains at least one subject and one predicate that fit together to make a statement, ask a question, or give a command.

Subject   The subject and the words that describe it are often called the *complete subject*. Within the complete subject, the word (or words) that serve as the focus of the sentence may be called the *simple subject*.

In the following examples, the complete subjects are underscored and the simple subjects are in boldface.

<u>The quick brown **fox**</u> *jumps over the lazy dog.*

<u>The huge black **clouds** in the west</u> *predicted a violent storm.*

A *compound subject* has two or more subjects joined by a

connecting word such as *and* or *but*.

*Thoughtful **acts** and kind **words** have distinguished his administrative career.*

Predicate

The predicate asserts something about the subject. The predicate, together with all the words that help make a statement about the subject, is often called the *complete predicate*. Within the complete predicate, the word (or words) that reports or states conditions, with all describing words removed, is called the *simple predicate* or the *verb*. A verb expresses action or a state of being.

In the following sentences, complete predicates are underlined and simple predicates (the *verbs*) are in boldface.

*The quick brown fox __**jumps** over the lazy dog__.*

*The huge black clouds in the west __**predicted** a violent storm__.*

*Thoughtful acts and kind words __**have** distinguished his administrative career__.*

In a *compound predicate*, a connecting word joins two or more verbs.

*The huge black clouds in the west __**predicted** a violent storm and **ended** our picnic__.*

Other Predicate Parts

In addition to verbs, complete predicates may also include sentence elements that modify, or help describe, other elements.

Direct objects The *direct object* tells who or what receives the action done by the subject and expressed by the verb. Not every sentence has a direct object, but transitive verbs (from the Latin *trans*, meaning "across") require one to complete their meaning. A transitive verb carries action from the subject across to the direct object. In the examples below, direct objects are in boldface; transitive verbs are underlined.

*Catholic missionaries __established__ the **school**.*

*I __have read__ that **story**.*

*We __heard__ the distant **voice**.*

A verb that does not carry action to a direct object is an intransitive verb. An *intransitive verb* reports action done by a subject, but it is not action done to anything. The following verbs are intransitive.

*The ship **sank** within three hours after the collision.*

*She **jogs** to keep fit.*

Indirect objects Sometimes, in addition to a direct object, a predicate also includes a noun or pronoun specifying to whom or for whom the action is done. This is the *indirect object*. It appears after the verb and before the direct object. Indirect objects are usually used with verbs such as *give, ask, tell, sing,* and *write*.

*The tenants gave the **manager** their complaints.*

*Tell the **teacher** your idea.*

*Jack asked **George** an embarrassing question.*

Phrases

A *phrase* is a group of related words without a subject and a predicate.

*They **were watching** the game.*

*The child ran **into the lake**.*

***Grinning happily**, she made a three-point shot.*

***To succeed in writing**, you must be willing to revise again and again.*

English sentences contain three basic types of phrases: prepositional phrases, verb phrases, and absolute phrases.

Prepositional phrases always begin with a preposition and always end with a noun or pronoun that serves as the object of the proposition. The noun or pronoun in the phrase can then help to describe something else in the sentence. A prepositional phrase generally serves as an adjective or an adverb in the sentence in which it occurs.

Adjective prepositional phrase: *The tree **in the yard** is an oak.*

Adverb prepositional phrase: *He arrived **before breakfast**.*

Verb phrases are combinations of verbs including a main verb and one or more auxiliary verbs. Verb phrases also can serve as *verbals*. Verbals include words formed from verbs that do not function as verbs in sentences. There are three kinds of verbals: infinitives, participials, and gerunds.

Infinitives and infinitive phrases The infinitive of any verb except the verb *to be* is formed when the infinitive marker *to* is placed before the common form of the verb in the first-person present tense.

Verb	Infinitive
go	to go
make	to make

Infinitives and infinitive phrases function as nouns, adjectives, and adverbs. In the sentences below, examine the various ways the infinitive phrase *to finish his novel* can function.

***To finish his novel** was his greatest ambition.* (noun, the subject of the sentence)

*He made many efforts **to finish his novel**.* (adjective modifying the noun *efforts*)

*He rushed **to finish his novel**.* (adverb modifying the verb *rushed*)

Participles and participial phrases *Present participles* suggest some continuing action. *Past participles* suggest completed action. To form the present participle of verbs add *–ing* to the common present form of the verb. (The present participle *being* is formed from the infinitive *to be*.) To form the past participle add *–ed* to the common present form of the verb. Past participles are frequently irregular. That is, some past participles are formed not by an added *–ed*, but by an added *–en* or by a change in the root of the verb.

Verb	Past Participle
bike	biked
drive	driven
fight	fought

Because they do represent action, participles serve in a wide variety of ways. They can be part of a verb phrase. Participles can act as adjectives. In the sentence below, the participial phrase modifies the subject.

***Insulted by the joke**, the team stormed out of the banquet.*

Gerunds and gerund phrases A *gerund* is the present participle used as a noun. A *gerund phrase* includes any words and phrases attached to the gerund so that the whole is a noun serving as a subject or an object.

***Walking** is one of life's great pleasures.* (subject)

*He worked hard at **typing the paper**.* (object)

Absolute phrases consist of a noun or pronoun attached to a participle without a helping verb. It modifies the whole sentence in which it appears. (Including a helping verb would make the participle part of a verb phrase.)

***Her body falling nearly a hundred miles an hour**, she pulled the ripcord and the parachute opened with a heavy jerk.*

***Falling nearly a hundred miles an hour**, she pulled the ripcord, and the parachute opened with a heavy jerk.*

*The storm came suddenly, **the clouds boiling across the sky**.*

Clauses   A *clause* is a group of grammatically related words containing both a subject and a predicate. An *independent clause* can usually stand by itself as a complete sentence. A *dependent*, or *subordinate*, clause often cannot stand by itself because it is introduced by a subordinating con-

junction or a relative pronoun and therefore the clause alone does not make sense. In the sentences below, the independent clauses are in boldface, the dependent clauses in italics.

***She ran in the marathon** because she wanted to test herself.*

*When we had done everything possible, **we left the wounded to the enemy**.*

Noun clauses   A *noun clause* is a clause that acts as a subject, object, or complement.

Subject: *That English is a flexible language is both its glory and its pain.*

Object: *He told me **that English is a flexible language**.*

Complement: *His response was **that English is a flexible language**.*

Adjective clauses   An *adjective* (or *adjectival*) *clause* modifies a noun or pronoun. A relative pronoun connects the adjective clause to the word it modifies.

*The contestant **whom he most wanted to beat** was his father.*

Here, the adjective clause modifies the noun *contestant*; the relative pronoun *whom*, which stands for its antecedent *contestant*, serves as the direct object of the infinitive *to beat*.

*The computer **that I wanted** cost too much money.*

Here the adjective clause modifies the noun *computer*; the relative pronoun *that* serves as the direct object of the verb *wanted*.

*The journey of Odysseus, **which is traceable even today on a map of Greece and the Aegean Sea**, made an age of giants and miracles seem close to the ancient Greeks.*

The adjective clause modifies *journey*; the relative pronoun *which* serves as the subject of the verb phrase *is visible*.

Adverb clauses   An *adverb* (or *adverbial*) *clause* serves as an adverb, frequently (but not always) modifying the verb in another clause. The subordinators *after, when, before, because, although, if, though, whenever, where,* and *wherever,* as well as many others, can introduce adverb clauses.

***After we had talked for an hour**, he began to look at his watch.* (The adverb clause modifies the verb *began*.)

*He ran as swiftly **as he could**.* (The adverb clause modifies the adverb *swiftly*.)

*The desert was more yellow **than he remembered**.* (The adverb clause modifies the adjective *yellow*.)

Sentence Types

Grammarians classify sentences by numbers of clauses and

how the clauses are joined. The basic sentence types in English are simple, compound, complex, and compound-complex. Another classification of sentences is by purpose: declarative, interrogative, imperative, and exclamatory.

Simple sentences

A simple sentence contains only one clause, and that clause is independent, able to stand alone grammatically. A simple sentence may have several phrases, a compound subject, and a compound verb. The following are simple sentences, each with one independent clause.

The bloodhound is the oldest known breed of dog.

He staked out a plot of high ground in the mountains, cut down the trees, and built his own house with a fine view of the valley below.

Historians, novelists, short-story writers, and playwrights write about characters, design plots, and usually seek the dramatic resolution of a problem.

Compound sentences

A compound sentence contains two or more independent clauses, usually joined by a comma and a coordinating conjunction such as *and, but, nor, or, for, yet,* or *so.* A compound sentence does not contain a dependent clause. Sometimes a semicolon, a dash, or a colon joins the independent clauses.

The sun blasted the earth, and the plants withered and died.

He asked directions at the end of every street; his wife sighed in frustration.

A compound sentence also may consist of a series of independent clauses joined by commas or semicolons, usually but not always with a conjunction before the last clause.

They searched the want ads, she visited real estate agents, he drove through neighborhoods seeking for-sale signs, and they finally located a house big enough for them and their pet rat-

tlesnakes.

The trees on the ridge behind our house change in September: the oaks redden; the maples pass from green to orange; the pines grow darker.

Complex sentences

A complex sentence contains one independent clause and one or more dependent clauses. In the following sentences, the dependent clause is in boldface type.

*He consulted the dictionary **because he did not know how to pronounce the word.***

*She asked people **if they approved of what the speaker said.***

Compound-complex sentences

A compound-complex sentence contains two or more independent clauses and at least one dependent clause. In the following sentences, boldface type indicates dependent clauses.

*She discovered a new world in international finance, but she worked so hard investing other people's money **that she had no time to invest any of her own.***

After Abraham Lincoln was killed,** the government could not determine **how many conspirators there were;** and **since John Wilkes Booth, the assassin, was himself soon killed,** he could not clarify the mystery, **which remains to this day.

Correct Verb Usage

Verbs can take a variety of forms, depending on how we use them.

Basic Tense   There are three basic tenses in English—present, past, and future.

Sentence Classification by Purpose

We also classify sentences by the kind of information they convey—by whether they are statements, questions, commands or exclamations. End punctuation helps identify the purpose of the sentence.

Sentence type	Meaning	Example	End Punctuation
Declarative	Makes a statement	*He stopped watching "Law and Order" reruns.*	Period
Interrogative	Asks a question	*Did he stop watching "Law and Order" reruns?*	Question mark
Imperative	Gives a command/ Makes a request	*Please stop watching "Law and Order" reruns.*	Period
Exclamatory	Expresses strong emotion	*I'll smash the TV if you don't stop watching "Law and Order" reruns!*	Exclamation point

Simple present The simple present of most verbs is the dictionary form, which is also called the present stem. Usually, to form the third-person singular from the simple present, add *–s* or *–es* to the present stem.

I run	we run	I go	we go
you run	you run	you go	you go
he runs	they run	she goes	they go

The simple present has several uses. It makes an unemphatic statement about something happening or a condition existing right now.

*The earth **revolves** around the sun.*

*The car **passes** in the street.*

It expresses habitual or continuous or characteristic action.

*Porters **carry** things.*

*Dentists **fill** teeth and sometimes **pull** them.*

It expresses a command indirectly, as a statement of fact.

*Periodicals **are** not to be taken out of the room.*

It reports the content of literature, documents, movies, musical compositions, works of art, or anything else that supposedly comes alive in the present each time it is experienced by an audience.

*Macbeth **is driven** by ambition, and he **is haunted** by ghosts.*

*The Parthenon in Athens **embodies** grace, beauty, and calm.*

Simple past To form the simple past of regular verbs, add *–d* or *–ed* to the present stem. The simple past does not change form.

I escaped	we escaped
you escaped	you escaped
he escaped	they escaped

Sometimes the simple past is irregular. Irregular verbs form the simple past tense not with *–d* or *–ed* but by some other change, often a change in an internal vowel.

Infinitive: *to run*

I ran	we ran	I brought	we brought
you ran	you ran	you brought	you brought
she ran	they ran	he brought	they brought

Simple future Use the helping verbs *shall* and *will* to make the simple future.

I shall go	we shall go
you will go	you will go
she will go	they will go

Traditional grammar holds that *shall* should be used for the first person, *will* for the second and third persons. In

practice, this distinction is often ignored; most people write: "I will be 25 years old on my next birthday."

The Three Perfect Tenses In addition to the simple present, past, and future, English verbs have three perfect tenses—the *present perfect*, the *past perfect*, and the *future perfect*. The *perfect* tense expresses an act that will be completed before an act reported by another verb takes place. For that reason, a verb in the *perfect tense* should always be thought of as paired with another verb, either expressed or understood.

Present perfect In the *present perfect* tense, the action of the verb started in the past. The present perfect is formed by the helping verb *has* or *have* plus the past participle.

*She **has loved** architecture for many years, and now she takes architecture courses in night school.*

*I **have worked** hard for this diploma.*

Past perfect The *past perfect* tense reports an action completed before another action took place. The past perfect is also formed with the past participle, but it uses the helping verb *had*.

*I **had worked** twenty years before I saved any money.*

The past perfect, like the present perfect, implies another act that is not always stated in the sentence.

*He **had told** me that he would quit if I yelled at him. I yelled at him, and he quit.*

Future perfect The *future perfect* tense reports an act that will be completed by some specific time in the future. It is formed by the helping verb *shall* or *will* added to *have* or *has* and the past participle.

*I **shall have worked** 50 years when I retire.*

*He **will have lived** with me 10 years next March.*

The Progressive Form The *progressive* form shows that an action continues during the time that the sentence reports, whether that time is past, present, or future. It is made with the present participle and a helping verb that is a form of *to be*.

Present progressive: *I am working.*
Past progressive: *I was working.*
Future progressive: *They will be working.*
Present perfect progressive: *She has been working.*
Past perfect progressive: *We had been working.*
Future perfect progressive: *They will have been working.*

Here are some more examples of progressive forms:

*I **am writing** a new book.*

*I **was making** soup in the kitchen when the house caught fire.*

*They **will be painting** the garage tomorrow afternoon.*

Principal Parts of the Most Common Irregular Verbs   Many verbs are *irregular*: their past tense and their past participle are not formed simply by an added *–ed*. If the verb is regular, a dictionary will list only the present form. Form both the past and the past participle by adding *–d* or *–ed* to this form. If the verb is irregular, a dictionary will give the forms of the principal parts.

The most important irregular verb is *to be*, often used as a helping verb. It is the only English verb that does not use the infinitive as the basic form for the present tense.

	Singular	**Plural**
Present:	I am	we are
	you are	you are
	she is	they are

Past:	I was	we were
	you were	you were
	it was	they were
Past perfect:	I had been	we had been
	you had been	you had been
	he had been	they had been

Mood   The mood of a verb expresses the attitude of the writer. Verbs have several moods—indicative, subjunctive, imperative and conditional.

Indicative mood   The indicative is used for simple statements of fact or for asking questions about fact. It is by far the most common mood of verbs in English.

*The tide **came** in at six o'clock and **swept** almost to the foundation of our house.*

Common Irregular Verbs

Present	Past	Past participle
awake	awoke	awoke/awakened
become	became	become
begin	began	begun
blow	blew	blown
break	broke	broken
bring	brought	brought
burst	burst	burst
choose	chose	chosen
cling	clung	clung
come	came	come
dive	dived	dived
do	did	done
draw	drew	drawn
drink	drank	drunk
drive	drove	driven
eat	ate	eaten
fall	fell	fallen
fly	flew	flown
forget	forgot	forgotten/forgot
forgive	forgave	forgiven
freeze	froze	frozen
get	got	gotten/got
give	gave	given
go	went	gone
grow	grew	grown
hang (things)	hung	hung
hang (people)	hanged	hanged
know	knew	known
lay (to put)	laid	laid
lie (to recline)	lay	lain

Present	Past	Past participle
lose	lost	lost
pay	paid	paid
ride	rode	ridden
ring	rang	rung
rise	rose	risen
say	said	said
see	saw	seen
set	set	set
shake	shook	shaken
shine	shone/shined	shone/shined
show	showed	shone
sing	sang	sung
sink	sank	sunk
sit	sat	sat
speak	spoke	spoken
spin	spun	spun
spit	spat/spit	spat/spit
steal	stole	stolen
strive	strove/strived	striven/strived
swear	swore	sworn
swim	swam	swum
swing	swung	swung
take	took	taken
tear	tore	torn
tread	trod	trod/trodden
wake	woke	waked/woke/wakened
wear	wore	worn
weave	wove	woven
wring	wrung	wrung
write	wrote	written

Subjunctive mood The subjunctive conveys a wish, a desire, or a demand in the first or third person, or it makes a statement contrary to fact.

*I wish I **were** a bird.*

*Helen wishes she **were** home.*

*He asked that she never **forget** him.*

*If only I **were** in Paris tonight!*

The subjunctive form for most verbs differs from the indicative only in the first and third person singular. The present subjunctive of the verb *to be* is *were* for the first, second, and third persons, singular and plural.

__Were__ she my daughter, I would not permit her to date a member of a motorcycle gang.

*If we **were** born with wings, we could learn to fly.*

When the subjunctive is used with the verb *to be* to express commands or wishes in the third person singular or the future tense in the first or third person, the verb form is *be.*

*If I **be** proved wrong, I shall eat my hat.*

*If this **be** treason, make the most of it!*

Use the subjunctive in clauses beginning with *that* after verbs that give orders or advice or express wishes or requests.

*He wishes that she **were** happier.*

*She asked that he **draw** up a marriage contract before the wedding.*

In the examples above, a request appears in a *that* clause. Since no one can tell whether a request will be honored or not, the verb clause is in the subjunctive. *Should* and *had* may also express the subjunctive.

__Should__ he step on a rattlesnake, his boots will protect him.

__Had__ he taken my advice, he would not have eaten raw cranberries.

Do not confuse the conditional with the past subjunctive:

Incorrect: *I wish we **would have** won the tournament.*

Correct: *I wish we **had** won the tournament.*

Imperative mood The imperative expresses a command or entreaty in the second person singular or plural, and the form of the verb is the same as the indicative.

In the imperative sentence, the *subject* of the verb is always *you,* but *you* is usually understood, not written out.

__Pass__ the bread.

__Watch__ your step!

Sometimes *you* is included for emphasis.

*You **give** me my letter this instant!*

Conditional mood The conditional makes statements that depend on one another; one is true on condition of the other's being true. A conditional sentence contains a clause that states the condition and another that states the consequence of the condition. Most conditional statements are introduced with *if.*

__If__ communist governments had been able to produce enough food for their people, they would not have collapsed in 1989.

__If__ you will be home tonight, I'll come to visit.

*Even **if** the strike is settled, the workers will still be angry.*

Like the indicative, the conditional requires no changes in ordinary verb forms. Distinguish the conditional from the subjunctive. Use the subjunctive only for conditions clearly contrary to fact.

If the circumstances are in the past, use the subjunctive for conditions that were clearly not factual and the indicative for conditions that may have been true. Use *would* or *could* as a helping verb for statements that give the supposed consequences of conditions that were not factual.

*If he **were** there that night, he **would have had** no excuse.*

He was not there; the *if* clause uses the subjunctive, and the clause stating the consequences uses *would.*

*If he **was** there, he **had** no excuse.*

He may have been there; we do not know. If he was indeed there, he had no excuse. The indicative mood is used in both clauses as a simple statement of fact.

Use the past perfect in past conditional statements when the condition states something that was not true.

*If Hitler **had stopped** in 1938, World War II **would not have come** as it did.*

Avoid using the conditional in both clauses.

Incorrect: *If she **would have gone** to Paris, she **would have had** a good time.*

Correct: *If she **had gone** to Paris, she **would have had** a good time.*

Do not confuse the conditional with the past subjunctive.

Incorrect: *I wish we **would have won** the tournament.*

Correct: *I wish we **had won** the tournament.*

Active and Passive Voice Use verbs in the active voice in most sentences; use verbs in the passive voice sparingly and only for good reason.

The voice of a transitive verb tells whether the subject is the actor in the sentence or is acted upon. (A transitive verb carries action from an agent to an object. A transitive verb can take a direct object; an intransitive verb does not take a direct object.) Intransitive verbs cannot be passive.

When transitive verbs are in the *active voice*, the subject does the acting. When transitive verbs are in the *passive voice*, an agent—either implied or expressed in a prepositional phrase—acts upon the subject.

Active: *He burned the* arroz con pollo.

Passive: *The* arroz con pollo **was burned** by him.

The arroz con pollo *was burned.*

Readers usually want to know the agent of an action; that is, they want to know *who* or *what* does the acting. Since the passive often fails to identify the agent of an action, it suggests evasion of responsibility.

Active: *The senator* **misplaced** *the memo.*

Passive: *The memo* **was misplaced.**

Use the passive when the recipient of the action in the sentence is much more important to the statement than the doer of the action.

My car **was stolen** *last night.*

Who stole your car is not known. The important thing is that the car was stolen.

Scientific researchers generally use the passive voice throughout reports on experiments to keep the focus on the experiment rather than on the experimenters.

When the bacteria **were isolated**, *they* **were treated** *carefully with nicotine and* **were observed** *to stop reproducing.*

Infinitives   The infinitive is the present tense of a verb with the marker *to*. Grammatically, the infinitive can complete the sense of other verbs, serve as a noun, and form the basis of some phrases.

The *present infinitive*, which uses the infinitive marker *to* along with the verb, describes action that takes place at the same time as the action in the verb the infinitive completes.

He wants **to go.**
He wanted **to go.**
He will want **to go.**

The *present perfect infinitive*, which uses the infinitive marker *to*, the verb *have* and a past participle, describes action prior to the action of the verb whose sense is completed by the infinitive. The present perfect infinitive often follows verb phrases that include *should* or *would*.

I would like **to have seen** *her face when she found the duck in her bathtub.*

An *infinitive phrase* includes the infinitive and the words that complete its meaning.

He studied **to improve his voice.**

Sometimes the infinitive marker is omitted before the verb, especially after such verbs as *hear, help, let, see* and *watch*.

They watched the ship **sail** *out to sea.*

In general, avoid split infinitives. A *split infinitive* has one or more words awkwardly placed between the infinitive marker *to* and the verb form. The rule against split infinitives is not absolute: some writers split infinitives and others do not. But the words used to split infinitives can usually go outside the infinitive, or they can be omitted altogether.

Split infinitive: *He told me* **to really try** *to do better.*

Enrique wanted **to completely forget** *his painful romance.*

Revised: *He told me* **to try** *to do better.*

Enrique wanted **to forget** *his painful romance completely.*

Correct Pronoun Usage

Pronouns take the places of nouns in sentences. Most pronouns require an antecedent to give them content and meaning. The *antecedent* is the word for which the pronoun substitutes. The antecedent usually appears earlier in the same sentence or in the same passage. In the following example, the antecedent for the pronoun *it* is *snow*.

The snow fell all day long, and by nightfall it was three feet deep.

Pronoun Reference   Rewrite sentences with pronouns that do not refer clearly to their antecedents or that are widely separated from them.

Confusing:
Albert was with Emanuel when **he** *got the news that* **his** *rare books had arrived.*

Who got the news? Did the rare books belong to Emanuel, or did they belong to Albert?

Improved:
When Albert got the news that **his** *rare books had arrived,* **he** *was with Emanuel.*

Generally, personal pronouns refer to the nearest previous noun, but don't risk a potentially unclear antecedent. Revise the sentence.

Pronoun Agreement   Pronouns must agree with their antecedents in number and gender. Singular antecedents require singular pronouns. Plural antecedents require plural pronouns.

*The house was dark and gloomy, and **it** sat in a grove of tall cedars that made **it** seem darker still.*

*The cars swept by on the highway, all of **them** doing more than 55 miles per hour.*

Use a singular pronoun when all the parts of a compound antecedent are singular and the parts are joined by *or* or *nor*. Notice, too, how the pronouns in the following examples also agree with their antecedents in *gender*, or sexual reference in grammar.

*Either Ted or John will take **his** car.*

*Neither Judy nor Linda will lend you **her** scalpel.*

Antecedents of unknown gender   Do not use the masculine singular pronoun to refer to a noun or pronoun of unknown gender.

Awkward:

*Any teacher must sometimes despair at the indifference of **his** students.*

*Everybody can have what **he** wants to eat.*

Such language, though grammatically correct, is now viewed as sexist. Avoid sexist language by changing nouns and pronouns to plural forms, or revise the sentence in some other way.

Improved:

Any teacher must sometimes despair at the indifference of students.

Teachers must sometimes despair at the indifference of their students.

When referring to the whole, collective nouns—*team, family, audience, majority, minority, committee, group, government, flock, herd* and many others—use singular pronouns.

*The team won **its** victory gratefully.*

*The committee disbanded when **it** finished its business.*

However, if the members of the group indicated by a collective noun are considered as individuals, use a plural pronoun.

Common Errors in Verbs

	Faulty	Correct
Irregular verbs		
Avoid confusing simple past with past participle.	*I **seen** her last night.*	*I **saw** her last night.*
	*He **done** it himself.*	*He **did** it himself.*
		*He **had done** it himself.*
Don't try to make irregular verbs regular.	*She **drawed** my picture.*	*She **drew** my picture.*
	*We **payed** for everything.*	*We **paid** for everything.*
Transitive and intransitive verbs		
Don't confuse *lay* (transitive) with *lie* (intransitive).	*I **lay** awake every night.*	*I **lie** awake every night.*
	*I **lay** my books on the desk when I came in.*	*I **laid** my books on the desk when I came in.*
	*I **laid** down for an hour.*	*I **lay** down for an hour.*
Don't confuse *set* (transitive) with *sit* (intransitive).	*He pointed to a chair, so I **set** down.*	*He pointed to a chair, so I **sat** down.*
	*She **sat** the vase on the table.*	*She **set** the vase on the table.*
Tense		
Don't shift tenses illogically.	*The car **bounced** over the curb and **comes** crashing through the window.*	*The car **bounced** over the curb and **came** crashing through the window.*
Mood		
Don't confuse conditional with past subjunctive.	*I wish he **would have** arrived sooner.*	*I wish he **had** arrived sooner.*
	*I would have been here if you **would have told** me you*	*I would have been here if you **had told** me you were performing.*

The hard-rock <u>band</u> broke up and began fighting among **themselves** *when* **their** *leader quit.*

Pronouns without references Pronouns such as *this, that, they, it, which* and *such* sometimes refer not to a specific antecedent, but to the general idea expressed by a whole clause or sentence. Using pronouns in this way is imprecise and often misleading.

> *Andy Warhol once made a movie of a man sleeping for a whole night, which was a tiresome experience.*

Was the movie tiresome to watch? Or was making the movie the tiresome experience?

"It" as Pronoun and Expletive The pronoun *it* always has an antecedent; the expletive *it* serves as a grammatical subject when the real subject comes after the verb or is understood.

> **Pronoun:**
> *In rural America when a barn burns,* **it** *often takes with* **it** *a year's hard work for a farm family.*

> **Expletive:**
> *In rural America, when a barn burns,* **it** *is difficult for a farm family to recover from the loss.*

The expletive *it* serves as the grammatical subject of the independent clause that it begins. Avoid using the expletive it and the pronoun it one after the other.

> **Weak:**
> *What will happen to the kite? If* **it** *is windy,* **it** *will fly.*

> **Improved:**
> *What will happen to the kite?* **It** *will fly if the wind blows.*

The expletive *it* does not require an antecedent. But other pronouns used without antecedents are both awkward and unclear.

Some Rules for Using Pronouns

❋ The subject of a dependent clause is always in the subjective case, even when the dependent clause serves as the object for another clause.

> *Dr. Hiromichi promised the prize to* **whoever** *made the best grades.*

> *Leave the message with* **whoever** *comes into the house first.*

❋ Objects of prepositions, direct objects, and indirect objects always take the objective case.

> *She called* **him** *and* **me** *fools.*

> *It was a secret between* **you** *and* **me.**

❋ When a noun follows a pronoun in an appositive con-

struction, use the case for the pronoun that you would use if the noun were not present. The presence of the noun does not change the case of the pronoun.

> *He gave the test to* **us** *students.*

> *We* *students said that the test was too hard.*

❋ *Than* and *as* often serve as conjunctions introducing implied clauses. In these constructions the idea that follows a pronoun at the end of a sentence is understood, not stated. The case of the pronoun depends on how the pronoun is used in the clause if it were written. (Implied clauses are sometimes called elliptical clauses.)

> *Throughout elementary school, Elizabeth was taller than* **he.**

> *The Sanchezes are much richer than* **they.**

❋ Pronouns that are the subjects or the objects of infinitives take the objective case.

> *I believe* **them** *to be tedious and ordinary.*

❋ Use the possessive case before a gerund (an *–ing* verb form used as a noun). Use the subjective or objective case with present participles used as adjectives.

> **Gerund:**
> **His** *returning the punt 96 yards for a touchdown spoiled the bets made by the gamblers.*

> **Present participle:**
> *They remembered* **him** *laughing as he said goodbye.*

❋ Pronouns agree in case with the nouns or pronouns with which they are paired.

> **Compound:**
> **She** *and Carla ran a design studio.*

> **Appositive:** *The captain chose two crew members,* **her** *and* **me,** *to attempt the rescue.*

> *The last two crew members on board, Carla and* **I,** *drew the first watch.*

Using Adjectives and Adverbs Correctly

Adverbs and Adjectives with Verbs of Sense Verbs of sense (*smell, taste, feel* and so on) can be linking or nonlinking. Decide whether the modifier after a verb of sense serves the verb (adverb) or the subject (adjective).

> **Adverb:** *I felt* **badly.** (referring to the sense of touch)

> **Adjective:** *I felt* **bad** *because she heard me say that her baby looked like a baboon.* (referring to emotions)

Distinguishing Adjectives and Adverbs Spelled Alike Not every adverb is an adjective with *–ly* tacked to the end of it. In standard English, many adverbs do not require the *–ly*, and some words have the same form whether they are used as adjectives or as adverbs.

Words that are both adjectives and adverbs: *fast, hard, only, right, straight.*

Using Adjectives and Adverbs for Comparison

Writers often use adjectives and adverbs to compare. Usually an *–er* or an *–est* ending on the word or the use of *more* or *most* along with the word indicates the degree, amount, or quality.

The simplest form of the adjective or the adverb is the positive degree, the form used when no comparison is involved. This is the form found in a dictionary.

To compare two things, use the *comparative* degree. Form the comparative degree of many adjectives by adding the suffix *–er*, or by using the adverb *more* or *less* with the positive form. Use the adverb *more* or *less* to form the comparative of most adverbs.

Use the *superlative* degree of both adjectives and adverbs to compare more than two things. Form the superlative of an adjective by adding the suffix *–est* to the positive form, or by using the adverb *most* or *least* with the positive form. The adverb *most* or *least* is used to form the superlative degree of an adverb.

Formal grammatical rules reserve the *–er* and *–est* endings for comparative and superlative degrees of adjectives and adverbs of no more than two syllables. Yet common usage for these modifiers of degree draws on suffix endings interchangeably with the forms *more* and *most, less* and *least.*

Irregular adjectives and adverbs
Some adjectives and adverbs are irregular; they change form to show degree.

Positive	Comparative	Superlative
bad	worse	worst
good	better	best
little	less	least
many/much	more	most
far	farther	farthest

Using degrees correctly

✳ Do not use the superlative for only two things or units.

Not: *Of the two brothers, John was the quickest.*

But: *Of the two brothers, John was the quicker.*

✳ Do not use the comparative and superlative degrees with absolute adjectives. *Absolutes* are words that in them-

selves mean something complete or ideal, such as *unique, half, infinite, impossible, perfect, round, square, destroyed,* and *demolished.* If something is unique, it is the only one of its kind. We cannot say, "Her dresses were more unique than his neckties." Either something is unique or it is not. No degrees of uniqueness are possible. "The answer to your question is *more impossible* than you think," is also wrong. Something is either possible or impossible; it cannot be *more* or *less* impossible.

✳ Avoid using the superlative when no comparison is stated.

Dracula *is the **scariest** movie!*

The scariest movie ever filmed? The scariest movie ever viewed? The scariest movie ever shown in town? In common speech expressions such as *scariest movie* or *silliest thing* often do not in fact compare the movie or the thing with anything else. In writing, such expressions take up space without conveying any precise meaning.

✳ Avoid adding an unnecessary adverb to the superlative degree of adjectives.

Not: *She was the very brightest person in the room.*

But: *She was the brightest person in the room.*

Not: *The interstate was the most shortest way to Nashville.*

But: *The interstate was the shortest way to Nashville.*

✳ Avoid making illogical comparisons with adjectives and adverbs. Illogical comparisons occur when writers leave out some necessary words.

Illogical: *The story of the* Titanic *is more interesting than the story of any disaster at sea.*

This comparison makes it seem that the story of the *Titanic* is one thing and that the story of any disaster at sea is something different. In fact, the story of the *Titanic* is about a disaster at sea. Is the story of the *Titanic* more interesting than itself?

Corrected: *The story of the* Titanic *is more interesting than the story of any other disaster at sea.*

Overuse of Adjectives and Adverbs
Too many adjectives or adverbs can weaken the force of a statement. Strong writers put an adjective before a noun or pronoun only when the adjective is truly needed. They rarely put more than one adjective before a noun unless they need to create some special effect or unless one of the adjectives is a number or part of a compound noun, such as *high school* or *living room.*

*The **clean** and **brightly lit** dining car left a **cold** and **snowy***

Moscow well stocked with **large** *and* **sweet fresh red** *apples,* **many** *oranges,* **long green** *cucumbers,* **delicious chocolate** *candy, and countless other* **well-loved** *delicacies.*

Improved: *The dining car left Moscow well stocked with* **fresh** *apples, oranges, cucumbers;* **chocolate** *candy; and* **other little** *delicacies.*

Use adverbs in the same careful way. Instead of piling them up, use strong verbs that carry the meaning.

Weak: *The train* **went very swiftly** *along the tracks.*

Improved: *The train* **sped** *along the tracks.*

Misplaced Modifiers

Most adjectives and adjectival clauses and phrases should stand as close as possible to the words that they modify. Misplacing the modifier can lead to unintended, and usually confusing and humorous, results.

In general it is easier to separate adverbs and adverbial phrases from the words that they modify than adjectives from the words that they modify.

Dangling Participles

Introductory participles and participial phrases must modify the grammatical subject of the sentence. Participles that do not modify the grammatical subject are called dangling or misplaced participles. A dangling participle lacks a noun to modify.

Incorrect:

Driving along Route 10, the sun shone in Carmela's face. (The sun is driving along Route 10?)

Using elaborate charts and graphs, the audience understood the plan. (The audience used the charts?)

Running down the street, the fallen lamppost stopped her suddenly. (The lamppost ran down the street?)

Revised:

Driving along Route 10, Carmela found the sun shining in her face.

or

As Carmela drove along Route 10, the sun shone in her face.

Using elaborate charts and graphs, the mayor explained the plan to the audience.

or

Because the mayor used elaborate charts and graphs, the audience understood the plan.

Running down the street, she saw the fallen lamppost, which stopped her suddenly.

or

As she ran down the street, the fallen lamppost stopped her suddenly.

Informal usage frequently accepts use of an introductory participle as a modifier of the expletive *it*, especially when the participle expresses habitual or general action.

Walking in the country at dawn, it is easy to see many species of birds.

The statement expresses something that might be done by anyone. Many writers and editors would prefer this revision: "Walking in the country at dawn is an easy way to see many species of birds."

Prepositional Phrases

Prepositional phrases used as adjectives seldom give trouble. Prepositional phrases used as adverbs, however, are harder to place in sentences, and misplaced adverbial phrases can lead readers astray.

Confusing:

He saw the first dive bombers approaching **from the bridge of the battleship.**

The multipurpose knife was introduced to Americans **on television.**

He ran the 10-kilometer race from the shopping mall through the center of town to the finish line by the monument **in his bare feet.**

Revised:

From the bridge of the battleship*, he saw the first dive bombers approaching.*

The multipurpose knife was introduced **on television** *to Americans.*

In his bare feet *he ran the 10-kilometer race from the shopping mall through the center of town to the finish line by the monument.*

or

From the shopping mall through the center of town to the finish line by the monument he ran the 10-kilometer race **in his bare feet.**

Clauses

A misplaced clause is one that modifies the wrong element of the sentence.

Confusing: *Professor Peebles taught the course on the English novel that most students dropped after three weeks.*

Revised: *Professor Peebles taught the course on the English* *novel, a course that most students dropped after three weeks.*

Placing Adverbs Correctly

Adverbs can modify what precedes or what follows them. Avoid the confusing adverb or adverbial phrase that seems to modify both the element that comes immediately before it and the element that comes immediately after it.

Confusing:

*To read a good book **completely** satisfies her.*

*To speak in public **often** makes her uncomfortable.*

Revised:

*She is **completely** satisfied when she reads a good book.*

or

*She is satisfied when she reads a good book **completely**.*

or

*When she speaks in public **often**, she feels uncomfortable.*

or

***Often** she feels uncomfortable when she speaks in public.*

Be cautious when you use adverbs to modify whole sentences. Some adverbs are much more ambiguous when they modify full sentences.

Confusing: *Hopefully he will change his job before this one gives him an ulcer.*

Who is doing the hoping?

Revised: *We hope he will change his job before this one gives him an ulcer.*

Confusing: *Briefly, Tom was the source of the trouble.*

Does the writer wish to say, briefly, that Tom was the source of the trouble? Or was Tom the source of the trouble, but only briefly?

Revised: *To put it briefly, Tom was the source of the trouble.*

Put Limiting Modifiers in Logical Places

In speaking, modifiers can work in illogical places because the sense is clear from tone of voice, gesture or general context. In writing, the lack of logic that results from misplacement of modifiers can cause confusion. Limiting modifiers, words such as *merely, completely, fully, perfectly, hardly, nearly, almost, even, just simply, scarcely* and *only,* must stand directly before the words or phrases they modify.

Confusing: *He **only** had one bad habit, but it **just** was enough to keep him in trouble.*

Revised: *He had **only** one bad habit, but it was **just** enough to keep him in trouble.*

Forming Degrees of Adjective and Adverb Modifiers

Modifier	Positive Degree (One object is)	Comparative Degree (Of two objects, one is)	Superlative Degree (Of three or more objects, one is)
fast (adjective)	*Pia's dog was fast.*	*Pia's dog was faster than Juan's cat.*	*Rebecca's snake was the fastest animal in the neighborhood.*
sophisticated (adjective)	*Joan's analysis of Moby-Dick was sophisticated.*	*Joan's analysis of Moby-Dick was more sophisticated than Emily's.*	*Joan's analysis of Moby-Dick was the most sophisticated in her class*
quickly (adverb)	*Eben ran quickly.*	*Rita ran more quickly than Eben.*	*Of the students in the class, Wilson ran most quickly.*
eloquently (adverb)	*The mayor spoke eloquently in support of the arts.*	*The governor spoke even more eloquently than the mayor.*	*The children's performance spoke most eloquently to support the City Art Center.*

Punctuation

Period

Use a period after a sentence that makes a statement, gives a mild command or makes a mild request, or asks a question indirectly. Simple statements end with a period.

Statement: *The building burned down last night*

Mild command: *Lend me a car, and I'll do the shopping.*

Indirect question:
She asked me where I had gone to college and who my adviser was.

Question Mark

Use a question mark after a direct question, but not after an indirect question.

Who wrote Wuthering Heights?

She wanted to know who wrote Wuthering Heights.

If a question ends with a quoted question, one question mark serves for both the question in the main clause and the question that is quoted.

What did Juliet mean when she cried, "O Romeo, Romeo! Wherefore art thou Romeo?"

For a quoted question before the end of a sentence that makes a statement, place a question mark before the last quotation mark and put a period at the end of the sentence.

"What did the president know and when did he know it?" became the great question of the Watergate hearings.

Occasionally a question mark changes a statement into a question.

You expect me to believe a story like that?

He drove my car into your kitchen?

Exclamation Point

Use exclamation points sparingly to convey surprise, shock, or some other strong emotion.

The land of the free! This is the land of the free! Why, if I say anything that displeases them, the free mob will lynch me, and that's my freedom. — D. H. Lawrence

Moon, rise! Wind, hit the trees, blow up the leaves! Up, now, run! Tricks! Treats! Gangway! — Ray Bradbury

Commands showing strong emotion also use exclamation points.

Stay away from the stove!

Help!

Avoid using too many exclamation marks.

Commas

With Independent Clauses   Use commas to set off independent clauses joined by the common coordinating conjunctions *and, but, or, nor, for, yet,* and *so.*

Her computer broke down, and she had to write with a pencil.

He won the Heisman Trophy, but no professional team drafted him.

The art majors could paint portraits, or they could paint houses.

Some writers do not separate short independent clauses with a comma.

He stayed at home and she went to work.

With Long Introductory Phrases and Clauses

Use commas after long introductory phrases and clauses.

After he had sat in the hot tub for three hours, the fire department had to revive him.

If you plan to lose 50 or more pounds, you should take the advice of a doctor.

A short opening phrase does not require a comma after the phrase.

After the game I drifted along with the happy crowd.

In their coffeehouses 18th-century Englishmen conducted many of their business affairs.

Always put a comma after an introductory subordinate clause.

When we came out, we were not on the busiest Chinatown street but on a side street across from the park. —Maxine Hong Kingston

Commas also set off introductory interjections, transitional expressions, and names in direct address.

Yes, a fight broke out after the game.

Nevertheless, we should look on the bright side.

Pablo, why are you doing this?

With Clauses and Phrases That Modify

Setting off absolutes An absolute is set off from the rest of the sentence by a comma. An absolute is a phrase that combines a noun with a present or past participle and that serves to modify the entire sentence.

The bridge now built*, the British set out to destroy it.*

The snake slithered through the tall grass, **the sunlight shining now and then on its green skin.**

Setting off participial modifiers Use commas to set off participial modifiers at the beginning or end of a sentence.

> *Having learned that she failed the test,* Marie had a sleepless night.

> We climbed the mountain, *feeling the spring sunshine and intoxicated by the view.*

With Nonrestrictive Clauses and Phrases Use

commas to set off nonrestrictive clauses and phrases. *Nonrestrictive clauses and phrases* can be lifted out of sentences without any resultant change in the primary meaning of the sentences. The paired commas that set off a nonrestrictive clause or phrase announce that these words provide additional information.

> *My dog Lady,* **who treed a cat last week,** *treed the mailman this morning.*

> *In the midst of the forest,* **hidden from the rest of the world,** *stood a small cabin.*

Setting off a phrase or a clause with commas can often change the meaning of a sentence. In this sentence the commas make the clauses nonrestrictive.

> *The commencement speaker, who was a sleep therapist, spoke for three hours.*

There was only one commencement speaker, and that speaker happened to be a sleep therapist.

> *The commencement speaker who was a sleep therapist spoke for three hours.*

In this sentence, the absence of commas means that there must have been more than one speaker. The clause is restrictive: it defines the noun and is essential to its meaning. The writer must single out the one who spoke for three hours.

With Items in a Series ("Serial Comma") Use com-

mas to separate items in a series. A *series* is a set of nouns, pronouns, adjectives, adverbs, phrases, or clauses joined by commas and a final coordinating conjunction. The serial comma, before the coordinating conjunction at the end of a series, is often necessary to avoid confusion so most style guides recommend using it. Newspaper style, including that of *The New York Times,* often omits the serial comma.

> **With:** *Winston Churchill told the English people that he had nothing to offer them but blood, toil, sweat, and tears.*

> **Without:** *Lincoln's great address commended government of the people, by the people and for the people.*

With Two or More Adjectives Use commas to separate two or more adjectives before a noun or a pronoun if you can use the conjunction *and* in place of the commas.

> *Lyndon Johnson flew a short, dangerous combat mission in the Pacific during World War II.*

> (*Lyndon Johnson flew a short* **and** *dangerous combat mission in the Pacific during World War II*)

With Direct Quotations Use a comma with quotation marks to set off a direct quotation from the clause that names the source of the quotation. When the source comes first, the comma goes before the quotation marks. When the quotation comes first, the comma goes before the last quotation mark.

> *She said, "I'm sorry, but all sections are full."*

> *"But I have to take the course to graduate," he said.*

Do not use a comma if the quotation ends in a question mark or an exclamation point.

> *"Do you believe in fate?" he asked.*

> *"Believe in it!" she cried. "It has ruled my life."*

In some cases, a colon can precede a quotation. (See *colons.*)

Parenthetical Elements are words, phrases or clauses that add further description to the main statement the sentence makes. Always set such elements off by paired commas: i.e., a comma at the beginning of the element and another at the end.

> *Brian Wilson, however, was unable to cope with the pressures of touring with the Beach Boys.*

> *Senator Cadwallader, responding to his campaign contributions from the coal industry, introduced a bill to begin strip-mining operations in Yellowstone National Park.*

With Numbers, Names, and Dates Use a pair of commas to separate parts of place names and addresses.

> *At Cleveland, Ohio, the river sometimes catches fire.*

Commas are used to separate the day from the year.

> *On October 17, 1989, the largest earthquake in America since 1906 shook San Francisco.*

No comma is necessary when the day of the month is omitted.

> Germany invaded Poland in September 1939.

Some writers use a form of the complete date that requires no comma at all.

> *She graduated from college on 5 June 1980.*

Checklist: Avoiding Unnecessary Commas

✳ A comma should not separate a subject from its verb or a verb from its object or complement unless a nonrestrictive clause or phrase intervenes.

Incorrect:

The tulips that I planted last year, suddenly died.

Revised:

The tulips that I planted last year, which grew rapidly, suddenly died.

✳ Do not separate prepositional phrases from what they modify. A prepositional phrase that serves as an adjective is not set off by commas from the noun or pronoun that it modifies.

Incorrect: *The book, about terrorists, was simplistic.*

✳ A prepositional phrase that serves as an adverb is not set off from the rest of the sentence by commas.

Incorrect: *He swam, with the current, rather than against it.*

✳ Do not divide a compound verb with a comma.

Incorrect: *He ran, and walked 20 miles.*

✳ But if the parts of a compound verb form a series, set off the parts of the verb with commas.

He ran, walked, and crawled 20 miles.

✳ Do not use a comma after the last item in a series unless the series concludes a clause or phrase set off by commas.

He loved books, flowers, and people and spent much of his time with all of them.

Three "scourges of modern life," as Roberts calls the automobile, the telephone, and the polyester shirt, are now ubiquitous.

✳ Avoid commas that create false parenthesis.

Incorrect: *A song called, "Faded Love," made Bob Wills famous.*

Semicolons

Semicolons are punctuation marks stronger than a comma, but weaker than a period. Use semicolons sparingly.

✳ Use a semicolon to join independent clauses that are closely related in meaning. A coordinating conjunction or a conjunctive adverb may precede the semicolon.

Silence is deep as eternity; speech is shallow as time.

— Thomas Carlyle

In the first draft I had Bigger going smack to the electric chair; but I felt that two murders were enough for one novel.

— Richard Wright

In the first sentence above, the semicolon helps stress the relation between the two clauses. In the second sentence the semicolon emphasizes the connection between the two independent clauses.

✳ Use a semicolon to join independent clauses separated by a conjunctive adverb, such as *however, nevertheless, moreover, then* and *consequently*. Conjunctive adverbs connect ideas between clauses, but these adverbs cannot work without appropriate punctuation. In these cases place a semicolon before the conjunctive adverb, and a comma after it.

He had biked a hundred miles in ten hours; nevertheless, he now had to do a marathon.

Sheila had to wait at home until the plumber arrived to fix the water heater; consequently, she was late for the exam.

✳ Use semicolons to separate various elements in a series when some of those elements contain commas.

They are aware of sunrise, noon and sunset; of the full moon and the new; of equinox and solstice; of spring and summer, autumn and winter. — Aldous Huxley

✳ Use semicolons to separate elements that contain other marks of punctuation as well.

The assignment will be to read Leviticus 21:1-20; Joshua 5:3-6; and Isaiah 55:1-10.

Apostrophes

Apostrophes form the possessive case of all nouns and of many pronouns. Apostrophes indicate omitted letters in words written as contractions. In only rare cases do apostrophes form plurals, so a good rule is not to use an apostrophe to make a word plural.

Forming a Possessive To form a possessive, add an apostrophe plus *s* to a noun or pronoun, whether it is singular or plural, unless the plural already ends in *s*; then add an apostrophe only.

Singular: *a baby's smile, the woman's hat*

Plural: *the men's club, the children's books, everyone's park, the robbers' plans*

Many writers add both an apostrophe and a final s to one-syllable singular nouns already ending in −s and to nouns of any number of syllables if the final s is a hard sound (as in *kiss*). *The New York Times Manual of Style and Usage* recommends this style as well.

Keats's poetry, Ross's flag, Elvis's songs, the kiss's power

However, other style manuals consider *Keats' poetry, Ross' play, Elvis' song, kiss' power* correct.

The *Times* suggests dropping the *s* after the apostrophe if a word ends in two sibilant sounds (*ch, sh, j, s,* or *z*) separated only by a vowel sound: *Kansas' climate, the sizes' range*).

Sometimes the thing possessed precedes the possessor. Sometimes the sentence may not name the thing possessed, but the reader easily understands its identity. Sometimes both the *of* form and an apostrophe plus *s* or a personal possessive pronoun can indicate possession.

The motorcycle is the student's.

Is the tractor Jan Stewart's?

I saw your cousin at Nicki's.

Other Common Uses of Apostrophes

Proper names of some geographical locations and organizations do not take apostrophes, even though possession is implied.

Kings Point, St. Marks Place, Harpers Ferry, Department of Veterans Affairs

For hyphenated words and compound words and word groups, add an apostrophe plus *s* to the last word only.

my father-in-law's job, the editor-in-chief's responsibilities

Use apostrophes with concepts of duration and monetary value.

An hour's wait, two minutes' work

To express joint ownership by two or more people, use the possessive form for the last name only; to express individual ownership, use the possessive form for each name.

McGraw-Hill's catalog

Felicia and Elias's house

Felicia's and Elias's houses

The city's and the state's finances

Showing omission

In a contraction—a shortened word or group of words formed when some letters or sounds are omitted—the apostrophe serves as a substitute for omitted letters.

it's	(for *it is* or *it has*)
weren't	(for *were not*)
here's	(for *here is*)
comin'	(for *coming*)
you're	(for *you are*)

Apostrophes can also substitute for omitted numbers: *The '50s were a decade of relative calm; the '60s were much more turbulent. The New York Times uses the apostrophe in these dates (1960's, 1970's).*

Special uses of apostrophes for plurals

The New York Times Manual of Style and Usage suggests the use of an apostrophe to show the plural form of an abbreviation, a

number or a letter:

two TV's, the new Delta 747's, mind your p's and q's

Many writers, however, omit the apostrophe in these cases.

Quotation Marks

Direct quotations

Use quotation marks, and other required punctuation, to indicate a direct quotation. A direct quotation repeats the exact words of a speaker or of a text. Direct quotations from written material may include whole sentences or only a few words or phrases.

James Baldwin wrote of his experiences during his childhood, "The only white people who came to our house were welfare workers and bill collectors."

In writing dialogue, use quotation marks to enclose everything a speaker says. When one person continues speaking, use quotation marks again if the quoted sentence is interrupted.

"I don't know what you're talking about," he said. "I did listen to everything you told me."

No comma precedes the quotation when it completes the meaning of the sentence and the existing initial capital letter in the quotation is made into a lowercase letter:

James Baldwin wrote of his childhood experiences that "the only white people who came to our house were welfare workers and bill collectors."

Indirect quotations

An indirect quotation is a paraphrase, that is, an expression in one's own words of the meaning of someone else's words. Do not use quotation marks with an indirect quotation.

Casey said that he enjoyed blowing the whistle more than anything else he did as a locomotive engineer.

Odette asked if she could borrow my car.

Single quotation marks set off quotations within quotations.

What happened when the faculty demanded an investigation of dishonest recruiting practices in the athletic department? The coach at the university said, "I know you're saying to me, 'We want an honest football team.' But I'm telling you this: 'I want a winning football team.'"

Placing punctuation with quotation marks

Convention calls for the placement of some marks of punctuation inside closing quotation marks. Other cases do require punctuation outside quotation marks.

✳ Periods always belong inside quotation marks.

✱ Commas always belong inside quotation marks.
✱ Semicolons always belong outside quotation marks.
✱ Exclamation points belong inside quotation marks if they are part of the statement or title quoted but outside quotation marks if they are end marks for the entire sentence.
✱ Question marks belong inside quotation marks if they are part of the question or title quoted but outside quotation marks if they are end marks for the entire sentence.

Enclosing Titles *The New York Times Manual of Style and Usage* recommends quotation marks around all titles and does not recommend italics for any titles. Most writers and publications use quotation marks only for certain titles, such as essays, book chapters or sections, short poems, short stories, songs, articles in periodicals, radio or television program episodes, and all unpublished works. They use italics for all other titles, including books, films, and artworks.

> *The chapter was called "Another Question of Location."*
> *Robert Herrick wrote the poem "Upon Julia's Clothes."*

Special Use of Quotation Marks Use quotation marks to show that someone else has used a word or phrase in a special way that others may not use or agree with completely.

> *George had the "privilege" of working his way through school by cleaning bathrooms.*
>
> *For them, getting "saved" is clearly only the first step.*
> — Frances Fitzgerald

Avoid quotation marks to apologize for the informality of certain expressions.

Apologetic:

> *Many people in California are "laid back."*
>
> *You can accomplish great things only if you "keep your nose to the grindstone."*
>
> *I thought he was "cute."*

It is better simply to avoid using slang, clichés, and expressions that call for an apology, and take time to think of a better way of expressing the thought.

Revised:

> *Many people in California pride themselves on living for pleasure without taking anything too seriously.*
>
> *You can accomplish great things only if you pay attention to what you are doing.*
>
> *I thought he was attractive.*

But if you have a good reason for using a cliché or a slang expression and are sure you can justify its use, use it—without quotation marks.

Italics

Italic, a typeface in which the characters slant to the right, is used to set off certain words and phrases.

Works of art and literature Many publications use italics for titles of books, magazines, journals, newspapers, plays, films, artworks, long poems, pamphlets, and other short works published separately, and for musical works. (Note that if surrounding text is italic, as here, the titles are set in roman, or plain text.)

> *Joan Didion, a former editor of* Vogue *and the* National Review, *received glowing reviews in* The New York Times *for her novel* A Book of Common Prayer.

Since newspapers use italics sparingly, *The New York Times Manual of Style and Usage* recommends quotation marks, not italics, for titles of works of art. According to the *Times*, names of newspapers and magazines take neither italics nor quotation marks.

Foreign terms Italicize most foreign words and phrases that are either absent from an English dictionary or included but labeled foreign.

> *They are wise to remember, however, one thing. He is Sinatra. The boss. Il Padrone.* — Gay Talese
>
> *Memphis, in fact, was definitely the mecca, yardstick and summum bonum.* — Terry Southern

Many common foreign words require no italics: rigor mortis (Latin), pasta (Italian), sombrero (Spanish), foie gras (French).

Some foreign words are still borderline, and some writers underline them while others do not. Examples are *ex nihilo* (Latin for "from nothing"), *imprimatur* (Latin for "Let it be printed"), and *Weltanschauung* (German for "worldview").

Dictionaries offer some help. By labeling as *French* a phrase like *mise-en-scène*, for example, a dictionary guides your decision to underline. Some dictionaries have special sections headed "Foreign Words." Others italicize foreign words when they appear. Use judgment about the borderline words. Consider the audience and the expectations that readers may bring to the writing. Be consistent in italicizing foreign words and phrases that appear more than once.

Words used as words Italicize words or phrases used

as words rather than for the meaning they convey.

> *And if the word* integration *means anything, this is what it means: that we, with love, shall force our brothers to see themselves as they are to cease fleeing from reality and begin changing it.* — James Baldwin

Letters used alone also require underlining to show italics.

> *The word bookkeeper has three sets of double letters: double* o, *double* k, *and double* e.

Some writers use quotation marks to show that words are being used as words.

> *When I was in graduate school in the late fifties, "criticism" was still a fighting word.* — Gerald Graff

Italics for emphasis Use italics sparingly to show the kind of emphasis desired if the words were spoken. An occasional word in italics helps emphasize a point.

> *That advertisers exploit women's subordination rather than cause it can be clearly seen now that* male *fashions and toiletries have become big business.* — Ellen Wills

In written dialogue, writers may use italics to emphasize words to show rhythms of speech used by characters.

> *The lady, however, regarded it very placidly. "I shouldn't have gone if she had* asked *me."* — Henry James

Other uses of italics By convention, the names of ships often appear in italics, as do the names of air and space vehicles. The names of trains do not. (*The New York Times Manual of Style and Usage* does not follow this convention.)

> *I packed my valise, and took passage on an ancient tub called the* Paul Jones *for New Orleans.* — Mark Twain

Many style manuals also recommend the use of italics for court cases. (*The New York Times Manual of Style and Usage* requires neither italics nor quotation marks for court cases.)

> *In* Brown v. Board of Education of Topeka *(1954), the U.S. Supreme Court ruled that segregation in public schools was unconstitutional.*

Dashes

The dash (—) sets off words, phrases, and sometimes whole sentences so that they receive special emphasis. Think of the dash as a very strong pause intended to give special emphasis to what follows—and sometimes to what comes immediately before.

> *I think this is the most extraordinary collection of human talent, of human knowledge, that has ever been gathered at the White House—with the possible exception of when Thomas Jefferson dined alone.* — John F. Kennedy

> *Coca-Cola, potato chips, and brevity—these are the marks of a good study session in the dorm.*

Sometimes dashes are paired—as in this sentence—and sometimes, as in the sentence above about study in the dorm, they are not.

When used in pairs, dashes serve to separate parenthetical statements more closely related to the sentence than parentheses would allow but less closely related than a pair of commas would imply.

> *What she gets—and enjoys—from me is a youthful perspective.* — Judith Viorst

> *A Wisconsin man traveling on horseback had the lower parts of his boots—brand new ones, be it noted—eaten by wolves, but managed to save his toes.* — Richard Erdoes

Colons

Colons can link independent clauses when the second clause restates or elaborates on the first. In this usage the colon emphasizes the second clause.

> *Until recently, women in Switzerland had an overwhelming political disadvantage: they could not vote.*

> *Of this I am sure: Martin will arrive late, talk loudly, and eat too much.*

Colons provide a formal way of introducing direct quotations. In this usage the colon provides additional separation between the statement before the quotation and the quotation itself.

> *"Don't speak of it," she said in a reciting voice and choosing her words sadly and carefully: "It was a stroke."*
> — V. S. Pritchett

Colons usually introduce block quotations, which are set off from regular text by spaces and indents, especially if the introduction previews the quotation.

> *Dickens had contempt for lazy people. Here is the way he introduces Mrs. Witterly in* Nicholas Nickleby:

> > *The lady had an air of sweet insipidity, and a face of engaging paleness; there was a faded look about her, and about the furniture, and about the house altogether.*

Colons also introduce itemized lists.

> *During its first four years the Virginia venture had failed to meet three basic needs: political stability, economic prosperity and peaceful Indian relations.* — Alden T. Vaughan

By convention, colons separate a main title from the subtitle. Capitalize the first word of the subtitle.

Doing Without: Meeting the Energy Crisis in the 1980's

Colons intervene between Bible chapters and verses.

Young writers should take Proverbs 12:1 as a motto.

Indicate the time of day using a colon between the hour and the minutes.

He woke up at 6:30 in the morning.

Colons follow salutations in business letters.

Dear Mr. Clinton:

Parentheses

Parentheses always work in pairs to set off information that breaks the flow of thought within a sentence or a paragraph. Parentheses enclose material that is not as important as material set off by commas or dashes.

The first money you get for a book will probably be your advance; as a rule, half of that is paid when you sign your con-

tract (or as soon thereafter as the legal department and the accounting department fill out the appropriate forms), and the other half comes due when you deliver a satisfactory manuscript.

When parentheses enclose a whole sentence, a period comes after the sentence but before the final parenthesis.

At another barrier a seaman held back Kathy Gilnagh, Kate Mullins and Kate Murphy. (On the Titanic *everyone seemed to be named Katherine.)* — Walter Lord

A sentence that appears inside parentheses within a sentence is neither capitalized nor ended with a period.

He was trying to memorize Kandahar (that's how he spent the long hours on the flight over), and one thing he knew for sure was that the city had lots of intersections.

— Mark Bowden

But a question mark or an exclamation point may follow a parenthetical sentence within a sentence.

John Henry (did he really swing a 40-pound hammer?) was a hero to miners fearing the loss of their jobs to machines.

Hyphen: Dos and Don'ts

Hyphenate	Do Not Hyphenate
compound adjectives preceding noun: *well-tailored suit; high-quality fabric*	modifiers following noun: *suit was well tailored; fabric is high quality*
after adjective ending in *ly: gravelly-voiced; grizzly-maned*	after adverb ending in *ly: highly paid job; newly married couple*
to avoid ambiguity: *unfair-practices charge; parochial-school teacher*	when meaning is clear: *sales tax bill; C minor concerto; foreign aid bill*
ages: *a three-year-old; two-year-old baby; eight-to-ten-year-olds*	ages: *She is three years old; they are eight and ten years old.*
colors: *bluish-green; black-and-white movie*	colors: *emerald green; dark red; navy blue; movie was in black and white*
noun+modifier: *tax-free; health- conscious*	noun+modifier: *commander in chief; secretary general*
numbers: *three-inch-high statue; ten-foot pole; 16th-century cathedral; second-best finish*	numbers: *it is three inches high; cathedral from 16th century; 20 percent; 20 percent increase*
three-, five-, and nine-inch snowfalls	*snowfalls of three, five, and nine inches*
nationality: *African-American man; Italian-American*	nationality: *He is African American; French Canadian; Jewish American*
noun+gerund: *A decision-making boss can be difficult.*	noun+gerund: *Decision making is difficult; decision maker*
relations: *great-grandfather; sister-in-law*	relations: *half brother; foster child; granddaughter; stepmother*
vice-chancellor	*vice president*
co-opt, co-worker, intra-arterial, multi-institutional, mid-July, pro-life, re-create, un-English	Close most words with prefixes such as: *ante, anti, co, intra, micro, mid, multi, non, post, pre, re, semi, sub, un*

Parentheses can enclose many kinds of numbers within a text. In some forms of annotation, parentheses enclose page numbers of a book referred to throughout a paper. Parentheses also can be used for numbered lists.

Stevens writes that the demands of their offices turn the best university presidents into machines (43).

Fernandez insists that (1) university presidents don't work as well as machines, (2) university presidents don't do any real work at all, and (3) universities would be better off if faculty committees ran them.

Use parenthetical numbers sparingly because the numbers interrupt the flow of thought.

Brackets

Use brackets to set off material within quoted matter that is not part of the quotation.

Samuel Eliot Morison has written, "This passage has attracted a good deal of scorn to the Florentine mariner [Verrazano], but without justice."

In this sentence, a writer is quoting Morison, whose sentence does not include the name of the "Florentine mariner." The writer adds the name—Verrazano—but places it in brackets.

Sometimes material in brackets explains or corrects a quotation.

Vasco da Gama's man wrote in 1487, "The body of the church [it was not really a church but a Hindu shrine] is as large as a monastery."

Brackets also surround words inserted within a quotation to make it fit the style or grammar of a sentence.

According to Ann Banks, he said, "I went back to the country and farmed a crop of tobacco with my dad that next year [but] I didn't make half as much as I'd been making at the factory."

The bracketed word *but* makes the sentence read smoothly. It eliminates the need for an ellipsis. (See *ellipses*.)

Brackets may enclose the word *sic* (Latin for "thus") after quoted matter that looks like a mistake. *Sic* lets the reader know that the quotation is presented exactly as it appears in its source and that the writer is aware of the error it contains.

The dean said, "Those kids is [sic] going to get kicked out of school for saying, 'I don't know no [sic] grammar.'"

Brackets are sometimes used to enclose editorial notes, page numbers, or other documentation inserted in a text.

Slashes

As a rule, use the slash only to show divisions between lines of poetry when you quote more than one line of a poem as part of a sentence. Poetry shown as a block quotation replicates the original lines and does not require slashes.

Sophocles wrote of the uncertainty of human knowledge: "No man can judge that rough unknown or trust in second sight/For wisdom changes hands among the wise."

Occasionally the slash shows that something happened over a couple of calendar years.

The book sold well in 1988/89.

But it is usually better to use this wording.

The book sold well in 1976 and 1977.

The book sold well in 1988–89.

Some writers use the slash to substitute for the conjunction *or* or as a marker between the words *and* and *or* when the words suggest options.

The winner will be chosen by lot, and he/she will drive a new car home.

You can buy the toaster oven and/or the microwave.

Most writers however, consider such usage awkward. It is usually better to paraphrase the sentence.

The winner, to be chosen by lot, will drive a new car home.

You can buy the toaster oven or the microwave, or both.

Do not use a slash to show alternative pronouns; it produces a clumsy sentence.

Ellipses

Use three spaced periods, called an ellipsis, to indicate words omitted from a quoted passage.

Full quotation:
In America, which is a successful society, we can all be celebrities in some little sphere, and we are very impressed with ourselves. — David Brooks

Edited quotation:
In his article on what he calls our superiority complex, Brooks argues that in America, "which is a successful society ... we are very impressed with ourselves."

In general, do not use ellipses to replace words left out at the beginning or the end of a quotation.

Use an ellipsis at the end of a sentence to suggest that the ending of the thought is either unclear or extremely obvious. Add a fourth spaced period for an ellipsis at the end of a sentence.

> *Oh God, I'm scared. I wish I could die right now with the feeling I have because I know Momma's going to make me mad and I'm going to make her mad, and me and Presley's gonna fight... "Richard, you get in here and put your coat on. Get in here or I'll whip you."* — Dick Gregory

Hyphens

✱ Use the hyphen in constructions like *three-mile hike* and *30-car train* and to avoid confusion in words like *re-form* (meaning form again).

✱ Do not use hyphens in compound modifiers when the meaning is clear without them: *sales tax bill; foreign aid plan; C minor concerto.* But: *pay-as-you-go plan* and *earned-income tax credit.* Hyphens inserted hastily or automatically can be misleading, since the first word may relate at least as much to the third word as to the second. For example: *airport departure lounge; fast breeder reactor; national health insurance.* Also, use no hyphen in these forms: *navy blue skirt; dark green paint.*

✱ In some compounds, the hyphen should be used to avoid ambiguity or absurdity: *unfair-practices charge,* not *unfair practices charge.* Note the separation of an otherwise solid compound in *small-business man* (not *small businessman*) and *parochial-school teacher* (not *parochial schoolteacher*).

✱ Never use a hyphen after an adverb ending in *ly: a newly married couple; an elegantly furnished house; a perfectly explicit instruction.* But an adjective ending in *ly* may take the hyphen if it is useful: *gravelly-voiced; grizzly-maned.*

✱ Use a hyphen with the modifiers *ill*(-) and *well*(-) when they precede a noun. An example: *He wore a well-tailored gray suit.* But omit the hyphen when the words follow the noun they modify: *The suit was well tailored.*

✱ Some other compound modifiers, typically those beginning with nouns, keep their hyphens regardless of position in a sentence: *They are health-conscious; The purchase was tax-free; The party describes itself as family-oriented; Stylebook editors are awe-inspiring.*

✱ Use no hyphens in a title consisting of a principal noun with modifiers: *commander in chief; lieutenant general; attorney general; director general; editor in chief; delegate at large; secretary general.* But use the hyphen in a title that joins two equal nouns: *secretary-treasurer.*

✱ When a modifier consisting of two or more words is bound together by quotation marks, the hyphen is redundant; thus *poison-pill defense* and *"poison pill" defense* are both acceptable, but *"poison-pill" defense* is not. A long phrase serving as a contrived modifier is best set off by quotation marks rather than hyphens: *her "fed up with business as usual" theme.*

✱ Use the *suspensive* hyphen, rather than repeat the second part of a modifier, in cases like this: *On successive days there were three-, five-, and nine-inch snowfalls.*

✱ Some house numbers in Queens take the hyphen: *107-71 111th Street.*

✱ Use the hyphen in a compound denoting national origin: *Italian-American; Japanese-American.* But *French Canadian* and *Jewish American,* for example, take no hyphen because both phrases denote current group membership rather than origin.

Joining Hyphens can join two nouns to make one compound word: *clerk-typist, scholar-poet, composer-conductor, writer-editor.*

Use a hyphen to link a noun with an adjective, an adverb, or another part of speech to form a compound noun: *accident-prone, cat-hater, break-in, first-rate.*

Hyphens also join nouns designating family relations and compounds of more than two words: *brother-in-law, stay-at-home, sister-in-law, stick-in-the-mud.*

In general, a compound that would be hard to decipher at a glance should be hyphenated. To avoid incongruity, a compound noun that is ordinarily solid should be separated when the first part is modified by an adjective: *businessman,* for example, becomes *small-business man; sailmaker* becomes *racing-sail maker; schoolteacher* becomes *public-school teacher.*

Modifiers Use hyphens to avoid confusion in meaning with modifiers.

> *She was a parochial school principal.* (meaning that her ideas were narrow)

> *She was a parochial-school principal.* (meaning that she was in charge of a parochial school)

When a compound modifier is formed by an adjective before a noun, it is usually hyphenated: *They wore well-tailored gray suits.* But the hyphen is sometimes omitted when the phrase follows what it modifies: *The suits were well tailored.*

Prefixes A hyphen joins a prefix and a capitalized word.

un-American, pre-Columbian

Some prefixes are attached with hyphens even though the main word is not capitalized.

all-conference, self-interest

Most prefixes, however, are not attached by hyphens. Simply join the prefix to the stem with no punctuation.

antisocial, nonjudgmental, superpower, atypical, postwar, undersea, extracurricular, preliterate

In some cases retain the hyphen to distinguish meanings or aid pronunciation.

anti-inflammatory, re-create

Some proper nouns that are joined to make an adjective are hyphenated.

a Mexican-American heritage, the Sino-Japanese agreement

Some numbers are hyphenated.

30-odd, twenty-five

Mechanics

Numbers

Style manuals have varying rules for when to spell out numbers and when to use figures. Many (including *The New York Times Manual of Style and Usage*) recommend spelling out the first nine *cardinal* and *ordinal* numbers. Some guides call for spelling out numbers up to one hundred and round numbers over one hundred but using figures for 100 and over.

Always try not to start a sentence with a number, but if you must, spell the number out.

Using Figures   Use figures for statistical comparisons, quantitative information, dates, times of day, and addresses.

In writing about some subjects where numbers are frequent, write them as figures.

The original plan for the house called for a dining room that would be 18 by 25 feet and a living room that would be 30 by 34 feet with plate-glass windows at each end.

In nontechnical writing, use figures to express percentages, but spell out *percent*.

Nearly 60 percent of those who went to the polls voted to reject the referendum.

Dates that include the year usually appear as figures, but some writers prefer to spell them out.

October 9, 1893   *the ninth of October 1893*

The 1960's or the 1960s   *the nineteen-sixties*

Always express the time of day in figures followed by the abbreviation A.M. or P.M. With the less technical forms *in the morning* or *in the evening*, spell out the numbers.

6:00 A.M., 8:15 P.M.

a quarter past eight in the evening

Street and highway numbers almost always appear as figures.

1 Park Avenue

Interstate 80

Abbreviations

As a general rule, spell out most words rather than abbreviate them.

Spell out the names of countries, cities, boroughs, and states and the words *Avenue, Boulevard, Highway, Street, River* and *Mountains* and words like them used as parts of proper names in formal writing.

The Catskill Mountains of New York flank the Hudson River.
Not: *The Catskill Mts. of N.Y. flank the Hudson Riv.*

Veterans Highway crosses Deer Park Avenue.

In addressing envelopes use street and state abbreviations as recommended in postal codes.

Spell out the names of months and days of the week, and spell out people's names.

Not: *In Sept. and Oct. Chas. visits the botanical gardens every Sun.*

But: *In September and October, Charles visits the botanical gardens every Sunday.*

Use an ampersand only if it is part of an official name.

The pistol was a Smith & Wesson.

Spell out the words *pages, chapter, volume,* and *edition* and the names of courses of study.

Chapter 16 in the 11th edition of the textbook presents new developments in open-heart surgery.

Freshman Composition 102 is a prerequisite for Communications 201.

Use abbreviations for *page, chapter,* and *edition* in footnotes, endnotes and bibliographical references in certain documentation systems such as the one set forth by the American Psychological Association. The APA requires the abbreviation *p* (for page) or *pp.* (for pages) in quoting a passage from a source and in citing an article in a monthly or bimonthly magazine on the references page.

The Hundred Words Most Frequently Misspelled	
1. accommodate	51. performance
2. achievement	52. personal
3. acquire	53. personnel
4. all right	54. possession
5. among	55. possible
6. apparent	56. practical
7. argument	57. precede
8. arguing	58. prejudice
9. belief	59. prepare
10. believe	60. prevalent
11. beneficial	61. principal
12. benefited	62. principle
13. category	63. privilege
14. coming	64. probably
15. comparative	65. proceed
16. conscious	66. procedure
17. controversy	67. professor
18. controversial	68. profession
19. definitely	69. prominent
20. definition	70. pursue
21. define	71. quiet
22. describe	72. receive
23. description	73. receiving
24. disastrous	74. recommend
25. effect	75. referring
26. embarrass	76. repetition
27. environment	77. rhythm
28. exaggerate	78. sense
29. existence	79. separate
30. existent	80. separation
31. experience	81. shining
32. explanation	82. similar
33. fascinate	83. studying
34. height	84. succeed
35. interest	85. succession
36. its, it's	86. surprise
37. led	87. technique
38. lose	88. than
39. losing	89. then
40. marriage	90. their
41. mere	91. there
42. necessary	92. they're
43. occasion	93. thorough
44. occurred	94. to, too, two
45. occurring	95. transferred
46. occurrence	96. unnecessary
47. opinion	97. villain
48. opportunity	98. women
49. paid	99. write
50. particular	100. writing

Unfamiliar Abbreviations Abbreviations may impair readability, since a general audience may be unfamiliar with them. But in some technical writing such as memos or reports intended for a limited audience, you may use abbreviations that are standard to that audience.

Not: *Dr. Ruth and SOL Dean Th. Luciano discussed the std. Rules about hab. Corp. proceedings in the pol. Cts. as they might apply to studs. arrested on DWI charges in the commercial dist. Alg. Mass. Ave.*

But: *Dr. Ruth Smith and Thomas Luciano, dean of the School of Law, discussed the standard rules about habeas corpus proceedings in the police courts as they might apply to students arrested on charges of driving while intoxicated in the commercial district along Massachusetts Avenue.*

Use the abbreviation *Inc., Corp., Co.,* or *Bros.* only when it is part of the official title of a company.

Tiffany & Co. sells extravagantly expensive jewelry.

Familiar Titles The general guideline about avoiding abbreviations does not apply to commonly abbreviated titles that always precede the person's name. These include *Mr., Mrs, Ms., Dr., St., the Rev., the Hon., Sen., Rep.,* and *Fr.*

Dr. Epstein and Dr. Kwang consulted on the operation.

The Rev. Dr. Karl Barth performed the marriage.

Many women prefer the title *Ms.* instead of *Miss* or *Mrs.* Strictly speaking, *Ms.* is not an abbreviation, since it does not stand for a word. But it is used in the same way *Mr.* and *Mrs.* are used—before a name. The title *Miss* is not an abbreviation, so it is not followed by a period. It always precedes the name.

Some abbreviations follow a proper name only. Usually they indicate academic or professional degrees or honors. Use a comma between the name and the abbreviation. A space follows the comma.

Robert Robinson, Jr.	*Elaine Leff, C.P.A., L.L.D.*
Kai-y Hsu, Ph.D.	*Michael Bartlett, Esq.*
Maria Tiante, M.D.	

But spell out titles used without proper names.

Mr. Carew asked if she had seen the doctor. (not dr.)

Notice that when an abbreviation ends a sentence, the period at the end of the abbreviation itself will serve as the period of the sentence. If a question mark or an exclamation point ends the sentence, use such a punctuation mark *after* the period in the abbreviation.

Is it true that he now wants to be called Stanley Martin, Esq.?

Acronyms   Abbreviate the name of an agency or organization named frequently, to make the repetition less tedious. Abbreviations of agency names that can be pronounced as words are called *acronyms*.

Many government agencies are regularly referred to by acronyms or abbreviations, especially in publications that mention them frequently. Often these abbreviations are so well known that they do not require any explanation.

The F.B.I. entered the case immediately at the request of the C.I.A.

The New York Times Manual for Style and Usage recommends the use of periods in abbreviations when the letters stand for separate words:

F.B.I., I.B.M., N.L.R.B.

However, in acronyms the *Times Manual* omits periods:

NASA, NATO

Broadcasting services, radio stations, and networks omit periods in all their abbreviations and call letters:

ABC, WOR, CNN, WNBC

Other Common Abbreviations   Abbreviate words typically used with times, dates and figures.

6:00 P.M.	*A.D. 1066*	*9:45 A.M.*
6000 r.p.m.	*498 B.C.*	

Note that instead of B.C., many writers now use B.C.E., "Before the Common Era." If a year stands alone, without B.C. or B.C.E., it is assumed to be A.D., although some writers still use C.E. when clarity requires it.

Latin Abbreviations   In text, use English translations rather than Latin abbreviations.

compare	not	cf.
for example	not	e.g.
and others	not	et al.
and so on,		
and so forth		
and the rest	not	etc.
in the same place	not	ibid.
that is	not	i.e.

Spelling

Important Spelling Rules

"ei" versus "ie"

The familiar rule is *i* before *e* except after *c* or when sounded like *a* as in *neighbor* or *weigh*.

In deciding between the combinations *ei* and *ie*, then, consider the previous letter and the sound of the word. When these letters sound like the *ee* in *see*, usually place the *i* before *e*.

believe, relieve, grief, chief, yield, wield

When the letters are preceded by *c*, the spelling is nearly always *ei*.

receive, deceive, ceiling, conceit

When the sound is like *ay* in *bay* or *May*, the spelling is nearly always *ei*.

neigh, feign, neighbor, weigh

Exceptions: *seize, caffeine, codeine, stein, weird, foreign, height, forfeit, pietism, sierra, pierce, pier, pie, pied, fiery, sieve*

Suffixes

Words ending in a silent —e   Before adding the suffix *—ing*, drop a final silent *—e* from the root word.

force/forcing,   surprise/surprising,   manage/managing,

hope/hoping,   scare/scaring,   come/coming,   pave/paving, become/becoming, fume/fuming

Exceptions:

dye/dyeing (to avoid confusion with *dying*)
hoe/hoeing (to avoid mispronunciation)
shoe/shoeing (to avoid mispronunciation and confusion with *showing*)

Always drop a final silent *—e* on a root word before the suffix *—ible*.

force/forcible

Some roots drop the *e* before the suffix *-able*; others retain the *e*.

observe/observable, advise/advisable, move/movable (sometimes *moveable*), *argue/arguable, debate/debatable*

knowledge/knowledgeable, manage/manageable, peace/peaceable, notice/noticeable, change/changeable, embrace/embraceable

In the second set of examples, the *e* is retained to keep the soft sound of the *c* and *g*.

Before adding a suffix, always drop a final silent *—e* preceded by another vowel.

argue/argument, true/truly

Words ending in —y   When adding the suffix *—ing* to a word ending in *—y*, retain the *—y*.

study/studying,   rally/rallying,   enjoy/enjoying,   cry/crying, ready/readying, steady/steadying, lay/laying

When a final –*y* follows a consonant in the root word, change the *y* to *i* before adding an ending other than –*ing*.

merry/merriment, merriest, merrier
happy/happier, happiness, happiest
rally/rallies, rallied, rallier

To form the past tense of verbs ending in a final –*y* preceded by a vowel, generally keep the final *y* and add the suffix –*ed*.

play/played, dismay/dismayed, enjoy/enjoyed

Exceptions: *pay/paid, say/said, lay/laid*

Words ending in a consonant With most words of one syllable ending in a consonant immediately preceded by a vowel, double the final consonant.

grip/gripping, quip/quipped, stun/stunning, quit/quitting, plan/planned, sad/saddest, scar/scarring

If the root word ends with two consecutive consonants or with a consonant preceded by two consecutive vowels, do not double the final consonant before suffixes that begin with vowels.

tight/tighter, stoop/stooping, straight/straightest, sing/singer, deep/deepened, creep/creeping, crawl/crawler

If the root word has more than one syllable, and if the accent of the root falls on the last syllable, usually double the final consonant.

occur/occurrence, refer/referred, rebut/rebutting, concur/concurring

But if the final consonant of the root is preceded by a consonant or by two consecutive vowels, or if the accent shifts from the final syllable of the root when the suffix is added, don't double the final consonant.

depart/departing, ferment/fermenting, repair/repairing, refer/reference

Spelling varies if the final consonant is –*l*. The increasing preference for the words listed below and others is not to double the final –*l*.

cancel/canceling, pencil/penciling, travel/traveled, unravel/unraveled

Prefixes are letters attached to the beginnings of words that change their meanings. Prefixes do not require changing the spelling or the root word.

appear/disappear	*create/procreate*
eminent/preeminent	*satisfy/dissatisfy*
operate/cooperate	*spell/misspell*
usual/unusual	

Before root words beginning with vowels, prefixes ending in vowels sometimes require a hyphen.

un-American   *co-op*

Forming Plurals To show plurality, simply add a final –*s*.

grove/groves, boat/boats, cobra/cobras, bank/banks, scientist/scientists, gasp/gasps

Exceptions based on endings When the singular of a noun ends in –*s*, -*x*, -*ch*, or –*sh*, add –*es* to form the plural.

kiss/kisses, Marx/the Marxes, Mr. Jones/the Joneses, church/churches, dish/dishes

If a noun ends in –*y* preceded by a consonant, change the *y* to *i* and add –*es* to form the plural; if the final *y* is preceded by a vowel, keep the *y* and add –*s* to make the plural.

beauty/beauties, sally/sallies, city/cities, ray/rays, boy/boys, joy/joys, valley/valleys

When a noun ends in –*o* in the singular, form the plural by adding –*s* or –*es*. The best practice here is to look these plurals up in the dictionary.

hero/heroes, solo/solos, tomato/tomatoes, folio/folios, flamingo/flamingos or flamingoes, piano/pianos

To form the plurals of some nouns ending in –*f*, change the final *f* to *v* and add –*es*. If a silent *e* follows the *f*, also change the *f* to *v*.

leaf/leaves, hoof/hooves, knife/knives

Many nouns ending in *f* form the plural by the standard addition of –*s*

chief/chiefs, roof/roofs

Irregular plurals Some nouns have irregular plurals formed by changes in internal vowels or the addition of endings that don't include –*s*.

child/children, goose/geese, man/men, woman/women, ox/oxen, tooth/teeth, mouse/mice

Some nouns are the same in the singular and plural.

deer/deer, fish/fish or fishes, fowl/fowl or fowls, moose/moose

Compound nouns generally form plurals by the addition of –*s* or –*es*.

babysitter/babysitters, millrace/millraces

But when the first element of the compound is the most important word, –*s* or –*es* is added to it.

attorney general/attorneys general, mother-in-law/mothers-in-law, father-in-law/fathers-in-law, court-martial/courts-martial, passerby/passersby

To form the plurals of many Latin and Greek words with the singular ending –*um* or –*on*, drop these endings and add –*a*.

addendum/addenda, criterion/criteria, datum/data, medium/media, phenomenon/phenomena

The plurals of a few nouns ending in *–is* are formed by changing this ending to *–es*.

analysis/analyses, basis/bases, crisis/crises, thesis/theses

Some words with Latin roots ending in a vowel and an *x* may change to *–ices* when the plural is formed.

appendix/appendices, index/indices (math), vortex/vortices

But *–es* is the preferred ending for the plurals of these words.

appendixes, indexes (book), vortexes

A few English words with Latin roots ending in *–us* form their plurals by changing the *–us* to *–i*.

alumnus/alumni, tumulus/tumuli, cumulus/cumuli, hippopotamus/hippopotami or hippopotamuses, calculus/calculi, cactus/cacti

Even fewer words with Latin roots ending in *–a* form their plurals by changing the *–a* to *–ae*.

alumna/alumnae

Homophones

The source of many spelling problems are homophones, words that sound alike or nearly alike but have different meanings and different spellings.

affect, effect	foreword, forward
all, awl	hear, here
complement, compliment	its, it's
council, counsel	lead, led
discreet, discrete	lightening, lightning
made, maid	sea, see
pail, pale	stationary, stationery
pair, pare	straight, strait
plain, plane	vain, vane, vein
principal, principle	way, weigh
rain, reign, rein	who's, whose

Words Commonly Confused and Misused

✦ A   An ✦

a: Use a when the next word begins with a consonant sound.

a book

an: Use an when the next word begins with a vowel sound.

an urgent request

Hint: It is the sound that counts, not the actual letter.

an hour   *a usual routine*

✦ Accept   Except ✦

accept: to receive, to agree to, to answer affirmatively

I accepted the parcel from the mail carrier.

except: excluding (when used as a preposition), to exclude (when used as a verb)

I liked everything about the concert except the music.

I except you from my criticism.

Hint: Except is usually used as a preposition.

✦ Adapt   Adept   Adopt ✦

adapt: change or adjust in order to make more suitable or in order to deal with new conditions

The dinosaur was unable to adapt to changes in its environment.

adept: skillful, handy, good at

Bill has always been adept at carpentry.

adopt: take or use as one's own, endorse

The Senate adopted the new resolution.

✦ Adolescence   Adolescents ✦

adolescence: refers to the teenage years

My adolescence was marked by religious questioning, parental snooping, and skin problems.

adolescents: teenagers

Adolescents pay outrageous rates for car insurance.

✦ Adverse   Averse to ✦

adverse: hostile, difficult, unfavorable

Adverse weather conditions have tormented farmers for the past decade.

averse to: someone's being unwilling or reluctant

John has always been averse to accepting other people's ideas.

✦ **Advice** **Advise** ✦

advice: a noun
*My **advice** to you is to leave well enough alone.*
advise: a verb
*I **advise** you to leave well enough alone.*

✦ **Affect** **Effect** ✦

affect: when used as a verb means to impress or influence; noun form is generally restricted to technical discussions of psychology, meaning an emotion
*This song always **affects** me powerfully.*
*Pete's **affect** was always sullen and perverse.*
effect: a noun meaning result; verb meaning to accomplish or produce is comparatively uncommon
*Many of our welfare programs have not had beneficial **effects**.*
*We hope this new program will **effect** a whole new atmosphere on campus.*

✦ **Ain't** ✦

ain't: is slang and used only in written English for humor or dialogue. Use of the phrase ain't I, when asking a question in conversational English is undesirable; as is the seemingly stylish but ungrammatical aren't I. Am I not is grammatically correct, but clumsy and stuffy.

✦ **All ready** **Already** ✦

all ready: all set, prepared
*The meal was **all ready** by six o'clock.*
already: previously, by the designated time
*Professor Willis has **already** told us that twice.*

✦ **All right** **Alright** ✦

Alright is nonstandard. **All right** is the preferred spelling.

✦ **All together** **Altogether** ✦

all together: joined in a group
*For once, the citizens are **all together** on an important issue.*
altogether: thoroughly, totally
*The character's motivations are **altogether** obscure.*

✦ **Allusion** **Illusion** ✦

allusion: an indirect mention or reference. The verb form is allude.
*The nominating speech **alluded** to every American hero from Jack Armstrong to Neil Armstrong.*
illusion: an idea not in accord with reality
*The patient suffered from the **illusion** that he was Napoleon.*

✦ **A lot of** ✦

a lot of: okay to use in conversation, but not usually in written English. **A lot** is two words. Do not confuse it with **allot,** meaning to give out or apportion. Do not use **lots** to mean "many" in writing.

✦ **Among** **Between** ✦

among: use when dealing with more than two units
between: use when dealing with only two units
Not: *The company president had to make an arbitrary decision among the two outstanding candidates for promotion,* but: *The company president had to make an arbitrary decision **between** the two outstanding candidates for promotion.*
Not: *Tension has always existed between my mother, my father, and me,* but: *Tension has always existed **among** my mother, my father, and me.*

✦ **Anxious** **Eager** ✦

anxious: suggests worry or fear
*I waited **anxiously** for the telephone to bring me news of Joan's safe arrival.*
eager: suggests enthusiasm
*The whole town waited **eagerly** to greet the triumphant hockey team.*

✦ **Anymore** **Any more** ✦

anymore: refers to time
*I don't eat apples **anymore**.*
any more: use in phrases
*I haven't **any more** apples.*

✦ **Anyone** **Any one** ✦

anyone: means anybody at all
***Anyone** can learn how to do simple electrical wiring.*
any one: singles out each person or thing within a group
***Any one** of these paintings is worth a small fortune.*

◆   Anyways   ◆

anyways: not standard written English. Use **anyway**.

◆   As   ◆

as: do not use as a substitute for because or since

Not: *I was late for my appointment as I missed the bus*, but: *I was late for my appointment **because** I missed the bus.*

◆   Awfully   ◆

awfully: does not mean "very"

Not: *He's an awfully nice person*, but: *He's a **very** nice person.*

◆   A while   Awhile   ◆

a while: a noun

*I thought I saw her **a while** ago.*

awhile: an adverb

*Success comes only to those who are prepared to wait **awhile**.*

◆   Bad   Badly   ◆

bad: an adjective

*I feel **bad**. She looks **bad**.*

badly: an adverb

*I play **badly**.*

Hint: In some sentences, the verbs look, feel, and seem function as linking verbs and must be followed by the adjectival form.

◆   Being as/as how   Being that   ◆

Not standard written English. Use because or since.

◆   Beside   Besides   ◆

beside: alongside of; other than or aside from

*He pulled in **beside** the Buick.*

*Your last statement is **beside** the point.*

besides: in addition to, moreover

*I'm starting to discover that I'll need something **besides** a big smile to get ahead.*

***Besides**, I'm not sure I really liked the dress in the first place.*

◆   Can   May   ◆

can: in formal English questions, asks if the ability is there

Can your baby speak yet?

may: in formal English questions, asks if the permission is there

May I intrude on your conversation?

(not can—anyone with a voice has the ability to intrude).

Hint: Outside of formal contexts, few people worry about the distinction.

◆   Can't hardly   ◆

can't hardly: a double negative. Use can hardly.

◆   Can't help but   ◆

can't help but: wordy and repetitious. Avoid this phrase in written English.

Not: *I can't help but worry about what winter will do to my old car*, but: *I **can't help** worrying about what winter will do to my old car.*

◆   Capital   Capitol   ◆

capital: refers to money, uppercase letters, and cities that are seats of government.

*Highly speculative investments can offer excellent opportunities for **capital** gains.*

*The poet e.e. cummings had an aversion to **capital** letters.*

*Madison is the **capital** of Wisconsin.*

capitol: a building in which major legislative bodies meet. With an uppercase C, Capitol refers to the building in Washington, D.C.

*Madison's **capitol** closely resembles the **Capitol** in Washington, D.C.*

◆   Casual   Causal   ◆

casual: informal, unplanned

*Bill is entirely too **casual** about his financial future.*

causal: having to do with a cause

*Karen understands the **causal** connection between cigarettes and lung disease is unmistakable.*

◆   Censor   Censure   ◆

censor: as a verb means to examine mail, art, etc., to see if it should be made public, or to cut out, ban. As a noun, means a person engaged in censoring.

*The school authorities **censored** parts of the movie.*

*The prison **censor** examines all mail.*

censure: can be a verb or a noun meaning condemn, or

condemnation; criticize adversely, or adverse criticism.

*The Citizens Committee recently **censured** the mayor.*

Critics have singled out Dickens's deathbed scenes for
***censure**.*

◆ **Center around** ◆

center around: since a center is a single point in the middle of something, center around is an illogical phrase. Use center on instead.

*The discussion **centered on** ways to increase productivity in the coming year.*

◆ **Cite** **Site** **Sight** ◆

cite: a verb meaning to mention

*He **cited** many examples to prove his point.*

site: a noun meaning location

*The **site** of a new housing project has been debated for more than a year.*

sight: a noun meaning something viewed, the ability to see, or the foreseeable future

*In her feather hat and seashell earrings she was quite a **sight**!*

◆ **Climactic** **Climatic** ◆

climactic: the adjective form of climax

*The hero's death is the **climactic** moment of the story.*

climatic: the adjective form of climate

***Climatic** conditions in the Dakotas go from one extreme to the other.*

◆ **Complected** ◆

complected: not standard English. Complexioned is preferable, but it's better to reword your sentence so you can avoid using either term.

Not: *He was a light-complexioned man,* but: *He had very fair skin.*

◆ **Complement** **Compliment** ◆

complement: a verb meaning to complete or bring to perfection

*Cheese and wine **complement** each other.*

compliment: praise, noun or verb

*I don't appreciate insincere **compliments**.*

◆ **Compose** **Comprise** ◆

compose: to make up, to constitute

*Thirteen separate colonies **composed** the original United States.*

comprise: to be made up of, to encompass

*The original United States **comprised** thirteen separate colonies.*

Hint: Never write "comprised of." The whole **comprises** the parts.

◆ **Conscience** **Conscientious** **Conscious** ◆

conscience: the inner voice that tells us right from wrong

*No one should ask you to act against your **conscience**.*

conscientious: painstaking, scrupulous, ruled by conscience, as in conscientious objector

*I've tried to do this work as **conscientiously** as possible.*

conscious: aware

*Jerry became **conscious** of a subtle change in Mary's attitude.*

◆ **Contemptible** **Contemptuous** ◆

contemptible: use to describe something or someone deserving of scorn

*Few crimes are more **contemptible** than child abuse.*

contemptuous: use to describe the expression of scorn

*Instead of shaking hands, she thumbed her nose and stuck out her tongue. Her **contemptuous** attitude was clear.*

◆ **Continual** **Continuous** ◆

continual: frequently repeated, but with interruptions or pauses

*He had a bad cold and blew his nose **continually**.*

continuous: completely uninterrupted, without any pause

*The **continuous** noise at the party next door kept us awake.*

Hint: **Continuous** ends in **o**(ne), **u**(ninterrupted), **s**(equence).

◆ **Could of** **Should of** **Would of** ◆

Not standard in written English. Use could have, should have, would have.

◆ **Council** **Counsel** ◆

council: a governing body or an advisory group

*The **council** met last week in a special emergency session.*

counsel: as a verb means to advise or recommend; as a noun means advice, recommendation, exchange of ideas
*Sarah knew she could rely on her father's friendly **counsel.***

✦ Credible   Creditable   Credulous ✦

credible: believable
*Their lame excuses were not **credible.***
creditable: worthy of praise
*Adam's behavior since his graduation has been **creditable.***
credulous: gullible, foolishly believing
*She's so **credulous** she still believes that the stork brings babies.*

✦ Data ✦

data: technically a plural word, the singular form of which is datum. The word's Latin origins, however, have nothing to do with its current usage. Many people believe that data works as singular in all levels of English.
Correct: *This data is accurate and helpful.*
Correct (but very formal): *These data are accurate and helpful.*

✦ Device   Devise ✦

device: a noun meaning, among other things, mechanism or special effect
*The safety pin is a simple but an extraordinarily clever **device.***
devise: a verb meaning to invent or plot
*The person who **devised** the safety pin is one of humanity's minor benefactors.*

✦ Different than   Different from ✦

Hint: **Different from** is preferable in all circumstances

✦ Discreet   Discrete ✦

discreet: tactful, reserved
***Discreet** silence is sometimes the most effective reply to an insult.*
discrete: separate, distinct
*Rising interest rates have several **discrete** effects on the economy.*

✦ Disinterested   Uninterested ✦

disinterested: impartial, unbiased
*A **disinterested** judge is necessary for a fair trial.*
uninterested: bored, indifferent
*An audience is **uninterested** in a poor play.*
Hint: These words are NOT synonyms.

✦ Each ✦

each: takes a singular verb and a singular pronoun. **Each other** refers to two persons. **One another** refers to more than two persons. See he, his, him, himself.
***Each** actress was told to practice her lines.*
***Each** of the Cleveland Indians is taking his turn at batting practice.*

✦ Economic   Economical ✦

economic: refers to business, finance, the science of economics, and so on
***Economic** conditions are improving in the textile industry.*
economical: inexpensive or thrifty
*The **economical** shopper looks for bargains.*

✦ Either ✦

either: only when dealing with two units
Not: *Either the Republican, the Democrat, or the Independent will be elected,* but: ***Either** Elaine or Tom will get the job.*
Hint: When either is the subject, it takes a singular verb and pronoun.
*The scientists are both qualified. **Either** is ready to give her best.*
See also **neither**.

✦ Elicit   Illicit ✦

elicit: to draw out
*The interviewer was unable to **elicit** a direct answer.*
illicit: improper or prohibited
*Our modern novelists often write about **illicit** romance.*

✦ Eminent   Imminent ✦

eminent: distinguished or noteworthy
*The **eminent** speaker delivered a disappointing address.*
imminent: about to happen
*After years of frustration, a peace treaty is **imminent.***

◆   Emigrate   Immigrate   ◆

emigrate: takes preposition *from*

*A century ago the people who did **emigrate** from Mexico did so without problems.*

immigrate: takes preposition *to*

*In order to **immigrate** to England, the Irish needed proof of their birthplace.*

◆   Ensure   Insure   ◆

Both words are used interchangeably, but use insure for references to financial guarantees against loss of life, health and property.

*The new screens **ensure** that insects stay outside where they belong.*

*If you **insure** your home or apartment, take photographs of all your most valuable possessions.*

◆   Equally as   ◆

equally as: not standard English. Eliminate the as or substitute just as.

Not: *My grades were equally as good,* but: *My grades were **equally** good.*

Not: *The style was equally as important as the plot,* but: *The style was **just as** important as the plot.*

◆   Etc.   ◆

etc.: Abbreviation of *et cetera* (Latin for "and so forth," "and other things"). Except where brevity is a major concern, avoid etc. It tends to convey the impression that the writer doesn't want to be bothered with being accurate and specific.

◆   Every   ◆

every: This adjective makes the noun it modifies take a singular verb and a singular pronoun. (See the entry below, "he, his, him, himself."

Every woman leader needs to learn how to deal with the prejudices of her male counterparts.

Every Denver Bronco is required to report his weight upon arrival at training camp.

◆   Every day   Everyday   ◆

every day: the common phrase used for references to time

*He loved her so much that he wanted to see her **every day**.*

everyday: an adjective meaning normal, ordinary, routine

*The **everyday** lives of many everyday people are filled with fears, tensions, and the potential for tragedy.*

◆   Expand   Expend   ◆

expand: to increase, enlarge, fill out

*The company needs to **expand** its share of the market.*

expend: to spend, use up

*Last night I had **expended** all my energy studying.*

◆   Explicit   Implicit   ◆

explicit: stated to shown directly

*Cheryl's mother gave **explicit** instructions to be home before dark.*

implicit: implied, not stated or shown directly

*My wife and I have an **implicit** understanding that the first one who can't stand the dirt any longer is the one who vacuums the rugs.*

◆   Farther   Further   ◆

farther: for geographic distance

*Allentown is five miles **farther** down the road.*

further: use for everything but geographic distance

Further changes improved the curriculum.

*Jim kissed her, but they were **further** apart than ever.*

◆   Faze   Phase   ◆

faze: disconcert, fluster

*No great artist is **fazed** by critical sneers.*

phase: a stage of development. Limit its use to contexts in which the passage of time is especially important.

Not: *One phase of the team's failure is poor hitting,* but: *the history of the team can be divided into three **phases**.*

◆   Fewer   Less   ◆

fewer: refers to amounts that can be counted individually, item by item

*Joe earned **fewer** dollars this year than he did five years ago.*

less: refers to general amounts or amounts that cannot be counted or measured

*Joe made **less** money this year than he did five years ago.*

◆   Flaunt   Flout   ◆

flaunt: to show off arrogantly or conspicuously

*They lost no opportunity to **flaunt** their newfound wealth.*

flout: to treat scornfully, to show contempt

*Those hoodlums **flout** all the basic decencies and then complain that we misunderstand them.*

✦ Foreword   Forward ✦

foreword: a preface or introduction

*The only interesting part of the book was the **foreword**.*

forward: opposite of backward; bold or impertinent

*Our mistakes are part of history. We must now look **forward**.*

*Amy's old-fashioned grandfather told her that she was a **forward** hussy.*

✦ Former ✦

former: first of the two

Not: *Grant, McKinley, and Harding were poor presidents. The former was the poorest,* but: *Grant, McKinley, and Harding were poor presidents. The first was the poorest. Grant and McKinley were poor presidents. The **former** was the poorer.*

Hint: Do not use **former** when dealing with more than two persons or items.

✦ Good   Well ✦

good: adjective that modifies a noun

*Mary was a **good** speaker.*

well: adverb that modifies a verb

*She spoke **well**.*

Hint: After a linking verb, always use good. Common linking verbs are to be (in all forms and tenses- am, is, are, was, were, have been, has been, had been, would be, will be, and so on), feel, look, sound, taste, appear, smell, and the like.

*Her voice sounded **good**.*

*The speech was **good**.*

*Mary felt **good**.*

✦ Hanged   Hung ✦

Hint: Both are past participles of hang; technically, they are interchangeable. Tradionally, however, hanged is reserved for references to executions and hung is used everywhere else.

*The spy was **hanged** the next morning.*

*All the pictures **hung** crookedly.*

✦ He His   Him   Himself ✦

Hint: English has no distinct singular pronoun to refer to both sexes. In the past, the masculine pronoun was used to refer to a singular subject of either sex or when sex was irrelevant of unknown.

*Each citizen can make **his** choice on Election Day.*

*Everybody should protect **himself** from the dangers of alcoholism.*

However, increased sensitivity to sexist language has caused this usage to disappear from contemporary published writing. The easiest and most common way to avoid sexist language is to change singular phrasing to plural whenever possible.

*All citizens can make **their** choice known on Election Day.*

*People should protect **themselves** from the dangers of alcoholism.*

Rephrase sentences that do not lend themselves to a plural approach. See **he/she, his/her, him/her, he or she, his or hers, him or her.**

✦ He/She His/Her   His or Hers ✦

Hint: Reserve these noble efforts to achieve sexual equality in language for legal contracts. Use a plural subject and pronoun whenever possible, or recast the sentence to eliminate sexist language.

Not: *Everyone needs to make early plans for his/her career.*

But: *People should make early plans for **their** careers.*

Not: *In cases of fatal illness, should a patient be told the truth about what is wrong with him or her?*

But: *In cases of fatal illness, should patients be told the truth about what is wrong with **them**?*

✦ Hoard   Horde ✦

hoard: verb means amass; noun means a large hidden supply

*As rumors of war increased, some citizens began to **hoard** food.*

*The old man's **hoard** of gold was concealed beneath the floorboards.*

horde: a large throng or crowd

*The **horde** of locusts totally destroyed last year's grain crop.*

✦ Hopefully ✦

Hint: **Hopefully** is an adverb, which means that it modifies and usually appears next to or close to a verb, adjective, or another adverb.

Not: *Hopefully, we can deal with this mess next weekend. The new driver's training program, hopefully, will cut down on traffic fatalities.*

But: *The farmers searched **hopefully** for a sign of rain. **Hopefully**, the children ran down the stairs on Christmas morning.*

In fairness, so many educated writers and speakers mishandle hopefully that the incorrect usage is likely to worm its way into standard English someday.

◆ I   Me ◆

I: functions as the subject of a sentence or clause, and as a complement in the very formal but grammatically correct *It is **I***.

me: the object of a verb or preposition

*He gave the book to **me**. Why does she like **me** so much?*

Hint: To determine which word to use in sentences like "Nobody is more enthusiastic than I" or "Nobody is more enthusiastic than me," simply complete the sentences with a verb and see which makes sense.

Not: *Nobody is more enthusiastic than me (am).*

But: *Nobody is more enthusiastic than **I** (am).*

◆ Imply   Infer ◆

imply: to suggest or hint at something without specifically stating it

*The editorial **implies** that our public officials have taken bribes.*

infer: to draw a conclusion

*I **inferred** from her standoffish attitude that she dislikes me.*

Hint: Imply and infer are not interchangeable.

◆ Incredible   Incredulous ◆

incredible: unbelievable

*The witness gave evidence that was utterly **incredible**.*

incredulous: unconvinced, nonbelieving

*I was **incredulous** at hearing those absurd lies.*

◆ Indict ◆

indict: to charge with a crime. It does not mean to arrest or convict.

*The grand jury **indicted** Fields for gambling.*

◆ Ingenious   Ingenuous ◆

ingenious: clever

*Sherlock Holmes was an **ingenious** detective.*

ingenuous: naïve, open

*Nothing could rival the **ingenuous** appeal of the little child's eyes.*

Hint: The noun forms are ingenuity and ingenuousness.

◆ Inter-   Intra- ◆

inter-: a prefix meaning "between different groups"

*Ohio State and Michigan fought bitterly for **intercollegiate** football supremacy.*

intra-: a prefix meaning "within the same group"

*The English faculty needs a new department head who can control **intradepartmental** bickering.*

◆ Irregardless ◆

Hint: Not standard. The proper word is **regardless**.

◆ It's   Its ◆

it's: it is   *It's too quiet. Tell us if **it's** true*
      it has   *It's been a week since I saw her.*

*Hint: **It's** always stands for it is or it has, and nothing else.*

its: possession or ownership by some nonhuman thing

*The Raggedy-Ann doll lost **its** stuffing.*

*As winter approached, the tree lost **its** leaves.*

Hint: Replace *its* with *his* or *her* to see if the possessive pronoun is correct in the sentence.

The tree lost his leaves.

(His gives the sense of ownership; since trees have no male or female qualities, *its* is correct in the sentence.)

Hint: The form **its'** does not exist.

◆ Kind of ◆

Hint: Means what it says- "a type of, a variety of." It does not mean "somewhat" or "rather" except in the most informal writing.

Not: *I was kind of curious about his answer.*

But: *She had a **kind of** honest stubbornness that could be very appealing.*

◆ Latter ◆

Hint: Means 'the second of the two.' Do not use latter when dealing with more than two items or people.

Not: *Washington, Jefferson and Lincoln were great presidents. The latter was the greatest.*

But: *Washington and Lincoln were great presidents. The latter was the greater.*

◆ Lay　　　　　　　　Lie ◆

lay: transitive verb
Hint: always takes an object or is expressed in the passive voice
Present: lay　Past: laid　Past Participle: laid　Present Participle: laying

*I **lay** my burden down forever.*

*The hen **laid** six eggs yesterday.*

*The mason has **laid** all the bricks.*

*The porter is **laying** down our suitcases.*

lie: intransitive verb
Hint: never takes an object, never is expressed in the passive voice. This problem-causing lie, by the way, means 'recline,' not 'fib.'
Present: lie　Past: lay　Past Participle: lain　Present Participle: lying

*Now I am going to **lie** down.*

*Yesterday he **lay** awake for five hours.*

*The refuse has **lain** there for weeks.*

*Homeless people are **lying** on park benches.*

◆ Lead　　　　　　　Led ◆

lead: 1. rhymes with *weed*. It means to show the way.

*A good instructor will **lead** you to discover important values.*

2. rhymes with *fed*. It is a grayish metal.

*A **lead** pencil contains graphite and no lead at all.*

led: rhymes with *fed*, too. This *led* is the past tense of *lead*. It means showed the way.

*He **led** us through the back alleys of Los Angeles.*

◆ Leave　　　　　　Let ◆

leave: to depart
let: to allow, permit
Not: *Leave us look more closely at this sonnet.*
But: ***Let** us look more closely at this sonnet.*

◆ Lend　　　　　　Loan ◆

lend: a verb
*Jack was kind enough to **lend** me ten dollars.*
loan: a noun
*High interest rates have interfered with **loans**.*

◆ Liable　　　　　　Libel ◆

liable: likely to, legally obligated
*After a few drinks, that man is **liable** to do anything.*
*The owner of the dog was **liable** for damages.*
libel: an unjust written statement exposing someone to public contempt
*Senator Green sued the newspaper for **libel**.*

◆ Like　　　　　　　As ◆

Hint: To use like or as (sometimes as if), look at the words that follow. If the words make up a clause (subject plus verb) use as; if not, use like. This rule is not foolproof, but it will solve most practical problems. Like in place of as is now fairly well accepted outside of formal written English.

*Even philosophers can sometimes act **like** fools.*

*Even philosophers can sometimes act **as** fools would act.*

*My boss treated me **like** dirt.*

*My boss treated me **as** if I were dirt.*

◆ Loath　　　　　　Loathe ◆

loath: an adjective meaning reluctant
*I am **loath** to express the full intensity of my feelings.*
loathe: a verb meaning to hate
*I **loathe** people who use old-fashioned words like loath.*

◆ Loose　　　　　　Lose ◆

loose: rhymes with *moose*. It means "not tight, freer;" sometimes it means "set free."
*A **loose** shoelace is dangerous.*
*You should **loose** the hand brake before driving your car.*
lose: rhymes with *whose*. It means "to misplace" or "not to win or keep."
*If you **lose** the registration form, you will have to pay another fee.*

◆ Majority　　　　Plurality ◆

Hint: A candidate who has a **majority** has more than half of the total votes. A candidate who has a **plurality** has won the election but received less than half the total votes.

◆ May be　　　　　Maybe ◆

may be: verb form meaning "could be, can be."
*I **may** be wrong, but I feel that* Light in August *is*

Faulkner's best novel.

maybe: adverb meaning "perhaps."

Maybe the railroad is best option.

 Medal   Metal   Mettle

medal: awarded to heroes or other celebrities

*The American team won most of its Olympic **medals** in swimming.*

metal: substance such as iron or copper

*Future **metal** exploration may take place more often beneath the sea.*

mettle: refers to stamina, enthusiasm, vigorous spirit

*Until the Normandy invasion, Eisenhower had not really proved his **mettle.***

♦ Moral   Morale ♦

moral: as an adjective means 'having to do with ethics' or 'honorable, decent, upright.' As a noun it means 'lesson, precept, teaching.'

*Not all **moral** issues are simple cases of right and wrong.*

*The story has a profound **moral.***

morale: refers to one's state of mind or spirit

*The new coach tried to improve the team's **morale.***

♦ More   Most ♦

more: use when comparing two things

*Between Sally and Phyllis, Sally was the **more** talented.*

most: use for any number over two

*Of all my teachers, Mr. Frederic was the **most** inspired.*

Hint: Never use most as a synonym for almost.

Not: *Most everyone showed up at the party.*

♦ Neither ♦

Hint: Use only when dealing with two units.

Not: *I like neither collies nor poodles nor dachshunds.*

But: *I like **neither** dogs nor cats.*

When **neither** is the subject, it takes a singular verb and pronoun.

*Both nations are responsible. **Neither** is doing its best for the environment.*

♦ None ♦

Hint: Means "no one" or "not one" and takes a singular verb and pronoun.

***None** of these women understands that she is a public servant.*

♦ Not hardly ♦

Hint: A double negative; not standard English. Use hardly.

Not: *He couldn't hardly see his hand in front of his face.*

But: *He could **hardly** see his hand in front of his face.*

♦ Only ♦

Hint: Make sure that it modifies only the word you want it to modify. "Only" can mean different things depending on where it is in the sentence.

Not: *I only felt a little unhappy.*

I only asked for a chance to explain.

But: *I felt **only** a little unhappy.*

*I asked **only** for a chance to explain.*

***Only** John went to the store.*

*John **only** went to the store.*

*John went to the **only** store.*

 Orientate   Orientated

Hint: Awkward versions of orient and oriented.

 Passed   Past

passed: the past of *pass*

*We **passed** them on the highway.*

past: used mainly as an adjective or noun

*Valerie had a mysterious **past.***

♦ Patience   Patients ♦

patience: not being in a hurry

*We expect the delivery tomorrow; our **patience** is almost at an end.*

patients: people seeking medical care or under medical attention

*The **patients** waited nervously in the doctor's office.*

♦ Perpetrate   Perpetuate ♦

perpetrate: to commit an evil, offensive or stupid act

*He **perpetrated** a colossal blunder.*

perpetuate: to preserve forever

*We resolved to **perpetuate** the ideals our leader stood for.*

♦ Personal   Personnel

personal: adjective meaning private, individual

*My love life is too **personal** for me to discuss.*

personnel: noun referring to the people employed in an organization. It can also refer to a department in the organization that oversees employee-based issues such as hiring and firing, morale, and processing of claims for benefits.

*Address all inquiries about the company's **personnel** to the **Personnel** Department.*

◆   Perspective   Prospective   ◆

perspective: has various meanings, most commonly "the logically correct relationships between the parts of something and the whole," or "the drawing techniques that give the illusion of space or depth."

*Inflation is not our only problem; we need to keep the economy in **perspective**.*

*Medieval painting reveals an almost complete indifference to **perspective**.*

prospective: "likely to become" or "likely to happen."

*The **prospective** jurors waited nervously for their names to be called.*

*None of the **prospective** benefits of the merger ever materialized.*

◆   Precede   Proceed   ◆

precede: to go before

*Years of struggle and poverty **preceded** her current success.*

proceed: to go on

*Let us **proceed** with our original plans.*

◆   Prejudice   Prejudiced   ◆

prejudice: ordinarily used as a noun
prejudiced: used as an adjective

Not: *The neighborhood is filled with prejudice people.*

But: *John is **prejudiced**. Legislation alone cannot prevent **prejudice**.*

◆   Prescribe   Proscribe   ◆

prescribe: to order, recommend, write a prescription

*The committee **prescribed** a statewide income tax.*

proscribe: to forbid

*The dean **proscribed** new fraternity housing.*

◆   Principal   Principle   ◆

principal: 1. a head person at a school

*The **principal** speaks to the students each day.*

2. a major sum of money

*The **principal** he invested earned $1,250 interest.*

3. a descriptive word that means "most important"

*Rice is still the **principal** food for many people.*

principle: a rule, a major belief, a basic idea or truth

*One **principle** for success is hard work.*

*As a woman of **principle**, she refused a bribe.*

Hint: *Principle* and *rule* both end in –*le*: if you use *principle*, make sure it means *rule*.

◆   Raise   Rise   ◆

raise: transitive verb

*The farmer **raises** corn and wheat.*

rise: an intransitive verb that never takes an object

*I always **rise** at 8:00 a.m.*

◆ Respectfully   Respectively   ◆

respectfully: with respect

*Everyone likes to be treated **respectfully**.*

respectively: each in the order named

*The speaker discussed education, medical research, and defense spending, **respectively**.*

◆   Robber   Thief   Burglar   ◆

robber: works by force
thief: works in secret
burglar: breaks in and enters with felonious intent

◆   Sadist   Masochist   ◆

sadist: enjoys hurting living creatures

*The way he treated his cat proved he was a **sadist**.*

masochist: enjoys being hurt

*She purposefully fell off the swings because she was a **masochist**.*

◆   Seeing as how   ◆

Hint: Not standard English. Use since or because.

◆   Seldom ever   ◆

Hint: Ever is unnecessary in this phrase. Avoid it.

Not: *He was seldom ever angry.*

But: *He was **seldom** angry.*

◆ Sensual   Sensuous ◆

sensual: negative; suggesting gross overindulgence in physical sensations

*Unlimited **sensual** abandon led to Ben's early death.*

sensuous: usually positive, refers to physical pleasure

*Jane felt that a hot tub and a glass of champagne were among life's great **sensuous** delights.*

◆ Set   Sit ◆

set: to place or to put

***Set** the table.*

***Set** down that chair.*

sit: is not the same as set

*We **sit** at the table. (Not: We set at the table.)*

***Sit** down in that chair. (Not: Set down in that chair.)*

◆ Shall   Will ◆

Hint: Elaborate rules differentiate between these words. Few people understand the rules, and no one remembers them. Our advice on this subject is to use will all the time except when shall obviously sounds more natural, as in some questions and traditional phrases.

***Shall** we dance?*

*We **shall** overcome.*

◆ Shone   Shown ◆

shone: the alternate past tense and past participle of shine. Same as shined.

*The **sun** shone brightly.*

shown: the alternate past participle of show. Same as showed.

*More shocking films are being **shown** in local theaters this spring.*

◆ So ◆

Hint: When so is used for emphasis, the full thought often needs to be completed by a clause. (See the entry below, "such.")

Not: *The coffee was so sweet. My sister is so smart.*

But: *The coffee was **so** sweet that it was undrinkable. My sister is **so** smart that she does my homework for me every night.*

◆ So-called ◆

Hint: Use so-called to complain about something that has been incorrectly or inaccurately named. Do not use it as a simple synonym for undesirable or unpleasant.

Not: *These so-called jet planes make too much noise. She wore a so-called wig.*

But: *Many of our **so-called** radicals are quite timid and conservative. These **so-called** luxury homes are really just mass-produced bungalows.*

◆ Somewheres ◆

Hint: Not standard English. Use somewhere.

◆ Sort of ◆

Hint: Means "a type of, a variety of." Do not use as a substitute for somewhat or rather. (See the entry below, "kind of.")

◆ Stationary   Stationery ◆

stationary: unmoving, unchanging

*The house was **stationary** despite the strong wind.*

stationery: paper for letter writing

*She wrote her love letters on personalized **stationery**.*

◆ Such ◆

Hint: When such is used for emphasis to mean "so much" or "so great," the full thought usually needs to be completed by a clause. (See the entry above, "so.")

Not: *He was such a wicked man. We had such fun at the picnic.*

But: *He was **such** a wicked man that everyone feared him. We had **such** fun at the picnic, we had to force ourselves to go home.*

◆ Then   Than ◆

then: at a certain time

*The folksinger performed, and **then** we left the party.*

than: a comparing word

*She is taller **than** her brother.*

◆ There   Their   They're ◆

there: a place

*Was it **there**?*

Hint: **There** often starts a sentence. It is sometimes followed by are, were, is, or some other verb.

***There** was a good movie at the Rialto.*

***There** are too many books, and **there** is too little time to read them.*

their: ownership (possession) by a group

> It's **their** car.
>
> Was it **their** house that burned?

they're: they are

Hint: They're always means they are. Substitute the two words for the contraction to see if the sentence is correct.

> **They're** late again! (They + are late again.)

◆   **Through   Thru**   ◆

Hint: Through is the standard spelling except, perhaps, on road signs where space and reading time merit special consideration

> We drove straight **through** to Buffalo.
>
> **Thru** traffic keep left.

◆   **Thusly**   ◆

Hint: Not standard English. Use thus.

◆   **Toward   Towards**   ◆

Hint: **Toward** is the American style. **Towards** is the British style.

◆   **Try and**   ◆

Hint: Acceptable in conversation, but undesirable in print. Use try to.

> Not: We must all try and improve our environment.
>
> But: We must all **try to** improve our environment.

◆   **Two   Too   To**   ◆

two: the number 2

too: 1. One meaning is "very," "more than enough," "excessively" or "in a great degree.

> The color is **too** dull.
>
> My cousin is **too** tall.

2. Too means "also" as well.

> Let me go, **too**.
>
> Will the mayor, **too**, speak at the luncheon?

Hint: When too (meaning "also") is an interrupting word or appears at the end of a sentence, use a comma before it.

> I shook President Carter's hand, **too**.

to: 1. To shows direction. It means "toward," "for," or "at."

> Carry the milk **to** the refrigerator.
>
> **To** me he is always fair.

2. To is the first word in an infinitive. (An infinitive is the starting point of any verb used in a sentence.)

> To run in track meets, you must begin to train your legs.
> infinitive   infinitive

◆   **Unique**   ◆

Hint: This word means "one of a kind." It cannot be made stronger than it already is, nor can it be qualified. Do not write "very unique, more unique, less unique, somewhat unique, rather unique, fairly unique."

◆   **Vain   Vane   Vein**   ◆

vain: refers to vanity or futility

> Jim is so **vain** that he dyes the gray hairs on his chest.

vane: most commonly another word for weathervane

> You can recognize the house by the rooster **vane** near the chimney.

vein: a blood vessel; has many figurative meanings as well

> The **vein** carries blood to the heart.
>
> Beneath the teasing runs a **vein** of deep tenderness.

◆   **Weather   Whether**   ◆

weather: has to do with climate

> The dark clouds indicate that the **weather** may soon change.

whether: has to do with choices and alternative possibilities

> Anita needs to decide **whether** to accept the most recent job offer.

◆   **When**   ◆

Hint: In using this word, make sure it refers to time, as in "It was ten years ago when we first fell in love."

> Not: Basketball is when five men on opposing teams...
>
> But: Basketball is a game **in which** five men on opposing teams...

◆   **Where**   ◆

Hint: When using this word, make sure it refers to a place, as in "This is the house where I used to live."

> Not: I am interested in seeing the movie where the motorcycle gang takes over the town.
>
> But: I'm interested in seeing the movie **in which** the motorcycle gang takes over the town.

✦ **Whether or not** ✦

Hint: The word *whether* means the same as *whether or not*, and is therefore preferable.

Not: *We wondered whether or not it would snow.*

But: *We wondered* **whether** *it would snow.*

✦ **Who   That   Which** ✦

Hint: Use *who* or *that* for people, preferably *who*, never *which*. Use *which* or *that* for things, preferably *that*, never *who*.

Keats is one of the many great writers **who** *died at an early age.*

There's the woman **that** *I was telling you about.*

Podunk is a town **that** *people always ridicule.*

The play, Othello, **which** *we are now studying, is incredibly difficult.*

✦ **Who   Whom** ✦

who: serves as the subject of verbs in dependent clauses

I dislike people **who** *can't take a joke.*

whom: used as the object in dependent clauses

The teacher **whom** *I feared so greatly last term has now become a great friend.*

Hint: Although the distinction between *who* and *whom* is no longer a major issue in the conversation of many educated speakers and in much informal writing, formal English still fusses about words.

The role played by *who* or *whom* in the dependent clause determines which word is right; don't be distracted by the connections that *who* or *whom* may appear to have with other parts of the sentence. In cases of doubt, a sometimes effective tactic is to substitute *he, she, they* or *him, her, them* for the word in question and see which makes better sense. If *he, she, they* works, use *who*. If *him, her, them* works, use *whom*.

I dislike people (who, whom) can't take a joke.

Take the dependent clause *(who, whom) can't take a joke.* Clearly, *they can't take a joke* works, and *them can't take a joke* does not work. Use *who*.

Special problems pop up when words intervene between *who* or *whom* and its verb. Don't be misled by expressions like *I think, they say, it seems, she feels,* and so on. These expressions should be thought of as interrupting words and do not affect the basic grammar of the clause.

The minority leader is the man **who** *I think should be the next president. (Who is the subject of should be.)*

No artist **who** *he said was brilliant ever impressed us. (Who is the subject of was.)*

Shortcuts:

Immediately after a preposition, use *whom*.

He asked to **whom** *I had been speaking.*

This is the person in **whom** *we must place our trust.*

At other times, use *who*.

In my home, it's the man **who** *does the cooking.*

Fred Smiley is the man **who** *Ethel chose.*

If *who* sounds "wrong" or unnatural, or if you are in a situation that demands formal writing and feel uncertain about the formal rules (the sample sentence about Fred and Ethel breaks the rules), try to eliminate the problem with one of these techniques:

Change *who* or *whom* to *that*.

Fred Smiley is the man **that** *Ethel chose.*

Remove *who* or *whom*.

Fred Smiley is the man Ethel chose.

✦ **Who's   Whose** ✦

who's: a contraction of who is or who has.

Who's *going to get the promotion?*

Fenton is a man **who's** *been in and out of jail all his life.*

whose: the possessive form of who

Quentin Tarantino is a filmmaker **whose** *place in movie history is still in doubt.*

✦ **Your   You're** ✦

your: ownership. It means "belonging to you."

Is that **your** *car?*

Give **your** *husband the car keys.*

you're: you are

When **you're** *out of town, call.*

Hint: You're always means *you are*. Substitute the two words for the contraction to see if the sentence is correct.

Using Capitals

The First Word of a Sentence   The capital letter at the beginning of a sentence signals the reader that a new unit of thought is about to begin. Together with the punctuation mark at the end of the previous sentence, it makes reading easier.

Chile and Peru are squabbling over strong liquor called pisco. Each country claims to be the parent country of the grape-based drink.

In sentence fragments used for special effects, capitalize the first word.

But aside from good hair grooming, they are oblivious to everything but each other. Everybody gives them a once-over. Disgusting! Amusing! How touching! — Tom Wolfe

After a Colon   Many writers do not capitalize the first word of an independent clause that follows a colon.

It should be clearly understood: facts can change, and new interpretations can, at any moment, alter our interpretations of them.

But some writers do capitalize the first word after a colon.

The answer is another question: How many days must go by before millions of people notice they are not eating?

The New York Times usually does not capitalize after a colon.

The first word in an independent clause following a semicolon is never capitalized unless it is a proper noun.

All in all, however, outside support counted for little; the men of the village did the work themselves.

Proper Nouns and Their Abbreviations   Proper nouns are the names of specific people, places, or things — names that set off the individual from the species. Proper nouns include names like *Melissa* (instead of the common noun *person*), *Spain* (instead of the common noun *country*) and *Empire State Building* (instead of the common noun *building*).

Names and nicknames of people Wolfgang Amadeus Mozart, Ella Fitzgerald, John F. Kennedy, Phish, Bugsy

Names of places Italy, the United States of America, the Panama Canal, Back Bay, the North Shore, the Irunia Restaurant, the Sierra Nevada, the Great Lakes

Official names of organizations, organized events, courses The Authors' Guild of America, the University of Notre Dame, Cumberland College, Ford Motor Company, the Roman Catholic Church, the American Red Cross, the NCAA, the N.A.A.C.P., History 351: Old South, and Civil War

Days of the week, months, special days Monday, July, Christmas, Labor Day, Yom Kippur, Pearl Harbor Day

Ethnic groups, nationalities, and their languages Greeks, Chinese, Americans, Turks, Chinese, English, Arabic. The words *blacks* and *whites* generally are not capitalized when they are used to refer to ethnic groups, but many writers follow individual choice in this matter.

Members of religious bodies and their sacred books and names Jews, Christians, Baptists, Holy Bible, God, Allah, Hindus, Jesus Christ, Holy Spirit, the Koran, the Torah.

Religious terms Many religious terms such as *sacrament, altar, priests, rabbi, preacher* and *holy water* are not capitalized. The word *Bible* is capitalized (though *biblical* is not), but it is never capitalized when it is used as a metaphor for an essential book.

*The Daily Racing Form was for many years called the **bible** of horse racing enthusiasts.*

Pronoun references to a deity worshiped by people in the present are sometimes capitalized, although some writers use capitals only to prevent confusion.

*God helped Abraham carry out **His** law.*

Do not capitalize pronoun references to deities no longer worshiped.

*The Roman god Jupiter led a tempestuous love life that often got **him** into deep trouble with **his** wife, Juno.*

Historical events, names of movements, and titles of works World War II, the Louisiana Purchase, Impressionism, the Bill of Rights, *Moby-Dick*

Other proper nouns Sometimes words not ordinarily capitalized take capitals when they are used as parts of proper names.

*My **aunt** is arriving this afternoon.*

*My **Aunt Lou** tells fantastic stories that I think she makes up.*

*I graduated from **high school** in 1989.*

✱ *Mother, Father, Cousin, Brother,* and *Sister* may replace proper names in speech and writing.

> *I still miss **Mother**, although she has been dead for years.*

> *I asked my **mother** to wake me at 5:00 A.M.*

✱ Some titles that may be capitalized before a proper name are often not capitalized when they are used after the name.

> *Everyone knew that **Governor** Cleveland was the most likely candidate for the Democratic nomination.*

> *The most likely candidate for the Democratic nomination was Grover Cleveland, **governor** of New York.*

Writers and editors do not agree on the capitalization of titles. *President of the United States,* or the *President* (meaning the chief executive of the United States), is frequently but not always capitalized. Practice varies with other titles also: *speak to the Governor, speak to the governor, the President of the university, the president of the university.*

In general, editors and writers are tending to capitalize less, but it is all-important to be consistent.

✱ Words derived from proper nouns generally keep the capitals of the original words.

> *Reaganomics, Siamese cat*

✱ When proper names describe or identify common nouns, the nouns that follow are generally not capitalized.

> *Russian history, French fries, Philadelphia cheese steak*

✱ Brand names and trademarks are capitalized

> *Apple computer, Band-Aid, Big Mac*

✱ Abbreviations used as parts of proper names usually take capitals.

> *T. S. Eliot; Sammy Davis, Jr.; Maria Lopez, M.D.*

Names of regions Capitalize names of regions if they are well established, like the Midwest and Central Europe, but do not capitalize directions, as in *turn south.*

Months and days of the week Capitalize names of months and days of the week; do not capitalize seasons, such as summer.

Capitalization in Dialogue and Quotations

Capitalize the first word in quoted spoken dialogue.

> *"Calm down," he shouted. "I spent just 30 minutes learning to drive this motorcycle, and we're already doing a hundred miles an hour."*

Indirect quotations and questions require no capitals for words attributed to a speaker or writer.

> *She said that jazz was one of the many contributions of blacks to world culture.*

Capitalize the first word of quotations from printed sources if the quotation is introduced as dialogue.

> *Jim, the narrator of* My Antonia, *concludes: "Whatever we had missed, we possessed together the precious, the incommunicable past."*

When a quotation from a printed source is only an element in a sentence, not a sentence on its own, do not capitalize the first word.

> *Jim took comfort in sharing with Antonia "the precious, the incommunicable past.*

AWARDS AND PRIZES

Academy Awards 1928–2010

The "Oscars" are officially known as the Academy of Motion Picture Arts and Sciences Awards. They were inaugurated in 1928 as part of Hollywood's drive to improve its less-than-respectable image. Academy librarian and eventual executive director Margaret Herrick remarked that the statuette looked like her uncle Oscar, and the nickname has stuck ever since. Membership in the Academy (currently over 6,000) is by invitation only, with members divided into 15 branches. Each branch selects up to five nominees for awards in its area of expertise; the entire membership makes "Best Picture" nominations and then votes on all the categories. Beginning in 2011, between five and 10 films can be nominated for Best Picture. Major awards are shown in the chart. The award for Best Cinematography is shown in a separate table. Awards for actors and directors are named for films winning Best Picture except where otherwise indicated.

Year	Best picture	Best director	Best actor	Best actress	Best supporting actor	Best supporting actress
1928	*Wings*	Frank Borzage, *Seventh Heaven* Lewis Milestone, *Two Arabian Knights*	Emil Jannings, *The Way of All Flesh, The Last Command*	Janet Gaynor, *Seventh Heaven, Sunrise, Street Angel*	No Awards Given	No Awards Given
1929	*The Broadway Melody*	Frank Lloyd, *The Divine Lady*	Warner Baxter, *In Old Arizona*	Mary Pickford, *Coquette*	No Awards Given	No Awards Given
1930	*All Quiet on the Western Front*	Lewis Milestone	George Arliss, *Disraeli*	Norma Shearer, *The Divorcee*	No Awards Given	No Awards Given
1931	*Cimarron*	Norman Taurog, *Skippy*	Lionel Barrymore, *A Free Soul*	Marie Dressler, *Min and Bill*	No Awards Given	No Awards Given
1932	*Grand Hotel*	Frank Borzage, *Bad Girl*	Wallace Beery, *The Champ* Fredric March, *Dr. Jekyll and Mr. Hyde*	Helen Hayes, *The Sin of Madelon Claudet*	No Awards Given	No Awards Given
1933	*Cavalcade*	Frank Lloyd	Charles Laughton *The Private Life of Henry VIII*	Katharine Hepburn, *Morning Glory*	No Awards Given	No Awards Given
1934	*It Happened One Night*	Frank Capra	Clark Gable	Claudette Colbert	No Awards Given	No Awards Given
1935	*Mutiny on the Bounty*	John Ford, *The Informer*	Victor McLaglen, *The Informer*	Bette Davis, *Dangerous*	No Awards Given	No Awards Given
1936	*The Great Ziegfeld*	Frank Capra, *Mr. Deeds Goes to Town*	Paul Muni, *The Story of Louis Pasteur*	Luise Rainer	Walter Brennan, *Come and Get It*	Gale Sondergaard, *Anthony Adverse*
1937	*The Life of Emile Zola*	Leo McCarey, *The Awful Truth*	Spencer Tracy, *Captains Courageous*	Luise Rainer, *The Good Earth*	Joseph Schildkraut,	Alice Brady, *In Old Chicago*
1938	*You Can't Take It With You*	Frank Capra	Spencer Tracy, *Boys Town*	Bette Davis, *Jezebel*	Walter Brennan, *Kentucky*	Fay Bainter, *Jezebel*

Year	Best picture	Best director	Best actor	Best actress	Best supporting actor	Best supporting actress
1939	*Gone With the Wind*	Victor Fleming	Robert Donat, *Goodbye, Mr. Chips*	Vivien Leigh	Thomas Mitchell, *Stagecoach*	Hattie McDaniel
1940	*Rebecca*	John Ford, *The Grapes of Wrath*	James Stewart, *The Philadelphia Story*	Ginger Rogers, *Kitty Foyle*	Walter Brennan, *The Westerner*	Jane Darwell, *The Grapes of Wrath*
1941	*How Green Was My Valley*	John Ford	Gary Cooper, *Sergeant York*	Joan Fontaine, *Suspicion*	Donald Crisp	Mary Astor, *The Great Lie*
1942	*Mrs. Miniver*	William Wyler	James Cagney, *Yankee Doodle Dandy*	Greer Garson	Van Heflin, *Johnny Eager*	Teresa Wright
1943	*Casablanca*	Michael Curtiz	Paul Lukas, *Watch On The Rhine*	Jennifer Jones, *The Song of Bernadette*	Charles Coburn, *The More the Merrier*	Katina Paxinou, *For Whom the Bell Tolls*
1944	*Going My Way*	Leo McCarey	Bing Crosby	Ingrid Bergman, *Gaslight*	Barry Fitzgerald	Ethel Barrymore, *None But the Lonely Heart*
1945	*The Lost Weekend*	Billy Wilder	Ray Milland	Joan Crawford, *Mildred Pierce*	James Dunn, *A Tree Grows in Brooklyn*	Anne Revere, *National Velvet*
1946	*The Best Years of Our Lives*	William Wyler	Fredric March	Olivia De Havilland, *To Each His Own*	Harold Russell	Anne Baxter, *The Razor's Edge*
1947	*Gentleman's Agreement*	Elia Kazan	Ronald Colman, *A Double Life*	Loretta Young, *The Farmer's Daughter*	Edmund Gwenn, *Miracle on 34th Street*	Celeste Holm
1948	*Hamlet*	John Huston, *The Treasure of the Sierra Madre*	Laurence Olivier	Jane Wyman, *Johnny Belinda*	Walter Huston, *The Treasure of the Sierra Madre*	Claire Trevor, *Key Largo*
1949	*All the King's Men*	Joseph L. Mankiewicz, *A Letter to Three Wives*	Broderick Crawford	Olivia De Havilland, *The Heiress*	Dean Jagger, *Twelve O'Clock High*	Mercedes McCambridge
1950	*All About Eve*	Joseph L. Mankiewicz	José Ferrer, *Cyrano de Bergerac*	Judy Holliday, *Born Yesterday*	George Sanders	Josephine Hull, *Harvey*
1951	*An American in Paris*	George Stevens, *A Place in the Sun*	Humphrey Bogart, *The African Queen*	Vivien Leigh, *A Streetcar Named Desire*	Karl Malden, *A Streetcar Named Desire*	Kim Hunter, *A Streetcar Named Desire*
1952	*The Greatest Show on Earth*	John Ford, *The Quiet Man*	Gary Cooper, *High Noon*	Shirley Booth, *Come Back, Little Sheba*	Anthony Quinn, *Viva Zapata!*	Gloria Grahame, *The Bad and the Beautiful*
1953	*From Here to Eternity*	Fred Zinnemann	William Holden, *Stalag 17*	Audrey Hepburn, *Roman Holiday*	Frank Sinatra	Donna Reed
1954	*On the Waterfront*	Elia Kazan	Marlon Brando	Grace Kelly, *The Country Girl*	Edmond O'Brien, *The Barefoot Contessa*	Eva Marie Saint
1955	*Marty*	Delbert Mann	Ernest Borgnine	Anna Magnani, *The Rose Tattoo*	Jack Lemmon, *Mister Roberts*	Jo Van Fleet, *East of Eden*

Year	Best picture	Best director	Best actor	Best actress	Best supporting actor	Best supporting actress
1956	*Around the World in 80 Days*	George Stevens, *Giant*	Yul Brynner, *The King And I*	Ingrid Bergman, *Anastasia*	Anthony Quinn, *Lust for Life*	Dorothy Malone, *Written on the Wind*
1957	*The Bridge on the River Kwai*	David Lean	Alec Guinness	Joanne Woodward, *The Three Faces of Eve*	Red Buttons, *Sayonara*	Miyoshi Umeki, *Sayonara*
1958	*Gigi*	Vincente Minnelli	David Niven, *Separate Tables*	Susan Hayward, *I Want to Live!*	Burl Ives, *The Big Country*	Wendy Hiller, *Separate Tables*
1959	*Ben-Hur*	William Wyler	Charlton Heston	Simone Signoret, *Room at the Top*	Hugh Griffith	Shelley Winters, *The Diary of Anne Frank*
1960	*The Apartment*	Billy Wilder	Burt Lancaster, *Elmer Gantry*	Elizabeth Taylor, *Butterfield 8*	Peter Ustinov, *Spartacus*	Shirley Jones, *Elmer Gantry*
1961	*West Side Story*	Jerome Robbins, Robert Wise	Maximilian Schell, *Judgment At Nuremberg*	Sophia Loren, *Two Women*	George Chakiris	Rita Moreno
1962	*Lawrence of Arabia*	David Lean	Gregory Peck, *To Kill a Mockingbird*	Anne Bancroft, *The Miracle Worker*	Ed Begley, *Sweet Bird of Youth*	Patty Duke, *The Miracle Worker*
1963	*Tom Jones*	Tony Richardson	Sidney Poitier, *Lilies of the Field*	Patricia Neal, *Hud*	Melvyn Douglas, *Hud*	Margaret Rutherford, *The V.I.P.s*
1964	*My Fair Lady*	George Cukor	Rex Harrison	Julie Andrews, *Mary Poppins*	Peter Ustinov, *Topkapi*	Lila Kedrova, *Zorba the Greek*
1965	*The Sound of Music*	Robert Wise	Lee Marvin, *Cat Ballou*	Julie Christie, *Darling*	Martin Balsam, *A Thousand Clowns*	Shelley Winters, *A Patch of Blue*
1966	*A Man for All Seasons*	Fred Zinnemann	Paul Scofield	Elizabeth Taylor, *Who's Afraid of Virginia Woolf?*	Walter Matthau, *The Fortune Cookie*	Sandy Dennis, *Who's Afraid of Virginia Woolf?*
1967	*In the Heat of the Night*	Mike Nichols, *The Graduate*	Rod Steiger	Katharine Hepburn, *Guess Who's Coming to Dinner*	George Kennedy, *Cool Hand Luke*	Estelle Parsons, *Bonnie and Clyde*
1968	*Oliver!*	Carol Reed	Cliff Robertson, *Charly*	Katharine Hepburn *The Lion in Winter* Barbra Streisand, *Funny Girl*	Jack Albertson, *The Subject Was Roses*	Ruth Gordon, *Rosemary's Baby*
1969	*Midnight Cowboy*	John Schlesinger	John Wayne, *True Grit*	Maggie Smith, *The Prime of Miss Jean Brodie*	Gig Young, *They Shoot Horses, Don't They?*	Goldie Hawn, *Cactus Flower*
1970	*Patton*	Franklin J. Schaffner	George C. Scott	Glenda Jackson, *Women in Love*	John Mills, *Ryan's Daughter*	Helen Hayes, *Airport*
1971	*The French Connection*	William Friedkin	Gene Hackman	Jane Fonda, *Klute*	Ben Johnson, *The Last Picture Show*	Cloris Leachman, *The Last Picture Show*
1972	*The Godfather*	Bob Fosse, *Cabaret*	Marlon Brando	Liza Minnelli, *Cabaret*	Joel Grey, *Cabaret*	Eileen Heckart, *Butterflies are Free*
1973	*The Sting*	George Roy Hill	Jack Lemmon *Save the Tiger*	Glenda Jackson, *A Touch of Class*	John Houseman, *The Paper Chase*	Tatum O'Neal, *Paper Moon*

Year	Best picture	Best director	Best actor	Best actress	Best supporting actor	Best supporting actress
1974	*The Godfather, Part II*	Francis Ford Coppola	Art Carney, *Harry And Tonto*	Ellen Burstyn, *Alice Doesn't Live Here Anymore*	Robert De Niro	Ingrid Bergman, *Murder on the Orient Express*
1975	*One Flew Over the Cuckoo's Nest*	Milos Forman	Jack Nicholson	Louise Fletcher	George Burns, *The Sunshine Boys*	Lee Grant, *Shampoo*
1976	*Rocky*	John G. Avildsen	Peter Finch, *Network*	Faye Dunaway, *Network*	Jason Robards, *All the President's Men*	Beatrice Straight, *Network*
1977	*Annie Hall*	Woody Allen	Richard Dreyfuss, *The Goodbye Girl*	Diane Keaton	Jason Robards, *Julia*	Vanessa Redgrave, *Julia*
1978	*The Deer Hunter*	Michael Cimino	Jon Voight, *Coming Home*	Jane Fonda, *Coming Home*	Christopher Walken	Maggie Smith, *California Suite*
1979	*Kramer vs. Kramer*	Robert Benton	Dustin Hoffman	Sally Field, *Norma Rae*	Melvyn Douglas, *Being There*	Meryl Streep, *Kramer vs. Kramer*
1980	*Ordinary People*	Robert Redford	Robert De Niro, *Raging Bull*	Sissy Spacek, *Coal Miner's Daughter*	Timothy Hutton	Mary Steenburgen, *Melvin and Howard*
1981	*Chariots of Fire*	Warren Beatty, *Reds*	Henry Fonda, *On Golden Pond*	Katharine Hepburn, *On Golden Pond*	John Gielgud, *Arthur*	Maureen Stapleton, *Reds*
1982	*Gandhi*	Richard Attenborough	Ben Kingsley	Meryl Streep, *Sophie's Choice*	Louis Gossett Jr., *An Officer and a Gentleman*	Jessica Lange, *Tootsie*
1983	*Terms of Endearment*	James L. Brooks	Robert Duvall, *Tender Mercies*	Shirley MacLaine	Jack Nicholson	Linda Hunt, *The Year of Living Dangerously*
1984	*Amadeus*	Milos Forman	F. Murray Abraham	Sally Field, *Places in the Heart*	Haing S. Ngor, *The Killing Fields*	Peggy Ashcroft, *A Passage to India*
1985	*Out of Africa*	Sydney Pollack	William Hurt, *Kiss of the Spider Woman*	Geraldine Page, *The Trip to Bountiful*	Don Ameche, *Cocoon*	Anjelica Huston, *Prizzi's Honor*
1986	*Platoon*	Oliver Stone	Paul Newman, *The Color of Money*	Marlee Matlin, *Children of a Lesser God*	Michael Caine, *Hannah and Her Sisters*	Dianne Wiest, *Hannah and Her Sisters*
1987	*The Last Emperor*	Bernardo Bertolucci	Michael Douglas, *Wall Street*	Cher, *Moonstruck*	Sean Connery, *The Untouchables*	Olympia Dukakis, *Moonstruck*
1988	*Rain Man*	Barry Levinson	Dustin Hoffman	Jodie Foster, *The Accused*	Kevin Kline, *A Fish Called Wanda*	Geena Davis, *The Accidental Tourist*
1989	*Driving Miss Daisy*	Oliver Stone, *Born on the Fourth of July*	Daniel Day-Lewis, *My Left Foot*	Jessica Tandy	Denzel Washington, *Glory*	Brenda Fricker, *My Left Foot*
1990	*Dances with Wolves*	Kevin Costner	Jeremy Irons, *Reversal of Fortune*	Kathy Bates, *Misery*	Joe Pesci, *Goodfellas*	Whoopi Goldberg, *Ghost*
1991	*The Silence of the Lambs*	Jonathan Demme	Anthony Hopkins	Jodie Foster	Jack Palance, *City Slickers*	Mercedes Ruehl, *The Fisher King*
1992	*Unforgiven*	Clint Eastwood	Al Pacino, *Scent of a Woman*	Emma Thompson, *Howards End*	Gene Hackman	Marisa Tomei, *My Cousin Vinny*

Year	Best picture	Best director	Best actor	Best actress	Best supporting actor	Best supporting actress
1993	*Schindler's List*	Steven Spielberg	Tom Hanks, *Philadelphia*	Holly Hunter, *The Piano*	Tommy Lee Jones, *The Fugitive*	Anna Paquin, *The Piano*
1994	*Forrest Gump*	Robert Zemeckis	Tom Hanks	Jessica Lange, *Blue Sky*	Martin Landau, *Ed Wood*	Dianne Wiest, *Bullets Over Broadway*
1995	*Braveheart*	Mel Gibson	Nicolas Cage *Leaving Las Vegas*	Susan Sarandon, *Dead Man Walking*	Kevin Spacey, *The Usual Suspects*	Mira Sorvino, *Mighty Aphrodite*
1996	*The English Patient*	Anthony Minghella	Geoffrey Rush, *Shine*	Frances McDormand, *Fargo*	Cuba Gooding Jr., *Jerry Maguire*	Juliette Binoche
1997	*Titanic*	James Cameron	Jack Nicholson, *As Good as it Gets*	Helen Hunt, *As Good as it Gets*	Robin Williams *Good Will Hunting*	Kim Basinger, *L.A. Confidential*
1998	*Shakespeare in Love*	Steven Spielberg, *Saving Private Ryan*	Roberto Benigni, *Life is Beautiful*	Gwyneth Paltrow	James Coburn, *Affliction*	Judi Dench
1999	*American Beauty*	Sam Mendes	Kevin Spacey	Hilary Swank, *Boys Don't Cry*	Michael Caine, *The Cider House Rules*	Angelina Jolie, *Girl, Interrupted*
2000	*Gladiator*	Steven Soderbergh, *Traffic*	Russell Crowe	Julia Roberts, *Erin Brockovich*	Benicio Del Toro, *Traffic*	Marcia Gay Harden, *Pollock*
2001	*A Beautiful Mind*	Ron Howard	Denzel Washington, *Training Day*	Halle Berry, *Monster's Ball*	Jim Broadbent, *Iris*	Jennifer Connelly
2002	*Chicago*	Roman Polanski	Adrien Brody	Nicole Kidman, *The Hours*	Chris Cooper, *Adaptation*	Catherine Zeta-Jones, *Chicago*
2003	*The Lord of the Rings: Return of the King*	Peter Jackson	Sean Penn, *Mystic River*	Charlize Theron, *Monster*	Tim Robbins, *Mystic River*	Renee Zellweger, *Cold Mountain*
2004	*Million Dollar Baby*	Clint Eastwood	Jamie Foxx, *Ray*	Hilary Swank	Morgan Freeman	Cate Blanchett, *The Aviator*
2005	*Crash*	Ang Lee, *Brokeback Mountain*	Philip Seymour Hoffman, *Capote*	Reese Witherspoon, *Walk the Line*	George Clooney, *Syriana*	Rachel Weisz, *The Constant Gardener*
2006	*The Departed*	Martin Scorsese	Forest Whitaker, *The Last King of Scotland*	Helen Mirren, *The Queen*	Alan Arkin, *Little Miss Sunshine*	Jennifer Hudson, *Dreamgirls*
2007	*No Country for Old Men*	Joel and Ethan Coen	Daniel Day-Lewis, *There Will Be Blood*	Marion Cotillard, *La Vie en Rose*	Javier Bardem	Tilda Swinton, *Michael Clayton*
2008	*Slumdog Millionaire*	Danny Boyle	Sean Penn, *Milk*	Kate Winslet, *The Reader*	Heath Ledger, *The Dark Knight*	Penelope Cruz, *Vicky Cristina Barcelona*
2009	*The Hurt Locker*	Kathryn Bigelow	Jeff Bridges, *Crazy Heart*	Sandra Bullock, *The Blind Side*	Christoph Waltz, *Inglourious Basterds*	Mo'Nique, *Precious*
2010	*The King's Speech*	Tom Hooper	Colin Firth	Natalie Portman, *Black Swan*	Christian Bale, *The Fighter*	Melissa Leo, *The Fighter*

Source: Academy of Motion Picture Arts & Sciences. www.oscars.org

Year	Cinematographer, Film
1928	Charles Rosher, Karl Struss, *Sunrise*
1929	Clyde DeVinna, White Shadows, *In the South Seas*
1930	Joseph T. Rucker, Willard Van Der Veer, *With Byrd at the South Pole*
1931	Floyd Crosby, *Tabu*
1932	Lee Garmes, *Shanghai Express*
1933	Charles Bryant Lang Jr., *A Farewell to Arms*
1934	Victor Milner, *Cleopatra*
1935	Hal Mohr, *A Midsummer Night's Dream*
1936	Gaetano Gaudio, *Anthony Adverse*
1937	Karl Freund, *The Good Earth*
1938	Joseph Ruttenberg, *The Great Waltz*
1939	Gregg Toland, *Wuthering Heights*
	Ernest Haller, Ray Rennahan, *Gone With the Wind*
1940	George Barnes, *Rebecca*
	George Perinal, *Thief of Baghdad*
1941	Arthur Miller, *How Green Was My Valley*
	Ernest Palmer, Ray Rennahan, *Blood & Sand*
1942	Joseph Ruttenberg, *Mrs. Miniver*
	Leon Shamroy, *The Black Swan*
1943	Arthur Miller, *The Song of Bernadette*
	Hal Mohr, W. Howard Greene, *The Phantom of the Opera*
1944	Joseph LaShelle, *Laura*
	Leon Shamroy, *Wilson*
1945	Harry Stradling, *The Picture of Dorian Gray*
	Leon Shamroy, *Leave Her to Heaven*
1946	Arthur Miller, *Anna and the King of Siam*
	Charles Rosher, Leonard Smith, Arthur Arling, *The Yearling*
1947	Guy Green, *Great Expectations*
1948	William Daniels, *The Naked City*
	Joseph Valentine, William V. Skall, Winton Hoch, *Joan of Arc*
1949	Paul C. Vogel, *Battleground*
	Winton Hoch, *She Wore a Yellow Ribbon*
1950	Robert Krasker, *The Third Man*
	Robert Surtees, *King Solomon's Mines*
1951	William C. Mellor, *A Place in the Sun*
	Alfred Gilks, John Alton (ballet), *An American in Paris*
1952	Robert Surtees, *The Bad and the Beautiful*
	Winton Hoch, Archie Stout, *The Quiet Man*
1953	Burnett Guffey, *From Here to Eternity*
	Loyal Griggs, *Shane*
1954	Boris Kaufman, *On the Waterfront*
	Milton Krasner, *Three Coins in the Fountain*
1955	James Wong Howe, *The Rose Tattoo*
	Robert Burks, *To Catch a Thief*
1956	Joseph Ruttenberg, *Somebody Up There Likes Me*
	Lionel Lindon, *Around the World in 80 Days*

Year	Cinematographer, Film
1957	Jack Hildyard, *The Bridge on the River Kwai*
1958	Sam Leavitt, *The Defiant Ones*
	Joseph Ruttenberg, *Gigi*
1959	William C. Mellor, *The Diary of Anne Frank*
	Robert L. Surtees, *Ben-Hur*
1960	Freddie Francis, *Sons and Lovers*
	Russell Metty, *Spartacus*
1961	Eugene Shuftan, *The Hustler*
	Daniel L. Fapp, *West Side Story*
1962	Jean Bourgoin, Walter Wottitz, *The Longest Day*
	Freddie Young, *Lawrence of Arabia*
1963	James Wong Howe, *Hud*
	Leon Shamroy, *Cleopatra*
1964	Walter Lassally, *Zorba the Greek*
	Harry Stradling, *My Fair Lady*
1965	Ernest Laszlo, *Ship of Fools*
	Freddie Young, *Dr. Zhivago*
1966	Haskell Wexler, *Who's Afraid of Virginia Woolf?*
	Ted Moore, *A Man for All Seasons*
1967	Burnett Guffey, *Bonnie and Clyde*
1968	Pasqualino De Santis, *Romeo and Juliet*
1969	Conrad Hall, *Butch Cassidy and the Sundance Kid*
1970	Freddie Young, *Ryan's Daughter*
1971	Oswald Morris, *Fiddler on the Roof*
1972	Geoffrey Unsworth, *Cabaret*
1973	Sven Nykvist, *Cries and Whispers*
1974	Fred Koenekamp, Joseph Biroc, *The Towering Inferno*
1975	John Alcott, *Barry Lyndon*
1976	Haskell Wexler, *Bound for Glory*
1977	Vilmos Zsigmond, *Close Encounters of the Third Kind*
1978	Nestor Almendros, *Days of Heaven*
1979	Vittorio Storaro, *Apocalypse Now*
1980	Geoffrey Unsworth, Ghislain Cloquet, *Tess*
1981	Vittorio Storaro, *Reds*
1982	Billy Williams, Ronnie Taylor, *Gandhi*
1983	Sven Nykvist, *Fanny & Alexander*
1984	Chris Menges, *The Killing Fields*
1985	David Watkin, *Out of Africa*
1986	Chris Menges, *The Mission*
1987	Vittorio Storaro, *The Last Emperor*
1988	Peter Biziou, *Mississippi Burning*
1989	Freddie Francis, *Glory*
1990	Dean Semler, *Dances With Wolves*
1991	Robert Richardson, *JFK*
1992	Philippe Rousselot, *A River Runs Through It*
1993	Janusz Kaminski, *Schindler's List*
1994	John Toll, *Legends of the Fall*
1995	John Toll, *Braveheart*
1996	John Seale, *The English Patient*
1997	Russell Carpenter, *Titanic*
1998	Janusz Kaminski, *Saving Private Ryan*

1999 Conrad L. Hall, *American Beauty*
2000 Peter Pau, *Crouching Tiger, Hidden Dragon*
2001 Andrew Lesnie, *The Lord of the Rings: The Fellowship of the Ring*
2002 Conrad L. Hall, *Road to Perdition* (posthumous)
2003 Gus Van Sant, *Elephant*
2004 Robert Richardson, *The Aviator*

2005 Dion Beebe, *Memoirs of a Geisha*
2006 Guillermo Navarro, *Pan's Labyrinth*
2007 Robert Elswit, *There Will Be Blood*
2008 Anthony Dod Mantle, *Slumdog Millionaire*
2009 Mauro Fiore, *Avatar*
2010 Wally Pfister, *Inception*

The Emmy Awards, 1951–2010

The Academy of Television Arts and Sciences, formed in 1946, presented the first Emmy Awards in 1949. The number and names of awards have changed over the years, but since 1965, the Academy has recognized an outstanding comedy and drama, as well as an actor and an actress in a comedy and in a drama.

Year	Comedy	Drama	Comedy Actor	Comedy Actress	Drama Actor	Drama Actress
1951	*The Red Skelton Show*	*Studio One*	Sid Caesar	Imogene Coca	(1)	(1)
1952	*I Love Lucy*	*Robert Montgomery Presents*	Thomas Mitchell	Helen Hayes	(1)	(1)
1953	*I Love Lucy*	*The U.S. Steel Hour*	Donald O'Connor, *Colgate Comedy Hour*	Eve Arden, *Our Miss Brooks*	(1)	(1)
1954	*Make Room for Daddy*	*The U.S. Steel Hour*	Danny Thomas, *Make Room for Daddy*	Loretta Young, *The Loretta Young Show*	(1)	(1)
1955	*The Phil Silvers Show*	*Producers' Showcase*	Phil Silvers, *The Phil Silvers Show*	Lucille Ball, *I Love Lucy*	(1)	(1)
1956	*The Phil Silvers Show*	*Requiem for a Heavyweight*	Sid Caesar, *Caesar's Hour*	Nanette Fabray, *Caesar's Hour*	Robert Young, *Father Knows Best*	Loretta Young, *The Loretta Young Show*
1957	*The Phil Silvers Show*	*Gunsmoke*	Robert Young, *Father Knows Best*	Jane Wyatt, *Father Knows Best*	(1)	(1)
1958 –59	*The Jack Benny Show*	(2)	Jack Benny, *The Jack Benny Show*	Jane Wyatt, *Father Knows Best*	Raymond Burr, *Perry Mason*	Loretta Young, *The Loretta Young Show*
1959 –60	"*Art Carney Special*"	*Playhouse 90*	Robert Stack, *The Untouchables*	Jane Wyatt, *Father Knows Best*	(1)	(1)
1960 –61	*The Jack Benny Show*	"*Macbeth*," *Hallmark Hall of Fame*	Raymond Burr, *Perry Mason*	Barbara Stanwyck, *The Barbara Stanwyck Show*	(1)	(1)
1961 –62	*The Bob Newhart Show*	*The Defenders*	E.G. Marshall, *The Defenders*	Shirley Booth, *Hazel*	(1)	(1)
1962 –63	*The Dick Van Dyke Show*	*The Defenders*	E.G. Marshall, *The Defenders*	Shirley Booth, *Hazel*	(1)	(1)
1963 –64	*The Dick Van Dyke Show*	*The Defenders*	Dick Van Dyke, *The Dick Van Dyke Show*	Mary Tyler Moore, *The Dick Van Dyke Show*	(1)	(1)
1964 –65	(3)	(3)	(3)	(3)	(3)	(3)
1965 –66	*The Dick Van Dyke Show*	*The Fugitive*	Dick Van Dyke, *The Dick Van Dyke Show*	Mary Tyler Moore, *The Dick Van Dyke Show*	Bill Cosby, *I Spy*	Barbara Stanwyck, *The Big Valley*

Year	Comedy	Drama	Comedy Actor	Comedy Actress	Drama Actor	Drama Actress
1966 –67	The Monkees	Mission: Impossible	Don Adams, Get Smart	Lucille Ball, The Lucy Show	Bill Cosby, I Spy	Barbara Bain, Mission: Impossible
1967 –68	Get Smart	Mission: Impossible	Don Adams, Get Smart	Lucille Ball, The Lucy Show	Bill Cosby, I Spy	Barbara Bain, Mission: Impossible
1968 –69	Get Smart	NET Playhouse (NET)	Don Adams, Get Smart	Hope Lange, The Ghost and Mrs. Muir	Carl Betz, Judd for the Defense	Barbara Bain, Mission: Impossible
1969 –70	My World & Welcome to It	Marcus Welby, M.D.	William Windom, My World & Welcome to It	Hope Lange, The Ghost and Mrs. Muir	Robert Young, Marcus Welby, M.D.	Susan Hampshire, The Forsyte Saga
1970 –71	All in the Family	The Senator (segment), The Bold Ones	Jack Klugman, The Odd Couple	Jean Stapleton, All in the Family	Hal Holbrook, The Senator (segment), The Bold Ones	Susan Hampshire, The First Churchills
1971 –72	All in the Family	"Elizabeth R" Masterpiece Theatre	Carroll O'Connor, All in the Family	Jean Stapleton, All in the Family	Peter Falk, Columbo	Glenda Jackson, "Elizabeth R" Masterpiece Theatre
1972 –73	All in the Family	The Waltons	Jack Klugman, The Odd Couple	Mary Tyler Moore, The Mary Tyler Moore Show	Richard Thomas, The Waltons	Michael Learned, The Waltons
1973 –74	M*A*S*H	"Upstairs, Downstairs," Masterpiece Theatre	Alan Alda, M*A*S*H	Mary Tyler Moore, The Mary Tyler Moore Show	Telly Savalas, Kojak	Michael Learned, The Waltons
1974 –75	The Mary Tyler Moore Show	"Upstairs, Downstairs," Masterpiece Theatre	Tony Randall, The Odd Couple	Valerie Harper, Rhoda	Robert Blake, Baretta	Jean Marsh, "Upstairs, Downstairs" Masterpiece Theater
1975 –76	The Mary Tyler Moore Show	Police Story	Jack Albertson, Chico & the Man	Mary Tyler Moore, The Mary Tyler Moore Show	Peter Falk, Columbo	Michael Learned, The Waltons
1977 –78	All in the Family	The Rockford Files	Carroll O'Connor, All in the Family	Jean Stapleton, All in the Family	Edward Asner, Lou Grant	Sada Thompson, Family
1978 –79	Taxi	Lou Grant	Carroll O'Connor, All in the Family	Ruth Gordon, Taxi	Ron Leibman, Kaz	Mariette Hartley, The Incredible Hulk
1979 –80	Taxi	Lou Grant	Richard Mulligan, Soap	Cathryn Damon, Soap	Ed Asner, Lou Grant	Barbara Bel Geddes, Dallas
1980 –81	Taxi	Hill Street Blues	Judd Hirsch, Taxi	Isabel Sanford, The Jeffersons	Daniel Travanti, Hill Street Blues	Barbara Babcock, Hill Street Blues
1981 –82	Barney Miller	Hill Street Blues	Alan Alda, M*A*S*H	Carol Kane, Taxi	Daniel Travanti, Hill Street Blues	Michael Learned, Nurse
1982 –83	Cheers	Hill Street Blues	Judd Hirsch, Taxi	Shelley Long, Cheers	Ed Flanders, St. Elsewhere	Tyne Daly, Cagney & Lacey
1983 –84	Cheers	Hill Street Blues	John Ritter, Three's Company	Jane Curtin, Kate & Allie	Tom Selleck, Magnum P.I.	Tyne Daly, Cagney & Lacey

Year	Comedy	Drama	Comedy Actor	Comedy Actress	Drama Actor	Drama Actress
1984 –85	*The Cosby Show*	*Cagney & Lacey*	Robert Guillaume, *Benson*	Jane Curtin, *Kate & Allie*	William Daniels, *St. Elsewhere*	Tyne Daly, *Cagney &Lacey*
1985 –86	*The Golden Girls*	*Cagney & Lacey*	Michael J. Fox, *Family Ties*	Betty White, *The Golden Girls*	William Daniels, *St. Elsewhere*	Sharon Gless, *Cagney &Lacey*
1986 –87	*The Golden Girls*	*L.A. Law*	Michael J. Fox, *Family Ties*	Rue McClanahan, *The Golden Girls*	Bruce Willis, *Moonlighting*	Sharon Gless, *Cagney &Lacey*
1987 –88	*The Wonder Years*	*thirtysomething*	Michael J. Fox, *Family Ties*	Beatrice Arthur, *The Golden Girls*	Richard Kiley, *A Year in the Life*	Tyne Daly, *Cagney &Lacey*
1988 –89	*Cheers*	*L.A. Law*	Richard Mulligan, *Empty Nest*	Candice Bergen, *Murphy Brown*	Carroll O'Connor, *In the Heat of the Night*	Dana Delany, *China Beach*
1989 –90	*Murphy Brown*	*L.A. Law*	Ted Danson, *Cheers*	Candice Bergen, *Murphy Brown*	Peter Falk, *Columbo*	Patricia Wettig, *thirtysomething*
1990 –91	*Cheers*	*L.A. Law*	Burt Reynolds, *Evening Shade*	Kirstie Alley, *Cheers*	James Earl Jones, *Gabriel's Fire*	Patricia Wettig, *thirtysomething*
1991 –92	*Murphy Brown*	*Northern Exposure*	Craig T. Nelson, *Coach*	Candice Bergen, *Murphy Brown*	Christopher Lloyd, *Avonlea*	Dana Delany, *China Beach*,
1992 –93	*Seinfeld*	*Picket Fences*	Ted Danson, *Cheers*	Roseanne Arnold, *Roseanne*	Tom Skerritt, *Picket Fences*	Kathy Baker, *Picket Fences*
1993 –94	*Frasier*	*Picket Fences*	Kelsey Grammer, *Frasier*	Candice Bergen, *Murphy Brown*	Dennis Franz, *NYPD Blue*	Sela Ward, *Sisters*
1994 –95	*Frasier*	*NYPD Blue*	Kelsey Grammer, *Frasier*	Candice Bergen, *Murphy Brown*	Mandy Patinkin, *Chicago Hope*	Kathy Baker, *Picket Fences*
1995 –96	*Frasier*	*E.R.*	John Lithgow, *Third Rock From the Sun*	Helen Hunt, *Mad About You*	Dennis Franz, *NYPD Blue*	Kathy Baker, *Picket Fences*
1996 –97	*Frasier*	*Law & Order*	John Lithgow, *Third Rock From the Sun*	Helen Hunt, *Mad About You*	Dennis Franz, *NYPD Blue*	Gillian Anderson, *The X-Files*
1997 –98	*Frasier*	*The Practice*	Kelsey Grammer, *Frasier*	Helen Hunt, *Mad About You*	Andre Braugher, *Homicide*	Christine Lahti, *Chicago Hope*
1998 –99	*Ally McBeal*	*The Practice*	John Lithgow, *Third Rock From the Sun*	Helen Hunt, *Mad About You*	Dennis Franz, *NYPD Blue*	Edie Falco, *The Sopranos*
1999 –2000	*Will and Grace*	*The West Wing*	Michael J. Fox, *Spin City*	Patricia Heaton, *Everybody Loves Raymond*	James Gandolfini, *The Sopranos*	Sela Ward, *Once and Again*
2000 –01	*Sex and the City*	*The West Wing*	Eric McCormack, *Will and Grace*	Patricia Heaton, *Everybody Loves Raymond*	James Gandolfini, *The Sopranos*	Edie Falco, *The Sopranos*
2001 –02	*Friends*	*The West Wing*	Ray Romano, *Everybody Loves Raymond*	Jennifer Aniston, *Friends*	Michael Chiklis, *The Shield*	Allison Janney, *The West Wing*
2002 –03	*Everybody Loves Raymond*	*The West Wing*	Tony Shalhoub, *Monk*	Debra Messing, *Will & Grace*	James Gandolfini, *The Sopranos*	Edie Falco, *The Sopranos*
2003 –04	*Arrested Development*	*The Sopranos*	Kelsey Grammer, *Frasier*	Sara Jessica Parker, *Sex and the City*	James Spader, *The Practice*	Allison Janney, *The West Wing*

Year	Comedy	Drama	Comedy Actor	Comedy Actress	Drama Actor	Drama Actress
2004 –05	*Everybody Loves Raymond*	*Lost*	Tony Shalhoub, *Monk*	Felicity Huffman, *Desperate Housewives*	James Spader, *Boston Legal*	Patricia Arquette, *Medium*
2005 –06	*The Office*	*24*	Tony Shalhoub, *Monk*	Julia Louis-Dreyfus, *The New Adventures of Old Christine*	Kiefer Sutherland, *24*	Mariska Hargitay, *Law & Order: SVU*
2006 –07	*30 Rock*	*The Sopranos*	Ricky Gervais, *Extras*	America Ferrera *Ugly Betty*	James Spader, *Boston Legal*	Sally Field, *Brothers and Sisters*
2007 –08	*30 Rock*	*Mad Men*	Alec Baldwin, *30 Rock*	Tina Fey, *30 Rock*	Bryan Cranston, *Breaking Bad*	Glenn Close, *Damages*
2008 –09	*30 Rock*	*Mad Men*	Alec Baldwin, *30 Rock*	Toni Colette, *United States of Tara*	Bryan Cranston, *Breaking Bad*	Glenn Close, *Damages*
2009 –10	*Modern Family*	*Mad Men*	Jim Parsons, *The Big Bang Theory*	Edie Falco, *Nurse Jackie*	Bryan Cranston, *Breaking Bad*	Kyra Sedgwick, *The Closer*

Notes: 1. Before 1965, the Academy did always not give separate acting awards for comedy and drama. 2. Playhouse 90 was best drama of one hour or longer; Alcoa-Goodyear Theatre was best drama of less than one hour. 3. In 1964, the Academy gave acting awards to Dick Van Dyke *for The Dick Van Dyke Show*, Lynn Fontaine and Alfred Lunt for "The Magnificent Yankee" *Hallmark Hall of Fame*, and Barbra Streisand for *My Name is Barbra*. It also gave Achievements in Entertainment awards to these programs. www.emmys.tv

The Tony Awards, 1947–2010

The Tony Awards are presented each year by the American Theatre Wing for distinguished achievement in the Broadway theater. Named for Antoinette Perry, an actress, producer, director, and chairman of the American Theatre Wing who died in 1946, the Tonys were first presented in 1947. Listed here is a selection of major awards for each year: best play (author), performance by an actor in a play, performance by an actress in a play, best musical (composer and lyricist), performance by an actor in a musical, performance by an actress in a musical.

PLAYS

Year	Best Play	Best Actor	Best Actress
1947	no award	José Ferrer, *Cyrano de Bergerac* Fredric March, *Years Ago*	Ingrid Bergman, *Joan of Lorraine* Helen Hayes, *Happy Birthday*
1948	*Mister Roberts*, Thomas Heggen and Joshua Logan	Henry Fonda, *Mister Roberts* Paul Kelly, *Command Decision* Basil Rathbone, *The Heiress*	Judith Anderson, *Medea*; Katharine Cornell, *Antony and Cleopatra*; Jessica Tandy, *A Streetcar Named Desire*
1949	*Death of a Salesman*, Arthur Miller	Rex Harrison, *Anne of the Thousand Days*	Martita Hunt, *The Madwoman of Chaillot*
1950	*The Cocktail Party*, T. S. Eliot	Sidney Blackmer, *Come Back, Little Sheba*	Shirley Booth, *Come Back, Little Sheba*
1951	*The Rose Tattoo*, Tennessee Williams	Claude Rains, *Darkness at Noon*	Uta Hagen, *The Country Girl*
1952	*The Fourposter*, Jan de Hartog	José Ferrer, *The Shrike*	Julie Harris, *I Am a Camera*
1953	*The Crucible*, Arthur Miller	Tom Ewell, *The Seven Year Itch*	Shirley Booth, *Time of the Cuckoo*

Year	Best Play	Best Actor	Best Actress
1954	*The Teahouse of the August Moon*, John Patrick	David Wayne, *The Teahouse of the August Moon*	Audrey Hepburn, *Ondine*
1955	*The Desperate Hours*, Joseph Hayes	Alfred Lunt, *Quadrille*	Nancy Kelly, *The Bad Seed*
1956	*The Diary of Anne Frank*, Frances Goodrich and Albert Hackett	Paul Muni, *Inherit the Wind*	Julie Harris, *The Lark*
1957	*Long Day's Journey Into Night*, Eugene O'Neill	Fredric March, *Long Day's Journey Into Night*	Margaret Leighton, *Separate Tables*
1958	*Sunrise at Campobello*, Dore Schary	Ralph Bellamy, *Sunrise at Campobello*	Helen Hayes, *Time Remembered*
1959	*J.B.*, Archibald Macleish	Jason Robards, *The Disenchanted*	Gertrude Berg, *A Majority of One*
1960	*The Miracle Worker*, William Gibson	Melvyn Douglas, *The Best Man*	Anne Bancroft, *The Miracle Worker*
1961	*Becket*, Jean Anouilh	Zero Mostel, *Rhinoceros*	Joan Plowright, *A Taste of Honey*
1962	*A Man for All Seasons*, Robert Bolt	Paul Scofield, *A Man for All Seasons*	Margaret Leighton, *Night of the Iguana*
1963	*Who's Afraid of Virginia Woolf*, Edward Albee	Arthur Hill, *Who's Afraid of Virginia Woolf*	Uta Hagen, *Who's Afraid of Virginia Woolf*
1964	*Luther,* John Osborne	Alec Guinness, *Dylan*	Sandy Dennis, *Any Wednesday*
1965	*The Subject Was Roses*, Frank Gilroy	Walter Matthau, *The Odd Couple*	Irene Worth, *Tiny Alice*
1966	*Marat/Sade*, Peter Weiss	Hal Holbrook, *Mark Twain Tonight!*	Rosemary Harris, *The Lion in Winter*
1967	*The Homecoming*, Harold Pinter	Paul Rogers, *The Homecoming*	Beryl Reid, *The Killing of Sister George*
1968	*Rosencrantz and Guildenstern are Dead*, Tom Stoppard	Martin Balsam, *You Know I Can't Hear You When the Water's Running*	Zoe Caldwell, *The Prime of Miss Jean Brodie*
1969	*The Great White Hope*, Howard Sackler	James Earl Jones, *The Great White Hope*	Julie Harris, *Forty Carats*
1970	*Borstal Boy*, Frank McMahon	Fritz Weaver, *Child's Play*	Tammy Grimes, *Private Lives* (R)
1971	*Sleuth*, Anthony Shaffer	Brian Bedford, *The School for Wives* (R)	Maureen Stapleton, *Gingerbread Lady*
1972	*Sticks and Bones*, David Rabe	Cliff Gorman, *Lenny*	Sada Thompson, *Twigs*
1973	*That Championship Season*, Jason Miller	Alan Bates, *Butley*	Julie Harris, *The Last of Mrs. Lincoln*
1974	*The River Niger*, Joseph A. Walker	Michael Moriarty, *Find Your Way Home*	Colleen Dewhurst, *A Moon for the Misbegotten* (R)
1975	*Equus*, Peter Shaffer	John Kani, *Sizwe Banzi Is Dead* Winston Ntshona, *The Island*	Ellen Burstyn, *Same Time, Next Year*
1976	*Travesties*, Tom Stoppard	John Wood, *Travesties*	Irene Worth, *Sweet Bird of Youth* (R)
1977	*The Shadow Box*, Michael Cristofer	Al Pacino, *The Basic Training of Pavlo Hummel*	Julie Harris, *The Belle of Amherst*
1978	*Da*, Hugh Leonard	Barnard Hughes, *Da*	Jessica Tandy, *The Gin Game*
1979	*The Elephant Man*, Bernard Pomerance	Tom Conti, *Whose Life Is It Anyway?*	Constance Cummings, *Wings* Carole Shelley, *The Elephant Man*
1980	*Children of a Lesser God*, Mark Medoff	John Rubinstein, *Children of a Lesser God*	Phyllis Frelich, *Children of a Lesser God*

Year	Best Play	Best Actor	Best Actress
1981	*Amadeus*, Peter Shaffer	Ian McKellen, *Amadeus*	Jane Lapotaire, *Piaf*
1982	*The Life and Adventures of Nicholas Nickleby*, David Edgar	Roger Rees, *The Life and Adventures of Nicholas Nickleby*	Zoe Caldwell, *Medea* (R)
1983	*Torch Song Trilogy*, Harvey Fierstein	Harvey Fierstein, *Torch Song Trilogy*	Jessica Tandy, *Foxfire*
1984	*The Real Thing*, Tom Stoppard	Jeremy Irons, *The Real Thing*	Glenn Close, *The Real Thing*
1985	*Biloxi Blues*, Neil Simon	Derek Jacobi, *Much Ado About Nothing* (R)	Stockard Channing, *Joe Egg* (R)
1986	*I'm Not Rappaport*, Herb Gardner	Judd Hirsch, *I'm Not Rappaport*	Lily Tomlin, *The Search for Signs of Intelligent Life in the Universe*
1987	*Fences*, August Wilson	James Earl Jones, *Fences*	Linda Lavin, *Broadway Bound*
1988	*M. Butterfly*, David Henry Hwang	Ron Silver, *Speed-The-Plow*	Joan Allen, *Burn This*
1989	*The Heidi Chronicles*, Wendy Wasserstein	Philip Bosco, *Lend Me a Tenor*	Pauline Collins, *Shirley Valentine*
1990	*The Grapes of Wrath*, Frank Galati	Robert Morse, *Tru*	Maggie Smith, *Lettice and Lovage*
1991	*Lost in Yonkers*, Neil Simon	Nigel Hawthorne, *Shadowlands*	Mercedes Ruhl, *Lost in Yonkers*
1992	*Dancing at Lughnasa*, Brian Friel	Judd Hirsch, *Conversations with My Father*	Glenn Close, *Death and the Maiden*
1993	*Angels in America: Millennium Approaches*, Tony Kushner	Ron Leibman, *Angels in America: Millennium Approaches*	Madeline Kahn, *The Sisters Rosensweig*
1994	*Angels in America: Perestroika*, Tony Kushner	Stephen Spinella, *Angels in America: Perestroika*	Diana Rigg, *Medea* (R)
1995	*Love! Valour! Compassion!*, Terrence McNally	Ralph Fiennes, *Hamlet* (R)	Cherry Jones, *The Heiress* (R)
1996	*Master Class*, Terrence McNally	George Grizzard, *A Delicate Balance* (R)	Zoe Caldwell, *Master Class*
1997	*Last Night of Ballyhoo*, Alfred Uhry	Christopher Plummer, *Barrymore*	Janet McTeer, *A Doll's House* (R)
1998	*Art*, Yasmina Reza	Anthony La Paglia, *A View From the Bridge* (R)	Marie Mullen, *The Beauty Queen of Leenane*
1999	*Side Man*, Warren Leight	Brian Dennehy, *Death of a Salesman* (R)	Judi Dench, *Amy's View*
2000	*Copenhagen*, Michael Frayn	Stephen Dillane, *The Real Thing*	Jennifer Ehle, *The Real Thing*
2001	*Proof*, David Auburn	Richard Easton, *The Invention of Love*	Mary-Louise Parker, *Proof*
2002	*The Goat or Who Is Sylvia?*, Edward Albee	Alan Bates, *Fortune's Fool*	Lindsay Duncan, *Private Lives* (R)
2003	*Take Me Out*, Richard Greenberg	Brian Dennehy, *Long Day's Journey Into Night* (R)	Vanessa Redgrave, *Long Day's Journey Into Night* (R)
2004	*I Am My Own Wife*, Doug Wright	Jefferson Mays, *I Am My Own Wife*	Phylicia Rashad, *A Raisin in the Sun*
2005	*Doubt*, John Patrick Shanley	Bill Irwin, *Who's Afraid of Virginia Woolf?*	Cherry Jones, *Doubt*
2006	*The History Boys*, Alan Bennett	Richard Griffiths, *The History Boys*	Cynthia Nixon, *Rabbit Hole*
2007	*The Coast of Utopia*, Tom Stoppard	Frank Langella, *Frost/Nixon*	Julie White, *The Little Dog Laughed*
2008	*August: Osage County*, Tracy Letts	Mark Rylance, *Boeing-Boeing* (R)	Deanna Dunagan, *August: Osage County*
2009	*God of Carnage*, Yasmina Reza	Geoffrey Rush, *Exit the King*	Marcia Gay Harden, *God of Carnage*
2010	*Red*, John Logan	Denzel Washington, *Fences*	Viola Davis, *Fences*

MUSICALS

Year	Best Musical	Best Actor	Best Actress
1947	no award	no award	no award
1948	no award	Paul Hartman, *Angel in the Wings*	Grace Hartman, *Angel in the Wings*
1949	*Kiss Me Kate*, Cole Porter (M&L)	Ray Bolger, *Where's Charley?*	Nanette Fabray, *Love Life*
1950	*South Pacific*, Richard Rodgers(M), Oscar Hammerstein (L)	Ezio Pinza, *South Pacific*	Mary Martin, *South Pacific*
1951	*Guys and Dolls*, Frank Loesser (M&L)	Robert Alda, *Guys and Dolls*	Ethel Merman, *Call Me Madam*
1952	*The King and I*, Richard Rodgers (M), Oscar Hammerstein (L)	Phil Silvers, *Top Banana*	Gertrude Lawrence, *The King and I*
1953	*Wonderful Town*, Leonard Bernstein (M), Betty Comden, and Adolph Green (L)	Thomas Mitchell, *Hazel Flagg*	Rosalind Russell, *Wonderful Town*
1954	*Kismet*, Alexander Borodin (M), adapted by Robert Wright and George Forrest (L)	Alfred Drake, *Kismet*	Dolores Gray, *Carnival in Flanders*
1955	*The Pajama Game*, Richard Adler and Jerry Ross (M&L)	Walter Slezak, *Fanny*	Mary Martin, *Peter Pan*
1956	*Damn Yankees*, Richard Adler and Jerry Ross (M&L)	Ray Walston, *Damn Yankees*	Gwen Verdon, *Damn Yankees*
1957	*My Fair Lady*, Frederick Loewe (M), Alan Jay Lerner (L)	Rex Harrison, *My Fair Lady*	Judy Holliday, *Bells Are Ringing*
1958	*The Music Man*, Meredith Willson (M&L)	Robert Preston, *The Music Man*	(tie) Thelma Ritter, Gwen Verdon, *New Girl in Town*
1959	*Redhead*, Albert Hague (M), Dorothy Fields (L)	Richard Kiley, *Redhead*	Gwen Verdon, *Redhead*
1960	(tie) *Fiorello*, Jerry Bock (M), Sheldon Harnick (L); *The Sound of Music*, Richard Rodgers (M), Oscar Hammerstein (L)	Jackie Gleason, *Take Me Along*	Mary Martin, *The Sound of Music*
1961	*Bye, Bye, Birdie*, Charles Strouse (M), Lee Adams (L)	Richard Burton, *Camelot*	Elizabeth Seal, *Irma la Douce*
1962	*How to Succeed in Business Without Really Trying*, Frank Loesser (M&L)	Robert Morse, *How to Succeed in Business Without Really Trying*	(tie) Anna Maria Alberghetti, *Carnival*; Diahann Carroll, *No Strings*
1963	*A Funny Thing Happened on the Way to the Forum*, Stephen Sondheim (M&L)	Zero Mostel, *A Funny Thing Happened on the Way to the Forum*	Vivien Leigh, *Tovarich*
1964	*Hello, Dolly!* Jerry Herman (M&L)	Bert Lahr, *Foxy*	Carol Channing, *Hello, Dolly!*
1965	*Fiddler on the Roof*, Jerry Bock (M), Sheldon Harnick (L)	Zero Mostel, *Fiddler on the Roof*	Liza Minnelli, *Flora, the Red Menace*
1966	*Man of La Mancha*, Mitch Leigh (M), Joe Darion (L)	Richard Kiley, *Man of La Mancha*	Angela Lansbury, *Mame*
1967	*Cabaret*, John Kander (M), Fred Ebb (L)	Robert Preston, *I Do! I Do!*	Barbara Harris, *The Apple Tree*
1968	*Hallelujah, Baby!*, Jule Styne (M), Betty Comden & Adolph Green (L)	Robert Goulet, *The Happy Time*	Patricia Routledge, *Darling of the Day* Leslie Uggams, *Hallelujah, Baby!*
1969	*1776*, Sherman Edwards (M&L)	Jerry Orbach, *Promises, Promises*	Angela Lansbury, *Dear World*
1970	*Applause*, Charles Strouse (M), Lee Adams (L)	Cleavon Little, *Purlie*	Lauren Bacall, *Applause*
1971	*Company*, Stephen Sondheim (M&L)	Hal Linden, *The Rothschilds*	Helen Gallagher, *No, No Nannette* (R)
1972	*Two Gentlemen of Verona* [best score: *Follies*, Stephen Sondheim (M&L)]	Phil Silvers, *A Funny Thing Happened on the Way to the Forum* (R)	Alexis Smith, *Follies*
1973	*A Little Night Music*, Stephen Sondheim (M&L)	Ben Vereen, *Pippin*	Glynis Johns, *A Little Night Music*
1974	*Raisin*, [best score: *Gigi*, Frederick Loewe (M), Alan Jay Lerner (L)]	Christopher Plummer, *Cyrano*	Virginia Capers, *Raisin*

Year	Best Musical	Best Actor	Best Actress
1975	*The Wiz*, Charlie Smalls (M&L)	John Cullum, *Shenandoah*	Angela Lansbury, *Gypsy* (R)
1976	*A Chorus Line*, Marvin Hamlisch (M), Edward Kleban (L)	George Rose, *My Fair Lady* (R)	Donna McKechnie, *A Chorus Line*
1977	*Annie*, Charles Strouse (M), Martin Charnin (L)	Barry Bostwick, *The Robber Bridegroom*	Dorothy Loudon, *Annie*
1978	*Ain't Misbehavin'* [best score: *On the Twentieth Century*, Cy Coleman (M) Betty Comden and Adolph Green (L)]	John Cullum, *On the Twentieth Century*	Liza Minnelli, *The Act*
1979	*Sweeney Todd*, Stephen Sondheim	Len Cariou, *Sweeney Todd*	Angela Lansbury, *Sweeney Todd*
1980	*Evita*, Andrew Lloyd Webber (M), Tim Rice (L)	Jim Dale, *Barnum*	Patti LuPone, *Evita*
1981	*42nd Street*, [best score: *Woman of the Year*, John Kander (M), Fred Ebb (L)]	Kevin Kline, *The Pirates of Penzance*	Lauren Bacall, *Woman of the Year*
1982	*Nine*, Maury Yeston (M&L)	Ben Harney, *Dreamgirls*	Jennifer Holliday, *Dreamgirls*
1983	*Cats*, Andrew Lloyd Webber (M), T.S. Eliot (L)	Tommy Tune, *My One and Only*	Natalia Makarova, *On Your Toes*
1984	*La Cage Aux Folles*, Jerry Herman (M&L)	George Hearn, *La Cage Aux Folles*	Chita Rivera, *The Rink*
1985	*Big River*, Roger Miller (M&L)	No award	No award
1986	*The Mystery of Edwin Drood*, Rupert Holmes (M&L)	George Rose, *The Mystery of Edwin Drood*	Bernadette Peters, *Song and Dance*
1987	*Les Misérables*, Claude-Michel Schönberg (M); Herbert Kretzmer & Alain Boublil (L)	Robert Lindsay, *Me and My Girl*	Maryann Plunkett, *Me and My Girl*
1988	*The Phantom of the Opera* [best score: *Into the Woods*, Stephen Sondheim (M&L)]	Michael Crawford, *The Phantom of the Opera*	Joanna Gleason, *Into the Woods*
1989	*Jerome Robbins' Broadway* [best score: no award]	Jason Alexander, *Jerome Robbins' Broadway*	Ruth Brown, *Black and Blue*
1990	*City of Angels*, Cy Coleman (M) David Zippel (L)	James Naughton, *City of Angels*	Tyne Daly, *Gypsy* (R)
1991	*The Will Rogers Follies*, Cy Coleman (M); Betty Comden and Adolph Green (L)	Jonathan Pryce, *Miss Saigon*	Lea Salonga, *Miss Saigon*
1992	*Crazy for You*, [best score: *Falsettos*, William Finn (M&L)]	Gregory Hines, *Jelly's Last Jam*	Faith Prince, *Guys and Dolls* (R)
1993	*Kiss of the Spider Woman* [best score: (tie) *Kiss of the Spider Woman*, John Kander (M) and Fred Ebb (L); *Tommy*, Pete Townshend (M&L)]	Brent Carver, *Kiss of the Spider Woman*	Chita Rivera, *Kiss of the Spider Woman*
1994	*Passion*, Stephen Sondheim (M&L)	Boyd Gaines, *She Loves Me* (R)	Donna Murphy, *Passion*
1995	*Sunset Boulevard*, Andrew Lloyd Webber (M&L)	Matthew Broderick, *How to Succeed in Business Without Really Trying* (R)	Glenn Close, *Sunset Boulevard*
1996	*Rent*, Jonathan Larson (M&L)	Nathan Lane, *A Funny Thing Happened on the Way to the Forum* (R)	Donna Murphy, *The King and I* (R)
1997	*Titanic*, Maury Yeston (M&L)	James McNaughton, *Chicago* (R)	Bebe Neuwirth, *Chicago* (R)
1998	*The Lion King*, [best score: *Ragtime*, Stephen Flaherty & Lynn Ahrens (M&L)]	Alan Cumming, *Cabaret* (R)	Natasha Richardson, *Cabaret* (R)

Year	Best Musical	Best Actor	Best Actress
1999	*Fosse*, [best score: *Parade*, Jason Robert Brown (M&L)]	Martin Short, *Little Me* (R)	Bernadette Peters, *Annie Get Your Gun* (R)
2000	*Contact* [best score: *Aida*, Elton John (M) and Tim Rice (L)]	Brian Stokes Mitchell, *Kiss Me Kate* (R)	Heather Headley, *Aida*
2001	*The Producers*, Mel Brooks (M&L)	Nathan Lane, *The Producers*	Christine Ebersole, *42nd Street* (R)
2002	*Thoroughly Modern Millie*, [best score: *Urinetown: The Musical*, Mark Hollmann (M); Mark Hollman and Greg Kotis (L)]	John Lithgow, *Sweet Smell of Success*	Sutton Foster, *Thoroughly Modern Millie*
2003	*Hairspray*, Scott Whittman, Marc Shaiman (M&L)	Harvey Fierstein, *Hairspray*	Marissa Jaret Winokur, *Hairspray*
2004	*Avenue Q*, Robert Lopez and Jeff Marx (M&L)	Hugh Jackman, *The Boy From Oz*	Idina Menzel, *Wicked*
2005	*Monty Python's Spamalot*	Norbert Leo Butz, *Dirty Rotten Scoundrels*	Victoria Clark, *A Light in the Piazza*
2006	*Jersey Boys*, Frankie Valli & The Four Seasons	John Lloyd Young, *Jersey Boys*	LaChanze, *The Color Purple*
2007	*Spring Awakening*, Duncan Sheik (M), Steven Sater (L)	David Hyde Pierce, *Curtains*	Christine Ebersole, *Grey Gardens*
2008	*In the Heights*, Lin-Manuel Miranda (M&L)	Paolo Szot, *South Pacific* (R)	Patti LuPone, *Gypsy* (R)
2009	*Billy Elliot, The Musical*, Elton John (M), Lee Hall (L)	David Alvarez, Trent Kowalik, Kiril Kurish, *Billy Elliot*	Alice Ripley, *Next to Normal*
2010	*Memphis*, David Bryan (M), Joe DiPietro & David Bryan (L)	Douglas Hodge, *La Cage Aux Folles* (R)	Catherine Zeta-Jones, *A Little Night Music* (R)

M = music; L = lyrics, R = revival. **Note:** Since 1971 "Musical" and "Score" have been separate categories. However, the winner of the Tony for Best Musical usually wins the award for Best Score, except where otherwise indicated.
Source: Isabelle Stevenson, The Tony Award 1989; American Theatre Wing.

The Grammys, 1958–2010

The "Grammys" are officially known as the National Academy of Recording Arts and Sciences Awards. Winners (in almost 70 categories) are selected yearly by the 6,000 or so voting members of the academy. The five award categories listed below have remained fairly constant over the years, although the overall "Best Vocal Performance" awards were phased out in 1968. From that year on, we list "Best Pop Vocal Performance" (male and female), except where indicated.

Year	Record of the year	Album of the year	Song of the year	Best male vocal performance	Best female vocal performance
1958	Domenico Modugno, "Nel Blu Dipinto di Blu (Volare)"	Henry Mancini, *The Music from Peter Gunn*	Domenico Modugno, "Nel Blu Dipinto di Blu (Volare)"	Perry Como, "Catch a Falling Star"	Ella Fitzgerald, *Ella Fitzgerald Sings the Irving Berlin Songbook*[2]
1959	Bobby Darin, "Mack the Knife"	Frank Sinatra, *Come Dance with Me*	Jimmy Driftwood, "The Battle of New Orleans"	Frank Sinatra, "Come Dance with Me"	Ella Fitzgerald, "But Not for Me"
1960	Percy Faith, "Theme from a Summer Place"	Bob Newhart, *Button-Down Mind*	Ernest Gold, "Theme from Exodus"	Ray Charles, "Georgia on My Mind"	Ella Fitzgerald, "Mack the Knife"
1961	Henry Mancini, "Moon River"	Judy Garland, *Judy at Carnegie Hall*	Henry Mancini, Johnny Mercer, "Moon River"	Jack Jones, "Lollipops and Roses"	Judy Garland, *Judy at Carnegie Hall*
1962	Tony Bennett, "I Left My Heart in	Vaughn Meader, *The First Family*	Leslie Bricusse, Anthony Newley,	Tony Bennett, "I Left My Heart in	Ella Fitzgerald, *Ella Swings*

Year	Record of the year	Album of the year	Song of the year	Best male vocal performance	Best female vocal performance
	San Francisco"		"What Kind of Fool Am I?"	San Francisco"	*Brightly with Nelson Riddle*
1963	Henry Mancini, "The Days of Wine and Roses"	Barbra Streisand, *The Barbra Streisand Album*	Henry Mancini, Johnny Mercer, "The Days of Wine and Roses"	Jack Jones, "Wives and Lovers"	Barbra Streisand, *The Barbra Streisand Album*
1964	Stan Getz, Astrud Gilberto, "The Girl from Ipanema"	Stan Getz, Astrud Gilberto, *Getz/Gilberto*	Jerry Herman, "Hello, Dolly!"	Louis Armstrong, "Hello, Dolly!"	Barbra Streisand, "People"
1965	Herb Alpert & the Tijuana Brass, "A Taste of Honey"	Frank Sinatra, *September of My Years*	Paul Francis Webster, Johnny Mandel, "The Shadow of Your Smile"	Frank Sinatra, "It Was a Very Good Year"	Barbra Streisand, *My Name is Barbra*
1966	Frank Sinatra, "Strangers in the Night"	Frank Sinatra, *A Man and His Music*	John Lennon, Paul McCartney, "Michelle"	Frank Sinatra, "Strangers in the Night"	Eydie Gorme, "If He Walked into My Life"
1967	5th Dimension, "Up, Up and Away"	The Beatles, *Sgt. Pepper's Lonely Hearts Club Band*	Jim Webb, "Up, Up, and Away"	Glen Campbell, "By the Time I Get to Phoenix"	Bobbie Gentry, "Ode to Billie Joe"
1968	Simon & Garfunkel, "Mrs. Robinson"	Glen Campbell, *By the Time I Get to Phoenix*	Bobby Russell, "Little Green Apples"	Jose Feliciano[3], "Light My Fire"	Dionne Warwick, "Do You Know the Way to San Jose?"
1969	5th Dimension, "Aquarius/Let the Sunshine In"	Blood, Sweat & Tears, *Blood, Sweat & Tears*	Joe South, "Games People Play"	Harry Nilsson[4], "Everybody's Talkin'"	Peggy Lee, "Is That All There Is?"
1970	Simon & Garfunkel, "Bridge Over Troubled Water"	Simon & Garfunkel, *Bridge over Troubled Water*	Paul Simon, "Bridge over Troubled Water"	Ray Stevens[4], "Everything is Beautiful"	Dionne Warwick, "I'll Never Fall in Love Again"
1971	Carole King, "It's Too Late"	Carole King, *Tapestry*	Carole King, "You've Got a Friend"	James Taylor[5], "You've Got a Friend"	Carole King, "Tapestry"
1972	Roberta Flack, "The First Time Ever I Saw Your Face"	George Harrison, Ravi Shankar, Bob Dylan et al, *Concert for Bangladesh*	Ewan McColl, "The First Time Ever I Saw Your Face"	Harry Nilsson, "Without You"	Helen Reddy, "I Am Woman"
1973	Roberta Flack, "Killing Me Softly with His Song"	Stevie Wonder, *Innervisions*	Norman Gimbel, Charles Fox, "Killing Me Softly with His Song"	Stevie Wonder, "You Are the Sunshine of My Life"	Roberta Flack, "Killing Me Softly with His Song"
1974	Olivia Newton-John, "I Honestly Love You"	Stevie Wonder, *Fulfillingness' First Finale*	Marilyn & Alan Bergman, Marvin Hamlisch, "The Way We Were"	Stevie Wonder, "Fulfillingness' First Finale"	Olivia Newton-John, "I Honestly Love You"
1975	Captain & Tennille, "Love Will Keep Us Together"	Paul Simon, *Still Crazy After All These Years*	Stephen Sondheim, "Send in the Clowns"	Paul Simon, "Still Crazy after All These Years"	Janis Ian, "At Seventeen"
1976	George Benson, "This Masquerade"	Stevie Wonder, *Songs in the Key of Life*	Bruce Johnston, "I Write the Songs"	Stevie Wonder, "Songs in the Key of Life"	Linda Ronstadt, "Hasten Down the Wind"
1977	The Eagles, "Hotel California"	Fleetwood Mac, *Rumours*	Barbra Streisand, Paul Williams, "Evergreen"	James Taylor, "Handy Man"	Barbra Streisand, "Evergreen"

Year	Record of the year	Album of the year	Song of the year	Best male vocal performance	Best female vocal performance
1978	Billy Joel, "Just the Way You Are"	Various artists, *Saturday Night Fever*	Billy Joel, "Just the Way You Are"	Barry Manilow, "Copacabana (At the Copa)"	Anne Murray, "You Needed Me"
1979	The Doobie Brothers, "What a Fool Believes"	Billy Joel, *52nd Street*	Kenny Loggins, Michael McDonald, "What a Fool Believes"	Billy Joel, "52nd Street"	Dionne Warwick, "I'll Never Love This Way Again"
1980	Christopher Cross, "Sailing"	Christopher Cross, *Christopher Cross*	Christopher Cross, "Sailing"	Kenny Loggins, "This Is It'	Bette Midler, "The Rose"
1981	Kim Carnes, "Bette Davis Eyes"	John Lennon/Yoko Ono, *Double Fantasy*	Donna Weiss, Jackie DeShannon, "Bette Davis Eyes"	Al Jarreau, "Breakin' Away"	Lena Horne, *The Lady and Her Music Live on Broadway*
1982	Toto, "Rosanna"	Toto, *Toto IV*	Johnny Christopher, Mark James, Wayne Carson, "Always on My Mind"	Lionel Richie, "Truly"	Melissa Manchester, "You Should Hear How She Talks About You"
1983	Michael Jackson, "Beat It"	Michael Jackson, *Thriller*	Sting, "Every Breath You Take"	Michael Jackson, "Thriller"	Irene Cara, *Flashdance... What a Feeling*
1984	Tina Turner, "What's Love Got to Do with It?"	Lionel Richie, *Can't Slow Down*	Graham Lyle, Terry Britten, "What's Love Got to Do with It?"	Phil Collins, "Against All Odds (Take a Look at Me Now)"	Tina Turner, "What's Love Got to Do with It?"
1985	USA for Africa, "We Are the World"	Phil Collins, *No Jacket Required*	Michael Jackson, Lionel Richie, "We Are the World"	Phil Collins, "No Jacket Required"	Whitney Houston, "Saving All My Love for You"
1986	Steve Winwood, "Higher Love"	Paul Simon, *Graceland*	Various, "That's What Friends Are For"	Steve Winwood, "Higher Love"	Barbra Streisand, *The Broadway Album*
1987	Paul Simon, "Graceland"	U2, *The Joshua Tree*	Linda Ronstadt, James Ingram, "Somewhere Out There"	Sting, "Bring on the Night"	Whitney Houston, "I Wanna Dance with Somebody (Who Loves Me)"
1988	Bobby McFerrin, "Don't Worry, Be Happy"	George Michael, *Faith*	Bobby McFerrin, "Don't Worry, Be Happy"	Bobby McFerrin, "Don't Worry, Be Happy"	Tracy Chapman, "Fast Car"
1989	Bette Midler, "Wind Beneath My Wings"	Bonnie Rait, *Nick of Time*	Bette Midler, "Wind Beneath My Wings"	Michael Bolton, "How Am I Supposed to Live Without You"	Bonnie Raitt, "Nick of Time"
1990	Phil Collins, "Another Day in Paradise"	Quincy Jones, *Back on the Block*	Julie Gold, "From a Distance"	Roy Orbison, "Oh, Pretty Woman"	Mariah Carey, *Vision of Love*
1991	Natalie Cole, "Unforgettable"	Natalie Cole, *Unforgettable*	Irving Gordon, "Unforgettable"	Michael Bolton, "When a Man Loves a Woman"	Bonnie Raitt, *Something to Talk About*
1992	Eric Clapton, "Tears in Heaven"	Eric Clapton, *Unplugged*	Eric Clapton, "Tears in Heaven"	Eric Clapton, "Tears in Heaven"	k.d. Lang, "Constant Craving"
1993	Whitney Houston, "I Will Always Love You"	Whitney Houston, *The Bodyguard*	Alan Menken and Tim Rice, " A Whole New World"	Sting, "If I Ever Lose My Faith in You"	Whitney Houston, "I Will Always Love You"
1994	Sheryl Crow, "All I Wanna Do"	Tony Bennett, *MTV Unplugged*	Bruce Springsteen, "Streets of Philadelphia"	Elton John, "Can You Feel the Love Tonight"	Sheryl Crow, "All I Wanna Do"

Year	Record of the year	Album of the year	Song of the year	Best male vocal performance	Best female vocal performance
1995	Seal, "Kiss From a Rose"	Alanis Morissette, *Jagged Little Pill*	Seal, "Kiss From a Rose"	Seal, "Kiss From a Rose"	Annie Lennox, *No More "I Love Yous"*
1996	Eric Clapton, "Change the World"	Celine Dion, *Falling Into You*	Wayne Kirkpatrick and Tommy Sims, "Change the World"	Eric Clapton, "Change the World"	Toni Braxton, "Unbreak My Heart"
1997	Shawn Colvin, "Sunny Came Home"	Bob Dylan, *Time Out of Mind*	Shawn Colvin and John Leventhal, "Sunny Came Home" 1997	Elton John, "Candle in the Wind"	Sarah McLachlan, "Building a Mystery"
1998	Celine Dion, "My Heart Will Go On"	Lauryn Hill, *The Miseducation of Lauryn Hill*	James Horner and Will Jennings, "My Heart Will Go On"	Eric Clapton, "My Father's Eyes"	Celine Dion, "My Heart Will Go On"
1999	Santana, "Smooth"	Santana, *Supernatural*	Itaal Shur and Rob Thomas, "Smooth"	Sting, "Brand New Day"	Sara McLachlan, "I Will Remember You"
2000	U2, "Beautiful Day"	Steely Dan, *Two Against Nature*	U2 "Beautiful Day"	Sting, "She Walks This Earth"	Macy Gray, "I Try"
2001	U2, "Walk On"	Various artists, *O Brother, Where Art Thou?*	Alicia Keys, "Fallin'"	James Taylor, "Don't Let Me Be Lonely Tonight"	Nelly Furtado, "I'm Like a Bird"
2002	Norah Jones, "Don't Know Why"	Norah Jones, *Come Away With Me*	Norah Jones, "Don't Know Why"	John Mayer, "Your Body is a Wonderland"	Norah Jones, "Don't Know Why"
2003	Coldplay, "Clocks"	Outkast, *Speakerboxxx/The Love Below*	Luther Vandross & Richard Marx, "Dance with My Father"	Justin Timberlake, "Cry Me a River"	Christina Aguilera "Beautiful"
2004	Ray Charles & Norah Jones, "Here We Go Again"	Ray Charles & Various Artists *Genius Loves Company*	John Mayer, "Daughters"	John Mayer, "Daughters"	Norah Jones, "Sunrise"
2005	Green Day, "Boulevard of Broken Dreams"	U2, *How to Dismantle an Atomic Bomb*	U2, "Sometimes You Can't Make it On Your Own"	Stevie Wonder, "From the Bottom of My Heart"	Kelly Clarkson, "Since U Been Gone"
2006	Dixie Chicks, "Not Ready to Make Nice"	Dixie Chicks, *Taking the Long Road*	Dixie Chicks, "Not Ready to Make Nice"	John Mayer, "Waiting On The World to Change"	Christina Aguilera, "Ain't No Other Man"
2007	Amy Winehouse, "Rehab"	Herbie Hancock, *River: The Joni Letters*	Amy Winehouse, "Rehab"	Justin Timberlake, "What Goes Around Comes Around"	Amy Winehouse, "Rehab"
2008	Robert Plant & Alison Krauss, "Please Read the Letter"	Robert Plant & Alison Krauss, *Raising Sand*	Coldplay, "Viva La Vida"	John Mayer, "Say"	Adele, "Chasing Pavements"
2009	Kings of Leon, "Use Somebody"	Taylor Swift, *Fearless*	Beyonce, "Single Ladies (Put A Ring On It)"	Jason Mraz, "Make it Mine"	Beyonce, "Halo"
2010	Lady Antebellum, "Need You Now"	Arcade Fire, *The Suburbs*	Lady Antebellum, "Need You Now"	Bruno Mars, "Just The Way You Are"	Lady Gaga, "Bad Romance"

Notes: 1. Awarded to the composer, rather than the performer, of the song. 2. Awarded for an album, rather than an individual song. 3. Award given for "Best Contemporary Pop Vocal Performance." 4. Award given for "Best Vocal Performance Contemporary." 5. From 1971 on, all awards are for "Best Pop Vocal Performance." **Source:** National Academy of Recording Arts and Sciences; www.grammy.com.

Pulitzer Prizes

Named for the man who created the endowment, Joseph Pulitzer (1847–1911), a Hungarian-born American newspaper publisher. He ran the *St. Louis Post-Dispatch* and the *New York World* at the end of the 19th century and helped to create many bedrock technologies of modern journalism—some good, some a bit sleazy. He also endowed the famous school of journalism at Columbia University. The Pulitzer Prize for Reporting is the oldest prize given in journalism and was first awarded in 1917 together with the Pulitzer Prizes for History and Biography.

Pulitzer Prize for Public Service in Newspaper Journalism, 1918–2011

Year	Paper	Year	Paper
1918	*The New York Times*	1958	*Arkansas Gazette*
1919	*Milwaukee Journal*	1959	*Utica Observer-Dispatch* and *Utica Daily Press* (N.Y.)
1920	No award	1960	*Los Angeles Times*
1921	*Boston Post*	1961	*Amarillo* (Tex.) *Globe-Times*
1922	*New York World*	1962	*Panama City* (Fla.) *News-Herald*
1923	*Memphis Commercial Appeal*	1963	*Chicago Daily News*
1924	*New York World*	1964	*St. Petersburg Times*
1925	No award	1965	*Hutchinson* (Kans.) *News*
1926	*Columbus* (Ga.) *Enquirer Sun*	1966	*Boston Globe*
1927	*Canton* (Ohio) *Daily News*	1967	*Louisville Courier Journal* and *Milwaukee Journal*
1928	*Indianapolis Times*	1968	*Riverside* (Calif.) *Press-Enterprise*
1929	*New York Evening World*	1969	*Los Angeles Times*
1930	No award	1970	*Newsday* (Garden City, N.Y.)
1931	*Atlanta Constitution*	1971	*Winston-Salem Journal and Sentinel*
1932	*Indianapolis News*	1972	*The New York Times*
1933	*New York World-Telegram*	1973	*Washington Post*
1934	*Medford* (Oreg.) *Mail Tribune*	1974	*Newsday* (Garden City, N.Y.)
1935	*Sacramento Bee*	1975	*Boston Globe*
1936	*Cedar Rapids Gazette*	1976	*Anchorage Daily News*
1937	*St. Louis Post-Dispatch*	1977	*Lufkin* (Tex.) *News*
1938	*Bismarck* (N.D.) *Tribune*	1978	*Philadelphia Inquirer*
1939	*Miami Daily News*	1979	*Point Reyes* (Calif.) *Light*
1940	*Waterbury* (Conn.) *Republican & American*	1980	*Gannett News Service*
1941	*St. Louis Post-Dispatch*	1981	*Charlotte Observer*
1942	*Los Angeles Times*	1982	*Detroit News*
1943	*Omaha* (Nebr.) *World-Herald*	1983	*Jackson* (Miss.) *Clarion-Ledger*
1944	*The New York Times*	1984	*Los Angeles Times*
1945	*Detroit Free Press*	1985	*Fort Worth Star-Telegram*
1946	*Scranton* (Pa.) *Times*	1986	*Denver Post*
1947	*Baltimore Sun*	1987	*Pittsburgh Press*
1948	*St. Louis Post-Dispatch*	1988	*Charlotte Observer*
1949	*Nebraska State Journal*	1989	*Anchorage Daily News*
1950	*Chicago Daily News* and *St. Louis Post-Dispatch*	1990	*Philadelphia Inquirer* and *Washington* (N.C.) *Daily News*
1951	*Miami Herald* and *Brooklyn Eagle*	1991	*Des Moines Register*
1952	*St. Louis Post-Dispatch*	1992	*Sacramento Bee*
1953	*Whiteville* (N.C.) *News Reporter* and *Tabor City* (N.C.) *Tribune*	1993	*Miami Herald*
1954	*Newsday* (Garden City, N.Y.)	1994	*Akron Beacon Journal*
1955	*Columbus* (Ga.) *Ledger* and *Sunday Ledger-Enquirer*	1995	*Virgin Islands Daily News*
1956	*Watsonville* (Calif.) *Register-Pajaronion*	1996	*Raleigh News and Observer*
1957	*Chicago Daily News*	1997	*New Orleans Times-Picayune*
		1998	*Grand Forks* (N.D.) *Herald*

1999   *Washington Post*
2000   *Washington Post*
2001   *The Oregonian* (Portland, Ore.)
2002   *The New York Times*
2003   *The Boston Globe*
2004   *The New York Times*
2005   *Los Angeles Times*

2006   *Times-Picayune* (New Orleans); *Sun Herald* (Biloxi-Gulfport, Miss.)
2007   *The Wall Street Journal*
2008   *The Washington Post*
2009   *Las Vegas Sun*
2010   *Bristol (VA) Herald Courier*
2011   *Los Angeles Times*

Pulitzer Prize for National Reporting, 1942–2011

Year	Winner, Newspaper
1942	Louis Stark, *The New York Times*
1943	No award
1944	Dewey L. Fleming, *Baltimore Sun*
1945	James B. Reston, *The New York Times*
1946	Edward A. Harris, *St. Louis Post-Dispatch*
1947	Edward T. Folliard, *Washington Post*
1948	Bert Andrews, *New York Herald Tribune* Nat S. Finney, *Minneapolis Tribune*
1949	C.P. Trussell, *The New York Times*
1950	Edwin O. Guthman, *Seattle Times*
1951	No award[1]
1952	Anthony Leviero, *The New York Times*
1953	Don Whitehead, *Associated Press*
1954	Richard Wilson, *Des Moines Register and Tribune*
1955	Anthony Lewis, *Washington Daily News*
1956	Charles L. Bartlett, *Chattanooga Times*
1957	James B. Reston, *The New York Times*
1958	Relman Morin, *Associated Press* Clark Mollenhoff, *Des Moines Register and Tribune*
1959	Howard Van Smith, *Miami News*
1960	Vance Trimble, *Scripps-Howard Newspaper Alliance*
1961	Edward R. Cony, *Wall Street Journal*
1962	Nathan G. Caldwell and Gene S. Graham, *Nashville Tennessean*
1963	Anthony Lewis, *The New York Times*
1964	Merriman Smith, *United Press International*
1965	Louis M. Kohlmeier, *Wall Street Journal*
1966	Haynes Johnson, *Washington Evening Star*
1967	Stanley Penn & Monroe Karmin, *Wall Street Journal*
1968	Howard James, *Christian Science Monitor* Nathan K. (Nick) Kotz, *Des Moines Register* and *Minneapolis Tribune*
1969	Robert Cahn, *Christian Science Monitor*
1970	William J. Eaton, *Chicago Daily News*
1971	Lucinda Franks and Thomas Powers, *United Press International*
1972	Jack Anderson, (Syndicated columnist)
1973	Robert Boyd and Clark Hoyt, *Knight Newspapers*
1974	James R. Polk, *Washington Star-News* Jack White, *Providence Journal and Evening Bulletin*
1975	Donald L. Bartlett and James B. Steele, *Philadelphia Inquirer*
1976	James Risser, *Des Moines Register*
1977	Walter Mears, *Associated Press*
1978	Gaylord D. Shaw, *Los Angeles Times*
1979	James Risser, *Des Moines Register*
1980	Bette Swenson Orsini and Charles Stafford, *St. Petersburg Times*
1981	John M Crewdson, *The New York Times*
1982	Rick Atkinson, *Kansas City Times*
1983	Staff, *Boston Globe*
1984	John Noble Wilford, *The New York Times*
1985	Thomas J. Knudson, *Des Moines Register*
1986	Arthur Howe, *Philadelphia Inquirer*; Craig Flournoy and George Rodrigues, *Dallas Morning News*
1987	Staff, *Miami Herald*; Staff, *The New York Times*
1988	Tim Weiner, *Philadelphia Inquirer*
1989	Donald L. Bartlett and James B. Steele, *Philadelphia Inquirer*
1990	Ross Anderson, Bill Dietrich, Mary Ann Gwinn, and Eric Nalder, *Seattle Times*
1991	Marji Lundstrom and Rochelle Sharpe, *Gannet News Service*
1992	Jeff Taylor and Mike McGraw, *Kansas City Star*
1993	David Maraniss, *Washington Post*
1994	Eileen Welsome, *Albuquerque Tribune*
1995	Tony Horwitz, *Wall Street Journal*
1996	Alix M. Freedman, *Wall Street Journal*
1997	Staff, *Wall Street Journal*
1998	Russell Carollo and Jeff Nesmith, *Dayton Daily News*
1999	Staff, *The New York Times*
2000	Staff, *Wall Street Journal*
2001	Staff, *The New York Times*
2002	Staff, *Washington Post*
2003	Alan Miller and Kevin Sack, *Los Angeles Times*
2004	Staff, *Los Angeles Times*
2005	Walt Bogdanich, *The New York Times*
2006	James Risen and Eric Lichtblau, *The New York Times*; Staffs of *San Diego Union-Tribune* and *Copley News Service*
2007	Charlie Savage, *The Boston Globe*
2008	Jo Becker and Barton Gellman, *The Washington Post*
2009	Staff, *St. Petersburg Times*
2010	Matt Richtel and staff, *The New York Times*
2011	Jesse Eisinger and Jake Bernstein, *ProPublica*

Pulitzer Prize for International Reporting, 1942–2011

Year	Winner, Newspaper
1942	Lawrence Edmund Allen, *Associated Press*
1943	Ira Wolfert, *North American Newspaper Alliance, Inc.*
1944	Daniel DeLuce, *Associated Press*
1945	Mark S. Watson, *Baltimore Sun*
1946	Homer William Bigart, *New York Herald Tribune*
1947	Eddy Gilmore, *Associated Press*
1948	Paul W. Ward, *Baltimore Sun*
1949	Price Day, *Baltimore Sun*
1950	Edmund Stevens, *Christian Science Monitor*
1951	Keyes Beech, *Chicago Daily News*
	Homer William Bigart, *New York Herald Tribune*
	Marguerite Higgins, *New York Herald Tribune*
	Relman Morin, *Associated Press*
	Fred Sparks, *Chicago Daily News*
	Don Whitehead, *Associated Press*
1952	John M. Hightower, *Associated Press*
1953	Austin Wehrwien, *Milwaukee Journal*
1954	Jim G. Lucas, *Scripps-Howard Newspaper Alliance*
1955	Harrison E. Salisbury, *The New York Times*
1956	William Randolph Hearst Jr., Kingsbury Smith, and Frank Conniff, *International News Service*
1957	Russell Jones, *United Press*
1958	Staff, *The New York Times*
1959	Joseph Martin and Philip Santora, *New York Daily News*
1960	A.M. Rosenthal, *The New York Times*
1961	Lynn Heinzerling, *Associated Press*
1962	Walter Lippmann, *New York Herald Tribune Syndicate*
1963	Hal Hendrix, *Miami News*
1964	Malcolm W. Browne, *Associated Press*
	David Halberstam, *The New York Times*
1965	J.A. Livingston, *Philadelphia Bulletin*
1966	Peter Arnett, *Associated Press*
1967	R. John Hughes, *Christian Science Monitor*
1968	Alfred Friendly, *Washington Post*
1969	William Tuohy, *Los Angeles Times*
1970	Seymour M. Hersh, *Dispatch News Service*
1971	Jimmie Lee Hoagland, *Washington Post*
1972	Peter R. Kann, *Wall Street Journal*
1973	Max Frankel, *The New York Times*
1974	Hedrick Smith, *The New York Times*
1975	William Mullen (reporter), Ovie Carter (photographer), *Chicago Tribune*
1976	Sydney H. Schanberg, *The New York Times*

Year	Winner, Newspaper
1977	No award
1978	Henry Kamm, *The New York Times*
1979	Richard Ben Cramer, *Philadelphia Inquirer*
1980	Joel Brinkley (reporter), Jay Mather (photographer), *Louisville Courier-Journal*
1981	Shirley Christian, *Miami Herald*
1982	John Darnton, *The New York Times*
1983	Thomas L. Friedman, *The New York Times*
	Loren Jenkins, *Washington Post*
1984	Karen Elliott House, *Wall Street Journal*
1985	Josh Friedman and Dennis Bell (reporters) and Ozier Muhammad (photographer), *Newsday* (Garden City, N.Y.)
1986	Lewis M. Simons, Pete Carey, and Katherine Ellison, *San Jose Mercury News*
1987	Michael Parks, *Los Angeles Times*
1988	Thomas L. Friedman, *The New York Times*
1989	Glenn Frankel, *Washington Post*
	Bill Keller, *The New York Times*
1990	Nicholas D. Kristof and Sheryl WuDunn, *The New York Times*
1991	Caryle Murphy, *Washington Post*
	Serge Schmemann, *The New York Times*
1992	Patrick J. Sloyan, *Newsday* (Garden City, N.Y.)
1993	John F. Burns, *The New York Times*
	Roy Gutman, *Newsday* (Garden City, N.Y.)
1994	Team of reporters, *Dallas Morning News*
1995	Mark Fritz, *Associated Press*
1996	David Rohde, *Christian Science Monitor*
1997	John F. Burns, *The New York Times*
1998	Staff, *The New York Times*
1999	Staff, *Wall Street Journal*
2000	Mark Schoofs, *Village Voice* (N.Y. City)
2001	Ian Johnson, *Wall Street Journal*
	Paul Salopek, *Chicago Tribune*
2002	Barry Bearak, *The New York Times*
2003	Kevin Sullivan and Mary Jordan, *Washington Post*
2004	Anthony Shadid, *Washington Post*
2005	Kim Murphy, *Los Angeles Times*
2006	Joseph Kahn, Jim Yardley, *The New York Times*
2007	Staff, *Wall Street Journal*
2008	Steve Fainaru, *Washington Post*
2009	Staff, *The New York Times*
2010	Anthony Shadid, *Washington Post*
2011	Clifford J. Levy and Ellen Barry, *The New York Times*

The Pulitzer Prize for Fiction, 1918–2011

Year	Author, Title
1918	Ernest Poole, *His Family*
1919	Booth Tarkington, *The Magnificent Ambersons*
1920	No award
1921	Edith Wharton, *The Age of Innocence*
1922	Booth Tarkington, *Alice Adams*
1923	Willa Cather, *One of Ours*
1924	Margaret Wilson, *The Able McLaughlins*
1925	Edna Ferber, *So Big*
1926	Sinclair Lewis, *Arrowsmith*
1927	Louis Bromfield, *Early Autumn*
1928	Thornton Wilder, *The Bridge of San Luis Rey*
1929	Julia Peterkin, *Scarlet Sister Mary*
1930	Oliver LaFarge, *Laughing Boy*
1931	Margaret Ayer Barnes, *Years of Grace*
1932	Pearl S. Buck, *The Good Earth*
1933	T.S. Stribling, *The Store*
1934	Caroline Miller, *Lamb in His Bosom*
1935	Josephine Winslow Johnson, *Now in November*
1936	Harold L. Davis, *Honey in the Horn*
1937	Margaret Mitchell, *Gone With the Wind*
1938	John Phillips Marquand, *The Late George Apley*
1939	Marjorie Kinnan Rawlings, *The Yearling*
1940	John Steinbeck, *The Grapes of Wrath*
1941	No award
1942	Ellen Glasgow, *In This Our Life*
1943	Upton Sinclair, *Dragon's Teeth*
1944	Martin Flavin, *Journey in the Dark*
1945	John Hersey, *A Bell for Adano*
1946	No award
1947	Robert Penn Warren, *All the King's Men*
1948[1]	James A. Michener, *Tales of the South Pacific*
1949	James Gould Cozzens, *Guard of Honor*
1950	A.B. Guthrie Jr., *The Way West*
1951	Conrad Richter, *The Town*
1952	Herman Wouk, *The Caine Mutiny*
1953	Ernest Hemingway, *The Old Man and the Sea*
1954	No award
1955	William Faulkner, *A Fable*
1956	MacKinlay Kantor, *Andersonville*
1957	No award
1958	James Agee, *A Death in the Family*
1959	Robert Lewis Taylor, *The Travels of Jaimie McPheeters*
1960	Allen Drury, *Advise and Consent*
1961	Harper Lee, *To Kill a Mockingbird*
1962	Edwin O'Connor, *The Edge of Sadness*
1963	William Faulkner, *The Reivers*
1964	No award
1965	Shirley Ann Grau, *The Keepers of the House*

Year	Author, Title
1966	Katherine Anne Porter, *Collected Stories*
1967	Bernard Malamud, *The Fixer*
1968	William Styron, *The Confessions of Nat Turner*
1969	N. Scott Momaday, *House Made of Dawn*
1970	Jean Stafford, *Collected Stories*
1971	No award
1972	Wallace Stegner, *Angle of Repose*
1973	Eudora Welty, *The Optimist's Daughter*
1974	No award
1975	Michael Shaara, *The Killer Angels*
1976	Saul Bellow, *Humboldt's Gift*
1977	No award
1978	James Alan McPherson, *Elbow Room*
1979	John Cheever, *The Stories of John Cheever*
1980	Norman Mailer, *The Executioner's Song*
1981	John Kennedy Toole, *A Confederacy of Dunces*
1982	John Updike, *Rabbit Is Rich*
1983	Alice Walker, *The Color Purple*
1984	William Kennedy, *Ironweed*
1985	Alison Lurie, *Foreign Affairs*
1986	Larry McMurtry, *Lonesome Dove*
1987	Peter Taylor, *A Summons to Memphis*
1988	Toni Morrison, *Beloved*
1989	Anne Tyler, *Breathing Lessons*
1990	Oscar Hijuelos, *The Mambo Kings Play Songs of Love*
1991	John Updike, *Rabbit at Rest*
1992	Jane Smiley, *A Thousand Acres*
1993	Robert Olen Butler, *A Good Scent From a Strange Mountain*
1994	E. Annie Proulx, *The Shipping News*
1995	Carol Shields, *The Stone Diaries*
1996	Richard Ford, *Independence Day*
1997	Steven Millhauser, *Martin Dressler: The Tale of an American Dreamer*
1998	Philip Roth, *American Pastoral*
1999	Michael Cunningham, *The Hours*
2000	Jhumpa Lahiri, *Interpreter of Maladies*
2001	Michael Chabon, *The Amazing Adventures of Kavalier & Clay*
2002	Richard Russo, *Empire Falls*
2003	Jeffrey Eugenides, *Middlesex*
2004	Edward P. Jones, *The Known World*
2005	Marilynne Robinson, *Gilead*
2006	Geraldine Brooks, *March*
2007	Cormac McCarthy, *The Road*
2008	Junot Diaz, *The Brief Wondrous Life of Oscar Wao*
2009	Elizabeth Stout, *Olive Kitteridge*
2010	Paul Harding, *Tinkers*
2011	Jennifer Egan, *A Visit from the Goon Squad*

In 1948, the name of the category was changed from "The Novel" to "Fiction." 2. Awarded posthumously.

The Pulitzer Prize for History, 1917–2011

Year	Author, Title
1917	J. J. Jusserand, *With Americans of Past and Present Days*
1918	James Ford Rhodes, *A History of the Civil War*
1920	Justin H. Smith, *The War with Mexico*
1921	William Sowden Sims, with Burton J. Hendrick, *The Victory at Sea*
1922	James Truslow Adams, *The Founding of New England*
1923	Charles Warren, *The Supreme Court in United States History*
1924	Charles Howard McIlwain, *The American Revolution*
1925	Frederic L. Paxson, *A History of the American Frontier*
1926	Edward Channing, *The History of the United States*
1927	Samuel Flagg Bemis, *Pinckney's Treaty*
1928	Vernon Louis Parrington, *Main Currents in American Thought*
1929	Fred Albert Shannon, *The Organization and Administration of the Union Army, 1861–1865*
1930	Claude H. Van Tyne, *The War of Independence*
1931	Bernadotte E. Schmitt, *The Coming of the War: 1914*
1932	John J. Pershing, *My Experiences in the World War*
1933	Frederick J. Turner, *The Significance of Sections in American History*
1934	Herbert Agar, *The People's Choice*
1935	Charles McLean Andrews, *The Colonial Period of American History*
1936	Andrew C. McLaughlin, *The Constitutional History of the United States*
1937	Van Wyck Brooks, *The Flowering of New England*
1938	Paul Herman Buck, *The Road to Reunion 1856–1900*
1939	Frank Luther Mott, *A History of American Magazines*
1940	Carl Sandburg, *Abraham Lincoln: The War Years*
1941	Marcus Lee Hansen, *The Atlantic Migration, 1607–1860*
1942	Margaret Leech, *Reveille in Washington*
1943	Esther Forbes, *Paul Revere and the World He Lived In*
1944	Merle Curti, *The Growth of American Thought*
1945	Stephen Bonsal, *Unfinished Business*
1946	Arthur Meier Schlesinger Jr., *The Age of Jackson*
1947	James Phinney Baxter III, *Scientists Against Time*
1948	Bernard DeVoto, *Across the Wide Missouri*
1949	Roy Franklin Nichols, *The Disruption of American Democracy*
1950	Oliver W. Larkin, *Art and Life in America*
1951	R. Carlyle Buley, *The Old Northwest*
1952	Oscar Handlin, *The Uprooted*
1953	George Dangerfield, *The Era of Good Feelings*
1954	Bruce Catton, *A Stillness at Appomattox*
1955	Paul Horgan, *Great River: The Rio Grande in North American History*
1956	Richard Hofstadter, *The Age of Reform*
1957	George F. Kennan, *Russia Leaves the War: Soviet American Relations, 1917–1920*
1958	Bray Hammond, *Banks and Politics in America*
1959	Leonard D. White, with Miss Jean Schneider, *The Republican Era: 1869–1901*
1960	Margaret Leech, *In the Days of McKinley*
1961	Herbert Feis, *Between War and Peace: The Potsdam Conference*
1962	Lawrence H. Gipson, *The Triumphant Empire: Thunder Clouds in the West*
1963	Constance McLaughlin Green, *Washington, Village and Capital, 1800–1878*
1964	Sumner Chilton Powell, *Puritan Village*
1965	Irwin Unger, *The Greenback Era*
1966	Perry Miller[1], *Life of the Mind in America*
1967	William H. Goetzmann, *Exploration and Empire*
1968	Bernard Bailyn, *The Ideological Origins of the American Revolution*
1969	Leonard W. Levy, *Origins of the Fifth Amendment*
1970	Dean Acheson, *Present at the Creation*
1971	James MacGregor Burns, *Roosevelt, The Soldier of Freedom*
1972	Carl N. Degler, *Neither Black Nor White*
1973	Michael Kammen, *People of Paradox*
1974	Daniel J. Boorstin, *The Americans: The Democratic Experience*
1975	Dumas Malone, *Jefferson and His Time*
1976	Paul Horgan, *Lamy of Santa Fe*
1977	David M. Potter[1], *The Impending Crisis*
1978	Alfred D. Chandler Jr., *The Visible Hand: The Managerial Revolution in American Business*
1979	Don E. Fehrenbacher, *The Dred Scott Case*
1980	Leon F. Litwack, *Been in the Storm So Long*
1981	Lawrence A. Cremin, *American Education*
1982	C. Vann Woodward (ed.), *Mary Chesnut's Civil War*
1983	Rhys L. Isaac, *The Transformation of Virginia, 1740–1790*
1985	Thomas K. McCraw, *Prophets of Regulation*
1986	Walter A. McDougall, *The Heavens and the Earth: A Political History of the Space Age*
1987	Bernard Bailyn, *Voyagers to the West*
1988	Robert V. Bruce, *The Launching of Modern American Science 1846–1876*

Year	Author, Title
1989	Taylor Branch, *Parting the Waters*
	James M. McPherson, *Battle Cry of Freedom: The Civil War Era*
1990	Stanley Karnow, *In Our Image*
1991	Laurel Thatcher Ulrich, *A Midwife's Tale*
1992	Mark E. Neely Jr., *The Fate of Liberty*
1993	Gordon S. Wood, *The Radicalism of the American Revolution*
1995	Doris Kearns Goodwin, *No Ordinary Time: Franklin and Eleanor Roosevelt*
1996	Alan Taylor, *William Cooper's Town*
1997	Jack N. Rakove, *Original Meanings: Politics and Ideas in the Making of the Constitution*
1998	Edward J. Larson, *Summer for the Gods: The Scopes Trial and America's Continuing Debate Over Science and Religion*
1999	Edwin G. Burrows and Mike Wallace, *Gotham: A History of New York City to 1898*
2000	David M. Kennedy, *Freedom From Fear: The American People in Depression*

Year	Author, Title
2001	Joseph P. Ellis, *Founding Brothers: The Revolutionary Generation*
2002	Louis Menand, *The Metaphysical Club: A Story of Ideas in America*
2003	Rick Atkinson, *An Army at Dawn: The War in North Africa, 1942–1943*
2004	Steven Hahn, *A Nation Under Our Feet: Black Political Struggles in the Rural South from Slavery to the Great Migration*
2005	David Hackett Fischer, *Washington's Crossing*
2006	David M. Oshinsky, *Polio: An American Story*
2007	Gene Roberts and Hank Klibanoff, *The Race Beat*
2008	David Walker Howe, *What God Hath Wrought: The Transformation of America, 1815–1848*
2009	Annette Gordon-Reed, *The Hemingses of Monticello: An American Family*
2010	Liaquat Ahmed, *Lords of Finance: The Bankers Who Broke the World*
2011	Eric Foner, *The Fiery Trial: Abraham Lincoln and American Slavery*

Notes: No award given in 1919, 1984, or 1994. 1. Awarded posthumously.

The Pulitzer Prize for Biography/ Autobiography, 1917–2011

Year	Author, Title
1917	Laura E. Richards and Maude Howe Elliott, with Florence Howe Hall, *Julia Ward Howe*
1918	William Cabell Bruce, *Benjamin Franklin, Self-Revealed*
1919	Henry Adams, *The Education of Henry Adams*
1920	Albert J. Beveridge, *The Life of John Marshall*
1921	Edward Bok, *The Americanization of Edward Bok*
1922	Hamlin Garland, *A Daughter of the Middle Border*
1923	Burton J. Hendrick, *The Life and Letters of Walter H. Page*
1924	Michael Idvorsky Pupin, *From Immigrant to Inventor*
1925	M.A. DeWolfe Howe, *Barrett Wendell and His Letter*
1926	Harvey Cushing, *The Life of Sir William Osler*
1927	Emory Holloway, *Whitman*
1928	Charles Edward Russell, *The American Orchestra and Theodore Thomas*
1929	Burton J. Hendrick, *The Training of an American. The Earlier Life and Letters of Walter H. Page*
1930	Marquis James, *The Raven*
1931	Henry James, *Charles W. Eliot*
1932	Henry F. Pringle, *Theodore Roosevelt*
1933	Allan Nevins, *Grover Cleveland*
1934	Tyler Dennett, *John Hay*
1935	Douglas S. Freeman, *R.E. Lee*
1936	Ralph Barton Perry, *The Thought and Character of William James*
1937	Allan Nevins, *Hamilton Fish*

Year	Author, Title
1938	Odell Shepard, *Pedlar's Progress*
	Marquis James, *Andrew Jackson*
1939	Carl Van Doren, *Benjamin Franklin*
1940	Ray Stannard Baker, *Woodrow Wilson, Life and Letters, vols. 7 & 8*
1941	Ola Elizabeth Winslow, *Jonathan Edwards*
1942	Forrest Wilson, *Crusader in Crinoline*
1943	Samuel Eliot Morison, *Admiral of the Ocean Sea*
1944	Carleton Mabee, *The American Leonardo: The Life of Samuel F.B. Morse*
1945	Russell Blaine Nye, *George Bancroft*
1946	Linnie Marsh Wolfe, *Son of the Wilderness*
1947	William Allen White, *The Autobiography of William Allen White*
1948	Margaret Clapp, *Forgotten First Citizen: John Bigelow*
1949	Robert E. Sherwood, *Roosevelt and Hopkins*
1950	Samuel Flagg Bemis, *John Quincy Adams and the Foundations of American Foreign Policy*
1951	Margaret Louise Coit, *John C. Calhoun*
1952	Merlo J. Pusey, *Charles Evan Hughes*
1953	David J. Mays, *Edmund Pendleton 1721-1803*
1954	Charles A. Lindbergh, *The Spirit of St. Louis*
1955	William S. White, *The Taft Story*
1956	Talbot Faulkner Hamlin, *Benjamin Henry Latrobe*
1957	John F. Kennedy, *Profiles in Courage*
1958	Douglas Southall Freeman, John Alexander Carroll,

Year	Author, Title
	Mary Wells Ashworth, *George Washington, vols. 1–4*; and *vol. 7, written after Dr. Freeman's death in 1953.*
1959	Arthur Walworth, *Woodrow Wilson, American Prophet*
1960	Samuel Eliot Morison, *John Paul Jones*
1961	David Donald, *Charles Sumner and the Coming of the Civil War*
1962	No award
1963	Leon Edel, *Henry James*
1964	Walter Jackson Bate, *John Keats*
1965	Ernest Samuels, *Henry Adams*
1966	Arthur M. Schlesinger Jr., *A Thousand Days*
1967	Justin Kaplan, *Mr. Clemens and Mark Twain*
1968	George F. Kennan, *Memoirs*
1969	Benjamin Lawrence Reid, *The Man From New York: John Quinn and His Friends*
1970	T. Harry Williams, *Huey Long*
1971	Lawrance Thompson, *Robert Frost*
1972	Joseph P. Lash, *Eleanor and Franklin*
1973	W.A. Swanberg, *Luce and His Empire*
1974	Louis Sheaffer, *O'Neill, Son and Artist*
1975	Robert A. Caro, *The Power Broker*
1976	R.W.B. Lewis, *Edith Wharton: A Biography*
1977	John E. Mack, *A Prince of Our Disorder: The Life of T.E. Lawrence*
1978	Walter Jackson Bate, *Samuel Johnson*
1979	Leonard Baker, *Days of Sorrow and Pain*
1980	Edmund Morris, *The Rise of Theodore Roosevelt*
1981	Robert K. Massie, *Peter the Great*
1982	William S. McFeely, *Grant: A Biography*
1983	Russell Baker, *Growing Up*
1984	Louis R. Harlan, *Booker T. Washington*
1985	Kenneth Silverman, *The Life and Times of Cotton Mather*

Year	Author, Title
1986	Elizabeth Frank, *Louise Bogan: A Portrait*
1987	David J. Garrow, *Bearing the Cross: Martin Luther King, Jr. and the Southern Christian Leadership Conference*
1988	David Herbert Donald, *Look Homeward: A Life of Thomas Wolfe*
1989	Richard Ellmann[1], *Oscar Wilde*
1990	Sebastian de Grazia, *Machiavelli in Hell*
1991	Steven Naifeh, Gregory White Smith, *Jackson Pollock*
1992	Lewis B. Puller Jr., *Fortunate Son*
1993	David McCullough, *Truman*
1994	David Levering Lewis, *W.E.B. DuBois*
1995	Joan D. Hedrick, *Harriet Beecher Stowe*
1996	Jack Miles, *God: A Biography*
1997	Frank McCourt, *Angela's Ashes*
1998	Katharine Graham, *Personal History*
1999	A. Scott Berg, *Lindbergh*
2000	Stacy Schiff, *Véra (Mrs. Vladimir Nabokov)*
2001	David Levering Lewis, *W.E.B. DuBois (vol. 2)*
2002	David McCullough, *John Adams*
2003	Robert A. Caro, *Master of the Senate*
2004	William Taubman, *Khruschev: The Man and His Era*
2005	Mark Stevens, Annalyn Swan *de Kooning: An American Master*
2006	Kai Bird, Martin J. Sherwin, *American Prometheus: The Triumph and Tragedy of J. Robert Oppenheimer*
2007	Debby Applegate, *The Most Famous Man in America*
2008	John Matteson, *Eden's Outcasts: The Story of Louisa May Alcott and Her Father*
2009	Jon Meacham, *American Lion: Andrew Jackson in the White House*
2010	T.J. Stiles, *The First Tycoon: The Epic Life of Cornelius Vanderbilt*
2011	Ron Chernow, *Washington: A Life*

Note: 1. Awarded posthumously.

The Pulitzer Prize for Poetry, 1922–2011

Year	Author, Title
1922	Edward Arlington Robinson, *Collected Poems*
1923	Edna St. Vincent Millay, *The Ballad of the Harp-Weaver; A Few Figs from Thistles; Eight Sonnets in American Poetry, 1922, A Miscellany*
1924	Robert Frost, *New Hampshire: A Poem with Notes and Grace Notes*
1925	Edward Arlington Robinson, *The Man Who Died Twice*
1926	Amy Lowell[1], *What's O'Clock*
1927	Leonora Speyer, *Fiddler's Farewell*
1928	Edward Arlington Robinson, *Tristram*
1929	Stephen Vincent Benét, *John Brown's Body*

Year	Author, Title
1930	Conrad Aiken, *Selected Poems*
1931	Robert Frost, *Collected Poems*
1932	George Dillon, *The Flowering Stone*
1933	Archibald MacLeish, *Conquistador*
1934	Robert Hillyer, *Collected Verse*
1935	Audrey Wurdemann, *Bright Ambush*
1936	Robert P. Tristram Coffin, *Strange Holiness*
1937	Robert Frost, *A Further Range*
1938	Marya Zaturenska, *Cold Morning Sky*
1939	John Gould Fletcher, *Selected Poems*
1940	Mark Van Doren, *Collected Poems*
1941	Leonard Bacon, *Sunderland Capture*

Year	Author, Title
1942	William Rose Benét, *The Dust Which Is God*
1943	Robert Frost, *A Witness Tree*
1944	Stephen Vincent Benét[1], *Western Star*
1945	Karl Shapiro, *V-Letter and Other Poems*
1947	Robert Lowell, *Lord Weary's Castle*
1948	W.H. Auden, *The Age of Anxiety*
1949	Peter Viereck, *Terror and Decorum*
1950	Gwendolyn Brooks, *Annie Allen*
1951	Carl Sandburg, *Complete Poems*
1952	Marianne Moore, *Collected Poems*
1953	Archibald MacLeish, *Collected Poems 1917–1952*
1954	Theodore Roethke, *The Waking*
1955	Wallace Stevens, *Collected Poems*
1956	Elizabeth Bishop, *Poems—North & South*
1957	Richard Wilbur, *Things of This World*
1958	Robert Penn Warren, *Promises: Poems 1954-1956*
1959	Stanley Kunitz, *Selected Poems 1928–1958*
1960	W.D. Snodgrass, *Heart's Needle*
1961	Phyllis McGinley, *Times Three: Selected Verse From Three Decades*
1962	Alan Dugan, *Poems*
1963	William Carlos Williams, *Pictures from Breughel*
1964	Louis Simpson, *At the End of the Open Road*
1965	John Berryman, *77 Dream Songs*
1966	Richard Eberhart, *Selected Poems*
1967	Anne Sexton, *Live or Die*
1968	Anthony Hecht, *The Hard Hours*
1969	George Oppen, *Of Being Numerous*
1970	Richard Howard, *Untitled Subjects*
1971	William S. Merwin, *The Carrier of Ladders*
1972	James Wright, *Collected Poems*
1973	Maxine Kumin, *Up Country*
1974	Robert Lowell, *The Dolphins*
1975	Gary Snyder, *Turtle Island*
1976	John Ashberry, *Self-Portrait in a Convex Mirror*

Year	Author, Title
1977	James Merrill, *Divine Comedies*
1978	Howard Nemerov, *Collected Poems*
1979	Robert Penn Warren, *Now and Then*
1980	Donald Justice, *Selected Poems*
1981	James Schuyler, *The Morning of the Poem*
1982	Sylvia Plath, *The Collected Poems*
1983	Galway Kinnell, *Selected Poems*
1984	Mary Oliver, *American Primitive*
1985	Carolyn Kizer, *Yin*
1986	Henry Taylor, *The Flying Change*
1987	Rita Dove, *Thomas and Beulah*
1988	William Meredith, *Partial Accounts: New and Selected Poems*
1989	Richard Wilbur, *New and Collected Poems*
1990	Charles Simic, *The World Doesn't End*
1991	Mona Van Duyn, *Near Changes*
1992	James Tate, *Selected Poems*
1993	Louise Glück, *The Wild Iris*
1994	Yusef Komunyakaa, *Neon Vernacular*
1995	Philip Levine, *Simple Truth*
1996	Jorie Graham, *The Dream of the Unified Field*
1997	Lisel Mueller, *Alive Together: New and Selected Poems*
1998	Charles Wright, *Black Zodiac*
1999	Mark Strand, *Blizzard of One*
2000	C.K. Williams, *Repair*
2001	Stephen Dunn, *Different Hours*
2002	Carl Dennis, *Practical Gods*
2003	Paul Muldoon, *Moy Sand and Gravel*
2004	Franz Wright, *Walking to Martha's Vineyard*
2005	Ted Kooser, *Delights & Shadows*
2006	Claudia Emerson, *Late Wife*
2007	Natasha Trethewey, *Native Guard*
2008	Robert Hass, *Time and Materials*
2009	W.S. Merwin, *The Shadow Series*
2010	Rae Armantrout, *Versed*
2011	Kay Ryan, *The Best of It: New and Selected Poems*

Note: No award given in 1946. 1. Awarded posthumously.

The Pulitzer Prize for General Nonfiction, 1962–2011

Year	Author, Title
1962	Theodore H. White, *The Making of the President, 1960*
1963	Barbara W. Tuchman, *The Guns of August*
1964	Richard Hofstadter, *Anti-Intellectualism in American Life*
1965	Howard Mumford Jones, *O Strange New World*
1966	Edwin Way Teal, *Wandering Through Winter*
1967	David Brion Davis, *The Problem of Slavery in Western Culture*
1968	Will and Ariel Durant, *Rousseau and Revolution*

Year	Author, Title
1969	René Jules Dubos, *So Human An Animal* Norman Mailer, *The Armies of the Night*
1970	Erik H. Erikson, *Gandhi's Truth*
1971	John Toland, *The Rising Sun*
1972	Barbara W. Tuchman, *Stilwell and the American Experience in China, 1911–45*
1973	Robert Coles, *Children of Crisis, vols. 2 & 3* Frances Fitzgerald, *Fire in the Lake*
1974	Ernest Becker[1], *The Denial of Death*
1975	Annie Dillard, *Pilgrim at Tinker Creek*

Year	Author, Title
1976	Robert N. Butler, *Why Survive? Being Old in America*
1977	William N. Warner, *Beautiful Swimmers*
1978	Carl Sagan, *The Dragons of Eden*
1979	Edward O. Wilson, *On Human Nature*
1980	Douglas R. Hofstadter, *Gödel, Escher, Bach: an Eternal Golden Braid*
1981	Carl E. Schorske, *Fin-de Siècle Vienna: Politics and Culture*
1982	Tracy Kidder, *The Soul of A New Machine*
1983	Susan Sheehan, *Is There No Place on Earth for Me?*
1984	Paul Starr, *The Social Transformation of American Medicine*
1985	Studs Terkel, *The Good War*
1986	Joseph Lelyveld, *Move Your Shadow* J. Anthony Lukas, *Common Ground*
1987	David K. Shipler, *Arab and Jew*
1988	Richard Rhodes, *The Making of the Atomic Bomb*
1989	Neil Sheehan, *A Bright and Shining Lie*
1990	Dale Maharidge, Michael Williamson, *And Their Children After Them*
1991	Bert Holldobler, Edward O. Wilson, *The Ants*
1992	Daniel Yergin, *The Prize: The Epic Quest for Oil, Money and Power*
1993	Garry Wills, *Lincoln at Gettysburg*
1994	David Remnick, *Lenin's Tomb: The Last Days of the Soviet Empire*
1995	Jonathan Weiner, *The Beak of the Finch*

Year	Author, Title
1996	Tina Rosenberg, *The Haunted Land*
1997	Richard Kluger, *Ashes to Ashes*
1998	Jared Diamond, *Guns, Germs, and Steel: The Fates of Human Societies*
1999	John McPhee, *Annals of the Former World*
2000	John W. Dower, *Embracing Defeat: Japan in the Wake of World War II*
2001	Herbert P. Bix, *Hirohito and the Making of Modern Japan*
2002	Diane McWhorter, *Carry Me Home: Birmingham, Alabama, the Climactic Battle of the Civil Rights Revolution*
2003	Samantha Power, *"A Problem From Hell": America and the Age of Genocide*
2004	Anne Applebaum, *Gulag: A History*
2005	Steve Coll, *Ghost Wars*
2006	Caroline Elkins, *Imperial Reckoning: The Untold Story of Britain's Gulag in Kenya*
2007	Lawrence Wright, *The Looming Tower*
2008	Saul Friedlander, *The Years of Extermination: Nazi Germany and the Jews*
2009	Douglas A. Blackmon, *Slavery by Another Name: The Re-Enslavement of Black Americans from the Civil War to World War II*
2010	David E. Hoffman, *The Dead Hand: The Untold Story of the Cold War Arms Race and Its Dangerous Legacy*
2011	Siddhartha Mukherjee, *The Emperor of All Maladies: A Biography of Cancer*

1. Awarded posthumously.

The Pulitzer Prize for Music, 1943–2011

Year	Author, Title
1943	William Schuman, *Secular Cantata No. 2, A Free Song*
1944	Howard Hanson, *Symphony No. 4, Opus 34*
1945	Aaron Copland, *Appalachian Spring*
1946	Leo Sowerby, *The Canticle of the Sun*
1947	Charles Ives, *Symphony No. 3*
1948	Walter Piston, *Symphony No. 3*
1949	Virgil Thomson, Music for the film, *Louisiana Story*
1950	Gian-Carlo Menotti, Music for the opera *The Consul*
1951	Douglas S. Moore, Music for the opera, *Giants in the Earth*
1952	Gail Kubik, *Symphony Concertante*
1953	No award
1954	Quincy Porter, *Concerto for Two Pianos and Orchestra*
1955	Gian-Carlo Menotti, *The Saint of Bleecker Street* (opera)
1956	Ernest Toch, *Symphony No. 3*
1957	Norman Dello Joio, *Meditations on Ecclesiastes*

Year	Author, Title
1958	Samuel Barber, *Vanessa* (opera)
1959	John LaMontaine, *Concerto for Piano and Orchestra*
1960	Elliott Carter, *Second String Quartet*
1961	Walter Piston, *Symphony No. 7*
1962	Robert Ward, *The Crucible* (opera)
1963	Samuel Barber, *Piano Concerto No. 1*
1964	No award
1965	No award
1966	Leslie Bassett, *Variations for Orchestra*
1967	Leon Kirchner, *Quartet No. 3*
1968	George Crumb, *Echoes of Time and the River* orchestral suite
1969	Karel Husa, *String Quartet No. 3*
1970	Charles Wuorinen, *Time's Encomium*
1971	Mario Davidovsky, *Synchronisms No. 6 for Piano and Electronic Sound*
1972	Jacob Druckman, *Windows*

Year	Author, Title
1973	Elliott Carter, *String Quartet No. 3*
1974	Donald Martino, *Notturno (chamber music)*
1975	Dominick Argento, *From the Diary of Virginia Woolf*
1976	Ned Rorem, *Air Music: Ten Etudes for Orchestra*
1977	Richard Wernick, *Visions of Terror and Wonder*
1978	Michael Colgrass, *Deja Vu for Percussion Quartet and Orchestra*
1979	Joseph Schwantner, *Aftertones of Infinity*
1980	David Del Tredici, *In Memory of a Summer Day*
1981	No award
1982	Roger Sessions, *Concerto for Orchestra*
1983	Ellen Taaffe Zwilich, *Symphony No. 1*
1984	Bernard Rands, *"Canti del Sole" for Tenor and Orchestra*
1985	Stephen Albert, *Symphony RiverRun*
1986	George Perle, *Wind Quintet IV*
1987	John Harbison, *The Flight Into Egypt*
1988	William Bolcom, *12 New Etudes for Piano*
1989	Roger Reynolds, *Whispers Out of Time*
1990	Mel Powell, *Duplicates: A Concerto for Two Pianos and Orchestra*
1991	Shulammit Ran, *Symphony*

Year	Author, Title
1992	Wayne Peterson, *The Face of the Night, The Heart of the Dark*
1993	Christopher Rouse, *Trombone Concerto*
1994	Gunther Schuller, *Of Reminiscences and Reflections*
1995	Morton Gould, *Stringmusic*
1996	George Walker, *Lilacs*
1997	Wynton Marsalis, *Blood on the Fields*
1998	Aaron Jay Kernis, *String Quartet No.2*
1999	Melinda Wagner, *Concerto for Flute, Strings, and Percussion*
2000	Lewis Spratalan, *Life is a Dream, Opera in Three Acts: Act II, Convert Version*
2001	John Corigliano, *Symphony No. 2 for String Orchestra*
2002	Henry Brant, *Ice Field*
2003	John Adams, *On the Transmigration of Souls*
2004	Paul Moravec, *Tempest Fantasy*
2005	Steven Stucky, *Second Concerto for Orchestra*
2006	Yehudi Wyner, *Piano Concerto: 'Chiavi in Mano'*
2007	Ornette Coleman, *Sound Grammar*
2008	David Lang, *The Little Match Girl Passion*
2009	Steve Reich, *Double Sextet*
2010	Jennifer Higdon, *Violin Concerto*
2011	Zhou Long, *Madame White Snake*

The Nobel Prizes

First awarded in 1901, the Nobel Prizes were established through a bequest of $9.2 million from Alfred Bernhard Nobel (1833–96), a Swedish chemical engineer and the inventor of dynamite and other explosives, and by a gift from the Bank of Sweden. Nobel's will directed that the interest from the fund be divided annually among people who have made significant discoveries or inventions in the fields of chemistry, physics, physiology or medicine, and literature, as well as to that individual or group that has "done the most or the best work for fraternity between nations, for the abolition or reduction of standing armies and for the holding and promotion of peace congresses." In 1968, an additional prize for outstanding work in the economic sciences was established; it was first granted the following year.

Nobel Peace Prize Recipients

Year	Recipient
1901	Jean-Henri Dunant (Switzerland)
1902	Elie Ducommun (Switzerland)
1903	Sir William R. Cremer (U.K.)
1904	Institute of International Law
1905	Baroness Bertha S.F. von Suttner (Austria)
1906	Theodore Roosevelt (U.S.)
1907	Ernesto T. Moneta (Italy); Louis Renault (France)
1908	Klas P. Arnoldson (Sweden); Fredrik Bajer (Denmark)
1909	Auguste M.F. Beernaert (Belgium); Paul H.B.B. D'Estournelles de Constant (Baron Constant de Rebecque) (France)
1910	Permanent International Peace Bureau
1911	Tobias M.C. Asser (Netherlands); Alfred H. Fried (Austria)
1912	Elihu Root (U.S.)
1913	Henri Lafontaine (Belgium)
1914–1916	No awards given.
1917	International Committee of the Red Cross
1918	No award.
1919	Woodrow Wilson (U.S.)
1920	Léon Victor A. Bourgeois (France)
1921	Karl H. Branting (Sweden); Christian L. Lange (Norway)
1922	Fridtjof Nansen (Norway)
1923–24	No award.
1925	Sir Austen Chamberlain (U.K.); Charles G. Dawes (U.S.)
1926	Aristide Briand (France) and Gustav Stresemann (Germany)
1927	Ferdinand Buisson (France); Ludwig Quidde (Germany)
1928	No award.
1929	Frank B. Kellogg (U.S.)

1930 L.O. Nathan Söderblom (Sweden)
1931 Jane Addams (U.S.); Nicholas M. Butler (U.S.)
1932 No award.
1933 Sir Norman Angell (Ralph Lane) (U.K.)
1934 Arthur Henderson (U.K.)
1935 Carol von Ossietzky (Germany)
1936 Carlos Saavedra Lamas (Argentina)
1937 Lord Edgar Algernon R.G. Cecil (U.K.)
1938 Nansen International Office for Refugees
1939–1943 No awards given.
1944 International Committee of the Red Cross
1945 Cordell Hull (U.S.)
1946 Emily G. Balch (U.S.); John R. Mott (U.S.)
1947 The Friends Service Council (U.K.) and The American Friends Service Committee (U.S.)
1948 No award.
1949 Lord John Boyd Orr (U.K.)
1950 Ralph Bunche (U.S.)
1951 Léon Jouhaux (France)
1952 Albert Schweitzer (France)
1953 George C. Marshall (U.S.)
1954 Office of the U.N. High Commissioner for Refugees
1955–1956 No awards given.
1957 Lester B. Pearson (Canada)
1958 Georges Pire (Belgium)
1959 Philip J. Noel-Baker (U.K.)
1960 Albert J. Lutuli (South Africa)
1961 Dag Hammarskjöld (Sweden)
1962 Linus C. Pauling (U.S.)
1963 International Committee of the Red Cross and League of Red Cross Societies
1964 Martin Luther King, Jr. (U.S.)
1965 United Nations Children's Fund (UNICEF).
1966–1967 No awards given.
1968 René Cassin (France)
1969 International Labour Organization
1970 Norman Borlaug (U.S.)
1971 Willy Brandt (Federal Republic of Germany)
1972 No award
1973 Henry A. Kissinger (U.S.) and Le Duc Tho (Democratic Republic of Viet Nam)
1974 Seán MacBride (Ireland); Eisaku Sato (Japan)
1975 Andrei Sakharov (USSR)
1976 Betty Williams, Mairead Corrigan (Northern Ireland)
1977 Amnesty International
1978 Anwar el-Sadat (Egypt) and Menachem Begin (Israel)
1979 Mother Teresa (India)
1980 Adolfo Pérez Esquivel (Argentina)
1981 Office of the United Nations High Commissioner for Refugees
1982 Alva Myrdal (Sweden) and Alfonso Garcia Robles (Mexico)

1983 Lech Walesa (Poland)
1984 Desmond M. Tutu (South Africa)
1985 Int'l Physicians for the Prevention of Nuclear War
1986 Elie Wiesel (U.S.)
1987 Oscar Arias Sánchez (Costa Rica)
1988 United Nations Peacekeeping Forces
1989 Dalai Lama (Tibet)
1990 Mikhail Gorbachev (USSR)
1991 Aung San Suu Kyi (Myanmar)
1992 Rigoberta Menchú (Guatemala)
1993 Pres. F. W. de Klerk and Nelson Mandela (South Africa)
1994 Yitzhak Rabin (Israel), Shimon Peres (Israel), Yasir Arafat
1995 Joseph Rotblat (U.K. b. Poland)
1996 Bishop Carlos Ximenes Belo (Australia, b. East Timor) and Jose Ramos-Horta (East Timor)
1997 The International Campaign to Ban Landmines and Jody Williams (U.S.)
1998 John Hume (Ireland) and David Trimble (Ireland)
1999 Doctors Without Borders (Médecins Sans Frontières)
2000 Kim Dae Jung (South Korea)
2001 United Nations and Kofi Annan (Ghana)
2002 Jimmy Carter (U.S.)
2003 Shirin Ebadi (Iran)
2004 Wangari Muta Maathai
2005 International Atomic Energy Agency (IAEA) and Mohamed ElBaradei
2006 Muhammad Yunus and Grameen Bank
2007 Intergovernmental Panel on Climate Change and Al Gore, Jr. (U.S.)
2008 Martti Ahtisaari (Finland)
2009 Barack Obama (U.S.)
2010 Liu Xiaobo (China)

Nobel Prizes in Physiology or Medicine

1901 Emil A. von Behring (Germany) Marburg Univ.
1902 Sir Ronald Ross (U.K.) University College
1903 Niels R. Finsen (Denmark) Finsen Medical Light Institute
1904 Ivan P. Pavlov (Russia) Military Medical Academy
1905 Robert Koch (Germany) Institute for Infectious Diseases
1906 Camillio Golgi (Italy) Pavia Univ., and Santiago Ramon Y Cajal (Spain) Madrid Univ.
1907 Charles L.A. Laveran (France) Institute Pasteur
1908 Il'ja I. Mecnikov (Russia) Institut Pasteur (Paris), and Paul Ehrlich (Germany) Goettingen Univ. and Royal Institute for Experimental Therapy
1909 Emil R. Kocher (Switzerland) Berne Univ.
1910 Albrecht Kossel (Germany) Heidelberg Univ.
1911 Allvar Gullstrand (Sweden) Uppsala Univ.

1912 Alexis Carrel (France) Rockefeller Institute for Medical Research (New York)

1913 Charles R. Richet (France)

1914 Robert Bárány (Austria) Vienna Univ.

1915–1918 No awards

1919 Jules Bordet (Belgium) Brussels Univ.

1920 Schack A.S. Krogh (Denmark) Copenhagen Univ.

1921 No award

1922 Sir Archibald V. Hill (U.K.) London Univ.; Otto F. Meyerhof (Germany) Kiel Univ.

1923 Sir Frederick G. Banting (Canada) Toronto Univ. and John J.R. Macleod (Canada) Toronto Univ.

1924 Willem Einthoven (Netherlands) Leyden Univ.

1925 No award

1926 Johannes A.G. Fibiger (Denmark) Copenhagen Univ.

1927 Julius Wagner-Jauegg (Austria) Vienna Univ.

1928 Charles J.H. Nicolle (France) Institut Pasteur

1929 Christiaan Eijkman (Netherlands) Utrecht Univ.; Sir Frederick G. Hopkins (U.K.) Cambridge Univ.

1930 Karl Landsteiner (Austria) Rockefeller Institute of Medical Research (New York)

1931 Otto H. Warburg (Germany) Kaiser-Wilhelm Institut

1932 Sir Charles S. Sherrington (U.K.) Oxford Univ. and Lord Edgar D. Adrian (U.K.) Cambridge Univ.

1933 Thomas H. Morgan (U.S.) California Institute of Technology

1934 George H. Whipple (U.S.) Rochester Univ., George R. Minot (U.S.) Harvard Univ., and William P. Murphy (U.S.) Harvard Univ.

1935 Hans Spemann (Germany) Univ. of Freiburg

1936 Sir Henry H. Dale (U.K.) National Institute for Medical Research, and Otto Loewi (Austria) Graz Univ.

1937 Albert von Szent-Györgyi Nagyrapolt (Hungary) Szeged Univ.

1938 Corneille J.F. Heymans (Belgium) Ghent Univ.

1939 Gerhard Domagk (Germany) Munster Univ.

1940–1942 No awards given.

1943 Henrik C.P. Dam (Denmark) Polytechnic Institut; Edward A. Doisy (U.S.) St. Louis Univ.

1944 Joseph Erlanger (U.S.) Washington Univ. and Herbert S. Gasser (U.S.) Rockefeller Institute for Medical Research

1945 Sir Alexander Fleming (U.K.) London Univ., Sir B. Chain (U.K.) Oxford Univ., and Lord Howard W. Florey (U.K.) Oxford Univ.

1946 Hermann J. Muller (U.S.) Indiana Univ.

1947 Carl F. Cori (U.S.) Washington Univ. and his wife Gerty T. Cori (U.S.) Washington Univ.; Bernardo A. Houssay (Argentina) Institute of Biology and Experimental Medicine

1948 Paul H. Müller (Switzerland) Laboratory of the J.R. Geigy Dye-Factory Co.

1949 Walter R. Hess (Switzerland) Zurich Univ.; Antonio Caetano de Abreu F.E. Moniz (Portugal) Univ. of Lisbon

1950 Edward C. Kendall (U.S.) Mayo Clinic, Tadeus Reichstein (Switzerland) Basel Univ., and Philip S. Hench (U.S.) Mayo Clinic

1951 Max Theiler (Union of South Africa) Laboratories Division of Medicine and Public Health, Rockefeller Foundation (New York)

1952 Selman A. Waksman (U.S.) Rutgers Univ.

1953 Sir Hans A. Krebs (U.K., b. Germany) Sheffield Univ.; Fritz A. Lipmann (U.S., b. Germany) Harvard Medical School and Massachusetts General Hospital

1954 John F. Enders (U.S.) Harvard Medical School and Research Division of Infectious Diseases, Children's Medical Center; Thomas H. Weller (U.S.) Research Division of Infectious Diseases, Children's Medical Center; and Frederick C. Robbins (U.S.) Western Reserve Univ.

1955 Axel H.T. Theorell (Sweden) Nobel Medical Institute

1956 Andre F. Cournand (U.S., b. France) Cardio-Pulmonary Laboratory, Columbia Univ. Division. Bellevue Hospital; Werner Forssman (Germany) Mainz Univ. and Bad Kreuznach; and Dickinson W. Richards (U.S.) Columbia Univ.

1957 Daniel Bovet (Italy, b. Switzerland) Chief Institute of Public Health

1958 George W. Beadle (U.S.) California Institute of Technology, and Edward L. Tatum (U.S.) Rockefeller Institute for Medical Research; Joshua Lederberg (U.S.) Wisconsin Univ.

1959 Severo Ochoa (U.S.) New York Univ. College of Medicine, and Arthur Kornberg (U.S.) Stanford Univ.

1960 Sir Frank M. Burnet (Australia) Walter and Eliza Hall Institute for Medical Research, and Sir Peter B. Medawar (U.K.) Univ. College

1961 Georg von Békésy (U.S., b. Hungary) Harvard Univ.

1962 Francis H.C. Crick (U.K.) Institute of Molecular Biology, James D. Watson (U.S.) Harvard Univ., and Maurice H.F. Wilkins (U.K.) University of London

1963 Sir John E. Eccles (Australia) Australian National Univ. Sir Alan L. Hodgkin (U.K.) Cambridge Univ., and Sir Andrew F. Huxley (U.K.) University of London

1964 Konrad Block (U.S., b. Germany) Harvard Univ. and Feodor Lymen (Germany) Max-Planck-Institut fur Zellchemie

1965 Francois Jacob (France), André Lwoff (France), and Jacques Monod (France), Institut Pasteur

1966 Peyton Rous (U.S.) Rockefeller Univ.; Charles B. Huggins (U.S.) Ben May Laboratory for Cancer Research, Univ. of Chicago

1967 Ragnar Granit (Sweden, b. Finland) Karolinska Institutet, Haldan K. Hartline (U.S.) Rockefeller Univ., and George Wald (U.S.) Harvard Univ.

1968 Robert W. Holley (U.S.) Cornell Univ., Har G. Khorana (U.S., b. India) Univ. of Wisconsin, and Marshall W. Nirenberg (U.S.) National Institutes of Health

1969 Max Delbrück (U.S., b. Germany) California Institute of Technology, Alfred D. Hershey (U.S.) Carnegie Institution of Washington, and Salvador Luria (U.S., b. Italy) M.I.T.

1970 Sir Bernard Katz (U.K.) University College, Ulf von Euler (Sweden) Karolinska Institutet, and Julius Axelrod (U.S.) National Institutes of Health

1971 Earl W. Sutherland, Jr. (U.S.) Vanderbilt Univ.

1972 Gerald M. Edelman (U.S.) Rockefeller Univ. and Rodney R. Porter (U.K.) Oxford Univ.

1973 Karl von Frisch (W. Germany) Zoologisches Institut der Universitat Munchen; Konrad Lorenz (Austria) Osterreichische Akademie der Wissenschaften, Institut fur vergleichende Verhaltensforschung, and Nikolaas Tinbergen (U.K.) University Museum

1974 Albert Claude (Belgium) Université Catholique de Louvain, Christian de Duve (Belgium) Rockefeller Univ. (New York), and George E. Palade (U.S., b. Romania) Yale Univ.

1975 David Baltimore (U.S.) M.I.T., Renato Dulbecco (U.S., b. Italy) Imperial Cancer Research Fund Laboratory (London), and Howard M. Temin (U.S.) Univ. of Wisconsin

1976 Baruch S. Blumberg (U.S.) Institute for Cancer Research, and D. Carleton Gajdusek (U.S.) National Institutes of Health

1977 Roger Guillemin (U.S., b. France) Salk Institute, and Andrew V. Schally (U.S., b. Poland) Veterans Administration Hospital, New Orleans; Rosalyn Yalow (U.S.) Veterans Administration Hospital, Bronx

1978 Werner Arber (Switzerland) Biozentrum der Universitat, Daniel Nathans (U.S.) John Hopkins Univ., and Hamilton O. Smith (U.S.) John Hopkins Univ.

1979 Alan M. Cormack (U.S., b. South Africa) Tufts Univ., and Sir Godfrey N. Hounsfield (U.K.) Central Research Laboratories, EMI

1980 Baruj Benacerraf (U.S., b. Venezuela) Harvard Medical School; Jean Dausset (France) Université de Paris, Laboratoire Immuno-Hemetologie; and George D. Snell (U.S.) Jackson Laboratory

1981 Roger W. Sperry (U.S.) California Institute of Technology; David H. Hubel (U.S., b. Canada) Harvard Medical School, and Torsten T. Wiesel (Sweden) Harvard Medical School

1982 Sune K. Bergström (Sweden) Karolinska Institute, Bengt I. Samuelsson (Sweden) Karolinska Institute, and Sir John R. Vane (U.K.) Wellcome Research Laboratories

1983 Barbara McClintock (U.S.) Cold Spring Harbor Laboratory

1984 Niels K. Jerne (Denmark) and Georges J.F. Köhler (W. Germany) of the Basel Institute for Immunology; and César Milstein (U.K. and Argentina) Medical Research Council Laboratory of Molecular Biology (Cambridge)

1985 Michael S. Brown (U.S.), and Joseph L. Goldstein (U.S.), Univ. of Texas Health Science Center at Dallas

1986 Stanley Cohen (U.S.) Vanderbilt Univ., and Rita Levi-Montalcini (Italy and U.S.) Institute of Cell Biology of the C.N.R. (Rome)

1987 Susumu Tonegawa (U.S.) MIT

1988 Sir James W. Black (U.K.) King's College Hospital Medical School, Gertrude B. Elion (U.S.) Wellcome Research Laboratories, and George H. Hitchings (U.S.) Wellcome Research Laboratories

1989 J. Michael Bishop and Harold E. Varmus (U.S.) Univ. of California, San Francisco

1990 Joseph E. Murray (U.S.) Brigham and Women's Hospital (Boston), and E. Donnall Thomas (U.S.), Fred Hutchinson Cancer Research Center (Seattle)

1991 Erwin Neher (Germany) Max-Planck Institute for Biophysical Chemistry, Göttingen, and Bert Sakmann (Germany) Max-Planck Institute for Medical Research, Heidelberg,

1992 Edmond H. Fischer (U.S.) and Edwin G. Krebs (U.S.), both of the Univ. of Washington

1993 Richard J. Roberts (U.K.), New England Bio Labs, and Phillip A. Sharp (U.S.), MIT

1994 Alfred G. Gilman (U.S.) Univ. of Texas Southwestern Medical Center, and Martin Rodbell (U.S.) National Institute of Environmental Health Sciences

1995 Edward B. Lewis (U.S.) California Institute of Technology, Eric F. Wieschaus (U.S.) Princeton Univ., and Christiane Nüsslein-Volhard (Germany) Max-Planck Institute in Tübingen

1996 Peter C. Doherty (Australia) St. Jude's Medical Center in Memphis, and Rolf Zinkernagel (Switzerland) University of Zurich

1997 Stanley B. Prusiner (U.S.), Univ. of California

1998 Robert F. Furchgott (U.S.), SUNY Health Science Center; Louis J. Ignarro (U.S.), UCLA School of Medicine; and Ferid Murad (U.S.), Univ. of Texas

1999 Günter Blobel (U.S., b. Germany), Rockefeller Univ.

2000 Arvid Carlsson (Sweden), Univ. of Gothenburg; Paul Greengard (U.S.), Rockefeller Univ., N.Y.; and Eric Kandel (U.S.), Columbia Univ.

2001 Leland H. Hartwell (U.S.), Fred Hutchinson Cancer Research Center, Seattle, and R. Timothy Hunt (U.K.) and Sir Paul M. Nurse (U.K.)

2002 Sydney Brenner, (U.K.), Molecular Sciences Institute, H. Robert Horvitz, (U.S.), M.I.T., and John E. Sulston, (U.K.), Wellcome Trust Sanger Institute

2003 Paul C. Lauterbur (U.S.) and Peter Mansfield (U.K.)

2004 Richard Axel (U.S.) and Linda B. Buck (U.S.)

2005 Barry J. Marshall (Australia) and J. Robin Warren (Australia)

2006 Andrew Z. Fire (U.S.) and Craig C. Mello (U.S.)

2007 Mario R. Capecchi (U.S.) University of Utah, Sir Martin J. Evans (U.K.) Cardiff University, and Oliver Smithies (U.S.) UNC Chapel Hill

2008 Francoise Barre-Sinoussi (France) Institut Pasteur, Paris, and Luc Montagnier (France) World Foundatiion for AIDS Research and Prevention, Paris

2009 Elizabeth H. Blackburn (U.S.) University of California, San Francisco, Carol W. Greider (U.S.) John Hopkins University School of Medicine and Jack W. Szostak (U.S.) Harvard Medical School, Mass. General Hospital, Howard Hughes Medical Institute

2010 Robert G. Edwards (U.K.) University of Cambridge

Nobel Prizes in Economic Sciences

1969 Ragnar Frisch (Norway) Oslo Univ. and Jan Tinbergen (Netherlands) Netherlands School of Economics

1970 Paul A. Samuelson (U.S.) M.I.T.

1971 Simon Kuznets (U.S.) Harvard Univ.

1972 Sir John R. Hicks (U.K.) All Souls College, and Kenneth J. Arrow (U.S.) Harvard Univ.

1973 Wassily Leontief (U.S.) Harvard Univ.

1974 Gunnar Myrdal (Sweden), Friedrich A. von Hayek (U.K.)

1975 Leonid Kantorovich (USSR) Academy of Sciences, and Tjalling C. Koopmans (U.S.) Yale Univ.

1976 Milton Friedman (U.S.) Univ. of Chicago

1977 Bertil Ohlin (Sweden) Stockholm School of Economics, and James E. Meade (U.K.) Cambridge Univ.

1978 Herbert A. Simon (U.S.) Carnegie-Mellon Univ.

1979 Theodore W. Schultz (U.S.) Univ. of Chicago, and Sir Arthur Lewis (U.K.) Princeton Univ.

1980 Lawrence R. Klein (U.S.) Univ. of Pennsylvania

1981 James Tobin (U.S.) Yale Univ.

1982 George J. Stigler (U.S.) Univ. of Chicago

1983 Gerard Debreu (U.S.) Univ. of California

1984 Sir Richard Stone (U.K.) Cambridge Univ.

1985 Franco Modigliani (U.S.) M.I.T.

1986 James M Buchanan Jr. (U.S.) Center for Study of Public Choice

1987 Robert M. Solow (U.S.) M.I.T.

1988 Maurice Allais (France) Centre d'analyse économique

1989 Trygve Haavelmo (Norway) Univ. of Oslo

1990 Harry Markowitz (U.S.) Baruch College (of the City Univ. of New York; William F. Sharpe (U.S.) Stanford Univ.; and Merton Miller (U.S.) Univ. of Chicago

1991 Ronald H. Coase (U.K.) Univ. of Chicago Law School

1992 Gary S. Becker (U.S.), Univ. of Chicago

1993 Robert W. Fogel (U.S.), Univ. of Chicago, and Douglass C. North (U.S.), Washington Univ.

1994 John F. Nash (U.S.) Princeton Univ., John C., Harsanyi (U.S., b. Hungary) Univ. of California, and Reinhard Selten (Germany) Univ. of Bonn

1995 Robert E. Lucas, Jr., (U.S.) Univ. of Chicago

1996 James A. Mirrlees (U.K.) Cambridge, Univ. and William Vickrey (U.S., b. Canada), Columbia Univ.

1997 Robert Merton (U.S.), Harvard University, and Myron Scholes (U.S.), Stanford University

1998 Amartya Sen (India), Cambridge Univ. and Harvard Univ.

1999 Robert A. Mundell (U.S.,b. Canada), Columbia University

2000 James J. Heckman (U.S.), Univ. of Chicago and Daniel L. McFadden (U.S.), Univ. of California

2001 George A. Akerlof (U.S.) Univ. of California, A. Michael Spence (U.S.), Stanford Univ., and Joseph E. Stiglitz (U.S.), Columbia Univ.

2002 Daniel Kahneman, (U.S. and Israel), Princeton University and Vernon L. Smith, (U.S.), George Mason University

2003 Robert F. Engle (U.S.), New York University, and Clive W. Granger (U.K.)

2004 Finn E. Kydland (Norway) and Edward C. Prescott (U.S.)

2005 Robert J. Aumann (Israel) and Thomas C. Schelling (U.S.)

2006 Edmund S. Phelps (U.S.)

2007 Leonid Hurwicz (U.S.) University of Minnesota, Eric S. Maskin (U.S.) Institute for Advanced Study and Roger B. Myerson (U.S.) University of Chicago

2008 Paul Krugman (U.S.) Princeton University

2009 Elinor Ostrom (U.S.) Indiana University, Arizona State University and Oliver E. Williamson (U.S.) University of California, Berkeley

2010 Peter A. Diamond (U.S.) MIT, Dale T. Mortensen (U.S.) Northwestern University, Aarhus University, Denmark and Christopher A. Pissarides (Cyprus) London School of Economics

Nobel Prizes in Chemistry

1901 Jacobus H. Van't Holt (Netherlands) Berlin Univ.

1902 Hermann E. Fischer (Germany)

1903 Svante A. Arrhenius (Sweden) Stockholm Univ.

1904 Sir William Ramsay (U.K.) London Univ.

1905 Johann F.W.A. von Baeyer (Germany) Munich Univ.

1906 Henri Moissan (France) Sorbonne Univ.

1907 Eduard Buchner (Germany) Agricultural College

1908   Lord Ernest Rutherfold (U.K.) Victoria Univ.

1909   Wilhelm Ostwald (Germany) Leipzig Univ.

1910   Otto Wallach (Germany) Goettingen Univ.

1911   Marie Curie (France) Sorbonne Univ.

1912   Victor Grignard (France) Nancy Univ.; Paul Sabatier (France) Toulouse Univ.

1913   Alfred Werner (Switzerland) Zurich Univ.

1914   Theodore W. Richards (U.S.) Harvard Univ.

1915   Richard M. Willstätter (Germany) Munich Univ.

1916–1917   No awards given.

1918   Fritz Haber (Germany) Kaiser-Wilhelm Institut

1919   No award

1920   Walther H. Nernst (Germany) Berlin Univ.

1921   Frederick Soddy (U.K.) Oxford Univ.

1922   Francis W. Aston (U.K.) Cambridge Univ.

1923   Fritz Pregl (Austria) Graz Univ.

1924   No award

1925   Richard A. Zsigmondy (Germany) Goettingen Univ.

1926   The (Theodor) Svedberg (Sweden) Uppsala Univ.

1927   Heinrich O. Wieland (Germany) Munich Univ.

1928   Adolf O.R. Windaus (Germany) Goettingen Univ.

1929   Sir Arthur Harden (U.K.) London Univ., Hans K.A. von Euler-Chelpin (Sweden)

1930   Hans Fischer (Germany) Institute of Technology

1931   Carl Bosch (Germany) Heidelberg Univ. I.G. Farbenindustrie A.G., and Fredrich Bergius (Germany) Heidelberg Univ. and I.G. Farbenindustrie A.G.

1932   Irving Langmuir (U.S.) General Electric Co.

1933   No award

1934   Harold C. Urey (U.S.) Columbia Univ.

1935   Frédéric Joliot and Iréne Joliot-Curie, (France) Institut du Radium

1936   Petrus (Peter) J.W. Debye (Netherlands) Berlin Univ. and Kaiser-Wilhelm-Institut (now Max-Planck-Institut)

1937   Sir Walter N. Haworth (U.K.) Birmingham Univ.; Paul Karrer (Switzerland) Zurich Univ.

1938   Richard Kuhn (Germany) Heidelberg Univ. and Kaiser-Wilhelm-Institut (now Max-Planck-Institut)

1939   Adolf F.J. Butenandt (Germany) Berlin Univ. and Kaiser-Wilhelm-Institut (now Max-Planck-Institut); Leopold Ruzicka (Switzerland) Federal Institute of Technology

1940–1942   No awards

1943   George de Hevesy (Hungary) Stockholm Univ.

1944   Otto Hahn (Germany) Kaiser-Wilhelm-Institut (now Max-Planck-Institut)

1945   Artturi I. Virtanen (Finland) Helsinki Univ.

1946   James B. Sumner (U.S.) Cornell Univ.; John H. Northrop (U.S.) Rockefeller Institute for Medical Research

1947   Sir Robert Robinson (U.K.) Oxford Univ.

1948   Arne W.K. Tiselius (Sweden) Uppsala Univ.

1949   William F. Giauque (U.S.) Univ. of California, Berkeley

1950   Otto P.H. Diels (Germany) Kiel Univ. and Kurt Alder (Germany) Cologne Univ.

1951   Edwin M. McMillan (U.S.) and Glenn T. Seaborg (U.S.) both of Univ. of California, Berkeley

1952   Archer J.P. Martin (U.K.) Nations Institute for Medical Research, and Richard L.M. Synge (U.K.) Rowett Research Institute (Scotland)

1953   Herman Staudinger (Germany) State Research Institute for Macromolecular Chemistry

1954   Linus C. Pauling (U.S.) California Institute of Technology

1955   Vincent du Vigneaud (U.S.) Cornell Univ.

1956   Sir Cyril N. Hinshelwood (U.K.) Oxford Univ. and Nikolaj N. Semenov (USSR) Institute for Chemical Physics of the Academy of Sciences of the USSR

1957   Lord Alexander R. Todd (U.K.) Cambridge Univ.

1958   Frederick Sanger (U.K.) Cambridge Univ.

1959   Jaroslav Heyrovsky (Czechoslovakia) Polaro-Institute of the Czechoslovakia Academy of Science

1960   Willard F. Libby (U.S.) Univ. of California, Los Angeles

1961   Melvin Calvin (U.S.) Univ. of California, Berkeley

1962   Max F. Perutz (U.K.) Laboratory of Molecular Biology, and Sir John C. Kendrew (U.K.) Laboratory of Molecular Biology

1963   Karl Ziegler (Germany) Max-Planck-Institute for Carbon Research, and Giulio Natta (Italy) Institute of Technology

1964   Dorothy C. Hodgkin (U.K.) Royal Society, Oxford Univ.

1965   Robert B. Woodward (U.S.) Harvard Univ.

1966   Robert S. Mulliken (U.S.) Univ. of Chicago

1967   Manfred Eigen (W. Germany) Max-Planck-Institut, Ronald G.W. Norrish (U.K.) Institute of Physical Chemistry, and Sir George Porter (U.K.) The Royal Institution

1968   Lars Onsager (U.S.) Yale Univ.

1969   Sir Derek H.R. Barton (U.K.) Imperial College of Science and Technology, and Odd Hassel (Norway) Kjemisk Institut

1970   Luis F. Leloir (Argentina) Institute for Biochemical Research

1971   Gerhard Herzberg (Canada) National Research Council of Canada

1972   Christian B. Anfinsen (U.S.) National Institutes of Health; Stanford Moore (U.S.) Rockefeller Univ. and William H. Stein (U.S.) Rockefeller Univ.

1973   Ernst O. Fischer (W. Germany) Technical Univ. of Munich, and Sir Geoffrey Wilkinson (U.K.) Imperial College

1974   Paul J. Flory (U.S.) Stanford Univ.

1975   Sir John W. Cornforth (Australia and U.K.) Univ. of Sussex; Vladimir Prelog (Switzerland) Eidgenossische Technische Hochschule

1976 William N. Lipscomb (U.S.) Harvard Univ.

1977 Ilya Prigogine (Belgium) Université Libre de Bruxelles, (Univ. of Texas, U.S.)

1978 Peter D. Mitchell (U.K.) Glynn Research Laboratories

1979 Herbert C. Brown (U.S.) Purdue Univ., and Georg Wittig (Germany) Univ. of Heidelberg

1980 Paul Berg (U.S.) Stanford Univ.; Walter Gilbert (U.S.) Biological Laboratories, and Frederick Sanger (U.K.) MRC Laboratory of Molecular Biology

1981 Kenichi Fukui (Japan) Kyoto Univ. and Roald Hoffman (U.S.) Cornell Univ.

1982 Aaron Klug (U.K.) MRC Laboratory of Molecular Biology

1983 Henry Taube (U.S.) Stanford Univ.

1984 Robert B. Merrifield (U.S.) Rockefeller Univ.

1985 Herbert A. Hauptman (U.S.) Medical Foundation of Buffalo, and Jerome Karle (U.S.) U.S. Naval Research Laboratory

1986 Dudley R. Herschbach (U.S.) Harvard Univ., Yuan T. Lee (U.S.) Univ. of California, and John C. Polanyi (Canada) Univ. of Toronto

1987 Donald J. Cram (U.S.) University of California, Los Angeles, Jean-Marie Lehn (France) Université Louis Pasteur, and Charles J. Pedersen (U.S.) Du Pont Laboratory

1988 Johann Deisenhofer (U.S.) Howard Hughes Medical Institute, Robert Huber (W. Germany) Max-Planck-Institut, and Hartmut Michel (W. Germany) Max-Planck-Institut

1989 Sidney Altman (U.S.) Yale Univ., and Thomas Cech (U.S.) Univ. of Colorado

1990 Elias James Corey (U.S.) Harvard Univ.

1991 Richard R. Ernst (Switzerland) Eidgenössische Technische Hochschule, Zurich

1992 Rudolph A. Marcus (U.S., b. Canada), Cal Tech.

1993 Kary B. Mullis (U.S.); and Michael Smith (Canada), Univ. of British Columbia

1994 George A. Olah (U.S., b. Hungary) Univ. of Southern California

1995 F. Sherwood Roland (U.S.) Univ. of California-Irvine, Mario Molina (U.S.) M.I.T., and Paul Crutzen (Netherlands) Max Planck Institute for Chemistry

1996 Robert F. Curl, Jr., (U.S.) and Richard E. Smalley (U.S.), of Rice University, and Harold W. Kroto (U.K.) of Univ. of Sussex

1997 Paul D. Boyer (U.S.), UCLA and John E. Walker (U.K.), Medical Research Council Laboratory of Molecular Biology; Jens C. Skou (Denmark), Aarhus Univ.

1998 Walter Kohn (U.S., b. Austria), Univ. of California, Santa Barbara; John A. Pople (U.S., b U.K.), Northwestern Univ.

1999 Ahmed H. Zewail (U.S., b. Egypt), CalTech,

2000 Alan J. Heeger (U.S.), Univ. of California at Santa Barbara; Alan G. MacDiarmid (U.S.), Univ. of Pennsylvania; and Hideki Shirakawa (Japan), Univ. of Tsukuba

2001 William S. Knowles (U.S.) and Ryoji Noyori, (Japan), Nagoya Univ.; K. Barry Sharpless (U.S.), Scripps Research Institute, La Jolla, Calif.

2002 John B. Fenn, (U.S.), Virginia Commonwealth University, and Koichi Tanaka, (Japan), Shimadzu Corp.; and Kurt Wüthrich, (Switzerland), Swiss Federal Institute of Technology Zürich, and The Scripps Research Institute, La Jolla, Calif.

2003 Peter Agre (U.S.), Johns Hopkins Univ.; Koichi Tanaka (U.S.), Rockefeller Univ.

2004 Aaron Ciechanover (Israel), Avram Hershko (Israel), and Irwin Rose (U.S.)

2005 Yves Chauvin (France), Robert H. Grubbs (U.S.) and Richard R. Schrock (U.S.)

2006 Roger D. Kornberg (U.S.)

2007 Gerhard Ertl (Germany) Fritz-Haber-Institut der Max-Planck-Gesellschaft

2008 Osamu Shimomura (Japan) Marine Biological Laboratory, Woods Hole, MA and Boston University, Martin Chalfie (U.S.) Columbia University and Roger Y. Tsein (U.S.) University of California at San Diego

2009 Venkatraman Ramakrishnan (U.K.) MRC Laboratory of Molecular Biology, Thomas A. Steitz (U.S.) Yale University Howard Hughes Medical Institute and Ada E. Yonath (Israel) Weizmann Institute of Science

2010 Richard F. Heck (U.S.) University of Delaware, Ei-ichi Negishi (China) Purdue University and Akira Suzuki (Japan) Hokkaido University

Nobel Prizes in Physics

1901 Wilhelm C. Röntgen (Germany) Munich Univ.

1902 Hendrik A. Lorentz (Netherlands) Leyden Univ., and Pieter Zeeman (Netherlands) Amsterdam Univ.

1903 Antoine H. Becquerel (France) Ecole Polytechnique; Pierre Curie (France) Municipal School of Industrial Physics and Chemistry and his wife, Marie Curie, (France, b. Poland)

1904 Lord Rayleigh (John W. Strutt) (U.K.) Royal Institution of U.K.

1905 Philipp E.A. Lenard (Germany) Kiel Univ.

1906 Sir Joseph J. Thomas (U.K.) Cambridge Univ.

1907 Albert A. Michelson (U.S.) Univ. of Chicago

1908 Gabriel Lippman (France) Sorbonne Univ.

1909 Guglielmo Marconi (Italy) Marconi Wireless Telegraph Co., Ltd., and Carl F. Braun (Germany) Strasbourg Univ.

1910 Johannes D. van der Waals (Netherlands) Amsterdam Univ.

1911 Wilhelm Wien (Germany) Würzburg Univ.

1912 Nils G. Dalén (Sweden) Swedish Gas-Accumulator Co.

1913 Heike Kamerlingh-Onnes (Netherlands) Leyden Univ.

1914 Max von Laue (Germany) Frankfurt-am-Main Univ.

1915 Sir William Henry Bragg (U.K.) London Univ. and his son Sir William Lawrence Bragg (U.K.) Victoria Univ.

1916 No award.

1917 Charles G. Barkla (U.K.) Edinburgh Univ.

1918 Max K.E.L. Planck (Germany) Berlin Univ.

1919 Johannes Stark (Germany) Greifswald Univ.

1920 Charles E. Guillaume (Switzerland) International Bureau of Weights and Measurers

1921 Albert Einstein (Germany) Kaiser-Wilhelm-Institut für Physik (now Max-Panck-Institut)

1922 Niels Bohr (Denmark) Copenhagen Univ.

1923 Robert A. Millikan (U.S.) California Institute of Technology)

1924 Karl M.G. Siegbahn (Sweden) Uppsala Univ.

1925 James Franck (Germany) Goettingen Univ., and Gustav Hertz (Germany) Halle Univ.

1926 Jean B. Perrin (France) Sorbonne Univ.

1927 Arthur H. Compton (U.S.) Univ. of Chicago; Charles T.R. Wilson (U.K.) Cambridge Univ.

1928 Sir Own W. Richardson (U.K.) London Univ.

1929 Prince Louis-Victor de Broglie (France) Sorbonne Univ.

1930 Sir Chandrasekhara V. Raman (India) Calcutta Univ.

1931 No award.

1932 Werner Heisenberg (Germany) Leipzig Univ.

1933 Edwin Schrödinger (Austria) Berlin Univ. and Paul A.M. Dirac (U.K.) Cambridge Univ.

1934 No award

1935 Sir James Chadwick (U.K.) Liverpool Univ.

1936 Victor F. Hess (Austria) Innsbruck Univ.; Carl D. Anderson (U.S.) California Institute of Technology

1937 Clinton J. Davisson (U.S.) Bell Telephone Laboratories, and Sir George P. Thomson (U.K.) London Univ.

1938 Enrico Fermi (Italy) Rome Univ.

1939 Ernest O. Lawrence (U.S.) Univ. of California, Berkeley

1940–1942 No awards given.

1943 Otto Stern (U.S.) Carnegie Institute of Technology

1944 Isidor I. Rabi (U.S.) Columbia Univ.

1945 Wolfgang Pauli (Austria) Princeton Univ.

1946 Percy W. Bridgman (U.S.) Harvard Univ.

1947 Sir Edward V. Appleton (U.K.) Dept. of Scientific and Industrial Research

1948 Lord Patrick M.S. Blackett (U.K.) Victoria Univ.

1949 Hideki Yukawa (Japan) Kyoto Imperial Univ.

1950 Cecil F. Powell (U.K.) Bristol Univ.

1951 Sir John D. Cockcroft (U.K.) Atomic Energy Research Establishment, and Ernest T.S. Walton (Ireland) Dublin Univ.

1952 Felix Block (U.S.) Stanford Univ., and Edward M. Purcell (U.S.) Harvard Univ.

1953 Frits (Frederik) Zernike (Netherlands) Groningern Univ.

1954 Max Born (U.K.) Edinburgh Univ.; Walther Bothe (Germany) Heidelbery Univ., Max-Planck-Institut

1955 Willis E. Lamb (U.S.) Stanford Univ.; Polykarp Kusch (U.S.) Columbia Univ.

1956 William Shockley (U.S. Semiconductor Laboratory of Beckman Instruments, Inc.), John Bardeen (U.S.) Univ. of Illinois, and Walter H. Brattain (U.S.) Bell Telephone Laboratories

1957 Chen N. Yang (China) Institute for Advanced Study (Princeton, NJ) and Tsung-Dao Lee (China) Columbia Univ.

1958 Pavel A. Cherenkov (USSR) Physics Institute of USSR Academy of Sciences, Il'ja M.Frank (USSR) Academy of Sciences, and Igor J. Tamm (USSR) Univ. of Moscow and Physics Institute of USSR Academy of Sciences

1959 Emillio G. Sergè (U.S.) Univ. of California, Berkeley, and Owen Chamberlain (U.S.) Univ. of California, Berkeley

1960 Donald A. Glaser (U.S.) Univ. of California, Berkeley

1961 Robert Hofstadter (U.S.) Stanford Univ.; Rudolf L. Mössbauer (Germany) Technische Hochschule (Munich), and California Institute of Technology

1962 Lev D. Landau (USSR) Academy of Sciences

1963 Eugene P. Wigner (U.S.) Princeton Univ.; Maria Goeppert-Mayer (U.S.) Univ. of California, La Jolla, and J. Hans D. Jensen (Germany) Univ. of Heidelberg

1964 Charles H. Townes (U.S.) M.I.T., Nikolai G. Basov (USSR) Lebedev Institute for Physics, and Aleksandre M. Prochorov (USSR) Lebedev Institute for Physics

1965 Schin'ichiro Tomonaga (Japan) Toyko Univ., Julian Schwinger (U.S.) Harvard Univ., and Richard P. Feynman (U.S.) California Institute of Technology

1966 Alfred Kastier (France) Ecole Normale Supérieure, Université de Paris

1967 Hans A. Bethe (U.S.) Cornell Univ.

1968 Luis W. Alvarez (U.S.) Univ. of California, Berkeley

1969 Murray Gell-Mann (U.S.) California Institute of Technology

1970 Hannes Alfvén (Sweden) Royal Institute of Technology; Louis Neel (France) Univ. of Grenoble

1971 Dennis Gabor (U.K.) Imperial College of Science and Technology

1972 John Bardeen (U.S.) Univ. of Illinois, Leon N. Cooper (U.S.) Brown Univ., and J. Robert Schrieffer (U.S.) Univ. of Pennsylvania

1973 Leo Esaki (Japan) IBM Thomas J. Watson Research Center (New York), and Ivar Giaever (U.S.) General Electric Co.; Brian D. Josephson (U.K.) Cambridge Univ.

1974 Sir Martin Ryle (U.K.) and Antony Hewish (U.K.), both of Cambridge Univ.

1975 Aage Bohr (Denmark) Niels Bohr Institute, Ben Mottelson (Denmark) Nordita, and James Rainwater (U.S.) Columbia Univ.

1976 Burton Richter (U.S.) Stanford Linear Accelerator Center, and Samuel C.C. Ting (U.S.) M.I.T.

1977 Philip W. Anderson (U.S.) Bell Laboratories, Sir Nevill F. Mott (U.K.) Cambridge Univ. and John H. van Vleck (U.S.) Harvard Univ.

1978 Peter L. Kapitsa (USSR) Academy of Sciences; Arno A. Penzias (U.S.) Bell Laboratories, and Robert W. Wilson (U.S.) Bell Laboratories

1979 Sheldon L. Glashow (U.S.) Lyman Laboratory, Harvard Univ., Abdus Salam (Pakistan) International Centre for Theoretical Physics (Italy) and Imperial College of Science and Technology (London), and Steven Weinberg (U.S.) Harvard Univ.

1980 James W. Cronin (U.S.) Univ. of Chicago, and Val L. Fitch (U.S.) Princeton Univ.

1981 Nicolaas Bloembergen (U.S.) Harvard Univ., and Arthur L. Schawlow (U.S.) Stanford Univ.; Kai M. Siegbahn (Sweden) Uppsala Univ.

1982 Kenneth G. Wilson (U.S.) Cornell Univ.

1983 Subrahmanyan Chandrasekhar (U.S.) Univ. of Chicago; William A. Fowler (U.S.) California Institute of Technology

1984 Carlo Rubbia (Italy) CERN (Switzerland), and Simon van der Meer (Netherlands) CERN (Switzerland)

1985 Klaus von Klitzing (W. Germany) Max-Planck-Institut for Solid State Research

1986 Ernst Ruska (W. Germany) Fritz-Haber-Institut der Max-Planck-Gesellschaft; Gerd Binnig (W. Germany) IBM Zurich Research Laboratory and Heinrich Rohrer (Switzerland) IBM Zurich Research Laboratory

1987 Georg J. Bednorz (Switzerland) IBM Zurich research Laboratory, and Dr. K. Alex Müller (Switzerland) IBM Zurich Research Laboratory

1988 Leon M. Lederman (U.S.) Fermi National Accelerator Laboratory, Melvin Schwartz (U.S.) Digital Pathways, Inc., and Jack Steinberger (Switzerland)

1989 Norman R. Ramsey (U.S.) Harvard Univ.; Hans G. Dehmelt (U.S.) Univ. of Washington, and Wolfgang Paul (W. Germany) Univ. of Bonn

1990 Richard E. Taylor (Can.), Stanford U.; Jerome I. Friedman (U.S.) MIT; and Henry W. Kendall (U.S.) MIT

1991 Pierre-Gilles de Gennes (France), Collège de France, Paris

1992 George Charpak (France, b. Poland), CERN

1993 Joseph H. Taylor (U.S.), Princeton Univ., and Russel A. Hulse (U.S.), Princeton Plasma Physics Laboratory

1994 Clifford G. Shull (U.S.) MIT, and Bertram N. Brockhouse (Canada) McMaster Univ.

1995 Martin L. Perl, (U.S.) Stanford Univ,, and Frederick Reines (U.S.) Los Alamos National Laboratory

1996 Robert C. Richardson (U.S.) and David M. Lee (U.S.) of Cornell Univ., and Douglas S. Osheroff (U.S.) Stanford Univ.

1997 Steven Chu (U.S.) Stanford Univ., Claude Cohen-Tannoudji (France), Collège de France, and William D. Phillips (U.S.), National Institute of Standards and Technology

1998 Robert B. Laughlin (U.S.), Stanford Univ., Horst L. Störmer (U.S.), Bell Laboratories; Daniel Tsui (U.S.), Princeton Univ.

1999 Gerardus 't Hooft (Netherlands), Univ. of Utrecht, and Martinus J.G. Veltman (Netherlands) Univ. of Michigan

2000 Jack S. Kilby (U.S.), Texas Instruments; Zhores I. Alferov (Russia), A.F. Ioffe Physico-Technical Institute, St. Petersburg, and Herbert Kroemer, (U.S.), Univ. of California at Santa Barbara

2001 Eric A. Cornell (U.S.) and Carl E. Wieman (U.S.) both of the Joint Institute for Laboratory Astrophysics, Boulder, Colo., and Wolfgang Ketterle (Germany), M.I.T.

2002 Raymond Davis Jr., (U.S.), University of Pennsylvania and Masatoshi Koshiba, (Japan), University of Tokyo; and Riccardo Giacconi, (U.S., B. Italy), University of Milan

2003 Alexei Abrikosov (U.S. and Russia), Argonne (Illinois) National Laboratory, Vitaly L. Ginzburg (Russia), P.N. Ledbedev Physical Institute, Moscow, and Anthony J. Leggett (U.S. and U.K.), Univ. of Illinois

2004 David J. Gross (U.S.), H. David Politzer (U.S.), and Frank Wilczek (U.S.)

2005 Roy J. Glauber (U.S.), John L. Hall (U.S.) and Theodor W. Hänsch (Germany)

2006 John C. Mather (U.S.) and George F. Smoot (U.S.)

2007 Albert Fret (France) Universite Paris-Sud, Orsay, France and Peter Grunberg (Germany) Forschungs-zentrum Julich, Julich, Germany

2008 Yoichiro Nambu (U.S.) Enrico Fermi Institute, Chicago, Makoto Kobayashi (Japan) High Energy Accelerator Research Organization, Tsukuba, Japan and Toshihide Maskawa (Japan) Kyoto University

2009 Charles K. Kao (China) Chinese University of Hong Kong, Willard S. Boyle (Canada) and George E. Smith (U.S.) Bell Laboratories

2010 Andre Geim (Russia) and Konstantin Novoselov (Russia) both of University of Manchester, England

Nobel Prizes in Literature

1901 Sully Prudhomme (France)

1902 Christian M.T. Mommsen (Germany)

1903 Bjørstjerne M. Bjørnson (Norway)

1904 Frédéric Mistral (France); José Echegaray y Eizaguirre (Spain)

1905 Henryk Sienkiewicz (Poland)

1906 Giosué Carducci (Italy)
1907 Rudyard Kipling (U.K.)
1908 Rudolf C. Eucken (Germany)
1909 Selma O.L. Lagerlöf (Sweden)
1910 Paul J.L. Heyse (Germany)
1911 Count Maurice (Mooris) P.M.B. Maeterlinck (Belgium)
1912 Gerhart J.R. Hauptmann (Germany)
1913 Rabindranath Tagore (India)
1915 Romain Rolland (France)
1916 Carl G.V. von Heidenstam (Sweden)
1917 Karl A. Gjellerup (Denmark); Henrik Pontoppidan (Denmark)
1919 Carl F.G. Spitteler (Switzerland)
1920 Knut P. Hamsun (Norway)
1921 Anatole France (France)
1922 Jacinto Benavente (Spain)
1923 William Butler Yeats (Ireland)
1924 Wladyslaw S. Reymont (Poland)
1925 George Bernard Shaw (U.K.)
1926 Grazia Deledda (pen name of Grazia Madesani (Italy)
1927 Henri Bergson (France)
1928 Sigrid Undset (Norway)
1929 Thomas Mann (Germany)
1930 Sinclair Lewis (U.S.)
1931 Erik A. Karlfeldt (Sweden)
1932 John Galsworthy (U.K.)
1933 Ivan A. Bunin (stateless domicile in France)
1934 Luigi Pirandello (Italy)
1936 Eugene G. O'Neill (U.S.)
1937 Roger Martin du Gard (France)
1938 Pearl Buck (pen name of Pearl Walsh) (U.S.)
1939 Frans E. Sillanpää (Finland)
1944 Johannes V. Jensen (Denmark)
1945 Gabriela Mistral (Chile)
1946 Hermann Hesse (Switzerland)
1947 André P.G. Gide (France)
1948 Thomas S. Eliot (U.K.)
1949 William Faulkner (U.S.)
1950 Earl (Bertrand) Russell (U.K.)
1951 Pär Fabian Lägerkvist (Sweden)
1952 François Mauriac (France)
1953 Sir Winston L.S. Churchill (U.K.)
1954 Ernest M. Hemingway (U.S.)
1955 Halldór K. Laxness (Iceland)
1956 Juan R. Jiménez (Puerto Rico, b. Spain)
1957 Albert Camus (France)
1958 Boris L. Pasternak (U.S.S.R.)
1959 Salvatore Quasimodo (Italy)
1960 Saint-John Perse (France)
1961 Ivo Andric (Yugoslavia)

1962 John Steinbeck (U.S.)
1963 Giorgos Seferis (Greece)
1964 Jean-Paul Sartre (France)
1965 Michail A. Sholokhov (U.S.S.R.)
1966 Shmuel U. Agnon (Israel); Nelly Sachs (Germany)
1967 Miguel A. Asturias (Guatemala)
1968 Yasunari Kawabata (Japan)
1969 Samuel Beckett (Ireland)
1970 Alexander Solzhenitsyn (U.S.S.R.)
1971 Pablo Neruda (Chile)
1972 Heinrich Böll (West Germany)
1973 Patrick White (Australia, b. U.K.)
1974 Eyvind Johnson (Sweden); Harry Martinson (Sweden)
1975 Eugenio Montale (Italy)
1976 Saul Bellow (U.S.)
1977 Vincente Aleixandre (Spain)
1978 Isaac Bashevis Singer (U.S., b. Poland)
1979 Odysseus Elytis (Greece)
1980 Czeslaw Milosz (U.S. and Poland)
1981 Elias Canetti (U.K., b. Bulgaria)
1982 Gabriel García Marquez (Colombia)
1983 William Golding (U.K.)
1984 Jaroslav Seifert (Czechoslovakia)
1985 Claude Simon (France)
1986 Wole Soyinka (Nigeria)
1987 Joseph Brodsky (U.S., b. U.S.S.R.)
1988 Naguib Mahfouz (Egypt)
1989 Camilo José Cela (Spain)
1990 Octavio Paz (Mexico)
1991 Nadine Gordimer (South Africa)
1992 Derek Walcott (West Indies, b. St. Lucia)
1993 Toni Morrison (U.S.)
1994 Kenzaburo Oe (Japan)
1995 Seamus Heaney (Ireland)
1996 Wislawa Szymborska (Poland)
1997 Dario Fo, (Italy)
1998 José Saramago (Portugal)
1999 Günter Grass (Germany)
2000 Gao Xingjian (France, b. China)
2001 V.S. Naipaul (U.K., b. Trinidad)
2002 Imre Kertész, (Hungary)
2003 J.M. Coetzee (South Africa)
2004 Elfriede Jelinek (Austria)
2005 Harold Pinter (U.K.)
2006 Orhan Pamuk (Turkey)
2007 Doris Lessing (U.K.)
2008 Jean-Marie Gustave Le Clezio (France)
2009 Herta Muller (Germany)
2010 Mario Vargas Llosa (Peru)

Note: No prizes awarded in 1914, 1918, 1935, 1940–43.

WEIGHTS AND MEASURES

Systems of Measurement

There are two widely used measurement systems. Most of the world uses a system known as the metric system, or the International System, abbreviated SI, from Système Internationale, its name in French. The United States continues to use a system called U.S. customary measure, which derives from (and differs from) the British imperial series of weights and measures. From time to time, our government has taken steps to change from the customary system to the International System, but these efforts have had limited success. Metric measure is legal in the United States, but nearly everyone continues to use the customary system in everyday life. The International System is generally used in scientific pursuits and increasingly in international trade.

Length or Distance

U.S. customary system

1 foot (ft.)	=	12 inches
1 yard (yd.)	=	3 feet = 36 inches
1 rod (rd.)	=	5.5 yards = 16.5 feet
1 furlong (fur.)	=	40 rods = 220 yards
	=	660 feet
1 mile (mi.)	=	8 furlongs =1,760 yards
	=	5,280 feet

An international nautical mile is 6,076.1155 feet.

International System   The basic unit of length is the meter, which is slightly longer than the yard. Other units of length are decimal subdivisions or multiples of the meter.

1 decimeter (dm)	=	10 centimeters
	=	0.1 meter
1 centimeter (cm)	=	0.01 meter
1 millimeter (mm)	=	0.1 centimeter
	=	0.001 meter
1 micrometer (μm)	=	0.001 millimeter
	=	0.0001 centimeter
	=	0.000001 meter
1 angstrom (Å)	=	0.0001 micrometers
	=	0.0000001 milimeter
1 dekameter (dam)	=	10 meters
1 hectometer (hm)	=	10 dekameters
	=	100 meters
1 kilometer (km)	=	10 hectometers
	=	100 dekameters
	=	1,000 meters

Conversions   In 1959 the relationship between between customary and international measures of length was officially defined as follows:

0.0254 meter (exactly)	=	1 inch
0.0245 meter x 12	=	0.3048 meter
	=	1 international foot

This definition, which makes many conversions simple, defines a foot that is shorter (by about 6 parts in 10 million) than the survey foot, which had earlier been defined as exactly 1200/3937, or 0.3048006, meter.

Following the international foot standard, the major equivalents are as listed below:

1 in.	=	2.54 cm = 0.0254 m
1 ft.	=	30.48 cm = .3048 m
1 yd.	=	91.44 cm = 0.9144 m
1 mi.	=	1,609.344 m = 1.609344 km
1 cm	=	0.3937 in.
1 m	=	1.093613 yd. = 3.28084 ft.
1 km	=	0.62137 mi.

Area

U.S. customary system   Areas are derived from lengths as follows:

1 square foot	=	144 square inches
1 square yard	=	9 sq. ft.
1 square rod (rd.2)	=	30.25 square yards
	=	272.25 square feet
1 acre	=	160 square rods
	=	4,840 square yards
	=	43,560 sq. ft.
1 square mile	=	640 acres
1 section	=	1 mile square
1 township	=	6 miles square
	=	36 square miles

International System

1 sq. millimeter (mm^2)	=	1,000,000 sq. micrometers
1 sq. centimeter (cm^2)	=	100 mm^2
1 sq. decimeter (dm^2)	=	100 cm^2
1 sq. meter (m^2)	=	10,000 cm^2
1 are (a)	=	100 m^2
1 hectare (ha)	=	100 ares
	=	10,000 m^2
1 sq kilometer (km^2)	=	100 hectares
	=	1,000,000 m^2

Conversions

1 square inch	=	6.4516 cm^2
1 square foot	=	929.0304 cm^2
	=	0.09290304 m^2
1 square yard	=	8,361.2736 cm^2
	=	0.83612736 m^2
1 acre	=	4,046.8564 m^2
	=	0.40468564 hectares
1 square mile	=	2,589,988.11 m^2
	=	258.998811 hectares
	=	2.58998811 km^2
1 cm^2	=	0.1550003 sq. in.
1 m^2	=	1,550.003 sq. in.
	=	10.76391 sq. ft.
	=	1.195990 sq. yds.
1 hectare	=	107,639.1 sq. ft.
	=	11,959.90 sq. yd.
	=	2.4710538 acres
1 km^2	=	247.10538 acres
	=	0.3861006 sq. mi

Cubic Measure

U.S. customary system

1 cu foot (ft.^{3})	=	1,728 cubic inches (in.^{3})
1 cubic yard (yd.^{3})	=	27 cubic feet (ft.^{3})

International System

1 cubic centimeter (cm^3)	=	1,000 cubic millimeters (mm^3)
1 cubic decimeter (dm^3)	=	1,000 cubic centimeters (cm^3)
1 cubic meter (m^3)	=	1,000 cubic decimeters (dm^3)
	=	1,000,000 cubic centimeters (cm^3)

Cubic centimeter is sometimes abbreviated cc and is used in fluid measure interchangeably with milliliter (ml).

Conversions

1 in.^{3}	=	16.387064 cm^3
1 ft.^{3}	=	28.316846592 cm^3
	=	0.028316847 cm^3
1 yd.^{3}	=	764,554.857984 cm^3
	=	0.764554858 m^3
1 cm^3	=	0.06102374 in.^{3}
1 m^3	=	61,023.74 in.^{3}
	=	35.31467 ft.^{3}
	=	1.307951 yd.^{3}

Fluid Volume

U.S. customary system

A gallon is equal to 231 cubic inches of liquid or capacity.

1 tablespoon (tbs.)	=	3 teaspoons (tsp.)
	=	0.5 fluid ounce (fl. oz).
1 cup	=	8 fl. oz.
1 pint (pt.)	=	2 cups = 16 fl. oz.
1 quart (qt.)	=	2 pt. = 4 cups
	=	32 fl. oz.
1 gallon (gal.)	=	4 qt. = 8 pt. = 16 cups
1 bushel (bu.)	=	8 gal. = 32 qt.

International System

Fluid-volume measurements are directly tied to cubic measure. One milliliter of fluid occupies a volume of 1 cubic centimeter. A liter of fluid (slightly more than the customary quart) occupies a volume of 1 cubic decimeter, or 1,000 cubic centimeters.

1 centiliter (cL)	=	10 mililiters (mL)
1 deciliter	=	10 cL = 100 mL
1 liter (L)	=	10 dL = 1,000 mL
1 dekaliter (daL)	=	10 L
1 hectoliter (hL)	=	10 daL = 100 L
1 kiloliter (kL)	=	10 hL = 1,000 L

Conversions

1 fluid ounce	=	29.573528 mL = 0.02957 L
1 cup	=	236.588 mL = 0.236588 L
1 pint	=	473.176 mL = 0.473176 L
1 quart	=	946.3529 mL = 0.9463529 L
1 gallon	=	3,785.41 mL = 3.78541 L
1 milliliter	=	0.0338 fluid ounce
1 liter	=	33.814 fluid ounces
	=	4.2268 cups = 2.113 pints
	=	1.0567 quarts = 0.264 gallon

Dry Volume

Conversions

1 pint, dry	=	33.600 cu. in. = 0.551 L
1 quart, dry	=	67.201 cu. in. = 1.101 L

Mass and Weight

Mass is a measure of the quantity of matter in an object and does not vary with changes in altitude or in gravitational force (as on the moon or another planet). Weight, on the other hand, is a measure of the force of gravity on an object and so does change with altitude or gravitational force.

U.S. customary system

In customary measure it is more common to measure weight than mass. The most common customary system of weight is avoirdupois:

1 pound (lb.)	=	16 ounces (oz.)
1 (short) hundred-weight (cwt.)	=	100 lb.
1 (short) ton	=	20 hundredweight
	=	2,000 lb.
1 long hundred-weight	=	112 lb.
1 long ton	=	2,240 lb.

A different system called troy weight is used to weigh precious metals. In troy weight the ounce is slightly larger than in avoirdupois, but there are only 12 ounces to the troy pound.

International System   Instead of weight, the International System uses measures of mass. The original basic unit was the gram, which was defined as the mass of 1 milliliter (= 1 cm^3) of water at 4 degrees Celsius (about 39°F). Today the official measure of mass is a specific metal object defined as the standard kilogram.

1 centigram (cg)	=	10 milligrams (mg)
1 decigram (dg)	=	10 cg = 100 mg
1 gram (g)	=	10 dg = 100 cg = 1,000 mg
1 kilogram (kg)	=	10 hectograms (hg)
	=	100 dekagrams (dag)
	=	1,000 grams
1 metric ton (t)	=	1,000 kg

Conversions   Since mass and weight are identical at standard conditions (sea level on Earth), grams and other International System units of mass are often used as measures of weight or converted into customary units of weight. Under standard conditions:

1 ounce	=	28.3495 grams
1 pound	=	453.59 grams
	=	0.45359 kilogram
1 short ton	=	907.18 kilograms
	=	0.907 metric ton
1 milligram	=	0.000035 ounce
1 gram	=	0.03527 ounce
1 kilogram	=	35.27 ounces
	=	2.2046 pounds
1 metric ton	=	2,204.6 pounds
	=	1.1023 short tons

Temperature

U.S. customary system   In the U.S, temperature is usually measured in degrees Fahrenheit: water freezes at 32°F and boils at 212°F. The basis of the Fahrenheit scale was 0°F, the coldest temperature that its originator, G. D. Fahrenheit (1686–1736), could obtain under laboratory conditions.

International System   The Swedish astronomer Anders Celsius (1701–44) devised the temperature scale that bears his name in 1742. On the Celsius scale, water freezes at 0°C and boils at 100°C. Very low temperatures are measured on the kelvin scale, named for William Thomson, Baron Kelvin (1824–1907). It is also called the absolute scale because absolute zero—0°K (–273.15° C)—is the temperature at which no body can give up heat. The interval of a kelvin equals the interval of a degree Celsius.

Conversions

Fahrenheit to Celsius: Subtract 32 from the temperature and multiply the difference by 5; then divide the product by 9. The formula is: C = $\frac{5}{9}$ (F – 32)

Celsius to Fahrenheit: Multiply the temperature by 1.8 (or $\frac{9}{5}$), then add 32. The formula is: F = $\frac{9}{5}$ C + 32

Celsius to Kelvin: Add 273.15 to the temperature. The formula is: K = C + 273.15

Force, Work/Energy, Power

U.S. customary system   The foot/pound/second system of reckoning includes the following units:

slug = mass to which a force of 1 poundal will give an acceleration of 1 foot per second per second (= approximately 32.17 lb.)

poundal = fundamental unit of force

foot-pound = work done when a force of 1 poundal produces a movement of 1 foot

foot-pound/second = unit of power equal to 1 foot/pound per second

Another common unit of power is horsepower, which is equal to 550 foot-pounds per second.

Thermal work or energy is often measured in British thermal units (Btu). One Btu is defined as the energy required to increase the temperature of 1 pound of water by 1 degree Fahrenheit. The Btu is equal to about 0.778 foot-pound.

International System   In physics, compound measurements of force, work or energy, and power are essential. There are two parallel systems using International System units: the centimeter/gram/second system (cgs) is used for small measurements, and the meter/kilogram/second system (mks) is used for larger measurements. The mks system is the official one for SI. They are described below.

Measurement of force

cgs unit	dyne (dy)	Force required to accelerate a mass of 1 g 1 cm/s^2 (cm/s^2 means "centimeter per second per second")
mks unit	newton (N)	Force required to accelerate a mass of 1 kg 1 m/s^2

Measurement of work or energy

cgs unit	erg	Dyne-centimeter, i.e., work done when a force of 1 dy produces a movement of 1 cm
mks unit	joule (j)	Newton-meter, i.e., work done when a force of 1 N produces a movement of 1 m (10,000,000 ergs)

Heat energy is also measured using the calorie (cal), which is defined as the energy required to increase the temperature of 1 cubic centimeter (1 ml) of water by 1 degree C. One calorie is equal to about 4.184 joules. The kilocalorie (Kcal or Cal) is equal to 1,000 calories and is the unit in which the energy values of food are measured. This more familiar unit, also commonly referred to as a Calorie, is equal to about 4,184 joules.

Measurement of power

cgs unit	erg/second	Rate of 1 erg per second
mks unit	watt (W)	Joule/second, i.e., a rate of 1 joule per second

Conversions

Measurement of force

1 poundal	=	13,889 dynes
	=	0.13889 newton
1 dyne	=	0.000072 poundal
1 newton	=	7.2 poundals

Measurement of work or energy

1 foot-pound	=	1,356 joules
British thermal unit	=	1,055 joules
	=	252 calories
1 joule	=	0.0007374 ft.-lbs.
1 calorie	=	0.003968 Btu
1 Kilocalorie	=	3.968 Btu

Measurement of power

1 foot-pound/second	=	1.3564 watts
1 horsepower	=	746 watts
	=	0.746 kilowatt
1 watt	=	0.73725 ft.-lb/sec.
	=	0.00134 horsepower
1 kilowatt	=	737.25 ft.-lb./sec.
	=	1.34 horsepower

Electrical Measure

Originally, the basic unit of quantity in electricity was the coulomb. A coulomb is equal to the passage of 6.25 x 10^18 electrons past a given point in an electrical system.

The unit of electrical flow is the ampere, which is equal to a coulomb/second, i.e., the flow of 1 coulomb per second. The ampere is analogous in electrical measure to a unit of flow such as gallons-per-minute in physical measure. In SI, the ampere is taken as the basic unit.

The unit for measuring electrical potential energy is the volt, which is defined as 1 joule/ coulomb, i.e., 1 joule of energy per coulomb of electricity. The volt is analogous to a measure of pressure in a water system.

The unit for measuring electrical power is the watt as defined in the previous section. Power in watts (P) is the product of the electrical flow in amperes (I) and the potential electrical energy in volts (E):

$$P = IE$$

Since the watt is such a small unit for practical applications, the kilowatt (= 1,000 watts) is often used. A kilowatt-hour is the power of 1,000 watts over an hour's time.

The unit for measuring electrical resistance is the ohm, which is the resistance offered by a circuit to the flow of 1 ampere being driven by the force of 1 volt. It is derived from Ohm's law, which defines the relationship between flow or current (amperes), potential energy (volts), and resistance (ohms). It states that the current in amperes (I) is proportional to potential energy in volts (E) and inversely proportional to resistance in ohms (R). Thus, when voltage and resistance are known, amperage can be calculated by the simple formula

$$I = \frac{E}{R}$$

Roman Numerals

Invented by the ancient Romans as a mathematical system of representation in which the Roman letters I, V, X, L, C, D and M represent the numbers 1, 5, 10, 50, 100, 500 and 1000. A letter placed after another of equal or greater value increases the value of the letter, and a letter placed before another of greater value subtracts from the letter's value, so that VI equals 6 and IV equals 4. A bar placed over a letter indicates that the value is multiplied by 1000. The number zero does not exist in the Roman method of counting. Roman numerals were commonly used in Europe until the 1200's, when the system of Arabic numerals and mathematics which is now employed became the preferred scholarly method of counting.

I = 1	X = 10	C = 100
II = 2	XX = 20	CC = 200
III = 3	XXX = 30	CCC = 300
IV = 4	XL = 40	CD = 400
V = 5	L = 50	D = 500
VI = 6	LX = 60	DC = 600
VII = 7	LXX = 70	DCC = 700
VIII = 8	LXXX = 80	M = 1000
IX = 9	XC = 90	$\overline{\text{MMD}}$ = 2,500
X = 10	C = 100	$\overline{\text{XV}}$ = 15,000

THE WONDERS OF THE WORLD

The Seven Wonders of the Ancient World

The seven wonders of the ancient world were majestic structures and sculptures built between 2500 and 200 B.C. They were described as the seven wonders by writers of classical antiquity, and were all located in the Greek world of the Mediterranean. While the wonders were described as far back as the 4th century B.C., the earliest known list is in a poem by Antipater of Sidon, about 140 B.C. A widely accepted list includes:

Great Pyramid at Giza Built over a period of perhaps 20 years during Egypt's Fourth Dynasty (about 2570 to 2500 B.C.), this pyramid was constructed as a tomb for pharaoh Khufu (Cheops in Greek). It is located west of Cairo near Giza, on the west bank of the Nile River. The Great Pyramid is made of approximately 2.3 million blocks of limestone, basalt and granite weighting several tons each. Its base covers 13 acres, and it originally rose to a height of 482 feet. Herodotus said that the pyramid's construction took 20 years and 100,000 men, but modern archeologists believe that it may have been built by as few as 20,000 workers. This pyramid is the oldest of the seven ancient wonders, and the only one still standing.

The Hanging Gardens of Babylon A collection of rooftop gardens resting on stepped terraces, they were located within the walls of the palace in the wealthy and powerful city of Babylon in what is now southern Iraq. The gardens were irrigated by water from the Euphrates River, and are said to have been built by King Nebuchadnezzar II (ruled 605–561 B.C.). The exact nature and extent of the gardens is in doubt, although they were described by Greek historians. It is supposed that they were destroyed in an earthquake after the 1st century B. C., following the decline of Babylon.

The Statue of Zeus Created by the Greek sculptor Phidias (who built the statue of Athena at the Parthenon) in about 430 B.C., the nearly 40-foot-tall statue of the Greek god was housed in the Temple of Zeus at Olympia, in western Greece. Of ivory with gold plating, the statue showed Zeus on an ornamented cedarwood throne, with a statue of Nike in his right hand, and an eagle perched on a sceptre in his left. The statue is thought to have been destroyed in the fire which destroyed the temple in 426 A.D.; alternatively, it may have been lost in a fire about 50 years later in Constantinople, to which the statue is said to have been moved.

The Temple of Artemis Originally built by King Croesus of Lydia (now western Turkey) in about 550 B.C., and later rebuilt after being burned down in 356 B.C., the temple at the city of Ephesus was renowned for its size and beauty. Roughly 350 by 180 feet, the temple was built for the non-Hellenic goddess Artemis, whom the Romans later referred to as Diana, the goddess of the hunt. The rebuilt temple was destroyed when the Goths invaded in 262 A.D.; fragments are housed in the British Museum.

The Mausoleum of Halicarnassus Built by the Lydian Queen Artemisia as a tomb for her husband and brother, King Mausolus of Caria, the mausoleum at Halicarnassus (now southwestern Turkey) was designed by the architect Pythius between 353 and 351 B.C. The tall, square building with a pyramidal roof was ornamented with sculpture by four renowned Greek artists: Scopas, Bryaxis, Leochares and Timotheus. Remnants of the sculpture are housed at the British Museum, including a long relief frieze depicting a battle between the Greeks and Amazons. The mausoleum is thought to have been destroyed in an earthquake sometime between the 11th and 15th century A.D., and its stones were reused, but the tomb's legacy remains in the form of the word mausoleum.

The Colossus of Rhodes This massive bronze statue of the sun god Helios stood beside the Mandrakion harbor of the Greek island of Rhodes, and was built by the

Greek sculptor Chares of Lyndus over the course of 12 years (294–282 B.C.). It is thought to have been 105 feet tall, and according to legend it straddled the entrance to the harbor, although that is now considered to have been impossible. The statue fell in an earthquake in 225/226 B.C., and in 654 A.D. the Arab Islamic forces seizing Rhodes destroyed the fallen god and sold the bronze.

The Pharos of Alexandria   Thought to have been more than 350 feet tall, this navigational marker and lighthouse on the island of Pharos in the harbor of Alexandria, Egypt, was built by the Hellenistic architect Sostratus of Cnidus and was completed during the reign of Ptolemy II around 280 B.C. Modern archeology supports the belief that the lighthouse was destroyed by an earthquake during the 14th century.

Other Wonders

While six of the seven classical wonders no longer exist, the desire to compile such lists has survived the centuries. Over the years, writers and historians have compiled their own lists of wonders, such as the seven wonders of the Middle Ages, the seven wonders of the Modern World, the seven natural wonders of the world, and other early wonders, some of which existed during Greek times but were unknown to the Greek world. Construction of these wonders depended, like the 7 Wonders of the World, on the use of human and animal power, enhanced by techniques such as ramps and hoists. These structures are special for their artistic, historical, and architectural interest; they are listed by geographic area and roughly by date. For the most part, the modern countries in which the wonders are located did not exist as national entities when the wonders were constructed. This compilation includes only human-created wonders, not natural wonders such as the Grand Canyon.

Africa and Middle East

Abu Simbel in Egypt   This archeological site in southern Egypt includes two temples that were carved from a sandstone cliff on the bank of the Nile during the reign of King Ramses II (1279–13 B.C.). Four massive (66 foot) sandstone statues of the seated Ramses guard the entrance to the larger temple. The temples were disassembled, moved to higher ground, and re-assembled to protect them from the rising waters of Lake Nasser with the construction of the Aswan High Dam (1970).

Throne Hall of Persepolis in Iran   Destroyed by Alexander the Great in 330 B.C., the ancient Persian capital city of Persepolis dates back to the 6th century. The Throne Hall, which features numerous doorways adorned with reliefs of throne scenes and combats, was commissioned by King Xerxes I in the 5th century and is thought to have been used for receptions for military commanders and representatives of subject nations.

Petra in Jordan   Carved into the pink sandstone hills and canyons of the Wadi Musa (Valley of Moses) in southwest Jordan more than 2,000 years ago, the city of Petra, or "Rock," was the capital city of the Nabataeans, an Arab tribe who were in the area after the 6th century B.C. and whose kingdom flourished from about the 2nd century B.C. A center for the spice trade, the city, with its extensive system of water supply channels, prospered until it fell to the Romans in 106 A.D. Many beautiful monuments and structures remain intact.

Great Zimbabwe   The extensive ruins at Great Zimbabwe, in the present-day country of Zimbabwe, are some of the oldest and largest structures located in Southern Africa. The ruins, which extend over some 1,800 acres, include the Great Enclosure, with walls as high as 36 feet, which is the largest ancient structure south of the Sahara Desert. Built between the 11th and 15th centuries A.D., by a Bantu-speaking people, the site was the center of an extensive trading kingdom.

Asia

Great Wall of China   Beginning as separate sections of fortification around the 7th Century B.C. and unified during the Qin dynasty in the 3rd century B.C., this wall, built of earth and rubble with a facing of brick or stone, runs from east to west across China for over 4,000 miles. Reconstructed several times over the course of some 20 centuries, and reaching its current form during the Ming dynasty (1368–1644), the wall is one of the largest construction projects ever undertaken.

Banaue Rice Terraces in the Philippines   Believed to have been constructed largely by hand by indigenous people 2,000 years ago, these terraces carved in the mountains of Ifugao Province on the island of Luzon are located about 5,000 feet above sea level and cover 4,000 square miles. They are fed by an ancient irrigation system from the rainforests above the terraces, and are part of the more extensive Rice Terraces of the Philippine Cordilleras.

Shwedagon Pagoda in Myanmar A symbol of Buddhism to the people of Myanmar, this roughly 2,500-year-old golden shrine sits on Singuttara Hill in the city of Yangon. Containing strands of the Buddha's hair, among other holy relics, the pagoda has an octagonal base, a bell-shaped dome, and a conical-shaped spire. The dome is covered with more than 40 tons of gold leaf; the tip of the spire is encrusted with 4,531 diamonds, rubbies, saphires, golden bells, and, at the very top, a 72-carat diamond.

Borobudur Temple in Indonesia Located in central Java and built between 778 and 850 A.D., this Buddhist temple of the Shailendra dynasty is pyramidal in form, rising in nine terraces from a square base. Relief sculptures cover the terrace walls, and the topmost terrace contains dozens of statues of the Buddha. The entire complex was buried under volcanic ash from about 1,000 A.D. until it was rediscovered and began to be excavated in 1814.

Angkor Wat in Cambodia Built by the Khmer Empire's King Suryavarman II (reigned 1131–50 A.D.), in honor of the Hindu god Vishnu, this temple complex in the ancient capital city of Angkor (northwestern Cambodia) features exquisite examples of Khmer Hindu art, most notably a frieze of sculptural reliefs extending for more than 2,600 feet around the base of the temple.

Taj Mahal in India Located on the southern bank of the Yamuna River in the city of Agra in northern India, this mausoleum complex was built by the Mughal emperor Shah Jahan (reigned 1628–58 A.D.) to honor his favorite wife. Consisting of a light-reflecting white marble mausoleum known for its five domes, a main gateway, garden, mosque and jawab ("answer," a building almost identical to the mosque), it is now a symbol of India.

Europe

Stonehenge in England One of the most famous prehistoric sites in the world, this massive circle of large standing stones surrounded by an earthen bank and ditch dates back to circa 3100 B.C. Construction continued over the course of many centuries to produce the complex known today. Located in southwest England, just north of Salisbury, Stonehenge was designed to incorporate several significant astronomical alignments (such as the direction of sunrise at the summer solstice) and is thought to have been a place of worship.

Parthenon in Greece The rectangular white marble temple of the Greek goddess Athena rests on the Acropolis in Athens. The most important surviving building of classical Greece, it was constructed between 447 B.C. and 432 B.C. under the direction of the Athenian statesman Pericles. Renowned for its colonnade of fluted columns and its intricate carvings and sculpture, the Parthenon was home to a massive ivory and gold statue of Athena Parthenos ("Athena the Virgin") which is thought to have been lost in a fire in the 5th century A.D.

Colosseum in Italy The freestanding stone amphitheatre begun between 70 and 72 A.D. under the Emperor Vespasian measures 620 by 513 feet and seats more than 40,000 people. Completed in 80 A.D., it was the scene of gladiatorial combats and public spectacles. The surviving parts of the building, which show the three stories of superimposed arcades, constitute one of the most notable and popular tourist sites in Rome.

Mont Saint-Michel in France Just off the coast of Normandy, France, and surrounded by vast sandbanks exposed to powerful tides, this fortified granite islet is home to a Gothic-style Benedictine abbey dedicated to the archangel St. Michael. The Benedictines were established on the island, where earlier church buildings had been constructed, in 966; the Abbey was built between the 11th and 16th centuries. The island is connected to the mainland by a causeway built in the 19th century.

Leaning Tower of Pisa in Italy Work began on this white marble bell tower in the city's cathedral complex in 1173, and by the time that three of its eight stories were completed, the tower had already begun to settle unevenly in the soft ground. Although the builders attempted to solve the problem, when construction was completed during the 14th century the tower (186 feet tall on its high side) was still leaning, and by the late 20th century it leaned at an angle of 5.5 degrees, or 15 feet. Soil extraction has since then stabilized the tower and reduced the lean slightly, and masonry repairs have also been undertaken; these interventions are believed to be sufficient to avoid a collapse of the tower.

Central and South America

Mayan Temples of Tikal in Guatemala The temples in the ancient ceremonial center of Tikal (now in the El Peten department of Guatemala) were constructed in lowland jungle between the 7th and early 9th centuries

A.D. Adorned with painted reliefs, they were built on the top of stepped pyramidal structures; the tallest is 230 feet high.   Tikal declined after the collapse of the Classic Mayan civilization after 900 A.D.

Temple of the Inscriptions in Mexico   This pyramidal temple is one of several large buildings in the Mayan site now called Palenque, in the southern state of Chiapas, Mexico. Most of Palenque's buildings were constructed in the 7th through 10th centuries, after which the city was abandoned. The Temple of the Inscriptions is known for its three large limestone tablets with hieroglyphics, and is one of the best-preserved Mayan temples.   It houses the sarcophagus of a Mayan ruler.

Aztec Temple in Mexico   The center of Aztec life, the Great Temple   sat in the heart of the Aztec capital city (now Mexico City) of Tenochtitlan on an island in Lake Texcoco. A pyramidal structure with steps leading to a ritual area at the top where human sacrifice was practiced, it was built soon after the Aztecs established their capital city around 1325 A.D. Tenochtitlan became the most pow-erful city in Mesoamerica, but was largely destroyed after the Spanish conquest of 1521.

Inca city of Machu Picchu in Peru   Probably built in the 15th century, Machu Picchu was an extensive city that was possibly a palace complex, royal retreat, or regional center.   The grey granite buildings are of Inca dry-stone wall construction, without mortar.   The city, located at about 8,000 feet in the Andes Mountains, was abandoned after the Spanish conquest, and rediscovered nearly intact in 1911 by the Yale archeologist Hiram Bingham (1875–1946).

Moai Statues in Rapa Nui (Easter Island), Chile The nearly 900 stone statues of human heads and torsos, or *moai*, which weigh on average 14 tons and are on average 14 feet 6 inches tall; they are cut from volcanic stone. Many of the statues are placed on stone platforms called *ahu* along the coasts, with their backs to the sea. The *moai* are believed to have been constructed between 1000 and 1500 A.D., and to have had both religious and political significance to the islanders.

Modern Wonders

Unlike earlier wonders, the construction of modern wonders has depended on sources of energy beyond human and animal muscle, inventions such as the elevator, and technological innovations in materials. Yet they still have the power to amaze people with their size, architectural beauty, and methods of construction.

Africa and Middle East

Suez Canal in Egypt   The Suez Canal connects the Mediterranean with the Red Sea. It is 101 miles long and is one of the busiest shipping lanes in the world. Running north-south across the Isthmus of Suez in Egypt, it stretches from Port Said to the city of Suez and is the shortest water route between Europe and the countries of the Indian and western Pacific Oceans. The canal was completed in 1869 under the leadership of Ferdinand de Lesseps (French, 1805–1894), under a concession granted by Said Pasha (1822–1863), the Ottoman viceroy of Egypt.

Aswan High Dam in Egypt   Completed in 1970, this rock-fill dam spans the Nile River at Aswan, Egypt and controls the annual Nile flood by impounding water in its reservoir, Lake Nasser. In addition to providing flood control and water for irrigation, the project produces hydro-electric energy. The dam has a height of 364 feet, a crest length of 12,562 feet and a volume of 57,940,000 cubic yards. The creation of the reservoir required the relocation of ancient monuments including the Abu Simbel temples.

Australia

Sydney Opera House   Located on Bennelong Point at the Sydney Harbor, this stunning example of modern architecture is based on a design by Danish architect Jorn Utzon (b. 1918).   It was opened by Queen Eliabeth II in 1973. Designed to resemble the shells and sails of the harbor, the pearlescent roof elements have made this structure Australia's most recognizable building.

Asia

Petronas Twin Towers in Malaysia   At 1,483 feet, these identical stainless steel and glass skyscrapers in Kuala Lumpur, Malaysia held the record for the world's tallest buildings from their completion in 1998 to 2003, when Taipei 101 was completed. Designed by architect Cesar Pelli (American, b. Argentina, 1926), the towers are eight-lobed circular structures topped with pyramidal pinnacles and slender steel spires, and are linked by a sky-bridge on the 41st and 42nd stories.

Three Gorges Dam, China The Three Gorges Dam on the Yangtze River in China is made of concrete and is about 1.4 miles long and 607 feet high. The dam was completed in 2006 and some of its hydroelectric generators began producing power at that time, but the project will not become fully operational until further hydroelectric generating facilities and a ship lift are constructed. The reservoir will be more than 375 miles long. The project is designed to provide flood control and hydrolelectric energy; when completed it will be the world's largest hydroelectric energy plant. The project has been controversial because of the need to relocate more than 1.3 million people and because of its environmental impacts.

Europe

The Clock Tower (Big Ben) in England St. Stephen's Tower, or the Clock Tower, is at the north-eastern end of the Houses of Parliament building in the Westminster district of London. It is popularly known as Big Ben, but this name is actually the nickname of the clock's main bell. The 316-foot-tall clock tower is part of the Houses of Parliament building erected after the destruction of the Palace of Westminster in 1834. The clock became operational in 1859, and has become a familiar symbol of London. The four dials of the clock are 23 feet square and the minute hands are 14 feet long. Big Ben is thought to be named after the commissioner of works, Sir Benjamin Hall.

Eiffel Tower in France Designed by engineer Alexandre Gustave Eiffel (French, 1832–1923), this 984-foot-tall open-lattice structural iron tower (1,056 feet including its television antenna) was built to celebrate the centenary of the French Revolution in 1889, and served as the entrance gate for the Universal Exposition held that year. Consisting of four piers that taper inward to form one tower, it was the tallest man-made structure in the world until the completion of New York City's Chrysler Building in 1930. It was originally intended as a temporary structure, to be taken down within 20 years, but it remained standing both in response to popular opinion and because of its use in communications.

Channel Tunnel Connecting southern England (Folkestone, near Dover) with northern France (Coquelles, near Calais), this 31-mile-long rail tunnel runs beneath the English Channel and is used for freight and passenger transportation. The undersea portion is the longest undersea tunnel in the world (24 miles). Work began in 1987 and the Chunnel, as it is often called, opened in May, 1994.

North America

Statue of Liberty in New York City A gift from the people of France to commemorate friendship between France and the United States and the centenary of American independence, the 305-foot-tall (including pedestal) statue on Liberty Island in the Upper New York Bay was designed by sculptor Frederic-Auguste Bartholdi (1834–1904) and paid for by public subscription. Alexandre Gustave Eiffel (1832–1923) designed the interior structure. The statue was constructed in France, disassembled, and shipped to New York in 1885. After being mounted on her pedestal, the copper-sheeted Liberty Enlightening the World, with a torch in her raised right hand and a tablet reading July 24, 1776 in her left, was dedicated by President Grover Cleveland on October 28, 1886. An extensive program of repairs and restoration was completed in time for the statue's centennial in 1986.

Empire State Building in New York City Completed in 1931, this 102-story steel-framed Art Deco icon in Manhattan is 1,250-feet tall (1,454 feet with its antenna). It was the tallest building in the world until the completion of the first tower of the World Trade Center in 1972. The architect was William Lamb of the firm Shreve, Lamb & Harmon, who modeled the building after a pencil's sleek lines. Contruction was completed in 1 year 45 days.

Hoover Dam in Arizona/Nevada Located 30 miles southeast of Las Vegas, Nevada, on the Arizona/Nevada border in the Black Canyon of the Colorado River, the dam is 726 feet tall and 1,244 feet long. It is the tallest solid concrete dam in the United States and impounds Lake Mead, the largest reservoir in the United States. Originally named Boulder Dam, it was built between 1930 and 1936 and was renamed Hoover Dam in honor of President Herbert Hoover in 1947. Hoover Dam provides hydroelectric energy, water for irrigation and other uses, and flood control.

Mount Rushmore National Memorial in South Dakota The 60-foot tall heads of Presidents George Washington, Thomas Jefferson, Theodore Roosevelt and Abraham Lincoln are carved into the granite southeast side of this mountain nestled in the Black Hills National Forest in southwestern South Dakota. Representing the United States' first 150 years, the memorial was constructed under the supervision of sculptor Gutzon Borglum (American, 1867–1941); work began in 1927 and was completed in 1941.

Golden Gate Bridge in San Francisco Connecting San Francisco to Marin County, California this 4,200-foot (main span) long suspension bridge extends over the Golden Gate strait; it is renowned for the physical beauty of both bridge and setting. Construction was completed in 1937; at that time, it was the world's longest suspension main span, a record it held until the completion of the Verrazano-Narrows Bridge in New York City in 1964. Bridge construction has developed to such an extent that the Golden Gate is only the 8th largest main span in the world today; the longest is the Akashi-Kaihyo Bridge on the Kobe-Naruto Route in Japan (main span 6,529 feet).

Gateway Arch in St. Louis This stainless steel arch rises 630 feet from the west bank of the Mississippi River; it was completed in 1965 to symbolize St. Louis' place as the gateway to the West. The arch was designed by architect Eero Saarinen (American b. Finland, 1910–1961), who won a national competition to design a monument for the Memorial. It is part of the Jefferson National Expansion Memorial built in 1935.

CN Tower in Canada The tallest freestanding structure in the world, this 1,815-foot-tall broadcast and communications tower in Toronto was built by the Canadian National railway company. The tower opened to the public in 1976; among its features for visitors are a revolving restaurant at 1,151 feet and the world's highest public observation deck at 1,465 feet.

South America

Statue of Christ the Redeemer in Brazil Overlooking Rio de Janeiro, the statue of Christ the Redeemer (Cristo Redentor in Portuguese) stands atop Corcovado Mountain at an altitude of 2,330 feet. The statue, which with its pedestal is 125 feet tall, was funded by public donations and inaugurated in 1931. The designer was the French monumental sculptor Paul Landowski (1875–1961), and overall construction supervision was by Brazilian engineer Heitor da Silva Costa (1873–1947). The statue, with its outstretched welcoming arms, is perhaps the most recognizable image of Brazil.

Itaipu Dam in Brazil/Paraguay Built by Paraguay and Brazil between 1975 and 1982, it is the largest hollow gravity dam in the world. Located on the Upper Parana River at the Brazil/Paraguay border, the dam is 643 feet tall and is part of a dam and spillway complex that spans almost five miles: The project's hydroelectric energy production is currently the largest in the world.

Panama Canal Opened in 1914, this canal connects the Atlantic and Pacific oceans through the Isthmus of Panama with a series of locks and lakes. Forty miles from shoreline to shoreline and 51 miles between the Atlantic and Pacific channel entrances, with a minimum depth of 41 feet, the canal brought enormous economic and strategic efficiencies to naval shipping. Built and originally owned by the United States on land leased from Panama, the canal has by treaty been fully controlled by the Republic of Panama since 1999.

The World Heritage Sites

In 1959, a campaign was launched to safeguard the ancient Abu Simbel temples in Egypt after construction plans for the Aswan High Dam threatened to destroy them. The campaign cost $80 million, and was funded in part by donations from some 50 countries. The campaign resulted in the dismantling, relocation, and re-assembling of the tombs, and its success soon led to other similar efforts. Consequently, the United Nations Educational, Scientific, and Cultural Organization (UNESCO) set about drafting a convention for the protection of cultural heritage. This convention—in coordination with a 1965 U.S. proposal for a "World Heritage Trust" that encompassed natural and scenic areas as well—was presented to the 1972 United Nations conference on Human Environment. What resulted was the Convention concerning the Protection of the World Cultural and Natural Heritage. As of June 2010, 187 member states of the U.N. had ratified the Convention.

The World Heritage List

The Convention defines what kind of sites can be considered for the World Heritage List, an ever-evolving list of properties that the World Heritage Committee "considers as having outstanding universal value." In 2010, there were 911 properties listed worldwide—the vast majority of which (704) were cultural sites. There were 180 natural and 27 mixed properties spread across 151 countries. If a site is threatened by either natural or human causes, it is added to the World Heritage in Danger list. There were 34 "In Danger" sites in 2010; the majority of which were in Africa and the Middle East. Web site: whc.unesco.org

Selected Sites

Cultural Landscape and Archaeological Remains of the Bamiyan Valley, Afghanistan　Remains found here represent cultural developments from the 1st to 13th centuries, including Buddhist edifices and fortified complexes from the Islamic period. Site of Taliban destruction of two enormous standing Buddhas, 2001. (In danger.)

M'Zab Valley, Algeria　Constructed in the 10th century, the five ksour (fortified cities) preserved in the M'Zab Valley are an early and influential example of sedentary living and urban planning.

Tassili n'Ajjer, Algeria　More than 15,000 cave drawings and engravings on area rocks record the evolution of human life on the edge of the Sahara from 6000 B.C. to the first centuries A.D.

Kasbah of Algiers, Algeria　This Islamic *medina* ("city") was the site of a Carthaginian trading post in the 4th century B.C. Includes a citadel, mosques, and Ottoman-style palaces.

Peninsula Valdes, Argentina　Marine breeding ground in Patagonia for endangered animals, including southern right whales, elephant seals, and sea lions.

Ischigualasto & Talampaya Natural Parks, Argentina　The most complete continental fossil record from the Triassic Period (245–208 million years ago), including mammals, dinosaurs, and plants.

Great Barrier Reef, Australia　The world's largest structure made by living organisms. Comprised of 2,100 barrier and 800 fringing reefs that began to form as early as the Miocene Epoch (23.7–5.3 million years ago).

Shark Bay, Western Australia, Australia　Contains the largest and richest sea-grass beds in the world; also boasts stromatolite colonies that are among oldest life-forms on Earth.

Sydney Opera House, Australia　Completed in 1973, this structure—at the tip of a peninsula in the Sydney Harbor—has had lasting influence on architecture for its unparalleled design and construction.

Historic Centre of City of Salzburg, Austria　Known for its Gothic art, this home of Wolfgang Amadeus Mozart has preserved its rich urban aesthetic, developed from the Middle Ages to the 19th century.

Walled City of Baku with the Shirvanshah's Palace and Maiden Tower, Azerbaijan　Site inhabited since Palaeolithic period reveals evidence of several cultures. Built and reconstructed over several centuries dating back to the 7th and 6th centuries B.C.

Gobustan Rock Art Cultural Landscape, Azerbaijan　Collection of 40,000 years of rock art; also remains of inhabited caves, settlements and burial grounds.

Ruins of the Buddhist Vihara at Paharpur, Bangladesh　Monastery-city that was influential to Buddhist architecture; renowned cultural center from 7th–12th century.

Struve Geodetic Arc; Belarus, Estonia, Finland, Latvia, Lithuania, Moldova, Norway, Russia, Sweden, Ukraine　Series of survey triangulations built in the 19th century that helped to establish exact size and shape of planet; important step in topographical mapping.

Neolithic Flint Mines at Spiennes (Mons), Belgium　The largest and earliest concentration of mines in Europe, dating back to 5th and 4th centuries B.C.

City of Potosi, Bolivia　Once the world's largest industrial complex, these hydraulic mills used to extract silver ore date back to the 16th century.

Tsodilo, Botswana　Known as the "Louvre of the Desert," this collection of some 4,500 paintings in the Kalahari give a chronological account of human and environment for 100,000 years.

Historic Centre of Salvador de Bahia, Brazil　Represents the blending of Euro-Afro-Amerindian cultures. First slave market in the New World, dating back to 1558.

Central Amazon Conservation Complex, Brazil　Largest protected area in the Amazon basin and one of world's most important regions in terms of biodiversity.

Angkor, Cambodia　Contains remains of different capitals of the Khmer Empire, 9th–15th century; profound influence in art and architecture in Southeast Asia.

Dinosaur Provincial Park, Alberta, Canada　Site of some of the most important fossil discoveries from the "Age of Reptiles," including 35 species of dinosaurs dating back 75 million years.

Imperial Palaces of Ming and Qing Dynasties in Beijing and Shenyang, China　These homes of the ruling family from 1416 to 1911 are a testimony to five centuries of Chinese culture. Includes Forbidden City in Beijing—the world's largest palace complex.

Mausoleum of the First Qin Emperor, China Not discovered until 1974, this site of Qin's burial (first unifier of China) is surrounded by hundreds of Terracotta Warriors; thousands more probably remain to be unearthed.

Peking Man Site at Zhoukoudian, China Remains of *homo sapiens sapiens* dating back to 18,000–11,000 B.C. Illustrates process of evolution.

The Great Wall, China Approximately 4,500 miles of wall extended from the Gulf of Chihli into central Asia, parts of which date back to 7th century B.C. This architectural feat was meant to protect the Chinese from invading peoples.

Historic Ensemble of the Potala Palace, Lhasa, Tibet (China) Winter palace of the Dalai Lama dating back to 7th century; symbolic of Tibetan Buddhism.

Dazu Rock Carvings, China Steep hillsides with Confucian, Daoist, and Buddhist carvings dating from 9th to 13th centuries A.D.

San Agustin Archaeological Park, Colombia Largest group of religious monuments and megalithic sculpture in South America; dating back to 1st–8th centuries A.D.

Cocos Island National Park, Costa Rica Only island in eastern Pacific with a tropical rainforest. First point of ocean current contact is ideal for biostudy and diving.

Old Havana and its Fortifications, Cuba Founded by the Spanish in 1519 and a major ship-building center in 17th century. Retains mix of Baroque and neoclassical architecture.

Paphos, Cyprus Inhabited since Neolithic times, this center of the cult of Aphrodite is one of the earliest settlements in the world.

Salonga National Park, Democratic Republic of the Congo Located at the central basin of the Congo River, Africa's largest tropical rainforest preserve is habitat to many endangered species. (In danger.)

Kronborg Castle, Denmark Built in 1574, this still-intact Renaissance castle is best known as Hamlet's Elsinore. Played a key role in European history during the 16th–18th centuries.

Galapagos Islands, Ecuador Best-known as the location where Charles Darwin was inspired to devise his theory of evolution by natural selection, these 19 islands are a "melting pot" of marine life.

Ancient Thebes with its Necropolis, Egypt Capital of Egypt during Middle and New Kingdom periods. Contains finest relics of ancient Egyptian art and religion, including a boulevard lined with sphinxes.

Historic Cairo, Egypt One of world's oldest Islamic cities, founded in the 10th century. Eastern bank of the Nile includes some 600 monuments dating from the 7th to 20th centuries A.D.

Memphis and its Necropolis—the Pyramid Fields from Giza to Dahshur, Egypt Some of the most recognizable sculptures in the world, these funerary monuments include rich information about ancient Egypt. The step pyramid, constructed entirely of limestone, is the oldest-known architectural structure of its kind.

Lower Valley of the Awash, Ethiopia Grouping of Paleolithic sites in Africa dating back 4 million years where some of most important hominid fossils have been found. One of these, "Lucy" provides the first evidence of hominid bipedal movement.

Mont-Saint-Michel and its Bay, France Built between the 11th and 16th centuries, this village and abbey is situated atop a rocky islet between Normandy and Brittany.

Palace and Park of Versailles, France Built by decadent King Louis XIV, this principal residence of French kings provided a model for royal European residences. Central chamber is the famed Hall of Mirrors, an impressive 17th century-construction feat.

Prehistoric Sites and Decorated Caves of the Vezere Valley, France The valley contains 25 decorated caves, the most famous of which is the Lascaux Cave discovered in 1940. The detailed hunting scenes are of great import to the study of prehistoric art.

Historic Center of Avignon: Papal Palace, Episcopal Ensemble and Avignon Bridge, France Temporary seat of papacy in the 14th century; influential example of Gothic architecture.

Frontiers of the Roman Empire, Germany and United Kingdom Wall border that represents Roman Empire at its greatest extent. Includes Hadrian's Wall, spanning over 73 miles and dating back to the 2nd century.

Messel Pit Fossil Site, Germany Richest site in the world for Eocene fossils (57–36 million years ago). Provides information about early evolution of mammals.

Luther Memorials in Eisleben and Wittenberg, Germany Sites in Saxony-Anhalt that are associated with Martin Luther, and consequently with the Protestant

Revolution. Includes church where Luther posted his 95 Theses.

Asante Traditional Buildings, Ghana Built of earth, wood, and straw in the 18th century, these are the last material remains of the Asante civilization.

Acropolis, Athens, Greece One of the most recognizable structures in the world, the Acropolis dates back to the 5th century B.C. Indicative of architectural and artistic legacy of Ancient Greece. Includes the Parthenon, a temple generally considered to be the high point of Doric construction.

Paleochristian and Byzantine Monuments of Thessalonika, Greece Port city founded in 315 B.C. that was one of first bases for the spread of Christianity.

Archaeological Site of Olympia, Greece Inhabited since prehistoric times, Olympia was a center for worship of Zeus in the 10th century B.C. It was also the site of the ancient Olympic Games, held every four years beginning in 776 B.C.

Archaeological Park and Ruins of Quirigua, Guatemala Mayan ruins essential for understanding the culture's sculptures and calendars. Inhabited since the 2nd century A.D.

Taj Mahal, India This 42-acre mausoleum complex—built almost entirely of white marble—is generally regarded as the finest example of Mughal architecture, completed in 1648.

Sun Temple, Konarak, India One of India's most important Brahman sanctuaries, built in the 13th century A.D. Includes 24 wheels decorated with symbolic designs.

The Jantar Mantar, Jaipur, India This astronomical observation site was built in the early 18th century and includes a set of 20 main fixed instruments.

Sangiran Early Man Site, Indonesia Site of discovery of the first hominid fossil during excavations from 1936 to 1941. Inhabited for the past 1.5 million years, this site is home to half of all world's hominid fossils.

Persepolis, Iran Impressive complex of palaces founded by Darius I in 518 B.C. Built on half-artificial, half-natural terrace.

Tabriz Historic Bazaar Complex, Iran A series of interconnected, brick-covered structures that served as an important center along Silk Road. Capital of Safavid Kingdom from 13th to 16th centuries A.D.

Hatra, Iraq Capital of first Arab Kingdom that withstood Roman invasions in 116 and 198 A.D.

Historic Center of Rome, the Properties of the Holy See in the City Enjoying Extraterritorial Rights and San Paolo Fuori le Mura, Italy and Holy See According to legend, Rome was founded in 753 B.C. The historical center includes the Forums, the Mausoleums of Augustus and Hadrian, religious and public buildings of the papacy, and the Pantheon.

Venice and Its Lagoon, Italy Venice was founded in the 5th century A.D. and is spread over 118 small islands. It was a major merchant and maritime powerhouse in the 10th century.

Archaeological Areas of Pompeii, Herculaneum and Torre Annunziata, Italy Pompeii and Herculaneum were buried by the eruption of Mt. Vesuvius in A.D. 79. The towns, frozen in time, have since been excavated and provide an unparalleled picture of life at the time.

Archaeological Area and the Patriarchal Basilica of Aquileia, Italy One of largest and most influential cities of Early Roman Empire, Aquileia was destroyed in the mid-5th century A.D. It represents the only archaeological reserve of its kind.

Historic Monuments of Ancient Kyoto, Japan Kyoto was built in 794 and was a center of Japanese culture for 1,000 years. Area monuments represent the development of wooden architecture and the art of Japanese gardens.

Hiroshima Peace Memorial, Japan The Genbaku Dome was the only building left standing after the first atomic bomb was dropped in 1945. It has since been preserved in the state immediately following the bombing.

Iwami Ginzan Silver Mine and its Cultural Landscape, Japan This cluster of mountains features archeological remains of mines and refineries that were in large part responsible for the economic developments of Japan and China in the 16th and 17th centuries.

Old City of Jerusalem and its Walls, site proposed by Jordan A holy city for Judaism, Christianity and Islam comprised of 220 historic monuments including the 7th-century Dome of the Rock, the Wailing Wall, and the Church of the Holy Sepulchre (site of Jesus Christ's tomb). (In danger.)

Petra, Jordan This caravan-city half carved into a rock has been inhabited since prehistoric times and was an important crossroads between Arabia, Egypt, and Phoenicia.

Complex of Koguryo Tombs, Democratic People's Republic of Korea (North) A property of about 30 tombs from the later period of the Koguryo Kingdom, one of the strongest between 3rd century B.C. and 7th century A.D. One of the only remains of this culture.

Haeinsa Temple Janggyeong Panjeon, the Depositories for the Tripitaka Koreana Woodblocks,

Republic of Korea (South)   The most complete collection of sacred Buddhist texts, dating between A.D. 1237 and 1248. Buildings housing the texts date from the 15th century.

Sulaiman-Too Sacred Mountain, Kyrgyzstan Represents pre-Islamic and Islamic sacred site. Most intact sacred mountain in the world, worshipped over several millennia with numerous places of worship, caves, and petroglyphs.

Anjar, Lebanon   Founded at beginning of 8th century A.D., these ruins reveal city planning under the Umayyads.

Baalbek, Lebanon   Phoenician city known as Heliopolis; one of finest examples of Roman architecture. Includes Temple of Jupiter with nearly 70-foot tall columns.

Timbuktu, Mali   An intellectual and religious capital in the 15th and 16th centuries that was a center for the spread of Islam in Africa.

Bikini Atoll Nuclear Test Site, Marshall Islands Site of 67 nuclear tests from 1946 to 1958, including explosion of first H-bomb. Tests had significant effect on geology and natural environment of the islands, and on the health of those exposed to radiation.

Pre-Hispanic city of Chichen-Itza, Mexico   Sacred site for the Mayans. Construction techniques reveal elements from central Mexico that make the site one of most important examples of Mayan-Toltec civilizations.

Earliest 16th-Century Monasteries on the Slope of Popocatepetl, Mexico   A collection of 14 monasteries that represent the architectural style of the first missionaries in "New Spain."

Agave Landscape and Ancient Industrial Facilities of Tequila, Mexico   Over 85,000 acres nestled in the foothills of the Tequila Volcano and the Rio Grande River valley, this landscape includes working distilleries and is a testimony to Teuchitlan cultures that shaped the area from A.D. 200–900.

Monarch Butterfly Biosphere Reserve, Mexico Site of migration for millions—perhaps billions—of monarch butterflies from wide areas of North America.

Orkhon Valley Cultural Landscape, Mongolia Site of numerous archeological remains dating back to 6th century A.D. Includes Kharkhorum, the 13th and 14th century capital of Genghis Khan's empire.

Medina of Fez, Morocco   Islamic city founded in 9th century A.D. and the home to first university in the world.

Kathmandu Valley, Nepal   These seven groups of monuments display the historic and artistic achievements of the region since the 3rd century B.C., and include Buddhist *stupas* (ceremonial mounds) and Hindu temples.

Osun-Osogbo Sacred Grove, Nigeria   Last surviving sacred grove of the Yoruba people. Regarded as abode of Osun, goddess of fertility.

Rock Art of Alta, Norway   Site of Nordic petroglyphs, evidence of a settlement dating back to 4200–500 B.C.

Archaeological Sites of Bat, Al-Khutm and Al-Ayn, Oman   Most complete collection of settlements in the world from 3000–2000 B.C.

Historic Sanctuary of Machu Picchu, Peru   An ancient Incan fortress city that spans five square miles. Most buildings are constructed of white granite and represent some of most advanced architecture from Incan society.

Sacred City of Caral-Supe, Peru   Oldest center of civilization in the Americas, dating back 5,000 years.

Rice Terraces of Philippine Cordilleras, Philippines   High rice fields of Ifugao that follow the contours of the mountain illustrates the marriage of humanity and environment dating back 2,000 years. (In danger.)

Auschwitz Birkenau, German Nazi Concentration and Extermination Camp, Poland The most notorious of six Nazi concentration camps where 1.5 million people are thought to have been murdered, the vast majority of them Jews.

Kremlin and Red Square, Moscow, Russia   The Kremlin complex is the heart of Moscow, and is inextricably linked to every major event in Russian history since the 13th century. Site of Moscow's first public library, university, printing house, and public theatre.

Western Caucasus, Russia   One of few mountain ranges in the world that never experienced significant human contact; features vast number of ecosystems.

Island of Goree, Senegal   Largest slave trading center on the African coast dating back to the 15th–19th centuries. Characterized by contrast between slave quarters and elegant houses of traders.

Vlkolinec, Slovakia   A settlement of 45 buildings that serves as the best example of a traditional European mountain town; earliest building dates back to 1376.

Fossil Hominid Sites of Sterkfontein, Swartkrans, Kromdraai, Environs, South Africa Includes Makapan Valley, where caves trace human occupation and evolution back more than 3 million years. Tuang skull discovered here in 1924.

Alhambra Generalife, and Albayzin, Spain
Residence of Islamic emirs who ruled this part of Spain in 13th–14th centuries. Situated on two hills above Granada, the site is a rich example of Moorish and Andalusian architecture.

Works of Antoni Gaudi, Spain   Seven properties built in the late 19th and early 20th centuries represent eclectic and creative contributions of Gaudi to the development of architecture.

Old Town of Segovia and its Aqueduct, Spain
Town is the site of an impressive Roman aqueduct built around A.D. 50.

Archaeological Site of Atapuerca, Spain   Caves contain earliest evidence of humanity in Europe, from nearly 1 million years ago.

Ancient City of Sigiriya, Sri Lanka   Ruins of old capital city built into a giant rock; staircases in sculpted lion's mouth provide access to the site.

Laponian Area, Sweden.   Home to the Saami (Lapp) people, one of the only remaining herding cultures in the world.

Swiss Alps Jungfrau-Aletsch, Switzerland
Example of formation of the High Alps that features the largest glacier in Eurasia. Landscape has played important role in European art, literature, and tourism.

Ancient City of Damascus, Syria   Founded around 3000 B.C., this was an important trade center in the Middle East and features roughly 125 monuments from different historical periods.

Serengeti National Park, Tanzania   1.5 million hectares of savannah, home to the annual migration of vast herds of herbivores and their predators.

Ban Chiang Archaeological Site, Thailand
Considered the most important prehistoric site in Southeast Asia, this site dating back to the 5th millennium B.C. presents the earliest evidence of farming and metalwork in the region.

Archaeological Site of Carthage, Tunisia   Founded in the 9th century B.C., Carthage was a trading empire covering most of the Mediterranean. Rival to Rome during long Punic Wars; Carthage was destroyed in 146 B.C. and rebuilt by Roman conquerors.

Great Mosque and Hospital of Divrigi, Turkey
Built by Emir Ahmet Shah in A.D. 1228–29, this mosque and its adjoining hospital are generally considered a masterpiece of Islamic architecture.

Hattusha: The Hittite Capital, Turkey   Former capital of the 14th century B.C. Hittite Empire; known for its preserved urban organization of temples, royal residence, and fortifications, in addition to the ornamentation of the Lions' Gate and Royal Gate.

Archaeological Site of Troy, Turkey   One of the most famous archaeological sites in the world—comprising 4,000 years of history—Troy is best known for its portrayal by Homer in *The Iliad*.

Stonehenge, Avebury and Associated Sites, Great Britain   These two sanctuaries consist of circles of giant menhirs whose astronomical significance is yet unknown.

Westminster Palace, Westminster Abbey and Saint Margaret's Church, Great Britain   The site of medieval remains, Westminster was rebuilt in 1840. The site is where all sovereigns since the 11th century have been crowned.

Tower of London, Great Britain   A typical example of Norman military structure founded in 1066, the Tower long-served as the gateway to the British capital. Its dungeons are known for brutal practices, and its courtyard saw many famous executions—including that of Queen Anne Boleyn.

Grand Canyon National Park, United States of America   Nearly 5,000 feet deep, the Grand Canyon was carved by the Colorado River and is the most impressive gorge in the world, revealing 2 billion years of geological history.

Chaco Culture, United States of America   A major center of ancestral Pueblo culture between 850 and 1250; known for its ancient urban ceremonial building.

Redwood National and State Parks, United States of America   Covering a region of coastal mountains in northern California, the Redwoods are the tallest trees in the world, a surviving remnant of the group of trees that existed for 160 million years.

Samarkand, Uzbekistan   Founded in the 7th century B.C., this ancient cultural melting pot includes important monuments such as the Registran Mosque and madrasas, and Ulugh-Beg's Observatory.

Old Walled City of Shibam, Yemen   Built in the 16th century, this is an early example of vertical urban planning known as the "Manhattan of the Desert."

Great Zimbabwe National Monument, Zimbabwe   The legendary capital of the Queen of Sheba, this monument is a testimony to the Bantu civilization of the lost Shona people between the 11th and 15th centuries.

U.S. STATES

U.S. States

This section is a compilation of history and statistics about the 50 United States and the District of Columbia. Included are the official motto and other emblems; a summary of geographic, demographic and economic facts; and a list of prominent natives. Statistical sources include the U.S. Census Bureau's 2000 decennial census, intercensal population estimates, and *The Statistical Abstract* (annual). The headings for demographic statistics conform to U.S. Census Bureau usage, except "Black" is used as short for Black or African-American, "Indian" is used for American Indian and Alaska Native, and "Pacific Islander" is used for Native Hawaiian and other Pacific Islander. Note that Hispanics may be of any race.

Alabama

www.alabama.gov.
Name Probably after Alabama tribe. **Nickname** Yellowhammer State, Heart of Dixie. **Capital** Montgomery. **Entered union** Dec. 14, 1819 (22nd). **Motto** "We dare defend our rights." **Emblems** *Bird* Yellowhammer. *Song* "Alabama." *Tree* Southern (longleaf) pine. **Land** Total area 52,419 sq. mi (30th), incl. 1,675 sq. mi. inland water. **Borders** Tenn., Ga., Fla., Gulf of Mexico, Miss. **Rivers** Alabama, Chattahoochee, Mobile, Tennessee, Tennessee-Tombigbee Waterway, Tensaw, Tombigbee. Lakes Guntersville, Pickwick, Wheeler, Wilson (all formed by Tennessee Valley Authority); Dannelly Res., Martin, Lewis Smith, Weiss. **Mountains** Cumberland, Lookout, Raccoon, Sand. **People** (July, 2009 est.) 4,709,000 (23rd). Race/Hispanic Origin (July, 2009 est.): White 70.9%. Black, 26.3%. Indian 0.5%. Asian 1.0%. Two or more races 1.1%. Hispanic 3.2%. **Cities** (2005) Birmingham 231,483. Montgomery 200,127. Mobile 191,544. Huntsville 166,313. Tuscaloosa 81,358. Hoover 67,469. Dothan 62,713. Decatur 54,909. Auburn 49,928. Gadsden 37,405. **Famous natives** Hank Aaron, baseball player. Tallulah Bankhead, actress. Wernher von Braun (b. Germany), rocket scientist. Nat "King" Cole, singer. Helen Keller, author. Coretta Scott (Mrs. Martin Luther) King, reformer. Harper Lee, author. Joe Louis, boxer. Jesse Owens, runner. George Wallace, politician. Hank Williams, singer. **Tourist information** 1-800-ALA-BAMA. www.800alabama.com

Alaska

www.state.ak.us
Name From Aleut alaska and Eskimo alakshak, both meaning "mainland." **Nickname** "The Last Frontier." **Capital** Juneau. **Entered union** Jan. 3, 1959 (49th). **Motto** "North to the future." **Emblems** *Bird* Willow ptarmigan. *Flower* Forget-me-not. *Song* "Alaska's Flag." *Tree* Sitka spruce. **Land** Total area 663,267 sq. mi (1st), incl. 91,316 sq. mi. inland water. **Borders** Arctic Ocean (Chukchi Sea, Beaufort Sea), Yukon, British Columbia, Pacific Ocean, Bering Strait. **Rivers** Colville, Porcupine, Noatak, Yukon, Susitna, Copper, Kobuk, Koyukuk, Kuskokwim, Tanana. **Mountains** Alaska Range (Mt. McKinley 20,320 ft., highest in North America), Aleutian Range, Brooks Range, Kuskokwim, St. Elias. **Other notable features** Aleutian Islands, Alexander Archipelago, Kodiak Island, Nunivak Island, Point Barrow (71°23'N), Pribilof Islands, Seward Peninsula, St. Lawrence Island. **People** (July, 2009 est.) 698,000 (47th). Race/Hispanic Origin (July, 2009 est.): White 70.3%. Black 4.2%. Indian 15.2%. Asian 5.0%. Pacific Islander 0.7%. Two or more races 4.7%. Hispanic 6.4%. **Cities** (2005) Anchorage 275,043. Fairbanks 31,324. Juneau 30,987. Sitka 8,986. Wasilla 8,471. Ketchikan 7,410. Kenai 7,464. Palmer 6,920. Kodiak 6,273. Bethel 6,262. **Famous natives** Aleksandr Baranov (b. Russia), first governor of Russian America. Vitus Bering (b. Denmark), explorer. Ernest Gruening (b. N.Y.), governor. Carl Ben Eielson, bush pilot. Walter Hickel (b. Kans.), governor. **Tourist information** 1-888-256-6784. www.travelalaska.com

Arizona

www.az.gov

Name Probably from the Pima or Papago for "place of small springs." **Nickname** Grand Canyon State. **Capital** Phoenix. **Entered union** Feb. 14, 1912 (48th). **Motto** Ditat deus (God enriches). **Emblems** *Bird* Cactus wren. *Flower* Blossom of the saguaro cactus. *Songs* "Arizona March Song," "Arizona." *Tree* Palo verde. **Land** Total area 113,998 sq. mi (6th), incl. 364 sq. mi. inland water. **Borders** Utah, Colo., N.Mex., Sonora, Baja California Norte, Calif., Nev. **Rivers** Colorado, Gila, Little Colorado, Salt, Zuni. **Lakes** Havasu, Mead, Mohave, Powell, Roosevelt, San Carlos. **Mountains** Black, Gila, Hualpai, Mohawk, San Francisco Peaks (Humphreys Peak 12,633 ft.). **Other notable features** Grand Canyon, Kaibab Plateau, Painted and Sonoran Deserts, Petrified Forest. **People** (July, 2009 est.) 6,596,000 (14th). Race/Hispanic Origin (July, 2009 est.): White 86.1%. Black 4.4%. Indian 4.9%. Asian 2.6%. Pacific Islander 0.2%. Two or more races 1.8%. Hispanic 30.8%. **Cities** (2005) Phoenix 1,461,575. Tucson 515,526. Mesa 442,780. Glendale 239,435. Scottsdale 226,013. Chandler 234,939. Gilbert 173,989. Tempe 161,143. Peoria 138,200. Yuma 84,688. **Famous natives** Bruce Babbitt, politician. Cesar Chavez, labor leader. Wyatt Earp (b. Ill.), lawman. Barry Goldwater, politician. Goyathlay (Geronimo), Apache chieftain. Carl T. Hayden, congressman. Eusebio Kino (b. Italy), missionary. Sandra Day O'Connor, jurist. William H. Rehnquist, jurist. **Tourist information** 1-866-275-5816. www.arizonaguide.com

Arkansas

www.arkansas.gov

Name From term for Quapaw tribe given by other Indians. **Nickname** Land of Opportunity. **Capital** Little Rock. **Entered union** June 15, 1836 (25th). **Motto** Regnat populus (Let the people rule). **Emblems** *Bird* Mockingbird. *Flower* Apple blossom. *Song* "Arkansas." *Tree* Pine. **Land** Total area 53,179 sq. mi (29th), incl. 1,110 sq. mi. inland water. **Borders** Mo., Tenn., Miss., La., Tex., Okla. **Rivers** Arkansas, Mississippi, Ouachita, Red, St. Francis, White. **Lakes** Beaver, Bull Shoals, Chicot, Dardanelle, Greers Ferry, Greeson, Norfolk, Ouachita. **Other notable features** Ozark Mts. **People** (July, 2009 est.) 2,889,000 (32nd). Race/Hispanic Origin (July, 2009 est.): White 80.6%. Black 15.8%. Indian 0.9%. Asian 1.2%. Pacific Islander 0.1%. Two or more races 1.5%. Hispanic 6.0%. **Cities** (2005) Little Rock 184,564. Fort Smith 82,481. Fayetteville 66,655. North Little Rock 58,803. Jonesboro 59,358. Pine Bluff 52,693. Springdale 60,096. Conway 51,999. Rogers 48,353. Hot Springs 37,847. **Famous natives** Maya Angelou, author. Linda Bloodworth-Thomason, television producer/director. Glen Campbell, singer. Hattie W. Caraway, first woman senator. Johnny Cash, singer. Eldridge Cleaver, author. Bill Clinton, U.S. president. William Fulbright (b. Mo.), politician. Douglas MacArthur, general. Dick Powell, actor. Brooks Robinson, baseball player. Winthrop Rockefeller (b. N.Y.), politician/philanthropist. Edward Durrell Stone, architect. C. Vann Woodward, historian. **Tourist information** 1-800-NATURAL. www.arkansas.com

California

www.ca.gov

Name Probably from mythical island in García Ordoñez de Montalvo's 16th-century romance, The Deeds of Esplandián. **Nickname** Golden State. **Capital** Sacramento. **Entered union** Sept. 9, 1850 (31st). **Motto** "Eureka" (I have found it). **Emblems** *Bird* California valley quail. *Flower* Golden poppy. *Song* "I Love You, California." *Tree* California redwood. **Land** Total area 163,696 sq. mi (3rd), incl. 7,736 sq. mi. inland water. **Borders** Oreg., Nev., Ariz., Baja California Norte, Pacific Ocean. **Rivers** American, Colorado, Colorado River Aqueduct, Eel, Friant-Kern Canal, Klamath, Russian, Sacramento, Salinas, San Joaquin. **Lakes** Clear, Goose, Honey, Mono, Owens, Salton Sea, Shasta, Tahoe. Mountains Coast Ranges, Klamath, Lassen Peak, Sierra Nevada (Mt. Whitney 14,494 ft.). Other notable features Catalina Islands, Death Valley (282 ft. below sea level), San Francisco Bay, San Joaquin Valley. **People** (July, 2009 est.) 36,962,000 (1st). Race/Hispanic Origin (July, 2009 est.): White 76.4%. Black 6.6%. Indian 1.2%. Asian 12.7%. Pacific Islander 0.4%. Two or more races 2.6%. Hispanic 37.0%. **Cities** (2005) Los Angeles 3,844,829. San Diego 1,255,540. San Jose 912,332. San Francisco 739,426. Long Beach 474,014. Fresno 461,116. Sacramento 456,441. Oakland 395,274. Santa Ana 340,368. Anaheim 331,804. **Famous natives** Ansel Adams, photographer. Dave Brubeck, musician. Luther Burbank (b. Mass.), horticulturist. John Cage, composer. Joe DiMaggio, baseball player. Robert Frost, poet. Ernest and Julio Gallo (b. Italy), vintners. Pancho Gonzales, tennis player. Samuel Ichiye Hayakawa, politician/educator. William Randolph Hearst, publisher. Steve Jobs, computer entrepreneur. Billie Jean King, tennis player. Allen Lockheed, aviator. Jack London, author. Marilyn Monroe, actress. John Muir (b. Scotland), naturalist. Richard M. Nixon, U.S. president. John Northrop, aviator. Adlai Stevenson, politician. John Steinbeck, author. Levi Strauss (b. Germany), clothier. Edward Teller (b. Hungary), nuclear physicist. Shirley Temple, actress. Earl Warren, politician/jurist. **Tourist information** 1-800-GOCALIF. www.visitcalifornia.com

Colorado

www.colorado.gov

Name For Spanish for the color red. **Nickname** Centennial State. **Capital** Denver. **Entered union** Aug. 1, 1876 (38th). **Motto** Nil sine numine (Nothing without providence). **Emblems** *Bird* Lark bunting. Flower Rocky Mountain Columbine. *Song* "Where the Columbines Grow." *Tree* Colorado blue spruce. **Land** Total area 104,094 sq. mi (8th), incl. 376 sq. mi. inland water. **Borders** Wyo., Nebr., Kans., N.Mex., Ariz., Utah. **Rivers** Arkansas, Colorado, Green, Platte, Rio Grande. **Lakes** Blue Mesa, Dillon, Granby. Mountains Front Range, Laramie, Sangre de Cristo, San Juan, Sawatch Range (Mt. Elbert 14,443 ft.). **People** (July, 2009 est.) 5,025,000 (22nd). Race/Hispanic Origin (July, 2009 est.): White 89.5%. Black 4.4%. Indian 1.2%. Asian 2.7%. Pacific Islander 0.2%. Two or more races 2.0%. Hispanic 20.3%. **Cities** (2005) Denver 557,917. Colorado Springs 369,815. Aurora 297,235. Lakewood 140,671. Fort Collins 128,026. Westminster 105,084. Pueblo 103,495. Arvada 103,966. Centennial 98,243. Boulder 91,685. **Famous natives** Charlie Bent (b. Va.), trapper. "Unsinkable" Molly Brown, Titanic survivor. Scott Carpenter, astronaut. Lon Chaney, actor. Jack Dempsey, boxer. Mamie Eisenhower, first lady. Douglas Fairbanks, actor. Scott Hamilton, ice skater. Anne Parrish, novelist. Lowell Thomas, journalist. Byron R. White, jurist. **Tourist information** 1-800-COLORADO. www.colorado.com

Connecticut

www.ct.gov

Name From Mahican word meaning "beside the long tidal river." **Nicknames** Constitution State, Nutmeg State. **Capital** Hartford. **Entered union** Jan. 9, 1788 (5th). **Motto** Qui transtulit sustinet (He who transplanted still sustains). **Emblems** *Bird* American robin. *Flower* Mountain laurel. *Song* "Yankee Doodle." *Tree* White oak. **Land** Total area 5,543 sq. mi (48th), incl. 699 sq. mi. inland water **Borders** Mass., R.I., Long Island Sound, N.Y. **Rivers** Connecticut, Housatonic, Mianus, Naugatuck, Thames. **Lakes** Bantam, Barkhamstead, Candlewood, Waramaug. Other notable features Berkshire Hills, Long Island Sound. **People** (July, 2009 est.) 3,518,000 (29th). Race/Hispanic Origin (July, 2009 est.): White 84.0%. Black 10.4%. Indian 0.4%. Asian 3.6%. Pacific Islander 0.1%. Two or more races 1.5%. Hispanic 12.3%. **Cities** (2005) Bridgeport 139,008. Hartford 124,397. New Haven 124,791. Stamford 120,045. Waterbury 107,902. Norwalk 84,437. Danbury 78,736. New Britain 71,254. Bristol 61,353. Meriden 59,653. **Famous natives** Benedict Arnold, traitor. P.T. Barnum, showman. Lyman Beecher, theologian. John Brown, abolitionist. Samuel Colt, inventor. Jonathan Edwards, theologian. Charles Goodyear, inventor. Nathan Hale, patriot. Katharine Hepburn, actress. Charles Ives, composer. J.P. Morgan, financier. Ralph Nader, consumer advocate. Frederick Law Olmsted, landscape architect. Harriet Beecher Stowe, author. John Trumbell, artist. Noah Webster, lexicographer. Eli Whitney, inventor. **Tourist information** 1-888-CTvisit. www.ctvisit.com

Delaware

www.delaware.gov

Name For Thomas West, Lord De La Warre, colonial governor of Virginia. **Nicknames** First State, Diamond State. **Capital** Dover. **Entered union** Dec. 7, 1787 (1st). **Motto** "Liberty and Independence." **Emblems** *Bird* Blue hen chicken. *Flower* Peach blossom. *Song* "Our Delaware." *Tree* American holly. **Land** Total area 2,489 sq. mi (49th), incl. 536 sq. mi. inland water. **Borders** Pa., N.J., Atlantic Ocean, Md. **Rivers** Chesapeake & Delaware Canal, Delaware, Nanticoke. **People** (July, 2009 est.) 885,000 (45th). Race/Hispanic Origin (July, 2009 est.): White 73.9%. Black 21.1%. Indian 0.4%. Asian 3.0%. Pacific Islander 0.1%. Two or more races 1.5%. Hispanic 7.2%. **Cities** (2005) Wilmington 72,786. Dover 34,288. Newark 30,060. **Famous natives** Valerie Bertinelli, actress. John Dickinson (b. Md.), Penman of the Revolution. Eleuthère I. du Pont, manufacturer. Pierre S. ("Pete") du Pont, politician. Morgan Edwards, founder of Brown University (R.I.). Thomas Macdonough, navy officer. Howard Pyle, illustrator. Edward R. Squibb, physician/manufacturer. Christopher Ward, historian. **Tourist information** (866) 284-7483. www.visitdelaware.com

District of Columbia

www.dc.gov

Name After Christopher Columbus; Columbia was commonly used for the U.S. before 1800. **Became capital** Dec. 1, 1800. **Motto** Justitia omnibus (Justice for all). **Emblems** *Bird* Wood thrush. *Flower* American beauty rose. *Tree* Scarlet oak. **Land** Total area 68 sq. mi., incl. 7 sq. mi. inland water. **Borders** Md., Va. **Rivers** Anacostia, Potomac. **People** (July, 2009 est.) 600,000 (50th) Race/Hispanic Origin (July, 2009 est.): White 40.6%. Black 54.0%. Indian 0.4%. Asian 3.2%. Pacific Islander 0.1%. Two or more races 1.6%. Hispanic 8.8%. **Famous natives** Edward Albee, playwright. Carl Bernstein, journalist. John Foster Dulles, politician. Duke Ellington, composer. J. Edgar Hoover, FBI director. **Tourist information** 1-800-422-8644. www.washington.org

Florida

www.myflorida.com
Name By Juan Ponce de León for Pascua Florida (Easter festival of the flowers). **Nickname** Sunshine State. **Capital** Tallahassee. **Entered union** Mar. 3, 1845 (27th). **Motto** "In God We Trust." **Emblems** *Bird* Mockingbird. *Flower* Orange blossom. *Song* "Old Folks at Home" ("Swanee River"). *Tree* Sabal palmetto palm. **Land** Total area 65,755 sq. mi (22nd), incl. 11,828 sq. mi. inland water. **Borders** Ga., Atlantic Ocean, Gulf of Mexico, Ala. **Rivers** Apalachicola, Caloosahatchee, Indian, Kissimmee, Perdido, St. Johns, St. Mary's, Suwanee, Withlacoochee. **Lakes** Apopka, George, Okeechobee, Seminole. Other notable features Everglades, Florida Keys, Okefenokee Swamp. **People** (July, 2009 est.) 18,538,000 (4th). Race/Hispanic Origin (July, 2009 est.): White 19.4%. Black 16.1%. Indian 0.5%. Asian 2.4%. Pacific Islander 0.1%. Two or more races 1.5%. Hispanic 21.5%. **Cities** (2005) Jacksonville 782,623. Miami 386,417. Tampa 325,989. St. Petersburg 248,232. Hialeah 220,485. Orlando 213,223. Fort Lauderdale 167,380. Tallahassee 158,500. Hollywood 139,357. Pembroke Pines 137,427. **Famous natives** Mary Bethune, educator/reformer. Faye Dunaway, actress. Chris Evert, tennis player. Zora Neale Hurston, writer. James Weldon Johnson, lawyer/novelist. Osceola, Seminole chief. Sidney Poitier, actor. A. Philip Randolph, labor leader. Edmund Kirby Smith, Confederate general. Joseph Warren "Vinegar Joe" Stillwell, army officer. Ben Vereen, actor/singer. **Tourist information** (888) 735-2872. www.visitflorida.com

Georgia

www.georgia.gov
Name For King George II of England 1732. **Nicknames** Empire State of the South, Peach State. **Capital** Atlanta. **Entered union** Jan. 2, 1788 (4th). **Motto** "Wisdom, justice, moderation." **Emblems** *Bird* Brown thrasher. *Flower* Cherokee rose. *Songs* "Georgia," "Georgia on My Mind." *Tree* Live oak. **Land** Total area 59,425 sq. mi (24th), incl. 1,519 sq. mi. inland water. **Borders** Tenn., N.C., S.C., Atlantic Ocean, Fla., Ala. **Rivers** Altamaha, Apalachicola, Chattahoochee, Flint, Ocmulgee, Oconee, Savannah, Suwanee. **Lakes** Clark Hill, Harding, Hartwell, Seminole, Sidney Lanier, Sinclair, Walter F. George, West Point Lake. Other notable features Blue Ridge Mountains (Mount Enotah 4,784 ft.), Okefenokee Swamp. **People** (July, 2009 est.) 9,829,000 (9th). Race/Hispanic Origin (July, 2009 est.): White 65%. Black 30.2%. Indian 0.4%. Asian 3.0%. Pacific Islander 0.1%. Two or more races 1.3%. Hispanic 8.3%. **Cities** (2005) Atlanta 470,688. Augusta 190,782. Columbus 185,271. Savannah 128,453. Athens 103,238. Macon 94,316. Roswell 85,920. Albany 75,394. Marietta 61,261. Warner Robins 57,907. **Famous natives** James Brown, singer. Erskine Caldwell, author. James Earl ("Jimmy") Carter, U.S. president. Ray Charles, musician. Ty Cobb, baseball player. James Dickey, poet. Martin Luther King, Jr., minister/reformer. Sidney Lanier, author. Little Richard, musician. Carson McCullers, author. Alexander McGillivray, Creek chief. Margaret Mitchell, author. Elijah Muhammad, religious leader. Flannery O'Connor, author. Burt Reynolds, actor. Jackie Robinson, baseball player. Tomochichi, Yamacraw chief. Ted Turner (b. Ohio), businessman. Joanne Woodward, actress. **Tourist information** 1-800-VISIT-GA. www.exploregeorgia.com

Hawaii

www.hawaii.gov
Name Of unknown origin, perhaps from Hawaii Loa, traditional discoverer of islands, or from Hawaiki, the traditional Polynesian homeland. **Nickname**s Aloha State, Paradise of the Pacific. **Capital** Honolulu. **Entered union** Aug. 21, 1959 (50th). **Motto** Ua mau ke ea o ka aina i ke pono (The life of the land is perpetuated in righteousness). **Emblems** *Bird* Nene (Hawaiian goose). *Flower* Pua aloalo (hibiscus). *Song* "Hawaii Ponoi." *Tree* Kukui (candlenut). **Land** Total area 10,931 sq. mi (43rd), incl. 4,508 sq. mi. inland water. Surrounded by Pacific Ocean. **Rivers** Kaukonahua Stream, Wailuku Stream. **Lakes** Halulu, Kolekole, Salt Lake, Waiia Res. Other notable features Pearl Harbor. Hualalai, Kilauea, Mauna Kea (13,796 ft.), and Mauna Loa volcanoes. Main islands Hawaii, Kauai, Lanai, Maui, Molokai, Oahu. **People** (July, 2009 est.) 1,295,000 (42nd). Race/Hispanic Origin (July, 2009 est.): White 30.2%. Black 3.2%. Indian 0.6%. Asian 38.8%. Pacific Islander 9.2%. Two or more races 18.0%. Hispanic 9.0%. **Cities** (2005) Honolulu 377,379. Hilo 40,759. Kailua 36,513. Kaneohe 34,970. Waipahu 33,108. Pearl City 30,976. Waimalu 29,371. Mililani Town 28,608. Kahului 20,146. Kihei 16,749. (Note: The Census Bureau does not keep statistics on cities other than Honolulu between decennial censuses because most Hawaiian cities are not incorporated). **Famous natives** Bernice P. Bishop, philanthropist. Sanford B. Dole, statehood advocate. Charlotte (b. Ohio) and Luther Halsey Gulick, Camp Fire Girls founders. Don Ho, singer. Daniel J. Inouye, politician. Duke Kahanamoku, swimmer. Victoria Kaiulani, last heiress presumptive to Hawaiian throne. Kamehameha I, king. Kamehameha III, king. Liliuokalani, queen. Bette Midler, singer. **Tourist information** 1-800-GOHAWAII. www.gohawaii.com

Idaho

www.state.id.us

Name Means "gem of the mountains." **Nickname** Gem State. **Capital** Boise. **Entered union** July 3, 1890 (43rd). **Motto** Esto perpetua (May it last forever). **Emblems** *Bird* Mountain bluebird. *Flower* Syringa. *Song* "Here We Have Idaho." *Tree* Western white pine. **Land** Total area 83,570 sq. mi (14th), incl. 823 sq. mi. inland water. **Borders** British Columbia, Mont., Wyo., Utah, Nev., Oreg., Wash. **Rivers** Bear, Clearwater, Payette, Salmon, Snake. **Lakes** American Falls Res., Coeur d'Alene, Pend Oreille. Mountains Bitterroot Range, Centennial, Clearwater, Salmon River, Sawtooth Range (Castle Peak 11,820 ft.), Wasatch Range. Other notable features Grand Canyon of the Snake River. **People** (July, 2009 est.) 1,546,000 (39th). Race/Hispanic Origin (July, 2009 est.): White 94.4%. Black 1.0%. Indian 1.6%. Asian 1.2%. Pacific Islander 0.1%. Two or more races 1.7%. Hispanic 10.7%. **Cities** (2005) Boise City 193,161. Nampa 71,713. Pocatello 53,372. Idaho Falls 52,338. Meridian 52,240. Coeur d'Alene 40,059. Twin Falls 38,630. Lewiston 31,081. Caldwell 34,433. Rexburg 26,265. **Famous natives** Joseph, Nez Percé chief. Ezra Taft Benson, politician. Gutzon Borglum, sculptor. Frank Church, politician. Ezra Pound, poet. Harmon Killebrew, baseball player. Jerry Kramer, football player. Sacagawea (Bird Woman), Shoshone interpreter. Lana Turner, actress. **Tourist information** 1-800-VISITID. www.visitidaho.org.

Illinois

www.illinois.gov

Name Corruption of iliniwek ("tribe of the superior men"), natives of region at time of earliest French explorations. **Nickname** Prairie State. **Capital** Springfield. **Entered union** Dec. 3, 1818 (21st). **Motto** "State sovereignty—national unity." Slogan "Land of Lincoln." **Emblems** *Bird* Cardinal. *Flower* Violet. *Song* "Illinois." *Tree* White oak. **Land** Total area 57,914 sq. mi (25th), incl. 2,331 sq. mi. inland water. **Borders** Wis., Lake Michigan, Ind., Ky., Mo., Iowa. **Rivers** Fox, Illinois, Illinois Waterway, Kankakee, Kaskaskia, Mississippi, Ohio, Rock, Vermillion, Wabash. **Lakes** Carlyle, Crab Orchard. Other notable features Charles Mound (1,235 ft.), Little Egypt. **People** (July, 2009 est.) 12,910,000 (5th). Race/Hispanic Origin (July, 2009 est.): White 79.0%. Black 14.9%. Indian 0.4%. Asian 4.4%. Pacific Islander 0.1%. Two or more races 1.3%. Hispanic 15.2%. **Cities** (2005) Chicago 2,842,518. Aurora 168,181. Rockford 152,916. Naperville 141,579. Joliet 136,208. Peoria 112,685. Springfield 115,668. Elgin 98,645. Waukegan 91,396. Cicero 82,741. **Famous natives** Jane Addams, reformer (Nobel Peace Prize, 1930). Ernie Banks, baseball player. Saul Bellow, author (Nobel Prize, 1976). Harry A. Blackmun, jurist. Ray Bradbury, author. Gwendolyn Brooks, poet. William Jennings Bryan, politician. Edgar Rice Burroughs, novelist. St. Frances Xavier Cabrini (b. Italy). Clarence Darrow, lawyer. Miles Davis, musician. John Dos Passos, novelist. Enrico Fermi (b. Italy), nuclear physicist (Nobel Prize, 1938). Robert Louis ("Bob") Fosse, choreographer. Milton Friedman, economist (Nobel Prize, 1976). Benny Goodman, musician. Ernest Hemingway, novelist. Charlton Heston, actor. William Holden, actor. Abraham Lincoln, U.S. President (b. Kentucky). Vachel Lindsay, poet. Archibald MacLeish, poet. Ludwig Mies van der Rohe (b. Germany), architect. Charles W. Post, cereal manufacturer. Ronald Reagan, U.S. president. Carl Sandburg, poet. Albert G. Spalding, merchant. John Paul Stevens, jurist. Gloria Swanson, actress. **Tourist information** 1-800-2CONNECT. www.enjoyillinois.com

Indiana

www.in.gov

Name For the land of Indians by early settlers, who found many distinct tribes living in region. **Nickname** Hoosier State. **Capital** Indianapolis. **Entered union** Dec. 11, 1816 (19th). **Motto** "The Crossroads of America." **Emblems** *Bird* Cardinal. *Flower* Peony. *Song* "On the Banks of the Wabash, Far Away." *Tree* Tulip tree. **Land** Total area 36,418 sq. mi (38th), incl. 551 sq. mi. inland water. **Borders** Lake Michigan, Mich., Ohio, Ky., Ill. **Rivers** Kankakee, Ohio, Tippecanoe, Wabash, White, Whitewater. **Lakes** Freeman, Shafer. **People** (July, 2009 est.) 6,423,000 (16th). Race/Hispanic Origin (July, 2009 est.): White 87.8%. Black 9.2%. Indian 0.3%. Asian 1.5%. Pacific Islander 0.1%. Two or more races 1.2%. Hispanic 5.5%. **Cities** (2005) Indianapolis 784,118. Fort Wayne 223,341. Evansville 115,918. South Bend 105,262. Gary 98,715. Hammond 79,217. Bloomington 69,017. Muncie 66,164. Lafayette 60,459. Anderson 57,500. **Famous natives** Larry Bird, basketball player. Hoagy Carmichael, composer. Eugene V. Debs, politician/organizer. Theodore Dreiser, author. Benjamin Harrison, U.S. president. Jimmy Hoffa, union leader. Michael Jackson, singer. David Letterman, comedian. Carole Lombard, actress. Cole Porter, composer. Ernie Pyle, journalist. Knute Rockne (b. Norway), football coach. Paul Samuelson, economist (Nobel Prize, 1960). Booth Tarkington, author. Kurt Vonnegut, author. Wendell L. Willkie, politician. **Tourist information** 1-888-EnjoyIN. www.in.gov/visitindiana.

Iowa

www.iowa.gov

Name For Iowa tribe. **Nickname** Hawkeye State. **Capital** Des Moines. **Entered union** Dec. 28, 1846 (29th). **Motto** "Our liberties we prize and our rights we will maintain." **Emblems** *Bird* Eastern goldfinch. *Flower* Wild rose. *Song* "The Song of Iowa." *Tree* Oak. **Land** Total area 56,272 sq. mi (26th), incl. 402 sq. mi. inland water. **Borders** Minn., Wis., Ill., Mo., Nebr., S.Dak. **Rivers** Big Sioux, Des Moines, Mississippi, Missouri. **Lakes** Okoboji, Rathbun Res., Red Rock, Saylorville Res., Spirit, Storm. Other notable features Ocheyedan Mound (1,675 ft.). **People** (July, 2009 est.) 3,008,000 (30th). Race/Hispanic Origin (July, 2009 est.): White 93.9%. Black 2.8%. Indian 0.4%. Asian 1.7%. Pacific Islander 0.1%. Two or more races 1.1%. Hispanic 4.5%. **Cities** (2005) Des Moines 194,163. Cedar Rapids 123,119. Davenport 98,845. Sioux City 83,148. Council Bluffs 59,568. Dubuque 57,798. Ames 52,263. West Des Moines 52,768. **Famous natives** Norman E. Borlaug, agronomist (Nobel Peace Prize, 1970). William F. ("Buffalo Bill") Cody, scout/showman. George Gallup, pollster. Josiah B. Grinnell (b. Vt.), abolitionist. Herbert Hoover, U.S. president. Harry L. Hopkins, politician. John L. Lewis, labor leader. John R. Mott, religious leader. Billy Sunday, baseball player/evangelist. John Wayne, actor. Meredith Wilson, composer. Grant Wood, painter. **Tourist information** 1-888-472-6035. www.traveliowa.com

Kansas

www.state.ks.gov

Name For Kansa or Kaw, "people of the south wind." **Nickname** Sunflower State. **Capital** Topeka. **Entered union** Jan. 29, 1861 (34th). **Motto** Ad astra per aspera ("To the stars through adversity"). **Emblems** *Bird* Western meadowlark. *Flower* Wild native sunflower. *Song* "Home on the Range." *Tree* Cottonwood. **Land** Total area 82,277 sq. mi (15th), incl. 462 sq. mi. inland water. **Borders** Nebr., Mo., Okla., Colo. **Rivers** Arkansas, Kansas, Missouri, Republican, Saline, Smoky Hill, Solomon. **Lakes** Kanapolis, Malvern, Perry, Pomona, Tuttle Creek, Waconda. Other notable features Flint Hills. **People** (July, 2009 est.) 2,819,000 (33rd). Race/Hispanic Origin (July, 2009 est.): White 88.5%. Black 6.2%. Indian 1.0%. Asian 2.3%. Pacific Islander 0.1%. Two or more races 1.9%. Hispanic 9.3%. **Cities** (2005) Wichita 354,865. Kansas City 144,210. Topeka 121,946. Olathe 111,334. Lawrence 81,816. Shawnee 57,628. Manhattan 48,668. Salina 45,956. Lenexa 43,434. **Famous natives** "Buffalo Bill" Cody. Walter Chrysler, carmaker. Robert Dole, politician. Amelia Earhart, aviator. Dwight David Eisenhower (b. Tex.), general/U.S. president. Dennis Hopper, actor. William Inge, playwright. Nancy Landon Kassebaum, politician. Alf Landon, politician. Edgar Lee Masters, poet. James Naismith, inventor of basketball. Carry Nation (b. Ky.), prohibitionist. Charlie ("Bird") Parker, musician. Damon Runyon, writer. Gale Sayers, football player. William Allen White, the Sage of Emporia, editor. **Tourist information** 1-800-2KANSAS. www.travelks.com

Kentucky, Commonwealth of

www.kentucky.gov

Name Corruption of the Iroquois kenta-ke (meadow land) or Wyandot kah-ten-tah-teh (land of tomorrow). **Nickname** Bluegrass State. **Capital** Frankfort. **Entered union** June 1, 1792 (15th). **Motto** "United we stand, divided we fall." **Emblems** *Bird* Cardinal. *Flower* Goldenrod. *Song* "My Old Kentucky Home." *Tree* Tulip poplar. **Land** Total area 40,409 sq. mi (37th), incl. 681 sq. mi. inland water. **Borders** Ind., Ohio, W.Va., Va., Tenn., Mo., Ill. **Rivers** Cumberland, Kentucky, Licking, Ohio, Tennessee. **Lakes** Barkley, Barren River Res., Dewey, Grayson Res., Laurel Res., Nolin Res., Rough Res. Mountains Appalachian (Black Mt., 4,145 ft.), Cumberland. Other notable features Tennessee Valley. **People** (July, 2009 est.) 4,314,000 (26th). Race/Hispanic Origin (July, 2009 est.): White 89.6%. Black 7.9%. Indian 0.3%. Asian 1.1%. Pacific Islander 0.1%. Two or more races 1.1%. Hispanic 2.7%. **Cities** (2005) Lexington-Fayette 268,080. Louisville 556,429. Owensboro 55,459. Bowling Green 52,272. Covington 42,811. Hopkinsville 28,821. Richmond 30,893. Henderson 27,666. Frankfort 27,210. Jeffersontown 26,100. **Famous natives** Muhammad Ali, boxer. Alben W. Barkley, politician. Daniel Boone (b. Pa.), frontiersman. Louis D. Brandeis, jurist. Kit Carson, frontiersman. Henry Clay, politician. Jefferson Davis, president of Confederate States of America. D.W. Griffith, director. John Marshall Harlan, jurist. Abraham Lincoln, U.S. president. Col. Harland Sanders, entrepreneur. Frederick M. Vinson, jurist. Robert Penn Warren, author. **Tourist information** 1-800-225-TRIP or 1-800-255-PARK. www.kytourism.com

Louisiana

www.louisiana.gov

Name For King Louis XIV. **Nickname** Pelican State. **Capital** Baton Rouge. **Entered union** Apr. 30, 1812 (18th). **Motto** "Union, justice, confidence." **Emblems** *Bird* Eastern brown pelican. *Flower* Magnolia. *Songs* "Give Me Louisiana," "You Are My Sunshine." *Tree* Bald cypress. **Land** Total area 51,840 sq. mi (31st), incl. 8,278 sq. mi. inland water. **Borders** Ark., Miss., Gulf of Mexico, Tex. **Rivers** Atchafalaya, Mississippi,

Ouachita, Pearl, Red, Sabine. **Lakes** Bistineau, Borgne, Caddo, Catahoula, Grand, Maurepas, Pontchartrain, Salvador, White. Other notable features Bayou Barataria, Bayou Bodcau, Bayou D'Arbonne, Driskill Mt. (535 ft.). **People** (July, 2009 est.) 4,492,000 (25th). Race/Hispanic Origin (July, 2009 est.): White 64.6%. Black 32.1%. Indian 0.6%. Asian 1.5%. Pacific Islander Z. Two or more races 1.1%. Hispanic 3.6%. **Cities** (2005) New Orleans 454,863. Baton Rouge 222,064. Shreveport 198,874. Lafayette 112,030. Lake Charles 70,555. Kenner 69,911. Bossier City 60,505. Monroe 51,914. Alexandria 45,693. New Iberia 32,495. **Famous natives** Louis "Satchmo" Armstrong, jazz musician. Pierre Beauregard, Confederate general. Terry Bradshaw, football player. Braxton Bragg, Confederate general. Truman Capote, author. Clyde Cessna, aviator. Michael DeBakey, surgeon. Fats Domino, singer. Lillian Hellman, author. Mahalia Jackson, singer. Jean Baptiste Le Moyne, sieur de Bienville (b. Canada), founded New Orleans. Jerry Lee Lewis, singer. Huey P. Long, senator. Ferdinand Joseph La Menthe "Jelly Roll" Morton, musician. Leonidas K. Polk, clergyman/Confederate general. Henry Miller Shreve (b. N.J.), riverboat captain. Edward D. White, Jr., jurist. **Tourist information** 1-800-99-GUMBO . www.louisianatravel.com

Maine

www.maine.gov
Name Either for Maine in France or to distinguish mainland from islands in the Gulf of Maine. **Nickname** Pine Tree State. **Capital** Augusta. **Entered union** Mar. 15, 1820 (23rd). **Motto** Dirigo (I direct). **Emblems** *Bird* Chickadee. *Flower* White pinecone and tassel. *Song* "State of Maine Song." *Tree* Eastern white pine. **Land** Total area 35,385 sq. mi (39th), incl. 4,523 sq. mi. inland water. **Borders** Quebec, New Brunswick, Atlantic Ocean, N.H. **Rivers** Alagash, Androscoggin, Aroostock, Kennebec, Machias, Penobscot, Piscataqua, Salmon Falls, St. John. **Lakes** Chamberlain, Chesuncook, Grand, Moosehead, Rangeley, Sebago. Other notable features Longfellow Mts. (Mt. Katahdin 5,268 ft.), Mt. Desert Island, Penobscot Bay. **People** (July, 2009 est.) 1,318,000 (41st). Race/Hispanic Origin (July, 2009 est.): White 96.1%. Black 1.2%. Indian 0.6%. Asian 1.0%. Two or more races 1.1%. Hispanic 1.4%. **Cities** (2005) Portland 63,889. Lewiston 36,050. Bangor 31,074. Auburn 23,602. Biddeford 22,072. Augusta 18,626. Saco 18,230. Westbrook 16,108. Waterville 15,621. **Famous natives** Cyrus H.K. Curtis, publisher. Hannibal Hamlin, politician. Sarah Orne Jewett, novelist. Henry Wadsworth Longfellow, poet. Sir Hiram and Hudson Maxim, inventors. Edna St. Vincent Millay, poet. Edmund S. Muskie, politician. John Knowles Paine, composer. Kenneth Roberts, novelist. Edward Arlington Robinson, poet. Nelson

Rockefeller, politician. Marguerite Yourcenar (b. France), author. **Tourist information** (888) 624-6345. www.visitmaine.com

Maryland

www.maryland.gov
Name For Henrietta Maria, queen consort of Charles I. **Nicknames** Old Line State, Free State. **Capital** Annapolis. **Entered union** Apr. 28, 1788 (7th). **Motto** Fatti maschii, parole femine (Manly deeds, womanly words). **Emblems** *Bird* Baltimore oriole. *Flower* Black-eyed Susan. *Song* "Maryland, My Maryland." *Tree* White oak. **Land** Total area 12,407 sq. mi (42nd), incl. 2,633 sq. mi. inland water. **Borders** Pa., Del., Atlantic Ocean, Va., D.C., W.Va. **Rivers** Chester, Choptank, Nanticoke, Patapsco, Patuxent, Pocomoke, Potomac, Susquehanna. Other notable features Allegheny Mts., Blue Ridge Mts., Chesapeake Bay. **People** (July, 2009 est.) 5,699,000 (19th). Race/Hispanic Origin (July, 2009 est.): White 63.0%. Black 29.7%. Indian 0.4%. Asian 5.2%. Pacific Islander 0.1%. Two or more races 1.7%. Hispanic 7.2%. **Cities** (2005). Baltimore 635,815. Gaithersburg 57,698. Frederick 57,907. Rockville 57,402. Bowie 53,878. Annapolis 36,300. College Park 25,171. Salisbury 26,295. Greenbelt 22,242. **Famous natives** Russell Baker, journalist. Benjamin Banneker, surveyor. Eubie Blake, pianist. Rachel Carson, biologist/author. Stephen Decatur, navy officer. Frederick Douglass, abolitionist. Billie Holiday, singer. Johns Hopkins, financier/philanthropist. Francis Scott Key, lawyer/"poet. Thurgood Marshall, jurist. H.L. Mencken, writer. Charles Willson Peale, artist. William Pinckney, statesman. James Rouse, urban planner. Babe Ruth, baseball player. Upton Sinclair, author. Roger B. Taney, jurist. Harriet Tub-man, abolitionist. John Waters, filmmaker. **Tourist Information** 1-866-639-3526 www.visitmaryland.org

Massachusetts, Commonwealth of

www.mass.gov
Name For Massachuset tribe, whose **name** means "at or about the great hill." **Nickname** Bay State. **Capital** Boston. **Entered union** Feb. 6, 1788 (6th). **Motto** Ense petit placidam sub libertate quietem (By the sword we seek peace, but peace only under liberty). **Emblems** *Bird* Chickadee. *Flower* Mayflower. *Song* "All Hail to Massachusetts." *Tree* American elm. **Land** Total area 10,555 sq. mi (44th), incl. 2,715 sq. mi. inland water. **Borders** Vt., N.H., Atlantic Ocean, R.I., Conn., N.Y. **Rivers** Cape Cod Canal, Connecticut, Merrimack, Taunton. Other notable features Buzzard's Bay, Cape Ann, Cape Cod, Cape Cod Bay, Connecticut Valley, Elizabeth Islands, Martha's Vineyard, Monomoy Island, Nantucket

Island. **People** (July, 2009 est.) 6,594,000 (15th). Race/Hispanic Origin (July, 2009 est.): White 85.9%. Black 7.1%. Indian 0.3%. Asian 5.1%. Pacific Islander 0.1%. Two or more races 1.5%. Hispanic 8.8%. **Cities** (2005) Boston 559,034. Worcester 175,898. Springfield 151,732. Lowell 103,111. Cambridge 100,135. Brockton 94,632. New Bedford 93,102. Fall River 91,802. Quincy 90,250. Lynn 88,792. **Famous natives** John Adams, U.S. president. John Quincy Adams, U.S. president. Samuel Adams, patriot. Horatio Alger, clergyman/author. Susan B. Anthony, suffragette. Clara Barton, nurse. Leonard Bernstein, composer. George Herbert Walker Bush, U.S. president. John ("Johnny Appleseed") Chapman, pioneer. Richard Cardinal Cushing, prelate. Bette Davis, actress. Emily Dickinson, poet. Ralph Waldo Emerson, author. Marshall Field, merchant. R. Buckminster Fuller, inventor/engineer. John Hancock, patriot. Oliver Wendell Holmes, jurist. Winslow Homer, painter. John F. Kennedy, U.S. president. Jack Kerouac, author. Cotton Mather, theologian. Samuel Eliot Morison, historian. Samuel Morse, inventor. Thomas P. "Tip" O'Neill, congressman. Edgar Allan Poe, poet/author. Paul Revere patriot/silversmith. Louis Sullivan, architect. Henry David Thoreau, author. **Tourist information** 1-800-227-MASS. www.massvacation.com

Michigan

www.michigan.gov

Name From the Fox mesikami, "large lake." **Nicknames** Wolverine State, Lake State. **Capital** Lansing. **Entered union** Jan. 26, 1837 (26th). **Motto** Si quaeris peninsulam amoenam circumspice (If you are looking for a beautiful peninsula, look around you). **Emblems** *Bird* Robin. *Flower* Apple blossom. *Song* "Michigan, My Michigan." *Tree* White pine. **Land** Total area 96,716 sq. mi (11th), incl. 39,912 sq. mi. inland water. **Borders** Lake Superior, Ontario, Lake Huron, Lake Erie, Ohio, Ind., Lake Michigan, Wisc. **Rivers** Brule, Detroit, Kalamazoo, Menominee, Montreal, Muskegon, St. Joseph, St. Mary's. **Lakes** Burt, Higgins, Houghton, Huron, Manistique, Michigan, Mullett, St. Clair, Superior. Other notable features Isle Royale, Mt. Curwood (1,980 ft.), Saginaw Bay, Traverse Bay, Whitefish Bay. **People** (July, 2009 est.) 9,970,000 (8th). Race/Hispanic Origin (July, 2009 est.): White 81.2%. Black 14.2%. Indian 0.6%. Asian 2.4%. Two or more races 1.6%. Hispanic 4.2%. **Cities** (2005) Detroit 886,671. Grand Rapids 193,780. Warren 135,311. Flint 118,551. Lansing 115,518. Ann Arbor 113,271. Livonia 97,977. Dearborn 94,090. Westland 85,623. **Famous natives** Ralph J. Bunche, statesman (Nobel Peace Prize, 1950). Paul de Kruif, bacteriologist. Thomas Dewey, politician. Herbert H. Dow (b. Canada), chemical manufacturer. Edna Ferber, author. Gerald

Ford (b. Neb.) U.S. president. Henry Ford, industrialist. Edgar Guest, journalist/poet. Robert Ingersoll, industrialist. Will Kellogg, business-man/philanthopist. Charles A. Lindbergh, aviator. Madonna, singer. Antoine de La Mothe, sieur de Cadillac (b. France), founded Detroit. Pontiac, Ottawa chief. William Upjohn, drug manufacturer. **Tourist information** 1-888-784-7328. www.michigan.org/travel

Minnesota

www.state.mn.us

Name From the Sioux minisota, "sky-tinted waters." **Nicknames** North Star State, Gopher State, **Land** of 10,000 Lakes. **Capital** St. Paul. **Entered union** May 11, 1858 (32rd). **Motto** L'étoile du nord (Star of the north). **Emblems** *Bird* Common loon. *Flower* Pink and white lady's slipper. *Song* "Hail, Minnesota!." *Tree* Red pine. **Land** Total area 86,939 sq. mi (12th), incl. 7,329 sq. mi. inland water. **Borders** Manitoba, Ontario, Lake Superior, Wisc., Iowa, S.Dak., N.Dak. **Rivers** Minnesota, Mississippi, Red River of the North, St. Croix. **Lakes** Itasca, Lake of the Woods, Leech, Mille Lacs, Red, Winnibigoshish. Other notable features Mesabi Range. **People** (July, 2009 est.) 5,266,000 (21st). Race/Hispanic Origin (July, 2009 est.): White 88.6%. Black 4.7%. Indian 1.3%. Asian 3.8%. Pacific Islander 0.1%. Two or more races 1.6%. Hispanic 4.3%. **Cities** (2005) Minneapolis 372,811. St. Paul 275,150. Rochester 94,950. Duluth 84,896 Bloomington 81,164. Brooklyn Park 68,550. Plymouth 69,701. Eagan 63,665. Coon Rapids 62,417. Burnsville 59,159. **Famous natives** Warren Burger, jurist. Bob Dylan, musician. F. Scott Fitzgerald, novelist. Judy Garland, actress. J. Paul Getty, businessman. Garrison Keillor, humorist. Sinclair Lewis, author (Nobel Prize, 1930). Paul Manship, sculptor. William and Charles Mayo, surgeons. Eugene McCarthy, politician. Walter F. Mondale, politician. Charles Schulz, cartoonist. Richard W. Sears, merchant. **Tourist information** 1-800-657-3700. www.exploreminnesota.com

Mississippi

www.mississippi.gov

Name From the Ojibwa misi sipi, "great river." **Nickname** Magnolia State. **Capital** Jackson. **Entered union** Dec. 10, 1817 (20th). **Motto** Virtute et armis (By virtue and arms). **Emblems** *Bird* Mockingbird. *Flower* Magnolia. *Song* "Go, Mississippi." *Tree* Magnolia. **Land** Total area 48,430 sq. mi (32nd), incl. 1,523 sq. mi. inland water. **Borders** Tenn., Ala., Gulf of Mexico, La., Ark. **Rivers** Big Black, Mississippi, Pearl, Tennessee, Yazoo. **Lakes** Arkabutla, Grenada, Ross Barnett Res., Sardis. Other notable features Pontotoc Ridge. **People** (July, 2009 est.) 2,952,000 (31st). Race/Hispanic

Origin (July, 2009 est.): White 60.5%. Black 37.2%. Indian 0.5%. Asian 0.9%. Two or more races 0.9%. Hispanic 2.5%. **Cities** (2005) Jackson 177,977. Gulfport 72,464. Biloxi 50,209. Hattiesburg 47,176. Greenville 38,724. Meridian 38,605. Southaven 38,840. Vicksburg 26,226. Pascagoula 25,990. **Famous natives** Medgar Evers, civil rights leader. William Faulkner, novelist. Shelby Foote, historian. Jim Henson, puppeteer. B.B. King, musician. Elvis Presley, singer. Leontyne Price, opera singer. Jerry Rice, football player. John C. Stennis, politician. Conway Twitty, singer. Muddy Waters, musician. Eudora Welty, novelist. Ben Ames Williams, novelist. Tennessee Williams, playwright. Richard Wright, author. **Tourist information** 1-866-SEE-MISS. www.visitmississippi.org

Missouri

www.state.mo.us

Name From the Iliniwek missouri, "owner of big canoes." **Nickname** Show Me State. **Capital** Jefferson City. **Entered union** Aug. 10, 1821 (24th). **Motto** Salus populi suprema lex esto (The welfare of the people shall be the supreme law). **Emblems** *Bird* Bluebird. *Flower* Hawthorne. *Song* "Missouri Waltz." *Tree* Dogwood. **Land** Total area 69,704 sq. mi (21st), incl. 818 sq. mi. inland water. **Borders** Iowa, Ill., Ky., Tenn., Ark., Okla., Kans., Nebr. **Rivers** Des Moines, Mississippi, Missouri, Osage, St. Francis. **Lakes** Bull Shoals, Clearwater, Lake of the Ozarks, Lake of the Woods, Table, Wappapella. Other notable features Ozark Mts. (Taum Sauk Mt. 1,772 ft.). **People** (July, 2009 est.) 5,988,000 (18th). Race/Hispanic Origin (July, 2009 est.): White 84.9%. Black 11.5%. Indian 0.5%. Asian 1.5%. Pacific Islander 0.1%. Two or more races 1.5%. Hispanic 3.4%. **Cities** (2005) Kansas City 444,965. St. Louis 344,362. Springfield 150,298. Indepen-dence 110,208. Columbia 91,814. Lee's Summit 80,338. St. Joseph 72,661. St. Charles 62,304. O'Fallon 69,694. St. Peters 54,209. **Famous natives** Thomas Hart Benton, painter. Yogi Berra, baseball player. George Caleb Bingham (b. Va.), painter. Omar Bradley, general. Adophus Busch (b. Germany), brewer. George Washington Carver, botanist. Walter Cronkite, journalist. Walt Disney, film producer. T.S. Eliot, poet. Walker Evans, photographer. Langston Hughes, poet. Jesse James, outlaw. Marianne Moore, poet. Reinhold Niebuhr, theologian. J.C. Penny, businessman. John J. "Black Jack" Pershing, soldier. Joseph Pulitzer (b. Hungary), publisher. Ginger Rogers, dancer. Casey Stengel, baseball player. Virgil Thompson, composer. Harry S Truman, U.S. president. Mark Twain, writer. Tom Watson, golfer. Shelley Winters, actress. **Tourist information** 1-800-519-2100. www.visitmo.com

Montana

www.mt.gov

Name From Spanish montaña, "mountainous." **Nicknames** Treasure State, Big Sky Country. **Capital** Helena. **Entered union** Nov. 8, 1889 (41st). **Motto** Oro y plata (Gold and silver). **Emblems** *Bird* Western meadowlark. *Flower* Bitterroot. *Song* "Montana." *Tree* Ponderosa pine. **Land** Total area 147,042 sq. mi (4th), incl. 1,490 sq. mi. inland water. **Borders** British Columbia, Alberta, Saskatchewan, N.Dak., S.Dak., Wyo., Idaho. **Rivers** Kootenai, Milk, Missouri, Musselshell, Powder, Yellowstone. **Lakes** Bighorn, Canyon Ferry, Elwell, Flathead, Ft. Peck. Mountains Absaroka Range, Beartooth Range (Granite Peak 12,799 ft.), Big Belt, Bitterroot Range, Centennial, Crazy, Lewis Range, Little Belt. Other notable features Continental Divide, Missoula Valley. **People** (July, 2009 est.) 975,000 (44th). Race/Hispanic Origin (July, 2009 est.): White 90.3%. Black 0.7%. Indian 6.4%. Asian 0.7%. Pacific Islander 0.1%. Two or more races 1.8%. Hispanic 3.1%. **Cities** (2005) Billings 98,721. Missoula 62,923. Great Falls 56,338. Butte-Silver Bow 32,282. Bozeman 33,535. Helena 27,383. Kalispell 18,480. Havre 9,390. Anaconda-Deer Lodge County 8,948 Miles City 8,162. **Famous natives** Gary Cooper, actor. Marcus Daly (b. Ireland), mine owner. Chet Huntley, journalist. Myrna Loy, actress. Mike Mansfield (b. N.Y.), politician/diplomat. Jeanette Rankin, politician/reformer. Charles M. Russell, artist. **Tourist information** 1-800-847-4868. www.visitmt.com

Nebraska

www.nebraska.gov

Name From the Oto nebrathka, "flat water." **Nickname** Cornhusker State. **Capital** Lincoln. **Entered union** Mar. 1, 1867 (37th). **Motto** "Equality before the law." **Emblems** *Bird* Western meadowlark. *Flower* Goldenrod. *Song* "Beautiful Nebraska." *Tree* Western cottonwood. **Land** Total area 77,354 sq. mi (16th), incl. 481 sq. mi. inland water. **Borders** S.Dak., Iowa, Mo., Kans., Colo., Wyo. **Rivers** Missouri, North Platte, Republican, South Platte. **Lakes** Harlan Co. Res., Lewis and Clark Lake. Other notable features Pine Ridge, Sand Hills. **People** (July, 2009 est.) 1,797,000 (38th). Race/Hispanic Origin (July, 2009 est.): White 91.1%. Black 4.6%. Indian 1.1%. Asian 1.7%. Pacific Islander 0.1%. Two or more races 1.3%. Hispanic 8.4%. **Cities** (2002) Omaha 399,357. Lincoln 232,362. Bellevue 46,217. Grand Island 43,010. Kearney 27,910. Fremont 25,188. Norfolk 24,183. Hastings 23,908. North Platte 23,674. Columbus 20,877. **Famous natives** Fred Astaire, dancer. Marlon Brando, actor. William Jennings Bryan, politician. Johnny Carson (b. Iowa), comedian. Willa Cather (b. Va.), author. Loren Eiseley, anthropologist. Henry Fonda, actor. Rollin Kirby, cartoonist. Melvin Laird, politician. Harold Lloyd, actor. Mahpiua Luta (Red Cloud), Oglala Sioux chief. Malcolm X, religious leader. Roscoe Pound, educator. **Tourist information** (877) NEBRASKA. www.visitnebraska.gov

Nevada

www.nv.gov

Name From Spanish, meaning "snow-covered sierra." **Nicknames** Sagebrush State, Silver State. **Capital** Carson City. **Entered union** Oct. 31, 1864 (36th). **Motto** "All for our country." **Emblems** *Bird* Mountain bluebird. *Flower* Sagebrush. *Song* "Home Means Nevada." *Tree* Single-leaf piñon. **Land** Total area 110,561 sq. mi (7th), incl. 735 sq. mi. inland water. **Borders** Oreg., Idaho, Utah, Ariz., Calif. **Rivers** Colorado, Humboldt. **Lakes** Pyramid, Walker, Winnemucca. Other notable features Black Rock Desert, Carson Sink, Humboldt Salt Marsh, Mojave Desert. **People** (July, 2009 est.) 2,643,000 (35th). Race/Hispanic Origin (July, 2009 est.): White 80.3%. Black 8.3%. Indian 1.5%. Asian 6.6%. Pacific Islander 0.5%. Two or more races 2.8%. Hispanic 26.5%. **Cities** (2005) Las Vegas 545,147. Henderson 232,146. Reno 203,550. Sparks 82,051. Carson City 56,062. Elko 16,685. Boulder City 15,177. Mesquite 13,523. **Famous natives** Andre Agassi, tennis player. Walter Van Tilburg Clark (b. Me.), author. Sarah Winnemucca Hopkins, interpeter/teacher. John William MacKay, miner. William Morris Stewart (b. N.Y.), lawyer/senator. **Tourist information** (800)NEVADA8. www.travelnevada.com

New Hampshire

www.nh.gov

Name For English county of Hampshire. **Nickname** Granite State **Capital** Concord **Entered union** June 21, 1788 (9th). **Motto** "Live free or die." **Emblems** *Amphibian* Spotted newt. *Flower* Purple lilac. *Gem* Smoke quartz. *Insect* Ladybug. *Mineral* Beryl. *Song* "Old New Hampshire." *Tree* White birch. **Land** Total area 9,350 sq. mi (46th), incl. 382 sq. mi. inland water. **Borders** Quebec, Maine, Atlantic Ocean, Mass., Vt. **Rivers** Connecticut, Merrimack, Piscataqua, Saco, Salmon Falls. **Lakes** First Connecticut, Francis, Newfound, Ossipee, Sunapee, Winnipesaukee. Other notable features Isles of Shoals, White Mts. (Mt. Washington 6,288 ft., highest peak in Northeast). **People** (July, 2009 est.) 1,325,000 (40th). Race/Hispanic Origin (July, 2009 est.): White 95.3%. Black 1.4%. Indian 0.3%. Asian 2.0%. Two or more races 1.1%. Hispanic 2.8%. **Cities** (2005) Manchester 109,691. Nashua 87,321. Concord 42,336. Rochester 30,004. Dover 28,486. Keene 22,778. Portsmouth 20,674. Laconia 17,060. Claremont 13,388. Lebanon 12,606. **Famous natives** Salmon P. Chase, jurist. Ralph Adams Cram, architect. Mary Baker Eddy, founder, Church of Christ, Scientist. Daniel Chester French, sculptor.

Horace Greeley, journalist. Sarah Buell Hale, author. Franklin Pierce, U.S. president. Augustus Saint-Gaudens (b. Ireland), sculptor. Alan Shepard, astronaut. Daniel Webster, politician. Eleazar Wheelock (b. Conn.), Dartmouth founder. **Tourist information** (800)FUN-IN-NH. www.visitnh.gov

New Jersey

www.state.nj.us

Name After English Channel Island of Jersey. **Nickname** Garden State. **Capital** Trenton. **Entered union** Dec. 18, 1787 (3rd). **Motto** "Liberty and prosperity." **Emblems** *Bird* Eastern goldfinch. *Flower* Violet. *Tree* Red oak. **Land** Total area 8,721 sq. mi (47th), incl. 1,304 sq. mi. inland water. **Borders** N.Y., Atlantic Ocean, Del., Pa. **Rivers** Delaware, Hackensack, Hudson, Passaic. **Lakes** Greenwood, Hopatcong, Round Valley Res., Spruce Run. Other notable features Delaware Water Gap, Kittatinny Mts., Palisades, Pine Barrens, Ramapo Mts. **People** (July, 2009 est.) 8,708,000 (11th). Race/Hispanic Origin (July, 2009 est.): White 75.8%. Black 14.5%. Indian 0.4%. Asian 7.8%. Pacific Islander 0.1%. Two or more races 1.4%. Hispanic 16.7%. **Cities** (2005) Newark 280,666. Jersey City 239,614. Paterson 149,843. Elizabeth 125,809. Trenton 84,639. Camden 80,010. Clifton 79,922. East Orange 68,190. Passaic 68,338. Union City 65,128. **Famous natives** Count Basie, jazz musician. William J. Brennan, jurist. Aaron Burr, politician. Grover Cleveland, U.S. president. James Fenimore Cooper, novelist/historian. Stephen Crane, author. Thomas Edison, inventor. Albert Einstein (b. Germany), nuclear physicist. Waldo Frank, author. Joyce Kilmer, poet. Jerry Lewis, actor. Jack Nicholson, actor. Zebulon Pike, explorer. Molly Pitcher, Revolutionary War heroine. Paul Robeson, actor/singer. Walter Schirra, astronaut. Frank Sinatra, singer. Alfred Stieglitz, photographer. Meryl Streep, actress. Aaron Montgomery Ward, merchant. William Carlos Williams, poet. **Tourist information** 1-800-VISITNJ. www.visitnj.org

New Mexico

www.newmexico.gov

Name By Spanish explorers after Mexico. **Nickname** Land of Enchantment. **Capital** Santa Fe. **Entered union** Jan. 6, 1912 (47th). **Motto** Crescit eundo (It grows as it goes). **Emblems** *Bird* Roadrunner (chaparral bird). *Flower* Yucca. *Songs* "O, Fair New Mexico," "Así es Nuevo Mejico." *Tree* Piñon. **Land** Total area 121,589 sq. mi (5th), incl. 234 sq. mi. inland water. **Borders** Colo., Okla., Tex., Chihuahua, Ariz. **Rivers** Gila, Pecos, Rio Grande, Zuni. **Lakes** Conchas Res., Eagle Nest, Elephant Butte Res., Navajo Res., Ute Res. Mountains Chuska, Guadalupe, Sacramento, San Andres,

Sangre de Cristo. Other notable features Carlsbad Caverns, Continental Divide, Staked Plain. **People** (July, 2009 est.) 2,010,000 (36th). Race/Hispanic Origin (July, 2009 est.): White 83.6%. Black 3.1%. Indian 9.7%. Asian 1.5%. Pacific Islander 0.2%. Two or more races 1.9%. Hispanic 45.6%. **Cities** (2005) Albuquerque 494,236. Las Cruces 82,671. Santa Fe 70,631. Rio Rancho 66,599. Roswell 45,199. Farmington 43,161. Alamogordo 36,245. Clovis 33,357. Hobbs 29,006. Carlsbad 25,300. **Famous natives** William "Billy the Kid" Bonney (b. N.Y.), outlaw. Peter Hurd, artist. Archbishop Jean Baptiste Lamy (b. France), missionary. Georgia O'Keeffe (b. Wis.), artist. Popé, Tewa Pueblo chief. Harrison Schmitt, astronaut. **Tourist information** 1-800-733-6396. www.newmexico.org

New York

www.ny.gov
Name For Duke of York, later James II, of England. **Nickname** Empire State. **Capital** Albany. **Entered union** July 26, 1788 (11th). **Motto** Excelsior (Higher). **Emblems** *Bird* Bluebird. *Flower* Rose. *Song* "I Love New York." *Tree* Sugar maple. **Land** Total area 54,556 sq. mi (27th), incl. 7,342 sq. mi. inland water. **Borders** Lake Ontario, Ontario, Quebec, Vt., Mass., Conn., Atlantic Ocean, N.J., Pa., Lake Erie. **Rivers** Allegheny, Delaware, Genesee, Hudson, Mohawk, New York State Barge Canal, Niagara, St. Lawrence, Susquehanna. **Lakes** Cayuga, Champlain, Chautauqua, Erie, George, Oneida, Ontario, Seneca. Mountains Adirondack (Mt. Marcy 5,344 ft.), Allegheny, Berkshire Hills, Catskill, Kittatinny, Ramapo. Other notable features Hudson Valley, Mohawk Valley, Niagara Falls, Palisades, Thousand Islands. **People** (July, 2009 est.) 19,541,000 (3rd). Race/Hispanic Origin (July, 2009 est.): White 73.4%. Black 17.2%. Indian 0.6%. Asian 7.1%. Pacific Islander 0.1%. Two or more races 1.6%. Hispanic 16.8%. **Cities** (2005) New York 8,143,197. Buffalo 279,745. Rochester 211,091. Yonkers 196,425. Syracuse 141,683. Albany 93,523. New Rochelle 72,967. Mount Vernon 67,924. Schenectady 61,280. Utica 59,336. **Famous natives** Woody Allen, director. John Jacob Astor (b. Germany), merchant. Humphrey Bogart, actor. George Burns, actor. Aaron Copland, composer. Agnes de Mille, choreographer. George Eastman, camera inventor. Millard Fillmore, U.S. president. Lou Gehrig, baseball player. George Gershwin, composer. Julia Ward Howe, reformer. Washington Irving, author. Henry James, author. Vince Lombardi, football coach. Groucho Marx, comedian. Herman Melville, author. Ogden Nash, poet/humorist. Eugene O'Neill, playwright. Otetiani "Red Jacket", Seneca chief. Channing E. Phillips, minister/reformer. John D. Rockefeller, industrialist. Norman Rockwell, illustrator. Richard Rodgers, composer. Franklin Delano Roosevelt, U.S. president. Theodore Roosevelt, U.S. president. Jonas Salk, physician. Elizabeth Ann Seton, first American saint. Elizabeth Cady Stanton, suffragette. James Johnson Sweeney, art critic. Martin Van Buren, U.S. president. Mae West, actress. E.B. White, author. Walt Whitman, poet. **Tourist information** 1-800-CALL-NYS. www.iloveny.com

North Carolina

www.ncgov.com
Name For King Charles I (Carolus is Latin for Charles). **Nicknames** Tarheel State, Old North State. **Capital** Raleigh. **Entered union** Nov. 21, 1789 (12th). **Motto** Esse quam videri (To be rather than to seem). **Emblems** *Bird* Cardinal. *Flower* Dogwood. *Song* "The Old North State." *Tree* Pine. **Land** Total area 53,819 sq. mi (28th), incl. 5,108 sq. mi. inland water. **Borders** Va., Atlantic Ocean, S.C., Tenn., Georgia. **Rivers** Pee Dee, Roanoke, Yadkin. **Lakes** Buggs Island, High Rock, Mattamuskeet, Norman, Waccamaw. Mountains Black, Blue Ridge, Great Smoky, Unaka. Other notable features Great Dismal Swamp, Mount Mitchell, Outer Banks, Pamlico Sound. **People** (July, 2009 est.) 9,381,000 (10th). Race/Hispanic Origin (July, 2009 est.): White 73.7%. Black 21.6%. Indian 1.3%. Asian 2.0%. Pacific Islander 0.1%. Two or more races 1.3%. Hispanic 7.7%. **Cities** (2005) Charlotte 610,949. Raleigh 341,530. Greensboro 231,962. Durham 204,845. Fayetteville 129,928. Cary 106,439. Wilmington 95,476. High Point 95,086. Asheville 72,231. **Famous natives** Benjamin Newton Duke and James Buchanan Duke, industrialists/philanthropists. Richard J. Gatling, inventor. Billy Graham, minister. Andy Griffith, actor. O. Henry, writer. Andrew Johnson, U.S. president. William Rufus King, politician. Charles Kuralt, journalist. Meadowlark Lemon, athlete. Dolley Madison, First Lady. Thelonius Monk, musician. Edward R. Murrow, journalist. James Knox Polk, U.S. president. Moses Waddell, Confederate general. Thomas Wolfe, author. **Tourist information** 1-800-VISIT-NC. www.visitnc.com

North Dakota

www.nd.gov
Name For northern section of Dakota territory; dakota is Sioux word for "allies." **Nicknames** Sioux State, Peace Garden State, Flickertail State. **Capital** Bismarck. **Entered union** Nov. 2, 1889 (39th). **Motto** "Liberty and union, now and forever, one and inseparable." **Emblems** *Bird* Western meadowlark. *Flower* Wild prairie rose. *Song* "North Dakota Hymn." *Tree* American elm. **Land** Total area 70,700 sq. mi (19th), incl.

1,724 sq. mi. inland water. **Borders** Saskatchewan, Manitoba, Minn., S.Dak., Mont. **Rivers** Missouri, Red River of the North. **Lakes** Ashtabula, Devils, Oahe, Sakakawea. Other notable features Geographical center of North America, Missouri Plateau, Red River Valley, Rolling Drift Prairie. **People** (July, 2009 est.) 647,000 (48th). Race/Hispanic Origin (July, 2009 est.): White 91.1%. Black 1.2%. Indian 5.6%. Asian 0.8%. Pacific Islander Z. Two or more races 1.2%. Hispanic 2.3%. **Cities** (2005) Fargo 90,672. Bismarck 57,377. Mandan 17,225. West Fargo 19,487. Dickinson 15,666. Jamestown 14,826. Williston 12,193. Wahpeton 8,220. **Famous natives** Angie Dickinson, actress. John Bernard Flannagan, sculptor. Louis L'Amour, novelist. Peggy Lee, singer. Roger Maris, baseball player. Vihjalmur Stefansson (b. Canada), ethnologist. Lawrence Welk, entertainer. **Tourist information** 1-800-HELLO-ND. www.ndtourism.com

Ohio

www.ohio.gov
Name From the Iroquois oheo, "beautiful." **Nickname** Buckeye State. **Capital** Columbus. **Entered union** Mar. 1, 1803 (17th). **Motto** "With God, all things are possible." **Emblems** *Bird* Cardinal. *Flower* Scarlet carnation. *Song* "Beautiful Ohio." *Tree* Buckeye. **Land** Total area 44,825 sq. mi (34th), incl. 3,877 sq. mi. inland water. **Borders** Mich., Lake Erie, Pa., W.Va., Ky., Ind. **Rivers** Cuyahoga, Maumee, Miami, Muskingum, Ohio, Sandusky, Scioto. **Lakes** Berlin Res., Dillon Res., Erie, Mosquito Res., St. Mary's. **People** (July, 2009 est.) 11,543,000 (7th). Race/Hispanic Origin (July, 2009 est.): White 84.7%. Black 12.1%. Indian 0.3%. Asian 1.6%. Two or more races 1.4%. Hispanic 2.8%. **Cities** (2005) Columbus 730,657. Cleveland 452,208. Cincinnati 308,728. Toledo 301,285. Akron 210,795. Dayton 158,873. Parma 81,469. Canton 79,478. Lorain 67,820. **Famous natives** Sherwood Anderson, writer. Neil Armstrong, astronaut. George Bellows, artist. Ambrose Bierce, author. George Armstrong Custer, army officer. Paul Laurence Dunbar, poet. Thomas A. Edison, inventor. James A. Garfield, U.S. president. John Glenn, astronaut/politician. Ulysses S. Grant, U.S. president/general. Zane Grey, author. Warren G. Harding, U.S. president. Benjamin Harrison, U.S. president. Rutherford B. Hayes, U.S. president. Bob Hope, entertainer. William McKinley, U.S. president. Annie Oakley, markswoman. Ransom Eli Olds, carmaker. Eddie Rickenbacker, pilot. William Sherman, army officer. William Howard Taft, U.S. president/chief justice. Art Tatum, pianist. Tecumseh, Shawnee chief. James Thurber, humorist. Orville Wright, airplane inventor. **Tourist information** (800)BUCKEYE. www.discoverohio.com

Oklahoma

www.ok.gov
Name From the Choctaw okla humma, "land of the red people." **Nickname** Sooner State. **Capital** Oklahoma City. **Entered union** Nov. 16, 1907 (46th). **Motto** *Labor omnia vincit* (Work overcomes all obstacles). **Emblems** *Bird* Scissor-tailed flycatcher. *Floral emblem* Mistletoe. *Song* "Oklahoma!" *Tree* Redbud. **Land** Total area 69,898 sq. mi (20th), incl. 1,231 sq. mi. inland water. **Borders** Kans., Mo., Ark., Tex., N.Mex., Colo. **Rivers** Arkansas, Canadian, Cimarron, Red. **Lakes** Canton, Lake o' the Cherokees, Oologah, Texoma. Other notable features Ouachita Mts., Ozark Plateau, Staked Plain, Wichita Mts. **People** (July, 2009 est.) 3,687,000 (28th). Race/Hispanic Origin (July, 2009 est.): White 78.0%. Black 8.1%. Indian 8.0%. Asian 1.7%. Pacific Islander 0.1%. Two or more races 4.1%. Hispanic 8.2%. **Cities** (2005) Oklahoma City 531,324. Tulsa 382,457. Norman 101,719. Lawton 90,234. Broken Arrow 86,228. Edmond 74,881. Enid 46,416. Moore 47,697. Stillwater 40,906. **Famous natives** Ralph Ellison, author. Woody Guthrie, refor-mer/musician. Patrick J. Hurley, diplomat. Karl Jansky, electrical engineer. Mickey Mantle, baseball player. Wiley Post, aviator. Tony Randall, actor. Oral Roberts, evangelist. Will Rogers, humorist. Maria Tallchief, ballerina. Jim Thorpe, athlete. **Tourist information** 1-800-652-6552. www.travelok.com

Oregon

www.oregon.gov
Name Unknown origin, first applied to Columbia River. **Nickname** Beaver State. **Capital** Salem. **Entered union** Feb. 14, 1859 (33rd). **Motto** "She flies with her own wings. **Emblems** *Animal* Beaver. *Bird* Western meadowlark. *Dance* Square dance. *Fish* Chinook salmon. *Flower* Oregon grape. *Song* "Oregon, My Oregon." *Stone* Thunderegg. *Tree* Douglas Fir. **Land** Total area 98,381 sq. mi (9th), incl. 2,384 sq. mi. inland water. **Borders** Wash., Idaho, Nev., Calif., Pacific Ocean. **Rivers** Columbia, Snake, Willamette. **Mountains** Cascade Range, Coast Range, Klamath. Other notable features Willamette Valley. **People** (July, 2009 est.) 3,826,000 (27th). Race/Hispanic Origin (July, 2009 est.): White 89.8%. Black 2.0%. Indian 1.6%. Asian 3.7%. Pacific Islander 0.3%. Two or more races 2.6%. Hispanic 11.2%. **Cities** (2005) Portland 533,427. Salem 148,751. Eugene 144,515. Greshem 96,072. Beaverton 85,775. Hillsboro 84,533. Medford 70,147. Bend 67,152. Springfield 55,641. Corvallis 49,553. **Famous natives** In-mut-too-yah-lat-lat (Joseph), Nez Percé chief. Ursula LeGuin (b. Calif.), author. Edwin Markham, poet. Dr. John McLoughlin, fur trader, "Father of Oregon". Linus Pauling, chemist. John Reed,

author. William Simon U'Ren (b. Wis.), lawyer/reformer. **Tourist information** 1-800-547-7842. www.traveloregon.com

Pennsylvania, Commonwealth of

www.state.pa.us

Name For Adm. William Penn, father of William Penn, founder of commonwealth. **Nickname** Keystone State. **Capital** Harrisburg. **Entered union** Dec. 12, 1787 (2nd). **Motto** "Virtue, liberty and independence." **Emblems** *Bird* Ruffed grouse. *Flower* Mountain laurel. *Tree* Hemlock. **Land** Total area 46,055 sq. mi (33rd), incl. 1,239 sq. mi. inland water. **Borders** N.Y., N.J., Del., Md., W.Va., Ohio, Lake Erie. **Rivers** Allegheny, Delaware, Juniata, Monongahela, Ohio, Schuylkill, Susquehanna. **Lakes** Allegheny Res., Erie, Pymatuning Res., Shenango Res. Mountains Allegheny, Kittatinny, Laurel Hills, Pocono. **People** (July, 2009 est.) 12,605,000 (6th). Race/Hispanic Origin (July, 2009 est.): White 85.2%. Black 10.9%. Indian 0.2%. Asian 2.5%. Two or more races 1.1%. Hispanic 5.1%. **Cities** (2005) Philadelphia 1,463,281. Pittsburgh 316,718. Allentown 106,992. Erie 102,612. Reading 80,855. Scranton 73,120. Bethlehem 72,895. Lancaster 54,757. Harrisburg 47,472. Altoona 47,176. **Famous natives** Louisa May Alcott, author. Maxwell Anderson, playwright. James Buchanan, U.S. president. Alexander Calder, sculptor. Andrew Carnegie (b. Scotland), industrialist/philanthropist. Mary Cassatt, painter. Wilt Chamberlain, basketball player. Bill Cosby, comedian/philanthropist. Stephen Foster, songwriter. Benjamin Franklin (b. Mass.), inventor/statesman. Robert Fulton, inventor. Milton S. Hershey, chocolatier. George C. Marshall, statesman. Andrew W. Mellon, financier/philanthropist. Robert E. Peary, explorer. Betsy Ross, patriot. Andy Warhol, artist. Johnny Weismuller, swimmer/actor. Benjamin West, painter. **Tourist information** 1-800-VISIT-PA. www.visitpa.com

Rhode Island and Providence Plantations

www.ri.gov

Name For Rhode Island in Narragansett Bay, named in turn for Mediterranean island of Rhodes. **Nicknames** Ocean State, Little Rhody. **Capital** Providence. **Entered union** May 29, 1790 (13th). **Motto** "Hope." **Emblems** *Bird* Rhode Island red. *Flower* Violet. *Song* "Rhode Island." *Tree* Red maple. **Land** Total area 1,545 sq. mi (50th), incl. 500 sq. mi. inland water. **Borders** Mass., Atlantic Ocean, Conn. **Rivers** Blackstone, Pawcatuck, Providence, Sakonnet. Other notable features Block Island, Narragansett Bay, Aquidneck Island. **People** (July, 2009 est.) 1,053,000 (43rd). Race/Hispanic Origin (July, 2009 est.): White 88.3%. Black 6.4%. Indian

0.6%. Asian 2.8%. Pacific Islander 0.1%. Two or more races 1.7%. Hispanic 12.1%. **Cities** (2005) Providence 176,862. Warwick 87,233. Cranston 81,614. Pawtucket 73,742. East Providence 49,515. Woonsocket 44,328. Newport 25,340. Central Falls 19,159. **Famous natives** George M. Cohan, actor/producer. Nathanael Greene, army officer. Galway Kinell, poet. Metacomet (King Philip), Wampanoag chief. Oliver H. Perry and Matthew C. Perry, naval officers. Gilbert Stuart, portraitist. **Tourist information** 1-800-250-7384. www.visitrhodeisland.com

South Carolina

www.sc.gov

Name For King Charles II (Carolus is Latin for Charles). **Nickname** Palmetto State. **Capital** Columbia. **Entered union** May 23, 1788 (8th). **Motto** *Animis opibusque parati* (Prepared in mind and deed); *Dum spiro spero* (While I breathe I hope). **Emblems** *Bird* Carolina wren. *Flower* Yellow jessamine. *Song* "Carolina." *Tree* Palmetto. **Land** Total area 32,020 sq. mi (40th), incl. 1,911 sq. mi. inland water. **Borders** N.C., Atlantic Ocean, Ga. **Rivers** Catawba, Congaree, Edisto, Pee Dee, Savannah, Tugalos, Wateree. **Lakes** Greenwood, Hartwell, Keowee, Marion, Murray, Santee Res., Wylie. Other notable features Blue Ridge Mts., Congaree Swamp, Sea Islands. **People** (July, 2009 est.) 4,561,000 (24th). Race/Hispanic Origin (July, 2009 est.): White 68.9%. Black 28.2%. Indian 0.4%. Asian 1.3%. Pacific Islander 0.1%. Two or more races 1.1%. Hispanic 4.5%. **Cities** (2005) Columbia 117,088. Charleston 106,712. North Charleston 86,313. Greenville 56,676. Rock Hill 59,554. Mount Pleasant 57,932. Sumter 39,679. Spartanburg 38,379. Hilton Head Island 34,497. **Famous natives** James F. Byrnes, politician/jurist. John C. Calhoun, politician. Dizzy Gillespie, musician. Althea Gibson, athlete. DuBose Heyward, author. Andrew Jackson, U.S. president. Eartha Kitt, singer. James Longstreet, army officer. Francis Marion, army officer/politician. Charles C. Pinckney and Thomas Pinckney, diplomats. Edward Rutledge and John Rutledge, politicians. Strom Thurmond, politician. **Tourist information** 1-866-224-9339. www.discoversouthcarolina.com

South Dakota

www.state.sd.us

Name For southern section of Dakota territory; dakota is Sioux word for "allies." **Nickname** Coyote State, Sunshine State. **Capital** Pierre. **Entered union** Nov. 2, 1889 (40th). **Motto** "Under God the people rule." **Emblems** *Bird* Chinese ring-necked pheasant. *Flower* Pasque . **Land** Total area 77,116 sq. mi (17th), incl. 1,232 sq. mi. inland water. **Borders** N.Dak., Minn., Iowa, Nebr., Wyo., Mont. **Rivers** Cheyenne, James, Missouri, Moreau, White. **Lakes** Belle Fourche Res., Big Stone, Traverse. Other notable features Badlands, Black Hills (Harney Peak 7,242 ft.). **People** (July, 2009 est.) 812,000 (46th). Race/Hispanic Origin (July, 2009 est.): White 87.9%. Black 1.2%. Indian 8.5%. Asian 0.9%. Pacific Islander 0.1%. Two or more races 1.5%. Hispanic 2.9%. **Cities** (2005) Sioux Falls 139,517. Rapid City 62,167. Aberdeen 24,098. Watertown 20,265. Brookings 18,715. Mitchell 14,696. Pierre 14,052. Yankton 13,716. Huron 11,086. Vermillion 9,964. **Famous natives** Tom Brokaw, journalist. Martha "Calamity" Jane Burk (b. Mo.), frontiers-woman. Alvin Hansen, economist. Hubert H. Humphrey, politician. Ernest O. Lawrence, physicist (Nobel Prize, 1939). George McGovern, politician. Ta-sunko-witko (Crazy Horse), Oglala Sioux chief. Tatanka Iyotake (Sitting Bull), Sioux chief. **Tourist information** 1-800-SDAKOTA. www.travelsd.com

Tennessee

www.tennesseeanytime.org

Name For Tenase, principal village of Cherokees. **Nickname** Volunteer State. **Capital** Nashville. **Entered union** June 1, 1796 (16th). **Motto** "Agriculture and commerce." Slogan "Tennessee—America at its best." Poet laureate Richard M. ("Pek") Gunn. **Emblems** *Bird* Mockingbird. *Flower* Iris. *Songs* "When It's Iris Time in Tennessee," "The Tennessee Waltz," My Homeland, Tennessee," "Rocky Top." *Tree* Tulip poplar. **Land** Total area 42,143 sq. mi (36th), incl. 926 sq. mi. inland water. **Borders** Ky., Va., N.C., Ga., Ala., Miss., Ark., Mo. **Rivers** Clinch, Cumberland, Mississippi, Tennessee. **Lakes** Boone, Center Hill, Cherokee, Dale Hollow, Douglass, J. Percy Priest, Watauga. Other notable features Cumberland Mts., Great Smoky Mts., Tennessee Valley, Unaka Mts. **People** (July, 2009 est.) 6,296,000 (17th). Race/Hispanic Origin (July, 2009 est.): White 80.2%. Black 16.8%. Indian 0.3%. Asian 1.4%. Pacific Islander 0.1%. Two or more races 1.2%. Hispanic 4.2%. **Cities** (2005) Memphis 672,277. Nashville-Davidson 549,110. Knoxville 180,130. Chattanooga 154,762. Clarksville 112,878. Murfreesboro 86,793. Jackson 62,099. Johnson City 58,718. Franklin 53,311. Kingsport 44,130. **Famous natives** James Agee, author. Davy Crockett, frontiersman. David Farragut, naval officer. Aretha Franklin, singer. Morgan Freeman, actor. Al Gore, (b. Washington, D.C.), politician. Cordell Hull, statesman (Nobel Peace Prize, 1945). Dolly Parton, singer. Sikawyi (Sequoya), Cherokee scholar. Alvin York, soldier. **Tourist information** 1-800-GO2-TENN. www.tnvacation.com

Texas

www.state.tx.us

Name From the Caddo *tavshas*, "friends." **Nickname** Lone Star State. **Capital** Austin. **Entered union** Dec. 29, 1845 (28th). **Motto** "Friendship." **Emblems** *Bird* Mockingbird. *Flower* Bluebonnet. *Songs* "Texas, Our Texas," "The Eyes of Texas." *Tree* Pecan. **Land** Total area 268,581 sq. mi (2nd), incl. 6,784 sq. mi. inland water. **Borders** Okla., Ark., La., Gulf of Mexico, Tamaulipas, Coahuila, Chihuahua, N.Mex. **Rivers** Brazos, Colorado, Natchez, Red, Rio Grande, Sabine, Trinity. **Lakes** Sam Rayburn Res., Texoma, Toledo Bend Res. Other notable features Balcones Escarpment, Diablo Sierra, Edwards Plateau, Guadalupe Mts., Staked Plain, Stockton Plateau. **People** (July, 2009 est.) 24,782,000 (2nd). Race/Hispanic Origin (July, 2009 est.): White 82.1%. Black 12.0%. Indian 0.8%. Asian 3.6%. Pacific Islander 0.1%. Two or more races 1.4%. Hispanic 36.9%. **Cities** (2005) Houston 2,016,582. Dallas 1,213,825. San Antonio 1,194,222. Austin 690,252. El Paso 598,590. Fort Worth 624,067. Arlington 362,805. Corpus Christi 283,474. Plano 250,096. Garland 216,346. **Famous natives** Stephen Austin (b. Va.), pioneer. James "Jim" Bowie (b. Ky.), army officer. Carol Burnett, comedian. J. Frank Dobie, folklorist. Dwight D. Eisenhower, U.S. president/general. Samuel Houston (b. Va.), president Republic of Texas/governor State of Texas. Howard Hughes, industrialist/aviator. Lyndon Baines Johnson, U.S. president. Janis Joplin, singer. Barbara Jordan, politician. Audie Murphy, soldier/actor. Chester Nimitz, navy officer. Katherine Anne Porter, author. Samuel T. Rayburn, politician. Mildred "Babe" Didrikson Zaharias, athlete. **Tourist information** 1-800-888-8TEX, ext. 728. www.traveltex.com

Utah

www.utah.gov

Name For Ute Indians. **Nickname**s Beehive State, Mormon State. **Capital** Salt Lake City. **Entered Union** Jan. 4, 1896 (45th). **Motto** "Industry." **Emblems** *Bird* California Gull. *Flower* Sego lily. *Song* "Utah, We Love Thee." *Tree* Blue spruce. **Land** Total area 84,899 sq. mi (13th), incl. 2,755 sq. mi. inland water. **Borders** Idaho, Wyo., Colo., Ariz., Nev. **Rivers** Bear, Colorado, Green, Sevier. **Lakes** Bear, Great Salt, Utah. Mountains La Sal, Uinta (Kings Peak 13,528 ft.) Wasatch Range. Other notable features Great Salt Lake Desert (Bonneville Salt Flats) Kaibab Plateau. **People** (July, 2009 est.) 2,785,000 (34th). Race/Hispanic Origin (July, 2009 est.): White 92.7%. Black 1.4%. Indian 1.4%. Asian 2.1%. Pacific Islander 0.8%. Two or more races 1.7%. Hispanic 12.3%. **Cities** (2005) Salt Lake City 178,097. Provo 113,459.

West Valley City 113,300. Sandy 89,664. Orem 89,713. Ogden 78,309. West Jordan 91,444. St. George 64,201. Layton 61,782. Taylorsville 58,009. **Famous natives** Maud Adams, actress. John Moses Browning, inventor. Philo Farnsworth, inventor of TV. Merlin Olsen, football player/actor. Brigham Young (b. Vt.), religious leader. Loretta Young, actress. **Tourist Information** 1-800-200-1160. www.utah.com

Vermont

www.vermont.gov

Name From French vert mont, "green mountain." **Nickname** Green Mountain State. **Capital** Montpelier. **Entered Union** Mar. 4, 1791 (14th). **Motto** "Freedom and unity." **Emblems** *Bird* Hermit thrush. *Flower* Red Clover. *Song* "Hail, Vermont!" *Tree* Sugar Maple. **Land** Total Area 9,614 sq. mi (45th), incl. 365 sq. mi. inland water. **Borders** Quebec, N.H., Mass., N.Y. **Rivers** Connecticut, Lamoille, Otter Creek, Poultney, White, Winooski. **Lakes** Bomoseen, Champlain, Memphremagog, Willoughby. Other Notable Features Grand Isle, Green Mts. (Mt. Mansfield 4,393 ft.), Taconic Mts. **People** (July, 2009 est.) 622,000 (49th). Race/Hispanic Origin (July, 2009 est.): White 96.2%. Black 1.0%. Indian 0.4%. Asian 1.2%. Two or more races 1.2%. Hispanic 1.5%. **Cities** (2002) Burlington 39,466. Rutland 17,098. South Burlington 15,870. **Famous natives** Ethan Allen (b. Conn.), army officer. Chester A. Arthur, U.S. President. Calvin Coolidge, U.S. president. John Deere, industrialist. George Dewey, naval officer. John Dewey, philosopher. Stephen Douglas, politician. James Fisk, financier. Robert Frost (b. Calif.), poet. Rudy Vallee, singer. **Tourist Information** 1-800-VERMONT. www.vermontvacation.com

Virginia, Commonwealth of

www.state.va.us

Name For Elizabeth I, called Virgin Queen. **Nicknames** Old Dominion, Mother of Presidents, Mother of States. **Capital** Richmond. **Entered union** June 25, 1788 (10th). **Motto** Sic semper tyrannis (Thus always to tyrants). **Emblems** *Bird* Cardinal. *Flower* Dogwood. *Song* "Carry Me Back to Old Virginia." *Tree* Dogwood. **Land** Total area 42,774 sq. mi (35th), incl. 3,180 sq. mi. inland water. **Borders** Md., D.C., Atlantic Ocean, N.C., Tenn., Ky., W.Va. **Rivers** James, Potomac, Rappahannock, Roanoke, Shenandoah, York. **Lakes** Buggs Island, Claytor, Gaston, Leesville. Mountains Allegheny, Blue Ridge, Cumberland, Unaka. Other notable features Great Dismal Swamp, Shenandoah Valley. **People** (July, 2009 est.) 7,883,000 (12th). Race/Hispanic Origin (July, 2009 est.): White 72.8%. Black 20.0%. Indian 0.4%. Asian 5.0%. Pacific Islander 0.1%. Two or more races 1.8%. Hispanic 7.2%. **Cities** (2005) Virginia Beach 438,415. Norfolk 231,954. Chesapeake 218,968. Richmond 193,777. Newport News 179,899. Hampton 145,579. Alexandria 135,337. Portsmouth 100,169. Roanoke 92,631. Suffolk 78,994. Famous natives Richard E. Byrd, explorer/aviator. William Clark, explorer. Jerry Falwell, evangelist. William Henry Harrison, U.S. president. Patrick Henry, Revolutionary patriot. Thomas Jefferson, U.S. president. Joseph E. Johnston, Confederate general. John Paul Jones (b. Scotland), navy officer. Robert E. Lee, Confederate general. Meriwether Lewis, explorer. James Madison, U.S. president. John Marshall, jurist. Cyrus Hall McCormick, inventor. James Monroe, U.S. president. Walter Reed, doctor. Pat Robertson, evangelist/politician. George C. Scott, actor. Thomas Sumter, army officer. Zachary Taylor, U.S. president. John Tyler, U.S. president. Booker T. Washington, educator. George Washington, U.S. president. Woodrow Wilson, U.S. president. **Tourist information** 1-800-VISIT-VA. www.virginia.org.

Washington

www.tourism.wa.gov

Name For George Washington. **Nickname** Evergreen State. **Capital** Olympia. **Entered union** Nov. 11, 1889 (42nd). **Motto** Alki (By and by). **Emblems** *Bird* Willow goldfinch. *Flower* Western rhododendron. *Song* "Washington, My Home." *Tree* Western hemlock. **Land** Total area 71,300 sq. mi (18th), incl. 4,756 sq. mi. inland water. **Borders** British Columbia, Idaho, Oreg., Pacific Ocean. **Rivers** Chehalis, Columbia, Pend Oreille, Snake, Yakima. **Lakes** Baker, Bank, Chelan, Franklin D. Roosevelt, Ross, Rufus Woods. Mountains Cascade Range, Coast Range, Kettle River Range, Olympic. Other notable features Puget Sound, San Juan Islands, Strait of Juan de Fuca. **People** (July, 2009 est.) 6,664,000 (13th). Race/Hispanic Origin (July, 2009 est.): White 83.8%. Black 3.9%. Indian 1.8%. Asian 7.0%. Pacific Islander 0.5%. Two or more races 3.1%. Hispanic 10.3%. **Cities** (2005) Seattle 573,911. Tacoma 195,898. Spokane 196,818. Vancouver 157,493. Bellevue 117,137. Everett 96,604. Federal Way 83,088. Kent 81,800. Yakima 81,214. Bellingham 74,547. **Famous natives** Harry L. "Bing" Crosby, singer. Merce Cunningham, choreographer. Bill Gates, businessman. Jimi Hendrix, guitarist. Robert Joffrey, choreographer. Gary Larson, cartoonist. Edward R. Murrow, reporter (b. North Carolina). Theodore Roethke (b. Mich.), poet. Marcus Whitman (b. N.Y.), missionary/pioneer. **Tourist information** 1-800-544-1800. www.experiencewa.com

West Virginia

www.wv.gov

Name for western part of Virginia. **Nickname** Mountain State. **Capital** Charleston. **Entered union** June 20, 1863 (35th). **Motto** *Montani semper liberi* (Mountaineers are always free). **Emblems** *Bird* Cardinal. *Flower* Rhododendron maximum (big laurel). *Songs* "The West Virginia Hills," "West Virginia, My Home Sweet Home," "This Is My West Virginia." *Tree* Sugar maple. **Land** Total area 24,230 sq. mi (41st), incl. 152 sq. mi. inland water. **Borders** Ohio, Pa., Md., Va., Ky. **Rivers** Big Sandy, Guayandotte, Kanawha, Little Kanawha, Monongahela, Ohio, Potomac. **Lakes** Summersville Dam. Mountains Allegheny, Blue Ridge, Cumberland. **People** (July, 2009 est.) 1,820,000 (37th). Race/Hispanic Origin (July, 2009 est.): White 94.4%. Black 3.7%. Indian 0.2%. Asian 0.7%. Pacific Islander Z. Two or more races 1.0%. Hispanic 1.2%. **Cities** (2005) Charleston 51,176. Huntington 49,198. Parkersburg 32,020. Wheeling 29,639. Morgantown 28,292. Weirton 19,544. Fairmont 19,049. Beckley 16,936. Clarksburg 16,439. Martinsburg 15,996. **Famous natives** Newton D. Baker, politician. Pearl Buck, novelist (Nobel Prize, 1938). John W. Davis, politician. Dwight Whitney Morrow, lawyer/"diplomat. Michael Owens, manufacturer. Walter Reuther, labor leader. Cyrus Vance, statesman. Jerry West, basketball player. Charles "Chuck" Yeager, pilot. **Tourist information** 1-800-CALL-WVA. www.wvtourism.com

Wisconsin

www.wisconsin.gov

Name From the Ojibwa wishkonsing, "place of the bearer." **Nickname** Badger State. **Capital** Madison. **Entered union** May 29, 1848 (30th). **Motto** "Forward." **Emblems** *Bird* Robin. *Flower* Wood violet. *Song* "On, Wisconsin!" *Tree* Sugar maple. **Land** Total area 65,498 sq. mi (23rd), incl. 11,188 sq. mi. inland water. **Borders** Minn., Lake Superior, Mich., Lake Michigan, Ill., Iowa. **Rivers** Black, Chippewa, Menominee, Mississippi, St. Croix, Wisconsin. **Lakes** Chippewa, Du Bay, Mendota, Michigan, Superior, Winnebago. Other notable features Apostle Islands, Door Peninsula, Green Bay. **People** (July, 2009 est.) 5,655,000 (20th). Race/Hispanic Origin (July, 2009 est.): White 89.4%. Black 6.2%. Indian 1.0%. Asian 2.2%. Two or more races 1.2%. Hispanic 5.3%.**Cities** (2005) Milwaukee 578,887. Green Bay 101,203. Madison 95,240. Kenosha 92,240. Racine 79,392. Appleton 70,217. Waukesha 67,658. Oshkosh 63,485. Eau Claire 62,570. Janesville 61,962. **Famous natives** King Camp Gillette, inventor/businessman. Eric Heiden, speed skater. Harry Houdini (b. Hungary), magician. Robert La Follette, politician. Liberace (Wladziu Valentino), pianist. Alfred Lunt, actor. Joseph R. McCarthy, politician. Spencer Tracy, actor. Thorstein Veblen, economist. Orson Welles, director. Laura Ingalls Wilder, novelist. Thornton Wilder, author. Frank Lloyd Wright, architect. **Tourist information** 1-800-432-TRIP or 1-800-432-8747. www.travelwisconsin.com

Wyoming

www.wyoming.gov

Name From the Delaware maugh-wau-wa-ma, "large plains" or "mountains and valleys alternating." **Nickname** Equality State. **Capital** Cheyenne. **Entered union** July 10, 1890 (44th). **Motto** "Equal rights." **Emblems** *Bird* Meadowlark. *Flower* Indian paintbrush. *Song* "Wyoming." *Tree* Cottonwood. **Land** Total area 97,814 sq. mi (10th), incl. 713 sq. mi. inland water. **Borders** Mont., S.Dak., Nebr., Colo., Utah, Idaho. **Rivers** Bighorn, Green, North Platte, Powder, Snake, Yellowstone. **Lakes** Bighorn, Yellowstone. Mountains Absaroka, Bighorn, Black Hills, Laramie, Owl Creek, Teton Range, Wind River Range, Wyoming Range. **People** (July, 2009 est.) 544,000 (51st). Race/Hispanic Origin (July, 2009 est.): White 93.5%. Black 1.4%. Indian 2.6%. Asian 0.8%. Pacific Islander 0.1%. Two or more races 1.5%. Hispanic 8.1%. **Cities** (2005) Cheyenne 55,731. Casper 51,738. Laramie 26,050. Gillette 22,685. Rock Springs 18,772. Sheridan 16,333. Green River 11,787. Evanston 11,459. **Famous natives** James Bridger (b. Va.), pioneer. J.C. Penney, businessman. Jackson Pollock, painter. Nellie Tayloe Ross (b. Mo.), politician. **Tourist information** 1-800-CALL-WYO. www.wyomingtourism.org

NATIONS OF THE WORLD

The following section presents major facts about all the nations of the world, including statistics on each nation's geography, people, government, and economy.

Sources include the United Nations, the U.S. Census Bureau, the U.S. Department of State, and the annual *World Factbook* published by the Central Intelligence Agency.

Afghanistan

Geography Location: Southern Asia, north and west of Pakistan, east of Iran. **Area:** 251,827 sq mi (652,230 sq km). **Border countries:** China, Iran, Pakistan, Tajikistan, Turkmenistan, Uzbekistan. **Natural resources:** natural gas, crude oil, coal, copper, talc. **People Population:** 29,835,392 (July 2011 est.). **Nationality:** *noun:* Afghan(s); *adj.:* Afghan. **Ethnic groups:** 42% Pashtun, 27% Tajik, 9% Hazara, 9% Uzbek. **Religions:** 80% Sunni Muslim, 19% Shi'a Muslim, 1% other. **Languages:** 50% Afghan Persian (Dari), 35% Pashtu, 11% Turkic langs. (primarily Uzbek and Turkmen), 4% minor langs. (30, primarily Balochi and Pashai); much bilingualism. **Government Government type:** Islamic republic. **Capital:** Kabul. **Independence:** 19 August 1919 (from U.K. control over Afghan foreign affairs). **National holiday:** Independence Day, 19 August (1919). **Economy G.D.P.:** purchasing power parity—$29.81 billion (2010 est.). **G.D.P.—per capita:** $1,000 (2010 est.). **Currency:** afghani (AFA).

Albania

Republic of Albania

Geography Location: Southeastern Europe, bordering the Adriatic Sea and Ionian Sea, between Greece, Serbia, and Montenegro. **Area:** 11,100 sq. mi. (28,750 sq km.). **Border countries:** Greece, The Former Yugoslav Republic of Macedonia, Montenegro, Serbia. **Natural resources:** crude oil, natural gas, coal, chromium, copper. **People Population:** 2,994,667 (July 2011 est.). **Nationality:** *noun:* Albanian(s); *adj.:* Albanian. **Ethnic groups:** 95% Albanian, 3% Greek, 2% Vlach, Gypsy, Serb, Bulgarian. **Religions:** 70% Muslim, 20% Albanian Orthodox, 10% Roman Catholic (all churches and mosques were closed in 1967 and religious observance prohibited; in November 1990, Albania began allowing private religious practice). **Languages:** Albanian (Tosk is official dialect), Greek, Vlach, Romani, Slavic dialects. **Government Government type:** Parliamentary democracy. **Capital:** Tirana. **Independence:** 28 November 1912 (from Ottoman Empire).

National holiday: Independence Day, 28 November (1912). **Economy G.D.P.:** purchasing power parity—$23.95 billion (2010 est.). **G.D.P.—per capita:** purchasing power parity—$8,000 (2010 est.). **Currency:** lek (ALL).

Algeria

People's Democratic Republic of Algeria

Geography Location: Northern Africa, bordering the Mediterranean Sea, between Morocco and Tunisia. **Area:** 919,595 sq. mi. (2,381,741 sq km). **Border countries:** Libya, Mali, Mauritania, Morocco, Niger, Tunisia, Western Sahara. **Natural resources:** crude oil, natural gas, iron ore, phosphates, uranium. **People Population:** 34,994,937 (July 2011 est.). **Nationality:** *noun:* Algerian(s); *adj.:* Algerian. **Ethnic groups:** 99% Arab-Berber, less than 1% European. **Religions:** 99% Sunni Muslim (state religion), 1% Christian and Jewish. **Languages:** Arabic (official), French, Berber dialects. **Government Government type:** republic. **Capital:** Algiers. **Independence:** 5 July 1962 (from France). **National holiday:** Revolution Day, 1 November (1954). **Economy G.D.P.:** purchasing power parity—$254.7 billion (2010 est.). **G.D.P.—per capita:** purchasing power parity—$7,400 (2010 est.). **Currency:** Algerian dinar (DZD).

Andorra

Principality of Andorra

Geography Location: Southwestern Europe, between France and Spain. **Area:** 174 sq mi (468 sq km). **Border countries:** France, Spain **Natural resources:** hydropower, mineral water, timber, iron ore, lead. **People Population:** 84,825 (July 2011 est.). **Nationality:** *noun:* Andorran(s); *adj.:* Andorran. **Ethnic groups:** 43% Spanish, 33% Andorran, 11% Portuguese, 7% French, 6% other. **Religions:** virtually all Roman Catholic. **Languages:** Catalan (official); many also speak some French and Castilian. **Government Government type:** parliamentary democracy. **Capital:** Andorra la Vella. **Independence:** 1278 (was formed under the joint suzerainty of the French count of Foix and the Spanish bishop of Urgel). **National holiday:** Our Lady of Meritxell Day, 8 September (1278). **Economy G.D.P.:** purchasing power parity—$4.22 billion (2008). **G.D.P.—per capita:** purchasing power parity—$44,900 (2008). **Currency:** euro (EUR).

Angola

Republic of Angola

Geography Location: Southern Africa, bordering the South Atlantic Ocean, between Namibia and Democratic Republic of the Congo. **Area:** 481,354 sq. mi. (1,246,700 sq km). **Border countries:** Democratic Republic of the Congo (of which 225 km is the boundary of discontiguous Cabinda Province), Republic of the Congo, Namibia, Zambia. **Natural resources:** petroleum, diamonds, iron ore, phosphates, copper. **People Population:** 13,338,541 (July 2011 est.). **Nationality:** *noun:* Angolan(s); *adj.:* Angolan. **Ethnic groups:** 37% Ovimbundu, 25% Kimbundu, 13% Bakongo, 2% Mestico, 1% European, 22% other. **Religions:** 47% indigenous beliefs, 38% Roman Catholic, 15% Protestant. **Languages:** Portuguese (official), Bantu and other African languages. **Government Government type:** republic, multiparty presidential regime. **Capital:** Luanda. **Independence:** 11 November 1975 (from Portugal). **National holiday:** Independence Day, 11 November (1975). **Economy G.D.P.:** purchasing power parity—$114.1 billion (2010 est.). **G.D.P.—per capita:** purchasing power parity—$8,700 (2010 est.). **Currency:** kwanza (AOA).

Antigua and Barbuda

Geography Location: Caribbean, islands between the Caribbean Sea and the North Atlantic Ocean, east-southeast of Puerto Rico. **Area:** 171 sq. mi. (442 sq km: Antigua 280 sq km; Barbuda 161 sq km). **Natural resources:** negligible; pleasant climate fosters tourism **People Population:** 87,884 (July 2011 est.). **Nationality:** *noun:* Antiguan(s), Barbudan(s); *adj.:* Antiguan, Barbudan. **Ethnic groups:** almost entirely of black African origin; some of British, Portuguese, Lebanese and Syrian origin. **Religions:** Anglican (predominant), other protestant sects, some Roman Catholic. **Languages:** English (official), local dialects. **Government Government type:** constitutional monarchy with U.K.-style parliament. **Capital:** Saint John's. **Independence:** 1 November 1981 (from U.K.). **National holiday:** Independence Day (National Day), 1 November (1981). **Economy G.D.P.:** purchasing power parity—$1.433 billion (2010 est.). **G.D.P.—per capita:** purchasing power parity—$16,500 (2010 est.). **Currency:** East Caribbean dollar (XCD).

Argentina

Argentine Republic

Geography Location: Southern South America, bordering the South Atlantic Ocean, between Chile and Uruguay. **Area:** 1,073,518 sq mi (2,780,400 sq km). **Border countries:** Bolivia, Brazil, Chile, Paraguay, Uruguay. **Natural resources:** fertile plains of the Pampas, lead, zinc, tin, copper, iron ore, petroleum. **People Population:** 41,769,726 (July 2011 est.). **Nationality:** *noun:* Argentine(s); *adj.:* Argentine. **Ethnic groups:** 97% white, 3% mestizo, Indian, and other nonwhite groups. **Religions:** 92% Roman Catholic (less than 20% practicing), 2% Protestant, 2% Jewish, 4% other. **Languages:** Spanish (official), English, Italian, German, French. **Government Government type:** republic. **Capital:** Buenos Aires. **Independence:** 9 July 1816 (from Spain). **National holiday:** Revolution Day, 25 May (1810). **Economy G.D.P.:** purchasing power parity—$596 billion (2010 est.). **G.D.P.—per capita:** purchasing power parity—$14,700 (2010 est.). **Currency:** Argentine peso (ARS).

Armenia

Republic of Armenia

Geography Location: Southwestern Asia, east of Turkey. **Area:** 11,484 sq mi (29,743 sq km). **Border countries:** Azerbaijan-proper, Azerbaijan-Naxcivan, Georgia, Iran, Turkey. **Natural resources:** small deposits of gold and copper. **People Population:** 2,967,975 (July 2011 est.). **Nationality:** *noun:* Armenian(s); *adj.:* Armenian. **Ethnic groups:** 98% Armenian, 1.3% Yezidi, .8% Russian and other. **Religions:** 95% Armenian Apostolic, 4% other Christian, 1% Yezidi. **Languages:** 98% Armenian, 1% Russian, 1% Yezidi. **Government Government type:** republic. **Capital:** Yerevan. **Independence:** 21 September 1991 (from Soviet Union). **National holiday:** Independence Day, 21 September (1991). **Economy G.D.P.:** purchasing power parity—$17.27 billion (2010 est.). **G.D.P.—per capita:** purchasing power parity—$5,800 (2010 est.). **Currency:** dram (AMD).

Australia

Commonwealth of Australia

Geography Location: Oceania, continent between the Indian Ocean and the South Pacific Ocean. **Area:** 2,988,902 sq mi (7,741,220 sq km). **Natural resources:** bauxite, coal, iron ore, copper, tin. **People Population:** 21,776,711 (July 2011 est.) . **Nationality:** *noun:* Australian(s); *adj.:* Australian. **Ethnic groups:** 92% Caucasian, 7% Asian, 1% aboriginal and other. **Religions:** 25.8% Roman Catholic, 18.7%

Anglican, 7.9% other Christian, 2.1% Buddhist, 1.7% Muslim, 18.7% none. **Languages:** English, Chinese, Italian, native languages. **Government Government type:** federal parliamentary democracy. **Capital:** Canberra. **Independence:** 1 January 1901 (federation of U.K. colonies). **National holiday:** Australia Day, 26 January (1788). **Economy G.D.P.:** purchasing power parity—$889.6 billion (2010 est.). **G.D.P.—per capita:** purchasing power parity—$41,300 (2010 est.). **Currency:** Australian dollar (AUD).

Austria

Republic of Austria

Geography Location: Central Europe, north of Italy and Slovenia. **Area:** 32,383 sq mi (83,871 sq km). **Border countries:** Czech Republic, Germany, Hungary, Italy, Liechtenstein, Slovakia, Slovenia, Switzerland. **Natural resources:** iron ore, crude oil, timber, magnesite, lead. **People Population:** 8,217,280 (July 2011 est.). **Nationality:** *noun:* Austrian(s); *adj.:* Austrian. **Ethnic groups:** 91% Austrian, 4% former Yugoslavs, 1.6% Turks, 1% German. **Religions:** 73% Roman Catholic, 5% Protestant, 4.2% Muslim, 17.5% other or unspecified. **Languages:** German, Turkish, Croatian (official in Burgenland). **Government Government type:** federal republic. **Capital:** Vienna. **Independence:** 976 (Margravate of Austria established). **National holiday:** National Day, 26 October (1955). **Economy G.D.P.:** purchasing power parity—$332.9 billion (2010 est.). **G.D.P.—per capita:** purchasing power parity—$40,300 (2010 est.). **Currency:** euro (EUR).

Azerbaijan

Geography Location: Southwestern Asia, bordering the Caspian Sea, between Iran and Russia, with a small European portion north of the Caucasus range. **Area:** 33,436 sq mi (86,600 sq km). **Border countries:** Armenia (with Azerbaijan-proper), Armenia (with Azerbaijan-Naxcivan exclave), Georgia, Iran (with Azerbaijan-proper), Iran (with Azerbaijan-Naxcivan exclave), Russia, Turkey. **Natural resources:** petroleum, natural gas, iron ore. **People Population:** 8,372,373 (July 2011 est.). **Nationality:** *noun:* Azerbaijani(s); *adj.:* Azerbaijani. **Ethnic groups:** 91% Azeri, 2.2% Dagestani Peoples, 1.8% Russian, 1.5% Armenian, 4.3% other. **Religions:** 93.4% Muslim, 2.5% Russian Orthodox, 2.3% Armenian Orthodox, 1.8% other. *note:* religious affiliation is still nominal in Azerbaijan; percentages for actual practicing adherents are much lower. **Languages:** 90.3% Azeri, 2.2% Lezgi, 1.8% Russian, 1.5% Armenian, 4.3% other. **Government Government type:** republic. **Capital:** Baku (Baki). **Independence:** 30 August 1991 (from Soviet Union).

National holiday: Founding of the Democratic Republic of Azerbaidzhan, 28 May (1918). **Economy G.D.P.:** purchasing power parity—$90.15 billion (2010 est.). **G.D.P.—per capita:** purchasing power parity—$11,000 (2010 est.). **Currency:** Azerbaijani manat (AZM).

Bahamas, The

Commonwealth of The Bahamas

Geography Location: Caribbean, chain of islands in the North Atlantic Ocean, southeast of Florida, northeast of Cuba. **Area:** 5,359 sq mi (13,880 sq km). **Natural resources:** ssalt, aragonite, timber. **People Population:** 313,312 (July 2011 est.) *note:* estimates for this country explicitly take into account the effects of excess mortality due to AIDS; this can result in lower life expectancy, higher infant mortality and death rates, lower population and growth rates, and changes in the distribution of population by age and sex than would otherwise be expected. **Nationality:** *noun:* Bahamian(s); *adj.:* Bahamian. **Ethnic groups:** 85% black, 12% white, 3% Asian and Hispanic. **Religions:** 35% Baptist, 15% Anglican, 14% Roman Catholic, 8% Pentecostal, 5% Church of God, 4% Methodist, 15% other Christian. **Languages:** English, some Creole among Haitian immigrants. **Government Government type:** constitutional parliamentary democracy. **Capital:** Nassau. **Independence:** 10 July 1973 (from U.K.). **National holiday:** Independence Day, 10 July (1973). **Economy G.D.P.:** purchasing power parity—$8.878 billion (2010 est.). **G.D.P.—per capita:** purchasing power parity—$28,600 (2010 est.). **Currency:** Bahamian dollar (BSD).

Bahrain

Kingdom of Bahrain

Geography Location: Middle East, archipelago in the Persian Gulf, east of Saudi Arabia. **Area:** 286 sq mi (741 sq km). **Border countries:** Saudi Arabia, Qatar. **Natural resources:** oil, associated and non-associated natural gas, fish. **People Population:** 1,214,705 *note:* includes 235,108 non-nationals (July 2011 est.). **Nationality:** *noun:* Bahraini(s); *adj.:* Bahraini. **Ethnic groups:** 62.4% Bahraini, 37.6% non-Bahraini. **Religions:** 81.2% Muslim (Shi'a and Sunni) 9% Christian, 9.8% other. **Languages:** Arabic, English, Farsi, Urdu. **Government Government type:** constitutional hereditary monarchy. **Capital:** Manama. **Independence:** 15 August 1971 (from U.K.). **National holiday:** National Day, 16 December (1971). **Economy G.D.P.:** purchasing power parity—$29.82 billion (2010 est.). **G.D.P.—per capita:** purchasing power parity—$40,400 (2010 est.). **Currency:** Bahraini dinar (BHD).

Bangladesh

People's Republic of Bangladesh

Geography Location: Southern Asia, bordering the Bay of Bengal, between Burma and India. **Area:** 55,598 sq mi (144,000 sq km). **Border countries:** Burma, India. **Natural resources:** natural gas, arable land, timber. **People Population:** 158,570,535 (July 2011 est.). **Nationality:** *noun:* Bangladeshi(s); *adj.:* Bangladeshi. **Ethnic groups:** 98% Bengali, tribal groups, non-Bengali Muslims. **Religions:** 83% Muslim, 16% Hindu, 1% Buddhist, Christian and others. **Languages:** Bangla (official); English widely used. **Government Government type:** parliamentary democracy. **Capital:** Dhaka. **Independence:** 16 December 1971 (from West Pakistan). **National holiday:** Independence Day, 26 March (1971). **Economy G.D.P.:** purchasing power parity—$259.3 billion (2010 est.). **G.D.P.—per capita:** purchasing power parity—$1,700 (2010 est.). **Currency:** taka (BDT).

Barbados

Geography Location: Caribbean, island in the North Atlantic Ocean, northeast of Venezuela. **Area:** 166 sq mi (431 sq km). **Natural resources:** crude oil, fish, natural gas. **People Population:** 286,705 (July 2011 est.). **Nationality:** *noun:* Barbadian(s) or Bajan (colloquial); *adj.:* Barbadian or Bajan (colloquial). **Ethnic groups:** 90% black, 4% white, 6% Asian and mixed. **Religions:** 63.4% Protestant, 4% Roman Catholic, 25% none or other. **Languages:** English. **Government Government type:** parliamentary democracy. **Capital:** Bridgetown. **Independence:** 30 November 1966 (from U.K.). **National holiday:** Independence Day, 30 November (1966). **Economy G.D.P.:** purchasing power parity—$6.196 billion (2010 est.). **G.D.P.—per capita:** purchasing power parity—$21,700 (2010 est.). **Currency:** Barbadian dollar (BBD).

Belarus

Republic of Belarus

Geography Location: Eastern Europe, east of Poland. **Area:** 80,154 sq. mi. (207,600 sq km). **Border countries:** Latvia, Lithuania, Poland, Russia, Ukraine. **Natural resources:** forest, peat, oil, natural gas. **People Population:** 9,577,552 (July 2011 est.). **Nationality:** *noun:* Belarusian(s); *adj.:* Belarusian. **Ethnic groups:** 81.2% Byelorussian, 11.4% Russian, 7.4% Polish, Ukrainian and other. **Religions:** 80% Eastern Orthodox. **Languages:** Byelorussian (official), Russian. **Government Government type:** republic in name, although in fact a dictatorship. **Capital:** Minsk. **Independence:** 25 August 1991 (from Soviet Union) **National holiday:** Independence Day, 3 July (1944).

Economy G.D.P.: purchasing power parity—$128.4 billion (2010 est.). **G.D.P.—per capita:** purchasing power parity—$13,400 (2010 est.). **Currency:** Belarusian ruble (BYB/BYR).

Belgium

Kingdom of Belgium

Geography Location: Western Europe, bordering the North Sea, between France and the Netherlands. **Area:** 11,787 sq mi (30,528 sq km). **Border countries:** France, Germany, Luxembourg, Netherlands. **Natural resources:** coal, natural gas. **People Population:** 10,431,477 (July 2011 est.). **Nationality:** *noun:* Belgian(s); *adj.:* Belgian. **Ethnic groups:** 58% Fleming, 31% Walloon, 11% mixed or other. **Religions:** 75% Roman Catholic, remainder Protestant or other. **Languages:** 60% Dutch, 40% French, less than 1% German (all three official); legally bilingual (Dutch and French). **Government Government type:** federal parliamentary democracy under a constitutional monarch. **Capital:** Brussels. **Independence:** 4 October 1830 a provisional government declared independence from the Netherlands; 21 July 1831 the ascension of King Leopold I to the throne. **National holiday:** Independence Day, 21 July (1831). **Economy G.D.P.:** purchasing power parity—$396.9 billion (2010 est.). **G.D.P.—per capita:** purchasing power parity—$37,900 (2010 est.). **Currency:** euro (EUR).

Belize

Geography Location: Central America, bordering the Caribbean Sea, between Guatemala and Mexico. **Area:** 8,867 sq mi (22,966 sq km). **Border countries:** Guatemala, Mexico. **Natural resources:** arable land potential, timber, fish. **People Population:** 321,115 (July 2011 est.). **Nationality:** *noun:* Belizean(s); *adj.:* Belizean. **Ethnic groups:** 49% mestizo, 25% Creole, 11% Maya, 6.1% Garifuna. **Religions:** 50% Roman Catholic, 27% Protestant. **Languages:** English (official), Spanish, Maya, Garifuna (Carib). **Government Government type:** parliamentary democracy. **Capital:** Belmopan. **Independence:** 21 September 1981 (from U.K.). **National holiday:** Independence Day, 21 September (1981). **Economy G.D.P.:** purchasing power parity—$2.652 billion (2010 est.). **G.D.P.—per capita:** purchasing power parity—$8,400 (2010 est.). **Currency:** Belizean dollar (BZD).

Benin

Republic of Benin

Geography Location: Western Africa, bordering the Bight of Benin, between Nigeria and Togo. **Area:** 43,484 sq mi

(112,622 sq km). **Border countries**: Burkina Faso, Niger, Nigeria, Togo. **Natural resources:** small offshore oil deposits, limestone, marble, timber. **People Population:** 9,325,032 (July 2011 est.) *note:* estimates for this country explicitly take into account the effects of excess mortality due to AIDS; this can result in lower life expectancy, higher infant mortality and death rates, lower population and growth rates, and changes in the distribution of population by age and sex than would otherwise be expected. **Nationality:** *noun:* Beninese (singular and plural); *adj.:* Beninese. **Ethnic groups:** 98.4% African (predominantly Fon, Adja, Yoruba, Bariba), 1.6% other and European. **Religions:** 42.8% Christian, 24.4% Muslim, 17.3% Vodoun, 15.5% other. **Languages:** French (official); Fon and Yoruba in south; at least six major tribal languages in north. **Government Government type:** republic. **Capital:** Porto-Novo is the official capital; Cotonou is the seat of government. **Independence:** 1 August 1960 (from France). **National holiday:** National Day, 1 August (1960). **Economy G.D.P.:** purchasing power parity—$14.2 billion (2010 est.). **G.D.P.—per capita:** purchasing power parity—$1,600 (2010 est.). **Currency:** Communaute Financiere Africaine franc (XOF).

Bhutan

Kingdom of Bhutan

Geography Location: Southern Asia, between China and India. **Area:** 14,824 sq mi (38,394 sq km). **Border countries**: China, India. **Natural resources:** timber, hydropower, gypsum, calcium carbide. **People Population:** 708,427 (July 2011 est.) **Nationality:** *noun:* Bhutanese (singular and plural); *adj.:* Bhutanese. **Ethnic groups:** 50% Bhote, 35% ethnic Nepalese, 15% indigenous or migrant tribes. **Religions:** 75% Lamaistic Buddhism, 25% Indian- and Nepalese-influenced Buddhism. **Languages:** Dzongkha (official), various Tibetan dialects, various Nepalese dialects. **Government Government type:** monarchy; special treaty relationship with India. **Capital:** Thimphu. **Independence:** 8 August 1949 (from India). **National holiday:** National Day (Ugyen Wangchuck became first hereditary king), 17 December (1907). **Economy G.D.P.:** purchasing power parity—$3.526 billion (2010 est.). **G.D.P.—per capita:** purchasing power parity—$5,000 (2010 est.). **Currency:** ngultrum (BTN); Indian rupee (INR).

Bolivia

Republic of Bolivia

Geography Location: Central South America, southwest of Brazil. **Area:** 424,164 sq mi (1,098,581 sq km). **Border** countries: Argentina, Brazil, Chile, Paraguay, Peru. **Natural resources:** tin, natural gas, crude oil, zinc, tungsten. **People Population:** 10,118,683 (July 2011 est.). **Nationality:** *noun:* Bolivian(s); *adj.:* Bolivian. **Ethnic groups:** 30% Quechua, 25% Aymara, 30% mixed, 15% white. **Religions:** 95% Roman Catholic; active Protestant minority, especially Methodist. **Languages:** Spanish (official), Quechua (official), Aymara (official). **Government Government type:** republic; *note:* the new constitution defines Bolivia as a "Social Unitarian State." **Capital:** La Paz (seat of government); Sucre (legal capital and seat of judiciary). **Independence:** 6 August 1825 (from Spain). **National holiday:** Independence Day, 6 August (1825). **Economy G.D.P.:** purchasing power parity—$47.98 billion (2010 est.). **G.D.P.—per capita:** purchasing power parity—$4,800 (2010 est.). **Currency:** boliviano (BOB).

Bosnia and Herzegovina

Geography Location: Southeastern Europe, bordering the Adriatic Sea and Croatia. **Area:** 19,767 sq mi (51,197 sq km). **Border countries**: Croatia, Serbia, Montenegro. **Natural resources:** coal, iron, bauxite, manganese, timber. **People Population:** 4,622,163 (July 2011 est.). **Nationality:** *noun:* Bosnian(s), Herzegovinian(s); *adj.:* Bosnian, Herzegovinian. **Ethnic groups:** 37% Serb, 48% Bozniak, 14% Croat; *note:* Bosniak has replaced Muslim as an ethnic term in part to avoid confusion with the religious term Muslim—an adherent of Islam. **Religions:** 40% Muslim, 31% Orthodox, 15% Catholic, 4% Protestant, 10% other. **Languages:** Croatian, Serbian, Bosnian. **Government Government type:** emerging federal democratic republic. **Capital:** Sarajevo. **Independence:** 1 March 1992. **National holiday:** National Day, 25 November (1943). **Economy G.D.P.:** purchasing power parity—$30.56 billion (2010 est.) *note:* large informal sector could be as much as 50% official G.D.P. **G.D.P.—per capita:** purchasing power parity—$6,600 (2010 est.). **Currency:** marka (BAM).

Botswana

Republic of Botswana

Geography Location: Southern Africa, north of South Africa. **Area:** 223,607 sq mi (581,730 sq km). **Border countries**: Namibia, South Africa, Zimbabwe. **Natural resources:** diamonds, copper, nickel, gold, coal, salt, soda, ash. **People Population:** 2,065,398 (July 2011 est.) *note:* estimates for this country explicitly take into account the effects of excess mortality due to AIDS; this can result in lower life expectancy, higher infant mortality and death rates, lower population and growth rates, and changes in the distribution of population by age and sex than would otherwise be expected. **Nationality:** *noun:* Motswana (singular), Batswana (plural) *adj.:* Motswana (singular), Batswana (plural). **Ethnic groups:** 79% Tswana, 11% Kalanga, 3% Basarwa, 7% other. **Religions:** 20.6% none, 71.6% Christian, 6% Badimo, 1.4% other. **Languages:** English (official), Setswana. **Government Government type:** parliamentary republic. **Capital:** Gaborone. **Independence:** 30 September 1966 (from U.K.). **National holiday:** Independence Day (Botswana Day), 30 September (1966). **Economy G.D.P.:** purchasing power parity—$26.56 billion (2010 est.). **G.D.P.—per capita:** purchasing power parity—$13,100 (2010 est.). **Currency:** pula (BWP).

Brazil

Federative Republic of Brazil

Geography   Location: Eastern South America, bordering the Atlantic Ocean. **Area:** 3,287,612 sq mi (8,514,877 sq km). **Border countries:** Argentina, Bolivia, Colombia, French Guiana, Guyana, Paraguay, Peru, Suriname, Uruguay, Venezuela. **Natural resources:** bauxite, gold, iron ore, manganese, nickel. **People Population:** 203,429,773 (July 2011 est.) *note:* estimates for this country explicitly take into account the effects of excess mortality due to AIDS; this can result in lower life expectancy, higher infant mortality and death rates, lower population and growth rates, and changes in the distribution of population by age and sex than would otherwise be expected. **Nationality:** *noun:* Brazilian(s); *adj.:* Brazilian; **Ethnic groups:** Portuguese, Italian, German, Japanese, black, Amerindian; 53.7% white, 38% mixed, 6% black, 1% other. **Religions:** 73.6% Roman Catholic, 15.4% Protestant, 2.6% other, 7.4% none. **Languages:** Portuguese (official), Spanish, English, French. **Government Government type:** federative republic. **Capital:** Brasilia. **Independence:** 7 September 1822 (from Portugal). **National holiday:** Independence Day, 7 September (1822). **Economy G.D.P.:** purchasing power parity—$2.194 trillion (2010 est.). **G.D.P.—per capita:** purchasing power parity—$10,900 (2010 est.). **Currency:** real (BRL).

Brunei

Negara Brunei Darussalam

Geography   Location: Southeastern Asia, bordering the South China Sea and Malaysia. **Area:** 2,225 sq mi (5,765 sq km). **Border countries:** Malaysia. **Natural resources:** petroleum, natural gas, timber. **People Population:** 401,890 (July 2011 est.). **Nationality:** *noun:* Bruneian(s); *adj.:* Bruneian. **Ethnic groups:** 66% Malay, 11.2% Chinese, 3.4% indigenous, 19.1% other. **Religions:** 67% Muslim (official), 13% Buddhist, 10% Christian, 10% indigenous and oth-

er. **Languages:** Malay (official), English, Chinese. **Government   Government type:** constitutional sultanate. **Capital:** Bandar Seri Begawan. **Independence:** 1 January 1984 (from U.K.). **National holiday:** National Day, 23 February (1984). **Economy G.D.P.:** purchasing power parity—$19.88 billion (2010 est.). **G.D.P.—per capita:** purchasing power parity—$50,300 (2010 est.). **Currency:** Bruneian dollar (BND).

Bulgaria

Republic of Bulgaria

Geography Location: Southeastern Europe, bordering the Black Sea, between Romania and Turkey. **Area:** 42,810 sq mi (110,879 sq km). **Border countries:** Greece, Macedonia, Romania, Serbia, Montenegro, Turkey. **Natural resources:** bauxite, copper, lead, zinc, gold. **People Population:** 7,093,635 (July 2011 est.). **Nationality:** *noun:* Bulgarian(s); *adj.:* Bulgarian. **Ethnic groups:** 83.9% Bulgarian, 9.4% Turk, 4.7% Roma, 2% other. **Religions:** 82.6% Bulgarian Orthodox, 12.2% Muslim, 1.2% Christian, 4% other. **Languages:** Bulgarian, Turkish, Roma. **Government Government type:** parliamentary democracy. **Capital:** Sofia. **Independence:** 3 March 1878 (from Ottoman Empire). **National holiday:** Liberation Day, 3 March (1878). **Economy G.D.P.:** purchasing power parity—$91.83 billion (2010 est.). **G.D.P.—per capita:** purchasing power parity—$12,800 (2010 est.). **Currency:** lev (BGL).

Burkina Faso

Geography Location: Western Africa, north of Ghana. **Area:** 105,869 sq. mi. (274,200 sq km). **Border countries:** Benin, Cote d'Ivoire, Ghana, Mali, Niger, Togo. **Natural resources:** manganese, limestone, marble, ; small deposits of gold, antimony, copper, nickel, bauxite. **People Population:** 16,751,455 (July 2011 est.) *note:* estimates for this country explicitly take into account the effects of excess mortality due to AIDS; this can result in lower life expectancy, higher infant mortality and death rates, lower population and growth rates, and changes in the distribution of population by age and sex than would otherwise be expected. **Nationality:** *noun:* Burkinabe (singular and plural); *adj.:* Burkinabe. **Ethnic groups:** over 40% Mossi; Gurunsi, Senufo, Lobi, Bobo, Mande, Fulani. **Religions:** 50% Muslim, 40% indigenous beliefs, 10% Christian (mainly Roman Catholic). **Languages:** French (official); native African languages spoken by 90% of the population. **Government Government type:** parliamentary republic. **Capital:** Ouagadougou. **Independence:** 5 August 1960 (from France). **National holiday:** Republic Day, 11 December (1958). **Economy G.D.P.:** purchasing power parity—

$20.06 billion (2010 est.). **G.D.P.—per capita:** purchasing power parity—$1,200 (2010 est.). **Currency:** Communaute Financiere Africaine franc (XOF); *note:* responsible authority is the Central Bank of the West African States.

Burundi

Republic of Burundi

Geography Location: Central Africa, east of Democratic Republic of the Congo. **Area:** 10,745 sq mi (27,830 sq km). **Border countries:** Democratic Republic of the Congo, Rwanda, Tanzania. **Natural resources:** nickel, uranium, rare earth oxide, peat, cobalt. **People Population:** 10,216,190 (July 2011 est.) *note:* estimates for this country explicitly take into account the effects of excess mortality due to AIDS; this can result in lower life expectancy, higher infant mortality and death rates, lower population and growth rates, and changes in the distribution of population by age and sex than would otherwise be expected. **Nationality:** *noun:* Burundian(s); *adj.:* Burundian. **Ethnic groups:** 85% Hutu (Bantu), 14% Tutsi (Hamitic), 1% Twa (Pygmy), 3,000 Europeans, 2,000 South Asians. **Religions:** 67% Christian (62% Roman Catholic, 5% Protestant), 23% indigenous beliefs, 10% Muslim. **Languages:** Kirundi and French (both official), Swahili (along Lake Tanganyika and in Bujumbura area). **Government Government type:** republic. **Capital:** Bujumbura. **Independence:** 1 July 1962 (from UN trusteeship under Belgian administration). **National holiday:** Independence Day, 1 July (1962). **Economy G.D.P.:** purchasing power parity—$3.418 billion (2010 est.). **G.D.P.— per capita:** purchasing power parity—$300 (2010 est.). **Currency:** Burundi franc (BIF).

Cambodia

Kingdom of Cambodia

Geography Location: Southeastern Asia, bordering the Gulf of Thailand, between Thailand, Vietnam, and Laos. **Area:** 69,898 sq mi (181,035 sq km). **Border countries:** Laos, Thailand, Vietnam. **Natural resources:** timber, gemstones, some iron ore, manganese, phosphates, hydropower potential. **People Population:** 14,701,717 (July 2011 est.) *note:* estimates for this country explicitly take into account the effects of excess mortality due to AIDS; this can result in lower life expectancy, higher infant mortality and death rates, lower population and growth rates, and changes in the distribution of population by age and sex than would otherwise be expected. **Nationality:** *noun:* Cambodian(s); *adj.:* Cambodian. **Ethnic groups:** 90% Khmer (Cambodian), 5% Vietnamese, 1% Chinese, 4% other minorities. **Religions:** 95% Theravada Buddhism. **Languages:** Khmer (official),

French, English. **Government Government type:** multiparty democracy under a constitutional monarchy. **Capital:** Phnom Penh. **Independence:** 9 November 1953 (from France). **National holiday:** Independence Day, 9 November (1953). **Economy G.D.P.:** purchasing power parity—$30.13 billion (2010 est.). **G.D.P.—per capita:** purchasing power parity—$2,000 (2010 est.). **Currency:** riel (KHR).

Cameroon

Republic of Cameroon

Geography Location: Western Africa, bordering the Bight of Biafra, between Equatorial Guinea and Nigeria. **Area:** 183,568 sq mi (475,440 sq km). **Border countries:** Central African Republic, Chad, Republic of the Congo, Equatorial Guinea, Gabon, Nigeria. **Natural resources:** crude oil, bauxite, iron ore, timber, hydropower potential. **People Population:** 19,711,291 (July 2011 est.) *note:* estimates for this country explicitly take into account the effects of excess mortality due to AIDS; this can result in lower life expectancy, higher infant mortality and death rates, lower population and growth rates, and changes in the distribution of population by age and sex than would otherwise be expected. **Nationality:** *noun:* Cameroonian(s); *adj.:* Cameroonian. **Ethnic groups:** 31% Cameroon Highlanders, 19% Equatorial Bantu, 11% Kirdi, 10% Fulani, 8% Northwestern Bantu, 7% Eastern Nigritic, 13% other African; less than 1% non-African. **Religions:** 40% indigenous beliefs, 40% Christian, 20% Muslim. **Languages:** English and French (both official); 24 major African language groups. **Government Government type:** unitary republic; multiparty presidential regime **Capital:** Yaounde. **Independence:** 1 January 1960 (from French-administered U.N. trusteeship). **National holiday:** Republic Day (National Day), 20 May (1972). **Economy G.D.P.:** purchasing power parity—$44.65 billion (2010 est.). **G.D.P.—per capita:** purchasing power parity—$2,300 (2010 est.). **Currency:** Communaute Financiere Africaine franc (XAF).

Canada

Geography Location: Northern North America, bordering the North Atlantic Ocean on the east, North Pacific Ocean on the west, and the Arctic Ocean on the north, north of the conterminous U.S. **Area:** 3,855,103 sq mi (9,984,670 sq km). **Border countries:** U.S. **Natural resources:** iron ore, nickel, zinc, copper, gold, lead. **People Population:** 34,030,589 (July 2011 est.). **Nationality:** *noun:* Canadian(s); *adj.:* Canadian. **Ethnic groups:** 28% British Isles origin, 23% French origin, 15% other European, 2% Amerindian, 6% other, mostly Asian, Arab, and African. **Religions:** 42.6% Roman Catholic, 23.3% Protestant, 14.1% other, 16% none. **Languages:**

59.3% English, 23.2% French (both official). **Government Government type:** confederation with parliamentary democracy. **Capital:** Ottawa. **Independence:** 1 July 1867 (from U.K.), 11 December 1931 independence recognized. **National holiday:** Canada Day, 1 July (1867). **Economy G.D.P.:** purchasing power parity—$1.335 trillion (2010 est.). **G.D.P.— per capita:** purchasing power parity—$39,600 (2010 est.). **Currency:** Canadian dollar (CAD).

Cape Verde

Republic of Cape Verde

Geography Location: Western Africa, group of islands in the North Atlantic Ocean, west of Senegal. **Area:** 1,557 sq mi (4,033 sq km). **Natural resources:** salt, basalt rock, pozzolana, limestone, kaolin, fish. **People Population:** 516,100 (July 2011 est.). **Nationality:** *noun:* Cape Verdean(s); *adj.:* Cape Verdean. **Ethnic groups:** 71% Creole (mulatto), 28% African, 1% European. **Religions:** Roman Catholicism fused with indigenous beliefs, Protestantism. **Languages:** Portuguese and Crioulo (blend of Portuguese and West African). **Government Government type:** republic. **Capital:** Praia. **Independence:** 5 July 1975 (from Portugal). **National holiday:** Independence Day, 5 July (1975). **Economy G.D.P.:** purchasing power parity—$1.861 billion (2010 est.). **G.D.P.—per capita:** purchasing power parity— $3,700 (2010 est.). **Currency:** Cape Verdean escudo (CVE).

Central African Republic

Central African Republic

Geography Location: Central Africa, north of Democratic Republic of the Congo. **Area:** 240,535 sq mi (622,984 sq km). **Border countries:** Cameroon, Chad, Democratic Republic of the Congo, Republic of the Congo, Sudan. **Natural resources:** diamonds, uranium, timber, gold, oil. **People Population:** 4,950,027 (July 2011 est.) *note:* estimates for this country explicitly take into account the effects of excess mortality due to AIDS; this can result in lower life expectancy, higher infant mortality and death rates, lower population and growth rates, and changes in the distribution of population by age and sex than would otherwise be expected. **Nationality:** *noun:* Central African(s); *adj.:* Central African. **Ethnic groups:** 33% Baya, 27% Banda, 13% Mandija, 10% Sara, 7% Mboum, 4% M'Baka; 2% other. **Religions:** 35% indigenous beliefs, 25% Protestant, 25% Roman Catholic, 15% Muslim; indigenous beliefs and practices strongly influence Christian majority. **Languages:** French (official), Sangho (lingua franca and national language), tribal languages. **Government Government type:** republic. **Capital:** Bangui. **Independence:** 13 August 1960 (from France). **National holiday:** Republic Day, 1 December (1958). **Economy G.D.P.:** purchasing power parity— $3.468 billion (2010 est.). **G.D.P.—per capita:** purchasing power parity—$700 (2010 est.). **Currency:** Communaute Financiere Africaine franc (XAF); *note:* responsible authority is the Bank of the Central African States.

Chad

Republic of Chad

Geography Location: Central Africa, south of Libya. **Area:** 495,793 sq mi (1,284,000 sq km). **Border countries:** Cameroon, Central African Republic, Libya, Niger, Nigeria, Sudan. **Natural resources:** small quantities of crude oil (unexploited but exploitation beginning), uranium, natron (sodium carbonate), kaolin, fish (Lake Chad). **People Population:** 10,758,945 (July 2011 est.). **Nationality:** *noun:* Chadian(s); *adj.:* Chadian. **Ethnic groups:** Sara, Arab, Mayo-Kebbie, Kanem-Bornou, Ouaddai, Hadjarai, Tandjile, Gorane, Fritri-Batha. **Religions:** 51% Muslim, 35% Christian, 7% Animist, 7% other. **Languages:** French and Arabic (both official); Sara and Sango in south; more than 120 different languages and dialects. **Government Government type:** republic. **Capital:** N'Djamena. **Indepen-dence:** 11 August 1960 (from France). **National holiday:** Independence Day, 11 August (1960). **Economy G.D.P.:** purchasing power parity—$18.56 billion (2010 est.). **G.D.P.—per capita:** purchasing power parity—$1,800 (2010 est.). **Currency:** Communaute Financiere Africaine franc (XAF); *note:* responsible authority is the Bank of the Central African States.

Chile

Republic of Chile

Geography Location: Southern South America, bordering the South Pacific Ocean, between Argentina and Peru. **Area:** 281,993 sq mi (756,102 sq km). **Border countries:** Argentina, Bolivia, Peru. **Natural resources:** copper, timber, iron ore, nitrates, precious metals. **People Population:** 16,888,760 (July 2011 est.). **Nationality:** *noun:* Chilean(s); *adj.:* Chilean. **Ethnic groups:** 95% white and white Amerindian, 3% Amerindian, 2% other. **Religions:** 70% Roman Catholic, 15.1% Evangelical, 1.1% Jehovah Witness, 4.6% other, 8.3% none. **Languages:** Spanish (official), English, Mapudungun, German. **Government Government type:** republic. **Capital:** Santiago. **Independence:** 18 September 1810 (from Spain). **National holiday:** Independence Day, 18 September (1810). **Economy G.D.P.:** purchasing power parity—$260 billion (2010 est.). **G.D.P.—per capita:** purchasing power parity—$15,500 (2010 est.). **Currency:** Chilean peso (CLP).

China

People's Republic of China

Geography Location: Eastern Asia, bordering the East China Sea, Korea Bay, Yellow Sea, and South China Sea, between North Korea and Vietnam. **Area:** 3,705,407 sq mi (9,596,961 sq km). **Border countries**: Afghanistan, Bhutan, Burma, Hong Kong, India, Kazakhstan, North Korea, Kyrgyzstan, Laos, Macau, Mongolia, Nepal, Pakistan, Russia (northeast), Russia (northwest), Tajikistan, Vietnam. **Natural resources:** coal, iron ore, crude oil, mercury, tin; world's largest hydropower potential. **People Population:** 1,336,718,015 (July 2011 est.). **Nationality:** *noun:* Chinese (singular and plural). *adj.:* Chinese. **Ethnic groups:** 91.5 % Han Chinese, 8.5% Zhuang, Uygur, Hui, Yi, Tibetan, Miao, Manchu, Mongol, Buyi, Korean, and numerous others. **Religions:** officially atheist, but traditionally pragmatic and eclectic; Taoism, Buddhism, 1–2% Muslim, 3–4% Christian. **Languages:** Standard Chinese or Mandarin (Putonghua, based on the Beijing dialect), Yue (Cantonese), Wu (Shanghaiese), Minbei (Fuzhou), Minnan (Hokkien-Taiwanese), Xiang, Gan, Hakka dialects, minority languages (see Ethnic groups entry). **Government Government type:** Communist state. **Capital:** Beijing. **Independence:** 221 B.C. (unification under the Qin or Ch'in Dynasty 221 B.C.; Qing or Ch'ing Dynasty replaced by the Republic on 12 February 1912; People's Republic established 1 October 1949). **National holiday:** Anniversary of the Founding of the People's Republic of China, 1 October (1949). **Economy G.D.P.:** purchasing power parity—$9.872 trillion (2010 est.). **G.D.P.—per capita:** purchasing power parity—$7,400 (2010 est.). **Currency:** yuan (CNY); *note:* currency is also referred to as Renminbi (RMB).

Colombia

Republic of Colombia

Geography Location: Northern South America, bordering the Caribbean Sea, between Panama and Venezuela, and bordering the North Pacific Ocean, between Ecuador and Panama. **Area:** 439,737 sq mi (1,138,914 sq km). **Border countries**: Brazil, Ecuador, Panama, Peru, Venezuela. **Natural resources:** crude oil, natural gas, coal, iron ore, nickel. **People Population:** 44,725,543 (July 2011 est.). **Nationality:** *noun:* Colombian(s); *adj.:* Colombian. **Ethnic groups:** 58% mestizo, 20% white, 14% mulatto, 4% black, 4% other. **Religions:** 90% Roman Catholic. **Languages:** Spanish. **Government Government type:** republic; executive branch dominates government structure. **Capital:** Bogota. **Independence:** 20 July 1810 (from Spain). **National holiday:** Independence Day, 20 July (1810). **Economy G.D.P.:** purchasing power parity—$431.9 billion (2010 est.). **G.D.P.—per capita:** purchasing power parity—$9,800 (2010 est.). **Currency:** Colombian peso (COP).

Comoros

Union of the Comoros

Geography Location: Southern Africa, group of islands at the northern mouth of the Mozambique Channel, about two-thirds of the way between northern Madagascar and northern Mozambique. **Area:** 863 sq mi (2,235 sq km). **Natural resources:** negligible. **People Population:** 794,683 (July 2011 est.). **Nationality:** *noun:* Comoran(s); *adj.:* Comoran. **Ethnic groups:** Antalote, Cafre, Makoa, Oimatsaha, Sakalava. **Religions:** 98% Sunni Muslim, 2% Roman Catholic. **Languages:** Arabic and French (both official), Shikomoro (a blend of Swahili and Arabic). **Government Government type:** republic. **Capital:** Moroni. **Independence:** 6 July 1975 (from France). **National holiday:** Independence Day, 6 July (1975). **Economy G.D.P.:** purchasing power parity—$789.4 million (2010 est.). **G.D.P.—per capita:** purchasing power parity—$1,000 (2010 est.). **Currency:** Comoran franc (KMF).

Congo, Democratic Republic of the

Democratic Republic of the Congo

Geography Location: Central Africa, northeast of Angola. **Area:** 905,355 sq mi (2,344,858 sq km). **Border countries**: Angola (of which 225 km is the boundary of Angola's discontiguous Cabinda Province), Burundi, Central African Republic, Republic of the Congo, Rwanda, Sudan, Tanzania, Uganda, Zambia. **Natural resources:** cobalt, copper, cadmium, crude oil, industrial and gem diamonds. **People Population:** 71,712,867 (July 2011 est.) *note:* estimates for this country explicitly take into account the effects of excess mortality due to AIDS; this can result in lower life expectancy, higher infant mortality and death rates, lower population and growth rates, and changes in the distribution of population by age and sex than would otherwise be expected. **Nationality:** *noun:* Congolese (singular and plural); *adj.:* Congolese or Congo. **Ethnic groups:** 45% of the people belong to one of four largest groups—Mongo, Luba, Kongo (all Bantu), and Mangbetu-Azande. **Religions:** 50% Roman Catholic, 20% Protestant, 10% Kimbanguist, 10% Muslim, 10% other syncretic sects and traditional beliefs. **Languages:** French (official), Lingala, Kingwana, Kikongo, Tshiluba. **Government Government type:** transitional government. **Capital:** Kinshasa. **Independence:** 30 June 1960 (from Belgium). **National holiday:** Independence Day, 30 June (1960). **Economy G.D.P.:** purchasing power parity—$22.92 billion (2010 est.). **G.D.P.—per capita:** purchasing power parity—$300 (2010 est.). **Currency:** Congolese franc (CDF).

Congo, Republic of the

Republic of the Congo

Geography **Location:** Western Africa, bordering the South Atlantic Ocean, between Angola and Gabon. **Area:** 132,047 sq mi (342,000 sq km). **Border countries:** Angola, Cameroon, Central African Republic, Democratic Republic of the Congo, Gabon. **Natural resources:** petroleum, timber, potash, lead, zinc. **People** **Population:** 4,243,929 (July 2011 est.) *note:* estimates for this country explicitly take into account the effects of excess mortality due to AIDS; this can result in lower life expectancy, higher infant mortality and death rates, lower population and growth rates, and changes in the distribution of population by age and sex than would otherwise be expected. **Nationality:** *noun:* Congolese (singular and plural); *adj.:* Congolese or Congo. **Ethnic groups:** 48% Kongo, 20% Sangha, 17% Teke, 12% M'Bochi; about 8,500 Europeans (may be half that number following 1997 civil war). **Religions:** 50% Christian, 48% Animist, 2% Muslim. **Languages:** French (official); many African languages with Lingala and Kikongo most widely used. **Government** **Government type:** republic. **Capital:** Brazzaville. **Independence:** 15 August 1960 (from France). **National holiday:** Independence Day, 15 August (1960). **Economy** **G.D.P.:** purchasing power parity—$17.45 billion (2010 est.). **G.D.P.—per capita:** purchasing power parity— $4,200 (2010 est.). **Currency:** Communaute Financiere Africaine franc (XAF); *note:* responsible authority is the Bank of the Central African States.

Costa Rica

Republic of Costa Rica

Geography **Location:** Middle America, bordering both the Caribbean Sea and the North Pacific Ocean, between Nicaragua and Panama. **Area:** 19,730 sq mi (51,100 sq km). **Border countries:** Nicaragua, Panama. **Natural resources:** hydropower potential. **People** **Population:** 4,576,562 (July 2011 est.). **Nationality:** *noun:* Costa Rican(s); *adj.:* Costa Rican. **Ethnic groups:** 94% white (including mestizo), 3% black, 1% Amerindian, 1% Chinese. **Religions:** 76.3% Roman Catholic, 13.7% Evangelical Protestant, other Protestant, Jehovah's Witness. **Languages:** Spanish (official), Jamaican dialect of English spoken around Puerto Limon. **Government** **Government type:** democratic republic. **Capital:** San Jose. **Independence:** 15 September 1821 (from Spain). **National holiday:** Independence Day, 15 September (1821). **Economy G.D.P.:** purchasing power parity—$51.3 billion (2010 est.). **G.D.P.—per capita:** purchasing power parity—$11,400 (2010 est.). **Currency:** Costa Rican colon (CRC).

Côte d'Ivoire

Republic of Cote d'Ivoire

Geography **Location:** Western Africa, bordering the North Atlantic Ocean, between Ghana and Liberia. **Area:** 124,502 sq mi (322,460 sq km). **Border countries:** Burkina Faso, Ghana, Guinea, Liberia, Mali. **Natural resources:** crude oil, diamonds, manganese, iron ore, cobalt. **People** **Population:** 21,504,162 (July 2011 est.) *note:* estimates for this country explicitly take into account the effects of excess mortality due to AIDS; this can result in lower life expectancy, higher infant mortality and death rates, lower population and growth rates, and changes in the distribution of population by age and sex than would otherwise be expected. **Nationality:** *noun:* Ivorian(s); *adj.:* Ivorian. **Ethnic groups:** 41% Akan, 18% Voltaiques or Gur, 17% Northern Mandes, 11% Krous, 10% Southern Mandes, 3% other (including 130,000 Lebanese and 20,000 French). **Religions:** 35–40% Muslim, 20–30% Christian, 25–40% indigenous beliefs. **Languages:** French (official); over 60 African languages and dialects with Dioula most widely spoken. **Government** **Government type:** *note:* the government was currently disputed as of early 2011, with both candidates from the runoff declaring victory. **Capital:** Yamoussoukro; *note:* although Yamoussoukro has been the official capital since 1983, Abidjan remains the commercial and administrative center; the U.S., like other countries, maintains its Embassy in Abidjan. **Independence:** 7 August (1960) (from France). **National holiday:** Independence Day, 7 August (1960). **Economy G.D.P.:** purchasing power parity—$37.8 billion (2010 est.). **G.D.P.—per capita:** purchasing power parity—$1,800 (2010 est.). **Currency:** Communaute Financiere Africaine franc (XOF); *note:* responsible authority is the Central Bank of the West African States.

Croatia

Republic of Croatia

Geography **Location:** Southeastern Europe, bordering the Adriatic Sea, between Bosnia and Herzegovina and Slovenia. **Area:** 21,851 sq mi (56,594 sq km). **Border countries:** Bosnia and Herzegovina, Hungary, Serbia, Montenegro, Slovenia. **Natural resources:** oil, coal, bauxite, low-grade iron ore, calcium. **People** **Population:** 4,483,804 (July 2011 est.). **Nationality:** *noun:* Croat(s), Croatian(s); *adj.:* Croatian. **Ethnic groups:** 90% Croat, 5% Serb, 0.5% Bosniak. **Religions:** 87.8% Catholic, 4.4% Orthodox, 1.3% Slavic Muslim. **Languages:** 96% Croatian. **Government** **Government type:** presidential/parliamentary democracy. **Capital:** Zagreb. **Independence:** 25 June 1991 (from Yugoslavia). **National holiday:** Independence Day, 8 October (1991). **Economy G.D.P.:** purchasing power parity—$78.52 billion (2010 est.). **G.D.P.—per capita:** purchasing power parity—$17,500 (2010 est.). **Currency:** kuna (HRK).

Cuba

Republic of Cuba

Geography   Location: Caribbean, island between the Caribbean Sea and the North Atlantic Ocean, 150 km south of Key West, Florida. **Area:** 42,803 sq mi (110,860 sq km). **Border countries:** U.S. Naval Base at Guantanamo Bay *note:* Guantanamo Naval Base is leased by the U.S. and thus remains part of Cuba. **Natural resources:** cobalt, nickel, iron ore, copper, manganese. **People Population:** 11,087,330 (July 2011 est.). **Nationality:** *noun:* Cuban(s); *adj.:* Cuban. **Ethnic groups:** 65.1% white, 24.8% mulatto/mestizo, 10.1% black. **Religions:** at least 85% Roman Catholic before Castro assumed power. **Languages:** Spanish. **Government** **Government type:** Communist state. **Capital:** Havana. **Independence:** 20 May 1902 (from Spain 10 December 1898; administered by the U.S. from 1898 to 1902). **National holiday:** Triumph of the Revolution, 1 January 1959. **Economy G.D.P.:** purchasing power parity—$114.1 billion (2010 est.). **G.D.P.—per capita:** purchasing power parity—$9,900 (2010 est.). **Currency:** Cuban peso (CUP) and Convertible peso (CUC).

Cyprus

Republic of Cyprus

Geography Location: Middle East, island in the Mediterranean Sea, south of Turkey. **Area:** 3,572 sq mi (9,251 sq km) (of which 3,355 sq km are in the Turkish Cypriot area). **Natural resources:** copper, pyrites, asbestos, gypsum, timber. **People Population:** 1,120,489 (July 2011 est.). **Nationality:** *noun:* Cypriot(s); *adj.:* Cypriot. **Ethnic groups:** 77% Greek, 18% Turk, 5% other. **Religions:** 78% Greek Orthodox, 18% Muslim. **Languages:** Greek, Turkish, English. **Government** **Government type:** republic. **Capital:** Nicosia. **Independence:** 16 August 1960 (from U.K.); *note:* Turkish Cypriot area proclaimed self-rule on 13 February 1975. **National holiday:** Independence Day, 1 October (1960); *note:*

Turkish Cypriot area celebrates 15 November (1983) as Independence Day. **Economy G.D.P.: Greek Cypriot area:** purchasing power parity—$23.18 billion (2010 est.); **Turkish Cypriot area:** purchasing power parity—$1.829 billion (2007 est.). **G.D.P.—per capita: Greek Cypriot area:** purchasing power parity—$21,000 (2010 est.); **Turkish Cypriot area:** purchasing power parity—$11,700 (2007 est.). **Currency: Greek Cypriot area:** Cypriot pound (CYP); **Turkish Cypriot area:** Turkish new lira (YTL).

Czech Republic

Geography   Location: Central Europe, southeast of Germany. **Area:** 30,451 sq mi (78,867 sq km). **Border countries:** Austria, Germany, Poland, Slovakia. **Natural resources:** coal, kaolin, clay, graphite. **People Population:** 10,190,213 (July 2011 est.). **Nationality:** *noun:* Czech(s); *adj.:* Czech. **Ethnic groups:** 90.4% Czech, 3.4% Moravian, 1.9% Slovak. **Religions:** 59% unaffiliated, 26.8% Roman Catholic, 2.1% Protestant. **Languages:** Czech. **Government** **Government type:** parliamentary democracy. **Capital:** Prague. **Independence:** 1 January 1993 (Czechoslovakia split into the Czech Republic and Slovakia). **National holiday:** Czech Founding Day, 28 October (1918). **Economy G.D.P.:** purchasing power parity—$261.5 billion (2010 est.). **G.D.P.—per capita:** purchasing power parity—$25,600 (2010 est.). **Currency:** Czech koruna (CZK) *note:* They planned to adopt the Euro in 2010 but the date keeps getting pushed back; 2015, or even as late as 2019, have been targeted.

Denmark

Kingdom of Denmark

Geography Location: Northern Europe, bordering the Baltic Sea and the North Sea, on a peninsula north of Germany (Jutland); also includes two major islands (Sjaelland and Fyn). **Area:** 16,639 sq mi (43,094 sq km). **Border countries:** Germany. **Natural resources:** crude oil, natural gas, fish, salt, limestone. **People Population:** 5,529,888 (July 2011 est.). **Nationality:** *noun:* Dane(s); *adj.:* Danish. **Ethnic groups:** Scandanavian, Inuit, Faroese, German. **Religions:** 95% Evangelical Lutheran, Protestant and Roman Catholic, Muslim. **Languages:** Danish, Faroese, English, Greenlandic (Eskimo dialect); small German speaking minority. **Government Government type:** constitutional monarchy. **Capital:** Copenhagen. **National holiday:** none designated; Constitution Day, 5 June is generally viewed as the National Day. **Economy G.D.P.:** purchasing power parity—$201.4 billion (2010 est.). **G.D.P.—per capita:** purchasing power parity—$36,700 (2010 est.). **Currency:** Danish krone (DKK).

Djibouti

Republic of Djibouti

Geography Location: Eastern Africa, bordering the Gulf of Aden and the Red Sea, between Eritrea and Somalia. **Area:** 8,494 sq mi (23,200 sq km). **Border countries**: Eritrea, Ethiopia, Somalia. **Natural resources:** geothermal areas. **People Population:** 757,074 (July 2011 est.). **Ethnic Groups:** 60% Somali, 35% Afar, 5% French, Arab, Ethiopian, Italian. **Religions:** 94% Muslim, 6% Christian. **Languages:** French and Arabic (official); Somali and Afar widely used. **Nationality:** *noun:* Djiboutian(s); *adj.:* Djiboutian. **Government   Government type:** republic. **Capital:** Djibouti. **Independence:** 27 June 1977 (from France). **National holiday:** Independence Day, 27 June (1977). **Economy G.D.P.:** purchasing power parity—$2.099 billion (2010 est.). **G.D.P.—per capita:** purchasing power parity—$2,800 (2010 est.). **Currency:** Djiboutian franc (DJF).

Dominica

Commonwealth of Dominica

Geography Location: Caribbean, island between the Caribbean Sea and the North Atlantic Ocean, about one-half of the way from Puerto Rico to Trinidad and Tobago. **Area:** 290 sq mi (750 sq km). **Natural resources:** timber, hydropower, arable land. **People Population:** 72,969 (July 2011 est.). **Nationality:** *noun:* Dominican(s); *adj.:* Dominican. **Ethnic groups:** black, Carib Amerindians, mixed, European, Syrian. **Religions:** 61.4% Roman Catholic, 6% Seventh Day Adventist, 23.4% other Christian, 1.3% Rastafarian, 6.1% none. **Languages:** English (official), French patois. **Government   Government type:** parliamentary democracy; republic within the Commonwealth. **Capital:** Roseau. **Independence:** 3 November 1978 (from U.K.). **National holiday:** Independence Day, 3 November (1978). **Economy G.D.P.:** purchasing power parity—$765.4 million (2010 est.). **G.D.P.—per capita:** purchasing power parity—$10,500 (2010 est.). **Currency:** East Caribbean dollar (XCD).

Dominican Republic

Geography Location: Caribbean, eastern two-thirds of the island of Hispaniola, between the Caribbean Sea and the North Atlantic Ocean, east of Haiti. **Area:** 18,792 sq mi (48,670 sq km). **Border countries**: Haiti. **Natural resources:** nickel, bauxite, gold, silver. **People Population:** 9,956,648 (July 2011 est.). **Nationality:** *noun:* Dominican(s); *adj.:* Dominican. **Ethnic groups:** 73% mixed, 16% white, 11% black. **Religions:** 95% Roman Catholic. **Languages:** Spanish. **Government   Government type:** democratic republic. **Capital:** Santo Domingo. **Independence:** 27 February 1844 (from Haiti). **National holiday:** Independence Day, 27 February (1844). **Economy G.D.P.:** purchasing power parity—$84.94 billion (2010 est.). **G.D.P.—per capita:** purchasing power parity—$8,600 (2010 est.). **Currency:** Dominican peso (DOP).

East Timor

Democratic Republic of Timor-Leste

Geography Location: Southeastern Asia, northwest of Australia in the Lesser Sunda Islands at the eastern end of the Indonesian archipelago; note: East Timor includes the eastern half of the island of Timor, the Oecussi (Ambeno) region on the northwest portion of the island of Timor, and the islands of Pulau Atauro and Pulau Jaco. **Area:** 7,336 sq mi (19,000 sq km). **Border countries:** Indonesia. **Natural resources:** gold, petroleum, natural gas, manganese, marble. **People Population:** 1,177,834 note: other estimates range as low as 800,000 (July 2011 est.) **Nationality:** *noun:* Timorese; *adj.:* Timorese. **Ethnic groups:** Austronesian (Malayo-Polynesian), Papuan, small Chinese minority. **Religions:** 90% Roman Catholic, 4% Muslim, 3% Protestant. **Languages:** Tetum and Portuguese (official); English, Indonesian. note: there are about 16 indigenous languages; Tetum, Galole, Mambae, and Kemak are spoken by significant numbers of people. **Government   Government type:** republic. **Capital:** Dili. **Independence:** 28 November 1975 (date of proclamation of independence from Portugal); note: 20 May 2002 is the official date of international recognition of East Timor's independence from Indonesia. **National holiday:** Independence Day, 28 November (1975). **Economy G.D.P.:** purchasing power parity—$3.004 billion (2010 est.). **G.D.P.—per capita:** purchasing power parity—$2,600 (2010 est.). **Currency:** Indonesian rupiah.

Ecuador

Republic of Ecuador

Geography Location: Western South America, bordering the Pacific Ocean at the Equator, between Colombia and Peru. **Area:** 109,484 sq mi (283,561 sq km). **Border countries**: Colombia, Peru. **Natural resources:** petroleum, fish, timber. **People Population:** 15,007,343 (July 2011 est.). **Nationality:** *noun:* Ecuadorian(s); *adj.:* Ecuadorian. **Ethnic groups:** 65% mestizo, 25% Amerindian, 7% Spanish, 3% black. **Religions:** 95% Roman Catholic. **Languages:** Spanish (official), Amerindian languages, especially Quechua. **Government Government type:** republic. **Capital:** Quito. **Independence:** 24 May 1822 (from Spain). **National holiday:** Independence Day (independence of

Quito), 10 August (1809). **Economy G.D.P.:** purchasing power parity—$114.7 billion (2010 est.). **G.D.P.—per capita:** purchasing power parity—$7,800 (2010 est.). **Currency:** U.S. dollar (USD).

Egypt

Arab Republic of Egypt

Geography   Location: Northern Africa, bordering the Mediterranean Sea, between Libya and the Gaza Strip, and the Red Sea north of Sudan, and includes the Asian Sinai Peninsula. **Area:** 386,662 sq mi (1,001,450 sq km). **Border countries:** Gaza Strip, Israel, Libya, Sudan. **Natural resources:** crude oil, natural gas, iron ore, phosphates, manganese. **People Population:** 82,079,636 (July 2011 est.). **Nationality:** *noun:* Egyptian(s); *adj.:* Egyptian. **Ethnic groups:** 99% Eastern Hamitic stock. **Religions:** 94% Muslim (mostly Sunni), 6% Coptic Christian and other. **Languages:** Arabic (official), English and French widely understood by educated classes. **Government Government type:** republic *note:* constitution dissolved by the military caretaker government in February, 2011. **Capital:** Cairo. **Independence:** 28 February 1922 (from U.K.). **National holiday:** Revolution Day, 23 July (1952). **Economy G.D.P.:** purchasing power parity—$500.9 billion (2010 est.). **G.D.P.—per capita:** purchasing power parity—$6,200 (2010 est.). **Currency:** Egyptian pound (EGP).

El Salvador

Republic of El Salvador

Geography   Location: Central America, bordering the North Pacific Ocean, between Guatemala and Honduras. **Area:** 8,124 sq mi (21,040 sq km). **Border countries:** Guatemala, Honduras. **Natural resources:** hydropower and geothermal power, crude oil. **People Population:** 6,071,774 (July 2011 est.). **Nationality:** *noun:* Salvadoran(s); *adj.:* Salvadoran. **Ethnic groups:** 90% mestizo, 1% Amerindian, 9% white. **Religions:** 83% Roman Catholic; extensive activity by Protestant groups throughout the country. **Languages:** Spanish, Nahua (among some Amerindians). **Government Government type:** republic. **Capital:** San Salvador. **Independence:** 15 September 1821 (from Spain). **National holiday:** Independence Day, 15 September (1821). **Economy G.D.P.:** purchasing power parity—$43.98 billion (2010 est.). **G.D.P.—per capita:** purchasing power parity—$7,300 (2010 est.). **Currency:** U.S. dollar (USD).

Equatorial Guinea

Republic of Equatorial Guinea

Geography   Location: Western Africa, bordering the Bight of Biafra, between Cameroon and Gabon. **Area:** 10,831 sq mi (28,051 sq km). **Border countries:** Cameroon, Gabon. **Natural resources:** timber, crude oil, small unexploited deposits of gold, manganese, uranium. **People Population:** 668,225 (July 2011 est.). **Nationality:** *noun:* Equatorial Guinean(s) or Equato-guinean(s); *adj.:* Equatorial Guinean or Equatoguinean. **Ethnic groups:** Fang, Bubi, Mdowe, Annobon, Bujeba. **Religions:** Christian, predominantly Roman Catholic; indigenous practices. **Languages:** Spanish (official), pidgin English, Fang. **Government Government type:** republic. **Capital:** Malabo. **Independence:** 12 October 1968 (from Spain). **National holiday:** Independence Day, 12 October (1968). **Economy G.D.P.:** purchasing power parity—$24.66 billion (2010 est.). **G.D.P.—per capita:** purchasing power parity—$37,900 (2010 est.). **Currency:** Communaute Financiere Africaine franc (XAF); *note:* responsible authority is the Bank of the Central African States.

Eritrea

State of Eritrea

Geography   Location: Eastern Africa, bordering the Red Sea, between Djibouti and Sudan. **Area:** 45,406 sq mi (117,600 sq km). **Border countries:** Djibouti, Ethiopia, Sudan. **Natural resources:** gold, potash, zinc, copper. **People Population:** 5,939,484 (July 2011 est.). **Nationality:** *noun:* Eritrean(s); *adj.:* Eritrean. **Ethnic groups:** 50% Tigrinya, 40% Tigre and Kunama, 4% Afar, 3% Saho. **Religions:** Muslim, Coptic Christian, Roman Catholic, Protestant. **Languages:** Afar, Amharic, Arabic, Tigre and Kunama, Tigrinya, minor ethnic group languages. **Government Government type:** transitional government. *note:* following a successful referendum on independence for the Autonomous Region of Eritrea on 23–25 April 1993, a National Assembly, composed entirely of the People's Front for Democracy and Justice or PFDJ, was established as a transitional legislature; a Constitutional Commission was also established to draft a constitution; ISAIAS Afworki was elected president by the transitional legislature; the constitution, ratified in May 1997, did not enter into effect, pending parliamentary and presidential elections; parliamentary elections had been scheduled to take place in December 2001, but were postponed indefinitely; currently the sole legal party is the People's Front for Democracy and Justice (PFDJ). **Capital:** Asmara (formerly Asmera). **Independence:** 24 May 1993 (from Ethiopia). **National holiday:** Independence Day, 24

May (1993). **Economy G.D.P.:** purchasing power parity—$4.178 billion (2010 est.). **G.D.P.—per capita:** purchasing power parity—$700 (2010 est.). **Currency:** nakfa (ERN).

Estonia

Republic of Estonia

Geography   Location: Eastern Europe, bordering the Baltic Sea and Gulf of Finland, between Latvia and Russia. **Area:** 17,463 sq mi (45,228 sq km). **Border countries:** Latvia, Russia. **Natural resources:** oil shale (world's number two producer), peat, phosphorites. **People Population:** 1,282,963 (July 2011 est.). **Nationality:** *noun:* Estonian(s); *adj.:* Estonian. **Ethnic groups:** 67.9% Estonian, 25.6% Russian, 2.1% Ukrainian. **Religions:** Lutheran, Orthodox Christian, others. **Languages:** Estonian (official), Russian, Ukrainian, English, Finnish, other. **Government Government type:** parliamentary republic. **Capital:** Tallinn. **Indepen-dence:** regained on 20 August 1991 (from Soviet Union). **National holiday:** Independence Day, 24 February (1918); *note:* 24 February 1918 was the date of independence from Soviet Russia, 20 August 1991 was the date of reindependence from the Soviet Union. **Economy G.D.P.:** purchasing power parity—$24.65 billion (2010 est.). **G.D.P.—per capita:** purchasing power parity—$19,000 (2010 est.). **Currency:** Estonian kroon (EEK).

Ethiopia

Federal Democratic Republic of Ethiopia

Geography   Location: Eastern Africa, west of Somalia. **Area:** 426,373 sq mi (1,104,300 sq km). **Border countries:** Djibouti, Eritrea, Kenya, Somalia, Sudan. **Natural resources:** small reserves of gold, platinum, copper, potash. **People Population:** 90,873,739 (July 2011 est.) *note:* estimates for this country explicitly take into account the effects of excess mortality due to AIDS; this can result in lower life expectancy, higher infant mortality and death rates, lower population and growth rates, and changes in the distribution of population by age and sex than would otherwise be expected. **Nationality:** *noun:* Ethiopian(s); *adj.:* Ethiopian. **Ethnic groups:** 40% Oromo, 32% Amhara and Tigrean, 9% Sidamo, 6% Shankella. **Religions:** 61% Christian, 33% Muslim, 4.6% traditional. **Languages:** Amharic, Tigrinya, Orominga, Guaraginga, Somali, Arabic, English (major foreign language taught in schools). **Government Government type:** federal republic. **Capital:** Addis Ababa. **Independence:** oldest independent country in Africa and one of the oldest in the world—at least 2,000 years. **National holiday:** National Day (defeat of Mengistu regime), 28 May (1991). **Economy G.D.P.:** purchasing

power parity—$84.02 billion (2010 est.). **G.D.P.—per capita:** purchasing power parity—$1,000 (2010 est.). **Currency:** birr (ETB).

Fiji

Republic of the Fiji Islands

Geography   Location: Oceania, island group in the South Pacific Ocean, about two-thirds of the way from Hawaii to New Zealand. **Area:** 7,056 sq mi (18,274 sq km). **Natural resources:** timber, fish, gold, copper, offshore oil potential. **People Population:** 883,125 (July 2011 est.). **Nationality:** *noun:* Fijian(s); *adj.:* Fijian. **Ethnic groups:** 55% Fijian, 38% Indian, 8% other. **Religions:** 64.5% Christian, 27.9% Hindu, 6.3% Muslim; Fijians are mainly Christian, Indians are Hindu with Muslim minority. **Languages:** English (official), Fijian, Hindustani. **Government Government type:** republic. **Capital:** Suva. **Independence:** 10 October 1970 (from U.K.). **National holiday:** Independence Day, second Monday of October (1970). **Economy G.D.P.:** purchasing power parity—$3.792 billion (2010 est.). **G.D.P.—per capita:** purchasing power parity—$4,300 (2010 est.). **Currency:** Fijian dollar (FJD).

Finland

Republic of Finland

Geography   Location: Northern Europe, bordering the Baltic Sea, Gulf of Bothnia, and Gulf of Finland, between Sweden and Russia. **Area:** 130,127 sq mi (338,145 sq km). **Border countries:** Norway, Sweden, Russia. **Natural resources:** timber, copper, iron ore, zinc, silver. **People Population:** 5,259,250 (July 2011 est.). **Nationality:** *noun:* Finn(s); *adj.:* Finnish. **Ethnic groups:** 93% Finn, 6% Swede; Sami, Roma, Tatar. **Religions:** 82.5% Lutheran Church of Finland, 1.1% Orthodox, 1.1% other Christian, 15.1% none. **Languages:** 91.5% Finnish, 5.5% Swedish (both official); small Sami- and Russian-speaking minorities. **Government Government type:** republic. **Capital:** Helsinki. **Independence:** 6 December 1917 (from Russia). **National holiday:** Independence Day, 6 December (1917). **Economy G.D.P.:** purchasing power parity—$187.6 billion (2010 est.). **G.D.P.—per capita:** purchasing power parity—$35,300 (2010 est.) **Currency:** euro (EUR).

France

French Republic

Geography   Location: Western Europe, bordering the Bay of Biscay and English Channel, between Belgium and Spain, southeast of the U.K.; bordering the Mediterranean Sea, between Italy and Spain. **Area:** 248,429 sq mi (643,427 sq km). **Border countries**: Andorra, Belgium, Germany, Italy, Luxembourg, Monaco, Spain, Switzerland. **Natural resources:** coal, iron ore, bauxite, fish, timber. **People Population:** 65,102,719 (July 2011 est.) France plus four overseas regions; metropolitan France is 62,814,233. **Nationality:** *noun:* Frenchman (men), Frenchwoman (women); *adj.:* French. **Ethnic groups:** Celtic and Latin with Teutonic, Slavic, North African, Indochinese, and Basque minorities. **Religions:** 83–88% Roman Catholic, 2% Protestant, 1% Jewish, 5–10% Muslim (North African workers), 4% unaffiliated. **Languages:** French (100% of the population); rapidly declining regional dialects (Provencal, Breton, Alsatian, Corsican, Catalan, Basque, Flemish). **Government Government type:** republic. **Capital:** Paris. **Independence:** 486 (unified by Clovis). **National holiday:** Bastille Day, 14 July (1789). **Economy G.D.P.:** purchasing power parity—$2.16 trillion (2010 est.). **G.D.P.—per capita:** purchasing power parity—$33,300 (2010 est.). **Currency:** euro (EUR).

Gabon

Gabonese Republic

Geography Location: Western Africa, bordering the Atlantic Ocean at the Equator, between Republic of the Congo and Equatorial Guinea. **Area:** 103,348 sq mi (267,670 sq km). **Border countries**: Cameroon, Republic of the Congo, Equatorial Guinea. **Natural resources:** crude oil, manganese, uranium, gold, timber, iron ore. **People Population:** 1,576,665 (July 2011 est.) *note:* estimates for this country explicitly take into account the effects of excess mortality due to AIDS; this can result in lower life expectancy, higher infant mortality and death rates, lower population and growth rates, and changes in the distribution of population by age and sex than would otherwise be expected. **Nationality:** *noun:* Gabonese (singular and plural); *adj.:* Gabonese. **Ethnic groups:** Bantu tribes, including four major tribal groupings (Fang, Nzebi, Obamba, Bapounou); 154,000 other Africans and Europeans, including 10,700 French and 11,000 dual nationality. **Religions:** 55–75% Christian, less than 1% Muslim, Animist. **Languages:** French (official), Fang, Myene, Bateke, Bapounou/Eschira, Bandjabi. **Government Government type:** republic; multiparty presidential regime (opposition parties legalized in 1990). **Capital:** Libreville. **Independence:** 17 August 1960 (from France). **National holiday:** Founding of the Gabonese Democratic Party (PDG), 12 March (1968). **Economy G.D.P.:** purchasing power pari-

ty—$22.54 billion (2010 est.). **G.D.P.—per capita:** purchasing power parity—$14,600 (2010 est.). **Currency:** Communaute Financiere Africaine franc (XAF); *note:* responsible authority is the Bank of the Central African States.

Gambia, The

Republic of The Gambia

Geography Location: Western Africa, bordering the North Atlantic Ocean and Senegal. **Area:** 4,363 sq mi (11,300 sq km). **Border countries**: Senegal. **Natural resources:** fish. **People Population:** 1,797,860 (July 2011 est.). **Nationality:** *noun:* Gambian(s); *adj.:* Gambian. **Ethnic groups:** African 99% (Mandinka 42%, Fula 18%, Wolof 16%, Jola 10%, Serahuli 9%, other 4%), non-African 1%. **Religions:** Muslim 90%, Christian 8%, indigenous beliefs 2%. **Languages:** English (official), Mandinka, Wolof, Fula, other indigenous vernaculars. **Government Government type**: republic. **Capital:** Banjul. **Independence**: 18 February 1965 (from U.K.). **National holiday**: Independence Day, 18 February (1965). **Economy G.D.P.:** purchasing power parity—$3.406 billion (2010 est.). **G.D.P.—per capita:** purchasing power parity—$1,900 (2010 est.). **Currency:** dalasi (GMD).

Georgia

Geography Location: Southwestern Asia, bordering the Black Sea, between Turkey and Russia. **Area:** 26,911 sq mi (69,700 sq km). **Border countries**: Armenia, Azerbaijan, Russia, Turkey. **Natural resources:** timber, hydropower, manganese deposits, iron ore, copper, minor coal and oil deposits; coastal climate and soils allow for important tea and citrus growth. **People Population:** 4,585,874 (July 2011 est.). **Nationality:** *noun:* Georgian(s); *adj.:* Georgian. **Ethnic groups:** Georgian 83.8%, Azeri 6.5%, Armenian 5.7%, Russian 1.5%, other 2.5% . **Religions:** Orthodox Christian 83.9%, Muslim 9.9%, Armenian-Gregorian 3.9%, Catholic 0.8%, other 0.8%, none 0.7%. **Languages:** Georgian 71% (official), Russian 9%, Armenian 7%, Azeri 6%, other 7% note: Abkhaz is the official language in Abkhazia. **Government Government type:** republic. **Capital:** T'bilisi. **Independence:** 9 April 1991 (from Soviet Union). **National holiday:** Independence Day, 26 May (1918); *note:* 26 May 1918 is the date of independence from Soviet Russia, 9 April 1991 is the date of independence from the Soviet Union. **Economy G.D.P.:** purchasing power parity—$22.32 billion (2010 est.). **G.D.P.—per capita:** purchasing power parity—$4,800 (2010 est.). **Currency:** lari (GEL).

Germany

Federal Republic of Germany

Geography Location: Central Europe, bordering the Baltic Sea and the North Sea, between the Netherlands and Poland, south of Denmark. **Area:** 137,847 sq mi (357,022 sq km). **Border countries:** Austria, Belgium, Czech Republic, Denmark, France, Luxembourg, Netherlands, Poland, Switzerland. **Natural resources:** coal, lignite, natural gas, iron ore, copper, nickel, uranium, potash, salt, construction materials, timber, arable land. **People Population:** 81,471,834 (July 2011 est.). **Nationality:** *noun:* German(s); *adj.:* German. **Ethnic groups:** German 91.5%, Turkish 2.4%, other 6.1% (made up largely of Greek, Italian, Polish, Russian, Serbo-Croatian, Spanish). **Religions:** Protestant 34%, Roman Catholic 34%, Muslim 3.7%, unaffiliated or other 28.3%. **Languages:** German. **Government Government type:** federal republic. **Capital:** Berlin. **Independence:** 18 January 1871 (German Empire unification); divided into four zones of occupation (U.K., U.S., U.S.S.R., and later, France) in 1945 following World War II; Federal Republic of Germany (FRG or West Germany) proclaimed 23 May 1949 and included the former U.K., U.S., and French zones; German Democratic Republic (GDR or East Germany) proclaimed 7 October 1949 and included the former U.S.S.R. zone; unification of West Germany and East Germany took place 3 October 1990; all four powers formally relinquished rights 15 March 1991. **National holiday:** Unity Day, 3 October (1990). **Economy G.D.P.:** purchasing power parity—$2.951 trillion (2010 est.). **G.D.P.—per capita:** purchasing power parity—$35,900 (2010 est.). **Currency:** euro (EUR).

Ghana

Republic of Ghana

Geography Location: Western Africa, bordering the Gulf of Guinea, between Cote d'Ivoire and Togo. **Area:** 92,100 sq. mi. (238,540 sq km). **Border countries:** Burkina Faso, Cote d'Ivoire, Togo. **Natural resources:** gold, timber, industrial diamonds, bauxite, manganese, fish, rubber, hydropower, petroleum, silver, salt, limestone. **People Population:** 24,791,073 (July 2011 est.) *note:* estimates for this country explicitly take into account the effects of excess mortality due to AIDS; this can result in lower life expectancy, higher infant mortality and death rates, lower population and growth rates, and changes in the distribution of population by age and sex than would otherwise be expected. **Nationality:** *noun:* Ghanaian(s); *adj.:* Ghanaian. **Ethnic groups:** Akan 45.3%, Mole-Dagbon 15.2%, Ewe 11.7%, Ga-Dangme 7.3%, Guan 4%, Gurma 3.6%, Grusi 2.6%, Mande-Busanga 1%, other tribes 1.4%, other 7.8% (2000 census). **Religions:** Christian 68.8% (Pentecostal/Charismatic 24.1%, Protestant 18.6%, Catholic 15.1%, other 11%), Muslim 15.9%, traditional 8.5%, other 0.7%, none 6.1% (2000 census). **Languages:** Asante 14.8%, Ewe 12.7%, Fante 9.9%, Boron (Brong) 4.6%, Dagomba 4.3%, Dangme 4.3%, Dagarte (Dagaba) 3.7%, Akyem 3.4%, Ga 3.4%, Akuapem 2.9%, other 36.1% (includes English (official)) (2000 census). **Government Government type:** constitutional democracy. **Capital:** Accra. **Independence:** 6 March 1957 (from U.K.). **National holiday:** Independence Day, 6 March (1957) **Economy G.D.P.:** purchasing power parity—$38.24 billion (2010 est.). **G.D.P.—per capita:** purchasing power parity—$1,600 (2010 est.). **Currency:** cedi (GHC).

Greece

Hellenic Republic

Geography Location: Southern Europe, bordering the Aegean Sea, Ionian Sea, and the Mediterranean Sea, between Albania and Turkey. **Area:** 50,949 sq mi (131,957 sq km). **Border countries:** Albania, Bulgaria, Turkey, Macedonia. **Natural resources:** lignite, petroleum, iron ore, bauxite, lead, zinc, nickel, magnesite, marble, salt, hydropower potential. **People Population:** 10,760,136 (July 2011 est.). **Nationality:** *noun:* Greek(s); *adj.:* Greek. **Ethnic groups:** Greek 93%, other (foreign citizens) 7% (2001 census). **Religions:** Greek Orthodox 98%, Muslim 1.3%, other 0.7%. **Languages:** Greek 99% (official), other 1% (includes English and French). **Government Government type:** parliamentary republic. **Capital:** Athens. **Independence:** 1829 (from the Ottoman Empire). **National holiday:** Independence Day, 25 March (1821). **Economy G.D.P.:** purchasing power parity—$321.7 billion (2010 est.). **G.D.P.—per capita:** purchasing power parity—$30,200 (2010 est.). **Currency:** euro (EUR).

Grenada

Geography Location: Caribbean, island between the Caribbean Sea and Atlantic Ocean, north of Trinidad and Tobago. **Area:** 131 sq mi (340 sq km). **Natural resources:** timber, tropical fruit, deepwater harbors. **People Population:** 108,419 (July 2011 est.). **Nationality:** *noun:* Grenadian(s); *adj.:* Grenadian. **Ethnic groups:** black 82%, mixed black and European 13%, European and East Indian 5%, and trace of Arawak/Carib Amerindian. **Religions:** Roman Catholic 53%, Anglican 13.8%, other Protestant 33.2%. **Languages:** English (official), French patois. **Government Government type:** parliamentary democracy. **Capital:** Saint George's. **Independence:** 7 February 1974 (from U.K.). **National holiday:** Independence Day, 7 February (1974). **Economy G.D.P.:** purchasing power parity—$1.127 billion (2010 est.). **G.D.P.—per capita:** purchasing power parity—$10,500 (2010 est.). **Currency:** East Caribbean dollar (XCD).

Guatemala

Republic of Guatemala

Geography   Location: Middle America, bordering the North Pacific Ocean, between El Salvador and Mexico, and bordering the Gulf of Honduras (Caribbean Sea) between Honduras and Belize. **Area:** 42,042 sq mi (108,890 sq km). **Border countries:** Belize, El Salvador, Honduras, Mexico. **Natural resources:** petroleum, nickel, rare woods, fish, chicle, hydropower. **People Population:** 13,824,463 (July 2011 est.). **Nationality:** *noun:* Guatemalan(s); *adj.:* Guatemalan. **Ethnic groups:** Mestizo (mixed Amerindian-Spanish—in local Spanish called Ladino) and European 59.4%, K'iche 9.1%, Kaqchikel 8.4%, Mam 7.9%, Q'eqchi 6.3%, other Mayan 8.6%, indigenous non-Mayan 0.2%, other 0.1% (2001 census). **Religions:** Roman Catholic, Protestant, indigenous Mayan beliefs. **Languages:** Spanish (official) 60%, Amerindian languages 40% (23 officially recognized Amerindian languages, including Quiche, Cakchiquel, Kekchi, Mam, Garifuna, and Xinca). **Government Government type:** constitutional democratic republic. **Capital:** Guatemala. **Independence:** 15 September 1821 (from Spain). **National holiday:** Independence Day, 15 September (1821). **Economy G.D.P.:** purchasing power parity—$70.31 billion (2010 est.). **G.D.P.—per capita:** purchasing power parity—$5,200 (2010 est.). **Currency:** quetzal (GTQ), U.S. dollar (USD), others allowed.

Guinea

Republic of Guinea

Geography   Location: Western Africa, bordering the North Atlantic Ocean, between Guinea-Bissau and Sierra Leone. **Area:** 94,927 sq. mi. (245,860 sq km). **Border countries:** Cote d'Ivoire, Guinea-Bissau, Liberia, Mali, Senegal, Sierra Leone. **Natural resources:** bauxite, iron ore, diamonds, gold, uranium, hydropower, fish, salt. **People Population:** 10,601,009 (July 2011 est.). **Nationality:** *noun:* Guinean(s); *adj.:* Guinean. **Ethnic groups:** Peuhl 40%, Malinke 30%, Soussou 20%, smaller ethnic groups 10%. **Religions:** Muslim 85%, Christian 8%, indigenous beliefs 7%. **Languages:** French (official), each ethnic group has its own language. **Government   Government type:** republic. **Capital:** Conakry. **Independence:** 2 October 1958 (from France). **National holiday:** Independence Day, 2 October (1958). **Economy G.D.P.:** purchasing power parity—$10.6 billion (2010 est.). **G.D.P.—per capita:** purchasing power

parity—$1,000 (2010 est.). **Currency:** Guinean franc (GNF).

Guinea-Bissau

Republic of Guinea-Bissau

Geography Location: Western Africa, bordering the North Atlantic Ocean, between Guinea and Senegal. **Area:** 13,946 sq. mi. (36,120 sq km). **Border countries:** Guinea, Senegal. **Natural resources:** fish, timber, phosphates, bauxite, clay, granite, limestone, unexploited deposits of petroleum. **People Population:** 1,596,677 (July 2011 est.). **Nationality:** *noun:* Guinean(s); *adj.:* Guinean. **Ethnic groups:** African 99% (includes Balanta 30%, Fula 20%, Manjaca 14%, Mandinga 13%, Papel 7%), European and mulatto less than 1%. **Religions:** Muslim 50%, indigenous beliefs 40%, Christian 10%. **Languages:** Portuguese (official), Crioulo, African languages. **Government Government type:** republic. **Capital:** Bissau. **Independence:** 24 September 1973 (unilaterally declared by Guinea-Bissau); 10 September 1974 (recognized by Portugal). **National holiday:** Independence Day, 24 September (1973). **Economy G.D.P.:** purchasing power parity—$1.769 billion (2010 est.). **G.D.P.—per capita:** purchasing power parity—$1,100 (2010 est.). **Currency:** Communaute Financiere Africaine franc (XOF); *note:* responsible authority is the Central Bank of the West African States; previously the Guinea-Bissau peso (GWP) was used.

Guyana

Co-operative Republic of Guyana

Geography   Location: Northern South America, bordering the North Atlantic Ocean, between Suriname and Venezuela. **Area:** 83,000 sq. mi. (214,970 sq km). **Border countries:** Brazil, Suriname, Venezuela. **Natural resources:** bauxite, gold, diamonds, hardwood timber, shrimp, fish. **People Population:** 744, 768 (July 2011 est.) note: estimates for this country explicitly take into account the effects of excess mortality due to AIDS; this can result in lower life expectancy, higher infant mortality and death rates, lower population and growth rates, and changes in the distribution of population by age and sex than would otherwise be expected. **Nationality:** *noun:* Guyanese (singular and plural); *adj.:* Guyanese. **Ethnic groups:** East Indian 43.5%, black (African) 30.2%, mixed 16.7%, Amerindian 9.1%, other 0.5% (2002 census). **Religions:** Hindu 28.4%, Pentecostal 16.9%, Roman Catholic 8.1%, Anglican 6.9%, Seventh Day Adventist 5%, Methodist 1.7%, Jehovah Witness 1.1%, other Christian 17.7%,

Muslim 7.2%, other 4.3%, none 4.3% (2002 census). **Languages:** English, Amerindian dialects, Creole, Caribbean Hindustani (a dialect of Hindi), Urdu. **Government Government type:** republic. **Capital:** Georgetown. **Independence:** 26 May 1966 (from U.K.). **National holiday:** Republic Day, 23 February (1970). **Economy G.D.P.:** purchasing power parity—$5.069 billion (2010 est.). **G.D.P.—per capita:** $6,800 (2010 est.) **Currency:** Guyanese dollar (GYD).

Haiti

Republic of Haiti

Geography Location: Caribbean, western one-third of the island of Hispaniola, between the Caribbean Sea and the North Atlantic Ocean, west of the Dominican Republic. **Area:** 10,714 sq mi (27,750 sq km). **Border countries:** Dominican Republic. **Natural resources:** bauxite, copper, calcium carbonate, gold, marble, hydropower. **People Population:** 9,719,932 (2011 est.) note: estimates for this country explicitly take into account the effects of excess mortality due to AIDS; this can result in lower life expectancy, higher infant mortality and death rates, lower population and growth rates, and changes in the distribution of population by age and sex than would otherwise be expected. **Nationality:** noun: Haitian(s); adj.: Haitian; **Ethnic groups:** black 95%, mulatto and white 5%. **Religions:** Roman Catholic 80%, Protestant 16% (Baptist 10%, Pentecostal 4%, Adventist 1%, other 1%), none 1%, other 3% note: roughly half of the population practices voodoo. **Languages:** French (official), Creole (official). **Government Government type:** republic. **Capital:** Port-au-Prince. **Independence:** 1 January 1804 (from France). **National holiday:** Independence Day, 1 January (1804). **Economy G.D.P.:** purchasing power parity—$11.18 billion (2010 est.). **G.D.P.—per capita:** purchasing power parity—$1,200 (2010 est.). **Currency:** gourde (HTG).

Holy See (Vatican City)

The Holy See (State of the Vatican City)

Geography Location: Southern Europe, an enclave of Rome (Italy). **Area:** 0.17 sq. mi. (0.44 sq km). **Border countries:** Italy. **Natural resources:** none. **People Population:** 832 (July 2011 est.). **Nationality:** noun: none; adj.: none. **Ethnic groups:** Italians, Swiss, other. **Religions:** Roman Catholic. **Languages:** Italian, Latin, French, various other languages. **Government Government type:** ecclesiastical. **Capital:** Vatican City. **Independence:** 11 February 1929 (from Italy). note: on 11 February 1929, three treaties were signed with Italy which, among other things, recognized the full sovereignty of the Vatican and established its territorial

extent; however, the origin of the Papal States, which over the years have varied considerably in extent, may be traced back to the 8th century. **National holiday:** Election Day of Pope Benedict XVI, April 19. **Economy** Overview: This unique, noncommercial economy is supported financially by an annual tax on Roman Catholic dioceses throughout the world, as well as by special collections (known as Peter's Pence); the sale of postage stamps, coins, medals, and tourist mementos; fees for admission to museums; and the sale of publications. Investments and real estate income also account for a sizable portion of revenue. The incomes and living standards of lay workers are comparable to those of counterparts who work in the city of Rome. **Currency:** euro (EUR).

Honduras

Republic of Honduras

Geography Location: Central America, bordering the Caribbean Sea, between Guatemala and Nicaragua and bordering the Gulf of Fonseca (North Pacific Ocean), between El Salvador and Nicaragua. **Area:** 43,278 sq. mi. (112,090 sq km). **Border countries:** Guatemala, El Salvador, Nicaragua. **Natural resources:** timber, gold, silver, copper, lead, zinc, iron ore, antimony, coal, fish, hydropower. **People Population:** 8,143,564 (July 2011 est.) note: estimates for this country explicitly take into account the effects of excess mortality due to AIDS; this can result in lower life expectancy, higher infant mortality and death rates, lower population and growth rates, and changes in the distribution of population by age and sex than would otherwise be expected. **Nationality:** noun: Honduran(s); adj.: Honduran. **Ethnic groups:** mestizo (mixed Amerindian and European) 90%, Amerindian 7%, black 2%, white 1%. **Religions:** Roman Catholic 97%, Protestant 3%. **Languages:** Spanish, Amerindian dialects. **Government Government type:** democratic constitutional republic. **Capital:** Tegucigalpa. **Independence:** 15 September 1821 (from Spain). **National holiday:** Independence Day, 15 September (1821). **Economy G.D.P.:** purchasing power parity—$33.77 billion (2010 est.). **G.D.P.—per capita:** purchasing power parity—$4,200 (2010 est.). **Currency:** lempira (HNL).

Hungary

Republic of Hungary

Geography Location: Central Europe, northwest of Romania. **Area:** 35,919 sq. mi. (93,030 sq km). **Border countries:** Austria, Croatia, Romania, Serbia and Montenegro, Slovakia, Slovenia, Ukraine. **Natural resources:** bauxite, coal, natural gas, fertile soils, arable land. **People Population:** 9,976,062 (July 2011 est.). **Nationality:** noun: Hungarian(s); adj.: Hungarian. **Ethnic groups:** Hungarian 92.3%, Roma

1.9%, other or unknown 5.8% (2001 census). **Religions:** Roman Catholic 51.9%, Calvinist 15.9%, Lutheran 3%, Greek Catholic 2.6%, other Christian 1%, other 11.1%, unaffiliated 14.5% (2001 census). **Languages:** Hungarian 93.6%, other/unspecified 6.4%. **Government Government type:** parliamentary democracy. **Capital:** Budapest. **Independence:** 1001 (unification by King Stephen I). **National holiday:** Saint Stephen's Day, 20 August. **Economy G.D.P.:** purchasing power parity—$190 billion (2010 est.). **G.D.P.—per capita:** purchasing power parity—$19,000 (2010 est.). **Currency:** forint (HUF).

Iceland

Republic of Iceland

Geography Location: Northern Europe, island between the Greenland Sea and the North Atlantic Ocean, northwest of the U.K. **Area:** 39,768 sq. mi. (103,000 sq km). **Natural resources:** fish, hydropower, geothermal power, diatomite. **People Population:** 311,058 (July 2011 est.). **Nationality:** *noun:* Icelander(s); *adj.:* Icelandic. **Ethnic groups:** homogeneous mixture of descendants of Norse and Celts 94%, population of foreign origin 6%. **Religions:** Lutheran Church of Iceland 80.7%, Roman Catholic Church 2.5%, Reykjavik Free Church 2.4%, Hafnarfjorour Free Church 1.6%, other religions 3.6%, unaffiliated 3%, other or unspecified 6.2% (2006 est.). **Languages:** Icelandic, English, Nordic languages, German widely spoken. **Government Government type:** constitutional republic. **Capital:** Reykjavik. **Independence:** 1 December 1918 (became a sovereign state under the Danish Crown); 17 June 1944 (from Denmark). **National holiday:** Independence Day, 17 June (1944). **Economy G.D.P.:** purchasing power parity—$11.86 billion (2010 est.). **G.D.P.—per capita:** purchasing power parity—$36,700 (2010 est.). **Currency:** Icelandic krona (ISK).

India

Republic of India

Geography Location: Southern Asia, bordering the Arabian Sea and the Bay of Bengal, between Burma and Pakistan. **Area:** 1,269,340 sq. mi. (3,287,590 sq km). **Border countries:** Bangladesh, Bhutan, Burma, China, Nepal, Pakistan. **Natural resources:** coal (fourth-largest reserves in the world), iron ore, manganese, mica, bauxite, titanium ore, chromite, natural gas, diamonds, petroleum, limestone, arable land. **People Population:** 1,189,172,906 (July 2011 est.). **Nationality:** *noun:* Indian(s); *adj.:* Indian. **Ethnic groups:** Indo-Aryan 72%, Dravidian 25%, Mongoloid and other 3% (2000). **Religions:** Hindu 80.5%, Muslim 13.4%, Christian 2.3%, Sikh 1.9%, other 1.8%, unspecified 0.1% (2001 census).

Languages: Hindi 41%, Bengali 8.1%, Telugu 7.2%, Marathi 7%, Tamil 5.9%, Urdu 5%, Gujarati 4.5%, Kannada 3.7%, Malayalam 3.2%, Oriya 3.2%, Punjabi 2.8%, Assamese 1.3%, Maithili 1.2%, other 5.9%. **Government Government type:** federal republic. **Capital:** New Delhi. **Independence:** 15 August 1947 (from U.K.). **National holiday:** Republic Day, 26 January (1950). **Economy G.D.P.:** purchasing power parity—$4.046 trillion (2010 est.). **G.D.P.—per capita:** purchasing power parity—$3,400 (2010 est.). **Currency:** Indian rupee (INR).

Indonesia

Republic of Indonesia

Geography Location: Southeastern Asia, archipelago between the Indian Ocean and the Pacific Ocean. **Area:** 741,097 sq. mi. (1,919,440 sq km). **Border countries:** East Timor, Malaysia, Papua New Guinea. **Natural resources:** petroleum, tin, natural gas, nickel, timber, bauxite, copper, fertile soils, coal, gold, silver. **People Population:** 245,613,043 (July 2011 est.). **Nationality:** *noun:* Indonesian(s); *adj.:* Indonesian. **Ethnic groups:** Javanese 40.6%, Sudanese 15%, Madurese 3.3%, Minangkabau 2.7%, Betawi 2.4%, Bugis 2.4%, Banten 2%, Banjar 1.7%, other or unspecified 29.9% (2000 census). **Religions:** Muslim 86.1% Protestant 5.7%, Roman Catholic 3%, Hindu 1.8%, other or unspecified 3.4% (2000 census). **Languages:** Bahasa Indonesia (official, modified form of Malay), English, Dutch, local dialects (the most widely spoken of which is Javanese). **Government Government type:** republic. **Capital:** Jakarta. **Independence:** 17 August 1945 (proclaimed independence; on 27 December 1949, Indonesia became legally independent from the Netherlands). **National holiday:** Independence Day, 17 August (1945). **Economy G.D.P.:** purchasing power parity—$1.033 trillion (2010 est.). **G.D.P.—per capita:** purchasing power parity—$4,300 (2010 est.). **Currency:** Indonesian rupiah (IDR).

Iran

Islamic Republic of Iran

Geography Location: Middle East, bordering the Gulf of Oman, the Persian Gulf, and the Caspian Sea, between Iraq and Pakistan. **Area:** 636,294 sq. mi. (1,648,000 sq km). **Border countries:** Afghanistan, Armenia, Azerbaijan-proper, Azerbaijan-Naxcivan exclave, Iraq, Pakistan, Turkey, Turkmenistan. **Natural resources:** petroleum, natural gas, coal, chromium, copper, iron ore, lead, manganese zinc, sulfur. **People Population:** 77,891,220 (July 2011 est.). **Nationality:** *noun:* Iranian(s); *adj.:* Iranian. **Ethnic groups:** Persian 51%, Azeri 24%, Gilaki and Mazandarani 8%, Kurd

7%, Arab 3%, Lur 2%, Baloch 2%, Turkmen 2%, other 1%. **Religions:** Muslim 98% (Shia 89%, Sunni 9%), other (includes Zoroastrian, Jewish, Christian, and Baha'i) 2%. **Languages:** Persian and Persian dialects 58%, Turkic and Turkic dialects 26%, Kurdish 9%, Luri 2%, Balochi 1%, Arabic 1%, Turkish 1%, other 2%. **Government Government type:** theocratic republic. **Capital:** Tehran. **Independence:** 1 April 1979 (Islamic Republic of Iran proclaimed). **National holiday:** Republic Day, 1 April (1979) note: additional holidays celebrated widely in Iran include Revolution Day, 11 February (1979); Noruz (New Year's Day), 21 March; Constitutional Monarchy Day, 5 August (1925). **Economy G.D.P.:** purchasing power parity—$863.5 billion (2010 est.). **G.D.P.—per capita:** purchasing power parity—$11,200 (2010 est.). **Currency:** Iranian rial (IRR).

Iraq

Republic of Iraq

Geography   Location: Middle East, bordering the Persian Gulf, between Iran and Kuwait. **Area:** 168,754 sq. mi. (437,072 sq km). **Border countries:** Iran, Jordan, Kuwait , Saudi Arabia, Syria, Turkey. **Natural resources:** petroleum, natural gas, phosphates, sulfur.   **People Population:** 30,399,572 (July 2011 est.). **Nationality:** noun: Iraqi(s); adj.: Iraqi. **Ethnic groups:** Arab 75–80%, Kurdish 15–20%, Turkoman, Assyrian, or other 5%. **Religions:** Muslim 97% (Shia 60–65%, Sunni 32–37%), Christian or other 3% note: while there has been voluntary relocation of many Christian families to northern Iraq, recent reporting indicates that the overall Christian population may have dropped by as much as 50 percent since the fall of Saddam Hussein regime in 2003, with many fleeing to Syria, Jordan, and Lebanon. **Languages:** Arabic (official), Kurdish (official in Kurdish regions), Turkoman (a Turkish dialect), Assyrian (Neo-Aramaic), Armenian. **Government Government type:** parliamentary democracy. **Capital:** Baghdad. **Independence:** 3 October 1932 (from League of Nations mandate under British administration). **National holiday:** Revolution Day, 17 July (1968). **Economy G.D.P.:** purchasing power parity—$117.7 billion (2010 est.). **G.D.P.—per capita:** purchasing power parity—$3,600 (2010 est.). **Currency:** new Iraqi dinar (NID).

Ireland

Geography   Location: Western Europe, occupying five-sixths of the island of Ireland in the North Atlantic Ocean, west of Great Britain. **Area:** 27,135 sq. mi. (70,280 sq km). **Border countries:** U.K. **Natural resources:** natural gas, peat, copper, lead, zinc, silver, barite, gypsum, limestone, dolomite. **People Population:** 4,670,976 (July 2011 est.). **Nationality:** noun: Irishman(men), Irishwoman(women), Irish (collective plural); adj.: Irish. **Ethnic groups:** Irish 87.4%, other white 7.5%, Asian 1.3%, black 1.1%, mixed 1.1%, unspecified 1.6% (2006 census). **Religions:** Roman Catholic 87.4%, Church of Ireland 2.9%, other Christian 1.9%, other 2.1%, unspecified 1.5%, none 4.2% (2006 census). **Languages:** English (official) is the language generally used, Irish (Gaelic or Gaeilge) (official) spoken mainly in areas along the west coast. **Government Government type:** republic, parliamentary democracy. **Capital:** Dublin. **Independence:** 6 December 1921 (from U.K. by treaty). **National holiday:** Saint Patrick's Day, 17 March. **Economy G.D.P.:** purchasing power parity—$172.3 billion (2010 est.). **G.D.P.—per capita:** purchasing power parity—$37,600 (2010 est.). **Currency:** euro (EUR).

Israel

State of Israel

Geography   Location: Middle East, bordering the Mediterranean Sea, between Egypt and Lebanon. **Area:** 8,522 sq mi (22,072 sq km). **Border countries:** Egypt, Gaza Strip, Jordan, Lebanon, Syria, West Bank. **Natural resources:** timber, potash, copper ore, natural gas, phosphate rock, magnesium bromide, clays, sand. **People Population:** 7,473,052 (July 2010 est.) note: approximately 296,700 Israeli settlers live in the West Bank (2009 est.); approximately 19,100 Israeli settlers live in the Golan Heights (2008 est.); approximately 192,800 Israeli settlers live in East Jerusalem (2008 est.). **Nationality:** noun: Israeli(s). adj.: Israeli. **Ethnic groups:** Jewish 76.4% (of which Israeli-born 67.1%, Europe/America-born 22.6%, Africa-born 5.9%, Asia-born 4.2%), non-Jewish 23.6% (mostly Arab) (2004). **Religions:** Jewish 75.5%, Muslim 16.8%, Christian 2.1%, Druze 1.7%, other 3.9% (2008). **Languages:** Hebrew (official), Arabic used officially for Arab minority, English most commonly used foreign language. **Government Government type:** parliamentary democracy. **Capital:** Jerusalem; note: Israel proclaimed Jerusalem as its capital in 1950, but the U.S., like nearly all other countries, maintains its Embassy in Tel Aviv. **Independence:** 14 May 1948 (from League of Nations mandate under British administration). **National holiday:** Independence Day, 14 May (1948); note: Israel declared independence on 14 May 1948, but the Jewish calendar is lunar and the holiday may occur in April or May. **Economy G.D.P.:** purchasing power parity—$217.1 billion (2010 est.). **G.D.P.—per capita:** purchasing power parity—$29,500 (2010 est.). **Currency:** new Israeli shekel (ILS).

Italy

Italian Republic

Geography **Location:** Southern Europe, a peninsula extending into the central Mediterranean Sea, northeast of Tunisia. **Area:** 116,305 sq. mi. (301,230 sq km). **Border countries:** Austria, France, Holy See (Vatican City), San Marino, Slovenia, Switzerland. **Natural resources:** zinc, barite, asbestos, pumice, mercury, potash, marble, sulfur, natural gas and crude oil reserves, fish, coal, fluorspar, feldspar, arable land. **People Population:** 61,016,804 (July 2011 est.). **Nationality:** *noun:* Italian(s); *adj.:* Italian. **Ethnic groups:** Italian (includes small clusters of German-, French-, and Slovene-Italians in the north and Albanian- and Greek-Italians in the south). **Religions:** Roman Catholic 90% (approximately; about one-third practicing), other 10% (includes mature Protestant and Jewish communities and a growing Muslim immigrant community). **Languages:** Italian (official), German (parts of Trentino-Alto Adige region are predominantly German speaking), French (small French-speaking minority in Valle d'Aosta region), Slovene (Slovene-speaking minority in the Trieste-Gorizia area). **Government** **Government type:** republic. **Capital:** Rome. **Independence:** 17 March 1861 (Kingdom of Italy proclaimed; Italy was not finally unified until 1870). **National holiday:** Republic Day, 2 June (1946). **Economy** **G.D.P.:** purchasing power parity—$1.782 trillion (2010 est.). **G.D.P.—per capita:** purchasing power parity—$30,700 (2010 est.). **Currency:** euro (EUR).

Jamaica

Geography **Location:** Caribbean, island in the Caribbean Sea, south of Cuba. **Area:** 4,243 sq. mi. (10,991 sq km). **Natural resources:** bauxite, gypsum, limestone. **People Population:** 2,868,380 (July 2011 est.). **Nationality:** *noun:* Jamaican(s); *adj.:* Jamaican. **Ethnic groups:** black 91.2%, mixed 6.2%, other or unknown 2.6% (2001 census). **Religions:** Protestant 62.5% (Seventh-Day Adventist 10.8%, Pentecostal 9.5%, Other Church of God 8.3%, Baptist 7.2%, New Testament Church of God 6.3%, Church of God in Jamaica 4.8%, Church of God of Prophecy 4.3%, Anglican 3.6%, other Christian 7.7%), Roman Catholic 2.6%, other or unspecified 14.2%, none 20.9% (2001 census). **Languages:** English, patois English. **Government** **Government type:** constitutional parliamentary democracy. **Capital:** Kingston. **Independence:** 6 August 1962 (from U.K.). **National holiday:** Independence Day, first Monday in August (1962). **Economy** **G.D.P.:** purchasing power parity—$23.93 billion (2010 est.). **G.D.P.—per capita:** purchasing power parity—$8,400 (2010 est.). **Currency:** Jamaican dollar (JMD).

Japan

Geography **Location:** Eastern Asia, island chain between the North Pacific Ocean and the Sea of Japan, east of the Korean Peninsula. **Area:** 145,882 sq. mi. (377,835 sq km). **Natural resources:** negligible mineral resources, fish. **People Population:** 126,475,664 (July 2011 est.). **Nationality:** *noun:* Japanese (singular and plural); *adj.:* Japanese. **Ethnic groups:** Japanese 98.5%, Koreans 0.5%, Chinese 0.4%, other 0.6% *note:* up to 230,000 Brazilians of Japanese origin migrated to Japan in the 1990's to work in industries; some have returned to Brazil (2004). **Religions:** Shintoism 83.9%, Buddhism 71.4%, Christianity 2%, other 7.8% *note:* total adherents exceeds 100% because many people belong to both Shintoism and Buddhism (2005). **Languages:** Japanese. **Government** **Government type:** constitutional monarchy with a parliamentary government. **Capital:** Tokyo. **Independence:** 660 B.C. (traditional founding by Emperor Jimmu). **National holiday:** Birthday of Emperor Akihito, 23 December (1933). **Economy** **G.D.P.:** purchasing power parity—$4.338 trillion (2010 est.). **G.D.P.—per capita:** purchasing power parity—$34,200 (2010 est.). **Currency:** yen (JPY).

Jordan

Hashemite Kingdom of Jordan

Geography **Location:** Middle East, northwest of Saudi Arabia. **Area:** 34,445 sq. mi. (89,213 sq km). **Border countries:** Iraq, Israel, Saudi Arabia, Syria, West Bank. **Natural resources:** phosphates, potash, shale oil. **People Population:** 6,508,271 (July 2011 est.). **Nationality:** *noun:* Jordanian(s); *adj.:* Jordanian. **Ethnic groups:** Arab 98%, Circassian 1%, Armenian 1%. **Religions:** Sunni Muslim 92%, Christian 6% (majority Greek Orthodox, but some Greek and Roman Catholics, Syrian Orthodox, Coptic Orthodox, Armenian Orthodox, and Protestant denominations), other 2% (several small Shia Muslim and Druze populations) (2001 est.). **Languages:** Arabic (official), English widely understood among upper and middle classes. **Government** **Government type:** constitutional monarchy. **Capital:** Amman. **Independence:** 25 May 1946 (from League of Nations mandate under British administration). **National holiday:** Independence Day, 25 May (1946). **Economy** **G.D.P.:** purchasing power parity—$33.79 billion (2010 est.). **G.D.P.—per capita:** purchasing power parity—$5,300 (2010 est.). **Currency:** Jordanian dinar (JOD).

Kazakhstan

Geography **Location:** Central Asia, northwest of China; a small portion west of the Ural River in eastern-most Europe.

Area: 1,049,151 sq. mi. (2,717,300 sq km). **Border countries:** China, Kyrgyzstan, Russia, Turkmenistan, Uzbekistan. **Natural resources:** major deposits of petroleum, natural gas, coal, iron ore, manganese, chrome ore, nickel, cobalt, copper, molybdenum, lead, zinc, bauxite, gold, uranium. **People Population:** 15,522,373 (July 2011 est.). **Nationality:** *noun:* Kazakhstani(s); *adj.:* Kazakhstani. **Ethnic groups:** Kazakh (Qazaq) 53.4%, Russian 30%, Ukrainian 3.7%, Uzbek 2.5%, German 2.4%, Tatar 1.7%, Uighur 1.4%, other 4.9% (1999 census). **Religions:** Muslim 47%, Russian Orthodox 44%, Protestant 2%, other 7%. **Languages:** Kazakh (Qazaq, state language) 64.4%, Russian (official, used in everyday business, designated the "language of interethnic communication") 95% (2001 est.). **Government Government type:** republic; authoritarian presidential rule, with little power outside the executive branch. **Capital:** Astana. **Independence:** 16 December 1991 (from the Soviet Union). **National holiday:** Independence Day, 16 December (1991). **Economy G.D.P.:** purchasing power parity—$193.8 billion (2010 est.). **G.D.P.—per capita:** purchasing power parity—$12,500 (2010 est.). **Currency:** tenge (KZT).

Kenya

Republic of Kenya

Geography   Location: Eastern Africa, bordering the Indian Ocean, between Somalia and Tanzania. **Area:** 224,962 sq. mi. (582,650 sq km). **Border countries:** Ethiopia, Somalia, Sudan, Tanzania, Uganda. **Natural resources:** limestone, soda ash, salt, gemstones, flourspar, zinc, diatomite, gypsum, wildlife, hydropower. **People Population:** 41,070,934 (July 2011 est.) *note:* estimates for this country explicitly take into account the effects of excess mortality due to AIDS; this can result in lower life expectancy, higher infant mortality and death rates, lower population and growth rates, and changes in the distribution of population by age and sex than would otherwise be expected. **Nationality:** *noun:* Kenyan(s); *adj.:* Kenyan. **Ethnic groups:** Kikuyu 22%, Luhya 14%, Luo 13%, Kalenjin 12%, Kamba 11%, Kisii 6%, Meru 6%, other African 15%, non-African (Asian, European, and Arab) 1%. **Religions:** Protestant 45%, Roman Catholic 33%, indigenous beliefs 10%, Muslim 10%, other 2% *note:* a large majority of Kenyans are Christian, but estimates for the percentage of the population that adheres to Islam or indigenous beliefs vary widely. **Languages:** English (official), Kiswahili (official), numerous indigenous languages. **Government Government type:** republic. **Capital:** Nairobi. **Independence:** 12 December 1963 (from U.K.). **National holiday:** Independence Day, 12 December (1963). **Economy G.D.P.:** purchasing power parity—$65.95 billion (2010 est.). **G.D.P.—per capita:** purchasing power parity—$1,600 (2010 est.). **Currency:** Kenyan shilling (KES).

Kiribati

Republic of Kiribati

Geography   Location: Oceania, group of 33 coral atolls in the Pacific Ocean, straddling the equator; the capital Tarawa is about one-half of the way from Hawaii to Australia; note—on 1 January 1995, Kiribati proclaimed that all of its territory lies in the same time zone as its Gilbert Islands group (GMT +12) even though the Phoenix Islands and the Line Islands under its jurisdiction lie on the other side of the International Date Line. **Area:** 277 sq. mi. (811 sq km). **Natural resources:** phosphate (production discontinued in 1979). **People Population:** 100,743 (July 2011 est.). **Nationality:** *noun:* I-Kiribati (singular and plural); *adj.:* I-Kiribati. **Ethnic groups:** Micronesian 98.8%, other 1.2% (2000 census). **Religions:** Roman Catholic 55%, Protestant 36%, Mormon 3.1%, Bahai 2.2%, Seventh-Day Adventist 1.9%, other 1.8% (2005 census). **Languages:** I-Kiribati, English (official). **Government Government type:** republic. **Capital:** Tarawa. **Independence:** 12 July 1979 (from U.K.). **National holiday:** Independence Day, 12 July (1979). **Economy G.D.P.:** purchasing power parity—$619.5 million (2010 est.). **G.D.P.—per capita:** purchasing power parity—$6,200 (2010 est.). **Currency:** Australian dollar (AUD).

Korea, North

Democratic People's Republic of Korea

Geography   Location: Eastern Asia, northern half of the Korean Peninsula bordering the Korea Bay and the Sea of Japan, between China and South Korea. **Area:** 46,541 sq. mi. (120,540 sq km). **Border countries:** China, South Korea, Russia. **Natural resources:** coal, lead, tungsten, zinc, graphite, magnesite, iron ore, copper, gold, pyrites, salt, fluorspar, hydropower. **People Population:** 24,457,492 (July 2011 est.). **Nationality:** *noun:* Korean(s); *adj.:* Korean. **Ethnic groups:** racially homogeneous; there is a small Chinese community and a few ethnic Japanese. **Religions:** traditionally Buddhist and Confucianist, some Christian and syncretic Chondogyo (Religion of the Heavenly Way); *note:* autonomous religious activities now almost nonexistent; government-sponsored religious groups exist to provide illusion of religious freedom. **Languages:** Korean. **Government Government type:** communist state, one-man dictatorship. **Capital:** Pyongyang. **Independence:** 15 August 1945 (from Japan). **National holiday:** Founding of the Democratic People's Republic of Korea (DPRK), 9 September (1948). **Economy G.D.P.:** purchasing power parity—$40 billion (2009 est.). **G.D.P.—per capita:** purchasing power parity—$1,800 (2009 est.). **Currency:** North Korean won (KPW).

Korea, South

Republic of Korea

Geography   Location: Eastern Asia, southern half of the Korean Peninsula bordering the Sea of Japan and the Yellow Sea. **Area:** 38,023 sq. mi. (98,480 sq km). **Border countries:** North Korea. **Natural resources:** coal, tungsten, graphite, molybdenum, lead, hydropower potential. **People Population:** 48,754,657 (July 2011 est.). **Nationality:** *noun:* Korean(s); *adj.:* Korean. **Ethnic groups:** homogeneous (except for about 20,000 Chinese). **Religions:** Christian 26.3% (Protestant 19.7%, Roman Catholic 6.6%), Buddhist 23.2%, other or unknown 1.3%, none 49.3% (1995 census). **Languages:** Korean, English widely taught in junior high and high school. **Government   Government type:** republic. **Capital:** Seoul. **Independence:** 15 August 1945 (from Japan). **National holiday:** Liberation Day, 15 August (1945). **Economy G.D.P.:** purchasing power parity—$1.467 trillion (2010 est.). **G.D.P.—per capita:** purchasing power parity—$1,800 (2009 est.). **Currency:** South Korean won (KRW).

Kuwait

State of Kuwait

Geography   Location: Middle East, bordering the Persian Gulf, between Iraq and Saudi Arabia. **Area:** 6,880 sq. mi. (17,820 sq km). **Border countries:** Iraq, Saudi Arabia. **Natural resources:** petroleum, fish, shrimp, natural gas. **People Population:** 2,595,628 *note:* includes 1,291,354 non-nationals (July 2011 est.). **Nationality:** *noun:* Kuwaiti(s); *adj.:* Kuwaiti. **Ethnic groups:** Kuwaiti 45%, other Arab 35%, South Asian 9%, Iranian 4%, other 7%. **Religions:** Muslim 85% (Sunni 70%, Shia 30%), other (includes Christian, Hindu, Parsi) 15%. **Languages:** Arabic (official), English widely spoken. **Government   Government type:** constitutional hereditary emirate. **Capital:** Kuwait City. **Independence:** 19 June 1961 (from U.K.). **National holiday:** National Day, 25 February (1950). **Economy G.D.P.:** purchasing power parity—$144.3 billion (2010 est.). **G.D.P.—per capita:** purchasing power parity—$51,700 (2010 est.). **Currency:** Kuwaiti dinar (KD).

Kyrgyzstan

Kyrgyz Republic

Geography   Location: Central Asia, west of China. **Area:** 76,641 sq. mi. (198,500 sq km). **Border countries:** China, Kazakhstan, Tajikistan, Uzbekistan. **Natural resources:** abundant hydropower; significant deposits of gold and rare earth metals; locally exploitable coal, oil, and natural gas; other deposits of nepheline, mercury, bismuth, lead, and zinc. **People Population:** 5,587,443 (July 2011 est.). **Nationality:**

noun: Kyrgyzstani(s); *adj.:* Kyrgyzstani. **Ethnic groups:** Kyrgyz 64.9%, Uzbek 13.8%, Russian 12.5%, Ukrainian 1%, Uighur 1%, Dungan 1.1%, other 5.7% (1999 census). **Religions:** Muslim 75%, Russian Orthodox 20%, other 5%. **Languages:** Kyrgyz 64.7% (official), Uzbek 13.6%, Russian 12.5% (official), Dungun 1%, other 8.2% (1999 census). **Government   Government type:** republic. **Capital:** Bishkek. **Independence:** 31 August 1991 (from Soviet Union). **National holiday:** Independence Day, 31 August (1991). **Economy G.D.P.:** purchasing power parity—$11.85 billion (2010 est.). **G.D.P.—per capita:** purchasing power parity—$2,200 (2010 est.). **Currency:** Kyrgyzstani som (KGS).

Laos

Lao People's Democratic Republic

Geography   Location: Southeastern Asia, northeast of Thailand, west of Vietnam. **Area:** 91,429 sq. mi. (236,800 sq km). **Border countries:** Burma, Cambodia, China, Thailand, Vietnam. **Natural resources:** timber, hydropower, gypsum, tin, gold, gemstones. **People Population:** 6,477,211 (July 2011 est.). **Nationality:** *noun:* Lao(s) or Laotian(s); *adj.:* Lao or Laotian. **Ethnic groups:** Lao 55%, Khmou 11%, Hmong 8%, other (over 100 minor ethnic groups) 26% (2005 census). **Religions:** Buddhist 67%, Christian 1.5%, other and unspecified 31.5% (2005 census). **Languages:** Lao (official), French, English, and various ethnic languages. **Government   Government type:** Communist state. **Capital:** Vientiane. **Independence:** 19 July 1949 (from France). **National holiday:** Republic Day, 2 December (1975). **Economy G.D.P.:** purchasing power parity—$15.68 billion (2010 est.). **G.D.P.—per capita:** purchasing power parity—$2,400 (2010 est.). **Currency:** kip (LAK).

Latvia

Republic of Latvia

Geography   Location: Eastern Europe, bordering the Baltic Sea, between Estonia and Lithuania. **Area:** 24,749 sq. mi. (64,100 sq km). **Border countries:** Belarus, Estonia, Lithuania, Russia. **Natural resources:** peat, limestone, dolomite, amber, hydropower, wood, arable land. **People Population:** 2,204,708 (July 2011 est.). **Nationality:** *noun:* Latvian(s); *adj.:* Latvian. **Ethnic groups:** Latvian 59.3%, Russian 27.8%, Belarusian 3.6%, Ukrainian 2.5%, Polish 2.4%, Lithuanian 1.3%, other 3.1% (2009). **Religions:** Lutheran 19.6%, Orthodox 15.3%, other Christian 1%, other 0.4%, unspecified 63.7% (2006). **Languages:** Latvian (official) 58.2%, Russian 37.5%, Lithuanian and other 4.3% (2000 census). **Government   Government type:** parliamentary democracy. **Capital:** Riga. **Independence:** 21 August 1991 (from Soviet Union). **National holiday:** Independence Day, 18 November (1918); *note:* 18 November 1918 is the date of independence from Soviet Russia, 21 August 1991 is the date of independence from the Soviet Union. **Economy G.D.P.:** purchasing power parity—$32.2 billion (2010 est.). **G.D.P.— per capita:** purchasing power parity—$14,300 (2010 est.). **Currency:** Latvian lat (LVL).

Lebanon

Lebanese Republic

Geography   Location: Middle East, bordering the Mediterranean Sea, between Israel and Syria. **Area:** 4,015 sq. mi. (10,400 sq km). **Border countries**: Israel, Syria. **Natural resources:** limestone, iron ore, salt, water-surplus state in a water-deficit region, arable land. **People Population:** 4,143,101 (July 2011 est.). **Nationality:** *noun:* Lebanese (singular and plural); *adj.:* Lebanese. **Ethnic groups:** Arab 95%, Armenian 4%, other 1% *note:* many Christian Lebanese do not identify themselves as Arab but rather as descendents of the ancient Canaanites and prefer to be called Phoenicians. **Religions:** Muslim 59.7% (including Shi'a, Sunni, Druze, Isma'ilite, Alawite or Nusayri), Christian 39% (including Maronite Catholic, Greek Orthodox, Melkite Catholic, Armenian Othodox, Syrian Catholic, Armenian Catholic, Protestant), other 1.3%; *note:* 17 religious sects recognized. **Languages:** Arabic (official), French, English, Armenian. **Government   Government type:** republic. **Capital:** Beirut. **Independence:** 22 November 1943 (from League of Nations mandate under French administration). **National holiday:** Independence Day, 22 November (1943). **Economy G.D.P.:** purchasing power parity—$58.65 billion (2010 est.). **G.D.P.—per capita:** purchasing power parity—$14,200 (2010 est.). **Currency:** Lebanese pound (LBP).

Lesotho

Kingdom of Lesotho

Geography   Location: Southern Africa, an enclave of South Africa. **Area:** 11,718 sq. mi. (30,350 sq km). **Border countries**: South Africa. **Natural resources:** water, agricultural and grazing land, diamonds, sand, clay, building stone. **People Population:** 1,924,886 (July 2011 est.) *note:* estimates for this country explicitly take into account the effects of excess mortality due to AIDS; this can result in lower life expectancy, higher infant mortality and death rates, lower population and growth rates, and changes in the distribution of population by age and sex than would otherwise be expected. **Nationality:** *noun:* Mosotho (singular), Basotho (plural); *adj.:* Basotho. **Ethnic groups:** Sotho 99.7%, Europeans, Asians, and other 0.3%. **Religions:** Christian 80%, indigenous beliefs 20%. **Languages:** Sesotho (southern Sotho), English (official),

Zulu, Xhosa. **Government   Government type:** parliamentary constitutional monarchy. **Capital:** Maseru. **Independence:** 4 October 1966 (from U.K.). **National holiday:** Independence Day, 4 October (1966). **Economy G.D.P.:** purchasing power parity—$3.31 billion (2010 est.). **G.D.P.—per capita:** purchasing power parity—$1,700 (2010 est.). **Currency:** loti (LSL); South African rand (ZAR).

Liberia

Republic of Liberia

Geography   Location: Western Africa, bordering the North Atlantic Ocean, between Cote d'Ivoire and Sierra Leone. **Area:** 43,000 sq. mi. (111,370 sq km). **Border countries**: Guinea, Cote d'Ivoire, Sierra Leone. **Natural resources:** iron ore, timber, diamonds, gold, hydropower. **People Population:** 3,786,764 (July 2011 est.). **Nationality:** *noun:* Liberian(s); *adj.:* Liberian. **Ethnic groups:** Kpelle 20.3%, Bassa 13.4%, Grebo 10%, Gio 8%, Mano 7.9%, Kru 6%, Lorma 5.1%, Kissi 4.8%, Gola 4.4%, other 20.1% (2008 census). **Religions:** Christian 85.6%, Muslim 12.2%, Traditional 0.6%, other 0.2%, none 1.4% (2008 census). **Languages:** English 20% (official), some 20 ethnic group languages, few of which can be written or used in correspondence. **Government   Government type:** republic. **Capital:** Monrovia. **Independence:** 26 July 1847. **National holiday:** Independence Day, 26 July (1847). **Economy G.D.P.:** purchasing power parity—$1.76 billion (2010 est.). **G.D.P.— per capita:** purchasing power parity—$500 (2010 est.). **Currency:** Liberian dollar (LRD).

Libya

Great Socialist People's Libyan Arab Jamahiriya

Geography   Location: Northern Africa, bordering the Mediterranean Sea, between Egypt and Tunisia. **Area:** 679,359 sq. mi. (1,759,540 sq km). **Border countries**: Algeria, Chad, Egypt, Niger, Sudan, Tunisia. **Natural resources:** petroleum, natural gas, gypsum. **People Population:** 6,597,960; *note:* includes 166,510 non-nationals (July 2011 est.). **Nationality:** *noun:* Libyan(s); *adj.:* Libyan. **Ethnic groups:** Berber and Arab 97%, other 3% (includes Greeks, Maltese, Italians, Egyptians, Pakistanis, Turks, Indians, and Tunisians). **Religions:** Sunni Muslim 97%, other 3%. **Languages:** Arabic, Italian, English, all are widely understood in the major cities. **Government   Government type:** Jamahiriya (a state of the masses) in theory, governed by the populace through local councils; in practice, an authoritarian state. **Capital:** Tripoli. **Independence:** 24 December 1951 (from U.N. trusteeship). **National holi-**

day: Revolution Day, 1 September (1969). **Economy G.D.P.:** purchasing power parity—$89.03 billion (2010 est.). **G.D.P.—per capita:** purchasing power parity—$13,800 (2010 est.). **Currency:** Libyan dinar (LYD).

Liechtenstein

Principality of Liechtenstein

Geography   Location: Central Europe, between Austria and Switzerland. **Area:** 62 sq. mi. (160 sq km). **Border countries**: Austria, Switzerland. **Natural resources:** hydroelectric potential, arable land. **People Population:** 35,236 (July 2011 est.). **Nationality:** *noun:* Liechtensteiner(s); *adj.:* Liechtenstein. **Ethnic groups:** Liechtensteiner 65.6%, other 34.4% (2000 census). **Religions:** Roman Catholic 76.2%, Protestant 7%, unknown 10.6%, other 6.2% (2002). **Languages:** German (official), Alemannic dialect. **Government   Government type:** constitutional monarchy. **Capital:** Vaduz. **Independence:** 23 January 1719 Imperial Principality of Liechtenstein established; 12 July 1806 established independence from the Holy Roman Empire. **National holiday:** Assumption Day, 15 August. **Economy G.D.P.:** purchasing power parity—$4.16 billion (2007). **G.D.P.—per capita:** purchasing power parity—$122,100 (2007 est.). **Currency:** Swiss franc (CHF).

Lithuania

Republic of Lithuania

Geography   Location: Eastern Europe, bordering the Baltic Sea, between Latvia and Russia. **Area:** 25,174 sq. mi. (65,200 sq km). **Border countries**: Belarus, Latvia, Poland, Russia (Kaliningrad). **Natural resources:** peat, amber, arable land. **People Population:** 3,535,547 (July 2011 est.). **Nationality:** *noun:* Lithuanian(s). *adj.:* Lithuanian. **Ethnic groups:** Lithuanian 84%, Polish 6.1%, Russian 4.9%, Belarusian 1.1%, other or unspecified 3.9% (2009). **Religions:** Roman Catholic 79%, Russian Orthodox 4.1%, Protestant (including Lutheran and Evangelical Christian Baptist) 1.9%, other or unspecified 5.5%, none 9.5% (2001 census). **Languages:** Lithuanian (official) 82%, Russian 8%, Polish 5.6%, other and unspecified 4.4% (2001 census). **Government   Government type:** parliamentary democracy. **Capital:** Vilnius. **Independence:** 11 March 1990 (independence declared from Soviet Union); 6 September 1991 (Soviet Union recognizes Lithuania's independence). **National holiday**: Independence Day, 16 February (1918); note—16 February 1918 is the date of independence from Soviet Russia, 11 March 1990 is the date of independence from the Soviet Union. **Economy   G.D.P.:** purchasing power parity—$56.22 billion (2010 est.). **G.D.P.—per capita:**

purchasing power parity—$15,900 (2010 est.). **Currency:** litas (LTL).

Luxembourg

Grand Duchy of Luxembourg

Geography   Location: Western Europe, between France and Germany. **Area:** 998 sq. mi. (2,586 sq km). **Border countries**: Belgium, France, Germany. **Natural resources:** iron ore (no longer exploited), arable land. **People Population:** 503,302 (July 2011 est.). **Nationality:** *noun:* Luxembourger(s); *adj.:* Luxembourg. **Ethnic groups:** Luxembourger 63.1%, Portuguese 13.3%, French 4.5%, Italian 4.3%, German 2.3%, other E.U. 7.3%, other 5.2% (2000 census). **Religions:** Roman Catholic 87%, other (includes Protestant, Jewish, and Muslim) 13% (2000). **Languages:** Luxembourgish (national language), German (administrative language), French (administrative language). **Government   Government type:** constitutional monarchy. **Capital:** Luxembourg. **Independence:** 1839 (from the Netherlands). **National holiday:** National Day (Birthday of Grand Duchess Charlotte) 23 June. **Economy G.D.P.:** purchasing power parity—$40.81 billion (2010 est.). **G.D.P.—per capita:** purchasing power parity—$81,800 (2010 est.). **Currency:** euro (EUR).

Macedonia, The Former Yugoslav Republic of

The Former Yugoslav Republic of Macedonia

Geography   Location: Southeastern Europe, north of Greece. **Area:** 9,781 sq. mi. (25,333 sq km). **Border countries**: Albania, Bulgaria, Greece, Serbia. **Natural resources:** low-grade iron ore, copper, lead, zinc, chromite, manganese, nickel, tungsten, gold, silver, asbestos, gypsum, timber, arable land. **People Population:** 2,077,328 (July 2011 est.). **Nationality:** *noun:* Macedonian(s); *adj.:* Macedonian. **Ethnic groups:** Macedonian 64.2%, Albanian 25.5%, Turkish 3.9%, Roma 2.7%, Serb 1.8%, other 2.2% (2002 census). **Religions:** Macedonian Orthodox 64.7%, Muslim 33.3%, other 2% (2002 census) **Languages:** Macedonian 66.5% (official), Albanian 25.1% (official), Turkish 3.5%, Roma 1.9%, Serbian 1.2%, other 1.8% (2002 census). **Government   Government type:** parliamentary democracy. **Capital:** Skopje. **Independence:** 8 September 1991 referendum by registered voters endorsing independence (from Yugoslavia). **National holiday:** Uprising Day, 2 August (1903); *note:* also known as Saint Elijah's Day and Ilinden. **Economy   G.D.P.:** purchasing power parity—$19.46 billion (2010 est.). **G.D.P.—per capita:** purchasing power parity—$9,400 (2010 est.). **Currency:** Macedonian denar (MKD).

Madagascar

Republic of Madagascar

Geography   Location: Southern Africa, island in the Indian Ocean, east of Mozambique. **Area:** 226,656 sq. mi. (587,040 sq km). **Natural resources:** graphite, chromite, coal, bauxite, salt, quartz, tar sands, semiprecious stones, mica, fish, hydropower. **People Population:** 21,926,221 (July 2011 est.). **Nationality:** *noun:* Malagasy (singular and plural); *adj.:* Malagasy. **Ethnic groups:** Malayo-Indonesian (Merina and related Betsileo), Cotiers (mixed African, Malayo-Indonesian, and Arab ancestry—Betsimisaraka, Tsimihety, Antaisaka, Sakalava), French, Indian, Creole, Comoran. **Religions:** Indigenous beliefs 52%, Christian 41%, Muslim 7%. **Languages:** French (official), Malagasy (official), English. **Government   Government type:** republic. **Capital:** Antananarivo. **Independence**: 26 June 1960 (from France). **National holiday**: Independence Day, 26 June (1960). **Economy G.D.P.:** purchasing power parity—$20.73 billion (2010 est.). **G.D.P.—per capita:** purchasing power parity—$1,000 (2010 est.). **Currency:** Madagascar ariary (MGA).

Malawi

Republic of Malawi

Geography   Location: Southern Africa, east of Zambia. **Area:** 45,745 sq. mi. (118,480 sq km). **Border countries**: Mozambique, Tanzania, Zambia. **Natural resources:** limestone, arable land, hydropower, unexploited deposits of uranium, coal, and bauxite. **People Population:** 15,879,252 (July 2011 est.) *note:* estimates for this country explicitly take into account the effects of excess mortality due to AIDS; this can result in lower life expectancy, higher infant mortality and death rates, lower population and growth rates, and changes in the distribution of population by age and sex than would otherwise be expected. **Nationality:** *noun:* Malawian(s); *adj.:* Malawian. **Ethnic groups:** Chewa, Nyanja, Tumbuka, Yao, Lomwe, Sena, Tonga, Ngoni, Ngonde, Asian, European. **Religions:** Christian 79.9%, Muslim 12.8%, other 3%, none 4.3% (1998 census). **Languages:** Chichewa 57.2% (official), Chinyanja 12.8%, Chiyao 10.1%, Chitumbuka 9.5%, Chisena 2.7%, Chilomwe 2.4%, Chitonga 1.7%, other 3.6% (1998 census). **Government   Government type:** multiparty democracy. **Capital:** Lilongwe. **Independence:** 6 July 1964 (from U.K.). **National holiday:** Independence Day (Republic Day), 6 July (1964). **Economy G.D.P.:** purchasing power parity—$13.51 billion (2010 est.). **G.D.P.—per capita:** purchasing power parity—$900 (2010 est.). **Currency:** Malawian kwacha (MWK).

Malaysia

Geography   Location: Southeastern Asia, peninsula and northern one-third of the island of Borneo, bordering Indonesia and the South China Sea, south of Vietnam. **Area:** 127,317 sq. mi. (329,750 sq km). **Border countries**: Brunei, Indonesia, Thailand. **Natural resources:** tin, petroleum, timber, copper, iron ore, natural gas, bauxite. **People Population:** 28,728,607 (July 2011 est.). **Nationality:** *noun:* Malaysian(s); *adj.:* Malaysian. **Ethnic groups:** Malay 50.4%, Chinese 23.7%, indigenous 11%, Indian 7.1%, other 7.8% (2004). **Religions:** Muslim 60.4%, Buddhist 19.2%, Christian 9.1%, Hindu 6.3%, Confucianism, Taoism, other traditional Chinese religions 2.6%, other or unknown 1.5%, none 0.8% (2000 census). **Languages:** Bahasa Malaysian (official), English, Chinese dialects (Cantonese, Mandarin, Hokkien, Hakka, Hainan, Foochow), Tamil, Telugu, Malayalam, Panjabi, Thai; *note:* in addition, in East Malaysia several indigenous languages are spoken, the largest are Iban and Kadazan. **Government   Government type:** constitutional monarchy, *note:* Malaya (what is now Peninsular Malaysia) formed 31 August 1957; Federation of Malaysia (Malaya, Sabah, Sarawak, and Singapore) formed 9 July 1963 (Singapore left the federation on 9 August 1965); nominally headed by the paramount ruler and a bicameral Parliament consisting of a nonelected upper house and an elected lower house; Peninsular Malaysian states—hereditary rulers in all but Melaka, George Town (Penang), Sabah, and Sarawak, where governors are appointed by the Malaysian Government; powers of state governments are limited by the federal constitution; under terms of the federation, Sabah and Sarawak retain certain constitutional prerogatives (e.g., the right to maintain their own immigration controls); Sabah—holds 25 seats in House of Representatives, with foreign affairs, defense, internal security, and other powers delegated to federal government; Sarawak—holds 28 seats in House of Representatives, with foreign affairs, defense, internal security, and other powers delegated to federal government. **Capital:** Kuala Lumpur. **Independence:** 31 August 1957 (from U.K.). **National holiday:** Independence Day/Malaysia Day, 31 August (1957). **Economy G.D.P.:** purchasing power parity—$416.4 billion (2010 est.). **G.D.P.—per capita:** purchasing power parity—$14,700 (2010 est.). **Currency:** ringgit (MYR).

Maldives

Republic of Maldives

Geography   Location: Southern Asia, group of atolls in the Indian Ocean, south-southwest of India. **Area:** 116 sq. mi. (300 sq km). **Natural resources:** fish. **People Population:**

394,999 (July 2011 est.). **Nationality:** *noun:* Maldivian(s); *adj.:* Maldivian. **Ethnic groups:** South Indians, Sinhalese, Arabs. **Religions:** Sunni Muslim. **Languages:** Dhivehi (official) (dialect of Sinhala, script derived from Arabic), English spoken by most government officials. **Government Government type:** republic. **Capital:** Male. **Independence:** 26 July 1965 (from U.K.). **National holiday:** Independence Day, 26 July (1965). **Economy G.D.P.:** purchasing power parity—$1.767 billion (2010 est.). **G.D.P.—per capita:** purchasing power parity—$4,500 (2010 est.). **Currency:** rufiyaa (MVR).

Mali

Republic of Mali

Geography Location: Western Africa, southwest of Algeria. **Area:** 478,765 sq. mi. (1,240,000 sq km). **Border countries:** Algeria, Burkina Faso, Guinea, Cote d'Ivoire, Mauritania, Niger, Senegal. **Natural resources:** gold, phosphates, kaolin, salt, limestone, uranium, hydropower, *note:* bauxite, iron ore, manganese, tin, and copper deposits are known but not exploited. **People Population:** 14,159 904 (July 2011 est.). **Nationality:** *noun:* Malian(s); *adj.:* Malian. **Ethnic groups:** Mande 50% (Bambara, Malinke, Soninke), Peul 17%, Voltaic 12%, Songhai 6%, Tuareg and Moor 10%, other 5%. **Religions:** Muslim 90%, indigenous beliefs 9%, Christian 1%. **Languages:** French (official), Bambara 80%, numerous African languages. **Government Government type:** republic. **Capital:** Bamako. **Independence:** 22 September 1960 (from France). **National holiday:** Independence Day, 22 September (1960). **Economy G.D.P.:** purchasing power parity—$16.74 billion (2010 est.). **G.D.P.—per capita:** purchasing power parity—$1,200 (2010 est.). **Currency:** Communaute Financiere Africaine franc (XOF); *note:* responsible authority is the Central Bank of the West African States.

Malta

Republic of Malta

Geography Location: Southern Europe, islands in the Mediterranean Sea, south of Sicily (Italy). **Area:** 124 sq. mi. (316 sq km). **Natural resources:** limestone, salt, arable land. **People Population:** 408,333 (July 2011 est.). **Nationality:** *noun:* Maltese (singular and plural); *adj.:* Maltese. **Ethnic groups:** Maltese (descendants of ancient Carthaginians and Phoenicians, with strong elements of Italian and other Mediterranean stock). **Religions:** Roman Catholic 98%. **Languages:** Maltese (official) 90.2%, English (official) 6%, multilingual 3%, other 0.8% (2005 census). **Government Government type:** republic. **Capital:** Valletta.

Independence: 21 September 1964 (from U.K.). **National holiday:** Independence Day, 21 September (1964). **Economy G.D.P.:** purchasing power parity—$10.21 billion (2010 est.). **G.D.P.—per capita:** purchasing power parity—$25,100 (2010 est.). **Currency:** euro (EUR).

Marshall Islands

Republic of the Marshall Islands

Geography Location: Oceania, group of atolls and reefs in the North Pacific Ocean, about one-half of the way from Hawaii to Australia. **Area:** 70 sq. mi. (181.3 sq km). **Natural resources:** coconut products, marine products, deep seabed minerals. **People Population:** 67,182 (July 2011 est.). **Nationality:** *noun:* Marshallese (singular and plural); *adj.:* Marshallese. **Ethnic groups:** Marshallese 92.1%, mixed Marshallese 5.9%, other 2% (2006). **Religions:** Protestant 54.8%, Assembly of God 25.8%, Roman Catholic 8.4%, Bukot nan Jesus 2.8%, Mormon 2.1%, other 4.6%, none 1.5% (1999 census). **Languages:** Marshallese 98.2%, other 1.8% *note:* English widely spoken as a second language, both English and Marshallese are official. **Government Government type:** constitutional government in free association with the U.S.; the Compact of Free Association entered into force 21 October 1986. The amended Compact entered into force in May 2004. **Capital:** Majuro. **Independence:** 21 October 1986 (from the U.S.-administered U.N. trusteeship). **National holiday:** Constitution Day, 1 May (1979). **Economy G.D.P.:** purchasing power parity—$133.5 million (2008 est.). **G.D.P.—per capita:** purchasing power parity—$2,500 (2008 est.). **Currency:** U.S. dollar (USD).

Mauritania

Islamic Republic of Mauritania

Geography Location: Northern Africa, bordering the North Atlantic Ocean, between Senegal and Western Sahara. **Area:** 397,954 sq. mi. (1,030,700 sq km). **Border countries:** Algeria, Mali, Senegal, Western Sahara. **Natural resources:** iron ore, gypsum, copper, phosphate, diamonds, gold, oil, fish. **People Population:** 3,281,634 (July 2011 est.). **Nationality:** *noun:* Mauritanian(s); *adj.:* Mauritanian. **Ethnic groups:** mixed Moor/black 40%, Moor 30%, black 30%. **Religions:** Muslim 100%. **Languages:** Arabic (official and national), Pulaar, Soninke, Wolof (all national languages), French, Hassaniya. **Government Government type:** military junta. **Capital:** Nouakchott. **Independence:** 28 November 1960 (from France). **National holiday:** Independence Day, 28

November (1960). **Economy G.D.P.:** purchasing power parity—$6.8 billion (2010 est.). **G.D.P.—per capita:** purchasing power parity—$2,100 (2010 est.). **Currency:** ouguiya (MRO).

Mauritius

Republic of Mauritius

Geography Location: Southern Africa, island in the Indian Ocean, east of Madagascar. **Area:** 718 sq. mi. (2,040 sq km). **Natural resources:** arable land, fish. **People Population:** 1,303,717 (July 2011 est.). **Nationality:** *noun:* Mauritian(s); *adj.:* Mauritian. **Ethnic groups:** Indo-Mauritian 68%, Creole 27%, Sino-Mauritian 3%, Franco-Mauritian 2%. **Religions:** Hindu 48%, Roman Catholic 23.6%, other Christian 8.6%, Muslim 16.6%, other 2.5%, unspecified 0.3%, none 0.4% (2000 census). **Languages:** Creole 80.5%, Bhojpuri 12.1%, French 3.4%, English (official, though spoken by less than 1% of the population), other 3.7%, unspecified 0.3% (2000 census). **Government Government type:** parliamentary democracy. **Capital:** Port Louis. **Independence:** 12 March 1968 (from U.K.). **National holiday:** Independence Day, 12 March (1968). **Economy G.D.P.:** purchasing power parity—$17.49 billion (2010 est.). **G.D.P.—per capita:** purchasing power parity—$13,500 (2010 est.). **Currency:** Mauritian rupee (MUR).

Mexico

United Mexican States

Geography Location: Central America, bordering the Caribbean Sea and the Gulf of Mexico, between Belize and the U.S. and bordering the North Pacific Ocean, between Guatemala and the U.S.. **Area:** 761,603 sq. mi. (1,972,550 sq km). **Border countries:** Belize, Guatemala, U.S. **Natural resources:** petroleum, silver, copper, gold, lead, zinc, natural gas. **People Population:** 113,724,226 (July 2011 est.). **Nationality:** *noun:* Mexican(s); *adj.:* Mexican. **Ethnic groups:** mestizo (Amerindian-Spanish) 60%, Amerindian or predominantly Amerindian 30%, white 9%, other 1%. **Religions:** Roman Catholic 76.5%, Protestant 6.3% (Pentecostal 1.4%, Jehovah's Witnesses 1.1%, other 3.8%), other 0.3%, unspecified 13.8%, none 3.1% (2000 census). **Languages:** Spanish only 92.7%, Spanish and indigenous languages 5.7%, indigenous only 0.8%, unspecified 0.8%; *note:* indigenous languages include various Mayan, Nahuatl, and other regional languages (2005). **Government Government type:** federal republic. **Capital:** Mexico City (Distrito Federal). **Independence:** 16 September 1810 (from Spain). **National holiday:** Independence Day, 16 September (1810). **Economy G.D.P.:** purchasing power parity—$1.56

trillion (2010 est.). **G.D.P.—per capita:** purchasing power parity—$13,800 (2010 est.). **Currency:** Mexican peso (MXN).

Micronesia, Federated States of

Federated States of Micronesia

Geography Location: Oceania, island group in the North Pacific Ocean, about three-quarters of the way from Hawaii to Indonesia. **Area:** 271 sq. mi. (702 sq km). **Natural resources:** timber, marine products, deep-seabed minerals, phosphate. **People Population:** 106,836 (July 2011 est.). **Nationality:** *noun:* Micronesian(s); *adj.:* Micronesian; Chuukese, Kosraen(s), Pohnpeian(s), Yapese. **Ethnic groups:** Chuukese 48.8%, Pohnpeian 24.2%, Kosraean 6.2%, Yapese 5.2%, Yap outer islands 4.5%, Asian 1.8%, Polynesian 1.5%, other 6.4%, unknown 1.4% (2000 census). **Religions:** Roman Catholic 52.7%, Congregational 40.1%, Baptist 0.9%, Seventh-Day Adventist 0.7%, other 3.8%, none or unspecified 0.8% (2000 census). **Languages:** English (official and common language), Chuukese, Kosrean, Pohnpeian, Yapese, Ulthian, Woleaian, Nukuoro, Kapingamarangi. **Government Government type:** constitutional government in free association with the U.S.; the Compact of Free Association entered into force 3 November 1986. The amended Compact entered into force in May 2004. **Capital:** Palikir. **Independence:** 3 November 1986 (from the U.S.-administered U.N. Trusteeship). **National holiday:** Constitution Day, 10 May (1979). **Economy G.D.P.:** purchasing power parity—$238.1 million (2008 est.) *note:* G.D.P. is supplemented by grant aid, averaging perhaps $100 million annually. **G.D.P.—per capita:** purchasing power parity—$2,200 (2008 est.). **Currency:** U.S. dollar (USD).

Moldova

Republic of Moldova

Geography Location: Eastern Europe, northeast of Romania. **Area:** 13,012 sq. mi. (33,700 sq km). **Border countries:** Romania, Ukraine. **Natural resources:** lignite, phosphorites, gypsum, arable land, limestone. **People Population:** 4,314,377 (July 2011 est.). **Nationality:** *noun:* Moldovan(s); *adj.:* Moldovan. **Ethnic groups:** Moldovan/Romanian 78.2%, Ukrainian 8.4%, Russian 5.8%, Bulgarian 1.9%, Gagauz 4.4%, other 1.3% (2004 census) *note:* internal disputes with ethnic Slavs in the Transnistrian region. **Religions:** Eastern Orthodox 98%, Jewish 1.5%, Baptist and other 0.5% (2000). **Languages:** Moldovan (official, virtually the same as the Romanian language), Russian (official), Gagauz (a Turkish dialect). **Government Government**

type: republic. **Capital:** Chisinau. **Independence:** 27 August 1991 (from Soviet Union). **National holiday:** Independence Day, 27 August (1991). **Economy G.D.P.:** purchasing power parity—$11.01 billion (2010 est.). **G.D.P.—per capita:** purchasing power parity—$2,500 (2010 est.). **Currency:** Moldovan leu (MDL).

Monaco

Principality of Monaco

Geography   Location: Western Europe, bordering the Mediterranean Sea on the southern coast of France, near the border with Italy. **Area:** 1.21 sq. mi. (1.95 sq km). **Border countries:** France. **Natural resources:** none. **People Population:** 30,539 (July 2011 est.). **Nationality:** noun: Monegasque(s) or Monacan(s); adj.: Monegasque or Monacan. **Ethnic groups:** French 47%, Monegasque 16%, Italian 16%, other 21%. **Religions:** Roman Catholic 90%, other 10%. **Languages:** French (official), English, Italian, Monegasque. **Government   Government type:** constitutional monarchy. **Capital:** Monaco. **Independence:** 1419 (beginning of the rule by the House of Grimaldi). **National holiday:** National Day (Prince of Monaco Holiday), 19 November. **Economy G.D.P.:** purchasing power parity—$976.3 million (2006 est.). **G.D.P.—per capita:** purchasing power parity—$30,000 (2006 est.) note: Monaco does not publish national income figures; the estimates are extremely rough. **Currency:** euro (EUR).

Mongolia

Geography   Location: Northern Asia, between China and Russia. **Area:** 604,247 sq. mi. (1,565,000 sq km). **Border countries:** China, Russia. **Natural resources:** oil, copper, molybdenum, tungsten, phosphates, tin, nickel, zinc, fluorspar, gold, silver, iron. **People Population:** 3,133,318 (July 2011 est.). **Nationality:** noun: Mongolian(s); adj.: Mongolian. **Ethnic groups:** Mongol (predominantly Khalkha) 94.9%, Turkic (of which Kazakh is the largest group) 5%, other (including Chinese and Russian) 0.1% (2000). **Religions:** Buddhist Lamaism 50%, none 40%, Shamanist and Christian 6%, Muslim 4% (2004). **Languages:** Khalkha Mongol 90%, Turkic, Russian (1999). **Government   Government type:** mixed parliamentary and presidential. **Capital:** Ulaanbaatar. **Independence:** 11 July 1921 (from China). **National holiday:** Independence Day/Revolution Day, 11 July (1921). **Economy G.D.P.:** purchasing power parity—$10.16 billion (2010 est.). **G.D.P.—per capita:** purchasing power parity—$3,300 (2010 est.). **Currency:** togrog/tugrik (MNT).

Montenegro

Republic of Montenegro

Geography   Location: Southeastern Europe, between the Adriatic Sea and Serbia. **Area:** 5,415 sq mi (14,026 sq km). **Border countries:** Albania, Bosnia and Herzegovina, Croatia, Serbia. **Natural resources:** bauxite, hydroelectricity. **People Population:** 661,807 (July 2011 est.). **Nationality:** noun: Montenegrin(s); adj.: Montenegrin. **Ethnic groups:** Montenegrin 43%, Serbian 32%, Bosniak 8%, Albanian 5%, other (Muslims, Croats, Roma) 12% (2003 census). **Religions:** Orthodox 74.2%, Muslim 17.7%, Catholic 3.5%, other 0.6%, unspecified 3%, atheist 1% (2003 census). **Languages:** Serbian 63.6%, Montenegrin (official) 22%, Bosnian 5.5%, Albanian 5.3%, unspecified 3.7% (2003 census). **Government   Government type:** republic. **Capital:** Podgorica. **Independence:** 3 June 2006 (from Serbia and Montenegro). **National holiday:** National Day 13 July (1878). **Economy G.D.P.:** purchasing power parity—$6.569 billion (2010 est.). **G.D.P.—per capita:** purchasing power parity—$9,900 (2010 est.). **Currency:** euro (EUR).

Morocco

Kingdom of Morocco

Geography   Location: Northern Africa, bordering the North Atlantic Ocean and the Mediterranean Sea, between Algeria and Western Sahara. **Area:** 172,413 sq. mi. (446,550 sq km). **Border countries:** Algeria, Western Sahara, Spain (Ceuta), Spain (Melilla). **Natural resources:** phosphates, iron ore, manganese, lead, zinc, fish, salt. **People Population:** 31,968,361 (July 2011 est.). **Nationality:** noun: Moroccan(s); adj.: Moroccan. **Ethnic groups:** Arab-Berber 99.1%, other 0.7%, Jewish 0.2%. **Religions:** Muslim 98.7%, Christian 1.1%, Jewish 0.2%. **Languages:** Arabic (official), Berber dialects, French often the language of business, government, and diplomacy. **Government   Government type:** constitutional monarchy. **Capital:** Rabat. **Independence:** 2 March 1956 (from France). **National holiday:** Throne Day (accession of King Mohamed VI to the throne), 30 July (1999). **Economy G.D.P.:** purchasing power parity—$153.8 billion (2010 est.). **G.D.P.—per capita:** purchasing power parity—$4,900 (2010 est.). **Currency:** Moroccan dirham (MAD).

Mozambique

Republic of Mozambique

Geography   Location: South-eastern Africa, bordering the Mozambique Channel, between South Africa and Tanzania.

Area: 309,494 sq. mi. (801,590 sq km). **Border countries:** Malawi, South Africa, Swaziland, Tanzania, Zambia, Zimbabwe. **Natural resources:** coal, titanium, natural gas, hydropower, tantalum, graphite. **People Population:** 22,948,858 (July 2011 est.) *note:* estimates for this country explicitly take into account the effects of excess mortality due to AIDS; this can result in lower life expectancy, higher infant mortality and death rates, lower population and growth rates, and changes in the distribution of population by age and sex than would otherwise be expected. **Nationality:** *noun:* Mozambican(s); *adj.:* Mozambican. **Ethnic groups:** African 99.66% (Makhuwa, Tsonga, Lomwe, Sena, and others), Europeans 0.06%, Euro-Africans 0.2%, Indians 0.08%. **Religions:** Catholic 23.8%, Muslim 17.8%, Zionist Christian 17.5%, other 17.8%, none 23.1% (1997 census). **Languages:** Emakhuwa 26.1%, Xichangana 11.3%, Portuguese 8.8% (official; spoke by 27% of the population as a second language), Elomwe 7.6%, Cisena 6.8%, Echuwabo 5.8%, other Mozambican languages 32%, other foreign languages 0.3%. **Government Government type:** republic. **Capital:** Maputo. **Independence:** 25 June 1975 (from Portugal). **National holiday:** Independence Day, 25 June (1975). **Economy G.D.P.:** purchasing power parity—$22.19 billion (2010 est.). **G.D.P.—per capita:** purchasing power parity—$1,000 (2010 est.). **Currency:** metical (MZM).

Myanmar

Union of Burma

Geography Location: Southeastern Asia, bordering the Andaman Sea and the Bay of Bengal, between Bangladesh and Thailand. **Area:** 261,969 sq. mi. (678,500 sq km). **Border countries:** Bangladesh, China, India, Laos, Thailand. **Natural resources:** petroleum, timber, tin, antimony, zinc, copper, tungsten, lead, coal, some marble, limestone, precious stones, natural gas, hydropower. **People Population:** 53,999,804 (July 2011 est.) *note:* estimates for this country take into account the effects of excess mortality due to AIDS; this can result in lower life expectancy, higher infant mortality and death rates, lower population and growth rates, and changes in the distribution of population by age and sex than would otherwise be expected. **Nationality:** *noun:* Burmese (singular and plural); *adj.:* Burmese. **Ethnic groups:** Burman, 68%, Shan 9%, Karen 7%, Rakhine 4%, Chinese 3%, Indian 2%, Mon 2%, Other 5%. **Religions:** Buddhist 89%, Christian 4%, Muslim 4%, Anamist 1%, Other 2%. **Languages:** Burmese (official), minor ethnic groups have their own languages. **Government Government type:** military junta. **Capital:** Rangoon (regime refers to the capital as Yangon). **Independence:** 4 January 1948 (from U.K.). **National holiday:** Independence Day, 4 January (1948).

Economy G.D.P.: purchasing power parity—$60.07 billion (2010 est.). **G.D.P.—per capita:** purchasing power parity—$1,100 (2010 est.). **Currency:** kyat (MMK).

Namibia

Republic of Namibia

Geography Location: Southern Africa, bordering the South Atlantic Ocean, between Angola and South Africa. **Area:** 318,259 sq. mi. (824,290 sq km). **Border countries:** Angola, Botswana, South Africa, Zambia. **Natural resources:** diamonds, copper, uranium, gold, silver, lead, tin, lithium, cadmium, tungsten, zinc, salt, hydropower, fish *note:* suspected deposits of oil, coal, and iron ore. **People Population:** 2,147,585 (July 2011 est.) *note:* estimates for this country explicitly take into account the effects of excess mortality due to AIDS; this can result in lower life expectancy, higher infant mortality and death rates, lower population and growth rates, and changes in the distribution of population by age and sex than would otherwise be expected. **Nationality:** *noun:* Namibian(s); *adj.:* Namibian. **Ethnic groups:** black 87.5%, white 6%, mixed 6.5% *note:* about 50% of the population belong to the Ovambo tribe and 9% to the Kavangos tribe; other ethnic groups include Herero 7%, Damara 7%, Nama 5%, Caprivian 4%, Bushmen 3%, Baster 2%, Tswana 0.5%. **Religions:** Christian 80% to 90% (Lutheran 50% at least), indigenous beliefs 10% to 20%. **Languages:** English 7% (official), Afrikaans common language of most of the population and about 60% of the white population, German 32%, indigenous languages 1% (includes Oshivambo, Herero, Nama). **Government Government type:** republic. **Capital:** Windhoek. **Independence:** 21 March 1990 (from South African mandate). **National holiday:** Independence Day, 21 March (1990). **Economy G.D.P.:** purchasing power parity—$14.64 billion (2010 est.). **G.D.P.—per capita:** purchasing power parity—$6,900 (2010 est.). **Currency:** Namibian dollar (NAD); South African rand (ZAR).

Nauru

Republic of Nauru

Geography Location: Oceania, island in the South Pacific Ocean, south of the Marshall Islands. **Area:** 8 sq. mi. (21 sq km). **Natural resources:** phosphates, fish. **People Population:** 9,322 (July 2011 est.). **Nationality:** *noun:* Nauruan(s); *adj.:* Nauruan. **Ethnic groups:** Nauruan 58%, other Pacific Islander 26%, Chinese 8%, European 8%. **Religions:** Nauru Congregational 35.4%, Roman Catholic 33.2%, Nauru Independent Church 10.4%, other 14.1%, none 4.5%, unspecified 2.4% (2002 census). **Languages:** Nauruan (official; a distinct Pacific Island language), English widely understood; spoken and used for most government and commercial purposes. **Government Government**

type: republic. **Capital:** no official capital; government offices in Yaren District. **Independence:** 31 January 1968 (from the Australia-, N.Z.-, and U.K.-administered U.N. trusteeship). **National holiday:** Independence Day, 31 January (1968). **Economy G.D.P.:** purchasing power parity—$60 million (2005 est.). **G.D.P.—per capita:** purchasing power parity—$5,000 (2005 est.). **Currency:** Australian dollar (AUD).

Nepal

Kingdom of Nepal

Geography   Location: Southern Asia, between China and India. **Area:** 54,363 sq mi (147,181 sq km). **Border countries:** China, India. **Natural resources:** quartz, water, timber, hydropower, scenic beauty, small deposits of lignite, copper, cobalt, iron ore. **People Population:** 29,391,883 (July 2011 est.). **Nationality:** *noun:* Nepalese (singular and plural); *adj.:* Nepalese. **Ethnic groups:** Chhettri 15.5%, Brahman-Hill 12.5%, Magar 7%, Tharu 6.6%, Tamang 5.5%, Newar 5.4%, Muslim 4.2%, Kami 3.9%, Yadav 3.9%, other 32.7%, unspecified 2.8% (2001 census). **Religions:** Hindu 80.6%, Buddhist 10.7%, Muslim 4.2%, Kirant 3.6%, other 0.9% (2001 census). **Languages:** Nepali (official) 47.8%, Maithali 12.1%, Bhojpuri 7.4%, Tharu (Dagaura/Rana) 5.8%, Tamang 5.1%, Newar 3.6%, Magar 3.3%, Awadhi 2.4%, other 10%, unspecified 2.5% (2001 census); *note:* many in government and business also speak English. **Government Government type:** federal democratic republic. **Capital:** Kathmandu. **Independence:** 1768 (unified by Prithvi Narayan Shah). **National holiday:** In 2006, Parliament abolished the birthday of King Gyanendra (7 July) and Constitution Day (9 November) as national holidays. **Economy G.D.P.:** purchasing power parity—$35.31 billion (2010 est.). **G.D.P.—per capita:** purchasing power parity—$1,200 (2010 est.). **Currency:** Nepalese rupee (NPR).

Netherlands

Kingdom of the Netherlands

Geography   Location: Western Europe, bordering the North Sea, between Belgium and Germany. **Area:** 14,413 sq. mi. (37,330 sq km). **Border countries:** Belgium, Germany. **Natural resources:** natural gas, petroleum, peat, limestone, salt, sand and gravel, arable land. **People Population:** 16,847,007 (July 2011 est.). **Nationality:** *noun:* Dutchman (men), Dutchwoman (women); *adj.:* Dutch. **Ethnic groups:** Dutch 80.7%, E.U. 5%, Indonesian 2.4%, Turkish 2.2%, Surinamese 2%, Moroccan 2%, Caribbean 0.8%, other 4.8% (2008 est.). **Religions:** Roman Catholic 30%, Dutch Reformed 11%, Calvinist 6%, other Protestant 3%, Muslim 5.8%, other 2.2%, none 42% (2006). **Languages:** Dutch (official language), Frisian (official language). **Government Government type:** constitutional monarchy. **Capital:** Amsterdam; The Hague is the seat of government. **Independence:** 1579 (from Spain); *note:* the northern provinces of the Low Country concluded the Union of Utrecht, but it was 1648 before Spain finally recognized their independence. **National holiday:** Queen's Day (Birthday of Queen-Mother Juliana in 1909 and accession to the throne of her oldest daughter Beatrix in 1980), 30 April. **Economy G.D.P.:** purchasing power parity—$680.4 billion (2010 est.). **G.D.P.—per capita:** purchasing power parity—$40,500 (2010 est.). **Currency:** euro (EUR).

New Zealand

Geography Location: Oceania, islands in the South Pacific Ocean, southeast of Australia. **Area:** 103,738 sq. mi. (268,680 sq km). **Natural resources:** natural gas, iron ore, sand, coal, timber, hydropower, gold, limestone. **People Population:** 4,290,347 (July 2011 est.). **Nationality:** *noun:* New Zealander(s); *adj.:* New Zealand. **Ethnic groups:** European 56.8%, Asian 8%, Maori 7.4%, Pacific Islander 4.6%, mixed 9.7%, other 13.5% (2006 census). **Religions:** Anglican 13.8%, Roman Catholic 12.6%, Presbyterian, Congregational, and Reformed 10%, Christian (no denomination specified) 4.6%, Methodist 3%, Pentecostal 2%, Baptist 1.4%, other Christian 3.8%, Maori Christian 1.6%, Hindu 1.6%, Buddhist 1.3%, other religions 2.2%, none 32.2%, other or unidentified 9.9% (2006 census). **Languages:** English 91.2% (official), Maori 3.9% (official), Samoan 2.1%, French 1.3%, Hindi 1.1%, Yue 1.1%, Northern Chinese 1%, other 12.9%, New Zealand Sign Language (official) note: shares sum to 114.6% due to multiple responses on census (2006 census). **Government   Government type:** parliamentary democracy. **Capital:** Wellington. **Independence:** 26 September 1907 (from U.K.). **National holiday:** Waitangi Day (Treaty of Waitangi established British sovereignty over New Zealand), 6 February (1840). **Economy G.D.P.:** purchasing power parity—$119.2 billion (2010 est.). **G.D.P.—per capita:** purchasing power parity—$28,000 (2010 est.). **Currency:** New Zealand dollar (NZD).

Nicaragua

Republic of Nicaragua

Geography   Location: Middle America, bordering both the Caribbean Sea and the North Pacific Ocean, between Costa Rica and Honduras. **Area:** 49,998 sq. mi. (129,494 sq km). **Border countries:** Costa Rica, Honduras. **Natural resources:** gold, silver, copper, tungsten, lead, zinc, timber, fish. **People Population:** 5,666,302 (July 2011 est.).

Nationality: *noun:* Nicaraguan(s); *adj.:* Nicaraguan. **Ethnic groups:** mestizo (mixed Amerindian and white) 69%, white 17%, black 9%, Amerindian 5%. **Religions:** Roman Catholic 58.5%, Evangelical 21.6%, Moravian 1.6%, Jehovah's Witness 0.9%, other 1.7%, none 15.7% (2005 census). **Languages:** Spanish 97.5% (official), Miskito 1.7%, other 0.8% (1995 census) *note:* English and indigenous languages on Atlantic coast. **Government Government type:** republic. **Capital:** Managua. **Independence:** 15 September 1821 (from Spain). **National holiday:** Independence Day, 15 September (1821). **Economy G.D.P.:** purchasing power parity—$17.34 billion (2010 est.). **G.D.P.—per capita:** purchasing power parity—$2,900 (2010 est.). **Currency:** gold cordoba (NIO).

Niger

Republic of Niger

Geography Location: Western Africa, southeast of Algeria. **Area:** 489,189 sq. mi. (1.267 million sq km). **Border countries:** Algeria, Benin, Burkina Faso, Chad, Libya, Mali, Nigeria. **Natural resources:** uranium, coal, iron ore, tin, phosphates, gold, molybdenum, gypsum, salt, petroleum. **People Population:** 16,468,886 (July 2011 est.). **Nationality:** *noun:* Nigerien(s); *adj.:* Nigerien. **Ethnic groups:** Haoussa 55.4%, Djerma Sonrai 21%, Tuareg 9.3%, Peuhl 8.5%, Kanouri Manga 4.7%, other 1.2% (2001 census). **Religions:** Muslim 80%, other (includes indigenous beliefs and Christian) 20%. **Languages:** French (official), Hausa, Djerma. **Government Government type:** republic. **Capital:** Niamey. **Independence:** 3 August 1960 (from France). **National holiday:** Republic Day, 18 December (1958). **Economy G.D.P.:** purchasing power parity—$10.58 billion (2010 est.). **G.D.P.—per capita:** purchasing power parity—$700 (2010 est.). **Currency:** Communaute Financiere Africaine franc (XOF); note—responsible authority is the Central Bank of the West African States.

Nigeria

Federal Republic of Nigeria

Geography Location: Western Africa, bordering the Gulf of Guinea, between Benin and Cameroon. **Area:** 356,668 sq. mi. (923,770 sq km). **Border countries:** Benin, Cameroon, Chad, Niger. **Natural resources:** natural gas, petroleum, tin, niobium, iron ore, coal, limestone, lead, zinc, arable land. **People Population:** 155,215,573 (July 2011 est.) *note:* estimates for this country explicitly take into account the effects of excess mortality due to AIDS; this can result in lower life expectancy, higher infant mortality and death rates, lower population and growth rates, and changes in the distribution of population by age and sex than would otherwise be expected. **Nationality:** *noun:* Nigerian(s); *adj.:* Nigerian. **Ethnic**

groups: Nigeria, which is Africa's most populous country, is composed of more than 250 ethnic groups; the following are the most populous and politically influential: Hausa and Fulani 29%, Yoruba 21%, Igbo (Ibo) 18%, Ijaw 10%, Kanuri 4%, Ibibio 3.5%, Tiv 2.5%. **Religions:** Muslim 50%, Christian 40%, indigenous beliefs 10%. **Languages:** English (official), Hausa, Yoruba, Igbo (ibo), Fulani, over 500 additional indigenous languages. **Government Government type:** federal republic. **Capital:** Abuja; note—on 12 December 1991 the capital was officially transferred from Lagos to Abuja; most federal government offices have now made the move to Abuja. **Independence:** 1 October 1960 (from U.K.). **National holiday:** Independence Day (National Day), 1 October (1960). **Economy G.D.P.:** purchasing power parity—$369.8 billion (2010 est.). **G.D.P.—per capita:** purchasing power parity—$2,400 (2010 est.). **Currency:** naira (NGN).

Norway

Kingdom of Norway

Geography Location: Northern Europe, bordering the North Sea and the North Atlantic Ocean, west of Sweden. **Area:** 125,182 sq mi (323,802 sq km). **Border countries:** Finland, Sweden, Russia. **Natural resources:** petroleum, natural gas, iron ore, copper, lead, zinc, titanium, pyrites, nickel, fish, timber, hydropower. **People Population:** 4,691,849 (July 2011 est.). **Nationality:** *noun:* Norwegian(s); *adj.:* Norwegian. **Ethnic groups:** Norwegian 94.4% (includes Sami, about 60,000), other European 3.6%, other 2% (2007 estimate). **Religions:** Church of Norway 85.7%, Pentecostal 1%, Roman Catholic 1%, other Christian 2.4%, Muslim 1.8%, other 8.1% (2004). **Languages:** Bokmal Norwegian (official), Nynorsk Norwegian (official), small Sami- and Finnish-speaking minorities; *note:* Sami is official in six municipalities. **Government Government type:** constitutional monarchy. **Capital:** Oslo. **Independence:** 7 June 1905 Norway declared the union with Sweden dissolved; 26 October 1905 Sweden agreed to the repeal of the union. **National holiday:** Constitution Day, 17 May (1814). **Economy G.D.P.:** purchasing power parity—$276.4 billion (2010 est.). **G.D.P.—per capita:** purchasing power parity—$59,100 (2010 est.). **Currency:** Norwegian krone (NOK).

Oman

Sultanate of Oman

Geography Location: Middle East, bordering the Arabian Sea, Gulf of Oman, and Persian Gulf, between Yemen and UAE. **Area:** 82,031 sq. mi. (212,460 sq km). **Border countries:** Saudi Arabia, United Arab Emirates, Yemen. **Natural resources:** petroleum, copper, asbestos, some marble, limestone, chromium, gypsum, natural gas. **People Population:** 3,027,959 *note:* includes 577,293 non-nationals (July 2011 est.). **Nationality:** *noun:* Omani(s); *adj.:* Omani. **Ethnic groups:** Arab, Baluchi, South Asian (Indian, Pakistani, Sri Lankan, Bangladeshi), African. **Religions:** Ibadhi Muslim 75%, Sunni Muslim, Shi'a Muslim, Hindu 25%. **Languages:** Arabic (official), English, Baluchi, Urdu, Indian dialects. **Government Government type:** monarchy. **Capital:** Muscat. **Independence:** 1650 (expulsion of the Portuguese). **National holiday:** Birthday of Sultan Qaboos, 18 November (1940). **Economy G.D.P.:** purchasing power parity—$76.53 billion (2010 est.). **G.D.P.—per capita:** purchasing power parity—$25,800 (2010 est.). **Currency:** Omani rial (OMR).

Pakistan

Islamic Republic of Pakistan

Geography Location: Southern Asia, bordering the Arabian Sea, between India on the east and Iran and Afghanistan on the west and China in the north. **Area:** 310,402 sq. mi. (803,940 sq km). **Border countries:** Afghanistan, China, India, Iran. **Natural resources:** land, extensive natural gas reserves, limited petroleum, poor quality coal, iron ore, copper, salt, limestone. **People Population:** 187,342,721 (July 2011 est.). **Nationality:** *noun:* Pakistani(s); *adj.:* Pakistani. **Ethnic groups:** Punjabi 44.68%, Pashtun (Pathan) 15.42%, Sindhi 14.1%, Sariaki 8.38%, Muhajirs 7.57%, Balochi 3.57%, other 6.28%. **Religions:** Muslim 95% (Sunni 75%, Shia 20%), other (includes Christian and Hindu) 5%. **Languages:** Punjabi 48%, Sindhi 12%, Siraiki (a Punjabi variant) 10%, Pashtu 8%, Urdu (official) 8%, Balochi 3%, Hindko 2%, Brahui 1%, English (official; lingu franca of Pakistani elite and most government ministries), Burushaski, and other 8%. **Government Government type:** federal republic. **Capital:** Islamabad. **Independence:** 14 August 1947 (from U.K.). **National holiday:** Republic Day, 23 March (1956). **Economy G.D.P.:** purchasing power parity—$451.2 billion (2010 est.). **G.D.P.—per capita:** purchasing power parity—$2,400 (2010 est.). **Currency:** Pakistani rupee (PKR).

Palau

Republic of Palau

Geography Location: Oceania, group of islands in the North Pacific Ocean, southeast of the Philippines. **Area:** 177 sq. mi. (458 sq km). **Natural resources:** forests, minerals (especially gold), marine products, deep-seabed minerals. **People Population:** 20,956 (July 2011 est.). **Nationality:** *noun:* Palauan(s); *adj.:* Palauan. **Ethnic groups:** Palauan

(Micronesian with Malayan and Melanesian admixtures) 70%, Filipino 15.3%, Chinese 4.9%, other Asian 2.4%, white 2%, Carolinian 1.4%, other 4.3% (2000 census). **Religions:** Roman Catholic 41.6%, Protestant 23.3%, Modekngei religion 8.8% (indigenous to Palau), Seventh-Day Adventist 5.3%, Jehovah's Witness 0.9%, Latter-Day Saints 0.6%, other 3.1%, unspecified or none 16.4% (2000 census). **Languages:** Palauan 64.7% (official in all islands except Sonsoral where Sonsoralese and English are official, Tobi where Tobi and English are official, and Angaur where Angaur, Japanese, and English are official), Filipino 13.5%, English 9.4%, Chinese 5.7%, Carolinian 1.5%, Japanese 1.5%, other Asian 2.3%, other languages 1.5% (2000 census). **Government Government type:** constitutional government in free association with the U.S.; the Compact of Free Association entered into force 1 October 1994. **Capital:** Melekeok. **Independence:** 1 October 1994 (from the U.S.-administered U.N. Trusteeship). **National holiday:** Constitution Day, 9 July (1979). **Economy G.D.P.:** purchasing power parity—164 million (July 2011 est.). **G.D.P.—per capita:** purchasing power parity—$8,100 (2008 est.). **Currency:** U.S. dollar (USD).

Panama

Republic of Panama

Geography Location: Middle America, bordering both the Caribbean Sea and the North Pacific Ocean, between Colombia and Costa Rica. **Area:** 30,193 sq. mi. (78,200 sq km). **Border countries:** Colombia, Costa Rica. **Natural resources:** copper, mahogany forests, shrimp, hydropower. **People Population:** 3,460,462 (July 2011 est.). **Nationality:** *noun:* Panamanian(s); *adj.:* Panamanian. **Ethnic groups:** Mestizo (mixed Amerindian and white) 70%, Amerindian and mixed (West Indian) 14%, white 10%, Amerindian 6%. **Religions:** Roman Catholic 85%, Portestant 15% (2000 census). **Languages:** Spanish (official), English 14%, *note:* many Panamanians bilingual. **Government Government type:** constitutional democracy. **Capital:** Panama City. **Independence:** 3 November 1903 (from Colombia; became independent from Spain 28 November 1821). **National holiday:** Independence Day, 3 November (1903). **Economy G.D.P.:** purchasing power parity—$43.48 billion (2010 est.). **G.D.P.—per capita:** purchasing power parity—$12,700 (2010 est.). **Currency:** balboa (PAB); U.S. dollar (USD).

Papua New Guinea

Independent State of Papua New Guinea

Geography Location: Oceania, group of islands including the eastern half of the island of New Guinea between the Coral Sea and the South Pacific Ocean, east of Indonesia. **Area:** 178,259 sq. mi. (462,840 sq km). **Border countries**: Indonesia. **Natural resources:** gold, copper, silver, natural gas, timber, oil, fisheries. **People Population:** 6,187,591 (July 2011 est.). **Nationality:** *noun:* Papua New Guinean(s); *adj.:* Papua New Guinean. **Ethnic groups:** Melanesian, Papuan, Negrito, Micronesian, Polynesian. **Religions:** Roman Catholic 27%, Evangelical Lutheran 19.5%, United Church 11.5%, Seventh-Day Adventist 10%, Pentecostal 8.6%, Evangelical Alliance 5.2%, Anglican 3.2%, Baptist 2.5%, other Protestant 8.9%, Bahai 0.3%, other 3.3% (2000 census). **Languages:** Tok Pisi, English, and Hiri Motu are official languages; some 860 indigenous languages spoken (over one-tenth of the world's total) *note:* Tok Pisin, a Creole language, is widely used and understood; English is spoken by 1–2%; Hiri Motu is spoken by less than 2%. **Government   Government type:** constitutional parliamentary democracy. **Capital:** Port Moresby. **Independence:** 16 September 1975 (from the Australian-administered U.N. trusteeship). **Economy G.D.P.:** purchasing power parity—$14.92 billion (2011 est.). **G.D.P.—per capita:** purchasing power parity—$2,500 (2011 est.). **Currency:** kina (PGK).

Paraguay

Republic of Paraguay

Geography   Location: Central South America, northeast of Argentina. **Area:** 157,046 sq. mi. (406,750 sq km). **Border countries**: Argentina, Bolivia, Brazil. **Natural resources:** hydropower, timber, iron ore, manganese, limestone. **People Population:** 6,459,058 (July 2011 est.). **Nationality:** *noun:* Paraguayan(s); *adj.:* Paraguayan. **Ethnic groups:** mestizo (mixed Spanish and Amerindian) 95%, other 5%. **Religions:** Roman Catholic 89.6%, Protestant 6.2%, other Christian 1.1%, other or unspecified 1.9%, none 1.1% (2002 census). **Languages:** Spanish (official), Guarani (official). **Government   Government type:** constitutional republic. **Capital:** Asuncion. **Independence:** 14 May 1811 (from Spain). **National holiday:** Independence Day, 14 May (1811). **Economy   G.D.P.:** purchasing power parity—$30.94 billion (2010 est.). **G.D.P.—per capita:** purchasing power parity—$4,900 (2010 est.). **Currency:** guarani (PYG).

Peru

Republic of Peru

Geography   Location: Western South America, bordering the South Pacific Ocean, between Chile and Ecuador. **Area:** 496,224 sq. mi. (1,285,220 sq km). **Border countries**:

Bolivia, Brazil, Chile, Colombia, Ecuador. **Natural resources:** copper, silver, gold, petroleum, timber, fish, iron ore, coal, phosphate, potash, hydropower, natural gas. **People Population:** 29,248,943 (July 2011 est.). **Nationality:** *noun:* Peruvian(s); *adj.:* Peruvian. **Ethnic groups:** Amerindian 45%, mestizo (mixed Amerindian and white) 37%, white 15%, black, Japanese, Chinese and other 3%. **Religions:** Roman Catholic 81.3%, Evangelical 12.5%, other 3.3%, unspecified or none 2.9% (2007 census). **Languages:** Spanish 84.1% (official), Quechua 13% (official), Aymara 1.7%, Ashaninka 0.3%, other native languages 0.7% (includes a large number of minor Amazonian languages), other 0.2% (2007 census). **Government   Government type:** constitutional republic. **Capital:** Lima. **Independence:** 28 July 1821 (from Spain). **National holiday:** Independence Day, 28 July (1821). **Economy G.D.P.:** purchasing power parity—$274.7 billion (2010 est.). **G.D.P.—per capita:** purchasing power parity—$9,200 (2010 est.). **Currency:** nuevo sol (PEN).

Philippines

Republic of the Philippines

Geography   Location: Southeastern Asia, archipelago between the Philippine Sea and the South China Sea, east of Vietnam. **Area:** 115,830 sq. mi. (300,000 sq km). **Natural resources:** timber, petroleum, nickel, cobalt, silver, gold, salt, copper. **People Population:** 101,833,938 (July 2011 est.). **Nationality:** *noun:* Filipino(s); *adj.:* Philippine. **Ethnic groups:** Tagalog 28.1%, Cebuano 13.1%, Ilocano 9%, Bisaya/Binisaya 7.6%, Hiligaynon Ilonggo 7.5%, Bikol 6%, Waray 3.4%, other 25.3% (2000 census). **Religions:** Roman Catholic 80.9%, Evangelical 2.8%, Iglesia ni Kristo 2.3%, Agilpayan 2%, other Christian 4.5%, Muslim 5%, other 1.8%, unspecified or none 0.7% (2000 census). **Languages:** Filipino (official; based on Tagalog) and English (official); eight major dialects—Tagalog, Cebuano, Ilocano, Hiligaynon or Ilonggo, Bicol, Waray, Pampango, and Pangasinan. **Government   Government type:** republic. **Capital:** Manila. **Independence:** 4 July 1946 (from U.S.). **National holiday:** Independence Day (from Spain), 12 June (1898); *note:* 12 June 1898 is the date of independence from Spain, 4 July 1946 is the date of independence from the U.S. **Economy G.D.P.:** purchasing power parity—$353.2 billion (2010 est.). **G.D.P.—per capita:** purchasing power parity—$3,500 (2010 est.). **Currency:** Philippine peso (PHP).

Poland

Republic of Poland

Geography   Location: Central Europe, east of Germany.

Area: 120,728 sq mi (312,685 sq km). **Border countries:** Belarus, Czech Republic, Germany, Lithuania, Russia (Kaliningrad Oblast), Slovakia, Ukraine. **Natural resources:** coal, sulfur, copper, natural gas, silver, lead, salt, amber, arable land. **People Population:** 38,441,588 (July 2011 est.). **Nationality:** *noun:* Pole(s); *adj.:* Polish. **Ethnic groups:** Polish 96.7%, German 0.4%, Ukrainian 0.6%, Belarusian 0.1%, other and unspecified 2.7% (2002 est.). **Religions:** Roman Catholic 89.8% (about 75% practicing), Eastern Orthodox 1.3%, Protestant 0.3%, unspecified 8.3%, other 0.3% (2002 census). **Languages:** Polish 97.8%, other and unspecified 2.2% (2002 census). **Government Government type:** republic. **Capital:** Warsaw. **Independence:** 11 November 1918 (independent republic proclaimed). **National holiday:** Constitution Day, 3 May (1791). **Economy G.D.P.:** purchasing power parity—$721.7 billion (2010 est.). **G.D.P.—per capita:** purchasing power parity—$18,800 (2010 est.). **Currency:** zloty (PLN).

Portugal

Portuguese Republic

Geography Location: Southwestern Europe, bordering the North Atlantic Ocean, west of Spain. **Area:** 35,552 sq. mi. (92,080 sq km). **Border countries:** Spain. **Natural resources:** fish, silver, gold, zinc, tin, clay, copper, forests (cork), gypsum, salt, tungsten, iron ore, uranium ore, marble, arable land, hydropower. **People Population:** 10,760,305 (July 2011 est.). **Nationality:** *noun:* Portuguese (singular and plural); *adj.:* Portuguese. **Ethnic groups:** homogeneous Mediterranean stock; citizens of black African descent who immigrated to mainland during decolonization number less than 100,000; since 1990 East Europeans have entered Portugal. **Religions:** Roman Catholic 84.5%, other Christian 2.2%, other 0.3%, unknown 9%, none 3.9% (2001 census). **Languages:** Portuguese (official), Mirandese (official, but locally used). **Government Government type:** parliamentary democracy. **Capital:** Lisbon. **Independence:** 1143 (independent republic proclaimed 5 October 1910). **National holiday:** Portugal Day, 10 June (1580). **Economy G.D.P.:** purchasing power parity—$247 billion (2010 est.). **G.D.P.—per capita:** purchasing power parity—$23,000 (2010 est.). **Currency:** euro (EUR).

Qatar

State of Qatar

Geography Location: Middle East, peninsula bordering the Persian Gulf and Saudi Arabia. **Area:** 4,247 sq. mi. (11,000 sq km). **Border countries:** Saudi Arabia. **Natural resources:** petroleum, natural gas, fish. **People Population:** 848,016 (July 2011 est.). **Nationality:** *noun:* Qatari(s); *adj.:* Qatari.

Ethnic groups: Arab 40%, Indian 18%, Pakistani 18%, Iranian 10%, other 14%. **Religions:** Muslim 77.5%, Christian 8.5%, other 14% (2004 census). **Languages:** Arabic (official), English commonly used as a second language. **Government Government type:** traditional emirate. **Capital:** Doha. **Independence:** 3 September 1971 (from U.K.). **National holiday:** Independence Day, 3 September (1971). **Economy G.D.P.:** purchasing power parity—$122.2 billion (2010 est.). **G.D.P.—per capita:** purchasing power parity—$145,300 (2010 est.). **Currency:** Qatari rial (QAR).

Romania

Geography Location: Southeastern Europe, bordering the Black Sea, between Bulgaria and Ukraine. **Area:** 91,699 sq. mi. (237,500 sq km). **Border countries:** Bulgaria, Hungary, Moldova, Serbia, Ukraine (north), Ukraine (east). **Natural resources:** petroleum (reserves declining), timber, natural gas, coal, iron ore, salt, arable land, hydropower. **People Population:** 21,904,551 (July 2011 est.). **Nationality:** *noun:* Romanian(s); *adj.:* Romanian. **Ethnic groups:** Romanian 89.5%, Hungarian 6.6%, Roma 2.5%, Ukrainian 0.3%, German 0.3%, Russian 0.2%, Turkish 0.2%, other 0.4% (2002). **Religions:** Eastern Orthodox (including all sub-denominations) 86.8%, Protestant 7.5%, Roman Catholic 4.7%, other (mostly Muslim and unspecified) 0.9%, none 0.1% (2002 census). **Languages:** Romanian 91% (official), Hungarian 6.7%, Romany (Gypsy) 1.1%, other 1.2%. **Government Government type:** republic. **Capital:** Bucharest. **Independence:** 9 May 1877 (independence proclaimed from Turkey; independence recognized 13 July 1878 by the Treaty of Berlin; kingdom proclaimed 26 March 1881; republic proclaimed 30 December 1947). **National holiday:** Unification Day (of Romania and Transylvania), 1 December (1918). **Economy G.D.P.:** purchasing power parity—$253.3 billion (2010 est.). **G.D.P.—per capita:** purchasing power parity—$11,500 (2010 est.). **Currency:** leu (RON).

Russia

Russian Federation

Geography Location: Northern Asia (that part west of the Urals is included with Europe), bordering the Arctic Ocean, between Europe and the North Pacific Ocean. **Area:** 6,592,745 sq. mi. (17,075,200 sq km). **Border countries:** Azerbaijan, Belarus, China (southeast), China (south), Estonia, Finland, Georgia, Kazakhstan, North Korea, Latvia, Lithuania (Kaliningrad Oblast), Mongolia, Norway, Poland (Kaliningrad Oblast), Ukraine. **Natural resources:** wide natural resource base including major deposits of oil, natural gas, coal, and many strategic minerals, reserves of rare earth elements, timber. **People Population:** 138,739,892 (July 2011 est.). **Nationality:** *noun:* Russian(s); *adj.:* Russian. **Ethnic groups:** Russian 79.8%, Tatar 3.8%, Ukrainian 2%, Chuvash 1.1%, Bashkir 1.2%, other or unspecified 12.1% (2002 census). **Religions:** Russian Orthodox 15–20%, Muslim 10–15%, other Christian 2% (2006 est.) *note:* estimates are of practicing worshippers; Russia has a large population of non-practicing believers and non-believers, a legacy of over seven decades of Soviet rule. **Languages:** Russian (official), many minority languages. **Government Government type:** federation. **Capital:** Moscow. **Independence:** 24 August 1991 (from Soviet Union). **National holiday:** Russia Day, 12 June (1990). **Economy G.D.P.:** purchasing power parity—$2.229 trillion (2010 est.). **G.D.P.—per capita:** purchasing power parity—$15,900 (2010 est.). **Currency:** Russian ruble (RUR).

Rwanda

Rwandese Republic

Geography Location: Central Africa, east of Democratic Republic of the Congo. **Area:** 10,170 sq. mi. (26,338 sq km). **Border countries:** Burundi, Democratic Republic of the Congo, Tanzania, Uganda. **Natural resources:** gold, cassiterite (tin ore), wolframite (tungsten ore), methane, hydropower, arable land. **People Population:** 11,370,425 (July 2011 est.) *note:* estimates for this country explicitly take into account the effects of excess mortality due to AIDS; this can result in lower life expectancy, higher infant mortality and death rates, lower population and growth rates, and changes in the distribution of population by age and sex than would otherwise be expected. *note:* Rwanda is the most densely populated country in Africa. **Nationality:** *noun:* Rwandan(s); *adj.:* Rwandan. **Ethnic groups:** Hutu (Bantu) 84%, Tutsi (Hamitic) 15%, Twa (Pygmy) 1%. **Religions:** Roman Catholic 56.5%, Protestant 26%, Adventist 11.1%, Muslim 4.6%, indigenous beliefs 0.1%, none 1.7% (2001). **Languages:** Kinyarwanda (official) universal Bantu vernacular, French (official), English (official), Kiswahili (Swahili) used in commercial centers. **Government Government type:** republic; presidential, multiparty system. **Capital:** Kigali. **Independence:** 1 July 1962 (from Belgium-administered U.N. trusteeship). **National holiday:** Independence Day, 1 July (1962). **Economy G.D.P.:** purchasing power parity—$11.84 billion (2010 est.). **G.D.P.—per capita:** purchasing power parity—$1,100 (2010 est.). **Currency:** Rwandan franc (RWF).

Saint Kitts and Nevis

Federation of Saint Kitts and Nevis

Geography Location: Caribbean, islands in the Caribbean Sea, about one-third of the way from Puerto Rico to Trinidad and Tobago. **Area:** 104 sq. mi. (261 sq km). **Natural resources:** arable land. **People Population:** 50,314 (July 2011 est.). **Nationality:** *noun:* Kittitian(s), Nevisian(s); *adj.:* Kittitian, Nevisian. **Ethnic groups:** predominantly black; some British, Portuguese, and Lebanese. **Religions:** Anglican, other Protestant, Roman Catholic. **Languages:** English (official). **Government Government type:** parliamentary democracy. **Capital:** Basseterre. **Independence:** 19 September 1983 (from U.K.). **National holiday:** Independence Day, 19 September (1983). **Economy G.D.P.:** purchasing power parity—$719.5 million (2010 est.). **G.D.P.—per capita:** purchasing power parity—$14,400 (2010 est.). **Currency:** East Caribbean dollar (XCD).

Saint Lucia

Geography Location: Caribbean, island between the Caribbean Sea and North Atlantic Ocean, north of Trinidad and Tobago. **Area:** 239 sq. mi. (620 sq km). **Natural resources:** forests, sandy beaches, minerals (pumice), mineral springs, geothermal potential. **People Population:** 161,557 (July 2011 est.). **Nationality:** *noun:* Saint Lucian(s); *adj.:* Saint Lucian. **Ethnic groups:** black 82.5%, mixed 11.9%, East Indian 2.4%, other or unspecified 3.1% (2001 census). **Religions:** Roman Catholic 67.5%, Seventh-Day Adventist 8.5%, Pentecostal 5.7%, Anglican 2%, Evangelical 2%, other Christian 5.1%, Rastafarian 2.1%, other 1.1%, unspecified 1.5%, none 4.5% (2001 census). **Languages:** English (official), French patois. **Government Government type:** parliamentary democracy. **Capital:** Castries. **Independence:** 22 February 1979 (from U.K.). **National holiday:** Independence Day, 22 February (1979). **Economy G.D.P.:** purchasing power parity—$1.789 billion (2010 est.). **G.D.P.—per capita:** purchasing power parity—$11,100 (2010 est.). **Currency:** East Caribbean dollar (XCD).

Saint Vincent and the Grenadines

Geography Location: Caribbean, islands between the Caribbean Sea and North Atlantic Ocean, north of Trinidad and Tobago. **Area:** 131 sq. mi. (340 sq km). **Natural resources:** hydropower, cropland. **People Population:** 103,869 (July 2011 est.). **Nationality:** noun: Saint Vincentian(s) or Vincentian(s); adj.: Saint Vincentian or Vincentian. **Ethnic groups:** black 66%, mixed 19%, East Indian 6%, European 4%, Carib Amerindian 2%, other 3%. **Religions:** Anglican 47%, Methodist 28%, Roman Catholic 13%, other (includes Hindu, Seventh-Day Adventist, other Protestant) 12%. **Languages:** English, French patois. **Government Government type:** parliamentary democracy. **Capital:** Kingstown. **Independence:** 27 October 1979 (from U.K.). **National holiday:** Independence Day, 27 October (1979). **Economy G.D.P.:** purchasing power parity—$1.107 billion (2010 est.). **G.D.P.—per capita:** purchasing power parity—$10,600 (2010 est.). **Currency:** East Caribbean dollar (XCD).

Samoa

Independent State of Samoa

Geography   Location: Oceania, group of islands in the South Pacific Ocean, about one-half of the way from Hawaii to New Zealand. **Area:** 1,104 sq. mi. (2,860 sq km). **Natural resources:** hardwood forests, fish, hydropower. **People Population:** 193,161 (July 2011 est.). **Nationality:** *noun:* Samoan(s); *adj.:* Samoan. **Ethnic groups:** Samoan 92.6%, Euronesians (persons of European and Polynesian blood) 7%, Europeans 0.4% (2001 census). **Religions:** Congregationalist 34.8%, Roman Catholic 19.6%, Methodist 15%, Latter-Day Saints 12.7%, Assembly of God 6.6%, Seventh-Day Adventist 3.5%, Worship Centre 1.3%, other Christian 4.5%, other 1.9%, unspecified 0.1% (2001 census). **Languages:** Samoan (Polynesian) (official), English. **Government   Government type:** mix of parliamentary democracy and constitutional monarchy. **Capital:** Apia. **Independence:** 1 January 1962 (from New Zealand-administered U.N. trusteeship). **National holiday:** Independence Day Celebration, 1 June (1962); *note:* 1 January 1962 is the date of independence from the New Zealand-administered U.N. trusteeship, 1 June 1962 is the date that independence is celebrated. **Economy G.D.P.:** purchasing power parity—$1.002 billion (2010 est.). **G.D.P.—per capita:** purchasing power parity—$5,200 (2010 est.). **Currency:** tala (SAT).

San Marino

Republic of San Marino

Geography   Location: Southern Europe, an enclave in central Italy. **Area:** 23 sq. mi. (61.2 sq km). **Border countries:** Italy. **Natural resources:** building stone. **People Population:** 31,817 (July 2011 est.). **Nationality:** *noun:* Sammarinese (singular and plural); *adj.:* Sammarinese. **Ethnic groups:** Sammarinese, Italian. **Religions:** Roman Catholic. **Languages:** Italian. **Government   Government type:** independent republic. **Capital:** San Marino. **Independence:** 3 September 301. **National holiday:** Founding of the Republic, 3 September (301). **Economy G.D.P.:** purchasing power parity—$1.662 billion (2007). **G.D.P.—per capita:** purchasing power parity—$41,900 (2007). **Currency:** euro (EUR).

Sao Tome and Principe

Democratic Republic of Sao Tome and Principe

Geography   Location: Western Africa, islands in the Gulf of Guinea, straddling the Equator, west of Gabon. **Area:** 371 sq. mi. (960 sq km). **Natural resources:** fish, hydropower. **People Population:** 179,506 (July 2011 est.). **Nationality:** *noun:* Sao Tomean(s); *adj.:* Sao Tomean. **Ethnic groups:** mestico, angolares (descendants of Angolan slaves), forros (descendants of freed slaves), servicais (contract laborers from Angola, Mozambique, and Cape Verde), tongas (children of servicais born on the islands), Europeans (primarily Portuguese). **Religions:** Catholic 70.3%, Evangelical 3.4%, New Apostolic 2%, Adventist 1.8%, other 3.1%, none 19.4% (2001 census). **Languages:** Portuguese (official). **Government   Government type:** republic. **Capital:** Sao Tome. **Independence:** 12 July 1975 (from Portugal). **National holiday:** Independence Day, 12 July (1975). **Economy G.D.P.:** purchasing power parity—$316.9 million (2010 est.). **G.D.P.—per capita:** purchasing power parity—$1,800 (2010 est.). **Currency:** dobra (STD).

Saudi Arabia

Kingdom of Saudi Arabia

Geography   Location: Middle East, bordering the Persian Gulf and the Red Sea, north of Yemen. **Area:** 756,982 sq mi (1,960,582 sq km). **Border countries:** Iraq, Jordan, Kuwait, Oman, Qatar, UAE, Yemen. **Natural resources:** petroleum, natural gas, iron ore, gold, copper. **People Population:** 26,131,703 *note:* includes 5,576,076 non-nationals (July 2011 est.). **Nationality:** *noun:* Saudi(s); *adj.:* Saudi or Saudi Arabian. **Ethnic groups:** Arab 90%, Afro-Asian 10%. **Religions:** Muslim 100%. **Languages:** Arabic (official). **Government   Government type:** monarchy. **Capital:** Riyadh. **Independence:** 23 September 1932 (Unification of the Kingdom). **National holiday:** Unification of the Kingdom, 23 September (1932). **Economy G.D.P.:** purchasing power parity—$622.5 billion (2010 est.). **G.D.P.—per capita:** purchasing power parity—$24,200 (2010 est.). **Currency:** Saudi riyal (SAR).

Senegal

Republic of Senegal

Geography   Location: Western Africa, bordering the North Atlantic Ocean, between Guinea-Bissau and Mauritania. **Area:** 74,749 sq mi (196,190 sq km). **Border countries:** The Gambia, Guinea, Guinea-Bissau, Mali, Mauritania. **Natural resources:** fish, phosphates, iron ore. **People Population:** 12,643,799 (July 2011 est.). **Nationality:** *noun:* Senegalese (singular and plural); *adj.*: Senegalese. **Ethnic groups:** Wolof 43.3%, Pular 23.8%, Serer 14.7%, Jola 3.7%, Mandinka 3%, Soninke 1.1%, European and Lebanese 1%, other 9.4%. **Religions:** Muslim 94%, Christian 5% (mostly Roman Catholic), indigenous beliefs 1%. **Languages:** French (official), Wolof, Pulaar, Jola, Mandinka. **Government Government type:** republic. **Capital:** Dakar. **Independence:** 4 April 1960 (from France); complete independence was achieved upon dissolution of federation with Mali on 20 August 1960. **National holiday:** Independence Day, 4 April (1960). **Economy G.D.P.:** purchasing power parity—$23.86 billion (2010 est.). **G.D.P.—per capita:** purchasing power parity—$1,900 (2010 est.). **Currency:** Communaute Financiere Africaine franc (XOF); *note*: responsible authority is the Central Bank of the West African States.

Serbia

Republic of Serbia

Geography Location: Southeastern Europe, between Macedonia and Hungary. **Area:** 39,517 sq mi (102,350 sq km). **Border countries:** Montenegro, Albania, Bosnia and Herzegovina, Bulgaria, Croatia (north), Croatia (south), Hungary, Macedonia, Romania. **Natural resources:** oil, gas, coal, iron ore, copper, zinc, antimony, chromite, gold, silver, magnesium, pyrite, limestone, marble, salt, arable land. **People Population:** 7,310,555 *note*: does not include the population of Kosovo (July 2011 est.). **Nationality:** *noun:* Serb(s); *adj.*: Serbian. **Ethnic groups:** Serb 82.9%, Hungarian 3.9%, Romany (Gypsy) 1.4%, Yugoslavs 1.1%, Bosniaks 1.8%, Montenegrin 0.9%, other 8% (2002 census). **Religions:** Serbian Orthodox 85%, Catholic 5.5%, Protestant 1.1%, Muslim 3.2%, unspecified 2.6%, other, unknown, or atheist 2.6% (2002 census). **Languages:** Serbian 88.3% (official), Hungarian 3.8%, Bosniak 1.8%, Romany (Gypsy) 1.1%, other 4.1%, unknown 0.9% (2002 census) *note*: Romanian, Hungarian, Slovak, Ukrainian, and Croatian all official in Vojvodina. **Government Government type:** republic. **Capital:** Belgrade. **Independence:** 5 June 2006 (from Serbia and Montenegro). **National holiday:** National Day, 15 February. **Economy G.D.P.:** purchasing power parity—$80.65 billion (2010 est.). **G.D.P.—per capita:** purchasing power parity—$11,000 (2010 est.). **Currency:** Serbian dinar (RSD).

Seychelles

Republic of Seychelles

Geography Location: Eastern Africa, group of islands in the Indian Ocean, northeast of Madagascar. **Area:** 176 sq. mi. (455 sq km). **Natural resources:** fish, copra, cinnamon trees. **People Population:** 89,188 (July 2011 est.). **Nationality:** *noun:* Seychellois (singular and plural); *adj.*: Seychellois.

Ethnic groups: mixed French, African, Indian, Chinese, and Arab. **Religions:** Roman Catholic 82.3%, Anglican 6.4%, Seventh-Day Adventist 1.1%, other Christian 3.4%, Hindu 2.1%, Muslim 1.1%, other/unspecified/none 3.6%. **Languages:** Creole 91.8%, English 4.9% (official), other 3.1%, unspecified 0.2% (2002 census). **Government Government type:** republic. **Capital:** Victoria. **Independence:** 29 June 1976 (from U.K.). **National holiday:** Constitution Day (National Day), 18 June (1993). **Economy G.D.P.:** purchasing power parity—$1.908 billion (2010 est.). **G.D.P.—per capita:** purchasing power parity—$21,600 (2010 est.). **Currency:** Seychelles rupee (SCR).

Sierra Leone

Republic of Sierra Leone

Geography Location: Western Africa, bordering the North Atlantic Ocean, between Guinea and Liberia. **Area:** 27,699 sq. mi. (71,740 sq km). **Border countries:** Guinea, Liberia. **Natural resources:** diamonds, titanium ore, bauxite, iron ore, gold, chromite. **People Population:** 5,363,669 (July 2011 est.). **Nationality:** *noun:* Sierra Leonean(s); *adj.*: Sierra Leonean. **Ethnic groups:** Temne 35%, Mende 31%, Limba 8%, Kono 5%, Kriole 2% (descendants of freed Jamaican slaves who were settled in the Freetown area in the late-18th century; also known as Kiro), Mandingo 2%, Loko 2%, other 15% (includes refugees from Liberia's recent civil war, and small numbers of Europeans, Lebanese, Pakistanis, and Indians) (2008 census). **Religions:** Muslim 60%, indigenous beliefs 30%, Christian 10%. **Languages:** English (official, regular use limited to literate minority), Mende (principal vernacular in the south), Temne (principal vernacular in the north), Krio (English-based Creole, spoken by the descendants of freed Jamaican slaves who were settled in the Freetown area, a lingua franca and a first language for 10% of the population but understood by 95%). **Government Government type:** constitutional democracy. **Capital:** Freetown. **Independence:** 27 April 1961 (from U.K.). **National holiday:** Independence Day, 27 April (1961). **Economy G.D.P.:** purchasing power parity—$4.812 billion (2010 est.). **G.D.P.—per capita:** purchasing power parity—$900 (2010 est.). **Currency:** leone (SLL).

Singapore

Republic of Singapore

Geography Location: Southeastern Asia, islands between Malaysia and Indonesia. **Area:** 244 sq. mi. (633 sq km). **Natural resources:** fish, deepwater ports. **People Population:** 4,740,737 (July 2011 est.). **Nationality:** *noun:* Singaporean(s); *adj.*: Singapore. **Ethnic groups:** Chinese 76.8%, Malay 13.9%, Indian 7.9%, other 1.4% (2000 census). **Religions:** Buddhist 42.5%, Muslim 14.9%, Taoist 8.5%,

Hindu 4%, Catholic 4.8%, other Christian 9.8%, other 0.7%, none 14.8% (2000 census). **Languages:** Mandarin (official) 35%, English (official) 23%, Malay (official) 14.1%, Hokkien 11.4%, Cantonese 5.7%, Teochew 4.9%, Tamil (official) 3.2%, other Chinese dialects 1.8%, other 0.9% (2000 census). **Government Government type:** parliamentary republic. **Capital:** Singapore. **Independence:** 9 August 1965 (from Malaysian Federation). **National holiday:** Independence Day, 9 August (1965). **Economy G.D.P.:** purchasing power parity—$292.4 billion (2010 est.). **G.D.P.—per capita:** purchasing power parity—$57,200 (2010 est.). **Currency:** Singapore dollar (SGD).

Slovakia

Slovak Republic

Geography Location: Central Europe, south of Poland. **Area:** 18,859 sq. mi. (48,845 sq km). **Border countries:** Austria, Czech Republic, Hungary, Poland, Ukraine. **Natural resources:** brown coal and lignite; small amounts of iron ore, copper and manganese ore; salt; arable land. **People Population:** 5,477,038 (July 2011 est.). **Nationality:** noun: Slovak(s); adj.: Slovak. **Ethnic groups:** Slovak 85.8%, Hungarian 9.7%, Roma 1.7%, Ruthenian and Ukrainian 1% other and unspecified 2.6% (2001 census). **Religions:** Roman Catholic 68.9%, Greek Catholic 4.1%, Protestant 10.8%, other/unspecified 3.2%, none 13% (2001 census). **Languages:** Slovak (official) 83.9%, Hungarian 10.7%, Roma 1.8%, Ukrainian 1%, other /unspecified 2.6% (2001 census). **Government Government type:** parliamentary democracy. **Capital:** Bratislava. **Independence:** 1 January 1993 (Czechoslovakia split into the Czech Republic and Slovakia). **National holiday:** Constitution Day, 1 September (1992). **Economy G.D.P.:** purchasing power parity—$121.3 billion (2010 est.). **G.D.P.—per capita:** purchasing power parity—$22,200 (2010 est.). **Currency:** Slovak koruna (SKK).

Slovenia

Republic of Slovenia

Geography Location: Central Europe, eastern Alpa bordering the Adriatic Sea, between Austria and Croatia. **Area:** 7,836 sq mi (20,296 sq km). **Border countries:** Austria, Croatia, Hungary, Italy. **Natural resources:** lignite coal, lead, zinc, building stone, hydropower, forests. **People Population:** 2,000,092 (July 2011 est.). **Nationality:** noun: Slovene(s); adj.: Slovenian. **Ethnic groups:** Slovene 83.1%, Serb 2%, Croat 1.8%, Bosniak 1.1%, other or unspecified 12% (2002 census). **Religions:** Catholic 57.8%, Muslim 2.4%, Orthodox 2.3%, other Christian 0.9%, unaffiliated 3.5%, other /unspecified 23%, none 10.1% (2002 census). **Languages:** Slovenian (official) 91.1%, Serbo-Croatian 4.5%, other or unspecified 4.4%, Italian (official), Hungarian (official), only

in municipalities where Hungarian national communities reside. **Government Government type:** parliamentary republic. **Capital:** Ljubljana. **Independence:** 25 June 1991 (from Yugoslavia). **National holiday:** Independence Day/Statehood Day, 25 June (1991). **Economy G.D.P.:** purchasing power parity—$56.81 billion (2010 est.). **G.D.P.—per capita:** purchasing power parity—$28,400 (2010 est.). **Currency:** euro (EUR).

Solomon Islands

Geography Location: Oceania, group of islands in the South Pacific Ocean, east of Papua New Guinea. **Area:** 10,985 sq. mi. (28,450 sq km). **Natural resources:** fish, forests, gold, bauxite, phosphates, lead, zinc, nickel. **People Population:** 571,890 (July 2011 est.). **Nationality:** noun: Solomon Islander(s); adj.: Solomon Islander. **Ethnic groups:** Melanesian 94.5%, Polynesian 3%, Micronesian 1.2%, other 1.1%, unspecified 0.2% (1999 census). **Religions:** Church of Melanesia 32.8%, Roman Catholic 19%, South Seas Evangelical 17%, Seventh-Day Adventist 11.2%, United Church 10.3%, Christian Fellowship Church 2.4%, other Christian 4.4%, other 2.4%, unspecified 0.3%, none 0.2% (1999 census). **Languages:** Melanesian pidgin in much of the country is lingua franca; English is official but spoken by only 1%–2% of the population. note: 120 indigenous languages. **Government Government type:** parliamentary democracy. **Capital:** Honiara. **Independence:** 7 July 1978 (from U.K.). **National holiday:** Independence Day, 7 July (1978). **Economy G.D.P.:** purchasing power parity—$1.559 billion (2010 est.). **G.D.P.—per capita:** purchasing power parity—$2,800 (2010 est.). **Currency:** Solomon Islands dollar (SBD).

Somalia

Geography Location: Eastern Africa, bordering the Gulf of Aden and the Indian Ocean, east of Ethiopia. **Area:** 246,201 sq. mi. (637,657 sq km). **Border countries:** Djibouti, Ethiopia, Kenya. **Natural resources:** uranium and largely unexploited reserves of iron ore, tin, gypsum, bauxite, copper, salt, natural gas, likely oil reserves. **People Population:** 9,925,640 (July 2011 est.). **Nationality:** noun: Somali(s); adj.: Somali. **Ethnic groups:** Somali 85%, Bantu and other non-Somali 15% (including Arabs 30,000). **Religions:** Sunni Muslim. **Languages:** Somali (official), Arabic, Italian, English. **Government Government type:** no permanent national government; transitional, parliamentary national government. **Capital:** Mogadishu. **Independence:** 1 July 1960 (from a merger of British Somaliland, which became independent from the U.K. on 26 June 1960, and Italian Somaliland, which became independent from the Italian-administered UN trusteeship on 1 July

1960, to form the Somali Republic). **National holiday:** Foundation of the Somali Republic, 1 July (1960); note: 26 June (1960) in Somaliland. **Economy G.D.P.:** purchasing power parity—$5.896 billion (2010 est.). **G.D.P.—per capita:** purchasing power parity—$600 (2010 est.). **Currency:** Somali shilling (SOS).

South Africa

Republic of South Africa

Geography   Location: Southern Africa, at the southern tip of the continent of Africa. **Area:** 471,444 sq. mi. (1,221,040 sq km). **Border countries:** Botswana, Lesotho, Mozambique, Namibia, Swaziland, Zimbabwe. **Natural resources:** gold, chromium, antimony, coal, iron ore, manganese, nickel, phosphates, tin, rare earth elements, uranium, gem diamonds, platinum, copper, vanadium, salt, natural gas. **People Population** 49,004,031 (July 2011 est.) note: estimates for this country explicitly take into account the effects of excess mortality due to AIDS; this can result in lower life expectancy, higher infant mortality and death rates, lower population and growth rates, and changes in the distribution of population by age and sex than would otherwise be expected. **Nationality:** noun: South African(s); adj.: South African. **Ethnic groups:** black African 79%, white 9.6%, colored 8.9%, Indian/Asian 2.5% (2001 census). **Religions:** Zionist Christian 11.1%, Pentecostal/Charismatic 8.2%, Catholic 7.1%, Methodist 6.8%, Dutch Reformed 6.7%, Anglican 3.8%, other Christian 36%, Muslim 1.5%, other 2.3%, unspecified 1.4%, none 15.1% (2001 census). **Languages:** IsiZulu (official) 23.8%, IsiXhosa (official) 17.6%, Afrikaans (official) 13.3%, Sepedi (official) 9.4%, English (official) 8.2%, Setswana (official) 8.2%, Sesotho (official) 7.9%, Xitsonga (official) 4.4%, other 7.2%, isiNdebele (official), Tshivenda (official), siSwati (official) (2001 census). **Government   Government type:** Republic. **Capital:** Pretoria; note: Cape Town is the legislative center and Johannesburg the judicial center. **Independence:** 31 May 1910 (from U.K.). **National holiday:** Freedom Day, 27 April (1994). **Economy G.D.P.:** purchasing power parity—$527.5 billion (2010 est.). **G.D.P.—per capita:** purchasing power parity—$10,700 (2010 est.). **Currency:** rand (ZAR).

Spain

Kingdom of Spain

Geography   Location: Southwestern Europe, bordering the Bay of Biscay, Mediterranean Sea, North Atlantic Ocean, and Pyrenees Mountains, southwest of France. **Area:** 194,884 sq. mi. (504,750 sq km). **Border countries:** Andorra, France, Gibraltar, Portugal, Morocco (Ceuta), Morocco (Melilla).

Natural resources: coal, lignite, iron ore, copper, lead, zinc, uranium, tungsten, mercury, pyrites, magnesite, fluorspar, gypsum, sepiolite, kaolin, potash, hydropower, arable land. **People Population:** 46,754,784 (July 2011 est.). **Nationality:** noun: Spaniard(s); adj.: Spanish. **Ethnic groups:** composite of Mediterranean and Nordic types. **Religions:** Roman Catholic 94%, other 6%. **Languages:** Castilian Spanish (official) 74%, Catalan 17%, Galician 7%, Basque 2% note: Castillian is the official language nationwide; the other languages are official regionally. **Government   Government type:** parliamentary monarchy. **Capital:** Madrid. **Independence:** the Iberian peninsula was characterized by a variety of independent kingdoms prior to the Moslem occupation that began in the early eighth century A.D. and lasted nearly seven centuries; the small Christian redoubts of the north began the reconquest almost immediately, culminating in the seizure of Granada in 1492; this event completed the unification of several kingdoms and is traditionally considered the forging of present-day Spain. **National holiday:** Hispanic Day, 12 October. **Economy G.D.P.:** purchasing power parity—$1.376 trillion (2010 est.). **G.D.P.—per capita:** purchasing power parity—$29,500 (2010 est.). **Currency:** euro (EUR).

Sri Lanka

Democratic Socialist Republic of Sri Lanka

Geography   Location: Southern Asia, island in the Indian Ocean, south of India. **Area:** 25,332 sq. mi. (65,610 sq km). **Natural resources:** limestone, graphite, mineral sands, gems, phosphates, clay, hydropower. **People Population:** 21,283,913 (July 2011 est.) note: since the outbreak of hostilities between the government and armed Tamil separatists in the mid-1980s, several hundred thousand Tamil civilians have fled the island; as of yearend 2000, approximately 65,000 were housed in 131 refugee camps in south India, another 40,000 lived outside the Indian camps, and more than 200,000 Tamils have sought refuge in the West. **Nationality:** noun: Sri Lankan(s); adj.: Sri Lankan. **Ethnic groups:** Sinhalese 73.8%, Indian Tamil 4.6%, Sri Lankan Moor 7.2%, Sri Lankan Tamil 3.9%, other 0.5%, unspecified 10% (2001 census). **Religions:** Buddhist 69.1%, Hindu 7.1%, Christian 6.2%, Muslim 7.6%, unspecified 10% (2001 census). **Languages:** Sinhala (official and national language) 74%, Tamil (national language) 18%, other 8% note: English is commonly used in government and is spoken competently by about 10% of the population **Government   Government type:** republic. **Capital:** Colombo; note: Sri Jayewardenepura Kotte is the legislative capital. **Independence:** 4 February 1948 (from U.K.). **National holiday:** Independence Day, 4 February (1948). **Economy G.D.P.:** purchasing power parity—$104.7 billion (2010 est.). **G.D.P.—per capita:** purchasing power parity—$4,900 (2010 est.). **Currency:** Sri Lankan rupee (LKR).

Sudan

Republic of the Sudan

Geography   Location: Northern Africa, bordering the Red Sea, between Egypt and Eritrea. **Area:** 967,495 sq. mi. (2,505,810 sq km). **Border countries:** Central African Republic, Chad, Democratic Republic of the Congo, Egypt , Eritrea, Ethiopia, Kenya, Libya, Uganda. **Natural resources:** petroleum; small reserves of iron ore, copper, chromium ore, zinc, tungsten, mica, silver, gold, hydropower. **People Population:** 45,047,502 (July 2011 est.). **Nationality:** *noun:* Sudanese (singular and plural); *adj.:* Sudanese. **Ethnic groups:** black 52%, Arab 39%, Beja 6%, foreigners 2%, other 1%. **Religions:** Sunni Muslim 70% (in north), indigenous beliefs 25%, Christian 5% (mostly in south and Khartoum). **Languages:** Arabic (official), Nubian, Ta Bedawie, diverse dialects of Nilotic, Nilo-Hamitic, Sudanic languages, English *note:* program of "Arabization" in process. **Government   Government type:** Government of National Unity (GNU)—the National Congress Party (NCP) and Sudan's People's Liberation Movement (SPLM) formed a power-sharing government under the 2005 Comprehensive Peace Agreement (CPA); the NCP, which came to power by military coup in 1989, is the majority partner; the agreement stipulated national elections in 2009, but these were subsequently rescheduled for April 2010; elections took place in April 2010 and the NCP was elected as the majority party; due to CPA stipulations, there is also an autonomous government in Southern Sudan where SPLM holds the majority of positions. **Capital:** Khartoum. **Independence:** 1 January 1956 (from Egypt and U.K.). **National holiday:** Independence Day, 1 January (1956). **Economy   G.D.P.:** purchasing power parity—$98.79 billion (2010 est.). **G.D.P.—per capita:** purchasing power parity—$2,200 (2010 est.). **Currency:** Sudanese dinar (SDD).

Note: In 2011, the nation divided peacefully, creating the new country of South Sudan.

Suriname

Republic of Suriname

Geography   Location: Northern South America, bordering the North Atlantic Ocean, between French Guiana and Guyana. **Area:** 63,039 sq. mi. (163,270 sq km). **Border countries:** Brazil, French Guiana, Guyana. **Natural resources:** timber, hydropower, fish, kaolin, shrimp, bauxite, gold, and small amounts of nickel, copper, platinum, iron ore. **People**

Population: 491,989 (July 2011 est.). **Nationality:** *noun:* Surinamer(s); *adj.:* Surinamese. **Ethnic groups:** Hindustani (also known locally as "East Indians"; their ancestors emigrated from northern India in the latter part of the 19th century) 37%, Creole (mixed white and black) 31%, Javanese 15%, "Maroons" (their African ancestors were brought to the country in the 17th and 18th centuries as slaves and escaped to the interior) 10%, Amerindian 2%, Chinese 2%, white 1%, other 2%. **Religions:** Hindu 27.4%, Muslim 19.6%, Roman Catholic 22.8%, Protestant 25.2% (predominantly Moravian), indigenous beliefs 5%. **Languages:** Dutch (official), English (widely spoken), Sranang Tongo (Surinamese, sometimes called Taki-Taki, is native language of Creoles and much younger population and is lingua franca among others), Caribbean Hindustani (a dialect of Hindi), Javanese. **Government   Government type:** constitutional democracy. **Capital:** Paramaribo. **Independence:** 25 November 1975 (from Netherlands). **National holiday:** Independence Day, 25 November (1975). **Economy   G.D.P.:** purchasing power parity—$4.794 billion (2010 est.). **G.D.P.—per capita:** purchasing power parity—$9,900 (2010 est.). **Currency:** Surinam dollar (SRD).

Swaziland

Kingdom of Swaziland

Geography   Location: Southern Africa, between Mozambique and South Africa. **Area:** 6,703 sq. mi. (17,363 sq km). **Border countries:** Mozambique, South Africa. **Natural resources:** asbestos, coal, clay, cassiterite, hydropower, forests, small gold and diamond deposits, quarry stone, and talc. **People Population:** 1,370,424 (July 2011 est.) *note:* estimates for this country explicitly take into account the effects of excess mortality due to AIDS; this can result in lower life expectancy, higher infant mortality and death rates, lower population and growth rates, and changes in the distribution of population by age and sex than would otherwise be expected. **Nationality:** *noun:* Swazi(s); *adj.:* Swazi. **Ethnic groups:** African 97%, European 3%. **Religions:** Zionist 40% (a blend of Christianity and indigenous ancestral worship), Roman Catholic 20%, Muslim 10%, other (includes Anglican, Bahai, Methodist, Mormon, Jewish) 30%. **Languages:** English (official, government business conducted in English), siSwati (official). **Government   Government type:** monarchy. **Capital:** Mbabane; *note:* Lobamba is the royal and legislative capital. **Independence:** 6 September 1968 (from U.K.). **National holiday:** Independence Day, 6 September (1968). **Economy G.D.P.:** purchasing power parity—$6.055 billion (2010 est.). **G.D.P.—per capita:** purchasing power parity—$4,500 (2010 est.). **Currency:** lilangeni (SZL).

Sweden

Kingdom of Sweden

Geography   Location: Northern Europe, bordering the Baltic Sea, Gulf of Bothnia, Kattegat, and Skagerrak, between Finland and Norway. **Area:** 173,731 sq. mi. (449,964 sq km). **Border countries:** Finland, Norway. **Natural resources:** zinc, iron ore, gold, tungsten, arsenic, lead, copper, silver, timber, uranium, feldpsar, hydropower. **People Population:** 9,088,728 (July 2011 est.). **Nationality:** *noun:* Swede(s); *adj.:* Swedish. **Ethnic groups:** indigenous population: Swedes with Finnish and Sami minorities; foreign-born or first-generation immigrants: Finns, Yugoslavs, Danes, Norwegians, Greeks, Turks. **Religions:** Lutheran 87%, other (includes Roman Catholic, Orthodox, Baptist, Muslim, Jewish, and Buddhist) 13%. **Languages:** Swedish; *note:* small Sami- and Finnish-speaking minorities. **Government   Government type:** constitutional monarchy. **Capital:** Stockholm. **Independence:** 6 June 1523 (Gustav Vasa elected king). **National holiday:** National Day, 6 June. **Economy G.D.P.:** purchasing power parity—$354 billion (2010 est.). **G.D.P.—per capita:** purchasing power parity—$39,000 (2010 est.). **Currency:** Swedish krona (SEK).

Switzerland

Swiss Confederation

Geography   Location: Central Europe, east of France, north of Italy. **Area:** 15,942 sq. mi. (41,290 sq km). **Border countries:** Austria, France, Italy, Liechtenstein, Germany. **Natural resources:** hydropower potential, timber, salt. **People Population:** 7,639,961 (July 2011 est.). **Nationality:** *noun:* Swiss (singular and plural); *adj.:* Swiss. **Ethnic groups:** German 65%, French 18%, Italian 10%, Romansch 1%, other 6%. **Religions:** Roman Catholic 41.8%, Protestant 35.3%, Orthodox 1.8%, other Christian 0.4%, Muslim 4.3%, other 1%, unspecified 4.3%, none 11.1% (2000 census). **Languages:** German (official) 63.7%, French (official) 20.4%, Italian (official) 6.5%, Serbo-Croatian 1.5%, Albanian 1.3%, Portuguese 1.2%, Spanish 1.1%, English 1%, Romansch 0.5%, other 2.8% (2000 census) *note:* German, French, Italian, and Romansch are all national languages, but only the first three are official languages. **Government   Government type:** formally a confederation, but similar in structure to a federal republic. **Capital:** Bern. **Independence:** 1 August 1291 (Founding of the Swiss Confederation). **National holiday:** Founding of the Swiss Confederation, 1 August (1291). **Economy G.D.P.:** purchasing power parity—$326.9 billion (2010 est.). **G.D.P.—per capita:** purchasing power parity—$42,900 (2010 est.). **Currency:** Swiss franc (CHF).

Syria

Syrian Arab Republic

Geography Location: Middle East, bordering the Mediterranean Sea, between Lebanon and Turkey. **Area:** 71,498 sq. mi. (185,180 sq km). **Border countries:** Iraq, Israel, Jordan, Lebanon, Turkey. **Natural resources:** petroleum, phosphates, chrome and manganese ores, asphalt, iron ore, rock salt, marble, gypsum, hydropower. **People Population:** 22,517,750 (July 2010 est.) *note:* approximately 19,100 Israeli settlers live in the Golan Heights (2008 est.). **Nationality:** *noun:* Syrian(s); *adj.:* Syrian. **Ethnic groups:** Arab 90.3%, Kurds, Armenians, and other 9.7%. **Religions:** Sunni Muslim 74%, other Muslim (includes Alawite, Druze) 16%, Christian (various denominations 10%, Jewish (tiny communities in Damascus, Al Qamishli, and Aleppo). **Languages:** Arabic (official); Kurdish, Armenian, Aramaic, Circassian widely understood; French, English somewhat understood. **Government   Government type:** rrepublic under an authoritarian, military-dominated regime. **Capital:** Damascus. **Independence:** 17 April 1946 (from League of Nations mandate under French administration). **National holiday:** Independence Day, 17 April (1946). **Economy G.D.P.:** purchasing power parity—$106.4 billion (2010 est.). **G.D.P.—per capita:** purchasing power parity—$4,800 (2010 est.). **Currency:** Syrian pound (SYP).

Taiwan

Geography   Location: Eastern Asia, islands bordering the East China Sea, Philippine Sea, South China Sea, and Taiwan Strait, north of the Philippines, off the southeastern coast of China. **Area:** 13,892 sq. mi. (35,980 sq km). **Natural resources:** small deposits of coal, natural gas, limestone, marble, and asbestos. **People Population:** 23,071,779 (July 2011 est.). **Nationality:** *noun:* Taiwan (singular and plural); *adj.:* Taiwan. **Ethnic groups:** Taiwanese (including Hakka) 84%, mainland Chinese 14%, indigenous 2%. **Religions:** mixture of Buddhist and Taoist 93%, Christian 4.5%, other 2.5%. **Languages:** Mandarin Chinese (official), Taiwanese (Min), Hakka dialects. **Government   Government type:** multiparty democracy. **Capital:** Taipei. **National holiday:** Republic Day (Anniversary of the Chinese Revolution), 10 October (1911). **Economy G.D.P.:** purchasing power parity—$807.2 billion (2010 est.). **G.D.P.—per capita:** purchasing power parity—$35,100 (2010 est.). **Currency:** new Taiwan dollar (TWD).

Tajikistan

Republic of Tajikistan

Geography   Location: Central Asia, west of China. **Area:** 55,251 sq. mi. (143,100 sq km). **Border countries:**

Afghanistan, China, Kyrgyzstan, Uzbekistan. **Natural resources:** hydropower, some petroleum, uranium, mercury, brown coal, lead, zinc, antimony, tungsten, silver, gold. **People Population:** 7,627,200 (July 2011 est.). **Nationality:** *noun:* Tajikistani(s); *adj.:* Tajikistani. **Ethnic groups:** Tajik 79.9%, Uzbek 15.3%, Russian 1.1%, Kyrgyz 1.1%, other 2.6% (2000 census). **Religions:** Sunni Muslim 85%, Shi'a Muslim 5%, other 10% (2003 est.). **Languages:** Tajik (official), Russian widely used in government and business. **Government Government type:** republic. **Capital:** Dushanbe. **Independence:** 9 September 1991 (from Soviet Union). **National holiday:** Independence Day (or National Day), 9 September (1991). **Economy G.D.P.:** purchasing power parity—$14.61 billion (2010 est.). **G.D.P.—per capita:** purchasing power parity—$2,000 (2010 est.). **Currency:** somoni (TJS).

Tanzania

United Republic of Tanzania

Geography Location: Eastern Africa, bordering the Indian Ocean, between Kenya and Mozambique. **Area:** 364,900 sq. mi. (945,087 sq km). **Border countries:** Burundi, Democratic Republic of the Congo, Kenya, Malawi, Mozambique, Rwanda, Uganda, Zambia. **Natural resources:** hydropower, tin, phosphates, iron ore, coal, diamonds, gemstones, gold, natural gas, nickel. **People Population:** 42,746,620 (July 2011 est.) *note:* estimates for this country explicitly take into account the effects of excess mortality due to AIDS; this can result in lower life expectancy, higher infant mortality and death rates, lower population and growth rates, and changes in the distribution of population by age and sex than would otherwise be expected. **Nationality:** *noun:* Tanzanian(s); *adj.:* Tanzanian. **Ethnic groups:** mainland—native African 99% (of which 95% are Bantu consisting of more than 130 tribes), other 1% (consisting of Asian, European, and Arab); Zanzibar—Arab, native African, mixed Arab and native African. **Religions:** mainland—Christian 30%, Muslim 35%, indigenous beliefs 35%; Zanzibar—more than 99% Muslim. **Languages:** Kiswahili or Swahili (official), Kiunguja (name for Swahili in Zanzibar), English (official, primary language of commerce, administration, and higher education), Arabic (widely spoken in Zanzibar), many local languages; *note:* Kiswahili (Swahili) is the mother tongue of the Bantu people living in Zanzibar and nearby coastal Tanzania; although Kiswahili is Bantu in structure and origin, its vocabulary draw on a variety of sources including Arabic and English; it has become the lingua franca of central and eastern Africa; the first language of most people is one of the local languages. **Government Government type:** republic. **Capital:** Dar es Salaam; *note:* legislative offices have been transferred to Dodoma, which is planned as the new national capital; the National Assembly now meets there on regular basis.

Independence: 26 April 1964; Tanganyika became independent 9 December 1961 (from U.K.-administered U.N. trusteeship); Zanzibar became independent 19 December 1963 (from U.K.); Tanganyika united with Zanzibar 26 April 1964 to form the United Republic of Tanganyika and Zanzibar; renamed United Republic of Tanzania 29 October 1964. **National holiday:** Union Day (Tanganyika and Zanzibar), 26 April (1964). **Economy G.D.P.:** purchasing power parity—$62.22 billion (2010 est.). **G.D.P.—per capita:** purchasing power parity—$1,500 (2010 est.). **Currency:** Tanzanian shilling (TZS).

Thailand

Kingdom of Thailand

Geography Location: Southeastern Asia, bordering the Andaman Sea and the Gulf of Thailand, southeast of Burma. **Area:** 198,456 sq. mi. (514,000 sq km). **Border countries:** Burma, Cambodia, Laos, Malaysia. **Natural resources:** tin, rubber, natural gas, tungsten, tantalum, timber, lead, fish, gypsum, lignite, fluorite, arable land. **People Population:** 66,720,153 (July 2011 est.) *note:* estimates for this country explicitly take into account the effects of excess mortality due to AIDS; this can result in lower life expectancy, higher infant mortality and death rates, lower population and growth rates, and changes in the distribution of population by age and sex than would otherwise be expected. **Nationality:** *noun:* Thai (singular and plural); *adj.:* Thai. **Ethnic groups:** Thai 75%, Chinese 14%, other 11%. **Religions:** Buddhist 94.6%, Muslim 4.6%, Christianity 0.7%, other 0.1% (2000 census). **Languages:** Thai, English (secondary language of the elite), ethnic and regional dialects. **Government Government type:** constitutional monarchy. **Capital:** Bangkok. **Independence:** 1238 (traditional founding date; never colonized). **National holiday:** Birthday of King Phumiphon, 5 December (1927). **Economy G.D.P.:** purchasing power parity—$580.3 billion (2010 est.). **G.D.P.—per capita:** purchasing power parity—$8,700 (2010 est.). **Currency:** baht (THB).

Togo

Togolese Republic

Geography Location: Western Africa, bordering the Bight of Benin, between Benin and Ghana. **Area:** 21,927 sq. mi. (56,785 sq km). **Border countries:** Benin, Burkina Faso, Ghana. **Natural resources:** phosphates, limestone, marble, arable land. **People Population:** 6,771,993 (July 2011 est.) *note:* estimates for this country explicitly take into account the effects of excess mortality due to AIDS; this can result in lower life expectancy, higher infant mortality and death rates, lower population and growth rates, and changes in the distribution of population by age and sex than would otherwise be expected. **Nationality:** *noun:* Togolese (singular and plural); *adj.:* Togolese. **Ethnic groups:** African (37 tribes; largest and most important are Ewe, Mina, and Kabre) 99%, European and Syrian-Lebanese less than 1%. **Religions:** Christian 29%, Muslim 20%, indigenous beliefs 51%. **Languages:** French (official and the language of commerce), Ewe and Mina (the two major African languages in the south), Kabye (sometimes spelled Kabiye) and Dagomba (the two major African languages in the north). **Government Government type:** republic under transition to multiparty democratic rule. **Capital:** Lome. **Independence:** 27 April 1960 (from French-administered U.N. trusteeship). **National holiday:** Independence Day, 27 April (1960). **Economy G.D.P.:** purchasing power parity—$5.927 billion (2010 est.). **G.D.P.—per capita:** purchasing power parity— $900 (2010 est.). **Currency:** Communaute Financiere Africaine franc (XOF) *note:* responsible authority is the Central Bank of the West African states.

Tonga

Kingdom of Tonga

Geography   Location: Oceania, archipelago in the South Pacific Ocean, about two-thirds of the way from Hawaii to New Zealand. **Area:** 289 sq. mi. (748 sq km). **Natural resources:** fish, fertile soil. **People Population:** 105,916 (July 2011 est.). **Nationality:** *noun:* Tongan(s); *adj.:* Tongan. **Ethnic groups:** Polynesian, European. **Religions:** Christian (Free Wesleyan Church claims over 30,000 adherents). **Languages:** Tongan (official), English (official). **Government   Government type:** constitutional monarchy. **Capital:** Nuku'alofa. **Independence:** 4 June 1970 (from U.K. protectorate). **National holiday:** Emancipation Day, 4 June (1970). **Economy G.D.P.:** purchasing power parity— $767 million (2010 est.). **G.D.P.—per capita:** purchasing power parity—$6,300 (2010 est.). **Currency:** pa'anga (TOP).

Trinidad and Tobago

Republic of Trinidad and Tobago

Geography   Location: Caribbean, islands between the Caribbean Sea and the North Atlantic Ocean, northeast of Venezuela. **Area:** 1,981 sq. mi. (5,128 sq km). **Natural resources:** petroleum, natural gas, asphalt. **People Population:** 1,227,505 (July 2011 est.). **Nationality:** *noun:* Trinidadian(s), Tobagonian(s); *adj.:* Trinidadian, Tobagonian. **Ethnic groups:** Indian (South Asian) 40%, African 37.5%, mixed 20.5%, other 1.2%, unspecified 0.8% (2000 census). **Religions:** Roman Catholic 26%, Hindu 22.5%, Anglican 7.8%, Baptist 7.2%, Pentecostal 6.8%, other Christian 5.8%, Muslim 5.8%, Seventh-Day Adventist 4%, other 10.8%, unspecified 1.4%, none 1.9% (2000 census). **Languages:**

English (official), Caribbean Hindustani (a dialect of Hindi), French, Spanish, Chinese. **Government Government type:** parliamentary democracy. **Capital:** Port-of-Spain. **Independence:** 31 August 1962 (from U.K.). **National holiday:** Independence Day, 31 August (1962). **Economy G.D.P.:** purchasing power parity—$27.1 billion (2010 est.). **G.D.P.— per capita:** purchasing power parity—$22,100 (2010 est.). **Currency:** Trinidad and Tobago dollar (TTD).

Tunisia

Tunisian Republic

Geography   Location: Northern Africa, bordering the Mediterranean Sea, between Algeria and Libya. **Area:** 63,170 sq. mi. (163,610 sq km). **Border countries:** Algeria, Libya. **Natural resources:** petroleum, phosphates, iron ore, lead, zinc, salt. **People Population:** 10,629,186 (July 2011 est.). **Nationality:** *noun:* Tunisian(s); *adj.:* Tunisian. **Ethnic groups:** Arab 98%, European 1%, Jewish and other 1%. **Religions:** Muslim 98%, Christian 1%, Jewish and other 1%. **Languages:** Arabic (official and one of the languages of commerce), French (commerce). **Government Government type:** republic. **Capital:** Tunis. **Independence:** 20 March 1956 (from France). **National holiday:** Independence Day, 20 March (1956). **Economy G.D.P.:** purchasing power parity—$100.3 billion (2010 est.). **G.D.P.—per capita:** purchasing power parity—$9,500 (2010 est.). **Currency:** Tunisian dinar (TND).

Turkey

Republic of Turkey

Geography Location: southeastern Europe and southwestern Asia (that portion of Turkey west of the Bosporus is geographically part of Europe), bordering the Black Sea, between Bulgaria and Georgia, and bordering the Aegean Sea and the Mediterranean Sea, between Greece and Syria. **Area:** 301,382 sq. mi. (780,580 sq km). **Border countries:** Armenia, Azerbaijan, Bulgaria, Georgia, Greece, Iran, Iraq, Syria. **Natural resources:** coal, iron ore, copper, chromium, antimony, mercury, gold, barite, borate, celestite (strontium), emery, feldspar, limestone, magnesite, marble, perlite, pumice, pyrites (sulfur), clay, arable land, hydropower. **People Population:** 78,785,548 (July 2011 est.). **Nationality:** *noun:* Turk(s); *adj.:* Turkish. **Ethnic groups:** Turkish 70–75%, Kurdish 18%, other minorities 7–12% (2008 est.). **Religions:** Muslim 99.8% (mostly Sunni), other 0.2% (mostly Christian and Jews). **Languages:** Turkish (official), Kurdish, other minority languages. **Government   Government type:** republican parliamentary democracy. **Capital:** Ankara. **Independence:** 29 October 1923 (successor state to the Ottoman Empire). **National holiday:** Independence Day, 29

October (1923). **Economy G.D.P.:** purchasing power parity—$958.3 billion (2010 est.). **G.D.P.—per capita:** purchasing power parity—$12,300 (2010 est.). **Currency:** Turkish lira (YTL).

Turkmenistan

Geography Location: Central Asia, bordering the Caspian Sea, between Iran and Kazakhstan **Area:** 188,456 sq. mi. (488,100 sq km). **Border countries:** Afghanistan, Iran, Kazakhstan, Uzbekistan. **Natural resources:** petroleum, natural gas, coal, sulfur, salt **People Population:** 4,997,503 (July 2011 est.). **Nationality:** *noun:* Turkmen(s) *adj.:* Turkmen. **Ethnic groups:** Turkmen 85%, Uzbek 5%, Russian 4%, other 6% (2003). **Religions:** Muslim 89%, Eastern Orthodox 9%, unknown 2%. **Languages:** Turkmen (official) 72%, Russian 12%, Uzbek 9%, other 7%. **Government Government type:** defines itself as a secular democracy and a presidential republic; in actuality displays authoritarian presidential rule, with power concentrated within the presidential administration. **Capital:** Ashgabat. **Independence:** 27 October 1991 (from the Soviet Union). **National holiday:** Independence Day, 27 October (1991). **Economy G.D.P.:** purchasing power parity—$36.64 billion (2010 est.). **G.D.P.—per capita:** purchasing power parity—$7,400 (2010 est.). **Currency:** Turkmen manat (TMM).

Tuvalu

Geography Location: Oceania, island group consisting of nine coral atolls in the South Pacific Ocean, about one-half of the way from Hawaii to Australia. **Area:** 10 sq. mi. (26 sq km). **Natural resources:** fish. **People Population:** 10,544 (July 2011 est.). **Nationality:** *noun:* Tuvaluan(s); *adj.:* Tuvaluan. **Ethnic groups:** Polynesian 96%, Micronesian 4%. **Religions:** Church of Tuvalu (Congregationalist) 97%, Seventh-Day Adventist 1.4%, Baha'i 1%, other 0.6%. **Languages:** Tuvaluan (official), English (official), Samoan, Kiribati (on the island of Nui). **Government Government type:** constitutional monarchy with a parliamentary democracy. **Capital:** Funafuti. **Independence:** 1 October 1978 (from U.K.). **National holiday:** Independence Day, 1 October (1978). **Economy G.D.P.:** purchasing power parity—$14.94 million (2002 est.). **G.D.P.—per capita:** purchasing power parity—$1,600 (2002 est.). **Currency:** Australian dollar (AUD); *note:* there is also a Tuvaluan dollar.

Uganda

Republic of Uganda

Geography Location: Eastern Africa, west of Kenya. **Area:** 91,135 sq. mi. (236,040 sq km). **Border countries:** Democratic Republic of the Congo, Kenya, Rwanda, Sudan, Tanzania. **Natural resources:** copper, cobalt, hydropower, limestone, salt, arable land, gold. **People Population:** 34,612,250 (July 2011 est.) *note:* estimates for this country explicitly take into account the effects of excess mortality due to AIDS; this can result in lower life expectancy, higher infant mortality and death rates, lower population and growth rates, and changes in the distribution of population by age and sex than would otherwise be expected. **Nationality:** *noun:* Ugandan(s); *adj.:* Ugandan. **Ethnic groups:** Baganda 16.9%, Banyakole 9.5%, Basoga 8.4%, Bakiga 6.9%, Iteso 6.4%, Langi 6.1%, Acholi 4.7%, Bagisu 4.6%, Lugbara 4.2%, Bunyoro 2.7%, other 29.6% (2002 census). **Religions:** Roman Catholic 41.9%, Protestant 42% (Anglican 35.9%, Pentecostal 4.6%, Seventh-Day Adventist 1.5%), Muslim 12.1%, other 3.1%, none 0.9% (2002 census). **Languages:** English (official national language, taught in grade schools, used in courts of law and by most newspapers and some radio broadcasts), Ganda or Luganda (most widely used of the Niger-Congo languages, preferred for native language publications in the capital and may be taught in school), other Niger-Congo languages, Nilo-Saharan languages, Swahili, Arabic. **Government Government type:** republic. **Capital:** Kampala. **Independence:** 9 October 1962 (from U.K.). **National holiday:** Independence Day, 9 October (1962). **Economy G.D.P.:** purchasing power parity—$41.7 billion (2010 est.). **G.D.P.—per capita:** purchasing power parity—$1,200 (2010 est.). **Currency:** Ugandan shilling (UGX).

Ukraine

Geography Location: Eastern Europe, bordering the Black Sea, between Poland and Russia. **Area:** 233,089 sq. mi. (603,700 sq km). **Border countries:** Belarus, Hungary, Moldova, Poland, Romania (south), Romania (west), Russia, Slovakia. **Natural resources:** iron ore, coal, manganese, natural gas, oil, salt, sulfur, graphite, titanium, magnesium, kaolin, nickel, mercury, timber, arable land. **People Population:** 45,134,707 (July 2011 est.). **Nationality:** *noun:* Ukrainian(s); *adj.:* Ukrainian. **Ethnic groups:** Ukrainian 77.8%, Russian 17.3%, Belarusian 0.6%, Moldovan 0.5%, Crimean Tatar 0.5%, Bulgarian 0.4%, Hungarian 0.3%, Romanian 0.3%, Polish 0.3%, Jewish 0.2%, other 1.8% (2001). **Religions:** Ukrainian Orthodox—Kyiv Patriarchate 50.4%, Ukrainian Orthodox—Moscow Patriarchate 26.1%, Ukrainian Greek Catholic 8%, Ukrainian Autocephalous Orthodox 7.2%, Roman Catholic 2.2%, Protestant 2.2%, Jewish 0.6%, other 3.2% (2006 est.). **Languages:** Ukrainian (official) 67%, Russian 24%, other 9% (includes small Romanian-, Polish-, and Hungarian-speaking minorities). **Government Government type:** republic. **Capital:** Kiev (Kyiv). **Independence:** 24 August 1991 (from the Soviet Union). **National holiday:** Independence Day, 24 August

(1991); the date of 22 January (1918), the day Ukraine first declared its independence (from Soviet Russia), is now celebrated as Unity Day. **Economy G.D.P.:** purchasing power parity—$306.3 billion (2010 est.). **G.D.P.—per capita:** purchasing power parity—$6,700 (2010 est.). **Currency:** hryvnia (UAH).

United Arab Emirates

United Arab Emirates

Geography Location: Middle East, bordering the Gulf of Oman and the Persian Gulf, between Oman and Saudi Arabia. **Area:** 31,969 sq mi (82,880 sq km). **Border countries:** Oman, Saudi Arabia. **Natural resources:** petroleum, natural gas. **People Population:** 5,148,664 note: estimate is based on the results of the 2005 census that included a significantly higher estimate of net immigration of non-citizens than previous estimates (July 2011 est.). **Nationality:** *noun:* Emirati(s); *adj.:* Emirati. **Ethnic groups:** Emirati 19%, other Arab and Iranian 23%, South Asian 50%, other expatriates (includes Westerners and East Asians) 8% (1982) *note:* less than 20% are UAE citizens (1982). **Religions:** Muslim 96% (Shi'a 16%), Christian, Hindu, and other 4%. **Languages:** Arabic (official), Persian, English, Hindi, Urdu. **Government Government type:** federation with specified powers delegated to the UAE federal government and other powers reserved to member emirates. **Capital:** Abu Dhabi. **Independence:** 2 December 1971 (from U.K.). **National holiday:** Independence Day, 2 December (1971). **Economy G.D.P.:** purchasing power parity—$199.8 billion (2010 est.). **G.D.P.—per capita:** purchasing power parity—$40,200 (2010 est.). **Currency:** Emirati dirham (AED).

United Kingdom

United Kingdom of Great Britain and Northern Ireland

Geography Location: Western Europe, islands including the northern one-sixth of the island of Ireland between the North Atlantic Ocean and the North Sea, northwest of France. **Area:** 94,525 sq. mi. (244,820 sq km). **Border countries:** Ireland. **Natural resources:** coal, petroleum, natural gas, tin, limestone, iron ore, salt, clay, chalk, gypsum, lead, silica, arable land. **People Population:** 62,698,362 (July 2011 est.). **Nationality:** *noun:* Briton(s), British (collective plural); *adj.:* British. **Ethnic groups:** English 83.6%, Scottish 8.6%, Northern Irish 2.9%, Welsh 4.9%, black 2%, Indian 1.8%, Pakistani 1.3%, mixed 1.2%, other 1.6% (2001 census). **Religions:** Christian (Anglican, Roman Catholic, Presbyterian, Methodist) 71.6%, Muslim 2.7%, Hindu 1%, other 1.6%, unspecified or none 23.1% (2001 census). **Languages:** English *note:* the following are recognized regional languages; Scots (about 30% of the population of Scotland), Welsh (about 20% of the population of Wales), Irish (about 10% of

the population of Northern Ireland), Cornish (some 2,000 to 3,000 in Cornwall). **Government Government type:** constitutional monarchy. **Capital:** London. **Independence:** England has existed as a unified entity since the 10th century; the union between England and Wales, begun in 1284 with the Statute of Rhuddlan, was not formalized until 1536 with an Act of Union; in another Act of Union in 1707, England and Scotland agreed to permanently join as Great Britain; the legislative union of Great Britain and Ireland was implemented in 1801, with the adoption of the name the United Kingdom of Great Britain and Ireland; the Anglo-Irish treaty of 1921 formalized a partition of Ireland; six northern Irish counties remained part of the United Kingdom as Northern Ireland and the current name of the country, the United Kingdom of Great Britain and Northern Ireland, was adopted in 1927. **National holiday:** the United Kingdom does not celebrate one particular national holiday. **Economy G.D.P.:** purchasing power parity—$2.189 trillion (2010 est.). **G.D.P.—per capita:** purchasing power parity—$35,100 (2010 est.). **Currency:** British pound (GBP).

United States

United States of America

Geography Location: North America, bordering both the North Atlantic Ocean and the North Pacific Ocean, between Canada and Mexico. **Area:** 3,717,797 sq mi (9,629,091 sq km). **Border countries:** Canada, Mexico. **Natural resources:** coal, copper, lead, molybdenum, phosphates, rare earth elements, uranium, bauxite, gold, iron, mercury, nickel, potash, silver, tungsten, zinc, petroleum, natural gas, timber. **People Population:** 313,232,044 (July 2011 est.). **Nationality:** *noun:* American(s); *adj.:* American. **Ethnic groups:** white 79.96%, black 12.85%, Asian 4.43%, Amerindian and Alaska native 0.97%, native Hawaiian and other Pacific islander 0.18%, two or more races 1.61% (July 2007 estimate); *note:* a separate listing for Hispanic is not included because the U.S. Census Bureau considers Hispanic to mean a person of Latin American descent (including persons of Cuban, Mexican, or Puerto Rican origin) living in the U.S. who may be of any race or ethnic group (white, black, Asian, etc.). **Religions:** Protestant 51.3%, Roman Catholic 23.9%, Mormon 1.7%, other Christian 1.6%, Jewish 1.7%, Buddhist 0.7%, Muslim 0.6%, other or unspecified 2.5%, unaffiliated 12.1%, none 4% (2007 est.). **Languages:** English 82.1%, Spanish 10.7%, other Indo-European 3.8%, Asian and Pacific Island 2.7%, other .7% (2000 census) *note:* Hawaiian is an official language in the state of Hawaii. **Government Government type:** Constitution-based federal republic; strong democratic tradition. **Capital:** Washington, DC. **Independence:** 4 July 1776 (from Great Britain). **National holiday:** Independence Day, 4 July (1776). **Economy G.D.P.:** purchasing power parity—$14.72 trillion (2010 est.).

G.D.P.—per capita: purchasing power parity—$47,400 (2010 est.). **Currency:** U.S. dollar (USD).

Uruguay

Oriental Republic of Uruguay

Geography   Location: Southern South America, bordering the South Atlantic Ocean, between Argentina and Brazil. **Area:** 68,039 sq. mi. (176,220 sq km). **Border countries:** Argentina, Brazil. **Natural resources:** arable land, hydropower, minor minerals, fish. **People   Population:** 3,308,535 (July 2011 est.) **Ethnic groups:** white 88%, mestizo 8%, black 4%, Amerindian (practically nonexistent). **Religions:** Roman Catholic 47.1%, non-Catholic Christians 11.1%, nondenominational 23.2%, Jewish 0.3%, atheist or agnostic 17.2%, other 1.1% (2006). **Languages:** Spanish (official), Portunol, Brazilero (Portuguese-Spanish mix on the Brazilian frontier). **Government   Government type:** constitutional republic. **Capital:** Montevideo. **Independence:** 25 August 1825 (from Brazil). **National holiday:** Independence Day, 25 August (1825). **Economy   G.D.P.:** purchasing power parity—$47.8 billion (2010 est.). **G.D.P.—per capita:** purchasing power parity—$13,600 (2010 est.). **Currency:** Uruguayan peso (UYU).

Uzbekistan

Republic of Uzbekistan

Geography   Location: Central Asia, north of Afghanistan. **Area:** 172,741 sq. mi. (447,400 sq km). **Border countries:** Afghanistan, Kazakhstan, Kyrgyzstan, Tajikistan, Turkmenistan. **Natural resources:** natural gas, petroleum, coal, gold, uranium, silver, copper, lead and zinc, tungsten, molybdenum. **People   Population:** 28,128,600 (July 2011 est.). **Ethnic groups:** Uzbek 80%, Russian 5.5%, Tajik 5%, Kazakh 3%, Karakalpak 2.5%, Tatar 1.5%, other 2.5% (1996 est.). **Religions:** Muslim 88% (mostly Sunnis), Eastern Orthodox 9%, other 3%. **Languages:** Uzbek (official) 74.3%, Russian 14.2%, Tajik 4.4%, other 7.1%. **Government   Government type:** republic; authoritarian presidential rule, with little power outside the executive branch. **Capital:** Tashkent (Toshkent). **Independence:** 1 September 1991 (from Soviet Union). **National holiday:** Independence Day, 1 September (1991). **Economy   G.D.P.:** purchasing power parity—$86.07 billion (2010 est.). **G.D.P.—per capita:** purchasing power parity—$3,100 (2010 est.). **Currency:** Uzbekistani sum (UZS).

Vanuatu

Republic of Vanuatu

Geography   Location: Oceania, group of islands in the South Pacific Ocean, about three-quarters of the way from Hawaii to Australia. **Area:** 5,699 sq. mi. (14,760 sq km). **Natural resources:** manganese, hardwood forests, fish. **People   Population:** 224,564 (July 2011 est.). **Nationality:** *noun:* Ni-Vanuatu (singular and plural); *adj.:* Ni-Vanuatu. **Ethnic groups:** Ni-Vanuatu 98.5%, other 1.5% (1999 census). **Religions:** Presbyterian 31.4%, Anglican 13.4%, Roman Catholic 13.1%, indigenous beliefs (including Jon Frum cargo cult) 5.6%, Seventh-Day Adventist 10.8%, other Christian 13.8%, other 9.6%, none 1%, unspecified 1.3% (1999 census). **Languages:** local languages (more than 100) 72.6%, pidgin (known as Bislama or Bichelama) 23.1%, English (official) 1.9%, French (official) 1.4%, other 0.3%, unspecified 0.7% (1999 census). **Government   Government type:** parliamentary republic. **Capital:** Port-Vila. **Independence:** 30 July 1980 (from France and U.K.). **National holiday:** Independence Day, 30 July (1980). **Economy   G.D.P.:** purchasing power parity—$1.216 billion (2010 est.). **G.D.P.—per capita:** purchasing power parity—$5,500 (2010 est.). **Currency:** vatu (VUV).

Venezuela

Bolivarian Republic of Venezuela

Geography   Location: Northern South America, bordering the Caribbean Sea and the North Atlantic Ocean, between Colombia and Guyana. **Area:** 352,144 sq. mi. (912,050 sq km). **Border countries:** Brazil, Colombia, Guyana. **Natural resources:** petroleum, natural gas, iron ore, gold, bauxite, other minerals, hydropower, diamonds. **People   Population:** 27,635,743 (July 2011 est.). **Nationality:** *noun:* Venezuelan(s); *adj.:* Venezuelan. **Ethnic groups:** Spanish, Italian, Portuguese, Arab, German, African, indigenous people. **Religions:** nominally Roman Catholic 96%, Protestant 2%, other 2%. **Languages:** Spanish (official), numerous indigenous dialects. **Government   Government type:** federal republic. **Capital:** Caracas. **Independence:** 5 July 1811 (from Spain). **National holiday:** Independence Day, 5 July (1811). **Economy   G.D.P.:** purchasing power parity—$344.2 billion (2010 est.). **G.D.P.—per capita:** purchasing power parity—$12,600 (2010 est.). **Currency:** bolivar (VEB).

Vietnam

Socialist Republic of Vietnam

Geography   Location: Southeastern Asia, bordering the Gulf of Thailand, Gulf of Tonkin, and South China Sea, alongside China, Laos, and Cambodia. **Area:** 127,243 sq. mi. (329,560 sq km). **Border countries:** Cambodia, China, Laos. **Natural resources:** phosphates, coal, manganese, bauxite, chromate, offshore oil and gas deposits, forests, hydropower. **People   Population:** 90,549,390 (July 2011 est.). **Nationality:** *noun:* Vietnamese (singular and plural); *adj.:* Vietnamese. **Ethnic groups:** Kinh (Viet) 86.2%, Tay

1.9%, Thai 1.7%, Muong 1.5%, Khome 1.4%, Hoa 1.1%, Nun 1.1%, Hmong 1%, others 4.1% (1999 census). **Religions:** Buddhist 9.3%, Catholic 6.7%, Hoa Hao 1.5%, Cao Dai 1.1%, Protestant .5%, Muslim .1%, none 80.8% (1999 census). **Languages:** Vietnamese (official), English (increasingly favored as a second language), some French, Chinese and Khmer; mountain area languages (Mon-Khmer and Malayo-Polynesian). **Government** **Government type:** Communist state. **Capital:** Hanoi. **Independence:** 2 September 1945 (from France). **National holiday:** Independence Day, 2 September (1945). **Economy G.D.P.:** purchasing power parity—$278.1 billion (2010 est.). **G.D.P.—per capita:** purchasing power parity—$3,100 (2010 est.). **Currency:** dong (VND).

Yemen

Republic of Yemen

Geography **Location:** Middle East, bordering the Arabian Sea, Gulf of Aden, and Red Sea, between Oman and Saudi Arabia. **Area:** 203,850 sq. mi. (527,970 sq km). **Border countries:** Oman, Saudi Arabia. **Natural resources:** petroleum, fish, rock salt, marble; small deposits of coal, gold, lead, nickel, and copper; fertile foil in west. **People Population:** 24,133,492 (July 2011 est.). **Nationality:** *noun:* Yemeni(s); *adj.:* Yemeni. **Ethnic groups:** predominantly Arab; but also Afro-Arab, South Asians, Europeans. **Religions:** Muslim including Shaf'i (Sunni) and Zaydi (Shia), small numbers of Jewish, Christian, and Hindu. **Languages:** Arabic (official). **Government** **Government type:** republic. **Capital:** Sanaa. **Independence:** 22 May 1990, Republic of Yemen established with merger of the Yemen Arab Republic [Yemen (Sanaa) or North Yemen] and the Marxist-dominated People's Democratic Republic of Yemen [Yemen (Aden) or South Yemen]; North Yemen had become independent in November 1918 (from the Ottoman Empire) and South Yemen on 30 November 1967 (from the U.K.). **National holiday:** Unification Day, 22 May (1990). **Economy G.D.P.:** purchasing power parity—$61.88 billion (2010 est.). **G.D.P.—per capita:** purchasing power parity—$2,600 (2010 est.). **Currency:** Yemeni rial (YER).

Zambia

Republic of Zambia

Geography **Location:** Southern Africa, east of Angola. **Area:** 290,583 sq. mi. (752,614 sq km). **Border countries:** Angola, Democratic Republic of the Congo, Malawi, Mozambique, Namibia, Tanzania, Zimbabwe. **Natural resources:** copper, cobalt, zinc, lead, coal, emeralds, gold, silver, uranium, hydropower. **People Population:** 13,881,336 (July 2011 est.) *note:* estimates for this country explicitly take

into account the effects of excess mortality due to AIDS; this can result in lower life expectancy, higher infant mortality and death rates, lower population and growth rates, and changes in the distribution of population by age and sex than would otherwise be expected. **Nationality:** *noun:* Zambian(s); *adj.:* Zambian. **Ethnic groups:** African 99.5% (includes Bemba, Tonga, Chewa, Lozi, Nsenga, Tumbuka, Ngoni, Lal, Kaonde, Lunda, and other African groups), other 0.5% (includes Europeans, Asians, and Americans) (2000 census). **Religions:** Christian 50%–75%, Muslim and Hindu 24%–49%, indigenous beliefs 1%. **Languages:** Bemba 30.1% (official), Nyanja 10.7% (official), Tonga 10.6% (official), Lozi 5.7% (official), Chewa 4.9%, Nsenga 3.4%, Tumbuka 2.5%, Lunda 2.2% (official), Kaonde 2% (official), Lala 2%, Luvale 1.7% (official). English 1.7% (official), other 22.5% (2000 census). **Government** **Government type:** republic. **Capital:** Lusaka. **Independence:** 24 October 1964 (from U.K.). **National holiday:** Independence Day, 24 October (1964). **Economy G.D.P.:** purchasing power parity—$20.03 billion (2010 est.). **G.D.P.—per capita:** purchasing power parity—$1,500 (2010 est.). **Currency:** Zambian kwacha (ZMK).

Zimbabwe

Republic of Zimbabwe

Geography **Location:** Southern Africa, between South Africa and Zambia. **Area:** 150,803 sq. mi. (390,580 sq km). **Border countries:** Botswana, Mozambique, South Africa, Zambia. **Natural resources:** coal, chromium ore, asbestos, gold, nickel, copper, iron ore, vanadium, lithium, tin, platinum group metals. **People Population:** 12,084,304 (July 2011 est.) *note:* estimates for this country explicitly take into account the effects of excess mortality due to AIDS; this can result in lower life expectancy, higher infant mortality and death rates, lower population and growth rates, and changes in the distribution of population by age and sex than would otherwise be expected. **Nationality:** *noun:* Zimbabwean(s); *adj.:* Zimbabwean. **Ethnic groups:** African 98% (Shona 82%, Ndebele 14%, other 2%) mixed and Asian 1%, white less than 1%. **Religions:** syncretic (part Christian, part indigenous beliefs) 50%, Christian 25%, indigenous beliefs 24%, Muslim and other 1%. **Languages:** English (official), Shona, Sindebele (the language of the Ndebele, sometimes called Ndebele), numerous but minor tribal dialects. **Government** **Government type:** parliamentary democracy. **Capital:** Harare. **Independence:** 18 April 1980 (from U.K.). **National holiday:** Independence Day, 18 April (1980). **Economy G.D.P.:** purchasing power parity—$4.395 billion (2010 est.). **G.D.P.—per capita:** purchasing power parity—$400 (2010 est.). **Currency:** Zimbabwean dollar (ZWD).

The United Nations

Pres. Franklin D. Roosevelt coined the name "United Nations," which was first used in the "Declaration by United Nations" of Jan. 1, 1942, during World War II, when representatives of 26 countries pledged their governments to continue fighting together against the Axis Powers. From August to October 1944, representatives of China, the Soviet Union, the United Kingdom and the United States met at Dumbarton Oaks, a mansion in Washington, D.C., to discuss creating an international peacekeeping organization. Out of these meetings came a general outline for the United Nations.

At the United Nations Conference on International Organization, which met at San Francisco from Apr. 25 to June 26, 1945, representatives from 50 countries drew up the United Nations Charter and signed it on June 26, 1945.

The United Nations officially came into existence on Oct. 24, 1945, when the charter was ratified by China, France, the Soviet Union, the United Kingdom, and the United States and by a majority of the other signatories.

Structure

Establishment Pres. Franklin D. Roosevelt coined the name "United Nations," which was first used in the "Declaration by United Nations" of Jan. 1, 1942, during World War II, when representatives of 26 countries pledged their governments to continue fighting together against the Axis Powers. From August to October 1944, representatives of China, the Soviet Union, the United Kingdom and the United States met at Dumbarton Oaks, a mansion in Washington, D.C., to discuss creating an international peacekeeping organization. Out of these meetings came a general outline for the United Nations.

At the United Nations Conference on International Organization, which met at San Francisco from Apr. 25 to June 26, 1945, representatives from 50 countries drew up the United Nations Charter and signed it on June 26, 1945. Poland, not present at the Conference, signed on October 15, 1945, and is considered one of the founding member states.

The United Nations officially came into existence on Oct. 24, 1945, when the charter was ratified by China, France, the Soviet Union, the United Kingdom, and the United States and by a majority of the other signatories.

U.N. Charter U.S. The Preamble to the Charter sets forth the hopes for the United Nations:

WE THE PEOPLES OF THE UNITED NATIONS DETERMINED

- to save succeeding generations from the scourge of war ...
- to reaffirm faith in fundamental human rights, in the dignity and worth of the human person, in the equal rights of men and women and of nations large and small . . .
- to establish conditions under which justice and respect for the obligations arising from treaties and other sources of international law can be maintained . . .
- to promote social progress and better standards of life in larger freedom.

AND FOR THESE ENDS

- to practice tolerance and live together in peace with one another as good neighbors
- to unite our strength to maintain international peace and security
- to ensure, by the acceptance of principles and the institution of methods, that armed force shall not be used, save in the common interest
- to employ international machinery for the promotion of the economic and social advancement of all peoples.

HAVE RESOLVED TO COMBINE OUR EFFORTS TO ACCOMPLISH THESE AIMS. Accordingly, our respective Governments, through representatives assembled in the city of San Francisco, who have exhibited their full powers found to be in good and due form, have agreed to the present Charter of the United Nations and do hereby establish an international organization to be known as the United Nations. [Full text of the Charter may be purchased for $3.00 from the United Nations, Sales Section, New York, NY 10017.]

Purposes The purposes of the United Nations are set forth in Article 1 of the Charter. They are: 1. To maintain international peace and security. 2. To develop friendly relations among nations based on respect for the principle of equal rights and self-determination of peoples. 3. To cooperate in solving international problems of an economic, social, cultural or humanitarian character, and in promoting respect for human rights and fundamental freedoms for all. 4. To be a center for harmonizing the actions of nations in the attainment of these common ends.

Official languages Originally, there were five official languages of the United Nations: Chinese, English, French, Russian and Spanish. Arabic was added to the General Assembly in 1973, to the Security Council in 1982 and to the Economic and Social Council in 1983. Major United Nations documents and all meetings of the General Assembly, the Security Council and the Economic and Social Council are translated into the six working languages.

United Nations headquarters United Nations, New York, NY 10017 U.S. U.N. headquarters covers a 16-acre site in New York City along the East River from 42nd to 48th Streets. It consists of the interconnected General Assembly, Secretariat and Dag Hammarskjöld Library buildings. Acquisition of the site was made possible by a gift of $8.5 million from John D. Rockefeller, Jr., and one-third of that amount from New York City. In 1951, the 39-story Secretariat building was completed and began functioning as the official home of the United Nations.

Permanent observers to the U.N. at New York headquarters cannot vote and do not have diplomatic privileges or immunities unless connected to the member nation's consulate. They do have free access to the public meetings and distribution of relevant documentation.

Non-member observers are the Holy See and Palestine.

Intergovernmental and other observer organizations: More than 25 organizations have observer status at the U.N. Following is a representative sample: Caribbean Community, Commonwealth of Independent States; Council of Europe; International Federation of Red Cross and Red Crescent Societies; League of Arab States; Organization of African Unity; Organization of American States; Organization of Islamic Conference.

Principal Organs

General Assembly The Assembly is the world's forum for discussing major issues facing the international community including world peace and security, human rights, global environment, disarmament, health issues including AIDS, and the rights of women and children.

The Assembly consists of all 192 member states, each having one vote. On important issues a two-thirds majority of those present and voting is required; other questions require a simple majority vote. It holds its annual session from September to December, and may call for extra sessions as needed. Its agenda of more than 150 matters for discussion is first dealt with in six main committees: Its agenda of more than 150 matters for discussion is first dealt with in six main committees: First Committee: Disarmament and International Security; Second Committee: Economic and Financial; Third Committee: Social, Humanitarian and Cultural; Fourth Committee: Special Political and De-colonization; Fifth Committee: Administrative and Budgetary; Sixth Committee: Legal. After discussing issues facing the world, it adopts recom-

mendations (called resolutions) but has no power to enforce its decisions (resolutions), except the power of world opinion.

The Assembly considers and approves U.N. budget and assesses member states according to their ability to pay.

Security Council The Council may investigate any dispute or situation that might lead to international friction, and may recommend methods for adjusting such disputes or terms for their settlement. While other organs of the U.N. make recommendations to governments, the Security Council alone has the power to take decisions that member states are obligated under the Charter to carry out.

The Security Council has 15 members: five permanent members, and the General Assembly elects 10 other members for two-year terms. They are not eligible for immediate re-election. The Council may be called into session at any time, and a representative of each member state must be present at U.N. headquarters at all times.

The five permanent members are China, France, Russia, the United Kingdom and the United States.

Decisions on matters of procedure require the approval of at least nine of the 15 members. Decisions on all other matters also require nine votes, including the concurring votes of all five permanent members. A negative vote by any permanent member on a non-procedural matter is often referred to as the "veto," which results in the rejection of the proposal. A state that is involved in a dispute may not vote.

Economic and Social Council (ECOSOC) The Council is the principal organ to co-ordinate the economic and social work of the U.N. and its specialized agencies. It makes recommendations and initiates activities relating to world trade, industrialization, natural resources, human rights, the status of women, population, social welfare, education, health and related matters, science and technology and many other economic and social questions.

ECOSOC has 54 members elected for three-year terms by the General Assembly.

International Court of Justice (World Court) The Court is the judicial organ of the U.N. and sits in The Hague, Netherlands. All U.N. member states are automatically members of the Court. The Court is not open to individuals. It issues judgments on all questions that states refer to it and all matters provided for in the U.N. Charter or in treaties or conventions in force. Both the General Assembly and the Security Council can ask the Court for an advisory opinion on any legal question as can other organs of the U.N. or specialized agencies, when authorized to do so by the Assembly.

Judges: The ICJ has 15 independent judges, of different nationalities, elected by both the General Assembly and the Security Council. Judges hold 9-year terms and may be re-elected. All questions are decided by a majority of the judges present; the president votes only in case of a tie.

Secretariat The Secretariat services the other organs of the U.N. and administers the programs and policies they develop. Headed by the Secretary-General, it consists of an international staff of more than 25,000 men and women from over 150 countries.

Secretaries-General: The General Assembly elects the Secretary-General to terms of office of five years (they may be re-elected). The Secretary-General, by tradition, does not come from one of the permanent member states of the Security Council—China, France, Russia, U.K. or the U.S. Those who have served in this post are:

Trygve Lie, Norway, Feb. 1, 1946, to Nov. 10, 1952;

Dag Hammarskjöld, Sweden, Apr. 11, 1953, to Sept. 17, 1961;

U Thant, Burma, Nov. 3, 1961, to Dec. 31, 1971;

Kurt Waldheim, Austria, Jan. 1, 1972, to Dec. 31, 1981;

Javier Perez de Cuellar, Peru Jan. 1, 1982 to Dec. 31, 1991

Boutros Boutros-Ghali, Egypt, Jan 1, 1992, to Dec. 31, 1996;

Kofi Annan, Ghana, Jan. 1, 1997 to 2006;

Ban Ki-Moon, Rep. of Korea, Jan 1. 2007 to present.

United Nations Programs

Each U.N. program was created by the General Assembly and reports to it through the Economic and Social Council (ECOSOC). Each member of the U.N. is a member of each Program. Below are the main programs:

United Nations Children's Fund (UNICEF) Estab.: 1946; **HQ:** UNICEF House, Three United Nations Plaza, New York, NY 10017, U.S. Provides care for children in developing countries by providing low-cost community-based services in maternal and child health, immunization, breast-feeding, growth monitoring, nutrition, clean water and sanitation, and education.

United Nations Conference on Trade and Development (UNCTAD) Estab.: 1964; **HQ:** Place des Nations, 8-14, Av. de la Paix, 1211 Geneva 10, Switzerland.

Works to bring developing countries into global trade by formulating international trade policies, mediating multilateral trade agreements and providing assistance to governments.

United Nations Development Programme (UNDP) Estab.: 1965; **HQ:** One United Nations Plaza, New York, NY 10017, U.S. Coordinates development activities within the U.N. Operates over 5,000 projects in 150 countries and territories to facilitate development in economic and social sectors, including: farming, fishing, forestry, mining, manufacturing, power, transport, communications, housing, trade, health and environmental sanitation, economic planning and public administration.

United Nations Environment Programme (UNEP) Estab.: 1972; **HQ:** United Nations Avenue, Gigiri, P.O. Box 30552, Nairobi, Kenya. Coordinates international environment issues, including international environment conventions, monitors significant changes in environment and coordinates sound environmental practices.

Office of the United Nations High Commissioner for Refugees (UNHCR) Estab.: 1950; **HQ:** Case Postale 2500, CH-1211 Geneve 2 Depot, Switzerland. Provides food, clothing and shelter for refugees and works with governments to establish safe conditions whereby refugees may return home and, when that is not possible, seeks to ensure that refugees receive asylum.

World Food Council (WFC) Estab.: 1974; **HQ:** Via delle Terme di Caracalla, 00100 Rome, Italy. Encourages developing countries to adopt a national food strategy whereby they assess their food situation needs, supply, potential for increasing production, storage, processing, transportation and distribution.

World Food Programme (WFP) (Joint program operated by U.N. and Food and Agriculture Organization (FAO)) **Estab.:** 1963; **HQ:** Via C.G.Viola 68/70, Parco dei Medici, 00148 Rome, Italy. Provides food to support development activities and in times of emergencies. Operates projects in forestry, soil erosion control, irrigation, land rehabilitation and rural settlements.

Specialized Agencies Of The U.N.

The specialized agencies associated with the United Nations are self-governing, independent organizations that work with the U.N. system and each other through the coordination machinery of the Economic and Social Council (ECOSOC). Each country affiliates with each agency on an individual basis. Membership in an agency is separate from

U.N. membership. Nongovernmental organizations (NGOs) having expertise in the area may affiliate with each agency on a separate basis. Below is a select list:

Food and Agriculture Organization of the United Nations (FAO) Member States: 174; **Estab.:** Oct. 16, 1945; **HQ:** Via delle Terme di Caracalla, 00100 Rome, Italy. Works to increase output of farmlands, forests and fisheries and to raise nutritional levels. Co-sponsors World Food Programme, which uses food, cash and services donated by member states for emergency situations.

International Atomic Energy Agency (IAEA) Member States: 127; **Estab.:** July 29, 1957; **HQ:** Vienna International Centre, P.O. Box 100, A-1400 Vienna, Austria. (Not regular specialized agency in that it does not report through ECOSOC but directly to General Assembly.) Fosters and guides development of peaceful uses of atomic energy, establishes standards for nuclear safety and environmental protection, aids member countries through technical cooperation, and fosters exchange of information on nuclear energy.

International Civil Aviation Organization (ICAO) Member States: 183; Estab.: Apr. 4, 1947; HQ: 999 University Street, Montreal, Quebec H3C 5H7, Canada. Works for safer air travel conditions worldwide. Establishes visual and instrument flight rules for pilots and crews; develops aeronautical charts for navigation; co-ordinates aircraft radio frequencies and works with customs procedures.

United Nations Educational, Scientific and Cultural Organization (UNESCO) Member States: 186; **Estab.:** Nov. 4, 1946; **HQ:** 7, Place de Fontenoy, 75007 Paris, France. Promotes literacy through teacher training, building schools, and developing textbooks. Natural science programs include Man and the Biosphere and Intergovernmental Oceanographic Commission. Undertakes study and development of cultures, and conservation of world's inheritance of books, art and monuments.

World Bank Group Group of five closely related institutions. HQ: 1818 H Street, N.W., Washington, D.C. 20433 **International Bank for Reconstruction and Development (IBRD) Member States:** 178; **Estab.:** Dec. 27, 1945, to provide loans and technical assistance to developing countries to assist in their reconstruction and development. **International Finance Corporation (IFC) Member States:** 165 (Membership is open only to World Bank members.); **Estab.:** July 20, 1956, to stimulate flow of private capital into productive investment in member countries. While closely associated with Bank, IFC is separate legal entity and its funds are distinct from those of Bank. **International Development Association (IDA) Member States:** 158; **Estab.:** Sept. 24, 1960. (Affiliate of the Bank, IDA has same directors and staff as Bank.) Lends money to poor countries with interest-free credits. Financial resources are from contributions by donor governments. **International Monetary Fund (IMF) Member States:** 181; Estab.: Dec. 27, 1945; **HQ:** 700 19th Street, N.W., Washington, D.C. 20431. Makes financing available to members in balance-of-payments difficulties and provides technical assistance to improve their economic management. **Multilateral Investment Guarantee Agency (MIGA) Member States:** 128; **Estab.:** 1988. Augments capacity of other insurers through coinsurance or reinsurance, thereby insuring investment in countries restricted or excluded by policies of other insurers.

World Health Organization (WHO) Member States: 190; **Estab.:** April 7, 1948; **HQ:** 20, avenue Appia, 1211 Geneva 27, Switzerland. Coordinates programs aimed at solving health problems by working with governments, other U.N. agencies and non-governmental organizations. See "World Health" section.

World Meteorological Organization (WMO) Member States: 179; **Estab.:** 1873. (became U.N. specialized agency Mar. 23, 1950); **HQ:** 7 bis Avenue de la Paix, CP 2300, 1211 Geneva 2, Switzerland. Facilitates exchange of weather reports among countries; "World Weather Watch" tracks global weather conditions.

Peacekeeping Operations

United Nations peacekeeping is the use of multinational forces, under U.N. command, to keep disputing countries or communities from fighting while efforts are made to help them negotiate a solution. It is undertaken only with the agreement of both hostile parties. United Nations Peacekeeping Forces received the Nobel Peace Prize in 1988. As of May 2011, the U.N. had more than 98,000 personnel serving in 14 peacekeeping operations. These operations were located in Western Sahara, Democratic Republic of the Congo, Sudan (two), Ivory Coast, Liberia, Haiti, East Timor, Cyprus, Kosovo, Syria, Lebanon, India and Pakistan, and the Middle East. One hundred fourteen countries contributed to the operations with Bangladesh making the largest contribution (10,589 personnel), followed by Pakistan (10,553) and India (8,488); the United States contributed 110 personnel.

How to Solve *The New York Times* Crossword Puzzle

By Will Shortz

A crossword puzzle is a battle between the puzzle maker and editor on one side and the solver on the other. But in this battle, unlike most battles, both sides have the same goal—for the solver to win. A perfect puzzle may put up lots of resistance. It may, in fact, seem impossible at first. Ideally, though, in the end the solver should triumph and think, Oh, how clever I am!

The perfect level of difficulty, of course, differs from person to person. This is why, as editor, I vary the difficulty of the weekday *Times* crossword from easy-medium on Monday up to what the actor and puzzle aficionado Paul Sorvino calls "the bitch mother of all crosswords" on Saturday. (He said this as a compliment.) The goal is to have something for everyone. I advise new solvers to begin on Monday and see how far through the week they can go. The *Sunday Times* puzzle, while larger than its weekday counterpart, averages only Thursday-plus in difficulty.

Step 1 in solving any crossword is to begin with the answers you're surest of and build from there. The fill-in-the-blank clues are easy to spot and often the easiest to solve. Focus in the early stages on the three-, four-, and five-letter words, because the English language has relatively few of these, and the same ones tend to repeat a lot in puzzles. This is especially so for vowel-heavy words like ALEE, IOTA, EEL, AGO, OREO, etc. Watch for the celebrity names (UMA, ARTE, ENO, AGEE) and geographical names (ADA, AMES, ELON, ORONO) that crop up with unusual frequency. Once you have a few crossing letters in the longer answers, you'll be more likely to get them from their clues.

Don't be afraid to guess. At the same time, don't be afraid to erase an answer that isn't working out. For the clue "Butcher's offering," I once watched a solver successively guess T-BONE, CHUCK, and STEAK before finally hitting upon the correct answer, SHANK. Don't assume that because you have a few crossing letters your answer is

necessarily correct. And if nothing seems to cross the answer you have filled in, be very wary.

Mental flexibility is a great asset in solving crosswords. Let your mind wander. The clue "Present time" might suggest NOWADAYS, but in a different sense it might lead to the answer YULETIDE. Similarly, "Life sentences" could be OBIT; "Inside shot" is X-RAY; and my all-time favorite clue, "It turns into a different story" (15 letters), results in the phrase SPIRAL STAIRCASE.

The *New York Times* crossword has not printed hints like "2 wds." and "3 wds." since the early 1950's, so be on your toes for multiword answers. One answer that always seems to trip solvers up is R-A-N-D-R, which was clued as "Leave time?" when it first appeared in a *Times* puzzle several years ago. Afterward lots of solvers called and wrote me saying that they couldn't find the word RANDR in their dictionaries, and where did I get it? I had to inform them gently that the answer was three words, R AND R, as in the time when one goes on leave.

A question mark at the end of a clue can mean several things. In the above clue for R AND R, it means "This clue is tricky! Be careful!" It can also indicate that the answer only loosely fits the clue. For example, "Cause for a head-slap?" (BONER). Making a boner may or may not be cause for slapping one's forehead. When question marks appear at the ends of the clues for all the long answers in a puzzle, usually the marks are signals for related puns.

No matter how tricky or misleading the clues, they will always follow a fairly strict set of rules. Most important, a clue and its answer will always be expressed in the same part of speech and as a rule must be interchangeable in a sentence, with the same meaning each way.

If a crossword answer is not a Standard English word, the clue will usually signal this fact. Thus, a slangy answer will have a slangy clue. The clue for an abbreviated answer will contain the tag "Abbr." or else a word that is not usually abbreviated ("Entrepreneur's deg." = M.B.A.). Similarly, words that are strictly foreign will be signaled either directly ("Boy: Sp." = NINO) or indirectly ("Son, in Sonora"). By convention, diacritical marks are ignored in American crosswords, so don't worry about that tilde in "niño."

True crossword cognoscenti observe the bylines on the crosswords and prepare themselves accordingly. Cathy Millhauser, a frequent *Times* constructor, is famous for puns. In a puzzle called "M-M-M" she changed N sounds to M's at the end of familiar phrases, like SAVINGS AND LOAM, AMERICA ON-LIME and AS CRAZY AS A LOOM. Knowing her tendencies helps you nail one or two of the long puns, and you have a big advantage in getting the others.

The constructor's age is sometimes reflected in a puzzle. The late Frances Hansen, one of *The Times*'s longest-running crossword contributors, produced elegant grids full of classical knowledge, while Brendan Emmett Quigley, 26, a guitarist for a rock band in Boston, conveys a younger, more pop-cultured sensibility.

If you get stuck on a puzzle, a time-honored technique is to put it aside and return later. Perhaps the brain works subconsciously on problems in the interim. Whatever the case, a fresh look at a tough puzzle almost always brings new answers.

A question I am asked often is this: "Is it cheating to use references?" In reply I always quote Will Weng, one of my predecessors as *Times* crossword editor: "It's your puzzle. Solve it any way you want." And is it cheating to call *The Times*'s 900 number to get answers? Well, of course! But what nobody knows won't hurt you.

Concise Crossword Dictionary

by Will Shortz

By their nature crossword puzzles tend to have shorter, more vowel-heavy words than the English language does as a whole. Short words are necessary to make the vocabulary in the grid interlock. And though most modern crosswords eschew obscurity, even well-made puzzles, by necessity, may have a few answers that ordinary people have never heard of. Below is a list of almost 600 short, difficult words that often appear in crosswords (words like these are sometimes called "crosswordese"), along with common clues that are used for them. The great majority of words in crosswords are ones you already know. Memorizing this modest list of rare but frequently encountered puzzle words will instantly make you a substantially better solver.

AAR	Swiss river (also AARE)	AGEE	Writer James
ABBE	French cleric	AGIO	Currency exchange premium
ABELE	White poplar	AGON	Literary conflict; Stravinsky ballet
ABIES	"____ Irish Rose"	AGORA	Ancient Greek marketplace
ABRI	Hillside shelter	AGRA	Taj Mahal city
ACER	Maple genus	AGUE	Chills and fever
ACIS	Galatea's beloved	AINU	Japanese aborigine
ACTA	Recorded proceedings	AIRE	River in Yorkshire
ADA	City in Oklahoma	AISNE	French river
ADAK	Alaskan island	AIT	River island
ADANO	Hersey's "A Bell for ____"	ALAE	Winglike part
ADAR	Jewish month	ALAI	Kyrgyzstan's ____ Mountains; jai ____
ADE	Fruit drink; humorist George	ALAR	Winged; banned apple spray
ADIT	Mine entrance	ALB	Church vestment
ADZ	Shaping tool (also ADZE)	ALEE	Toward shelter
AEDES	Mosquito genus	ALETA	Prince Valiant's wife
AERIE	Eagle's nest (also AERY)	ALGA	Tiny pond plant
AESIR	Pantheon in Norse mythology	ALOP	Askew
AGA	Turkish leader (also AGHA)	ALOU	Baseball family name
AGANA	Guam's capital, old-style	ALTAI	Asia's ____ Mountains
AGAR	Culture medium; journalist-writer Herbert	ALUM	Astringent; graduate, for short

ALVA	Thomas Edison's middle name	AVAL	Grandparental
AMAH	Oriental nurse	AWN	Grain bristle
AMATI	Italian violinmaker	AXEL	Skater's jump
AMES	Iowa university town; singer Ed	AXIL	Leaf angle
A MOI	Belonging to me, in France	AXON	Nerve-cell process
AMUR	River in northeastern Asia	AYIN	Hebrew letter
ANA	Literary collection; Santa ____	AYN	Author Rand
ANAIS	Diarist Nin	BAHT	Thai money
ANI	Black cuckoo	BEDE	"Venerable" monk
ANIL	Indigo-yielding plant	BELEM	Brazilian city
ANILE	Old-womanish	BEY	Governor in the Ottoman Empire
ANION	Negatively charged particle	BOLA	Gaucho's weapon
ANO	Year in Spain	BOLO	Philippine knife; ____ tie
ANOA	Celebes ox	BRAE	Scottish hillside
ANSA	Looped handle	BREN	Clip-fed machine gun
ANTA	Theater group	CAEN	Normandy city
ANYA	Author Seton	CANA	Where Jesus performed his first miracle
APIA	Samoa's capital	CANEA	Former capital of Crete
APIS	Sacred bull of ancient Egypt	CARIB	West Indies native
APOD	Footless animal	CHA	Oriental tea
APSE	Church recess	CEBU	Philippine island
ARA	Southern constellation; coach Parseghian	CERE	Cover with wax: Obs.
ARAL	Asia's ____ Sea	CERES	Goddess of agriculture; largest asteroid
ARAM	Composer Khachaturian	CLIO	Muse of history
ARAN	Ireland's ____ Islands	COHO	Great Lakes salmon
ARECA	Betel palm	COIR	Coconut fiber
ARETE	Mountain rdge	CONTE	French story
ARI	Shipping magnate Onassis; former White House spokesman Fleischer	COR	Heart
ARIL	Seed covering	COS	Type of lettuce; business grps.
ARON	Elvis Presley's middle name	CREE	Algonquian Indian
ARRAS	Tapestry	CREEL	Fisher's basket
ARTEL	Old Soviet peasants' cooperative	DACE	Carplike fish
ARUM	Calla lily family	DADA	Art movement
ASANA	Yoga position	DADO	Part of a pedestal
ASE	Peer Gynt's mother; enzyme suffix	DAG	Former U.N. Secretary General ____ Hammarskjöld
ASOR	Ancient Hebrew musical instrument	DAIL	Irish parliament
ASSAI	Very, in music	DEE	Scottish river; actress Ruby or Sandra
ASSAM	State in northeastern India	DELE	Remove, to a typesetter
ASTA	Nick and Nora Charles's dog in *The Thin Man*	DENE	Sand hill
ASTI	Italian wine region	DEVA	Hindu deity
ATLE	Tamarisk salt tree	DEY	Former Algerian ruler; actress Susan
ATLI	Norse king	DIDO	Queen of Carthage; prank
ATON	Egyptian solar diety (also ATEN)	DOGE	Old Venetian magistrate
ATRI	Italian bell town	DREI	German four
ATTU	Westernmost of the Aleutian Islands	DUMA	Russian legislature
AUDE	French river	DYAD	Pair
AUGER	Hole-boring tool	DYNE	Unit of force

EBON	Black, in poetry
EBRO	Spanish river
ECCE	Behold, in old Rome
ECLAT	Brilliant display
ECOLE	French place of learning
ECRU	Beige
ECTO	Outer: Prefix
ECU	Old French coin
EDA	Author LeShan
EDDA	Icelandic literary work
EDE	Dutch city
EDEMA	Swelling
EDER	German river
EDH	Old English letter (also ETH)
EDIE	Singer Adams
EDILE	Old Roman magistrate
EDO	Former name of Tokyo
EDOM	Biblical country
EER	Always, in poetry
EERO	Architect Saarinen
EFT	Young newt
EGER	German river
EGIS	Protection (also AEGIS)
EIN	German article (also EINE)
EIS	Frozen water: Ger.
E LA	Guido's note
ELAM	Biblical kingdom
ELATER	Click beetle
ELATH	Israeli port on the Gulf of Aqaba (also ELAT, EILAT)
ELBA	Island of Napoleon's exile
ELBE	German river
ELD	Antiquity
ELEA	Zeno of ____
ELEMI	Fragrant resin
ELEVE	French student
ELI	Biblical high priest
ELIA	Charles Lamb's pen name
ELIS	Home of the ancient Olympics; Yale students
ELL	Building wing; pipe joint
ELOI	*The Time Machine* people
ELON	North Carolina university
ELS	Overhead trains; golfer Ernie
ELSA	*Born Free* lioness; Lohengrin's love
ELUL	Jewish month
ELVER	Young eel
ELY	English cathedral town; Tarzan player Ron
EME	Scottish uncle

EMIR	Mideast leader (also EMEER, AMIR, AMEER)
EMO	Comic Philips
EMS	German spa; type widths
ENA	Bambi's aunt; Alfonso's queen
ENERO	January: Sp.
ENG	Chang's conjoined twin; H.S. class
ENID	City in Oklahoma; Arthurian lady; author Bagnold
ENNA	Sicilian city
ENNS	Austrian river
ENO	Rock musician Brian
ENOL	Organic compounds
ENOS	Son of Seth
ENS	Type widths; nav. officer
ENTO	Inner: Prefix
ENYO	Ares' mother
EOS	Greek goddess of the dawn
EOSIN	Rose-colored dye
EPEE	Fencing sword
EPHAH	Hebrew measure
EPI	Finial ornament; prefix with center
EPODE	Lyric poem
EPOS	Grand poetry
ERATO	Muse of lyric poetry
ERDA	Norse earth goddess
ERE	Before
ERG	Energy unit
ERGOT	Plant fungus
ERI	Silkworm (also ERIA); "____ Tu" (aria)
ERIS	Goddess of discord
ERN	Sea eagle (also ERNE)
EROS	Greek god of love
ERS	Bitter vetch; hesitation sounds
ERSE	Scottish Gaelic
ESAU	Twin brother of Jacob
ESKER	Glacial ridge
ESNE	Anglo-Saxon slave
ESS	Double curve; feminine suffix
ESSE	Existence
ESSENE	Dead Sea scrolls writer
ESTE	Italian commune; Renaissance family name
ESTER	Organic compounds
ESTES	____ Park, Colo.; Sen. Kefauver
ESTOP	Prevent by law
ETAH	Greenland settlement
ET AL	And others: Lat.
ETAPE	Public warehouse

ETE	French summer
ETNA	Sicilian volcano
ETO	W.W. II zone: Abbr.
ETON	English college; type of jacket or collar
ETTA	Singer James or Jones
ET TU	"____, Brute!"
ETUDE	Practice piece in music
ETUI	Needle case
EVOE	Bacchanalian cry
EWER	Pitcher
EXE	River in Devon
FALA	F.D.R.'s dog
FARO	Card game
FRA	Monk
GAEA	Mother of the Titans
GAM	Attractive leg, slangily; school of whales
GAR	Needlefish
GARE	Railway station: Fr.
GASPE	Canadian peninsula
GAT	Gangster's gun
GHEE	Liquid butter, in India
GNAR	Snarl, growl
GNU	African antelope
GOA	Former Portuguese colony in India
HARI	W.W. I spy Mata ____
HEBE	Greek goddess of youth
HEL	Loki's daughter
HEMO	Blood: Prefix (also HEMA)
HEART	Afghanistan city
HESSE	German state; *Steppenwolf* author
HOREB	Biblical mountain
IAGO	*Othello* villain
IAMB	Verse foot
IBEX	Wild goat
IBO	Nigerian tribesman
ICI	Here: Fr.
IDA	Mountain on Crete
IDEO	Thought: Prefix
IGLU	Eskimo home: Var.
ILA	Dockworkers' org.
ILE	____ de France
ILIA	Hip bones
ILO	Worldwide workers' grp.
INEE	Arrow poison
INGE	Dramatist William
INO	Daughter of Cadmus, in Greek mythology
IN RE	Concerning
IOLA	Kansas town

IOLE	Hercules' captive
IONA	Scottish isle; New Rochelle college
IONIA	Asia Minor district
IPSE	____ dixit
IRADE	Muslim decree
ISAK	Author Dinesen
ISER	Czech river
ISERE	French river
ISSEI	Japanese-American
ISTLE	Rope fiber
ITEA	Virginia willow
ITER	Roman road
ITO	Japanese statesman; Simpson judge Lance
IYAR	Hebrew month
JETE	Ballet jump
KEIL	German canal
KEPI	Military cap
KOLA	Nut with caffeine
KRAAL	Enclosure for cattle in South Africa
KRONA	Icelandic money
KUDU	African antelope
LAC	Resin in sealing wax; Fond du ____, Wis.
LAE	New Guinea port
LAIC	Secular
LAR	Roman household god
LEA	Meadow
LEDA	Mother of Castor and Pollux
LEHR	Glassmaker's oven
LEK	Albanian money
LEN	Author Deighton
LENA	Russian river; singer Horne
LENE	Smooth sound
LER	Celtic god of the sea
LETO	Apollo's mother
LETT	Native of Latvia
LEU	Romanian money
LEV	Bulgarian coin
LEVI	Jacob's son
LEYTE	Philippine island
LIANA	Tropical climbing plant (also LIANE)
LIRA	Turkish money; former Italian currency
LIS	French flower
LOBO	Timber wolf
LODI	Town in New Jersey or California
LOKI	Mischief-making Norse god
LST	W.W. II craft: Abbr.
LYS	French/Belgian river
MAKO	Variety of shark

MARL	Crumbly soil	ODIN	Supreme Norse deity
MARU	Japanese ship name	OGEE	Double curve, in molding
MEDE	Ancient Persian	OHM	Unit of resistance
MENE	Part of writing on a wall, in Daniel	OISE	River of France
MERL	Blackbird	OKA	Russian river
MHO	Unit of electrical conductance	OKAPI	Relative of the giraffe
MIL	Wire measure	OKIE	Migratory Dust Bowl worker
MISE	____ en scene (the staging of a play)	OLAND	Warner ____, Charlie Chan portrayer
MITER	Bishop's headdress	OLID	Foul-smelling
MOA	Extinct flightless bird	OLIO	Medley
MORO	Philippine tribesman; 1960's–70's Italian P.M. Aldo ____	OLLA	Earthenware jar
		OLOR	Swan genus
NACRE	Mother-of-pearl	OMAR	Persian poet and mathematician
NAE	Scottish refusal	OMER	Ancient Hebrew measure
NAHA	Okinawa port	OMOO	Melville novel
NAIAD	Water nymph	OMRI	Ahab's father; actor Katz
NANA	Zola novel; child's caretaker	ONDE	French wave
NARD	Aromatic plant that yields an ointment	ONER	Unique person or thing
NEB	Bird's beak	OONA	Mrs. Charlie Chaplin
NEBO	Biblical mount	OPA	W.W. II ration board agcy.; ____-Locka, Fla.
NEE	Born: Fr.	OPAH	Colorful moonfish
NEF	Ship clock	OPE	Unlock: Poetic
NENE	Hawaiian goose	OPS	Roman goddess of plenty; photo ____
NESS	Headland; Eliot in *The Untouchables*	ORA	Mouths
NEVA	Leningrad's river	ORAN	Algerian port
NEVE	Glacial snowfield; actress Campbell	ORCA	Killer whale
NEY	Napoleon's marshal at Waterloo	ORD	California's Fort ____
NEZ	____ Percé Indians; pince-____	ORDO	Church calendar
NIB	Pen point	OREL	Russian city; pitcher Hershiser
NIDE	Brood of pheasants	ORIEL	Bay window
NIDI	Nests of eggs	ORLE	Heraldic bearing
NIPA	East Indian palm	ORNE	French department
NISAN	Hebrew month	ORO	Spanish gold
NISI	Not yet final, at law	ORONO	Maine university town
NOH	Japanese drama	ORT	Table scrap
NONES	Canonical hour	OSAR	Glacial ridge
NORIA	Waterwheel	OSIER	Willow
NORN	One of the three Norse Fates	OSS	C.I.A. predecessor
OAST	Kiln	OSSA	Greek mountain
OBE	British award: Abbr.	OSTIA	Port of ancient Rome
OBEAH	Witchcraft	OTHO	Holy Roman emperor
OBI	Japanese sash	OTIC	Ear-related
OBOL	Ancient Greek coin	OTO	Oklahoma tribe (also OTOE)
OCA	Edible root in South America	OUSE	English river
ODA	Harem room	OVA	Eggs
ODEA	Concert halls	PACA	Spotted brown rodent
ODER	German-Polish border river	PAS	Dance step; fathers
ODETS	Playwright Clifford	PEKOE	Black tea

PELEE	Martinique volcano
PERI	Persian sprite
PES	Footlike part
PHON	Loudness measure
PHOT	Light unit
PIA	____ mater (brain cover); actress Zadora
PICA	Type measure
PIMA	Arizona Indian; strong-fibered cotton
PLIE	Ballet bend
POI	Hawaiian dish
POILU	French soldier in W.W. I
PROA	Malay outrigger
PTAH	Egyptian deity
PULE	Whimper
PULI	Hungarian dog
PYE	English poet laureate
QADI	Muslim magistrate (also CADI)
RAE	Arctic explorer John; actress Charlotte
RAGA	Indian music
RALE	Harsh breathing
RAMA	Incarnation of Vishnu
RAMIE	Sturdy cloth fiber
RANA	Indian prince
RANI	Hindu queen (also RANEE)
RAO	Indian novelist
RAREE	____ show (amusing spectacle)
RATEL	Nocturnal animal of Africa and India
RAVI	Sitarist Shankar
REBEC	Medieval musical instrument
REN	Stimpy's partner in cartoons
RENI	Italian painter Guido
REO	Antique auto
RES	Thing at law; musical notes
RET	Soak flax
RETE	Network
RHEA	Ostrichlike bird
RHEE	First president of Korea
RIA	Narrow inlet
RIAL	Mideast money (also RIYAL)
RIATA	Gaucho's lariat (also REATA)
RIEN	Nothing: Fr.
RIGA	Latvia's capital
RIVA	Kentucky Derby winner ____ Ridge
ROC	Fabled bird of *The Arabian Nights*
ROE	Caviar; ____ v. Wade
ROO	Aussie hopper; *Winnie-the-Pooh* baby
ROTA	Roster
ROTI	Roasted: Fr.

ROTO	Old newspaper section
RUR	Karel Capek drama
RYA	Scandinavian rug
SABRA	Native Israeli
SAC	Algonquian Indian; pouch
SAGO	Starchy foodstuff
SAKI	H. H. Munro's pen name
SANA	Capital of Yemen (also SANAA)
SARD	Semiprecious stone
SARI	Hindu dress
SEC	Dry, as wine; part of a min.
SEGO	Utah's state flower
SEL	Salt: Fr.
SERA	Antitoxins; evening in Italy
SERAC	Glacial ridge
SERAI	Mideast inn
SERE	Dry and withered
SERT	Spanish muralist José María ____
SES	French possessive
SETA	Bristle
SETI	One of two Egyptian pharaohs
SHEM	Son of Noah
SIENA	City of Tuscany
SIMI	California's ____ Valley
SIVA	Hindu god (also SHIVA)
SLOE	Blackthorn fruit; ____ gin fizz
SMA	Wee, in Scotland
SMEE	Captain Hook's assistant
SMEW	Eurasian diving duck
SNA	Scottish snow
SNEE	Old-fashioned dagger
SOMA	*Brave New World* drug
SORA	Marsh bird
SPEE	Graf ____ (historic German battleship)
SRA	Mrs.: Spanish
SRI	Hindu honorific
SRO	Theater box-office sign
SRTA	Spanish miss: Abbr.
STELE	Inscribed pillar (also STELA)
STEN	British submachine gun
STERE	Cubic dry measure
STET	"Let it stand," to a typesetter
STILE	Set of steps over a fence or wall
ST. LO	Normandy town
STOA	Greek portico
STOAT	Brown ermine
STOL	Aircraft acronym
STRAD	Classic violin

SURA	Chapter in the Koran
SUSA	Capital of ancient Elam
SUVA	Fiji's capital
TABU	Forbidden: Var.
TAEL	Oriental weight
TARA	*Gone With the Wind* plantation
TARE	Weight allowance
TARN	Mountain lake
TARO	Tropical tuber
TASS	Soviet news agency
TASSE	French cup
TAT	Make lace
TAV	Hebrew letter
TEC	Gumshoe
TERA	Trillion: Prefix
TIA	Aunt: Sp.
TIC	Spasm; ____-tac-toe
TIKI	Polynesian carving; "Kon-____"
TIO	Spanish uncle
TITI	Small South American monkey
TIU	Teutonic deity
TOLE	Lacquered metalware
TOPEE	Pith helmet (also TOPI)
TOR	Craggy hill
TORI	Geometric doughnuts; actress Spelling
TORTE	Rich cake
TRE	Italian three
TRET	Waste allowance
TYPEE	Melville novel

UBER	Over: Ger.
UDO	Japanese vegetable
UELE	River to the Ubangi
UKASE	Edict
ULAN	____ Bator, Mongolia
ULEE	Peter Fonda title role
ULU	Eskimo knife
UMBO	Projecting stud at the center of a shield
UNA	Heroine of Spenser's *The Faerie Queene*; Spanish article
UNAU	Two-toed sloth
UNCAS	*The Last of the Mohicans* character
U NU	Burma's first prime minister
UPAS	Javanese poison tree
URAL	Russian river or mountain
URE	River in Yorkshire
UREY	Chemistry Nobelist Harold
URI	Swiss canton; mentalist Geller
URIAH	Dickens's "____ Heep"
UTE	Colorado Indian; sport ____ (vehicle)
UVEA	Iris layer
VOLE	Short-tailed rodent
WADI	Dry river bed
WEIR	Small dam
WEN	Cyst
YALU	Korean river
YSER	Belgian river
ZARF	Coffee cup holder
ZED	Last letter, in England and Canada

Calendar of the Year

Understanding Calendars

The Day Earth turns at a fairly steady pace about the imaginary line that defines the North and South Poles. This line through the poles is called Earth's axis. Each turn about the axis, called a rotation, takes slightly less than 24 hours. Since Earth is also traveling around the Sun, however, the time from noon to noon is longer than the time it takes for one rotation—about 3 minutes and 56 seconds longer, or almost exactly 24 hours. The time from noon to noon changes slightly during the year, depending on where Earth is in its path. If you average all the days in a year, the mean time from noon to noon is exactly 24 hours.

The Year All the planets of the solar system travel in nearly circular paths, called orbits, around the Sun. Each trip around the Sun is called a revolution. The planets all revolve in the same direction, which can be observed from Earth by noting the position the Sun has among the background stars, which are traditionally grouped into constellations. (Since you can't see the Sun and stars at the same time, you can observe where the Sun rises or sets each day and then note the stars that appear in the same region.) Over the course of a year, the Sun appears to pass through the 12 constellations that make up the zodiac.

Earth's trip around the Sun, reflected in the Sun's trip through the zodiac, takes about 365.25 days. This varies slightly from time to time, so astronomers add or delete a second in some years to keep their records in tune with Earth's motion. (see also "Precession of the equinoxes" below).

Seasons The seasons mark the change in the pattern of daylight over the course of the year. Because the Earth is tilted with respect to its path around the Sun, different parts receive different amounts of sunlight during Earth's annual orbit, the time we know as a year. Between late September (around the 21st) and late March, Earth's Northern Hemisphere is tilted away from the Sun. This period constitutes the fall and winter seasons for the Northern Hemisphere, during which there are fewer than 12 hours of daylight each day. For the rest of the year, spring and summer, the Northern Hemisphere is tilted toward the Sun, and daylight hours constitute more than half of each day. In the Southern Hemisphere, this situation is reversed: spring and summer last from late September to late March, while fall and winter make up the other half of the year.

At the points of transition from long days and short nights to short days and long nights and vice versa, the equinoxes occur—the two days of the year when periods of daylight and darkness are equal. The vernal equinox, marking the first day of spring, takes place on or around March 21 in the Northern Hemisphere, while the autumnal equinox, marking the beginning of fall, is on or around September 21. Officially, summer begins on the day of the longest daytime during the year, about June 21 in the Northern Hemisphere, called the summer solstice. The winter solstice, about December 21 in the Northern Hemisphere, has the shortest amount of daylight and the longest night of the year. The word solstice means "standing still Sun." These two days are so called because the apparent movement of where the Sun rises or sets reaches its extreme positions on the solstices and then reverses direction.

Lunar Calendar There is some evidence that very early humans (c. 25,000 B.C.) used marks on bone to indicate the passage of time, which they may have measured by the Moon's phases. A calendar for the year can be based upon the Moon's phases, which gives a year of 12 periods from new moon to new moon (hence the word month) lasting about 354 days. This is about 11 days shorter than the time it takes Earth to revolve around the Sun. The Chinese, who still use a version of this calendar, resolve the discrepancy by inserting extra months at fixed intervals to bring the lunar and solar years into alignment. The Chinese year is divided into months that are either 29 or 30 days long, since the time from new moon to new moon is approximately 29.5 days. The New Year begins at the first new moon over China between Jan. 21 and Feb. 19, and is celebrated for a four-day period. Each year has both a number and a name. The year 2007, or 4704 in the Chinese era, is the Year of the Rat.

Solar Calendar   The ancient Egyptians were the first people known to have instituted a solar calendar. In actuality, their calendar might be called a stellar calendar, since the year began with the rising of Sirius (the brightest star in the sky) at the same place the Sun rises, which generally happened at the same time the Nile flooded. The Egyptians determined that a year was 365 days, about one-quarter of a day short of the true solar year, so gradually the Egyptian calendar no longer coincided with the seasons. Historical records reveal when the Egyptian calendar and the rising of Sirius coincided, from which astronomers inferred that the Egyptian calendar must have been instituted in either 4241 B.C. or 2773 B.C. The Egyptian calendar had 12 months of 30 days and five days of festival, a system adopted by various early cultures, although some continued to use lunar calendars.

Julian Calendar   In 46 B.C., Julius Caesar realized that various parts of the land controlled by Rome used different calendars, so he asked the astronomer Sosigenes to develop a uniform calendar. Sosigenes proposed that since the year was 365.25 days long (though not exactly), a

365-day calendar be kept with one day added (a leap day) every fourth year. When Caesar introduced the new system, he also added days to the year 46 B.C. to bring the seasons in line with the calendar. With a total of 445 days, 46 B.C. is the longest calendar year on record. A year at that time began in what we call March, and the months were numbered. September, October, November, and December derive from this system and mean "seventh," "eighth," "ninth," and "tenth" months respectively.

There was a little further adjustment of the calendar, however, by Augustus Caesar, the first Roman emperor. The name of the fifth month was changed from Quintilis to July to honor Julius Caesar, and Augustus named the sixth month August after himself. So that August would not be shorter than 31-day July, Augustus borrowed a day from February.

Because of the Roman Empire's great sphere of influence, the Julian calendar became the ordinary calendar of Western nations.

Gregorian Calendar   From at least A.D. 730, it was known that the solar year—measured from vernal equinox to vernal equinox—was somewhat short of 365.25 days. Each century the solar year gets about half a second shorter. In 1990 the solar year was calculated at 365 days, 5 hours, 48 minutes, and 45.5 seconds long, not 365 1 / 4 days, which is what the Julian calendar assumes. Because the date of Easter was slipping, Pope Gregory XIII instituted calendar reform in 1582. He proclaimed that the day following Oct. 4 would be Oct. 15, which dropped 10 days

Chinese Years, 1900–2019

The Chinese New Year is the second New Moon after the winter solstice. The Chinese Year 4704 began on February 18, 2007.

Year of the Rat	1900	1912	1924	1936	1948	1960	1972	1984	1996	2008
...Ox	1901	1913	1925	1937	1949	1961	1973	1985	1997	2009
...Tiger	1902	1914	1926	1938	1950	1962	1974	1986	1998	2010
...Hare (Rabbit)	1903	1915	1927	1939	1951	1963	1975	1987	1999	2011
...Dragon	1904	1916	1928	1940	1952	1964	1976	1988	2000	2012
...Snake	1905	1917	1929	1941	1953	1965	1977	1989	2001	2013
...Horse	1906	1918	1930	1942	1954	1966	1978	1990	2002	2014
...Sheep(Goat)	1907	1919	1931	1943	1955	1967	1979	1991	2003	2015
...Monkey	1908	1920	1932	1944	1956	1968	1980	1992	2004	2016
...Rooster	1909	1921	1933	1945	1957	1969	1981	1993	2005	2017
...Dog	1910	1922	1934	1946	1958	1970	1982	1994	2006	2018
...Pig	1911	1923	1935	1947	1959	1971	1983	1995	2007	2019

from the year. Furthermore, on the advice of astronomer Christoph Clavius, the new calendar would be kept in line by omitting the leap year in century years unless they were divisible by 400. Thus 1900 was not a leap year in the Gregorian calendar, but 2000 was.

Most Roman Catholic countries and some other Western countries adopted the new system, but England did not. Finally, in 1752, England and its colonies adopted the Gregorian calendar, but they had to drop 11 days to fit common Western practice. It was at this time that New Year's Day in England was moved from Mar. 25 to Jan. 1,

changing the number of the year for the almost three months affected. Thus George Washington was born according to the Julian calendar on Feb. 11, 1731, but he came to celebrate his birthday on Feb. 22, 1732 according to the Gregorian calendar.

Because the solar year is shortening, astronomers today keep the Gregorian calendar in line by making a one-second adjustment, as needed, usually on Dec. 31 at midnight, whenever the error's accumulation nears one second.

Holy Days

Christian Holy Days

Christmas   is the celebration of Christ's birth. The exact date of his birth is unknown, but the date of December 25 was probably chosen because it coincided with the ancient mid-winter celebrations honoring pagan deities. The 12 days of Christmas fall between Christmas and Epiphany (January 6), the day the Wise Men visited the Christ child.

Advent, a religious season that begins on the Sunday nearest Nov. 30 and lasts until Christmas, both celebrates the birth of Jesus and anticipates His second coming. At one time Advent was a solemn season observed by fasting, but this is no longer the case.

Easter   is the most important holy day in the Christian religion. It is the celebration of Christ's Resurrection from the dead, which gave Christians the hope of salvation and eternal life. Although Easter is only one day, the full observance of the holy day spans from Septuagesima Sunday (70 days before Easter Sunday), which may fall as early as January, to Pentecost, which can occur as late as June.

Easter always falls on the first Sunday after the first full moon after the vernal equinox on March 21. Thus, Easter can fall no earlier than March 23 (if the first full moon is a Saturday March 22) and no later than April 24 (if the first full moon is a Sunday, April 17).

Mardi Gras (Shrove Tuesday; Fat Tuesday) Originally a day of penance, the last day before the beginning of Lent is now celebrated with feasting and merrymaking.

Ash Wednesday derives its name from the rite of

burning the palms carried on the Palm Sunday of the year before and using the ashes to mark worshippers' foreheads with a cross.

Lent, a 40-day period of fasting and penitence beginning on Ash Wednesday and ending on Easter Sunday, Lent is traditionally observed by fasting, performing acts of charity, and by giving up certain pleasures and amusements.

Palm Sunday, the Sunday before Easter, celebrates Jesus' triumphant entry into Jerusalem where palm branches were spread before Him to honor His path.

Holy (Maundy) Thursday, is the anniversary of the Last Supper. The traditional services mark three events that occurred during the week before Jesus was crucified: He washed the feet of His 12 disciples; He instituted the Eucharist (the sacrament of Holy Communion); and He was arrested and imprisoned.

Good Friday marks the day of Christ's Crucifixion. The holy day is observed with fasting, mourning, and penance.

Holy Saturday is the day that anticipates the Resurrection. In the Catholic church, special vigils are held on Holy Saturday evening.

Easter Sunday marks the day of Christ's Resurrection. Many worshippers celebrate the holy day with sunrise services, a custom believed to be inspired by the example of Mary Magdalene, who went to Christ's tomb "early, while it was yet dark."

Pentecost (literally, "fiftieth day") is the end of the full ecclesiastical observance of Easter. It takes place on the seventh Sunday after Easter Sunday and commemorates the descent of the Holy Spirit upon the Apostles.

The Annunciation   This holy day marks the

archangel Gabriel's announcement to Mary that she would conceive and give birth to Jesus. It is celebrated by Roman Catholics on March 25; it is not observed by Protestant denominations.

Trinity Sunday The Sunday after Pentecost, this occasion honors the Father, Son and Holy Spirit. It was declared a part of the church calendar in 1334 by Pope John XXII and is observed by Roman Catholics and by some Protestant denominations.

Corpus Christi This feast celebrates the presence of the body (corpus) of Christ in the Eucharist. At one time this was the principal feast of the church year, but today it is observed only by Catholic churches. Corpus Christi is celebrated on the Thursday following Trinity Sunday.

All Saints' Day, celebrated on November 1, honors all of the Christian saints. In America, many churches mark the Sunday nearest November 1 as a day to pay tribute to those who have died during the year. All Saints' Day is observed primarily by Roman Catholics.

Holy Days of Obligation are feast days in the Catholic calendar observed by attendance at Mass and rest from unnecessary work. Six holy days of obligation are observed in the United States:

1. Solemnity of Mary, Jan. 1 (formerly, Christ's circumcision, the first shedding of his blood, was commemorated on this day).

2. Ascension (of Jesus to Heaven), 40 days after Easter

3. Assumption of the Blessed Virgin into Heaven, Aug. 15

4. All Saints' Day, Nov. 1

5. Mary's Immaculate Conception (honoring the Mother of God as the only person conceived without original sin), Dec. 8

6. Christmas, Dec. 25

The Jewish Calendar

The months of the Jewish year are Tishri, Heshvan, Kislev, Tebet, Shebat, Adar, Nisan, Iyar, Sivan, Tammuz, Ab and Elul. The Jewish era dates from the year of the creation (anno mundii or a.m.), which is equal to 3761 B.C.), thus 5768 began in 2007 and ends in 2008 of the Gregorian calendar. (Tishri, the first month of the Jewish year, falls in either September or October of the Gregorian calendar.)

Because the Jewish calendar is a blend of solar and lunar calendars, there are intercalated months to keep the lunar and solar years in alignment. (Intercalation is the insertion of an extra day, month, or other unit—February 29 in a leap year, for example—into a calendar). The intercalated month is called Adar Sheni or Veadar—Second Adar.

Jewish Holy Days

Sabbath is the first and most important Jewish holy day, occurring each week from sundown Friday to sundown Saturday. It is a day of rest and spiritual growth, given to men and women so they will remember the sweetness of freedom and keep it. Sabbath takes precedence over all other observances.

Rosh Hashanah (New Year) held to be the birthday of the world, is also called the Day of Judgment and Remembrance, and the day of the shofar—a ram's horn—which is blown to remind Jews of Abraham's willingness to sacrifice his son Isaac. The holiday takes place on the first and second days of Tishri (in September or October).

Yom Kippur (Day of Atonement) concludes the 10 days of repentance that Rosh Hashanah begins and takes place from sundown on the ninth day of Tishri until sundown on the 10th. The observance begins with the recitation of the most famous passage in the Jewish liturgy—Kol Nidre—which nullifies unfulfilled vows made in the past year. The entire day is spent praying and fasting.

Sukkoth (Tabernacles) is a harvest festival celebrated from the 15th through the 22nd of Tishri. Sukkoth also commemorates the journey of the Jewish people through the wilderness to the land of Israel. Jewish families take their meals this week in a roughly constructed sukkah (booth)—a reminder of an agricultural society, of the Exodus, and of how precarious and fragile life can be. On the Simchath Torah, the 23rd of Tishri, a congregation finishes reading the last book of the Torah and immediately starts again with the first.

Hanukkah (Chanukah, Feast of Dedication; Festival of Lights) The importance of the eight-day feast, which begins on the 25th day of Kislev, is its commemoration of the first war in human history fought in the cause of religious freedom. The Maccabees vanquished not just the military threat to Judaism, but the internal forces for assimilation into the Hellenistic culture of Israel's rulers. Jews light candles for eight nights to mark a miracle: a day's supply of oil, found in the recaptured Temple, which according to religious myth, burned for eight days.

Purim (Feast of Lots) set on the 14th day of Adar, is another celebration of survival, noting the events described in the Book of Esther. At Purim, Jews rejoice at Queen Esther's and her cousin Mordecai's defeat of Haman, the Persian King Ahaseurus's advisor who plotted to slaughter all the Persian Jews around 400 B.C.

Pesach (Passover) beginning on the 15th day of Nisan and lasting seven days, commemorates the exodus of the Hebrews from Egypt in about 1300 B.C. The name, Passover, also recalls God's sparing (passing over) the Jewish first-born during the plagues upon the land brought by God through Moses. The holiday is marked by eating only unleavened foods, participating in a seder, or special meal, and reading the Haggadah, the story of the Hebrews' deliverance from Egypt.

Shabuoth (Feast of Weeks) is observed on the sixth or seventh day of Sivan. Originally an agricultural festival, Shabuoth is a celebration of the revelation of the Torah at Mt. Sinai, by which God established his covenant with the Jewish people.

The Islamic Calendar

The 12 months of the Islamic year are: Muharram, Safar, Rab'i I, Rab'i II, Jomada I, Jomada II, Rajab, Sha'ban, Ramadan, Shawwal, Dhu al-Qa'dah, Dhu al-Hijja. The Islamic calendar is based on a lunar year of 12 months of 30 and 29 days (alternating every month) and the year is equal to 354 days. It runs in cycles of 30 years, of which the 2nd, 5th, 7th, 10th, 13th, 16th, 18th, 21st, 24th, 26th, and 29th are leap years. Leap years have 355 days, the extra day being added to the last month, Dhu al-Hijja. There are no intercalated months or leap years, so the Islamic year does not keep a constant relationship to the solar year—which dictates the seasons—and months occur about 10 or 11 days earlier than in the year before.

The caliph Abu Bakr adopted A.D. 622, the year of the hejira (Mohammed's migration from Mecca to Medina), as the first year of Islam. However, dating of the Muslim era varies throughout the Islamic world. In some countries, the year of the Muslim era is obtained by subtracting 622 from the Gregorian year; 2004 A.D. equals 1382 A.H. (anno hegirae, in the year of the hejira).

Other countries (Saudi Arabia, Yemen, and the principalities of the Persian Gulf) continue to use a purely lunar year. To approximate the Muslim era equivalent of the Gregorian year, subtract 622 (the year of hejira in the Gregorian calendar) from the current year, and multiply the result by 1.031 (days in the year of the Gregorian calendar divided by days in the lunar year): 2005 A.D. = (2005−622) x 1.031 = 1426 A.H. The accompanying calendar uses this method of calculation.

Muslim Holy Days

Ramadan the ninth month of the Islamic calendar, is the Islamic faith's holiest period. To honor the month in which the Koran was revealed, all adult Muslims of sound body and mind fast, eschewing food, water, or even a kiss between the hours of sunrise and sunset. Exempted from the fast are women in menstruation or childbirth bleeding, the chronically ill, or people on a journey, all of whom must make up the fast days at a later date.

Id al-Fitr This day of feasting is celebrated at the end of Ramadan. To mark the fast's break, worshippers also attend an early morning service, Salat-ul-'Id, at which they give alms in staple foodstuffs or their monetary value.

Id al-Adha The Feast of Sacrifice takes place on the 10th day of Dhu al-Hijja, the last month of the year and the season of the haj, or pilgrimage. The day begins with a service in the mosques or other places of gathering, and for those who are not pilgrims, continues with the ritual slaughter of a sheep in commemoration of God's ransom of Abraham's son from sacrifice. At least a third of the meat of the animal is to be given in charity.

Fridays At noontime, Muslims attend mosque or comparable gathering places to say the congregational Friday prayer that ends the week. While Friday is the holy day of the weekly Muslim calendar, it is not a Sabbath comparable to Christian Sundays or Jewish Saturdays, and there are no restrictions on work or other worldly enterprises.

The Hindu Year

The Hindu year consists of 12 months: Caitra, Vaisakha, Jyaistha, Asadha, Sravana, Bhadrapada, Asvina, Karttika, Margasivsa, Pansa, Magha and Phalguna. Calendrically, holidays are of two types, lunar and solar.

Solar holidays in the Hindu calendar include:

Mesasamkranti The beginning of the new astrological year, when the Sun enters the constellation Aries.

Makaraj-Samkranti The winter solstice, when the sun enters the constellation Capricorn.

Mahavisuva Day is New Year's Eve.

Principal holidays determined by the lunar year are:

Ramanavami (Caitra 9), celebrates the birth of Rama, in Hindu folklore, the epitome of chivalry, courage and obedience to sacred law. Considered an incarnation of Vishnu, his name is synonymous with God.

Rathayatra (Asadha 2), the pilgrimage of the chariot festival of Orissa.

Janmastami (Sravana 8), The birthday of Krishna, an incarnation of the supreme deity, Vishnu, celebrated as a philosopher-king and hero.

Dasahra (Asvina 7-10), commemorates Rama's victory over the demon Ravana.

Laksmipuja (Asvina 15), honors Laksmi, goddess of good fortune.

Dipavali (Karttika 15), festival of lights and exchanging of presents.

Mahasivaratri (Magha 13), which honors the god Shiva, one of the three supreme Hindu gods. Shiva, whose name means "Auspicious One," is a god of both reproduction and destruction.

Calendar of Christian Holy Days, 2011–16

Year A.D.	Ash Wednesday	Good Friday	Easter Sunday	Pentecost	Trinity Sunday	Advent
2011	Mar. 9	Apr. 22	Apr. 24	June 12	June 19	Nov. 27
2012	Feb. 22	Apr. 6	Apr. 8	May 27	June 3	Dec. 2
2013	Feb. 13	Mar. 29	Mar. 31	May 19	May 26	Dec. 1
2014	Mar. 5	Apr. 18	Apr. 20	June 8	June 15	Nov. 30
2015	Feb. 18	Apr. 3	Apr. 5	May 24	May 31	Nov. 29
2016	Feb. 10	Mar. 25	Mar. 27	May 15	May 22	Nov. 27

Calendar of Muslim Holy Days, 1432–36

Year A.H. (A.D.)	New Year's Day 1 Muharram	1 Ramadan	Id al-Fitr, 1 Shawwal	Id al-Adha, 10 Dhu al-Hijja
1432 (2010–11)	Dec. 7, 2010	Aug. 1, 2011	Aug. 30, 2011	Nov. 6, 2011
1433 (2011–12)	Nov. 26, 2011	July 20, 2012	Aug. 19, 2012	Oct. 26, 2012
1434 (2012–13)	Nov. 15, 2012	July 9, 2013	Aug. 8, 2013	Oct. 15, 2013
1435 (2013–14)	Nov. 4, 2013	June 28, 2014	July 28, 2014	Oct. 4, 2014
1436 (2014–15)	Nov. 3, 2014	June 18, 2015	July 17, 2015	Sept. 23, 201

Note: The Islamic calendar is based on calculation and depends on actual sighting of the moon. Therefore the dates above are estimates. For exact dates, contact your local masjid, organization, or scholar. **Source:** Islamic Shura Council of North America.

Calendar of Jewish Holy Days, 5771–77

Year A.M.	Rosh Hashanah[1]	Yom Kippur	Sukkoth[1]	Hanukkah[1]	Purim	Pesach[1]	Shabuoth[1]
5771	Sept. 9, 2010	Sept. 18, 2010	Sept. 23, 2010	Dec. 2, 2010	Mar. 20, 2011	Apr. 19, 2011	June 8, 2011
5772	Sept. 29, 2011	Oct. 8, 2011	Oct. 13, 2011	Dec. 21, 2011	Mar. 8, 2012	Apr. 7, 2012	Mar. 27, 2102
5773	Sept. 17, 2012	Sept. 26, 2012	Oct. 1, 2012	Dec. 9, 2012	Feb. 24, 2013	Mar. 26, 2013	May 15, 2013
5774	Sept. 5, 2013	Sept. 14, 2013	Sept. 19, 2013	Nov. 28, 2013	Mar. 16, 2014	Apr. 15, 2014	June 4, 2014
5775	Sept. 25, 2014	Oct. 4, 2014	Oct. 9, 2014	Dec. 17, 2014	Mar. 5, 2015	Apr. 4, 2015	May 24, 2015
5776	Sept. 14, 2015	Sept. 23, 2015	Sept. 28, 2015	Dec. 7, 2015	Mar. 24, 2016	Apr. 23, 2016	June 12, 2016
5777	Oct. 3, 2016	Oct. 12, 2016	Oct. 17, 2016	Dec. 25, 2016	Mar. 12, 2017	Apr. 10, 2017	May 30, 2017

Note: The Jewish day begins and ends at sundown. Thus, all holidays begin at sundown of the day preceding the date shown.
1. Multi-day holiday; first day of holiday shown. **Source:** B'nai B'rith.

BIOGRAPHICAL DICTIONARY

Aaron, Hank (Henry), *b. Mobile, Ala., 1934.* Baseball player. Aaron smacked 755 round-trippers in a 23-year (1954–76) career with the Milwaukee and Atlanta Braves and the Milwaukee Brewers. "Hammerin' Hank" ranks second on the all-time list for career homers and first for runs batted in (2,297) and total bases (6,856). An outstanding all-around player, he repeatedly led the National League in multiple hitting categories and won three Gold Glove awards for his play in the outfield. Aaron appeared in a record-tying 24 All-Star Games and was named the NL's M.V.P. in 1957.

Abdul-Jabbar, Kareem (Lew Alcindor), *b. New York, N.Y., 1947.* Basketball player. Kareem Abdul-Jabbar combined height, skill, and athletic ability to become one of the top "big men" in basketball. As a collegian, the 7'2" center led UCLA to three straight NCAA titles, earning All-America honors three times and honored as College Player of the Year twice. As an N.B.A. star with the Milwaukee Bucks and Los Angeles Lakers, he scored the most points in league history (38,387) and was named M.V.P. a record six times. His teams won six N.B.A. championships (1971, 1980, 1982, 1985, 1987, 1988).

Abelard, Pierre, *b. Le Pallet, France, 1079; d. 1142.* Philosopher and theologian. Born into a wealthy family, Abelard gave up his aristocratic life to devote himself to the study of philosophy. Early on he distinguished himself with his work on the concept of universals. Later, he fell in love with and secretly married his student, Heloise. After incurring the anger of her uncle, Heloise entered a convent, and Abelard entered the monastic life, where he developed the use of dialectical analysis in philosophical argument.

Acheson, Dean, *b. Middletown, Conn., 1893; d. 1971.* American diplomat and lawyer. As secretary of state (1949–53) under President Harry S. Truman, Acheson helped shape the postwar policy of containment of Soviet expansionism, including the Marshall Plan for rebuilding Europe and the North Atlantic Treaty Organization to oppose the Soviets militarily. Critics, however, faulted him for failures in Asia, including the Communist victory in China in 1949 and the invasion of South Korea by North Korea in 1950.

Adams, Ansel, *b. San Francisco, Calif., 1902; d. 1984.* Photographer. Best known for his technical expertise and innovations, and for documenting and preserving the landscape of the American West, Adams helped found the famous photography group f/64, was granted three Guggenheim Fellowships to photograph America's national parks and monuments, and spent much of his career working with the Sierra Club. Adams developed the zone system of metering and exposure, one of the most important photographic innovations of the 20th century. His best-known works include *Moonrise, Hernandez, New Mexico* (1942); *Mount Williamson* (1945); and countless images of Yosemite.

Adams, Henry, *b. Boston, Mass., 1838; d. 1918.* Historian. A direct descendant of two U.S. presidents, he eschewed politics in favor of law, then journalism, then history. His nine-volume *History of the United States of America* (1889–91), which covered the Jefferson and Madison administrations, was acclaimed as one of the finest pieces of historical writing. But he is best remembered for his Pulitzer Prize–winning autobiography, *The Education of Henry Adams* (1918).

Adams, John Coolidge, *b. Worcester, Mass., 1947.* American composer and conductor. Adams began composing as a teenager and at Harvard and he was the first student to submit a musical composition as his senior honors thesis. Drawing on a range of sources from jazz, pop and electronic music, his work is characterized by the minimalist techniques of repetition and simplicity. He is best-known for his operas, including *Nixon in China* (1987), *The Death of Klinghoffer* (1991), and *Doctor Atomic* (2005). In 2003 Adams won the Pulitzer Prize for Music for *On the Transmigration of Souls*, a work for orchestra and two choruses, commissioned by the New York Philharmonic in the aftermath of the 9/11 attacks.

Adams, John Quincy, *b. Braintree, Mass. 1767; d. 1848.* Sixth U.S. president, 1825–29. The first president's son to become president, John Quincy Adams spent his teens in Europe with his father, John Adams, on diplomatic missions for the new nation. As James Monroe's secretary of state, he purchased Florida from Spain, patched relations with Britain, and conceived the Monroe Doctrine. In 1824

Adams was chosen for the presidency by the House of Representatives, after losing both the popular vote and the electoral vote to Andrew Jackson. He was an unpopular president and failed to win a second term. Adams returned to politics in 1830 as congressman from Massachusetts, remaining a powerful antislavery leader until he collapsed and died on the House floor at age 80.

Adams, John, b. *Braintree, Mass., 1735; d. 1826.* Second U.S. president, 1797–1801. Adams gained attention by defending British soldiers brought to trial for the Boston Massacre in 1770. During the Revolution, he persuaded the Continental Congress to commission George Washington as commander in chief, declare independence, and put stars and stripes on the flag. Adams wrote the Massachusetts state constitution (1779), negotiated peace with Britain (1782), and served under Washington as the nation's first vice president. Elected president as a Federalist in 1796, Adams built up the navy and kept the peace, while also signing the controversial Alien and Sedition Acts (1798), which permitted the government to deport foreign-born residents and indict anyone who published "false, scandalous, and malicious" writings. Adams lived to see his son John Quincy Adams elected the sixth president in 1824.

Adams, Samuel, b. *Boston, 1722; d. 1803.* Leader in American Revolution, governor of Massachusetts. Second cousin to John Adams, he was an early voice in the fight against taxation without representation, helping to encourage the Stamp Act riots. A skillful propagandist, Adams was leader of the Massachusetts radicals and made independence his goal. He helped organize the Boston Tea Party, and he was a member of the provincial congress of Massachusetts and the First Continental Congress, in which capacity he signed the Declaration of Independence. Adams also helped draft the Massachusetts constitution of 1780 and served as both lieutenant governor and governor of the state.

Addams, Jane, b. *Cedarville, Ill., 1860; d. 1935.* Social reformer. In 1889, Addams founded Hull House, a pioneering facility that offered education, vocational training, child care, legal aid, and recreational facilities to anyone in need. Her success inspired the settlement house movement, which brought social services to poor urban areas throughout the United States. Addams also spoke out on women's suffrage and labor reform, lobbying for more humane laws governing child labor, juvenile justice, industrial safety, and exploitation of immigrants. A committed peace activist, she campaigned against U.S. entry into World War I and won the Nobel Peace Prize in 1931.

Adler, Alfred, b. *Rudolfsheim, Austria, 1870; d. 1937.* Austrian psychiatrist and founder of the school of individual psychology. A devoted acolyte of Sigmund Freud, Adler later disagreed with him over his emphasis on sex as the cause of neurosis. Instead, Adler focused on childhood feelings of inferiority as the cause of psychopathology. Adler's humanistic approach assumes that an individual is capable of self-determination and the ability to cope with society. Adlerian therapy is encouraging and optimistic, and designed to help the individual reach a state of social maturity. Adler taught in the United States in the 1930's. His key published works include *Understanding Human Nature* (1927) and *What Life Should Mean to You* (1931).

Aeschylus, b. *Eleusis, 524 B.C.; d. 456 B.C.* Playwright. The oldest of the three great playwrights of ancient Greece. Aeschylus's *Oresteia* (458 B.C.) trilogy is considered his masterpiece, exemplifying his concerns with justice, cycles of violence, and the importance of civic law. Of his more than 90 plays, only seven survive intact. These include *The Persians* (472 B.C.), *The Suppliants* (c. 463 B.C.), and *Prometheus Bound* (undated). Aeschylus is credited with introducing a second actor to the Greek stage, which in turn allowed dialogue to take place between actors rather than only with the chorus.

Akbar (Abu al-Fath Jalal al-Din Muhammad Akbar), b. *Umarkot, India, 1542; d. 1605.* Mogul emperor. Akbar, who assumed power in 1556, was the greatest of the Mogul emperors. The Moguls were descended from the Mongolian tribesmen who had conquered much of Asia in the 13th century. By the 16th century, the Moguls had accepted Islam and were enthusiastic patrons of literature and the arts. At first, Akbar ruled a small area—Punjab and the area around Delhi—but his power quickly spread across the entire Indian subcontinent. He introduced administrative reforms that increased centralization, and he insisted that subject peoples were treated fairly, with religious tolerance for all.

Akhenaton, d. *1334 B.C.* Egyptian pharaoh, 1351–34 B.C.. An 18th-dynasty (New Kingdom) king, Amenhotep IV changed his name to Akhenaton—"He who serves the Aton"—to reflect his worship of a unitary god which, unusually for Egyptian deities, had no human or animal form. Although particulars of the worship are not known, Aton is often regarded as the first manifestation of a monotheistic god. Akhenaton and his wife, Nefertiti, moved from Thebes to Tell el-Amarna, and the empire declined during his rule, because of Akhenaton's preoccupation with his worship of Aton. He was succeeded by his more traditionalist son-in-law, Tutankhamen.

Albee, Edward (Franklin), *b. Washington, D.C. , 1928.* Playwright. An adopted member of the Albee theater management family, Albee rose to prominence with such plays as the one-act "The Zoo Story" (1959) and "The American Dream" (1961), and the full-length *Who's Afraid of Virginia Woolf* (1962), that plumb the emotional and intellectual depths of individuals trapped together and trapped within American society. The sustained, brilliant but corrosive dialogue of *Virginia Woolf* established him as a major American dramatist. It was followed by *Tiny Alice* (1964). Three later plays, *A Delicate Balance* (1966), *Seascape* (1975), and *Three Tall Women* (1991), won Pulitzer Prizes.

Albertus Magnus, *b. Lauingen an der Donau, Germany, ca. 1200; d. 1280.* Philosopher, canonized 1931. The teacher of St. Thomas Aquinas, Albertus, a Dominican bishop, was a philosopher as well as an innovator in the study of the natural world. He brought Aristotelian knowledge to contemporary scientific thought, creating a precedent for the study of science within the Christian church.

Aldrin, Buzz (Edwin Eugene Aldrin, Jr.), *b. Montclair, N.J., 1930.* Astronaut. An Air Force pilot who flew dozens of combat missions in Korea, Aldrin earned a Ph.D. from M.I.T. before joining the U.S. space program. As part of the 1966 Gemini 12 flight, Aldrin took a historic 5 1/2-hour walk in space, demonstrating that humans could survive in its vacuum. In 1969, Aldrin, Neil Armstrong, and Michael Collins formed the crew of Apollo 11. In a separate landing vehicle, Armstrong and Aldrin touched down near the Sea of Tranquillity and became the first humans to walk on the moon.

Alexander the Great, *b. Pelle, Macedonia, 356 B,C,: d. 323 B.C.* Macedonian king. Alexander, who became king of Macedonia in 336 B.C., was one of the greatest military leaders in history. He conquered Greece in 335 B.C., then invaded Persia at the head of a Greek and Macedonian army. He defeated the Persians at the battle of Issus (in modern Turkey) in 333 B.C. The next year Alexander seized Egypt. In 331 B.C., he again defeated the Persians and marched east, arriving in 326 B.C. on the banks of the Indus River. On his death, at age 33, his empire collapsed into several warring states ruled by his generals, who continued Alexander's policy of hellenizing subject populations.

Ali, Muhammad (Cassius Clay), *b. Louisville, Ky., 1942.* Boxer. After winning a gold medal at the 1960 Olympics, he won the heavyweight crown with a surprise knockout of Sonny Liston in 1964. A Black Muslim, he changed his name to Muhammad Ali and was stripped of his title for refusing to fight in the Vietnam War (a decision that was eventually reversed in court). Ali won back the belt in 1974 (defeating George Foreman in Zaire in the heavily hyped "Rumble in the Jungle") and again in 1978. Career highlights included three classic bouts with Joe Frazier, including the "Thrilla in Manila" in 1975. Parkinson's disease eventually robbed Ali of the irrepressible wit and graceful motion that were his trademarks.

Allen, Woody (Allen Stewart Konigsberg), *b. Brooklyn, N.Y., 1935.* American movie director, writer, and actor. After writing jokes for television and doing stand-up comedy, he directed film comedies of angst and sex. His multiple Oscar-winner *Annie Hall* (1977) marked a turn toward more sophisticated romantic fare, including *The Purple Rose of Cairo* (1985), *Hannah and Her Sisters* (1986), and *Radio Days* (1987). In a scenario of life imitating art, his messy breakup with Mia Farrow became tabloid fodder.

Altman, Robert, *b. Kansas City, Mo., 1925; d. 2006.* Film director. According to *The New York Times*, he was "one of the most adventurous and influential American directors of the late 20th century." He is most famous for movies that reflected the disillusionment of the 1970's: *M*A*S*H* (1970), *McCabe and Mrs. Miller* (1971), *Images* (1972), *The Long Goodbye* (1973), *California Split* (1974), and *Nashville* (1975). Hallmarks of his movies included an improvisational style, multiple narratives, and multilayered soundtracks that struck viewers at the time as a refreshing depiction of reality in all its complexity. Toward the end of his life, Altman regained critical attention with *Gosford Park* (2001) and *A Prairie Home Companion* (2006). He received an honorary Academy Award for lifetime achievement in 2006.

Ambrose (Saint), *b. Trier, Gaul, 339 or 340; d. 397.* Bishop, theologian, Father of the Roman Catholic Church. Raised and educated in Rome, Ambrose became a provincial governor and, though a layman, was persuaded to become bishop of Milan in 374. He then took holy orders and became a great defender of the faith against the Arian heresy, which denied the divinity of Christ. He also established the authority of the church over the emperors in issues of faith and morality. Though Ambrose was not a speculative theologian, his powerful sermons critically influenced Augustine's conversion and were incorporated into books of biblical commentary, including the *Hexaemeron*. His hymns, original in form, helped establish that Christian musical tradition.

Amundsen, Roald, *b. Borge, Norway, 1872; d. 1928.* **Polar explorer.** In 1897–99, Amundsen sailed with Adrien de Gerlachei's *Belgica* expedition—the first to winter in Antarctica—to locate the southern magnetic pole. He was the first person to transit the Northwest Passage (1903–06). In 1910, Amundsen sailed the *Fram* to the coast of Antarctica and with four companions was the first to reach the South Pole, on December 16, 1911. He later transited the Northeast Passage from Norway to Alaska (1918–20), and in 1925 he flew a dirigible over the North Pole. He died when another dirigible crashed in the Arctic.

Anderson, Marian, *b. Philadelphia, Pa., 1897; d. 1993.* **Singer.** Considered the greatest contralto of her era, Anderson was barred from many U.S. venues because she was black. In 1939, after successful European tours, Anderson planned a concert in Washington's Constitution Hall, owned by the Daughters of the American Revolution. When the D.A.R. refused Anderson, Eleanor Roosevelt resigned from the organization in protest. Denied her stage, Anderson performed at the Lincoln Memorial for 75,000 fans. In 1955, she became the first African American to perform with New York's Metropolitan Opera. Anderson became a goodwill ambassador for the United States and won the Presidential Medal of Freedom (1963).

Anderson, Sherwood, *b. Camden, Ohio, 1876; d. 1941.* **Writer.** Short-story writer whose work influenced writers such as Ernest Hemingway and William Faulkner. His fiction, characterized by patterns of everyday speech and a deep connection to place, is exemplified by his most famous work, *Winesburg, Ohio* (1919), a series of interrelated short stories narrated by a newspaper reporter and all taking place in the fictionalized town of its title.

Ando, Tadao, *b. Osaka, Japan, 1941.* **Architect.** Ando is self-taught and has no degree in architecture but has read deeply—especially the works of Le Corbusier—and traveled widely, filling sketchbooks with what he has seen. His early buildings were houses, including Azuma House (1977), a small row house in Osaka. Later buildings embody concrete cast in stark geometrical forms and include the Chikatsu-Asuka Historical Museum (1990–94) in Osaka and Church of the Light (1989) in Ibaraki. He won the Pritzker Prize in 1995.

Angelico, Fra (Fra Giovanni da Fiesole; Guido di Piero da Mugello), *b. near Vicchio, Italy, c. 1395–1400; d. 1455.* **Painter, illuminator and Dominican friar.** Fra Angelico was one of Florence's most sought-after artists of the early Renaissance. His style, though somewhat conservative, was influenced by Masaccio, and he is admired for strong three-dimensional spatial compositions. He is best known for fresco cycles at the Vatican and St. Peter's in Rome, as well as his fresco of *The Annunciation* (c. 1440–50) at the monastery of S. Marco in Florence.

Angelou, Maya, (Marguerite Johnson), *b. St. Louis, Mo., 1928.* **Poet and memoirist.** Honored throughout her long and prolific career for her poetry, autobiographical work, and contributions to the chronicling of the African-American experience, Angelou, in her early life, also worked as an actor and dancer, traveling throughout Europe and living for a time in Egypt and Ghana, where she worked on the *African Review.* Her memoir, *I Know Why the Caged Bird Sings* (1970), details the racial oppression and violence of her childhood in rural Arkansas. Later memoirs include *The Heart of a Woman* (1981), and *All God's Children Need Traveling Shoes* (1986).

Anthony, Susan B., *b. Adams, Mass., 1820; d. 1906.* **Feminist social reformer.** Working with Elizabeth Cady Stanton, Anthony campaigned successfully to expand New York's Married Women's Property Law (1848), which granted women the right to own property. During the Civil War, they formed the first national women's organization, which also lobbied for a constitutional amendment guaranteeing freedom to African Americans. In 1869, they founded the National Woman Suffrage Association. Anthony cast a ballot in the 1872 presidential election, an act of defiance that landed her in jail. Her crusade for female suffrage succeeded 14 years after her death.

Antony, Mark (Latin: Marcus Antonius), *b. ca. 82 B.C.; d. 30 B.C.* **Roman general and statesman.** Mark Antony was a general under Julius Caesar and a member of the Second Triumvirate along with Octavian (Augustus) and Lepidus after Caesar's assassination. Antony formed an alliance with Cleopatra in Egypt (41 B.C.), but returned to Rome and married Octavian's sister. In 32 B.C. the triumvirate defeated Brutus and Cassius and divided the empire among themselves. When the triumvirate disintegrated, Antony fled to Egypt. He and Cleopatra were defeated by Octavian's forces in the battle of Actium in 31 B.C. and he committed suicide the next year after being falsely told of Cleopatra's death. She too subsequently committed suicide.

Aquinas, Thomas (Saint), *b. Rocca Secca (by Naples), c. 1225; d. 1274.* **Theologian and philosopher.** The greatest figure of scholasticism, a saint of the church, and the founder of what Pope Leo XIII (1879) declared to be the official philosophy of Roman Catholicism. His system, as expressed in the *Summa Theologica* (1267–73) and other writings, is based on the works of Aristotle. The universe is seen as an ordered construct of things, ascending to God, the only necessary and self-sufficient being. The truths of faith and reason are complementary; there are no conflicts between theology and science or philosophy.

Arafat, Yasir (Muhammad 'Abd ar-Ra'uf al-Qudwah al-Husayni), *b. Cairo?, 1929; d. 2004.* **Palestinian political leader.** The founder of Fatah, one of the main military components of the Palestinian Liberation Organization, Arafat became PLO chairman in 1969, and leader of its political arm in 1973. His efforts at diplomacy in the Middle East won him a share of the Nobel Peace Prize (in 1994, with Israel's Yitzhak Rabin and Shimon Peres) and the presidency of the Palestinian Authority (in 1996), but never a lasting peace with Israel nor a full transition to Palestinian self-rule.

Archimedes, *b. ca. 287 B.C.; d. ca. 212 B.C.* **Greek mathematician, physicist, and inventor.** Archimedes spent most of his life in Syracuse (on Sicily). He developed the mathematical theory of simple machines, such as the lever and pulley, as well as the basic law of hydrostatics and applied these laws to build practical devices. Archimedes showed how to write numbers as great as one could desire and how to find the areas bounded by parabolic curves. He considered his greatest achievement to be the discovery of how to calculate the volume of a sphere by comparing it with a similar-sized cylinder.

Aristophanes, *b. ca. 448 B.C.; d. ca. 388 B.C.* **Greek playwright.** Considered the greatest comic poet of his time, Aristophanes wrote the only complete existing examples of Greek Old Comedy. Little is known about his life, but Athens became his home and its politics, society, and prominent figures were the subjects of his satire. Aristophanes parodied everything from Socrates and the sophists in *The Clouds* (423 B.C.) to the Peloponnesian War in *Lysistrata* (411 B.C.), in which the women of Athens boycott their husbands until a peace is reached. The other nine of his 11 surviving plays, out of 50 attributed to him, are *The Acharnians* (425 B.C.), *The Knights* (424 B.C.), *The Wasps* (422 B.C.), *The Peace* (421 B.C.), *The Birds* (414 B.C.), *The Thesmophoriazusae* (*The Women at Demeter's Festival*, 411 B.C.), *The Frogs* (405 B.C.), *The Ecclesiazusae* (*The Women in Politics*, 392 B.C.), and *The Plutus* (388 B.C.).

Aristotle, *b. Stagira, Chalcidice, Greece, 384 B.C.; d. 322 B.C.* **Ancient Greek philosopher and scientist.** One of the greatest figures in Western intellectual history, Aristotle was a pupil and colleague of Plato for 20 years, and served as tutor to the future Alexander the Great when Alexander was a boy of 13. Aristotle is considered the founder of formal logic and in six works known as the Organon, set out a system that survived for centuries. Aristotle pioneered the study of zoology, and established the Lyceum in Athens, the world's first institution with a research library. Unlike Plato's Academy, the Lyceum offered lectures free of charge to the general public. Aristotle's wide-ranging writings on ethics (*The Nicomachean Ethics*), politics (*Politics*), rhetoric, poetry (*Ars Poetica*), and science (*Physics*) made such a significant contribution to human knowledge that Dante dubbed him "the master of those who know."

Armstrong, Louis Daniel, *b. New Orleans, La., 1901; d. 1971.* **Jazz trumpeter and vocalist.** Also known as "Pops" and "Satchmo." The first important soloist and arguably the most influential musician in the history of jazz. Armstrong's virtuoso trumpet playing, beginning with his Hot Five and Hot Seven ensembles, featured dynamic, brassy, highly imaginative improvisation. He was also the first singer to scat sing on record ("Heebie Jeebies," 1926), when he purportedly dropped his lyric sheet while recording and was forced to improvise nonsense lyrics. Other important recordings include "Muskrat Ramble" (1926), "West End Blues" (1928), "Chinatown, My Chinatown" (1932), and "When the Saints Go Marching In" (1939).

Armstrong, Neil Alden *b. Wapakoneta, Ohio, 1930.* **Astronaut.** A Navy pilot during the Korean War, Armstrong became a test pilot for the National Advisory Committee for Aeronautics, which developed into the National Aeronautics and Space Administration (NASA). Armstrong piloted the first manual docking in space as commander of *Gemini* 8 in 1966. Three years later, on July 20th, Armstrong made world history by becoming the first man to set foot on the surface of the Moon, declaring the accomplishment "…one small step for man, one giant leap for mankind."

Arnold, Benedict, *b. Norwich, Conn., 1741; d. 1801.* **American military leader in the Revolutionary War.** Arnold distinguished himself in engagements against the English but became embittered over slow promotions and fell into debt. He offered his services to the English in 1779 in exchange for a high command and a substantial fee. His treason was discovered, and he went over to the English, commanding engagements in Virginia and Connecticut. After the war he was shunned by London society and his name became synonymous with treason.

Arnold, Matthew, *b. Laleham, England, 1822; d. 1888.* **Poet, critic, essayist.** Arnold composed one of the most beloved English poems, "Dover Beach" (ca. 1851), emblematic of the Victorians' loss of spiritual certainty, as well as "The Forsaken Merman" (1849), "The Scholar Gypsy" (1853), and "Thyrsis" (1866). As a poet he expressed alienation, but as a critic—in *Essays in Criticism* (1865, 1888) and *The Study of Poetry* (1880)—he praised uplifting literature that gives value to human life. He wrote extensively about society and culture (*Culture and Anarchy*, 1869). "Culture" was for him encompassed an openness of mind and appreciation of the arts necessary to combat middle-class "Philistinism."

Arthur, Chester A., *b. Fairfield, Vt., 1829; d. 1886.* **Twenty-first U.S. president, 1881–85.** A true machine politician, Arthur worked for Republican candidates in New York and enjoyed several patronage jobs during the Civil War. President Grant appointed him collector of the port of New York in 1871, and Arthur prospered there until 1879. In 1880 "Half-Breed" Republicans nominated him for vice president; he acceded to the presidency on Sept. 19, 1881, after James A. Garfield was assassinated. Arthur rooted out post office graft and signed the Pendleton Civil Service Act (1883) that established the tradition of permanent federal employment based on merit rather than party affiliation, but Democrats in Congress thwarted the rest of Arthur's initiatives.

Astaire, Fred (Fredrick E. Austerlitz Jr.), *b. Omaha, Neb., 1899; d. 1987.* **Dancer, actor, singer, and film star.** Astaire began his career as a child star working with his sister, Adele. In 1917–31, they were regulars on Broadway, starring in a number of classic shows, including *Oh, Lady Be Good* (1924) and *Funny Face* (1927). Astaire went to Hollywood in 1933, where he was partnered with Ginger Rogers, and the two became icons in a series of dance-musicals, notably *Top Hat* (1935), which established Astaire's debonair image. Astaire's success continued with a number of partners after World War II, on film, record, and television. His seemingly effortless style inspired thousands to study in the ballroom studios that bore his name.

Ataturk, Kemal (Mustafa Kemal), *b. 1881 Salonika (now Thessaloníki); d. 1938.* **Turkish leader.** Ataturk, whose last name means "father of Turks," founded the Republic of Turkey and was its first president (1922–38).

As a soldier, he patched together the Turkish forces of the vanquished Ottoman Empire at the end of World War I and repelled invasions by Greece, Britain, France, and Italy. As president, he encouraged national and ethnic pride while simultaneously implementing reforms that laid the groundwork for democracy, modernization of the legal and educational systems, and adoption of the Latin alphabet and European-style names.

Attila, *b. Hunnic Empire, ca. 406; d. 453.* **King of the Huns, 434–53.** Attila the Hun, also called the Scourge of God, ruled a vast territory extending at one time from Germany well into Asia. Attila ruled from 434 to 445 with his brother, whom he murdered, and then alone until his own death in 453. Attila is best known for his savagery and ongoing conflicts with the Roman Empire, particularly his invasions of Gaul (451) and northern Italy (452). Although he was defeated in Gaul, he moved on to sack many cities in northern Italy; he nearly invaded Rome but for a shortage of provisions and the mediation of Pope Leo I. After Attila's death his empire disintegrated.

Auden, W(ystan) H(ugh), *b. York, England, 1907; d. 1973.* **English-American poet.** In his early career Auden was one of a group of English poets dedicated to new techniques and leftist politics. He attacked his country's social and economic system before settling in New York, where he wrote his famous ruminative poem on the outbreak of World War II, "September 1st, 1939." He was a poet of versatile style, simple yet haunting diction, and a range of themes from love to art to politics; his sensibility combined modern psychological insight and homosexual orientation with Catholic faith. Other noted poems are "Spain 1937," "Lay Your Sleeping Head, My Love," "Musée des Beaux Arts," and "In Memory of W. B. Yeats."

Augustine (of Hippo), *b. 354, Tagaste, Numidia, North Africa; d. 430.* **Roman Catholic theologian, saint, Church father, and doctor.** In his youth, Augustine took a mistress and joined the Manichaean sect—a period lamented in his *Confessions* (401). In Italy after 376, Augustine was influenced by Plato, and, inspired by St. Ambrose, Bishop of Milan, he embraced Christianity in 387. He became a priest and was bishop of Hippo, in Africa, about 395. A strenuous apologist in a sectarian age, he produced profuse writings that are fundamental to Christian teaching, emphasizing the Fall of Man and his dependence on God's saving grace. *City of God* (413–26) is his great apologetic work and treatise on God and history. *On the Trinity* (400–16) is his greatest dogmatic work.

Augustus, (Gaius Octavius, or Octavian) *b. 63 B.C.; d. A.D. 14.* Great-nephew and heir of Julius Caesar, became the first Roman emperor in 27 B.C. His reign ushered in a period of peace and prosperity for Rome and the golden age of Latin literature. Upon Caesar's murder by the Roman Senate in 44 B.C., Octavian returned to Rome to avenge Caesar's death. He joined Mark Antony and Lepidus to form the Second Triumvirate and defeat their rivals Brutus and Cassius in 42 B.C. When Antony joined forces with Cleopatra in Egypt, Octavian fought and defeated him at the Battle of Actium in 31 B.C., becoming sole ruler, although he kept up the guise of republican rule as *princeps civitatis,* or "first citizen," until 27 B.C., when he was renamed Augustus. After his death he was deified, leaving behind a system of government that remained in place for centuries.

Aung San Suu Kyi, *b. Rangoon, Burma (now Yangon, Myanmar) 1945.* Nonviolent political activist, winner of the 1991 Nobel Prize for Peace. Suu Kyi began her fight for democracy and human rights in 1988 in response to the brutal military regime of U Ne Win. She went on to serve as general-secretary of the National League for Democracy (N.L.D.), which sought multiparty, parliamentary elections in hopes of overturning the military government. The N.L.D. won 82 percent of the parliamentary seats, but the results were ignored by the government. Suu Kyi was placed under house arrest in 1989 and was released in 1995 after vigorous protests from the world community. She and the N.L.D. continue to be harassed, and she was returned to house arrest in 2003.

Austen, Jane, *b. Steventon, Hampshire, England,1775; d. 1817.* Novelist. Austen lived and wrote almost anonymously in her family's home. Focusing on young women and their families and the urgency of arranging appropriate marriages, her novels are revered for their precision of language and form; skillful, often satirical, delineation of character and society; and combination of comic intelligence and moral seriousness are fully achieved within a small frame. Her first book, *Sense and Sensibility,* begun in her early twenties, was not published until 1811. It was followed by *Pride and Prejudice* (1813), *Mansfield Park* (1814), *Emma* (1816), *Persuasion,* and *Northanger Abbey* (both 1818).

Austin, Stephen Fuller, *b. Wythe County, Tex., 1793; d. 1836.* American political leader in early Texas. Austin founded a settlement in Texas in 1822 and in 1833 went to Mexico City to persuade the Mexican government to grant the settlers self-government. The Mexicans jailed him when he urged the settlers not to wait but to set up their own government. He returned to Texas in 1835 and went to Washington, D.C., where he won military and financial support for the Republic of Texas. He was secretary of state in Sam Houston's cabinet in 1836.

Avedon, Richard, *b. New York City, 1923; d. 2004.* Photographer. Best known to the general public for his photographs of the rich and famous, Avedon started at *Harper's Bazaar.* He shot the French collections in Paris from 1947 to 1984 for *Harper's* and later for *Vogue.* He became the first staff photographer for *The New Yorker* in 1992. Throughout his career, Avedon collaborated with writers such as James Baldwin and Truman Capote on publications that featured their work. His photographs of the civil rights movement and of the Vietnam War are also famous. He received many honors, including the International Center of Photography's Master of Photography Award, and was named one of the world's ten greatest photographers by *Popular Photography* magazine.

Bach, Carl Philipp Emanuel, *b. Weimar, Germany, 1714; d. 1788.* Composer. The second surviving son of Johann Sebastian Bach, C. P. E. Bach was a successful musician and composer in his own right. He served as court harpsichordist for Frederick II of Prussia, and then he succeeded his godfather, Georg Telemann, as *Kantor* of the Hamburg Johanneum. His *Essay on the True Art of Playing Keyboard Instruments* (1744) influenced musicians for several generations. C. P. E. Bach composed nearly 150 keyboard sonatas, including the "Prussian" Sonatas (1740), and 20 symphonies. Although he wrote two oratorios, and almost 250 pieces of sacred music, he was most interested in keyboard composition, and between 1779 and 1787 he published *Sonatas, Fantasias,* and *Rondos for Connoisseurs and Amateurs.*

Bach, Johann Christian, *b. Leipzig, Germany, 1735; d. 1782.* Composer. The 11th son of Johann Sebastian Bach received his musical training from his father and his brother Carl Philipp Emanuel Bach. Known as the "London" Bach, he achieved his fame there, and helped to usher in the "classical" era of music by writing 90 symphonies, many operas, and chamber pieces. In addition to composing, he served as music master to Queen Sophie Charlotte, and accompanied George III when the king played the flute. He taught the eight-year-old Mozart, and the two were inseparable during Mozart's stay in London. His influence can be heard in several of Mozart's piano sonatas and concertos.

Bach, Johann Sebastian, *b. Eisenach, 1685; d. 1750.* German composer and organist of the Baroque period. Bach was the most important member of a large musical family. He was married twice and fathered 20 children, including his sons Carl Philipp Emanuel and Johann Christian, also noted composers. During his life he was best known as an organist and as music director in Leipzig. Later generations discovered that his musical genius perfectly balanced technical mastery, intellectual control, and an almost limitless inventiveness. Notable works include the *Brandenburg Concertos*, Concerto in D Minor for Two Violins, Toccata and Fugue in D Minor, *Die Kunst der Fuge* (*The Art of Fugue*), *Die Wohltemperierte Klavier* (*The Well-Tempered Klavier*), *Goldberg Variations*, *St. John Passion*, *St. Matthew Passion*, Cantata No. 140 (*Wachet auf*) (he wrote over 300 cantatas), and Mass in B Minor.

Bacon, Francis, *b. London, 1561; d. 1626.* Philosopher, writer, statesman. In public life Bacon became lord chancellor (1618) at the court of James I; dismissed because of bribery charges, he retired to his estate to write. His philosophical work, a foundation of the scientific revolution, is found in the *Novum Organum* (1620) and other books. In opposition to older a priori methods of scholasticism, Bacon championed the inductive method of science, arguing that scientific theories should arise only from careful observation and experiment. His best-known literary works are the *Essays* (1597–1625).

Baker, James Addison, III, *b. Houston, Tex., 1930.* American statesman. Baker became under secretary of commerce under President Gerald R. Ford in 1975 and was White House chief of staff (1981–85) under President Ronald Reagan. He was secretary of the treasury (1985–88) in the second Reagan administration and became secretary of state under President George H. W. Bush (1989–92). As secretary of state he served during the Persian Gulf War (1990–91) and organized a Middle East peace conference in 1991.

Balanchine, George (Georgi Melitonovich Balanchivadze), *b. St. Petersburg, Russia, 1904; d. 1983.* Choreographer and co-founder of the New York City Ballet. Balanchine studied at Russia's Imperial Theater, first choreographing as a student in 1919. He made his first European tour in 1924 as a dancer/choreographer with Diaghilev's Ballets Russes, remaining with the company for five years. In 1933, he was invited to the U.S. by dance promoter Lincoln Kirstein; a year later, they co-founded the School of American Ballet. The two formed a number of short-lived companies through the 1930's and early 1940's until finally, in 1948, they successfully estab-lished the New York City Ballet, for which Balanchine became principal choreographer. Among Balanchine's best known dances are *Serenade* (1934), *Orpheus* (1948), *Agon* (1957), *Jewels* (1967), and *Union Jack* (1976).

Balboa, Vasco Núñez de, *b. Jerez de los Caballeros, Spain, 1475; d. 1519.* Explorer and conquistador. Balboa arrived on the Caribbean coast of South America in 1501. In 1510, he founded Darien, Panama, the oldest permanent European settlement on the American mainland. In 1513, he led an expedition across the mountains of Panama and was the first European to see the Pacific; he claimed it and all the lands it touched for Spain. In 1516, he led another expedition that transported two ships from the Caribbean to the Pacific. Accused of treason, he and four allies were beheaded in Panama in 1519.

Baldwin, James, *b. New York City, 1924; d. 1987.* Novelist, essayist, and playwright. Baldwin was the child of a poor African-American family in Harlem. He left New York City for Paris in 1948 and first rose to literary prominence in 1953 with the publication of his autobiographical *Go Tell It on the Mountain,* one of the first novels to reveal the pain of racism. Returning off and on to the United States until the time of his death, Baldwin was a participant in the civil rights movement; most of his essays (collected in *Notes of a Native Son,* 1955; *The Fire Next Time,* 1963) and dramatic works (*Blues for Mr. Charlie,* 1964) are powerful commentaries on civil rights and racism.

Ball, Lucille, *b. Jamestown, N. Y., 1911; d. 1989.* Actress. One of television's best-loved entertainers, Lucille Ball was also one of most powerful executives in show business. She started out as a Ziegfeld girl, then moved to Hollywood and worked her way up from bit parts to lead roles in B-movies. Stardom seemed to have passed her by, but at the age of 40 she moved from movies to television and starred with her husband, Desi Arnaz, in the pioneering sitcom *I Love Lucy* (1951–57), in which she was finally able to display her genius for slapstick comedy. As owner of Desilu Productions, she was the first woman to head a Hollywood studio.

Balzac, Honoré de, *b. Tours, France, 1799; d. 1850.* Novelist and short story writer. A prolific novelist, Balzac wrote for years under various pseudonyms before publishing his first novel under his own name (*Les Chouans,* 1829). He is considered the founder of realism and an innovator in the use of the omniscient point of view, and his work displayed keen observations about French society. His works are collected in the 24 volume *Comédie humaine* (1869–76).

Baraka, Amiri (LeRoi Jones), b. *Newark, N.J., 1934.* Poet and Playwright. Baraka first rose to prominence in the 1960's with his collection of poetry, *Preface to a Twenty Volume Suicide Note* (1961), and his play *Dutchman* (1964). His early work focused on African-American rage at racial oppression, and on black nationalism. He went on to found the Black Arts Repertory Theatre in Harlem in 1965. He has published prolifically, counting among his works several volumes of poetry, plays, collections of essays, and short stories.

Barber, Samuel, b. *West Chester, Pa., 1910; d. 1981.* 20th century American composer. In 1936 Barber composed his *String Quartet*, subsequently known as the famous *Adagio for Strings*. In addition to two symphonies and a violin concerto, Barber wrote a *Piano Sonata* (1949), which is considered a landmark of 20th century American piano music, and a *Piano Concerto* (1962) for which he won a Pulitzer Prize. He composed song settings from texts by a range of writers, notably *Dover Beach*, to the Victorian poem by Matthew Arnold. In 1958 his opera *Vanessa*, with a libretto by his lifelong partner Gian Carlo Menotti, was awarded a Pulitzer Prize.

Bardeen, John, b. *Madison, Wis. 1908; d. 1991.* American physicist. In 1947 at Bell Telephone Laboratories, Bardeen, with William Bradford Schockley and Walter H. Brittain, developed the first transistor that eventually replaced larger vacuum tubes, which consumed more power, in electronic applications from consumer products to the emerging computer industry. The three received the Nobel Prize in Physics in 1956. Bardeen's later studies of superconductivity won him a second Nobel Prize in 1972, making him only the scientist to receive two Nobel Prizes in the same field.

Barnard, Christiaan, b. *South Africa, 1922; d. 2001.* Surgeon. At Groote Schuur Hospital in Cape Town, Barnard caused an international sensation in 1967 when he performed the world's first heart transplant on a human being. His patient, a middle-aged diabetic with incurable heart disease, received the heart of a young accident victim and died 18 days later. But the surgery was a milestone, and its success rate improved markedly by the 1980's, after new drugs were developed to fight the body's rejection of donor organs.

Barnum, P. T. (Phineas Taylor), b. *Bethel, Conn., 1810; d. 1891.* American showman. In 1841 Barnum bought Scudder's American Museum in New York City, where he exhibited the midget General Tom Thumb, and the Siamese twins Chang and Eng. In 1871 he created an inno-

vative traveling circus with animals, including Jumbo the elephant, and freaks, and called it "The Greatest Show on Earth." He merged his circus in 1881 with another owned by James Anthony Bailey. The Barnum and Bailey Circus traveled in the United States and abroad and became known internationally.

Barrymore, Ethel (Ethel Blythe), b. *Philadelphia, Pa. 1879; d. 1959.* Actress. The "first lady of American theater," Ethel Barrymore had style and wit that made her a star of stage, screen, vaudeville, radio, and television. Her best-known stage roles were in *Alice Sit by the Fire* (1905) and *The Corn Is Green* (1940–42). She won an Academy Award for her supporting role in *None but the Lonely Heart* (1944). In 1928, she appeared in *The Kingdom of God*, the first production staged at New York's Ethel Barrymore Theater.

Barrymore, Lionel (Lionel Blythe), b. *Philadelphia, Pa. 1878; d. 1954.* Actor. The oldest son in the first family of American theater, Lionel Barrymore was a star of stage, screen, and radio, as well as a musician and artist. A well-regarded character actor, he is remembered for screen roles in *Captains Courageous* (1937), *Key Largo* (1948), and more than a dozen Dr. Kildare films. He won an Academy Award as Best Actor of 1931 for *A Free Soul*.

Barton, Clara (Clarissa), b. *Oxford, Mass., 1821; d. 1912.* Founder of the American Red Cross. During the Civil War, Barton was the "angel of the battlefield," nursing the wounded and navigating enemy lines to deliver supplies. Relief work in Europe during the Franco-German War introduced Barton to the International Red Cross. She returned home in 1873, and successfully lobbied for the U.S. to sign the Geneva Convention, allowing medics to treat those wounded in battle and mandating humane treatment for prisoners of war. In 1881, Barton organized the American Association of the Red Cross. She served as its president until 1904, expanding its mission to assist victims of natural disasters.

Baruch, Bernard Mannes, b. *Camden, S.C., 1870; d. 1965.* American financier. Speculating on Wall Street (1891–1912), Baruch became immensely wealthy; he then had the leisure to consult on financial and other matters with several generations of American political leaders, beginning with Woodrow Wilson. Before and during World War I he helped find ways of financing war industries, and later, in the administration of Franklin D. Roosevelt, he helped shape economic policies. He continued to offer advice during World War II and in 1946 President Harry S. Truman appointed him ambassador to the United Nations Atomic Energy Commission.

Baryshnikov, Mikhail, *b. Riga, Latvia, 1948.* Ballet star. Baryshnikov studied in Riga and then at the Vaganova School in Leningrad, becoming a principal dancer with the Kirov Ballet in 1967–74. He defected while touring Canada in 1974 and was immediately engaged by American Ballet Theatre as a principal dancer; with the exception of one year at New York City Ballet (1978–79), he remained with ABT through 1989, becoming its artistic director in 1980. In 1990, he founded the White Oak Dance Project. He has also appeared in several Hollywood films, and on television as a dramatic actor.

Baudelaire, Charles Pierre, *b. Paris, 1821; d. 1867.* **Poet and critic.** Baudelaire published only one book of poems, *Les Fleurs du Mal* (*Flowers of Evil*), which appeared in 1857 and was expanded in 1861 and 1868. Its bold, sensuous contents introduced French symbolism and defined the beginning of modernism in French poetry. In it he developed a theory of "correspondences" among the senses, and, as its title suggests, explored beauty's evanescence and closeness to decay and evil. Six of its poems were banned as obscene. Baudelaire, whose life was troubled by spiritual, physical and financial turmoil, was also an important critic of literature and art. A volume of his prose poems was published posthumously.

Beardsley, Aubrey (Vincent), *b. Brighton, England, 1872; d. 1898.* **Draftsman and writer.** Beardsley was mentored by the artist Sir Edward Burne-Jones and was a member of the aesthetic movement. His black-and-white ink drawings were influenced by the pre-Raphaelites, art nouveau, and Japanese prints, and often shocked critics with their curious combination of sensual and grotesque elements. Beardsley died of tuberculosis. His work includes *Hamlet patris manem sequiiur* [sic] ("Hamlet following the Ghost of His Father"), (1891), *Salome* (1892), and *A Footnote* (self-portrait) (1896).

Becker, Gary, *b. Pottsville, Pa., 1930.* **Economist.** A professor of economics and sociology at the University of Chicago, Becker is noted for applying the principles of economic theory to other aspects of human behavior, such as crime, family life, addictions, and racial discrimination. His seminal work on education, *Human Capital* (1964), argued that investing in education and training is analogous to investing in business equipment. In 1992 Becker was awarded the Nobel Prize in Economics, and in 2000 he received the National Medal of Science for his work in social policy.

Becket, Thomas á, (Thomas of London), *b. London, c. 1118; d. 1170.* **Chancellor of England, 1155–62 and archbishop of Canterbury, 1162–70.** As chancellor, he was a favorite of King Henry II. But after his consecration, believing he had to answer to a higher authority, Becket publicly opposed the king's attempt to exert royal authority over the Catholic Church. Becket lived in exile in France (1164–70), but on his return to Canterbury, he was murdered by knights of Henry's court. The matyred Becket was canonized in 1173; his shrine was the object of Catholic pilgrimages for centuries until Henry VIII had it destroyed.

Beckett, Samuel, *b. Dublin, Ireland, 1906; d. 1989.* **Playwright, novelist, short-story writer.** Considered the leading "absurdist writer," Beckett won the Nobel Prize in Literature in 1969. He first achieved worldwide recognition with the production of his play *Waiting for Godot* (1952). Equally facile writing in both English and French, Beckett proved an innovator not only in the sparseness and abstractness of the worlds he created, but also in his sense of wordplay and his ability to create comedy while exploring man's existential isolation and futile quest for meaning. Notable works include the plays *Endgame* (1957) and *Krapp's Last Tape* (1958), the short stories collected in *More Pricks Than Kicks* (1934), and the novels *Murphy* (1938) and the trilogy *Molloy* (1951), *Malone Dies*, and *The Unnameable* (1953).

Bede (Saint) (the Venerable), *b. Jarrow, Northumbria, England 672 or 673; d. 735.* **Monk, historian, theologian; Doctor of the Church.** The Anglo-Saxon Benedictine monastery at Jarrow, where Bede was brought up and which he later joined, was a center of learning, and there he became the greatest historian and leading scholar of the early Middle Ages. His *Ecclesiastical History of the English People*, ending in 731, is celebrated for its thoroughness and accuracy, and in it he introduced into the West the practice dividing dating before and after Christ's birth. He wrote a *History of the Abbots;* an encyclopedia, *De natura reru;,* commentaries on scripture and the Church Fathers; and treatises on astronomy.

Beethoven, Ludwig van, *b. Bonn , 1770; d. 1827.* **German composer and pianist of the late Classical period.** In early 1790's Vienna he drew attention as both a pianist and composer, but his writing was considered odd and difficult. His career began to flourish around 1800, the year of his first symphony. From 1801 to 1811 he grew progressively deaf, but the handicap never inhibited his development as one of the very greatest Western composers. Notable works include Piano Sonatas No. 14, Op. 27, in C♯ Minor (*Moonlight*) (1800–1), Symphony No. 3 in E♭ (*Eroica*), Op. 55 (1803–04), Symphony No. 5 in C Minor, Op. 67 (1804–08), Symphony No. 6 in F (*Pastorale*), Op. 68 (1807–08), Piano Concerto No. 5 in E♭ (*Emperor*), Op. 73 (1809), Symphony No. 9 in D Minor, Op. 125 (1817–23), and Mass in D Major (*Missa Solemnis*), Op. 123, (1819–22). He wrote one opera, *Fidelio* (1805, 1814). Beethoven composed abundantly, with a depth and expansiveness that permanently changed musical form. Considered course in manner, appearance and temperament, he never married.

Begin, Menachem Wolfovitch, b. *Brest-Litovsk, Russia (now Belarus) 1913; d. 1992.* Zionist leader and prime minister of Israel, 1977–83. During World War II he fled from Europe to Palestine, where he became a military leader and commander of the Irgun, a resistance force that used terrorist tactics against the British. After Israel's independence he became head of the opposition Herut Party (1948–67). He was elected prime minister of Israel. In 1977, and though he steadfastly refused to end Israel's occupation of the West Bank and Gaza Strip, he agreed to return the Sinai Peninsula to Egypt. For his role in the historic Camp David Accords, Begin shared the 1978 Nobel Peace Prize with Egyptian President Anwar Sadat.

Bell, Alexander Graham, b. *Edinburgh, Scotland, 1847; d. 1922.* Scottish-born American inventor. On March 7, 1876, the U.S. Patent office issued a patent on Bell's device that sent intelligible words over a wire by converting sound waves to a varying current of electricity. Some have called it the single most valuable patent in history. Though Bell is generally credited with the invention of the telephone, others made substantial contributions to its invention and subsequent development.

Bellow, Saul, b. *Lachine, near Montreal, Canada, 1915; d. 2005.* American author. The winner of the Nobel Prize for Literature in 1976, Bellow was the dean of a group of Jewish-American writers whose work had great influence on postwar American literature. His heroes are often eccentric, Jewish intellectual rogues. Three of his books won the National Book Award. *The Adventures of Augie March* (1953), *Herzog* (1964), and *Mr. Sammler's Planet* (1971). *Humboldt's Gift* (1975), won the Pulitzer Prize for fiction (1976).

Benedict (Saint), b. *Nursia (Norcia), Italy, ca. 480; d. ca. 547.* Founder of the Benedictine monastic order. Benedict is the most important figure in the history of

organized monasticism because he wrote and established the guide—called "The Rule of St. Benedict"—under which monks of his and other orders have been organized ever since. It provided for strong authority under an abbot, combined with prescriptions for all aspects of community life, including daily prayer and manual labor. Benedict emerged from a period as a hermit to organize 12 monasteries with 12 monks each and then, ca. 520, his great monastery at Monte Cassino, between Rome and Naples, where he imposed his rule and lived out his life.

Benedict XVI (Joseph Alois Ratzinger), b. *Marktl, Germany, 1927.* Pope, 2005–present. After serving as a close advisor to Pope John Paul II for more than two decades, Ratzinger was elected Pope in 2005, becoming the oldest newly elected pope in the last few centuries. A respected theologian, his views on the future of the church were of a similarly conservative nature as those of the previous pope's, and like John Paul II, he reached out to other religions and countries around the world. Benedict XVI's papacy encountered several problems, including a decline in church attendance and, most notably, a number of sexual and physical abuse cases brought against priests which bishops in Europe and the U.S. covered up.

Benny, Jack, (Benjamin Kubelsky) b. *Chicago, Ill., 1894 ; d. 1974.* Comedian. Star of stage, radio, television, and film (*The Horn Blows at Midnight*, 1945). Benny got his start in show business while he was still in high school, playing violin for the orchestra of a vaudeville theater. He starred in numerous programs for NBC Radio in the 1930's and 1940's, becoming famous for his miserliness, his screechy violin, and his twenty-year-long mock feud with a fellow comedian, Fred Allen. As host of *The Jack Benny Show* from 1950 to 1965, he was one of a group of ex-vaudevillians and radio stars who came to represent the "golden age" of television.

Bentham, Jeremy, b. *London, 1748; d. 1832.* Philosopher and political theorist. The founder of utilitarianism, Bentham held that the fundamental moral principle is the greatest happiness of the greatest number of people, and that actions and policies should be judged in accordance with this principle. In Bentham's view, public welfare was bound up with personal happiness. His major work is *Introduction to the Principles of Morals and Legislation*, (1789). Many 19th-century legislative and legal reforms in criminal law, the justice system, and the extension of the political franchise were influenced by Bentham and his followers.

Benton, Thomas Hart, *b. Neosho, Mo., 1889; d. 1975.* Painter, illustrator, and lithographer. An American scene painter, or regionalist, Benton was part of a movement of socially conscious and nationalist artists who rejected academic styles and European modernism. He embraced an illustrational style, seeking to document American life in works such as *City Building,* from the mural series *America Today* (1930); and *The Ballad of the Jealous Lover of Lone Green Valley* (1934).

Benz, Karl, *b. Karlsruhe, Germany, 1844; d. 1929.* Automotive pioneer. In 1885, Benz built a three-wheeled vehicle that was the world's first practical automobile powered by an internal combustion engine. Benz & Company started manufacturing four-wheeled cars in 1893, and merged with Daimler-Motoren-Gesellschaft in 1926 to become Daimler-Benz, maker of Mercedes-Benz cars.

Berg, Alban, *b. Vienna, 1885; d. 1935.* Austrian composer. While embracing both atonality and the 12-tone method, Berg brought a welcome emotionality to what were often perceived as cold and calculating forms; he became one of the most influential composers of the early 20th century. His early studies with Schoenberg, along with a friendship with another composer, Webern, influenced Berg's entry into the avant-garde. Notable works include *Altenberglieder* (1912); Chamber Concerto for pianoforte, violin, and 14 wind instruments (1923–25); *Lyric Suite* for string quartet (1925–26); *Der Wein* (1929); Violin Concerto (1935); and the operas *Wozzeck* (1914–22) and *Lulu* (1929–35).

Bergman, Ingmar, *b. Uppsala, Sweden, 1918; d. 2007.* Film and stage director. A superb visual stylist, Bergman became a master at using film to analyze human psychology as well as to depict such grand themes as alienation, isolation, and the search for God. He first won international acclaim for his explorations of the metaphysical, as in *The Seventh Seal* (1957) and *Virgin Spring* (1960), but then grew fascinated with female psychology, as revealed in *Persona* (1966) and *Cries and Whispers* (1972). In 1982, an older, softer Bergman reaffirmed the positive values of life and love in *Fanny and Alexander.*

Bergman, Ingrid, *b. Stockholm, Sweden, 1915; d. 1982.* Actress. In her best-known roles, Ingrid Bergman struck the perfect balance between naturalness and exoticism, self-assurance and vulnerability. She was already a star in Sweden when David O. Selznik brought her to the United States to remake *Intermezzo* in 1939. Bergman gained international stardom as Ilsa Lund, in *Casablanca* (1942), fol-

lowed by *For Whom the Bell Tolls* (1943), *Notorious* (1946), and *Joan of Arc* (1948). She abandoned Hollywood and her family for the Italian director Roberto Rossellini, with whom she had three children including the actress Isabella Rossellini. Her later films include *Murder on the Orient Express* (1974), for which she won her third Oscar.

Berle, Milton, *b. New York, N.Y., 1908; d. 2002.* Comedian, early television star. Dubbed "Mr. Television" and "Uncle Miltie," Berle achieved fame on television with his immensely popular variety show, *Texaco Star Theater* (1948–54). A slapstick comic who grew up in vaudeville and was known for his rapid delivery and trademark cigar, he appeared in 19 films between 1937 and 1968, notably *Let's Make Love* (1960) and *It's a Mad Mad Mad Mad World* (1963), and was a regular television presence until 1966. In 1984 he was among the first to be inducted into the Television Hall of Fame.

Berlin, Irving, (**Israel Isidore Baline**), *b. Tumen, Russia, 1888; d. 1989.* Popular composer. One of the most successful practitioners of American popular song before World War II, with thousands of songs to his credit, Berlin could not read or write music; but employed a secretary to notate the compositions he plunked out on the black keys of his piano. Memorable compositions include "Alexander's Ragtime Band" (1911), "God Bless America" (1918), "Puttin' on the Ritz" (1929), "Cheek to Cheek" (1933), "Isn't This a Lovely Day (To Be Caught in the Rain)" (1935), "Let's Face the Music and Dance" (1936), "White Christmas" (1942), and "There's No Business Like Show Business" (1946).

Berners-Lee, Sir Tim, *b. London, 1955.* Computer scientist. Credited with having invented the World Wide Web, Berners-Lee began working in computer science in the 1970's. In the 1980's he developed a program that provided links between files (later known as hypertext). Between 1990 and 1991, he wrote the programs for the first web server and first web browser.

Bernini, Giovanni Lorenzo, *b. Naples, 1598; d. 1680.* Italian architect, sculptor, painter, and poet of the Baroque. His enormous baldacchino (begun in 1624), the canopy over the altar in Saint Peter's in Rome , helped to establish his reputation at an early age. *The Ecstasy of St. Teresa* (1646), his statue in the Cornaro Chapel, Santa Maria della Vittoria, Rome, is an example of his mastery of Baroque sculpture. Bernini designed a number of Baroque churches, including San Andrea al Quirinale (1678) in

Rome, but he is best known for the magnificent colonnade (1655–67) that forms the piazza in front of the entrance facade of Saint Peter's.

Berra, Yogi (Lawrence), b. *St. Louis, Mo., 1925*. Baseball player and wordsmith. The Yankee catcher was one of the best to ever play his position but he is just as famous for his "Yogi-isms," colorful, sometimes convoluted sayings that contain the ring of truth like "it ain't over til it's over," and "the future ain't what it used to be." Berra played from 1947 through 1963, and he holds the record for the most World Series games played (75). He was named Most Valuable Player three times and was elected to the National Baseball Hall of Fame in 1972.

Berry, Chuck (Charles Edward Anderson Berry), b. *St. Louis, Mo, 1926*. Rock 'n' roll guitarist, vocalist, and songwriter. Berry defined the instrumental voice of rock 'n' roll, in particular its guitar sound and the straight-ahead 4/4 rock beat. He was also a key shaper of the rock 'n' roll song form, and a surprisingly intelligent lyricist. Key recordings include: "Maybellene" (1955), "Roll Over Beethoven" (1956), "Rock and Roll Music" (1957), "School Day" (1957), "Sweet Little Sixteen" (1958), "Johnny B. Goode" (1958), "Memphis, Tennessee" (1964), and "No Particular Place to Go" (1965).

Bethe, Hans, b. *Strassburg, Germany (now Strasbourg, France), 1906; d. 2005*. Physicist. A theoretical physicist who was a central figure in quantum physics, he won the Nobel Prize in Physics in 1967 for his work on the production of energy in stars. He is more familiarly known for his work with atomic weapons. In 1943 he headed the theoretical division of the Los Alamos Laboratory, which was part of the Manhattan Project. He later designed the hydrogen bomb, but he came to believe that such a weapon was immoral, and he became an outspoken advocate for nuclear arms control. His later years were marked by political activism and his desire to develop nuclear power as an alternative to fossil fuels.

Bettleheim, Bruno, b. *Vienna, 1903; d. 1990*. Psychologist. Imprisoned at Dachau and Buchenwald during the Nazi occupation of Austria, he emigrated to the U.S. in 1939 and published a shocking psychological study of concentration camp prisoners' behavior. A psychology professor at the University of Chicago and director of the Orthogenic School for Children (1944–73), Bettelheim developed a widely accepted theory of autism that blamed parents. After Bettelheim's death by suicide, many of his theories were discredited.

Bevin, Ernest, b. *Winsford, U.K., 1881; d. 1951*. English labor leader and statesman. Beginning with a series of manual jobs, Bevin joined the labor movement and in 1911 became a full time official of the Dockers' Union. For the next three decades he was active in labor organizing and in 1940 he joined the cabinet of Winston Churchill as minister of labor and national service. In 1945 he became secretary of state for foreign affairs in the cabinet of the Labour prime minister Clement Atlee, where he helped organize the Berlin airlift and the North Atlantic Treaty Organization.

Bezos, Jeff, b. *Albuquerque, N.M., 1964*. Founder and C.E.O. of Amazon.com. After graduating from Princeton with degrees in electrical engineering and computer science, he worked a string of jobs before landing at D.E. Shaw & Co., a New York based investment bank. He quit the bank in 1994 and opened a virtual bookstore out of his garage and in July 1995 Amazon.com sold its first book. Bezos went on to create a diversified online business that sold everything from apparel, consumer electronics, and hardware. In 2007 Amazon.com released the Kindle, a handheld e-reader that helped create the explosion in the e-book market and by 2010 revenue for the whole company had reached over $34 billion.

Billy the Kid (Henry McCarty), b. *New York City(?), 1859; d. 1881*. American outlaw. McCarty adopted many names, and only near the end of his life was he known as Billy the Kid. At an early age he took up petty crime in New Mexico. He fought in the Lincoln County War of 1878 and was one of six who ambushed and killed Sheriff William Brady. Captured in 1880, he was convicted of Brady's murder, escaped before being hanged, but was tracked down by Sheriff Pat Garrett and shot in his bedroom at Fort Sumner on July 14, 1881.

bin Laden, Osama, b. *Riyadh, Saudi Arabia, 1957; d. 2011*. al-Qaeda founder, terrorist. The founder and leader of the militant Islamic group al-Qaeda, which was responsible for the September 11, 2001 attacks on the World Trade Center and the Pentagon, as well as other terrorist acts including the bombing of the American warship the *USS Cole* in Yemen in 2000. Following 9/11 and the overthrow of the Taliban in Afghanistan, bin Laden evaded U.S. forces and went into hiding. He was eventually found in a secure compound near Islamabad, Pakistan, and was killed by U.S. forces on May 2, 2011.

Bird, Larry, *b. West Baden, Ind., 1956.* Basketball player. Never a great natural athlete, the "hick from French Lick" became one of basketball's all-time greats, with unmatched court sense and passing skills, and a deadly accurate outside shot. After leading Indiana State to the NCAA finals in 1979 against Magic Johnson and Michigan State, Bird signed with the Boston Celtics and was named Rookie of the Year. In his 12-year career (1980–92), the 6'9" forward led Boston to NBA championships in 1981, 1984, and 1986, and was a three-time league Most Valuable Player (1984, 1985, and 1986).

Birdseye, Clarence, *b. Brooklyn, N.Y., 1886; d. 1956.* American inventor and entrepreneur. Birdseye is best known for his method of quick-freezing food to preserve freshness and taste. While in Labrador (1912–17) he observed that fish caught at temperatures of 50 degrees below zero instantly froze and retained their freshness for several months. Though he was not the first to realize the value of quick-freezing he perfected the process for fish and later vegetables and successfully commercialized frozen foods.

Bismarck, Otto von (Otto Eduard Leopold), *b. Schönhausen, Prussia (now Germany), 1815; d. 1898.* First chancellor of the German Empire, 1871–90. He was known as the Iron Chancellor for his assertion, upon taking office as Prussian prime minister, that German problems would be solved with "blood and iron." As Prussian prime minister, and later as chancellor, Bismarck transformed the weakest of the major European powers into a German empire with Prussia at its head. He presided over 20 years of peace in western Europe, yet managed to redraw the map of the continent with a powerful, unified Germany in its center.

Black, Hugo LaFayette, *b. Harlan, Ala., 1886; d. 1971.* American jurist. As a young lawyer, Black joined the Ku Klux Klan in 1923, but he resigned to run for the U.S. Senate in 1926. He campaigned for Franklin D. Roosevelt in 1932 and backed New Deal legislation in the Senate. Roosevelt appointed him to the Supreme Court in 1937, and after a contentious process he was confirmed. Black believed strongly in the literal meaning of the Constitution and argued for the absolute right of free speech. For three decades on the court he moved far from his early racist roots and was a champion of equal rights for all citizens.

Blackstone, William, *b. London, 1723; d. 1780.* English jurist and legal scholar. In 1758 Blackstone was appointed the first professor of English law at Oxford University where his lectures were widely praised. He collected his lectures in four volumes (1765–69) and, though they have been criticized by legal scholars, his *Commentaries* became standard reading for generations of law students. He served in Parliament (1761–70) and was appointed a justice of the Common Pleas in 1770.

Blair, Anthony Charles Lynton, (Tony), *b. Edinburgh, 1953.* Scottish-born English statesman. Elected to Parliament in the Labour Party in 1983, Blair rose quickly as he worked to free the party from its close ties to labor unions and give it a broader appeal. He became head of the Labour Party in 1994 and prime minister in the election of 1997 at the age of 44. He oversaw better relations with the European Union, separate parliaments for Scotland and Wales, and peace talks with Northern Ireland. He joined with the United States in the invasion of Iraq in 2003.

Blake, William, *b. London, 1757; d. 1827.* Poet and artist. Blake, a romantic who preceded the Romantic era, was trained as an engraver, and all his books after *Poetical Sketches* (1783) were composites of art and poetry. His early lyrics, *Songs of Innocence* (1789) and *Songs of Experience* (1794), are beloved for their simple diction and rhythms and haunting images; but his later long, symbolic, prophetic poems can be difficult reading. Blake was a visionary who developed his own mythical system. He is seen as both a political revolutionary and religious mystic. His prophetic poems include the satirical *Marriage of Heaven and Hell* (ca. 1793), *America* (1793), *The Book of Urizon* (1794), and *Jerusalem* (1804–20).

Boccaccio, Giovanni, *b. Paris, 1313; d. 1375.* Italian writer. Born illegitimately, Boccaccio spent his youth in Florence and Naples and became a writer against his merchant father's wishes. His early works were *Il Filocolo* (ca. 1336–38), a prose romance; the narrative poem *Il Filostrato* (ca. 1338–40), based on the Troilus and Cressida legend, and an epic, *Teseida* (1341). His grand achievement was the *Decameron* (1348–53), a volume of prose tales, both tragic and comic, some bawdy, taking place during the Black Death. This panoramic treatment of bourgeois life is one of the first and greatest works of Italian humanism and helped usher in vernacular Italian as a literary language.

Bogart, Humphrey, *b. New York City, 1899; d. 1957.* American movie actor. "Bogie" began on the Broadway stage playing society types; went on to Hollywood, where he had a series of routine tough-guy roles; and reached his prime in *High Sierra* (1941), *The Maltese Falcon* (1941), and

Casablanca (1942), playing introspective outsiders. Movie magic developed when he was paired with Lauren Bacall (later his wife) in *To Have and Have Not* (1944) and *The Big Sleep* (1946). He won an Oscar for *The African Queen* (1951).

Bohr, Niels *b. Copenhagen, 1885; d. 1962* Danish physicist. Bohr's analysis of the hydrogen atom in 1913 explained the spectrum of glowing hydrogen gas in terms of sudden "quantum leaps" of an electron from one orbit to another. From 1918 to 1943 Bohr led the Copenhagen Institute of Theoretical Physics, which became the principal incubator of quantum theory. Bohr himself developed the philosophical basis of the theory. In 1939 his water-drop model of the nucleus of heavy elements was used to predict the properties of uranium-235, the basis of one type of atomic bomb.

Boleyn (Bullen), Anne, *b. London, England, 1507?; d. 1536.* Second wife of England's King Henry VIII and mother of Queen Elizabeth I. The daughter of Sir Thomas Boleyn, who was the Earl of Wiltshire and then Ormonde, Anne Boleyn lived in Henry's court from 1522. Henry's decision to annul his marriage to Catherine of Aragon, his first wife, led to his break with the Catholic Church and the start of the English Reformation. He married Anne in 1533. In 1536, after Anne had suffered a miscarriage and a stillbirth, Henry had her charged with adultery and incest. She was convicted and beheaded.

Bolivar, Simon, *b. Caracas, New Granada (now Venezuela), 1783; d. 1830.* South American soldier and statesman. "*El Libertador*" (The Liberator) led independence movements against Spanish rule throughout South America. His daring attack in 1819 liberated Colombia, and led to independence for Venezuela (1821) and Ecuador (1822). Elected president of the Colombian Republic (1821–30), he preferred the soldier's life. He routed the Spanish army in Ayacucho in 1824, adding president of Peru (1824–29) to his resume, and in 1825, he freed Upper Peru, which renamed itself Bolivia in his honor. A better liberator than a president—his authoritarian constitution gave him dictatorial powers—he resigned after several revolts and an assassination attempt.

Bonds, Barry, *b. Riverside, Calif., 1964.* Star of modern major-league baseball. Bonds claimed one of the game's most cherished records by smashing 73 home runs in 2001; his slugging percentage that year (.863) also established a new single-season high. In 2002, the San Francisco Giants outfielder won his first batting title with a .370 average, set records for walks (197) and on-base percentage (.582), and was named National League M.V.P. In 2003, he won an unprecedented sixth M.V.P. title.

Bonnard, Pierre, *b. Fontenay-aux-Roses, France, 1867; d. 1947.* Painter, printmaker, and photographer. A member of the Nabis and later the Intimists, Bonnard was known for his decorative style and distinctive use of color. In his still lifes, nudes, interior scenes, and images of Montmartre, he documented France's Belle Époque. Later in his career he became interested in landscape scenes and studied French classisist painting. His work includes *The Dining Room* (1913), *The Abduction of Europa* (1919), and *Bowl of Fruit* (c.1933).

Bono (Paul David Hewson), *b. Dublin, Ireland, 1960.* Lead singer of the Irish rock band U2. Formed in 1976, U2 has won 22 Grammy awards for socially and politically charged lyrics, which were initially inspired by political strife in Ireland. Almost all of these are written by Bono, and include the hit singles "Sunday Bloody Sunday," "Pride (In the Name of Love)," "With or Without You," "One," "Beautiful Day," and "I Still Haven't Found What I'm Looking For." Bono also won a Golden Globe for "The Hands that Built America," from the film *Gangs of New York*. Bono is widely known for his humanitarian work in Africa, and for it was named Man of the Year by *Time* and granted honorary knighthood by Queen Elizabeth II.

Boone, Daniel *b. Berks County, Pa. 1734; d. 1820.* American frontiersman. A hunter and trapper, in 1775 Boone blazed the Wilderness Road through Cumberland Gap in the Appalachians in Kentucky, making possible the first settlements in the so-called West. After Kentucky became a county of Virginia, Boone was made captain of the militia. In 1778 he used his own capture and subsequent adoption by the Shawnee to successfully warn and defend Boonesborough against an attack by the British and Indians. Boone was famous even during his own life, especially owing to a feature in Lord Byron's *Don Juan*, as well as popular legends.

Borges, Jorge Luis, *b. Buenos Aires, 1899; d. 1986.* Short-story writer, poet, essayist. Educated in Switzerland, Borges later joined the Ultraist "pure poetry" movement in Spain, and, returning to Argentina, published several books of poems. His primary achievement, however, was his short stories, beginning with the sketches in *A Universal History of Infamy* (1935), followed by *Ficciones* (1944). Many of his tales are fantasies or allegories, including those in *The Book of Imaginary Beings*

(1967), *Dr. Brodie's Report* (1970), and *The Book of Sand* (1975).

Borgia, Alfonso, *b. near Jativa, Aragon, 1378; d. 1458.* A member of the Aragonese court. Was made cardinal in 1444, thereby establishing the family's Italian basis. He became Pope Calixtus III in 1455, and established the Feast of the Transfiguration in 1457. He was resented for his preferential treatment of family members, which included the appointment of his nephew **Rodrigo Borgia** (*b. Jativa, 1431; d. 1503*) to the positions of cardinal (1456) and generalissimo of the papal forces. Rodrigo amassed great wealth and enjoyed the elaborate lifestyle of a Renaissance prince. He was named Pope Alexander VI in 1492. The politically ambitious pope fought the Ottoman Turks, forced the French to abandon their claim to Naples, and cemented his Spanish alliance by granting King Ferdinand and Queen Isabella exclusive exploratory rights to parts of the New World in 1493. He patronized the arts, establishing a center for the University of Rome, restoring the Castel Sant'Angelo, and convincing Michaelangelo to draw plans to rebuild St. Peter's Basilica.

His illegitimate son **Cesare Borgia** (*b. probably Rome, 1475/76; d. 1507*) was named a cardinal in 1493 by his father when he was only 17. His search for power and his worldly lifestyle contributed to his legacy as a pope of low moral regard, and he is considered partly responsible for the ensuing Protestant Reformation. Cesare resigned from the position of cardinal in 1498 to marry a French noblewoman and ally the Borgias with King Louis XII, who was granted a marriage annulment by the pope in exchange. Cesare served as the duke of the Romagna and the captain general of the armies of the church. His use of siege and assassination in his conquest of Northern Italy, and his attempt to establish his own secular kingdom in central Italy, led Niccolò Machiavelli to use Cesare as the model for his book *The Prince*. The pope's daughter and Cesare's sister, **Lucrezia Borgia** (*b. Rome, 1480; d. 1519*), was once notorious for political intrigue, but now she is viewed as more of a political pawn. Her three marriages to Italian noblemen were used to further the family's political power, and the first two were abruptly ended—her second husband was murdered by Cesare's servant—when the pope changed his alliances. Following the death of her third husband, the duke of Ferrarra, she lived quietly as a patron of the arts at the court of Ferrarra, where the great artist Titian found support.

Borlaug, Norman Ernest, *b. Cresco, Iowa, 1914; d. 2009.* American agricultural scientist. His early work on pathology and genetic mutations in plants helped him develop short-stemmed wheat, a high yield, disease resistant variety. This "dwarf" wheat, planted in Mexico, Pakistan, and India, yielded tremendous increases in wheat production and led to the Green Revolution and a drastic reduction in the problem of hunger in those regions. Borlaug received the 1970 Nobel Prize for Peace for his work and is credited with helping reduce starvation worldwide. Later in life he spent most of his time focusing on the hunger problems in Africa.

Bosch, Hieronymous (Hieronimus, Jérôme, Jheronimus), *b. Netherlands ca. 1450; d. 1516.* Painter and draftsman. One of the most distinctive artists of his time, Bosch is known for epic and chaotic scenes that illustrate moral lessons. His detailed compositions, filled with fantastic characters in idiosyncratic landscapes, have been difficult to interpret and have produced much speculation. His works include *The Carrying of the Cross* (ca. 1510), *The Garden of Delights* (ca. 1510–15) and *The Temptation of St. Anthony* (middle period).

Boswell, James, *b. Edinburgh, Scotland, 1740; d. 1795.* Biographer. Boswell is famous chiefly for his exhaustively detailed biography of the philosopher Samuel Johnson, considered the definitive biography of all time. He also kept detailed journals chronicling his own daily life that are considered examples of excellent writing. It is his use of details within the *Life of Johnson* that allows Johnson to emerge as a fully rounded, complex human being.

Botticelli, Sandro (Filipepi, Alessandro), *b. Florence, Italy, 1444–45; d. 1510.* Painter and draftsman. In his lifetime, Botticelli was one of Italy's most admired and innovative painters, but by the time of his death, with the onset of the High Renaissance, his reputation was waning. He did not regain popularity until the 1890's. His most famous painting is *Birth of Venus* (ca. 1484), in which a nude Venus rises from the water on a clamshell. Focusing on mythological and religious scenes, Botticelli combined classical aesthetics with contemporary courtly style. Other well-known images are *Primavera* (1478) and *Mars and Venus* (1485).

Bougainville, Louis-Antoine, Comte de, *b. Paris, 1729; d. 1811.* French navigator. Author of a treatise on calculus before joining the army, Bougainville helped negotiate the surrender of Quebec in 1763. He commanded three voyages to the Falkland Islands, where he established a

French colony. In 1766, he led the first French circumnavigation of the world. The expedition discovered or rediscovered dozens of Pacific islands and returned with more than 3,000 plant and animal specimens, together with opinions of Tahitian culture that profoundly shaped Enlightenment thinking. Bougainville later served in the French navy during the American and French Revolutions.

Bourke-White, Margaret, b. *Bronx, N.Y., 1904; d. 1971.* Photographer. One of the most prominent photojournalists in America, Bourke-White was known for covering difficult, dangerous, and epic events around the world. As a principal photographer for both *Fortune* and *Life* magazines, she developed and mastered the photo-essay form. Her work included coverage of the Dust Bowl and the American South in the 1930's, the birth of India and Pakistan, the bombing of Moscow in 1941, and the end of World War II in Germany. Bourke-White was also the first female war photographer for the U.S. armed forces, and the first woman to fly on a combat mission.

Boyle, Robert, b. *Lismore, Ireland, 1627; d. 1691.* Irish scientist. Boyle's experiments with an air pump led to his postulation of the existence of a vacuum and an understanding of the elastic properties of air. Boyle's Law, published in 1662, states that the pressure of a given mass of gas is inversely proportional to its volume when temperature is held constant. He was also a proponent of the theory that matter is composed of corpuscles, or atoms, that are themselves composed of smaller particles.

Bradbury, Ray, b. *Waukegan, Ill, 1920.* Science-fiction writer. A master of social commentary through science fiction, Bradbury is known both for short-story collections and for novels. Among his short story collections are *The Martian Chronicles* (1950), *The Illustrated Man* (1951), and *The Golden Apples of the Sun* (1953). His novels include *Fahrenheit 451* (1953) and *Something Wicked This Way Comes* (1962). Many of his stories and novels have been adapted for the screen.

Bradstreet, Anne, b. *Northampton, England, ca. 1612; d. 1672.* Poet. Bradstreet was born into a Puritan family and moved to the Massachusetts colony when she was eighteen. She wrote poems that focus on domestic and spiritual matters and became one of the first English poets to write in America. Bradstreet's verse was written for her family, and her first volume, *The Tenth Muse Lately Sprung Up in America* (1650) was published in England without her knowledge. Her sequence *Contemplations*, considered today the finest example of her work, was not published until the mid-19th century.

Brahe, Tycho, b. *Knudstrup, Denmark (now Sweden), 1546; d. 1601.* Astronomer. Prior to the invention of the telescope he designed and built improved astronomical instruments and made precise measurements of the positions of planets and stars, providing an empirical basis for Kepler's laws of planetary motion. His advanced observatory at Uranienborg was funded by Frederick II of Denmark. Among many other things, he studied a supernova (1572) and the varied inclination of the moon's orbit. Brahe did not fully accept the Copernican heliocentric system, proposing instead that the sun revolved around the Earth and the five known planets revolved around the sun. Out of favor with a later Danish king, he spent his last years in Prague.

Brahms, Johannes, b. *Hamburg, 1833; d. 1897.* German composer and pianist of the Romantic era. Brahms's best-received works were his piano pieces, lieder, and other art music; in these genres, he was regarded as the logical successor to Schubert and Schumann (with whose wife, Clara, he fell in love). Notable works include Piano Sonata No. 3 in F Minor, Op. 5 (1853); Symphony No. 1 in C Minor, Op. 68 (1855–76); *Ein Deutsches Requiem* (*German Requiem*), Op. 45 (1857–68); *Liebeslieder Waltzes*, Op. 52 (1868–9); *Hungarian Dances* (1873); Violin Concerto in D Major, Op. 77 (1878); and Piano Concerto No. 2 in B♭ Major, Op. 83 (1878–81).

Brancusi, Constantin, b. *Hobitza, Gorj, Romania, 1876; d. 1957.* French sculptor, painter and photographer. An influential modernist sculptor, known for his primitive aesthetic and his sleek abstracted biomorphic forms, he often reworked a single theme, such as an egg, in stone, wood, marble, and bronze, and he was particularly interested in subjects relating to the cycle of birth, life, and death. Among his famous works are *The Kiss* (1909), *Sleeping Muse* (1909–10), *The Newborn* (1915) and *Bird in Space* (1928).

Brandeis, Louis Dembitz, b. *Louisville, Ky., 1856; d. 1941.* American attorney and jurist. In his law practice Brandeis represented many who lacked power against corporations or the state and became known as the "people's attorney." He fought for the right to organize unions and for wage and hour laws. In 1916 he was the first Jew nominated to the Supreme Court; soon he was dissenting in cases decided by the conservative court. During the 1930's he supported New Deal legislation when it came before the court. He retired in 1939.

Brando, Marlon, *b. Omaha, Neb., 1924; d. 2004.* Actor. Brando grew up in Omaha and Los Angeles. He became a student of Stella Adler at New York's Actor's Studio, and epitomized her "Method" acting style with his performance as Stanley Kowalski in the Broadway production of *A Streetcar Named Desire* in 1947, a role he brought to film in 1951. Movie roles followed: *Viva Zapata!* (1952), Shakespeare's *Julius Ceasar* (1953) and the musical *Guys and Dolls* (1955). He won an Oscar for *On the Waterfront,* and starred in the original biker film, *The Wild One* (both 1954). Brando's reputation declined during the 1960's, but was revived by legendary performances in *The Godfather* (1972) and *Last Tango in Paris* (1973). Long at odds with the film industry, he lived many years in Tahiti, and refused a 1972 Academy Award.

Brecht, Bertolt, *b. Augsburg, Germany, 1898; d. 1956.* Playwright and director. Brecht was the founder of the Berliner Ensemble and creator of "epic theater," which saw theater as a forum for social change. Brecht's plays were politically charged and called for a style of heightened theatricality. Brecht collaborated with the composer Kurt Weill on a ballad opera, the *Threepenny Opera* (1928). Other notable works include *The Caucasian Chalk Circle* (1944), *Mother Courage and Her Children* (1941), and *The Good Woman of Setzuan* (1943).

Brennan, William Joseph, Jr., *b. Newark, N.J., 1906; d. 1997.* American jurist. A Democrat, Brennan was appointed by the Republican president Dwight D. Eisenhower to the Supreme Court in 1956 after private law practice and service on the New Jersey Supreme Court. His expansive view that the Constitution guaranteed human dignity for all suited the court under Chief Justice Earl Warren and he wrote a number of important decisions. But under Warren's successors he often dissented on the more conservative court. He retired in 1990.

Breton, André, *b. Tinchebray, France, 1896; d. 1966.* Poet, essayist, critic, and editor. One of the leaders of the Surrealist movement, and a participant in Dada, its predecessor, Breton, a onetime medical student, was interested in mental illness and was influenced by Freud's ideas about the unconscious. With Louis Aragon and Philippe Soupault he founded the journal *Littérature* which promoted the technique of automatic writing. His best-known works include *Manifeste du surréalisme* (1924), the novel *Nadja* (1928), and *Poèmes* (1948).

Brin, Sergey, *b. Moscow, Russia, 1973.* Co-founder of Google. While a graduate student at Stanford University, Brin and fellow student Larry Page formed the idea that would one day become Google, one of the most powerful and successful Internet sites. Page assumed C.E.O. duties and Brin was named president of technology. By mid-1998 they had raised over $1 million in financing and Google was officially formed as a company. In 1999 Google was processing 500,000 searches per day. On Aug 19, 2004 Google issued its first IPO, netting Brin more than $3.8 billion. In 2010 Google processed over 3 billion searches per day and had over $29 billion in revenue.

Britten, Benjamin (Edward Benjamin Britten, Baron Britten of Aldeburgh), *b. Lowestoft, Suffolk, England, 1913; d. 1976.* British composer of mid-20th century. Britten began his formal studies at age 12, first with composer Frank Bridge and later at the Royal College of Music in London. In 1937, *Variations on a Theme of Frank Bridge* brought him to international notice. *Paul Bunyan,* his first operetta, was performed in the U.S. in 1941 and his reputation as an important opera composer was firmly established with *Peter Grimes* (1945), followed by *Billy Budd* (1951). His *War Requiem* (1962), based on the Latin mass and the poems of Wilfred Owen, is often performed today.

Brontë, Charlotte *(1816–55)* and **Emily** *(1818–48), b. Thornton, Yorkshire, England.* Novelists. The Brontë family was ravaged by tuberculosis. After Mrs. Brontë's early death, the two eldest sisters died while still children. Their only brother, Patrick Branwell, and the youngest daughter, Anne, a novelist less talented than her sisters, died between the ages 29 and 31. Charlotte did not reach 40. Charlotte and Emily studied in Brussels and failed at running a school home. They and Anne then published a poetry collection under pseudonyms; and, using these same names, all published novels in 1847. Of these, Charlotte's *Jane Eyre,* about a governess's love for her employer; and Emily's *Wuthering Heights,* describing the tempestuous, tragic relationship between the genteel Catherine Earnshaw and the elemental Heathcliff, are enduring romantic gems. Charlotte's other novels include *Villette* (1853).

Brooks, Gwendolyn, *b. Topeka, Kan., 1917; d. 2000.* Poet. The first African-American poet to win the Pulitzer Prize (*Annie Allen,* 1949), Brooks' work, often narrative in nature, addressed the everyday lives of urban blacks. Among her many collections are *The Bean Eaters* (1960), *In the Mecca* (1968), and *Children Coming Home* (1991). In addition to her collections of poetry, Brooks published novels (*Maud Martha,* 1953), memoirs, and children's books. In 1989 Brooks received a lifetime achievement award from the National Endowment for the Arts.

Brooks, Mel, (**Melvin Kaminsky**), *b. Brooklyn, New York, 1926.* Writer, director, actor. Brooks started out doing standup comedy then became a gag writer for the television comedian Sid Caesar in 1950. In the 1960's, he made the award-winning 2000-Year-Old Man comedy records with Carl Reiner, created the television spy spoof *Get Smart* with Buck Henry, and directed his first film, *The Producers* (1968), about the improbable success of a Broadway musical based on the life of Hitler. His most popular films were two genre spoofs made in 1974, *Blazing Saddles* and *Young Frankenstein.* Later parodies of Hitchcock thrillers, *Star Wars*, *Robin Hood*, and *Dracula* were less successful.

Brown, James, *b. Barnwell, South Carolina, 1933; d. 2006.* Singer, songwriter, bandleader. In a career that lasted half a century, the "godfather of soul" introduced the percussive genre of funk to the masses. With an innovative sound that influenced pop and R&B and laid the foundation for hip-hop, he sold millions of records. His trademark shuffles, spins, knee-drops, and splits were often imitated. His best-known hits include "I Got You (I Feel Good)" (1965), the Grammy Award–winning "Papa's Got a Brand New Bag" (1965), and the civil rights anthem "Say It Loud—I'm Black and I'm Proud" (1968). He received many Grammys, and a Grammy Lifetime Achievement Award in 1992.

Brown, Jim, *b. St. Simon Island, Ga., 1936.* Football player. Brown dominated the National Football League during the 1950's and early 1960's, and is considered the greatest running back in the history of the sport. An All-America player at Syracuse, he was N.F.L. Rookie of the Year in 1957. He led the league in rushing that year as well, as he did in seven of the next eight seasons. By the time he retired in 1965 (to launch a career in Hollywood), Brown had rushed for a record 12,739 yards and 126 touchdowns.

Brown, John, *b. Torrington, Conn., 1800; d. 1859.* American abolitionist. Brown was strongly influenced by his father's opposition to slavery and while he sought to make a living from tanning, farming, and wool, he was involved in numerous actions against slavery, notably in Kansas. Deciding that slavery could be destroyed by a military attack, Brown organized a raid that seized the U.S. arsenal in Harper's Ferry, Va., on October 16, 1859. But his small group of 21 was easily defeated by a force led by Robert E. Lee and he was tried and hanged that same year.

Browning, Elizabeth Barrett, *b. Durham, England, 1806; d. 1861.* Poet. Chiefly known for her collection *Sonnets from the Portuguese* (1850), which chronicles her love affair with her husband, Robert Browning, Elizabeth Barrett Browning began publishing in 1838 (*Seraphim and Other Poems*). Although ill and a recluse for much of her early life, Browning quickly became well known in literary circles. After their marriage, the Brownings moved to Italy, where Elizabeth spent the rest of her life.

Browning, Robert, *b. Camberwell, England, 1812; d. 1889.* Poet. Browning, once a less-known poet than his wife, Elizabeth Barrett, is now recognized as one of the greatest Victorian poets. He failed as a dramatist but mastered the dramatic monologue to express powerful irony and psychological insight in poems such as "My Last Duchess," "Andrea del Sarto," and "Fra Lippo Lippi." His often colloquial and discordant style affected later poets. Other important poems are *Pippa Passes* (1841), "Love Among the Ruins" (1852), and the long, great narrative, *The Ring and the Book* (1868–69).

Brubeck, Dave, *b. Concord, Calif., 1920.* Jazz pianist and composer. He brought a refined intellectualism to the cool jazz idiom, in part from his classical training. Brubeck's style combined complex harmonies with odd time signatures. The Dave Brubeck Quartet had several successful albums, including *Jazz Goes to College* (1954), *Dave Digs Disney* (1957), and *Time Out* (1960). Key recordings include "In Your Own Sweet Way" (1956), "Take Five" (1960), "Blue Rondo a la Turk" (1960), and "Three to Get Ready" (1960).

Bruegel I, Pieter (**the Elder**), *b. Breda, Netherlands, ca. 1525–30; d. 1569.* Painter and draftsman. The head of a family of artists who were active for four generations, Bruegel painted highly detailed compositions that include many figures in large spaces. He was one of the first painters of his time to portray common people and nonreligious subjects, as in his famous *Peasant Wedding* (ca. 1568), and he strongly influenced landscape and genre artists of the later 16th century and 17th century. His most important works also include *Battle between Carnival and Lent* (1559) and *Parable of the Blind* (1568).

Brunelleschi, Filippo, *b. Florence, 1377; d. 1446.* Italian architect, goldsmith, and sculptor of the Renaissance. Apprenticed as a goldsmith, he also studied geometry and helped to devise the methods for representing perspective on a flat surface. His growing interest in architecture led him to enter the competition to design a dome for the cathedral of Santa Maria del Fiori in Florence in 1418. Brunelleschi's dome was selected to be built and is considered a masterpiece of design and construction, blending a Renaissance dome with a Gothic cathedral. Among his other buildings were the Ospedale degli Innocenti (Foundlings' Hospital, 1419–99), and the churches of San Lorenzo (begun 1418) and Santo Spirito (begun 1436).

Bryan, William Jennings, *b. Salem, Ill., 1860; d. 1925.* **Politician and orator.** Nicknamed the "boy orator of the Platte," Bryan provided a voice for the American heartland throughout his long political career. He sought populist reforms as a congressman from Nebraska but was ousted from office in 1894. Bryan rebounded in 1896, when he railed against the gold standard in his "Cross of Gold" speech, one of the hallmarks of American oratory. The speech swept him to the Democratic presidential nomination. Bryan ran twice more in 1900 and 1908, losing both times. He was secretary of state in the Wilson administration.

Bryant, William Cullen, *b. Cummington, Mass., 1794; d. 1878.* **American poet and journalist.** Bryant wrote the first draft of his best-known poem, "Thanatopsis," when he was 16 and published *Poems*, his widely praised collected work, when he was 27. Moving to New York in 1825 to work in journalism, he became editor in chief and part owner of the *New York Evening Post* in 1829. His paper was an ardent champion of free speech, workers' rights, free trade, and the abolition of slavery, and he helped organize the Republican Party.

Buchanan, James, *b. Mercersburg, Pa., 1791; d. 1868.* **Fifteenth U.S. president, 1857–61.** Considered one of the worst presidents because of his lack of good judgment and moral courage, Buchanan compiled more than 40 years of public service as legislator and diplomat. As president, Buchanan favored "popular sovereignty" over slavery in the territories and was the last of the Doughfaces, or northern politicians submissive to the South. The secession crisis paralyzed Buchanan, who denied both the southern right to secede and the federal government's right to do anything about it; he was relieved to hand Abraham Lincoln the reins in 1860.

Buck, Pearl, *b. Hillsboro, W. Va., 1892; d. 1973.* **Novelist.** Winner of the Nobel Prize for Literature in 1938, She is best known for her novel *The Good Earth* (1931), which

was awarded the Pulitzer Prize in 1932. The daughter of missionaries, Buck was raised in China. Buck's novels, among them *Sons* (1932), *A House Divided* (1935), and *The Good Deed* (1969), often address the struggles of Chinese peasants.

Buddha (Gautama, Siddhartha), *b. Nepal, ca. 563 B.C.; d. ca. 483 B.C.* **"The Enlightened One," the founder of Buddhism.** According to writings from 200 years after he lived, Siddhartha was born in a royal household and grew up in luxury. But seeing death, illness, and old age, at 29 he became an ascetic. Sitting beneath a pipal tree, he passed through the four stages of insight and achieved enlightenment: there is no soul seeking rescue, but only the process of change and death. He spent the rest of his life wandering with a growing band of disciples.

Buffalo Bill (William F. Cody), *b. Scott County, Iowa, 1846; d. 1917.* **Pioneer of the American West.** The legendary Buffalo Bill was a trapper, stagecoach driver, Pony Express rider, and showman. Nicknamed for his skill at hunting buffalo to feed railroad workers, he was also a remarkably adept scout for the Fifth Cavalry as it clamped down on Indian resistance in the West (1868–72). Buffalo Bill's exploits won adulation from journalists and novelists, and persuaded him to cash in on his celebrity. His Wild West Show, featuring a stagecoach robbery, a buffalo hunt, and marksmanship displays, drew audiences worldwide for a decade.

Buffett, Warren Edward, *b. Omaha, Neb., 1930.* **American businessman and philanthropist.** After working as a stockbroker for several years, he formed several investment partnerships and in 1965 took majority control of Berkshire Hathaway Inc., a textile manufacturer, and by 1967 he had expanded into the insurance industry among other investments. Buffett helped Berkshire Hathaway's shares rise an average of 11 percent annually for over thirty years. Dubbed the "Oracle of Omaha," he became devoted to the theories known as "value investing" so he consistently bucked common investment trends. He amassed a fortune of over $50 billion dollars by 2011, making him the world's third richest person. A regular contributor to philanthropic causes related to education and world health, in 2010 Buffett pledged that 99 percent of his wealth would go to charity upon his death.

Bunche, Ralph Johnson, *b. Detroit, Mich., 1904; d. 1971.* **American scholar and statesman.** Bunche contributed to the landmark book *An American Dilemma: The Negro Problem and Modern Democracy*, published in 1944 and edited by Gunnar Myrdal. He participated in organizing the United Nations and in 1946 was appointed to the U.N. Secretariat. When the Arab-Israeli War (1948–49) broke out, he negotiated peace agreements which ended the conflict and for which he received the Nobel Peace Prize in 1950. He later directed peacekeeping in the Suez crisis of 1956 and the Congo in 1960.

Bunshaft, Gordon, *b. Buffalo, 1909; d. 1990.* **American architect.** In 1937 Bunshaft joined the firm of Skidmore & Owings—later Skidmore, Owings and Merrill. He rose in the firm to become a full partner in 1949. The firm became known for its command of the modernist idiom with the glass-faced Lever House (1952) on Park Avenue in New York, designed by Bunshaft. His later work included the glass-walled Manufacturers' Trust Company Bank (1954), the Chase Manhattan Bank (1961), and the Union Carbide Corporation building (1960), all in New York; and the Beinike Rare Book and Manuscript Library (1963) at Yale University.

Burger, Warren Earl, *b. St. Paul, Minn., 1907; d. 1995.* **American jurist.** Burger practiced and taught law until 1953, when he became an assistant attorney general in the Justice Department. In 1956 he was appointed to the U.S. Court of Appeals in Washington, D.C., and in 1969 he became Chief Justice of the U.S. Supreme Court. His professed goal was to repeal many of the decisions of the Warren Court but in this he largely failed. In fact, in *Roe v. Wade*, which legalized abortion, he reluctantly concurred, though his court rendered one of its most far-reaching and controversial decisions.

Burke, Edmund, *b. Dublin, 1729; d. 1797.* **Statesman and political writer.** He became private secretary to the British prime minister in 1765 and entered parliament the same year. He was among the first to argue for the value of political parties (*Thoughts on the Cause of the Present Discontents,* 1770) and was interested in reform domestically as well as overseas. He called for compromise with the American colonists and spoke in favor of repealing the Stamp Act. His most famous work, *Reflections on the Revolution in France* (1790), opposed the revolution; his work has influenced conservative thought ever since.

Burns, Robert, *b. Alloway, Ayrshire, Scotland, 1759; d. 1796.* **Poet.** Burns, regarded as Scotland's national poet, is the best-known writer of poetic songs in English. A farmer much of his life, he wrote mostly in the Scots-English dialect—a fresh infusion of colloquial verse into a neo-

classical age. A scandalous womanizer, he produced illegitimate children and famous love poems, first published in 1786 in *Poems, Chiefly in the Scottish Dialect,* and continuing with such compositions as "Afton Water" (1789) and "A Red, Red Rose" (1796). He is best known for another song, "Auld Lang Syne," but he also wrote excellent satires and the well-regarded narrative "Tam o' Shanter."

Burr, Aaron, *b. Newark, N.J., 1756; d. 1836.* **American politician.** After serving with distinction in the Revolutionary War, Burr practiced law in New York City where he clashed with Alexander Hamilton. He ran as Thomas Jefferson's vice presidential candidate in 1800, but both received the same number of electoral votes and under the Constitution at the time the election was thrown into the House of Representatives which elected Jefferson. Angered by Hamilton's opposition to his later political aspirations, Burr challenged him to a duel on July 11, 1804, in Weehawken, N.J., and killed him. Burr fled a murder charge to the Louisiana Territory, where he hoped to execute a mysterious plan to invade Mexico and establish a separate republic. The plan failed, and he was arrested and tried for treason in 1807, but was acquitted.

Burton, Richard, (**Richard Walter Jenkins**) *b. Pantrhdyfen, Wales, 1925; d. 1984.* **Actor.** One of the brightest stars of the British stage during the 1940's and 1950's, and a sensation on Broadway in the role of King Arthur in *Camelot* in 1960, Richard Burton never quite managed to transfer his considerable talent from the stage to the screen. He costarred with Elizabeth Taylor in *Cleopatra* (1963); their subsequent affair and stormy marriage gave him a tabloid immortality. Burton was nominated for seven Oscars and won none.

Bush, George H. W., *b. Milton, Mass., 1924.* **Forty-first U.S. president, 1989–93.** George Herbert Walker Bush served as congressman, senator, and director of the C.I.A. before serving as Ronald Reagan's vice president and then winning the 1988 presidential election. with a pledge of "no new taxes." Despite being criticized for a lack of leadership, he ordered the invasion of Panama (1989) and Operation Desert Storm (1990) to liberate Kuwait from Iraqi occupation. He also helped oversee the peaceful dismantling of the Soviet Union (1991), and worked with Mikhail Gorbachev to end the arms race. A poor economy contributed to his defeat in the 1992 election; his son George W. Bush later became the nation's 43rd president.

Bush, George W., *b. New Haven, Conn., 1946.* **Forty-third U.S. president.** A former governor of Texas, George

Walker Bush was the second son of a former president to ascend to the top office, winning the controversial 2000 election despite losing the popular vote to the sitting vice president, Al Gore. Bush didn't capture a majority in the Electoral College until five weeks after the election, when the U.S. Supreme Court voted 5–4 to suspend recounts in Florida, which Bush appeared to win by fewer than 1,000 votes. Despite running as a "compassionate conservative," he pushed a pro-business agenda, deep tax cuts (with resulting high deficits), and, after the terrorist attacks of 9/11, an aggressive military policy in Afghanistan and Iraq. Mounting controversies surrounding the buildup to and the aftermath of the Iraq war clouded the final days of his first term, and a vicious civil war there and failure to help victims of a huge hurricane on the Gulf Coast helped to sink his approval ratings and destroy his credibility.

Bush, Vannevar, *b. Chelsea, Mass., 1890; d. 1974.* **Scientist.** A star in M.I.T.'s electrical engineering department, where he built a differential analyzer and an early analog computer, Bush convinced President Roosevelt to mobilize military research in support of U.S. forces in World War II. As director of the new federal Office of Scientific Research and Development, he institutionalized the relationship between business, government, and the scientific community. Bush's Memex concept, introduced in a groundbreaking *Atlantic Monthly* article called "As We May Think," pioneered the idea of hypertext research—a theory that shaped development of the World Wide Web.

Byrd, Richard Evelyn, *b. Winchester, Va., 1888; d. 1957.* **Aviator and polar explorer.** Byrd and Floyd Bennett made the first flights over the Greenland icecap, in 1924–25; and over the North Pole, from Spitsbergen, in 1926. Byrd led two expeditions to Antarctica (1929–30 and 1933–35), during which he made the first flight over the South Pole and wintered alone at a camp in the interior. He subsequently commanded three expeditions to Antarctica in 1939–41, 1947–48 (Operation High Jump), and 1956–57 (Operation Deep Freeze), and flew twice more over the South Pole. He also promoted peaceful international cooperation in Antarctic exploration.

Byron, George Gordon (Lord), *b. London, 1788; d. 1824.* **Poet.** Clubfooted but legendarily handsome, Byron had affairs with perhaps 200 women, including his half-sister, and several men. His notoriety led to exile in Switzerland and Italy. His great poetic gift was for narra-

tive and satire, written with mastery of English verse forms. The first two cantos of *Childe Harold* (1812) made him famous, and subsequent poems introduced the "Byronic hero," the individualistic, iconoclastic immoralist who reappears definitively in his tragedy *Manfred* (1817). Byron's greatest poem, *Don Juan,* a comic, epic satire written 1819–24, was his last. He died in Greece while training troops for that country's war of independence.

Caesar, Gaius Julius, *b. Rome ca. 100 B.C.; d. 44 B.C.* **Roman general, political leader, dictator.** Born into the aristocratic Julii clan, Caesar pursued power and influence throughout his life. His brilliant military successes enabled him to become an effective political leader, and he became consul of Rome in 59 B.C. He undertook the conquest of Gaul's powerful tribes in 58 B.C. and subdued them by 50 B.C. He also subdued Britain in 54 B.C. Fearing Caesar's growing power, the senate told him to resign his command but he refused and in 49 B.C. illegally crossed the Rubicon river and crushed all opposition, eventually defeating Pompey at Pharsalus in 48 B.C. Over the next four years Caesar ruled Rome as a dictator, destroying his enemies but also reforming the calendar in 46 B.C, and introducing social reform before being assassinated in 44 B.C

Caesar, Sid (Isaac Sidney), *b. Yonkers, N.Y., 1922.* **U.S. comedian.** Although his first love was music, and he studied the saxophone at the Juilliard School, Caesar turned to comedy during World War II. After appearing in the Broadway review *Make Mine Manhattan* (1948), Caesar became the star of TV's *Admiral Broadway Review,* a big-budget variety show that famously paired him with Imogene Coca. Together they went on to star in *Your Show of Shows,* a Saturday night fixture from 1950 to 1954 that featured brilliant comedy sketches with Caesar playing a wide variety of eccentric characters. Caesar won the Emmy Award for Best Comedian in 1956 and received the Lifetime Achievement Award from the American Comedy Awards in 1987.

Cagney, James, *b. 1899, New York City; d. 1986.* **Actor.** The epitome of the Warner Brothers gangster, Cagney's performances are distinguished for their intensity and unpredictability. He started out as a song-and-dance man in vaudeville and began his Hollywood career with supporting roles in a variety of genres before getting his big break as *The Public Enemy* (1931), in which he hit Mae Clarke in the face with a grapefruit. In addition to gangsters, he played fighter pilots, G-men, boxers, and Bottom the Weaver in *A Midsummer Night's Dream* (1935). He returned to the gangster film in the classic *White Heat* (1949), in which he slugged prison guards while keening for his mother.

Calder, Alexander, *b. Philadelphia, Pa., 1898; d. 1976.* Sculptor, painter, illustrator, printmaker, and designer. Calder is best known for his kinetic sculptures, or mobiles—delicately balanced arrangements of conjoined hanging pieces that move in response to air currents. Calder was influenced by the surrealists' affinity for incorporating the element of chance. His constructions usually feature abstracted organic shapes, as in *Lobster Trap and Fish Tail* (1939). Other well-known works include *A Universe* (1934) and *Constellation with Red Object* (1943).

Calhoun, John Caldwell, *b. Abbeville, N.C., 1782; d. 1850.* American politician and political theorist. In 1817 Calhoun became secretary of war in the cabinet of President James Monroe; he later served as vice president under Andrew Jackson and secretary of state under John Tyler. As United States senator from South Carolina 1832, he championed states' rights and the institution of slavery. In 1832 he challenged a tariff with a theory of a states' right to nullification of bills they felt harmful. His essays on minority rights in majority rule and pluralism are considered important contributions to political theory.

Caligula *b. Rome, 12; d. 41.* **Roman emperor from 37 to 41.** Gaius Caesar, called Caligula from a childhood nickname meaning "little boot," succeeded Tiberius. His reign was marked by savagery and madness of a legendary nature, some true, some exaggerated, and some outright fabricated, such as the story that he appointed his horse consul. Many scholars believe that a seven-month illness shortly after he came into power left him insane, resulting in mass executions, cruelty, delusions of divinity, and a questionable relationship with his sister, Drusilla, whom he deified after her death. Having squandered a vast amount of Rome's fortune, Caligula was assassinated at the Palatine Games by conspirators in 41. His wife and daughter were also killed.

Callas, Maria, *b. New York City, 1923; d. 1977.* Greek-American soprano. Callas was an international opera star whose wide-ranging performances and many recordings were mainly responsible for restoring early 19th-century bel canto opera to the popular repertoire in the 1950's. Notable roles include Bellini's Norma and Donizetti's Lucia, as well as Verdi's Violetta and Giordano's Maddalena. Her fiery temperament and makeover into a svelte beauty brought jet-set celebrity at the cost of vocal problems. She made only seven Metropolitan Opera appearances.

Calvin, John, *b. 1509, Noyon, France; d. 1564.* Protestant reformer. A conversion experience in 1533 propelled Calvin into the cause of Protestant reform. His *Institutes of Christian Religion* (1536) followed Luther in rejecting papal authority and embracing justification by faith alone and belief in predestined salvation. He was banished from Geneva in 1538 but welcomed back in 1541; he then achieved a full reform of the city under ecclesiastical codes of law and conduct harmonious with industrial society. Calvin exceeded Luther in his diminution of Catholic sacraments, and Protestantism soon split into Lutheran and "Reformed" sects. By his death, Calvin had spread his influence from Scotland to the Netherlands.

Camus, Albert, *b. Mondovi, Algeria, 1913; d. 1960.* Algerian-French novelist, playwright, and essayist. Because of his view that life is absurd, Camus is linked, against his wish, with the philosophical existentialist movement. After being involved in a theater group in Algiers, he became a journalist in Paris during World War II and joined the French Resistance. In 1942 his essay "The Myth of Sisyphus" and his short, terse novel *The Stranger* expressed his theory of the absurd. Other novels are *The Plague* (1947), which dramatizes his belief that humanity can act nobly in the face of meaningless death, and *The Fall* (1956). *The Rebel* (1951) is a collection of essays. Plays include *Caligula* (1944) and *State of Siege* (1948).

Cantor, Georg, *b. St. Petersburg, Russia, 1845; d. 1918* German mathematician. Cantor was the first mathematician to cope directly with infinity. He determined how to compare the sizes of different infinite sets, proving that the set of rational numbers (fractions) is the same size as the set of whole numbers (1895). But both the set of real numbers (any numbers represented by decimals, including infinite decimals) and the set of points in a plane, although equal in size to each other, have more members than the whole numbers. Cantor's work solved problems concerning infinite series but also introduced paradoxes not yet completely resolved.

Capra, Frank, *b. Bisacquino, Sicily 1897; d. 1991.* **Film director.** Frank Capra made hugely entertaining movies in a variety of genres but always returned to the populist social comedy, in which honesty, optimism, and compassion defeat cynicism and corruption. Among his most important films are the classic screwball comedy *It Happened One Night* (1934), *Mr. Smith Goes to Washington* (1939), and the perennial Christmas favorite, *It's a Wonderful Life* (1946). He also produced and directed a series of famous wartime propaganda films, *Why We Fight*.

Caravaggio, Michelangelo Merisi da (Merisi, Michelangelo), b. *Milan or Caravaggio, Italy, 1571; d. 1610.* Painter. After an early career painting portraits, still lifes, and genre scenes, Caravaggio turned to religious subjects, espousing a bold style that emphasized the contrast between light and shade. Rejecting the formality of his Mannerist predecessors, he painted common people rather than idealized beauties. Caravaggio repeatedly ran into trouble with the law, culminating in a murder he committed in 1600. His paintings, which influenced later European artists such as Rubens and Velázquez, include *The Lute-Player* (ca. 1595–97) and *The Calling of St. Matthew* (1599–1602).

Carlyle, Thomas, b. *Ecclefechan, Scotland, 1795; d. 1881.* Author. Educated in Scotland and later resident in London (1834), he was an expert on German literature and philosophy. His *Sartor Resartus* (1833–4) is a complex spiritual autobiography. Carlyle, influenced by transcendentalism, had a religious outlook without conventional Christian belief. *The French Revolution: A History* (1837), was an acclaimed interpretation of an event that spoke to the fears and hopes of the day. In his later work he alienated former allies such as John Stuart Mill by attacking parliamentary systems and glorifying autocratic "heroes" such as Cromwell and Frederick the Great.

Carnegie, Andrew, b. *Dunfermline, Scotland, 1835; d. 1919.* Scottish born American industrialist and philanthropist. Carnegie's father, in search of factory work, moved his family to Pittsburgh in 1848. After working in a mill and as a telegraph operator, Carnegie became a railroad superintendant. He entered the steel business in 1864 and built up the business through mergers and acquisitions, often with his competitors. A violently supressed strike at the Homestead Plant in 1892 sullied his reputation. In 1901, unsatisfied with his life, Carnegie sold his company and began to give away his money in ways of direct benefit to society. By the time of his death he had given away nine-tenths of his enormous wealth to philanthropic causes including public libraries and New York's Carnegie Hall.

Carothers, Wallace Hume, b. *Burlington, Iowa, 1896; d. 1937.* American chemist. Carothers, working at the DuPont chemical corporation, established by experiment the theory of how polymers, the chemical basis of plastics, form. He applied this to developing neoprene (1932), an artificial rubber that resists the degradation caused in natural rubber by heat, light, or chemicals. Carothers next turned to artificial fibers, and produced nylon in 1934. Not only has nylon replaced silk for some types of clothing and wool for durable rugs, but it is also used as a strong solid plastic.

Carson, Johnny, b. *Corning, Iowa, 1925; d. 2005.* Late-night television host, comedian. The king of late-night television, Carson hosted *The Tonight Show* for nearly 30 years (1962–92), shaping the format for the television chat show with his guest couch and studio band. One of the most popular and powerful television performers of his era, he was admired for his charm, self-depreciating humor, and comic timing, and he helped to launch the careers of many celebrities. Winner of four Emmy Awards, he was inducted into the Television Hall of Fame in 1987, and received the Presidential Medal of Freedom in 1992.

Carter, Elliott, b. *New York City, N.Y., 1908.* 20th century American composer. In 1971 Aaron Copland nominated Elliot Carter for the Gold Medal of the National Institute of Arts and Letters for Eminence in Music, calling him "one of America's most distinguished creative artists in any field." He is considered one of the great innovators of 20th century music, known for his atonal, rhythmically complex pieces, winning his first Pulitzer Prize in 1960 for his *Second String Quartet*. In 1973 he won his second Pulitzer Prize for *String Quartet No. 3*. Carter was the first composer to receive the United States National Medal of Arts in 1985. Still productive in his later years, Carter published 40 works after turning 90 years old, and three after his 100th birthday in 2008.

Carter, Jimmy (James Earl), b. *Plains, Ga., 1924.* Thirty-ninth U.S. president, 1977–81. Carter grew up on a farm with no plumbing or electricity but realized his dream of attending the U.S. Naval Academy, after which he joined the submarine fleet and studied nuclear physics. He left the Navy in 1953 to run the family peanut business, was elected to the Georgia state senate in 1962, and became governor in 1970. Carter's, homespun style and vows of honesty struck a chord with voters after Watergate, and he defeated the incumbent, Gerald R. Ford, for the presidency in 1976. Lack of Washington connections helped his candidacy but not his presidency, as congress ignored Carter's pleas for tax reform and a long-range energy policy. When oil prices doubled, most

Americans blamed Carter for runaway inflation; this, combined with the Iran hostage crisis, led to his landslide defeat in the 1980 election. In later years he became a trusted figure around the world, often monitoring contentious elections.

Cartier, Jacques, *b. Saint-Malo, France, 1491; d. 1557.* **French navigator.** Cartier may have sailed with Giovanni da Verrazano to North America and to Brazil (1524–27). He persuaded Francis I to sponsor a search for the Northwest Passage, and in 1534 he explored Canada between Newfoundland and New Brunswick. A second expedition the next year sailed up the St. Lawrence River as far as the Huron settlement of Hochelaga (Montreal). On his third and probably last voyage (1541–42), to help establish a French colony in Canada, Cartier reached the Lachine Rapids above Hochelaga.

Cartier-Bresson, Henri, *b. Chanteloup, France, 1908; d. 2004.* **Photographer.** After studying to be a painter, Cartier-Bresson chose photography as his art form, and, using simple technique and equipment, black-and-white film, and realistic, unstaged conditions, he became the 20th century's leading photojournalist. Beginning with his creation of an underground photography unit during the World War II French resistance, he captured historic events and conditions of life around the world. He was also famous for his photographic portraits of the world's most famous people (Gandhi, Sartre, Matisse, et al.). Among several books of his collected photographs, the best-known is *The Decisive Moment* (1952), a title that expresses his artistic purpose.

Cash, Johnny, (**John R.**) *b. Kingsland, Ark., 1932; d. 2003.* **Country vocalist and songwriter, also known as "The Man in Black."** Cash was one of the most respected and influential figures in modern country music. His deep baritone voice perfectly complemented his earnest compositions, most which combined the emotional honesty of folk music, the rebelliousness of rock and roll, and the world-weariness of country. Key recordings include "Folsom Prison Blues" (1956/1968), "I Walk the Line" (1956), "Ring of Fire" (1963), "Jackson" (1967), and "A Boy Named Sue" (1969).

Cassatt, Mary (**Stevenson**), *b. Allegheny City (now Pittsburgh), Pa., 1844; d. 1926.* **American painter and printmaker, active in France.** In her early career, Cassatt worked primarily as a genre painter, exhibiting regularly in the U.S. and at the Paris Salon. As her style became looser and more innovative, Degas invited her to join the Impressionist circle, in which she had considerable success with her portraits of women and children. After being forced to retire in 1915 because of cataracts, she continued to advise younger artists. Her works include *Woman in a Loge* (1879) and *The Bath* (1891).

Cassini, Gian Domenico, *b. Perinaldo, Italy, 1625; d. 1712.* **Astronomer.** At Bologna he studied the sun and planets, determining the periods of rotation around their own axes of Jupiter, Mars, and Venus. At Paris, where he was director of the Royal Observatory, he discovered four satellites of Saturn and studied its ring system; he also initiated the mapping of the geographic meridian passing through Paris.

Castro, Fidel Ruz, *b. near Birán, Cuba, 1926 or 1927.* **Cuban dictator.** Castro seized power in 1959, when his army of 800 guerrillas routed Gen. Fulgencio Batista's 30,000 government troops. He began turning Cuba into the first communist state in the Western Hemisphere, cutting ties with the U.S. and opening trade and arms agreements with the Soviet Union. In 1961, the U.S.-led Bay of Pigs invasion failed to overthrow Castro. Cuba remained communist even after the fall of the Soviet Union, but in the 1990's, Castro began permitting Cubans to leave the country; thousands fled to the United States.

Cather, Willa, *b. Winchester, Va., 1873; d. 1947.* **Novelist.** The child of a pioneer family, Cather grew up in frontier Nebraska and went on to become a magazine editor in New York before turning to the writing of fiction. Cather's best-known novels, of which *O Pioneers!* (1913) and *My Antonia* (1918) are considered her finest, depict the life of the pioneer as a celebration of spirit and courage. Other novels include *One of Ours* (1922), which won the Pulitzer Prize, and *Obscure Destinies* (1932).

Catherine the Great (**Sophie Fredericke Auguste von Anhalt-Zerbst**), *b. Stettin, Prussia (now Szczecin, Poland), 1729; d. 1796.* As empress for more than 30 years, she molded Russia into a modern European superpower. Months after her husband Peter took the throne in 1762, Catherine had him deposed and murdered. Under her reign, Russia seized vast new territories and was swiftly modernized and westernized (often at the expense of the serfs). A patron of the arts, she founded the Hermitage Museum and many academies and libraries. Though her sexual escapades have been exaggerated, she did take many lovers, including state advisors.

Catullus *b. Verona, Italy, ?84 B.C.; d. ?54 B.C.* **Roman lyric poet.** A contemporary of Caesar, Cicero, and Pompey,

Catullus is considered one of the finest lyric poets. He arrived in Rome around 62 B.C. and established himself as an aristocrat and prominent figure. His poems, 116 of which survive, were often short, sometimes satirical, and always skillful. His most famous works are passionate poems addressing Lesbia, the pseudonym for his mistress, probably Clodia, the sister of a well-known Roman statesman.

Cavendish, Henry, *b. Nice, France, 1731; d. 1810.* English physicist and chemist. Reclusive and taciturn, Cavendish was one of the great scientists of his day. His most important contributions lay in his research into the chemical properties of gases, by which he isolated hydrogen and through his research on air, discovered (as did James Watt, independently) that water is a compound, not an element. Cavendish also made major contributions to electrical theory, anticipating the work of Faraday, Coulomb, and Ohm. In his seventies, he devised the Cavendish experiment to determine the gravitational constant and measure the density of the Earth.

Cervantes (Saavedra), Miguel de, *b. Alcala de Henares, Spain, 1547; d. 1616.* Novelist, poet, playwright. He was wounded at the battle of Lepanto in 1571, enslaved by Barbary pirates, impoverished, and briefly imprisoned. Cervantes took up writing poetry, stories, and plays, and in 1605 he produced the first part of the most internationally popular work of Spanish literature, *Don Quixote* (Part II, 1615), a long burlesque of chivalric romance, featuring an aging, gaunt, self-proclaimed knight who sets out, in the company of his round, earthy squire, on a series adventures to impose his idealism on Spanish society. It has often been called the world's first novel. Cervantes continued to publish—stories, stage-pieces, and a romance—until his death.

Cézanne, Paul, *b. Aix-en-Provence, France, 1839; d. 1906.* Painter. His early work featured dark, fantastical subjects, but Cézanne later adopted the Impressionists' colorful, rhythmic brushstrokes and love of nature. Departing from the Impressionists' ambition to capture fleeting moments, however, Cézanne aspired to portray permanence and solidity in his images, and is therefore considered a Postimpressionist. His still lifes, landscapes, and portraits are seen as precursors to important developments in 20th-century artwork, particularly Cubism. Not fully recognized during his lifetime, Cézanne has become famous for images such as *Still Life with Apples* (1879–82) and *Mont Sainte-Victoire* (ca. 1885–87).

Chamberlain, Wilt, *b. Philadelphia, Pa., 1936; d. 1999.*

The dominant basketball player of his generation. Chamberlain compiled 31,419 points and 23,924 rebounds in a storied N.B.A. career (1959–73). He ranks third on the all-time N.B.A. list in scoring and first in rebounding. Chamberlain's records also include single-season scoring average (50.4 in 1962) and most points in one game (100). Known as "Wilt the Stilt," the 7'1" center was named M.V.P. four times (1960, 1966–68) and won championships in 1967 with the Philadelphia '76ers and in 1972 with the Los Angeles Lakers.

Champlain, Samuel de, *b. Brouage, France, 1567; d. 1635.* Explorer. Champlain's first major voyage (1599–1602) took him to the West Indies, Mexico, and Panama. In 1603 Champlain was invited to explore the St. Lawrence River in Canada. During his second voyage (1604–07) he made multiple surveys of what would become eastern Canada and the northeastern United States. On his third voyage in 1608, he mapped the Great Lakes region, discovered the lake that today bears his name (1609), and founded a fur-trading settlement on the St. Lawrence River that became Québec City. Forming alliances with the Hurons and the Algonquins, Champlain engaged in several skirmishes with the Iroquois, beginning a legacy of violence that would linger for many decades. Champlain's later years were spent formalizing the administration of "New France" and expanding the fur trade.

Chaplin, Charlie (Charles Spencer Chaplin) *b. London, England, 1889; d. 1977.* Silent film comedian and director. His Dickensian childhood inspired his screen character, the Little Tramp, who embodied the dreams and disappointments of the lower social classes. Chaplin was a superb pantomimist; his forte was his graceful handling of props to define character and reveal emotions. The Little Tramp emerged in the short *Kid Auto Races at Venice* (1914) and was fully formed by *The Tramp* (1915). Chaplin, who directed himself, moved to feature-length films with the *The Kid* (1921) and *The Gold Rush* (1925), his masterpiece. Other classics include *Modern Times* (1931) and *The Great Dictator* (1940). He won special-achievement Oscars in 1929 and 1972.

Charlemagne (Carolus Magnus, Charles the Great), *b. ca. 742; d. 814.* King and emperor. As king of the Franks in 768, Charlemagne fought successful military campaigns throughout Western Europe, extending Frankish possessions in modern France to include much of Germany, Italy, and Spain. In 800, Pope Leo III crowned him emperor of a restored western Roman

Empire which later became the Holy Roman Empire. At his court in Aachen Charlemagne sponsored a revival of the arts and learning known as the Carolingian renaissance.

Charles, Ray (Ray Charles Robinson), *b. Albany, Ga., 1930; d. 2004.* **Blues and soul vocalist, pianist, and composer.** Charles merged 1950's R&B, gospel-powered vocals, and hints of jazz, blues, and pop to create the genre known as soul music. Blind since the age of six (from glaucoma), he helped to popularize black music to an integrated audience; he even incorporated country music in his 1962 album, *Modern Sounds in Country and Western Music.* Key recordings include "What'd I Say" (1959), "Georgia" (1960), "Hit the Road Jack" (1961), "Unchain My Heart" (1961), "One Mint Julep" (1961), "I Can't Stop Loving You" (1962), and "Busted" (1963).

Chaucer, Geoffrey, *b. London, ca. 1343; d. 1400.* **Narrative poet.** The first great, and greatest medieval, English poet, spent most of his life around the English court in government service. Being both commoner and aristocrat, he understood people of every station. After he completed an elegy, *The Book of the Duchess,* in 1370, diplomatic travels to Italy acquainted him with the writing of Boccaccio, which influenced Chaucer's greatest works, *Troilus and Criseide,* (ca. 1385) and *The Canterbury Tales* begun about 1386 and never completed.

Chekhov, Anton (Pavlovich), *b. Taganrog, Ukraine, 1860; d. 1904.* **Playwright, novelist, short story writer.** Considered a master of the short-story and one of the founders of modern drama, Chekhov wrote more than 50 short stories, notably "Neighbors" (1892), "An Anonymous Story" (1893), "The Black Monk" (1894), and "Ward Number Six" (1892); some were later adapted for the stage as one-act farces. His full-length plays often show the isolation and frustrations of intellectuals living in the provinces of Russia; famous works include *The Seagull* (1898), *Uncle Vanya* (1899), *Three Sisters* (1901), and *The Cherry Orchard* (1904).

Cheney, Dick (Richard Bruce), *b. Lincoln, Neb., 1941.* **U.S. vice president.** Although always known for his hawkish views, Cheney received five draft deferments during the Vietnam War and never served in the military. He was President Gerald Ford's chief of staff before being elected to Congress from Wyoming in 1978. In 1989 President George H. W. Bush named Cheney secretary of defense. During the 1990's, Cheney became chairman and CEO of Halliburton (a firm that would later receive enor- mous no-bid contracts to serve the military when Cheney returned to the executive branch). Upon becoming vice president under George W. Bush in 2000, Cheney greatly expanded the powers of his office. He has been criticized for excessive secrecy, for hyping the threat posed by Iraq, and for continuing to insist that 9/11 and Iraq were linked. In 2006 Cheney accidentally shot a hunting companion in the face. In 2007 Cheney's chief of staff, Lewis "Scooter" Libby, was convicted of perjury and obstruction of justice for his role in leaking the identity of an undercover C.I.A. agent.

Chiang Kai-shek, (Mandarin pronunciation Jiang Jieshi), *b. Zhejiang Province, China, 1887; d. 1975.* **Chinese nationalist leader.** Chiang received a military education under the Qing dynasty and became a follower of Sun Yat-sen after the Revolution of 1911. Chiang became party leader after Sun's death in 1925. Chiang's Northern Expedition of 1926–28, which reunified the warlord-riven country, included an "extermination campaign" designed to wipe out the Chinese Communist Party. He was later criticized for fighting communism rather than concentrating on the invading Japanese. His wartime alliance with the United States was facilitated by the diplomacy of Mme. Chiang (Soong Meiling, 1898–2003). Defeated by Mao Zedong's forces in the civil war of 1946–49, Chiang's government retreated to Taiwan, where he remained president until his death.

Chief Joseph (In-mut-too-yah-lat-lat), *b. Wallowa Valley, Ore., 1840?; d. 1904.* **American Indian chief.** After becoming chief of the Nez Perce in 1871, he resisted the takeover of his homeland by white settlers. When the U.S. government attempted to force the tribe onto an Idaho reservation, Chief Joseph led his people on a brilliantly executed 1,400-mile retreat toward Canada, winning four major battles along the way. The Nez Perce were ultimately forced to surrender, and were resettled in Oklahoma, where many died of disease. In 1885, Chief Joseph was sent to a reservation in Washington.

Chomsky, Noam, *b. Philadelphia, Pa., 1928.* **Linguist and activist.** Chomsky was educated at the University of Pennsylvania and has been on the faculty of MIT since 1955. His theory of transformational grammer, which proposes that humans have an innate ability to learn language, has influenced generations of linguists. Since the 1960's, Chomsky has been known for his political activism in support of left-wing causes and opposition to American interventions especially in Latin America.

Chopin, Frédéric, b. *Zelazowa Wola, duchy of Warsaw, 1810; d. 1849.* Pianist and composer. A virtuoso pianist, Chopin also wrote many enduring works for piano, notably his waltzes, preludes, nocturnes, and études. Although he wrote two piano concertos, his best-known works were for solo piano, most famously the *Polonaise in A-Flat Major* ("Heroic"), the *"Minute" Waltz*, and *Fantaisie-Impromptu in C*, the second section of which was popularized as "I'm Always Chasing Rainbows" in 1918. Chopin's compositions were innovative in their use of harmony, inspiring many composers from Franz Liszt to Sergei Rachmaninov.

Churchill, Winston Leonard Spencer, b. *Blenheim Palace, Oxfordshire, Britain, 1874; d. 1965.* English statesman and man of letters. Son of the Tory statesman Randolph Churchill, Winston saw war in India and Africa as an officer and journalist. In 1900 he was elected to the House of Commons, where he remained until 1964 except for two years. He served as home secretary (1910–11) and first lord of the Admiralty (1911–15), a tenure that ended after the disastrous defeat at Gallipoli. He rejoined the army and between the world wars, served in several more cabinet posts. His greatest achievements began when he became prime minister in 1940 at the beginning of World War II. His inspiring oratory, his alliance with the United States, and his understanding of geopolitics helped to guide England through its most challenging era. His prodigious literary output included *The Second World War* (six volumes) and *The History of the English Speaking Peoples* (four volumes). He was awarded the Nobel Prize in Literature in 1953.

Cicero, (Marcus Tullius Cicero) b. *106 B.C.; d. 43 B.C.* Roman orator and statesman. More of Cicero's writings survive than those of any other Roman of his time, most notably the Phillipics, a series of attacks on Mark Antony. Cicero held the positions of aedile, praetor, and consul during his long and contentious political career. He was responsible for prosecuting Catiline in 61 B.C. and was exiled for having five of Catiline's supporters illegally executed. He returned in 57 B.C. and remained in public life, supporting Pompey in the civil war against Julius Caesar. His opposition to Mark Antony was at the root of his undoing. After Caesar's assassination and the formation of the second triumvirate—Octavian, Lepidus, and Mark Antony—Cicero was executed in 43 B.C.

Clarke, Arthur C., b. *Somerset, England, 1917; d. 2008..* Novelist and essayist. As a young writer, Clarke developed a vision of the future that proved, from the start, to be startlingly prescient—in 1945 he predicted a satellite system that in fact came into use two decades later. Author of more than 70 books, Clarke began publishing science-fiction novels in 1953, when *Childhood's End* appeared, followed by *The City and the Stars* (1956). His novels *Rendezvous with Rama* (1973) and *The Fountains of Paradise* (1979) both won the Nebula and the Hugo awards. The 1968 film *2001:A Space Odyssey* is based on Clarke's work.

Claudius b. *10 B.C.; d. A.D. 54* Roman emperor. Kept out of public life largely by his grandfather, Augustus, because of his physical disabilities and unattractiveness, Claudius studied and wrote historical works until the assassination of his nephew Caligula in A.D. 41. Claudius is said to have been hiding out in the palace, fearful that he, too, would be murdered, when the Praetorian Guard discovered him and proclaimed him emperor. His reign saw expansion to Britain, Mauritania, and Thrace, although Claudius is historically considered a pawn of the army and other influences. He was poisoned and killed in A.D. 54, probably by his fourth wife, Agrippina, who had persuaded Claudius to make her son, Nero, successor.

Clay, Henry b. *Hanover County., Va., 1777; d. 1852.* American statesman. Called the Great Pacificator and the Great Compromiser, Clay began as a highly successful Kentucky lawyer. He served as a Jeffersonian Republican, in the state legislature and U.S. House of Representatives where he worked to precipitate the war of 1812 and pass the Missouri Compromise in 1820. He became a leader of the Whig Party, and opposed war with Mexico, which cost him the presidency in 1844. He was U.S. secretary of state (1825–29) and served several senate terms. There he was instrumental in the passage of several important treaties and compromises that balanced free and slave states' rights, including the compromise tariff of 1833, which resolved the nullification crisis over South Carolina's attempt to secede.

Cleisthenes, b. *ca. 570; d. ca. 507 B.C.* Athenian statesman. A member of an old Athenian family, Cleisthenes spent much of his life in exile owing to a combination of curses against his family and political tumult at Athens. He served as chief archon in 525–524, and led opposition to the tyrant Hippias in 512–511 B.C. In 508 he persuaded the Assembly to expand the democratizing measures instituted by Solon. He reorganized the body politic into ten tribes of ten demes (or townships), giving preference to citizenship of a place rather than membership in a tribe, and encouraging greater participation in Athenian politics.

Clemenceau, Georges, *b.* *Mouilleron-en-Pareds, France, 1841; d. 1929.* French statesman and journalist. As a senator in 1913, "Le Tigre" feared German aggression, and founded a newspaper, *L'Homme Libre* ("The Free Man"), to publicize his opinion. When World War I began a year later, he urged the United States to join the fight. Clemenceau's elevation to prime minister (1917–20) of France's Third Republic was instrumental in the Allied victory. He also was a major player in negotiating the difficult terms of the Treaty of Versailles, including the return of Alsace-Lorraine to France and the disarmament of Germany.

Clemens, Roger, *b. Dayton, Ohio, 1962.* Baseball pitcher. Nicknamed "Rocket," the accomplished power pitcher struck out 20 batters in a single game, a record at the time, on two occasions (1986, 1996). He is the first pitcher to win the Cy Young Award seven times. Over the course of his career he pitched for the Boston Red Sox, the Toronto Blue Jays, the New York Yankees, and the Houston Astros, achieving his 300th career win and his 4,000th strikeout in 2003. After testifying before Congress in 2008 about his alleged performance-enhancing drug use, Clemens was indicted on six counts, including perjury and obstruction.

Cleopatra, *b. Alexandria, 69 B.C.; d. 30 B.C.* Queen of Egypt. Probably the most frequently referenced woman in the ancient world, Cleopatra VII and her brother, Ptolemy XIII, were left to rule Egypt in 51 B.C. after the death of their father. She was exiled by supporters of her brother and formed an alliance with Julius Caesar, with whom she had a son, Caesarion. After Caesar was assassinated, she returned to Egypt. Mark Antony went to her with charges of supporting his enemies, but ended up forming a romantic relationship with her instead. She bore him three children, though he married Octavian's sister, Octavia. When the alliance between Octavian and Mark Antony disintegrated, Octavian declared war on them. Mark Antony committed suicide on mistakenly hearing of Cleopatra's death after their defeat in the Battle of Actium in 31 B.C. Cleopatra committed suicide in 30 B.C. after a failed attempt to negotiate with Octavian, reportedly dying from the bite of an asp.

Cleveland, Grover, *b. Caldwell, N.J., 1837; d. 1908.* Twenty-second and twenty-fourth president, 1885–89; 1893–97. The only president to serve two non-consecutive terms, Stephen Grover Cleveland showed scant interest in politics until Buffalo elected him mayor in 1881; the next year he became governor. His war on corrupt Tammany Hall made Cleveland the perfect Democratic reform candidate for president in 1884. After winning the election, he pushed for civil service reform and lower tariffs, seized 81 million acres of unused land from railroads, and signed the Interstate Commerce Act (1887). He was defeated in the 1888 election, but four years later he won a rematch with Benjamin Harrison.

Clinton, Bill (William Jefferson), *b. Hope, Ark., 1946.* Forty-second U.S. president, 1993–2001. As governor of Arkansas, William Jefferson Clinton became a leading figure among so-called New Democrats, who called for welfare reform and smaller government; in 1992, he beat the incumbent president, George Bush, in a three-way race. Clinton found little support for his domestic programs, however, although the decade's economic prosperity and booming stock market generated so much tax income that the Reagan-Bush deficits turned to surpluses by 1998. During his second term, the ongoing Whitewater scandal unearthed evidence of an affair between Clinton and a young White House intern, Monica Lewinsky. His lies under oath about the relationship led the Republican-controlled House to approve two articles of impeachment, although neither article mustered enough votes to pass.

Clinton, Hillary Rodham, *b. Chicago, Ill., 1947.* U.S. Secretary of State, Senator, and First Lady. After graduating from Wellesley College she received a law degree from Yale where she met her future husband, Bill Clinton, who became governor of Arkansas. After serving as an influential first lady, Clinton embarked on her own successful political career. She represented New York in the U.S. Senate from 2001–2009, making history as the only first lady to be elected to the U.S. Senate, and focusing on issues including children's rights, health care reform, and the health concerns of 9/11 first responders. In 2008 Clinton pursued the Democratic presidential nomination, but after a tight race, lost the nomination to Barack Obama. Once elected to the presidency, Obama appointed Clinton to the office of Secretary of State.

Cobb, Ty, *b. Narrows, Ga., 1886; d. 1961.* Baseball player. Although not the most beloved player in the annals of baseball, Cobb is one of the game's all-time greats. In 24 seasons (1905–28), most with the Detroit Tigers, the "Georgia Peach" compiled the highest career batting average (.367) and second-most hits (4,197) in major-league history. His career totals rank in the top five of virtually every offensive category except home runs. A fiercely aggressive competitor, Cobb batted over .400 three times, hit .300 or better 23 times, and won 12 American League batting titles.

Coetzee, J. M. (John Maxwell), *b. Cape Town, South Africa, 1940.* Novelist and critic. Known for his novels about the effects of colonization, Coetzee won the Nobel Prize in Literature in 2003. Among his acclaimed books are *Waiting for the Barbarians* (1980) and *Life and Times of Michael K* (1983), which won the Booker Prize. With the publication of *Disgrace* (1999), he became the first author to win the Booker Prize twice. Although he was a vigorous opponent of apartheid, he returned to live in South Africa after his application for permanent residence in the United States was denied. In 2002 Coetzee immigrated to Australia, where he holds an honorary position at the University of Adelaide

Coleman, Ornette, *b. Fort Worth, Tex., 1930.* Jazz saxophonist and composer. A leading proponent of avant-garde jazz, Coleman burst on the scene in 1959 with a series of dynamic quartet albums. His improvisational alto sax playing dispensed almost completely with traditional harmony, and served to influence other free jazz players, including John Coltrane. Key albums include *The Shape of Jazz to Come* (1959), *Change of the Century* (1959), *This Is Our Music* (1960), and *Free Jazz* (1960).

Coleridge, Samuel Taylor, *b. Ottery St. Mary, Devonshire, England, 1772; d. 1834.* Poet and essayist. After Coleridge's impulsive, dreamy, scholarly youth, his poetic career took shape when he and William Wordsworth collaborated on *Lyrical Ballads* (1798), which initiated what we call English Romanticism. The collection contained Coleridge's most famous poem, *The Rime of the Ancient Mariner,* whose mysterious, supernatural qualities also flavored his "Kubla Khan" and *Christabel,* both written early but published in 1816. Coleridge also excelled in writing more sober, meditative poems such as "Frost at Midnight" (1798) and "Dejection: An Ode" (1802). His output was constricted by physical suffering and opium addiction. Later philosophical writings and very important literary criticism were collected in *Biographia Literaria* (1817).

Collins, Michael, *b. Clonakilty, Ireland, 1890; d. 1922.* Irish Nationalist. Collins took part in the Easter Rising of 1916 and was held in detention for several months. After the Irish Assembly voted for independence in 1918, he was responsible for numerous attacks on the police and others from 1919 to 1921. He was one of the principal negotiators of a peace that in 1921 gave Ireland self-government within the British Empire. This did not satisfy more radical leaders, like Eamon DeValera, who organized resistance to the new government. Collins took charge of crushing the insurgency in 1922. Shortly thereafter, he was ambushed and killed by insurgents.

Colt, Samuel, *b. Hartford, Conn., 1814; d. 1862.* Inventor. Colt devised the first remotely controlled explosive and utilized the first underwater telegraph cable, but he is best known as the inventor of the revolver that bore his name. After the U.S. military ordered a large supply of the new guns for use in the Mexican War, Colt established a manufacturing plant where he developed the concepts of interchangeable parts and a mass production line. The Colt .45 became the signature sidearm of the American West.

Coltrane, John William, *b. Hamlet, N.C., 1926; d. 1967.* Jazz saxophonist and composer. One of the most controversial figures in the history of jazz, Coltrane was a great hard bop player with a Herculean style who moved beyond traditional musical forms and helped develop the genre known as free jazz. His later playing employed both soprano and tenor sax in the pursuit of a radically experimental style. Important recordings include "Giant Steps" (1960), "My Favorite Things" (1961), "Chasin' the Trane" (1962), "A Love Supreme" (1965), and "Ascension" (1965).

Columbus, Christopher, *b. Genoa, 1451; d. 1506.* Italian explorer. Columbus commanded the first ships to cross the mid-Atlantic from Europe to the Americas. His fleet sailed from Spain to the Azores and on to the Bahamas, where the Spanish landed on October 12, 1492. They later visited Cuba and Hispaniola, where one ship was lost, and returned to Spain on March 15, 1493. Columbus made three more voyages (1493–96, 1498–1500 and 1502–04), reaching mainland South America and Central America on the third and fourth voyages. Dogged but politically inept, he died wealthy but embittered at the lack of support from his royal patrons.

Comte, Auguste, *b. Montpellier, France, 1798; d. 1857.* Philosopher and sociologist. Founder of the philosophical school of positivism, which holds that only scientific knowledge is valid and that metaphysical questions are unanswerable; and of the discipline of sociology, to which he gave its name. A social reformer and early collaborator of Henri de Saint-Simon, Comte held that all sciences led to and contributed to sociology, which would provide the basis for a reformed and harmonious society. His detailed plans for such a society, however, were attacked as hierarchical and undemocratic.

Confucius, *b. Shandong Province, China, ca. 551 B.C.; d. ca. 479 B.C.;* Chinese philosopher. He was born to the minor aristocracy at a time of intense sociopolitical change in ancient China. Confucius is a latinized form of Kongfuzi, "great master Kong." He aspired to high office in his native state of Lu so that he could put into practice his theory of government by a natural elite of the virtuous. Thwarted, he gathered disciples to whom he taught his principles of hierarchy and filial piety (the state modeled on the patriarchal family), harmony, and personal self-cultivation; his teachings are preseved in the *Lunyu* ("Analects of Confucius"). His view of the ideal society and how to achieve it dominated Chinese political philosophy for over two thousand years.

Conrad, Joseph, (Jozef Konrad Korzeniowski) *b. Poland, 1857; d. 1924.* English novelist. Conrad learned English at sea and became one of the great English novelists and prose stylists. Many of his works are set at sea, among them *The Nigger of the Narcissus* (1897); *Lord Jim* (1900), which introduces his innovative technique of an intermediate narrator and tells the story from multiple points of view; and several superb novellas, including *Heart of Darkness* (1902) and *The Secret Sharer* (1909). Other major works. such as *Nostromo* (1904), *The Secret Agent* (1907), and *Under Western Eyes* (1911), have political contexts. His characters confront moral isolation, corruption and the complexity of human interaction.

Constantine I (The Great), *b. Naissus, Moesia, ?280; d. 337.* First Christian emperor of Rome. Constantine was hailed caesar after the death of his father, Constantius, in A.D. 306. Ruling only in Gaul at that time, Constantine invaded Italy and defeated Maxentius at the Milvian Bridge in 312, taking control of the western empire. Attributing his victory to the christian God, Constantine granted christians freedom to practice their religion in the Edict of Milan in 313. After he gained control of the whole empire, the major events in his reign were the Nicene Creed of 325, which proclaimed the basic doctrine of Christianity that persists to this day, and the move of the seat of power in 330 from Rome to the eastern city of Byzantium, thereafter known as Constantinople until the 20th century.

Cook, James, *b. Marton-in-Cleveland, England, 1728; d. 1779.* English explorer. A self-taught navigator, Captain Cook entered the Royal Navy at 27 and was quickly recognized for his abilities. His survey of the St. Lawrence River in 1759–60 helped ensure the British victory at Quebec, and in 1763–66 he charted Newfoundland. He led three circumnavigations of the world (1768–71, 1772–75, and 1776–80), during which he sailed around Antarctica; charted Australia, New Zealand, and many Pacific and Southern Ocean islands; and visited the Pacific Northwest, Alaska, Siberia, and Hawaii, where on his second visit he was killed in a skirmish on the beach.

Coolidge, Calvin, *b. Plymouth, Vt., 1872; d. 1933.* Thirtieth U.S. president, 1923–29. Coolidge entered Republican politics in 1899, rose through a succession of state offices, and was elected governor of Massachusetts in 1918. He was the Republican vice presidential nominee in 1920 and assumed office after Warren G. Harding's death. "Silent Cal" was the butt of jokes for his laconic utterances, but his minimalist approach to government restored respectability to a White House tainted by Harding's corrupt appointees. Pronouncing that the "business of America is business," he ushered in the heady years of "Coolidge prosperity" as the stock market soared higher and higher.

Cooper, Gary, (Frank James Cooper) *b. Helena Montana, 1901; d. 1961.* American movie actor. More than any other star, Cooper came to represent the image Americans wished to project to the world. *The Virginian* (1929) established him as a western star, but thanks to a childhood spent moving between Montana and England, Cooper could be just as convincing in a business suit as in a cowboy hat. He was Lou Gehrig in *Pride of the Yankees* (1942), Mr. Deeds and John Doe for Frank Capra, and the upright sheriff in *High Noon* (1952). His career spanned 35 years during which he appeared in more than 100 films.

Copernicus, Nicolas, *b. Torun, Poland 1473; d. 1543.* Astronomer. He studied astronomy and other subjects in Poland and Italy, and became canon of the cathedral in Frauenburg, East Prussia (1512). His great work *On the Revolutions of the Heavenly Spheres* (completed, in Latin, about 1530, published 1543) described a heliocentric system of sun and planets, where for the first time the sun rather than the earth was placed at the center. However, his belief that the planetary orbits are circular necessitated complex adjustments called epicycles. His work paved the way for Kepler's laws of planetary motion.

Coppola, Francis Ford, *b. Detroit, Mich, 1939.* Director. One of the most successful directors to emerge from the "film school" generation of the 1970's, Coppola started out working for Roger Corman's B-movie factory and earning a degree in film studies from UCLA. After a number of apprentice works, he struck critical and commercial gold with *The Godfather* (1971), which was followed by two sequels, *The Godfather II* (1974) and *The Godfather III* (1990). His Vietnam epic, *Apocalypse Now* (1979), became a legend. Coppola has been at least as influential a close-up producer as director, backing films by George Lucas, and Paul Schrader, among others.

Cortés, Hernán (Hernando), *b. Medellin, Spain, 1485; d. 1547.* Spanish conquistador. Cortés was an experienced soldier when he reached the Americas in 1504. He took part in the conquest of Cuba in 1511, and in 1518 he commanded an expedition to explore the Yucatán Peninsula. Burning his fleet at Veracruz in August 1519, he led his 500 men and their Indian allies inland to Tenochtitlán, capital of Montezuma's Aztec empire (now Mexico City). Overcoming numerous obstacles, including other Spaniards, Cortés (and smallpox) defeated the Aztecs in 1521. He served as captain-general of New Spain (1521–28) and retired to Spain in 1540.

Coulomb, Charles *b. Angoulême, France 1736; d. 1806.* French physicist. Coulomb made critical discoveries about the nature of magnetism and electricity after retiring as a military engineer in 1789. His inventions of the magnetometer, magnetoscope and torsion balance led to his formulation of Coulomb's law which stated that the force between two electric charges could be measured from the product of the charges and the distance between them. This clarified knowledge of attraction and repulsion between unlike and like charges, as well as the bonds that hold atoms and molecules together. The coulomb, or unit of electric charge (one ampere enduring for one second), is named for him.

Coward, Noel, *b. Teddington, England, 1899; d. 1973.* Playwright, actor, and composer. Coward began appearing on the stage at the age of twelve. His successful plays, the drama *The Vortex* (1924) and the comedy *Hay Fever* (1925), established him as one of the most popular playwrights of twentieth century. Coward's comedies (among them *Private Lives,* 1930; *Design for Living,* 1933; and *Blithe Spirit,* 1941), witty and sophisticated, capture the speech and manners of the post–World War I British upper class. Coward also wrote musicals and short stories. He produced, directed, and performed in many of his works.

Crawford, Joan (Lucille le Sueur), *b. San Antonio, Tex., 1908; d. 1977.* American movie actress. Her early years working as a department store clerk and a Broadway chorine set the pattern for many of her early roles; *Our Dancing Daughters* (1928) made her a star. After notable dramatic roles in *Grand Hotel* (1932) and *The Women* (1939), she won an Oscar for *Mildred Pierce* (1945). *Johnny Guitar* (1954) and *What Ever Happened to Baby Jane?* (1962) have become cult favorites. After her fourth husband's death in 1959, she took over his director's position with Pepsi-Cola.

Crazy Horse (Ta-sunko-witko or Tashunca-Uitco), *b. Rapid Creek, Lakota Nation (S.D.), 1842?; d. 1877.* American Indian chief. Celebrated for his ferocity and his vision, Crazy Horse was determined to preserve his Oglala Lakota people's way of life. He scored his most memorable triumph in 1876, when he joined forces with Sitting Bull and Chief Gall to massacre General George Armstrong Custer's Seventh Cavalry at Little Bighorn. After his fighters were forced to surrender to U.S. authorities in 1877, he was killed by a soldier's bayonet while resisting arrest.

Crick, Francis Harry Compton, *b. Northampton, Britain, 1916; d. 2004.* English molecular biologist. Crick and James Dewey Watson at Cambridge University discovered the structure of deoxyribonucleic acid, DNA, that carries genetic information in living organisms. Their paper of 1953 described the double-helix structure of DNA and the coding system within it. Crick and Watson, together with Maurice Wilkins, were awarded the Nobel Prize in Physiology or Medicine in 1962.

Crockett, David (Davy), *b. Greene County, Tenn., 1786; d. 1836.* American frontiersman, politician, folk hero. Crockett, the son of a backwoods farmer, had only 100 days of formal schooling. He was elected to the Tennessee legislature in 1821, and served intermittently in the U.S. House of Representatives in the 1820's and 1830's. After his final congressional defeat in 1835, he joined the American forces fighting General Santa Anna in Texas, where he died a hero at the Alamo. With his coonskin cap and his tales of hunting and Indian fighting, Crockett was an iconic figure of frontier independence. His legend continued into the 1950's, when he was portrayed in a Disney television series starring Fess Parker.

Cromwell, Oliver, *b. Huntingdon, England, 1599; d. 1658.* English soldier and political leader. A fiery Puritan in his youth, Cromwell led the parliamentary forces in the English Civil War in overthrowing the Stuart monarchy of

King Charles I. But his reign (1653–58) as lord protector of the republican Commonwealth of England was marked by religious tolerance. He restored England to a position of power in Europe not seen since the death of Queen Elizabeth I. He refused an offer to become king, but was also unable to share power with Parliament, which he twice dismissed. After Cromwell's death and the restoration of the monarchy (in 1660), his body was disinterred and his head impaled on a pole atop Westminster Hall, where it stayed for more than 20 years.

Crosby, Bing (Harry Lillis Crosby), *b. Tacoma, Wash., 1903; d. 1977.* **Actor, singer.** A fixture of Hollywood musicals throughout the 1930's, Bing Crosby had an easygoing manner and mellow voice made him America's best-loved crooner. Among jazz critics he is considered one of the great performers. In 1940 he appeared in *The Road to Singapore* with Bob Hope and Dorothy Lamour, inaugurated a series of equally popular *Road* movies throughout the 1940's. Crosby won an Oscar for his dramatic performance as a Catholic priest in *Going My Way* (1944).

cummings, e. e. (Edward Estlin), *b. Cambridge, Mass., 1894; d. 1962.* **Poet.** One of the most popular American poets of his time, Cummings is best recognized for the idiosyncratic shaping of his verse and his elimination of uppercase letters, even in his own name. In 15 volumes he wrote, often with humor, sometimes in poems without beginnings or ends, or with quirky phrasing ("pity this monster, manunkind," "all ignorance toboggans into know") of joy and sadness, of love, and (rather explicitly) of sex. He was also an accomplished painter and wrote a successful memoir of his imprisonment during World War I, *The Enormous Room* (1922).

Cunningham, Merce (Mercier Philip Cunningham), *b. Centralia, Wash., 1919; d. 2009.* **Innovative modern dance choreographer.** While in California Cunningham met composer John Cage, who became his longtime companion and artistic collaborator. Cunningham danced with the Martha Graham Company in 1939–45, giving his first independent concert in 1942; he danced his own works as a soloist 1945–53, then formed his company. Notable works include *Suite by Chance* (1952), *Summerspace* (1958), and *Rainforest* (with sets by Andy Warhol, 1968). He began choreographing with the computer in the later 1980's, in works such as *Trackers* (1991), and continued performing until the early 1990's, when arthritis ended his career.

Curie, Marie, *b. Warsaw, Poland, 1867; d. 1934.* **Chemist/physicist.** Marie Curie and her husband Pierre expanded scientific understanding of uranium rays and coined the term "radioactivity." They shared the 1903 Nobel Prize for Physics with, fellow researcher, Henri Becquerel. After Pierre's death in 1906, Marie assumed his professorship, becoming the first woman to teach at the Sorbonne. In 1911, she won an unprecedented second Nobel Prize, this time in chemistry. Working with her daughter Irène (a future Nobel Prize winner), she created x-ray vans at the French front lines during World War I. Her research paved the way for advanced nuclear physics and cancer therapies.

Custer, George Armstrong, *b. New Rumley, Ohio, 1839; d. 1876.* **American military leader.** Custer graduated from the U.S. Military Academy at West Point in 1861 and entered the Civil War. A bold cavalry officer, he became a brigadier general at the age of 23, the youngest general in the Union Army, and continued to distinguish himself throughout the war. After the war he fought in the Indian wars; and in the battle of the Little Bighorn in Montana on June 25, 1876, he and his troops were vastly outnumbered, defeated, and killed by Sioux warriors.

Cyrus II (The Great) *b. Media (now in Iran), ?590-580 B.C.; d. ca. 529 B.C.* **King and founder of the ancient Achaemenian Persian empire.** Most of what is know of Cyrus' life and reign comes from Greek historian Herodotus and later Xenophon in more legendary form. He was portrayed as a model ruler with a perfect balance of might and mercy. The son of Cambyses and a Medean princess, Cyrus overthrew his maternal grandfather, Astyages, ca. 550 B.C., taking control of the empire of the Medes. He went on to overthrow Croesus, king of Lydia (ca. 546 B.C.) and then Nabonidus in Babylonia (538 B.C.). A great conciliator, Cyrus was credited in the Bible with sending the captive Jews in Babylonia back to their homelands and blending Achaemenian culture with that of the people he conquered.

Dalai Lama (Lhamo Dhondrub), *b. Tsinghai province, China, 1935.* **Religious leader.** Born to a peasant family, the 14th Dalai Lama was declared by Buddhist leaders at the age of two as the latest reincarnation of the Bodhisattva of Compassion. He assumed a role as head of the Tibetan government when Chinese forces invaded Tibet in 1950. After a full-fledged uprising was crushed by the Chinese in 1959, the Dalai Lama fled to India, where he set up a government-in-exile. Revered worldwide for his spiritual teachings, he won the 1989 Nobel Peace Prize for his advocacy of nonviolent means to end the Chinese occupation.

Dalí, Salvador , *b. Figueres, Spain, 1904; d. 1989.* **Painter, draftsman, illustrator, sculptor, writer and filmmaker.** One of the most famous of the surrealist group, and a prolific artist, Dalí created imaginary worlds in which reality is grotesquely distorted. His fantastic, often nightmarish landscapes and monsterlike figures are rendered in a smooth, detailed, almost photographic style. His best-known works include *Accommodations of Desire* (1929), *The Persistence of Memory* (1931), and *Soft Construction with Boiled Beans: Premonitions of Civil War* (1936).

Dante Alighieri, *b. Florence, 1265; d. 1321.* **Poet.** Dante, the greatest Italian poet, was a nobleman intimately involved in the tumultuous politics of Florence. After the death of his beloved Beatrice, he celebrated her, and ideal love, in *The New Life* (1292). In 1302 he was banished from Florence; afterward, it is believed, he composed *The Divine Comedy,* one of the greatest works of world literature. Intricately rhymed in the Tuscan dialect, it is a three-book account of the poet's tour, guided by Virgil and Beatrice, of hell, purgatory, and paradise—a vivid, symbolic, meditative investigation of a medieval Christian's understanding of God.

Danton, Georges-Jacques, *b. Arcis-sur-Aube, France, 1759; d. 1794.* **French Revolutionary leader.** Although his role in the overthrow of the French monarchy was unclear, he nonetheless took credit for it. His opportunism resulted in his election to the Legislative Assembly, where his oratorical skills and decisiveness allowed him to shape the First French Republic. As president of the First Committee of Public Safety (1793), he led the moderate opposition, which tried, unsuccessfully, to pursue a path of negotiation and compromise. His disapproval of Robespierre's Reign of Terror led first to his withdrawal from politics, and later to his own death at the guillotine.

Darwin, Charles, *b. Shrewsbury, Shropshire, England, 1809; d. 1882.* **English naturalist.** Darwin was educated at the University of Edinburgh and Christ's College, Cambridge. His five-year voyage on the HMS *Beagle* (1831–36) to South America, the Galápagos, Tahiti, New Zealand, and other places, changed the history of science forever. His fossil discoveries and observations of plant and animal life led him to formulate his theory of evolu-

tion which he revealed to the public in 1859 when he published *On the Origin of Species by Means of Natural Selection.* Darwin's central idea that the human species evolved from lower forms of animals including monkeys and apes brought vicious criticism of him and his work. Criticism continues today, although virtually all biologists accept the theory, which is based on voluminous evidence from the fossil record.

David, *b. Bethlehem, Judah, d. 926 B.C.* Second Israelite king (ca. 1000–962 B.C.). A popular warrior for his legendary slaying of the giant Goliath, David was anointed by the prophet Samuel to be the future king. He united the tribes of Israel and extended his dominion to Jerusalem (the "city of David"). He brought the ark of the Covenant (holder of the Ten Commandments) to Jerusalem, which he made the capital of his empire. Author of many of the biblical psalms, David was said to be chosen by God to be a great king of Israel; his reign was considered ancient Israel's golden age.

David, Jacques-Louis, *b. Paris, 1748; d. 1825.* **Painter.** David developed a neoclassical style influenced by the painter Poussin and the principles of the Enlightenment, rejecting the luxuriant rococo aesthetic popular in his time. Having participated in the French Revolution, David painted *The Death of Marat* (1793), documenting the murder of a revolutionary political leader who was attacked in his bathtub. Another well-known work is the *Coronation of Napoleon in Notre-Dame* (1805–07). Although David's technique was groundbreaking during his lifetime, his style became so influential that it was later considered rigid and conservative.

Davis, Bette (Ruth Elizabeth Davis), *b. Lowell, Mass., 1908; d. 1989.* **American movie actress.** Her magnetic eyes and bearing made an indelible mark on the screen for more than 50 years. Her early Oscars were for *Dangerous* (1935) and *Jezebel* (1938). She was a top star in the 1940's playing spirited women, then experienced a decline in popularity but turned it around with an iconic performance as an aging stage star, Margo Channing, in *All About Eve* (1950). Later roles included a blowsy housewife in *The Catered Affair* (1956) and a grotesque silent film fossil in *What Ever Happened to Baby Jane?* (1962).

Davis, Jefferson, *b. Fairview, Ky., 1808; d. 1889.* **President of the Confederate States of America.** As senator from Mississippi (1847–51; 1857–61), and secretary of war (1853–57), Davis vocally defended slavery, but opposed secession. When seven states seceded, however, he quit the Senate and was elected Confederate president (1862). A lack of supplies, money, and international allies spelled the Confederacy's doom. After Robert E. Lee surrendered, Davis fled Richmond in April 1865 and was captured six weeks later. He was indicted for treason, but was never tried; he was released in 1867.

Davis, Miles (Miles Dewey Davis III) *b., Alton, Ill., 1926; d. 1991.* Jazz trumpeter and composer. A brilliant musician, he drove jazz through a staggering variety of styles, from cool to hard bop to modal to fusion. Davis's trumpet playing was in turns lyrical and introspective; he often employed a Harmon mute for a more intimate sound. His bands frequently included sidemen (including Bill Evans, Herbie Hancock, Freddie Hubbard, and Tony Williams) who went on to solo careers. Influential albums include *Birth of the Cool* (1949), *Round About Midnight* (1955), *Miles Ahead* (1958), *Kind of Blue* (1959), *Sketches of Spain* (1960), *In a Silent Way* (1969), and *Bitches Brew* (1970).

Davy, Sir Humphry, *b. Penzance, Cornwall, 1778; d. 1829.* English chemist. Davy was one of the foremost scientists of his day. His first discovery was on the effects of inhaling nitrous oxide. He subsequently published a work on the physiological effects of different gases and went on to devise the means of isolating by electrolysis chemical elements including potassium, sodium, and calcium. His work for the Society for Preventing Accidents in Coal Mines led to his invention of the miner's lamp.

de Beauvoir, Simone, *b. Paris, 1908; d. 1986.* French feminist writer. Her best-known work, *The Second Sex* (1949), is a landmark in feminist literature, arguing for the emancipation of women from their subjugation by men. She was a close companion of fellow existentialist writer, Jean-Paul Sartre, for more than 60 years; together, they founded and edited the monthly journal *Le Temps Modernes*. Her novel *The Mandarins* (1954), which tells the story of sheltered intellectuals turning to political activism, won the *Prix Goncourt*.

de Gaulle, Charles André Joseph Marie, *b. Lille, France, 1890; d. 1970.* French soldier and statesman. After the German victory over France in 1940, de Gaulle led the government-in-exile in London. He served as president of France's provisional government (1944–46) after liberation. He resigned when he realized that the constitution for the Fourth Republic severely curtailed the president's powers. By 1958, France's failures in Indochina and Algiers led to a popular outcry for de Gaulle's return, entreaties he refused until he was allowed to draft a new

constitution. His Fifth Republic pursued independence from both the U.S. and the Soviet Union. Instead, he sought an alliance with Germany that helped to create the European Union.

de Kooning, Willem, *b. Rotterdam, Netherlands, 1904; d. 1997.* Painter and sculptor. A leading figure in the abstract expressionist movement in post–World War II New York, de Kooning is known for his painterly, semi-abstract images, many of them featuring women. In his painting *Woman I* (1950–52) the figure barely emerges from the background, and is shaped with wild, energetic brushstrokes that have been characterized as both violent and erotic. De Kooning gradually shifted his interests to include semiabstracted landscape. Other well-known works include *Woman and Bicycle* (1952–53) and *Two Figures in a Landscape* (1967).

Debs, Eugene Victor, *b. Terre Haute, Ind., 1855; d. 1926.* American labor leader and Socialist. Debs organized and became president of the American Railway Union in 1893 and in 1894 won a strike against the Great Northern Railway. The same year, after shutting down the western railroads, he was arrested and jailed because the action interrupted the mails. In jail he read books on socialism and in 1898 he organized the Social Democratic Party, running unsuccessfully for president several times. He was sentenced to ten years in prison during World War I for pacifist beliefs, but his sentence was commuted in 1921.

Defoe, Daniel, *b. London, England, 1660; d. 1731.* Novelist. As a young man Defoe was a merchant, but went bankrupt and later took up journalism, a field in which he was an important innovator, working feverishly for many outlets and publishing his own *Review* of international affairs. Not until late in life did he publish the books for which he is most famous, *Robinson Crusoe* (1719) and *Moll Flanders* (1722), realistic and episodic tales that are often considered the first English novels. Other important works are *Colonel Jack*, another work of fiction, and *A Journal of the Plague Year*, an account of 1665 London.

Degas, Edgar, *b. Paris, 1834; d. 1917.* Painter, sculptor, photographer, and collector. A founding member of the Impressionist movement, considered a realist within the group, Degas was trained classically and believed in the importance of drawing. He wanted to document modern life and had a preference for artificial light and urban subjects, particularly female workers and ballerinas. His works include *The Star (Dancer on a Stage*, ca. 1878) and *The Glass of Absinthe* (1876). After 1886, Degas rarely showed his work.

DeMille, Cecil. B., *b. Ashfield, Mass., 1881; d. 1959.* Film producer and director. A master showman, DeMille became famous for elaborate films with luxurious settings, colorful costumes, and large casts. In 1913 he formed a partnership with Jesse Lasky, resulting in one of the first films shot in Hollywood, *Squaw Man* (1914). Their company became Paramount, where DeMille spent his entire career. His major films, including *The Ten Commandments* (1923) and *Sign of the Cross* (1932), carefully balanced the depiction of explicit sin with traditional morals. His last film was a remake of his own *Ten Commandments* (1956).

Dempsey, Jack, *b. Manassa, Colo., 1895; d. 1983.* Boxer. Nicknamed the "Manassa mauler," Dempsey was one of the best and most popular heavyweight fighters of the 20th century. He became champion in 1919 by knocking out Jess Willard but lost the title to Gene Tunney in 1926. Their controversial rematch in 1927 remains one of the most famous fights in history. Dempsey knocked down Tunney in the seventh round but since he failed to immediately return to a neutral corner, the referee delayed the count. The "long count" enabled Tunney to come back and win. Dempsey never fought again and retired with a record of 64 wins, 6 losses, and 9 draws.

Deng Xiaoping *b. Sichuan Province, China, 1904; d. 1997.* Chinese political leader. In 1924 Deng joined the Chinese Communist Party while studying in France. An early supporter of Mao Zedong, Deng benefited from Mao's rise to the party chairmanship during the Long March (1934–35). After long service as an army political commissar, he became general secretary of the party in 1956. Although he was purged in 1969 during the Cultural Revolution, and again in 1976 after the death of his patron Zhou Enlai, Deng returned to power in 1977 and became China's de facto supreme leader until his death. Deng crushed the Tiananmen Square democracy movement (1989), but his economic reform policies ("the Four Modernizations," 1978) set the stage for China's emergence as a world economic power.

Descartes, René, *b. La Haye, France, 1596; d. 1650.* Philosopher, mathematician, and scientist. His many mathematical contributions include the development of Cartesian coordinates and analytic geometry. He is regarded as a founder of modern philosophy; his ideas are set out in *Discourse on Method* (1637) and *Meditations* (1641). He began with the undoubted knowledge of self (*cogito, ergo sum*: I think, therefore I am), and went on to expand knowledge, including knowledge of God. He regarded the physical world as mechanistic and entirely divorced from the mind, a position called dualism; the two realms are connected only by the intervention of God.

Dewey, John, *b. 1859, Burlington, Vt., d. 1952.* Educator and philosopher. One of the leading educators of his day, Dewey opposed authoritarian methods of teaching and was influential in progressive education based on experiment and practice. His approach was instrumentalism. Forms of human activity are instruments to solve social and personal problems; and since problems change, the instruments to confront them must also change. Democracy is a fundamental value, and truth is seen as not transcendental but evolving, accessible to all who inquire. Dewey was also active in social and political reform, including women's suffrage. His many books include *The School and Society* (1899), *Experience and Nature* (1925), and *Freedom and Culture* (1939).

Dickens, Charles, *b. Portsmouth, England, 1812; d. 1870.* Novelist. Dickens is unsurpassed as a creator of vivid, idiosyncratic, often comic, characters. His rich descriptions of poverty and suffering were informed by an impoverished childhood. His first books were collections, *Sketches by Boz* (1836) and *Pickwick Papers* (1837), which brought him fame; and the novel *Oliver Twist* (1838). His famous short novel, *A Christmas Carol*, was published in 1843. Dickens wrote long books quickly in installments for magazines, and even the best could lack finish. These best include *Dombey and Son* (1848), *David Copperfield* (1850), *Bleak House* (1853), *Hard Times* (1854), *Great Expectations* (1861), and *Our Mutual Friend* (1865). Dickens was a father of 10; his marriage was complicated by close friendships with his wife's sisters.

Dickinson, Emily, *b. 1830, Amherst, Mass.; d. 1886.* Poet. Daughter of a onetime congressman, Dickinson seems to have lived a normal life until her late twenties, when she began to withdraw into a lifelong reclusiveness in her Amherst home. There she developed into one of the greatest and most influential American poets, unrecognized until, after her death, her sister discovered more than 1,500 of her poems. These poems, plain in diction but original in imagery, meter, and their irregular rhyming, revealed a quietly passionate woman sensitive to nature, in love with an unnamed man, and troubled by the specter of death and uncertainty about faith and immortality.

Diderot, Denis, *b. Langres, France, 1713; d. 1784.* Philosopher and encyclopedist. One of the foremost figures of the European Enlightenment, Diderot made a meager living as a hack writer, essayist, novelist, playwright, and translator. Approached for a translation of the British *Chambers' Cyclopaedia*, he expanded on that assignment to edit and publish the magisterial *Encyclopédie* (1751–72; 17 volumes of text and 11 of plates), a work of sublime erudition and revolutionary opinions. It contributors included his partner, the mathematician Jean Le Rond d'Alembert; and the philosophers Jean-Jacques Rousseau and Voltaire.

Didrikson, Babe (Mildred Didrikson Zaharias), *b. Port Arthur, Tex., 1911; d. 1956.* **Athlete.** Considered by many to be the best all-around female athlete in history, Babe Didrickson was accomplished in track, swimming, basketball, boxing, bowling, golf, and tennis. She was muscular and competitive—traits that were considered shocking for female athletes in her era. She began as a basketball All-American before winning three medals in track-and-field events at the 1932 Los Angeles Olympics. Didrikson reached the apex of her career as a brilliant golfer, winning dozens of tournaments. She co-founded the Ladies Professional Golf Association (L.P.G.A.) in 1949. The Associated Press voted her the greatest female athlete of the first half of the 20th century.

Dietrich, Marlene (Maria Magdalene Dietrich), *b. Berlin, Germany, 1901; d. 1992.* **Film actress.** An exotic glamour queen who sometimes dressed in men's clothing, Dietrich was a uniquely erotic addition to Hollywood during the 1930's. She was discovered in Germany by Josef von Sternberg, who constructed her image as the mysterious femme fatale for *The Blue Angel* (1930). They made six more films together in Hollywood, including *Shanghai Express* (1932) and *The Devil Is a Woman* (1935). Though her film career faltered in the 1950's, she reinvented herself as a nightclub performer.

Diocletian *b. Salonae, Dalmatia (now Solin, Croatia), 245; d. 316.* **Roman emperor, 284–305.** Known for restoring order to the Roman Empire and waging a persecution of the Christians later in his reign, Diocletian came into power through his military service and the death of Numerian, brother of the emperor Carinus. After his soldiers hailed him emperor in 284 and Carinus was killed by his own soldiers, Diocletian rendered the senate and other remnants of the republic virtually powerless. He divided the empire with Maximian, who ruled the western half, in 286. In 293 he further divided the empire, naming four caesars to govern. He abdicated in 305, leaving the empire in disarray until Constantine I took power.

Disney, Walt (Walter Elias Disney), *b. Chicago, Illinois, 1901; d. 1966.* **Animator, producer.** The world's most successful producer of children's entertainment, Walt Disney trained and worked as a commercial artist in Kansas City and then, in 1923, moved to Hollywood, where he created Mickey Mouse and Donald Duck. He made *Steamboat Willie* (1928), the first animated cartoon to use synchronized sound; and *Snow White and the Seven Dwarfs* (1937), the first feature-length cartoon. In the 1950's, Disney expanded into live-action features, television series, and a theme park, Disneyland, that has become one of America's most popular tourist attractions.

Disraeli, Benjamin, first Earl of Beaconsfield, *b. London, 1804; d. 1881.* **English statesman and man of letters.** Disraeli was elected to the House of Commons in 1837; after a brief term as prime minister in 1868 he regained the post from 1874 to 1880. As prime minister he guided legislation to aid the working class, borrowed money to gain controll over the Suez Canal, and gave Queen Victoria the title empress of India. He also wrote novels that reflected his experience in the workings of politics.

Djerassi, Carl, *b. Vienna, Austria, 1923.* **Chemist.** Djerassi invented the first oral contraceptive for women (the Pill). His honors include the National Medal of Science, the National Medal of Technology, and the Priestley Medal. Turning to writing later in life, Djerassi published his first novel, *Cantor's Dilemma*, in 1991. He is the author of several plays, novels, and works of autobiography including *The Pill, Pygmy Chimps, and Degas' Horse* (1992).

Dominic, Saint (Santo Domingo de Guzman), *b. Caleruega, Castile, Spain, ca. 1170; d. 1221.* **Founder of the Order of Friars Preachers (Dominicans).** The patron saint of astronomers, St. Dominic preached against the Cathar heretics and followed the pope's army for seven years during the Albigensian Crusade. He founded an order devoted to the conversion of the Albigensians, which was approved by Pope Honorius III in 1216. The order was extremely effective in conversion work because of its concept of blending intellectual and popular needs. Dominic was canonized in 1234 and is venerated in the Catholic and Lutheran churches. His feast day is August 8.

Donatello (Donato di Niccolo di Betto Bardi), *b. Florence, 1386 or 1387; d. 1466.* **Sculptor.** Donatello worked under Ghiberti and became the most innovative and versatile sculptor of the early Renaissance. Moving away from the conventions of the late Gothic period, he sought inspiration from the classical sculptors of antiquity. His remarkably lifelike statues include *David* (ca. 1425–30), depicted as a nearly nude adolescent, and the armored *St. George* (ca. 1415–17); his bronze work includes *The Feast of Herod* (ca. 1425), on the baptismal font in Siena Cathedral. Donatello invented the shallow *schiacciato* method of relief. He was patronized and supported by Cosimo de' Medici, who had Donatello buried beside him in the family vault.

Donne, John, *b. London, 1572; d. 1631,* **Poet.** Donne, the first "metaphysical" poet, introduced a new poetic style— witty, colloquial, almost perverse in its leaps of thought and imagery—that strongly influenced poets of the 20th century. Donne left the Catholic Church, joined military expeditions, became a courtier, and pursued ladies; then in 1615 he became an Anglican priest. He is at once a great poet of physical love ("The Ecstasy," "The Canonization") and religious devotion. Keenly conscious of death, he composed several elegies, as well as satires and celebrated prose sermons. Nearly all of Donne's poetry was published posthumously.

Dos Passos, John, *b. Chicago, 1896; d. 1970.* **Novelist.** Dos Passos traveled as a newspaper correspondent in Europe after World War I before settling in the United States to write novels that addressed the social and economic conditions of the day. His naturalistic novels, sometimes called documentary novels, are characterized by strict realism and the accumulation of material, such as newspaper headlines and popular songs, taken from the real world. These novels include the *U.S.A.* trilogy: (*The 42nd Parallel* (1930), *1919* (1932), and *The Big Money* (1936).

Dostoyevsky, Fyodor, *b. Moscow, 1821; d. 1881.* **Novelist.** Dostoyevsky's father was killed by his own serfs; this event informed the psychological searching, violence, and examination of guilt in the son's novels. Dostoyevsky's own time in a penal colony for socialist activities left him with epilepsy and a deep Russian Orthodox faith, which influenced his development into the greatest of all religious novelists in his most important works: *Crime and Punishment* (1866), a tale of violent sin and redemption; *The Idiot* (1868), a portrait of a Christlike figure; *The Possessed* (1872), a rejection of socialist revolutionary ideas; and *The Brothers Karamazov* (1880), his investigation of evil and faith.

Douglas, Stephen, *b. Brandon, Vt., 1813; d. 1861.* **Politician.** The "Little Giant" became known for his soar- ing oratory during his stint as a Democratic congressman from Illinois (1843–47). In 1847 he was elected to the U.S. Senate, where he crafted legislation that greatly expanded U.S. territory. He was responsible for the concept of "popular sovereignty," a compromise measure that allowed the residents of new U.S. territories and states to decide for themselves whether to permit slavery. In 1858 Douglas squared off with Abraham Lincoln in a historic series of debates; Lincoln's superb performance against the acclaimed orator sealed his national reputation. In 1860 Lincoln defeated Douglas in the presidential election. Despite his defeat, Douglas was loyal to the new president, rallying support for the Union cause until his death in 1861

Douglass, Frederick (Frederick Augustus Washington Bailey), *b. Tuckahoe, Md., 1818; d. 1895.* **Abolitionist.** Born to a slave mother and a white father, he spent his childhood in slavery but secretly learned to read. As a teenager, he was hired out to a brutal overseer before escaping to the North. Douglass became a powerful orator and a leading voice in the struggle against slavery. In 1845, his autobiography was published to great acclaim, and during the Civil War he served as a consultant to President Lincoln. He was U.S. minister to Haiti from 1889 to 1891.

Doyle, Sir Arthur Conan, *b. Edinburgh, Scotland, 1859; d. 1930.* **Author.** Trained as a medical student and fascinated by forensic diagnosis, Conan Doyle became famous as a fiction writer when he created one of the world's most memorable literary characters, the fastidious and eminently logical detective Sherlock Holmes. Conan Doyle turned out dozens of wildly popular Sherlock Holmes short stories, which gave birth to hundreds of radio, television, and movie dramatizations. He also produced historical novels and military chronicles; he devoted much of his later life to essays and nonfiction expounding on his deep belief in spiritualism.

Drake, Sir Francis, *b. Tavistock, England, 1540; d. 1596.* **English privateer and navigator.** In 1569–70, Drake sailed with his cousin to trade illegally in the Spanish Caribbean, where their ships were ambushed by the Spanish. In 1577–80, he commanded the *Golden Hind* on the first English circumnavigation of the globe, for which accomplishment he was knighted by Elizabeth I. In 1586, he rescued survivors of Sir Walter Raleigh's failed Roanoke colony. Drake played a leading role in England's struggle with Spain, and he sailed as vice admiral during the defeat of the Spanish Armada (1588). He died of dysentery while privateering in the Caribbean.

Du Bois, W. E. B. (William Edward Burghardt), *b. Great Barrington, Mass.; 1868; d. 1963.* Author and civil rights leader. A Ph.D. from Harvard (1895), Du Bois conducted pioneering empirical studies of black society. He advocated full black political and civil rights and was an early leader in the Pan-African movement and in cultural nationalism. He helped found the National Association for the Advancement of Colored People (N.A.A.C.P.), where he was research director and editor (1910–34) of *The Crisis*. Disillusioned with the U.S., he late in life joined the Communist Party (1961), moved to Ghana, and renounced American citizenship.

Duchamp (Henri-Robert-) Marcel, *b. Blainville, France, 1887; d. 1968.* Painter, sculptor, writer. A groundbreaking and extremely influential artist, Duchamp became involved with the Dadaist movement (1915–22), which explored irrationality, chance, and the unconscious, as well as with Dada's successor, Surrealism, which was influenced by psychoanalytic theory. In the wake of these movements Duchamp invented the ready-made or found object sculpture; his piece *Bicycle Wheel* (1913), a single wheel mounted on a household stool, is a famous example of this playful yet highly theoretical genre. Other works include *Nude Descending a Staircase No. 2* (1912) and *Fountain* (1917).

Dulles, John Foster, *b. Washington, D.C., 1888; d. 1959.* American statesman. After serving as a U.S. adviser to the founding of the United Nations in 1945, and negotiating the peace treaty with Japan (1951), Dulles was appointed secretary of state by President Eisenhower in 1953. Pursuing a strong anticommunist strategy, he negotiated mutual defense treaties in Southeast Asia and the Middle East, and promoted the European Defense Community. His announced threat of "massive retaliation" with nuclear weapons against communist aggression was widely criticized as "brinkmanship."

Dumas, Alexandre, *b. Villers-Cotteret, France, 1802; d. 1870.* Novelist. The illegitimate son of an aristocratic father and a Haitian slave, Dumas, with little education, became an extraordinarily popular and wealthy Romantic novelist. He began as a playwright, first achieving success with *Henri III* in 1829. Turning to novels, he worked with collaborators and did not succeed until *The Three Musketeers* (1844), followed by two sequels, as well as *The Count of Monte Cristo* (1845) and *The Black Tulip* (1850).

Duncan, Isadora (Dora Angelica Duncan), *b. San Francisco, Calif., 1877; d. 1927.* Legendary modern dancer and choreographer. Largely self-educated in dance, Duncan began performing as a child, managed by her mother, who took her to New York in the mid-1890's. Isadora began giving solo recitals for wealthy New Yorkers, making a sensation with her barefoot, free-flowing performances, given in a loose-fitting tunic. In 1900, she traveled to London, where she was an immediate sensation, and a trip to Greece inspired her to begin "recreating" its ancient dances. She toured Europe and in 1921 she opened a school in Russia. A final U.S. tour was a failure, and she moved to Paris in 1925; two years later, she died in a freak automobile accident.

Dürer, Albrecht, *b. Nuremberg, Germany, 1471; d. 1528.* Painter, printmaker, and writer. Considered one of the greatest German artists, Dürer traveled to Italy early in his life, where he studied the work Renaissance masters. He made major contributions to the development of printmaking, and his most important works include a series of 15 woodcuts on the Book of Revelation, *The Apocalypse* (1496–98). His best-known pieces include *Death and the Devil* (1513), *Melencolia I* (1514) and *Four Apostles* (1526). Dürer was interested in the mathematical principles of images, and his writings include a treatise on proportion

Dvořák, Antonín, *b. Nelahozeves, Bohemia, 1841; d. 1904.* Czechoslovakian (Bohemian) composer of the late Romantic era. One of the great nationalist European composers of the 19th century, Dvořák was a natural melodist; many of his works evoke Bohemian and American folk songs. Notable works include Romance for Violin and Orchestra, Op. 11 (1873–77); Serenade in E Major for Strings, Op. 22 (1875); *Slavonic Dances*, Op. 46 (1878); Symphony No. 7 in D Minor (1884–85) Op. 70; Symphony No. 9 in E minor (*From the New World*) (1893) Op. 95; String Quartet No. 12 in F Major ("American"), Op. 96 (1893); and Cello Concerto in B Minor, Op. 104 (1894–95).

Dylan, Bob (Robert Allen Zimmerman), *b. Duluth, Minn., 1941.* Folk and rock songwriter and vocalist. One of the most influential songwriter of the 1960's, Dylan pioneered several different schools of songwriting, including the confessional singer-songwriter and stream-of-consciousness narrative styles. Throughout his career he embraced and popularized several styles, from the folk revival of the early 1960's through electric folk-rock and country rock. Important compositions include "Blowin' in the Wind" (1963), "The Times They Are A-Changin'" (1964), "Mr. Tambourine Man" (1964), and "Like a Rolling Stone" (1965); albums include

Highway 61 Revisited (1965), *Blonde on Blonde* (1966), *Nashville Skyline* (1969), and *Blood on the Tracks* (1975).

Earhart, Amelia, *b. Atchison, Kan., 1897; disappeared 1937.* **Aviator.** Earhart initially made an impression in 1928 as the first woman to fly across the Atlantic Ocean as a passenger. Determined to win fame for her own achievements, she set out to cross the Atlantic again as a solo pilot, completing the journey in just under 15 hours. In 1935, she made an even longer solo flight from Hawaii to California, marking the first time anyone, male or female, had safely navigated this route. She set off on a round-the-world flight in 1937 but vanished mysteriously over the Pacific.

Eastman, George, *b. Waterville, N.Y., 1854; d. 1932.* **Inventor and industrialist.** Eastman's many innovations included a dry-plate photographic process, roll film, the Kodak camera (1888), and, late in his life, a color film (1928). He successfully incorporated his inventions into a well-organized, efficient manufacturing process for photographic equipment, and as a result was instrumental in transforming photography from a complex, expensive enterprise to a mass pursuit. He was active as a philanthropist in Rochester, where his production facilities were located, and elsewhere.

Eastwood, Clint, *b. San Francisco, 1930.* **American movie actor and director.** He began acting in B pictures and in *Rawhide* on televison (1959–66) and became a star in Italian westerns such as *The Good, the Bad, and the Ugly* (1966). With *Dirty Harry* (1971) he went on to play a string of taciturn action heroes, then turned to directing. He won an Oscar for best director for *Unforgiven* (1992).

Edison, Thomas Alva, *b. Milan, Ohio, 1847; d. 1931.* **American inventor and entrepreneur.** Edison devoted his life to developing practical inventions that could be commercialized. Beginning in 1876 he produced a stream of inventions that included improvements in the telegraph system, the phonograph, the incandescent electric light, electric dynamos, a motion picture camera, a storage battery, and a multitude of other devices he commercialized. He pioneered the organized invention process itself that has become the standard in most industries today.

Edwards, Jonathan, *b. East Windsor, Conn., 1703; d. 1758.* **American preacher and religious philosopher.** In 1729 Edwards became pastor in Northampton, Mass. The position provided a forum for his eloquent sermons and influential writings in support of a rigorous Calvinism. Together with other preachers, he brought about the Great Awakening, a religious revival in the American colonies.

But his censorious views and actions in Northampton resulted in his being dismissed from the church in 1750. Until his death he continued to preach and write on questions of free will and determinism in Christian faith.

Einstein, Albert, *b. Ulm, Germany, 1879; d. 1955.* **German-American theoretical physicist.** Einstein was educated and began teaching in Zurich. In 1905 he published three papers that changed the history of physical science, introducing revolutionary concepts regarding the nature of light-particles (photons), the existence and nature of molecules (and Brownian motion), and the electrodynamics of moving bodies (special theory of relativity). In 1914 he accepted a professorship at Berlin's Kaiser Wilhelm Institute and in 1921 was awarded the Nobel Prize in Physics. In 1934, when the Nazi regime stripped the Jewish Einstein of citizenship and property, he moved to a post at Princeton University, soon to become an American citizen. A pacifist and humanitarian, he nonetheless encouraged President Roosevelt to pursue development of an atomic bomb, to preempt the Germans. One of the greatest synthesizers of scientific thought, Einstein helped develop quantum physics, but never accepted it as a unifying theory, and never realized his quest to find one.

Eisenhower, Dwight D., *b. Denison, Tex., 1890; d. 1969.* **Thirty-fourth U.S. president, 1953–61.** After graduating from West Point Dwight David Eisenhower spent World War I as a tank-training instructor, and in World War II he rose rapidly through the ranks, becoming commander of U.S. forces in Europe in 1942 and the country's first five-star general. Famous for his role in planning D-Day he served as army chief of staff until 1948, was named commander of NATO forces in 1950, and accepted the Republican nomination for president in 1952. "Ike" became one of the most popular presidents in U.S. history, though many questioned his lax work habits and detached management style. He ended the Korean War but aggressively pursued a strong military response to Soviet and communist expansion.

Eisenstein, Sergei, *b. Riga, Latvia, 1898; d. 1948.* **Film director and theoretician.** His experiments with the manipulative powers of editing expanded the perimeters of Russian montage and influenced filmmakers around the world. Eisenstein theorized that editing together two unrelated shots could result in an abstract idea or metaphor, a technique now called intellectual montage. Though evident in his first film, *Strike* (1925), Eisenstein's ideas took full shape in the groundbreaking *Battleship Potemkin* (1925). Denounced by Stalin for being too formalistic, he made few films in his later years; those included *Alexander Nevsky* (1938) and *Ivan the Terrible, I and II* (1944–46).

Eleanor of Aquitaine, *b. Fontevrault, France, c. 1122; d. 1204.* Queen of both France, 1137–52, and England, 1152–1204. Eleanor was considered the most influential woman in Europe in the 12th century. She inherited from her father, more French land than possessed was by the French king, Louis VII, whom she married in 1137. She retook possession of Aquitaine when the marriage was annulled in 1152, and then married Henry Plantagenet, heir to the British throne. When he acceded, as Henry II, he ruled England, Normandy, and western France. She was mother of Richard I (Richard the Lion-Heart) and John I.

Elgar, Edward (Sir Edward William Elgar), *b. Broadheath, Worcestershire, England, 1857; d. 1934.* 19th century English composer. Although he was an excellent violinist and also played the bassoon and organ, Elgar had no formal training in composition. His earliest large choral piece was the oratorio, *Lux Christi* (1896; *The Light of Life*) written shortly before he began work on his most popular orchestral work, *Enigma Variations.* His oratorio, *The Dream of Gerontius,* based on a poem by John Henry Cardinal Newman is considered by many to be his masterpiece. The world over, graduates best know Elgar as the composer of *Pomp and Circumstance* (1901).

Eliot, George (pseudonym of Mary Ann Evans), *b. 1819, Warwickshire, England; d. 1880.* Novelist. Mary Ann (or Marian) Evans grew up in a devout evangelical home but renounced religion and lived with a married man, G. H. Lewes. Her first novel was *Adam Bede* (1859), followed by *The Mill on the Floss* (1860), and her best-known, *Silas Marner* (1861). Writing mainly of rural life, she keenly observed society and was deeply concerned with moral responsibility. Other novels are *Romola,* a historical romance (1863); *Felix Holt* (1866); *Middlemarch,* her masterpiece (1872); and *Daniel Deronda* (1876).

Eliot, T. S. (Thomas Stearns), *b. St. Louis, 1888; d. 1965.* American-English poet, dramatist, and critic. Eliot moved permanently to England in 1914 and soon published an entirely new kind of poetry for the 20th century, beginning with the ironic, anxiously edged, uneven-lined monologue, "The Love Song of J. Alfred Prufrock" in 1915. With *The Waste Land* (1922), a long, allusive, diverse poem, he established himself as a great poet who had found the voice and prosody to capture the barren and broken condition of Western civilization after World War I. He later expressed Christian faith in poems such as "Ash Wednesday" (1930) and the *Four Quartets* (1943). Eliot was a particularly astute critic of Elizabethan and Jacobean poetry and drama. After his historical drama, *Murder in the Cathedral* (1935), he wrote plays with contemporary settings, including *The Cocktail Party* (1950).

Elizabeth I, *b. Greenwich, England, 1533; d. 1603.* Queen of England, 1558–1603. The 45-year reign of the "Virgin Queen" was known as the Elizabethan age, an era in which England became a major power in European politics and the arts. The daughter of Henry VIII and Anne Boleyn, she succeeded her half-sister Mary I, who had reinstated Catholicism as the law of the land. Elizabeth's coronation was publicly and prominently celebrated as the return of Protestant Reformation. In 1588, the queen's navy stunned the mighty Spanish Armada, catapulting England to the rank of world power. Elizabeth never married and died without heirs.

Ellington, Duke (Edward Kennedy Ellington), *b. Washington, D.C., 1899; d. 1974.* Jazz composer, arranger, pianist, and bandleader. Ellington was one of the most important composer in the history of jazz, and the leader of one of its longest-lasting and most influential big bands. He used his band as a laboratory for his new compositions, and often shaped his writing to showcase the talents of individual band members. Important songs include "East St. Louis Toodle-Oo" (1926), "Black and Tan Fantasy" (1928), "Mood Indigo" (1931), "It Don't Mean a Thing (If It Ain't Got That Swing)" (1932), "Sophisticated Lady" (1933), "Caravan" (1937), "Take the 'A' Train" (1941), "I Got It Bad (And That Ain't Good)" (1941), and "Don't Get Around Much Anymore" (1943).

Ellison, Ralph, *b. Oklahoma City, Okla., 1914; d. 1994.* American author and teacher. Ellison is best known for the only novel he published in his lifetime, *Invisible Man,* which won the National Book Award for Fiction in 1953. When it was published, Ellison offered a new type of African-American protagonist, who, unlike the characters in novels written by his mentor Richard Wright, was educated and eloquent. Ellison strove to present black culture as complex and developed, rather than the oppressed world presented by his literary predecessors. His views influenced the civil rights movement, but because of his alienation from the black community after his success, Ellison was never a leader in the movement. *Shadow and Act* (1964) and *Flying Home and Other Stories* (1986) are his two short-story collections.

Emerson, Ralph Waldo, *b. Boston, 1803; d. 1882.* Poet and essayist. Emerson, like his father, was a Unitarian minister, but his unorthodox views led to an early end to his clerical career and ostracism by Harvard Divinity School. He took up a literary (and lecturing) career and expressed, beginning with the essay "Nature" in 1836, a philosophy to be known as "Transcendentalism" that became an important literary movement. It held that God was immanent in man and nature, and emphasized individual freedom. His lecture "American Scholar" (1837) was a historic call for cultural independence from Europe. *Essays* (1841) contained the famous "Self-Reliance"; his other books include *Representative Men* (1850) and *The Conduct of Life* (1860). Noted poems are "The Rhodora" (1834), "Concord Hymn" (1837), and "Threnody" (1846).

Engels, Friedrich, *b. Barmen, Germany, 1820; d. 1895.* Revolutionary and social philosopher. He managed a factory in Manchester, England, and wrote *The Condition of the Working Class in England* (1845). In 1844, he met Karl Marx and began a close lifelong collaboration. They published the *Communist Manifesto* (1848), predicting the overthrow of capitalism and the triumph of communism. After the failure of the revolutions in 1848 in Europe, Engels moved back to England, where, as a successful businessman, he supported Marx's work on *Das Kapital.* He edited the second and third volumes after Marx's death.

Epicurus, *b. Samos, Greece, 341 B.C.; d. 270 B.C.* Greek philosopher. Schooled by his father in the teachings of Plato and Democritus, Epicurus taught throughout Asia Minor before establishing an academy in Athens in 306 B.C. Here he taught that intellectual pleasure was the highest good, and prescribed a social system based on honesty, prudence, and justice as the path to serenity. Although today his name is associated with the pursuit of hedonistic pleasures, his philosophy recommended a life of austerity and seclusion.

Erasmus, Desiderius, *b. Rotterdam, ca. 1466; d. 1536.* Humanist, scholar, and Roman Catholic priest. He was one of the leading figures of the Renaissance, widely known for his editions of Greek and Latin classics and the church fathers, his translation of the New Testament into Latin from the original Greek, and his personal humor and tolerance. His own writings were mainly critical and satirical works, the latter including *In Praise of Folly* (1509). Although he had attacked clerical abuses and favored Church reform, he opposed the Reformation and became a bitter enemy of Martin Luther.

Ericsson, Leif ("the Lucky"), *b. Iceland, ca. 970; d. ca. 1020.* Norse-Icelandic explorer. Ericsson and his father, Eric "the Red" Thorvaldsson, settled in Greenland ca. 985. While returning from a visit to Norway ca. 1001, he was blown off course and apparently sailed as far west as Labrador or Newfoundland, previously visited by Bjarni Herjulfsson in the 980's. Around 1001, Ericsson sailed for lands he called Helluland, Markland, and Vinland, possibly Baffin Island, Labrador, or Newfoundland. Around 1005 his brother attempted to colonize Vinland, possibly at L'Anse aux Meadows, Newfoundland, but the colony was abandoned after he was killed.

Euclid, *b. birthplace unknown, Greece, ca. 300 B.C.* Working in Alexandria, Euclid organized what was known about mathematics in his time into a complete axiomatic system in a work called *Elements.* His selection of axioms and postulates, although criticized for a few unstated assumptions, shows great sophistication. Many theorems in *Elements* are thought to be original, especially those in number theory.

Euler, Leonhard, *b. Basel, Switzerland, 1707; d. 1783.* Swiss mathematician. Euler created much of the calculus that is taught in colleges today, including many specific sequences and series; advanced trigonometry; and much of standard notation, such as $f(x)$ for a function. More than a dozen well-known results bear his name and e, the base of the natural logarithms, is called Euler's number. Euler contributed to all branches of mathematics, including number theory and geometry. It is calculated that Euler averaged about 800 pages of new mathematics each year from the time he was 16 until the day of his death.

Euripides, *b. Athens, 484 B.C.; d. 406 B.C.* Playwright. One of the three great tragic playwrights of ancient Greece, Euripides created psychological but realistic dramas in which complex characters are responsible for their fate. Of a total of 92 plays, only 19 still exist. Among them are *Medea* (431 B.C.), *The Trojan Women* (415 B.C.), and *The Bacchae* (c. 406 BC).

Evert, Chris (Chris Evert Lloyd), *b. Fort Lauderdale, Fla., 1954.* Tennis player. Noted for her poise on the court, her strong two-handed backhand, and her nearly flawless baseline game, she won at least one Grand Slam title every year from 1974 to 1986. She won seven French Open titles (1974–75, 1979–80, 1983, 1985–86), six U.S. Open titles (1975–78, 1980, 1982), three Wimbledon titles (1974, 1976, 1981), and two Australian Open titles (1982, 1984).

Eyck, Jan van, *b. Maaseick, Netherlands, ca. 1395; d. 1441.* Painter. Beginning his career as an illuminator, van Eyck perfected the fine technique and small scale that characterize his paintings. One of the first artists in northern Europe to promote oil painting, he is known for vibrant colors and a polished finish. Van Eyck worked for John III, count of Holland; and was court painter to Philip the Good. His works, which include *Man in a Red Chaperon* (1433) and *Giovanni Arnolfini* and *Giovanna Cenami* (1434), influenced later artists in Italy and northern Europe.

Fairbanks, Douglas, Sr., (Douglas Elton Ulman) *b. Denver, Colo., 1883; d. 1939.* Silent film actor. In the silent era, he created the icon of the American film hero—attractive, morally courageous, and action-oriented. Fairbanks's physical agility and devil-may-care attitude made him a top star in such stunt-filled adventures as *The Mark of Zorro* (1920), *The Thief of Bagdad* (1924), and *The Black Pirate* (1926). To combat the increasing power of the big studios, Fairbanks, Mary Pickford, Charlie Chaplin, and D. W. Griffith formed United Artists in 1919 to distribute their films. Fairbanks and Pickford married the following year, enhancing their star power.

Faraday, Michael, *b. Newington, England, 1791; d. 1867.* Physicist and chemist. The discoverer of electromagnetic induction, Faraday was fascinated with electricity from a young age. His first scientific achievements were in chemistry. In 1825 he isolated benzene. He later turned to physics, inventing the first electric motor and dynamo, and developing laws of electrochemistry.

Farragut, David Glasgow, *b. Campbell's Station, Tenn., 1801; d. 1870.* U.S. Navy officer. Adopted son a of U.S. Navy captain, David Porter, Farragut joined the navy at age nine and served in the War of 1812 and the Mexican War. At the start of the Civil War, Farragut commanded the West Gulf Blockading Squadron, with which he seized New Orleans on April 25, 1862. On July 4, 1863, Farragut's riverine fleet helped capture Vicksburg, Miss., and in August 1864 his ships captured the approaches to Mobile, Ala. To honor Farragutís accomplishments, Congress created the ranks of rear admiral, vice admiral, and admiral.

Faulkner, William, *b. New Albany, Miss., 1897; d. 1962.* Novelist. Faulkner is regarded as the greatest southern writer. His four most important novels were written in a short span: *The Sound and the Fury* (1929), *As I Lay Dying* (1930), *Light in August* (1932), and *Absalom, Absalom!* (1936). In them he created an imaginary Mississippi county, Yoknapatawpha, with recurring characters, in which the traditional southern family and society are racked by intense psychological and historical strain. In content they are vividly emotional, graphic, and often violent. Faulkner later focused three novels—*The Hamlet* (1940), *The Town* (1957), and *The Mansion* (1959)—on the Snopeses, a family of ascendent "poor whites." *Intruder in the Dust* (1948), which deals harshly with racism, led to his winning the Nobel Prize in Literature in 1949.

Feller, Bob (Robert), *b. Van Meter, Iowa, 1918; d. 2010.* Baseball player. An Iowa farm boy, Feller became one of the most intimidating fastball pitchers of his day. He spent his entire career with the Cleveland Indians, amassing 266 wins despite missing almost four seasons in the military. Feller was the first major-league player to enlist after the attack on Pearl Harbor and was highly decorated for his service. "Rapid Robert" won 20 or more games in six different seasons, threw three no-hitters, and led the American League in strikeouts seven times. Feller was elected to the Baseball Hall of Fame in 1962.

Fellini, Federico, *b. Rimini, Italy, 1920; d. 1974.* Film director. Mixing autobiography and neorealism, Fellini fashioned a style that was personal in content but universal in theme. He began as a screenwriter for the neorealist director Roberto Rossellini; and his first films—*Variety Lights* (1951), *The White Sheik* (1952), and *I Vitelloni* (1953)—had neorealist characteristics. With *La Strada* (1954), starring his wife and muse Guilietta Masina, he embraced a more personal style, reaching his peak with *La Dolce Vita* (1960) and *8 1/2* (1963). Four of Fellini's films won Oscars as best foreign film: *La Strada*, *The Nights of Cabiria* (1957), *8 1/2*, and *Amarcord* (1973).

Fermat, Pierre de *b. Beaumont de Lomagne, France, 1601; d. 1665.* French mathematician. Fermat was a lawyer by profession but discovered analytic geometry a year before Descartes and employed some of the main ideas of calculus before either Newton or Leibniz. His main fame today, however, comes from many discoveries about number relationships. Fermat's "last theorem," that for natural numbers there is no number n greater than 2 for which $xn + yn = zn$ is true, is especially well known. Fermat claimed a proof of this theorem, but did not reveal it. It was finally proved in 1995.

Fermi, Enrico, *b. Rome, Italy, 1901 d. 1954.* Italian-American physicist. Fermi is the only physicist of the 20th century whose experimental work and theoretical work are equally valuable. In the 1920's he developed the first mathematical treatment of how electrons and similar particles of matter—now called fermions—interact physically. This work with electrons became the basis of the modern theory of conductivity. Fermi also showed experimentally that slow-moving neutrons can change one element or isotope into another. In 1942 Fermi was the chief designer of the first working nuclear reactor, based on using slow neutrons and techniques that he had developed to control nuclear fission in uranium.

Feynman, Richard, *b. Far Rockaway, N.Y., 1918; d. 1988.* **American physicist.** Feynman was one of the leading developers of quantum physics, the theory of subatomic particle behavior that expanded Einstein's theory of relativity—and, specifically, of quantum electrodynamics, for which work he was a co-winner of a 1965 Nobel Prize. He was also a lucid explicator, known for the Feynman diagram (1949), which depicted the paths and interactions of particles in space and time. Feynman was one of the youngest of the major participants in the Manhattan Project that developed the atomic bomb, and four decades later identified the cause—faulty "O-rings"—of the *Challenger* spaceship disaster.

Fielding, Henry, *b. Somerset, England, 1707; d. 1754.* **Novelist and playwright.** Fielding is considered, with Samuel Richardson, to be a founder of the English novel. His first novel, *Shamela* (1741), is a parody of Richardson's *Pamela* (1740). Although other of his novels also began as parodies, Fielding quickly found in the novel a form for social criticism. His most famous work, *Tom Jones* (1749), is masterful in its social commentary and established the novel as a literary form.

Fields, W. C. (William Claude Dukinfield) *b. Philadelphia, 1879; d. 1946.* **Comic actor.** Starting out in vaudeville, he became a Ziegfeld star with his juggling and monologues, then went on to make many silent movies in the 1920's. His gnarled face and matching voice made his screen nastiness uproarious in later films such as *It's a Gift* and *The Man on the Flying Trapeze* (both 1934); a sole dramatic success came with *David Copperfield* (1935) in which he played Mr. Micawber. His movie with Mae West, *My Little Chickadee*, (1939) had brought him long-lasting fame. Fields wrote many of the stories for his comic movies.

Fillmore, Millard, *b. Locke Township, N.Y., 1800; d. 1874.* **Thirteenth U.S. president, 1850–53.** The son of a poor farmer, Fillmore entered politics as an Anti-Mason and was a four-term congressman when the Whigs made him Zachary Taylor's vice president in 1848. Dignified

good looks were Fillmore's main political asset; he was quite unprepared for the presidency when Taylor died suddenly in 1850. Fillmore delayed civil war another decade by signing the Compromise of 1850, but he lost the nomination in 1852 when the Whigs turned to Gen. Winfield Scott, yet another genial war hero and the party's last candidate.

Fischer, Bobby, *b. Chicago, Ill., 1943; d. 2008.* The only American ever to become world chess champion, the quixotic Fischer was 15 when he became the world's youngest grandmaster. He won an unprecedented 20 straight matches in the Interzonal and Candidates' matches of 1970 and 1971 to win the right to challenge the champion, Boris Spassky. After overwhelming Spassky in 1972, Fischer refused to play another match in public, and forfeited his world title in 1975.

Fitzgerald, F. Scott, *b. St. Paul, Minn., 1896; d. 1940.* **Novelist.** Fitzgerald left Princeton without graduating, joined the army, and then wrote his first novel, *This Side of Paradise* (1920), about college life, which was an immediate success; he followed it with *The Beautiful and the Damned* (1922). He married an Alabama belle, Zelda Sayre, and they lived prodigally in New York City. *The Great Gatsby* (1925), set in the "jazz age" of that time and place, is his most famous novel. *Tender Is the Night* (1934), is set among American expatriates in France, a life he and Zelda also lived. The romance of his own life was scuttled by alcoholism and Zelda's mental illness. Dead at 44 of a heart attack, he left an unfinished novel, *The Last Tycoon.*

Flaubert, Gustave, *b. Rouen, France, 1821; d. 1880.* **Novelist.** A surgeon's son, Flaubert was a master of realism who wrote of French middle-class life with controlled, if scornful, objectivity and legendary stylistic precision. His first and best-known novel, *Madame Bovary* (1857), describes the adulterous adventures of an unhappy provincial woman, and led to his trial for immorality, of which he was acquitted. Of equal merit is *Sentimental Education* (1870), in which romance and other aspirations are swallowed by mercenary conditions of French society. Flaubert suffered from epilepsy and lived mostly with his mother. Other works are the novels *Salammbô* (1863) and *The Temptation of St. Anthony* (1874).

Fleming, Sir Alexander, *b. Lochfield, Ayr, Scotland, 1881; d. 1955.* **Bacteriologist.** A researcher and university professor, Fleming discovered the antibiotic properties of the *Penicillium notatum* mold while studying *Staphylococcus* bacteria in 1928, and published his work on penicillin the following year. In its raw form, penicillin is unstable, and Fleming dropped his research. In 1940, the Oxford scientists Howard Florey and Ernst Chain isolated and purified penicillin and devised means for its mass production. The three shared the 1945 Nobel Prize for Physiology or Medicine "for the discovery of penicillin and its curative effect in various infectious diseases."

Fonda, Henry, b. *Grand Island, Neb., 1905; d. 1982.* Actor. Tall, slim, slow, and steady, Henry Fonda started out doing Community Theater in Omaha, before moving east to join the Cape Cod University Players, where he was soon joined by James Stewart. His film career began with a series of honest country-boy roles in the late 1930's. For John Ford, he starred in *Young Mr. Lincoln* (1939) and *The Grapes of Wrath* (1940), and he played the legendary Wyatt Earp in *My Darling Clementine* (1946). His greatest stage success was 1948's *Mister Roberts*, and he split his career between Broadway and Hollywood from the 1950's on. He won the Oscar for Best Actor for his last film, *On Golden Pond* (1982). His other important films include *The Lady Eve* (1941), *The Oxbow Incident* (1943), *The Wrong Man* (1957), and *12 Angry Men* (1952).

Fonda, Jane, b. *1937, New York City.* Actress. The daughter of actor Henry Fonda, Jane was an art student and model before beginning studies at the Actors Studio in 1958. In 1965, she married the French director Roger Vadim for whom she made the sci-fi live-action comic strip movie *Barbarella* (1968). She graduated from sexpot to serious actress with *They Shoot Horses, Don't They* (1969), and won Best Actress Oscars for *Klute* (1971) and *Coming Home,* (1978). Her antiwar activities, including a trip to North Vietnam in 1972, earned her the nickname "Hanoi Jane."

Ford, Gerald R., b. *Omaha, Neb., 1913; d. 2006.* Thirty-eighth U.S. president, 1974–77. The only vice president and president never elected to either office, Ford served in Congress from 1949 until he was appointed to the vice presidency in December 1973, replacing Spiro T. Agnew under the 25th Amendment. From 1965 to 1973 he was Republican minority leader. Richard Nixon's resignation made Ford the new president on August 9, 1974. Ford announced that "our long national nightmare is over," but a month later he shocked the nation by giving Nixon a blanket pardon. He sought reelection in 1976 but lost to Jimmy Carter in the first defeat of an incumbent president since Herbert Hoover's.

Ford, Henry, b. *Springwells Township, Mich., 1863; d. 1947.* American industrialist and automotive pioneer. In 1903 Ford founded the Ford Motor Company to build the first mass-produced car for a mass market. He adopted the assembly line to lower the cost of production and allow him to price his cars low, and the company became the world's largest auto producer. The first Model T was shipped in 1908 and revolutionized transportation. In 1914 Ford began paying his workers the extraordinary wage of $5 for an eight-hour day, and offered them a share of the profits. By 1927 more than 15 million Model T's had been sold, but after that he lost his domination of the market to General Motors. His reputation was tarnished by anti-Semitic writings in his *Dearburn Independent* and by his anti-union policies.

Ford, John, (**Sean Aloysius O'Fearna or O'Feeney**) b. *Cape Elizabeth, Me., 1895; d. 1973.* Film director. Ford's personal vision was remarkably consistent during his 50-year career. His deceptively simple narratives embodied larger American experiences, and his protagonists represented the pioneer spirit of individualism. He went to Hollywood in 1917 and directed his first major silent film, *The Iron Horse* in 1924. His first successful "talkie" ws the *The Informer* (1935), set in revolutionary Ireland. He made John Wayne a star with *Stagecoach* (1939), beginning an association that yielded such western classics as *The Searchers* (1956) and *The Man Who Shot Liberty Valance* (1962). Though acclaimed for westerns, Ford won directing Oscars for his other work: *The Informer* (1935), *The Grapes of Wrath* (1940), *How Green Was My Valley* (1941), and *The Quiet Man* (1952).

Foreman, George, b. *Marshall, Tex., 1948.* Heavyweight boxer. A gold medalist at the Olympics of 1968. Foreman won his first 34 pro fights to earn a title shot in 1973 against Joe Frazier, whom he knocked down six times in two rounds. His first loss came in 1974 in Zaire to Muhammad Ali. Foreman retired in 1977 and was ordained as a minister, but he began a comeback in 1987 at age 39. In 1994, he became the oldest champion in any weight division by defeating Michael Moorer.

Forster, E. M. (**Edward Morgan**), b. *London, 1879; d. 1970.* Novelist. A traditional novelist but technically and stylistically superb, Forster published all his novels between 1905 and 1924. They include *A Room with a View* (1908), *Howards End* (1910); and *Maurice*, finished in 1914 but not published until 1971 because the relationships it explores are homosexual. In *A Passage to India* (1924), Forster's last novel, the relationships concern British colonials and native residents. Forster's major theme is the difficulty of forming meaningful human relationships, in society and in love. His *Aspects of the Novel* (1927) is an important work of literary criticism.

Fortas, Abe, *b. Memphis, Tenn., 1910; d. 1982.* U.S. Supreme Court justice. Founder of a prestigious law firm, Fortas won acclaim by defending a client facing interrogation by Senator Joseph McCarthy, and by representing Clarence Earl Gideon before the Supreme Court. President Lyndon Johnson named Fortas to the Supreme Court in 1965, and in 1968 chose him for the newly vacant post of chief justice. But conservatives in the Senate greeted the move with hostility. Upon discovering that Fortas had accepted fees for speaking, they filibustered his nomination, defeating it. The next president, Richard Nixon, named Warren Burger as chief justice. Fortas remained on the Court until 1969, when it was revealed that he had accepted retainer fees from a former client under investigation for securities fraud. Fortas denied wrongdoing, but resigned to avoid impeachment.

Fox, Charles James, *b. London, England, 1749; d. 1806.* British political leader. An inveterate gambler in his youth, Fox became a leader of the Whig party in the House of Commons and built a reputation as a champion of individual rights. He supported American independence and opposed British intervention during the French Revolution. Although he was almost always in opposition to the ruling party, he became the first foreign secretary in English history. In 1792, he proposed the Libel Act which gave juries the right to determine what constituted libel and whether someone was guilty of it; and he presented to Parliament a resolution to abolish the slave trade, an act that was passed in 1807, shortly after his death.

Francis I (Francis of Angoulême), *b. Cognac, France, 1494; d. 1547.* King of France, 1515–47. Crowned at age 20, Francis I immediately waged a war to recapture the duchy of Milan (1515–16); he had himself knighted after the bloody victory. But the accession of Charles V as Holy Roman Emperor marked the end of Francis's power. Already king of Spain, Charles now surrounded France and had his sights on all of Europe. The enmity between the two kings set off a war that lasted more than two decades (1521–44). Captured at the Battle of Pavia (1525), Francis never again wielded influence in Europe.

Francis of Assisi, (Francesco di Pietro di Bernardone) *b. Giovanni Bernardone, Assisi, Italy, 1181/82?; d. 1226.* Roman Catholic saint, founder of the Franciscan monastic order. He was the son of a wealthy merchant. As a young soldier, Francis was imprisoned, then stricken ill, and experienced a sudden conversion during an expedition, about 1205. He embraced absolute poverty and became a hermit but was inspired to travel and preach. He attracted a small band of followers, which grew into an order of several thousand mendicant friars during his lifetime. His devotee, St. Clare, founded an order of nuns. Francis endured his hardships joyfully, loving all God's creation and, famously, preaching to animals and birds. He traveled to France, Spain, and Palestine, winning concessions for Christians from the sultan of Egypt. During his last years, Francis yielded active leadership of his order and is said to have received the wounds of Christ's crucifixion, or the stigmata.

Francis Xavier (Saint), *b. Xavier Castle, Navarre, Spain, 1506; d. 1552.* Jesuit missionary, patron saint of Roman Catholic missions. Francis Xavier, a nobleman and knight, was one of the first Jesuit priests, an associate of the order's founder, St. Ignatius of Loyola. After working with Ignatius in Rome, he went to Lisbon; from there, in 1541, he embarked on a Portuguese mission to Goa—and a career that would earn him the sobriquet "apostle to the Indies." A noted preacher, skilled in relating to people within their own cultures, he traveled to India, Ceylon, Malacca, the Moluccas, and Japan, and is estimated to have converted about 30,000 to Christianity. He died while sailing to China.

Franklin, Benjamin, *b. Boston, 1706; d. 1790.* Printer and publisher, writer, inventor and scientist, statesman. Franklin was a man of many talents and experiences. Among his best-known published works is *Poor Richard's Almanack* (1732–57). His inventions included the efficient Franklin (wood) stove and bifocal glasses. The lightning rod was a result of his famous experiments into the nature of electricity. Franklin's ideas for community resources included a library, fire department, insurance company, police, hospital, and an academy, that later became the University of Pennsylvania. Franklin was deputy postmaster general for the northern colonies (1753–74); Pennsylvania delegate to the Albany Congress; London (Parliament) agent for Pennsylvania, Georgia, New Jersey, and Massachusetts; delegate to the Second Continental Congress (helping draft the Declaration of Independence); and commissioner to France, securing military and economic aid for the American Revolution. Franklin was a member of the Constitutional Convention of 1787, which wrote the United States Constitution.

Frazier, Joe, *b. Beaufort S.C., 1944.* **Boxer.** Nicknamed "Smokin' Joe" for his relentless punching style, Frazier was a 1964 Olympic gold medalist and heavyweight champion from 1970 to 1973. But many in boxing did not consider him the champ until 1971, when he defeated Muhammad Ali, who had been stripped of his title in 1967. Frazier lost the title two years later in a stunning second-round knockout by George Foreman. Frazier later lost two wildly hyped bouts to Ali, including a 14th-round knockout in 1975 in the "Thrilla in Manila," one of the greatest fights of all time.

Frederick the Great (Frederick II), *b. Berlin, 1712; d. 1786.* **King of Prussia.** Soon after Frederick became king in 1740, he seized Silesia (now in southwestern Poland), which Austria ceded to him in 1745. Austria remained unreconciled to its loss. In 1756, Frederick launched a preemptive war, which ended in 1763 with Frederick still in control of Silesia. Frederick's greatest diplomatic triumph was to persuade Austria and Russia to join him in the first partition of Poland in 1772. Frederick was a domestic reformer and a patron of the arts and letters, who, like many of his contemporary rulers, believed in "enlightened despotism."

Freud, Sigmund, *b. Freiburg, Moravia, 1856; d. 1939.* **Physician, founder of psychoanalysis.** Freud moved to Vienna at age four, and would live and work there nearly all his life. He studied medicine, which was one of the few professions open to Jews. Influenced by Josef Breuer, Freud became interested in using hypnosis to treat hysteria; then, working with J. M. Charcot in Paris, he moved toward a theoretical understanding of psychopathology, with emphasis on sexual causes. Hypnosis gave way to his technique of "free association," by which patients revealed repressed feelings believed to be the sources of neurotic symptoms. Freud developed a complex dynamic theory of the mind, dividing it into the unconscious id, containing irrational (including sexual) impulses; and the civilizing ego and conscientious superego. He published his groundbreaking first book, *The Interpretation of Dreams,* in 1900, followed by *The Psychopathology of Everyday Life* (1904). Other important works are *Totem and Taboo* (1913), *Beyond the Pleasure Principle* (1919), *The Ego and the Id* (1923), and, on religion, *The Future of an Illusion* (1927). After the Nazi annexation of Austria, Freud spent his last year in London.

Friedan, Betty, *b. Peoria, Ill., 1921; d. 2006.* **American feminist and author.** Friedan burst onto the scene in 1963 with *The Feminine Mystique,* whch argued that American women are stifled by domesticity and limited career options. Her book ignited the modern feminist movement. In 1966 Friedan cofounded the National Organization for Women (NOW), and in 1969 she cofounded the National Association for the Repeal of Abortion Laws (NARAL). She campaigned tirelessly for sexual, political, and economic equality.

Friedman, Milton, *b. New York City, 1912; d. 2006.* **American economist.** From 1946 to 1976, Friedman taught at the University of Chicago, where he was the leading voice of the Chicago school of monetary economics, arguing that the Federal Reserve should regulate the supply of money to achieve economic stability during business cycles. He strongly advocated a free market system with emphasis on individual freedom. Among his important books are *A Theory of the Consumption Function* (1957), *Capitalism and Freedom* (1962), *A Monetary History of the United States, 1867–1960* (1963) with Anna Schwartz, *A Theoretical Framework for Monetary Analysis* (1971), and *Free to Choose* (1980), with his wife, Rose Friedman. He was awarded the Nobel Prize in Economic Science in 1976.

Frost, Robert Lee, *b. San Francisco, 1874; d. 1963.* **Poet.** Frost moved to Lawrence, Mass., at age 10, and is considered the quintessential 20th-century New England poet. After withdrawing from Harvard, he lived meanly as a New Hampshire farmer, then moved to England and published his first books of poetry, *A Boy's Will* (1913) and *North of Boston* (1914). Their success brought him back home, where he became America's most famous poet. His use of traditional verse patterns, colloquial diction, and natural settings in lyrical poems like "Mending Wall," "After Apple Picking" (both 1914), and "Stopping by Woods on a Snowy Evening" (1923), make them appealing, yet closer reading reveals inklings of mystery and danger. Important narrative poems include "The Death of the Hired Man," "Home Burial" (both 1914), and "Two Tramps in Mud Time" (1936). His style was consistent throughout many volumes of poems, for which he won four Pulitzer Prizes.

Gable, Clark, *b. Cadiz, Ohio, 1901; d. 1960.* **American movie actor.** "The King" with his knowing grin that signaled rugged force made more than 65 films, many with the beautiful stars of succeeding generations: Joan Crawford, Jean Harlow, Hedy Lamarr, Lana Turner, Grace Kelly, and Marilyn Monroe. He won an Oscar for a comic performance in *It Happened One Night* (1934) and is best known as Rhett Butler in *Gone With the Wind* (1939). In *The Misfits* (1960)—his last film, made shortly after his death—he played a tough, aging cowboy.

Galbraith, John Kenneth, *b. Iona Station, Ont., Canada, 1908; d. 2006.* Economist. One of the leading economists of his generation, Galbraith taught at Harvard University for decades. He advised several Democratic candidates and presidents, and served as John Kennedy's ambassador to India. Galbraith worked with President Lyndon Johnson in designing the Great Society program before breaking with Johnson over the Vietnam War. An unabashed liberal in a largely conservative field, Galbraith wrote dozens of influential books, including *The Affluent Society* (1958). This seminal work argued that America's obsession with frivolous consumer goods was damaging the environment and preventing the nation from caring for the poor and investing in the public sector.

Galen (Galenos), *b. Pergamum, Mysia, Anatolia [now Bergama, Turkey) 129; d. ca. 216.* Greek physician, writer, and philosopher. Galen spent most of his career in Rome. A prolific author and unabashed promoter of his theories, he was an early advocate of dissection, which he used to expand knowledge of the nervous system and demonstrate that arteries carry blood, rather than air, as had been thought for centuries. But because he could work only with animals (human dissection was forbidden), he often mistook animal anatomy for human. Although his conclusions were often wrong, his methods of observation and investigation, described in copius writings, were sound, and his influence on medicine lasted for centuries.

Galileo (Galileo Galilei), *b. 156; d. 1642.* Italian astronomer, physicist, inventor, mathematician. Galileo taught at the University in Pisa and Padua and worked in Florence as a Medici patron. After developing the first astronomical telescopes, Galileo discovered the moons of Jupiter, the phases of Venus, the mountains and plains of the Moon, sunspots, and the individual stars of the Milky Way. In physics his experiments showed that all bodies would fall at the same distance in the same amount of time in a vacuum and that objects in motion continue to move in a straight line unless a force acts against them. He also contributed to the study of mathematical infinity and invented the first way to measure temperature. Galileo promoted Copernican views as early as 1604 and did not stop when in 1616 the church declared such ideas to be heresy. Galileo, who had enjoyed close relations with

Church officials was put before the Inquisition and informed that he must recant or be tortured; he recanted, but spent the last years of his life under house arrest.

Gandhi, Indira, *b. Allahabad, India, 1917; d. 1984.* Prime minister of India. Daughter of Jawaharlal Nehru, India's first prime minister, she herself became India's head of state in 1966. She made strides in modernizing India but never quelled its political turmoil. In 1971, Gandhi provided military support for the secession of East Bengal from Pakistan, creating Bangladesh. She won the election of 1972 in a landslide, but courts later upheld charges of election fraud in 1975. Gandhi responded by jailing her opponents and suspending civil liberties. In 1977, she was toppled from power, later regaining her post as prime minister in 1980. After quashing a Sikh uprising in 1984 she was assassinated by her Sikh bodyguards. Her son Rajiv succeeded her, and he, too, was assassinated in 1991.

Gandhi, Mahatma (Mohandas Karamchand Gandhi), *b. Porbandar, India 1869; d. 1948.* Indian revolutionary. Gandhi studied law in London and practiced in South Africa, where his spirituality deepened and he first exercised nonviolent resistance. He returned to India in 1915 and became involved in national affairs. Considered the father of modern India—Mahatma means "Great Soul"—Mohandas Gandhi used the tactics of nonviolent protest to throw off British rule and establish an independent India in 1947. His invention of *satyagraha*, or devotion to truth, encompassed civil disobedience, sit-ins, fasting, and other forms of nonviolent resistance. Weeks after fostering a truce between rioting Hindus and Muslims in Delhi, Gandhi was assassinated by Nathuram Godse, a Hindu fanatic.

Garbo, Greta, (Greta Louisa Gustafsson) *b. Stockholm, Sweden, 1905; d. 1990.* Film actress. Garbo became one of Hollywood's enduring legends when she created her star image as an enigmatic woman of mystery. Discovered by the Swedish director Mauritz Stiller, she came to Hollywood during the silent era to make *The Torrent* (1926) for MGM. She successfully survived the coming of sound with *Anna Christie* (1930), then moved on to such classic dramas as *Anna Karenina* (1935) and *Camille* (1937), generally playing an aloof, remote woman pained by love. She retired in 1941 and received a career Oscar in 1954.

Garcia Marquez, Gabriel, *b. 1928, Aracataca, Colombia.* Novelist, short-story writer. Garcia Marquez worked as a journalist before publishing his first book of fiction, *Leafstorm and Other Stories*, in 1955. In that, a subsequent collection, and an internationally popular novel, *One Hundred Years of Solitude*, he developed into the best-known practitioner of Latin-American "magical realism," which combines realistic narrative with myth and fantasy. Although he has lived largely in Mexico and Spain, his writing focuses on Colombia, and deals with the tension between solitude and love. Other novels are *Autumn of the Patriarch* (1975), *Love in the Time of Cholera* (1985), and *The General in His Labyrinth* (1989).

Garfield, James A., *b. Orange, Ohio, 1831; d. 1881.* Twentieth U.S. president, 1881. Garfield was a classics professor, president of Hiram College, a lawyer, and at age 30 the youngest Union general in the Civil War. He left the battlefield in 1864 to enter Congress, where he remained until the Republicans nominated him for president in 1880. Garfield won the fall election, but after only four months in office was shot in a Washington, D.C., railroad station by Charles J. Guiteau, a disappointed office-seeker. He died 80 days later.

Garibaldi, Giuseppe, *b. Nice, France, 1807; d. 1882.* Italian patriot. A merchant seaman by trade, Garibaldi was a radical advocate of Italian unification, women's rights, workers, and racial equality. In exile from Italy (1836–48) he fought for Brazilian and Uruguayan independence movements. In 1860, he helped usher in the kingdom of Italy with his invasion of Sicily and Naples. Governments kept him at arm's length, but he led the campaign of 1866 that took Venice from Austria. An attack on Rome failed owing to French resistance, but he fought for the French in the Franco-Prussian War (1870–71) before retiring to Caprera Island.

Garland, Judy (Frances Ethel Gumm), *b. Grand Rapids, Minn., 1922; d. 1969.* Singer and movie actress. Raised in vaudeville, she became a star as Dorothy in *The Wizard of Oz* (1939), singing her signature "Over the Rainbow." After several spirited "let's put on a show" pictures with Mickey Rooney, she grew into adult roles in such notable musicals as *Meet Me in St. Louis* (1944), *The Harvey Girls* (1945), and *Easter Parade* (1948). Fired by MGM in 1950, she made a glamorous comeback in *A Star Is Born* (1954), then went on to successful worldwide concerts and a turbulent year on television.

Garrison, William Lloyd, *b. Newburyport, Mass., 1805; d. 1879.* Abolitionist. Publisher of *The Liberator* (beginning in 1831), a newspaper famous for its searing moral attacks on the institution of slavery, Garrison advocated immediate and complete abolition. His self-righteous tone and demand for overnight reform alienated many. He advocated secession of the North from the Union because the Constitution permitted slavery, and he opposed the Civil War until Lincoln issued the Emancipation Proclamation. Garrison served as president of the American Anti-Slavery Society for more than two decades.

Garvey, Marcus, *b. Saint Ann's Bay, Jamaica, 1887; d. 1940.* Black nationalist leader. Garvey's experience as a printer in Jamaica inspired him to lead blacks into better economic conditions and give them pride in their African heritage. In 1914 he founded the Universal Negro Improvement Association (U.N.I.A.), moving to New York City in 1916. He espoused a "Back to Africa" movement and founded the Black Star Line in 1919 to transport blacks to Africa. But mismanagement doomed the enterprise, and he was charged with mail fraud in 1922, convicted, and jailed in 1925. His sentence was commuted in 1927, and he was deported to Jamaica, where he was unable to rebuild the U.N.I.A.

Gates, Bill (William Henry Gates III), *b. Seattle, Wash., 1955.* Businessman. At age 19, Gates and his childhood friend Paul Allen founded the Microsoft Company. In 1980 they began producing MS-DOS, the operating system for IBM's first personal computer. DOS and subsequent programs, including Windows, made Microsoft the world's largest software producer. Aggressive marketing earned Microsoft billions in profits (and persistent accusations of antitrust violations). One of the world's richest men, Gates also founded Corbis, a massive digital archive of art and photography; and he endowed a $24 billion philanthropic foundation to tackle global health and education issues.

Gauguin, Paul, *b. Paris, France, 1848; d. 1903.* Painter, printmaker, sculptor, ceramicist. After a successful stint as a stockbroker, Gauin left his wife and five children to pursue a life devoted to art. Inspired by Impressionism, Gauguin developed a unique style of Symbolism that incorporated elements from primitive Polynesian culture, and spent several years in Tahiti, developing an "untamed" aesthetic. With the artist Emile Bernard, Gauguin invented a method of rendering pictoral space that uses large patches of flat color and thick line; these techniques influenced early 20th-century artists. Gauguin's works include *Vision after the Sermon: Jacob Wrestling with the Angel* (1888), *Mahana no atua (Day of the God)* (1814), and *Savage Tales* (1902).

Gauss, Carl Friedrich b. *Brunswick, Germany, 1777, d. 1855* German mathematician and physical scientist. Between the ages of 19 and 28 Gauss discovered the first major new geometric construction since Greek times (1796) and developed the first proof that all polynomial equations have a solution, the fundamental theorem of algebra (1799); completely restructured number theory (1801); and invented a way to calculate the path of a planet from a few observations (1809). Later he created the theory that mathematically describes properties of surfaces (1827) and also became the first to establish a non-Euclidean geometry. Gauss also studied Earth's magnetic field and with a collaborator built one of the first working telegraphs (1833).

Gehry, Frank Owen, b. *Toronto, 1929.* Architect. His early houses included the Davis Studio and Residence (1968–72) in Malibu and his own house in Santa Monica (1977–78, and 1991–2002) and exhibit his imaginative use of industrial materials in incongruous settings. The Guggenheim Museum (1991–97) in Bilbao, Spain, with its billowing titanium exterior walls, gained him world attention and put the city of Bilbao on the tourist map. Gehry demonstrated his inventiveness with the DG Bank building (1995–2001) in Berlin. The exterior of the Walt Disney Concert Hall (1987–2003) in Los Angeles, is a variation in stainless steel of the sweeping curves of the Bilbao Guggenheim.

Gell-Mann, Murray, b. *New York City, 1929.* American physicist. In 1963 Gell-Mann showed that some short-lived subatomic particles do not decay as fast as predicted, because of a quality Gell-Mann named "strangeness." Gell-Mann developed a theory called the eightfold way that enabled him to predict the properties of a previously unknown particle, later discovered and named the omega-minus. In 1964 Gell-Mann proposed that mesons, protons, and other heavy subatomic particles are constructed from smaller particles called quarks, an idea now generally accepted as proved by experiment.

Genghis Khan (Chinggis, Jenghiz), b. *Mongolia, ca. 1162; d. 1227.* World conquerer. The orphan Temujin assembled a band of comrades to kill his father's murderers. A natural leader, he then set about assembling larger and larger coalitions of Mongol tribes for raiding and conquest. He was confirmed as great leader of all the tribes at an assembly in 1206, and took the name Genghis Khan ("oceanlike ruler"). In an unending cycle of conquest marked by both strategic genius and great brutality, his armies subdued a vast territory from northern China across Central Asia to west of the Caspian Sea and into south-central Russia. He died from injuries from a riding accident while on campaign; his secret tomb has never been found.

George III, b. *London, 1738; d. 1820.* King of Great Britain and Ireland, elector of Hanover and king of Hanover. George succeeded to the throne in 1760 and was determined to be an active ruler. But his policies helped to provoke the American Revolution, and the English defeat nearly forced him to abdicate. A mental condition, possibly porphyria, caused a progressive dementia, and in 1811 it had become so severe that his son, later George IV, was appointed regent until his death.

Geronimo (Goyathlay), b. *present-day site of Clifton, Ariz., 1829; d. 1909.* American Indian warrior. Renowned as a great medicine man and spiritual leader, Geronimo was one of the last holdouts against the inexorable white settlement of North America. His elite band of Apache warriors raided white settlements in what is now Arizona and New Mexico before being captured and forced onto a reservation in 1876. Geronimo escaped and eluded U.S. troops for a decade. Forced to surrender in 1886, he was shipped to Florida for imprisonment. Geronimo was ultimately settled in Oklahoma and never saw his homeland again.

Gershwin, George (Jacob Gershvin) b. *New York City, 1898; d. 1937.* Popular composer. Gershwin was both a talented songwriter in the Tin Pan Alley tradition (usually collaborating with his lyricist brother Ira) and a composer of serious classical music. Noteworthy compositions include the popular songs "Swanee" (1919), "Someone to Watch Over Me" (1926), "I Got Rhythm" (1927), "But Not for Me" (1927), "Embraceable You" (1927), "They Can't Take That Away from Me" (1937), and "Let's Call the Whole Thing Off" (1937); the classical compositions "Rhapsody in Blue" (1924) and "American in Paris" (1928); and the opera *Porgy and Bess* (1935).

Gibson, Althea, b. *Silver, S.C., 1927; d. 2003.* Tennis player. When Gibson launched her career, tennis was a strictly segregated sport. Her appearance at the U.S. Championships in 1950 broke the color barrier; she later became the first black player to compete at Wimbledon. In 1956 Gibson won the French championship, the first of 11 Grand Slam titles she would claim. She was often shunned at tennis clubs and denied hotel rooms, even while competing at the highest levels of her sport. In 1957 Gibson became the first African-American to be honored by the Associated Press as Female Athlete of the Year; she won the award again in 1958. She was inducted into the International Tennis Hall of Fame in 1971.

Gibson, Bob, *b. Omaha, Neb., 1935.* Baseball player. Playing for the St. Louis Cardinals (1959–75), Gibson was baseball's best pitcher from 1964 to 1970, intimidating hitters with inside pitches. His 1.12 earned true average in 1968 is the lowest seasonal mark in National League history. He led the league in victories, strikeouts, and ERA only once, but he won 20 games five times and routinely struck out 200 batters per season. His World Series record is 9–2 (including two victories in game 7), 1.89 ERA, and 92 strikeouts in 81 innings. Gibson was elected to the Hall of Fame in 1981.

Gillespie, Dizzy, (John Birks Gillespie) *b. Cheraw, S.C., 1917; d. 1993.* Jazz trumpeter and composer. Dizzy was one of the most complex jazz trumpeters of all time. Along with the saxophonist Charlie Parker, he defined and popularized the bebop style; he also helped to popularize Afro-Cuban (Latin) jazz. With his puffed-out cheeks, bent trumpet, and easy wit, Dizzy was a particularly popular performer. Recordings include "Salt Peanuts" (1944), "Shaw Nuff" (1945), "A Night in Tunisia" (1946), and "Manteca" (1948).

Ginsberg, Allen, *b. Newark, N.J., 1926; d. 1997.* Poet. A member of the Beat movement and one of the most famous American poets of the late 20th century, Ginsberg rose to prominence in the 1950's with the publication of his epic poem *Howl* (1956). Deeply influenced by Buddhism, Ginsberg's poems show a concern with ordinary language and natural speech patterns. Among his collections are *Kaddish and Other Poems* (1961), and *The Fall of America: Poems of These States, 1965–1971* (1972), which won the National Book Award.

Giotto (di Bondone), *b. Vespignano, Italy, ca. 1267; d. 1337.* Painter and designer. Regarded as the first artist in the Gothic tradition to have depicted nature in a convincingly realistic manner, Giotto represents a crucial turning point in the progression of western art toward the illusionism of the Renaissance. To his contemporaries, Giotto's, life-like paintings were considered revolutionary. He is best known for his frescoes in the Arena Chapel in Padua, which include *The Lamentation* (1305–06), as well as for small panel paintings such as *Madonna* (ca. 1310). In 1334 Giotto was appointed head of the Florence Cathedral workshop.

Gish, Lillian, *b. Springfield, Ohio, 1896; d. 1993.* Actress. The "first lady of the silver screen," Gish was part of D. W. Griffith's stock company of film actors, who developed a credible style of screen acting less exaggerated than stage performance. She and her sister, Dorothy, began working for Griffith in 1912 on *An Unseen Enemy*. She became his favorite actress, starring in his major feature films such as *The Birth of a Nation* (1915) and *Broken Blossoms* (1919). She also acted in films by other directors, before returning to the stage in the 1930's. She received a career achievement Oscar in 1970 and made her last screen appearance in *The Whales of August* (1987).

Gladstone, William Ewart, *b. Liverpool, England, 1809; d. 1898.* Statesman and man of letters. As a young Tory in Parliament, Gladstone served in several national posts under Robert Peel and became an advocate for free trade; he ultimately joined and led the Liberal Party. During the first of his four terms as prime minister (1868–74), Gladstone passed a series of reform bills on education, the judiciary, and civil service. During his later terms (1880–1885, 1886, and 1892–94), he continued to press measures for social reform. Throughout his life he wrote about political issues and contributed literary criticism to reviews and magazines. Long a supporter of Irish causes, he fought within his own party for Irish home rule. Though greatly controversial in his time, he is considered by many the moral conscience of Victorian Britain.

Glass, Philip, *b. Baltimore, Md., 1937.* Innovative American composer. Now considered one of the most influential composers of the late 20th century, Glass studied composition at the Juilliard School of Music. His acquaintance with Ravi Shankar, the Indian sitarist, had a profound influence on his compositional style. Glass defines his style not as minimalist, but as "music with repetitive structures." In 25 years he has composed more than 20 operas. His first, *Einstein on the Beach* (1976) earned him international acclaim and was followed by *Satyagraha* (1980), which portrays the early life of Mohandas Gandhi. Glass is also well known for his film scores , three of which have been nominated for Academy Awards, including *The Hours, Kundun, Notes on a Scandal,* and *The Fog of War,* the Errol Morris documentary about the Vietnam War.

Gleason, Jackie (Herbert John Gleason), *b. Brooklyn, N.Y., 1916; d. 1987.* Actor and comedian. Gleason was one of television's early giants. His career began when he hosted *Cavalcade of Stars* (1950–52) and then the enormously popular *Jackie Gleason Show* (1952–55). Here he introduced a series of comic characters, including Ralph Kramden, a Brooklyn bus driver; Ralph's wife, Alice, played by Audrey Meadows; and his friend Ed Norton, played by Art Carney. Called "The Honeymooners," these brief sketches were so popular that in 1955–56, *The Honeymooners* became a half-hour series. Gleason won a Tony Award for *Take Me Along* (1959), and an Oscar nomination for best supporting actor for his role as Minnesota Fats in *The Hustler* (1961).

Glenn, John Herschel, Jr. *b. Cambridge, Ohio, 1921.* **Astronaut, senator.** A Marine pilot during World War II and the Korean War, Glenn was recruited as one of the first seven astronauts for Project Mercury, and became the first man to orbit the Earth on February 20, 1962, in the Friendship 7 space capsule. In 1964 Glenn retired from the space program, and in 1978 he was elected U.S. senator from Ohio, serving four terms. He returned to space aboard the Discovery in 1998, at age 77, the oldest person ever to do so, as part of research into weightlessness and the aging process.

Gluck, Christoph Willibald, *b. Erasbach, Bavaria (Germany), 1714; d. 1787.* **Opera composer.** Although his family intended him to be a forester, Gluck left home to pursue his music, becoming one of the great figures in 18th-century opera. He traveled widely, studying in Italy, London, and Paris and finally settling in Vienna, where he remained until the end of his life. With *Orfeo ed Euridice* (1762), Gluck changed the face of opera by blending dramatic acting with musical elements for the first time. Though rarely performed, his last work, *Iphigénie in Tauride* (1779), is considered his masterpiece. His operas marked the beginning of the modern music drama, and influenced such composers as Berlioz and Wagner.

Godard, Jean-Luc, *b. Paris, 1930.* **Film Director.** The most controversial member of the French New Wave, Godard is known for the radical form and political content of his films. Beginning with his first feature, *Breathless* (1959), he broke away from filmmaking norms, preferring the roughness of jump cuts and handheld camera to established techniques. Later, attempting to use film as a political instrument, he stripped down his narrative structures and cast aside dramatic form, as in *Masculine Feminine* (1966), *Weekend* (1968), and *Wind from the East* (1969). During the 1980's, he returned to conventional filmmaking but remained controversial (*Hail Mary*, 1985).

Goddard, Robert Hutchings, *b. Worcester Mass., 1882; d. 1945* **Physicist and rocket pioneer.** He designed and built early high-altitude rockets, including the first liquid-fueled rocket (1926). His inventions included an automatic rocket-steering system and many other rocket devices. He developed a general theory of rocket action and demonstrated rocket propulsion in a vacuum. Goddard was a professor of physics at Clark University.

Gödel, Kurt, *b. Brunn, Austrian Empire, 1906; d. 1978.* **Austrian-American logician.** Gödel's first major work demonstrated that every statement in the most basic form of logic can either be proved or disproved (1930). His proof in 1931 that any system that contains the arithmetic of whole numbers is either not complete or not consistent—known as Gödel's incompleteness theorem—is his most famous result. In the 1940's and 1950's, Gödel and Albert Einstein became friends, leading Gödel to formulate a mathematical framework for Einstein's theories.

Goebbels, Paul Joseph, *b. 1897, Rheydt, Germany; d. 1945.* **German politician.** The premier propagandist for Adolf Hitler and the Nazi Party, with which he was associated from 1924, Goebbels held a doctorate in philosophy from Heidelberg University. Under the Nazis, he headed the National Ministry for Public Enlightenment and Propaganda, the Ministry of Culture, and, in 1944, the Reich Plenipotentiary for the Total War Effort, among other positions. He killed himself, his wife, and their six children in Hitler's bunker the day after succeeding Hitler as chancellor of the Reich upon the latter's suicide.

Goëthe, Johann Wolfgang von, *b. Frankfurt, 1749; d. 1832.* **Poet, dramatist, and novelist.** Goëthe began writing as part of the romantic *Sturm und Drang* movement, to which he contributed the popular novel *The Sorrows of Young Werther* (1774). More classical writings followed: the dramas *Iphigenie in Tauris* (1787) and *Egmont* (1788) and the epic poem *Hermann and Dorothea* (1797). His novel *The Apprenticeship of Wilhelm Meister* (1796) is the first bildungsroman, or novel of a young man's development. Goëthe's masterwork is the poetic drama *Faust*, published in two parts in 1808 and 1832. Based on the legend of a learned man's bargain with the devil, it is a profound investigation of the human condition and the soul's struggle for salvation.

Goldwater, Barry Morris, *b. Phoenix, Ariz., 1909; d. 1998.* **American politician.** After service in World War II, Goldwater entered politics as a Republican and was elected to the U.S. Senate in 1952. He advocated conservative policies of states' rights, free enterprise, and anti-communism. In 1964 he became the Republican candidate for president and although he was defeated decisively by Lyndon. B. Johnson that campaign is considered the beginning of the conservative "revolution" in American politics. He returned to the Senate and served intermittedly until in 1986.

Goldwyn, Samuel (Schmuel Gelbfisz, later Samuel Goldfish) *b. Warsaw, Poland, 1882; d. 1974.* Film producer. Known for his cantankerous nature and quotable malapropisms ("Include me out"), Goldwyn was one of Hollywood's most successful independent producers during the studio era. He was a glove salesman before going into the film business with his brother-in-law, Jesse L. Lasky, in 1913, and founded Samuel Goldwyn Productions in 1923. It merged with Metro Pictures and Louis B. Mayer's company to become Goldwyn-Mayer (MGM) in 1925. As an independent producer, his most important films were directed by William Wyler, including *The Best Years of Our Lives,* which won the Oscar for Best Picture in 1946.

Gompers, Samuel, *b. London, 1850; d. 1924.* American labor leader. Gompers moved with his family to the United States in 1863 and became active in the labor movement. He worked to organize a national federation of unions, which in 1886 became the American Federation of Labor, and he became its president. He advocated moderate policies rather than strikes and resisted militant unions in the A.F.L. He used the power of the A.F.L. to influence legislation favorable to workers. After World War I he traveled abroad to internationalize the policies of the A.F.L.

Goodall, Jane, *b. London, 1934.* British Naturalist. Mentored by the renowned paleontologist and anthropologist Louis Leakey, Goodall, at age 26, began years of lonely work monitoring wild chimpanzees on the shores of Africa's Lake Tanganyika. Her observations, based on years of painstaking observation, transformed human knowledge of chimpanzee behavior and raised fascinating questions about the evolution of humans. Her decades of fieldwork, frequently profiled by *National Geographic,* shaped all future studies of primates. A prolific author, Goodall is an international spokesperson for conservation.

Goodman, Benny (Benjamin David Goodman) *b. Chicago, Ill., 1909; d. 1986.* Jazz clarinetist and bandleader. Dubbed "the king of swing," Goodman was the most celebrated bandleader of the swing era. His distinc-

tive clarinet playing gave an identity both to his popular big band and to the smaller groups he led. Goodman also showcased black performers to white audiences, in particular two band members, Lionel Hampton and Teddy Wilson. His recordings include "Moon Glow" (1934), "Stompin' at the Savoy" (1935), "Sing, Sing, Sing" (1935), "Avalon" (1938), "One O'Clock Jump" (1938), and "And the Angels Sing" (1939).

Goodyear, Charles, *b. New Haven, Conn., 1800; d. 1860.* American inventor. Goodyear began working on the problems of converting rubber into useful goods in the early 1830's. It was soft when heated and brittle when cold. After many experiments, in 1838 he accidentally discovered that when combined with sulfur and heated to a high temperature rubber remained flexible when hot or cold. The process was named "vulcanization." But he was never able to successfully commercialize his discovery and spent years fighting patent infringement suits. Periodically in debtors' prison, he died in poverty.

Gorbachev, Mikhail, *b. Privolnoye, U.S.S.R, 1931.* Russian politician. Born to a peasant family, Gorbachev joined the Communist Party in 1952 and later received a law degree. Rising through the ranks, he was general secretary (head) of the Communist Party (1985–92). In an effort to revive the Soviet Union's enervated economy, he endorsed policies of *glastnost* (openness), *perestroika* (reform) and democratization. Partial reform proved impossible, and he oversaw the transformation of the Soviet Union into the Commonwealth of Independent States in 1991. He received the 1990 Nobel Peace Prize for his efforts to end the cold war and the Soviet intervention in Afghanistan.

Gordimer, Nadine, *b. Springs, South Africa, 1923.* Author. One of South Africa's leading writers, Gordimer has produced novels, plays, short stories, and nonfiction works. Her work has consistently addressed the moral and political tensions surrounding race. An ardent opponent of apartheid, Gordimer joined the African National Congress when the organization was deemed illegal. Several of her works were banned by the South African government during the apartheid era. Her novel *The Conservationist,* which juxtaposed Zulu culture with the world of white elites, won the 1974 Booker Prize. Her other works include *Burger's Daughter* (1979) and *July's People* (1981). In 1991 she was awarded the Nobel Prize in Literature. In postapartheid South Africa, Gordimer has become a leading activist against HIV/AIDS.

Goya, Francisco, *b. Fuendetodos, Spain, 1746; d. 1828.* Painter. Considered one of the greatest painters of the emotionally expressive Romantic movement, Goya was a highly esteemed court painter, despite the fact that he produced mercilessly unflattering portraits such as *The Family of Charles IV* (1800). Goya's gruesome *The Third of May, 1808* (1814–15) portrays the execution of Madrid citizens by Napoleon's Army. Toward the end of his life, having lived through turbulent political times, Goya grew more reclusive, and his work grew darker. Eighty-two prints, called *Disasters of War* (1810–20), recall moments during the Peninsular War (1808–1814), and the nightmarish painting *Saturn* (1820–23) depicts the devouring of a human figure. In 1824 Goya left Spain for Paris, and eventually Bordeaux.

Graham, Billy (William Franklin Graham, Jr.), *b. Charlotte, N.C., 1918.* Evangelist. At the age of 16, Graham declared his "decision for Christ" and after attending Bob Jones University and Florida Bible College, he was ordained as a Southern Baptist minister in 1939. His reputation grew during World War II, and by 1950 he was regarded as the leader of the fundamentalist Christian movement. Harry Truman invited him to the White House in 1949; this was the first of many visits and friendships with U.S. presidents. Graham's "crusades" drew thousands seeking personal salvation, and he is considered by many as America's spiritual counselor. He was awarded the Congressional Gold Medal in 1996 and in 1999 was chosen as one of *Time's* 100 most important people of the 20th century.

Graham, Martha, *b. Allegheny, Pa., 1894; d. 1991.* Innovative modern dancer and choreographer. Graham studied with the dancer-choreographers Ruth St. Denis and Ted Shawn from 1916–23 and also danced in New York revues. She founded her company in 1926, and gained attention for her innovative choreography and magnetic dancing. Among her best-known solos was *Lamentation* (1930); well-known group dances included *Primitive Mysteries* (1931) and *Appalachian Spring* (1944). From the 1950's through the end of her career, Graham turned to Greek myth and biblical stories for inspiration. She won numerous awards, including a Kennedy Center Honor in 1979.

Grange, Red (Harold Edward), *b. Forksville, Pa., 1903; d. 1991.* Football player. Credited with making professional football a major spectator sport, the "Galloping Ghost" was a thrilling and elusive broken-field runner. He won All-America honors three times (1923–25) at the University of Illinois and set off a major controversy by turning pro before graduation. A 17-game barnstorming tour attracted large crowds at every stop. Grange played for the New York Yankees of the American Football League and the Chicago Bears of the National Football League until 1934.

Grant, Cary (Archibald Alexander Leach) *b. Bristol, England, 1904; d. 1986.* Actor. Witty and debonair without ever being effete, Grant owed his impeccable comic timing to his early training as an acrobat and juggler. He ran away from home at age 13 to join Bob Pender's traveling show, and was appearing in Broadway musicals by the 1920's. His first big screen role was *She Done Him Wrong* (1933) with Mae West. His best films were directed by Howard Hawks (*Bringing Up Baby*, 1938; *His Girl Friday*, 1940), George Cukor (*The Philadelphia Story*, 1940), and Alfred Hitchcock (*Notorious*, 1946; *North by Northwest*, 1959). He retired from movies in 1966.

Grant, Ulysses S., *b. Point Pleasant, Ohio, 1822; d. 1885.* Eighteenth U.S. president, 1869–77. A graduate of West Point he fought in the Mexican War under Gen. Zachary Taylor. During the Civil War Grant rose rapidly to brigadier general during and acquired the nickname "Unconditional Surrender" for his string of western victories, notably at Vicksburg and Chattanooga. Once Lincoln made him supreme commander in 1864, Grant opened a relentless offensive that quickly ended the war; he personally accepted Gen. Robert E. Lee's surrender at Appomattox in 1865. Elected president in 1868, he pressed radical Reconstruction in the South to mixed results. His presidency was marred by corruption, notably the Jay Gould (1869), Crèdit Mobilier (1872), and Whiskey Ring (1875) scandals. His memoirs are considered among the finest writing about war.

Grass, Günter, *b. Danzig (now Gdansk), Poland, 1927.* Novelist and playwright. With the publication of his first novel, *The Tin Drum* (1956), Grass quickly rose to prominence as the voice of the German postwar generation. His work, overtly political, addressing topics such as the rise of Naziism, the threat of nuclear war, the destruction of the environment, and German reunification, includes *Cat and Mouse* (1961), *Dog Years* (1963), *The Rat* (1986), and *My Century* (1999). He received the Nobel Prize for Literature in 1999.

Greco, El (Doménikos Theotokópoulos), *b. Candia, now Herakleion, Greece, ca. 1541; d. 1614.* Greek painter, active in Italy and Spain. After living in Crete, painting in a Byzantine style, El Greco went to Venice, Rome, and eventually Toledo, becoming one of the most original artists in Europe. It was in Italy, where he lived from 1567 to 1577, that he was first called "Il Greco." He absorbed the use of rich color and light typical of the Venetian school, but rejected some of the Western norms of perspective and proportion. His dramatic compositions include the portrait of Cardinal Fernando Niño de Guevura (ca. 1600) and *Burial of the Count of Orgaz* (1586–88).

Greene, Graham, *b. Berkhamsted, England, 1904; d. 1991.* Novelist, short-story writer, journalist, and playwright. Deeply inspired by his Catholic faith, Greene separated his more serious literary novels from novels that he labelled "entertainments," which are thrillers, such as *This Gun for Hire* (1936), spy stories such as *The Quiet American* (1955), and comic novels such as *Our Man In Havana* (1958), and *Travels With My Aunt* (1969). His most important novels have religious themes, presenting characters in often sordid, morally decayed settings caught between grace and damnation. These include *Brighton Rock* (1938) *The Power and the Glory* (1940), and *The Heart of the Matter*, (1948). Greene wrote much journalism, short fiction, several plays, and film scripts including *The Third Man* (1950).

Gregory I (Saint) (Gregory the Great), *b. ca. 540, Rome; d. 604.* Pope, doctor of the church. A wealthy Roman prefect, Gregory donated his property for the building of monasteries, joined the Benedictine order, and reluctantly answered calls to be an abbot, deacon of Rome, church ambassador, papal advisor, and, in 590, pope. Yet he established the institution of the medieval papacy, opposing the Donatist heresy, reinforcing papal supremacy, and centralizing church administration. By defending Rome against a Lombard invasion and negotiating for peace, he enhanced the temporal authority of the papacy. He conformed and improved liturgical practice and his name was given to "Gregorian chant." Gregory wrote books on scripture, church leadership, and a life of St. Benedict.

Gretzky, Wayne, *b. Brantford, Ontario, Canada, 1961.* Hockey player. Wayne Gretzky is widely regarded as the greatest player in the history of ice hockey. In a 20-year NHL career (1979–99), he set all-time records for goals (894), assists (1,963), and total points (2,857). Known as "the great one," the smooth-skating center topped the league in scoring 10 times, won M.V.P. honors nine times,

and led the Edmonton Oilers to four Stanley Cups. His single-season records include most goals (92 in 1982), assists (163 in 1986), and points (215 in 1986).

Griffith, D. W., (David Lewelyn Wark Griffith) *b. LaGrange, Ky., 1875; d. 1948.* Director. Griffith pioneered many techniques still used by filmmakers today. His innovations in editing formed the basis of Hollywood continuity editing, and his developments in lighting and camera movement influenced others to expand further. He developed his craft at American Biograph from 1908 to 1913, beginning with the one-reel *Adventures of Dollie* and ending with the four-reel *Judith of Bethulia*. His mastery over filmmaking techniques is evident in the epic *The Birth of a Nation* (1915) but its racist content forever marred his reputation. Later features include *Intolerance* (1916) and *Broken Blossoms* (1919).

Griffith-Joyner, Florence, *b. Los Angeles, Calif., 1959; d. 1998.* Runner. Viewers on television immediately identified "Flo-Jo" by her long flowing hair, brightly colored outfits, and dazzlingly painted long fingernails, but her competition rarely saw anything but her back. At the 1988 U.S. Olympic trials, she set a world record for the 100-meters dash and a U.S. record for the 200-meters, and went on to win both events easily at the Seoul Olympiad. She also won a gold medal on the 4x100 relay team and a silver on the 4x400 relay team.

Grimm, Jacob (1785–1863) and **Wilhelm (1786–1859),** *b. Hanau, Germany.* Linguists and folklorists. Wilhelm was the virtual founder of philology, the comparative study of languages, and conceived "Grimm's law," governing the shifts of consonants in Indo-European languages. As a related interest, the brothers collected the folktales told by German country people, and, with the help of Dorothea, Wilhelm's wife, published them, often in edited form, as *Household and Nursery Tales* in three volumes (1812, 1815, 1822). The stories, translated into more than 70 languages, include "Cinderella," Sleeping Beauty," "Snow White," "Hansel and Gretel," "Little Red Riding Hood" and "Rumpelstilskin." The brothers also began the work on the definitive German dictionary.

Gropius, Georg Walter Adolf, *b. Berlin, 1883; d. 1969.* German-born American architect and educator. Gropius's early fame rests on his role in founding the Bauhaus in Weimar, Germany, in 1919; this was a school that combined craftsmanship with design and brought together artisans, painters, sculptors, and architects. In

1926 Gropius moved the Bauhaus to Dessau, into a radical new building complex he had designed and that was an icon of what came to be called the International Style. He came to America and in 1938 became chairman of the department of architecture at Harvard University. He continued to design works including the Bauhaus-like Harvard Graduate Center (1949).

Guevara, Che (Ernesto Guevara de la Serna), *b. Rosario, Argentina, 1928; d. 1967.* **Revolutionary and author.** Guevara left Argentina to foment socialist reform throughout Latin America. In 1954, he joined forces in Mexico with Fidel Castro, who was plotting to overthrow the Cuban dictator Fulgencio Batista. An initial defeat left their forces decimated, but made Guevara one of Castro's closest confidants. After the Communist victory, Guevara was a key figure in the new government. He chronicled the revolution in *Reminiscences of the Cuban Revolutionary War* (1963) and the fledgling Communist nation in *Man and Socialism in Cuba* (1965). He was executed by government troops in Bolivia, where he led a guerilla uprising.

Gustavus II (Gustavus Adolphus), *b. Stockholm, Sweden, 1594; d. 1632.* **King of Sweden.** Gustav became king in 1611. Under his rule, Sweden became a major European power. Assisted by his chancellor, Oxenstierna, he also transformed the Swedish state by instituting a variety of reforms. Supported by French subsidies, he invaded Germany during the Thirty Years' War on behalf of the beleaguered Protestants, who were being pressed by the Hapsburgs and their Catholic allies. He won major victories in 1632 at Breitenfeld and Luetzen but was killed at the height of his power.

Gutenberg, Johannes, *b. Mainz, Germany, ca. 1395; d. 1468.* **Inventor and printer.** Around 1450 the German goldsmith Guttenberg became the first European to mass-produce books and documents. His method was based on movable type, a smudge-resistant ink he had developed, paper (the first German paper mill was about 50 years old), and a wine press used as a printing press. Although movable type had been invented earlier in China, Gutenberg is credited with developing techniques for manufacturing hundreds of identical letters and aligning them so that they produced a flat surface for printing. His 42-line Bible, so called for the length of its columns, is still considered one of printing's masterpieces.

Guthrie, Woody (Woodrow Wilson Guthrie), *b. Okemah, Okla., 1912; d. 1967.* **American folksinger and songwriter.** During the Great Depression Guthrie was

unable to support his family so he went west to California. In 1937 he landed his first spot on the radio and turned his attention increasingly towards songwriting. By the time he landed in New York City in 1940, Guthrie had become an important musical spokesman for labor and populist sentiments. He was one of the main songwriters for the Almanac Singers, a group of activist performers that included Pete Seeger and Lead Belly. His most popular songs were "This Land Is Your Land," and "Tom Joad." Guthrie had an enormous influence on the American folk revival of the 1960's.

Halsey, William F., Jr. (Bull), *b. Elizabeth, N.J., 1882; d. 1959.* **Naval commander.** Halsey was an early advocate of air power and became an aviator in 1935, when he was over 40. After Pearl Harbor, his carrier group was virtually the only operational unit in the Pacific available for combat. In early 1942, his group launched the planes that participated in Doolittle's air raid on Tokyo. Halsey showed a unique ability to coordinate naval and air support of land operations at Guadalcanal, at Okinawa, and elsewhere.

Hamilton, Alexander, *b. Nevis, West Indies, 1755; d. 1804.* **American statesman and political theorist.** Hamilton attended King's College (Columbia) in New York (1773–74), then served in the Revolution as an artillery captain and Washington's aide-de-camp. Back in New York he was a successful trial-lawyer and delegate to the Continental Congress, (1782–83). At the Constitutional Convention in 1787 he was a leading advocate for a strong central government and for the ratification of the Constitution as drafted. He was a principal contributor to the Federalist Papers and a central figure in the Federalist party. As the nation's first treasury secretary, (1789–95), he created the national bank. In 1800, when the popular election resulted in a tie between Thomas Jefferson and Aaron Burr, Hamilton influenced Congress to elect Jefferson president. His again blocking Burr from becoming New York governor led to a pistol duel between them, at which Hamilton was mortally wounded.

Hammerstein, Oscar, II *b. New York City, 1895; d. 1960.* **Lyricist.** Working with the composer Richard Rodgers, Hammerstein helped to redefine the Broadway musical by integrating songs into the plot. Before teaming up with Rodgers, he wrote lyrics for the musicals *Show Boat* (1928) and *Sweet Adeline* (1929), and collaborated with other notable composers, including George Gershwin and Jerome Kern. His best-known songs include "Ol' Man River" (1928), "Lover, Come Back to Me" (1928), "All the Things You Are" (1939), "People Will

Say We're in Love" (1943), "Some Enchanted Evening" (1949), and "Getting to Know You" (1951).

Handel, George Frideric, *b. Halle, Germany, 1685; d. 1759.* German-born composer and organist of the Baroque period. Handel spent most of his life in England, where he was acknowledged as one of the greatest composers of his age. He contributed to every musical genre of his time, with operas dominating his early career; he spent his later years focusing on large-scale vocal works, such as the English oratorio, which he invented. Handel's most famous composition is the oratorio *The Messiah* (1741). He wrote more than 20 oratorios, along with nearly 50 operas and a large number of concerti grossi and orchestral pieces. Notable works include *Water Music* (ca. 1717), the *Coronation Anthems* (1727), Trio Sonatas op. 2 (1722–33) and op. 5 (1739), Concerto Grosso op. 6 (1739), and *Music for Royal Fireworks* (1749).

Hannibal *b. 247 B.C.; d. ?182 B.C.* Carthaginian general. Son of the general Hamilcar Barca, Hannibal was a sworn enemy of Rome from childhood. He set out to avenge Carthage's losses in the First Punic War, first taking over Spain and then mounting his famous invasion of Italy after trekking over the Pyrenees with thousands of soldiers, cavalry, and elephants in the Second Punic War (218–202). He lost thousands at the Alps but invaded northern Italy with success until he was eventually forced to retreat. He was finally defeated by Scipio Africanus in Carthage at Zama in 202 B.C. He went on to reform his own government while paying tribute to Rome until forced into exile where he poisoned himself.

Harding, Warren Gamaliel, *b. Blooming Grove, Ohio, 1865; d. 1923.* Twenty-ninth U.S. president, 1921–23. Harding taught, studied law, and sold insurance before following his father into the newspaper business. He was a staunch Republican whose pro-business editorials for the *Marion Star* got him elected state senator, lieutenant governor, and U.S. senator. Elected to the presidency by an unprecedented 61 percent majority, Harding promised a return to "normalcy" for Americans tired of war and Woodrow Wilson. His administration featured higher tariffs, lower taxes, and immigration restriction—but also pervasive corruption and incompetence by Harding's crooked appointees. Harding died suddenly of an embolism on August 2, 1923; scandals involving secret love affairs, official graft, and the vast Teapot Dome swindle erupted soon thereafter.

Hardy, Thomas, *b. Upper Bockhampton, Dorset, England, 1840, d. 1928.* Novelist and poet. Hardy's pessimistic fiction is set in his native Dorsetshire, renamed Wessex, and concerns the strivings of provincial people for happiness against the forbidding forces of nature and cosmic fate. Important novels include *Return of the Native* (1878), *Tess of the D'Urbervilles* (1891), and *Jude the Obscure* (1896). After the last was criticized as immoral, he treated the same themes in poetry of plain language but stark power. He wrote mostly lyrics, including the somber "The Darkling Thrush" to usher in the 20th century, but also an "epic-drama" of the Napoleonic Wars, *The Dynasts* (1908).

Harrison, Benjamin, *b. North Bend, Ohio, 1833; d. 1901.* Twenty-third president, 1889–93. The grandson of the ninth president, William Henry Harrison, Benjamin Harrison was a prominent Republican in Indiana, where he was elected senator in 1881. A colorless compromise candidate for president, Harrison won the 1888 election despite receiving fewer popular votes than Grover Cleveland. The McKinley Tariff, the Sherman Anti-Trust Act, the Sherman Silver Purchase Act (all 1890), and Secretary of State James G. Blaine's vigorous foreign policy were hallmarks of Harrison's administration, which oversaw the admission of six new states.

Harrison, George, *b. Liverpool, England, 1943; d. 2001.* Rock-pop vocalist, guitarist, and songwriter. As the Beatles' lead guitarist, Harrison had a sparse but lyrical style of playing. As a songwriter, he made infrequent memorable contributions ("Something," "While My Guitar Gently Weeps," "Here Comes the Sun"). Post-Beatles, Harrison embraced social causes and Indian music; he organized the Concert for Bangladesh (1971),, one of the first all-star charity concerts. His post-Beatles recordings include "My Sweet Lord" (1970), "Isn't It a Pity?" (1970), "Give Me Love (Give Me Peace on Earth)" (1973), "All Those Years Ago" (1981), and the triple album *All Things Must Pass* (1970).

Harrison, John, *b. Foulby, England, 1693; d. 1776.* English clockmaker. In 1714, the British Parliament established the Board of Longitude and offered £20,000 for a timepiece accurate enough to enable navigators to determine longitude (one's position east or west of a given point) to within half a degree after a voyage to the West Indies. Harrison built his first chronometer, weighing 72 pounds, in 1735. The accuracy of his fourth, a pocket watch called H4 completed in 1759, exceeded the requirement. Parliament balked at awarding the prize—even after Captain James Cook praised it—and did so only slowly.

Harrison, William Henry, *b. Charles City County, Va., 1773; d. 1841.* Ninth U.S. president, 1841. Son of a signatory of the Declaration of Independence, Harrison had an illustrious military career and served in both the house (1816–19) and the Senate (1825–28). He received the Whig nomination for president in 1840; in the first election full of hoopla and hype, the slogan "Tippecanoe and Tyler Too" linked Harrison's most famous military victory with his obscure running mate. Harrison caught a cold at his inauguration from which he never recovered, and succumbed to pneumonia 31 days later. His grandson, Benjamin Harrison, was the 23rd president.

Harvey, William, *b. Folkestone, Kent, England, 1578; d. 1657.* Physician. A graduate of Cambridge University and the University of Padua in Italy, Harvey served as physician extraordinary to James I and was later personal physician to Charles I. He is best remembered for his groundbreaking research into the circulation of the blood, first widely articulated in his *On the Motion of the Heart and Blood in Animals* (1628), which explained the function of heart valves, arteries, veins, and pulmonary circulation,

Hatshepsut Maatkare, *(dates unknown).* Egyptian pharaoh, 1458–47 B.C. One of the most powerful women known from antiquity, Hatshepsut was the daughter of Thutmose I and wife of her half-brother, Thutmose II. After her husband's death, she took the unusual step for a woman of ruling as a pharaoh during the minority of her nephew and stepson, Thutmose III. She is best remembered for her temple at Deir el-Bahri (Luxor). After her death, Thutmose III had virtually all references to her name obliterated.

Hawking, Stephen, *b. Oxford, England, 1942.* English physicist. In 1974 Hawking calculated that black holes emit a form of energy now known as Hawking radiation. Since then he has analyzed the shape and fate of the universe in technical studies and popular books. Although Hawking has been afflicted with severe progressive muscle degeneration since the early 1960's, he manages with the use of a speech synthesizer to continue as Lucasian Professor of Mathematics at Cambridge University (since 1979), the chair once held by Isaac Newton.

Hawks, Howard, *b. Goshen, Ind., 1896; d. 1977.* Film director. Hawks excelled at crafting tightly structured stories in almost any genre. He began as a prop master during the silent era, then worked his way up to film cutter, assistant director, and story editor. He directed his first film, *The Road to Glory,* in 1925. After the coming of sound, Hawks made his best films, *Scarface* (1932), *Bringing Up Baby* (1938), *The Big Sleep* (1946), *Red River* (1948), and *Gentlemen Prefer Blondes* (1953). He received a career Oscar in 1975.

Hawthorne, Nathaniel, *b. Salem, Mass, 1804.; d. 1864.* Novelist, short-story writer. Hawthorne was a secluded child who became a secluded writer. His first novel, *Fanshawe* (1829), was unsuccessful, but *Twice-Told Tales* (1837, 1842) gained recognition. Of Puritan stock, Hawthorne searched into human darkness, examining moral issues through the lens of symbolism. His greatest novel, *The Scarlet Letter* (1850), a tale of adultery, guilt, and revenge, is set in 17th-century Puritan Salem. It was followed by *The House of the Seven Gables* (1851) and *The Blithedale Romance* (1852). He served as a port official in Salem and a consul in England. Living in Italy influenced his last novel, *The Marble Faun* (1860).

Haydn, Franz Joseph, *b. Rohrau, Austria, 1732; d. 1809.* Composer. The most celebrated composer of his time, Haydn is known as the "father of the symphony," having composed 104 symphonic works; he also helped to develop the string quartet and contributed to the development of the sonata and to sonata form. Notable works include the opera *Orfeo ed Euridice* (1791), Symphony No. 94 in G (*Surprise*) (1791), Symphony No. 100 in G (*Military*) (1794), Symphony No. 101 in D (*Clock*) (1794), Symphony No. 104 in D (*London*) (1795), Concerto in E flat for Trumpet and Orchestra (1796), *Die Schöpfung* (*The Creation*) (1797–8), and *Die Jahreszeiten* (*The Seasons*) (1798–1801).

Hayek, Friedrich August von *b. Vienna, Austria-Hungary, 1899; d. 1992.* Economist and social philosopher. A central figure in the Austrian school of economics, Hayek was a prolific thinker who made important contributions to technical aspects of economics. But he is generally remembered for his strong support for capitalism and opposition to socialist planning. Hayek argued that the self-regulating capitalistic system was far more efficient in allocating resources and elaborated this view in his now famous book, *The Road to Serfdom* (1944,) which sells more copies today than ever before. Conservatives and Libertarians have cited Hayek in calling for minimizing the size of government and limiting its reach into the workings of the marketplace, though some of his views run contrary to theirs. He was awarded the Nobel Prize in Economic Science in 1974.

Hayes, Rutherford B., *b. Delaware, Ohio, 1822; d. 1893.* Nineteenth U.S. president, 1877–81. A decorated Civil War veteran, Hayes founded the Ohio Republicans, served as governor of Ohio, and was nominated as a scandal-free presidential candidate in 1876. Although he lost the election to the Democrat Samuel Tilden, congressional Republicans disputed enough state vote totals to put "Rutherfraud" in office. Hayes never overcame the resulting stigma of political bargain, even though he effectively ended Reconstruction in the South by removing federal troops; he also put the nation back on the gold standard, put down railroad strikes, and reformed the civil service. He kept his promise to serve only one term.

Heaney, Seamus, *b. Derry, Ireland, 1939.* **Poet.** A Nobel laureate in 1995, Heaney is regarded as the finest Irish poet since Yeats. His early books of poetry, *Death of a Naturalist* (1966), *Door into the Dark* (1969) and *Wintering Out* (1972), focused on rural Ireland, but with *North* (1975) he began to address his country's political and religious "troubles." In *Station Island* (1984), he incorporates his own experience as an Ulster native into his country's bitter history. Technically brilliant, musical, and poignant, Heaney's poetic volumes include *Field Work* (1979), *The Haw Lantern* (1987), *Seeing Things* (1991), *The Spirit Level* (1996), and a translation of *Beowulf* (2000).

Hearst, William Randolph, *b. San Francisco, 1863; d. 1951.* **American publisher, and politician.** In 1887 when Hearst was 23 his father put him in charge of the *San Francisco Examiner;* thereafter he helped to reshape a large segment of American newspapers into vehicles of sensationalism called "yellow journalism." He acquired many other papers and magazines, and he controlled a newsreel and a movie company. His grandiose political ambitions resulted in only two terms in Congress.

Hegel, Georg Wilhelm Friedrich, *b. Stuttgart, Germany, 1770; d. 1831.* **Philosopher.** A clerk's son, Hegel was an undistinguished theology student who persevered to become a teacher at the University of Jena—and, ultimately, one of the greatest systematic philosophers. His first great work, *The Phenomenology of Mind* (1807), established him as an idealist, for whom all reality was spiritual, a manifestation of the "Absolute," or infinite God. His system for understanding all reality, all history, was the "dialectic," a progressive, rational process in which each thesis incorporates its antithesis to develop a synthesis. Hegel's later career was spent at the University of Berlin. His most comprehensive work is *Encyclopedia of the Philosophical Sciences* (1817); *Philosophy of Right* (1821) sums up his whole philosophy.

Heidegger, Martin, *b. Messkirch, Germany, 1889; d. 1976.* **Philosopher.** Generally regarded as a founder of existentialism, he disliked the attribution. He was influenced by the phenomenology of Edmund Husserl. His major work is *Being and Time* (1927). His concern was with the problem of being; he investigated aspects of human existence and the individual's relationship to death; he attributed the difficulties of society to individuals' awareness of their own temporality. He was a supporter of Hitler during the latter's early years in power, and as a result was banned from teaching after World War II.

Heine, Heinrich, *b. Dusseldorf, Prussia, 1797; d. 1856.* **Poet.** The best-known poet of Germany's Romantic movement, Heine was born into a Jewish family but later reluctantly converted to Protestantism. Heine rose to prominence in 1827 with the publication of *The Book of Songs* (1827), a series of poems, often set to music, that explore the schism between the artistic sensibility and reality. Heine's late collection, *Romanzero* (1851), contains some of his most powerful work.

Heisenberg, Werner Karl, *b. Würzburg, Germany, 1901; d. 1976.* **Physicist.** At the age of 23, Heisenberg published his theory of quantum mechanics, which showed that the position, velocity, and other mechanical quantities of atomic particles can be described only by abstract mathematical "matrices" and not by ordinary numbers. For this he received the 1932 Nobel Prize in Physics. In 1927, Heisenberg defined his principle of uncertainty, which states that it is impossible to measure exactly the position and velocity of any object, particularly at the atomic and subatomic level.

Hemingway, Ernest, *b. Oak Park, Ill., 1899; d. 1961.* **Novelist and short-story writer.** Hemingway was wounded in World War I, then settled in Paris and wrote a book of stories, *In Our Time* (1925), and two very successful novels, *The Sun Also Rises* (1926) and *A Farewell to Arms* (1929). These introduced a new American prose style, terse and rhythmically repetitious, and a writer whose literature overlapped with a life of confronting danger and proving manhood. His stories, in volumes such as *Men Without Women* (1927) and *The Snows of Kilimanjaro* (1936), and the novel *For Whom the Bell Tolls* (1940), are much admired. The novella *The Old Man and the Sea* (1952) led to the Nobel Prize in Literature. Hemingway killed himself in 1961.

Henry II (**Henry Plantagenet, Henry of Anjou, Henry Curtmantle**), *b. LeMans, England, 1133; d. 1189.* **King of England, 1154–89.** His marriage to Eleanor of Aquitaine (1152) greatly expanded his kingdom to Normandy and western France. But his public dispute with Thomas à

Becket, archbishop of Canterbury, concerning the power of church courts over royal authority (which culminated in Becket's murder) made him enemies in Rome. His quarrels with his wife and his sons ultimately put his own life in jeopardy. These squabbles obscured his great accomplishment: trial by judge and jury, a practice that was in existence at the time, but not routinely used.

Henry V, *b. Monmouth, Wales, 1387; d. 1422.* King of England, 1413–22. His victory over the French at Agincourt (1415) during the Hundred Years' War made England one of the most influential European powers. It also allowed him to join forces with the Holy Roman emperor Sigismund to end the papal schism with the election of Pope Martin V (1417). His marriage (1420) to Catherine of Valois made him heir to the French throne as well, but he died of camp fever during the sieges of Melun and Meaux before he had the chance to accede.

Henry VIII, *b. Greenwich, England, 1491; d. 1547.* King of England, 1509–47. Henry's long reign influenced English history for centuries. His first wife, Catherine of Aragon, failed to provide him with a male heir, so he sought an annulment from Pope Clement VII. But when the pope refused, the king instead divorced the English Church from Rome, and declared himself its leader on Earth. He married Anne Boleyn, then annulled the marriage to Catherine, earning himself an excommunication from the pope. The breach with Rome marked the beginning of the English Reformation. Though he married six times, he only produced one male heir. He ordered the beheading of two of his wives and of the advisor, Thomas Cromwell, who arranged one of his marriages.

Henry, Patrick, *b. Studley, Va., 1736; d. 1799.* Orator, statesman. A self-taught lawyer, Henry excelled in criminal law. As a member of the Virginia colonial legislature, he eloquently opposed the British Stamp Act, and went on to become a delegate to the Continental Congresses of 1774 and 1775, where he delivered his most famous line "[G]ive me liberty or give me death." Henry served as the Virginia's first governor and as a member of the state legislature. He strongly opposed ratification of the U.S. Constitution, believing it neglected state and individual rights, but he was a central figure in the development of the Bill of Rights.

Hepburn, Katharine, *b. Hartford, Conn., 1907; d. 2003.* Movie actress. One of the last of Hollywood's golden age, she played strong, independent women on stage and screen for 60 years, winning an early Oscar for *Morning Glory* (1933) and going on to win a record four with *Guess*

Who's Coming to Dinner (1967), *The Lion in Winter* (1968), and *On Golden Pond* (1981). In Spencer Tracy she found her perfect foil (and real-life love) in the nine films they made together. *The Philadelphia Story*, which she commissioned for the stage, was also the film (1940) that brought her renewed popularity.

Herodotus *b. Halicarnassus, Asia Minor, ca. 484 B.C.; d. ca. 425 B.C.* Greek historian. Herodotus is known as the father of history, and his work serves as the precursor to studies of history, anthropology, and geography. Herodotus spent his life traveling and writing about the people and places he saw and the cultures, histories, and legends of those regions.

Hertz, Heinrich, *b. Hamburg, Germany, 1857; d. 1894.* Physicist. Proving the theory of the British scientist John Clerk Maxwell, Hertz was the first person to transmit and receive electromagnetic waves. In honor of this achievement—the high point in his distinguished academic career—the unit of measurement for the frequency of radio waves was given the name "hertz." His findings were published in his book Investigations on the Propagation of Energy, considered one of the most important scientific works ever published. His experiments with electric waves led to the invention of the radio, television, and radar.

Herzl, Theodor, *b. Budapest, Hungary, 1860; d. 1904.* Founder of political Zionism. Herzl was not the first to advocate a Jewish state—Napoleon suggested it as early as 1799—but his pamphlet *The Jewish State* (1896) gave the idea strength by suggesting that it was a political question to be determined by an international council. A tireless organizer, Herzl created the World Zionist Organization and was its first president. He died 40 years before the creation of Israel, but he believed he had created the political movement and laid the groundwork that would eventually lead to a Jewish homeland.

Hill, George Roy, *b. Minneapolis, Minn., 1922; d. 2002.* Film director. Hill began his career as a musician and actor, turning to directing after World War II when he worked on popular live television series such as *Studio One* and *Kraft Television Theater*. His movie career began in 1962 with *A Period of Adjustment*, and he was the reliable director of commercial hits such as *The World of Henry Orient* (1964) and *Hawaii* (1967). His breakthrough came in 1969 when he cast and directed Paul Newman and Robert Redford in *Butch Cassidy and the Sundance Kid*, for which he received an Oscar nomination for best director. In 1973, he went on to win the Academy Award for *The Sting*, which reunited that popular duo.

Himmler, Heinrich, *b. Munich, Germany, 1900; d. 1945.* German politician. Close associate of Adolf Hitler's from the time of the Munich Putsch in 1923, Himmler was head of the SS (*Schutzstaffel*, "Protective Corps," Hitler's bodyguard). After Hitler was elected chancellor, Himmler became second in command of the Gestapo (secret police). He was the primary architect for the "final solution" to annihilate European Jewry, and he oversaw the death camps of Eastern Europe. Hitler ordered his arrest for negotiating secretly with the Allies in April 1945. Later caught by the Allies, Himmler killed himself before he could be brought to trial.

Hippocrates, *b. Cos, Greece, ca. 460 B.C.; d. 377 B.C.* Physician; the "father of medicine." Hippocrates was a physician and teacher renowned for his writings on various diseases, including *Epidemics*, *The Sacred Disease* (epilepsy), *Prognostics*, and *Aphorisms*. In antiquity, his writings—and many written around his time but probably not by him—were compiled into the *Hippocratic Collection* (*Corpus Hippocraticum*). The so-called Hippocratic oath, attributed to him, establishes the reciprocal obligations of students and teachers, and enjoins practitioners among other things to prescribe beneficial treatments, discourage abortion and assisted suicide, and respect patient confidentiality.

Hitchcock, Alfred, *b. London, England, 1899; d. 1980.* Film Director. The master of suspense, Hitchcock elevated the mystery thriller to the level of art by infusing his films with universal themes of guilt and moral consequence. He began as an intertitle designer, then worked as a screenwriter, assistant director, and art director. In 1925 he directed his first feature, *The Pleasure Garden*, but *The Lodger* was his first thriller (1926) followed by *The Thirty-nine Steps* (1935). In 1939, he moved to Hollywood to direct *Rebecca* (1940). Among the highlights of his remarkably consistent career are *Notorious* (1946), *Strangers on a Train* (1951), *Rear Window* (1954), *Vertigo* (1958), *North by Northwest* (1959), *Psycho* (1960), *The Birds* (1963), and *Frenzy* (1972).

Hitler, Adolf, *b. Braunau, Austria, 1889; d. 1945.* German dictator. Originally an artist, Hitler moved to Germany in 1913. After serving in the army in World War I, he joined the National Socialist (Nazi) Party in 1919, articulating virulent anti-Semitism and calling for a revival of German militarism and revenge for the penalties imposed on Germany at the end of World War I. Elected chancellor

in 1933, he became Fuhrer (leader) the next year. His invasion of Poland in 1939 started World War II. German success was compromised by Hitler's inept strategic choices, including the invasion of Russia and declaring war on the United States. He killed himself in Berlin in April 1945.

Ho Chi Minh (born Nguyen That Thanh), *b. Hoang Tru, Vietnam, 1890; d. 1969.* Vietnamese political leader. He left Vietnam when he was only 21 years old and lived in the U.S., England, and France where he joined the French Communist Party. He lived in Moscow and China and returned to Vietnam in 1941, changing his name to Ho Chi Minh ("he who enlightens") and the revolutionary movement's to Viet Minh. In 1945, with the help of the U.S., he expelled Japanese forces from Vietnam and declared independence. As president (1945–69) of the Democratic Republic of Vietnam, he battled first France and then the United States to maintain his country's freedom from colonialism.

Hobbes, Thomas, *b. Westport, England, 1588; d. 1679.* Philosopher. His materialistic, pessimistic philosophy is evident in *Leviathan* (1651) in which he paints a dismal picture of the state of nature, where life is "nasty, brutish, and short." Hobbes argued that people give up their natural rights, in fear of the violence of the state of nature, in exchange for protection from an absolute ruler; once the subjects contract to trade their rights, the ruler's power is absolute. Later writers such as Rousseau (and, in the 20th century, John Rawls) had a broader, less authoritarian view of the social contract.

Hoffa, James Riddle, *b. Brazil, Ind., 1913; d. 1975?.* American labor leader. In 1934 "Jimmy" Hoffa took the local union he had organized in 1930 in Detroit into the International Brotherhood of Teamsters. Thereafter he worked to conclude a national contract for all teamsters that would give the union enormous power over the trucking industry. But he was dogged by charges of corruption and ties to organized crime. He was convicted of jury tampering, fraud, and conspiracy in 1964 and sentenced to a federal penitentiary. Pardoned in 1971, he disappeared on July 30, 1975 and it is widely believed that he was assassinated by organized crime.

Hogan, Ben, *b. Dublin, Tex., 1912; d. 1997.* American golfer. Hogan dominated professional golf during the 1940's and 1950's. Hogan ranks third on the list of career P.G.A. Tour victories, with 63. Known for his precise, controlled play, the 5'7" Texan won the U.S. Open four times, the Masters and P.G.A. championship twice, and the

British Open once. He was named P.G.A. Player of the Year four times (1948, 1950–51, 1953). Hogan suffered a near-fatal automobile accident in 1949 but overcame permanent leg injuries to play his best golf after returning the following year.

Holbein (the Younger), Hans, b. *Augsburg, Germany, 1497–98; d. 1543.* Painter, and designer. Active in Switzerland and England, Holbein began his career in Basel, creating altarpieces and woodcuts. He went on to become the most important portrait painter in England during the Reformation, working mainly under the patronage of King Henry VIII and his courtiers. Holbein's most famous paintings include *The Ambassadors* (1533) and *Henry VIII* (1540).

Holiday, Billie (Elinore Harris), b *Philadelphia, Pa., 1915; d. 1959.* American jazz singer. In 1933 at the age of 18, "Lady Day" made her first recordings with Benny Goodman and two years later her works with Teddy Wilson launched her career as the leading jazz singer of her time. She toured with Count Basie and Artie Shaw and made hundreds of recordings notably "Strange Fruit," "God Bless the Child," and "Lover Man." Holiday struggled with heroin addiction and in 1947 was arrested for drug possession. After spending a year in a rehabilitation center, "Lady Day" packed Carnegie Hall just 10 days after her release. Her remaining years were marked by drug and alcohol abuse before she died at 44.

Holmes, Oliver Wendell, Jr., b. *Boston, 1841; d. 1935.* U.S. Supreme Court justice. The son of the acclaimed 19th-century poet and leading physician Oliver Wendell Holmes, Sr., he enlisted with the Union forces and saw heavy action during the Civil War. A noted attorney and brilliant legal scholar, Holmes was nominated to the Supreme Court in 1902 by President Theodore Roosevelt, who was later sorely disappointed that Holmes failed to support his administration's positions. In his three decades on the Court, Holmes was known for concise and elegant opinions. A towering figure in American jurisprudence, he is perhaps best known for his doctrine of "judicial restraint," which holds that judges must refrain from letting their personal opinions influence their decisions. He also articulated the "clear and present danger" rule, which allows for restrictions on the First Amendment when public safety is in jeopardy.

Homer, Winslow, b. *Boston, Mass., 1836; d. 1910.* Painter, illustrator. One of the most admired late 19th-century American artists, Homer was a landscape painter who shared many of the attitudes of the Hudson River school. Known for bold, fluid brushwork and strong compositions, he worked extensively in watercolor, helping to popularize the medium in paintings such as *Adirondack Guide* (1894). Homer depicted unsentimental images of the relationship between man and nature. Important works include *The Morning Bell* (1870) and *Snap the Whip* (1872).

Hoover, Herbert Clark, b. *West Branch, Iowa, 1874; d. 1964.* Thirty-first U.S. president, 1929–33. Hoover became a world-famous mining engineer and a multimillionaire by age 40. In World War I he helped rescue Americans stranded in Europe, distributed food supplies to occupied Belgium, and persuaded the nation to save food ("Hooverize") for the war effort. Hoover was Woodrow Wilson's economic adviser at Versailles, and earned prominence as the secretary of commerce in the 1920's. He was elected president on the promise of a "chicken in every pot," but the Wall Street crash brought on the Great Depression. Paralyzed by his conservative instincts, Hoover could not halt the spread of bank failures, bankruptcy, and unemployment; shantytowns across the country were dubbed Hoovervilles. Massively defeated by Franklin D. Roosevelt in 1932, Hoover was blamed for decades for the depression but salvaged his reputation with more relief work after World War II. Hoover later chaired two bipartisan commissions on government reorganization, issuing many important recommendations for federal reform.

Hoover, J. (John) Edgar b. *Washington, D.C., 1895; d. 1972.* Director of the F.B.I. Hoover first made his name in the Justice Department by compiling an enormous list of suspected communists and anarchists, 10,000 of whom were arrested in 1919 in the Palmer Raids. In 1924, Hoover assumed the helm at the Federal Bureau of Investigation, building the bureau's storied image by taking on gangsters such as John Dillinger and Machine Gun Kelly. But in later years, Hoover avoiding fighting the Mafia, instead using surveillance techniques to harass anyone he considered politically radical including Martin Luther King, Jr. Paranoid and vengeful, he kept secret files on hundreds of left-leaning celebrities, politicians, and journalists.

Hope, Bob (Leslie Townes Hope), b. *Eltham, England, 1903; d. 2003.* Actor and comedian. Famous for his ski-slope nose and rapid-fire comic delivery, Bob Hope was already a big radio star when he made his movie debut singing "Thanks for the Memory" on *The Big Broadcast* of 1938. He made more than 30 movies, the most successful of which were the six *Road* movies (starting with *Road to Singapore*) that he made with Bing Crosby and Dorothy Lamour between 1940 and 1952. He entertained American troops with his U.S.O. shows during every major conflict from World War II to the first Gulf War, starred in numerous television specials, and frequently hosted the Academy Awards in the 1950's and 1960's.

Hopkins, Gerard Manley, *b. Stratford, Essex, England, 1844, d. 1889.* **Poet.** One of the most original English poets, Hopkins introduced diction, syntax, and rhythm embraced in the 20th century. He converted to Catholicism in 1866 and was ordained a Jesuit priest in 1877. After burning his early poems, he resumed writing with "The Wreck of the Deutschland" (1876), a meditational narrative concerning the drowning of five nuns. Many of his poems are devotional sonnets and other lyrics that praise the God revealed in nature, such as "God's Grandeur," "The Windhover," and "Pied Beauty," each written in 1877 but like all his work not published until 1918. In other sonnets, such as "Carrion Comfort" and "No Worst, There Is None" (both 1885), he struggles with spiritual despair.

Hopper, Edward, *b. Nyack, N.Y., 1882; d. 1967.* **Painter, and illustrator.** In a plain, realist style, Hopper's paintings depict scenes of urban isolation, featuring quiet, solitary figures and documenting an everyday American life of movie theaters, storefronts, and city streets. A pupil of the painter Robert Henri, Hopper was profoundly influenced by several trips to Europe. His most famous images include *Night Shadow* (1924) *Early Sunday Morning* (1930), *Gas* (1940), *Nighthawks* (1942), and *Second-Story Sunlight* (1960).

Horace (Quintus Horatius Faccus) *b. Venusia, Italy, 65 B.C.; d. 8 B.C.* **Roman poet.** Horace is considered the greatest Roman lyric poet of his time. Having been written under the patronage of Virgil and Maecenas, much of Horace's work is in praise of the emperor Augustus and the state. His great works are *Satires, Epodes, Odes, Epistles* (including the famous *Ars Poetica*), and *Secular Hymn*.

Housman, A. E. (Alfred Edward), *b. Fockbury, England, 1859; d. 1936.* **Poet.** In pessimistic though romantic and occasionally ironical verse, Housman demonstrated a mastery of alliteration, parallelism, and mood. In Houseman's first collection, *A Shropshire Lad*

(1896), he assumed the persona of a farm laborer. His most popular poems include "When I was One-and-Twenty" and "To an Athlete Dying Young," from *A Shropshire Lad*. Housman was equally renowned as a scholar and translator of Latin texts.

Howe, Gordie, *b. Floral, Saskatchewan, Canada, 1928.* **Hockey player.** Gordie Howe, known as "Mr. Hockey," was the NHL's all-time leading scorer with 801 goals until Wayne Gretzky passed him in 1994. The brilliant right wing joined the Detroit Red Wings in 1946 and played professional hockey through the 1979–80 season (though he retired for two seasons in the 1970's before returning to play with his sons in the World Hockey Association). Howe won the Hart Trophy, annually awarded to hockey's best player, six times. His teams won the Stanley Cup five times.

Hubble, Edwin Powell, *b. Marshfield, Mo., 1899; d. 1953.* **American astronomer.** Although he studied law and joined the Kentucky bar, Hubble became bored with his practice and returned to his true interest, astronomy. After World War II, he began work at the Mount Wilson Observatory in California, where he founded the study of extragalactic astronomy. His many contributions included the discovery that not all nebulae are part of the Milky Way galaxy, and in 1929 he formulated Hubble's law allowing astronomers to determine the age of the universe and to prove that the universe is expanding. Hubble was one of the designers of the Hale telescope, set up at the Mount Palomar Observatory, where he continued to work until his death. NASA's Hubble telescope, currently orbiting in space, is named in his honor.

Hudson, Henry, *b. England, ca. 1550; d. 1611.* **Explorer.** Of obscure origin, Hudson made his first known voyages in command of Muscovy Company expeditions to find the Northeast Passage; he discovered Jan Mayen Island (1607) and explored Novaya Zemlya (1608). The Dutch East India Company hired Hudson to find the Northeast Passage in 1609. Frustrated by the ice, he turned west and ascended the Hudson River as far as Albany. While the Dutch established New Amsterdam the next year, Hudson sailed north for the English Northwest Company and discovered Hudson Strait and Hudson Bay, where his mutinous crew marooned him.

Hughes, Howard, *b. Humble, Tex., 1905; d. 1976.* **Businessman and aviator.** Heir to an oil industry fortune, Hughes spent his life and money in a variety of pursuits. As a pilot, he set numerous speed records in the 1930's; and his firm, Hughes Aircraft Company, produced several models through the years, none more famous than the *Spruce Goose*, a cargo aircraft made from birch. (It was flown only once.) He also directed movies, including *Hell's Angels* and the original *Scarface*. Later in life, Hughes, one of the world's richest men, withdrew completely from the public eye.

Hughes, Langston, *b. Joplin, Mo., 1902; d. 1967.* **Poet, short story writer, and translator.** A member of the Harlem Renaissance group of writers that included Zora Neale Hurston and Jean Toomer, Hughes wrote of the black experience in America. He achieved critical success early on—his poem "The Negro Speaks of Rivers" was published in 1921, when he was only 19. His books include *The Weary Blues* (1926), *Fine Clothes to the Jew* (1927), and the short-story collection *The Ways of White Folks* (1934).

Hugo, Victor, *b. Besancon, France, 1802; d. 1885.* **Poet, novelist, dramatist.** Hugo was already a well-known Romantic poet when his play *Hernani* (1830) introduced Romanticism into drama and stirred a riot in the theater. Other plays are *Le Roi s'amuse* (1832), and *Ruy Blas* (1838). His best-known novels, are *Notre Dame de Paris* (*The Hunchback of Notre Dame*) (1832); and *Les Misérables* (1862). Hugo's opposition to Napoleon III caused his banishment from 1851 to 1870. He returned to France a hero and was elected to the Senate.

Hurston, Zora Neale, *b. Notasulga, Ala., 1891; d. 1960.* **Folklorist and novelist.** A member, with Langston Hughes, of the Harlem Renaissance. Hurston's work was concentrated primarily on preserving the folklore of African Americans in the South. After dropping out of school at age 13, Hurston went on to graduate from Howard University and Barnard University, and to pursue graduate studies in anthropology at Columbia University. Her first novel, *Jonah's Gourd Vine,* was published in 1934; her most famous novel, *Their Eyes Were Watching God,* was published in 1937.

Hussein, Saddam, *b. Tikrit, Iraq, 1937; d. 2006.* **President of Iraq.** After helping the Ba'ath party seize power in a 1968 revolt, Saddam ruled oil-rich Iraq for over two decades. Hussein's leadership was characterized by violent suppression of his own people, and failed invasions of other Arab nations. He came to power in 1979, and in 1980 invaded Iran, starting a war that ended in stalemate in 1988. In 1990 Saddam's army invaded Kuwait with the intention of annexing the small but strategic nation. Hussein's refusal to withdraw resulted in the six-week-long Persian Gulf War, led by American forces, which successfully drove Iraq out of Kuwait. Iraq was subsequently banned from making or having chemical, biological, or nuclear weapons. The U.S. claim that he had a nuclear program led to an American bombing and invasion of Iraq. Hussein went into hiding but he was captured and tried by the Iraqi High Tribunal, who sentenced him to death for brutality against his own people, and he was executed in 2006.

Huston, John, *b. Nevada, Mo., 1906; d. 1987.* **Screenwriter and director.** Huston specialized in directing tales of social misfits and rebels, who were brought to life through well-crafted dialogue. He began as a screenwriter and directed his first film, *The Maltese Falcon,* in 1941. His collaboration with the star Humphrey Bogart resulted in their best work, including *Treasure of the Sierra Madre* (1948), *Key Largo* (1948), and *The African Queen* (1951). Later films include *Fat City* (1973) and *The Man Who Would Be King* (1975). An Oscar winner for both writing and directing, John was the son of the actor Walter Huston and father of the actress Anjelica Huston.

Hutton, James, *b. Edinburgh, Scotland, 1726; d. 1797.* **Scottish geologist, chemist, and naturalist.** He is considered the "father of modern geology" for originating the principle of uniformitarianism, stating that geological phenomena observed in the present, such as erosion and sedimentation, are the same as those that occurred in the past, making it possible to estimate the length of time it took to create the Earth's surfaces. His theory, presented in *A Theory of the Earth* (1785), became one of the fundamental principles of geology, explaining the Earth's physical processes without reference to the Bible. Hutton's work had a profound influence on scientists of the nineteenth century, including Charles Darwin.

Ibsen, Henrik, *b. Skien, Norway, 1828; d. 1906.* **Playwright.** Ibsen is one of the great social dramatists and Norway's most internationally famous writer. Ibsen's early plays are drawing room dramas; some look to Norwegian folklore (*Peer Gynt*, 1867) for inspiration. His later works, beginning with the revolutionary *A Doll's House* (1879), which is thought to have ushered in modern drama, focus on psychology and social issues. Other works include *Ghosts* (1881), *The Wild Duck* (1884), and *Hedda Gabler* (1890).

Ignatius of Loyola (Saint), *b. Azpeitia, Guipuzcoa, Spain, 1491; d. 1556.* **Religious leader, founder of the Jesuits.** Ignatius was a nobleman and soldier who experienced a conversion while reading a life of Christ after being wounded. He wrote *Spiritual Exercises* which became the basic text of his followers. In 1534 at the University of Paris, he formed the Society of Jesus (the Jesuits), confirmed by the pope as a religious order in 1538. Ignatius spent the rest of his life establishing schools and universities all over the world. The Jesuit emphasis on education, contemplation, and purity reinvigorated the Catholic Church during the Counter-Reformation. He was canonized in 1622.

Imhotep, *fl. 27th century B.C.* **Egyptian architect.** Imhotep designed the tomb complex and pyramid of the pharaoh Zozer, for whom he was chancellor, at Saqqara ca. 2680 B.C. The size and scope of the complex are unprecedented for its time in Egypt, and the monumental stepped pyramid marks the beginning of the pyramid form in the tombs of later pharaohs. Imhotep's name is cut into the stone of the pyramid, where he is called "first after the king of Upper and Lower Egypt." Later he was deified as one of a trinity with Horus and Isis.

Ingres, Jean-Auguste-Dominique, *b. Montauban, France, 1780; d. 1867.* **Painter.** A French neoclassicist and pupil of the painter David, Ingres lived in Italy for 18 years and championed history painting. He was an accomplished draftsman and portrait painter, able to combine psychological insight with perfectionist physical accuracy. Highly interested in myths about the Orient, Ingres is famous for such polished, sensuous images as *Turkish Bath* (1863) and *Odalisque* (1814).

Innocent III (Lothair of Segni), *b. Campagna di Roma, Papal States, 1160; d. 1216.* **Pope, 1198–1216.** His Fourth Lateran Council (1215) brought the medieval papacy's influence and prestige to their zenith. It required confession at least annually, and communion every Easter. He endorsed the vows of poverty and itinerant preaching favored by St. Dominic and St. Francis of Assisi. He disapproved of the Fourth Crusade (1202–04) on Constantinople, but agreed to it in hopes of reuniting the Eastern and Western churches. The bloody Albigensian Crusade (1209), to convert heretics in southern France, bore his approval.

Ivan the Terrible (Ivan IV; Ivan Vasilyevich; Ivan Grozny), *b. Kolomenskoye, Russia, 1530; d. 1584.* **First czar of Russia, 1547–84, and grand prince of Moscow, 1533–84.** After proclaiming himself czar Ivan worked to limit the power of the greatest nobles ("boyars"); he established a general council (1566) that included merchants and the lower ranks of nobility. Ivan's dream of bringing Russia closer to Europe by obtaining access to the Baltic encouraged him to wage brutal, costly wars

against Sweden and Poland that nearly bankrupted Russia. His vision of a vast Russian empire with Moscow at its center and non-Slav states surrounding it was more successful, though it necessitated a reign of terror against the nobility of his own country.

Ives, Charles, *b. Danbury, Conn., 1874; d. 1954.* **American composer.** Ives was an influential figure in the history of music, his work foreshadowing the innovations of younger avant-garde composers. He was fascinated with clashing rhythms and tonalities, as exemplified by two bands playing different tunes or different sections of the orchestra playing in different keys. Notable works include *Variations on a National Hymn, "America"* (1891), Psalm 67 (1893), *Song for Harvest Season* (1893), Symphony No. 3 (*The Camp Meeting*) (1904–11), *New England Holidays* (1904–13), *The Unanswered Question* (1906, rev. ca. 1932).

Jackson, Andrew, *b. Waxhaw, S.C., 1767; d. 1845.* **Seventh U.S. president, 1829–37.** The first first-generation American to become president, Jackson was elected to Congress in 1796 but soon resigned, disgusted with Washington politics. In Tennessee, Jackson became a respected judge and honorary major general of the militia, and in the War of 1812 he led troops to victory at the Battle of New Orleans (1815). Now a national icon, "Old Hickory" reentered the Senate in 1823 and unsuccessfully ran for president in 1824; he won the 1828 election as the "people's choice" reform candidate. As president, Jackson aggrandized the power of his office by expanding suffrage, rotating officeholders (the "spoils system"), and economizing in government by vetoing federal road-building and blocking the renewal of the charter of the Bank of the United States.

Jackson, Michael Joseph, *b. Gary, Ind., 1958; d. 2009.* **Pop-rock vocalist and songwriter.** As a child, Jackson was the lead singer in a successful Motown group the Jackson 5; he grew up to become the biggest pop star of the 1980's. Jackson's style combined elements of soul, rock, and dance music; his album *Thriller* in 1982 became the biggest-selling album of all time, and he was the first black artist to find stardom on MTV. His solo recordings include "Got to Be There" (1971), "Rock with You" (1979), "Thriller" (1982), "Billie Jean" (1982), "Beat It" (1982), "Bad" (1987), and "Black or White" (1991).

Jackson, Thomas, "Stonewall," *b. Clarksburg, now W.Va., 1824; d. 1863.* **American general of the Confederacy.** A graduate of West Point he served bravely in the Mexican War. Jackson joined the Confederate army in 1861 and rose quickly to become brigadier general and the most trusted commander under General Robert E. Lee. Getting his nickname at the first battle of Bull Run (1861), he helped win the seven days battle of Richmond (1862), the second battle of Bull Run (1862), and the battle of Fredricksburg (1862). His role was decisive in the victory at Chancellorsville (1863), but he was accidentally shot and killed by one of his own men.

James I, *b. Edinburgh, Scotland, 1566; d. 1625.* **King of Scotland (James IV) and first Stuart king of England and Ireland.** The only son of Mary Stuart, (Queen of Scots), James became king of Scotland on her abdication in 1567. After an alliance with Queen Elizabeth I of England, he became king of England on her death in 1603. Convinced that kings rule by divine right, he feuded with parliament for power. He initiated a new translation of the Bible that came to be called the King James Version, or the Authorized Version in Great Britain.

James II, *b. London, 1633; d. 1701.* **Stuart king of England, Ireland, and Scotland.** Son of King Charles I, James became king on the death of his older brother Charles II in 1685. His Catholic beliefs provoked wide opposition and in the bloodless Glorious Revolution of 1688–89 he was deposed and replaced by William III, called William of Orange who was married to James' daughter, Mary. The revolution established the constitutional monarchy, giving parliament greater power. James died in exile in France.

James, Henry, *b. New York City, 1843; d. 1916.* **American-English novelist and critic.** James, brother of the philosopher-psychologist William, settled in England in 1876. In the novels of his first period, such as *The Portrait of a Lady* (1881), he examined the tensions between American innocence and European tradition. He turned then to social and political themes in *The Princess Casamassima* (1886) and other novels, and, after a failed trial as a playwright, wrote short drama-like novels, including *The Turn of the Screw* (1898). The fiction of his last and greatest period (*The Ambassadors*, 1903; *The Golden Bowl*, 1904) again took up the international theme, with psychological intricacy in a dense style.

James, William, *b. New York City, 1842; d. 1910.* **Philosopher and psychologist.** Trained as a doctor, he taught at Harvard first in physiology and then in psychology and philosophy. In his groundbreaking *Principles of Psychology* (1890) he shaped the modern discipline of psychology, placing it among the laboratory sciences based on experimental method. In his influential philosophical works, James developed and expounded pragmatism, according to which the truth of ideas is found only in their correspondence with experiential consequences. William James was the brother of the novelist Henry James.

Jay, John, *b. New York City, 1745; d. 1829.* **American statesman and jurist.** Elected to the Continental Congress in 1774 and 1775, Jay advocated a strong national central government and with James Madison and Alexander Hamilton he wrote *The Federalist* papers. George Washington appointed him the first chief justice of the United States Supreme Court in 1789, and in 1794 he concluded Jay's Treaty settled territorial and commercial differences with England. In 1795 he resigned from the court to serve two terms as governor of New York.

Jefferson, Thomas, *b. Albemarle County, Va., 1743; d. 1826.* **Third U.S. president, 1801–09.** Jefferson joined the Virginia House of Burgesses in 1769; as a delegate to the Continental Congress in 1776, he drafted the Declaration of Independence. Congress sent him to Europe in 1784 as minister to France; he later served under Washington as secretary of state, and under Adams as vice president, after losing the 1796 election. Chosen president by the House of Representatives in 1800 (after a tie in the electoral vote with Aaron Burr), Jefferson slashed the budget, lowered taxes, reduced the national debt, and sent marines to fight Barbary pirates. His greatest feat as president was the Louisiana Purchase from France in 1803; which doubled the size of the United States. Retiring to Monticello in 1809, Jefferson busied himself with inventions and designing the University of Virginia; his broad interests spanned music, science, architecture, agronomy, and the classics. Jefferson was an early opponent of the slave trade but was himself a slaveholder and allegedly fathered several children with the slave Sally Hemings.

Jenner, Edward, *b. Berkeley, Gloucestershire, England, 1749; d. 1823.* **Physician; inventor of smallpox vaccination.** Apprenticed to a surgeon at the age of 13, Jenner is best known for his discovery that matter from cowpox—a relatively benign disease that humans could contract from contact with infected cows—could be used to inoculate people to render them immune from smallpox. This procedure, which takes its name from *vacca*, Latin for "cow," has since been adopted for developing numerous vaccines against other diseases.

Jerome, *b. Stridon, Dalmatia, 347; d. 420.* Saint, theologian, translator, and father and doctor of the church. A contemporary of St. Augustine, Jerome renounced secular scholarship after converting to christianity and retired to the desert to devote himself to scriptural and linguistic studies. He later was secretary to Pope Damasus I. A great scholar, he is best known for preparing the Vulgate, the Latin translation of the Old and New Testaments. He also translated Origen and wrote biographies, histories, biblical commentaries, letters, and tracts against heresy.

Jesus (Jesus Christ; Jesus of Nazareth), *b. Bethlehem, ca. 4 B.C.; d. ca. 30 A.D.* Jewish teacher and prophet, founder of Christianity. The main sources for his life are the four Gospels, based on earlier traditions, written A.D. 70–95. He was born the son of Mary of the tribe of Judah and of Joseph, a carpenter. Little is known of his life until he was about 30, when after baptism by John he began his ministry. He preached the coming of God's kingdom and the need to love God and one's neighbor, attacked the priestly elite, and healed the sick. In the third year of his ministry he was betrayed by Judas, one of his disciples, in Jerusalem and crucified by the Romans. In Christian belief he rose from the dead and ascended into heaven. In Christianity (*Christ* = anointed), he is the Son of God.

Jinnah, Mohammed Ali, *b. Gujarat, India, 1876; d. 1948.* Indo-Pakistani politician; founder of Pakistan. Educated in law in England, Jinnah entered Indian politics in 1906. Interested in greater Indian nationhood and Hindu-Muslim unity, he joined the All-India Muslim League in 1913. He withdrew from politics in response to Gandhi's "Non-Cooperation Movement" in 1920, and in 1930 over differences within the Muslim League. After Muslims fared poorly in India's elections in 1937, Jinnah called for a separate Muslim state, an idea rejected by Gandhi, Nehru, and the British authorities, but realized in the partition of 1947. Jinnah was first governor-general of independent Pakistan.

Joan of Arc, *b. Domremy, Champagne, France, 1412; d. 1431.* French saint and military heroine. As a girl, Joan of Arc heard the voices of St. Michael, St. Catherine, and St. Margaret, who directed her to assist the dauphin of France in his attempt to claim his throne against the English. Her military victories at Orléans and Patay brought him to power as Charles VII. When taken by the English and tried by a papal court, Joan eventually admitted heresy, then recanted, and was burned at the stake. Decades later, she was exonerated by a court under Charles.

Jobs, Steve, *b. San Francisco, 1955.* One of the founders of the personal computer industry. Jobs and Stephen Wozniak helped launch the personal computer revolution by introducing the Apple computer in 1976. Jobs successfully established Apple's Macintosh as an elegant, innovative, and user-friendly alternative to traditional PCs. He was forced out of Apple in 1985 in a corporate power struggle. In 1986, he cofounded Pixar, an animation studio that has produced some of the most successful animated films in Hollywood history. In 1997, Jobs returned as C.E.O. of Apple, where he helped to pioneer a new business model for downloading music.

John XXIII (Angelo Giuseppe Roncalli), *b. Sotto il Monte, Italy, 1881; d. 1963.* Pope, 1958–63. A compromise candidate expected to serve only as interim pontiff, he became one of the most popular popes ever because of the Second Vatican Council (1962–65), which brought the Roman Catholic Church into the modern era. Vatican II, as it was known, permitted vernacular, rather than Latin, in the celebration of the mass. It suggested that lay members could find God even outside the church, and permitted opportunities for them to do so, such as Bible study groups and social justice organizations. John was beatified in 2000.

John the Baptist, *d. ca. 30.* Saint. Said to be a cousin of Jesus Christ, John acts in the Gospels as Jesus' prophet and forerunner. He baptized many people in the Jordan River, calling them to repent and prepare for the coming of the Messiah. Recognizing Jesus as the savior and "Lamb of God," John baptized him, and Scripture reports that God the Father appeared in the sky to bless the event. When John denounced King Herod's marriage to his brother's wife Herodias, Herod imprisoned him. At the request of Herodias's daughter Salome, John was beheaded, and his head was served on a platter.

John, Elton (Reginald Dwight) *b. Middlesex, England, 1947.* Pop-rock vocalist, pianist, and songwriter. Elton John was the pop superstar of the early 1970's, known for his melodic songwriting (often with the lyricist Bernie Taupin) and his outlandish stage performances. His albums *Madman Across the Water, Don't Shoot Me I'm Only the Piano Player,* and *Goodbye Yellow Brick Road* helped to define album-oriented FM radio of the era. His recordings include "Your Song" (1970), "Tiny Dancer" (1971), "Levon" (1971), "Rocket Man" (1972), and "Daniel" (1973); his song "Candle in the Wind" (1973) became the fastest-selling single of all time following his performance of the tune at Princess Diana's funeral in 1997.

John Paul II (Karol Józef Wojtyla), *b. Wadowice, Poland, 1920; d. 2005.* Pope, 1978–2005. The first pope from a Slavic country and the first pope of the global age, he has worked to broaden the Roman Catholic Church's reach with more than 90 papal visits to countries around the world. He supported the Polish Solidarity movement and pressured the Soviet Union on human rights issues. In 2000, he made a historic trip to the Holy Land in an effort to find common ground among the world's major religions. He staunchly opposed such reforms as the ordination of women and allowing priests to marry.

Johns, Jasper, *b. Augusta, Ga., 1930.* Painter, sculptor, printmaker. A key figure in the Pop Art movement, Johns became famous for painting images of well-known objects such as targets and the American flag. He worked closely with the painter Robert Rauschenberg, and both artists were able to combine figurative imagery with some of the painting techniques developed by the Abstract Expressionists. Influenced by Duchamp's ready-mades, Johns created sculptures that replicated everyday objects such as lightbulbs, raising questions about the role of the artist and the process of creation. His works include *Target with Four Faces* (1955) and *Three Flags* (1958).

Johnson, Andrew, *b. Raleigh, N.C., 1808; d. 1875.* Seventeenth U.S. president, 1865–69. The first president to be impeached, Johnson served as a state legislator, congressman, governor, and senator. Alone among 22 southern senators, Johnson stayed loyal to the Union in 1861, and he was nominated for vice president on the "National Union" ticket in 1864. Suddenly made president by Lincoln's assassination, Johnson vowed to carry on Lincoln's policy of leniency toward the South, but radical Republican opposition and his own coarse ineptitude led to serious clashes with Congress. Impeached in the House for defying the Tenure of Office Act, Johnson was tried in the Senate—and acquitted by a single vote.

Johnson, Lyndon B., *b. Stonewall, Texas, 1908; d. 1973.* Thirty-sixth U.S. president, 1963–69. A powerful and persuasive politician, Lyndon Baines Johnson was elected to Congress in 1937, and to the Senate in 1948 where he was majority leader from 1955 unil he accepted John F. Kennedy's offer of the vice presidency in 1960. He was made president after Kennedy was assassinated. Johnson vowed to continue Kennedy's programs, pushing them through Congress with surprising ease—most notably the Civil Rights Act and the Equal Opportunity Act. After his reelection in 1964, Johnson unveiled plans for a "Great Society" free from poverty and discrimination, but his presidency unraveled as American losses in Vietnam mounted, antiwar protests grew strident, and race riots exploded in inner cities across the nation.

Johnson, Magic (Earvin, Jr.), *b. Lansing, Mich., 1959.* Basketball player. An all-time N.B.A. great, Johnson first came to national prominence when he led Michigan State to the N.C.A.A. title over Larry Bird's Indiana State team. As a member of the Los Angeles Lakers, Magic appeared in the N.B.A. finals nine times and won five championships. He was named league M.V.P. three times. After testing positive for HIV in 1991, he retired. He returned to win a gold medal on the 1992 U.S. Olympic Dream Team and later to briefly coach and play for the Lakers. He retired in 1996.

Johnson, Philip Cortelyou, *b. Cleveland, Ohio, 1906; d. 2005.* Architect. Johnson's first important work was his own Glass House (1949) in New Canaan, Conn., inspired by Ludwig Mies van der Rohe's Farnsworth House. He collaborated with Mies on the Seagram Building (1954–58) in New York, and went on to produce a number of buildings in variations of the modernist idiom; but he responded creatively when modernism began to go out of style. He readily adapted to the postmodern movement in his AT&T Building (1979) in New York with its Chippendale top, and in many later works.

Johnson, Samuel, *b. 1709, Lichfield, England; d. 1784.* Essayist, critic, and poet. Dr. Johnson was his century's leading literary scholar and one of England's greatest critics and literary personalities. He struggled as a magazine writer, poet ("The Vanity of Human Wishes," 1749), and dramatist (*Irene*, 1749), until he completed his groundbreaking *Dictionary of the English Language* in 1755. He published essays in his own periodicals, *The Rambler*, (1750–52) and *Idler*, (1758–60), and criticism in his edition of *Shakespeare* (1765) and *Lives of the Poets* (1779, 1781). In the prose romance *Rasselas* (1759) he expressed a pessimistic view of humanity, but his decency, openness, faith, and legendary wit were recorded in James Boswell's enduring contemporary biography.

Johnson, Walter, *b. Humboldt. Kan., 1887; d. 1946.* Baseball player. In a long career with the Washington Senators, Johnson amassed one of the most impressive pitching records in major-league history. Possessed of a legendary fastball, the "Big Train" won 417 games (second only to Cy Young's 511). The right-hander notched a record 110 shutouts and won 20 or more games 10 years in a row.

He led the American League in strikeouts 12 times and earned run average five times. His lifetime record was 417-279, with a 2.17 E.R.A. and 3,508 strikeouts.

Jones, Bobby, *b. Atlanta, Ga., 1902; d. 1971.* Golfer. Though he competed for only eight years (1923–30) and remained an amateur throughout his career, Jones is considered one of the greatest golfers of all time. He won the U.S. Open at age 21, going on to capture 13 of the 27 majors he entered, including three U.S. Opens, four U.S. Amateurs, and one British Open. After sweeping the U.S. Open, the British Open, the U.S. Amateur, and the British Amateur in 1930, Jones retired at age 28 to practice law.

Jones, John Paul, *b. Kirkcudbright, Scotland, 1747; d. 1792.* American naval officer. A founding father of the U.S. Navy, Jones sailed in merchant ships for 15 years before being commissioned a lieutenant in the Continental Navy (1775). His most celebrated victory was fought in the French-built *Bonhomme Richard*, which sank after fighting HMS *Serapis* in September 1779. After the Revolution, Jones served as an admiral in the Russian navy of Catherine the Great (1788–90). He died and was buried in Paris. In 1906, President Theodore Roosevelt ordered his remains exhumed for interment at the U.S. Naval Academy in Annapolis, Maryland.

Jones, Inigo, *b. London, 1573; d. 1652.* Architect and stage designer of the Renaissance. From 1605 to 1640 he designed sets for more than 50 dramatic presentations. During a trip to Italy in 1613–14 he carefully studied ancient buildings, often with a copy of the *Four Books on Architecture* by Palladio at hand; this experience shaped his subsequent career as an architect. He brought the Renaissance ideals of classical architecture to England together with the teachings of Palladio and changed the course of English architecture. His Banqueting House in London (1619–21) and the Queen's House in Greenwich (1616–35) were entirely new to England in their restrained classicism and exquisite proportioning.

Jonson, Ben, *b. London, 1572; d., 1637.* Playwright and poet. Jonson is considered by many to be, the second-greatest playwright of the Elizabethan and Jacobean periods. His plays are characterized by vibrant characters, by one overarching side of their personality; witty dialogue and careful plotting. Jonson's plays include *Volpone* (1606), *The Alchemist* (1610), and *Bartholomew Fair* (1614).

Jordan, Michael, *b. Brooklyn, N.Y., 1963.* Basketball player. Widely regarded as the greatest basketball player of all time, Michael Jordan led the N.B.A. in scoring a record 10 times (1987–93, 1996–98), earned the M.V.P. award five times (1988, 1991–92, 1996, 1998), and won six championships with the Chicago Bulls (1991-93, 1996-98). Dubbed "Air Jordan" for his remarkable leaping ability, Jordan thrilled spectators with his acrobatic dunks and game-winning shots. Off the court, Jordan became a celebrity and one of the most sought-after commercial spokesmen in the world.

Joyce, James, *b. Dublin, 1882; d. 1941.* Novelist. Joyce is one of the towering figures of modern literature. His four major works, set in Dublin, which he left in his early twenties, are progressively innovative. *Dubliners* (1915), a volume of stories, was succeeded by *A Portrait of the Artist as a Young Man* (1916), a powerful autobiographical novel that takes expressionistic leaps in style. *Ulysses* (1922), composed with stream-of-consciousness technique that merges interior life and external context, is an account, modeled on Homer's *Odyssey*, of one day in Dublin, June 16, 1904. The dense, multilingual wordplay and character transformations in *Finnegans Wake* (1939) make it a seldom-read masterpiece.

Jung, Carl Gustav, *b. Kresswil, Switzerland, 1875; d. 1961.* Psychoanalytic theorist. As a young psychiatrist in Switzerland, Jung published *The Psychology of Dementia Praecox* (schizophrenia) in 1906, which led to an association with Sigmund Freud. But *Psychology of the Unconscious* (1911–12) began a break with Freud by challenging the exclusively sexual character of the libido drive. Jung's "analytic psychology" incorporated mythology and religion. He believed that individuals have both a personal and a collective unconscious, that each psyche contains an "archetype" of the opposite sex, and that the goal of analysis is "individuation," a wholeness harmonizing the conscious and unconscious. Jung also introduced the theory of introverted and extroverted personality types. His other books include *Psychology and Religion* (1937).

Justinian I (Flavius Justinianus; Petrus Sabbatius), *b. Tauresium, Dardania (now probably Serbia), 483; d. 565.* Roman Emperor of Byzantium, 527–65. Justinian and his ambitious wife Theodora set out to reclaim much of Rome's western empire for Constantinople, succeeding in reestablishing dominion over Spain, North Africa, and much of Italy. His greatest legacies are the *Codex Justinianus* (534), a codification of the Roman laws, which had immeasurable influence on succeeding legal systems; and the church of Hagia Sophia in

Constantinople, the crown jewel of his extensive building program, still extant in Istanbul.

Kafka, Franz, *b. Prague, 1883; d. 1924.* Novelist, short-story writer. A middle-class Jew, Kafka earned a law degree and worked for years in the insurance business. He wrote in German and published little while he was alive. *The Metamorphosis* (1916), a story in which a man wakes up one morning as an insect is his most famous work. Kafka's surrealistically isolated characters, described in clear, straightforward prose, strongly influenced 20th-century literature. His own life was pained by romantic disappointment and the tuberculosis that brought early death. His novels were all published posthumously: *The Trial* (1925), *The Castle* (1926), and *Amerika* (1927).

Kahlo, Frida, *b. Mexico City, Mexico, 1907; d. 1954.* Painter. Kahlo began painting while recovering from an accident that crippled her. She is known for riveting self-portraits that use fantasy and a semi-primitive style to explore her physical and psychological circumstances. She drew on popular Mexican art and often pointedly clothed herself in Mexican rather than European or American garments. Kahlo was married to the artist Diego Rivera. Her works include *Frida and Diego Rivera* (1931), *Henry Ford Hospital* (1932), and *The Two Fridas* (1939).

Kahneman, Daniel, *b. Tel Aviv, Israel, 1934.* Economist. A research psychologist by training, Kahneman analyzes economics from a behavioral perspective. His "prospect theory" considers how people manage risk and make decisions in uncertain conditions. A professor at Princeton University, Kahneman received the 2002 Nobel Prize in Economics.

Kant, Immanuel, *b. Konigsberg (Kaliningrad), 1724; d. 1804.* Philosopher. One of the great figures of metaphysics, Kant held that only phenomena, objects of experience, can be known; things beyond experience, noumena, cannot be known or scientifically demonstrated. In his *Critique of Pure Reason* (1781), he argued that God, immortality and freedom are unknowable by scientific thought, but he also held that belief in them is required by morality. Kant's famous moral imperative is: act only according to that rule which you can at the same time will to become a universal law.

Kazan, Elia (Elia Kazanjoglous), *b. Constantinople, Ottoman Empire (now Istanbul, Turkey), 1909, d. 2003.* Turkish-born American director and author. After attending the Drama School at Yale University, Kazan studied with Lee Strasberg and Harold Clurman in New York. He directed his first Broadway play in 1934 and later won acclaim for such productions as Tennessee Williams's *A Streetcar Named Desire* (1947), and Arthur Miller's *All My Sons* (1947) and *Death of a Salesman* (1949), for which he won a Tony Award for best director. Known for his socially relevant films, Kazan won Academy Awards for directing *Gentleman's Agreement* (1947) and *On the Waterfront* (1954), and continued to direct in spite of his controversial decision to cooperate with the House Committee on Un-American Activities in 1952. He received an Academy Award for lifetime achievement in 1999.

Keaton, Buster, (Joseph Francis Keaton) *b. Piqua, Kans., 1895; d. 1966.* Silent film comedian. Keaton created a screen persona dubbed the "Great Stone Face" because of his deadpan expression despite all adversity. Keaton's youth as a part of his family's vaudeville act served as his training ground in acrobatics and physical comedy, which became the basis of the large-scale stunts in his films. His first film role was in *The Butcher Boy* (1917). Keaton starred in and directed his best work during the 1920's, including *Sherlock Jr.* (1924) and his masterpiece, *The General* (1927).

Keats, John, *b. London, 1795; d. 1821.* Poet. Keats produced more great writing in a comparably brief period than any other English poet. Important early poems included "On First Looking into Chapman's Homer" and *Endymion*. Then, in 1819, poor, sickly, and unhappily in love, he wrote an astonishing series of superior poems, including his six great odes, published in *Lamia, Isabella, The Eve of St. Agnes and Other Poems*. He also composed some of the finest English sonnets and two aborted but celebrated "epics," *Hyperion* and *The Fall of Hyperion*. In melodious, exquisitely sensuous, beautifully phrased verse, Keats expressed the tension between the richness and sadness of physical and emotional experience.

Kennan, George, *b. Milwaukee, Wis., 1904; d. 2005.* Diplomat and author. Stationed in many of Europe's hot spots during World War II, Kennan amassed decades of experience in the U.S. foreign service. In the war's aftermath, Kennan provided a blunt and detailed assessment of the threat posed by Stalin—an 8,000-word missive known as the "Long Telegram"—that caused a sensation in Washington. Kennan subsequently developed a policy of "containment" that prevented Soviet expansion and defined America's approach to the cold war. After leaving the State Department in 1953, Kennan wrote 17 books, simultaneously winning the Pulitzer Prize and the National Book Award for both *Russia Leaves War* (1956) and *Memoirs, 1925–1950* (1967).

Kennedy, John Fitzgerald, *b. Brookline, Mass., 1917; d. 1963.* Thirty-fifth U.S. president, 1961–63. The youngest man elected president, the only Roman Catholic, and the first born in the 20th century, Kennedy served three undistinguished terms in Congress before he was elected to the Senate in 1952. In 1960, he won the presidency over vice president Richard M. Nixon by just 118,000 votes out of 69 million cast. Just after taking office, Kennedy approved the disastrous Bay of Pigs invasion, and a year later, he confronted the Soviets over the presence of their nuclear missiles in Cuba. As racial unrest spread in the turbulent early 1960's, Kennedy cautiously supported the civil rights movement, introducing sweeping legislation that would not pass in his lifetime—nor would his plans for aid to education and medical care for the elderly reach fruition before his death. In a motorcade in Dallas, Tex. on November 22, 1963, Kennedy was fatally shot by Lee Harvey Oswald, a left-wing ex-marine who was in turn murdered by Jack Ruby two days later.

Kennedy, Joseph P., *b. East Boston, Mass., 1888; d. 1969.* American businessman and diplomat. Father of President John F. Kennedy, and senators Robert F. Kennedy and Edward M. Kennedy, he amassed a fortune during Prohibition and the Depression, in businesses ranging from banking to shipbuilding to motion picture distribution. The patriarch of the Kennedy clan used his power and influence to secure political office for his sons. As ambassador to Great Britain (1937–40), he supported Chamberlain's policy of appeasement. Persistent rumors of links with organized crime surrounded him but were never proved.

Kennedy, Robert F. (Bobby), *b. Brookline, Mass., 1925; d. 1968.* U.S. politician. Younger brother of President John F. Kennedy, Bobby served as the most trusted advisor of his brother's administration. As U.S. attorney general, he attacked organized crime and staunchly supported civil rights. During the Cuban missile crisis, he advocated a naval blockade, rather than a military response. After his brother's assassination, he resigned from Lyndon Johnson's cabinet and won a Senate seat from New York (1964). In 1968, he made his own bid for the presidency, but he was slain by Sirhan Sirhan in Los Angeles, hours after winning California's Democratic primary.

Kepler, Johannes, *b. Weil der Stadt, Germany, 1571; d. 1630.* Astronomer. Kepler, influenced by Copernicus' teachings, became Tycho Brahe's assistant in 1600. He published (1609) Brahe's calculations of the orbit of Mars, adding the first two of his own laws: that planetary

orbits are elliptical, not circular, and that a planet's speed increases as its distance from the sun decreases. His third law relates the average distance of a planet from the sun and the time it takes to complete its orbit. Kepler's work was instrumental in Newton's development of the laws of motion and gravity.

Keynes, John Maynard, *b. Cambridge, England, 1883; d. 1946.* Economist. Keynes gained prominence with *The Economic Consequences of the Peace* (1919), which predicted accurately that the onerous reparations levied against Germany after World War I would drive it into dangerous economic nationalism and militarism. During the Great Depression he published *The General Theory of Employment, Interest and Money* (1936), a vastly influential book expounding a revolutionary view that prolonged recessions are not self-correcting but require government spending to stimulate economic growth. Its thesis became known as Keynsian economics and shaped government policies in a number of countries. In 1944 at the Bretton Woods Conference he helped to establish the postwar system of exchange rates, the International Monetary Fund, and the International Bank for Reconstruction and Development (World Bank).

Khrushchev, Nikita, *b. Kalinovka, Kursk Province, Russia, 1894; d. 1971.* Premier of the Soviet Union, 1958–64. Born a peasant, Khrushchev rapidly rose through Communist Party ranks and, with Nikolai Bulganin, seized power after Stalin's death in 1953. In 1956, he denounced the worst excesses of Stalin's regime (omitting his own role). Although he released thousands of political prisioners, he crushed budding independence movements in Hungary and Poland. In 1958, Khrushchev became prime minister and assumed control over both state and party. Despite his attempted reforms, the Soviet economy soured and individual liberties remained limited. Even as he pursued the arms race, he acknowledged the dangers of the cold war and called for "peaceful coexistence." Khrushchev was ousted in 1964 after the Cuban missile crisis and a bitter ideological split with China.

Kierkegaard, Søren, *b. Copenhagen, Denmark, 1813; d. 1855.* Philosopher and religious writer. He was a precursor of the existentialists and a major influence on Protestant theology. He argued that advancing through the three stages of the aesthetic, the ethical and the religious by means of an "existential dialectic" brings the individual closer to God. A leap of faith is required; reason is not a help. But awareness of the relationship to God leads to despair as the individual contrasts temporality with eternal truth. His major works include *Either/Or*

(1843) and *Fear and Trembling* (1843).

Killy, Jean-Claude, b. *Saint-Cloud, France, 1943.* French skier. Killy became a national hero and earned a place in Olympic history by sweeping the men's Alpine events—downhill, slalom, and giant slalom—at the 1968 Winter Games in Grenoble, France. In a stellar career, Killy also won the World Championship combined title twice (1965–66) and the World Cup overall championship twice (1967–68).

King, Martin Luther Jr., b. *Atlanta, 1929; d. 1968.* Minister and social activist. The foremost leader of the civil rights movement of the 1960's, King employed non-violence to end legal segregation of blacks in the United States, especially in the South. His leadership during the Montgomery bus boycott (1955–56) drew national attention, and persuaded him to start the Southern Christian Leadership Conference. From this pulpit, he organized sit-ins and protest marches against segregation, notably the 1963 March on Washington, at which he delivered his famous "I Have a Dream" speech. His words moved the nation and led to the passage of the Civil Rights Act of 1964, the same year he was awarded the Nobel Peace Prize. King's march on Selma, Alabama, led to the Voting Rights Act of 1965. He was assassinated by a sniper, James Earl Ray, at a motel in Memphis on April 4, 1968.

Kinsey, Alfred, b. *Hoboken, N.J., 1894; d. 1956.* Biologist. A professor of zoology and botany, Kinsey shocked the United States in 1948 with his publication of *Sexual Behavior in the Human Male*, the first academic inquiry into people's sexual habits. Based on more than 18,000 interviews, Kinsey's report revealed levels of bisexuality and masturbation that were much higher than previously thought. Although his *Sexual Behavior in the Human Female* (1953) was less controversial and less successful, Kinsey's research changed public perception of sexuality, contributing to the sexual revolution of the 1960's.

Kipling, Rudyard, b. *Bombay, India, 1865; d. 1936.* Poet, novelist, and short-story writer. Forever associated with the spirit of imperialism that existed before World War I, Kipling's works drew from his experience in the colonies of the British Empire. His *Barrack-Room Ballads* (1892)—which included "Gunga Din"—proved a popular edition of poetry, and he followed it with the children's favorite, *The Jungle Book* (1894). Kipling collected several short children's tales in *Just-So Stories* (1902), and he published a critically acclaimed novel, *Kim* (1902). He won the Nobel Prize for Literature in 1907.

Kissinger, Henry Alfred, b. *Fürth, Germany, 1923.* German-born American statesman and scholar. Emigrating from Germany in 1938, Kissinger taught government at Harvard University from 1954 to 1969 when President Richard Nixon appointed him national security advisor. In this post, and after 1973 as secretary of state, he arranged President Nixon's trip to mainland China and the Soviet Union in 1972, negotiated a cease-fire in the Vietnam War in 1973, and helped arrange a cease-fire in the Arab-Israeli war of 1973. He shared the Nobel Peace Prize with Le Duc Tho of North Vietnam in 1973. His critics accuse him of being involved in the suppression of socialist revolutions in Latin America and elsewhere.

Klee, Paul, b. *Münchenbuchsee, near Berne, Switzerland, 1879; d. 1940.* Painter, printmaker. While his work is highly theoretical (he drew inspiration from music, poetry, and color theory), Klee strove to achieve qualities found in the art of the untrained, children, and the insane. He developed unique methods of picture-making, including such oil transfer drawings as his *Twittering Machine* (1922), in which simplified forms mock modern machinery. Klee was revered by the surrealists and the abstract expressionists and was targeted by the Nazi regime. Well-known works include *Around the Fish* (1926) and *Park Near Lu(cerne)* (1938).

Klimt, Gustav, b. *Vienna, Austria, 1862; d. 1918.* Austrian painter. began his career as a muralist after studying at the Vienna School of Decorative Arts. In 1897 he founded the Vienna Secession, which worked in a style similar to art nouveau. His work was often criticized as being too erotic, but today his paintings are considered among the most important to come out of Vienna. His most famous works include *The Kiss* (1907–08) and *Frau Adele Bloch-Bauer* (1907), one of several Klimt paintings stolen by the Nazis from the Bloch-Bauer family. In 2006 the works were returned to the family and sold to the Neue Gallery in New York City.

Koufax, Sandy (Sanford), b. *Brooklyn, N.Y., 1935.* Baseball player. Koufax spent his entire 11-year career with the Brooklyn and Los Angeles Dodgers and was one of the most dominant pitchers of his era. His blazing fastball made him a three-time 25-game winner, and he posted the game's lowest E.R.A. in five straight seasons. He threw no-hitters in four consecutive seasons, the last a perfect game in 1965. Koufax appeared in four World Series, compiling a minuscule E.R.A. of 0.95. He led the Dodgers to three world championships and was twice named World Series M.V.P. Koufax was the National

League M.V.P. in 1963, and won three Cy Young Awards. He was elected to the Baseball Hall of Fame in 1972.

Kublai Khan, *b. 1215, d. 1294.* **Mongol leader.** Kublai, the grandson of Genghis Khan, was chosen as leader of the Mongols in 1260. From the beginning, Kublai evinced an interest in China, and he proclaimed his own dynasty, in the Chinese style, the Yuan. Kublai finally defeated the ruling Chinese dynasty, the Sung, in 1279, reuniting China, which had been divided between north and south since the end of the Tang dynasty. Kublai fought a number of wars with neighboring kingdoms, including Burma and Japan, with mixed success.

Kubrick, Stanley, *b. Bronx, New York, 1928; d. 1999.* **Film director.** A filmmaker known for his visual boldness, black humor, and pessimistic outlook, his acclaimed indictment of military justice, *Paths of Glory* (1956), led to an invitation to complete the wide-screen epic *Spartacus* (1961). Unhappy with Hollywood, he moved to England, where he made the films that polarized his fans and critics: *Dr. Strangelove* (1964), *2001: A Space Odyssey* (1968), and *A Clockwork Orange* (1971). His work continued to be controversial up until his final film, *Eyes Wide Shut* (1999).

Kurosawa, Akira, *b. Tokyo, Japan, 1910; d. 1998.* **Film director.** The first Japanese director to become famous in the West, Kurosawa astounded audiences with both historical films about honor among the samurai (*Seven Samurai,* 1954) and modern tales of great humanism (*Ikiru,* 1952). His directed his first film, *Judo Saga,* in 1943, but it was *Drunken Angel* (1948) that announced him as a serious talent and *Rashomon* (1951) that secured his reputation. *Drunken Angel* began a lifelong collaboration with the star Toshiro Mifune. Among his best films are *Throne of Blood* (1957) based on *Macbeth*; *Yojimbo,* (1961) a Japanese western; and *Ran* (1985), based on *King Lear.*

Lafayette, Marquis de, *b. near Le Puy-en-Velay, France, 1757; d. 1834.* **Military officer.** A French aristocrat, Lafayette became so inspired by the ideals of the American Revolution that he journeyed overseas and volunteered his military skills. The young Frenchman became a loyal confidant of George Washington, with whom he shared the hardships of the long winter at Valley Forge. Returning to France after the American victory, Lafayette played a significant role in the revolution sweeping his homeland. As a member of the fledgling National Constituent Assembly, he drafted the Declaration of the Rights of Man. When the French Revolution deteriorated, Lafayette's fortunes fell; he was arrested by the Jacobins and spent five years in prison. After his release, he returned to America, where he was hailed as a hero.

La Follette, Robert M. (Sr.), *b. Primrose, Wis., 1855; d. 1925.* **Politician.** In a long career that included stints as a U.S. senator and representative as well as governor of his native Wisconsin, La Follette earned the nickname "Fighting Bob" for his ceaseless campaigns against corruption and his support for public causes. His reforms advanced such issues as open primary elections, unemployment compensation, and progressive income taxation. When criticized for his vote against the United States' entry into World War I in 1917, he defended the right to free speech in wartime. Although he was a Republican for most of his career, La Follette ran for president on the Progressive ticket in the election of 1924.

Lamarck, Jean-Baptiste Pierre Antoine de Monet, Chevalier de, *b. Bazantin, France, 1744; d. 1829.* **Naturalist.** Lamarck studied and classified invertebrates, worked in botany, and developed invertebrate paleontology. He is known today for his idea that life-forms have changed over geologic time as a result of needs created by the environment. This evolutionary approach was a forerunner of Darwin's, but Lamarck's proposed mechanism of change, the inheritance of acquired characteristics, was rejected as the principles of heredity were developed.

Lancaster, Burt, *b. New York City, 1913; d. 1994.* **Movie actor.** Trained as a circus acrobat, he defined swashbuckling, whether playing the title role in *The Crimson Pirate* (1952) or an obstinately romantic old man in *Atlantic City* (1980). He is remembered for his debut in *The Killers* (1946) and a career of more than 65 films, notably *From Here to Eternity* (1953), *Sweet Smell of Success* (1957), and *Birdman of Alcatraz* (1962).

Lang, Fritz, *b. Vienna, Austria, 1890; d. 1976.* **Film director.** A legendary German Expressionist filmmaker, Lang excelled at using composition, set design, and lighting to convey his themes of fate and destiny. Though trained as an architect, he preferred writing screenplays for the busy German film industry after World War I. He directed his first film, *Halbblut,* in 1919; it was followed by several critical successes, including *Metropolis* (1927) and *M* (1931). He emigrated to America in the 1930's, directing his first Hollywood film, *Fury,* in 1936. His best Hollywood films include *You Only Live Once* (1937), *Scarlet Street* (1945), and *The Big Heat* (1953).

Laozi *(dates unknown).* **Chinese philosopher.** The historical reality of an individual known as Laozi ("Old Master") is doubtful; the conventional identification of

Laozi with Lao Dan, a figure of the sixth century B.C. is almost certainly wrong. *The Book of Laozi* (also known as the *Daodejing*, "The Way and Its Power"), a fundamental text of Taoist philosophy and religion, was compiled from earlier materials ca. 300 B.C. Envisioning a primitive agrarian society ruled by a sage-king empowered by his possession of the dao (the "Way"), it poses a radical challenge to Confucian social theory and imperial-bureaucratic government. Laozi was later regarded as an immortal and as one of the high gods of religious Taoism.

Lavoisier, Antoine Laurent, *b. Paris, 1743; d. 1794.* **Chemist and physicist.** Lavoisier was a founder of modern chemistry. He introduced effective quantitative methods in chemistry, explained combustion, elucidated the role of oxygen in respiration, and established the composition of water and many other compounds. In his classification of substances he suggested the modern distinction between chemical elements and compounds. His famous textbook, called in English *Elements of Chemistry*, was published in 1789. Active as a government expert and official, he was executed during the revolution in France.

Lawrence, D. H. (David Herbert), *b. Eastwood, Nottinghamshire, England, 1885; d. 1930.* **English novelist and poet.** Lawrence's largely autobiographical first major novel, *Sons and Lovers* (1913), introduced his themes of the unhealthy separation of man from nature, and the stifling effects of social convention, and intellectualism. With *The Rainbow* (1915) and *Women in Love* (1921), he achieved his highest art and received much criticism for their sexually explicit content. After World War I, his notoriety and that of his previously married German wife, Frieda, caused them to leave England and live in the southwestern United States, Mexico, Australia, and other places. His most famous novel, *Lady Chatterley's Lover,* (1928), was banned in the U.S. and U.K. because of sexual content. His short-stories (including "Rocking Horse" and "Odor of Chyrysanthemums,") are highly regarded and his poetry, including "Snake," "Figs," and "Blue Gentians" increasingly appreciated.

Leakey, Louis S. B., *b. Kabete, Kenya, 1903; d. 1972.* **Kenyan archaeologist and anthropologist.** The son of missionary parents, Leakey began his archaeological research in East Africa in 1924. His fossil discoveries led him to conclude that human evolution was centered in Africa rather than Asia. His findings concerning the links between apes and early man were considered significant, and although many scientists questioned his interpretations, later fossil finds proved him correct. Leakey encour-

aged Jane Goodall, Dian Fossey, and Birute Galdikas to study chimpanzees, gorillas, and orangutans in their natural habitats. The Louis Leakey Memorial Institute for African Prehistory was established in Nairobi as a fossil repository and to foster further study.

Le Corbusier (Charles-Edouard Jeanneret-Gris), *b. La Chaux-de-Fonds, Switzerland, 1887; d. 1965.* **Architect, painter, and theorist.** Considered by many the most influential architect of the 20th century, he designed one of the great works of modern architecture, the Villa Savoye in Poissy, France (1928–30). In a seminal book, *Toward a New Architecture* (1923), he delivered his famous dictum, "The house is a machine for living in"; but his houses were elegant, with hints of classicism. He produced work of astonishing diversity, including the Unite d'Habitation (1946–52), an apartment building in Marseilles, France; the pilgrimage church of Notre-Dame-du-Haut (1950–55) in Ronchamp, France; and the principal public buildings for the capital of Punjab in Chandigarh (1951–65), India.

Lee, Robert Edward, *b. Stratford, Va., 1807; d. 1870.* **American general of the Confederacy.** The son of a Revolutionary War hero, Lee attended West Point and later served in the Mexican War. He became superintendant at West Point, and later led the troops who captured John Brown at Harpers Ferry. In 1862, Lee was given command of the Army of Northern Virginia. Thereafter he led the Confederate forces brilliantly in historic Civil War battles, including the second Bull Run, Antietam, Chancellorsville, and Fredericksburg; but at Gettysburg he suffered the defeat that spelled the beginning of the end of the Civil War. He surrendered to General Ulysses S. Grant at Appomattox courthouse on April 9, 1865.

Leibniz, Gottfried Wilhelm, Baron von, *b. Leipzig, 1646; d. 1716.* **German philosopher and mathematician.** An impressive scientist and scholar who also held diplomatic posts under various German princes, his main contributions are now regarded as those in mathematics and logic. He invented the calculus at the same time as, but independently of, Newton, and he was one of the founders of symbolic logic. His philosophy was an optimistic, consistent rationalism. He held that the universe was made up of monads, infinite in number, nonmaterial, and hierarchically arranged, and that divine guidance made the existing world the best of possible worlds.

Lemieux, Mario, *b. Montreal, Canada, 1965.* **Hockey player.** Lemieux burst onto the scene with the Pittsburgh

Penguins in 1984, scoring 100 points and winning the Calder trophy for outstanding rookie. He won the M.V.P. award in 1988 and led the Penguins to back-to-back Stanley Cup championships in 1991 and 1992. In 1993, he was diagnosed with Hodgkin's disease, and after missing 20 games for treatment, "Super Mario" returned, scored 160 points in just 60 games, and won his second M.V.P. Lemieux has been the league's leading scorer six times; he reentered the NHL in 2000 after a three-year retirement.

Lenin (Vladimir Ilyich Ulyanov), *b. Simbirsk, Russia, 1870; d. 1924.* **Russian political leader.** Inspired by the writings of Karl Marx, Lenin founded Russia's Communist Party and orchestrated the Bolshevik revolution (1917). When it succeeded, he became the first leader of the new Soviet state (1917–24). Under his leadership, the Bolsheviks withdrew from World War I, distributed land to the peasants, and granted independence to Finland, Poland, and the Baltic republics. The promise of Soviet Communism ended even before Lenin's death, as the state began brutally quashing dissent and civil war ravaged the country.

Lennon, John Winston, *b. Liverpool, England, 1940; d. 1980.* **Rock-pop vocalist, guitarist, and songwriter; member of the Beatles.** As half of the Lennon-McCartney songwriting team, he wrote or cowrote many of the great popular songs of the 1960's, most notably "Norwegian Wood," "Revolution," "In My Life," "Strawberry Fields Forever," and "A Day in the Life." Post-Beatles, Lennon's success was spreading. He was shot and killed outside his New York apartment building on December 8, 1980, by Mark David Chapman. Lennon's solo recordings include "Give Peace a Chance" (1969), "Cold Turkey" (1969), "Instant Karma" (1970), "Imagine" (1971), and "(Just Like) Starting Over" (1980).

Leo I (Saint) (Leo the Great), *b. Tuscany, ca. 400; d. 461.* **Pope, 440-61, Doctor of the Church.** Leo was one of the most important figures in the establishment of the bishop of Rome as pope and supreme leader of the Christian church, specifically by securing an edict from Emperor Valentinian III that recognized the pope's authority over other bishops. Leo also effectively battled the Manichaean and Nestorian heresies; and in his *Tome of Leo* and at the Council of Chalcedon (451), he led the condemnation of Eutyches's doctrine that Christ has one divine nature. His successful negotiation with Attila the Hun to prevent an attack on Rome in 452 was a critical event in the development of the papacy's temporal rule.

Leonardo da Vinci, *b. Anchiano, Italy, 1452; d. 1519.* **Painter, sculptor, architect, designer, theorist, engineer, scientist.** Founder of the High Renaissance movement, and painter of the *Mona Lisa* (1503–5), arguably the most famous and influential image in Western art. Other well-known works include *The Last Supper* (1495–98). Leonardo's radical technical and conceptual innovations established an unprecedented standard of realism in painting. He mastered a method of modeling figures using light and shade called *chiaroscuro*, and his paintings have a luminous, hazy quality referred to as *sfumato*. Committed to a study of nature, Leonardo left behind hundreds of drawings and notes; he developed the technique of modern scientific illustration, and his many inventions include machinery and military engineering.

Lewis, Carl, *b. Birmingham, Ala., 1961.* **U.S. track-and-field star.** Lewis won a record-tying nine gold medals and one silver medal in appearances at the 1984, 1988, 1992, and 1996 Olympic Games. A sprinter and long jumper, he equaled Jesse Owens's feat of 1936 by taking gold in the 100-meter, 200-meter, long jump, and 4x100 relay at the 1984 Olympics in Los Angeles.

Lewis, Sinclair, *b. Sauk Centre, Minn., 1885; d. 1951.* **Author.** Lewis's satirical novels deftly skewered capitalism and the conformity of American middle-class life. *Babbitt* (1922), his masterpiece, is a devastating portrait of a narrow and complacent midwestern businessman. *Elmer Gantry* (1927) took on hypocritical charlatans in the church. Many critics were offended that Lewis refused to glorify traditional American values, and his work was banned in several U.S. cities. In 1930 Lewis became the first American to win the Nobel Prize in Literature. His novel, *It Can't Happen Here* (1935), explored the possibility of fascism's taking root in the United States. Lewis's output declined in his later years, as he succumbed to alcoholism.

Lichtenstein, Roy, *b. New York, N.Y., 1923; d. 1997.* **Painter, sculptor, printmaker, decorative artist.** A central figure in the Pop Art movement, Lichtenstein is famous for paintings that mimic comic books. Using simplified color schemes and black outlines, and representing tonal variation with tiny dots, he invites the viewer to examine everyday aspects of American culture. In his later career Lichtenstein put his comic book technique to use in renderings of such famous painting styles as Cubism and Abstract Expressionism. Well-known works include *Whaam!* (1963), *Hopeless* (1963), and *Brushstrokes in Flight* (1984).

Lincoln, Abraham, *b. Hodgenville, Ky., 1809; d. 1865.* Sixteenth U.S. president, 1861–65. Lincoln was born in a log cabin and accumulated barely a year's total education while growing up. Family moves took him to Indiana and then to Illinois by the time he was 21; a failed storekeeper, Lincoln worked at odd jobs while he taught himself law, sometimes walking 20 miles to borrow books. He was elected to the Illinois state legislature (as a Whig) in 1834 and to Congress in 1846, and unsuccessfully ran for the Senate in 1858, drawing national attention in debates with Stephen A. Douglas, the nation's leading Democrat. He was rewarded with the Republican party's nomination for president in 1860, and defeated three opponents to win the general election. As southern states left the Union, Lincoln preached conciliation, although he vowed to crush secession and forced the issue at Fort Sumter. After early reverses in the Civil War, Lincoln decided that slavery had to be abolished altogether to restore the Union, and he issued the Emancipation Proclamation (1862). Five days after the war's end, Lincoln was shot and killed by John Wilkes Booth, an arch-Confederate. Lincoln's prestige has grown with time, until many have come to regard him as the nation's greatest president.

Lindbergh, Charles A., *b. Detroit, 1902; d. 1974.* American aviator. On May 20–21, 1927, he made the first nonstop solo flight across the Atlantic in a small plane, "The Spirit of St. Louis." After completing the journey from New York to Paris in 33.5 hours, Lindbergh immediately became an international hero. In 1929, he married the writer Anne Morrow. Their infant son was kidnapped and murdered in 1932 in a crime that received worldwide attention. His support of fascist governments caused him to lose his heroic stature but his 1953 account of his flight, *The Spirit of St. Louis*, won a Pulitzer Prize.

Linnaeus, Carolus, *b. Råshult, Sweden, 1707; d. 1778.* Botanist and taxonomist. Linnaeus originated the system of classification of animals and plants, in which organisms are placed on the basis of natural characteristics into a hierarchy of groups. From the broadest to narrowest these are kingdom, phylum (in botany, division), class, order, family, genus, and species. Linnaeus also developed the binomial naming system. For each organism the genus is given first and then the species, e.g. lion: *Panthera leo*. Modified by the influence of evolutionary theory and new scientific discoveries, Linnaeus's work remains the basis of modern taxonomy.

Lloyd George, David, *b, Manchester, England, 1863; d. 1945.* British politician. First elected to parliament in 1890 as a Liberal, he served as a minister in several governments. He rose to prominence when he introduced the National Insurance Act of 1911, which established health and unemployment insurance for English workers and marked the beginning of the modern welfare state. He was immensely popular as prime minister (1916–22), especially during World War I, when he devised a solution to the food shortages caused by German submarine attacks. At the negotiations for the Treaty of Versailles, he lobbied for a peace that was less punitive to Germany than the one sought by France's Georges Clemenceau.

Locke, John, *b. Wrington, England, 1632; d. 1704.* Philosopher. Considered the founder of British empiricism, his two main works, *Essay Concerning Human Understanding* (1690) and *Two Treatises on Civil Government* (1690), made him the leading philosopher of freedom. Against Hobbes, he held that the state of nature was happy, and that all humans were equal and free to pursue "life, health, liberty and possessions." The social contract forms the state, which is guided by natural law and guarantees inalienable rights. Locke also developed the idea of checks and balances found in the U.S. Constitution.

Lodge, Henry Cabot, *b. Boston, 1850; d. 1924.* U.S. Senator. Born to an illustrious Massachusetts family, Lodge was a prolific historian. He served in the House of Representatives from 1887 to 1893, when he was elected senator. During the three decades that Cabot served, he was one of the most powerful Republicans in Congress; he was a fierce supporter of immigration restrictions, supported U.S. imperialist adventures, and backed the development of a strong military. A stubborn foe of President Woodrow Wilson, Lodge fought to block American participation in the League of Nations, arguing that the United States should not be bound by international peacekeeping commitments. (Ironically, his grandson would later serve as the U.S. ambassador to the United Nations.)

Longfellow, Henry Wadsworth, *b. Portland, Me., 1807; d. 1882.* Poet. Longfellow published his first book of verse, *Voices of the Night*, and a prose romance, *Hyperion*, in 1839. Highly popular in both America and England during his lifetime, he composed some of America's best-known poems, both short and long. Among the former are "The Village Blacksmith" and "The Wreck of the Hesperus" (both 1841). *Poems on Slavery*, revealing abolitionist sentiment, was published in 1842. His long narrative poems, set in his country's past and written in intricate, "antique" rhythms, include *Evangeline* (1847), *The Song of Hiawatha* (1855), *The Courtship of Miles Standish* (1858), and *Paul Revere's Ride* (1861).

Lorca, Federico García, *b. Fuente Vaqueros, Spain, 1898; d. 1936.* **Poet and playwright.** Responsible for revitalizing the drama and literature of Spain in the early 20th century, Lorca was strongly influenced by the folk traditions and social conditions of his native Andalusia as well as by surrealism and expressionism. His poems look back to the Gypsy ballads and romances of classical Spain, and his plays, among them *Blood Wedding* (1933) and *The House of Bernarda Alba* (1936), explore the search for love within a restrictive society. Lorca, a revolutionary during the Spanish Civil War, was arrested and executed in 1936.

Louis IX (St. Louis) *b. Poissy, France, 1214; d. 1270.* **King of France, 1226–70.** The only French king to be canonized by the Roman Catholic Church (1297), Louis IX was an immensely popular king who led the Seventh Crusade into the Holy Land, which had fallen under Muslim control. Though the military operation failed, Louis negotiated several important alliances that made the endeavor a success. He also achieved a lasting peace with England (1258) and sponsored the first great encyclopedia. He died on a crusade to Tunisia.

Louis XIV (Louis the Great), *b. Saint-Germain-en-Laye, France, 1638; d. 1715.* **King of France, 1643–1715.** One of the great monarchs of European history, the "Sun King" attempted to rule through divine right. He built lavish palaces for himself, including the one that still stands at Versailles, where he moved the seat of government in 1682. He greatly expanded his domain into the Netherlands (1667–78) and parts of the Hapsburg empire on France's eastern border. But he earned the enmity of Protestants when he revoked (1685) the Edict of Nantes, which had guaranteed their freedom of worship.

Louis XV (Louis the Well-Beloved), *b. Versailles, France, 1710; d. 1774.* **King of France, 1715–74.** He ascended to the throne at age five because both his parents and his brother had died three years earlier. He took little interest in politics, causing the monarchy's authority to wane. In the Seven Years' War (1756–63), Louis allied France with Austria against England and Prussia, resulting in the loss of almost all French colonial possessions in India and North America.

Louis XVI, *b. Versailles, 1754; d. 1793.* **King of France, 1774-92.** Louis, the last Bourbon king, came to the throne in a time of fiscal crisis and popular ferment. He appointed capable ministers to stabilize government and economy, but failed to gain the cooperation of the aristocracy, who refused to be taxed and prevailed on him to summon the long-dormant Estates General in 1789. Louis stifled the influence of the third, or popular, estate, which then declared itself the National Assembly. Rumors of suppression of this body were a cause of the storming of Bastille prison on July 14, 1789, the focal date of the French Revolution. Louis and his queen were confined to the Tuileries palace, and his attempt to escape, his refusal to implement the Constitution of 1791 and his alliances with foreign armies against the revolution led to his conviction for treason and his beheading.

Louis, Joe (Joseph Louis Barrow), *b. Lafayette, Ala., 1914; d. 1981.* **Boxer.** The longest-reigning heavyweight champion in history the "Brown Bomber" won the title in 1937 and successfully defended it 25 times before retiring in 1949. His most famous bout was a first-round knockout of the German heavyweight Max Schmeling (Hitler's symbol of Aryan racial supremacy) in 1938. During the height of his career, Louis enlisted in the army, a move that helped in desegregating U.S. armed services. Louis won 68 of 71 career fights, 54 by knockout. Generous to a fault, Louis fell deep into debt, eventually owing the I.R.S. more than $1 million.

Lucas, George, *b. Modesto, Calif., 1944.* **Screenwriter, director, and founder of Industrial Light and Magic (ILM).** As creator of *Star Wars*, one of the most successful film series of all time, Lucas helped push the Hollywood industry toward action-driven genres. He directed his first film, *THX 1138*, in 1971, and the financial success of his second feature, *American Graffiti* (1973), made *Star Wars* (1977) possible. *The Empire Strikes Back* (1980) and *The Return of the Jedi* (1983) completed the first *Star Wars* trilogy, which combined old-fashioned Hollywood storytelling with ideas from mythology.

Ludendorff, Erich, *b. near Poznan, Poland, 1865; d. 1937.* **German military leader.** Prior to World War I, he was attached to the German general staff and was responsible for revisions to the Schlieffen Plan. At the start of the war, he was assigned to Paul von Hindenburg in the east, where they won a great victory at Tannenberg in 1914. In 1916, the team was given supreme military command and assumed a virtual dictatorship over the German state.

Fearing American involvement in the war, Ludendorff launched a series of offenses in the west in 1918 that came close to succeeding but ultimately failed. After the war, he did much to undermine the Weimar Republic and for a time was an associate of Adolf Hitler.

Luther, Martin, b. *Eisleben, Saxony, 1483; d. 1546.* Protestant reformer. A Catholic monk and theology professor, Luther became discontented with the church about 1510, when he observed in Rome the widespread sale of indulgences, which reduced the spiritual penalties for sins. Luther believed salvation was God's free gift, and when a papal indulgence was offered in Saxony in 1517, he nailed 95 theses of objection to the Wittenberg church door. He soon published writings rejecting the authority of the pope, and in 1521 he was excommunicated and condemned at the imperial diet (assembly) at Worms. The articles of faith of his Lutheran Church were established in the Augsburg Confession of 1530. Luther translated the Bible into German and for the rest of his life was a central figure of the Reformation.

MacArthur, Douglas, b. *Little Rock, Ark., 1880: d. 1964.* Military leader. MacArthur became U.S. Army chief of staff in 1930 and was military adviser to the Philippines from 1935 to 1941. He fought a delaying action in the Philippines after World War II broke out. Recalled to Australia, he was made commander of the southwest Pacific theater in 1942. As Allied governor of Japan from 1945 to 1951, he radically reformed Japanese society. He was chosen to command United Nations forces in Korea when war began there in 1950, but was relieved of command by President Truman for insubordination in 1951.

Machiavelli, Niccolo, b. *Florence, Italy, 1469; d. 1527.* Political philosopher, statesman, and author. A senior official of the Florentine Republic, he undertook vital diplomatic missions to France, the Vatican, and Germany, and replaced mercenaries with a citizens' militia. He lost his office with the return of Medici rule (1512). Machiavelli's most famous work, *The Prince* (1532), describes the ways, amoral and calculating, in which a prince may maintain power, but his *Discourses* (1531) displays his republican principles; he also wrote poems, plays, and histories.

Macmillan, Harold, b. *London, 1894; d. 1986.* English statesman. Elected to Parliament in 1924, Macmillan served, with a break (1929–1931), to 1963. He held posts in the wartime cabinet of Winston Churchill and later in other cabinets. He became prime minister in 1957 and

signed the the Nuclear Test Ban Treaty with the United States and the Soviet Union in 1963. However, he failed to have England admitted into the European Economic Community, and he resigned in 1963 amid a scandal involving his war secretary, John Profumo.

Madison, James, b. *Port Conway, Va., 1751; d. 1836.* Fourth U.S. president, 1809–17. A graduate of Princeton, Madison was the youngest member of the Continental Congress in 1780, when he led the movement to revise the Articles of Confederation. At the Constitutional Convention in Philadelphia in 1787, Madison's Virginia Plan became the pivot of discussion; he (with John Jay and Alexander Hamilton) was a coauthor of *The Federalist* papers, drafted the Bill of Rights, and cofounded the Democratic-Republican party. After ascending to the presidency, Madison successfully led the country in the fight against the British in the War of 1812.

Madonna (Ciccone, Madonna Louise), b. *Rochester, Mich., 1958.* Musician, actress. In a career spanning two decades, the "Material Mom" is the highest-paid female singer of all time. Her provocative lyrics and dance moves carved her a niche in history; her singles include "Like a Virgin," "Material Girl," and "Papa Don't Preach." Madonna began her film career with *Desperately Seeking Susan* (1985) and then, notably, worked on *Dick Tracy* (1990) and *A League of Their Own* (1992). She won an Academy Award for her song "You Must Love Me," which she performed in the title role in *Evita* (1996). Madonna also manages her own label, Maverick Records, and has published two children's books.

Magellan, Ferdinand, b. *Oporto, Portugal, 1480; d. 1521.* Navigator. Magellan spent six years in Portuguese Asia, voyaging to India, Malacca, and perhaps the Spice Islands. He approached Spain's Charles I with a plan to sail from South America to the Spice Islands. His were the first ships to transit the Strait of Magellan (1519) and to cross the Pacific, taking fourteen weeks to reach the Mariana Islands (1520). Magellan was killed in 1521, in the Philippines. Under Juan Sebastian de Elcano, the first circumnavigation of the world was completed on September 6, 1522.

Magritte, René, b. *Lessines, Hainaut, Belgium, 1898; d. 1967.* Painter, sculptor, photographer, filmmaker. Magritte was one of the founding members in 1926 of the Belgian Surrealist group, which developed independently from the French surrealists. Not wanting the style of his paintings to detract from the subject, he created a straightforward, unembellished visual language, which he used to depict scenes in which reality is pointedly skewed. His painting *Red Model* (1935), for example, shows a pair of shoes with human toes. Other important works include *Threatened Assassin* (1927), *Treachery of Images* (1929), and *Empire of Light* (1950).

Mahler, Gustav, *b. Kalist, Bohemia, 1860; d. 1911*. **Austrian composer, conductor, and pianist.** Educated in Vienna, Mahler conducted several orchestras in Europe and the New York Philharmonic (1909–11) and Metropolitan Opera (1908–10). Mahler's music combined romantic eloquence with subtle chromaticism and polyphony, anticipating the coming avant-garde movement. Notable works include Symphonies No. 1 in D Major (1884-88), No. 2 in C Minor (*Resurrection*) (1888–94), No. 4 in G Major (1899–1900), No. 5 in C♯ Minor (1901–02), No. 6 in A Minor (1903–05), and No. 9 in D Major (1909–10); *Das Lied von der Erde* (*The Song of the Earth*) (1907–09); and the song cycles *Lieder eines Fahrenden Gesellen* (*Songs of a Wayfarer*) (1884) and *Des Knaben Wunderhorn* (*The Youth's Magic Horn*) (1888–99).

Mailer, Norman, *b. Long Branch, N.J., 1923; d. 2007*. **Non-fiction writer, and novelist.** Mailer, an uncommonly gifted and prolific writer, has published nonfiction books, novels, essays, articles, poems, plays, and more. An early practicioner of the New Journalism of the 1960's, Mailer had already gained fame for *The Naked and the Dead* (1948), a novel recounting his experience in World War II. Other well-known non-fiction works include *Miami and the Siege of Chicago* (1968), *Of a Fire on the Moon* (1971), and *Marilyn* (1973). He won two Pulitzer prizes, one in nonfiction for *The Armies of the Night* (1968) and one in fiction for *The Executioner's Song* (1979).

Maimonides, Moses (Rambam), *b. Cordova, Spain, 1135; d. 1204*. **Jewish philosopher, jurist, and physician.** Maimonides was the most important Jewish scholar of the medieval period. He and his family were forced into exile by a fanatical Islamic sect, and eventually settled in Egypt. When he was 23, Maimonides wrote a commentary on the *Mishna*, the compendium of Jewish laws. This major work was following by *Mishne Torah—The Torah Reviewed* (1178) and *Moreh nevukhim—The Guide for the Perplexed* (1191), which is considered a classic work of religious philosophy. Maimonides emerged as a leader of the Jewish community in Egypt and became the court physician to the great sultan Saladin (1137–93) and his family.

Maki, Fumihiko, *b. Tokyo, 1929*. **Japanese architect.** Maki calls himself a modernist, but his buildings, in their human scale and use of diverse materials, do not reflect a strict modernist style. His vast Makuhari Messe Exhibition Center (1986–89) in Tokyo and Kirishima International Concert Hall (1994) make use of modern industrial materials softened by a plastic approach to form. The Center for the Arts, Yerba Buena Gardens (1991–93), in San Francisco is an important work in the United States. Maki was a winner of the 1993 Pritzker prize.

Malthus, Thomas Robert, *b. near Guilford, Britain, 1766; d. 1834*. **English economist.** Malthus is best known for his theory of population in his *Essay on Population*, first published in 1798 and revised in several subsequent editions. He argued that population increases geometrically while the food supply increases arithmetically. Population growth is limited by famine, disease, and war when it outstrips the food supply, but these undesirable forces can be mitigated by abstinence and birth control. The thesis was influential and came to be known as Malthusianism.

Mandela, Nelson, *b. Qunu, Transkei region, South Africa, 1918*. **Political leader.** After South Africa's white government banned the African National Congress resistance movement in 1961, its leader, Nelson Mandela, continued his political activities underground. He was eventually arrested and imprisoned for 27 years. During his captivity, his fame spread abroad, and "free Nelson Mandela" became an international rallying cry. In 1990, President F. W. de Klerk lifted the ban on the A.N.C. and released Mandela. Mandela and de Klerk shared the 1993 Nobel Peace Prize. In 1994, Mandela was elected South Africa's first black president.

Manet, Édouard, *b. Paris, 1832; d. 1883*. **Painter.** A realist who influenced and was influenced by the Impressionists of the 1870's, in his lifetime Manet's avant-gardism was often ill–received. Images such as *Déjeuner sur l'herbe* (1863) and *Olympia* (1863) were thought to bring a vulgar modernity to classical subjects. Influenced by Velázquez and Japanese woodblock prints, Manet's paintings are characterized by flatly applied tones. *Boating* (1874) demonstrates the high color value and broken brushwork also typical of the Impressionists. Manet sought to document contemporary Parisian life, as he did in *Bar at the Folies-Bergère* (1882).

Mann, Thomas, *b. Lubeck, Germany, 1875; d. 1955.* Novelist and essayist. Mann explored several themes in his fiction, including the clash between the rational and the irrational and between liberal and conservative values, and above all the place of the artist in a rapidly changing society. His first novel *Buddenbrooks* (1901) described the decay and fall of a prominent family; *Death in Venice* (1912) depicted the conflict between death and art. Other notable works are *The Magic Mountain* (1924) and the tetralogy *Joseph and His Brethren* (1933–43). Mann received the Nobel Prize for Literature in 1929. Also a distinguished political and literary essayist, he left Nazi Germany in 1933 and lived 14 years in the U.S.

Mantle, Mickey (Charles) *b. Spavinaw, Okla., 1931; d. 1995.* Baseball player. The switch-hitting New York Yankees center fielder possessed a rare combination of speed and power that made him one of the game's most exciting players. He was the American League M.V.P. three times. Though slowed by various injuries throughout his 18-year career, Mantle ended up with 536 career home runs. He added a record 18 career World Series home runs. Mantle played for seven World Series winning teams and was elected to the National Baseball Hall of Fame in 1974.

Mao Zedong, *b. Hunan Province, China, 1893; d. 1976.* Chinese Communist leader. Mao was born to a prosperous peasant family and moved to Beijing in 1918, where he studied Marxism. A revolutionary activist and founding member of the Chinese Communist Party (Shanghai, 1921), Mao had unorthodox ideas about peasant-based revolution that marginalized him within the party. During the Long March (1934–35) Mao was elected party chairman. Vindicated, he used the party base at Yan'an as a laboratory of Maoist ideology in action. After victory over the Nationalists in the Civil War (1946–49), Mao quickly solidified Communist control, quashing all opposition. Despite the catastrophic Great Leap Forward (1958–60) and the disruptive Cultural Revolution (1966–76), Mao remained chairman until his death, which was followed by an era of post-Mao economic and social reform.

Marciano, Rocky (Rocco Marchegiano), *b. Brockton, Mass., 1923; d. 1969.* World heavyweight boxing champion, 1952–56. Marciano began to box in the army during World War II and did not turn professional until age 23 in 1947. His impressive knockout record raised him through the heavyweight ranks and he became the leading title contender when he knocked out former longtime champion Joe Louis in 1951. He took the title with a 13th-round knockout of Jersey Joe Walcott on Sept. 23, 1952,

and defended it successfully six times before retiring in 1956. Marciano won all 49 of his professional fights, 43 of them by knockout. He was killed in a plane crash in Iowa.

Marconi, Guglielmo, *b. 1874, d. 1937.* Italian inventor. Marconi learned in 1894 that Heinrich Hertz (b. 1857, d. 1894) had produced invisible waves that travel through space. Marconi thought such waves could be used to send wireless communications similar to the dot-and-dash messages sent by telegraph. Within a year he was sending and detecting signals over distances of more than a mile (1.6 km). On December 12, 1901, Marconi showed that he could decipher signals sent across the Atlantic Ocean. Marconi was awarded the 1909 Nobel Prize in Physics for his invention of wireless telegraphy ("wireless"), the first form of radio.

Marcus Aurelius *b. 121; d. 180.* Roman emperor. The adopted son of emperor Antonius Pius, Marcus Aurelius took power after his father's death in 161. He made his adoptive brother, Lucius Verus, co-emperor. Marcus largely overshadowed his brother and is regarded as one of Rome's most wise and just emperors, respected for instituting political and social reforms, as well as writing *Meditations*, a work of Stoic philosophy. His reign was marred by ongoing wars, and he left his son Commodus, a notoriously brutal leader, as successor.

Marie Antoinette, *b. Vienna, 1755; d. 1793.* Queen of France. The daughter of the Austrian emperor of the Holy Roman Empire, Marie married the French dauphin in 1770. Indecisive and unprepared to rule, he ascended to the French throne in 1774 as Louis XVI. While discontent was percolating throughout France, Marie's extravagant lifestyle infuriated the public. As the French Revolution exploded in 1789, a mob descended on the lavish palace at Versailles, demanding that Marie and Louis move to Paris, where they became virtual prisoners in the Tuileries. In 1792, the royal family was arrested for treason. Marie followed her husband to the guillotine in 1793.

Marlborough, First Duke of (John Churchill) *b. Ashe, England, 1650; d. 1722.* English military leader. A brilliant general who never lost a battle, Marlborough made his reputation during the War of the Spanish Succession. In 1702 Queen Anne rewarded him with a duchy and later with Blenheim Palace, named for his decisive victory over Louis XIV of France near a town of that name in Bavaria. An important political figure in the Tory party, he lost influence as the Whig party took control. He retired after being condemned by the House of Commons for misappropriation of public money.

Marlowe, Christopher, *b. Canterbury, England (?), 1564; d. 1593.* Poet and playwright. Considered to be the finest English playwright before Shakespeare, he was a great innovator in the development of blank verse, in which unrhymed iambic pentameter is used to dramatic effect, Marlowe exerted a lasting influence on, among others, Shakespeare and Milton. His plays include *Tamburlaine the Great* (1587), *Edward II* (1594), *Doctor Faustus* (1604), and *The Jew of Malta* (1633). He was killed in a barroom fight, perhaps because he had been acting as an agent of Queen Elizabeth. His unfinished poem *Hero and Leander* was published in 1598.

Marshall, George C., *b. Uniontown, Pa., 1880; d. 1959.* American military leader and statesman. A career army officer, he graduated from Virginia Military Institute, served in World War I, and rose to the rank of five-star general (1944) and chief of staff of the U.S. Army during World War II. But he is best remembered for the European Recovery Program—better known as the Marshall Plan (1947)—which brought U.S. aid to a war-ravaged Europe. As secretary of state (1947–49) and secretary of defense (1950–51), he laid the groundwork for the formation of NATO. In 1953, he became the first professional soldier to win the Nobel Peace Prize.

Marshall, John, *b. near Germantown, Va., 1755; d. 1835.* American statesman and jurist. After the American Revolution, Marshall practiced law in Richmond, Va., and served in the Virginia Assembly, the U.S., House of Representatives, and as secretary of state in President John Adams's cabinet. In 1801 he was appointed the fourth chief justice of the Supreme Court, where he had a profound impact on constitutional law. In *Marbury v. Madison* (1803) the court asserted a power to overrule legislation it deemed unconstitutional. Other decisions further increased the power of the Supreme Court, including decisions in conflicts between the states and the federal government.

Marx, Groucho (Julius Henry Marx) *New York City, 1890; d. 1977.* Comedian. His greasepaint mustache and funny walk brought ironic reality to the madcap antics of his brothers Harpo and Chico, first in their Broadway successes *The Cocoanuts* and *Animal Crackers*, then in Hollywood in such notable movies as *Duck Soup* (1933) and *A Night at the Opera* (1935). The Marx Brothers continued making movies into the 1950's; Groucho went on to fame on TV as the wacky host of the quiz show *You Bet Your Life.*

Marx, Karl, *b. Trier (Treves), Prussia, 1818; d. 1883.* German political and economic theorist and philosopher. Trained in law and a doctor of philosophy, Marx, along with his longtime collaborator and patron, Friedrich Engels, employed Hegel's dialectical system to develop his theory of dialectical materialism, an economic view of history that saw the triumph of the working class over capitalist control as inevitable. Committed to action as well as theory—to the cause of class struggle—the two men enunciated their beliefs in the concise *Communist Manifesto* ("Workers of the world, unite!") in 1848, the same year as the failed revolutions in Europe. He then worked as a journalist in Cologne but when the paper was suppressed, he settled permanently with his family in London in 1849, where he was a correspondent for the *New York Tribune.* Here he wrote his magnum opus, *Das Kapital,* published, with the help of Engels, especially after Marx's death, in three volumes from 1867 to 1894. Marx was a founder and leader of the International Workingmen's Association (the First International, 1864-72).

Mary, Queen of Scots (Mary Stuart), *b. Linlithgow, Scotland, 1542; d. 1587.* Queen of Scotland. Daughter of James V, king of Scotland, Mary became queen as an infant. She married the dauphin of France in 1559 but his death in 1560 brought her back to Scotland in 1561 as queen. But she was a Catholic ruling a Protestant government and her marriages to Lord Darnley and the Earl of Bothwell increased opposition to her rule. Her armies were defeated by Scottish nobles in 1567 and 1568. and she fled to the English court of Elizabeth I. She was beheaded after being involved in Catholic plots to assassinate Elizabeth.

Masaccio (Tommaso di Ser Giovanni di Mone Cassai), *b. San Giovanni Val d'Arno, Italy, 1401; d. 1428.* Painter. Regarded as the founder of Italian Renaissance painting, Masaccio was the first painter of his time to employ Brunelleschi's system of linear perspective. Also inspired by Giotto, Masaccio created mathematically proportioned spaces, fully three-dimensional figures, and a realistic depiction of light, all of which were significant developments for his time. His fresco *Trinity* (ca. 1425–27) was groundbreaking for placing the crucifixion scene in an illusionistic architectural setting. Other well-known works include *The Tribute Money* (ca. 1427), a fresco in the Brancacci Chapel.

Mathewson, Christy (Christopher), *b. Factoryville, Pa., 1880; d. 1925.* Baseball player. One of baseball's early pitching greats, Mathewson amassed 373 victories over 17 seasons, almost all spent with the New York Giants. In an era of hard-drinking baseball players, the clean-cut, college-educated Mathewson stood out as the "Christian gentleman." He posted four 30-win seasons, and in 1908 he won 37 games. Mathewson appeared in four World Series, throwing 10 complete games. The Giants won the 1905 World Series on the strength of his arm, as he pitched three shutouts in just six days. With his playing career winding down, Mathewson enlisted in the army during World War I. He was exposed to poison gas and later developed tuberculosis. In 1936 "Matty" became one of the inaugural members of the Baseball Hall of Fame.

Matisse, Henri, b. *Le Cateau-Cambrésis, France, 1869; d. 1954.* **Painter, sculptor.** Matisse came to painting late in life, having earned a degree as a lawyer. He became a leading figure in the Fauvist movement and one of the most influential artists of the 20th century. The Fauvists, or "wild beasts," produced paintings radical in their simplicity, with bold distortions and a primitive use of colors in high value. Matisse's best-known work is perhaps *Joy of Life* (1905–06), a modern interpretation of a classical Bacchanalian scene; other important work includes *The Red Studio* (1911).

Maxwell, James Clerk, b. *Edinburgh, 1831; d. 1879.* **Scottish physicist.** In 1857 he showed that Saturn's rings must consist of small particles. Three years later, he determined the statistical distribution of moving molecules in gases, explaining diffusion and conduction of heat. Maxwell was the first to show that the primary colors of light are red, green, and blue, and in 1861 he demonstrated the first color photograph based on this idea. From 1856 through 1873 he developed laws showing that light is a form of electromagnetic wave and predicted the rest of the electromagnetic spectrum.

Mayer, Louis (Eliezar Mayer) B., b. *Minsk, Russia 1885; d. 1957.* **Film producer.** One of the most powerful moguls of the Hollywood studio system, he was in the scrap-iron business when he bought his first movie theater in Haverhill, Mass., in 1907. He soon branched out into film distribution and production and moved to Hollywood in 1918. Mayer was the studio head at Metro-Goldwyn-Mayer (MGM) from its formation in 1924 until he was forced out in 1951. During this time, MGM films became known for their glamorous stars, high production values, and wholesome subject matter.

Mays, Willie, b. *Westfield, Ala.; 1931.* **Baseball player.** After his major league debut at age 19, Mays quickly emerged as one of baseball's most exciting and talented players. In 22 seasons, most with the New York and San Francisco Giants, the "Say Hey Kid" hit 660 home runs, fourth on the all-time list. He also ranks among the top 10 in career hits, runs, runs batted in, and total bases. A superb center fielder, Mays won a Gold Glove in each of the first 12 seasons it was awarded. He was twice named National League M.V.P. (1954, 1965) and played in a record-tying 24 All-Star Games.

McCain, John Sidney III, b. *Panama Canal Zone, 1936.* **U.S. Senator.** A Vietnam War hero, John McCain served as a naval pilot when he was shot down over Hanoi in 1967 and was a prisoner of war for five and a half years where he was beaten and tortured. He served two-terms (1983–87) as a member of the U.S. House of Representatives from Arizona, before being elected to the U.S. Senate in 1986. Considered an unconventional conservative, he took a traditionally conservative stance on most issues, but differed from the Republican mainstream on points including immigration reform, health care, the financing of elections and global warming. With controversial Alaskan governor Sarah Palin as his vice-presidential running mate in 2008, McCain made a strong showing, but lost the election when Democratic nominee Barack Obama won almost 53 percent of the popular vote.

McCarthy, Joseph Raymond, b. *near Appleton, Wis., 1908; d. 1957.* **American politician.** Elected to the U.S. Senate in 1946, McCarthy began an anti-communist campaign that defined his career as a senator. He claimed in 1950 to have a list of 205 communists who worked in the State Department—though he never produced the list. In 1952 he accused Secretary of Defense George C. Marshall of being a traitor and Secretary of State Dean Acheson of Communist sympathies. But his investigation of the army was his undoing in 1953 and the Senate censured him in 1954. The term "McCarthyism" became synonymous with witch-hunting.

McCartney, Paul (James Paul), b., *Liverpool, England, 1942.* **Rock-pop vocalist, bassist, guitarist, and songwriter; member of the Beatles.** Along with bandmate John Lennon, he wrote or cowrote most of the group's hit songs, including "All My Loving," "Yesterday," "Eleanor Rigby," "Here, There, and Everywhere," "Penny Lane," "Let It Be," and "The Long and Winding Road." His post-Beatles career includes both solo recordings and stints with the group Wings. Recordings include "Maybe I'm Amazed" (1970), "Another Day" (1971), "Band on the Run" (1973), and "Silly Love Songs" (1976).

McClintock, Barbara, *b. Hartford, Conn., 1902; d. 1992.* American scientist. McClintock discovered her lifework in graduate school when she identified and analyzed individual corn chromosomes, and was coauthor of a paper that proved chromosomes formed the basis of genetics. While working at the Cold Spring Harbor Laboratory in Long Island, New York, she discovered "jumping genes," which move along the chromosome, changing the behavior of neighboring genes. Her work was considered radical and was ignored by her colleagues for many years, but in the 1970's her findings were verified by fellow scientists. McClintock received the 1983 Nobel Prize in Physiology or Medicine for her discoveries and was the first woman to be the sole winner of the award.

McKinley, William, *b. Niles, Ohio, 1843; d. 1901.* Twenty-fifth president 1897–1901. The last Civil War veteran to become president, William McKinley was elected to Congress in 1876, where he wrote the record-high McKinley Tariff of 1890. He then served two terms as governor; he won the presidency in 1896. Strongly pro-business, McKinley raised the tariff still higher and reluctantly led the country into the Spanish-American War (1898). By acquiring the Philippines and other islands, America became a world power, and McKinley went on to proclaim the open-door policy in China. He was enjoying great popularity when the anarchist Leon Czolgosz shot and killed him in Buffalo, N.Y.

McLuhan, Marshall (Herbert Marshall McLuhan), *b. Edmonton, Canada, 1911; d. 1980.* Communications theorist. A communication professor at the University of Toronto and elsewhere in Canada and the U.S., McLuhan predicted the enormous impact of the electronic age in his book *Understanding Media: The Extensions of Man,* (1964). He proclaimed that "the medium is the message" and predicted the death of the printed page. Regarded by many as the "high priest of pop culture," he coined the terms "media" and "global village." As one of the first media critics, McLuhan was concerned with how technology influenced social interactions, warning that "we become what we behold."

McNamara, Robert Strange, *b. San Francisco, 1916; d. 2009.* Business executive; U.S. secretary of defense. After serving in the Pentagon during World War II, and rising to president of the Ford Motor Company, McNamara was appointed secretary of defense by President Kennedy in 1961. He brought his analytic skills to the management of the Pentagon but is best remembered for his role in the U.S. involvement in the Vietnam War. Initially in favor of the war, he came to believe that it was wrong but obeyed President Johnson's orders to send 500,000 U.S. troops and expand the war. He resigned in 1968 to become president of the World Bank (1968–81).

McPherson, Aimee Semple (Aimee Elizabeth Kennedy), *b. Salford, Ont., Canada, 1890; d. 1944.* Evangelist. "Sister Aimee" was a wildly popular Pentacostal preacher who toured the nation, holding tent revivals that drew enormous crowds. In 1923 she opened a huge domed church in Los Angeles, creating a denomination called the Church of the Foursquare Gospel. In addition to starting her own newspaper and magazine, McPherson launched a radio station for broadcasting sermons. In 1926, at the height of her fame, McPherson disappeared for more than a month. The public assumed she had drowned at the beach, but she reappeared in the desert, claiming that she had escaped from kidnappers. Her story was full of holes, and when the suspicion arose that she had disappeared to enjoy a tryst, she was accused of obstructing justice. The charges were eventually dropped, but the media circus ruined McPherson's reputation.

Mead, Margaret, *b. Philadelphia, Pa. 1901; d. 1978.* Anthropologist. Her first and most important book, *Coming of Age in Samoa* (1928), became a perennial bestseller and made her a celebrity. Based on her observations of natives in American Samoa, the book promotes the theory of cultural determinism, or the idea that cultural demands can influence an individual's development. It caused controversy for intimating that the so-called civilized world might learn something from more primitive societies. Among her other books are *Sex and Temperament in Three Primitive Societies* (1935) and *Male and Female* (1949) Awarded the Presidential Medal of Freedom in 1979, Mead was an outspoken advocate for women's rights, population control, and environmental causes.

Meany, George, *b. New York, 1894; d. 1980.* Labor leader. As president of the American Federation of Labor from 1948 to 1979, he oversaw the organization through its complicated merger with the Congress of Industrial Organizations (in 1955). Under his powerful leadership, the combined AFL-CIO used lobbying and arbitration, rather than the traditional tools of strikes and marches, to achieve its goals. Meany's support for civil rights in the workplace was instrumental in the passage of the 1964 Civil Rights Act. He was awarded the Presidential Medal of Freedom in 1977.

Medici Family. Powerful ecclesiastical, political and banking family in Italy, 14th–17th centuries Descendants of Tuscan peasants, the Medici ruled Florence and later Tuscany for most of the period between 1434 and 1737, turning the region into the center of the Italian Renaissance. After founding the Medici bank in 1422, the family members used their wealth to commission extravagant and inspired works of Renaissance art and architecture, serving as patrons to artists and architects such as Michelangelo, Raphael, Donatello, Leonardo da Vinci, Botticelli, and Brunelleschi. The Medici lines produced four popes—Leo X, Clement VII, Pius IV and Leon XI—and two queens of France: Catherine de' Medici and Marie de' Medici.

The line of **Cosimo the Elder** ruled as the unofficial princes of Florence during the 15th century and the early 16th century, the apex of the Medici rule. **Giovanni di Bicci de' Medici** (*b. 1360; d. 1429*) established the Medici bank and was appointed banker to the papacy, bringing great wealth to the family. Giovanni's son **Cosimo the Elder** (*b. 1389; d. 1464*) was the leading citizen of Florence owing to his position on the Florentine board of war and his patronage of Renaissance architecture such as the church of San Lorenzo and the monastery of Saint Mark. His grandson **Lorenzo** (*b. 1449; d. 1492*), Il Magnifico, was a poet and patron of Botticelli and Leonardo da Vinci, among others. He became the de facto ruler of Florence, and his learning, tolerant attitude, and generosity brought him such enormous popularity that Pope Sixtus IV felt threatened and helped to plot a futile assasination attmept in 1478. Lorenzo's son **Giovanni** (*b. 1475; d. 1521*) became **Pope Leo X** (1513–21) and turned Rome into a cultural and political center. However, he drained the papal treasure patronizing the arts, and paid little attention to the stirring of the Protestant Reformation that tore the Catholic Church apart throughout Europe. His cousin became **Pope Clement VII** (*b. Giulio de' Medici, 1478; d. 1534*) in 1523 as the Reformation continued to spread. The line died when Clement VII's supposed illegitimate son **Alessandro** (*b. 1511; d. 1537*), the duke of Florence, was assassinated.

The final line, the grand dukes of Tuscany, ruled Tuscany from 1569 until 1738, bringing stability to the region. When Alessandro was murdered in 1537, **Cosimo de' Medici** (*b. 1519; d. 1574*), a descendant of Cosimo the Elder's brother, became the grand duke of Tuscany in 1569, establishing the dynasty of grand dukes. He continued the tradition of patronage and his granddaughter **Marie de' Medici** (*b. 1573; d. 1642*) became queen of France when she married Henry IV in 1589. **Giovanni**

Angelo de' Medici (*b. 1499; d. 1565*) reigned as **Pope Pius IV** from 1559 to 1565. The last Medici, **Anna Marie Luisa** (*b. 1667; d. 1743*) bequeathed the Medici family art to the grand duchy and Florence. In 1738 the European powers transferred the grand duchy to the dukes of Lorraine.

Meier, Richard Alan, b. *Newark, N.J. 1934.* **Architect.** Early in his career he established a vocabulary of impeccably white buildings, composed mostly of abstract rectilinear forms, such as the Smith House (1965) on Long Island, New York. Acknowledging a debt to Le Corbusier, Frank Lloyd Wright, and Mies van der Rohe. Meier has been a prolific designer of a wide variety of buildings that reflect his sensitivity to the play of light and shadow on white surfaces and in clearly articulated spaces. Among his larger works are the High Museum in Atlanta (1980–83); the city hall and Central Library (1986–95), The Hague, Netherlands; and the Getty Center complex (1989–97) in Los Angeles. He won the Pritzker Prize in 1984.

Melville, Herman, b. *New York City, 1819; d. 1891.* **Novelist, and poet.** As a young seaman, he was captured in the South Pacific by cannibals and imprisoned for mutiny; these experiences provided material for a series of dramatic and profitable romances, beginning with *Typee* (1846). Though not popular, *Moby-Dick* (1851) was his masterpiece—a long, profound, intricate, symbolic tale of a captain's vengeful quest for the whale that had taken his leg. Its failure, and that of *Pierre* (1852) and *The Confidence Man* (1857), required him to work as a customs inspector in New York. An important novella, *Billy Budd*, was completed in his last year but not published until 1924. Poems include *Battle-Pieces* (1866) and a long narrative, *Clarel* (1876).

Mencken, H. L. (Henry Louis) b. *Baltimore, 1880; d. 1956.* **Journalist and social critic.** Mencken was a writer for the *Baltimore Sun* for much of his life. He and George Jean Nathan coedited the influential literary magazine *The Smart Set* (1914–23), and cofounded (in 1924) *The American Mercury*. No subject was safe from Mencken's barbs: women, religion, the South, the middle class, Prohibition, even democracy itself. His most famous quotes include "No one ever went broke underestimating the taste of the American public," and "Freedom of the press is limited to those who own one."

Mendel, Gregor Johann, b. *Hyncice, Czech Republic, 1822; d. 1884.* **Roman Catholic monk and experimental geneticist.** He was the first to develop, through careful pollination techniques and statistical analysis, a clear analysis of heredity. He showed that inherited characteristics are determined by a combination of genes from both parents, and that genes can be either dominant or recessive. He carried out his experiments on garden peas and other plants at the Augustinian monastery at Brno.His work, published in 1866, was ignored in his lifetime but rediscovered independently by three researchers in 1900.

Mendelssohn, Felix, *b. Hamburg, 1809; d. 1847.* German composer, pianist, organist, and conductor. Mendelssohn's father, Abraham, son of the Jewish intellectual Moses Mendelssohn, converted to Christianity. Felix was a child prodigy who began composing seriously at 17. Mendelssohn's music bridged the Classical and Romantic periods, serving as a "lovely interlude" (Nietzsche, 1886) between Beethoven and Wagner in German music. Notable works include *A Midsummer Night's Dream*, Op. 21 (1826); *Hebrides Overture (Fingal's Cave)*, Op. 26 (1830); Symphony No. 3 in A Minor, Op. 56 (*Scotch*) (1830–42); Symphony No. 5 in D Minor, Op. 107 (*Reformation*) (1830-2); Concerto No. 1 in G Minor for Piano and Orchestra, Op. 25 (1832); Symphony No. 4 in A, Op. 90 (*Italian*) (1833); Violin Concerto in E Minor, Op. 64 (1844); and the oratorio *Elijah*, Op. 70 (1846).

Messier, Mark, *b. Edmonton, Alberta, Canada, 1961.* Hockey player. Famous for his leadership, Messier is also one of the most prolific goal scorers in NHL history. He figured prominently in six Stanley Cup winning teams. He was drafted by the Edmonton Oilers in 1979 and won five Stanley Cups in Edmonton, four alongside Wayne Gretzky. In 1994, he led the New York Rangers to their first Cup in 54 years. He retired in 2004 with 1,756 games played, second only to Gordie Howe; and 1,887 points, second only to his old teammate Gretzky.

Metternich, Klemens, Furst von, *b. Koblenz, Germany, 1773; d. 1859.* Austrian diplomat and statesman. The son of an Austrian envoy, Metternich studied diplomacy, although his studies were interrupted by the advance of French revolutionary armies. As minister to France and later minister of foreign affairs (1809–48), Metternich sought to minimize Austrian exposure during the Napoleonic Wars. He was chief architect of the Congress of Vienna (1814–15), where he sought a balance of power in Europe that helped prevent a major war for 100 years, but his policies were repressive and led to the revolutions of 1848.

Michelangelo Buonarroti (Michelagnolo di Lodovico Buonarroti Simoni), *b. Caprese, Italy, 1475; d. 1564.* Sculptor, painter, draftsman, architect. A chief figure in the Roman High Renaissance, prolific in all his endeavors, Michelangelo thought of himself primarily as a sculptor. His monumental marble sculptures include the placid yet powerful *David* (1501–04) and the figure of *Moses* (ca. 1513–15) from the unfinished tomb of Julius II. Michelangelo's masterpiece is thought to be the series of frescoes on the Sistine Chapel Ceiling (1508–12) in the Vatican, which depict scenes from the book of Genesis. For the last 18 years of his life (1546–64) he served as the chief architect for St. Peter's in Rome.

Mies van der Rohe, Ludwig, *b. Aachen, Germany, 1886; d. 1969.* Architect. Mies van der Rohe intensely studied new building materials, their aesthetic potential, and the plasticity of architectural space. His Tugendhat House (1928–30) in Brno, Czech Republic, and the German Pavilion (1929) at the Barcelona International Exposition were the culmination of his European work. Mies van der Rohe emigrated to America and in 1938 became director of the architectural department at Illinois Institute of Technology, where he planned the campus and designed the major buildings (1938–56). There he worked out the simplification of architectural elements that he summed up in his famous phrase, "Less is more." Later buildings were the glass-walled concrete-and-steel Farnsworth House (1945–50) and the bronze Seagram Building (1954–58), New York, with Philip Cortelyou Johnson.

Mill, John Stuart, *b. London, 1806; d. 1873.* English philosopher and economist. Mill learned the theory of utilitarianism from his father, John Mill (1773–1836); and from Jeremy Bentham. His *Utilitarianism* (1863) systematically founded knowledge on empirical experience and reason. He is probably best known for his essay "On Liberty" (1859), which argued the paramount importance of individual liberty to oppose political and social tyranny. In later years he softened his utilitarian views and advocated women's equality, proportional voting representation, and labor unions. Other important books were *System of Logic* (1843), *Principles of Political Economy* (1848), and his *Autobiography* (1873).

Miller, Arthur, *b. New York City, 1915; d. 2005.* Playwright. Miller is considered one of America's greatest modern playwrights. His plays of the 1940's and 1950's were meditations on issues of social justice. In works such as *All My Sons* (1947) and *Death of a Salesman* (1949, winner of the Pulitzer Prize) Miller explored the ravages of society on the individual. *The Crucible* (1953), an even more overtly political play, used the Salem witch trials as an allegory for McCarthyism.

Milton, John, *b. London, 1608; d. 1674.* Poet. One of the greatest English poets, Milton was also a political and religious activist and tract writer. He served as foreign secretary in Cromwell's Puritan government. Blind after 1651, he wrote some of the finest English sonnets, but his towering stature rests on the long, biblically-based poems of his later years: the epics *Paradise Lost* (1667) and *Paradise Regained* (1671), and the "closet" drama *Samson Agonistes* (1671). *Paradise Lost* dramatizes the rebellion and defeat of Satan and the fall of Adam and Eve. *Paradise Regained* presents Christ's contrasting triumph over Satan in the wilderness.

Modigliani, Franco, *b. Rome, 1918; d. 2003.* Italian-born American economist. Modigliani was strongly influenced by the ideas of John Maynard Keynes, and his early study of savings rates demonstrated the "life-cycle" theory that individuals save most when they are earning the most—usually during their middle years—and then consume savings in later years. The theory influenced pension plans and the Social Security system. With Merton Miller he argued that investors value companies not by the amount of their debt-to-equity ratio but by their anticipated earnings, and his technique for calculating a company's future earnings became a standard tool in corporate finance. He was awarded the Nobel Prize in Economic Science in 1985.

Molière (Jean-Baptiste Poquelin), *baptized Paris, 1622; d. 1673.* Playwright. Considered France's greatest comic playwright, Molière was well educated, but left the life of the court to become a traveling actor and playwright. His comedies, exuberant farces that skewer the behavior of irrational characters, include *Tartuffe* (1664), *The Misanthrope* (1666), *The Miser* (1668), and *The Imaginary Invalid* (1673). Molière's acting company, Theatre Illustre, exists today as the Comedie Francaise.

Mondrian, Piet, *b. Amersfoort, Netherlands, 1872; d. 1944.* Painter. Regarded as one of the founders of abstract art, Mondrian is best known for works that feature geometric patterns, often involving a grid of horizontal and vertical lines with a limited palette. Mondrian hoped his paintings would convey the vitality that he saw in modern cities and in modern jazz. He was influenced by the Cubist movement. His best-known works include *Composition with Red, Blue, and Yellow* (1930) and *Broadway Boogie-Woogie* (1942–43).

Monet, Claude, *b. Paris, 1840; d. 1926.* Painter. Monet's paintings epitomize the Impressionist style, which when first introduced was criticized as sloppy and unfinished but has grown to enjoy great popularity. Influenced by Manet's concept of the color patch, Monet devoted his life to exploring the shifting qualities of light and atmosphere and is thought of as the leader of the Impressionist group. He painted landscapes *en plein air*, and in the 1890's he began producing series paintings, working at one time on a number of canvases that depicted the same site. His most famous works include *Gare St-Lazare* (1877), *Rouen Cathedral: The Portal (In Sun)* (1894), and *Water Lillies, Giverny* (1907).

Monroe, James, *b. Westmoreland County, Va., 1758; d. 1831.* Fifth U.S. president, 1817–25. The last Revolutionary hero and member of the "Virginia Dynasty" to become president, Monroe learned law as an aide to Thomas Jefferson. He served as minister to France in 1794 and governor of Virginia from 1799 to 1802; he later negotiated the Louisiana Purchase and served as both secretary of state and secretary of war under James Madison. As president, Monroe presided over the "era of good feelings," a period marked by minimal sectional or partisan discord. In 1823 he proclaimed American opposition to European encroachment in the Western Hemisphere; his policy became known as the Monroe Doctrine.

Monroe, Marilyn (Norma Jean Baker), *b. Los Angeles, 1926; d. 1962.* Movie actress. Her seductive figure and breathy voice made her the outstanding sex symbol of the 1950's, but she always felt unfulfilled as an actress. Brief roles in *The Asphalt Jungle* and *All About Eve* (both 1950) led to stardom in many films, notably *The Seven-Year Itch* (1955) and *Some Like It Hot* (1959). She married the baseball legend Joe DiMaggio and later the playwright Arthur Miller, who wrote her last film, *The Misfits* (1960).

Montaigne, Michel de, *b. near Bordeaux, France, 1533; d. 1592.* French author. A great French Renaissance thinker, Montaigne was the master of the essay as a literary form. His three-volume work *Essais* (*Essays*), published between 1580 and 1595, began as a series of self-portraits, examining his opinions on a range of subjects ("I am myself the matter of my book," he wrote), but the work grew into a study of human nature in general. Montaigne had a skeptical attitude toward human behavior and a distrust of commonly accepted ideas, though he ultimately believed in the human capacity for honesty and compassion. His work influenced many philosophers, including Descartes, Voltaire, and Rousseau, and readers around the world still turn to his essays for enlightenment and wisdom.

Montana, Joe, *b. Monongahela, Pa., 1956.* Football player. Montana led the San Francisco 49ers to four Super Bowl championships (after the 1981, 1984, 1988, and 1989 seasons) and was M.V.P. in three of them. He ended his career (1979–94) among the top five quarterbacks in most major passing categories; Montana completed a remarkable 63 percent of his passes and threw nearly two touchdowns for every interception. He was elected to seven Pro Bowls. In 1993 he was traded to the Kansas City Chiefs, where he played two more years before retiring.

Montezuma II, *b. 1466; d. 1520.* Aztec emperor. The ninth Aztec emperor, Montezuma ascended the throne of an empire that extended from Mexico to Nicaragua in 1502. His reign was one of almost incessant warfare against subject tribes, which made them willing to support Hernando Cortez in 1519. Montezuma believed Cortez to be the god Quetzacóatl, but failed to appease him. Cortez took Montezuma hostage at Tenochtitlán and attempted to rule the Aztecs through him. He was killed in 1520—by the Spanish according to Aztec accounts, by the Aztecs according to the Spanish.

More, Thomas, *b. London, 1478; d. 1535.* Statesman, author, and Catholic saint. A distinguished lawyer, More was drafted into diplomatic service by King Henry VIII, knighted, and appointed lord chancellor in 1529. A devout Catholic, he disapproved of the king's first divorce, and when he refused to swear to the Act of Succession and Supremacy naming Henry head of the church in England, he was imprisoned and executed. More, a humanist, was the author of the brilliant satirical tale *Utopia* (1516), a description of a mythical, totally rational, propertyless realm, which introduced a new literary genre. More also wrote biographies, including *A History of Richard III*, poetry, and devotional works.

Morgan, John Pierpont, *b. Hartford., Conn., 1837; d. 1913.* American financier. Morgan worked three years in New York before joining his father's London-based bank. Soon he was a partner in his own bank and invested in railroads, including railroad mergers that stifled competition. This became J.P. Morgan and Co. in 1895. Other investments included Thomas Edison's incandescent light and generation plants, and in 1892 the creation of General Electric. In 1901 he combined a number of steel companies into the United Steel Corporation, the largest industrial company in the world. He stopped the U.S. gold crisis of 1894–95 and led the rescue of the banking system in 1907.

Morrison, Toni, *b. Lorain, Ohio, 1931.* Novelist and essayist. Morrison won the Nobel Prize for Literature in 1993. She began publishing fiction in 1970 with her novel *The Bluest Eye.* From the start her work, which chronicles the African-American experience, has been characterized by poetic language, dazzling intellect, and innovative storytelling. Other novels include *Sula* (1973), *Song of Solomon* (1977), *Tar Baby* (1981), *Beloved* (1987, winner of the Pulitzer Prize), and *Paradise* (1998). *Playing in the Dark: Whiteness and the Literary Imagination* was published in 1992.

Morse, Samuel Finley Breese, *b. Charlestown, Mass., 1791; d. 1872.* American inventor. Morse was an accomplished artist, known especially as a portrait painter, before becoming invovled with electricity. In 1844 he successfully tested his device to send electrical impulses through a wire that drove another device to inscribe a series of dots and dashes on a moving strip of paper at the other end. He also devised a code for the letters of the alphabet, the Morse Code. The telegraph came to dominate long-distance telegraphic communications in a wide range of applications.

Moses, Grandma (Anna Mary Robertson), *b. Greenwich, N.Y., 1860; d. 1961.* Painter. In her seventies, after a life of farming in Virginia and upstate New York, and with no formal training, Grandma Moses began to paint rural scenes, such as *Wash Day* (1945) and *Hoosick Falls, N.Y. in Winter* (1944). Her treatment of figures and buildings is considered primitive yet charming; details are often borrowed from Currier & Ives prints and magazines. She was discovered when a collector found some of her pictures at the Women's Exchange of a drugstore in Hoosick Falls.

Mozart, Wolfgang Amadeus, *b. Salzburg, 1756; d. 1791.* Austrian composer, keyboard player, violinist, violist, and conductor. A child prodigy, he was taught the harpsichord, violin, and organ by his father, who when the boy was six began to present him in concerts before the royalty of Europe. By the time Mozart was 13 he had written symphonies, concertos, and sonatas, and was known throughout the world of music. By the time of his death at age 35 he had produced more than 600 works—symphonies, operas, concertos, quartets, cantatas—almost all of them of the most astonishing quality. He is regarded by many as the world's greatest natural musical genius; his mature compositions are distinguished by their melodic beauty, formal elegance, and richness of harmony and texture. Notable works include Piano Concerto No. 21 in C (K.

467, 1785), Serenade No. 13 in G for Strings (*Eine kleine Nachtmusik*, K. 525, 1787), Symphony No. 40 in G Minor (K. 550, 1788), Symphony No. 41 in C (*Jupiter*, K. 551, 1788), and the operas *Le Nozze de Figaro* (*The Marriage of Figaro*, 1785–86); *Don Giovanni* (1787); *Cosi fan tutti* (1790); and *Die Zauberflöte* (*The Magic Flute*) (K. 620, 1790-1).

Muhammad, *b. Mecca,   ca. 570; d. 632.* **Prophet of Islam.** Muhammed was employed by the widow Khadijah (whom he later married) to take caravans to Syria, where he met Christians and Jews. He struggled with ideas of monotheism in contrast to the polytheism of Mecca. Finally he concluded that there is but one God, whose prophet he was; in a visitation, he was told to recite, words ultimately collected in the Koran. With the hejira (flight) to Yathrib (now Medina) in 622 (the Muslim calendar's first year) he established his theocratic state, later conquering Mecca and purifying it of idols.

Muir, John, *b. Dunbar, Scotland, 1838; d. 1914.* **U.S. naturalist.** Muir was instrumental in the creation of the National Park System. His writings about nature and his friendship with President Theodore Roosevelt led to federal protection for Yosemite (1890), Sequoia (1890), Mount Rainier (1899), Petrified Forest (1906), and Grand Canyon (1908) National Parks. In 1892, he led a group of naturalists in forming the Sierra Club, and he served as the group's first president until his death. Muir's camping trip with Roosevelt at Yosemite persuaded the president to set aside more than 148 million acres of additional national forest.

Murdoch, Rupert (Keith Rupert Murdoch), *b. Melbourne, Australia, 1931.* **Media entrepreneur, founder and head of the News Corporation, Ltd.** After briefly working on the London *Daily Express*, where he honed his skills as a sensational journalist, Murdoch returned to Australia to run the *Sunday Mail* and *The News* in Adelaide. His recipe for success was a combination of scandal, sex, and human interest stories, which he applied to the *New York Post*, the *Boston Herald*, and others, as he built his American newspaper empire. In the 1980's and 1990's, he created Fox, Inc., which became a major TV network known for its conservative editorializing. His other holdings include HarperCollins Publishers and British Sky Broadcasting.

Musial, Stan, *b. Donora, Pa., 1920.* **Baseball player.** In more than two decades with the St. Louis Cardinals, "Stan the Man" made his mark as one of the all-time great slugging outfielders. With his distinctive corkscrew batting stance, he was known for remarkable consistency at the plate (his 3,630 hits still rank fourth in baseball history). Musial won seven batting titles, was named the National League's M.V.P. three times, and was a 24-time All-Star. After his playing career ended, Musial spent the 1967 season as general manager of the Cardinals, orchestrating a World Series title. He was inducted into the Baseball Hall of Fame in 1969.

Mussolini, Benito, *b. Predappio, Italy, 1883; d. 1945.* **Italian dictator.** Mussolini began his career as a journalist and socialist labor agitator with a penchant for violence. During World War I, he became a fierce nationalist, and in 1919 he founded the Fasci di Combattimento—Europe's first fascist party. He became prime minister in 1922 and instituted a program of salutary public works. His foreign policy proved disastrous, from the widely condemned invasion of Abyssinia (Ethiopia) to his support of Nazi Germany. Arrested in 1943, he was rescued by German paratroopers, only to be killed attempting to flee Italy in disguise.

Nabokov, Vladimir, *b. St. Petersburg, Russia, 1899; d. 1977.* **Russian-American novelist.** Nabokov left Russia after the revolution of 1917, studied in England, and settled in the United States in 1940. His early novels were in Russian, and he began writing in English in 1938. *Bend Sinister* (1947) was followed by one of the most famous— and infamous—books of the century, *Lolita* (1955). An ironic, comic-serious, self-reflectively artistic account of an earnest madman's love for a 12-year old girl, it was banned in America for three years. Nabokov is considered one of the geniuses of 20th-century fiction—an erudite, allusive, verbally adroit weaver of meanings. Other novels include *Pnin* (1957), *Pale Fire* (1957), and *Ada* (1969).

Namath, Joe, *b. Beaver Falls, Pa., 1943.* **Football player.** Namath burst onto the scene with the New York Jets, earning AFL rookie of the year honors in 1965 and leading the league in passing in 1966 and 1967. His high-flying lifestyle and cocksure attitude earned him the nickname "Broadway Joe" and made him a celebrity. In 1969, he guaranteed that his Jets of the upstart AFL would upset the heavily favored Baltimore Colts in Super Bowl III, and he won the M.V.P. award in New York's 16–7 win. Knee and shoulder injuries limited Namath in later years, and he retired in 1977. He was elected to the Hall of Fame in 1985.

Napoléon I (Napoléon Bonaparte; Napoleon), *b. 1769, Ajaccio, Corsica; 1821.* **French emperor.** A brilliant soldier, Napoleon distinguished himself in the French Revolutionary Wars and was a general by 24.

Though defeated in Egypt and Syria in 1798–99, in the latter year he became supreme ruler in France and proclaimed himself emperor in 1804. His important and long-lasting reforms in education, civil law, and military organization were offset by his aggressive expansionism. His brilliant victories over a coalition of European powers at Austerlitz (1805), Jena (1806), and Borodino (1812) gave him an aura of invincibility. His invasion of Russia (1812) proved his undoing, and in 1814 he was exiled to Elba. He returned in 1815, but was defeated at the Battle of Waterloo and exiled to remote St. Helena.

Napoléon III (Louis-Napoléon), *b. Paris, 1808; d. 1873*. **French emperor.** Nephew of Napoléon I, Louis Napoléon was raised in exile but developed a keen interest in politics and military affairs. Attempts to usurp power in France ended in exile in the U.S. and England before he became president (1848) and emperor (1852). He promoted social welfare and industrialization domestically, sought rapprochement with England and promoted the Suez Canal. France's humiliating defeat in the Franco-Prussian War forced him into exile in England.

Nasser, Gamal Abdel, *b. Alexandria, 1918; d. 1970*. **Egyptian president.** One of the most important figures in modern Arab history, Nasser foughtin the 1948 Arab-Israeli War. After leading two coups in 1952 and 1954, he was elected president in 1956. His nationalization of the Suez Canal succeeded when the U.S. failed to support Britain and France. Nasser's effort to create a pan-Arab state, the United Arab Republic (1958–61)was a failure. The 1967 Six-Day War ended in Egypt's defeat and the loss of the Sinai Peninsula. Nasser also promoted the Soviet-funded AswanHigh Dam on the Nile River (1960–70).

Navratilova, Martina, *b. Prague, Czech Republic, 1956*. **Tennis player.** Shortly after turning pro, Martina Navratilova defected to the United States. A serve-and-volley player, she added a jolt of pure power to the women's game. She enjoyed a historic run as the most dominant female player in tennis, ranked number one in the world for more than six straight years. Navratilova won 18 singles and 40 doubles Grand Slam titles (many of the doubles events were won alongside Pam Shriver). She holds a record nine Wimbledon singles championships. In the 1980's Navratilova came out as a lesbian, and she has frequently advocated for gay rights. She was inducted into the International Tennis Hall of Fame in 2000. ESPN ranked her 19th among the 100 Greatest Athletes of the 20th century.

Nebuchadnezzar, *b. Babylon, ca. 630; d. 562 B.C.* **Chaldaean king.** Second ruler of the Chaldaean Empire founded by his father, he was an able military commander who succeeded his father in 605. He campaigned extensively in Syria, Palestine, and northern Arabia and against Egypt, and he became a major figure in the diplomacy of the Near East generally. In 586 he captured Jerusalem and took many of its leading citizens in captivity to Babylon—a city he had done much to improve—though he is viewed in a generally positive light by the authors of the Hebrew Bible.

Nehru, Jawaharlal, *b. Allahabad, India, 1889; d. 1964*. **Indian politician.** The English-educated Nehru joined the Indian National Congress in 1919, serving as general secretary (1923–25, 1927–29) and president (from 1929). During World War II, Nehru favored support for Britain but sided with Gandhi; both were jailed, Nehru for the ninth time. He split with Gandhi over the idea of partition with Pakistan, and he became India's first prime minister in 1947. An advocate of Democrat Socialism, he favored non-alignment in foreign policy. His daughter Indira Gandhi and grandson Rajiv Gandhi also served as prime minister.

Nelson, Horatio (Viscount Nelson), *b. Burnham Thorpe, England, 1758; d. 1805*. **Naval commander.** Nelson was knighted for his imaginative tactics at the battle of Cape St. Vincent in 1797. In 1798, at the battle of the Nile, he annihilated the French fleet that had transported Napoleon to Egypt. In 1801, he destroyed the Danish fleet at the battle of Copenhagen. In 1805, he had his greatest triumph, defeating a combined French and Spanish fleet at the battle of Trafalgar, where he was killed.

Nero (Lucius Domitus Ahenobarbus) *b. 37 A.D.; d. 68*. **Roman emperor (54–68).** Nero owed his rise to power to his mother Agrippina, sister of Caligula and great-granddaughter of Augustus. She urged her new husband, the emperor Claudius, to make her son his successor and then murdered Claudius. Under the tutelage of Seneca the Younger, Nero began his reign with political and social reforms. His reputation as a mad tyrant arose after he had his mother killed, in 59, and later his wife. At this point, he began to dwell on obscure religious pursuits, and developed delusions of artistic greatness. During this period a great fire destroyed half of Rome (64) and Nero blamed the Christians, whom he subsequently persecuted. He killed himself in 68, having been abandoned by his army and political supporters.

Neruda, Pablo, *b. Parral, Chile, 1904; d. 1973*. **Poet.** Neruda, awarded the Nobel Prize for Literature in 1971, stands as one of the great poets of the 20th century. He published one of his best-known works, *Twenty Love Poems and a Song of Despair* (1924) at a young age, and he traveled the world as a diplomat for his native Chile. A political activist, Neruda sided with the Republicans in the Spanish Civil War and returned to Chile as an elected member of the Communist Party. His other works include *Spain in the Heart* (1937) and *Canto General* (1950).

Netanyahu, Benjamin, *b. Tel Aviv, Israel, 1949.* Prime Minister of Israel. Netanyahu served two terms as Israeli prime minister, from 1996–99, and again beginning in 2009. Elected to the Knesset (Israeli parliament) in 1988, he became leader of the Likud party in 1993. In 1996 he became the youngest Israeli prime minister. During his first term, Israel's relationship with Syria worsened, and tension over the West Bank led to violent protests and bombings. In 1993 Netanyahu had opposed the Israel-PLO peace accords and Israeli withdrawals from the West Bank and Gaza Strip, but as prime minister he fluctuated in his position on control of the West Bank. His 1998 decision to give the Palestinians control of as much as 40 percent of the West Bank prompted several factions of his government to quit, leading the Knesset to dissolve the government. In his second term as prime minister he and Likud became firm supporters of the large number of Israeli settlements in former areas held by Palestinians, putting him in direct confrontation with U.S. policies.

Newman, Paul, *b. Cleveland, Ohio, 1925; d. 2008.* Actor. Coming from Broadway and TV, he made his mark playing cocky outsiders in such films as *The Hustler* (1961) and *Hud* (1963), and craven heroes in Tennessee Williams's *Cat on a Hot Tin Roof* (1958) and *Sweet Bird of Youth* (1962). Later films revealed his versatility Butch Cassidy and *The Sundance Kid* (1969), *The Sting* (1973), *The Verdict* (1982), and *The Color of Money* (1986), for which he finally won an Oscar. He founded Newman's Own, a line of food products, and he donated the profits to charity.

Newton, Sir Isaac, *b. Lincolnshire, England, 42. d. 1727* English physicist and mathematician. Newton was a student at Cambridge University when a plague epidemic caused Cambridge to close during 1665–66. During this period, he first developed new methods in mathematics—extending the binomial theorem, finding a useful method for approximating solutions to equations, and inventing the calculus. He also experimented with light, finding that white light is a mixture of all colors, and began to think about gravity. Instead of publishing his work, however, he circulated manuscripts to friends. After he built the first

reflecting telescopes, the Royal Society elected him a fellow. He began to communicate some of his discoveries more widely. He was urged to publish his theory explaining the motions of planets, and Newton's *Principia* (1687) contained his laws of motion and gravity as well as such topics as artificial satellites. He wrote a full account of his study of light, called *Opticks* (1704). Although Newton devoted a major portion of his life to alchemy, the predecessor of chemistry, he did not publish any results.

Nicklaus, Jack, *b. Columbus, Ohio, 1940.* Golfer. The "Golden Bear" compiled one of the most impressive record in the annals of golf. With his mammoth drives and clutch shot-making, he claimed a record 18 victories in major PGA events—six Masters, five PGA Championships, four U.S. Opens, and three British Opens. Nicklaus won more than 100 tournaments in all, including 70 on the PGA Tour (second only to Sam Snead). He was named Player of the Year five times and was the tour's leading money winner eight times.

Nicholson, Jack, *b. Neptune, N.J., 1937.* Movie actor. After 10 years in B movies, he became a star in *Easy Rider* (1969). Since then his bad-boy grin and devilish eyebrows have lit up comedies and dramas. He has won Oscars for *One Flew Over the Cuckoo's Nest* (1975), *Terms of Endearment* (1983), and *As Good as It Gets* (1997). Other notable films include *Chinatown* (1974) and *Batman* (1989).

Nietszche, Friedrich Wilhelm, *b. Roecken, Prussia, 1844; d. 1900,* Philosopher. Originally a professor of classical languages, Nietzsche wrote his philosophical works over 20 years, before suffering a mental breakdown in 1889. He argued for a new, heroic mentality that would reject the "slave morality" of Christianity, part of the bourgeois Western civilization that he rejected with passion. A group of "supermen," with a will to power, would lead the mass of inferior humanity. His main works are *Thus Spake Zarathustra* (1883–91) and *Beyond Good and Evil* (1886). His doctrines were later used to justify Nazi racial and national ideology, but most scholars regard this as a perversion of Nietzsche's own thought.

Nijinsky, Vaslav, *b. Kiev, Russia, 1889; d. 1950.* Dancer-choreographer. Nijinsky studied in St. Petersburg at the Imperial Theatre from 1898–1907, making his professional debut a year before his graduation. He joined the Maryinsky Theatre Ballet from 1907–1911, and from 1909 danced with Diaghilev's Ballet Russes. Diaghilev encouraged him to choreograph, and Nijinsky created his famous *L'Après Midi d'un faune* in 1912 and *Le Sacre du Printemps*, with a score by Igor Stravinsky, a year later; *Sacre* caused riots on its Paris premiere. He left the company in 1913, beginning to show the effects of his coming mental illness; he last performed in 1919, and he spent the rest of his life primarily in institutions for treatment of his schizophrenia.

Nimitz, Chester W., *b. Fredericksburg, Tex., 1885; d. 1966.* Naval commander. After Pearl Harbor, Nimitz became commander of the U.S. Pacific fleet and eventually the supreme Allied commander for the Pacific. Under his direction, the outnumbered U.S. Navy won major victories over the Japanese navy at the battles of the Coral Sea and Midway in 1942. He was also in charge of the amphibious operation in the Pacific that culminated in the capture of Iwo Jima and Okinawa in 1945. He ended his career as chief of Naval Operations.

Nixon, Richard M., *b. Yorba Linda, Calif., 1913; d. 1994.* Thirty-seventh U.S. president, 1969–74. The only president to resign from office, Richard Milhous Nixon rode into Congress on the Republican wave of 1946, and gained fame in the anticommunist trial of Alger Hiss. He entered the Senate in 1950 and was chosen as Eisenhower's running mate in 1952. After losing the 1960 presidential election to John F. Kennedy, Nixon staged a comeback and won the presidency in 1968. Seeking "peace with honor" in Vietnam, Nixon built up the South Vietnamese army and withdrew U.S. troops—while massively escalating bombing of North Vietnam. During his reelection campaign in 1972, five burglars were arrested in the Democratic Party headquarters, and the ensuing "Watergate" scandal exposed the Nixon administration's rampant corruption, obstruction of justice, and abuse of power. The House began impeachment proceedings, and on August 9, 1974, Nixon resigned the presidency.

Nurmi, Paavo, *b. Finland, 1897; d. 1973.* Track star. Nurmi established his reputation as the greatest distance runner in the history of the modern Olympics by winning nine gold and three silver medals at the games of 1920, 1924, and 1928. Known as the "Flying Finn," he won six individual golds in 1,500m, 5,000m, 10,000m, and cross-country events. He was barred from the 1932 Olympics for accepting expense money while on tour.

Obama, Barack H. II, *b. Honolulu, Hawaii, 1961.* Forty-fourth U.S. president. Obama was born to an American mother and Kenyan father, who left the family when Barack was two. After his mother remarried, he spent several years living in Indonesia before returning to Hawaii. Obama attended Occidental College before trans-ferring to Columbia University, where he received his bachelor's degree. After spending several years as a community organizer on Chicago's South Side, Obama earned his law degree from Harvard University, where he served as the first African American president of *Harvard Law Review.* Upon returning to Chicago he became active in politics, winning an Illinois Senate seat in 1996. Eight short years later Obama had been elected to the United States Senate and delivered the keynote speech at the 2004 Democratic National Convention. In 2009, Obama became the first African American president of the United States. Barack Obama won the 2009 Nobel Peace Prize.

O'Connor, Flannery, *b. Savannah, Ga., 1925; d. 1964.* Short-story writer, novelist. O'Connor's literary works are few but her contributions are significant. After being diagnosed with lupus while in her twenties, O'Connor returned to her family's home in Milledgeville, Ga., where she lived for the remainder of her life. She was a devout Catholic and her short stories are remarkable for their moral, ironic, and comic qualities. Her works include two short-story collections, *A Good Man Is Hard to Find* (1955) and *Everything That Rises Must Converge* (1964); along with two novels, *Wise Blood* (1952) and *The Violent Bear It Away* (1960).

O'Higgins, Bernardo, *b. Chillán, Chile, 1776; d. 1842.* South American revolutionary leader and first Chilean head of state. O'Higgins commanded the military forces that won independence from Spain. As general in chief of Chile's defensive forces, he fought unsuccessfully against the invading Peruvian army and was forced into exile. In 1817, O'Higgins helped to reconquer Chile from the Spanish, and he served as the country's supreme director for the next six years. O'Higgins was associated with an Argentine-sponsored scheme of continental independence, and in 1823 he was forced to resign in the face of growing Chilean nationalism.

O'Keeffe, Georgia, *b. San Prairie, Wisc., 1887; d. 1986.* Painter. A highly influential figure in American art, O'Keeffe developed a unique style that borrowed from naturalism, realism, symbolism, abstraction, and photography. She was married to the photographer Alfred Stieglitz. O'Keeffe is best known for semiabstracted large close-up flower paintings, such as *Black Iris* (1926). Other works include *Cow's Skull with Calico Roses* (1931). She is also known for her cityscapes and images from New Mexico, where she moved in 1949. After going blind in 1971, she learned to be a ceramist.

Olivier, Laurence, *b. Dorking, England, 1907; d. 1989.* Actor, director, and producer. He made his stage debut in Shakespearean repertory at Stratford-on-Avon in 1922 and made his first film in 1930. His refined looks, magnetic voice, and athletic versatility made him a Renaissance man of stage and screen, notably in major Shakespearean roles at London's Old Vic and then at the National Theatre. He was appointed as first director of the National Theatre in 1962. He also directed and performed in three Shakespeare films: *Henry V* (1945), the Oscar-winning *Hamlet* (1948), and *Richard III* (1955). Always changing—from his dashing Heathcliff in *Wuthering Heights* (1939) to his seedy Archie Rice in *The Entertainer* (1960) to the dying Lord Marchmain in TV's *Brideshead Revisited* (1981)—yet always Olivier.

Onassis, Jacqueline Bouvier, *b. Southampton, N.Y., 1929; d. 1994.* **American first lady and socialite.** Wife of John Fitzgerald Kennedy, she entered the White House with him in 1961 on his election as president. She became known for her stylish fashions and redecoration of the White House. After President Kennedy's assassination, she retired to private life, and later married the Greek shipping magnate Aristotle Onassis in 1968. One of her most memorable personal achievements was the preservation of Grand Central Station in New York.

O'Neal, Shaquille, *b. Newark, N.J., 1972.* **Basketball player.** Beginning in 1992, the 7'1" O'Neal used all of his 300 pounds to dominate the low post, and helped transform the Orlando Magic from a mediocre expansion team to a playoff contender. O'Neal was an even more dominating presence off the court as a marketing giant who capitalized on his amiable personality to capture the attention of a new generation of teenagers. After joining the Los Angeles Lakers, he was named M.V.P. of the N.B.A. finals three times in a row while leading the team to consecutive championships (2000–02).

O'Neil, Buck (John Jordan), *b. Carrabell, Fla., 1911; d. 2006.* **Baseball player.** A slick-fielding first baseman in the Negro Leagues, O'Neil barnstormed with Satchel Paige, won a batting title, and successfully managed the Kansas City Monarchs. By the time Jackie Robinson broke the color barrier in major league baseball, O'Neil was too old to make the transition. But he became a scout (signing Ernie Banks and Lou Brock) and was eventually hired as a bench coach by the Cubs, becoming the first African-American coach in the majors. O'Neil made it his mission to preserve the legacy of the great African-American players of his era, serving as chairman of the Negro Leagues Baseball Museum in Kansas City.

O'Neill, Eugene, *b. New York City, 1888; d. 1953.* **Playwright.** O'Neill was a four-time Pulitzer Prize winner and winner of the Nobel Prize in Literature in 1936, His most famous plays were often intensely personal, drawing on the combative relationship of his parents, his brother's alcoholism, and his own depression. O'Neill was a master of many different styles, employing the techniques of expressionism, symbolism, and realism to explore psychology. His major works include *The Emperor Jones* (1920), *The Hairy Ape* (1922), *Mourning Becomes Electra* (1931), *The Iceman Cometh* (1939), and *Long Day's Journey Into Night* (1943).

Orr, Bobby, *b. Parry Sound, Ont., Canada, 1947.* **Hockey player.** The first hockey defenseman to take an active role on offense, he revolutionized the game. He joined the Boston Bruins in 1966 as an 18-year-old, signing a two-year contract for $75,000, an unheard-of amount for a rookie. Orr became the only defenseman to win the scoring title (1970 and 1975) and the first player to record more than 100 assists in a season (1971). He led the Bruins to Stanley Cup championships in 1970 and 1972 and was the NHL's M.V.P. three straight years (1970–72) before injuries forced his retirement at age 30 in 1978.

Orwell, George (Eric A. Blair), *b. Bengal, India, 1903; d. 1950.* **English essayist and novelist.** At 19 Orwell became a policeman in Burma, the setting for his first novel, *Burmese Days* (1934), and one of his best essays, "Shooting an Elephant" (1936), both indictments of British imperialism. He embraced socialism and joined the Republican forces in the Spanish Civil War, where he recognized the tyranny of Soviet communism, described in *Homage to Catalonia* (1938). His two most famous books extended this view: *Animal Farm* (1945), a fable exposing the corruption of the Soviet system; and *Nineteen Eighty-Four* (1949), a novel depicting a nightmarish world under an enslaving dictatorship. Orwell's lucid prose is a modern English model.

Otto, Nikolaus August, *b. 1832, d. 1891.* **German inventor.** Otto learned in the early 1860's that a balky internal combustion engine running on coal gas had been introduced in France by Jean-Joseph Lenoir. Otto developed a more improved version, which he exhibited at the Paris World's Fair in 1867. While manufacturing and selling that engine, he designed a much improved four-stroke internal combustion engine (1876), which remains the basis of the most common type of engine today. Variations on Otto's engines were used in the first motorbikes and automobiles.

Owens, Jesse, b. *Danville, Ala., 1913; d. 1980.* Track-and-field star. The son of sharecroppers, Jesse Owens turned in the most memorable performance in the history of the Olympics by winning four gold medals—in the 100-meter, 200-meter, long jump, and 4x100 relay—at the 1936 games in Berlin. The stunning performance by an African American embarrassed Adolf Hitler, who had declared the Berlin Games a showcase for Aryan supremacy. The previous year, at Ohio State University, Owens tied the world record for the 100-yard dash and set new marks in the 220-yard dash, 220-yard hurdles, and long jump—all one day.

Ovid (Pulius Ovidius Naso) b. *Sulmona, Italy, 43 B.C.; d. ?17 A.D.* Roman poet. Although his father urged him to study law, Ovid was a natural poet. Even his earliest works, the *Amores*, notably *The Art of Love*, display extraordinary skill with meter and verse. Emperor Augustus morally objected to Ovid's subject matter and exiled him just after he completed what most consider his masterpiece, *Metamorphoses*, an epic containing 15 books of mythology. In exile, Ovid completed many works, including *Fasti* concerning the Roman calendar.

Page, Larry (Lawrence Edward Page), b. *East Lansing, Mich., 1973.* Co-founder of Google. Page earned a computer engineering degree from the University of Michigan (1995) before entering the doctorate program at Stanford University. Here he met Sergey Brin, and together they would create one of the most successful Internet sites to date. Google, an Internet search engine, was created out of Page's dorm room and by 1998 they had raised enough money to officially form as a company. Google went public in 2004 earning Page over $3.8 billion dollars. He stayed active in the company helping them to acquire You Tube in 2006 and in 2011 was reinstated as the C.E.O. Page remains committed to finding sources of alternative energy, funding numerous projects through Google.org, the company's philanthropic arm.

Paine, Thomas b. *Thetford, Norfolk, England, 1737; d. 1809.* English-American writer. Born in England, Paine moved to America in 1774; there he published political articles against slavery and in support of American independence. "Common Sense" (1776) greatly influenced the Declaration of Independence. Paine argued for "a continental constitution" that would lay out a strong central government for the independent colonies. In 1787 he went to Europe where he wrote *Rights of Man* (1791) in support of the French Revolution. His arguments against monarchy and for social welfare gained him a indictment of trea-son in England. In France, he was jailed by Robespierre's repressive regime for his criticism of its terror tactics. Paine became (inaccurately) known as an atheist after publishing *The Age of Reason* (1794).

Palestrina, Giovanni Pierluigi da, b. *Palestrina, ca. 1525; d. 1594.* Composer. Prolific Italian composer of masses (104), motets (more than 300), and madrigals (more than 140). He was one of the primary musical figures of the late 16th century, and one of the few Italian musicians of that era who assimilated the polyphonic techniques of their French and Flemish predecessors. Notable works include *Missa Papae Marcelli* (c. 1562), *Missa Brevis* (1570), *Jesu Rex Admirabilis*, *Litaniae de Beata Virgine Maria*, *Magnificat*, *Missa Tu Es Petrus*, and *Stabat Mater*.

Palladio, Andrea, b. *Padua, 1508; d. 1580.* Italian architect and architectural theorist of the Renaissance. Of all his contemporaries, he had the longest-lasting influence. In 1536 he was given an opportunity to study the ancient classical buildings in Rome, and his careful measurements, calculations of proportions, and drawings formed the basis of his later seminal buildings and writings. He designed grand houses and churches in Vicenza and Venice, but it is his villas in and around Vicenza that have had the most influence. Among these are the Villa Capra (1560's), known as the Rotonda, and the Villa Barbaro (1550's) in Maser. "Palladian" has entered the lexicon as a term to describe countless buildings ever since. His influence was also spread by his *Four Books on Architecture*, a theoretical work of idealized buildings that ranks among the most important written works in architecture.

Palmer, Arnold, b. *Latrobe, Pa., 1929.* Golfer. Palmer's popularity is widely credited for the explosive growth of golf during the 1960's. His personal charisma and exciting style of play attracted throngs of followers, referred to as "Arnie's army," wherever he played and brought golf to the masses through the new medium of television. Palmer won a total of 61 PGA events, including seven majors (four Masters, two British Opens, and one U.S. Open), from 1955 to 1973. He was named Player of the Year in 1960 and 1962.

Parker, Charlie, (Charles Christopher Parker, Jr.) b. *Kansas City, Kan., 1920; d. 1955.* Jazz saxophonist, also known as "Bird." Perhaps the greatest jazz saxophonist of all time and (along with the trumpeter Dizzy Gillespie and pianist Bud Powell) the founder of the modern bebop style. Parker could play remarkably fast lines on his alto sax, employing intricate extended harmonies, but every note made sense in relation to the song's chord structure. He suffered from heroin addiction, and died at age 34. His recordings include "Ornithology" (1945), "Ko Ko" (1945), "Yardbird Suite" (1945), "Parker's Mood" (1948), and "Scrapple from the Apple" (1949).

Parnell, Charles Stewart, b. *Avondale, Ireland, 1846; d. 1891.* Irish statesman and nationalist. Elected to Parliament in 1875, Parnell was a strong proponent of home rule for Ireland. He supported the Liberal prime minister William Gladstone in the election of 1880 but broke with him over the Land Act. He was jailed in 1881–82 for advocating disobedience to the act and was released by Gladstone when he renounced these policies. His political career was shattered in 1890 by the revelation of an illicit affair with Katherine O'Shea, wife of one of his lieutenants.

Pascal, Blaise, b. *Clermont-Ferrand, France 1623; d. 1662.* Mathematician, physicist, and philosopher. Pascal extended the principles of hydrostatics (1648), creating the theory behind the hydraulic press. In mathematics he helped found probability theory (1654) and analyzed infinite series and the geometry of curves. Pascal invented the first mechanical calculator, a machine that used gears. The first working model of his adding machine, the pascaline, appeared for sale in 1642. He is considered a major French philosopher and author for his books *Provincial Letters* (1656) and *Pensées* (1670), a classic work of Christian apologetics in which he argued that mankind can achieve glory only through Jesus Christ.

Pasteur, Louis, b. *Dole, France, 1822; d. 1895.* French chemist. Leading a scientific life of rigorous experimentation, Pasteur made fundamental contributions to the study of organic and mineral molecules, bacterial contamination and its elimination ("pasteurization"), the germ theory of diseases, sanitary practices, and vaccines. Pasteur's breakthroughs, derived from his studies of fermentation were critical to the success of beer and dairy industries, and because his research on silkworm diseases, the silk industry. The vaccines developed to fight anthrax and rabies changed the way that medicine is practiced.

Patrick (Saint), b. *Britain, ca. 387; d. 461.* Patron saint of Ireland. Patrick's family were Christians and Roman citizens. At 16, he was kidnapped by Irish marauders and taken to Ireland to work as a herder for six years. In his own account, the *Confessio*, he described a dream that allowed him to escape to Gaul, and another dream—after he had entered a monastery and returned to Britain—in which he

was instructed to Christianize Ireland. In 432, after years of study under Bishop Germanus of Auxerre, he was sent to Ireland, accommodating his message to tribal structures and laws, was extraordinarily successful, converting nearly the entire nation by the time of his death.

Patton, George S., b. *San Gabriel, Calif., 1885; d. 1945.* American military leader. Early on Patton appreciated the potential of tank warfare. Given command of an armored division in 1940, he saw action in North Africa and Sicily. He was relieved of command for striking a hospitalized soldier but was eventually given command of the Third Army, which raced across northern France in 1944 following the invasion of Normandy. That army helped relieve Americans surrounded at Bastogne during the battle of the Bulge. Patton, whose nickname was "Old Blood and Guts," died in a car crash in Heidelberg after the war's end.

Paul (Saint), b. *Tarsus, Asia Minor; d. ca. 64–67.* Christian missionary and writer. Paul, originally Saul, was a Jewish rabbi who persecuted early Christians. About the year 35, riding on the road to Damascus, he was reportedly knocked from his horse, heard God's voice, and converted to Christianity. After retiring to the desert for many years to study and meditate, he became the most important figure in early Christianity. Reaching out to non-Jews, he was the church's greatest missionary and its first, and most important, theologian. He set up communities throughout Greece and Asia Minor, and wrote them his Epistles, which explicated such fundamental Christian doctrines as grace and resurrection.

Pavarotti, Luciano, b. *Modena, Italy, 1935; d. 2007.* Tenor. After his debuts in Italy (1961) and in the United States (1967), the "king of the high C's" became a worldwide favorite in such notable roles as Donizetti's Nemorino, Puccini's Rodolfo and Cavarodossi, and Verdi's Riccardo, often performing at the Metropolitan Opera. He has made numerous concert recordings with great sopranos and was one of the "Three Tenors"—a venture that brought him mounting fame and fortune.

Paz, Octavio, b. *1914, Mexico City; d. 1998.* Poet and essayist. After publishing poems as a university student (*Forest Moon* 1933) Paz visited his father's native Spain and wrote a successful book of poems reflecting that country's revolution: *Beneath Your Clear Shadow and Other Poems* (1937). Paz was Mexico's leading literary figure of the 20th century, and a Nobel laureate. His poetry approached politics (from a liberal-leftist direction), religion (he was influenced by Hinduism and Buddhism) and physical love. Volumes include *The Sun Stone* (1957), *The Violent Condition,* (1958) *East Slope* (1971), and *A Tree Within* (1987). Paz was Mexico's ambassador to India from 1962 to 1968.

Peary, Robert Edwin, *b. Cresson, Pa., 1856; d. 1920.* **American polar explorer.** Peary made four expeditions to Greenland between 1886 and 1900. In 1902, he attempted to reach the North Pole with his African-American valet Matthew Henson, and an Inuit guide, but drifting ice pushed them from their goal. They made a second attempt (1905–06) in the steamer *Roosevelt,* which was damaged by ice 200 miles from the pole. On a third attempt, Peary claimed that he, Henson, and the Inuit Egingwah, Seeglo, Ootah, and Ooqueah reached the North Pole on April 6, 1908, an assertion that is widely considered suspect.

Peck, (Eldred) Gregory, *b. La Jolla, Calif., 1916; d. 2003.* **Film actor.** Best known for his portrayal of Atticus Finch in the film *To Kill a Mockingbird* (1962), for which he won the Academy Award for best actor, Peck was a premed student turned highly successful Hollywood actor. After studying with the Neighborhood Playhouse in New York, he made his Broadway debut in 1942 in *Morning Star,* which led to his first Hollywood film, the war film *Days of Glory* (1944). Appearing in 60 films in a career spanning six decades, he was also a four-time nominee for the Academy Award for the following: The *Keys of the Kingdom* (1944), *The Yearling* (1946), *Gentleman's Agreement* (1947), and *Twelve O'Clock High* (1949). Peck is remembered for his good looks, his durability, his quiet and sympathetic ways, and his suburb ability to play ordinary men faced with extraordinary moral challenges.

Pei, Ioeh Ming, *b. Canton, China, 1917.* **American architect.** An early work was the Mile High Center (1952–56) in Denver, which brought him to prominence. With his partners he designed the sharply angular East Building (1968–78) of the National Gallery of Art in Washington D.C.; the Morton Myerson Symphony Center (1981–89), in Dallas; and the extension of the Musée du Louvre (1983–93) with its glass pyramid in the courtyard, below which he rationalized the circulation patterns that lead into different sections of a complex museum.

Pelé (Edson Arantes do Nascimento), *b. Brazil, 1940.* **Soccer player.** Brazilian soccer player who is widely acknowledged as the greatest player in the history of the sport. A professional by age 15, he became the only player to participate in four World Cups and to win three (1958, 1962, 1970). He scored a total of 1,281 goals in his career, most of it spent with Brazil's Santos club. He played his last three seasons (1975–77) with the New York Cosmos of the North American Soccer League.

Penn, William, *b. London, 1644; d. 1718.* **English Quaker and founder of Pennsylvania.** Penn became a Quaker in 1667 and thereafter served several short terms in prison in England for his beliefs. Hoping to found a society in America that guaranteed freedom of conscience to believers in God, and to free himself of debt, he received a charter to Pennsylvania in 1681 from King Charles II. He established a legislature and sold land for farms, but he fell further into debt, and his dream of an ideal society was dashed by boundary disputes and conflicts within the colony.

Pericles *b. Athens, ca. 495 B.C.; d. 429 B.C.* **Athenian statesman.** From 454 B.C. for about 30 years, Pericles was elected and reelected *strategos,* or "general," by the Athenian people. Pericles oversaw the Delian League's power and the prosperity, influence, and military dominance that this grouping of Greek city-states enjoyed. He was responsible for promoting the arts in Athens, the building of the Parthenon, and various political reforms, including salaries for all government officials, and making dual Athenian parentage required for citizenship. Near to the end of his life, war broke out between Athens and Sparta, the glory of Athens flagged, and Pericles was deposed. Thucydides reported Pericles' most famous oration appealing to Athenian pride. He was soon reinstated but died of the plague shortly afterward.

Peter (Saint) *b. Bethsaida, Galilee; d. ca. 64.* **Apostle of Jesus.** According to the Gospels, Peter, originally Simon, was a fisherman called by Jesus. When Simon recognized Jesus as Messiah, Jesus renamed him Cephas ("Peter" in Greek), signifying the "rock" upon which he would build his church. Despite Peter's primacy among the apostles, Jesus predicted, with apparent accuracy, that Peter would deny him. After his master's death, Peter was a church leader at Antioch and a missionary in Asia Minor. He is believed to have to have become the first bishop of Rome—to Roman Catholics, the first pope—and to have been martyred there under Emperor Nero.

Peter I, the Great, *b. Moscow, Russia, 1672; d. 1725.* **Russian czar and emperor.** Peter ruled in a co-regency with his half-brother, Ivan V (1682–96), and thereafter alone. A man of wide practical interests, Peter traveled extensively in western Europe (1697–98) to learn firsthand ways of modernizing Russian industry and government. His reforms strengthened the monarchy and weakened the church and nobility. Peter also founded the

Russian navy and expanded Russia's access to ice-free ports on the Black Sea and Baltic, through war with Ottoman Turkey (1696–99) and the Great Northern War with Sweden (1700–21). He became emperor in 1721.

Petrarch (Francesco Petrarca), *b. Arezzo, Tuscany, Italy, 1304; d. 1374.* **Poet.** Petrarch's poetry was a bridge from the Middle Ages to the Renaissance and an important factor in the development of vernacular literature. He spent much of his life in France but returned to Italy for his last two decades. A classicist and the original humanist, he discovered Roman manuscripts and linked Greek and Roman tradition to Christian culture. He was the first great writer of sonnets; his were addressed to a woman named Laura. His ode *Italia Mia* expresses his advocacy of Italian unity. His Latin poems include the epic *Africa*, about the Second Punic War, and *Eclogues*.

Phelps, Michael, *b. Baltimore, Md., 1985.* **Swimmer.** Phelps was already a prolific Olympian before the 2008 Beijing games, having won six gold and two bronze medals at Athens in 2004. He dominated the swimming competition winning a record eight gold medals in a single Olympics and setting world records in seven of his eight events. His overall total of 16 medals is second all-time and he holds the record for most individual gold's with nine. By April 2011 he had broken 39 world records.

Phidias, *b. Athens, ca. 490 B.C.; d. ca. 430 B.C.* **Sculptor.** Considered the greatest classical sculptor, Phidias is best known for creating a statue of Zeus that stood in Olympia; this colossal work was one of the seven wonders of the ancient world. According to accounts written by Plutarch, Phidias worked closely with Pericles to beautify Athens, overseeing construction of the Parthenon. He created many of the city's notable statues, including a large bronze figure of Athena. Unfortunately, no confirmed originals exist today. The reputation of Phidias largely rests on written descriptions and the powerful influence he exerted on generations of sculptors.

Philip II, *b. Valladolid, Spain, 1527; d. 1598.* **Spanish king.** When he became King of Spain in 1556, Philip inherited one of Europe's most extensive empires from his father the Hapsburg emperor Charles V, with holdings in Italy, the Netherlands, France, and the Spanish Americas. This legacy, coupled with his four marriages (including one to England's Mary I), embroiled him in European politics of the day. A leader of the Counter-Reformation, he sought to suppress the Dutch independence movement (1568–1609) and to undermine its English allies, against

whom he launched the disastrous Spanish Armada (1588). He also fought the Ottoman Empire, and upon the death of his heirless nephew, Sebastian, became king of Portugal in 1580.

Piaget, Jean, *b. Neuchâtel, Switzerland, 1896; d. 1980.* **Child psychologist.** A pioneer in developmental psychology, Piaget devised the first systematic study of the way children reason and acquire understanding. According to Piaget's theory of "genetic epistemology," children's minds evolve as they grow older. Because their mental growth is inextricably linked with their physical development, Piaget believed that children cannot develop certain thought processes until they reach the proper age.

Piano, Renzo, *b. Genoa, Italy 1937.* **Architect.** Piano's first major work was the influential Pompidou Center (1971–77) art museum in Paris with the English architect Richard Rogers; they exposed the viscera of the building—trusses, pipes, ducts, exhaust vents—as its primary aesthetic experience. Later work exhibits great diversity in building types and includes the Menil Collection Exhibition Building (1981–86) in Houston; the football stadium (1987–90) in Bari, Italy; and the Kansai air terminal (1988–94), built on an artificial island in Osaka Bay. Piano won a Pritzker Prize in 1998.

Picasso, Pablo, *b. Málaga, Spain, 1881; d. 1973.* **Painter, sculptor, printmaker, decorative artist, writer.** One of the most influential figures in 20th-century art, Picasso produced works in an astonishing range of styles, from neoclassical portraits to aggressively inventive abstracted images. Together with the artist Georges Braque, he is credited with developing Cubism, a style of painting that breaks the picture plane into collagelike fragments. Picasso lived much of his life in Paris and other parts of France, and was influenced by the Postimpressionists as well as by African and Oceanic art. Among his many famous works are *Gertrude Stein* (1906), *Les Demoiselles d'Avignon* (1907), and *Guernica* (1937).

Pickford, Mary (Gladys Smith) *b. Toronto, Canada, 1893; d. 1979.* **Silent film actress.** Dubbed "America's Sweetheart," Pickford's screen image as an innocent, energetic adolescent made her an international star. She began as a child performer on the stage but turned to movies in 1909. She starred in several shorts for D. W. Griffith, including *The Lonely Villa.* One of the first major movie stars, she moved from studio to studio, increasing her salary each time. Her popular feature films included *The Foundling* (1916), *Pollyanna* (1920), and *My Best Girl*

(1927). In 1919 Pickford joined her husband Douglas Fairbanks, Griffith, and Charlie Chaplin to form the studio United Artists.

Pierce, Franklin, b. *Hillsboro, N.H., 1804; d. 1869.* Fourteenth U.S. president, 1853–57. A leader of Jacksonian Democrats in Congress in the 1830's, Pierce had been absent from national politics for a decade when the deadlocked Democratic convention nominated him for president in 1852. A dark horse candidate, Pierce won enough southern votes to become the youngest president as of that date. He greatly hastened the coming of the Civil War by signing the Kansas-Nebraska Act (1854), which repealed the Missouri Compromise and reopened the dangerous issue of expanding slavery. In 1856 Pierce became the only elected president to be denied his own party's renomination.

Pinter, Harold, b. *London, England, 1930; d. 2008.* Playwright and screenwriter. Born into a working class family, Pinter became an actor before turning to playwriting. With the production of his first full-length play, *The Birthday Party*, in 1958, Pinter revealed the characteristics of his work: psychological exploration taking precedence over plot; dialogue that relies on silence and subtext; and characters disrupted in their behavioral patterns by the arrival of a stranger. Other plays of note are *The Caretaker* (1960), *The Homecoming* (1965), and *Betrayal* (1978).

Pissarro, Camille, b. *Charlotte Amalie, St. Thomas, Danish Virgin Islands, 1830; d. 1903.* Painter and printmaker. Sometimes cited as the father of the Impressionist movement, Pissarro was the only artist to show in all of the Impressionist exhibitions. By the early 1870's he was using a bright palette in patches of unmixed color; after meeting Signac and Seurat in 1885, he began to paint in a method similar to pointillism, which he ultimately found constricting. He then returned to a purer Impressionist style. His well-known works include *Versailles Road at Louveciennes* (1870) and *Wooded Landscape at l'Hermitage, Pontoise* (1878).

Pitt, William, First Earl of Chatham ("Pitt the Elder"), b. *Westminster, 1708; d. 1778.* Statesman. Pitt came from a family that had become wealthy in India. As a young and contentious member of Parliament, he was an enemy of King George II, but his eloquence and popularity led to his becoming secretary of state in 1756, effectively prime minister at the time. He attacked the French empire, winning Canada, a section of America, and the French West Indies, and later expelling French power

from India. In 1761 he resigned, but in 1766 he formed a new government that ended in failure in 1768.

Pitt, William ("Pitt the Younger"), b. *Hayes, 1759; d 1806.* English statesman. Second son of William Pitt, he became the youngest prime minister ever at the age of 24, remaining in office for 18 years. He restored England's economy and pride after defeat in the American Revolution, but resigned in 1801 over King George III's opposition to Catholic emancipation in Ireland. He was brought back in 1804 and died in office in 1806.

Pius IX (Pio Nono), b. *Senigallia, Italy, 1792; d. 1878.* Pope, 1846–78. Pius IX's tenure, the longest in church history, was roiled by international events that transformed him from a reformer to a political and theological reactionary. Opposing a nationalist takeover of Rome, he fled the city in 1848. Backed by France, he returned in 1850, but could not prevent—or accept—his ultimate loss of temporal authority and control of the papal states. In 1854 Pius declared the doctrine of the Immaculate Conception of the Virgin Mary, and in 1869 he summoned the Vatican council, at which the pope was declared infallible when speaking *ex cathedra* on faith and morals.

Pizarro, Francisco, b. *Trujillo, Spain, 1476; d. 1541.* Conquistador. Pizarro arrived in the Americas in 1509 and took part in Balboa's expedition of 1513 to the Pacific. After Balboa's execution (in which he conspired) in 1519, Pizarro explored the Pacific coast between Panama and Peru until 1528. Returning to Spain, he persuaded Charles I to sponsor his expedition of 1531 against the Incas; during this expedition he marched inland from the coast of Ecuador, captured the cities of Cajamarca and Cuzco, and seized and executed the emperor Atahualpa in 1533. Two years later he founded Lima, Peru, where he was assassinated.

Plato, b. *ca. 427 B.C.; d. 347 B.C.* Philosopher. Plato was a pupil and friend of Socrates; his early dialogues have Socrates in conversations that illustrate the unity of virtue and knowledge and virtue and happiness. In the *Republic* and other writings, Plato explains his ideas on the relationships between the individual, the state (to be ruled by the philosopher-king), and the cosmos.

Poe, Edgar Allan, b. *Boston, 1809; d. 1849.* Poet, short-story writer, critic. Poe's parents died before he was three, and he was raised by an uncle and aunt. He published *Tamerlane and Other Poems* at 18, then became a magazine editor and writer in several eastern cities, contributing poems, stories, and literary criticism. His vivid, surrealistic, often macabre tales, such as "The Tell-Tale Heart," "The Fall of the House of Usher," and "The Cask of "Amontillado," were complemented by detective stories ("Murders in the Rue Morgue," "The Purloined Letter"), a genre he invented. His poem "The Raven" (1845) made him famous. He died after a drinking spree in Baltimore while en route to his second wedding.

Polk, James Knox, b. *Mecklenburg County, N.C., 1795; d. 1849.* Eleventh U.S. president, 1845–49. A star orator in Tennessee politics, Polk was Speaker of the House and governor of Tennessee before he won the presidency in 1844 as a dark horse candidate. From his inaugural address onward he pursued expansion in the West. When Mexico attacked U.S. troops in disputed Texas territory, Polk called it an invasion, and the ensuing Mexican War (1846–48) won California and the Southwest for the United States. Polk declined a second term, having fulfilled the nation's "Manifest Destiny" to span the continent.

Pollock, (Paul) Jackson, b. *Cody, Wyo., 1912; d. 1956.* Painter. A pioneer in the Abstract Expressionist movement, which flourished in New York after World War II, Pollock is often called an "action painter." His earlier work is based on figurative images, but he began producing his famous abstract poured paintings in 1947. With sticks and other tools, he threw drips of paint onto large canvases in loose, energetic patterns. Well-known works include *Autumn Rhythm: Number 30* (1950) and *Male and Female* (1942). Pollock was married to the artist Lee Krasner. He suffered from alcoholism and was killed in a car accident.

Polo, Marco, b. *Venice (?), 1254; d. 1324.* Venetian merchant and explorer. Marco Polo joined his father and uncle on their second journey to China in 1271. Traveling from Palestine through Asia Minor, Iran, and Afghanistan and along the Silk Road to China, they reached the court of Kublai Khan around 1274. They remained in the Orient for about seventeen years and returned by sea as escorts of a Mongol princess betrothed to a Persian khan. Polo later dictated his memoirs while in a Genoese prison after being captured in a naval battle. His *Travels* have enjoyed immense popularity ever since.

Pompey (The Great; Gnaeus Pompeius), b. *Rome, 106 B.C.; d. 48 B.C.* Roman general and statesman. After an illustrious military performance in the civil war, siding with the victor Sulla against Gaius Marius, Pompey was elected consul in 70 B.C. and then went on to military service in the Mediterranean. In 59 B.C. Pompey, Julius Caesar, and Marcus Crassus formed the First Triumvirate and took control of Rome. After Crassus died the political bonds began to dissolve. Caesar returned from Gaul in 49 B.C. and crossed the river Rubicon to fight Pompey's forces. Pompey was finally defeated at Pharsalus and fled to Egypt, where he was killed by Ptolemy.

Pope, Alexander, b. *London, 1688; d. 1744.* English poet. A tubercular child, Pope grew to be just 4 feet 6 inches. Denied educational and economic advantages because of his Catholicism, he became wealthy from his translations of Homer. Pope was a brilliant wit, master of the rhyming heroic couplet, and the greatest English verse satirist. Important works include: *An Essay on Criticism* (1711); *The Rape of the Lock* (1714), a nonpareil mock-epic satirizing high society; *The Dunciad* (1728), which attacked his mostly inferior literary enemies; the philosophical *An Essay on Man* (1734); and *Epistle to Dr. Arbuthnot* (1735).

Porter, Cole, b. *Peru, Ind, 1891; d. 1964.* Popular composer. Along with George Gershwin and Irving Berlin, Porter was one of America's great songwriters. He wrote both music and lyrics; and his songs were featured in numerous Broadway and Hollywood musicals and have become true standards. Important compositions include "Love for Sale" (1930), "Night and Day" (1932), "Anything Goes" (1934), "I Get a Kick Out of You" (1934), "You're the Top" (1934), "Begin the Beguine" (1935), "I've Got You Under My Skin" (1936), "I Love Paris" (1952), and "All of You" (1954).

Pound, Ezra, b. *Hailey, Idaho, 1885; d. 1972.* Poet. Pound moved to Europe in 1908. He was one of the most influential modern poets, but his aesthetic theories were bound up with antidemocratic political and economic views that drove him, ultimately, to Mussolini's Italy, which he supported. His poetry, rooted in spare "imagism," expanded into longer poems such as *Hugh Selwyn Mauberly* (1920), which were fragmented to express the dissolution of civilization. Thereafter he composed only his *Cantos*, 116 in all, which he saw as one long poem merging his life, his mind, and history. Pound was arrested for treason in 1945 and committed to a sanatorium in Washington for 13 years.

Presley, Elvis Aaron, b. *Tupelo, Miss., 1935; d. 1977.* Rock 'n' roll vocalist. Arguably the most important figure in 20th-century popular music, Elvis was the musician most responsible for popularizing rock 'n' roll on an international level. He was the first performer to fuse country and blues music into the style known as rockabilly, and the first white vocalist to sing in a "black" style. His recordings include "Heartbreak Hotel" (1956), "Hound Dog" (1956), "Love Me Tender" (1956), "All Shook Up" (1957), "Little Sister" (1961), "Suspicious Minds" (1969), "In the Ghetto" (1969), "Kentucky Rain" (1970), and "Burning Love" (1972).

Priestley, Joseph, *b. Fieldhead, England, 1733; d. 1804.* Chemist, philosopher, and educator. A Unitarian minister, Priestley was an intellectual giant, a master of languages, an incisive philosopher, and a scientific innovator. With the encouragement of his friend Benjamin Franklin, he conducted experiments with electricity, but he is best known for his work in isolating gases and discovering oxygen. Priestley's radical books on religious philosophy, some of which attempted to disprove the doctrine of the Trinity, generated storms of controversy. In 1791 a mob burned down his house and laboratory. In 1794 he immigrated to the United States, where he helped to found the nation's first Unitarian Church (attended by John Adams).

Proust, Marcel, *b. Auteuil, outside Paris, 1871; d. 1922.* French Novelist. Proust was weakened from childhood by asthma. Although as a young man he moved amid Parisian society and joined the army, he became a recluse after his mother's death in 1905. After publishing an unsuccessful collection of short pieces in 1896, Proust turned to his magisterial work, *Remembrance of Things Past,* a seven-novel sequence, beginning with *Swann's Way* (1913). This cycle, much of it published posthumously, is one of the greatest and most influential works of modern fiction—a semiautobiographical, profound, sensuous monologue that explores the meaning of human experience as lived and remembered in time.

Ptolemy (Claudius Ptolemaeus), *b. Rome, ca. A.D. 100; d. ca. 170.* Mathematician, geographer, astronomer, and astrologer. Little is known about Ptolemy, who was probably a Roman citizen in Roman-ruled Alexandria. He was the author of an array of scientific treatises, including the *Almagest,* which synthesized the astronomical knowledge and theories of the ancient world. His earth-centric view of the universe held sway until it was debunked by Copernicus in the 16th century. Ptolemy's *Geographia* advanced cartography and compiled all that was known about world geography during the Roman Empire. His computational methods were used by navigators for centuries. Ptolemy also wrote influential texts on astrology, music theory, and optics.

Puccini, Giacomo, *b. Lucca, 1858; d. 1924.* Italian opera composer. Puccini's first opera (*Edgar,* commissioned in 1889) was a failure, but his second (*Manon Lescaut*) was a triumph, and led to further successes. His operas are marvels of characterization, sentiment, and craftsmanship; and his mastery of melody and genius for orchestration have made his works among the most popular and beloved in the repertoire. His later works included influences from contemporaries such as Debussy and Schoenberg. Notable works include *Manon Lescaut* (1890–92), *La Bohème* (1894–95), *Tosca* (1898–99), *Madama Butterfly* (1901–1903), *La rondine* (The Swallow) (1914–16), and *Turandot* (1920–26).

Pushkin, Aleksandr, *b. Moscow, 1799; d. 1837.* Poet. Most celebrated of Russian poets, Pushkin had a brief career marked by political and romantic strife. His early satires on the upper class and his "Ode to Liberty" led to exile in southern Russia, and another freedom-embracing poem, *The Gypsies,* brought further confinement. He is best known for narrative poetry, including *The Bronze Horseman* (1833), in praise of Peter the Great; *Eugene Onegin,* (1831) a "verse novel" dealing with contemporary society; and the tragic historical drama *Boris Godunov* (published 1831). Pushkin was killed in a duel by a Frenchman accused of being the lover of the poet's wife.

Putin, Vladimir, *b. St. Petersburg, Russia, 1952.* Russian politician. Putin graduated with a law degree from Leningrad State University and subsequently worked with the Foreign Intelligence Service and on the Leningrad–St. Petersburg City Council. In 1994–96, he was first deputy chairman of the city government and chairman of the committee for external relations. He joined Boris Yeltsin's staff and served as deputy chief of staff and, from 1998, director of the Federal Security Service and secretary of the Security Council. In 1999 he was appointed acting prime minister. He won election as president of the Russian Federation in 2000 and 2004.

Pynchon, Thomas, *b. Glen Cove, N. Y., 1937.* Novelist and short-story writer. Pynchon first rose to prominence in 1963 with the publication of his absurdist first novel, *V.* In novels characterized by a fanciful, satirical, postmodern worldview such as *The Crying of Lot 49* (1966), *Gravity's Rainbow* (1973), and *Vineland* (1990). Pynchon has continually pushed the boundaries of the literary novel, exploring such genres as science fiction and magical realism.

Pythagoras, *b. Samos, Greece, ca. 580 B.C.; d. ca. 500 B.C.* Mathematician and philosopher. Pythagoras founded a Greek colony in southern Italy, where his supporters formed a secretive religious and philosophical movement known as Pythagoreanism. They adhered to a rigorous and ascetic lifestyle, while refining their belief in the transmigration of souls. The sect carried out extensive mathematical studies, concentrating on odd and even numbers, prime numbers, and square numbers; they believed that numbers held the key to order and harmony. Pythogoras is largely remembered today for the theorem that bears his name; it states that in any right triangle, the square of the hypotenuse is equal to the sum of the squares of the other two sides. The sect was among the first set of scientific thinkers to consider that the Earth might revolve around the Sun.

Qin Shihuangdi, *b. Shaanxi Province, China, 258 B.C.; d. 210 B.C.* **Chinese emperor.** Prince Zheng came to the throne of the ancient Chinese state of Qin in 245 B.C., at a time of incessant warfare among the independent royal states of the time. Assisted by able advisers, he transformed Qin into a highly mobilized military-agrarian state that defeated and absorbed all rivals by 221. As self-proclaimed Qin Shihuangdi ("First Emperor of Qin"), he built the Great Wall, promulgated a code of laws, standardized weights and measures, and instituted administrative reforms. Repressive and despotic, his regime provoked popular unrest; the Qin dynasty was overthrown in 206, four years after the First Emperor's death. His tomb near Xi'an, guarded by some 7,000 life-sized terra-cotta soldiers, is one of the archaeological wonders of the world.

Rabin, Yitzhak, *b. Jerusalem, 1922; d. 1995.* **Israeli prime minister.** During the 1967 Six-Day War, Rabin led Israel to victory over Egypt, Syria, and Jordan, tripling Israel's territory. He became prime minister in 1974, achieving an agreement with Egypt that led to the Camp David Accords. Ousted as prime minister in 1977, he was reelected in 1992. He negotiated with Yasir Arafat, offering Palestinian self-rule in the Gaza Strip, Jericho, and the West Bank. Rabin, Shimon Peres, and Yasir Arafat shared the 1994 Nobel Peace Prize. Rabin also negotiated a full peace treaty with Jordan. In 1995, Rabin was assassinated by a right-wing Jewish student.

Racine, Jean, *baptized, La Ferté-Milon, France, 1639; d. 1699.* **Playwright and poet.** Considered the master of the French neoclassical tragedy, Racine is noted for fusing the metaphysical concerns of 17th-century France with the style and structure of Greek tragedy. Notable works include *Andromaque* (1667), *Britannicus* (1669), and *Berenice* (1670). Throughout his life Racine struggled to reconcile his interest in theater with his religious beliefs, and he gave up writing secular drama altogether after the premiere of his masterpiece, *Phèdre,* in 1677. During the last 20 years of his life, Racine wrote only religious poetry and drama.

Raphael (Santi, Raffaello; Sanzio, Raffaello), *b. Urbino, Italy, 1483; d. 1520.* **Painter, architect.** Although he was not the most inventive artist of his period, Raphael was able to synthesize all of its developments in highly illusionistic representation, resulting in what is thought of as the definitive High Renaissance style. Raphael produced devotional paintings, altarpieces, and portraits. Some of his well-known works are *Madonna of the Meadow* (1505); *The School of Athens* (1510–12), which depicts Greek philosophers gathered around Plato and Aristotle in a grand architectural setting; and *Galatea* (1513).

Rawls, John, *b. Baltimore, Md., 1921; d. 2002.* **Political philosopher.** A Harvard professor and a powerful advocate for liberalism, Rawls was one of the preeminent political thinkers of the 20th century. His seminal work, *A Theory of Justice* (1971), argued for a society based on equality and individual rights. He emphasized that the first duty of the state is to safeguard the basic civil liberties of the individual, and that the interests of the majority cannot be used to justify a loss of freedom for the minority.

Reagan, Ronald, *b. Tampico, Ill., 1911; d. 2004.* **Fortieth U.S. president, 1981–89.** Ronald Wilson Reagan was a B-movie actor who, despite his lack of experience, was elected governor of California in 1966. His good humor and optimistic outlook charmed voters, and he won the presidency in a landslide in 1980. His "Reaganomics" resulted in massive tax cuts that caused a meteoric rise in the national debt; he called the Soviet Union an "evil empire" and applied military pressure to end decades of communist rule. In 1987 his invincible popularity finally succumbed to the Iran-Contra scandal: White House staffers had secretly sold arms to Iran and used the profits to illegally fund Contra fighters in Nicaragua.

Redford, Robert, *b. Santa Monica, Calif., 1937.* **Actor and director.** A cautious actor who sometimes seems at odds with his movie-star good looks, he became a real star with *Butch Cassidy and the Sundance Kid* (1969) and *The Sting* (1973). Other notable films include *All the President's Men* (1976) and *The Natural* (1984). He won an Oscar as best director for *Ordinary People* (1980). In 1981 he founded the Sundance Institute, with its annual festival featuring the work of young and independent filmmakers.

Rehnquist, William, b. *Milwaukee, Wis., 1924; d. 2005.* U.S. Supreme Court justice. Rehnquist began his career by clerking for Supreme Court Justice Robert Jackson. As a lawyer in Phoenix, Rehnquist became a Republican party official, establishing himself as a conservative stalwart. He later moved to Washington and served in the Justice Department. President Richard Nixon nominated Rehnquist to the Supreme Court to succeed John Marshall Harlan, and he was seated in early 1972. In his early days on the Court, he was often the lone dissenter from his colleagues' more liberal opinions; he felt they were attempting to shape public policy by expanding the scope of the Court. After Chief Justice Warren Burger retired in 1986, President Ronald Reagan made Rehnquist the chief justice. The Rehnquist Court strengthened police authority, restricted habeas corpus, permitted indirect government funding of religion, and—most notably—decided the presidential election of 2000.

Rembrandt (Harmenszoon) van Rijn, b. *Leiden, Netherlands, 1606; d. 1669.* Painter. At the center of what is thought to be the Dutch golden age, Rembrandt painted landscapes, figures, animals, history, and mythology, particularly Old Testament subjects such as *The Blinding of Samson* (1636) and *The Blessing of Jacob* (1656). He was also a sought-after portraitist and executed many self-portraits. His works are characterized by Baroque sumptuousness and a fascination with glowing light. Famous images include a group portrait of a military company known as *The Night Watch* (1642), *Aristotle Contemplating the Bust of Homer* (1653), and *The Jewish Bride* (ca. 1665).

Renoir, Pierre Auguste, b. *Limoges, France, 1841; d. 1919.* Painter, printmaker, sculptor. One of the founders of the Impressionist movement, Renoir produced some of the group's best-known images, which often focus on leisure activities. His painting *Ball at the Moulin de la Galette* (1876) is an ambitious rendering of the crowd at an outdoor dance hall, depicting the complex effects of dappled light and shade. Other well-known works include *Two Young Girls at the Piano* (1892). Renoir departed from the Impressionist circle in 1878, adopted a more classical style, and became a society painter.

Renoir, Jean, b. *Paris, France, 1894; d. 1979.* Film director. Son of the Impressionist painter Auguste Renoir, Jean used money inherited from his father to set up a film production company. Self-taught, he directed his first feature, *La Fille d'Eau,* in 1925. Social consciousness became his primary focus in the 1930's, as in *Boudu Saved from Drowning* (1932), *The Crime of Monsieur Lange* (1936), *Grand*

Illusion (1937), and his masterpiece *Rules of the Game* (1939). During World War II, he directed several films in Hollywood, including *The Southerner* (1945). After returning to Europe, Renoir became eclectic in style and in subject, experimenting with color and form.

Rhodes, Cecil (John), b. *Hertfordshire, England, 1853; d. 1902.* British financier, statesman, and effective founder of Rhodesia (now Zimbabwe). The son of a vicar, Rhodes traveled to South Africa as a young man, for his health. He enhanced his wealth mining the Kimberley diamond mines, and in 1888 he formed his own company, De Beers Consolidated Mines. Rhodes became prime minister of the Cape Colony in 1890, but resigned in 1896 amid controversy over raids into neighboring Transvaal by a colleague. His will established the Rhodes Scholarships, which enable foreign nationals to study at Oxford.

Ricardo, David, b. *London, 1772; d. 1823.* English economist. Influenced by the work of Adam Smith, Ricardo held that the economy follows scientific laws, and he systematized classical economics with his theories of value, rent, and international trade. His major work was *The Principles of Political Economy and Taxation* (1817), in which he argued that the value of a good is determined by the amount of labor required to produce it, a theory that influenced Karl Marx. He also formulated the law of diminishing returns, a major contribution to economic thought.

Richard III, b. *Fotheringhay Castle, 1452; d. 1485.* Last of the Plantagenet kings of England. Richard became king in 1483 after his brother, King Edward IV, died and Parliament declared on dubious grounds that Edward's young son, Edward V, was illegitimate. Richard's reign of two years was cut short when he was defeated and killed at the battle of Bosworth Field fighting against Henry Tudor, later Henry VII, the first Tudor king. Richard's villainous portrayal in Shakespeare's *Richard III* is generally considered to be exaggerated.

Richelieu, Cardinal (Armand-Jean du Plessis), b. *Richelieu, Poitou, 1585; d. 1642.* French cardinal and politician. Known as the "Red Eminence," Richelieu entered the priesthood at 22. Politically adept, he was appointed secretary of state at 31, and by 1614 was chief minister to Louis XIII. Among his primary aims was to check Spanish Hapsburg power in Europe and to quell Huguenot opposition to the crown in France; this policy led to French involvement in the Thirty Years' War. At home, he supported French trading companies and industries, laid the foundation for the French navy, and founded the French Academy.

Riefenstahl, Leni (Berta Helene Amalie Riefenstahl) *b. Berlin, 1902; d. 2003.* Actress, film director, photographer. She was a ballet dancer before she began acting in a series of melodramatic "mountain films" in the late 1920's. On the strength of *The Blue Light*, which she wrote and directed in 1932, Hitler commissioned her to record the 1934 Nuremburg rally (*Triumph of the Will*, 1935) and the 1936 Berlin Olympics (*Olympiad*, 1938). Blacklisted from filmmaking after the war, she continued to depict physical and natural beauty, without political overtones, in her photographic studies of African tribesmen and of undersea life.

Riemann, Bernhard *b. Breselenz, Germany, 1826; d. 1866.* German mathematician. Riemann's work made mathematics more general or abstract and put the integral calculus on a firmer basis. He invented a new way to show functions of complex numbers on a plane (1851) and developed the mathematics to handle such representations. He rethought the foundations of geometry in spaces of *n* dimensions (1854), suggesting new non-Euclidean geometries. The truth of his conjecture about a complex function called the zeta function (1859) remains among the main unresolved issues of mathematics.

Rilke, Rainer Maria, *b. Prague, 1875; d. 1926.* Czech-German poet. Rilke was a an unhappy child and had a restless life. Married only briefly, often ill, he moved frequently around Europe and Russia and sought stability and meaning in his art. Considered the best German lyric poet of the 20th century, he wrote poems that are strongly imagistic, often erotic; and his search for meaning led him to explore God, mysticism, and death. In *New Poems* (1907–08), he introduced the "object-poem," which sought to reach the core reality of physical things. Other volumes are *Sonnets to Orpheus* (1921) and his most optimistic work, *Duino Elegies* (1922).

Rimbaud, Arthur, *b. Charleville, France, 1854; d. 1891.* Poet. An important French Symbolist, Rimbaud was an original poet who wrote most or all of his poems before he was 20. At 16 he began an amorous relationship with the poet Paul Verlaine that ended when Verlaine shot and wounded Rimbaud. Rimbaud's poetry is dreamlike, rushing headlong from image to image and dipping into the subconscious. A successful effort to match poetic form with visionary content is "The Drunken Boat." Somewhat more restrained are the personal poems in *Last Verses*. *Illuminations* contains 40 innovative prose-poems, and *A Season in Hell* (1873) is a confessional renunciation, in prose and verse, of his wicked life .

Robbins, Jerome (Jerome Rabinowitz), *b. New York City, 1918; d. 1998.* Broadway and ballet choreographer. Robbins was educated at N.Y.U. (1935–38), danced on Broadway from 1938–40, and joined Ballet Theatre in 1940–44. His first major ballet, *Fancy Free*, inspired the musical *On the Town*, which he also choreographed. From 1949 to 1959, Robbins was a member of the New York City Ballet, but continued to work on Broadway, choreographing a series of major hits: *The King and I* (1951), the classic *West Side Story* (1957), *Gypsy* (1959),and *Fiddler on the Roof* (1964). Robbins returned to New York City Ballet in 1969, and created several of the company's signature works including "Dances at a Gathering" (1969) and "The Goldberg Variations" (1971).

Robert the Bruce (Robert I), *b. 1274; d. 1329.* King of Scotland. Crowned king in 1306, Robert fought throughout his reign to free Scotland from English rule. In 1314, he won a decisive victory over the English at Bannockburn. The English finally agreed to Scottish independence in 1328.

Roberts, John G. Jr., *b. Buffalo, N.Y., 1955.* U.S. Supreme Court Chief Justice. Appointed the 17th chief justice of the United States by President George W. Bush in 2005, John Roberts was originally nominated to fill the vacancy left by Justice Sandra Day O'Connor after her retirement, but instead was appointed to replace chief justice William H. Rehnquist who died just before Roberts' confirmation hearings were to begin. Roberts had extensive legal experience, having clerked for Rehnquist, served as special assistant to the Attorney General and associate counsel to President Reagan, worked as deputy solicitor general during the George W. Bush administration, and having been appointed to the D.C. Circuit Court of Appeals in 2003. Although the Senate confirmed Roberts with bipartisan support on September 29, 2005, some questioned whether his Roman Catholic faith and conservative legal history would improperly influence his judicial decisions.

Robertson, Oscar, *b. Charlotte, Tenn., 1938.* Basketball player. The "Big O" was a star at the University of Cincinnati before becoming the prototypical NBA guard, paving the way for the likes of Magic Johnson and Michael Jordan. Robertson starred for the Cincinnati Royals and the Milwaukee Bucks during a career that spanned the years 1960 through 1974. He scored 26,710 points and held the NBA record for assists with 9,887 until Johnson and later John Stockton passed him. He won a gold medal in the 1960 Olympics, was named Rookie of the Year in 1961, and was named the league M.V.P. in 1964.

Robespierre, Maximilien (François-Marie-Isidore de), *b. Arras, France, 1758; d. 1794.* **French revolutionary leader.** A lawyer by training, Robespierre was appointed to the Estates General and joined the Jacobins in 1789. In 1792 he was elected to the National Assembly (successor to the Estates General), where he called for Louis XVI's execution. A member of the extremist Montagnards, in 1793 he joined the Committee of Public Safety. Although he abetted the Reign of Terror, he deplored its most extreme abuses. Perceived both as a dictator and as a moderate, he was indicted by the Legislative Assembly and executed together with more than 100 supporters.

Robinson, Jackie, *b. Cairo, Ga., 1919; d. 1972.* **Baseball player.** Robinson was a star athelete at UCLA before he changed the face of society when he was signed by the Brooklyn Dodgers and became the first African American to play modern major-league baseball. Although harassed and threatened by fans and opposing players in his debut season of 1947, the infielder batted .297, won Rookie of the Year honors, and became a symbol of personal courage. Known for his daring on the base paths—he stole home 19 times—Robinson led the Dodgers to the National League pennant in six of his 10 years. He was named M.V.P. in 1949, leading the league in batting (.342) and stolen bases (37), while knocking in 124 runs.

Rockefeller, John Davison, *b. Richford, N.Y., 1839; d. 1937.* **Industrialist and philanthropist.** Starting out in Cleveland, Rockefeller and his partners built an oil refinery in 1863 and set up business in the Pennsylvania oil patch. In 1870 Rockefeller organized the Standard Oil Company to end the volatility in the industry by buying up smaller companies and combining them into a company large enough to control the market. By 1879 the company controlled 90 percent of America's refining capacity. In 1911 the Supreme Court dissolved the Standard Oil Trust and reorganized it into 38 companies. Rockefeller withdrew from the company in 1896 and devoted the rest of his life to philanthropy.

Rockne, Knute, *b. Voss, Norway, 1888; d. 1931.* **Football player and coach.** A legendary figure in American football, he is best known as the coach of the University of Notre Dame from 1918 to 1930. Sparked by his inspirational halftime speeches—his "Win one for the Gipper" speech was immortalized in the 1940 film *Knute Rockne,- All American*—the "Fighting Irish" enjoyed five undefeated seasons and compiled a record of 105-12-5 during the Rockne era. As players, in 1913, "Rock" and Notre Dame quarterback Gus Dorais first established the forward pass as an effective offensive weapon.

Rockwell, Norman, *b. New York City, 1984; d. 1978.* **Illustrator and painter.** Best known for his magazine illustrations, Rockwell contributed to publications such as *The Saturday Evening Post, Boy's Life*, and *Look*. He was a realist, influenced by the narrative genre style of artists, and he documented optimistic images of American life. His works include *Freedom from Want* (1943) and *Rosie the Riveter* (1943), the wartime working woman. Rockwell's work of the 1960's reflects the changes and conflicts of the time—pictures of the desegregation of schools, astronauts, and Peace Corps volunteers.

Rodgers, Richard, *b. Hammels Station, NY, 1902; d. 1979.* **Popular composer.** Arguably the most successful composer for the Broadway theater he collaborated with the lyricists Lorenz Hart and Oscar Hammerstein II. His later works redefined the musical form by using music to advance the plot, instead of as stand-alone vignettes. His musicals include *Babes in Arms* (1937), *Pal Joey* (1940), *Oklahoma!* (1943), *Carousel* (1945), *South Pacific* (1949), *The King and I* (1951), *Flower Drum Song* (1958), and *The Sound of Music* (1959); important songs include "Isn't It Romantic?" (1932), "Blue Moon" (1934), "My Romance" (1935), "The Lady Is a Tramp" (1937), "My Funny Valentine" (1937), "You'll Never Walk Alone" (1945), "Some Enchanted Evening" (1949) and "My Favorite Things" (1959).

Rodin, Auguste, *b. Paris, 1840; d. 1917.* **Sculptor.** Regarded as one of the greatest sculptors of the modern age, Rodin came from a working-class background and for 20 years labored as a craftsman and ornamenter. He relied on models for inspiration, and becaused he encouraged the reproduction of his work in bronze and marble editions, he is well represented in collections all over the world. His most famous works include *The Thinker* and *The Kiss*.

Roosevelt, Eleanor, *b. New York City, 1884; d. 1962.* **First lady and social activist.** Born to a socially prominent family, she married her fifth cousin, Franklin Delano Roosevelt. When he became president in 1933, Eleanor expanded the role of first lady beyond its ceremonial duties, holding weekly press conferences with female reporters, writing a syndicated newspaper column, broadcasting her own radio program, and visiting U.S. troops worldwide. Uncompromising on civil rights, she publicly ignored segregation laws and resigned from the Daughters of the American Revolution when the organization barred the black singer Marian Anderson from performing in its hall. After Franklin Roosevelt's death in 1945, she continued a life of public service and Democratic party politics.

Appointed to the U.S. delegation to the U.N., she chaired the U.N. Commission on Human Rights and helped to draft the U.N. Declaration of Human Rights.

Roosevelt, Franklin Delano, *b. Hyde Park, N.Y., 1882; d. 1945.* **Thirty-second U.S. president, (1933–45).** The cousin of Theodore Roosevelt, Franklin Delano Roosevelt was paralyzed by polio in 1921. His success as governor of New York helped him win the 1932 presidential election by a landslide, assuring Americans they had "nothing to fear but fear itself." His first 100 days saw the enactment of the New Deal, which established the federal government's responsibility for protecting farmers, workers, and the unemployed while actively regulating the economy to prevent another crash. Roosevelt won an unprecedented third term in 1940 and, as war loomed in Europe, used his mastery of public opinion to lead Americans away from isolation. After Pearl Harbor, World War II occupied his full attention as he orchestrated the mammoth war effort, and he won his fourth election in 1944. Just after the Yalta Conference of 1945, Roosevelt died suddenly of a cerebral hemorrhage, days before the war ended in Europe.

Roosevelt, Theodore, *b. New York City, 1858; d. 1919.* **Twenty-sixth U.S. president, (1901–09).** During the Spanish-American War, Roosevelt left a job at the Navy Department to lead the Rough Riders volunteer regiment in Cuba, achieving glory at the battle of San Juan Hill. After serving as governor of New York, Roosevelt was named William McKinley's running mate in 1900, and assumed the presidency after McKinley's assassination. The youngest president at 42, "T.R." promised a Square Deal to close the gap between capital and labor, and signed progressive laws to regulate railroads and inspect food and drugs. He became the first American to win the Nobel Peace Prize, for helping to end the Russo-Japanese War, although he considered beginning the Panama Canal his greatest achievement. Roosevelt kept his pledge not to seek a third term in 1908—but in 1912 he ran against his chosen successor, William Howard Taft, who had leanings toward big business. Denied his party's nomination, Roosevelt won more than 4 million votes as the Progressive, or Bull Moose, candidate, which threw the election to Democrat Woodrow Wilson.

Rossetti, Dante Gabriel, *b. London, England, 1828; d. 1882.* **Painter and poet.** He was the most famous member of the Pre-Raphaelite Brotherhood, whose work was championed by Ruskin; Rossetti urged an adherence to nature found in Italian artwork before Raphael. Rossetti's own art was characterized by symbolism and often illus-trated scenes from literature. In his later life he published translations of Dante and several collections of his own poetry.

Roth, Philip, *b. Newark, N.J., 1933.* **Novelist, and short-story writer.** After extensive study and work as a college teacher, Roth looked to his Jewish roots for inspiration in his early fiction. He won the National Book Award for his debut, *Goodbye, Columbus* (1959), a collection of the titular novella and five short stories. *Portnoy's Complaint* (1969) was a funny and sometimes shocking story of a young Jewish man's sexual education. The prolific writer later captured the Pulitzer Prize for Fiction with *American Pastoral* (1997) and followed that with *The Human Stain* (2000).

Rothko, Mark (Marcus Rothkowitz), *b. Dvinsk, Russia (now Daugavpils, Latvia), 1903; d. 1970.* **American painter.** A major figure in the Abstract Expressionist movement who is also considered a color-field painter, Rothko migrated to the U.S. in 1913. His most famous paintings feature blurred rectangles of color resting on an abstract ground; they include *White and Greens in Blue* (1957) and *Ochre and Red on Red* (1954). Toward the final years of his career, his palette grew darker, and his life ended in suicide.

Rousseau, Jean-Jacques, *b. Geneva, 1712; d. 1778.* **Philosopher and political theorist.** After a desultory early life Rousseau met an older woman who became his patron and moving with her to Paris, began to write for Diderot's *Encyclopédie*. Rousseau was one of the Enlightenment figures who most profoundly affected French Revolutionary thought, Romanticism, and philosophy to the present day. In the *Discourse on the Inequalities of Men* (1754) and the *Social Contract* (1762), he argued that men were good and equal in the state of nature, but were corrupted by the rise of property, agriculture, commerce, and science. They entered into a "social contract" to create government to correct the inequities of civilization. He also wrote on education (*Emile*, 1762), and his autobiography (*Confessions*, 1781).

Rubens, Peter Paul, *b. Siegen, Flanders, 1577; d. 1640.* **Painter and diplomat.** Rubens developed his extremely influential Baroque style after visiting Italy, where he studied ancient sculpture, the High Renaissance, and the paintings of Caravaggio. Images like *The Raising of the Cross* (1609–10), *Rape of the Daughters of Leucippus* (1617), *Venus and Adonis* (ca. 1635) and *The Garden of Love* (ca. 1638) combine a southern European approach to color, brushwork, and light with a typically Flemish attention to meticulous, realistic detail. His paintings are characterized by swirling compositions, rosy coloring, and sensuous, fleshy figures.

Rushdie, Salman, *b. Bombay, 1947.* Indian-English novelist. A middle-class Muslim, Rushdie was educated in England, and settled there. He attracted notice with the novel *Midnight's Children* in 1981, a dreamlike allegory, set in India, that placed him in the magical realist movement. It was followed by *Shame* (1983), set in Pakistan, and *Satanic Verses* (1988), another allegorical and adventure novel whose treatment of the Prophet Muhammad aroused a call for Rushdie's death by Iran's Ayatollah Khomeini. Forced into hiding, Rushdie continued to write essays, stories, and a novel. After the death sentence was lifted in 1998, he published the novel *The Ground Beneath Her Feet* in 1999.

Rusk, (David) Dean, *b. Cherokee County, Ga., 1909; d. 1994.* Statesman. From 1946 to 1952 Rusk served in a number of posts in the State Department, and in 1952, became president of the Rockefeller Foundation. He was appointed secretary of state in 1961 by President Kennedy. After Kennedy's assassination, he continued under President Lyndon Baines Johnson and played a leading role in the escalation of U.S. involvement in the Vietnam War.

Ruskin, John, *b. London, 1819; d. 1900.* Critic. In sharp, energetic prose, Ruskin advanced the art of criticism by turning his eye initially to the works of Turner and later to art of the Middle Ages and then the work of the Pre-Raphaelites. His works on architecture include *The Seven Lamps of Architecture* (1849) and *The Stones of Venice* (1851 and 1853). His works of cultural criticism include *The Work of Iron in Nature, Art, and Policy* (1859).

Russell, Bertrand, *b. Trelleck, Wales, 1872; d. 1970.* Philosopher, mathematician, and social reformer. His most important works are *Principles of Mathematics* (1903) and, with Alfred North Whitehead, *Principia Mathematica* (3 vol., 1910-13). In these works he attempted to illustrate how the laws of mathematics can be deduced from the fundamental axioms of logic. He was an ardent realist, convinced of the dependence of knowledge on the data of experience. A social activist, he was imprisoned for being a pacifist in World War I and vigorously opposed nuclear weapons and U.S. involvement in Vietnam. He won the Nobel Prize for Literature in 1950. Other influential books include *History of Western Philosophy* (1945), *Human Knowledge: Its Scope and Limits* (1948), and his *Autobiography* (1967–69).

Ruth, Babe (George Herman Ruth), *b. Baltimore, Md., 1895; d. 1948.* Baseball player. Though some of his records have been eclipsed, Babe Ruth remains the greatest player in baseball history. As a pitcher for Boston (1914–19), the "Bambino" compiled a record of 89-46 and twice led the majors in homers. The Red Sox traded the slugging pitcher to the then-hapless New York Yankees (1920–35), who made Ruth an everyday player. His prodigious clouts ended baseball's "dead-ball era" and revived the game after the Black Sox scandal of 1919. The "Sultan of Swat" led the Bronx Bombers to seven pennants and four World Series championships. Ruth's single-season record of 60 homers, set in 1927, stood for 34 years; his career total of 714 went unsurpassed until 1974.

Rutherford, Ernest, *b. Brightwater, New Zealand, 1871; d. 1937.* New Zealander-Canadian-English physicist. Early in the 20th century, he showed that radioactivity consists of alpha particles (helium nuclei), beta radiation (electrons), and gamma rays (high-energy electromagnetic waves). Rutherford and coworkers established that radioactive elements change into other elements. They showed that the atom has a positive nucleus surrounded by negative electrons (1911); this finding resulted in Rutherford's discovery of the proton. In the 1920's he was the first to "smash" atoms, breaking up light atoms with alpha particles. In the 1930's he demonstrated fusion of atoms of heavy hydrogen (deuterium) into tritium (hydrogen with two neutrons).

Ryan, Nolan, *b. Refugio, Tex., 1947.* Baseball player. Baseball's all-time strikeout leader (5,712), Ryan was the only pitcher to throw seven no-hitters. He struck out more than 300 batters five times (1972, 1973, 1974, 1976, and 1977) over a 28-year career (1966–93). Even in his best strikeout seasons, Ryan sometimes lost more games than he won. But his winning percentage increased as he aged, and he continued to puzzle hitters well into his 40's.

Sadat, Anwar, *b. Mit Abul Kom, Egypt, 1918; d. 1981.* President of Egypt. Sadat joined Gamal Abdel Nasser to depose King Farouk in 1952, and became president when Nasser died in 1970. An economy ruined by war and discontent among the poor persuaded Sadat to seek peace with Israel. But in 1973, after Israel rejected Sadat's peace proposal, he attacked Israeli forces in the Sinai, recapturing land lost during the Six-Day War of 1967. In 1977, he made history with a visit to Israel that led to the Camp David Accords in 1979. He and Prime Minister Menachem Begin of Israel shared the 1978 Nobel Peace Prize. Sadat was assassinated in 1981 by Muslim extremists who opposed his peace initiatives.

Saladin (in Arabic, Salah Ad-din Yusuf Ibn Ayyub) *b. Tikrit, Mesopotamia, ca. 1137–38; d. 1193.* Muslim sultan of Egypt, Syria, Yemen, and Palestine. Saladin founded the Ayyubid dynasty and is the most famous of Muslim heroes. He was born into a prominent Kurdish family, and at the age of 31 was appointed vizier and commander of the Syrian troops in Egypt. Inspired by the notion of jihad, Saladin fought to unite the Muslim territories of Syria, northern Mesopotamia, Palestine, and Egypt. In 1187 his armies defended his lands against the Christian armies of the Third Crusade and took the kingdom of Jerusalem.

Samuelson, Paul Anthony, *b. Gary, Ind., 1915; d. 2009.* Economist. In his seminal book *Foundations of Economic Analysis* (1947), Samuelson used mathematical analysis to describe equilibrium and dynamics in new and innovative ways and ushered in the modern era of using sophisticated mathematics to study economics. His pioneering work explored a broad range of topics in microeconomics and macroeconomics in which he made groundbreaking contributions. His best-selling textbook, *Economics,* first published in 1948 and revised many times, was based on the theories of John Maynard Keynes. He was the first American awarded the Nobel Prize in Economic Science, in 1970.

Sanger, Margaret (Margaret Louisa Higgins), *b. Corning, N.Y., 1879; d. 1966.* Founder of the U.S. birth control movement. As an obstetrical nurse, Sanger saw countless deaths from childbirth and botched abortions; this experience persuaded her to dedicate her life to birth control, a term she coined. Her birth-control clinic, the first of its kind, led to her arrest in 1917 for creating a "public nuisance," but it swayed public opinion in favor of birth control. In 1921 she founded the American Birth Control League, which evolved into Planned Parenthood Federation of America; Sanger was its first honorary chairman.

Sappho *b. Lesbos, Asia Minor, ca. 610 B.C.; d. ?580 B.C.* Greek lyric poet. Little is known of Sappho's life, and only fragments of her work survive. She was probably married to an aristocrat with whom she had a daughter, but spent most of her adult life as a poet and teacher to an association of women in Mytilene on the island of Lesbos. These associations were common for young, unmarried aristocratic women at the time, but Sappho's group was thought to be superior. Her work is of a very personal nature, often expressing passionate emotions toward other women, but whether or not she was actually homosexual is unknown. Her work was extolled by her contemporaries and later poets and thinkers in the ancient world.

Sargent, John Singer, *b. Florence, Italy, 1856; d. 1925.* American painter active in England. Sargent was influenced by the Impressionists and the Barbizon school, and became the most sought-after portrait painter in both England and the United States. His best-known works include the dramatic *Madame Gautreau* ("Madame X") (1884), and *Carnation, Lily, Lily, Rose* (1885–86). In 1894 Sargent accepted a commission to create a series of murals for the Boston Public Library; this and another commission at the Boston Museum of Fine Arts occupied much of his energy for the rest of his career.

Sartre, Jean-Paul, *b. Paris, 1905; d. 1980.* Philosopher and author. Sartre was a leading philosopher of existentialism whose work achieved popular success after World War II. His works include his definitive philosophical book *Being and Nothingness* (1943), plays, such as *No Exit* (1944), and several novels. He portrays the individual adrift in a meaningless universe, possessed of a frightening freedom of choice. He declined to accept the 1964 Nobel Prize in Literature. With Bertrand Russell, he opposed U.S. involvement in Vietnam.

Schiller, Friedrich, *b. Marbach, Germany, 1759; d. 1805.* Playwright and poet. Along with Goethe, his friend and contemporary, Schiller figured prominently in the German Romantic period. Through his plays and poems, Schiller displayed a revolutionary mind; he also wrote a history of the revolt of the Netherlands. Schiller's plays include *The Robbers* (1781), the *Wallenstein* trilogy (1796–99), and *William Tell* (1804). His most famous poem, "Ode to Joy," provided the words sung in the fourth movement of Beethoven's Ninth Symphony.

Schoenberg, Arnold, *b. Vienna, 1874; d. 1951.* Composer, conductor, and teacher. One of the most influential figures in the history of music, Schoenberg developed the revolutionary 12-tone system of composition, in which each of the 12 notes in an octave are played in a set order, resulting in a rigid atonality. Notable works include *Pelleas und Melisande,* Op. 5 (1902–03); *3 Pieces for Pianoforte,* Op. 11 (1909); *Das Buch der Hängenden Gärten,* Op. 15 (1908–09); *Five Orchestral Pieces,* Op. 16 (1909); *Pierrot Lunaire,* Op. 21 (1912); *Five Piano Pieces,* Op. 23 (1920–23), *Serenade,* Op. 24 (1920–23); and *Suite for piano,* Op. 25 (1921).

Schopenhauer, Arthur, *b. Danzig, Prussia, 1788; d. 1860.* Philosopher. He taught at the University of Berlin but failed to gain a following, in part because of his surly temperament. After 1831 he lived reclusively in Frankfurt am Main. His emphasis on the primacy of the will, enunciated in *The World as Will and Representation* (1819), places him in opposition to Hegel and German idealism and as a significant influence on Wagner, Nietzsche, Tolstoy, and Freud. To him the will was greater than reason or spirit, but because the individual will cannot be satisfied and comes into conflict with others, the will must be negated. Relief from its frustrations can be found in art.

Schrödinger, Erwin, *b. Vienna, 1887; d. 1961.* Physicist. Schrödinger is known primarily as the creator in 1926 of the wave equation for quantum mechanics, a year after Werner Heisenberg's development of quantum mechanics. Schrödinger's equation allows physicists to compute energy levels for electrons and remains an important tool in particle physics. After World War II, Schrödinger considered fundamental problems in biology, expressing his views in the philosophical book *What Is Life?* (1944).

Schubert, Franz, *b. Vienna, 1797; d. 1828.* Composer of the early Romantic era. Schubert is best known for his contributions in chamber music, piano music, and German lieder. Notable works include Quintet in A Major (*Trout*) for Piano and Strings (1819); *Fantasia* in C (*Wanderer*) (1822); Symphony No. 8 in B Minor (*Unfinished*) (1822); the song cycle *Die Schöne Müllerin* (1823); String Quartet No. 14 in D Minor (*Death and the Maiden*) (1824); Symphony No. 9 in C Major (*Great*) (1825); Piano Trio No. 1 (*lieder*) in B^b (1827); and more than 500 individual songs.

Schumann, Robert, *b. Zwickau, Germany, 1810; d. 1856.* German composer, pianist, conductor, and critic of the Romantic era. Husband of the composer and pianist Clara Schumann (1819–96), his duel interest in literature and music led him to develop historically informed music criticism, as well as a musical style deeply indebted to literary models. Notable works include *Carnaval: Scènes Mignonnes sur 4 notes*, Op. 9 (1834–4); *Fantasy in C*, Op. 17 (1836); *Kinderscenen*, Op. 15 (1838); the song cycle *Dichterliebe*, Op. 48 (1840); Symphony No. 4 in D Minor (1841), Op. 120; and Piano Concerto in A Minor, Op. 54 (1841-5).

Schumpeter, Joseph Alois, *b. Triesch, now the Czech Republic, 1883; d. 1950.* Economist. Schumpeter first worked in Austria and later in the U.S. He is best known for his theory of entrepreneurship, first articulated in *Theory of Economic Development* (1911). In it he argued that economic growth depends on individual entrepreneurs

who innovate in pursuit of profit. Later books, including *Business Cycles* (1939) and *Capitalism, Socialism, and Democracy* (1942), concluded that capitalism was doomed to be destroyed by government, leading to socialism. His *History of Economic Thought* (1954) was published posthumously.

Scorsese, Martin, *b. Flushing, N.Y., 1942.* American film director. Abandoning his plan to enter the Roman Catholic priesthood, Scorsese went on to earn degrees in filmmaking from New York University. His first film was released in 1968, but he achieved critical notice in 1973 with *Mean Streets*, the first of many successful collaborations with Robert DeNiro. Although he directed musicals (*New York, New York*, 1977), and romances (*The Age of Innocence*, 1993), Scorsese is best known for his violent depictions of American culture, including *Taxi Driver* (1976), *Raging Bull* (1980), *Goodfellas* (1990), *Casino* (1995) and *Gangs of New York* (2002). Nominated six times for awards for writing and directing, Scorsese won his first Academy Award for best director in 2006 for *The Departed*, which was also named best picture. He received the American Film Institute's Life Achievement Award in 1997.

Scott, Walter, *b. Edinburgh, 1771; d. 1832.* Poet and novelist. Scott was a very popular and extraordinarily productive writer. He wrote short lyrical poems and ballads (e.g., "Lochinvar,") and long narrative poems influenced by medieval romance (*The Lay of the Last Minstrel*, 1805; *The Lady of the Lake*, 1810) and was an originator of the regional and the historical novel. His first fictional efforts were the "Waverley novels," a series of colorful, well-plotted narratives set in Scotland, including *Waverley* (1814), *Rob Roy*, and *The Heart of Midlothian* (both 1818). *Ivanhoe* (1820), set in 12th-century England, was his first historical novel, followed by *Kenilworth* (1821) and several others.

Selznick, David O., *b. Pittsburgh, Pa., 1902; d. 1965.* Film producer. The most successful independent producer of the golden age of Hollywood, Selznick worked for MGM, Paramount, and RKO before forming Selznick International in 1936. He brought Ingrid Bergman and Alfred Hitchcock to America, and he produced the first major films of George Cukor and Katharine Hepburn. In 1939, he guided *Gone with the Wind* through three directors and fifteen screenwriters; one of the most expensive productions of its time, it became one of the most profitable films in history.

Sen, Amartya, *b. Santiniketan, India, 1933.* Economist. As a boy in Bengal, Sen witnessed the horrific famine of 1943—an experience that informed his lifework in economics, which has focused on human rights, poverty, inequality, and hunger. In 1981 Sen wrote *Poverty and Famines*, which explained why the poor may starve even when there is adequate food production. Sen was instrumental in creating and refining the United Nations Human Development Index, which measures the well-being of each country. The first Asian to head an Oxbridge college—Trinity College, Cambridge—Sen has taught at many of the world's most prestigious universities. He received the Nobel Prize in Economics in 1998.

Seuss, Dr. (Geisel, Theodore Seuss), *b. Springfield, Mass., 1904; d. 1991.* Children's writer and illustrator. Geisel was originally an illustrator for magazines such as *Life* and *Vanity Fair*, and later worked in advertising. He became an immensely popular writer and illustrator of children's books. Among his most popular books are *How the Grinch Stole Christmas* (1957), *The Cat in the Hat* (1957), and *Green Eggs and Ham* (1960). Geisel's work is characterized by an enormous vocabulary of nonsense words and by the introduction of chaos to ordered life.

Seward, William, *b. Florida, N.Y., 1801; d. 1872.* Politician. As governor (1839–43) and senator from New York (1849–61), Seward led the antislavery arm of the Whig Party. He joined the Republicans in 1855 as the Whigs' influence waned. Seward lost the Republican presidential nomination in 1860, then campaigned hard for Abraham Lincoln, who appointed him secretary of state. He was stabbed the same night Lincoln was assassinated, but survived and returned to his position, holding the government together during a national crisis. In 1867, he negotiated the purchase of Alaska from Russia for $7.2 million.

Shaka, *b. ca. 1787; d. 1828.* Zulu leader. An outcast at birth, Shaka proved himself a brilliant warrior and became head of the Zulus in 1816. Under his leadership, the foundations of a Zulu empire in southern Africa were laid, based on strict discipline and standardized tactics and weapons. After his mother died in 1827, he became increasingly erratic and was murdered.

Shakespeare, William. *b. Stratford-on-Avon, 1564; d. 1616.* Playwright and poet. Considered the greatest of all English playwrights, Shakespeare was the author of 38 plays—13 comedies, 10 histories, 10 tragedies, and five romances—dramatic poems, and a sequence of 154 sonnets. (see pp. 377–79 for a full discussion of his life.)

Shannon, Claude, *b. Petoskey, Mich., 1916; d. 2001.* American Mathematician and electrical engineer. Widely known as "the father of Information Theory," Shannon's M.I.T. master's thesis, *A Symbolic Analysis of Relay and Switching Circuits* (1940) is considered one of the most important papers of the 20th century due to its influence on modern computing and telecommunications. Using Boolean algebra, he introduced the theoretical ideas behind digital circuits. After graduating he worked at Bell Labs, helping the war effort with his work in cryptography and missile control systems. His 1948 paper "A Mathematical Theory of Communication," laid the framework for the field of information theory, which is described as "a mathematical representation of the conditions and parameters affecting the transmission and processing of information."

Shaw, Artie (Arthur Jacob Arshawsky), *b. New York, N.Y., 1910; d. 2004.* Clarinetist. A leading musician of the swing era, Shaw toured with dance bands from 1926 to 1937, when he formed the Artie Shaw Orchestra. His hit of 1938, Cole Porter's "Begin the Beguine," launched his career. A reluctant idol, he withdrew from the public eye in 1939 and resurfaced in Hollywood, where he was as famous for his marriages to Ava Gardner and Lana Turner as he was for his music. His hits during this period included "Star Dust," "Moon Glow," and "Dancing in the Dark." In the 1940's and 1950's he organized several groups and big bands and issued recordings including "Little Jazz" with Roy Eldridge, now considered a classic. Shaw was a superb technical musician, at home with classical music as well as jazz, and he performed with numerous symphony orchestras and chamber groups.

Shaw, George Bernard, *b. Dublin, 1856; d. 1950.* Playwright and critic. Shaw settled in London in 1816 and became England's leading social critic, art critic, and one of the great modern playwrights. A socialist, he wrote plays with a broad range of historical and social settings but specialized in witty comedies that satirized English middle-class pretension and convention. An early play, *Mrs. Warren's Profession* (1893), dealt humorously with prostitution. *Candida* (1896) presented the first of Shaw's great heroines, a type that took fullest form with *Saint Joan* (1923). Other plays are *The Devil's Disciple* (1897), *Caesar and Cleopatra* (1899), *Man and Superman* (1904), *Major Barbara* (1905), *Pygmalion* (1913), and his melancholy World War I play, *Heartbreak House* (1917).

Shelley, Percy Bysshe, *b. Horsham, Sussex, England, 1792; d. 1822.* Poet. Born to wealth, Shelley was attracted to nonconformity and radical causes. His first significant poem, *Queen Mab*, advocated the toppling of established institutions. With Mary Wollstonecraft Godwin, the novelist, he fled to France, then Italy, where he created his finest works before drowning at age 30. These include his masterpiece, the verse drama *Prometheus Unbound*; a tragedy, *The Cenci* (both 1819); *Epipsychidion* (1821); and *Adonais* (1821), his elegy for John Keats. Famous shorter poems are the ironic "Ozymandias" and the lyric "Ode to the West Wind." Shelley was a moral and philosophical poet who hoped for human redemption through the power of love.

Sherman, William Tecumseh, *b. Lancaster, Ohio, 1820; d. 1891.* **Civil War general.** An 1840 West Point graduate, Sherman served in the Mexican War. A strong supporter of the Union, Sherman was a reluctant military leader who was promoted to major general after several successes, especially at the battle of Shiloh. His famous capture of Atlanta and subsequent "march to the sea" introduced a "total warfare," or the complete destruction of the general infrastructure and countryside through which he marched, thus reducing the Confederacy's ability to wage war. In 1869 he became commanding general of the army and used his position to enact a policy of forcing Indian tribes onto separate reservations, again using his tactic of economic destruction. Reported to have said, "War is hell."

Shockley, William Bradford, *b. London, 1910; d. 1989.* **American physicist.** With his collaborators John Bardeen (1908–91) and Walter H. Brittain, Shockey developed the first transistor, which eventually replaced larger vacuum tubes that consumed more power in electronic applications for consumer products, a crucial development in the emerging computer industry. The three received the Nobel Prize in Physics in 1956. In his later years Shockley was accused of racism for his views on eugenics and inherited intelligence.

Sinatra, Frank (Francis Albert Sinatra) *b. Hoboken, N.J. 1915; d. 1998.* **American singer and actor.** The "chairman of the board" started out in the 1940's as a big band crooner who sent teenage girls into shrieking hysterics at Times Square's Paramount; his smooth style and sophisticated way with lyrics in many recordings made him an enduring star. His early films were musicals, notably *On the Town* (1949); then he was reborn as a dramatic actor, winning an Oscar for *From Here to Eternity* (1953). Later films include *The Manchurian Candidate* (1962) and *The Detective* (1968).

Sitting Bull (Tatanka Iyotaka), *b. Grand River, Lakota Nation (S. D.), ca. 1831; d. 1890.* **American Indian chief.** Known for his resistance to U.S. power and promises, Sitting Bull became head chief of the Lakota nation around 1868. After joining with Chief Gall and Crazy Horse to massacre General George Armstrong Custer's Seventh Cavalry at Little Bighorn (1876), Sitting Bull fled to Canada. The near-extinction of buffalo in Canada forced him to surrender to U.S. authorities in 1881. In 1885, he joined Buffalo Bill's Wild West Show. In 1890, he was arrested by Lakota police and was killed during a gunfight when his acolytes tried to rescue him.

Smith, Adam, *b. Kirkcaldy, Scotland, 1723; d. 1790.* **Economist and philosopher.** With the publication of *An Inquiry into the Nature* and *Causes of the Wealth of Nations* (1776), Smith laid the foundations of classical economics. He rejected the prevailing policy of mercantilism and argued instead that if individuals are left to pursue their self-interest without government interference they will act, in Smith's famous words, as if "led by an invisible hand" to benefit society as a whole. He also explored the concepts of the division of labor, specialization, free trade, the determination of price and value, the distribution of income, and the accumulation of capital.

Smith, Emmitt, *b. Pensacola, Fla., 1969.* **Football player.** In 2002–03, his 13th season in the NFL, running back Emmitt Smith broke Walter Payton's all-time rushing record of 16,726 yards. Already the career leader in rushing touchdowns, Smith reached the landmark 150th of his career later that season. Despite his small stature (5'9"), the quick, powerful running back was an All-America at the University of Florida in 1989. As a pro, he won four rushing titles, three Super Bowls, and one Player of the Year award (1993) with the Cowboys. He is considered a certain member of the Pro Football Hall of Fame.

Smith, Kate, *b. Greenville, Va., 1907; d. 1986.* **American popular singer.** In a career that spanned over 50 years from the 1920's to the early 70's, she was one of the most popular entertainers in the history of radio and television. Blessed with a powerful but pleasing contralto voice, Smith is best known for her rendition of "God Bless America." During World War II she performed constantly for the soldiers and raised more money for the war effort than any other celebrity. Her famous theme song "When the Moon Comes Over the Mountain" was written by her.

Socrates, *b. Athens, 469 B.C.; d. 399 B.C.* Philosopher. One of the greatest philosophers, he is known from the works of his pupil Plato and those of Xenophon. Socrates eagerly discussed justice, piety, and virtue with his fellow citizens, seeking wisdom about correct conduct to help guide the affairs of Athens. He used the dialectic (or Socratic) method, posing questions and examining the implications of responses. Socrates looked upon the soul as the seat of consciousness and character, equating virtue with the knowledge of true self. His trial and death with the cup of poison hemlock are described by Plato.

Solon, *b. ca. 630 B.C.; d. ca. 560 B.C.* Athenian statesman; one of the seven wise men of Greece. Solon ended exclusive aristocratic control of the government, substituted control by the wealthy, and introduced a more humane code of law. His reforms included forbidding mortgages on bodies; repealing the laws of Dracon, which punished even small offenses with death; creating a supreme court; and forming the council of 400, with 100 members each from the four tribes in Athens. Solon was also a noted poet, using poetry to forward his ideas to the populace.

Solzhenitsyn, Aleksandr, *b. Kislovodsk, Russia, 1918; d. 2008.* Novelist and historian. In 1945 Solzhenitsyn was sent to a labor camp for eight years for criticizing Stalin. His novel about the camps, *One Day in the Life of Ivan Denisovich,* was published with the blessing of Premier Khrushchev in 1962. Later critical novels, *The First Circle* and *The Cancer Ward* (both 1968), led to restrictions of his freedom, and *The Gulag Archipelago* (1973), about the Stalinist prison system, led to his expulsion from the Soviet Union in 1974. After living in Vermont, he returned to Russia in 1994. Other books are the novel *August 1914* and the nonfiction *The Oak and the Calf* and *The Mortal Danger* (both 1980).

Sondheim, Stephen, *b. New York City, 1930.* Broadway musical composer/lyricist. In his long career he has won the Tony, the Oscar, the Grammy and the Pulitzer Prize. Mentored by Oscar Hammerstein II, he wrote the lyrics for two landmark musicals, *West Side Story* (1957) and *Gypsy* (1959) while still in his 20s. With *A Funny Thing Happened on the Way to the Forum* (1962) and thereafter he created both the clever words and sometimes challenging music for such hits as *Company* (1970), *Follies* (1971), *A Little Night Music* (1973, featuring the popular song "Send in the Clowns"), *Sweeny Todd* (1979), *Sunday in the Park with George* (1984), *Into the Woods* 1987), and *Passion* (1994). An annotated collection of his lyrics, *Finishing the Hat,* was published in 2010.

Sophocles, *b. Colonus, Greece, ca. 496 B.C.; d. 406* B.C. Playwright. Sophocles is thought to have written 123 plays, of which only seven survive. As exemplified in his masterpieces, *Oedipus Rex, Antigone, Electra, Philoctetes,* and *Ajax,* his plays demonstrate an economy of events and characters and a sense of inexorable movement toward a tragic fate. Chief among his innovations in theater were introducing a third actor to the stage and increasing the size of the chorus from 12 to 15 members.

Soyinka, Wole (Akinwande Oluwole), *b. Obeokuta, Nigeria, 1934.* Dramatist, novelist, essayist. Soyinka, the first black African to win the Nobel Prize in Literature, writes in English. After founding theater companies, he was imprisoned in the 1960's for his support of Biafran secession. He wrote *Poems from Prison* and a prose account, *The Man Died* (1972), about the experience. Some of his plays, such as the early *Dance of the Forest* (1960), are comically satirical; others are more seriously critical of Nigerian society and government. These include *Kongi's Harvest* (1965), *Death and the King's Horseman* (1975), and *From Zia with Love* (1992). He has written literary essays, an autobiography, *Ake* (1981); and novels, including *The Interpreters* (1965).

Spelling, Aaron, *b. Dallas, Tex., 1923; d. 2006.* American television producer. Spelling began his prolific career as an actor in the 1950's, before moving into production with the *Zane Grey Theater* in 1960. After his first runaway hit, *The Mod Squad* (1968), he produced many hit shows, including *Starsky and Hutch, Love Boat, Charlie's Angels, Dynasty, Beverly Hills 90210* and *Melrose Place.* He produced more than 200 television series and movies, which tended to be disliked by critics and loved by audiences.

Spenser, Edmund, *b. London, 1552/3; d. 1599.* Poet. Spenser is deemed the leading nondramatic Elizabethan poet and was a great originator of verse patterns. His first important work, *The Shepheardes Calendar* (1579), was a series of Virgilian pastoral eclogues. In 1580 he became secretary to the lord deputy of Ireland and there composed his greatest, though unfinished, work, *The Faerie Queene* (1590–96), an allegorical and fiercely anti-Catholic epic-romance, structured in beautiful nine-line "Spenserian stanzas." Other works include his sonnet sequence, *Amoretti;* a marriage poem, *Epithalamion,* and *Astrophel,* his elegy for Sir Philip Sidney, all published in 1595.

Spielberg, Steven, b. *Cincinnati, Ohio, 1947.* Film director and producer. A skilled craftsman and storyteller, Spielberg specializes in genre action-driven films which he imbues with universal themes and emotional resonance. Crowd-pleasers such as *Raiders of the Lost Ark* (1981), *E.T.* (1982), and *Jurassic Park* (1992) have shattered worldwide box-office records; and his more thoughtful films have become cultural touchstones, as with *Schindler's List* (1993) and *Saving Private Ryan* (1998). In 1994 Spielberg formed a studio, Dreamworks SKG, in partnership with two other industry heavyweights.

Spinoza, Baruch, b. *Amsterdam, 1632; d. 1677.* Philosopher. Spinoza was a member of the Amsterdam's Sephardic Jewish community, from which he was expelled for heresy. He was by trade a lens grinder but achieved great philosophical fame in his own day. The major work published in his lifetime is *A Treatise on Religious and Political Philosophy* (1670). For Spinoza, truth (like geometry) follows from first principles; ideas and physical things are the aspects of a single substance, God and Nature, where God is Nature in its fullness. A virtuous person acts out of understanding, and his ambition is the intellectual love of God.

Spitz, Mark, b. *Modesto, Calif., 1950.* Swimmer. Spitz won an unprecedented seven gold medals—four in individual events and three in relays, all in world-record time—at the 1972 Olympics in Munich. It was the most dominant performance by any swimmer in the history of the games. Combined with his haul in 1968, Spitz won a total of 11 Olympic medals (9 gold, 1 silver, 1 bronze). Spitz swam for four national collegiate championship teams at Indiana University. He set a total of 33 world records and 38 U.S. records during his career.

Spock, Benjamin McLane (Dr. Spock), b. *New Haven, Conn., 1903; d. 1998.* Pediatrician and author. *Dr. Spock's Common Sense Book of Baby and Child Care* (1946) has been the bible of new parents since its publication, which coincided with the start of the U.S. baby boom. It has sold nearly 50 million copies and has been translated into dozens of languages. While most pediatricians of his era stressed rigid feeding schedules and discouraged parents from publicly showing affection for their children, Spock urged permissiveness and flexibility. He was convicted for counseling draft evaders during the Vietnam War but the conviction was later overturned.

Springsteen, Bruce Frederick, b. *Freehold, N.J., 1949.* Rock-pop vocalist, guitarist, and songwriter. Springsteen was hailed by critics of the mid-1970's as the "savior of rock and roll." His music embodies all the best aspects of rock, combining driving rhythms, majestic "wall of sound" production values, and thoughtful lyrics. His roots-oriented rock has enjoyed enormous popularity through three decades, with his concerts with the E Street Band approaching the fervor of religious revivals. His albums include *Born to Run* (1975), *Darkness on the Edge of Town* (1978), *The River* (1980), *Nebraska* (1982), *Born in the U.S.A.* (1984), and *The Rising* (2002).

Stalin, Joseph (Josif Vissarionovich Dzhugashvili), b. *Gori, Georgia, 1879; d. 1953.* Soviet dictator. A Bolshevik from 1903, Stalin outmaneuvered his rivals to assume Lenin's mantle as leader of the Soviet Union in 1924. His implementation of successive agricultural and industrial five-year plans proved economically ruinous, and his extreme paranoia led to the execution of millions suspected of being bourgeois, counterrevolutionary, or otherwise a threat to his power. His nonaggression pact with Hitler proved short-lived, and Germany's invasion in 1940 resulted in catastrophic losses. Nonetheless, Stalin managed to build a powerful military that was instrumental in defeating Germany. After the war he brought Eastern Europe into the Soviet sphere and developed atomic weapons thereby precipitating the 50-year-long cold war.

Stanton, Elizabeth Cady, b. *Johnstown, N.Y., 1815; d. 1902.* Feminist social reformer. In 1848 she helped to organize the first women's rights convention in the U.S. and she was a driving force in the women's movement for 50 years. She and Susan B. Anthony formed the National Woman Suffrage Association, with Stanton as president. Stanton published *Revolution*, a feminist newspaper; was coauthor of the first three volumes of the *History of Woman Suffrage* (1881–86); and produced the *Women's Bible*, which recast many biblical passages that Stanton found derogatory to women.

Stein, Gertrude, b. *Allegheny, Pa., 1874; d. 1946.* Novelist and poet. Stein was a key figure of the artistic world of the early 20th century, not so much for her own works as through her association with numerous authors and painters. Her flat in Paris served as a salon for such people as Picasso, F. Scott Fitzgerald, and Ernest Hemingway. In her own writing, she experimented with techniques such as the cubist styles seen in the poems of *Tender Buttons* (1914), or in perspective, as evidenced in the *Autobiography of Alice B. Toklas* (1933), the story of her own life as seen through the eyes of her longtime companion.

Steinbeck, John, b. *Salinas, Calif., 1902; d. 1968.* Novelist and short-story writer. One of the great American authors of the 20th century, he won the Pulitzer Prize for his novel, *The Grapes of Wrath* (1939), which follows a poor Oklahoma farming family as they seek work in California during the Depression. A former reporter and fruit picker, Steinbeck lived and worked with Oklahoma migrants for two years (1937–1939) prior to the novel's release. Much of his work explores the human condition, the California landscape, and the exploitation of the poor and underprivileged, as is reflected in his first successful novel, *Tortilla Flat* (1935), and other well-known novels such as *Of Mice and Men* (1937) and *East of Eden* (1952). He also wrote the memoir *Travels with Charley* (1962) and served as a foreign correspondent during World War II and Vietnam. He was awarded the Nobel Prize in Literature in 1962.

Steinem, Gloria, b. *Toledo, Ohio, 1934.* Feminist writer. Steinem began her career as a journalist with an attention-grabbing article called "I Was a Playboy Bunny" (1963), recounting her experience as a waitress at Hugh Hefner's Playboy Club. In 1971, she helped found the National Women's Political Caucus, she also launched *Ms.* magazine, which covered current events from a feminist viewpoint. She is the author of *Outrageous Acts and Everyday Rebellions* (1983), a collection of essays; and *Revolution from Within* (1992), a nonfiction work on women's self-esteem.

Stendhal (Marie-Henri Beyle), b. *Grenoble, France, 1783; d. 1842.* Novelist. Stendhal, a self-proclaimed egotist, called this same trait in his characters "Beylism," after himself. At odds with his father and the Catholic Church, he joined Napoleon's army and began writing in Milan after the emperor's final defeat in 1814. Following the unsuccessful novel *Armance* (1827), he published his most famous novel, *The Red and the Black*, in 1831, about a young, ambitious priest who engages in a tempestuous adulterous affair. His other great novel is *The Charterhouse of Parma* (1839), featuring a quintessential passionate egotist. In the 1830's Stendhal served as French consul at Trieste and Civitavecchia.

Stevens, Wallace, b. *Reading, Pa., 1879; d. 1955.* Poet. The imaginative variety in Stevens's poetry is remarkable, considering that for much of his life he was an executive at an insurance company in Hartford, Conn., and maintained little contact with the literary world. Nevertheless, Stevens stands as a major poet of the early 20th century.

His most famous poems, "Sunday Morning" and "Thirteen Ways of Looking at a Blackbird," exhibit his characteristic symbolism and love for the imagination. His editions include *Harmonium* (1923), *Notes Towards a Supreme Fiction* (1942), and *Collected Poems* (1954) which won the Pulitzer Prize.

Stewart, James, b. *Indiana, Pa., 1908; d. 1997.* American movie actor. His likable persona moved easily from stage to screen and gave us the drawling innocent guy he personified in *Mr. Smith Goes to Washington* (1939), *The Shop Around the Corner* (1940) and the Capra classic *It's a Wonderful Life* (1946). He won an Oscar for *The Philadelphia Story* (1940). Darker roles and a newfound intensity replaced the shy charm in several westerns, such as *The Naked Spur* (1953), *The Man Who Shot Liberty Valence* (1962), *Rear Window* (1954), and *Vertigo* (1958).

Stieglitz, Alfred, b. *Hoboken, N.J., 1864; d. 1946.* Photographer. One of America's most influential photographers, Stieglitz promoted photography as art and was a great supporter of modern art in the United States. Stieglitz founded and led a succession of photography groups, publications, and galleries, including Photo-Secession, *Camera Work*, and the "291" gallery. His most notable works include *Sun's Rays—Paula, Berlin* (1889), *Steerage* (1907), and a series of his wife, the painter Georgia O'Keeffe. His *Equivalents* series, composed mainly of cloud and sky photographs, was revolutionary in conveying emotion through form instead of subject.

Stiglitz, Joseph, b. *Gary, Ind., 1943.* Economist. Stiglitz, a critic of globalization, served as a member of President Clinton's Council of Economic Advisors. Stiglitz was chief economist for the World Bank from 1997 to 2000, until he resigned under pressure for refusing to refrain from open disagreements with the institution's policies. A professor at Columbia University, Stiglitz received the 2001 Nobel Prize in Economics for his advanced theoretical work on the "economics of information," focusing specifically on markets in which the players have "asymmetric information."

Stirling, James Frazer, b. *Glasgow, 1926; d. 1992.* Scots architect. Stirling's early work in collaboration with James Gowan included the Engineering Building (1959–63) at the University of Leicester, which brought him to prominence. Later, in collaboration with Michael Wilford, he designed the Music School and Theater Academy (1977–84) in Stuttgart, Germany, which combines the materials and planning of a prior 18th-century museum into a new configuration of geometric forms in harmony with its site; and the Performing Arts Center (1983–88) at Cornell University.

Stowe, Harriet Beecher, *b. Litchfield, Conn., 1811; d. 1896.* **Author/abolitionist.** Sister of the famous preacher and abolitionist Henry Ward Beecher, she is best known as the author of *Uncle Tom's Cabin* (1852), an abolitionist novel that ignited a storm of controversy. Its vivid depiction of the brutality of slavery was dismissed by critics as propaganda, but the novel galvanized the national debate. Abraham Lincoln referred to her as "the little lady who made this big war."

Strauss, Richard, *b. Munich, 1864; d. 1949.* **German composer, conductor, and pianist.** Equally adept at conducting and composing, Strauss was a master of several musical forms, most notably operas and orchestral tone poems; his richly melodic work embraced a fading romanticism in stark contrast to the increasingly atonal musical environment of the 20th century. Notable works include the tone poems *Tod und Verklärung* (1888–89); *Till Eulenspiegels Lustige Streiche* (1894–95); *Also sprach Zarathustra* (1896); and *Don Juan* (1898); the operas *Salome* (1903–05); *Elektra* (1906–08); and *Der Rosenkavalier* (1909–10); and the symphonic works *Metamorphosen* (1945); and *Vier Letzte Lieder (Four Last Songs)* (1947–48).

Stravinsky, Igor, *b. Oranienbaum, Russia, 1882; d. 1971.* **Russian-born composer, conductor, pianist, and writer.** One of the most widely performed and influential composers of the 20th century, Stravinsky explored a variety of musical styles over the course of his career. His most notorious composition, the ballet *The Rite of Spring* (1911–3), shocked audiences with its abrasive harmonies and jagged rhythms. Notable works include *The Firebird* (1909–10); *Petrushka* (1910–11); *Les Noces* (1914–17); *L'histoire du soldat (The Soldier's Tale)* (1918); *Symphonies of Wind Instruments* (1918–20); *Oedipus Rex* (1926–7); *Symphony of Psalms* (1930); *Symphony in C* (1938–40); *Symphony in Three Movements* (1942–5); and *Orpheus* (1947).

Streep, Meryl, *b. Summit, N.J., 1949.* **Movie actress.** After Yale Drama School and some Broadway and TV roles, she made her mark in films with prodigious skill at accents and a presence at once cool and intense. Notable films include *Silkwood* (1983) and *A Cry in the Dark* (1988). She had Oscar-winning roles in *Kramer vs. Kramer* (1979) and *Sophie's Choice* (1982), and performed in *Angels in America* (2004).

Streisand, Barbra, *b. Brooklyn, N.Y., 1942.* **Singer and actress.** After early nightclub stints, she won wider attention on Broadway in *I Can Get for You Wholesale* (1962) and became a star playing Fanny Brice in *Funny Girl* onstage and winning an Oscar for the film (1968). Numerous recordings "Evergreen", "People" and "Don't Rain on My Parade", and "The Way We Were"—have given her dynamic voice wide popularity, as has her resolute self-importance in such films as *The Way We Were* (1973), *A Star Is Born* (1976)—and *Yentl* (1983), which she also directed.

Strindberg, August (Johan), *b. Stockholm, Sweden, 1849; d. 1912.* **Playwright, novelist, short-story writer.** Strindberg's early work, characterized by naturalistic dialogue, fascination with psychology, and starkness of setting as exemplified in the play *Miss Julie* (1888), turned a radical, critical eye on Swedish society, exploring issues of social class and relations between the sexes. His later work, such as *A Dream Play* (1902) and *The Ghost Sonata* (1907), rely on symbols rather than realistic depiction of events to explore the internal world.

Styron, William, *b. Newport News, Va., 1925; d. 2006.* **Novelist.** His first novel, *Lie Down in Darkness* (1951), established him as a distinctive southern voice in the tradition of Faulkner. In 1968 he won the Pulitzer Prize for his controversial novel *The Confessions of Nat Turner* (1967), a fictional account of the violent slave rebellion of 1831. With his best seller, *Sophie's Choice* (1979), he moved beyond those limitations, telling the story of a female Polish Catholic Holocaust survivor struggling to come to terms with a heartbreaking decision. The novel was made into an opera and a highly successful film (1982), for which Meryl Streep won the Academy Award for best actress.

Suharto, Thojib N J, *b. Java, Dutch East Indies (now Indonesia), 1921; d. 2008.* **President of Indonesia, 1967–98.** Suharto had a successful military career, rising through the ranks of the Indonesian army following the country's independence to become a major general in 1962. In 1965 he helped crush a left-wing coup. He took control of the Indonesian government in 1966 and was appointed president the following year. Three decades of uninterrupted rule followed, giving Indonesia much-needed political stability and sustained economic growth. In 1998, Suharto's authoritarian regime fell victim to an economic downturn and its own internal corruption.

Sukarno, *b. Java, Dutch East Indies (now Indonesia), 1901; d. 1970.* Leader of the Indonesian independence movement and the country's first president (1945–67). Sukarno spent two years in a Dutch jail and eight years in exile for challenging colonialism. In 1945 he defined the *pantjasila* ("five principles") of nationalism, internationalism, democracy, social prosperity, and belief in God, which became the state doctrine. That same year, Sukarno declared Indonesia's independence and became president of the new republic, eventually suppressing the country's original parliamentary system in favor of an authoritarian "guided democracy." He was deposed in 1966 by Suharto's coup d'état.

Sulayman the Magnificent (Sulayman I), *b. ca. 1495; d. 1566.* Becoming sultan of the Ottoman Empire in 1520, he undertook campaigns that led to its naval dominance in the eastern Mediterranean and extended its military power into central Europe. Sulayman also undertook campaigns in the east that succeeded in bringing Iraq under Ottoman control, but he failed to conquer Persia. In 1551, he conquered Tripoli, in modern Libya. Sulayman was a noted patron of architecture and the arts in general.

Sulla, Lucius Cornelius, *b. 138 B.C.; d. 78 B.C.* Roman general and politician. Sulla was dictator of Rome from 82 to 79 B.C. He began his career under Gaius Marius; after fighting several victorious wars abroad, Sulla returned to Rome and was declared a public enemy by Marius's ruling party. Sulla's march on Rome launched the empire's first civil war, which ended with his victory at Colline Gate in 82. As the new dictator, he chose the name Felix. During his rule he reorganized the senate and judiciary and strengthened the Roman Empire.

Sullivan, Louis Henri , *b. Boston, 1856; d 1924.* American architect. With his partner, Dankmar Adler (1844–1900), Sullivan realized that the skyscraper, made desirable by rising real estate prices and made possible by modern building materials, required a new aesthetic celebrating verticality. His Wainright Building in St. Louis (1890–1991) epitomizes his famous statement that a tall building "must be every inch a proud and soaring thing." Other important works included the Guaranty Building (1894–96), Buffalo, and the Schlesinger-Mayer department Store (1898–1904, now the Carson-Pirie-Scott store), Chicago. The maxim "form follows function"— that is, the look of a building must be subordinate to its purpose—is also attributed to Sullivan and was later taken up by other 20th-century architects.

Sun Yat-sen, *b. Guangdong Province, China, 1866; d. 1925.* Chinese Revolutionary Leader. Sun's name is the Cantonese Yixian pronunciation of Mandarin Yixian; he is usually known in China by his nom de guerre Sun Zhongshan. Of peasant background, the future "father of the chinese revolution" earned a medical degree in Hong Kong, but abandoned medicine for revolutionary politics in the 1890's. Sun traveled extensively overseas, visiting Chinese communities, raising funds, and plotting to overthrow the Qing dynasty. When the Revolution of 1911 broke out, he returned to China and briefly became provisional president; soon ousted, he repudiated the republic's corrupt and undemocratic government. Thereafter he led the Nationalist Party's opposition regime in Canton and formulated its core doctrine, the "three principles of the people" (nationalism, socialism, democracy).

Swift, Jonathan, *b. Dublin, 1667; d. 1745.* Poet and-satirist. Swift lived in both England and Ireland and served his last three decades as Anglican dean of St. Patrick's Cathedral, Dublin. He wrote witty poems and love poems but became England's supreme prose satirist, beginning with *A Tale of a Tub* and *The Battle of the Books* (both published 1704). He wrote powerfully against English policy toward Ireland; his "Drapier Letters" (1724), opposing the debasement of currency, and his ironic classic, "A Modest Proposal" (1729), made him a permanent Irish hero. *Gulliver's Travels* (1726), an account of a journey to four fanciful lands, is regarded as the greatest (and fiercest) English satire.

Tacitus (Cornelius Tacitus), *b. A.D. 56; d. ca. 120.* Roman historian. Little is known about the life of Tacitus, author of the *Annals*, which cover the lives of emperors Tiberius, Claudius, and Nero. He was a friend of Pliny the Younger and consul for a time. Other works include *Agricola*, a biography of his father-in-law; and *De Origine et Situ Germanorum* (also called *Germania*), which discusses German tribal customs.

Taft, William Howard, *b. Cincinnati, Ohio, 1857; d. 1930.* Twenty-seventh U.S. president, (1909–13). Taft tried to carry on Theodore Roosevelt's policies, but he wrecked the Republican party by alienating progressives over tariff and conservation issues. Although he initiated the income tax and pursued antitrust suits against big business, Taft generally sided with wealthy interests. In 1921, Taft was appointed chief justice of the United States; he served with distinction, alternating liberal nationalism in economic affairs with political and social conservatism.

Talbot, William Henry Fox, *b. Dorset, England, 1800; d.1877.* English inventor. Fox Talbot has the best claim among several pioneers of having invented photography, which he first thought of in October 1833. After several years of experiments creating images with silver nitrate on paper, he described his invention to the Royal Society on January 31, 1839. Later that year he developed the first form of photographic negatives, patenting the process early in 1841. Fox Talbot's early photographs of scenes and people around Lacock Abbey in England are still effective and are often reprinted.

Talleyrand(-Périgord), Charles-Maurice de (Prince de Bénévent), *b. 1754, Paris; d. 1838.* French statesman. A master of political survival, Talleyrand held important offices during the French Revolution, under Napoleon, and during the Bourbon Restoration. Elected to the National Assembly in 1789, he was soon denounced and fled to England and then the U.S. He served as foreign minister for the Directory (1797) and Napoleon, who appointed him grand chamberlain. Having abandoned Napoleon by 1808, he was the restored Louis XVIII's foreign minister at the Congress of Vienna, though royalists secured his removal. Under Louis-Philippe, he served as ambassador to Britain (1830–34).

Taylor, Elizabeth, *b. London, England, 1932; d. 2011.* Actress. Famous for her eight marriages, two to Richard Burton, Taylor made the difficult leap from child star (*National Velvet*, 1944; *Little Women*, 1948) to romantic lead (*Father of the Bride*, 1950; *A Place in the Sun*, 1951), before solidifying her reputation with two adaptations of plays by Tennessee Williams, *Cat on a Hot Tin Roof* (1958) and *Suddenly, Last Summer* (1959). Her tempestuous relationship with Burton began on the set of *Cleopatra* (1963). Together, they made *Who's Afraid of Virginia Woolf?* (1966), for which she won her second Oscar (the first had been for *Butterfield 8*, 1960).

Taylor, Zachary, *b. Montebello, Va., 1784; d. 1850.* Twelfth U.S. president, 1849–50. Taylor was the first president to have no previous political experience. He served as a professional soldier for nearly 40 years; his finest hour came during the Mexican War, when he captured Monterrey and smashed General Santa Ana's much larger army at the battle of Buena Vista (1847). "Old Rough and Ready" was the last Whig to be elected president, in 1848. Taylor died suddenly of acute indigestion after a long, hot Fourth of July ceremony at the Washington Monument.

Tchaikovsky, Pyotr, *b. Votkinsk, 1840; d. 1893.* Russian composer and conductor of the Romantic era. Tchaikovsky was the first composer to assimilate the traditions of Western European symphonic music into the Russian national style, in the process ushering in a new age of serious music composed specifically for dramatic dance. Notable works include *Romeo and Juliet* (1869); *Capriccio*, Op. 8 (1870); *Swan Lake*, Op. 20 (1875-6); Violin Concerto in D, Op. 35 (1878); *1812, Ceremonial Overture*, Op. 49 (1880); *The Sleeping Beauty*, Op. 66 (1888–9); *The Nutcracker*, Op. 71 (1891–2); and Symphony No. 6 in B Minor, Op. 74 (*Pathétique*) (1893). He wrote 11 operas including *Eugene Onegin* (1879), and *The Queen of Spades* (1890).

Tecumseh, *b. (modern) Clark Co., Ohio, 1768; d. 1813.* Shawnee chief. Tecumseh was a great orator and won fame by calling for an end to the torture of whites. He was chosen as leader of his band, and in 1795 he rejected the Treaty of Greenville for giving away land, which he believed to be a communal right. Tecumseh then served as the Indians' spokesman at the Ohio great councils. Turning to action, he helped the Shawnee fight against the U.S., and he joined with the British in the War of 1812, organizing a massive Indian force to enable the taking of Detroit. He was killed in battle when William Henry Harrison led troops into Canada.

Telemann, Georg Philipp, *b. Magdeburg, Germany, 1681; d. 1767.* Composer. Self-taught in music, Telemann was one of the most prolific composers of the Baroque era. Although not as famous as his contemporaries Bach and Handel, he wrote more than 1,000 cantatas, oratorios, Masses, and psalms, as well as 50 concertos for different solo instruments. His *Concerto in G* is the first such work written for the viola and is still performed regularly today. He served as *kapellmeister* in several courts in Germany, and ultimately gained the coveted post of *Kantor* of the Hamburg Johanneum, directing the music of Hamburg's five principal churches. He remained in this position until his death and was succeeded by his godson, Carl Philipp Emanuel Bach.

Teller, Edward, *b. Budapest, Hungary, 1908; d. 2003.* Hungarian-born American nuclear physicist. Educated in Germany, Teller also studied with Niels Bohr in Copenhagen before moving to George Washington University. In 1943 he was recruited by J. Robert Oppenheimer to join the Los Alamos Scientific Laboratory, where he worked on the first atomic bomb and began development on the hydrogen bomb. Teller felt strongly that the United States should remain ahead of the Soviet Union in the nuclear arms race and opposed the Nuclear Test Ban Treaty in 1963. He remained a government adviser on nuclear weapons and was awarded the Presidential Medal of Freedom in 2003.

Tennyson, Alfred (Lord), *b. Lincolnshire, England, 1809; d. 1892.* Poet. The most popular Victorian poet, he had composed fine poems, such as "The Lotos-Eaters," by 1833, when the death of his friend Arthur Hallam deepened his poetic sensibility. His pessimism about 19th-century progress and the quest for religious faith are evident in *Poems* (1842), which includes "Ulysses," and in *Morte d'Arthur* (poems characteristically based on literature of the past). His long, contemplative elegy for Hallam, *In Memoriam A.H.H.*, was published in 1850, the year he was appointed poet laureate. In poems widely varied in length, meter, and setting, Tennyson sustained throughout his long career an uncommon ability to enchant the ear.

Tesla, Nikola, *b. Smiljan, Croatia, 1856; d. 1943.* Physicist and inventor. After building the first alternating-current electric motor in 1883, Tesla migrated to the United States and worked for Thomas Edison whose fledgling electric power plants were based on direct current (DC). In 1887 Tesla established his own company which produced patents in alternating-current (AC) technology. George Westinghouse bought many of his patents and brought them to commercial fruition and AC became the global standard. Tesla designed the first hydroelectric powerplant at Niagara Falls (1895). Tesla's difficult personality created problems with those he worked with, and helped to delay recognition of the technology that revolutionized electric power. After about 1913 he lived in seclusion in New York City. He held over 700 patents.

Thackeray, William Makepeace, *b. Calcutta, 1811; d. 1863.* English novelist. Like his contemporary, Dickens, Thackeray wrote novels serially in magazines. He was a satirist who attacked hypocrisy and burlesqued other novelists. His greatest and most famous novel, *Vanity Fair* (1848), is a masterly satire of the English upper class, featuring Becky Sharp, a clever, crooked, successful schemer who is one of the major figures in English fiction. It was followed by the partly biographical *Pendennis* (1850) and the historical novels *Henry Esmond* (1852) and *The Virginians* (1857–59). Thackeray worked feverishly to support his family after his wife went insane around 1840, and he lectured widely in Britain and America.

Thatcher, Margaret, *b. Grantham, England, 1925.* British prime minister. A grocer's daughter, Maggie Thatcher won a seat in Parliament at age 34, and quickly climbed the ranks of Britain's Conservative Party. She assumed the party leadership in 1975, and in 1979 she was elected Britain's first female prime minister. She promptly dismantled many social welfare programs, cut taxes for the wealthy, reduced government spending, battled trade unions, and privatized nationalized industries. Thatcher was a major foreign-policy partner of Ronald Reagan. Her introduction of a poll tax eroded her support, and she resigned in 1990. In 1992, she became a baroness, and entered the House of Lords.

Thomas, Dylan, *b. Swansea, Wales, 1914; d. 1953.* Poet and playwright. In many ways, Thomas was a Romantic poet born a century too late. His flamboyant personality and notorious drinking brought him public attention, and like Byron and Keats, he died at a relatively young age. In his most famous poems, "Do Not Go Gentle into That Good Night" and "Fern Hill," Thomas displays a fierce love of life and a sense of nostalgia. His works include *18 Poems* (1934), *Collected Poems* (1952), and the play *Under Milk Wood* (published posthumously in 1954).

Thomson, J. J. (Joseph John), *b. Manchester, England, 1856; d. 1940* English physicist. In 1897 Thomson discovered the electron. He later showed that the electron's mass is much smaller than that of any atom and that atoms contain electrons. Thomson also invented the first version of a mass spectrometer (a device that separates ions by mass) and used it to discover two different-mass atoms of neon, the first physical proof that isotopes (different forms of the same element) exist.

Thoreau, Henry David, *b. Concord, Mass., 1817; d. 1862.* Author and poet. Thoreau was Ralph Waldo Emerson's protegé and a main figure in the Transcendental movement. An advocate of individualism and antimaterialism and a keen observer of nature, he lived alone for two years in a cabin on Walden Pond near Concord, and recorded his natural and philosophical observations in the classic *Walden* (1854). Other books include *A Week on the Concord and Merrimac Rivers* (1849) and *The Maine Woods*, published posthumously. His essay "Civil Disobedience," (1849) written after he was jailed for not paying a poll tax to support the Mexican War, has had an international influence on civil rights movements.

Thorpe, Jim, *b. Prague, Okla., 1888; d. 1953.* Athlete. Thorpe was voted the greatest male athlete of the first half of the 20th century by the Associated Press. A Native American, he won All-America honors in football in 1911 and 1912 at the Carlisle (Pa.) Indian School, also competing in baseball, track, and lacrosse. At the 1912 Olympics in Stockholm, Thorpe won gold medals in both the pentathlon and the decathlon. He was stripped of the medals in 1913 for violating the rules of amateurism—he had played professional football and baseball—but they were restored posthumously in 1982.

Thucydides, *b. ca. 460 B.C.; d. ca. 404 B.C.* Greek historian of the Peloponnesian War (431–404 B.C.). Thucydides was not only a pivotal figure for the study of history but possibly the first journalist in the modern sense. His firsthand account of the Peloponnesian War covers everything from military details to profiles of the participants. Little is known of his life, but he was a general in exile for a military failure during much of the writing of his account, leaving it somewhat biased. He is thought to have returned to Athens after its defeat in 404 B.C. His account was never completed and ends in 411 B.C.

Thutmose III Menkheperre, *(dates unknown)* Egyptian pharaoh, ca. 1479–25 B.C. Assuming the throne as a minor, Thutmose reigned jointly with his aunt, Hatshepsut (probably Egypt's most powerful woman), until her death in 1457. Shortly thereafter, Thutmose led his army into Palestine and won a major victory at Megiddo, the first battle in history recorded in detail, on a wall at Karnak in Thebes. It was the first of Thutmose's 17 campaigns, which brought Egypt to the height of its imperial reach in Palestine, Syria, and Nubia (Sudan). During his reign, Egypt also received tribute from Minoan Crete, the Hittites, and Mesopotamia.

Tiberius (Tiberius Claudius Nero Caesar), *b. 42 B.C.; d. A.D. 37.* Roman emperor. Tiberius was the stepson and successor of Augustus, taking power after his death in A.D. 14 at age 54. He spent his early life as a prominent figure in Roman politics and then became disillusioned and retired for a period. He returned to Rome in 6 B.C. after the death of Augustus' other heirs and regained power. The early part of his 23-year reign was marked by peace, prosperity, and social reform. However, after the death of his son Drussus in 23 A.D, Tiberius became infamous for executions, brutality, and torture. He died on Capri, probably killed by the head of his praetorian guard, leaving Caligula as his successor.

Timur (also known as Tamerlane, Tamburlaine, or Timur Lenk), *b. Kesh, Transoxania (now in Uzbekistan), 1336; d. 1405.* Turkic conqueror. Timur is remembered for the barbarity of his conquests. He established dominion over the Transoxania lands by 1366, and for the next 10 years fought against the khans of Jatah and Khorezm. His troops occupied Moscow, defeated the Lithuanians near Poltava, conquered Persia (1383), and invaded India (1398). The poverty, bloodshed, and desolation caused by his campaigns gave rise to many legends, which in turn inspired such works as Christopher Marlowe's *Tamburlaine the Great.*

Titian (Tiziano Vecellio or Vecelli,), *b. Pieve di Cadore, Italy, ca. 1488/90; d. 1576.* Painter. A chief figure in the High Renaissance, thought of as the greatest artist of the Venetian school, Titian painted scenes from history and mythology, religious subjects, and allegories, as well as portraits. He helped to establish the 16th-century style, with its looser brushwork and subtler colors. His well-known works include a scene of pagan revelry, *Bacchanal of the Andrians* (mid-1520's), *Venus of Urbino* (1538), and *Pietà* (1573–76).

Tobin, James, *b. Champaign, Ill., 1918; d. 2002.* Economist. One of America's leading Keynesian economists, Tobin developed advanced theories to describe how financial markets affect employment, prices, and individuals' decisions about spending and investment. His "portfolio theory" held that diversification lessens risk for investors. A Yale professor and a member of President Kennedy's Council of Economic Advisors, he was awarded the Nobel Prize in Economics in 1981.

Tocqueville, Alexis de, *b. Verneuil-sur-Seine, France, 1805; d. 1859.* Political philosopher and historian. Born into an aristocratic family, Tocqueville was a prominent figure in French politics. He was intrigued by the American Revolution and became convinced that the ideals of democracy and equality would supplant the old European aristocratic traditions. He is best known as the author of *Democracy in America* (1835), an in-depth sociological study of the United States published after an extensive observational tour. This remarkably prescient two-volume work describes a young and vibrant democracy and reports on the customs and manners of the people, revealing how different they were from Europeans. It also sounds a warning about the threats posed by consumerism, corruption, and the tyranny of the majority.

Tolstoy, Leo, *b. near Tula, Russia, 1828; d. 1910.* Novelist and philosopher. Count Tolstoy grew up on an estate and was orphaned at nine. He lived aimlessly before joining the army at 23. His army service contributed to a successful collection of stories, *Sevastapol Sketches* (1855–56); a short novel, *The Cossacks* (1863) and his long epic of the Napoleonic Wars, *War and Peace* (1865–69), one of the greatest narrative achievements in literature. Another great novel, *Anna Karenina* (1874–77), tells the parallel stories of an adulterous love between a passionate woman and a military officer, and of an introspective estate owner. After converting to what has been called Christian anarchy, Tolstoy lived a life of pacifism, poverty, and moral searching. Other fictional works include the novellas *The Death of Ivan Ilych* (1886) and *The Kreutzer Sonata* (1889).

Trotsky, Leon (Lev Davidovitch Bronstein), *b. Yanovka, Ukraine, 1879; d. 1940.* Russian politician. A first- generation Russian Communist leader, Trotsky was twice exiled to Siberia by the czarist government (1898 and 1905). He collaborated with Lenin as early as 1902. Instrumental in the Bolsheviks' rise to power during the October Revolution (1917), he subsequently served as commissar of war in the final months of World War I. Losing to Stalin in a struggle to head the Communist Party after Lenin's death in 1924, he was eventually stripped of his party membership. He was murdered in Mexico on Stalin's orders.

Truffaut, François, *b. Paris, 1932; d. 1984.* Screenwriter and director. Truffaut's humanist films made him the most popular director of the French New Wave. He had been mentored by the film theorist André Bazin, who hired him to write for the magazine *Cahiers du cinéma*. One of his articles was the basis for the auteur theory. Truffaut's first feature was *The Four Hundred Blows* (1959), the first of a cycle of autobiographical films, which include *Love at 20* (1962) and *Stolen Kisses* (1968). Other films by Truffaut films are *Jules and Jim* (1961), *Wild Child* (1970), and *Day for Night* (1972).

Truman, Harry S, *b. Lamar, Mo., 1884; d. 1972.* Thirty-third U.S. president (1945–53). A plain-spoken midwesterner who was a World War I artilleryman, Harry S Truman (the S does not stand for a middle name) entered politics as a Democrat in the 1920's after his Kansas City haberdashery failed. The local Pendergast machine arranged his election to the Senate as a New Dealer in 1934, and he was chosen for the vice presidency in 1944. After only a few weeks in office, Truman had the presiden-

cy thrust upon him by Roosevelt's sudden death; utterly unprepared, he vowed to carry on Roosevelt's policies—and proved to be a remarkably capable chief executive. In his first four months, Truman approved the United Nations, accepted the German surrender, met with Allied leaders at Potsdam, and ordered atomic bombs dropped on Japan. In 1947 he proclaimed the Truman Doctrine, promising U.S. aid to threatened countries, and the Marshall Plan to aid European recovery. He also committed the country to the NATO alliance and sent troops to South Korea when Communist armies invaded in 1950.

Tubman, Harriet (Araminta Ross), *b. Dorchester county, Md., ca. 1820; d. 1913.* Escaped slave, abolitionist, and "conductor" on the Underground Railroad. A slave from birth, she married John Tubman, a free black, in 1844. But when she heard she was to be sold, she fled to Philadelphia. In 1850, she returned to Baltimore to help her mother and two sisters escape slavery. She made 18 additional trips into Maryland to guide more than 300 fugitive slaves along the Underground Railroad into Canada. Abolitionists deemed her the "Moses of her people," while slaveholders offered $40,000 in rewards for her capture.

Turgenev, Ivan, *b. Orel, Russia, 1818; d. 1883.* Novelist, short-story writer, playwright. Born to landed wealth, Turgenev advocated westernization for Russia, wrote a book of stories, *A Sportsman's Sketches* (1852), that influenced the end of serfdom; and, after being banished to his estate in the 1850's, lived mainly in Paris. His greatest novel, *Fathers and Sons* (1862), was controversial for its sympathetic characterization of a nihilist (a term he invented) who opposes the Russian upper class. Other novels include *Rudin* (1855), *A Nest of Gentlefolk* (1859), and *Virgin Soil* (1877). His plays include *A Month in the Country* (1850), and among his highly esteemed stories is "First Love" (1870).

Turing, Alan, *b. London, England, 1912; d. 1954.* British mathematician and logician. After studying mathematics at the University of Cambridge, Alan Turing earned his Ph. D. in mathematical logic from Princeton University. In his early career he invented the Turing machine, which became the basis for all subsequent digital computers. Recruited by his country during WW II, Turing helped invent the Bombe, a code-breaking machine designed to crack the German's Enigma code. Due to this success he was made an officer of the Order of the British Empire. After some pioneering efforts in the fields of cognitive science and artificial intelligence, Turing was prosecuted in 1952 for homosexuality. He soon lost his security clearance, and in 1954 he committed suicide.

Turner, J. M. W. (Joseph Mallord William), b. *Chelsea (now in London), England, 1775; d. 1851.* Painter and printmaker. Turner dominated the field of landscape painting in the first half of the 19th century. Interested in history and the sublime, he saw himself as a modern master in the tradition of Claude and Poussin, although some of his later studies of light have led to comparisons with the Impressionists. In 1804 he opened a gallery to show his paintings. His best-known works include *The Slave Ship* (1840) and *The Decline of the Carthaginian Empire* (1817).

Turner, Nat, b. *Southampton County, Va., 1800; d. 1831.* American slave leader. Turner, born into slavery in Virginia, believed he had been selected by God to lead his fellow slaves to freedom. In the uprising of 1831, Turner and his followers killed several dozen slave owners before being defeated by government forces. Many of the participants were summarily executed, and Turner was subsequently captured, tried, and sentenced to death for his role. His life served as the inspiration for *The Confessions of Nat Turner*, a work of historical fiction by William Styron that won the Pulitzer Prize in 1968.

Tutankhamen Nebkheperre, *(dates unknown)* Egyptian pharaoh, ca. 1333–23 B.C. Originally named Tutankhaten, "Living image of the Aten," Tutankhamen changed his name as part of a repudiation of the monotheistic Aten-worship of his father-in-law, Akhenaton. He also moved his capital and encouraged worship of the old gods. Tutankhamen died aged about 18. Memory of his reign was obliterated in the 19th dynasty, and his small burial tomb in the Valley of the Kings was unknown to grave robbers until 1922, when its elaborate contents were revealed to the world by Howard Carter. Tutankhamen's fame today depends entirely on his obscurity in antiquity.

Tutu, Desmond, b. *Klerksdorp, South Africa, 1931.* Anglican cleric who won the Nobel Peace Prize in 1984 for his opposition to apartheid. Ordained an Anglican priest in 1961, he was the first black to serve as dean of St. Mary's Cathedral in Johannesburg in 1975. He was appointed general secretary of the South African Council of Churches in 1978, and in this position was an outspoken advocate for the rights of black South Africans, seeking "a democratic and just society without racial divisions." He encouraged nonviolent protest and urged

world leaders to apply economic pressure to South Africa to end apartheid. He was later elected archbishop of Cape Town. In 1995 he became the head of the Truth and Reconciliation Committee, investigating human rights abuses during the apartheid era.

Twain, Mark (Samuel Langhorne Clemens) b. *Florida, Mo., 1835; d. 1910.* Author, novelist. Twain is regarded as the greatest American humorist. His experience as a Mississippi River pilot provided his pseudonym (slang for "two fathoms of water"). His first book, *The Innocents Abroad* (1869), recounted a trip around the Mediter-ranean. His most famous books are novels based on his Missouri boyhood, *The Adventures of Tom Sawyer* (1876) and *Adventures of Huckleberry Finn* (1884). After his marriage in 1870, Twain settled in Hartford, Conn. Bad investments plummeted him into debt, and in the 1890's he lectured around the world. Other books are *Life on the Mississippi* (1883), and the novel *A Connecticut Yankee in King Arthur's Court* (1889).

Tyler, John, b. *Charles City County, Va., 1790; d. 1862.* Tenth U.S. president, (1841–45). Tyler was the first vice president to become president by succession. He had been a Virginia legislator, congressman, senator, and governor before the Whigs chose him as William Henry Harrison's running mate in 1840. As president after Harrison's death, "His Accidency" earned the Whig party's ire by changing parties. In 1842 his cabinet resigned, his party expelled him, and outraged members of Congress called for his impeachment. This was the first time impeachment proceedings were introduced in Congress, although the proposal was eventually defeated.

Unitas, Johnny, b. *Pittsburgh, Pa., 1933; d. 2002.* Football player. He was the premier quarterback of his era, who over 18 seasons (1956–73)—all except one with the Baltimore Colts—led his team to four NFL championships and earned league Player of the Year honors three times (1959, 1964, 1967). By the time he retired, "Johnny U" had appeared in 10 Pro Bowls and set career records (all since surpassed) in virtually every major passing category.

Updike, John, b. *Shillington, Pa., 1932; d. 2009.* Novelist, essayist, and short story writer. A prominent figure in contemporary American letters, Updike has had a varied career and has written novels, short stories, poetry, and many articles and book reviews for *The New Yorker*. He won Pulitzer Prizes in fiction for *Rabbit is Rich* (1981) and *Rabbit at Rest* (1991), two in a series of four novels that track the life of Rabbit Angstrom, a former high school basketball star who finds little glory as an adult. In these novels and others, (*The Poorhouse Fair*, 1959; *Couples*, 1968) Updike examines the moral foibles of modern American society especially its middle class.

Valentino, Rudolph (Rodolfo Alfonzo Raffaele Pierre Philibert Guglielmi), *b. Castellaneta, Italy, 1895; d. 1926.* Silent film actor. Darkly handsome, passionate, and graceful, Valentino epitomized the exotic lover so popular in the silent era's adventure fantasies. He began as a dancer in nightclubs and dance halls before landing work as a Hollywood extra. The screenwriter June Mathis discovered him and cast him in *Four Horsemen of the Apocalypse* (1921), which skyrocketed him to stardom. He followed with starring roles in *The Sheik* (1921) and *Blood and Sand* (1922). His premature death drove fans into a mass frenzy, which reflected the star worship of the era.

Van Buren, Martin, *b. Kinderhook, N.Y., 1782; d. 1862.* Eighth U.S. president, 1837–41. Van Buren's staunch party loyalty elevated him to the Senate in 1821; his brief service as governor of New York ended when Andrew Jackson appointed him secretary of state in 1829. He helped build the Democratic Party, and Jackson made him vice president in 1832. He ascended to the presidency in 1836, but two months after he took office the Panic of 1837 launched a severe economic depression and he was limited to one term. In 1844 Van Buren lost the Democratic nomination, then guaranteed a Democratic defeat by founding the Free Soil party, which split the decisive New York vote.

Van Gogh, Vincent (Willem), *b. Zundert, Netherlands, 1853; d. 1890.* Painter. Van Gogh was unrecognized during his lifetime, but his life and work have become legendary. He was inspired to paint peasants in the style of Millet, as demonstrated in his early work *The Potato-Eaters* (1885), but later he abandoned the dark tones of that piece for vibrant colors and thick, textured layers of busy brushwork. Van Gogh is thought of as Postimpressionist, and he was influenced Japanese woodcuts. Tormented by mental illness, epilepsy, and he famously cut off part of his ear late in life. He was supported by his brother Theo, and left behind prolific correspondence before committing suicide. His most famous works include *The Night Café* (1888), *Starry Night* (1889), and *Crows in a Wheat-Field* (1890).

Veblen, Thorstein, *b. Manitowoc County, Wisconsin, 1857; d. 1929.* American economist and social scientist.

A brilliant scholar, Veblen began teaching at the University of Chicago in 1892. His first and most famous book, *The Theory of the Leisure Class* (1899), applied Darwinian principles of evolution to the study of business and economics. Veblen coined the phrase "conspicuous consumption," which is still in use today. The book brought him literary fame, but not academic success, although his ideas about the American system of business were vindicated during the Depression in the 1930's.

Velázquez, Diego (Rodríguez de Silva y), *b. Seville, Spain, 1599; d. 1660.* Painter. After early successes such as *The Water Carrier of Seville* (ca. 1619), Velázquez was appointed court painter in Madrid in 1623; he spent most of his life producing portraits of the royal family. As well as the famous *Pope Innocent X* (1650). His masterpiece is *Las Meninas* (1656), one of the best-known works of the Baroque period; a group portrait that includes the young Princess Margarita, it is considered a superb study of light, color, and space.

Venter, Craig (John Craig Venter), *b. Salt Lake City, Utah, 1946.* Biochemist. In 1995, working with Hamilton Smith of Johns Hopkins University, Venter sequenced the DNA of the entire genome of Hemophilus influenzae, marking the first time that all the genetic material of a living organism had been deciphered. Frustrated by the time-consuming techniques used at the National Institutes of Health (NIH) for identifying genes, Venter founded Celera Genomics, a commercial venture that ran a parallel version of the Human Genome Project. In 2002 Venter and Francis Collins of the NIH jointly announced the mapping of the human genome, no doubt completed so quickly because of the competition between the two. In 2005 Venter cofounded a company devoted to producing alternative fuels from genetically modified microorganisms.

Venturi, Robert, *b. Philadelphia, Pa. 1925.* Architect, theorist, and educator. Venturi rejected the "modernist" idiom. His influence derives from both his designs and his writings. His books, *Complexity and Contradiction in Architecture* (1966, 2nd edition 1977) and *Learning from Las Vegas* (1972, 2nd edition 1977) written with his wife, Denise Scott Brown, set forth his critique of modern architecture. His designs, include his early Guild House (1960–63) in Philadelphia and the Vanna Venturi House (1963) in Chestnut Hill, Pa., and the later Seattle Art Museum (1984–91). He won the Pritzker Prize in 1991.

Verdi, Guiseppe, *b. Le Roncole, near Busseto, Parma, Italy, 1813; d. 1901.* Composer of the Romantic era. Born into an ordinary family, Verdi composed some of the most popular and critically acclaimed operas of all time. Because of his technical mastery of the operatic form and his unsurpassed powers of characterization his work remains extremely popular today. He wrote 30 operas, including *Macbeth* (1846–7), *Rigoletto* (1850–1), *Il trovatore* (1851–2), *La traviata* (1852-3), *Don Carlos* (1867), *Aida* (1870), *Otello* (1884–6), and *Falstaff* (1889–92); his *Requiem* mass (1874) is highly regarded.

Verlaine, Paul, *b. Metz, France, 1844; d. 1896.* Poet. After publishing two volumes of lyric poetry as a young bohemian in Paris, Verlaine, with the publication of *Songs Without Words* (1874), joined the Symbolist movement, which advocated freedom from conventional poetic form. A younger Symbolist, Arthur Rimbaud, became his lover, and Verlaine was imprisoned for shooting and wounding him. After prison, he wrote religious poetry in the volume *Sagesse* (1881). He was later associated with the end-of-the-century decadent poets, as his life became more dissipated. Verlaine's poetry is highly regarded for its sensuality and musicality. His later volumes include *Jadis et Naguère* (1884) and *Parallèlement* (1889).

Vermeer, Johannes (Jan), *b. Delft, Netherlands, 1632; d. 1675.* Painter. Best known for portraits of women engaged in domestic, often solitary activities, Vermeer was fascinated by the quality of light in interior spaces. Works such as *Woman with a Water Jug* (1662–25) and *Head of a Girl with a Pearl Earring* (ca. 1665) depict a tranquil beauty in everyday life. The solemn, nonnarrative qualities in his compositions set him apart from other Dutch genre painters in the Baroque period. Because his working process was painstaking, his output was limited, and only 35 of his paintings survive.

Victoria (Alexandrina Victoria), *b. Kensington Palace, England, 1819; d. 1901.* Queen of Great Britain, 1837–1901. She gave her name to an era, the Victorian age. Alexandrina Victoria was the only child of the fourth son of King George III; when her uncle William IV died childless in 1837, she became queen of England. She married her cousin, Prince Consort Albert of Saxe-Coburg-Gotha, in 1840; they had nine children, through whose marriages were descended many of the royal families of Europe. During Victoria's reign, the longest of any English monarch, the monarchy took on its modern ceremonial character.

Villa, Pancho (Doroteo Arango), *b. San Juan del Rio, Mexico, 1878; d. 1923.* Revolutionary and guerrilla leader. Villa, joined Francisco Madero's uprising against the dictator Porfirio Diaz in 1909. He was imprisoned by General Victoriano Huerta in 1912 but escaped and formed a band of several thousand men, known as the División del Norte. Revolting against Huerta's dictatorship, he joined with Venustiano Carranza and defeated Huerta in June 1914. He then broke with Carranza and engaged in banditry and various guerrilla activities, receiving an official pardon only after the overthrow of Carranza's government in 1920.

Virgil (Publius Vergilius Maro), *b. Andes (near Mantua), Italy, 70 B.C.; d. 19 B.C.* Roman poet. Virgil is considered by many to be the greatest Roman poet. Educated in Rome, he was befriended and patronized by Maecenas, Augustus' chief imperial minister. Virgil's major works include the *Eclogues* and *Georgics*, books of pastoral poems; but by far his most lauded and important work is the *Aeneid*. Considered one of the great epics of all time, the *Aeneid*, published posthumously and unfinished, tells of the adventures of the Trojan Aeneas and how he went on to found Rome after the Trojan War.

Vivaldi, Antonio, *b. Venice, 1678; d. 1741.* Composer and violinist of the Baroque period. The son of a violinist, Vivaldi was ordained as a priest (1703) but his love of life and music brought him into conflict with church leaders so he frequently traveled throughout Europe. A contemporary of J. S. Bach, he was known primarily for his string concertos, but recent scholarship shows he wrote over 45 operas, (16 survive) 73 sonatas, 33 cantatas—nearly 800 works in all. Notable works include Op. 3, *L'Estro Armonico*, 12 concertos for various instruments (1711); Op. 4, *La Stravaganza*, 12 violin concertos (1714); Op. 8, *Il cimento dell'Armonia e Dell' inventione*, 12 violin concertos, the first four (E, G minor, F, and F minor) known as *The Four Seasons* (1725); Op. 10, six flute concertos (1728); and *Gloria* in D.

Volta, Alessandro, *b. Como, Italy, 1745; d. 1827.* Physicist. Volta is remembered for his invention in 1799 of the electric battery, which used a chemical reaction to produce the first electric current—previously only static electricity had been known. About 25 years earlier, Volta had also perfected the electrophorus, a device still used today for creating a large amounts of static electricity. In 1778 he became the first to recognize methane, the gas released from marshes. The "volt" measure of electric potential is named for him.

Voltaire, (Francois Marie Arouet de), *b. Paris, 1694; d. 1778*. Philosopher and author. Voltaire was one of the leading figures of the Enlightenment. He began writing in earnest while in prison in 1717 for remarks about the regent actually made by someone else. Once more unjustly imprisoned and he was banished to England in 1726, where he learned to admire English liberalism and in *Letters Concerning the English Nation* (1733) helped bring English philosophy and science to the French Enlightenment. A stay at the court of Frederick II in Prussia (1749–53) was discordant, and he returned to live near Geneva. He wrote *Philosophical Dictionary* (1764) and many plays and histories and polemical writings. His most widely read work today is his satirical novel *Candide* (1759).

Wagner, Richard, *b. Leipzig, 1813; d. 1883*. Composer, conductor, poet, and author. He is one of the key figures in the history of music particularly in opera which he elevated to epic proportions through the use of larger orchestras, more prominent instrumental passages, "endless melody"—eliminating arias—and organically conceived, through-composed structures. Later composers, including Richard Strauss and Gustav Mahler, regarded his music as the source of their own. His writings on music and drama have remained influential while his virulent anti-semitic screeds have permanently damaged him. Notable musical works include *Der fliegende Holländer* (The Flying Dutchman) (1841); *Tannhauser* (1844) *Tristan und Isolde* (1857–9); *Die Meistersinger von Nürnberg* (The Mastersingers of Nuremberg) (1862–7); *Siegfried Idyll* (1870); *Parsifal* (1878–82); and the fifteen-hour opera cycle *Der Ring des Nibelungen* (The Nibelung's Ring): *Das Rheingold* (The Rhine Gold) (1853–4), *Die Walküre* (The Valkyrie) (1854–6), *Siegfried* (1856–7), and *Götterdämmerung* (Twilight of the Gods) (1869–74).

Walcott, Derek, *b. St. Lucia, 1930*. Poet and playwright. Although his poetry focuses on themes from his native Caribbean, Walcott's body of work surpasses the merely regional and has earned worldwide acclaim, including the Nobel Prize for Literature in 1992. His volumes include *In a Green Night* (1962) and *Omeros* (1990), an epic poem that melds Homeric legend and Caribbean folklore. A background and lifelong interest in painting also influenced his poetry. In addition, he has written a number of plays.

Walesa, Lech, *b. Popowo, Poland, 1943*. Trade union activist and president of Poland. An electrician in the Gdansk shipyards, Walesa was fired in 1976 for antigovernment union activities. But in 1980, as massive strikes paralyzed Poland, Walesa returned to lead the protests and form Solidarity, a coalition of workers' groups. The communist government outlawed Solidarity and imposed martial law in 1981. Walesa was harrassed by Poland's secret police for years, even after winning the 1983 Nobel Peace Prize. In 1989, the Communist Party allowed parliamentary elections; Solidarity candidates triumphed and Walesa became Poland's first non-communist president. He was defeated in a reelection bid in 1995.

Warhol, Andy (Andrew Warhola), *b. Pittsburgh, Pa., 1928; d. 1987*. Painter, sculptor, illustrator. After a career as a commercial artist, Warhol began painting symbols and scenes borrowed from popular culture and became a main figure in the Pop Art movement. His images of consumer goods, ads, newspaper headlines, and famous faces are among the best-known pieces of American art. Such works include *Gold Marilyn Monroe* (1962) and *Campbell's Soup Cans* (1962). Warhol made himself a prominent public persona, enlisting the help of a studio of assistants known as the Factory.

Warren, Earl, *b. Los Angeles, 1891; d. 1974*. Politician and jurist. As attorney general of California (1938–1942) and as governor (1942–1953) Warren championed clean government but also supported the internment of Japanese-Americans after the attack on Pearl Harbor. In 1953 President Dwight D. Eisenhower appointed him chief justice of the Supreme Court; during his tenure the court rendered decisions of far-reaching importance, including *Brown v. Board of Education of Topeka* (1954), which outlawed segregated schools. Other decisions upheld the rights of the accused, legislative apportionment, voting rights, and freedom of the press. He headed the commission on the assassination of President John F. Kennedy (1963) and retired in 1969.

Warren, Robert Penn, *b. Guthrie, Ky., 1905; d. 1989*. Novelist and poet. Warren distinguished himself as a novelist, poet, and critic in a career largely spent in academia. During his teaching career, he cowrote two influential textbooks, *Understanding Poetry* (1938) and *Understanding Fiction* (1943). Warren won the Pulitzer prize in fiction for *All the King's Men* (1947), a work loosely based on the life of Louisiana's governor Huey Long. Later, he captured two Pulitzer Prizes in poetry for *Promises* (1958) and *Now and Then* (1979).

Washington, Booker T., *b. Franklin County, Va., 1856; d. 1915*. Educator and leader. Born into slavery, Washington was a prominent figure in black America until his death. He is best known for his administration of the Tuskegee Institute in Tuskegee, Ala., where he developed an educational system for blacks that focused on the development of practical industrial skills. Washington served as an adviser on African-American issues to two presidents, and his autobiography, *Up from Slavery* (1901), was a best seller.

Washington, George, b. *Westmoreland County, Va., 1732; d. 1799.* First U.S. president, 1789–97. Washington first joined the Virginia militia in 1753 and fought in the French and Indian War; in 1775 he was appointed by the Continental Congress to command the Continental Army, and he prevailed over the British. Washington retired to his Mount Vernon estate but later presided over the Constitutional Convention in Philadelphia in 1787, which framed the presidency with him in mind. His first act as president was to urge adoption of the Bill of Rights; other notable achievements included quelling the Whiskey Rebellion, bolstering the treasury with a national bank, settling Jay's Treaty of commerce with Britain, and maintaining neutrality in the French Revolution.

Watson, James Dewey, b. *Chicago, 1928.* American molecular biologist. Watson and Francis Harry Compton Crick at Cambridge University discovered the structure of deoxyribonucleic acid, DNA, which carries genetic information in living organisms. Their paper of 1953 described the double-helix structure of DNA and the coding system within it. Crick and Watson, together with Maurice Wilkins, were awarded the Nobel Prize in Physiology or Medicine in 1962. Watson published his personal memoir, *The Double Helix*, in 1968.

Watt, James, b. *Greenock, Scotland, 1736; d. 1819.* Scottish inventor. Working on a model of Thomas Newcomen's steam engine, Watt produced a series of inventions that vastly improved the efficiency and range of applications of the steam engine. In 1781 he patented a rotary engine that could power factories and ships, and the critical new mode of transportation, the railroad. Watt's design for the steam engine was major factor in the transformation of industry in the Industrial Revolution.

Waugh, Evelyn, b. *Hampstead, England, 1903; d. 1966.* Novelist. During his early career, Waugh, a professed reactionary and a convert to Catholicism, specialized in tearing apart contemporary society with razor-sharp comic wit, clever use of irony, and stylish prose. His novels include *Decline and Fall* (1928), *A Handful of Dust* (1934), *Brideshead Revisited* (1945), *The Loved One* (1948) and a World War II trilogy, *Men at Arms* (1952), *Officers and Gentlemen* (1955), and *Unconditional Surrender* (1961).

Waugh also wrote travel books, two biographies; and his own autobiography, *A Little Learning* (1964).

Wayne, John (Marion Michael Morrison), b. *Winterset, Iowa, 1907; d. 1979.* Movie actor. "The Duke" projected an enduring image of tough survival from westerns of the 1930's to the Vietnam era and beyond. His many roles as cowboys and soldiers—notably in such films as *Stagecoach* (1939), *Fort Apache*, and *Red River* (both 1948), and *The Searchers* (1956)—set his swaggering image. Criticized by some, praised by others for his right-wing politics, he won sympathy fighting cancer and finally won an Oscar for *True Grit* (1969).

Weber, Max, b. *Erfurt, Germany, 1864; d. 1930.* Economist and social historian. Weber rejected the rigid economic determinism of Karl Marx in his famous book *The Protestant Ethic and the Spirit of Capitalism* (1904–05), and argued for the importance of religious values, ethical principles, and charismatic leaders in shaping society. He maintained that the Protestant work ethic played a major role in the rise of Western capitalism. By contrast, in the three volumes of his series *Religions of the East* (1920–21), he sought to show that capitalism failed to develop in Eastern societies because of their religious and philosophical beliefs.

Webster, Daniel b. *Salisbury, N.H., 1782; d. 1852.* Lawyer, orator, politician. In 1812 Webster was elected to the House of Representatives from New Hampshire. He won fame as a lawyer in several important cases including *McCulloch v. Maryland*. In 1827 he became a senator from Massachusetts and later served as secretary of state under William Harrison and John Tyler. He was famous as an orator and for his rejoinder in a debate with a southerner advocating secession "Liberty and Union, now and forever, one and inseparable!"

Webster, Noah, b. *West Hartford, Conn., 1758; d. 1843.* Lexicographer. His *American Dictionary of the English Language* (1828) gave American English an equal footing with its British counterpart. He believed that rules of spelling, grammar, and punctuation should evolve as the spoken language changes, rather than hew to prescribed rules, and his books reflect that belief. His *American Spelling Book* (1783), known as the "Blue-Backed Speller," has never been out of print; its sales, estimated by some at more than 100 million, made Webster a rich man.

Weill, Kurt, b. *Dessau, Germany, 1900; d. 1950.* Composer. A German-American composer for the stage, Weill found success in the worlds of both classical and popular music. His first opera, *The Protagonist*, was performed in Germany in 1926. He then collaborated with the lyricist Bertolt Brecht on a series of works for musical theater that incorporated a popular song style, the most notable of which was *The Threepenny Opera* (1928). After fleeing Nazi Germany for America in 1933, Weill composed numerous operettas, scores for Hollywood films, and musicals, including *Lady in the Dark* (1941, with Moss Hart and Ira Gershwin) and *Street Scene* (1947, with Elmer Rice and Langston Hughes). Weill's song "Mack the Knife" (from *The Threepenny Opera*) became a standard, performed by jazz artist Louis Armstrong and the popular singer Bobby Darrin, among others. Over the years, Weill's greatest interpreter was his wife, the actress and singer Lotte Lenya.

Welles, Orson (George), *b. Kenosha, Wis., 1915; d. 1985.* Actor, screenwriter, director. Originally a stage actor and director, he gained notoriety with a radio broadcast of "War of the Worlds" in 1938 that frightened many listeners. Welles signed with RKO Studios in 1940, creating his first feature film, *Citizen Kane* (1941) which stretched the boundaries of the classic narrative style with his inventive narrative structure and deep-focus photography. The box-office failure of *Kane* and *The Magnificent Ambersons* (1942) resulted in his dismissal from RKO. Though stylish and inventive, his subsequent films suffered from studio interference, as with *The Lady from Shanghai* (1948) and *Touch of Evil* (1959); or from lack of sufficient funds, as with *Othello* (1952).

Wellesley, Arthur, First Duke of Wellington, *b. Dublin, Ireland, 1769; d. 1852.* British army commander and politician. Nicknamed the "Iron Duke," Wellington first earned a military reputation in India. In 1808, he was sent to Portugal. He fought the French throughout the Iberian Peninsula until 1814. Among his most important victories were Talavera in 1809 and Salamanca in 1812. In 1815, he defeated Napoleon at Waterloo, in modern Belgium. He entered politics, serving as prime minister from 1828 to 1830. Although a Tory, he pragmatically supported both Catholic emancipation (1829) and parliamentary reform (1832).

Wells, H. G., *b. Bromley, England, 1866; d. 1946.* Novelist and historian. One of the fathers of science fiction, Wells popularized the genre with such works as *The Time Machine* (1895), *The Invisible Man* (1897), and *The War of the Worlds* (1898). In other books, he described how humans might travel to the moon and predicted the calamitous possibilities of the airplane. Later in his career, Wells turned to social criticism—particularly of the Victorian era—and nonfiction, including *The Outline of History* (1920) and *The Science of Life* (1929).

Welty, Eudora, *b. Jackson, Miss., 1909; d. 2001.* Novelist and short-story writer. A photographer for the WPA before turning to fiction, Welty is one of the great Southern regional writers. Her work focused on Mississippi, where she spent almost her entire life. Among her short-story collections is *A Curtain of Green* (1941), which includes, "Why I Live at the PO." Her novels include *Delta Wedding* (1946) and *The Optimist's Daughter* (1972), which won the Pulitzer Prize.

West, Mae, *b. Brooklyn, N.Y., 1892; d. 1980.* Stage and movie star. Like tiny Shirley Temple, buxom, 40-year-old Mae West sashayed into movies and helped save her studio in the financially challenged 1930's. She grew up in vaudeville and went on to the theater as the author and star of *Sex* and *Diamond Lil* in the 1920's. Hollywood called and she answered with comic innuendo, tilted smiles, and her trademark swinging gait, making America laugh at sex. Notable films include *She Done Him Wrong* (1933) with Cary Grant, *Klondike Annie* (1936), and *My Little Chickadee* (1939) with W.C. Fields.

Wharton, Edith, *b. New York City, 1862; d. 1937.* Novelist and short-story writer. Born into a well-to-do family of the leisure class, Wharton turned her penetrating eye toward high society in two of her best-known works, *The House of Mirth* (1905) and *The Age of Innocence* (1920), for which she won the Pulitzer Prize. Her popular novel *Ethan Frome* appeared in 1911. A prolific writer of novels and short stories, Wharton was widely honored during her lifetime, and she now stands as one of the foremost novelists in American literature.

Whistler, James (Abbot) McNeill, *b. Lowell, Mass., 1834; d. 1903.* American painter, printmaker, designer, and active in England and France. Inspired by the realism of Courbet and Manet, and by Japonisme, Whistler became a member of the Aesthetic Movement. He used musical terms such as *symphony* in the titles of his work, emphasizing the abstract features of their compositions rather than their subjects. His most famous painting is *Arrangement in Grey* and *Black No. 1: Portrait of the Artist's Mother* (1872). When the critic John Ruskin insulted his work in 1877, Whistler famously sued him for libel.

Whitehead, Alfred North, *b. Ramsgate, Kent, England, 1861; d. 1947.* English mathematician and philosopher. Best known for collaborating with Bertrand Russell on *Principia Mathematica* (1910-13), Whitehead also wrote for a general audience, including *An Introduction to Mathematics* (1911), still in print and considered one of the best books of its kind. In 1916 he delivered an influential address that inspired teachers throughout the English-speaking world, "The Aims of Education: A Plea for Reform" stating that the purpose of education was not to bombard students with scraps of information, but to guide their self-development. He ended his career at Harvard University, establishing himself as a leading metaphysician, comparable in stature to Leibniz and Hegel.

Whitman, Walt, *b. West Hills, N.Y., 1819; d. 1892.* Poet. Whitman is widely considered the greatest American poet. He grew up in Brooklyn, where he worked for several newspapers as a reporter and editor, and where he published *Leaves of Grass* (1855). In theme (the poet as the embodiment of common humanity), form ("free verse," without rhyme or fixed meter), and content (vivid scenes, depicting nudity and evoking sexuality), it broke new ground, and it became one of American literature's most influential works. Whitman continually expanded it, publishing eight more editions through 1892. His *Drum-Taps* and *Sequel to Drum-Taps* (1865) reflect his service as a Civil War army nurse. His final book of poetry was *November Boughs* (1888), his principal prose works are *Democratic Vistas* (1871) and *Specimen Days* (1881).

Whitney, Eli, *b. Westboro, Mass., 1765; d. 1825.* Inventor and manufacturer. Whitney is famous for his invention of the cotton gin (1793), a hand-cranked engine (or "gin") that separates cotton fibers from seeds, increasing the output of a worker 50-fold. His introduction of special machines and interchangeable parts for his musket factory (1798), however, was as important to American industry as the cotton gin. He also developed the milling machine, a modified lathe that turns out irregularly shaped parts.

Wiener, Norbert, *b. Columbia, Mo., 1894; d. 1964.* Mathematician; established science of cybernetics. A child prodigy, he received his Harvard Ph.D. by age 18 and he taught math at MIT where he worked on problems of mathematical analysis. During World War II, Wiener helped soldiers with the problem of aiming gunfire at a moving target. After the war he published *Extrapolation, Interpolation, and Smoothing of Stationary Time Series* and as a result was named co-discoverer of the theory on the prediction of stationary time series. This work led to his groundbreaking book *Cybernetics; or, Control and Communication in the Animal and the Machine.* While remaining a passionate supporter of cybernetics, Wiener stayed active in a wide range of scientific subjects including quantum theory and mathematical prediction theory. He was awarded the National Medal of Science in 1963.

Wiesel, Elie (Eliezer), *b. Sighet, Romania, 1928.* Writer, political activist. A Holocaust survivor, he has dedicated his life to ensuring that its horrors are never forgotten. Deported to Auschwitz with his family at 16, he lost both of his parents and a sister before he was liberated in April 1945. He then studied at the Sorbonne, writing for French and Israeli newspapers before arriving in the United States in 1956. That year he published his first book, *Night,* which is based on his experiences at Auschwitz and is considered one of the most powerful pieces of Holocaust literature. He wrote several novels, including *Dawn* (1961) and *Twilight* (1987), as well as plays and collections of biblical and Hasidic tales, and taught at both City College of New York and Boston University. In 1986 he was awarded the Nobel Peace Prize.

Wilberforce, William, *b. Hull, England, 1759; d. 1833.* British abolitionist and member of Parliament. After serving in Parliament, Wilberforce converted to Christianity and endeavored to honor his religious convictions by fighting for social reform. For years he led a stubborn parliamentary campaign to abolish the British slave trade, which sent captives from Africa to the West Indies. Shortly before his death, a bill was passed that freed all the slaves in the British Empire, an act that had a major effect on America's antislavery movement. Wilberforce is buried in Westminster Abbey.

Wilde, Oscar, *b. Dublin, 1854; d. 1900.* Playwright, poet, novelist. Known in London as a great dandy and wit, Wilde published a book of poems in 1881 and, in 1891, the novel *The Picture of Dorian Gray,* concerning a young man whose pursuit of beauty leads to corruption. His most successful achievements were his plays, including *Salome* (1893), *Lady Windemere's Fan* (1892), *An Ideal Husband* (1895), and the enormously witty comedy of manners *The Importance of Being Earnest* (1895). He lost a libel suit he had filed in response to a charge of homosexual behavior, and served two years in prison. Out of this experience he wrote the poem *Ballad of Reading Gaol* (1898) and the posthumously published memoir-apology *De Profundis.*

Wilder, Billy (Samuel Wilder), b. *Vienna, Austria, 1906; d. 2002.* Screenwriter, director, producer. Famous for his cynical wit, Wilder was a master at creating morally flawed characters who spoke in literate dialogue. He began as a screenwriter, partnering with Charles Brackett in 1938. Their collaboration resulted in such hits as *Ninotchka* (1939) and *Ball of Fire* (1942). In 1942 he directed his first film, *The Major and the Minor,* which was followed by *Double Indemnity* (1944) and *The Lost Weekend* (1945). The 1950's proved to be Wilder's most productive period; among his films were *Sunset Boulevard* (1950), *The Seven Year Itch* (1955), and *Some Like It Hot* (1959).

Wilder, Thornton, b. *Madison, Wis., 1897; d. 1975.* Playwright, and novelist. A writer of diverse talents, Wilder won three Pulitzer prizes, one for his novel *The Bridge of San Luis Rey* (1927), and two in drama, for *Our Town* (1938) and *The Skin of Our Teeth* (1942). In *Our Town,* Wilder depicted the lives of the citizens of Grover's Corners, New Hampshire, a fictional town represented onstage by a minimalist set. The play, still a popular production, focuses on the theme that we should savor each moment of our lives.

William III, (William of Orange) b. *The Hague, Holland, 1650; d. 1702.* King of England and stadtholder of the Netherlands. Son of William II, prince of Orange and stadtholder (chief magistrate) of the Netherlands, William married Mary, eldest daughter of the future King James II of England, in 1677. Fearful of the growth of Roman Catholic power under James II, his opponents secretly invited William to invade England in 1688, leading to the bloodless Glorious Revolution, and William's proclamation by Parliament to the monarchy together with his wife in 1689. In 1690 he defeated Irish supporters of James; thereafter he opposed the territorial ambitions of Louis XIV of France.

William the Conqueror (William I), b. *Falaise, France, ca. 1028; d. 1087.* In 1035, William became duke of Normandy. Edward the Confessor, king of England and William's cousin, died childless in 1066, and William sailed for England, claiming that Edward had named him as heir. At the battle of Hastings in the same year, William defeated the Anglo-Saxons under Harold Godwineson and was crowned king. The rest of his life involved a series of campaigns both in England and on the continent to bolster his rule. His most famous administrative accomplishment was the compilation of an economic census of England known as the Domesday Book.

Williams, Tennessee (Thomas Lanier), b. *Columbus, Miss., 1911; d. 1983.* Playwright. In plays that explore the clash of a deluded, romantic vision of the world with the world's harsh reality and show broken characters yearning for their former grandeur, Williams created a vision of the American South as a place fraught with an undercurrent of sex and violence, of a once genteel society now in a state of ruin. Williams's first commercial success was *The Glass Menagerie* (1944); *Summer and Smoke* (1948), *The Rose Tatoo* (1950), and *Camino Real* (1953) are other well-known works. He later won the Pulitzer Prize for *A Streetcar Named Desire* (1947), and *Cat on a Hot Tin Roof* (1955).

Williams, William Carlos, b. *Rutherford, N. J., 1883; d. 1963.* Poet. A poet who also practiced medicine throughout his adult life, Williams is known for extreme simplicity and naturalism of style, particularly in his early work, exemplified by the poem "Red Wheelbarrow" (1923) and "This is Just to Say" (1934). In his later career, Williams used his poetry to critique the world. *Paterson* (5 vols., 1946–58), the great poem of his later years, looks at the complexity of the city as a metaphor for the complexity of man.

Wilson, Woodrow, b. *Staunton, Va., 1856; d. 1924.* Twenty-eighth U.S. president, 1913–21. Thomas Woodrow Wilson attracted the attention of Democratic bosses after he was elected president of Princeton in 1902, and they persuaded him to run for governor of New Jersey in 1910. A strong progressive, Wilson won easily—and then turned on party bosses by sponsoring antimachine reforms. He won the presidency for the Democrats in 1912, after Taft and Roosevelt split the Republican vote. Wilson remained neutral on the war in Europe until Germany spurned his attempts at mediation and resumed attacks on Allied shipping. In April 1917, Congress declared war at Wilson's behest; after the armistice in November 1918, Wilson became the first president to visit Europe when he attended the Paris peace conference that produced the Versailles Treaty. Wilson's dream of "peace without vengeance" was frustrated at Versailles, where he compromised away his Fourteen Points to obtain the League of Nations for collective security. In October 1919 he suffered a paralytic stroke; Wilson's second wife, Edith Bolling Galt, shielded the disabled president from the press and politicians until the end of his term in 1921.

Winfrey, Oprah, b. *Kosciusko, Miss., 1954.* Media mogul. Ranked as the highest-paid person in television in 2006, Winfrey got her start in Nashville as the youngest and first African-American woman to be a news anchor. In 1984, she moved to *AM Chicago*, which within a year was renamed *The Oprah Winfrey Show*. By 1986, it was the highest-rated talk show in television history, and in 2006 it had remained so for 20 seasons. In addition to Oprah's Book Club, *O, The Oprah Magazine*, and her work as a theater producer and actress, Winfrey is known for her philanthropic efforts with education in Africa through the Oprah Winfrey Foundation.

Winthrop, John, *b. Edwardstone, England, 1588; d. 1649.* **Historian and first governor of Massachusetts.** In 1629 the Massachusetts Bay Company appointed Winthrop governor to settle the colony. He governed under the patent granted to the company, but disputes arose frequently over powers he claimed for himself and a small inner circle and those claimed by the settlers. He served four terms (1629–34, 1637–40, 1642–44, 1646–49) and is generally credited with creating the institutions that ensured the colony's survival. His journal, published as *History of New England 1630–49* (1825–26), is an important document of Puritanism in early America.

Wittgenstein, Ludwig, *b. Vienna, 1889; d. 1951.* **Philosopher.** He argued in *Tractatus Logico-Philosophicus* (1921) that language and thought act as pictures of the real world, and that to understand any sentence one must understand the relationship of its components to each other and to the real. There are, however, things beyond language, the unsayable, and here Wittgenstein allowed for the possibility of a metaphysics, unlike the *logical positivism* movement. His later work in Cambridge, England, influenced "ordinary-language" philosophy, which holds that philosophical questions arise from the ambiguities of language.

Woods, Tiger (Eldrick Woods), *b. Cypress, Calif., 1975.* **Golfer.** Tiger Woods established himself as the game's top player and one of the all-time greats while still in his twenties. A child prodigy, Woods was the first golfer to win three consecutive U.S. Amateur titles (1994–96). After attending Stanford, he turned pro in 1996 and the following year became the youngest player ever to win the Masters. Tiger claimed 34 P.G.A. victories—including eight majors—through 2002. That year he also won his unprecedented fourth straight P.G.A. Player of the Year award. In 2009, after a domestic incident involving his wife, several women came forward to allege affairs with Woods, leading to the breakup of his marriage and a steep decline in production. Tiger had no victories in 2010, the first time in his career.

Woolf, Virginia, *b. London, 1882; d. 1941.* **Novelist.** The daughter of the critic and philosopher Leslie Stephen, Virginia Woolf and her husband, Leonard, were the hosts of the Bloomsbury Group of writers and artists. Like James Joyce, she developed the stream-of-consciousness technique, taking it in a more lyrical direction, and emphasizing neither plot nor character but experience. From *Jacob's Room* (1922) through *Mrs. Dalloway*, (1925), *To the Lighthouse* (1927), and *The Waves* (1931), this style became freer and more experimental as she examined time and change pressing upon personal development and human relationships. A victim of recurring mental traumas, Woolf drowned herself at age 59.

Wordsworth, William, *b. Cockermouth, Cumberland, England, 1770; d. 1850.* **Poet.** Wordsworth grew up in the English Lake District, the beauty of which inspired his poetic career. A trip to France in 1790 fired him with democratic sentiment and helped influence a radically new direction in English poetry, charted with Samuel Taylor Coleridge in *Lyrical Ballads* (1798). With simple diction, Wordsworth described humble people and celebrated nature. It included his great picturesque and meditative poem "Tintern Abbey." Within a decade Wordsworth had done most of his best work, including the extended *The Ruined Cottage* (1799) and *Michael* (1800), "Ode: Intimations of Immortality" (1807), and many well-known lyrics and sonnets. His 14-book autobiographical poem, *The Prelude*, considered his masterpiece, was completed by 1805 but not published until after his death.

Wren, Christopher, *b. East Knoyle, England, 1632; d. 1723.* **Architect and scientist of the Renaissance.** His early scientific studies were admired by Isaac Newton but his fame rests on his later prolific work as an architect. The great fire of London in 1666 gave him the opportunity to create ingeniously differing designs for many parish churches as well as Saint Paul's cathedral (1675–1710), with its monumental western facade, splendid dome, and vaulted interior. His important works include the Naval Hospital in Greenwich (1682–89); the Library at Trinity College (1676–84), Cambridge; and Marlborough House (1709–11), London.

Wright, Frank Lloyd, *b. Richland Center, Wisc., 1867; d. 1959.* **American architect.** Considered by many the greatest architect of the 20th century, Wright's works have had a profound influence on its architecture. After serving an apprenticeship with Louis Sullivan, he began developing his distinctive "prairie houses" with their open plans arranged around large central fireplaces; they included the Robie House (1906–10) in Chicago. Wright also produced two major large works: Unity Temple (1904) in Oak Park, and the Larkin Company Administration Building (1903–06, since demolished) in Buffalo. He lived almost to 92 and designed some of his greatest works after age 60, including Fallingwater (1936–38) in Mill Run, Pennsylvania; and the Johnson Wax Building (1936–37) in Racine, Wisconsin. But his Usonian houses, designed in the 1930's as affordable for middle-class owners, were perhaps his most important achievement.

Wright, Orville *b. Dayton, Ohio, 1871; d. 1948* and **Wilbur**, *b. Millville, Ind., 1867; d. 1912.* **American inventors and aviation pioneers.** The Wrights were bicycle mechanics who used the tools and materials in their Dayton shop for their early aeronautic constructions. They began the study of aeronautics in 1886 and experimented with gliders at Kitty Hawk, N.C., in 1900, 1901, and 1902. On December 17, 1903, at Kitty Hawk they flew four times in an engine-powered craft and became the first ever to develop and fly an airplane in sustained and controlled flight. They continued to advance their inventions, developing biplanes and forming a company that, after Wilbur's death, Orville sold in 1915.

Wright, Richard, *b. Natchez, Miss., 1908; d. 1960.* **American novelist and short-story writer.** The grandson of slaves, Wright was born into poverty in rural Mississippi. His first collection of short stories, *Uncle Tom's Children* (1938), addressed the impossibility of living in a racist world. *Native Son* (1940), his greatest work, follows the life of a young African-American man, Bigger Thomas, who, after the accidental killing of a white girl, must flee through a hostile world. Among Wright's other works are the existential novel *The Outsider* (1953) and the memoir *Black Boy* (1945). A member of the Communist Party from 1932 to 1944, Wright lived as an expatriate in Paris from the end of World War II until his death.

Yeats, William Butler, *b. Dublin, 1865; d. 1939.* **Poet and playwright.** Yeats is regarded as the 20th century's greatest English-language poet. His early poetry—e.g., "The Stolen Child" (1889), and "The Lake Isle of Innisfree" (1893)—has a dreamy, musical quality derived partly from Irish folklore. In midlife he embraced the Irish nationalist cause in "Easter 1916" (1921), and "Meditations in Time of Civil War" (1928) and helped establish the Irish National Theater. Yeats incorporated a complex symbolic spiritual system into his mature poetry—as in "The Tower" (1928) and "Byzantium" (1933)—yet his work is almost always approachable, rooted in vivid imagery and physical reality, and phrased with startling beauty.

Yeltsin, Boris, *b. Sverdlovsk, Russia, 1931; d. 2007.* **Russian politician.** Yeltsin joined the Communist Party in 1960 and worked his way through the ranks to become first secretary of the Communist Party in Moscow in 1985. Ousted in 1987 for criticizing the slow pace of Gorbachev's reforms, in 1989 he was elected to the Supreme Soviet. When the Russian Soviet Federated Socialist Republic became independent, he was elected president in June 1991. Two months later, he gained worldwide acclaim for facing down an attempted coup by the army. His tenure as president was less inspired, and he resigned his post in 1999.

Young, Brigham, *b. Whittingham, Vt., 1801; d. 1877.* **American religious leader.** In 1832 Young converted to the Church of Jesus Christ of Latter-Day Saints (Mormons), founded by Joseph Smith. To escape religious persecution, he moved with Smith and their followers from Ohio first to Missouri and later to Illinois. After Smith was imprisoned and murdered in 1844, Young organized a migration west and settled in the Salt Lake Valley in Utah in 1847. From then until his death he worked to build a society based on Mormon principles that succeeded in spite of hostility from the federal government and others.

Young, Cy (Denton True Young), *b. Gilmore, Ohio., 1867; d. 1955.* **Baseball player.** Professional baseball's first major star, Cy Young remains the all-time statistical leader in several major pitching categories: wins (511), losses (316), complete games (749), and innings (7,356). In a 22-year career (1890–1911), the right-hander topped 30 wins five times and 20 wins 15 times. He pitched three no-hitters, one of them a perfect game. In 1903, Young won two games for Boston in the first modern World Series. Today, the annual award given to the most outstanding pitcher in each league is named in his honor.

Zapata, Emiliano, *b. Anenecuilco, Mexico, 1879; d. 1919.* **Mexican revolutionary and national hero.** Zapata campaigned for the restoration of village lands confiscated by *hacendados*, with the slogan "Tierra y libertad." In 1910, he played an important role in the fight against the dictator Porfirio Diaz; after the revolution, Zapata became disillusioned with Francisco Madero's land reforms and continued his guerrilla fight for land and liberty. His Plan of Ayala called for seizure of foreign-owned land and confiscation of one-third of all land held by "friendly" *hacendados*. In 1919, he was killed in a trap perpetrated by one of Venustiano Carranza's generals.

Zátopek, Emil, *b. Koprivinice, Czechoslovakia, 1922; d. 2000.* **Runner.** The Czech long-distance runner accomplished one of the most remarkable feats in Olympic history by winning the 5,000 m, 10,000 m, and marathon at the 1952 games in Helsinki. In his Olympic debut four years earlier, he won a gold medal in the 10,000 and a silver medal in the 5,000. Before ending his career in 1956, Zátopek had set 18 world records at nine different distances, including five in the 10,000.

Zhou Enlai, *b. Jiangsu Province, China, 1898; d. 1976.* **Statesman.** Zhou was born into a scholar-official family and had a privileged upbringing. He studied abroad in Japan and Europe, joining the Chinese Communist Party in France in 1922. His political, administrative, and diplomatic skills propelled his rapid rise in party ranks; he was careful always to be an ally, not a rival, of Mao Zedong. Zhou was elected to the Politburo in 1927, served as China's premier from the founding of the People's Republic in 1949 until his death, and was never demoted or purged. His was the reasonable face that Chinese communism showed to the outside world, so he played a large role in President Nixon's rapprochement with China in the early 1970's.

Zola, Emile, *b. Paris, 1840; d. 1902.* **Novelist.** Zola was the premier French writer in the naturalist movement, which presented life with scientific realism, focusing on mean physical, social, and psychological conditions. His first novel in this manner was *Therese Raquin* (1867). From 1871 to 1893 he composed a series of novels known as the "Rougon-Macquart Cycle," investigating lower-class and laboring-class conditions and revealing the effects of heredity as well as environment. The best-known of these is *Nana* (1880). In 1898 Zola famously wrote a public letter, known as "J'accuse" ("I accuse"), in which he indicted the French army leadership for anti-semitism in the Dreyfus affair.

Zoroaster (Persian: Zarathushtra), *b. Persia, ca. 628 B.C.; d. ca. 551 B.C.* **Religious teacher and prophet.** Founder of Zorastrianism, a religion with holy writings (*Avesta* = law) in old Iranian, akin to Vedic Sanskrit. Little is known of Zoroaster's life. He divided traditional Persian deities into the good (led by Ahura Mazdah), who will ultimately prevail, and the evil (led by Ahriman); individuals by their conduct help one or the other side and go to the realm of light or perdition accordingly.

Zuckerberg, Mark, *b. Dobbs Ferry, N.Y., 1984.* **Cofounder and CEO of Facebook.** In 2004, Harvard University student Zuckerberg launched a social networking Web site called thefacebook.com, later renamed Facebook. Designed to allow users to create a profile by posting pictures and personal information onto a predesigned template, Facebook's focus was on creating a network of friends, and friends of friends, thereby building connections between people and their interests. Initially only available to Harvard students, Facebook has since expanded to allow user access to anyone with an email address. By 2011, the number of active Facebook users had risen to more than 500 million, and Forbes Magazine estimated Zuckerberg's personal net worth at $13.5 billion, making the 27-year-old the 19th wealthiest person in the United States, and one of the world's youngest billionaires.

INDEX